Standard Catalog of® WORLD PAPER MONEY

Modern Issues • 1961-Present

22nd Edition

Special Contributors

**Thomas Augustsson, Miloš Kudweis,
Juozas Minikevicius, David Murcek,
Ray Recher, Ludek Vostal**

Published by

Krause Publications, a division of F+W Media, Inc.
700 East State Street • Iola, WI 54990-0001
715-445-2214 • 888-457-2873
www.krausebooks.com

To order books or other products call toll-free 1-800-258-0929
or visit us online at www.shopnumismaster.com

ISSN 1538-2028
ISBN-13: 978-1-4402-4656-2
ISBN-10: 1-4402-4656-4

Book designed by Sandi Carpenter
Edited by Maggie Judkins

Printed in the United States of America

10 9 8 7 6 5 4 3 2 1

Introduction

Welcome to this 22nd edition of the *Standard Catalog of World Paper Money, Modern Issues*.

Many new issues, date varieties and signature combinations, as well as expanded text descriptions and price updates, have been made. Foreign Exchange Certificates, Military use notes and Regional notes are now presented in the *Standard Catalog of World Paper Money, Specialized Issues* volume, now in its 12th edition.

In our constant endeavor to provide as much detail as possible, we have expanded our detailed signature variety information. For the ease of identification, notes are listed under their historic country identification (British Honduras is no longer hidden within Belize). North Korea and South Korea are now under N and S, respectively, not under K. Northern Ireland is under N. Please consult the country index or bank issuer index if you continue to experience difficulty.

Notes of a particular bank are listed in release date order, and then grouped in ascending denomination order. In the cases of countries where more than one issuing authority is in effect at a single time, follow the bank headings in the listings and it will become apparent if that country's listing are by date or alphabetical by issuing authority. In the cases where a country has changed from a kingdom to a republic, all the bank notes of the kingdom's era would be listed before that of the republic.

If you wish to contribute images, please contact us first and follow the guidelines as set forth in the information notice. We can accept them as JPGs, and preferably on a disc, rather than as an email attachment. But please contact us first before you do a lot of work, which could be duplicating items already in progress for inclusion in future editions.

Table of Contents

An Invitation

Users of this catalog may find a helpful adjunct to be the *Bank Note Reporter*, the only monthly newspaper devoted exclusively to North American and world paper money. Each issue presents up-to-date news, feature articles and valuable information. All purchasers of this catalog are invited to subscribe to the *Bank Note Reporter*. See www.shopnumismaster.com.

A review of modern paper money collecting

Paper money collecting is probably as old as paper money itself. However, this segment of the numismatic hobby did not begin to reach a popularity approaching that of coin collecting until the latter half of the 1970s. While coins and paper money are alike in that both served as legal obligations to facilitate commerce, longtime paper money enthusiasts know the similarity ends there.

Coins were historically guaranteed by the intrinsic value of their metallic content - at least until recent years when virtually all circulating coins have become little more than legal tender tokens, containing little or no precious metal - while paper money possesses a value only when it is accepted for debts or converted into bullion or precious metals. With many note issues, this conversion privilege was limited and ultimately negated by the imposition of redemption cutoff dates.

The development of widespread collector interest in paper money of most nations was inhibited by a near total absence of adequate documentation. No more than four decades ago, collectors could refer to only a few catalogs and dealer price lists of limited scope, most of which were difficult to acquire, or they could build their own knowledge through personal collecting pursuits and contact with fellow collectors.

The early catalogs authored by Albert Pick chronicled issues of Europe and the Americas and were assembled as stepping-stones to the ultimate objective, which became reality with publication of the first *Standard Catalog of World Paper Money* in 1975. That work provided collectors with fairly complete listings and up-to-date valuations of all recorded government note issues of the 20th century, incorporating Pick's previously unpublished manuscripts on Africa, Asia and Oceania, plus many earlier issues.

This completely revised and updated 22nd Edition of Modern Issues, along with the companion 15th Edition of General Issues, presents a substantial extension of the cataloging effort initiated in 1975. As the most comprehensive world paper money references ever assembled, they fully document the many and varied legal tender paper currencies issued and circulated by more than 380 past and current government issuing authorities of the world from the 1300s to present.

Maggie Judkins
Editor

Acknowledgements

Over time, contributor enhancements to this catalog have been many and varied, and to recognize them all would be a volume in itself. Accordingly, we wish to acknowledge the following individuals who have exhibited a special enthusiasm for this edition.

Dundar Acikalin
Esko Ahlroth
Paulo Almeida
Thomas Augustsson
Keith Austin
Oksana Bandriuska
Adriaan C.F. Beck
Dan Bellan
Jan Bendix
Milt Blackburn
Joseph E. Boling
Wilfried A. Bracke
Jean Bricaud
Alejandro Brill
Mahdi Bseiso
Christopher J. Budesa
Lance K. Campbell
David F. Cieniewicz
Mark C. Clark
Scott E. Cordry
Guido Crapanzano
Ray Czahor
Howard A. Daniel III
Antonio de Albergaria
Michel Dufour
Arnoldo Efron
Wilhelm R. Eglseer

Ricardo Faillace
Wolfgang A. Frick
Yves Gilles
Flemming Lyngbeck Hansen
Anton Holt
Armen Hovsepian
Yu Jian Hua
Edouard Jean-Pierre
Alex Kaglyan
Luis A.A. Karmy
Olaf Kiener
Ladislav Klaus
Michael E. Knabe
Tristan Kolm
Miloš Kudweis
Michael Kvasnica
Samson K.C. Lai
Michael Lang
Akos Ledai
C. K. Leong
David Leong
Owen Linzmayer
Alan Luedeking
Stu Lumsden
Dr. Dennis Lutz
Martin Mac Daid

Ma Tak Wo
Arthur C. Matz
Ali Mehilba
James Michaelsen
Juozas Minikevicius
Jon Morowitz
David Murcek
Tanju Mutlu
William Myers
Fred O'Connell
Francisco Orozco
Frank Passic
Antonio E. Pedraza
Miguel Pratt
Yahya J. Qureshi
Kavan Ratnatunga
Mircea Raicopol
Jay Recher
Bob Reis
Ilan Rinetzky
John Rishel
Kerry A. Rodgers
William Rosenblum
Juri Rudich
Remy Said
Sergio Sanchez
Jacco Scheper

Harmut Schoenawa
Christian Selvais
Victor F. Seper Jr.
Joel Shafer
Neil Shafer
Gary F. Snover
Jeremy Steinberg
Tim Steiner
Georg H. Stocker
Zeljko Stojanovic
Peter Symes
Frank Tesson
Anthony Tumonis
W. J. van der Drift
Norbert von Euw
Michael Vort-Ronald
Ludek Vostal
Evangelos Vyzas
Wakim Wakim
James Warmus
Pam West
Luke Wilson
Peter Zapf
Joseph Zaffern
Christof Zellweger

Special Thanks

Heritage Auctions
International Bank Note Society
Monetary Research Institute
Paper Money Guaranty

Country Index

Issuer and Bank Index

How To Use This Catalog

Catalog listings consist of all regular and provisional notes attaining wide circulation in their respective countries for the period covered. Notes have been listed under the historical country name. Thus Dahomey is not under Benin, as had been the case in some past catalogs. The listings continue to be grouped by issue range rather than by denomination, and the listing format should make the bank name, issue dates as well as catalog numbers and denominations easier to locate. These improvements have been made to make the catalog as easy to use as possible for you.

The editors and publisher make no claim to absolute completeness, just as they acknowledge that some errors and pricing inequities will appear. Correspondence is invited with interested persons who have notes previously unlisted or who have information to enhance the presentation of existing listings in succeeding editions of this catalog.

Catalog Format

Listings proceed generally according to the following sequence: country, geographic or political, chronology, bank name and sometimes alphabetically or by date of first note issue. Release within the bank, most often in date order, but sometimes by printer first.

Catalog number — The basic reference number at the beginning of each listing for each note. For this Modern Issues volume the regular listings require no prefix letters except when 'a' or 'b' appear within the catalog number as a suffix or variety letter. (Military and Regional prefixes are explained later in this section.)

Denomination — the value as shown on the note, in western numerals. When denominations are only spelled out, consult the numerics chart.

Date — the actual issue date as printed on the note in day-month-year order. Where more than one date appears on a note, only the latest is used. Where the note has no date, the designation ND is used, followed by a year date in parentheses when it is known. If a note is dated by the law or decree of authorization, the date appears with an L or D.

Descriptions of the note are broken up into one or more items as follows:

Color — the main color(s) of the face, and the underprint are given first. If the colors of the back are different, then they follow the face design description.

Design — The identification and location of the main design elements if known. Back design elements identified if known.

Printer — often a local printer has the name shown in full. Abbreviations are used for the most prolific printers. Refer to the list of printer abbreviations elsewhere in this introduction.

Valuations — are generally given under the grade headings of Good, Fine and Extremely Fine for early notes; and Very Good, Very Fine and Uncirculated for the later issues. Listings that do not follow these two patterns are clearly indicated. UNC followed by a value is used usually for specimens and proofs when lower grade headings are used for a particular series of issued notes.

Catalog suffix letters

A catalog number followed by a capital 'A', 'B' or 'C' indicated the incorporation of a listing as required by type or date it may indicate newly discovered lower or higher denominations to a series which needed to be fit into long standing listings. Listings of notes for regional circulation are distinguished from regular national issues with the prefix letter 'R'; military issues use a 'M' prefix; foreign exchange certificates are assigned a 'FX' prefix. These are now presented in the *Standard Catalog of World Paper Money, Specialized Issues Volume, 12th Edition*. Varieties, specific date or signature listings are shown with small letters 'a' following a number within their respective entries. Some standard variety letters include: 'ct' for color trials, 'p' for proof notes, 'r' for remainder notes, 's' for specimen notes and 'x' for counterfeits or errors.

Denominations

The denomination as indicated on many notes issued by a string of countries stretching from eastern Asia, through western Asia and on across northern Africa, often appears only in unfamiliar non-Western numeral styles. With the listings that follow, denominations are always indicated in Western numerals.

A comprehensive chart keying Western numerals to their non-Western counterparts is included elsewhere in this introduction as an aid to the identification of note types. This compilation features not only the basic numeral systems such as Arabic, Japanese and Indian, but also the more restricted systems such as Burmese, Ethiopian, Siamese, Tibetan, Hebrew, Mongolian and Korean. Additionally, the list includes other localized variations that have been applied to some paper money issues.

In consulting the numeral systems chart to determine the denomination of a note, one should remember that the actual numerals styles employed in any given area, or at a particular time, may vary significantly from these basic representations. Such variations can be deceptive to the untrained eye, just as variations from Western numeral styles can prove deceptive to individuals not acquainted with the particular style employed.

Dates and Date Listing Policy

In previous editions of this work it was the goal to provide a sampling of the many date varieties that were believed to exist. In recent times, as particular dates (and usually signature combinations) were known to be scarcer, that particular series was expanded to include listings of individual dates. At times this idea has been fully incorporated, but with some series it is not practicable, especially when just about every day in a given month could have been an issue date for the notes.

Accordingly, where it seems justifiable that date spans can be realistically filled with individual dates, this has been done. In order to accommodate the many new dates, the idea of providing variety letters to break them up into narrower spans of years has been used. If it appears that there are too many dates for a series, with no major differences in value, then a general inclusive date span is used (beginning and ending) and individual dates within this span are not shown.

For those notes showing only a general date span, the only important dates become those that expand the range of years, months or days earlier or later. But even they would have no impact on the values shown.

Because a specific date is not listed does not necessarily mean it is rare. It may be just that it has not been reported. Those date varieties known to be scarcer are cataloged separately. Newly reported dates in a wide variety of listings are constantly being reported. This indicates that research into the whole area is very active, and a steady flow of new dates is fully expected upon publication of this edition.

Valuations

Valuations are given for most notes in three grades. Earlier issues are usually valued in the grade headings of Good, Fine and Extremely Fine; later issues take the grade headings of Very Good, Very Fine and Uncirculated. While it is true that some early notes cannot be valued in Extremely Fine and some later notes have no premium value in Very Good, it is felt that this coverage provides the best uniformity of value data to the collecting community. There are exceptional cases where headings are adjusted for either single notes or a series that really needs special treatment.

Valuations are determined generally from a consensus of individuals submitting prices for evaluation. Some notes have NO values; this does not necessarily mean they are expensive or even rare, but it shows that no pricing information was forthcoming. A number of notes have a 'Rare' designation, and no values. Such notes are generally not available on the market, and when they do appear the price is a matter between buyer and seller. No book can provide guidance in these instances except to indicate rarity.

Valuations used in this book are based on the IBNS grading standards and are stated in U.S. dollars. They serve only as aids in evaluating paper money since actual market conditions throughout the worldwide collector community are constantly changing. In addition, particularly choice examples of many issues listed often bring higher premiums than values listed. Users should remember that a catalog such as this is only a guide to values.

FV (for Face Value) is used as a value designation on new issues as well as older but still redeemable legal tender notes in lower conditions. FV may appear in one or both condition columns before Uncirculated, depending on the relative age and availability of the note in question. Some non-current notes which are still exchangeable carry FV designations.

Collection care

The proper preservation of a collection should be of paramount importance to all in the hobby - dealers, collectors and scholars. Only a person who has housed notes in a manner giving pleasure to him or herself and others will keep alive the pleasure of collecting for future generations. The same applies to the way of housing as to the choice of the collecting specialty: it is chiefly a question of what most pleases the individual collector.

Arrangement and sorting of a collection is most certainly a basic requirement. Storing the notes in safe paper envelopes and filing boxes should, perhaps, be considered only when building a new section of a collection, for accommodating varieties or for reasons of saving space when the collection has grown quickly.

Many paper money collections are probably housed in some form of plastic-pocketed album, which are today manufactured in many different sizes and styles to accommodate many types of world paper money. Because the number of bank note collectors has grown continually over the past thirty-five years, some specialty manufacturers of albums have developed a paper money selection. The notes, housed in clear plastic pockets, individually or in groups, can be viewed and exchanged without difficulty. These albums are not cheap, but the notes displayed in this manner do make a lasting impression on the viewer.

A word of concern: certain types of plastic and all vinyl used for housing notes may cause notes to become brittle over time, or cause an irreversible and harmful transfer of oils from the vinyl onto the bank notes.

The high demand for quality that stamp collectors make on their products cannot be transferred to the paper money collecting fraternity. A postage stamp is intended for a single use, then is relegated to a collection. With paper money, it is nearly impossible to acquire uncirculated specimens from a number of countries because of export laws or internal bank procedures. Bends from excessive counting, or even staple holes, are commonplace. Once acquiring a circulated note, the collector must endeavor to maintain its state of preservation.

The fact that there is a classification and value difference between notes with greater use or even damage is a matter of course. It is part of the opinion and personal taste of the individual collector to decide what is considered worthy of collecting and what to pay for such items.

For the purposed of strengthening and mending torn paper money, under no circumstances should one use plain cellophane tape or a similar material. These tapes warp easily, with sealing marks forming at the edges, and the tape frequently discolors. Only with the greatest of difficulty (and often not at all) can these tapes be removed, and damage to the note or the printing is almost unavoidable. The best material for mending tears is an archival tape recommended for the treatment and repair of documents.

There are collectors who, with great skill, remove unsightly spots, repair badly damaged notes, replace missing pieces and otherwise restore or clean a note. There is a question of morality by tampering with a note to improve its condition, either by repairing, starching, ironing, pressing or other methods to possibly deceive a potential future buyer. Such a question must, in the final analysis, be left to the individual collector.

IBNS Grading Standards For World Paper Money

The following introduction and Grading Guide is the result of work prepared under the guidance of the Grading Committee of the International Bank Note Society (IBNS). It has been adopted as the official grading standards of that society.

Introduction

Grading is the most controversial component of paper money collecting today. Small differences in grade can mean significant Vdifferences in value. The process of grading is so subjective and dependent on external influences such as lighting, that even a very experienced individual may well grade the same note differently on separate occasions.

To facilitate communication between sellers and buyers, it is essential that grading terms and their meanings be as standardized and as widely used as possible. This standardization should reflect common usage as much as practicable. One difficulty with grading is that even the actual grades themselves are not used everywhere by everyone. For example, in Europe the grade 'About Uncirculated' (AU) is not in general use, yet in North America it is widespread. The European term 'Good VF' may roughly correspond to what individuals in North America call 'Extremely Fine' (EF).

The grades and definitions as set forth below cannot reconcile all the various systems and grading terminology variants. Rather, the attempt is made here to try and diminish the controversy with some common-sense grades and definitions that aim to give more precise meaning to the grading language of paper money.

How to look at a banknote

In order to ascertain the grade of a note, it is essential to examine it out of a holder and under a good light. Move the note around so that light bounces off of it at different angles. Try holding the note obliquely, so the note is even with your eye as you look up at the light. Hard-to-see folds or slight creases will show up under such examination. Some individuals also lightly feel along the surface of the note to detect creasing.

Cleaning, Washing, Pressing of Banknotes

a) Cleaning, washing or pressing paper money is generally harmful and reduces both the grade and the value of a note. At the very least, a washed or pressed note may lose its original sheen and its surface may become lifeless and dull. The defects a note had, such as folds and creases, may not necessarily be completely eliminated and their telltale marks can be detected under a good light. Carelessly washed notes may also have white streaks where the folds or creases were (or still are).

b) Processing of a note which started out as Extremely Fine will automatically reduce it at least one full grade.

Unnatural Defects

Glue, tape or pencil marks may sometimes be successfuly removed. While such removal will leave a cleaned surface, it will improve the overall appearance of the note without concealing any of its defects. Under such circumstances, the grade of that note may also be improved.

The words "pinholes", "staple holes", "trimmed", "graffiti", "writing on face", "tape marks" etc. should always be added to the description of a note. It is realized that certain countries routinely staple their notes together in groups before issue. In such cases, the description can include a comment such as "usual staple holes" or something similar. After all, not everyone knows that certain notes cannot be found otherwise.

The major point of this section is that one cannot lower the overall grade of a note with defects simply because of the defects. The value will reflect the lowered worth of a defective note, but the description must always include the specific defects.

Grading

Definitions of Terms

UNCIRCULATED: A perfectly preserved note, never mishandled by the issuing authority, a bank teller, the public or a collector.

Paper is clean and firm, without discoloration. Corners are sharp and square without any evidence of rounding. (Rounded corners are often a tell-tale sign of a cleaned or "doctored" note.)

Note: Some note issues are most often available with slight evidence of very light counting folds which do not "break" the paper. Also, French-printed notes usually have a slight ripple in the paper. Many collectors and dealers refer to such notes as AU-UNC.

ABOUT UNCIRCULATED: A virtually perfect note, with some minor handling. May show very slight evidence of bank counting folds at a corner or one light fold through the center, but not both. An AU note canot be creased, a crease being a hard fold which has usually "broken" the surface of the note.

Paper is clean and bright with original sheen. Corners are not rounded.

Note: Europeans will refer to an About Uncirculated or AU note as "EF-Unc" or as just "EF". The Extremely Fine note described below will often be referred to as "GVF" or "Good Very Fine".

EXTREMELY FINE: A very attractive note, with light handling. May have a maximum of three light folds or one strong crease.

Paper is clean and firm, without discoloration. Corners are sharp and square without any evidence of rounding. (Rounded corners are often a tell-tale sign of a cleaned or "doctored" note.)

VERY FINE: An attractive note, but with more evidence of handling and wear. May have several folds both vertically and horizontally.

Paper may have minimal dirt, or possible color smudging. Paper itself is still relatively crisp and not floppy.

There are no tears into the border area, although the edges do show slight wear. Corners also show wear but not full rounding.

FINE: A note that shows considerable circulation, with many folds, creases and wrinkling.

Paper is not excessively dirty but may have some softness.

Edges may show much handling, with minor tears in the border area. Tears may not extend into the design. There will be no center hole because of excessive folding.

Colors are clear but not very bright. A staple hole or two would would not be considered unusual wear in a Fine note. Overall appearance is still on the desirable side.

VERY GOOD: A well used note, abused but still intact.

Corners may have much wear and rounding, tiny nicks, tears may extend into the design, some discoloration may be prsent, staining may have occurred, and a small hole may sometimes be seen at center from excessive folding.

Staple and pinholes are usually present, and the note itself is quite limp but NO pieces of the note can be missing. A note in VG condition may still have an overall not unattractive appearance.

GOOD: A well worn and heavily used note. Normal damage from prolonged circulation will include strong multiple folds and creases, stains, pinholes and/or staple holes, dirt, discoloration, edge tears, center hole, rounded corners and an overall unattractive appearance. No large pieces of the note may be missing. Graffiti is commonly seen on notes in G condition.

FAIR: A totally limp, dirty and very well used note. Larger pieces may be half torn off or missing besides the defects mentioned under the Good category. Tears will be larger, obscured portions of the note will be bigger.

POOR: A "rag" with severe damage because of wear, staining, pieces missing, graffiti, larger holes. May have tape holding pieces of the note together. Trimming may have taken place to remove rough edges. A Poor note is desirable only as a "filler" or when such a note is the only one known of that particular issue.

A word on crimps to otherwise uncirculated notes.

Due to inclusion of wide security foils, crimps appear at the top and bottom edge during production or counting. Thus notes which are uncirculated have a crimp. Examples without these crimps are beginning to command a premium.

Bank Note Printers

Printers' names, abbreviations or monograms will usually appear as part of the frame design or below it on face and/or back. In some instances the engraver's name may also appear in a similar location on a note. The following abbreviations identify printers for many of the notes listed in this volume:

ABNC	American Bank Note Company (USA)
BABN(C)	British American Bank Note Co., Ltd. (Canada)
B&S	Bouligny & Schmidt (Mexico)
BDDK	Bunddesdruckerei (Germany)
BEPP	Bureau of Engraving & Printing, Peking (China)
BF	Banque de France (France)
BFL	Barclay & Fry, Ltd. (England)
BWC	Bradbury, Wilkinson & Co. (England)
CABB	Compania Americana de Billetes de Banco (ANBC)
CBC	Columbian Banknote Co. (US)
CBNC	Canadian Bank Note Company (Canada)
CC	Ciccone Calcografica S.A. (Italy)
CCBB	Compania Columbiana de Billetes de Banco (CDC)
CdM-	Casa de Moeda (Brazil)
CdM-	Casa de Moeda (Argentina, Chile, etc.)
CHB	Chung Hua Book Co. (China)
CMN	Casa de Moneda de la Nacion (Argentina)
CMPA	Commercial Press (China)
CNBB	Compania Nacional de billetes de Banco (NBNC)
CONB	Continental Bank Note Company (US)
CPF	Central Printing Factory (China)
CSABB	Compania Sud/Americana de billetes de Banco (Argentina)
CS&E	Charles Skipper & East (England)
DLR or (T)DLR	De La Rue (England)
DTB	Dah Tung Book Co., and Ta Tung Printing (China)
F&C	Evans & Cogswell (CSA)
EAW	F.A. Wright (US)
FLBN	Franklin-Lee Bank Note Company (US)
FNMT	Fabrica Nacional de Moneda y Timbre (Spain)
G&D	Giesecke & Devrient (Germany)
HBNC	Hamilton Bank Note Company (USA)
HKB	Hong Kong Banknote (Hong Kong)
HKP	Hong Kong Printing Press (Hong Kong)
H&L	Hoyer & Ludwig, Richmond, Virginia (CSA)
HLBNC	Homer Lee Bank Note Co. (US)
H&S	Harrison & Sons, Ltd. (England)
IBB	Imprenta de Billetes-Bogota (Colombia)
IBSFB	Imprenta de Billetes-Santa Fe de Bogota (Colombia)
IBNC	International Bank Note Company (US)
JBNC	Jeffries Bank Note Company (US)
JEZ	Joh, Enschede en Zonen (Netherlands)
K&B	Keatinge & Ball (CSA)
KBNC	Kendall Bank Note Company, New York (USA)
LN	Litographia Nacional (Colombia)
NAL	Nissen & Arnold (England)
NBNC	National Bank Note Company (US)
OCV	Officina Carte-Valori (Italy)
OBDI	Officina Della Banca D'Italia (Italy)
OFZ	Orell Fÿssli, Zurich (Switzerland)
P&B	Perkins & Bacon (England)
PBC	Perkins, Bacon & Co. (England)
PB&P	Perkins, Bacon & Petch (England)
SBNC	Security Banknote Company (US)
TDLR or (T)DLR	Thomas De La Rue (England)
UPC	Union Printing Co., Ltd. (China)
UPP	Union Publishers & Printers Fed. Inc. (China)
USBNC	United States Banknote Corp. (US)
WDBN	Western District Banknote Fed. Inc.
W&S	Waterlow & Sons Ltd. (England)
WPCo	Watson Printing Co. (China)
WWS	W.W. Sprague & Co. Ltd. (England)

Standard International Grading Terminology and Abbreviations

U.S. and ENGLISH SPEAKING LANDS	UNCIRCULATED	EXTREMELY FINE	VERY FINE	FINE	VERY GOOD	GOOD	POOR
Abbreviation	UNC	EF or XF	VF	FF	VG	G	PR
BRAZIL	(1) DW	(3) S	(5) MBC	(7) BC	(8)	(9) R	UTGeG
DENMARK	O	O1	1+	1	1÷	2	3
FINLAND	0	01	1+	1	1?	2	3
FRANCE	NEUF	SUP	TTB or TB	TB or TB	B	TBC	BC
GERMANY	KFR	II / VZGL	III / SS	IV / S	V / S.g.E.	VI / G.e.	G.e.s.
ITALY	FdS	SPL	BB	MB	B	M	—
JAPAN	未 使 用	極 美 品	美 品	並 品	—	—	—
NETHERLANDS	FDC	Pr.	Z.F.	Fr.	Z.g.	G	—
NORWAY	0	01	1+	1	1+	2	3
PORTUGAL	Novo	Soberbo	Muito bo	—	—	—	—
SPAIN	Lujo	SC, IC or EBC	MBC	BC	—	RC	MC
SWEDEN	0	01	1+	1	1?	2	—

BRAZIL

FE	— Flor de Estampa
S	— Soberba
MBC	— Muito Bem Conservada
BC	— Bem Conservada
R	— Regular
UTGeG	— Um Tanto Gasto e Gasto

DENMARK

O	— Uncirkuleret
01	— Meget Paent Eksemplar
1+	— Paent Eksemplar
1	— Acceptabelt Eksemplar
1	—Noget Slidt Eksemplar
2	— Darlight Eksemplar
3	— Meget Darlight Eskemplar

FINLAND

00	— Kiiltolyönti
0	— Lyöntiveres
01	— Erittäin Hyvä
1+	— Hyvä
1?	— Heikko
2	— Huono

FRANCE

NEUF	— New
FDC	— Fleur De Coin
SPL	— Splendide
SUP	— Superbe
TTB	— Très Très Beau
TB	— Très Beau
B	— Beau
TBC	— Tres Bien Conserve
BC	— Bien Conserve

GERMANY

VZGL	— Vorzüglich
SS	— Sehr schön
S	— Schön
S.g.E.	— Sehr gut erhalten
G.e.	— Gut erhalten
G.e.S.	— Gering erhalten Schlecht

ITALY

Fds	— Fior di Stampa
SPL	— Splendid
BB	— Bellissimo
MB	— Molto Bello
B	— Bello
M	— Mediocre

JAPAN

未 使 用	— Mishiyo
極 美 品	— Goku Bihin
美 品	— Bihin
並 品	— Futuhin

NETHERLANDS

Pr.	— Prachtig
Z.F.	— Zeer Fraai
Fr.	— Fraai
Z.g.	— Zeer Goed
G	— Goed

NORWAY

0	— Usirkuleret eks
01	— Meget pent eks
1+	— Pent eks
1	— Fullgodt eks
1-	— Ikke Fullgodt eks
2	— Darlig eks

ROMANIA

NC	— Necirculata (UNC)
FF	— Foarte Frumoasa (VF)
F	— Frumoasa (F)
FBC	— Foarte Bine Conservata (VG)
BC	— Bine Conservata (G)
M	— Mediocru Conservata (POOR)

SPAIN

EBC	— Extraordinariamente Bien Conservada
SC	— Sin Circular
IC	— Incirculante
MBC	— Muy Bien Conservada
BC	— Bien Conservada
RC	— Regular Conservada
MC	— Mala Conservada

SWEDEN

0	— Ocirkulerat
01	— Mycket Vackert
1+	— Vackert
1	— Fullgott
1?	— Ej Fullgott
2	— Dalight

Foreign Exchange Table

The latest foreign exchange rates below apply to trade with banks in the country of origin. The left column shows the number of units per U.S. dollar at the official rate. The right column shows the number of units per dollar at the free market rate. Rates recorded March 10, 2016.

COUNTRY	#/$	#/$
Afghanistan (New Afghani)	.68	–
Albania (Lek)	.123	–
Algeria (Dinar)	.108	–
Andorra uses Euro	0.910	–
Angola (Readjust Kwanza)	.158	–
Anguilla uses E.C. Dollar	2.70	–
Antigua uses E.C. Dollar	2.70	–
Argentina (Peso)	15.4	–
Armenia (Dram)	.491	–
Aruba (Florin)	1.79	–
Australia (Dollar)	1.34	–
Austria (Euro)	0.910	–
Azerbaijan (New Manat)	1.62	–
Bahamas (Dollar)	0.993	–
Bahrain Is. (Dinar)	0.374	–
Bangladesh (Taka)	.77	–
Barbados (Dollar)	2.00	–
Belarus (Ruble)	21,068	–
Belgium (Euro)	0.910	–
Belize (Dollar)	1.95	–
Benin uses CFA Franc West	519	–
Bermuda (Dollar)	1.00	–
Bhutan (Ngultrum)	.67	–
Bolivia (Buliviano)	6.66	–
Bosnia-Herzegovina (Conv. marka)	1.78	–
Botswana (Pula)	11.0	–
British Virgin Islands uses U.S. Dollar	1.00	–
Brazil (Real)	3.73	–
Brunei (Dollar)	1.36	–
Bulgaria (Lev)	1.77	–
Burkina Faso uses CFA Franc West	.597	–
Burma (Kyat)	1,199	–
Burundi (Franc)	1,540	–
Cambodia (Riel)	3,912	–
Cameroon uses CFA Franc Central	.597	–
Canada (Dollar)	1.34	–
Cape Verde (Escudo)	.100	–
Cayman Islands (Dollar)	0.816	–
Central African Rep.	.597	–
CFA Franc Central	.597	–
CFA Franc West	.597	–
CFP Franc	.109	–
Chad uses CFA Franc Central	.597	–
Chile (Peso)	.669	–
China, P.R. (Renminbi Yuan)	6.52	–
Colombia (Peso)	3,110	–
Comoros (Franc)	.441	–
Congo uses CFA Franc Central	.597	–
Congo-Dem.Rep. (Congolese Franc)	.914	–
Cook Islands (Dollar)	1.48	–
Costa Rica (Colon)	.523	–
Croatia (Kuna)	6.85	–
Cuba (Peso)	.22	27
Cyprus (Euro)	0.910	–
Czech Republic (Koruna)	.24	–
Denmark (Danish Krone)	6.79	–
Djibouti (Franc)	.178	–
Dominica uses E.C. Dollar	2.70	–
Dominican Republic (Peso)	.45	–
East Caribbean (Dollar)	2.70	–
East Timor (U.S. Dollar)	1.00	–
Ecuador (U.S. Dollar)	1.00	–
Egypt (Pound)	7.81	–
El Salvador (U.S. Dollar)	1.00	–
Equatorial Guinea uses CFA Franc Central	.597	–
Eritrea (Nafka)	15.0	–
Estonia (Euro)	0.910	–
Ethiopia (Birr)	.21	–
Euro	0.910	–
Falkland Is. (Pound)	0.704	–

COUNTRY	#/$	#/$
Faroe Islands (Krona)	6.79	–
Fiji Islands (Dollar)	2.08	–
Finland (Euro)	0.910	–
France (Euro)	0.910	–
French Polynesia uses CFP Franc	.108	–
Gabon (CFA Franc)	.597	–
Gambia (Dalasi)	.39	–
Georgia (Lari)	2.45	–
Germany (Euro)	0.910	–
Ghana (New Cedi)	3.84	–
Gibraltar (Pound)	0.704	–
Greece (Euro)	0.910	–
Greenland uses Danish Krone	6.79	–
Grenada uses E.C. Dollar	2.70	–
Guatemala (Quetzal)	7.52	–
Guernsey uses Sterling Pound	0.704	–
Guinea Bissau uses CFA Franc West	.597	–
Guinea Conakry (Franc)	7,571	–
Guyana (Dollar)	.198	–
Haiti (Gourde)	.61	–
Honduras (Lempira)	.22	–
Hong Kong (Dollar)	7.77	–
Hungary (Forint)	.282	–
Iceland (Krona)	.127	–
India (Rupee)	.62	–
Indonesia (Rupiah)	13,123	–
Iran (Rial)	30,195	–
Iraq (Dinar)	1,150	–
Ireland (Euro)	0.910	–
Isle of Man uses Sterling Pound	0.704	–
Israel (New Sheqel)	3.90	–
Italy (Euro)	0.910	–
Ivory Coast uses CFA Franc West	.597	–
Jamaica (Dollar)	.120	–
Japan (Yen)	.113	–
Jersey uses Sterling Pound	0.704	–
Jordan (Dinar)	0.706	–
Kazakhstan (Tenge)	.343	–
Kenya (Shilling)	.100	–
Kiribati uses Australian Dollar	1.34	–
Korea-PDR (Won)	.135	–
Korea-Rep. (Won)	1,211	–
Kuwait (Dinar)	0.300	–
Kyrgyzstan (Som)	.73	–
Laos (Kip)	7,910	–
Latvia (Lats)	0.640	–
Lebanon (Pound)	1,472	–
Lesotho (Maloti)	15.4	–
Liberia (Dollar)	.90	–
Libya (Dinar)	1.36	–
Liechtenstein uses Swiss Franc	0.998	–
Lithuania (Litas)	3.14	–
Luxembourg (Euro)	0.910	–
Macao (Pataca)	7.82	–
Macedonia (New Denar)	.55	–
Madagascar (Ariary)	3,170	–
Malawi (Kwacha)	.715	–
Malaysia (Ringgit)	4.11	–
Maldives (Rufiya)	14.9	–
Mali uses CFA Franc West	.597	–
Malta (Euro)	0.910	–
Marshall Islands uses U.S.Dollar	1.00	–
Mauritania (Ouguiya)	.337	–
Mauritius (Rupee)	.34	–
Mexico (Peso)	17.9	–
Moldova (Leu)	19.7	–
Monaco uses Euro	0.910	–
Mongolia (Tugrik)	2,038	–
Montenegro uses Euro	0.910	–
Montserrat uses E.C. Dollar	2.70	–
Morocco (Dirham)	9.82	–
Mozambique (New Metical)	.49	–
Namibia (Rand)	15.4	–
Nauru uses Australian Dollar	1.34	–
Nepal (Rupee)	.106	–
Netherlands (Euro)	0.910	–

COUNTRY	#/$	#/$
Netherlands Antilles (Gulden)	2.00	–
New Caledonia uses CFP Franc	.109	–
New Zealand (Dollar)	1.48	–
Nicaragua (Cordoba Oro)	.28	–
Niger uses CFA Franc West	.597	–
Nigeria (Naira)	.197	–
Northern Ireland uses Sterling Pound	0.704	–
Norway (Krone)	8.56	–
Oman (Rial)	0.384	–
Pakistan (Rupee)	.103	–
Palau uses U.S.Dollar	1.00	–
Panama (Balboa) uses U.S.Dollar	1.00	–
Papua New Guinea (Kina)	2.98	–
Paraguay (Guarani)	5,591	–
Peru (Nuevo Sol)	3.39	–
Philippines (Peso)	.47	–
Poland (Zloty)	3.93	–
Portugal (Euro)	0.910	–
Qatar (Riyal)	3.64	–
Romania (New Leu)	4.06	–
Russia (Ruble)	.72	–
Rwanda (Franc)	.739	–
St. Helena (Pound)	0.624	–
St. Kitts uses E.C. Dollar	2.70	–
St. Lucia uses E.C. Dollar	2.70	–
St. Vincent uses E.C. Dollar	2.70	–
Samoa (Tala)	2.27	–
San Marino uses Euro	0.910	–
Sao Tome e Principe (Dobra)	22,298	–
Saudi Arabia (Riyal)	3.75	–
Scotland uses Sterling Pound	0.704	–
Senegal uses CFA Franc West	.597	–
Serbia (Dinar)	.112	–
Seychelles (Rupee)	11.8	–
Sierra Leone (Leone)	4,027	–
Singapore (Dollar)	1.38	–
Slovakia (Euro)	0.910	–
Slovenia (Euro)	0.910	–
Solomon Islands (Dollar)	8.10	–
Somalia (Shilling)	.579	–
Somaliland (Somali Shilling)	.579	4,000
South Africa (Rand)	15.4	–
Spain (Euro)	0.910	–
Sri Lanka (Rupee)	.142	–
Sudan (Pound)	6.06	–
Surinam (Dollar)	3.96	–
Swaziland (Lilangeni)	15.4	–
Sweden (Krona)	8.47	–
Switzerland (Franc)	0.998	–
Syria (Pound)	.220	–
Taiwan (NT Dollar)	.33	–
Tajikistan (Somoni)	7.87	–
Tanzania (Shilling)	2,143	–
Thailand (Baht)	.35	–
Togo uses CFA Franc West	.597	–
Tonga (Pa'anga)	2.30	–
Transdniestra (Ruble)	.72	–
Trinidad & Tobago (Dollar)	6.41	–
Tunisia (Dinar)	2.03	–
Turkey (New Lira)	2.91	–
Turkmenistan (Manat)	3.49	–
Turks & Caicos uses U.S. Dollar	1.00	–
Tuvalu uses Australian Dollar	1.34	–
Uganda (Shilling)	3,327	–
Ukraine (Hryvnia)	.26	–
United Arab Emirates (Dirham)	3.67	–
United Kingdom (Sterling Pound)	0.704	–
Uruguay (Peso Uruguayo)	.32	–
Uzbekistan (Sum)	2,846	–
Vanuatu (Vatu)	.111	–
Vatican City uses Euro	0.910	–
Venezuela (New Bolivar)	6.28	35
Vietnam (Dong)	22,003	–
Yemen (Rial)	.215	–
Zambia (Kwacha)	11.3	–
Zimbabwe (Dollar)	.373	–

Standard International Numeral Systems

Prepared especially for the *Standard Catalog of World Paper Money*© 2015 by Krause Publications

Western	0	½	1	2	3	4	5	6	7	8	9	10	50	100	500	1000
Roman			I	II	III	IV	V	VI	VII	VIII	IX	X	L	C	D	M
Arabic-Turkish	٠	١/٢	١	٢	٣	٤	٥	٦	٧	٨	٩	١٠	٥٠	١٠٠	٥٠٠	١٠٠٠
Malay-Persian	٠	١/٢	١	٢	٣	۴	۵	۶	٧	٨	٩	١٠	۵٠	١٠٠	۵٠٠	١٠٠٠
Eastern Arabic	٥	½	١	٢	٣	٤	५	५	٧	٦	٩	١٥	٤٥٥	١٥٥	٤١٥٥	١٥٥٥
Hyderabad Arabic	٥	١/٢	١	٢	٣	٤	٥	٧	٧	٨	٩	١٥	٥٥	١٥٥	٥٥٥	١٥٥٥
Indian (Sanskrit)	०	½	१	२	३	४	५	६	७	८	९	१०	४०	१००	४००	१०००
Assamese	০	½	১	২	৩	৪	৫	৬	৭	৮	৯	১০	৫০	১০০	৫০০	১০০০
Bengali	০	৴৹	১	২	৩	৪	৫	৬	৭	৮	৯	১০	৫০	১০০	৫০০	১০০০
Gujarati	૦	૫	૧	૨	૩	૪	૫	૬	૭	૮	૯	૧૦	૫૦	૧૦૦	૫૦૦	૧૦૦૦
Kutch	૦	½	૧	૨	૩	૪	૫	૬	૭	૮	૯	10	40	100	400	1000
Devavnagri	०	½	१	२	३	४	५	६	७	८	९	१०	४०	१००	४००	१०००
Nepalese	०	⅓	१	२	३	४	५	६	७	८	९	१०	४०	१००	४००	१०००
Tibetan	༠	⅞	༡	༢	༣	༤	༥	༦	༧	༨	༩	༡༠	༤༠	༡༠༠	༤༠༠	༧༠༠༠
Mongolian	᠐	⅗	᠑	᠒	᠓	᠔	᠕	᠖	᠗	᠘	᠙	᠑᠐	᠕᠐	᠑᠐᠐	᠕᠐᠐	᠙᠐᠐᠐
Burmese	၀	⅔	၁	၂	၃	၄	၅	၆	၇	၈	၉	၁၀	၅၀	၁၀၀	၅၀၀	၁၀၀၀
Thai-Lao	๐	⅖	๑	๒	๓	๔	๕	๖	๗	๘	๙	๑๐	๕๐	๑๐๐	๕๐๐	๑๐๐๐
Lao-Laotian	໐		໑	໒	໓	໔	໕	໖	໗	໘	໙	໑໐				
Javanese	꧐		꧑	꧒	꧓	꧔	꧕	꧖	꧗	꧘	꧙	꧑꧐	꧕꧐	꧑꧐꧐	꧕꧐꧐	꧑꧐꧐꧐
Ordinary Chinese Japanese-Korean	零	半	一	二	三	四	五	六	七	八	九	十	十五	百	百五	千
Official Chinese			壹	貳	參	肆	伍	陸	柒	捌	玖	拾	拾伍	佰	佰伍	仟
Commercial Chinese			〡	〢	〣	乂	〥	〦	〧	〨	夊	十	〥十	一百	〥百	一千
Korean		반	일	이	삼	사	오	육	칠	팔	구	십	오십	백	오백	천
Georgian			ა	ბ	გ	დ	ე	ვ	ზ	ჱ	თ	ი	ჲ	რ	ფ	ჰ
Georgian (tens/hundreds)			კ²⁰	ლ³⁰	მ⁴⁰	ნ⁶⁰	ჟ⁷⁰	ჲ⁸⁰	ჳ⁹⁰	პ²⁰⁰	ჟ³⁰⁰	ჯ⁴⁰⁰	ჴ⁶⁰⁰	ჶ⁷⁰⁰	ჷ⁸⁰⁰	
Ethiopian	◆		፩	፪	፫	፬	፭	፮	፯	፰	፱	፲	፶	፻	፭፻	፲፻
Ethiopian (tens)			፳²⁰	፴³⁰	፵⁴⁰	፷⁶⁰	፸⁷⁰	፹⁸⁰	፺⁹⁰							
Hebrew			א	ב	ג	ד	ה	ו	ז	ח	ט	י	נ	ק	תק	תת
Hebrew (tens/hundreds)			כ²⁰	ל³⁰	מ⁴⁰	ס⁶⁰	ע⁷⁰	פ⁸⁰	צ⁹⁰	ר²⁰⁰	ש³⁰⁰	ת⁴⁰⁰	תר⁶⁰⁰	תש⁷⁰⁰	תת⁸⁰⁰	
Greek			Α	Β	Γ	Δ	Ε	Ζ	Η	Θ	Ι		Ν	Ρ	Φ	Α
Greek (tens/hundreds)			Κ²⁰	Λ³⁰	Μ⁴⁰	Ξ⁶⁰	Ο⁷⁰	Π⁸⁰		Σ²⁰⁰	Τ³⁰⁰	Υ⁴⁰⁰	Χ⁶⁰⁰	Ψ⁷⁰⁰	Ω⁸⁰⁰	

A Guide To International Numerics

	ENGLISH	CZECH	DANISH	DUTCH	ESPERANTO	FRENCH
1/4	quarter	jedna ctvrina	én kvart	een-kwart	unu-kvar'ono	quart
1/2	half	jedna polovinal	én halv	halve	unu-du'one	demi
1	one	jedna	én	een	unu	un
2	two	dve	to	twee	du	deux
3	three	tri	tre	drie	tri	trois
4	four	ctyri	fire	vier	kvar	quatre
5	five	pet	fem	vijf	kvin	cinq
6	six	sest	seks	zes	ses	six
7	seven	sedm	syv	zeven	sep	sept
8	eight	osm	otte	acht	ok	huit
9	nine	devet	ni	negen	nau	neuf
10	ten	deset	ti	tien	dek	dix
12	twelve	dvanáct	tolv	twaalf	dek du	douze
15	fifteen	patnáct	femten	vijftien	dek kvin	quinze
20	twenty	dvacet	tyve	twintig	du'dek	vingt
24	twenty-four	dvacetctyri	fireogtyve	vierentwintig	du'dek kvar	vingt-quatre
25	twenty-five	dvacetpet	femogtyve	vijfentwintig	du'dek kvin	vingt-cinq
30	thirty	tricet	tredive	dertig	tri'dek	trente
40	forty	ctyricet	fyrre	veertig	kvar'dek	quarante
50	fifty	padesát	halvtreds	vijftig	kvin'dek	cinquante
60	sixty	sedesát	tres	zestig	ses'dek	soixante
70	seventy	sedmdesát	halvfjords	zeventig	sep'dek	soixante-dix
80	eighty	ösemdesát	firs	tachtig	ok'dek	quatre-vingt
90	ninety	devadesát	halvfems	negentig	nau'dek	quatre-vingt-dix
100	one hundred	sto	hundrede	honderd	unu-cento	cent
1000	thousand	tis'c	tusind	duizend	mil	mille

	GERMAN	HUNGARIAN	INDONESIAN	ITALIAN	NORWEGIAN	POLISH
1/4	viertel	egy-negyed	satu per empat	quarto	en-fjeerdedel	POLISH
1/2	halb	fél	satu per dua	mezzo	halv	jedna czwarta
1	ein	egy	satu	uno	en	podowa
2	zwei	kettö	dua	due	to	jeden
3	drei	három	tiga	tre	tre	dwa
4	vier	négy	empat	quattro	fire	trzy
5	fünf	öt	lima	cinque	fem	cztery
6	sechs	hat	enam	sei	seks	piec'
7	sieben	hét	tujuh	sette	sju	szes'c'
8	acht	nyolc	delapan	otto	atte	siedem
9	neun	kilenc	sembilan	nove	ni	osiem
10	zehn	t'z	sepuluh	dieci	ti	dziewioc'
12	zwölf	tizenkettö	dua belas	dodici	tolv	dziesiec'
15	fünfzehn	tizenöt	lima belas	quindici	femten	dwanas'cie
20	zwanzig	hász	dua puluh	venti	tjue or tyve	piotnas'cie
24	vierundzwanzig	hászonnégy	dua puluh empat	ventiquattro	tjue-fire or tyve-fire	dwadzies'cia
25	fünfundzwanzig	huszonöt	dua puluh lima	venticinque	tjue-fem or tyve-fem	dwadzies'cia-cztery
30	dreissig	harminc	tiga puluh	trenta	tredve	dwadzies'cia-piec
40	vierzig	negyven	empat puluh	quaranta	forti	trydzies'ci
50	fünfzig	ötven	lima puluh	cinquanta	femti	czterdries'ci
60	sechzig	hatvan	enam puluh	sessanta	seksti	piec'dzlesiat
70	siebzig	hetven	tujuh pulu	settanta	sytti	szes'c'dziesiat
80	achtzig	nyolcyan	delapan puluh	ottonta	syttl	siedemdziesiat
90	neunzig	kilencven	sembilan puluh	novanta	nitti	osiemdziesiat
100	hundert	száz	seratus	cento	hundre	dziewiec'dzlesiat
1000	tausend	ezer	seribu	mille	tusen	jeden-sto
						tysiac

	PORTUGUESE	ROMANIAN	SERBO-CROATIAN	SPANISH	SWEDISH	TURKISH
1/4	quarto	un-sfert	jedna ceturlina	carto	en-fjördedel	bir ceyrek
1/2	meio	o-jumatate	jedna polovina	medio	hölft	bir yarim
1	um	un	jedan	uno	en	bir
2	dois	doi	dva	dos	tva	iki
3	trÉs	trei	tri	tres	tre	üc
4	quatro	patru	cetiri	cuatro	fyra	dört
5	cinco	cinci	pet	cinco	fem	bes
6	seis	sase	sest	seis	sex	alti
7	sete	sapte	sedam	siete	sju	yedi
8	oito	opt	osam	ocho	åtta	sekiz
9	nove	noua	devet	nueve	nio	dokuz
10	dez	zece	deset	diez	tio	on
12	doze	doisprezece	dvanaest	doce	tolv	oniki
15	quinze	cincisprezece	petnaest	quince	femton	onbes
20	vinte	douazeci	dvadeset	veinte	tugu	yirmi
24	vinte-quatro	douacei si patru	dvadeset cetiri	veinticuatro	tjugu fyra	jirmidört
25	vinte-cinco	douacei si cinci	dvadeset pet	veinticinco	tjugu fem	yirmibes
30	trinta	treizeci	trideset	treinta	trettio	yirmibes
40	quarenta	patruzeci	cetrdeset	cuarenta	fyrtio	otuz
50	cinquenta	cincizeci	padeset	cincuenta	femtio	kirk
60	sessenta	saizeci	sezdeset	sesenta	sextio	elli
70	setenta	saptezeci	sedamdeset	setenta	sjuttio	altmis
80	oitenta	optzeci	osamdeset	ochenta	åttio	yetmis
90	noventa	nouazeci	devedeset	noventa	nittio	seksen
100	cem	suta	sto	cien	hundra	doksan
1000	mil	mie	Serbo hiljada	mil	tusen	yüz
						bin

Dating

Determining the date of issue of a note is a basic consideration of attribution. As the reading of dates is subject not only to the vagaries of numeric styling, but to variations in dating roots caused by the observation of differing religious eras or regal periods from country to country, making this determination can sometimes be quite difficult. Most countries outside the North African and Oriental spheres rely on Western date numerals and the Christian (AD) reckoning, although in a few instances note dating has been tied to the year of a reign or government.

Countries of the Arabic sphere generally date their issues to the Muslim calendar that commenced on July 16, 622 AD when the prophet Mohammed fled from Mecca to Medina. As this calendar is reckoned by the lunar year of 354, its is about three percent (precisely 3.3 percent) shorter than the Christian year. A conversion formula requires you to subtract that percent from the AH date, and then add 621 to gain the AD date.

A degree of confusion arises here because the Muslim calendar is not always based on the lunar year (AH). Afghanistan and Iran (Persia) used a calendar based on a solar year (SH) introduced around 1920. These dates can be converted to AD by simply adding 621. In 1976, Iran implemented a solar calendar based on the founding of the Iranian monarchy in 559 BC. The first year observed on this new system was 2535(MS) which commenced on March 20, 1976.

Several different eras of reckoning, including the Christian (AD) and Muslim (AH), have been used to date paper money of the Indian subcontinent. The two basic systems are the Vikrama Samvat (VS) era that dates from October 18, 58 BC,. and the Saka (SE) era, the origin of which is reckoned from March 3, 78 AD.

Dating according to both eras appears on notes of several native states and countries of the area.

Thailand (Siam) has observed three different eras for dating. The most predominant is the Buddhist (BE) era originating in 543 BC. Next is the Bangkok or Ratanakosind-sok (RS) era dating from 1781 AD (and consisting of only 3 numerals), followed by the Chula-Sakarat (CS) era dating from 638 AD, with the latter also observed in Burma.

Other calendars include that of the Ethiopian (EE) era that commenced 7 years, 8 months after AD dating, and that of the Hebrew nation beginning on October 7, 3761 BC. Korea claims a dating from 2333 BC which is acknowledged on some note issues.

The following table indicates the years dating from the various eras that correspond to 2012 by Christian (AD) calendar reckoning. It must be remembered that there are overlaps between the eras in some instances:

Christian Era (AD)	— 2012
Mohammedan era (AH)	— AH1433
Solar year (SH)	— SH1391
Monarchic Solar era (MS)	— MS2571
Vikrama Samvat era (VS)	— SE2068
Saka era (SE)	— Saka 1933
Buddhist era (BE)	— BE2555
Bangkok era (RS)	— RS301
Chula-Sakarat era (CS)	— CS1374
Ethiopian era (EE)	— EE2004
Jewish era	— 5772
Korean era	— 4345

Paper money of Oriental origin - principally Japan, Korea, China, Turkestan and Tibet - generally date to the year of the government, dynastic, regnal or cyclical eras, with the dates indicated in Oriental characters usually reading from right to left. In recent years some dating has been according to the Christian calendar and in Western numerals reading from left to right.

More detailed guides to the application of the less prevalent dating systems than those described, and others of strictly local nature, along with the numeral designations employed, are presented in conjunction with the appropriate listings.

Some notes carry dating according to both the locally observed and Christian eras. This is particularly true in the Arabic sphere, where the Muslim date may be indicated in Arabic numerals and the Christian date in Western numerals.

In general the date actually shown on a given paper money issue is indicated in some manner. Notes issued by special Law or Decree will have L or D preceding the date. Dates listed within parentheses may differ from the date appearing on the note; they have been documented by other means. Undated notes are listed with ND, followed by a year only when the year of actual issue is known.

Timing differentials between the 354-day Muslim and the 365-day Christian year cause situations whereby notes bearing dates of both eras have two date combinations that may overlap from one or the other calendar system.

China - Republic 9th year, 1st month, 15th day (15.1.1920), read r. to l.

Russia-1 October 1920

Poland - 28 February 1919

Thailand (Siam) - 1 December 2456

Israel - 1973, 5733

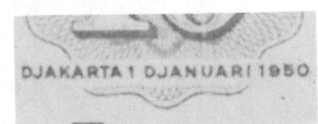

Indonesia - 1 January 1950

Egypt - 1967 December 2

Korea - 4288 (1955)

Greece - 5 March 1943

Afghanistan - Solar Year 1356

HEJIRA DATE CONVERSION CHART

HEJIRA (Hijira, Hegira), the name of the Muslim era (A.H. = Anno Hegirae) dates back to the Christian year 622 when Mohammed "fled" from Mecca, escaping to Medina to avoid persecution from the Koreish tribemen. Based on a lunar year the Muslim year is 11 days shorter.

*=Leap Year (Christian Calendar)

AH Hejira	AD Christian Date	AH Hejira	AD Christian Date	AH Hejira	AD Christian Date	AH Hejira	AD Christian Date	AH Hejira	AD Christian Date
1010	1601, July 2	1088	1677, March 6	1179	1765, June 20	1270	1853, October 4	1361	1942, January 19
1011	1602, June 21	1089	1678, February 23	1180	1766, June 9	1271	1854, September 24	1362	1943, January 8
1012	1603, June 11	1090	1679, February 12	1181	1767, May 30	1272	1855, September 13	1363	1943, December 28
1013	1604, May 30	1091	1680, February 2*	1182	1768, May 18*	1273	1856, September 1*	1364	1944, December 17*
1014	1605, May 19	1092	1681, January 21	1183	1769, May 7	1274	1857, August 22	1365	1945, December 6
1015	1606, May 9	1093	1682, January 10	1184	1770, April 27	1275	1858, August 11	1366	1946, November 25
1016	1607, April 28	1094	1682, December 31	1185	1771, April 16	1276	1859, July 31	1367	1947, November 15
1017	1608, April 17	1095	1683, December 20	1186	1772, April 4*	1277	1860, July 20*	1368	1948, November 3*
1018	1609, April 6	1096	1684, December 8*	1187	1773, March 25	1278	1861, July 9	1369	1949, October 24
1019	1610, March 26	1097	1685, November 28	1188	1774, March 14	1279	1862, June 29	1370	1950, October 13
1020	1611, March 16	1098	1686, November 17	1189	1775, March 4	1280	1863, June 18	1371	1951, October 2
1021	1612, March 4	1099	1687, November 7	1190	1776, February 21*	1281	1864, June 6*	1372	1952, September 21*
1022	1613, February 21	1100	1688, October 26*	1191	1777, February 1	1282	1865, May 27	1373	1953, September 10
1023	1614, February 11	1101	1689, October 15	1192	1778, January 22	1283	1866, May 16	1374	1954, August 30
1024	1615, January 31	1102	1690, October 5	1193	1779, January 19	1284	1867, May 5	1375	1955, August 20
1025	1616, January 20	1103	1691, September 24	1194	1780, January 8*	1285	1868, April 24*	1376	1956, August 8*
1026	1617, January 9	1104	1692, September 12*	1195	1780, December 28*	1286	1869, April 13	1377	1957, July 29
1027	1617, December 29	1105	1693, September 2	1196	1781, December 17	1287	1870, April 3	1378	1958, July 18
1028	1618, December 19	1106	1694, August 22	1197	1782, December 7	1288	1871, March 23	1379	1959, July 7
1029	1619, December 8	1107	1695, August 12	1198	1783, November 26	1289	1872, March 11*	1380	1960, June 25*
1030	1620, November 26	1108	1696, July 31*	1199	1784, November 14*	1290	1873, March 1	1381	1961, June 14
1031	1621, November 16	1109	1697, July 20	1200	1785, November 4	1291	1874, February 18	1382	1962, June 4
1032	1622, November 5	1110	1698, July 10	1201	1786, October 24	1292	1875, February 7	1383	1963, May 25
1033	1623, October 25	1111	1699, June 29	1202	1787, October 13	1293	1876, January 28*	1384	1964, May 13*
1034	1624, October 14	1112	1700, June 18	1203	1788, October 2*	1294	1877, January 16	1385	1965, May 2
1035	1625, October 3	1113	1701, June 8	1204	1789, September 21	1295	1878, January 5	1386	1966, April 22
1036	1626, September 22	1114	1702, May 28	1205	1790, September 10	1296	1878, December 26	1387	1967, April 11
1037	1627, September 12	1115	1703, May 17	1206	1791, August 31	1297	1879, December 15	1388	1968, March 31*
1038	1628, August 31	1116	1704, May 6*	1207	1792, August 19*	1298	1880, December 4*	1389	1969, March 20
1039	1629, August 21	1117	1705, April 25	1208	1793, August 9	1299	1881, November 23	1390	1970, March 9
1040	1630, August 10	1118	1706, April 15	1209	1794, July 29	1300	1882, November 12	1391	1971, February 27
1041	1631, July 30	1119	1707, April 4	1210	1795, July 18	1301	1883, November 2	1392	1972, February 16*
1042	1632, July 19	1120	1708, March 23*	1211	1796, July 7*	1302	1884, October 21*	1393	1973, February 4
1043	1633, July 8	1121	1709, March 13	1212	1797, June 26	1303	1885, October 10	1394	1974, January 25
1044	1634, June 27	1122	1710, March 2	1213	1798, June 15	1304	1886, September 30	1395	1975, January 14
1045	1635, June 17	1123	1711, February 19	1214	1799, June 5	1305	1887, September 19	1396	1976, January 3*
1046	1636, June 5	1124	1712, February 9*	1215	1800, May 25	1306	1888, September 7*	1397	1976, December 23*
1047	1637, May 26	1125	1713, January 28	1216	1801, May 14	1307	1889, August 28	1398	1977, December 12
1048	1638, May 15	1126	1714, January 17	1217	1802, May 4	1308	1890, August 17	1399	1978, December 2
1049	1639, May 4	1127	1715, January 7	1218	1803, April 23	1309	1891, August 7	1400	1979, November 21
1050	1640, April 23	1128	1715, December 27	1219	1804, April 12*	1310	1892, July 26*	1401	1980, November 9*
1051	1641, April 12	1129	1716, December 16*	1220	1805, April 1	1311	1893, July 15	1402	1981, October 30
1052	1642, April 1	1130	1717, December 5	1221	1806, March 21	1312	1894, July 5	1403	1982, October 19
1053	1643, March 22	1131	1718, November 24	1222	1807, March 11	1313	1895, June 24	1404	1983, October 8
1054	1644, March 10	1132	1719, November 14	1223	1808, February 28*	1314	1896, June 12*	1405	1984, September 27*
1055	1645, February 27	1133	1720, November 2*	1224	1809, February 16	1315	1897, June 2	1406	1985, September 16
1056	1646, February 17	1134	1721, October 22	1225	1810, February 6	1316	1898, May 22	1407	1986, September 6
1057	1647, February 6	1135	1722, October 12	1226	1811, January 26	1317	1899, May 12	1408	1987, August 26
1058	1648, January 27	1136	1723, October 1	1227	1812, January 16*	1318	1900, May 1	1409	1988, August 14*
1059	1649, January 15	1137	1724, September 19	1228	1813, January 6	1319	1901, April 20	1409	1988, August 14*
1060	1650, January 4	1138	1725, September 9	1229	1813, December 24	1320	1902, April 10	1410	1989, August 3
1061	1650, December 25	1139	1726, August 29	1230	1814, December 14	1321	1903, March 30	1411	1990, July 24
1062	1651, December 14	1140	1727, August 19	1231	1815, December 3	1322	1904, March 18*	1412	1991, July 13
1063	1652, December 2	1141	1728, August 7*	1232	1816, November 21*	1323	1905, March 8	1413	1992, July 2*
1064	1653, November 22	1142	1729, July 27	1233	1817, November 11	1324	1906, February 25	1414	1993, June 21
1065	1654, November 11	1143	1730, July 17	1234	1818, October 31	1325	1907, February 14	1415	1994, June 10
1066	1655, October 31	1144	1731, July 6	1235	1819, October 20	1326	1908, February 4*	1416	1995, May 31
1067	1656, October 20	1145	1732, June 24*	1236	1820, October 9*	1327	1909, January 23	1417	1996, May 19*
1068	1657, October 9	1146	1733, June 14	1237	1821, September 28	1328	1910, January 13	1418	1997, May 9
1069	1658, September 29	1147	1734, June 3	1238	1822, September 18	1329	1911, January 2	1419	1998, April 28
1070	1659, September 18	1148	1735, May 24	1239	1823, September 8	1330	1911, December 22	1420	1999, April 17
1071	1660, September 6	1149	1736, May 12*	1240	1824, August 26*	1331	1912, December 11	1421	2000, April 6*
1072	1661, August 27	1150	1737, May 1	1241	1825, August 16	1332	1913, November 30	1422	2001, March 26
1073	1662, August 16	1151	1738, April 21	1242	1826, August 5	1333	1914, November 19	1423	2002, March 15
1074	1663, August 5	1152	1739, April 10	1243	1827, July 25	1334	1915, November 9	1424	2003, March 5
1075	1664, July 25	1153	1740, March 29*	1244	1828, July 14*	1335	1916, October 28*	1425	2004, February 22*
1076	1665, July 14	1154	1741, March 19	1245	1829, July 3	1336	1917, October 17	1426	2005, February 10
1077	1666, July 4	1155	1742, March 8	1246	1830, June 22	1337	1918, October 7	1427	2006, January 31
1078	1667, June 23	1156	1743, February 25	1247	1831, June 12	1338	1919, September 26	1428	2007, January 20
1079	1668, June 11	1157	1744, February 15*	1248	1832, May 31*	1339	1920, September 15*	1429	2008, January 10*
1080	1669, June 1	1158	1745, February 3	1249	1833, May 21	1340	1921, September 4	1430	2008, December 29
1081	1670, May 21	1159	1746, January 24	1250	1834, May 10	1341	1922, August 24	1431	2009, December 18
1082	1671, May 10	1160	1747, January 13	1251	1835, April 29	1342	1923, August 14	1432	2010, December 8
1083	1672, April 29	1161	1748, January 2	1252	1836, April 18*	1343	1924, August 2*	1433	2011, November 27*
1084	1673, April 18	1162	1748, December 22*	1253	1837, April 7	1344	1925, July 22	1434	2012, November 15
1085	1674, April 7	1163	1749, December 11	1254	1838, March 27	1345	1926, July 12	1435	2013, November 5
1086	1675, March 28	1164	1750, November 30	1255	1839, March 17	1346	1927, July 1	1436	2014, October 25
1087	1676, March 16*	1165	1751, November 20	1256	1840, March 5*	1347	1928, June 20*	1437	2015, October 15*
		1166	1752, November 8*	1257	1841, February 23	1348	1929, June 9	1438	2016, October 3
		1167	1753, October 29	1258	1842, February 12	1349	1930, May 29	1439	2017, September 22
		1168	1754, October 18	1259	1843, February 1	1350	1931, May 19	1440	2018, September 12
		1169	1755, October 7	1260	1844, January 22*	1351	1932, May 7*	1441	2019, September 1*
		1170	1756, September 26*	1261	1845, January 10	1352	1933, April 26	1442	2020, August 20
		1171	1757, September 15	1262	1845, December 30	1353	1934, April 16	1443	2021, August 10
		1172	1758, September 4	1263	1846, December 20	1354	1935, April 5	1444	2022, July 30
		1173	1759, August 25	1264	1847, December 9	1355	1936, March 24*	1445	2023, July 19*
		1174	1760, August 13*	1265	1848, November 27*	1356	1937, March 14	1446	2024, July 8
		1175	1761, August 2	1266	1849, November 17	1357	1938, March 3	1447	2025, June 27
		1176	1762, July 23	1267	1850, November 6	1358	1939, February 21	1448	2026, June 17
		1177	1763, July 12	1268	1851, October 27	1359	1940, February 10*	1449	2027, June 6*
		1178	1764, July 1*	1269	1852, October 15*	1360	1941, January 29	1450	2028, May 25

Country / Bank Identification Guide

Afghanistan / Bank of Afghanistan

Belarus / Belarus National Bank

Algeria / Banque Centrale D' Algerie

Bulgaria / Bulgarian National Bank

Armenia / Armenia Republic Bank

Cambodia / National Bank of Cambodia

Armenia / Armenia Republic Bank

Georgia / Georgian National Bank

Belarus / Belarus National Bank

Greece / Bank of Greece

Kazakhstan / Kazakhsta National Bank

Mongolia / Mongol Bank

North Korea / Korean Central Bank

Nepal / State Bank

Kyrgystan / Kyrgyz Bank

Thailand / Bank of Thailand

Lao / Bank of the Lao PDR

Transnistria / Banka Nistriana

Libya / Bank of Libya

Uzbekistan / Central Bank of Uzbekistan Republic

Macedonia / National Bank of the Republic of Macedonia

Ukraine / Unkranian National Bank

International Bank Note Society

The International Bank note Society (IBNS) was formed in 1961 to promote the study and collecting of world paper money. A membership of almost 2,000 in over 90 nations draws on the services of the Society for advancing their knowledge and their collections.

The benefits of the society include the quarterly IBNS Journal, a full color, 80-page magazine featuring learned writings on the notes of the world, their history, artistry and technical background. Additionally each member receives a directory, which lists members by name—with their contact details and collecting interests—as well as by geographic location. The Society conducts auctions in which all members may participate.

One of the greatest strengths of IBNS membership is the facility for correspondence with other members around the world for purposes of exchanging notes, and for obtaining information and assistance with research projects or the identification of notes. Information about the Society can be found at www.theIBNS.org

Application for Membership in the International Bank Note Society

Name: _____

Address: _____

City: _____

Province/State: _____

Postal/Zip Code: _____

Country: _____

Telephone: _____

E-mail: _____

Website: _____

Collecting Interest: _____

Do you want your postal address and web site published in the printed Membership Directory? ☐ Yes ☐ No

Do you want your e-mail address published in the printed Membership Directory? ☐ Yes ☐ No

Do you want your postal address and web site published in the PDF version of the Membership Directory? ☐ Yes ☐ No

Do you want your email address published in the PDF version of the Membership Directory? ☐ Yes ☐ No

Do you want your e-mail address to appear on the IBNS website? ☐ Yes ☐ No

Are you a banknote dealer? ☐ Yes ☐ No

Type of Membership:

Individual	☐ $US33.00	☐ £20.00	☐ €25
Group	☐ $US33.00	☐ £20.00	☐ €25
Junior (Under 18)	☐ $US16.50	☐ £10.00	☐ €12.50
Family	☐ $US33.00	☐ £20.00	☐ €25

Application for membership must be completed on line at:
www.theIBNS.org

For further information please contact **us-secretary@ibns.biz** or **uk-secretary@ibns.biz**

Specimen notes

To familiarize private banks, central banks, law enforcement agencies and treasuries around the world with newly issued currency, many nations provide special "Specimen" examples of their notes. Specimens are actual bank notes, complete with dummy or all zero serial numbers and signatures bearing the overprinted and/or perforated word "SPECIMEN" in the language of the country of origin itself or where the notes were printed.

Some countries have made specimen notes available for sale to collectors. These include Cuba, Czechoslovakia, Poland and Slovakia after World War II and a special set of four denominations of Jamaica notes bearing red matched star serial numbers. Also, in 1978, the Franklin Mint made available to collectors specimen notes from 15 nations, bearing matching serial numbers and a Maltese cross device used as a prefix. Several other countries have also participated in making specimen notes available to collectors at times.

Aside from these collectors issues, specimen notes may sometimes comand higher prices than regular issue notes of the same type, even though there are far fewer collectors of specimens. In some cases, notably older issues in high denominations, specimens may be the only form of such notes available to collectors today. Specimen notes are not legal tender or redeemable, thus have no real "face value".

The most unusual forms of specimens were produced by Waterlow and Sons. They printed special off colored notes for salesman's sample books adding the word SPECIMEN and their seal.

Some examples of how the word "SPECIMEN" is represented in other languages or on notes of other countries follow:

AMOSTRA: Brazil
CAMPIONE: Italy
CONTOH: Malaysia
EKSEMPLAAR: South Africa
ESPƒCIME: Portugal and Colonies
ESPECIMEN: Various Spanish-speaking nations
GIAY MAU: Vietnam
MINTA: Hungary
MODELO: Brazil
MODEL: Albania
MUSTER: Austria, Germany
MUESTRA: Various Spanish-speaking nations
NUMUNDEDIR GECMEZ: Turkey
ORNEKTIR GECMEZ: Turkey
ОБРАЗЕЦ or **ОБРАЗЕЦЪ:** Bulgaria, Russia, U.S.S.R.
PARAUGS: Latvia
PROFTRYK: Sweden
UZORAK: Croatia
WZOR: Poland
ЗАГВАР: Mongolia

Language	January	February	March	April	May	June	July	August	September	October	November	December
English	January	February	March	April	May	June	July	August	September	October	November	December
Albanian	Kallnuer	Fruer	Mars	Prill	Maj	Qershuer	Korrik	Gusht	Shtatuer	Tetuer	Nanduer	Dhetuer
Czech	Leden	Únor	Brezen	Duben	Kveten	Cerven	Cervenec	Srpen	Zári	Rijen	Listopad	Prosinec
Danish	Januar	Februar	Maart	April	Maj	Juni	Juli	August	September	Oktober	November	December
Dutch	Januari	Februari	Maart	April	Mei	Juni	Juli	Augustus	September	Oktober	November	December
Estonian	Jaanuar	Veebruar	Marts	Aprill	Mai	Juuni	Juuli	August	September	Oktoober	November	Detsember
French	Janvier	Fevrier	Mars	Avril	Mai	Juin	Jillet	Août	September	Octobre	Novembre	Decembre
Finnish	Tammikuu	Helmikuu	Maaliskuu	Huhtikuu	Toukokuu	Kesakuu	Heinakuu	Elokuu	Syyskuu	Lokakuu	Marraskuu	Joulukuu
German	Januar	Februar	Marz	April	Mai	Juni	Juli	August	September	Oktober	November	Dezember
Hungarian	Januar	Februar	Marcius	Aprilis	Majus	Junius	Julius	Augusztus	Szeptember	Oktober	November	December
Indonesian	Djanuari	Februari	Maret	April	Mai	Djun	Djuli	Augustus	September	Oktober	Nopember	Desember
Italian	Gennaio	Fabbraio	Marzo	Aprile	Maggio	Giugno	Lugio	Agosto	Settembre	Ottobre	Novembre	Dicembre
Lithuanian	Sausis	Vasaris	Kovas	Balandis	Geguzis	Birzeis	Lepos	Rugpiutis	Rugsejis	Spalis	Lapkritis	Gruodis
Norwegian	Januar	Februar	Mars	April	Mai	Juni	Juli	August	September	Oktober	November	Desember
Polish	Styczen	Luty	Marzec	Kwiecien	Maj	Cerwec	L piec	Sierpien	Wrzesien	Pazdziernik	Listopad	Grudzien
Portuguese	Janerio	Fevereiro	Marco	Abril	Maio	Junho	Julho	Agcsto	Setembro	Outubro	Novembro	Dezembro
Romanian	Ianuarie	Februarie	Martie	Aprilie	Mai	Iunie	Iulie	August	Septembrie	Octombrie	Noiembrie	Decembrie
Croatian	Sijecanj	Veljaca	Ozujak	Travanj	Svibanj	Lipanj	Srpanj	Kolovoz	Rujan	Listopad	Studeni	Prosinac
Spanish	Enero	Febrero	Marzo	Abril	Mayo	Junio	Julio	Agosto	Septiembre	Octubre	Noviembre	Diciembre
Swedish	Januari	Februari	Mars	April	Maj	Juni	Jli	Augusti	September	Oktober	November	December
Turkish	Ocak	Subat	Mart	Nisan	Mayis	Haziran	Tammuz	Agusto	Eylul	Ekim	Kasim	Aralik
Arabic-New (condensed)	يناير	فبراير	مارس	أبريل	مايو	يونيو	يوليو	أغسطس	سبتمبر	أكتوبر	نوفمبر	ديسمبر
(extended)	كانون الثاني	شباط	آذار	نيسان	أيار	حزيران	تموز	آب	أيلول	تشرين الأول	تشرين الثاني	كانون الأول
Persian (Solar)	فروردین	اردیبهشت	خرداد	تیر	مرداد	شهریور	مهر	آبان	آذر	دی	بهمن	اسفند
(Lunar)	محرم	صفر	ربیع الأول	ربیع الثاني	جمادى الأول	جمادى الثاني	رجب	شعبان	رمضان	شوال	ذو القعدة	ذو الحجة
Chinese	正月	二月	三月	四月	五月	六月	七月	八月	九月	十月	十一月	十二月
Japanese	一月	二月	三月	四月	五月	六月	七月	八月	九月	十月	十一月	十二月
Greek	Ιανουάριος	Φεβρουάριος	Μάρτιος	Απρίλιος	Μάιος	Ιούνιος	Ιούλιος	Αύγουστος	Σεπτέμβριος	Οκτώβριος	Νοέμβριος	Δεκέμβριος
Russian	ЯНВАРЬ	ФЕВРАЛЬ	МАРТ	АПРЕЛЬ	МАЙ	ИЮНЬ	ИЮЛЬ	АВГУСТ	СЕНТЯБРЬ	ОКТЯБРЬ	НОЯБРЬ	ДЕКАБРЬ
Serbian	Jануар	Фебруар	Март	Април	Мај	Jун	Jул	Август	Септембар	Октобар	Новембар	Децембар
Ukranian	Січень	Лютий	Березень	Квітень	Травень	Червень	Липень	Серпень	Вересень	Жовтень	Листопад	Грудень
Yiddish	יאַנואַר	פֿעברואַר	מערץ	אַפּריל	מיי	יוני	יולי	אויגוסט	סעפּטעמבער	אָקטאָבער	נאָוועמבער	דעצעמבער
Hebrew (Israeli)	ינואר	פברואר	מרץ	אפריל	מאי	יוני	יולי	אוגוסט	ספטמבר	אוקטובר	נובמבר	דצמבר

Note: Word spellings and configurations as represented on actual notes may vary significantly from those shown on this chart.

Security Devices

ASCENDING SIZE SERIAL NUMBER - A serial number with each digit slightly increasing in height and width. Both horizontal and vertical formats have been used. Czech Republic and Slovakia are among the countries where this may be found.

BAR CODE AND NUMERALS - Used mainly by banks for checks. Some countries have used these on banknotes. Scotland has a bar code, and Canada has used it with serial numbers. Sometimes magnetic.

COLORED FIBERS - Fibers usually red, blue or green, that are added either into the pulp mix to be randomly flowed onto the paper as it is made, or distributed onto the drying paper in particular areas of the page forming 'bars' of colored fibers, quite visible to the naked eye.

EMBEDDED SECURITY THREAD - A high strength thread, sometimes magnetic, embedded into the paper at the beginning of the drying stage. Looks to the eye as a solid dark strip within the paper.

FACE-BACK OPTICAL REGISTRATION DESIGN (TRANSPARENT REGISTER) - A design technique where half of an image in a framed area is printed on the face, and the other half is printed on the back, in exact register, so when held to a light, the two half images form one full image.

FOIL IMPRINTS - Shaped metal foil applied to the printed note, usually with an adhesive. Sometimes the foil is embossed with an image.

HOLOGRAM - Shiny application to the note containing an image that changes in design and color depending upon the viewing angle.

INVISIBLE PRINTING - Designs printed with inks detectable only when viewed under bright sunlight or ultraviolet light. Sometimes used to replace the more expensive watermark on low value notes.

LATENT IMPRESSIONS - Portions of the note containing sculptured engraving, making some legends or designs visible only when held to the light at certain angles.

KINEGRAM(r) - Similar to a foil imprint, the design and color changes at different viewing angles.

METALLIC INK - An ink with very fine granules of metal, thus giving the ink a metallic sheen.

MICRO PRINTING - Very small letters added to an intaglio printing plate, sometimes as single lines, or in multiple repeating lines forming a larger block in the underprint design. Intaglio printing keeps the design sharp and clear, but if the note is counterfeit the microprinted area usually becomes muddy and unclear.

OPTICAL VARIABLE DEVICE (OVD) - A foil that displays a three-dimensional image when viewed under proper lighting conditions. Similar to foil imprints.

OPTICALLY VARIABLE INK - An ink when printed in a special pattern changes shades when viewed and then tilted slightly.

PLANCHETTES - Tiny multicolored discs of paper embedded into the pulp mix or randomly sprinkled throughout the paper as it is drying.

RAISED MARKS - A type of braille design in notes, enabling blind people to identify note values.

SEGMENTED SECURITY THREAD - A continuous security thread, usually wide and with lettering, that is added into the paper during the drying process. Once added, a special tool is used to scrape the wet paper off only above the thread, and usually in a particular pattern, thus exposing alternate areas of the embedded thread.

UV-ULTRAVIOLET (FLOURESCENT) - When viewed in a darkened area, and exposed to a special low or high frequency UV light, a design, value, or paper fibers will glow.

WATERMARK - Extensively used as a security measure, the watermark is created by a raised design on a drying cylinder applied towards the end of the paper manufacturing process. The raised design causes a thin area in the paper which when held to the light reveals an image. This image can be words, design, or a portrait. Recent developments have made graduations available. Thus, rather than a light/dark watermark, a gradual light to dark fade can be achieved.

AFGHANISTAN

The Islamic Republic of Afghanistan, which occupies a mountainous region of Southwest Asia, has an area of 647,500 sq. km. and a population of 32.74 million. Capital: Kabul. It is bordered by Iran, Pakistan, Tajikistan, Turkmonistan, Uzbekistan and Peoples Republic of China's Sinkiang Province. Agriculture and herding are the principal industries; textile mills and cement factories are recent additions to the industrial sector. Cotton, wool, fruits, nuts, sheepskin coats and hand-woven carpets are exported but foreign trade has been sporadic since 1979.

Ahmad Shah Durrani unified the Pashtun tribes and founded Afghanistan in 1747. The country served as a buffer between the British and Russian empires until it won independence from national British control in 1919. A brief experiment in democracy ended in a 1973 coup and a 1978 Communist counter-coup. The Soviet Union invaded in 1979 to support the tottering Afghan Communist regime, touching off a long and destructive war. The USSR withdrew in 1989 under relentless pressure by internationally supported anti-Communist mujahedin rebels. A series of subsequent civil wars saw Kabul finally fall in 1996 to the Taliban, a hardline Pakistani-sponsored movement that emerged in 1994 to end the country's civil war and anarchy. Following the 11 September 2001 terrorist attacks in New York City, a US, Allied, and anti-Taliban Northern Alliance military action toppled the Taliban for sheltering Osama Bin Ladin. The UN-sponsored Bonn Conference in 2001 established a process for political reconstruction that included the adoption of a new constitution, a presidential election in 2004, and National Assembly elections in 2005. In December 2004, Hamid Karzai became the first democratically elected president of Afghanistan and the National Assembly was inaugurated the following December. Despite gains toward building a stable central government, a resurgent Taliban and continuing provincial instability - particularly in the south and the east - remain serious challenges for the Afghan Government.

RULERS:

Amanullah, SH1298-1307/1919-1929AD

Habibullah Ghazi (rebel, known as Baccha-i-Saqao) AH1347-1348/1929AD

Muhammad Nadir Shah, SH1308-1312/1929-1933AD

Muhammad Zahir Shah, SH1312-1352/1933-1973AD

MONETARY SYSTEM:

1 Rupee = 100 Paise to 1925

1 Rupees = 10 Afghani, 1925-

1 Afghani = 100 Pul

1 Amani = 20 Afghani

1 "new" Afghani = 1000 "old" Afghani, 2002-

KINGDOM - POST REBELLION

Bank of Afghanistan

1961-63 Issues

37   10 Afghanis

SH1340 (1961). Brown on multicolor underprint. King Muhammad Zahir (third portrait) at left. Back: Mosque of Khwajeh Mohammad Abu-Nasr Parsa in Balkh at center. Watermark: Muhammad Zahir. Printer: TDLR.

		VF	UNC
a. Issued note.		1.00	6.00
s. Specimen.		—	75.00

38   20 Afghanis

SH 1340 (1961). Blue on multicolor underprint. King Muhammad Zahir (third portrait) at left. Back: Independence monument in Kabul at center. Watermark: Muhammad Zahir. Printer: TDLR.

VF	UNC
1.00	9.00

39   50 Afghanis   **VF   UNC**

SH1340 (1961). Green on multicolor underprint. King Muhammad Zahir (third portrait) at left. Back: Mausoleum of King Nadir Shah in Kabul at center. Watermark: Muhammad Zahir. Printer: TDLR.

	VF	UNC
a. Issued note.	1.50	15.00
s. Specimen.	—	75.00

40   100 Afghanis   **VF   UNC**

SH1340 (1961). Red on multicolor underprint. King Muhammad Zahir (third portrait) at left. Watermark: Muhammad Zahir. Printer: TDLR.

VF	UNC
7.50	32.50

40A   500 Afghanis   **VF   UNC**

SH1340 (1961). Orange on multicolor underprint. King Muhammad Zahir (third portrait) at left. Watermark: Muhammad Zahir. Printer: TDLR.

	VF	UNC
a. Issued note.	50.00	250
s. Specimen.	—	125

41   500 Afghanis   **VF   UNC**

SH1340 (1961); SH1342 (1963). Olive-brown on multicolor underprint. King Muhammad Zahir (third portrait) at left. Watermark: Muhammad Zahir. Printer: TDLR.

	VF	UNC
a. 8 digit serial #. SH1340.	25.00	150
b. Serial # with prefix. SH1342.	30.00	150
s. Specimen.	—	125

42   1000 Afghanis   **VF   UNC**

SH1340 (1961); SH1342 (1963), Blue-gray on multicolor underprint. King Muhammad Zahir (third portrait) at left. Back: Arch of Qila'-e Bost in Lashkargah at right. Watermark: Muhammad Zahir. Printer: TDLR.

	VF	UNC
a. 8 digit serial #. SH1340.	35.00	200
b. Prefix serial #. SH1342.	20.00	150

1967 Issue

43 50 Afghanis
SH1346 (1967). Green on multicolor underprint. King Muhammad Zahir at left. Back: Arg-e Shahi, King's palace at center right. Watermark: Muhammad Zahir. Printer: TDLR without imprint.

		VF	UNC
a. Issued note.		1.50	6.00
s. Specimen.		—	75.00

44 100 Afghanis
SH 1346 (1967). Lilac on multicolor underprint. King Muhammad Zahir at left. Back: Mosque in Kabul at center right. Watermark: Muhammad Zahir. Printer: TDLR without imprint.

		VF	UNC
a. Issued note.		2.50	9.00
s. Specimen.		—	75.00

45 500 Afghanis
SH1346 (1967). Black and dark blue on multicolor underprint. King Muhammad Zahir at left. Back: Qandahar Airport at right. Watermark: Muhammad Zahir. Printer: TDLR without imprint.

		VF	UNC
a. Issued note.		12.50	50.00
s. Specimen.		—	75.00

46 1000 Afghanis
SH1346 (1967). Brown on multicolor underprint. King Muhammad Zahir at left. Watermark: Muhammad Zahir. Printer: TDLR without imprint.

		VF	UNC
a. Issued note.		15.00	80.00
s. Specimen.		—	75.00

REPUBLIC
Bank of Afghanistan
1973-78 Issue

47 10 Afghanis
SH1352 (1973); SH1354 (1975); SH1356 (1977). Green on multicolor underprint. President Muhammad Daud at left. Back: Arch of Qila'-e Bost in Lashkargah at center. Watermark: Muhammad Daud.

		VF	UNC
a. SH1352 (1973).		0.50	2.25
b. SH1354 (1975).		0.50	2.25
c. SH1356 (1977).		0.50	2.25
s. Specimen.		—	50.00

48 20 Afghanis
SH1352 (1973); SH1354 (1975); SH1356 (1977). Purple on multicolor underprint. President Muhammad Daud at left. Back: Canal at right. Watermark: Muhammad Daud.

		VF	UNC
a. SH1352 (1973).		0.50	3.00
b. SH1354 (1975).		0.50	3.00
c. SH1356 (1977).		0.50	3.00
s. Specimen.		—	50.00

49 50 Afghanis
SH1352 (1973); SH1354 (1975); SH1356 (1977). Green on multicolor underprint. President Muhammad Daud at left. Back: Men riding yaks at center. Watermark: Muhammad Daud.

		VF	UNC
a. SH1352 (1973).		1.00	5.00
b. SH1354 (1975).		1.00	5.00
c. SH1356 (1977).		1.00	5.00
s. Specimen.		—	50.00

50 100 Afghanis
SH1352 (1973); SH1354 (1975); SH1356 (1977). Brown-lilac on multicolor underprint. President Muhammad Daud at left. Back: Friday Mosque in Herât at center right. Watermark: Muhammad Daud.

	VF	UNC
a. SH1352 (1973).	2.00	14.00
b. SH1354 (1975).	2.00	14.00
c. SH1356 (1977).	2.00	14.00
s. Specimen.	—	50.00

51 500 Afghanis
SH1352 (1973); SH1354 (1975). Blue on multicolor underprint. President Muhammad Daud at left. Back: Fortified tribal village at center right. Watermark: Muhammad Daud.

	VF	UNC
a. SH1352 (1973).	3.00	30.00
b. SH1354 (1975).	3.00	30.00
s. Specimen.	—	50.00

52 500 Afghanis
SH1356 (1977). Brown on multicolor underprint. President Muhammad Daud at left. Back: Fortified tribal village at center right. Watermark: Muhammad Daud.

	VF	UNC
a. Issued note.	5.00	25.00
s. Specimen.	—	50.00

53 1000 Afghanis
SH1352 (1973); SH1354 (1975); SH1356 (1977). Brown on multicolor underprint. President Muhammad Daud at left. Back: Mosque of Mazâr-e Sharf, the Noble Shrine at center right. Watermark: Muhammad Daud.

	VF	UNC
a. SH1352 (1973).	3.50	25.00
b. SH1354 (1975).	3.50	25.00
c. SH1356 (1977).	3.50	25.00

KHALQ DEMOCRATIC REPUBLIC
Da Afghanistan Bank
1978 Issue

53A 20 Afghanis
AH1357 (1978). Purple on multicolor underprint. With Khalq Government emblem from flag at top left. Back: Fortress at center.

	VF	UNC
s. Specimen. Overprint: SPECIMEN. Punched hole cancelled.	—	125

54 50 Afghanis
SH1357 (1978). Blue-green on multicolor underprint. With Khalq Government emblem from flag at top right center. Back: Dar-al-Aman Palace in Kabul.

	VF	UNC
	3.00	20.00

DEMOCRATIC REPUBLIC
Da Afghanistan Bank
1979 Issue

55 10 Afghanis
SH1358 (1979). Green and blue on multicolor underprint. Bank arms with horseman at top center right. Back: Mountain road scene at center.

	VF	UNC
a. Issued note.	0.20	1.00
s. Specimen. Punch hole cancelled, overprint: *SPECIMEN.*	—	8.00

56 20 Afghanis
SH 1358 (1979). Purple on multicolor underprint. Bank arms with horseman at top center right. Signature varieties. Back: Building and mountains at center.

	VF	UNC
a. Issued note.	0.25	1.25
s. Specimen. Punch hole cancelled, overprint *SPECIMEN.*	—	20.00

57 50 Afghanis
SH 1358-70 (1979-91). Greenish black with black text on multicolor underprint. Bank arms with horseman at top center left. Back: Dar-al-Aman Palace in Kabul.

	VF	UNC
a. SH1358 (1979). 2 signature varieties.	0.20	1.00
b. SH1370 (1991).	0.25	1.00
s. Specimen. As a. Punch hole cancelled, overprint: *SPECIMEN.*	—	40.00

58 100 Afghanis

SH1358-70 (1979-91). UV: threads fluoresce blue, values yellow. Deep red-violet on multicolor underprint. Bank arms with horseman at top center. Farm worker in wheat field at right. Back: Hydroelectric dam in mountains at center.

	VF	UNC
a. SH1358 (1979). 2 signature varieties.	0.50	1.00
b. SH1369 (1990).	0.50	1.00
c. SH1370 (1991).	0.25	1.00

59 500 Afghanis

SH1358 (1979). Violet and dark blue on multicolor underprint. Bank arms with horseman at top center; horsemen competing in Buzkashi at right. Back: Fortress at Kabul at left center.

	VF	UNC
	2.00	12.00

60 500 Afghanis

SH1358-70 (1979-91). UV: threads fluoresce blue. Reddish-brown, deep green and deep brown on multicolor underprint. Bank arms with horseman at top center; horsemen competing in Buzkashi at right. Back: Fortress at Kabul at left center.

	VF	UNC
a. SH1358 (1979).	0.75	2.00
b. SH1369 (1990).	1.00	2.00
c. SH1370 (1991).	0.25	1.00

61 1000 Afghanis

SH1358-70 (1979-91). Dark brown and deep red-violet on multicolor underprint. Bank arms with horseman at top center; Mosque at Mazar-e-Sharif at right. Back: Victory Arch near Kabul at left center.

	VF	UNC
a. SH1358 (1979).	2.50	3.00
b. SH1369 (1990).	0.50	2.50
c. SH1370 (1991). UV: Face value fluoresce orange. One or two letter characters in series denominator.	0.25	1.25

62 5000 Afghanis

	VF	UNC
SH1372 (1993). UV: Fibers fluoresce green, red; face: value yellow, serial #s red, security thread red. Violet and blue-black on multicolor underprint. Mosque with minaret at right. Bank arms with horseman at top center. Back: Tomb of King Habibullah, Jalalabad at center. Watermark: Bank arms.	0.50	3.00

63 10,000 Afghanis

SH1372 (1993). UV: Fibers fluoresce green, red; face: value green, serial #s red. Black, deep olive-green and deep blue-green on multicolor underprint. Bank arms with horseman at top left center; gateway between minarets at right. Back: Arched gateway at Bost in center. Watermark: Bank arms.

	VF	UNC
a. Without small space between *Da* and *Afghanistan* on back.	0.75	2.50
b. With small space between *Da* and *Afghanistan* on back.	0.50	2.00

REPUBLIC (2001)

Da Afghanistan Bank

2002 Issue

1000 'old' afghani = 1 'new' afghani.

64 1 Afghani

SH1381 (2002); SH1383 (2004). Purple on multicolor underprint. Bank arms with horseman at top left center; bank name around ancient coin, cornucopia pair below. Back: Mosque at Mazar-i Sharif at center. Watermark: Bank arms. 131x55mm.

	VF	UNC
a. SH1381 (2002).	FV	0.50
b. SH1383 (2004).	FV	0.50

65 2 Afghanis

SH1381 (2002); SH1383 (2004). Slate blue on multicolor underprint. Bank name around ancient coin, cornucopia pair below. Back: Victory Arch in Paghman Gardens near Kabul. 131x55mm.

	VF	UNC
a. SH1381 (2002).	FV	0.50
b. SH1383 (2004).	FV	0.50
s. Specimen.	—	10.00

66 5 Afghanis

VF   UNC

SH1381 (2002); SH1383 (2004). Olive on multicolor underprint. Bank name around ancient coin, cornucopia pair below. Back: Bala Hissar Fortress in Kabul at center. 131x55mm.

a. SH1381 (2002). FV 0.75
b. SH1383 (2004). FV 0.75

67 10 Afghanis

VF   UNC

SH1381 (2002); SH1383 (2004). Segmented security thread. Green and brown on multicolor underprint. Ahmed Shah Durrashi Mausoleum in Kandahar at right. Back: Victory Arch in Paghman Gardens near Kabul at center. 136x56mm.

a. SH1381 (2002). FV 1.25
b. SH1383 (2004). FV 1.25

67A 10 Afghanis

VF   UNC

SH1387 (2008). Similar to #67 but different gilloche at bottom center. FV 1.25

68 20 Afghanis

VF   UNC

SH1381 (2002)-. Green and purple on multicolor underprint. Rowza Sultan Mahmud of Ishazni's Tomb at right. Back: Arg-e Shahi, King's Palace at center. 140x58mm.

a. SH1381 (2002). FV 1.50
b. SH1383 (2004). FV 1.50
c. SH1387 (2008). Printer TDLR. FV 1.25
d. SH1387 (2008). Cornerstones added to watermark. Signature: Abdul Qadeeer Fitrat and Omar Zakhilwal. 0.40 1.50

69 50 Afghanis

VF   UNC

SH1381 (2002)-. Green and brown on multicolor underprint. Shah Do Shamira Mosque at right. Back: Salang Pass at center. 144x60mm.

a. SH1381 (2002). FV 4.00
b. SH1383 (2004). Signatures: Noorullah Delawari and Anwar ul-Haq Ahady. FV 4.00
c. SH1387 (2008). Cornerstone watermarks. Slight color change in center. FV 3.50
d. SH1389 (2010). FV 3.50
e. SH1391 (2012). FV 3.00

70 100 Afghanis

VF   UNC

SH1381 (2002); SH1383 (2004). Pule Khighti Mosque at right. Back: Arch at Qila'-e Bost. 148x62mm.

a. SH1381 (2002). FV 5.00
b. SH1383 (2004). FV 5.00

71 500 Afghanis

VF   UNC

SH 1381 (2002); SH1383 (2004). Violet and blue on multicolor underprint. Khwaja Abdullah Ansari in Herat at right, bank seal above. Back: Kandahar Airport control tower at center. Printer: G&D. 152x64mm.

a. SH 1381 (2002). FV 17.50

72 1000 Afghanis

VF   UNC

SH 1381 (2002); SH 1383 (2004). Orange and brown on yellow and multicolor underprint. Mazaz e-Sharif Shrine of Hazrat Ali at right, bank seal above. Back: Mausoleum of Ahmad Shah Durani in Kandahar at center. Printer: G&D. 156x66mm.

a. SH 1381 (2002). FV 35.00

2004 Issue

73 500 Afghanis

VF   UNC

SH1383 (2004). Violet and blue on multicolor underprint. Masjid-i Jami' (Friday Mosque) in Herat at right, bank seal above. Left end value at top. Back: Kandahar Airport control tower at center. Printer: G&D. 152x64mm. FV 17.50

74 1000 Afghanis

VF   UNC

SH1383 (2004). Orange and brown on yellow and multicolor underprint. Blue Mosque in Mazari Sharif at right, bank seal above. Left end value at top. Signatrue varieties. Back: Mausoleum ofr Ahmad Shah Durrani in Kandahar at center. Printer: G&D. 158x66mm. FV 35.00

2004; 2008 Issue

75   100 Afghanis   **VF   UNC**
SH 1387 (2008)-. Purple and multicolor. Pul-e Khishti Mosque in Kabul at right,
bank seal above. Segmented security thread. Back: Arch at Qila'-e Bost at center.
Printer: TDLR. 148x62mm.
    a. SH 1387 (2008).   FV   7.50
    b. SH 1389 (2010).   FV   5.00
    c. SH 1381 (2012).   FV   4.00

76   500 Afghanis   **VF   UNC**
SH 1387 (2008)-. Blue and multicolor. Masjid-i Jami' (Friday Mosque) in Herat
at right, bank seal above. Holographic strip at left center. Back: Kandahr Airport
control tower at center. Windowed security thread. Printer: TDLR. 152x64mm.
    a. SH1387 (2008).   FV   32.50
    b. SH1389 (2010).   FV   30.00
    c. SH1391 (2012).   FV   15.00

77   1000 Afghanis   **VF   UNC**
SH 1387 (2008); SH 1389 (2010). Orange and multicolor. Blue Mosque in Mazari
Sharif at right, bank seal above. 12mm Holographic strip at left center, 3mm wide
windowed security thread. Color changing ink at center. Back: Mausoleum of Ah-
mad Shah Durrani in Kandahar at center. Windowed security thread. Watermark:
Value and ornament added. Printer: TDLR. 158x66mm.
    a. SH 1387 (2008).   FV   50.00
    b. SH 1389 (2010).   FV   45.00

78   1000 Afghanis   **VF   UNC**
SH1391 (2012). Orange and multicolor. Blue Mosque in Mazari Sharuf at right,
bank scene above. New holographic strip at left center. Back: Mausoleum of
Ahmad Shah Durrani in Kandahar at center. 158x66mm.   FV   30.00

ALBANIA

The Republic of Albania, a balkan republic bounded by the Montenegro, Macedonia, Greece and the
Adriatic Sea, has an area of 11,100
sq. mi. (28,748 sq. km.) and a population of 3.5 million. Capital: Tirana.
The country is mostly agricultural,
although recent progress has been
made in manufacturing and mining
sectors. Petroleum, chrome, iron,
copper, cotton textiles, tobacco and
wood products are exported.

Since it had been part of the Greek and Roman Empires, little is known of the eary history of Albania.
After Roman rule it was overrun by Goths, Brzantines, Venetians and Turks. Skanderbeg, the national hero,
resisted the Turks and established an independent Albania in 1443. In 1468 the country again fell to the Turks
and remained part of the Ottoman Empire for the next 400 years.

Independence was re-established by revolt in 1912, and the present borders established in 1913 by a
conference of European powers which, in 1914, placed Prince William of Wied on the throne - popular discontent forced his abdication within months. In 1920, following World War I and occupancy by several nations, a
republic was set up. Ahmet Zogu seized the presidency in 1925, and in 1928, proclaimed him self king with the
title Zog I. At the start of World War II, when Albania was invaded by Italy, Zog fled. Victor Emanuel of Italy ruled
for a time. Upon the surrender of Italy to the Allies in 1943, German troops occupied the country. They withdrew
in 1944, and communist partisans seized power, naming Gen. Enver Hoxha provisional president. IN 1946,
following a vicotry by the communist front in 1945 elections, a new constitution modeled on that of the Soviet
Union was adopted. In accordance with the 1976 constitution the official name of the country was changes
from the Peoples Republic of Albania to the Peoples Socialist Republic of Albania. A general strike by trade
unions in 1991 forced the communist government to resign. A new government was elected in March 1992.
In 1997 Albania had a major financial crisis which caused civil distrubances and the fall of the administration.

    MONETARY SYSTEM:
    1 "heavy" Lek = 10 old Lekë, 1965-
    1 Lek Valutë = 50 Lekë, 1992-1993

PEOPLES REPUBLIC
Banka e Shtetit Shqiptar
1964 Issue

33   1 Lek   **VF   UNC**
1964. Green and deep blue on multicolor underprint. Peasant couple at center.
Back: Shkoder fortress at left center; arms at upper right. Watermark: Curved
BSHSH repeated.
    a. Issued note.   1.00   4.00
    s. Specimen overprint: *MODEL* or *SPECIMEN*.   —   3.00

34   3 Lekë   **VF   UNC**
1964. Brown and lilac on multicolor underprint. Woman with basket of grapes
at left. Back: Vlora view at left center; arms at upper right. Watermark: Curved
BSHSH repeated.
    a. Issued note.   1.00   6.00
    s. Specimen overprint: *MODEL* or *SPECIMEN*.   —   4.00

35   5 Lekë   **VF   UNC**
1964. Purple and dark blue on multicolor underprint. Truck and steam passenger
train crossing viaduct at left center. Back: Ship at left; arms at upper right. Watermark: Curved BSHSH repeated.
    a. Issued note.   2.00   8.00
    s. Specimen overprint: *MODEL* or *SPECIMEN*.   —   5.00

36   10 Lekë   **VF   UNC**

1964. Dark green on multicolor underprint. Woman working with cotton spinning
frame. Back: People outside the palace of culture at left center. Naim Frashëre
portrait and arms at upper right. Watermark: Curved BSHSH repeated.

    a. Issued note.   3.00   10.00
    s. Specimen overprint: *MODEL* or *SPECIMEN*.   —   6.00

37   25 Lekë   **VF   UNC**

1964. Blue-black on multicolor underprint. Peasant woman with sheaf at left,
combine and truck at center. Back: Farm tractor at left center. Watermark: Curved
BSHSH repeated.

    a. Issued note.   4.00   15.00
    s. Specimen overprint: *MODEL* or *SPECIMEN*.   —   7.50

38   50 Lekë   **VF   UNC**

1964. Red-brown on multicolor underprint. Soldiers on parade at left center, bust
of Skanderbeg at upper right. Back: Rifle and pick axe at left, modern apartment
building under construction at left center; arms at upper right. Watermark: Curved
BSHSH repeated.

    a. Issued note.   8.00   25.00
    s. Specimen overprint: *MODEL* or *SPECIMEN*.   —   8.50

39   100 Lekë   **VF   UNC**

1964. Brown-lilac. Worker and boy at hydroelectric dam at left center. Back: Steel
worker and well rigger at center; arms at upper right. Watermark: Curved BSHSH
repeated.

    a. Issued note.   15.00   40.00
    s. Specimen overprint: *MODEL* or *SPECIMEN*.   —   10.00

PEOPLES SOCIALIST REPUBLIC

Banka e Shtetit Shqiptar

1976 Issue

40   1 Lek   **VF   UNC**

1976. Green and deep blue on multicolor underprint. Peasant couple at center.
Back: Shkodor fortress at left center. Arms at upper right. Watermark: Bank name
around radiant star, repeated.

    a. Issued note.   0.50   2.00
    s1. Red overprint: *SPECIMEN* with all zeros serial #.   —   3.50
    s2. Red overprint: *SPECIMEN* with normal serial #.   —   0.50
    s3. Large blue overprint: *SPECIMEN* on face. Black overprint: *E PRAN-*   —   —
       UESHME on back.

Note: #40 with large blue overprint: *SPECIMEN* on face and black rectangular overprint for bank
    25th anniversary on back is a private issue.

41   3 Lekë   **VF   UNC**

1976. Brown and lilac on multicolor underprint. Woman with basket of grapes
at left. Back: Saranda view at left center. Arms at upper right. Watermark: Bank
name around radiant star, repeated.

    a. Issued note.   0.50   3.00
    s1. Red overprint: *SPECIMEN* with all zeros serial #.   —   4.00
    s2. Red overprint: *SPECIMEN* with normal serial #.   —   0.75

42 **5 Lekë** | VF | UNC
1976. Lilac and blue on multicolor underprint. Truck and steam passenger train crossing viaduct at left center. Back: Ship at left; arms at upper right. Watermark: Bank name around radiant star, repeated.

	VF	UNC
a. Issued note.	1.00	5.00
s1. Red overprint: SPECIMEN with all zeros serial #.	—	4.50
s2. Red overprint: SPECIMEN with normal serial #.	—	1.00
s3. Large blue overprint: SPECIMEN on face. Black overprint: E PRAN-UESHME on back.	—	—

Note: #42 with large blue overprint: SPECIMEN on face and black rectangular overprint for bank 25th anniversary on back is a private issue.

43 **10 Lekë** | VF | UNC
1976. Dark green on multicolor underprint. Woman working with cotton spinning frame. Back: People at left center, male portrait at upper right. Arms at upper right. Watermark: Bank name around radiant star, repeated.

	VF	UNC
a. Issued note.	1.00	8.00
s1. Red overprint: SPECIMEN with all zeros serial #.	—	5.50
s2. Red overprint: SPECIMEN with normal serial #.	—	1.25

44 **25 Lekë** | VF | UNC
1976. Blue-black on multicolor underprint. Peasant woman with sheaf at left. Combine and truck at center. Back: Farm tractor at left center. Arms at upper right. Watermark: Bank name around radiant star, repeated.

	VF	UNC
a. Issued note.	2.00	10.00
s1. Red overprint: SPECIMEN with all zeros serial #.	—	6.50
s2. Red overprint: SPECIMEN with normal serial #.	—	1.75

45 **50 Lekë** | VF | UNC
1976. Red-brown on multicolor underprint. Soldiers on parade at left center, bust of Skanderbeg at upper right. Back: Rifle and pick axe at left, modern building under construction at left center. Arms at upper right. Watermark: Bank name around radiant star, repeated.

	VF	UNC
a. Serial # prefix without serifs. Chinese printing.	2.00	15.00
b. Serial # prefix with serifs. Crossbar of 4 is thicker than bottom serif. (1st European printing).	2.50	20.00
c. Serial # prefix with serifs. Crossbar of 4 is same thickness as bottom serif. (2nd European printing).	2.00	15.00
s1. Red overprint: SPECIMEN with all zeros serial #.	—	7.50
s2. Red overprint: SPECIMEN with normal serial #.	—	2.50
s3. Large blue overprint: SPECIMEN on face. Black overprint: E PRAN-UESNHME on back.	—	—

Note: #45 with large blue overprint: SPECIMEN on face and black rectangular overprint for bank's 25th anniversary on back is a private issue.

46 **100 Lekë** | VF | UNC
1976. Brown-lilac on multicolor underprint. Worker and boy at hydroelectric dam at left center. Back: Steel worker and well rigger at center. Arms at upper right. Watermark: Bank name around radiant star, repeated.

	VF	UNC
a. Issued note.	3.00	20.00
s1. Red overprint: SPECIMEN with all zeros serial #.	—	8.50
s2. Red overprint: SPECIMEN with normal serial #.	—	3.00

ND Issue

46A **100 Lekë** | VF | UNC
ND. Steel workers at left, steel mill at center. Back: Oil well derricks at left center, arms at upper right.

	VF	UNC
s1. Blue and dull red on light green and light yellow underprint. Specimen only.	—	250
s2. Brown and dull red on light green and light yellow underprint. Specimen only.	—	250

1991 Issue

47 **100 Lekë** | VF | UNC
1991. Deep brown and deep purple on pale orange and multicolor underprint. Steel workers at left, steel mill at right. Back: Refinery at left center; arms at upper right. Watermark: Bank name around radiant star, repeated.

	VF	UNC
a. Issued note.	3.00	15.00
s. Specimen.	—	5.00

50 — 50 Lek Valutë (= 2500 Lekë)

ND (1992). Deep brown-violet and gray-green on multicolor underprint. Steelworker at center. Back: Electrical transmission towers at left, arms at upper center, hydroelectric generator at right. Watermark: B.SH.SH. below star, repeated.

	VF	UNC
a. With serial #.	20.00	60.00
b. Without serial #.	6.00	25.00
s. Specimen.	—	25.00

#51 not assigned.

REPUBLIC

Banka e Shqiperise
1992 Issue

48 — 500 Lekë

1991;1996. Purple, red and blue-green on light blue and light orange underprint. Peasant woman by sunflowers at left center. Back: Evergreen trees, mountains at left center, arms at upper right. Watermark: Bank name around radiant star, repeated.

	VF	UNC
a. 1991.	FV	25.00
b. 1996. Enhanced UV printing.	FV	10.00

1992 ND Issue

52 — 200 Lekë

1992. Deep reddish-brown on multicolor underprint. Ismail Qemali at left. Back: Citizens portrayed in double-headed eagle outline. Watermark: Repeated ring of letters B.SH.SH. 162x78mm.

	VF	UNC
a. Issued note.	4.00	15.00
s. Specimen.	—	—

48A — 1 Lek Valutë (= 50 Lekë)

ND (1992). (Not issued). Purple and gray-green on multicolor underprint. Steelworker at center. Back: Electrical transmission towers at left, arms at upper center, hydroelectric generator at right. Watermark: B.SH.SH. below star, repeated.

VF UNC — FV 40.00

53 — 500 Lekë

1992. Deep blue on blue and multicolor underprint. Naim Frashëri at left. Back: Poetry of Frashëri: Rural mountains at left, candle at center. Watermark: Repeated ring of letters B.SH.SH. 170x78mm.

	VF	UNC
a. Issued note.	8.00	25.00
s. Specimen.	—	—

49 — 10 Lek Valutë (= 500 Lekë)

ND (1992). Deep green and purple on multicolor underprint. Steelworker at center. Back: Electrical transmission towers at left, arms at upper center, hydroelectric generator at right. Watermark: B.SH.SH. below star, repeated.

	VF	UNC
a. With serial #.	5.00	20.00
b. Without serial #.	5.00	20.00
s. Specimen.	—	—

Note: Many examples of #49 have mismatched serial numbers. No additional premium is attached to them.

54 — 1000 Lekë

1992. Deep green and green on multicolor underprint. Skanderbeg at left. Back: Kruja Castle at left, crowned arms at center. Watermark: Repeated ring of letters B.SH.SH. 178x78mm.

	VF	UNC
a. Issued note.	18.00	40.00
s. Specimen.	—	12.00

1993-94 Issue

		VF	**UNC**
55	**100 Lekë**		

1993-96. Purple on multicolor underprint. L. Kombetar at left. Back: Mountain peaks at left center, Lanner Falcon at center. 154x72mm.

		VF	**UNC**
a. 1993.		7.50	30.00
b. 1994.		4.00	8.00
c. 1996. Enhanced U-V printing.		3.50	5.00
s. Specimen. Red overprint: SPECIMEN on each side.		—	40.00

		VF	**UNC**
56	**200 Lekë**		

1994. Deep reddish brown on multicolor underprint. Ismail Qemali at left. Back: Citizens portrayed in double-headed eagle outline. 162x78mm.

		VF	**UNC**
a. Issued note.		3.00	10.00
s. Specimen.		—	6.00

		VF	**UNC**
57	**500 Lekë**		

1994. Deep blue on blue and multicolor underprint. Naim Frashëri at left. Back: Frashëri poetry: Rural mountains at left, candle at center. 170x78mm.

		VF	**UNC**
a. Issued note.		8.00	20.00
s. Specimen.		—	10.00

		VF	**UNC**
58	**1000 Lekë**		

1994. Deep green on green and multicolor underprint. Skanderbeg at left. Back: Kruja Castle at left, crowned arms at center. 178x78mm.

		VF	**UNC**
a. Issued note.		18.00	40.00
s. Specimen.		—	12.50

1995-96 Issue

		VF	**UNC**
59	**200 Lekë**		

1996. Deep reddish brown on multicolor underprint. Ismail Qemali at left. Segmented foil over security thread. Back: Citizens portrayed in double-headed eagle outline. 162x78mm.

		VF	**UNC**
a. Issued note.		3.00	10.00
s. Specimen. Red overprint: SPECIMEN.		—	40.00

		VF	**UNC**
60	**500 Lekë**		

1996. Deep blue on blue and multicolor underprint. Naim Frashëri at left. Segmented foil over security thread. Back: Frashëri poetry: Rural mountains at left, candle at center. 170x78mm.

		VF	**UNC**
a. Issued note.		8.00	15.00
s. Specimen. Red overprint: SPECIMEN.		—	50.00

		VF	**UNC**
61	**1000 Lekë**		

1995-96. Deep green and green on multicolor underprint. Skanderbeg at left. Segmented foil over security thread. Back: Kruja Castle at left, crowned arms at center. 178x78mm.

		VF	**UNC**
a. 1995. Olive-green signature.		18.00	30.00
b. 1995. Black signature.		18.00	20.00
c. 1996. Black signature.		18.00	20.00
s. Specimen. As c. Red overprint: SPECIMEN.		—	90.00

1996 Issue

		VF	**UNC**
62	**100 Lekë**		

1996 (1997). UV: Fibers fluoresce blue, yellow; security strip green; Face: value in box green, central design orange, green. Purple, dark brown and orange on multicolor underprint. Fan S. Noli at left. Back: First Albanian parliament building at upper right. Watermark: Fan S. Noli. 130x66mm.

		VF	**UNC**
a. Issued note.		1.50	3.00
s. Specimen. Red overprint: SPECIMEN and perforation squares at ends.		—	200

		VF	**UNC**
63	**200 Lekë**		

1996 (1997). Brown and brown-orange on multicolor underprint. Niam Frasheri at left. Back: Frasheri's birthplace at upper right. Watermark: Niam Frasheri. 138x69mm.

		VF	**UNC**
a. Issued note.		1.50	4.00
s. Specimen. Red overprint: SPECIMEN.		—	35.00

64 500 Lekë

1996 (1997). Dark blue, purple and brown on multicolor underprint. Ismail Qemali at left. Back: Conference table and movie projector at center, Independence house in Vlora at upper right. Watermark: Ismail Qemali. 146x69mm.

	VF	UNC
a. Issued note.	5.00	10.00
s. Specimen. Red overprint: *SPECIMEN*.	—	60.00

65 1000 Lekë

1996 (1997); 1999. Green and dark green on multicolor. Pjeter Bogdani at left. Back: Church of Vau i Dejes at upper right. Watermark: Pjeter Bogdani. 153x72mm.

	VF	UNC
a. 1996.	12.50	20.00
b. 1999.	12.50	20.00

66 5000 Lekë

1996 (1999). Olive green and multicolor. Skanderbeg at left. Back: Kruja castle, equestrian statue, and crown. Watermark: Skanderbeg. 160x72mm.

	VF	UNC
a. Issued note.	40.00	120
s. Specimen. Red overprint: *SPECIMEN*.	—	225

2001 Issue

67 200 Lekë

2001. Brown and brown-orange on multicolor underprint. N. Frasheri at left. Back: Frasheri's birthplace at upper right. Watermark: N. Frasheri. 138x69mm.

	VF	UNC
	FV	3.00

68 500 Lekë

2001. Dark blue, purple and brown on multicolor underprint. I. Qemali at left. Back: Independence House at upper right, conference table and movie projector at center. Watermark: I. Qemali. 146x69mm.

	VF	UNC
	FV	8.00

69 1000 Lekë

2001. Green and dark green on multicolor underprint. P. Bogadani at left. Back: Sun at center, Church of Vau i Dejes at upper right . Watermark: P. Bogadani. 153x72mm.

	VF	UNC
	FV	18.00

70 5000 Lekë

2001 (2004). Olive green and multicolor. Skanderbeg at left. Back: Kruja castle, equestrian statue, and crown. Watermark: Skanderbeg. 160x72mm.

	VF	UNC
	FV	110

2007 Issue

71 200 Lekë

2007; 2012. Brown on multicolor underprint. Naim Frasheri at left. Back: Poem manuscript and Frasheri's birthplace. Watermark: N. Frasheri. Printer: TDLR. 138x69mm.

	VF	UNC
a. 2007. Narrow windowed security thread.	FV	4.00
b. 2012. Wide window security thread.	FV	4.00

72 500 Lekë

2007. Blue on multicolor underprint. Ismail Qemali at left. Back: House were Independence was declared. Watermark: I. Qemali. Printer: TDLR. 145x68mm.

	VF	UNC
	FV	7.00

73 1000 Lekë

2007, 2011. Green on multicolor underprint. Pjeter Bogdani at left, sunburst at center. Back: Bogdani's heliocentric system, church in Vau i Dejës. Watermark: P. Bogdani. Printer: TDLR. 151x72mm.

	VF	UNC
a. 2007.	FV	20.00
b. 2011.	FV	25.00

74 2000 Lekë

2007; 2012. Violet and brown on multicolor underprint. Mbreti Gent at left. Back: Butrint amphitheater near Sarandë at right. Watermark: M. Gent. Printer: TDLR. 160x72mm.

	VF	UNC
a. 2007.	FV	30.00
b. 2012.	FV	30.00

75 5000 Lekë

2007; 2013. Brown and yellow on multicolor underprint. Gjergi Kastrioti at left. Back: Kruja Castle at right. Watermark: Skanderbeg. Printer: TDLR. 160x72mm.

	VF	UNC
a. 2007.	FV	80.00
b. 2013.	FV	80.00

ALGERIA

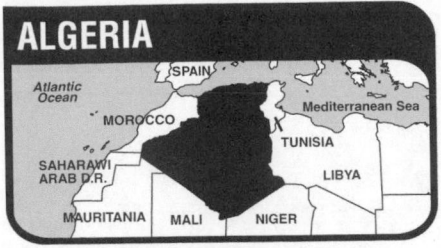

The People's Democratic Republic of Algeria, a North African country fronting on the Mediterranean Sea between Tunisia and Morocco, has an area of 2.382 million sq. km. and a population of 33.77 million. Capital: Algiers. Most of the country's working population is engaged in agriculture although industrial diversification, financed by oil revenues, is making steady progress. Wines, fruits, iron and zinc ores, phosphates, tobacco products, liquified natural gas, and petroleum are exported.

After more than a century of rule by France, Algerians fought through much of the 1950s to achieve independence in 1962. Algeria's primary political party, the National Liberation Front (FLN), has dominated politics ever since. Many Algerians in the subsequent generation were not satisfied, however, and moved to counter the FLN's centrality in Algerian politics. The surprising first round success of the Islamic Salvation Front (FIS) in the December 1991 balloting spurred the Algerian army to intervene and postpone the second round of elections to prevent what the secular elite feared would be an extremist-led government from assuming power. The army began a crackdown on the FIS that spurred FIS supporters to begin attacking government targets. The government later allowed elections featuring pro-government and moderate religious-d parties, but did not appease the activists who progressively widened their attacks. The fighting escalated into an insurgency, which saw intense fighting between 1992-98 and which resulted in over 100,000 deaths - many attributed to indiscriminate massacres of villagers by extremists. The government gained the upper hand by the late-1990s and FIS's armed wing, the Islamic Salvation Army, disbanded in January 2000. However, small numbers of armed militants persist in confronting government forces and conducting ambushes and occasional attacks on villages. The army placed Abdelaziz Bouteflika in the presidency in 1999 in a fraudulent election but claimed neutrality in his 2004 landslide reelection victory. Longstanding problems continue to face Bouteflika in his second term, including the ethnic minority Berbers' ongoing autonomy campaign, large-scale unemployment, a shortage of housing, unreliable electrical and water supplies, government inefficiencies and corruption, and the continuing activities of extremist militants. The 2006 merger of the Salafist Group for Preaching and Combat (GSPC) with al-Qaida (followed by a name change to al-Qaida in the Lands of the Islamic Maghreb) signaled an increase in bombings, including high-profile, mass-casualty suicide attacks targeted against the Algerian government and Western interests. Algeria must also diversify its petroleum-d economy, which has yielded a large cash reserve but which has not been used to redress Algeria's many social and infrastructure problems.

RULERS:
French to 1962

MONETARY SYSTEM:
1 Franc = 100 Centimes to 1960
1 Nouveau Franc = 100 Old Francs, 1959-64
1 Dinar = 100 Centimes, 1964-

FRENCH ADMINISTRATION

Banque de l'Algérie

1959 Issue

118   5 Nouveaux Francs   VF   UNC

1959. Green and multicolor. Ram at bottom center, Bacchus at right. Back: Like #106.

a. 31.7.1959; 18.12.1959.   85.00   340
s. Specimen. 31.7.1959.   —   175

119   10 Nouveaux Francs   VF   UNC

1959-61. Brown and yellow. Isis at right. Back: Like #104.

a. 31.7.1959-2.6.1961.   100   350
s. Specimen. 31.7.1959.   —   185

120   50 Nouveaux Francs   VF   UNC

1959. Multicolor. Pythian Apollo at left, penal code shows at bottom center. Back: Like #109.

a. 31.7.1959; 18.12.1959.   175   550
s. Specimen. 31.7.1959.   —   400

121 100 Nouveaux Francs   VF UNC
1959-61. Blue and multicolor. Seagulls with city of Algiers in background. Back: Like #110.
  a. 31.7.1959; 18.12.1959.   225   600
  b. 3.6.1960; 25.11.1960; 10.2.1961; 2.6.1961; 29.9.1961.   115   425
  s. Specimen. 31.7.1959.   —   200

REPUBLIC
Banque Centrale d'Algérie
1964 Issue

122 5 Dinars   VF UNC
1.1.1964. Two styles of numerals in date and serial number. Purple and lilac. Griffon vulture, tawny eagle perched on rocks at left center. Back: Sheep herder and native objects. Watermark: Amir Abd el-Kader.
  a. Issued note.   50.00   250
  s. Specimen.   —   100

123 10 Dinars   VF UNC
1.1.1964. 2 styles of numerals in date and serial #. Lilac and multicolor. Pair of storks and minaret. Back: Carpert weavers. Watermark: Amir Abd el-Kader.
  a. Issued note.   20.00   100
  s. Specimen.   —   100

124 50 Dinars   VF UNC
1.1.1964. Light brown and multicolor. 2 mountain sheep. Back: Camel caravan. Watermark: Amir Abd el-Kader.
  a. Issued note.   25.00   100
  s. Specimen.   —   150

125 100 Dinars   VF UNC
1.1.1964. 2 styles of numerals in date and serial #. Multicolor. Port of d'Algers harbor scene. Back: Modern building complex at left center on back. Watermark: Amir Abd el-Kader.
  a. Issued note.   20.00   80.00
  s. Specimen.   —   200

1970 Issue

126 5 Dinars   VF UNC
1.11.1970. Signature varieties. Blue and multicolor. Warrior with shield and sword at center right. Back: Ruppel's sand fox at left center, village in background at center right. Watermark: Amir Abd el-Kader.
  a. Issued note.   6.00   20.00
  s. Specimen.   —   30.00

1977; 1981 Issue

127 10 Dinars
1.11.1970. Red-brown and multicolor. Sheep at left, peacock at right. Back: Seated elderly man at left, ornate building at right. Minor plate varieties in French text. Watermark: Amir Abd el-Kader.

	VF	UNC
a. Penal Code with serif font. Series 001-014.	6.00	25.00
b. Penal Code in sans serif font. Series 015-054.	6.00	25.00
s. Specimen.	—	30.00

130 50 Dinars
1.11.1977. Dark green on multicolor underprint. Shepherd with flock at lower left center. 3 Signature varieties. Back: Farm tractor. Watermark: Amir Abd el-Kader.

	VF	UNC
a. Issued note.	2.50	10.00
s. Specimen.	—	25.00

131 100 Dinars
1.11.1981. Dark blue and aqua on light blue underprint. Village with minarets at left. 3 Signature varieties. Back: Man working with plants at center. Watermark: Amir Abd el-Kader.

	VF	UNC
a. Issued note.	4.00	12.50
s. Specimen.	—	50.00

128 100 Dinars
1.11.1970. Brown, brown-orange, blue-gray and pale yellow-orange. Two men at at left, airport at center, wheat ears at right. Back: Scenery with edmi gazelle at right.

	VF	UNC
a. Deep brown.	12.50	55.00
b. light brown.	10.00	45.00
s. Specimen.	—	50.00

1982-83 Issue

132 10 Dinars
2.12.1983. UV: security strip fluoresce blue. Black on brown and blue-green underprint. Diesel passenger train at center. Back: Mountain village at center. Watermark: Amir Abd el-Kader.

	VF	UNC
a. Issued note.	0.75	3.50
s. Specimen.	—	25.00

133 20 Dinars
2.1.1983. Red-brown on ochre underprint. Vase at left center, handcrafts at right. Back: Tower at center. Watermark: Amir Abd el-Kader.

	VF	UNC
a. Issued note.	1.00	5.00
s. Specimen.	—	40.00

129 500 Dinars
1.11.1970. Purple. View of city. Back: Galleon and fortress.

	VF	UNC
a. Issued note.	20.00	75.00
s. Specimen.	—	50.00

134 100 Dinars

8.6.1982. Pale blue and gray. Similar to #131 but without bird at upper right. Back: Man working with plants at center. Watermark: Amir Abd el-Kader.

	VF	UNC
a. Issued note.	17.50	50.00
s. Specimen.	—	75.00

135 200 Dinars

23.3.1983. Brown and dark green on multicolor underprint. Back: Monument to the Algerian martyrs at left, bridge over canyon at center, amphora at right. Watermark: Amir Abd el-Kader.

	VF	UNC
a. Issued note.	5.00	20.00
s. Specimen.	—	100

#136 not assigned

Banque d'Algérie
1992 Dated (1995; 1996) Issue

137 100 Dinars

21.5.1992 (1996). Dark blue with black text on pale blue and multicolor underprint. Battle of El Harrach, army charging at right. Back: Seal with horsemen charging at left, ancient galley at center. Watermark: Horse's head. 131x72mm.

VF	UNC
FV	7.50

138 200 Dinars

21.5.19921996). UV: security strip fluoresce blue; back: design elements green. Dark brown and red-brown on multicolor underprint. Back: Koranic school at center right, building at center. Watermark: Horse's head. 141x72mm.

VF	UNC
FV	12.50

139 500 Dinars

21.5.1992 (1996). Deep purple, violet and red-violet on multicolor underprint. Hannibal's troops and elephants engaging the Romans at center right. Back: Waterfalls at left, tomb ruins of Numid King Massinissa at left center, elephant mounted troops at center right. Watermark: Elephant heads. 151x72mm.

VF	UNC
FV	30.00

140 1000 Dinars

21.5.1992 (1995). Red-brown and orange on multicolor underprint. Tassili cave carvings of animals at lower center, water buffalo's head at right. Back: Hoggar cave painting of antelope at left, ruins at center. Watermark: Water buffalo head. 160x72mm.

VF	UNC
FV	50.00

1998 Dated (2000) Issue

141   500 Dinars

	VF	UNC
	FV	20.00

10.6.1998. UV: security strip fluoresce blue; face: either side of foil yellow, design elements pink. Deep purple, violet and red-violet on multicolor underprint. Hannibal's troops and elephants engaging the Romans at center right, waterfalls at left, tomb ruins of Numid King Massinissa at left center. Holographic band at left center. 2 Signature varieties. Back: Elephant mounted troops at center right. 151x72mm.

142   1000 Dinars

	VF	UNC

1992; 1998. Red-brown, grey-green and orange on multicolor underprint. Tassili cave carvings of animals at lower center, water buffalo's head at right. Holographic band at left center. Back: Hoggar cave painting of antelope at left, ruins at center. 160x72mm.

	VF	UNC
a. 21.5.1992.	15.00	60.00
b. 6.10.1998. 2 Signature varieties.	FV	35.00

2005 Commemorative Issue

143   1000 Dinars

	VF	UNC
	FV	45.00

22.3.2005. Arab League's 60th Anniversary seal and holographic band added. Red-brown and orange on multicolor underprint. 160x72mm.

2011 Issue

144   2000 Dinars

	VF	UNC
	FV	65.00

24.3.2011. Blue-green and multicolor.

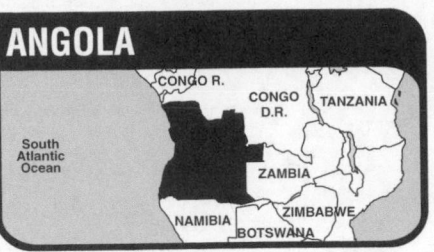

ANGOLA

The Peoples Republic of Angola, a country on the west coast of southern Africa bounded by Zaïre, Zambia and Namibia (South-West Africa), has an area of 1.25 million sq. km. and a population of 12.53 million, predominantly Bantu in origin. Capital: Luanda. Most of the people are engaged in subsistence agriculture. However, important oil and mineral deposits make Angola potentially one of the richest countries in Africa. Iron and diamonds are exported.

Angola is rebuilding its country after the end of a 27-year civil war in 2002. Fighting between the Popular Movement for the Liberation of Angola (MPLA), led by Jose Eduardo Dos Santos, and the National Union for the Total Independence of Angola (UNITA), led by Jonas Savimbi, followed independence from Portugal in 1975. Peace seemed imminent in 1992 when Angola held national elections, but UNITA renewed fighting after being beaten by the MPLA at the polls. Up to 1.5 million lives may have been lost - and 4 million people displaced - in the quarter century of fighting. Savimbi's death in 2002 ended UNITA's insurgency and strengthened the MPLA's hold on power. President Dos Santos has announced legislative elections will be held in September 2008, with presidential elections planned for sometime in 2009.

RULERS:
Portuguese to 1975

MONETARY SYSTEM:
1 Escudo = 100 Centavos, 1954-77
1 Kwanza = 100 Lwei, 1977-95
1 Kwanza Reajustado = 1,000 "old" Kwanzas, 1995-
1 Kwanza = 1,000,000 Kwanzas Reajustados, 1999-

	SIGNATURE VARIETIES	
	Governor	Administrator
1		
	Governor	Administrator
2		
	Governor	Administrator
3		
	Governor	Vice-Governor
4		
	Governor	Vice-Governor
5		
	Governor	Vice-Governor
6		
	Governor	Administrator
7		
	Governor	Administrator
8		
	Governor	Administrator
9		
	Governor	Administrator
10		
	Governor	Vice-Governor
11		

SIGNATURE VARIETIES

	Governor	Administrator
12		

	Governor	Administrator
13		

	Governor	Vice-Governor
14		

	Governor	Vice-Governor
15		

	Governor	Vice-Governor
16		

	Governor	Vice-Governor
17		

	Governor	Vice-Governor
18		

	Governor	Vice-Governor
19		

	Governor	Administrator
20		

PORTUGUESE ADMINISTRATION

Banco de Angola

1962 Issue

92   20 Escudos
10.6.1962. Black on multicolor underprint. Portrait of Americo Tomas at right, dock at left. Signature 1. Back: Gazelles running. Printer: TDLR.   VF 10.00   UNC 40.00

93   50 Escudos
10.6.1962. Light blue on multicolor underprint. Portrait of Americo Tomas at right, airport at left. Signature 2. Back: Various animals at water hole. Printer: TDLR.   VF 12.50   UNC 50.00

94   100 Escudos
10.6.1962. Lilac on multrcolor underprint. Portrait of Americo Tomas at right, Salazar bridge at left. Signature 3. Back: Elephants at watering hole.   VF 30.00   UNC 125

95   500 Escudos
10.6.1962. Red on multicolor underprint. Portrait of Americo Tomas at left or right, Port of Luanda at center. Signature 4. Back: 2 Black rhinoceros. Printer: TDLR.   VF 50.00   UNC 325

96   1000 Escudos
10.6.1962. Blue on multicolor underprint. Portrait of Americo Tomas at left or right, dam at center. Signature 4. Back: Herd. Printer: TDLR.   VF 45.00   UNC 260

1970 Issue

97   500 Escudos
10.6.1970. Red on multicolor underprint. Portrait of Americo Tomas at left, Port of Luanda at center. Signature 5. Back: 2 Rhinoceros. Printer: TDLR.   VF 40.00   UNC 215

98   1000 Escudos
10.6.1970. Blue on multicolor underprint. Portrait of Americo Tomas at left or right, dam at center. Signature 5. Back: Herd. Printer: TDLR.   VF 45.00   UNC 225

1972 Issue

99   20 Escudos
24.11.1972. Red and brown on multicolor underprint. Arms at left, M. Carmona at center right. Signature 7. Back: Flowers. Watermark: M. Carmona. Printer: TDLR.   VF 1.25   UNC 6.50

100   50 Escudos
24.11.1972. Green and brown on multicolor underprint. Arms at left, M. Carmona at center right. Signature 8. Back: Plants. Watermark: M. Carmona. Printer: TDLR.   VF 1.25   UNC 6.50

105 50 Escudos   VF UNC
10.6.1973. Blue and brown on multicolor underprint. Luiz de Camoes at right.
Signature 9. Back: Plant. Watermark: Luiz de Camoes.
    a. Issued note.   1.00   5.00
    s. Specimen.   —   75.00
    ct. Color trial. Blue, purple and green on multicolor underprint.   —   225

101 100 Escudos   VF UNC
24.11.1972. Light and dark brown on multicolor underprint. Arms at left, M.   1.50   6.50
Carmona at center right. Signature 7. Back: Tree and plants. Watermark: M.
Carmona. Printer: TDLR.

106 100 Escudos   VF UNC
10.6.1973. Brown, black and maroon on multicolor underprint. Luiz de Camoes at   1.50   7.50
right. Signature 10. Back: Tree at left. Watermark: Luiz de Camoes.

102 500 Escudos   VF UNC
24.11.1972. Blue on multicolor underprint. Arms at left, M. Carmona at center   5.00   20.00
right. Signature 6. Back: Rock formation at Pungo Andongo at center right.
Watermark: M. Carmona. Printer: TDLR.

107 500 Escudos   VF UNC
10.6.1973. Dark brown, violet and purple on multicolor underprint. Luiz de Camoes   4.50   20.00
at right. Signature 11. Back: High rock formation. Watermark: Luiz de Camoes.

103 1000 Escudos   VF UNC
24.11.1972. Purple on multicolor underprint. Arms at left, M. Carmona at center   6.00   37.50
right. Signature 5. Back: Waterfall. Watermark: M. Carmona. Printer: TDLR.

108 1000 Escudos   VF UNC
10.6.1973. Olive and blue on multicolor underprint. Luiz de Camoes at right.   9.00   35.00
Signature 11. Back: Waterfall. Watermark: Luiz de Camoes.

1973 Issue

PEOPLES REPUBLIC

Banco Nacional de Angola
1976 Issue

104 20 Escudos   VF UNC
10.6.1973. Blue, purple and green on multicolor underprint. Luiz de Camoes at
right. Signature 10. Back: Cotton plant. Watermark: Luiz de Camoes.
    a. Issued note.   5.00   32.50
    s. Specimen.   —   75.00
    ct. Color trial.   —   225

109 20 Kwanzas   VF UNC
11.11.1976. Brown, green and orange. Antonio Agostinho Neto at right. Signature
12. Back: Arms at lower left, soldiers in field.
    a. Issued note.   3.50   12.75
    s. Specimen.   —   20.00

110   50 Kwanzas

11.11.1976. Purple, brown and black. Antonio Agostinho Neto at right. Signature 12. Back: Field workers, arms at lower left.
    VF   UNC

  a. Issued note.   2.00   9.50
  s. Specimen.   —   30.00

111   100 Kwanzas

11.11.1976. Green on multicolor underprint. Antonio Agostinho Neto at right. Signature 12. Back: Textile factory workers, arms at lower left.
    VF   UNC

  a. Issued note.   1.50   15.00
  s. Specimen.   —   40.00

112   500 Kwanzas

11.11.1976. Blue on multicolor underprint. Antonio Agostinho Neto at right. Signature 12. Back: Cargo ships dockside, arms at lower left.
    VF   UNC

  a. Issued note.   6.00   30.00
  s. Specimen.   —   50.00

113   1000 Kwanzas

11.11.1976. Red on multicolor underprint. Antonio Agostinho Neto at right. Signature 12. Back: School class, arms at lower left.
    VF   UNC

  a. Issued note.   9.50   40.00
  s. Specimen.   —   50.00

1979 Issue

114   50 Kwanzas

14.8.1979. Purple, brown and black. Antonio Agostinho Neto at right, 2 serial numbers, signature titles, date of independence added under bank name. Signature 13. Back: Field workers, arms at lower left.
    VF   UNC
    2.50   10.00

115   100 Kwanzas

14.8.1979. Green on multicolor underprint. Antonio Agostinho Neto at right, 2 serial numbers, signature titles, date of independence added under bank name. Signature 13. Back: Textile factory workers, arms at lower left.
    VF   UNC

  a. Issued note.   1.75   7.50
  s. Specimen. Red overprint: SPECIMEN once on face.   —   75.00

116   500 Kwanzas

14.8.1979. Blue on multicolor underprint. Antonio Agostinho Neto at right, 2 serial numbers, signature titles, date of independence added under bank name. Signature 13. Back: Cargo ships dockside, arms at lower left.
    VF   UNC
    17.50   75.00

117   1000 Kwanzas

14.8.1979. Red on multicolor underprint. Antonio Agostinho Neto at right, 2 serial numbers, signature titles, date of independence added under bank name. Signature 13. Back: School class, arms at lower left.
    VF   UNC

  a. Issued note.   10.00   47.50
  s. Specimen.   —   75.00

1984-87 Issue

Replacement notes: Serial # prefixes ZA, ZB, ZC, etc.

118   50 Kwanzas

7.1.1984. Deep brown and green on light green and tan underprint. Conjoined busts of José Eduardo dos Santos and Antonio Agostinho Neto at right. Signature 14. Back: Classroom and teacher, arms at lower left. Watermark: Bird, (weak).
    VF   UNC
    1.25   5.00

Note: #118 dated 11.11.1987 may exist but requires confirmation (see #122).

119   100 Kwanzas

7.1.1984;11.11.1987. Deep blue, violet and brown on light blue and multicolor underprint. Conjoined busts of José Eduardo dos Santos and Antonio Agostinho Neto at right. Signature 14. Back: Picking cotton, arms at lower left. Watermark: Bird, (weak).
    VF   UNC
    10.00   35.00

Note: #119 dated 1987 was issued only with overprint. (see #125).

120   500 Kwanzas

7.1.1984; 11.11.1987 Brown, red-brown and red on lilac and multicolor underprint. Conjoined busts of José Eduardo dos Santos and Antonio Agostinho Neto at right. Back: Offshore oil platform at left, worker at right, arms at lower left. Watermark: Bird (weak).
    VF   UNC

  a. Signature 14. 7.1.1984.   11.00   50.00
  b. Signature 15. 11.11.1987.   10.00   60.00

121 1000 Kwanzas
7.1.1984; 11.11.1987 Purple, blue-black and blue on light blue and multicolor underprint. Conjoined busts of Josè Eduardo dos Santos and Antonio Agostinho Neto at right. Back: Soldiers embarking dockside at left center and soldier at right, arms at lower left. Watermark: Bird (weak).

	VF	UNC
a. Signature 14. 7.1.1984.	12.50	65.00
b. Signature 15. 11.11.1987.	11.00	45.00

1991 Provisional Issue

123 500 Novo Kwanza on 500 Kwanzas
ND (-old date 11.11.1987). Conjoined busts of Josè Eduardo dos Santos and Antonio Agostinho Neto at right. Back: Arms at lower left. Watermark: Conjoined busts of Josè Eduardo dos Santos and Antonio Agostinho Neto.

VF 13.00 — UNC 65.00

124 1000 Novo Kwanza on 1000 Kwanzas
ND (-old date 11.11.1987). Conjoined busts of Josè Eduardo dos Santos and Antonio Agostinho Neto at right. Back: Arms at lower left. Watermark: Conjoined busts of Josè Eduardo dos Santos and Antonio Agostinho Neto.

VF 13.00 — UNC 65.00

125 5000 Novo Kwanza on 100 Kwanzas
ND (-old date 11.11.1987). Conjoined busts of Josè Eduardo dos Santos and Antonio Agostinho Neto at right. Signature 15. Back: Arms at lower left. Watermark: Conjoined busts of Josè Eduardo dos Santos and Antonio Agostinho Neto.

VF 100 — UNC 285

1991 Issue

126 100 Kwanzas
4.2.1991. Purple, green and brown. Conjoined busts of Josè Eduardo dos Santos and Antonio Agostinho Neto at right. Signature 16. Back: Rock formation at Pungo Andongo at left center, tribal mask at right, arms at lower left. Watermark: Conjoined busts of Josè Eduardo dos Santos and Antonio Agostinho Neto.

VF 1.25 — UNC 5.75

127 500 Kwanzas
4.2.1991. Specimen. Blue and violet. Conjoined busts of Josè Eduardo dos Santos and Antonio Agostinho Neto at right. Back: Rock formation at Pungo Andongo at left center, tribal mask at right, arms at lower left. Watermark: Conjoined busts of Josè Eduardo dos Santos and Antonio Agostinho Neto.

VF — — UNC —

128 500 Kwanzas
4.2.1991. Purple and deep blue-green on multicolor underprint. Conjoined busts of Josè Eduardo dos Santos and Antonio Agostinho Neto at right. Back: Serra da Leba at left center, native pot at right, arms at lower left. Watermark: Conjoined busts of Josè Eduardo dos Santos and Antonio Agostinho Neto.

	VF	UNC
a. Signature 16.	5.00	25.00
b. Signature 17.	2.50	10.00
c. Signature 18.	3.25	12.50

129 1000 Kwanzas
4.2.1991. Brown, orange, purple and red-violet on multicolor underprint. Conjoined busts of Josè Eduardo dos Santos and Antonio Agostinho Neto at right. Back: Banco Nacional at left center, native doll at right, arms at lower left. Watermark: Conjoined busts of Josè Eduardo dos Santos and Antonio Agostinho Neto.

	VF	UNC
a. Signature 16.	7.50	37.50
b. Signature 17.	2.75	12.75
c. Signature 18.	5.00	16.00

130 5000 Kwanzas
4.2.1991. Dark green, blue-green and dark brown on multicolor underprint. Conjoined busts of Josè Eduardo dos Santos and Antonio Agostinho Neto at right. Back: Waterfall and stylized statue of "The Thinker", arms at lower left. Watermark: Conjoined busts of Josè Eduardo dos Santos and Antonio Agostinho Neto.

	VF	UNC
a. Signature 16.	15.00	50.00
b. Signature 17.	5.00	20.00
c. Signature 18.	7.50	22.50

131 10,000 Kwanzas
4.2.1991. Red, olive-green and purple on multicolor underprint. Conjoined busts of Josè Eduardo dos Santos and Antonio Agostinho Neto at right. Back: Sable antelope herd and shell, arms at lower left. Watermark: Conjoined busts of Josè Eduardo dos Santos and Antonio Agostinho Neto.

	VF	UNC
a. Signature 17.	15.00	80.00
b. Signature 18.	3.25	12.50

132 50,000 Kwanzas
4.2.1991. Bright green, yellow-green and dark brown on multicolor underprint. Conjoined busts of Josè Eduardo dos Santos and Antonio Agostinho Neto. Signature 18. Back: Waterfall and stylized statue of "The Thinker", arms at lower left. Watermark: Conjoined busts of Josè Eduardo dos Santos and Antonio Agostinho Neto.

	VF	UNC
	5.00	20.00

133 100,000 Kwanzas
4.2.1991 (1993). Orange and aqua on emerald green and multicolor underprint. Conjoined busts of Josè Eduardo dos Santos and Antonio Agostinho Neto at right. Signature 18. Back: Sable antelope herd and shell, arms at lower left. Watermark: Conjoined busts of Josè Eduardo dos Santos and Antonio Agostinho Neto.

		VF	UNC
a.	Microprint around watermark area reads: *100000 BNA*, latent print: *100000 CEM MIL.* watermark: *100000*.	5.00	9.50
x.	Microprint around watermark. area reads: *10000 BNA*, latent print: *10000 DEZ MIL.* watermark: *10,000.* (error).	15.00	57.50

134 500,000 Kwanzas
4.2.1991 (1994). Red, brown and violet on multicolor underprint. Conjoined busts of Josè Eduardo dos Santos and Antonio Agostinho Neto at right. Signature 19. Back: Rhinoceros at left, arms at lower left. Watermark: Conjoined busts of Josè Eduardo dos Santos and Antonio Agostinho Neto.

	VF	UNC
	2.00	6.50

1995 Issue

135 1000 Kwanzas Reajustados
1.5.1995. Black and blue on multicolor underprint. Conjoined busts of Josè Eduardo dos Santos and Antonio Agostinho Neto at right. Signature 20. Back: Sable antelope at left, arms at lower left, mask at upper right. Watermark: Sculpture.

	VF	UNC
	1.50	3.75

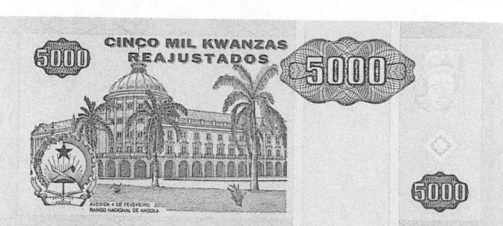

136 5000 Kwanzas Reajustados
1.5.1995. Green and brown on multicolor underprint. Conjoined busts of Josè Eduardo dos Santos and Antonio Agostinho Neto at right. Signature 20. Back: Banco Nacional at left, arms at lower left, mask at upper right. Watermark: Sculpture.

	VF	UNC
	2.25	9.00

137 10,000 Kwanzas Reajustados
1.5.1995. Red and purple on multicolor underprint. Conjoined busts of Josè Eduardo dos Santos and Antonio Agostinho Neto at right. Signature 20. Back: Off shore oil platform at left, arms at lower left, mask at upper right. Watermark: Sculpture.

	VF	UNC
	2.25	9.50

138 50,000 Kwanzas Reajustados
1.5.1995. Orange and green on multicolor underprint. Conjoined busts of Josè Eduardo dos Santos and Antonio Agostinho Neto at right. Signature 20. Back: Telecommunications station in Luanda at left center, arms at lower left, mask at upper right. Watermark: Sculpture.

	VF	UNC
	1.75	9.00

139 100,000 Kwanzas Reajustados
1.5.1995 UV: Fibers fluoresce green; face: logo and value yellow. Dark blue and brown-violet on multicolor underprint. Conjoined busts of Josè Eduardo dos Santos and Antonio Agostinho Neto at right. Signature 20. Back: Mask and pottery at left center, arms at lower left, mask at upper right. Watermark: Sculpture.

	VF	UNC
	1.75	6.50

140 500,000 Kwanzas Reajustados
1.5.1995. Dark brown and red-brown on multicolor underprint. Conjoined busts of Josè Eduardo dos Santos and Antonio Agostinho Neto at right. Signature 20. Back: Matala dam at left center, arms at lower left, mask at upper right. Watermark: Sculpture.

	VF	UNC
	3.00	4.50

141   1,000,000 Kwanzas Reajustados

VF   UNC

1.5.1995. Bright blue and red-brown on multicolor underprint. Conjoined busts
of Josè Eduardo dos Santos and Antonio Agostinho Neto at right. Signature 20.
Back: School girl at left center, arms at lower left, mask at upper right. Watermark:
Sculpture.

3.50   8.50

142   5,000,000 Kwanzas Reajustados

VF   UNC

1.5.1995. Violet and red-brown on multicolor underprint. Conjoined busts of Josè
Eduardo dos Santos and Antonio Agostinho Neto at right. Signature 20. Back:
Serra da Leba at left center, arms at lower left, mask at upper right. Watermark:
Sculpture.

7.50   35.00

1999; 2003 Issue

143   1 Kwanza

VF   UNC

Dark brown, pink and light blue on multicolor underprint. Conjoined busts of
Josè Eduardo dos Santos and Antonio Agostinho Neto at right Signature 21.
Back: Women picking cotton, arms at lower left, mask at upper right. Watermark:
Sculpture. Printer: FCO.

FV   1.00

144   5 Kwanzas

VF   UNC

10.1999; 5.2010. Purple, light-blue and dark blue on multicolor underprint.
Conjoined busts of Josè Eduardo dos Santos and Antonio Agostinho Neto at
right. Signature 21. Back: Mountain pass, arms at lower left, mask at upper right.
Watermark: Sculpture. Printer: FCO. 138x66mm.

	VF	UNC
a. 10.1999.	FV	3.00
b. 5.2010.	FV	2.00
c. 1.2011.	FV	2.00

145   10 Kwanzas

VF   UNC

10.1999; 5.2010; 1.2011. Brown, orange and purple on multicolor underprint.
Conjoined busts of Josè Eduardo dos Santos and Antonio Agnostinho Neto at
right. Signature 21. Back: Two antelope, arms at lower left, mask at upper right.
Watermark: Sculpture. Printer: FCO. 144x66mm.

	VF	UNC
a. 10.1999.	FV	4.00
b. 5.2010.	FV	3.00
c. 1.2011.	FV	3.00

146   50 Kwanzas

VF   UNC

10.1999; 5.2010; 1.2011. UV: Fibers fluoresce green; face: logo, value and legend
green; lower serial # orange. Conjoined busts of Josè Eduardo dos Santos and
Antonio Agnostinho Neto at right. Back: Off-shore oil rig. Watermark: Sculpture.
Printer: FCO. 160x66mm.

	VF	UNC
a. 10.1999.	FV	5.00
b. 5.2010.	FV	4.00
c. 1.2011	FV	4.00

147   100 Kwanzas

VF   UNC

10.1999; 1.2011. Olive and multicolor underprint. Back: Banco Nacional building.
160x66mm.

	VF	UNC
a. 10.1999.	FV	10.00
b. 1.2011.	FV	3.00

148   200 Kwanzas
11.2003; 1.2011. Mauve, aqua, pink and orange on multicolor underprint. Signature 22. Back: Aerial view of Luanda's coastline boulevard. 160x66mm.

	VF	UNC
a. 11.2003.	FV	10.00
b. 1.2011.	FV	6.00

149   500 Kwanzas
11.2003; 1.2011. Mauve, yellow and green on multicolor underprint. Signature 22. Back: Cotton harvesting scene. 160x66mm.

	VF	UNC
a. 11.2003.	FV	20.00
b. 1.2011.	FV	15.00

150   1000 Kwanzas
11.2003; 1.2011. Red, orange, blue and purple on multicolor underprint. Signature 22. Back: Coffee plantation. 163x66mm.

	VF	UNC
a. 11.2003.	FV	60.00
b. 1.2011.	FV	30.00

151   2000 Kwanzas
11.2003; 1.2011. Light and dark green on multicolor underprint. Back: Seashore. 165x66mm.

	VF	UNC
a. 11.2003.	FV	110
b. 1.2011.	FV	60.00

2012 Issue

152   50 Kwanzas
10.2012. Ochre and brown. Conjoined busts of José Eduardo dos Santos and Antonio Agnostinho Neto at right center. Back: Cuemba waterfall.

VF	UNC
FV	2.50

153   100 Kwanzas
10.2012. Ochre and brown. Conjoined busts of José Eduardo dos Santos and Antonio Agnostinho Neto at right center. Back: Binga waterfall.

VF	UNC
FV	5.00

154   200 Kwanzas
10.2012. Blue and brown. Conjoined busts of José Eduardo dos Santos and Antonio Agnostinho Neto at right center. Back: Tchimbue waterfall.

VF	UNC
FV	7.50

155   500 Kwanzas   **VF   UNC**
10.2012. Brown and tan. Conjoined busts of José Eduardo dos Santos and   FV   10.00
Antonio Agnostinho Neto at right center. Back: Andulo waterfall.

156   1000 Kwanzas   **VF   UNC**
10.2012. Lilac and brown. Dos Santos and Neto heads at right center. Back: FV   17.50
Waterfall. 163x66mm.

157   2000 Kwanzas   **VF   UNC**
10.2012 Green, brown and rose. Dos Santos and Neto at right center. Back: FV   30.00
Waterfall. 165x66mm.

158   5000 Kwanzas   **VF   UNC**
10.2012 Lilac. Dos Santos and Neto at right center. Back: Dam. 167x66mm.   FV   45.00

ARGENTINA

The Argentine Republic, located in South America, has an area of 2.76 million sq. km. and a population of 40.48 million. Capital: Buenos Aires. Its varied topography ranges from the subtropical lowlands of the north to the towering Andean Mountains in the west and the windswept Patagonian steppe in the south. The rolling, fertile pampas of central Argentina are ideal for agriculture and grazing, and support most of the republic's population. Meat packing, flour milling, textiles, sugar refining and dairy products are the principal industries. Oil is found in Patagonia, but most of the mineral requirements must be imported.

In 1816, the United Provinces of the Rio Plata declared their independence from Spain. After Bolivia, Paraguay, and Uruguay went their separate ways, the area that remained became Argentina. The country's population and culture were heavily shaped by immigrants from throughout Europe, but most particularly Italy and Spain, which provided the largest percentage of newcomers from 1860 to 1930. Up until about the mid-20th century, much of Argentina's history was dominated by periods of internal political conflict between Federalists and Unitarians and between civilian and military factions. After World War II, an era of Peronist authoritarian rule and interference in subsequent governments was followed by a military junta that took power in 1976. Democracy returned in 1983, and has persisted despite numerous challenges, the most formidable of which was a severe economic crisis in 2001-02 that led to violent public protests and the resignation of several interim presidents. The economy has recovered strongly since bottoming out in 2002.

MONETARY SYSTEM:
1 Peso (m/n) = 100 Centavos to 1970
1 'New' Peso (Ley 18.188) = 100 'Old' Pesos (m/n), 1970-83
1 Peso Argentino = 10,000 Pesos, (Ley 18.188) 1983-85
1 Austral = 100 Centavos = 1000 Pesos Argentinos, 1985-92
1 Peso = 10,000 Australes, 1992-
1 Peso = 8 Reales = 100 Centavos

REPLACEMENT NOTES:
#260d onward: R prefix before serial #.

SIGNATURE TITLES:
A - GERENTE GENERAL

B - SUBGERENTE GENERAL

C - GERENTE GENERAL and PRESIDENTE

D - SUBGERENTE GENERAL and VICE-PRESIDENTE

E - SUBGERENTE GENERAL and PRESIDENTE

F - VICE PRESIDENTE and PRESIDENTE

G - PRESIDENTE B.C.R.A. and PRESIDENTE H.C. SENADORES

H - PRESIDENTE B.C.R.A. and PRESIDENTE H.C. DIPUTADOS

I - VICE PRESIDENTE and GERENTE GENERAL

REPUBLIC
Banco Central de la Republica Argentina
1960-69 ND Issue

275   5 Pesos   **VF   UNC**
ND (1960-62). Brown on yellow underprint. General José de San Martin in uniform
at right. 3 signature varieties. Serie A. Back: People gathering before building.
Printer: CMN.
   a. Signature titles: D.   1.50   6.00
   b. Signature titles: C.   3.00   12.50
   c. Signature titles: E.   1.75   5.50

276   50 Pesos
	VF	UNC
ND (1968-69). Green. General José de San Martin in uniform at right, *SERIE D.* 2 signature varieties. Signature titles: C. Back: Army in mountain pass. | 1.25 | 5.00 |

277   100 Pesos
	VF	UNC
ND (1967-69). Red-brown. General José de San Martín in uniform at right. 2 signature varieties. *SERIES E, F, G.* Signature titles: C. Back: Spanish and Indians. | 1.25 | 4.00 |

278   500 Pesos
	VF	UNC
ND (1964-69). Blue on blue and gold underprint. Portrait of elderly General José de San Martín not in uniform at right. 4 signature varieties. Serie A. Back: Grand Bourg House in France. | | |
a. Signature titles: E. | 10.00 | 17.50 |
b. Signature titles: C. | 4.00 | 10.00 |

279   1000 Pesos
	VF	UNC
ND (1966-69). Purple. Portrait young General José de San Martín in uniform at right. 3 signature varieties. Serie C, D. Back: Sailing ship. | | |
a. Signature titles: E. | 3.75 | 15.00 |
b. Signature titles: C. | 3.25 | 10.00 |

280   5000 Pesos
	VF	UNC
ND (1962-69). Brown on yellow-green underprint. Portrait young General José de San Martín in uniform. 6 signature varieties. Serie A. Back: Capitol. | | |
a. Signature titles: E. | 15.00 | 50.00 |
b. Signature titles: C. | 12.50 | 37.50 |
s. As a. Specimen. | — | 200 |

281   10,000 Pesos
	VF	UNC
ND (1961-69). Deep red on blue and yellow underprint. Portrait elderly General José de San Martín not in uniform at right. 5 signature varieties. Serie A, B. Back: Armies in the field. | | |
a. Signature titles: E. Serie A, B. | 15.00 | 50.00 |
b. Signature titles: C. Serie B. | 12.50 | 35.00 |
s. As a. Specimen. | — | 200 |

1969 ND Provisional Issue

282   1 Peso on 100 Pesos
	VF	UNC
ND (1969-71). Red-brown. Portrait General José San Martin in uniform at right. Overprint of new denomination on #277 in watermark area. Signature titles: C. Series G. Back: Spanish and Indians. | 3.00 | 10.00 |

283 5 Pesos on 500 Pesos
ND (1969-71). Blue on blue and gold underprint. Overprint of new denomination on #278 in watermark area. 2 signature varieties. Signature titles: C. *Series A*.

VF UNC
7.50 22.50

284 10 Pesos on 1000 Pesos
ND (1969-71). Purple. Overprint of new denomination on #279 in watermark area. Signature titles:C. *SERIES D, E*.

VF UNC
7.50 22.50

285 50 Pesos on 5000 Pesos
ND (1969-71). Brown on yellow green underprint. Overprint of new denomination on #280 in watermark area. *SERIES A*.

VF UNC
12.50 37.50

286 100 Pesos on 10,000 Pesos
ND (1969-71). Deep red on blue and yellow underprint. Overprint of new denomination on #281 in watermark area. *SERIES B*. 2 signature varieties. Signature titles: C.

VF UNC
22.50 75.00

Ley 18.188; 1970-73 ND Issue

#287-292 Replacement notes: Serial # suffix *R*.

287 1 Peso
ND (1970-73). Without colored threads in white or grayish tint paper. UV: face: background details fluoresce pink. Orange on multicolor underprint. General Manuel Belgrano at right. *SERIES A-E*. 5 signature varieties. Back: Scene of Bariloche-Llao-Llao at center. Watermark: Varieties. Printer: CMN.

VF UNC
0.40 1.50

288 5 Pesos
ND (1971-73). Without colored threads in white or grayish tint paper. Multicolor underprint. General Manuel Belgrano at right. 2 signature varieties. Back: Monument to the Flag at Rosario at center. Watermark: Varieties. Printer: CMN.

VF UNC
1.00 4.50

289 10 Pesos
ND (1970-73). Without colored threads in white or grayish tint paper. Purple on multicolor underprint. General Manuel Belgrano at right. *SERIES A, B*. 6 signature varieties. Back: Waterfalls at Iguazu at center. Watermark: Varieties. Printer: CMN.

VF UNC
0.30 2.00

290 50 Pesos
ND (1972-73). Colored threads in paper. Black and brown on multicolor underprint. General José de San Martin at right. 3 signature varieties. Back: Hot springs at Jujuy at center. Watermark: Arms.

VF UNC
3.00 15.00

291   100 Pesos

	VF	UNC
ND (1971-73). Colored threads in paper. Red on multicolor underprint. General
José de San Martin at right. *SERIE A, B.* 4 signature varieties. Back: Coastline at
Ushuaia at center. Watermark: Arms.   5.00   20.00

292   500 Pesos

	VF	UNC
ND (1972-73). Colored threads in paper. Green on multicolor underprint. Josè de
San Martin at right. 2 signature varieties. Back: Army monument at Mendoza at
center. Watermark: Arms.   10.00   30.00

Decreto-Ley 18.188/69; 1973-76 ND Issue

#293-299 Replacement notes: Serial # suffix: *R.*

293   1 Peso

	VF	UNC
ND (1974). Without colored threads in paper (varieties). Orange on multicolor
underprint. General Manuel Belgrano at right. *SERIE E,F.* Signature varieties.
Back: Scene of Bariloche-Llao-Llao at center. Watermark: Arms.   0.50   1.50

294   5 Pesos

	VF	UNC
ND (1974-76). Without colored threads in paper (varieties). Blue on multicolor
underprint. General Manuel Belgrano at right.*SERIE A,B.* 2 signature varieties.
Back: Monument to the Flag at Rosario at center. Watermark: Arms.   0.40   1.25

295   10 Pesos

	VF	UNC
ND (1973-76). Without colored threads in paper (varieties). Purple on multicolor
underprint. General Manuel Belgrano at right. *SERIE C,D.* 4 signature varieties.
Back: Waterfall at Iguazu at center. Watermark: Arms.   0.50   2.50

296   50 Pesos

	VF	UNC
ND (1974-75). Colored threads in paper. Black and brown on multicolor under-
print. General José San Martin at right. *SERIE A, B.* 2 signature varieties. Back:
Hot springs at Jujuy at center. Watermark: Arms.   0.50   1.50

297   100 Pesos

	VF	UNC
ND (1973-76). Colored threads in paper. Red on multicolor underprint. General
José de San Martin at right. *SERIE B, C.* 3 signature varieties. Back: Ushuaia
Harbor scene at center. Watermark: Arms.   1.00   3.50

298   500 Pesos

	VF	UNC
ND (1974-75). Colored threads in paper. Green on multicolor underprint. General
José de San Martin at right. 2 signature varieties. Back: Army monument at
Mendoza at center. Watermark: Arms.		
a. Signature titles: C.	3.00	10.00
b. Signature titles: F.	2.00	7.50
c. Signature titles : I.	3.00	10.00

299　1000 Pesos

	VF	UNC
ND (1973-76). Colored threads in paper. Brown on multicolor underprint. General José de San Martin at right. *SERIE A-C.* 3 signature varieties. Back: *Plaza de Mayo* in Buenos Aires at center. Watermark: Arms. | 5.00 | 12.50 |

1976-83 ND Issue

W/o Decreto or Ley #301-310 Replacement notes: Serial # suffix: *R.*

300　10 Pesos

	VF	UNC
ND (1976). Purple on multicolor underprint. General Manuel Belgrano at right. *SERIES D, E.* Back: Waterfall at Iguazu at center. Watermark: Arms. | 0.20 | 1.00 |

301　50 Pesos

	VF	UNC
ND (1976-78). Engraved or lithographed back. Black on multicolor underprint. General José de San Martin at right. *SERIE B, C.* 2 signature varieties. Back: Hot springs at Jujuy at center. Watermark: Arms. | | |
a. Without colored threads in paper. | 5.00 | 10.00 |
b. Colored threads in paper. | 0.20 | 0.75 |

302　100 Pesos

	VF	UNC
ND (1976-78). Red on multicolor on underprint. General José de San Martin at right *SERIE C-E.* Signature varieties. Back: Coastline at Ushuaia at center. Watermark: Arms. | | |
a. Without colored threads in paper. 2 signature varieties. | 0.50 | 2.50 |
b. Colored threads in paper. 2 signature varieties. | 0.30 | 1.00 |

303　500 Pesos

	VF	UNC
ND (1977-82). UV: face: design elements fluoresce orange. Green on multicolor underprint. General José de San Martin at right. *SERIE A-D.* 4 signature varieties.. Back: Army monument at Mendoza at center. | | |
a. Watermark: Arms. without colored threads in paper. | 0.20 | 1.50 |
b. Watermark: Arms. Colored threads in paper. | 0.50 | 2.50 |
c. Watermark: Multiple sunbursts. Colored threads. Back lithographed. *SERIE C, D.* UV: threads fluoresce blue. | 0.20 | 0.75 |

304　1000 Pesos

	VF	UNC
ND (1976-83). Color varieties in underprint: yellow or green, maroon or ochre. Brown on multicolor underprint. General José de San Martin at right *SERIE C-I.* 5 signature varieties. Back: *Plaza de Mayo* in Buenos Aires at center. | | |
a. Watermark: Arms. without colored threads in paper. | 0.30 | 2.00 |
b. Watermark: Arms. Colored threads in paper. 2 signature varieties. | 0.20 | 1.50 |
c. Watermark: Multiple sunbursts. Back engraved. | 0.20 | 1.00 |
d. Watermark: Multiple sunbursts. Back lithographed. *SERIE I.* | 0.15 | 0.75 |

305　5000 Pesos

	VF	UNC
ND (1977-83). Color varieties in underprint: yellow or green, maroon or ochre. Blue and olive-green on multicolor underprint. General José de San Martin at right. Back: Coastline of Mar del Plata. | | |
a. Watermark: Arms. 2 signature varieties. *SERIE A, B.* | 0.40 | 2.00 |
b. Watermark: Multiple sunbursts. 2 signature varieties. *SERIE B.* | 0.20 | 1.00 |

306　10,000 Pesos

	VF	UNC
ND (1976-83). With colored threads. Orange and red on multicolor underprint. General José de San Martin at right. 4 signature varieties. Back: National park on back. Watermark: Varieties. | | |
a. Watermark: Arms. 3 signature varieties. *SERIE A-G.* | 0.75 | 3.00 |
b. Watermark: Multiple sunbursts. *SERIE G.* | 0.50 | 1.50 |

307 50,000 Pesos
ND (1979-83). With colored threads. Brown on multicolor underprint. General José
de San Martin at right. 2 signature varieties. Back: Banco Central building at left
center. Watermark: Arms.

	VF	UNC
	1.00	3.00

308 100,000 Pesos
ND (1979-83). With colored threads. Gray and red on multicolor underprint.
General José de San Martin at right. Signature varieties. Back: Mint building at left
center. Watermark: Varieties.

	VF	UNC
a. Watermark: Arms. *SERIE A, B.*	2.00	10.00
b. Watermark: Multiple sunbursts. *SERIE B.*	1.00	3.00

309 500,000 Pesos
ND (1980-83). With colored threads. Green, brown and blue on multicolor under-
print. General José de San Martin at right. 2 signature varieties. Back: Founding of
Buenos Aires at left center. Watermark: Multiple sunbursts.

	VF	UNC
	1.00	5.00

310 1,000,000 Pesos
ND (1981-83). Blue and pink on multicolor underprint. General José de San Martin
at right. *SERIE A, B.* 3 signature varieties. Back: Independence Declaration with
25 de Mayo at left center. Watermark: Multiple sunbursts.

	VF	UNC
	7.50	17.50

1983-85 ND Issue

#311-319 Replacement notes: Serial # suffix: *R.*

311 1 Peso Argentino
ND (1983-84). UV: fibers fluoresce green. Red-orange and purple on blue
and multicolor underprint. General José de San Martin at right. *SERIE A, B.* 2
signature varieties. Colored threads. Back: Scene of Bariloche-Llao-Llao at center.
Watermark: Multiple sunbursts. Printer: CdM.

	VF	UNC
a. Issued note.	0.15	0.75
s. Specimen. Overprint: *MUESTRA* twice on both sides.	—	25.00

312 5 Pesos Argentinos
ND (1983-84). With colored threads. Brown-violet and black on multicolor underprint. General José de San Martin at right. 2 signature varieties. Back: Monument
to the Flag at Rosario at center. Watermark: Multiple sunbursts. Printer: CdM.

	VF	UNC
a. Issued note.	0.15	0.75
s. Specimen. Overprint: *MUESTRA* twice on both sides.	—	25.00

313 10 Pesos Argentinos
ND (1983-84). With colored fibers. UV: Fibers fluoresce green. Black and red on
green and multicolor underprint. General José de San Martin at right. *SERIE A,
B.* 2 signature varieties. Back: Waterfall at Iguazu at center. Watermark: Multiple
sunbursts. Printer: CdM.

	VF	UNC
a. Issued note.	0.15	0.75
s. Specimen. Overprint: *MUESTRA* twice on both sides.	—	25.00

317   1000 Pesos Argentinos   **VF   UNC**

ND (1983-85). With colored threads. Blue-green and brown on multicolor
underprint. General José de San Martin at right. Back: *El Paso de los Andes* battle
scene. Watermark: Varieties.

   a. *SERIE A, B.* 2 signature varieties.   1.50   7.00
   b. Watermark: Multiple sunbursts (1984). *SERIE C, D.*   0.50   1.50
   s1. As a. Specimen. Overprint: *MUESTRA* on each side.   —   25.00
   s2. As b. Specimen. Overprint.: *MUESTRA* on each side.   —   25.00

314   50 Pesos Argentinos   **VF   UNC**

ND (1983-85). With colored fibers. UV: Fibers fluoresce blue. Brown on green and
multicolor underprint. General José de San Martin at right. 2 signature varieties.
Back: Hot springs at Jujuy at center. Watermark: Multiple sunbursts. Printer: CdM.

   a. Issued note.   0.15   0.75
   s. Specimen. Overprint: *MUESTRA* twice on both sides.   —   25.00

318   5000 Pesos Argentinos   **VF   UNC**

ND (1984-85). With colored threads. Red-brown on multicolor underprint. J. B.
Alberdi at right. *SERIES A, B.* Back: Constitutional meeting of 1853. Watermark:
Young San Martín.

   a. Issued note.   2.00   10.00
   s. Specimen. Overprint: MUESTRA on each side.   —   25.00

315   100 Pesos Argentinos   **VF   UNC**

ND (1983-85). With colored threads. Blue on multicolor underprint. General José
de San Martin at right. *SERIE A, B.* 2 signature varieties. Back: Coastline at
Ushuaia at center. Watermark: Multiple sunbursts. Printer: CdM.

   a. Issued note.   0.50   1.50
   s. Specimen. Overprint: *MUESTRA* twice on both sides.   —   25.00

316   500 Pesos Argentinos   **VF   UNC**

ND (1984). With colored threads. Purple on multicolor underprint. General José
de San Martin at right. Back: Town meeting of May 22, 1810. Watermark: Multiple
sunbursts. Printer: CdM.

   a. Issued note.   0.50   1.50
   s. Specimen. Overprint: *MUESTRA* on each side.   —   25.00

319   10,000 Pesos Argentinos   **VF   UNC**

ND (1985). With colored threads. Blue-violet on multicolor underprint. M. Belgrano
at right. Back: Creation of Argentine flag. Watermark: Young San Martín.

   a. Issued note.   3.50   15.00
   s. Specimen. Overprint: *MUESTRA* on each side.   —   25.00

1985 ND Provisional Issue

#320-322 Rectangle overprint in watermark area on face of Peso Argentino notes.

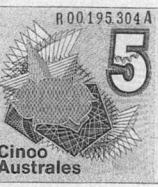

320   1 Austral VF   UNC

ND (1985). New denomination overprint in numeral and wording in box, green   0.50   2.50
on face and blue on back of #317b. Series D. Rectangle on watermark area.
Watermark: Sunburst.

321   5 Australes VF   UNC

ND (1985). New denomination overprint as #320, purple on face and brown on   2.00   5.00
back of #318, Series B. Rectangle on watermark area. Watermark: San Martin.

322   10 Australes VF   UNC

ND (1985). New denomination overprint as #320 on #319. Rectangle in watermark
area.

	VF	UNC
a. Blue overprint on face and back. Watermark: San Martín. Series A; B.	4.00	9.00
b. Blue overprint on face and back. Watermark: Multiple sunbursts. Series A-C.	1.75	6.00
c. Blue overprint on face, light olive-green overprint on back. Series B; C. Watermark San Martin.	1.75	5.00
d. Like c., but watermark Multiple sunbursts.	1.75	6.00
e. Series B without overprint. Watermark: Multiple sunbursts.	30.00	60.00
s. As b. Specimen.	—	25.00

1985-91 ND Issue

323   1 Austral VF   UNC

ND (1985-89). UV: threads fluoresce green; back: design elements pink. Blue-
green and purple on multicolor underprint. B. Rivadavia at center, latent image
"BCRA". Signature varieties. Back: Liberty (Progreso) with torch and shield seated
at left center. Watermark: Multiple sunbursts. Printer: CdM.

	VF	UNC
a. Signature titles E. Series A.	0.75	3.00
b. Signature titles C. Series B; C. 2 Signature varieties.	0.15	0.40
s. Signature titles C. Series A. Specimen.	—	25.00

324   5 Australes VF   UNC

ND (1985-89). UV: threads fluoresce green; black design elements orange. Brown
and deep olive-green on multicolor underprint. J. J. de Urquiza at center, latent
image "BCRA". Signature varieties. Back: Liberty (Progreso) with torch and shield
seated at left center. Watermark: Multiple sunbursts. Printer: CdM.

	VF	UNC
a. Signature titles F. Series A.	0.25	2.00
b. Signature titles C. Series A.	0.15	0.10

325   10 Australes VF   UNC

ND (1985-89). UV: threads fluoresce green; back: design elements pink, orange.
Dark blue and purple on multicolor underprint. S. Derqui at center, latent image
"BCRA". Signature varieties. Back: Liberty (Progreso) with torch and shield seated
at left center. Watermark: Multiple sunbursts. Printer: CdM.

	VF	UNC
a. Coarse portrait in heavy horizontal wavy lines. Signature titles E. Series A.	0.75	3.50
b. Modified portrait in finer horizontal wavy lines. Signature titles C. Series A; B; C.	0.15	0.40

326   50 Australes VF   UNC

ND (1986-89). UV: threads fluoresce green; back: design elements orange. Purple
and deep brown on multicolor underprint. B. Mitre at center, latent image "BCRA".
Signature varieties. Back: Liberty (Progreso) with torch and shield seated at left
center. Watermark: Multiple sunbursts. Printer: CdM.

	VF	UNC
a. Signature titles E. Series A.	6.00	20.00
b. Signature titles C. Series A. 3 Signature varieties.	0.15	0.50
s. As b. Specimen.	—	25.00

327 100 Australes

	VF	UNC
ND (1985-90). UV: threads fluoresce green. Dark red and purple on multicolor underprint. D. F. Sarmiento at center, latent image "BCRA". Signature varieties. Back: Liberty (Progreso) with torch and shield seated at left center. Watermark: Multiple sunbursts. Printer: CdM.		
a. Signature titles E. Series A.	4.00	15.00
b. Signature titles C. Engraved back. Series A; B. 3 signature varieties.	0.20	0.75
c. Signature titles C. Back pink and lithographed; without purple and blue. Series C; D.	0.15	0.50
s. As b. Specimen.	—	25.00

330 5000 Australes

	VF	UNC
ND (1989-91). Dark brown and red-brown on multicolor underprint. M. Juarez at center, latent image "BCRA". Signature varieties. Back: Liberty (Progreso) with torch and shield seated at left center. Printer: CdM.		
a. Green shield design at upper center r. Sign titles: E. Watermark: Liberty. Series A.	3.00	12.50
b. Green shield design at upper center r. Sign titles: C. Watermark: Liberty. Series A.	5.00	17.50
c. Dark brown shield design at upper center r. signature titles: E. Watermark: Liberty. Series B.	2.50	8.00
d. Dark brown shield designature signature titles: C. Watermark: Liberty. Series B.	2.00	7.00
e. Dark brown shield designature signature titles: F. Lithographed back. Watermark: Multiple sunbursts. Series C.	1.00	4.00
f. Series D (1991).	60.00	125

1989; 1991 ND Provisional Issue

328 500 Australes

	VF	UNC
ND (1988-90). Pale olive-green on multicolor underprint. N. Avellaneda at center, latent image "BCRA". Signature titles: C. 2 signature varieties. Back: Liberty (Progreso) with torch and shield seated at left center. Printer: CdM.		
a. Metallic green guilloche by *500*. Back olive-green, black and multicolor. Watermark: Liberty. Series A. (1988).	0.50	2.00
b. Dark olive-green guilloche by *500*. Back pale olive-green and multicolor; lithographed (without black). Watermark: Multiple sunbursts. Series A. (1990).	0.25	0.85
s. As a. Specimen.	—	25.00

331 10,000 Australes

	VF	UNC
ND (1989). Black-blue, deep blue-green and brown on multicolor underprint. San Martin at right, overprint value in olive-green in box at left, word "PESOS" at center blocked out. Signature titles: C. Back: Denomination repeated in lines of text and overprint value at right. Watermark: Multiple sunbursts. Printer: CdM-A.	7.50	25.00

329 1000 Australes

	VF	UNC
ND (1988-90). Violet-brown and purple on multicolor underprint. J. A. Roca at center, latent image"BCRA". Signature titles: *GERENTE GENERAL* and *PRESIDENTE*. Signature varieties. Back: Liberty (Progreso) with torch and shield seated at left center. Printer: CdM.		
a. Vertical green guilloche near *1000*. Watermark: Liberty. Series A.	0.20	0.75
b. Vertical brown-violet guilloche near *1000*. Watermark: Liberty. Series B.	0.25	1.00
c. Like b. but watermark: Multiple sunbursts.	0.25	1.00
d. Like c. but signature titles: F. Series C.	0.50	2.00
s. As a. Specimen.	—	25.00

332 50,000 Australes

	VF	UNC
ND (1989). Deep olive-green and blue on multicolor underprint. San Martin at right, overprint value in violet in box at left, word "PESOS" at center blocked out. Series M. Signature titles: E. Back: Denomination repeated in lines of text and overprint value at right, value in light brown at right. Watermark: Multiple sunbursts. Printer: CdM-A.	8.00	27.50

333 500,000 Australes

	VF	UNC
ND (1990). Black, purple and red on multicolor underprint. San Martin at right, overprint value in box at left, word "PESOS" at bottom right blocked out. Signature titles: F. Signature varieties. Series M. Back: Denomination repeated in lines of text and overprint value at right. Watermark: Multiple sunbursts. Printer: CdM-A.	30.00	75.00

1989-91 ND Issue

334 10,000 Australes   **VF UNC**
ND (1989-91). Black on deep blue, brown and multicolor underprint with brown diamond design at upper center right. C. Pellegrini at center. Back: Liberty (Progreso) with torch and shield seated at left center. Watermark: Liberty head. Printer: CdM-A.

    a. Signature titles: C. Series A; B.   1.25   3.50
    b. Signature titles: F. Series C. Watermark: sunbursts.   1.50   6.00

335 50,000 Australes   **VF UNC**
ND (1989-91). Black on ochre, olive-green and multicolor underprint with black flower design at upper center right Saenz Peña at center, signature titles: C. Series A; B. Back: Liberty (Progreso) with torch and shield seated at left center. Watermark: Liberty head. Printer: CdM-A.   6.00   25.00

336 100,000 Australes   **VF UNC**
ND (1990-91). Dark brown and reddish brown on pale brown and multicolor underprint. Coarsely engraved portrait of J. Evaristo Uriburu at center. Black signature titles: F. Series A; B. Back: Liberty (Progreso) with torch and shield seated at left center. Watermark: Liberty head. Printer: CdM-A.   10.00   45.00

337 100,000 Australes   **VF UNC**
ND (1991). Dark brown and reddish brown on brown and multicolor underprint. Finely engraved portrait of J. Evaristo Uriburu at center. Brown signature titles. Series B. Back: Liberty (Progreso) with torch and shield seated at left center. Watermark: Liberty head. Printer: CdM-A.   8.00   50.00

338 500,000 Australes   **VF UNC**
ND (1991). Black-violet, red and blue on multicolor underprint. M. Quintana at center. Series A, B. 2 signature varieties. Back: Liberty (Progreso) with torch and shield seated at left center. Watermark: Liberty head. Printer: CdM-A.   25.00   75.00

1991-92 ND Issue

#339-345 replacement notes: Serial # prefix *R*.

339 1 Peso   **VF UNC**
ND (1992-94). Dark blue and violet-brown on multicolor underprint. C. Pellegrini at right. Back: National Congress building at left center. Watermark: Multiple sunbursts. Printer: CdM-A. 155x65mm.

    a. Signature titles: F. (1992). Series A, B.   FV   3.00
    b. Signature titles: G. (1993). Series B, C, D.   FV   2.50
    c. Signature titles as a. Serial # prefix L. (1994).   FV   5.00

340 2 Pesos   **VF UNC**
ND (1992-97). Deep blue and red-violet on multicolor underprint. B. Mitre at right. Back: Mitre Museum at left center. Watermark: Multiple sunbursts. Printer: CdM-A.

    a. Signature titles: F. (1992). Series A.   FV   5.00
    b. Signature titles: H. (1993). Series A-C.   FV   4.00

341 5 Pesos

ND (1992-97). Deep olive-green and red-orange on multicolor underprint. General José de San Martín at right. Back: Monument to the Glory of Mendoza at left center. Watermark: Multiple sunbursts. Printer: CdM-A.

		VF	UNC
a. Signature titles: F. (1992). Series Λ.		FV	8.00
b. Signature titles: G. (1993). Series A-C.		FV	9.00
c. Signature titles as a. Serial # prefix L. (1994).		FV	10.00

Uncut sheets and partial sheets exist of this note.

342 10 Pesos

ND (1992-97). Deep brown and dark green on multicolor underprint. M. Belgrano at right. Back: M. Belgrano at right. Monument to the Flag at Rosario with city in background at left center. Watermark: Liberty head. Printer: CdM-A.

		VF	UNC
a. Signature titles: F. (1992). Series A-B.		FV	20.00
b. Signature titles: H. (1993). Series C-E.		FV	17.50

Uncut sheets and partial sheets exist of this note.

343 20 Pesos

ND (1992-97). Carmine and deep blue on multicolor underprint. J. Manuel de Rosas at right. Back: *Vuelta de Obligado* battle scene at left center. Watermark: Liberty head. Printer: CdM-A.

		VF	UNC
a. Signature titles: F. (1992). Series A.		FV	30.00
b. Signature titles: G. (1993). Series A-B.		FV	25.00

344 50 Pesos

ND (1992-97). Black and red on multicolor underprint. D. Faustino Sarmiento at right. Back: Plaza de Mayo in Buenos Aires at left center. Watermark: D. Faustino Sarmiento.

		VF	UNC
a. Signature titles: F. (1992). Series A.		FV	65.00
b. Signature titles: H. (1993). Series A-B.		FV	60.00

Uncut sheets and partial sheets exist of this note.

345 100 Pesos

ND (1992-97). Violet, lilac and green on multicolor underprint. J. A. Roca at right. Back: *La Conquista del Desierto* scene at left center. Watermark: J. A. Roca.

		VF	UNC
a. Signature titles: F. (1992). Series A.		FV	125
b. Signature titles: G. (1993). Series A-D.		FV	110

1997-2000 ND Issue

#346-351 Replacement notes: Serial # prefix *R*.

346 2 Pesos

ND (1997-2002). Uncut sheets and partial sheets exist. Deep blue and brown-violet on multicolor underprint. B. Mitre at right, ornate gate at center. Ascending size serial number at upper right. Signature titles: H. 2 signature varieties. Series A-D. Back: Mitre Museum at left center. Printer: CdM-A. 155x65mm.

	VF	UNC
	FV	3.00

347 5 Pesos

ND (1998-2003). Uncut sheets and partial sheets exist. Deep olive-green and purple on multicolor underprint. General José de San Martín at right and on horseback with troops at center. Signature titles: G. 4 signature varieties. Series A-C. Ascending size serial number at upper right. Back: Monument to the Glory at Mendoza at left center. Printer: CdM-A. 155x65mm.

	VF	UNC
	FV	7.00

348 10 Pesos

ND (1998-2003). Uncut sheets and partial sheets exist. Deep brown and dark green on multicolor underprint. M. Belgrano at right, Liberty with flag at center, ascending size serial number at upper right. Signature titles: H. 3 signature varieties. Series A-E. Back: Monument to the Flag at Rosario with city in background at left center. Watermark: M. Belgrano. Printer: CdM-A. 155x65mm.

	VF	UNC
	FV	15.00

349 20 Pesos
ND (1999-2003). Red-brown and purple on multicolor underprint. J. Manuel de Rosas at right, ascending size serial number at upper right. Signature titles: G. 4 signature varieties. Series A, B. Back: *Vuelta de Obligado* battle scene at left center. Watermark: J. Manuel de Rosas. Printer: CdM-A. 155x65mm.

VF UNC
FV 30.00

Uncut sheets and partial sheets exist of this note.

350 50 Pesos
ND (1999-2003). Multicolor. D. Faustino Sarmiento at right , ascending size serial number at upper right. Signature titles: H. 3 signature varieties. Series A. Back. Government office with monuments, palm trees in foreground at left center. Watermark: D. Faustino Sarmiento. Printer: CdM-A. 155x65mm.

VF UNC
FV 65.00

Uncut sheets and partial sheets exist of this note.

351 100 Pesos
ND (1999-2002). Uncut sheets and partial sheets exist. Multicolor. J. A. Roca at right, ascending size serial number at upper right Signature titles: G. 4 signature varieties. Series A, B.. Back: *La Conquista del Desierto* scene at left center. Watermark: J. A. Roca. Printer: CdM-A. 155x65mm.

VF UNC
FV 120

2002-03 ND Issue

352 2 Pesos
ND (2002). No clause: *CONVERTIBLES DE CURSO LEGAL.* B. Mitre at right, ascending size serial number at upper right, ornate gate at center. Series D-L. 5 signature varieties. Back: Mitre Museum at left center. 155x65mm.

VF UNC
FV 3.00

353 5 Pesos
ND (2003). No clause: *CONVERTIBLES DE CURSO LEGAL.* Gen. J. de San Martin at right and on horseback with troops at center. Ascending size serial numbers at upper right. Series C-G. 3 signature varieties. Back: Monument to the Glory at Mendoza at left center. 155x65mm.

VF UNC
FV 7.00

354 10 Pesos
ND (2003). No clause: *CONVERTIBLES DE CURSO LEGAL.* M. Belgrano at right, Liberty with flag at center, ascending size serial number at upper right.Series E-N. 3 signature varieties. Back: Monument to the Flag at Rosario with city in background at left center. Watermark: M. Belgrano. 155x65mm.

VF UNC
FV 7.00

355 20 Pesos
ND (2003). No clause: *CONVERTIBLES DE CURSO LEGAL.* J. Manuel de Rosas at right, ascending size serial numbers at upper right. Series B-D. 3 signature varieties. Back: Vuelta de Obligado battle scene at left center. Watermark: J. Manuel de Rosas. 155x65mm.

VF UNC
FV 20.00

356 50 Pesos
ND (2003). No clause: *CONVERTIBLES DE CURSO LEGAL.* D. Faustino Sarmiento at right, ascending size serial numbers at upper right. Series A-G. Signature varieties. Back: Government office with monuments, palm trees in foreground at left center. Watermark: D. Faustino Sarmiento. 155x65mm.

VF UNC
FV 55.00

357 100 Pesos
ND (2003). No clause: *CONVERTIBLES DE CURSO LEGAL.* J. A. Roca at right, ascending size serial numbers at upper right. Series B-J. 3 signature varieties. Back: La Conquista del Desierto scene at left center. Watermark: J. A. Roca. 155x65mm.

VF UNC
FV 100

2012 Commemorative Issue

358   100 Pesos   **VF   UNC**

ND (2012). Violet and multicolor. Eva Peron profile at right. Back: Allegorical
woman and two children. Watermark: Eva Peron.

    a. 100 at left edge in center. Serial # suffix A.   FV   40.00

    b. 100 at left edge in center. Serial # suffix B.   FV   30.00

Commemorates the 60th Anniversary of her death.

2015 ND Issue

359   5 Pesos   **VF   UNC**

1.10.2015. Green, light blue, violet and yellow. Handshake as registration device,   FV   7.00
sunburst, branch with flowers, statue, Gen. J. de San Martin and standing soldier
at right. Back: José Artigas, Simón Bolívar, José de San Martín and Bernardo
O'Higgins; flags, flames and presidential seal; coat of arms; handshake. No
security thread. Watermark: Gen. J. de San Martin and electrotype JSM. Printer:
S.E. CASA DE MONEDA. 155x65mm.

ARMENIA

The Republic of Armenia is
bounded to the north by Georgia,
to the east by Azerbaijan and to the
south and west by Turkey and Iran.
It has an area of 29,743 sq. km and
a population of 2.97 million. Capital:
Yerevan. Agriculture including cotton,
vineyards and orchards, hydroelec-
tricity, chemicals - primarily synthetic
rubber and fertilizers, and vast mineral deposits of copper, zinc and
aluminum and production of steel and
paper are major industries.

    Armenia prides itself on being the first nation to formally adopt Christianity (early 4th century). Despite
periods of autonomy, over the centuries Armenia came under the sway of various empires including the Roman, Byzantine, Arab, Persian, and Ottoman. During World War I in the western portion of Armenia, Ottoman Turkey instituted a policy of forced resettlement coupled with other harsh practices that resulted in an
estimated 1 million Armenian deaths. The eastern area of Armenia was ceded by the Ottomans to Russia in
1828; this portion declared its independence in 1918, but was conquered by the Soviet Red Army in 1920.
Armenian leaders remain preoccupied by the long conflict with Muslim Azerbaijan over Nagorno-Karabakh,
a primarily Armenian-populated region, assigned to Soviet Azerbaijan in the 1920s by Moscow. Armenia and
Azerbaijan began fighting over the area in 1988; the struggle escalated after both countries attained independence from the Soviet Union in 1991. By May 1994, when a cease-fire took hold, Armenian forces held not
only Nagorno-Karabakh but also a significant portion of Azerbaijan proper. The economies of both sides have
been hurt by their inability to make substantial progress toward a peaceful resolution. Turkey imposed an
economic blockade on Armenia and closed the common border because of the Armenian separatists' control
of Nagorno-Karabakh and surrounding areas.

MONETARY SYSTEM:

    1 Dram = 100 Lumma

REPUBLIC

Armenian Republic Bank

1993 Bond - Coupon Issue

32A   5000 Dram   **VF   UNC**

    1993. Multicolor   —   —

1993-95 Issue

33   10 Dram   **VF   UNC**

1993. Dark brown, light blue and pale orange on multicolor underprint. Statue of
David from Sasoun at upper center right, main railway station in Yerevan at upper
left center. Back: Mount Ararat at upper center right. Watermark: Crude outlined
arms, or refined arms. Printer: G&D (without imprint).

    a. Issued note.   0.50   2.00

    s. Specimen. Red overprint: SPECIMEN on both sides.   FV   75.00

34   25 Dram   **VF   UNC**

1993. Brown and light red on multicolor underprint. Frieze with lion from Erebuni
Castle at center right, cuneiform tablet at upper left center. Back: Arched ornament
at upper center right. Watermark: Crude outlined arms, or refined arms. Printer:
G&D (without imprint).

    a. Issued note.   1.00   3.00

    s. Specimen. Red overprint: SPECIMEN on both sides.   —   75.00

35 50 Dram

1993. Dark blue on pink and multicolor underprint. State Museum of History and National Gallery at upper left center. Back: Parliament building at upper center right . Watermark: Crude outlined arms, or refined arms. Printer: G&D (without imprint).

	VF	UNC
a. Issued note.	2.00	4.00
s. Specimen. Red overprint: SPECIMEN on both sides.	—	75.00

36 100 Dram

1993. Purple, light blue and light red on multicolor underprint. Mt. Ararat at upper left center, Church of Zvarnots at center right. Back: Opera and ballet theater in Yerevan at upper center right. Printer: G&D (without imprint).

	VF	UNC
a. Watermark: Crude outline arms.	3.00	6.00
b. Watermark: Refined arms.	3.00	6.00
s. Specimen. Red overprint: SPECIMEN on both sides.	—	75.00

37 200 Dram

1993. Brown, green and red on multicolor underprint. Church of St. Hripsime in Echmiadzin at center right. Back: Circular design at upper center right. Printer: G&D (without imprint).

	VF	UNC
a. Watermark: Crude outline arms.	4.00	9.00
b. Watermark: Refined arms.	4.00	9.00
s. Specimen. Red overprint: SPECIMEN on both sides.	—	75.00

38 500 Dram

1993. Dark green and red-brown on multicolor underprint. Tetradrachm of King Tigran II the Great aat center right, Mt. Ararat at upper left. Back: Center Open book and quill pen at upper center right. Printer: G&D (without imprint).

	VF	UNC
a. Watermark: Crude outline arms.	7.00	16.00
b. Watermark: Refined arms.	7.00	16.00
s. Specimen. Red overprint: SPECIMEN on both sides.	—	75.00

39 1000 Dram

1994. Dark brown and brown on multicolor underprint. Statue of Mesrop Mashtotz at left. Back: Matenadaran façade at right. Watermark: Arms.

	VF	UNC
a. Issued note.	FV	20.00
s. Specimen. Red overprint: SPECIMEN on both sides.	FV	75.00

40 5000 Dram

1995. Temple of Garni at center. Back: Goddess Anahit.

	VF	UNC
	FV	50.00

Central Bank of the Republic of Armenia
1998-99 Issue

#41, 42, 44 replacement notes serial # first digit is 9.

41 50 Dram

1998. Brownish pink and slate blue on multicolor underprint. Aram Khachaturian at left, opera house at right. Back: Scene from *Gayaneh* Ballet and Mt. Ararat. Printer: TDLR (without imprint).

	VF	UNC
	0.50	2.00

42 100 Dram

1998. UV: threads fluoresce blue and yellow; value at left yellow; vertical serial # red. Light and dark blue on multicolor underprint. Victor Hambartsumyan at left, solar system map at right. Back: Byurakan Observatory on Mt. Arakadz. Watermark: Victor Hambartsumyan. Printer: TDLR (without imprint).

	VF	UNC
	0.50	3.00

#43 Not assigned.

44   500 Dram
1999 (2000). Black on red and multicolor underprint. Alexander Tamanyan and city plan. Back: House of the Government in Yerevan at left center. Watermark: A. Tamanyan. Printer: TDLR (without imprint). 129x72mm.

	VF	UNC
	2.00	5.00

45   1000 Dram
1999. Aqua and green on multicolor underprint. Yeghishe Charents at left, lines of poetry at right. Back: Old Yerevan city scene. Watermark: Y. Charents. Printer: TDLR (without imprint). 136x72mm.

	VF	UNC
	3.50	12.00

46   5000 Dram
1999 (2000). Dark and light brown on green, gold and multicolor underprint H. Tumanyan at left. Back: Saryan's picture of Lory mountains. Watermark: H. Tumanyan. Printer: JEZ. 143x72mm.

	VF	UNC
	FV	40.00

47   20,000 Dram
1999. Brown and yellow on multicolor underprint. Martiros Saryan, painter at left, abstract painting in center. Hologram at right. Back: Saryan painting *Armenia*. Watermark: M. Saryan. 150x72mm.

	VF	UNC
	FV	100

2001 Commemorative Issue
#48, 1700 years of Christianity in Armenia

48   50,000 Dram
2001. 1700 years of Christianity in Armenia. Brown and multicolor. Cathedral of Holy Echmiatzin at center, holographic strip at left with commemorative text vertically. Back: St Gregory and King Tiridat holding church. Akhachkar at right. Watermark: Portrait. Printer: TDLR (without imprint). 160x79mm.

	VF	UNC
	FV	200

#49 Not assigned.

2001; 2003 Issue

50   1000 Dram
2001 (2002). Aqua and green on multicolor underprint. Yeghishe Charents at left, lines of poetry at right, additional security features. Back: Old Yerevan city scene. Watermark: Y. Charents. 136x72mm.

		VF	UNC
a. 2001. Printer: OEBS.		FV	7.50
b. 2001. Printer: G&D.		FV	7.50

51   5000 Dram
2003, 2005, 2009. H. Tumanyuan at left. Back: Saryan's picture of Lory Mountains. Watermark: H. Tumanyuan. 143x72mm.

		VF	UNC
a. 2003.		FV	35.00
b. 2005.		FV	35.00
c. 2009.		FV	35.00

52   10,000 Dram   **VF   UNC**

2003; 2006; 2008. Purple and light violet on multicolor unpt. Avetik Isahakyan
(poet) at left, Mt. Aragats at center. Back: Gyumri city view. Watermark: A.
Isahakyan. 151x72mm.

   a. 2003.   FV   55.00
   b. 2006.   FV   50.00
   c. 2008.   FV   50.00

53   20,000 Dram   **VF   UNC**

2007, 2009. Brown and yellow on multicolor underprint. Martiros Saryan, painter,
at left, abstract painting at center. Holographic foil at left. Back: Saryan painting
Armenia. Watermark: M. Saryan. 150x72mm.

   a. 2007.   FV   125
   b. 2009.   FV   125

54   100,000 Dram   **VF   UNC**

2009 Slate blue, brown and multicolor. King Abgar V standing at left, 1st century
map at center. Back: St. Thaddeus transfers the painting of Jesus Christ to Abgar
V of Edessa. Watermark: Abgar V. Printer: TDLR. 160x72mm.

   a. Issued note.   FV   350
   s. Specimen.   —   450

2011-12 Issue

55   1000 Dram   **VF   UNC**

2011. Aqua and green on multicolor underprint. Yeghishe Charents at left, lines   FV   7.50
of poetry at right. Foil strip at left. Back: Old Yerevan city scene. Watermark:
Yeghishe Charents.

56   5000 Dram   **VF   UNC**

2012. Green and brown on multicolor underprint. H. Tumanyuan at left. Back: FV   35.00
Saryan's pictre of Lory Mountains. Watermark: H. Tumanyuan.

57   10,000 Dram   **VF   UNC**

2012. Lilac and black on multicolor underprint. Avetik Isahakyan at left, foil strip at   FV   55.00
left. Back: Gyumri city view. Watermark: A. Isahakyan

58   20,000 Dram   **VF   UNC**

2012. Brown and multicolor. Martiros Saryan at left, foil strip at left. Back: Saryan   FV   125
painting *Armenia*. Watermark: M. Saryan.

Aruba was the second-largest island of the Netherlands Antilles and is situated near the Venezuelan coast. The island has an area of 193 sq. km. and a population of 101,500. Capital: Oranjestad, named after the Dutch royal family.Discovered and claimed for Spain in 1499, Aruba was acquired by the Dutch in 1636. The island's economy has been dominated by three main industries. A 19th century gold rush was followed by prosperity brought on by the opening in 1924 of an oil refinery. The last decades of the 20th century saw a boom in the tourism industry. Aruba seceded from the Netherlands Antilles in 1986 and became a separate, autonomous member of the Kingdom of the Netherlands. Movement toward full independence was halted at Aruba's request in 1990.

MONETARY SYSTEM:
1 Florin = 100 Cents

DUTCH ADMINISTRATION
Banco Central di Aruba
1986 Issue

		VF	**UNC**
1	**5 Florin**	FV	55.00

1.1.1986. Green. Flag at left, coastal hotels at center. Back: Arms of Aruba at center. Printer: JEZ. 146x66mm.

		VF	**UNC**
2	**10 Florin**	FV	70.00

1.1.1986. Green. Flag at left, coastal hotels at center. Back: Arms of Aruba at center. Printer: JEZ. 147x66mm.

		VF	**UNC**
3	**25 Florin**	FV	125

1.1.1986. Green. Flag at left, coastal hotels at center. Back: Arms of Aruba at center. Printer: JEZ. 147x66mm.

		VF	**UNC**
4	**50 Florin**	FV	180

1.1.1986. Green. Flag at left, coastal hotels at center. Back: Arms of Aruba at center. Printer: JEZ. 147x66mm.

		VF	**UNC**
5	**100 Florin**	FV	370

1.1.1986. Green. Flag at left, coastal hotels at center. Back: Arms of Aruba at center. Printer: JEZ. 147x66mm.

Centrale Bank van Aruba
1990 Issue

		VF	**UNC**
6	**5 Florin**	FV	47.50

1.1.1990. Purple and multicolor. Tortuga Blanco (sea turtle) at center right. Back: Geometric forms with pre-Columbian Aruban art. Watermark: Stylized tree. Printer: JEZ. 147x66mm.

		VF	**UNC**
7	**10 Florin**	FV	60.00

1.1.1990. Blue and multicolor. Calco Indian conch (Melongena melongena) at center right. Back: Geometric forms with pre-Columbian Aruban art. Watermark: Stylized tree. Printer: JEZ. 147x66mm.

8   25 Florin
1.1.1990. Brown and multicolor. Rattlesnake *(Crotalus durissus unicolor)* at right.
Back: Geometric forms with pre-Columbian Aruban art. Watermark: Stylized tree.
Printer: JEZ. 147x66mm.

VF UNC
FV 70.00

9   50 Florin
1.1.1990. Red-brown and multicolor. Burrowing owl *(Speotyto cunicularia
arubensis)* at center right. Back: Geometric forms with pre-Columbian Aruban art.
Watermark: Stylized tree. Printer: JEZ. 147x66mm.

VF UNC
FV 95.00

10   100 Florin
1.1.1990. Olive-green and multicolor. Frog *(Pleurodema brachyops)* at center
right. Back: Geometric forms with pre-Columbian Aruban art. Watermark: Stylized
tree. Printer: JEZ. 147x66mm.

VF UNC
FV 350

1993 Issue

11   10 Florin
16.7.1993. With additional security features and new signatures. Blue and multicolor. Calco Indian conch *(Melongona melongena)* at center right, with text: *Wettig
Betaalmiddel* (legal tender). Back: Geometric forms with pre-Columbian Aruban
art. Watermark: Stylized tree. Printer: JEZ. 147x66mm.

VF UNC
FV 50.00

12   25 Florin
16.7.1993. With additional security features and new signatures. Brown and
multicolor. Rattlesnake *(Speotyto cunicularia arubensis)* at right, with text: *Wettig
Betaalmiddel* (legal tender). Back: Geometric forms with pre-Colombian Aruban
art. Watermark: Stylized tree. Printer: JEZ. 147x66mm.

VF UNC
FV 50.00

13   50 Florin
16.7.1993. With additional security features and new signatures. Red-brown
and multicolor. Burrowing owl *(Speotyto cunicularia arubensis)* at center right,
with text: *Wettig Betaalmiddel* (legal tender). Back: Geometric forms with pre-
Colombian Aruban art. Watermark: Stylized tree. Printer: JEZ. 147x66mm.

VF UNC
FV 85.00

14   100 Florin
16.7.1993. With additional security features and new signatures. Olive-green
and multicolor. Frog at center right, with text: *Wettig Betaalmiddel* (legal tender).
Back: Geometric forms with pre-Colombian Aruban art. Watermark: Stylized tree.
Printer: JEZ. 147x66mm.

VF UNC
FV 210

15   500 Florin
16.7.1993. With additional security features and new signatures. Blue and
multicolor. Grouper fish *(Epinephelus morio)* at center right, with text: *Wettig
Betaalmiddel* (legal tender). Back: Geometric forms with pre-Colombian Aruban
art. Watermark: Stylized tree. Printer: JEZ. 147x66mm.

VF UNC
FV 625

2003 Issue

16   10 Florin   VF   UNC
1.12.2003; 1.7.2008; 1.12.2012. With additional security features. Blue and
multicolor. Calco Indian conch *(Melongena melongena)* at center right with text:
Wettig Betaalmiddel (legal tender). Back: Geometric forms with pre-Colombian
Aruban art. Printer: JEZ. 147x66mm.
   a. 1.12.2003.   FV   25.00
   b. 1.7.2008. New right hand signature.   FV   22.50
   c. 1.12.2012.   FV   22.50

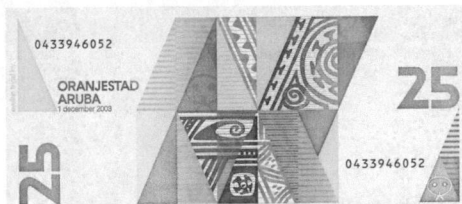

17   25 Florin   VF   UNC
1.12.2003; 1.7.2008; 12.1.2012. With additional security features. Brown and
multicolor. Rattlesnake *(Crotalus durissus unicolor)* at right, with text: *Wettig
Betaalmiddel* (legal tender). Back: Geometric forms with pre-Colombian Aruban
art. Watermark: Stylized tree. Printer: JEZ. 147x66mm.
   a. 1.12.2003.   FV   45.00
   b. 1.7.2008. New right hand signature.   FV   40.00
   c. 12.1.2012.   FV   40.00

18   50 Florin   VF   UNC
1.12.2003; 1.7.2008; 1.12.2012. With additional security features. Red-brown
and multicolor. Burrowing owl (Speotyto cunicularia arubensis) at center right,
with text: *Wettig Betaalmiddel* (legal tender). Back: Geometric forms with pre-
Colombian Aruban art. Watermark: Stylized tree. Printer: JEZ. 147x66mm.
   a. 1.12.2003.   FV   75.00
   b. 1.7.2008. New right hand signature.   FV   70.00
   c. 1.12.2012   FV   70.00

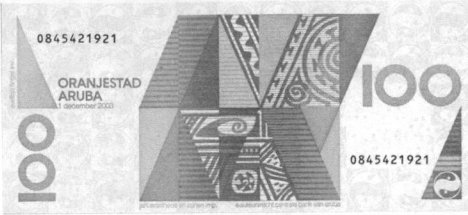

19   100 Florin   VF   UNC
1.12.2003; 1.7.2008; 12.1.2012. With additional security features. Olive-green
and multicolor. Frog *(Pleurodema brachyops)* at center right, with text: *Wettig
Betaalmiddel* (legal tender). Back: Geometric forms with pre-Colombian Aruban
art. Watermark: Stylized tree. Printer: JEZ. 147x66mm.
   a. 1.12.2003.   FV   275
   b. 1.7.2008. New right hand signature.   FV   190
   c. 12.1.2012.   FV   190

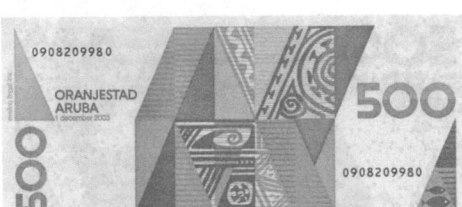

20   500 Florin   VF   UNC
1.12.2003. With additional security features. Blue and multicolor. Grouper fish   FV   585
(Epinephelus morio) at center right, with text: *Wettig Betaalmiddel* (legal tender).
Back: Geometric forms with pre-Colombian Aruban art. Watermark: Stylized tree.
Printer: JEZ. 147x66mm.

COLLECTOR SERIES
Centrale Bank van Aruba
1990 Issue

CS1   1990 5-100 Florin   Mkt. Value
  #6-10 with low matched serial numbers housed in a six-page special presentation   710
  folder. 200 sets produced.

AUSTRALIA

The Commonwealth of Australia, the smallest continent and largest island in the world, is located south of Indonesia between the Indian and Pacific oceans. It has an area of 7.68 million sq. km. and a population of 21 million. Capital: Canberra. Due to its early and sustained isolation, Australia is the habitat of such curious and unique fauna as the kangaroo, koala, platypus, wombat and barking lizard. The continent possesses extensive mineral deposits, the most important of which are gold, coal, silver, nickel, uranium, lead and zinc. Livestock raising, mining and manufacturing are the principal industries. Chief exports are wool, meat, wheat, iron ore, coal and nonferrous metals.

Aboriginal settlers arrived on the continent from Southeast Asia about 40,000 years before the first Europeans began exploration in the 17th century. No formal territorial claims were made until 1770, when Capt. James Cook took possession in the name of Great Britain. Six colonies were created in the late 18th and 19th centuries; they federated and became the Commonwealth of Australia in 1901. The new country took advantage of its natural resources to rapidly develop agricultural and manufacturing industries and to make a major contribution to the British effort in World Wars I and II. In recent decades, Australia has transformed itself into an internationally competitive, advanced market economy. It boasted one of the OECD's fastest growing economies during the 1990s, a performance due in large part to economic reforms adopted in the 1980s. Long-term concerns include climate-change issues such as the depletion of the ozone layer and more frequent droughts, and management and conservation of coastal areas, especially the Great Barrier Reef.

RULERS:
British

MONETARY SYSTEM:
1 Shilling = 12 Pence
1 Pound = 20 Shillings = 2 Dollars
1 Pound = 20 Shillings; to 1966
1 Dollar = 100 Cents, 1966

COMMONWEALTH OF AUSTRALIA

Reserve Bank
1960-61 ND Issue

33   10 Shillings   VF   UNC

ND (1961-65). Dark brown on orange and green underprint. Arms at lower left, portrait Matthew Flinders at right. Signature H. C. Coombs with title: *GOVERNOR / RESERVE BANK of AUSTRALIA* below lower left, signature R. Wilson. Back: Old Parliament House in Canberra. Watermark: Capt. James Cook.

a. Issued note. | 100 | 400
r. Serial # suffix *, replacement. | 2,500 | 25,000
s. Specimen. | 20,000 | 60,000

34   1 Pound   VF   UNC

ND (1961-65). Black on green and yellow underprint. Arms at upper center, cameo portrait Queen Elizabeth II at right. Signature H. C. Coombs with title: *GOVERNOR / RESERVE BANK of AUSTRALIA* below lower left, signature R. Wilson. Back: Facing portrait Charles Sturt and Hamilton Hume. Watermark: Capt. James Cook.

a. Issued note. | 60.00 | 300
r. Serial # suffix *, replacement. | 3,000 | 30,000
s. Specimen. | 17,500 | 45,000

35   5 Pounds   VF   UNC

ND (1960-65). Black on blue underprint. Arms at upper left, portrait Sir John Franklin at right. Signature H. C. Coombs and R. Wilson with title *GOVERNOR / RESERVE BANK of AUSTRALIA* below lower left signature. Like #31. Back: Cattle, sheep and agricultural products across center. Watermark: Capt. James Cook.

a. Issued note. | 150 | 500
r. Serial # suffix *, replacement. | 5,000 | 20,000
s. Specimen. | 8,000 | 60,000

36   10 Pounds   VF   UNC

ND (1960-65). Black on red underprint. Arms at top center, portrait Gov. Arthur Philip at left. Signature H. C. Coombs and R. Wilson with title *GOVERNOR / RESERVE BANK of AUSTRALIA* below lower left signature. Like #32. Back: Symbols of science and industry. Watermark: Capt. James Cook.

a. Issued note. | 300 | 1,000
s. Specimen. | 10,000 | 75,000

1966-67 ND Issue

37　1 Dollar

ND (1966-72). Dark brown on orange and multicolor underprint. Arms at center, Queen Elizabeth II at right, with text: *COMMONWEALTH OF* in heading. Back: Stylized aboriginal figures and animals. Watermark: Capt. James Cook. 140x70mm.

	VF	UNC
a. Signature H. C. Coombs and R. Wilson. (1966).	20.00	80.00
b. Signature H. C. Coombs and R. J. Randall. (1968).	170	850
c. Signature J. G. Phillips and R. J. Randall. (1969).	15.00	65.00
d. Signature J. G. Phillips and F. H. Wheeler. (1972).	16.00	70.00
s1. Specimen in oval on each side.	3,000	10,000
s2. Specimen eight times each side.	6,000	25,000
s3. Specimen twice diagonally each side.	8,000	35,000
ar. As a, serial # suffix *, replacement.	600	3,000
br. As b, serial # suffix *, replacement.	2,000	8,500
cr. As c, serial # suffix *, replacement.	650	3,500

38　2 Dollars

ND (1966-72). Black on green, blue and yellow multicolor underprint. John MacArthur at right, sheep at center, with text: *COMMONWEALTH OF* in heading. Back: William Farrer at left, wheat at center. Watermark: Capt. James Cook. 145x71mm.

	VF	UNC
a. Signature H. C. Coombs and R. Wilson. (1966).	20.00	80.00
b. Signature H. C. Coombs and R. J. Randall. (1967).	50.00	200
c. Signature J. G. Phillips and R. J. Randall. (1968).	20.00	80.00
d. Signature J. G. Phillips and F. H. Wheeler. (1972).	20.00	80.00
s1. As a. Specimen.	3,000	10,000
ar. As a, serial # suffix *, replacement.	750	3,500
br. As b, serial # suffix *, replacement.	2,000	8,500
cr. As c, serial # suffix *, replacement.	100	400

39　5 Dollars

ND (1967-72). Deep purple on multicolor underprint. Sir Joseph Banks at right, plants at center, with text: *COMMONWEALTH OF* in heading. Back: Caroline Chisholm, ship, buildings, and women. Watermark: Capt. James Cook. 152x76mm.

	VF	UNC
a. Signature H. C. Coombs and R. J. Randall. (1967).	50.00	275

	VF	UNC
b. Signature J. G. Phillips and R. J. Randall. (1969).	50.00	265
c. Signature J. G. Phillips and F. H. Wheeler. (1972).	45.00	240
s1. As a. Specimen in oval each side.	3,000	10,000
s2. As b. Specimen eight time each side.	6,500	26,500
s3. As c. Specimen twice diagonally each side.	9,000	36,500
ar. As a, serial # suffix *, replacement.	2,000	9,000
br. As b, serial # suffix *, replacement.	2,500	11,000

40　10 Dollars

ND (1966-72). Black on blue, orange and multicolor underprint. Francis Greenway at right, village scene at center, with text: *COMMONWEALTH OF* in heading. Back: Henry Lawson and buildings. Watermark: Capt. James Cook. 155x76mm.

	VF	UNC
a. Signature H. C. Coombs and R. Wilson. (1966).	20.00	80.00
b. Signature H. G. Coombs and R. J. Randall. (1967).	150	700
c. Signature J. G. Phillips and R. J. Randall. (1968).	30.00	130
d. Signature J. G. Phillips and F. H. Wheeler. (1972).	25.00	90.00
s1. As a. Specimen in oval each side.	3,000	10,000
s2. As b. Specimen eight time each side.	6,750	28,000
s3. As c. Specimen twice diagonally each side.	10,000	38,000
ar. As a, serial # suffix *, replacement.	1,000	4,500
br. As b, serial # suffix *, replacement.	2,000	8,000
cr. As c, serial # suffix *, replacement.	1,250	5,500

41　20 Dollars

ND (1966-72). Black on red, yellow and multicolor underprint. Sir Charles Kingsford-Smith at right, with text: *COMMONWEALTH OF* in heading. Back: Lawrence Hargrave at left, aeronautical devices. Watermark: Capt. James Cook. 160x81mm.

	VF	UNC
a. Signature H. C. Coombs and R. Wilson. (1966).	30.00	90.00
b. Signature H. G. Coombs and R. J. Randall. (1968).	1,000	7,500
c. Signature J. G. Phillips and R. J. Randall. (1968).	50.00	300
d. Signature J. G. Phillips and F. H. Wheeler. (1972).	50.00	325
s1. As a. Specimen in oval each side.	3,000	12,000
s2. As b. Specimen eight times each side.	6,750	10,000
s3. As c. Specimen twice diagonally each side.	1,400	28,000
cr. As c, serial # suffix *, replacement.	4,000	12,000

Australia, Reserve Bank
1973; 1984 ND Issue

42   1 Dollar

	VF	UNC

ND (1974-83). Dark brown on orange and multicolor underprint. Arms at center, Queen Elizabeth II at right, without text: *COMMONWEALTH OF* in heading. Back: Stylized aboriginal figures and animals. Watermark: Capt. James Cook. 140x70mm.

	VF	UNC
a. Signature J. G. Phillips and F. H. Wheeler. (1974).	15.00	60.00
b1. Signature H. M. Knight and F. H. Wheeler. (1976). Center security thread.	8.00	35.00
b2. As b1. Side security thread.	8.00	25.00
b3. KW test note DBP.	40.00	190
c. Signature H. M. Knight and J. Stone. (1979).	5.00	15.00
d. Signature R. A. Johnston and J. Stone. (1983).	2.00	7.00
s1. As a. Specimen twice diagonally each side.	—	12,500
s2. As b1. Specimen twice diagonally each side.	—	25,000

43   2 Dollars

	VF	UNC

ND (1974-85). Black on green, blue and yellow underprint. John MacArthur at right, sheep at center, without text: *COMMONWEALTH OF* in heading. Back: William Farrer at left, wheat at center. Watermark: Capt. James Cook. 145x71mm.

	VF	UNC
a. Signature J. G. Phillips and F. H. Wheeler. (1974).	15.00	70.00
b1. Signature H. M. Knight and F. H. Wheeler. (1976). Gothic serial # .	40.00	170
b2. Signature H. M. Knight and F. H. Wheeler. (1976). Ocrb serial # . Center thread.	30.00	100
b3. Signature H. M. Knight and F. H. Wheeler. (1976). Ocrb serial # . Side thread.	8.00	40.00
c. Signature H. M. Knight and J. Stone. (1979).	5.00	17.00
d. Signature R. A. Johnston and J. Stone. (1983).	5.00	17.00
e. Signature R. A. Johnston and B. W. Fraser. (1985).	2.00	8.00
s1. As a. Specimen twice diagonally each side.	5,000	10,000
s2. As b. Specimen twice diagonally each side.	—	15,000

44   5 Dollars

	VF	UNC

ND (1974-91). Deep purple on multicolor underprint. Sir Joseph Banks at right, plants at center, without text: *COMMONWEALTH OF* in heading. Back: Caroline Chisholm, ship, buildings and women. Watermark: Capt. James Cook. 152x76mm.

	VF	UNC
a. Signature J. G. Phillips and F. H. Wheeler. (1974).	40.00	220
b1. H.M. Knight and F.H. Wheeler. Centre metal thread.	20.00	80.00
b2. H.M. Knight and F.H. Wheeler. Side metal thread.	15.00	70.00
b3. H.M. Knight and F.H. Wheeler. Ocrb (last type) serials.	15.00	60.00
c. Signature H. M. Knight and J. Stone. (1979).	12.00	35.00
d. Signature R. A. Johnston and J. Stone. (1983).	12.00	35.00
e. Signature R. A. Johnston and B. W. Fraser. (1985). 2 serial # varieties.	10.00	30.00
f. Signature B. W. Fraser and C. I. Higgins. (1990).	10.00	30.00
g. Signature B. W. Fraser and A. S. Cole. (1991).	8.00	25.00
s1. As a. Specimen twice diagonally each side.	5,000	10,000
s2. As b1. Specimen twice diagonally each side.	—	15,000

45   10 Dollars

	VF	UNC

ND (1974-91). Black on blue and orange underprint. Francis Greenway at right, village scene at center, without text: *COMMONWEALTH OF* in heading. Back: Henry Lawson and buildings. Watermark: Capt. James Cook. 155x76mm.

	VF	UNC
a. Signature J. G. Phillips and F. H. Wheeler. (1974).	55.00	220
b. Signature H. M. Knight and F. H. Wheeler. (1976).	50.00	200
c. Signature H. M. Knight and J. Stone. (1979). 2 serial # varieties.	30.00	100
d. Signature R. A. Johnston and J. Stone. (1983).	25.00	95.00
e. Signature R. A. Johnston and B. W. Fraser. (1985).	15.00	40.00
f. Signature B. W. Fraser and C. I. Higgins. (1990).	18.00	45.00
g. Signature B. W. Fraser and A. S. Cole. (1991).	15.00	40.00
s1. As a. Specimen.	5,500	11,000

46   20 Dollars

	VF	UNC

ND (1974-94). Black on red, yellow and multicolor underprint. Sir Charles Kingsford-Smith at right, without text: *COMMONWEALTH OF* in heading. Back: Lawrence Hargrave at left, aeronautical devices. Watermark: Capt. James Cook. 160x81mm.

	VF	UNC
a. Signature J. G. Phillips and F. H. Wheeler. (1974).	75.00	375
b. Signature H. M. Knight and F. H. Wheeler. (1975).	50.00	300
c. Signature H. M. Knight and J. Stone. (1979). 2 serial # varieties.	65.00	220
d. Signature R. A. Johnston and J. Stone. (1983).	40.00	180
e. Signature R. A. Johnston and B. W. Fraser. (1985) 2 serial # varieties.	30.00	90.00
f. Signature M. J. Phillips and B. W. Fraser. (1989).	35.00	125
g. Signature B. W. Fraser and C. I. Higgins. (1989).	30.00	105
h. Signature B. W. Fraser and A. S. Cole. (1991).	28.00	90.00
i. Signature B. W. Fraser and E. A. Evans. (1994).	28.00	90.00
s1. As a. Specimen.	5,000	10,000

47 50 Dollars   VF UNC

ND (1973-94). Dark brown and black on multicolor underprint. Teaching implements at center, Lord Howard Walker Florey at right, without text: *COMMON-WEALTH OF* in heading. Back: Ian Clunies-Ross at left, space research at center. Watermark: Capt. James Cook. 165x82mm.

	VF	UNC
a. Signature J. G. Phillips and F. H. Wheeler. (1973).	120	300
b. Signature H. M. Knight and F. H. Wheeler. (1975).	120	325
c. Signature H. M. Knight and J. Stone. (1979).	100	250
d. Signature R. A. Johnston and J. Stone. (1983).	90.00	230
e. Signature R. A. Johnston and B. W. Fraser. (1985). 2 serial # varieties.	100	250
f. Signature M. J. Phillips and B. W. Fraser. (1989).	80.00	200
g. Signature B. W. Fraser and C. I. Higgins. (1989).	100	250
h. Signature B. W. Fraser and A. S. Cole. (1991).	65.00	140
i. Signature B. W. Fraser and E. A. Evans. (1994).	70.00	150

48 100 Dollars   VF UNC

ND (1984-92). Blue and gray on multicolor underprint. Sir Douglas Mawson at center, without text: *COMMONWEALTH OF* in heading. Back: J. Tebbutt at left center. Watermark: Capt. James Cook. 172x83mm.

	VF	UNC
a. Signature R. A. Johnston and J. Stone. (1984).	125	250
b. Signature R. A. Johnston and B. W. Fraser. (1985).	125	250
c. Signature B. W. Fraser and C. I. Higgins. (1990).	125	250
d. Signature B. W. Fraser and A. S. Cole. (1992).	125	250

1988 ND Commemorative Issue

49 10 Dollars   VF UNC

1988; ND. Polymer plastic. Brown and green on multicolor underprint. Captain James Cook OVD at upper left, colonists across background; Cook's ship *Supply* at lower right shoreline. Signature R. A. Johnston and B. W. Fraser. Back: Aboriginal youth, rock painting and ceremonial *Morning Star* pole at center. Printer: NPA.

	VF	UNC
a. Serial # prefix AA. 26.1.1988. Issued in folder.	15.00	40.00
b. Issued note. Serial # prefix AB. ND.	15.00	45.00

1992-2001 Issues

50 5 Dollars   VF UNC

ND (1992); (19)93. UV: serial # fluoresce yellow; Face: blue. Black, red and blue on multicolor underprint. Branch at left, Queen Elizabeth II at center right, issue dates are indicated by the first two digits of the serial number. Back: Old and new Parliament Houses in Canberra at center, gum flower OVD at lower right. Printer: NPA. 130x65mm.

	VF	UNC
a. Signature B. W. Fraser and A. S. Cole. (1992).	10.00	35.00
b. Signature B. W. Fraser and E. A. Evans. (1993).	10.00	40.00

51 5 Dollars   VF UNC

(19)95-(20)01. Black, red and bright purple. Branch at left, Queen Elizabeth II at center right. Orientation bands in upper and lower margins, gum flower OVD at lower right, issue dates are indicated by the first two digits of the serial number. Back: Old and new Parliament Houses in Canberra at center. Printer: NPA. 130x65mm.

	VF	UNC
a. With 4 diagonal white lines in orientation band at lower left signature B. W. Fraser and E. A. Evans. (1995-96).	15.00	35.00
b. As a, but with 11 diagonal white lines in orientation band at lower left Plate error. (1995).	25.00	50.00
c. Signature I. Macfarlane and E. A. Evans. (1996-98) 2002-03.	15.00	35.00

52 10 Dollars   VF UNC

(19)93-(20)01. Dark blue and purple on multicolor underprint. Man on horseback at left, A. B. "Banjo" Paterson at center, windmill OVD in transparent window at lower right, issue dates are indicated by the first two digits of the serial number. Back: Dame Mary Gilmore at center right. Printer: NPA. 137x65mm.

	VF	UNC
a. Signature B. W. Fraser and E. A. Evans. (1993-94).	30.00	35.00
b. Signature I. Macfarlane and E. A. Evans. (1996-98).	28.00	35.00

53 20 Dollars   VF UNC

(19)94-(20)01. Blaack and red on orange and pale green underprint. Mary Reiby at center, sailing ship at left, compass OVD in treansparent window at lower right, issue dates are indicated by the first two digits of the serial number. Back: Biplane at left, Rev. John Flynn at center right, camel at right. Printer: NPA. 144x65mm.

	VF	UNC
a. Signature B. W. Fraser and E. A. Evans. (1994-96).	40.00	75.00
b. Signature I. Macfarlane and E. A. Evans. (1997-98).	30.00	55.00

54 50 Dollars

VF UNC

(19)95-(20)01. Black and deep purple on yellow-brown, green and multicolor underprint. David Unaipon at left center, Mission Church at Point McLeay at lower left, patent drawings at upper center right, Southern Cross constellation OVD in transparent window at lower right, issue dates are indicated by the first two digits of the serial number. Back: Edith Cowan, foster mother with children at center, W. Australia's Parliament House at upper left, Cowan at lectern at right. Printer: NPA. 151x65mm.

a. Signature B. W. Fraser and E. A. Evans. (1995-96)	75.00	150
b. Signature I. Macfarlane and E. A. Evans. (1997-98).	70.00	120

55 100 Dollars

VF UNC

(19)96-(20)01. Black and green on orange and multicolor underprint. Opera stage at left, Dame Nellie Melba at center, stylized peacock OVD in transparent window at lower right, issue dates are indicated by the first two digits of the serial number. Back: Sir John Monash and WWI battle scenes and insignia. Printer: NPA. 158x65mm.

a. Signature B. W. Fraser and E. A. Evans. (1996).	135	200
b. Signature I. Macfarlane and E. A. Evans. (1998-2001).	120	175

2001 Commemorative Issue

#56, Centennial of the Commonwealth

56 5 Dollars

VF UNC

1.1.2001. UV: back branch of leaves and 5 fluoresce yellow. Black, violet and blue on multicolor underprint. Sir Henry Parkes at center, issue date is the first two digits of the serial number. Back: Catherine Helen Spence at center. Printer: NPA. 130x65mm.

10.00 20.00

2002-09 Issue

57 5 Dollars

VF UNC

(20)03-(20)12. Black, red and blue on multicolor un derprint. Branch at left, Queen Elizabeth II at center right with name under portrait. Issue dates are first two digits of serial number. Back: Old and new Parliament Houses in Canberra at center. Printer: NPA. 130x05mm.

a. (20)02. Signature I. Macfarlane and K. Henry.	7.50	12.50
b. (20)03. Signature I. Macfarlane and K. Henry.	7.50	12.50
c. (20)05. Signature I. Macfarlane and K. Henry.	6.00	10.00
d. (20)06. Signature I. Macfarlane and K. Henry.	FV	9.00
e. (20)07. Signature Glenn R. Stevens and K. Henry.	FV	9.00
f. (20)08. Signature Glenn R. Stevens and K. Henry.	FV	8.00
g. (20)12. Signatures Glenn R. Stevens and Martin Parkinson.	FV	8.00
h. (20)13. Signatures Glenn R. Stevens and Martin Parkinson.	FV	8.00

58 10 Dollars

VF UNC

(20)02-03; (20)06-07; (20)12. Polymer plastic. Dark blue and purple on multicolor underprint. Man on horseback at left, A. B. "Banjo" Paterson at center with name below, windmill OVD in transparent window at lower right, issue date is first two digits of the serial number. Back: Dame Mary Gilmore at center right. Printer: NPA. 137x65mm.

a. (20)02. Signature I. Macfarlane and K. Henry.	15.00	25.00
b. (20)03. Signature I. Macfarlane and K. Henry.	15.00	25.00
c. (20)06. Signature I. Macfarlane and K. Henry.	15.00	25.00
d. (20)07. Signature Glenn R. Stevens and K. Henry.	FV	20.00
e. (20)08. Signature Glenn R. Stevens and K. Henry.	FV	20.00
f. (20)12. Signature Glenn R. Stevens and Martin Parkinson.	FV	17.50
g. (20)13. Signatures Glenn R. Stevens and Martin Parkinson.	FV	17.50

59 20 Dollars   **VF   UNC**

(20)02-03; (20)05-10. Polymer plastic. Black and red on orange and pale green underprint. Mary Reiby at center, name below, sailing ship at left, compass OVD in transparent window at lower right, issue date is first two digits of the serial number. Back: Biplane at left, Rev. John Flynn at center right, camel at right. Printer: NPA. 144x65mm.

		VF	UNC
a.	(20)02. Signature I. Macfarlane and K. Henry.	25.00	35.00
b.	(20)03. Signature I. Macfarlane and K. Henry.	25.00	35.00
c.	(20)05. Signature I. Macfarlane and K. Henry.	25.00	35.00
d.	(20)06. Signature I. Macfarlane and K. Henry.	25.00	35.00
e.	(20)07. Signature Glenn R. Stevens and K. Henry	25.00	35.00
f.	(20)08. Signature Glenn R. Stevens and K. Henry.	25.00	35.00
g.	(20)10. Signature Glenn R. Stevens and K. Henry.	25.00	35.00
h.	(20)13. Signatures Glenn R. Stevens and Martin Parkinson.	25.00	35.00

60 50 Dollars   **VF   UNC**

(20)03-(20)12. Black and deep purple on yellow-brown, green and multicolor. David Unaipon at left center, name below. Mission church at Point McLeay at lower left, patent drawings at upper center. Southern Cross OVD in transparent window at lower right. Back: Edith Cowan, foster mother with children at center. W. Australia's Parliament House at upper left. Printer: NPA. 151x65mm.

		VF	UNC
a.	(20)03. Signature I. Macfarlane and K. Henry.	65.00	75.00
b.	(20)04. Signature I. Macfarlane and K. Henry.	65.00	75.00
c.	(20)05. Signature I. Macfarlane and K. Henry.	65.00	75.00
d.	(20)06. Signature I. Macfarlane and K. Henry.	65.00	75.00
e.	(20)07. Signature I. Macfarlane and K. Henry.	65.00	75.00
f.	(20)08. Signatures Glenn R. Stevens and K. Henry.	FV	75.00
g.	(20)09. Signatures Glenn R. Stevens and K. Henry.	FV	75.00
h.	(20)10. Signatures Glenn R. Stevens and K. Henry.	FV	75.00
i.	(20)11. Signatures Glenn R. Stevens and K. Henry.	FV	75.00
j.	20(12). Signatures Glenn R. Stevens and Martin Parkinson.	FV	75.00
k.	(20)13. Signatures Glenn R. Stevens and Martin Parkinson.	FV	75.00

61 100 Dollars   **VF   UNC**

(20)08; (20)10. Black and green on orange and multicolor underprint. Opera stage at left, Dame Nellie Melba at center, name below. Stylized peacock OVD in transparent window at lower right. Back: Sir John Monash with WWI battle scenes and insignia. 158x65mm.

		VF	UNC
a.	(20)08. Signatures Glenn R. Stevens and Ken Henry.	FV	115
b.	(20)10. Signatures Glenn R. Stevens and K. Henry.	FV	115
c.	20(11). Signatures Glenn R. Stevens and K. Henry.	FV	115
d.	20(13). Signatures Glenn R. Stevens and Martin Parkinson.	FV	115

The Republic of Austria (Oesterreich), a parliamentary democracy located in mountainous central Europe, has an area of 83,870 sq. km. and a population of 8.2 million. Capital: Vienna. Austria is primarily an industrial country. Machinery, iron and steel, textiles, yarns and timber are exported.

Once the center of power for the large Austro-Hungarian Empire, Austria was reduced to a small republic after its defeat in World War I. Following annexation by Nazi Germany in 1938 and subsequent occupation by the victorious Allies in 1945, Austria's status remained unclear for a decade. A State Treaty signed in 1955 ended the occupation, recognized Austria's independence, and forbade unification with Germany. A constitutional law that same year declared the country's "perpetual neutrality" as a condition for Soviet military withdrawal. The Soviet Union's collapse in 1991 and Austria's entry into the European Union in 1995 have altered the meaning of this neutrality. A prosperous, democratic country, Austria entered the EU Economic and Monetary Union in 1999.

MONETARY SYSTEM:
1 Gulden = 60 Kreuzer, 1754-1857
1 Gulden = (Florin) = 100 Kreuzer, 1857-1892
1 Krone = 100 Heller, 1892-1924
1 Schilling = 100 Groschen, 1924-1938, 1945-2002
1 Euro = 100 Cents, 2002-

REPUBLIC

Oesterreichische Nationalbank

AUSTRIAN NATIONAL BANK

1956-65 Issues

136 20 Schilling   **VF   UNC**

2.7.1956. Brown on red-brown and multicolor underprint. Carl Auer Freiherr von Welsbach at right, arms at left. Back: Village Maria Rain, church and Karawanken mountains.

		VF	UNC
a.	Issued note.	10.00	25.00
s.	Specimen.	—	50.00

137 50 Schilling   **VF   UNC**

2.7.1962 (1963). Purple on multicolor underprint. Richard Wettstein at right, arms at bottom center. Back: Mauterndorf castle in Salzburg.

		VF	UNC
a.	Issued note.	12.50	25.00
s.	Specimen.	—	50.00

138   100 Schilling

1.7.1960 (1961). Dark green on multicolor underprint. Violin and music at lower left, Johann Strauss at right, arms at left. Back: Schönbrunn Castle.

		VF	UNC
a. Issued note.		10.00	50.00
s. Specimen.		—	75.00

139   500 Schilling

1.7.1965 (1966). Red-brown on multicolor underprint. Josef Ressel at right. Back: Steam powered screw propeller ship *Civetta* at left, arms at lower right. 155x80mm.

	VF	UNC
a. Issued note.	75.00	150
s. Specimen. Red overprint: *MUSTER* on face and *SPECIMEN* on back.	—	500

140   1000 Schilling

2.1.1961 (1962). Dark blue on multicolor underprint. Viktor Kaplan at right. Back: Dam and Persenburg Castle, arms at right. 148x75mm.

	VF	UNC
a. Issued note. Rare.	—	—
s. Specimen.	500	1,000

Note: #140 was in use for only 11 weeks.

141   1000 Schilling

2.1.1961 (1962). Dark blue on multicolor underprint with blue lines up to margin. Viktor Kaplan at right. Back: Dam and Persenburg Castle, arms at right. 158x85mm.

	VF	UNC
a. Issued note.	150	300
s. Specimen. Overprint and perforated: *Muster*.	—	1,500

1966-70 Issues

142   20 Schilling

2.7.1967 (1968). Brown on olive and lilac underprint. Carl Ritter von Ghega at right, arms at lower center. Back: Semmering Railway bridge over the Semmering Pass (986 meters). 132x65mm.

	VF	UNC
a. Issued note.	2.50	4.50
s. Specimen.	—	250

143   50 Schilling

2.1.1970 (1972). Purple on multicolor underprint. Ferdinand Raimund at right, arms at left. Back: Burg Theater in Vienna at left center.

	VF	UNC
a. Issued note.	6.00	12.00
s. Specimen. Overprint: *Muster*.	—	500

144   50 Schilling

2.1.1970 (1983). Ferdinand Raimund at right, arms at left, with overprint 2. *AUFLAGE* (2nd issue) at lower left center. Back: Burg Theater in Vienna at left center.

	VF	UNC
	6.00	12.00

145   100 Schilling

2.1.1969 (1970). Dark green on multicolor underpritn. Angelika Kauffmann at right. Back: Large house.

	VF	UNC
a. Issued note.	10.00	22.50
s. Specimen. Overprint: *Muster*.	—	750

146 100 Schilling   VF UNC

2.1.1969 (1981). Angelika Kauffmann at right, with overprint; *2 AUFLAGE* (2nd issue) at upper left. Back: Large house.

    a. Issued note.   12.00 22.50
    s. Specimen.   — 250

147 1000 Schilling   VF UNC

1.7.1966 (1970). Blue-violet on multicolor underprint. Bertha von Suttner at center right, arms at right. Back: Leopoldskron Castle and Hohensalzburg Fortress.

    a. Issued note.   90.00 275
    s. Specimen. Overprint: *Muster*.   — 1,250

1983-88 Issue

148 20 Schilling   VF UNC

1.10.1986 (1988). UV: Fibers fluoresce blue; security strip yellow; back: bottom serial # orange. Dark brown and brown on multicolor underprint. Federal arms at upper left, Moritz Daffinger at right. Back: Vienna's *Albertina* Museum at left center. Watermark: Federal arms and parallel vertical lines. 123x62mm.   FV 3.25

149 50 Schilling   VF UNC

2.1.1986 (1987). Purple and violet on multicolor underprint. Federal arms at upper left, Sigmund Freud at right. Back: Vienna's *Josephinum* Medical School at left center. Watermark: Federal arms and parallel vertical lines. 130x65mm.   FV 7.00

150 100 Schilling   VF UNC

2.1.1984 (1985). Dark green, gray and dark brown on multicolor underprint. Federal arms at upper left, Eugen Böhm v. Bawerk at right. 3 serial number varieties. Back: Wissenschaften Academy in Vienna at left center. Watermark: Federal arms and parallel vertical lines. 137x69mm.   FV 17.50

151 500 Schilling   VF UNC

1.7.1985 (1986). Dark brown, deep violet and orange-brown on multicolor underprint Federal arms at upper left, Architect Otto Wagner at right. Back: Vienna's Post Office Savings Bank at left center. Watermark: Federal arms and parallel vertical lines. 144x72mm.   FV 75.00

152 1000 Schilling   VF UNC

3.1.1983. Dark blue and purple on multicolor underprint. Federal arms at upper left, Erwin Schrödinger at right. Back: Vienna University at left center. Watermark: Federal arms and parallel vertical lines. 152x72mm.   FV 150

153 5000 Schilling   VF UNC

4.1.1988 (1989). Light brown and purple on multicolor underprint. Federal arms at upper left, Woflgang Amadeus Mozart at right, kinegram of Mozart's head at lower left. Back: Vienna Opera House at center. Watermark: Federal arms and parallel vertical lines. 160x80mm.

    a. Issued note.   FV 675
    s. Specimen. Overprint *MUSTER.* in red.   — 850

1997 Issue

154 500 Schilling
1.1.1997. Brown on multicolor underprint. Rosa Mayreder at left. Back: Rosa and Karl Mayreder with group at right. 147x72mm.
VF UNC
FV 70.00

155 1000 Schilling
1.1.1997. Blue on multicolor underprint. Karl Landsteiner at left. Back: Landsteiner working in his laboratory in Licenter at right. 154x72mm.
VF UNC
FV 135

Note: For later issues used in Austria, see European Union listings.

AZERBAIJAN

The Republic of Azerbaijan includes the Nakhichevan Autonomous Republic and Nagorno-Karabakh Autonomous Region (which was abolished in 1991). Situated in the eastern area of Transcaucasia, it is bordered in the west by Armenia, in the north by Georgia and the Russian Federation of Dagestan, to the east by the Caspian Sea and to the south by Iran. It has an area of 86,600 sq. km. and a population of 8.18 million. Capital: Baku. The area is rich in mineral deposits of aluminum, copper, iron, lead, salt and zinc, with oil as its leading industry. Agriculture and livestock follow in importance.

Azerbaijan - a nation with a majority-Turkic and majority-Muslim population - was briefly independent from 1918 to 1920; it regained its independence after the collapse of the Soviet Union in 1991. Despite a 1994 cease-fire, Azerbaijan has yet to resolve its conflict with Armenia over the Azerbaijani Nagorno-Karabakh enclave (largely Armenian populated). Azerbaijan has lost 16% of its territory and must support some 600,000 internally displaced persons as a result of the conflict. Corruption is ubiquitous, and the government has been accused of authoritarianism. Although the poverty rate has been reduced in recent years, the promise of widespread wealth from development of Azerbaijan's energy sector remains largely unfulfilled.

MONETARY SYSTEM:
1 Manat = 10 Soviet Rubles, to 1992
1 New Manat = 5,000 Old Manat, 2005-

REPUBLIC
Azerbaycan Milli Banki
1992 ND Issue

In 1993, due to a cash crisis, bonds of the State Loan of Azerbaijan Republic were officially used as currency; however, they were not freely accepted in the local bazaars. The acceptance term of these bonds in the branches of the State Savings Bank was until 1 June 2000.

11 1 Manat
ND (1992). Deep olive-green on multicolor underprint. Baku's Maiden Tower at center.
VF UNC
3.00 7.50

12 10 Manat
ND (1992). Deep brown-violet on multicolor underprint. Baku's Maiden Tower at center.
VF UNC
7.50 15.00

13 250 Manat
ND (1992). UV: threads fluoresce blue. AMB yellow, 250 green; back design elements green. Deep blue-gray on multicolor underprint. Baku's Maiden Tower at center.
VF UNC
a. First issue with fraction prefix. 25.00 75.00
b. Second issue with 2 prefix letters. 2.50 5.00

Azerbaycan Republic State Loan Bonds
1993 Issue

13A   250 Manat
1993. Olive-green on multicolor underprint. Printer: Goznak.   VF UNC
                                                                                 —   —
13B   500 Manat
1993. Pinkish-red on multicolor underprint. Printer: Goznak.   VF UNC
                                                                                 —   —
13C   1000 Manat
1993. Steel-blue on multicolor underprint. Printer: Goznak.   VF UNC
                                                                                 —   —

Azerbaycan Milli Banki (resumed)
1993 ND; 1994-95 Issue

#13b, 17b, 18b, 19b, 20b replacement notes: Serial # prefix BZ.

14   1 Manat   VF   UNC
ND (1993). UV: AMB fluoresce yellow; back: design elements yellow. Deep blue   FV   5.00
on tan, dull orange and green underprint. Baku's Maiden Tower ruins at center.
Back: Ornate "value". Watermark: 3 flames.

15   5 Manat   VF   UNC
ND (1993). Deep brown on lilac and multicolor underprint. Baku's Maiden Tower   FV   7.00
ruins at center. Back: Ornate "value". Watermark: 3 flames.

16   10 Manat   VF   UNC
ND (1993). Deep grayish blue-green on pale blue and multicolor underprint.   FV   10.00
Baku's Maiden Tower ruins at center. Back: Ornate "value". Watermark: 3 flames.

17   50 Manat   VF   UNC
ND (1993). Red on ochre and multicolor underprint. Baku's Maiden Tower ruins at
center. Back: Ornate "value". Watermark: 3 flames.
    a. First issue with fraction prefix.   5.00 15.00
    b. Second issue with 2 prefix letters.   1.00   2.00

18   100 Manat   VF   UNC
ND (1993). Red-violet on pale blue and multicolor underprint. Baku's Maiden
Tower ruins at center. Back: Ornate "value". Watermark: 3 flames.
    a. First issue with fraction prefix.   5.00 20.00
    b. Second issue with 2 prefix letters.   1.00   3.00

19   500 Manat   VF   UNC
ND (1993). Deep brown on pale blue, pink and multicolor underprint. Portrait N.
Gencevi at right. Back: Ornate "value". Watermark: 3 flames.
    a. First issue with fraction prefix.   7.00 25.00
    b. Second issue with 2 prefix letters.   1.00   5.00

20   1000 Manat   VF   UNC
ND (1993). Dark brown and blue on pink and multicolor underprint. M. E. Resul-
zado at right. Back: Ornate "value". Watermark: 3 flames.
    a. First issue with fraction prefix.   5.00 20.00
    b. Second issue with 2 prefix letters.   1.00   5.00

21   10,000 Manat   VF   UNC
1994. Dull dark brown and pale violet on multicolor underprint. Shirvansha's
Palace at center right. Watermark: AMB repeated.
    a. Security thread.   20.00 60.00
    b. Segmented foil over security thread.   2.00 15.00

22   50,000 Manat
1995. Segmented foil over security thread. Blue-green and light brown on multicolor underprint. Mausoleum in Nachziban at center right. Back: Carpet design at left.

	VF	UNC
	FV	50.00

2001 Issue

23   1000 Manat
2001. UV: fibers fluoresce yellow, blue; Face: value in box green, lower serial # orange, background elements yellow. Slate blue on light blue and multicolor underprint. Oil rigs and pumps at center right. Back: Value.

	VF	UNC
	FV	6.00

2005 Issue

24   1 Manat
2005. Olive gray on yellow. Azerbaijani folk musical instruments. Back: Map and carpets 119x70mm.

	VF	UNC
	FV	3.00

#25 not assigned.

26   5 Manat
2005. Yellowish-brown. Writers, poets and books. Back: Map. 127x70mm.

	VF	UNC
	FV	12.00

27   10 Manat
2005. Slate blue and blue. Old Baku City view, Sharvanshah's Palace, Maiden Tower. Back: Map. 130x70mm.

	VF	UNC
	FV	24.00

28   20 Manat
2005. Green on light orange. Sword, helmet and shield. Back: Map. 141x70mm.

	VF	UNC
	FV	45.00

29   50 Manat
2005. Olive green, blue and multicolor. Stairs. Back: Map. 148x70mm.

	VF	UNC
	FV	100

30   100 Manat
2005. Lilac, brown on blue and multicolor. 155x70mm.

	VF	UNC
	FV	200

Azerbaycan Merkezi Banki

2009 Issue

31   1 Manat
2009.

	VF	UNC
	FV	3.00

32   5 Manat
2009. Orange and multicolor. Literature personalities, ancient books and a part of the national anthem. Back: Map of Europe at lower left, Qobustan rock hieroglyphs, Orhon-Yenisei alphabet and modern writing; Map of Azerbaijan at right. Watermark: Quill pen and book and 5 127x70mm.

	VF	UNC
	FV	12.00

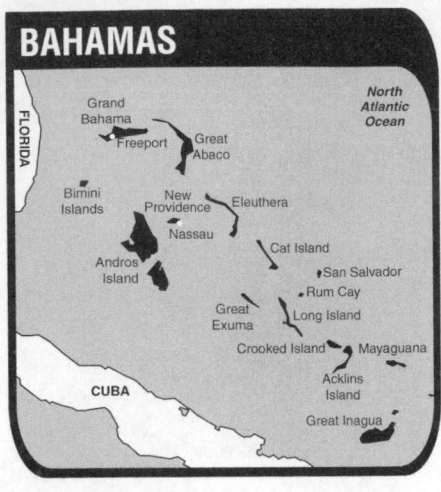

BAHAMAS

The Commonwealth of The Bahamas is an archipelago of about 3,000 islands, cays and rocks located in the Atlantic Ocean east of Florida and north of Cuba. The total land area of the chain of islands is 10,070 sq. km. They have a population of 307,400. Capital: Nassau. The Bahamas imports most of their food and manufactured products and exports cement, refined oil, pulpwood and lobsters. Lucayan Indians inhabited the islands when Christopher Columbus first set foot in the New World on San Salvador in 1492. British settlement of the islands began in 1647; the islands became a colony in 1783. Since attaining independence from the UK in 1973, The Bahamas have prospered through tourism and international banking and investment management.

RULERS:
British

MONETARY SYSTEM:
1 Shilling = 12 Pence
1 Pound = 20 Shillings to 1966
1 Dollar = 100 Cents 1966-

COMMONWEALTH

Bahamas Government

1965 Currency Note Act

Replacement notes: Serial # prefix *Z*.

17   1/2 Dollar   **VF   UNC**

L.1965. Purple on multicolor underprint. Queen Elizabeth II at left. Back: Straw market, arms at right. Watermark: Shellfish. Printer: TDLR. 156x67mm.

a. 2 signatures.	15.00	80.00
b. 3 signatures.	13.00	70.00
s. Specimen.	—	280

18   1 Dollar   **VF   UNC**

L.1965. Green on multicolor underprint. Queen Elizabeth II at left. Back: Sea garden, arms at right. Watermark: Shellfish. Printer: TDLR. 156x67mm.

a. 2 signatures.	40.00	180
b. 3 signatures.	55.00	200
s. As b. Specimen.	—	370

19   3 Dollars   **VF   UNC**

L.1965. Red on multicolor underprint. Queen Elizabeth II at left. Back: Paradise Beach, arms at right. Watermark: Shellfish. Printer: TDLR. 156x67mm.

a. 2 signatures, Sands and Higgs.	45.00	200
b. 3 signatures.	55.00	200
s. Signature Francis and Higgs. Specimen.	—	470

20   5 Dollars   **VF   UNC**

L.1965. Green on multicolor underprint. Queen Elizabeth II at left. Back: Government House, arms at right. Watermark: Shellfish. Printer: TDLR. 156x67mm.

a. 2 signatures.	80.00	380
b. 3 signatures.	100	450
s. Specimen.	—	360

21   5 Dollars   **VF   UNC**

L.1965. Orange on multicolor underprint. Queen Elizabeth II at left. Back: Government House, arms at right. Watermark: Shellfish. Printer: TDLR. 156x67mm.

a. 2 signatures.	175	700
b. 3 signatures.	450	1,300
s. Specimen.	—	600

22   10 Dollars   **VF   UNC**

L.1965. Dark blue on multicolor underprint. Queen Elizabeth II at left. Back: Flamingos, arms at right. Watermark: Shellfish. Printer: TDLR. 156x67mm.

a. 2 signatures.	300	1,350
b. 3 signatures.	500	2,400
s. Specimen.	—	820

23   20 Dollars   **VF   UNC**

L.1965. Dark brown on multicolor underprint. Queen Elizabeth II at left. Back: Surrey, arms at right. Watermark: Shellfish. Printer: TDLR. 156x67mm.

a. 2 signatures.	680	3,300
b. 3 signatures.	800	4,200
s. Specimen. 3 signatures.	—	800

24   50 Dollars   **VF   UNC**

L.1965. Brown on multicolor underprint. Queen Elizabeth II at left. Back: Produce market, arms at right. Watermark: Shellfish. Printer: TDLR. 156x67mm.

a. Issued note.	1,650	8,400
s. Specimen. 3 signatures.	—	850

25   100 Dollars   **VF   UNC**

L.1965. Blue on multicolor underprint. Queen Elizabeth II at left. Signature varieties. Back: Deep sea fishing, arms at right. Watermark: Shellfish. Printer: TDLR. 156x67mm.

a. 2 signatures.	2,900	14,000
b. 3 signatures.	5,200	—
s. Specimen. 3 signatures.	—	1,200

Bahamas Monetary Authority

1968 Monetary Authority Act

#26-33 Replacement notes: Serial # prefix *Z*.

26 1/2 Dollar   **VF UNC**

L.1968. Purple on multicolor underprint. Queen Elizabeth II at left. Back: Straw market, arms at right. Watermark: Shellfish. Printer: TDLR. 156x67mm.

  a. Issued note.   9.00   40.00

  s. Specimen.   —   120

27 1 Dollar   **VF UNC**

L.1968. Green on multicolor underprint. Queen Elizabeth II at left. Back: Sea garden, arms at right. Watermark: Shellfish. Printer: TDLR. 156x67mm.

  a. Issued note.   20.00   95.00

  s. Specimen.   —   120

28 3 Dollars   **VF UNC**

L.1968. Red on multicolor underprint. Queen Elizabeth II at left. Back: Paradise Beach, arms at right. Watermark: Shellfish. Printer: TDLR. 156x67mm.

  a. Issued note.   50.00   140

  s. Specimen.   —   120

29 5 Dollars   **VF UNC**

L.1968. Orange on multicolor underprint. Queen Elizabeth II at left. Back: Government House, arms at right. Watermark: Shellfish. Printer: TDLR. 156x67mm.

  a. Issued note.   80.00   360

  s. Specimen. Overprint: *SPECIMEN* on each side.   —   160

30 10 Dollars   **VF UNC**

L.1968. Dark blue on multicolor underprint. Queen Elizabeth II at left. Back: Flamingos, arms at right. Watermark: Shellfish. Printer: TDLR. 156x67mm.

  a. Issued note.   500   3,000

  s. Specimen. Overprint: *SPECIMEN* on each side.   —   210

31 20 Dollars   **VF UNC**

L.1968. Dark brown on multicolor underprint. Queen Elizabeth II at left. Back: Surrey, arms at right. Watermark: Shellfish. Printer: TDLR. 136x67mm.

  a. Issued note.   1,000   8,750

  s. Specimen. Overprint: *SPECIMEN* on each side.   —   300

32 50 Dollars   **VF UNC**

L.1968. Brown on multicolor underprint. Queen Elizabeth II at left. Back: Produce market, arms at right. Watermark: Shellfish. Printer: TDLR. 156x37mm.

  a. Issued note.   1,500   6,000

  s. Specimen. Overprint: *SPECIMEN* on each side.   —   570

33 100 Dollars   **VF UNC**

L.1968. Blue on multicolor underprint. Queen Elizabeth II at left. Back: Deep sea fishing, arms at right. Watermark: Shellfish. Printer: TDLR. 156x67mm.

  a. Issued note.   3,000   15,000

  s. Specimen. Overprint: *SPECIMEN* on each side.   —   500

#34 not assigned.

Central Bank of the Bahamas
1974 Central Bank Act

#35-41 Replacement notes: Serial # prefix *Z*.

35 1 Dollar   **VF UNC**

L.1974. Dark blue-green on multicolor underprint. Queen Elizabeth II at left. Back: Sea garden, arms at right. Watermark: Shellfish. Printer: TDLR. 156x67mm.

  a. Signature T. B. Donaldson.   18.00   85.00

  b. Signature W. C. Allen.   20.00   130

  r. Replacement note. Serial # prefix Z.   100   200

  s. Specimen.   —   —

#36 not assigned.

37 5 Dollars   **VF UNC**
L.1974. Orange on multicolor underprint. Queen Elizabeth II at left. Government House, arms at right. Watermark: Shellfish. Printer: TDLR. 156x67mm.

	VF	UNC
a. Signature T. B. Donaldson.	80.00	350
b. Signature W. C. Allen.	130	570
r. Replacement note. Serial # prefix Z.	—	—
s. Specimen.	—	—

38 10 Dollars   **VF UNC**
L.1974. Dark blue on multicolor underprint. Queen Elizabeth II at left. Back: Flamingos, arms at right. Watermark: Shellfish. Printer: TDLR. 156x37mm.

	VF	UNC
a. Signature T. B. Donaldson.	215	930
b. Signature W. C. Allen.	350	1,600
r. Replacement note. Serial # prefix Z.	300	640
s. Specimen.	—	—

39 20 Dollars   **VF UNC**
L.1974. Dark brown on multicolor underprint. Queen Elizabeth II at left. Back: Surrey, arms at right. Watermark: Shellfish. Printer: TDLR. 156x67mm.

	VF	UNC
a. Signature T. B. Donaldson.	310	1,300
b. Signature W. C. Allen.	450	2,000
r. Replacement note. Serial # prefix Z.	—	—
s. Specimen.	—	—

40 50 Dollars   **VF UNC**
L.1974. Brown on multicolor underprint. Queen Elizabeth II at left. Back: Produce market, arms at right. Watermark: Shellfish. Printer: TDLR. 156x67mm.

	VF	UNC
a. Signature T. B. Donaldson.	850	3,900
b. Signature W. C. Allen.	1,300	5,700
r. Replacement note. Serial # prefix Z.	—	—
s. Specimen.	—	—

41 100 Dollars   **VF UNC**
L.1974. Blue on multicolor underprint. Queen Elizabeth II at left. Back: Deep sea fishing, arms at right. Watermark: Shellfish. Printer: TDLR. 156x67mm.

	VF	UNC
a. Signature T. B. Donaldson.	1,200	5,400
b. Signature W. C. Allen.	1,550	7,000
s. Specimen.	—	—

1974 Central Bank Act; 1984 ND Issue

#42-49 Replacement notes: Serial # prefix Z.

42 1/2 Dollar   **VF UNC**
L.1974 (1984). UV: 1/2 in box fluoresce orange. Green on multicolor underprint. Baskets at left, map at center left, mature portrait of Queen Elizabeth II at center right. Signature W. C. Allen. Back: Sister Sarah in Nassau market, arms at right. Watermark: Sailing ship. Printer: TDLR. 156x67mm.

	VF	UNC
a. Issued note.	4.00	20.00
r. Replacement note. Serial # prefix Z.	19.00	90.00
s. Specimen.	—	220

43 1 Dollar   **VF UNC**
L.1974 (1984). UV: value in box fluoresce orange. Deep green on multicolor underprint. Fish at loft, map at center left, mature portrait of Queen Elizabeth II at center right. Back: Royal Bahamas Police band at center, arms at right. Watermark: Sailing ship. Printer: TDLR. 156x67mm.

	VF	UNC
a. Signature W. C. Allen.	7.00	32.50
b. Signature James H. Smith. 2 horizontal serial #.	12.00	50.00
r. Replacement note. Serial # prefix: Z.	40.00	100

44 3 Dollars   **VF UNC**
L.1974 (1984). UV: value in box fluoresce orange. Red-violet on multicolor underprint. Paradise Beach at left, map at center left, mature portrait of Queen Elizabeth II at center right. Back: Family Island sailing regatta, arms at right. Watermark: Sailing ship. Printer: TDLR. 156x67mm.

	VF	UNC
a. Signature W.C. Allen.	15.00	60.00
b. Signature James H. Smith.	15.00	60.00
r. Replacement note. Serial # prefix Z.	50.00	180
s. Specimen.	—	—

45 5 Dollars   **VF UNC**
L.1974 (1984). Orange on multicolor underprint. Statue at left. map at center left, mature portrait of Queen Elizabeth II at center right. Back: Local dancers *Junkanoo* at center, arms at right. Watermark: Sailing ship. Printer: TDLR. 156x67mm.

	VF	UNC
a. Signature W. C. Allen.	50.00	215
b. Signature James H. Smith. 2 horizontal serial #.	37.50	135
r. Replacement note. Serial # prefix Z.	67.50	295
s. Specimen.	—	—

46 10 Dollars   **VF UNC**
L.1974 (1984). Pale blue on multicolor underprint. Two flamingos at left, map at center left, mature portrait of Queen Elizabeth II at center right. Back: Lighthouse and Abaco Settlement, arms at right. Watermark: Sailing ship. Printer: TDLR. 156x67mm.

	VF	UNC
a. Signature W. C. Allen.	75.00	340
b. Signature James H. Smith. 2 horizontal serial #.	125	540
r. Replacement note. Serial # prefix Z.	—	—

47 20 Dollars
                               VF UNC
L.1974 (1984). Red and black on multicolor underprint. Horse and carriage at left, map at center left, mature portrait of Queen Elizabeth II at center right. Back: Nassau harbor scene, four ships in horizontal format. Arms at right. Watermark: Sailing ship. Printer: TDLR. 156x67mm.
  a. Signature W. C. Allen. — 120 — 520
  b. Signature James H. Smith. 2 horizontal serial #. — 85.00 — 380
  s. Specimen. — — —

48 50 Dollars
    VF UNC
L.1974 (1984). Purple, orange and green on multicolor underprint. Lighthouse at left, map at center left, mature portrait of Queen Elizabeth II at center right. Back: Central Bank, arms at right. Watermark: Sailing ship. Printer: TDLR. 156x67mm.
  a. Signature W. C. Allen. — 500 — 1,400
  b. Signature James H. Smith. 2 horizontal serial #. — 930 — 4,300
  s. Specimen. — — —

49 100 Dollars
    VF UNC
L.1974 (1984). Purple, deep blue and red-violet on multicolor underprint. Sailboat at left, map at center left, mature portrait of Queen Elizabeth II at center right. Signature W. C. Allen. Back: Blue marlin, arms at right. Watermark: Sailing ship. Printer: TDLR. 156x67mm.
  a. Issued note. — 480 — 2,100
  s. Specimen. — — —

1992 Commemorative Issue
#50, Quincentennial of First Landfall by Christopher Columbus

50 1 Dollar
    VF UNC
ND (1992). UV: fibers fluoresce red and yellow. $1 at right and design elements yellow. Dark blue and deep violet on multicolor underprint. Commercial seal at left, bust of Christopher Columbus right with compass face behind. Signature James H. Smith. Back: Flamingos, rose-throated parrots, lizard, islands, ships across back with arms at lower right. Printer: CBNC. 156x67mm.
  a. Issued note. — FV — 27.50
  s. Specimen. — — 250

1974 Central Bank Act; 1992-95 ND Issue
51 1 Dollar
    VF UNC
L.1974 (1992). Deep green on multicolor underprint. Map at left center, mature portrait Queen Elizabeth II at center. Signature James H. Smith. Fish at left. Vertical and horizontal serial #. Back: Police band at center. Watermark: Caravel sailing ship. Printer: BABN 156x67mm. — FV — 30.00

52 5 Dollars
    VF UNC
L.1974 (1995). Dark brown, brown and orange on multicolor underprint Statue of Columbus at left, Wallace-Whitfield at right. Signature James H. Smith. Back: Local dancers *Junkanoo* at center, arms at right. Watermark: Caravel sailing ship. Printer: TDLR. 156x67mm.
  a. Issued note. — FV — 105
  s. Specimen. — — —

53 10 Dollars
    VF UNC
L.1974 (1992). Pale blue on multicolor underprint. Two flamingos at left, map at center left, mature portrait of Queen Elizabeth II at center right. Signature James H. Smith. 1 serial number vertical and horizontal. Back: Lighthouse and Abaco Settlement, arms at right. Watermark: Caravel sailing ship. Printer: BABN. 156x67mm. — 50.00 — 230

53A 20 Dollars
    VF UNC
L.1974 (1993). Red and black on multicolor underprint. Sir Milo B. Butler at right, horse drawn surrey at left. Back: Nassau harbor scene, four ships in horizontal format. Arms at right. Watermark: Sailing ship. 156x67mm. — 200 — 750

54 20 Dollars
    VF UNC
L.1974 (1993). Black and red on multicolor underprint. Sir Milo B. Butler at right, horse drawn surrey at left. Signature James H. Smith. Back: Aerial view of ships in Nassau's harbor at center, Ships docked in a vertical format. Arms at right. Watermark: Caravel sailing ship. Printer: TDLR. 156x67mm.
  a. Issued note. — 60.00 — 280
  r. Replacement note. Serial # prefix Z. — 150 — 300
  s. Specimen. — — —

55   50 Dollars   VF   UNC
L.1974 (1992). Brown, blue-green and orange on multicolor underprint. Lighthouse at left, map at center left, mature portrait of Queen Elizabeth II at center
right. Signature James H. Smith, 1 vertical and horizontal serial number. Back:
Central Bank, arms at right. Watermark: Caravel sailing ship. Printer: TDLR.
156x67mm.

    a. Issued note.   130   550
    s. Specimen.

56   100 Dollars   VF   UNC
L.1974 (1992). Purple, deep blue and red-violet on multicolor underprint. Sailboat
at left, map at center left, mature portrait of Queen Elizabeth II at center right. Signature James H. Smith. 1 vertical and horizontal serial number. Back: Blue marlin,
arms at right. Watermark: Caravel sailing ship. Printer: TDLR. 156x67mm.

    a. Issued note.   320   1,400
    s. Specimen.   —   —

1974 Central Bank Act; 1996 Series

57   1 Dollar   VF   UNC
1996. Deep green on multicolor underprint. Fish at left, map at center left, mature
bust of Queen Elizabeth II at center right. Vertical and ascending size horizontal
serial number at lower left. Signature James H. Smith. Back: Royal Bahamas
Police band aat center, arm at right. Watermark: Caravel sailing ship. Printer:
BABN. 156x67mm.

    a. Issued note.   FV   30.00
    s. Specimen.   —   —

#58 *Deleted*. See #63.

59   10 Dollars   VF   UNC
1996. Deep blue-green, green and violet on multicolor underprint. Two flamingos
at left, map at center left, mature bust of Queen Elizabeth II at center right. Vertical
and ascending size horizontal serial number at lower left. Signature James H.
Smith Back: Lighthouse and Abaco Settlement, arms at right. Watermark: Caravel
sailing ship. Printer: TDLR. 156x67mm.

    a. Issued note.   FV   150
    s. Specimen.   —   —

#60 not assigned.

61   50 Dollars   VF   UNC
1996. Red-brown and deep green on multicolor underprint. Lighthouse at left,
map at center left, mature bust of Queen Elizabeth II at center right. Vertical and
ascending size horizontal serial number at lower left. Signature James H. Smith.
Back: Central Bank, arms at right. Watermark: Caravel sailing ship. Printer: TDLR.
156x67mm.

    a. Issued note.   FV   425
    s. Specimen.   —   —

Note: The following notes were stolen and are not redeemable. Serial # G101,001-103,000;
    G104,001-G105,000; G108,001-G109,000.

62   100 Dollars   VF   UNC
1996. Purple, deep blue and violet on multicolor underprint. Sailboat at left, map at
center left, mature bust of Queen Elizabeth II at center right. Vertical and ascending size horizontal serial number. Signature James H. Smith. Back: Blue marlin,
arms at right. Watermark: Caravel sailing ship. Printer: BABN. 156x67mm.

    a. Issued note.   400   1,000
    s. Specimen.   —   —

Note: The following notes were stolen and are not redeemable. Serial # G541,001-G548,000.

1974 Central Bank Act; 1997; 2000-01 Series

63   5 Dollars   VF   UNC
1997; 2001. UV: threads fluoresce green. 5 in box green. Back: center design and
flowers yellow. Dark brown, brown and orange on multicolor underprint. Statue of
Columbus at left, Wallace-Whitfield at right. Vertical and ascending size horizontal
serial numbers. Signature J. W. Francis. Back: Local dancers *Junkanoo* at center,
arms at right. Watermark: Caravel sailing ship. Printer: TDLR. 156x67mm.

    a. 1997. *GOVERNOR* title in orange.   FV   105
    b. 2001. *GOVERNOR* in black.   FV   70.00

64 10 Dollars

		VF	UNC
2000. Deep blue-green, green and violet on multicolor underprint. Sir Stafford Sands and OVD at right, pair of flamingos at left. Vertical and ascending size horizontal serial numbers. Signature J. W. Francis. Printer: TDLR. 156x67mm.		35.00	115

65 20 Dollars

		VF	UNC
1997. Multicolor. Sir Milo B. Butler at right, Vertical and ascending size horizontal serial numbers. Back: Aerial view of ships in Nassau's Harbor at center. Printer: TDLR. 156x67mm.			
a. 1997. 2 signature varieties.		FV	210
r. Replacement note.		FV	340

65A 20 Dollars

		VF	UNC
2000. Multicolor. Sir Milo B. Butler at right. Vertical and ascending size serial #. Signature J.W. Francis. Back: Aerial view of ships in Nassau's harbor at center. Printer: TDLR 156x67mm.		FV	190

66 50 Dollars

		VF	UNC
2000. Sir Roland Symonette and OVD at right, lighthouse at left. Vertical and ascending size horizontal serial numbers. Signature J. W. Francis. Printer: TDLR. 156x67mm.		100	300

67 100 Dollars

		VF	UNC
2000. Multicolor. Queen Elizabeth II, OVD at right. Vertical and ascending size horizontal serial numbers. Signature J. W. Francis. Back: Blue marlin, arms at lower right. Printer: TDLR. 167x67mm.		200	600

2000 Central Bank Act; 2001 Series

68 1/2 Dollar

		VF	UNC
2001. UV: value in box fluoresce green, background elements orange; back: background elements green. Slate blue and green on tan and multicolor underprint. Queen Elizabeth II at right, baskets at left. Vertical and sscending size horizontal serial numbers. Signature J. W. Francis. Back: Sister Sarah In Nassau market. Printer: TDLR. 156x67mm.		FV	8.50

69 1 Dollar

		VF	UNC
2001. Green, brown and multicolor. Sir Lynden O. Pindling at right. Vertical and ascending size horizontal serial numbers. Signature J. W. Francis. Back: Royal Bahamas Police band at center, arms at right. Printer: TDLR. 156x67mm.		FV	12.50

2000 Central Bank Act; 2002 Series

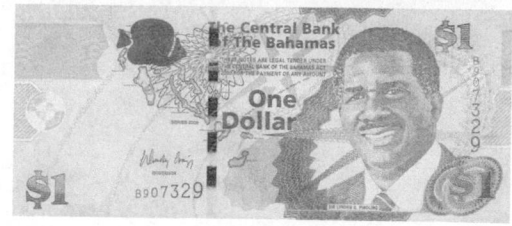

70 1 Dollar

		VF	UNC
2002. Segmented foil security strip. Emergency issue of 6 million notes. Reuse of P#43 design. Deep green on multicolor underprint. Fish at left, map at center left, mature portrait of Queen Elizabeth II at center right. Signature J. W. Francis. Back: Royal Bahamas Police band at center, arms at right. Watermark: Sailing ship. Printer: TDLR. 156x67mm.		FV	30.00

2000 Central Bank Act; 2005-2015 CRISP Series

71 **1 Dollar**
2008. Green on multicolor underprint. Sir Lynden O. Pindling at right. Signature W. Craigg. Back: Royal Bahamas Police band at center. Printer: FC-O. 156x67mm.

VF FV UNC 7.50

71A **1 Dollar**
2015. Green on multicolor underprint. Sir Lynden O. Pindling at right. Islands at center updated. Signature W. Craigg. Back: Royal Bahamas Police band at center. Printer: TDLR. 156x67mm.

VF FV UNC 7.50

72 **5 Dollars**
2007. Multicolor. Wallace-Whitfield at right. Signature W. Craigg. Back: Local dancers *Junkanoo* at center. Printer: TDLR. 156x67mm.

VF FV UNC 27.50

72A **5 Dollars**
2013. Multicolor. Wallace-Whitfield at right. Signature W. Craigg. Back: Local dancers *Junkanoo* at center. 156x67mm.

VF FV UNC 20.00

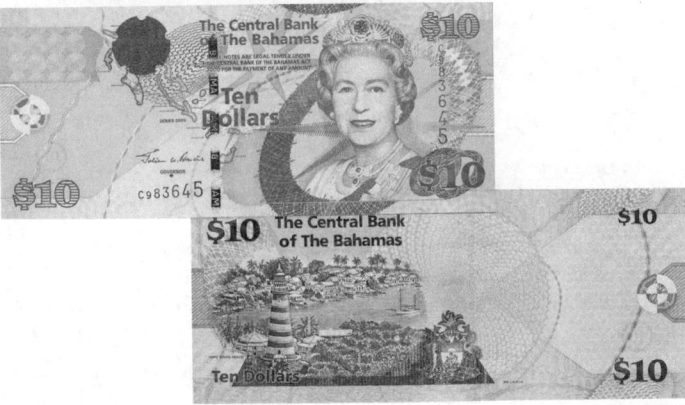

73 **10 Dollars**
2005. Blue on multicolor underprint. Queen Elizabeth II at right. Signature J. W. Francis. Printer: TDLR. 156x67mm.

VF UNC

   a. Issued note | FV | 85.00
   r. Replacement note. Serial # prefix Z. | 60.00 | 130

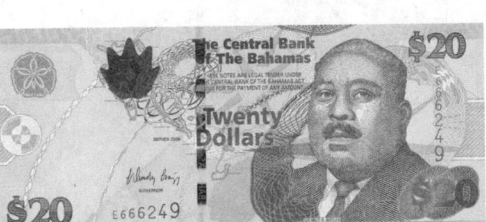

73A **10 Dollars**
2009. Dark blue, dark green and maroon on multicolor underprint. Sir Stafford Sands at right. Signature W. Craigg. Back: Hope town, lighthouse at left. Watermark: S. Sands. Printer: (T)DLR. 156x67mm.

VF FV UNC 50.00

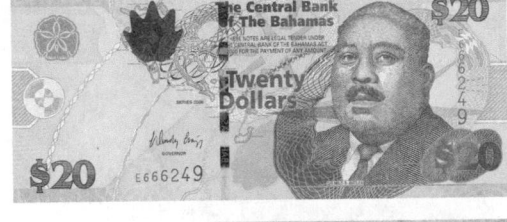

74 **20 Dollars**
2006. Multicolor. Sir Milo B. Butler at right. Signature W. Craigg. Printer: FC-O. 156x67mm.

VF FV UNC 95.00

74A **20 Dollars**
2010. Sir Milo B. Butler at right. Signature W. Craigg. Printer: G&D.

VF UNC

   a. Issued note. | FV | 85.00
   r. Replacement note. Serial # prefix: Z. | — | 150

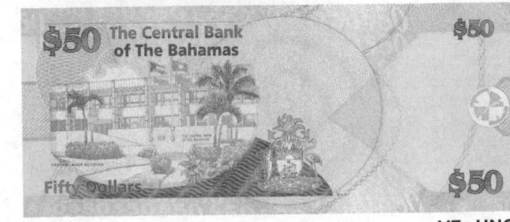

75 **50 Dollars**
2006. Multicolor. Sir Roland T. Symonette at right. Signature W. Craigg. Printer: FC-O. 156x67mm.

VF FV UNC 145

75A **50 Dollars**
2012. Multicolor. Sir Roland T. Symonette at right. Signature W. Craigg. Printer: G+D. 156x67mm.

VF FV UNC 145

76   100 Dollars
2009. Multicolor. Queen Elizabeth II at right. Signature W. Craigg. Back: Blue marlin at center. Printer: TDLR. 156x67mm.

	VF	UNC
a. Issued note.	FV	250
r. Replacement note. Z serial # prefix.	150	375

COLLECTOR SERIES

Bahamas Government

1965 Issue

CS1   1/2-100 Dollars
#17-25 overprint: *SPECIMEN*. (100 sets). *L.1965*.

Mkt. Value 7,100

Bahamas Monetary Authority

1968 Issues

CS2   1/2-100 Dollars
#26-33 overprint: *SPECIMEN*, punch hole cancelled. *L.1968*.

Mkt. Value 1,600

CS3   1/2-100 Dollars
#26-33 overprint: *SPECIMEN*, punched hole cancelled. In blue presentation book. *L.1968*.

Mkt. Value 2,600

BAHRAIN

The State of Bahrain, a group of islands in the Persian Gulf off Saudi Arabia, has an area of 665 sq. km. and a population of 718,300. Capital: Manama. Prior to the depression of the 1930s, the economy was based on pearl fishing. Petroleum and aluminum industries and transit trade are the vital factors in the economy today.

In 1783, the al-Khalifa family captured Bahrain from the Persians. In order to secure these holdings, it entered into a series of treaties with the UK during the 19th century that made Bahrain a British protectorate. The archipelago attained its independence in 1971. Bahrain's small size and central location among Persian Gulf countries require it to play a delicate balancing act in foreign affairs among its larger neighbors. Facing declining oil reserves, Bahrain has turned to petroleum processing and refining and has transformed itself into an international banking center. King Hamad bin Isa al-Khalifa, after coming to power in 1999, pushed economic and political reforms to improve relations with the Shia community. Shia political societies participated in 2006 parliamentary and municipal elections. Al Wifaq, the largest Shia political society, won the largest number of seats in the elected chamber of the legislature. However, Shi'a discontent has resurfaced in recent years with street demonstrations and occasional low-level violence.

RULERS:
Isa Bin Sulman al-Khalifa, 1961-1999
Hamad bin Isa al-Khalifa, 1999-

MONETARY SYSTEM:
1 Dinar = 1000 Fils

KINGDOM

Bahrain Currency Board

Authorization 6/1964

#1-6 For specimen notes with a maltese cross serial # prefix, see #CS1 at the end of the country listing.

1   100 Fils
L.1964. Ochre on multicolor underprint. Dhow at left, arms at right. Back: Palm trees at center. Watermark: Falcon's head.

	VF	UNC
a. Issued note.	4.00	22.00
s. Specimen.	—	50.00

2   1/4 Dinar
L.1964. Brown on multicolor underprint. Dhow at left, arms at right. Back: Oil derricks. Watermark: Falcon's head.

	VF	UNC
a. Issued note.	6.00	30.00
s. Specimen.	—	60.00

3   1/2 Dinar
L.1964. Purple on multicolor underprint. Dhow at left, arms at right. Back: Ships at the Mina Sulman Jetty. Watermark: Falcon's head.

	VF	UNC
a. Issued note.	9.00	40.00
s. Specimen.	—	80.00

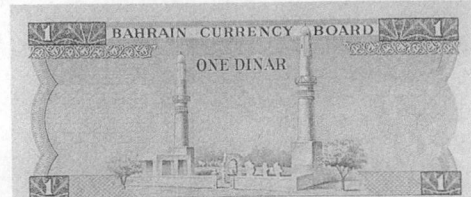

4   **1 Dinar**   **VF   UNC**

L.1964. Brownish red on multicolor underprint. Dhow at left, arms at right. Back:
Ruins of the Suq al-Khamis mosque, dominated by two minarets. Watermark:
Falcon's head.

    a. Issued note.   13.00   50.00
    s. Specimen.   —   100

5   **5 Dinars**   **VF   UNC**

L.1964. Blue-black on multicolor underprint. Dhow at left, arms at right. Back: Two
pearling dhows. Watermark: Falcon's head.

    a. Issued note.   100   650
    s. Specimen.   —   275

6   **10 Dinars**   **VF   UNC**

L.1964. Green on multicolor underprint. Dhow at left, arms at right. Back: Aerial
view of the town of Isa. Watermark: Falcon's head.

    a. Issued note.   80.00   550
    s. Specimen.   —   225

Bahrain Monetary Agency
Authorization 23/1973

7   **1/2 Dinar**   **VF   UNC**

L.1973. UV: Arabic value twice fluoresces orange. Brown on multicolor underprint.   6.00   12.00
Cast copper head of bull at lower left. Map at left, dhow at center, arms at right.
Back: Smelting works of Aluminium Bahrain at left. Watermark: Falcon's head.

8   **1 Dinar**   **VF   UNC**

L.1973. UV: Arabic value twice fluoresces orange. Red on multicolor underprint.   6.00   14.00
Minaret of the Manama Mosque at left, map at left, dhow at center, arms at right.
Back: Headquarters of Bahrain Monetary Agency at left. Watermark: Falcon's
head.

8A   **5 Dinars**   **VF   UNC**

L.1973. UV: Arabic value twice fluoresces orange. Dark blue on multicolor un-   28.00   75.00
derprint. Minaret of the Suq al-Khamis mosque at left, map at left, dhow at center,
arms at right. Back: Pearling dhows at left. Watermark: Falcon's head.

9   **10 Dinars**   **VF   UNC**

L.1973. Green on multicolor underprint. Wind tower and map at left, dhow at
center, arms at right. Back: Dry dock at left. Watermark: Falcon's head.

    a. 2 horizontal serial #.   55.00   100
    b. Serial # vertical and horizontal.   60.00   110

10   **20 Dinars**   **VF   UNC**

L.1973. Reddish-brown on multicolor underprint. Minaret of the al-Fadhel mosque
and map at left, dhow at center, arms at right. Back: Government House at left.
Watermark: Falcon's head.

    a. Issued note.   100   275
    s. Specimen.   —   —

11 20 Dinars VF UNC
L.1973. Also various color differences. Map at left, dhow at center, arms at right, symbol changed at right of map. Silvering added at lower left denomination. Back: Open frame and symbol around watermark area. Watermark: Falcon's head.
a. 2 horizontal serial #. 100 220
b. Serial # vertical and horizontal. 110 250

Authorization 23/1973; 1993 ND Issue

12 1/2 Dinar VF UNC
L.1973 (1986). Dark brown and violet on violet on multicolor underprint. Red shield of arms at center, man weaving at right, outline map at left. Back: Aluminum Bahrain" facility at left center. Watermark: Antelope's head.
3.50 8.00

13 1 Dinar VF UNC
L.1973 (1993). Violet and red-orange on multicolor underprint. Ancient Dilmun seal at right, arms at center, outline map at left. Back: Bahrain Monetary Agency building at left center. Watermark: Antelope's head.
6.00 15.00

14 5 Dinars VF UNC
L.1973 (1993). Dark blue and deep blue-green on multicolor underprint. Riffa Fortress at right, arms at center, outline map at left. Back: Bahrain International Airport at left center. Watermark: Antelope's head.
24.00 95.00

15 10 Dinars VF UNC
L.1973 (1993). Deep olive-green and green on multicolor underprint. Dhow at right, arms at center, outline map at left. Back: Aerial view of King Fahad Causeway at left center. Watermark: Antelope's head.
65.00 120

16 20 Dinars VF UNC
L.1973 (1993). Purple and violet multicolor underprint. Bab al-Bahrain gate at right, arms at center, outline map at left. Back: Ahmed al-Fateh Islamic Center at left center. Watermark: Antelope's head.
95.00 250

Note: A second printing was ordered using a false authorization. These are easily distinguished by a space between the 2 Arabic letters in the serial # prefix and are not redeemable. Collector value is approximately $10.00.

Authorization 23/1973; 1996 ND Issue

17 1/2 Dinar VF UNC
L.1973 (1996). Narrow security thread. Deep brown, violet and brown with deep brown shield at center. Arms at center, outline map at left, man weaving at right. Back: Aluminum Bahrain" facility at left center. Watermark: Antelope's head. 142x72mm.
FV 9.00

Authorization 23/1973; 1998 ND Issue

18 1/2 Dinar VF UNC
L.1973 (1998). Wide security thread. No microprinting. Deep brown, violet and brown. Deep brown shield of arms at lower center, man weaving at right, outline map at left. Back: Aluminum Bahrain" facility at left center. Watermark: Antelope's head. 142x72mm.
FV 8.00

19 1 Dinar VF UNC
L.1973 1998. Wide security thread. Violet and red-orange on multicolor underprint. Ancient Dilmun seal at right, arms at lower center, outline map at left. Back: Bahrain Monetary Agency building at left center. Watermark: Antelope's head. 142x72mm.
a. With *BMA* microprinting on security thread. FV 15.00
b. Without microprinting on security thread. FV 12.00

20 5 Dinars VF UNC
L.1973 (1998). Wide security thread. Hologram at lower left. Blue on multicolor underprint. Arms at lower center, outline map at left, Riffa Fortress at right. Back: Bahrain International Airport at left center. Watermark: Antelope's head. 142x72mm.
a. With *BMA* microprinting on security thread. 55.00 90.00
b. Without microprinting on security thread. 50.00 65.00

21　10 Dinars　　　　　　　　　　　　　　　　　　**VF　UNC**
L.1973 (1998). Hologram at lower left. Green on multicolor underprint. Arms at center, outline map at left, dhow at right. Back: Aerial view of King Fahad Causeway at left center. Watermark: Antelope's head. 142x72mm.
　　a. With *BMA* microprinting on security thread.　　　　　85.00　　150
　　b. Without microprinting on security thread.　　　　　　　FV　　90.00

22　20 Dinars　　　　　　　　　　　　　　　　　　**VF　UNC**
L.1973 (1998). With hologram and wide micro-printed security thread. Purple on　280　　600
multicolor underprint. Bab al-Bahrain gate at right, arms at center, outline map at left. Back: Ahmed al-Fateh Islamic Center at left center. Watermark: Antelope's head. 142x72mm.

23　20 Dinars　　　　　　　　　　　　　　　　　　**VF　UNC**
L. 1973 (1998). Hologram at lower left. Orange and black on multicolor underprint.　95.00　　220
Bab al-Bahrain gate at right, arms at center, outline map at left. Back: Ahmed al-Fateh Islamic Center at left center. Watermark: Antelope's head. 142x72mm.

Authorization 23/1973; 2001 ND Issue

24　20 Dinars　　　　　　　　　　　　　　　　　　**VF　UNC**
ND (2001). Orange on multicolor underprint. Shaikh Hamad bin Issa al Khalifa,　FV　　150
King of Bahrain at right. 142x72mm.

Central Bank of Bahrain
2007 ND First Issue

25　1/2 Dinar　　　　　　　　　　　　　　　　　　**VF　UNC**
ND (2008). UV: bottom corner device and box at lower center yellow, vertical　FV　　4.00
serial # orange; back: background elements blue, orange. Orange and brown on multicolor underprint. Old Bahrain Court building at left. Back: Bahrain International Circuit Court building. 155x74mm.

26　1 Dinar　　　　　　　　　　　　　　　　　　**VF　UNC**
ND (2008). Red and rose on multicolor underprint. Al Hedaya al Khaliflya School　FV　　7.00
at left. Back: Arabian horses and the Sail and Pearl Monument. 155x74mm.

27　5 Dinars　　　　　　　　　　　　　　　　　　**VF　UNC**
ND (2008). Light and dark blue on multicolor underprint. Sheik Isa House in Mu-　FV　　35.00
harraq at left and Riffa Fort at bottom. Back: First oil well in Bahrain and Aluminum Bahrain plant. 155x74mm.

28　10 Dinars　　　　　　　　　　　　　　　　　　**VF　UNC**
ND (2008). Brown, green and tan on multicolor underprint. King Hamad bin isa al　FV　　45.00
Khalifa at left. Back: Sheik isa bin al Khalifa causeway. 155x74mm.

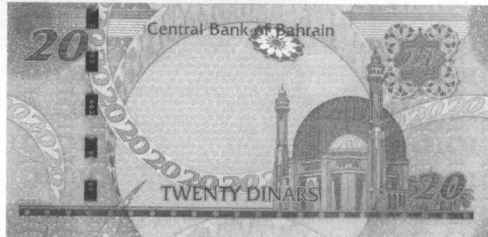

29   20 Dinars
ND (2008). Brown and dark green on multicolor underprint. King Hamad bin isa al Khalifa at left. Back: Al Fateh Islamic Center. 155x74mm.

	VF	UNC
	FV	85.00

COLLECTOR SERIES
Bahrain Monetary Agency
Authorization 23/1973

CS1   100 Fils - 20 Dinars
ND (1978). #1-6 and 10 with overprint: *SPECIMEN* and Maltese cross serial # prefix.

	Mkt. Value
	80.00

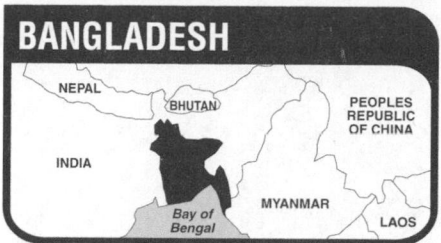

BANGLADESH

The Peoples Republic of Bangladesh (formerly East Pakistan), a parliamentary democracy located on the Bay of Bengal bordered by India and Burma, has an area of 144,000 sq. km. and a population of 153.55 million. Capital: Dhaka (Dacca). The economy is predominantly agricultural. Jute products and tea are exported.

Europeans began to set up trading posts in the area of Bangladesh in the 16th century; eventually the British came to dominate the region and it became part of British India. In 1947, West Pakistan and East Bengal (both primarily Muslim) separated from India (largely Hindu) and jointly became the new country of Pakistan. East Bengal became East Pakistan in 1955, but the awkward arrangement of a two-part country with its territorial units separated by 1,600 km left the Bengalis marginalized and dissatisfied. East Pakistan seceded from its union with West Pakistan in 1971 and was renamed Bangladesh. A military-backed caretaker regime suspended planned parliamentary elections in January 2007 in an effort to reform the political system and root out corruption; the regime has pledged new democratic elections by the end of 2008. About a third of this extremely poor country floods annually during the monsoon rainy season, hampering economic development.

MONETARY SYSTEM:
   1 Rupee = 100 Paise to 1972
   1 Taka = 100 Paisas 1972-

REPUBLIC
Peoples Republic of Bangladesh
1971 ND Provisional Issue

#1-3 The Bangladesh Bank never officially issued any Pakistan notes with overprints. These are considered locally issued by some authorities.

1   1 Rupee
ND (1971). Four different overprints are documented. Blue. Purple overprint *BANGLADESH* on Pakistan #9.

	VF	UNC
	30.00	90.00

1A   1 Rupee
ND (1971). Two different overprints are documented. Blue. Purple Bengali overprint on Pakistan #9.

	VF	UNC
	30.00	90.00

2   5 Rupees
ND (1971). Brown-violet. Purple Bengali overprint on Pakistan #15.

	VF	UNC
	32.50	100

2A   5 Rupees
ND (1971). Purple Bengali overprint on Pakistan #9.

	VF	UNC
	32.50	100

3A 5 Rupees   VF   UNC
ND (1971). English overprint on Pakistan #15.   75.00 175

3 10 Rupees   VF   UNC
ND (1971). Brown. Purple Bengali overprint on Pakistan #19. 35.00 120

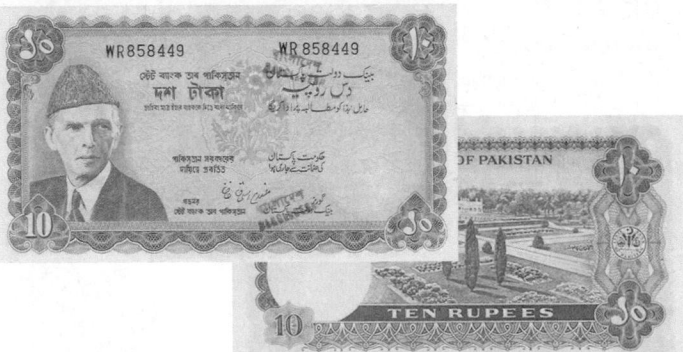

3B 10 Rupees   VF   UNC
ND (1971). English overprint on Pakistan #16.   125   225

3C 50 Rupees   VF   UNC
ND (1971). English/Bengali overprint on Pakistan #17. —   —

3D 100 Rupees   VF   UNC
ND (1971). English overprint on Pakistan #18.   —   —

3E 500 Rupees   VF   UNC
ND (1971). English overprint on Pakistan #19.   —   —

1972-89 ND Issues

4 1 Taka   VF   UNC
ND (1972). Brown on orange and blue underprint. Map of Bangladesh at left. 7.00 25.00

5 1 Taka   VF   UNC
ND (1973). Purple and ochre. Hand holding rice plants at left. Back: Arms at right.
  a. With watermark: Tiger's head.   1.00 9.00
  b. Without watermark. (2 signature varieties). 1.00 8.00

6 1 Taka   VF   UNC
ND (1973). Purple on ochre and blue underprint. Woman preparing grain at left.
Back: Hand holding rice plants at center, arms at right. Watermark: Tiger's head.
  a. Issued note.   0.60 7.00
  s. Specimen.   —   100

6A 1 Taka   VF   UNC
ND (1979). Purple on multicolor underprint. Arms at right. Back: Deer at left 0.50 4.50
center. Watermark: Tiger's head.

6B 1 Taka   VF   UNC
ND (1982). Purple on multicolor underprint. Arms at right, no printing on watermark area at left. Back: Deer at left center. Watermark: Modified tiger.
  a. Signature title in Bengali: *FINANCE SECRETARY*. Solid security thread. Six 0.10 2.00
    signature varieties.
  b. Signature title in Bengali: *PRINCIPAL FINANCE SECRETARY*. Solid 0.10 1.00
    security thread.
  c. Signature title in Bengali: *FINANCE SECRETARY*. Micro-printed security 0.10 1.00
    thread.

6C 2 Taka   VF   UNC
ND (1988-). Gray-green on orange and green underprint. Shahid Minar, Martyr's
Monument at right. Back: Dhyal or Magpie-robin at left. Watermark: Tiger's head.
100x60mm.
  a. Solid security thread. 4 signature varieties. 0.50 4.00
  b. Security thread reads: *BANGLADESH BANK* in Bengali. 0.50 2.50
  c. Security thread reads: *GOVERNMENT OF BANGLADESH* in Bengali. One 0.50 2.50
    signature variety.
  d. As c. but smaller watermark.   0.50 2.50
  e. 2002 date on back. Security thread reads: Government of Bangladesh. 0.50 2.00
  f. 2003 date on back. Signature in brown ink. 0.50 2.00
  g. 2003. Signature in black ink.   0.50 2.00
  h. 2004 date on back.   0.50 2.00
  i. 2006 date on back.   0.25 1.00
  j. 2007. 3mm wide segmented security thread. 0.25 1.00
  k. 2007. Embedded microprinted security thread. 0.25 1.00
  l. 2008.   0.25 1.00
  m. 2009.   0.25 1.00
  n. 2010.   0.25 1.00

Bangladesh Bank
1972 ND Issue

7 5 Taka   VF   UNC
ND (1972). Purple on multicolor underprint. Map of Bangladesh at left, portrait of 3.00 17.50
Mujibur Rahman at right.

8 10 Taka   VF   UNC
ND (1972). Blue on multicolor underprint. Map of Bangladesh at left, portrait of 6.00 32.50
Mujibur Rahman at right.

9 **100 Taka**   **VF**   **UNC**
ND (1972). Green on multicolor underprint. Map of Bangladesh at left, portrait of
Mujibur Rahman at right.
     a. Serial # panel at upper right with a blue backgorund.   8.00   75.00
     b. Serial # panel at upper right with a brown tint background   8.00   75.00

1973 ND Issue

10 **5 Taka**   **VF**   **UNC**
ND (1972). Red on multicolor underprint. Mujibur Rahman at left. Back: Lotus
plants at center right. Watermark: Tiger's head.
     a. Issued note.   1.50   10.00
     s. Specimen.   —   —

11 **10 Taka**   **VF**   **UNC**
ND (1972). Green on multicolor underprint. Mujibur Rahman at left. Back: River
scene. Watermark: Tiger's head.
     a. Serial # in Western numerals.   4.00   17.50
     b. Serial # in Bengali numerals.   7.50   25.00
     s. Specimen.   —   —

12 **100 Taka**   **VF**   **UNC**
ND (1972). Brown on multicolor underprint. Mujibur Rahman at left. Back: River
scene. Watermark: Tiger's head.
     a. Serial # in western numerals.   5.00   25.00
     b. Serial # in Bengali numerals.   50.00   100

1974 ND Issue

13 **5 Taka**   **VF**   **UNC**
ND (1973). Red on multicolor underprint. Mujibur Rahman at right. 2 signature
varieties. Back: Aerial view of factory. Watermark: Tiger's head.
     a. Issued note.   1.50   12.50
     s. Specimen.   —   110

14 **10 Taka**   **VF**   **UNC**
ND (1973). Green on multicolor underprint. Mujibur Rahman at right. 2 signature
varieties. Back: Rice harvesting scene at left center.
     a. Issued note.   1.00   10.00
     s. Specimen.   —   110

1976; 1977 ND Issue

15 **5 Taka**   **VF**   **UNC**
ND (1977). Light brown on multicolor underprint. Star mosque in Dhaka at right.
Back: Aerial view of factory. Watermark: Tiger's head.
     a. Issued note.   1.50   7.50
     s. Specimen.   —   100

16 **10 Taka**   **VF**   **UNC**
ND (1977). Violet on multicolor underprint. Star mosque in Dhaka at right. Back:
Rice harvesting scene at left center. Watermark: Tiger's head.
     a. Issued note.   2.00   17.50
     s. Specimen.   —   110

17   50 Taka   VF   UNC

ND (1976). Orange on multicolor underprint. Star mosque in Dhaka at right. Back:
Harvesting scene. Watermark: Tiger's head.

    a. Issued note.   5.00   25.00
    s. Specimen.   —   100

18   100 Taka   VF   UNC

ND (1976). Blue-violet on multicolor underprint. Star mosque in Dhaka at left.   10.00   50.00
Back: River scene. Watermark: Tiger's head.

19   500 Taka   VF   UNC

ND (1976). Blue and lilac on multicolor underprint. Star mosque in Dhaka at right.   90.00   250
Back: High Court in Dhaka. Watermark: Tiger's head.

Note: For similar 500 Taka but w/o printing on wmk. area, see #30.

1978-82 ND Issue

20   5 Taka   VF   UNC

ND (1978). Brown on multicolor underprint. Mihrab in *Kushumba* mosque at right.
Back: Aerial view of factory. Watermark: Tiger's head. 119x64mm.

    a. Issued note.   1.00   5.50
    s. Specimen.   —   100

21   10 Taka   VF   UNC

ND (1978). Violet on multicolor underprint. *Atiya Jam-e* mosque in Tangali at right.
Back: Rice harvesting scene at left center. Watermark: Tiger's head.

    a. Issued note.   2.00   9.00
    s. Specimen.   —   110

22   20 Taka   VF   UNC

ND (1979). Micro-printed security thread. Dark blue-green on multicolor under-   4.00   20.00
print. *Chote Sona* mosque at right. Underprint over watermark area at left. Back:
Harvesting scene. Watermark: Tiger's head.

23   50 Taka   VF   UNC

ND (1979). Orange on multicolor underprint. Sat Gamnbuj Mosque in Dhaka at   2.50   20.00
right. Back: Women harvesting tea. Watermark: Tiger's head.

24   100 Taka   VF   UNC

ND (1977). Blue-violet, deep brown and orange on multicolor underprint. Star   6.00   30.00
mosque in Dhaka at right, underprint throughout watermark area at left. Back:
Ruins of Lalbagh Fort at left center. Watermark: Tiger's head.

1982-88 ND Issue

25 5 Taka

ND (1981). Mihrab in *Kushumba* mosque at right, without printing on watermark area at left. Back: Industrial landscape scene at left center. Watermark: Modified tiger's head. 119x64mm.

		VF	UNC
a.	Solid security thread. Black signature Large serial #.	2.00	7.50
b.	Micro-printed security thread. Black signature Small serial #. 2 signature varieties.	1.00	6.00
c.	Micro-printed security thread. Brown signature Small serial #. 3 signature varieties.	0.75	3.50
s.	Specimen.	—	50.00

26 10 Taka

ND (1982). Violet and red-violet on multicolor underprint. *Atiya Jam-e* mosque in Tangail at right, without printing in watermark area. Back: Spillway of Kaptai Dam at left center. Watermark: Modified tiger's head.

		VF	UNC
a.	With curved line of text above and below mosque. Solid security thread.	2.50	12.50
b.	Without curved line of text above mosque. Solid security thread. 2 signature varieties.	2.50	10.00
c.	Micro-printed security thread. 3 signature varieties.	2.00	7.50

27 20 Taka

ND (1988); 2002. Blue-green on multicolor underprint. *Chote Sona* mosque at right, without printing on watermark area. Signature varieties. Back: Harvesting scene. Watermark: Modified tiger's head.

		VF	UNC
a.	Black signature Large serial #. 2 signature varieties.	2.50	9.00
b.	Green signature Small serial #. 2 signature varieties.	2.00	7.50
c.	Foil security thread. Green signature small serial #.	1.00	5.00

28 50 Taka

ND (1987). Black, red and deep green on multicolor underprint. National Monument at Savar at center. Back: National Assembly building at center. Watermark: Modified tiger's head.

		VF	UNC
a.	7-digit serial #.	2.75	12.50
b.	8-digit serial #.	2.75	12.50
c.	Different tiger in watermark. Clouds on back have been re-engraved. Underprint colors changed.	2.75	12.50

29 100 Taka

ND (1981). Blue-violet, deep brown and orange on multicolor underprint. Star mosque in Dhaka at right, without printing on watermark area at left. Signature varieties. Back: Ruins of Lalbagh Fort at left center. Watermark: Modified tiger's head.

VF 3.50   UNC 17.50

31 100 Taka

ND (1983). Star mosque in Dhaka at right, without printing on watermark area at left. Circular toothed border added around watermark area. Back: Ruins of Lalbagh Fort at left center. Circular toothed order added around watermark area. Watermark: Modified tiger's head.

		VF	UNC
a.	Solid security thread. 2 signature varieties.	FV	6.50
b.	Micro-printed security thread. 2 signature varieties.	FV	6.00
c.	Segmented foil security thread. 2 signature varieties.	FV	6.00
d.	Segmented foil thread with micro-printing.	FV	6.00
e.	Solid foil thread with micro-printing.	FV	6.00

30   500 Taka   VF UNC
ND (1982). Gray, blue and violet on multicolor underprint. Star mosque in dhaka at right, without printing on watermark area at left. Signature varieties. Back: High Court in Dhaka. Watermark: Modified tiger's head.
    a. Without segmented foil. 2 signature varieties.   FV 55.00
    b. With segmented foil over security thread. 2 signature varieties.   FV 30.00
    c. Eight numerals in serial #.   FV 30.00

1996 ND Commemorative Issue

#35, Victory Day. Ovpt: *VICTORY DAY SILVER JUBILEE '96* in lower l. wmk. area.

32   10 Taka   VF UNC
ND (1996). Violet on multicolor underprint. Commemorative overprint on #26b in   FV 2.50
lower left watermark area. 2 signature varieties.

1997 ND Issue

33   10 Taka   VF UNC
ND (1997). Dark brown and deep blue-green on multicolor underprint. Mujibur   FV 3.00
Rahman at right. 2 signature varieties. Back: Arms at left, Lalbagh fort mosque at left center. Watermark: Mujibur Rahman.

1998 ND Issue

34   500 Taka   VF UNC
ND (1998). Brown, blue, purple and red on multicolor underprint. National Monu-   FV 30.00
ment in Savar at center right. Back: High Court building in Dhaka.

2000-01 Issue

35   10 Taka   VF UNC
2000. Polymer plastic. Brown, red and multicolor. Mujibur Rahman at left. Back: FV 2.00
National Assembly building. 152x64mm.

36   50 Taka   VF UNC
ND (2000). Brown and blue on multicolor underprint. National Assembly building   FV 3.00
at left. Back: Bagha Mosque of Rajshahi at right.

37   100 Taka   VF UNC
2001. Dark blue on light red-brown underprint. Mujibur Rahman at left, Sixty Dome   FV 5.00
Mosque at right. Back: Bangabandhu Bridge.

38   500 Taka   VF UNC
2000. Brownish purple on multicolor underprint. Mujibur Rahman at right, *Sat*   FV 22.50
Gambuj mosque in center. Back: High Court building in Dhaka. 152x65mm.

2002 Issue

39   10 Taka   VF UNC
2002-2005. Brown, red and multicolor. National emblem at left; Baitul Mukarram at lower right. Back: National Assembly building, Jatiyo Sangshad Bhaban. 130x60mm.
    a. 2002.   FV 2.00
    b. 2003.   FV 2.00
    c. 2004.   FV 2.00
    d. 2005.   FV 2.00

39A   10 Taka   VF UNC
2006-08. Brown, red and multicolor. National emblem at left, building at lower right. Only blue signature surrounded in white. Back: National Assembly building. 123x60mm.
    a. 2006.   FV 2.00
    b. 2007.   FV 2.00

40   20 Taka
2002-08. Reduced size. Enhanced security features. Blue-green on multicolor underprint. *Chote Sona* mosque at right. Underprint in watermark area at left. Back: Washing jute scene. 130x60mm.

	VF	UNC
a. 2002.	FV	3.50
b. 2003.	FV	3.50
c. 2004.	FV	3.50
d. 2005.	FV	3.50
e. 2006.	FV	3.50
f. 2008.	FV	3.50

41   50 Taka
2003-10. Reduced size. Iridescent security thread, sight impaired features. Brown and blue on multicolor underprint. National Assembly building at left. Back: Bagha Mosque of Rajshahi at right. 130x60mm.

	VF	UNC
a. 2003.	FV	4.00
b. 2004.	FV	4.00
c. 2005. Signature 8.	FV	4.00
d. 2005. Signature 9.	FV	4.00
e. 2008.	FV	4.00
f. 2010. Signature 10.	FV	4.00

42   100 Taka
2002-04. Dark blue on light red-brown underprint. National monument at Savar at center. Back: Bangabandhu Bridge. 152x65mm.

	VF	UNC
a. 2002.	FV	5.00
b. 2003.	FV	5.00
c. 2004.	FV	5.00

43   500 Taka
2002; 2003. Value line in solid ink. Brownish purple on multicolor underprint. National Monument at Savar at right, *Sat Gambuj* mosque in center. Back: High Court building in Dhaka. 152x65mm.

	VF	UNC
a. 2002.	FV	22.50
b. 2003.	FV	22.50

2004-05 Issue

44   100 Taka
2005. Multicolor. National monument at Savar at center, value in upper left is a solid color. Back: Jamuna Bridge. 152x65mm.   FV   5.00

45   500 Taka
2003-08. Value at upper left is in solid color. Value in text is in color shifting ink. National monument at Savar at right, *Sat Gambuj* Mosque in center. Back: High Court building in Dhaka. 152x65mm.

	VF	UNC
a. 2003.	FV	22.50
b. 2004.	FV	22.50
c. 2005. Signature 8.	FV	22.50
d. 2005. Signature 9.	FV	22.50
e. 2006.	FV	22.50
f. 2007.	FV	22.50
g. 2008.	FV	22.50

2006-07 Issue

46   5 Taka
2006. Brown on orange and tan underprint. Kusumbag mosque in Rajshahi at right. Back: Riverfront industrial scene. 119x62mm.
a. 2006. Segmented security thread.   FV   1.50

46A   5 Taka
2007; 2009; 2010. Brown on orange and tan underprint. Kusumbag mosque in Rajshahi at right. Back: Riverfont industria scene.

	VF	UNC
a. 2007. Segmented security thread.	FV	1.50
b. 2009.	FV	1.50
c. 2010.	FV	1.50

47   10 Taka
2008; 2009; 2010. Brown, red and multicolor. National emblem at left; building at lower right. Text in center and signature surrounded in white. Back: National Assembly building. 120x60mm.

	VF	UNC
a. 2008.	FV	2.00
b. 2009.	FV	2.00
c. 2010.	FV	2.00

48   20 Taka
2006; 2008; 2009; 2011. Like #40 but reduced size. Blue-green on multicolor underprint. *Chote Sona* mosque at right. Segmented security thread. Back: Harvesting scene. 127x60mm.

	VF	UNC
a. 2006. Signature 9.	FV	3.50
b. 2008.	FV	3.50
c. 2009. Signature 10.	FV	3.50
d. 2011.	FV	3.50

49   100 Taka   VF   UNC

2006-10. Like #44 but reduced size. Multicolor. National monument at Savar at right, *Sat Gambuj* mosque in center. Back: High court building in Dhaka. 140x62mm.

a. 2006. Signature 9. Bengali digits in serial #.	FV	3.50
b. 2007.	FV	3.50
c. 2008.	FV	3.50
d. 2009.	FV	3.50
e. 2009. Signature 10.	FV	4.00
f. 2009. Signature 10. New name of bridge on back.	FV	5.00
g. 2010.	FV	3.50

50   500 Taka   VF   UNC

2009; 2010. Purple and brown on multicolor underprint. Mujibur Rahman at right. Back: Supreme Court. 153x66mm.

a. 2009.	FV	17.50
b. 2010.	FV	17.50

51   1000 Taka   VF   UNC

2008-10. Rose on light blue underprint. Shahid Minar Monument. Serial # font varieties. Back: Curzon Hall, Dhaka University 160x72mm.

a. 2008. Signature 9.	FV	25.00
b. 2009. Signature 10.	FV	25.00
c. 2010.	FV	25.00

2011 Issue

52   2 Taka   VF   UNC

2011; 2012; 2013; 2015. Green and tan.

a. 2011.	FV	0.25
b. 2012.	FV	0.25
c. 2013.	FV	0.25
d. 2015.	FV	0.25

53   5 Taka   VF   UNC

2011; 2012. Brown and tan on multicolor underprint. Muhibur Rahman at left, National Martyr's Monument in Savar at center. Back: Naogaon Kusumba mosque at center. 117x60mm.

a. 2011. Dark portrait.	FV	0.30
a. 2014.	FV	0.30
b. 2011. Light portrait.	FV	0.30
b. 2015.	FV	0.30
c. 2012.	FV	0.30

53A   5 Taka   VF   UNC

2014; 2015. Like #53 but olive green and brown color, white margins. Muhibur Rahman at left, National Martyr's Monument in Savar at center. 117x60mm.

a. 2014.	FV	0.30
b. 2015.	FV	0.30

54   10 Taka   VF   UNC

2012; 2013; 2014. Brown on light purple underprint. Muhibur Rahman at left, National Martyr's Monument in Savar at center. Back: Baitul Mukarraqm, the national mosque in Dhaka at center. Watermark: Mujibur Rahman. 122x60mm.

a. 2012.	FV	0.50
b. 2013.	FV	0.50
c. 2014. Bengali digits in serial #.	FV	0.50
d. 2014. Western digits in serial # lower left.	FV	0.50
e. 2015.	FV	0.50

55   20 Taka   VF   UNC

2012. Dark green on light green andmulticolor underprint. Muhibur Rahman at left, National Martyr's Monument in Savar at center. Back: Shaat Gambuj Masjid, the Sixty Dome Mosque in Bagerhat at center. Watermark: Mujibur Rahman and 20. 127x60mm.

a. Black vertical lathework on face at right end.	FV	1.00
b. Green vertical lathework on face at right end.	FV	1.00

55A   20 Taka   VF   UNC

2012; 2013; 2014. Dark green on light green andmulticolor underprint. Muhibur Rahman at left, National Martyr's Monument in Savar at center. Orange vertical lathework at right. Back: Sixty Dome Mosque at center. 127x60mm.

a. 2012.	FV	1.00
b. 2013.	FV	1.00
c. 2014. Lower left serial # in Western digits.	FV	1.00

56   50 Taka   VF   UNC

2011; 2012; 2013; 2014. Brown on multicolor underprint. Muhibur Rahman at left, National Martyr's Monument in Savar at center. Back: Shilpacharya Jaqinul Abedin's painting "Ploughing." Watermark: Muhibur Rahman and 50. 130x60mm.

a. 2011. Spelling error in artist's name on back (eight blocks of letters).	FV	3.00
b. 2012. Corrected artist's name on back (six blocks of letters).	FV	2.50
c. 2013.	FV	3.00
d. 2014. Lower left serial # in Western digits.	FV	3.00

57   100 Taka   VF   UNC

2011-. Slate black on blue underprint. Muhibur Rahman at left, National Martyr's Monument in Savar at center. Back: Star Mosque in Dhaka on back. 140x62mm.

a. 2011.	FV	5.00
b. 2012.	FV	5.00
c. 2013.	FV	5.00
d. 2014.	FV	5.00
e. 2015.	FV	5.00

58   500 Taka   **VF   UNC**
2011-. Slate black, green and blue on multicolor underprint. Muhibur Rahman at
left, National Martyr's Monument in Savar at center. Back: Farmers plowing field at
riverbank. 152x65mm.
   a. 2011.   FV   15.00
   b. 2012.   FV   15.00
   c. 2013.   FV   15.00

59   1000 Taka   **VF   UNC**
2011-. Slate black and violet on multicolor underprint. Muhibur Rahman at left,
National Martyr's Monument in Savar at center. Back: National Parliament buildign
at center. 160x70mm.
   a. 2011.   FV   30.00
   b. 2012.   FV   30.00
   c. 2013.   FV   30.00
   d. 2014.   FV   30.00

2011 Commemorative Issue

60   40 Taka   **VF   UNC**
2011. Violet, orange and green on multicolor underprint. Mujibur Rahman with   FV   2.50
hand raised at left, National Martyr's Monument in Savar at right. Back: Six men
holding rifles aloft. 122x60mm.

61   60 Taka   **VF   UNC**
2012. Multicolor. Shaheed Minar, Martyrs' Monument of the Language Movement   FV   3.50
in Dhaka at center. Back: Flowering branch, Five portraits and obelisk monument
at center. Watermark: Mujibur Rahman. 130x60mm.

2013 Commemorative Issues

62   25 Taka   **VF   UNC**
26.1.2013. Purple and blue on multicolor underprint. National monument at Savar   FV   2.00
at left, montage of banknotes at center. Back: Security Printing Company building.
123x60mm.

63   100 Taka   **VF   UNC**
2013. Red-brown and multicolor. 18th century terra-cotta fragment depicting a
horse rider. Signature Atiur Rahman. Back: Bangladesh National Museum building. Watermark: Sheikh Mujibur Rahman. 140x62mm.
   a. Issued note. 100,000 pieces.   FV   4.50
   b. Commemorative folder. 11,000 pieces.   —   6.00

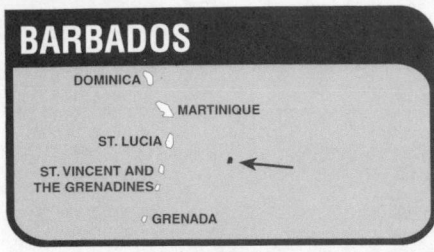

BARBADOS

DOMINICA
MARTINIQUE
ST. LUCIA
ST. VINCENT AND
THE GRENADINES
GRENADA

Barbados, an independent state within the British Commonwealth, is located in the Windward Islands of the West Indies east of St. Vincent. The coral island has an area of 431 sq. km and a population of 281,900. Capital: Bridgetown.

The island was uninhabited when first settled by the British in 1627. Slaves worked the sugar plantations established on the island until 1834 when slavery was abolished.

The economy remained heavily dependent on sugar, rum, and molasses production through most of the 20th century. The gradual introduction of social and political reforms in the 1940s and 1950s led to complete independence from the UK in 1966. In the 1990s, tourism and manufacturing surpassed the sugar industry in economic importance.

RULERS:
British to 1966

MONETARY SYSTEM:
1 British West Indies Dollar = 4 Shillings - 2 Pence
5 British West Indies Dollars = 1 Pound - 10 Pence
1 Dollar = 100 Cents, 1950-

STATE

Central Bank of Barbados

1973 ND Issue

#29-35 Replacement notes: serial # prefix Z1.

29   1 Dollar   **VF   UNC**
ND (1973). Red on multicolor underprint. Portrait S. J. Prescod at right, arms at left center. Signature C. Blackman. Back: Trafalgar Square in Bridgetown. Watermark: Map of Barbados. Printer: (T)DLR. 150x65mm.
    a. Issued note.   5.00   27.50
    s. Specimen.   —   90.00

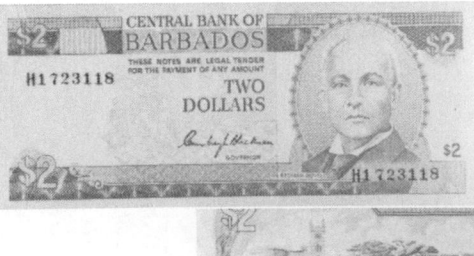

30   2 Dollars   **VF   UNC**
ND (1980). Blue on multicolor underprint. Portrait J. R. Bovell at right, arms at left center. Signature C. Blackman. Back: Trafalgar Square in Bridgetown. Watermark: Map of Barbados. Printer: (T)DLR. 150x65mm.
    a. Issued note.   6.00   37.50
    s. Specimen.   —   90.00

31   5 Dollars   **VF   UNC**
ND (1973). Green on multicolor underprint. Portrait S. J. Prescod at right, arms at left center. Signature C. Blackman. Back: Trafalgar Square in Bridgetown. Watermark: Map of Barbados. Printer: (T)DLR. 150x65mm.
    a. Issued note.   15.00   70.00
    s. Specimen.   —   90.00

32   5 Dollars   **VF   UNC**
ND (1975). Dark green on multicolor underprint. Portrait Sir. F. Worrell at right, arms at left center. Signature C. Blackman. Back: Trafalgar Square. Watermark: Map of Barbados. Printer: (T)DLR. 150x65mm.
    a. Issued note.   14.00   60.00
    s. Specimen.   —   120

33   10 Dollars   **VF   UNC**
ND (1973). Dark brown on multicolor underprint. Portrait C. D. O'Neal at right, arms at left center. Signature C. Blackman. Back: Trafalgar Square. Watermark: Map of Barbados. Printer: (T)DLR. 150x65mm.
    a. Issued note.   19.00   85.00
    s. Specimen. Overprint: SPECIMEN on each side.   —   180

34   20 Dollars   **VF   UNC**
ND (1973). Purple on multicolor underprint. Portrait S. J. Prescod at right, arms at left center. Signature C. Blackman. Back: Trafalgar Square. Watermark: Map of Barbados. Printer: (T)DLR. 150x65mm.
    a. Issued note.   30.00   110
    s. Specimen. Overprint: SPECIMEN on each side.   —   225

35   100 Dollars   **VF   UNC**
ND (1973). Gray and blue on multicolor underprint. Portrait Sir. G. H. Adams at right, arms at left center. Signature C. Blackman. Serial number to E3 200000. Back: Trafalgar Square, treetops are grayish blue. 150x65mm.
    a. Issued note.   95.00   320
    s. Specimen. Overprint: SPECIMEN on each side.   —   480

1986 ND Issue

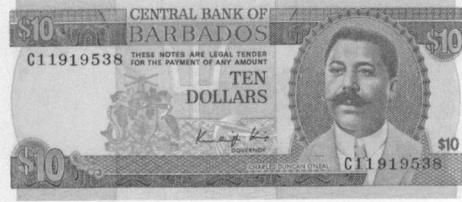

35A   10 Dollars   **VF   UNC**
ND. Dark brown and green on multicolor underprint. Portrait C. D. O'Neal at right, arms at left center, without seahorse at left. Signature K. King. Back: Trafalgar Square in Bridgetown, seahorse at right. Watermark: Map of Barbados. Printer: (T)DLR.   17.50   75.00

35B 100 Dollars   **VF UNC**

ND. Brown, purple and gray-blue on multicolor underprint. Portrait Sir. G. H.   95.00 285
Adams at right, arms at left center, seahorse emblem at right. Signature C. Blackman. Serial number above E3 200000. Back: Trafalgar Square in Bridgetown,
seahorse emblem at left, treetops are green. Watermark: Map of Barbados.
Printer: (T)DLR.

1986-89 ND Issue

#36-41 Replacement notes: serial # prefix *Z1*.

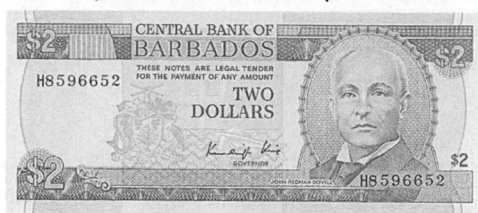

36 2 Dollars   **VF UNC**

ND (1986). Blue on multicolor underprint. Portrait J. R. Bovell at right. Signature K.   7.00 37.50
King. Printer: (T)DLR. 150x65mm.

37 5 Dollars   **VF UNC**

ND (1986). Dark green on multicolor underprint. Portrait Sir. F. Worrell at right.   12.00 52.50
Signature K. King. Printer: (T)DLR. 150x65mm.

38 10 Dollars   **VF UNC**

ND (1988). Dark Brown and green on multicolor underprint. Portrait C. D. O'Neal   14.00 70.00
at right, arms at left center, seahorse in rectangle at left. Signature K. King. Back:
Trafalgar Square in Bridgetown. Watermark: Map of Barbados. Printer: (T)DLR.
150x65mm.

39 20 Dollars   **VF UNC**

ND (1988). Purple on multicolor underprint. Portrait of S. J. Prescod at right, arms   23.00 105
at left center, bird emblem in rectangle at left. Signature K. King. Back: Trafalgar
Square in Bridgetown. Watermark: Map of Barbados. Printer: (T)DLR. 150x65mm.

40 50 Dollars   **VF UNC**

ND (1989). Orange, blue and gray on multicolor underprint. Portrait Prime Minister
E. W. Barrow at right, trident emblem at left. Signature K. King. Printer: (T)DLR.
150x65mm.

    a. Issued note.   52.50 170
    r. Replacement note. Serial # prefix: Z/1.   85.00 255

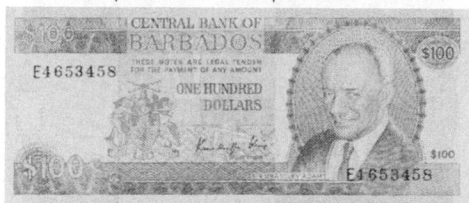

41 100 Dollars   **VF UNC**

ND (1989). Brown, purple and gray-blue on multicolor underprint. Portrait of Sir.   87.50 295
G. H. Adams at right, arms at left center, seahorse emblem at right. Signature K.
King. Back: Trafalgar Square at Bridgetown, treetops are green. Watermark: Map
of Barbados. Printer: (T)DLR. 150x65mm.

1993-94 ND Issue

#42-45 Replacement notes: serial # prefix *Z1*.

42 2 Dollars   **VF UNC**

ND (1993). Blue on multicolor underprint. Portrait J. R. Bovell at right, arms at   FV 35.00
left center. Signature C. M. Springer. Back: Trafalgar Square in Bridgetown.
Watermark: Map of Barbados. Printer: (T)DLR. 150x65mm.

43 5 Dollars   **VF UNC**

ND (1993). Dark green on multicolor underprint. Portrait Sir. F. Worrell at   FV 45.00
right, arms at left center. Signature C. M. Springer. Back: Trafalgar Square in
Bridgetown. Watermark: Map of Barbados. Printer: (T)DLR. 150x65mm.

44 20 Dollars   **VF UNC**

ND (1993). Portrait S. J. Prescod at right, arms at left center. Signature C. M.   FV 100
Springer. Back: Trafalgar Square in Bridgetown. Watermark: Map of Barbados.
Printer: (T)DLR. 150x65mm.

45 100 Dollars   **VF UNC**

ND (1994). Brown, purple and gray-blue multicolor underprint. Portrait Sir. G.   FV 320
H. Adams at right, arms at left center. Signature C. M. Springer. Back: Trafalgar
Square in Bridgetown. Watermark: Map of Barbados. Printer: (T)DLR. 150x65mm.

1995-96 ND Issue

#46-49 Replacement notes: serial # prefix *Z1*.

46 2 Dollars   **VF UNC**

ND (1995). Enhanced security features. Blue on multicolor underprint. Portrait J.   FV 32.50
R. Bovell at right, arms at left center, ascending size serial number at upper left.
Signature C. M. Springer. Back: Trafalgar Square in Bridgetown. Watermark: Map
of Barbados. Printer: (T)DLR. 150x65mm.

47   5 Dollars

	VF	UNC
	FV	37.50

ND (1996). Enhanced security features. Dark green on multicolor underprint. Portrait Sir. F. Worrell at right, arms at left center, ascending size serial number at upper left. Signature C. M. Springer. Back: Trafalgar Square in Bridgetown. Watermark: Map of Barbados. Printer: (T)DLR. 150x65mm.

48   10 Dollars

	VF	UNC
	FV	57.50

ND (1995). Enhanced security features. Dark brown and green on multicolor underprint. Portrait C. D. O'Neal at right, arms at left center, seahorse in rectangle at left, asceding size serial number at upper left. Signature C. M. Springer. Back: Trafalgar Square in Bridgetown. Watermark: Map of Barbados. Printer: (T)DLR. 150x65mm.

49   20 Dollars

	VF	UNC
	FV	90.00

ND (1996). Enhanced security features. Red-violet and purple on multicolor underprint. Portrait of S. J. Prescod at right, arms at left center, bird emblem in rectangle at left, ascending size serial number at upper left. Signature C. M. Springer. Back: Trafalgar Square in Bridgetown. Watermark: Map of Barbados. Printer: (T)DLR. 150x65mm.

1996-97 ND Issue

#50-52 Replacement notes: serial # prefix Z1.

50   20 Dollars

	VF	UNC
	FV	80.00

ND (1997). Red-violet and purple on multicolor underprint. Portrait of S. J. Prescod at right, arms at left center, bird emblem in rectangle at left, ascending size serial number and enlarged denomination numerals at upper left. Signature C. M. Springer. Back: Trafalgar Square in Bridgetown. Watermark: Map of Barbados. Printer: (T)DLR. 150x65mm.

51   50 Dollars

	VF	UNC
	FV	155

ND (1997). Orange, blue and gray on multicolor underprint. Portrait Prime Minister E. W. Barrow at right, trident emblem at left, enlarged denomination numerals at upper left. Signature C. M. Springer. Watermark: Map of Barbados. Printer: (T) DLR. 150x65mm.

52   100 Dollars

	VF	UNC
	—	—

ND (1996). Brown, purple and blue-gray on multicolor underprint. Portrait Sir. G. H. Adams at right, arms at left center, enlarged denomination numerals at upper left. Signature C. M. Springer. Back: Trafalgar Square in Bridgetown. Watermark: Map of Barbados. Printer: (T)DLR. 150x65mm.

1997 ND Commemorative Issue

#53, 25th Anniversary Central Bank.

53   100 Dollars

	VF	UNC

ND (1997). Brown, purple and blue-gray on multicolor underprint. Portrait Sir G. H. Adams at right, arms at left center, enlarged denomination numerals at upper left. Signature C. M. Springer. Back: Trafalgar Square in Bridgetown. Watermark: Map of Barbados. Printer: (T)DLR. 150x65mm.

a. Issued note.	FV	290
r. Replacement note.	FV	395
s. Specimen.	—	525

1998 ND Issue

#54-59 Replacement notes: serial # prefix Z1.

54   2 Dollars

	VF	UNC

ND (1998). Enhanced security features. Blue on multicolor underprint. Portrait J. R. Bovell at right, arms at left center, ascending size serial number at upper left. Signature W. Cox. Back: Trafalgar Square in Bridgetown. Watermark: Map of Barbados. Printer: (T)DLR. 150x65mm.

a. ND (1998). Face-to-back register device of surveyors target with quadrants all white.	FV	30.00
b. ND (1999). Face-to-back register device of surveyors target with two quadrants filled in.	FV	25.00

55   5 Dollars   **VF   UNC**
ND (1999). Enhanced security features. Dark green on multicolor underprint.   FV   30.00
Portrait Sir. F. Worrell at right, arms at left center, ascending size serial number at
upper left. Signature W. Cox. Back: Trafalgar Square in Bridgetown. Watermark:
Map of Barbados. Printer: (T)DLR. 150x65mm.

56   10 Dollars   **VF   UNC**
ND (1999). Enhanced security features. Dark brown and green on multicolor un-   FV   40.00
derprint. Portrait C. D. O'Neal at right, arms at left center, seahorse in rectangle at
left, ascending size serial number at upper left. Signature W. Cox. Back: Trafalgar
Square in Bridgetown. Watermark: Map of Barbados. Printer: (T)DLR. 150x65mm.

57   20 Dollars   **VF   UNC**
ND (1999). Enhanced security features. Red-violet and purple on multicolor   FV   70.00
underprint. Portrait of S. J. Prescod at right, arms at left center, bird emblem
in rectangle at left, ascending size serial number and enlarged denomination
numerals at upper left. Signature W. Cox. Back: Trafalgar Square in Bridgetown.
Watermark: Map of Barbados. Printer: (T)DLR. 150x65mm.

58   50 Dollars   **VF   UNC**
ND (1999). Enhanced security features. Orange, blue and gray on multicolor   FV   140
underprint. Portrait Prime Minister E. W. Barrow at right, trident emblem at left,
enlarged denomination numerals at upper left. Signature W. Cox. Back: Trafalgar
Square in Bridgetown. Watermark: Map of Barbados. Printer: (T)DLR. 150x65mm.

59   100 Dollars   **VF   UNC**
ND (1999). Enhanced security features. Brown, purple and blue-gray on multicolor   FV   230
underprint. Portrait Sir. G. H. Adams at right, arms at left center, enlarged
denomination numerals at upper left. Signature W. Cox. Back: Trafalgar Square in
Bridgetown. Watermark: Map of Barbados. Printer: (T)DLR. 150x65mm.

2000 ND Issue
#60-65 Replacement notes: Serial # prefix *Z1*.

60   2 Dollars   **VF   UNC**
ND (2000). Enhanced security features. UV: value in box fluoresce green, arms   FV   20.00
in multicolor, background elements and serial #s green. Blue on multicolor underprint. Portrait J. R. Bovell at right, arms at left center, ascending size serial number
at upper left. Signature M. Williams. Back: Trafalgar Square in Bridgetown.
Watermark: Map of Barbados. Printer: (T)DLR. 150x65mm

61   5 Dollars   **VF   UNC**
ND (2000). Enhanced security features. Dark on multicolor underprint. Portrait Sir.   FV   25.00
Frank Worrell at right, arms at left center, ascending size serial number at upper
left. Signature M. Williams. Back: Trafalgar Square in Bridgetown. Printer: (T)DLR.
150x65mm.

62   10 Dollars   **VF   UNC**
ND (2000). Enhanced security features. Dark brown and green on multicolor   FV   35.00
underprint. Portrait C. D. O'Neal at right, arms at left center, seahorse in rectangle
at left, ascending size serial number at upper left. Signature M. Williams. Back:
Trafalgar Square in Bridgetown. Watermark: Map of Barbados. Printer: (T)DLR.
150x65mm.

63A **20 Dollars**   VF UNC
ND (2000). Enhanced security features. Red-violet and purple on multicolor underprint. Portrait of S. J. Prescod at right, arms at left center, bird emblem in rectangle at left, ascending size serial number and enlarged denomination numerals at upper left. Signature M. Williams. Back: Trafalgar Square in Bridgetown. Watermark: Map of Barbados. Printer: (T)DLR. 150x65mm.   FV 60.00

63B **20 Dollars**   VF UNC
ND (2006). Enhanced security features, narrow segmented security foil. Red-violet and purple on multicolor underprint. Portrait of J.S. Prescod at right, arms at left center, bird emblem in rectangle at left, ascending size serial number and enlarged denomination numerals at upper left. Signature M. Williams Back: Trafalgar Square in Bridgetown. Watermark: Map of Barbados. Printer: (T)DLR. 150x65mm.   FV 115

64 **50 Dollars**   VF UNC
ND (2000). Enhanced security features. Orange, blue and gray on multicolor underprint. Portrait Prime Minister E. W. Barrow at right, trident emblem at left, enlarged denomination numerals at upper left. Signature M. Williams. Back: Trafalgar Square in Bridgetown. Watermark: Map of Barbados. Printer: (T)DLR. 150x65mm.   FV 115

65 **100 Dollars**   VF UNC
ND (2000). Enhanced security features. Brown, purple and blue-gray on multicolor underprint. Portrait Sir. G. H. Adams at right, arms at left center, enlarged denomination numerals at upper left. Signature M. Williams. Back: Trafalgar Square in Bridgetown. Watermark: Map of Barbados. Printer: (T)DLR. 150x65mm.   FV 185

2002 Commemorative Issue

65A **5 Dollars**   VF UNC
ND (2002). Note was issued glued on the back into a 4-page folder. 1000 presented to Central Bank employees. Not sold to the public. Dark green on multicolor underprint. Portrait Sir Frank Worrell at right, arms at left center. Signature M. Williams. Back: Trafalgar Square in Bridgetown. Printer: (T)DLR. 150x65mm.   — 190

2007; 2012 Issue

66 **2 Dollars**   VF UNC
1.5.2007; 2.5.2012. Wide segmented security foil. Blue on multicolor underprint. Portrait J. R. Bovell at right, arms at left center, ascending size serial number at upper left. Back: Trafalgar Square in Bridgetown. Watermark: Map of Barbados. Printer: (T)DLR. 150x65mm.
     a. Signature M. Williams (2007).   FV 12.00
     b. Signature Delisle Worrell (2009).   FV 10.00
     c. 2.5.2012.   FV 13.00

67 **5 Dollars**   VF UNC
1.5.2007; 2.5.2012. Wide segmented security foil. Dark green on multicolor underprint. Portrait Sir F. Worrell at right, arms at left center, ascending size serial number at upper left. Back: Trafalgar Square in Bridgetown. Watermark: Map of Barbados. Printer: (T)DLR. 150x65mm.
     a. Signature M. Williams.   FV 20.00
     b. Signature Delisle Worrell (2009).   FV 14.00
     c. 2.5.2012.   FV 18.00

68 **10 Dollars**   VF UNC
1.5.2007; 2.5.2012. Wide segmented security foil. Dark brown and green on multicolor underprint. Portrait C. D. O'Neal at right, arms at left center, seahorse in rectangle at left, ascending size serial number at upper left. Back: Trafalgar Square in Bridgetown. Watermark: Map of Barbados. Printer: (T)DLR. 150x65mm.
     a. Signature M. Williams.   FV 25.00
     b. Signature Delisle Worrell (2009).   FV 20.00
     c. 2.5.2012.   FV 23.00

69 **20 Dollars**   VF UNC
1.5.2007. Wide segmented security foil. Red-violet and purple on multicolor underprint. Portrait S. J. Prescod at right, arms at left center, bird emblem in rectangle at left, ascending size serial number and enlarged denomination numerals at upper left. Back: Trafalgar Square in Bridgetown. Watermark: Map of Barbados. Printer: (T)DLR. 150x65mm.
     a. Signature M. Williams.   FV 42.50
     b. Signature Delisle Worrell (2009).   FV 35.00

70 **50 Dollars**   VF UNC
1.5.2007. Wide segmented security foil. Orange, blue and gray on multicolor underprint. Portrait Prime Minister E. W. Barrow at right, trident emblem at left, enlarged denomination numerals at upper left. Back: Trafalgar Square in bridgetown. Watermark: Map of Barbados. Printer: (T)DLR. 150x65mm.
     a. Signature M. Williams.   FV 90.00
     b. Signature Delisle Worrell (2009).   FV 80.00

71 **100 Dollars**   VF UNC
1.5.2007. Brown, purple and blue-gray on multicolor underprint. Portrait Sir G. H. Adams at right, arms at left center. Signature M. Williams. Back: Trafalgar Square in Bridgetown. Watermark: Map of Barbados Printer: (T)DLR. 150x65mm.
     a. Signaturre M. Williams.   FV 140
     b. Signature Delisle Worrell (2009).   FV 130

2012 Commemorative Issue

72 20 Dollars   **VF UNC**
2.5.2012. Red-violet and purple on multicolor underprint. Portrait S. J. Prescod at   FV   45.00
right, arms at center. Back: Trafalgar Square in Bridgetown. Watermark: Map of
Barbados. Printer: (T)DLR. 150x65mm.

2013 Issue

73 2 Dollars   **VF UNC**
2.5.2013. Light and dark blue on multicolor underprint. John R. Bovell at right.   FV   4.00
Back: Morgan Lewis windmill, St. Andrew, at left. Watermark: John Bovell and 2.
150x65mm.

74 5 Dollars   **VF UNC**
2.5.2013. Printer: DLR.   —   9.00

75 10 Dollars   **VF UNC**
2.5.2013. Brown on multicolor underprint. Charles D. O'Neal at right. Back: O'Neil   —   15.00
bridge over the Careenage in Bridgetown. Watermark: Charles O'Neal and 10.
Printer: DLR. 150x65mm.

76 20 Dollars   **VF UNC**
2.5.2013. Light and dark pruple on multicolor underprint. Samuel J. Prescod at   FV   30.00
right. Back: Parliament buildings, Bridgetown. Watermark: Samuel Prescod and
20. Printer: DLR. 150x65mm.

77 50 Dollars   **VF UNC**
2.5.2013. Blue and tan on multicolor underprint. Prime Minister Errol W. Barrow at   FV   60.00
right. Back: Independence Squire, Bridgetown. Watermark: Errol Barrow and 50.
Printer: DLR. 150x65mm.

78 100 Dollars   **VF UNC**
2.5.2013. Brown, purple and gray on multicolor underprint. Grantley Adams at   FV   125
right and Pride of Barbados flowers. Back: Grantley Adams International Airport.
Watermark: Grantley Adams and 100. 150x65mm.

Belarus is bounded in the west by Poland, to the north by Latvia and Lithuania, to the east by Russia and the south by the Ukraine. It has an area of 207,600 sq. km. and a population of 9.68 million. Capital: Minsk. Peat, salt, agriculture including flax, fodder and grasses for cattle breeding and dairy products, along with general manufacturing industries comprise the economy.

After seven decades as a constituent republic of the USSR, Belarus attained its independence in 1991. It has retained closer political and economic ties to Russia than any of the other former Soviet republics. Belarus and Russia signed a treaty on a two-state union on 8 December 1999 envisioning greater political and economic integration. Although Belarus agreed to a framework to carry out the accord, serious implementation has yet to take place. Since his election in July 1994 as the country's first president, Alexandr Lukashenko has steadily consolidated his power through authoritarian means. Government restrictions on freedom of speech and the press, peaceful assembly, and religion continue.

MONETARY SYSTEM:
1 Ruble = 100 Kapeek
1 New Ruble = 1,000 Rubles, 2000-

REPUBLIC
КУПОН РЭСПУБЛІКА БЕЛАРУСЬ
Belarus Republic
1991 First Ruble Control Coupon Issue

A1 20 Rublei   **VF UNC**
ND (1991). Uniface. Blue.
    a. Full sheet of 12 coupons and registry.   2.00   6.00
    b. Single coupon.   0.10   0.15

A2 50 Rublei   **VF UNC**
ND (1991). Light blue.
    a. Full sheet of 28 coupons and registry.   2.00   6.00
    b. Single coupon.   0.10   0.15

A3 75 Rublei   **VF UNC**
ND (1991). Blue.
    a. Full sheet of 28 coupons and registry.   2.00   6.00
    b. Single coupon   0.10   0.15

A4 75 Rublei   **VF UNC**
ND (1991). Light green-blue.
    a. Full sheet of 28 coupons and registry.   2.00   6.00
    b. Single coupon.   0.10   0.15

A5 100 Rublei
ND (1991). Red.

	VF	UNC
a. Full sheet of 28 coupons and registry.	2.00	6.00
b. Single coupon.	0.10	0.15

A6 100 Rublei
ND (1991). Pink.

	VF	UNC
a. Full sheet of 28 coupons and registry.	2.00	6.00
b. Single coupon.	0.10	0.15

A7 200 Rublei
ND (1991). Light pink.

	VF	UNC
a. Full sheet of 28 coupons and registry.	2.00	6.00
b. Single coupon.	0.10	0.15

A8 300 Rublei
ND (1991). Pink.

	VF	UNC
a. Full sheet of 28 coupons and registry.	2.00	6.00
b. Single coupon.	0.10	0.15

A9 300 Rublei
ND (1991). Red.

	VF	UNC
a. Full sheet of 28 coupons and registry.	2.00	6.00
b. Single coupon.	0.10	0.15

1992 Second Ruble Control Coupon Issue

A10 20 Rublei
ND (1992). Dark yellow.

	VF	UNC
a. Full sheet of 12 coupons and registry.	2.00	6.00
b. Single coupon.	0.10	0.15

A11 50 Rublei
ND (1992). Light blue without corner markings.

	VF	UNC
a. Full sheet of 28 coupons and registry.	2.00	6.00
b. Single coupon.	0.10	0.15

A12 50 Rublei
ND (1992). Dark blue without corner markings.

	VF	UNC
a. Full sheet of 28 coupons and registry.	2.00	6.00
b. Single coupon.	0.10	0.15

A13 50 Rublei
ND (1992). Violet without corner markings.

	VF	UNC
a. Full sheet of 28 coupons and registry.	2.00	6.00
b. Single coupon.	0.10	0.15

A14 50 Rublei
ND (1992). Blue without corner markings.

	VF	UNC
a. Full sheet of 28 coupons and registry.	2.00	6.00
b. Single coupon.	0.10	0.15

A15 75 Rublei
ND (1992). Violet with black text.

	VF	UNC
a. Full sheet of 28 coupons and registry.	2.00	6.00
b. Single coupon.	0.10	0.15

A16 75 Rublei
ND (1992). Light violet with black text.

	VF	UNC
a. Full sheet of 28 coupons and registry.	2.00	6.00
b. Single coupon.	0.10	0.15

A17 75 Rublei
ND (1992). Dark violet with black text.

	VF	UNC
a. Full sheet of 28 coupons and registry.	2.00	6.00
b. Single coupon.	0.10	0.15

A18 75 Rublei
ND (1992). Light violet with brown text.

	VF	UNC
a. Full sheet of 28 coupons and registry.	2.00	6.00
b. Single coupon.	0.10	0.15

A19 100 Rublei
ND (1992). Light pink without corner markings.

	VF	UNC
a. Full sheet of 28 coupons and registry.	2.00	6.00
b. Single coupon.	0.10	0.15

A20 100 Rublei
ND (1992). Pink without corner markings.

	VF	UNC
a. Full sheet of 28 coupons and registry.	2.00	6.00
b. Single coupon.	0.10	0.15

A21 100 Rublei
ND (1992). Orange.

	VF	UNC
a. Full sheet of 28 coupons and registry.	2.00	6.00
b. Single coupon.	0.10	0.15

A22 200 Rublei
ND (1992). Pink.

	VF	UNC
a. Full sheet of 28 coupons and registry.	2.00	6.00
b. Single coupon.	0.10	0.15

A23 200 Rublei
ND (1992). Light pink.

	VF	UNC
a. Full sheet of 28 coupons and registry.	2.00	6.00
b. Single coupon.	0.10	0.15

A24 300 Rublei
ND (1992). Orange.

	VF	UNC
a. Full sheet of 28 coupons and registry.	2.00	6.00
b. Single coupon.	0.10	0.15

A25 300 Rublei
ND (1992). Red.

	VF	UNC
a. Full sheet of 28 coupons and registry.	2.00	6.00
b. Single coupon.	0.10	0.15

A26 500 Rublei
ND (1992). Violet-yellow.

	VF	UNC
a. Full sheet of 28 coupons and registry.	2.00	6.00
b. Single coupon.	0.10	0.15

1992 Third Ruble Control Coupon Issue

A27 20 Rublei
ND (1992). Blue.

	VF	UNC
a. Full sheet of 28 coupons and registry.	2.00	6.00
b. Single coupon.	0.10	0.15

1992-94 Privatisation Checks

A28 100 Rublei
ND (1992).

	VF	UNC
	—	—

A29 500 Rublei
ND (1992).

	VF	UNC
	—	—

A30 1000 Rublei
ND (1992).

	VF	UNC
	—	—

A31 5000 Rublei
ND (1992).

	VF	UNC
	—	—

НАЦЫЯНАЛЬНАГА БАНКА БЕЛАРУСІ

BELARUS NATIONAL BANK

1992-96 РАЗЛІКОВЫ БІЛЕТ - Exchange Note Issue

1 50 Kapeek

	VF	UNC
1992. red and brown-orange on pink underprint. *"Pagonya"* warrior on horseback at center. Back: Squirrel at center right. Watermark: Interlocked S's. 105x53mm.	0.10	2.00

2 1 Ruble VF UNC
1992. Blue-green and blue. *"Pagonya"* warrior on horseback at center. Back: Rabbit at center. Watermark: Interlocked S's. 105x53mm. 1.00 5.00

3 3 Rublei VF UNC
1992. UV: fibers fluoresce red; back: serial #s orange. Green, red-orange and pale olive-green on multicolor underprint. *"Pagonya"* warrior on horseback at center. Back: Two beavers at center right. Watermark: Interlocked S's. 105x53mm. 1.00 5.00

4 5 Rublei VF UNC
1992. UV: fibers fluoresce red; back: serial #s orange. Deep blue on light blue, lilac, violet and multicolor underprint. *"Pagonya"* warrior on horseback at center. Back: Two wolves at center right. Watermark: Interlocked S's. 105x53mm. 0.50 3.00

5 10 Rublei VF UNC
1992. UV: fibers fluoresce red; back: serial #s orange. Deep green on light green, orange and multicolor underprint. *"Pagonya"* warrior on horseback at center. Back: Lynx with kitten at center right. Watermark: Interlocked S's. 105x53mm. 0.30 2.00

6 25 Rublei VF UNC
1992. UV: fibers fluoresce red; back: serial #s orange. Violet on red, green and multicolor underprint. *"Pagonya"* warrior on horseback at center. Back: Moose at center right. Watermark: Interlocked S's. 105x52mm.
a. Horizontal watermark. 0.10 1.00
b. Horizontal watermark. 0.10 1.00

7 50 Rublei VF UNC
1992. Deep purple on red and green underprint. *"Pagonya"* warrior on horseback at center. Back: Bear at center right. Watermark: Interlocked S's. 105x53mm. 0.20 1.00

8 100 Rublei VF UNC
1992. UV: fibers fluoresce red; back: serial #s orange. Brown, gray and tan on multicolor underprint. *"Pagonya"* warrior on horseback at center. Back: Wisent (European Bison) at center. Watermark: Interlocked S's. 105x53mm. 0.20 1.00

9 200 Rublei VF UNC
1992. Deep brown-violet, orange, green and ochre on multicolor underprint. *"Pagonya"* warrior on horseback at center. Back: City view at center right. Watermark: Interlocked S's. 105x53mm. 1.00 7.00

10 500 Rublei VF UNC
1992. Violet, tan, light blue and orange on multicolor underprint. *"Pagonya"* warrior on horseback at center. Back: Victory Plaza in Minsk at center right. Watermark: Interlocked S's. 105x53mm. 1.50 10.00

11 1000 Rublei VF UNC
1992 (1993). Light blue, pale olive-green and pink. *"Pagonya"* warrior on horseback at center. Back: Academy of Sciences building at center right. 105x53mm. 1.00 3.00

12 5000 Rublei VF UNC
1992 (1993). Purple and red-violet on multicolor underprint. *"Pagonya"* warrior on horseback at center. Back: Buildings in Minsk lower city at center right. 105x53mm. 1.00 4.00

1994-96 Issue

13 20,000 Rublei VF UNC
1994. Dark brown on multicolor underprint. National Bank building at left center. Back: *"Pagonya"* warrior on horseback. Watermark: Tower and tree. 150x69mm. 1.00 6.00

14   50,000 Rublei
1995. Dark brown on multicolor underprint. Brest's tower, Holmsky Gate at left, tapestry at center right. Back: Star shaped war memorial gateway at center right. 150x69mm.

		VF	UNC
a.	Security thread with bank initials.	3.00	12.00
b.	Security thread with bank initials and value.	3.00	12.00

15   100,000 Rublei   VF   UNC
1996. Deep blue and violet on multicolor underprint. Bolshoi Opera and Ballet Theatre at center, tapestry at left. Back: Scene from Glebov's ballet *Vibrannitsa* at center. 150x69mm.

		VF	UNC
a.	Security thread with bank initials.	4.00	18.00
b.	Security thread with bank initials and value.	4.00	18.00

1998 Issue

16   1000 Rublei   VF   UNC
1998. Light blue, pale olive-green and pink. Single value moved to oval replacing *Pagonya*, warrior on horseback at left center. Back: Academy of Sciences building at center right. Watermark: Paper. 110x60mm.   0.50   2.00

1998-99 Issue

17   5000 Rublei   VF   UNC
1998. Multicolor. Back: Buildings in Minsk lower city at center right. 110x60mm.   0.50   2.00

18   500,000 Rublei   VF   UNC
1998. Light red and green on yellow underprint. Palace of Culture building at center. Back: Façade fragment. 150x69mm.   5.00   22.00

19   1,000,000 Rublei   VF   UNC
1999. Green on multicolor underprint. National Museum of Art at center. Back: 5.00   27.00
Artwork: *Wife's Portrait with Flowers and Fruits*. 150x69mm.

20   5,000,000 Rublei   VF   UNC
1999. Purple and green on multicolor underprint. Minsk sports complex at center. 10.00 40.00
Back: Winter sports complex. 150x69mm.

2000 Issue

21   1 Ruble   VF   UNC
2000. Green on multicolor underprint. Back: Academy of Sciences building at   0.25   1.00
center right. 110x60mm.

22   5 Rublei   VF   UNC
2000. Pale red and violet on multicolor underprint. Back: Buildings in Minsk lower 0.25   1.00
city at center right. 110x60mm.

23   10 Rublei   VF   UNC
2000. Lilac on multicolor underprint. Back: National Library at right. 110x60mm.   0.25   1.00

24   20 Rublei

VF   UNC

2000. Brown on multicolor underprint. National Bank building at left center. Back: 0.25   1.50
Interior view. 150x69mm.

25   50 Rublei

VF   UNC

2000; 2010. UV: fibers fluoresce red, blue security thread yellow; back: upper
serial # red, "50" yellow in watermark area. Red-borwn on multicolor underprint.
Brest's tower, Holmsky Gate at left, tapestry at center right. Back: Star shaped war
memorial gateway at center right. 150x69mm.

   a. Solid security thread with bank initials. Old spelling of 50 with a 3E (2000).   0.50   2.00
   b. Without security thread. New spelling of 50 (2010).   0.50   2.00

26   100 Rublei

VF   UNC

2000; 2011. UV: fibers fluoresce red, blue; security thread yellow, value yellow;
back: upper serial # red. Green on multicolor underprint. Bolshoi Opera and
Ballet Theater at center, tapestry at left. Back: Scene from ballet *Vibrannitsa*.
Watermark: Ballerina. 150x69mm.

   a. Solid security thread (2000).   0.25   3.00
   b. Without security thread (2011).   0.25   3.00

27   500 Rublei

VF   UNC

2000. Brown and green on tan underprint. Palace of Culture. Back: Façade
fragment. 150x74mm.

   a. Solid security thread with bank initials (2000).   1.50   6.00
   b. Segmented security thread with bank initials.(2011).   1.50   3.00

28   1000 Rublei

VF   UNC

2000. UV: fibers fluoresce red, blue security thread yellow; back: upper serial #
red, value yellow. Blue on yellow underprint. National Museum of Art at left center.
Back: Flowers and fruits still-life. 150x74mm.

   a. Solid security thread with bank initials (2000).   2.50   8.00
   b. Segmented security thread with bank initials (2011).   2.50   4.00

29   5000 Rublei

VF   UNC

2000. UV: fibers fluoresce red, blue; security thread yellow; vlaue yellow; back:
upper serial # red. Purple and slate gray on multicolor underprint. Minsk Sports
complex at center. Back: Winter sports complex (three ski jump hills). 150x74mm.

   a. Solid security thread with bank initials (2000).   FV   14.00
   b. Segmented security thread with bank initials (2011).   FV   6.00

30   10,000 Rublei

VF   UNC

2000 (2001). Orange and blue on multicolor underprint. Viciebsk city view. Back:
Amphitheater in Viciebsk. 150x74mm.

   a. Solid security thread with bank initials.   FV   20.00
   b. Segmented security thread with bank initials.   FV   10.00

31   20,000 Rublei   **VF   UNC**
2000 (2001). Olive on multicolor underprint. Palace in Gomel at center. Back:
Mountain top palace. 150x74mm.
    a. Solid security thread with bank initials.   FV   30.00
    b. Segmented security thread with bank initials.   FV   15.00

32   50,000 Rublei   **VF   UNC**
2000 (2002). Blue, gray, lilac on multicolor underprint. Mir castle at left center.
Back: Details of Mir castle. Printer: Goznak. 150x74mm.
    a. Old spelling of 50,000 with 3E. Solid security thread with bank initials.   FV   70.00
    b. New spelling of 50,000. Segmented security thread (2010).   FV   70.00

2001 Commemorative Issue

#33, 10th Anniversary National Bank of Belarus

33   20 Rublei   **VF   UNC**
2001. #24 with OVD denomination at upper center right and gold-stamped
dates 1991-2001 with bank initials at right. Issued in a special folder. Brown on
multicolor underprint. 150x74mm.   1.50   6.00

2005 Issue

34   100,000 Rublei   **VF   UNC**
ND (2005). Brown on rose and multicolor underprint. Radziwill Castle in Neswizh
at center. Back: Castle. 150x74mm.
    a. ND (2005).   FV   80.00
    b. ND (2014). Cross on castle.   FV   60.00

2011 Commemorative Issue

35   20,000 Rublei   **VF   UNC**
2011. Olive on multicolor underprint. Palace in Gomel at center. Back: Mountain   FV   35.00
top palace. Printer: Goznak. 150x74mm.

2012 Issue

36   200,000 Rublei   **VF   UNC**
2000 (2012). Green, orange, blue and yellow. Mogilev Byalynitski-Birulya Art Mu-   FV   70.00
seum at left center. Back: Architectural elements from the museum. Watermark:
Architectural elements and bank initials. 150x74mm.

COLLECTOR SERIES

Belarus National Bank

2000 Commemorative

CS1   Rublei - Various Amounts   **Mkt. Value**
    10-piece set of notes in blue folder. Set consists of #21-30 dated 2000 and with   25.00
matching serial #. Back: The 20 Rublei and higher include an overprint: MILLEN-
NIUM at the lower left.

BELGIUM

The Kingdom of Belgium, a constitutional monarchy in northwest Europe, has an area of 30,528 sq. km. and a population of 10.40 million, chiefly Dutch-speaking Flemish and French-speaking Walloons. Capital: Brussels. Agriculture, dairy farming, and the processing of raw materials for re-export are the principal industries. "Beurs voor Diamant" in Antwerp is the world's largest diamond trading center. Iron and steel, machinery, motor vehicles, chemicals, textile yarns and fabrics comprise the principal exports.

Belgium became independent from the Netherlands in 1830; it was occupied by Germany during World Wars I and II. The country prospered in the past half century as a modern, technologically advanced European state and member of NATO and the EU. Tensions between the Dutch-speaking Flemings of the north and the French-speaking Walloons of the south have led in recent years to constitutional amendments granting these regions formal recognition and autonomy.

RULERS:

Leopold I, 1831-1865
Leopold II, 1865-1909
Albert I, 1909-34
Leopold III, 1934-51
Baudouin I, 1952-93
Albert II, 1993-

MONETARY SYSTEM:

1 Franc = 100 Centimes to 2001
1 Belga = 5 Francs
1 Euro = 100 Cents, 2002-

GOUVERNEURS de la BANQUE NATIONALE de BELGUIQUE		DIRECTEURS GÉNÉRAUX de la TRÉSORERIE	
1	Hubert Ansiaux 08.08.1957 - 17.02.1971	17	Maurice Williot 02.04.1956 - 31.01.1963
2	Robert Vandeputte 01.03.1971 - 25.02.1975	18	Marcel d'Haeze 01.02.1963 - 31.05.1975
3	Cecil de Strijcker 26.02.1975 - 28.02.1982	19	Maurice Esselens 01.06.1975 - 30.09.1976
4	Jean Godeaux 01.03.1982 - 02.07.1989	20	Emiel Kestens 01.10.1976 - 31.11.1984
5	Alfons Verplaetse 03.07.1989 -	21	René Lauwerijns 01.12.1984 - 31.03.1988
		22	Edgard Van De Pontseele 01.04.1988 - 31.10.1990
		23	Gregoire Brouhns 01.11.1990 -
TREASURERS			
6	Jean Jacques Vincent 01.07.1953 - 19.02.1960	11	Maurice Demanet 17.11.1982 - 30.09.1984
7	René Magdonelle 19.02.1960 - 30.10.1968	12	Georges Lakière 01.10.1984 - 21.12.1986
8	Maurice Jordens 30.10.1968 - 02.06.1977	13	Paul Génie 25.12.1986 - 02.08.1989
9	Raymond Simonis 03.06.1977 - 03.10.1979	14	Jacques Van Droogenbroeck 03.08.1989 - 28.02.1992

GOUVERNEURS de la BANQUE NATIONALE de BELGUIQUE		DIRECTEURS GÉNÉRAUX de la TRÉSORERIE	
10	Pol Dasin 04.10.1979 - 17.11.1982	15	Bertholomé 01.03.1992 -

KINGDOM - 1944-PRESENT

Banque Nationale de Belgique

NATIONALE BANK VAN BELGIE

1961-71 Issue

134	100 Francs	VF	UNC

1.2.1902-2.6.1977. Violet on multicolor underprint. Lambert Lombard at left. 4 signature varieties. Back: Allegorical figure at center. Watermark: King Baudouin I. 138x69mm.

a. Serial # 00001 A 001 to 10000 Z 999. Signature (1 and 7), (1 and 8). — 4.00 — 13.00
b. Serial # 1001 A 0001 to 2350 Z 999. Signature (1 and 8), (2 and 8) and (3 and 8). — 4.00 — 13.00
c. Series 3000. Coated with plastic. Signature (2 and 8). — 25.00 — 75.00

#135-137 replacement notes: Serial # prefix I.

135	500 Francs	VF	UNC

2.5.1961-28.4.1975. Blue-gray and multicolor. Bernard Van Orley at center. 4 signature varieties. Back: Margaret of Austria and Malines Palace façade at right. Watermark: King Baudouin I. 147x74mm.

a. Serial # 0001 A 001 to 2500 Z 999. signature (1 and 7) and (1 and 8). — 30.00 — 80.00
b. Serial # 251 A 0001 to 556 Z 9999. signature (1 and 8), (2 and 8) and (3 and 8). — 30.00 — 80.00
s. Specimen. — — — 600

136   1000 Francs

VF   UNC

2.1.1961-8.12.1975. Brown and blue. Gérard Kremer (called Mercator) at left. 4 signature varieties. Back: Atlas holding globe. Watermark: King Baudouin I. 157x79mm.

a. Serial # 0001 A 001 to 10400 Z 999. signature (1 and 7).   50.00   100

b. Serial # 1041 A 0001 to 1877 Z 999. signature (1 and 8), (2 and 8) and (3 and 8).   50.00   100

s. Specimen.   —   600

137   5000 Francs

VF   UNC

6.1.1971-15.9.1977. Green. André Vesalius at center. Signature (1 and 8), (2 and 8), (3 and 8) and (3 and 9). Back: Escapelus statue and temple of Epidaure. Watermark: King Baudouin I. 167x84mm.

a. Issued note.   275   400

s. Specimen.   —   600

KINGDOM
Royaume de Belgique - Koninkrijk Belgie
1964-66 Issue

#138 and 139 replacement notes: Serial # prefix Z/1.

138   20 Francs

VF   UNC

15.6.1964. Black on blue, orange and multicolor underprint. King Baudouin I at left, arms at lower right. Signature 18, 19, 20. Back: Atomium complex in Brussels at right. Watermark: King Baudouin I.   0.50   3.00

139   50 Francs

VF   UNC

16.5.1966. Brown-violet and orange-brown on multicolor underprint. Arms at lower left center, King Baudouin I and Queen Fabiola at right. Signature 18, 19, 20, 21. Back: Parliament building in Brussels. Watermark: King Baudouin I.   2.00   4.00

Banque Nationale de Belgique - Continued
1978; 1980 ND Issue

140   100 Francs

VF   UNC

ND (1978-81). UV: Back, central design fluoresces yellow. Maroon, blue and olive-green on multicolor underprint. Hendrik Beyaert at center right. Architectural view and plan at left. Signature (3 and9), (3 and 10) only on face. Back: Geometric design. Watermark: King Baudouin I. 142x76mm.

a. Issued note.   10.00   30.00

s. Specimen.   —   —

141   500 Francs

VF   UNC

ND (1980-81). Signature on face only. Deep blue-violet and deep green on blue and multicolor underprint. Constantin Meunier at left center underprint of two coal miners and mine conveyor tower at center right. Signature (3 and 8). Back: Five circular designs. Watermark: King Baudouin I. 147x76mm.

a. Issued note.   50.00   90.00

s. Specimen.   —   —

1981-82 ND Issue

142   100 Francs

VF   UNC

ND (1982-94). Signature on face and back. Hendrik Beyaert at center right. Architectural view and plan at left. Signature (3 and 10), (4 and 10), (4 and 11), (4 and 12), (4 and 13), (5 and 14), (5 and 15). Back: Geometric design. Watermark: King Baudouin I. 142x76mm.

a. Issued note.   6.00   10.00

s. Specimen.   —   —

143 500 Francs | VF | UNC

ND (1982-98). Signature on face and back. Deep blue-violet and deep green on blue and multicolor underprint. Constantine Meunier at left center, underprint of two coal miners and mine conveyor tower at center right. Signature (3 and 10), (4 and 10), (4 and 11), (4 and 12), (4 and 13), (5 and 14), (5 and 15). Back: Five circular designs. Watermark: King Baudouin I. 147x76mm.

    a. Issued note. — 25.00   60.00

    s. Specimen. — —   —

144 1000 Francs | VF | UNC

ND (1980-96). Brown and green on multicolor underprint. André Gretry at left center, bass violin center right in background. Signature (3 and 10), (4 and 10), (4 and 11), (4 and 12), (4 and 13), (5 and 14), (5 and 15). Back: Tuning forks and view of inner ear. Watermark: King Baudouin I. 154x76mm.

    a. Name as: *ANDRÉ ERNEST MODESTE GRETRY. 1741-1813.* — 50.00   90.00

    s. Specimen. — —   300

    x1. Name as: *ERNEST MODESTE.* — 120   300

    x2. Name as: *ANDRÉ ERNEST MODESTE TRY.* — 75.00   180

145 5000 Francs | VF | UNC

ND (1982-92). Green on multicolor underprint. Guido Gezelle at left center, tree and stained glass window behind. Signature (4 and 10), (4 and 11), (4 and 12), (4 and 13), (5 and 14). Back: Dragonfly and leaf at center. Watermark: King Baudouin I. 160x76mm.

    a. Issued note. — 225   400

    s. Specimen. — —   400

1992 ND Issue

146 10,000 Francs | VF | UNC

ND (1992-97). Grayish purple on multicolor underprint. King Baudouin I and Queen Fabiola at left , aerial map as underprint. Signature (5 and 15). Back: Flora and greenhouses at Laeken (royal residence) at center. Watermark: King Baudouin I and Queen Fabiola. 166x76mm. — 475   900

1994-97 ND Issue

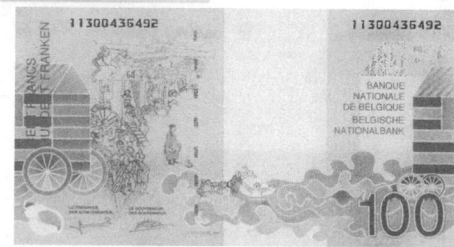

147 100 Francs | VF | UNC

ND (1995-2001). Red-violet and black on multicolor underprint. James Ensor at left and as watermark, masks at lower center and at right. Signature (5 and 15), (6 and 16). Back: Beach scene at left. 139x76mm. — 5.00   7.50

148 200 Francs | VF | UNC

ND (1995). Black and brown on yellow and orange underprint. Adolphe Sax at left, saxophone at right. Signature (5 and 15). Back: Saxophone players outlined at left, church, houses in Dinant outlined at lower right. Watermark: Adolphe Sax. 144x76mm. — 10.00   25.00

149 500 Francs | VF | UNC

ND (1998). Blue-black, purple and blue-green on multicolor underprint. René Magritte at left, birds in plants at lower center, tree at right. Signature (5 and 15). Back: Six men, chair at left, men at center right. Watermark: René Magritte. 150x76mm. — 25.00   50.00

150   1000 Francs
ND (1997). Dark brown on multicolor underprint. Constant Permeke at left, sailboat at center. Signature (5 and 15). Back: *Sleeping Farmer* painting at left. Watermark: Constant Permeke. 154x76mm.

	VF	UNC
	40.00	80.00

151   2000 Francs
ND (1994-2001). Purple and blue-green on multicolor underprint. Baron Victor Horta at left. Signature (5 and 15). Back: *Flora* and *Art Nouveau* design at left. Watermark: Baron Victor Horta. 159x76mm.

	VF	UNC
	80.00	110

152   10,000 Francs
ND (1997). Deep purple on multicolor underprint. King Albert II and Queen Paola at left, aerial view of Parliamentary chamber at right. Signature (5 and 15). Back: Greenhouses at Laeken (royal residence). Watermark: King Albert II. 169x76mm.

	VF	UNC
	375	600

Note: For later issues used in Belgium, see European Union listings.

BELIZE

Belize (formerly British Honduras) is situated in Central America south of Mexico and east and north of Guatemala. It has an area of 22,965 sq. km. and a population of 301,300. Capital: Belmopan. Sugar, citrus fruits, chicle and hard woods are exported.

Belize was the site of several Mayan city states until their decline at the end of the first millennium A.D. The British and Spanish disputed the region in the 17th and 18th centuries; it formally became the colony of British Honduras in 1854. Territorial disputes between the UK and Guatemala delayed the independence of Belize until 1981. Guatemala refused to recognize the new nation until 1992. Tourism has become the mainstay of the economy.

MONETARY SYSTEM:
1 Dollar = 100 Cents

Government of Belize
1974-75 Issue

33   1 Dollar
1974-76. Green on multicolor underprint. Portrait of Queen Elizabeth II at right, arms at left.

	VF	UNC
a. 1.1.1974.	20.00	100
b. 1.6.1975.	15.00	85.00
c. 1.1.1976.	15.00	80.00
s. Specimen, punch hole cancelled. Red overprint: SPECIMEN OF NO VALUE and SPECIMEN on both sides.	—	250
ct. Color trial. Blue, green and pale orange.	—	225

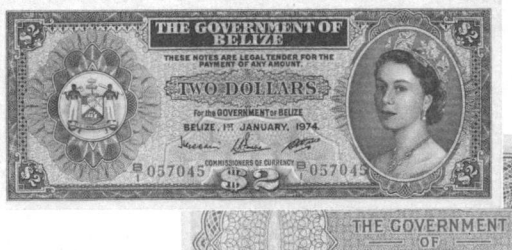

34   2 Dollars
1974-76. Violet on lilac and multicolor underprint. Portrait of Queen Elizabeth II at right, arms at left.

	VF	UNC
a. 1.1.1974.	35.00	175
b. 1.6.1975.	25.00	125
c. 1.1.1976.	20.00	110
s. Specimen. Red overprint: SPECIMEN OF NO VALUE and SPECIMEN. Punch hole cancelled.	—	300
ct. Color trial. Brown, orange and red.	—	325

35   5 Dollars — VF UNC
1975; 1976. Red on multicolor underprint. Portrait of Queen Elizabeth II at right, arms at left.
  a. 1.6.1975. — 60.00 / 300
  b. 1.1.1976. — 50.00 / 250
  s. Specimen. Red overprint SPECIMEN OF NO VALUE and SPECIMEN. Punch hole cancelled. — — / 350
  ct. Color trial. Red on multicolor underprint. — — / 425

36   10 Dollars — VF UNC
1974-76. Black on multicolor underprint. Portrait of Queen Elizabeth II at right, arms at left.
  a. 1.1.1974. — 600 / 3,300
  b. 1.6.1975. — 200 / 950
  c. 1.1.1976. — 250 / 1,000
  s. Specimen, punch hole cancelled. — — / 950
  ct. Color trial. Green and orange. — — / 725

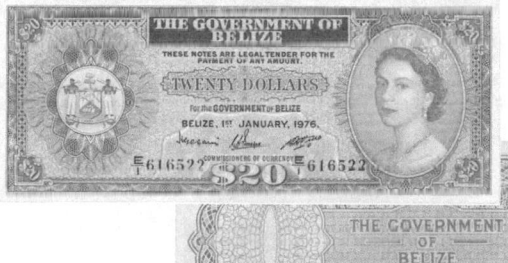

37   20 Dollars — VF UNC
1974-76. Brown on multicolor underprint. Portrait of Queen Elizabeth II at right, arms at left.
  a. 1.1.1974. — 375 / 1,650
  b. 1.6.1975. — 250 / 1,100
  c. 1.1.1976. — 250 / 1,000
  s. Specimen, punch hole cancelled. — — / 900
  ct. Color trial. Blue, green and pale yellow. — — / 1,250

Monetary Authority of Belize
Ordinance No. 9 of 1976; 1980 Issue

38   1 Dollar — VF UNC
1.6.1980. Green on multicolor underprint. Linear border on arms in upper left corner, Queen Elizabeth II at center right 3/4 looking left, underwater scene with reef and fish in center background. Back: House of Representatives at center. Jabiu stork at right. Watermark: Carved head of the "sleeping giant".
  a. Issued note. — 15.00 / 60.00
  r. Replacement note. Serial # prefix: Z/1. — 35.00 / 100
  s. Specimen. — — / —

39   5 Dollars — VF UNC
1.6.1980. Red on multicolor underprint. Linear border on arms in upper left corner, Queen Elizabeth II at center right 3/4 looking left, underwater scene with reef and fish in center background. Back: House of Representatives at center. Jabiu stork at right. Watermark: Carved head of the "sleeping giant".
  a. Issued note. — 35.00 / 125
  r. Replacement note. Serial # prefix: Z/1. — 65.00 / 200
  s. Specimen. — — / —

40   10 Dollars — VF UNC
1.6.1980. Violet on multicolor underprint. Linear border on arms in upper left corner, Queen Elizabeth II at center right 3/4 looking left, underwater scene with reef and fish in center background. Back: House of Representatives at center. Jabiu stork at right. Watermark: Carved head of the "sleeping giant".
  a. Issued note. — 75.00 / 275
  s. Specimen. — — / —

41   20 Dollars — VF UNC
1.6.1980. Brown on multicolor underprint. Linear border on arms in upper left corner, Queen Elizabeth II at center right 3/4 looking left, underwater scene with reef and fish in center background. Back: House of Representatives at center. Jabiu stork at right. Watermark: Carved head of the "sleeping giant". — 150 / 650

42   100 Dollars — VF UNC
1.6.1980. Blue on multicolor underprint. Linear border on arms in upper left corner, Queen Elizabeth II at center right 3/4 looking left, underwater scene with reef and fish in center background. Back: House of Representatives at center. Jabiu stork at right. Watermark: Carved head of the "sleeping giant". — 500 / 2,000

Central Bank of Belize
Act 1982; 1983 Issue

43   1 Dollar — VF UNC
1.7.1983. Green on multicolor underprint. Wreath border on arms in upper left corner, Queen Elizabeth II at center right 3/4 looking left, underwater scene with reef and fish in center background. Back: House of Representatives at center. Jabiu stork at right. Watermark: Carved head of the "sleeping giant". — 10.00 / 50.00

44 10 Dollars

1.7.1983. Black on red and multicolor underprint. Wreath border on arms in upper left corner, Queen Elizabeth II at center right 3/4 looking left, underwater scene with reef and fish in center background. Back: House of Representatives at center. Jabiu stork at right. Watermark: Carved head of the "sleeping giant".

	VF	UNC
a. Issued note.	50.00	175
s. Specimen.	—	125

45 20 Dollars

	VF	UNC
	140	550

1.7.1983. Brown on multicolor underprint. Wreath border on arms in upper left corner, Queen Elizabeth II at center right 3/4 looking left, underwater scene with reef and fish in center background. Back: House of Representatives at center. Jabiu stork at right. Watermark: Carved head of the "sleeping giant".

Act 1982; 1983-87 Issue

46 1 Dollar

1983-87. Green on multicolor underprint. Wreath border on arms with large tree behind in upper left corner, Queen Elizabeth II at center right 3/4 looking left, underwater scene with reef and fish in center background. Signature varieties. Back: House of Representatives at center. Jabiu stork at right. Watermark: Carved head of the "sleeping giant".

	VF	UNC
a. 1.11.1983.	8.00	35.00
b. 1.1.1986.	7.00	30.00
c. 1.1.1987.	6.00	25.00
s. Specimen.	—	75.00

47 5 Dollars

1987; 1989. Red on multicolor underprint. Wreath border on arms with large tree behind in upper left corner, Queen Elizabeth II at center right 3/4 looking left, underwater scene with reef and fish in center background. Signature varieties. Back: House of Representatives at center. Jabiu stork at right. Watermark: Carved head of the "sleeping giant".

	VF	UNC
a. 1.1.1987.	100	350
b. 1.1.1989.	25.00	85.00

48 10 Dollars

1987; 1989. Black on red and multicolor underprint. Wreath border on arms with large tree behind in upper left corner, Queen Elizabeth II at center right 3/4 looking left, underwater scene with reef and fish in center background. Signature varieties. Back: House of Representatives at center. Jabiu stork at right. Watermark: Carved head of the "sleeping giant".

	VF	UNC
a. 1.1.1987.	50.00	200
b. 1.1.1989.	150	550

49 20 Dollars

1986; 1987. Brown on multicolor underprint. Wreath border on arms with large tree behind in upper left corner, Queen Elizabeth II at center right 3/4 looking left, underwater scene with reef and fish in center background. Signature varieties. Back: House of Representatives at center. Jabiu stork at right. Watermark: Carved head of the "sleeping giant".

	VF	UNC
a. 1.1.1986.	110	350
b. 1.1.1987.	50.00	150

50 100 Dollars

1983; 1989. Blue on multicolor underprint. Wreath border on arms with large tree behind in upper left corner, Queen Elizabeth II at center right 3/4 looking left, underwater scene with reef and fish in center background. Signature varieties. Back: House of Representatives at center. Jabiu stork at right. Watermark: Carved head of the "sleeping giant".

	VF	UNC
a. 1.11.1983.	225	850
b. 1.1.1989.	250	950
r. Replacement note. Serial # prefix: Z/1.	FV	1,250

Act 1982; 1990 Issue

#51-57 older facing portr. of Qn. Elizabeth II at r. Wmk: Carved head of the "sleeping giant." Printer: TDLR. Replacemetn ntoes: serial # prefix *AZ*.

51 1 Dollar

1.5.1990. Green on light brown, blue and multicolor underprint. Mature facing portrait of Queen Elizabeth II at right, lobster at left. Back: Marine life of Belize across center. Watermark: Carved head of the "sleeping giant". Printer: TDLR. 158x69mm.

	VF	UNC
	5.00	27.50

55   20 Dollars

1.5.1990. Upper left dog-like bat; lower left Kinkajou; upper center Black Howler Monkey; lower center left Collared Peccary; upper center right Northern Tamandua; lower center right Red Brocket; upper right Ringtail; lower right Jaguar. Dark brown on multicolor underprint. Jaguar at left, mature portrait of Queen Elizabeth II at right. Back: Fauna of Belize. Watermark: Carved head of the "sleeping giant". Printer: TDLR. 158x69mm.

	VF	UNC
	30.00	125

52   2 Dollars

1990; 1991. UV: fish and stork fluoresce yellow, reial #s and right design orange. Back: value green. Purple on light green, blue and multicolor underprint. Mature facing portrait ot Queen Elizabeth II at right, carved stone pillar at left. Back: Mayan ruins of Belize. Watermark: Carved head of the "sleeping giant". Printer: TDLR. 158x69mm.

	VF	UNC
a. 1.5.1990.	6.00	37.50
b. 1.6.1991.	5.00	37.50

56   50 Dollars

1990; 1991. Purple, brown and red on multicolor underprint. Mature facing portrait of Queen Elizabeth II at right, boats at left. Back: Bridges of Belize. Watermark: Carved head of the "sleeping giant". Printer: TDLR. 158x69mm.

	VF	UNC
a. 1.5.1990.	65.00	240
b. 1.6.1991.	60.00	215

53   5 Dollars

1990; 1991. Red-orange, orange and violet on multicolor underprint. Mature facing portrait of Queen Elizabeth II at right, C. Columbus medallion at left, silver tiger fish below. Back: St. George's Caye, coffin, outline map and building. Watermark: Carved head of the "sleeping giant". Printer: TDLR. 158x69mm.

	VF	UNC
a. 1.5.1990.	12.50	60.00
b. 1.6.1991.	10.00	52.50

57   100 Dollars

1990-94. The birds on the back include: jabiru stork, brown pelican, red-footed booby, magnificent frigate bird, yellow-heded parrot and king vulture. Blue-violet, orange and red on multicolor underprint. Keel-billed toucan at left, mature portrait of Queen Elizabeth II at right. Back: Birds of Belize. Watermark: Carved head of the "sleeping giant". Printer: TDLR. 158x69mm.

	VF	UNC
a. 1.5.1990.	150	475
b. 1.6.1991.	150	500
c. 1.5.1994.	140	410

54   10 Dollars

1990; 1991. Black, olive-brown and deep blue-green on multicolor underprint. Court House clock tower at left, mature facing portrait of Queen Elizabeth II at right. Back: Government House, Court House and St. John's Cathedral. Watermark: Carved head of the "sleeping giant". Printer: TDLR. 158x69mm.

	VF	UNC
a. 1.5.1990.	20.00	90.00
b. 1.6.1991.	17.00	75.00

Act 1982; 1996 Issue

58 5 Dollars

1.3.1996. Red-orange, orange and violet on multicolor underprint. Mature facing portrait of Queen Elizabeth II at right, C. Columbus medallion at left, silver tiger fish below. Segmented foil over security strip and ascending size serial number at upper right. Back: St. George's Caye, coffin, outline map and building. Watermark: Carved head of the "sleeping giant". Printer: TDLR. 158x69mm.

	VF	UNC
	11.00	52.50

59 10 Dollars

1.3.1996. Black, olive brown and deep blue-green on multicolor underprint. Court House clock tower at left, mature facing portrait of Queen Elizabeth II at right. Segmented foil over security strip and ascending size serial number at upper right. Back: Government House, Court House and St. John's Cathedral. Watermark: Carved head of the "sleeping giant". Printer: TDLR. 158x69mm.

	VF	UNC
	15.00	85.00

1997-2002 Issues

60 2 Dollars

1999; 2002. Reduced size. Purple on light green, blue and multicolor underprint. Mature facing portrait of Queen Elizabeth II at right, carved stone pillar at left. Back: Mayan ruins of Belize. Watermark: Carved head of the "sleeping giant". Printer: TDLR. 140x70mm.

	VF	UNC
a. 1.1.1999.	FV	35.00
b. 1.1.2002.	FV	32.50
r. Replacement note. 1.1.1999. Serial # prefix: CZ.	25.00	110

61 5 Dollars

1999; 2002. Reduced size. Red-orange, orange and violet on multicolor underprint. Mature facing portrait of Queen Elizabeth II at right, C. Columbus medallion at left, silver tiger fish below. Back: St. George's Caye, coffin, outline map and building. Watermark: Carved head of the "sleeping giant". Printer: TDLR. 140x70mm.

	VF	UNC
a. 1.1.1999.	FV	50.00
b. 1.1.2002.	FV	42.50

62 10 Dollars

1997; 2001. Reduced size. Black, olive-brown and deep blue-green on multicolor underprint. Court House clock tower at left, mature facing portrait of Queen Elizabeth II at right. Segmented foil over security strip and ascending size serial number at upper right. Back: Government House, Court House and St. John's Cathedral. Watermark: Carved head of the "sleeping giant". Printer: TDLR. 140x70mm.

	VF	UNC
a. 1.6.1997.	FV	82.50
b. 1.2001. (no day)	FV	70.00

63 20 Dollars

1997; 2000. Upper left dog-like bat; lower left Kinkajou; upper center Black Howler Monkey; lower center left Collared Peccary; upper center right Northern Tamandua; lower center right Red Brocket; upper right Ringtail; lower right Jaguar. Reduced size. Dark Brown on multicolor underprint. Jaguar at left, mature portrait of Queen Elizabeth II at right. Back: Fauna of Belize. Watermark: Carved head of the "sleeping giant". Printer: TDLR. 140x70mm.

	VF	UNC
a. 1.6.1997.	FV	125
b. 1.10.2000.	FV	100

64 50 Dollars

1997; 2000. Reduced size. Purple, brown and red on multicolor underprint. Mature facing portrait of Queen Elizabeth Ii at right, boats at left. Back: Bridges of Belize. Watermark: Carved head of the "sleeping giant". Printer: TDLR. 150x75mm.

	VF	UNC
a. 1.6.1997.	FV	220
b. 1.9.2000.	FV	195

65   100 Dollars   **VF   UNC**

1.6.1997. The birds on the back include: jabiru stork, brown pelican, red-footed   FV   380
booby, magnificent frigate bird, yellow-headed parrot and king vulture. Reduced
size. Blue-violet, orange and red on multicolor underprint. Keel-billed toucan at
left, mature portrait of Queen Elizabeth II at right. Back: Birds of Belize. Watermark: Carved head of the "sleeping giant". Printer: TDLR. 150x75mm.

2003-10 Issues

66   2 Dollars   **VF   UNC**

2003; 2005; 2007; 2011. With additional security features. Multicolor. Mature facing portrait of Queen Elizabeth II at right, carved stone pillar at left. Back: Mayan
ruins of Belize. Watermark: Carved head of the "sleeping giant". Printer: TDLR.
140x70mm.

		VF	UNC
a. 1.6.2003.		FV	25.00
b. 1.1.2005.		FV	18.00
c. 1.9.2007.		FV	12.00
d. 1.11.2011.		FV	12.00
e. 1.11.2014.		FV	12.00

67   5 Dollars   **VF   UNC**

2003-11. With additional security features. Mature facing portrait of Queen
Elizabeth II at right, C. Columbus medallion at left, silver tiger fish below. Back: St.
George's Caye, Columbus's tomb, outline map and building. Watermark: Carved
head of the "sleeping giant". Printer: TDLR. 140x70mm.

	VF	UNC
a. 1.6.2003.	FV	40.00
b. 1.1.2005.	FV	32.50
c. 1.9.2007.	FV	25.00
d. 1.7.2009.	FV	20.00
e. 11.1.2011.	FV	15.00
r. 1.1.2005. Replacement. Serial # prefix: Z.	FV	105

68   10 Dollars   **VF   UNC**

2003; 2005; 2007; 2011. With additional security features. Court House clock
tower at left, mature facing portrait of Queen Elizabeth II at right. Segmented foil
over security strip and ascending size serial number at upper right. Back: Government House, Court House and St. John's Cathedral. Watermark: Carved head of
the "sleeping giant". Printer: TDLR. 140x70mm.

	VF	UNC
a. 1.3.2003.	FV	60.00
b. 1.1.2005.	FV	40.00
c. 1.9.2007.	FV	35.00
d. 11.1.2011.	FV	25.00

69   20 Dollars   **VF   UNC**

2003; 2005; 2007; 2010. With additional security features. Upper left dog-like bat;
lower left Kinkajou; upper center Black Howler Monkey; lower center left Collared
Peccary; upper center right Northern Tamandua; lower center right Red Brocket;
upper right Ringtail; lower right Jaguar. Jaguar at left, mature portrait of Queen
Elizabeth II at right. Back: Fauna of Belize. Watermark: Carved head of the "sleeping giant". Printer: TDLR. 140x70mm.

	VF	UNC
a. 1.1.2003.	FV	90.00
b. 1.1.2005.	FV	75.00
c. 1.9.2007.	FV	65.00
d. 1.8.2010.	FV	55.00
e. 1.11.2014.	FV	45.00

70   50 Dollars   **VF   UNC**

2003; 2006; 2009; 2010. With additional security features. Mature facing portrait
of Queen Elizabeth Ii at right, boats at left. Back: Bridges of Belize. Watermark:
Jaguar's head. Printer: TDLR. 150x75mm.

	VF	UNC
a. 1.3.2003.	FV	175
b. 1.11.2006	FV	145
c. 1.2.2009.	FV	125
d. 1.8.2010.	FV	115
e. 1.11.2014.	FV	110

71   100 Dollars   VF UNC
2003; 2006. The birds on the back include: jabiru stork, brown pelican, red-footed booby, magnificent frigate bird, yellow-headed parrot and king vulture. Multicolor. Keel-billed toucan at left, mature portrait of Queen Elizabeth II at right. With additional security features. Back: Birds of Belize. Watermark: Carved head of the "sleeping giant". Printer: TDLR. 150x75mm.

    a. 1.1.2003.   FV 255
    b. 1.11.2006.   FV 210

2012 Commemorative Issue

72   20 Dollars   VF UNC
1.1.2012. Brown and orange on multicolor underprint. Jaguar at left, mature   FV 75.00
portrait of Elizabeth II at right. Back: Tapir; keel-billed toucan and Baird's tapir; Central Bank building at right center. Printer: DLR 140x70mm.

COLLECTOR SERIES

Central Bank of Belize
1984 ND Issue

Note: The Central Bank of Belize will no longer exchange these notes for regular currency. (It is illegal to export the currency afterwards). Value is thus speculative.

CS1   ND (1984) Collection   Mkt. Value
    Stamped from paper bonded within gold foil. Denominations: $1 (1 pc.), $2 (2   375
pcs.) $5 (3 pcs.), $10 (4 pcs.), $20 (2 pcs.), $25 (6 pcs.), $50 (7 pcs.), $75 (5 pcs.), $100 (6 pcs.). Total 36 pcs. Queen Elizabeth II and building. Back: Diffrerent animals, ships, fish, birds etc.

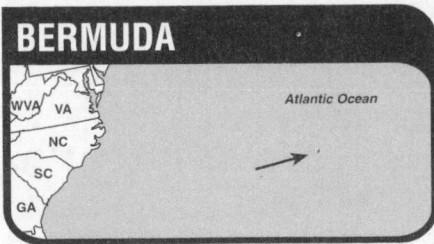

BERMUDA

The Parliamentary British Colony of Bermuda, situated in the western Atlantic Ocean 1,062 km. east of North Carolina, has an area of 53.3 sq. km. and a population of 66,500. Capital: Hamilton. Concentrated essences, beauty preparations, and cut flowers are exported.

Bermuda was first settled in 1609 by shipwrecked English colonists headed for Virginia. Tourism to the island to escape North American winters first developed in Victorian times. Tourism continues to be important to the island's economy, although international business has overtaken it in recent years. Bermuda has developed into a highly successful offshore financial center. Although a referendum on independence from the UK was soundly defeated in 1995, the present government has reopened debate on the issue.

RULERS:
  British

MONETARY SYSTEM:
  1 Shilling = 12 Pence
  1 Pound = 20 Shillings, to 1970
  1 Dollar = 100 Cents, 1970-

BRITISH ADMINISTRATION

Bermuda Government
1952 Issue

18   5 Shillings   VF UNC
1952; 1957. Brown on multicolor underprint. Portrait Queen Elizabeth II at upper center, Hamilton Harbor in frame at bottom center. Back: Royal crest. Printer: BWC.

    a. 20.10.1952.   65.00 225
    b. 1.5.1957.   50.00 150
    s. As b. Specimen.   — —

1952-66 Issue

19   10 Shillings   VF UNC
1952-66. Red on multicolor underprint. Portrait Queen Elizabeth II at upper center, Gate's Fort in St. George in frame at bottom center. Back: Arms at center. Printer: BWC.

    a. 20.10.1952.   75.00 425
    b. 1.5.1957.   40.00 200
    c. 1.10.1966.   60.00 250
    s. As b. Specimen.   — —

20   **1 Pound**   VF   UNC

1952-66. Blue on multicolor underprint. Queen Elizabeth II at right. Bridge at left. Back: Arms at center. Printer: BWC.

a. 20.10.1952.	100	550
b. 1.5.1957. Without security strip.	75.00	400
c. 1.5.1957. With security strip.	70.00	350
d. 1.10.1966.	60.00	275
s. As d. Specimen.	—	—
ct. Green on multicolored underprint.	—	1,000

21   **5 Pounds**   VF   UNC

1952-66. Orange on multicolor underprint. Portrait Queen Elizabeth II at right, large value at left, ship entering Hamilton Harbor at left. Back: Arms at center. Printer: BWC.

a. 20.10.1952.	1,250	2,500
b. 1.5.1957. Without security strip.	1,000	2,000
c. 1.5.1957. With security strip.	1,125	2,250
d. 1.10.1966.	1,250	2,500

22   **10 Pounds**   VF   UNC

28.7.1964. Purple on multicolor underprint. Portrait Queen Elizabeth II at right. Back: Arms at center. Printer: BWC.   600   2,750

1970 Issue

23   **1 Dollar**   VF   UNC

6.2.1970. Dark blue on tan and aqua underprint. Queen Elizabeth II at right looking 3/4 to left, arms at left center, bermuda petrel or cahow at center. Back: Sailboats at left center, buildings at upper right. Watermark: Tuna fish.

a. Issued note.	4.00	27.50
s. Specimen.	—	25.00

24   **5 Dollars**   VF   UNC

6.2.1970. Red-violet on aqua and multicolor underprint. Queen Elizabeth II at right looking 3/4 to left, arms at left center. Back: Lighthouse at left, buildings at center right. Watermark: Tuna fish.

a. Issued note.	10.00	45.00
s. Specimen.	—	25.00

25   **10 Dollars**   VF   UNC

6.2.1970. Purple on brown and multicolor underprint. Queen Elizabeth II at right looking 3/4 to left, arms at left center. Back: Bermuda petrel and seashell at center, beach at left. Watermark: Tuna fish.

a. Issued note.	15.00	95.00
s. Specimen.	—	25.00

26   **20 Dollars**   VF   UNC

6.2.1970. Green on multicolor underprint. Queen Elizabeth II at right looking 3/4 to left, arms at left center. Back: Building, sailboat and bridge at left center. Watermark: Tuna fish.

a. Issued note.	30.00	150
s. Specimen. Overprint: *SPECIMEN* on each side. Punch hole cancelled in each corner.	—	35.00

27   **50 Dollars**   VF   UNC

6.2.1970. Brown on multicolor underprint. Queen Elizabeth II at right looking 3/4 to left, arms at left center. Back: Lighthouse at left, map at upper right. Watermark: Tuna fish.

a. Issued note.	80.00	300
s. Specimen. Overprint: *SPECIMEN* on each side. Punch hole cancelled in each corner.	—	60.00

Bermuda Monetary Authority
1974-82 Issue

28   **1 Dollar**   VF   UNC

1975-88. Dark blue on tan and aqua underprint. Queen Elizabeth II at right looking 3/4 to left, arms at left center, bermuda petrel or cahow at center. Back: Sailboats at left center, buildings at upper right. Watermark: Tuna fish.

a. Signature titles: *CHAIRMAN* and *MANAGING DIRECTOR*. 1.7.1975; 1.12.1976.	5.00	35.00
b. 1.4.1978; 1.9.1979; 2.1.1982; 1.5.1984.	3.00	17.50
c. Signature titles: *CHAIRMAN* and *GENERAL MANAGER*. 1.1.1986.	3.50	17.50
d. Signature titles: *CHAIRMAN* and *DIRECTOR*. 1.1.1988.	3.00	17.50
s. Specimen, punch hole cancelled. Red overprint: SPECIMEN on both sides.	—	30.00

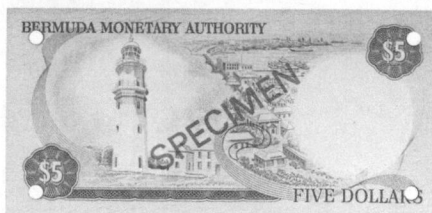

29   **5 Dollars**   VF   UNC

1978-88. Red-violet on aqua and multicolor underprint. Queen Elizabeth II at right looking 3/4 to left, arms at left center. Back: Lighthouse at left, buildings at center right. Watermark: Tuna fish.

a. Signature titles: *CHAIRMAN* and *MANAGING DIRECTOR*. 1.4.1978.	8.00	45.00

	VF	UNC
b. 2.1.1981.	7.50	40.00
c. Signature titles: *CHAIRMAN* and *GENERAL MANAGER*. 1.1.1986.	7.50	37.50
d. Signature titles: *CHAIRMAN* and *DIRECTOR*. 1.1.1988.	7.50	35.00
s. Specimen, punch hole cancelled in each corner. Red overprint: SPECIMEN on both sides.	—	25.00

1988-89 Issue

30 10 Dollars

	VF	UNC

1978; 1982. Purple on brown and multicolor underprint. Queen Elizabeth II at right looking 3/4 to left, arms at left center. Back: Bermuda petrel and seashell at center, beach at left. Watermark: Tuna fish.

a. 1.4.1978.	45.00	200
b. 2.1.1982.	40.00	165
s. Specimen, punch hole cancelled in two corners. Red overprint: SPECIMEN on both sides.	—	30.00

34 2 Dollars

	VF	UNC

1988; 1989. UV: sea gull fluoresces orange. Blue-green on green and multicolor underprint. Mature bust of Queen Elizabeth II at right. Signature titles: *CHAIRMAN* and *DIRECTOR*. Back: Dockyards clock tower building at upper left, map at center, arms at center right. Stylistic changes Watermark: Tuna fish.

a. Serial # prefix: *B/1*. 1.10.1988.	FV	10.00
b. Serial # prefix: *B/2*. 1.8.1989.	FV	9.50

31 20 Dollars

	VF	UNC

1974-86. Green on multicolor underprint. Queen Elizabeth II at right looking 3/4 to left, arms at left center. Back: Building, sailboat and bridge at left center.

a. 1.4.1974.	125	550
b. 1.3.1976.	50.00	200
c. 2.1.1981; 1.5.1984.	25.00	100
d. Signature title: *GENERAL MANAGER* at right. 1.1.1986.	25.00	100
s. Specimen, punch hole cancelled in each corner. Red overprint: SPECIMEN on both sides.	—	—

35 5 Dollars

	VF	UNC

20.2.1989. Stylistic changes on back. Red-violet and purple on multicolor underprint. Mature bust of Queen Elizabeth II at right. Signature titles: *CHAIRMAN* and *DIRECTOR*. Back: Lighthouse at left, buildings at center right, arms at upper left. Watermark: Tuna fish.

a. Signature title: *DIRECTOR* on silver background at bottom center Serial # prefix: *B/1*.	7.00	27.50
b. Signature title: *DIRECTOR* without silver background. Serial # prefix: *B/1*, *B/2*.	FV	12.50
r. Replacement.	15.00	50.00

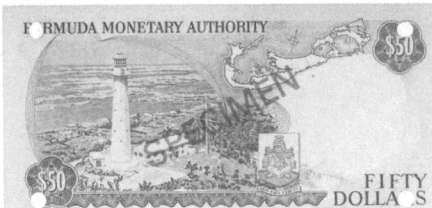

32 50 Dollars

	VF	UNC

1974-82. Brown on multicolor underprint. Queen Elizabeth II at right looking 3/4 left., arms at left center. Back: Lighthouse at left, map at upper right.

a. 1.5.1974.	350	1,950
b. 1.4.1978; 2.1.1982.	100	450
s. Specimen, punch hole cancelled in each corner. Red overprint: SPECIMEN on both sides.	—	95.00

36 10 Dollars

	VF	UNC
	FV	25.00

20.2.1989. Purple, blue and ochre on multicolor underprint. Mature bust of Queen Elizabeth II at right. signature titles: *CHAIRMAN* and *DIRECTOR*. Back: Bermuda petrel and seashell at center, beach at left, arms at upper left. Watermark: Tuna fish.

33 100 Dollars

	VF	UNC

1982-86. Orange and brown on multicolor underprint. Queen Elizabeth II at right looking 3/4 left. Back: House of Assembly at left, Camden building at upper center right. Watermark: Tuna fish.

a. 2.1.1982.	FV	900
b. Signature title: *GENERAL MANAGER* overprint at right. 14.11.1984.	FV	875
c. Signature title: *GENERAL MANAGER* at right. 1.1.1986.	FV	800
s. Specimen, punch hole cancelled in each corner. Red overprint SPECIMEN on both sides.	—	85.00

37 20 Dollars

	VF	UNC

20.2.1989. Stylistic changes on back. Green and red on multicolor underprint. Mature bust of Queen Elizabeth II at right. Signature titles: *CHAIRMAN* and *DIRECTOR*. Back: Building, sailboat and bridge at left center, arms at upper left. Watermark: Tuna fish.

a. Serial # prefix: *B/1*.	FV	42.50
b. Serial # prefix: *B/2*.	FV	40.00

38 50 Dollars
VF UNC
20.2.1989. Stylistic changes on back. Brown and olive on multicolor underprint.
Mature bust of Queen Elizabeth II at right. Signature titles: *CHAIRMAN* and
DIRECTOR. Back: Lighthouse at left, map at upper right, arms at upper left.
Watermark: Tuna fish.
FV 100

39 100 Dollars
VF UNC
20.2.1989. Stylistic changes on back. Orange, brown and violet on multicolor
underprint. Mature bust of Queen Elizabeth II at right. Signature titles: *CHAIRMAN*
and *DIRECTOR*. Back: House of Assembly at left, Camden building at upper
center right, arms at upper left. Watermark: Tuna fish.
FV 185

1992 Commemorative Issue; Act 1969
#40, Quincentenary of Christopher Columbus

40 50 Dollars
VF UNC
12.10.1992. Dark blue, brown and red on multicolor underprint. Mature bust
of Queen Elizabeth II at right, commemorative details. Maltese cross as serial
number prifix at upper left, c/c fractional prefix at right, and overprint: *Christopher
Columbus / Quincennary 1492-1992* at left. Back: Scuba divers, shipwreck at left,
island outline at upper center right above arms. 140x68mm.
a. Issued note. — FV 120
s. Specimen. Overprint:*SPECIMEN,* punch hole cancelled. — 125

Act 1969; 1992-96 Issue

40A 2 Dollars
VF UNC
1996-97. Blue and green on multicolor underprint. Mature bust of Queen Elizabeth
II at right, Authorization text in 3 lines at center. Signature titles: *CHAIRMAN* and
DIRECTOR. Back: Dockyards clock tower building at upper left, map at center,
arms at center right. Watermark: Tuna fish. 140x68mm.
a. 29.2.1996. FV 10.00
b. 6.6.1997. FV 5.00

41 5 Dollars
VF UNC
1992-97. Red-violet and purple on multicolor underprint. Mature bust of Queen
Elizabeth II at right. Authorization text in 3 lines at center. Signature titles: *CHAIR-
MAN* and *DIRECTOR*. Back: Lighthouse at left, buildings at center right, arms at
upper left. Watermark: Tuna fish. 140x68mm.
a. 12.11.1992. FV 12.50
b. 25.3.1995. FV 11.00
c. 20.2.1996. FV 10.00
d. 10.6.1997. FV 10.00

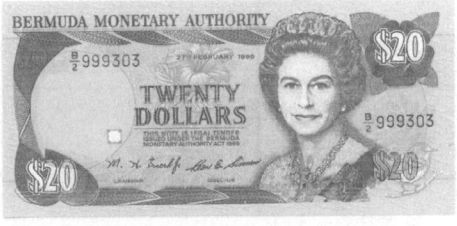

42 10 Dollars
VF UNC
1993-99. Purple, deep blue and orange on multicolor underprint. Mature bust of
Queen Elizabeth II at right. Authorization text in 3 lines at center. Signature titles:
CHAIRMAN and *DIRECTOR*. Back: Bermuda petrol and cedar hall at center, beach
at left, arms at upper left. Watermark: Tuna fish. 140x68mm.
a. 4.1.1993. FV 22.50
b. 15.3.1996. FV 20.00
c. 17.6.1997. FV 20.00
d. 31.5.1999. With security strip. FV 20.00

43 20 Dollars
VF UNC
1996; 1999. Green and red on multicolor underprint. Mature bust of Queen Elizabeth II at right. Authorization text in 3 lines at center. Signature titles: *CHAIRMAN*
and *DIRECTOR*. Back: Building, sailboat and bridge at left center, arms at upper
left. Watermark: Tuna fish. 140x68mm.
a. 27.2.1996. FV 40.00
b. 13.5.1999. With security strip. FV 37.50

44 50 Dollars
VF UNC
1992-96. Dark blue, brown and red on multicolor underprint. Mature bust of
Queen Elizabeth II at right. Authorization text in 3 lines at center. Signature titles:
CHAIRMAN and *DIRECTOR*. Back: Scuba divers, shipwreck at left, island outline
at upper center right above arms. Watermark: Tuna fish. 140x68mm.
a. 12.10.1992. FV 100
b. 25.3.1995. FV 90.00
c. 23.2.1996. FV 85.00

45 100 Dollars — VF UNC

14.2.1996. Orange, brown and violet on multicolor underprint. Mature bust of Queen Elizabeth II at right. Authorization text in 3 lines at center. Signature titles: *CHAIRMAN* and *DIRECTOR*. Back: House of Assembly at center, Camden building at upper center right, arms at upper left. Watermark: Tuna fish. 140x68mm. — FV 175

1994 Commemorative Issue

#46, 25th Anniversary Bermuda Monetary Authority

46 100 Dollars — VF UNC

20.2.1994. Orange, brown and violet on multicolor underprint. Mature bust of Queen Elizabeth II at right. Authorization text in 3 lines at center, overprint: *25th Anniversary....* Signature titles: *CHAIRMAN* and *DIRECTOR*. Back: Arms at upper left, House of Assembly at left, Camden building at upper center right. Watermark: Tuna fish. 140x68mm.

    a. Issued note. — FV 170

    s. Specimen. Red overprint: *SPECIMEN,* punch hole cancelled. — — 150

1997 Commemorative Issue

#47, Opening of Burnaby House

47 20 Dollars — VF UNC

17.1.1997. Green and red on multicolor underprint. Mature bust of Queen Elizabeth II at right. Overprint on #43. *To commemorate the opening of Burnaby House...* in watermark area at left. Authorization text in 3 lines at center. Signature titles Back: Building, sailboat and bridge at left center. Watermark: Tuna fish. 140x68mm. — FV 37.50

1997 Regular Issue

48 50 Dollars — VF UNC

6.6.1997. Segmented foil over security thread. Dark blue, brown and red on multicolor underprint. Mature bust of Queen Elizabeth II at right. Authorization text in 3 lines at center. Signature titles: *CHAIRMAN* and *DIRECTOR*. Back: Scuba divers, shipwreck at left, island outline at upper right above arms. Watermark: Tuna fish. 140x68mm. — FV 87.50

---

49 100 Dollars — VF UNC

30.6.1997. Segmented foil over security thread. Orange and brown on multicolor underprint. Mature bust of Queen Elizabeth II at right. Authorization text in 3 lines at center. Signature titles: *CHAIRMAN* and *DIRECTOR*. Back: Arms at upper left, House of Assembly at left, Camden building at upper center right. Watermark: Tuna fish. 140x68mm. — FV 165

2000 Issue

50 2 Dollars — VF UNC

24.5.2000; 7.5.2007. Blue and green on multicolor underprint. Mature portrait of Queen Elizabeth II at right. Sea horse at center. Back: Boats and building at left, island map at center. Watermark: Tuna fish. 140x68mm.

    a. 24.5.2000. — FV 4.00

    b. 7.5.2007. — FV 4.00

    s. As a. Specimen. Overprint: *SPECIMEN* on each side. Punch hole cancelled in three corners. — — 75.00

51 5 Dollars — VF UNC

25.5.2000. Purple and burgundy on multicolor underprint. Mature portrait of Queen Elizabeth II at right. Shell and fish at center. Back: Lighthouse at left, bay view at center. Watermark: Tuna fish. 140x68mm.

    a. Issued note. — FV 8.50

    s. As a. Specimen. Overprint: *SPECIMEN* on each side. Punch hole cancelled in three corners. — — 75.00

52 10 Dollars — VF UNC

24.5.2000; 7.5.2007. Dark blue and mauve on multicolor underprint. Mature portrait of Queen Elizabeth II at right. Flower and Bermuda Petrel at center. Back: Bay scene, Bermuda Petrel and shell. Watermark: Tuna fish. 140x68mm.

    a. 24.5.2000. — FV 17.00

    b. 7.5.2007. — FV 17.00

    s. As a. Specimen. As a. Overprint: *SPECIMEN* on each side. Punch hole cancelled in three corners. — — 75.00

53 20 Dollars VF UNC

24.5.2000. Green and red on multicolor underprint. Mature portrait of Queen Elizabeth II at right, building at center. Back: Bridge and harbor scene. Watermark: Tuna fish. 140x68mm.

    a. Issued note. FV 37.50

    s. As a. Specimen. Overprint: *SPECIMEN* on each side. Punch hole cancelled — 75.00
       in three corners.

53A 20 Dollars VF UNC

24.5.2000 (2008). Green and red on multicolor underprint. Mature portrait of Queen Elizabeth II at right. Flower and foil patch. Serial # prefix: *D/2*. Back: Bridge and harbor scene. Printer: (T)DLR. 140x68mm. FV 37.50

54 50 Dollars VF UNC

24.5.2000; 7.5.2007. Bluish black, red and brown on multicolor underprint. Mature portrait of Queen Elizabeth II at right, building at center. Back: Scuba divers and wreck at left, map at upper center. Watermark: Tuna fish. 140x68mm.

    a. 24.5.2000. FV 85.00

    b. 7.5.2007. FV 85.00

    r. Replacement note: Serial # prefix *Z*. FV 150

    s. As a. Specimen. Overprint: *SPECIMEN* on each side. Punch hole cancelled — 75.00
       in three corners.

55 100 Dollars VF UNC

24.5.2000. Red-orange and brown on multicolor underprint. Mature portrait of Queen Elizabeth II at right, flowers and shell at center. Back: House of Assembly at left, Camden building at upper center right, arms at upper left. Watermark: Tuna fish. 140x68mm.

    a. Issued note. FV 165

    r. Replacement note: Serial # prefix: *Z*. FV 250

    s. As a. Specimen. Overprint: *SPECIMEN* on each side. Punch hole cancelled — 75.00
       in three corners.

2003 Commemorative Issue

56 50 Dollars VF UNC

2.6.2003. Mature portrait of Queen Elizabeth II at right, golden crown at right with overprint: *TO COMMEMORATE THE CORONATION OF QUEEN ELIZABETH II 1953-2003*. 140x68mm. FV 95.00

2009 Issue

57 2 Dollars VF UNC

1.1.2009. Blue and multicolor. Bluebird and flowers. Back: Dockyard clocktower, statue of Nepture. Watermark: Hibiscus flower and sail boat. Printer: TDLR. 69x136mm.

    a. Issued note. FV 9.00

    s. Specimen. Overprint *SPECIMEN* and punch hole cancelled. — 50.00

58 5 Dollars VF UNC

1.1.2009. Vertical format. Rose and multicolor. Blue marlin and flowers. Back: Horshoe Bay Beach, Somerset Bridge with boat passing below. Watermark: Hibiscus flower and sail boat. Printer: TDLR. 69x136mm.

    a. Issued note. FV 20.00

    s. Specimen. Overprint *SPECIMEN* and punch hole cancelled. — 50.00

59 10 Dollars VF UNC

1.1.2009. Vertical format. Violet and multicolor. Blue angel fish and flowers. Back: Commissioner's House in Somerset Parish and the H.M.S. Deliverance. Watermark: Hibiscus flower and sail boat. Printer: TDLR. 69x136mm.

    a. Issued note. FV 35.00

    s. Specimen. Overprint *SPECIMEN* and punch hole cancelled. — 75.00

60 20 Dollars VF UNC

1.1.2009. Vertical format. Green and multicolor. Whistling frog and flowers. Back: St. Mark's Chruch steeple, Gibbs Hill lighthouse in Southampton Parish. Watermark: Hibiscus flower and sail boat. Printer: TDLR. 69x136mm.

    a. Issued note. FV 55.00

    s. Specimen. Overprint *SPECIMEN* and punch hole cancelled. — 75.00

61 50 Dollars VF UNC

1.1.2009. Vertical format. Light orange and multicolor. Red-billed longtail tropic bird and flowers. Back: St. Peter's church in St. George. Watermark: Hibiscus flower and sail boat. Printer: TDLR. 136x69mm.

    a. Issued note. FV 65.00

    s. Specimen. Overprint *SPECIMEN* and punch hole cancelled. — 100

61A 50 Dollars   VF   UNC
1.1.2009 (2012). Yellow and multicolor White longtail tropic bird. Back: St. Peter's   FV   100
Church in Saint George. 69x136mm.

62 100 Dollars   VF   UNC
1.1.2009. Vertical format. Rose and multicolor. Cardinal on branch, flowers. Back:
House of Assembly in Hamilton. Watermark: Hibiscus flower and sail boat. Printer:
TDLR. 136x69mm.
   a. Issued note.   FV   175
   s. Specimen. Overprint *SPECIMEN* and punch hole cancelled.   —   125

COLLECTOR SERIES
Bermuda Monetary Authority
1978-84 Dated Issue (1985)

CS1 1978-84 1-100 Dollars   Mkt. Value
#22-33 with normal serial #, punched hole cancelled, overprint: *SPECIMEN*   65.00
(1985). (Often seen with mixed dates).

1981-82 Issue (1985)

CS2 1981-82 1-100 Dollars   Mkt. Value
#28-33 with all zero serial #, punched hole cancelled in all 4 corners, overprint: 65.00
SPECIMEN (1985).

2000 Issue

CS3 2000 2-100 Dollars   Mkt. Value
#50-55 with all zerio serial #, punched hole cancelled in three corners. 2000.   75.00

BHUTAN

The Kingdom of Bhutan, a land-locked Himalayan country bordered by Tibet, India, and Sikkim, has an area of 47,000 sq. km. and a population of 682,300. Capital: Thimphu. Virtually the entire population is engaged in agricultural and pastoral activities. Rice, wheat, barley, and yak butter are produced in sufficient quantity to make the country self-sufficient in food.

In 1865, Britain and Bhutan signed the Treaty of Sinchulu, under which Bhutan would receive an annual subsidy in exchange for ceding some border land to British India. Under British influence, a monarchy was set up in 1907; three years later, a treaty was signed whereby the British agreed not to interfere in Bhutanese internal affairs and Bhutan allowed Britain to direct its foreign affairs. This role was assumed by independent India after 1947. Two years later, a formal Indo-Bhutanese accord returned the areas of Bhutan annexed by the British, formalized the annual subsidies the country received, and defined India's responsibilities in defense and foreign relations. A refugee issue of over 100,000 Bhutanese in Nepal remains unresolved; 90% of the refugees are housed in seven United Nations Office of the High Commissioner for Refugees (UNHCR) camps. In March 2005, King Jigme Singye Wangchuck unveiled the government's draft constitution - which would introduce major democratic reforms - and pledged to hold a national referendum for its approval. In December 2006, the King abdicated the throne to his son, Jigme Khesar Namgyel Wangchuck, in order to give him experience as head of state before the democratic transition. In early 2007, India and Bhutan renegotiated their treaty to allow Bhutan greater autonomy in conducting its foreign policy, although Thimphu continues to coordinate policy decisions in this area with New Delhi. In July 2007, seven ministers of Bhutan's ten-member cabinet resigned to join the political process, and the cabinet acted as a caretaker regime until democratic elections for seats to the country's first parliament were completed in March 2008. The king ratified the country's first constitution in July 2008.

RULERS:
Jigme Dorji Wangchuk, 1952-1972
Jigme Singye Wangchuk, 1972-2006
Jigme Khesar Namgyel Wangchuck, 2006-

MONETARY SYSTEM:
1 Ngultrum (= 1 Indian Rupee) = 100 Chetrums, 1974-

SIGNATURES			
1	Chairman *Ashi Sonam Wangchuck*	2	Bank of Bhutan *Yeshe Dorji*
3	Chairman *Dorji Tsering*		

KINGDOM
Royal Government of Bhutan
1974-78 ND Issue

1 1 Ngultrum   VF   UNC
ND (1974). Blue on multicolor underprint. Dragon design at left and right. Watermark: 4-petaled symbol, called a *dorje,* the Buddhist of a thunderbolt.   2.50   6.00

2 5 Ngultrum   VF   UNC
ND (1974). Red-brown on multicolor underprint. Portrait J. Singye Wangchuk at center. Back: Simtokha Dzong palace center right. Watermark: 4-petaled symbol, called a *dorje,* the Buddhist of a thunderbolt.   15.00   50.00

3 10 Ngultrum

	VF	UNC
ND (1974). Blue-violet on multicolor underprint. Portrait J. Dorji Wangchuk at top center. Back: Paro Dzong palace center right. Watermark: 4-petaled symbol, called a *dorje*, the Buddhist of a thunderbolt. — 30.00 — 200

4 100 Ngultrum

	VF	UNC
ND (1978). Green and brown on multicolor underprint. Portrait J. Singye Wangchuk at center, circle with 8 good luck symbols at right. Back: Tashichho Dzong palace at left center. Watermark: 4-petaled symbol, called a *dorje*, the Buddhist of a thunderbolt. — 2,000 — —

1981 ND Issue

5 1 Ngultrum

	VF	UNC
ND (1981). Blue on multicolor underprint. Royal emblem between facing dragons at center, serial number at upper left and right. Back: Simtokha Dzong palace at center. — 0.25 — 3.00

6 2 Ngultrum

	VF	UNC
ND (1981). Brown and green on multicolor underprint. Royal emblem between facing dragons at center, serial number at upper left and right. Back: Simtokha Dzong palace at center. — 0.50 — 4.50

7 5 Ngultrum

	VF	UNC
ND (1981). Brown on multicolor underprint. Royal emblem between facing birds at center, serial number at upper left and right. Back: Paro Dzong palace at center. — 2.50 — 10.00

8 10 Ngultrum

	VF	UNC
ND (1981). Purple on multicolor underprint. Royal emblem at left, portrait J. Singye Wangchuk at right, serial number at left and right. Back: Paro Dzong palace at center. — 5.00 — 17.50

9 20 Ngultrum

	VF	UNC
ND (1981). Olive on multicolor underprint. Facing portrait Jigme Dorji Wangchuk at right, royal emblem at left, serial number at left and right. Back: Punakha Dzong palace at center. — 7.50 — 30.00

10 50 Ngultrum

	VF	UNC
ND (1981). Purple, violet and brown on multicolor underprint. Facing portrait Jigme Dorji Wangchuk at right, royal emblem at left, serial number at left and right. Back: Tongsa Dzong palace at center. — 15.00 — 75.00

11   100 Ngultrum   VF   UNC
ND (1981). Dark green, olive-green and brown-violet on multicolor underprint. Bird   27.50   150
at center, portrait J. Singye Wangchuk at right, royal emblem at left, serial number
at left and right. Back: Tashichho Dzong palace at center.

Royal Monetary Authority of Bhutan
1985-92 ND Issue

12   1 Ngultrum   VF   UNC
ND (1986; 1990). Reduced size. Blue on multicolor underprint. Royal emblem
between facing dragons at center. 2 signature varieties. Serial number at lower left
and upper right. Back: Simtokha Dzong palace at center.
    a. ND (1986). Signature 1.   FV   0.50
    b. ND (1990). Signature 3.   FV   0.50

13   2 Ngultrum   VF   UNC
ND (1986). Reduced size. Brown and green on multicolor underprint. Royal   FV   0.75
emblem between facing dragons at center, serial number at lower left and upper
right. Back: Simtokhan Dzong palace at center.

14   5 Ngultrum   VF   UNC
ND (1985; 1990). Reduced size. Brown on multicolor underprint. Royal emblem
between facing birds at center, serial number at lower left and upper right. Back:
Paro Dzong palace at center. 130x62mm.
    a. ND (1985). Signature 1.   FV   1.50
    b. ND (1990). Signature 3.   FV   1.50

15   10 Ngultrum   VF   UNC
ND (1986; 1992). Reduced size. Purple on multicolor underprint. Royal emblem at
left, portrait of J. Singye Wangchuk at right, serial number at lower left and upper
right. Back: Paro Dzong palace at center. 139x69mm.
    a. Fractional serial # prefix. (1986).   FV   1.75
    b. 2 letter serial # prefix (Chinese printer.) (1992).   FV   2.00

16   20 Ngultrum   VF   UNC
ND (1986; 1992). Olive on multicolor underprint. Facing portrait Jihme Dorji
Wangchuk at right, royal emblem at left, serial number at lower left and upper
right. Back: Punakha Dzong palace at center. 152x69mm.
    a. Serial # prefix fractional style. (1986).   FV   4.00
    b. Serial # prefix 2 large letters (Chinese printer.) (1992).   FV   3.50

17   50 Ngultrum   VF   UNC
ND (1985; 1992). Violet and brown on multicolor underprint. Facing portrait Jihme
Dorji Wangchuk at right, royal emblem at left, serial number at lower left and upper
right. Back: Tongsa Dzong palace at center. 154x70mm.
    a. Serial # prefix fractional style. (1986).   3.00   15.00
    b. Serial # prefix letters 2 large letters (Chinese printer.) (1992).   2.00   6.50

18   100 Ngultrum   VF   UNC
ND (1986; 1992). Green and brown on multicolor underprint. Bird at center, royal
emblem left, portrait of J. Singye Wangchuk at right, serial number at lower left
and right. Back: Tashichho Dzong palace at center. 160x70mm.
    a. Serial # prefix fractional style. (1986).   5.00   25.00
    b. Serial # prefix 2 large letters (Chinese printer.) (1992).   4.00   17.50

1994 ND Issue

19   50 Ngultrum   **VF UNC**
ND (1994). Purple, violet and brown on multicolor underprint. Facing portrait Jihme Dorji Wangchuk at right, royal emblem at left, serial number at lower left and upper right. Modified underprint including floral diamond shaped registry design at upper center. Back: Tongsa Dzong palace at center. Watermark: Wavy *ROYAL MONETARY AUTHORITY* repeated. 154x70mm.   FV   6.00

20   100 Ngultrum   **VF UNC**
ND (1994). Green and brown on multicolor underprint. Bird at center, royal emblem left, portrait of J. Singye Wangchuk at right, serial number at lower left and right. Modified underprint including floral diamond shaped registry design at upper center. Back: Tashichho Dzong palace at center. Watermark: Wavy *ROYAL MONETARY AUTHORITY* repeated. 160x70mm.   FV   9.00

1994 ND Commemorative Issue

#21, National Day

21   500 Ngultrum   **VF UNC**
ND (1994). Red-orange on multicolor underprint. Portrait King Jigme Singye Wangchuk in headdress at right. Both serial numbers ascending size. Back: Punakha Dzong palace. Watermark: 4-petaled symbol. 160x70mm.   FV   40.00

2000-01 ND Issue

22   10 Ngultrum   **VF UNC**
ND (2000). Purple and blue on multicolor underprint. Royal emblem at left, portrait King Jigme Singye Wangchuk at right. Back: Paro Dzong palace at center. 140x70mm.   FV   1.75

23   20 Ngultrum   **VF UNC**
ND (2000). Olive on multicolor underprint. Facing portrait Jigme Dorji Wangchuk at right, royal emblem at left. Signature 3. Back: Punakha Dzong palace at center. 152x69mm.   FV   4.00

24   50 Ngultrum   **VF UNC**
ND (2000). Violet and brown on multicolor underprint. Facing portrait Jihme Dorji Wangchuk at right, royal emblem at left, serial number at lower left and upper right. Modified underprint including floral diamond shaped registry design at upper center. Back: Tongsa Dzong palace at center. Watermark: Wavy *ROYAL MONETARY AUTHORITY* repeated. 154x70mm.   FV   6.50

25   100 Ngultrum   **VF UNC**
ND (2000). Green and brown on multicolor underprint. Portrait King Jigme Singye Wangchuk at right, vertical serial # at right, both ascending size. Back: Tashichho Dzong palace at center. Watermark: 4-petaled symbol. 160x70mm.   FV   17.50

26   500 Ngultrum   **VF UNC**
ND (2000). Red-orange on multicolor underprint. Portrait King Jigme Singye Wangchuk in headdress at right. Back: Punakha Dzong palace. 160x70mm.   FV   32.50

2006 Series

27   1 Ngultrum   **VF   UNC**
2006; 2013. Dark blue and orange on multicolor underprint. Circle flanked by two
dragons. Back: Simtokha Dzong palace.
  a. 2006.   FV   0.50
  b. 2013.   FV   0.50

28   5 Ngultrum   **VF   UNC**
2006; 2011; 2013. Brown and orange on yellow and multicolor underprint. Circle
flanked by two mythological birds. Back: Taktsang palace. 125x60mm.
  a. 2006.   FV   1.00
  b. 2011.   FV   1.00
  c. 2013.   FV   1.00

29   10 Ngultrum   **VF   UNC**
2006; 2013. Blue-violet on tan and green underprint. King Jigme Dorji Wangchick
at right. Back: Paro Dzong palace at center. 125x65mm.
  a. 2006.   FV   2.50
  b. 2013.   FV   2.50

30   20 Ngultrum   **VF   UNC**
2006; 2013. Green on yellow and multicolor underprint. King Jigme Doriji Wangchuk at right. Back: Punakha Dzong palace. 132x66mm.
  a. 2006.   FV   4.00
  b. 2013.   FV   4.00

31   50 Ngultrum   **VF   UNC**
2006; 2013. King Jihme Doriji Wangchuk at right. Back: Tongsa Dzong palace at
left center. 146x70mm.
  a. 2006.   FV   6.50
  b. 2013.   FV   6.50

32   100 Ngultrum   **VF   UNC**
2006; 2011; 2013; 2015. Black and green on multicolor underprint. King Jigme
Doriji Wangchuk at right. Back: Paru Rirpung Dzong palace. 146x70mm.
  a. 2006.   FV   17.50
  b. 2011.   FV   17.50
  c. 2013.   FV   17.50
  d. 2015.   FV   17.50

33   500 Ngultrum   **VF   UNC**
2006; 2011; 2013. Orange on multicolor underprint. King Jigme Singye Wangchuk
at right. Back: Prinakha Dzong palace. 154x70mm.
  a. 2006.   FV   32.50
  b. 2011.   FV   32.50
  c. 2013.   FV   32.50

34   1000 Ngultrum   **VF   UNC**
2008; 2013. Dark green on yellow and tan underprint. King Jigme Khesar
Namgyel Wangchuck at right. Signature 6. Back: Tashchho Dzong at center.
Watermark: Jigme Khesar Namgyel Wangchuck. Printer: G&D. 165x70mm.
  a. 2008.   FV   55.00
  b. 2013.   FV   55.00
  s. Specimen.   —   150

2012 Royal Wedding Commemorative

35   100 Ngultrum   **VF   UNC**
2011. Black and green on multicolor underprint Portraits at right, design at center.   FV   25.00
Back: Punakha Dzong palace at center. 145x70mm.

BIAFRA

On May 27, 1967, Gen. Yakubu Gowon, head of the Federal Military Government of Nigeria, created three states from the Eastern Region of the country. Separation of the region, undertaken to achieve better regional and ethnic balance, caused Lt. Col. E. O. Ojukwu, Military Governor of the Eastern Region, to proclaim on May 30, 1967, the independence of the Eastern Region as the "Republic of Biafra." Fighting broke out between the Federal Military Government and the forces of Lt. Col. Ojukwu and continued until Biafra surrendered on Jan. 15, 1970. Biafra was then reintegrated into the Republic of Nigeria as three states: East-Central, Rivers, and South-Eastern. For additional history, see Nigeria.

MONETARY SYSTEM:
1 Shilling = 12 Pence
1 Pound = 20 Shillings

REPUBLIC

Bank of Biafra

1967 ND Issue

1   5 Shillings   **VF   UNC**
ND (1967). Blue on lilac underprint. (Rising sun color varies from orange to yellow.) Palm tree, large rising sun at left. Back: Four girls at right.   3.00   15.00

2   1 Pound   **VF   UNC**
ND (1967). Blue and orange. Palm tree, large rising sun at left. Back: Arms at right.   25.00   100

1968 ND Issue

3   5 Shillings   **VF   UNC**
ND (1968-69). Blue on green and orange underprint. Palm tree and small rising sun at top left center. Back: Four girls at right.
  a. Issued note.   5.00   17.50
  b. Without serial #.   12.50   40.00

4   10 Shillings   **VF   UNC**
ND (1968-69). Dark green on blue and and orange underprint. Palm tree and small rising sun at top left center. Back: Buildings at right.   1.50   4.50

5   1 Pound   **VF   UNC**
ND (1968-69). Dark brown on green, brown and orange underprint. Palm tree and small rising sun at top left center. Back: Arms at right.
  a. Issued note.   0.25   1.50
  b. Without serial #.   5.00   20.00

6   5 Pounds   **VF   UNC**
ND (1968-69). Purple on green and orange underprint. Palm tree and small rising sun at top left center. Back: Arms at left, weaving at left center.
  a. Issued note.   17.50   70.00
  b. Without serial #.   7.00   30.00

7   10 Pounds   **VF   UNC**
ND (1968-69). Black on blue, brown and orange underprint. Palm tree and small rising sun at top left center. Back: Arms at left, carver at left center.
  a. Issued note.   15.00   85.00
  b. Without serial #.   7.50   40.00

BOLIVIA

The Republic of Bolivia, a land-locked country in west central South America, has an area of 1,098,580 sq. km. and a population of 9.25 million. Capitals: La Paz (administrative); Sucre (constitutional). Mining is the principal industry and tin the most important metal. Minerals, petroleum, natural gas, cotton and coffee are exported.

Bolivia, named after independence fighter Simon Bolivar, broke away from Spanish rule in 1825; much of its subsequent history has consisted of a series of nearly 200 coups and countercoups. Democratic civilian rule was established in 1982, but leaders have faced difficult problems of deep-seated poverty, social unrest, and illegal drug production. In December 2005, Bolivians elected Movement Toward Socialism leader Evo Morales president - by the widest margin of any leader since the restoration of civilian rule in 1982 - after he ran on a promise to change the country's traditional political class and empower the nation's poor majority. However, since taking office, his controversial strategies have exacerbated racial and economic tensions between the Amerindian populations of the Andean west and the non-indigenous communities of the eastern lowlands.

MONETARY SYSTEM:
1 Peso Boliviano = 100 Centavos, 1962-1987
1 Boliviano = 100 Centavos, 1987-

SPECIMEN NOTES:
All *SPECIMEN, MUESTRA, MUESTRA SIN VALOR* and *ESPECIMEN* notes always have serial #'s of zero.

REPUBLIC

Banco Central de Bolivia

Ley de 13 de Julio de 1962 - First Issue

152   1 Peso Boliviano   VF   UNC

L.1962. Black on multicolor underprint. Portrait Campesino at right, arms at left. Signature varieties. Series A-E. Back: Agricultural scene at center right, old and new denomination at botom. Printer: TDLR.

a. Issued note.	7.50	20.00
p. Proof.	—	750
s. Specimen with red overprint: *SPECIMEN.* Series A.	—	20.00

153   5 Pesos Bolivianos   VF   UNC

L.1962. Blue on multicolor underprint. Portrait Mayor Gualberto Villarroel Lopez at right, arms at left. Signature varieties. Series A-B1. Back: Petroleum refinery, old and new denomination at bottom. Printer: TDLR.

a. Issued note.	3.00	12.00
b. Uncut sheet of 4 signed notes.	—	100
s. Specimen. Red overprint: *SPECIMEN* on both sides. Series A; T; Z.	—	50.00

154   10 Pesos Bolivianos   VF   UNC

L.1962. Olive-green on multicolor underprint. Portrait Colonel Germán Busch Becerra at right, arms at left. Series A-U3. 18 signature varieties. Back: Mountain of Potosí, old and new denomination at bottom. Printer: TDLR.

a. Issued note.	0.20	0.75
b. Uncut sheet of 4 signed notes. Series U2.	—	30.00
s1. Specimen. Red overprint: *SPECIMEN.* Series A.	—	35.00
s2. As s1. Specimen, but with punched hole cancellation and TDLR oval stamp. Series A.	—	50.00
s3. Specimen. Red overprint: *SPECIMEN* on both sides. Series U2.	—	80.00
s4. Uncut sheet of 4 specimen notes. Series U2.	—	35.00

155   20 Pesos Bolivianos   VF   UNC

L.1962. Purple on multicolor underprint. Portrait Pedro Domingo Murillo at right, arms at left. Series A. Signature varieties. Back: La Paz mountain, old and new denomination at bottom. Printer: TDLR.

a. Issued note.	15.00	50.00
s. Specimen with red overprint: *SPECIMEN.* Series A.	—	20.00

156   50 Pesos Bolivianos   VF   UNC

L.1962. Orange on multicolor underprint. Portrait Antonio Jose de Sucre at right, arms at left. Series A. Signature varieties. Back: Puerta del Sol, old and new denomination at bottom. Printer: TDLR.

a. Issued note.	85.00	225
s. Specimen with red overprint: *SPECIMEN.* Series A.	—	20.00

157 100 Pesos Bolivianos   VF UNC

L.1962. Red on multicolor underprint with green at left, blue at right. Portrait
Simón Bolívar at right. Red serial #, and security thread at left center, arms at left.
Series A. Signature varieties. Back: Engraved, scene of the declaration of the
Bolivian Republic. Old and new denomination at bottom. Printer: TDLR.

	VF	UNC
a. Issued note. Large, wide, dark signatures.	85.00	225
b. Issued note. Small, thin, light signatures.	75.00	185
s. Specimen with red overprint: *SPECIMEN.* Series A.	—	20.00

Ley de 13 de Julio de 1962 - Second Issue

158 1 Peso Boliviano   VF UNC

L.1962. Black on multicolor underprint. Portrait Campesino at right, arms at left.
Series F-F1. 7 signature varieties. Back: Agricultural scene, new denomination
only. Printer: TDLR.

	VF	UNC
a. Issued note.	0.75	8.00
s. Specimen with red overprint: *SPECIMEN.* Series Y.	—	25.00

#159, 160 not assigned.

161 20 Pesos Bolivianos   VF UNC

L.1962. Purple on multicolor underprint. Portrait Pedro Domingo Murillo at right,
arms at left. Series B H. 4 signature varieties. Back: La Paz mountain, new
denomination only. Printer: TDLR.

	VF	UNC
a. Issued note.	1.00	10.00
s. Specimen with red overprint: *SPECIMEN.* Series E.	—	25.00

#162-164 replacement notes: Serial # prefixes: *ZX; ZY; ZZ.*

162 50 Pesos Bolivianos   VF UNC

L.1962. Orange on multicolor underprint. Portrait Antonio Jose de Sucre at
right, arms at left. Series A-W7. 22 signature varieties. Back: Puerta del Sol, new
denomination only. Printer: TDLR.

	VF	UNC
a. Issued note.	0.25	1.00
b. Uncut sheet of 4 signed notes. Series L2, Y2.	—	10.00
r. Uncut sheet of 4 unsigned notes. Series AZ.	—	20.00
s1. Specimen with red overprint: *SPECIMEN.* Series F; X; D1.	—	50.00
s2. As s1 but with punched hole cancellation (in left signature area) and TDLR oval stamp. Series C.	—	125
bx. Uncut sheet of 4 notes with signature at top of notes. Series L2; Y2. (error).	—	10.00

163 100 Pesos Bolivianos   VF UNC

L.1962. Red on multicolor underprint. Portrait Simón Bolívar at right, arms at left,
red serial number and security thread at left center. Lower number prefixes (from
B to T9). 19 signature varieties. Back: Engraved, scene of the declaration of the
Bolivian Republic, new denomination only. Printer: TDLR.

	VF	UNC
a. Issued note. Prefix Z2.	0.25	1.00
b. Uncut sheet of 4 signed notes. Series X4; D5; U5.	—	12.50
r. Uncut sheet of 4 unsigned notes. Series AZ.	—	—
s. Specimen with red overprint: *SPECIMEN.* Series G.	—	50.00

164 100 Pesos Bolivianos   VF UNC

L.1962 (1983). Red on multicolor underprint. Portrait Simón Bolívar at right, arms
at left, red serial number and security thread at left center. Lower number prefixes
(from B to T9). 19 signature varieties. Back: Engraved, scene of the declaration of
the Bolivian Republic, new denomination only.

	VF	UNC
a. Back dull red, lithographed with poor detail. Black serial #. without security thread. Prefixes #10E-13D. 2 signature varieties.	0.75	4.00
b. As a. but with solid black security thread.	0.75	5.00
c. As a. but with segmented security thread.	2.00	8.00
r. Unsigned remainder. Prefix #12H		17.50
s. Specimen with red overprint: *SPECIMEN.* Prefix #10E.	—	75.00

164A 100 Pesos Bolivianos   VF UNC

L.1962. Red on multicolor underprint. Portrait Simón Bolívar at right, arms at
left, red serial number and security thread at left center. Higher number prefixes
(13E-19T). 2 signature varieties. Back: Engraved, scene of the declaration of the
Bolivian Republic, new denomination only. Printer: TDLR.   0.25 2.00

1981-84 Various Decrees ND Issue

#165-171 replacement notes: Serial # prefixes: *Z; ZY; ZZ.*

165 500 Pesos Bolivianos   VF UNC

D. 1.6.1981. Deep blue, blue-green and black on multicolor underprint. Arms at
center, portrait Eduardo Avaroa at right. Series A. Back: View of Puerto de Antofagasta, ca. 1879 at center. Watermark: Eduardo Avaroa Printer: ABNC.

	VF	UNC
a. Issued note. 2 signature varieties.	0.25	2.00
r. Remainder without series, decreto or signature printing.	45.00	75.00
s. Specimen with red overprint: *MUESTRA.*	—	75.00

166 500 Pesos Bolivianos   VF UNC

D. 1.6.1981. Deep blue, blue-green and black on multicolor underprint. Arms
at center, portrait Eduardo Avaroa at right. Series B; C. Back: View of Puerto de
Antofagasta, ca. 1879 at center. Watermark: Eduardo Avaroa. Printer: TDLR.

	VF	UNC
a. Issued note.	0.30	1.25
b. Specimen with red overprint: *SPECIMEN.* Series B.	—	50.00

167　1000 Pesos Bolivianos　　　　　　　　　　　　　VF　UNC
D. 25.6.1982. UV: fibers fluoresce red, serial #s and value orange, left design
gren. Back security thread blue. Black on multicolor underprint. Arms at center,
portrait Juana Azurday de Padilla at right. Series A1-Z9; (6 digits) A-L; (8 digits)
each only to 49,999,999. 3 signature varieties. Back: House of Liberty. Watermark:
Juana Azurday de Padilla. Printer: TDLR.
　　a. Issued note.　　　　　　　　　　　　　　　　　　　0.30　1.00
　　s. Specimen with red overprint: *SPECIMEN*. Series A1.　　—　25.00

168　5000 Pesos Bolivianos　　　　　　　　　　　　　VF　UNC
D. 10.2.1984. UV: threads fluorese blue and yellow. Value blue and orange. Back:
security thread and value blue. Deep brown on multicolor underprint. Arms at
center, Marshal J. Ballivian y Segurola at right . Series A. Back: Stylized condor
and leopard. Watermark: Marshal J. Ballivian y Segurola. Printer: BDDK.
　　a. Issued note. signature varieties.　　　　　　　　　1.00　2.00
　　s1. Specimen with red overprint: *MUESTRA SIN VALOR*. Series A.　—　25.00
　　s2. Specimen pin-holed cancelled: *SPECIMEN*.　　　　—　25.00

169　10,000 Pesos Bolivianos　　　　　　　　　　　　VF　UNC
D. 10.2.1984. UV: threads fluoresce blue, red and yellow. Security strip blue;
Value blue, BCB blue. Back: central design wavy stripes yellow. Blackish purple
and purple with dark green arms on multicolor underprint. Arms at center portrait
Marshal Andres de Santa Cruz at right. Series A. Back: Legislative palace at
center. Watermark: Marshal Andres de Santa Cruz. Printer: BDDK.
　　a. Issued note.　　　　　　　　　　　　　　　　　　0.20　0.75
　　s. Specimen with red overprint: *MUESTRA SIN VALOR*. Series A.　—　25.00

170　50,000 Pesos Bolivianos　　　　　　　　　　　　VF　UNC
D. 5.6.1984. UV: central design fluoresces green. Deep green on multicolor
underprint. Arms at left, portrait Gualberto Villarroel Lopez at right. Series A; B.
Back: Petroleum refinery. Printer: TDLR.
　　a. Issued note. 2 signature varieties.　　　　　　　　0.25　1.00
　　s. Specimen with red overprint: *MUESTRA SIN VALOR*. Series A.　—　50.00

171　100,000 Pesos Bolivianos　　　　　　　　　　　VF　UNC
D. 5.6.1984. UV: planchettes fluoresce orange, fibers blue and yellow. Brown-
violet on multicolor underprint. Arms at left, portrait Campesino at right. Series A;
B. Back: Agricultural scene at center right. Printer: TDLR.
　　a. Issued note. 2 signature varieties.　　　　　　　　0.50　2.00
　　s. Specimen with red overprint: *MUESTRA SIN VALOR*. Series A.　—　50.00

1982-86 MONETARY EMERGENCY
Banco Central de Bolivia
Decreto Supremo No. 19078, 28 Julio 1982
Cheque de Gerencia Issue

172　5000 Pesos Bolivianos　　　　　　　　　　　　VF　UNC
D.1982.
　　a. Stub with text attached at right.　　　　　　　　　—　8.00
　　b. Without stub at right.　　　　　　　　　　　　　　—　7.00

173　10,000 Pesos Bolivianos　　　　　　　　　　　VF　UNC
D.1982.
　　a. Stub with text attached at right.　　　　　　　　　—　10.00
　　b. Without stub at right.　　　　　　　　　　　　　　—　9.00
#174 and 175 not assigned.

Santa Cruz
1984 Cheque de Gerencia Issue

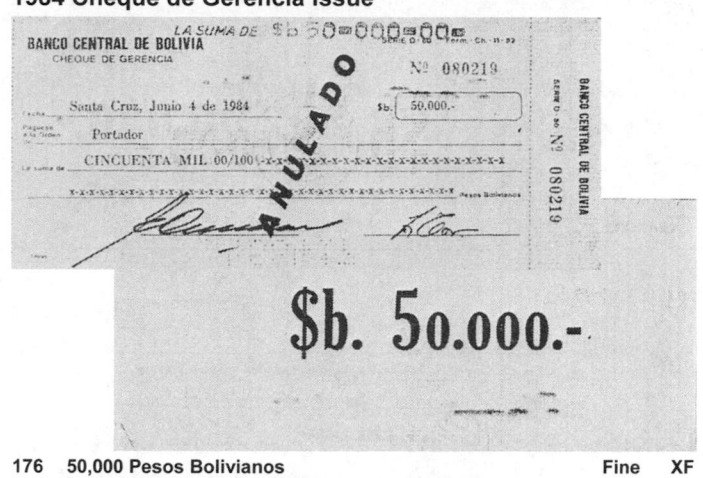

176   50,000 Pesos Bolivianos

	Fine	XF
4.6.1984; 7.6.1984. Black. Mercury in green circular underprint at center.		
a. Issued note.		
b. Overprint: *ANULADO* (cancelled) across face.	90.00	200

#177 not assigned.

178   1,000,000 Pesos Bolivianos

	Fine	XF
4.6.1984; 7.6.1984. Black. Mercury in green circular underprint at center.		
a. Issued note.	—	—
b. Overprint: *ANULADO* (cancelled) across face.	100	250

#179 not assigned.

1984 Cheque de Gerencia Issue

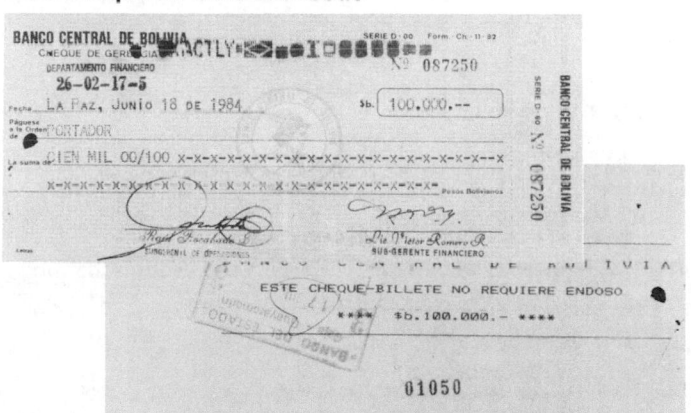

180   100,000 Pesos Bolivianos

	Fine	XF
18.6.1984. Olive-green text on pale green underprint. Mercury in green circular underprint at center. Back: Black text.		
a. Issued note.	—	—
b. Overprint: *ANULADO* across face.	100	210
c. Paid. Punched hole cancelled.	150	275

181   500,000 Pesos Bolivianos

	Fine	XF
4.6.1984; 18.6.1984. Black. Mercury in green circular underprint at center.		
a. Issued note.	—	—
b. Overprint: *ANULADO* across face.	110	225
c. Paid. Punched hole cancelled.	175	300

182   1,000,000 Pesos Bolivianos

	Fine	XF
18.6.1984. Black. Mercury in green circular underprint at center.		
a. Issued note.	—	—
b. Overprint: *ANULADO* across face.	120	240
c. Paid. Punched hole cancelled.	210	425

Decreto Supremo No. 20272, 5 Junio 1984, First Issue

#183-185 Underprint of "B.C.B." and denomination boxes easily fade from pink to light tan to pale yellow.

183   10,000 Pesos Bolivianos

	VF	UNC
D.1984. Brown on pink underprint. Mercury at upper left. Series A. Back: Usable for 90 days after date of issue (Spanish text at lower right). Printer: JBNC.	7.00	20.00

184   20,000 Pesos Bolivianos

	VF	UNC
D.1984. Brown on pink underprint. Mercury at upper left. Series A. Back: Usable for 90 days after date of issue (Spanish text at lower right). Printer: JBNC.	50.00	125

185   50,000 Pesos Bolivianos

	VF	UNC
D.1984. Brown on pink underprint. Mercury at upper left. Series A. Back: Usable for 90 days after date of issue (Spanish text at lower right). Printer: JBNC.	5.00	17.50

Decreto Supremo No. 20272, 5 Junio 1984, Second Issue

186   10,000 Pesos Bolivianos VF UNC
D.1984. Light blue on pink underprint. Mercury at upper left. Series A. Back: 2.50 8.00
Without 90-day use restriction text. Printer: JBNC.

187   20,000 Pesos Bolivianos VF UNC
D.1984. Green on pink underprint. Mercury at upper left. Series A. Back: Without 2.50 8.50
90-day use restriction text. Printer: JBNC.

188   100,000 Pesos Bolivianos VF UNC
21.12.1984. UV: threads fluoresce blue. Reddish brown on light blue and light 0.75 3.00
reddish brown underprint. Series A. Imprint: CdMB. Back: 90 day usage clause at
lower right. Watermark: CdMB.

Decreto Supremo No. 20272, de 5 de Junio de 1984

189   500,000 Pesos Bolivianos VF UNC
D.1984. Deep green on green and peach underprint. Back: Without 90-day 0.75 3.50
clause. Printer: CdMB without imprint.

Decreto Supremo No. 20732, 8 Marzo 1985; First Issue

190   1 Million Pesos Bolivianos VF UNC
D.1985. Blue on yellow and pale blue underprint. Similar to previous issue. Series
A. Back: Without 90-day restriction clause at lower right. Printer: CdMB without
imprint.
   a. Issued note. 1.00 5.50
   s. Specimen perforated: *SPECIMEN*. — —

191   5 Million Pesos Bolivianos VF UNC
D.1985. Brown-orange and red-brown on multicolor underprint. Similar to previous issues but higher quality printing and appearance. Series A. Back: Bank initials in ornate guilloche at center, without 90-day restriction clause. Printer: G&D.
   a. Issued note. 1.50 8.00
   s. Specimen overprint: *SPECIMEN*. — 25.00

192   10 Million Pesos Bolivianos VF UNC
D.1985. Rose, violet and purple on multicolor underprint. Similar to previous
issues but higher quality printing and appearance. Series A. Back: Bank initials in
ornate guilloche at center, without 90-day restriction clause. Printer: G&D.
   a. Issued note. 8.00 20.00
   s1. Specimen. Overprint: *SPECIMEN*. — 35.00
   s2. Specimen. Black overprint: MUESTRA on face. — 35.00

Decreto Supremo No. 20732, 8 Marzo 1985; Second Issue

192A   5 Million Pesos Bolivianos VF UNC
D.1985. Brown-orange and red-brown on multicolor underprint. Similar to 2.00 7.50
previous issues but higher quality printing and appearance. Series B. Back: Bank
initials in ornate guilloche at center, without 90-day restriction clause. Printer:
CdM-Brazil.

192B 10 Million Pesos Bolivianos
D.1985. Rose, violet and purple on multicolor underprint. Similar to previous
issues but higher quality printing and appearance. Series B. Back: Bank initials in
ornate guilloche at center, without 90-day restriction clause. Printer: CdM-Brazil.

VF 3.50 / UNC 10.00

Decreto Supremo No. 20732, 8 Marzo 1985; Third Issue

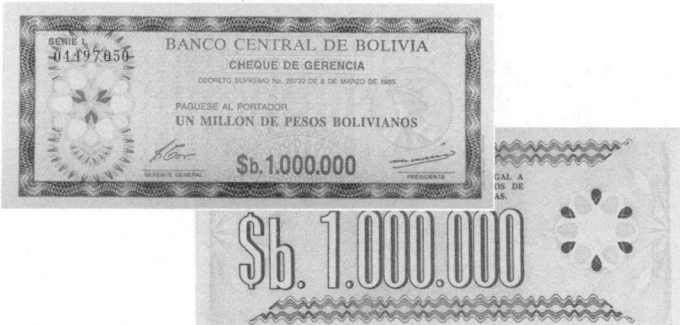

192C 1 Million Pesos Bolivianos
D.1985. Blue and multicolor. Large guilloche at left, Mercury head in underprint at
right. Series left. Printer: CdM-Argentina.

a. Issued note. — 0.75 / 3.25
s. Specimen with black overprint: *MUESTRA*. — 15.00

193 5 Million Pesos Bolivianos
D.1985. Brown with reddish brown text on multicolor underprint. Large guilloche
at left, Mercury head in underprint at right. Series N. Printer: CdM-Argentina.

a. Issued note. — 3.25 / 7.50
s. Specimen. Black overprint: *MUESTRA* on face. — 30.00

194 10 Million Pesos Bolivianos
D.1985. Violet with lilac text on multicolor underprint. large guilloche at left,
Mercury head in underprint at right. Series M. Printer: CdM-Argentina.

a. Issued note. — 4.00 / 20.00
s. Specimen. Black overprint: *MUESTRA*. — 40.00

REPUBLIC, 1986-
Banco Central de Bolivia
1987 ND Provisional Issue

195 1 Centavo on 10,000 Pesos Bolivianos
ND (1987). UV: threads fluoresce blue, red and yellow. Security strip blue; Value
blue, BCB blue. Back: central design wavy stripes yellow. Back: Overprint at right
on back of #169.

VF 0.25 / UNC 1.00

196 5 Centavos on 50,000 Pesos Bolivianos
ND (1987). Back: Overprint at right on back of #170.

VF 0.50 / UNC 2.25

196A 10 Centavos on 100,000 Pesos Bolivianos
ND (1987). Back: Overprint at right on back of #171.

VF 1.50 / UNC 7.00

197 10 Centavos on 100,000 Pesos Bolivianos
ND (1987). Back: Overprint at right on back of #188.

VF 0.50 / UNC 3.00

198 50 Centavos on 500,000 Pesos Bolivianos
ND (1987). Back: Overprint at right on back of #189.

VF 0.75 / UNC 3.25

199 1 Boliviano on 1,000,000 Pesos Bolivianos
ND (1987). Back: Overprint at right on back of #192C.

	VF	UNC
	0.50	2.50

200 5 Bolivianos on 5,000,000 Pesos Bolivianos
ND (1987). Back: Overprint at left on back of #192A.

	VF	UNC
a. Issued note.	1.25	6.00
x1. Error. Inverted overprint on left end.	6.00	15.00
x2. Error. Overprint on right end.	—	—

Note: Several varieties of "errors" have been reported and all should be looked upon as suspect.

201 10 Bolivianos on 10,000,000 Pesos Bolivianos
ND (1987), Back: Overprint at left on back of #192B.

	VF	UNC
	4.00	20.00

Ley 901 de 28.11.1986;1987-2001 ND Issues

#202-208 Series A signature titles: *PRESIDENTE BCB* and *MINISTRO DE FINANZAS.* Serial # suffix *A*. Series B signature titles: *PRESIDENTE DEL B.C.B.* and *GERENTE GENERAL B.C.B.* Serial # suffix *B*. Series E signature titles: *PRESIDENTE BCB* and *GERENTE GENERAL BCB.* Serial # suffix *E*.

202 2 Bolivianos
L.1986. (1987; 1990). Black on multicolor underprint. Antonio Vaca Diez at right, arms at lower center. Back: Trees and buildings at center. Watermark: Simón Bolívar. Printer: F-CO.

	VF	UNC
a. Series A (1987). With control #.	FV	3.50
b. Series B. (1990). With control #.	FV	4.00
s. As a. Specimen with red overprint: *ESPECIMEN*.	—	25.00

203 5 Bolivianos
L.1986. (1987; 1990; 1998). Olive-green on multicolor underprint. Adela Zamudio at right, arms at lower left. Back: Religious shrine at left center. Watermark: Simón Bolívar. Printer: F-CO.

	VF	UNC
a. Series A (1987). With control #.	FV	6.00
b. Series B (1990). With control #.	FV	6.50
c. Series E (1998). Without control #.	FV	4.00
s. As a. Specimen with red overprint: *ESPECIMEN*.	—	25.00

204 10 Bolivianos
L.1986. (1987-97). Blue-black on multicolor underprint. Cecilio Guzman de Rojas at right, arms at lower left. Back: Figures overlooking city view. Watermark: Simón Bolívar. Printer: F-CO.

	VF	UNC
a. Series A (1987). With control #.	FV	9.50
b. Series B (1990). With control #.	FV	12.50
c. Series E (1997). Without control #.	FV	5.00
s. As a. Specimen with red overprint: *ESPECIMEN*.	—	50.00

205 20 Bolivianos
L.1986. (1987; 1990; 1997). Orange on multicolor underprint. Pantaleon Dalence at right, arms at lower center. Back: Building at center. Watermark: Simón Bolívar. Printer: F-CO.

	VF	UNC
a. Series A (1987). With control #.	FV	20.00
b. Series B (1990). With control #.	FV	25.00
c. Series E (1997). Without control #.	FV	8.50
s. As a. Specimen with red overprint: *ESPECIMEN*.	—	75.00

206 50 Bolivianos
L.1986 (1987; 1997). Purple on multicolor underprint. Melchor Perez de Holguin at right, arms at lower center. Back: Tall building at center. Watermark: Simón Bolívar. Printer: F-CO.

	VF	UNC
a. Series A (1987). With control #.	FV	50.00
b. Series E (1997). Without control #.	FV	17.50
s. As a. Specimen with red overprint: *ESPECIMEN*.	—	100

207 100 Bolivianos

L.1986 (1987; 1997). Red-violet and orange on multicolor underprint. Gabriel Rene Moreno at right, arms at lower right. Back: University building at center. Watermark: Simón Bolívar. Printer: F-CO.

		VF	UNC
a.	Watermark: Simon Bolívar.	FV	110
b.	Series E (1997). Without control #. Watermark: Gabriel Reno Morono.	FV	35.00
s.	As a. Specimen with red overprint: *ESPECIMEN*.	—	150

208 200 Bolivianos

L.1986 (1987; 1997). Brown and dark brown on multicolor underprint. Franz Tamayo at right, arms at lower center. Back: Ancient statuary. Watermark: Simón Bolívar. Printer: F-CO.

		VF	UNC
a.	Serles A (1987). With control #.	FV	225
b.	Series E (1997). Without control #. Watermark: F. Tamayo.	FV	60.00
s.	As a. Specimen with red overprint: *ESPECIMEN*.	—	200

Ley 901 de 28.11.1986; 1993 ND Issue

209 5 Bolivianos

	VF	UNC
	FV	17.50

L.1986 (1993). Olive-green on multicolor underprint. Adela Zamudio at right, arms at lower left. Series C. Signature titles: *PRESIDENTE BCB* and *GERENTE GENERAL BCB*. Serial number suffix C. Back: Religious shrine at left center. Watermark: Simón Bolívar. Printer: FNMT.

210 10 Bolivianos

	VF	UNC
	FV	6.50

l.1986(1993). Blue-black on multicolor underprint. Cecilio Guzman de Rojas at right, arms at lower left. Series C. Serial number suffix C. Signature titles: *PRESIDENTE BCB* and *GERENTE GENERAL BCB*. Back: Figures overlooking city view. Watermark: Simón Bolívar. Printer: FNMT.

211 20 Bolivianos

	VF	UNC
	FV	10.00

L.1986(1993). Orange on multicolor underprint. Pantaleon Dalence at right, arms at lower center. Series C. Serial number suffix C. Signature titles: *PRESIDENTE BCB* and *GERENTE GENERAL BCB*. Back: Building at center. Watermark: Simón Bolívar. Printer: FNMT.

212 50 Bolivianos

	VF	UNC
	FV	22.50

L.1986(1993). Purple on multicolor underprint. Melchor Perez de Holguin at right, arms at lower center. Series C. Serial number suffix C. Signature titles: *PRESIDENTE BCB* and *GERENTE GENERAL BCB*. Back: Tall buiding at center. Watermark: Simón Bolívar. Printer: FNMT.

213 100 Bolivianos

	VF	UNC
	FV	45.00

L.1986(1993). Red and ornage on multicolor underprint. Gabriel Rene Moreno at right, arms at lower right. Series C. Serial number suffix C. Signature titles: *PRESIDENTE BCB* and *GERENTE GENERAL BCB*. Back: University building at center. Printer: FNMT.

214 **200 Bolivianos**
L.1986(1993). Brown and dark brown on multicolor underprint. Franz Tamayo at right, arms at lower center. Series C. Serial number suffix C. Signature titles: *PRESIDENTE BCB* and *GERENTE GENERAL BCB*. Back: Ancient statuary. Printer: FNMT.

	VF	UNC
	FV	90.00

Ley 901 de 28.11.1986; 1995 ND Interim Issue

215 **5 Bolivianos**
L.1986 (1995). Olive-green on multicolor underprint. Adela Zamudio at right, arms at lower left. Series C. Signature titles: *PRESIDENTE BCB* and *GERENTE GENERAL BCB*. Serial number suffix C. Back: Religious shrine at left center. Watermark: Simón Bolívar. Printer: TDLR.

	VF	UNC
a. Issued note.	FV	6.00
s. Specimen with red overprint: *MUESTRA SIN VALOR*.	—	25.00

216 **10 Bolivianos**
L.1986 (1995). Blue-black on multicolor underprint. Cecilio Guzman de Rojas at right, arms at lower left.Series C. Serial number suffix C.Signature titles: *PRESIDENTE BCB* and *GERENTE GENERAL BCB*. Back: Figures overlooking city view. Watermark: Simón Bolívar. Printer: TDLR. 140x69mm.

	VF	UNC
a. Issued note.	FV	12.00
s. Specimen with red overprint: *MUESTRA SIN VALOR*.	—	25.00

Ley 901 de 28.11.1986; 1995-96 ND Issue

217 **5 Bolivianos**
L.1986(1995). Olive-green on multicolor underprint. Adela Zamudio at right, arms at lower left. Series D. Signature titles: *PRESIDENTE BCB* and *GERENTE GENERAL BCB*. Back: Religious shrine at left center. Watermark: Simón Bolívar. Printer: TDLR. 140x69mm.

	VF	UNC
	FV	3.50

218 **10 Bolivianos**
L.1986(1995). Blue-black on multicolor underprint. Cecilio Guzman de Rojas at right, arms at lower left. Series D. Signature titles: *PRESIDENTE BCB* and *GERENTE GENERAL BCB*. Back: Figures overlooking city view. Watermark: Simón Bolívar. Printer: TDLR. 140x69mm.

	VF	UNC
	FV	5.00

219 **20 Bolivianos**
L.1986(1995). Orange on multicolor underprint. Pantaleon Dalence at right, arms at lower left. Series D. Signature titles: *PRESIDENTE BCB* and *GERENTE GENERAL BCB*. Back: Building at center. Watermark: Simón Bolívar. Printer: TDLR. 140x69mm.

	VF	UNC
	FV	9.00

220 **50 Bolivianos**
L.1986(1995). Purple on multicolor underprint. Melchor Perez de Holguin at right, arms at lower left. Series D. Signature titles: *PRESIDENTE BCB* and *GERENTE GENERAL BCB*. Back: Tall building at center. Watermark: Simón Bolívar. Printer: TDLR. 140x69mm.

	VF	UNC
a. Issued note.	FV	20.00
s. Specimen with red overprint: *MUESTRA SIN VALOR*.	—	50.00

221 **100 Bolivianos**
L.1986(1996). Red and orange on multicolor underprint. Gabriel Rene Moreno at right, arms at lower left. Series D. Signature titles: *PRESIDENTE BCB* and *GERENTE GENERAL BCB*. Back: University building at center. Watermark: Gabriel Rene Moreno. Printer: TDLR.

	VF	UNC
	FV	35.00

222 **200 Bolivianos**
L.1986(1996). Brown and dark brown on multicolor underprint. Franz Tamayo at right, arms at lower lef. Series D. Signature titles: *PRESIDENTE BCB* and *GERENTE GENERAL BCB*. Back: Ancient statuary. Watermark: Franz Tamayo.

	VF	UNC
	FV	65.00

Note: For Series E, see #203a-208a.

Ley 901 de 28.11.1986; 2001 ND Issue

229 20 Bolivianos
VF UNC
L.1986 (2005). With value in numerals vertically. Orange and brown-orange on
multicolor underprint. Pantaleon Dalence at right, arms at lower left. Series G.
Signature titles: *PRESIDENTE BCB* and *GERENTE GENERAL BCB*. Raised
marks for the blind and narrow clear text security thread. Back: Building at center.
Watermark: Pantaleon Dalence. Printer: F-CO.
FV 7.00

223 10 Bolivianos
VF UNC
L.1986 (2001). Blue-black on multicolor underprint. Cecilio Guzman de Rojas
at right, arms at lower left. Series F. Signature titles: *PRESIDENTE BCB* and
GERENTE GENERAL BCB. Raised marks for the blind and narrow clear text
security thread Back: Figures overlooking city view. Watermark: Simón Bolívar.
Printer: F-CO. 140x69mm.
FV 4.00

224 20 Bolivianos
VF UNC
L.1986 (2001). Orange and brown-orange on multicolor underprint. Pantaleon
Dalence at right, arms at lower left. Series F. Signature titles: *PRESIDENTE BCB*
and *GERENTE GENERAL BCB*. Raised marks for the blind and narrow clear
text security thread. Back: Building at center. Watermark: Simón Bolívar. Printer:
F-CO.
FV 7.00

225 50 Bolivianos
VF UNC
L.1986 (2001). Purple on multicolor underprint. Melchor Perez de Holguin at right,
arms at lower left. Series F. Signature titles: *PRESIDENTE BCB* and *GERENTE
GENERAL BCB*. Raised marks for the blind and narrow clear text security threa
Back: Tall building at center. Watermark: Simón Bolívar. Printer: F-CO.
FV 15.00

230 50 Bolivianos
VF UNC
L.1986(2005). With value in numerals vertically. Purple on multicolor underprint.
Melchor Perez de Holguin at right, arms at lower left. Series G. Signature titles:
PRESIDENTE BCB and *GERENTE GENERAL BCB*. Raised marks for the blind
and wide clear text security thread. Back: Tall building at center. Watermark:
Melchor Perez de Holguin. Printer: F-CO.
FV 15.00

226 100 Bolivianos
VF UNC
L.1986 (2001). Like 207b; Series E (1997). Red-violet and orange on multicolor
underprint. Gabriel Rene Moreno at right, arms at lower left. Series F. Signature
titles: *PRESIDENTE BCB* and *GERENTE GENERAL BCB*. Raised marks for the
blind and narrow clear text security thread. Back: University building at center.
Watermark: Gabriel Rene Moreno. Printer: F-CO.
FV 30.00

227 200 Bolivianos
VF UNC
L.1986 (2001). Like 208b; Series E (1997). Brown and dark brown on multicolor
underprint. Franz Tamayo at right, arms at lower left. Series F. Signature titles:
PRESIDENTE BCB and *GERENTE GENERAL BCB*. Raised marks for the blind
and narrow clear text security thre Back: Ancient statuary. Watermark: Franz
Tamayo. Printer: F-CO.
FV 60.00

Ley 901 de 28.11.1986; 2005 ND Issue

228 10 Bolivianos
VF UNC
L.1986 (2005). With value in numerals vertically. Blue-black on multicolor under-
print. Cecilio Guzman de Rojas at right, arms at lower left. Series G. Signature
titles: *PRESIDENTE BCB* and *GERENTE GENERAL BCB*. Raised marks for the
blind. Back: Figures overlooking city view. Watermark: Cecilio Guzman de Rojas.
Printer: F-CO.
FV 4.00

231 100 Bolivianos
VF UNC
L.1986(2005). With value in numerals vertically. Red-violet and orange on
multicolor underprint. Gabriel Rene Moreno at right, arms at lower left. Series
G. Signature titles: *PRESIDENTE BCB* and *GERENTE GENERAL BCB*. Raised
marks for the blind and wide clear text security thread. Back: University building at
center. Watermark: Gabriel Rene Moreno. Printer: F-CO.
FV 30.00

232 200 Bolivianos
VF UNC
L.1986 (2005). With value in numerals vertically. Brown and dark brown on mul-
ticolor underprint. Franz Tomayo at right, arms at lower left. Series G. Signature
titles: *PRESIDENTE BCB* and *GERENTE GENERAL BCB*. Raised marks for
the blind and wide clear text security thread. Back: Ancient statuary. Watermark:
Franz Tomayo. Printer: F-CO.
FV 60.00

Ley 901 de 28.11.1986; 2007 ND Issue

233 10 Bolivianos
VF UNC
ND (2007). Blue-black on multicolor underprint. Cecilio Guzman de Rojas at right,
arms at lower left. Series H. Back: Figures overlooking city view Watermark:
Cecilio Guzman de Rojas Printer: F-CO.
FV 4.00

234 20 Bolivianos
VF UNC
ND (2007). Orange and brown-orange on multicolor underprint. Pantaleon
Dalence at right, arms a lower left. Series H. Back: Building at center. Watermark:
Pantaleon Dalence. Printer: F-CO.
FV 7.00

235 50 Bolivianos
VF UNC
ND (2007). Purple on multicolor underprint. Melchor Perez de Holguin at right,
arms at lower left. Series H. Back: Tall building at center. Watermark: Melchor
Perez de Holguin. Printer: F-CO.
FV 15.00

236 100 Bolivianos
VF UNC
ND (2007). Red-violet and orange on multicolor underprint. Gabriel Rene Moreno
at right, arms at lower left. Series H. Back: University building at center. Water-
mark: Gabriel Rene Moreno. Printer: F-CO.
FV 30.00

237 200 Bolivianos
VF UNC
ND (2007). Brown and dark brown on multicolor underprint. Franz Tomayo at right,
arms at lower left. Series H. Back: Ancient statuary. Watermark: Franz Tomayo.
Printer: F-CO.
FV 60.00

BOSNIA - HERZEGOVINA

The Republic of Bosnia-Herzegovina borders Croatia to the north and west, Serbia to the east and Montenegro in the southeast with only 12.4 miles of coastline. The total land area is 51,209 sq. km. It has a population of 4.59 million. Capital: Sarajevo. Electricity, mining and agriculture are leading industries.

Bosnia and Herzegovina's declaration of sovereignty in October 1991 was followed by a declaration of independence from the former Yugoslavia on 3 March 1992 after a referendum boycotted by ethnic Serbs. The Bosnian Serbs - supported by neighboring Serbia and Montenegro - responded with armed resistance aimed at partitioning the republic along ethnic lines and joining Serb-held areas to form a "Greater Serbia." In March 1994, Bosniaks and Croats reduced the number of warring factions from three to two by signing an agreement creating a joint Bosniak/Croat Federation of Bosnia and Herzegovina. On 21 November 1995, in Dayton, Ohio, the warring parties initialed a peace agreement that brought to a halt three years of interethnic civil strife (the final agreement was signed in Paris on 14 December 1995). The Dayton Peace Accords retained Bosnia and Herzegovina's international boundaries and created a joint multi-ethnic and democratic government charged with conducting foreign, diplomatic, and fiscal policy. Also recognized was a second tier of government comprised of two entities roughly equal in size: the Bosniak/Croat Federation of Bosnia and Herzegovina and the Bosnian Serb-led Republika Srpska (RS). The Federation and RS governments were charged with overseeing most government functions. The Office of the High Representative (OHR) was established to oversee the implementation of the civilian aspects of the agreement. In 1995-96, a NATO-led international peacekeeping force (IFOR) of 60,000 troops served in Bosnia to implement and monitor the military aspects of the agreement. IFOR was succeeded by a smaller, NATO-led Stabilization Force (SFOR) whose mission was to deter renewed hostilities. European Union peacekeeping troops (EUFOR) replaced SFOR in December 2004; their mission is to maintain peace and stability throughout the country. EUFOR's mission changed from peacekeeping to civil policing in October 2007, with its presence reduced from nearly 7,000 to 2,500 troops.

MONETARY SYSTEM:
1 Dinar = 100 Para 1992-1998
1 Convertible Marka = 1 Deutschemark
1 Convertible Marka = 100 Convertible Pfeniga, 1998-

REPUBLIKA BOSNA I HERCEGOVINA

Moslem Republic

НАРОДНА БАНКА БОСНЕ И ХНРЦЕГОВИНЕ

NARODNA BANKA BOSNE I HERCEGOVINE
Bank was transformed into the Central Bank of Bosnia and Herzegovina on August 11, 1997.

W/o Branch

1992 First Provisional Issue

1	**500 Dinara**	**Fine**	**XF**
	ND (1992). 27mm or 31mm handstamp on Yugoslavia #109. Violet handstamp: NARODNA BANKA BOLNE I HERCEGOVINE, also in Cyrillic around Yugoslav arms, on Yugoslav regular issues. Handstamp varieties exist.		
	a. Handstamp without numeral.	30.00	100
	b. Handstamp with numeral: 1.	30.00	100
	c. Handstamp with numeral: 2.	30.00	100
	d. Handstamp: Tuzla.	30.00	100

2	**1000 Dinara**	**Fine**	**XF**
	ND (1992). 48mm handstamp on Yugoslavia #110. Violet handstamp: NARODNA BANKA BOLNE I HERCEGOVINE, also in Cyrillic around Yugoslav arms, on Yugoslav regular issues. Handstamp varieties exist. 165x80mm.		
	a. Handstamp without numeral.	25.00	125
	b. Handstamp with numeral 1.	25.00	125
	c. Handstamp with numeral 2.	25.00	125
	d. Handstamp: Tuzla.	25.00	125

#3 and 4 not assigned.

1992 Second Provisional Novcani Bon Issue

#6-9 issued in various Central Bosnian cities. Example without indication of city of issue are remainders.

6	**100 Dinara**	**Fine**	**XF**
	1992. Deep pink on gray and yellow underprint. Peace dove at upper left center.		
	a. Handstamped: BREZA on back.	25.00	100
	b. Circular red handstamp: FOJNICA on back.	10.00	50.00
	c. Rectangular purple handstamp on face, circular purple hand-stamp: KRESEVO on back.	20.00	80.00
	d. Handstamped: TESANJ on back.	20.00	80.00
	e. Handstamped: VARES on back.	35.00	110
	f1. Handstamped: VISOKO 31mm on back.	6.00	30.00
	f2. Handstamped: VISOKO 20mm on back.	10.00	55.00
	g. Circular red overprint: ZENICA, 11.5.1992. on back right with printed signature at either side.	3.00	9.00
	h. Rectangular handstamp: OSNOVA ZAJEDNICA on face. Circular hand-stamp: BOS. PETROVAC on back.	3.00	10.00
	i. Large circular purple handstamp: SARAJEVO and 16.6.1993 on back.	3.00	10.00
	r. Remainder, without handstamp or overprint.	3.00	10.00

7	**500 Dinara**	**Fine**	**XF**
	1992. Pale greenish-gray and yellow underprint. Peace dove at upper left center.		
	a. Handstamped: BREZA on back.	17.50	70.00
	b. Circular red handstamp: FOJNICA on back.	17.50	70.00
	c. ZRectangular purple handstamp on face. Handstamped: KRESEVO on back.	45.00	120
	d. Handstamped: TESANJ on back.	7.50	35.00
	e. Handstamped: VARES on back.	17.50	70.00
	f1. Circular 31mm red handstamp: VISOKO on back.	12.50	40.00
	f2. Circular 20mm red handstamp: VISOKO on back.	12.50	40.00
	g. Circular red handstamp on back: ZENICA (small or large), 11.5.1992. Printed signature at either side.	2.00	7.00
	h. Rectangular handstamp: OSNOVA ZAJEDNICA on face. Circular hand-stamp: BOS. PETROVAC on back.	12.50	40.00
	i. Circular large purple handstamp: SARAJEVO and 16.6.1993 on back.	12.50	40.00
	r. Remainder without handstamp or overprint.	2.00	7.00

8	**1000 Dinara**	**Fine**	**XF**
	1992. Blue on gray underprint. Peace dove at upper left center.		
	a. Handstamped: BREZA on back.	15.00	65.00
	b. Handstamped: FOJNICA on back.	15.00	65.00
	c. Rectangular purple handstamp on face. Circular purple handstamp: KRESEVO on back.	30.00	90.00
	d. Handstamped: TESANJ on back.	20.00	75.00
	e. Handstamped: VARES on back.	20.00	75.00
	f1. Handstamped: VISOKO 31mm on back.	9.00	35.00
	f2. Handstamped: VISOKO 20mm on back.	30.00	100
	g. Circular handstamp: ZENICA on face, no date on stamping.	25.00	75.00
	h. Circular red overprint on back: ZENICA, 11.5.1992. Pinted signature at either side.	2.00	10.00
	i. Rectangular handstamp: OSNOVA ZAJEDNICA on front. Circular hand-stamp: BOS. PETROVAC on back.	20.00	75.00
	j. Circular large purple handstamp: SARAJEVO and 16.6.1993 on back.	20.00	75.00
	r. Remainder without handstamp or overprint.	2.00	10.00

9   5000 Dinara

		Fine	XF
1992. Dull brown on gray and yellow underprint. Peace dove at upper left center.			
a.	Handstamped: *BREZA* on back.	10.00	35.00
b.	Circular red handstamp: *FOJNICA* on back.	8.00	30.00
c.	Handstamped: *KRESEVO* on back.	50.00	125
d.	Handstamped: *TESANJ* on back.	85.00	350
e.	Handstamped: *VARES* on back.	20.00	75.00
f1.	Handstamped: *VISOKO* 31mm on back.	30.00	90.00
f2.	Handstamped: *VISOKO* 20mm on back.	10.00	35.00
g.	Circular red handstamp: *ZENICA* and 11.5.1992 with printed signature at each side on back.	22.50	65.00
h.	Rectangular handstamp: *OSNOVA ZAJEDNICA* on front. Circular handstamp *BOS. PETROVAC* on back	2.00	7.50
i.	Circular large purple handstamp: *SARAJEVO* and 16.6.1993 on back.	10.00	35.00
r.	Remainder, without handstamp or overprint	5.00	20.00

1992-93 Issues

10   10 Dinara   VF   UNC

1.7.1992. Purple on pink underprint. Guilloche at left center, serial number varieties. Back: Mostar stone arch bridge at right. Watermark: Repeated diamonds. Printer: Cetis (Celje, Slovenia). 145x73mm.

a. Issued note.	0.25	1.00
s. Specimen.	—	30.00

11   25 Dinara   VF   UNC

1.7.1992. Blue-black on light blue underprint. Guilloche at left center, serial number varieties. Back: Crowned arms at center right. Watermark: Repeated diamonds. Printer: Cetis (Celje, Slovenia). 145x73mm.

a. Issued note.	0.20	1.25
s. Specimen.	—	30.00

12   50 Dinara   VF   UNC

1.7.1992. Blue-black on red-violet underprint. Guilloche at left center, serial number varieties. Back: Mostar stone arch bridge at right. Watermark: Repeated diamonds. Printer: Cetis (Celje, Slovenia). 145x73mm.

a. Issued note.	0.50	1.50
s. Specimen.	—	30.00

13   100 Dinara   VF   UNC

1.7.1992. Dull black on olive-green underprint. Guilloche at left center, serial number varieties. Back: Crowned arms at center right. Watermark: Repeated diamonds. Printer: Cetis (Celje, Slovenia). 145x73mm.

a. Issued note.	0.50	1.75
s. Specimen.	—	30.00

14   500 Dinara   VF   UNC

1.7.1992. Dull violet-brown on pink and ochre underprint. Guilloche at left center, serial number varieties. Back: Crowned arms at center right. Watermark: Repeated diamonds. Printer: Cetis (Celje, Slovenia). 145x73mm.

a. Issued note.	0.75	3.50
s. Specimen.	—	30.00

15   1000 Dinara   VF   UNC

1.7.1992. Deep purple on light green and lilac underprint. Guilloche at left center, serial number varieties. Back: Mostar stone arch bridge at right. Watermark: Repeated diamonds. Printer: Cetis (Celje, Slovenia). 145x73mm.

a. Issued note.	1.00	4.50
s. Specimen.	—	30.00

16   5000 Dinara   **VF   UNC**

25.1.1993. Pale olive-green on yellow-orange underprint. Guilloche at left center,
serial number varieties. Back: Grayish blue shield with fleur-de-lis at center right.
Printer: Printed in Zenica. 110x61mm.

    a. Issued note.   3.00   7.50
    b. With overprint: *SDK..ZENICA* on back as a handstamp or machine printing.   5.00   15.00
    s. Specimen.   —   10.00

17   10,000 Dinara   **VF   UNC**

25.1.1993. Brown on pink underprint. Guilloche at left center, serial number
varieties. Back: Grayish blue shield with fleur-de-lis at center right. Printer: Printed
in Zenica. 110x61mm.

    a. Issued note.   3.50   8.50
    b. With overprint: *SDK..ZENICA* on back as a handstamp or machine printing.   5.00   15.00
    s. Specimen.   —   10.00

1992-94 Bon Issue

**#21-33 Issued during the seige of Sarajevo. Grayish green or yellow unpt. on
back.**

21   10 Dinara   **VF   UNC**

1.8.1992. Violet. Back: Shield at left.

    a. Issued note.   6.00   35.00
    s. Specimen.   —   30.00

22   20 Dinara   **VF   UNC**

1.8.1992. Blue-violet. Back: Shield at left.

    a. Issued note.   5.00   30.00
    s. Specimen.   —   30.00

23   50 Dinara   **VF   UNC**

1.8.1992. Pink. Back: Shield at left.

    a. Issued note.   6.00   35.00
    s. Specimen.   —   30.00

24   100 Dinara   **VF   UNC**

1.8.1992. Green. Back: Shield at left.

    a. Issued note.   25.00   125
    s. Specimen.   —   30.00

25   500 Dinara   **VF   UNC**

1.8.1992. Orange. Back: Shied at left.

    a. Issued note.   8.00   40.00
    s. Specimen.   —   30.00

26   1000 Dinara   **VF   UNC**

1.8.1992. Brown. Back: Shield at left.

    a. Issued note.   6.00   35.00
    s. Specimen.   —   30.00

27   5000 Dinara   **VF   UNC**

1.8.1992. Violet. Back: Shield at left.

    a. Issued note.   6.00   35.00
    s. Specimen.   —   30.00

28   10,000 Dinara   **VF   UNC**

6.4.1993. Light blue. Back: Shield at left.

    a. Issued note.   6.00   35.00
    s. Specimen.   —   30.00

29   50,000 Dinara   **VF   UNC**

1.5.1993. Pink. Back: Shield at left.

    a. Issued note.   10.00   40.00
    s. Specimen.   —   30.00

30 100,000 Dinara VF UNC

1.8.1993. Green on multicolor underprint. Back: Shield at left text below.
a. Issued note. 5.00 30.00
s. Specimen. — 25.00

31 100,000 Dinara VF UNC

1.8.1993. Green. Back: Shield at left, value below.
a. Issued note. 5.00 30.00
s. Specimen. — 30.00

32 500,000 Dinara VF UNC

1.1.1994. Brown. Back: Shield at left.
a. Issued note. 5.00 25.00
s. Specimen. — 30.00

33 1,000,000 Dinara VF UNC

1.1.1994. Red. Back: Shield at left.
a. Issued note. 5.00 25.00
s. Specimen. — 30.00

1993 Novcani Bon Emergency Issue

34 100,000 Dinara VF UNC

1993 (-old date 1.7.1992). Rectangular crenalated framed overprint: *NOVCANI BON 100,000...* Back: Mostar stone arch bridge at right.
a. Purple overprint. 1.9.1993. 7.50 17.50
b. Blue overprint and signature overprint. 10.11.1993. 7.50 17.50

35 1,000,000 Dinara VF UNC

10.11.1993 (old date-1.7.1992).
a. Purple overprint. 1.9.1993. 8.00 20.00
b. Blue overprint and signature overprint. 10.11.1993. 3.50 9.00
c. Blue-violet overprint (not issued). — —

36 10,000,000 Dinara VF UNC

10.11.1993 (old date-1.7.1992). Blue-violet overprint on #12. (Not issued) 4.00 12.50

37 100,000,000 Dinara VF UNC

10.11.1993 (old date-1.7.1992).
a. Blue-violet overprint on #13. (Not issued) 4.00 12.50
b1. As a. but without overprint 100000000 at lower right on front. — —

1994 Issue

Currency Reform, 1994 1 New Dinar = 10,000 Old Dinara

39 1 Dinar VF UNC

15.8.1994. Purplish gray on red-violet and pale green underprint. Back: Shield at center right. Watermark: Block design. Printer: DD "Dom Stampe" Zenica.
a. Issued note. 0.15 0.75
s. Specimen. — —

40	**5 Dinara**		**VF**	**UNC**

15.8.1994. Purplish gray on lilac, red and orange underprint. Back: Mostar bridge at center rightl Watermark: Block design. Printer: DD "Dom Stampe" Zenica.

a. Issued note. — 0.15 0.75
s. Specimen. — —

41	**10 Dinara**		**VF**	**UNC**

15.8.1994. Pruple on red, orange and red-violet underprint. Back: Shield at center right. Watermark: Block design. Printer: DD "Dom Stampe" Zenica.

a. Issued note. — 0.25 1.00
s. Specimen. — —

42	**20 Dinara**		**VF**	**UNC**

15.8.1994. Brown on violet, red and yellow underprint. Back: Mostar stone bridge at center right. Watermark: Block design. Printer: DD "Dom Stampe" Zenica.

a. Issued note. — 0.50 1.50
s. Specimen. — —

43	**50 Dinara**		**VF**	**UNC**

15.8.1994. Purplish gray on red-violet and pale purple underprint. Back: Shield at center right. Watermark: Block design. Printer: DD "Dom Stampe" Zenica.

a. Issued note. — 0.50 2.00
s. Specimen. — —

44	**100 Dinara**		**VF**	**UNC**

15.8.1994. Dull black on aqua, yellow and olive-green underprint. Back: Mostar stone bridge at center right. Watermark: Block design. Printer: DD "Dom Stampe" Zenica.

a. Issued note. — 0.50 2.25
s. Specimen. — —

45	**500 Dinara**		**VF**	**UNC**

15.8.1994. Dull brown on lilac and yellow underprint. Back: Shield at center right. Watermark: Block design. Printer: DD "Dom Stampe" Zenica.

a. Large #'s. — 1.50 6.00
b. Small #'s. — 1.50 6.00
s. Specimen. — —

46	**1000 Dinara**		**VF**	**UNC**

15.8.1994. Blue-gray on gray-green, red-violet and light green underprint. Back: Mostar stone bridge at center right. Watermark: Block design. Printer: DD "Dom Stampe" Zenica.

a. Large #'s. — 4.50 12.50
b. Small #'s. — 4.50 12.50
s. Specimen. — —

1995 ND Issue

#47-47C Printed in London but unable to be delivered.

47	**50 Dinara**		**VF**	**UNC**

ND (1995). Purple on pink and ochre underprint. Back: Bridge at right. Watermark: Lis. — 6.00 20.00

47A	**100 Dinara**		**VF**	**UNC**

ND (1995). (Not issued). Back: Bridge at right.

47B	**500 Dinara**		**VF**	**UNC**

ND (1995). (Not issued). Back: Bridge at right. — —

47C	**1000 Dinara**		**VF**	**UNC**

ND (1995). (Not issued). Back: Bridge at right. — —

1992 ND Novcani Bon Issue

48	**200 Dinara**		**VF**	**UNC**

ND (1992). Orange. Plain design with value at center. Back: Plain design with value at center, handstamp at right.

a. Handstamped: *TRAVNIK*. 10.00 40.00
b. Handstamped: *NOVI TRAVNIK*. 20.00 80.00
c. Handstamped: *VITEZ*. 35.00 110
r. Remainder without handstamp. 10.00 40.00

49	**500 Dinara**		**VF**	**UNC**

ND (1992). Brown. Plain design with value at center. Back: Plain design with value at center, handstamp at right.

a. Handstamped: *TRAVNIK*. 15.00 55.00
b. Handstamped: *NOVI TRAVNIK*. 30.00 95.00
c. Handstamped: *VITEZ*. 45.00 120
r. Remainder without handstamp. 15.00 55.00

50   1000 Dinara

		VF	UNC
ND (1992). Lilac. Plain design with value at center. Back: Plain design with value at center, handstamp at right.			
a. Handstamped: *TRAVNIK*.		8.00	30.00
b. Handstamped: *NOVI TRAVNIK*.		18.00	70.00
c. Handstamped: *VITEZ*.		25.00	95.00
r. Remainder without handstamp.		8.00	30.00

 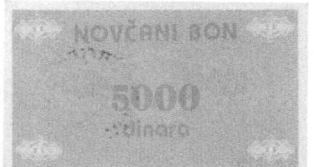

51   5000 Dinara

		VF	UNC
ND (1992). Light blue. Plain design with value at center. Back: Plain design with value at center.			
a. Handstamped: *TRAVNIK*.		70.00	500
b. Handstamped: *NOVI TRAVNIK*. Rare.		—	—
c. Handstamped: *VITEZ*. Rare.		—	—
r. Remainder without handstamp.		30.00	80.00

52   10,000 Dinara

		VF	UNC
ND (1992). Red on blue underprint. Plain design with value at center. Back: Plain design with value at center, handstamp at right.			
a. Handstamped: *TRAVNIK*.		15.00	45.00
b. Handstamped: *NOVI TRAVNIK*		25.00	95.00
c. Handstamped: *VITEZ*.		35.00	110
r. Remainder without handstamp.		15.00	45.00

52A   20,000 Dinara

		VF	UNC
ND (1992). Red on underprint.			
a. Handstamped: *TRAVNIK*.		70.00	300
b. Handstamped: *NOVI TRAVINK*.		100	600
c. Handstamped: *VITEZ*.		120	700
r. Remainder wihtout handstamp.		35.00	70.00

1993 Emergency Issue

#53-56 like #10-13 w/additional 3 solid zeroes printed after large value on face w/Travnik Branch dated handstamp.

53   10,000 Dinara

		VF	UNC
1993. Red on yellow underprint. Guilloche at left center 145x73mm., 3 additional solid zeroes printed after large value. Handstamp. Back: Mostar stone arch bridge at right. Watermark: Repeated diamonds. Printer: Cetis (Celje, Slovenia).			
a. 15.10.1993. Short green zeroes. Travnik.		2.50	7.50
b. 15.10.1993. Short red zeroes. Travnik.		2.50	7.50
c. 24.12.1993. Tall green zeroes. Travnik.		2.50	7.50
d. 24.12.1993. Tall red zeroes. Travnik.		2.50	7.50
e. 15.10.1993. Short green zeroes. Sarajevo.		2.50	7.50
f. 15.10.1993. Short red zeros. Sarajevo.		2.50	7.50
g. 24.12.1993. Tall green zeroes. Sarajevo.		2.50	7.50
h. 24.12.1993. Tall red zeroes. Sarajevo.		2.50	7.50

54   25,000 Dinara

		VF	UNC
1993. Green on blue underprint. Guilloche at left center 145x73mm., 3 additional solid zeroes printed after large value. Handstamp. Back: Crowned arms at center right. Watermark: Repeated diamonds. Printer: Cetis (Celje, Slovenia).			
a. 15.10.1993. Short green zeroes. Travnik.		2.50	7.50
b. 15.10.1993. Short red zeroes. Travnik.		2.50	7.50
c. 24.12.1993. Tall green zeroes. Travnik.		2.50	7.50
d. 24.12.1993. Tall red zeroes. Travnik.		2.50	7.50
e. 15.10.1993. Short green zeroes. Sarajevo.		2.50	7.50
f. 15.10.1993. Short red zeroes. Sarajevo.		2.50	7.50
g. 24.12.1993. Tall green zeroes. Sarajevo.		2.50	7.50
h. 24.12.1993. Tall red zeroes. Sarajevo.		2.50	7.50

55   50,000 Dinara

		VF	UNC
1993. Red. Guilloche at left center 145x73mm., 3 additional solid zeroes printed after large value. Handstamp. Back: Mostar stone arch bridge at right. Watermark: Repeated diamonds. Printer: Cetis (Celje, Slovenia).			
a. 15.10.1993. Short green zeroes. Travnik.		2.50	7.50
b. 15.10.1993. Short red zeroes. Travnik.		2.50	7.50
c. 24.12.1993. Tall green zeroes. Travnik.		2.50	7.50
d. 24.12.1993. Tall red zeroes. Travnik.		2.50	7.50
e. 15.10.1993. Short green zeroes. Sarajevo.		2.50	7.50
f. 15.10.1993. Short red zeroes. Sarajevo.		2.50	7.50
g. 24.12.1993. Tall green zeroes. Sarajevo.		2.50	7.50
h. 24.12.1993. Tall red zeroes. Sarajevo.		2.50	7.50

56   100,000 Dinara

		VF	UNC
1993. Green. Guilloche at left center 145x73mm., 3 additional solid zeroes printed after large value. Handstamp. Back: Crowned arms at center right. Watermark: Repeated diamonds. Printer: Cetis (Celje, Slovenia).			
a. 15.10.1993. Short green zeroes. Travnik.		2.50	7.50
b. 15.10.1993. Short red zeroes. Travnik.		2.50	7.50
c. 24.12.1993. Tall green zeroes. Travnik.		2.50	7.50

	VF	UNC
d. 24.12.1993. Tall red zeroes. Travnik.	2.50	7.50
e. 15.10.1993. Short green zeroes. Sarajevo.	2.50	7.50
f. 15.10.1993. Short red zeroes. Sarajevo.	2.50	7.50
g. 21.10.1993. Tall green zeroes. Sarajevo.	2.50	7.50
h. 21.10.1993. Tall red zeroes. Sarajevo.	2.50	7.50
i. 24.12.1993. Tall green zeroes. Sarajevo.	2.50	7.50
j. 24.12.1993. Tall red zeroes. Sarajevo.	2.50	7.50
k. 24.8.1993. Short green zeroes. Donji Vakuf.	2.50	7.50
l. 15.10.1993. Short red zeroes. Donji Vakuf.	2.50	7.50

ЦЕНТРАЛНА БАНКА БОСНЕ И ХНРЦНгОВИНЕ

CENTRALNA BANKA BOSNE I HERCEGOVINE

Established in Sarajevo on Aug. 11, 1997.

1998 ND Issue

57   50 Convertible Pfeniga   VF   UNC

ND (1998). Alternating texts of bank name and denominations. Dark blue on blue
and lilac underprint. Portrait S. Kulenovic at right. Back: *Stecak Zgosca* fragment
at left center. Watermark: Central Bank monogram repeated vertically. Printer:
F-CO (without imprint).

    a. Issued note.   FV   0.75
    s. Specimen. Red overprint: SPECIMEN on face and perforated UZORAK.   —   30.00

58   50 Convertible Pfeniga   VF   UNC

ND (1998). Alternating texts of bank name and denominations. Dark blue on
blue and lilac underprint. Portrait B. Copic at right. Back: Open book, cabin at left
center. Watermark: Central Bank monogram repeated vertically. Printer: F-CO
(without imprint).

    a. Issued note.   FV   0.75
    s. Specimen. Red overprint: SPECIMEN on face and perforated UZORAK.   —   30.00

59   1 Convertible Marka   VF   UNC

ND (1998). Alternating texts of bank name and denominations. Dark green
on green and yellow-green underprint. I. F. Jukic at right. Back: *Stecak Stolac*
fragment at left center. Watermark: Central Bank monogram repeated vertically.
Printer: F-CO (without imprint).

    a. Issued note.   FV   1.50
    s. Specimen. Red overprint: SPECIMEN on face and perforated UZORAK.   —   30.00

60   1 Convertible Marka   VF   UNC

ND (1998). Alternating texts of bank name and denominations. Dark green on
green and yellow-green underprint. I. Andric at right. Back: Bridge at left center.
Watermark: Central Bank monogram repeated vertically. Printer: F-CO (without
imprint).

    a. As prepared. Not issued. Some examples were stolen from stock and have   —   —
       been offered at about 80-100 dollars.
    s. Specimen. Red overprint: SPECIMEN on face and perforated UZORAK.   —   30.00

61   5 Convertible Maraka   VF   UNC

ND (1998). Alternating texts of bank name and denominations. Violet on multicolor
underprint. M. Selimovic at right. Back: Trees at left center. English letters in bank
name as top line Watermark: Central Bank monogram repeated vertically. Printer:
F-CO (without imprint). 123x62mm.

    a. Issued note.   FV   7.50
    s. Specimen. Red overprint: SPECIMEN on face and perforated UZORAK.   —   30.00

62   5 Convertible Maraka   VF   UNC

ND (1998). Alternating texts of bank name and denominations. Violet on multicolor
underprint. M. Selimovic at right. Back: Trees at left center. Cyrillic bank name and
denomination as top line. Watermark: Central Bank monogram repeated vertically.
Printer: F-CO (without imprint). 123x62mm.

    a. Issued note.   FV   7.50
    s. Specimen. Red overprint: SPECIMEN on face and perforated UZORAK.   —   30.00

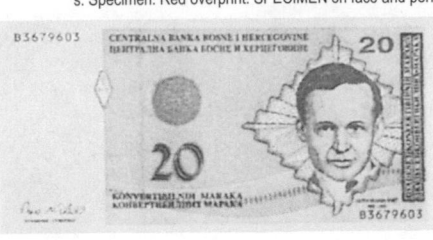

63   10 Convertible Maraka   VF   UNC

ND (1998). Alternating texts of bank name and denominations. Orange-brown
on dull purple and orange-brown underprint. M. M. Dizdar at right. Back: *Stecak
Radimlja* fragment at left center. Watermark: Central Bank monogram repeated
vertically. Printer: F-CO (without imprint). 130x65mm.

    a. Issued note.   FV   12.50
    s. Specimen. Red overprint: SPECIMEN on face and perforated UZORAK.   —   30.00

64   10 Convertible Maraka   VF   UNC

ND (1998). Alternating texts of bank name and denominations. Orange-brown on
dull purple and orange-brown underprint. A. Santic at right. Back: Loaf of bread at
left center. Watermark: Central Bank monogram repeated vertically. Printer: F-CO
(without imprint). 130x65mm.

    a. Issued note.   FV   12.50
    s. Specimen. Red overprint: SPECIMEN on face and perforated UZORAK.   —   30.00

65   20 Convertible Maraka VF UNC

ND (1998). Alternating texts of bank name and denominations. Dark brown on multicolor underprint. A. B. Simic at right. Back: *Stecak Radimilja* fragment at left center, variable optical device at upper left center. Watermark: Central Bank monogram repeated vertically. Printer: F-CO (without imprint). 138x68mm.

    a. Issued note.   FV   20.00

    s1. Specimen. Red overprint: SPECIMEN. All zero serial #.   —   75.00

    s2. Specimen. Red overprint: SPECIMEN on face and perforated UZORAK.   —   30.00

66   20 Convertible Maraka VF UNC

ND (1998). Alternating texts of bank name and denominations. Dark brown on multicolor underprint. F. Visjic at right. Back: Gusle" musical instrument at left center, variable optical device at upper left center. Watermark: Central Bank monogram repeated vertically. Printer: F-CO (without imprint). 138x68mm.

    a. Issued note.   FV   20.00

    s1. Specimen. Red overprint: SPECIMEN. All zero serial #.   —   75.00

    s2. Specimen. Red overprint: SPECIMEN on face and perforated UZORAK.   —   30.00

67   50 Convertible Maraka VF UNC

ND (1998); 2002. Alternating texts of bank name and denominations. Purple on lilac and multicolor underprint. M. C. Catic at right. Back: Stone relief at left center, variable optical device at upper left center. Watermark: Central Bank monogram repeated vertically. Printer: F-CO (without imprint). 146x71mm.

    a. ND (1998).   FV   60.00

    b. 2002. Windowed security thread.   FV   55.00

    s1. Specimen. Red overprint: SPECIMEN. All zero serial #.   —   75.00

    s2. Specimen. As a. Regular serial #. Red overprint: SPECIMEN on face and perforated UZORAK.   —   30.00

    s3. Specimen. As b. Regular serial #. Red overprint: SPECIMEN on face and perforated UZORAK.   —   30.00

68   50 Convertible Maraka VF UNC

ND (1998); 2002. Alternating texts of bank name and denominations. Purple on lilac and multicolor underprint. I. Ducic at right. Back: Pen, glasses and book at left center, variable optical device at upper left center. Watermark: Central Bank monogram repeated vertically. Printer: F-CO (without imprint). 146x71mm.

    a. ND (1998).   FV   120

    b. 2002.   FV   100

    s1. Specimen. As a. Red overprint: SPECIMEN. Zero serial #.   —   75.00

    s2. Specimen. As a. Regular serial #. Red overprint: SPECIMEN on face and perforated UZORAK.   —   30.00

    s3. Specimen. As b. Regular serial #. Red overprint: SPECIMEN on face and perforated UZORAK.   —   30.00

69   100 Convertible Maraka VF UNC

ND (1998); 2002. Alternating texts of bank name and denominations. Dark brown on yellow and multicolor underprint. N. Sop at right. Back: "Stecak Sgosca" fragment at left center, variable optical device at upper left center. Watermark: Central Bank monogram repeated vertically. Printer: F-CO (without imprint). 154x74mm.

    a. NS (1998).   FV   100

    b. 2002.   FV   100

    s1. Specimen. Red overprint: SPECIMEN. All zero serial #.   —   75.00

    s2. Specimen. As a. Regular serial #. Red overprint: SPECIMEN on face and perforated UZORAK.   —   30.00

    s3. Specimen. As b. Regular serial #. Red overprint: SPECIMEN on face and perforated UZORAK.   —   —

70   100 Convertible Maraka VF UNC

ND (1998); 2002. Alternating texts of bank name and denominations. Dark brown on yellow and multicolor underprint. P. Kocic at right. Back: Pen, glasses and book at left center, variable optical device at upper left center. Watermark: Central Bank monogram repeated vertically. Printer: F-CO (without imprint). 154x74mm.

    a. ND (1998).   FV   100

    b. 2002.   FV   85.00

    s1. Specimen. Zero serpial #.   —   —

    s2. Specimen. As a. Regular serial #. Red overprint: SPECIMEN on face and perforated UZORAK.   —   30.00

    s3. Specimen. As b. Regular serial #. Red overprint: SPECIMEN on face and perforated UZORAK.   —   30.00

71 200 Convertible Maraka | | VF | UNC
ND (2002). Blue. 156x76mm.
a. Issued note. | | FV | 165
s. Specimen. Red overprint: SPECIMEN on both sides. | | — | 200

2008 ND Issue

72 10 Convertible Maraka | | VF | UNC
2008.
a. Issued note. | | FV | 12.50
s. Specimen. | | — | —

73 10 Convertible Maraka | | VF | UNC
2008.
a. Issued note. | | FV | 12.50
s. Specimen. | | — | —

74 20 Convertible Maraka | | VF | UNC
2008.
a. Issued note. | | FV | 20.00
s. Specimen. | | FV | 75.00

75 20 Convertible Maraka | | VF | UNC
2008.
a. Issued note. | | FV | 20.00
s. Specimen. | | — | 75.00

76 50 Convertible Maraka | | VF | UNC
2007; 2008, 2009. Purple on Lilac and multicolor underprint. M. C. Catic at right. Windowed security thread. Back: Stone relief at left center. 146x71mm.
a. 2007. | | FV | 75.00
b. 2008. | | FV | 55.00
c. 2009. | | FV | 55.00
s. Specimen. | | — | —

77 50 Convertible Maraka | | VF | UNC
2007; 2008; 2009.
a. 2007. | | FV | 75.00
b. 2008. | | FV | 55.00
c. 2009. | | FV | 55.00
s. Specimen. | | — | —

78 100 Convertible Maraka | | VF | UNC
2007; 2008. Dark brown on yellow and multicolor underprint. P. Kocic at right. Window security thread. Back: Pen, glass and book at left center. 154x74mm.
a. 2007. | | FV | 150
b. 2008. | | FV | 100
s. Specimen. | | — | —

79 100 Convertible Maraka | | VF | UNC
2007; 2008.
a. 2007. | | FV | 150
b. 2008. | | FV | 100
s. Specimen. | | — | —

2012 Issue

80 10 Convertible Maraka | | VF | UNC
2012. M.M. Dizar at right.
a. Issued note. | | FV | 12.50
s. Specimen. | | — | 50.00

81 10 Convertible Maraka | | VF | UNC
2012. A. Santic at right.
a. Issued note. | | FV | 12.50
s. Specimen. | | — | 50.00

82 20 Convertible Maraka | | VF | UNC
2012. A.B. Simic at right.
a. Issued note. | | FV | 20.00
s. Specimen. | | — | 50.00

83 20 Convertible Maraka | | VF | UNC
2012. F. Visjic at right.
a. Issued note. | | FV | 20.00
s. Specimen. | | — | 50.00

84 50 Convertible Maraka | | VF | UNC
2012. M.C. Catric at right. Wide segmented security thread.
a1. Issued note. | | FV | 50.00
s. Specimen. | | — | 50.00

85 50 Convertible Maraka | | VF | UNC
2012. I. Ducic at right. Wide segmented security thread.
a. Issued note. | | FV | 50.00
s. Specimen. | | — | 50.00

86 100 Convertible Maraka | | VF | UNC
2012. N. Sop at right. Wide segmented security thread.
a. Issued note. | | FV | 100
s. Specimen. | | — | 50.00

87 100 Convertible Maraka | | VF | UNC
2012. P. Kocic at right. Wide segmented security thread.
a. Issued note. | | FV | 130
s. Specimen. | | FV | 50.00

SRPSKA (SERBIAN) REPUBLIC

НАРОДНА БАНКА СРПСКЕ РЕПУБЛИКЕ БОСНЕ И ХЕРЦЕГОВИНЕ

NARODNA BANKA SRPSKE REPUBLIKE BOSNE I HERCEGOVINE
Ceased operations in August 1997.

1992-93 Banja Luka Issue

133 10 Dinara | | VF | UNC
1992. Deep brown or orange and silver underprint. Arms at left, numerals in heart-shaped design below guilloche at center right. Back: Curved artistic design at left center, arms at right. Watermark: Portrait of a young girl. 139x66mm.
a. Issued note. | | 0.50 | 1.50
s. Specimen. | | — | 5.00

134 50 Dinara | | VF | UNC
1992. Deep olive-gray on ochre and multicolor underprint. Arms at left, numerals in heart-shaped design below guilloche at center right. Back: Curved artistic design at left center, arms at right. Watermark: Portrait of a young girl. 139x66mm.
a. Issued note. | | 0.50 | 1.50
s. Specimen. | | — | 5.00

135   100 Dinara   VF   UNC
1992. Dark blue on lilac and silver underprint. Arms at left, numerals in heart-
shaped design below guilloche at center right. Back: Curved artistic design at left
center, arms at right. Watermark: Portrait of a young girl. 139x66mm.
    a. Issued note.   1.00   3.00
    s. Specimen.   —   5.00

136   500 Dinara   VF   UNC
1992. Dark blue on pink and multicolor underprint. Arms at left, numerals in heart-
shaped design below guilloche at center right. Back: Curved artistic design at left
center, arms at right. Watermark: Portrait of a young boy. 147x70mm.
    a. Issued note.   1.50   4.50
    s. Specimen.   —   5.00

137   1000 Dinara   VF   UNC
1992. Slate gray on peach and tan underprint. Arms at left, numerals in heart-
shaped design below guilloche at center right. Back: Curved artistic design at left
center, arms at right. Watermark: Portrait of a young boy. 147x70mm.
    a. Issued note.   1.25   3.75
    s. Specimen.   —   5.00

138   5000 Dinara   VF   UNC
1992. Violet on lilac and light blue underprint. Arms at left, numerals in heart-
shaped design below guilloche at center right. Back: Curved artistic design at left
center, arms at right. Watermark: Portrait of a young boy. 147x70mm.
    a. Issued note.   2.50   10.00
    s. Specimen.   —   5.00

139   10,000 Dinara   VF   UNC
1992. Gray on tan and light blue underprint. Arms at left, numerals in heart-
shaped design below guilloche at center right. Back: Curved artistic design at left
center, arms at right. Watermark: Portrait of a young boy. 147x70mm.
    a. Issued note.   2.50   10.00
    s. Specimen.   —   5.00

140   50,000 Dinara   VF   UNC
1993. Brown on olive-green and multicolor underprint. Arms at left, numerals in
heart-shaped design below guilloches at center right. Back: Curved artistic design
at left center, arms at right. Watermark: Portrait of a young boy. 147x70mm.
    a. Issued note.   8.00   30.00
    s. Specimen.   —   7.50

Note: For similar notes to #136-140 but differing only in text at top, signature, and Knin as place of
issue, see Croatia-Regional listings in the *Standard Catalog of World Paper Money, Specialized Issues* volume.

141   100,000 Dinara   VF   UNC
1993. Purple on brown and multicolor underprint. Arms at left, numerals in heart-
shaped design below guilloche at center right. Back: Curved artistic design at left
center, arms at right. Watermark: Portrait of a young woman with head covering.
151x73mm.
    a. Issued note.   1.50   4.00
    s. Specimen.   —   7.50

142   1 Million Dinara   VF   UNC
1993. Deep purple on pink, yellow and multicolor underprint. Arms at left, numerals in heart-shaped design below guilloche at center right. Watermark: Portrait of
a young girl. 139x66mm.
    a. Issued note.   8.00   40.00
    s. Specimen.   —   7.50

143   5 Million Dinara   VF   UNC
1993. Dark brown on light blue and yellow-orange underprint. Arms at left, numerals in heart-shaped design below guilloche at contor right. Back: Curved artistic
design at left center, arms at right. Watermark: Portrait of a young girl. 139x66mm.
    a. Issued note.   1.00   3.00
    s. Specimen.   —   7.50

144   10 Million Dinara   VF   UNC
1993. Dark blue-violet on loive-green and yellow-orange underprint. Arms at left,
numerals in heart-shaped design below guilloche at center right. Back: Curved
artistic design at left center, arms at right. Watermark: Portrait of a young girl.
139x66mm.
    a. Issued note.   1.50   4.50
    s. Specimen.   —   7.50

НАРОДНА БАНКА РНПУБЛИКЕ СРПСКЕ
Narodna Banka Republike Srpske
National Bank of the Serbian Republic
1993 Banja Luka First Issue

145   50 Million Dinara   VF   UNC
1993. Dark brown on pink and gray underprint. Arms at left, numerals in heart-
shaped design below guilloche at center right. Back: Curved artistic desing at left
center, arms at right. 139x66mm.
    a. Issued note.   2.50   7.50
    s. Specimen.   —   5.00

146   100 Million Dinara

	VF	UNC
1993. Pale blue-gray on light blue and gray underprint. Arms at left, numerals in heart-shaped design below guilloche at center right. Back: Curved artistic design at left center, arms at right. 139x66mm.

	VF	UNC
a. Issued note.	1.50	4.00
s. Specimen.	—	5.00

147   1 Milliard Dinara

1993. Orange on pale blue and light orange underprint. Arms at left, numerals in heart-shaped design below guilloche at center right. Back: Curved artistic design at left center, arms at right. 139x66mm.

	VF	UNC
a. Issued note.	1.50	5.00
s. Specimen.	—	5.00

148   10 Milliard Dinara

1993. Black on pink and pale orange underprint. Arms at left, numerals in heart-shaped design below guilloche at center right. Back: Curved artistc design at left center, arms at right. 139x66mm.

	VF	UNC
a. Issued note.	1.50	5.00
s. Specimen.	—	5.00

1993 Banja Luka Second Issue

1,000,000 old dinars = 1 new Dinar.

149   5000 Dinara

	VF	UNC
1993. Red-violet and purple on pale blue-gray underprint. Petar Kocic, novelist, at left. Back: Serbian arms at center right. Watermark: Greek design repeated. 139x66mm.

	VF	UNC
a. Issued note.	1.00	3.00
s. Specimen.	—	7.50

150   50,000 Dinara

	VF	UNC
1993. Brown and dull red on ochre underprint. Petar Kocic, novelist, at left. Back: Serbian arms at center right. Watermark: Greek design repeated. 139x66mm.

	VF	UNC
a. Issued note.	1.00	3.00
s. Specimen.	—	7.50

151   100,000 Dinara

	VF	UNC
1993. Violet and blue-gray on pink underprint. Petar Kocic, novelist, at left. Back: Serbian arms at center right. Watermark: Greek design repeated. 139x66mm.

	VF	UNC
a. Issued note.	1.00	3.00
s. Specimen. Red overprint SPECIMEN on both sides.	—	15.00

152   1,000,000 Dinara

	VF	UNC
1993. Black and blue-gray on pale purple underprint. P. Kocic at left. Back: Serbian arms at center right. Watermark: Greek design repeated.

	VF	UNC
a. Issued note.	1.50	5.00
s. Specimen.	—	7.50

153   5,000,000 Dinara

	VF	UNC
1993. Orange and gray-blue on pale orange underprint. P. Kocic at left. Back: Serbian arms at center right. Watermark: Greek design repeated.

	VF	UNC
a. Issued note.	1.50	5.00
s. Specimen.	—	7.50

154 100,000,000 Dinara **VF UNC**
1993. Dull grayish green and pale olive-brown on light blue underprint. P. Kocic at left. Back: Serbian arms at center right. Watermark: Greek design repeated.
    a. Issued note. 1.50 5.00
    s. Specimen. — 7.50

155 500,000,000 Dinara **VF UNC**
1993. Brown-violet and grayish green on pale olive-brown underprint. P. Kocic at left. Back: Serbian arms at center right. Watermark: Greek design repeated.
    a. Issued note. 1.50 5.00
    s. Specimen. — 7.50

156 10,000,000,000 Dinara **VF UNC**
1993. Blue and red.
    a. As prepared. Not issued. — 100
    s. Specimen. — 50.00

157 50,000,000,000 Dinara **VF UNC**
1993. Brown.
    a. As prepared. Not issued. — 100
    s. Specimen. — 50.00

158 10,000,000 Dinara **VF UNC**
1993. Overprint on #133.
    a. As prepared. Black overprint. Not issued. — 100

159 50,000,000 Dinara **VF UNC**
1993. Overprint on #134.
    a. As prepared. Dark purple overprint. Not issued. — 100
    b. As prepared. Dark green overprint. Not issued. — 100

160 100,000,000 Dinara **VF UNC**
1993. Overprint on #135.
    a. As prepared. Black overprint. Not issued — 100

BOTSWANA

The Republic of Botswana, located in south central Africa between Namibia and Zimbabwe has an area of 600,370 sq. km. and a population of 1.84 million. Capital: Gaborone. The economy is primarily pastoral with a rapidly developing mining industry, of which diamonds, copper and nickel are the chief elements. Meat products and diamonds comprise 85 percent of the exports.

Formerly the British protectorate of Bechuanaland, Botswana adopted its new name upon independence in 1966. Four decades of uninterrupted civilian leadership, progressive social policies, and significant capital investment have created one of the most dynamic economies in Africa. Mineral extraction, principally diamond mining, dominates economic activity, though tourism is a growing sector due to the country's conservation practices and extensive nature preserves.

MONETARY SYSTEM:
1 Pula (Rand) = 100 Thebe (Cents)

	MINISTER OF FINANCE	GOVERNOR
1	Sir Q.K.J. Masire	Q. Hermans
2	Sir Q.K.J. Masire	B.C. Leavitt
3	P.S. Mmusi	F.G. Mogae
4	P.S. Mmusi	C. Kilonoyogo
5	P.S. Mmusi	Q. Hermans
6a	F.G. Mogae	Q. Hermans
6b	F.G. Mogae	Q. Hermans
7a	P.H.K. Kedikilwe	B. Gaolatihe
7b	P.H.K. Kedikilwe	B. Gaolatihe
8a	B. Gaolatihe	Mrs. L.K. Mohohlo
8b	B. Gaolatihe	Mrs. L.K. Mohohlo

REPUBLIC

Bank of Botswana

1976-79 ND Issue

#1-5 For specimen notes with a maltese cross serial # prefix see the CS1 listing at the end of the country.

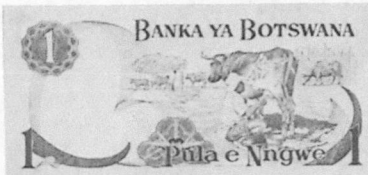

1 Pula

1   1 Pula   VF   UNC

ND (1976). Brown on multicolor underprint. Sir Seretse Khana at left, bird at center, arms at upper right. Back: Farmer milking cow at center right. Watermark: Rearing Zebra. Printer: TDLR.

  a. Issued note.   2.50   12.00
  s. Specimen. Overprint: SPECIMEN on both sides. Punch hole cancelled.   —   95.00
    Serial # prefix: A/1.

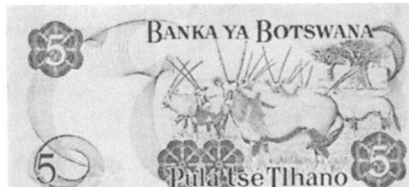

2   2 Pula   VF   UNC

ND (1976). Blue on multicolor underprint. Sir Seretse Khana at left, bird at center, arms at upper right. Back: Various workers at center right. Watermark: Rearing Zebra. Printer: TDLR.

  a. Issued note.   6.00   25.00
  s. Specimen. Overprint: SPECIMEN on both sides. Punch hole cancelled.   —   95.00
    Serial # prefix: B/1.

3   5 Pula   VF   UNC

ND (1976). Purple on multicolor underprint. Sir Seretse Khana at left, bird at center, arms at upper right. Back: Gemsbok antelope at center right. Watermark: Rearing Zebra. Printer: TDLR.

  a. Issued note.   12.00   50.00
  s. Specimen. Overprint: SPECIMEN on both sides. Punch hole cancelled.   —   90.00
    Serial # prefix: C/1.

4   10 Pula   VF   UNC

ND (1976). Green on multicolor underprint. Sir Seretse Khana at left, bird at center, arms at upper right. Back: Large building at center right. Watermark: Rearing Zebra. Printer: TDLR.

  a. Signature 1.   30.00   180
  b. Signature 2.   45.00   300
  s1. As a. Specimen. Overprint: SPECIMEN on both sides. Punch hole cancelled. Serial # prefix: D/1.   —   95.00
  s2. As b. Specimen. Overprint: SPECIMEN on both sides. Punch hole cancelled. Serial # prefix: D/4.   —   95.00

5   20 Pula   VF   UNC

ND (1979). Red, pruple and brown on multicolor underprint. Sir Seretse Khana at left, bird at center, arms at upper right. Back: Mining conveyors at center right. Watermark: Rearing Zebra. Printer: TDLR.

  a. Signature 1.   50.00   300
  b. Signature 2.   55.00   400
  s1. As a. Specimen. Overprint: SPECIMEN on both sides. Punch hole cancelled. Serial # prefix: E/1.   —   95.00
  s2. As b. Specimen. Overprint: SPECIMEN on both sides. Punch hole cancelled. Serial # prefix: E/2.   —   95.00

1982-83 ND Issue

6   1 Pula   VF   UNC

ND (1983). Dark brown. President Q. K. J. Masire at left wearing coarsely striped pinstripe suit. Signature 4. Back: Cattle, arms and plants. Printer: TDLR.

  a. Issued note.   1.00   5.00
  s. Specimen. Red overprint: SPECIMEN on both sides. Punch hole cancelled. Serial # prefix: A/1.   —   70.00

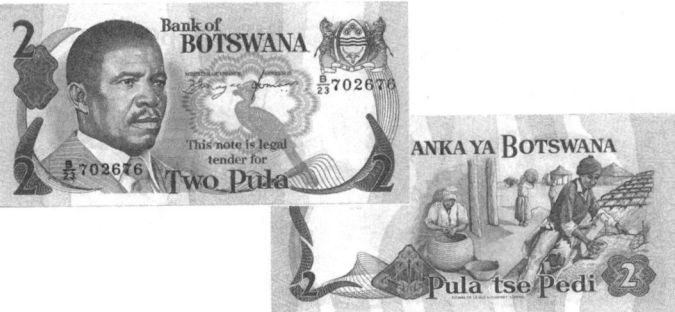

7   2 Pula   VF   UNC

ND (1982). Blue on multicolor. President Q. K. J. Masire at left wearing coarsely striped pinstripe suit, Grey Lourie at center, arms at upper right. Back: Various workers at center right. Watermark: Rearing Zebra. Printer: TDLR.

  a. Signature 3.   2.50   16.00
  b. Signature 4.   1.00   8.50
  c. Signature 5.   5.00   20.00
  d. Signature 6a.   1.00   7.00
  s1. As a. Specimen. Red overprint: SPECIMEN on both sides. Punch hole cancelled. Serial # prefix B/6.   —   70.00
  s2. As b. Specimen. Red overprint: SPECIMEN on both sides. Punch hole cancelled. Serial # prefix B/7.   —   70.00
  s3. As c. Specimen. Red overprint: SPECIMEN on both sides. Punch hole cancelled. Serial # prefix B/16.   —   70.00
  s4. As d. Specimen. Red overprint: SPECIMEN on both sides. Punch hole cancelled. Serial # prefix B/21.   —   70.00

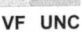

8 5 Pula

ND (1982). Deep violet on multicolor underprint. President Q. K. J. Masire at left wearing coarsely striped pinstripe suit, Helmeted guinea fowl at center, arms at upper right. Back: Gemsbok antelope at center right. Watermark: Rearing Zebra. Printer: TDLR.

		VF	UNC
a.	Signature 3.	5.00	35.00
b.	Signature 4.	5.00	35.00
c.	Signature 5.	3.00	18.00
s1.	As a. Specimen. Red overprint: SPECIMEN on both sides. Punch hole cancelled. Serial # prefix C/5.	—	70.00
s2.	As b. Specimen. Red overprint: SPECIMEN on both sides. Punch hole cancelled. Serial # prefix C/6.	—	70.00
s3.	As c. Specimen. Red overprint: SPECIMEN on both sides. Punch hole cancelled. Serial # prefix C/10.	—	70.00

9 10 Pula

ND (1982). Green on multicolor underprint. President Q. K. J. Masire at left wearing coarsely striped pinstripe suit, crowned hornbill at center, arms at upper right. Back: Large building at center right. Watermark: Rearing Zebra. Printer: TDLR.

		VF	UNC
a.	Signature 3.	10.00	50.00
b.	Signature 4.	8.00	35.00
c.	Signature 5.	8.00	40.00
d.	Signature 6a.	8.00	35.00
s1.	As a. Specimen. Red overprint: SPECIMEN on both sides. Punch hole cancelled. Serial # prefix: D/7.		70.00
s2.	As b. Specimen. Red overprint: SPECIMEN on both sides. Punch hole cancelled. Serial # prefix: D/12.	—	70.00
s3.	As c. Specimen. Red overprint: SPECIMEN on both sides. Punch hole cancelled. Serial # prefix: D/21.	—	70.00
s4.	As d. Specimen. Red overprint: SPECIMEN on both sides. Punch hole cancelled.	—	70.00

10 20 Pula

ND (1982). Red, purple and brown on multicolor underprint. President Q. K. J. Masire at left wearing coarsely striped pinstripe suit, Ostrich at center, arms at upper right. Back: Mining conveyors at center right. Watermark: Rearing Zebra. Printer: TDLR.

		VF	UNC
a.	Signature 3.	17.50	70.00
b.	Signature 4.	17.50	70.00
c.	Signature 5.	17.50	70.00
d.	Signature 6a.	17.50	70.00
s1.	As a. Specimen. Red overprint: SPECIMEN on both sides. Punch hole cancelled. Serial # prefix: E/2.	—	70.00
s2.	As b. Specimen. Red overprint: SPECIMEN on both sides. Punch hole cancelled. Serial # prefix: E/5.	—	70.00
s3.	As c. Specimen. Red overprint: SPECIMEN on both sides. Punch hole cancelled. Serial # prefix: E/9.	—	70.00
s4.	As d. Specimen. Red overprint: SPECIMEN on both sides. Punch hole cancelled. Serial # prefix: E/13.	—	70.00

1992-95 ND Issue

11 5 Pula

ND (1992). Deep violet on multicolor underprint. President Q. K. J. Masire at left wearing pinstripe suit, helmeted guinea fowl at center, arms at upper right. Signature 6a. Back: Gemsbok antelope at center right. Watermark: Rearing Zebra. Printer: Harrison.

		VF	UNC
a.	Issued note.	3.00	10.00
s.	C/18, C/19, C/27.	—	125

12 10 Pula

ND (1992). Green on multicolor underprint. President Q. K. J. Masire at left wearing pinstripe suit, crowned hornbill at center, arms at upper right. Signature 6a. Back: Large building at center right. Watermark: Rearing Zebra. Printer: Harrison.

		VF	UNC
a.	Issued note.	5.00	20.00
s.	Specimen. Serial # prefix: D/45, D/46.	—	135

13 20 Pula

ND (1993). Red, purple and brown on multicolor underprint. President Q. K. J. Masire at left wearing pinstripe suit, Ostrich at center, arms at upper right. Signature 6a. Watermark: Rearing Zebra. Printer: Harrison.

		VF	UNC
a.	Issued note.	8.00	25.00
s.	Specimen. Serial # prefix: E/21, E/29.	—	150

14 50 Pula   VF   UNC

ND (ca. 1992). Dark brown and dark green on multicolor underprint. President Q. K. J. Masire at left wearing pinstripe suit, Malachite Kingfisher at center, arms at upper right. Signature 6b. Back: Man in canoe and African fish eagle at center right. Watermark: Rearing Zebra. Printer: Fidelity Printers (Zimbabwe - Harare), without imp

     a. Issued note.   20.00   80.00
     s1. Specimen. Serial # *F000000A*.   —   60.00
     s2. Specimen. Serial # *F000000A*. Punch-hole cancelled.   —   60.00

#15 has is now #19

16 100 Pula   VF   UNC

ND (1993). Blue-violet and ochre on multicolor underprint. President Q. K. J. Masire at left wearing pinstripe suit, diamond and fish eagle at center, arms at upper right Back: Worker sorting rough diamonds at center right. Watermark: Rearing Zebra. Printer: TDLR.

     a. Issued note.   FV   85.00
     b. Specimen. Serial # prefix *G/1, G/6*.   —   60.00

1997 ND Issue

17 10 Pula   VF   UNC

ND (1997). Green on multicolor underprint. President Q. K. J. Masire at left wearing finer striped pinstripe suit, crowned hornbill at center, arms at upper right. Signature 6a. Back: Large building at center right. Watermark: Rearing Zebra. Printer: TDLR, LIMITED.

     a. Issued note. signature 6a.   4.00   18.00
     s. Specimen. Serial # prefix *D/54*.   —   60.00

18 20 Pula   VF   UNC

ND (1997). Red, purple and brown on multicolor underprint. President Q. K. J. Masire at left wearing finer striped pinstripe suit, Ostrich at center, arms at upper right. Back: Mining conveyors at center right. Watermark: Rearing Zebra. Printer: TDLR, LIMITED.

     a. Issued note. signature 6a.   5.00   22.50
     s. Specimen. Serial # prefix *E/33*.   —   60.00

19 50 Pula   VF   UNC

ND (1997). Dark brown and dark green on multicolor underprint. President Q. K. J. Masire at left wearing finer striped pinstripe suit, Malachite Kingfisher at center, arms at upper right. Signature 6b. Back: Man in canoe and African fish eagle at center right. Watermark: Rearing Zebra. Printer: TDLR, LIMITED.

     a. Issued note. signature 6b.   12.50   42.50
     s. Specimen. Serial # prefix *F/13*.   —   60.00

1999-2000 ND Issue

20 10 Pula   VF   UNC

ND (1999). Green on multicolor underprint. President F. Mogae at left, Hornbill at center, arms at upper right. Back: Parliament building. Watermark: Rearing Zebra. Printer: F-CO. 138x69mm.

     a. Signature 7a.   FV   12.00
     b. Signature 8a.   FV   7.00
     s1. As a. Specimen. Serial # prefix *D/62*.   —   60.00
     s2. As b. Specimen. Serial # prefix *D/72*.   —   60.00

21 20 Pula   VF   UNC

ND (1999). Red, purple and brown on multicolor underprint. K. Motsete at left, Ostrich at center, arms at upper right. Back: Mining conveyors at center right. Watermark: Rearing Zebra. Printer: SABN. 144x72mm.

     a. Signature 7b.   FV   16.00
     s1. As a. Specimen. Serial # prefix *E/42*.   —   60.00

22 50 Pula   VF   UNC

ND (2000). Dark brown and dark green on multicolor underprint. Sir Seretse Khama at left, Malachite Kingfisher at center, arms at upper right. Optical variable ink star at right. Back: Man in canoe and fish eagle at center right. Watermark: Rearing Zebra. Printer: F-CO. 150x75mm.

     a. Signature 8a.   FV   22.50
     s. As a. Specimen. Serial # prefix *F/18*.   —   60.00

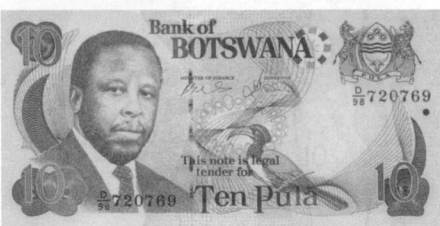

23 100 Pula   VF   UNC

ND (2000). Blue-violet and ochre on multicolor underprint. Three chiefs: Sebeli I, Bathoen I and Khama III at left, fisheagle at center, arms and optical variable ink diamond at right. Back: Worker sorting rough diamonds at center. Watermark: Rearing Zebra. Printer: F-CO. 156x78mm.

     a. Signature 8a.   FV   52.50
     s. As a. Specimen. Serial # prefix *G/11*.   —   60.00

2002 ND Issue

24 10 Pula

2002; 2007. Wide security thread. Green on multicolor underprint. President F. Mogae at left, hornbill at center, arms at upper right. Back: Parliament building. Watermark: Rearing Zebra. Printer: DLR. 138x69mm.

	VF	UNC
a. 2002. Signature 8b.	FV	6.50
b. 2007	FV	6.50
s. As a. Specimen. Serial # prefix *D/82*.	—	60.00

26 20 Pula

2002; 2008. Wide security thread. Red, purple and brown on multicolor underprint. K. Motsete at left, ostrich at center, arms at upper right. Back: Mining conveyors at center right. Watermark: Rearing Zebra. 144x72mm.

	VF	UNC
a. 2002. Signature 8b.	FV	12.00
b. 2008	FV	7.50
s. As a. Specimen. Serial # prefix *E/52*.	—	60.00

#26 has is renumbered to 24b.

2004-07 Issue

27 20 Pula

2004; 2006. Red, purple and brown on multicolor underprint. K. Motsete at left, ostrich at center, arms at upper right. Wide segmented security foil. Back: Mining conveyors at center right. Printer: F-CO. 144x72mm.

	VF	UNC
a. 2004	FV	12.00
b. 2006	FV	10.00

28 50 Pula

2005. Dark brown and dark green on multicolor underprint. Sir Serese Khama at left, Malachite Kingfisher at center. Hologram. Back: Man in canoe, fish-eagle and Ikavango Delta. Watermark: Rearing Aebra. Printer: DLR. 150x75mm.

	VF	UNC
a. Issued note.	FV	18.50
s. Specimen.	—	50.00

29 100 Pula

2004; 2005. Blue-violet and ochre on multicolor underprint. Three chiefs: Sebeli I, Bathoen I and Khama III at left, fish eagle at center, arms and variable ink diamond at right, circular Kinegram at lower right. Signature 8a. Back: Worker sorting rough diamonds at center. Printer: TDLR. 156x78mm.

	VF	UNC
a. 2004	FV	52.50
b. 2005	FV	50.00

2009 ND Issue

30 10 Pula

2009; 2010; 2012. Light green, dark green and tan. President Seretse Khama Ian Khama at left center. Back: National Assembly building in Gaborone. Watermark: Rearing zebra and 10. Printer: DLR. 132x66mm.

	VF	UNC
a. 2009.	FV	2.50
b. 2010	FV	2.50
c. 2012.	FV	2.50

31 20 Pula

2009; 2010; 2012; 2014. Purple and rose on multicolor underprint. Dr. Kgalemang Motsete at left center. Back: Mining conveyors at center right. Watermark: Rearing zebra and 20. 138x69mm.

	VF	UNC
a. 2009.	FV	5.00
b. 2010	FV	5.00
c. 2012.	FV	5.00
d. 2014.	FV	2.50

32 50 Pula   VF   UNC
2009; 2012; 2014. Brown and tan on multicolor underprint. Sir Seretse Khama at
left center. Back: Okawango Delta wetlands. Watermark: Rearing zebra and 50.
Printer: DLR. 144x72mm.

		VF	UNC
a. 2009.		FV	10.00
b. 2012.		FV	12.00
c. 2014.		FV	12.00

33 100 Pula   VF   UNC
2009; 2010; 2012. Slate black, blue-violet and ochre on multicolor underprint.
Three chiefs: Sebeli I, Bathoen I and Khama III at left, arms at upper right. Back:
Worker sorting rough diamonds at center. Watermark: Rearing zebra and 100.
150x75mm.

		VF	UNC
a. 2009.		FV	30.00
b. 2010		FV	30.00
c. 2012.		FV	30.00

34 200 Pula   VF   UNC
2009; 2010; 2012; 2014. Purple, brown and violet on green and multicolor underprint. Female teaching children to read at left center, arms at upper center. Back:
Herd of zebras at waterhole. Watermark: Rearing zebra and 200. 156x78mm.

		VF	UNC
a. 2009.		FV	60.00
b. 2010		FV	60.00
c. 2012.		FV	60.00
d. 2014.		FV	60.00

COLLECTOR SERIES

Bank of Botswana

1979 ND Issue

CS1 ND (1979) 1-20 Pula   Mkt. Value
#1-3, 4a, 5a. overprint: *SPECIMEN* and Maltese cross serial # prefix.   40.00

BRAZIL

The Federative Republic of Brazil, which comprises half the continent
of South America, is the only Latin
American country deriving its culture
and language from Portugal. It has an
area of 8,511,965 sq. km. and a population of 196.34 million. Capital: Bra-
sília.Following three centuries under
the rule of Portugal, Brazil became
an independent nation in 1822 and
a republic in 1889. By far the largest
and most populous country in South
America, Brazil overcame more than
half a century of military intervention
in the governance of the country when
in 1985 the military regime peacefully
ceded power to civilian rulers. Brazil
continues to pursue industrial and
agricultural growth and development
of its interior. Exploiting vast natural
resources and a large labor pool, it
is today South America's leading economic power and a regional leader.
Highly unequal income distribution
and crime remain pressing problems.

SIGNATURE VARIETIES

8	Sebastião P. Almeida	Carlos A. Carrílho
9	Clemente Mariani	Carlos A. Carrílho
10	Walter M. Salles	Reginaldo F. Nunes
11	Reginaldo F. Nunes, 1962	Walter M. Salles
12	Reginaldo F. Nunes, 1963	Miguel Calmon
13	Reginaldo F. Nunes, 1964	Octávio Gouvex Bulhões
14	Sérgio Augusto Ribeiro, 1964-66	Octávio Gouvex Bulhões
15	Dénio Nogueira, 1966-67	Octávio Gouvex Bulhões
16	Ruy Leme, 1967	Antônio Delfim Netto
17	Ername Galveas, 1967-72	Antônio Delfim Netto
18	Mário Henrique Simonsen, 1974-79	Paulo H.P. Lira
19	Karlos Rischbieter, 1979-80	Ernane Galveas

SIGNATURE VARIETIES

20	Emane Galvêas, 1980-81	Carlos P. Langoni
21	Emane Galvêas, 1983-85	Alfonso C. Pastore
22	Francisco Dornélles, 1985	Antonio Lengruber
23	Dilson Funaro, 1985-86	Fernao C.B. Bracher
24	Dilson Funaro, 1987	Francisco Gross
25	Luiz Carlos Bresser Pereira, 1987	Fornando M. Oliveria
26	Maílson Ferreira Da Nóbrega, 1988-89	Elmo Camões
27	Maílson Ferreira Da Nóbrega, 1989-90	Wadico Bucchi
28	Zélia Cardoso De Mello, 1990	Ibrahim Éris
29	Marcílio M. Moreira, 1991-92	Francisco Gross
30	Paulo R. Haddad, 1993	Gustavo Loyola
31	Elizeu Resende, 1993	Paulo Ximenes
32	Fernando H. Cardoso, 1993	Paulo Ximenes
33	Fernando H. Cardoso, 1993-94	Pedro Malan
34	Rubens Ricúpero, 1994	Pedro Malan
35	Ciro Gomes, 1994	Pedro Malan
36	Pedro Malan, 1995	Pérsio Arida
37	Pedro Malan, 1995-97	Gustavo Loyola

SIGNATURE VARIETIES

38	Pedro Malan, 1998	Gustavo Franco
39	Pedro Malan, 1999-	Arminia Fraganeto
40	Antonio Palocci Filho, 2003-	Henrique De Campos Meirelles

SIGNATURE VARIETIES

Affonso Almino	Afonso Celso Pastore	Antonio Delfin Netto
Carlos Augusto Carrilho	Carlos Geraldo Langoni	Claudionor de Souza Lemos
Clemente Mariani	Dênio Nogueira	Dilson Funaro
Eilcou Reoende	Elmo Camões	Ernane Galveas
Eugenio Gudin	Fernando Henrique Cardoso	Fernando Milliet de Oliveira
Fernão Bracher	Francisco Dornelles	Francisco Gross
Gustavo J.L. Loyola	Horácio Lafer	Ibrahim Éris
José Maria Alkimin	José Maria Whytaker	Karlos Rischbieter
Lucas Lopes	Luiz Carlos Bresser Pereira	Mailson Ferreira da Nóbrega
Marcílio Marques Moreira	Mário Henrique Simonsen	Miguel Calmon
Oswaldo Aranha	Octávio Gouvêa de Bulhões	Paulo Henrique Pereira Lira
Paulo R. Haddad	Paulo Ximenes	Pedro Malan
Reginaldo Fernandes Nunes	Ruy Leme	Sebastião Paes de Almeida
Sérgio Augusto Ribeiro	Wadico Bucchi	Walter Moreira Salles
Zélia Cardoso de Mello		

REPUBLIC

Tesouro Nacional, Valor Recebido
Estampa 3; 1961 ND Issue

166   5 Cruzeiros

ND (1961-62). Dark brown and brown. Raft with sail at left, male Indian at right. Back: Flower. Printer: CdM-B.

		VF	UNC
a. Signature 8. Series #1-75.		0.50	2.00
b. Signature 10. Series #76-111.		0.25	1.25

Estampa 1a; 1961 ND Issue

167   10 Cruzeiros

ND (1961-63). Dark blue on microcolor underprint. Portrait G. Vargas at center. 2 printed signatures. Back: Allegory of "Industry" at center. Printer: ABNC.

		VF	UNC
a. Signature 9. Series #331-630. (1961).		0.50	2.00
b. Signature 12. Series #631-930. (1963).		0.50	1.75
s. As a or b. Specimen.		—	125

168   20 Cruzeiros

ND (1961-63). Dark blue on microcolor underprint. Portrait D. da Fonseca at center. 2 printed signatures. Back: Allegory of "the Republic" at center. Printer: ABNC.

		VF	UNC
a. Signature 9. Series #461-960. (1961).		0.50	2.25
b. Signature 12. Series #961-1260. (1963).		0.50	2.00
s. As a or b. Specimen.		—	135

169   50 Cruzeiros

ND (1961). Dark blue on microcolor underprint. Portrait Princess Isabel at center. 2 printed signatures. Signature 9. Series # 721-1220. Back: Allegory of "Law" at center. Printer: ABNC.

		VF	UNC
a. Issued note.		1.50	7.50
s. Specimen.		—	135

170   100 Cruzeiros

ND (1961-64). Dark blue on microcolor underprint. Portrait D. Pedro at center. 2 printed signatures. Back: Allegory of "National Culture" at center. Printer: ABNC.

		VF	UNC
a. Signature 9. Series #761-1160. (1961).		2.25	9.00
b. Signature 13. Series #1161-1360. (1964).		1.00	4.50
c. Signature 14. Series #1361-1560. (1964).		2.00	8.00
s. As a, b or c. Specimen.		—	150

171   200 Cruzeiros

ND (1961-64). Dark blue on microcolor underprint. Portrait D. Pedro at center. 2 printed signatures. Back: Battle scene at center. Printer: ABNC.

		VF	UNC
a. Signature 9. Series #671-1070. (1961).		3.50	15.00
b. Signature 13. Series #1071-1370. (1964).		3.00	12.00
c. Signature 14. Series #1371-1570. (1964).		3.00	12.00
s. As a, b or c. Specimen.		—	150

172   500 Cruzeiros
<table>
<tr><td></td><td></td><td>VF</td><td>UNC</td></tr>
</table>
ND (1961-62). Dark blue on microcolor underprint. Portrait D. Joao VI at center. 2 printed signatures. Back: Allegory of "Maritime Industry" at center. Printer: ABNC.

		VF	UNC
a. Signature 9. Series #261-660. (1961).		5.00	25.00
b. Signature 11. Series #661-1460. (1962).		4.00	20.00
s. As a, b. Specimen.		—	125

173   1000 Cruzeiros   VF   UNC
ND (1961-63). Dark blue on microcolor underprint. Portrait P. Alvares Cabral at center. 2 printed signatures. Back: Scene of the "First Mass" at center. Printer: ABNC.

		VF	UNC
a. Signature 9. Series #1331-1730. (1961).		8.00	50.00
b. Signature 11. Series #1731-3030. (1962).		6.00	40.00
c. Signature 12. Series #3031-3830. (1963).		7.00	45.00
s. As a, b or c. Specimen.		—	135

174   5000 Cruzeiros   VF   UNC
ND (1963-64). Blue-gray on multicolor underprint. Portrait Tiradentes at right. Back: Tiradentes in historical scene at center. Printer: ABNC.

		VF	UNC
a. Signature 12. Series #1-400. (1963).		5.00	35.00
b. Signature 13. Series #401-1400. (1964).		4.50	30.00
c. Signature 14. Series #1401-1650. (1965).		8.00	50.00
s. As a, b or c. Specimen.		—	150

Estampa 2a; 1962-63 ND Issue

#175 *Deleted,* **see #182B.**

176   5 Cruzeiros   VF   UNC
ND (1962-64). Brown on multicolor underprint. Portrait Barao do Rio Branco at center. 2 printed signatures. Printer: TDLR.

		VF	UNC
a. Signature 11. Series #2301-3500. (1962).		0.25	1.00
b. Signature 12. Series #3501-3700. (1963).		0.25	2.50
c. Signature 13. Series #3701-3748; 4149-4180; 4201-4232. (1964).		0.25	5.00
d. Signature 14. Series #3749-4148; 4181-4200; 4233-4700. (1964).		0.25	0.75

177   10 Cruzeiros   VF   UNC
ND (1962). Green on multicolor underprint. Portrait G. Vargas at center. 2 printed signatures Back: Allegory of "Industry" at center Printer: TDLR.

		VF	UNC
a. Signature 10. Series # 2365-3055.		0.25	1.50
b. Signature 11. Series # 2394A.		0.25	1.50

178   20 Cruzeiros   VF   UNC
ND (1962). Red-brown on multicolor underprint. Portrait D. da Fonseca at center. 2 printed signatures. Signature 11. Series # 1576-2275. Back: Allegory of "the Republic" at center. Printer: TDLR.
0.50   2.25

179   50 Cruzeiros   VF   UNC
ND (1963). Purple on multicolor underprint. Portrait Princess Isabel at center. 2 printed signatures. Signature 12. Series # 586-785. Back: Allegory of "Law" at center. Printer: TDLR.
1.00   4.00

180   100 Cruzeiros   VF   UNC
ND (1963). Red on multicolor underprint. Portrait D. Pedro at center. 2 printed signatures. Signature 12. Series # 216-415. Back: Allegory of "National Culture" at center. Printer: TDLR.
2.00   9.00

181   1000 Cruzeiros   VF   UNC
ND (1963). Orange on multicolor underprint. Portrait P. Alvares Cabral at center. 2 printed signatures. Signature 12. Series # 791-1590. Back: Scene of the "First Mass" at center. Printer: TDLR.
3.00   15.00

182   5000 Cruzeiros   VF   UNC
ND (1963-64(. Red on multicolor underprint. Portrait Tiradentes at right. 2 printed signatures. Signature at left with title: *Director Caixa de Amortizacao.* Back: Tiradentes in historical scene at center. Printer: TDLR.

		VF	UNC
a. Signature 12. Series #1-400. (1963).		4.50	30.00
b. Signature 13. Series #401-1400. (1964).		4.00	25.00
c. Signature 14. Series #1401-1700. (1964).		6.00	40.00

Banco Central do Brasil
1965; 1966 ND Issue

182A 5000 Cruzeiros   VF   UNC
ND (1965). Red on multicolor underprint. Portrait Tiradentes at right. 2 printed signatures. Signature D. Nogueira with title: *Presidente do Banco Central* and O. Gouvea de Bulhões. Signature 15. Series # 1701-2200. Back: Tiradentes in historical scene at center. Printer: ABNC.
5.00   35.00

182B 10,000 Cruzeiros

	VF	UNC

ND (1966). Gray on multicolor underprint. Portrait S. Dumont at right. Signature
15. Back: Early airplane at right. Printer: ABNC.

	VF	UNC
a. Series #1-493.	17.50	70.00
b. Series #561-590.	175	350
s. As a. Specimen.	—	375

1966; 1967 ND Provisional Issue

Feb. 1967 Monetary Reform: 1 Cruzeiro Novo = 1,000 Cruzeiros

183 1 Centavo on 10 Cruzeiros

	VF	UNC

ND (1966-67). Overprint on #177. UV: planchettes fluorese yellow. Green on multicolor underprint. Black circular overprint: *BANCO CENTRAL* and new currency
unit in black circle. Signature 15.

	VF	UNC
a. Error: *Minstro* below right signature (2 types of 1 in overprint.) (1966). Series #3056-3151.	0.20	1.00
b. *Ministro* below right signature (1967). Series # 3152-4055.	0.20	1.00
s. As b. Specimen overprint: *MODELO*.	—	—

184 5 Centavos on 50 Cruzeiros

	VF	UNC

ND (1966-67). Overprint on #179. Purple on multicolor underprint. Black circular
overprint: *BANCO CENTRAL* and new currency unit in black circle. Signature 15.

	VF	UNC
a. Type of #183a. Series #786-1313.	0.25	1.50
b. Type of #183b. Series #1314-1885.	0.25	1.50

185 10 Centavos on 100 Cruzeiros

	VF	UNC

ND (1966-67). Overprint on #180. UV: planchettes fluoresce yellow. Red on multicolor underprint. Black circular overprint: *BANCO CENTRAL* and new currency
unit in black circle. Signature 15.

	VF	UNC
a. Type of #183a. Series #416-911.	0.25	2.00
b. Type of #183b. Series #912-1515.	0.25	1.75

186 50 Centavos on 500 Cruzeiros

	VF	UNC

ND (1967). Overprint on #172. Blue on multicolor underprint. Black circular
overprint: *BANCO CENTRAL* and new currency unit in black circle. Signature 15.
Series # 1461-2360.

	VF	UNC
a. Issued note.	2.00	4.50
s. Specimen.	—	150

187 1 Cruzeiro Novo on 1000 Cruzeiros

	VF	UNC

ND (1966-67). Overprint on #173. Blue on multicolor underprint. Black circular
overprint: *BANCO CENTRAL* and new currency unit in black circle.

	VF	UNC
a. Signature 14. Series #3831-3930.	7.50	22.50
b. Signature 15. Series #3931-4830.	2.50	7.50
s. As b. Specimen.	—	150

188 5 Cruzeiros Novos on 5000 Cruzeiros

	VF	UNC

ND (1966-67). Overprint on #174. Blue-green on multicolor underprint. Black
circular overprint: *BANCO CENTRAL* and new currency unit in black circle.

	VF	UNC
a. Signature 14. Series #1651-1700.	30.00	60.00
b. Signature 15. Series #1701-2900.	8.00	22.50
s. As b. Specimen.	—	150

189 10 Cruzeiros Novos on 10,000 Cruzeiros

	VF	UNC

ND (1966-67). Bold or semi-bold overprint on #182B. Gray on multicolor underprint. Black circular overprint: *BANCO CENTRAL* and new currency unit in black
circle. Printer: ABNC.

	VF	UNC
a. Signature 15. Series #494-560 and 591-700. (1966).	25.00	85.00
b. Signature 16. Series #701-1700. (1967).	6.00	25.00
c. Signature 17. Series #1701-2700. (1967).	5.00	20.00
s. As b. Specimen.	—	175

190 10 Cruzeiros Novos on 10,000 Cruzeiros

	VF	UNC

ND (1967). Brown on pink and multicolor underprint. Black circular overprint:
BANCO CENTRAL and new currency unit in black circle. Portrait S. Dumont at
right. Signature 15. Back: Early airplane at right. Printer: TDLR.

	VF	UNC
a. Signature 16. Series #1-1000.	3.50	15.00
b. Signature 17. Series #1001-2100.	2.25	10.00

1970 ND Issues

191 1 Cruzeiro

ND (1970-72). Dark green and blue on ochre and green underprint with medallic. Liberty head at right in brown. Series number prefix A. 5 digit series number above serial number. Signature 17. Back: Banco Central building at left. Watermark: Liberty head. Printer: CdM-B.

		VF	UNC
a. Series #1-3000.		0.50	2.00
s1. Specimen. Overprint: *MODELO*.		—	25.00
s2. Specimen. Overprint: *SEM VALOR* and perforated *MODELO*.		—	60.00

191A 1 Cruzeiro

ND (1972-80). Dark green and blue with medallic. Liberty head in green. Series number prefix B. 5 digit series number above serial number. Back: Banco Central building at left. Watermark: Liberty head. Printer: CdM-B.

		VF	UNC
a. Signature 17. Series #1-3781 (1972).		0.25	1.00
b. Signature 18. Series #3782-13194 (1975).		0.15	0.75
c. Signature 20. Series #13195-18094 (1980).		0.10	0.50
s. As a. Specimen. Red overprint: *MODELO*, perforated: *MODELO* and number		—	75.00

192 5 Cruzeiros

ND (1970-80). Blue on orange and green underprint. Portrait D. Pedro I at right. 5 digit series number above serial number. Back: Parade square at left. Watermark: D. Pedro I. Printer: CdM-B.

		VF	UNC
a. Back darkly printed. Signature 17. Series # prefix A. Series #1-107 (1970-71).		5.00	20.00
b. Back lightly printed. Signature 17. Series # prefix B. Series #1-2467 (1973).		0.25	1.25
c. Signature 18. Series #2468-6050 (1974).		0.25	1.50
d. Signature 19. Series #6051-6841 (1979).		0.25	2.00
s1. As a. Specimen overprint: *SEM VALOR*, and perforated: *MODELO*.		—	100
s2. Specimen. Black overprint: MUESTRA on face.		—	25.00
s3. Specimen. Black overprint: MODELO on both sides. Perforated number.		—	100

193 10 Cruzeiros

ND (1970-80). Grayish purple and dark brown on orange-brown, blue-green and multicolor underprint. Portrait D. Pedro II at right. 5 digit series number above serial number. Back: Statue of the Prophet Daniel. Watermark: D. Pedro II. Printer: CdM-B.

		VF	UNC
a. Back darkly printed. Signature 17. Series # prefix A. Series #1-1429 (1970).		2.50	15.00
b. As a. signature 18. Series #1430-7745 (1974).		0.50	1.75
c. Back lightly printed. Signature 18. Series # prefix B. Series #1-2394 (1979).		1.00	5.00
d. As c. Signature 19. Series #2395-2870 (1980).		0.50	2.50
e. As d. Signature 20. Series #2871-5131 (1980).		0.50	2.00
s1. Specimen. Overprint: *MODELO* and pin hole cancelled.		—	80.00
s2. Specimen. Black overprint: MUESTRA on face.		—	25.00

194 50 Cruzeiros

ND (1970-81). Black, purple, blue-black and violet on lilac and multicolor underprint. Portrait D. da Fonseca at right. 5 digit series number above serial number. Back: Coffee loading. Watermark: D. da Fonseca. Printer: CdM-B. 161x76mm.

		VF	UNC
a. Signature 17. Series #1-1260 (1970).		3.00	20.00
b. Signature 18. Series #1251-3841 (1974).		0.50	3.00
c. Signature 20. Series #3842-5233 (1980).		0.50	2.50
s1. Specimen. As a. Overprint: *SEM VALOR* and perforated: *MODELO*.		—	125
s2. Specimen. Black overprint: MUESTRA on face.		—	25.00

195 100 Cruzeiros

ND (1970-81). Purple and violet on pink and multicolor underprint. Portrait Marshal F. Peixoto at right. Signature 17 (with imprint CdM-B). Series number 1-01358. 5 digit series number above serial number. Back: National Congress at left. Watermark: Marshal F. Peixoto. Printer: TDLR.

		VF	UNC
a. Issued note.		6.00	35.00
s. Specimen. Overprint: *SEM VALOR* on both sides.		—	75.00

Note: The difference between #195 and 195A is in the watermark.

195A   100 Cruzeiros   VF   UNC
ND (1974-81). Purple and violet on pink and multicolor underprint. Portrait
Marshal F. Peixoto at right. Signature 17 (with imprint CdM-B). Series number
1-01358. 5 digit series number above serial number. Back: National Congress at
left. Printer: CdM-B.

a. Signature 18. Series #01359-10455 (1974).	0.75	6.00
b. Signature 20. Series #10456-12681 (1981).	0.75	6.00
s. Specimen.	—	25.00

Note: The difference between #195 and 195A is in the watermark.

1972 Commemorative Issue

#196, 196A, 150th Anniversary of Brazilian Independence

196   500 Cruzeiros   VF   UNC
1972 (1972-74). Dark olive-green and brown on violet and multicolor underprint.
Portrait of five men of differing racial groups. Back: 5 different maps of Brazil.
Watermark: Dates *1822 1972* in clear area at left. Printer: CdM-B.

a. Signature 17. Series # prefix A. #1-90 (1972).	100	300
b. As a. Signature 18. Series #91-2636 (1974).	5.00	35.00
s1. Specimen. Signature 17. Red overprint: *MODELO* and perforated number.	—	175
s2. Specimen. Signature 18. Red overprint: *MODELO* and perforated number.	—	150

196A   500 Cruzeiros   VF   UNC
1972 (1979-80). Dark olive-green and brown on violet and multicolor underprint.
Portrait of five men of differing racial groups, watermark area has vertical lines.
Back: 5 different maps of Brazil, watermark area has vertical lines. Watermark:
Dates *1822 1972* in clear area at left. Printer: CdM-B.

a. Signature 18. Series # prefix B. #1-1401 (1979).	4.00	25.00
b. As a. Signature 19. Series #1402-1959 (1979).	4.00	25.00
c. As a. Signature 20. Series #1960-2763 (1980).	4.00	25.00
s. Specimen. Black overprint: SIN VALOR, grey overprint: MODELO and perforated number.	—	175

1978 ND Issue

197   1000 Cruzeiros   VF   UNC
ND (1978-80). Green and brown. Double portrait B. do Rio Branco, *BANCO
CENTRAL DO BRASIL* in two lines. The first 4 digits of the serial number
represent the series number. Back: Double view of machinery. Watermark: B. do
Rio Branco.

a. Signature 18. Series #1-665 (1978).	8.00	50.00
b. Signature 19. Series #666-2072 (1979).	6.00	32.50
c. Signature 20. Series #2073-3297 (1980).	6.00	35.00
s. Specimen. Grey overprint: MODELO twice on face. Perforated number.	—	150

1981-85 ND Issue

198   100 Cruzeiros   VF   UNC
ND (1981-84). Red and purple on multicolor underprint. Double portrait D. de
Caxias at center. The first 4 digits of the serial number represent the series
number. Back: Double view of a battle scene and sword at center. Watermark: D.
de Caxias. Printer: CdM-B.

a. Signature 20. Series #1-4081 (1981).	0.15	0.50
b. Signature 21. Series #4082-8176 (1984).	0.15	0.50
s. Specimen. Black overprint: MODELO twice on face. Perforated number.	FV	100

199   200 Cruzeiros   VF   UNC
ND (1981-84). Green and violet on multicolor underprint. Double portrait of Princess Isabel at center. The first 4 digits of the serial number represent the series
number. Back: Double view of two women cooking outdoors. Watermark: Princess
Isabel. Printer: CdM-B.

a. Signature 20. Series #1-2996 (1981).	0.15	0.50
b. Signature 21. Series #2997-4960 (1984).	0.15	0.50

200   500 Cruzeiros   VF   UNC
ND (1981-85). Blue and brown on multicolor underprint. Double portrait of D.
da Fonseca at center. The first 4 digits of the serial number represent the series
number. Back: Double view of a group of legislators Watermark: D. da Fonseca.
Printer: CdM-B.

    a. Signature 20. Series #1-3510 (1981).   0.20   1.00
    b. Signature 21. Series #3511-4238 (1985).   0.15   0.75
    s1. Specimen. Black overprint: MODELO twice on face. Perforated number.   FV   65.00
    s2. Specimen. Red overprint: MODELO on face and SEM VALOR on back.   FV   225
        Perforated number.

201   1000 Cruzeiros   VF   UNC
ND (1981-86). Brown and dark olive on multicolor underprint. Double portrait B.
do Rio Branco, *BANCO CENTRAL DO BRASIL* in two lines. The first 4 digits of
the serial number represent the series number. Back: Double view of machinery.
Watermark: B. do Rio Branco. Printer: CdM-B.

    a. Signature 20. Series # prefix A, #1-5733 (1981)   0.50   2.50
    b. As a. Signature 21. Series #5734-7019 (1984).   0.15   0.75
    c. As b. Signature 22. Series #7020-9999 (1985).   0.15   0.75
    d. Signature 22. Series # prefix B, #1-788 (1986).   0.15   0.75

202   5000 Cruzeiros   VF   UNC
ND (1981-85). Purple and brown on multicolor underprint. Double portrait of C.
Branco at center. The first 4 digits of the serial number represent the series num-
ber. Back: Double view of antennas. Watermark: C. Branco. Printer: CdM-B.

    a. Signature 20. Series # prefix A, #1-9205 (1981)   0.75   6.50
    b. As a. Signature 21. Series #9206-9999 (1983).   0.25   1.50
    c. Signature 21. Series # prefix B, #1-2118 (1984).   0.25   1.00
    d. As c. Signature 22. Series #2119-2342 (1985).   0.50   2.00

203   10,000 Cruzeiros   VF   UNC
ND (1984-85). Brown on multicolor underprint. Desk top at center, Rui Barbosa at
center. The first 4 digits of the serial number represent the series number. Back:
Conference scene. Watermark: Rui Barbosa. Printer: CdM-B.

    a. Signature 21. Series #1-3619 (1984).   1.25   4.50
    b. Signature 22. Series #3620-3696 (1985).   4.00   22.50

204   50,000 Cruzeiros   VF   UNC
ND (1984-86). Purple on multicolor underprint. Microscope at center, O. Cruz at
right. The first 4 digits of the serial number represent the series number. Back: O.
Cruz Institute at center. Watermark: O. Cruz. Printer: CdM-B.

    a. Signature 21. Series #1-1673 (1984).   3.75   20.00
    b. Signature 22 (reversed). Series #1674-2170 (1985).   5.00   15.00
    c. Signature 22 (corrected). Series #2171-3248 (1985).   1.75   7.00
    d. Signature 23. Series #3249-3290 (1986).   2.00   12.50

205   100,000 Cruzeiros   VF   UNC
ND (1985). Black on blue, gold and multicolor underprint. Electric power station at
center, Pres. J. Kubitschek at right. Signature 23. Series number 1-4347. The first
4 digits of the serial number represent the series number. Back: Old and modern
buildings at center. Watermark: Pres. J. Kubitschek. Printer: CdM-B.

    a. Issued note.   2.50   5.50
    s. Specimen. Red overprint MODELO twice on face. Perforated number.   —   175

1986 ND Provisional Issue

Feb. 1986 Monetary Reform: 1 Cruzado = 1,000 Cruzeiros

206   10 Cruzados on 10,000 Cruzeiros   VF   UNC
ND (1986). Black circular overprint: *Banco Central Do Brasil* and new currency   0.20   1.50
unit on #203. Signature 23. Series number 3697-5124.

207   50 Cruzados on 50,000 Cruzeiros   VF   UNC
ND (1986). Black circular overprint: *Banco Central Do Brasil* and new currency
unit on #204. Signature 23. Series number 3291-4592.

    a. Issued note.   0.75   2.50
    s. Specimen. Red overprint: MODELO on face. Perforated number.   —   125

208   100 Cruzados on 100,000 Cruzeiros

	VF	UNC

ND (1986). Black circular overprint: *Banco Central Do Brasil* and new currency unit on #205. Signature 23. Series number 4348-6209.

	VF	UNC
a. Issued note.	0.75	5.00
s. Specimen. Red overprint: MODELO on face. Perforated number.	—	175

1986 ND Issue

209   10 Cruzados

	VF	UNC

ND (1986-87). Brown on multicolor underprint. Desk top at center, portrait of Rui Barbosa at center right. Back: Conference scene. Watermark: Rui Barbosa. Printer: CdM-B.

	VF	UNC
a. Signature 23. Series #1-1155 (1986).	0.20	1.00
b. Signature 25. Series #1156-1505 (1987).	0.15	0.50

210   50 Cruzados

	VF	UNC

ND (1986-88). Purple on multicolor underprint. Microscope at center, O. Cruz at right. Back: Cruz Institute at center. Watermark: O. Cruz. Printer: CdM-B.

	VF	UNC
a. Signature 23. Series #1-1617 (1986).	0.20	0.75
b. Signature 25. Series #1618-2044 (1987).	0.20	0.75
c. Signature 26. Series #2045-2051 (1988).	15.00	100

211   100 Cruzados

	VF	UNC

ND (1986-88). Black on blue, gold and multicolor underprint. Electric power station at center, Pres. J. Kubitschek at right. Back: Old and modern buildings at center. Watermark: President J. Kubitschek. Printer: CdM-B.

	VF	UNC
a. Signature 23. Series #1-1176 (1986).	0.40	2.00
b. Signature 24. Series #1177-1582 (1987).	0.40	2.00
c. Signature 25. Series #1583-3045 (1987).	0.15	0.50
d. Signature 26. Series #3046-3059 (1988).	3.00	17.50
s. Specimen. As a. Red overprint: MODELO. Perforated number.	—	125

1986 ND Commemorative Issue

#212, Birth Centennial of H. Villa-Lobos

212   500 Cruzados

	VF	UNC

ND (1986). Blue-green on green and multicolor underprint. H. Villa-Lobos at center. Back: Villa-Lobos conducting at left center. Watermark: H. Villa-Lobos. Printer: CdM-B.

	VF	UNC
a. Signature 23. Series #1-2352 (1986).	0.50	3.00
b. Signature 24. Series #2353-2842 (1987).	0.50	2.50
c. Signature 25. Series #2843-7504 (1987).	0.15	0.50
d. Signature 26. Series #7505-8309 (1988).	0.20	1.00
s. Specimen. As a. Red overprint: MODELO. Perforated number.	—	150

1987 ND Regular Issue

213   1000 Cruzados

	VF	UNC

ND (1987-88). Purple and brown-violet on multicolor underprint. J. Machado at right. Series numbers are first 4 digits of serial number. Back: Street scene from old Rio de Janeiro. Watermark: J. Machado. Printer: CdM-B.

	VF	UNC
a. Signature 25. Series #1-2744 (1987).	1.00	6.00
b. Signature 26. Series #2745-9919 (1988)	0.15	0.75
s. Specimen. As a. Red overprint: MODELO. Perforated number.	—	125

214   5000 Cruzados

ND (1988). Blue on multicolor underprint. Portion of mural at left center, C. Portinari at right. Series numbers are first 4 digits of serial number.Signature 26. Series # 1-1757. Back: Portinari painting at center. Watermark: C. Portinari. Printer: CdM-B.

	VF	UNC
a. Issued note.	1.00	4.00
s. Specimen. Red overprint: *MODELO*. Perforated number.	—	150

215   10,000 Cruzados

ND (1989). Red and brown on multicolor underprint. C. Chagas at right. Signature 26. Series # 1-1841. Series numbers are first 4 digits of serial number. Back: Chagas with lab instruments. Watermark: C. Chagas. Printer: CdM-B.

	VF	UNC
a. Issued note.	1.00	7.00
s. Specimen. Red overprint: *MODELO* on face. Perforated number.	—	200

1989 ND Provisional Issue

Jan. 1989 Monetary Reform: 1 Cruzado Novo = 1,000 Cruzados

216   1 Cruzado Novo on 1000 Cruzados

ND (1989). Purple and brown-violet on multicolor underprint. J. Machado at right. Series numbers are first 4 digits of serial number. Back: Street scene from old Rio de Janeiro. Watermark: J. Machado. Printer: CdM-B.

	VF	UNC
a. Signature 26. Series # prefix A, #9920-9999 (1989).	0.50	2.00
b. Signature 26. Series # prefix B, #1-1617 (1989).	0.15	0.50
c. As b. signature 27. Series #1618-1792 (1989).	0.25	1.25
s. Specimen. Red overprint: MODELO on face. Perforated number.	—	125

217   5 Cruzados Novos on 5000 Cruzados

ND (1989). Blue on multicolor underprint. Portion of mural at left center, C. Portinari at right. Signature 26. Series number 1-1757. Series numbers are first 4 digits of serial number. Back: Portinari painting at center. Printer: CdM-B.

	VF	UNC
a. Signature 26. Series #1758-3531 (1989).	0.50	1.75
b. Signature 27. Series #3532-3818 (1989).	0.50	1.75
s. Specimen. Red overprint: MODELO and number perforated.	FV	135

218   10 Cruzados Novos on 10,000 Cruzados

ND (1989-90). Red and brown on multicolor underprint. C. Chagas at right. Signature 26. Series number 1-1841. Series numbers are first 4 digits of serial number. Back: Chagas with lab instruments. Watermark: C. Chagas. Printer: CdM-B.

	VF	UNC
a. Signature 26. Series #1842-4171 (1989).	0.25	1.50
b. Signature 27. Series #4172-4502 (1990).	0.50	2.50
s. Specimen. Red overprint: MODELO on face. Perforated number.	FV	125

1989 ND Issue

219   50 Cruzados Novos

ND (1989-90). Brown and black on multicolor underprint. C. Drummond de Andrade at right. Back: de Andrade writing poetry. Watermark: Liberty head. Printer: CdM-B.

	VF	UNC
a. Signature 26. Series #1-3340 (1989).	0.25	1.50
b. Signature 27. Series #3341-3358 (1990).	2.00	15.00
s. Specimen. Red overprint: MODELO on face. Perforated number.	—	125

220   100 Cruzados Novos

ND (1989). Orange, purple and green on multicolor underprint. C. Meireles at right. Back: Child reading and people dancing. Watermark: Liberty head. Printer: CdM-B.

	VF	UNC
a. Signature 26. Series #1-6772.	0.75	1.50
b. Signature 27. Series #6773-8794.	1.00	5.00
s. Specimen. As a. Red overprint: *MODELO*. Perforated number.	—	150

1989 ND Commemorative Issue

#221, Republic Centennial

221   200 Cruzados Novos

ND (1989). Blue and black on multicolor underprint. Political leaders at center, sculpture of the Republic at center right, arms at right. Signature 27. Series # 1-1964. Back: Oil painting *Patria* by P. Bruno with flag being embroidered by a family. Watermark: Liberty head. Printer: CdM-B.

	VF	UNC
a. Issued note.	1.00	5.00
s. Specimen. Red overprint: *MODELO*. Perforated number.	—	200

1990 ND Issue

222 500 Cruzados Novos

ND (1990). Green and purple on multicolor underprint. Orchids at center, A. Ruschi at right. Signature 27. Series # 1-3700. Back: Swallow-tailed hummingbird, orchids and Ruschi at center. Watermark: Liberty head.

		VF	UNC
a. Issued note.		2.00	7.50
s. Specimen. Red overprint: *MODELO.* Perforated number.		—	250

1990 ND Provisional Issue

March 1990 Monetary Reform: 1 Cruzeiro = 1 Cruzado Novo

223 50 Cruzeiros on 50 Cruzados Novos

ND (1990). UV: fibers fluoresce blue. Brown and black on multicolor underprint. C. Drummond de Andrade at right. Series number 3359-5338. Signature 27. Back: C. Drummond de Andrade writing poetry. Watermark: Liberty head. Printer: CdM-B.

VF	UNC
0.15	0.50

224 100 Cruzeiros on 100 Cruzados Novos

ND (1990). Orange, purple and green on multicolor underprint. C. Meireles at right. Signature 27. Back: Child reading and people dancing. Watermark: Liberty head. Printer: CdM-B.

	VF	UNC
a. Series #8601.	50.00	140
b. Series #8795-9447.	0.40	1.50

225 200 Cruzeiros on 200 Cruzados Novos

ND (1990). UV: fibers fluoresce blue. Blue and black on multicolor underprint. Political leaders at center, sculpture of the Republic at center right, arms at right. Signature 27. Back: Oil painting *Patria* by P. Bruno with flag being embroidered by a family. Watermark: Liberty head. Printer: CdM-B.

	VF	UNC
a. Series #1725.	75.00	175
b. Series #1965-2668.	0.50	1.00

226 500 Cruzeiros on 500 Cruzados Novos

ND (1990). Green and pruple on multicolor underprint. Orchids at center, A. Ruschi at right. Signature 27. Back: Swallow-tailed hummingbird, orchids and Ruschi at center. Watermark: Liberty head.

	VF	UNC
a. Series #3111.	35.00	100
b. Series #3701-7700.	0.25	0.75

1992 ND Emergency Issue

227 5000 Cruzeiros

ND (1990). Deep olive-green and deep brown on multicolor underprint. Liberty head in green at right. Signature 28. Series # 1-1520. Back: Arms at left. Watermark: Liberty head. Printer: CdM-B.

	VF	UNC
a. Issued note.	0.75	2.00
s. Specimen. Red overprint: MODELO on both sides. Perforated number.	FV	150

1990-93 ND Regular Issue

228 100 Cruzeiros

ND (1990). UV: fibers fluoresce blue. Orange, purple and green on multicolor underprint. C. Meireles at right. Signature 28. Series # 1-1045. Back: Child reading and people dancing. Watermark: Liberty head. Printer: CdM-B.

VF	UNC
0.20	0.50

229 200 Cruzeiros

ND (1990). UV: fibers fluoresce blue. Blue and black on multicolor underprint. Political leaders at center, sculpture of the Republic at center right, arms at right. Signature 28. Series # 1-1646. Back: Oil painting "Patria" by P. Bruno with flag being embroidered by a family. Watermark: Liberty head. Printer: CdM-B.

VF	UNC
0.15	0.50

230 500 Cruzeiros VF UNC
ND (1990). Green and purple on multicolor underprint. Orchids at center, A. Ruschi at right. Signature 28. Series # 1-0210. Back: Swallow-tailed hummingbird, orchids and Ruschi at center. Watermark: Liberty head. Printer: CdM-B.
  a. Issued note. 0.75 3.00
  s. Specimen. Red overprint: MODELO. Perforated number. — 150

231 1000 Cruzeiros VF UNC
ND (1990-91). UV: fibers fluoresce blue. Dark brown, brown, violet and black on multicolor underprint. C. Rondon at right, native hut at center, map of Brazil in background. Back: Two Indian children and local food from Amazonia. Watermark: Liberty head. Printer: CdM-B.
  a. Signature 28. Upper Signature title: MINISTRO DA ECONOMIA,... Series #1-4268 (1990). 0.40 2.50
  b. Upper signature title: MINISTRA DA ECONOMIA,... Series #4269-6796 (1990). 0.30 2.00
  c. Signature 29. Series #6797-8453 (1991). 0.15 0.50
  s. Specimen. As b. Red overprint: MODELO on both sides. Perforated number. 150

232 5000 Cruzeiros VF UNC
ND (1990-93). UV: fibers fluoresce blue. Blue-black, black and deep brown on light blue and multicolor underprint. C. Gomes at center right, Brazilian youths at center. Back: Statue of Gomes seated, grand piano in background at center. Printer: CdM-B.
  a. Signature 28. Series #1-4489 (1990). 0.50 2.00
  b. Signature 29. Series #4490-5501 (1992). 0.25 1.50
  c. Signature 30. Series #5502-6041 (1993). 0.20 1.00
  s. Specimen. As a. Red overprint: MODELO on both sides. Perforated number. — 175

233 10,000 Cruzeiros VF UNC
ND (1991-93). UV: fibers fluoresce blue. Black and brown-violet on multicolor underprint. Extracting poisonous venom at center, V. Brazil at right. Back: One snake swallowing another at center. Watermark: V. Brazil. Printer: CdM-B.
  a. Signature 28. Series #1-3136 (1991). 0.50 3.00
  b. Signature 29. Series #3137-6937 (1992). 0.25 1.25
  c. Signature 30. Series #6938-7365 (1993). 0.15 1.00

234 50,000 Cruzeiros VF UNC
ND (1992). UV: fibers fluoresce blue. Dark brown and red-orange on multicolor underprint. C. Cascudo at center right, two men on raft in background at left center. Signature 29. Series # 1-6289. Back: Folklore dancers at left center. Printer: CdM-B.
  a. Issued note. 0.25 1.25
  s. Specimen. Overprint: MODELO. Perforated number. — 150

235 100,000 Cruzeiros VF UNC
ND (1992-93). Brown, green and purple on multicolor underprint. Hummingbird feeding nestlings at center, butterfly at right. Back: Butterfly at left, Iguaçú cataract at center. Watermark: Sculptured head of Brasilia. Printer: CdM-B.
  a. Signature 29. Series #1-6052 (1992). 0.50 6.00
  b. Signature 30. Series #6053-6226 (1993). 0.50 5.00
  c. Signature 31. Series #6227-6290 (1993). 0.50 5.00
  d. Signature 32. Series #6291-6733 (1993). 0.25 1.25
  s. Specimen. As a. Red overprint: MODELO on face and SEM VALOR on back. Perforated number. — 175

236 500,000 Cruzeiros VF UNC
ND (1993). Red-violet, brown and deep purple on multicolor underprint. M. de Andrade at right, native Indian art in underprint. Back: Building; de Andrade teaching children at center. Watermark: Sculptured head of Brasilia. Printer: CdM-B.
  a. Signature 30. Series #1-3410 (1993). 2.50 12.00
  b. Signature 31. Series #3411-4404 (1993). 2.00 10.00
  c. Signature 32. Series #4405-8291 (1993). 0.50 4.00

1993 ND Provisional Issue

August 1993 Monetary Reform: 1 Cruzeiro Real = 1,000 Cruzeiros

237 50 Cruzeiros Reais on 50,000 Cruzeiros

VF UNC

ND (1993). Dark brown and red-orange on multicolor underprint. C. Cascudo at center right, two men on raft in background at left center. Signature 32. Series # 6290-6591. Back: Folklore dancers at left center. Printer: CdM-B.

0.20 1.00

238 100 Cruzeiros Reais on 100,000 Cruzeiros

VF UNC

ND (1993). Brown, green and purple on multicolor underprint. Hummingbird feeding nestlings at center, butterfly at right. Signature 32. Series # 6291-6733. Back: Butterfly at left, Iguaçú cataract at center. Watermark: Sculptured head of *Brasilia*.

0.20 1.00

239 500 Cruzeiros Reais on 500,000 Cruzeiros

VF UNC

ND (1993). UV: fibers fluoresce blue. Red-violet, brown and deep purple on multicolor underprint. M. de Andrade at right, native Indian art in underprint. Signature 32. Series # 4405-8291. Back: Building; de Andrade teaching children a center. Watermark: Sculpture head of *Brasilia*.
a. Series prefix A, #8292-9999. 0.50 3.00
b. Series prefix B, #1-717. 0.25 2.25

1993-94 ND Issue

240 1000 Cruzeiros Reais

VF UNC

ND (1993). Black, dark blue and brown on multicolor underprint. A. Teixeira at center right. "Parque" school at left center. Signature 33. Series numbers 1-2515. Back: Children and workers. Watermark: Sculptured head of *Brasilia*. Printer: CdM-B.
a. Issued note. 0.50 2.00
s. Specimen. Red overprint: MODELO on face and SEM VALOR on back. FV 175
Perforated number.

241 5000 Cruzeiros Reais

VF UNC

ND (1993). Black, red-brown and dark olive-green on multicolor underprint. Gaucho at center right, urins of São Miguel das Missões at left center. Signature 33. Series numbers 1-9999. Back: Vertical format; gaucho on horseback roping steer at center. Watermark: Sculptured head of *Brasilia*. Printer: CdM-B.

2.50 12.50

242 50,000 Cruzeiros Reais

VF UNC

ND (1994). Deep purple and brown-violet on multicolor underprint. Dancer at left center, Baiana at center right. Signature 33. Series numbers 1-1200. Back: Vertical format; Baina do Acarajé priparing food at center. Watermark: Sculptured head of *Brasilia*. Printer: CdM-B.

25.00 50.00

1994 ND Issue

July 1994 Monetary Reform: 1 Real = 2750 Cruzeiros Reals

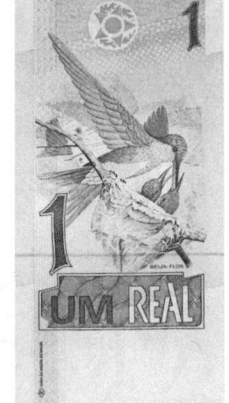

243 1 Real

VF UNC

ND (1994-97). Black, olive-green and blue-green on aqua and pale green underprint. Sculpture of the Republic at center right. Series # is the first 4 digits of serial #. Back: Vertical format; white-necked jacobin hummingbirds at center. Printer: CdM-B or with additional imprint. 140x65mm.
a. Signature 33. without text *DEUS SEJA LOUVADO*, Series #1-2409 (1994). Serial #A-A. 1.00 6.00
b. Signature 34. Series 2410-3833 (1994). 1.00 6.00
c. Signature 34. with text: *DEUS SEJA LOUVADO* at lower left Series #3834-6568. 1.00 6.00
d. Signature 35. Series 6569-7019. 1.00 9.00
e. Signature 37. Series 7020-9999. 1.00 5.00
f. Signature 37. Series 0001-0072, serial #A-B. 2.00 17.50

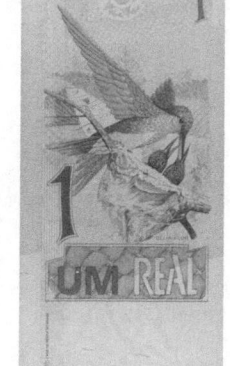

243A 1 Real

ND (1997-). UV: fibers fluoresce blue. Black,olive-green on aqua and pale green underprint. Sculpture of the Republic at center right. Series # is the first 4 digits of serial #. Serial # A-B, B-B or C-B. Back: Vertical format. White-necked jacobin hummingbirds at center. Watermark: Flag. Printer: CdM-B or with additional imprint.

	VF	UNC
a. Signature 37. Series #0001-3247.	1.00	4.00
b. Signature 38. Series #3248-7561.	1.00	4.00
c. Signature 39. Series #7562-0948.	1.00	6.00
d. Signature 39. Series #8949-9999.	1.00	4.00
e. Signature 39. Series #0001-9999, series B-B.	FV	3.00
f. Signature 39. Serial C-B. Series #0001-3382.	FV	2.00
g. Signature 40. Series 3383-4505.	FV	2.00

244 5 Reais

ND(1994-97). Violet, dark brown and blue on lilac underprint. Sculpture of the Republic at center right. Series # is the first 4 digits of serial #. Serial # A-A. Back: Vertical format: great egret at center. Watermark: Republic. Printer: CdM-B or with additional imprint. 140x65mm.

	VF	UNC
a. Signature 33. without text: *DEUS SEJA LOUVADO.* Series #0001-1411.	5.00	22.50
b. Signature 33. without text. Printer: G & D. Series A-B,#1-1000.	20.00	55.00
c. Signature 34. without text. Series A-A: #1412-1609.	50.00	130
d. Signature 34. with text: *DEUS SEJA LOUVADO. Series #1610-4093.*	5.00	17.50
e. Signature 35. with text. Series 4094-5378.	5.00	17.50
f. Signature 36. with text. Series 5379-5798.	5.00	22.50
g. Signature 37. with text. Series #5799-8232.	5.00	17.50

244A 5 Reais

ND (1997-). Violet, dark brown and blue on lilac underprint. Sculpture of the Republic at center right. Series # is the first 4 digits of serial #. Back: Vertical format. Great egret at center. Watermark: Flag. Printer: CdM-B or with additional imprint. 140x65mm.

	VF	UNC
a. Signature 37. Series #0001-1504.	5.00	17.50
b. Signature 38. Series #1505-3034.	5.00	17.50
c. Signature 39. Series #3035-3196.	7.50	22.50
d. Signature 39. Series #3197-8817.	2.00	6.00
e. Signature 40. Series #8818-9999.	FV	5.00
f. Signature 40. Series #B0001-5158.	FV	5.00
g. Signature 41. 1st signature variety. Series #B5159-B7387.	FV	5.00
h. Signatrue 41. 2nd signature variety. Series #B7388-.	FV	5.00

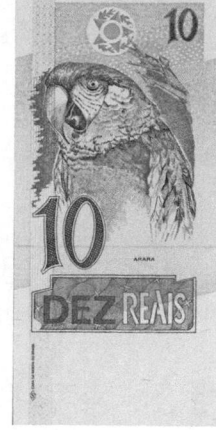

245 10 Reais

ND (1994). Dark brown, brown-violet and brown-orange on lilac and pale orange underprint. Sculpture of the Republic at center right. Series # is the first 4 digits of serial #. Back: Vertical format. Macaw at center. Watermark: Republic. Printer: CdM-B or with additional imprint. 140x65mm.

	VF	UNC
a. Signature 33. without text: *DEUS SEJA LOUVADO.* Series A-A: #1-0713.	10.00	45.00
b. Signature 33. Printer: TDLR. Series #A-B: #0001-1200.	15.00	55.00
c. Signature 34. without text: *DEUS SEJA LOUVADO* at lower left Series #0714-1817.	10.00	30.00
d. Signature 34. with text at lower left Series #1818-3403.	10.00	30.00
e. Signature 35. Series #3404-6102.	10.00	30.00
f. Signature 36. Series #6103-6714.	15.00	55.00
g. Signature 37. Series #6715-9999.	10.00	30.00
h. Signature 37. Series #0001-4844. Serial A-B.	15.00	55.00

245A 10 Reais

ND (1997-). UV: fibers fluoresce blue. Dark brown, brown-violet and brown-orange on lilac and pale orange underprint. Sculpture of the Republic at center right. Series # is the first 4 digits of serial #. Back: Vertical format. Macaw at center. Watermark: Flag. Printer: CdM-B or with additional imprint. 140x65mm.

	VF	UNC
a. Signature 37. Series #0001-4571. Serial A-C.	7.00	22.50
b. Signature 38. Series #4572-9179.	7.00	22.50
c. Signature 39. Series #9180-9999.	7.00	22.50
d. Signature 39. Series #0001-0075. Serial B-C.	10.00	27.50
e. Signature 39. Series #0076-9999.	5.00	12.50
f. Signature 39. Serial C-C. Series #0001-1136.	FV	8.00
g. Signature 40. Series #1137-9999.	FV	8.00
h. Signature 40. Series #D0001-D3438.	FV	8.00
i. Signature 41. 1st signature variety. Series #D3439-D9100.	FV	8.00
j. Signature 41. 2nd signature variety. Series #D9101-D9999.	FV	8.00
k. Signature 41. 2nd signature variety. Series #E0001-.	FV	8.00

246 50 Reais

ND (1994-). Dark brown and red-brown on multicolor underprint. Sculpture of
the Republic at center right. Series # is the first 4 digits of serial #. Back: Vertical
format, Jaguar. Printer: CdM-B or with additional imprint. 140x65mm.

	VF	UNC
a. Signature 33. Without text: *DEUS SEJA LOUVADO*. Series A-A: #0001-1249.	50.00	115
b. Signature 33. Without text. Printer: F-CO. Series A-B: #0001-0400.	50.00	165
c. Signature 34. Without text. Series #1250-1338.	40.00	135
d. Signature 34. With text. Series #1339-1438.	50.00	165
e. Signature 36. Series #1439-1636.	100	550
f. Signature 37. Series #1637-8405.	50.00	120
g. Signature 38. Series #8406-9999.	40.00	135
h. Signature 38. Series #0001-1004. Serial #B-A.	40.00	135
i. Signature 39. Series #1005-1483. Serial #B-A.	40.00	135
j. Signature 39. Series #1484-9057.	25.00	60.00
k. Signature 40. Series #9058-9999.	FV	30.00
l. Signature 40. Series #C0001-C8342.	FV	30.00
m. Signature 41. 1st signature variety. Series #C8343-C9999.	FV	30.00
n. Signature 41. 1st signature variety. Series #D0001-D2492.	FV	30.00
o. Signature 41. 2nd signature variety. Series #D2493-.	FV	30.00

247 100 Reais

ND(1994-). Blue-green and purple on multicolor underprint. Sculpture of the Republic at center right. Series # is the first 4 digits of serial #. Back: Vertical format.
Garoupa fish. Printer: CdM-B or with additional imprint. 140x65mm.

	VF	UNC
a. Signature 33. Without text: *DEIS SEJA LOUVADO*. Series #0001-1198.	100	175
b. Signature 34. Series #1199-1201.	150	325
c. Signature 34. Series #1202-1301. With text: *DEUS SEJA LOUVADO* at lower left.	125	225
d. Signature 37. Series #A1302-A1310.	125	225
e. Signature 41. 1st signature variety. Series #A1311-A2818.	125	225
f. Signature 41. 2nd signature variety. Series #A2819-.	125	225

2000 Commemorative Issue

#248, 500th Anniversary of the Discovery of Brazil

248 10 Reais

ND (2000). Polymer plastic. Dark Blue, blue and orange. Pedro Alvares Cabral at
center, compass to left. Back: Map and many portraits. 140x65mm.

	VF	UNC
a. Name as: *PEDRO A. CABRAL*. Series #0001-0586.	FV	15.00
b. Name as: *PEDRO ALVARES CABRAL*. Series #0587-2536.	FV	10.00

#248 Series #0001 was also available in a special folder, value $20.00.

2001-02 Issue

249 2 Reais

ND (2001-). UV: fibers fluoresce blue. Blue-green and black on multicolor underprint. Back: Tartaruga Marinha turtles. 140x65mm.

	VF	UNC
a. Signature 39. Series #0001-2798.	FV	2.50
b. Signature 40. Series #2799-7980.	FV	2.50
c. Signature 41. 1st signature variety. Series #A7981-A9999.	FV	2.50
d. Signature 41. 1st signature variety. Series #B0001-B2036.	FV	2.50
e. Signature 41. 2nd signature variety. Series #B2037-.	FV	2.50
s. Specimen. Red overprint: SEM VALOR on face.	—	225

250 20 Reais

ND (2002-). Yellow and rose on multicolor underprint. Back: Lion monkey.
140x65mm.

	VF	UNC
a. Signature 39. Series #0001-2125.	FV	12.50
b. Signature 40. Series #2126-7521.	FV	10.00
c. Signature 41. 1st signature variety. Series #A7522-A9398.	FV	10.00
d. Signature 41. 2nd signature variety. Series #A9399-A9999.	FV	10.00
e. Signature 41. 2nd signature variety. Series #B0001-.	FV	10.00
s. Specimen. Red overprint SEM VALOR on face.	—	250

REPUBLICA FEDERATIVA DO BRAZIL
Banco Central do Brazil
2003 Issue

251   1 Real   VF   UNC
ND (2003-). Black, olive-green and blue-green on aqua and pale green underprint.
Sculpture of the Republic at center right. Series # is first 4 digits of serial #. Serial
A-C. Back: Vertical format. White-necked jacobin hummingbirds at center.
Watermark: Flag. Printer: CdM-B. 140x65mm.
   a. Signature 40. Series 0001-3995.   FV   2.00

252   2 Reals   VF   UNC
2010. Sculpture of the Republic. Back: Turtles. Watermark: Turtles and 2.   FV   2.50
121x65mm.

253   5 Reais   VF   UNC
2010. Violet. Sculpture of the Republic. Back: Heron. Watermark: Heron and 5.
128x65mm.
   a. 2010.   FV   5.00

254   10 Reais   VF   UNC
2010. Brown and rose on multicolor underprint Republica head at right. Back: FV   8.00
Arara (macaw) bird at left, two in flight at right. Watermark: Macaw and 10.
135x65mm.

255   20 Reais   VF   UNC
ND. Orange on yellow and multicolor underprint Republica head at right. Back: FV   10.00
Lion Monkey at left and right. 156x70mm.

256   50 Reais   VF   UNC
2010. Dark brown. 149x70mm.   FV   25.00

257   100 Reais   VF   UNC
2010. Blue on multicolor underprint. 156x70mm.   FV   50.00

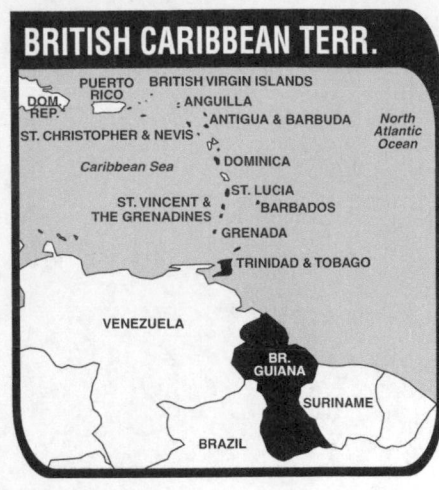

BRITISH CARIBBEAN TERR.

The British Caribbean Territories (Eastern Group), a currency board formed in 1950, comprised the British West Indies territories of Trinidad and Tobago; Barbados; the Leeward Islands of Anguilla, St. Christopher, Nevis and Antigua; the Windward Islands of St. Lucia, Dominica, St. Vincent and Grenada; British Guiana and the British Virgin Islands. As time progressed, the members of this Eastern Group varied. For later issues see East Caribbean States listings in Volume 3, Modern issues.

RULERS:
British

MONETARY SYSTEM:
1 Dollar = 100 Cents

BRITISH ADMINISTRATION

British Caribbean Territories, Eastern Group

1953 Issue

7	**1 Dollar**	**VF**	**UNC**
	1953-64. Red on multicolor underprint. Map at lower left, portrait of Queen Elizabeth II at right. Back: Arms in all four corners. Printer: BWC.		
	a. Watermark: Sailing ship. 5.1.1953.	100	400
	b. Watermark: Queen Elizabeth II. 1.3.1954-2.1.1957.	40.00	275
	c. 2.1.1958-2.1.1964.	40.00	275

8	**2 Dollars**	**VF**	**UNC**
	1953-64. Blue on multicolor underprint. Map at lower left, portrait of Queen Elizabeth II at right. Back: Arms in all four corners. Printer: BWC.		
	a. Watermark: Sailing ship. 5.1.1953.	550	1,750
	b. Watermark: Queen Elizabeth II. 1.3.1954-1.7.1960.	100	700
	c. 2.1.1961-2.1.1964.	100	700

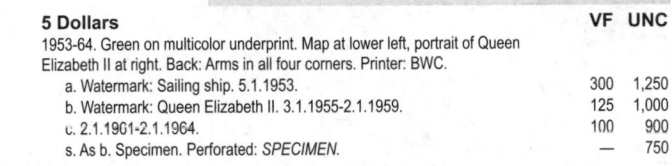

9	**5 Dollars**	**VF**	**UNC**
	1953-64. Green on multicolor underprint. Map at lower left, portrait of Queen Elizabeth II at right. Back: Arms in all four corners. Printer: BWC.		
	a. Watermark: Sailing ship. 5.1.1953.	300	1,250
	b. Watermark: Queen Elizabeth II. 3.1.1955-2.1.1959.	125	1,000
	c. 2.1.1961-2.1.1964.	100	900
	s. As b. Specimen. Perforated: *SPECIMEN*.	—	750

10	**10 Dollars**	**VF**	**UNC**
	1953-64. Brown on multicolor underprint. Map at lower left, portrait of Queen Elizabeth II at right. Back: Arms in all four corners. Printer: BWC.		
	a. Watermark: Sailing ship. 5.1.1953.	400	—
	b. Watermark: Queen Elizabeth II. 3.1.1955-2.1.1959.	250	2,000
	c. 2.1.1961; 2.1.1962; 2.1.1964.	200	1,800

11	**20 Dollars**	**VF**	**UNC**
	1953-64. Purple on multicolor underprint. Map at lower left, portrait of Queen Elizabeth II at right. Back: Arms in all four corners. Printer: BWC.		
	a. Watermark: Sailing ship. 5.1.1953.	600	—
	b. Watermark: Queen Elizabeth II. 2.1.1957-2.1.1964.	300	—

12	**100 Dollars**	**VF**	**UNC**
	1953-63. Black on multicolor underprint. Map at lower left, portrait of Queen Elizabeth II at right. Back: Arms in all four corners. Printer: BWC.		
	a. Watermark: Sailing ship. 5.1.1953.	6,000	—
	b. Watermark: Queen Elizabeth II. 1.3.1954.	4,000	—
	c. 2.1.1957.	8,800	—
	d. 2.1.1963.	4,000	—
	s. As b. Specimen.	—	2,500

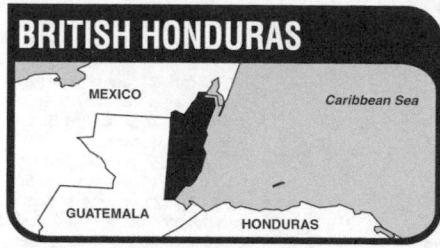

BRITISH HONDURAS

MEXICO

Caribbean Sea

GUATEMALA

HONDURAS

The former British colony of British Honduras is now Belize, a self-governing dependency of the United Kingdom situated in Central America south of Mexico and east and north of Guatemala, has an area of 8,867 sq. mi. (22,965 sq. km.) and a population of 209,000. Capital: Belmopan. Sugar, citrus fruits, chicle and hard woods are exported. The area, site of the ancient Mayan civilization, was sighted by Columbus in 1502, and settled by shipwrecked English seamen in 1638. British buccaneers settled the former capital of Belize in the 17th century. Britain claimed administrative right over the area after the emancipation of Central America from Spain, and declared it a colony subordinate to Jamaica in 1862. It established as the separate Crown Colony of British Honduras in 1884. The anti-British People's United Party, which attained power in 1954, won a constitution, effective in 1964 which established self-government under a British appointed governor. British Honduras became Belize on June 1, 1973, following the passage of a surprise bill by the Peoples United Party, but the constitutional relationship with Britain remained unchanged. In Dec. 1975, the U.N. General Assembly adopted a resolution supporting the right of the people of Belize to self-determination, and asking Britain and Guatemala to renew their negotiations on the future of Belize. Belize obtained independence on Sept. 21, 1981.

RULERS:
British

MONETARY SYSTEM:
1 Dollar = 100 Cents

Government of British Honduras
1952-53 Issue

28	1 Dollar		VF	UNC
	1953-73. Green on multicolor underprint. Arms at left, portrait of Queen Elizabeth II at right.			
	a. 15.4.1953-1.10.1958.		125	500
	b. 1.1.1961-1.5.1969.		75.00	400
	c. 1.6.1970-1.1.1973.		75.00	300
	s. As a, b, c. Specimen. Overprint: *SPECIMEN,* Punch hole cancelled.		—	100

29	2 Dollars		VF	UNC
	1953-73. Purple on multicolor underprint. Arms at left, portrait of Queen Elizabeth II at right.			
	a. 15.4.1953-1.10.1958.		100	750
	b. 1.10.1960-1.5.1965.		60.00	500
	c. 1.1.1971-1.1.1973.		40.00	350
	s. As a, b, c. Specimen. Overprint: *SPECIMEN,* Punch hole cancelled.		—	125

30	5 Dollars		VF	UNC
	1953-73. Red on multicolor underprint. Arms at left, portrait of Queen Elizabeth II at right.			
	a. 15.4.1953-1.10.1958.		150	1,000
	b. 1.3.1960-1.5.1965.		85.00	700
	c. 1.1.1970-1.1.1973.		75.00	500
	s. As a, c. Specimen. Overprint: *SPECIMEN,* Punch hole cancelled.		—	150

31	10 Dollars		VF	UNC
	1958-73. Black on multicolor underprint. Arms at left, portrait of Queen Elizabeth II at right.			
	a. 15.4.1953-1.11.1961.		300	—
	b. 1.4.1964-1.5.1969.		175	1,300
	c. 1.1.1971-1.1.1973.		125	1,200
	s. As a, c. Specimen. Overprint: *SPECIMEN,* Punch hole cancelled.		—	200

32	20 Dollars		VF	UNC
	1952-73. Brown on multicolor underprint. Arms at left, portrait of Queen Elizabeth II at right.			
	a. 1.12.1952-1.10.1958.		500	—
	b. 1.3.1960-1.5.1969.		350	2,800
	c. 1.1.1970-1.1.1973.		300	2,500
	s. As a, c. Specimen. Overprint: *SPECIMEN,* Punch hole cancelled.		—	400

Note: For similar notes but with the *BELIZE* heading, see Belize country listings.

BRITISH WEST AFRICA

British West Africa was an administrative grouping of the four former British colonies of Gambia, Sierra Leone, Nigeria and Gold Coast (now Ghana). All are now independent republics and members of the British Commonwealth of Nations. These four colonies were supplied with a common currency by the West African Currency Board from 1907 through 1962. Also see Gambia, Ghana, Nigeria and Sierra Leone for related currency and for individual statistics and history.

RULERS:
British to 1952

MONETARY SYSTEM:
1 Shilling = 12 Pence
1 Pound = 20 Shillings

BRITISH ADMINISTRATION

West African Currency Board

1962 Issue

		VF	UNC
12	**20 Shillings**		
	17.4.1962. Black and red. River scene with palm trees at left. Back: Harvesting scene. Printer: TDLR.	75.00	400

BRUNEI

Negara Brunei Darussalam (The State of Brunei), a member of the British Commonwealth is located on the northwest coast of the island of Borneo, has an area of 5,770 sq. km. and a population of 381,370. Capital: Bandar Seri Begawan.

The Sultanate of Brunei's influence peaked between the 15th and 17th centuries when its control extended over coastal areas of northwest Borneo and the southern Philippines. Brunei subsequently entered a period of decline brought on by internal strife over royal succession, colonial expansion of European powers, and piracy. In 1888, Brunei became a British protectorate; independence was achieved in 1984. The same family has ruled Brunei for over six centuries. Brunei benefits from extensive petroleum and natural gas fields, the source of one of the highest per capita GDPs in Asia.

RULERS:
Sultan Sir Omar Ali Saifuddin III, 1950-1967
Sultan Hassanal Bolkiah I, 1967-

MONETARY SYSTEM:
1 Dollar = 100 Sen to 1967
1 Ringgit (Dollar) = 100 Sen, 1967-

STATE

Kerajaan Brunei

GOVERNMENT OF BRUNEI

1967 Issue

		VF	UNC
1	**1 Ringgit**		
	1967. Dark blue on multicolor underprint. Sultan Omar Ali Saifuddin III with military cap at right. Back: Mosque. Watermark: Sultan Omar Ali Saifuddin III. Printer: BWC.		
	a. Issued note.	35.00	70.00
	s. Specimen.	—	—

		VF	UNC
2	**5 Ringgit**		
	1967. Dark green on multicolor underprint. Sultan Omar Ali Saifuddin III with military cap at right. Back: Mosque. Watermark: Sultan Omar Ali Saifuddin III. Printer: BWC.		
	a. Issued note.	50.00	175
	s. Specimen.	—	—

		VF	UNC
3	**10 Ringgit**		
	1967. Red on multicolor underprint. Sultan Omar Ali Saifuddin III with military cap at right. Back: Mosque. Watermark: Sultan Omar Ali Saifuddin III. Printer: BWC.		
	a. Issued note.	125	250
	s. Specimen.	—	—

4   50 Ringgit
1967. Dark brown on multicolor underprint. Sultan Omar Ali Saifuddin III with
military cap at right. Back: Mosque. Watermark: Sultan Omar Ali Saifuddin III.
Printer: BWC.

	VF	UNC
	200	400

5   100 Ringgit
1967. Blue on multicolor underprint. Sultan Omar Ali Saifuddin III with military cap
at right. Back: Mosque. Watermark: Sultan Omar Ali Saifuddin III. Printer: BWC.

	VF	UNC
	350	700

1972-79 Issue

6   1 Ringgit
1972-88. Blue on multicolor underprint. Sultan Hassanal Bolkiah I in military uniform at right. Back: Mosque. Watermark: Sultan Hassanal Bolkiah I. Printer: BWC.

	VF	UNC
a. 1972; 1976; 1978.	6.00	30.00
b. 1980; 1982.	6.00	22.50
c. 1983-1986.	5.00	20.00
d. 1988	4.00	15.00
s. Specimen.	—	130

7   5 Ringgit
1979-86. Green on multicolor underprint. Sultan Hassanal Bolkiah I in military uniform at right. Back: Mosque. Watermark: Sultan Hassanal Bolkiah I. Printer: BWC.

	VF	UNC
a. 1979; 1981.	15.00	90.00
b. 1983; 1984; 1986.	12.50	75.00
s. Specimen.	—	150

8   10 Ringgit
1976-86. Red on multicolor underprint. Sultan Hassanal Bolkiah I in military uniform at right. Back: Mosque. Watermark: Sultan Hassanal Bolkiah I. Printer: BWC.

	VF	UNC
a. 1976; 1981.	30.00	175
b. 1983; 1986.	27.50	100
s. Specimen.	—	225
x. Issued note, double printed.	175	—

9   50 Ringgit
1973-86. Dark brown on multicolor underprint. Sultan Hassanal Bolkiah I in
military uniform at right. Back: Mosque. Watermark: Sultan Hassanal Bolkiah I.
Printer: BWC.

	VF	UNC
a. 1973	100	200
b. 1977; 1982.	90.00	175
c. 1981	110	150
d. 1986	70.00	225
s. Specimen.	—	400

10   100 Ringgit
1972-88. Blue on multicolor underprint. Sultan Hassanal Bolkiah I in military uniform at right. Back: Mosque. Watermark: Sultan Hassanal Bolkiah I. Printer: BWC.

	VF	UNC
a. 1972; 1976.	150	400
b. 1978; 1980.	140	375
c. 1982; 1983; 1988.	130	350
s. Specimen.	—	400

1979; 1987 Issue

11   500 Ringgit
1979; 1987. Orange on multicolor underprint. Sultan Hassanal Bolkiah I in royal
uniform at right. Back: Mosque at center. Watermark: Sultan Hassanal Bolkiah I.
Printer: BWC.

	VF	UNC
a. 1979	450	1,500
b. 1987	425	1,200
s. Specimen.	—	1,100

12   1000 Ringgit   **VF   UNC**

1979; 1986; 1987. Gray, brown and greenish blue. Sultan Hassanal Bolkiah I in
royal uniform at right. Back: Brunei Museum. Watermark: Sultan Hassanal Bolkiah
I. Printer: BWC.

	VF	UNC
a. 1979	1,400	2,000
b. 1986-87.	1,300	1,800
s. Specimen.	1,200	1,750

Negara Brunei Darussalam
1989 Issue

13   1 Ringgit   **VF   UNC**

1989-95. Purple on multicolor underprint. Sultan Hassanal Bolkiah I at right. Back:
Aerial view of Bandar Seri. Watermark: Sultan Hassanal Bolkiah I.

	VF	UNC
a. 1989; 1991; 1992.	4.00	10.00
b. 1994-95.	3.00	9.00

14   5 Ringgit   **VF   UNC**

1989-91; 1993; 1995. Blue-gray and deep green on multicolor underprint. Sultan
Hassanal Bolkiah I at right. Back: Houses and boats. Watermark: Sultan Hassanal
Bolkiah I.   15.00   20.00

15   10 Ringgit   **VF   UNC**

1989-92; 1995. Purple and red-orange on multicolor underprint. Sultan Hassanal
Bolkiah I at right. Back: Waterfront village with mosque. Watermark: Sultan Hassanal Bolkiah I.   20.00   35.00

16   50 Ringgit   **VF   UNC**

1989-91;1994; 1995. Brown, olive-green and orange on multicolor underprint.
Sultan Hassanal Bolkiah I at right. Back: People in power launch. Watermark:
Sultan Hassanal Bolkiah I. Printer: TDLR.

	VF	UNC
a. Issued note.	FV	110
s. 1989. Specimen. Punch hole cancelled. Red oval DLR stamps.	—	500

17   100 Ringgit   **VF   UNC**

1989-92; 1994. Blue and violet on ulticolor underprint. Sultan Hassanal Bolkiah I
at right. Back: River scene. Watermark: Sultan Hassanal Bolkiah I.   FV   200

18   500 Ringgit   **VF   UNC**

1989-92. Red-orange, purple olive and black on multicolor underprint. Sultan
Hassanal Bolkiah I at right, houses at left center. Back: Padian woman paddling
her boat in Kampong Ayer. Watermark: Sultan Hassanal Bolkiah I.   FV   900

19 1000 Ringgit

VF UNC

1989-91. Red-violet, purple, olive and blue-green on multicolor underprint. Sultan Hassanal Bolkiah I at right. Back: Waterfront village of Kampong Ayer and Istana Nurul Iman. Watermark: Sultan Hassanal Bolkiah I.

FV 1,500

20 10,000 Ringgit

VF UNC

1989. Dark brown and dark green on multicolor underprint. Sultan Hassanal Bolkiah I at right. Back: Aerial view of Bandar Seri Begawan harbor. Watermark: Sultan Hassanal Bolkiah I.

a. Issued note.	FV	13,000
s. Specimen. Overprint: *CONTOH SPECIMEN* in two lines.	—	4,500

1992 Commemorative Issue

#21, 25th Anniversary of Accession

21 25 Ringgit

VF UNC

1992. Brown, lilac, green and multicolor. Royal procession at center, Sultan Hassanal Bolkiah I at right. Back: Crown at left, coronation at center. Dates *1967* and *1992* with text at top. Watermark: Sultan Hassanal Bolkiah I.

50.00 75.00

1996 Issue

22 1 Ringgit

VF UNC

1996; 2007; 2008. Polymer plastic. Blue-black and deep green on multicolor underprint. Sultan Jam'Asr Hassan Bolkiah I at right. Riverside simpur plant at left center. Back: Rain forest waterfall at left center, arms at upper left. Printer: NPA (without imprint). 141x69mm.

a. 1996	FV	4.00
b. 2007	FV	3.75
c. 2008	FV	3.00

23 5 Ringgit

VF UNC

1996; 2002. Polymer plastic. Black on green and multicolor underprint. Sultan Jam'Asr Hassan Bolkiah I at right, pitcher plant at left center. Back: Rain forest floor, arms at upper left. Printer: NPA (without imprint). 141x69mm.

FV 10.00

24 10 Ringgit

VF UNC

1996; 1998; 2008. Polymer plastic. Dark brown and brown on red and multicolor underprint. Sultan Jam'Asr Hassan Bolkiah I at right, purple-leafed forest yam at left center. Back: Rain forest canopy, arms at upper left. Printer: NPA (without imprint). 141x69mm.

a. 1996	FV	20.00
b. 1998	FV	17.50
c. 2008	FV	15.00

25   50 Ringgit
1996. Brown, blue and purple on multicolor underprint. Sultan Jam'Asr Hassan
Bolkiah I at right. Back: Offshore oil rig.

VF   UNC
FV   75.00

26   100 Ringgit
1996. Brown and orange on multicolor underprint. Sultan Jam'Asr Hassan Bolkiah
I at right. Back: Brunei International Airport.

VF   UNC
FV   125

27   500 Ringgit
2000. Deep orange and brown on multicolor underprint. Sultan Jam'Asr Hassan
Bolkiah I at right. Back: Bolkiah Mosque.

VF   UNC
FV   650

2004 Commemorative Issue

28   50 Ringgit
15.7.2004. Polymer plastic. Brown, green and blue on multicolor underprint.
Kantan medicinial flower at center. 158x75mm.

VF   UNC
FV   100

29   100 Ringgit
15.7.2004; 2008. Polymer plastic. Brown, orange and yellow on multicolor underprint. Kjojk medicinial flower at center. 158x75mm.

VF   UNC

    a. 15.7.2004.   FV   125
    b. 2008. (Date at lower right on back.)   FV   120

2006-7 Issue

31   500 Ringgit
2006; 2013. Polymer plastic. Brown on green and rose underprint. Sultan Omar Ali
Saifuddin III at right, java tea flowers at center. Back: Omar Ali Saifuddin mosque
in Bandar Seri Begawan. Watermark: Sultan Omar Ali Saifuddin III Printer: NPA.
175x80mm.

VF   UNC

    a. 2006   FV   500
    b. 2013   FV   500
    s. Specimen.   —   650

32   1000 Ringgit
2006. Polymer plastic. Black and tan on multicolor underprint. Sultan Hassanal
Bolkiah at right, akar bilaran flower at center. Back: Ministry of Finance building
in Bandar Seri Begawan. Watermark: Sultan Hassanal Bolkiah. Printer: NPA.
175x80mm.

VF   UNC

    a. Issued note.   FV   1,000
    s. Specimen.   FV   1,250

33   10,000 Ringgit
2006. Polymer plastic. Green and brown. Sultan Haji Hassanal Bolkiah at right,
pangarus timun dendang flower at center. Back: Legslative Council building in
Bandar Seri Begawan at center. Watermark: Sultan Haji Hassanal Bolkiah. Printer:
NPA. 180x90mm.

VF   UNC

    a. Issued note.   —   9,500
    s. Specimen.   — 10,000

2007 Commemorative Issue

34 20 Ringgit   **VF UNC**
2007. Polymer plastic. Orange. Sultan Hassanal Bolkiah at right, Ipomoea pescapre plant at center. Back: Singapore skyline and Sultan Ali Saifuddien mosque. Watermark: Sultan Hassanal Bolkiah and HB. 149x72mm.

  a. Serial # prefix A.   FV 30.00
  b. Serial # prefix BND.   FV 35.00
  s. Specimen.   — 125

2011 Polymer Issue

35 1 Ringgit   **VF UNC**
2011. Polymer plastic. Dark and light blue on multicolor underprint. Sultan Hassanal Bolkiah at right. Back: Bandar Seri Begawan at center 141x69mm.   FV 3.00

36 5 Ringgit   **VF UNC**
2011. Polymer plastic. Olive and green on multicolor underprint. Sultan Hassanal Bolkiah at right, pitcher plant at center. Back: Lapau - Royal Ceremonial Hall at center 141x69mm.   FV 10.00

37 10 Ringgit   **VF UNC**
2011. Polymer plastic. Brown and rose on multicolor underprint. Sultan Hassanal Bolkiah at right, leafed forest yam at center. Back: Jame Asr Hassanii Bolkiah Mosque at center 141x69mm.   FV 18.00

BULGARIA

The Republic of Bulgaria (formerly the Peoples Republic of Bulgaria), a Balkan country on the Black Sea in southeastern Europe, has an area of 110,910 sq. km. and a population of 7.26 million. Capital: Sofia. Agriculture remains a key component of the economy but industrialization, particularly heavy industry, has been emphasized since the late 1940's. Machinery, tobacco and cigarettes, wines and spirits, clothing and metals are the chief exports.

The Bulgars, a Central Asian Turkic tribe, merged with the local Slavic inhabitants in the late 7th century to form the first Bulgarian state. In succeeding centuries, Bulgaria struggled with the Byzantine Empire to assert its place in the Balkans, but by the end of the 14th century the country was overrun by the Ottoman Turks. Northern Bulgaria attained autonomy in 1878 and all of Bulgaria became independent from the Ottoman Empire in 1908. Having fought on the losing side in both World Wars, Bulgaria fell within the Soviet sphere of influence and became a People's Republic in 1946. Communist domination ended in 1990, when Bulgaria held its first multiparty election since World War II and began the contentious process of moving toward political democracy and a market economy while combating inflation, unemployment, corruption, and crime. The country joined NATO in 2004 and the EU in 2007.

MONETARY SYSTEM:
1 Lev = 100 Stotinki until 1999
1 Lev = 1,000 "Old" Lev, 1999
Silver Lev = Lev Srebro
Gold Lev = Lev Zlato

PEOPLES REPUBLIC
БЪЛГАРСКА НАРОДНА БАНКА
BULGARIAN NATIONAL BANK
1962 Issue

88 1 Lev   **VF UNC**
1962. Brown-lilac on multicolor underprint. Arms at left. Back: Monument for the Battle of Shipka Pass (1877) at left center. Printer: Gosnak.

  a. Issued note.   0.25 2.00
  s1. Specimen. Serial # as 000000.   — 60.00
  s2. Specimen. Serial # as 240xxx.   — 50.00

89 2 Leva   **VF UNC**
1962. Black and blue on green underprint. Arms at left. Back: Woman picking grapes in vineyard at right. Printer: Gosnak.

  a. Issued note.   0.40 3.00
  s1. Specimen. Serial # as 000000.   — 60.00
  s2. Specimen. Serial # as 040xxx.   — 50.00

90 5 Leva   **VF UNC**
1962. Red on blue and multicolor underprint. Arms at left. Back: Coastline village. Printer: Gosnak.

  a. Issued note.   0.50 6.00
  s1. Specimen. Serial # as 000000.   — 60.00
  s2. Specimen. Serial # as 600xxx.   — 50.00

91 10 Leva VF UNC
1962. Black on blue and multicolor underprint. G. Dimitrov at left, arms at upper
center. Back: Factory. Printer: Gosnak.
    a. Issued note. 0.50 9.00
    s1. Specimen. Serial # as 000000. — 80.00
    s2. Specimen. Serial # as 225xxx. — 70.00

92 20 Leva VF UNC
1962. Brown-lilac on multicolor underprint. G. Dimitrov at left, arms at upper right
center. Back: Factory. Printer: Gosnak.
    a. Issued note. 0.50 14.00
    s1. Specimen. Serial # as 000000. — 90.00

1974 Issue

93 1 Lev VF UNC
1974. Brown on multicolor underprint. Modified arms with dates at left. Back:
Monument for the battle of Shipka Pass (1877) at keft center. Watermark: Decorative design.
    a. Issued note. 0.20 1.00
    s1. Specimen. 6-digit serial #. 000000. — 50.00
    s2. Specimen. 7-digit serial #. 0000000. — 50.00

94 2 Leva VF UNC
1974. Black and blue on green underprint. Modified arms with dates at left. Back:
Woman picking grapes in vineyard at right. Watermark: Decorative design.
    a. Issued note. 0.25 2.00
    s1. Specimen. 6-digit serial #. 000000. — 50.00
    s2. Specimen. 7-digit serial #. 0000000. — 50.00

95 5 Leva VF UNC
1974. Red on blue and multicolor underprint. Modified arms with dates at left.
Back: Coastline village. Watermark: Decorative design.
    a. Issued note. 0.50 3.00
    s1. Specimen. 6-digit serial #. 000000. — 50.00
    s2. Specimen. 7-digit serial #. 0000000. — 50.00

96 10 Leva VF UNC
1974. Black on blue and multicolor underprint. G. Dimitrov at left, modified arms at
upper center. Back: Factory. Watermark: Hands holding hammer and sickle.
    a. Issued note. 0.50 6.00
    s1. Specimen. 6-digit serial #. 000000. — 70.00
    s2. Specimen. 7-digit serial #. 0000000. — 70.00

97 20 Leva VF UNC
1974. Brown-lilac on multicolor underprint. G. Dimitrov at left, modified arms at
upper center. Back: Factory. Watermark: Hands holding hammer and sickle.
    a. Issued note. 1.00 10.00
    s1. Specimen. 6-digit serial #. 000000. — 80.00
    s2. Specimen. 7-digit serial #. 0000000. — 80.00

1989; 1990 Issues

98 50 Leva VF UNC
1990. Brown and daark blue on multicolor underprint. Arms at left. center. Back:
Castle ruins at center right. Watermark: Hands holding hammer and sickle.
    a. Issued note. 3.00 12.00
    s. Specimen. — 120
#98 was withdrawn from circulation shortly after its release.

99 100 Leva VF UNC
1989. (Not issued). Purple on lilac underprint. Arms at left center. Back: Horseman — 150
with two dogs at center right. Watermark: Rampant lion.
#99 carries the name of the Bulgarian Peoples Republic, which could be the reason it was not
released. An estimated 500-600 pieces were *liberated* during the distruction process.

REPUBLIC
БЪЛГАРСКА НАРОДНА БАНКА
BULGARIAN NATIONAL BANK
1991-94 Issue

100 20 Leva   **VF UNC**

1991. UV: fibers fluoresce blue. Blue-black and blue-green on multicolor underprint. Dutchess Sevastokratoritza Desislava at left center. Back: Boyana Church at right. Watermark: Arms (lion). Printer: Wertpapierdruckerei-Germany.

		VF	UNC
a. Issued note		0.50	1.00
s1. Specimen.		FV	150

101 50 Leva   **VF UNC**

1992. UV: fibers fluoresce blue. Purple and violet on multicolor underprint. Khristo G. Danov at left. Back: Platen printing press at right. Watermark: Arms (lion).

		VF	UNC
a. Issued note.		0.50	1.00
s. Specimen.		FV	150

102 100 Leva   **VF UNC**

1991; 1993. UV: fibers fluoresce yellow and blue. Dark brown and maroon on multicolor underprint. Zhary Zograf (artist) at left center. Back: Wheel of Life at right. Watermark: Arms (lion).

		VF	UNC
a. 1991.		1.00	5.00
b. 1993.		0.50	1.00
s1. As a. Specimen.		—	150
s2. As b. Specimen.		—	200

103 200 Leva   **VF UNC**

1992. UV: fibers fluoresce blue Deep violet and brown-orange on multicolor underprint. Ivan Vazov at left, village in underprint. Back: Lyre with laurel wreath at right. Watermark: Arms (lion).

		VF	UNC
a. Issued note.		FV	1.00
s. Specimen.		—	150

104 500 Leva   **VF UNC**

1993. Dark green and black on multicolor underprint. D. Christov at left. Back: Opera house in Varna at center right, herring gulls at lower right. Watermark: D. Christov.

		VF	UNC
a. Issued note.		FV	1.50
s. Specimen.		—	200

105 1000 Leva   **VF UNC**

1994; 1997. Dark green and olive-brown on multicolor underprint. V. Levski at left, Liberty with flag, sword and lion at upper center right. Back: Monument and writings of Levski at center right. Watermark: V. Levski. Printer: G&D.

		VF	UNC
a. Issued note.		FV	2.00
s. Specimen.		—	150

1994-96 Issue

106 1000 Leva   **VF UNC**

1996. Dark green and olive-brown on multicolor underprint. V. Levski at left, Liberty with flag, sword and lion at upper center right. Wide hologram foil strip at left. Back: Monument and writings of Levski at center right. Watermark: V. Levski.

		VF	UNC
a. Issued note.		FV	12.00
s. Specimen.		—	150

107 2000 Leva   **VF UNC**

1994; 1996. Black and dark blue on multicolor underprint. N. Ficev at left, building outlines at center, wide hologram foil strip at left. Back: Steeple, building plans at center right. Watermark: N. Ficev.

		VF	UNC
a. 1994.		2.00	15.00
b. 1996.		2.00	15.00
s1. As a. Specimen.		—	150
s2. As b. Specimen.		—	150

108   5000 Leva

1996. Violet on multicolor underprint. Z. Stoyanov at left, quill pen at center right. Back: Monument (two views) at center, and *1885 Proclamation to the Bulgarian People* at right. Watermark: Z. Stoyanov.

	VF	UNC
a. Issued note.	4.00	9.00
s. Specimen.	—	150

109   10,000 Leva

1996. Brown and purple on multicolor underprint. V. Dimitrov at left, palette, brushes, Academy of the Arts at center, wide hologram foil strip at left. Back: Sketches at center, *Bulgarian Madonna* at right. Watermark: V. Dimitrov.

	VF	UNC
a. Issued note.	8.00	20.00
s. Specimen.	—	200

#110 Renumbered, see #105.

1997 Issue

111   5000 Leva

1997. Violet on multicolor underprint. Z. Stoyanov at left, quill pen at center, without wide hologram foil strip. Back: Monument (two views) at center, and *1885 Proclamation to the Bulgarian People* at right. Watermark: Z. Stoyanov. Printer: G&D.

	VF	UNC
a. Issued note.	4.00	9.00
s. Specimen.	—	200

112   10,000 Leva

1997. Reduced size. Multicolor. Dr. P. Beron at left, wide hologram foil strip at left. Back: Telescope at right.

	VF	UNC
a. Issued note.	7.00	12.00
s. Specimen.	—	200

113   50,000 Leva

1997. Purple on multicolor underprint. St. Cyril at left, St. Methodius at center right, with wide hologram foil strip at left. Back: Architectural monuments of the ancient Bulgarian capitals of Pliska and Preslav.

	VF	UNC
a. Issued note.	35.00	60.00
s. Specimen.	—	250

1999-2003 Issue

Monetary Reform: 1 Lev = 1000 "Old" Leva.

114   1 Lev

1999. Red and blue on yellow underprint. Icon of St. John of Rila at left, holographic strip at left. Back: Rila Monastery. 112x60mm.

	VF	UNC
	FV	1.00

115   2 Leva

1999; 2005. Violet and pink on light blue underprint. Paisii Hilendarski at left, holographic strip at left. Back: Heraldic lion. 116x64mm.

	VF	UNC
a. 1999.	FV	1.75
b. 2005.	FV	1.75

116   5 Leva

1999; 2009. Red, brown and green on multicolor undeerprint. Ivan Milev at left, holographic strip at left. Back: Parts of paintings. 121x67mm.

	VF	UNC
a. 1999.	FV	4.50
b. 2009.	FV	4.50

117   10 Leva

1999; 2008. UV: fibers fluoresce yellow and blue, series of 10 fluoresce yellow at left end. Dark green on ochre underprint. Dr. Peter Beron at left, holographic strip at left. Back: Astronomy sketches and telescope. 126x70mm.

	VF	UNC
a. 1999.	FV	10.00
b. 2008. Improved security devices.	FV	9.00

118 20 Leva VF UNC
1999; 2007. Blue on multicolor underprint. S. Stambolov at left, holographic strip
at left. Back: National Assembly building and Eagles' and Lions' Bridges in Sofia.
131x72mm.
  a. 1999. FV 17.50
  b. 2007. Bank initials added to watemark. FV 17.50

119 50 Leva VF UNC
1999, 2006. Brown and yellow on multicolor underprint. Pencho Slaveykov at left,
holographic strip at left. Back: Illustrations from his poetry works. 136x76mm.
  a. 1999. Building in circle at lower center. Serial number prefix A. FV 45.00
  b. 2006. Solid device at lower center. Serian number prefix B. FV 45.00

120 100 Leva VF UNC
2003. Green on multicolor underprint. Aleka Konstantinov at left. Back: His FV 85.00
character "Uncle Ganyo".

2005 Commemorative Issue

121 20 Leva VF UNC
2005. Purple and yellow on multicolor underprint. Architectural renderings, three FV 25.00
shields at bottom. Back: Bank building and bank notes. 134x74mm.

BURMA

The Socialist Republic of the Union of Burma (now called Myanmar), is a country of Southeast Asia fronting on the Bay of Bengal and the Andaman Sea, has an area of 261,228 sq. mi. (676,577 sq. km.) and a population of 49.34 million. Capital: Rangoon. The first European to reach Burma, about 1435, was Nicolo Di Conti, a merchant of Venice. During the beginning of the reign of Bodawpaya (1782-1819AD) the kingdom comprised most of the same area as it does today including Arakan which was taken over in 1784-85. The British East India Company, while unsuccessful in its 1612 effort to establish posts along the Bay of Bengal, was enabled by the Anglo-Burmese Wars of 1824-86 to expand to the whole of Burma and to secure its annexation to British India. In 1937, Burma was separated from India, becoming a separate British colony with limited self-government. The Japanese occupied Burma in 1942, and on Aug. 1, 1943 Burma became an "independent and sovereign state" under Dr. Ba Maw who was appointed the Adipadi (head of state). This puppet state later collapsed with the surrender of Japanese forces. Burma became an independent nation outside the British Commonwealth on Jan. 4, 1948, the constitution of 1948 providing for a parliamentary democracy and the nationalization of certain industries. However, political and economic problems persisted, and on March 2, 1962, Gen. Ne Win took over the government, suspended the constitution, installed himself as chief of state, and pursued a socialistic program with nationalization of nearly all industry and trade. On Jan. 4, 1974, a new constitution adopted by referendum established Burma as a "socialist republic" under one-party rule. The country name was changed formally to the Union of Myanmar in 1989. For later issues refer to Myanmar.

MONETARY SYSTEM:
  1 Kyat = 100 Pyas, 1943-45, 1952-89

REPUBLIC

Peoples Bank of Burma

1965 ND Issue

#52-55 Replacement notes have special Burmese characters with serial #.

52 1 Kyat VF UNC
ND(1965). Purple and blue-gray on multicolor underprint. Portrait of General Aung 0.30 1.00
San at center. Serial # varieties. Back: Fisherman at center, arms at upper left.
Watermark: Pattern throughout paper. Printer: East Berlin.

53 5 Kyats VF UNC
ND (1965). Green and light blue. Portrait of General Aung San at center. Back: 1.00 2.50
Man with ox, arms at upper left. Watermark: Pattern throughout paper. Printer:
East Berlin.

58   10 Kyats   VF   UNC
ND (1973). Red and violet on multicolor underprint. Military portrait of General   0.50   1.00
Aung San at left. Back: Native ornaments at left center. Watermark: General Aung
San.

54   10 Kyats   VF   UNC
ND (1965). Red-brown and violet. Portrait of General Aung San at center. Back: 1.50   5.00
Woman picking cotton at right, arms at upper left. Watermark: Pattern throughout
paper. Printer: East Berlin.

59   25 Kyats   VF   UNC
ND (1972). Brown and tan on multicolor underprintl Military portrait of General   0.75   1.50
Aung San at left. Back: Mythical winged creature at center. Watermark: General
Aung San.

55   20 Kyats   VF   UNC
ND (1965). Brown and tan. Portrait of General Aung San at center. Back: Farmer   2.50   8.00
on tractor at center right, arms at upper left. Watermark: Pattern throughout paper.
Printer: East Berlin.

Union of Burma Bank
1972-79 ND Issue

56   1 Kyat   VF   UNC
ND (1972). UV: fibers fluoresce blue. Green and blue on multicolor underprint.   0.15   0.40
Military portrait of General Aung San at left. Back: Ornate native wheel assembly
at right. Watermark: General Aung San.

60   50 Kyats   VF   UNC
ND (1979). Brown and violet on multicolor underprintl Military portrait of General   10.00   25.00
Aung San at left. Back: Mythical dancer at left center. Watermark: General Aung
San.

57   5 Kyats   VF   UNC
ND (1973). Blue and purple on multicolor underprint. Military portrait of General   0.25   1.00
Aung San at left. Back: Palm tree at left center. Watermark: General Aung San.

61   100 Kyats

ND (1976). Blue and green on multicolor underprint. Military portrait of General
Aung San at left. Back: Native wheel and musical string instrument at left center.
Watermark: General Aung San.

	VF	UNC
a. Issued note.	4.00	15.00
s. Specimen. Overprint and rubber stamped: *SPECIMEN*.	—	—

1985-87 ND Issue

62   15 Kyats

ND (1986). Reduced size. Blue-gray and green on multicolor underprint. Portrait
of General Aung San at left center. Back: Mythical dancer at left. Watermark:
General Aung San.

VF — FV   UNC — 2.00

63   35 Kyats

ND (1986). Reduced size. Brown-violet and purple on multicolor underprint.
General Aung San in military hat at left center. Back: Mythical dancer at left.
Watermark: General Aung San.

VF — 0.50   UNC — 1.50

64   45 Kyats

ND (1987). Reduced size. Blue-gray and blue on multicolor underprint. Po Hla Gyi
at right. Back: Two workers with rope and bucket at left center, oil field at center.
Watermark: General Aung San.

VF — FV   UNC — 4.00

65   75 Kyats

ND (1985). Reduced size. Brown on multicolor underprint. General Aung San at
left center. Back: Dancer at left. Watermark: General Aung San.

VF — 0.75   UNC — 2.75

66   90 Kyats

ND (1987). Reduced size. Brown, green and blue on multicolor underprint. Seya
San at right. Back: Farmer plowing with oxen at left center, rice planting at upper
right. Watermark: General Aung San.

VF — FV   UNC — 6.00

NOTE: FOR LATER ISSUES SEE MYANMAR.

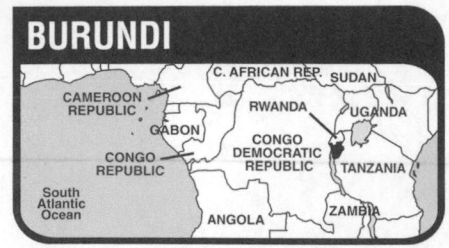

The Republic of Burundi, a landlocked country in central Africa, east of Lake Taganyila has an area of 27,830 sq. km. and a population of 8.69 million. Capital: Bujumbura. Burundi has a predominantly agricultural economy. Coffee, tea and cotton are exported.

Burundi's first democratically elected president was assassinated in October 1993 after only 100 days in office, triggering widespread ethnic violence between Hutu and Tutsi factions. More than 200,000 Burundians perished during the conflict that spanned almost a dozen years. Hundreds of thousands of Burundians were internally displaced or became refugees in neighboring countries. An internationally brokered power-sharing agreement between the Tutsi-dominated government and the Hutu rebels in 2003 paved the way for a transition process that led to an integrated defense force, established a new constitution in 2005, and elected a majority Hutu government in 2005. The new government, led by President Pierre Nkurunziza, signed a South African brokered ceasefire with the country's last rebel group in September of 2006 but still faces many challenges.

RULERS:
    Mwambutsa IV, 1962-1966
    Ntare V, 1966

MONETARY SYSTEM:
    1 Franc = 100 Centimes

KINGDOM
Banque du Royaume du Burundi
1964 ND Provisional Issue

1	5 Francs	Fine	XF
	ND (1964 - old dates 15.5.1961; 15.4.1963). Light brown. Large black overprint on Rwanda-Burundi #1.	45.00	200

2	10 Francs	Fine	XF
	ND (1964 - old date 5.10.1960). Gray. Large red overprint on Rwanda-Burundi #2.	75.00	250

3	20 Francs	Fine	XF
	ND (1964 - old date 5.10.1960). Green. Large black overprint on Rwanda-Burundi #3.	75.00	250

4	50 Francs	Fine	XF
	ND (1964 - old dates 15.9.1960-1.10.1960). Red. Large black overprint on Rwanda-Burundi #4.	75.00	250

5	100 Francs	Fine	XF
	ND (1964 - old dates 1.10.1960; 31.7.1962). Blue. Large red overprint on Rwanda-Burundi #5.	65.00	235
6	500 Francs	Fine	XF
	ND (1964 - old dates 15.9.1960-15.5.1961). Lilac brown. Large black overprint on Rwanda-Burundi #6.	650	1,150

7	1000 Francs	Fine	XF
	ND (1964 - old date 31.7.1962). Green. Large black overprint on Rwanda-Burundi #7.	400	1,250

1964; 1965 Regular Issue

8	5 Francs	VF	UNC
	1.10.1964; 1.12.1964; 1.5.1965. Light brown on gray-green underprint. Two young men picking coffee beans at left. Back: Arms at center.	10.00	30.00

9	10 Francs	VF	UNC
	20.11.1964; 25.2.1965; 20.3.1965; 31.12.1965. Dark brown on lilac-brown underprint. Cattle at center. Back: Arms at center.	10.00	35.00

10	20 Francs	VF	UNC
	20.11.1964; 25.2.1965; 20.3.1965. Blue-green. Dancer. Back: Arms at center.	35.00	125

11 50 Francs

1964-66. Red-orange. View of Bujumbura. Back: Arms at center.

		VF	UNC
a. Signature titles: *LE VICE-PRESIDENT* and *LE PRESIDENT*. 1.10.1964-31.12.1965.		65.00	200
b. Signature titles: *L'ADMINISTRATEUR* and *LE PRESIDENT*. 1.7.1966.		—	—
ct. Color trial. Purple on light blue underprint. Punch hole cancelled. 1.10.1964.		—	750

Note: #11b was prepared but apparently not released without overprint. See #16b.

12 100 Francs

1964-66. Bluish pruple. Prince Rwagasore at center. Back: Arms at center.

		VF	UNC
a. Signature titles: *LE VICE-PRESIDENT* and *LE PRESIDENT*. 1.10.1964; 1.12.1964; 1.5.1965.		65.00	200
b. Signature titles: *L'ADMINISTRATEUR* and *LE PRESIDENT*. 1.7.1966.		—	—
ct. Color trial. Rose. Punch hole cancelled. 1.10.1964.		—	750

13 500 Francs

5.12.1964; 1.8.1966. Brown on yellow underprint. Bank at right. Back: Arms at center.

	VF	UNC
	175	—

14 1000 Francs

1.2.1965. Green on multicolor underprint. King Mwami Mwambutsa IV at right. Back: Arms at center.

	VF	UNC
	625	—

REPUBLIC

Banque de la République du Burundi

1966 ND Provisional Issue

15 20 Francs

ND (1966 - old date 20.3.1965). Dancer at center, black overprint. Back: Arms at center.

	VF	UNC
	55.00	200

16 50 Francs

ND (1966 - old dates 1.5.1965; 31.12.1965; 1.7.1966). Black overprint.

	VF	UNC
a. Overprint on #11a.	75.00	250
b. Overprint on #11b.	85.00	275

Note: Overprint has letters either 3.2 or 2.6mm high.

17 100 Francs

ND (1966). Black overprint.

	VF	UNC
a. Overprint on #12a. (- old date 1.5.1965).	55.00	200
b. Overprint on #12b. (- old date 1.7.1966).	55.00	200

Note: Overprint has letters either 3.2 or 2.6mm high.

18 500 Francs

ND (1966 - old dates 5.12.1964; 1.8.1966). Bank at right, black overprint. Back: Arms at center.

	VF	UNC
	250	—

19 1000 Francs

ND (1966 - old date 1.2.1965). King Mwami Mwambutsa IV at right, black overprint. Back: Arms at center.

	VF	UNC
	725	—

1968-75 Issues

20 10 Francs

1968; 1970. Red on green and blue underprint. *Place de la Revolution* monument at right. Signature titles: *L'ADMINISTRATEUR* and *LE PRESIDENT*.

	VF	UNC
a. 1.11.1968.	5.00	15.00
b. 1.4.1970.	1.50	7.50

21 20 Francs VF UNC
1968-73. Blue on green and violet underprint. Dancer at center, signature varieties. Back: Text.

a. Signature titles: *LE PRESIDENT* and *LE VICE-PRESIDENT*. 1.11.1968. 10.00 40.00
b. Signature titles:*LE PRESIDENT* and *L'ADMINISTRATEUR*. 1.4.1970; 7.00 30.00
   1.11.1971; 1.7.1973.

22 50 Francs VF UNC
1968-73. UV: $1 and central emblem fluoresces green. Pale red on multicolor underprint. Watermark: Drummer at left center. Signature varieties.

a. Signature titles: *LE VICE-PRESIDENT* and *LE PRESIDENT*. 15.5.1968. 25.00 100
   1.10.1968.
b. Signature titles: *ADMINISTRATEUR* and *PRESIDENT*. 1.2.1970; 1.8.1971; 15.00 40.00
   1.7.1973.
s. Specimen. — 200

22A 50 Francs VF UNC
1.6.1975. Brown on multicolor underprint. Drummer at left center, signature titles: *ADMINISTRATEUR and PRESIDENT*.

a. Issued note. 35.00 115
s. Specimen. — —

23 100 Francs VF UNC
1968-75. Brown on pale orange, lilac and blue underprint. Prince Rwagasore at right.

a. Signature titles: *LE VICE-PRESIDENT* and *LE PRESIDENT*. 15.5.1968; 50.00 150
   1.10.1968.
b. Signature titles: *ADMINISTRATEUR* and *LE PRESIDENT*. 1.2.1970; 30.00 100
   1.8.1971; 1.7.1973; 1.6. 1975.
s. Specimen. — 200

24 500 Francs VF UNC
1968-75. Brown. Bank building at right.

a. Signature titles: *LE PRESIDENT* and *LE VICE-PRESIDENT*.1.8.1968. 250 900
b. Signature titles: *LE PRESIDENT* and *L'ADMINISTRATEUR*. 1.4.1970; 200 750
   1.8.1971.
c. Signature titles: *LE PRESIDENT* and *LE VICE-PRESIDENT*. 1.7.1973; 200 750
   1.6.1975.
s. Specimen. — —

25 1000 Francs VF UNC
1968-75. Blue and multicolor. Paradise whydah and flowers. Back: Cattle at center.

a. Signature titles: *L'ADMINISTRATEUR* and *LE PRESIDENT*. 1.4.1968; 175 550
   1.5.1971; 1.2.1973.
b. Signature title: *LE VICE-PRESIDENT* 1.6.1975; 1.9.1976. 150 500
s. Specimen. — 850

26 5000 Francs VF UNC
1968; 1971; 1973. Blue. President Micombero in military uniform at right. Back: Loading at dockside.

a. Signature titles: *LE VICE-PRESIDENT* and *LE PRESIDENT*. 1.4.1968; 500 1,500
   1.7.1973.
b. Signature title: *L'ADMINISTRATEUR*. 1.5.1971. 500 1,750
ct. As a. Color trial in purple. Punch hole cancelled. — 1,000

1975-78 Issue

27 20 Francs VF UNC
1977-2007. Red on multicolor underprint. Dancer at center. Signature titles: *LE GOUVERNEUR* and *L'ADMINISTRATEUR*. Back: Arms at center.

a. 1.7.1977; 1.6.1979; 1.12.1981. 1.00 5.00
b. 1.12.1983; 1.12.1986; 1.5.1988; 1.10.1989. 0.50 2.00
c. 1.10.1991; 25.5.1995. FV 1.25
d. Signature titles: *LE GOUVERNEUR* and *LE 2e VICE-GOUVERNEUR*. FV 0.75
   5.2.1997; 1.8.2001; 1.7.2003; 5.2.2005; 1.11.2007
s. Specimen. — 100

28 50 Francs VF UNC
1977-93. Brown on multicolor underprint. Drummer at left center. Back: Arms at center.

a. 1.7.1977; 1.5.1979. 1.50 7.50
b. 1.12.1981; 1.12.1983. 1.00 5.00
c. 1.5.1988; 1.10.1989; 1.10.1991; 1.5.1993. 0.75 4.00
s. Specimen. — 100

29 100 Francs

	VF	UNC
1977-93. Purple on multicolor underprint. Prince Rwagasore at right. Signature titles: *L'ADMINISTRATEUR* and *LE GOUVERNEUR*. Back: Arms at center.		
a. 1.7.1977; 1.5.1979.	1.00	3.50
b. 1.1.1981; 1.7.1982; 1.11.1984; 1.11.1986.	0.75	3.00
c. 1.5.1988; 1.7.1990; 1.5.1993.	FV	2.00
s. Specimen. Red overprint on both sides. Punch hole cancelled.	—	100

30 500 Francs

	VF	UNC
1977-88. Dark blue on multicolor underprint. Bank building at right, numeral and date style varieties. Signature titles: *LE GOUVERNEUR* and *LE VICE-GOUVERNEUR*. Back: Arms at center.		
a. 1.7.1977; 1.9.1981.	10.00	40.00
b. 1.7.1985; 1.9.1986.	7.00	20.00
c. 1.5.1988.	5.00	12.50
s. Specimen. 1.1.1980; 1.7.1985.	—	175

31 1000 Francs

	VF	UNC
1977-91. Dark green on multicolor underprint. Paradise whydah and flowers. Back: Cattle at center.		
a. Signature titles: *LE VICE-GOUVERNEUR* and *LE GOUVERNEUR*.1.7.1977; 1.1.1978; 1.5.1979; 1.1.1980.	15.00	50.00
b. 1.1.1981; 1.5.1982; 1.1.1984; 1.12.1986.	12.50	35.00
c. Signature titles: *L'ADMINISTRATEUR* and *LE VICE-GOUVERNEUR*. 1.6.1987.	20.00	65.00
d. Signature titles: *LE VICE-GOUVERNEUR* and *LE GOUVERNEUR*. 1.5.1988; 1.10.1989; 1.10.1991.	7.50	12.50
s. Specimen.	—	175

32 5000 Francs

	VF	UNC
1978-95. Dark brown and grayish purple on multicolor underprint. Arms at upper center; building at lower right. Back: Ship dockside. 179x79mm		
a. 1.7.1978; 1.10.1981.	60.00	200
b. 1.1.1984; 1.9.1986.	30.00	100
c. 1.10.1989; 1.10.1991.	20.00	80.00
d. Sign titles: *LE 1ER VICE-GOUVERNEUR* and *LE GOUVERNEUR*. 19.5.1994; 25.5.1995.	FV	62.60

1979-81 Issues

#33 and 34 replacement notes: Serial # prefix *Z*.

33 10 Francs

	VF	UNC
1981-2007. Blue-green on tan underprint. Map of Burundi with arms superimposed at center. Back: Text.		
a. Signature titles: *LE GOUVERNEUR* and *ADMINISTRATEUR*. 1.6.1981; 1.12.1983.	FV	2.50
b. 1.12.1986; 1.5.1988; 1.10.1989; 1.10.1991.	FV	1.25
c. 25.5.1995.	FV	0.75
d. Signature titles: *LE GOUVERNEUR* and *LE 2eme VICE-GOUVERNEUR*. 5.2.1997; 1.8.2001; 1.7.2003.	FV	0.50
e. Signature titles: *LE GOUVERNEUR* and *LE 2E VICE GOUVERNEUR*. 5.2.2005; 1.11.2007.	FV	0.50

34 500 Francs

	VF	UNC
1.6.1979; 1.1.1980. Tan, blue-black, purple and green on multicolor underprint. Bank building at right. Signature titles: *LE GOUVERNEUR* and *LE VICE-GOUVERNEUR*.		
a. 1.6.1979.	12.50	50.00
b. 1.1.1980.	12.50	50.00

1993-97 Issue

#35 not assigned.

36   50 Francs   **VF   UNC**

1994-. Dull brown-violet on multicolor underprint. Man in dugout canoe at left,
arms at lower center. Back: Four men with canoe at center, hippopotamus at
lower right.

a. 19.5.1994.		FV	2.00
b. 5.2.1999.		FV	2.00
c. 1.8.2001.		FV	2.00
d. 1.7.2003.		FV	2.00
e. 5.2.2005.		FV	2.00
f. 1.5.2006.		FV	2.00
g. 1.11.2007.		FV	2.00

39   1000 Francs   **VF   UNC**

1994-. Greenish black and brown-violet on multicolor underprint. Cattle at left,
arms at lower center. Signature titles: *LE GOUVERNEUR* and *LE 1ER VICE-
GOUVERNEUR*. Back: Monument at center. Watermark: President Micombero.
170x76mm.

a. 19.5.1994.		FV	17.50
b. 1.12.1997.		FV	9.00
c. 1.7.2000.		FV	9.00
d. 1.5.2006.		FV	9.00
e. 1.5.2009.		FV	9.00

37   100 Francs   **VF   UNC**

1993-. Dull purple on multicolor underprint. Archway at left center, Prince
Rwagasore at right. Signature titles: *LE 2eme VICE-GOUVERNEUR* and *LE
GOUVERNEUR.*. Back: Arms at lower left, home construction at center.

a. 1.10.1993.		FV	3.00
b. 1.12.1997.		FV	3.00
c. 1.8.2001.		FV	3.00
d. 1.5.2004.		FV	3.00
e. 1.5.2006.		FV	3.00
f. 1.10.2007.		FV	3.00
s. Specimen.		—	125

37A   500 Francs   **VF   UNC**

5.2.1995 (2005). Blue and lilac on multicolor underprint. President facing at left.   FV   7.50
Back: Bank building at center.

40   5000 Francs   **VF   UNC**

5.2.1997. Olive-green and dark green on multicolor underprint. Arms at upper   FV   55.00
center, building at lower right, date at left, segmented foil over security thread.
Back: Ship dockside. 179x79mm.

1999-2001 Issue

38   500 Francs   **VF   UNC**

1995-. Gray and violet on multicolor underprint. Native painting at left. Back: Bank
building at center, arms at right. Watermark: Ox. 160x73mm.

a. 1.5.1997.		FV	7.50
b. 5.2.1999.		FV	7.50
c. 1.7.2003.		FV	6.00
d. 1.10.2007.		FV	6.00
e. 1.5.2009.		FV	6.00

41   2000 Francs   **VF   UNC**

2001. Blue and green on multicolor underprint. Harvest scene at right. Back: Lake
and dam. 176x77mm.

a. 25.6.2001.		FV	15.00

42 5000 Francs   **VF   UNC**
1999; 2003; 2005. Green, olive and light red on multicolor underprint. Arms at upper center, building at lower right, date at left, printed bull's head with OVD ink at lower left center. Segmented foil over security thread. Back: Ship dockside. 179x70mm.

a. 5.2.1999.	FV	40.00
b. 1.7.2003.	FV	25.00
c. 5.2.2005.	FV	25.00

43 10,000 Francs   **VF   UNC**
2004; 2006. Multicolor. Prince Rwagasore and President Ndadaye at lower left. Back: Three students at desks at center. 150x75mm.

a. 25.10.2004.	FV	60.00
b. 1.5.2006.	FV	60.00

2008 Issue

44 100 Francs   **VF   UNC**
1.5.2010; 9.11.2011. Purple on multicolor underprint. Prince Ragawasore at right. Back: Home construction 125x65mm.

a. 1.5.2010.	FV	0.50
b. 9.11.2011.	FV	0.50

45 500 Francs   **VF   UNC**
1.5.2009; 1.9.2011; 31.10.2013. Dark blue and multicolor. Bas relief of natives, trees and couldron. Back: Central Bank of Burundi building at center. 132x67mm.

a. 1.5.2009.	FV	2.00
b. 1.9.2011.	FV	1.50
c. 31.10.2013	FV	1.50

46 1000 Francs   **VF   UNC**
1.5.2009. Multicolor. Three cattle at left. Back: Monument with fountain at center. Watermark: Cattle. 137x69mm.   FV   3.00

47 2000 Francs   **VF   UNC**
1.12.2008. Blue and green on multicolor underprint. Harvest scene at right. Silver foil bull's head at lower center. Back: Lake and dam. Watermark: Cattle. 140x71mm.   FV   5.00

48 5000 Francs   **VF   UNC**
1.12.2008; 1.9.2011; 31.10.2013. Green, olive and light red on multicolor underprint. Arms at upper center, building at lower right, date a left. Bull's head hologram at lower left. Back: Ship dockside. Watermark: Cattle Printer: TDLR (without imprint). 145x73mm.

a. 1.12.2008.	FV	9.00
b. 1.9.2011	FV	9.00
c. 31.10.2013	FV	9.00

49 10,000 Francs   **VF   UNC**
1.7.2009; 31.10.2013. Multicolor. Prince Rwagasore and President Ndadaye at lower left. Eagle hologram above. Back: Three students at desks at center.

a. 1.7.2009	FV	60.00
b. 31.10.2013	FV	60.00

2015 Issue

50 500 Francs   **VF   UNC**
15.1.2015. Orange. Coffee plant at right. Back: Map of Burundi, boat.   FV   1.50

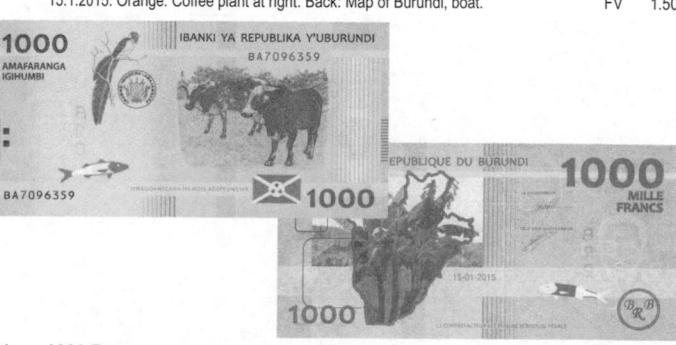

51 1000 Francs   **VF   UNC**
15.1.2015. Green. Fish as registration device. Cattle at right. Watermark: Prince Louis Rwagasore and electrotype BRB. 125x65mm.   FV   3.00

52 2000 Francs   **VF   UNC**
15.1.2015. Pink. Pineapple at right. Back: Map of Burundi, farmer.   FV   5.00

53 5000 Francs   **VF   UNC**
15.1.2015. Blue. Dancers with drums at right. Back: Map of Burundi.   FV   9.00

54 10,000 Francs   **VF   UNC**
15.1.2015. Yellow. M. Ndadaye and L. Rwagasore at right. Back: Map of Burundi.   FV   60.00

CAMBODIA

Kingdom of Cambodia, formerly known as Democratic Kampuchea, People's Republic of Kampuchea, and the Khmer Republic, a land of paddy fields and forest-clad hills located on the Indo-Chinese peninsula fronting on the Gulf of Thailand, has an area of 181,040 sq. km. and a population of 14.24 million. Capital: Phnom Penh. Agriculture is the major part of the economy, with rice the chief crop. Native industries include cattle breeding, weaving and rice milling. Rubber, cattle, corn, and timber are exported.

Most Cambodians consider themselves to be Khmers, descendants of the Angkor Empire that extended over much of Southeast Asia and reached its zenith between the 10th and 13th centuries. Attacks by the Thai and Cham (from present-day Viet Nam) weakened the empire, ushering in a long period of decline. The king placed the country under French protection in 1863 and it became part of French Indochina in 1887. Following Japanese occupation in World War II, Cambodia gained full independence from France in 1955

In April 1975, after a five-year struggle, communist Khmer Rouge forces captured Phnom Penh and evacuated all cities and towns. At least 1.5 million Cambodians died from execution, forced hardships, or starvation during the Khmer Rouge regime under Pol Pot. A December 1978 Vietnamese invasion drove the Khmer Rouge into the countryside, began a 10-year Vietnamese occupation, and touched off almost 13 years of civil war.

The 1991 Paris Peace Accords mandated democratic elections and a ceasefire, which was not fully respected by the Khmer Rouge. UN-sponsored elections in 1993 helped restore some semblance of normalcy under a coalition government. Factional fighting in 1997 ended the first coalition government, but a second round of national elections in 1998 led to the formation of another coalition government and renewed political stability. The remaining elements of the Khmer Rouge surrendered in 1998.

The colition governments parliament decided to restore the constitutional monarchy on September 24, 1993 and King Sihanouk became chief of state. He abdicated on October 6, 2004 and one of his sons, Prince Norodom Sihamoni, now sits on the throne.

RULERS:
Norodom Suramarit, 1955-1960
Norodom Sihanouk (as Chief of State), 1960-1970
Lon Nol, 1970-1975
Pol Pot, 1975-1979
Heng Samrin, 1979-1985
Hun Sen, 1985-1991
Norodom Sihanouk (as Chairman, Supreme National Council), 1991-1993
Norodom Sihanouk (as King), 1993-2002
Boromneath Norodom Sihamoni, 2004-

MONETARY SYSTEM:
1 Riel = 100 Sen

REPLACEMENT NOTES:
#4b-c, 5b, 7b use 3 special Cambodian prefix characters (equivalent to Z90).

SIGNATURES

	Governor	Chief Inspector	Advisor	Date
1				28.10.1955
2				1956
3				1956
4				Late 1961
5				Mid 1962
6				1963
7				1965
8				1968
9				1968
10				1969
11				1970
12				1972
13				1972
14				1974
15				March 1975 (printed 1974)

KINGDOM OF CAMBODIA
Banque Nationale du Cambodge
1956; 1958 ND Second Issue

4   1 Riel   VF   UNC

ND (1956-75). Grayish green on multicolor underprint. Boats dockside in port of Phnom-Penh. Back: Royal palace throne room. Printer: BWC (without imprint).

		VF	UNC
a.	Signature 1; 2.	3.00	15.00
b.	Signature 6; 7; 8; 10; 11.	0.25	3.00
c.	Signature 12.	0.15	1.00
r.	Replacement note. As b, c. Cambodian characters equivalent to Z90.	2.00	5.00
s.	Specimen. Signature 1. Perforated and printed: *SPECIMEN*.	—	150
ct.	Color trial. Purple and blue. Specimen.	—	—

5   20 Riels   VF   UNC

ND (1956-75). Brown on multicolor underprint. Combine harvester at right. Back: Phnom Penh pagoda. Watermark: Buddha. Printer: BWC (without imprint).

		VF	UNC
a.	Signature 3.	1.00	10.00
b.	Signature 6.	0.75	4.00
c.	Signature 7; 8; 10.	0.50	3.00
d.	Signature 12.	0.25	1.00
r.	Replacement note. As b. Cambodian characters equivalent to Z90.	2.00	5.00
ct.	Color trial. Green. Specimen.	—	—

#6 not assigned.

7   50 Riels   VF   UNC

ND (1956-75). Blue and orange. Fishermen fishing from boats with Large nets in Lake Tonle Sap at left and right. Back: Angkor Wat complex. Watermark: Buddha. Printer: TDLR (without imprint).

		VF	UNC
a.	Western numeral in plate block designator. Signature 3.	3.00	20.00
b.	Cambodian numeral in plate block designator. 5-digit serial #. Signature 7; 10.	1.00	4.00
c.	As b. Signature 12.	0.50	1.00
d.	Cambodian serial # 6-digits. Signature 12.	0.20	1.00
r.	Replacement note. As b. Cambodian characters equivalent to Z90.	0.00	5.00
s1.	As a. Specimen.	—	150
s2.	As c. Specimen. (TDLR).	—	150

8   100 Riels **VF   UNC**

ND (1957-75). Brown and green on multicolor underprint. Statue of Lokcovara at left. Back: Long boat. Watermark: Buddha.

a. Imprint: *Giesecke & Devrient AG, Munchen*. Signature 3.	3.00	20.00
b. As a. Signature 7; 8; 11.	1.00	4.00
c. Imprint: *Giesecke & Devrient-Munchen*. Signature 12; 13; 15.	0.50	2.00
s. Specimen. As a. Signature 3. Perforated *Specimen. Uniface printings.*	—	200

9   500 Riels **VF   UNC**

ND (1958-70). Green and brown on multicolor underprint. Sculpture of two royal women dancers - *Devatas* at left. Back: Two royal dancers in ceremonial costumes. Watermark: Buddha. Printer: G&D.

a. Signature 3.	50.00	150
b. Signature 6.	35.00	100
c. Signature 9.	3.00	12.50
s. As a. Signature 3. Specimen.	—	—
x. Counterfeit.	2.00	5.00

Note: This banknote was withdrawn in March 1970 due to extensive counterfeiting.

1962-63 ND Third Issue

10   5 Riels **VF   UNC**

ND (1962-75). Red on multicolor underprint. Bayon stone 4 faces of Avalokitesvara at left. Back: Royal Palace Entrance - Chanchhaya at right. Watermark: Buddha. Printer: BWC (without imprint).

a. Signature 4; 6.	3.00	20.00
b. Signature 7; 8; 11.	0.50	4.00
c. Signature 12.	0.25	1.00
s. Specimen. Signature 4, 8. Perforated *SPECIMEN*.	—	200
ct. Color trial. Green. Specimen.	—	—

11   10 Riels **VF   UNC**

ND (1962-75). Red-brown on multicolor underprint. Temple of Banteay Srei at right. Back: Central Market building at Phnom-Penh at left. Watermark: Buddha. Printer: TDLR (without imprint).

a. Signature 5; 6.	3.00	20.00
b. Signature 7; 8; 11.	0.50	3.00
c. Signature 12. 5 digit serial #.	0.25	1.00
d. As c. 6 digit serial #.	0.50	2.00
s. Specimen. Signature 5, 6, 8. TDLR.	—	125

12   100 Riels **VF   UNC**

ND (1963-72). Blue-black, dark green and dark brown on multicolor underprint. Sun rising behind Temple of Preah Vihear at left. Back: Aerial view of the Temple of Preah Vihear. Watermark: Buddha. Printer: G&D.

a. Signature 6.	3.00	20.00
b. Signature 13. (Not issued).	0.20	1.00
s. Specimen. Signature 6.	—	200

13   100 Riels **VF   UNC**

ND (1956-1972). Blue on light blue underprint. Two oxen at right. Back: Three ceremonial women.

a. Printer: ABNC with imprint on lower margins, face and back. Signature 3.	20.00	100
b. Without imprint on either side. Signature 12.	0.25	2.00
p. Uniface proofs.	FV	75.00
s. As a. Specimen. Signature 3.	—	300

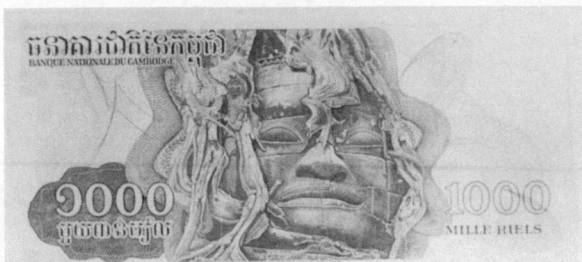

14 **500 Riels** VF UNC
ND (1958-1970). Multicolor. Farmer plowing with two water buffalo. Back: Pagoda at right, doorway of Preah Vihear at left. Watermark: Buddha. Printer: BdF (without imprint).
a. Signature 3. 4.00 30.00
b. Signature 5; 7. 2.00 10.00
c. Signature 9. 1.50 9.00
d. Signature 12. 1.00 5.00
x1. Lithograph counterfeit; watermark. barely visible. Signature 3; 5. 70.00 120
x2. As x1. Signature 7; 9. 60.00 100
x3. As x1. Signature 12. 45.00 80.00

17 **1000 Riels** VF UNC
ND. (Not issued). Green on multicolor underprint. School children. Signature 13. 0.20 1.00
Back: Head of Lokecvara at Ta Som. Watermark: School girl. Printer: BWC.

KHMER REPUBLIC
Banque Nationale du Cambodge
1973 ND Issue

15 **100 Riels** VF UNC
ND. (Not issued). Replacement notes: Series # 90. Purple and violet on multicolor underprint. Carpet weaving. Back: Angkor Wat. Watermark: Man's head. Printer: TDLR (without imprint).
a. Signature 13. 0.35 2.00
b. Signature 14. 1.25 7.50
r. Replacement note. 2.00 5.00

17A **5000 Riels** VF UNC
ND (1974). Unissued. Only released starting in 2005. Brown, tan, yellow and — 7.50
green. Male bust at right. Back: Building.

State Bank of Democratic Kampuchea
1979 Issue

16 **500 Riels** VF UNC
ND(1973-75). Green and black on multicolor underprint. Girl with vessel on head at left. Back: Rice paddy scene. Watermark: Man's head. Printer: TDLR (without imprint).
a. Signature 13; 14. 2.00 10.00
b. Signature 15. 0.20 1.00
r. Replacement note. 2.00 5.00
s. As a. Specimen. — —

25 **0.1 Riel (1 Kak)** VF UNC
1979. Olive-green on light blue underprint. Arms at center. Back: Water buffalos.
a. Issued note. 0.15 0.50
s. Specimen. Overprint *SPECIMEN* in red on both sides. — 25.00

26 **0.2 Riel (2 Kak)** VF UNC
1979. Grayish green on tan underprint. Arms at center. Back: Rice workers.
a. Issued note. 0.20 0.50
s. Specimen. Overprint *SPECIMEN* in red on both sides. — 25.00

27 **0.5 Riel (5 Kak)** VF UNC
1979. Red-orange on tan and gray underprint. Arms at left, modern passenger train at right. Back: Men fishing from boats with nets.
a. Issued note. 0.20 1.00
s. Specimen. Overprint *SPECIMEN* in red on both sides. — 35.00

28   1 Riel   VF   UNC

1979. UV: fibers fluoresce blue. Brown on yellow and multicolor underprint. Arms
at center. Back: Women harvesting rice.
    a. Issued note.   0.20   0.50
    s. Specimen. Overprint *SPECIMEN* in red on both sides. 2 serial # var.   —   35.00

29   5 Riels   VF   UNC

1979. UV: fibers fluoresce blue. Dark brown on light green and multicolor underprint. Four people at left, arms at right. Back: Independence from France (now
Victory) monument.
    a. Issued note.   0.30   2.00
    s. Specimen. Overprint *SPECIMEN* in red on both sides.   —   35.00
    x. Counterfeit (contemporary).   1.00   3.00

30   10 Riels   VF   UNC

1979. UV: fibers fluoresce blue. Dark gray on lilac and multicolor underprint. Arms
at left, harvesting fruit trees at right. Back: School.
    a. Issued note.   0.50   4.00
    s. Specimen. Overprint *SPECIMEN* in red on both sides.   —   35.00

31   20 Riels   VF   UNC

1979. Purple on pink and multicolor underprint. Arms at left. Back: Water buffalos
hauling logs. Watermark: Arms.
    a. Issued note.   0.35   5.00
    s. Specimen. Overprint *SPECIMEN* in red on both sides.   —   35.00
    x. Counterfeit (contemporary).   2.00   4.00

32   50 Riels   VF   UNC

1979. Deep red on yellow-green and multicolor underprint. Arms at left, Bayon
stone head at center. Back: Angkor Wat. Watermark: Arms.
    a. Issued note.   0.35   7.50
    s. Specimen. Overprint *SPECIMEN* in red on both sides.   —   35.00

1987 Issue

33   5 Riels   VF   UNC

1987. UV: fibers fluoresce blue. Back serial # fluoresce orange. Red and brown   0.35   2.00
on light yellow and light green underprint. Four people at left, arms at right. Back:
Independence from France (now Victory) monument.

34   10 Riels   VF   UNC

1987. Green on light blue and multicolor underprint. Arms at left, harvesting fruit   0.35   2.00
trees at right. Back: School.

STATE OF CAMBODIA

Peoples National Bank of Cambodia
1990-92 Issue

35   50 Riels   VF   UNC

1992. Dull brown on multicolor underprint. Arms at center, male portrait at right.
Back: Ships dockside. Watermark: Stylized lotus flowers. Printer: NBC (without
imprint).
    a. Issued note.   0.25   2.00
    s. Specimen. Overprint *SPECIMEN* in red on both sides.   —   75.00

36 **100 Riels** VF UNC

1990. Dark green and brown on light blue and lilac underprint. Independence from France (now Victory) monument at left center, male portrait at right. Back: Rubber trees. Watermark: Styilized lotus flowers.

    a. Issued note. 0.50 3.00
    s. Specimen. Red overprint *SPECIMEN* on both sides. — 65.00

37 **200 Riels** VF UNC

1992-93 Dull olive-green and tan on multicolor underprint. Floodgates at right. Back: Bayon sculpture in Angkor Wat center. Watermark: Styilized lotus flowers. Printer: NBC.

    a. Issued note. 0.50 2.00
    s. Specimen. 1993. Red overprint: SPECIMEN on each side. — 100

38 **500 Riels** VF UNC

1991. Red, purple and brown-violet on multicolor underprint. Arms above Angkor Wat at center. Back: Animal statue at left, cultivating with tractors at center. Watermark: Sculptured heads.

    a. Issued note. 0.50 3.00
    s. Specimen. Overprint *SPECIMEN* in red on both sides. (Two different serial — 65.00
       # varieties.)

39 **1000 Riels** VF UNC

1992. (Not released). Dark green, brown and black on multicolor underprint. Bayon Temple ruins in Angkor Wat. Back: Fishermen fishing in boats with large nets in Lake Tonle Sap. Watermark: Chinze. — 10.00

40 **2000 Riels** VF UNC

1992. (Not released). Black, deep blue and violet-brown on multicolor underprint. King N. Sihanouk at left. Back: Temple portal at Preah Vihear at right. Watermark: King N. Sihanouk. — 10.00

National Bank of Cambodia
1995 Issue

SIGNATURE VARIETIES		
	Le Gouverneur	Le Caissier Général
16	Thor Peng Leath, 1995-	Tieng Seng, 1998-
17	Chea Chanto, 1999-	Tieng Seng, 1999-2005
18	Chea Chanto, 1999-	Tha Yao, 2007-

41 **100 Riels** VF UNC

1995; 1998. UV: fibers fluoresce blue. Back 100 in Cambodian fluoresce yellow at right. Grayish green and brown on multicolor underprint. Chinze, Independence from France (Now Victory) monument at right, arms at upper left. Back: Tapping rubber trees. Watermark: Styilized lotus flowers. Printer: NBC.

    a. 1995. Signature 16. 0.20 2.00
    b. 1998. Signature 16; 17. 0.20 0.50
    s. Specimen. Overprint *SPECIMEN* in red either on face or on both sides. — 45.00
       1995; 1998.

42 **200 Riels** VF UNC

1995; 1998. Dark olive-green and brown on multicolor underprint. Floodgates at right, but smaller size, arms at upper left. Back: Bayon sculpture in Angkor Wat, center. Watermark: Styilized lotus flowers. Printer: NBC.

    a. 1995. Signature 16. FV 2.00
    b. 1998. Signature 16; 17. FV 0.35
    s. Specimen. Overprint *SPECIMEN* in red on face.1995. — 45.00

43 500 Riels

VF UNC

1996, 1998. Red and purple on multicolor underprint. Angkor Wot at right, arms at upper left. Back: Mythical animal at left, rice fields at center. Watermark: Stiyilized lotus flowers. Printer: NBC.

		VF	UNC
a. 1996. Signature 16.		FV	1.00
b. 1998. Signature 16; 17.		FV	1.00
s. Specimen. Overprint *SPECIMEN* in red on face or both sides. 1996, 1998.		—	35.00

#44-50 Replacement notes have an *0* at the end of the serial # prefix, eg. *A0*.

44 1000 Riels

VF UNC

ND (1995). Blue-green on gold and multicolor underprint. Bayon stone four faces of Avalokitesvara at left. Back: Prasat Chan Chaya at right. Watermark: Cube design. Printer: F-CO.

		VF	UNC
a. ND (1995).		FV	2.00
r. Replacement note. Zero after prefix letter.		2.00	5.00
s. Specimen. Overprint *SPECIMEN* in rectangle in red on both sides.		—	50.00

45 2000 Riels

VF UNC

ND (1995). Reddish brown on multicolor underprint. Fishermen fishing from boats with nets in Lake Tonie Sap at left and right. Back: Temple ruins at Angkor Wat. Watermark: Cube design. Printer: F-CO.

		VF	UNC
a. Issued note.		FV	3.50
r. Replacement note. Zero after prefix letter.		3.00	7.50
s. Specimen. Overprint *SPECIMEN* in rectangle in red on both sides.		—	40.00

46 5000 Riels

VF UNC

ND (1995); 1998. Deep purple and blue-black with black text on multicolor underprint. King N. Sihanouk at right, Temple of Banteai Srei at lower left center. Back: Central market in Phnom-Penh. Watermark: King N. Sihanouk. Printer: F-CO.

		VF	UNC
a. ND (1995). Signature 16.		FV	10.00
b. 1998. Signature 16, 17.		FV	6.50
r. Replacement note. Zero after prefix letter.		4.00	12.50
s. Specimen. Overprint *SPECIMEN* in red on both sides. ND (1995) Signature 16; 1998, Signature 17.		—	50.00

47 10,000 Riels

VF UNC

ND (1995); 1998. Blue-black, black and dark green on multicolor underprint. King N. Sihanouk at right, statue of Lokecvara at lower left center. Back: People rowing long boat during the water festival at lower center. Watermark. King N. Sihanouk. Printer: F-CO.

		VF	UNC
a. ND (1995). Signature 16.		FV	12.50
b. 1998. Signature 16, 17.		FV	12.00
r. Replacement note. Zero after prefix letter.		7.00	15.00
s. Specimen. Overprint *SPECIMEN* in red on both sides. ND (1995) Signature 16; 1998, signature 17.		—	50.00

48 20,000 Riels

VF UNC

ND (1995). Violet and red on multicolor underprint. King N. Sihanouk at right, boats dockside in Port of Phnom-Penh at center. Signature 16. Back: Throne Room in National Palace. Watermark: King N. Sihanouk. Printer: F-CO.

		VF	UNC
a. Issued note.		FV	30.00
r. Replacement note. Zero after prefix letter.		15.00	35.00
s. Specimen. Overprint *SPECIMEN* in red on both sides.		—	55.00

49 50,000 Riels

VF UNC

ND (1995); 1998. Dark brown, brown and deep olive-green on multicolor underprint. Preah Vihear Temple at center. Back: Road to Preah Vihear Temple. Watermark: King N. Sihanouk. Printer: F-CO.

		VF	UNC
a. ND (1995). Signature 16.		FV	52.50
b. 1998. Signature 16, 17.		FV	50.00
r. Replacement note. Zero after prefix letter.		25.00	55.00
s. Specimen. ND (1995); 1998, signature 16, 17. Overprint SPECIMEN with or without linear frame.		—	75.00

50 100,000 Riels   VF   UNC

ND (1995). Green, blue-green and black on multicolor underprint. Chief and First Lady at right. Signature 16. Back: Chief and First Lady receiving homage of people at center right. Watermark: Chief and First Lady. Printer: F-CO.

	VF	UNC
a. Issued note.	FV	95.00
r. Replacement note. Zero after prefix letter.	45.00	100
s. Specimen. Perforated: SPECIMEN.	—	85.00

1999 Issue

51 1000 Riels   VF   UNC

1999. Dark brown and dark olive-green on multicolor underprint. Temples at center right, signature 17. Back: Construction site at center.

	VF	UNC
a. Issued note.	FV	1.25
s. Specimen. Overprint SPECIMEN in red on both sides.	—	30.00

2001-02 Issue

52 50 Riels   VF   UNC

2002. Dark brown and tan on multicolor underprint. Preah Vihear temple at center, naga heads sculpture at lower left center. Signature 17. Back: Dam at center. Watermark: Bayon sculpture in Angkor Wat.

	VF	UNC
a. Issued note.	FV	0.35
s. Specimen. Overprint SPECIMEN in red on both sides.	—	25.00

53 100 Riels   VF   UNC

2001. UV: fibers fluoresce blue. Back 100 in Cambodian fluoresce yellow at right. Purple, brown and green. Independence monument at right, naga heads sculpture at lower left center. Signature 17. Back: Students and school. Watermark: Multiple lines of text.

	VF	UNC
a. Issued note.	FV	0.50
s. Specimen. Overprint SPECIMEN in red on both sides.	—	15.00

54 500 Riels   VF   UNC

2002; 2004. Red and purple on multicolor underprint. Angkor Wat temple at center, naga heads sculpture at lower left center. Signature 17. Back: Bridge spanning Mekong river at Kampong Cham at center. Watermark: Baylon sculpture in Angkor Wat.

	VF	UNC
a. 2002. Dark sky on back.	FV	1.50
b. 2004. Light sky on back.	FV	1.00
s. Specimen. Overprint SPECIMEN in red on both sides. 2002; 2004.	FV	15.00

55 5000 Riels   VF   UNC

2001-. Green and gray. King Norodom Sihanouk at right, signature 17. Back: Bridge of Kampong Kdei in Siemreap Province.

	VF	UNC
a. 2001.	FV	5.00
b. 2002.	FV	5.00
c. 2004.	FV	4.00
d. 2007.	FV	3.00
s. Specimen. As a. Overprint SPECIMEN in red on face.	—	50.00

56 10,000 Riels   VF   UNC

2001; 2005. Violet, brown and blue. King Norodom Sihanouk at right, signature 17. Back: Water festival before Royal Palace.

	VF	UNC
a. 2001.	FV	6.00
b. 2005.	FV	5.00
s. Specimen. As a. Overprint SPECIMEN in red on face.	—	50.00

57   50,000 Riels   VF   UNC
2001. Violet, brown and blue. King Norodom Sihanouk at right, signature 17.
Back: Angkor Wat temple.
  a. Issued note.   FV   40.00
  s. Specimen. Overprint: SPECIMEN.   —   75.00

2005-13 Issue

58   1000 Riels   VF   UNC
2005; 2007. Brown and lilac on multicolor underprint. Temple at center. Back:
Cargo ships.
  a. 2005.   FV   2.25
  b. 2007.   FV   2.25
  s. Specimen. Overprint *SPECIMEN* in red on both sides. 2005.   —   40.00

59   2000 Riels   VF   UNC
2007. Dark and light green on multicolor underprint. Portal ruins at the Preah
Vihear Temple. Back: Female farm worker in rice fields and Angkopr Wat temple
complex in distance. Watermark: Bayon sculpture. 146x68mm.
  a. Issued note.   FV   2.00
  s. Specimen. Perforated *SPECIMEN*.   —   50.00

60   20,000 Riels   VF   UNC
2008. Purple and violet on multicolor underprint. King Norodom Sohamoni at right.
Back: Aerial view of Angkor Thom Temple complex at center, Four faced Buddah
in bayon temple at right. Watermark: Bayon sculpture. 155x72mm.
  a. Issued note.   FV   9.00
  s. Specimen. Perforated SPECIMEN vertically at left end.   FV   100

61   50,000 Riels   VF   UNC
2013. Brown and tan on multicolor underprint. Norodom Sihanouk at right.
150x70mm.
  a. Issued note.   FV   30.00
  s. Specimen.   —   —

62   100,000 Riels   VF   UNC
2012. Slate grey and green on multicolor underprint. King Norodom Sihanouk
and Queen Norodom Monineath Sihanouk at right center. Back: King-Father and
Queen-Mother and King Norodom Sihamoni. 170x77mm.
  a. Issued note.   FV   65.00
  s. Specimen. Pin hole cancelled: *SPECIMEN*.   —   150

2013 Issue

63 1000 Riels   VF   UNC
2012. Brown and blue on multicolor underprint. The late King Samdech Preah
Norodom Sihanouk at right center. Back: Royal boat parade float at right center.
Watermark: Lotus flower. 146x68mm.
     a. Issued note.   FV   5.00
     s. Specimen. Pin hole cancelled: *SPECIMEN*.   —   50.00

64 2000 Riels   VF   UNC
2013. Black, green and grey on multicolor underprint. King Norodom Sihanouk   FV   1.00
at right, mythical snake, coat of arms. Watermark: Rhombic flower pattern.
146x68mm.

65 100 Riels   VF   UNC
2014. Norodom Sihanouk as young monk.   FV   0.50

66 500 Riels   VF   UNC
2014. Norodom Sihamoni at right.   FV   1.00

67 10,000 Riels   VF   UNC
2015. Blue. Naga, mythical snake; King Norodom Sihamoni. Back: Temple on   FV   7.00
circular island, stone statue. Holographic stripe. Solid security thread with demetalized *NBC*. Watermark: Floral pattern. 155x72mm.

COLLECTOR SERIES

National Bank of Cambodia
1995 ND Issue

CS1 1000 - 100,000 Riels   Mkt. Value
ND (1995). #44-50. Specimen.   250
Note: Issued in a special folder w/notes laminated in plastic including 50, 100, 200 and 500 Riels
     coins dated BE2538 (1994).

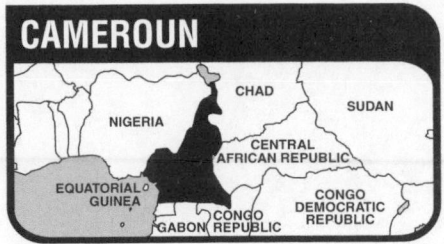

CAMEROUN

The United Republic of Cameroun, located in west-central Africa
on the Gulf of Guinea, has an area
of 475,440 sq. km. and a population
of 18.46 million. Capital: Yaounde.
About 90 percent of the labor force
is employed on the land; cash crops
account for 80 percent of the country's export revenue. Cocoa, coffee,
aluminum, cotton, rubber and timber
are exported.

The former French Cameroon
and part of British Cameroon merged
in 1961 to form the present country. Cameroon has generally enjoyed stability, which has permitted the development of agriculture, roads, and railways, as well as a petroleum industry. Despite a slow movement toward
democratic reform, political power remains firmly in the hands of President Paul Biya.

MONETARY SYSTEM:
     1 Franc = 100 Centimes

SIGNATURE VARIETIES:
     Refer to introduction of Central African States.

RÉPUBLIQUE DU CAMEROUN

Banque Centrale
1961 ND Issue
#7-9 denominations in French only, or French and English.

			Fine	XF
7	**1000 Francs**	ND (1961). Multicolor. Man with basket harvesting cocoa. Signature 1A.	750	1,850
8	**5000 Francs**	ND (1961). Multicolor. President A. Ahidjo at right. Signature 1A.	300	1,500

			Fine	XF
9	**5000 Francs**	ND. Multicolor. President A. Ahidjo at right. Signature 1A, denomination in English words at lower left.	600	2,000

RÉPUBLIQUE FÉDÉRALE DU CAMEROUN

Banque Centrale
1962 ND Issue

10 100 Francs
ND (1962). Multicolor. President of the Republic at left, denomination in French
and English. Signature 1A. Back: Ships. Watermark: Antelope's head.

	VF	UNC
a. Issued note.	30.00	125
s. Specimen. Overprint: *SPECIMEN* in black and perforated.	—	300

11 500 Francs
ND (1962). Engraved (intaglio) and lithographic varieties. Multicolor. Man with
2 oxen, denomination in French and English. Signature 1A. Back: Man with bananas at left, truck on road at center right, two ships in background at upper right.

VF 150 UNC 475

12 1000 Francs
ND (1962). Multicolor. Denominations in French and English. Signature 1A. Back:
Like #7 but with title: *RÉPUBLIQUE FÉDÉRALE* .

	VF	UNC
a. Issued note. Engraved.	250	750
b. Issued note. Lithographic.	250	750
s. Specimen. Overprint: *SPECIMEN* in black and perforated.	—	750

13 5000 Francs
ND (1962). Multicolor. Denominations in French and English. Signature 1A. Back:
Like #9 but with title: *RÉPUBLIQUE FÉDÉRALE* .

	VF	UNC
a. Issued note.	500	1,650
s. Specimen. Overprint: *SPECIMEN* in black and perforated.	—	1,250

1972 ND Issue

14 10,000 Francs
ND (1972). Multicolor. President A. Ahidjo at left, fruit at center, wood carving at
right. Signature 2. Back: Statue at left and right, tractor plowing at center.

VF 125 UNC 375

RÉPUBLIQUE UNIE DU CAMEROUN
Banque des États de l'Afrique Centrale
1974 ND Issue

15 500 Francs
ND (1974; 1984); 1978-83. Red-brown and multicolor. Woman wearing hat at left,
aerial view of modern buildings at center. Back: Mask at left, students and chemical testing at center, statue at right.

	VF	UNC
a. Signature titles: *LE DIRECTEUR GÉNÉRAL* and *UN CENSEUR*. Engraved. watermark: Antelope in half profile. Signature 3. ND (1974).	75.00	250
b. As a. signature 5.	12.50	45.00
c. Signature titles: *LE GOUVERNEUR* and *UN CENSEUR*. watermark: Antelope in profile. Signature 10. 1.4.1978.	8.00	35.00
d. Signature 12. 1.6.1981; 1.1.1983.	6.00	25.00
e. Signature 12. 1.1.1982.	25.00	75.00

18   10,000 Francs

VF   UNC

ND (1974; 1978; 1981). Multicolor. President A. Ahidjo at left. Back: Statue at left and right, tractor plowing at center.

a. Signature titles: *LE DIRECTEUR GÉNÉRAL* and *UN CENSEUR*. Signature 5. ND (1974).   100   400

b. Signature titles: *LE GOUVERNEUR* and *UN CENSEUR*. Signature 11; 12. ND (1978; 1981).   75.00   300

1981 ND Issue

19   5000 Francs

VF   UNC

ND (1981). Brown and multicolor. Mask at left, woman carrying bundle of fronds at right, signature 12. Back: Plowing and mine ore conveyor.

a. Issued note.   25.00   100

s. Specimen. Overprint: *SPECIMEN* in black and perforated.   —   750

16   1000 Francs

VF   UNC

ND (1974); 1978-83. Blue and multicolor. Hut at center, girl with plaits at right. Back: Mask at left, trains, planes and bridge at center, statue at right.

a. Signature titles: *LE DIRECTEUR GÉNÉRAL* and *UN CENSEUR*. Engraved. watermark: Antelope in half profile. Signature 5. ND (1974).   15.00   60.00

b. Signature titles like a. Lithographed. watermark. like c. Signature 8. ND (1978).   55.00   175

c. Signature titles: *LE GOUVERNEUR* and *UN CENSEUR*. Lithographed. watermark: Antelope in profile. Signature 10. 1.4.1978, 1.7.1980.   10.00   40.00

d. Signature 12. 1.6.1981; 1.1.1982; 2; 1.1.1983.   8.00   35.00

s. As a. Specimen.   —   —

20   10,000 Francs

VF   UNC

ND (1981). Brown, green and multicolor. Stylized antelope heads at left, woman at right, signature 12. Back: Loading of fruit onto truck at left.   50.00   175

RÉPUBLIQUE DU CAMEROUN

Banque des États de l'Afrique Centrale
1984 ND Issue

17   5000 Francs

VF   UNC

ND (1974). Brown and multicolor. President A. Ahidjo at left, railway loading equipment at right. Back: Mask at left, industrial college at center, statue at right.

a. Signature titles: *LE DIRECTEUR GÉNÉRAL* and *UN CENSEUR*. Engraved. Signature 3. ND (1974).   175   550

b. Like a. signature 5.   100   350

c. Signature titles: *LE GOUVERNEUR* and *UN CENSEUR*. Signature 11; 12.   80.00   250

s. As a. Specimen. Overprint: *SPECIMEN* in black and perforated.   —   1,000

21   1000 Francs

VF   UNC

1.6.1984. Blue and multicolor. Hut at center, girl with plaits at right, signature 12. Back: Mask at left, trains, planes, and bridge at center, statue at right.   7.50   30.00

22   5000 Francs

VF   UNC

ND (1984; 1990; 1992). Brown and multicolor. Mask at left, woman carrying bundle of fronds at right, signature 12; 13; 15. Back: Plowing and mine ore conveyor.   25.00   100

23 10,000 Francs   VF   UNC
ND (1984; 1990). Brown, green and multicolor. Styilized antelope heads at left,   50.00   175
woman at right, signature 12; 13. Back: Loading of fruit onto truck at left.

1985-86 Issue

24 500 Francs   VF   UNC
1985-90. Brown on multicolor underprint. Carving and jug at center. Back: Man
carving mask at left center. Watermark: Carving.
   a. Signature 12. 1.1.1985-1.1.1988.   5.00   20.00
   b. Signature 13. 1.1.1990.   4.00   15.00

25 1000 Francs   VF   UNC
1.1.1985. Dark blue on multicolor underprint. Carving at left, small figurines at   10.00   40.00
center, man at right, incomplete map of Chad at top. Back: Elephant at left, carving at right. Watermark: Carving.

26 1000 Francs   VF   UNC
1986-92. Dark blue on multicolor underprint. Carving at left, small figurines at
center, man at right, completed outline map of Chad at top center. Back: Elephant
at left, carving at right. Watermark: Carving.
   a. Signature 12. 1.1.1986-1.1.1989.   8.00   35.00
   b. Signature 13. 1.1.1990.   7.00   30.00
   c. Signature 15.1.1.1992.   6.00   25.00

CANADA

Canada is located to the north of the United States, and spans the full breadth of the northern portion of North America from Atlantic to Pacific oceans, except for the State of Alaska. It has a total area of 9,984,670 sq. km. and a population of 33.21 million. Capital: Ottawa.

A land of vast distances and rich natural resources, Canada became a self-governing dominion in 1867 while retaining ties to the British crown. Economically and technologically the nation has developed in parallel with the US, its neighbor to the south across an unfortified border. Canada faces the political challenges of meeting public demands for quality improvements in health care and education services, as well as responding to separatist concerns in predominantly francophone Quebec. Canada also aims to develop its diverse energy resources while maintaining its commitment to the environment.

RULERS:
   French 1534-1763
   British 1763-

MONETARY SYSTEM:
   French:
      12 Deniers = 1 Sou (sols)
      20 Sous or Sols = 1 Livre Coloniale
      1 Liard = 3 Deniers
      1 Ecu = 6 Livres
      1 Louis D'or = 4 Ecus
   English:
      4 Farthings = 1 Penny
      12 Pence = 1 Shilling
      20 Shillings = 1 Pound
   Canadian Decimal Currency
      100 Cents = 1 Dollar

REPLACEMENT NOTES:
   #66-70A and 74b, asterisk in front of fractional prefix letters. #76, 78-81, triple letter prefix ending
      in X (AAX, BAX, etc.). Exceptions: #82, no asterisk but serial number starts with 510 or 516;
      #83, serial number starts with 31 (instead of 30).
   #84-90, as #76 and 78-81.

DOMINION
Banque du Canada / Bank of Canada
1954 Modified Hair Style Issue

74 1 Dollar   VF   UNC
1954 (1955-72). Black on green underprint. Like #66 but Queen's hair in modified
style. Back: Western prairie scene. Printer: CBNC.
   a. Signature Beattie-Coyne. (1955-61).   2.50   15.00
   b. Signature Beattie-Rasminsky. (1961-72).   2.00   12.50

75   1 Dollar   VF   UNC
1954 (1955-74). Black on green underprint. Queen's hair in modified style. Like #74. Back: Western prairie scene. Printer: BABNC.

a. Signature Beattie-Coyne. (1955-61).	2.50	40.00
b. Signature Beattie-Rasminsky. (1961-72).	2.00	12.50
c. Signature Bouey-Rasminsky. (1972-73).	2.00	10.00
d. Signature Lawson-Bouey. (1973-74).	2.00	10.00

76   2 Dollars   VF   UNC
1954 (1955-75). UV: planchettes fluoresce blue. Black on red-brown underprint. Like #67 but Queen's hair in modified style. Back: Quebec scenery. Printer: BABNC.

a. Signature Beattie-Coyne. (1955-61).	8.00	55.00
b. Signature Beattie-Rasminsky. (1961-72).	3.00	12.50
c. Signature Bouey-Rasminsky. (1972-73).	3.00	15.00
d. Signature Lawson-Bouey. (1973-75).	3.00	15.00

77   5 Dollars   VF   UNC
1954 (1955-72). Black on blue underprint. Like #68 but Queen's hair in modified style. Back: River in the north country. Printer: CBNC.

a. Signature Beattie-Coyne. (1955-61).	15.00	70.00
b. Signature Beattie-Rasminsky. (1961-72).	10.00	45.00
c. Signature Bouey-Rasminsky. (1972).	10.00	35.00

78   5 Dollars   VF   UNC
1954 (1955-61). Black on blue underprint. Queen's hair in modified style. Like #77. Signature Beattie-Coyne. Back: River in the north country. Printer: BABNC.

	12.50	70.00

79   10 Dollars   VF   UNC
1954 (1955-71). Black on purple underprint. Like #69 but Queen's hair in modified style. Back: Rocky Mountain scene. Printer: BABNC.

a. Signature Beattie-Coyne. (1955-61).	15.00	85.00
b. Signature Beattie-Rasminsky. (1961-71).	13.00	60.00

80   20 Dollars   VF   UNC
1954 (1955-70) Black on olive olive-green underprint. Like #70 but Queen's hair in modified style. Back: Laurentian hills in winter. Printer: CBNC.

a. Signature Beattie-Coyne. (1955-61).	25.00	150
b. Signature Beattie-Rasminsky. (1961-70).	25.00	100

81   50 Dollars   VF   UNC
1954 (1955-75). Black on orange underprint. Like #71 but Queen's hair in modified style. Back: Atlantic coastline. Printer: CBNC.

a. Signature Beattie-Coyne. (1955-61).	75.00	400
b. Signature Beattie-Rasminsky. (1961-72).	75.00	300
c. Signature Lawson-Bouey. (1973-75).	75.00	350

82   100 Dollars   VF   UNC
1954 (1955-76). Black on brown underprint. Queen's hair in modified style. Back: Mountain lake. Printer: CBNC.

a. Signature Beattie-Coyne. (1955-61).	125	375
b. Signature Beattie-Rasminsky. (1961-72).	125	300
c. Signature Lawson-Bouey. (1973-76).	125	350

83 **1000 Dollars**

1954 (1955-87). Black on rose underprint. Like #73 but Queen's hair in modified style. Back: Central Canadian landscape.

	VF	UNC
a. Signature Beattie-Coyne. (1955-61).	1,400	4,500
b. Signature Beattie-Rasminsky. (1961-72).	1,100	2,750
c. Signature Bouey-Rasminsky. (1972).	1,100	2,250
d. Signature Lawson-Bouey. (1973-84).	1,075	1,500
e. Signature Thiessen-Crow. (1987).	1,250	2,250

1967 Commemorative Issue

#84, Centennial of Canadian Confederation

84 **1 Dollar** VF UNC

1967. Centennial of Canadian Confederation. UV: planchettes fluoresce blue. Black on green underprint. Queen Elizabeth II at right. Signature Beattie-Rasminsky. Back: First Parliament Building.

	VF	UNC
a. Centennial dates: 1867-1967 replaces serial #.	1.50	4.00
b. Regular serial #'s.	2.00	7.50

1969-75 Issue

85 **1 Dollar** VF UNC

1973. UV: planchettes fluoresce blue. Black on light green and multicolor underprint. Queen Elizabeth II at right, arms at left. Back: Parliament Building as seen from across the Ottawa River.

	VF	UNC
a. Engraved back. signature Lawson-Bouey.	1.00	5.00
b. Lithographed back. signature as a. Serial # prefix: AFF-.	1.00	6.00
c. Signature Crow-Bouey.	1.00	3.50

Note: Two formats of uncut 40-note sheets of #85b were sold to collectors in 1988 (BABN) and again in 1989 (CBNC). BABN format: 5x8 notes regular serial # prefixes BFD, BFK, BFL and replacement prefix BAX. CBNC format: 4x10 notes regular serial # prefixes ECP, ECR, ECV, ECW and replacement prefix EAX.

86 **2 Dollars** VF UNC

1974. UV: planchettes fluoresce blue. Red-brown on multicolor underprint. Queen Elizabeth II at right, arms at left. Back: Inuits preparing for hunt.

	VF	UNC
a. Signature Lawson-Bouey.	2.25	12.50
b. Signature Crow-Bouey.	2.25	12.00

Note: Two formats of uncut 40-note sheets of #86b were sold to collectors in 1995-96. BABN format: 5x8 notes. CBNC format: 4x10 notes.

87 **5 Dollars** VF UNC

1972. UV: planchettes and fibers fluoresce blue. Blue on multicolor underprint. Sir Wilfred Laurier at right, serial # on face, arms at left. Back: Salmon fishing boat at Vancouver Island.

	VF	UNC
a. Signature Bouey-Rasminsky.	6.00	40.00
b. Signature Lawson-Bouey.	6.00	37.50

88 **10 Dollars** VF UNC

1971. Purple on multicolor underprint. Sir John A. MacDonald at right, arms at left. Back: Oil refinery at Sarnia, Ontario.

	VF	UNC
a. Signature Beattie-Rasminsky.	12.50	70.00
b. Signature Bouey-Rasminsky.	15.00	85.00
c. Signature Lawson-Bouey.	FV	45.00
d. Signature Crow-Bouey.	FV	40.00
e. Signature Thiessen-Crow.	FV	42.50

89 **20 Dollars** VF UNC

1969. Green on multicolor underprint. Queen Elizabeth II at right, serial # on face, arms at left. Back: Alberta's Lake Moraine and Rocky Mountains.

	VF	UNC
a. Signature Beattie-Rasminsky.	25.00	95.00
b. Signature Lawson-Bouey.	22.50	90.00

90 **50 Dollars**

1975. Red on multicolor underprint. William Lyon MacKenzie King at right, arms at left. Back: Mounted Police in *Dome* formation (from their Musical Ride program).

		VF	UNC
a. Signature Lawson-Bouey.		65.00	220
b. Signature Crow-Bouey.		55.00	185

91 **100 Dollars**

1975. Brown on multicolor underprint. Sir Robert Borden at right, arms at left. Back: Lunenburg, Nova Scotia harbor scene.

		VF	UNC
a. Signature Lawson-Bouey.		105	250
b. Signature Crow-Bouey.		100	225

1979 Issue

92 **5 Dollars**

1979. Blue on multicolor underprint. Sir Wilfred Laurier at right, arms at left, different design element at upper center. Back: Salmon fishing boat at Vancouver Island, serial #.

		VF	UNC
a. Signature Lawson-Bouey.		FV	35.00
b. Signature Crow-Bouey.		FV	40.00

93 **20 Dollars**

1979. UV: planchettes fluoresce blue. Deep olive-green on multicolor underprint. Queen Elizabeth II at right, arms at left, similar to # 89, but different guilloches. Back: Alberta's Lake Moraine and Rocky Mountains, serial number.

		VF	UNC
a. Signature Lawson-Bouey.		FV	75.00
b. Signature Crow-Bouey.		FV	70.00
c. Signature Thiessen-Crow.		FV	50.00

1986-91 Issue

#94-100 Replacement notes: Third letter of serial # prefix is *X*.

94 **2 Dollars**

1986. Replacement notes: Third letter of serial # prefix is X. Brown on multicolor underprint. Queen Elizabeth II, Parliament building at right, arms at upper left center. Back: Pair of robins.

		VF	UNC
a. Signature Crow-Bouey.		FV	8.50
b. Signature Thiessen-Crow.		FV	4.00
c. Signature Bonin-Thiessen.		FV	4.00

95 **5 Dollars**

1986. Blue-gray on multicolor underprint. Sir Wilfrid Laurier, Parliament buildings at right, arms at upper left center. Back: Kingfisher.

		VF	UNC
a1. Signature Crow-Bouey. Yellow plate # on back.		5.50	35.00
a2. Signature Crow-Bouey. Blue plate # on back.		FV	27.50
b. Signature Thiessen-Crow.		FV	15.00
c. Signature Bonin-Thiessen.		FV	12.00
d. Signature Knight-Thiessen.		FV	11.00
e. Signature Knight-Dodge.		FV	10.00

96 **10 Dollars**

1989. Purple on multicolor underprint. Sir John A. Macdonald, Parliament buildings at right, arms at upper left center. Back: Osprey in flight.

		VF	UNC
a. Signature Thiessen-Crow.		FV	20.00
b. Signature Bonin-Thiessen.		FV	18.50
c. Signature Knight-Thiessen.		FV	17.50

97 20 Dollars VF UNC

1991. Note: The letter "I" in the serial # prefix exists serif and sans-serif. Deep olive-green and olive-green on multicolor underprint. Green foil optical device with denomination at upper left, Queen Elizabeth II, Parliament library at right, arms at upper left center. Back: Common loon.

    a. Signature Thiessen-Crow. FV 35.00
    b. Signature Bonin-Thiessen. FV 35.00
    c. Signature Knight-Thiessen. FV 32.50
    d. Signature Knight-Dodge. FV 32.50

100 1000 Dollars VF UNC

1988. Pink on multicolor underprint. Queen Elizabeth II, Parliament library at right, Optical device with denomination at upper left, arms at upper left center. Back: Pine grosbeak pair on branch at right.

    a. Signature Thiessen-Crow. FV 1,650
    b. Signature Bonin-Thiessen. FV 1,500

2001-03 Issue

98 50 Dollars VF UNC

1988. Red on multicolor underprint. William Lyon MacKenzie King, Parliament building at right, gold optical device with denomination at upper left, arms at upper left center. Back: Snowy owl.

    a. Signature Thiessen-Crow. FV 95.00
    b. Signature Bonin-Thiessen. FV 100
    c. Signature Knight-Thiessen. FV 85.00
    d. Signature Knight-Dodge. FV 80.00

101 5 Dollars VF UNC

2002. Blue and tan-yellow. Sir Wilfrid Laurier at left, west block of Parliament at center. Back: Winter sports - children skating, tobogganing, and playing hockey.

    a. 2002/2001. Signature Knight-Dodge. FV 8.50
    b. 2002/2003. Signature Knight-Dodge. FV 8.50
    c. 2002/2004. Signature Jenkins-Dodge. FV 8.50
    d. 2002/2005. Signature Jenkins-Dodge. FV 8.50

99 100 Dollars VF UNC

1988. Dark brown on multicolor underprint. Sir Robert Borden, Parliament building at right, green optical device with denomination at upper left, arms at upper left center. Back: Canadian geese.

    a. Signature Thiessen-Crow. FV 175
    b. Signature Bonin-Thiessen. FV 225
    c. Signature Knight-Thiessen. FV 150
    d. Signature Knight-Dodge. FV 135

101A 5 Dollars VF UNC

2006-. Blue and tan-yellow. Sir Wilfrid Laurier at left, west block of Parliament at center, holographic strip at left. Back: Winter sports - children skating, tobogganing, and playing hockey.

    a. 2006/2006. Signature Jenkins-Dodge. FV 8.00
    b. 2006/2008. Signature Jenkins-Carney. FV 7.50
    c. 2006/2009. Signature Jenkins-Carney. FV 7.50
    d. 2006/2010. Signature Jenkins-Carney. FV 7.50
    e. 2006/2011. Signature Macklem-Carney. FV 7.50

102 10 Dollars VF UNC

2001. Purple and tan on multicolor underprint. Sir John A. Macdonald at left, Parliament Library at center. Back: Veteran and children at memorial at right, peacekeeper with binoculars at center, poppies and doves.

    a. 2001/2000. Signature Knight-Thiessen. FV 15.00
    b. 2001/2001. Signature Knight-Dodge. FV 13.50
    c. 2001/2002. Signature Knight-Dodge. FV 13.50
    d. 2001/2003. Signature Jenkins-Dodge. FV 17.50
    e. 2001/2004. Signature Jenkins-Dodge. FV 17.50

102A 10 Dollars

VF UNC

2005-. Purple and tan on multicolor underprint. Sir John A. Macdonald at left, Parliament Library at center, holographic strip at left. Back: Veteran and children at memorial at right, peacekeeper with binoculars at center, poppies and doves.

a. 2005/2004. Signature Jenkins-Dodge.	FV	14.00
b. 2005/2005. Signature Jenkins-Dodge.	FV	14.00
c. 2005/2007. Signature Jenkins-Dodge.	FV	14.00
d. 2005/2008. Signature Jenkins-Carney.	FV	13.00
e. 2005/2009. Signature Jenkins-Carney.	FV	12.00

103 20 Dollars

VF UNC

2004-. Green and tan on multicolor underprint. Queen Elizabeth II at left. Back: Westcoast native art theme.

a. 2004/2004. Signature Jenkins-Dodge.	FV	30.00
b. 2004/2005. Signature Jenkins-Dodge.	FV	27.50
c. 2004/2006. Signature Jenkins-Dodge.	FV	27.50
d. 2004/2007. Signature Jenkins-Dodge.	FV	27.50
e. 2004/2008. Signature Jenkins-Dodge.	FV	25.00
f. 2004/2009. Signature Jenkins-Carney.	FV	25.00
g. 2004/2010. Signature Jenkins-Carney.	FV	25.00
h. 2004/2011. Signature Maclem-Carney	FV	22.50

104 50 Dollars

VF UNC

2004-. Red-orange and tan on multicolor underprint. William Lyon MacKenzie King at left. Back: Accomplishments of the Famous Five and Thérèse Casgrain. 152x69mm.

a. 2004/2004. Signature Jenkins-Dodge.	FV	80.00
b. 2004/2006. Signature Jenkins-Dodge.	FV	75.00
c. 2004/2008. Signature Jenkins-Carney.	FV	75.00
d. 2004/2011. Signature Maclem and Carney.	FV	70.00

105 100 Dollars

VF UNC

2004-. Brown and green on multicolor underprint. Sir Robert Borden at right. Back: Historic and satellite maps of Canada.

a. 2004/2004. Signature Jenkins-Dodge.	FV	150
b. 2004/2005. Signature Jenkins-Dodge.	FV	140
c. 2004/2006. Signature Jenkins-Dodge.	FV	140
d. 2004/2009. Signature Jenkins-Carney.	FV	135

2011-13 Polymer Issue

106 5 Dollars

VF UNC

2013 Polymer plastic. Light and dark blue and multicolor. Sir Wilfrid Laurier and west block of Parliament Building. Back: Canadarm2 at right center. 152x69mm.

a. Signature: Macklem-Carney.	FV	7.50
b. Signature Macklem-Poloz.	FV	7.50

107 10 Dollars

VF UNC

2013 Polymer plastic. Light and dark purple and multicolor. Sir John A. MacDonald and Parliament library Back: VIA rail train in rockies at right center. 152x69mm.

a. Signature Macklem-Carney.	FV	15.00
b. Signature Macklem-Poloz. Polymer.	FV	15.00

108 20 Dollars

VF UNC

2012 Polymer plastic. Light and dark green and multicolor. Elizabeth II at left center. Back: Canadian WWI VIMY memorial. 152x69mm.

a. Signature: Maclem-Carney.	FV	25.00
b. Signature Wilkins-Poloz. Polymer.	FV	25.00

109 50 Dollars

VF UNC

2012 Polymer plastic. Light and dark red and multicolor. W. L. Mackenzie at left center. Back: CCGS Amudsen, research icebreaker. 152x69mm.

a. Signature Maclem-Carney.	FV	60.00
b. Signature Wilkins-Poloz. Polymer.	FV	60.00

110 100 Dollars

VF UNC

2011. Light and dark brown and multicolor. Sir Robert L. Borden at left center. Back: Researcher using microscope. 152x69mm.

a. Signature Macklem-Carney.	FV	115
b. Signature Macklem-Poloz. Polymer.	FV	115

CAPE VERDE

The Republic of Cape Verde, is located in the Atlantic Ocean, about 370 miles (595 km.) west of Dakar, Senegal off the coast of Africa. The 14-island republic has an area of 4,033 sq. km. and a population of 427,000. Capital: Praia. Fishing is important and agriculture is widely practiced, but the Cape Verdes are not self-sufficient in food. Fish products, salt, bananas, coffee, peanuts and shellfish are exported.

The uninhabited islands were discovered and colonized by the Portuguese in the 15th century; Cape Verde subsequently became a trading center for African slaves and later an important coaling and resupply stop for whaling and transatlantic shipping. Following independence in 1975, and a tentative interest in unification with Guinea-Bissau, a one-party system was established and maintained until multi-party elections were held in 1990. Cape Verde continues to exhibit one of Africa's most stable democratic governments. Repeated droughts during the second half of the 20th century caused significant hardship and prompted heavy emigration. As a result, Cape Verde's expatriate population is greater than its domestic one. Most Cape Verdeans have both African and Portuguese antecedents.

RULERS:
Portuguese to 1975

MONETARY SYSTEM:
1 Mil Reis = 1000 Reis
1 Escudo = 100 Centavos, 1911-

STEAMSHIP SEALS

Type I	Type II	Type III
LOANDA	LISBOA	C.C.A

C,C,A = Colonias, Commercio, Agricultura.

PORTUGUESE ADMINISTRATION

Banco Nacional Ultramarino
1971; 1972 Issue

52 20 Escudos   **VF UNC**
4.4.1972. Security thread. Green on multicolor underprint. Portrait of S. Pinto at right, bank seal at left, arms at lower center. Two signature varieties. Signature titles: *ADMINISTRATOR* and *VICE-GOVERNADOR*. Back: Allegorical woman with ships.
    a. Issued note.   150   400
    s. Specimen.   —   250

53 50 Escudos   **VF UNC**
4.4.1972. Security thread. Blue on multicolor underprint. Portrait of S. Pinto at right, bank seal at left, arms at lower center. Signature titles: *ADMINISTRATOR* and *VICE-GOVERNADOR*. Back: Allegorical woman with ships.
    a. Issued note.   175   500
    s. Specimen.   —   325

53A 500 Escudos   **VF UNC**
16.6.1971; 20.6.1971. Olive-green on multicolor underprint. Infante D. Henrique at right.
    a. Issued note.   225   600
    s. Specimen.   —   500
    ct. Color trial. Blue on multicolor underprint.   —   650

REPUBLIC

Banco de Cabo Verde
1977 Issue

54 100 Escudos   **VF UNC**
20.1.1977. Red and multicolor. Bow and musical instruments at left, A. Cabral with native hat at right. Back: Mountain at left center. Watermark: A. Cabral. Printer: BWC.
    a. Issued note.   7.50 25.00
    s1. Specimen. Overprint: *ESPECIME* in red on both sides. Punch hole cancelled.   —   95.00
    s2. Specimen. Overprint: *ESPECIME* in black. Punch hole cancelled.   —   95.00
    s3. Specimen. Overprint: *SPECIMEN*. in red. Punch hole cancelled.   —   95.00

55 500 Escudos VF UNC
20.1.1977. Blue and multicolor. Shark at left, A. Cabral with native hat at right.
Back: Harbor at Praia. Watermark: A. Cabral. Printer: BWC.

    a. Issued note. 15.00 40.00
    s1. Specimen. Overprint: *ESPECIMEN* in red on both sides. Punch hole — 95.00
       cancelled.
    s2. Specimen. Overprint: *SPECIMEN* on both sides. Punch hole cancelled. — 95.00

58 200 Escudos VF UNC
20.1.1989. Green and black on multicolor underprint. A. Cabral at right, Serial
number black at left, red at right. Back: Modern airport collage in vertical format.
Watermark: A. Cabral. Printer: TDLR.

    a. Issued note. FV 10.00
    s. Specimen. Overprint: *ESPECIMEN* in red on both sides. Punch hole — 35.00
       cancelled.

56 1000 Escudos VF UNC
20.1.1977. Brown and multicolor. Electrical appliance at left, A. Cabral with
native hat at right. Back: Workers at quarry at left center, banana stalk at right.
Watermark: A. Cabral. Printer: BWC.

    a. Issued note. 27.50 75.00
    s1. Specimen. Red overprint: *ESPECIMEN* on both sides. Punch hole — 100
       cancelled.
    s2. Specimen. Overprint: *SPECIMEN* on both sides. Punch hole cancelled. — 200

59 500 Escudos VF UNC
20.1.1989. Blue on multicolor underprint. A. Cabral at right, serial number black at
left, red at right. Back: Shipyard. Watermark: A. Cabral. Printer: TDLR.

    a. Issued note. FV 20.00
    s. Specimen. — 40.00

1989 Issue

57 100 Escudos VF UNC
20.1.1989. Red and dark purple on multicolor underprint. A. Cabral at right, serial
number black at left, red at right. Back: Festival at left center. Watermark: A.
Cabral. Printer: TDLR.

    a. Issued note. FV 6.00
    s. Specimen. Overprint: *ESPECIMEN* in red on both sides. Punch hole — 25.00
       cancelled.

60 1000 Escudos VF UNC
20.1.1989. Brown and red-brown on multicolor underprint. A Cabral at right,
serial number black at left, red at right. Back: Insects at left center. Watermark: A.
Cabral. Printer: TDLR.

    a. Issued note. FV 35.00
    s. Specimen. — 50.00

61   2500 Escudos   VF   UNC

20.1.1989. Violet on multicolor underprint. A. Cabral at right, serial number black
at left, red at right. Back: Palace of National Assembly. Watermark: A. Cabral.
Printer: TDLR.

   a. Issued note.   FV   70.00

   s. Specimen. Overprint: *ESPECIMEN* in red on both sides. Punch hole   —   75.00
   cancelled.

1992 Issue

63   200 Escudos   VF   UNC

8.8.1992. Black and blue-green on multicolor underprint. Sailing ship *Ernestina* at
center right. Back: Modern airport collage in vertical format. Watermark: A. Cabral.
Printer: TDLR.

   a. Issued note.   FV   6.00

   s. Specimen. Overprint: *ESPECIME* in red on both sides. Punch hole   —   35.00
   cancelled.

64   500 Escudos   VF   UNC

23.4.1992; 1.7.2002. Purple, blue and dark brown on multicolor underprint. Doctor
B. Lopes da Silva at center right. Back: Shipyard. Watermark: A. Cabral. Printer:
TDLR

   a. 23.4.1992.   FV   15.00
   b. 1.7.2002.   FV   12.50
   s1. Specimen. As a. Overprint: *ESPECIME* in thin letters on both sides. Punch   —   100
   hole cancelled.
   s2. Specimen. As b. Red overprint: *ESPECIMEN* in thick letters on both sides.   —   100
   Punch hole cancelled.

65   1000 Escudos   VF   UNC

5.6.1992; 1.7.2002. Dark brown, red-orange and purple on multicolor underprint.
Cape Verde warbler at center right. Back: Insects at left center. 145x68mm.

   a. 5.6.1992.   FV   25.00
   b. 1.7.2002.   FV   22.50
   s1. Specimen. As a. Red overprint: *ESPECIME* in thin letters on both sides.   —   60.00
   Punch hole cancelled.
   s2. Specimen. As b. Red overprint: *ESPECIMEN* in thick letters on both sides.   —   60.00
   Punch hole cancelled.

1999-2000 Issue

66   2000 Escudos   VF   UNC

1.7.1999. Brown, green, red and multicolor. Eugenio Tavares at bottom. Back:
Cardeal flower and stanza from poem *Morna de Aguada*.

   a. Issued note.   FV   35.00
   s. Specimen. Red overprint: *ESPECIME* in thin letters on both sides. Punch   —   100
   hole cancelled.

67   5000 Escudos   VF   UNC

5.7.2000. Orange, red and multicolor. Woman carrying stones. Back: Fortress
details.

   a. Issued note.   FV   75.00
   s. Specimen. Overprint: *ESPECIME* in red on both sides. Punch hole   —   120
   cancelled.

2005 Issue

68 200 Escudos

20.1.2005. Vertical format. Sailing ship *Ernestina*. Back: Modern airport collage.
Printer: DLR

	VF	UNC
a. Issued note.	FV	7.50
s. Specimen. Red overprint: *ESPECIMEN*.	FV	75.00

69 500 Escudos

25.2.2007. Vertical format. Green, yellow, red and multicolor. Roberto Duarte
Silva at bottom. Back: Sugar cain press on the island of Santa Antáo. Watermark:
Roberto Duarte Silva Printer: F-CO. 130x65mm.

	VF	UNC
a. Issued note.	FV	12.50
s. Specimen. Red overprint: *ESPECIMEN*.	FV	75.00

70 1000 Escudos

25.9.2007. Violet, blue and rose onmulticolor underprint. Antonio Aurelio Con-
çalves at bottom. Back: Dragon tree.

	VF	UNC
a. Issued note.	FV	20.00
s. Specimen. Overprint: *ESPECIME* in red on both sides.	FV	125

71 200 Escudos

5.7.2014. Red, purple and yellow. H.T. Teixeira de Sousa at right. Back: Pico de
Fogo volcano.

	VF	UNC
	FV	4.50

72 500 Escudos

5.7.2014. Green, red and purple. Jorge Barbosa at right. Back: Poilaco Dam.
Watermark: Jorge Barbosa with electrotype typewriter and Cornerstones. Printer:
TDLR. 131x65mm.

	VF	UNC
	FV	8.00

73 1000 Escudos

25.9.2007. Violet, blue and rose onmulticolor underprint. Antonio Aurelio Con-
çalves at bottom. Back: Dragon tree.

	VF	UNC
	FV	20.00

74 2000 Escudos

5.7.2014. Orange, blue and red. Cesaria Evora at right. Back: Violin.

	VF	UNC
	FV	40.00

75 5000 Escudos

5.7.2014. Purple, blue and red. A.M. Pereira at right. Back: Factory with chimney.
Watermark: A.M. Pereira and electrotype torch with Cornerstones. Printer: TDLR.
148x74mm.

	VF	UNC
	FV	80.00

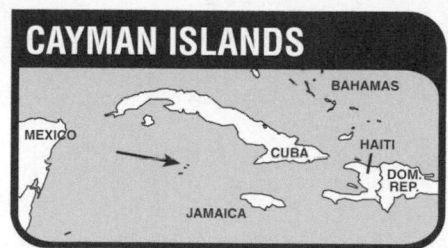

CAYMAN ISLANDS

The Cayman Islands, a British Crown Colony situated about 290 km. northwest of Jamaica, consists of three islands: Grand Cayman, Little Cayman and Cayman Brac. The islands have an area of 262 sq. km. and a population of 47,900. Capital: Georgetown. Seafaring, commerce, banking and tourism are the principal industries.

The Cayman Islands were colonized from Jamaica by the British during the 18th and 19th centuries, and were administered by Jamaica after 1863. In 1959, the islands became a territory within the Federation of the West Indies, but when the Federation dissolved in 1962, the Cayman Islands chose to remain a British dependency.

RULERS:
British

MONETARY SYSTEM:
1 Dollar = 100 Cents

BRITISH ADMINISTRATION
Cayman Islands Currency Board
1971 Currency Law

1 **1 Dollar**		**VF**	**UNC**

L.1971 (1972). Blue on multicolor underprint. Arms at upper center, Queen Elizabeth II at right. Back: Fish, coral at center. Watermark: Tortoise. Printer: TDLR.

a. Serial # Prefix *A/1*.	30.00	140
b. Serial # Prefix *A/2*.	25.00	130
c. Serial # Prefix *A/3*.	25.00	125
r. Replacement. Serial # Prefix *Z/1*.	40.00	175
s. Specimen.	—	220

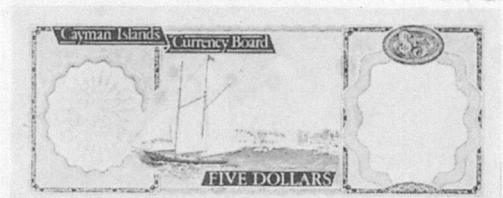

2 **5 Dollars**		**VF**	**UNC**

L.1971 (1972). Green on multicolor underprint. Arms at upper center, Queen Elizabeth II at right. Back: Sailboat at center. Watermark: Tortoise. Printer: TDLR.

a. Issued note.	45.00	225
r. Replacement. Serial # prefix *Z/l*.	55.00	290
s. Specimen.	—	275

3 **10 Dollars**	**VF**	**UNC**
	115	530

L.1971 (1972). Red on multicolor underprint. Arms at upper center, Queen Elizabeth II at right. Back: Beach scene at center. Watermark: Tortoise. Printer: TDLR.

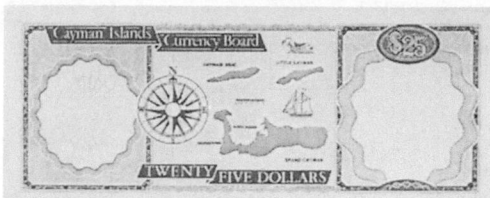

4 **25 Dollars**		**VF**	**UNC**
		335	1,625

L.1971 (1972). Brown on multicolor underprint. Arms at upper center, Queen Elizabeth II at right. Back: Compass and map at center. Watermark: Tortoise. Printer: TDLR.

1974 Currency Law

5 **1 Dollar**		**VF**	**UNC**

L.1974 (1985). UV: back left design fluoresce green. Blue on multicolor underprint. Arms at upper center, Queen Elizabeth II at right. Back: Fish, coral at center. Watermark: Tortoise. Printer: TDLR.

a. Signature as SCWPM #1 illustration. Serial # prefix *A/3*.	25.00	130
b. Signature Jefferson. Serial # prefix *A/3*.	23.00	110
c. Signature Jefferson. Serial # prefix *A/4*.	12.00	95.00
d. Signature Jefferson. Serial # prefix *A/5*.	8.00	70.00
e. Signature Jefferson. Serial # prefix *A/6*.	8.00	65.00
f. Signature Jefferson. Serial # prefix *A/7*.	8.00	60.00
r1. Replacement. As a. Serial # prefix *Z/1*.	35.00	190
r2. Replacement. As b. Serial # prefix *Z/1*.	35.00	170
s. Specimen. As. a.	—	210

6 **5 Dollars**		**VF**	**UNC**

L.1974.. Green on multicolor underprint. Arms at upper center, Queen Elizabeth II at right. Back: Sailboat at center. Watermark: Tortoise. Printer: TDLR.

a. Issued note.	25.00	125
r. Replacement. Serial # prefix *Z/1*.	40.00	180
s. Specimen.	—	280

7 **10 Dollars**		**VF**	**UNC**

L.1974. Red on multicolor underprint. Arms at upper center, Queen Elizabeth II at right. Back: Beach scene at center. Watermark: Tortoise. Printer: TDLR.

a. Issued note.	70.00	285
r. Replacement. Serial # prefix *Z/1*.	100	560
s. Specimen.	—	330

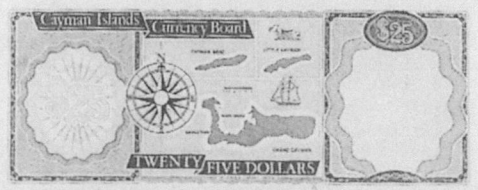

8   25 Dollars   VF UNC

L.1974. Brown on multicolor underprint. Arms at upper center, Queen Elizabeth II at right. Back: Compass and map at center. Watermark: Tortoise. Printer: TDLR.

    a. Issued note.   60.00   325
    r. Replacement. Serial # prefix *Z/1.*   80.00   435
    s. Specimen.   —   420

9   40 Dollars   VF UNC

L.1974 (1981). Purple on multicolor underprint. Arms at upper center, Queen Elizabeth II at right. Back: Pirates' Week Festival (crowd on beach) at center. Watermark: Tortoise. Printer: TDLR.

    a. Issued note.   80.00   320
    r. Replacement. Serial # prefix *Z/1.*   100   430

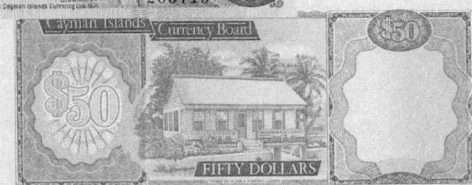

10   50 Dollars   VF UNC

L.1974 (1987). Blue on multicolor underprint. Arms at upper center, Queen Elizabeth II at right. Back: Government House at center. Watermark: Tortoise. Printer: TDLR.

    a. Issued note.   120   480
    r. Replacement. Serial # prefix *Z/1.*   270   940

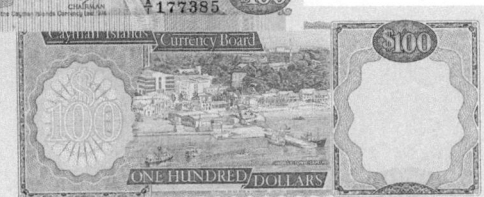

11   100 Dollars   VF UNC

L.1974 (1982). Deep orange on multicolor underprint. Arms at upper center, Queen Elizabeth II at right. Back: Seacoast view of George Town at center. Watermark: Tortoise. Printer: TDLR.   235   1,050

1991 Issue

12   5 Dollars   VF UNC

1991. Dark green, blue-green and olive-brown on multicolor underprint. Arms at upper center, Queen Elizabeth II at right, treasure chest at lower left center. Back: Sailboat in harbor waters at center, red coral at left. Watermark: Tortoise. Printer: TDLR.

    a. Issued note.   17.50   75.00
    r. Replacement. Serial # prefix *Z/1.*   45.00   150

13   10 Dollars   VF UNC

1991. Red and purple on multicolor underprint. Arms at upper center, Queen Elizabeth II at right, treasure chest at lower left center. Back: Open chest, palm tree along coastline at center, red coral at left. Watermark: Tortoise. Printer: TDLR.

    a. Golden colors around conch shell on back.   FV   155
    b. Orange colors around conch shell on back.   FV   175

14   25 Dollars   VF UNC

1991. Deep brown, tan and orange on multicolor underprint. Arms at upper center, Queen Elizabeth II at right, Treasure chest at lower left center. Back: Island outlines and compass at center, red coral at left. Watermark: Tortoise. Printer: TDLR.   FV   155

15   100 Dollars   VF UNC

1991. Orange and dark brown on multicolor underprint. Arms at upper center, Queen Elizabeth II at right, treasure chest at lower left center. Back: Harbor view at center, red coral at left. Watermark: Tortoise. Printer: TDLR.   FV   380

1996 Issue

16   1 Dollar

1996. Purple, orange and deep blue on multicolor underprint. Queen Elizabeth II
at right. Back: Fish, coral at center. Watermark: Tortoise. Printer: TDLR.

		VF	UNC
a. Serial # prefix *R/1*		6.00	37.50
b. Serial # prefix *B/2*.		5.00	35.00

17   5 Dollars

1996. Dark green, blue-green and olive-brown on multicolor underprint. Queen
Elizabeth II at right. Back: Sailboat in harbor waters at center, red coral at left.
Watermark: Tortoise. Printer: TDLR.

VF UNC
FV 70.00

18   10 Dollars

1996. Red and purple on multicolor underprint. Queen Elizabeth II at right. Back:
Open chest, palm trees along coastline at center, red coral at left.(Two varieties in
color of conch shell at upper center, red coral at left. Watermark: Tortoise. Printer:
TDLR.

		VF	UNC
a. Serial # prefix *B/I*.		FV	80.00
b. Serial # prefix *X/I*. Experimental paper. (100,000 pieces issued).		1,650	—

19   25 Dollars

1996. Deep brown, tan and orange on multicolor underprint. Queen Elizabeth II at
right. Back: Island outines and compass at center. Watermark: Tortoise. Printer:
TDLR.

VF UNC
FV 135

20   100 Dollars

1996. Orange and brown on multicolor underprint. Queen Elizabeth II at right.
Back: Harbor view at center. Watermark: Tortoise. Printer: TDLR.

VF UNC
160 325

Cayman Islands Monetary Authority
1998 Issue; 1996 Law

21   1 Dollar

1998. Segmented foil over security thread. Purple, orange and deep blue on
multicolor underprint. Queen Elizabeth II at right. Back: Fish, coral at center.
Watermark: Tortoise. Printer: (T)DLR.

		VF	UNC
a. Serial # prefix *C/1*.		4.00	32.50
b. Serial # prefix *C/2*.		4.00	30.00
r. Replacement. Serial # prefix *Z/1*.		20.00	110

22   5 Dollars

1998. Segmented foil over security thread. Olive-green and blue-green on
multicolor underprint. Queen Elizabeth II at right. Back: Sailboat in harbor waters
at center, red coral at left. Watermark: Tortoise. Printer: (T)DLR.

		VF	UNC
a. Issued note.		12.00	55.00
r. Replacement. Serial # prefix *Z/I*		30.00	140

23 **10 Dollars** VF UNC

1998. Segmented foil over security thread. Red and purple on multicolor underprint. Queen Elizabeth II at right. Back: Open chest, palm tree along coastline at center,(two varieties in color of conch shell at upper center, red coral at left. Watermark: Tortoise. Printer: (T)DLR. — 22.50 80.00

24 **25 Dollars** VF UNC

1998. Segmented foil over security thread. Deep brown, tan and orange on multicolor underprint. Queen Elizabeth II at right. Back: Island outlines and compass at center, red coral at left. Watermark: Tortoise. Printer: (T)DLR. — FV 150

25 **100 Dollars** VF UNC

1998. Segmented foil over security thread. Orange and brown on multicolor underprint. Queen Elizabeth II at right. Back: Harbor view at center, red coral at left. Watermark: Tortoise. Printer: (T)DLR. — FV 265

2001 Issue; 2001 Law Revision

26 **1 Dollar** VF UNC

2001. Segmented foil over security thread. Multicolor. Queen Elizabeth II at right. Back: Fish, coral at center. Watermark: Tortoise and CIMA. Printer: (T)DLR.

		VF	UNC
a. Serial # prefix: C/2.		FV	29.00
b. Serial # prefix: C/3.		FV	27.50
c. Serial # prefix: C/4.		FV	25.00
r. Replacement. Serial # prefix Z/1.		17.50	110
s. Specimen.		—	165

27 **5 Dollars** VF UNC

2001. Segmented foil over security thread. Multicolor. Queen Elizabeth II at right. Back: Sailboat in harbor waters at center, red coral at left. Watermark: Tortoise and CIMA. Printer: (T)DLR.

		VF	UNC
a. Issued note.		FV	37.50
s. Specimen.		—	165

28 **10 Dollars** VF UNC

2001. Segmented foil over security thread. Multicolor. Queen Elizabeth II at right. Back: Open chest, palm tree along coastline at center, (two varieties in color of conch shell at upper center, red coral at left. Watermark: Tortoise and CIMA. Printer: (T)DLR.

		VF	UNC
a. Issued note.		FV	60.00
s. Specimen.		—	175

29 **50 Dollars** VF UNC

2001. Segmented foil over security thread. Multicolor. Queen Elizabeth II at right. Watermark: Tortoise and CIMA. Printer: (T)DLR.

		VF	UNC
a. Issued note.		FV	210
r. Replacement. Serial # prefix Z/1.		105	375
s. Specimen.		—	325

2003 Commemorative Issue; 2002 Law Revision
500th Anniversary of discovery.

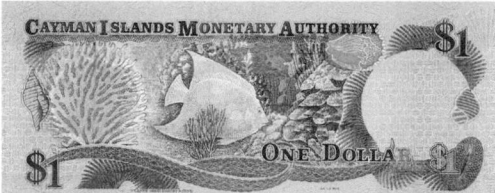

30   1 Dollar   VF   UNC

2003. UV: face right crab fluoresces green. Back: Left sea turtle, CIMA, and center
design all fluoresce green. Multicolor. Signature titles: *FINANCIAL SECRETARY*
and MANAGING DIRECTOR.

a. Issued note.	FV	35.00
b. Issued note in presentation folder (4000 made).	—	75.00
r. Replacement note. Serial # prefix *Z/1*.	15.00	85.00
s. Specimen.	—	225

2003 Issue; 2002 Law Revision

31   25 Dollars   VF   UNC

2003. Multicolor. Signature titles: *FINANCIAL SECRETARY* and *MANAGING
DIRECTOR.*

a. Issued note.	FV	85.00
s. Specimen.	—	240

32   50 Dollars   VF   UNC

2003. Multicolor. Signature titles: *FINANCIAL SECRETARY* and *MANAGING
DIRECTOR.*

a. 2003. Serial # prefix: *C/1*.	FV	225
b. 2003 (2007). Serial # prefix: *C/2*.	FV	150
s. Specimen.	—	325

2005-2006 Issue; 2004 Law Revision

33   1 Dollar   VF   UNC

2006. Blue on multicolor underprint. Signature titles: *FINANCIAL SECRETARY*
and *MANAGING DIRECTOR*. Watermark: Design in each corner.

a. Serial # prefix *C/4*.	3.00	20.00
b. Serial # prefix: *C/5*.	2.50	15.00
c. Serial # prefix *C/6*.	2.50	14.00
d. Serial # prefix *C/7*.	FV	10.00
r. Replacement note. As d.	10.00	65.00
s. Specimen.	—	155

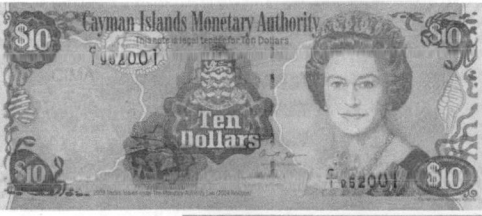

34   5 Dollars   VF   UNC

2005. Green on peach and multicolor underprint. Signatue titles: *FINANCIAL
SECRETARY* and *MANAGING DIRECTOR*. Watermark: Design in each corner.

a. Serial # prefix *C/1*.	FV	40.00
b. Serial # prefix *C/2*. (2009).	FV	20.00
s. Specimen.	—	170

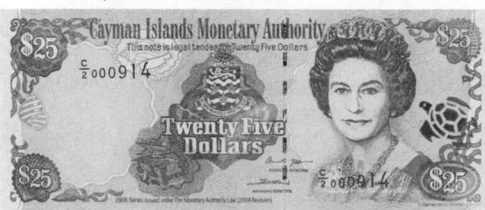

35   10 Dollars   VF   UNC

2005. Rose on blue and multicolor underprint. Signatue titles: *FINANCIAL SEC-
RETARY* and *MANAGING DIRECTOR*. Watermark: Design in each corner.

a. Issued note.	FV	35.00
r. Replacement note. Serial # prefix *Z/1*.	55.00	215
s. Specimen.	—	240

36   25 Dollars   VF   UNC

2006. Multicolor. Signatue titles: *FINANCIAL SECRETARY* and *MANAGING
DIRECTOR*. Watermark: Design in each corner.

a. Issued note.	FV	72.50
r. Replacement note.	70.00	280
s. Specimen.	—	315

37   100 Dollars   **VF   UNC**
2006. Multicolor. Signatue titles: *FINANCIAL SECRETARY* and *MANAGING DIRECTOR*. Watermark: Design in each corner.
    a. Issued note.   FV   205
    s. Specimen.   —   380

2010 Series

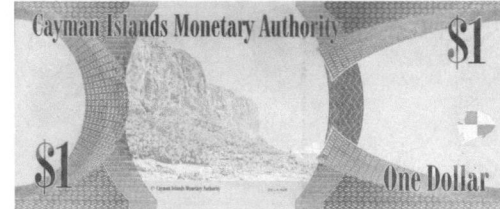

38   1 Dollar   **VF   UNC**
2011. Blue and violet on multicolor underprint. Queen Elizabeth II at right. Back: Cliffs. Printer: DLR. 156x66mm.
    a. Series D/1.   FV   8.00
    b. Series D/2.   —   7.50
    c. Series D/3.   —   —
    s. Specimen.   —   150

39   5 Dollars   **VF   UNC**
2010. Green and peach on multicolor underprint. Queen Elizabeth II at right. Back: Pair of parrots at center. Printer: DLR. 156x66mm.
    a. Issued note.   FV   17.50
    s. Specimen.   —   180
40   10 Dollars   **VF   UNC**
2010. Rose adn blue on multicolor underprint. Queen Elizabeth II at right. Printer: DLR. 156x66mm.
    a. Issued note.   FV   30.00
    s. Specimen.   —   240

41   25 Dollars   **VF   UNC**
2010. Brown and tan on multicolor underprint. Queen Elizabeth II at right. Printer: DLR. 156x66mm.
    a. Issued note.   FV   60.00
    s. Specimen.   —   275
42   50 Dollars   **VF   UNC**
2010. Multicolor. Queen Elizabeth II at right. Printer: DLR. 156x66mm.
    a. Issued note.   FV   115
    s. Specimen.   FV   340
43   100 Dollars   **VF   UNC**
2010. Multicolor. Queen Elizabeth II at right. Printer: DLR. 156x66mm.
    a. Issued note.   FV   175
    s. Specimen.   FV   400

COLLECTOR SERIES

Cayman Islands Currency Board
1974 Currency Law Issue

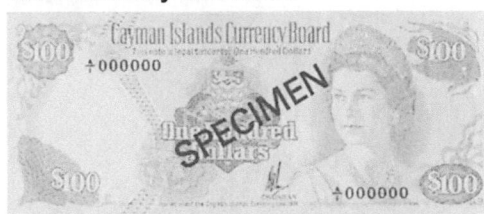

CS1   *L.1974.*   1-100 Dollars   **Mkt. Value**
    #5-11 overprint: *SPECIMEN*. (300 sets.)   3,400

1991 Issue

CS2   1991 5-100 Dollars   **Mkt. Value**
    #12-15 overprint: *SPECIMEN*. (300 sets.)   1,700

1996 Issue

CS3   1996 1-100 Dollars   **Mkt. Value**
    #16-20 overprint: *SPECIMEN*. (300 sets.)   1,600

1998 Issue

CS4   1998 1-100 Dollars   **Mkt. Value**
    #21-25 overprint: *SPECIMEN*. (100 sets.)   2,350

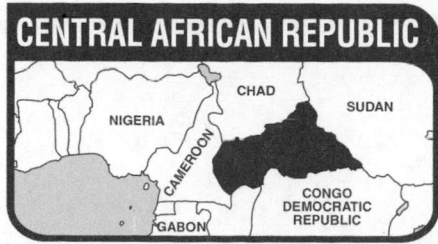

CENTRAL AFRICAN REPUBLIC

The Central African Republic, a landlocked country in Central Africa, bounded by Chad on the north, Cameroon on the west, Democratice Republic of the Congo and the Republic of the Congo on the south, and The Sudan on the east, has an area of 622,984 sq. km. and a population of 4.44 million. Capital: Bangui. Deposits of uranium, iron ore, manganese and copper remain to be developed. Diamonds, cotton, timber and coffee are exported.

The former French colony of Ubangi-Shari became the Central African Republic upon independence in 1960. After three tumultuous decades of misrule - mostly by military governments - civilian rule was established in 1993 and lasted for one decade. President Ange-Felix Patasse's civilian government was plagued by unrest, and in March 2003 he was deposed in a military coup led by General Francois Bozize, who established a transitional government. Though the government has the tacit support of civil society groups and the main parties, a wide field of candidates contested the municipal, legislative, and presidential elections held in March and May of 2005 in which General Bozize was affirmed as president. The government still does not fully control the countryside, where pockets of lawlessness persist. Unrest in neighboring nations, Chad, Sudan, and the DRC, continues to affect stability in the Central African Republic as well. It is a member of the "Union Monetaire des Etats de l'Afrique Centrale." See also Central African States, Equatorial African States, and French African States.

RULERS:

Emperor J. B. Bokassa I, 1976-79

MONETARY SYSTEM:

1 Franc = 100 Centimes

SIGNATURE VARIETIES:

Refer to introduction to Central African States.

RÉPUBLIQUE CENTRAFRICAINE

Banque des États de l'Afrique Centrale

1974-76 ND Issue

1	**500 Francs**		**VF**	**UNC**
	ND (1974). Lilac-brown and multicolor. President J.B. Bokassa at right, landscape at center, signature 6. Back: Mask at left, students and chemical testing at center, statue at right. Watermark: Antelope's head.		40.00	175

2	**1000 Francs**		**VF**	**UNC**
	ND (1974). Blue and multicolor. President J.B. Bokassa at right, rhinoceros at left, water buffalo at center, signature 6. Back: Mask at left, trains, planes and bridge at center, statue at right. Watermark: Antelope's head.		60.00	250

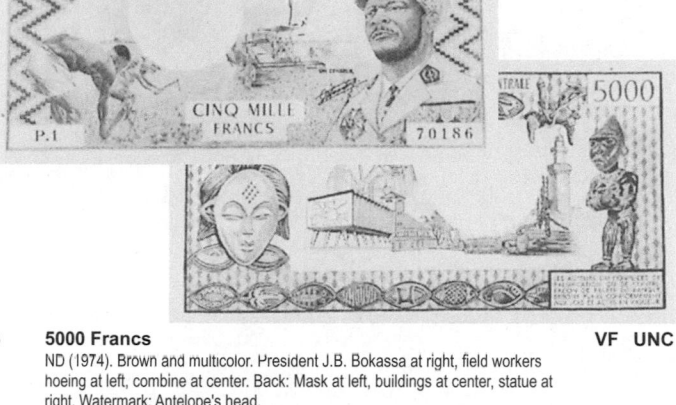

3	**5000 Francs**	**VF**	**UNC**
	ND (1974). Brown and multicolor. President J.B. Bokassa at right, field workers hoeing at left, combine at center. Back: Mask at left, buildings at center, statue at right. Watermark: Antelope's head.		
	a. Signature 4.	150	600
	b. Signature 6.	125	550

4	**10,000 Francs**	**VF**	**UNC**
	ND (1976). Multicolor. President J.B. Bokassa at right, sword hilts at left and center, signature 6. Back: Mask at left, tractor cultivating at center, statue at right. Watermark: Antelope's head.	300	900

EMPIRE CENTRAFRICAIN

Banque des États de l'Afrique Centrale

1978-79 Issue

5	**500 Francs**	**VF**	**UNC**
	1.4.1978. Specimen. Lilac-brown and multicolor. Emperor J.B. Bokassa I at right, landscape at center. Back: Mask at left, students and chemical testing at center, statue at right. Watermark: Antelope's head.	—	2,000

6	**1000 Francs**	**VF**	**UNC**
	1.4.1978. Blue and multicolor. Emperor J.B. Bokassa I at right, rhinoceros at left, water buffalo at center, signature 9. Back: Mask at left, trains, planes and bridge at center, statue at right. Watermark: Antelope's head.	200	800

7   5000 Francs
ND (1979). Brown and multicolor. Emperor J.B. Bokassa I at right, field workers hoeing at left, combine at center, signature 9. Back: Mask at left, buildings at center, statue at right. Watermark: Antelope's head.

VF	UNC
225	900

8   10,000 Francs
ND (1978). Multicolor. Emperor J.B. Bokassa I at right, sword hilts at left and center, signature 6. Back: Mask at left, tractor cultivating at center, statue at right. Watermark: Antelope's head.

VF	UNC
200	800

RÉPUBLIQUE CENTRAFRICAINE (RESUMED)

Banque des États de l'Afrique Centrale
Note: For notes with similar back designs see Cameroon Republic, Chad, Congo (Brazzaville) and Gabon. #9-10 wmk: Antelope's head.

1980 Issue

9   500 Francs
1.1.1980; 1.7.1980; 1.6.1981. Lithographed. Red and multicolor. Woman weaving basket at right, signature 9. Back: Mask at left, students and chemical testing at center, statue at right.

VF	UNC
7.50	25.00

10   1000 Francs
1.1.1980; 1.7.1980; 1.6.1981; 1.1.1982; 1.6.1984. Lithographed. Blue and multicolor. Butterfly at left, waterfall at center, water buffalo at right, signature 9. Back: Mask at left, trains, planes, and bridge at center, statue at right.

VF	UNC
10.00	35.00

11   5000 Francs
1.1.1980. Similar to Equatorial African States #6. Brown and multicolor. Girl at left, village scene at center, signature 9. Back: Carving at left, airplane, train crossing bridge and tractor hauling logs at center, man with pipe at right.

VF	UNC
50.00	250

1983-84 ND Issue

12   5000 Francs
ND (1984). Brown and multicolor. Mask at left, woman with bundle of fronds at right. Back: Plowing and mine ore conveyor.

	VF	UNC
a. Signature 9.	35.00	150
b. Signature 14.	25.00	100
s. Specimen. Perforated *SPECIMEN*.	—	150

13   10,000 Francs
ND (1983). Brown, green and multicolor. Stylized antelope heads at left, woman at right, signature 9. Back: Loading fruit onto truck at left.

VF	UNC
50.00	200

1985 Issue

14	**500 Francs**		**VF**	**UNC**

1985-91. Brown on orange and multicolor underprint. Carving and jug at center, signature 9. Back: Man carving mark at left center. Watermark: Carving.

	a. 1.1.1985.	6.00	25.00
	b. 1.1.1986.	5.00	20.00
	c. 1.1.1987.	5.00	20.00
	d. 1.1.1989; 1.1.1991.	5.00	20.00
	s. Specimen. 1.1.1985. Red overprint: SPECIMEN in box on face.	—	80.00

15	**1000 Francs**		**VF**	**UNC**

1.1.1985. Dull blue-violet on multicolor underprint. Carving at left, map at center, General Kolingba at right, incomplete map of Chad at top center, signature 9. Back: Elephant at left, animals at center, carving at right. Watermark: Carving.   10.00 40.00

1986 Issue

16	**1000 Francs**		**VF**	**UNC**

1.1.1986-1.1.1990. Dull blue-violet on multicolor underprint. Carving at left, map at center, General Kolingba at right, complete outline map of Chad at top center, signature 9. Back: Elephant at left, animals at center, carving at right. Watermark: Carving.   8.00 30.00

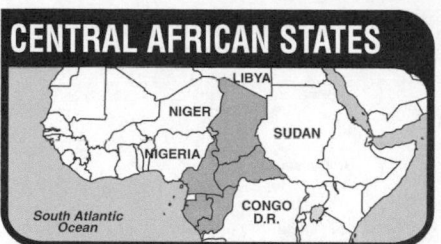

The Bank of the Central African States (BEAC) is a regional central bank for the monetary and customs union formed by Cameroun, Central African Republic, Chad, Congo (Brazzaville), Gabon, and (since 1985) Equatorial Guinea. It succeeded the Equatorial African States Bank in 1972-73 when the latter was reorganized and renamed to provide greater African control over its operations. The seat of the BEAC was transferred from Paris to Yaounde in 1977 and an African governor assumed responsibility for direction of the bank in 1978. The BEAC is a member of the franc zone with its currency denominated in CFA francs and pegged to the French franc at a rate of 50-1. BEAC notes carry country names on the face and the central bank name on the back. The 1974-84 series had common back designs but were face-different. A new series begun in 1983-85 uses common designs also on the face except for some 1000 franc notes. The notes carry the signatures of *LE GOUVERNEUR (LE DIRECTEUR GENERAL* prior to 1-4-78) and *UN CENSEUR* (since 1972). Cameroun, Gabon, and France each appoint one censeur and one alternate. Cameroun and Congo notes carry the Cameroun censeur signature. Central African Republic, Equatorial Guinea, and Gabon notes carry the Gabon censeur signature. Chad notes have been divided between the two. Prior to 1978, all BEAC notes were printed by the Bank of France. Since 1978, the 500 and 1000 franc notes have been printed by the private French firm F. C. Oberthur. The Bank of France notes are engraved and usually undated. The F. C. Oberthur notes are lithographed and most carry dates. See individual member countries for additional note listings. Also see Equatorial African States and French Equatorial Africa.

CONTROL LETTER or CODE		
	1993-2001	**2002 Onward**
Cameroun	E	U
Central African Republic	F	M
Chad	P	C
Congo	C	I
Equatorial Guinea	N	F
Gabon	L	A

SIGNATURE VARIETIES			
1	Le Directeur-Genera / Panouillot	Le President / Gautier	
1a	Le Directeur-Genera / Panouillot	Un Censeur / Duouedi	
2	Le Directeur-Genera / Panouillot	Un Censeur / Koulla	1955-72
3	Le Directeur-Genera / Joudiou	Un Censeur / Koulla	1961-72
4	Le Directeur-Genera / Joudiou	Un Censeur / Renombo	1972-73
5	Le Directeur-Genera / Joudiou	Un Censeur / Ntang	1974-77
6	Le Directeur-Genera / Joudiou	Un Censeur / Ntoutoume	1974-78
7	Le Directeur-Genera / Joudiou	Un Censeur / Beke Bihege	1977
8	Le Directeur-Genera / Joudiou	Un Censeur / Kamgu	1978

SIGNATURE VARIETIES

	Le Gouverneur	Un Censeur	
9	Oye Mba	Ntoutoume	1979-90
10	Le Gouverneur Oye Mba	Un Censeur Kamgueu	1978-86
11	Le Gouverneur Oye Mba	Un Censeur Kamgueu	1978-80
12	Le Gouverneur Oye Mba	Un Censeur Tchepannou	1981-89
13	Le Gouverneur Oye Mba	Un Censeur Dang	1990
14	Le Gouverneur Mamalepot	Un Censeur Ntoutoume	1991
15	Le Gouverneur Mamalepot	Un Censeur Mebara	1991-93
16	Le Gouverneur Mamalepot	Un Censeur Ognagna	1994
17	Le Gouverneur Mamalepot	Un Censeur Kaltjob	1994-
18	Le Gouverneur Mamalepot		
19	Le Gouverneur Mamalepot		
20	Le Gouverneur Mamalepot		

CENTRAL AFRICAN STATES

Banque des États de l'Afrique Centrale

1993; 1994 Issue

101C 500 Francs   VF   UNC

(19)93-(20)00. Dark brown and gray on multicolor underprint. Shepherd at right, zebus at center, map of Central African states at lower left center. Back: Baobab, antelopes and Kota mask. Watermark: Shepherd.

	VF	UNC
a. Signature 15. (19)93.	FV	5.00
b. Signature 16. (19)94.	FV	4.50
c. Signature 16. (19)95.	FV	4.50
d. Signature 16. (19)97.	FV	4.00
e. Signature 16. (19)98.	FV	4.00
f. Signature 16. (19)99.	FV	4.00
g. Signature 19. (20)00.	FV	4.00
h. Signature 19. (20)02.	FV	4.00

102C 1000 Francs   VF   UNC

(19)93-(20)00. Dark brown and red with black text on multicolor underprint. Young man at right, harvesting coffee beans at center, map of Central African States at lower left center. Back: Forest harvesting, Okoume raft and Bakele wood mask. Watermark: Young man.

	VF	UNC
a. Signature 15. (19)93.	FV	9.00
b. Signature 16. (19)94.	FV	8.00
c. Signature 16. (19)95.	FV	8.00
d. Signature 16. (19)97.	FV	7.50
e. Signature 16. (19)98.	FV	7.50
f. Signature 16. (19)99.	FV	7.50
g. Signature 19. (20)00.	FV	7.00
h. Signature 19. (20)02.	FV	7.50

103C 2000 Francs   VF   UNC

(19)93-(19)99. Dark brown and green with black text on orange and multicolor underprint. Woman's head at right, surrounded by tropical fruit, map of Central African States at lower left center. Back: Exchange of passengers and produce with ship at left center. Watermark: Woman's head.

	VF	UNC
a. Signature 15. (19)93.	FV	14.00
b. Signature 16. (19)94.	FV	12.50
c. Signature 16 (19)95.	FV	12.00
d. Signature 16. (19)97.	FV	12.00
e. Signature 16. (19)98.	FV	12.00
f. Signature 16. (19)99.	FV	12.00
g. Signature 19. (20)00.	FV	9.00
h. Signature 19. (20)02.	FV	10.00

104C 5000 Francs   VF   UNC

(19)94-(20)00. Dark brown, brown and blue with violet text on multicolor underprint. Laborer wearing hard hat at center right, riggers with well drill at right. Back: Woman with head basket at lower left, gathering cotton at center.

	VF	UNC
a. Signature 16. (19)94.	FV	27.50
b. Signature 16. (19)95.	FV	27.50
c. Signature 16. (19)97.	FV	25.00
d. Signature 16. (19)98.	FV	25.00
e. Signature 16. (19)99.	FV	25.00
f. Signature 16. (20)00.	FV	25.00

105C 10,000 Francs   VF   UNC

(19)94-(20)00. Dark brown and blue with blue-black text on multicolor underprint. Modern building at center, young woman at right. Back: Fisherman, boats and villagers along shoreline at left center.

	VF	UNC
a. Signature 16. (19)94.	FV	47.50
b. Signature 16. (19)95.	FV	45.00
c. Signature 16. (19)97.	FV	42.50
d. Signature 16. (19)98.	FV	45.00
e. Signature 16. (19)99.	FV	45.00
f. Signature 19. (20)00.	FV	45.00
g. Signature 19. (20)02.	FV	45.00

2002 Issue

106T 500 Francs   VF   UNC

2002. Signature 19.	FV	4.00

107T 1000 Francs   VF   UNC

2002. Signature 19.	FV	7.00

108T 2000 Francs   VF   UNC

2002. Signature 19.	FV	10.00

109T	5000 Francs		VF	UNC
	2002. Signature 19.		FV	25.00
110T	10,000 Francs		VF	UNC
	2002. Signature 19.		FV	45.00

E for Cameroun (1993-2001)

1993; 1994 Issue

201E	500 Francs		VF	UNC
	(19)90-(20)02. Dark brown and gray on multicolor underprint. Shepherd at right, map of Central African States at lower left center. Back: Baobab, antelopes and Kota mask. Watermark: Shepherd.			
	a. Signature 15. (19)93.		FV	5.00
	b. Signature 17. (19)94.		FV	4.50
	c. Signature 17. (19)95.		FV	4.50
	d. Signature 17. (19)97.		FV	4.50
	e. Signature 18. (19)98.		FV	4.50
	f. Signature 18. (19)99.		FV	4.50
	g. Signature 20. (20)00.		FV	4.00
	h. Signature 20. (20)02.		FV	4.00

202E	1000 Francs		VF	UNC
	(19)93-(20)02. Dark brown and red with black text on green and multicolor underprint. Young man at right, harvesting coffee beans at center, map of Central African States at lower left center. Back: Forest harvesting, Okoume raft and Bakele wood mask. Watermark: Young man.			
	a. Signature 15. (19)93.		FV	9.00
	b. Signature 17. (19)94.		FV	8.00
	c. Signature 17. (19)95.		FV	8.00
	d. Signature 17. (19)97.		FV	8.00
	e. Signature 18. (19)98.		FV	8.00
	f. Signature 18. (19)99.		FV	7.00
	g. Signature 20. (20)00.		FV	6.50
	h. Signature 20. (20)02.		FV	6.50

203E	2000 Francs		VF	UNC
	(19)93-(20)02. Dark brown and green with black text on orange and multicolor underprint. Woman's head at right, surrounded by tropical fruit, map of Central African States at lower left center. Back: Exchange of passengers and produce with ship at left center. Watermark: Woman's head.			
	a. Signature 15. (19)93.		FV	15.00
	b. Signature 17. (10)04.		FV	12.50
	c. Signature 17. (19)95.		FV	12.50
	d. Signature 17. (19)97.		FV	12.00
	e. Signature 18. (19)98.		FV	11.00
	f. Signature 18. (19)99.		FV	12.00
	g. Signature 20. (20)00.		FV	12.00
	h. Signature 20. (20)02.		FV	12.00
204E	5000 Francs		VF	UNC
	(19)94-(20)02. Dark brown, brown and blue with violet text on multicolor underprint. Laborer wearing hard hat at center right, riggers with well drill at right. Back: Woman with head basket at lower left, gathering cotton at center.			
	a. Signature 17. (19)94.		FV	27.50
	b. Signature 17. (19)95.		FV	27.50
	c. Signature 17. (19)97.		FV	25.00
	d. Signature 18. (19)98.		FV	25.00
	e. Signature 18. (19)99.		FV	25.00
	f. Signature 20. (20)00.		FV	22.00
	g. Signature 20. (20)02.		FV	22.00
205E	10,000 Francs		VF	UNC
	(19)94-(20)00. Dark brown and blue with blue-black text on multicolor underprint. Modern building at center, young woman at right. Back: Fisherman, boats and villagers along shoreline at left center.			
	a. Signature 17. (19)94.		FV	45.00
	b. Signature 17. (19)95.		FV	45.00
	c. Signature 17. (19)97.		FV	45.00
	d. Signature 18. (19)98.		FV	45.00
	e. Signature 18. (19)99.		FV	45.00
	f. Signature 20. (20)00.		FV	45.00
	h. Signature 20. (20)02.		FV	45.00

2002 Issue

206U	500 Francs		VF	UNC
	2002. Signature 20.		FV	4.00

207U 1000 Francs
2002. Signature 20.

	VF	UNC
	FV	7.00

208U 2000 Francs
2002. Signature 20.

	VF	UNC
	FV	10.00

209U 5000 Francs
2002. Signature 20.

	VF	UNC
	FV	25.00

210U 10,000 Francs
2002. Signature 20.

	VF	UNC
	FV	45.00

1993; 1994 Issue

301F 500 Francs

	VF	UNC

(19)93-(19)99. Dark brown and gray on multicolor underprint. Shepherd at right, zebus at center, map of Central African States at lower left center. Back: Baobab, antelopes and Kota mask. Watermark: Shepherd.

a. Signature 15. (19)93.	FV	6.00
b. Signature 16. (19)94.	FV	5.00
c. Signature 16. (19)95.	FV	5.00
d. Signature 16. (19)97.	FV	4.00
e. Signature 16. (19)98.	FV	4.00
f. Signature 16. (19)99.	FV	4.00
g. Signature 19. (20)00.	FV	4.00

302F 1000 Francs

	VF	UNC

(19)93-(19)99. Dark brown and red with black text on green and multicolor underprint. Young man at right, harvesting coffee beans at center, map of Central African States at lower left center. Back: Forest harvesting, Okoume raft and Bakele wood mask. Watermark: Young man.

a. Signature 15. (19)93.	FV	9.00
b. Signature 16. (19)94.	FV	8.50
c. Signature 16. (19)95.	FV	8.00
d. Signature 16. (19)97.	FV	7.50
e. Signature 16. (19)98.	FV	7.00
f. Signature 16. (19)99.	FV	7.00

303F 2000 Francs

	VF	UNC

(19)93-(19)99. Dark brown and green with black text on orange and multicolor underprint. Woman's head at right, surrounded by tropical fruit, map of Central African States at lower left center. Back: Exchange of passengers and produce with ship at left center. Watermark: Woman's head.

a. Signature 15. (19)93.	FV	17.50
b. Signature 16. (19)94.	FV	15.00
c. Signature 16. (19)95.	FV	13.00
d. Signature 16. (19)97.	FV	13.00
e. Signature 16. (19)98.	FV	13.00
f. Signature 16. (19)99.	FV	12.00

304F 5000 Francs

	VF	UNC

(19)94-(19)99. Dark brown, brown and blue with violet text on multicolor underprint. Laborer wearing hard hat at center right, riggers with well drill at right. Back: Woman with head basket at lower left, gathering cotton at center.

a. Signature 16. (19)94.	FV	32.50
b. Signature 16. (19)95.	FV	30.00
c. Signature 16. (19)97.	FV	25.00
d. Signature 16. (19)98.	FV	25.00
e. Signature 16. (19)99.	FV	25.00

305F 10,000 Francs

	VF	UNC

(19)94-(19)99. Dark brown and blue with blue-black text on multicolor underprint. Modern building at center, young woman at right. Back: Fisherman, boats and villagers along shoreline at left center.

a. Signature 16. (19)94.	FV	55.00
b. Signature 16. (19)95.	FV	50.00
c. Signature 16. (19)97.	FV	45.00
d. Signature 16. (19)98.	FV	45.00
e. Signature 16. (19)99.	FV	45.00
f. Signature 19. (20)00.	FV	45.00

2002 Issue

306M 500 Francs

	VF	UNC
2002. Signature 19.	FV	4.00

307M 1000 Francs

	VF	UNC
2002. Signature 19.	FV	7.00

308M 2000 Francs

	VF	UNC
2002. Signature 19.	FV	10.00

309M 5000 Francs

	VF	UNC
2002. Signature 19.	FV	25.00

310M 10,000 Francs

	VF	UNC
2002. Signature 19.	FV	45.00

1993; 1994 Issue

401L 500 Francs
    (19)93-(20)00. Dark brown and gray on multicolor underprint. Shepherd at right,
zebus at center, map of Central African States at lower left center. Back: Baobab
antelopes and Kota mask. Watermark: Shepherd.

	VF	UNC
a. Signature 15. (19)93.	FV	5.00
b. Signature 16. (19)94.	FV	4.50
c. Signature 16. (19)95.	FV	4.50
g. Signature 16. (20)00.	FV	4.50

402L 1000 Francs   VF   UNC
    (19)93-(20)00. Dark brown and red with black text on green and multicolor
underprint. Young man at right, harvesting coffee beans at center, map of Central
African States at lower left center. Back: Forest harvesting, Okoume raft and
Bakele wood mask. Watermark: Young man

	VF	UNC
a. Signature 15. (19)93.	FV	8.50
b. Signature 16. (19)94.	FV	8.00
c. Signature 16. (19)95.	FV	7.50
d. Signature 16. (19)97.	FV	7.50
e. Signature 16. (19)98.	FV	7.50
f. Signature 16. (19)99.	FV	7.50
g. Signature 19. (20)00.	FV	7.50
h. Signature 19. (20)02.	FV	7.50

403L 2000 Francs   VF   UNC
    (19)93-(20)00. Dark brown and green with black text on orange and multicolor
underprint. Woman's head at right, surrounded by tropical fruit, map of Central
African States at lower left center. Back: Exchange of passengers and produce
with ship at left center. Watermark: Woman's head.

	VF	UNC
a. Signature 15. (19)93.	FV	15.00
b. Signature 16. (19)94.	FV	15.00
c. Signature 16. (19)95.	FV	15.00
d. Signature 16. (19)97.	FV	12.50
e. Signature 16. (19)98.	FV	12.50
f. Signature 16. (19)99.	FV	12.50
g. Signature 19. (20)00.	FV	12.50
h. Signature 19. (20)02.	FV	7.50

404L 5000 Francs   VF   UNC
    (19)94-(20)00. Dark brown, brown and blue with violet text on multicolor under-
print. Laborer wearing hard hat at center right, riggers with well drill at right. Back:
Woman with head basket at lower left, gathering cotton at center.

	VF	UNC
a. Signature 16. (19)94.	FV	25.00
b. Signature 16. (19)95.	FV	25.00
c. Signature 16. (19)97.	FV	25.00
d. Signature 16. (19)98.	FV	25.00
e. Signature 16. (19)99.	FV	25.00
f. Signature 16. (20)00.	FV	25.00

405L 10,000 Francs   VF   UNC
    (19)94-(20)00. Dark brown and blue with blue-black text on multicolor underprint.
Modern building at center, young woman at right. Back: Fisherman, boats and
villagers along shoreline at left center.

	VF	UNC
a. Signature 15. (19)94.	FV	52.50
b. Signature 16. (19)95.	FV	47.50
c. Signature 16. (19)97.	FV	45.00
d. Signature 16. (19)98.	FV	45.00
e. Signature 16. (19)99.	FV	45.00
f. Signature 19. (20)00.	FV	45.00
g. Signature 19 (20)02.	FV	45.00

A for Gabon (2002-)

2002 Issue

406A 500 Francs   VF   UNC
    2002. Signature 19.   FV   4.00
407A 1000 Francs   VF   UNC
    2002. Signature 19.   FV   7.00

408A 2000 Francs   VF   UNC
    2002. Signature 19.   FV   10.00
409A 5000 Francs   VF   UNC
    2002. Signature 19.   FV   25.00
410A 10,000 Francs   VF   UNC
    2002. Signature 19.   FV   45.00

N for Equatorial Guinea (1993-2001)

1993; 1994 Issue

501N 500 Francs   VF   UNC
    (19)93-(20)00. Dark brown and gray on multicolor underprint. Shepherd at right,
zebus at center, map of Central African States at lower left center. Back: Baobab,
antelopes and Kota mask. Watermark: Shepherd.

	VF	UNC
a. Signature 15. (19)93.	FV	6.00
b. Signature 16. (19)94.	FV	6.00
c. Signature 16. (19)95.	FV	6.00
d. Signature 16. (19)97.	FV	4.50
f. Signature 16. (19)99.	FV	4.50
g. Signature 19. (20)00.	FV	4.50

502N 1000 Francs   VF   UNC
    (19)93-(20)00. Dark brown and red with black text on multicolor underprint. Young
man at right, harvesting coffee beans at center, map of Central African States at
lower left center. Back: Forest harvesting, Okoume raft and Bakele wood mask.
Watermark: Young man.

	VF	UNC
a. Signature 15. (19)93.	FV	9.00
b. Signature 16. (19)94.	FV	8.00
c. Signature 16. (19)95.	FV	7.50
d. Signature 16. (19)97.	FV	7.50
e. Signature 16. (19)98.	FV	7.50
f. Signature 16. (19)99.	FV	7.50
g. Signature 16. (20)00.	FV	7.00
h. Signature 19. (20)00.	FV	7.50

503N 2000 Francs   **VF**   **UNC**

(19)93-(20)00. Dark brown and green with black text on multicolor underprint. Woman's head at right, surrounded by tropical fruit. map of Central African States at lower left center. Back: Exchange of passengers and produce with ship at left center. Watermark: Woman's head.

	VF	UNC
a. Signature 15. (19)93.	FV	15.00
b. Signature 16. (19)94.	FV	15.00
c. Signature 16. (19)95.	FV	15.00
d. Signature 16. (19)97.	FV	12.50
g. Signature 19. (20)00.	FV	12.50

504N 5000 Francs   **VF**   **UNC**

(19)94-(20)00. Dark brown, brown and blue with violet text on multicolor underprint. Laborer wearing hard hat at center right, riggers and well drill at right. Back: Woman with head basket at lower left, gathering cotton at center.

	VF	UNC
a. Signature 16. (19)94.	FV	25.00
b. Signature 16. (19)95.	FV	25.00
d. Signature 16. (19)98.	FV	25.00
e. Signature 16. (19)99.	FV	25.00
f. Signature 19. (20)00.	FV	25.00

505N 10,000 Francs   **VF**   **UNC**

(19)94-(20)00. Dark brown and blue with blue-black text on multicolor underprint. Modern building at center, young woman at right. Back: Fisherman, boats and villagers along shoreline at left center.

	VF	UNC
a. Signature 16. (19)94.	FV	47.50
b. Signature 16. (19)95.	FV	47.50
c. Signature 16. (19)97.	FV	45.00
d. Signature 16. (19)98.	FV	47.50
e. Signature 16. (19)99.	FV	45.00
f. Signature 19. (20)00.	FV	45.00

F for Equatorial Guinea (2002-)

2002 Issue

506F 500 Francs   **VF**   **UNC**

2002. Signature 19.   FV   4.00

507F 1000 Francs   **VF**   **UNC**

2002. Signature 19.   FV   7.00

508F 2000 Francs   **VF**   **UNC**

2002. Signature 19.   FV   10.00

509F 5000 Francs   **VF**   **UNC**

2002. Signature 19.   FV   25.00

510F 10,000 Francs   **VF**   **UNC**

2002. Signature 19.

	VF	UNC
a. 2002.	FV	45.00
b. 2003.	FV	45.00

P for Chad (1993-2001)

1993; 1994 Issue

601P 500 Francs   **VF**   **UNC**

(19)93-(20)00. Dark brown and gray on multicolor underprint. Shepherd at right, zebus at center, map of Central African States at lower left center. Back: Baobab, antelopes and Kota mask. Watermark: Shepherd.

	VF	UNC
a. Signature 15. (19)93.	FV	6.00
b. Signature 16. (19)94.	FV	5.00
c. Signature 16. (19)95.	FV	5.00
d. Signature 16. (19)97.	FV	5.00
e. Signature 16. (19)98.	FV	4.50
f. Signature 16. (19)99.	FV	4.50
g. Signature 19. (20)00.	FV	4.50

602P 1000 Francs   **VF**   **UNC**

(19)93-(20)00. Dark brown and red with black text on green and multicolor underprint. Young man at right, harvesting coffee beans at center, map of Central African States at lower left center. Back: Forest harvesting, Okoume raft and Bakele wood mask. Watermark: Young man.

	VF	UNC
a. Signature 15. (19)93.	FV	8.50
b. Signature 16. (19)94.	FV	7.50
c. Signature 16. (19)95.	FV	7.00
d. Signature 16. (19)97.	FV	7.00
e. Signature 16. (19)98.	FV	7.50
f. Signature 16. (19)99.	FV	7.50
g. Signature 19. (20)00.	FV	7.50

603P 2000 Francs   **VF**   **UNC**

(19)93-(20)00. Dark brown and green with black text on orange and multicolor underprint. Woman's head at right, surrounded by tropical fruit, map of Central African States at lower left center. Back: Exchange of passengers and produce with ship at left center. Watermark: Woman's head.

	VF	UNC
a. Signature 15. (19)93.	FV	15.00
b. Signature 16. (19)94.	FV	15.00
c. Signature 16. (19)95.	FV	12.50
d. Signature 16. (19)97.	FV	12.50
e. Signature 16. (19)98.	FV	12.50
f. Signature 16. (19)99.	FV	12.50
g. Signature 16. (20)00.	FV	12.50

604P 5000 Francs   **VF UNC**

(19)94-(20)00. Dark brown, brown and blue with violet text on multicolor underprint. Laborer wearing hard hat at center right, riggers with well drill at right. Back: Woman with head basket at lower left, gathering cotton at center.

a. Signature 16. (19)94.	FV	30.00
b. Signature 16. (19)95.	FV	27.50
c. Signature 16. (19)97.	FV	27.50
d. Signature 16. (19)98.	FV	25.00
e. Signature 16. (19)99.	FV	25.00
f. Signature 19. (20)00.	FV	25.00

605P 10,000 Francs   **VF UNC**

(19)94-(20)00. Dark brown and blue with blue-black text on multicolor underprint. Modern building at center, young woman at right. Back: Fisherman, boats and villagers along shoreline at left center.

a. Signature 16. (19)94.	FV	50.00
b. Signature 16. (19)95.	FV	50.00
c. Signature 16. (19)97.	FV	47.50
d. Signature 16. (19)98.	FV	45.00
e. Signature 16. (19)99.	FV	45.00
f. Signature 19. (20)00.	FV	45.00

C for Chad (2002-)

2002 Issue

606C 500 Francs   **VF UNC**
2002. Signature 19.   FV 4.00

607C 1000 Francs   **VF UNC**
2002. Signature 19.   FV 7.00

608C 2000 Francs   **VF UNC**
2002. Signature 19.   FV 10.00

609C 5000 Francs   **VF UNC**
2002. Signature 19.   FV 25.00

610C 10,000 Francs   **VF UNC**
2002. Signature 19.   FV 45.00

U for Cameroun (2015-)

2015 Issue

611U 500 Francs   **VF UNC**
2015. Signature Lucas Nchama and Salomon Francis Meke. 130x70mm.   FV 4.00

612U 1000 Francs   **VF UNC**
2015. Signature Lucas Nchama and Salomon Francis Meke. 135x75mm.   FV 7.00

613U 2000 Francs   **VF UNC**
2015. Signature Lucas Nchama and Salomon Francis Meke. 140x75mm.   FV 10.00

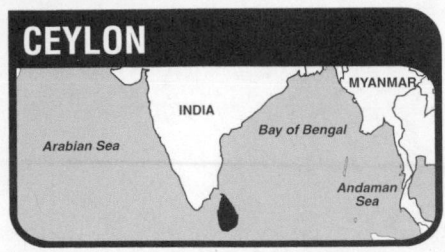

Ceylon (later to become The Democratic Socialist Republic of Sri Lanka) is an island situated in the Indian Ocean 18 miles (29 km.) southeast of India. It has an area of 65,610 sq. km. and a population of 21.13 million. Capital: Colombo. The economy is chiefly agricultural. Tea, rubber and coconut products are exported. The earliest known inhabitants are the Veddahs. The first Sinhala arrived in Lanka late in the 5th century BCE, probably from northern India. The coastal areas of the island were controlled by China for 30 years from 1408, the Portuguese from 1505 and the Dutch from 1658. The island was ceded to the British in 1796, became a crown colony in 1802, and the independent Kingdom of Kandy in the central part of the island was united under British rule by 1815, as Ceylon. Constitutional changes in 1931 granted Ceylon a parliamentary form of government. It became independent in 1948. Its name in English was changed to Sri Lanka on 1972 May 22 with the adoption of a Republican constitution. For later issues, see Sri Lanka.

RULERS:
Dutch to 1796
British, 1796-1972

MONETARY SYSTEM:
1 Rix Dollar = 48 Stivers
1 Rupee = 100 Cents

Note: Certain listings encompassing issues circulated by various bank and regional authorities are contained in Volume 1.

STATE

Central Bank of Ceylon

1956 Issue

56   1 Rupee   VF   UNC
1956-63. Blue on orange, green and brown underprint. Arms of Ceylon at left.
Back: Ornate stairway. Watermark: Chinze. Printer: BWC. 108x60mm.

		VF	UNC
a. 30.7.1956. Signature: Stanley de Soysa and A. G. Ranasingha.		7.00	25.00
b. 31.5.1957; 9.4.1958; 7.11.1958.		5.00	15.00
c. With security strip. 11.9.1959.		2.00	7.50
d. 18.8.1960; 29.1.1962. Signatures: Felix R. Dias Bandaranaike and W. Rajapatirana.		2.00	7.50
e. 6..5.1963. Signature: T. B. Illangaratne and W. Rajapatirana.		2.00	7.50

57   2 Rupees   VF   UNC
1956-62. Brown and lilac on blue and green underprint. Arms of Ceylon at left.
Back: Pavilion. Watermark: Chinze. Printer: BWC. 121x67mm.

		VF	UNC
a. 30.7.1956; 31.5.1957; 6.10.1958; 7.11.1958. Signature: Stanley de Soysa and A. G. Ranasingha. Without security strip.		12.00	40.00
b. 11.9.1959; Signature: Stanley de Soysa and W. Rajapatirana. With security strip.		12.00	40.00
c. 18.8.1960; 29.1.1962. Signature: Felix R. Dias Bandaranaike and W. Rajapatirana.		10.00	30.00

58   5 Rupees   VF   UNC
1956-62. Orange on aqua, green and brown underprint. Arms of Ceylon at left.
Back: Standing figure. Watermark: Chinze. Printer: BWC. 133x73mm.

		VF	UNC
a. 30.7.1956; 31.5.1957; 10.6.1958. Signature: Stanley de Soysa and A. G. Ranasingha. Without security strip.		20.00	120
b. 1.7.1959; 11.9.1959. Signature: Stanley de Soysa and W. Rajapatirana. With security strip.		20.00	120
c. 18.8.1960; 29.1.1962. Signarues: Felix R. Dias Bandaranaike and W. Rajapatirana.		15.00	75.00

59   10 Rupees   VF   UNC
1956-63. Green on violet, brown and blue underprint. Arms of Ceylon at left. Back: Ceremonial figures. Watermark: Chinze. Printer: BWC. 146x76mm.

		VF	UNC
a. 30.7.1956; 7.11.1957; 7.11.1958. Signatures Stanley de Soysa and A. G. Ranasingha. Without security strip.		25.00	100
b. 11.9.1959. With security strip.		25.00	100
c. 18.8.1960; 7.4.1961; 5.6.1963. Signatures Felix R. Dias Bandaranaike and W. Rajapatirana.		15.00	75.00

60   50 Rupees   VF   UNC
30.7.1956; 9,4,1958; 7.11.1958; 11.9.1959. Blue and violet on multicolor underprint. Arms of Ceylon at left. Back: Ornate stairway. Watermark: Chinze. Printer: BWC. 159x89mm.

		VF	UNC
a. 30.7.1956; 9.4.1958; 7.11.1958. Signatures: Stanley de Soysa and A. G. Ranasingha.		90.00	300
b. 11.9.1959. Signatures: Stanley de Soysa and W. Rajapatirana.		90.00	300

61   100 Rupees   VF   UNC
24.10.1956. Brown on multicolor underprint. Arms of Ceylon at left. Signature: Stanley de Soysa and A. G. Ranasingha. Back: Two women in national dress. Watermark: Chinze. Printer: BWC. 171x98mm.
                                                                                 200   800

1962-65 Issue

62   2 Rupees   **VF   UNC**

1962-65. Light brown on lilac, green and blue underprint. S. W. R. D. Bandaranaike at right. Back: Pavilion at left center. Watermark: Chinze. Printer: BWC. 114x59mm.

- a. Signature P. B. G. Kalugalla and D. W. Rajapatirana. 8.11.1962.   10.00   25.00
- b. Signature T. B. Illangaratue and D. W. Rajapatirana. 11.4.1964; 12.6.1964.   15.00   40.00
- c. Signature U. B. Wanninayake and D. W. Rajapatirana. 6.4.1965.   12.00   35.00

63   5 Rupees   **VF   UNC**

1962; 1964. Orange and brown on multicolor underprint. S. W. R. D. Bandaranaike at right. Back: Standing figure at center. Watermark: Chinze. Printer: BWC. 125x64mm.

- a. Signature P. B. G. Kalugalla and D. W. Rajapatirana. 8.11.1962.   9.00   35.00
- b. Signature N. M. Perera and D. W. Rajapatirana. 12.6.1964.   20.00   60.00

64   10 Rupees   **VF   UNC**

12.6.1964; 20.6.1964; 19.9.1964. Green and purple on orange and blue underprint. S. W. R. D. Bandaranaike at right. Signatures: N. M. Perera and W. Rajapatirana. Back: Ceremonial figures. Watermark: Chinze. Printer: BWC. 140x70mm.   10.00   70.00

65   50 Rupees   **VF   UNC**

1961-65. Blue and purple on multicolor underprint. S. W. R. D. Bandaranaike at right. Back: Ornate stairway. Watermark: Chinze. Printer: BWC. 151x79mm.

- a. Signature: Felix R. Dias Bandaranaike and W. Rajapatirana. 2.11.1961.   30.00   120
- b. Signature: T. B. Illangaratne and W. Rajapatirana. 5.6.1963.   25.00   90.00
- c. Signature: U. B. Wanninayake and W. Rajapatirana. 6.4.1965.   20.00   80.00
- d. Signature: N. M. Perera and W. Rajapatirana. 12.6.1964. (Not released and destroyed).   —   —

66   100 Rupees   **VF   UNC**

5.6.1963. Brown and blue on multicolor underprint. S. W. R. D. Bandaranaike at right. Signatures: T. B. Illangaratne and W. Rajapatirana. Back: Two women in national dress. Watermark: Chinze. Printer: BWC. 171x98mm.   55.00   225

1965-68 Issue

67   2 Rupees   **VF   UNC**

1965-68. Light brown on lilac, light green and blue underprint. Statue of King Parakkrama at right. Back: Pavilion. Watermark: Chinze. Printer: BWC. 114x59mm.

- a. Signature U. B. Wanninayake and D. W. Rajapatirana. 9.9.1965; 15.7.1967.   3.00   9.00
- b. Signature U. B. Wanninayake and W. Tennekoon. 10.1.1968.   2.50   7.00

68   5 Rupees   **VF   UNC**

1965-68. Orange and brown on multicolor underprint. Statue of King Parakkrama at right. Back: Standing figure. Watermark: Chinze. Printer: BWC. 125x64mm.

- a. Signature U. B. Wanninayake and D. W. Rajapatirana. 9.9.1965; 15.7.1967.   3.00   20.00
- b. Signature U. B. Wanninayake and W. Tennekoon. 1.9.1967; 10.1.1968.   2.00   17.50

69   10 Rupees   **VF   UNC**

10.1.1968. Green and purple on orange and blue underprint. Statue of King Parakkrama at right. Signatures: U. B. Wanninayake and William Tennekoon. Back: Ceremonial figures. Watermark: Chinze. Printer: BWC. 140x70mm.   12.00   50.00

70   50 Rupees   **VF   UNC**

1967; 1968. Blue and purple on multicolor underprint. Statue of King Parakkrama at right. Back: Ornate stairway. Watermark: Chinze. Printer: BWC. 151x79mm.

- a. Signature U. W. Wanninayake and D. W. Rajapatirana. 7.3.1967.   70.00   300
- b. Signature U. B. Wanninayake and W. Tennekoon. 10.1.1968.   60.00   225

71   100 Rupees   **VF   UNC**

1966-68. Brown and blue on multicolor underprint. Statue of King Parakkrama at right. Back: Two women in national dress. Watermark: Chinze. Printer: BWC. 171x98mm.

- a. Signature U. W. Wanninayake and D. W. Rajapatirana. 20.5.1966; 22.11.1966.   50.00   250
- b. Signature U. B. Wanninayake and W. Tennekoon. 10.1.1968.   40.00   200

1969-77 Issue

Central Bank of Ceylon text in English and Tamil.

72   2 Rupees   **VF   UNC**

1969-72. Light brown on lilac, light green and blue underprint. Statue of King Parakkrama at right. Back: Pavilion. Watermark: Chinze. Printer: BWC. 114x59mm.

- a. Signature U. B. Wanninayake and W. Tennekoon. 10.5.1969.   2.00   9.00
- b. Signature N. M. Perera and W. Tennekoon. 1.6.1970; 1.2.1971; 7.6.1971.   2.00   6.00
- c. Signature N. M. Perera and W. Tennekoon. 12.5.1972   2.00   6.00

73   5 Rupees   **VF   UNC**

1969-71. Orange and brown on multicolor underprint. Statue of King Parakkrama at right. Back: Standing Figure. Watermark: Chinze. Printer: BWC. 125x64mm.

- a. Signature U. B. Wanninayake and W. Tennekoon. 10.5.1969.   5.00   15.00
- b. Signature N. M. Perera and W. Tennekoon. 1.6.1970; 1.2.1971.   4.00   10.00
- ct. Color trial.   —   150

74   10 Rupees   **VF   UNC**

1969-71. Green and purple on orange and blue underprint. Statue of King Parakkrama at right. Back: Ceremonial figures. Watermark: Chinze. Printer: BWC. 140x70mm.

- a. Signature U. B. Wanninayake and W. Tennekoon. 20.10.1969.   15.00   50.00
- b. Signature N. M. Perera and W. Tennekoon. 1.6.1970; 1.2.1971; 7.6.1971.   5.00   15.00
- ct. Color trial.   —   175

75   50 Rupees   **VF   UNC**

20.10.1969. Blue and purple on multicolor underprint. Statue of King Parakkrama at right. Back: Ornate stairway. Watermark: Chinze. Printer: BWC. 151x79mm.

- a. Signature: U. B. Wanninayake and William Tennekoon. 20.10.1969.   90.00   300
- b. Signature: N. M. Perera and William Tennekoon. 1.6.1970. (Not released and destroyed).   —   —

76   100 Rupees   VF   UNC
10.5.1969. Brown and blue on multicolor underprint. Statue of King parakkrama
at right. Back: Two women in national dress. Watermark: Chinze. Printer: BWC.
162x86mm.
    a. Signature: U. B. Wanninayake and William Tennekoon. 10.5.1969.   40.00   150
    b. Signature: N. M. Perera and William Tennekoon. 1.6.1970.(Not released   —   —
      and destroyed).

1970 Issue

77   50 Rupees   VF   UNC
26.10.1970; 29.12.1970. Blue on lilac, yellow and brown underprint. Smiling
President S. W. R. D. Bandaranaike with raised hand. Signature: N. M. Perera
and William Tennekoon. Serial # prefix D. Back: Monument. Watermark: Chinze.
Printer: TDLR. 151x79mm.
    a. 26.10.1970.   20.00   100
    b. 9.12.1970.   40.00   150
    r. Replacement note: Serial # Prefix W/1.   —   —

78   100 Rupees   VF   UNC
26.10.1970; 9.12.1970. Red-violet on multicolor underprint. Smiling President S.
W. R. D. Bandaranaike with raised hand. Signature: N. M. Perera and William
Tennekoon. Serial # prefix: E. Back: Female dancers. Watermark: Chinze. Printer:
TDLR. 162x86mm.
    a. 26.10.1970.   60.00   250
    b. 9.12.1970.   70.00   300
    r. Replacement note. Serial # prefix: V/1.   —   —
80   100 Rupees   VF   UNC
1971-75 Brown and purple on multicolor underprint. Smiling President W. R. D.
Bandaranaike without raised hand. Back: Ornate stairway. Watermark: Chinze.
Printer: BWC. 162x86mm.
    a. Signature N. M. Perera and H. E. Tennekoon. 18.12.1971.   17.50   100

For later issues, see Sri Lanka.

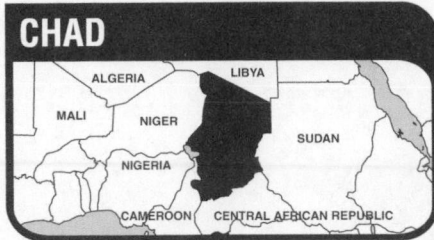

The Republic of Chad, a land-locked country of central Africa, is the largest country of former French Equatorial Africa. It has an area of 1.284 million sq. km. and a population of 10.11 million. Capital. N'Djaména. An expanding livestock industry produces camels, cattle and sheep. Cotton (the chief product), ivory and palm oil are important exports.

Chad, part of France's African holdings until 1960, endured three decades of civil warfare as well as invasions by Libya before a semblance of peace was finally restored in 1990. The government eventually drafted a democratic constitution, and held flawed presidential elections in 1996 and 2001. In 1998, a rebellion broke out in northern Chad, which has sporadically flared up despite several peace agreements between the government and the rebels. In 2005, new rebel groups emerged in western Sudan and made probing attacks into eastern Chad, despite signing peace agreements in December 2006 and October 2007. Power remains in the hands of an ethnic minority. In June 2005, President Idriss Deby held a referendum successfully removing constitutional term limits and won another controversial election in 2006. Sporadic rebel campaigns continued throughout 2006 and 2007, and the capital experienced a significant rebel threat in early 2008. For later issues, see Central African States.

MONETARY SYSTEM:
  1 Franc = 100 Centimes

SIGNATURE VARIETIES:
  Refer to introduction to Central African States.

RÉPUBLIQUE DU TCHAD

Banque Centrale
1971 Issue

1   10,000 Francs   VF   UNC
ND (1971). Multicolor. President Tombalbaye at left, cattle watering at center right,   1,750   3,750
signature 1. Back: Mask at left, tractor plowing at center, statue at right.

Banque des États de l'Afrique Centrale
1974-78; ND Issue

2   500 Francs   VF   UNC
ND (1974); 1978. Brown and red on multicolor underprint. Woman at left, flamingos, crowned cranes, abdim's stork at center and at right. Back: Mask at left, students and chemical testing at center, statue at right.
    a. Signature titles and watermark like #3a. Signature 6. (1974).   12.50   40.00
    b. Signature titles, watermark and date like #3c. Signature 10. 1.4.1978.   75.00   200
    s1. As a. Specimen. Overprinted and perforated: SPECIMEN.   —   400
    s2. As b. Specimen. Overprinted and perforated: SPECIMEN..   —   750

3 1000 Francs   **VF UNC**
ND; 1.4.1978. Blue and brown on multicolor underprint. Woman at right. Back:
Mask at left, trains, planes and bridge at center, statue at right.

    a. Signature titles: *LE DIRECTEUR GÉNÉRAL* and *UN CENSEUR*. Engraved.   85.00   100
      Watermark: Antelope in half profile. Signature 5; 7.
    b. Signature titles: *LE DIRECTEUR GÉNÉRAL* and *UN CENSEUR*. Litho-   20.00   75.00
      graphed. Watermark: Antelope in profile. Signature 8.
    c. Signature titles: *LE GOUVERNEUR* and *UN CENSEUR*. Signature 10.   12.50   50.00
      1.4.1978.
    s. As a. Specimen. Overprinted and perforated: *SPECIMEN*.   —   250

4 5000 Francs   **VF UNC**
ND (1974). Brown-orange on multicolor underprint. President Tombalbaye at left,   500   2,000
signature 4. Back: Mask at left, industrial collage at center, statue at right.

5 5000 Francs   **VF UNC**
ND. Brown on multicolor underprint. Woman at left. Back: Mask at left, industrial
collage at center, statue at right.

    a. Signature 6. (1976).   75.00   275
    b. Signature 9. (1978).   70.00   250
    s. As a. Specimen. Overprinted and perforated: *SPECIMEN*.   —   750

1980 Issue

6 500 Francs   **VF UNC**
1.6.1980; 1.6.1984. Red and brown on multicolor underprint. Woman weaving   10.00   45.00
basket at right, signature 10. Back: Mask at left, students and chemical testing at
center, statue at right.

7 1000 Francs   **VF UNC**
1.6.1980; 1.6.1984. Blue and dull purple on multicolor underprint. Water buffalo   15.00   60.00
at right, signature 9; 10. Back: Mask at left, trains, planes and bridge at center,
statue at right.

8 5000 Francs   **VF UNC**
1.1.1980. Similar to Central African Republic #11 and others. Brown and   60.00   250
multicolor. Girl at lower left, village scene at center, signature 9. Back: Carving,
airplane, train, tractor and man smoking pipe.

1984-85; ND Issue

For notes with similar back designs see Cameroun Republic, Central African Republic, Congo (Brazzaville) and Gabon.

9   500 Francs

		VF	UNC
1985-92. Brown on multicolor underprint. Carved statue and jug at center. Back: Man carving mask at left center. Watermark: Carving.			
a. Signature 10. 1.1.1985; 1.1.1986.		5.00	25.00
b. Signature 12. 1.1.1987.		5.00	20.00
c. Signature 13. 1.1.1990.		5.00	20.00
d. Signature 15. 1.1.1991.		5.00	20.00
e. Signature 15. 1.1.1992.		5.00	20.00

10   1000 Francs

	VF	UNC
1.1.1985. Dull blue-violet on multicolor underprint. Animal carving at lower left, map at center, starburst at lower right, incomplete outline map of Chad at top center, signature 9. Back: Elephants at left, statue at right. Watermark: Animal carving.	60.00	125

#10 was withdrawn shortly after issue because of the incompleteness of the map at top.

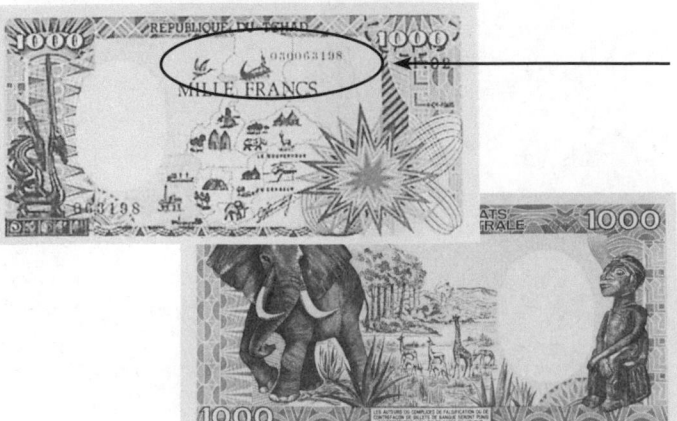

10A   1000 Francs

		VF	UNC
1985-92. Dull violet-blue on multicolor underprint. Animal carving at lower left, map at center, starburst at lower right, complete outine map of Chad at top center. Back: Elephants at left, statue at right. Watermark: Animal carving.			
a. Signature 9. 1.1.1985; 1.1.1988; 1.1.1989; 1.1.1990.		7.50	30.00
b. Signature 15. 1.1.1991.		15.00	40.00
c. Signature 15. 1.1.1992.		7.50	30.00

11   5000 Francs

	VF	UNC
ND (1984-91). Brown on multicolor underprint. Mask at left, woman with bundle of fronds at right, signature 9; 15. Back: Plowing and mine ore conveyor.	35.00	150

12   10,000 Francs

		VF	UNC
ND (1984-91). Black, brown and dark green on multicolor underprint. Stylized antelope heads at left, woman at right. Back: Loading fruit onto truck at left. Watermark: Woman.			
a. Signature 9.		50.00	200
b. Signature 15.		40.00	175

Note: For notes with similar back designs see Cameroun Republic, Central African Republic, Congo (Brazzaville) and Gabon.

CHILE

The Republic of Chile, a ribbon-like country on the Pacific coast of southern South America, has an area of 756,950 sq. km. and a population of 16.45 million. Capital: Santiago. Copper, of which Chile has about 25 percent of the world's reserves, has accounted for a major portion of Chile's export earnings in recent years. Other important exports are iron ore, iodine, fruit and nitrate of soda.

Prior to the coming of the Spanish in the 16th century, northern Chile was under Inca rule while Araucanian Indians (also known as Mapuches) inhabited central and southern Chile. Although Chile declared its independence in 1810, decisive victory over the Spanish was not achieved until 1818. In the War of the Pacific (1879-83), Chile defeated Peru and Bolivia and won its present northern regions. It was not until the 1880s that the Araucanian Indians were completely subjugated. A three-year-old Marxist government of Salvador Allende was overthrown in 1973 by a military coup led by Augusto Pinochet, who ruled until a freely elected president was installed in 1990. Sound economic policies, maintained consistently since the 1980s, have contributed to steady growth, reduced poverty rates by over half, and have helped secure the country's commitment to democratic and representative government. Chile has increasingly assumed regional and international leadership roles befitting its status as a stable, democratic nation.

MONETARY SYSTEM:
  1 Peso = 100 Centavos
  1 Condor = 100 Centavos = 10 Pesos to 1960
  1 Escudo = 100 Centesimos, 1960-75
  1 Peso = 100 "old" Escudos, 1975-

REPLACEMENT NOTES:
  #140, 143, 145-148 w/R next to serial #.
  #149-158 w/R near to plate position #.

PROVINCIAL
  Province of Valdivia #S101-S102

REPUBLIC

Banco Central de Chile
1960 ND Provisional Issue
1 Escudo = 1000 Pesos (= 100 Centesimos)

124 1/2 Centesimo on 5 Pesos   **VF UNC**
ND (1960-61). Rare. Blue. Portrait Bernard O'Higgins at left, signature titles: *PRESIDENTE* and *GERENTE GENERAL*. Watermark: D. Diego Portales. Printer: CdM-Chile.

— —

125 1 Centesimo on 10 Pesos   **VF UNC**
ND (1960-61). Red-brown. Portrait Manuel Bulnes at left. Series F. Signature titles: *PRESIDENTE* and *GERENTE GENERAL*. Watermark: D. Diego Portales. Printer: CdM-Chile.   2.50 12.50

126 5 Centesimos on 50 Pesos   **VF UNC**
ND (1960-61). Green. Portrait Anibal Pinto at left. Series C. 3 signature varieties. Signature titles: *PRESIDENTE* and *GERENTE GENERAL*. Watermark: D. Diego Portales. Printer: CdM-Chile.
   a. Imprint on face 25mm wide.   1.00 2.50
   b. Imprint on face 22mm wide.   0.20 2.00
   s. Specimen.   — 12.50

127 10 Centesimos on 100 Pesos   **VF UNC**
ND (1960-61). Red. Portrait Arturo Prat at left. 3 signature varieties. Series C-K. Signature titles: *PRESIDENTE* and *GERENTE GENERAL*. Watermark: D. Diego Portales. Printer: CdM-Chile.
   a. Issued note.   1.00 3.00
   s. Specimen.   — 12.50

128 50 Centesimos on 500 Pesos   **VF UNC**
ND (1960-61). Blue. Portrait Manuel Montt at right. Series A. Signature titles: *PRESIDENTE* and *GERENTE GENERAL*. Watermark: D. Diego Portales. Printer: CdM-Chile.   2.50 15.00

129 1 Escudo on 1000 Pesos   **VF UNC**
ND (1960-61). Dark brown. Portrait Manuel Blanco Encalada at left. Series A. Signature titles: *PRESIDENTE* and *GERENTE GENERAL*. Watermark: D. Diego Portales. Printer: CdM-Chile.   2.00 12.50

130 5 Escudos on 5000 Pesos   **VF UNC**
ND (1960-61). Brown-violet. Portrait Manuel Antonio Tocornal at left. 2 signature varieties. Series J. Signature titles: *PRESIDENTE* and *GERENTE GENERAL*. Watermark: D. Diego Portales. Printer: CdM-Chile.   5.00 25.00

131 10 Escudos on 10,000 Pesos   **VF UNC**
ND (1960-61). Purple on light blue underprint. Portrait Jose Manuel Balmaceda at left. Series F. Signature titles: *PRESIDENTE* and *GERENTE GENERAL*. Watermark: D. Diego Portales at left, words *DIEZ MIL* at right. Printer: CdM-Chile.   10.00 40.00

132 10 Escudos on 10,000 Pesos   **VF UNC**
ND (1960-61). Red-brown. Portrait Jose Manuel Balmaceda at left. Similar to #131. Series F. Signature titles: *PRESIDENTE* and *GERENTE GENERAL*. Watermark: D. Diego Portales. Printer: CdM-Chile.   15.00 55.00

133 50 Escudos on 50,000 Pesos   VF   UNC
ND (1960-61). Blue-green and brown on multicolor underprint. Portrait Arturo Ales-   25.00   75.00
sandri at left. Series A. Signature titles: *PRESIDENTE* and *GERENTE GENERAL*.
Watermark: D. Diego Portales. Printer: CdM-Chile.

SIGNATURES 1962-1975			
Gerente Gral		**Presidente**	
Francisco Ibáñez 1962-70		Louis MacKenna 1962-70	
Sergio Molina 1964-67			
Carlos Massad 1967-70			
Alfonso Inostroza 1970-73		Jamie Barrios 1970-73	
Carlos Matus 1973		Carlos Trucco 1973	
Eduardo Cano 1973-75		Carlos Molina 1973-85	
Pablo Baraona 1975-76			

1962-75 ND Issue

134 1/2 Escudo   VF   UNC
ND. Dark blue on pale orange and light blue underprint. Portrait General Bernardo
O'Higgins at center, signature varieties. Back: Explorer on horseback at left center.
Red serial #. Watermark: D. Diego Portales P. Printer: CdM-Chile.
   a. Paper of #122. Series A. 3 signature varieties.   0.50   3.00
   b. Paper of #121. Series B. 2 signature varieties.   0.50   3.00
   s. Specimen.   —   15.00

134A 1/2 Escudo   VF   UNC
ND. Dark blue on pale orange on tan underprint. Portrait of General Bernardo
O'Higgins at center, signature varieties. Back: Explorer on horseback at left center.
Black serial #. Watermark: D. Diego Portales P. Printer: CdM-Chile.
   a. Paper of #121. Series B-G.   0.25   2.00
   s. Specimen.   —   17.50

135 1 Escudo   VF   UNC
ND. Engraved. Brown-violet with lilac guilloche on tan underprint. Portrait Arturo
Prat at center, signature varieties. Back: Red-brown arms with founding of
Santiago. Watermark: Balmaceda. Printer: CdM-Chile.
   a. Large and small brown serial #. Watermark: *1000* at right. Series A.   3.00   10.00
   b. Large and small black serial #. Watermark: *500* at right. Series A.   5.00   20.00
   c. Without watermark at right. Series A; B.   1.50   5.00
   d. Small black serial #. Without watermark. at right. Arms in red-brown at left   0.50   2.00
     on back.
   s. As c. Specimen.   —   17.50

135A 1 Escudo   VF   UNC
ND. Brown-violet with lilac guilloche on tan underprint. Portrait Arturo at center,
2 signature varieties. Series A; B. Back: Olive arms at left, founding of Santiago.
Printer: CdM-Chile.
   a. Series G-I. Without watermark at right.   0.20   1.00
   b. With *V* under portrait Paper of #121. Series J-N.   0.20   1.00

136 1 Escudo   VF   UNC
ND (1964). Lithographed. 6 or 7 digit serial #. Series N; P; Q. Dull violet on tan   0.25   1.00
underprint. Portrait Arturo Prat, 3 signature varieties. Back: Light olive arms with
founding of Santiago. Watermark: D. Diego Portales P. Printer: CdM-Chile.

137 5 Escudos

ND. Reddish brown on multicolor underprint. Portrait Manuel Bulnes at center,
signature varieties. Back: Battle of Rancagua at center, yellow-orange arms at left.
Watermark: D. Diego Portales P. Printer: CdM-Chile.

		VF	UNC
a. Series A.		2.00	12.50
s. Specimen.		—	17.50

138 5 Escudos

ND (1964). 6 or 7 digit serial #. Series A-E. Red and brown-violet on multicolor underprint. Portrait Manuel Bulnes at center, 4 signature varieties. Back: Red-brown
arms at left. Watermark: D. Diego Portales P. Printer: CdM-Chile.

VF: 0.25 UNC: 2.00

139 10 Escudos

ND. Violet, blue-gray and dull purple on multicolor underprint. Portrait Jose
Manuel Balmaceda at center, 3 signature varieties. Back: Dark or light brown
arms at left, soldiers meeting at center. Watermark: D. Diego Portales P. Printer:
CdM-Chile.

		VF	UNC
a. Series A-G.		0.75	5.00
s. Specimen.		—	25.00

140 50 Escudos

ND. Dark green and olive-brown on multicolor underprint. Portrait Arturo Ales-
sandri at center. 5 signature varieties. Back: Banco Central building. Watermark:
D. Diego Portales P. Printer: CdM-Chile.

		VF	UNC
a. Series A-D.		1.75	8.00
b. Series E-F.		0.25	3.00
s. Specimen.		—	25.00

141 100 Escudos

ND. Blue-gray and violet-brown on tan underprint. Portrait Manuel Regifo at right.
2 signature varieties. Back: Sailing ships at center, arms at left. Watermark: D.
Diego Portales P. Printer: CdM-Chile.

		VF	UNC
a. Series A-G.		0.75	4.00
s. Specimen.		—	25.00

1967-76 ND Issues

#142-148 Replacement notes: Serial # suffix *R* or *R* in area of sheet position #.

142 10 Escudos

ND (1970). Engraved. Gray-green, violet-brown and blue-gray on multicolor
underprint. Portrait Jose Manuel Balmaceda at right, 2 signature varieties. Series
A. Back: Red-brown lower margin. Watermark: D. Diego Portales P. Printer:
CdM-Chile.

VF: 0.50 UNC: 2.00

142A 10 Escudos

ND. Lithographed. Grey-green, violet-brown and blue-grey on multicolor underprint. Portrait Jose Manuel Balmaceda at right, signature varieties. Back: Green
lower margin. Watermark: D. Diego Portales P. Printer: CdM-Chile.

		VF	UNC
a. Series B.		0.50	2.00
s. Specimen.		—	20.00

147   5000 Escudos   VF   UNC
ND. Dark green and brown on multicolor underprint. Jose Miguel Carrera at left,
signature varieties. Back: Carrera House at center right. Watermark: D. Diego
Portales P. Printer: CdM-Chile.
  a. Back with deep green vignette. Lithographed. Series A.   1.50   5.00
  b. Back with dark olive-green vignette. Partially engraved. Series B. 2   0.75   3.00
     signature varieties.

143   10 Escudos   VF   UNC
ND. Lithographed. Grayish brown on tan underprint. Portrait Jose Manuel Bal-   0.25   1.50
maceda at right, 3 signature varieties. Series A. Back: Red-brown lower margin.
Watermark: D. Diego Portales P. Printer: CdM-Chile.

144   500 Escudos   VF   UNC
1971. Nationalization of iron and copper mines commemorative. Red-brown on   —   —
multicolor underprint. Copper worker at left. Back: Strip mining at center right.
Without 3-line text: *NO DEBEMOS CONSENTIR...* at bottom. Watermark: D.
Diego Portales P. Printer: CdM-Chile.

148   10,000 Escudos   VF   UNC
ND. Orange-brown on multicolor underprint. General Bernardo O'Higgins at left.   3.50   6.00
Blue serial #. 2 signature varieties. Series A. Back: Battle of Rancagua. Water-
mark: D.Diego Portales P. Printer: CdM-Chile.

SIGNATURES 1975-1999			
Gerente Gral		**Presidente**	
Carlos Molina 1973-85		Pablo Baraona 1975-76	
		Alvaro Bardón 1977-81	
		Sergio de La Cuadra 1981-82	
		Miguel Kast 1982	
		Carlos Cáceres 1982-83	
		Hermán Ezzázuriz 1984-85	
		Francisco Ibáñez 1984-85	
Jorge Court 1985-86		Enrique Sequel 1985-89	
Jorge Correa 1986-89			
Julio Acevedo 1990		Manuel Concha 1989	
Juan Rodriguez 1989-90 (Interum)		Andrés Bianchi 1989-91	
Enrique Tassara 1990-91 (Interum)		Roberto Zahler 1991-97	
Enrique Marshall 1991-94		Carlos Massad 1997-	
Camilo Carrasco 1994-			

145   500 Escudos   VF   UNC
1971. Nationalization of iron and copper mines commemorative. Red-brown on   0.50   2.50
multicolor underprint. Copper worker at left, 2 signature varieties. Series A; B.
Back: Strip mining at center right, 3-line text: *NO DEBEMOS CONSENTIR...*at
bottom. Watermark: D. Diego Portales P. Printer: CdN-Chile.

146   1000 Escudos   VF   UNC
ND. Purple and violet on multicolor underprint. Jose Miguel Carrera at left. 2   0.50   3.00
signature varieties. Series A; B. Back: Carrera House at center right. Watermark:
D. Diego Portales P. Printer: CdM-Chile.

1975-89 Issues
#149-152 Replacement notes: *R* serial # suffix.

149 5 Pesos

	VF	UNC
1975-76. Green on olive underprint. Jose Miguel Carrera at right. Signature varieties. Back: Carrera House at center right. Watermark: D. Diego Portales P. Printer: CdM-Chile.		
a. 1975.	2.00	7.50
b. 1976.	25.00	55.00
s. As a. Specimen.	—	25.00

150 10 Pesos

	VF	UNC
1975-76. Red on multicolor underprint. General Bernardo O'Higgins at right. Signature varieties. Back: Battle of Rancagua. Watermark: General Bernardo O'Higgins. Printer: CdM-Chile		
a. B. O'HIGGINS under portrait 1975.	1.75	8.00
b. LIBERTADOR B. O'HIGGINS under portrait 1975; 1976.	1.00	7.50
s. As a. Specimen.	—	25.00

151 50 Pesos

	VF	UNC
1975-81. Dark blue and aqua on green and light blue underprint. Portrait Captain Arturo Prat at right. 3 signature varieties. Back: Sailing ships at center. Watermark: D. Diego Portales P. Printer: CdM-Chile.		
a. 1975; 1976; 1977; 1978.	0.50	3.00
b. 1980; 1981 (2 signature varieties.)	0.25	2.00
s. Specimen. 1975.	—	25.00

152 100 Pesos

	VF	UNC
1976-84. Purple and red-violet on multicolor underprint. Diego Portales at right. 6 signature varieties. Back: 1837 meeting at left center. Watermark: D. Diego Portales P. Printer: CdM-Chile.		
a. Normal serial # without prefix letter. Series A. 1976.	4.00	10.00
b. Electronic sorting serial # with prefix letter. 1976-77, 1979-84. 6 signature varieties (2 for 1981).	0.50	3.00
s. Specimen. 1976.	—	25.00

153 500 Pesos

	VF	UNC
1977-2000. Dark brown and brown-violet with black text on multicolor underprint. Pedro de Valdivia at right. 11 signature varieties. Back: Founding of Santiago at center. Watermark: Ignacio Carrera Pinto.		
a. 1977; 1978.	1.50	7.50
b. 1980-82; 1985-90.	FV	4.50
c. Signature titles: PRESIDENTE and GERENTE GENERAL INTERINO. 1991.	2.00	7.50
d. 1991-93.	FV	4.00
e. 1994-2000. (1000 without imprint).	FV	3.00
s. Specimen. 1977.	—	25.00

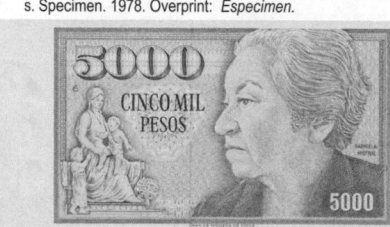

154 1000 Pesos

	VF	UNC
1978-. Deep blue-green, dark olive-brown on multicolor underprint. Ignacio Carrera Pinto at right, military arms at center. 12 signature varieties. Back: Monument to Chilean heroes. Watermark: Ignacio Carrera Pinto.		
a. Signature titles: PRESIDENTE and GERENTE GENERAL. 1978-80.	4.00	25.00
b. 1982.	FV	10.00
c. 1984-90.	FV	9.50
d. Signature titles: PRESIDENTE and GERENTE GENERAL INTERINO. 1990.	FV	9.00
e. Signature titles as a. 1991-94. (2 Signature varieties in 1994).	FV	7.50
f. Designer's names omitted from lower left and right. 1995-2005. (without imprint 1999; 2001-2002, 2004-6).	FV	5.00
g. One horizontal bar added to assist sight impaired. 2006; 2007; 2008; 2009.	FV	5.00
s. Specimen. 1978. Overprint: Especimen.	—	50.00

155 5000 Pesos VF UNC

1981-. Brown and red-violet on multicolor underprint. Allegorical woman with musical instrument, seated male at center. 9 signature varieties. Back: Statue of woman with children at left center, Gabriela Mistral at right. Watermark: Gabriela Mistral.

    a. Signature titles: *PRESIDENTE* and *GERENTE GENERAL*. 1981. Plain security thread.   FV   70.00

    b. 1986-90.   FV   50.00

    c. Signature titles: *PRESIDENTE* and *GERENTE GENERAL INTERINO*. 1991.   FV   35.00

    d. Signature titles: *PRESIDENTE* and *GERENTE GENERAL*. 1991-94.   FV   27.50

    e. As d but with segmented foil security thread. 1994-2005. (without imprint, 2002-2005).   FV   20.00

    f. Two horizontal bars added to assist sight impaired. 2006; 2007.   FV   20.00

    g. 2008.   FV   17.50

    s. Specimen. 1981; 1993.   —   100

156 10,000 Pesos VF UNC

1989-94. Dark blue and dark olive-green on multicolor underprint. Captain Arturo Prat at right. 5 signature varieties. Back: Statue of Liberty at left, Hacienda San Agustin de Punual Cuna at left center. Watermark: Captain Arturo Prat.

    a. Plain security thread. 1989-93.   FV   60.00

    b. As a. 1994.   FV   50.00

    s. Specimen. 1994.   —   100

1994 Issue

157 10,000 Pesos VF UNC

1995-99; 2001-08. Dark blue and deep olive-green on multicolor underprint. Captain Arturo Prat at right. 2 signature varieties. Back: Statue of Liberty at left, Hacienda San Agustin de Punual Cuna at left center. Watermark: Captain Arturo Prat. Printer: TDLR.

    a. Plain security thread. TDLR imprint. 1994.   FV   35.00

    b. Segmented security thread. TDLR. 1994-2001.   FV   35.00

    c. Without imprint. 2001-6; 2008.   FV   35.00

    s. 1998. Specimen. Red overprint: *ESPECIMEN*.   —   100

1997 Issue

158 2000 Pesos VF UNC

1997; 1999 (with imprint); 2001-03 (without imprint). Purple and dark brown on multicolor underprint. Manuel Rodríguez E. at right, statue of Manuel Rodríguez on horseback at center. Back: Iglesia de los Dominicos (church) at center. Watermark: Manuel Rodríguez E. Printer: CdM-C.

    a. Issued note.   FV   9.00

    s. 1998. Specimen. Red overprint: *ESPECIMEN*.   —   50.00

1998 Issue

159 20,000 Pesos VF UNC

1998-. Lilac brown, green and multicolor. Don Andres Bello at right. Back: University building. Printer: CdM-C.

    a. 1998-2005.   FV   60.00

    b. Circle added to assist slight impaired. 2006-.   FV   60.00

    s. 1998. Specimen. Red overprint: *ESPECIMEN*.   —   100

2004 Polymer Issue

160 2000 Pesos VF UNC

2004-. Polymer plastic. Lilac and brown on multicolor underprint. Manuel Rodríguez E. at right and as statue on horseback. Back: Iglesia de los Dominicos (church) at center. Watermark: Manuel Rodriguez E. Printer: CdM-C.

    a. 2004. Signature V. Corbo and C.A. Carrasco.   FV   7.50

    b. 2007. Signature V. Corbo and A.Z. Silva.   FV   7.50

    c. 2008. Signature J. de Gregorio Rebeco and A. Z. Silva.   FV   7.50

2009 Polymer Issue

161 1000 Pesos VF UNC

2011; 2012. Green. 120x70mm.

    a. 2011.   FV   4.00

    b. 2012.   FV   4.00

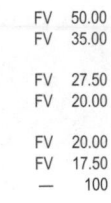

162 2000 Pesos   **VF**   **UNC**

2009; 2012. Black on purple and rose underprint. Manuel Rodriguez at left center.
Back: Nalcas National Reserve.

     a. 2009.   FV   7.50
     b. 2012.   FV   7.50

163 5000 Pesos   **VF**   **UNC**

2009; 2011; 2013. Rose on blue underprint. Gabriela Mistral facing at center.
Back: Chilean palm trees in the La Campana National Park; Tucúquere bird.
Printer: NPA.

     a. 2009.   FV   17.50
     b. 2011.   FV   17.50
     c. 2013.   FV   17.50

164 10,000 Pesos   **VF**   **UNC**

2009; 2013. Blue. Arturo Prat at center. Back: Alberto de Agostini National Park.

     a. 2009.   FV   35.00
     b. 2013.   FV   35.00

165 20,000 Pesos   **VF**   **UNC**

2009. Brown and orange. Andres Bello at left center. Back: Salar de Surire Natural
Monument.   FV   70.00

CHINA

The Republic of China, comprising Taiwan (an island located 90 miles (145 km.) off the southeastern coast of mainland China), the offshore islands of Quemoy and Matsu and nearby islets of the Pescadores chain, has an area of 14,000 sq. mi. (35,981 sq. km.) and a population of 20.2 million. Capital: Taipei. During the past decade, manufacturing has replaced agriculture in importance. Fruits, vegetables, plywood, textile yarns and fabrics and clothing are exported. Chinese migration to Taiwan began as early as the sixth century. The Dutch established a base on the island in 1624 and held it until 1661, when they were driven out by supporters of the Ming dynasty who used it as a base for their unsuccessful attempt to displace the ruling Manchu dynasty of mainland China. After being occupied by Manchu forces in 1683, Taiwan remained under the suzerainty of China until its cession to Japan in 1895. It was returned to China following World War II. On December 8, 1949, Taiwan became the last remnant of Sun Yatsen's Republic of China when Chiang Kai-shek moved his army and government from mainland China to the island following his defeat by the Communist forces of Mao Tse-tung.

MONETARY SYSTEM:
   1 Chiao = 10 Fen (Cents)
   1 Yuan (Dollar) = 10 Chiao

MONETARY UNITS

Yuan	圓 ᵒʳ 圜
Pan Yuan	圓 半
5 Jiao	角 伍
1 Jiao	角 壹
1 Fen	分 壹

NUMERICAL CHARACTERS

No.	CONVENTIONAL			FORMAL	
1	一	正	元	壹	弌
2	二			弍	貳
3	三			弎	叁
4	四			肆	
5	五			伍	
6	六			陸	
7	七			柒	
8	八			捌	
9	九			玖	
10	十			拾	什
20	十 二	廿		拾貳	念
25	五 十 二	五廿		伍拾貳	
30	十 三	卅		拾叁	
100	百 一			佰壹	

NUMERICAL CHARACTERS

No.	CONVENTIONAL		FORMAL	
1,000	千一		仟壹	
10,000	萬一		萬壹	
100,000	萬十	億一	萬拾	億壹
1,000,000	萬百一		萬佰壹	

PEOPLES REPUBLIC OF CHINA

Peoples Bank of China

行銀民人國中
Chung Kuo Jen Min Yin Hang

中國人民銀行
Zhong Guo Ren Min Yin Hang

1953 Second Issue

860　1 Fen　　　　　　　　　　　　　　　**VF　UNC**
1953. Brown on yellow-orange underprint. Produce truck at right. Back: Arms at center.
- a. Roman control numerals and serial #. 　　　　2.00　10.00
- b. 3 Roman control numerals only. 　　　　　　　—　0.50
- c. 2 Roman control numerals. 　　　　　　　　　—　0.20

861　2 Fen　　　　　　　　　　　　　　　**VF　UNC**
1953. Dark blue on light blue underprint. Airplane at right. Back: Arms at center.
- a. Roman control numerals and serial #. 　　　　5.00　35.00
- b. Roman control numerals only. 　　　　　　　0.20　0.50

862　5 Fen　　　　　　　　　　　　　　　**VF　UNC**
1953. Dark green on green underprint. Cargo ship at right. Back: Arms at center.
- a. Roman control numerals and serial #. 　　　　20.00　100
- b. Roman control numerals only. 　　　　　　　0.30　1.00

1962; 1965 Issue

877　1 Jiao　　　　　　　　　　　　　　　**VF　UNC**
1962. Brown on multicolor underprint. Workers at left. Back: Arms at right.
- a. Back brown and green and light orange underprint. Without watermark. 　100　350
- b. As a, watermark: stars. 　　　　　　　　　　800　2,500
- c. Serial # prefix: 3 blue Roman numerals. Back brown. Without watermark. 　0.50　2.00
- d. Like c, serial # prefix: 2 blue Roman numerals. 　0.50　2.00
- e. Back brown, partially engraved. Serial # prefix: 3 red Roman numerals. Watermark: Stars. 　0.50　2.00
- f. Like e but lithographed, serial # prefix: 2 red Roman numerals. Without watermark. 　0.30　1.00

878　2 Jiao　　　　　　　　　　　　　　　**VF　UNC**
1962. Green. Bridge over Yangtze River at left. Back: Arms at right.
- a. Engraved face. Serial # prefix: 3 Roman numerals. 　5.00　20.00
- b. Lithographed face. Serial # prefix: 3 Roman numerals. 　0.50　2.00
- c. As b. Serial # prefix: 2 Roman numerals. 　0.30　1.00
- x. As b. Red back. Post production chemical alteration. 　1.00　3.50

879　10 Yüan　　　　　　　　　　　　　　**VF　UNC**
1965. Black on multicolor underprint. Representatives of the National Assembly at center. Back: Arms at right, palace gate at left. Watermark: Great Hall with rays.
- a. Serial # prefix: 3 Roman numerals. 　　　　10.00　30.00
- b. Serial # prefix: 2 Roman numerals. 　　　　5.00　20.00

1972 Issue

880　5 Jiao　　　　　　　　　　　　　　　**VF　UNC**
1972. Purple and multicolor. Women working in textile factory. Back: Arms at right.
- a. Engraved bank title and denomination. Serial # prefix: 3 Roman numerals. Watermark: Stars. 　3.00　9.00
- b. As a, but lithographed face. With watermark. 　15.00　60.00
- c. Lithographed face. Without watermark. 　0.30　1.00

1980 Issue

881　1 Jiao　　　　　　　　　　　　　　　**VF　UNC**
1980. Brown and dark brown on multicolor underprint. A *Gaoshan* and a *Man* ethnic group member at left. Back: Arms at center. 115x52mm.
- a. Issued note. 　　　　　　　　　　　　　FV　0.50
- s. Specimen. 　　　　　　　　　　　　　　—　25.00

882　2 Jiao　　　　　　　　　　　　　　　**VF　UNC**
1980. Grayish olive-green on multicolor underprint. Native *Pu Yi* and Korean youth at left. Back: Arms at center. 120x55mm.
- a. Issued note. 　　　　　　　　　　　　　FV　0.50
- s. Specimen. 　　　　　　　　　　　　　　—　25.00

883　5 Jiao　　　　　　　　　　　　　　　**VF　UNC**
1980. Purple and red-violet on multicolor underprint. *Miao* and *Zhuang* children at left. Back: Arms at center. 125x58mm.
- a. Issued note. 　　　　　　　　　　　　　FV　0.75
- s. Specimen. 　　　　　　　　　　　　　　—　25.00

884 1 Yüan

1980; 1990; 1996. Brown-violet on multicolor underprint. *Dong* and *Yao* youths at right. Arms at upper left. Stylized birds in underprint at center, braille dot at lower left for the poor of sight. Back: Great Wall at center. Watermark: Ancient *Pu* (pants) coin repeated. 140x63mm.

	VF	UNC
a. Engraved. dark blue serial #. watermark: Ancient *Pu* (pants) coin repeated. 1980.	0.50	3.00
b. Partially engraved. watermark: as a. Black serial #. 1990.	0.30	1.00
c. Litho. watermark: Stars. Black serial #. 1996.	FV	0.50
s. As a. Specimen.	—	50.00

885 2 Yüan

1980; 1990. Dark olive-green on multicolor underprint. *Uygur* and *Yi* youths at right. Arms at upper left. Stylized birds in underprint at center. Braille dots at lower left for poor of sight. Back: Pillar of South Heaven in the South China Sea. Watermark: Ancient *Pu* (pants) coin repeated. 145x63mm.

	VF	UNC
a. Engraved back. 1980.	FV	5.00
b. Litho. back. 1990.	FV	3.00
s. As a. Specimen.	—	50.00

886 5 Yüan

1980. Dark brown on multicolor underprint. Old Tibetan man and young *Hui* woman at right. Arms at upper left. Stylized birds in underprint at center. Braille dots at lower left for poor of sight. Back: Wu Gorge of the Changjiang (Yangtse) River. Watermark: Ancient *Pu* (pants) coin repeated. 150x70mm.

	VF	UNC
a. Issued note.	FV	3.00
s. Specimen.	—	50.00

887 10 Yüan

1980. Black on blue and multicolor underprint. Elder Han and youthful Mongolian man at right. Arms at upper left. Stylized birds in underprint at center. Braille dots at lower left for poor of sight. Back: Mount Qomolangma (Mount Everest) at center. Watermark: Young Mongolian man. 155x70mm.

	VF	UNC
a. Issued note.	FV	5.00
s. Specimen.	—	50.00

888 50 Yüan

1980; 1990. Black on light green and multicolor underprint. Intellectual, farm girl and industrial male worker at center. Stylized birds in underprint at center. Braille dots at lower right for poor of sight. Back: HuKo Waterfall on the Yellow River. Arms at upper left. Watermark: Steel worker. 160x77mm.

	VF	UNC
a. 1980	60.00	300
b. Security thread at right. 1990.	20.00	50.00
s. As a. Specimen.	—	250

889 100 Yüan

1980; 1990. Black on multicolor underprint. Four profiles: Zhu De, Liu Shaoqi, Zhow Enlai, Mao Zedong at center. Stylized birds in underprint at center. Braille dots at lower right for poor of sight. Back: Main peak of the Jinggang Mountains (starting point of the "Long March"). Arms at upper left. Watermark: Bust of Mao Zedong. 165x77mm.

	VF	UNC
a. 1980	50.00	200
b. 1990. Security thread at right.	30.00	30.00
s. As a. Specimen.	—	150

890 500 Yüan

1990. Used for inter-bank transfers only. Black on multicolor underprint.

VF	UNC
—	—

1999 Commemorative Issue

891, 50th Anniversary of Revolution

891　50 Yüan　　　　　　　　　　　　　　　　　　　　**VF　UNC**
1999. Red on multicolor underprint. Mao Tse-tung delivering speech. Braille dots　25.00　90.00
at lower left for poor of sight. Back: Five pigeons in flight, carvings to left and right.
Arms at upper left.

#892-894 not assigned.

1999 Regular Issue

895　1 Yüan　　　　　　　　　　　　　　　　　　　　　**VF　UNC**
1999. Mao Tse-tung at right, flora at lower center. Watermark: Flora.
　　a. Serial # prefix format as: Letter, letter, number, number.　　FV　1.00
　　b. Serial # prefix format as: Letter, number, letter, number　　FV　1.00
　　c. Serial # prefix format as: Letter, number, number, letter, number.　　FV　1.00

#896 not assigned.

897　5 Yüan　　　　　　　　　　　　　　　　　　　　　**VF　UNC**
1999 (2002). . Purple on multicolor underprint. Mao Tse-tung at right, flora at lower　FV　2.00
center. Back: Mountain valley view. Watermark: Flora.

898　10 Yüan　　　　　　　　　　　　　　　　　　　　**VF　UNC**
1999 (2000). Slate blue and multicolor. Mao Tse-tung at right, flora at lower center.　FV　4.00
Back: Three gorges of Yangtze river. Watermark: Flora.

899　20 Yüan　　　　　　　　　　　　　　　　　　　　**VF　UNC**
1999. Brown on multicolor underprint. Mao Tse-tung at right, flora at lower center.　FV　5.00
Back: River scene. Watermark: Flora.

900　50 Yüan　　　　　　　　　　　　　　　　　　　　**VF　UNC**
1999 (2001). Green and multicolor. Mao Tse-tung at right, flora at lower center.　FV　20.00
Back: Potala of Tibet. Watermark: Flora.

901　100 Yüan　　　　　　　　　　　　　　　　　　　　**VF　UNC**
1999. Red and multicolor. Mao Tse-tung at right, flora at lower center. Back: Hall　FV　25.00
of the People. Watermark: Flora.

2000 Commemorative Issue

#902, Year 2000 commemorative

902　100 Yüan　　　　　　　　　　　　　　　　　　　　**VF　UNC**
2000. Polymer plastic. The clear window is a lotent hologram, shine a laser
pointer through it and view the character "Zhong. Orange, red and green. Dragon
at center, clear window with image at lower left, OVD at upper right. Back: Millenium monument, Beijing.
　　a. Series I. Replacement note.　　FV　800
　　b. Series J.　　FV　500

2005 Issue

903 5 Yüan VF UNC
2005. Purple on multicolor underprint. Mao Tse-Tung at right. Back: Mountain valley view. FV 1.00

904 10 Yüan VF UNC
2005. Slate blue on multicolor underprint. Mao Tse-Tung at right. Back: Three gorges of the Yangtze river. FV 2.50

905 20 Yüan VF UNC
2005. Brown on peach and multicolor underprint. Mao Tse-Tung at right. Back: River scene. FV 5.00

906 50 Yüan VF UNC
2005. Multicolor. Mao Tse-Tung at right. Back: Potala of Tibet at left center. FV 10.00

907 100 Yüan VF UNC
2005. Red on multicolor underprint. Mao Tse-Tung at right. Back: Hall of the People. FV 20.00

2008 Commemorative Issue

908 10 Yüan VF UNC
2008. Light and dark green. The "Bird's Nest" olympic stadium. Back: Discus thrower statue.
a. Issued note. — 700

Also issued in a folder with Macau commemorative.

2015 Issue

909 100 Yüan VF UNC
12.11.2015. Red on multicolor underprint. Mao Tse-Tung at right. Back: Hall of the People. FV 20.00

2015 Commemorative Issue

910 100 Yüan VF UNC
26.11.2015. Blue on multicolor underprint. Shenzhou-9 capsule docking with the Tiangong-1 space lab. Back: Satellite reminiscent of Chang'e 1 lunar satellite. Printer: China Banknote Printing and Minting. 155x77mm. FV 25.00

CHINESE ADMINISTRATION OF TAIWAN
Bank of Taiwan

行銀灣臺

T'ai Wan Yin Hang

PORTRAIT ABBREVIATIONS

SYS = DR. SUN YAT-SEN, 1867-1925
President of Canton Government, 1917-25

CKS = CHIANG KAI-SHEK, 1886-1975
President in Nanking, 1927-31
Head of Formosa Government, Taiwan,
1949-1975

Note: Because of the frequency of the above appearing in the following listings, their initials are used only in reference to their portraits.

PRINTERS

CPF:
(Central Printing Factory)

CPFT:
(Central Printing Factory, Taipei)

FPFT:
(First Printing Factory)

PFBT:
(Printing Factory of Taiwan Bank)

廠製印央中
廠北台廠製印央中
廠刷印一第
所刷印行銀灣臺

1961 Issue

		VF	UNC
1971	**1 Yüan**		
	1961. Dark blue-green and purple on multicolor underprint. Portrait SYS at left, steep coastline at right. Printer: PFBT.		
	a. Engraved.	0.75	5.00
	b. Lithographed. (1972).	1.50	3.00

		VF	UNC
1972	**5 Yüan**		
	1961. Red on multicolor underprint. Portrait SYS at left, house with tower at right. Printer: CPF.	0.75	4.00

		VF	UNC
1973	**5 Yüan**		
	1961. Brown on multicolor underprint. Portrait SYS at left, house with tower at right. Printer: CPF.	1.50	10.00
1974	**50 Yüan**	VF	UNC
	1961. Purple on multicolor underprint. Portrait SYS at left. Printer: CPF.	3.00	20.00

1964 Issue

		VF	UNC
1976	**50 Yüan**		
	1964. Purple on multicolor underprint. Portrait SYS at left. Printer: CPF.	2.00	15.00

1961 Issue

		VF	UNC
1975	**100 Yüan**		
	1961. Green on multicolor underprint. Portrait SYS at left. Printer: CPF.	3.25	22.00

1964 Issue

		VF	UNC
1977	**100 Yüan**		
	1964. Green on multicolor underprint. Portrait SYS at left. Printer: CPF.	3.00	20.00

Republic of China-Taiwan Bank

行銀灣臺　國民華中
Chung Hua Min Kuo-T'ai Wan Yin Hang

1969 Issue

		VF	UNC
1978	**5 Yüan**		
	1969. Blue on multicolor underprint. Portrait SYS at left. Printer: CPF.		
	a. Issued note.	0.40	3.00
	s. Specimen. Uniface impression of each side.	—	150

		VF	UNC
1979	**10 Yüan**		
	1969. Red on multicolor underprint. Portrait SYS at left. Printer: CPF.		
	a. Without plate letter.	0.50	3.00
	b. Plate letter A at lower right. on face.	0.35	2.50
	s. As a. Specimen. Uniface printing of each side.	—	150

1970 Issue

1980 50 Yüan | **VF** | **UNC**
1970. Purple on multicolor underprint. Portrait SYS at left. Printer: CPF. | 2.25 | 10.00

1981 100 Yüan | **VF** | **UNC**
1970. Green on multicolor underprint. Portrait SYS at left. Printer: CPF. | 4.50 | 15.00

1972 Issue

1982 50 Yüan | **VF** | **UNC**
1972. Purple and light blue on multicolor underprint. Portrait SYS at left. Wide margin with guilloche at right. Back: Chungshan building. Printer: CPF.
  a. Issued note. | 2.00 | 6.00
  s. Specimen. Uniface printing of each side. | — | 150

1983 100 Yüan | **VF** | **UNC**
1972. Dark green, light green and orange on multicolor underprint. Portrait SYS at left. Wide margin with guilloche at right. Back: Presidential Palace. Printer: CPF.
  a. Issued note. | 3.50 | 8.00
  s. Specimen. Uniface printing of each side. | — | 150

1976 Issue

1984 10 Yüan | **VF** | **UNC**
1976. Red on multicolor underprint. Portrait SYS at left. Back: Presidential Palace. Printer: CPF. | 0.50 | 2.00

1985 500 Yüan | **VF** | **UNC**
1976. Olive, purple and multicolor. CKS at left. Back: Chungshan building. Without watermark at right. Printer: CPF. | 20.00 | 45.00

1986 1000 Yüan | **VF** | **UNC**
1976. Blue-black, olive-brown and violet on multicolor underprint. CKS at left. Back: Presidential Palace. Without watermark at right. Printer: CPF.
  a. Issued note. | 40.00 | 120
  s. Specimen. | — | 600

1981 Issue

1987 500 Yüan | **VF** | **UNC**
1981. Brown and red-brown on multicolor underprint. CKS at left. Back: Presidential Palace. Watermark: CKS. Printer: CPF. | FV | 40.00

1988 1000 Yüan | **VF** | **UNC**
1981. Blue-black on multicolor underprint. CKS at left. Back: Presidential Palace. Watermark: CKS. Printer: CPF. | FV | 80.00

1987 Issue

1989 100 Yüan | **VF** | **UNC**
1987 (1988). Red, red-brown and brown-violet on multicolor underprint. SYS at left. Back: Chungshan building. Watermark: SYS. | FV | 7.00

1999 Commemorative Issue

1990   50 Yüan   VF   UNC

Polymer plastic. 50th Anniversary of Taiwan. Red on multicolor underprint. Currency and high-speed train at left. Back: Bank building.   FV   4.00

1999; 2001 Issue

1991   100 Yüan   VF   UNC

2001. Red on tan underprint. Sun-Yat Sen at right. Back: Chungshan Building.   FV   7.50

1992   200 Yüan   VF   UNC

2001. Dark green on light green and tan underprint. Chaing Kai-shek at right. Back: Presidential Palace.   FV   8.50

1993   500 Yüan   VF   UNC

1999; 2001. Brown and rose on multicolor underprint. Boy's baseball team at center, Professional Pitcher at right. Back: Formosan Sika Deer family and Mt. Dabajian.

   a. 1999   FV   25.00
   b. 2001   FV   25.00

1994   1000 Yüan   VF   UNC

1999. Light and dark blue on light green underprint. School children studying globe at center. Back: Two Mikado Pheasant and mountian vista.   FV   40.00

1995   2000 Yüan   VF   UNC

2002. Purple and lilac on multicolor underprint. Satellite Dishes and rocket. Back: Two salmon and Mt. Nanhu.   FV   80.00

2005 Issue

1996   500 Yüan   VF   UNC

2005. Wide security foil at right. Brown and rose on multicolor underprint. Boy's baseball team at center, Professional Pitcher at right. Back: Formosan Sika Deer family.   FV   25.00

1997   1000 Yüan   VF   UNC

2005. With wide security foil at right. Light and dark blue on light green underprint. School children studying globe at center. Back: Two Mikado Pheasant and mountain vista.   FV   40.00

OFF-SHORE ISLAND CURRENCY

Bank of Taiwan

T'ai Wan Yin Hang

Kinmen (Quemoy) Branch

Notes of the Bank of Taiwan and later notes of the Republic of China/Bank of Taiwan w/ovpt:

1949-51 (1963; 1967) Issue

R101 1 Yüan — VF UNC
1949 (1963). Vertical format. Green on multicolor underprint. Portrait SYS at upper center. Printer: CPF. — 2.00 10.00

1950-51 Issues

R106 10 Yüan — VF UNC
1950 (1963). Vertical format. Blue. Portrait SYS at upper center. Printer: CPF. — 1.50 18.00

R107 50 Yüan — VF UNC
1951 (1967). Vertical format. Green. Portrait SYS at upper center. Printer: FPFT. — 20.00 120

1955-72 Issues

R109 5 Yüan — VF UNC
1966 Vertical format. Violet-brown. Portrait SYS at upper center. Printer: CPF. — 3.00 20.00

R110 10 Yüan — VF UNC
1969 (1975). Red on multicolor underprint. — 2.00 10.00

R111 50 Yüan — VF UNC
1969 (1970). Dark blue on multicolor underprint. SYS at right. — 3.50 25.00

R112 100 Yüan — VF UNC
1972 (1975). — 7.50 40.00

1976; 1981 Issue

R112A 10 Yüan — VF UNC
1976 — 0.75 10.00

R112B 100 Yüan — VF UNC
1981 — 8.00 30.00

R112C 1000 Yüan — VF UNC
1981 — 50.00 200

Matsu Branch

Notes of the Bank of Taiwan and later notes of the Republic of China/Bank of Taiwan w/ovpt:

1950-51 Dated (1964; 1967) Issue

R117 10 Yüan — VF UNC
1950 (1964). Vertical format. Blue on multicolor underprint. Portrait SYS at upper center. Printer: CPF. — 3.00 25.00

R118 50 Yüan — VF UNC
1951 (1967). Vertical format. Green on multicolor underprint. Portrait SYS at upper center. Printer: FPFT. — 8.00 80.00

Matsu Branch
1969; 1972 Issue

		VF	UNC
R122	**10 Yüan**		
	1969 (1975). Red on multicolor underprint. Printer: CPF.	1.00	10.00

		VF	UNC
R123	**50 Yüan**		
	1969 (1970). Violet on multicolor underprint. Printer: CPF.	4.00	30.00
R124	**100 Yüan**		
	1972 (1975). Dark green, light green and orange on multicolor underprint. Printer: CPF.	10.00	80.00

Matsu Branch
1976; 1981 Issue

		VF	UNC
R125	**10 Yüan**		
	1976 Red on multicolor underprint.	1.00	8.00
R126	**500 Yüan**		
	1981 Brown and red-brown on multicolor underprint.	20.00	80.00
R127	**1000 Yüan**		
	1981 Blue-black on multicolor underprint.	37.50	200

COLOMBIA

The Republic of Colombia, located in the northwestern corner of South America, has an area of 1.139 million sq. km. and a population of 45.01 million. Capital: Bogotá. The economy is primarily agricultural with a mild, rich coffee the chief crop. Colombia has the world's largest platinum deposits and important reserves of coal, iron ore, petroleum and limestone; precious metals and emeralds are also mined. Coffee, crude oil, bananas, sugar, coal and flowers are exported.

Colombia was one of the three countries that emerged from the collapse of Gran Colombia in 1830 (the others are Ecuador and Venezuela). A 40-year conflict between government forces and anti-government insurgent groups and illegal paramilitary groups - both heavily funded by the drug trade - escalated during the 1990s. The insurgents lack the military or popular support necessary to overthrow the government, and violence has been decreasing since about 2002, but insurgents continue attacks against civilians and large swaths of the countryside are under guerrilla influence. More than 32,000 former paramilitaries had demobilized by the end of 2006 and the United Self Defense Forces of Colombia (AUC) as a formal organization had ceased to function. Still, some renegades continued to engage in criminal activities. The Colombian Government has stepped up efforts to reassert government control throughout the country, and now has a presence in every one of its administrative departments. However, neighboring countries worry about the violence spilling over their borders.

MONETARY SYSTEM:
    1 Real = 1 Decimo = 10 Centavos, 1870's
    1 Peso = 10 Decimos = 10 Reales, 1880's
    1 Peso = 100 Centavos 1993
    1 Peso Oro = 100 Centavos to 1993

REPLACEMENT NOTES:
    Earlier issues, small R just below and between signatures. Larger R used later. Some TDLR printings have R preceding serial number. Later Colombian-printed notes use circled asterisk usually close to sign. or a star at r. of upper serial #. Known replacements: #389-407, 409, 413-15, 417-19, 421-22, 425-29, 431-433, 436-41, 443, 445-48.

REGULAR ISSUES, 1904-1960
1943 Pesos Oro Issue

		VF	UNC
392	**20 Pesos Oro**		
	1943-63. Purple and multicolor. Bust of Francisco José de Caldas at left, bust of Simon Bolívar at right. Back: Liberty at center. Printer: ABNC.		
	a. Series U in red. 20.7.1943.	200	500
	b. Series U in purple. 20.7.1944; 1.1.1945.	60.00	200
	c. Series U. Prefix A. 7.8.1947.	15.00	80.00
	d. Series DD. 1.1.1950; 1.1.1951.	7.50	50.00
	e. Series DD. 2.1.1963.	7.50	50.00
	s. Specimen.	—	65.00

REPUBLIC
Banco de la República
1953 Pesos Oro Issue

		VF	UNC
400	**10 Pesos Oro**		
	1953-61. Blue on multicolor underprint. Similar to #377, but palm trees at right instead of watermark. Portrait General Antonio Nariño with Mercury alongside at left. Back: Bank building at Cali. Series N. Printer: TDLR.		
	a. 1.1.1953.	7.50	50.00
	b. 1.1.1958; 1.1.1960.	7.50	50.00
	c. 2.1.1961.	7.50	50.00
	s1. Specimen. With red TDLR and *SPECIMEN* overprint. Punched hole cancelled.	—	100
	s2. Specimen. Red overprint: *SPECIMEN*.	—	100

1959-60 Pesos Oro Issue

401 20 Pesos Oro

1953-65. Red-brown on multicolor underprint. Similar to #378, but Liberty in circle at right instead of watermark. Portrait Francisco José de Caldas and allegory at left. Series O. Back: Newer bank building at Barranquilla on back. Printer: TDLR.

	VF	UNC
a. 1.1.1953.	7.50	45.00
b. 1.1.1960.	7.50	45.00
c. 2.1.1961; 2.1.1965.	6.00	40.00
s1. Specimen. With red TDLR overprint and *SPECIMEN*. Punched hole cancelled.	—	100
s2. Specimen. Red overprint; *SPECIMEN*. Punched hole cancelled.	—	65.00

1958 Pesos Oro Issue

402 50 Pesos Oro

1958-67. Light brown on multicolor underprint. Portrait Antonio José de Sucre at lower left. Series Z. Back: Liberty at center. Printer: ABNC.

	VF	UNC
a. 20.7.1958; 7.8.1960.	10.00	100
b. 1.1.1964; 12.10.1967.	8.00	70.00
s1. Specimen.	—	135
s2. Specimen. Red overprint: *SPECIMEN*. Punched hole cancelled.	—	150

403 100 Pesos Oro

1958-67. Gray on multicolor underprint. Portrait General Francisco de Paula Santander at right. Series Y. Back: Liberty at center. Printer: ABNC.

	VF	UNC
a. 7.8.1958.	8.00	70.00
b. 1.1.1960; 1.1.1964.	6.00	90.00
c. 20.7.1965; 20.7.1967.	6.00	90.00
p1. Face proof. Without date, signatures, series or serial #. Punched hole cancelled.	—	150
s. Specimen.	—	125

404 1 Peso Oro

1959-77. Blue on multicolor underprint. Portrait Simón Bolívar at left, portrait General Francisco de Paula Santander at right. Back: Liberty head and condor with waterfall and mountain at center. Printer: Imprenta de Billets-Bogota.

	VF	UNC
a. Security thread. 12.10.1959.	2.50	12.50
b. Security thread. 2.1.1961; 7.8.1962; 2.1.1963; 12.10.1963; 2.1.1964; 12.10.1964.	2.00	9.00
c. As b. 20.7.1966.	10.00	40.00
d. Without security thread. 20.7.1966; 20.7.1967; 1.2.1968, 2.1.1969.	1.25	6.00
e. Without security thread. 1.5.1970; 12.10.1970; 7.8.1971; 20.7.1972; 7.8.1973; 7.8.1974.	0.50	4.00
f. As c. 1.1.1977.	5.00	35.00
s1. Specimen.	—	60.00
s2. Specimen. Red overprint: *ESPECIMEN*. on face	—	60.00

1961-64 Issue

#406-407 replacement notes: Serial # prefix *R* or *.

406 5 Pesos Oro

1961-81. Deep greenish black and deep brown on multicolor underprint. Condor at left, José María Córdoba at right. Back: Fortress at Cartagena at center.

	VF	UNC
a. Security thread. 2.1.1961; 1.5.1963; 2.1.1964.	6.00	30.00
b. Security thread. 11.11.1965; 12.10.1967; 20.7.1968.	3.00	15.00
c. Security thread. 20.7.1971.	2.50	10.00
d. As c. 1.1.1973.	50.00	200
e. Without security thread. 1.1.1973; 20.7.1974; 20.7.1975; 20.7.1976; 20.7.1977.	1.00	5.50
f. Without security thread. 1.10.1978; 1.4.1979; 1.1.1980; 1.1.1981.	0.75	4.00
s. Specimen. As a. Red overprint: ESPECIMEN on both sides.	—	75.00

407 10 Pesos Oro VF UNC

1963-80. Lilac and slate blue on green and multicolor underprint. General Antonio Nariño at left, condor at right. Back: Archaeological site with monoliths.

a. Security thread. 20.7.1963.	10.00	40.00
b. As a. 20.7.1964.	4.00	25.00
c. 20.7.1965; 20.7.1967; 2.1.1969.	4.00	17.50
d. As c. with segmented security thread. 12.10.1970; 1.1.1973.	2.00	10.00
e. As d. 20.7.1974.	75.00	300
f. Without security thread. 20.7.1974; 1.1.1975; 20.7.1976; 1.1.1978.	0.75	6.00
g. As f. 7.8.1979; 7.8.1980.	0.35	4.00
h. Like f., but *SERIE AZ* at left center and upper right. on face. 7.8.1980. *Serie AZ*.	0.50	5.00
s. Specimen. Red overprint ESPECIMEN on both sides.	—	90.00

408 500 Pesos Oro VF UNC

20.7.1964. Series *AA*. Olive-green on multicolor underprint. Portrait Simon Bolívar at right. Back: No open space under Liberty head. Printer: ABNC.

a. Six digit serial #.	200	750
b. Seven digit serial #.	50.00	200
s. Specimen. Overprint *MUESTRA* and punched hole cancelled.	—	175

1966-68 Issue

#409 replacement note: Serial # prefix *R* or *.

409 20 Pesos Oro VF UNC

1966-83. Brown, gray and green on multicolor underprint. Francisco José de Caldas with globe at right. Back: *Balsa Muisca* from the Gold Museum.

a. Security thread. 12.10.1966; 2.1.1969; 1.5.1972; 1.5.1973.	4.00	30.00
b. As a. 20.7.1974.	150	400
c. Without security thread. 20.7.1974; 20.7.1975; 20.7.1977.	2.50	15.00
d. As c. 1.4.1979; 1.1.1981; 1.1.1982; 1.1.1983.	2.00	10.00
s. Specimen.	—	50.00

410 100 Pesos Oro VF UNC

1968-71. Blue on multicolor underprint. General Francisco de Paula Santander at right. Series Y. Back: Capitol at Bogotá. Watermark: Simon Bolívar. Printer: TDLR.

a. 1.1.1968.	12.50	50.00
b. 2.1.1969.	7.50	40.00
c. 1.5.1970; 20.7.1971.	5.00	30.00
s. Specimen. As b, c. Red overprint: SPECIMEN on each side. Some punch hole cancelled.	—	110

411 500 Pesos Oro VF UNC

1968; 1971. Green on multicolor underprint. Simón Bolívar at right. Series A. Back: Zipaquirá subterranean salt cathedral at center. Watermark: Liberty head. Printer: ABNC.

a. 1.1.1968.	30.00	125
b. 12.10.1971.	40.00	125
s. Specimen. Red overprint: MUESTRA twice on both sides. Punch hole cancelled.	—	150

1969 Issue

412 50 Pesos Oro VF UNC

1969-70. Purple on pale blue, lilac and pink underprint. Blue design without border at left, Camilo Torres at right. Back: Arms and flowers. Watermark: Camilo Torres. Printer: TDLR.

a. 2.1.1969.	FV	45.00
b. 12.10.1970.	FV	30.00
s. Specimen. Red overprint: SPECIMEN on both sides. Punched hole cancelled.	—	175

1972-73 Issue

#413-415 replacement notes: Serial # prefix *R* or *.

413 2 Pesos Oro

1972-77. Purple on multicolor underprint. Policarpa Salavarietta at left. Back: *El Dorado* from the Gold Museum.

	VF	UNC
a. Large size serial #, and # at right. near upper border. 1.1.1972; 20.7.1972; 1.1.1973.	FV	5.00
b. Small size serial #, and # at right. far from upper border. 20.7.1976; 1.1.1977; 20.7.1977.	FV	5.00
s. Specimen. Red overprint: MUESTRA twice on each side. Punch hole cancelled.	—	90.00

414 50 Pesos Oro

20.7.1973; 20.7.1974. Purple on pale blue, lilac and pink underprint. Curved dark border added at left and right, Camilo Torres at right. Back: Curved dark border at right, Arms and flowers. Watermark: Camilo Torres. Printer: TDLR.

	VF	UNC
	FV	20.00

415 100 Pesos Oro

20.7.1973; 20.7.1974. Blue on multicolor underprint. Curved dark border added at left and right, General Francisco de Paula Santander at right. Series Y. Back: Curved dark border at right, Capital at Bagota. Printer: TDLR.

	VF	UNC
a. Issued note.	FV	30.00
s. Specimen. Overprint: *SPECIMEN* in red on both sides. Punched hole cancelled.	—	165

416 500 Pesos Oro

7.8.1973. Red on multicolor underprint. Simón Bolívar at right. Series A. Back: Zipaquirá subterranean salt cathedral at center. Watermark: Liberty head. Printer: ABNC.

	VF	UNC
a. Issued note.	FV	100
s. Specimen.	—	100

1974 Issue

#417 replacement note: Serial # prefix *R*.

417 200 Pesos Oro

1974; 1975. Green on multicolor underprint. Simón Bolívar at center right, church at right. *BOGOTÁ COLOMBIA* at lower left center. Back: Man picking coffee beans. Watermark: Simón Bolívar. Printer: TDLR.

	VF	UNC
a. 20.7.1974.	FV	50.00
b. 7.8.1975.	FV	20.00
s. Specimen. As b. Overprint: *SPECIMEN* in red on both sides. Punched hole cancelled.	—	165

1977-79 Issue

#418-420 replacement notes: Serial # prefix *R* or *.

418 100 Pesos Oro

1977-80. Purple and black on multicolor underprint. General Francisco de Paula Santander at center right. Back: Capitol at Bogotá. Watermark: Liberty head. Printer: TDLR.

	VF	UNC
a. 1.1.1977.	FV	10.00
b. 1.1.1980. Numerals at upper center and upper right are darker, as is the word *CIEN*.	FV	8.00
c. As b. Serial # prefix *A-C*. 1.1.1980.	FV	6.00
s1. Specimen.	—	75.00
s2. Specimen. Red overprint: *SPECIMEN*. Punch hole cancelled.	—	200

419 200 Pesos Oro

20.7.1978; 1.1.1979; 1.1.1980. Green on multicolor underprint. Simón Bolívar at center right, church at right. *COLUMBIA* at lower left center. Back: Man picking coffee beans. Watermark: Simón Bolívar. Printer: TDLR.

	VF	UNC
	FV	10.00

420 500 Pesos Oro   VF   UNC

1977; 1979. Olive and multicolor. General Francisco de Paula Santander at left. Back: Subterranean church and Liberty head. Watermark: General Francisco de Paula Santander in profile. Printer: ABNC.

a. 20.7.1977.	FV	40.00
b. 1.4.1979.	FV	30.00
s1. Specimen. As a. Specimen. Overprint: *MUESTRA* in red on both sides. Punched hole cancelled.	—	100
s2. Specimen. As b. Red overprint: MUESTRA SIN VALOR twice on both sides.	—	150

423 500 Pesos Oro   VF   UNC

1981-86. Brown, dark green and red-brown on multicolor underprint. General Francisco de Paula Santander at left. Back: Bogotá; screw coinage press at lower right. Watermark: General Francisco de Paula Santander in profile. Printer: TDLR.

a. 20.7.1981.	FV	30.00
b. 20.7.1984; 20.7.1985.	FV	15.00
c. 12.10.1985; 20.7.1986.	FV	10.00
s1. Specimen. 20.7.1981; 20.7.1984; 12.10.1985; 20.7.1986. Overprint: *SPECIMEN* in red on both sides. Punched hole cancelled.	—	200
s2. Specimen. Overprint: *MUESTRA SIN VALOR* in red on both sides. Punched hole cancelled.	—	100
s3. Specimen. 20.7.1986. Overprint in black: *MUESTRA SIN VALOR* once on each side.	—	100

421 1000 Pesos Oro   VF   UNC

1.4.1979. Black and multicolor. José Antonio Galan at right. Back: Nariño Palace. Watermark: José Antonio Galan. Printer: ABNC.

a. Issued note.	FV	10.00
s. Specimen. Specimen. Overprint: *SPECIMEN* in red on both sides. Punched hole cancelled.	—	200

424 1000 Pesos Oro   VF   UNC

1982-87. Deep blue and olive-brown on multicolor underprint. Simón Bolívar at left. Back: Scene honoring 1819 battle heroes. Watermark: Simón Bolívar. Printer: TDLR.

a. 1.1.1982.	FV	20.00
b. 7.8.1984.	FV	12.50
c. 1.1.1986; 1.1.1987.	FV	10.00
s. Specimen. As a, b, c. Overprint: *SPECIMEN* in red on both sides. Punched hole cancelled.	—	100

1980-82 Issues

#422 replacement note: Serial # prefix *.

1982-84 Issues

#425-430 replacement notes: Serial # prefix circled-*.

422 50 Pesos Oro   VF   UNC

1980-83. Purple on pale blue, lilac and pink underprint. *COLOMBIA* added near border at upper left center. Printer: TDLR (without imprint).

a. 1.1.1980; 7.8.1981.	1.00	7.50
b. 1.1.1983.	0.75	5.00
s. Specimen. Red overprint: MUESTRA SIN VALOR on each side. Punch hole cancelled.	—	200

425 50 Pesos Oro   VF   UNC

1984-86. Purple on pale blue, lilac and pink underprint. Camillo Torres at right, curved dark border added at left and right. Back: Curved dark border added at right, Arms and flowers. Printer: IBB.

a. 12.10.1984; 1.1.1985.	FV	6.00
b. 1.1.1986.	FV	5.00
s. Specimen. 1.1.1985. Red overprint: *MUESTRA SIN VALOR* on both sides.	—	100

426   100 Pesos Oro

	VF	UNC
1983-91. Violet, brown, orange and dark red on multicolor underprint. General Antonio Nariño at left. Back: Villa de Leyva; flat bed letterpress at lower right. Watermark: General Antonio Nariño. Printer: IBB.		
a. 1.1.1983; 12.10.1984.	1.00	7.50
b. 12.10.1985; 1.1.1986; 12.10.1986.	FV	7.00
c. Larger stylized serial #. 12.10.1986; 1.1.1987; 12.10.1988.	FV	6.00
d. Back colors slightly off shade from earlier issues. 7.8.1989.	FV	4.00
e. Signature titles: *GERENTE* and *SECRETARIO*. 1.1.1990; 1.1.1991.	FV	3.00
s. Specimen. 1.1.1983; 12.10.1984; 1.1.1986; 12.10.1986; 1.1.1987. Black or red overprint: *MUESTRA SIN VALOR* in on both sides. Punch hole cancelled.	—	120

426A   100 Pesos Oro

	VF	UNC
7.8.1991. Violet, brown, orange and dark red on multicolor underprint. General Antonio Nariño at left. Back: Villa de Leyva; flat bed letterpress at lower right. Watermark: General Antonio Nariño. Printer: IBSFB.	FV	1.00

427   200 Pesos Oro

	VF	UNC
1.1.1982. Green on multicolor underprint. Simón Bolívar at center right, church at right, COLUMBIA at lower left center. Back: Man picking coffee beans. Watermark: Simón Bolívar. Printer: IBB.		
a. Issued note.	FV	5.00
s. Specimen. Red overprint: MUESTRA SIN VALOR on each side. Punch hole cancelled.	—	115

428   200 Pesos Oro

	VF	UNC
1.4.1983. Deep green and black on multicolor underprint. Church and Fr. José Celestino Mutis at left, arms at upper right. Back: Monastery of Nuestra Señora del Rosario at right. Watermark: Church and Fr. José Celestino Mutis. Printer: TDLR.		
a. Issued note.	FV	10.00
s. Specimen. Overprint: *SPECIMEN* in red on both sides. Punched hole cancelled.	—	150

429   200 Pesos Oro

	VF	UNC
1983-91. Deep green and black on multicolor underprint. Church and Fr. José Celestino Mutis at left, Arms at upper right. Back: Monastery of Nuestra Señora del Rosario at right. Watermark: Church and Fr. José Celestino Mutis. Printer: TDLR.		
a. Printer: IBB. 1.4.1983; 20.7.1984.	FV	25.00
b. 20.7.1984; 1.11.1984; 1.4.1985.	FV	10.00
c. 1.11.1985.	FV	7.00
d. Larger stylized and bold serial #. 1.4.1987; 1.4.1988; 1.11.1988; 1.4.1989; 1.11.1989; 1.4.1991.	FV	4.00
s. Specimen. 1.4.1987. Red overprint: *MUESTRA SIN VALOR*. Punch hole cancelled.	—	100

429A   200 Pesos Oro

	VF	UNC
10.8.1992. Dark brown and brown-orange on multicolor underprint. Simón Bolívar at left, *EL* deleted from title, *ORO* deleted from value. Back: Scene at *Peso del Paramo de Pisba* at center right. Printer: IBSFB.	FV	4.00

430   2000 Pesos Oro

	VF	UNC
1983-86. Dark brown and brown-orange on multicolor underprint. Simón Bolívar at left. Back: Scene at *Paso del Paramo de Pisba* at center right. Watermark: Simón Bolívar. Printer: TDLR.		
a. 24.7.1983.	FV	35.00
b. 24.7.1984.	FV	20.00
c. 17.12.1985.	FV	15.00
d. 17.12.1986.	FV	10.00
s. Specimen. Red overprint SPECIMEN on both sides. Some punched hole cancelled.	—	75.00

1986-87 Issue

#431-433 replacement notes: Serial # prefix *.

431   500 Pesos Oro

	VF	UNC
20.7.1986; 12.10.1987; 20.7.1989; 12.10.1990. Brown, dark green and red-brown on multicolor underprint. General Francisco de Paula Santander at left. Back: Bogotá scene; screw coinage press at lower right. Watermark: General Francisco de Paula Santander in profile. Printer: IBB.	FV	5.00

431A 500 Pesos Oro

	VF	UNC
2.3.1992; 4.1.1993. Brown, dark green and red-brown on multicolor underprint. General Francisco de Paula Santander at left. Back: Bogotá; screw coinage press at lower right. Watermark: General Francisco de Paula Santander in profile. Printer: IBSFB.	FV	3.00

432 1000 Pesos Oro

	VF	UNC
1.1.1987; 1.1.1990; 1.1.1991. Black, blue-green and deep olive-brown on multicolor underprint. Simón Bolívar at left. Back: Scene honoring 1819 battle heroes. Watermark: Simón Bolívar. Printer: IBB.		
a. Issued note.	FV	9.00
s. Specimen. Red overprint: MUESTRA SIN VALOR on each side. Punch hole cancelled.	—	150

432A 1000 Pesos Oro

	VF	UNC
31.1.1992; 1.4.1992; 4.1.1993. Black, blue-green and deep olive-brown on multicolor underprint. Simón Bolívar at left. Back: Scene honoring 1819 battle heroes. Watermark: Simón Bolívar. Printer: IBSFB.	FV	5.00

433 2000 Pesos Oro

	VF	UNC
17.12.1986; 17.12.1988; 17.12.1990. Dark brown and brown-orange on multicolor underprint. Simón Bolívar at left, redesigned 2's in denomination. Back: Scene at Paso del Paramo de Pisba at center right. Watermark: Simón Bolívar. Printer: IBB.		
a. 17.12.1986.	FV	9.00
b. 17.12.1988.	FV	9.00
c. 17.12.1990.	FV	9.00

433A 2000 Pesos Oro

	VF	UNC
1992. Dark brown and brown-orange on multicolor underprint. Simón Bolívar at left, redesigned 2's in denomination. Back: Scene at Paso del Paramo de Pisba at center right. Watermark: Simón Bolívar. Printer: IBSFB.		
a. 2.3.1992; 1.4.1992.	FV	5.00
b. 3.8.1992.	FV	50.00

1986 Commemorative Issue
#434, Centennial of the Constitution

434 5000 Pesos Oro

	VF	UNC
5.8.1986. Deep violet and red-violet on multicolor underprint. Rafael Nuñez at left. Back: Statue of Miguel Antonio Caro at center right. Watermark: Rafael Nuñez. Printer: BDDK.		
a. Issued note.	FV	50.00
s. Specimen. Red serial # at upper right. Overprint: SPECIMEN in red on both sides. Punched hole cancelled.	—	165

1987 Issue

435 5000 Pesos Oro

	VF	UNC
5.8.1987; 5.8.1988; 1.1.1990. Deep violet and red-violet on multicolor underprint. Rafael Nuñez at left. Back: Statue of Miguel Antonio Caro at center right. Watermark: Rafael Nuñez. Printer: IPS-Roma.		
a. 5.8.1987.	FV	40.00
b. 5.8.1988.	FV	40.00
c. 1.1.1990.	FV	35.00
s. Specimen. As a, b. Overprint: SPECIMEN in red on both sides. Punched hole cancelled.	—	140

1990 Issue

#436 replacement note: Serial # prefix *.

436 5000 Pesos Oro   **VF UNC**
1.1.1990. Deep violet and red-violet on multicolor underprint. Rafael Nuñez at left.   FV   25.00
Back. Statue of Miguel Antonio Caro at center right. Watermark: Rafael Nuñez.
Printer: IBB.

436A 5000 Pesos Oro   **VF UNC**
31.1.1992. 4.1.1993. Deep violet and red-violet on multicolor underprint. Rafael   FV   25.00
Nuñez at left. Back: Statue of Miguel Antonio Caro at center right. Watermark:
Rafael Nuñez. Printer: IBSFB.

1992 Commemorative Issue

#437, Quincentennial of Columbus' Voyage, 12.10.1492

437 10,000 Pesos Oro   **VF UNC**
1992. The birds are left to right: greater flamingo, andean condor, green
honeycreeper, andean cock of the rock, blue and yellow macaw, hotzin, scarlet
ibis, yellow-hooded blackbird, metallic green tanager, white pelican, magnificent
frigatebird, keel-billed toucan, baltimore oriole, scarlet macaw, yellow crowned
parrot, red-capped cardinal. Light and dark brown on multicolor underprint. Early
sailing ships at center, youthful woman *Mujer Embera* at center right, native gold
statue at right. Back: Native birds around antique world map at left center, Santa
Maria sailing ship at lower right. Watermark: youthful woman *Mujer Embera*.
Printer: BDM.
     a. Issued note.   FV   60.00
     s. Specimen.   —   100

1993 Issue

437A 10,000 Pesos Oro   **VF UNC**
1993; 1994. The birds are left to right: greater flamingo, andean condor, green   FV   40.00
honeycreeper, andean cock of the rock, blue and yellow macaw, hotzin, scarlet
ibis, yellow-hooded blackbird, metallic green tanager, white pelican, magnificent
frigatebird, keel-billed toucan, baltimore oriole, scarlet macaw, yellow crowned
parrot, red-capped cardinal. Deep brown and black on multicolor underprint. Early
sailing ships at center, youthful woman *Mujer Embera* at center right, native gold
statue at right. Back: Native birds around antique world map at left center, Santa
Maria sailing ship at lower right. Watermark: Youthful woman *Mujer Embera*.
Printer: IBSFB.

Note: 1,000,000 pieces of #437A dated 1993 were stolen in 1994.

1993-95 Issues

Peso System

438 1000 Pesos   **VF UNC**
3.1.1994; 1.11.1994; 1.7.1995; 2.8.1995; 2.10.1995. Black, blue-green and deep   FV   5.00
olive-brown on multicolor underprint. Simón Bolívar at left. *EL* omitted from title
and *ORO* omitted from value. Back: Scene honoring 1819 battle heroes. Watermark: Simón Bolívar. Printer: IBSFB.

439 2000 Pesos   **VF UNC**
1993-94. Dark brown and brown-orange on multicolor underprint. Simón Bolívar
at left, *EL* deleted from title, *ORO* deleted from value. Back: Scene at *Peso del
Paramo de Pisba* at center right. Watermark: Simón Bolívar. Printer: IBSFB.
     a. 1.7.1993.   FV   10.00
     b. Orange omitted from back. 1.7.1994; 1.11.1994; 17.12.1994.   FV   8.00

Note: 1,700,000 pieces of #439a were stolen in 1994.

440   5000 Pesos   **VF   UNC**
3.1.1994; 4.7.1994; 2.1.1995. Deep violet and red-violet on multicolor underprint.   FV   20.00
Rafael Nuñez at left, *EL* deleted from the title, *ORO* deleted from the value. Back:
Statue of Miguel Antonio Caro at center right. Watermark: Rafael Nuñez. Printer:
IBSFB.

Note: 2,200,000 pieces of #440 dated 3.1.1994 were stolen in 1994.

441   5000 Pesos   **VF   UNC**
1.3.1995; 1.3.1996. Dark brown, brown and deep blue-green on multicolor
underprint. José Asunción Silva and bug at upper right, trees at left and center.
Back: Woman, trees and monument at center. Watermark: Asunción Silva. Printer:
IBSFB.
    a. Issued note.   FV   20.00
    s. Specimen.   —   75.00

442   5000 Pesos   **VF   UNC**
1.7.1995. Dark brown, brown and deep blue-green on multicolor underprint. José
Asunción Silva and bug at upper right, trees at left and center. Back: Woman,
trees and monument at center. Watermark: Portrait. Printer: TDLR.
    a. Issued note.   FV   25.00
    s. Specimen.   —   75.00

443   10,000 Pesos   **VF   UNC**
1.3.1995; 1.8.1996; 23.7.1997; 6.1.1998; 23.7.1998; 23.7.1999; 17.12.1999;
1.6.2001. The birds are left to right: greater flamingo, andean condor, green
honeycreeper, andean cock of the rock, blue and yellow macaw, hotzin, scarlet
ibis, yellow-hooded blackbird, metallic green tanager, white pelican, magnificent
frigatebird, keel-billed toucan, baltimore oriole, scarlet macaw, yellow crowned
parrot, red-capped cardinal. Deep brown and black on multicolor underprint.
Youthful woman *Mujer Embera* at center right, native gold statue at right. *EL* omitted from title, *ORO* omitted from value, different signature and titles. Back: Native
birds around antique world map at left center, Santa Maria sailing ship at lower
right. Watermark: Portrait. Printer: IBSFB.
    a. Issued note.   FV   20.00
    s. Specimen.   —   75.00

1995 Commemorative Issue

**#444, 200th Anniversary of Policarpa Salavarrieta *"La Pola"* Replacement
note: Serial # prefix *.**

444   10,000 Pesos   **VF   UNC**
1.7.1995; 1.8.1995. Red-brown and green on multicolor underprint. Policarpa
Salavarrieta at right. Back: Village of Guaduas (ca. 1846) at left center. Printer:
TDLR.
    a. Issued note.   FV   30.00
    s. Specimen.   —   75.00

1996-97, 2000 Issue

445   2000 Pesos   **VF   UNC**
1996-99. Dark olive-green, red-brown and dark brown on multicolor underprint.
General Francisco de Paula Santander at right. Back: Casa de Moneda building,
entrance at left center. Watermark: General Francisco de Paula Santander.
Printer: IBSFB.
    a. 2.4.1996.   FV   6.00
    b. 6.5.1997.   FV   6.00
    c. 6.1.1998.   FV   6.00
    d. 7.8.1998.   FV   6.00
    e. 9.4.1999.   FV   6.00
    s. Specimen.   —   50.00

446   5000 Pesos   **VF   UNC**
2.1.1997. Dark brown and deep blue-green on multicolor underprint. José Asunción Silva and bug at upper right, trees at left and center. Back: Woman, trees and
monument at center. Watermark: Asunción Silva. Printer: IBSFB.
    a. Issued note.   FV   15.00
    s. Specimen.   —   75.00

447   5000 Pesos

1997-99. Deep violet and red-violet on multicolor underprint. José Asunción Silva and bug at upper right, trees at left and center, bank seal at bottom right. Back: Woman, trees and monument at center. Watermark: José Asunción Silva. Printer: IBSFB.

		VF	UNC
a. 12.10.1997.		FV	10.00
b. 2.4.1998.		FV	10.00
c. 23.7.1999.		FV	10.00
d. 12.10.1999.		FV	10.00
s. Specimen.		—	75.00

448   20,000 Pesos

1996-2000. Black, deep green and dark blue on multicolor underprint. Julio Garavito Armero at right. View of the moon at center. Back: Satellite view of earth at center right, moon's surface along bottom, geometric forms in underprint. Watermark: Julio Garavito Armero. Printer: IBSFB.

		VF	UNC
a. 23.7.1996.		FV	25.00
b. 6.1.1998.		FV	25.00
c. 7.8.1998.		FV	25.00
d. 6.5.1999.		FV	25.00
e. 1.5.2000.		FV	25.00
f. 12.10.2000.		FV	25.00
s. Specimen.		—	60.00

449   50,000 Pesos

7.8.2000. Vertical format. Purple, green and light orange on multicolor underprint. Jorge Isaacs at lower center. Maria, character from book, at center. Back: *Hacienda el Paraiso.* Printer: IBSFB.

		VF	UNC
a. Issued note.		FV	50.00
s. Specimen.		—	100

2001 Issue

450   1000 Pesos

2001-05. UV: fibers fluoresce yellow and blue. Car in box yellow, serial #s green. Back: security thread blue, bottom right design green. Brown and orange on multicolor underprint. Crowd at center, Jorge Elíecer Gaitán at right. Back: Gaitán with right arm raised, crowd behind at center. Watermark: Jorge Elíecer Gaitán Printer: IBBR. 140x70mm.

		VF	UNC
a. 7.8.2001.		FV	2.00
b. 27.9.2001.		FV	2.00
c. 17.12.2001.		FV	2.00
d. 7.5.2002.		FV	2.00
e. 30.5.2003.		FV	2.00
f. 16.2.2004.		FV	2.00
g. 17.2.2004.		FV	2.00
h. 2.3.2005.		FV	2.00
i. 3.3.2005		FV	2.00
s. Specimen.		—	50.00

451   2000 Pesos

2000-05. Dark olive-green, red-brown and dark brown on multicolor underprint. General Francisco de Paula Santander at right. Back: Casa de Moneda building, entrance at left center. Watermark: General Francisco de Paula Santander. Printer: IBBR. 140x70mm.

		VF	UNC
a. 12.10.2000.		FV	4.00
b. 23.7.2001.		FV	4.00
c. 12.10.2001.		FV	4.00
d. 11.11.2001.		FV	4.00
e. 8.5.2002.		FV	4.00
f. 13.5.2002.		FV	4.00
g. 2.6.2003.		FV	4.00
h. 18.2.2004.		FV	4.00
i. 19.2.2004. Triangles added at left front for visually impaired.		FV	4.00
j. 7.3.2005.		FV	4.00
s. Specimen.		—	50.00

452 5000 Pesos   VF   UNC

2001-13. UV: security strip fluoresces blue. Value, logo, and design elements at left and right yellow. Deep violet and red-violet on multicolor underprint. José Asunción Silva and bug at upper right, trees at left and center, bank seal at center. Back: Woman, trees and monument at center. Watermark: José Asunción Silva. Printer: IBBR.

	VF	UNC
a. 11.11.2001.	FV	7.50
b. 17.12.2001.	FV	7.50
c. 9.5.2002.	FV	6.00
d. 6.6.2003.	FV	6.00
e. 20.2.2004.	FV	5.00
f. 2.11.2005.	FV	5.00
g. 4.2.2006.	FV	5.00
h. 15.11.2006.	FV	5.00
i. 18.8.2007.	FV	5.00
j. 31.8.2008.	FV	5.00
k. 21.8.2009. Braille 5 added at left near frog.	FV	5.00
l. 31.7.2010.	FV	5.00
m. 1.9.2010.	FV	5.00
n. 20.8.2012.	FV	5.00
o. 31.8.2013.	FV	5.00
s. Specimen.	—	50.00

453 10,000 Pesos   VF   UNC

2001-12. Deep brown and black on multicolor underprint. Youthful woman *Mujer Embera* at center right, native gold statue at right. *EL* omitted from title, *ORO* omitted from value, different signature and titles. Back: Native birds around antique world map at left center, Santa Maria sailing ship at lower right. Watermark: Portrait. 140x70mm.

	VF	UNC
a. 1.6.2001. Printer: IBSFB.	FV	15.00
b. 20.7.2001. Printer: IBBR.	FV	15.00
c. 10.5.2002.	FV	15.00
d. 20.11.2002.	FV	15.00
e. 25.11.2002.	FV	15.00
f. 9.6.2003.	FV	15.00
g. 21.2.2004.	FV	15.00
h. 16.11.2006.	FV	15.00
i. 17.11.2006.	FV	15.00
j. 19.8.2007.	FV	15.00
k. 20.8.2007.	FV	15.00
l. 1.9.2008.	FV	15.00
m. 27.8.2009.	FV	12.00
n. 2.8.2010.	FV	12.00
o. 21.8.2012.	FV	12.00
p. 22.8.2012.	-20.00	12.00
s. Specimen.	—	75.00

454 20,000 Pesos   VF   UNC

2001-09. Black, deep green and dark blue on multicolor underprint. Julio Garavito Armero at right. View of the moon at center. Back: Satellite view of earth at center right, moon's surface along bottom, geometric forms in underprint. Watermark: Julio Garavito Armero. Printer: IBBR.

	VF	UNC
a. 1.6.2001.	FV	25.00
b. 23.7.2001.	FV	25.00
c. 7.8.2001.	FV	25.00
d. 14.5.2002.	FV	25.00
e. 20.11.2002.	FV	25.00
f. 13.6.2003.	FV	25.00
g. 16.6.2003.	FV	25.00
h. 21.9.2004.	FV	25.00
i. 22.9.2004.	FV	25.00
j. 8.3.2005.	FV	25.00
k. 3.11.2005.	FV	25.00
l. 5.2.2006.	FV	25.00
m. 20.11.2006.	FV	20.00
n. 21.11.2006.	FV	20.00
o. 22.11.2006.	FV	20.00
p. 21.8.2007.	FV	20.00
q. 3.9.2008.	FV	20.00
r. 23.8.2009.	FV	20.00
s. Specimen.	—	75.00

455 50,000 Pesos   VF   UNC

2001-13. Vertical format. Purple, green and light orange on multicolor underprint. Jorge Isaacs at lower center. Maria, character from book, at center. Back: *Hacienda el Paraiso*. Printer: IBBR.

	VF	UNC
a. 1.5.2001.	FV	40.00
b. 23.7.2001	FV	40.00
c. 15.5.2002.	FV	40.00
d. 20.6.2003.	FV	37.50
e. 9.3.2005.	FV	37.50
f. 20.7.2005.	FV	37.50
g. 6.2.2006.	FV	37.50
h. 23.11.2006.	FV	37.50
i. 24.11.2006.	FV	37.50
j. 22.8.2007.	FV	37.50
k. 4.9.2008.	FV	37.50
l. 6.9.2008.	FV	37.50
m. 25.8.2009.	FV	37.50
n. 26.8.2009.	FV	37.50
o. 7.9.2013.	FV	37.50
s. Specimen.	—	100

2005 Issue

456 1000 Pesos

2005-. Brown and orange on multicolor underprint. Crown at center. Jorge Elíecer Gaitán at right. Back: Gaitán with right arm raised, crowd behind at center. Watermark: Jorge Elíecer Gaitán. 130x65mm.

	VF	UNC
a. 1.11.2005.	FV	1.50
b. 31.1.2006.	FV	1.50
c. 1.2.2006.	FV	1.50
d. 7.11.2006.	FV	1.50
e. 8.11.2006.	FV	1.00
f. 9.11.2006.	FV	1.00
g. 13.8.2007.	FV	1.00
h. 14.8.2007.	FV	1.00
i. 15.8.2007.	FV	1.00
j. 27.8.2008.	FV	1.00
k. 28.8.2008.	FV	1.00
l. 28.8.2008.	FV	1.00
m. 23.11.2010.	FV	1.00
n. 10.6.2011.	FV	1.00
o. 11.6.2011.	FV	1.00
p. 13.6.2011.	FV	1.00
q. 27.8.2014.	FV	1.00
s. Specimen. Punch hole cancelled.	—	50.00

457 2000 Pesos

2006-. Darf olive-green, red-brown and dark brown on multicolor underprint, General Francisco de Paula Santander at right. Green tint over watermark area. Back: Casa de Moneda building, entrance at left center. Watermark: Francisco de Paula Santander. 130x65mm.

2006-. Darf olive-green, red-brown and dark brown on multicolor underprint. General Francisco de Paula Santander at right. Green tint over watermark area. Back: Casa de Moneda building, entrance at left center. Watermark: Francisco de Paula Santander. 130x65mm.

2006-. Darf olive-green, red-brown and dark brown on multicolor underprint. General Francisco de Paula Santander at right. Green tint over watermark area. Back: Casa de Moneda building, entrance at left center. Watermark: Francisco de Paula Santander. 130x65mm.

	VF	UNC
	FV	2.00
	FV	2.00
a. 2.2.2006.	FV	2.00
b. 3.2.2006.	FV	2.00
c. 10.11.2006.	FV	2.00
d. 14.11.2006.	FV	2.00
e. 20.11.2006.	FV	2.00
f. 16.8.2007.	FV	2.00
g. 17.8.2007.	FV	2.00
h. 29.8.2008.	FV	2.00
i. 30.8.2008.	FV	2.00
j. 19.8.2009.	FV	2.00
k. 20.8.2009.	FV	2.00
l. 22.7.2010.	FV	2.00
m. 28.7.2010.	FV	2.00
n. 29.7.2010.	FV	2.00
o. 25.8.2011.	FV	2.00
p. 15.8.2012.	FV	2.00
q. 17.8.2012.	FV	2.00
r. 28.8.2013.	FV	2.00
s. 29.8.2013.	FV	2.00
t. 29.7.2014.	FV	2.00

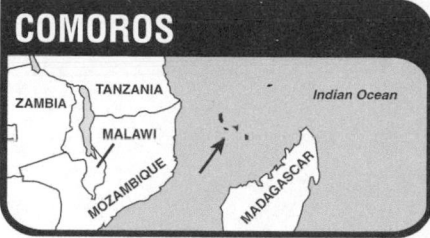

The Union of the Comoros, a volcanic archipelago located in the Mozambique Channel of the Indian Ocean 483 km. northwest of Madagascar, has an area of 2,170 sq. km. and a population of 731,800. Capital: Moroni. The economy of the islands is based on agriculture. There are practically no mineral resources. Vanilla, essence for perfumes, copra and sisal are exported.

Comoros has endured more than 20 coups or attempted coups since gaining independence from France in 1975. In 1997, the islands of Anjouan and Moheli declared independence from Comoros. In 1999, military chief Col. Azali seized power in a bloodless coup, and helped negotiate the 2000 Fomboni Accords power-sharing agreement in which the federal presidency rotates among the three islands, and each island maintains its own local government. Azali won the 2002 Presidential election, and each island in the archipelago elected its own president. Azali stepped down in 2006 and President Sambi took office. Since 2006, Anjouan's President Mohamed Bacar has refused to work effectively with the Union presidency. In 2007, Bacar effected Anjouan's de-facto secession from the Union, refusing to step down in favor of fresh Anjouanais elections when Comoros' other islands held legitimate elections in July. The African Union (AU) initially attempted to resolve the political crisis by applying sanctions and a naval blockade on Anjouan, but in March 2008, AU and Comoran soldiers seized the island. The move was generally welcomed by the island's inhabitants. Its present status is that of a French Territorial Collectivity. Euro coinage and currency circulates there.

RULERS:
French to 1975

MONETARY SYSTEM:
1 Franc = 100 Centimes

REPUBLIC

Banque de Madagascar et des Comores
1960 ND Provisional Issue

2 50 Francs

ND (1960-63). Brown and multicolor. Woman with hat at right. Back: Man.

	VF	UNC
a. Signature titles: *LE CONTROLEUR GAL.* and *LE DIRECTEUR GAL.* ND (1960).	—	—
b. Signature titles: *LE DIRECTEUR GAL. ADJOINT* and *LE PRESIDENT DIRECTEUR GAL.* ND (1963). 2 sign varieties.	30.00	105
s. Specimen.	—	—

3 100 Francs

ND (1960-63). Multicolor. Woman at right, palace of the Queen of Tananariva in background. Back: Woman, boats and animals.

	VF	UNC
a. Signature titles: *LE CONTROLEUR GAL.* and *LE DIRECTEUR GAL.* ND (1960).	60.00	175
b. Signature titles: *LE DIRECTEUR GAL. ADJOINT* and *LE PRESIDENT DIRECTEUR GAL.* ND (1963).	18.00	70.00
s. Specimen.	—	—

4   500 Francs   **VF   UNC**
ND (1960-63). Multicolor. Man with fruit at center.
   a. Signature titles: *LE CONTROLEUR GAL.* and *LE DIRECTEUR GAL.* - old   170   550
      date 30.6.1950; 9.10.1952 (1960).
   b. Signature titles: *LE DIRECTEUR GAL. ADJOINT* and *LE PRESIDENT*   110   380
      DIRECTEUR GAL. ND (1963).

5   1000 Francs   **VF   UNC**
ND (1960-63). Multicolor. Woman and man at left center. Back: Center Ox cart.
   a. Signature titles: *LE CONTROLEUR GAL.* and *LE DIRECTEUR GAL.* - old   220   650
      date 1950-52; 9.10.1952 (1960).
   b. Signature titles: *LE DIRECTEUR GAL. ADJOINT* and *LE PRESIDENT*   130   425
      DIRECTEUR GAL. ND (1963).

6   5000 Francs   **VF   UNC**
ND (1960-63). Multicolor. Portrait Gallieni at upper left, young woman at right.
Back: Huts at left, woman with baby at right.
   a. Signature titles: *LE CONTROLEUR GAL.* and *LE DIRECTEUR GAL.* - old   450   1,000
      date 30.6.1950 (1960).
   b. Signature titles: *LE DIRECTEUR GAL. ADJOINT* and *LE PRESIDENT*   350   850
      DIRECTEUR GAL. ND (1963).
   c. Signature titles: *LE DIRECTEUR GÉNÉRAL* and *LE PRÉSIDENT*   350   850
      DIRECTEUR GAL.

Institut d'Émission des Comores
1976 ND Issue

7   500 Francs   **VF   UNC**
ND (1976). Blue-gray, brown and red on multicolor underprint. Building at center,
young woman wearing a hood at right. Two signature varieties. Back: Two women
at left, boat at right. Watermark: Cresent on Maltese cross.
   a. Issued note.   10.00   40.00
   s. Specimen.   —   50.00

8   1000 Francs   **VF   UNC**
ND (1976). Blue-gray, brown and green on multicolor underprint. Woman at right,
palm trees at water's edge in background. Back: Women. Watermark: Cresent on
Maltese cross.
   a. Issued note.   20.00   85.00
   s. Specimen.   —   60.00

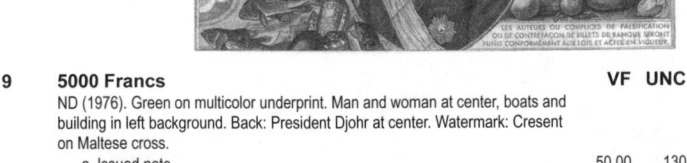

9   5000 Francs   **VF   UNC**
ND (1976). Green on multicolor underprint. Man and woman at center, boats and
building in left background. Back: President Djohr at center. Watermark: Cresent
on Maltese cross.
   a. Issued note.   50.00   130
   s. Specimen.   —   1,200

Banque Centrale des Comores
1984-86 ND Issue

10 500 Francs
ND (1986-). Blue-gray, brown and red on multicolor underprint. Building at center, young woman wearing a hood at right. Two signature varieties. Back: Two women at left, boat at right. Watermark: Maltese cross with cresent.

		VF	UNC
a. Partially engraved. signature titles: *LE DIRECTEUR GÉNÉRAL* and *LE PRÉSIDENT DU CONSEIL D'ADMINISTRATION* (1986).		5.00	20.00
b. Offset. signature titles: *LE GOUVERNEUR* and *PRÉSIDENT DU...* (1994). (2 signature varieties.)		4.00	18.00

11 1000 Francs
ND (1984-). Blue-gray, brown and green on multicolor underprint. Woman at right, palm trees at water's edge in background. Back: Women. Watermark: Maltese cross with cresent.

		VF	UNC
a. Partially engraved. signature titles: *LE DIRECTEUR GÉNÉRAL* and *LE PRÉSIDENT DU CONSEIL D'ADMINISTRATION.* (1986).		15.00	60.00
b. Offset. signature titles: *LE GOUVERNEUR* and *PRÉSIDENT DU...* (1994). (2 signature varieties.)		10.00	30.00

12 5000 Francs
ND (1984-). Engraved. Green on multicolor underprint. Man and woman at center, boats and building in left background. Back: President Djohr at center. Watermark: Maltese cross with cresent.

		VF	UNC
a. Signature titles: *LE DIRECTEUR GÉNÉRAL* and *LE PRÉSIDENT DU CONSEIL D'ADMINISTRATION.*		25.00	125
b. Signature titles: *LE GOVERNEUR* and *LE PRESIDENT...*		20.00	115

1997 ND Issue

13 2500 Francs
ND (1997). Purple and blue on multicolor underprint. Woman wearing colorful scarf at left. Back: Sea turtle at lower left center. Watermark: Four stars below cresent (arms).

	VF	UNC
	10.00	155

14 10,000 Francs
ND (1997). Yellow, brown and blue on multicolor underprint. Two seated women weaving baskets at center. Back: Al-Habib Seyyid Q. Bin Sumeit at left, mosque at center. Watermark: Four stars below cresent (arms).

	VF	UNC
	35.00	185

2005-06 Issue

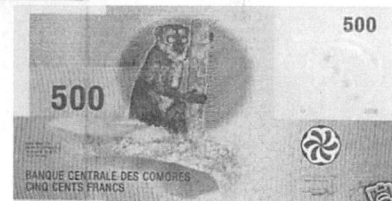

15 500 Francs
2006. Pink, green and multicolor. Lemur at upper center. Back: Orchard. 120x66mm.

	VF	UNC
	FV	8.00

16 1000 Francs
2005. Blue and multicolor. Fish. Back: Man in outrigger canoe. 126x65mm.

	VF	UNC
	FV	9.00

17   2000 Francs   **VF   UNC**
2005. Green and multicolor. Mosque and market scene. Back: Village huts.   FV   11.50
132x65mm.

18   5000 Francs   **VF   UNC**
2006. Purple on lilac and multicolor. Portrait. Back: Tree.   FV   30.50

19   10,000 Francs   **VF   UNC**
2006. Brown, yellow on multicolor underprint. Friday Mosque in Moroni at left,   FV   66.00
al-Habib Seyyid O. bin Sumeit at center. Back: Cananga tree, ylang-ylanf flowers
and turtle. Watermark: Four stars and crescent. 144x73mm.

The Congo Democratic Republic (formerly Zaïre), located in the south-central part of Africa, has an area of 2.345 million sq. km. and a population of 66.51 million. Capital: Kinshasa. The mineral-rich country produces copper, tin, diamonds, gold, zinc, cobalt and uranium.

Established as a Belgian colony in 1908, the Republic of the Congo gained its independence in 1960, but its early years were marred by political and social instability. Col. Joseph Mobutu seized power and declared himself president in a November 1965 coup. He subsequently changed his name - to Mobutu Sese Seko - as well as that of the country - to Zaire. Mobutu retained his position for 32 years through several sham elections, as well as through the use of brutal force. Ethnic strife and civil war, touched off by a massive inflow of refugees in 1994 from fighting in Rwanda and Burundi, led in May 1997 to the toppling of the Mobutu regime by a rebellion backed by Rwanda and Uganda and fronted by Laurent Kabila. He renamed the country the Democratic Republic of the Congo (DRC), but in August 1998 his regime was itself challenged by a second insurrection again backed by Rwanda and Uganda. Troops from Angola, Chad, Namibia, Sudan, and Zimbabwe intervened to support Kabila's regime. A cease-fire was signed in July 1999 by the DRC, Congolese armed rebel groups, Angola, Namibia, Rwanda, Uganda, and Zimbabwe but sporadic fighting continued. Laurent Kabila was assassinated in January 2001 and his son, Joseph Kabila, was named head of state. In October 2002, the new president was successful in negotiating the withdrawal of Rwandan forces occupying eastern Congo; two months later, the Pretoria Accord was signed by all remaining warring parties to end the fighting and establish a government of national unity. A transitional government was set up in July 2003. Joseph Kabila as president and four vice presidents represented the former government, former rebel groups, the political opposition, and civil society. The transitional government held a successful constitutional referendum in December 2005 and elections for the presidency, National Assembly, and provincial legislatures in 2006. Kabila was inaugurated president in December 2006. The National Assembly was installed in September 2006. Its president, Vital Kamerhe, was chosen in December. Provincial assemblies were constituted in early 2007, and elected governors and national senators in January 2007. A change to a Francs-Congolese currency has been considered, but meanwhile "hard" currencies such as U.S. dollars circulate freely.

See also Rwanda, Rwanda-Burundi, and Zaïre.

MONETARY SYSTEM:
1 Franc = 100 Centimes to 1967
1 Zaïre = 100 Makuta, 1967-71
1 Franc = 100 Centimes, 1997-

CONGO (KINSHASA)

République du Congo Conseil Monétaire de la République du Congo

1962-63 Issue

1   100 Francs   **VF   UNC**
1.6.1963-8.7.1963. Green and multicolor. Dam at left. Signature varieties. Back:
Dredging at right.
    a. Issued note.   40.00   160
    s. Specimen. Punch hole cancelled.   85.00   145
    ct. Color trial. Blue on multicolor underprint.   —   175

2   1000 Francs   **VF   UNC**

15.2.1962. Purple on multicolor underprint. Portrait African man at left. Text: *EMIS-SION DU CONSEIL MONÉTAIRE DE LA REPUBLIQUE DU CONGO* in place of watermark. Signature varieties. Back: Waterbuck drinking in stream.

    a. Issued note.   100   525
    s. Specimen.   —   385

5   50 Francs   **VF   UNC**

1.9.1961-1.7.1962. Green. Lion at left, bridge and lake at center right in back-ground. Signature 1. Back: Long building at bottom.

    a. Issued note.   25.00   145
    s. Specimen. Punch hole cancelled.   —   100
    ct. Color trial. Brown on multicolor underprint.   150

6   100 Francs   **VF   UNC**

1.9.1961-1.8.1964. Dark brown on multicolor underprint. J. Kasavubu at left, two crowned cranes at right. Sinature 1. Back: Long building at bottom. Printer: TDLR.

    a. Issued note.   15.00   110
    s. Specimen.   —   00.00

3   5000 Francs   **VF   UNC**

1.12.1963. Gray-green. Portrait African woman at left. Signature varieties. Back: Standing oarsmen.

    a. Issued note.   1,800   —
    s. Specimen. Punch hole cancelled.   —   4,000
    ct. Color trial. Blue on multicolor underprint.   —   4,500

7   500 Francs   **VF   UNC**

15.10.1961; 1.12.1961; 1.1.1962; 1.8.1964. Lilac. Mask at left. Signature 1. Back: Long building at bottom. Watermark: Bird.

    a. Issued note.   40.00   180
    s. Specimen.   —   150

Banque Nationale du Congo
1961 Issue

4   20 Francs   **VF   UNC**

15.11.1961-15.9.1962. Green, blue and brown. Girl seated at right. Signature 1. Back: Stylized tree at center. Watermark: Seated girl. Printer: JEZ.

    a. Issued note.   15.00   80.00
    s. Specimen.   —   80.00

8   1000 Francs   **VF   UNC**

15.10.1961; 15.12.1961; 1.8.1964. Dark blue on multicolor underprint. J. Kasavubu at left, carving at right. Signature 1. Back: Long building at bottom. Watermark: Antelope's head. Printer: TDLR.

    a. Issued note.   30.00   150
    s. Specimen.   —   100

1967 Issue

#9-13 Replacement notes: Serial # prefix ZZ.

9   10 Makuta   **VF   UNC**

2.1.1967; 1.9.1968; 14.1.1970; 21.1.1970. Blue on olive-green and multicolor underprint. Stadium at left, Mobutu at right. Signature 1. Back: Long building. Printer: TDLR.

    a. Issued note.   12.50   60.00
    s. Specimen.   —   40.00

10   20 Makuta   **VF   UNC**

1967-70. Black on green, blue and multicolor underprint. Man with flag at center, P. Lumumba at right. Signature varieties. Back: People in long boat at left center. Watermark: Antelope's head. Printer: TDLR.

    a. Signature 1. 24.11.1967; 21.1.1970.   32.50   140
    b. Signature 2. 1.10.1970.   30.00   140
    s. Specimen. 21.1.1970.   —   170

11   50 Makuta   **VF   UNC**

1967-70. Red on olive-green and multicolor underprint. Stadium at center left, Mobutu at right. Signature varieties. Back: Gathering coconuts. Printer: TDLR.

    a. Signature 1. 2.1.1967; 1.9.1968; 21.1.1970.   30.00   145
    b. Signature 2. 1.10.1970.   30.00   145
    s1. Specimen. 1.9.1968.   —   100
    s2. Specimen. 21.1.1970.   —   100

12   1 Zaïre = 100 Makuta   **VF   UNC**

1967-70. Brown and green on multicolor underprint. Stadium at left, Mobutu at right. Signature varieties. Back: Mobutu's "time to work" to gathering of people at left center. Watermark: Antelope's head. Printer: TDLR.

    a. Signature 1. 2.1.1967; 24.11.1967; 1.9.1968.   25.00   100
    b. Signature 2. 21.1.1970; 1.10.1970.   25.00   100
    s1. Specimen. 24.11.1967.   —   100
    s2. Specimen. 1.9.1968.   —   100
    s3. Specimen. 21.1.1970. Red overprint: SPECIMEN on both sides. —   165
    s4. Specimen. 1.10.1970. Overprint: *SPECIMEN* in red on both sides. —   165

13   5 Zaïres = 500 Makuta   **VF   UNC**

1967-70. Green and multicolor. Mobutu at right. Signature varieties. Back: Long building at left center. Watermark: Antelope's head. Printer: TDLR.

    a. Signature 1 above title: *LE GOUVERNEUR*. Green date. 2.1.1967; 24.6.1967. 95.00   385
    b. Signature 2 below title: *LE GOUVERNEUR*. Black date. 2.1.1967; 24.11.1967; 1.9.1968; 21.1.1970. 75.00   285
    s1. Specimen. 2.1.1967.   —   200
    s2. Specimen. 1.9.1968.   —   200
    s3. Specimen. 21.1.1970.   —   200

1971 Issue

#14 and 15 Replacement notes: Serial # suffix Z.

14   5 Zaïres   **VF   UNC**

24.11.1971. Green, black and multicolor. Portrait Mobuta at left, leopard at lower right facing right. Signature 2. Back: Carving at left center, hydroelectric dam at center right. Watermark: Mobuta. Printer: G&D.

    a. Issued note.   60.00   300
    s. Specimen. Red overprint: SPECIMEN on each side.   —   175

15   10 Zaïres   **VF   UNC**

30.6.1971. Blue, brown and multicolor. Portrait Mobuta at left, leopard at lower right facing right. Signature 2. Back: Arms with yellow star. Watermark: Mobuta. Printer: G&D.

    a. Issued note.   60.00   300
    s. Specimen. Red overprint: SPECIMEN on each side.   —   175

DEMOCRATIC REPUBLIC

Banque Centrale du Congo

1997 Issue

80   1 Centime   **VF   UNC**

1.11.1997. UV: fibers fluoresce yellow and blue, upper right serial # red. Deep olive-green, violet and dark brown on multicolor underprint. Woman harvesting coffee beans at left. Bank monogram at center. Back: Nyiragongo volcano erupting at right. Watermark: Single Okapi head or multiple heads repeated vertically. Printer: ATB.

    a. Issued note.   FV   1.00
    s. Specimen. Overprint: *SPECIMEN* in red on both sides.   —   12.50

81   5 Centimes   **VF   UNC**
1.11.1997. UV: fibers fluoresce yellow and blue, upper right serial # red. Purple on multicolor underprint. Suku mask at left. Bank monogram at center. Back: Zande Harp at center right. Watermark: Single Okapi head or multiple heads repeated vertically. Printer: G&D.
a. Issued note.   FV   1.00
s. Specimen. Overprint: *SPECIMEN* in red on both sides.   —   15.00

82   10 Centimes   **VF   UNC**
1.11.1997. UV: fibers fluoresce blue, upper right serial # red, security strip interrupted blue. Red-violet and dark brown on multicolor underprint. Pende mask at left. Bank monogram at center. Back: Pende dancers at center right. Watermark: Single Okapi head or multiple heads repeated vertically. Printer: ATB.
a. Issued note.   FV   1.25
s. Specimen. Overprint: *SPECIMEN* in red on both sides.   —   17.50

83   20 Centimes   **VF   UNC**
1.11.1997. Blue-green and black on multicolor underprint. Waterbuck at left. Bank monogram at center. Back: Waterbuck herd by large tree at center right. Watermark: Single Okapi head or multiple heads repeated vertically. Printer: ATB.
a. Issued note.   FV   1.25
s. Specimen. Overprint: *SPECIMEN* in red on both sides.   —   20.00

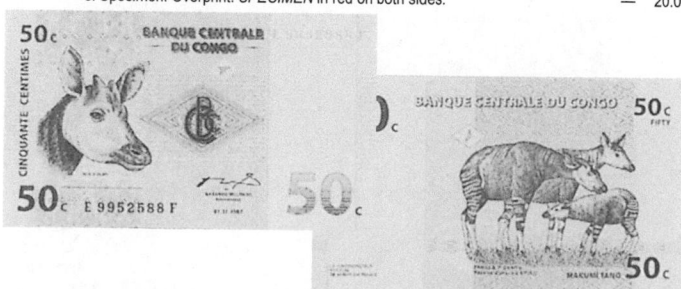

84   50 Centimes   **VF   UNC**
1.11.1997. UV: fibers fluoresce orange, upper right serial # red, security strip interrupted blue. Dark brown and brown on multicolor underprint. Okapi's head at left. Bank monogram at center. Back: Family of Okapis at left center. Watermark: Single Okapi head or multiple heads repeated vertically. Printer: G&D.
a. Issued note.   FV   1.75
s. Specimen.   —   15.00
84A   50 Centimes   **VF   UNC**
1.11.1997. Serial # prefix: E; suffix: A-E, T. Dark brown and brown on multicolor underprint. Okapi's head at left. Bank monogram at center. Back: Family of Okapis at left center. Watermark: Single Okapi head or multiple heads repeated vertically. Printer: ATB.   FV   1.75

85   1 Franc   **VF   UNC**
1.11.1997 (1998). Deep purple and blue-violet on multicolor underprint. Large mining complex at left. Bank monogram at center. Back: Prisoners Lumumba and two companions at center right. Watermark: Single Okapi head or multiple heads repeated vertically. Printer: G&D.
a. Issued note.   35.00   100
s. Specimen. Red overprint: SPECIMEN on each side.   —   40.00

86   5 Francs   **VF   UNC**
1.11.1997 (1998). Purple and black on multicolor underprint. White rhinoceros at left. Bank monogram at center. Back: Kamwanga Falls at center right. Watermark: Single Okapi head or multiple heads repeated vertically. Printer: NBBPW.
a. Issued note.   FV   65.00
s. Specimen. Red overprint: SPECIMEN on each side.   —   20.00
86A   5 Francs   **VF   UNC**
1.11.1997 (1998). Purple and black on multicolor underprint. White rhinoceros at left. Bank monogram at center. Back: Kamwanga Falls at center right. Watermark: Single Okapi head or multiple heads repeated vertically. Printer: HdM.   FV   65.00

87   10 Francs   **VF   UNC**
1.11.1997 (1998). Serial # prefix: *H*; suffix: *A*. Olive-brown, olive-green and deep blue-green on multicolor underprint. *Apui-tete Chef Luba* carving of a couple at left. Bank monogram at center. Back: *Coupe en Bois Luba* carving at right. Watermark: Single Okapi head or multiple heads repeated vertically. Printer: NBBPW.
a. Issued note.   4.00   15.00
s. Specimen. Overprint: *SPECIMEN* in red on both sides.   —   22.50
87A   10 Francs   **VF   UNC**
1.11.1997. Serial # prefix: H; suffix: B-E. Olive-brown, olive-green and deep blue-green on multicolor underprint. Apui-tete Chef Luba" carving of a couple at left. Bank monogram at center. Back: Coupe en Bois Luba" carving at right. Watermark: Single Okapi head or multiple heads repeated vertically. Printer: G&D.   5.00   17.50
87B   10 Francs   **VF   UNC**
1.11.1997. Olive-brown, olive-green and deep blue-green on multicolor underprint. Apui-tete Chef Luba" carving of a couple at left. Bank monogram at center. Back: Coupe en Bois Luba" carving at right. Watermark: Single Okapi head or multiple heads repeated vertically. Printer: HdM.   FV   15.00

88   20 Francs   VF   UNC
1.11.1997 (1998). Brown-orange and red-orange on multicolor underprint. Male lion's head at left. Bank monogram at center. Back: Lioness lying with two cubs at center right. Watermark: Single Okapi head or multiple heads repeated vertically. Printer: NBBPW.
   a. Issued note.   5.00   20.00
   s. Specimen.   —   17.50

88A   20 Francs   VF   UNC
1.11.1997 (1998). Brown-orange and red-orange on multicolor underprint. Male lion's head at left. Bank monogram at center. Back: Lioness lying with two cubs at center right. Watermark: Single Okapi head or multiple heads repeated vertically. Printer: HdM.   4.00   15.00

89   50 Francs   VF   UNC
1.11.1997 (1998). Olive-green. Head at left. Bank monogram at center. Back: Village scene. Watermark: Single Okapi head or multiple heads repeated vertically. Printer: NBBPW.
   a. Issued note.   10.00   50.00
   s. Specimen. Overprint: *SPECIMEN* in red on both sides.   —   30.00

90   100 Francs   VF   UNC
1.11.1997 (1998). Brown. Elephant at left. Bank monogram at center. Back: Dam. Watermark: Single Okapi head or multiple heads repeated vertically. Printer: NBBPW.
   a. Issued note.   17.50   90.00
   s. Specimen.   —   30.00

90A   100 Francs   VF   UNC
1.11.1997. Brown. Elephant at left. Bank monogram at center. Back: Dam. Watermark: Single Okapi head or multiple heads repeated vertically. Printer: HDM.   FV   90.00

2000 Issue

91   50 Francs   VF   UNC
4.1.2000. Lilac brown. Head at left. Bank monogram at center. Back: Village scene. Watermark: Single Okapi head or multiple heads repeated vertically. Printer: G&D.
   a. Issued note.   FV   10.00
   s. Specimen.   —   15.00

91A   50 Francs   VF   UNC
4.1.2000. Lilac brown. Head at left. Bank monogram at center. Back: Village scene. Watermark: Single Okapi head or multiple heads repeated vertically. Printer: HDM.   FV   10.00

92   100 Francs   VF   UNC
4.1.2000. Slate blue. Elephant at left. Bank monogram at center. Back: Dam. Watermark: Single Okapi head or multiple heads repeated vertically. Printer: G&D.
   a. Issued note.   FV   15.00
   s. Specimen.   —   10.00

92A   100 Francs   VF   UNC
4.1.2000. Slate blue. Elephant at left. Bank monogram at center. Back: Dam. Watermark: Single Okapi head or multiple heads repeated vertically. Printer: HdMZ.   FV   15.00

2003 Issue

93   10 Francs   VF   UNC
30.6.2003. Serial # prefix: *H*; suffix: *A*. Brown and red on orange and blue multicolor underprint. *Apui-tete Chef Luba* carving of a couple at left. Bank monogram at center. Back: *Coupe en Bois Luba* carving at right. Watermark: Single Okapi head or multiple heads repeated vertically. Printer: G&D.
   a. Issued note.   FV   3.00
   s. Specimen.   —   10.00

94   20 Francs   VF   UNC
30.6.2003. Blue-green on green multicolor underprint. Male lion's head at left. Back: Lioness lying with two cubs at center right. Printer: HdM-B.O.C.
   a. Issued note.   FV   5.00
   s. Specimen.   —   10.00

94A   20 Francs   VF   UNC
30.6.2003. Blue-green on green multicolor underprint. Male lion's head at left. Back: Lioness lying with two cubs at center right. Printer: G&D.   FV   6.00

95 200 Francs VF UNC
30.6.2000 (2003). Lilac and olive green on multicolor underprint. Two farmers at left. Back: Four men working on logs. Printer: G&D.
  a1. Issued note. FV 6.00
  s. Specimen. — 10.00

95A 200 Francs VF UNC
30.6.2000 (2006). Like #95. Lilac and olive green on multicolor underprint. Two farmers at left. Back: Four men working on logs. Printer: HdM. -20.00 12.00

96 500 Francs VF UNC
4.1.2002 (2004). Blue on multicolor underprint. Miners and diamond at left. 3 diamonds at right. Printer: G&D.
  a. Issued note. FV 12.00
  s. Specimen. — 10.00
96A 500 Francs VF UNC
4.1.2002 (2004). Like #96, but without 3 diamonds on front. Blue on multicolor underprint. Miners and diamond at left. Printer: G&D. -20.00 12.00

2007 Issue

97 50 Francs VF UNC
31.7.2007. Serial # prefix KA or KB, suffix A. Printer: G&D.
  a. Issued note. FV 5.00
  s. Specimen. — 15.00

97A 50 Francs VF UNC
30.6.2013. Like #97. Serial # prefix KA or KB, suffix A. Printer: HdM. FV 5.00
98 100 Francs VF UNC
31.7.2007. Serial # prefix MA, suffix T-X. Printer: HdM.
  a. Issued note. FV 5.00
  s. Specimen. — 15.00
98A 100 Francs VF UNC
31.7.2007. Like #98. Serial # prefix MA, suffix T-X. Printer: G&D. FV 5.00

99 200 Francs VF UNC
31.7.2007. Serial # prefix N, suffix W. Printer: G&D. 162x70mm.
  a. Issued note. FV 5.00
  s. Specimen. — 15.00

2010-2012 Issue

100 500 Francs VF UNC
30.6.2010. Light and dark green. Port of Matadi at right center. Back: Kinsuka bridge. 50th Anniversary of Independence logo at lower right. Printer: G&D. 151x70mm.
  a. Issued note. FV 5.00
  s. Specimen. — 15.00

101 1000 Francs VF UNC
2.2.2005 (2012); 30.6.2013. Green and gray. Two okapi at center, Kanioka carved box at right two seated human figures and two lizards on lid at right. Back: Field of corn, parrot on branch at center. Watermark: Okapi head. 141x72mm.
  a. 2.2.2005. Signature Jean-Claude Masangu Mulongo. FV 5.00
  b. 30.6.2013. Signature Deogratias Mutombo Mwana Nyembo. FV 5.00
  s. Specimen. — 15.00

102 5000 Francs VF UNC

2.2.2005 (2012); 30.6.2013. Brown and orange-brown. Zebras at center, Hemba statuette at right. Back: Food bundles and two Congo Peafowl birds. Watermark: Okapi head. 146x72mm.

    a. 2.2.2005. Signature Jean-Claude Masangu Mulongo. FV 8.00
    b. 30.6.2013. Signature Deogratias Mutombo Mwana Nyembo. FV 8.00
    s. Specimen. — 15.00

103 10000 Francs VF UNC

18.2.2006 (2012); 30.6.2013. Lilac, violet and gray. Two water buffalo and carved statuette. Back: Trees, bird on branch. 151x70mm.

    a. 18.2.2006. Signature Jean-Claude Masangu Mulongo. FV 15.00
    b. 30.6.2013. Signature Deogratias Mutombo Mwana Nyembo. FV 15.00
    s. Specimen. — 15.00

104 20000 Francs VF UNC

2.18.2006 (2012). Yellow and brown. Two giraffes and carved head. Back: Palm trees, date clusters, two gray crowned crane (Balearica regulorum) birds. Watermark: Leopard head. 157x72mm.

    a. 18.2.2006. SIgnature Jean-Claude Masangu Mulongo. FV 55.00
    s. Specimen. — 15.00

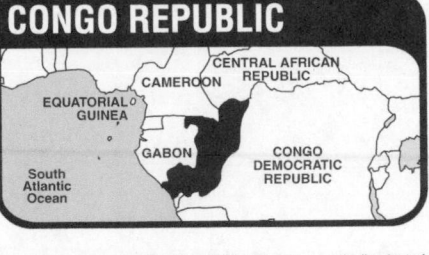

CONGO REPUBLIC

The Republic of the Congo is located on the equator in west-central Africa, has an area of 342,000 sq. km. and a population of 3.90 million. Capital: Brazzaville. Agriculture forestry, mining, and food processing are the principal industries. Timber, industrial diamonds, potash, peanuts, and cocoa beans are exported.

Upon independence in 1960, the former French region of Middle Congo became the Republic of the Congo. A quarter century of experimentation with Marxism was abandoned in 1990 and a democratically elected government took office in 1992. A brief civil war in 1997 restored former Marxist President Denis SASSOU-NGUESSO, and ushered in a period of ethnic and political unrest. Southern-based rebel groups agreed to a final peace accord in March 2003, but the calm is tenuous and refugees continue to present a humanitarian crisis. The Republic of Congo was once one of Africa's largest petroleum producers, but with declining production it will need new offshore oil finds to sustain its oil earnings over the long term.

RULERS:
    French to 1960

MONETARY SYSTEM:
    1 Franc = 100 Centimes

SIGNATURE VARIETIES:
    Refer to introduction of Central African States.

RÉPUBLIQUE POPULAIRE DU CONGO

Banque Centrale

1971 Issue

1 10,000 Francs VF UNC

ND (1971). Multicolor. Young Congolese woman at left, people marching with sign at center. Signature 1. Back: Statue at left and right, tractor plowing at center. 1,000 2,750

Banque des États de l'Afrique Centrale

1974 ND Issue

2 500 Francs VF UNC

ND (1974)-1983. Lilac-brown and multicolor. Woman at left, river scene at center. Back: Mask at left, students and chemical testing at center, statue at right.

    a. Signature titles: *LE DIRECTEUR GENERAL* and *UN CENSEUR*. Engraved. 15.00 50.00
        Signature 5. ND (1974).
    b. Signature titles: *LE GOUVERNEUR* and *UN CENSEUR*. Lithographed. 25.00 90.00
        Signature 10. 1.4.1978.
    c. Titles as b. signature 10; 1.7.1980. 7.50 25.00
    d. Titles as b. signature 12. 1.6.1981; 1.1.1982; 1.1.1983; 1.6.1984. 6.00 25.00

3   1000 Francs

ND (1974)-1984. Blue and multicolor. Industrial plant at center, man at right. Back: Mask at left, trains, planes and bridge at center, statue at right.

	VF	UNC
a. Signature titles: *LE DIRECTEUR GENERAL* and *UN CENSEUR*. Engraved. watermark: Antelope head in half profile. Signature 3. ND (1974).	40.00	200
b. Like a. signature 5.	12.50	75.00
c. Signature titles: *LE DIRECTEUR GENERAL* and *UN CENSEUR*. Litho-graphed. watermark: Antelope head in profile. Signature 8. ND (1978).	12.50	50.00
d. Signature titles: *LE GOUVERNEUR* and *UN CENSEUR*. Lithographed. watermark: like b. Signature 10. 1.4.1978.	10.00	40.00
e. Titles as d. signature 12; 1.6.1981; 1.1.1982; 1.1.1983; 1.6.1984.	8.00	35.00

4   5000 Francs

ND (1974; 1978). Brown. Man at left. Back: Mask at left, buildings at center, statue at right.

	VF	UNC
a. Signature titles: *LE DIRECTEUR GENERAL* and *UN CENSEUR*. Signature 3. ND (1974).	100	450
b. Like a. signature 5.	75.00	300
c. Signature titles: *LE GOUVERNEUR* and *UN CENSEUR*. Signature 11; 12. ND (1978).	50.00	250

5   10,000 Francs

ND (1974-81). Multicolor. Young Congolese women at left, people marching with sign at center. Signature 1. Back: Statue at left and right, tractor plowing at center, new bank name.

	VF	UNC
a. Signature titles: *LE DIRECTEUR GENERAL* and *UN CENSEUR*. Signature 5; 7. ND (1974; 1977).	125	500
b. Signature titles: *LE GOUVERNEUR* and *UN CENSEUR*. Signature 11; 12. ND (1978; 1981).	100	400

1983-84 ND Issue

6   5000 Francs

ND (1984; 1991). Brown and multicolor. Mask at left, woman with bundle of fronds at right. Back: Plowing and mine ore conveyor.

	VF	UNC
a. Signature 12. (1984).	50.00	200
b. Signature 15. (1991).	40.00	150

7   10,000 Francs

ND (1983). Brown, green and multicolor. Stylized antelope heads at left, woman at right. Signature 12. Back: Loading fruit onto truck at left.

	VF	UNC
	50.00	200

1985-87 Issues

Note: For issues w/similar back designs see Cameroun Republic, Central African Republic, Chad and Gabon.

8   500 Francs

1985-91. Brown on multicolor underprint. Statue at left center, jug at center. Signature titles: *LE GOUVERNEUR* and *UN CENSEUR*. Back: Man carving mask at left center. Watermark: Statue.

	VF	UNC
a. Signature 12. 1.1.1985; 1.1.1987; 1.1.1989.	4.00	15.00
b. Signature 12. 1.1.1988.	—	—
c. Signature 13. 1.1.1990.	4.00	12.50
d. Signature 15. 1.1.1991.	4.00	12.50

1985-87 Issues

Note: For issues w/similar back designs see Cameroun Republic, Central African Republic, Chad and Gabon.

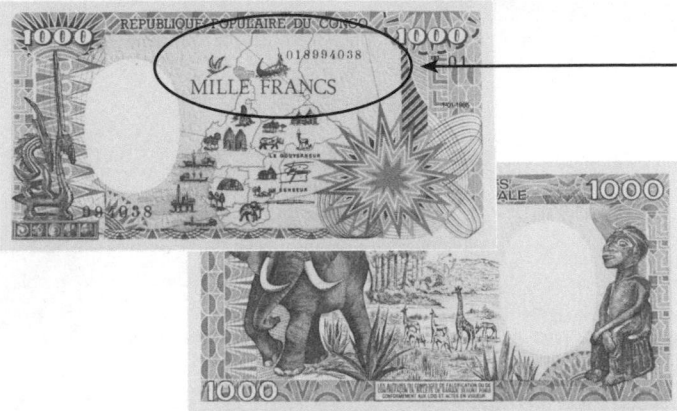

9   1000 Francs

1.1.1985. Dull blue-violet on multicolor underprint. Animal carving at lower left, map of 6 member states at center. Unfinished map of Chad at upper center. Signature Titles: *LE GOUVERNEUR* and *UN CENSEUR*. Signature 12. Back: Elephant at left, animals at center, carving at right. Watermark: Animal carving.

VF	UNC
10.00	35.00

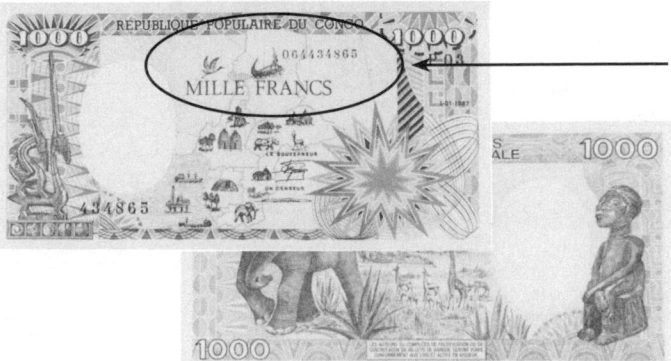

10   1000 Francs

1987-91. Dull blue-violet on multicolor underprint. Animal carving at lower left, map of 6 member states at center. Completed map of Chad at upper center. Signature Titles: *LE GOUVERNEUR* and *UN CENSEUR*. Signature 12. Back: Elephant at left, animals at center, carving at right. Watermark: Animal carving.

	VF	UNC
a. Signature 12. 1.1.1987; 1.1.1988; 1.1.1989.	6.00	25.00
b. Signature 13. 1.1.1990.	5.00	20.00
c. Signature 15. 1.1.1991.	5.00	20.00

RÉPUBLIQUE DU CONGO

Banque des États de l'Afrique Centrale
1992 Issue

11   1000 Francs

1.1.1992. Dull blue-violet on multicolor underprint. Animal carving at lower left, map of 6 member states at center. Unfinished map of Chad at upper center. Signature Titles: *LE GOUVERNEUR* and *UN CENSEUR*. Signature 15. Back: Elephant at left, animals at center, carving at right, new country name.

VF	UNC
5.00	17.50

1992 ND Issue

12   5000 Francs

ND (1992). Black text and brown on pale yellow and multicolor underprint. African mask at left, woman carrying bundle of cane at right. Signature 15. Back: African string instrument at far left, farm tractor plowing at left center, mineshaft cable ore bucket lift at right. Watermark: African mask.

VF	UNC
25.00	100

13   10,000 Francs

ND (1992). Greenish-black text, brown on pale green and multicolor underprint. Artistic antelope masks at left, woman's head at right. Signature 15. Back: Loading produce truck with bananas at left. Watermark: Woman's head.

VF	UNC
40.00	150

For later issues, see Central African States.

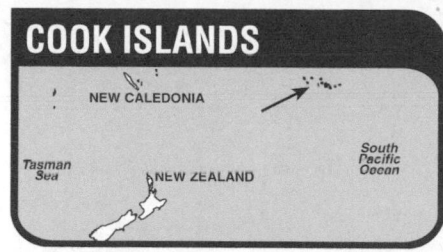

COOK ISLANDS

Cook Islands, a political dependency of New Zealand consisting of 15 islands located in the South Pacific Ocean about 3,218 km. northeast of New Zealand, has an area of 236.7 sq. km. and a population of 12,270. Capital: Avarua. The United States claims the islands of Danger, Manahiki, Penrhyn and Rakahanga atolls. Citrus, canned fruits and juices, copra, clothing, jewelry and mother-of-pearl shell are exported.

Named after Captain Cook, who sighted them in 1770, the islands became a British protectorate in 1888. By 1900, administrative control was transferred to New Zealand; in 1965, residents chose self-government in free association with New Zealand. The emigration of skilled workers to New Zealand and government deficits are continuing problems.

Note: In June 1995 the Government of the Cook Islands began redeeming all 10, 20 and 50 dollar notes in exchange for New Zealand currency while most coins originally intended for circulation along with their 3 dollar notes will remain in use.

RULERS:
New Zealand, 1901-

MONETARY SYSTEM:
1 Shilling = 12 Pence
1 Pound = 20 Shillings, to 1967
1 Dollar = 100 Cents, 1967-

NEW ZEALAND ADMINISTRATION

Government of the Cook Islands

1987 ND Issue

3   3 Dollars   VF   UNC
ND (1987). Deep green, blue and black on multicolor underprint. Ina and the shark at left. Back: Fishing canoe and statue of the god of Te-Rongo.
    a. Issued note.   3.00   6.50
    s. Specimen. Overprint: SPECIMEN on each side.   —   40.00

4   10 Dollars   VF   UNC
ND (1987). Violet-brown, blue and black on multicolor underprint. Ina and the shark at left. Back: Pantheon of gods.
    a. Issued note.   8.50   17.50
    s. Specimen. Overprint: SPECIMEN on each side.   —   40.00

5   20 Dollars   VF   UNC
ND (1987). Blue, black and purple on multicolor underprint. Ina and the shark at left. Back: Conch shell, turtle shell and drum.
    a. Signature T. Davis.   17.50   37.50
    b. Signature M. J. Fleming   17.50   35.00
    s. Specimen. Overprint: SPECIMEN on each side.   —   40.00

1992 Commemorative Issue

#6, 6th Festival of Pacific Arts, Rarotonga, Oct. 16-27, 1992

6   3 Dollars   VF   UNC
Oct. 1992. Black commemorative text overprint at left on back of #3.   3.00   6.00

1992 ND Issue

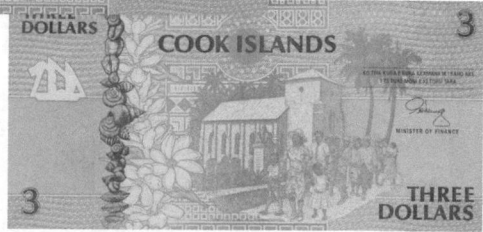

7   3 Dollars   VF   UNC
ND (1992). UV: center design fluoresces yellow. Back: value and rectangles yellow, serial #s orange. Lilac and green on multicolor underprint. Worshipers at church with cemetery at center. Back: AITUTAKI at upper center, local drummers at left, dancers at center, blue lorikeet and fish a Watermark: Sea turtle.
    a. Issued note.   FV   6.00
    s. Specimen. Red overprint: SPECIMEN on each side.   —   50.00

8 10 Dollars   **VF UNC**
ND (1992). Green and olive on multicolor underprint. Worshippers at church with
cemetery at center. Back: Cook Islands Fruit Dove. *RAROTONGA* above hillside
gathering. Watermark: Sea turtle.

a. Issued note.	FV	12.50
s. Specimen. Red overprint: SPECIMEN on each side.	—	50.00

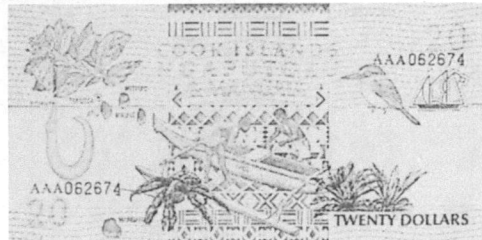

9 20 Dollars   **VF UNC**
ND (1992). Brown-orange and olive on multicolor underprint. Worshippers at
church with cemetery at center. Back: *NGAPUTORU & MANGAIA* above two
islanders with canoe at center. Mangaia kingfisher at right. Watermark: Sea turtle.

a. Issued note.	FV	22.50
s. Specimen. Red overprint: SPECIMEN on each side.	—	50.00

10 50 Dollars   **VF UNC**
ND (1992). Blue and green on multicolor underprint. Worshippers at church with
cemetery at center. Back: Three islanders in canoe at left, *NORTHERN GROUP*
above two seated women weaving at center, s Watermark: Sea turtle.

a. Issued note.	FV	55.00
s. Specimen. Red overprint: SPECIMEN on each side.	—	50.00

COLLECTOR SERIES
Government of the Cook Islands
1987 ND Issue

CS1 ND (1987) 3-20 Dollars   **VF UNC**
#3-5 with matched serial # in special pack.   0.00   0.00

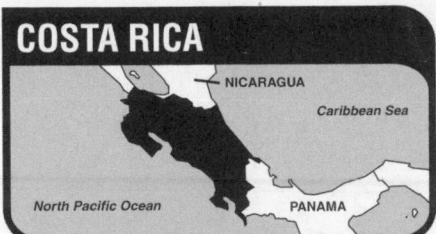

COSTA RICA

The Republic of Costa Rica,
located in southern Central America
between Nicaragua and Panama,
has an area of 51,100 sq. km. and
a population of 4.19 million. Capital:
San Jose. Agriculture predominates;
coffee, bananas, beef and sugar contribute heavily to the country's export
earnings.

Although explored by the Spanish early in the 16th century, initial
attempts at colonizing Costa Rica
proved unsuccessful due to a combination of factors, including: disease from mosquito-infested swamps, brutal heat, resistance by natives, and pirate raids. It was not until 1563 that a permanent settlement of Cartago
was established in the cooler, fertile central highlands. The area remained a colony for some two and a half
centuries. In 1821, Costa Rica became one of several Central American provinces that jointly declared their
independence from Spain. Two years later it joined the United Provinces of Central America, but this federation
disintegrated in 1838, at which time Costa Rica proclaimed its sovereignty and independence. Since the late
19th century, only two brief periods of violence have marred the country's democratic development. Although
it still maintains a large agricultural sector, Costa Rica has expanded its economy to include strong technology
and tourism industries. The standard of living is relatively high. Land ownership is widespread.

MONETARY SYSTEM:
    1 Peso = 100 Centavos to 1896
    1 Colon = 100 Centimos

REPUBLIC
Banco Central de Costa Rica
1951; 1952 Issue - Series A

220 5 Colones   **VF UNC**
1951-58. Green on multicolor underprint. Portrait B. Carillo at right. Back: Coffee
worker. Printer: ABNC.

a. *POR* (for) added to left of signature title at right. 20.11.1952.	15.00	66.00
b. Without signature title changes. 2.7.1952-6.8.1958.	15.00	60.00
c. Signature title: *SUB-GERENTE* overprint at right. 11.7.1956.	15.00	50.00
d. *POR* added to left of signature title at left. 12.9.1951; 26.5.1954.	15.00	50.00
s. Specimen. Punch hole cancelled.	—	150

221 10 Colones   **VF UNC**
1951-62. Blue on multicolor underprint. Portrait A. Echeverria at center. Back:
Ox-cart at center. Printer: W&S.

a. *POR* added to left of sign title at left. 24.10.1951; 8.11.1951; 19.11.1951; 5.12.1951; 29.10.1952.	25.00	120
b. *POR* added to both signature titles. 28.11.1951.	25.00	100
c. Without *POR* title changes. 2.7.1952; 28.10.1953-27.6.1962.	25.00	100
d. *POR* added to left of signature title at right. 20.11.1952.	25.00	100

222 20 Colones

1952-64. Red on multicolor underprint. Portrait C. Picado at center. Back: University building at center. Printer: W&S.

	VF	UNC
a. Date at left center, without signature title changes. 26.2.1952; 11.6.1952; 11.8.1954; 14.10.1955; 13.2.1957; 10.12.62.	50.00	200
b. Signature title: *SUB-GERENTE* overprint at right. 20.4.1955	50.00	175
c. Date at lower left 7.11.1957-9.9.1964.	50.00	175
d. *POR* added at left of signature title at left. 25.3.1953; 25.2.1954.	50.00	175

223 50 Colones

1952-64. Olive on multicolor underprint. Portrait right. F. Guardia at center. Back: National Library at center. Printer: W&S.

	VF	UNC
a. 10.6.1952-25.11.1959.	50.00	225
b. 14.9.1960-9.9.1964.	45.00	200

224 100 Colones

1952-60. Black on multicolor underprint. Portrait J. R. Mora at center. Back: Statue of J. Santamaria at center.

	VF	UNC
a. Without signature title changes: 11.6.1952-29.4.1960.	35.00	240
b. Signature title: *SUB-GERENTE* overprint at right. 27.3.1957.	35.00	200

225 500 Colones

1951-77. Purple on multicolor underprint. Portrait M. M. Gutiérrez at right. Back: National Theater at center. Printer: ABNC.

	VF	UNC
a. 10.10.1951-6.5.1969.	300	850
b. 7.4.1970-26.4.1977.	250	500
s. Specimen. Punch hole cancelled.	—	1,000

226 1000 Colones

1952-74. Red on multicolor underprint. Portrait J. Pena at left. Back: Central and National Bank at center. Printer: ABNC.

	VF	UNC
a. 11.6.1952-6.10.1959.	500	1,350
b. 25.4.1962-6.5.1969.	350	850
c. 7.4.1970-12.6.1974.	150	300
s. Specimen. Punch hole cancelled.	—	600

1958 Issue

227 5 Colones

29.10.1958-8.11.1962. Green on multicolor underprint. Portrait B. Carrillo at center. Series B. Back: Coffee worker at center. Printer: W&S.

VF	UNC
15.00	50.00

1963-70 Issues

228 5 Colones

3.10.1963-29.5.1967. Green on multicolor underprint. Portrait B. Carrillo at center. Series C. Back: Coffee worker at center. Printer: TDLR.

	VF	UNC
a. Issued note.	10.00	30.00
s. Specimen. Overprint: *MUESTRA* twice.	—	—

229 10 Colones

19.9.1962-9.10.1967. Blue on multicolor underprint. Portrait Echeverria at center. Series B. Back: Ox-cart at center. Printer: TDLR.

VF	UNC
20.00	60.00

230   10 Colones

1969-70; ND. Blue on multicolor underprint. Portrait right. Facio Brenes at right.
Series C. Back: Banco Central building at center. Printer: ABNC.

	VF	UNC
a. 4.3.1969; 17.6.1969.	8.50	40.00
b. 30.6.1970.	6.00	30.00
s. Specimen. overprint *MUESTRA*. Punch hole cancelled.	—	—
x. Without date or signature	—	—

Note: It is reported that 10,000 pieces of #230x mistakenly reached circulation.

231   20 Colones

11.11.1964-30.6.1970. Brown on multicolor underprint. Portrait Picado at center.
Series B. Back: University building at center. Printer: TDLR.

	VF	UNC
a. Issued note.	15.00	60.00
s. Specimen.	—	—

232   50 Colones

9.6.1965-30.6.1970. Greenish-brown on multicolor underprint. Portrait Guardia at
center. Series B. Back: National Library at center. Printer: TDLR.

	VF	UNC
	30.00	125

233   100 Colones

1961-66. Black on multicolor underprint. Portrait J. R. Mora at center. Series B.
Back: Statue of J. Santamaría at center. Printer: TDLR.

	VF	UNC
a. Brown underprint. 18.10.1961-3.12.1964.	40.00	150
b. Olive underprint. and with security thread. 9.6.1965; 14.12.1965; 27.4.1966.	30.00	150

234   100 Colones

29.8.1966-27.8.1968. Black on multicolor underprint. Portrait Mora at center,
without *C* in corners or at right. Series C. Back: Statue of J. Santamaría at center.
Printer: TDLR.

	VF	UNC
a. Issued note.	30.00	135
s. Specimen. Overprint: *MUESTRA*.	125	500

1967 Provisional Issue

#235 ovpt: *BANCO CENTRAL DE COSTA RICA/SERIE PROVISIONAL* **on
Banco Nacional notes.**

235   2 Colones

5.12.1967. Black overprint on #203 (Vol. 2). Series F.

	VF	UNC
	15.00	50.00

1968-72 Issues

236   5 Colones

1968-92. UV: fibers fluoresce orange. Deep green and lilac on multicolor
underprint. Rafael Yglesias Castro at left, flowers at right. Series D. Back: National
Theater scene. Printer: TDLR.

	VF	UNC
a. Date at center. Watermark: *BCCR CINCO*. Security thread. Error name *T. VILLA* on back. 20.8.1968; 11.12.1968.	5.00	25.00
b. Date at right center. With watermark and security thread. Error name *T. VILLA* on back. 1.4.1969; 30.6.1970; 24.5.1971; 8.5.1972.	1.25	10.00
c. Date at right center. Watermark and security thread. Corrected name *J. VILLA* on back. 4.5.1973-4.5.1976.	0.75	7.00
d. Without watermark or security thread. Changed signature titles. 28.6.1977-4.10.1989.	FV	5.00
e. As d. 24.1.1990-15.1.1992.	FV	3.50
s. As d. Specimen. Overprint: *MUESTRA*.	—	50.00
x. As d. but with error date: 7.4.1933 (instead of 1983).	10.00	30.00

237 10 Colones
1972-87. Dark blue on multicolor underprint. University building at left, Rodrigo Facio Brenes at right. Series D. Back: Central Bank. Watermark: *BCCR 10.* Printer: ABNC (without imprint).

	VF	UNC
a. Security thread. 6.9.1972-1977.	3.00	10.00
b. Without security thread. 26.4.1977-18.2.1987.	1.00	6.50
s. As a. Specimen. Overprint: *MUESTRA.*	—	60.00

238 20 Colones
1972-03. Dark brown on multicolor underprint. President Cleto González Víquez at left, buildings and trees at right. Series C. Back: Allegorical scene of Justice. Printer: ABNC (without imprint).

	VF	UNC
a. Watermark: *BCCR 20.* (error). *BARBA* - etc. text under buildings at center. Signature titles: *EL PRESIDENTE DE LA JUNTA DIRECTIVA* and *EL GERENTE DEL BANCO.* Date at upper right, with security strip. 10.7.1972; 6.9.1972.	7.50	25.00
b. Watermark as a. Text and signature as a, date position at upper center, with security strip. 13.11.1972-26.4.1977.	3.00	12.00
c. Without watermark. Light brown. Signature titles: *PRESIDENTE EJECUTIVO* and *GERENTE.* (corrected). *BARVA...* etc. text under buildings at center. Date at upper right center or upper center. 1.6.1978-7.4.1983.	1.50	10.00
s1. Specimen. Overprint: *MUESTRA.* 1.6.1978.	—	80.00
s2. Specimen. ND.	—	80.00

Note: For 20 Colones dated 28.6.1983 Series Z, printed on Tyvek, see #252.

239 50 Colones
6.9.1972-26.4.1977. Olive-green multicolor underprint. Meeting scene at left, M. M. de Peralta y Alfaro at right. Series C. Back: Casa *Amarilla* (Yellow House). Printer: TDLR (without imprint).

VF	UNC
7.50	30.00

240 100 Colones
26.8.1969-26.4.1977. Black on multicolor underprint. Ricardo Jimenez O. at left, cows and mountains at center. Series D. Back: Supreme Court at left center, figures at right. Printer: TDLR.

	VF	UNC
a. Issued note.	12.50	54.00
s. Specimen. Overprint: *MUESTRA.*	—	—

1971 Commemorative Issue

#241-246 circular ovpt: 150 *AOS DE INDEPENDENCIA* **1821-1971**

241 5 Colones
24.5.1971. Series D.

VF	UNC
10.00	50.00

242 10 Colones
24.5.1971. Series C.

VF	UNC
25.00	125

243 50 Colones
24.5.1971. Series B.

VF	UNC
75.00	325

244   100 Colones
24.5.1971; 13.12.1971. Series D.

	VF	UNC
	100	350

245   500 Colones
24.5.1971. Series A.

	VF	UNC
	500	1,250

246   1000 Colones
24.5.1971. Series A.

	VF	UNC
	650	1,000

1975 Commemorative Issue

247   5 Colones
20.3.1975. Series D.

	VF	UNC
	12.50	50.00

1975-79 Issue

248   100 Colones
1977-88. Black on multicolor underprint. Ricardo Jimenez O. at left. Series E.
Printer: TDLR.
a. 26.4.1977-24.12.1981.
b. 18.5.1982-9.11.1988.

	VF	UNC
a.	4.00	20.00
b.	3.00	15.00

249   500 Colones
1979-85. Purple on multicolor underprint. M. M. Gutiérrez at right. Series B. Back:
National Theatre at center right. Printer: TDLR.
a. Red serial #. 4.6.1979-12.3.1981.
b. Black serial #. 17.9.1981; 24.12.1981; 18.5.1982; 7.8.1984; 20.3.1985.

	VF	UNC
a.	15.00	75.00
b.	12.50	40.00

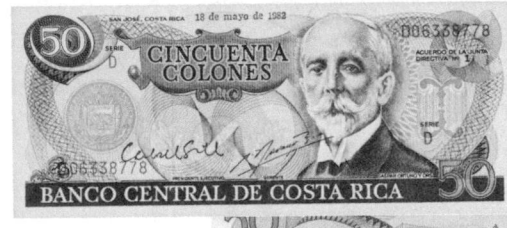

250   1000 Colones
9.6.1975; 13.11.1978; 24.12.1981; 8.7.1982; 4.11.1982; 7.4.1983; 2.10.1984;
20.3.1985. Red on multicolor underprint. T. Soley Guell at left. Series B. Back:
National Insurance Institute at center right. Printer: ABNC.

	VF	UNC
	10.00	75.00

1978 Commemorative Issue
#251, Centennial - Bank of Costa Rica 1877-1977

251   50 Colones
1978-86. Olive-green and multicolor. Obverse of 1866-dated 50 Centimos coin
at left, Gaspar Ortunoy Ors at right. Series D. Back: Old bank, reverse of 50 Centimos coin and commemorative text: *1877-CENTENARIO...* Printer: TDLR.
a. 30.10.1978; 30.4.1979; 18.3.1980; 2.4.1981.
b. 18.5.1982; 28.8.1984; 22.11.1984; 20.3.1985; 2.4.1986.

	VF	UNC
a.	7.50	40.00
b.	5.00	27.00

1983-88 Issue

252 20 Colones

28.6.1983. Printed on Tyvek. Without watermark. Light brown. Signature titles: *PRESIDENTE EJECUTIVO* and *GERENTE*. Without security thread. (corrected). *BARVA*... etc. text under buildings at center. Date at up

		VF	UNC
a.	Issued note.	5.00	80.00
s.	Specimen. Punch hole cancelled.	—	400

253 50 Colones

15.7.1987; 26.4.1988. Olive-green on multicolor underprint. Obverse of 1866-dated 50 Centimos coin at left, Gaspar Ortunoy Ors at right. Series E. Back: Old bank, reverse of 50 Centimos coin and commemorative text: *ANTIGUO EDIFICIO*... Watermark: *BCCR 50* with security thread. Printer: CdM-Brazil.

	VF	UNC
	2.00	10.00

1986; 1987 Issue

254 100 Colones

30.11.1988; 4.10.1989; 5.10.1990. Black on multicolor underprint. Ricardo Jimenez O. at left. Series F. Printer: ABNC.

		VF	UNC
a.	Issued note.	2.50	15.00
s.	Specimen.	—	350

255 500 Colones

21.1.1987; 14.6.1989. Brown-orange, brown and olive-brown on multicolor underprint. M. M. Gutiérrez at right. Series C. Clear watermark area at left. Back: National Theatre at center right. Printer: TDLR.

	VF	UNC
	4.00	20.00

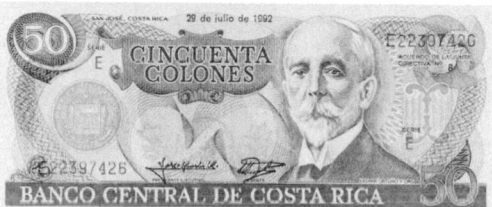

256 1000 Colones

19.11.1986; 17.6.1987; 6.1.1988; 17.1.1989. Red on multicolor underprint. T. Soley Guell at left. Series C. Back: National Insurance Institute at center right. Printer: ABNC.

		VF	UNC
a.	Issued note. Large C.	7.50	40.00
b.	Issued note. Small C.	7.50	35.00
s.	Specimen.	—	125

1990-92 Issue

257 50 Colones

19.6.1991; 28.8.1991; 29.7.1992; 2.6.1993; 7.7.1993. Olive-green on multicolor underprint. Obverse of 1866-dated 50 Centimos coin at left, Gaspar Ortunoy Ors at right. Series E. Without security thread. Back: Old bank, reverse of 50 Centimos coin and commemorative text: *ANTIGUO EDIFICIO*... Printer: TDLR.

		VF	UNC
a.	Issued note.	0.75	10.00
s.	Specimen. Overprint: *MUESTRA*.	—	120

258 100 Colones

17.6.1992. Black on multicolor underprint. Ricardo Jimenez O. at left. Series G. Printer: CdM-Brazil.

	VF	UNC
	2.50	12.50

259 1000 Colones

1990-94. Red on multicolor underprint. T. Soley Guell at left. Series C. Back: National Insurance Institute at center right. Printer: USBN.

		VF	UNC
a.	24.4.1990; 3.10.1990; 23.10.1991.	4.00	35.00
b.	2.2.1994; 20.4.1994; 15.6.1994; 10.10.1994.	FV	35.00

260　5000 Colones

	VF	UNC

1991-95. Dark blue, blue and dark brown on multicolor underprint. Local sculpture at left center. Series A. Back: Toucan, leopard, local carving, foliage and sphere. Printer: TDLR.

	VF	UNC
a. 28.8.1991;11.3.1992; 29.7.1992.	20.00	70.00
b. 4.5.1994; 18.1.1995.	FV	55.00

1993-97 Issue

261　100 Colones

	VF	UNC

28.9.1993. Black on multicolor underprint. Ricardo Jimenez O. at left. Series H. Watermark: *BCCR-100* (repeated). Printer: ABNC.

	VF	UNC
a. Issued note.	0.75	7.00
s. Specimen. Overprint: *MUESTRA.* 28.9.1993.	—	125

262　500 Colones

	VF	UNC

6.7.1994. Brown-orange, brown and olive-brown on multicolor underprint. M. M. Gutièrrez at right, printing in watermark area at left. Series D. Ascending size serial # at lower left. Back: National Theatre at center right. Printer: TDLR.

	VF	UNC
a. Issued note.	FV	18.00
s. Specimen. Overprint: *MUESTRA.* 6.7.1994.	—	150

#263 *Renumbered. See #259.*

264　1000 Colones

	VF	UNC

1997-99; 2003-05. Red on multicolor underprint. T. Soley Guell at left. Series D. Ascending size serial # at upper right. Back: National Insurance Institute at center right. Printer: F-CO. 146x67mm.

	VF	UNC
a. 23.7.1997.	FV	10.00
b. 23.9.1998.	FV	10.00
c. 24.2.1999.	FV	10.00
d. 9.4.2003.	FV	10.00
e. 27.9.2004.	FV	10.00
f. 14.9.2005.	FV	10.00
s. Specimen. Overprint: *MUESTRA.* 23.7.1997.	—	200

265　2000 Colones

	VF	UNC

1997-99; 2003-05. Brown-orange and dark brown on multicolor underprint. C. Picado T. at center right, Coco Island in underprint at center. Series A. Back: Hammerhead shark at left, dolphin at lower center. Watermark: C. Picado T. Printer: F-CO.

	VF	UNC
a. 30.7.1997 (1998).	FV	25.00
b. 16.9.1998.	FV	25.00
c. 9.4.1999.	FV	25.00
d. 9.4.2003.	FV	25.00
e. 14.9.2005.	FV	25.00
s. Specimen. Overprint: *MUESTRA* or *MUESTRA SIN VALOR.* 30.7.1997.	—	375

266　5000 Colones

	VF	UNC

1996; 2004-05. Dark blue and dark brown on multicolor underprint. Local sculpture at left center. Series B, C. Ascending size serial #. Back: Toucan, leopard, local carving, foliage and sphere. Printer: TDLR.

	VF	UNC
a. 27.3.1996 (1997).	FV	45.00
b. 27.9.2004.	FV	45.00
c. 14.9.2005.	FV	45.00
s. Specimen. Overprint: *MUESTRA* or *MUESTRA SIN VALOR.* 27.3.1996.	—	300

267 10,000 Colones   VF   UNC
1997; 2004-05; 2007. Dark blue and deep blue-green on multicolor underprint.
E. Gamboa A. at center right, volcanoes in underprint at center. Series A. Back:
Puma at upper center. Watermark: E. Gamboa A. Printer: F-CO. 146x67mm.
a. 30.7.1997 (1998).	FV	85.00
b. 20.3.2002.	FV	85.00
c. 27.9.2004.	FV	85.00
d. 14.9.2005.	FV	85.00
e. 26.9.2007.	FV	85.00
s. Specimen. Overprint: *MUESTRA* or *MUESTRA SIN VALOR*. 30.7.1997.	—	500

1999 Issue

267A 1000 Colones   VF   UNC
1999. Multicolor.   FV   10.00

268 5000 Colones   VF   UNC
24.2.1999. Dark blue and dark brown on multicolor underprint. Local sculpture at
left center. Series C. Ascending size serial #. Microprinting and security thread
added. Back: Toucan, leopard, local carving, foliage and sphere. Printer: TDLR.
146x67mm.
a. Issued note.	FV	45.00
s. Specimen. Overprint: *MUESTRA* or *MUESTRA SIN VALOR*.	—	400

268A 5000 Colones   VF   UNC
24.2.1999; 14.9.2005. Dark blue and dark brown on multicolor underprint. Local
sculpture at left center. Back: Toucan, leopard, local carving, foliage and sphere.
Printer: FC-O. 146x67mm.
a. 24.2.1999.	FV	45.00
b. 14.9.2005.	FV	45.00

2000 Commemorative Issue

50th Anniversary Banco Central #269-273 as #262-267 but w/commemorative
ovpt. *50 BCCR ANIVERSARIO* added at lower r. 10,000 notes of each denomination were overprinted, but not all on uncirculated notes. All of #269-271
were sold as collectors' items; however, approximately 1/3 of #272-73 were
put into general circulation.

269 500 Colones   VF   UNC
6.7.1994. Brown-orange, brown on multicolor underprint. M. M. Gutiérrez at right,   FV   20.00
printing in watermark area at left. Series D. Ascending size serial # at lower left.
Commemorative overprint added at lower right. Back: National Theatre at center
right. Printer: TDLR.

270 1000 Colones   VF   UNC
23.9.1998. Red on multicolor underprint. T. Soley Guell at left. Series D. Ascend-   FV   50.00
ing size serial number at upper right. Commemorative overprint added at lower
right. Back: National Insurance Institute at center right. Printer: F-CO.

271 2000 Colones   VF   UNC
30.7.1997. Brown-orange and dark brown on multicolor underprint. C. Picado   FV   60.00
T. at center right, Coco Island in underprint at center. Series A. Commemorative
overprint added at lower right. Back: Hammerhead shark at left, dolphin at lower
center. Printer: F-CO.

272 5000 Colones   VF   UNC
24.2.1999. Dark blue and dark brown on multicolor underprint. Local sculpture   FV   75.00
at left center. Series C. Ascending size serial number. Commemorative overprint
added at lower right. Back: Toucan, leopard, local carving, foliage and sphere.
Printer: F-CO.

273 10,000 Colones   VF   UNC
30.7.1997. Dark blue and deep blue-green on multicolor underprint. E. Gamboa
A. at center right, volcanoes in underprint at center. Series A. Commemorative
overprint added at lower right. Back: Puma at upper center. Printer: F-CO.
a. Issued note.	FV	150
s. Specimen.	—	—

2010 Issue

274   1000 Colones   **VF   UNC**
2.9.2009. Polymer plastic. Red and multicolor. Braulio Carrillo Colina at left. Back: FV   9.00
Tree, cactus and white-tailed deer. Printer: OT. 125x67mm.

275   2000 Colones   **VF   UNC**
2.9.2009. Blue and multicolor. Mauro Ferandez Acuna at left. Back: Bull shark,   FV   16.00
fish, coral reef star fish, turtles at right center. Printer: OT. 132x67mm.

276   5000 Colones   **VF   UNC**
9.2.2009. Yellow and multicolor. Alfredo Gonzalez Flores Back: Mangrove swamp,   FV   25.00
monkey, crab at right center. Printer: OT. 139x67mm.

277   10,000 Colones   **VF   UNC**
2.9.2009. Green and multicolor. Jose Figueres Ferrer at left. Back: Rainforest,   FV   45.00
orchid, three-toed sloth at right center. 146x67mm.

278   20,000 Colones   **VF   UNC**
2.9.2009. Orange and multicolor. Maria I. Carvajal "Carmen Lyra" at left. Back: FV   175
Chispita hummingburg at right center. Printer: OT 153x67mm.

279   50,000 Colones   **VF   UNC**
2.9.2009. Purple and multicolor. Ricardo Jimenez Oremuno at left. Back: Cloud   FV   250
forest, mushroom flowers and Morpho butterfly at right center. Printer: OT.
160x67mm.

CROATIA

The Republic of Croatia (Hrvatska), has an area of 56,542 sq. km. and a population of 4.49 million. Capital: Zagreb.

The lands that today comprise Croatia were part of the Austro-Hungarian Empire until the close of World War I. In 1918, the Croats, Serbs, and Slovenes formed a kingdom known after 1929 as Yugoslavia. Following World War II, Yugoslavia became a federal independent Communist state under the strong hand of Marshal Tito. Although Croatia declared its independence from Yugoslavia in 1991, it took four years of sporadic, but often bitter, fighting before occupying Serb armies were mostly cleared from Croatian lands. Under UN supervision, the last Serb-held enclave in eastern Slavonia was returned to Croatia in 1998.

Local Serbian forces supported by the Yugoslav Federal Army had developed a military stronghold and proclaimed an independent "SRPSKE KRAJINA" state in the area around Knin, located in southern Croatia. In August 1995 Croat forces overran this political-military enclave.

RULERS:
Austrian, 1527-1918
Yugoslavian, 1918-1941

MONETARY SYSTEM:
1 Dinar = 100 Para 1918-1941, 1945-
1 Kuna = 100 Banica 1941-1945
1 Kuna = 100 Lipa, 1994-
1 Dinar = 100 Para

REPUBLIC

Republika Hrvatska

REPUBLIC OF CROATIA

1991-93 Issue

16	1 Dinar	VF	UNC

8.10.1991. UV: fibers fluoresce yellow. Dull orange-brown on multicolor underprint. R. Boskovic at center, geometric calculations at upper right. 4.5mm serial number. Back: Vertical back with Zagreb cathedral and artistic rendition of city buildings behind. Watermark: Lozenges. Printer: Swedish.

a. Issued note.	0.50	1.00
s. Specimen.	—	15.00

17	5 Dinara	VF	UNC

8.10.1991. UV: fibers fluoresce yellow. Pale purple on multicolor underprint. R. Boskovic at center, geometric calculations at upper right. 4mm serial number. Back: Vertical back with Zagreb cathedral and artistic rendition of city buildings behind. Watermark: Lozenges. Printer: Swedish.

a. Issued note.	0.50	1.00
s. Specimen.	—	15.00

18	10 Dinara	VF	UNC

8.10.1991. Pale red-brown on multicolor underprint. R. Boskovic at center, geometric calculations at upper right. 4.5mm serial number. Back: Vertical back with Zagreb cathedral and artistic rendition of city buildings behind. Watermark: Lozenges. Printer: Swedish.

a. Issued note.	1.00	1.50
s. Specimen.	—	20.00

19	25 Dinara	VF	UNC

8.10.1991. Dull purple on multicolor underprint. R. Boskovic at center, geometric calculations at upper right. Buff paper with 2.8mm serial #. (Printed in Sweden). Back: Vertical back with Zagreb cathedral and artistic rendition of city buildings behind. Watermark: 5's in crossed wavy lines. Printer: Swedish.

a. Issued note.	1.50	2.00
b. Inverted watermark.	15.00	35.00
s. Specimen.	—	20.00

Note: The watermark paper actually used in the production for #19 was originally prepared for printing Sweden 5 Kroner, #51.

20	100 Dinara	VF	UNC

8.10.1991. Pale green on multicolor underprint. R. Boskovic at center, geometric calculations at upper right. Back: Vertical back with Zagreb cathedral and artistic rendition of city buildings behind. Printer: Swedish.

a. Issued note.	2.50	4.00
s. Specimen.	—	35.00

21	500 Dinara	VF	UNC

8.10.1991. Lilac on multicolor underprint. R. Boskovic at center, geometric calculations at upper right. Back: Vertical back with Zagreb cathedral and artistic rendition of city buildings behind. Watermark: Baptismal font. Printer: Swedish.

a. Issued note.	3.50	12.00
s. Specimen.	—	35.00

22	1000 Dinara	VF	UNC

8.10.1991. Pale blue-violet on multicolor underprint. R. Boskovic at center, geometric calculations at upper right. Back: Vertical back with Zagreb cathedral and artistic rendition of city buildings behind. Watermark: Baptismal font. Printer: Swedish.

a. Issued note.	4.50	15.00
s. Specimen.	—	35.00

23   2000 Dinara
15.1.1992. Deep brown on multicolor underprint. R. Boskovic at center, geometric
calculations at upper right. Back: Statue of seated Glagolica *Mother Croatia* at
center. Watermark: Baptismal font. Printer: Swedish.

VF   UNC

    a. Issued note.   2.50   8.00
    s. Specimen.   —   40.00

24   5000 Dinara
15.1.1992. Dark gray on multicolor underprint. R. Boskovic at center, geometric
calculations at upper right. Back: Statue of seated Glagolica *Mother Croatia* at
center. Watermark: Baptismal font. Printer: Swedish.

VF   UNC

    a. Issued note.   2.50   10.00
    s. Specimen.   —   40.00

25   10,000 Dinara
15.1.1992. Olive-green on multicolor underprint. R. Boskovic at center, geometric
calculations at upper right. Back: Statue of seated Glagolica *Mother Croatia* at
center. Watermark: Baptismal font. Printer: Swedish.

VF   UNC

    a. Issued note.   4.00   15.00
    s. Specimen.   —   40.00

26   50,000 Dinara
30.5.1993. Deep red on multicolor underprint. R. Boskovic at center, geometric
calculations at upper right. Back: Statue of seated Glagolica *Mother Croatia* at
center. Watermark: Baptismal font. Printer: Swedish.

VF   UNC

    a. Issued note.   1.00   3.50
    s. Specimen.   —   25.00

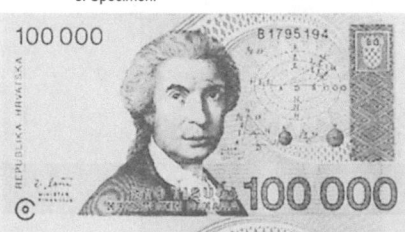

27   100,000 Dinara
30.5.1993. UV: left shield fluoresces yellow. Back, right design yellow and orange.
Dark blue-green on multicolor underprint. R. Boskovic at center, geometric
calculations at upper right. Back: Statue of seated Glagolica *Mother Croatia* at
center. Printer: Swedish.

VF   UNC

    a. Issued note.   1.50   6.50
    s. Specimen.   —   25.00

Narodna Banka Hrvatske
1993 Issue

28   5 Kuna
31.10.1993 (1994). Dark green and green on multicolor underprint. F. K. Frankopan and P. Zrinski at right, shield at upper left center. Back: Fortress in Varazdin at
left center. Watermark: F. K. Frankopan and P. Zrinski. Printer: G&D.

VF   UNC

    a. Issued note.   3.00   5.00
    s. Specimen.   —   20.00
    x. Error without date or signature   30.00   60.00

29   10 Kuna
31.10.1993 (1994). Purple and violet on multicolor underprint. J. Dobrila at right,
shield at upper left center. Back: Pula arena at left center. Watermark: J. Dobrila.
Printer: G&D.

VF   UNC

    a. Issued note.   4.00   7.00
    s. Specimen.   —   20.00

30   20 Kuna
31.10.1993 (1994). Brown, red and violet on multicolor underprint. J. Jelacic at
right, shield at upper left center. Back: Pottery dove and castle of Count Eltz in
Vukovar at left center. Watermark: J. Jelacic. Printer: G&D.

VF   UNC

    a. Issued note.   5.00   10.00
    s. Specimen.   —   25.00

31   50 Kuna   VF   UNC
31.10.1993 (1994). Dark blue and blue-green on multicolor underprint. I. Gundulic at right, shield at upper left center. Back: Aerial view of old Dubrovnik at left center. Watermark: I. Gundulic. Printer: G&D.
    a. Issued note.   8.00   20.00
    s. Specimen.   —   25.00

32   100 Kuna   VF   UNC
31.10.1993 (1994). Red-brown and brown-orange on multicolor underprint. I. Mazuranic at right, shield at upper left center. Back: Plan of and church of St. Vitus in Rijeka at left center. Watermark: I. Mazuranic. Printer: G&D.
    a. Issued note.   10.00   25.00
    s. Specimen.   —   30.00
    x. Error without serial #.   25.00   50.00

33   200 Kuna   VF   UNC
31.10.1993 (1994). Dark brown and brown on multicolor underprint. S. Radic at right, shield at upper left center. Back: Town command in Osijek at left center. Watermark: S. Radic. Printer: G&D.
    a. Issued note.   15.00   30.00
    s. Specimen.   —   30.00

34   500 Kuna   VF   UNC
31.10.1993 (1994). Dark brown and olive-brown on multicolor underprint. M. Marulic at right, shield at upper left center. Back: Palace of Diocletian in Spit at left center. Watermark: M. Marulic. Printer: G&D.
    a. Issued note.   35.00   80.00
    s. Specimen.   —   35.00

35   1000 Kuna   VF   UNC
31.10.1993 (1994). Dark brown and purple on multicolor underprint. Ante Starcevic at right, shield at upper left center. Back: Equestrian statue of King Tomislav at left center, Zagreb Cathedral at center right. Watermark: Ante Starcevic. Printer: G&D.
    a. Issued note.   100   185
    s. Specimen.   —   40.00

1995 Issue

36   10 Kuna   VF   UNC
15.1.1995. Black and brown on green and multicolor underprint. J. Dobrilla at right, shield at upper left center. Back: Pula arena at left center. Watermark: J. Dobrilla. Printer: G&D.
    a. Issued note.   0.25   2.00
    s. Specimen.   —   40.00

Hrvatska Narodna Banka
2001 Issue

37   5 Kuna   VF   UNC
7.3.2001. Multicolor. F. K. Frankopan and P. Zrinski at right, shield at upper left center. Back: Fortress in Varazdin at left center. Watermark: F. K. Frankopan and P. Zrinski. Printer: G&D.
    a. Issued note.   0.25   2.00
    s. Specimen.   —   25.00

38 10 Kuna   **VF UNC**

7.3.2001; 9.7.2012. Multicolor. J. Dobrila at right, shield at upper left center. Back: Pula arena at left center. Watermark: J. Dobrila. Printer: G&D. 126x63mm.

		VF	UNC
a. 7.3.2001.		0.50	2.50
b. 9.7.2012.		0.50	2.50
s. Specimen.		—	25.00

39 20 Kuna   **VF UNC**

7.3.2001; 9.7.2012. Multicolor. J. Jelacic at right, shield at upper left center. Back: Pottery dove and castle of Count Eltz in Vukovar at left center. Watermark: J. Jelacic. Printer: G&D. 130x65mm.

		VF	UNC
a. 7.3.2001.		0.50	5.00
b. 9.7.2012.		0.50	5.00
s. Specimen.		—	25.00

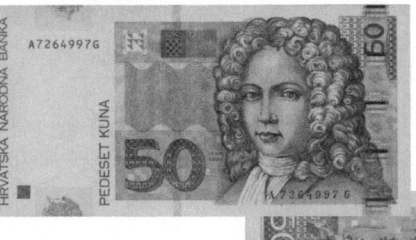

40 50 Kuna   **VF UNC**

7.3.2002. Multicolor. I. Gundulic at right, shield at upper left center. Back: Aerial view of old Dubrovnik at left center. Watermark: I. Gundulic. Printer: OEBS. 134x67mm.

		VF	UNC
a. Issued note.		1.75	10.00
s. Specimen.		—	25.00

41 100 Kuna   **VF UNC**

7.3.2002; 9.7.2012. Multicolor. I. Mazuranic at right, shield at upper left center. Back: Plan of and church of St. Vitus in Rijeka at left center. Watermark: I. Mazuranic. Printer: OEBS. 138x69mm.

		VF	UNC
a. 7.3.2002.		2.50	20.00
b. 9.7.2012.		2.50	20.00
s. Specimen.		—	50.00

42 200 Kuna   **VF UNC**

7.3.2002; 9.7.2012. Brown on multicolor underprint. S. Radic at right, shield at upper left center. Back: Town command in Osijek at left center. Watermark: S. Radic. Printer: OEBS. 142x71mm.

		VF	UNC
a. 7.3.2002.		5.00	35.00
b. 9.7.2012.		5.00	35.00
s. Specimen.		—	50.00

2004 Commemorative Issue

#45, 10th Anniversary of the National Bank of Croatia.

43 10 Kuna   **VF UNC** 1.00 5.00

30.5.2004. Multicolor. J. Dobrilla at right, shield at upper left center. Back: Pula arena at left center. Watermark: J. Dobrilla. Large 10 added. Printer: G&D.

44 20 Kuna   **VF UNC** 0.50 5.00

Like #39 but additional guilloche front left. Multicolor. 130x65mm.

COLLECTOR SERIES

Republic of Croatia

1998 Issue

Note: #CS1 and CS2 are sold by the Croatian National Bank.

CS1	**1991-93 1-100,000 Dinara**	**Mkt Value**
	#16-27 with matched serial # (50,000).	—
CS2	**1993 5-1000 Kuna**	**Mkt Value**
	#28-36 with matched serial # (50,000).	—

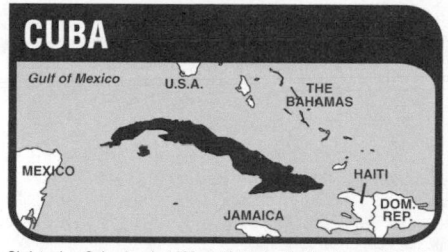

CUBA

The Republic of Cuba, situated at the northern edge of the Caribbean Sea about 145 km. south of Florida, has an area of 110,860 sq. km. and a population of 11.4 million. Capital: Havana. The Cuban economy is based on the cultivation and refining of sugar, which provides 80 percent of export earnings.

The native Amerindian population of Cuba began to decline after the European discovery of the island by Christopher Columbus in 1492 and following its development as a Spanish colony during the next several centuries. Large numbers of African slaves were imported to work the coffee and sugar plantations, and Havana became the launching point for the annual treasure fleets bound for Spain from Mexico and Peru. Spanish rule, marked initially by neglect, became increasingly repressive, provoking an independence movement and occasional rebellions that were harshly suppressed. It was US intervention during the Spanish-American War in 1898 that finally overthrew Spanish rule. The subsequent Treaty of Paris established Cuban independence, which was granted in 1902 after a three-year transition period. Fidel Castro led a rebel army to victory in 1959; his iron rule held the subsequent regime together for nearly five decades. He stepped down as president in February 2008 in favor of his younger brother Raul Castro. Cuba's Communist revolution, with Soviet support, was exported throughout Latin America and Africa during the 1960s, 1970s, and 1980s. The country is now slowly recovering from a severe economic downturn in 1990, following the withdrawal of former Soviet subsidies. Cuba portrays its difficulties as the result of the US embargo in place since 1961.

MONETARY SYSTEM:
1 Peso = 100 Centavos
1 Peso Convertible = 1 U.S.A. Dollar, 1995-

REPUBLIC

Banco Nacional de Cuba

NATIONAL BANK OF CUBA

1961 Issue

94	1 Peso	VF	UNC
	1961-65. Olive-green on ochre underprint. Portrait J. Martí at center, denomination at left and right. Signature titles: *PRESIDENTE DEL BANCO* at left, *MINISTRO DE HACIENDA* at right. Back: F. Castro with rebel soldiers entering Havana in 1959. Printer: STC-P (without imprint).		
a.	1961	3.00	17.00
b.	1964	2.50	10.00
c.	1965	1.75	8.00
s.	As a. Specimen.	—	9.00

95	5 Pesos	VF	UNC
	1961-65. Dull deep green on pink underprint. Portrait A. Maceo at center, denomination at left and right. Signature titles: *PRESIDENTE DEL BANCO* at left, *MINISTRO DE HACIENDA* at right. Back: Invasion of 1958. Printer: STC-P (without imprint).		
a.	1961	3.75	19.00
b.	1964	3.00	12.50
c.	1965	2.50	10.00
s.	As a. Specimen.	—	6.00

96	10 Pesos	VF	UNC
	1961-65. Brown on tan and yellow underprint. Portrait M. Gómez at center, denomination at left and right. Signature titles: *PRESIDENTE DEL BANCO* at left, *MINISTRO DE HACIENDA* at right. Back: Castro addressing crowd in 1960. Printer: STC-P (without imprint).		
a.	1961	5.00	23.00
b.	1964	4.50	17.50
c.	1965	4.00	15.00
s.	As a. Specimen.	—	6.00

97	20 Pesos	VF	UNC
	1961-65. Blue on pink underprint. Portrait C. Cienfuegos at center, denomination at left and right. Signature titles: *PRESIDENTE DEL BANCO* at left, *MINISTRO DE HACIENDA* at right. Back: Soldiers on the beach in 1956. Printer: STC-P (without imprint).		
a.	1961	12.50	60.00
b.	1964	8.00	35.00
c.	1965	7.50	30.00
s.	As a. Specimen.	—	8.00
x.	U.S.A. counterfeit. Series F69; F70, 1961.	20.00	100

Note: Each member of the *Bay of Pigs* invasion force was reportedly issued one hundred each of #97x. They are found with or without an added serial #.

98 50 Pesos VF UNC

1961. Purple on green underprint. Portrait C. García Iñiguez at center, denomination at left and right. Signature titles: *PRESIDENTE DEL BANCO* at left, *MINISTRO DE HACIENDA* at right. Back: Nationalization of international industries. Printer: STC-P (without imprint).

a. Issued note. 35.00 150
s. Specimen. Red overprint: SPECIMEN on face. — 50.00

99 100 Pesos VF UNC

1961. Light red on orange underprint. Portrait C. M. de Céspedes at center, denomination at left and right. Signature titles: *PRESIDENTE DEL BANCO* at left, *MINISTRO DE HACIENDA* at right. Back: Attack on Moncada in 1953. Printer: STC-P (without imprint).

a. Issued note. 60.00 210
s. Specimen. Red overprint: SPECIMEN on face. — 100

Note: #98 and 99 were recalled shortly after release. A small hoard appeared in the marketplace and has since been dispursed.

1966 Issue

100 1 Peso VF UNC

1966. Olive-green on ochre underprint. Portrait J. Martí at center. Denomination at left and right. Signature titles: *PRESIDENTE DEL BANCO* at left and right. Back: F. Castro with rebel soldiers entering Havana in 1959. Printer: STC-P (without imprint).

a. Issued note. 1.25 5.00
s. Specimen. — 6.00

101 10 Pesos VF UNC

1966. Brown on tan and yellow underprint. Portrait M. Gómez at center, denomination at left and right. Signature titles: *PRESIDENTE DEL BANCO* at left and right. Back: Castro addressing crowd in 1960. Printer: STC-P (without imprint).

a. Issued note. 7.50 20.00
s. Specimen. — 6.00

1967; 1971 Issue

102 1 Peso VF UNC

1967-88. Olive-green on ochre underprint. Portrait J. Martí at center, denomination at left. Signature title: *PRESIDENTE DEL BANCO* at lower right. Back: F. Castro with rebel soldiers entering Havana in 1959. Printer: STC-P (without imprint).

a. 1967-70; 1972. 1.00 5.00
b. 1978-85. 0.50 3.50
c. 1986 0.50 3.00
d. 1988 0.50 2.50
s1. Specimen. As a, b. Overprint: SPECIMEN in red on both sides. — 10.00
s2. Specimen. As b. Overprint: MUESTRA in red on both sides. — 10.00
s3. Specimen. As d. Overprint: MUESTRA in red twice on both sides. — 10.00
s4. Specimen. Red overprint: ESPECIMEN on each side. — 10.00

103 5 Pesos VF UNC

1967-90. Dull deep green on pink underprint. Portrait A. Maceo at center, denomination at left. Signature title: *PRESIDENTE DEL BANCO* at lower right. Back: Invasion of 1958. Printer: STC-P (without imprint).

a. 1967-68. 1.00 15.00
b. 1970; 1972. 0.75 12.50
c. 1984-87. 0.75 10.00
d. 1988; 1990. 0.50 4.00
s. Specimen. Red overprint: SPECIMEN on face. — 8.00

104 10 Pesos VF UNC

1967-89. Brown on tan and yellow underprint. Portrait M. Gómez at center, denomination at left. Signature title: *PRESIDENTE DEL BANCO* at lower right. Back: Castro addressing crowd in 1960. Printer: STC-P (without imprint). 150x70mm.

a. 1967-71. 1.00 15.00
b. 1978 1.00 15.00
c. 1983-84; 1986-87. 1.00 10.00
d. 1988-89. 1.00 10.00
s. Specimen. Overprint: MUESTRA in red on both sides. — 20.00

105 20 Pesos VF UNC

1971-90. Blue on pink underprint. Portrait C. Cienfuegos at center, denomination at left. Signature title: *PRESIDENTE DEL BANCO* at lower right. Back: Soldiers on the beach in 1956. Printer: STC-P (without imprint).

a. 1971 3.50 20.00
b. 1978 3.50 20.00
c. 1983 3.50 15.00
d. 1987-90. 3.50 10.00
s. Specimen. — 6.00

1975 Commemorative Issue

#106, 15th Anniversary Nationalization of Banking

106	**1 Peso**	VF	UNC

1975. Olive on violet underprint. Portrait J. Martí at left, arms at right. Back: Ship dockside.

	a. Issued note.	1.25	5.00
	s. Specimen.	—	5.00

1983 Issue

107	**3 Pesos**	VF	UNC

1983-89. Red on multicolor underprint. Portrait E. "Che" Guevara at center. Back: Che" cutting sugar cane at center.

	a. 1983-86.	1.00	5.00
	b. 1988-89.	1.00	2.00
	s1. 1983. Specimen with black overprint: *MUESTRA* once on each side.	—	20.00
	s2. 1983. Specimen with black overprint: *MUESTRA* twice on each side.	—	10.00

1990; 1991 Issue

Replacement notes: #108-112: *EX, DX, CX, BX, AX* **series #, by denomination.**

108	**5 Pesos**	VF	UNC

1991. Deep green and blue on multicolor underprint. A. Maceo at right. Back: Conference between A. Maceo and Spanish General A. Martínez Campos at Mangos de Baraguá in 187 Watermark: J. Martí.

	a. Issued note.	0.50	1.25
	s. Specimen. Red overprint: SPECIMEN twice on each side.	—	15.00

109	**10 Pesos**	VF	UNC

1991. Deep brown and olive-green on multicolor underprint. M. Gómez at right. Back: Guerra de todo el Pueblo" at left center Watermark: J. Marti.

	a. Issued note.	FV	2.50
	s. Specimen. Red overprint: SPECIMEN twice on each side.	—	15.00

110	**20 Pesos**	VF	UNC

1991. Blue-black and purple on multicolor underprint. Camilio Cienfuegos at right. Back: Agricultural scenes at left center. Watermark: Celia Sánchez Manduley.

	a. Issued note.	FV	5.00
	s. Specimen. Red overprint: SPECIMEN twice on each side.	—	15.00

111	**50 Pesos**	VF	UNC

1990. Deep violet and dark green on multicolor underprint. Arms at center. C. García Iñiguez at right center. Back: Genetic Engineering and Biotechnology at left center. Watermark: Celia Sánchez Manduley.

	a. Issued note.	FV	6.00
	s. Specimen. Red overprint: SPECIMEN twice on each side.	—	15.00

1995 Issue

112   1 Peso   VF   UNC
1995. Dull olive-green and orange on light blue and multicolor underprint. J. Martí   FV   1.00
at left, arms at upper center right. Back: F. Castro with rebel soldiers entering
Havana in 1959.

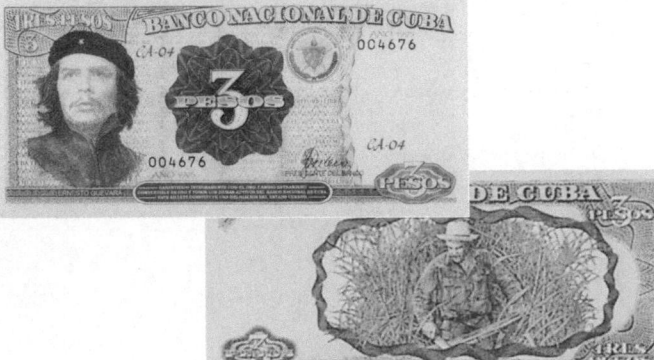

113   3 Pesos   VF   UNC
1995. Red-brown, purple and green on multicolor underprint. E. *Che* Guevara at   FV   2.00
left. Arms at upper center right. Back: Guevara cutting sugar cane.

1995 Dual Commemorative Issue
**#114, 45th anniversary of central banking in Cuba and 100th of death of José
Martí**

114   1 Peso   VF   UNC
1995. Specimen. Black and olive-green on green and brown underprint. J. Martí   —   200
at left, arms and commemorative text at center right. Back: Horseback riders at
center, commemorative text and dates at left.

Note: It is reported that only 1300 examples of #114 were printed, only as specimens. The value is
thus speculative.

Banco Central de Cuba
**Established in 1997 to replace the Banco Nacional as issuer of coins and
paper currency. #115 not assigned.**

1997-98 Issue

116   5 Pesos   VF   UNC
1997-. Green on multicolor underprint. A. Maceo at right. Back: Conference
between A. Maceo and Spanish General A. Martínez Campos at Mangos de
Baraguá in 187 Watermark: J. Marti.

a. 1997	FV	2.00
b. 1998	FV	2.00
c. 2000	FV	2.00
d. 2001	FV	2.00
e. 2002	FV	2.00
f. 2003	FV	2.00
g. 2004	FV	2.00
h. 2005	FV	2.00
i. 2006	FV	2.00
j. 2007	FV	2.00
k. 2009	FV	2.00
l. 2011	FV	2.00
m. 2012	FV	2.00
n. 2014	FV	2.00

117   10 Pesos   VF   UNC
1997-. Brown on multicolor underprint. M. Gómez at right. Back: *Guerra de todo
el Pueblo* at left center.

a. 1997. Watermark: J. Marti.	FV	4.00
b. 1998	FV	4.00
c. 2000	FV	4.00
d. 2001	FV	3.00
e. 2002. Watermark BCC	FV	3.00
f. 2003	FV	3.00
g. 2004	FV	3.00
h. 2005	FV	3.00
i. 2007	FV	3.00
j. 2008. Watermark bust.	FV	3.00
k. 2009	FV	3.00
l. 2010	FV	3.00
m. 2011	FV	3.00
n. 2012	FV	3.00
o. 2013	FV	3.00
p. 2014	FV	3.00

118   20 Pesos   VF   UNC
1998-2002. Blue-black and light blue on violet and blue underprint. C. Cienfuegos
at right. Back: Agricultural scenes at left center. Watermark: Celia Sánchez
Manduley.

a. 1998	FV	5.00
b. 2000	FV	5.00
c. 2001	FV	5.00
d. 2002	FV	5.00

119   50 Pesos
1998; 1999; 2001. Light purple on green underprint. C. Garcia Iñiguez at right center. Back: Genetic Engineering and Biotechnology at left center. Watermark: Celia Sánchez Manduley.

		VF	UNC
		FV	6.00

2000 Commemorative Issue

#120, 50th anniversary of central banking in Cuba

120   100 Pesos
2002. Reddish brown on yellow underprint. Carlos Manuel de Cespedes at right, commemorative symbol and text at left. Back: Martí and scene of Havana. Watermark: National heroine.

	VF	UNC
	FV	8.00

2001-02 Issue

121   1 Peso
2001-. Black and olive green. J. Martí at right. Back: Fidel Castro and victory parade scene.

	VF	UNC
a. 2001. Series prefix in red.	FV	1.25
b. 2002. Series prefix in red.	FV	1.25
c. 2003. Series prefix in olive green.	FV	1.25
d. 2004. Series prefix in red.	FV	1.25
e. 2005. Series prefix in red.	FV	1.25
f. 2006. Series prefix in red.	FV	1.25
g. 2007. Series prefix in red. Watermark: Bust.	FV	1.25
h. 2008. Series prefix in red.	FV	1.25
i. 2009. Series prefix in red.	FV	1.25
j. 2010	FV	1.25
k. 2011	FV	1.25

122   20 Pesos
2004-. Blue-black and light blue on violet and blue underprint. C. Cienfuegos at right. Back: Agricultural scenes at left center. Watermark: Celia Sanchez Manduley

		VF	UNC
a. 2004		FV	5.00
b. 2005		FV	5.00
c. 2006		FV	5.00
d. 2007		FV	5.00
e. 2008		FV	5.00
f. 2009		FV	5.00
g. 2012		FV	5.00
h. 2013		FV	5.00
i. 2014		FV	5.00

123   50 Pesos
2002-. Light purple on green underprint. C. Garcia Iniguez at right center. Braile added to top right. Back: Genetic Engineering and Biotechnology building at left center. Watermark: Celia Canchez Manduley.

	VF	UNC
a. 2002	FV	7.50
b. 2003	FV	7.50
c. 2005	FV	7.60
d. 2007	FV	7.50
e. 2008	FV	7.50
f. 2009	FV	7.50
g. 2012	FV	7.50
h. 2013	FV	10.00
i. 2014. Watermark: Calixto Garcia Iniguez.	FV	10.00
j. 2015	FV	10.00

124   100 Pesos
2001. Reddish brown on yellow underprint. Carlos Manuel de Cespedes at right, without commemorative overprint. Back: Martì and scene of Havana. Watermark: National heroine.

	VF	UNC
	FV	15.00

2003 First Commemorative Issue

150th Anniversary birth of Jose Martí.

125	1 Peso	VF	UNC
	2003. José Martí at right. Back: Martí's birthplace.	FV	1.50

2003 Second Commemorative Issue
#122A 50th Anniversary of the Moncada Assault.

126	20 Peso	VF	UNC
	2003. Violet, blue and rose. Camilo Cienfuegos	FV	8.00

2004 Commemorative Issue

127	3 Pesos		VF	UNC
	2004-2005. Brown on tan underprint. E. "Che" Guevara at right. Back: View of Guevara in sugar cane fields.			
	a. 2004		FV	2.00
	b. 2005		FV	2.00

2004 Issue

128	1 Peso		VF	UNC
	2004; 2005; 2007. Multicolor. José Martí at right. Back: Martí's birthplace.			
	a. 2004.		FV	1.50
	b. 2005.		FV	1.50
	c. 2007.		FV	1.50

129	100 Pesos		VF	UNC
	2004. Multicolor. Carlos Manuel de Cespedes at right. Braile at upper right. Back: Martí and scene of Havana. 150x70mm.			
	a. 2004		FV	20.00
	b. 2005		FV	20.00
	c. 2007		FV	20.00
	d. 2008		FV	20.00
	e. 2013		FV	20.00
	f. 2014		FV	20.00

130	200 Pesos	VF	UNC
	2010. Brown. I.P. Garcia at right. Back: School buildings in Santiago de Cuba.	FV	40.00

131	500 Pesos	VF	UNC
	2010. Green, blue. I. Agramonte y Loynaz at right. Back: Constituent Assembly.	FV	100

132	1000 Pesos	VF	UNC
	2010. Purple, yellow, brown. J.A. Mella McPartland at right. Back: University of Habana.	FV	200

COLLECTOR SERIES
Banco Nacional de Cuba
1961-1995 Issues

The Banco Nacional de Cuba had been selling specimen notes regularly of the 1961-1989 issues. Specimen notes dated 1961-66 have normal block # and serial # while notes from 1967 to date all have normal block # and all zero serial #.

		Mkt. Value
CS1	1961 1-100 Pesos	
	Overprint: *SPECIMEN* on #94a-97a, 98, 99.	110
CS2	1964 1-20 Pesos	Mkt. Value
	Overprint: *SPECIMEN* on #94b-97b.	20.00
CS3	1965 1-20 Pesos	Mkt. Value
	Overprint: *SPECIMEN* on #94c-97c.	14.00
CS4	1966 1, 10 Pesos	Mkt. Value
	Overprint: *SPECIMEN* on #100, 101.	7.00
CS5	1967 1-10 Pesos	Mkt. Value
	Overprint: *SPECIMEN* on #102a-104a.	10.00
CS6	1968 1-10 Pesos	Mkt. Value
	Overprint: *SPECIMEN* on #102a-104a.	10.00
CS7	1969 1, 10 Pesos	Mkt. Value
	Overprint: *SPECIMEN* on #102a, 104a.	7.00
CS8	1970 1-10 Pesos	Mkt. Value
	Overprint: *SPECIMEN* on #102a, 103b, 104a.	7.00
CS9	1971 10, 20 Pesos	Mkt. Value
	Overprint: *SPECIMEN* on #104a, 105a.	8.00
CS10	1972 1, 5 Pesos	Mkt. Value
	Overprint: *SPECIMEN* on #102a, 103b.	7.00
CS11	1975 1 Peso	Mkt. Value
	Overprint: *SPECIMEN* on #106.	10.00
CS12	1978 1, 10, 20 Pesos	Mkt. Value
	Overprint: *ESPECIMEN* on #102b, 104b, 105b.	11.00
CS13	1979 1 Peso	Mkt. Value
	Overprint: *ESPECIMEN* on #102b.	3.00
CS14	1980 1 Peso	Mkt. Value
	Overprint: *ESPECIMEN* on #102b.	3.00
CS15	1981 1 Peso	Mkt. Value
	Overprint: *ESPECIMEN* on #102b.	3.00
CS16	1982 1 Peso	Mkt. Value
	Overprint: *MUESTRA* on #102b.	3.00
CS17	1983 3, 10, 20 Pesos	Mkt. Value
	Overprint: *MUESTRA* on #104c, 105c, 107a.	12.00
CS18	1984 3, 5, 10 Pesos	Mkt. Value
	Overprint: *MUESTRA* on #103c, 104c, 107a.	12.00
CS19	1985 1, 3, 5 Pesos	Mkt. Value
	Overprint: overprint: *MUESTRA* on #102b, 103c, 107a.	12.00
CS20	1986 1-10 Pesos	Mkt. Value
	Overprint: *MUESTRA* on #102b, 103c, 104c, 107a.	12.50
CS21	1987 5, 10, 20 Pesos	Mkt. Value
	Overprint: *MUESTRA* on #103c-105c.	12.00
CS22	1988 1-20 Pesos	Mkt. Value
	Overprint: *MUESTRA* on #102c, 103d-105d, 107b.	12.50
CS23	1989 3, 20 Pesos	Mkt. Value
	Overprint: *MUESTRA* on #105d, 107b.	7.00
CS24	1990 5, 20, 50 Pesos	Mkt. Value
	Overprint: *SPECIMEN* on #103d, 105d, 111.	10.00
CS25	1991 5, 10, 20 Pesos	Mkt. Value
	Overprint: *SPECIMEN* on #108-110.	10.00
CS26	1994 1-100 Peso Convertibles	Mkt. Value
	Overprint: *MUESTRA* on FX37-FX43.	60.00
CS27	1995 1, 3 Pesos	Mkt. Value
	Overprint: *MUESTRA* on #112 and 113.	5.00

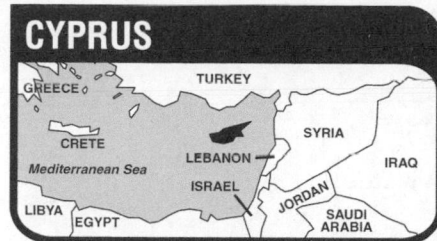

CYPRUS

The Republic of Cyprus lies in the eastern Mediterranean Sea 71 km. south of Turkey and 97 km. west of Syria. It is the third largest island in the Mediterranean Sea, having an area of 9,250 sq. km. and a population of 792,600. Capital: Nicosia. Agriculture and mining are the chief industries. Asbestos, copper, citrus fruit, iron pyrites and potatoes are exported.

A former British colony, Cyprus became independent in 1960 following years of resistance to British rule. Tensions between the Greek Cypriot majority and Turkish Cypriot minority came to a head in December 1963, when violence broke out in the capital of Nicosia. Despite the deployment of UN peacekeepers in 1964, sporadic intercommunal violence continued forcing most Turkish Cypriots into enclaves throughout the island. In 1974, a Greek Government-sponsored attempt to seize control of Cyprus was met by military intervention from Turkey, which soon controlled more than a third of the island. In 1983, the Turkish-held area declared itself the "Turkish Republic of Northern Cyprus" (TRNC), but it is recognized only by Turkey. The latest two-year round of UN-brokered talks - between the leaders of the Greek Cypriot and Turkish Cypriot communities to reach an agreement to reunite the divided island - ended when the Greek Cypriots rejected the UN settlement plan in an April 2004 referendum. The entire island entered the EU on 1 May 2004, although the EU acquis - the body of common rights and obligations - applies only to the areas under direct government control, and is suspended in the areas administered by Turkish Cypriots. However, individual Turkish Cypriots able to document their eligibility for Republic of Cyprus citizenship legally enjoy the same rights accorded to other citizens of European Union states. The election of a new Cypriot president in 2008 served as the impetus for the UN to encourage both the Turkish and Cypriot Governments to reopen unification negotiations.

RULERS:
British to 1960

MONETARY SYSTEM:
1 Shilling = 9 Piastres
1 Pound = 20 Shillings to 1963
1 Shilling = 50 Mils
1 Pound = 1000 Mils, 1963-83
1 Pound = 100 Cents, 1983-2007,
1 Euro = 100 cents, 2008 -

DEMOCRATIC REPUBLIC

ΚΥΠΡΙΑΚΗ ΔΗΜΟΚΡΑΤΙΑ

Kıbrıs Cumhuriyeti

1961 Issue

37   250 Mils   VF   UNC
1.12.1961. Blue on multicolor underprint. Fruit at left, arms at right, map at lower right. Back: Mine. Watermark: Eagle's head. Printer: BWC (without imprint).

		VF	UNC
a. Issued note.		40.00	225
s. Specimen.		—	170

38   500 Mils   VF   UNC
1.12.1961. Green on multicolor underprint. Arms at right, map at lower right. Back: Mountain road lined with trees. Watermark: Eagle's head. Printer: BWC (without imprint).

		VF	UNC
a. Issued note.		95.00	440
s. Specimen.		—	180

39   1 Pound   VF   UNC
1.12.1961. Brown on multicolor underprint. Arms at right, map at lower right. Back: Viaduct and pillars. Watermark: Eagle's head. Printer: BWC (without imprint).

		VF	UNC
a. Issued note.		60.00	260
s. Specimen.		—	190

40   5 Pounds   VF   UNC
1.12.1961. Dark green on multicolor underprint. Arms at right, map at lower right. Back: Embroidery and floral design. Watermark: Eagle's head. Printer: BWC (without imprint).

		VF	UNC
a. Issued note.		100	525
s. Specimen.		—	195

ΚΕΝΤΡΙΚΗ ΤΡΑΠΕΖΑ ΤΗΣ ΚΥΠΡΟΥ

Kıbrıs Merkez Bankası

1964-66 Issue

41   250 Mils   VF   UNC
1964-82. Blue on multicolor underprint. Fruit at left, arms at right, map at lower right. Signature varieties. Back: Mine. Watermark: Eagle's head. Printer: BWC (without imprint).

		VF	UNC
a. 1.12.1964-1.12.1969; 1.9.1971.		35.00	160
b. 1.3.1971; 1.6.1972; 1.5.1973, 1.6.1974.		27.50	130
c. 1.7.1975-1.6.1982.		20.00	115
s. Specimen. Punch hole cancelled.		—	250
ct. Color trial. Brown on multicolor underprint.		—	370

42   500 Mils   VF   UNC
1964-79. Green on multicolor underprint. Arms at right, map at lower right. Signature varieties. Back: Mountain road lined with trees. Watermark: Eagle's head. Printer: BWC (without imprint).

		VF	UNC
a. 1.12.1964-1.6.1972.		45.00	215
b. 1.5.1973; 1.6.1974; 1.7.1975; 1.8.1976.		35.00	180
c. 1.6.1979; 1.9.1979.		30.00	150
s. Specimen. Punch hole cancelled.		—	250

46   1 Pound

1.6.1979. Dark brown and brown on multicolor underprint. Mosaic of nymph Acme at right, arms at top left center. Back: Bellapais Abbey. Watermark: Moufflon (ram's) head. Printer: TDLR (without imprint).

	VF	UNC
	17.50	75.00

43   1 Pound

1966-78. Brown on multicolor underprint. Arms at right, map at lower right. Signature varieties. Back: Viaduct and pillars. Watermark: Eagle's head. Printer: BWC (without imprint).

	VF	UNC
a. 1.8.1966-1.6.1972.	60.00	300
b. 1.11.1972; 1.5.1973; 1.6.1974; 1.7.1975.	37.50	165
c. 1.8.1976; 1.5.1978.	30.00	150
s. Specimen. Punch hole cancelled.	—	260

47   5 Pounds

1.6.1979. Violet on multicolor underprint. Limestone head from Hellenistic period at left, arms at upper center right. Back: Ancient Theater at Salamis. Watermark: Moufflon (ram's) head. Printer: TDLR (without imprint).

	VF	UNC
	42.50	175

44   5 Pounds

1966-76. Blue on multicolor underprint. Arms at right, map at lower right. Signature varieties. Back: Embroidery and floral design. Watermark: Eagle's head. Printer: BCW (without imprint).

	VF	UNC
a. 1.8.1966; 1.9.1967; 1.12.1969.	80.00	350
b. 1.6.1972; 1.11.1972; 1.5.1973.	55.00	255
c. 1.6.1974; 1.7.1975; 1.8.1976.	50.00	230

48   10 Pounds

1977-85. Dark green and blue-black on multicolor underprint. Archaic bust at left, arms at right. Back: Two Cyprus warblers. Watermark: Moufflon (ram's) head. Printer: BWC (without imprint).

	VF	UNC
a. 1.4.1977; 1.5.1978; 1.6.1979.	70.00	300
b. 1.7.1980; 1.10.1981; 1.6.1982; 1.9.1983; 1.6.1985.	65.00	275
s. As a. Specimen.	—	240

1977-82 Issue

1982-87 Issue

45   500 Mils

1.6.1982. Light brown on green and multicolor underprint. Woman seated at right, arms at top left center. Back: Yermasoyia Dam. Watermark: Moufflon (ram's) head. Printer: BWC (without imprint).

	VF	UNC
a. Issued note.	27.50	130
s. Specimen. Punch hole cancelled.	—	215

49   50 Cents

1.10.1983; 1.12.1984. Brown and multicolor. Woman seated at right, arms at top left center. Back: Yermasoyia Dam. Watermark: Moufflon (ram's) head. Printer: BWC (without imprint).

	VF	UNC
a. Issued note.	9.00	40.00
s. Specimen.	—	205

50   1 Pound

	VF	UNC
1.2.1982; 1.11.1982; 1.3.1984; 1.11.1985. Dark brown and multicolor. Mosaic of nymph Acme at right, arms at top left center, bank name in outlined (white) letters by dark underprint. Back: Bellapais Abbey. Watermark: Moufflon (ram's) head. Printer: TDLR (without imprint).	13.50	65.00

51   10 Pounds

	VF	UNC
1.4.1987; 1.10.1988. Dark green and blue-black on multicolor underprint. Archaic bust at left, date above at left of modified arms on right. Back: Two Cyprus warblers. Watermark: Moufflon (ram's) head. Printer: TDLR (without imprint).	60.00	260

1987-92 Issue

52   50 Cents

	VF	UNC
1.4.1987; 1.10.1988; 1.11.1989. Brown and multicolor. Woman seated at right, arms at top left center, bank name in micro-printing alternately in Greek and Turkish just below upper frame. Back: Yermasoyia Dam. Watermark: Moufflon (ram's) head. Printer: BABN (without imprint).	7.00	30.00

53   1 Pound

		VF	UNC
1987-96. Dark brown and multicolor. Mosaic of nymph Acme at right, arms at top left center, bank name in unbroken line of micro-printing with Greek at left and Turkish at right just below upper frame. Back: Bellapais Abbey. Watermark: Moufflon (ram's) head. Printer: TDLR (without imprint).			
a. Without light beige underprint color on back. Micro-print line under dark bar at top. Printer: TDLR (Without imprint). 1.4.1987; 1.10.1988; 1.11.1989.		FV	65.00
b. Light beige color added to center underprint on back for security. Printer: F-CO (without imprint). 1.11.1989; 1.2.1992.		FV	40.00
c. Dot added near upper left corner. 1.3.1993; 1.3.1994.		FV	37.50
d. 1.9.1995.		FV	32.50
e. 1.10.1996.		10.00	50.00

54   5 Pounds

	VF	UNC
1990; 1995. Violet on multicolor underprint. Limestone head from Hellenistic period at left, arms at upper center right, line of micro printing added within bank titles. Back: Ancient Theater at Salamis. Watermark: Moufflon (ram's) head. Printer: TDLR (without imprint).		
a. 1.10.1990.	FV	160
b. 1.9.1995.	FV	140

55   10 Pounds

	VF	UNC
1989-95. Dark green and blue-black on multicolor underprint. Archaic bust at left, arms at right, enhanced security features and micro-printing. Back: Two Cyprus warblers. Watermark: Moufflon (ram's) head. Printer: TDLR (without imprint).		
a. 1.11.1989; 1.10.1990.	FV	260
b. 1.2.1992.	FV	225
c. 1.6.1994.	FV	210
d. 1.9.1995.	FV	195

56   20 Pounds   VF   UNC

1992; 1993. Deep blue on multicolor underprint. Bust of Aphrodite at left, arms at upper center, ancient bird (pottery art) at right. Enhanced designs with micro-printing. Back: Kyrenia boat at center, ancient pottery jugs at lower right. Watermark: Moufflon (ram's) head. Printer: TDLR (without imprint).

    a. Error: No dot over 'i' in *YIRMI LIRA*. 1.2.1992.   95.00   390
    b. Corrected: *YiRMi LiRA*. 1.3.1993.   80.00   295

1997 First Issue

57   1 Pound   VF   UNC

1.2.1997. Brown on pink and multicolor underprint. Cypriot girl at left, arms at upper center. Thin security thread. Back: Handcrafts and Kato Drys village scene in background. Watermark: Bust of Aphrodite. Printer: F-CO (without imprint).   FV   32.50

58   5 Pounds   VF   UNC

1.2.1997. Purple and violet on multicolor underprint. Archaic limestone head of young man at left, arms at upper center. Thin security thread. Back: Peristerona church and Turkish mosque. Watermark: Bust of Aphrodite. Printer: F-CO (without imprint).   FV   80.00

59   10 Pounds   VF   UNC

1.2.1997. Olive-green and blue-green on multicolor underprint. Marble head of Artemis at left, arms at upper center. Thin security thread. Back: Ruppell's warbler green turtle, butterfly, moufflon, tulip and cyclamen plants. Watermark: Bust of Aphrodite. Printer: F-CO (without imprint).   FV   140

1997-2001 Issue

60   1 Pound   VF   UNC

1.10.1997; 1.12.1998; 1.2.2001; 1.4.2004. Wide security foil. Brown on light tan and multicolor underprint. Cypriot girl at left, arms at upper center with slightly modified colors. Back: Handcrafts and Kato Drys village scene in background. Watermark: Bust of Aphrodite. Printer: F-CO (without imprint).

    a. 1.10.1997.   FV   27.50
    b. 1.12.1998.   FV   23.00
    c. 1.2.2001.   FV   21.00
    d. 1.4.2004. Signature: Chr. Christodoulou.   FV   12.50

61   5 Pounds   VF   UNC

1.2.2001; 1.9.2003. Wide security foil. Purple and violet on multicolor underprint. Archaic limestone head of young man at left, arms at upper center. Back: Peristerona church and Turkish mosque. Watermark: Bust of Aphrodite.

    a. 1.2.2001. Printer: F-CO (without imprint).   FV   75.00
    b. 1.9.2003. Printer: TDLR (without imprint). Signature: Chr. Christodoulou.   FV   50.00

62   10 Pounds   VF UNC

1.10.1997; 1.12.1998; 1.2.2001; 1.9.2003. Wide security foil. Olive-green and
blue-green on multicolor underprint. Marble head of Artemis at left, arms at upper
center. Back: Ruppell's warbler green turtle, butterfly, moufflon, tulip and cyclamen
plants Watermark: Bust of Aphrodite.

   a. 1.10.1997. Printer: F-CO (without imprint).   FV   155
   b. 1.12.1998. Printer: F-CO (without imprint).   FV   145
   c. 1.2.2001. Printer: F-CO (without imprint).   FV   135
   d. 1.9.2003. Printer: TDLR (without imprint). Signature: Chr. Christodoulou.   FV   100
   e. 1.4.2005.   FV 85.00

63   20 Pounds   VF UNC

1.10.1997; 1.10.2001; 1.4.2004. Wide security foil. Deep blue on multicolor
underprint. Bust of Aphrodite at left, arms at upper center, ancient bird (pottery
art) at right. Enhanced designs with micro-printing. Corrected: *YiRMi LiRA*. Back:
Kyrenia boat at center, ancient pottery jugs at lower right. Watermark: Bust of
Aphrodite. Printer: TDLR (without imprint).

   a. 1.10.1997.   FV   255
   b. 1.10.2001.   FV   235
   c. 1.4.2004. Signature: Chr. Christodoulou.   FV   150

In January 2008 the Cypriot Pound was replaced by the Euro.

The Czech Republic is bordered
to the west by Germany, to the north
by Poland, to the east by Slovakia and
to the south by Austria. It consists of 3
major regions: Bohemia, Moravia and
Silesia. It has an area of 78,866 sq.
km. and a population of 10.22 million.
Capital: Prague (Praha). Industrial
production in cities and agriculture
and livestock in the rural areas are
chief occupations while coal deposits
are the main mineral resources.

Following the First World War,
the closely related Czechs and Slovaks of the former Austro-Hungarian Empire merged to form Czechoslovakia. During the interwar years, the new country's leaders were frequently preoccupied with meeting the
demands of other ethnic minorities within the republic, most notably the Sudeten Germans and the Ruthenians
(Ukrainians). After World War II, a truncated Czechoslovakia fell within the Soviet sphere of influence. In 1968,
an invasion by Warsaw Pact troops ended the efforts of the country's leaders to liberalize Communist party
rule and create "socialism with a human face." Anti-Soviet demonstrations the following year ushered in a
period of harsh repression. With the collapse of Soviet authority in 1989, Czechoslovakia regained its freedom
through a peaceful "Velvet Revolution." On 1 January 1993, the country underwent a "velvet divorce" into its
two national components, the Czech Republic and Slovakia. The Czech Republic joined NATO in 1999 and
the European Union in 2004.

MONETARY SYSTEM:
   1 Czechoslovak Koruna (Kcs) = 100 Haleru Jan. - Feb. 1993
   1 Czech Koruna (Kc) = 100 Haleru since Feb. 1993

REPUBLIC
Ceská Národní Banka
CZECH NATIONAL BANK
1993 ND Provisional Issue

#1-3 were released 8.2.1993 having adhesive revalidation stamps affixed
(later a printed *1000* was also circulated). Valid until 31.8.1993 but could be
exchanged in deposits until 31.5.1994. Old Czechoslovak notes of 100 Korun
and higher denominations became obsolete on 7.2.1993. Smaller denominations remained in circulation until 30.11.1993. Note: In 1997 the CNB made
available uncirculated examples of #1-3a and 3b to collectors. The notes are
without cancellation marks and have regular serial #.

1   100 Korun   VF UNC

ND (1993-old date 1961). . Dark green. *C-100* adhesive stamp affixed to Czechoslovakia #91a or 91b.

   a. Stamp on Czechslovakia #91a.   50.00   100
   b. Stamp on Czechslovakia #91b.   12.50 30.00
   c. Stamp on Czechslovakia #91c.   5.00 27.50

2   500 Korun   VF UNC

ND (1993-old date 1973). Dark green. *D-500* adhesive stamp affixed to Czecho-   15.00 50.00
slovakia #93. Series prefixes: U, W, Z.

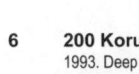

3   1000 Korun   VF   UNC
ND (1993-old date 1985). Deep green. *M-1000* revalidation stamp on Czecho-slovakia #98.
   a. Adhesive stamp affixed. Series prefixes: C, U.   40.00   155
   b. Stamp image printed. Series prefix: U.   40.00   155

1993 Regular Issue

#4-7 replacement notes: Serial # prefix *Z*.

4   50 Korun   VF   UNC
1993. Violet and black on pink and gray underprint. St. Agnes of Bohemia at right with crown, arms at center right. Serial number prefix *A*. Back: Large A within gothic window frame at left center. Watermark: St. Agnes of Bohemia with crown. Printer: TDLR. 134x64mm.
   a. Issued note.   4.00   14.00
   r. Serial # prefix *Z*, replacement.   50.00   150

5   100 Korun   VF   UNC
1993. Blue-green, green and blue-black on lilac and multicolor underprint. King Karel IV at right, arms at center right. Serial number prefix *A*. Back: Large seal of Charles University at left center. Watermark: King Karel IV. Printer: TDLR. 140x69mm.
   a. Issued note.   11.00   35.00
   r. Serial # prefix *Z*, replacement.   35.00   80.00

6   200 Korun   VF   UNC
1993. Deep brown on light orange and light green underprint. Jan Ámos Komen-sky at right, arms at center right. Serial number prefix *A*. Back: Hands outreached at left center. Watermark: Jan Ámos Komensky. Printer: STC-P. 146x69mm.
   a. Security filament with *200 KCS*.   18.00   65.00
   b. Security filament with *200 KC*.   16.00   27.50
   x. Error. Security filament reads: *REPUBLIQUE DU ZAÏRE*.   2,000   3,500

7   500 Korun   VF   UNC
1993. Dark brown, brown & brown-violet on pink and tan underprint. Rose in underprint at upper center, Bozena Nemcova at right, arms at center right. Serial number prefix *A*. Back: Laureate young woman's head at left center. Watermark: Bozena Nemcová. Printer: TDLR. 152x69mm.
   a. Issued note.   38.00   52.50
   r. Serial # prefix *Z*, replacement.   60.00   150
   s. Specimen.   —   —

8   1000 Korun   VF   UNC
1993. Purple and lilac on multicolor underprint. Frantisek Palacky, arms at center right. Serial number prefix *A; B*. Back: Eagle and Kromeriz Castle. Watermark: Frantisek Palacky. Printer: STC-P. 158x74mm. Note: Foil segments vary somewhat in position.
   a. Issued ntoe.   70.00   100
   s. Specimen.   —   —

9   5000 Korun   VF   UNC
1993. Black, blue-gray and violet on pink and light gray underprint. President To-   350   450
mas Garrigue Masaryk at right, arms at center right. Serial number prefix *A*. Back:
Montage of Prague Gothic and Baroque buildings. Printer: STC-P. 170x74mm.

1994-96 Issue

10   20 Korun   VF   UNC
1994. Blue-black and gray on light blue underprint. King Premysl Otakar I at right.
Back: Crown with seal above at center, stylized crown at lower right. Watermark:
King Premysl Otakar I. Printer: STC-P. 128x64mm.
    a. Serial # prefix *A; B*. Security filament at center (74mm from left edge).   FV   6.00
       (1994).
    b. Serial # prefix *B*. Security filament at left center (50mm from left edge).   FV   3.50
       (1995).

11   50 Korun   VF   UNC
1994. Violet and black on multicolor underprint. St. Agnes of Bohemia with crown   FV   7.50
at right , arms at center right, without gray in underprint. Serial number prefix *B*.
Back: Stylized heart at lower right. Watermark: St. Agnes of Bohemia. Printer:
STC-P. 134x64mm.

12   100 Korun   VF   UNC
1995. Blue-green, green and blue-black on lilac and multicolor underprint. King   FV   14.00
Karel IV at right. Serial number prefix *B*. Back: Large seal of Charles University at
left center with stylized *K* in circle at lower right. Watermark: King Karel IV. Printer:
STC-P. 140x69mm.

13   200 Korun   VF   UNC
1996. Deep brown on pale orange and light green underprint. Jan Ámos Komen-   FV   18.00
sky at right. Serial number prefix *B*. Back: Hands outreached at left center, stylized
open book at lower right. Watermark: Jan Ámos Komensky. Printer: STC-P.

14   500 Korun   VF   UNC
1995. Dark brown, brown and brown-violet on pink and tan underprint. Bozena   FV   42.50
Nemcová at right, arms at center right. Serial number prefix *B*. Back: Laureate
young woman's head at left center, stylized rose at lower right. Watermark:
Bozena Nemcová. Printer: STC-P. 152x69mm.

15   1000 Korun   VF   UNC
1996. Purple and lilac on multicolor underprint. Frantisek Palacky with metallic   FV   110
linden leaf at upper center. Serial number prefix *C, D, E, F*. Back: Eagle and
Kromeriz Castle, stylized *P* and tree at lower right. Watermark: Frantisek Palacky.
Printer: STC-P. 158x74mm.

16   2000 Korun   VF   UNC
1996. Dark olive-green, gray and violet on tan underprint. Ema Destinnová at   FV   220
right, lyre at at upper left in spray. Serial number prefix *A*. Back: Muse of music
and lyric poetry Euterpe at left center, violin and cello and a large *D*, stylized lyre
at lower right. Printer: STC-P. 164x74mm.

1997-99 Issue

17 50 Korun

1997. Violet and purple on multicolor underprint. St. Agnes of Bohemia with crown at right , arms at center right, without gray in underprint. Serial number prefix *C, D, E*. Back: Stylized heart at lower right. Watermark: St. Agnes of Bohemia. Printer: STC-P. 134x64mm.

VF UNC
FV 5.50

18 100 Korun

1997. Dark green, dark olive-green and black on multicolor underprint. King Karel IV at right. Serial number prefix *C, D, E, F*. Back: Large seal of Charles University at left center with stylized *K* in circle at lower right. Watermark: King Karel IV. Printer: STC-P. 140x69mm.

VF UNC
FV 10.00

19 200 Korun

1998. Fibers added in the paper. Deep brown on pale orange and light green underprint. Jan Ámos Komensky at right, arms at center right. Stylized open book at lower right. Serial number prefix *C, D, E*. Back: Hands outreached at left center, stylized open book at lower right. Watermark: Jan Ámos Komensky. Printer: STC-P. 146x69mm.

VF UNC
FV 20.00

20 500 Korun

1997. Fibers added in the paper. Dark brown, brown and brown-violet on pink and tan underprint. Bozena Nemcová at right, arms at center right. Serial number prefix *C, D*. Back: Laureate young woman's head at left center, stylized rose at lower right. Watermark: Bozena Nemcová. Printer: STC-P. 152x69mm.

VF UNC
FV 42.50

#21 not assigned.

22 2000 Korun

1999. Fibers added in the paper. Dark olive-green and violet on tan underprint. Ema Destinnová at right, lyre at upper left in spray. Three metallic vertical bars in lyre at top center. Serial number prefix *B*. Back: Muse of music and lyric poetry Euterpe at left center, violin, cello, large D, stylized lyre at lower right. Printer: STC-P. 164x74mm.

VF UNC
FV 200

23 5000 Korun

1999. Fibers added in the paper. Black, blue-gray and violet on pink and light gray underprint. President Tomas Garrigue Masaryk at right. Metallic hexagon emblem at top center. Serial number prefix *B*. Back: Montage of Prague Gothic and Baroque buildings. Linden leaf in watermark area. 170x74mm.

VF UNC
FV 425

2007-09 Issue

24 500 Korun

2009. Dark brown, brown and brown-violet on pink and tan. Bozena Nemcová at right. Back: Laureate young woman's head at center. Watermark: Bozena Nemcová. Printer: STC-P 152x69mm.

VF UNC
FV 40.00

25 1000 Korun
2008. Purple and lilac on multicolor underprint. Frantisek Palacky at right. Series G. Wide security thread. Back: Eagle and Kromeriz Castle. Printer: STC-P. 157x74mm.

	VF	UNC
a. 2008.	FV	80.00

26 2000 Korun
2007. Dark olive-green and violet on tan underprint. Ema Destinnova at right, lyre at upper left in spray. Three metallic vertical bars in lyre at top center. Serial number prefix *C*. Back: Muse of music and lyric poetry Euterpe at left center, violin, cello, large D, stylized lyre at lower right. Printer: STC-P 164x74mm.

	VF	UNC
	FV	160

27 5000 Korun
2009. Black, blue-gray and violet on pink and light gray underprint. President Tomas Garrigue Masaryk at right. Back: MOntage of Prague Gothic and Baroque architecture. Printer: STC-P. 170x74mm.

	VF	UNC
	FV	425

The Republic of Czechoslovakia, located in central Europe, had an area of 49,365 sq. mi. (127,859 sq. km.). Capital: Prague (Praha). Industrial production in the cities and agriculture and livestock in the rural areas were the chief occupations. The Czech lands to the west were united with the Slovak to form the Czechoslovak Republic on October 28, 1918 upon the dissolution of the Austrian-Hungarian Empire. Tomas G. Masaryk was the first president. In the 1930s Hitlet provoked Czechoslovakia's German minority in the Sudetenland to agitate for autonomy. The territory was broken up for the benefit of Germany, Poland and Hungary by the Munich agreement signed by the United Kingdom, France, Germany and Italy on September 29, 1938. On March 15, 1939, Germany invaded Czechoslovakia and incorporated the Czech lands into the Third Reich as the "Protectorate of Bohemia and Moravia." eastern Slovakia, was constituted as a republic under Nazi inulence. A government-in-exile was set up in London in 1940. The Soviet and American forces liberated the area by May 1945. After World War II the physical integrity and independence of Czechoslovakia was re-established, while bringing it within the Russian sphere of influence. On February 23-25, 1948, the Communists seized control of the government in a *coup d'etat,* and adopted a constitution making the country a "people's republic." A new constitution adopted June 11, 1960, converted the country into a "socialist republic." Communist infulence increased steadily while pressure for liberalization culminated in the overthrow of the Stalinist leader Antonçin Novotny and his associates in January, 1968. The Communist Party then introduced far reaching reforms which received warnings from Moscow, followed by occupation of Warsaw Pact forces on August 21, 1968 resulting in stationing of Soviet troops. Student demonstrations for reform began in Prague on November 17, 1989. The Federal Assembly abolished the Communist Party's sole right to govern. In December, 1989, communism was overthrown. In January, 1990 the Czech and Slovak Federal Republic (CSFR) was formed. The movement for a democratic Slovakia was apparent in the June 1992 elections with the Slovak National Council adopting a declaration of sovereignty. The CSFR was disolved on December 31, 1992, and both new republics came into being on January 1, 1993. See the Czech Republic and Slovakia sections for additional listings.

MONETARY SYSTEM:
1 Koruna = 100 Haleru

SPECIMEN NOTES:
Large quantities of specimens were made available to collectors. Notes issued after 1945 are distinguished by a perforation consisting of three small holes or a letter S (for Solvakia). Since the difference in value between issued notes and specimen notes is frequently very great, both types of notes are valued. Earlier issues recalled from circulation were perforated: *SPECIMEN* or *NEPLATNE* or with a letter S for collectors. Caution should be exercised while examining notes as examples of perforated notes having the holes filled in are known.

NOTE AVAILABILITY:
The Czech National Bank in 1997 made available to collectors uncirculated examples of #78-98, as a full set or in issue groups. As the notes were demonetized they had no cancellation holes nor were overprinted. These notes have regular serial #'s and thus can not be distinguished from regular uncirculated notes of the period.

SOCIALIST REPUBLIC
Ceskoslovenská Socialistická Republika
CZECHOSLOVAK SOCIALIST REPUBLIC
1961 Issue

81 3 Koruny
1961. Blue on blue-green underprint. Large three at center and upper corners. Back: Socialist arms at center. Watermark: Star in circle, repeated. Printer: STC-P. 113x56mm.

	VF	UNC
a. Issued note. Serial # prefix 2.5mm in height.	1.00	3.00
b. Issued note. Serial # prefix 3mm in height.	1.00	3.00
s. Perforated with 3 holes or *SPECIMEN*.	0.50	3.00

82 5 Korun
1961. Dull black on pale green underprint. Text in frame. Back: Socialist arms at center. Watermark: Star in circle, repeated. Printer: STC-P. 123x60mm.

	VF	UNC
a. Issued note. Serial # prefix 2.5mm in height.	1.00	3.00
b. Issued note. Serial # prefix 3mm in height.	1.00	3.00
s. Perforated with 3 holes or *SPECIMEN*.	0.50	3.00

Státní Banka Ceskoslovenská

CZECHOSLOVAK STATE BANK

1960-64 Issue

88   10 Korun   **VF   UNC**

1960. Brown on multicolor underprint. Two girls with flowers at right. Back: Orava Dam. Watermark: Star and linden leaf. Printer: STC-Prague. 133x65mm.

    a. Series prefix: H; F (wet photogravure printing). (Smaller image area).   20.00   50.00

    b. Series prefixes: E, J, L, M, S, X (dry photogravure printing).   1.50   6.00

    s. Specimen.   —   3.00

89   25 Korun   **VF   UNC**

1961 (1962). Blue-black on light blue underprint. Arms at left center. Portrait Jan Zizka at right. Back: Tábor town square. Printer: STC-Prague. 138x70mm.

    a. Series prefix: E. (wet printing).   50.00   200

    b. Series prefix: Q. (dry printing)   5.00   20.00

    s. Perforated: SPECIMEN.   —   2.00

90   50 Korun   **VF   UNC**

1964 (1965). Red-brown. Arms at left, Russian soldier and partisan at right. Back: Slovnaft refinery in Bratislava. Printer: STC-Prague. 150x74mm.

    a. Series prefix: K. (wet printing).   100   500

    b. Series prefix: A; N; G; J (dry printing).   5.00   15.00

91   100 Korun   **VF   UNC**

1961. Deep green on multicolor underprint. Factory at lower left, farm couple at right. Back: Charles Bridge and Hradcany in Prague. Watermark: Star and linden leaf. Printer: STC-Prague. 164x80mm.

    a. Watermark: Star within linden leaf, repeated. Series prefix: B01-40; C; D (wet printing).   30.00   60.00

    b. As a. Series prefix: B41-99; P; R; T; Z; X01-24 (dry printing).   10.00   20.00

    c. Reissue watermark: Multiple stars and linden leaves. Series prefix: X25-96; G; M. (1990-92).   5.00   10.00

Note: #91b or #91c w/added C-100 adhesive stamp, see Czech Republic. With SLOVENSKÁ REPUBLIKA adhesive stamp, see Slovakia.

1970; 1973 Issue

92   20 Korun   **VF   UNC**

1970 (1971). Blue on light blue and multicolor underprint. Arms at center, Jan Zizka at right. Series prefix: F, H, L, M. Back: Husite soldiers. Printer: STC-Prague. 132x58mm.   1.00   2.50

93   500 Korun   **VF   UNC**

1973. Deep brown-violet and multicolor. Soldiers at right. Series prefix: U, W, Z. Back: Medieval shield at lower center, mountain fortress ruins at Devin at right. Printer: STC-Prague. 154x68mm.   10.00   30.00

Note: For #93 with additional "D-500" adhesive stamp, see Czech Republic. SLOVENSKÁ REPUBLIKA adhesive stamp, see Slovakia.

1985-89 Issue

94   10 Korun   **VF   UNC**

1986. Deep brown on blue and multicolor underprint. Pavol Orszag-Hviezdoslav at right. Series prefix: J, P, V. Back: Bird at lower left, view of Orava mountains. Printer: STC-Prague. 132x67mm.   0.50   2.00

95 20 Korun   **VF UNC**

1988. Blue and multicolor. Jan Ámos Komensky at right, circular design with open book at left. Series prefix: E, H. Back: Alphabet at left, Tree of life growing from book at center, young couple at right. Printer: STC-Prague. 137x67mm.   0.75   2.50

Note: For #95 with additional *SLOVENSKÁ REPUBLIKA* adhesive stamp, see Slovakia.

96 50 Korun   **VF UNC**

1987. Brown-violet and blue on red and orange underprint. Ludovít Stúr at right, shield and spotted eagle at right. Back: Bratislava castle and town view. Printer: STC-Prague. 142x67mm.

  a. Series prefix: *F.*   1.50   5.00
  b. Series prefix: *I.*   2.50   8.00

Note: For #96 with additional *SLOVENSKÁ REPUBLIKA* adhesive stamp, see Slovakia.

97 100 Korun   **VF UNC**

1989. Dark green on green and red underprint. Klement Gottwald at right. Series prefix: A. Back: Hradcany in Prague. Printer: STC-Prague.   5.00   12.00

Note: #97 was in circulation only from 1.10.1989 to 31.12.1990.

98 1000 Korun   **VF UNC**

1985. Blue-black, blue and purple on multicolor underprint. Bedrich Smetana at right. Back: Vysehrad Castle at left. Printer: SCT-Prague. 157x67mm.

  a. Serial # prefix *C.*   20.00   50.00
  b. Serial # prefix *U.*   30.00   100

Note: For #98 w/additional "M-1000" adhesive stamp or printed, see Czech Republic. With *SLOVENSKÁ REPUBLIKA* adhesive stamp, see Slovakia.

DENMARK

The Kingdom of Denmark, a constitutional monarchy located at the mouth of the Baltic Sea, has an area of 43,094 sq. km. and a population of 5.48 million. Capital: Copenhagen. Most of the country is arable. Agriculture, which used to employ the majority of the people, is now conducted by large farms served by cooperatives. The largest industries are food processing, iron and metal, and shipping. Machinery, meats (chiefly bacon), dairy products and chemicals are exported.

Once the seat of Viking raiders and later a major north European power, Denmark has evolved into a modern, prosperous nation that is participating in the general political and economic integration of Europe. It joined NATO in 1949 and the EEC (now the EU) in 1973. However, the country has opted out of certain elements of the European Union's Maastricht Treaty, including the European Economic and Monetary Union (EMU), European defense cooperation, and issues concerning certain justice and home affairs.

RULERS:
Frederik IX, 1947-1972
Margrethe II, 1972-

MONETARY SYSTEM:
1 Kronc (1/2 Rigsdaler) = 100 re 1874-

REPLACEMENT NOTES:
#42-45 although dated (19)50, they were issued from 1952 onwards.
#42-47, suffix OJ (for whole sheets) or OK (for single notes).

KINGDOM

Danmarks Nationalbank

1944-46 Issue

#35-41 first signatrue: Svendsen for 1944-45. Halberg for 1945-49. Riim for 1948-62.

41 500 Kroner   **VF UNC**

1944-62. Orange-red. Farmer with horses at center, plowing a field. Back: Arms. 175x108mm.

  a. 1944. Prefix D. Left signature: Svendsen.   700   2,000
  b. 1945. Prefix D. Left signature: Halberg.   950   2,300
  c. 1948. Prefix D. Left signature: Halberg.   950   2,300
  d. 1948. Prefix D. Left signature: Riim.   950   2,300
  e. 1951. Prefix D. Left signature: Riim.   1,200   2,700
  f. 1953. Prefix D. Left signature: Riim.   1,200   2,700
  g. 1954. Prefix D. Left signature: Riim.   1,400   3,200
  h. 1956. Prefix D. Left signature: Riim.   850   2,300
  i. 1959. Prefix D. Left signature: Riim.   725   1,900
  j. 1961. Prefix D. Left signature: Riim.   1,100   2,500
  k. 1962. Prefix D. Left signature: Riim.   850   2,400
  s. Specimen.   —   —

1950 (1952)-63 Issue

Law of 7.4.1936 #42-47 first signatrue changes. Usually there are 3 signatrue combinations per prefix A0, A1, A2 etc. Second signature Riim, (19)51-68 for #42, 43, 44a-f, (19)51-68 for #42, 43, 44a-f, 45a-b, 46a-b, 47. Valeur for (19)69 for #44g-h, 45c and 46b. The prefixes mentioned in the listings refer to the first two characters of the left serial #. The middle two digits indicate the year date of issue, and the last two characters indicate the sheet position of the note. Replacement Notes: #42-47, Serial # suffix: OJ (for whole sheet replacements) or OK (for single note replacements).

42 5 Kroner

(19)50; (19)52; (19)54-60. Blue-green. Portrait Bertil Thorvaldsen at left, three Graces at right. Back: Kalundborg city view with five spire church at center. Watermark: *5* repeated. 125x65mm.

	VF	UNC
a. 5 in the watermark 11mm high. Without dot after 7 in law date. (19)52. Prefix A0; A1.	30.00	120
b. As a. (19)52. Prefix A2.	60.00	235
c. As a, but with dot after 7 in law date. (19)52. Prefix A2.	40.00	150
d. As c. (19)52. Prefix A3.	70.00	250
e. As c. (19)54. Prefixes A3-A5.	35.00	135
f. As c. (19)54. Prefix A6.	45.00	180
g. As c. (19)55. Prefixes A7-A8.	35.00	135
h. As c. (19)55. Prefix A9.	45.00	180
i. 5 in the watermark 13mm high. Prefix B0.	20.00	80.00
j. As i. (19)55. Prefix B1.	45.00	180
k. As i. (19)56. Prefix B1.	40.00	150
l. As i. (19)56. Prefixes B2-B3.	30.00	120
m. As i. (19)56. Prefix B4.	60.00	240
n. As i. (19)57. Prefixes B4-B6.	12.00	35.00
o. As i. (19)58-59. Prefixes B7-B9, C0.	12.00	34.00
p. As i. (19)59. Prefix C1.	8.00	28.00
q. As i. (19)59. Prefix C3.	400	800
r. As i. (19)60. Prefixes C3.	8.00	28.00
r1. Replacement note. (19)50. Prefixes as e, g. suffix 0J.	70.00	180
r2. Replacement note. (19)50. Prefixes as f, h, j, m,q, suffix 0J.	100	280
r3. Replacement note. (19)50. Prefixes as i, l, suffix 0J.	60.00	160
r4. Replacement note. (19)50. Prefixes as n, o, suffix 0J.	45.00	110
r5. Replacement note. (19)60. Prefixes as p, r, s, suffix 0J.	30.00	80.00
r6. Replacement note. (19)50. Prefixes as a, suffix 0K.	450	—
r7. Replacement note. (19)50. Prefixes as e, suffix 0K.	450	—
r8. Replacement note. (19)60. Prefixes as f, suffix 0K.	450	—
r9. Replacement note (19)50. Prefixes as o, suffix 0K.	450	900
r10. Replacement note. (19)60. Prefixes as s, suffix 0K.	450	—
s. As i. (19)60. Prefix C4.	10.00	32.00
s1. Specimen.	—	350

43 10 Kroner

(19)50-52. Black and olive-brown. Portrait Hans Christian Andersen at left, white storks in nest at right. Back: Green landscape of Egeskov Mølle Fyn at center. Watermark: *10* repeated. 125x65mm.

	VF	UNC
a. (19)51. Prefix A0.	60.00	220
b. (19)51. Prefix A3.	125	400
c. (19)51. Prefix A4.	90.00	275
d. (19)52. Prefix A1-A2; A5-A8.	50.00	180
e. (19)52. Prefix A9.	550	—
f. (19)52. Prefix B0.	115	325
g. (19)52. Prefix B1.	150	450
r1. (19)51. Replacement note. Suffix 0K.	650	—
r2. (19)52. Replacement note. Suffix 0K.	550	—

44 10 Kroner

(19)50; (19)54-74. Black and brown. Portrait Hans Christian Andersen at left, white storks in nest at right, text line added in upper and lower frame. Portrait Hans Christian Andersen at left. Back: Black landscape at center. 125x71mm.

	VF	UNC
a. Top and bottom line in frame begins with *10*. Watermark: *10* repeated, 11mm high. (19)54. Prefix C0.	30.00	120
b. As a. Prefix C1.	60.00	200
c. As a. Watermark 13mm high. (19)54. Prefix C1.	60.00	200
d. As c. (19)54-55. Prefixes C2-D5.	27.00	110
e. As c. (19)55. Prefix D6.	100	275
f. As c. (19)56. Prefix D6.	80.00	240
g. As a. (19)56. Prefix D6.	100	275
h. As a. (19)56. Prefix D7.	70.00	240
i. As a. (19)56. Prefix D8.	70.00	220
j. As c. (19)56. Prefixes D8-E1.	24.00	90.00
k. As c. (19)56. Prefix E2.	350	750
l. As c. (19)57. Prefixes E2-E4.	22.00	85.00
m. Top and bottom line in frame begins with *Ti*. (19)57. Prefix E4.	350	750
n. As m. (19)57. Prefixes E5-E6.	22.00	85.00
o. As m. (19)58. Prefixes E7-F3.	20.00	75.00
p. As m. (19)57. Prefix E7.	180	450
q. As m. (19)58. Prefix F4.	22.00	85.00
r. As m. (19)59. Prefix F4.	27.00	110
r1. Replacement note. (19)50. Prefixes as d. Suffix 0J.	100	200
r2. Replacement note. (19)50. Prefixes as e-i, m. Suffix 0J.	150	400
r3. Replacement note. (19)50. Prefixes as j, l. Suffix 0J.	95.00	220
r4. Replacement note. (19)50, (19)60. Prefixes as n, p-s. Suffix 0J.	50.00	135
r5. Replacement note. (19)60. Prefixes as t. Suffix 0J.	45.00	110
r6. Replacement note. (19)61-64. Prefixes as u, w. Suffix 0J.	35.00	70.00
r7. Replacement note. (19)62. Prefixes as v. Suffix 0J.	50.00	140
r8. Replacement note. (19)64. Prefixes as x. Suffix 0J.	40.00	90.00
r9. Replacement note. (19)65-69. Prefixes as y-ac. Suffix 0J.	15.00	40.00
r10. Replacement note. (19)70-71. Prefixes as ae. Suffix 0J.	12.00	30.00
r11. Replacement note. (19)69, (19)71. Prefixes as ad, af. Suffix 0J.	200	425
r12. Replacement note. (19)74. Prefixes as ag, ai. Suffix 0J.	9.00	22.00
r13. Replacement note. (19)74. Prefix as aj. Suffix 0J.	11.00	25.00
r14. Replacement note. (19)50. Prefixes as d. Suffix 0K.	650	—
r15. Replacement note. (19)62-64. Prefixes as u-w. Suffix 0K.	550	—
r16. Replacement note. (19)65-69. Prefix as y-ac. Suffix 0K.	350	—
r17. Replacement note. (19)69, (19)71. Prefixes as ad, af. Suffix 0K.	400	—
r18. Replacement note. (19)70-73. Prefixes as ae, ag. Suffix 0K.	175	350
r19. Replacement note. (19)74. Prefixes as ai-aj. Suffix 0K.	250	450
s. As m. (19)59. Prefixes F5-F8.	20.00	75.00
t. As m. (19)60. Prefixes F9-G3.	18.00	60.00
u. As m. (19)61-62. Prefixes G4-H1.	16.00	50.00
v. As m. (19)62. Prefix H2.	27.00	110
w. As m. (19)63-64. Prefixes H2-J3.	14.00	40.00
x. As m. (19)64. Prefix J4.	25.00	75.00
y. As m. (19)65-67. Prefixes J5-K9.	12.00	30.00
z. As m. (19)68. Prefixes A0-A3.	8.00	25.00
aa. As m. (19)68. Second signature: Riim. Prefix A4.	11.00	22.50
ab. As m. (19)69. Second signature: Valear. Prefix A4.	11.00	22.50
ac. As aa. (19)69. Prefixes A5-A8.	9.00	18.00
ad. As aa. (19)69. Prefix A9.	120	300
ae. As aa. (19)70-71. Prefixes A9-B9.	5.00	14.00
af. As aa. (19)71. Prefix C0.	120	300
ag. As aa. (19)72-73. Prefixes C0-C9.	4.75	12.50
ah. As aa. (19)74. Prefix C9.	120	300
ai. As aa. (19)74. Prefixes D0-D5.	4.00	10.00
aj. As aa. (19)74. Prefix D6.	5.00	14.00
s1. Specimen.	—	500

45   50 Kroner

(19)50; (19)56-70. Blue on green underprint. Portrait Ole Rømer at left, Round Tower in Copenhagen at right. Back: Stone Age burial site Dolmen of Stenvad, Djursland at center. 153x78mm.

	VF	UNC
a. Handmade paper. Watermark: Crowns and 50 (19)56, Prefix A1.	140	350
b. As a. (19)57. Prefix A1.	140	350
c. As a. (19)57. Prefix A2.	165	400
d. As a. (19)58. Prefix A2.	75.00	250
e. As a. (19)58. Prefix B0.	600	1,250
f. As a. (19)60. Prefix A2.	1,500	
g. Machine made paper. Watermark: Rhombuses and 50. (19)61/1962. Prefix A4.	75.00	250
h. As f. (19)62. Prefix A4.	80.00	260
i. As f. (19)63. Prefix A4.	70.00	250
j. As f. (19)63. Prefix A5.	60.00	120
k. As f. (19)66. Prefix A6-A7.	40.00	85.00
l. As f. (19)66. Prefix A8.	80.00	160
m. As g. (19)70. Prefix A8-A9.	35.00	80.00
r1. As a. Replacement note. (19)50/1956. Suffix 0J.	120	300
r2. As b. Replacement note. (19)50/1957. Suffix 0J.	120	300
r3. As c. Replacement note. (19)57. Suffix 0J.	150	375
r4. As d. Replacement note. (19)50/1958. Suffix 0J.	90.00	275
r5. As f. Replacement note. Prefixes A2-A3. (19)60.	75.00	250
r6. As g-j. Replacement note. (19)61-63. Suffix 0J.	80.00	250
r7. As k. Replacement note. (19)66. Suffix 0J.	50.00	140
r8. As l. Replacement note. (19)66. Suffix 0J.	90.00	200
r9. As m. Replacement note. (19)70. Suffix 0J.	40.00	90.00
r10. As b. Replacement note. (19)50/1957. Suffix 0K.	550	1,500
r11. As d. Replacement note. (19)50/1958. Suffix 0K.	700	1,750
r12. As f. Replacement note. (19)60. Suffix 0K.	550	1,500
r13. As k-l. Replacement note. (19)66. Suffix 0K.	450	1,250
r14. As m. Replacement note. (19)70 Suffix 0K.	400	1,000
s. Specimen.	—	600

#45g shows date in lower left corner as 1962, while the date in the left serial number shows (19)61. On the replacements r1-r4 and r10-r11, the date in the lower left corner shows the actual date, while the date in the left serial number shows (19)50.

46   100 Kroner

(19)61-70. Red-brown on red-yellow underprint. Portrait Hans Christian Ørsted at left, compass card at right. Back: Kronborg castle in Elsinore. 155x84mm.

	VF	UNC
a. Handmade paper. Watermark: Close wavy lines and compass. (19)61. Prefix A0.	400	1,000
b. Machine made paper. Watermark: 100. (19)61. Prefix A2-A3.	75.00	265
c. (19)62. Prefix A4-A5.	90.00	300
d. (19)65. Prefix A6-B1.	50.00	130
e. (19)65. Prefix B2.	120	425
f. (19)70. Prefix B2-B4.	40.00	100
r1. As a. Replacement note. (19)61. Suffix 0J.	45.00	400

	VF	UNC
r2. As b. Replacement note. (19)62. Suffix 0J.	80.00	300
r3. As c. Replacement note. (19)62. Suffix 0J.	110	350
r4. As d. Replacement note. (19)65. Suffix 0J.	60.00	150
r5. As d. Replacement note. (19)65. Suffix 0J.	120	400
r6. As f. Replacement note. (19)70. Suffix 0J.	40.00	110
r7. As a. Replacement note. (19)61. Suffix 0K.	650	1,250
r8. As d. Replacement note. (19)65. Suffix 0K.	650	1,250
r9. As f. Replacement note. (19)70. Suffix 0K.	650	1,250
s. Specimen.	—	600

47   500 Kroner

1963-67. Green. Portrait C.D.F. Reventlow at left, farmer plowing at right. Small date at lower right. Back: Roskilde city view. 175x90mm.

	VF	UNC
a. 1963. Prefix A0.	300	800
b. 1965. Prefix A0.	300	900
c. 1967. Prefix A0.	200	525
d. 1967. Prefix A1.	240	575
r1. As a. Replacement note. (19)63. Suffix 0J.	325	900
r2. As b. Replacement note. (19)65. Suffix 0J.	340	1,050
r3. As c. Replacement note. (19)67. Suffix 0J.	225	650
r4. As d. Replacement note. (19)67. Suffix 0J.	240	575
s. Specimen.	—	900

1972; 1979 Issue

Issued under *L. 1936*. **The year of issue is shown by the 2 middle numerals within the alpha-numeric series code at lower left or right. Signature varieties.**

48   10 Kroner

(19)72-78. Black on olive and multicolor underprint. Portrait Catherine Sophie Kirchhoff by Jens Juel at right. Back: Eider duck at left, *SERIE* 1972 at lower right. Printer: Nationalbanken, Copenhagen (without imprint). 125x67mm.

	VF	UNC
a. (19)72. Prefix A0-A2.	7.00	20.00
b. (19)72. Prefix A3.	25.00	80.00
c. (19)75. Prefix A4. Blight security thread.	5.00	12.00
d. (19)75. Prefix A4. Light-colored security thread.	35.00	90.00
e. (19)75. Prefixes A5-A7.	4.00	9.00
f. (19)76. Prefixes A8-A9, B10.	3.00	6.00
g. (19)77. Prefixes B1-B7.	FV	4.00
h. (19)78. Prefix B8.	FV	4.00

49 20 Kroner

(19)79-88. Dark blue on brown and multicolor underprint. Portrait PaulineTutein by Jens Juel at right. Back: Male and female House Sparrow at left center, *SERIE* 1972 at lower right. Watermark: Painter's palette, brushes and *20*. Printer: Nationalbanken, Copenhagen (without imprint). 125x72mm.

		VF	UNC
a. (19)79. Prefix A0-A4.		4.50	12.00
b. (19)80. Prefix A5.		5.50	16.00
c. (19)81. Prefix A6, C0-C1.		5.00	14.00
d. (19)83. Prefix C2.		5.00	14.00
e. (19)84. Prefix C3-C4.		FV	12.00
f. (19)85. Prefix C5.		FV	12.00
g. (19)87. Prefix C6.		FV	8.00
h. (19)88. Prefix C7-C8.		FV	7.00

51 100 Kroner

(19)72-93. Black and red on multicolor underprint. Jens Juel's self-portrait (ca.1773-74) at right. Back: Danish Red Order Ribbon moth at left, *SERIE* 1972 at lower right. Printer: Nationalbanken, Copenhagen (without imprint). 150x78mm.

		VF	UNC
a. (19)72. Prefix A0-A2.		50.00	200
b. (19)75. Prefix A3-A5.		45.00	150
c. (19)76. Prefix A6.		37.50	100
d. (19)77. Prefix A7.		70.00	275
e. (19)78. Prefixes A8-A9, B0.		35.00	90.00
f. (19)79. Prefixes B1-B3.		32.00	85.00
g. (19)81. Prefix B4.		170	425
h. (19)81. Prefixes C0-C1.		25.00	70.00
i. (19)82. Prefix C2.		30.00	80.00
j. (19)83. Prefix C3-C4.		25.00	70.00
k. (19)84. Prefixes C5-C6.		25.00	70.00
l. (19)84. Prefix C7.		30.00	80.00
m. (19)85. Prefixes C8-C9.		22.50	60.00
n. (19)85. Prefix H0.		100	350
o. (19)86. Prefix D0-D2.		22.50	60.00
p. (19)86. Prefix R1.		85.00	300
q. (19)87. Prefixes D3-D4.		20.00	50.00
r. (19)88. Prefixes D5-D6.		FV	45.00
s. (19)89. Prefix D7.		FV	40.00
t. (19)90. Prefixes D8-D9, E0.		FV	37.50
u. (19)91. Prefix E1.		FV	32.50
v. (19)91. Prefix E2.		30.00	80.00
w. (19)93. Prefix E3-E4.		FV	32.50
s1. Specimen.		—	500

50 50 Kroner

(19)72-98. Dark gray on pale blue, dull purple and pale green underprint. Portrait Mrs. Ryberg by Jens Juel at right. Back: *Carassius-Carassius* fish at left, *SERIE* 1972 at lower right. Printer: Nationalbanken, Copenhagen (without imprint). 139x72mm.

		VF	UNC
a. (19)72. Prefix A0-A1.		50.00	150
b. (19)76. Prefix A2-A3.		40.00	125
c. (19)78. Prefix A4-A5.		27.50	75.00
d. (19)79. Prefix A6.		35.00	100
e. (19)82. Prefix C0-C1.		27.50	75.00
f. (19)84. Prefix C2-C3.		25.00	65.00
g. (19)85. Prefix C4.		20.00	45.00
h. (19)89. Prefix C5.		16.00	30.00
i. (19)90. Prefixes C6-C7.		12.00	23.00
j. (19)92. Prefixes C8-C9.		12.00	23.00
k. (19)94. Prefix D0.		12.50	25.00
l. (19)95. Prefix D1.		27.50	75.00
m. (19)96. Prefixes D2-D3.		11.00	18.00
n. (19)97. Prefix D4.		FV	16.00
o. (19)98. Prefix D5.		FV	16.00
s. Specimen.		—	400

52 500 Kroner

(19)72-88. Black on green and multicolor underprint. *Unknown Lady* portrait by Jens Juel, possibly von Qualen at right. Back: Lizard, *SERIE* 1972 at lower right. Watermark: Jens Juel and *500* repeated. Printer: Nationalbanken, Copenhagen (without imprint). 164x85mm.

		VF	UNC
a. (19)72. Prefix A0-A1.		160	300
b. (19)76. Prefix A2.		140	275
c. (19)80. Prefix A3-A5.		125	235
d. (19)88. Prefix C0-C1.		FV	220

53 1000 Kroner VF UNC

(19)72-92. Black on gray and multicolor underprint. Portrait Thomasine Heiberg by Jens Juel at right. Back: European or Red squirrel, *SERIE* 1972 at lower right. Watermark: Double portrait Jens Juel and his wife and *1000*. Printer: Nationalbanken, Copenhagen (without imprint). 176x94mm.

a. (19)72. Prefixes A0-A1.	300	600
b. (19)77. Prefix A2.	275	500
c. (19)80. Prefix A3.	250	400
d. (19)80. Prefix C0.	230	350
e. (19)81. Prefix C1.	250	400
f. (19)86. Ptrefixes C2-C3.	FV	290
g. (19)02. Prefixes C4-C5.	FV	270

1972A Issue

54 100 Kroner VF UNC

(19)94-98. Black and orange on multicolor underprint. Jens Juel's self-portrait (ca.1773-74) at right. Additional security devices. Back: Danish Order Ribbon moth at left, *SERIE* 1972 at lower right. Additional security devices. Watermark: Jens Juul and 100. 150x78mm.

a. (19)94. Prefix F0.	20.00	40.00
b. (19)95. Prefix F1.	20.00	40.00
c. (19)95. Prefix F2.	FV	30.00
d. (19)95. Prefix F3.	FV	35.00
e. (19)95. Prefixes F4-F5.	FV	30.00
f. (19)96. Prefix F6.	FV	35.00
g. (19)97. Prefix F7.	FV	30.00
h. (19)97. Prefix F8.	40.00	100
i. (19)98. Prefixes F9-G0.	FV	27.50

1997-2001 Issue

55 50 Kroner VF UNC

(19)99-(20)02. Black and deep purple on multicolor underprint. Green latent image at upper left, Karen Blixen at right. Back: Centaur stone relief from Landet Church, Tåsinge at left center. Watermark: Karen Blixen. 125x72mm.

a. (19)99. Prefixes A0-A1.	FV	22.00
b. (20)00. Prefixes A2-A3.	FV	22.00
c. (20)01. Prefixes A4-A6.	FV	16.00
d. (20)01. Prefix A7.	20.00	65.00
e. (20)02. Prefix A8.	FV	16.00
f. (20)02. Prefix A9.	FV	20.00

56 100 Kroner VF UNC

(19)99-(20)01. Black and red-brown on orange and multicolor underprint. Blue latent image at upper left, Carl Nielsen at right. Back: Basilisk stone relief from Tømmerby Church in Thy at left center. Watermark: Carl Nielsen. 135x72mm.

a. (19)99. Prefixes A0-A2.	FV	32.50
b. (20)00. Prefixes A3-A4.	FV	32.50
c. (20)00. Prefix A5.	30.00	100
d. (20)01. Prefixes A6-A7.	FV	27.50
e. (20)01. Prefix A8.	30.00	100

57 200 Kroner VF UNC

(19)97; (20)00. Black and dark blue on turquoise green and multicolor underprint. Pale red-violet latent image at upper left, J. L. Heiberg at right. Back: Stone lion relief from Viborg Cathedral at left center. Watermark: J. L. Heiberg. 145x72mm.

a. (19)97. Prefixes A0-A1.	FV	60.00
b. (20)00. Prefix A2.	FV	65.00

58 500 Kroner VF UNC

(19)97-(20)03. Black on blue, orange and multicolor underprint. Niels Bohr at right. Back: Knight and dragon relief from Lihme Church at left center. Watermark: Niels Bohr. 155x72mm.

		VF	UNC
a.	(19)97. Prefix A0.	FV	160
b.	(19)97. Prefix A1.	100	200
c.	(19)99. Prefix A2.	100	200
d.	(20)00. Prefix A3.	FV	140
e.	(20)00. Prefix A4.	100	200
f.	(20)03. Prefix A5.	95.00	190

59 1000 Kroner VF UNC

(19)98. Violet, dark red-brown and green. Green latent image at upper left, Anna and Michael Ancher at right. Serial number prefix A0-A1. Back: Tournament scene relief from Bislev Church at left center. Watermark: Anna Archer. 165x72mm.

		VF	UNC
a.	(19)98. Prefix A0.	FV	250
b.	(19)98. Prefix A1.	FV	250

2002 Issue

60 50 Kroner VF UNC

(20)04-(20)07. Black and deep purple on multicolor underprint. Karen Blixen at right. iridescent metallic strip. Hologram at upper left. Back: Centaur stone relief from Landet Church, Tåsinge at left center. Watermark: Karen Blixen. 125x72mm.

		VF	UNC
a.	(20)04. Prefixes B0-B1.	FV	18.00
b.	(20)05. Prefix B2.	FV	20.00
c.	(20)06. Prefix B3.	FV	16.00
d.	(20)07. Prefix B4.	FV	16.00
e.	(20)07. Preifx B5.	FV	22.50
f.	(20)07. Preifx B6.	FV	20.00

61 100 Kroner VF UNC

(20)02-(20)08. Black and red-brown on orange and multicolor underprint. Carl Nielsen at right. Iridescent metallic strip. Hologram at upper left. Back: Basilisk stone relief from Tømmerby Church in Thy at left center. Watermark: Carl Nielsen. 135x72mm.

		VF	UNC
a.	(20)02. Prefixes B0-B6.	FV	25.00
b.	(20)03. Prefixes B7-B8.	FV	27.50
c.	(20)04. Prefixes B9-C0.	FV	27.50
d.	(20)04. Prefix C1.	FV	40.00
e.	(20)05. Prefix C2.	FV	30.00
f.	(20)06. Prefixes C3-C5.	FV	25.00
g.	(20)07. Prefixes C6-C9.	FV	22.50
h.	(20)07. Prefix D0.	60.00	200
i.	(20)08. Prefix D2.	FV	40.00
j.	(20)08. Prefix D3.	FV	35.00

Prefix D1 was not issued.

62 200 Kroner VF UNC

(20)03-(20)08. Black and dark blue on turquoise green and multicolor underprint. J. L. Heiberg at right. Iridescent metallic strip. Hologram at upper left. Back: Stone lion relief from Viborg Cathedral at left center. Watermark: J.L. Heiberg. 145x72mm.

		VF	UNC
a.	(20)03. Prefixes B0-B1.	FV	55.00
b.	(20)03. Prefixes B2.	FV	65.00
c.	(20)04. Prefixes B3-B4.	FV	45.00
d.	(20)05. Prefixes B5-B8.	FV	45.00
e.	(20)07. Prefix C0.	FV	45.00
f.	(20)08. Prefix C1-C2.	FV	45.00
g.	(20)08. Prefix C4.	FV	50.00

Prefixes B9 and C3 were not issued.

63 500 Kroner VF UNC

(20)03-(20)08. Black on blue, orange and multicolor underprint. Niels Bohr at right. Iridescent metallic strip. Hologram at upper left. Back: Knight and dragon relief from Lihme Church at left center. Watermark: Niels Bohr. 155x72mm.

		VF	UNC
a.	(20)03. Prefixes B0-B2.	FV	130
b.	(20)03. Prefix B3.	FV	155
c.	(20)06. Prefixes B4-B6.	FV	130
d.	(20)06. Prefix B7.	FV	165
e.	(20)08. Prefix B8.	FV	145

64 1000 Kroner

		VF	**UNC**

(20)04-(20)06. Violet, dark red-brown and green. Anna and Michael Ancher at right. Iridescent metallic strip. Hologram at upper left. Back: Tournament scene relief from Bislev Church at left center. Watermark: Anna Ancher. 165x72mm.

		VF	**UNC**
a. (20)04. Prefix B0.		FV	235
b. (20)04. Prefix B1.		FV	250
c. (20)06. Prefix B2.		FV	235
d. (20)06. Prefix B3.		FV	235

2009-2010 Issue

65 50 Kroner

		VF	**UNC**

(20)09-(20)13. Violet brown and blue. Bridge of Sallingsund at right, hologram at lower left. Back: Stone age jar from Skarpsalling on landscape of Oudrup Moor at left. Map of sailing at right. Watermark: Viking ship and 50. 125x72mm.

		VF	**UNC**
a. (20)09. Prefixes A0, A2-A3.		FV	16.00
b. (20)09. Prefix A4.		60.00	200
c. (20)09. Prefixes A5-A6.		FV	16.00
d. (20)11. Prefix A7-A8.		FV	16.00
e. (20)12. Prefix A9.		FV	16.00
f. (20)13.		FV	16.00

Prefix A1 not issued.

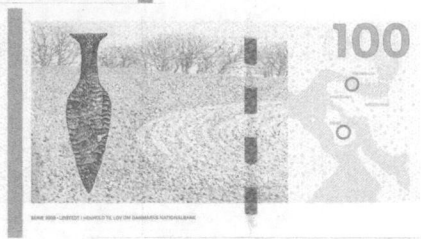

66 100 Kroner

		VF	**UNC**

(20)09-(20)13. Orange-yellow on multicolor underprint. Little Belt Bridge at right. Hologram at lower left. Back: Stone age flint dagger - The Hindsgavl dagger from the island of Faenø at left. 135x72mm.

		VF	**UNC**
a. (20)09. Prefixes A0-A2.		FV	27.00
b. (20)10. Prefixes A3-A6.		FV	27.00
c. (20)13. Prefix A8.		FV	25.00

67 200 Kroner

		VF	**UNC**

(20)10-(20)13. Black, green and blue. Knippel Bridge in Copenhagen at right center. Hologram at lower left. Back: Bronze-age belt plate from Langstrip in North Zealand at center left. 145x72mm.

		VF	**UNC**
a. (20)10. Prefixes A0-A3.		FV	45.00
b. (20)11. Prefix A4.		FV	45.00
c. (20)12. Prefix A5.		FV	45.00
d. (20)13.		FV	45.00

68 500 Kroner

		VF	**UNC**

(20)10-(20)12. Black, blue and brown. Queen Alexandrine Bridge / Møn Bridge at center right. Hologram at lower left. Back: Bronze age bucket of Greek/Thracian origin found in Keldby. 155x72mm.

		VF	**UNC**
a. (20)10. Prefix A2.		FV	120
b. (20)11. Prefixes A0-A1.		FV	120
c. (20)11. Prefix A3.		FV	140
d. (20)12. Prefix A4.		FV	120

Prefix A2 was printed before A0 and A1.

69 1000 Kroner

		VF	**UNC**

(20)11-(20)12. Black, red and green. Great-Belt Bridge at center right. Back: Sun chariot found at Trundholm in NW Zealand at center left. 165x72mm.

		VF	**UNC**
a. (20)11. Prefixes A0-A2.		FV	225
b. (20)12. Prefix A3-A4.		FV	225

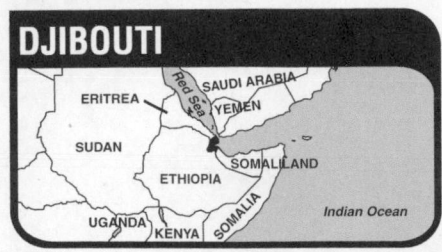

DJIBOUTI

The Republic of Djibouti is located in northeast Africa at the Bab el Mandeb Strait connecting the Suez Canal and the Red Sea with the Gulf of Aden and the Indian Ocean, has an area of 23,000 sq. km. and a population of 506,200. Capital: Djibouti. The nation has very little arable land and few natural resources. The commercial activities of the trans-shipment port of Djibouti and the Addis Ababa-Djibouti railroad are the basis of the economy also French and American military activity. Salt, fish and hides are exported.

The French Territory of the Afars and the Issas became Djibouti in 1977. Hassan Gouled Aptidon installed an authoritarian one-party state and proceeded to serve as president until 1999. Unrest among the Afars minority during the 1990s led to a civil war that ended in 2001 following the conclusion of a peace accord between Afar rebels and the Issa-dominated government. In 1999, Djibouti's first multi-party presidential elections resulted in the election of Ismail Omar Guelleh; he was re-elected to a second and final term in 2005. Djibouti occupies a strategic geographic location at the mouth of the Red Sea and serves as an important transshipment location for goods entering and leaving the east African highlands. The present leadership favors close ties to France, which maintains a significant military presence in the country, but also has strong ties with the US.

MONETARY SYSTEM:
1 Franc = 100 Centimes

REPUBLIC OF DJIBOUTI

Banque Nationale de Djibouti

1979; 1984 ND Issue

36	500 Francs	VF	UNC
	ND (1979; 1988). Multicolor. Man at left, rocks in sea, storks at right. Back: Stern of ship at right.		
	a. Blue underprint. Without signature. (1979).	15.00	40.00
	b. Pale blue underprint. Signature title: *LE GOUVERNEUR* added. (1988).	12.00	37.50

37	1000 Francs	VF	UNC
	ND (1979; 1988). Brown and multicolor. Woman at left, people by diesel passenger trains at center. Back: Trader with camels at center.		
	a. Long Arabic text on back. Without signature. Engraved. (1979).	22.00	50.00
	b. Signature title: *LE GOUVERNEUR* added above *MILLE*. Short Arabic text at top on back. Lithographed. (1988).	18.00	45.00
	c. Long Arabic text on back. (1991).	15.00	42.00
	d. As c. but with security thread. 2 signature varieties.	10.00	30.00
	e. as d. but bluish microprint frame on both sides.	FV	28.00

38	5000 Francs	VF	UNC
	ND (1979). Multicolor. Man at right, forest scene at center. Back: Aerial view at center.		
	a. Without signature.	50.00	150
	b. With signature.	45.00	150
	c. As b. but with security thread.	35.00	125
	d. As c. but fluorescent security stripe.	FV	85.00

39	10,000 Francs	VF	UNC
	ND (1984). Brown and red on yellow and green. Woman holding baby at left, goats in tree at right. Back: Fish and harbor scene.		
	a. Signature title: *TRÉSORIER*.	110	235
	b. Signature title: *GOUVERNEUR*. with security thread.	FV	160

1997; 1999 ND Issue

40   2000 Francs   VF   UNC
ND (1997). Dark blue, blue-black and black on yellow and multicolor underprint.   FV   40.00
Young girl at right, camel caravan at center. Wide security overprint at right center.
Back: Statue with spear and shield at lower left, government building at center.
170x80mm.

Reportedly a commemorative for the 20th Anniversary of Independence.

41   10,000 Francs   VF   UNC
ND (1999). Blue and multicolor. President Hassan Gouled Aptidon at right,   FV   145
undersea life at center. Back: Central Bank building at center.

44   5000 Francs   VF   UNC
ND (2002). Purple and multicolor. Central bank building and M. Harbi. Back: Three   FV   55.00
females dancing with swords, rock landscape.

45   10,000 Francs   VF   UNC
ND (2005). president Hassan Gouled Aptidon at right, undersea wildlife at center.   FV   100
Back: Central Bank building at center.

Banque Centrale de Djibouti
2002 ND Issue

42   1000 Francs   VF   UNC
ND (2005). Reddish brown and multicolor.
  a. Issued note.   FV   16.00
  r. Replacement note. Z prefix.   FV   55.00

43   2000 Francs   VF   UNC
ND (2005). Dark blue, blue-black and black on yellow and multicolor underprint.   FV   28.00
Young woman and camel caravan. Back: Statue and palace. 170x80mm.

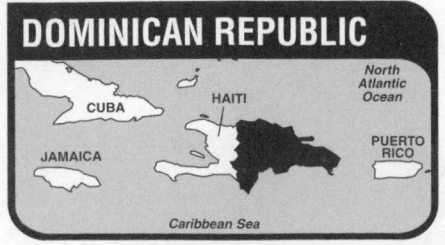

DOMINICAN REPUBLIC

The Dominican Republic, occupying the eastern two-thirds of the island of Hispañiola, has an area of 48,730 sq. km. and a population of 9.50 million. Capital: Santo Domingo. The agricultural economy produces sugar, coffee, tobacco and cocoa.

Explored and claimed by Christopher Columbus on his first voyage in 1492, the island of Hispaniola became a springboard for Spanish conquest of the Caribbean and the American mainland. In 1697, Spain recognized French dominion over the western third of the island, which in 1804 became Haiti. The remainder of the island, by then known as Santo Domingo, sought to gain its own independence in 1821, but was conquered and ruled by the Haitians for 22 years; it finally attained independence as the Dominican Republic in 1844. In 1861, the Dominicans voluntarily returned to the Spanish Empire, but two years later they launched a war that restored independence in 1865. A legacy of unsettled, mostly non-representative rule followed, capped by the dictatorship of Rafael Leonidas Trujillo from 1930-61. Juan Bosch was elected president in 1962, but was deposed in a military coup in 1963. In 1965, the United States led an intervention in the midst of a civil war sparked by an uprising to restore Bosch. In 1966, Joaquin Balaguer defeated Bosch in an election to become president. Balaguer maintained a tight grip on power for most of the next 30 years when international reaction to flawed elections forced him to curtail his term in 1996. Since then, regular competitive elections have been held in which opposition candidates have won the presidency. Former President (1996-2000) Leonel Fernandez Reyna won election to a second term in 2004 following a constitutional amendment allowing presidents to serve more than one term.

MONETARY SYSTEM:
  1 Peso Oro = 100 Centavos Oro
  1 Peso Dominicano = 100 Centavos, 2010-

SPECIMEN NOTES:
  In 1998 the Banco Central began selling various specimens over the counter to the public.
  REPLACEMENT NOTES:
  #53-61: Z prefix and suffix (TDLR printings).
  #117-124: Z prefix and suffix (TDLR printings).

REPUBLIC

Banco Central de la República Dominicana
1961 ND Issues

85	**10 Centavos Oro**	**VF**	**UNC**
	ND (1961). Blue and black. Banco de Reservas in round frame at center. Printer: ABNC.		
	a. Issued note.	3.50	15.00
	s. Specimen.	—	20.00

86	**10 Centavos Oro**	**VF**	**UNC**
	ND (1961). Black on light blue-green safety paper. Banco de Reservas in oval frame at center. Printer: Banco Central.		
	a. Issued note.	10.00	40.00
	s. Specimen.	—	25.00

87	**25 Centavos Oro**	**VF**	**UNC**
	ND (1961). Red and black. Entrance to the Banco Central in rectangular frame at center. Printer: ABNC.		
	a. Issued note.	4.00	12.50
	s. Specimen.	—	20.00

88	**25 Centavos Oro**	**VF**	**UNC**
	ND (1961). Black. Entrance to the Banco Central in oval frame at center. Printer: Banco Central.		
	a. Pink safety paper.	10.00	50.00
	b. Plain cream paper.	10.00	50.00
	s. Specimen.	—	30.00

89	**50 Centavos Oro**	**VF**	**UNC**
	ND (1961). Purple and black. Palacio Nacional in circular frame at center. Printer: ABNC.		
	a. Issued note.	4.00	15.00
	s. Specimen.	—	20.00

90	**50 Centavos Oro**	**VF**	**UNC**
	ND (1961). Black on yellow safety paper. Palacio Nacional in oval frame at center. Printer: Banco Central.		
	a. Issued note.	25.00	80.00
	s. Specimen.	—	30.00

1962 ND Issue

91	**1 Peso Oro**	**VF**	**UNC**
	ND (1962-63). Red. Portrait J. P. Duarte at center, text over seal: *SANTO DOMINGO / DISTRITO NACIONAL / REPúBLICA DOMINICANA*. Back: Medallic portrait of Liberty head at left, arms at right. Printer: ABNC.		
	a. Issued note.	25.00	100
	s. Specimen.	—	175

92   5 Pesos Oro   VF   UNC
ND (1962). Red. Portrait J. Sánchez at right center, text over seal: *SANTO
DOMINGO / DISTRITO NACIONAL / REPúBLICA DOMINICANA*. Back: Medallic
portrait of Liberty head at left, arms at right. Printer: ABNC.

   a. Issued note.   40.00   150
   s. Specimen.   —   250

93   10 Pesos Oro   VF   UNC
ND (1962). Red. Portrait Mella at center, text over seal: *SANTO DOMINGO /
DISTRITO NACIONAL / REPúBLICA DOMINICANA*. Back: Medallic portrait of
Liberty head at left, arms at right. Printer: ABNC.

   a. Issued note.   65.00   250
   s. Specimen.   —   300

94   20 Pesos Oro   VF   UNC
ND (1962). Red. *Puerta del Conde* at center, text over seal: *SANTO DOMINGO
/ DISTRITO NACIONAL / REPúBLICA DOMINICANA*. Back: Medallic portrait of
Liberty head at left, arms at right. Printer: ABNC.

   a. Issued note.   125   350
   s. Specimen.   —   400

95   50 Pesos Oro   VF   UNC
ND (1962). Red. Tomb of Columbus at center, text over seal: *SANTO DOMINGO
/ DISTRITO NACIONAL / REPúBLICA DOMINICANA*. Back: Medallic portrait of
Liberty head at left, arms at right. Printer: ABNC.

   a. Issued note.   250   750
   s. Specimen.   —   400

96   100 Pesos Oro   VF   UNC
ND (1962). Red. Woman with coffee pot and cup at center, text over seal: *SANTO
DOMINGO / DISTRITO NACIONAL / REPúBLICA DOMINICANA*. Back: Medallic
portrait of Liberty head at left, arms at right. Printer: ABNC.

   a. Issued note.   275   800
   s. Specimen.   —   400

97   500 Pesos Oro   VF   UNC
ND (1962). *Obelisco de Ciudad Trujillo* at center, text over seal: *SANTO
DOMINGO / DISTRITO NACIONAL / REPúBLICA DOMINICANA*. Back: Medallic
portrait of Liberty head at left, arms at right. Printer: ABNC.

   a. Issued note.   1,000 2,000
   s. Specimen.   —   500

98   1000 Pesos Oro   VF   UNC
ND (1962). Minor Basilica of Santa Maria at center, text over seal: *SANTO
DOMINGO / DISTRITO NACIONAL / REPúBLICA DOMINICANA*. Back: Medallic
portrait of Liberty head at left, arms at right. Printer: ABNC.

   a. Issued note. Unique.   1,750 5,000
   s. Specimen.   —   500

1964 ND Issue

99   1 Peso Oro   VF   UNC
ND (1964-73). Black on multicolor underprint. Portrait J. P. Duarte at center with
eyes looking left, white bow tie. Orange bank seal at right. Signature varieties.
Back: Medallic portrait of Liberty head at left, arms at right. Printer: TDLR.
156x67mm.

   a. Issued note.   7.50 30.00
   s1. Specimen. Black overprint: *MUESTRA* twice on face.   —   140
   s2. Specimen. Black overprint: *MUESTRA* once on face.   —   140
   s3. Specimen. Black overprint: *MUESTRA* once on each side. — 140

100　5 Pesos Oro　　　　　　　　　　　　　　　　**VF　UNC**
ND (1964-74). Brown on multicolor underprint. Portrait J. Sánchez at center.
Orange bank seal at right. Signature varieties. Back: Medallic portrait of Liberty
head at left, arms at right. Printer: TDLR. 156x67mm.
　　a. Issued note.　　　　　　　　　　　　　　　　10.00　40.00
　　s1. Specimen. Black overprint: *MUESTRA* twice on each side. Punch hole　—　100
　　　　cancelled.
　　s2. Specimen. Black overprint: *ESPECIMEN* once on each on each side.　—　100
　　　　Punch hole cancelled.
　　s3. Specimen. Black overprint: *MUESTRA* once on face.　　　　—　100
　　s4. Specimen. Black overprint: *MUESTRA* once on each side.　　　—　100

101　10 Pesos Oro　　　　　　　　　　　　　　　　**VF　UNC**
ND (1964-74). Deep green on multicolor underprint. Portrait Mella at center.
Orange bank seal at right. Signature varieties. Back: Medallic portrait of Liberty
head at left, arms al right. Printer: TDLR. 156x67mm.
　　a. Issued note.　　　　　　　　　　　　　　　　17.50　60.00
　　s1. Specimen. Black overprint: *MUESTRA* once on each side.　　　—　100
　　s2. Specimen. Black overprint: *MUESTRA* twice on each side. Punch hole　—　100
　　　　cancelled.
　　s3. Specimen. Black overprint: *ESPECIMEN* once on each side. Punch hole　—　100
　　　　cancelled.

102　20 Pesos Oro　　　　　　　　　　　　　　　　**VF　UNC**
ND (1964-74). Dark brown on multicolor underprint. *Altar de la Patria* at center.
Orange bank seal at right. Signature varieties. Back: Medallic portrait of Liberty
head at left, arms at right. Printer: TDLR. 156x67mm.
　　a. Issued note.　　　　　　　　　　　　　　　　30.00　125
　　s1. Specimen. Black overprint: *MUESTRA* twice on each side.　　　—　100
　　s2. Specimen. Black overprint: *MUESTRA* once on each side.　　　—　100
　　s3. Specimen. Black overprint: *ESPECIMEN* once on each side. Punch hole　—　100
　　　　cancelled.

103　50 Pesos Oro　　　　　　　　　　　　　　　　**VF　UNC**
ND (1964-74). Purple on multicolor underprint. Ox cart at center. Orange bank
seal at right. Signature varieties. Back: Medallic portrait of Liberty head at left,
arms at right. Printer: TDLR. 156x67mm.
　　a. Issued note.　　　　　　　　　　　　　　　　75.00　175
　　s1. Specimen. Black overprint: *MUESTRA* once on each side.　　　—　100
　　s2. Specimen. Black overprint: *MUESTRA* twice on each side. Punch hole　—　100
　　　　cancelled.
　　s3. Specimen. Black overprint: *ESPECIMEN* once on each side. Punch hole　—　100
　　　　cancelled.

104　100 Pesos Oro　　　　　　　　　　　　　　　　**VF　UNC**
ND (1964-74). Orange-brown on multicolor underprint. Banco Central at center.
Orange bank seal at right. Signature varieties. Back: Medallic portrait of Liberty
head at left, arms at right. Printer: TDLR. 156x67mm.
　　a. Issued note.　　　　　　　　　　　　　　　　125　300
　　s1. Specimen. Black overprint: *ESPECIMEN* on both sides. Punch hole　—　100
　　　　cancelled.
　　s2. Specimen. Black overprint: *MUESTRA* twice on both sides. Punch hole　—　100
　　　　cancelled.
　　s3. Specimen. Black overprint: *MUESTRA* once on both sides.　　　—　100
　　s4. Specimen. Black overprint: *MUESTRA* once on both sides. Punch hole　—　100
　　　　cancelled.

105　500 Pesos Oro　　　　　　　　　　　　　　　　**VF　UNC**
ND (1964-74). Dark blue on multicolor underprint. Columbus tomb and cathedral
at center. Orange bank seal at right. Signature varieties. Back: Medallic portrait of
Liberty head at left, arms at right. Printer: TDLR. 156x67mm.
　　a. Issued note.　　　　　　　　　　　　　　　　450　1,200
　　s1. Specimen with black overprint: *MUESTRA* once on each side.　　—　175
　　s2. Specimen with black overprint: *MUESTRA* twice on each side. Punch hole　—　190
　　　　cancelled.

106　1000 Pesos Oro　　　　　　　　　　　　　　　　**VF　UNC**
ND (1964-74). Red and multicolor underprint. National Palace at center. Orange
bank seal at right. Signature varieties. Back: Medallic portrait of Liberty head at
left center, arms at right center. Printer: TDLR. 156x67mm.
　　a. Issued note.　　　　　　　　　　　　　　　　1,250　3,000
　　s1. Specimen. Black overprint: *ESPECIMEN* once on both sides. Punch hole　—　100
　　　　cancelled.
　　s2. Specimen. Black overprint: *MUESTRA* twice on both sides. Punch hole　—　100
　　　　cancelled.
　　s3. Specimen. Black overprint: *MUESTRA* once on each sides. Punch hole　—　250
　　　　cancelled.

1973 ND Issue

107　1 Peso Oro　　　　　　　　　　　　　　　　**VF　UNC**
ND (1973-74). Black on light green and pinkish tan underprint. Portrait J. P. Duarte
with eyes looking front, black bow tie. Orange bank seal at right. Signature varieties. Back: Medallic portrait of Liberty head at left, arms at right. Printer: TDLR.
156x67mm.
　　a. Issued note.　　　　　　　　　　　　　　　　2.00　10.00
　　s. Specimen with black overprint: *ESPECIMEN* once on each side. Punch　—　35.00
　　　　hole cancelled.

1975 Issue

108 1 Peso Oro

1975-78. Black on light green and pinkish tan underprint. Portrait J. P. Duarte with eyes looking front, black bow tie. Orange bank seal at right. Signature varieties. Back: Medallic portrait of Liberty head at left, arms at right. Dates at center in upper margin. Printer: TDLR. 156x67mm.

	VF	UNC
a. Issued note.	1.50	7.50
s. Specimen. Black overprint: *ESPECIMEN* on each side. Punch hole cancelled.	—	35.00

109 5 Pesos Oro

1975-76. Brown on light green and lilac underprint. Portrait J. Sánchez at right center. Orange bank seal at right. Signature varieties. Back: Medallic portrait of Liberty head at left, arms at right. Dates at center in upper margin. Printer: TDLR. 156x67mm.

	VF	UNC
a. Issued note.	5.00	20.00
s. Specimen with black overprint: *ESPECIMEN* once on each side. Punch hole cancelled.	—	50.00

110 10 Pesos Oro

1975-76. Green on light green and lilac underprint. Portrait Mella at center. Orange bank seal at right. Signature varieties. Back: Medallic portrait of Liberty head at left, arms at right. Dates at center in upper margin. Printer: TDLR. 156x67mm.

	VF	UNC
a. Issued note.	10.00	35.00
s. Specimen.	—	50.00

111 20 Pesos Oro

1975-76. Brown on light green and blue underprint. *Altar de la Patria* at center. Orange bank seal at right. Signature varieties. Back: Medallic portrait of Liberty head at left, arms at right. Dates at center in upper margin. Printer: TDLR. 156x67mm.

	VF	UNC
a. 1975.	15.00	55.00
b. 1976.	15.00	55.00
s. 1975. Specimen. Black overprint: *ESPECIMEN* once on each side. Punch hole cancelled.	—	50.00
s2. 1976. Specimen. Black overprint: *ESPECIMEN* once on each side. Punch hole cancelled.	—	50.00

112 50 Pesos Oro

1975-76. Purple on multicolor underprint. Ox cart at center. Orange bank seal at right. Signature varieties. Back: Medallic portrait of Liberty head at left, arms at right. Dates at center in upper margin. Printer: TDLR. 156x67mm.

	VF	UNC
a. 1975	35.00	110
b. 1976.	35.00	110
s1. 1975. Specimen. Black overprint: *ESPECIMEN* once on each side. Punch hole cancelled.	—	75.00

113 100 Pesos Oro

1975-76. Orange-brown on multicolor underprint. Banco Central at center. Orange bank seal at right. Signature varieties. Back: Medallic portrait of Liberty head at left, arms at right. Dates at center in upper margin. Printer: TDLR. 156x67mm.

	VF	UNC
a. 1975.	60.00	190
b. 1976.	60.00	190
s1. 1975. Specimen with black overprint: *ESPECIMEN* on both sides. Punch hole cancelled.	—	100
s2. 1976. Specimen with black overprint: *ESPECIMEN* on both sides. Punch hole cancelled.	—	100

114 500 Pesos Oro

1975. Dark blue on multicolor underprint. Columbus tomb and cathedral at center. Orange bank seal at right. Signature varieties. Back: Medallic portrait of Liberty head at left, arms at right. Dates at center in upper margin. Printer: TDLR. 156x67mm.

	VF	UNC
a. Issued note.	250	750
s. Specimen with black overprint: *ESPECIMEN* once on each side. Punch hole cancelled.	—	100

115 1000 Pesos Oro

1975-76. Red on multicolor underprint. National Palace at center. Orange bank seal at right. Signature varieties. Back: Medallic portrait of Liberty head at left center, arms at right center. Dates at center in upper margin. Printer: TDLR. 156x67mm.

	VF	UNC
a. 1975.	500	1,500
b. 1976.	500	1,500
s1. 1975. Specimen. Black overprint: *ESPECIMEN* once on both sides. Punch hole cancelled.	—	125
s2. 1976. Specimen. Black overprint: *ESPECIMEN* once on both sides. Punch hole cancelled.	—	125

1977-80 Issues

#116-124 Replacement notes: Serial # prefix and suffix Z.

116 1 Peso Oro
1978-79. Black, dark green and dark brown on multicolor underprint. J. P. Duarte at right, orange seal at left. Back: Sugar refinery, dates in upper margin. Printer: ABNC. 156x67mm.

		VF	UNC
a.	Issued note.	1.00	5.00
s.	Specimen with red overprint: *MUESTRA / SIN VALOR.* 1978; 1980. Punch hole cancelled.	—	35.00

117 1 Peso Oro
1980-82. Black, dark green and dark brown on multicolor underprint. J. P. Duarte at right, orange bank seal at left. Back: Sugar refinery, dates (lightly printed) in upper margin. Printer: TDLR. 156x67mm.

		VF	UNC
a.	1980.	1.00	4.50
b.	1981.	1.00	4.50
c.	1982.	1.00	4.50
s1.	Specimen. Black overprint: *ESPECIMEN* on both sides. 1980. Punch hole cancelled.	—	35.00
s2.	Specimen. Black overprint: *ESPECIMEN* on both sides. 1981. Punch hole cancelled.	—	35.00
s3.	Specimen. Black overprint: *ESPECIMEN* on both sides. 1982. Punch hole cancelled.	—	35.00

118 5 Pesos Oro
1978-88. Deep brown, red-brown and red on multicolor underprint. J. Sánchez at right, arms at center. Orange bank seal at left. Back: Hydroelectric dam, dates in upper margin. Printer: TDLR. 156x67mm.

		VF	UNC
a.	1978.	3.00	12.50
b.	1980-82.	2.50	9.00
c.	1984; 1985; 1987; 1988.	1.50	8.00
s1.	Specimen with black overprint: *ESPECIMEN.* 1978; 1980; 1981. Punch hole cancelled.	—	15.00
s2.	Specimen with red overprint: *MUESTRA SIN VALOR* and TDLR oval seals. 1985; 1987.	—	15.00
s3.	Specimen with black overprint: *MUESTRA SIN VALOR* and red overprint: TDLR oval seals. 1988.	—	15.00
s4.	Specimen with pinhole cancellation: *MUESTRA SIN VALOR.* TDLR oval.	0.00	15.00

119 10 Pesos Oro
1978-88. Black and green on multicolor underprint. Mella at right, medallic Liberty head at center. Orange bank seal at left. Back: Quarry mining scene, dates in upper margin. Printer: TDLR. 156x67mm.

		VF	UNC
a.	1978.	5.00	25.00
b.	1980-82.	4.00	20.00
c.	1985; 1987; 1988.	3.00	17.50
s1.	Specimen with black overprint: *ESPECIMEN* once on each side. 1978; 1980; 1981; 1982.	—	20.00
s2.	Specimen with red overprint: *MUESTRA SIN VALOR* and TDLR oval seals. 1985; 1987.	—	25.00
s3.	Specimen with black overprint: *MUESTRA SIN VALOR* and red overprint: TDLR oval seals. 1988.	—	25.00

120 20 Pesos Oro
1978-88. Black, dark brown and olive-brown on multicolor underprint. *Altar de la Patria* at center. Orange bank seal at left. Back: *Puerta del Conde*, dates in upper margin. Printer: TDLR. 156x67mm.

		VF	UNC
a.	1978.	8.00	40.00
b.	1980-82.	6.00	30.00
c.	1985; 1987; 1988.	5.00	20.00
s1.	Specimen. Black overprint: *ESPECIMEN* once on each side. 1978; 1980; 1981, 1982.	—	20.00
s2.	Specimen. Red overprint: *MUESTRA SIN VALOR* and TDLR oval seals. 1985; 1987.	—	22.50
s3.	Specimen. Black overprint: *MUESTRA SIN VALOR* and red overprint: TDLR oval seals. 1988.	—	22.50

121 50 Pesos Oro
1978-87. Black and purple on multicolor underprint. Basilica at center, orange bank seal at left. Back: First cathedral in America at center right, dates in upper margin. Printer: TDLR. 156x67mm.

		VF	UNC
a.	Watermark: Indian head. 1978; 1980; 1981.	25.00	65.00
b.	Watermark: J. P. Duarte. 1985; 1987.	30.00	70.00
s1.	As a. Specimen with black overprint: *ESPECIMEN.* 1978; 1980; 1981. Punch hole cancelled.	—	22.50
s2.	As b. Specimen with perforated *MUESTRA SIN VALOR* and red overprint: TDLR oval seals. 1985; 1987.	—	25.00
s3.	As b. Specimen with red overprint: *MUESTRA SIN VALOR* on both sides. TDLR oval. Punch hole cancelled.	—	25.00

122   100 Pesos Oro   VF   UNC
1977-87. Violet, brown-orange and yellow-orange on multicolor underprint.
Entrance to 16th century mint at center, orange bank seal at left. Back: Banco
Central at center right, dates in upper margin. Printer: TDLR. 156x67mm.
  a. Watermark: Indian head. 1977; 1978; 1980; 1981.   50.00   145
  b. Watermark: J.P. Duarte. 1984; 1985; 1987.   60.00   175
  s1. As a. Specimen with black overprint: *ESPECIMEN.* 1978; 1980; 1981.   —   30.00
  s2. As b. Specimen with perforated: *MUESTRA SIN VALOR* and red TDLR   —   25.00
      oval seals. 1984; 1985; 1987.
  s3. As b. Specimen with black overprint: *MUESTRA SIN VALOR* and red   —   25.00
      TDLR oval seals. 1987.

123   500 Pesos Oro   VF   UNC
1978-87. Deep blue, blue and brown on multicolor underprint. National Theater
at center, orange bank seal at left. Back: Fort San Felipe at center right, dates in
upper margin. Printer: TDLR. 156x67mm.
  a. Watermark: Indian head. 1978; 1980; 1981.   225   450
  b. Watermark: J. P. Duarte. 1985; 1987.   200   400
  s1. As a. Specimen with black overprint: *ESPECIMEN.* 1978; 1980; 1981.   —   40.00
  s2. As b. Specimen with perforated: *MUESTRA SIN VALOR* and red overprint: —   40.00
      TDLR oval seals. 1985; 1987.
  s3. As b. Specimen with black overprint: *MUESTRA SIN VALOR* and red   —   40.00
      overprint: TDLR oval seals. Punch hole cancelled. 1987.

124   1000 Pesos Oro   VF   UNC
1978-87. Red, purple and violet on multicolor underprint. National Palace at
center, orange bank seal at left. Back: Columbus' fortress at center right, dates in
upper margin. Printer: TDLR. 156x67mm.
  a. Watermark: Indian head. 1978; 1980.   275   550
  b. Watermark: J. P. Duarte. 1984; 1985; 1987.   225   450
  s1. As a. Specimen with black overprint: *ESPECIMEN.* 1978; 1980; 1981.   —   50.00
      Punch hole cancelled.
  s2. As b. Specimen with perforated: *MUESTRA SIN VALOR* and red overprint: —   50.00
      TDLR oval seals. 1984; 1985; 1987.
  s3. As b. Specimen with red overprint: *ESPECIMEN / MUESTRA SIN VALOR*   —   50.00
      once on each side and red TDLR oval in two corners.

1978 Commemorative Issue

#125, Inauguration of new Banco Central building.

125   100 Pesos Oro   VF   UNC
15.8.1978 (- old date 1977). 1977; 1978; 1980; 1981. Specimen in red folder.   —   200
Violet, brown-orange and yellow-orange on multicolor underprint. Entrance to 16th
century mint at center, orange bank seal at left. Back: Banco Central at center
right, dates in upper margin. Watermark: Indian head. Printer: TDLR. 156x67mm.

1982 Commemorative Issue

#125A, 35th Anniversary Banco Central, 1947-1982

125A 100 Pesos Oro   VF   UNC
22.10.1982 (old dates 1978, 1981). 1977; 1978; 1980; 1981. Violet, brown-orange
and yellow-orange on multicolor underprint. Entrance to 16th century mint at
center, orange bank seal at left. Back: Banco Central at center right, dates in
upper margin. Watermark: Indian head. Printer: TDLR.
  s1. Old date 1978. Face without adhesive stamp or handstamp. Specimen.   —   135
  s2. Old date 1981. Banco Central commemorative adhesive stamp affixed at   —   150
      left, handstamp with date 22.10.1982 at center left. Specimen.

1984 Issue

126   1 Peso Oro   VF   UNC
1984; 1987; 1988. UV: UNO, five 1s and seal fluoresce orange. Black and brown
on multicolor underprint. New portrait J. P. Duarte at right. Back: Sugar refinery,
dates (lightly printed) in upper margin. Printer: TDLR. 156x67mm.
  a. 1984.   FV   4.00
  b. 1987.   FV   4.00
  c. 1988.   FV   4.00
  s1. 1984. Specimen. Perforated: *MUESTRA SIN VALOR.* and TDLR oval seal.   —   10.00
  s2. 1987. Specimen. Red overprint: *MUESTRA SIN VALOR* and TDLR oval   —   10.00
      seals.
  s3. 1988. Specimen Black overprint: *MUESTRA SIN VALOR* and red over-   —   10.00
      print: TDLR oval seals. Punch hole cancelled.

1988 Issue

127   50 Pesos Oro   VF   UNC
1988; 1990. Black and purple on multicolor underprint. Basilica at center, orange
bank seal at left. Back: First cathedral in America at center right, dates in upper
margin. Watermark: Duarte (profile). Printer: USBNC.
  a. 1988.   FV   17.50
  b. 1990.   FV   17.50
  s. Specimen with red overprint: *ESPECIMEN / MUESTRA SIN VALOR* once   —   20.00
     on each side.

128   100 Pesos Oro   VF   UNC
1988; 1990. Violet, brown-orange and brown on multicolor underprint. Entrance
to 16th century mint at center, orange bank seal at left. Back: Banco Central at
center right, dates in upper margin. Watermark: Duarte (profile). Printer: USBNC.
156x67mm.
  a. 1988.   FV   25.00
  b. 1990.   FV   25.00
  s1. 1988. Specimen with red overprint: *ESPECIMEN / MUESTRA SIN VALOR*   —   22.50
      on both aides.
  s2. 1990. Specimen with red overprint: *ESPECIMEN / MUESTRA SIN VALOR*   —   22.50
      on both aides.

129 500 Pesos Oro | **VF UNC**

1988. Deep blue, blue, and brown on multicolor underprint. National Theater at center, orange bank seal at left. Back: Fort San Felipe at center right, dates in upper margin. Watermark: Duarte (profile). Printer: USBNC. 156x67mm.

a. Issued note. — FV 75.00
s. Specimen with red overprint: *ESPECIMEN / MUESTRA SIN VALOR* once on each side. — — 35.00

130 1000 Pesos Oro | **VF UNC**

1988; 1990. Purple, red-violet and violet on multicolor underprint. National Palace at center, orange bank seal at left. Back: Columbus' fortress at center right, dates in upper margin. Watermark: Duarte (profile). Printer: USBNC. 156x67mm.

a. 1988. — FV 135
b. 1990. — FV 135
s1. 1988. Specimen with red overprint: *ESPECIMEN / MUESTRA SIN VALOR* once on each side. — — 45.00
s2. 1990. Specimen with red overprint: *ESPECIMEN / MUESTRA SIN VALOR* once on each side. — — 45.00

1990 Issue

131 5 Pesos Oro | **VF UNC**

1990. Deep brown, red-brown and red on multicolor underprint. J. Sánchez at right, arms at center. Orange bank seal at left. Silver leaf-like underlays at left and right. Back: Hydroelectric dam, dates in upper margin. Printer: H&S. 156x67mm. | FV 5.00

132 10 Pesos Oro | **VF UNC**

1990. Deep green and black on multicolor underprint. Mella at right, medallic Liberty head at center. Orange bank seal at left. Silver leaf-like underlays at left and right. Back: Quarry mining scene, dates in upper margin. Printer: H&S. 156x67mm. | FV 7.50

133 20 Pesos Oro | **VF UNC**

1990. Deep brown and brown on multicolor underprint. *Altar de la Patria* at center. Orange bank seal at left. Silver leaf-like underlays at left and right. Back: *Puerta del Conde*, dates in upper margin. Printer: H&S. 156x67mm. | FV 12.50

134 500 Pesos Oro | **VF UNC**

1990. Deep blue-green, black and brown on multicolor underprint. National Theater at center, orange bank seal at left. Silver leaf-like underlays at left and right. Back: Fort San Felipe at center right, dates in upper margin. Printer: H&S. 156x67mm. | FV 75.00

1991 Issue

135 50 Pesos Oro | **VF UNC**

1991; 1994. Black and purple on multicolor underprint. Basilica at center, orange bank seal at left. Back: First cathedral in America at center right, dates in upper margin. Watermark: Columbus. Printer: TDLR. 156x67mm.

a. 1991. — FV 15.00
b. 1994. — FV 10.00
s1. 1991. Specimen. Overprint: *MUESTRA SIN VALOR* in black and TDLR oval seals in red. Punch hole cancelled. — — 20.00
s2. 1994. Specimen. Overprint: *MUESTRA SIN VALOR* in black and TDLR oval seals in red. Punch hole cancelled. — — 20.00

136 100 Pesos Oro | **VF UNC**

1991; 1994. Orange and violet on multicolor underprint. Entrance to 16th century mint at center, orange bank seal at left. Back: Banco Central at center right, dates in upper margin. Printer: TDLR. 156x67mm.

a. 1991. — FV 25.00
b. 1994. — FV 20.00
s1. 1991. Specimen with black overprint: *MUESTRA SIN VALOR* and red overprint: TDLR oval seals. Punch hole cancelled. — — 35.00
s2. 1994. Specimen with black overprint: *MUESTRA SIN VALOR* and red overprint: TDLR oval seals. Punch hole cancelled. — — 35.00

137 500 Pesos Oro | **VF UNC**

1991; 1994. Deep blue, blue and dark brown on multicolor underprint. National Theater at center, orange bank seal at left. Silver leaf-like underlays at left and right. Back: Fort San Felipe at center right, dates in upper margin. Printer: TDLR. 156x67mm.

a. 1991. — FV 65.00
b. 1994. — FV 65.00
s1. 1991. Specimen with black overprint: *MUESTRA SIN VALOR* and red overprint: TDLR oval seals. — — 35.00
s2. 1994. Specimen with black overprint: *MUESTRA SIN VALOR* and red overprint: TDLR oval seals. — — 35.00

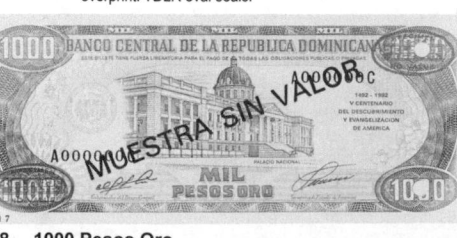

138 1000 Pesos Oro | **VF UNC**

1991; 1992; 1994. Purple, red-violet and violet on multicolor underprint. National Palace at center, orange bank seal at left. Back: Columbus' fortress at center right, dates in upper margin. Printer: TDLR. 156x67mm.

a. 1991. — FV 125
b. 1992. — FV 125
c. 1994. — FV 125
s1. 1991. Specimen with black overprint: *MUESTRA SIN VALOR* and red overprint: TDLR oval seals. Punch hole cancelled. — — 50.00
s2. 1992. Specimen with black overprint: *MUESTRA SIN VALOR* and red overprint: TDLR oval seals. Punch hole cancelled. — — 50.00
s3. 1994. Specimen with black overprint: *MUESTRA SIN VALOR* and red overprint: TDLR oval seals. Punch hole cancelled. — — 50.00

1992 Commemorative Issue

#139-142, Quincentennial of First Landfall by Christopher Columbus, 1992

139   20 Pesos Oro   VF   UNC
1992. Deep brown and brown on multicolor underprint. *Altar de la Patria* at center.
Orange bank seal at left. Silver leaf-like underlays at left and right. Brown commemorative text: *1492-1992 V Centenario...* at left over orange seal. Back: *Puerta
del Conde*, dates in upper margin. Printer: BABNC. 156x67mm.
    a. Issued note.   FV   8.00
    s. Specimen with red overprint: *ESPECIMEN* in red in upper corners and black   —   50.00
       overprint: *ESPECIMEN / MUESTRA SIN VALOR* once on each side.

140   500 Pesos Oro   VF   UNC
1992. Brown and blue-black on multicolor underprint. Sailing ships at center, C.
Columbus at center right. Back: Arms at left, Columbus Lighthouse, placement of
Cross of Christianity and map outline at center. Watermark: C. Columbus. Printer:
CBNC. 156x67mm.
    a. Issued note.   FV   110
    s1. Specimen with black overprint: *MUESTRA SIN VALOR* and red overprint: —   110
       TDLR oval seals.
    s2. Specimen with red overprint: *MUESTRA*.   —   100

141   500 Pesos Oro   VF   UNC
1992. Deep blue, blue and dark brown on multicolor underprint. National Theater
at center, orange bank seal at left. Silver leaf-like underlays at left and right. Back:
Fort San Felipe at center right, dates in upper margin. Watermark: C. Columbus.
Printer: TDLR. 156x67mm.
    a. Issued note.   FV   110
    s. Specimen with black overprint: *MUESTRA SIN VALOR* and red overprint: —   50.00
       TDLR oval seals. Punch hole cancelled.

142   1000 Pesos Oro   VF   UNC
1992. Purple, red-violet and violet on multicolor underprint. National Palace at
center, orange bank seal at left. Back: Columbus' fortress at center right, dates in
upper margin. Watermark: C. Columbus. Printer: TDLR. 156x67mm.
    a. Issued note.   FV   150
    s. Specimen with black overprint: *MUESTRA SIN VALOR* and red overprint: —   50.00
       TDLR oval seals. Punch hole cancelled.

1993 Regular Issue

143   5 Pesos Oro   VF   UNC
1993. Deep brown, red-brown and red on multicolor underprint. J. Sánchez at
right, arms at center. Orange bank seal at left. Silver leaf-like underlays at left
and right. Back: Hydroelectric dam, dates in upper margin. Printer: USBNC.
156x67mm.
    a. Issued note.   FV   2.00
    s. Specimen. Black overprint: *ESPECIMEN / MUESTRA SIN VALOR* on each   —   50.00
       side.

144   100 Pesos Oro   VF   UNC
1993. Orange and violet on multicolor underprint. Entrance to 16th century mint
at center, orange bank seal at left. Back: Banco Central at center right, dates in
upper margin. Printer: FNMT. 156x67mm.
    a. Issued note.   FV   17.50
    s. Specimen. Black overprint: *ESPECIMEN / MUESTRA SIN VALOR* on each   —   50.00
       side. Punch hole cancelled.

145   1000 Pesos Oro   VF   UNC
1993. Red, purple and violet on multicolor underprint. National Palace at center,
orange bank seal at left. Back: Columbus' fortress at center right, dates in upper
margin. Printer: FNMT. 156x67mm.
    a. Issued note.   FV   120
    s. Specimen. Black overprint: *ESPECIMEN / MUESTRA SIN VALOR* once on   —   50.00
       each side. Punch hole cancelled.

1994 Issue

146   5 Pesos Oro   VF   UNC
1994. Deep brown, red-brown and red on multicolor underprint. J. Sánchez at
right, arms at center. Orange bank seal at left. Silver leaf-like underlays at left and
right. Back: Hydroelectric dam, dates in upper margin. Printer: TDLR.
    a. Issued note.   FV   1.75
    s. Specimen with black overprint: *MUESTRA SIN VALOR* once on each side.   —   50.00
       Punch hole cancelled. TDLR oval.

1995 Issue

147   5 Pesos Oro   VF   UNC
1995. Deep brown, red-brown and red on multicolor underprint. J. Sánchez at
right, bright colored arms at center. Orange bank seal at left. Silver leaf-like underlays at left and right. Back: Hydroelectric dam, dates in upper margin. Printer:
F-CO. 156x67mm.
    a. Issued note.   FV   1.25
    s. Specimen with black overprint: *ESPECIMEN / MUESTRA SIN VALOR* once   —   25.00
       on each side. Punch hole cancelled.

148 10 Pesos Oro

1995. Deep green and black on multicolor underprint. Mella at right, medallic Liberty head at center. Orange bank seal at left. Silver leaf-like underlays at left and right. Back: Quarry mining scene, dates in upper margin. Printer: F-CO. 156x67mm.

		VF	UNC
a. Issued note.		FV	3.00
s. Specimen with black overprint: *ESPECIMEN / MUESTRA SIN VALOR* once on each side. Punch hole cancelled.		—	20.00

149 50 Pesos Oro

1995. Purple and black on multicolor underprint. Basilica at center, orange bank seal at left. Back: First cathedral in America at center right, dates in upper margin. Printer: F-CO. 156x67mm.

		VF	UNC
a. Issued note.		FV	7.00
s. Specimen with black overprint: *ESPECIMEN / MUESTRA SIN VALOR.* Punch hole cancelled.		—	20.00

150 100 Pesos Oro

1995. Orange, violet and brown on multicolor underprint. Entrance to 16th century mint at center, orange bank seal at left, silver overlays at left and right, purple design with *RD* also at right. Back: Banco Central at center right, dates in upper margin. Luminescent strip at right with text. Printer: F-CO. 156x67mm.

		VF	UNC
a. Issued note.		FV	12.50
s. Specimen with black overprint: *ESPECIMEN / MUESTRA SIN VALOR* on each side. Punch hole cancelled.		—	30.00

151 500 Pesos Oro VF UNC

1995. Deep blue, blue and brown on multicolor underprint. National Theater at center, orange bank seal at left. Silver overlays at loft and right, gold design with *RD* also at right. Back: Fort San Felipe at center right, dates in upper margin. Luminescent strip at right with text. Printer: F-CO. 156x67mm.

		VF	UNC
a. Issued note.		FV	70.00
s. Specimen with black overprint: *ESPECIMEN / MUESTRA SIN VALOR* once on each side. Punch hole cancelled.		—	60.00

1996-97 Issue

152 5 Pesos Oro VF UNC

1996; 1997. Deep brown, red-brown and red on multicolor underprint. J. Sánchez at right, bright colored arms at center. Date under orange bank seal at left. Silver leaf-like underlays at left and right. Back: Hydroelectric dam, dates in upper margin. Printer: F-CO. 156x67mm.

		VF	UNC
a. 1996.		FV	2.00
b. 1997.		FV	2.00
s1. 1996. Specimen. Black overprint *ESPECIMEN MUESTRA SIN VALOR* once on each side. Punch hole cancelled.		—	25.00
s2. 1997. Specimen. Black overprint *ESPECIMEN MUESTRA SIN VALOR* once on each side. Punch hole cancelled.		—	25.00

153 10 Pesos Oro VF UNC

1996; 1997; 1998. Deep green and black on multicolor underprint. Mella at right, medallic Liberty head at center. Date under orange bank seal at left. Silver leaf-like underlays at left and right. Back: Quarry mining scene, dates in upper margin. Printer: F-CO. 156x67mm.

		VF	UNC
a. Issued note.		FV	3.00
s. Specimen. Black overprint: *ESPECIMEN / MUESTRA SIN VALOR* once on each side. Punch hole cancelled.		—	25.00

154 20 Pesos Oro VF UNC

1997; 1998. Deep brown and brown on multicolor underprint. *Altar de la Patria* at center. Date under orange bank seal at left. Silver leaf-like underlays at left and right. Back: *Puerta del Conde,* dates in upper margin. Printer: F-CO. 156x67mm.

		VF	UNC
a. 1997.		FV	5.00
b. 1998.		—	5.00
s1. 1997. Specimen. Black overprint: *ESPECIMEN / MUESTRA SIN VALOR* once on each side. Punch hole cancelled.		—	10.00
s2. 1998. Specimen Black overprint: *ESPECIMEN / MUESTRA SIN VALOR* once on each side. Punch hole cancelled.		—	10.00

155 50 Pesos Oro   **VF UNC**

1997; 1998. Purple and black on multicolor underprint. Basilica at center, date under orange bank seal at left. Back: First cathedral in America at center right, dates in upper margin. Watermark: Daurte. Printer: F-CO. 156x67mm.

a. 1997.	FV	10.00
b. 1998.	FV	10.00
s1. 1997. Specimen. Overprint: *ESPECIMEN / MUESTRA SIN VALOR* in black on each side. Punch hole cancelled.	—	15.00
s2. 1998. Specimen. Overprint: *ESPECIMEN / MUESTRA SIN VALOR* in black on each side. Punch hole cancelled.	—	15.00

156 100 Pesos Oro   **VF UNC**

1997; 1998. Orange and violet on multicolor underprint. Entrance to 16th century mint at center, date under orange bank seal at left, silver overlays at left and right, purple design with *RD* also at right. Back: Banco Central at center right, dates in upper margin. Luminescent strip at right with text. Watermark: Duarte. Printer: F-CO. 156x67mm.

a. 1997.	FV	17.50
b. 1998.	FV	17.50
s1. 1997. Specimen with black Overprint: *ESPECIMEN / MUESTRA SIN VALOR* on each side. Punch hole cancelled.	—	20.00
s2. 1998. Specimen with black Overprint: *ESPECIMEN / MUESTRA SIN VALOR* on each side. Punch hole cancelled	—	20.00

157 500 Pesos Oro   **VF UNC**

1996; 1997; 1998. Deep blue, blue and brown on multicolor underprint. National Theater at center, date under orange bank seal at left. Silver overlays at left and right, gold design with *RD* also at right. Back: Fort San Felipe at center right, dates in upper margin. Luminescent strip at right with text. Watermark: Duarte. Printer: F-CO. 156x67mm.

a. 1996.	FV	55.00
b. 1997.	FV	55.00
c. 1998.	FV	55.00
s1. 1996. Specimen with black overprint: *ESPECIMEN / MUESTRA SIN VALOR* on each side. Punch hole cancelled.	—	25.00
s2. 1997. Specimen with black overprint: *ESPECIMEN / MUESTRA SIN VALOR* on each side. Punch hole cancelled.	—	25.00
s3. 1998. Specimen with black overprint: *ESPECIMEN / MUESTRA SIN VALOR* on each side. Punch hole cancelled.	—	25.00

158 1000 Pesos Oro   **VF UNC**

1996; 1997; 1998. Red, purple, violet on multicolor underprint. National Palace at center, date under orange bank seal at left. Back: Columbus' fortress at center right, dates in upper margin. Watermark: Duarte. Printer: F-CO. 156x67mm.

a. 1996.	FV	120
b. 1997.	FV	120
c. 1998.	FV	120
s1. 1996. Specimen. Overprint in black: *ESPECIMEN / MUESTRA SIN VALOR* once on both sides. Punch hole cancelled.	—	30.00
s2. 1997. Specimen. Overprint in black: *ESPECIMEN / MUESTRA SIN VALOR* once on both sides. Punch hole cancelled.	—	30.00
s3. 1998. Specimen. Overprint in black: *ESPECIMEN / MUESTRA SIN VALOR* once on both sides. Punch hole cancelled.	—	30.00

2000 Issue

159 10 Pesos Oro   **VF UNC**

2000. Dark green on multicolor underprint. Matí as Ramón Mella at right. Back: *Altar de la Patria*. Printer: BABN. 156x67mm.

a. Issued note.	FV	3.00
s. Specimen. Black overprint: *ESPECIMEN MUESTRA SIN VALOR* in two lines once on each side. Punch hole cancelled.	—	25.00

160 20 Pesos Oro   **VF UNC**

2000. Brown on multicolor underprint. Gregorio Luperon at right. Back: *Panteón Nacional* at left. Printer: F-CO. 156x67mm.

a. Issued note.	FV	4.00
s. Specimen with black overprint: *ESPECIMEN / MUESTRA SIN VALOR* once on both sides. Punch hole cancelled.	—	10.00

161 50 Pesos Oro   **VF UNC**

2000. Purple and dark brown on multicolor underprint. Santa Maria la Menor Cathedral at right. Back: Basilica de Nuestra Señora de la Altagracia at left. Watermark: Duarte. Printer: F-CO. 156x67mm.

a. Issued note.	FV	9.00
s. Specimen. With black overprint: *ESPECIMEN / MUESTRA SIN VALOR* on both sides. Punch hole cancelled.	—	12.50

162 500 Pesos Oro   **VF   UNC**

2000. Dark brown and aqua on multicolor underprint. Salome Ureña de Henriquez and Pedro Henriquez Ureña at right. Back: Banco Central building at left. Watermark: Duarte. Printer: F-CO. 156x67mm.

   a. Issued note.   FV   45.00
   s. Specimen. With black overprint: *ESPECIMEN / MUESTRA SIN VALOR* on   —   35.00
      both sides. Punch hole cancelled.

163 1000 Pesos Oro   **VF   UNC**

2000. Red and deep lilac on multicolor underprint. *Palacio Nacional* at right. Back: Alcazar de Don Diego Colon at left. Watermark: Duarte. Printer: F-CO. 156x67mm.

   a. Issued note.   FV   125
   s. Specimen with black overprint: *ESPECIMEN / MUESTRA SIN VALOR* once   —   75.00
      on both sides. Punch hole cancelled.

164 2000 Pesos Oro   **VF   UNC**

2000. Black and blue on multicolor underprint. Emillo Prud-Homme and José Reyes at right. Back: *Teatro Nacional*. 156x67mm.

   a. Issued note.   FV   220
   s. Specimen. Overprint in black: *ESPECIMEN / MUESTRA SIN VALOR* in two   —   —
      lines once on each side. Punch hole cancelled.

Note: #166 has a special rendition of the date and a millennium commemorative text.

2000-01 Issue

165 10 Pesos Oro   **VF   UNC**

2000; 2001. Dark green on multicolor underprint. Matías Ramón Mella at right. Back: *Altar de la Patria*. Printer: F-CO. 156x67mm.

   a. 2000.   FV   3.00
   b. 2001.   FV   3.00
   s1. 2000. Specimen with black overprint: *ESPECIMEN / MUESTRA SIN*   —   25.00
      VALOR once on each side. Punch hole cancelled.
   s2. 2001. Specimen with black overprint: *ESPECIMEN / MUESTRA SIN*   —   25.00
      VALOR once on each side. Punch hole cancelled.

166 20 Pesos Oro   **VF   UNC**

2000; 2001. The 2000 note has a special rendition of the date and a millennium commemorative text. Brown on multicolor underprint. Gregorio Luperon at right. Back: *Panteón Nacional* at left. Watermark: Duarte. Printer: BABN. 156x67mm.

   a. 2000.   FV   4.00
   b. 2001.   FV   4.00
   s. Specimen.   —   10.00

167 100 Pesos Oro   **VF   UNC**

2000; 2001. Dark brown and orange on multicolor underprint. F. R. Sanches, J. P. Duarte and M. R. Mella at right. Back: *Puerta del Conde* at left. Watermark: Duarte. Printer: BABN. 156x67mm.

   a. 2000.   FV   20.00
   b. 2001.   FV   20.00
   s1. 2000. Specimen with black overprint: *ESPECIMEN / MUESTRA SIN*   —   20.00
      VALOR on each side. Punch hole cancelled
   s2. 2001. Specimen with black Overprint: *ESPECIMEN / MUESTRA SIN*   —   20.00
      VALOR on each side. Punch hole cancelled

2001-02 Issue

168 10 Pesos Oro   **VF   UNC**

2001; 2002; 2003. Dark green on multicolor underprint. Matí as Ramón Mella at right. Wide border printing at upper center right. Back: *Altar de la Patria*. Printer: (T)DLR. 156x67mm.

   a. 2001. Yellow to left on both sides.   FV   2.00
   b. 2002. Green to left on face.   FV   2.00
   c. 2003. Green to left on face.   FV   2.00
   s1. 2001. Specimen. Overprint in black: *ESPECIMEN / MUESTRA SIN*   —   25.00
      VALOR on both sides. Punch hole cancelled.
   s2. 2002. Specimen. Overprint in black: *ESPECIMEN / MUESTRA SIN*   —   25.00
      VALOR on both sides. Punch hole cancelled.
   s3. 2003. Specimen. Overprint in black: *ESPECIMEN / MUESTRA SIN*   —   25.00
      VALOR on both sides. Punch hole cancelled.

169 20 Pesos Oro   **VF   UNC**

2001-04. Brown on peach, green and multicolor underprint. Gregorio Luperon at right. Wide border printing at upper center right. Back: *Panteón Nacional* at left. Printer: (T)DLR. 156x67mm.

   a. 2001. Yellow to left on both sides.   FV   3.00
   b. 2002. Pink to left on face.   FV   3.00
   c. 2003. Pink to left on face.   FV   3.00
   d. 2004. Pink to left on face.   FV   3.00
   s1. Specimen. 2001. Overprint: *ESPECIMEN / MUESTRA SIN VALOR* in   —   10.00
      black on both sides. Punch hole cancelled.

	VF	UNC
s2. Specimen. 2002. Overprint: *ESPECIMEN / MUESTRA SIN VALOR* in black on both sides. Punch hole cancelled.	—	10.00
s3. Specimen. 2003. Overprint: *ESPECIMEN / MUESTRA SIN VALOR* in black on both sides. Punch hole cancelled.	—	10.00
s4. Specimen. 2004. Overprint: *ESPECIMEN / MUESTRA SIN VALOR* in black on both sides. Punch hole cancelled.	—	10.00

170 50 Pesos Oro

2001; 2002; 2003; 2004. Purple and dark brown on multicolor underprint. Santa Marla la Menor Cathedral at right. Wide border printing at upper center right. Back: Basilica de Nuestra Señora de la Altagracia at left. Watermark: Duarte. Printer: (T)DLR. 156x67mm.

	VF	UNC
a. 2001.	FV	8.00
b. 2002. Violet to left on face.	FV	8.00
c. 2003. Violet to left on face.	FV	8.00
d. 2004. Violet to left on face.	FV	8.00
s1. 2001. Specimen. Overprint: *ESPECIMEN / MUESTRA SIN VALOR* in black on each side. Punch hole cancelled.	—	12.50
s2. 2002. Specimen. Overprint: *ESPECIMEN / MUESTRA SIN VALOR* in black on each side. Punch hole cancelled.	—	12.50
s3. 2003. Specimen. Overprint: *ESPECIMEN / MUESTRA SIN VALOR* in black on each side. Punch hole cancelled.	—	12.50
s4. 2004. Specimen. Overprint: *ESPECIMEN / MUESTRA SIN VALOR* in black on each side. Punch hole cancelled.	—	12.50

171 100 Pesos Oro

2001; 2002; 2003; 2004. Dark brown and orange on multicolor underprint. F. R. Sanches, J. P. Duarte and M. R. Mella at right. Wide border printing at upper center right. Back: *Puerta del Conde* at left. Watermark: Duarte. Printer: (T)DLR. 156x67mm.

	VF	UNC
a. 2001. Yellow to left on face and back.	FV	17.50
b. 2002. Green to left on face.	FV	17.50
c. 2003. Green to left on face.	FV	17.50
d. 2004. Green to left on face.	FV	17.50
s1. 2001. Specimen. Overprint: *ESPECIMEN / MUESTRA SIN VALOR* in black on both sides. Punch hole cancelled.	—	20.00
s2. 2002. Specimen. Overprint: *ESPECIMEN / MUESTRA SIN VALOR* in black on both sides. Punch hole cancelled.	—	20.00
s3. 2003. Specimen. Overprint: *ESPECIMEN / MUESTRA SIN VALOR* in black on both sides. Punch hole cancelled.	—	20.00
s4. 2004. Specimen. Overprint: *ESPECIMEN / MUESTRA SIN VALOR* in black on both sides. Punch hole cancelled.	—	20.00

172 500 Pesos Oro

2002; 2003; 2004. Placement of security strip varies slightly. Dark brown and aqua on multicolor underprint. Salome Ureña de Henriquez and Pedro Henriquez Ureña at right. Wide border printing at upper center right. Back: Banco Central building at left. Watermark: Duarte. Printer: (T)DLR. 156x67mm.

	VF	UNC
a. 2002.	FV	40.00
b. 2003.	FV	40.00
c. 2004.	FV	40.00

	VF	UNC
s1. 2002. Specimen. Overprint in black: *ESPECIMEN / MUESTRA SIN VALOR* on both sides. Punch hole cancelled.	—	20.00
s2. 2003. Specimen. Overprint in black: *ESPECIMEN / MUESTRA SIN VALOR* on both sides. Punch hole cancelled.	—	20.00
s3. 2004. Specimen. Overprint in black: *ESPECIMEN / MUESTRA SIN VALOR* on both sides. Punch hole cancelled.	—	20.00

173 1000 Pesos Oro

2002; 2003; 2004. Red and deep lilac on multicolor underprint. *Palacio Nacional* at right. Wide border printing at upper center right. Back: Alcazar de Don Diego Colon at left. Watermark: Duarte. Printer: (T)DLR. 156x67mm.

	VF	UNC
a. 2002.	FV	105
b. 2003.	FV	105
c. 2004.	FV	105
s1. 2002. Specimen. Overprint in black: *ESPECIMEN / MUESTRA SIN VALOR* once on each side. Punch hole cancelled.	—	30.00
s2. 2003. Specimen. Overprint in black: *ESPECIMEN / MUESTRA SIN VALOR* once on each side. Punch hole cancelled.	—	30.00
s3. 2004. Specimen. Overprint in black: *ESPECIMEN / MUESTRA SIN VALOR* once on each side. Punch hole cancelled.	—	30.00

174 2000 Pesos Oro

2002. Black and blue on multicolor underprint. Emillo Prud-Homme and José Reyes at right. Wide border printing at upper center right. Back: *Teatro Nacional*. Watermark: Duarte. Printer: (T)DLR. 156x67mm.

	VF	UNC
a. 2002.	FV	200
b. 2003.	FV	200
c. 2004.	FV	200
s1. 2002. Specimen. Overprint in black: *ESPECIMEN / MUESTRA SIN VALOR* once on each side. Punch hole cancelled.	—	40.00
s2. 2003. Specimen. Overprint in black: *ESPECIMEN / MUESTRA SIN VALOR* once on each side. Punch hole cancelled.	—	40.00
s3. 2004. Specimen. Overprint in black: *ESPECIMEN / MUESTRA SIN VALOR* once on each side. Punch hole cancelled.	—	40.00

2002 Commemorative Issue

#175, 55th Anniversary of the Central Bank.

175   100 Pesos Oro
2002. Dark Brown and orange on multicolor underprint. F. R. Sanches, J. P. Duarte and M. R. Mella at right. Wide border printing at upper center right. Back: *Puerta del Conde* at left. Commemorative overprint. Watermark: Duarte. Printer: (T)DLR. 156x67mm.

	VF	UNC
a. 2002.	FV	17.50
s1. 2002. Specimen. Overprint: *ESPECIMEN / MUESTRA SIN VALOR* in black on both sides. Punch hole cancelled.	—	50.00

2006 Issue

176   50 Pesos Oro
2006; 2008. Clear text security thread. Printer: (T)DLR. 156x67mm.

	VF	UNC
a. 2006. Upper right background border engraving has flat bottom.	FV	8.00
b. 2008. Upper right background border engraving has curved bottom.	FV	8.00
s1. 2006. Specimen. Overprint: *ESPECIMEN / MUESTRA SIN VALOR* in black on both sides. Punch hole cancelled.	—	25.00
s2. 2008. Specimen. Overprint: *ESPECIMEN / MUESTRA SIN VALOR* in black on both sides. Punch hole cancelled.	—	25.00

177   100 Pesos Oro
2006; 2009; 2010. Dark brown and orange on multicolor underprint. F.R. Sanches, J.P. Duarte and M.R. Mella at right. Clear text security thread. Back: *Puerta del Conde* at left. Watermark: J.P. Duarte and 100. Printer: (T)DLR. 156x67mm.

	VF	UNC
a. 2006.	FV	8.00
b. 2009.	FV	8.00
c. 2010.	FV	8.00
s1. 2006. Specimen. Overprint: *ESPECIMEN / MUESTRA SIN VALOR* in black on both sides. Punch hole cancelled.	—	20.00
s2. 2009. Specimen. Overprint: *ESPECIMEN / MUESTRA SIN VALOR* in black on both sides. Punch hole cancelled.	—	20.00
s3. 2010. Specimen. Overprint: *ESPECIMEN / MUESTRA SIN VALOR* in black on both sides. Punch hole cancelled.	—	20.00

178   200 Pesos Oro
2007. Violet on multicolor underprint. Three women at right. Back: Monument at left center. Watermark: Value added to watermark. 156x67mm.

	VF	UNC
	FV	35.00

179   500 Pesos Oro
2006; 2009; 2010. Watermark: Value added, Printer: (T)DLR. 156x67mm.

	VF	UNC
a. 2006.	FV	17.50
b. 2009.	FV	17.50
c. 2010.	FV	17.50
s1. 2006. Specimen. Overprint in black: *ESPECIMEN / MUESTRA SIN VALOR* on both sides. Punch hole cancelled.	—	50.00
s2. 2009. Specimen. Overprint in black: *ESPECIMEN / MUESTRA SIN VALOR* on both sides. Punch hole cancelled.	—	50.00
s3. 2010. Specimen. Overprint in black: *ESPECIMEN / MUESTRA SIN VALOR* on both sides. Punch hole cancelled.	—	50.00

180   1000 Pesos Oro
2006; 2009; 2010. Red and deep lilac on multicolor underprint. *Palacio Nacional* at right. Back: Alcazae de Don Diego Colon at left. Watermark: Duarte and value. 156x67mm.

	VF	UNC
a. 2006.	FV	55.00
b. 2009.	FV	55.00
c. 2010.	FV	55.00
s1. 2006. Specimen. Overprint in black: *ESPECIMEN / MUESTRA SIN VALOR* once on each side. Punch hole cancelled.	—	40.00
s2. 2009. Specimen. Overprint in black: *ESPECIMEN / MUESTRA SIN VALOR* once on each side. Punch hole cancelled.	—	40.00
s3. 2010. Specimen. Overprint in black: *ESPECIMEN / MUESTRA SIN VALOR* once on each side. Punch hole cancelled.	—	40.00

181   2000 Pesos Oro
2006; 2009; 2010. Black and blue on multicolor underprint. Emilo Prud Homme and José Reyes at right. Back: *Teatro Nacional* at left. Watermark: Duarte and value. 156x67mm.

	VF	UNC
a. 2006.	FV	100
b. 2009.	FV	100
c. 2010.	FV	100
s1. 2006. Specimen. Overprint in black: *ESPECIMEN / MUESTRA SIN VALOR* once on each side. Punch hole cancelled.	—	50.00
s2. 2009. Specimen. Overprint in black: *ESPECIMEN / MUESTRA SIN VALOR* once on each side. Punch hole cancelled.	—	50.00
s3. 2010. Specimen. Overprint in black: *ESPECIMEN / MUESTRA SIN VALOR* once on each side. Punch hole cancelled.	—	50.00

2010 Polymer Issue

182   20 Pesos Oro
2009. Polymer plastic. Brown, orange and green on multicolor underprint. Gregorio Luperon at right. Back: Panteon Nacional. Printer: F-CO. 156x67mm.

	VF	UNC
a. Issued note.	FV	3.00
s. Specimen. Overprint: *ESPECIMEN / MUESTRA SIN VALOR* in black on both sides. Punch hole cancelled.	—	50.00

2011 Pesos Dominicanos Issue

183   50 Pesos Dominicanos
2010-2012. Santa Maria la Menor Cathedral at right. Printer: F-CO.

	VF	UNC
a. 2010.	FV	8.00
b. 2011.	FV	8.00
c. 2012.	FV	8.00
s. Specimen. Overprint in black: *ESPECIMEN / MUESTRA SIN VALOR* once on each side. Punch hole cancelled.	—	30.00

184 100 Pesos Dominicanos
2010. F.dR. Sanchez, J.P. Duarte and M.R. Mella at right. Printer: F-CO.

		VF	UNC
a. 2010.		FV	16.00
b. 2011.		FV	16.00
c.		FV	16.00
s. Specimen. Overprint in black: *ESPECIMEN / MUESTRA SIN VALOR* once on each side. Punch hole cancelled.		—	50.00

185 200 Pesos Dominicanos
2013. Violet on multicolor underprint. Three women at right. Back: Monument at left center. 156x67mm.

VF	UNC
FV	22.50

185A 200 Pesos Dominicanos
2014. Like #185 but with redesigned images and enhanced security features. Printer: (T)DLR.

VF	UNC
FV	22.50

186 500 Pesos Dominicanos
2010. S.U. de Heriquez and P.H. Quziurena at right. Printer: F-CO.

		VF	UNC
a. 2010.		FV	25.00
b. 2011.		FV	25.00
s. Specimen. Overprint in black: *ESPECIMEN / MUESTRA SIN VALOR* once on each side. Punch hole cancelled.		—	50.00

187 1000 Pesos Dominicanos
2010. Palacio Nacional at right. Printer: F-CO.

		VF	UNC
a. 2010.		FV	50.00
b. 2011.		FV	50.00
s. Specimen. Overprint in black: *ESPECIMEN / MUESTRA SIN VALOR* once on each side. Punch hole cancelled.		—	75.00

188 2000 Pesos Dominicanos
2011. E.P. Homme and J. Reyes at right.

		VF	UNC
a. Issued note.		FV	100
s. Specimen. Overprint in black: *ESPECIMEN / MUESTRA SIN VALOR* once on each side. Punch hole cancelled.		—	75.00

189 50 Pesos Dominicanos
2014. Violet and dark green. Santa Maria la Menor Cathedral at right center. Back: Modern church at center. Printer: DLR. 156x67mm.

VF	UNC
FV	8.00

190 100 Pesos Dominicanos
2014. Orange and gray. F.dR. Sanchez, J.P. Duarte and M.R. Mella at right. Back: Puerta del Conde at center. 156x67mm.

VF	UNC
FV	16.00

191 100 Pesos Dominicanos
2014. Expected new issue. Printer: DLR. 156x67mm.

VF	UNC
—	—

192 500 Pesos Dominicanos
2014. Marine blue and gray. S.U. de Heriquez and P.H. Quziurena at right. Back: Banco Central building at center. Printer: DLR. 156x67mm.

VF	UNC
FV	17.50

193   1000 Pesos Dominicanos

2014. Red, violet, yellow. Bank seal, Rose of Bayahibe flowers, Palacio Nacional building in Santo Domingo. Back: Alcázar de Colón museum building in Santo Domingo. Windowed security thread with demetalized MIL PESOS DOMINICA-NOS. Watermark: Juan Pablo Duarte. Printer: DLR. 156x67mm.

	VF	UNC
	FV	40.00

194   2000 Pesos Dominicanos

2014. Blue and black. E.P. Homme and J. Reyes at right. Back: Teatro Nacional at center. 156x67mm.

	VF	UNC
	FV	80.00

COLLECTOR SERIES

Banco Central de la República Dominicana

1974 Issues

CS1   1-1000 Pesos Oro

ND(1974). #99-106. Overprint: *MUESTRA* twice on face.

Mkt. Value
450

CS2   1-1000 Pesos Oro

ND(1974). #99-106. Overprint: *MUESTRA* on face and back.

Mkt. Value
450

1978 Issues

CS3   Pesos Oro

1978. #116, 118-124. Overprint: *MUESTRA / SIN VALOR* on face, *ESPECIMEN* on back.

Mkt. Value
235

EAST AFRICA

East Africa was an administrative grouping of several neighboring British territories: Kenya, Tanganyika, Uganda and Zanzibar. The common interest of Kenya, Tanzania and Uganda invited cooperation in economic matters and consideration of political union. The territorial governors, organized as the East Africa High Commission, met periodically to administer such common activities as taxation, industrial development and education. The authority of the Commission did not infringe upon the constitution and internal autonomy of the individual colonies. The common monetary system circulated for the territories by the East African Currency Board and was also used in British Somaliland and the Aden Protectorate subsequent to the independence of India (1947) whose currency had previously circulated in these two territories. Also see British Somaliland, Zanzibar, Kenya, Uganda and Tanzania. Also see Somaliland Republic, Kenya, Uganda and Tanzania.

RULERS:
   British

MONETARY SYSTEM:
   1 Rupee = 100 Cents to 1920
   1 Florin = 100 Cents, 1920-1921
   1 Shilling = 100 Cents

BRITISH ADMINISTRATION

East African Currency Board, Nairobi

1961 ND Issue

41   5 Shillings

ND (1961-63). Various. Brown on light red underprint. Portrait Queen Elizabeth II at upper left. Three signatures at left and four at right. Printer: TDLR.

	VF	UNC
a. Top left signature: E. B. David. (1961).	20.00	250
b. Top left sign: A. L. Adu. (1962-63).	15.00	200

42   10 Shillings

ND (1961-63). Various. Green on multicolor underprint. Portrait Queen Elizabeth II at upper left. Three signatures at left and four at right. Printer: TDLR.

	VF	UNC
a. Top left signature: E. B. David. (1961).	25.00	350
b. Top left signature: A. L. Adu. (1962-63).	20.00	300

43   20 Shillings

ND (1961-63). Various. Blue on light pink underprint. Portrait Queen Elizabeth II at upper left. Three signatures at left and four at right. Printer: TDLR.

	VF	UNC
a. Top left signature: E. B. David. (1961).	75.00	500
b. Top left signature: A. L. Adu. (1962-63).	50.00	350

44   100 Shillings
ND (1961-63). Various. Red on multicolor underprint. Portrait Queen Elizabeth II
at upper left. Three signatures at left and four at right. Printer: TDLR.

		VF	UNC
a. Top left signature: E. B. David. (1961).		150	1,000
b. Top left signature: A. L. Adu. (1962-63).		100	750

1964 ND Issue

45   5 Shillings
ND (1964). Brown on multicolor underprint. Sailboat at left center. Back. Various
plants. Watermark: Rhinoceros.

	VF	UNC
	15.00	100

48   100 Shillings
ND (1964). Deep red on multicolor underprint. Sailboat at left center. Back: Various plants. Watermark: Rhinoceros.

	VF	UNC
a. Issued note.	50.00	260
s. Specimen. Punched hole cancelled.	—	400

46   10 Shillings
ND (1964). Green on multicolor underprint. Sailboat at left center. Back: Various
plants. Watermark: Rhinoceros.

	VF	UNC
a. Issued note.	25.00	150
s. Specimen, punch hole cancelled.	—	250

47   20 Shillings
ND (1964). Blue on multicolor underprint. Sailboat at left center. Back: Various
plants. Watermark: Rhinoceros.

	VF	UNC
a. Issued note.	40.00	400
s. Specimen. Punched hole cancelled.	—	600

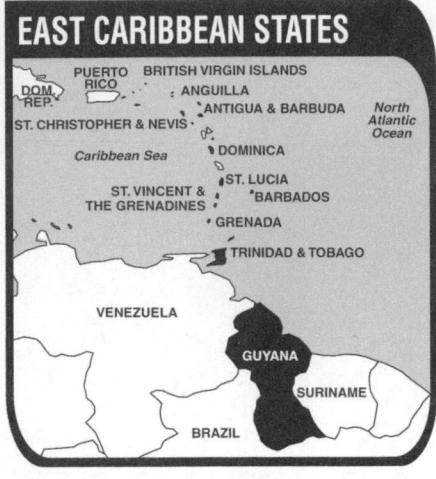

EAST CARIBBEAN STATES

The East Caribbean States, formerly the British Caribbean Territories (Eastern Group), a currency board formed in 1950, comprised the British West Indies territories of Trinidad and Tobago, Barbados, the Leeward Islands of Anguilla, St. Christopher, Nevis and Antigua; the Windward Islands of St. Lucia, Dominica, St. Vincent and Grenada; British Guiana and the British Virgin Islands. As time progressed, the member countries varied and is reflected on the backs of #13-16. The first issue includes Barbados but not Grenada, while the second issue includes both Barbados and Grenada and the third issue retains Grenada while Barbados is removed. Barbados attained self-government in 1961 and independence on Nov. 30, 1966. On May 26, 1966 British Guiana became independent as Guyana which later became a cooperative Republic on Feb. 23, 1970. The British Virgin Islands became a largely self-governing dependent territory of the United Kingdom in 1967. United States currency is the official medium of exchange. St. Christopher and Nevis became fully independent on Sept. 19, 1983. Trinidad & Tobago became an independent member state of the Commonwealth on August 31, 1962.

RULERS:
British

MONETARY SYSTEM:
1 Dollar = 100 Cents

ISLAND PARTICIPATION

| Variety I | Variety II | Variety III |

Variety I: Listing of islands on back includes Barbados but not Grenada.
Variety II: Listing included Barbados and Grenada.
Variety III: Listing retains Grenada while Barbados is denied.

SIGNATURE VARIETIES

(Signature varieties table showing pairs 1–10, each with Chairman signature and three Director signatures)

BRITISH ADMINISTRATION
East Caribbean Currency Authority
1965 ND Issue

#13-16 Replacement notes: Serial # prefix *Z1*. Beginning in 1983, #13-16 were overprinted with circled letters at left indicating their particular areas of issue within the Eastern Group.

13	**1 Dollar**		VF	UNC

ND (1965). Red on multicolor underprint. Fish at center, map at left, Queen Elizabeth II at right. Signature varieties. Back: Coastline with rocks and trees at left center. Watermark: Queen Elizabeth II. Printer: TDLR. 145x69mm.

		VF	UNC
a. Signature 1; 2. Back variety 1.		25.00	135
b. Signature 3. Back variety 2.		14.00	75.00
c. Signature 4.		36.00	200
d. Signature 5; 6; 7.		14.00	75.00
e. Signature 8. Back variety 3.		12.00	65.00
f. Signature 9; 10. Darker red on back as previous varieties, to Series B82.		9.00	50.00
g. Signature 10. Brighter red on back. Series B83-B91.		9.00	50.00
h. overprint: *A* in circle.		9.00	50.00
i. overprint: *D* in circle.		10.00	55.00
j. overprint: *G* in circle.		9.00	50.00
k. overprint: *K* in circle.		9.00	50.00
l. overprint: *L* in circle.		10.00	55.00
m. overprint: *M* in circle.		9.00	50.00
n. overprint: *U* in circle.		9.00	50.00
o. overprint: *V* in circle.		9.00	50.00
s. As a, j-n. Specimen.		—	230

14	**5 Dollars**		VF	UNC

ND (1965). Green on multicolor underprint. Flying fish at center, map at left, Queen Elizabeth II at right. Signature varieties. Back: Coastline with rocks and trees at left center. Watermark: Queen Elizabeth II. Printer: TDLR. 145x69mm.

		VF	UNC
a. Signature 1. Back variety 1.		60.00	320
b. Signature 2.		60.00	320
c. Signature 3. Back variety 2. Reported not confirmed.		—	—
d. Signature 4.		45.00	260
e. Signature 5; 6.		28.00	155
f. Signature 7.		28.00	155
g. Signature 8. Back variety 3.		18.00	100
h. Signature 9; 10.		14.00	75.00
i. overprint: *A* in circle.		14.00	75.00
j. overprint: *D* in circle.		15.00	85.00
k. overprint: *G* in circle.		14.00	75.00
l. overprint: *K* in circle.		14.00	75.00
m. overprint: *L* in circle.		40.00	220
n. overprint: *M* in circle.		15.00	85.00
o. overprint: *U* in circle.		14.00	80.00
p. overprint: *V* in circle.		14.00	80.00
s. As a, b. Specimen.		—	390

1985-87 ND Issue

#17-25 Replacement notes: Serial # prefix *Z1*. #17-20 do not have name Anguilla at island near top of map at right.

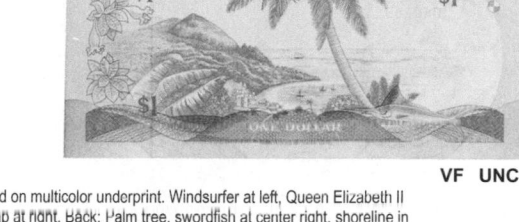

15	20 Dollars	VF	UNC

ND (1965). Purple on multicolor underprint. Turtles at center, map at left, Queen Elizabeth II at right. Signature varieties. Back: Coastline with rocks and trees at left center. Watermark: Queen Elizabeth II. Printer: TDLR. 145x69mm.

		VF	UNC
a. Signature 1. Back variety 1.		270	1,500
b. Signature 2.		230	1,250
c. Signature 3. Back variety 2. Reported not confirmed.		—	—
d. Signature 4.		125	600
e. Signature 5; 6; 7.		90.00	560
f. Signature 8. Back variety 3.		30.00	170
g. Signature 9; 10.		26.00	145
h. overprint: *A* in circle.		24.00	135
i. overprint: *D* in circle.		26.00	145
j. overprint: *G* in circle.		26.00	145
k. overprint: *K* in circle.		45.00	260
l. overprint: *L* in circle.		27.00	150
m. overprint: *M* in circle.		27.00	150
n. overprint: *U* in circle.		27.00	150
o. overprint: *V* in circle.		27.00	150
s. As a; e; g. Specimen.		—	800

17	1 Dollar	VF	UNC

ND (1985-88). Red on multicolor underprint. Windsurfer at left, Queen Elizabeth II at center right, map at right. Back: Palm tree, swordfish at center right, shoreline in background. Watermark: Queen Elizabeth II. Printer: TDLR. 145x69mm

	VF	UNC
a. Suffix letter *A*.	7.00	37.50
d. Suffix letter *D*.	7.00	37.50
g. Suffix letter *G*.	7.00	37.50
k. Suffix letter *K*.	7.00	37.50
l. Suffix letter *L*.	7.00	37.50
m. Suffix letter *M*.	7.00	37.50
u. overprint: *U* in circle on suffix letter *V* issue (1988).	7.00	37.50
v. Suffix letter *V*.	7.00	37.60

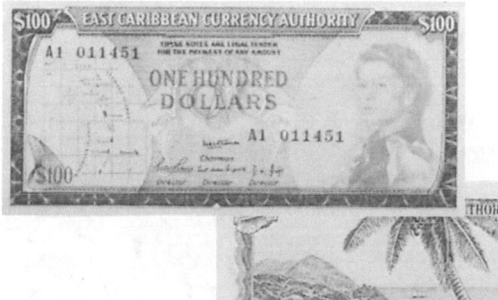

16	100 Dollars	VF	UNC

ND (1965). Black on multicolor underprint. Sea horses at center, map at left, Queen Elizabeth II at right. Signature varieties. Back: Coastline with rocks and trees at left center. Watermark: Queen Elizabeth II. Printer: TDLR. 145x69mm.

	VF	UNC
a. Signature 1. Back variety 1.	650	3,600
b. Signature 2. Reported not confirmed.	—	—
c. Signature 5. Back variety 2.	685	3,800
d. Signature 3; 4; 6; 7. Reported not confirmed.	—	—
e. Signature 8. Back variety 3. Reported not confirmed.	—	—
f. Signature 9; 10.	160	1,300
g. overprint: *A* in circle.	160	880
h. overprint: *D* in circle.	290	1,600
i. overprint: *G* in circle.	200	1,100
j. overprint: *K* in circle.	260	1,450
k. overprint: *L* in circle.	160	880
l. overprint: *M* in circle.	160	880
m. overprint: *U* in circle.	160	880
n. overprint: *V* in circle.	160	880
s. As a. Specimen.	—	1,100

18	5 Dollars	VF	UNC

ND (1986-88). Deep green on multicolor underprint. Windsurfer at left, Queen Elizabeth II at center right, map at right. Back: Palm tree, swordfish at center right, shoreline in background. Watermark: Queen Elizabeth II. Printer: TDLR. 145x69mm.

	VF	UNC
a. Suffix letter *A*.	11.00	60.00
d. Suffix letter *D*.	11.00	60.00
g. Suffix letter *G*.	11.00	60.00
k. Suffix letter *K*.	11.00	60.00
l. Suffix letter *L*.	11.00	60.00
m. Suffix letter *M*.	11.00	60.00
u. overprint: *U* in circle on suffix letter *V* issue (1988).	11.00	60.00
v. Suffix letter *V*.	11.00	60.00
ur. Replacement note. Z/1 serial # prefix.	25.00	140

19	20 Dollars	VF	UNC

ND (1987-88). Purple and brown on multicolor underprint. Windsurfer at left, Queen Elizabeth II at center right, map at right. Back: Palm tree, swordfish at center right, shoreline in background. Watermark: Queen Elizabeth II. Printer: TDLR. 145x69mm.

	VF	UNC
a. Suffix letter *A*.	37.50	210
d. Suffix letter *D*.	37.50	210
g. Suffix letter *G*.	37.50	210
k. Suffix letter *K*.	37.50	210
l. Suffix letter *L*.	37.50	210
m. Suffix letter *M*.	37.50	210
u. overprint: *U* in circle.	37.50	210
v. Suffix letter *V*.	37.50	210

Eastern Caribbean Central Bank

SIGNATURE VARIETIES			
	Governor		Governor
1	*signature*	2	K. Dwight Venner

20 100 Dollars | | VF | UNC
ND (1986-88). Black and orange on multicolor underprint. Windsurfer at left, Queen Elizabeth II at center right, map at right. Back: Palm tree, swordfish at center right, shoreline in background. Watermark: Queen Elizabeth II. Printer: TDLR. 145x69mm.

	VF	UNC
a. Suffix letter *A*.	145	800
d. Suffix letter *D*.	145	800
g. Suffix letter *G*.	145	800
k. Suffix letter *K*.	145	800
l. Suffix letter *L*.	145	800
m. Suffix letter *M*.	145	800
u. overprint: *U* in circle on suffix letter *V* issue (1988).	145	800
v. Suffix letter *V*.	145	800

1985-88 ND Issue

21 1 Dollar VF UNC
ND (1988-89). Red on multicolor underprint. Windsurfer at left, Queen Elizabeth II at center right, map at right. *Anguilla island* named near top of map at right. Signature 1. Back: Harbor at St. Lucia. Watermark: Queen Elizabeth II. Printer: TDLR. 145x69mm.

	VF	UNC
a. Suffic letter *A*.	9.00	50.00
d. Suffix letter *D*.	9.00	50.00
k. Suffix letter *K*.	9.00	50.00
l. Suffix letter *L*.	9.00	50.00
m. Suffix letter *M*.	9.00	50.00
u. Suffix letter *U*.	9.00	50.00
ur. Suffix letter *U*. Replacement note. Serial # prefix *Z*.	20.00	110

22 5 Dollars VF UNC
ND (1988-93). Deep green on multicolor underprint. Windsurfer at left, Queen Elizabeth II at center right, map at right. *Anguilla island* named near top of map at right. Back: Harbor at St. Lucia. Watermark: Queen Elizabeth II. Printer: TDLR. 145x69mm.

	VF	UNC
a1. Suffix letter *A*. Signature 1.	10.00	55.00
a2. Like a1. Signature 2.	10.00	55.00
d. Suffix letter *D*. Signature 1.	10.00	55.00
g1. Suffix letter *G*. Signature 1.	10.00	55.00
g2. Like g1. Signature 2.	10.00	55.00
k1. Suffix letter *K*. Signature 1.	10.00	55.00
k2. Like k1. Signature 2.	10.00	55.00
l1. Suffix letter *L*. Signature 1.	10.00	55.00
l2. Like l1. Signature 2.	10.00	55.00
m. Suffix letter *M*. Signature 1.	10.00	55.00
u. Suffix letter *U*. Signature 1.	10.00	55.00
v2. Suffix letter *V*. Signature 2.	10.00	55.00
v1. Suffix letter *V*. Signature 1.	10.00	55.00

23 10 Dollars VF UNC
ND (1985-93). Blue on multicolor underprint. Windsurfer at left, Queen Elizabeth II at center right, map at right. *Anguilla island* named near top of map at right. Back: Harbor at Grenada, sailboats at left and center. Watermark: Queen Elizabeth II. Printer: TDLR. 145x69mm.

	VF	UNC
a1. Suffix letter *A*. signature 1.	19.00	105
a2. Like a1. signature 2.	19.00	105
d1. Suffix letter *D*. signature 1.	19.00	105
d2. Like d1. signature 2.	19.00	105
g. Suffix letter *G*. signature 1.	19.00	105
k1. Suffix letter *K*. signature 1.	19.00	105
k2. Like k1. signature 2.	19.00	105
l1. Suffix letter *L*. signature 1.	19.00	105
l2. Like l1. signature 2.	19.00	105
m. Suffix letter *M*. signature 1.	19.00	105
u. Suffix letter *U*. signature 1.	19.00	105
v1. Suffix letter *V*. signature 1.	19.00	105
v2. Like v1. signature 2.	19.00	105
ar. As a2. Replacement note. Serial # prefix: *Z*.	36.00	200

24 20 Dollars VF UNC
ND (1988-93). Purple and brown on multicolor underprint. Windsurfer at left, Queen Elizabeth II at center right, map at right. *Anguilla island* named near top of map at right. Back: Harbor at St. Lucia. Watermark: Queen Elizabeth II. Printer: TDLR. 145x69mm.

	VF	UNC
a1. Suffix letter *A*. Signature 1.	32.00	180
a2. Like a1. Signature 2.	32.00	180
d1. Suffix letter *D*. Signature 1.	32.00	180
d2. Like d1. signature 2.	32.00	180
g1. Suffix letter *G*. Signature 1.	32.00	180
g2. Like g1. Signature 2.	32.00	180
k1. Suffix letter *K*. Signature 1.	32.00	180
k2. Like k1. Signature 2.	32.00	180
l1. Suffix letter *L*. Signature 1.	32.00	180
l2. Like l1. Signature 2.	32.00	180
m1. Suffix letter *M*. Signature 1.	32.00	180
m2. Like m1. Signature 2.	32.00	180
u. Suffix letter *U*. Signature 1.	32.00	180
v. Suffix letter *V*. Signature 1.	32.00	180

25 100 Dollars | | VF | UNC

ND (1988-93). Black and orange on multicolor underprint. Windsurfer at left, Queen Elizabeth II at center right, map at right. *Anguilla island* named near top of map at right. Back: Harbor at St. Lucia. Watermark: Queen Elizabeth II. Printer: TDLR. 145x69mm.

	VF	UNC
a1. Suffix letter *A*. signature 1.	200	1,100
a2. Like a1. signature 2.	200	1,100
d1. Suffix letter *D*. signature 1.	200	1,100
d2. Like d1. signature 2.	200	1,100
g. Suffix letter *G*. signature 1.	200	1,100
k1. Suffix letter *K*. signature 1.	200	1,100
k2. Like k1. signature 2.	200	1,100
l1. Suffix letter *L*. signature 1.	200	1,100
l2. Like l1. signature 2.	200	1,100
m1. Suffix letter *M*. signature 1.	200	1,100
m2. Like m1. signature 2.	200	1,100
u. Suffix letter *U*. signature 1.	200	1,100
v. Suffix letter *V*. signature 1.	200	1,100

Antigua (A)	▮ ▮ ▮ ▮	St. Lucia (L)	▮ ▮ ▮
Dominica (D)	▮ ▮ ▮	Montserrat (M)	▮ ▮ ▮ ▮
Grenada (G)	▮ ▮	Anguilla (U)	▮ ▮ ▮ ▮
St. Kitts (K)	▮ ▮ ▮	St. Vincent (V)	▮ ▮ ▮ ▮

1993 ND Issue

26 5 Dollars | | VF | UNC

ND (1993). Dark green, black and violet on multicolor underprint. Queen Elizabeth II at center right, turtle at lower center, green-throated carib at top right. Signature 2. Back: Admiral's House in Antigua and Barbuda at left, Trafalgar Falls in Dominica at right, island map at center. Watermark: Queen Elizabeth II. Printer: TDLR. 145x69mm.

	VF	UNC
a. Suffix letter *A*.	FV	60.00
d. Suffix letter *D*.	FV	60.00
g. Suffix letter *G*.	FV	60.00
k. Suffix letter *K*.	FV	60.00
l. Suffix letter *L*.	FV	60.00
m. Suffix letter *M*.	FV	80.00
u. Suffix letter *U*.	FV	60.00
v. Suffix letter *V*.	FV	60.00

27 10 Dollars | | VF | UNC

ND (1993). Dark blue, black and red on multicolor underprint. Queen Elizabeth II at center right, turtle at lower center, green-throated carib at top right. Signature 2. Back: Admiralty Bay in St. Vincent and Grenadines at left, sailing ship *Warspite* and brown pelican at right center, island map at right center. Watermark: Queen Elizabeth II. Printer: TDLR. 145x69mm.

	VF	UNC
a. Suffix letter *A*.	FV	90.00
d. Suffix letter *D*.	FV	90.00
g. Suffix letter *G*.	FV	90.00
k. Suffix letter *K*.	FV	90.00
l. Suffix letter *L*.	FV	90.00
m. Suffix letter *M*.	FV	140
u. Suffix letter *U*.	FV	90.00
v. Suffix letter *V*.	FV	90.00

28 20 Dollars | | VF | UNC

ND (1993). Brown violet, blue-gray and orange on multicolor underprint. Queen Elizabeth II at center right, turtle at lower center, green-throated carib at top right. Signature 2. Back: Government House in Montserrat at left, nutmeg in Grenada at right, island map at center. Watermark: Queen Elizabeth II. Printer: TDLR. 145x69mm.

	VF	UNC
a. Suffix letter *A*.	FV	130
d. Suffix letter *D*.	FV	130
g. Suffix letter *G*.	FV	130
k. Suffix letter *K*.	FV	130
l. Suffix letter *l*.	FV	130
m. Suffix letter *M*.	FV	200
u. Suffix letter *U*.	FV	130
v. Suffix letter *V*.	FV	130

29 50 Dollars | | VF | UNC

ND (1993). Purple and olive-green on multicolor underprint. Queen Elizabeth II at center right, turtle at lower center, green-throated carib at top right. Signature 2. Back: Brimstone Hill in St. Kitts at left, Les Pitons mountains in St. Lucia and sooty tern at right, island map at center. Watermark: Queen Elizabeth II. Printer: TDLR. 145x69mm.

	VF	UNC
a. Suffix letter *A*.	FV	260
d. Suffix letter *D*.	FV	260
g. Suffix letter *G*.	FV	260
k. Suffix letter *K*.	FV	260
l. Suffix letter *L*.	FV	260
m. Suffix letter *M*.	65.00	370
u. Suffix letter *U*.	FV	260
v. Suffix letter *V*.	FV	260

30 100 Dollars

ND (1993). Dark brown, dark olive-green and tan on multicolor underprint. Queen Elizabeth II at center right, turtle at lower center, green-throated carib at top right. Signature 2. Back: Sir Arthur Lewis at left, E.C.C.B. Central Bank building and Lesser Antillean Swift at right, island map at center. Watermark: Queen Elizabeth II. Printer: TDLR. 145x69mm.

	VF	UNC
a. Suffix letter A .	65.00	380
d. Suffix letter D .	65.00	380
g. Suffix letter G .	65.00	380
k. Suffix letter K .	65.00	380
l. Suffix letter L .	65.00	380
m. Suffix letter M .	85.00	470
u. Suffix letter U .	65.00	380
v. Suffix letter V .	65.00	380

1994 ND Issue

#31-35 like #26-30 but w/clear bold values at upper l. and lower r. Thin security thread. Sign. 2. Replacement notes: Serial # prefix Z are scarce and command a premium.

31 5 Dollars

ND (1994). Thin security thread. Dark green, black and violet on multicolor underprint. Queen Elizabeth II at center right, turtle at lower center, green-throated carib at top right. Clear bold values at upper left and lower right. Signature 2. Back: Admiral's House in Antigua and Barbuda at left, Trafalgar Falls in Dominica at right, island map at center. Watermark: Queen Elizabeth II. Printer: TDLR. 145x69mm.

	VF	UNC
a. Suffix letter A .	FV	50.00
d. Suffix letter D .	FV	50.00
g. Suffix letter G .	FV	50.00
k. Suffix letter K .	FV	50.00
l. Suffix letter L .	FV	50.00
m. Suffix letter M .	14.00	80.00
u. Suffix letter U .	FV	50.00
v. Suffix letter V .	FV	50.00

32 10 Dollars

ND (1994). Thin security thread. Dark blue, black and red on multicolor underprint. Queen Elizabeth II at center right, turtle at lower center, green-throated carib at top right. Clear bold values at upper left and lower right. Signature 2. Back: Admiralty Bay in St. Vincent and Grenadines at left, sailing ship *Warspite* and brown pelican at right center, island map at center. Watermark: Queen Elizabeth II. Printer: TDLR. 145x69mm.

	VF	UNC
a. Suffix letter A .	FV	70.00
d. Suffix letter D .	FV	70.00
g. Suffix letter G .	FV	70.00
k. Suffix letter K .	FV	70.00
l. Suffix letter L .	FV	70.00
m. Suffix letter M .	20.00	110
u. Suffix letter U .	FV	70.00
v. Suffix letter V .	FV	70.00

33 20 Dollars

ND (1994). Thin security thread. Brown-violet, blue-gray and orange on multicolor underprint. Queen Elizabeth II at center right, turtle at lower center, green-throated carib at top right. Clear bold values at upper left and lower right. Signature 2. Back: Government House in Montserrat at left, nutmeg in Grenada at right, island map at center. Watermark: Queen Elizabeth II. Printer: TDLR. 145x69mm.

	VF	UNC
a. Suffix letter A .	FV	110
d. Suffix letter D .	FV	110
g. Suffix letter G .	FV	110
k. Suffix letter K .	FV	110
l. Suffix letter L .	FV	110
m. Suffix letter M .	35.00	190
u. Suffix letter U .	FV	110
v. Suffix letter V .	FV	110

34 50 Dollars

ND (1994). Thin security thread. Tan, red-orange and green on multicolor underprint. Queen Elizabeth II at center right, turtle at lower center, green-throated carib at top right. Clear bold values at upper left and lower right. Signature 2. Back: Brimstone Hill in St. Kitts at left, Les Pitons mountains in St. Lucia and sooty tern at right , island map at center. Watermark: Queen Elizabeth II. Printer: TDLR. 145x69mm.

	VF	UNC
a. Suffix letter A .	40.00	220
d. Suffix letter D .	40.00	220
g. Suffix letter G .	40.00	220
k. Suffix letter K .	40.00	220
l. Suffix letter L .	40.00	220
m. Suffix letter M .	80.00	450
u. Suffix letter U .	40.00	220
v. Suffix letter V .	40.00	220

35 100 Dollars

VF UNC

ND (1994). Thin security thread. Dark brown and dark green on multicolor underprint. Queen Elizabeth II at center right, turtle at lower center, green-throated carib at top right. Clear bold values at upper left and lower right. Signature 2. Back: Sir Arthur Lewis at left, E.C.C.B. Central Bank building and Lesser Antillean Swift at right, island map at center. Watermark: Queen Elizabeth II. Printer: TDLR. 145x69mm.

a. Suffix letter A.	60.00	330
d. Suffix letter D.	60.00	330
g. Suffix letter G.	60.00	330
k. Suffix letter K.	60.00	330
l. Suffix letter L.	60.00	330
m. Suffix letter M.	90.00	510
u. Suffix letter U.	60.00	330
v. Suffix letter V.	60.00	330

1998 ND Issue

#36 Building rendering is long, partially covering signature. Printer: (T)DLR.

36 100 Dollars

VF UNC

ND (1998). Gold foil flower enhanced colors and segmented foil over security thread. Dark brown and dark green on multicolor underprint. Queen Elizabeth II at center right, turtle at lower center, green-throated carib at top right. Signature 2. Back: Sir Arthur Lewis at left, Central Bank building and Lesser Antillean Swift at right, island map at center. Watermark: Queen Elizabeth II. Printer: (T)DLR. 145x69mm.

a. Suffix letter A.	55.00	270
d. Suffix letter D.	55.00	270
g. Suffix letter G.	55.00	270
k. Suffix letter K.	55.00	270
l. Suffix letter L.	55.00	270
m. Suffix letter M.	80.00	360
u. Suffix letter U.	55.00	270
v. Suffix letter V.	55.00	270

2000 ND Issue

#37-41. Modified security features. Segmented security thread. Gold foil devices in upper r. of face. Shorter building rendering above signature.

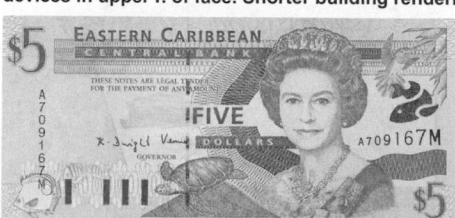

37 5 Dollars

VF UNC

ND (2000). Green, dark green, slate blue on multicolor underprint. Queen Elizabeth II at center right, turtle at lower center, green-throated carib at top right. Signature 2. Gold foil fish at right. Back: Admiral's House in Antigua and Barbuda at left, Trafalgar Falls in Dominica at right, island map at center. Watermark: Queen Elizabeth II. Printer: TDLR. 145x69mm.

a. Suffix letter A.	FV	37.50
d1. Suffix letter D.	FV	37.50
d2. Suffix letter D. FIVE in burgundy color.	10.00	50.00
g. Suffix letter G.	FV	37.50
k1. Suffix letter K.	FV	37.50
k2. Suffix letter K. FIVE in burgundy color.	10.00	50.00
l. Suffix letter L.	FV	37.50
m. Suffix letter M.	FV	42.50
u. Suffix letter U.	FV	40.00
v. Suffix letter V.	FV	37.50

38 10 Dollars

VF UNC

ND (2000). Blue and black on multicolor underprint. Queen Elizabeth II at center right, turtle at lower center, green-throated carib at top right. Signature 2. Gold foil fish at right. Back: Admiralty Bay in St. Vincent and Grenadines at left, sailing ship *Warspite* and brown pelican at right, island map at center. Watermark: Queen Elizabeth II. Printer: TDLR. 145x69mm.

a. Suffix letter A.	FV	55.00
d. Suffix letter D.	FV	55.00
g. Suffix letter G.	FV	55.00
k. Suffix letter K.	FV	55.00
l. Suffix letter l.	FV	55.00
m. Suffix letter M.	FV	72.50
u. Suffix letter U.	FV	60.00
v. Suffix letter V.	FV	55.00

39 20 Dollars

VF UNC

ND (2000). Purple and slate blue on multicolor underprint. Queen Elizabeth II at center right, turtle at lower center, green-throated carib at top right. Signature 2. Gold foil butterfly at right. Back: Government House in Montserrat at left, nutmeg in Grenada at right, island map at center. Watermark: Queen Elizabeth II. Printer: TDLR. 145x69mm.

a. Suffix letter A.	FV	80.00
d. Suffix letter D.	FV	80.00
g. Suffix letter G.	FV	80.00
k. Suffix letter K.	FV	80.00
l. Suffix letter L.	FV	80.00
m. Suffix letter M.	FV	120
u. Suffix letter U.	FV	85.00
v. Suffix letter V.	FV	80.00

40　50 Dollars

ND (2000). Bronze and orange on multicolor underprint. Queen Elizabeth II at center right, turtle at lower center, green-throated carib at top right. Signature 2. Gold foil flower at right. Back: Brimstone Hill in St. Kitts at left, Les Pitons mountains in St. Lucia and sooty tern at right , island map at center. Watermark: Queen Elizabeth II. Printer: TDLR. 145x69mm.

	VF	UNC
a. Suffix letter *A*.	FV	170
d. Suffix letter *D*.	FV	170
g. Suffix letter *G*.	FV	170
k. Suffix letter *K*.	FV	170
l. Suffix letter *L*.	FV	170
m. Suffix letter *M*.	FV	280
u. Suffix letter *U*.	FV	175
v. Suffix letter *V*.	FV	170

41　100 Dollars

ND (2000). Dark brown and dark green on multicolor underprint. Queen Elizabeth II at center right, turtle at lower center, green-throated carib at top right. Gold foil flower at upper right. Signature 2. Back: Sir Arthur Lewis at left, Central Bank building and Lesser Antillean Swift at right, island map at center. Watermark: Queen Elizabeth II. Printer: TDLR. 145x69mm.

	VF	UNC
a. Suffix letter *A*.	FV	235
d. Suffix letter *D*.	FV	235
g. Suffix letter *G*.	FV	235
k. Suffix letter *K*.	FV	235
l. Suffix letter *L*.	FV	235
m. Suffix letter *M*.	FV	290
u. Suffix letter *U*.	FV	240
v. Suffix letter *V*.	FV	235

2003 ND Issue

42　5 Dollars

ND (2003). Silver foil devices in the upper right of the face and wide security thread. Fish at lower left has a brown eyeball. Green, dark green, slate blue on multicolor underprint. Queen Elizabeth II at center right, turtle at lower center, green-throated carib at top right. Signature 2. Gold foil fish at right. Back: Admiral's House in Antigua and Barbuda at left, Trafalgar Falls in Dominica at right, island map at center. Watermark: Queen Elizabeth II. Printer: TDLR. 145x69mm.

	VF	UNC
a. Suffix letter *A*.	FV	15.00
d. Suffix letter *D*.	FV	29.00
g. Suffix letter *G*.	FV	29.00
k. Suffix letter *K*.	FV	29.00
l. Suffix letter *L*.	FV	29.00
m. Suffix letter *M*.	FV	37.50
u. Suffix letter *U*.	FV	32.50
v. Suffix letter *V*.	FV	29.00
ur. Suffix letter *U*. Replacement note. Serial # prefix *Z/1*.	20.00	115

42A　5 Dollars

ND (2003). Fish at lower left has a green eyeball. Green, dark green, slate blue on multicolor underprint. Queen Elizabeth II at center right, turtle at lower center, Signature 2. Back: Admiral's House in Antigua and Barbuda at left, Trafalgar Falls in Dominica at right, island map at center. Printer: TDLR. 145x69mm.

	VF	UNC
a. Suffix letter *A*.	FV	35.00
l. Suffix letter *L*.	FV	35.00
m. Suffix letter *M*.	FV	42.50
v. Suffix letter *V*.	FV	35.00

43　10 Dollars

ND (2003). Silver foil devices in the upper right of the face and wide security thread. Blue and black on multicolor underprint. Queen Elizabeth II at center right, turtle at lower center, green-throated carib at top right. Signature 2. Gold foil fish at right. Back: Admiralty Bay in St. Vincent and Grenadines at left, sailing ship *Warspite* and brown pelican at right center, island map at center. Watermark: Queen Elizabeth II. Printer: TDLR. 145x69mm.

	VF	UNC
a. Suffix letter *A*.	FV	42.50
d. Suffix letter *D*.	FV	42.50
g. Suffix letter *G*.	FV	42.50
k. Suffix letter *K*.	FV	25.00
l. Suffix letter *L*.	FV	42.50
m. Suffix letter *M*.	FV	47.50
u. Suffix letter *U*.	FV	47.50
v. Suffix letter *V*.	FV	25.00

44　20 Dollars

ND (2003). Silver foil devices in the upper right of the face and wide security thread. Purple and slate blue on multicolor underprint. Queen Elizabeth II at center right, turtle at lower center, green-throated carib at top right. Signature 2. Gold foil butterfly at right. Back: Government House in Montserrat at left, nutmeg in Grenada at right, island map at center. Watermark: Queen Elizabeth II. Printer: TDLR. 145x69mm.

	VF	UNC
a. Suffix letter *A*.	FV	62.50
d. Suffix letter *D*.	FV	35.00
g. Suffix letter *G*.	FV	62.50
k. Suffix letter *K*.	FV	62.50
l. Suffix letter *L*.	FV	62.50
m. Suffix letter *M*.	FV	82.50
u. Suffix letter *U*.	FV	70.00
v. Suffix letter *V*.	FV	62.50

45   50 Dollars   VF   UNC

ND (2003). Silver foil devices in the upper right of the face and wide security thread. Bronze and orange on multicolor underprint. Queen Elizabeth II at center right, turtle at lower center, green-throated carib at top right. Signature 2. Gold foil flower at right. Back: Brimstone Hill in St. Kitts at left, Les Pitons mountains in St. Lucia and sooty tern at right, island map at center. Watermark: Queen Elizabeth II. Printer: TDLR. 145x69mm.

    a. Suffix letter *A*.   FV   137
    d. Suffix letter *D*.   FV   137
    g. Suffix letter *G*.   FV   137
    k. Suffix letter *K*.   FV   137
    l. Suffix letter *L*.   FV   137
    m. Suffix Letter *M*.   FV   190
    u. Suffix letter *U*. Not issued.   —   —
    v. Suffix letter *V*.   FV   137

48   10 Dollars   VF   UNC

ND (2008). Blue and black on multicolor underprint. Queen Elizabeth II at center right, turtle at lower center, green-throated carib at top right. Back: Admiralty Bay in St. Vincent and Grenadines at left, sailing ship *Warspite*. Printer: DLR. 145x69mm.   FV   22.50

46   100 Dollars   VF   UNC

ND (2003). Silver foil devices in the upper right of the face and wide security thread. Black Brown and dark green on multicolor underprint. Queen Elizabeth II at center right, turtle at lower center, green-throated carib at top right. Signature 2. Back: Sir Arthur Lewis at left, Central Bank building and Lesser Antillean Swift at right, island map at center. Watermark: Queen Elizabeth II. Printer: TDLR. 145x69mm.

    a. Suffix letter *A*.   FV   215
    d. Suffix letter *D*.   FV   215
    g. Suffix letter *G*.   FV   215
    k. Suffix letter *K*.   FV   215
    l. Suffix letter *L*.   FV   215
    m. Suffix letter *M*.   FV   275
    u. Suffix letter *U*. Not issued.   —   —
    v. Suffix letter *V*.   FV   215

49   20 Dollars   VF   UNC

ND (2008). Purple and slate blue on multicolor underprint. Queen Elizabeth II at center right, turtle at lower center, green-throated carib at top right. Back: Government House in Monserrat at left, nutmeg in Grenada at right. Printer: DLR. 145x69mm.   FV   30.00

2008 ND Issue

47   5 Dollars   VF   UNC

ND (2008). Green, dark green and slate blue on multicolor underprint. Queen Elizabeth II at center right, turtle at lower center. Back: Admiral's House in Antigua and Barbuda at left, Trafalgar falls in Dominica at right. Printer: DLR. 145x69mm.

    a. Issued note.   FV   8.50
    r. Replacement note. Serial # prefix *Z1*.   FV   85.00

50   50 Dollars   VF   UNC

ND (2008). Bronze and orange on multicolor underprint. Queen Elizabeth II at center right, turtle at lower center, green-throated carib at top right. Back: Brimstone Hill in St. Kitts at left. Les Pitons mountains in St. Lucia and sooty tern at right. Printer: DLR. 145x69mm.   FV   60.00

51   100 Dollars   VF   UNC

ND (2008). Black, brown and dark green on multicolor underprint. Queen Elizabeth II at center right, turtle at lower center, green-throated carib at top right. Back: Sir Arthur Lewis at left, Central Bank Building and Lesser Antillean Swift at right center. Printer: DLR. 145x69mm.   FV   110

2012 ND Issue, Tactile markings added

52 10 Dollars

ND (2012). Blue and black on multicolor underprint. Queen Elizabeth II at center right, turtle at lower center. Tactile markings at lower left. Back: Admiralty Bay in St. Vincent and Grenadines at left, sailing ship *Warspite*. Printer: DLR. 145x69mm.

	VF	UNC
	FV	12.50

53 20 Dollars

ND (2012). Purple and slate blue on multicolor underprint. Queen Elizabeth II at center right, turtle at lower center. Tactile markings at lower left. Back: Government House in Monserrat at left, nutmeg in Grenada at right. Printer: DLR. 145x69mm.

	VF	UNC
	FV	22.50

54 50 Dollars

ND (2012). Bronze and orange on multicolor underprint. Queen Elizabeth II at center right, turtle at lower center. Tactile markings at lower left. Back: Brimstone Hill in St. Kitts at left, Les Pitons mountains in St. Lucia and sooty tern at right. Printer: DLR. 145x69mm.

	VF	UNC
	FV	60.00

55 100 Dollars

ND (2012). Black, brown and dark green on multicolor underprint. Queen Elizabeth II at center right, turtle at lower center. Tactile markings at lower left. Back: Sir Arthur Lewis at left, Central Bank Building and Lesser Antillean Swift at right center. Printer: DLR. 145x69mm.

	VF	UNC
	FV	110

COLLECTOR SERIES

Government of Antigua and Barbuda

1983 ND Issue

This set is made with thin gold and silver foil bonded to paper.

CS1 30 Dollars — Mkt. Value

ND (1983). 12 different notes showing various flowers and animals.

	Mkt. Value
a. Hibiscus / Egret. Beauties of the islands.	25.00
b. Hummingbird / Yellow elder. The search for nectar.	25.00
c. Green Turtle / Yellow Goatfish. Food from the sea.	25.00
d. Queen Angel Fish / Coral. Wonders of the sea garden.	25.00
e. Petrea Butterfly / Caribbean Buckeye. Brilliance in the bushes.	25.00
f. Sea Horse / Shells. Underwater treasures.	25.00
g. Dolphins. Seafearubg symbols.	25.00
h. Iguana. Newcomer to a new nation.	25.00
i. Brown Pelican. Endangered coastal bird.	25.00
j. Clown Fish / Anemone. The prefect relationship.	25.00
k. Zebra Butterfly / Jacaranda. Tropical Beauties.	25.00
l. Spiny Lobster. Delacy of the sea.	25.00
m. Full set of 12 notes.	300

1984 ND Issue

CS2 30 Dollars — Mkt. Value

ND (1984). 12 different notes showing various animals and plants.

	Mkt. Value
a. Red-billed Tropic Bird. Beauty over the sea.	25.00
b. White-spotted Octopus. Hermit of the Sea.	25.00
c. Humpback Whale. Playful singer of the deep.	25.00
d. Queen Conch, Helmet Shell, Triton Trumpet shells.	25.00
e. Blue Euphonia Bird / Blue Passion-Flower. Beauties in blue.	25.00
f. Butterfly Fish / Sea Fan, Sea Rod. Colorful sea creatures	25.00
g. Black Skimmer Shore Bird. One of a kind.	25.00
h. Bananaquit Bird / Banana Tree. Tropical treasures.	25.00
i. Queen of the Night Cactus. Startling splendor	25.00
j. Sailfish. Popular sport fish.	25.00
k. Frigatebird. Pirate of the tropical seas.	25.00
l. Stilt Bird. Long-legged wader.	25.00
m. Set of 12 notes.	300

1985 ND Issue

CS3 30 Dollars — Mkt. Value

ND (1985). 6 different notes showing various animals and plants.

	Mkt. Value
a. Monarch Butterfly / Lantana Flower. Famous and familiar wanderer	25.00
b. Queen Triggerfish. Vivid underwater beauty.	25.00
c. Mangrove Cuckoo Bird. Elusive bird of the tropics.	25.00
d. Squirrelfish, Soldierfish / Fanworms. Colorful reef fish.	25.00
e. Mountain Dove / Tree of Life. Colorful tropic sights.	25.00
f. Man of War Fish / Portuguese Man of War. Unusual pair.	25.00
g. Set of 6 notes.	225

CS4 50 Dollars

ND (1985) 30 different notes showing various captains and ships.

	Mkt. Value
a. Captain Howell Davis and the *King James*.	30.00
b. Captain Edward Low and his brigantine.	30.00
c. Jean LaFfite and the *Pride*.	30.00
d. Francois l'Ollonois attacks Puerto Caballos.	30.00
e. Captain Charles Gibb's schooner *Maria*.	30.00
f. Admiral Plet Heyn and the *Amsterdam*.	30.00
g. Captain Jean Fleury and the *Dieppe*.	30.00
h. Easton Attacks on the Newfoundland coast.	30.00
i. Captain henry Avery and the *Gang-i-Saway*.	30.00
j. Captain William Dampier and the *St. George*.	30.00
k. Bartolomeo the Portuguese and his barque.	30.00
l. Captain Henry Mainwaring and the *Resistance*.	30.00
m. Pierre Legrand captures the Vice-Admiral's ship.	30.00
n. Captain Thomas Anstis and the *Good Fortune*.	30.00
o. Ann Bonny boards John Halman's sloop.	30.00
p. Captain Thomas Tew and the *Amity*.	30.00
q. Captain WilliamTaylor and the *Victory*.	30.00
r. Captain Samuel Bellamy and the *Whidah*.	30.00
s. Calico Jack Rackam and his *Merchantman*.	30.00
t. Captain Kidd and the *Adventure Galley*.	30.00
u. Sir Henry morgan captures the *Marquesa*.	30.00
v. Captain Thomas Cocklyn and the *Bird Galley*.	30.00
w. Captain Edward England and the *Cassandra*.	30.00
x. Sir Francis Drake and the *Golden Hind*.	30.00
y. Captain George Lowther and the *Happy Delivery*.	30.00
z. Benito de Soto and the *Black Joke*.	30.00
aa. Sede Bonnet's sloop *Royal James*.	30.00
ab. Charles Vane's ship challenges *HMS Buck*.	30.00
ac. Bartholomew Robert's *Royal Fortune*.	30.00
ad. Blackbeard's *Queen Ann's Revenge*.	30.00
ae. Set of 30 ntoes.	1,100

CS5 100 Dollars

11.1981 (1988). 30 different notes showing various pirate and treasure sailing ships. (20,000 sets).

	Mkt. Value
a. Jean LaFfite / The *Pride*.	40.00
b. Howell Davis / *King James*.	40.00
c. Captian Kidd / *Adventure Galley*.	40.00
d. Thomas Cocklyn / *Bird Galley*.	40.00
e. Sir Francis Drake / *Golden Hind*.	40.00
f. Stede Bonnetts / *Royal James*.	40.00
g. Charles Vane / *Challenges* (HMS Buck).	40.00
h. George Lowther / *Happy Delivery*.	40.00
i. Edward England / *Cassandra*.	40.00
j. Henry Avery / *Gaing-I-Saway*.	40.00
k. Piet Heyn / *Amsterdam*.	40.00
l. William Taylor / *Victory*.	40.00
m. Anne Bonny / John Halmans Sloop.	40.00
n. Bartolomeo the Portuguese / *Barque*.	40.00
o. Bartholomew Robert / *Royal Fortune*.	40.00
p. Blackbeard / *Queen Ann's Revenge*.	40.00
q. Benito de Soto / *Black Jake*.	40.00
r. Calico Jack Rackman / *Merchantman*.	40.00
s. Charles Gibbs / *Maria*.	40.00
t. Henry Mainwaring / *Resistance*.	40.00
u. Edward Low / Brigantine.	40.00
v. Jean Fleury / *Dieppe*.	40.00
w. Thomas Anstis / *Good Fortune*.	40.00
x. Thomas Tew / *Amity*.	40.00
y. Easton Attacks on the Newfoundland Coast.	40.00
z. François l'Ollonois Attacks Puerto Caballos.	40.00
aa. Pierre LeGrand Captures the Vice-Admiral's ship.	40.00
ab. Sir Henry Morgan Captures the Marquesa.	40.00
ac. Samuel Bellamy / *Whidah*.	40.00
ad. William Dampier / The *St. George*.	40.00
ae. Set of 30 notes.	1,100

ECUADOR

The Republic of Ecuador, located astride the equator on the Pacific coast of South America, has an area of 283,560 sq. km. and a population of 13.93 million. Capital: Quito. Agriculture is the mainstay of the economy but there are appreciable deposits of minerals and petroleum. It is the world's largest exporter of bananas and balsa wood. Coffee, cacao and shrimp are also valuable exports.

What is now Ecuador formed part of the northern Inca Empire until the Spanish conquest in 1533. Quito became a seat of Spanish colonial government in 1563 and part of the Viceroyalty of New Granada in 1717. The territories of the Viceroyalty - New Granada (Colombia), Venezuela, and Quito - gained their independence between 1819 and 1822 and formed a federation known as Gran Colombia. When Quito withdrew in 1830, the traditional name was changed in favor of the "Republic of the Equator." Between 1904 and 1942, Ecuador lost territories in a series of conflicts with its neighbors. A border war with Peru that flared in 1995 was resolved in 1999. Although Ecuador marked 25 years of civilian governance in 2004, the period has been marred by political instability. Protests in Quito have contributed to the mid-term ouster of Ecuador's last three democratically elected Presidents. In 2007, a Constituent Assembly was elected to draft a new constitution; Ecuador's twentieth since gaining independence.

MONETARY SYSTEM:
- 1 Peso = 8 Reales
- 1 Peso = 100 Centavos
- 1 Sucre = 10 Decimos = 100 Centavos
- 1 Condor = 25 Sucres
- 1 USA Dollar = 25,000 Sucres (March 2001)

REPUBLIC

Banco Central del Ecuador
1944-67 Issue

96 500 Sucres

1944-66. Black on multicolor underprint. Mercury seated at center. With text:*CAPITAL AUTORIZADO 20,000,000 SUCRES*. 3 signatures. Printer: ABNC.

	VF	UNC
a. Signature title overprint: *PRESIDENTE* at left. 12.5.1944; 27.6.1944.	400	—
b. Signature title overprint: *GERENTE GENERAL* at left, *VOCAL* at right. 31.7.1944; 7.9.1944.	375	—
c. Signature title overprint: *GERENTE GENERAL* at right. 12.1.1945-12.7.1947.	300	—
d. As c. 21.4.1961-17.11.1966.	300	—
s. Specimen. ND.	—	700

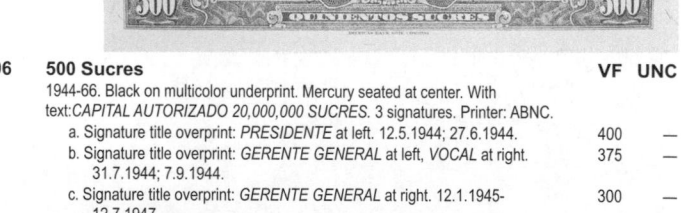

97 1000 Sucres

1944-67. Black on multicolor underprint. Woman reclining ("Telephone Service") at center. With text:*CAPITAL AUTORIZADO 20,000,000 SUCRES*. 3 signatures. Printer: ABNC.

	VF	UNC
a. Signature title overprint: *PRESIDENTE* at left. 12.5.1944; 27.6.1944.	650	—
b. Signature title overprint: *GERENTE GENERAL* at left, *VOCAL* at right. 31.7.1944; 7.9.1944.	550	—

	VF	UNC
c. Signature title overprint: *PRESIDENTE* at left, *GERENTE GENERAL* at right. 12.1.1945.	500	—
d. Signature title overprint: *GERENTE GENERAL* at right. 16.10.1945; 12.7.1947.	450	—
e. As d. 21.4.1961; 27.2.1962; 4.3.1964; 23.7.1964; 17.11.1966; 6.4.1967.	350	—
s. Specimen. ND.		850

The following reduced size notes are listed by printer.1950 Issue (1950-59) (TAB)#98-99 printer: W&S. 1950-71 Issue (1950-74) (TAB)#100-107 printer: ABNC. 1975-80 Issue (1975-83) (TAB)#108-112 printer: ABNC. 1957-71 Issue (1957-82) (TAB)#113-118 printer: TDLR.

1950 Issue - Reduced Size Notes

98   5 Sucres   VF   UNC

1950-55. Black on green underprint. Portrait Antonio Jose de Sucre at center. Date at left or right. Back: Arms at center. Printer: W&S.

a. 11.5.1950-13.7.1953.	15.00	75.00
b. Signature title overprint: *SUBGERENTE GENERAL* at left. 21.9.1953.	20.00	85.00
c. 31.5.1954-28.11.1955.	12.50	55.00

99   50 Sucres   VF   UNC

1950-59. Black on green underprint. National monument at center with buildings in background. Back: Arms at center. Printer: W&S.

a. 11.5.1950; 26.7.1950; 13.10.1950; 3.4.1951; 26.9.1951.	50.00	150
b. Signature title overprint: *SUBGERENTE GENERAL* at left. 3.9.1952; 8.10.1954; 24.9.1957.	50.00	150
c. 10.12.1953; 19.6.1956; 25.11.1957; 25.11.1958; 8.4.1959.	40.00	125
s1. Specimen. Black overprint: *ESPÉCIMEN* on both sides. ND, with 0000 serial #, unsigned.	—	175
s2. Specimen. Red overprint: *MUESTRA* twice on both sides. ND, without serial # or signs. Punched hole cancelled.	—	175

1950-71 Issue

100   5 Sucres   VF   UNC

1956-73. Several varieties in signature title overprints and serial # styles. Black on multicolor underprint. Portrait Antonio Jose de Sucre at center. Back: Arms 31mm. wide, without flagpole stems below. Printer: ABNC.

a. 19.6.1956; 28.8.1956; 2.4.1957; 19.6.1957; 19.7.1957.	5.00	40.00
b. Signature title overprint: *SUBGERENTE GENERAL*. 24.9.1957; 2.1.1958.	5.00	40.00
c. 2.2.1958; 1.1.1966.	2.50	20.00
d. 27.2.1970; 3.9.1973. Serial # varieties.	1.50	3.50

101   10 Sucres   VF   UNC

1950-1955. Several varieties in signature title overprints and serial # styles. Black on multicolor underprint. Portrait Sebastian de Benalcazar at center. Plain background. Back: Arms 31mm. wide, without flagpole stems below. Printer: ABNC.

a. 14.1.1950-28.11.1955.	8.00	45.00
b. 21.9.1953; 16.3.1954; 3.10.1955. Overprint: *SUB GERENTE GENERAL*.	10.00	50.00
s. Specimen.	—	150

101A   10 Sucres   VF   UNC

1956-74; 24.12.1957. UV: fibers fluoresce blue and yellow. Black on multicolor underprint. Portrait Sebastian de Benalcazar at center, with different guilloches and ornate background. Signature title overprint varieties. Serial # varieties. Back: Arms 31 mm. wide, without flagpole stems below. Printer: ABNC.

a. 15.6.1956-27.4.1966.	7.50	35.00
b. 24.5.1968-2.1.1974.	3.00	15.00
s. Specimen.	—	150

Note: #101A with date of 24.12.1957 has signature title overprint: *SUB GERENTE GENERAL*.

102   20 Sucres   VF   UNC

28.2.1950-28.7.1960. Several varieties in signature title overprints and serial # styles. Black on multicolor underprint. Church façade at center. Back: Arms 31 mm. wide, without flagpole stems below. Printer: ABNC.

a. Issued note.	15.00	50.00
s. Specimen. Overprint: *SPECIMEN* in red on face.	—	80.00

103   20 Sucres   VF   UNC

1962-73. Several varieties in signature title overprints, and serial # styles. Black on multicolor underprint. Church façade at center, different guilloches and darker underprint. Back: Arms 31 mm. wide, without flagpole stems below. Printer: ABNC.

a. 12.12.1962-4.10.1967.	5.00	25.00
b. 24.5.1968-3.9.1973.	3.00	15.00
s. Specimen. ND.	—	175

104   50 Sucres   VF   UNC

1968-76. UV: planchettes fluoresce pink. Black on multicolor underprint. National monument at center with buildings in background. Signature title overprint varieties. Serial # varieties. Back: Arms 31 mm. wide, without flagpole stems below. Printer: ABNC.

a. 24.5.1968; 5.11.1969.	5.00	30.00
b. 20.5.1971; 10.8.1976.	4.00	20.00
s. Specimen. ND.	—	50.00

104A   100 Sucres   VF   UNC

1952-57. Several varieties, signature title overprints, and serial # styles. Black on multicolor underprint. Portrait Simón Bolívar at center. Back: Arms 31 mm. wide, without flagpole stems below. Printer: ABNC.

a. 3.9.1952-19.6.1957.	75.00	220
b. Signature title: *SUBGERENTE*. 3.9.1952; 10.12.1953.	75.00	220

105   100 Sucres   VF   UNC

27.6.1964-7.7.1970. Several varieties, signature title overprints, and serial # styles. Black on multicolor underprint. Portrait Simón Bolívar at center with different guilloches. Back: Arms 31 mm. wide, without flagpole stems below. Printer: ABNC.

a. Issued note.	10.00	50.00
s. Specimen. Overprint: *SPECIMEN* in red on face.	—	80.00

107   1000 Sucres   VF   UNC

30.5.1969-20.9.1973. Several varieties, signature title overprints, and serial # styles. Black on multicolor underprint. Banco Central building at center. Back: Arms 31 mm. wide, without flagpole stems below. Printer: ABNC.

a. Issued note.	85.00	250
s. Specimen. ND.	—	75.00

108 5 Sucres VF UNC

1975-83. UV: planchettes fluoresce red, fibers yellow. Black on multicolor underprint. Portrait Antonio Jose de Sucre at center. Back: New rendition of arms. 29mm. wide with flag-pole stems below. Printer: ABNC.

a. 14.3.1975; 29.4.1977.	1.50	9.00
b. 20.8.1982; 20.4.1983.	1.00	6.00

109 10 Sucres VF UNC

14.3.1975; 10.8.1976; 29.4.1977; 24.5.1978. Black on multicolor underprint. Portrait Sebastian de Benalcazar at center. Back: New rendition of arms. 29mm. wide with flag-pole stems below. Printer: ABNC.

2.00 12.50

110 20 Sucres VF UNC

10.8.1976. Black on multicolor underprint. Church facade at center. Back: New rendition of arms. 29mm. wide with flag-pole stems below. Printer: ABNC.

2.50 17.50

111 50 Sucres VF UNC

10.8.1976. Black on multicolor underprint. National monument at center with buildings in background. Back: New rendition of arms. 29mm. wide with flag-pole stems below. Printer: ABNC.

a. Issued note.	4.00	27.50
s. Specimen.	—	100

112 100 Sucres VF UNC

24.5.1980. Black on multicolor underprint. Portrait Simón Bolívar at center with different guilloches. Back: New rendition of arms. 29mm. wide with flag-pole stems below. Printer: ABNC.

a. Issued note.	1.50	15.00
s. Specimen. Overprint: *MUESTRA* in red twice on both sides. Punch hole cancelled.	—	80.00

112A 100 Sucres VF UNC

ND (ca. 1980). Printed on tyvek as a test note. Black on multicolor undeprint. Printer: ABNC.

— 500

1957-71 Issue

113 5 Sucres VF UNC

1958-88. Black on multicolor underprint. Portrait Antonio Jose de Sucre at center. Back: New rendition of arms. Printer: TDLR.

a. 2.1.1958-7.11.1962.	4.00	17.50
b. 23.5.1963-27.2.1970.	1.00	12.50
c. 25.7.1979-24.5.1980.	0.50	7.50
d. 20.4.1983; 22.11.1988.	0.25	3.00
s. Specimen. ND; 24.5.1968; 25.7.1979; 24.5.1980. Overprint: *MUESTRA SIN VALOR* in red on both sides.	—	125

114 10 Sucres VF UNC

1968-83. Black on multicolor underprint. Portrait Sebastian de Benalcazar at center. Back: New rendition of arms. Printer: TDLR.

a. 24.5.1968; 20.5.1971.	3.00	20.00
b. 24.5.1980; 30.9.1982; 20.4.1983.	1.00	12.50
s1. Specimen. 24.5.1968. Series KV. Overprint: *MUESTRA SIN VALOR* in red on both sides.	—	100
s2. Specimen. 20.5.1971. Series KY.	—	100
s3. Specimen. 30.9.1982. Series LI.	—	100

115 20 Sucres

1961-83. Black on multicolor underprint. Church facade at center. Back: New rendition of arms. Printer: TDLR.

	VF	UNC
a. 7.6.1961; 29.8.1961; 27.2.1962; 6.7.1962; 7.11.1962; 12.12.1962.	5.00	35.00
b. 1.5.1978; 24.5.1980; 20.4.1983.	2.50	17.50
s1. Specimen. ND. Series JR. Overprint: *SPECIMEN* in black on both sides.	—	80.00
s2. Specimen. Series LE. 24.5.1980.	—	80.00

116 50 Sucres

1957-82. Black on multicolor underprint. National monument at center. Back: New rendition of arms. Printer: TDLR.

	VF	UNC
a. 2.4.1957; 7.7.1959.	15.00	60.00
b. 7.11.1962; 29.10.1963; 27.6.1964; 29.1.1965; 6.8.1965.	8.00	35.00
c. 1.1.1966; 27.4.1966; 17.11.1966.	4.00	25.00
d. 4.10.1967; 30.5.1969; 17.7.1974.	2.00	15.00
e. 24.5.1980; 20.8.1982.	1.25	10.00
s1. Specimen. ND; 1.1.1966. Overprint: *SPECIMEN* in red on both sides.	—	80.00
s2. Specimen. 20.8.1982. Overprint: *MUESTRA SIN VALOR* in red on both sides.	—	100

117 100 Sucres

29.8.1961-6.8.1965. Black on multicolor underprint. Crude portrait Simón Bolívar at center with light clouds behind. Back: New rendition of arms. Printer: TDLR.

	VF	UNC
a. Issued note.	20.00	50.00
s. Specimen. Without signature. Series TW.	—	75.00

118 100 Sucres

1971-77. UV: planchetts fluoresce yellow. Black on multicolor underprint. Finer portrait Simón Bolívar at center with dark clouds behind. Back: New rendition of arms. Printer: TDLR.

	VF	UNC
a. 20.5.1971; 17.7.1974.	8.00	40.00
b. 10.8.1976; 10.8.1977.	5.00	25.00
s. Specimen. 20.5.1971. Overprint: *MUESTRA SIN VALOR* in red on both sides.	—	80.00

1976 Issue

119 500 Sucres

1976-82. Black, violet-brown and dark olive on multicolor underprint. Dr. Eugenio de Santa Cruz y Espejo at left. Back: Arms at center. Watermark: Arms. Printer: TDLR.

	VF	UNC
a. 24.5.1976; 10.8.1977; 9.10.1978; 25.7.1979.	12.50	50.00
b. 20.7.1982.	7.50	30.00
s1. Specimen. ND. Series AB. Overprint: *MUESTRA SIN VALOR* in red on both sides.	—	85.00
s2. Specimen. 20.7.1982.	—	85.00

120 1000 Sucres

1976-82. Dark green and red-brown on multicolor underprint. Ruminahui at right. Back: Arms at center. Watermark: Arms. Printer: TDLR.

	VF	UNC
a. 24.5.1976-25.7.1979.	7.50	50.00
b. 24.5.1980; 20.7.1982.	5.00	25.00
s1. Specimen. ND. Series AB. Overprint: *MUESTRA SIN VALOR* in red on both sides.	—	80.00
s2. Specimen. Series HP. 24.5.1980. Overprint: *MUESTRA SIN VALOR* in red on both sides.	—	100

1984-88 Issues

#120A-125 w/o text: *SOCIEDAD ANONIMA* **below bank title.**

120A 5 Sucres VF UNC

121 10 Sucres

29.4.1986; 22.11.1988. Black on multicolor underprint. Portrait Sebastian de Benalcazar at center. Back: New rendition of arms. Printer: TDLR without imprint.

	VF	UNC
	0.75	3.50

121A 20 Sucres VF UNC

1986-88. Black on multicolor underprint. Church façade at center. Back: New rendition of arms. Printer: TDLR without imprint.

a. 29.4.1986; 22.11.1988.	0.75	5.00
s1. Specimen. 29.4.1986. Series LM.	—	20.00
s2. Specimen. 22.11.1988. Series LP. Overprint: *MUESTRA SIN VALOR* in red on both sides.	—	80.00

122 50 Sucres VF UNC

5.9.1984; 22.11.1988. Black on multicolor underprint. National monument at center. Back: New rendition of arms. Printer: TDLR without imprint.

a. Issued note.	1.00	7.50
s. Specimen. 5.9.1984. Overprint: *MUESTRA SIN VALOR* in red on both sides.	—	100

123 100 Sucres VF UNC

29.4.1986; 20.4.1990. Black, dark blue or light blue serial number. Black on multicolor underprint. Finer portrait Simón Bolívar at center with dark clouds behind. Back: New rendition of arms. Printer: TDLR without imprint. 2.00 15.00

123A 100 Sucres VF UNC

1988-97. Plate differences on face and back. Serial # style varieties. Black on multicolor underprint. Finer portrait Simón Bolívar at center with dark clouds behind. Back: New rendition of arms. Printer: TDLR without imprint.

a. Blue serial #. 8.6.1988; 21.6.1991; 11.10.1991.	0.50	5.00
b. 9.3.1992; 4.12.1992; 20.8.1993.	0.50	5.00
c. Black serial #. 21.2.1994.	0.50	5.00
d. As c. 3.4.1997.	0.50	5.00
p. Proof. Without serial #, signatures. Punch hole cancelled.	—	65.00
s1. As a. Specimen. 8.6.1988. Punched hole cancelled.	—	35.00
s2. As b. Specimen. 21.6.1991; 20.8.1993. Series WF. Overprint: *ESPECIMEN SIN VALOR* in red on both sides.	—	100

124 500 Sucres VF UNC

5.9.1984. Black, violet-brown and dark olive on multicolor underprint. Dr. Eugenio de Santa Cruz y Espejo at left. Signature varieties. Back: Arms at center. Watermark: Arms. Printer: TDLR without imprint.

a. Issued note.	2.00	15.00
s. Specimen. Overprint: *MUESTRA SIN VALOR* in red on both sides.	—	110

124A 500 Sucres VF UNC

8.6.1988. Many minor plate differences from #124. Black, violet-brown and dark olive on multicolor underprint. Dr. Eugenio de Santa Cruz y Espejo at left. Signature varieties. Back: Arms at center. Printer: TDLR.

a. Issued note.	1.25	10.00
s. Specimen. Overprint: *SPECIMEN* in red on face.	—	100

125 1000 Sucres VF UNC

1984-88. UV: planchetts fluoresce red and yellow. Value and central design orange. Dark green and red-brown on multicolor underprint. Ruminahui at right. Without *EL* in bank title. Serial # style varieties. Back: Arms at center. Watermark: Arms. Printer: TDLR.

a. 5.9.1984; 29.9.1986.	2.00	15.00
b. 8.6.1988.	1.50	10.00
s1. Specimen. 5.9.1984. Overprint: *MUESTRA SIN VALOR* in red on both sides.	—	100
s2. Specimen. Overprint: *ESPECIMEN SIN VALOR* in red on both sides.	—	100

Note: Later dates of #123A-#125 were made by different printers (w/o imprint) and vary slightly.

126 5000 Sucres VF UNC

1.12.1987. Purple and brown on multicolor underprint. Juan Montalvo at left, arms at center. Back: Flightless cormoran, Galapagos penguin and Galapagos tortoise. Watermark: Juan Montalvo. Printer: BCdE.

a. Issued note.	2.00	25.00
s. Specimen. Series AB. Overprint: *MUESTRA SIN VALOR* in red on both sides.	—	100

Note: #126 was designed in Mexico.

127   10,000 Sucres

1988-98. Serial # varieties exist. Dark brown and reddish brown on multicolor underprint. Vicente Rocafuerte at left. Back: Arms upper left center, Independence monument in Quito at center right. Watermark: Vicente Rocafuerte. Printer: BCdE.

		VF	UNC
a. Signature title by itself at left: *VOCAL.* 30.7.1988; 21.2.1994; 13.10.1994.		2.00	15.00
b. Signature title at lleft: *PRESIDENTE JUNTA MONETARIA.* 6.2.1995; 8.3.1995; 8.8.1995; 4.1.1996; 23.9.1996.		2.00	15.00
c. Signature title at lleft: *PRESIDENTE DEL DIRECTORIO.* 14.12.1998.		0.75	10.00
d. Signatrue title left: *VOCAL* in black; signature title right in brown. 4.1.1996; 23.9.1996.		0.75	10.00
e. Signature title left: *PRESIDENTE DEL DIRECTORIO* in black; signature title right in black. 14.12.1998.		0.75	10.00
s1. As a. Specimen. Series AB. Overprint: *ESPECIMEN SIN VALOR* in red on face.		—	100
s2. As a. Specimen. 13.10.1994 Series AH.		—	100
s3. As b. Specimen. 8.3.1995. Series AL. Overprint: *ESPECIMEN / MUESTRA SIN VALOR* in red on both sides.		—	100
s4. As e. Specimen. Overprint: *ESPECIMEN SIN VALOR* in red on both sides.		—	100

1991-95 Issue

128   5000 Sucres

1991-99. UV: planchetts fluoresce yellow and red. Value and design yellow. Purple and brown on multicolor underprint. Juan Montalvo at left, arms at center. Repositioned signature and both serial number horizontal. Back: Flightless cormoran, Galapagos penguin and Galapagos tortoise. Watermark: Juan Montalvo. Printer: BCdE.

		VF	UNC
a. Signature title by itself at left: *VOCAL.* 21.6.1991; 17.3.1992; 22.6.1992; 20.8.1993.		1.25	10.00
b. Signature title at left: *PRESIDENTE JUNTA MONETARIA.* 31.1.1995; 8.8.1995; 13.1.1996; 31.10.1996.		1.25	7.50
c. Signature title at left: *PRESIDENTE DEL DIRECTORIO.* 26.3.1996; 6.3.1999; 26.3.1999; 12.7.1999.		1.25	7.50
s1. Specimen. 21.6.1991. Series AG. Overprint: *MUESTRA SIN VALOR* in red on both sides.		—	100
s2. As a. Specimen. 17.3.1992. Series AJ. Overprint: *MUESTRA SIN VALOR* in red on both sides.		—	100
s3. As b. Specimen. 31.1.1995.		—	100
s4. Handstamp: *PRUEBA* in red on face.		—	60.00

129   20,000 Sucres

1995-99. Brown, black and deep blue on multicolor underprint. Dr. Gabriel Garcia Moreno at right . Back: Arms at center. Watermark: Dr. Gabriel Garcia Moreno.

		VF	UNC
a. Signature title at right: *PRESIDENTE JUNTA MONETARIA.* 31.1.1995; 20.11.1995.		2.00	20.00
b. Signature title at right: *PRESIDENTE JUNTA MONETARIA.* 2.6.1997.		1.50	15.00
c. Signature title at right: *VOCAL.* 1.6.1998.		7.50	30.00
e. Without security thread. signature title at right: *PRESIDENTE DEL DIRECTORIO.* 5.10.1999.		1.50	7.50
f. Two security threads. signature title at right: *PRESIDENTE DEL DIRECTORIO.* 5.10.1998; 26.3.1999; 12.7.1999.		1.50	10.00
s1. As a. Specimen. 31.1.1995. Overprint: *ESPECIMEN SIN VALOR* in red on both sides. With or without punch holes.		—	110
s2. As b. Specimen. 2.6.1997. Series AD.		—	100
s3. As c. 10.3.1999.		—	100

130   50,000 Sucres

1995-99. Segmented foil over security thread. Gray and red-brown on multicolor underprint. Eloy Alfaro at right. Back: Arms. Watermark: Eloy Alfaro.

		VF	UNC
a. Two security threads. signature title at left: *PRESIDENTE JUNTA MONETARIA.* 31.1.1995; 2.6.1997; 20.4.1998; 6.3.1999; 26.3.1999.		2.50	15.00
b. 2 security threads. 6.3.1999.		2.50	10.00
c. Decreased security features. Windowed security thread. Signature title at left: *GERENTE GENERAL.* 10.3.1999; 26.3.1999.		2.50	10.00
d. Embedded security thread. 12.7.1999.		2.50	10.00
s1. As a. Specimen. 31.1.1995; 2.6.1997. Series AB. Overprint: *MUESTRA SIN VALOR* in red on both sides.		—	150
s2. Specimen. 31.1.1995, without series. Overprint: *SPECIMEN* in red on both sides. Punch hole cancelled.		—	75.00
s3. Specimen. 31.1.1995, Series AB. Overprint: *MUESTRA SIN VALOR* in red on both sides. Punch hole cancelled.		—	75.00

Note: Since September 7, 2000, the U.S. Dollar became legal tender, and the sucre was redeemable until March 30, 2001 at the rate of 25,000 Sucres per U.S. Dollar.

EGYPT

The Arab Republic of Egypt, located on the northeastern corner of Africa, has an area of 1,001,450 sq. km. and a population of 81.71 million. Capital: Cairo. Although Egypt is an almost rainless expanse of desert, its economy is predominantly agricultural. Cotton, rice and petroleum are exported.

The regularity and richness of the annual Nile River flood, coupled with semi-isolation provided by deserts to the east and west, allowed for the development of one of the world's great civilizations. A unified kingdom arose circa 3200 B.C., and a series of dynasties ruled in Egypt for the next three millennia. The last native dynasty fell to the Persians in 341 B.C., who in turn were replaced by the Greeks, Romans, and Byzantines. It was the Arabs who introduced Islam and the Arabic language in the 7th century and who ruled for the next six centuries. A local military caste, the Mamluks took control about 1250 and continued to govern after the conquest of Egypt by the Ottoman Turks in 1517. Following the completion of the Suez Canal in 1869, Egypt became an important world transportation hub, but also fell heavily into debt. Ostensibly to protect its investments, Britain seized control of Egypt's government in 1882, but nominal allegiance to the Ottoman Empire continued until 1914. Partially independent from the UK in 1922, Egypt acquired full sovereignty with the overthrow of the British-backed monarchy in 1952. The completion of the Aswan High Dam in 1971 and the resultant Lake Nasser have altered the time-honored place of the Nile River in the agriculture and ecology of Egypt. A rapidly growing population (the largest in the Arab world), limited arable land, and dependence on the Nile all continue to overtax resources and stress society. The government has struggled to meet the demands of Egypt's growing population through economic reform and massive investment in communications and physical infrastructure.

MONETARY SYSTEM:
1 Pound (Junayh) = 100 Piastres, 1916

REPLACEMENT NOTES:
Starting in 1969, 2 types exist. Earlier system uses a single Arabic letter as series prefix instead of normal number/letter prefix. Known notes: #38-. Later system has the equivalent of English "200" or "300" in front of a single Arabic series letter. Known notes: #46-.

SIGNATURE VARIETIES

11	A. El-Refay, 1961-63	12	A. Zendo, 1962-66
13	A. Nazmy A. A El Hamed, 1967-70	14	A. Zendo, 1972-75
15	M. Ibrahim, 1976-81	16	M.S.A. Shalaby, 1981-84
17	A. Negm, 1985	18	A. Hamed, 1986
19	I.H. Mohamed	20	M. Abou El-Oyoun
21	Farouk Abdel Baky El Okda 1st kind	22	Farouk Abdel Baky El Okda 2nd kind
23	Hisham Ramez, Abdel Hafez		

REPUBLIC
Central Bank of Egypt
1961-64 Issues

35 25 Piastres — VF UNC
1.11.1961-18.8.1966. Blue on multicolor underprint. U. A. R. arms at right.
 a. 1.11.1961-24.4.1963. Signature 11. Series #1-18. 2.00 6.00
 b. 3.7.1965-18.8.1966. Signature 12. Series #19-42. 2.00 6.00
 s. Specimen. — —

36 50 Piastres — VF UNC
1.11.1961-14.8.1966. Blackish green multicolor underprint. U. A. R. arms at right. Watermark: U. A. R. arms.
 a. 1.11.1961-13.4.1963. Signature 11. Series #1-18. 3.00 15.00
 b. 6.2.1965-14.8.1966. Signature 12. Series #19-42. 3.00 15.00
 s. Specimen. — —

37 1 Pound — VF UNC
1.11.1961-23.2.1967. Blue-green on lilac and multicolor underprint. Tutankhamen's mask at right. Signature 11; 12; 13. Watermark: Arms.
 a. Issued note. 2.50 6.00
 s. Specimen. — —

38 **5 Pounds** | | VF | UNC
1.11.1961-12.11.1961. Green and brown on multicolor underprint. Circular guilloche at left, Tutankhamen's mask at right. Signature 11. Back: Value at left and right. Watermark: Flower. — 25.00 150

39 **5 Pounds** | | VF | UNC
13.11.1961-16.6.1964. Green and brown on multicolor underprint. Clear watermark area at left, Tutankhamen's mask at right. Guilloche at bottom center. Signature 11; 12. Back: Value at left, clear watermark area at right. Watermark: Arms.
  a. Issued note. 7.50 27.50
  s. Specimen. — —

40 **5 Pounds** | | VF | UNC
17.6.1964-13.2.1965. Lilac and brown on multicolor underprint. Clear circular area at left, Tutankhamen's mask at right. Guilloche at bottom center. Signature 12. Back: Value at left, clear watermark area at right. Watermark: Arms. 5.00 22.50

41 **10 Pounds** | | VF | UNC
1.11.1961-13.2.1965. Dark green and dark brown on multicolor underprint. Tutankhamen's mask at right. Signature 11; 12. Watermark: Arms. 7.50 30.00

1967-69 Issue

#42-46 Replacement notes: Serial # prefix single Arabic letter.

42 **25 Piastres** | | VF | UNC
6.2.1967-4.1.1975. Blue, green and brown on multicolor underprint. Sphinx with statue at left center. Signature 13; 14. Back: U.A.R. arms at center. Watermark: Archaic Egyptian scribe. 0.50 3.00

43 **50 Piastres** | | VF | UNC
2.12.1967-28.1.1978. Red-brown and brown on multicolor underprint. Al Azhar mosque at right. Signature 13; 14; 15. Back: Ramses II at center right. Watermark: Archaic Egyptian scribe.
  a. Issued note. 1.00 3.50
  s. Specimen. — —

44 1 Pound

12.5.1967-19.4.1978. Brown and black on multicolor underprint. Sultan Quayet Bey mosque at left center. Signature 12; 13; 14; 15. Back: Archaic statues. Watermark: Archaic Egyptian scribe.

VF UNC

    a. Issued note.   1.00   5.00

    s. Specimen.   —   —

45 5 Pounds

1.1.1969-78. Black on blue and multicolor underprint. Ahmad ibn Tulun mosque at Cairo at center right. Signature 13; 14; 15. Back: Ruins at left, frieze at center right. Watermark: Archaic Egyptian scribe.

VF UNC

    a. Issued note.   3.50 20.00

    s. Specimen. Black overprint: *ANNULE* and *CANCELLED*.   —   750

46 10 Pounds

1.9.1969-78. Red-brown and brown on multicolor underprint. Sultan Hassan Mosque at Cairo at left center. Signature 13; 14; 15. Back: Pharaoh and pyramids. Watermark: Archaic Egyptian scribe.

VF UNC

6.00 25.00

1976 Issue

#47 and 48 replacement notes: Serial # prefix single Arabic letter.

47 25 Piastres

12.4.1976-9.6.1978; 12.6.1978; 28.8.1978. Blue, green and grayish brown on blue and orange underprint. Sphinx with statue at left center. Signature 15. Back: A. R. E. arms. Watermark: Archaic Egyptian scribe.

VF UNC

    a. Issued note.   1.00   4.00

    s. Specimen.   —   —

Confirmation of additional dates are requested.

48 20 Pounds

5.7.1976; 1978. Green and black on multicolor underprint. Mohammed Ali mosque at left, Arabic legends at right. Signature 15. Back: Archaic war chariot at left center, frieze at center right. Watermark: Archaic Egyptian scribe.

VF UNC

10.00 35.00

1978-79 Issue

#40-62 no longer have conventional dates with Arabic day, month and year. In place of this are six Arabic numerals, the first and last making up the year, the second and third the day, the fourth and fifth the month of issue; YDD-MMY; i.e. 025029 will be 25 Feb. 1989. Replacement notes: Serial # prefix. Arabic *200* or *300* before single Arabic letter.

49 25 Piastres

2.1.-11.5.(19)79. Black and brown on gray, pale blue and orange underprint. Al-Sayida Aisha mosque at center. Signature 15. Back: Stylized A. R. E. arms, cotton, wheat and corn plants at center. Watermark: Tutankhamen's mask.

VF UNC

0.50   2.00

50	**1 Pound**	**VF**	**UNC**

(19)78-2008. Brown, purple and deep olive-green on multicolor underprint. Sultan Qait Bey mosque at left center. Back: Statues from the Abu Simbel Temple. Watermark: Tutankhamen's mask. 140x70mm.

		VF	UNC
a.	Back deep brown. Solid security thread. 29.5.1978-15.8.1981. Series #1-129. Signature 15.	FV	1.50
b.	3.4.1982-6.3.1984. Series #130-150. Signature 16.	FV	1.50
c.	2.5.1985-2.1.1986. Series #151-165. Signature 17.	FV	1.50
d.	Back pale brown. Solid security thread or segmented security thread with bank name repeated. 16.11.1986-1.6.1992. Series #166-246. Signature 18.	FV	1.50
e.	17.10.1993-25.2.2001. Series #247-380. Signature 19.	FV	1.50
f.	22.11.2001-14.8.2003. Series #381-428. Signature 20.	FV	1.50
g.	23.12.2003. Series #429-432. Signature 21.	FV	1.50
h.	23.12.2003. Series #432-; 12.4.2005. Signature 22.	FV	1.50
i.	7.7.(20)04; 4.1.2005; 17.4.2005. Signature 25.	FV	1.50
j.	5.3.2006. Signature 25.	FV	1.50
k.	31.1.2007. Signature 25.	FV	1.50
l.	25.3.2007.	FV	1.50
m.	15.5.2008.	FV	1.50
s.	Specimen. Red overprint in Arabic script. Punch hole cancelled.	—	500

51	**10 Pounds**	**VF**	**UNC**

24.6.(19)78-27.9.(20)00. Red-brown and brown-violet on multicolor underprint. Al-Rifai mosque at center. Signature 15; 16; 17; 18; 19. Back: Pharaoh. Watermark: Tutankhamen's mask. 150x70mm. | FV | 10.00

52	**20 Pounds**	**VF**	**UNC**

6.9.(19)78-92. Black, gray-violet and deep green on multicolor underprint. Muhammed Ali mosque at center. Back: Archaic sculptures from Chapel of Sesostris I and archaic war chariot. Watermark: Tutankhamen's mask. 175x70mm.

		VF	UNC
a.	Date below watermark. Solid security thread. 6.9.(19)78-22.4.(19)82. Signature 15; 16.	5.00	35.00
b.	Date at lower right of watermark. Solid security thread. 9.12.(19)86; 3.3.(19)87; 4.10.(19)87. Signature 18.	FV	20.00
c.	Segmented security thread with bank name repeated. (19)88-(19)92. Signature 19.	FV	17.50

53	**100 Pounds**	**VF**	**UNC**

(19)78; (19)92. Blue and green on multicolor underprint. Al-Sayida Zainab mosque at center. Back: Pharaoh's mask above frieze at center of vertical format. Watermark: Tutankhamen's mask.

		VF	UNC
a.	Series 1-6.(19)78. Signature 15.	30.00	100
b.	(19)92. Signature 18.	22.50	90.00

1980-81 Issue

Replacement notes: Serial # prefix Arabic *200* or *300* before single Arabic series letter.

54	**25 Piastres**	**VF**	**UNC**

17.1.(19)80-10.1(19)84. Dark green on light green, orange and blue underprint. Al-Sayida Aisha mosque at center. Signature 15; 16. Back: Stylized A. R. E. arms, cotton, wheat and corn plants at center. Watermark: Tutankhamen's mask. | 0.30 | 1.50

55	**50 Piastres**	**VF**	**UNC**

1.1.(19)81-10.6.(19)83. Green and brown on multicolor underprint. Al Azhar mosque at center. Signature 15; 16. Back: Sculptured wall design at left, Ramses II at center, archaic seal at right. Watermark: Tutankhamen's mask. | 0.50 | 3.00

56   5 Pounds   VF   UNC

(19)81; (19)86; (19)87. Olive-black and blue-black on multicolor underprint. Ibn Toulon mosque at center. Back: Design symbolizing bounty of the Nile River at center. Watermark: Tutankhamen's mask. 145x70mm.

- a. 1.2.(19)81. Signature 15. Top left serial # above border design and close to top edge of paper. Series 1.   5.00   35.00
- b. 2.2.(19)81. Signature 15. Top left serial # below border design. Series 2.   5.00   35.00
- c. (19)86; 6.1.(19)87. Signature 16; 17; 18.   3.00   15.00

1985 Issue

Replacement notes: Serial # prefix Arabic *200* or *300* before single Arabic series letter.

57   25 Piastres   VF   UNC

(19)85-2007. Purple and pale blue on pale lilac and multicolor underprint. Al-Sayida Aisha mosque at center. Signature 15. Back. Standard A. R. E. arms at left center. Watermark: Tutankhamen's mask.

- a. Solid security thread. 12.1.(19)85-30.1.(19)89. Signature 17; 18.   FV   1.00
- b. Segmented security thread with bank name repeated. 5.12.(19)90-(19)99. Signature 18; 19.   FV   0.75
- c. 8.1.(20)01. Signature 19.   FV   0.75
- d. Solid security thread. 22.1.(20)02. 21.1.2003. Signature 20.   FV   0.75
- e. 3.8.2004.   FV   0.75
- f. 12.9.2004; 31.10.2005. Signature 22.   FV   0.75
- g. 24.9.2006.   FV   0.75
- h. 27.6.2007.   FV   0.75
- s. Specimen. Red overprint in Arabic script.   —   500

58   50 Piastres   VF   UNC

(19)85-94. UV: security strip fluoresces orange. Black on pale orange, pink and multicolor underprint. Al Azhar mosque at center right. Back: Sculptured wall design at left, Ramses II at center, archaic seal at right. Watermark: Tutankhamen's mask.

- a. No text line at lower left on face. Solid security thead. 2.7.(19)85-(19)87. Signature 17; 18.   0.25   2.00
- b. Text line added at lower left on face. 1.2.(19)87-17.8.(19)89. Signature 18.   FV   1.25
- c. Segmented security thread with bank name repeated. 5.1.(19)90-15.8.(19)94. Signature 18, 19.   FV   1.00
- s. As a. Specimen. Overprinted in Arabic and English.   —   400

1989-94 Issue

Replacement notes: Serial # prefix Arabic *200* or *300* before single Arabic series letter.

59   5 Pounds   VF   UNC

2.4.(19)89-1.2.(20)01. Multicolor scrollwork added in underprint and into water-mark area. Black and blue-black on multicolor underprint. Multicolor scrollwork added in underprint. Ibn Toulon mosque at center. Signature 18; 19; 20. Back: Archaic design over watermark area at right. Watermark: Tutankhamen's mask. 145x70mm.   FV   6.00

60   50 Pounds   VF   UNC

9.2.(19)93-18.11.(19)99. Brown, violet and multicolor. Abu Hariba Mosque at right. Signature 18; 19. Back: Isis above archaic boat, interior view of Edfu temple at left center. Watermark: Tutankhamen's mask. 160x70mm.   12.50   35.00

61   100 Pounds   VF   UNC

14.9.(19)94; (19)97. Dark brown and brown-violet on multicolor underprint. Sultan Hassan Mosque at lower left center. Signature 19. Back: Sphinx at center. Watermark: Tutankhamen's mask. 165x70mm.   25.00   80.00

1995 Issue

62   50 Piastres   **VF UNC**

23.8.(19)94-2007. Dull olive-gray on multicolor underprint. Al Azhar mosque at center right. Signature 19; 20; 22. Back: Sculptured wall design at left, Ramses II at center, archaic seal at right. Watermark: Tutankhamen's mask.

a. 23.8.(19)94.	FV	0.75
b. 6.7.(19)95.	FV	0.75
c. 9.7.(19)95.	FV	0.75
d. 28.5.1997.	FV	0.75
e. 14.7.1999.	FV	0.75
f. 17.7.2002.	FV	0.75
g. 25.12.2003.	FV	0.75
h. 3.8.2004.	FV	0.75
i. 12.5.2005.	FV	0.75
j. 21.7.2005.	FV	0.75
k. 14.11.2006.	FV	0.75

2000-03 Issue

#63-64 w/wide segmented silver security strip and added rosette printed in optical variable ink.

63   5 Pounds   **VF UNC**

2001-. Dark blue and green on multicolor underprint. Ahmed Ibn Touloun Mosque at center. Back: Archaic Egyptian wall drawing. 145x70mm.

a. 4.2.2001; 21.2.2002; 16.12.2002. Signature 20.	FV	4.00
b. 6.1.2004; 11.1.2004; 13.1.2004; 16.2.2005; 5.9.2006; 18.8.2008. Signature 22.	FV	3.00
c. 2.5.2009.	FV	3.00
d. 2.8.2010.	FV	3.00
e. 26.2.2013; 27.2.2013.	FV	3.00
f. 31.3.2014. Signature 23.	FV	3.00
g. 20.04. 2015. Latent image at upper right front. Wider windowed security thread to left of vignette on front.	FV	3.00

64   10 Pounds   **VF UNC**

2003-. Brown and violet on multicolor underprint. Mosque. 158x70mm.

a. 19.8.2003; 28.8.2003. Signature 20.	FV	5.00
b. 12.8.2003; 31.8.2003. Signature 21.	FV	5.00
c. 13.6.2004; 28.12.2004; 22.11.2006; 5.12.2009; 27.4.2012. Signature 22.	FV	4.00
d. 10.3.2013; 27.04.2014.	FV	4.00
e. 18.08.2014. Latent image at lower left front. Wider windowed security thread to right of vignette on front.	FV	4.00

65   20 Pounds   **VF UNC**

3.10.2001-. Black, gray-violet and deep green on multicolor underprint. Muhammed Ali mosque at center. Signature 19, 20, 21, 22, 23. Back: Archaic sculptures from Chapel of Sesostris I and archaic war chariot. Watermark: Tutankhamen's mask. 175x70mm.

a. Signature 19.	FV	8.00
b. Signature 20.	FV	8.00
c. 10.12.2003. Signature 21.	FV	7.00
d. 7.11.2004; 11.11.2004; 26.1.2006. Signature 22.	FV	7.00
e. 14.8.2006.	FV	7.00
f. 16.1.2008.	FV	7.00
g. 15.3.2009.	FV	7.00
h. 16.5.2013.	FV	7.00
i. 26.5.2013.	FV	7.00
j. 9.2.2014.	FV	7.00
k. 14.01.2015. Signature 23.	FV	7.00

66   50 Pounds   **VF UNC**

2001-. Multicolor. Mosque. Signature 20, 21, 22, 23. Back: Temple and Nile boat. 160x70mm.

a. 25.11.2001.	FV	17.50
b. 2003.	FV	17.50
c. 28.9.2004. Signature 22.	FV	17.00
d. 2005.	FV	17.00
e. 16.4.2007.	FV	16.00
f. 3.3.2008.	FV	16.00
g. 25.3.2009.	FV	16.00
h. 16.9.2009.	FV	16.00
i. 27.10.2009.	FV	16.00
j. 11.4.2012.	FV	16.00
k. 17.6.2013.	FV	16.00
l. 25.6.2013.	FV	16.00

67 100 Pounds   VF UNC
2000-. Dark brown and brown-violet on multicolor underprint. Sultan Hassan Mosque at lower left center. Signature 19; 20; 21, 22; 23. Back: Sphinx at center. Watermark: Tutankhamen's mask and value. 165x70mm.

		VF	UNC
a.	4.10.2000. Signature 19. Narrow value in watermark.	FV	35.00
b.	Signature 19. Wide value in watermark.	FV	35.00
c.	Signature 20.	FV	32.50
d.	29.12.2003. Signature 21.	FV	32.50
e.	18.4.2006.	FV	32.50
f.	4.6.2006.	FV	32.50
g.	13.6.2007.	FV	30.00
h.	18.6.2009.	FV	30.00
i.	5.12.2012.	FV	30.00
j.	11.2.2013.	FV	30.00

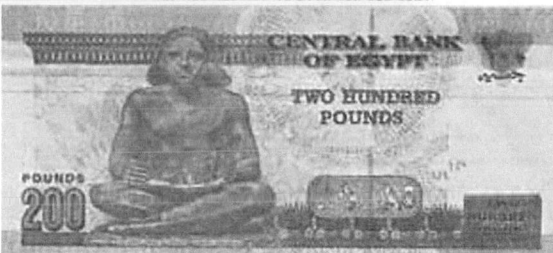

68 200 Pounds   VF UNC
3.4.2007-. Violet, brown and green on multicolor underprint. Qani-Bay Mosque at right center. Back: Seated scribe. 176x80mm.

		VF	UNC
a.	3.4.2007 - 28.5.2008.	FV	80.00
r.	Replacement note. 3.4.2007.	—	85.00

69 200 Pounds   VF UNC
3.4.2007-. Violet, brown and green on multicolor underprint. Qani-Bay Mosque at right center. Back: Seated scribe. Watermark: Seated scribe. 165x74mm.

		VF	UNC
a.	12.1.2009 - 28.11.2012. Signature 22.	FV	75.00
b.	4.2.2013 - 8.9.2013. Signature 23.	FV	75.00
r.	Replacement note. 3.4.2007.	FV	85.00

70 5 Pounds   VF UNC
28.12.2013. Signature 23.   FV   3.00

71 10 Pounds   VF UNC
18.8.2014. Signature 23.   FV   4.00

72 100 Pounds   VF UNC
8.10.2014 - 15.4.2015. Signature 23. Like #67, but with SPARK patch at left.   FV   30.00

73 200 Pounds   VF UNC
10.9.2013 - 28.4.2015. Signature 23. Like #69, but with SPARK patch at left.   FV   75.00

CURRENCY NOTES
United Arab Republic
1961 ND Issue

180 5 Piastres   VF UNC
L.1940. Lilac. Queen Nefertiti at right. Watermark: *U A R.*

	VF	UNC
a. Signature Baghdady with titles: *VICE-PRESIDENT AND MINISTER OF TREASURY.* Series 15-16.	6.00	30.00
b. Signature Kaissouni with titles: *MINISTER OF TREASURY AND PLANNING.* Series 16-18.	3.00	15.00
c. Signature Daif with titles: *MINISTER OF TREASURY.* Color lilac to blue. Watermark 3mm tall. Series 18-22.	2.00	12.00
d. Signature and titles as c. Watermark 5mm tall. Series 22-26.	2.00	12.00
e. Signature Hegazy with titles as d. Series 26-33.	2.00	12.00

180A 5 Piastres   VF UNC
L.1940. . Series 16. Lilac. Queen Nefertiti at right. Back: Signature Kaissouni with title: *MINISTER OF TREASURY* (error). Watermark: *U A R.*   60.00   175

181 10 Piastres   VF UNC
L.1940. Black. Group of militants with flag having only two stars.

	VF	UNC
a. Signature Baghdady with titles: *VICE-PRESIDENT AND MINISTER OF TREASURY.* Series 16.	15.00	45.00
b. Signature Kaissouni with titles: *MINISTER OF TREASURY AND PLANNING.* Series 16-18.	3.00	17.50
c. Signature Kaissouni with titles: *MINISTER OF TREASURY.* Series 16.	50.00	175
d. Signature Daif with title as c. Series 18-24.	3.00	15.00
e. Signature Hegazy with title as c. Series 24-29.	3.00	15.00

Arab Republic of Egypt
1971 ND Issue

182 5 Piastres   VF UNC
L.1940. Imprint: Survey of Egypt. Lilac. Queen Nefertiti at right. Watermark: *U A R.*

	VF	UNC
a. Signature Hegazy with title: *MINISTER OF TREASURY.* Watermark: *U A R.* Series 33-34.	5.00	20.00
b. Signature Hegazy with title: *MINISTER OF TREASURY.* Watermark: *A R E.* Series 34-36.	4.00	15.00
c. Signature Ibrahim with title: *MINISTER OF FINANCE.* Watermark: *A R E.* Series 36-37.	1.50	6.00
d. Signature El Nashar with title as c. Series 37.	2.50	10.00
e. Signature Ismail. with title as c. Series 37-40.	0.75	3.00
f. Signature M. S. Hamed. Series 40-42.	1.00	4.00
g. Signature Loutfy. Series 42-47.	0.75	3.00
h. Signature Meguid. Series 47-50.	0.60	3.00
i. Signature Hamed. Series. 50.	6.00	25.00
j. Like c. Printer: Postal Printing House. Signature Hamed. Series 50-72.	0.50	2.50
k. Signature El Razaz. Series 72.	1.00	5.00

183   10 Piastres

	VF	UNC

L.1940. Black. Group of militants with flag having only two stars. Printer: Survey Authority.

		VF	UNC
a.	Signature Hegazy with title: *MINISTER OF TREASURY.* Watermark: *U A R.* Series 29-30.	10.00	45.00
b.	Signature Hegazy with title: *MINISTER OF TREASURY.* Watermark: *A R E.* Series 30-31.	5.00	25.00
c.	Signature Ibrahim with title: *MINISTER OF FINANCE.* Watermark: *A R E.* Series 31-32.	2.00	9.00
d.	Signature El Nashar with titles as c. Series 32-33.	4.00	15.00
e.	Signature Ismail with titles as c. Series 33-35.	1.00	4.00
f.	Signature M. S. Hamed with titles as c. Series 35-38.	1.75	7.00
g.	Signature Loutfy with titles as c. Series 38-43.	1.00	4.00
h.	Signature Meguid with titles as c. Series 43-46.	0.75	3.00
i.	Signature Hamed with titles as c. Series 46.	8.00	30.00

184   10 Piastres

	VF	UNC

L.1940. Black. Group of militants, new flag with eagle. Signature title: *MINISTER OF FINANCE.*

		VF	UNC
a.	Signature Hamed. Series 46-69.	0.50	2.50
b.	Signature El Razaz. Series 69-75.	0.75	3.00

Note: Transitional series numbers from one signature to the next are generally much scarcer and command a premium. As of July, 1991 all Egyptian currency notes had been demonetized and withdrawn from circulation. A new series was released recently because of a coinage shortage.

1997; 1998 ND Issue

Law 50 of 1940.

185   5 Piastres

	VF	UNC
	0.25	1.25

L.1940. Green and orange. Queen Nefertiti at right. Signature El-Ghareeb with title: *MINISTER OF FINANCE.* Arabic Series 1-2. Watermark: Tutankhamen's mask. Printer: Postal Printing House.

186   5 Piastres

	VF	UNC
	3.00	12.50

L.1940. Mule issue with signature Salah Hamad with title: *MINISTER OF FINANCE* on back. Green and orange. Queen Nefertiti at right. Signatrue El-Ghareeb with title: *MINISTER OF FINANCE.* Arabic Series 1-2. Back: Mule issue with signature Salah Hamad with title: *MINISTER OF FINANCE.*

187   10 Piastres

	VF	UNC
	0.50	1.50

L.1940. Black and orange. Sphinx, pyramids at right. Signature El Ghareeb with title: *MINISTER OF FINANCE.* Arabic Series 1-2. Back: Mosque of Mohamed Ali at Citadel at left. Watermark: Tutankhamen's mask.

Note: Because of the error note the production of #185-187 ceased.

1998; 1999 ND Issue

Law 50 of 1940

188   5 Piastres

	VF	UNC
	0.25	1.25

L.1940. Blue-gray on blue and lilac underprint. Queen Nefertiti at right. Signature El-Ghareeb with title: *MINISTER OF FINANCE.* Arabic Series 1-6. Watermark: Tutankhamen's mask. Printer: Postal Printing House.

189   10 Piastres

	VF	UNC

L.1940. Dull purple and blue on multicolor underprint. Sphinx, pyramids at right. Signature El Ghareeb with title: *MINISTER OF FINANCE.* Arabic Series 1-2. Back: Mosque of Mohamed Ali at Citadel at left. Watermark: Tutankhamen's mask.

		VF	UNC
a.	Signature El Ghareeb.	0.25	1.00
b.	Signature.	0.25	1.00

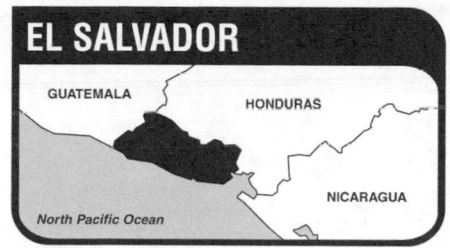

EL SALVADOR

The Republic of El Salvador, a Central American country bordered by Guatemala, Honduras and the Pacific Ocean, has an area of 21,040 sq. km. and a population of 7.07 million. Capital: San Salvador. This most intensely cultivated country of Latin America produces coffee (the major crop), sugar and balsam for export. Gold, silver and other metals are largely unexploited.

El Salvador achieved independence from Spain in 1821 and from the Central American Federation in 1839. A 12-year civil war, which cost about 75,000 lives, was brought to a close in 1992 when the government and leftist rebels signed a treaty that provided for military and political reforms.

On January 1, 2001, a monetary reform established the U.S. dollar as the accounting unit for all financial transactions, and fixed the exchange rate as 8.75 colones per dollar. In addition, the Central Reserve Bank has indicated that it will cease issuing coins and notes.

MONETARY SYSTEM:
1 Peso = 100 Centavos to 1919
1 Colón = 100 Centavos 1919-

REPUBLIC

Banco Central de Reserva de El Salvador

1962; 1963 Issue

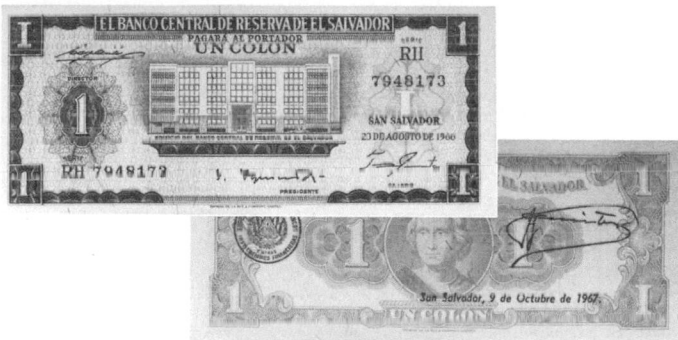

100   1 Colón   VF   UNC
12.3.1963; 25.1.1966; 23.8.1966. Black on multicolor underprint. Central Bank at center. Back: Portrait of Christopher Columbus at center left. Printer: TDLR.
    a. Issued note.   10.00   35.00
    s. Specimen. 12.3.1963,   —   150

101   2 Colones   VF   UNC
15.2.1962; 9.6.1964. Black on multicolor underprint. Coffee bush at left, workers at left center. Back: Portrait of Christopher Columbus at center left. Printer: TDLR.
    a. Issued note.   15.00   75.00
    s. Specimen. 15.2.1962. Red overprint: *MUESTRA SIN VALOR* on both sides.   —   185

102   5 Colones   VF   UNC
15.2.1962; 12.3.1963. Black on multicolor underprint. Woman with basket of fruit on her head at left. Back: Portrait of Christopher Columbus at center left. Printer: TDLR.
    a. Issued note.   15.00   80.00
    s. Specimen. 15.2.1962. Red overprint: MUESTRA SIN VALOR on each side.   —   350

103   10 Colones   VF   UNC
15.2.1962; 9.6.1964; 27.12.1966. Black on multicolor underprint. Portrait Manuel José Arce at center, serial number at lower left and upper right. Back: Portrait of Christopher Columbus at center left. Printer: TDLR.
    a. Issued note.   20.00   100
    s. Specimen. 15.2.1962; 9.6.1964. Red overprint: *MUESTRA SIN VALOR* on both sides.   —   200

104   25 Colones   VF   UNC
1963; 1966. . Black on multicolor underprint. Fifth of November Dam at center. Back: Portrait of Christopher Columbus at center left. Printer: TDLR.
    a. 12.3.1963.   25.00   130
    b. 27.12.1966.   25.00   110
    s1. As a. Specimen. Red overprint: *MUESTRA SIN VALOR* on both sides.   —   200
    s2. As b. Specimen.   —   75.00

1964; 1965 Issue

105   1 Colón   VF   UNC
8.9.1964. Black on pink and green underprint. Farmer plowing at center, *SAN SALVADOR* at upper left. Black serial number and series letters. Back: Portrait of Christopher Columbus at center left. Printer: ABNC.
    a. Issued note.   7.50   30.00
    s. Specimen.   —   125

106 5 Colones

8.9.1964. Black on green and multicolor underprint. José Matías Delgado addressing crowd at center, *SAN SALVADOR* at upper left. Black serial number at lower left and upper right. Back: Portrait of Christopher Columbus at center left. Printer: ABNC.

		VF	UNC
a. Issued note.		10.00	50.00
s. Specimen.		—	150

107 100 Colones

12.1.1965. Brown and green underprint. Independence monument at center but *SAN SALVADOR* at upper left. Serial number at lower left and upper right. Back: Portrait of Christopher Columbus at center left. Printer: ABNC.

		VF	UNC
a. Issued note.		75.00	250
s. Specimen. Red overprint: *MUESTRA SIN VALOR* twice on both sides. Punch hole cancelled.		—	325

1967 Commemorative Issue

#108-109 These notes are reportedly commemoratives for the Bicentennial of the Birth of José Cañas.

108 1 Colón

20.6.1967. Black on multicolor underprint. Juan José Cañas at right, *UN COLON* at center *SAN SALVADOR* and date at right. Back: Portrait of Christopher Columbus at center left. Printer: TDLR.

		VF	UNC
a. Issued note.		4.00	25.00
s. Specimen. Punched hole cancelled.		—	40.00

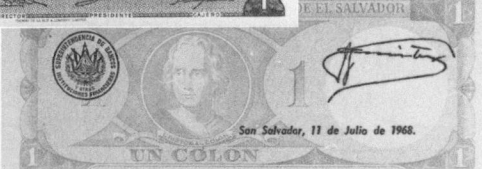

109 5 Colones

20.6.1967. Black on pink and green underprint. Scene of Juan José Cañas freeing the slaves, *31.12.1823* at center. Back: Portrait of Christopher Columbus at center left. Printer: TDLR.

		VF	UNC
a. Issued note.		125	325
s. Specimen.		—	100

1968-70 Issue

110 1 Colón

1968; 1970. Black on light orange and pale blue underprint. Juan José Cañas at right, *1 COLON* at center. Back: Portrait of Christopher Columbus at center left. Printer: USBNC.

		VF	UNC
a. Signature title: *CAJERO* at right. 13.8.1968.		5.00	25.00
b. Signature title: *GERENTE* at right. 12.5.1970.		5.00	22.50
s1. As a. Specimen.		—	35.00
s2. As b. Specimen.		—	35.00

111 5 Colones

1968-70. Black on green and ochre underprint. José Matías Delgado addressing crowd at center, *5 COLONES* at right. Back: Portrait of Christopher Columbus at center left. Printer: USBNC.

		VF	UNC
a. Signature title: *CAJERO* at right. 13.8.1968; 4.2.1969.		7.50	35.00
b. Signature title: *GERENTE* at right. 12.5.1970.		6.00	30.00
s1. As a. Specimen. 13.8.1968; 4.2.1969.		—	35.00
s2. As b. Specimen.		—	35.00

112 10 Colones

13.8.1968. Black on tan and pale blue underprint. Manuel José Arce at right, *10 COLONES* at center. Back: Portrait of Christopher Columbus at center left. Printer: USBNC.

		VF	UNC
a. Issued note.		15.00	60.00
s. Specimen.		—	40.00

113 25 Colones   **VF   UNC**
12.5.1970. Black on light orange and pale blue underprint. Fifth of November Dam
at right. Back: Portrait of Christopher Columbus at center left. Printer: USBNC.
    a. Issued note.   25.00   90.00
    s. Specimen.   —   50.00

114 100 Colones   **VF   UNC**
12.5.1970. Black on pink and pale olive-green underprint. Independence monument at center. Back: Portrait of Christopher Columbus at center left. Printer:
USBNC.
    a. Issued note.   75.00   250
    s. Specimen. Red overprint: *MUESTRA SIN VALOR* twice on both sides.   —   275

1971; 1972 Issue

115 1 Colón   **VF   UNC**
31.8.1971; 24.10.1972. Black on multicolor underprint. *SAN SALVADOR* and
date at left, *UN COLON* at center, Juan José Cañas at right. Back: Portrait of
Christopher Columbus at center left. Printer: TDLR.
    a. Issued note.   2.00   12.50
    s. Specimen. 31.8.1971; 24.10.1972.   —   30.00

116 2 Colones   **VF   UNC**
1972; 1974. Black on multicolor underprint. Colonial church of Panchimalco at
center, *DOS COLONES* at right. Back: Portrait of Christopher Columbus at center
left. Printer: TDLR.
    a. 24.10.1972.   3.00   17.50
    b. 15.10.1974.   2.50   15.00
    s. As a, b. Specimen.   —   30.00
Note: #116 w/o wmk. is reported, not confirmed.

117 5 Colones   **VF   UNC**
31.8.1971-24.6.1976. Black on pale blue and multicolor underprint. José Matías
Delgado addressing crowd at center. Back: Portrait of Christopher Columbus at
center left. Printer: TDLR.
    a. Issued note.   4.00   25.00
    s. Specimen. 31.8.1971; 24.10.1972; 15.10.1974.   —   30.00

118 10 Colones   **VF   UNC**
31.8.1971-23.12.1976. Black on multicolor underprint. *DIEZ COLONES* at center,
Manuel José Arce at right. Back: Portrait of Christopher Columbus at center left.
Printer: TDLR.
    a. Issued note.   7.50   40.00
    s. Specimen. 31.8.1971; 24.10.1972; 15.10.1974.   —   35.00

119 25 Colones   **VF   UNC**
31.8.1971. Black on multicolor underprint. Fifth of November Dam at center. Back:
Portrait of Christopher Columbus at center left. Printer: TDLR.
    a. Issued note.   15.00   75.00
    s. Specimen.   —   32.50

1974 Issue

120 1 Colón
                                                                   VF UNC
15.10.1974. Black on multicolor underprint. Cerron Grande Dam at center, without *UN COLON* at left. Back: Portrait of Christopher Columbus at center left. Printer: TDLR.   3.00 15.00

121 25 Colones   **VF UNC**
15.10.1974; 24.6.1976; 23.12.1976. Black on multicolor underprint. Aerial view of Acajutla port. Back: Portrait of Christopher Columbus at center left. Printer: TDLR.
    a. Issued note.   12.50 55.00
    s. Specimen. 15.10.1974.   — 150

122 100 Colones   **VF UNC**
1974-79. Black on multicolor underprint. Indian pyramid at Tazumal at center, arms at lower right. Back: Portrait of Christopher Columbus at center left. Printer: TDLR.
    a. Regular serial #. 15.10.1974-11.5.1978.   20.00 100
    b. Electronic sorting serial #. 3.5.1979.   17.50 80.00
    s. As a. Specimen. 15.10.1974.   — 60.00

1976 Issue

123 1 Colón   **VF UNC**
28.10.1976. Black on multicolor underprint. Cerron Grande Dam at center, *UN COLON* at left. Back: Portrait of Christopher Columbus at center left. Printer: TDLR.
    a. Issued note.   2.00 12.50
    s. Specimen.   — 30.00

124 2 Colones   **VF UNC**
24.6.1976. Black on multicolor underprint. Colonial church of Panchimalco at center, *DOS COLONES* at left and right. Denomination added at left. Back: Portrait of Christopher Columbus at center left. Printer: TDLR.
    a. Issued note.   1.75 17.50
    s. Specimen. Red overprint: MUESTRA SIN VALOR on each side.   — 100

1977-79 Issues

125 1 Colón   **VF UNC**
1977-80. Black on multicolor underprint. Cerron Grande Dam at center, *UN COLON* at left. Underprint in margins. Back: Portrait of Christopher Columbus at center left. Printer: TDLR.
    a. Regular style serial #. 7.7.1977; 11.5.1978.   1.50 11.00
    b. Electronic sorting serial #. 3.5.1979; 19.6.1980.   1.00 8.50
    s. As b. Specimen.   — 75.00

126 5 Colones   **VF UNC**
6.10.1977. Black on multicolor underprint. José Matías Delgado addressing crowd at center. *5 COLONES* at left and right. Underprint in margins. Back: Portrait of Christopher Columbus at center left. Printer: TDLR.
    a. Issued note.   3.50 22.50
    s. Specimen.   — 32.50

Note: For similar 5 Colones dated 19.6.1980, see #132A.

127 10 Colones   **VF UNC**
7.7.1977. Black on multicolor underprint. *DIEZ COLONES* at center, Manuel José Arce at center right. Back: Portrait of Christopher Columbus at center left. Printer: ABNC.
    a. Issued note.   5.00 30.00
    s. Specimen.   — 125

128 10 Colones   **VF UNC**
13.10.1977. Black on multicolor underprint. *DIEZ COLONES* at center, Manuel José Arce at center right. Blue arms added. Back: Portrait of Christopher Columbus at center left. Blue arms added. Printer: ABNC.
    a. Issued note.   5.00 25.00
    s. Specimen.   — 125

129 10 Colones   **VF UNC**
1978-80. Black on multicolor underprint. Manuel José Arce at right. Underprint in margins. Back: Portrait of Christopher Columbus at center left. Printer: TDLR.
    a. Regular serial #. 11.5.1978.   3.00 17.50
    b. Electronic sorting serial #. 3.5.1979; 21.7.1980.   2.00 15.00
    s. As b. Specimen. 3.5.1979.   — 35.00

133 100 Colones — VF / UNC
17.7.1980. Black on multicolor underprint. Indian pyramid at Tazumal at center, arms at lower right. Flag below, date at upper left. Back: Portrait of Christopher Columbus at center left. Printer: TDLR. — 17.50 / 60.00

1982; 1983 Issue

#133A-137 w/o sign. title *GERENTE* at r.

130 25 Colones — VF / UNC
1978-80. Black on multicolor underprint. Aerial view of Acajutla port. Underprint in margins. Back: Portrait of Christopher Columbus at center left. Printer: TDLR.
a. Regular serial #. 11.5.1978. — 5.00 / 40.00
b. Electronic sorting serial #. 3.5.1979; 19.6.1980. — 3.00 / 25.00
s. As b. Specimen. 19.6.1980. Red overprint: *MUESTRA SIN VALOR* on both sides. — — / 90.00

133A 1 Colón — VF / UNC
3.6.1982. Black on multicolor underprint. Cerron Grande Dam at center, *UN COLON* at left. Back: Portrait of Christopher Columbus at center left. Printer: TDLR.
a. Issued note. — FV / 10.00
s. Specimen. Red overprint: MUESTRA SIN VALOR on each side. — — / 100

131 50 Colones — VF / UNC
1979; 1980. Purple on multicolor underprint. Large building and statue at left, Captain General Gerardo Barrios at right. Back: Ships at left, Christopher Columbus at center. Printer: TDLR.
a. 3.5.1979. — 8.00 / 60.00
b. 19.6.1980. — 5.00 / 30.00
s1. As a. Specimen. — — / 30.00
s2. As b. Specimen. Red overprint: MUESTRA SIN VALOR on both sides. — — / 75.00

134 5 Colones — VF / UNC
1983; 1988. Like #132A. Black on multicolor underprint. Back: Portrait of Christopher Columbus at center left. Printer: ABNC.
a. 25.8.1983. — FV / 12.00
b. 17.3.1988. — FV / 10.00
s1. As a. Specimen. Red overprint: MUESTRA SIN VALOR on both sides. Punch hole cancelled. — — / 125
s2. As b. Specimen. — — / 100

132 100 Colones — VF / UNC
7.7.1977. Deep olive-green on multicolor underprint. Independence monument at right. Back: Portrait of Christopher Columbus at center left. Printer: ABNC.
a. Issued note. — 20.00 / 100
s. Specimen. — — / 300

1980 Issue

135 10 Colones — VF / UNC
1983; 1988. Black on multicolor underprint. *DIEZ COLONES* at center, Manuel José Arce at center right. Back: Portrait of Christopher Columbus at center left. Printer: ABNC.
a. 25.8.1983. — FV / 15.00
b. 17.3.1988. — FV / 12.50
s1. As a. Specimen. Red overprint: *MUESTRA SIN VALOR* twice on face. — — / 125
s2. As b. Specimen. — — / 100

132A 5 Colones — VF / UNC
19.6.1980 (1992). Like #134. Black on multicolor underprint. Back: Portrait of Christopher Columbus at center left. Printer: ABNC. — FV / 10.00

136 25 Colones   VF   UNC
29.9.1983. Black on multicolor underprint. Bridge and reservoir at center. Back:
Portrait of Christopher Columbus at center left. Printer: ABNC.
     a. Issued note.   FV   35.00
     s. Specimen.   —   35.00

137 100 Colones   VF   UNC
1983; 1988. Deep olive-green on multicolor underprint. Independence monument
at right. Back: Portrait of Christopher Columbus at center left. Printer: ABNC.
     a. 29.9.1983.   FV   45.00
     b. 17.3.1988.   FV   50.00
     s1. As a. Specimen. Overprint: MUESTRA SIN VALOR twice on face.   —   100
     s2. As b. Specimen.   —   27.50

1990-93 Issues

138 5 Colones   VF   UNC
16.5.1990. Without signature title: *GERENTE* at right, with electronic sorting serial
number. Black on multicolor underprint. José Matías Delgado addressing crowd
at center. *5 COLONES* at left and right. Underprint in margins. Back: Portrait of
Christopher Columbus at center left. Printer: TDLR.
     a. Issued note.   FV   10.00
     s. Specimen.   —   35.00

#139 *Renumbered.* See #132A.

140 100 Colones   VF   UNC
12.3.1993; 22.12.1994; 26.5.1995. Black, blue-green and violet on pink, blue and
pale green underprint. Indian pyramid at Tazumal at center, arms at upper left, flag
at lower right. Underprint in margins. Back: Portrait of Christopher Columbus at
center left. Printer: TDLR.
     a. Issued note.   FV   40.00
     s. Specimen. Red overprint: MUESTRA SIN VALOR on each side.   FV   75.00

1995 Issue

141 10 Colones   VF   UNC
26.5.1995. Black on multicolor underprint. Manuel José Arce at right. Underprint in
margins. Ascending size serial number at upper right. Back: Portrait of Christopher Columbus at center left. Watermark: Christophor Columbus wearing hat. Printer: TDI R.
     a. Issued note.   FV   10.00
     s. Specimen.   —   40.00

142 25 Colones   VF   UNC
26.5.1995; 9.2.1996. Without signature title: *GERENTE* at right. Black on multicolor underprint. Aerial view of Acajutla port. Underprint in margins. Ascending
size serial number at upper right. Back: Portrait of Christopher Columbus at center
left. Watermark: Christopher Columbus wearing hat. Printer: TDLR.
     a. Issued note.   FV   20.00
     s. Specimen. Red overprint: *MUESTRA SIN VALOR* on both sides.   —   70.00

143 50 Colones   VF   UNC
26.5.1995. Without signature, title: *GERENTE* at right. Purple on multicolor
underprint. Large building and statue at left, Captain General Gerardo Barrios at
right. Ascending size serial number at upper right. Back: Ships at left, Christopher
Columbus at center. Watermark: Christopher Columbus wearing hat. Printer: TDLR.
     a. Issued note.   FV   30.00
     s. Specimen.   —   40.00

1996 Issue

144 10 Colones   VF   UNC
9.2.1996. Black on multicolor underprint. Manuel José Arce at right. Underprint in
margins. Ascending size serial number at upper right. Back: Portrait of Christopher Columbus at center left. Watermark: Christopher Columbus wearing hat. Printer: CBNC.
     a. Issued note.   FV   10.00
     s. Specimen. Red overprint: MUESTRA SIN VALOR on face.   —   75.00

145 50 Colones   **VF UNC**
9.2.1996. Segmented foil over security thread. Purple on multicolor underprint. Large building and statue at left, Captain General Gerardo Barrios at right. Ascending size serial number at upper right. Back: Portrait of Christopher Columbus at center left. Watermark: Christopher Columbus wearing hat. Printer: CBNC.
    a. Issued note.   FV 27.50
    s. Specimen. Red overprint: MUESTRA SIN VALOR on each side.   — 75.00

146 100 Colones   **VF UNC**
9.2.1996. Segmented foil over security thread. Black, blue-green and violet on pink, blue and pale green underprint. Indian pyramid at Tazumal at center, arms at upper left, flag at lower right. Underprint in margins. Back: Portrait of Christopher Columbus at center left. Watermark: Christopher Columbus wearing hat. Printer: CBNC.
    a. Issued note.   FV 37.50
    c. Specimen.   — 50.00

1997 Issue

147 5 Colones   **VF UNC**
18.4.1997; 2.3.1998. Black, dark green and brown on multicolor underprint. National Palace at center right. Special marks for the poor of sight above arms at left center. Signature titles: *PRESIDENTE* and *DIRECTOR*. Back: Christopher Columbus wearing hat at left, continents over his three ships at center. Watermark: Christopher Columbus wearing hat.
    a. Issued note. Series D, E, K.   FV 7.50
    s. Specimen. Series A.   — 22.50

148 10 Colones   **VF UNC**
18.4.1997; 2.3.1998. Dark blue-violet, brown and deep blue-green on multicolor underprint. Izalco volcano at center right. Special marks for the poor of sight above arms at left center. Signature titles: *PRESIDENTE* and *DIRECTOR*. Back: Christopher Columbus wearing hat at left, continents over his three ships at center. Watermark: Christopher Columbus wearing hat.
    a. Issued note. Series A; C.   FV 10.00
    s. Specimen. Series A.   — 22.50

149 25 Colones   **VF UNC**
1997; 1998. Black, brown and blue-black on multicolor underprint. San Andres pyramid at center right. Special marks for the poor of sight above arms at left center. Signature titles: *PRESIDENTE* and *DIRECTOR*. Back: Christopher Columbus wearing hat at left, continents over his three ships at center. Watermark: Christopher Columbus wearing hat.
    a. Issued note. Series A-D. 18.4.1997.   FV 15.00
    b. Issued note. Series F. 2.3.1998.   FV 12.00
    s. Specimen. Series A.   — 22.50

150 50 Colones   **VF UNC**
18.4.1997. Purple, brown and blue-black on multicolor underprint. Lake Coatepeque at center right. Special marks for the poor of sight above arms at left center. Signature titles: *PRESIDENTE* and *DIRECTOR*. Back: Christopher Columbus wearing hat at left, continents over his three ships at center. Watermark: Christopher Columbus wearing hat.
    a. Issued note. Series A-G.   FV 20.00
    s. Specimen. Series A.   — 50.00

151 100 Colones   **VF UNC**
18.4.1997; 4.5.1998. Deep olive-green and dark brown on multicolor underprint. Tazumal pyramid at center right. Special marks for the poor of sight above arms at left center. Signature titles: *PRESIDENTE* and *DIRECTOR*. Back: Christopher Columbus wearing hat at left, continents over his three ships at center. Watermark: Christopher Columbus wearing hat.
    a. Issued note. Series A.   FV 27.50
    s. Specimen. Series A.   — 27.50

152 200 Colones

VF UNC

1997-98. Brown, red-violet and purple on multicolor underprint. *EL SALVADOR DEL MUNDO* monument at center right. Special marks for the poor of sight above arms at left center. Signature titles: *PRESIDENTE* and *DIRECTOR*. Back: Christopher Columbus wearing hat at left, continents over his three ships at center. Watermark: Christopher Columbus wearing hat.

a. 1997; 1998. Series B. — FV 45.00
s. Specimen. Series A. — 35.00

1999 Issue

153 5 Colones

VF UNC

19.4.1999. Added security features. Green and olive on multicolor underprint. National Palace at center right. Special marks for the poor of sight above arms at left center. Signature titles: *PRESIDENTE* and *DIRECTOR*. Back: Christopher Columbus wearing hat at left, continents over his three ships at center. Watermark: Christopher Columbus wearing hat.

a. Issued note. FV 5.00
s. Specimen. Overprint: *MUESTRA SIN VALOR*. — —

154 10 Colones

VF UNC

19.4.1999. Added security features. Purple and green on multicolor underprint. Izalco volcano at center right. Special marks for the poor of sight above arms at left center. Signature titles: *PRESIDENTE* and *DIRECTOR*. Back: Christopher Columbus wearing hat at left, continents over his three ships at center. Watermark: Christopher Columbus wearing hat.

a. Issued note. FV 7.50
s. Specimen. Overprint: *MUESTRA SIN VALOR*. — —

155 25 Colones

VF UNC

19.4.1999. Added security features. Brown and green on multicolor. San Andres pyramid at center right. Special marks for the poor of sight above arms at left center. Signature titles: *PRESIDENTE* and *DIRECTOR*. Back: Christopher Columbus wearing hat at left, continents over his three ships at center. Watermark: Christopher Columbus wearing hat.

a. Issued note. FV 12.50
s. Specimen. Overprint: *MUESTRA SIN VALOR*.

156 50 Colones

VF UNC

19.4.1999. Added security features. Violet and orange on multicolor underprint. Lake Coatepeque at center right. Special marks for the poor of sight above arms at left center. Signature titles: *PRESIDENTE* and *DIRECTOR*. Back: Christopher Columbus wearing hat at left, continents over his three ships at center. Watermark: Christopher Columbus wearing hat.

a. Issued note. FV 25.00
s. Specimen. Overprint: *MUESTRA SIN VALOR*. — —

157 100 Colones

VF UNC

19.4.1999. Added security features. Dark green and light green on multicolor underprint. Tazumal pyramid at center right. Special marks for the poor of sight above arms at left center. Signature titles: *PRESIDENTE* and *DIRECTOR*. Back: Christopher Columbus wearing hat at left, continents over his three ships at center. Watermark: Christopher Columbus wearing hat.

a. Issued note. FV 37.50
s. Specimen. Overprint: *MUESTRA SIN VALOR*.

158 200 Colones

VF UNC

19.4.1999. Added security features. Brown, red and multicolor. *EL SALVADOR DEL MUNDO* monument at center right. Special marks for the poor of sight above arms at left center. Signature titles: *PRESIDENTE* and *DIRECTOR*. Back: Christopher Columbus wearing hat at left, continents over his three ships at center. Watermark: Christopher Columbus wearing hat.

a. Issued note. FV 60.00
s. Specimen. Overprint: *MUESTRA SIN VALOR*.

Note: U.S. Dollars have replaced Salvadorian Colones.

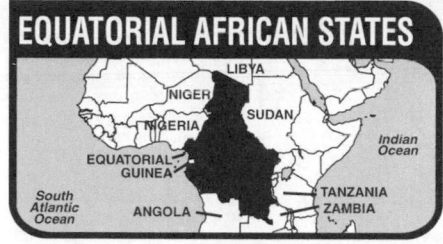

Equatorial African States (Central African States), a monetary union comprising the former French possessions and now independent states of the Republic of Congo (Brazzaville), Gabon, Central African Republic, Chad and Cameroon, issues a common currency for the member states from a common central bank. The monetary unit, the African Financial Community Franc, is tied to and supported by the French franc. In 1960, an abortive attempt was made to form a union of the newly independent republics of Chad, Congo, Central Africa and Gabon. The proposal was discarded when Chad refused to become a constituent member. The four countries then linked into an Equatorial Customs Unit, to which Cameroon became an associate member in 1961. A more extensive cooperation of the five republics, identified as the Central African Customs and Economic Union, was entered into force at the beginning of 1966. In 1974 the Central Bank of the Equatorial African States, which had issued coins and paper currency in its own name and with the names of the constituent member nations, changed its name to the Bank of the Central African States.

MONETARY SYSTEM:
1 Franc (C.F.A.) = 100 Centimes

CONTROL LETTER or SYMBOL CODE

Country	1961-72
Cameroun	*
Cameroun	*
Central African Republic	B
Chad	A
Congo	C
Equatorial Guinea	
Gabon	D

EQUATORIAL AFRICAN STATES

Banque Centrale des États de l'Afrique Équatoriale et du Cameroun

1961 ND Issues

1   100 Francs   **VF   UNC**

ND (1961-62). Blue and multicolor. Portrait of Governor Felix Eboue at center, woman with jug at left, people in canoe at right. Back: Cargo ships at center, man at right.

a. Code letter A.	125	450
b. Code letter B.	150	500
c. Code letter C.	125	450
d. Code letter D.	125	450
e. * for Cameroun.	200	750
f. Without code letter.	40.00	300
s. Specimen. Prefix letter O, serial #0000000s	—	500

2   100 Francs   **VF   UNC**

ND (1961-62). Multicolor. Portrait of Governor Felix Eboue at center, woman with jug at left, people in canoe at right. Denomination also in English with * for Cameroun. Back: Cargo ships at center, man at right.   150   500

Note: For similar 100 Francs w/FRANÇAISE in the title see French Equatorial Africa #32. (Vol. II).

Banque Centrale États de l'Afrique Équatoriale

1963 ND Issue

3   100 Francs   **VF   UNC**

ND (1963). Brown and multicolor. Musical instrument at left, hut at left center, man at right. Back: Elephant at left, tools at right.

a. Code letter A.	40.00	125
b. Code letter B.	50.00	150
c. Code letter C.	40.00	125
d. Code letter D.	40.00	125

4   500 Francs   **VF   UNC**

ND (1963). Green and multicolor. Girl wearing bandana at right, track mounted crane with ore bucket in background. Back: Radar unit at left, man on camel at right.

a. Engraved. Code letter A. Block #1-4.	70.00	260
b. As a. Code letter B.	125	400
c. As a. Code letter C.	70.00	260
d. As a. Code letter D.	70.00	260
e. Lithographed. Code letter A. Block #5-.	55.00	240
f. As e. Code letter B.	65.00	260
g. As e. Code letter C.	55.00	240
h. As e. Code letter D.	55.00	240
s. Specimen. Black overprint *SPECIMEN* and perforated.	—	750

5 **1000 Francs**
ND (1963). Multicolor. People gathering cotton. Back: Young men logging.

	VF	UNC
a. Engraved. Code letter *A*. Block #1-5.	125	400
b. As a. Code letter *B*.	150	450
c. As a. Code letter *C*.	125	400
d. As a. Code letter *D*.	125	400
e. Lithographed. Code letter *A*. Block #7-.	100	350
f. As e. Code letter *B*.	125	400
g. As e. Code letter *C*.	100	350
h. As e. Code letter *D*.	100	350

6 **5000 Francs**
ND (1963). Multicolor. Girl at left, village scene at center. Back: Carving at left, airplane, train crossing bridge and tractor hauling logs at center, man smoking a pipe at right.

	VF	UNC
a. Code letter *A*.	375	1,150
b. Code letter *B*.	375	1,150
c. Code letter *C*.	375	1,150
d. Code letter *D*.	375	1,150
s. As a. Specimen. Overprinted and perforated: *SPECIMEN*.	—	1,000

7 **10,000 Francs**
ND (1968). Multicolor. President Bokassa at right, Rock Hotel, Bangui, C.A.R. in background, arms of the Central African Republic at lower left.

	VF	UNC
a. Issued note.	3,500	10,000
s. Specimen. Serial #00000.	—	8,000

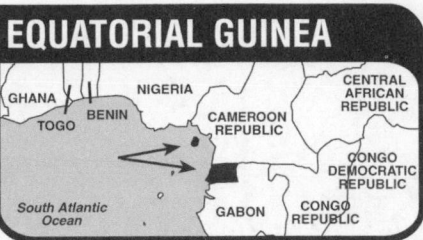

EQUATORIAL GUINEA

The Republic of Equatorial Guinea consists of Rio Muni, located on the coast of west-central Africa between Cameroon and Gabon, and several offshore islands, principally Isla de Corisco and Isla de Bioko. The country has an area of 28,051 sq. km. and a population of 616,460. Capital: Malabo. The economy is based on agriculture and forestry. Cacao, wood and coffee are exported.

Equatorial Guinea gained independence in 1968 after 190 years of Spanish rule. This tiny country, composed of a mainland portion plus five inhabited islands, is one of the smallest on the African continent. President Teodoro Obiang Nguema Mbasogo has ruled the country since 1979 when he seized power in a coup. Although nominally a constitutional democracy since 1991, the 1996 and 2002 presidential elections - as well as the 1999 and 2004 legislative elections - were widely seen as flawed. The president exerts almost total control over the political system and has discouraged political opposition. Equatorial Guinea has experienced rapid economic growth due to the discovery of large offshore oil reserves, and in the last decade has become Sub-Saharan Africa's third largest oil exporter. Despite the country's economic windfall from oil production resulting in a massive increase in government revenue in recent years, there have been few improvements in the population's living standards.

Additional listings can be found under Central African States.

MONETARY SYSTEM:
    1 Peseta Guineana = 100 Centimos to 1975
    1 Ekuele = 100 Centimos, 1975-80
    1 Epkwele (pl. Bipkwele) = 100 Centimos, 1980-85
    1 Franc (C.F.A.) = 100 Centimes, 1985-
    1 Franco (C.F.A.) = 4 Bipkwele

REPUBLIC

Banco Central

1969 Issue

1 **100 Pesetas Guineanas**
12.10.1969. Red-brown on light tan underprint. Banana tree at left. Back: Shoreline and man with boat. Watermark: Woman's head. Printer: FNMT.

VF	UNC
10.00	40.00

2 **500 Pesetas Guineanas**
12.10.1969. Green on multicolor underprint. Derrick loading logs at left, shoreline at center. Back: Woman with bundle on head at right. Watermark: Man's head. Printer: FNMT.

VF	UNC
15.00	60.00

3   1000 Pesetas Guineanas   **VF   UNC**
12.10.1969. Blue on multicolor underprint. President M. Nguema Biyogo at center.   20.00   85.00
Back: Tree at left, arms at center. Watermark: King and queen. Printer: FNMT.

Banco Popular
1975 First Dated Issue
#4-8 Replacement notes: Serial # prefix Z1.

4   25 Ekuele   **VF   UNC**
7.7.1975. Purple on light orange and green underprint. Trees at center. Portrait of   4.00   15.00
President M. N. Biyogo at right. Name underneath: *PUENTE MACIAS NGUEMA
BIYOGO*. Back: Arms at left, bridge at center. Watermark: M. N. Biyogo. Printer:
TDLR.

5   50 Ekuele   **VF   UNC**
7.7.1975. Brown on green and pink underprint. Plants at center. Portrait of Presi-   4.00   15.00
dent M. N. Biyogo at right. Name underneath: *MACIAS NGUEMA BIYOGO*. Back:
Arms at left, logging at center. Watermark: M. N. Biyogo. Printer: TDLR.

6   100 Ekuele   **VF   UNC**
7.7.1975. Green on pink and multicolor underprint. Arms at center. Portrait of   4.00   15.00
President M. N. Biyogo at right. Name underneath: *MACIAS NGUEMA BIYOGO*.
Back: Bridge and boats. Watermark: M. N. Biyogo. Printer: TDLR.

7   500 Ekuele   **VF   UNC**
7.7.1975. Blue on multicolor underprint. Arms at center. Portrait of President M. N.   8.00   30.00
Biyogo at right. Name underneath: *MACIAS NGUEMA BIYOGO*. Back: National
Palace. Watermark: M. N. Biyogo. Printer: TDLR.

8   1000 Ekuele   **VF   UNC**
7.7.1975. Red on multicolor underprint. Arms at center. Portrait of President M.   10.00   40.00
N. Biyogo at right. Name underneath: *MACIAS NGUEMA BIYOGO*. Back: Bank.
Watermark. M. N. Biyogo. Printer: TDLR.

1975 Second Dated Issue
#9-13 Replacement notes: Serial # prefix Z1.

9   25 Ekuele   **VF   UNC**
7.7.1975. Purple on light orange and green underprint. Trees at center. Portrait   4.00   15.00
of President M. N. Biyogo at right. Name underneath: *MAISE NGUEMA BIYOGO
NEGUE NDONG* . Back: Arms at left, bridge at center. Watermark: M. N. Biyogo.
Printer: TDLR.

10   50 Ekuele   **VF   UNC**
7.7.1975. Brown on green and pink underprint. Plants at center. Portrait of   4.00   15.00
President M. N. Biyogo at right. Name underneath: *MAISE NGUEMA BIYOGO
NEGUE NDONG* . Back: Arms at left, logging at center. Watermark: M. N. Biyogo.
Printer: TDLR.

11   **100 Ekuele**

     7.7.1975. Green on pink and multicolor underprint. Arms at center. Portrait of President M. N. Biyogo at right. Name underneath: *MAISE NGUEMA BIYOGO NEGUE NDONG* . Back: Bridge and boats. Watermark: M. N. Biyogo. Printer: TDLR.

	VF	UNC
	4.00	15.00

12   **500 Ekuele**

     7.7.1975. Blue on multicolor underprint. Arms at center. President M. N. Biyogo at right. Back: National Palace. Watermark: M. N. Biyogo. Printer: TDLR.

	VF	UNC
	5.00	20.00

13   **1000 Ekuele**

     7.7.1975. Red on multicolor underprint. Arms at center. Portrait of President M. N. Biyogo at right. Back: Central Bank building. Watermark: M. N. Biyogo. Printer: TDLR.

	VF	UNC
	6.00	25.00

Banco de Guinea Ecuatorial
1979 Issue

14   **100 Bipkwele**

     3.8.1979. Dark olive-green and multicolor. Arms at center, T. E. Nkogo at right. Back: Boats along pier of Puerto de Bata. Watermark: T. E. Nkogo. Printer: FNMT.

	VF	UNC
	6.00	25.00

15   **500 Bipkwele**

     3.8.1979. Black on green and pink underprint. Arms at center right. Uganda at right. Back: Sailboat, shoreline and trees at left center. Watermark: T. E. Nkogo. Printer: FNMT.

	VF	UNC
	25.00	100

16   **1000 Bipkwele**

     3.8.1979. Brown, black and multicolor. Arms at center right. Bioko at right. Back: Men cutting food plants at left center. Watermark: T. E. Nkogo. Printer: FNMT.

	VF	UNC
	25.00	100

17   **5000 Bipkwele**

     3.8.1979. Blue-gray on multicolor underprint. Arms at center, E. N. Okenve at right. Back: Logging scene at center. Watermark: T. E. Nkogo. Printer: FNMT.

	VF	UNC
	20.00	80.00

1980 Provisional Issue

18   **1000 Bipkwele on 100 Pesetas**

     21.10.1980 (-old date 12.10.1969). Red-brown on light tan underprint. Banana tree at left. Back: Shoreline and man with boat. Watermark: Woman's head. Printer: FNMT.

	VF	UNC
	9.00	35.00

19   **5000 Bipkwele on 500 Pesetas**

     21.10.1980 (-old date 12.10.1969). Green on multicolor underprint. Derrick loading logs at left, shoreline at center. Back: Woman with bundle on head at right. Watermark: Man's head. Printer: FNMT.

	VF	UNC
	12.50	50.00

Note: #18 and 19 were prepared for issue but not released to circulation. Shortly afterwards, Equatorial Guinea began the use of CFA franc currency. #3 was not ovprinted because it carries the portrait of the former president.

Banque des États de l'Afrique Centrale
1985 Issue

#20-22 For signature chart see Central African States listings.

20   **500 Francos**

     1.1.1985. Brown on multicolor underprint. Carving and jug at center. Signature 9. Back: Man carving mask at left center. Watermark: Carving (as printed on notes).

	VF	UNC
	4.00	15.00

21   1000 Francos

1.1.1985. Dark blue on multicolor underprint. Animal carving at lower left, map at center, starburst at lower right. Incomplete map of Chad at upper center. Signature 9. Back: Elephant at left, statue at right. Watermark: Carving (as printed on notes).

	VF	UNC
	8.00	30.00

22   5000 Francos

1.1.1985; 1.1.1986. Brown, yellow and multicolor. Carved mask at left, woman carrying bundle at right. Signature 9. Back: Farmer plowing with tractor at left, ore lift at right. Watermark: Carving (as printed on notes).

	VF	UNC
a. 1.1.1985.	35.00	140
b. 1.1.1986.	30.00	125

ERITREA

The State of Eritrea, a former Ethiopian province fronting on the Red Sea, has an area of 121,320 sq. km. and a population of 5.50 million.

Eritrea was awarded to Ethiopia in 1952 as part of a federation. Ethiopia's annexation of Eritrea as a province 10 years later sparked a 30-year struggle for independence that ended in 1991 with Eritrean rebels defeating governmental forces; independence was overwhelmingly approved in a 1993 referendum. A two-and-a-half-year border war with Ethiopia that erupted in 1998 ended under UN auspices in December 2000. Eritrea currently hosts a UN peacekeeping operation that is monitoring a 25 km-wide Temporary Security Zone (TSZ) on the border with Ethiopia. An international commission, organized to resolve the border dispute, posted its findings in 2002. However, both parties have been unable to reach agreement on implementing the decision. On 30 November 2007, the Eritrea-Ethiopia Boundary Commission remotely demarcated the border by coordinates and dissolved itself, leaving Ethiopia still occupying several tracts of disputed territory, including the town of Badme. Eritrea accepted the EEBC's "virtual demarcation" decision and called on Ethiopia to remove its troops from the TSZ which it states is Eritrean territory. Ethiopia has not accepted the virtual demarcation decision.

MONETARY SYSTEM:
1 Nakfa = 100 Cents

REPUBLIC

Bank of Eritrea

1997 Issue

#1-6 Notes designed by Clarence Holbert of the U.S. Bureau of Engraving and Printing.

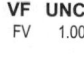

1   1 Nakfa

24.5.1997. UV: fibers fluoresce yellow and blue. Dark brown and black on multicolor underprint. Three girls at center. Flag raising at left. Back: Children in bush school at center right. Watermark: Camel's head. Printer: G&D (without imprint). 140x70mm.

	VF	UNC
	FV	1.00

2   5 Nakfa

24.5.1997. Dark brown and black on multicolor underprint. Young boy, young and old man at center. Flag raising at left. Kinnegram vertical foil strip at left. Back: Cattle grazing under huge Jacaranda tree at center right. Watermark: Camel's head. Printer: G&D (without imprint). 140x70mm.

	VF	UNC
	FV	3.50

3   10 Nakfa   **VF   UNC**
  24.5.1997. Dark brown and black on multicolor underprint. Three young women at   FV   7.50
  center. Flag raising at left. Kinnegram vertical foil strip at left. Back: Truck on rails
  hauling box cars across viaduct over the Dogali River at center right. Watermark:
  Camel's head. Printer: G&D (without imprint). 140x70mm.

4   20 Nakfa   **VF   UNC**
  24.5.1997. Dark brown and black on multicolor underprint. Three young girls   FV   12.50
  at center. Flag raising at left. Kinnegram vertical foil strip at left. Back: Farmer
  plowing with camel, woman harvesting, woman on farm tractor at center right.
  Watermark: Camel's head. Printer: G&D (without imprint). 140x70mm.

5   50 Nakfa   **VF   UNC**
  24.5.1997. Dark brown and black on multicolor underprint. Three young women   FV   25.00
  at center. Flag raising at left. Kinnegram vertical foil strip at left. Back: Ships in
  Port of Masawa at center right. Watermark: Camel's head. Printer: G&D (without
  imprint). 140x70mm.

6   100 Nakfa   **VF   UNC**
  24.5.1997. Dark brown and black on multicolor underprint. Three young girls   FV   45.00
  at center. Flag raising at left. Kinnegram vertical foil strip at left. Back: Farmers
  plowing with oxen at center right. Watermark: Camel's head. Printer: G&D (without
  imprint). 140x70mm.

2004 Issue

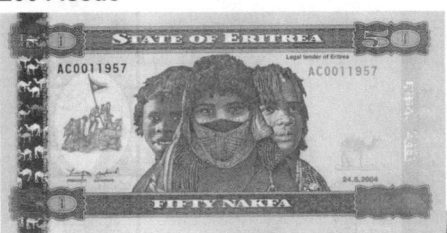

7   50 Nakfa   **VF   UNC**
  24.5.2004 Brown- red on pale yellow underprint. Three young women at center.   FV   20.00
  Back: Ships in Port of Masawa at right center. 140x70mm.

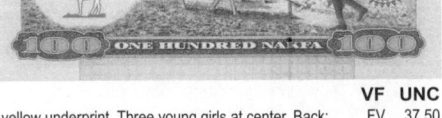

8   100 Nakfa   **VF   UNC**
  24.5.2004. Slate blue on pale yellow underprint. Three young girls at center. Back: FV   37.50
  Farmers plowing with oxen at center right. 140x70mm.

2011 Issues

9   50 Nakfa   **VF   UNC**
  24.5.2011. Purple and green on multicolor underprint. Three young women at   FV   20.00
  center. Back: Ships in port of Masawa at right center.

10   50 Nakfa   **VF   UNC**
  24.5.2011. Green and olive on multicolor underprint. Three young women at   FV   20.00
  center. Back: Ships in port of Masawa at right center.

11   100 Nakfa   **VF   UNC**
  24.5.2011.   FV   37.50

12   10 Nakfa   **VF   UNC**
  24.5.2012.   FV   7.50

13   20 Nakfa   **VF   UNC**
  24.5.2012.   FV   12.50

The Republic of Estonia is the northernmost of the three Baltic states in eastern Europe. It has an area of 45,226 sq. km. and a population of 1.31 million. Capital: Tallinn. Agriculture and dairy farming are the principal industries. Butter, eggs, bacon, timber are exported.

After centuries of Danish, Swedish, German, and Russian rule, Estonia attained independence in 1918. Forcibly incorporated into the USSR in 1940 - an action never recognized by the US - it regained its freedom in 1991, with the collapse of the Soviet Union. Since the last Russian troops left in 1994, Estonia has been free to promote economic and political ties with Western Europe. It joined both NATO and the EU in the spring of 2004.

MONETARY SYSTEM
1 Mark = 100 Penni to 1928
1 Kroon = 100 Senti

REPUBLIC

Eesti Pank

BANK OF ESTONIA

1991-92 Issue

#69-71 replacement notes: Serial # prefix *.

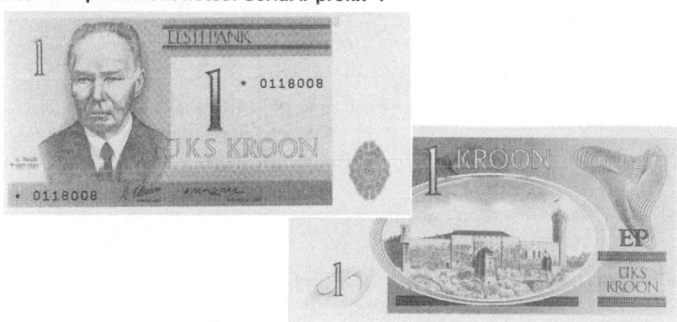

69   1 Kroon VF   UNC
1992. UV; fibers fluoresce blue, value orange. Brownish black on yellow-orange and dull violet-brown underprint. K. Raud at left. Back: Toompea castle with Tall Hermann (national landmarks). Watermark: Fortress. 140x70mm.

    a. Issued note. Serial # prefix A.   1.00   5.00
    r. Replacement note. Serial # prefix *.   5.00   25.00
    s. Specimen.   —   45.00

70   2 Krooni VF   UNC
1992. Black on light blue-violet and grayish green underprint. K. E. von Baer at left. Back: Tartu University building at center. Watermark: Fortress. 140x70mm.

    a. Issued note. Serial # prefix A.   1.00   4.00
    r. Replacement note. Serial # prefix *.   8.00   30.00
    s. Specimen.   —   45.00

71   5 Krooni VF   UNC
1991 (92); 1992 (94). Black and tan on multicolor underprint. P. Keres at center, chessboard and arms at upper right. Back: Teutonic fortress along Narva River, church. Watermark: Arms (three lions). 140x70mm.

    a. 1991. Serial # prefix A.   1.00   6.00
    b. 1992. Serial # prefix B.   1.00   6.00
    s. Specimen.   —   60.00

72   10 Krooni VF   UNC
1991 (92); 1992 (94). Purple and red on multicolor underprint. J. Hurt at left center. Back: Tamme-lauri oak tree at Urvaste at right. Watermark: Arms (three lions). 140x70mm.

    a. 1991. Serial # prefix A.   1.00   8.00
    b. 1992. Serial # prefix B.   1.00   5.00
    s. Specimen.   —   60.00

73   25 Krooni VF   UNC
1991 (92); 1992 (94). Deep olive-green on multicolor underprint. A. Hansen-Tammsaare at left center, wilderness in background at right. Back: Early rural log construction farm; view of Vargamäe. Watermark: Arms (three lions). 140x70mm.

    a. 1991. Serial # prefix A.   2.00   15.00
    b. 1992. Serial # prefix A.   2.00   10.00
    s. Specimen.   —   70.00

74   100 Krooni VF   UNC
1991 (92); 1992 (94). Black and deep blue on light blue and multicolor underprint. L. Koidula at left center, cuckoo bird at lower right. Back: Waves breaking against rocky cliffs of north coast at center to right. Watermark: Arms (three lions). 140x70mm.

    a. 1991. Serial # prefix A.   5.00   20.00
    b. 1992. Serial # prefix A.   5.00   30.00
    s. Specimen.   —   85.00

75   500 Krooni   **VF   UNC**

1991 (92). Blue-black and purple on multicolor underprint. C. R. Jakobson at
left center, harvest between two farmers with Sakala above at right. Back: Barn
swallow in flight over rural pond at right, value at upper right. Watermark: Arms
(three lions). 140x70mm.

    a. 1991. Serial # prefix A.   FV   120
    b. 1992. Serial # prefix A.   FV   100
    s. Specimen.   —   200

1994 Issue

76   5 Krooni   **VF   UNC**

1994 (97). Black and tan on multicolor underprint. P. Keres at center, chessboard
and arms at upper right. Modified design at lower right. Ascending size serial number at right. Back: Teutonic fortress along Narva River, church. Modified design at
lower left. Watermark: Arms (three lions). 140x70mm.

    a. Serial # prefix B, C.   1.00 4.00
    s. Specimen.   —   60.00

77   10 Krooni   **VF   UNC**

1994 (97). Purple and red on multicolor underprint. J. Hurt at left center. Modified
design at lower right. Ascending size serial number at right. Back: Tamme-lauri
oak tree at Urvaste at right. Modified design at lower left. Watermark: Arms (three
lions). 140x70mm.

    a. Serial # prefix B.   1.00 5.00
    s. Specimen.   —   60.00

78   50 Krooni   **VF   UNC**

1994; 1995. Green and black on multicolor underprint. R. Tobias at left center,
gates at lower center right. Ascending size serial number at right. Back: Opera
house in Tallinn at center right. 140x70mm.

    a. 1994. Serial # prefix A.   FV   15.00
    b. 1995. Serial # prefix A.   FV   12.00
    s. Specimen.   —   60.00

79   100 Krooni   **VF   UNC**

1994. Black and dark blue on multicolor underprint. L. Koidula at left center,
cuckoo bird at lower right. Gray seal at upper right. Ascending size serial number
at right. Back: Waves breaking against rocky cliffs of north coast at center to right.
Different rosette at lower left. Watermark: Arms (three lions). 140x70mm.

    a. 1994. Serial # prefix B.   FV   25.00
    b. 1995. Serial # prefix B, C.   FV   20.00
    s. Specimen.   —   75.00

80   500 Krooni   **VF   UNC**

1994; 1995. Blue-black and purple on multicolor underprint. C. R. Jakobson at left
center, harvest between two farmers with Sakala above at right. Dark gray bank
seal at upper right. Ascending size serial number at right. Back: Barn swallow in
flight over rural pond at right, value at upper right. Different rosette at lower left.
Watermark: Arms (three lions). 140x70mm.

    a. 1994. Serial # prefix A.   FV   100
    b. 1995. Serial # prefix B, C.   FV   90.00
    s. Specimen.   —   200

1996 Issue

81   500 Krooni   **VF   UNC**

1996; 1997. Blue, black and purple on multicolor underprint. C. R. Jakobson at left
center, harvest between two farmers with Sakala above at right. Dark gray bank
seal at upper right, hologram at upper left. Back: Barn swallow in flight over rural
pond at right, value at upper right. Different rosette at lower left. Watermark: Arms
(three lions). 140x70mm.

    a. 1996. Serial # prefix A.   FV   90.00
    b. 1997. Serial # prefix B, C.   FV   85.00
    s. Specimen.   —   200

1999-2000 Issue

82   100 Krooni   VF   UNC

1999. Blue on light blue and multicolor underprint. L. Koidula at left center, cuckoo bird at lower center. Holographic band at left. Gray seal at upper right. Back: Waves breaking against rocky cliffs of north coast at center to right. Watermark: Arms (three lions). 140x70mm.

    a. 1999. Serial # prefix C.   FV   20.00
    s. Specimen with overprint: *PROOV*.   —   35.00

83   500 Krooni   VF   UNC

2000. Dark blue and blue on multicolor underprint. C. R. Jakobson at left. Back. Barn swallow. Watermark: C. R. Jakobson. 140x70mm.

    a. Serial # prefix A.   FV   100
    s. Specimen.   —   125

2002 Issue

84   25 Krooni   VF   UNC

2002. Green, black and lilac on multicolor underprint. Anton Hansen-Tammsaare at left, arms at upper right. Wide holographic band at left. Back: Estonian farm view Vargamae. 140x70mm.

    a. Serial # prefix B, C.   FV   15.00
    s. Specimen.   —   50.00

2006 Issue

85   2 Krooni   VF   UNC

2006-. Black on light blue-violet and grayish green underprint. K. E. von Baer at left. Back: Tartu University buildign at center. Watermark: K. E. von Baer. 140x70mm.

    a. 2006   FV   2.00
    b. 2007   FV   3.00

86   10 Krooni   VF   UNC

2006; 2007. Purple and red on multicolor underprint. Jacob Hurt at left center. Back. Tamme-lauri oak tree at Urvaste at right. Watermark: Jacob Hurt. 140x70mm.

    a. 2006   FV   5.00
    b. 2007   FV   6.00

87   25 Krooni   VF   UNC

2007. Deep olive-green on multicolor underprint. A. Hansen-Tammsaare at left center. Back: Early rural log construction farm. Watermark: A. Jansen-Tammsaare. Printer: G&D. 140x70mm.

    a. 2007   FV   10.00

88   100 Krooni   VF   UNC

2007. Light and dark blue on multicolor underprint. L. Koidula at left center. Back: Waves breaking against rocky cliff at right. Watermark: L. Koidula. 140x70mm.

    a. 2007   FV   20.00

89   500 Krooni   VF   UNC

2007. Blue-black and purple on multicolor underprint. C. R. Jakobson at left center. Back: Barn swallow in flight over rural pond. Watermark: C. R. Jakobson. 140x70mm.   FV   90.00

2008 Commemorative Issue

		VF	UNC
90	**10 Krooni**		

2008 Sold in Bank packet. Blue on tan underprint. Female holding wheat at left. Back: Oak tree. 140x70mm. — 50.00

For future listings of Estonia, see European Union listings.

COLLECTOR SERIES

Eesti Pank

BANK OF ESTONIA

1999 Collector's Set

80th Anniversary of Bank

		Mkt. Value
CS1	**100 Krooni**	

Set includes: 100 Krooni specimen note (#82), 5 Krooni coin, and 4 stamps. 3,000 pcs. 1999. 80.00

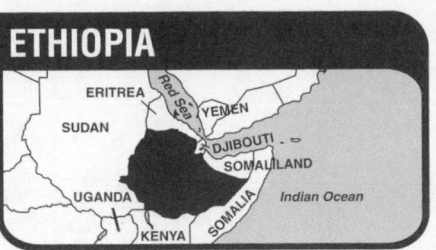

ETHIOPIA

The Federal Republic of Ethiopia is located in east-central Africa. The country has an area of 1.13 million sq. km. and a population of 82.54 million people. Capital: Addis Ababa. The economy is predominantly agricultural and pastoral. Gold and platinum are mined and petroleum fields are being developed. Coffee, oil, seeds, hides and cereals are exported.

Unique among African countries, the ancient Ethiopian monarchy maintained its freedom from colonial rule with the exception of the 1936-41 Italian occupation during World War II. In 1974, a military junta, the Derg, deposed Emperor Haile Selassie (who had ruled since 1930) and established a socialist state. Torn by bloody coups, uprisings, wide-scale drought, and massive refugee problems, the regime was finally toppled in 1991 by a coalition of rebel forces, the Ethiopian People's Revolutionary Democratic Front (EPRDF). A constitution was adopted in 1994, and Ethiopia's first multiparty elections were held in 1995. A border war with Eritrea late in the 1990s ended with a peace treaty in December 2000. The Eritrea-Ethiopia Border Commission in November 2007 remotely demarcated the border by geographical coordinates, but final demarcation of the boundary on the ground is currently on hold because of Ethiopian objections to an international commission's finding requiring it to surrender territory considered sensitive to Ethiopia.

RULERS:
Menelik II, 1889-1913
Lij Yasu, 1913-1916
Zauditu, Empress, 1916-1930
Haile Selassie I, 1930-1936, 1941-1974

MONETARY SYSTEM:
1 Birr = 1 Thaler = 16 Gersh (Piastres) to 1930
1 Birr = 1 Thaler = 100 Matonas, 1931-1935
1 Birr (Dollar) = 100 Santeems (Cents), since 1944

EMPIRE

State Bank of Ethiopia

1961 ND Issue

		VF	UNC
18	**1 Dollar**		

ND (1961). Green on lilac and light orange underprint. Coffee bushes at left. Emperor Haile Selassie at right. Back: Arms at center. Printer: BWC.

a. Issued note.	18.00	60.00
s. Specimen. Punched hole cancelled.	—	50.00

		VF	UNC
19	**5 Dollars**		

ND (1961). Orange on green and multicolor underprint. Addis Ababa University (old palace) at left. Emperor Haile Selassie at right. Back: Arms at center. Printer: BWC.

a. Issued note.	35.00	130
s. Specimen. Punched hole cancelled.	—	80.00

		VF	UNC
20	**10 Dollars**		

ND (1961). Red on multicolor underprint. Harbor at Massawa at left. Emperor Haile Selassie at right. Back: Arms at center. Printer: BWC.

a. Issued note.	75.00	200
s. Specimen. Punched hole cancelled.	—	150

21 20 Dollars

	VF	UNC
ND (1961). Brown on multicolor underprint. Ancient stone monument (Axum) at left. Emperor Haile Selassie at right. Back: Arms at center. Printer: BWC.		
a. Issued note.	110	325
s. Specimen. Punched hole cancelled.	—	140

22 50 Dollars

	VF	UNC
ND (1961). Blue on multicolor underprint. Bridge over Blue Nile at left. Emperor Haile Selassie at right. Back: Arms at center. Printer: BWC.		
a. Issued note.	150	500
s. Specimen. Punched hole cancelled.	—	200

23 100 Dollars

	VF	UNC
ND (1961). Purple on multicolor underprint. Trinity Church at Addis Ababa at left. Emperor Haile Selassie at right. Back: Arms at center. Printer: BWC.		
a. Signature title: GOVERNOR.	175	600
b. Signature title: ACTING GOVERNOR.	150	550
s. Specimen.	—	200

24 500 Dollars

	VF	UNC
ND (1961). Dark green on multicolor underprint. Fasilides castle at Gondar at left. Emperor Haile Selassie at right. Back: Arms at center. Printer: BWC.		
a. Issued note.	450	1,200
s. Specimen. Punched hole cancelled.	—	300

ARMS VARIETIES

Type A 1975-1987	Type B 1987-	Type C	Type D

SIGNATURE VARIETIES

1	Teferra Deguefe, 1974-76 CHAIRMAN OF THE BOARD	2	Tadesse G. Kidan, 1978-87 ADMINISTRATOR
3	Bekele Tamirat, 1987-91 ADMINISTRATOR	4	Leikun Berhanu, 1991-97 GOVERNOR
5	Thbale Tala, 1997-98 GOVERNOR	6	Teklewold Atnafu, 1998- GOVERNOR

National Bank of Ethiopia
1966 ND Issue

25 1 Dollar

	VF	UNC
ND (1966). Dark green on multicolor underprint. Aerial view of Massawa harbor, city at left. Emperor Haile Selassie at right. Back: Arms at center. Printer: TDLR.		
a. Issued note.	7.50	20.00
s. Specimen.	—	50.00

26 5 Dollars

	VF	UNC
ND (1966). Brown on multicolor underprint. Bole Airport, Addis Ababa at left. Emperor Haile Selassie at right. Back: Arms at center. Printer: TDLR.		
a. Issued note.	25.00	80.00
r. Replacement note. Serial # prefix X.	30.00	140
s. Specimen.	—	50.00

27 10 Dollars

	VF	UNC
ND (1966). Dark red on multicolor underprint. National Bank at Addis Ababa at left. Emperor Haile Selassie at right. Back: Arms at center. Printer: TDLR.		
a. Issued note.	15.00	60.00
s. Specimen.	—	60.00

28   **50 Dollars**   **VF**   **UNC**
ND (1966). Blue on multicolor underprint. Koka High Dam on the Awash River at
left. Emperor Haile Selassie at right. Back: Arms at center. Printer: TDLR.
     a. Issued note.   40.00   150
     s. Specimen.   —   165

29   **100 Dollars**   **VF**   **UNC**
ND (1966). Purple on green and multicolor underprint. Rock church *Bet Giorgis*
in Lalibela at left. Emperor Haile Selassie at right. Back: Arms at center. Printer:
TDLR.
     a. Issued note.   40.00   150
     s. Specimen.   —   125

PEOPLES DEMOCRATIC REPUBLIC

National Bank of Ethiopia

EE 1969 (1987) Issue

**Law EE Meskerem 1969 (September 1976 AD). EE date in Ethiopian figures
only. Replacement notes: Serial # prefix** *ZZ*.

30   **1 Birr**   **VF**   **UNC**
L.EE1969 (1976). Black and dark green on light brown and green underprint.
Young man at center right, longhorns at right. Map at left, lion's head in underprint
at left center. Back: White-throated bee-eaters and Tisisat waterfalls of Blue Nile.
Arms (Type A) at right. 135x60mm.
     a. Signature 1.   2.00   7.00
     b. Signature 2.   1.50   4.00

31   **5 Birr**   **VF**   **UNC**
L.EE1969 (1976). Black and brown-orange on multicolor underprint. Man picking
coffee beans at center right, plant at right. Map at left, lion's head in underprint at
left center. Back: Kudu, caracal and Semien Mountains. Arms (Type A) at right.
140x65mm.
     a. Signature 1.   3.25   12.50
     b. Signature 2.   2.75   10.00

32   **10 Birr**   **VF**   **UNC**
L.EE1969 (1976). Brown-violet and red on multicolor underprint. Woman weaving
basket at center right, wicker work dining table with lid at right. Map at left, lion's
head in underprint at left center. Back: Plowing with tractor. Arms (Type A) at right.
142x67mm.
     a. Signature 1.   6.00   20.00
     b. Signature 2.   4.00   15.00

33   **50 Birr**   **VF**   **UNC**
L.EE1969 (1976). . Blue-black and dark brown on lilac and multicolor underprint.
Science students at center right, musical instrument at right. Map at left, lion's
head in underprint at left center. Back: Fasilides Castle at Gondar. Arms (Type
A) at right.
     a. Signature 1.   30.00   110
     b. Signature 2.   25.00   90.00

34   **100 Birr**   **VF**   **UNC**
L.EE1969 (1976). Purple, violet and dark brown on multicolor underprint. Warrior
standing at center right, flowers at right. Map at left, lion's head in underprint at left
center. Back: Young man with microscope. Arms (Type A) at right. 147x72mm.
     a. Signature 1.   50.00   150
     b. Signature 2.   40.00   125

EE 1969 (1987) Issue

**Law EE Meskerem 1969 (September 1976 AD). EE date in Ethiopian figures
only. Replacement notes: Serial # prefix** *ZZ*.

36   **1 Birr**   **VF**   **UNC**
L.EE1969 (1987). Black and green on light brown and green underprint. Young   1.00   3.00
man at center right, longhorns at right. Map at left, lion's head in underprint at left
center. Signature 3. Back: White-throated bee-eaters and Tisisat waterfalls of Blue
Nile. Arms (Type A) at right. Ornate design 135x60mm.

37   **5 Birr**   **VF**   **UNC**
L.EE1969 (1987). Black and brown-orange on multicolor underprint. Man picking   3.00   10.00
coffee beans at center right, plant at right. Map at left, lion's head in underprint at
left center. Signature 3. Back: Kudu, caracal and Semien Mountains. Arms (Type
A) at right. Ornate design at ends. 140x65mm.

38   **10 Birr**   **VF**   **UNC**
L.EE1969 (1987). Brown-violet and red on multicolor underprint. Woman weaving   5.00   15.00
basket at center right, wicker work dining table with lid at right. Map at left, lion's
head in underprint at left center. Signature 3. Back: Plowing with tractor. Arms
(Type A) at right. Ornate design at ends. 142x67mm.

39   **50 Birr**   **VF**   **UNC**
L.EE1969 (1987). Blue-black and dark brown on lilac and multicolor underprint.   20.00   40.00
Science students at center right, musical instrument at right. Map at left, lion's
head in underprint at left center. Signature 3. Back: Fasilides Castle at Gondar.
Arms (Type A) at right. Ornate design at ends.

40   **100 Birr**   **VF**   **UNC**
L.EE1969 (1976). Purple, violet and dark brown on multicolor underprint. Warrior   40.00   135
standing at center right, flowers and dark silvered shield at right. Map at left, lion's
head in underprint at left center. Signature 3. Back: Young man with microscope.
Arms (Type A) at right. Ornate design at ends. 147x72mm.

FEDERAL DEMOCRATIC REPUBLIC

National Bank of Ethiopia

EE 1969 (1991) Issue

Law EE Meskerem 1969 (September 1976 AD). EE date in Ethiopian figures only.

41 1 Birr

VF UNC

L.EE1969 (1991). Dark green on light brown and green underprint. Young man at center right, longhorns at right. Map at left, lion's head in underprint at left center. Signature 3. Back: White-throated bee-eaters and Tisisat waterfalls of Blue Nile. Arms (Type D) at right. Ornate design 135x60mm.

		VF	UNC
a.	Signature 3 with title in Amharic script. Serial # prefix larger sans-serif letters.	1.00	2.50
b.	Signature 4 with title: *GOVERNOR* and also in Amharic script.	1.00	2.50
c.	As b. but with serial # prefix smaller serif letters.	0.75	2.00

42 5 Birr

VF UNC

L.EE1969 (1991). Black and brown-orange on multicolor underprint. Man picking coffee beans at center right, plant at right. Map at left, lion's head in underprint at left center. Signature 3. Back: Kudu, caracal and Semien Mountains. Arms (Type D) at right. Ornate design at ends. 135x60mm.

		VF	UNC
a.	Sign 3 with title in Amharic script. Arms Type B.	3.00	6.00
b.	Signature 4 with title *GOVERNOR* and also in Amharic script. Arms Type C.	3.00	6.00
c.	As b. Arms Type D. Reported not confirmed.	—	—

43 10 Birr

VF UNC

L.EE1969 (1991). Brown-violet and red on multicolor underprint. Woman weaving basket at center right, wicker work dining table with lid at right. Map at left, lion's head in underprint at left center. Signature 3. Back: Plowing with tractor. Arms (Type D) at right. Ornate design at ends. 142x67mm.

		VF	UNC
a.	Signature 3 with title in Amharic script.	3.75	7.50
b.	Signature 4 with title: *GOVERNOR* and also in Amharic script.	3.00	6.00

44 50 Birr

VF UNC

L.EE1969 (1991). Blue-black and dark brown on lilac and multicolor underprint. Science students at center right, musical instrument at right. Map at left, lion's head in underprint at left center. Signature 3. Back: Fasilides Castle at Gondar. Arms (Type D) at right. Ornate design at ends.

		VF	UNC
a.	Signature 3 with title in Amharic script. Arms Type B.	25.00	60.00
b.	Signature 4 with title: *GOVERNOR* and also in Amharic script. Arms Type C.	25.00	50.00
c.	As b. Arms Type D.	25.00	40.00

45 100 Birr

VF UNC

L.EE1969 (1991). Purple, violet and dark brown on multicolor underprint. Warrior standing at center right, flowers and dark silvered shield at right. Map at left, lion's head in underprint at left center. Signature 3. Back: Young man with microscope. Arms (Type D) at right. Ornate design at ends. 147x72mm.

		VF	UNC
a.	Signature 3 with title in Amharic script.	30.00	60.00
b.	Signature 4 with title: *GOVERNOR* and also in Amharic script.	25.00	50.00
s.	Specimen. Red overprint: SPECIMEN on both sides.	—	70.00

1997/EE1989 Issue

46 1 Birr

VF UNC

1997/EE1989-. Black on multicolor underprint. Young man at center right, longhorns at right. Map at left, lion's head in underprint at left center. Latent image (map of Ethiopia) with value at left. Back: White-throated bee-eaters and Tisisat waterfalls of Blue Nile. Ornate design at ends. 135x60mm.

		VF	UNC
a.	1997/EE 1989. Signature 5.	FV	1.50
b.	2000/EE 1992. Signature 6.	FV	1.50
c.	2003/EE 1995. Signature 6.	FV	1.50
d.	2006/EE 1998.	FV	1.50
e.	2008/EE 2000.	FV	1.50

47 5 Birr

1997/EE1989-. Dark blue on multicolor underprint. Man picking coffee beans at center right, plant at right. Map at left, lion's head in underprint at left center. Latent image (map of Ethiopia) with value at left. Segmented foil security thread. Back: Kudu, caracal and Semien Mountains. Ornate design at ends. 140x65mm.

	VF	UNC
a. 1997/EE1989. Signature 5.	FV	4.00
b. 2000/EE1992. Signature 6.	FV	3.50
c. 2003/EE 1995. Signature 6.	FV	3.00
d. 2006/EE 1998.	FV	2.50
e. 2008/EE 2000.	FV	2.50
f. 2013/EE2005.	FV	2.50
g. 2007/2015.	FV	2.50

48 10 Birr

1997/EE1989-. Deep brown, red and green on multicolor underprint. Woman weaving basket at center right, wicker work dining table with lid at right. Map at left, lion's head in underprint at left center. Latent image (map of Ethiopia) with value at left. Segmented fo Back: Plowing with tractor. Ornate design at ends. 142x67mm.

	VF	UNC
a. 1997/EE 1989. Signature 5.	FV	5.00
b. 2000/EE 1992. Signature 6.	FV	4.50
c. 2003/EE 1995. Signature 6.	FV	4.50
d. 2006/EE 1998.	FV	3.50
e. 2008/EE 2000.	FV	2.00
f. 2015/EE2007	FV	2.00

49 50 Birr

1997/EE1989; 2000/EE1992. Tan and orange-brown on multicolor underprint. Farmer plowing with oxen at center. Lion's head in underprint at left center. Latent image (map of Ethiopia) with value at left. Segmented foil security thread. Back: Fasilides Castle at Gondar.

	VF	UNC
a. 1997/EE1989. Signature 5.	FV	25.00
b. 2000/EE1992. Signature 6.	FV	20.00

50 100 Birr

1997/EE1989; 2000/EE1992. Deep blue-green, olive-green and dark green on multicolor underprint. Farmer plowing with oxen at center. Lion's head in underprint at left center. Latent image (map of Ethiopia) with value at left. Segmented foil security thread. Back: Young man with microscope. 147x72mm.

	VF	UNC
a. 1997/EE1989. Signature 5.	FV	40.00
b. 2000/EE1992. Signature 6.	FV	33.00

2003/EE1995; 2004/EE1997; 2006/EE1998 Issue

51 50 Birr

2003/EE 1996-. Increased security features. Tan and orange-brown on multicolor underprint. Farmer plowing with oxen at center.

	VF	UNC
a. 2003/EE 1996.	FV	15.00
b. 2004/EE 1997.	FV	12.00
c. 2006/EE 1998.	FV	10.00
d. 2008/EE 2000.	FV	8.00
e. 2011/EE 2003.	FV	8.00
f. EE2004/2012.	FV	8.00

52 100 Birr

2003/EE1995-. Increased security features. Deep blue-green, olive-green and dark green on multicolor underprint. 147x72mm.

	VF	UNC
a. 2003/EE 1995.	FV	30.00
b. 2004/EE 1997.	FV	25.00
c. 2006/EE 1998.	FV	22.50
d. 2008/EE 2000.	FV	22.50
e. 2011/EE 2003.	FV	22.50
f. 2012/EE 2004.	FV	20.00

EUROPEAN UNION

The Treaty of Rome (1958) declared a common European market as a European objective with the aim of increasing economic prosperity and contributing to an ever closer union among the peoples of Europe. The Single European Act (1986) and the Treaty on European Union (1992) have built on this, introducing the Economic and Monetary Union and laying the foundations for the single currency. In January 1999 the exchange rate was irrevocably set for the original participating countries. These were: Austria, Belgium, Finland, France, Germany, Ireland, Italy, Luxembourg, Netherlands, Portugal and Spain. Greece became a participating member in January 2001. Denmark, Sweden and the United Kingdom, although members of the European Union, decided not to participate in the single currency at its inception. The currency was introduced on January 1, 2002. Since the original group Cyprus, Estonia, Malta, Latvia, Slovenia and Slovakia have introduced Euro notes. The French overseas departments: French Guiana, Guadeloupe, Martinique; these dependencies: Saint Martin, Saint Barthélemy; and territories: Saint Pierre et Miquelon and Mayotte all use the Euro Currency, and are depicted on the map section on the notes along with Réunion and the Canary Islands.

MONETARY SYSTEM:
1 Euro = 100 Cent

EUROPEAN UNION

European Central Bank
2002 Issue, Signature 1, Duisenberg.

		VF	UNC
1	**5 Euro**		
2002. Gray and multicolor. Classical architecture, arch. Signature Willem F. Duisenberg. Printer code by RO in EURO. Back: Bridges, map of Europe and European Union flag. 120x62mm.			
l. Serial # prefix *L*.		FV	14.00
m. Serial # prefix *M*.		FV	11.00
n. Serial # prefix *N*.		FV	10.00
p. Serial # prefix *P*.		FV	10.00
s. Serial # prefix *S*.		FV	10.00
t. Serial # prefix *T*.		FV	11.00
u. Serial # prefix *U*.		FV	10.00
v. Serial # prefix *V*.		FV	11.00
x. Serial # prefix *X*.		FV	10.00
y. Serial # prefix *Y*.		FV	10.00
z. Serial # prefix *Z*.		FV	11.00

		VF	UNC
2	**10 Euro**		
2002. Red and multicolor. Romanesque architecture, arch. Signature Willem F. Duisenberg. Printer code in star at 8 o'clock. Back: Bridges, map of Europe and European Union flag. 127x67mm.			
l. Serial # prefix *L*.		FV	25.00
m. Serial # prefix *M*.		FV	22.50
n. Serial # prefix *N*.		FV	20.00
p. Serial # prefix *P*.		FV	21.50
s. Serial # prefix *S*.		FV	20.00
t. Serial # prefix *T*.		FV	20.00
u. Serial # prefix *U*.		FV	20.00
v. Serial # prefix *V*.		FV	21.50
x. Serial # prefix *X*.		FV	25.00
y. Serial # prefix *Y*.		FV	20.00
z. Serial # prefix *Z*.		FV	20.00

		VF	UNC
3	**20 Euro**		
2002. Blue and multicolor. Gothic architecture, window. Signature Willem F. Duisenberg. Printer code in star at 9 o'clock. Back: Bridges, map of Europe and European Union flag. 133x72mm.			
l. Serial # prefix *L*.		FV	45.00
m. Serial # prefix *M*.		FV	42.50
n. Serial # prefix *N*.		FV	37.50
p. Serial # prefix *P*.		FV	37.50
s. Serial # prefix *S*.		FV	37.50
t. Serial # prefix *T*.		FV	37.50
u. Serial # prefix *U*.		FV	42.50
v. Serial # prefix *V*.		FV	37.50
x. Serial # prefix *X*.		FV	45.00
y. Serial # prefix *Y*.		FV	37.50
z. Serial # prefix *Z*.		FV	37.50

		VF	UNC
4	**50 Euro**		
2002. Orange and multicolor. Renaissance architecture, arch. Signature Willem F. Duisenberg. Printer code above OVD at right. Back: Bridges, map of Europe and European Union flag. 140x77mm.			
l. Serial # prefix *L*.		FV	100
m. Serial # prefix *M*.		FV	95.00
n. Serial # prefix *N*.		FV	90.00
p. Serial # prefix *P*.		FV	90.00
s. Serial # prefix *S*.		FV	90.00

	VF	UNC
t. Serial # prefix *T*.	FV	90.00
u. Serial # prefix *U*.	FV	90.00
v. Serial # prefix *V*.	FV	100
x. Serial # prefix *X*.	FV	100
y. Serial # prefix *Y*.	FV	90.00
z. Serial # prefix *Z*.	FV	90.00

5   100 Euro

	VF	UNC

2002. Green and multicolor. Baroque and Rococo architecture, arch. Signature Willem F. Duisenberg. Printer code in star at 10 o'clock. Back: Bridges, map of Europe and European Union flag. 147x82mm.

l. Serial # prefix *L*.	FV	185
m. Serial # prefix *M*.	FV	180
n. Serial # prefix *N*.	FV	175
p. Serial # prefix *P*.	FV	175
s. Serial # prefix *S*.	FV	175
t. Serial # prefix *T*.	FV	175
u. Serial # prefix *U*.	FV	175
v. Serial # prefix *V*.	FV	180
x. Serial # prefix *X*.	FV	175
y. Serial # prefix *Y*.	FV	175
z. Serial # prefix *Z*.	FV	175

6   200 Euro

	VF	UNC

2002. Yellow-brown and multicolor. Iron and glass architecture, window. Signature Willem F. Duisenberg. Printer code vertically between 7 and 8 o'clock stars. Back: Bridges, map of Europe and European Union flag. 153x82mm.

l. Serial # prefix *L*.	FV	360
n. Serial # prefix *N*.	FV	350
p. Serial # prefix *P*.	FV	335
s. Serial # prefix *S*.	FV	335
u. Serial # prefix *U*.	FV	335
v. Serial # prefix *V*.	FV	350
x. Serial # prefix *X*.	FV	350
y. Serial # prefix *Y*.	FV	335
z. Serial # prefix *Z*.	FV	335

7   500 Euro

	VF	UNC

2002. Purple and multicolor. Modern 20th century architecture, window. Signature Willem F. Duisenberg. Printer code in star at 9 o'clock. Back: Bridges, map of Europe and European Union flag. 160x82mm.

l. Serial # prefix *L*.	FV	900
n. Serial # prefix *N*.	FV	875
p. Serial # prefix *P*.	FV	850
s. Serial # prefix *S*.	FV	850
t. Serial # prefix *T*.	FV	850
u. Serial # prefix *U*.	FV	850
v. Serial # prefix *V*.	FV	875
x. Serial # prefix *X*.	FV	850
y. Serial # prefix *Y*.	FV	850
z. Serial # prefix *Z*.	FV	850

2002 Issue, Signature 2, J. C. Trichet.

8   5 Euro

	VF	UNC

2002. Gray and multicolor. Classical architecture, arch. Signature Jean-Claude Trichet. Printer code by RO in EURO. Back: Bridges, map of Europe and European Union flag. 120x62mm.

e. Serial # prefix *E*.	FV	14.00
f. Serial # prefix *F*.	FV	14.00
g. Serial # prefix *G*.	FV	14.00
h. Serial # prefix *H*.	FV	11.00
l. Serial # prefix *L*.	FV	14.00
m. Serial # prefix *M*.	FV	11.00
n. Serial # prefix *N*.	FV	10.00
p. Serial # prefix *P*.	FV	10.00
t. Serial # prefix *T*.	FV	11.00
u. Serial # prefix *U*.	FV	10.00
v. Serial # prefix *V*.	FV	11.00
x. Serial # prefix *X*.	FV	10.00

9   10 Euro

	VF	UNC

2002. Red and multicolor. Romanesque architecture, arch. Signature Jean-Claude Trichet. Printer code in star at 8 o'clock. Back: Bridges, map of Europe and European Union flag. 127x67mm.

m. Serial # prefix *M*.	FV	22.50
n. Serial # prefix *N*.	FV	20.00
p. Serial # prefix *P*.	FV	21.50
s. Serial # prefix *S*.	FV	20.00
t. Serial # prefix *T*.	FV	20.00
u. Serial # prefix *U*.	FV	20.00
x. Serial # prefix *X*.	FV	20.00
y. Serial # prefix *Y*.	FV	20.00

10   20 Euro

	VF	UNC

2002. Blue and multicolor. Gothic architecture, window. Signature Jean-Claude Trichet. Printer code in star at 9 o'clock. Back: Bridges, map of Europe and European Union flag. 133x72mm.

e. Serial # prefix *E*.	FV	45.00
f. Serial # prefix *F*.	FV	45.00
g. Serial # prefix *G*.	FV	45.00
h. Serial # prefix *H*.	FV	42.50
l. Serial # prefix *L*.	FV	45.00
m. Serial # prefix *M*.	FV	42.50
n. Serial # prefix *N*.	FV	37.50
p. Serial # prefix *P*.	FV	37.50
s. Serial # prefix *S*.	FV	37.50
t. Serial # prefix *T*.	FV	37.50
u. Serial # prefix *U*.	FV	37.50
v. Serial # prefix *V*.	FV	37.50
x. Serial # prefix *X*.	FV	37.50
y. Serial # prefix *Y*.	FV	37.50

11   50 Euro

	VF	UNC

2002. Orange and multicolor. Renaissance architecture, arch. Signature Jean-Claude Trichet. Printer code above 50 OVD at right. Back: Bridges, map of Europe and European Union flag. 140x77mm.

p. Serial # prefix *P*.	FV	90.00
s. Serial # prefix *S*.	FV	90.00
v. Serial # prefix *V*.	FV	100
x. Serial # prefix *X*.	FV	90.00
y. Serial # prefix *Y*.	FV	90.00
z. Serial # prefix *Z*.	FV	90.00

12   100 Euro

	VF	UNC

2002. Green and multicolor. Baroque architecture, arch. Signature Jean-Claude Trichet. Printer code in star at 10 o'clock. Back: Bridges, map of Europe and European Union flag. 147x82mm.

l. Serial # prefix *L*.	FV	180
n. Serial # prefix *N*.	FV	175
p. Serial # prefix *P*.	FV	175
s. Serial # prefix *S*.	FV	175
x. Serial # prefix *X*.	FV	175

13   200 Euro

	VF	UNC

2002. Yellow-brown and multicolor. Iron and glass architecture, window. Signature Jean-Claude Trichet. Printer code vertically between 7 and 8 o'clock stars. Back: Bridges, map of Europe and European Union flag. 153x82mm.

x. Serial # prefix *X*.	FV	335

14 500 Euro VF UNC
2002. Purple and multicolor. Modern 20th Century architecture, window. Signature Jean-Claude Trichet. Printer code in star at 9 o'clock. Back: Bridges, map of Europe and European Union flag. 160x82mm.
  n. Serial # prefix N. FV 850
  x. Serial # prefix X. FV 850

2002 Issue, Signatrue 3, M. Draghi

15 10 Euro VF UNC
2002. Red and multicolor. Romanesque architecture, arch. Signature M. Draghi. Printer code in star at 8 o'clock. Back: Bridges, map of Europe and European Union flag. 127x67mm.
  x. Serial # prefix X. FV 20.00

16 20 Euro VF UNC
2002. Blue and multicolor. Gothic architecture, window. Signature M. Draghi. Printer code in star at 9 o'clock. Back: Bridges, mape of Europe and European Union flag. 133x72mm.
  d. Serial # prefix D. FV 40.00
  e. Serial # prefix E. FV 40.00
  f. Serial # prefix F. FV 40.00
  g. Serial # prefix G. FV 40.00
  h. Serial # prefix H. FV 40.00
  l. Serial # prefix L. FV 40.00
  p. Serial # prefix P. FV 40.00
  s. Serial # prefix S. FV 40.00
  u. Serial # prefix U. FV 40.00
  x. Serial # prefix X. FV 40.00
  y. Serial # prefix Y. FV 40.00

17 50 Euro VF UNC
2002. Orange and multicolor. Renaissance architecutre, arch. Signature M. Draghi. Printer code abovo 50 OVD at right. Back: Bridges, map of Europe and European Union flag. 140x77mm.
  p. Serial # prefix P. FV 90.00
  s. Serial # prefix S. FV 90.00
  v. Serial # prefix V. FV 90.00
  x. Serial # prefix X. FV 90.00
  z. Serial # prefix Z. FV 90.00

18 100 Euro VF UNC
2002. Green and multicolor. Baroque architecutre, arch. Signature M. Draghi. Printer code in star at 10 o'clock. Back: Bridges, map of Europe and European Union flag. 147x82mm.
  x. Serial # prefix X. FV 175

19 200 Euro VF UNC
2002. Yellow-brown and multicolor. Iron and glass architecture, arch. Signature M. Draghi. Pringter code vertially better 7 and 8 o'clock stars. Back: Bridges, map of Europe and European Union flag. 153x82mm.
  x. Serial # prefix X. FV 350

2013-19 Issue, Signature 3, M. Draghi

20 5 Euro VF UNC
2002. Gray and multicolor. Classical architecutre, arch. Signature M. Draghi. Printer code at top right near foil. Back: Viaduct bridge at top left, map of Europe within circle of stars at lower left center. Watermark: Europa. 120x62mm.
  n. Serial # prefix N. FV 10.00
  s. Serial # prefix S. FV 10.00
  u. Serial # prefix U. FV 10.00
  v. Serial # prefix V. FV 10.00
  z. Serial # prefix Z. FV 10.00

21 10 Euro VF UNC
Expected new issue. — —

22 20 Euro VF UNC
Expected new issue. — —

23 50 Euro VF UNC
Expected new issue. — —

24 100 Euro VF UNC
Expected new issue. — —

25 200 Euro VF UNC
Expected new issue. — —

26 500 Euro VF UNC
Expected new issue. — —

FAEROE ISLANDS

The Faroes, a self-governing community within the kingdom of Denmark, are situated in the North Atlantic between Iceland and the Shetland Islands. The 17 inhabited islets and reefs have an area of 1,399 sq. km. and a population of 46,668. Capital: Thorshavn. The principal industries are fishing and grazing. Fish and fish products are exported.

The population of the Faroe Islands is largely descended from Viking settlers who arrived in the 9th century. The islands have been connected politically to Denmark since the 14th century. A high degree of self government was attained in 1948.

RULERS:
Danish

MONETARY SYSTEM:
1 Króne = 100 re

DANISH ADMINISTRATION

Føroyar

1964-74 Issue

#16-18 Replacement notes: Serial # suffix *OJ; OK.*

16 10 Krónur VF UNC
L.1949 (19)74. Green. Shield with ram at left. Coded year date in the upper right seriel # (the two middle digits). Signature: Leif Groth and Atli P. Dam. Back: Rural scene at center. Watermark: Anchor chain. 125x67mm.
  a. Issued note. FV 9.00
  s. Specimen. — 100

17 50 Krónur VF UNC
L.1949 (19)67. Black on light blue and blue-green underprint. Portrait Nölsoyar Pall at left. Coded year dates in the left series number (the two middle digits). Signature: M. Wahl and P. M. Dam. Back: Drawing of homes and church in Nólsoy village across center. Watermark: Anchor chain. 155x79mm.
  a. (19)67. Issued note. 20.00 90.00
  r1. Replacement note. Suffix 0J. 30.00 105
  r2. Replacement note. Suffix 0K. 500 —

18   100 Krónur   VF   UNC

L.1949 (19)64; 69; 72; 75. Black on pink and gold underprint. Portrait V. U. Hammershaimb at left. Coded year dates in the left series (the two middle digits). Back: Drawing of house and mountains. Watermark: Anchor chain. 155x84mm.

	VF	UNC
a. (19)75. Signature L. Groth and A.P. Dam.	35.00	90.00
r1. (19)64. Signature M. Wahl and H. Djurhuus. Suffix 0J.	65.00	225
r2. (19)64. As r1 but suffix 0K.	700	—
r3. (19)69. Signature M. Wahl and Kr. Djurhuus. Suffix 0J.	50.00	175
r4. (19)72. Signature as r3. Suffix 0J.	45.00	175
r5. (19)75. Signature L. Groth and Atli P. Dam. Suffix 0J.	35.00	90.00
s. Specimen. As a.	—	250

1978-86 Issue

#19-23 Replacement notes: Serial # suffix *OJ; OK.*

19   20 Krónur   VF   UNC

L.1949 (19)86; (19)88. Deep purple on pink and aqua underprint. Shephard at right. Coded year dates in upper right serial # (the two middle digits). Back: Drawing of animals at center. Watermark: Anchor chain. 125x72mm.

	VF	UNC
a. Signature N. Bentsen and A. P. Dam. (19)86.	6.00	15.00
b. Signature B. Klinte and A. P. Dam. (19)88.	15.00	30.00
r. Replacement note. As a. Suffix 0J.	30.00	100

20   50 Krónur   VF   UNC

L.1949 (19)78-94. Reduced size. Black on light blue and gray underprint. Portrait Nólsoyar Pall at left. Coded year dates in the left series number (the two middle digits). Back: Drawing of homes and church in Nólsoy village across center. Watermark: Chain links. 140x72mm.

	VF	UNC
a. Signature L. Groth and A. P. Dam. (19)78.	30.00	90.00
b. Signature as a. (19)87.	40.00	130
c. Signature N. Bentsen and A. P. Dam. (19)87.	25.00	50.00
d. Signature B. Klinte and E. Joensen (19)94.	15.00	30.00
s. Specimen. As a.	—	200

21   100 Krónur   VF   UNC

L.1949 (19)78-94. Reduced size. Black on tan underprint. Portrait V. U. Hammershaimb at left. Coded year dates in the left series (the two middle digits). Back: Drawing of house and mountains. Watermark: Chain links. 150x78mm.

	VF	UNC
a. Signature L. Groth and A. P. Dam. (19)78.	30.00	100
b. Signature N. Bentsen and P. Ellefsen. (19)83.	25.00	85.00
c. Signature N. Bentsen and A. P. Dam. (19)87.	35.00	120
d. Signature B. Klinte and A. P. Dam. (19)88.	22.50	60.00
e. Signature B. Klinte and J. Sunstein. (19)90.	24.00	70.00
f. Signature B. Klinte and E. Joensen. (19)94.	FV	37.50
s. Specimen. As a.	—	400

22   500 Krónur   VF   UNC

L.1949 (19)78; (19)94. Black on green and dull purple underprint. Sketch of fisherman at right. Coded year dates in the left series number (the two middle digits). Back: Sketch of fishermen in boat at sea. Watermark: Anchor chain. 164x85mm.

	VF	UNC
a. Signature L. Groth and A. P. Dam. (19)78.	FV	190
b. Signature B. Klinte and E. Joensen. (19)94.	FV	190

23 1000 Krónur VF UNC
L.1949 (19)78; 83; 87; 89; 94. Blue-green, black and green. J. H. O. Djurhuus at left. Coded year dates in the left series number (the two middle digits). Back: Tórshaven street scene sketch. Watermark: Anchor chain. 176x94mm.

	VF	UNC
a. Signature L. Groth and A. P. Dam. (19)78.	300	750
b. Signature N. Bentsen and P. Ellefsen. (19)83.	270	650
c. Signature N. Bentsen and A. P. Dam. (19)87.	260	575
d. Signature B. Klinte and A. P. Dam. (19)89.	FV	350
e. Signature B. Klinte and M. Petersen. (19)94.	FV	300

2001-2005 Issue

24 50 Krónur VF UNC
(20)01. Black on gray underprint. Ram's horn and lilac segmented security strip at right. Back: Hillside in Sumba. Watermark: Ram's head. 125x72mm. FV 18.00

25 100 Krónur VF UNC
(20)02. Dull yellow. Codfish tail at right. Back: View of Klaksvík. Watermark: Ram's head. 135x72mm. FV 27.00

26 200 Krónur VF UNC
(20)03. Dull purple. Ghost Moth at right. Back: View of Tindhólmur near Vágur. Watermark: Ram's head. 145x72mm. FV 50.00

27 500 Krónur VF UNC
(20)04. Dull green. Beach Crab's claw at right. Back: View of Hvannasundi. Watermark: Ram's head. 155x72mm. FV 140

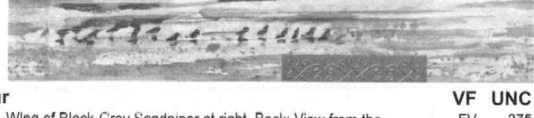

28 1000 Krónur VF UNC
(20)05. Dull red. Wing of Black-Grey Sandpiper at right. Back: View from the island of Sandoy. Watermark: Ram's head. 165x72mm. FV 275

2011 Issue

29 50 Krónur VF UNC
(20)11. Black on gray underprint. Ram's horn, circular face-to-back registry device at top left and lilac segmented security strip. Back: Hillside in Sumba. Watermark: Ram's head. 125x72mm. FV 16.00

30 100 Krónur VF UNC
(20)11. Dull yellow. Codfish tail at right, circular face-to-back registry device at top left. Back: View of Klaksvík. Watermark: Ram's head. 135x72mm. FV 25.00

31 200 Krónur VF UNC
(20)11. Dull purple. Ghost Moth at right. Back: View of Tindhólmur near Vágur. Watermark: Ram's head. 145x72mm. FV 45.00

32 500 Krónur VF UNC
(20)11. Dull green. Beach Crab's claw at right. Back: View of Hvannasundi. Watermark: Ram's head. 155x72mm. FV 125

33 1000 Krónur VF UNC
(20)11. Dull red. Wing of Black-Grey Sandpiper at right. Back: View of the island of Sandoy. Watermark: Ram's head. 165x72mm. FV 230

FALKLAND ISLANDS

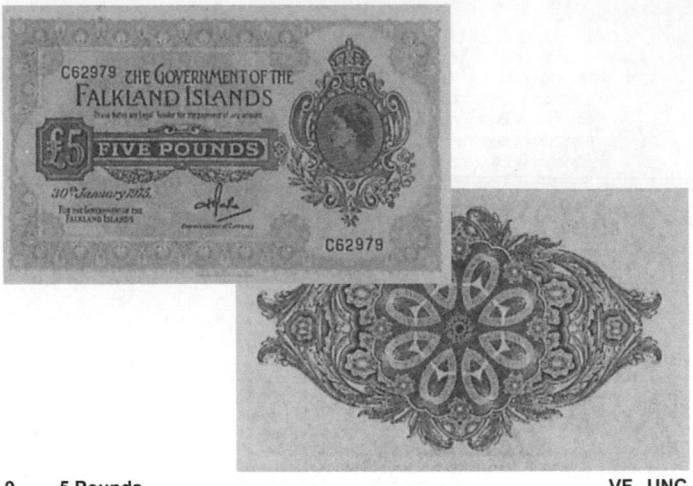

The Colony of the Falkland Islands and Dependencies, a British colony located in the South Atlantic about 500 miles northeast of Cape Horn, has an area of 12,173 sq. km. and a population of 3,140. East Falkland, West Falkland, South Georgia, and South Sandwich are the largest of the 200 islands. Capital: Port Stanley. Fishing and sheep are the industry. Wool, whale oil, and seal oil are exported.

Although first sighted by an English navigator in 1592, the first landing was by the English almost a century later in 1690, and the first settlement was by the French in 1764. The colony was turned over to Spain two years later and the islands have since been the subject of a territorial dispute, first between Britain and Spain, then between Britain and Argentina. The UK asserted its claim to the islands by establishing a naval garrison there in 1833. The Islands were important in the days of sail and steam shipping as a location to re-stock fresh food and fuel, and make repairs after trips around Cape Horn. In April 1982 Argentine forces invaded and after a short military campaign Britain regained control in June 1982. In 1990 the Argentine congress declared the Falklands and Dependencies as the province Tierra del Fuego.

RULERS:
British

MONETARY SYSTEM:
1 Shilling = 12 Pence
1 Pound = 20 Shillings to 1966
1 Pound = 100 Pence, 1966-

BRITISH ADMINISTRATION

Government of the Falkland Islands

1960-67 Issue

7	**10 Shillings**	**VF**	**UNC**
	10.4.1960. Brown on gray underprint. Portrait of Queen Elizabeth II at right. Printer: TDLR.		
	a. Issued note.	300	900
	s. Specimen.	—	850

8	**1 Pound**	**VF**	**UNC**
	1967-82. Blue on gray-green and lilac underprint. Portrait of Queen Elizabeth II at right. Printer: TDLR.		
	a. 2.1.1967. Signature L. Gleadell.	45.00	190
	b. 20.2.1974. Signature H. T. Rowlands.	27.50	135
	c. 1.12.1977. Signature H. T. Rowlands.	70.00	310
	d. 1.1.1982. Signature H. T. Rowlands.	25.00	120
	e. 15.6.1982. Signature H. T. Rowlands.	25.00	110
	s. Specimen. As a-e.	—	330

9	**5 Pounds**	**VF**	**UNC**
	1960; 1975. Red on green underprint. Portrait of Queen Elizabeth II at right. Printer: TDLR.		
	a. Signature L. Gleadell. 10.4.1960.	250	1,000
	b. Signature H. T. Rowlands. 30.1.1975.	200	900
	s. Specimen. As a, b.	—	1,075

1969; 1975 Issue

10	**50 Pence**	**VF**	**UNC**
	1969; 1974. Brown on gray underprint. Portrait of Queen Elizabeth II at right. Printer: TDLR.		
	a. Signature L. Gleadell. 25.9.1969.	21.00	115
	b. Signature H. T. Rowlands. 20.2.1974.	18.00	100
	s. Specimen. As a, b.	—	250

11	**10 Pounds**	**VF**	**UNC**
	1975-82. Green on light orange and yellow-green underprint. Portrait of Queen Elizabeth II at right. Signature H. T. Rowlands. Printer: TDLR.		
	a. 5.6.1975.	300	900
	b. 1.1.1982.	350	1,075
	c. 15.6.1982.	275	850
	s. Specimen. As a.	—	850

1983 Commemorative Issue
#12, 150th Anniversary of English rule, 1833-1983

12	5 Pounds		VF	UNC

14.6.1983. Red on multicolor underprint. Queen Elizabeth II at right, King penguins and shield at left, seals at right. Commemorative legend at lower center. Back: Governor's home and church. 145x75mm.

	a. Issued note.	FV	90.00
	s. Specimen.	—	210

1984-90 Regular Issue

13	1 Pound	VF	UNC

1.10.1984. Blue on brown and yellow underprint. Queen Elizabeth II at right, King penguins and shield at left, seals at right. Back: Governor's home and church. 145x75mm.

	a. Issued note.	15.00	75.00
	s. Specimen.	—	210

14	10 Pounds	VF	UNC

1.9.1986. Green on blue and multicolor underprint. Queen Elizabeth II at right, King penguins and shield at left, seals at right. Back: Governor's home and church. 145x75mm.

	a. Issued note.	FV	95.00
	s. Specimen.	—	210

15	20 Pounds		VF	UNC

1.10.1984. Brown on multicolor underprint. Queen Elizabeth II at right. King penguins and shield at left, seals at right. Back: Governor's home and church. 145x75mm.

	a. Issued note.	45.00	125
	s. Specimen.	—	270

16	50 Pounds	VF	UNC

1.7.1990. Blue on multicolor underprint. Queen Elizabeth II at right, King penguins and shield at left, seals at right. Back: Governor's home and church. 145x75mm.

	a. Issued note.	FV	250
	s. Specimen.	—	440

2005 Issue

17	5 Pounds	VF	UNC

14.6.2005. Like #12 but without commemorative legend. Red on multicolor underprint. King penguins at left, island map at center, Queen Elizabeth II at right center, seals at right. Three signatures. Back: Government House and Christ Church Cathedral in Stanley. 145x75mm.

	a. Issued note.	FV	40.00
	s. Specimen.	—	290

2011 Issue

18	10 Pounds	VF	UNC
	1.1.2011.	FV	60.00

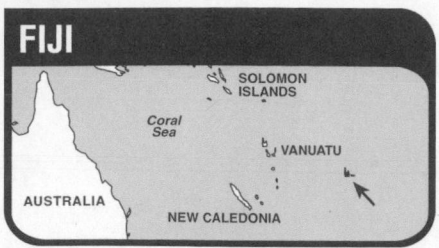

FIJI

The republic of Fiji consists of about 320 islands located in the southwestern Pacific 1,770 km. north of New Zealand. The islands have a combined area of 18,270 sq. km. and a population of 931,750. Capital: Suva, on the island of Viti Levu. Fiji's economy is based on agriculture, tourism and mining. Sugar, fish, timber, coconut products, and gold are exported.

Fiji became independent in 1970, after nearly a century as a British colony. Democratic rule was interrupted by two military coups in 1987, caused by concern over a government perceived as dominated by the Indian community (descendants of contract laborers brought to the islands by the British in the 19th century). The coups and a 1990 constitution that cemented native Melanesian control of Fiji, led to heavy Indian emigration; the population loss resulted in economic difficulties, but ensured that Melanesians became the majority. A new constitution enacted in 1997 was more equitable. Free and peaceful elections in 1999 resulted in a government led by an Indo-Fijian, but a civilian-led coup in May 2000 ushered in a prolonged period of political turmoil. Parliamentary elections held in August 2001 provided Fiji with a democratically elected government led by Prime Minister Laisenia Qarase. Re-elected in May 2006, Qarase was ousted in a December 2006 military coup led by Commodore Voreqe Bainimarama, who initially appointed himself acting president. In January 2007, Bainimarama was appointed interim prime minister. In Sptember 2009 Fiji was suspended from the British Commonwalth.

RULERS:
Thakombau (Cakobau), until 1874
British, 1874-1970.

MONETARY SYSTEM:
1 Dollar = 100 Cents, 1871-73
1 Shilling = 12 Pence
1 Pound = 20 Shillings to 1969
1 Dollar = 100 Cents, 1969-

REPLACEMENT NOTES:
#64-85: Z/1 prefix; #96-108: Z prefix; #109-114: ZA prefix.

BRITISH ADMINISTRATION

Fiji Government

1953-67 Issue

51	**5 Shillings**	**VF**	**UNC**
	1957-65. Gray-blue on lilac, green and blue underprint. Arms at upper center, portrait of Queen Elizabeth II at right. Watermark: Fijian youth's bust. Printer: BWC.		
	a. 1.6.1957. Signature Davidson, Griffiths, Marais.	75.00	550
	b. 28.4.1961. Signature Bevington, Griffiths, Cruickshank.	75.00	550
	c. 1.12.1962. Signature Ritchie, Griffiths, Cruickshank.	60.00	525
	d. 1.9.1964. Signature Ritchie, Griffiths, Cruickshank.	50.00	475
	e. 1.10.1965. Signature Ritchie, Griffiths, Cruickshank.	40.00	400
	s. Specimen. Various dates.	—	750
	cs. Commercial (false color) specimen.	—	550

52	**10 Shillings**	**VF**	**UNC**
	1957-65. Brown on green, pink and yellow underprint. Arms at upper center, portrait of Queen Elizabeth II at right. Watermark: Fijian youth's bust. Printer: BWC.		
	a. 1.6.1957. Signature Davidson, Griffiths, Marais.	100	750
	b. 28.4.1961. Signature Bevington, Griffiths, Cruickshank.	120	800
	c. 1.12.1962. Signature Ritchie, Griffiths, Cruickshank.	80.00	750
	d. 1.9.1964. Signature Ritchie, Griffiths, Cruickshank.	125	500
	e. 1.10.1965. Signature Ritchie, Griffiths, Cruickshank.	75.00	600
	s. Specimen. Various dates.	—	850
	cs. Commercial (false color) specimen.	—	700

53	**1 Pound**	**VF**	**UNC**
	1954-67. Green on yellow and blue underprint. Arms at upper center, portrait of Queen Elizabeth II at right. Watermark: Fijian youth's bust. Printer: BWC.		
	a. 1.7.1954. Signature Davidson, Donovan, Davis.	130	825
	b. 1.6.1957. Signature Davidson, Griffiths, Marais.	145	875
	c. 1.9.1959. Signature Bevington, Griffiths, Marais.	130	825
	d. 1.12.1961. Signature Ritchie, Griffiths, Cruickshank.	145	900
	e. 1.12.1962. Signature Ritchie, Griffiths, Cruickshank.	145	925
	f. 20.1.1964. Signature Ritchie, Griffiths, Cruickshank.	140	825
	g. 1.5.1965. Signature Ritchie, Griffiths, Cruickshank.	130	750
	h. 1.12.1965. Signature Ritchie, Griffiths, Cruickshank.	135	725
	i. 1.1.1967. Signature Ritchie, Griffiths, Cruickshank.	125	725
	s. Specimen. Various dates.	—	1,050
	cs. Commercial (false color) specimen.	—	900

54	**5 Pounds**	**VF**	**UNC**
	1954-67. Purple on orange, green and purple underprint. Arms at upper center, portrait of Queen Elizabeth II at right. Watermark: Fijian youth's bust. Printer: BWC.		
	a. 1.7.1954. Signature Davidson, Donovan, Davis.	850	1,950
	b. 1.9.1959. Signature Bevington, Griffiths, Marais.	900	2,150
	c. 1.10.1960. Signature Bevington, Griffiths, Cruickshank.	850	1,950
	d. 1.12.1962. Signature Ritchie, Griffiths, Cruickshank.	825	1,900
	e. 20.1.1964. Signature Ritchie, Griffiths, Cruickshank.	800	1,950
	f. 1.1.1967. Signature Ritchie, Griffiths, Cruickshank.	800	1,800
	s. Specimen. Various dates.	—	1,400
	cs. Commercial (false color) specimen.	—	1,050

55	**10 Pounds**	**VF**	**UNC**
	1954-65. Blue on blue, orange and green underprint. Arms at upper center, portrait of Queen Elizabeth II at right. Watermark: Fijian youth's bust. Printer: BWC.		
	a. 1.7.1954. Signature Davidson, Donovan, Davis.	1,250	2,750
	b. 1.9.1959. Signature Bevington, Griffiths, Marais.	1,250	2,500
	c. 1.10.1960. Signature Bevington, Griffiths, Cruickshank.	1,100	3,250
	d. 20.1.1964. Signature Ritchie, Griffiths, Cruickshank.	1,000	2,250
	e. 11.6.1965. Signature Ritchie, Griffiths, Cruickshank.	900	2,100
	f. 1.5.1965. Signature Ritchie, Griffiths, Cruickshank. Not released.	—	—
	s. Specimen. Various dates.	—	2,250
	cs. Commercial (false color) specimen.	—	1,100

56	**20 Pounds**	**VF**	**UNC**
	1953. Black and purple on purple underprint. Arms at upper center, portrait of Queen Elizabeth II at right. Watermark: Fijian youth's bust. Printer: BWC.		
	a. 1.1.1953. Signature Davidson, Donovan, Smith.	1,850	8,250
	s. Specimen.	—	4,250
	cs. Commercial (false color) specimen.	—	2,750

57 20 Pounds | VF | UNC
1954 58. Red on red and green underprint. Arms at upper center, portrait of
Queen Elizabeth II at right. Watermark: Fijian youth's bust. Printer: BWC.

- a. 1.7.1954. Signature Davidson, Donovan, Davis. — 2,000 — 6,500
- b. 1.11.1958. Signature Bevington, Griffiths, Marais. — 2,000 — 6,500
- s. Specimen. — — — 4,000
- cs. Commercial (false color) specimen. — — — 2,000

1969 Commissioners of Currency Issue

58 50 Cents | VF | UNC
ND (1969). . Blue-green on multicolor underprint. Queen Elizabeth at right, arms
and heading: *GOVERNMENT OF FIJI* at upper center. Signature Ritchie and
Barnes. Back: Thatched bure (house) and coconut palms on back. Watermark:
Profile Fijian head. Printer: TDLR.

- a. Issued note. — 4.00 — 25.00
- s1. Specimen. Red seals. Signatures punched out. — — — 150
- s2. Specimen. No seals. Corners punched out. — — — 100

59 1 Dollar | VF | UNC
ND (1969). Brown on brown, green and pink underprint. Queen Elizabeth at right,
arms and heading: *GOVERNMENT OF FIJI* at upper center. Signature Ritchie and
Barnes. Back: Yanuca beach scene in Yasewas. Watermark: Profile Fijian head.
Printer: TDLR.

- a. Issued note. — 7.50 — 55.00
- s1. Specimen. Red seals. Signatures punched out. — — — 200
- s2. Specimen. No seals. Corners punched out. — — — 150

60 2 Dollars | VF | UNC
ND (1969). Green on brown and light blue underprint. Queen Elizabeth at right,
arms and heading: *GOVERNMENT OF FIJI* at upper center. Signature Ritchie and
Barnes. Back: Geometric lathe pattern. Watermark: Profile Fijian head. Printer:
TDLR.

- a. Issued note. — 15.00 — 110
- s1. Specimen. Red seals. Signatures punched out. — — — 300
- s2. Specimen. No seals. Corners punched out. — — — 250

61 5 Dollars | VF | UNC
ND (1970). Orange on purple and gray underprint. Queen Elizabeth at right, arms
and heading: *GOVERNMENT OF FIJI* at upper center. Signature Ritchie and
Barnes. Back: Geometric lathe pattern. Watermark: Profile Fijian head. Printer:
TDLR.

- a. Issued note. — 22.50 — 250
- s1. Specimen. Red seals. Signatures punched out. — — — 400
- s2. Specimen. No seals. Corners punched out. — — — 350

62 10 Dollars | VF | UNC
ND (1969). Purple on orange and purple underprint. Queen Elizabeth at right,
arms and heading: *GOVERNMENT OF FIJI* at upper center. Signature Ritchie and
Barnes. Back: Geometric lathe pattern. Watermark: Profile Fijian head. Printer:
TDLR.

- a. Issued note. — 55.00 — 800
- s1. Specimen. Red seals. Signatures punched out. — — — 500
- s2. Specimen. No seals. Corners punched out. — — — 450

63 20 Dollars | VF | UNC
ND (1969). Blue on light green, orange and blue underprint. Queen Elizabeth
at right, arms and heading: *GOVERNMENT OF FIJI* at upper center. Signature
Ritchie and Barnes. Back: Geometric lathe pattern. Watermark: Profile Fijian
head. Printer: TDLR.

- a. Issued note. — 125 — 1,350
- s1. Specimen. Red seals. Signatures punched out. — — — 750
- s2. Specimen. No seals. Corners punched out. — — — 600

1971-73 Ad-interim Currency Board Issue

64	50 Cents	VF	UNC

ND (1971). Blue-green on multicolor underprint. Queen Elizabeth at right, arms and heading: *GOVERNMENT OF FIJI* at upper center. One signature. Back: Thatched bure (house) and coconut palms. Watermark: Profile Fijian head. Printer: TDLR.

		VF	UNC
a.	Signature Wesley Barrett.	4.00	25.00
b.	Signature C. A. Stinson.	3.50	22.50
s1.	Specimen. As a.	—	200
s2.	Specimen. As b.	—	175
ar.	As a. Replacement *Z/1* prefix.	35.00	125
br.	As b. Replacement *Z/l* prefix.	20.00	90.00

68	10 Dollars	VF	UNC

ND (1971). Purple on orange and purple underprint. Queen Elizabeth at right, arms and heading: *GOVERNMENT OF FIJI* at upper center. One signature. Back: Geometric lathe pattern. Watermark: Profile Fijian head. Printer: TDLR.

		VF	UNC
a.	Signature Wesley Barrett.	100	850
b.	Signature C. A. Stinson.	75.00	750
s1.	Specimen. As a.	—	850
s2.	Specimen. As b.	—	750
ar.	As a. Replacement. *Z/1* prefix.	550	1,250
br.	As b. Replacement. *Z/l* prefix.	400	1,500

65	1 Dollar	VF	UNC

ND (1971). Brown on brown, green and pink underprint. Queen Elizabeth at right, arms and heading: *GOVERNMENT OF FIJI* at upper center. One signature. Back: Yanuca beach scene in Yasewas. Watermark: Profile Fijian head. Printer: TDLR.

		VF	UNC
a.	Signature Wesley Barrett.	7.50	75.00
b.	Signature C. A. Stinson.	15.00	60.00
s1.	Specimen. As a.	—	250
s2.	Specimen. As b.	—	250
ar.	As a. Replacement. *Z/l* prefix.	50.00	350
br.	As b. Replacement. *Z/l* prefix.	35.00	250

69	20 Dollars	VF	UNC

ND (1971). Blue on light green, orange and blue underprint. Queen Elizabeth at right, arms and heading: *GOVERNMENT OF FIJI* at upper center. One signature. Back: Geometric lathe pattern. Watermark: Profile Fijian head. Printer: TDLR.

		VF	UNC
a.	Signature Wesley Barrett.	350	1,200
b.	Signature C. A. Stinson.	250	1,050
s1.	Specimen. As a.	—	1,000
s2.	Specimen. As b.	—	900
ar.	As a. Replacement. *Z/l* prefix.	1,250	2,000
br.	As b. Replacement. *Z/l* prefix.	800	1,750

Central Monetary Authority
1974 ND Issue

70	50 Cents	VF	UNC

ND (1974). Blue-green on multicolor underprint. Queen Elizabeth at right, arms and heading *FIJI* at top center. Issuing authority name across lower center. Back: Thatched bure (house) and coconut palms . Watermark: Profile Fijian head. Printer: TDLR. 156x67mm.

		VF	UNC
a.	Signature D. J. Barnes and R. J. Earland. (Not issued.)	—	—
s.	Specimen.	—	1,000

66	2 Dollars	VF	UNC

ND (1971). Green on brown and light blue underprint. Queen Elizabeth at right, arms and heading: *GOVERNMENT OF FIJI* at upper center. One signature. Back: Geometric lathe pattern. Watermark: Profile Fijian head. Printer: TDLR.

		VF	UNC
a.	Signature Wesley Barrett.	10.00	125
b.	Signature C. A. Stinson. Not issued.	—	—
s1.	Specimen. As a.	—	450
s2.	Specimen. As b.	—	400
ar.	As a. Replacement. *Z/l* prefix.	100	450
br.	As b. Replacement. *Z/l* prefix. Not issued.	—	—

71	1 Dollar	VF	UNC

ND (1974). Brown on brown, green and pink underprint. Queen Elizabeth at right, arms and heading *FIJI* at top center. Issuing authority name across lower center. Back: Yanuca beach scene in Yasewas. Watermark: Profile Fijian head. Printer: TDLR. 156x67mm.

		VF	UNC
a.	Signature D. J. Barnes and R. J. Earland.	3.00	22.50
b.	Signature D. J. Barnes and H. J. Tomkins.	3.00	20.00
s1.	Specimen. As a.	—	300
s2.	Specimen. As b.	—	200
ar.	As a. Replacement. *Z/l* prefix.	9.00	40.00
br.	As b. Replacement. *Z/l* prefix.	7.50	30.00

67	5 Dollars	VF	UNC

ND (1971). Orange on purple and gray underprint. Queen Elizabeth at right, arms and heading: *GOVERNMENT OF FIJI* at upper center. One signature. Back: Geometric lathe pattern. Watermark: Profile Fijian head. Printer: TDLR.

		VF	UNC
a.	Signature Wesley Barrett.	25.00	300
b.	Signature C. A. Stinson.	22.50	250
s1.	Specimen. As a.	—	650
s2.	Specimen. As b.	—	550
ar.	As a. Replacement. *Z/l* prefix.	350	850
br.	As b. Replacement. *Z/l* prefix.	300	750

72 2 Dollars   **VF**   **UNC**
ND (1974). Green on brown and light blue underprint. Queen Elizabeth at right, arms
and heading *FIJI* at top center. Issuing authority name across lower center. Back:
Geometric lathe pattern. Watermark: Profile Fijian head. Printer: TDLR. 156x67mm.

	VF	UNC
a. Signature D. J. Barnes and I. A. Craik.	25.00	100
b. Signature D. J. Barnes and R. J. Earland.	7.00	37.50
c. Signature D. J. Barnes and H. J. Tomkins.	7.00	35.00
s1. Specimen. As a.	—	450
s2. Specimen. As b.	—	350
s3. Specimen. As c.	—	300
ar. As a. Replacement. *Z/I* prefix.	150	850
br. As b. Replacement. *Z/I* prefix.	25.00	135
cr. As c. Replacement. *Z/I* prefix.	15.00	100

73 5 Dollars   **VF**   **UNC**
ND (1974). Orange on purple and gray underprint. Queen Elizabeth at right, arms
and heading *FIJI* at top center. Issuing authority name across lower center. Back:
Geometric lathe pattern. Watermark: Profile Fijian head. Printer: TDLR. 156x67mm.

	VF	UNC
a. Signature D. J. Barnes and I. A. Craik.	85.00	850
b. Signature D. J. Barnes and R. J. Earland.	45.00	250
c. Signature D. J. Barnes and H. J. Tomkins.	45.00	225
s1. Specimen. As a.	—	650
s2. Specimen. As b.	—	600
s3. Specimen. As c.	—	550
ar. As a. Replacement. *Z/I* prefix.	350	1,250
br. As b. Replacement. *Z/I* prefix.	225	750
cr. As c. Replacement. *Z/I* prefix.	95.00	400

74 10 Dollars   **VF**   **UNC**
ND (1974). Purple on orange and purple underprint. Queen Elizabeth at right, arms
and heading *FIJI* at top center. Issuing authority name across lower center. Back:
Geometric lathe pattern. Watermark: Profile Fijian head. Printer: TDLR. 156x67mm.

	VF	UNC
a. Signature D. J. Barnes and I. A. Craik.	275	1,500
b. Signature D. J. Barnes and R. J. Earland.	35.00	350
c. Signature D. J. Barnes and H. J. Tomkins.	85.00	300
s1. Specimen. As a.	—	750
s2. Specimen. As b.	—	650
s3. Specimen. As c.	—	600
ar. As a. Replacement *Z/1* prefix.	450	2,000
br. As b. Replacement *Z/1* prefix.	225	800
cr. As c. Replacement *Z/1* prefix.	125	650

75 20 Dollars   **VF**   **UNC**
ND (1974). Blue on light green, orange and blue underprint. Queen Elizabeth at
right, arms and heading *FIJI* at top center. Issuing authority name across lower
center. Back: Geometric lathe pattern. Watermark: Profile Fijian head. Printer:
TDLR. 156x67mm.

	VF	UNC
a. Signature D. J. Barnes and I. A. Craik.	675	2,000
b. Signature D. J. Barnes and R. J. Earland.	100	600
c. Signature D. J. Barnes and H. J. Tomkins.	100	600
s1. Specimen. As a.	—	850
s2. Specimen. As b.	—	750
s3. Specimen. As c.	—	700
ar. As a. Replacement. *Z/I* prefix.	650	3,000
br. As b. Replacement. *Z/I* prefix.	225	1,000
cr. As c. Replacement. *Z/I* prefix.	200	1,200

1980 ND Issue

76 1 Dollar   **VF**   **UNC**
ND (1980). Denomination figures are 8 mm high. Brown on multicolor underprint.
Queen Elizabeth II at right center, arms at center, artifact at right. Signatures; D.
J. Barnes and H. J. Tomkins. Back: Open air Suva markets at center. Watermark:
Profile Fijian head. Printer: TDLR. 156x67mm.

	VF	UNC
a. Issued note.	3.00	25.00
r. As a. Replacement. *Z/I* prefix.	12.50	75.00
s1. Specimen. Signatures punch hole cancelled.	—	300
s2. Specimen. Corners punch hole cancelled.	—	225

77 2 Dollars   **VF**   **UNC**
ND (1980). Denomination figures are 8 mm high. Green on multicolor underprint.
Queen Elizabeth II at right center, arms at center, artifact at right. Signatures;
D. J. Barnes and H. J. Tomkins. Back: Train and sugar cane harvest at center.
Watermark: Profile Fijian head. Printer: TDLR. 156x67mm.

	VF	UNC
a. Issued note.	5.00	45.00
r. As a. Replacement. *Z/I* prefix.	18.50	125
s1. Specimen. Signatures punched hole cancelled.	—	400
s2. Specimen. Corners punched hole cancelled.	—	300

78 5 Dollars   **VF**   **UNC**
ND (1980). Denomination figures are 8 mm high. Orange on multicolor underprint.
Queen Elizabeth II at right center, arms at center, artifact at right. Signatures; D.
J. Barnes and H. J. Tomkins. Back: Fishing group with net at center. Watermark:
Profile Fijian head. Printer: TDLR. 156x67mm.

	VF	UNC
a. Issued note.	7.50	80.00
r. As a. Replacement. *Z/I* prefix.	35.00	250
s1. Specimen. Signatures punch hole cancelled.	—	450
s2. Specimen. Corners punched hole cancelled.	—	350

79 10 Dollars   **VF**   **UNC**
ND (1980). Denomination figures are 8 mm high. Purple on multicolor underprint.
Queen Elizabeth II at right center, arms at center, artifact at right. Signatures;
D. J. Barnes and H. J. Tomkins. Back: Ceremonial tribal dance scene at center.
Watermark: Profile Fijian head. Printer: TDLR. 156x67mm.

	VF	UNC
a. Issued note.	25.00	225
r. As a. Replacement. *Z/I* prefix.	75.00	400
s1. Specimen. Signatures punched hole cancelled.	—	550
s2. Specimen. Corners punched hole cancelled.	—	450

80 20 Dollars

	VF	UNC

ND (1980). Denomination figures are 8 mm high. Blue on multicolor underprint. Queen Elizabeth II at right center, arms at center, artifact at right. Signatures; D. J. Barnes and H. J. Tomkins. Back: Fijian bure (house) at center. Watermark: Profile Fijian head. Printer: TDLR. 156x67mm.

		VF	UNC
a.	Issued note.	50.00	350
r.	As a. Replacement. Z/I prefix.	100	600
s.	Specimen. Signatures punched hole cancelled.	—	650
s2.	Specimen. Corners punch hole cancelled.	—	550

1983-86 ND Issue

81 1 Dollar

	VF	UNC

ND (1983). Denomination figures 9.5 mm high. Gray on multicolor underprint. Queen Elizabeth II at right center, arms at center, artifact at right. Signatures; D. J. Bares and S. Siwatibau. Back: Open air Suva markets at center, lithographed. Watermark: Profile Fijian head. Printer: TDLR. 156x67mm.

		VF	UNC
a.	Issued note.	2.00	9.00
r.	As a. Replacement. Z/I prefix.	10.00	45.00
s1.	Specimen. Signatures punched out.	0.00	200
s2.	Specimen. Corners punched out.	—	125

82 2 Dollars

	VF	UNC

ND (1983). Denominatiion figures 9.5 mm high. Green on multicolor underprint. Queen Elizabeth II at right center, arms at center, artifact at right. Signatures; D. J. Bares and S. Siwatibau. Back: Sugar cane harvest at center, lithographed. Watermark: Profile Fijian head. Printer: TDLR. 156x67mm.

		VF	UNC
a.	Issued note.	4.50	15.00
r.	As a. Replacement. Z/I prefix.	22.50	150
s1.	Specimen. Signatures punched out.	—	275
s2.	Specimen. Corners punched out.	—	175

83 5 Dollars

	VF	UNC

ND (1986). Denomination figures 9.5 mm high. Orange on multicolor underprint. Queen Elizabeth II at right center, arms at center, artifact at right. Signatures; D. J. Bares and S. Siwatibau. Back: Circle of fishermen with net at center, lithographed. Watermark: Profile Fijian head. Printer: TDLR. 156x67mm.

		VF	UNC
a.	Issued note.	6.00	55.00
r.	As a. Replacement. Z/I prefix.	30.00	185
s1.	Specimen. Signatures punched out.	—	300
s2.	Specimen. Corners punched out.	—	225

84 10 Dollars

	VF	UNC

ND (1986). Denomination figures 9.5 mm high. Purple on multicolor underprint. Queen Elizabeth II at right center, arms at center, artifact at right. Signatures; D. J. Bares and S. Siwatibau. Back: Ceremonial dance scene at center, lithographed. Watermark: Profile Fijian head. Printer: TDLR. 156x67mm.

		VF	UNC
a.	Issued note.	12.50	100
r.	As a. Replacement. Z/I prefix.	50.00	275
s1.	Specimen. Signatures punched out.	—	400
s2.	Specimen. Corners punched out.	—	285

85 20 Dollars

	VF	UNC

ND (1986). Denomination figures 9.5 mm high. Blue on multicolor underprint. Queen Elizabeth II at right center, arms at center, artifact at right. Signatures; D. J. Bares and S. Siwatibau. Back: Fijian bure (house) at center, lithographed. Watermark: Profile Fijian head. Printer: TDLR. 156x67mm.

		VF	UNC
a.	Issued note.	20.00	175
r.	As a. Replacement. Z/I prefix.	85.00	350
s1.	Specimen. Signatures punched out.	—	500
s2.	Specimen. Corners punched out.	—	350

Reserve Bank of Fiji
1987-88 ND Issue
#86-88 No replacement notes.

86 1 Dollar

	VF	UNC

ND (1987). Gray on multicolor underprint. Modified portrait of Queen Elizabeth II at right, arms at center, artifact at right. Signature S. Siwatibau. Back: Open air Suva markets at center. Watermark: Profile Fijian head. Printer: BWC. 156x67mm.

		VF	UNC
a.	Issued note.	FV	8.00
s1.	Specimen. Signature punched out.	—	100
s2.	Specimen. No punch cancellation.	—	75.00

87 2 Dollars

	VF	UNC
ND (1988). UV: native design and value fluoresce orange. Green on multicolor underprint. Modified portrait of Queen Elizabeth II at right, arms at center, artifact at right. Signature S. Siwatibau. Back: Sugar cane harvest at center. Watermark: Profile Fijian head. Printer: BWC. 156x67mm.

	VF	UNC
a. Issued note.	FV	20.00
s1. Specimen. Signature punched out.	—	125
s2. Specimen. No punch cancellation.	—	100

88 20 Dollars

ND (1988). Blue on multicolor underprint. Modified portrait of Queen Elizabeth II at right, arms at center, artifact at right. Signature S. Siwatibau. Back: Fijian bure (house) at center. Watermark: Profile Fijian head. Printer: BWC. 156x67mm.

	VF	UNC
a. Issued note.	15.00	110
s1. Specimen. Signature punched out.	—	200
s2. Specimen. No punch cancellation.	—	175

1991 ND Issue

#89-92 No replacement notes.

89 1 Dollar

ND (1993). Gray on multicolor underprint. Modified portrait of Queen Elizabeth II at right, arms at center, artifact at right. Signature J. Kuabuabola. Back: Open air Suva markets at center. Watermark: Profile Fijian head. Printer: TDLR. 156x67mm.

	VF	UNC
a. Issued note.	FV	4.00
s1. Specimen. Signature punched out.	—	125
s2. Specimen. No punch cancellation.	—	85.00

90 2 Dollars

ND (1995). Green on multicolor underprint. Modified portrait of Queen Elizabeth II at right, arms at center, artifact at right. Signature J. Kuabuabola. Back: Sugar cane harvest at center. Watermark: Profile Fijian head. Printer: TDLR. 156x67mm.

	VF	UNC
a. Issued note.	FV	15.00
s1. Specimen. Signature punched out.	—	150
s2. Specimen. No punch cancellation.	—	100

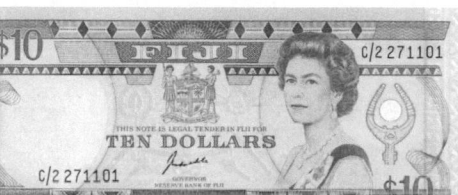

91 5 Dollars

ND (1989). Orange on multicolor underprint. Modified portrait of Queen Elizabeth II at right, arms at center, artifact at right. Signature J. Kuabuabola. Back: Circle of fishermen with net at center. Watermark: Profile Fijian head. Printer: TDLR. 156x67mm.

	VF	UNC
a. Issued note.	7.50	40.00
s1. Specimen. Signature punched out.	—	200
s2. Specimen. No punch cancellation.	—	175

92 10 Dollars

ND (1989). Purple on multicolor underprint. Modified portrait of Queen Elizabeth II at right, arms at center, artifact at right. Signature J. Kuabuabola. Back: Ceremonial dance scene at center. Watermark: Profile Fijian head. Printer: TDLR. 156x67mm.

	VF	UNC
a. Issued note.	10.00	55.00
s1. Specimen. Signature punched out.	—	250
s2. Specimen. No punch cancellation.	—	225

1992 ND Issue

93 5 Dollars

ND (1992). Orange and violet on multicolor underprint. Modified portrait of Queen Elizabeth II at right, arms at center, artifact at right. Signature J. Kuabuabola. Vertical and horizontal serial number. Back: Circle of fishermen with net at center. Watermark: Profile Fijian head. Printer: TDLR. 146x67mm.

	VF	UNC
a. Issued note.	5.00	40.00
s1. Specimen. Signature punched out.	—	185
s2. Specimen. No punch cancellation.	—	150

94 10 Dollars

Purple and brown on multicolor underprint. Modified portrait of Queen Elizabeth II at right, arms at center, artifact at right. Signature J. Kuabuabola. Vertical and horizontal serial number. Back: Ceremonial dance scene at center. Watermark: Profile Fijian head. Printer: TDLR. 146x67mm.

	VF	UNC
a. Issued note.	10.00	60.00
s1. Specimen. Signature punched out.	—	200
s2. Specimen. No punch cancellation.	—	185

95 20 Dollars VF UNC

ND (1992). Blue and black on multicolor underprint. Modified portrait of Queen Elizabeth II at right, arms at center, artifact at right. Signature J. Kuabuabola. Vertical and horizontal serial number. Back: Fijian bure (house) at center. Watermark: Profile Fijian head. Printer: TDLR. 146x67mm.

a. Issued note.	15.00	95.00
s1. Specimen. Signature punched out.	—	250
s2. Specimen. No punch cancellation.	—	200

1992-95 ND Issue

96 2 Dollars VF UNC

ND (1996). UV: value in box fluoresces yellow; back design elements at left and right orange. Green, blue and gold on multicolor underprint. Mature bust of Queen Elizabeth II at right, arms at upper right. Kaka (Masked Shining Parrot) at lower left. Segmented foil security thread. Back: Culturally diverse group of five at left center. Watermark: Profile Fijian head. Printer: TDLR. 156x67mm.

a. Single letter prefix.	FV	6.00
b. Double letter prefix. Amended security thread.	FV	4.00
s. Specimen.	—	100
ar. As a. Replacement. Z prefix.	3.00	15.00
br. As b. Replacement. X prefix.	3.00	10.00

97 5 Dollars VF UNC

ND (1995). Red, orange and maroon on multicolor underprint. Mature bust of Queen Elizabeth II at right, arms at upper right. Bunedamu (White-throated Pigeon) at lower left. Segmented foil security thread. Back: Aerial view Nadi International Airport at center, ferry boat at lower center right. Watermark: Profile Fijian head. Printer: TDLR. 156x67mm.

a. Issued note.	FV	12.50
r. Replacement. Z prefix.	12.50	65.00
s. Specimen.	—	250

98 10 Dollars VF UNC

ND (1996). Purple, violet and brown onmulticolor underprint. Mature bust of Queen Elizabeth II at right, arms at upper right. Kikau (Orange-breasted Myzomela) at lower left. Segmented foil security thread. Back: Traditional boat with thatched shelter at center. Watermark: Profile Fijian head. Printer: TDLR. 156x67mm.

a. Single letter prefix.	—	45.00
b. Double letter prefix.	FV	25.00
r. Replacement. Z prefix.	35.00	125
s. Specimen.	—	300

99 20 Dollars VF UNC

ND. Blue, purple and dark blue on multicolor underprint. Mature bust of Queen Elizabeth II at right, arms at upper right. Manusa (Fantail) at lower left. Segmented foil security thread. Back: Parliament House at left, Reserve Bank building at center right. Watermark: Profile Fijian head. Printer: TDLR. 156x67mm.

a. Single letter prefix.	FV	55.00
b. Double letter prefix.	FV	40.00
r. Replacement. Z prefix.	60.00	185
s. Specimen.	—	450

100 50 Dollars VF UNC

ND (1996). Black, red, orange and violet on multicolor underprint. Mature bust of Queen Elizabeth II at right, arms at upper right. Kaka (Petrel) at lower left. Segmented foil security thread. Novel serial numbers at left only. Back: Flag raising ceremony at left, signing of Deed of Cession, Cession Stone. Watermark: Profile Fijian head. Printer: TDLR. 156x67mm.

a. Single letter prefix. Signature J. Kuabuabola.	30.00	185
b. Signature Savenaca Narube.	50.00	450
r1. As a. Replacement. Z prefix.	300	750
r2. As b. Replacement. Z prefix.	450	900
s1. Specimen as a. Signature J. Kuabuabola.	—	600
s2. Specimen as b. Signature Savenaca Narube.	—	900

1998 ND Issue

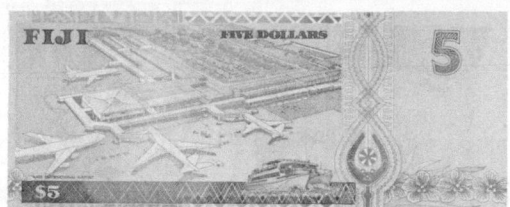

101 5 Dollars VF UNC

ND. Brown on multicolor underprint. Mature bust of Queen Elizabeth II at right, arms at upper right. Bunedamu bird (White-throated Pigeon) at lower left. Back: Aerial view Nadi International Airport at left center, ferry boat at lower center right. Watermark: Profile Fijian head. 156x67mm.

a. Signature J. Kuabuabola.	FV	12.50
b. Signature Savenaca Narube.	FV	15.00
s1. As a. Specimen.	—	50.00
s2. As b. Specimen.	—	65.00
ar. As a. Replacement. Z prefix.	30.00	125
br. As b. Replacement. Z prefix.	50.00	200

2000 Commemorative Issue

102 2 Dollars VF UNC

2000. UV: value in box fluoresces yellow. Green, blue and brown on multicolor underprint. Kaka (Parrot) at left, Sir Penaia Ganilau at right, arms at upper right, y2k at center. Segmented foil security thread. Back: Culturally diverse group and turtle. Watermark: Profile Fijian head. Printer: TDLR. 156x67mm.

a. Issued note.	FV	2.00
b. Uncut pair.	FV	5.00
c. Uncut sheet of 20.	—	75.00
d. Uncut sheet of 32.		150
s. Specimen.	—	100

103 2000 Dollars VF UNC

2000. Blue and gold on multicolor underprint. Sir Kamisese Mara at right, Kulawaj (Parrot) at lower left, arms at upper right, y2k at center. Segmented foil security thread. Back: Earth, rising sun, island map, shells. Watermark: Profile Fijian head. Printer: TDLR.

a. Isused note.	FV	2,500
s. Specimen, individually numbered.	—	800

2002 ND Issue

104 2 Dollars VF UNC

ND (2002). Additional security features. Green, blue and gold on multicolor underprint. Mature bust of Queen Elizabeth II at right, arms at upper right. Kaka (Masked Shining Parrot) at lower left. Novel serial #. Signature Savenaca Narube. Back: Culturally diverse group of five at left center. Watermark: Profile Fijian head. Printer: TDLR. 156x67mm.

a. Double letter prefix.	FV	3.00
r. Replacement. Z prefix.	4.00	10.00
s. Specimen.	—	45.00

105 5 Dollars VF UNC

ND (2002). Additional security features. Brown on multicolor underprint. Mature bust of Queen Elizabeth II at right, arms at upper right. Bunedamu (White-throated Pigeon) at lower left. Novel serial #. Signature Savenaca Narube. Back: Aerial view Nadi International Airport at left center, ferry boat at lower center right. Watermark: Profile Fijian head. Printer: TDLR. 156x67mm.

a. Single letter prefix.	FV	10.00
b. Double letter prefix.	FV	5.00
r. Replacement. Z prefix.	7.00	20.00
s. Specimen.	—	85.00

106 10 Dollars VF UNC

ND (2002). Additional security features. Purple, violet and brown on multicolor underprint. Mature bust of Queen Elizabeth II at right, arms at upper right. Novel serial #. Kikau at lower left. Signature Savenaca Narube. Back: Traditional boat with thatched shelter at center. Watermark: Profile Fijian head. Printer: TDLR. 156x67mm.

a. Double letter prefix.	FV	17.50
r. Replacement. Z prefix.	17.50	30.00
s. Specimen.	—	180

107 20 Dollars

ND (2002). Additional security features. Blue, purple and dark blue on multicolor underprint. Mature bust of Queen Elizabeth II at right, arms at upper right. Novel serial #. Manusa at lower left. Signature Savenaca Narube. Back: Parliament House at left, Reserve Bank building at center right. Watermark: Profile Fijian head. Printer: TDLR. 156x67mm.

		VF	UNC
a. Double letter prefix.		FV	35.00
r. Replacement. Z prefix.		22.50	85.00
s. Specimen.		—	250

108 50 Dollars

ND (2002). Black, red, orange and violet on multicolor underprint. Mature bust of Queen Elizabeth II at right, arms at upper right. Novel serial #. Kaka at lower left. Additional security features. Signature Savenaca Narube. Back: Flag raising ceremony at left, signing of Deed of Cession, Cession Stone. Watermark: Profile Fijian head. Printer: TDLR. 156x67mm.

		VF	UNC
a. Single letter prefix.		FV	75.00
r. Replacement. Z prefix.		30.00	180
s. Specimen.		—	400

2007 ND Issue

109 2 Dollars

ND (2007; 2012). Green on multicolor underprint. Mature bust Queen Elizabeth II at right, arms at upper right. Novel numbering on both serial #. Mohar (sovereign locket) at lower left. Back: Faces of diverse group of children during school games. Fiji National Stadium at left; Mount Korobasanasaga at center right. Printer: TDLR. 131x67mm.

		VF	UNC
a. Signature Savenaca Narube. Signature title: Governor.		FV	2.00
b. Signature Barry Whiteside. Signature title: Acting Governor.		FV	2.00
r1. As a. Replacement note. Serial # prefix: ZA.		3.00	7.50
r2. As b. Replacement note. Serial # prefix: ZA.		2.50	10.00
s. As a. Specimen.		—	45.00
s2. As b. Specimen.		—	45.00

110 5 Dollars

ND (2007; 2012). Brown on multicolor underprint. Mature bust Queen Elizabeth II at right, arms at upper right. Novel numbering on both serial #. Kato ni Masima (salt basket) at lower left. Back: Crested Iguana at left, Balaka palm center, Masiratu flower at right, Mount Valili at far left. Printer: TDLR. 136x67mm.

		VF	UNC
a. Signature Savenaca Narube. Signature title: Governor.		FV	5.00
b. Signature: Barry Whiteside. Signature title: Acting Governor.		FV	5.00
r1. As a. Replacement note. Serial # prefix: ZA.		5.00	15.00
r2. As b. Replacement note. Serial # prefix: ZA.		4.00	15.00
s1. As a. Specimen.		—	85.00
s2. As b. Specimen.		—	85.00

111 10 Dollars

ND (2007; 2012). Purple on multicolor underprint. Mature bust Queen Elizabeth II at right, arms at upper right. Novel numbering on both serial #. i Buburau ni Bete (dish) at lower left. Foil security insert with motion. Back: Grand Pacific Hotel at right center. Joske's Thumb at left center. Printer: TDLR. 141x67mm.

		VF	UNC
a. Signature Savenaca Narube. Signature title: Governor.		FV	10.00
b. Signature: Barry Whiteside. Signature title: Acting Governor.		FV	10.00
r1. As a. Replacement note. Serial # prefix: ZA.		10.00	25.00
r2. As b. Replacement note. Serial # prefix: ZA.		8.50	20.00
s1. As a. Specimen.		—	125
s2. As b. Specimen.		—	125

112 20 Dollars

ND (2007). Blue on multicolor underprint. Mature bust Queen Elizabeth II at right, arms at upper right. Novel numbering on both serial #. Foa (coconut scraper) at lower left. Fan shaped hologram at right. Signature Savenaca Narube. Back: Sugarcane, fishery, forestry and mining scenes. Mount Uluinabukelevu at right center. Printer: TDLR. 146x67mm.

		VF	UNC
a. Issued note.		FV	22.50
r. Replacement note. Serial # prefix: ZA.		20.00	100
s. Specimen.		—	150

113 50 Dollars

VF UNC

ND (2007). Orange on multicolor underprint. Mature bust Queen Elizabeth II at right, arms at upper right. Novel numbering on both serial #. Wasekaseka (whale tooth necklace) at lower left. Turtle-shaped hologram at right. Signature Savenaca Narube. Back: Ceremonial presentation of tabua and yaqona. Printer: TDLR. 151x67mm.

	FV	55.00
a. Issued note.	FV	55.00
r. Replacement note. Serial # prefix: ZA.	50.00	150
s. Specimen.	—	200

114 100 Dollars

VF UNC

ND (2007). Yellow. Mature bust Queen Elizabeth II at right, arms at upper right. Novel numbering on both serial #. Buli Kula (Golden Cowry) at lower left. OPTIKS 18mm wide security foil at right. Signature Savenaca Narube. Back: Tourism: map, smiling faces, cruise boat, snorkeling. Printer: TDLR. 156x67mm.

a. Issued note.	FV	110
r. Replacement note. Serial # prefix: ZA.	100	250
s. Specimen.	—	300

2012 Issue

115 5 Dollars

VF UNC

ND (2013). Polymer plastic. Green on multicolor underprint. Endemic Kulawai (Red-throated Lorikeet) at right, arms at upper right. Clear window with images of i-Taukei at left, Kato ni Masima (salt basket) at lower left. Signature Barry Whiteside. Back: Crested Iguana at left, Balaka Palm at cener. Masiratu flower at right, Mount Valili at far left. 136x67mm.

a. Issued note.	FV	5.00
r. Replacement note: Serial # prefix: ZZA.	5.00	6.50
s. Specimen.	—	45.00

116 10 Dollars

VF UNC

ND (2013). Purple on multicolor underprint. Beli fish (Lever's Goby) at right, arms upper right. i Buburau-ni-bete (duck dish) at lower left. Signature Bary Whiteside. Back: Grand Pacific Hotel at right center, Joske's Thumb at left. Printer: DLR. 141x67mm.

a. Issued note.	FV	10.00
r. Replacement note. Serial # prefix: ZZA.	10.00	15.00
s. Specimen.	—	85.00

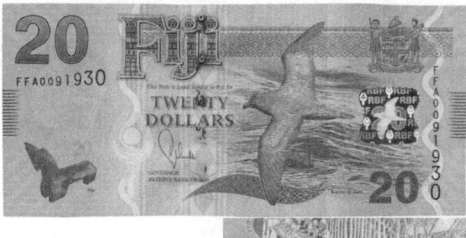

117 20 Dollars

VF UNC

ND (2013). Blue on multicolor underprint. Kacnu ni Gau bird (Fiji Petrol) at right, arms at upper right. Foa (coconut scraper) at lower left. Signature Barry Whiteside. Back: Fishing, Forestry, sugarcane and mining scenes, Mt. Uluinabukelevu at upper right center. Printer: DLR. 146x67mm.

a. Issued note.	FV	20.00
r. Replacement note. Serial # prefix: ZZA.	20.00	30.00
s. Specimen.	—	135

118 50 Dollars

VF UNC

ND (2013). Orange and yellow on multicolor underprint. Tagimoucia flowers at right, arms at upper right. Wasekaseka (whale's tooth necklace) at lower left. Signature Barry Whiteside. Back: Ceremonial Tabua presentation and Yaqona ceremony. Printer: DLR. 151x67mm.

a. Issued note.	FV	50.00
r. Replacement note. Serial # prefix: ZZA.	50.00	75.00
s. Specimen.	—	185

119 100 Dollars

VF UNC

ND (2013). Yellow on multicolor underprint. Nanai (cicada) at center right, arms at upper right. Buli kula (Golden Cowrie) at lower left. Signature Barry Whiteside. Back: International dateline at rigth center, tourism scenes, three welcoming Fijian host at left. Printer: DLR. 156x67mm.

a. Issued note.	FV	100
r. Replacement note: Serial # prefix: ZZA.	100	150
s. Specimen.	—	300

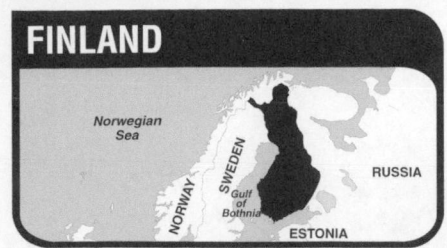

FINLAND

Norwegian Sea
NORWAY
SWEDEN
Gulf of Bothnia
RUSSIA
ESTONIA

The Republic of Finland, the second most northerly state of the European continent, has an area of 338,145 sq. km. and a population of 5.24 million. Capital: Helsinki. Electrical, optical equipment, shipbuilding, metal and woodworking are the leading industries. Paper, wood pulp, plywood and telecommunication equipment are exported.

Finland was a province and then a grand duchy under Sweden from the 12th to the 19th centuries, and an autonomous grand duchy of Russia after 1809. It won its complete independence in 1917. During World War II, it was able to successfully defend its freedom and resist invasions by the Soviet Union - albeit with some loss of territory. In the subsequent half century, the Finns made a remarkable transformation from a farm/forest economy to a diversified modern industrial economy; per capita income is now among the highest in Western Europe. A member of the European Union since 1995, Finland was the only Nordic state to join the euro system at its initiation in January 1999.

RULERS:
Gustaf III, 1771-1792, of Sweden
Gustaf IV Adolph, 1792-1809
Alexander I, 1809-1825, of Russia
Nicholas I, 1825-1855
Alexander II, 1855-1881
Alexander III, 1881-1894
Nicholas II, 1894-1917

MONETARY SYSTEM:
(With Sweden to 1809)
1 Riksdaler Specie = 48 Skilling Specie
(With Russia 1809-1917)
1 Ruble = 100 Kopeks, 1809-1860
1 Markka = 100 Penniä, 1860-1963
1 Markka = 100 "Old" Markkaa, 1963-2001
1 Euro = 100 Cents, 2002-

REPLACEMENT NOTES:
Replacement notes were introduced in 1955. Until 1980, replacement notes have an asterisk after the serial number. Series 1986 show 2nd and 3rd digits of serial # as 99.

REPUBLIC

Suomen Pankki - Finlands Bank

1963 Dated Issue

98   1 Markka   VF   UNC
1963. Lilac-brown on olive underprint. Wheat ears. Back: Arms at center.
   a. Issued note.   0.50   2.00
   r. Replacement note. Serial # suffix *.   8.00   25.00
   s. Specimen.   —   100

99   5 Markkaa   VF   UNC
1963. Blue and blue-green. Conifer branch. Back: Arms at center.
   a. Issued note.   3.00   12.50
   r. Replacement note. Serial # suffix *.   20.00   40.00
   s. Specimen.   —   125

100   10 Markkaa   VF   UNC
1963. Dark green and blue. Juho Kusti Paasikivi at left. Back: Arms at center right. Watermark: Juho Kusti Paasikivi, (direction varies).
   a. Issued note.   15.00   30.00
   r. Replacement note. Serial # suffix *.   250   500
   s. Specimen.   —   150

101   50 Markkaa   VF   UNC
1963. Brown. Kaarlo Juho Ståhlberg at left. Back: Arms at center right. Watermark: Kaarlo Juho Ståhlberg (direction varies).
   a. Issued note.   20.00   50.00
   r. Replacement note. Serial # suffix *.   700   1,000
   s. Specimen.   —   175

102   100 Markkaa   VF   UNC
1963. Violet. Juhana Vilhelm Snellman at left. Back: Arms at center right.
   a. Issued note.   25.00   60.00
   r. Replacement note. Serial # suffix *.   350   1,000
   s. Specimen.   —   200

1963 Dated Issue, Litt. A

103   5 Markkaa   VF   UNC
1963. Blue and blue-green. Conifer branch, border and date designs are more detailed. Back: Arms at center.
   a. Issued note.   3.00   13.00
   r. Replacement note. Serial # suffix *.   5.00   30.00

104   10 Markkaa   VF   UNC
1963. Dark green and blue. Juho Kusti Paasikivi at left. Back: Arms at center right. Watermark: Juho Kusti Paasikivi, (position varies).
   a. Issued note.   3.00   9.00
   r. Replacement note. Serial # suffix *.   5.00   10.00

105   50 Markkaa   VF   UNC
   1963. Brown. Kaarlo Juho Ståhlberg at left. Back: Arms at center right.
     a. Issued note.   20.00   50.00
     r. Replacement note. Serial # suffix *.   250   400

106   100 Markkaa   VF   UNC
   1963. Violet. Juhana Vilhelm Snellman at left. Back: Arms at center right.
     a. Issued note.   25.00   40.00
     r. Replacement note. Serial # suffix *.   40.00   75.00

1963 Dated Issue, Litt. B

106A   5 Markkaa   VF   UNC
   1963. Blue and blue-green. Conifer branch. Back: Arms at center.
     a. Issued note.   1.50   4.00
     r1. Replacement note. Serial # suffix *.   5.00   8.00
     r2. Replacement note. Serial # suffix *I*.   75.00   150
107   50 Markkaa   VF   UNC
   1963. Brown. Kaarlo Juho Ståhlberg at left. Back: Arms at center right. Watermark: Kaarlo Juho Ståhlberg (direction varies).
     a. Issued note.   15.00   35.00
     r. Replacement note. Serial # suffix *.   30.00   60.00

1975-77 Issue

108   50 Markkaa   VF   UNC
   1977. Brown and multicolor. Kaarlo Juho Ståhlberg at left. Watermark: Kaarlo
   Juho Ståhlberg, (position and direction varies).
     a. Issued note.   12.50   20.00
     r1. Replacement note. Serial # suffix *.   20.00   40.00
     r2. Replacement note. Serial # suffix *I*.   300   600
     s. Specimen.   —   200

109   100 Markkaa   VF   UNC
   1976. Violet. Juhana Vilhelm Snellman at left. Watermark: Juhana Vilhelm Snellman, (position and direction varies).
     a. Issued note.   25.00   35.00
     r1. Replacement note. Serial # suffix *.   25.00   48.00
     r2. Replacement note. Serial # suffix *I*.   150   300

110   500 Markkaa   VF   UNC
   1975. Blue and violet. Urho Kaleva Kekkonen at left. Back: Arms and nine small
   shields. Watermark: Urho Kaleva Kekkonen at left, (position varies).
     a. Thin metallic security thread.   150   200
     b. Broad yellow plastic security thread.   100   150
     r1. As a. Replacement note. Serial # suffix *.   400   750
     r2. As b. Replacement note. Serial # suffix *.   250   350
     r3. As b. Replacement note. Serial # suffix *I*.   800   1,200
     s. Specimen.   —   350

1980 Issue

111   10 Markkaa   VF   UNC
   1980. Green and brown on orange and multicolor underprint. Juho Kusti Paasikivi
   at left, four raised discs at right center for denomination identification by the blind.
   Back: Arms at center right. Watermark: Juho Kusti Paasikivi.
     a. Issued note.   3.00   8.00
     r1. Replacement note. Serial # suffix *.   5.00   14.00
     r2. Replacement note. Serial # suffix *I*.   75.00   150

1980 Issue; Litt. A

112   10 Markkaa   VF   UNC
   1980. Green and brown on orange and multicolor underprint. Juho Kusti Paasikivi
   at left, date under portrait, five small circles at bottom center. *Litt. A.* Back: Arms at
   center right. Watermark: Juho Kusti Paasikivi.
     a. Issued note.   3.00   6.00
     r. Replacement note. *99* as 2nd and 3rd numerial in serial #.   5.00   10.00

1986 Issue

#113-115, and 117 replacement notes: w/*99* as 2nd and 3rd digits in serial #.

113 10 Markkaa   **VF UNC**

1986. Deep blue and green underprint. Paavo Nurmi at left, circles above lower right serial number. Back: Helsinki Olympic Stadium. Watermark: Paavo Nurmi.

     a. Issued note.   2.50   6.00
     r. Replacement note.   4.00   12.50

114 50 Markkaa   **VF UNC**

1986. Black on red-brown and multicolor underprint. Alvar Aalto at left, four raised circles above lower right serial number. Back: Finlandia Hall. Watermark: Alvar Aalto.

     a. Issued note.   12.50   25.00
     r. Replacement note.   30.00   50.00

115 100 Markkaa   **VF UNC**

1986. Black on green and multicolor underprint. Jean Sibelius at left, three raised circles above lower right serial number. Back: Whooper Swans. Watermark: Jean Sibelius.

     a. Issued note.   25.00   40.00
     r. Replacement note.   40.00   60.00

116 500 Markkaa   **VF UNC**

1986. Black on red, brown and yellow underprint. Elias Lönnrot at left, two circles above lower right serial number. Back: Punkaharju. Watermark: Elias Lönnrot.

     a. Issued note.   125   175
     r. Replacement note.   150   200

117 1000 Markkaa   **VF UNC**

1986. Blue and purple on multicolor underprint. Anders Chydenius at left, one circle above lower right serial number. Back: King's gate, sea fortress of Suomenlinna in Helsinki harbor, seagulls. Watermark: Anders Chydenius.

     a. Issued note.   200   300
     r. Replacement note.   250   325

1986 Dated (1991) Issue, Litt. A

118 50 Markkaa   **VF UNC**

1986 (1991). Latent image at upper right. Black on red-brown and multicolor underprint. Alvar Aalto at left, *Litt. A* above denomination at lower left, 4 raised circles above bank name, optical variable device (OVD) at upper right. Back: Finlandia Hall. Watermark: Alvar Aalto.   10.00   20.00

119 100 Markkaa   **VF UNC**

1986 (1991). Latent image at upper right. Black on green and multicolor underprint. Jean Sibelius at left, *Litt. A* above denomination at lower left, 3 raised circles above bank name, optical variable device (OVD) at upper right. Back: Whooper Swans. Watermark: Jean Sibelius.   17.50   27.50

120 500 Markkaa   **VF UNC**

1986 (1991). Black on red, brown and yellow underprint. Elias Lönnrot at left, *Litt. A* above denomination at lower left, 2 raised circles above bank name, optical variable device (OVD) at upper right. Back: Punkaharju. Watermark: Elias Lönnrot.   135   160

121 1000 Markkaa

VF UNC

1986 (1991). Blue and purple on multicolor underprint. Anders Chydenius at left, *Litt. A* above denomination at lower left, 1 raised circle above bank name, optical variable device (OVD) at upper right. Back: King's gate, sea fortress of Suomenlinna in Helsinki harbor, seagulls. Watermark: Anders Chydenius.

250 300

1993 Issue

122 20 Markkaa

VF UNC

1993. Black on blue and gold underprint. Väinö Linna at left, latent image at upper right, four circles above bank name at lower center. Back: Tampere street scene. Watermark: Väinö Linna.

7.50 12.50

1993 Dated (1997) Issue; Litt. A.

123 20 Markkaa

VF UNC

1993 (1997). Black on blue and green underprint. Väinö Linna at left, four circles above bank name at lower center, with optical variable device at upper right. *Litt. A.* at lower left. Back: Tampere street scene. Watermark: Väinö Linna.

5.00 8.00

Note: For later issues made for use in Finland see European Union listings.

The French Republic, largest of the West European nations, has an area of 547,026 sq. km. and a population of 64.05 million. Capital: Paris. Agriculture, manufacturing and tourism are the most important elements of France's diversified economy. Textiles and clothing, iron and steel products, machinery and transportation equipment, agricultural products and wine are exported.

Although ultimately a victor in World Wars I and II, France suffered extensive losses in its empire, wealth, manpower, and rank as a dominant nation-state. Nevertheless, France today is one of the most modern countries in the world and is a leader among European nations. Since 1958, it has constructed a hybrid presidential-parliamentary governing system resistant to the instabilities experienced in earlier more purely parliamentary administrations. In recent years, its reconciliation and cooperation with Germany have proved central to the economic integration of Europe, including the introduction of a common exchange currency, the euro, in January 1999. At present, France is at the forefront of efforts to develop the EU's military capabilities to supplement progress toward an EU foreign policy.

MONETARY SYSTEM:

1 Livre = 20 Sols (Sous)
1 Ecu = 6 Livres
1 Louis D'or = 4 Ecus to 1794
1 Franc = 10 Decimes = 100 Centimes, 1794-1959
1 Nouveau Franc = 100 "old" Francs, 1959-1962
1 Franc = 100 Centimes, 1962-2002
1 Euro = 100 Cents, 2002-

REPUBLIC

Banque de France

1959 Issue

141 5 Nouveaux Francs

VF UNC

5.3.1959-5.11.1965. Blue, orange and multicolor. Panthéon in Paris at left, Victor Hugo at right, denomination: *NOUVEAUX FRANCS* (NF). Back: Vosges place at right, Victor Hugo at left.

a. Issued note. 55.00 530
s. Specimen. 340 1,250

142   10 Nouveaux Francs VF UNC

5.3.1959-4.1.1963. Multicolor. *Palais Royal* across bottom, Armand du Plessis,
Cardinal Richelieu at right, denomination: *NOUVEAUX FRANCS* (NF). Back: Town
gate (of Richelieu, in *Indre et Loire*) at right.

a. Issued note.	23.00	390
s. Specimen.	340	1,250

143   50 Nouveaux Francs VF UNC

5.3.1959-6.7.1961. Multicolor. Henry IV at center, Paris' *Pont Neuf* bridge in
background, denomination: *NOUVEAUX FRANCS* (NF). Back: Henry IV at center,
Château de Pau at left.

a. Issued note.	175	1,500
s. Specimen.	450	2,800

144   100 Nouveaux Francs VF UNC

5.3.1959-2.4.1964. Multicolor. Arc de Triomphe at left, Napoléon Bonaparte at
right, denomination: *NOUVEAUX FRANCS* (NF). Back: Paris' *Church of the
Invalides* at right, Bonaparte at left.

a. Issued note.	55.00	1,250
s. Specimen.	450	2,000

145   500 Nouveaux Francs VF UNC

1959-66. Multicolor. Jean Baptiste Poquelin called Molière at center Paris' *Palais
Royal* in background, denomination: *NOUVEAUX FRANCS* (NF). Back: Theater
in Versailles.

a. Signature G. Gouin D'Ambrières, R. Tondu and P. Gargam. 2.7.1959-8.1.1965.	460	—
b. Signature H. Morant, R. Tondu and P. Gargam. 6.1.1966.	500	—
s. Specimen. As b.	625	2,270

1962-66 Issue

146   5 Francs VF UNC

1966-70. Brown, purple and multicolor. Louis Pasteur at left, Pasteur Institute in
Paris at right. Back: Laboratory implements, man fighting a rabid dog, Pasteur
at right.

a. Signature R. Tondu, P. Gargam and H. Morant. 5.5.1966-4.11.1966.	25.00	285
b. Signature R. Tondu, H. Morant and G. Bouchet. 5.5.1967-8.1.1970.	32.00	325
s. Specimen. As a. Overprint and perforated: *SPECIMEN*.	285	1,130

147   10 Francs VF UNC

1963-73. Red and multicolor. Paris' *Palais des Tuileries* at center, Voltaire at right.
Back: Château de Cirey at right, Voltaire at left. Watermark: Voltaire.

a. Signature G. Gouin D'Ambrières, P. Gargam and R. Tondu. 4.1.1963-2.12.1965.	22.00	175
b. Signature H. Morant, P. Gargam and R. Tondu. 6.1.1966-6.4.1967.	11.00	95.00
c. Signature G. Bouchet, H. Morant and R. Tondu. 6.7.1967-4.2.1971.	8.50	60.00
d. Signature G. Bouchet, H. Morant and P. Vergnes. 3.6.1971-6.12.1973.	7.00	55.00
s. Specimen. As a-c. Overprint and perforated: *SPECIMEN*.	285	850

148   50 Francs VF UNC

1962-76. Multicolor. Port Royal des Champs Abbey at center, Jean Racine at
right. Back: Jean Racine at left, view of La Ferté-Milon.

a. Signature G. Gouin d'Ambrières, R. Tondu and P. Gargam. 7.6.1962-4.3.1965.	27.00	200
b. Signature H. Morant, R. Tondu and P. Gargam. 2.2.1967.	35.00	225
c. Signature H. Morant, R. Tondu and G. Bouchet. 7.12.1967-5.11.1970.	25.00	225
d. Signature G. Bouchet, P. Vergnes and H. Morant. 3.6.1971-3.10.1974.	18.50	170
e. Signature G. Bouchet, J. J. Tronche and H. Morant. 6.3.1975-2.10.1975.	17.00	145
f. Signature P. A. Strohl, G. Bouchet and J. J. Tronche. 2.1.1976-3.6.1976.	19.00	145
s. Specimen. Overprint and perforated: *SPECIMEN*.	340	900

149   100 Francs VF UNC

1964-79. Multicolor. Pierre Corneille at center, Theater in Versailles around. Back:
Corneille's bust in cartouche at center, View of Rouen.

a. Signature R. Tondu. G. Gouin D'Ambrières and P. Gargam. 2.4.1964-2.12.1965.	45.00	220
b. Signature R. Tondu, H. Morant and P. Gargam. 3.2.1966-6.4.1967.	33.50	180
c. Signature R. Tondu, G. Bouchet and H. Morant. 5.10.1967-1.4.1971.	30.00	175
d. Signature P. Vergnes, G. Bouchet and H. Morant. 1.7.1971-3.10.1974.	26.00	135
e. Signature J. J. Tronche, G. Bouchet and H. Morant. 6.2.1975-6.11.1975.	27.50	135
f. Signature P. A. Strohl, G. Bouchet and J. J. Tronche. 2.1.1976-1.2.1979.	26.00	100
s. Specimen. Overprint and perforated: *SPECIMEN*.	340	900

1968-81 Issue

150   10 Francs VF UNC

1972-78. Red, brown and olive. Hector Berlioz at right, conducting in the Chapelle
des Invalides. Back: Berlioz at left, musical instrument at right and Rome's Villa
Medici in background.

a. Signature H. Morant, G. Bouchet and P. Vergnes. 23.11.1972-3.10.1974.	6.50	65.00
b. Signature H. Morant, G. Bouchet and J. J. Tronche. 6.2.1975-4.12.1975.	5.50	45.00
c. Signature P. A. Strohl, G. Bouchet and J. J. Tronche. 2.1.1976-6.7.1978.	4.50	30.00
s. Specimen. As b. Overprint and perforated: *SPECIMEN*.	285	795

151 20 Francs

		VF	UNC
1980-97. Dull violet, brown and multicolor. Claude Debussy at right, sea scene in background (*La Mer*). Back: Claude Debussy at left, lake scene in background. Watermark: Claude Debussy. 140x75mm.			
a. Without security thread. Signature P. A. Strohl, J. J. Tronche and B. Dentaud. 1980-86.		4.00	30.00
b. Signature P. A. Strohl, D. Ferman and B. Dentaud. 1987.		3.00	28.50
c. Signature D. Ferman, B. Dentaud and A. Charriau. 1988; 1989.		7.00	31.00
d. With security thread. Signature as c. 1990.		—	17.00
e. Signature D. Bruneel, B. Dentaud and A. Charriau. 1991.		—	17.00
f. Signature D. Bruneel, J. Bonnardin and A. Charriau. 1992; 1993.		—	13.50
g. Signature D. Bruneel, J. Bonnardin and C. Vigier. 1993.		—	13.50
h. Signature as g. New *Ley* (law) on back. 1995.		—	13.50
i. Signature D. Bruneel, J. Bonnardin and Y. Barroux. 1997.		4.50	22.00
s. Specimen. Overprint and perforated. *SPECIMEN*.		170	740

152 50 Francs

		VF	UNC
1976-92. Deep blue-black on multicolor underprint. Maurice Quentin de la Tour at center right, and Palace of Versailles at left center in background. Back: Quentin de la Tour and St.Quentin City Hall at center right in background. Watermark: Maurice Quentin de la Tour.			
a. Signature P. A. Strohl, G. Bouchet and J. J. Tronche. 1976-79.		7.00	50.00
b. Signature P. A. Strohl, J. J. Tronche and B. Dentaud. 1979-86.		6.50	44.00
c. Signature P. A. Strohl, D. Ferman and B. Dentaud. 1987.		5.50	45.00
d. Signature D. Ferman, B. Dentaud and A. Charriau. 1988; 1989.		5.50	35.00
e. Signature D. Bruneel, B. Dentaud and A. Charriau. 1990; 1991.		5.50	35.00
f. Signature D. Bruneel, J. Bonnardin and A. Charriau. 1992.		5.50	35.00
s. Specimen. Overprint and perforated: *SPECIMEN*.		285	680

153 100 Francs

	VF	UNC
1978. Brown. Eugène Delacroix at left center, Marianne holding tricolor, part of Delacroix's painting *La Liberté Guidant le Peuple* at right. Signature P. A. Strohl, G. Bouchet and J. J. Tronche. Back: Delacroix at right with quill pen. Watermark: Eugène Delacroix.	25.00	150

154 100 Francs

		VF	UNC
1978-95. Brown. Eugène Delacroix at left center. Marianne holding tricolor, park of Delacroix's painting *La Liberté Guident le Peuple* at right. Like #153 but 100 *CENT FRANCS* retouched with heavier diagonal lines at upper left. Back: Delacroix at right holding quill pen.			
a. Signature P. A. Strohl, G. Bouchet and J. J. Tronche. 1978-79.		21.00	120
b. Signature P. A. Strohl, J. J. Tronche and B. Dentaud. 1979-86.		8.50	57.00
c. Signature P. A. Strohl, D. Ferman and B. Dentaud. 1987.		7.00	50.00
d. Signature D. Ferman, B. Dentaud and A. Charriau. 1988-90.		11.00	42.00
e. Signature D. Bruneel, B. Dentaud and A. Charriau. 1990-91.		30.00	145
f. Signature D. Bruneel, J. Bonnardin and A. Charriau. 1991.		25.00	130
g. Signature D. Bruneel, J. Bonnardin and C. Vigier. 1993.		14.00	70.00
h. Signature as g. New Ley (law) on back. 1994; 1995.		9.00	55.00
s. Specimen. Overprint and perforated: *SPECIMEN*.		225	900

155 200 Francs

		VF	UNC
1981-94. Blue-green, yellow and multicolor. Figure with staff at at left, Charles Baron de Montesquieu at right. Back: Montesquieu at left, Castle of Labrède on back (Montesquieu's birthplace). Watermark: Charles Baron de Montesquieu.			
a. Signature P. A. Strohl, J. J. Tronche and B. Dentaud. 1981-86.		35.00	140
b. Signature P. A. Strohl, D. Ferman and B. Dentaud. 1987.		17.00	85.00
c. Signature D. Ferman, B. Dentaud and A. Charriau. 1988; 1989.		15.00	75.00
d. Signature D. Bruneel, B. Dentaud and A. Charriau. 1990; 1991.		17.00	105
e. Signature D. Bruneel, J. Bonnardin and A. Charriau. 1992.		11.50	65.00
f. Signature D. Bruneel, J. Bonnardin and C. Vigier. New Ley (law) on back. 1994.		45.00	210
s. Specimen. Overprint and perforated: *SPECIMEN*.		285	795

156 500 Francs

VF UNC

1968-93 Yellow-brown and dark brown. Tower of St. Jacques in Paris at left, Blaise Pascal at center. Back: Blaise Pascal at left, abbey of Port Royal.

		VF	UNC
a.	Signature G. Bouchet, R. Tondu and H. Morant. 4.1.1968-8.1.1970.	65.00	850
b.	Signature G. Bouchet, P. Vergnes and H. Morant. 5.8.1971-5.9.1974.	60.00	565
c.	Signature G. Bouchet, J. J. Tronche and H. Morant. 5.12.1974-6.11.1975.	40.00	310
d.	Signature P. A. Strohl, G. Bouchet and J. J. Tronche. 1.4.1976-7.6.1979.	42.00	215
e.	Signature P. A. Strohl, J. J. Tronche and B. Dentaud. 7.6.1979-6.2.1986.	25.00	155
f.	Signature P. A. Strohl, D. Ferman and B. Dentaud. 8.1.1987; 22.1.1987; 5.11.1987.	11.50	85.00
g.	Signature of D. Ferman, B. Dentaud and A. Charriau. 3.3.1988-1.2.1990.	21.00	135
h.	Signature D. Bruneel, B. Dentaud and A. Charriau. 5.7.1990-2.5.1991.	17.00	115
i.	Signature D. Bruneel, J. Bonnardin and A. Charriau. 3.10.1991-7.1.1993.	16.00	110
j.	Signature D. Bruneel, J. Bonnardin and C. Vigier. 2.9.1993.	85.00	355
s.	Specimen. Overprint and perforated: *SPECIMEN*.	400	1,590

1993-97 Issue

#157-160 Many technical anti-counterfeiting devices added

157 50 Francs

VF UNC

1992-93. Purple and dark blue on blue, green and multicolor underprint. Drawing of *le Petit Prince* at left. Old airplane at top left, topographical map of Africa at center, Antoine de Saint-Exupéry at right. Back: Breguet XIV biplane. Name as Éxupéry, old law clause. Watermark: Antoine de Saint-Exupéry. 123x80mm.

		VF	UNC
a.	Signature D. Bruneel, J. Bonnardin and A. Charriau. 1992.	50.00	205
b.	Signature D. Bruneel, J. Bonnardin and C. Vigier. 1993.	5.00	30.00
s.	Specimen.	255	795

157A 50 Francs

VF UNC

1994-99. Drawing of *le Petit Prince* at left. Old airplane at top left, topographical map of Africa at center, Antoine de Saint-Exupéry at right. Back: Breguet XIV biplane. Name as Exupéry, new law clause. 123x80mm.

		VF	UNC
a.	Signature D. Bruneel, J. Bonnardin and C. Vigier. 1994. 8 cardinal points in compass solid. Underline *al.* in signature titles.	5.00	20.00
b.	Signature D. Bruneel, J. Bonnardin and C. Vigier. 1994. 8 cardinal points in compass striped. without underlined *al.* in signature title.	5.00	20.00
c.	Signature D. Bruneel, J. Bonnardin and Y. Barroux. 1996.	7.00	30.00
d.	Signature as c. 1997, 1999.	4.50	20.00

158 100 Francs

VF UNC

1997; 1998. Deep brown on orange, pink and light green underprint. Paul Cézanne at right. Signature D. Bruneel, J. Bonnardin and Y. Barroux. Back: Painting of fruit at left. Watermark: Paul Cézanne. 133x80mm.

		VF	UNC
a.	Issued note.	4.50	28.50
s.	Specimen.	200	680

159 200 Francs

VF UNC

1995-99. Brown and pink on multicolor underprint. Gustave Eiffel at right, observatory at upper left center, Eiffel tower truss at center. Back: View through tower base across exhibition grounds at left. Watermark: Gustave Eiffel. 145x80mm.

		VF	UNC
a.	Signature D. Bruneel, J. Bonnardin and C. Vigier. 1995; 1996.	14.00	75.00
b.	Signature D. Bruneel, J. Bonnardin and Y. Barroux. 1996; 1997.	12.50	65.00
c.	Signature D. Bruneel, J. Bonnardin and Y. Barroux. 1999.	8.50	45.00
s.	Specimen.	225	1,020

160 500 Francs

VF UNC

1994-2000. Dark green and black on multicolor underprint. Marie and Pierre Curie at center right. Segmented foil strip at left. Back: Laboratory utensils at left center. Watermark: Marie Curie. 154x80mm.

		VF	UNC
a.	1994-95. Signature D. Bruneel, J. Bonnardin and C. Vigier.	17.00	68.00
b.	1996. Signature D. Bruneel, J. Bonnardin and C. Vigier.	40.00	225
c.	1998. Signature D. Bruneel, J. Bonnardin and Y. Barroux.	17.00	68.00
d.	2000. Signature Y. Barroux, J. Bonnardin, A. Vienney.	23.00	170
s.	2000. Signature Y. Barroux, J. Bonnardin, A. Vienney.	255	1,135

Note: For later issues made for use in France see European Union listings.

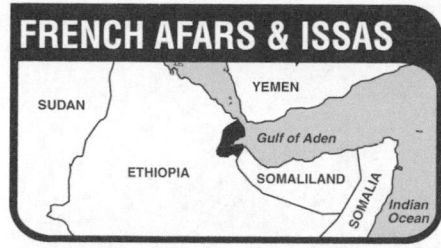

FRENCH AFARS & ISSAS

The French Overseas Territory of Afars and Issas (formerly French Somaliland, later to be independent as Djibouti) is located in northeast Africa at the Bab el Mandeb Strait connecting the Suez Canal and the Red Sea with the Gulf of Aden and the Indian Ocean, has an area of 8,494 sq. mi. (22,000 sq. km.) and a population of 542,000. Capital: Djibouti. The tiny nation has less than one sq. mi. of arable land, and no natural resources except salt, sand and camels. The commercial activities of the trans-shipment port of Djibouti and the Addis Ababa-Djibouti railroad are the basis of the economy. Salt, fish and hides are exported. French interest in former French Somaliland began in 1839 with concessions obtained by a French naval lieutenant from the provincial sultans. French Somaliland was made a protectorate in 1884 and its boundaries were delimited by the Franco-British and Ethiopian accords of 1887 and 1897. It became a colony in 1896 and a territory within the French Union in 1946. In 1958, it voted to join the new French Community as an overseas territory, and reaffirmed that choice by a referendum in March 1967. Its name was changed from French Somaliland to the French Territory of Afars and Issas on July 5, 1967. The French Tricolor, which had flown over the strategically important territory for 115 years, was lowered for the last time on June 27, 1977, when French Afars and Issas became Djibouti. Note: For later issues see Djibouti.

RULERS:
French to 1977

MONETARY SYSTEM:
1 Franc = 100 Centimes

FRENCH ADMINISTRATION

Trésor Public, Territoire Français des Afars et des Issas

1969 ND Issue

30   5000 Francs   **VF   UNC**
ND (1969.). Multicolor. Aerial view of Djibouti harbor at center. Back: Ruins at   275   750
center.

1973; 1974 ND Issue

31   500 Francs   **VF   UNC**
ND (1973). Multicolor. Ships at left center. Back: Rearing antelope at center.   50.00   185

32   1000 Francs   **VF   UNC**
ND (1974). Multicolor. Woman holding jug at left center. Back: Woman holding jug,   80.00   325
reversed image of note's face.

1975 ND Issue

33   500 Francs   **VF   UNC**
ND (1975). Multicolor. Man at left, rocks in sea, storks at right. Back: Stern of ship   20.00   80.00
at right.

34   1000 Francs   **VF   UNC**
ND (1975). Multicolor. Woman at left, people by diesel passenger trains at center.   35.00   150
Back: Trader with camels.

35   5000 Francs   **VF   UNC**
ND (1975). Multicolor. Man at right, forest scene at center. Back: Aerial view at   85.00   350
center.

FRENCH ANTILLES

French Antilles is made up of three French overseas departments, Guiana, Guadeloupe and Martinique, which issued a common currency from 1961-1975. It has an area of 1,609 sq. km., and a population of 842,247. Since 1975, Bank of France notes have circulated.

RULERS:
French

MONETARY SYSTEM:
1 Nouveau Franc = 100 "old" Francs
1 Franc = 100 Centimes
1 Euro = 100 Cents

SIGNATURE VARIETIES		
	Le Directeur Général	Le Président du Conseil de Surveillance
1	*André POSTEL-VINAY*	*Pierre CALVET 1959-1965*
2	*André POSTEL-VINAY*	*Bernard CLAPPIER 1966-1972*

FRENCH ADMINISTRATION

Institut d'Emission des Départements d'Outre-Mer
1961 ND Provisional Issue
Nouveau Franc System

1   1 Nouveau Franc on 100 Francs   VF   UNC
ND (1961). Multicolor. La Bourdonnais at left. Signature 1. Back: Woman at right.
  a. Issued note.   250   750
  s. Specimen.   —   600

2   10 Nouveaux Francs on 1000 Francs   VF   UNC
ND (1961). Multicolor. Fishermen from the Antilles. Signature 1.   1,000   3,000

3   50 Nouveaux Francs on 5000 Francs   VF   UNC
ND (1961). Multicolor. Woman with fruit bowl at center right. Signature 1.
  a. Issued note.   1,250   3,500
  s. Specimen.   —   2,000

Second 1961 ND Provisional Issue

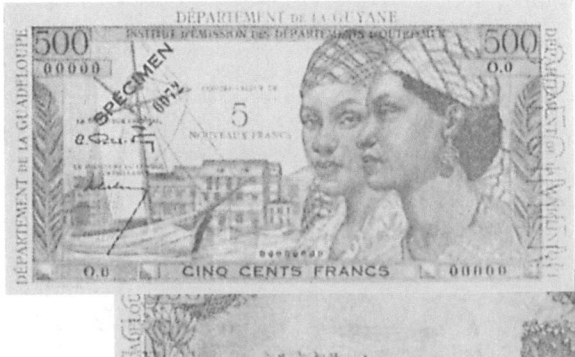

4   5 Nouveaux Francs on 500 Francs   VF   UNC
ND (1961). Brown on multicolor underprint. Sailboat at left, two women at right.
Signature 1. Back: Men with carts containing plants and wood.
  a. Issued note.   650   2,000
  s. Specimen.   —   2,500

Institut d'Emission des Départements d'Outre-Mer
République Francaise
1963 ND Issue

5	10 Nouveaux Francs	VF	UNC

ND (1963). Brown and green on multicolor underprint. Girl at right, coastal scenery in background. Signature 1. Back: People cutting sugar cane.

	a. Issued note.	200	650
	s. Specimen.	—	550

6	50 Nouveaux Francs	VF	UNC

ND (1963). Green on multicolor underprint. Banana harvest. Signature 1. Back: Shoreline with houses at left, man and woman at right.

	a. Issued note.	325	1,100
	s. Specimen.	—	1,000

1964 ND Issue

7	5 Francs	VF	UNC

ND (1964). Like #4, but smaller size. Brown on multicolor underprint. Sailboat at left, two women at right. Back: Men with carts containing plants and wood.

	a. Signature 1.	300	1,100
	b. Signature 2.	250	950
	s. As b. Specimen.	—	—

8	10 Francs	VF	UNC

ND (1964). Green on multicolor underprint. Banana harvest. Back: Shoreline with houses at left, man and woman at right.

	a. Signature 1.	185	600
	b. Signature 2.	150	500

9	50 Francs	VF	UNC

ND (1964). Banana harvest. Back: Shoreline with houses at left, man and woman at right.

	a. Signature 1.	300	1,000
	b. Signature 2.	275	900

10	100 Francs	VF	UNC

ND (1964). Brown and multicolor. General Schoelcher at center right. Back: Schoelcher at left center, various arms and galleon around.

	a. Signature 1.	500	1,500
	b. Signature 2.	450	1,350

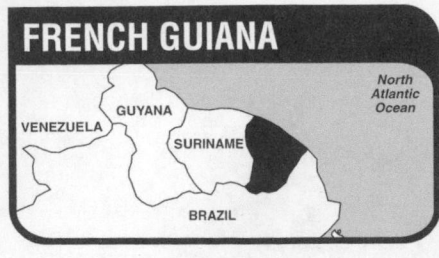

FRENCH GUIANA

The French Overseas Department of French Guiana, located on the northeast coast of South America, bordered by Surinam and Brazil, has an area of 32,252 sq. mi. (91,000 sq. km.) and a population of 173,000. Capital: Cayenne. Placer gold mining and shrimp processing are the chief industries. Shrimp, lumber, gold, cocoa and bananas are exported. The coast of Guiana was sighted by Columbus in 1498 and explored by Amerigo Vespucci in 1499. The French established the first successful trading stations and settlements, and placed the area under direct control of the French Crown in 1674. Portuguese and British forces occupied French Guiana for five years during the Napoleonic Wars. Devil's Island, the notorious penal colony in French Guiana where Capt. Alfred Dreyfus was imprisoned, was established in 1852 - and finally closed in 1947. When France adopted a new constitution in 1946, French Guiana voted to remain within the French Union as an overseas department.

Note: For later issues see French Antilles.

RULERS:
French

MONETARY SYSTEM:
1 Franc = 10 Decimes = 100 Centimes to 1960
1 Nouveau (new) Franc = 100 "old" Francs, 1961-
1 Euro = 100 Cents

FRENCH ADMINISTRATION

Caisse Centrale de la France d'Outre-Mer

1961 ND Provisional Issue

		VF	UNC
29	**1 Nouveau Franc on 100 Francs** ND (1961). Multicolor. La Bourdonnais at left, women at right. Back: B. d'Esnambuc at left, sailing ship at right.	45.00	325
30	**5 Nouveaux Francs on 500 Francs** ND (1961). Overprint on #24. Multicolor. Sailboat at left, two women at right.	165	675
31	**10 Nouveaux Francs on 1000 Francs** ND (1961). Overprint on #27. Multicolor. Fishermen.	500	1,300
32	**10 Nouveaux Francs on 1000 Francs** ND. Overprint on #25. Multicolor. Two women at right. Back: Woman at right.	350	900
33	**50 Nouveaux Francs on 5000 Francs** ND. Multicolor. Woman with fruit bowl.	800	1,800

Note: For later issues see French Antilles.

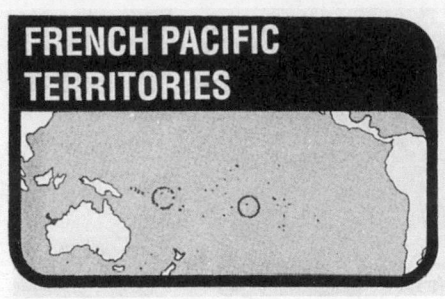

FRENCH PACIFIC TERRITORIES

The French Pacific Territories include French Polynesia, New Caledonia and formerly the New Hebrides Condominium. Area is 1,359 sq. mi. (3,521 sq. km.), and population is 268,270. For earlier issues also refer to French Oceania and Tahiti.

MONETARY SYSTEM:
1 Franc (CFP) = 100 Centimes

SIGNATURE VARIETIES

W.P.M.	Directeur Général	President du Conseil de surveillance	Directeur Délégué or Directeur
1	Yves Roland-Billecart 1985-1989	Jacques Waitzenegger 1985-1990	
2	Philippe Jurgensen 1989-1995	Denis Ferman 1990-2000	
3	Philippe Jurgensen 1989-1995	Denis Ferman 1990-2000	Olivier Beugnot 1992-1995
4	Antoine Pouillieute 1995-2002	Denis Ferman 1990-2000	Olivier Beugnot 1992-1995
5	Antoine Pouillieute 1995-2002	Denis Ferman 1990-2000	Gilles Audren 1995-2002
5B	Antoine Pouillieute 1995-2002	Denis Ferman 1990-2000	Gilles Audren 1995-2002
6	Antoine Pouillieute 1995-2002	Jean Paul Redoiun 2000-2006	Gilles Audren 1995-2002
7	Antoine Pouillieute 1995-2002	Jean Paul Redoiun 2000-2006	Teyssere 2002-2003
8	Severoni 2002-2006	Jean Paul Redoiun 2000-2006	Teyssere 2002-2003
9	Severoni 2002-2006	Jean Paul Redoiun 2000-2006	T. Comaille 2003-2006
10	Severoni 2002-2006	j.p. Landau 2007-2010	Patrick Besse 2006-
11	A. Vienney 2008-2010	j.p. Landau 2007-2010	Patrick Besse 2006-
12	Yves Barroux 2010-2012	Christian Noyer 2010-	Patrick Besse 2006-
13	de Seze 2012-	Christian Noyer 2010-	Patrick Besse 2006-

FRENCH ADMINISTRATION
Institut d'Emission d'Outre-Mer
1985-96 ND Issue

Notes like those of New Caledonia or New Hebrides but without *NOUMEA* **or** *PAPEETE. Valued in CPF francs (change frans Pacifique). Common currency of French Polynesia, New Caledonia, and Wallis & Futuna Islands. Signature varieties correspond to those used for New Caledonia and New Hebrides issues.*

1	500 Francs	VF	UNC
	ND (1992). Multicolor. Sailboat at center, fisherman at right. Back: Man at left, objects at right. 150x80mm.		
	a. 2 signatures. Without security thread. Signature 2.	FV	25.00
	b. 3 Signatures. With security thread. Signature 3.	FV	20.00
	c. Signature 5b. Error Law.	FV	20.00
	d. Signature 8. Law corrected.	FV	20.00
	e. Signature 9.	FV	20.00
	f. Signature 11.	FV	20.00
	g. Signature 12.	FV	20.00
	h. Signature 13.	FV	20.00

2	1000 Francs	VF	UNC
	ND (1996). Multicolor. Hut in palm trees at left, girl at right. 160x85mm.		
	a. Signature 3.	FV	32.50
	b. Signature 4.	FV	30.00
	c. Signature 5.	FV	30.00
	d. Signature 5B.	FV	30.00
	e. Signature 6.	FV	30.00
	f. Signature 7	FV	30.00
	g. Signature 8.	FV	30.00
	h. Signature 9.	FV	30.00
	i. Signature 10.	FV	30.00
	j. Signature 11.	FV	30.00
	k. Signature 12.	FV	30.00
	l. Signature 13.	FV	13.00

3	5000 Francs	VF	UNC
	ND (1996). Multicolor. Bougainville at left, sailing ships at center. 172x90mm.		
	a. Signature 3.	FV	140
	b. Signature 4.	FV	140
	c. Signature 5.	FV	140
	d. Signature 5B.	FV	140
	e. Signature 6.	FV	140
	f. Signature 8.	FV	140
	g. Signature 9.	FV	140
	h. Signature 11.	FV	140
	i. Signature 12.	FV	140
	s. Specimen. Perforated cancelled.	—	750

4	10,000 Francs	VF	UNC
	ND (1985). Multicolor. Tahitian girl with floral headdress at upper left topuristic bungalows at center. Back: Fish at center, Melanesian girl wearing flower at right on back. Watermark: Two ethnic heads. 172x92mm.		
	a. 2 signatures. Without security thread. Signature 1.	FV	250
	b. 3 signatures. With security thread and new law on back. Signature 5.	FV	225
	c. Signature 5B.	FV	225
	d. Signature 8.	FV	225
	e. Signature 9.	FV	225
	f. Signature 11.	FV	225
	g. Signature 12.	FV	225
5	**500 Francs**	**VF**	**UNC**
	ND (2014). Kava leaves.	FV	20.00
6	**1000 Francs**	**VF**	**UNC**
	ND (2014). Tortoise.	FV	30.00
7	**5000 Francs**	**VF**	**UNC**
	ND (2014). Coralfish.	FV	140
8	**10,000 Francs**	**VF**	**UNC**
	ND (2014). Hut and palm trees.	FV	225

GABON

The Gabonese Republic, a member of the French Community, straddles the equator on the west coast of Africa. The hot and humid rain forest country has an area of 267,667 sq. km. and a population of 1.48 million, almost all of Bantu origin. Capital: Libreville. Extravagantly rich in resources, Gabon exports crude oil, manganese ore, gold and timbers.

Only two autocratic presidents have ruled Gabon since independence from France in 1960. The current president of Gabon, El Hadj Omar Bongo Ondimba - one of the longest-serving heads of state in the world - has dominated the country's political scene for four decades. President Bongo introduced a nominal multiparty system and a new constitution in the early 1990s. However, allegations of electoral fraud during local elections in 2002-03 and the presidential elections in 2005 have exposed the weaknesses of formal political structures in Gabon. Gabon's political opposition remains weak, divided, and financially dependent on the current regime. Despite political conditions, a small population, abundant natural resources, and considerable foreign support have helped make Gabon one of the more prosperous and stable African countries.

Note: For related currency, see the Equatorial African States.

RULERS:
French to 1960

MONETARY SYSTEM:
1 Franc = 100 Centimes

SIGNATURE VARIETIES:
Refer to introduction to Central African States.

RÉPUBLIQUE GABONAISE
Banque Centrale
1971 ND Issue

		VF	UNC
1	**10,000 Francs**		
	ND (1971). Multicolor. President O. Bongo at right, mask at left, mine elevator at center. Signature 1. Back: Statue at left and right, tractor plowing at center.		
	a. Issued note.	200	750
	s. Specimen. Overprinted and perforated: *SPECIMEN*.	—	850

Banque des États de l'Afrique Centrale
1974 ND Issue

		VF	UNC
2	**500 Francs**		
	ND (1974); 1978. Lilac-brown on multicolor underprint. Woman wearing kerchief at left, logging at center. Back: Mask at left, students and chemical testing at center, statue at right.		
	a. Engraved. Signature 6. ND (1974).	7.00	30.00
	b. Lithographed. Signature 9. 1.4.1978.	5.00	20.00

		VF	UNC
3	**1000 Francs**		
	ND (1974; 1978); 1978-84. Red and blue on multicolor underprint. Ship and oil refinery at center, President O. Bongo at right. Back: Mask at left, trains, planes and bridge at center, statue at right.		
	a. Signature 4 with titles: *LE DIRECTEUR GÉNÉRAL* and *UN CENSEUR*. Engraved. Watermark: Antelope head in half profile. ND (1974).	150	350
	b. Like a. Signature 6.	25.00	80.00
	c. Signature 6 with titles: *LE DIRECTEUR GÉNÉRAL* and *UN CENSEUR*. Lithographed. Watermark: Antelope head in profile. ND (1978).	15.00	50.00
	d. Signature 9 with titles: *LE GOUVERNEUR* and *UN CENSEUR*. Lithographed. Watermark: Antelope head in profile. 1.4.1978; 1.1.1983; 1.6.1984.	10.00	35.00

		VF	UNC
4	**5000 Francs**		
	ND (1974; 1978). Brown. Oil refinery at left, open pit mining and President O. Bongo at right. Back: Mask at left, buildings at center, statue at right.		
	a. Signature 4 with titles: *LE DIRECTEUR GENERAL* and *UN CENSEUR*. ND (1974).	100	400
	b. Like a. Signature 6.	50.00	200
	c. Signature 9 with titles: *LE GOUVERNEUR* and *UN CENSEUR*. ND (1978).	50.00	200
	x1. Error. As a. Without signature.	60.00	200
	x2. Error. As c. Without signature.	50.00	200

5   10,000 Francs   VF   UNC
ND (1974; 1978). Multicolor. President O. Bongo at right, mask at left, mine
elevator at center. Back: Statue at left and right, tractor polwing at center, new
bank name.
   a. Signature 6 with titles: *LE DIRECTEUR GÉNÉRAL* and *UN CENSEUR.*   75.00   250
     ND (1974).
   b. Signature 9 with titles: *LE GOUVERNEUR* and *UN CENSEUR.* ND (1978).   50.00   200
   s. Specimen. Perforated and overprint *SPECIMEN..*   —   350

1983; 1984 ND Issue

6   5000 Francs   VF   UNC
ND (1984-91). Brown on multicolor underprint. Mask at left, woman with fronds at
right. Back: Plowing and mine ore conveyor.
   a. Signature 9. (1984).   20.00   75.00
   b. Signature 14. (1991).   15.00   50.00
   s. As a. Specimen. Overprinted and perforated: *SPECIMEN.*   —   250

7   10,000 Francs   VF   UNC
ND (1983-91). Brown and green on multicolor underprint. Stylized antelope heads
at left, woman at right. Back: Loading fruit onto truck at left.
   a. Signature 9. (1984).   35.00   150
   b. Signature 14. (1991).   25.00   100
   s. Specimen. Perforated and overprint *SPECIMEN.*   —   150

1985 Issue

8   500 Francs   VF   UNC
1.1.1985. Brown on orange and multicolor underprint. Carving and jug at center.   4.00   15.00
Signature 9. Back: Man carving mask at left center. Watermark: Carving.

9   1000 Francs   VF   UNC
1.1.1985. Deep blue on multicolor underprint. Carving at left, map at center, Presi-   9.50   35.00
dent O. Bongo at right. Incomplete outline map of Chad at top center. Signature
9. Back: Elephant at left, animals at center, man carving at right. Watermark:
Carving.

1986 Issue

10   1000 Francs   VF   UNC
1986-91. Deep blue on multicolor underprint. Carving at left, map at center,
President O. Bongo at right. Complete outline map of Chad at top center. Back:
Elephant at left, animals at center, man carving at right.
   a. Signature 9. 1.1.1986; 1.1.1987; 1.1.1990.   7.50   30.00
   b. Signature 14. 1.1.1991.   7.00   25.00

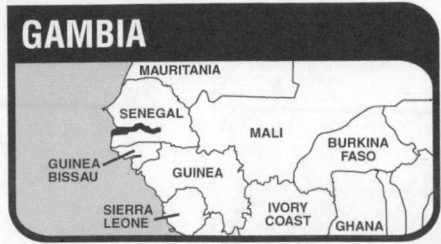

GAMBIA

The Republic of The Gambia, an independent member of the British Commonwealth, occupies a long strip of land encompassing both sides of West Africa's Gambia River, and completely surrounded by Senegal. The republic, one of Africa's smallest, has an area of 11,300 sq. km. and a population of 1.76 million. Capital: Banjul. Agriculture and tourism are the principal industries. Peanuts constitute 95 per cent of export earnings.

The Gambia gained its independence from the UK in 1965. Geographically surrounded by Senegal, it formed a short-lived federation of Senegambia between 1982 and 1989. In 1991 the two nations signed a friendship and cooperation treaty, but tensions have flared up intermittently since then. Yahya A. J. J. Jammeh led a military coup in 1994 that overthrew the president and banned political activity. A new constitution and presidential elections in 1996, followed by parliamentary balloting in 1997, completed a nominal return to civilian rule. Jammeh has been elected president in all subsequent elections, including most recently in late 2006.

RULERS:
British to 1970

MONETARY SYSTEM:
1 Shilling = 12 Pence
1 Pound = 20 Shillings to 1970
1 Dalasi = 100 Bututs 1970-

REPLACEMENT NOTES:
#13-16, Z prefix.

	SIGNATURE VARIETIES				
1	*J.B. Loynes* CHAIRMAN	*[sig]* DIRECTOR	**10**	*[sig]* GENERAL MANAGER	*[sig]* GOVERNOR
2	*[sig]* GENERAL MANAGER	*[sig]* GOVERNOR	**11**	*[sig]*	*[sig]*
3	*[sig]*	*S.S. Sisay*	**12**	*[sig]*	*[sig]*
4	*[sig]*	*S.S. Sisay*	**13**	*[sig]*	*[sig]*
5	*[sig]*	*S.S. Sisay*	**14**	*H.Salla*	*[sig]*
6	*[sig]*	*S.S. Sisay*	**15**		
8	*[sig]*	*D.A.Senghore*	**16**		
9	*[sig]* GENERAL MANAGER	*D.A.Senghore* GOVERNOR			

BRITISH ADMINISTRATION

The Gambia Currency Board
1965 ND Issue
Pound System

1   10 Shillings   VF   UNC
ND (1965-70). Green and brown on multicolor underprint. Sailboat at left. Signature 1. Back: Workers in field. Watermark: Crocodile's head.
a. Issued note.	25.00	150
s. Specimen.	—	200
ct. Color trial. Blue and green on multicolor underprint.	—	350

2   1 Pound   VF   UNC
ND (1965-70). Red and brown on multicolor underprint. Sailboat at left. Signature 1. Back: Loading sacks at dockside. Watermark: Crocodile's head.
a. Issued note.	40.00	205
s. Specimen.	—	290
ct. Color trial. Brown and gray on multicolor underprint.	—	400

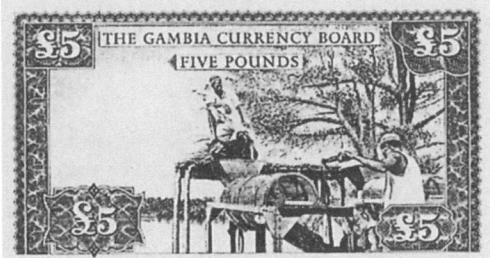

3   5 Pounds   VF   UNC
ND (1965-70). Blue and green on multicolor underprint. Sailboat at left. Signature 1. Back: Man and woman operating agricultural machine at center right. Watermark: Crocodile's head.
a. Issued note.	90.00	125
s. Specimen.	—	525
ct. Color trial. Gray-brown and green on multicolor underprint.	—	450

REPUBLIC

Central Bank of The Gambia
1971; 1972 ND Issue
Dalasi System

4   1 Dalasi   VF   UNC
ND (1971-87). Purple on multicolor underprint. Sailboat at left, Pres. D. Kairaba Jawara at right. Back: Workers in field. Watermark: Crocodile's head.
a. Signature 2.	35.00	100
b. Signature 3.	45.00	105
c. Signature 4.	15.00	52.50
d. Signature 5.	10.00	31.00
e. Signature 6.	4.75	14.00
f. Signature 7.	4.50	8.75
g. Signature 8.	9.00	14.50
p. Proof.	—	500
s. Specimen. Overprint: *SPECIMEN* and Punch hole cancelled.	—	170

5 5 Dalasis   **VF UNC**

ND (1972-86). Red on multicolor underprint. Sailboat at left, Pres. D. Kairaba Jawara at right. Back: Loading sacks at dockside. Watermark: Crocodile's head.

	VF	UNC
a. Signature 2.	75.00	185
b. Signature 4.	15.00	90.00
c. Signature 6.	10.00	48.00
d. Signature 7.	9.00	30.00
s. Specimen. Overprint: *SPECIMEN* and Punch hole cancelled.	—	145

6 10 Dalasis   **VF UNC**

ND (1972-86). Green on multicolor underprint. Sailboat at left, Pres. D. Kairaba Jawara at right. Back: Fishermen in boat with net. Watermark: Crocodile's head.

	VF	UNC
a. Signature 3.	30.00	145
b. Signature 6.	15.00	65.00
c. Signature 7	15.00	60.00
s. Specimen. Overprint: *SPECIMEN* and Punch hole cancelled.	—	300
ct. Color trial. Purple-brown on multicolor underprint.	—	400

7 25 Dalasis   **VF UNC**

ND (1972-83). Blue on multicolor underprint. Sailboat at left, Pres. D. Kairaba Jawara at right. Back: Man and woman operating agricultural machine at left center. Watermark: Crocodile's head.

	VF	UNC
a. Signature 2.	150	700
b. Signature 6.	40.00	150
s. As a, b. Specimen. Overprint: *SPECIMEN* and Punch hole cancelled.	—	550
ct. Color trial. Slate on multicolor underprint.	—	750

1978 ND Commemorative Issue

#8, Opening of Central Bank on 18.2.1978

8 1 Dalasi   **VF UNC**

ND (1978). Purple on multicolor underprint. Sailboat at left, Pres. D. Kairaba Jawara at right. Signature 5. Back: Central Bank building on back; commemorative legend beneath. Watermark: Crocodile's head.

	VF	UNC
a. Issued note.	30.00	190
s. Specimen. Overprint: *SPECIMEN* and Punch hole cancelled.	—	200

1987 ND Issue

9 5 Dalasis   **VF UNC**

ND (1987-90). Red and orange on multicolor underprint. Sailboat at left, President D. Kairaba Jawara at right, line of microprint under text: *PROMISE TO PAY*. Back: Fishermen in boat with net. Watermark: Crocodile's head.

	VF	UNC
a. Signature 8.	8.00	41.00
b. Signature 10.	7.00	20.00

10 10 Dalasis   **VF UNC**

ND (1987-90). Green on multicolor underprint. Sailboat at left, Pres. D. Kairaba Jawara at right, line of microprint under text: *PROMISE TO PAY*. Back: Fishermen in boat with net. Watermark: Crocodile's head.

	VF	UNC
a. Signature 8 with title: *GOVERNOR* at right.	10.00	35.00
b. Signature 9 with title: *ACTING GOVERNOR* at right.	10.00	26.00

11 25 Dalasis   **VF UNC**

ND (1987-90). Blue on multicolor underprint. Sailboat at left, Pres. D. Kairaba Jawara at right, line of microprint under text: *PROMISE TO PAY*. Back: Man and woman operating agricultural machine at left center. Watermark: Crocodile's head.

	VF	UNC
a. Signature 8 with title: *GOVERNOR* at right.	30.00	175
b. Signature 9 with title: *ACTING GOVERNOR* at right.	22.50	100
c. Signature 10.	17.00	90.00
s. Specimen.	—	300

1989-91 ND Issue

#12-15 Replacement notes: serial # prefix *Z/1*.

12 5 Dalasis   **VF UNC**

ND (1991-95). Red and orange on multicolor underprint. Giant Kingfisher at center, Pres. D Kairaba Jawara at right. Microprinting of bank name above and below title. Back: Herding cattle. Watermark: Crocodile's head. 132x69mm.

	VF	UNC
a. Signature 10.	4.00	22.00
b. Signature 11.	5.50	8.00
s. Specimen.	—	90.00

13   10 Dalasis   VF   UNC

ND (1991-95). Dark green, green and olive-green on multicolor underprint. Sacred Ibis at center, Pres. D Kairaba Jawara at right. Microprinting of bank name above and below title. Back: Abuko Earth satellite station at left center. Watermark: Crocodile's head. 138x72mm.

a. Signature 10.	7.00	12.00
b. Signature 11.	6.00	10.75
s. Specimen.	—	90.00

14   25 Dalasis   VF   UNC

ND (1991-95). Dark blue-violet, black and blue on multicolor underprint. Carmine Bee Eater at center, Pres. D Kairaba Jawara at right. Microprinting of bank name above and below title. Signature 10. Back: Government house at left center. Watermark: Crocodile's head. 144x75mm.

a. Issued note.	9.00	23.00
s. Specimen.	—	200

15   50 Dalasis   VF   UNC

ND (1989-95). Purple and violet on multicolor underprint. Hoopoe birds at center, Pres. D. Kairaba Jawara at right. Microprinting of bank name above and below title. Signature 10. Back: Stone circles at Wassu. Watermark: Crocodile's head. 154x78mm.

a. Issued note.	25.00	50.00
s. Specimen.	—	145

1996 ND Issue

#16-19 Replacement notes: Serial # prefix *Z.*

16   5 Dalasis   VF   UNC

ND (1996). Red, orange and dark brown on multicolor underprint. Giant Kingfisher at center, young girl a right. Signature 12. Back: Herding cattle. Watermark: Crocodile's head, without imprint. 132x69mm.

a. Issued note.	3.50	5.00
s. Specimen.	—	90.00

17   10 Dalasis   VF   UNC

ND (1996). Dark green, bright green and olive-green on multicolor underprint. Sacred Ibis at center, young boy at right. Signature 12. Back: Abuko Earth satellite station at left center. Watermark: Crocodile's head, without imprint. 138x72mm.

a. Issued note.	4.25	8.00
s. Specimen.	—	90.00

18   25 Dalasis   VF   UNC

ND (1996). Deep blue-violet, black and blue on multicolor underprint. Carmine Bee Eater at center, man at right. Signature 12. Back: Government house at left center. Watermark: Crocodile's head, without imprint. 144x75mm.

a. Issued note.	9.00	35.00
s. Specimen.	—	125

19   50 Dalasis   VF   UNC

ND (1996). Purple and violet on multicolor underprint. Hoopoe birds at center, woman at right. Signature 12. Back: Stone circles a Wassu. Watermark: Crocodile's head, without imprint. 154x78mm.

a. Issued note.	17.50	35.00
s. Specimen.	—	95.00

2001 ND Issue

20   5 Dalasis   VF   UNC
ND (2001). Multicolor. Giant Kingfisher at center, young girl at right. Signature
12. Ascending size vertical serial number. Back: Herding cattle. Watermark:
Crocodile's head, without imprint. 132x69mm.
  a. Signature 13.   FV   4.00
  b. Signature 14.   FV   3.50
  c. Signature 15.   FV   2.50

21   10 Dalasis   VF   UNC
ND (2001). Multicolor. Sacred Ibis at center, young boy at right. Signature 12.
Ascending size vertical serial number. Back: Abuko Earth satellite station at left
center. Watermark: Crocodile's head, without imprint. 138x72mm.
  a. Signature 13.   FV   7.50
  b. Signature 14.   FV   4.50
  c. Signature 15.   FV   3.00

22   25 Dalasis   VF   UNC
ND (2001). Multicolor. Carmine Bee Eater at center, man at right. Ascending
size vertical serial number. Signature 12. Back: Government house at left center.
Watermark: Crocodile's head, without imprint. 144x75mm.
  a. Signature 13.   FV   15.00
  b. Signature 14.   FV   8.00
  c. Signatrure 15.   FV   5.00

23   50 Dalasis   VF   UNC
ND (2001). Multicolor. Hoopoe birds at center, woman at right. Ascending
size vertical serial number. Signature 12. Back: Stone circles at Wassu.
Watermark: Crocodile's head, without imprint. 154x78mm.
  a. Signature 13.   10.00   14.00
  b. Signature 14.   7.50   10.00
  c. Signature 15.   FV   6.00

24   100 Dalasis   VF   UNC
ND (2001). Multicolor. Senegal Parrot at center, male bust facing at right. Watermark: Crocodile's head, without imprint. 157x81mm.
  a. Signature 13.   12.50   20.00
  b. Signature 14.   15.00   38.00
  c. Signature 15.   FV   8.50

2006 ND Issue

25   5 Dalasis   VF   UNC
2006. Multicolor. Giant Kingfisher at center, young girl at right. Signature 15. Back: FV   2.00
Hearding cattle. 132x69mm.

26   10 Dalasis   VF   UNC
2006. Multicolor. Sacred Ibis at center, young boy at right. Signature 15. Back:
Abuko Earth satellite station at left center. 138x72mm.
  a. Signature 15.   FV   3.00
  b. Signature 16.   FV   3.00
  c. Signature 17.   FV   8.00

27   25 Dalasis   VF   UNC
2006. Multicolor. Carmine Bee Eater at cetner, man at right. Signature 15. Back:
Government house at left center. 144x75mm.
  a. Signature 15.   FV   4.00
  b. Signature 16.   FV   4.00
  c. Signature 17.   FV   4.00

28   50 Dalasis

2006. Multicolor. Hoopoe birds at center, woman at right. Back: Stone circles at
Wassu. 154x78mm.

		VF	UNC
a. Signature 15.		FV	6.00
b. Signature 16.		FV	6.00
c. Signature 17.		FV	6.00

29   100 Dalasis

2006; 2010. Multicolor. Back: Arch 22 Monument. 157x81mm.

		VF	UNC
a. Signature 15. Hologram with value at left center.		FV	10.00
b. Signature 16. Hologram with man's head.		FV	9.00

2014 Commemorative Issue

30   20 Dalasis   VF   UNC

22.7.2014. Green. Y. Jammeh at right. 20th Anniversary of Revolution.   FV   3.50

2015 ND Issue

31   5 Dalasis   VF   UNC

ND (2015). Red. Y. Jammeh at right. 132x69mm.   FV   2.00

32   10 Dalasis   VF   UNC

ND (2015). Green. Y. Jammeh at right. 138x72mm.   FV   3.00

33   20 Dalasis   VF   UNC

ND (2015). Blue. Y. Jammeh at right.   FV   3.50

34   50 Dalasis   VF   UNC

ND (2015). Purple. Y. Jammeh at right. 154x78mm.   FV   6.00

35   100 Dalasis   VF   UNC

ND (2015). Green, brown, blue. Y. Jammeh at right. 157x81mm.   FV   11.00

36   200 Dalasis   VF   UNC

ND (2015). Brown. Y. Jammeh at right.   FV   20.00

GEORGIA

Georgia is bounded by the Black Sea to the west and by Turkey, Armenia and Azerbaijan. It occupies the western part of Transcaucasia covering an area of 69,700 sq. km. and a population of 4.63 million. Capital: Tbilisi. Hydro-electricity, minerals, forestry and agriculture are the chief industries.

The region of present-day Georgia contained the ancient kingdoms of Colchis and Kartli-Iberia. The area came under Roman influence in the first centuries A.D. and Christianity became the state religion in the 330s. Domination by Persians, Arabs, and Turks was followed by a Georgian golden age (11th-13th centuries) that was cut short by the Mongol invasion of 1236. Subsequently, the Ottoman and Persian empires competed for influence in the region. Georgia was absorbed into the Russian Empire in the 19th century. Independent for three years (1918-1921) following the Russian revolution, it was forcibly incorporated into the USSR until the Soviet Union dissolved in 1991. An attempt by the incumbent Georgian government to manipulate national legislative elections in November 2003 touched off widespread protests that led to the resignation of Eduard Shevardnadze, president since 1995. New elections in early 2004 swept Mikheil Saakashvili into power along with his National Movement party. Progress on market reforms and democratization has been made in the years since independence, but this progress has been complicated by Russian assistance and support to the breakaway regions of Abkhazia and South Ossetia. Georgian military action in South Ossetia in early August 2008 led to a Russian military response that not only occupied the breakaway areas, but large portions of Georgia proper as well. Russian troops pulled back from most occupied Georgian territory, but in late August 2008 Russia unilaterally recognized the independence of Abkhazia and South Ossetia. This action was strongly condemned by most of the world's nations and international organizations.

MONETARY SYSTEM:
1 Lari = 100 Thetri to 1995
1 Lari = 1,000,000 'old' Laris, 1995

REPUBLIC OF GEORGIA

Georgian National Bank

First 1993 *KUPONI* ND Issue

#25-32 Fractional serial # prefix w/1 as denominator.

25	5 (Laris)	VF	UNC

ND (1993). Dull brown on lilac underprint. View of Tbilisi at center right with equestrian statue of King V. Gorgosal in foreground, Mount Tatzminda in background. Rosettes at sides of value. Back: Cave dwellings at left center. Rosettes at sides of value. Watermark: Hexagonal design repeated. 1.00 / 4.00

26	10 (Laris)	VF	UNC

ND (1993). Yellow-brown on lilac underprint. View of Tbilisi at center right with equestrian statue of King V. Gorgosal in foreground, Mount Tatzminda in background. Back: Cave dwellings at left center. Watermark: Hexagonal design repeated. 1.00 / 6.00

27	50 (Laris)	VF	UNC

ND (1993). Light blue on lilac underprint. View of Tbilisi at center right with equestrian statue of King V. Gorgosal in foreground, Mount Tatzminda in background. Back: Cave dwellings at left center. Watermark: Hexagonal design repeated. 1.00 / 8.00

28	100 (Laris)	VF	UNC

ND (1993). Greenish gray and light brown on lilac underprint. View of Tbilisi at center right with equestrian statue of King V. Gorgosal in foreground, Mount Tatzminda in background. Back: Cave dwellings at left center. Watermark: Hexagonal design repeated. 1.00 / 10.00

29	500 (Laris)	VF	UNC

ND (1993). Purple on lilac underprint. View of Tbilisi at center right with equestrian statue of King V. Gorgosal in foreground, Mount Tatzminda in background. Back: Cave dwellings at left center. Watermark: Hexagonal design repeated. 2.00 / 12.00

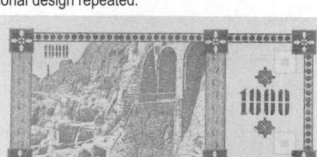

30	1000 (Laris)	VF	UNC

ND (1993). Blue-gray and brown on lilac underprint. View of Tbilisi at center right with equestrian statue of King V. Gorgosal in foreground, Mount Tatzminda in background. Back: Cave dwellings at left center. Watermark: Hexagonal design repeated. 3.00 / 15.00

31	5000 (Laris)	VF	UNC

ND (1993). Green and brown on lilac underprint. View of Tbilisi at center right with equestrian statue of King V. Gorgosal in foreground, Mount Tatzminda in background. Back: Cave dwellings at left center. Watermark: Hexagonal design repeated. 3.00 / 10.00

32	10,000 (Laris)	VF	UNC

ND (1993). Violet on lilac and brown underprint. View of Tbilisi at center right with equestrian statue of King V. Gorgosal in foreground, Mount Tatzminda in background. Back: Cave dwellings at left center. Watermark: Hexagonal design repeated. 5.00 / 20.00

Second 1993 *KUPONI* ND Issue

#33-38 Fractional serial # prefix w/2 as denominator.

33	1 (Laris)	VF	UNC

ND (1993). Red-orange and light brown on lilac underprint. View of Tbilisi at center right with equestrian statue of King V. Gorgosal in foreground, Mount Tatzminda in background. Ornate triangular design at left of large value in box at left center. Back: Cave dwellings at left center. Ornate triangular design at sides of value at right. Watermark: Hexagonal design repeated. 0.50 / 2.00

34	3 (Laris)	VF	UNC

ND (1993). Purple and light brown on lilac underprint. View of Tbilisi at center right with equestrian statue of King V. Gorgosal in foreground, Mount Tatzminda in background. Ornate triangular design at left of large value in box at left center. Back: Cave dwellings at left center. Ornate triangular design at sides of value at right. Watermark: Hexagonal design repeated. 0.50 / 2.00

35 5 (Laris)

VF UNC
0.50 3.00

ND (1993). Dull brown on lilac underprint. View of Tbilisi at center right with equestrian statue of King V. Gorgosal in foreground, Mount Tatzminda in background. Ornate triangular designat left of large value in box at left center. Back: Cave dwellings at left center. Ornate triangular design at sides of value at right. Watermark: Hexagonal design repeated.

36 10 (Laris)

VF UNC
0.50 2.00

ND (1993). Yellow-brown on lilac underprint. View of Tbilisi at center right with equestrian statue of King V. Gorgosal in foreground, Mount Tatzminda in background. Ornate triangular design at left of large value in box at left center. Back: Cave dwellings at left center. Ornate triangular design at sides of value at right. Watermark: Hexagonal design repeated.

37 50 (Laris)

VF UNC
0.50 2.00

ND (1993). Light blue on lilac underprint. View of Tbilisi at center right with equestrian statue of King V. Gorgosal in foreground, Mount Tatzminda in background. Ornate triangular design at left of large value in box at left center. Back: Cave dwellings at left center. Ornate triangular design at sides of value at right. Watermark: Hexagonal design repeated.

38 100 (Laris)

VF UNC
1.00 4.00

ND (1993). Greenish gray and light brown on lilac underprint. View of Tbilisi at center right with equestrian statue of King V. Gorgosal in foreground, Mount Tatzminda in background. Ornate triangular design at left of large value in box at left center. Back: Cave dwellings at left center. Ornate triangular design at sides of value at right. Watermark: Hexagonal design repeated.

Third 1993 Dated Issue

#39-42 Fractional serial # prefix w/3 as denominator.

39 10,000 (Laris)

VF UNC
1.00 8.00

1993. Violet on lilac and brown underprint. View of Tbilisi at center right with equestrian statue of King V. Gorgosal in foreground, Mount Tatzminda in background. Back: Cave dwellings at left center. Watermark: Hexagonal design repeated.

40 25,000 (Laris)

VF UNC
3.00 10.00

1993. Orange and dull brown on lilac underprint. View of Tbilisi at center right with equestrian statue of King V. Gorgosal in foreground, Mount Tatzminda in background. Back: Cave dwellings at left center. Watermark: Hexagonal design repeated.

41 50,000 (Laris)

VF UNC
2.00 6.00

1993. Pale red-brown and tan on lilac underprint. View of Tbilisi at center right with equestrian statue of King V. Gorgosal in foreground, Mount Tatzminda in background. Back: Cave dwellings at left center. Watermark: Hexagonal design repeated.

42 100,000 (Laris)

VF UNC
2.00 8.00

1993. Olive-green and brown on lilac underprint. View of Tbilisi at center right with equestrian statue of King V. Gorgosal in foreground, Mount Tatzminda in background. Back: Cave dwellings at left center. Watermark: Hexagonal design repeated.

Fourth 1993 Dated Issue

43 250 (Laris)

VF UNC

1993. Dark blue on green, lilac and light blue underprint. Griffin at left and right of ornate round design at center. Back: Two bunches of grapes with vine above and below value on vertical format. Watermark: Isometric rectangular design.
  a. With security thread.   0.50   2.00
  b. Without security thread.   —   —

44 2000 (Laris)

VF UNC
1.00 4.00

1993. Green and blue on gold and green underprint. Griffin at left and right of ornate round design at center. Back: Two bunches of grapes with vine above and below value on vertical format. Watermark: Isometric rectangular design.

45 3000 (Laris)

VF UNC
1.00 4.00

1993. Brown and yellow on light brown underprint. Griffin at left and right of ornate round design at center. Back: Two bunches of grapes with vine above and below value on vertical format. Watermark: Isometric rectangular design.

46   20,000 (Laris)

1993; 1994. Purple on light red and blue underprint. Griffin at left and right of ornate round design at center. Back: Two bunches of grapes with vine above and below value on vertical format. Watermark: Isometric rectangular design.

	VF	UNC
a. Large watermark. 1993.	2.00	6.00
b. With security foil printing at left edge of signature. Small watermark. 1994.	1.00	3.00

1994 Issue

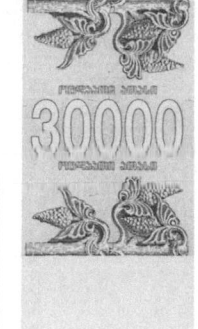

47   30,000 (Laris)   VF 2.00 UNC 6.00

1994. Dull red-brown on pale orange and light gray underprint. Griffin at left and right of ornate round design at center. Security foil at left. Back: Two bunches of grapes with vine above and below value on vertical format. Watermark: Isometric rectangular design repeated.

48   50,000 (Laris)   VF 2.00 UNC 6.00

1994. Dark olive-green and dull black on pale olive-green and tan underprint. Griffin at left and right of ornate round design at center. Security foil at left. Back: Two bunches of grapes with vine above and below value on vertical format. Watermark: Isometric rectangular design repeated.

48A   100,000 (Laris)   VF UNC

1994. Dark gray on light blue and light gray underprint. Griffin at left and right of ornate round design at center. Security foil at left. Back: Two bunches of grapes with vine above and below value on vertical format.

	VF	UNC
a. With security thread. Large watermark.	2.00	6.00
b. Without security thread. Small watermark.	2.00	6.00

49   150,000 (Laris)   VF 2.00 UNC 7.00

1994. Dark blue-green on pale blue, light gray and lilac underprint. Griffin at left and right of ornate round design at center. Security foil at left. Back: Two bunches of grapes with vine above and below value on vertical format. Watermark: Isometric rectangular design repeated.

50   250,000 (Laris)   VF 2.00 UNC 7.00

1994. Brown-orange on pale orange and light green underprint. Griffin at left and right of ornate round design at center. Security foil at left. Back: Two bunches of grapes with vine above and below value on vertical format. Watermark: Isometric rectangular design repeated.

51   500,000 (Laris)   VF 2.00 UNC 7.00

1994. Deep violet on pale purple and pink underprint. Griffin at left and right of ornate round design at center. Security foil at left. Back: Two bunches of grapes with vine above and below value on vertical format. Watermark: Isometric rectangular design repeated.

52   1 Million (Laris)   VF 2.00 UNC 7.00

1994. Red on pink and pale yellow-brown underprint. Griffin at left and right of ornate round design at center. Security foil at left. Back: Two bunches of grapes with vine above and below value on vertical format. Watermark: Isometric rectangular design repeated.

1994 Privatization Check Voucher Issue

52A   Various Denominations   VF 10.00 UNC 30.00

1994. Orange, black and multicolor.

1995 Issue

53   1 Lari   VF FV UNC 5.00

1995. Dull purple on multicolor underprint. N. Pirosmani between branches at center, arms at upper left center. Back: View of Tbilisi, painting of deer at center right. 115x61mm.

54   2 Lari
1995. Deep olive-green on multicolor underprint. Arms above bars of music at
left, Z. Paliashvili at center right. Back: Opera House in Tbilisi at center right.
115x61mm.

VF	UNC
FV	8.00

55   5 Lari
1995. Brown on multicolor underprint. Arms at upper left, I. Javakhishvili at center.
Back: Map above ornate lion statue at left center, Tbilisi State University above
open book at right. 115x61mm.

VF	UNC
FV	15.00

56   10 Lari
1995. Blue-black on multicolor underprint. Flowers at left, arms at upper center,
A. tsereteli and barn swallow at center right. Back: Woman seated on stump
while spinning yarn with a crop spindle between ornamental branches at center
Watermark: Arms repeated vertically. 125x63mm.

VF	UNC
FV	25.00

57   20 Lari
1995. Dark brown on multicolor underprint. Open book and newspaper at upper
left, arms at lower left, I. Chavchavadze at center. Back: Statue of King V. Gorgosal between views of Tbilisi at center right. Watermark: Griffin. 130x65mm.

VF	UNC
FV	40.00

58   50 Lari
1995. Dark brown and deep blue-green on multicolor underprint. Griffin at left,
arms at upper left, Princess Tamara at center right. Back: Mythical figure at center
right. Watermark: Griffin. 135x66mm.

VF	UNC
FV	90.00

59   100 Lari
1995. Dark brown, purple and black on multicolor underprint. Carved bust of S.
Rustaveli at center right, arms at upper left center. Back: Frieze at upper center
right. Watermark: Griffin. 140x67mm.

VF	UNC
FV	150

60   500 Lari
1995. (Not issued). Deep purple on multicolor underprint. King David *the Builder*
with building at center. Back: Early Georgian inscriptions, cross on back.

VF	UNC
—	800

1999 Issue

61   1 Lari
1999. Deep purple on multicolor underprint. N. Pirosmani between branches at
center, arms at upper left center. Country name in English; *GEORGIA*. Back: View
of Tbilisi, painting of deer at center right. 115x61mm.

VF	UNC
FV	2.00

62   2 Lari
1999. Deep olive-green on multicolor underprint. Arms above bars of music at left,
Z. Paliashvili at center right. Country name in English; *GEORGIA*. Back: Opera
House in Tbilisi at center right. 115x61mm.

VF	UNC
FV	5.00

63   5 Lari
1999. Brown on multicolor underprint. Arms at upper left, I. Javakhishvili at center.
Country name in English; *GEORGIA*. Back: Map above ornate lion statue at left
center, Tbilisi State University above open book at right. 115x61mm.

VF	UNC
FV	12.50

64   10 Lari
1999. Similar to #56. Blue-black on multicolor underprint. Flowers at left, arms
at upper center, A. tsereteli and barn swallow at center right. Country name in
English; *GEORGIA*. Back: Woman seated on stump while spinning yarn with a
crop spindle between ornamental branches at center 125x63mm.

VF	UNC
FV	25.00

65   20 Lari
1999. Dark brown on multicolor underprint. Open book and newspaper at upper
left, arms at lower left, I. Chavchavadze at center. Country name in English;
GEORGIA. Back: Statue of King V. Gorgosal between views of Tbilisi at center
right. Watermark: Griffin. 130x65mm.

VF	UNC
FV	35.00

66   50 Lari
1999. Dark brown and deep blue-green on multicolor underprint. Griffin at left,
arms at upper left, Princess Tamara at center right. Back: Mythical figure at center
right. Watermark: Griffin. 135x66mm.

VF	UNC
FV	65.00

67 100 Lari
1999. Dark brown, purple and black on multicolor underprint. Carved bust of S. Rustaveli at center right, arms at upper left center. Country name in English; *GEORGIA*. Back: Frieze at upper center right. 140x67mm.

	VF	UNC
	FV	125

2002; 2004 Issue

68 1 Lari
2002; 2007. Deep purple on multicolor underprint. Niko Pirosmani at center. Back: Deer and view of Tbilisi. 115x61mm.

	VF	UNC
a. 2002.	FV	2.00
b. 2007.	FV	2.00

69 2 Lari
2002. Deep olive-green on multicolor underprint. Zakaria Paliashvili at right center. Back: Opera House in Tbilisi. 115x61mm

	VF	UNC
	FV	5.00

70 5 Lari
2002-. Brown on multicolor underprint. Ivane Javakhishvili at center. Back: Tbilisi State University Building at right, map at upper left. 115x61mm.

	VF	UNC
a. 2002.	FV	10.00
b. 2008.	FV	10.00
c. 2011.	FV	7.50
d. 2013.	FV	7.50

71 10 Lari
2002-. Blue-black on multicolor underprint. Akaki Tsereteli at left center. Back: Woman weaving. 125x63mm.

	VF	UNC
a1. 2002. Vertical denomination on back: Fen Lari.	FV	24.00
a2. 2002. Vertical denomination on back reads: Ten Lari.	FV	20.00
b. 2007.	FV	20.00
c. 2008.	FV	20.00
d. 2012.	FV	20.00

72 20 Lari
2002-. Dark brown on multicolor underprint. Ila Chavchavadze. Back: King Vakhtang Gorasale, founder of Tbilisi. 130x65mm.

	VF	UNC
a. 2002.	FV	30.00
b. 2008.	FV	30.00
c. 2011.	FV	30.00
d. 2013.	FV	30.00

73 50 Lari
2004-. Brown and multicolor underprint. Statue of Queen at left center. Back: Ancient mythical drawing. 135x66mm.

	VF	UNC
a. 2004.	FV	60.00
b. 2008.	FV	55.00
c. 2011.	FV	55.00
d. 2013.	FV	55.00

74 100 Lari
2004-. Green on multicolor underprint. Ancient statue Back: Medevial carving. 140x67mm.

	VF	UNC
a. 2004.	FV	110
b. 2008.	FV	110
c. 2012. Signatures; Giorgi Kadagidze adn Dmitri Gvindadze.	FV	110
d. 2014. Signature Giorgi Kadagidze and Nodar Khaduri.	FV	110

75 200 Lari
2006. Brown and yellow on multicolor underprint. Kakutsa Choloashvili at left center. Back: Seaside town view. 146x72mm.

	VF	UNC
	FV	200

GERMANY-DEMOCRATIC REP.

The German Democratic Republic (East Germany), located on the great north European plain, ceased to exist in 1990. During the closing days of World War II in Europe, Soviet troops advancing into Germany from the east occupied the German provinces of Mecklenburg, Brandenburg, Saxony-Anhalt, Saxony and Thuringia. These five provinces comprised the occupation zone administered by the Soviet Union after the cessation of hostilities. The other three zones were administered by the United States, Great Britain and France. Under the Potsdam agreement, questions affecting Germany as a whole were to be settled by the commanders in chief of the occupation zones acting jointly and by unanimous decision. When Soviet intransigence rendered the quadripartite commission inoperable, the three western zones were united to form the Federal Republic of Germany, May 23, 1949. Thereupon the Soviet Union dissolved its occupation zone and established it as the Democratic Republic of Germany, Oct. 7, 1949. East and West Germany became reunited as one country on Oct. 3, 1990.

MONETARY SYSTEM:
1 Mark = 100 Pfennig

DEMOCRATIC REPUBLIC

Deutsche Notenbank
1964 Issue

#22-26 replacement notes: Serial # prefix *YA-YZ; ZA-ZZ.*

22   5 Mark   **VF   UNC**
1964. Brown on multicolor underprint. Alexander von Humboldt at right. Back: Humboldt University in Berlin at left center, arms at left. Watermark: Hammer and compass.
    a. Issued note.   5.00   10.00
    s. Specimen.   —   150

23   10 Mark   **VF   UNC**
1964. Green on multicolor underprint. Friedrich von Schiller at right. Back: Zeiss factory in Jena at left center, arms at upper center right. Watermark: Hammer and compass.
    a. Issued note.   9.00   20.00
    s. Specimen.   —   200

24   20 Mark   **VF   UNC**
1964. Red-brown on multicolor underprint. Johann Wolfgang von Goethe at right. Back: National Theater in Weimar at left center, arms at upper center right. Watermark: Johann Wolfgang von Goethe.
    a. Issued note.   10.00   25.00
    s. Specimen.   —   150

25   50 Mark   **VF   UNC**
1964. Deep green on multicolor underprint. Friedrich Engels at right. Back: Wheat threshing at left center, arms at left. Watermark: Friedrich Engels.
    a. Issued note.   10.00   25.00
    r. Replacement note. Serial # prefix ZA-ZE.   20.00   35.00
    s. Specimen.   —   225

26   100 Mark   **VF   UNC**
1964. Blue on multicolor underprint. Karl Marx at right. Back: Brandenburg Gate in Berlin at left center, arms at upper center right. Watermark: Karl Marx.
    a. Issued note.   15.00   30.00
    r. Replacement note. Serial # prefix ZA, ZB.   20.00   35.00
    s. Specimen.   —   225

Staatsbank der DDR
1971-85 Issue

#27-31 Replacement notes: Serial # prefix *YA-YI, YZ, ZA-ZQ.*

27   5 Mark
1975. Purple on multicolor underprint. Thomas Müntzer at right, arms at upper left.
Back: Harvesting scene, arms at left. Watermark: Thomas Müntzer.

		VF	UNC
a.	6 digit wide serial #.	2.00	7.00
b.	6 digit narrow serial #. (1987).	2.00	7.00
s.	As b. Specimen.	—	50.00
x.	Mismatched serial number.	60.00	—

28   10 Mark
1971. Brown on multicolor underprint. Clara Zetkin at right, arms at upper left.
Back: Woman at radio station, arms at left. Watermark: Clara Zetkin.

		VF	UNC
a.	6 digit wide serial #.	4.00	6.00
b.	7 digit narrow serial #. (1985).	2.00	4.00
s.	As a. Specimen.	—	125

29   20 Mark
1975. Green on multicolor underprint. Johann Wolfgang von Goethe at right, arms
at upper left. Back: Children leaving school, arms at left. Watermark: Johann
Wolfgang von Goethe.

		VF	UNC
a.	6 digit wide serial #.	4.00	7.00
b.	7 digit narrow serial #. (1900).	6.00	9.00
s.	As b. Specimen.	—	175

30   50 Mark
1971. Dark red on multicolor underprint. Friedrich Engels at right, arms at upper
left. Back: Oil refinery, arms at left. Watermark: Friedrich Engels.

		VF	UNC
a.	7 digit wide serial #.	5.00	10.00
b.	7 digit narrow serial #. (1986).	5.00	10.00
s.	Specimen.	—	225

31   100 Mark
1975. Blue on multicolor underprint. Karl Marx at right, arms at upper left. Back:
Street scene in East Berlin, arms at left. Watermark: Karl Marx.

		VF	UNC
a.	7 digit wide serial #.	7.00	10.00
b.	7 digit narrow serial #. (1986).	10.00	17.50
s.	Specimen.	—	175

32   200 Mark   VF   UNC
1985. (Not issued.) Dark olive-green and dark brown on multicolor underprint.   —   25.00
Family at right. Back: Teacher dancing with children in front of modern school
building at center. Watermark: Dove.

33   500 Mark   VF   UNC
1985. (Not issued.) Dark brown on multicolor underprint. Arms at right. Back.   —   25.00
Government Building Staatsrat (in Berlin) at center. Watermark: Arms.

COLLECTOR SERIES
Staatsbank der DDR
1989 Commemorative Issue
#CS1, Opening of Brandenburg Gate, 1989. Not legal tender.

CS1   20 Mark 22.12.1989   Mkt. Value
Black and purple on multicolor underprint. Brandenburg Gate in Berlin at center.   500
Note: As stated on this item, #CS1 was never intended to be legal tender.

GERMANY-FEDERAL REP.

The Federal Republic of Germany (formerly West Germany), located in north-central Europe, since 1990 with the unification of East Germany, has an area of 137,782 sq. mi. (356,854 sq. km.) and a population of 82.69 million. Capital: Berlin. The economy centers about one of the world's foremost industrial establishments. Machinery, motor vehicles, iron, steel, chemicals, yarns and fabrics are exported. During the post-Normandy phase of World War II, Allied troops occupied the western German provinces of Schleswig-Holstein, Hamburg, Lower Saxony, Bremen, North Rhine-Westphalia, Hesse, Rhineland-Palatinate, Baden-Wurttemberg, Bavaria and Saarland. The conquered provinces were divided into American, British and French occupation zones. Five eastern German provinces were occupied and administered by the forces of the Soviet Union. The western occupation forces restored the civil status of their zones on Sept. 21, 1949, and resumed diplomatic relations with the provinces on July 2, 1951. On May 5, 1955, nine of the ten western provinces, organized as the Federal Republic of Germany, became fully independent. The tenth province, Saarland, was restored to the republic on Jan. 1, 1957. The post-WW II division of Germany ended on Oct. 3, 1990, when the German Democratic Republic (East Germany) ceased to exist and its five constituent provinces were formally admitted to the Federal Republic of Germany. An election Dec. 2, 1990, chose representatives to the united federal parliament (Bundestag), which then conducted its opening session in Berlin in the old Reichstag building.

MONETARY SYSTEM:
1 Deutsche Mark (DM) = 100 Pfennig, 1948-2001
1 Euro = 100 Cents, 2002-

FEDERAL REPUBLIC

Deutsche Bundesbank

1960 Issue

#18-24 Replacement notes: Serial # prefix *Y, Z.* #18-22 with or without ultra-violet sensitive features.

18	**5 Deutsche Mark**		**VF**	**UNC**
	2.1.1960. Green on multicolor underprint. *Young Venetian Woman* by Albrecht Dürer (1505) at right. Back: Oak sprig at left center. Watermark: Young Venetian woman. 120x60mm.			
	a. Issued note.		8.50	17.50
	s. Specimen.		—	150

19	**10 Deutsche Mark**		**VF**	**UNC**
	2.1.1960. Blue on multicolor underprint. *Young Man* by Albrecht Dürer at right. Back: Sail training ship *Gorch Fock*. Watermark: Young man. 130x65mm.			
	a. Issued note.		15.00	50.00
	s. Specimen.		—	150

20	**20 Deutsche Mark**		**VF**	**UNC**
	2.1.1960. Black and green on multicolor underprint. *Elsbeth Tucher* by Albrecht Dürer (1499) at right. Back: Violin, bow and clarinet. Watermark: Elsbeth Tucher. 140x70mm.			
	a. Issued note.		65.00	100
	s. Specimen.		—	150

21	**50 Deutsche Mark**		**VF**	**UNC**
	2.1.1960. Brown and olive-green on multicolor underprint. *Hans Urmiller* by Barthel Beham (about 1525) at right. Back: Holsten-Tor gate in Lübeck. Watermark: Hans Urmiller. 150x75mm.			
	a. Issued note.		55.00	135
	s. Specimen.		—	150

22	**100 Deutsche Mark**		**VF**	**UNC**
	2.1.1960. Blue on multicolor underprint. *Master Sebastian Münster* by Christoph Amberger (1552) at right. Back: Eagle. Watermark: Sebastian Münster. 160x80mm.			
	a. Issued note.		125	250
	s. Specimen.		—	250

23 500 Deutsche Mark VF UNC
2.1.1960. Brown-lilac on multicolor underprint. Male portrait by Hans Maler zu Schwaz. Back: Eltz Castle. Watermark: Male portrait. 170x85mm.
    a. Issued note. — 750 1,500
    s. Specimen. — 800

24 1000 Deutsche Mark VF UNC
2.1.1960. Dark brown on multicolor underprint. Astronomer Johann Schöner by Lucas Cranach the Elder (1529) at right. Back: Cathedral of Limburg on the Lahn. Watermark: Johan Schöner. 180x90mm.
    a. Issued note. 1,250 2,000
    s. Specimen. — 1,200

Bundeskassenschein
1967 ND Issue

#25-29A small change notes. Printed for use in a coin shortage which never developed. Not issued. Replacement notes: Serial # prefix 4 petals (+).

25 5 Pfennig VF UNC
ND. (Not issued). Black and dark green on lilac underprint. Value at center and in underprint. Printer: BDDK, without imprint. — 110

26 10 Pfennig VF UNC
ND. (Not issued). Dark brown on tan underprint. Value at center and in underprint. Printer: BDDK, without imprint. — 15.00

27 50 Pfennig VF UNC
ND. (Not issued). Dark brown. Value at center and in underprint. Printer: BDDK, without imprint. — 4,200

28 1 Deutsche Mark VF UNC
ND. (Not issued). Brown and blue on multicolor underprint. Value at center and in underprint. Printer: BDDK, without imprint. — 150

29 2 Deutsche Mark VF UNC
ND. (Not issued). Purple and tan on multicolor underprint. Value at center and in underprint. Printer: BDDK, without imprint. — 35.00

29A 5 Deutsche Mark VF UNC
1.7. 1963. (Not issued). Brown. Young Venetian woman by Albrecht Dürer. Back: Oak sprig at left center. Printer: BDDK, without imprint. — —

Deutsche Bundesbank (Cont.)
1970-80 Issue

#30-36 Replacement notes: Serial # prefix *Y, Z, YA-, ZA-*. Values are significantly higher.

30 5 Deutsche Mark VF UNC
1970; 1980. Green on multicolor underprint. Young Venetian woman by Albrecht Dürer. Back: Oak sprig at left center. Watermark: Portrait. 120x60mm.
    a. 2.1.1970. 25.00 70.00
    b. With *DEUTSCHE BUNDESBANK 1963* on back. 2.1.1980. 7.00 12.00
    s. Specimen. As a. — 100

31 10 Deutsche Mark VF UNC
1970-80. Blue on multicolor underprint. Young man by Albrecht Dürer at right. Back: Sail training ship *GORCH FOCK*. Watermark: Portrait. 130x65mm.
    a. 2.1.1970. Letters of serial # either 2.8 or 3.3mm in height. 15.00 30.00
    b. 1.6.1977. 10.00 15.00
    c. Without notice. 2.1.1980. 25.00 45.00
    d. With *DEUTSCHE BUNDESBANK 1963* on back. 2.1.1980. 7.50 15.00
    s. Specimen. — 100

32 20 Deutsche Mark VF UNC
1970-80. Black and green on multicolor underprint. *Elsbeth Tucher* by Albrecht Dürer (1499) at right. Back: Violin, bow and clarinet. Watermark: Portrait. 140x70mm.
    a. 2.1.1970. Letters of serial # either 2.8 or 3.3mm in height. 30.00 70.00
    b. 1.6.1977. 25.00 60.00
    c. Without notice. 2.1.1980. 45.00 100
    d. With *DEUTSCHE BUNDESBANK 1961* on back. 2.1.1980. 20.00 40.00
    s. Specimen. — 100

33 50 Deutsche Mark

VF UNC

1970-80. Brown and olive-green on multicolor underprint. Portrait of *Hand Urmiller* by Barthel Beham (about 1525) at right. Back: Holsten-Tor gate in Lübeck. Watermark: Portrait. 150x75mm.

	VF	UNC
a. 2.1.1970. Letters of serial # either 2.8 or 3.3mm in height.	40.00	90.00
b. 1.6.1977.	40.00	90.00
c. Without notice. 2.1.1980.	55.00	210
d. With *DEUTSCHE BUNDESBANK 1962* on back. 2.1.1980.	55.00	125
s. Specimen.	—	100

34 100 Deutsche Mark

VF UNC

1970-80. Blue on multicolor underprint. *Master Sebastian Münster* by Christoph Amberger (1552) at right. Back: Eagle. Watermark: Portrait. 160x80mm.

	VF	UNC
a. 2.1.1970. Letters of serial # either 2.8 or 3.3mm in height.	75.00	170
b. 1.6.1977.	85.00	170
c. Without notice. 2.1.1980.	180	275
d. With *DEUTSCHE BUNDESBANK 1962* on back. 2.1.1980.	100	160
s. Specimen.	—	100

35 500 Deutsche Mark

VF UNC

1970-80. Brown-lilac on multicolor underprint. Male portrait by Hans Maler zu Schwaz. Back: Eltz Castle. Watermark: Portrait. 170x85mm.

	VF	UNC
a. 2.1.1970.	775	110
b. 1.6.1977.	700	950
c. 2.1.1980.	900	1,250
s. Specimen.	—	700

36 1000 Deutsche Mark

VF UNC

1977-80. Dark brown on multicolor underprint. Astronomer Johannes Schöner by Lucas Cranach the elder (1529) at right. Back: Cathedral of Limburg on the Lahn. Watermark: Portrait. 180x90mm.

	VF	UNC
a. 1.6.1977.	1,300	1,800
b. 2.1.1980.	1,450	1,900
s. Specimen.	—	1,000

1989-91 Issue

#37-44 replacement notes: Serial # prefix *ZA; YA.*

37 5 Deutsche Mark

VF UNC

1.8.1991. Green and olive-green on multicolor underprint. Bettina von Arnim (1785-1859) at right, Signature Schlesinger-Tietmeyer. Back: Bank scal and Brandenburg Gate in Berlin at left center, script on open envelope at lower right. 122x62mm.

7.50   10.00

38 10 Deutsche Mark

VF UNC

1989-99. Purple, violet and blue on multicolor underprint. Carl Friedrich Gauss (1777-1855) at right. Back: Sextant at left center, mapping at lower right. 130x65mm.

	VF	UNC
a. Signature Pöhl-Schlesinger. 2.1.1989.	8.00	25.00
b. Signature Schlesinger-Tietmeyer. 1.8.1991.	7.00	20.00
c. Signature Tietmeyer-Gaddum. 1.10.1993.	5.00	15.00
d. Signature Welteke-Stark. 1.9.1999.	6.00	20.00
e. Uncut sheet of 54 notes, signature as c or d.	—	500

39 20 Deutsche Mark

VF UNC

1991; 1993. Green and red-violet on multicolor underprint. Annette von Droste-Hülshoff (1797-1848) at right. Back: Quill pen and beech-tree at left center, open book at lower right. 138x68mm.

	VF	UNC
a. Signature Schlesinger-Tietmeyer. 1.8.1991.	15.00	35.00
b. Signature Tietmeyer-Gaddum. 1.10.1993.	15.00	30.00

40 50 Deutsche Mark

VF UNC

1989-93. Dark brown and red-brown on multicolor underprint. Balthasar Neuman (1687-1753) at right. Back: Architectural drawing of Bishop's residence in Würz-burg at left center, blueprint at lower right in watermark area. 146x71mm.

	VF	UNC
a. Signature Pöhl-Schlesinger. 2.1.1989.	70.00	125
b. Signature Schlesinger-Tietmeyer. 1.8.1991.	55.00	85.00
c. Signature Tietmeyer-Gaddum. 1.10.1993.	45.00	70.00

41   100 Deutsche Mark

1989-93. Deep blue and violet on multicolor underprint. Clara Schumann (1819-1896) at center right. Back: Building at left in background, grand piano at center, multiple tuning forks at lower right in watermark area. 154x74mm.

		VF	UNC
a. Signature Pöhl-Schlesinger. 2.1.1989.		125	170
b. Signature Schlesinger-Tietmeyer. 1.8.1991.		110	170
c. Signature Tietmeyer-Gaddum. 1.10.1993.		100	145

42   200 Deutsche Mark

2.1.1989. Red-orange and blue on multicolor underprint. Paul Ehrlich (1854-1915) at right. Signature Pöhl-Schlesinger. Back: Microscope at left center, medical science symbol at lower right. 162x77mm.

	VF	UNC
	300	400

43   500 Deutsche Mark

1991; 1993. Red-violet and blue on multicolor underprint. Maria Sibylla Merian (1647-1717) at right. Back: Dandelion with butterfly and caterpillar at center, flower at lower right. 170x80mm.

		VF	UNC
a. Signature Schlesinger-Tietmeyer. 1.8.1991.		450	650
b. Signature Tietmeyer-Gaddum. 1.10.1993.		500	725

44   1000 Deutsche Mark

1.8.1991; 1.10.1993. Deep brown-violet and blue-green on multicolor underprint. City drawing at center, Wilhelm and Jakob Grimm (1786-1859 and 1785-1863) at center right. Back: Bank seal at left, book frontispiece of *Deutches Würterbuch* over entry for freedom at left center, child collecting falling stars at lower right in watermark area. 178x83mm.

		VF	UNC
a. Signature Schlesinger-Tietmeyer. 1.8.1991.		825	1,100
b. Signature Tietmeyer-Gaddum. 1.10.1993.		825	1,100

1996 Issue

45   50 Deutsche Mark

2.1.1996. Dark brown and red-brown on multicolor underprint. Balthasar Neuman (1687-1753) at right. Square-shaped Kinegram foil at left center. Signature Tietmeyer-Gaddum. Back: Architectural drawing of Bishop's residence in Würzburg at left center, blueprint at lower right. 146x71mm.

VF	UNC
35.00	65.00

46   100 Deutsche Mark

2.1.1996. Deep blue and violet on multicolor underprint. Clara Schumann (1819-1896) at center right. Lyre-shaped Kinegram foil at left center. Signature: Tietmeyer-Gaddum. Back: Building at left in background, grand piano at center, multiple tuning forks at lower right. 154x74mm.

VF	UNC
60.00	120

47   200 Deutsche Mark

2.1.1996. Red-orange and blue on multicolor underprint. Paul Ehrlich (1854-1915) at right. Double hexagon-shaped Kinegram foil. Signature; Tietmeyer-Gaddum. Back: Microscope at left center, medical science symbol at lower right. 162x77mm.

VF	UNC
150	350

Note: For later issues made for use in Germany see European Union listings.

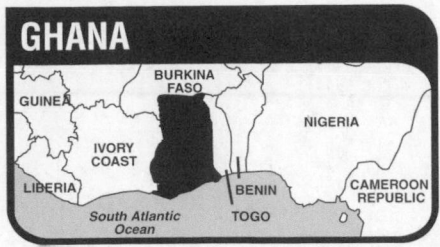

GHANA

The Republic of Ghana, a member of the British Commonwealth situated on the West Coast of Africa between the Ivory Coast and Togo, has an area of 239,460 sq. km. and a population of 23,38 million, almost entirely African. Capital: Accra. Traditional exports include cocoa, coffee, timber, gold, industrial diamonds, maganese and bauxite. Additional exports include pineapples, bananas, yams, tuna, cola and salt.

Formed from the merger of the British colony of the Gold Coast and the Togoland trust territory, Ghana in 1957 became the first sub-Saharan country in colonial Africa to gain its independence. Ghana endured a long series of coups before Lt. Jerry Rawlings took power in 1981 and banned political parties. After approving a new constitution and restoring multiparty politics in 1992, Rawlings won presidential elections in 1992 and 1996, but was constitutionally prevented from running for a third term in 2000. John Kufuor succeeded him and was reelected in 2004. Kufuor is constitutionally barred from running for a third term in upcoming Presidential elections, which are scheduled for December 2008.

Ghana's monetary denomination of "cedi" is derived from the word "sedie" meaning cowrie, a shell money commonly employed by coastal tribes.

MONETARY SYSTEM:
1 Shilling = 12 Pence
1 Pound = 20 Shillings to 1965
1 Cedi = 100 Pesewas, 1965-

REPUBLIC
Bank of Ghana
1958-63 Issue

1	10 Shillings	VF	UNC
	1958-63. Green and brown on multicolor underprint. Bank of Ghana building in Accra at center right. Back: Star. Watermark: *GHANA* in star.		
	a. 1.7.1958. 2 signatures. Printer: TDLR.	30.00	90.00
	b. 1.7.1961. Without imprint.	22.50	70.00
	c. 1.7.1962. Without imprint.	35.00	100
	d. 1.7.1963. 1 signature.	15.00	50.00
	s. As a. Specimen.	—	200

2	1 Pound	VF	UNC
	1958-62. Red-brown and blue on multicolor underprint. Bank of Ghana building in Accra at center. Back: Cocoa pods in two heaps. Watermark: *GHANA* in star.		
	a. 1.7.1958. Printer: TDLR.	18.00	60.00
	b. 1.4.1959. Printer: TDLR.	15.00	45.00
	c. 1.7.1961. Without imprint.	12.50	45.00
	d. 1.7.1962. Without imprint.	8.00	25.00
	s. As a. Specimen.	—	75.00

3	5 Pounds	VF	UNC
	1.7.1958-1.7.1962. Purple and orange on multicolor underprint. Bank of Ghana building in Accra at center. Back: Cargo ships, logs in water. Watermark: *GHANA* in star.		
	a. 1.7.1958.	75.00	250
	b. 1.4.1959.	60.00	225
	c. 1.7.1961.	50.00	200
	d. 1.7.1962.	20.00	70.00
	s1. Specimen. 1.7.1958.	—	225
	s2. Specimen. Perforated: *CANCELLED*.		350

4	1000 Pounds	VF	UNC
	1.7.1958. Used in interbank transactions only. Blackish brown. Bank of Ghana building in Accra at lower right. Back: Ornate design. Watermark: *GHANA* in star.	150	500

1965 Issue

5	1 Cedi	VF	UNC
	ND (1965). Blue on multicolor underprint. Portrait Kwame Nkrumah at upper right. Back: Bank. Watermark: Kwame Nkrumah.		
	a. Issued note.	8.50	17.50
	s. Specimen, punch hole cancelled.	—	80.00
	ct. Color trial. Red multicolor underprint.	—	350

9   100 Cedis   **VF   UNC**
ND (1965). Purple on multicolor underprint. Portrait Kwame Nkrumah at upper right. Signature 3. Back: Hospital. Watermark: Kwame Nkrumah.
- a. Issued note.   65.00   130
- s. Specimen.   —   150
- ct. Color trial. Brown multicolor underprint.   —   500

6   5 Cedis   **VF   UNC**
ND (1965). Dark brown on multicolor underprint. Portrait Kwame Nkrumah at upper right. Signature 3. Back: Parliament House at left center. Watermark: Kwame Nkrumah.
- a. Issued note.   9.00   27.50
- s. Specimen, punch hole cancelled.   —   80.00
- ct. Color trial. Green multicolor underprint.   —   350

9A   1000 Cedis   **VF   UNC**
ND(1965). Black. Large star at upper left. Signature 3. Back: Bank of Ghana building in Accra at right.
- a. Issued note.   275   700
- s. Specimen.   —   700
- ct. Color trial. Purple.   —   1,250

7   10 Cedis   **VF   UNC**
ND (1965). Green on multicolor underprint. Portrait Kwame Nkrumah at upper left. Signature 3. Back: Independence Square at center. Watermark: Kwame Nkrumah.
- a. Issued note.   15.00   45.00
- s. Specimen, punch hole cancelled.   —   80.00
- ct. Color trial. Dark blue multicolor underprint.   —   375

1967 Issue

Replacement notes: Serial # prefix Z/99.

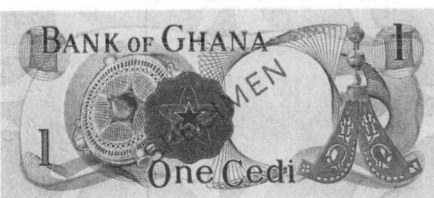

10   1 Cedi   **VF   UNC**
23.2.1967; 8.1.1969; 1.10.1970; 1.10.1971. UV: fibers fluoresce blue, value 10 orange. Blue on multicolor underprint. Cacao tree with pods at right. Signature 4, 5. Back: Shield and ceremonial sword. Watermark: Arms-Eagle's head above star.
- a. 23.2.1967.   5.00   10.00
- b. 8.1.1969.   8.00   17.50
- c. 1.10.1970.   4.00   9.00
- d. 1.10.1971.   3.50   9.00
- s. Specimen. Red overprint: SPECIMEN once on each side.   —   50.00

8   50 Cedis   **VF   UNC**
ND (1965). Red on multicolor underprint. Portrait Kwame Nkrumah at upper left. Signature 3. Back: Island and coconut trees. Watermark: Kwame Nkrumah.
- a. Issued note.   32.50   90.00
- s. Specimen, punch hole cancelled.   —   85.00
- ct. Color trial. Light blue on multicolor underprint.   —   400

11   5 Cedis   **VF   UNC**
23.2.1967; 8.1.1969. Dark brown on multicolor underprint. Wood carving of a bird at right. Signature 4, 5. Back: Animal carvings. Watermark: Arms-Eagle's head above star.
- a. 23.2.1967.   17.50   60.00
- b. 8.1.1969.   17.50   55.00
- s. Specimen. Red overprint: SPECIMEN once on each side.   —   50.00

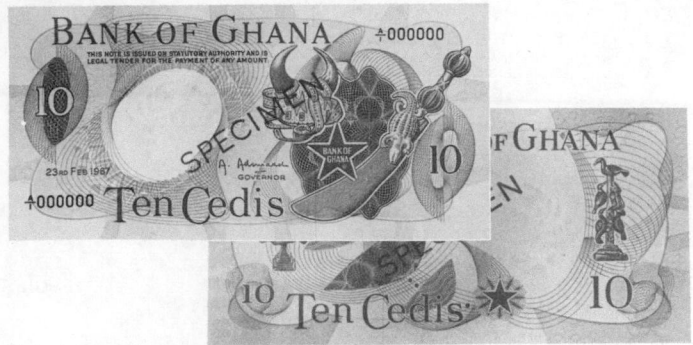

12   10 Cedis   **VF   UNC**

23.2.1967; 8.1.1969; 1.10.1970. Red on multicolor underprint. Art products at right. Signature 4, 5. Back: Small statuettes. Watermark: Arms-Eagle's head above star.

a. 23.2.1967.   17.50   60.00
b. 8.1.1969.   20.00   65.00
c. 1.10.1970.   6.50   27.50
s. Specimen. Red overprint: SPECIMEN once on each side.   —   60.00

1972-73 Issue

13   1 Cedi   **VF   UNC**

1973-76. UV: value 1 fluoresces orange. Dark blue, deep green and purple on multicolor underprint. Young boy with slingshot at right. Signature 5, 6, 7. Back: Man cutting Cacao pods from tree at left center. Watermark: Arms-Eagle's head above star.

a. 2.1.1973.   3.00   9.00
b. 2.1.1975.   2.50   7.50
c. 2.1.1976. Two minor varieties in length of "2nd" as part of date.   2.00   6.00
d. 2.1.1978.   1.00   5.00
s. As a. Specimen. Red overprint: SPECIMEN on both sides.   —   55.00

14   2 Cedis   **VF   UNC**

1972-78. Green on multicolor underprint. Young man with hoe at right. Signature 5, 6, 7. Back: Workers in field at left center. Watermark: Arms-Eagle's head above star.

a. 21.6.1972. Signature J. J. Ansah.   5.00   18.00
b. 21.6.1972. Signature G. Nikoi.   4.00   13.00
c. 2.1.1977; 2.1.1978.   1.25   6.00
s. As a. Specimen.   —   65.00

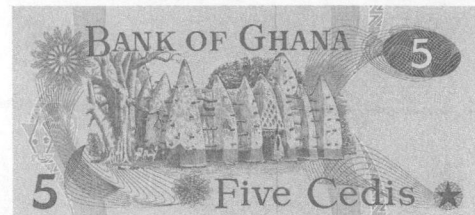

15   5 Cedis   **VF   UNC**

1973-78. UV: value 5 fluoresces orange. Brown on multicolor underprint. Woman wearing large hat at right. Signature 5, 6, 7. Back: Huts. Watermark: Arms-Eagle's head above star.

a. 2.1.1973; 2.1.1975; 2.1.1976.   1.50   9.00
b. 2.1.1977; 4.7.1977, 2.1.1978.   1.25   7.50
s. As a. Specimen.   —   65.00

16   10 Cedis   **VF   UNC**

1973-78. UV: value 10 fluoresces orange. Red, violet and dark brown on multicolor underprint. Elderly man smoking a pipe a right. Signature 5, 6, 7. Back: Dam. Watermark: Arms-Eagle's head above star.

a. 2.1.1973. Serial # prefix A/1.   5.50   10.00
b. 2.1.1973. Serial # prefix B/1-.   5.00   10.00
c. 2.1.1975.   6.50   12.00
d. 2.1.1976.   2.50   7.50
e. 2.1.1977.   2.50   7.50
f. 2.1.1978.   1.50   6.00
s. As a. Specimen.   —   65.00

1979 Issue

#17-22 Replacement notes: Serial # prefix XX; ZZ.

17   1 Cedi   **VF   UNC**

7.2.1979; 6.3.1982. Green and multicolor. Young man at right. Signature 7. 2 serial number varieties. Back: Man weaving at center right. Watermark: Arms-Eagle's head above star.

a. 7.2.1979.   2.00   7.50
b. 6.3.1982.   1.50   4.25
s. As b. Specimen. Red overprint: SPECIMEN on both sides.   —   90.00

18   2 Cedis   VF   UNC

7.2.1979; 2.1.1980; 2.7.1980; 6.3.1982. UV: country name and value 2 fluoresces orange. Blue and multicolor. School girl at right. Signature 7. 2 serial number varieties. Back: Workers tending plants in field at center right. Watermark: Arms-Eagle's head above star.

a. 7.2.1979.	1.25	7.50
b. 2.1.1980.	2.00	8.00
c. 2.7.1980.	1.00	6.00
d. 6.3.1982.	1.50	7.50
s. Specimen.	—	70.00

19   5 Cedis   VF   UNC

7.2.1979; 2.1.1980; 6.3.1982 Elderly man at right, Signature 7. 2 serial number varieties. Back: Man cutting log at left center. Watermark: Arms-Eagle's head above star.

a. 7.2.1979.	3.00	11.00
b. 2.1.1980.	2.75	10.00
c. 6.3.1982.	2.50	8.00
s. Specimen.	—	75.00

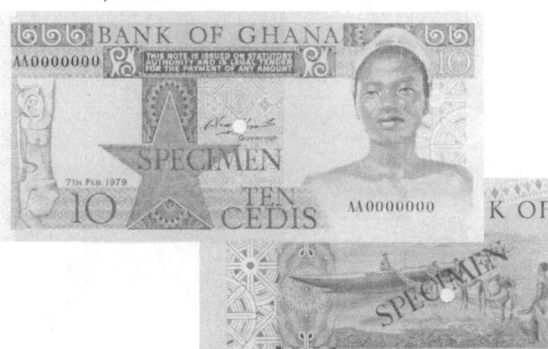

20   10 Cedis   VF   UNC

7.2.1979; 2.1.1980; 2.7.1980; 6.3.1982. Purple, green and multicolor. Young woman at right. Signature 7. 2 serial number varieties. Back: Fishermen with long net at left center. Watermark: Arms-Eagle's head above star.

a. 7.2.1979.	7.50	25.00
b. 2.1.1980.	5.75	17.00
c. 2.7.1980.	6.00	20.00
d. 6.3.1982.	6.50	22.00
s. Specimen.	—	100

21   20 Cedis   VF   UNC

7.2.1979; 2.7.1980; 6.3.1982. Green and multicolor. Miner at right. Signature 7. 2 serial number varieties. Back: Man weaving at center right. Watermark: Arms-Eagle's head above star.

a. 7.2.1979.	9.50	35.00
b. 2.7.1980.	8.50	27.50
c. 6.3.1982.	8.00	25.00
s. Specimen.	—	100

22   50 Cedis   VF   UNC

7.2.1979; 2.7.1980. Brown and multicolor. Oil man at right. Signature 7. 2 serial number varieties. Back: Men splitting cacao pods. Watermark: Arms-Eagle's head above star.

a. 7.2.1979.	5.50	16.00
b. 2.7.1980.	5.00	14.00
s. Specimen.	—	120

1983-91 Issue

#23-31 Replacement notes: Serial # prefix Z/1.

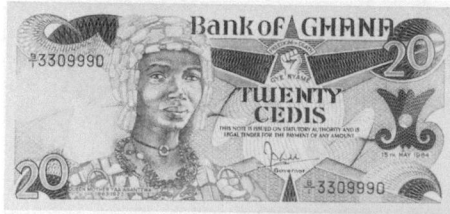

23   10 Cedis   VF   UNC

15.5.1984. Purple and multicolor. W. Larbi, F. Otoo, E. Nukpor at left, arms at top center right. Signature 8. Without security thread. Back: People going to rural bank at center.

a. Issued note.	1.75	6.50
s. Specimen.	—	40.00

24   20 Cedis   VF   UNC

15.5.1984; 15.7.1986. Shades of green and aqua. Queen Mother Yaa Asantewa at left, arms at top center right. Signature 8. Back: Workers and flag procession. Watermark: Arms-Eagle's head above star.

a. Issued note.	2.00	9.00
s. Specimen. Red overprint: *SPECIMEN* on each side.	—	45.00

25   50 Cedis   **VF   UNC**
1.4.1983; 15.5.1984; 15.7.1986. Brown, violet and multicolor. Boy with hat at   2.00   10.00
left center, arms at top center right. Signature 8. Back: Drying grain at center.
Watermark: Arms-Eagle's head above star.

26   100 Cedis   **VF   UNC**
1983-91. Purple, blue and multicolor. Woman at left center, arms at top center
right. Signature 8, 9. Back: Loading produce onto truck at center. Watermark:
Arms-Eagle's head above star.
    a. Signature J. S. Addo. 1.4.1983; 15.5.1984; 15.7.1986.   4.25   18.00
    b. Signature G. K. Agama. 19.7.1990; 19.9.1991.   2.25   10.00
    s. As a. 1983. Specimen. Red overprint SPECIMEN on each side.   —   70.00

27   200 Cedis   **VF   UNC**
1983-93. Light brown, orange and multicolor. Old man at left center, arms at top
center right. Signature 8, 9. Back: Children in classroom at center. Watermark:
Arms-Eagle's head above star.
    a. Signature J. S. Addo. 1.4.1983; 15.5.1984; 15.7.1986.   3.50   14.00
    b. Signature G. K. Agama. 20.4.1989; 19.7.1990; 19.9.1991; 14.10.1992;   2.00   7.00
       10.8.1993.
    s. Specimen. 1.4.1983.   —   100

28   500 Cedis   **VF   UNC**
1986-94. Purple and blue-green on multicolor underprint. Arms at right. Signature
8, 9. Back: Cacao trees with cacao pods and miner at center. Watermark: Arms-
Eagle's head above star.
    a. Signature J. S. Addo. 31.12.1986.   5.00   30.00
    b. Signature G. K. Agama. 20.4.1989; 19.7.1990.   3.50   10.00
    c. Signature G. K. Agama. 19.9.1991; 14.10.1992; 10.8.1993; 10.6.1994.   3.50   8.00
    s. Specimen.   —   100

29   1000 Cedis   **VF   UNC**
1991-96. Dark brown, dark blue and dark green on multicolor underprint. Jewels
at right, arms at lower left. Signature 9, G. K. Agama. Back: Harvesting, splitting
cacao pods at left center. Watermark: Arms-Eagle's head above star.
    a. 22.2.1991.   4.00   18.00
    b. Segmented foil security thread. 22.7.1993; 6.1.1995; 23.2.1996.   2.25   10.00

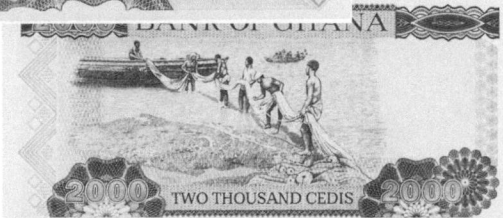

30   2000 Cedis   **VF   UNC**
1994-96. Red-brown, green and multicolor. Suspension bridge at right, arms at
lower right. Signature 9, G. K. Agama. Back: Fisherman loading nets into boat at
left center. Watermark: Arms-Eagle's head above star.
    a. 15.6.1994.   5.00   20.00
    b. 6.1.1995.   5.00   20.00
    c. 23.1.1996.   5.00   20.00

31   5000 Cedis

1994-96. Green and red-orange on multicolor underprint. Large stars in underprint at center, supported shield of arms at upper right, arms at lower left. Signature 9, G. K. Agama. Back: Map at left center, freighter in harbor at center, log flow in foreground. Watermark: Arms-Eagle's head above star.

		VF	UNC
a. 26.6.1994.		12.00	50.00
b. 6.1.1995.		9.00	35.00
c. 23.2.1996.		9.00	30.00

1996 Issue

34   5000 Cedis

1996-. Reduced size. Green and red-orange on multicolor underprint. Large stars in underprint at center, supported shield of arms at upper right, arms at lower left. Signature 9, 10, 11. Back: Map at left ceneter, freighter in harbor at center, log flow in foreground. Watermark: Arms-Eagle's head above star.

	VF	UNC
a. 5.12.1996.	FV	11.00
b. 1.12.1997.	FV	11.00
c. 2.5.1998.	FV	11.00
d. 1.7.1999.	FV	11.00
e. 1.7.2000.	FV	10.00
f. 3.9.2001.	FV	10.00
g. 22.10.2001.	FV	9.00
h. 2.9.2002.	FV	9.00
i. 4.8.2003.	FV	9.00
j. 4.8.2006.	FV	9.00

32   1000 Cedis

1996-2003. Reduced size. Dark brown, dark blue and dark green on multicolor underprint. Jewels at right, arms at lower left. Signature 9, 10, 11. Back: Harvesting, splitting cacao pods at left center. Watermark: Arms-Eagle's head above star.

	VF	UNC
a. 5.12.1996.	3.00	7.60
b. 1.12.1997.	2.50	6.50
c. 2.5.1998.	2.50	6.50
d. 1.7.1999.	2.50	6.50
e. 1.7.2000.	2.50	6.50
f. 3.9.2001.	4.50	18.00
g. 22.10.2001.	FV	4.50
h. 2.9.2002.	FV	4.50
i. 4.8.2003.	FV	4.50
s. Specimen. 1.7.2000.	—	55.00

2002 Issue

35   10,000 Cedis

2002-03; 2006. Purple and red-yellow on multicolor underprint. Kwame Nkrumah and five other leaders at right. Signature 11.

	VF	UNC
a. 2.9.2002.	FV	14.00
b. 4.8.2003.	FV	10.00
c. 4.8.2006.	FV	10.00

33   2000 Cedis

1996-. Reduced size. Red-brown, green and multicolor. Suspension bridge at right, arms at lower left. Signature 9, 10, 11. Back: Fisherman loading nets into boat at left center. Watermark: Arms-Eagle's head above star.

	VF	UNC
a. 5.12.1996.	FV	8.00
b. 1.12.1997.	FV	7.00
c. 2.5.1998.	FV	6.00
d. 1.7.1999.	FV	5.00
e. 1.7.2000.	FV	5.00
f. 3.9.2001.	FV	5.00
f. 22.10.2001.	FV	5.00
g. 2.9.2002.	FV	5.00
h. 4.8.2003.	FV	5.00
i. 4.8.2006.	FV	5.00
s. Specimen. 2.5.1998.	—	55.00

36   20,000 Cedis

2002-03; 4.8.2006. Red-orange and pink-yellow on multicolor underprint. Ephraim Amu, musician, at right. Signature 11.

	VF	UNC
a. 2.9.2002.	FV	22.50
b. 4.8.2003.	FV	19.00
c. 4.8.2006.	FV	13.50

2007 Issue

37   1 Cedi   **VF UNC**

1.7.2007-. Red and rose on multicolor underprint. Kwame Nkrumah and five other leaders at right. Back: Dam and water spillway. 137x65mm.

		VF	UNC
a.	1.7.2007.	FV	4.00
b.	6.3.2010. Without "1" in watermark.	FV	4.00
c.	6.3.2010. With "1" in watermark.	FV	4.00
d.	6.3.2013. Signature Henry Kofi Wampah.	FV	4.00

37A   2 Cedis   **VF UNC**

6.3.2010-. Olive brown on yellow and orange underprint. Kwame Nkrumah at right. Back: Old and new Parliament buildings. 140x67mm.

		VF	UNC
a.	6.3.2010. Birth Centennial legend at top center.	FV	4.50
b.	6.3.2013. Without Birth Centennial legend at top center. Signature Henry Kofi Wampah.	FV	4.50
c.	7.1.2014.	FV	4.50

38   5 Cedis   **VF UNC**

1.7.2007-. Light and dark blue and tan on multicolor underprint. Kwame Nkrumah and five other leaders at right. Back: Buildings and monuments. 141x68mm.

		VF	UNC
a.	1.7.2007.	FV	5.00
b.	6.3.2010.	FV	5.00
c.	7.1.2011.	FV	5.00
d.	6.3.2013. Signature Henry Kofi Wampah.	FV	5.00

39   10 Cedis   **VF UNC**

1.7.2007-. Light and dark green and peach on multicolor underprint. Kwame Nkrumah and five other leaders at right. Back: Bank of Ghana building. 145x71mm.

		VF	UNC
a.	1.7.2007.	FV	10.00
b.	6.3.2010.	FV	10.00
c.	1.7.2011.	FV	10.00
d.	6.3.2013. Signature Henry Kofi Wampah.	FV	10.00

40   20 Cedis   **VF UNC**

1.7.2007-. Violet on multicolor underprint. Kwame Nkrumah and five other leaders at right. Back: Government Building. 149x65mm.

		VF	UNC
a.	7.1.2007.	FV	17.50
b.	3.6.2010.	FV	17.50
c.	7.1.2011.	FV	17.50
d.	6.3.2013. Signature Henry Kofi Wampah.	FV	17.50

41   50 Cedis   **VF UNC**

1.7.2007; 6.3.2010. Brown and tan on multicolor underprint. Kwame Nkrumah and five other leaders at right. Back: Buildings. 153x77mm.

		VF	UNC
a.	1.7.2007.	FV	45.00
b.	6.3.2010.	FV	45.00

42   50 Cedis   **VF UNC**

2.1.2012. Brown and tan on multicolor underprint. Kwame Nlkrumah and five other leaders at right. Cocoa pod in green color shifting ink at bottom right center. Back: Buildings. 153x77mm.   FV 45.00

COLLECTOR SERIES

Bank of Ghana
1977 Issue

CS1   1977 1-10 Cedis   **Mkt. Value**

#13b, 14c, 15b, 16d. with overprint: *SPECIMEN* and Maltese cross prefix serial #.   50.00

GIBRALTAR

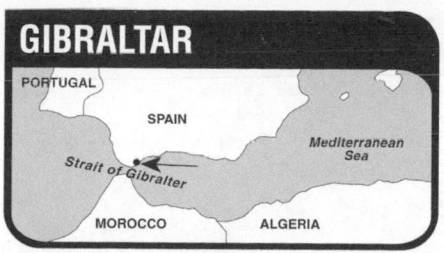

The British Colony of Gibraltar, located at the southernmost point of the Iberian Peninsula, has an area of 6.5 sq. km. and a population of 28,000. Capital (and only town): Gibraltar.

Strategically important, Gibraltar was reluctantly ceded to Great Britain by Spain in the 1713 Treaty of Utrecht; the British garrison was formally declared a colony in 1830. In a referendum held in 1967, Gibraltarians voted overwhelmingly to remain a British dependency. The subsequent granting of autonomy in 1969 by the UK led to Spain closing the border and severing all communication links. A series of talks were held by the UK and Spain between 1997 and 2002 on establishing temporary joint sovereignty over Gibraltar. In response to these talks, the Gibraltar Government called a referendum in late 2002 in which the majority of citizens voted overwhelmingly against any sharing of sovereignty with Spain. Since the referendum, tripartite talks on other issues have been held with Spain, the UK, and Gibraltar, and in September 2006 a three-way agreement was signed. Spain agreed to remove restrictions on air movements, to speed up customs procedures, to implement international telephone dialing, and to allow mobile roaming agreements. Britain agreed to pay increased pensions to Spaniards who had been employed in Gibraltar before the border closed. Spain will be allowed to open a cultural institute from which the Spanish flag will fly. A new noncolonial constitution came into effect in 2007, but the UK retains responsibility for defense, foreign relations, internal security, and financial stability.

RULERS:
British

MONETARY SYSTEM:
1 Shilling = 12 Pence
1 Pound = 20 Shillings to 1971
1 Pound = 100 New Pence, 1971-

BRITISH ADMINISTRATION
Government of Gibraltar
1934 Ordinance; 1958 Issue

17 10 Shillings VF UNC
3.10.1958; 1.5.1965. Blue on yellow-brown underprint. Rock of Gibraltar at left. 100 380
Back: Arms at center. Printer: TDLR.

18 1 Pound VF UNC
1958-75. Green on yellow-brown underprint. Rock of Gibraltar at bottom center.
Back: Arms at center. Printer: TDLR.
 a. Signature title: *FINANCIAL SECRETARY.* 3.10.1958; 1.5.1965. 27.50 150
 b. Signature title: *FINANCIAL AND DEVELOPMENT SECRETARY.* 22.50 115
  20.11.1971.
 c. 20.11.1975. 45.00 230
 s. Specimen. As a-c. — —

19 5 Pounds VF UNC
1958-75. Brown. Rock of Gibraltar at bottom center. Back: Arms at center. Printer: TDLR.
 a. Signature title: *FINANCIAL SECRETARY.* 3.10.1958; 1.5.1965. 155 800
 b. Signature title: *FINANCIAL AND DEVELOPMENT SECRETARY.* 1.5.1965; 120 640
  20.11.1971; 20.11.1975.
 s. Specimen. As a-b. — —

1975; 1986 Issue; Ordinance CAP 39

20 1 Pound VF UNC
1975-88. Brown and red on multicolor underprint. Queen Elizabeth II at center right. Three signature varieties. Back: The Covenant of Gibraltar at left center. Watermark: Queen Elizabeth II. Printer: TDLR.
 a. 20.11.1975 (1978). 20.00 120
 b. 15.9.1979. 19.00 110
 c. 10.11.1983. 10.00 105
 d. 21.10.1986. 11.00 86.00
 e. 4.8.1988. FV 30.00
 s. Specimen. As a; b; d. — 260

21 5 Pounds VF UNC
1975; 1988. Green on multicolor underprint. Queen Elizabeth II at right. Signature varieties. Back: The Covenant of Gibraltar at left center. Watermark: Queen Elizabeth II. Printer: TDLR.
 a. 20.11.1975. 35.00 185
 b. 4.8.1988. 16.00 80.00

22 10 Pounds VF UNC
1975; 1986. Deep violet, dark brown and deep blue-green on multicolor underprint. Queen Elizabeth II at right. Signature varieties. Back: Governor's house. Watermark: Queen Elizabeth II. Printer: TDLR.
 a. 20.11.1975 (1977). 55.00 260
 b. 21.10.1986. FV 130

23   20 Pounds

1975-86. Light brown on multicolor underprint. Queen Elizabeth II at right. Signature varieties. Back: Governor's house. Watermark: Queen Elizabeth II. Printer: TDLR.

	VF	UNC
a. 20.11.1975 (1978).	185	630
b. 15.9.1979.	175	570
c. 1.7.1986.	110	350

24   50 Pounds

27.11.1986. Purple on multicolor underprint. Queen Elizabeth II at right. Signature varieties. Back: Rock of Gibraltar. Watermark: Queen Elizabeth II. Printer: TDLR.

VF	UNC
125	380

1995 Issue

25   5 Pounds

1.7.1995. Green and purple on multicolor underprint. Mature image of Queen Elizabeth II at right, shield of arms at left. Urn above gateway at left center. Back: Tavik ibn Zeyad with sword at right, Moorish castle at upper left. Watermark: Queen Elizabeth II. 135x70mm.

	VF	UNC
a. Issued note.	FV	65.00
s. Specimen.	—	140

26   10 Pounds

1.7.1995. Orange-brown and violet on multicolor underprint. Mature image of Queen Elizabeth II at right, shield of arms at left. Lighthouse above cannon at left center. Back: Portrait General Eliott at right, scene of *The Great Siege, 1779-85* at upper left center. Watermark: Queen Elizabeth II. 142x75mm.

	VF	UNC
a. Issued note.	FV	115
s. Specimen.	—	250

27   20 Pounds

1.7.1995. Purple and violet on multicolor underprint. Mature image of Queen Elizabeth II at right, shield of arms at left, bird above cannon at left center. Back: Portrait Admiral Nelson at right, H.M.S. Victory at upper left center. Watermark: Queen Elizabeth II. 150x80mm.

	VF	UNC
a. Issued note.	FV	185
s. Specimen.	—	330

28   50 Pounds

1.7.1995. Red and violet on multicolor underprint. Mature image of Queen Elizabeth II at right, shield of arms at left. Gibraltar monkey above horse and carriage at left center. Back: Portrait W. Churchill at upper right, Spitfire airplanes at the North Front, 1942 at upper left center. Watermark: Queen Elizabeth II. 157x85mm.

	VF	UNC
a. Issued note.	150	480
s. Specimen.	—	580

Note: #28 also honored the 30th anniversary of the death of Churchill.

2000 Issue
#29, Millennium Commemorative

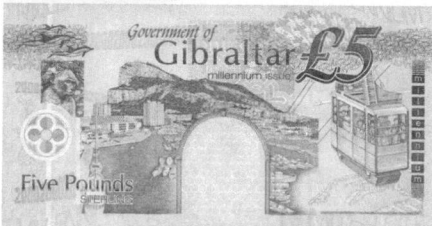

		VF	**UNC**
29	**5 Pounds**		

2000. Green on multicolor underprint. Mature image of Queen Elizabeth at right. shield of arms at lower left, urn above gateway at left center. Enhanced security devices. Back: Gibraltar monkey at left, city & harbor view at center, gondola on right. 135x70mm.   FV   57.50

		VF	**UNC**
30	**10 Pounds**		

10.9.2002. Orange-brown and violet on multicolor underprint. Mature image of Queen Elizabeth II at right. Back: Large square with butterflies and grouse within. 142x72mm.   FV   110

2004 Commemorative Issue

		VF	**UNC**
31	**20 Pounds**		

4.8.2004. Mauve, tan and black on multicolor underprint. Mature image of Queen Elizabeth II at right. Back: John Mackintosh Square at center, 19th century townfolk at right edge. 150x80mm.
    a. Issued note.   FV   175
    s. Specimen.   —   300

2006 Issue

		VF	**UNC**
32	**10 Pounds**		

1.12.2006. Reprint of #26a with new date and signature. Orange-brown and violet on multicolor underprint. Mature image of Queen Elizabeth II at right. Back: Large square. 142x75mm.
    a. Issued note.   FV   50.00
    s. Specimen.   —   240

		VF	**UNC**
33	**20 Pounds**		

1.12.2006. Reprint of #27a with new date and signature. Purple and violet on multicolor underprint. Mature image of Queen Elizabeth II at right. Back: Portrait Admiral Nelson at right, H.M.S. Victory at upper left center. 150x80mm.
    a. Issued note.   FV   160
    s. Specimen.   —   285

		VF	**UNC**
34	**50 Pounds**		

1.12.2006. Reprint of #28a with new date and signature. Red and violet on multicolor underprint. Mature image of Queen Elizabeth II at right. Back: Winston Churchill at right, Spitfire airplanes at the North Front. 157x85mm.
    a. Issued note.   FV   230
    s. Specimen.   —   525

2010 Issue

35 5 Pounds

1.1.2011. Green on multicolor underprint. Queen Elizabeth II at left center. Back: Upper Ward and Tower of Homage of the Moorish Castle. Printer: TDLR (without imprint). 133x70mm.

	VF	UNC
	FV	30.00

36 10 Pounds

1.1.2010. Blue on multicolor underprint. Queen Elizabeth II at left center. Back: John Trumbull's painting "Sortie made by the Garrison of Gibraltar. Printer: TDLR (without imprint.) 142x75mm.

	VF	UNC
	FV	55.00

37 20 Pounds

1.1.2011. Orange and purple on multicolor underprint. Queen Elizabeth II at left center. Back: H.M.S. Victory returning to Gibraltar being towed by H.M.S. Neptune after Battle of Trafalgar. Printer: TDLR (without imprint). 150x80mm.

	VF	UNC
	FV	100

38 50 Pounds

1.1.2010. Red and brown on multicolor underprint. Queen Elizabeth II at left center. Back: Casemates Square buildings. 157x85mm.

	VF	UNC
	FV	225

39 100 Pounds

1.1.2011. Purple on multicolor underprint. Queen Elizabeth II at left center. Back: King's Bastion. Printer: TDLR (without imprint). 164x90mm.

	VF	UNC
	FV	350

COLLECTOR SERIES

Government of Gibraltar

1975 Issue

CS1 1975 1-20 Pounds

#20a, 21a, 22, 23a. with overprint: *SPECIMEN* and serial # prefix: Maltese cross.

Mkt. Value
350

GREAT BRITAIN

North Atlantic Ocean · IRELAND · North Sea · NORWAY · SWEDEN · DENMARK · Baltic Sea · English Channel · GERMANY

The United Kingdon of Great Britain and Northern Ireland, (including England, Scotland, Wales and Norhtern Ireland) is located off the northwest coast of the European continent, has an area of 94,227 sq. mi. (244,046 sq. km.), and a population of 59.45 million. Capital: London. The economy is based on industrial activity, trading and financial services. Machinery, motor vehicles, chemicals and textile yarns and fabrics are exported. After the departure of the Romans, who brought Britain into an active relationship with Europe, Britain fell prey to invaders from Scandinavia and the Low Countries who drove the original Britons into Scotland and Wales, and established a profusion of kingdoms that finally united in the 11th century under the Danish King Canute. Norman rule, following the conquest of 1066, stimulated the development of those institutions which have since distinguished British life. Henry VIII (1509-47) turned Britain from continental adventuring and faced it to the sea - a decision that made Britain a world power during the reign of Elizabeth I (1558-1603). Strengthened by the Industrial Revolution and the defeat of Napoleon, 19th century Britain turned to the remote parts of the world and established a colonial empire of such extent and prosperity that the world has never seen its like. World Wars I and II sealed the fate of the Empire and relegated Britain to a lesser role in world affairs by draining her resources and inaugurating a worldwide movement toward national self-determination in her former colonies. By the mid-20th century, most of the former British Empire had gained independence and had evolved into the Commonwealth of Nations. This association of equal and and autonomous states, set out to agree views and special relationships with one another (appointing High Commissioners rather than Ambassadors) for mutual benefit, trade interests, etc. The Commonwealth is presently (1999) composed of 54 member nations, Including the United Kingdom. All recognize the monarch as Head of the Commonwealth; 16 continue to recognize Queen Elizabeth II as Head of State. In addition to the United Kingdom, they are: Antigua & Barbuda, Australia, The Bahamas, Barbados Belize, Canada, Grenada, Paupa New Guinea, St. Christopher & Nevis, St. Lucia, St. Vincent & the Grenadines, Solomon Islands.

RULERS:
Elizabeth II, 1952-

MONETARY SYSTEM:
1 Shilling = 12 Pence
1 Pound = 20 Shillings to 1971
1 Pound = 100 (New) Pence, 1971-

REPLACEMENT NOTES.
#368, ##A series prefix. #369, S-S or S-T, #373-376, letter M as one of the letters in series prefix. #377-380, Page sign. only, M## or ##M series prefix.

KINGDOM
Bank of England
1957-61 ND Issue

371 5 Pounds — VF UNC
ND (1957-61). Blue and multicolor. Helmeted Britannia head at left, St. George and dragon at lower center. Signature L.K. O'Brien. Back: Lion standing left. Denomination *5* in blue print on back. 159x88mm.
- a. Issued note. — 65.00 — 150
- s. Specimen. — — 1,500

372 5 Pounds — VF UNC
ND (1961-63). Blue and multicolor. Helmeted Britannia head at left, St. George and dragon at lower center. Signature L. K. O'Brien at left. Back: Denomination *5* in white on back. 159x88mm.
- a. Issued note. — 65.00 — 150
- s. Specimen. — — 1,500

1960-64 ND Issue

373 10 Shillings — VF UNC
ND (1961-70). Brown on multicolor underprint. Portrait Queen Elizabeth II at right. Back: Britannia seated with shield in circle at center right. Watermark: Laureate heads in continuous vertical row at left. 140x67mm.
- a. Signature L. K. O'Brien. (1961-62). — 5.00 — 16.00
- b. Signature J. Q. Hollom. (1962-66). — 4.50 — 14.00
- c. Signature J. S. Fforde. (1966-70). — 4.00 — 12.50
- s. Specimen. As a-c. — — 1,000

374 1 Pound — VF UNC
ND (1960-78). Deep green on multicolor underprint. Portrait Queen Elizabeth II at right. Watermark: Laureate heads in continuous vertical row at left. Back: Britannia seated with shield in circle at center right. Watermark: Laureate heads in continuous vertical row at left. 150x72mm.
- a. Signature L. K. O'Brien. (1960-61). — 5.00 — 14.00
- b. Signature as a. Small letter *R* (for Research) at lower left center on back. (Notes printed on web press.) Serial # prefixes A01N; A05N; A06N. — 400 — 1,250
- c. Signature J. Q. Hollom (1962-66). — 4.00 — 12.00
- d. Signature as c. Letter *G* at lower left center on back. (Printed on the experimental German Goebel Press.) — 12.50 — 27.50
- e. Signature J. S. Fforde. (1966-70). — 4.00 — 12.00
- f. Signature as e. Letter *G* at lower center on back. — 14.00 — 32.50
- g. Signature J. B. Page. (1970-77). — 4.00 — 10.00
- s. Specimen. As a, e, g. — — 1,100

375 5 Pounds — VF UNC
ND (1963-71). Deep blue on multicolor underprint. Portrait of Queen Elizabeth II at right. Back: Britannia seated with shield in 8-petalled pattern at center. Watermark: Laureate heads in continuous vertical row. 140x85mm.
- a. Signature J. Q. Hollom. (1963-66). — 27.50 — 80.00
- b. Signature J. S. Fforde. (1966-70). — 25.00 — 70.00
- c. Signature J. B. Page. (1970-71). — 27.50 — 80.00
- s. Specimen. As a, b. — — 1,500

376   10 Pounds

VF UNC

ND (1964-75). Deep brown on multicolor underprint. Portrait of Queen Elizabeth II at right. Back: Lion facing left at center. Watermark: Queen Elizabeth II. 151x93mm.

	VF	UNC
a. Signature J. Q. Hollom. (1964-66).	45.00	110
b. Signature J. S. Fforde. (1966-70).	45.00	110
c. Signature J. B. Page. (1970-75).	40.00	100
r. As c. Replacement note. Serial # prefix *M*.	60.00	135
s. Specimen. As a; b; c.	—	1,800

1971-82 ND Issue

377   1 Pound

VF UNC

ND (1978-84). Deep green on multicolor underprint. Queen Elizabeth II in court robes at right. Back: Sir Isaac Newton at center right, guilloches gray at lower left and right corners. Watermark: Sir Isaac Newton. 135x67mm.

	VF	UNC
a. Green signature J. B. Page. (1978-80).	4.00	10.00
b. Black signature D. H. F. Somerset. Back guilloches are light green at lower left and right. (1981-84).	4.00	10.00
s. Specimen. As a; b.	—	1,500

378   5 Pounds

VF UNC

ND (1971-91). Blue-black and blue on multicolor underprint. Queen Elizabeth II in court robes at right. Back: Arthur Wellesley, Duke of Wellington at center right, battle scene in Spain at left center. Watermark: Wellington's head. 145x77mm.

	VF	UNC
a. Blue-gray signature. J. B. Page. (1971-72).	17.50	50.00
b. Black signature. J. B. Page. Litho back with small *L* at lower left (1973-80).	17.50	50.00
c. Black signature. D. H. F. Somerset. (1980-87). Thin security thread.	15.00	40.00
d. As c. Without signature.	120	350
e. Signature D. H. F. Somerset. Wide security thread. (1987-88).	18.00	55.00
f. Signature G. M. Gill (1988-91).	15.00	40.00
s. Specimen. As a; e.	—	1,400

379   10 Pounds

VF UNC

ND (1975-92). Deep brown on multicolor underprint. Queen Elizabeth II in court robes at right. Back: Florence Nightingale at center right, hospital scene with Florence Nightingale as the *Lady with l* Watermark: Florence Nightingale. 150x85mm.

	VF	UNC
a. Signature J. B. Page. (1975-80).	35.00	90.00
b. Signature D. H. F. Somerset (1980-84).	40.00	110
c. Signature D. H. F. Somerset. Litho printing with *L* at lower left on back. (1984-86).	25.00	75.00
d. Signature D. H. F. Somerset. Segmented security thread. (1987-88).	30.00	85.00
e. Signature G. M. Gill (1988-91).	25.00	75.00
f. Signature G. E. A. Kentfield (1991-92).	40.00	115
r. As a. Replacement note. Serial # prefix *M*.	110	325
s. Specimen. As a; d.	—	1,700

380   20 Pounds

VF UNC

ND (1970-91). Purple on multicolor underprint. Queen Elizabeth II in court robes at right. Back: William Shakespeare statue at center right. Watermark: William Shakespeare. 160x90mm.

	VF	UNC
a. Watermark: Queen Elizabeth II. Signature J. S. Fforde. (1970).	190	600
b. Watermark as a. Signature J. B. Page. (1970-80).	60.00	185
c. Watermark as a. Signature D. H. F. Somerset. (1981-84).	70.00	225
d. Watermark: Shakespeare. Modified background colors. Segmented security thread. D. H. F. Somerset. (1984-88).	55.00	175
e. Signature G. M. Gill (1988-91).	55.00	165
s1. Specimen. As a.	—	2,000
s2. Specimen. As d.	—	1,800

381   50 Pounds

VF UNC

ND (1981-93). Olive-green and brown on multicolor underprint. Queen Elizabeth II in court robes at right. Back: View and plan of St. Paul's Cathedral at left, Sir C. Wren at center right. Watermark: Queen Elizabeth II. 169x95mm.

	VF	UNC
a. Black signature. D. H .F. Somerset (1981-88).	140	350
b. Modified background and guilloche colors. Segmented foil on security thread on surface. Signature G. M. Gill (1988-91).	160	425
c. Signature G. E. A. Kentfield (1991-93).	150	375
s. Specimen. As a; b.	—	1,900

387 20 Pounds VF UNC

©1993 (1993-2006). Black, teal-violet and purple on multicolor underprint. Queen Elizabeth II at right, Britannia at left, dark 20 value symbol at upper left corner and at upper right corner. Segmented vertical foil strip at left. Back: M. Faraday with students at left, portrait at right, 20 value symbol at top right. Watermark: Queen Elizabeth II. 150x80mm.

    a. Signature G. E. A. Kentfield (1993-98).   FV   100
    b. Signature M. Lowther (1999).   FV   155

382 5 Pounds VF UNC

©1990 (1990-2002). Dark brown and deep blue-green on multicolor underprint. Queen Elizabeth II at right, crown at upper right corner, Britannia seated at upper left center. Back: Rocket locomotive at left, George Stephenson at right. Watermark: Queen Elizabeth II. 135x70mm.

    a. Signature G. M. Gill (1990-91). Light and dark signature varieties.   FV   40.00
    b. Signature G. E. Kentfield (1991-98).   FV   25.00
    c. Signature M. Lowther (1999-2002).   FV   25.00
    s1. Specimen. As a.   —   1,750
    s2. Specimen. As b.   —   1,600

383 10 Pounds VF UNC

©1992 (1992-93). Black, brown and red on multicolor underprint. Queen Elizabeth II at right, crown at upper right corner, Britannia at left. Signature G. E. A. Kentfield (1992). Back: Cricket match at left, Charles Dickens at right. Watermark: Queen Elizabeth II. 142x75mm.

    a. Issued note.   FV   60.00
    s. Specimen.   —   1,600

384 20 Pounds VF UNC

©1991 (1991-93). Queen Elizabeth II, crown at upper right corner, Britannia at left. Segmented vertical foil strip and purple optical device at left center.Serial # olive-green to maroon at upper left and dark blue at Back: M. Faraday with students at left, portrait at right. Watermark: Queen Elizabeth II. 150x80mm.

    a. Signature G. M. Gill (1990-91).   FV   115
    b. Signature G. E. A. Kentfield (1991-93).   FV   125
    s. Specimen. As a.   —   1,800

#385 not assigned.

1993 Modified Issue

388 50 Pounds VF UNC

©1994 (1993-). Brownish-black, red and violet on multicolor underprint. Queen Elizabeth II at right, Allegory in oval in underprint at left, 50 value at upper right corner. Back: Bank gatekeeper at lower left, his house at left and Sir J. Houblon at right. Watermark: Queen Elizabeth II. 156x85mm.

    a. Signature G. E. A. Kentfield (1993-98).   FV   240
    b. Signature M. Lowther (1999-2003).   FV   225
    c. Signature A. Bailey (2006-).   FV   190

Note: #388 also honors the 300th anniversary of the Bank of England.

1999-2000 Issue

386 10 Pounds VF UNC

©1993 (1993-2000). Black, brown and red on multicolor underprint. Queen Elizabeth II at right, Britannia at left, enhanced symbols for value 10 at upper right. Back: Cricket match at left, Charles Dickens at right, value symbol at top right. Watermark: Queen Elizabeth II. 142x75mm.

    a. Signature G. E. A. Kentfield (1993-98).   FV   60.00
    b. Signature M. Lowther (1999-2000).   FV   55.00

389 10 Pounds VF UNC

© 2000. (2000-12). Brown, orange and multicolor. Queen Elizabeth II at right. Back: Charles Darwin at right, Hummingbird magnifying glass and flora to left. 142x75mm.

    a. Copyright notice reads: *THE GOVERNOR AND THE COMPANY...* signature M. Lowther (2000).   FV   50.00
    b. Copyright notice reads: *THE GOVERNOR AND COMPANY...* signature M. Lowther (2000-03).   FV   42.50
    c. Signature A. Bailey (2004).   FV   35.00
    d. Signature Chris Salmon (2012).   FV   35.00

390 20 Pounds   VF UNC

© 1999 (1999-2004). Brown and purple on red and green underprint. Queen Elizabeth II at right, 20 and Britannia in OVD, modified top left and right value numerals. Back: Worcester Cathedral at left, Sir Edward Elgar at right. 150x80mm.

    a. Signature M. Lowther (1999-2003).   FV 75.00
    b. Signature A. Bailey (2004).   FV 70.00

2002 Issue

391 5 Pounds   VF UNC

© 2002. Brown and green on multicolor underprint. Queen Elizabeth II at right. Back: Elizabeth Fry at right, scene of women and children in workhouse at left. 135x70mm.

    a. Serial # on varnished paper, easily rubbed off. Withdrawn. From serial # prefix: HA 01. Signature M. Lowther (2002).   FV 40.00
    b. Serial # prefix on paper, varnished. From serial # prefix: HC 01. Signature M. Lowther (2002-03).   FV 20.00
    c. Signature A. Bailey (2004).   FV 17.50
    d. Signature Chris Salmon (2012).   FV 17.50

2006 Issue

392 20 Pounds   VF UNC

© 2006 (2007-12). Deep violet, purple and black on multicolor underprint. Queen Elizabeth II at right, façade of Buckingham Palace at lower center. Britannia at lower left. Back: Adam Smith at left and pin factory at center. Watermark: Adam Smith. 150x80mm.

    a. Sign. A. Bailey. (2006).   FV 65.00
    b. Signature Chris Salmon (2012).   FV 65.00

393 50 Pounds   VF UNC

(2011). Queen Elizabeth II at right. Back: Matthew Boulton and James Watt.; staem engine and the Soho (Birmingham) Factory. 156x85mm.

    a. Signature: Andrew Bailey.   FV 185
    b. Signature Chris Salmon.   FV 175

COLLECTOR SERIES

Bank of England

1995 Issue

#CS1 and CS2, 200th Anniversary of the First 5 Pound Note

CS1 5 Pounds   Mkt. Value
    Uncut sheet of three notes #385 in folder. Serial #AB16-AB18. Last sheet printing.   170

CS2 5 Pounds   Mkt. Value
    Uncut sheet of three notes #385 in folder. Serial #AC01-AC03. First web printing.   170

CS3 10 Pounds   Mkt. Value
    As #386 with serial #HM70. 70th Birthday of Queen Elizabeth II. Issued in a case with 5 Proof coin. 2,000 sets.   140

CS4 20 Pounds   Mkt. Value
    Uncut pair of #384b. Kentfield first issue. 1000 pair in folder.   460

1996 Issue

CS5 5 Pounds   Mkt. Value
    As #386 with serial # prefix *HM70* for the 70th Birthday of Queen Elizabeth II. Limited to 5000.   80.00

CS6 5 Pounds   Mkt. Value
    Uncut sheet of 8 of #382b. Limited to 5000 sheets.   220

1997 Issue

CS7 5 Pounds   Mkt. Value
    As #385a with serial # prefix HK issued commemorating the Return of Hong Kong to the People's Republic of China.
        a. Single note in a special card.   25.00
        b. Uncut sheet of 12.   440
        c. Uncut sheet of 35.   700

CS8 5, 10, 20 Pounds   Mkt. Value
    As #385b, 386b, 387b with serial # prefix BE98 with matching numbers. Limited to 1888.   160

1999 Issue

CS9 5, 10, 20, 50 Pounds   Mkt. Value
    New Lowther issue. In folder: #385b, 386b, 387b and 388b.   600

2000 Issue

CS10 5 Pounds   Mkt. Value
    As 385b but with serial # prefix *YR20*. Millenium. Limited to 1500.   40.00

CS12 5 Pounds   Mkt. Value
    As #385b with serial # prefix *QM10*. With CN crown in folder. Queen Mother's 100th birthday. Limited to 10,000.   60.00

CS13 5 Pounds   Mkt. Value
    As #CS12 with 5 pound stamp in folder. Limited to 1000.   80.00

CS11 10 Pounds   Mkt Value
    As #386b with serial # prefix *YR20*.Millenium. Limited to 1500.   65.00

GREECE

The Hellenic Republic of Greece is situated in southeastern Europe on the southern tip of the Balkan Peninsula. The republic includes many islands, the most important of which are Crete and the Ionian Islands. Greece (including islands) has an area of 131,940 sq. km. and a population of 10.72 million. Capital: Athens. Greece is still largely agricultural. Tobacco, cotton, fruit and wool are exported.

Greece achieved independence from the Ottoman Empire in 1829. During the second half of the 19th century and the first half of the 20th century, it gradually added neighboring islands and territories, most with Greek-speaking populations. In World War II, Greece was first invaded by Italy (1940) and subsequently occupied by Germany (1941-44); fighting endured in a protracted civil war between supporters of the king and Communist rebels. Following the latter's defeat in 1949, Greece joined NATO in 1952. A military dictatorship, which in 1967 suspended many political liberties and forced the king to flee the country, lasted seven years. The 1974 democratic elections and a referendum created a parliamentary republic and abolished the monarchy. In 1981, Greece joined the EC (now the EU); it became the 12th member of the European Economic and Monetary Union in 2001.

RULERS:
Paul I, 1947-1964
Constantine II, 1964-1973

MONETARY SYSTEM:
1 Drachma = 100 Lepta, 1841-2001
1 Euro = 100 Cents, 2002-

REPLACEMENT NOTES:
#195-: OOA prefix.

GREEK ALPHABET

A	α	Alpha	(ă)	I	ι	Iota	(ē)	P	ρ	Rho	(r)
B	β	Beta	(b)	K	κ	Kappa	(k)	Σ	σ	Sigma	(s)6
Γ	γ	Gamma	(g)	Λ	λ	Lambda	(l)	T	τ	Tau	(t)
Δ	δ	Delta	(d)	M	μ	Mu	(m)	Y	υ	Upsilon	(oo)
E	ε	Epsilon	(e)	N	ν	Nu	(n)	Φ	φ	Phi	(f)
Z	ζ	Zeta	(z)	Ξ	ξ	Xi	(ks)	X	χ	Chi	(H)
H	η	Eta	(ā)	O	o	Omicron	(o)	Ψ	ψ	Psi	(ps)
Θ	θ	Theta	(th)	Π	π	Pi	(p)	Ω	ω	Omega	(ū)

KINGDOM

ΤΡΑΠΕΖΑ ΤΗΣ ΕΛΛΑΔΟΣ

BANK OF GREECE

1964-70 Issue

195   50 Drachmai   VF   UNC
1.10.1964. Blue on multicolor underprint. Arethusa at left, galley at bottom right. Back: Shipyard. Watermark: Ephebus.
    a. Issued note.   1.25   10.00
    s. Specimen.   —   90.00

196   100 Drachmai   VF   UNC
1966-67. Red-brown on multicolor underprint. Demokritos at left, building and atomic symbol at right. Back: University at center. Watermark: Ephebus.
    a. Signature Zolotas as Bank President. 1.7.1966.   40.00   150
    b. Signature Galanis as Bank President. 1.10.1967.   2.00   10.00
    s. Specimen. As b.   —   90.00

197   500 Drachmai   VF   UNC
1.11.1968. Olive on multicolor underprint. Relief of Elusis at center. Back: Relief of animals at bottom left, fruit at bottom center. Watermark: Ephebus.
    a. Issued note.   6.00   28.00
    s. Specimen.   —   90.00

198   1000 Drachmai   VF   UNC
1.11.1970. Brown on multicolor underprint. Zeus at left, stadium at bottom center. Back: Woman at left and view of city Hydra on the Isle of Hydra.
    a. Watermark: Aphrodite of Knidus (hair in knot at top of head) profile (1970).   23.00   80.00
    b. Watermark: Ephebus of Anticythera in 3/4 profile (1972).   1.00   4.00
    s. As b. Specimen.   —   90.00

REPUBLIC - 1970S

ΤΡΑΠΕΖΑ ΤΗΣ ΕΛΛΑΔΟΣ

BANK OF GREECE

1978 Issue

199   50 Drachmai   VF   UNC
8.12.1978. Blue on multicolor underprint. Poseidon at left. Back: Sailing ship at left center, man and woman at right. Watermark: Charioteer Polyzalos of Delphi.
    a. Issued note.   0.75   2.50
    r. Replacement note. Series 00A.   FV   25.00
    s. Specimen.   —   90.00

200 100 Drachmai

VF UNC

8.12.1978. Brown and violet on multicolor underprint. Athena Peiraios at left.
Back: A. Koraes at left, Church of Arkadi Monastery in Crete at bottom right.
Watermark: Charioteer Polyzalos of Delphi. 158x67mm.

a. Original issue. Without *L* at lower left on back.	—	1.00
b. Second issue. With *L* at lower left on back.	—	1.00
r. As b. Replacement note. Series *00A*.	FV	25.00
s. Specimen.	—	115

1983-87 Issue

201 500 Drachmaes

VF UNC

1.2.1983. Deep green on multicolor underprint. I. Capodistrias at left center, his
birthplace at lower right. Back: Fortress overlooking Corfu. Watermark: Charioteer
Polyzalos of Delphi. 158x72mm.

a. Issued note.	1.00	3.50
r. Replacement note. Series *00A*.	FV	115
s. Specimen.	—	115

202 1000 Drachmaes

VF UNC

1.7.1987. Brown on multicolor underprint. Apollo at center right, ancient coin
at bottom left center. Back: Discus thrower and Hera Temple ruins at Olympia.
Watermark: Charioteer Polyzalos of Delphi. 158x77mm.

a. Issued note.	1.00	4.00
r. Replacement note. Series *00A*.	FV	70.00
s. Specimen.	—	115

203 5000 Drachmaes

VF UNC

23.3.1984. Deep blue on multicolor underprint. T. Kolokotronis at left, Church of
the Holy Apostles at Calamata at bottom center right. Back: Landscape and view
of town of Karytaina at center right. Watermark: Charioteer Polyzalos of Delphi.
163x81mm.

a. Issued note.	5.00	25.00
r. Replacement note. Series *00A* .	FV	135
s. Specimen.	—	160

1995-98 Issue

204 200 Drachmaes

VF UNC

2.9.1996. Deep orange on multicolor underprint. R. Velestinlis-Feraios at left.
Velestinlis-Feraios singing his patriotic song at lower right. Back: Secret school
run by Greek priests (during the Ottoman occupation) at center right. Watermark:
Philip of Macedonia. 129x65mm.

a. Issued note.	—	2.50
s. Specimen.	—	115

205 5000 Drachmaes | **VF** | **UNC**

1.6.1997. Reduced size. Purple and yellow-green on multicolor underprint. T. Kolokotronis at left, Church of the Holy Apostles at Calamata at bottom center right. Back: Landscape and view of town of Karytaina at center right. Watermark: Philip of Macedonia. 147x74mm.

	VF	UNC
a. Issued note.	8.00	30.00
r. Replacement note. Serie *00A*.	FV	160
s. Specimen.	—	160

206 10,000 Drachmaes | **VF** | **UNC**

16.1.1995. Deep purple on multicolor underprint. Dr. Georgios Papanikolaou at left center, microscope at lower center right. Back: Medical care frieze at bottom center, statue of Asklepios at center right. 153x77mm.

	VF	UNC
a. Issued note.	10.00	45.00
r. Replacement note. Series *00A*.	FV	225
s. Specimen.	—	225

Note: For later issues made for use in Greece see European Union listings.

GREENLAND

Greenland, an integral part of the Danish realm, is a huge island situated between the North Atlantic Ocean and the Polar Sea, almost entirely within the Artic Circle. It has an area of 2.166 million sq. km. and a population of 57,564. Capital: Nuuk (Godthab). Greenland is the world's only source of natural cryolite, a fluoride of sodium and aluminum important in making aluminum. Fish products and minerals are exported.

Greenland, the world's largest island, is about 81% ice-capped. Vikings reached the island in the 10th century from Iceland; Danish colonization began in the 18th century, and Greenland was made an integral part of Denmark in 1953. It joined the European Community (now the EU) with Denmark in 1973, but withdrew in 1985 over a dispute centered on stringent fishing quotas. Greenland was granted self-government in 1979 by the Danish parliament; the law went into effect the following year. Denmark continues to exercise control of Greenland's foreign affairs in consultation with Greenland's Home Rule Government.

RULERS:
Danish

MONETARY SYSTEM:
1 Rigsbankdaler = 96 Skilling to 1874
1 Krone = 48 Skilling
1 Krone = 100 Öre, 1874-

DANISH ADMINISTRATION
Den Kongelige Grønlandske Handel
1953 Issue

18 5 Kroner | **VF** | **UNC**

ND (1953-67). Green. Polar bear on ice at center. *DEN KONGELIGE GRNLANDSKE HANDEL* at left and right margin, across bottom. Back: *DEN KONGELIGE GRNLANDSKE HANDEL* around map at center.

	VF	UNC
a. Signature: Hans C. Christensen. Size: 84x125mm.	90.00	200
b. Signature: Hans C. Christensen. Size: 84x130mm.	90.00	200
s. Specimen.	—	200

19 10 Kroner

ND (1953-67). Brown. Hump-back whale at center. *DEN KONGELIGE GRNLANDSKE HANDEL* at left and right margin, across bottom. Back: *DEN KONGELIGE GRNLANDSKE HANDEL* around map at center.

		VF	UNC
a.	Serial number with serifs. Signature: Hans C. Christensen.	180	400
b.	Serial number without serifs. Signature: Hans C. Christensen.	100	250
s1.	Specimen. As a.	200	—
s2.	Specimen. As b.	—	200

20 50 Kroner

ND (1953-67). Lilac. Clipper ship at center. *DEN KONGELIGE GRNLANDSKE HANDEL* at left and right margin, across bottom. Back: *DEN KONGELIGE GRNLANDSKE HANDEL* around map at center.

		VF	UNC
a.	Signature: Hans C. Christensen.	375	700
s.	Specimen.	—	475

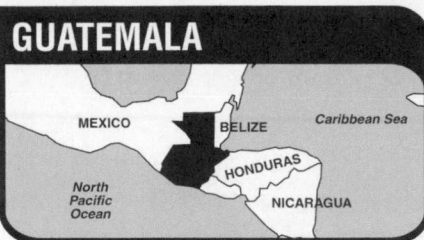

GUATEMALA

The Republic of Guatemala, the northernmost of the five Central American republics, has an area of 108,800 sq. km. and a population of 13 million. Capital: Guatemala City. The economy of Guatemala is heavily dependent on resources which are being developed. Coffee, cotton and bananas are exported.

The Mayan civilization flourished in Guatemala and surrounding regions during the first millennium A.D. After almost three centuries as a Spanish colony, Guatemala won its independence in 1821. During the second half of the 20th century, it experienced a variety of military and civilian governments, as well as a 36-year guerrilla war. In 1996, the government signed a peace agreement formally ending the conflict, which had left more than 100,000 people dead and had created, by some estimates, some 1 million refugees.

MONETARY SYSTEM:
1 Peso = 100 Centavos to 1924
1 Quetzal = 100 Centavos, 1924-

REPUBLIC

Banco de Guatemala

1957-63 Issue

35 1/2 Quetzal
	VF	UNC
22.1.1958. Brown on multicolor underprint. Hermitage of Cerro del Carmen at left. Signature title: *JEFE DE...* Back: Two Guatemalans. Printer: ABNC.	20.00	100

36 1 Quetzal
1957-58. Green on multicolor underprint. Palace of the Captains General at left. Signature title: *JEFE DE...* Back: Lake Atitlan. Printer: ABNC.

		VF	UNC
a.	16.1.1957.	15.00	90.00
b.	22.1.1958.	15.00	90.00

37 5 Quetzales
22.1.1958. Purple. Vase *Vasija de Uaxactum* at left. Signature title: *JEFE DE...* Back: Mayan-Spanish battle scene. Printer: ABNC.

		VF	UNC
a.	Issued note.	35.00	175
s.	Specimen.	—	50.00

38 10 Quetzales
1958; 1962-64. Red. Round stone carving *Ara de Tikal* at left. Signature title: *JEFE DE...* Back: Founding of old Guatemala. Printer: ABNC.

		VF	UNC
a.	22.1.1958.	65.00	225
b.	12.1.1962.	65.00	225
c.	9.1.1963.	65.00	225
d.	8.1.1964.	65.00	225

39 20 Quetzales
1963-65. Blue. Landivar at left. Signature title: *JEFE DE...* Back: Meeting of Independence. Printer: ABNC.

		VF	UNC
a.	9.1.1963.	75.00	275
b.	8.1.1964.	75.00	275
c.	15.1.1965.	75.00	275

1959-60 Issues

40 1/2 Quetzal
	VF	UNC
18.2.1959. Printed area 2mm smaller than #41. Signature title: *JEFE DE...* at right. Lighter brown shadings around value guilloche at left. 6-digit serial #. Signature varieties. Printer: W&S.	15.00	100

47 10 Quetzales
1959-1961. Similar to #46 but redesigned guilloche. Round stone in brown.
Signature title: *JEFE DE...* at right. Signature varieties. Printer: W&S.

	VF	UNC
a. 18.2.1959.	35.00	175
b. 13.1.1960.	35.00	175
c. 18.1.1961.	35.00	175
s. Specimen.	—	—

41 1/2 Quetzal
1959-1961. Signature title: *JEFE DE...* at right. Darker brown shadings around
value guilloche at left. 7-digit serial #. Signature varieties. Printer: W&S.

	VF	UNC
a. 18.2.1959.	10.00	45.00
b. 13.1.1960.	10.00	45.00
c. 18.1.1961.	10.00	45.00
s. Specimen.	—	30.00

42 1 Quetzal
18.2.1959. Signature title: *JEFE DE...* at right. Building at center right. Green
palace. 6-digit serial #. Signature varieties. Printer: W&S.

	VF	UNC
a. Issued note.	10.00	75.00
s. Specimen.	—	80.00

43 1 Quetzal
1959-1964. Signature title: *JEFE DE...* at right. Black palace. 7-digit serial #.
Signature varieties. Printer: W&S.

	VF	UNC
a. 18.2.1959.	7.50	45.00
b. 13.1.1960.	7.50	45.00
c. 18.1.1961.	7.50	45.00
d. 12.1.1962.	7.50	45.00
e. 9.1.1963.	7.50	45.00
f. 8.1.1964.	7.50	45.00
s. Specimen.	—	80.00

48 20 Quetzales
1960-65. Blue. Signature title: *JEFE DE...* at right. Portrait at right Landivar at
right. Signature varieties. Printer: W&S.

	VF	UNC
a. 13.1.1960.	65.00	200
b. 18.1.1961.	65.00	200
c. 12.1.1962.	65.00	200
d. 9.1.1963.	65.00	200
e. 8.1.1964.	65.00	200
f. 15.1.1965.	65.00	200
s. Specimen.	—	—

49 100 Quetzales
18.2.1959. Dark blue. Signature title: *JEFE DE...* at right. *Indio de Nahuala* in blue
at center. Signature varieties. Printer: W&S.

	VF	UNC
	250	650

44 5 Quetzales
18.2.1959. Value at left center. Vase in purple. Signature title: *JEFE DE...* at right.
Signature varieties. Printer: W&S.

	VF	UNC
	50.00	200

50 100 Quetzales
1960-65. Dark blue. Signature title: *JEFE DE...* at right. Portrait *Indio de Nahuala*
in brown at right. Signature varieties. Printer: W&S.

	VF	UNC
a. 13.1.1960.	250	500
b. 18.1.1961.	250	500
c. 12.1.1962.	250	500
d. 9.1.1963.	250	500
e. 8.1.1964.	250	500
f. 15.1.1965.	250	500
s. Specimen.	—	—

1964-67 Issue

51 1/2 Quetzal
1964-1972. Signature varieties. Brown on multicolor underprint. Signature title:
JEFE DE... at right. Darker brown shadings around value guilloche at left. 7-digit
serial #. Hermitage of Cerro del Carmen at left. Back: Two Guatemalans at center.
Printer: TDLR.

	VF	UNC
a. 8.1.1964.	10.00	40.00
b. 15.1.1965.	15.00	40.00
c. 21.1.1966.	15.00	40.00
d. 13.1.1967.	15.00	40.00
e. 3.1.1968.	15.00	40.00
f. 3.1.1969.	15.00	40.00
g. 7.1.1970.	15.00	40.00
h. 6.1.1971.	15.00	40.00
i. 5.1.1972.	15.00	40.00

45 5 Quetzales
1959-1964. Redesigned guilloche. Value at center. Vase in brown. Signature title:
JEFE DE... at right. Signature varieties. Printer: W&S.

	VF	UNC
a. 18.2.1959.	25.00	100
b. 13.1.1960.	25.00	100
c. 18.1.1961.	25.00	100
d. 12.1.1962.	25.00	100
e. 9.1.1963.	25.00	100
f. 8.1.1964.	25.00	100
s. Specimen.	—	—

46 10 Quetzales
18.2.1959. Signature title: *JEFE DE...* at right. Round red stone at right. Signature
varieties. Printer: W&S.

	VF	UNC
a. Issued note.	70.00	250
s. Specimen.	—	135

52   1 Quetzal   VF   UNC

1964-1972. Black and green on multicolor underprint. Palace of the Captains General at center right. Signature varieties. Back: Lake Atitlan Printer: TDLR.

a. 8.1.1964.	7.50	37.50
b. 15.1.1965.	7.50	37.50
c. 21.1.1966.	7.50	37.50
d. 13.1.1967.	7.50	37.50
e. 3.1.1968.	7.50	37.50
f. 3.1.1969.	7.50	37.50
g. 7.1.1970.	7.50	37.50
h. 6.1.1971.	7.50	37.50
i. 5.1.1972.	7.50	37.50

53   5 Quetzales   VF   UNC

1964-1971. Purple on multicolor underprint. Vase *Vasija de Uaxactum* at right. Signature varieties. Watermark: 2 varieties. Printer: TDLR.

a. 8.1.1964.	10.00	60.00
b. 15.1.1965.	10.00	60.00
c. 21.1.1966.	10.00	60.00
d. 13.1.1967.	10.00	60.00
e. 3.1.1968.	10.00	60.00
f. 3.1.1969.	10.00	60.00
g. 7.1.1970.	10.00	60.00
h. 6.1.1971.	10.00	60.00

54   10 Quetzales   VF   UNC

1965-1970. Red on multicolor underprint. Round carved stone *Arade Tikal* at right. Signature varieties. Back: Mayan-Spanish battle scene. Watermark: 2 varieties. Printer: TDLR.

a. 15.1.1965.	25.00	120
b. 21.1.1966.	25.00	120
c. 13.1.1967.	25.00	120
d. 3.1.1968.	25.00	120
e. 3.1.1969.	25.00	120
f. 7.1.1970.	25.00	120

55   20 Quetzales   VF   UNC

1965-1971. Blue on multicolor underprint. R. Landivar at right. Signature varieties. Back: Founding of Guatemala. Watermark: 2 varieties. Printer: TDLR.

a. 15.1.1965.	45.00	200
b. 21.1.1966.	45.00	200
c. 13.1.1967.	45.00	200
d. 3.1.1968.	45.00	200
e. 3.1.1969.	45.00	200
f. 7.1.1970.	45.00	200
g. 6.1.1971.	45.00	200

56   50 Quetzales   VF   UNC

1967-1973. Orange and blue on multicolor underprint. General J. M. Orellana at right. Signature varieties. Back: Bank at center. Watermark: 2 varieties. Printer: TDLR.

a. 13.1.1967.	175	450
b. 3.1.1968.	175	450
c. 3.1.1969.	175	450
d. 7.1.1970.	175	450
e. 6.1.1971.	175	450
f. 5.1.1972.	175	450
g. 5.1.1973.	175	450

57   100 Quetzales   VF   UNC

1966-1970. Blue-black and brown on pale green and multicolor underprint. *Indio de Nahuala* at right. Signature varieties. Back: City and mountain in valley Antihua. Watermark: 2 varieties.

a. 21.1.1966.	150	400
b. 13.1.1967.	150	400
c. 3.1.1968.	150	400
d. 3.1.1969.	150	400
e. 7.1.1970.	150	400

1969-75 Issue

58   1/2 Quetzal   VF   UNC

1972-83. Brown on multicolor underprint. Tecun Uman (national hero) at right. Quetzal bird at upper center. Signature varieties. Back: Tikal temple. Printer: TDLR. 156x68mm.

a. Without security (flourescent) imprint. 5.1.1972; 5.1.1973.	1.75	20.00
b. Security (flourescent) imprint on back. 2.1.1974; 3.1.1975; 7.1.1976; 20.4.1977.	1.50	17.00
c. 4.1.1978; 3.1.1979; 2.1.1980; 7.1.1981; 6.1.1982; 6.1.1983.	1.50	14.00
s. Specimen. As c.	—	10.00

59   1 Quetzal   VF   UNC

1972-83. Green on multicolor underprint. General J. M. Orellana at right, Quetzal bird at upper center. Signature varieties. Back: Banco de Guatemala building. Printer: TDLR. 156x68mm.

a. Security (flourescent) imprint on face. Date at lower right. 5.1.1972; 5.1.1973.	2.50	25.00
b. Security imprint as a. on face and back. 2.1.1974; 3.1.1975; 7.1.1976.	2.00	17.00
c. Date at center r. 5.1.1977; 20.4.1977; 4.1.1978; 3.1.1979; 2.1.1980; 7.1.1981; 6.1.1982; 6.1.1983; 30.12.1983.	1.25	15.00
s. Specimen. As c.	—	10.00

60   5 Quetzales   **VF   UNC**
1969-83. Purple on multicolor underprint. General (later President) J. R. Barrios
at right, Quetzal bird at upper center. Signature varieties. Back: Classroom scene.
Watermark: Tecun Uman. Printer: TDLR. 156x68mm.

a. 3.1.1969; 6.1.1971; 5.1.1972; 5.1.1973.	6.00	35.00
b. 2.1.1974; 3.1.1975; 7.1.1976; 5.1.1977; 20.4.1977.	4.00	25.00
c. 4.1.1978; 3.1.1979; 2.1.1980; 7.1.1981; 6.1.1982; 6.1.1983.	3.00	20.00
s. Specimen. As c. ND.	—	10.00

61   10 Quetzales   **VF   UNC**
1971-83. Red on multicolor underprint. General M. G. Granados at right, Quetzal
bird at upper center. Signature varieties. Back: National Assembly session of
1872. Watermark: Tecun Uman. Printer: TDLR. 156x68mm.

a. 6.1.1971; 5.1.1972; 3.1.1973.	10.00	60.00
b. 2.1.1974; 3.1.1975; 7.1.1976; 5.1.1977; 20.4.1977.	7.50	45.00
c. 4.1.1978; 3.1.1979; 2.1.1980; 7.1.1981; 6.1.1982; 6.1.1983.	5.00	35.00
s. Specimen. As c. ND.	—	10.00

62   20 Quetzales   **VF   UNC**
1972-83; 1988. Blue on multicolor underprint. Dr. M. Galvez at right, Quetzal bird
at upper center. Signature varieties. Back: Granting of Independence to Central
America. Watermark: Tecun Uman. Printer: TDLR. 156x68mm.

a. 5.1.1972; 5.1.1973.	15.00	100
b. 2.1.1974; 3.1.1975; 7.1.1976; 5.1.1977; 20.4.1977.	10.00	75.00
c. 4.1.1978; 2.1.1979; 2.1.1980; 7.1.1981; 6.1.1982; 6.1.1983.	10.00	55.00
d. 6.1.1988.	7.00	40.00

63   50 Quetzales   **VF   UNC**
1974; 1981-83. Orange on multicolor underprint. C. O. Zachrisson at right,
Quetzal bird at upper center. Signature varieties. Back: Crop workers. Watermark:
Tecun Uman. Printer: TDLR. 156x68mm.

a. 2.1.1974.	45.00	275
b. 1.4.1978; 7.1.1981; 6.1.1982; 6.1.1983.	35.00	200

64   100 Quetzales   **VF   UNC**
1972-83. Brown on multicolor underprint. F. Marroquin at right, Quetzal bird at
upper center. Signature varieties. Back: University of San Carlos de Borromeo.
Watermark: Tecun Uman. Printer: TDLR. 156x68mm.

a. 5.1.1972.	75.00	350
b. 3.1.1975; 7.1.1976; 1.4.1978; 3.1.1979.	60.00	275
c. 6.1.1982; 6.1.1983.	45.00	200

1983 Issue

65   1/2 Quetzal   **VF   UNC**
6.1.1983-4.1.1989. Brown on multicolor underprint. Tecun Uman at right, Quetzal   FV   14.00
bird at upper center. Back. Tikal temple. Watermark: Tecun Uman. Printer: G&D.
156x68mm.

66   1 Quetzal   **VF   UNC**
30.12.1983-4.1.1989. UV: fibers fluoresce yellow, design on left green. Back: left   FV   14.00
and right ends orange. Blue-green and green on multicolor underprint. General J.
Orellana at right, Quetzal bird at upper center. Back: Banco de Guatemala building. Watermark: Tecun Uman. Printer: G&D. 156x68mm.

67   5 Quetzales   **VF   UNC**
6.1.1983-6.1.1988. Purple on multicolor underprint. J. R. Barrios at right, Quetzal   2.50   20.00
bird at upper center. Back: Classroom scene. Watermark: Tecun Uman. Printer:
G&D. 156x68mm.

68   10 Quetzales   VF   UNC
30.12.1983-6.1.1988. Red and red-brown on multicolor underprint. General M. G.   5.00   30.00
Granados at right, Quetzal bird at upper center. Back: National Assembly session
of 1872. Watermark: Tecun Uman. Printer: G&D. 156x68mm.

69   20 Quetzales   VF   UNC
6.1.1983-7.1.1987. Blue on multicolor underprint. Dr. M. Galvez at right, Quetzal   10.00   45.00
bird at upper center. Back: Granting of Independence to Central America. Watermark: Tecun Uman. Printer: G&D. 156x68mm.

70   50 Quetzales   VF   UNC
30.12.1983-7.1.1987. Orange and yellow-orange on multicolor underprint. C. O.   24.00   125
Zachrisson at right, Quetzal bird at upper center. Back: Crop workers. Watermark:
Tecun Uman. Printer: G&D. 156x68mm.

71   100 Quetzales   VF   UNC
30.12.1983-7.1.1987. Brown on multicolor underprint. F. Marroquin at right, Quet-   35.00   175
zal bird at right. Back: University of San Carlos de Borromeo. Watermark:
Tecun Uman. Printer: G&D. 156x68mm.

1989; 1990 Issue

72   1/2 Quetzal   VF   UNC
1989; 1992. Brown on multicolor underprint. Tecun Uman at right, Quetzal bird at
upper center. Signature varieties. Back: Tikal temple. Printer: CBN. 156x68mm.
    a. 4.1.1989.   FV   6.00
    b. 14.2.1992.   FV   5.00

73   1 Quetzal   VF   UNC
1990-92. UV: fibers fluoresce blue and green. Back, value 1 yellow. Blue-green
on multicolor underprint. General J. Orellana at right, Quetzal bird at upper
center. Signature varieties. Back: Banco de Guatemala building. Printor: CBN.
156x68mm.
    a. 3.1.1990.   FV   6.00
    b. 6.3.1991.   FV   6.00
    c. 22.1.1992.   FV   6.00
    d. 14.2.1992.   FV   6.00

74   5 Quetzales   VF   UNC
1990-92. Purple on multicolor underprint. J. R. Barrios at right, Quetzal bird at upper center. Signature varieties. Back: Classroom scene. Printer: CBN. 156x68mm.
    a. 3.1.1990.   FV   12.00
    b. 6.3.1991.   FV   12.00
    c. 22.1.1992.   FV   12.00

75   10 Quetzales   VF   UNC
1989; 1990; 1992. Brown-violet and red on multicolor underprint. General M. G.
Granados at right, Quetzal bird at upper center. Signature varieties. Vertical serial
number at left. Back: National Assembly session of 1872. Watermark: Tecun
Uman. Printer: TDLR. 156x68mm.
    a. 4.1.1989.   FV   17.00
    b. 3.1.1990.   FV   17.00
    c. 22.1.1992.   FV   17.00

76   20 Quetzales   VF   UNC
1989; 1990; 1992. Blue-black, purple and blue on multicolor underprint. Dr. M.
Galvez at right, Quetzal bird at upper center. Signature varieteis. Vertical serial
number at left. Back: Granting of Independence to Central America. Watermark:
Tecun Uman. Printer: TDLR. 156x68mm.
    a. 4.1.1989.   FV   24.00
    b. 3.1.1990.   FV   24.00
    c. 22.1.1992.   FV   24.00

77 50 Quetzales

1989-92. Orange and green on multicolor underprint. C. O. Zachrisson at right, Quetzal bird at upper center. Signature varieties. Vertical serial number at left. Back: Crop workers. Watermark: Tecun Uman. Printer: TDLR. 156x68mm.

	VF	UNC
a. 4.1.1989.	7.50	55.00
b. 3.1.1990.	7.50	55.00
c. 1.22.1992.	7.50	55.00

78 100 Quetzales

1989; 1990; 1992. Brown and red-brown on multicolor underprint. F. Marroquin at right, Quetzal bird at upper center. Signature varieties. Vertical serial number at left. Back: University of San Carlos de Borromeo. Watermark: Tecun Uman. Printer: TDLR. 156x68mm.

	VF	UNC
a. 4.1.1989.	20.00	90.00
b. 3.1.1990.	20.00	90.00
c. 22.1.1992.	20.00	90.00

1992 Issue

79 1/2 Quetzal

16.7.1992. Brown on multicolor underprint. Tecun Uman at right, Quetzal bird at upper center. Signature varieties. Back: Tikal temple. Printer: F-CO. 156x68mm.

VF	UNC
FV	4.00

80 1 Quetzal

16.7.1992. Blue green on multicolor underprint. General J. Orellana at right, Quetzal bird at upper center. Signature varieties. Back: Banco de Guatemala building. Printer: F-CO. 156x68mm.

VF	UNC
FV	5.00

81 5 Quetzales

16.7.1992. Purple on multicolor underprint. J. R. Barrios at right, Quetzal bird at upper center. Signature varieties. Back: Classroom scene. Printer: F-CO. 156x68mm.

VF	UNC
FV	10.00

82 10 Quetzales

16.7.1992. Brown-violet and red on multicolor underprint. General M. G. Granados at right, Quetzal bird at upper center. Signature varieties. Back: National Assembly session of 1872. Watermark: Tecun Uman. 156x68mm.

VF	UNC
FV	14.00

83 20 Quetzales

12.8.1992. Blue-black, purple and blue on multicolor underprint. Dr. M. Galvez at right, Quetzal bird at upper center. Signature varieties. Back: Granting of Independence to Central America. Watermark: Tecun Uman. Printer: BABN. 156x68mm.

VF	UNC
FV	20.00

84 50 Quetzales

12.8.1992. Orange and green on multicolor underprint. C. O. Zachrisson at right, Quetzal bird at upper center. Signature varieties. Back: Crop workers. Watermark: Tecun Uman. Printer: BABN. 156x68mm.

VF	UNC
6.00	40.00

85 100 Quetzales

27.5.1992. Brown on multicolor underprint. F. Marroquin at right, Quetzal bird at upper center., date at lower left, gold colored device at right. Signature varieties. Back: University of San Carlos de Borromeo. Watermark: Tecun Uman. Printer: BABN. 156x68mm.

VF	UNC
10.00	60.00

1993; 1995 Issue

86 1/2 Quetzal

1993-95. Brown on multicolor underprint. Tecun Uman at right, Quetzal bird at upper center. Signature varieties. Back: Tikal temple. Printer: CBNC. 156x68mm.

	VF	UNC
a. 27.10.1993.	FV	3.00
b. 27.9.1994.	FV	2.50
c. 6.9.1995.	FV	2.50

87 1 Quetzal

1993-95. Dark green on green and multicolor underprint. General J. Orellana at right, Quetzal bird at upper center. Signature varieties. Back: Banco de Guatemala building. Printer: CBNC. 156x68mm.

	VF	UNC
a. 27.10.1993	FV	4.00
b. 6.9.1994.	FV	3.50
c. 6.9.1995.	FV	3.50

88 5 Quetzales

1993; 1995. UV: fibers fluoresce blue, quetzal green. Back value 5 orange. Purple on multicolor underprint. J. R. Barrios at right, Quetzal bird at upper center. Signature varieties. Back: Classroom scene. Printer: CBNC. 156x68mm.

	VF	UNC
a. 27.10.1993.	1.50	7.50
b. 16.6.1995.	1.50	7.50
c. Without imprint. 16.6.1995.	FV	5.00

89   10 Quetzales
16.6.1995. Large and small printer imprint on back. Brown-violet and red on
multicolor underprint. General M. G. Granados at right, Quetzal bird at upper
center. Signature varieties. Back: National Assembly session of 1872. Printer:
CNBC. 156x68mm.

	VF	UNC
	FV	12.50

1994; 1995 Issue

90   1 Quetzal
27.9.1994. Dark green on green and multicolor underprint. General J. Orellana at
right, Quetzal bird at upper center. Signature varieties. Back: Banco de Guatemala
building. Printer: F-CO. 156x68mm.

	VF	UNC
	FV	2.50

92   5 Quetzales
29.6.1994. Orange and green on multicolor underprint. J. R. Barrios at right,
Quetzal bird at upper center. Signature varieties. Back: Classroom scene. Printer:
TDLR. 156x68mm.

	VF	UNC
	FV	5.00

91   10 Quetzales
29.6.1994. Brown-violet and red on multicolor underprint. General M. G. Granados
at right, Quetzal bird at upper center. Signature varieties. Vertical serial number at
left. Back: National Assembly session of 1872. Printer: F-CO. 156x68mm.

	VF	UNC
	FV	10.00

93   20 Quetzales
16.6.1995. Blue-black, purple and blue on multicolor underprint. Dr. M. Galvez
at right, Quetzal bird at upper center. Back: Granting of Independence to Central
America. Printer: G&D. 156x68mm.

	VF	UNC
	FV	14.00

94   50 Quetzales
16.6.1995. Orange and green on multicolor underprint. Similar to #77. 156x68mm.

	VF	UNC
	FV	30.00

95   100 Quetzales
1994-95. Brown on multicolor underprint. F. Marroquin at right, Quetzal bird at
upper center. Signature varieties. Vertical serial number at left. Back: University of
San Carlos de Borromeo. Printer: TDLR. 156x68mm.

	VF	UNC
a. 29.6.1994.	FV	50.00
b. 16.6.1995.	FV	50.00

1996 Issue

96   1/2 Quetzal
28.8.1006. Brown on multicolor underprint. Tecun Uman at right, Quetzal bird at
upper center. Signature varieties. Back: Tikal temple. Printer: H&S. 156x68mm.

	VF	UNC
a. Issued note.	FV	1.50
s. Specimen.	—	75.00

97   1 Quetzal
28.1.1996. Dark green on green and multicolor underprint. General J. Orellana at
right, Quetzal bird at upper center. Signature varieties. Back: Banco de Guatemala
building. Printer: H&S. 156x68mm.

	VF	UNC
a. Issued note.	FV	2.50
s. Specimen.	—	75.00

1998-99 Issue

98   1/2 Quetzal
9.1.1998. Brown on multicolor underprint. Tecun Uman at right, Quetzal bird at
upper center. Signature varieties. Back: Tikal temple. Printer: (T)DLR. 156x68mm.

	VF	UNC
	FV	1.00

99   1 Quetzal
9.1.1998. Dark green and green on multicolor underprint. General J. Orellana at
right, Quetzal bird at upper center. Signature varieties. Back: Banco de Guatemala
building. Printer: (T)DLR 156x68mm.

	VF	UNC

100   5 Quetzales
29.7.1998. Purple on multicolor underprint. J. R. Barrios at right, Quetzal bird at
upper center. Signature varieties. Back: Classroom scene. 156x68mm.

	VF	UNC
	FV	3.00

101   10 Quetzales
29.7.1998. Brown-violet and red on multicolor underprint. General M. G. Granados
at right, Quetzal bird at upper center. Signature varieties. Vertical serial number at
left. Back: National Assembly session of 1872. Printer: BABN. 156x68mm.

	VF	UNC
	FV	6.50

102   20 Quetzales   **VF   UNC**
    17.6.1999. Blue-black, purple and blue on multicolor underprint. Dr. M. Galvez at   FV   15.00
    right, Quetzal bird at upper center. Signature varieties. Back: Granting of Indepen-
    dence to Central America. Printer: TDLR. 156x68mm.

103   100 Quetzales   **VF   UNC**
    29.7.1998. Multicolor. F. Marroquin at right. Back: University of San Carlos de   FV   40.00
    Borromeo. Printer: BABN. 156x68mm.

2001 Issue

104   100 Quetzales   **VF   UNC**
    2001; 2006-07. Multicolor. F. Marroquin at right. Back: University of San Carlos de
    Borromeo. Printer: G&D. 156x68mm.
    a. 9.4.2001.   FV   30.00
    b. 25.8.2006.   FV   30.00
    c. 24.1.2007.   FV   30.00

2001 Second Issue

105   50 Quetzales   **VF   UNC**
    9.4.2001. Orange and green on multicolor underprint. C. O. Zachrisson at right.   FV   20.00
    Back: Crop workers. Watermark: Mayan head. Printer: G&D. 156x68mm.

2003 Issue

106   5 Quetzales   **VF   UNC**
    2003; 2006; 2007. Purple on multicolor underprint. J. R. Barrios at right. Back:
    Classroom scene. Printer: F-CO. 156x68mm.
    a. 12.2.2003.   FV   3.50
    b. 22.11.2006.   FV   3.50
    c. 17.1.2007.   FV   3.50

107   10 Quetzales   **VF   UNC**
    12.2.2003. Brown-violet and red on multicolor underprint. General M. G. Granados   FV   6.00
    at right. Back: National Assembly session of 1872. Printer: F-CO. 156x68mm.

108   20 Quetzales   **VF   UNC**
    12.2.2003. Blue-black, purple and blue on multicolor underprint. Dr. M. Galves   FV   10.00
    at right. Back: Granting of Independence to Central America. Printer: FC-O.
    156x68mm.

2006 Issue

109   1 Quetzal   **VF   UNC**
    20.12.2006. Polymer plastic. Green on multicolor underprint. General J. Orellana   FV   1.00
    at right. Back: Banco de Guatemala building. Printer: CBNC. 156x68mm.

#110 Not assigned.

111   10 Quetzales   **VF   UNC**
    2006-07. Brown-violet and red on multicolor underprint. General M. G. Granados
    at right. Back: National Assembly session of 1872. Watermark: Denomination
    added. Printer: CBNC. 156x68mm.
    a. 25.8.2006.   FV   4.50
    b. 17.1.2007.   FV   4.50

112 20 Quetzales VF UNC
25.8.2006; 24.1.2007. Blue-black, purple and blue on multicolor underprint. Dr. M.
Galvez at right. Back: Granting of Independence to Central America. Watermark:
Denomination added. Printer: DLR. 156x68mm.
a. 25.8.2006. FV 6.50
b. 24.1.2007. FV 5.00

113 50 Quetzales VF UNC
15.11.2006. Orange and green on multicolor underprint. C. O. Zachrisson ar right.
Back: Crop workers. Watermark: Denomination added. Printer: DLR. 156x68mm. FV 25.00

114 100 Quetzales VF UNC
2006-07. Brown on multicolor underprint. F. Marroquin at right. Back: University
of San Carlos de Borromeo. Watermark: Denomination added. Printer: G&D.
156x68mm.
a. 25.8.2006. FV 40.00
b. 24.1.2007. FV 35.00

2008 Issue

115 1 Quetzal VF UNC
12.3.2008. Polymer plastic. Green on multicolor undeprint. General J. Orellana at
right. Back: Banco de Guatemala building. Printer: FC-O. 156x68mm.
a. 12.3.2008. FV 1.00
b. 2.5.2012. FV 1.00

116 5 Quetzales VF UNC
12.3.2008. Purple and tan on multicolor underprint. General J. Rufino Barrios at FV 1.50
right. Back: Classroom. Printer: FC-O. 156x68mm.

117 10 Quetzales VF UNC
12.3.2008. Red and tan on multicolor underprint. General M. Garcis Granados at FV 2.50
right. Back: National Assembly of 1872. Printer: FC-O. 156x68mm.

118 20 Quetzales VF UNC
12.3.2008. Blue and rose on multicolor underprint. Dr. M. Galvez at right. Back: FV 10.00
Granting of Independence to Central America. Printer: F-CO

119 100 Quetzales VF UNC
12.3.2008. Brown and tan on multicolor underprint. Bishop Francisco Marroquin at FV 30.00
right. Back: Universidad de San Carlos. Printer: Enschede. 156x68mm.

120 200 Quetzales
18.2.2009. Blue and brown on multicolor underprint. Sebastian Hurtado, Mariano Valverde and German Alcantara at right. Back: Score of "La Flor del Cafe", Marimba cromatica and "Noche de luna entre ruinas. Printer: FC-O. 156x68mm.

	VF	UNC
	FV	40.00

2010-13 Issue

122 5 Quetzales
19.5.2010-. Polymer plastic. Violet and purple on multicolor underprint. Back: Classroom. Printer: CBN.

	VF	UNC
a. 19.5.2010.	FV	1.50
b. 11.5.2011.	FV	1.50

123 10 Quetzales
19.5.2010-. Red on multicolor underprint. Back: National Assembly of 1872. Printer: CBN.

	VF	UNC
a. 19.5.2010.	FV	2.50
b. 11.5.2011.	FV	2.50

125 10 Quetzales
20.3.2013. Red on multicolor underprint. Braille (10) at left front in watermark area. Prefix D. Suffix D. Printer: PWPW S.A.

	VF	UNC
	FV	2.50

124 20 Quetzales
17.10.2012. Blue and rose on multicolor underprint. Dr. M. Galvez at right. Braille (20) at left front in watermark area. Windowed security thread with demetalized BANCO DE GUATEMALA 20. Prefix E. Suffix C. Back: Granting of Independence to Central America. Printer: Joh. Enschedé.

	VF	UNC
	FV	0.00

126 100 Quetzales
20.3.2013. Brown and tan on multicolor underprint. Bishop Francisco Marroquin at right. Braille at lower left front. Back: Universidad de San Carlos. Printer: OBERTHUR FIDUCIARE. 156x68mm.

	VF	UNC
	FV	30.00

GUERNSEY

The Bailiwick of Guernsey, a British crown dependency located in the English Channel 48 km. west of Normandy, France, has an area of 78 sq. km., including the Isles of Alderney, Jethou, Herm, Brechou and Sark, and a population of 58,681. Capital: St. Peter Port. Agriculture and cattle breeding are the main occupations.

Guernsey and the other Channel Islands represent the last remnants of the medieval Dukedom of Normandy, which held sway in both France and England. The islands were the only British soil occupied by German troops in World War II. Guernsey is a British crown dependency, but is not part of the UK. However, the UK Government is constitutionally responsible for its defense and international representation. United Kingdom bank notes and coinage circulate concurrently with Guernsey money as legal tender.

RULERS:
British to 1940, 1944-
German Occupation, June 1940-June 1944

MONETARY SYSTEM:
1 Penny = 8 Doubles
1 Shilling = 12 Pence
5 Shillings = 6 Francs
1 Pound = 20 Shillings to 1971
1 Pound = 100 New Pence 1971-

BRITISH ADMINISTRATION
States of Guernsey
1945; 1956 Issue

42 10 Shillings   VF   UNC
1945-66. Lilac on light green underprint. Value at center and in underprint. Printer: PBC.

	VF	UNC
a. 1.8.1945-1.9.1957.	225	600
b. 1.7.1958-1.3.1965.	100	325
c. 1.7.1966.	45.00	125
s. As c. Specimen.	—	—

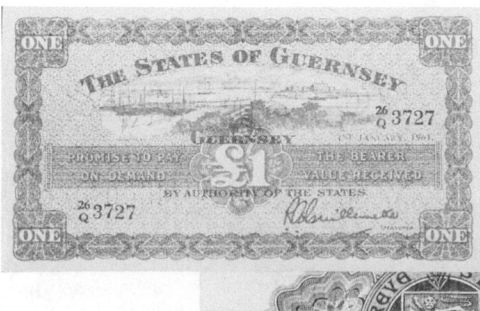

43 1 Pound   VF   UNC
1945-66. Purple on green underprint. Harbor entrance across top center. Printer: PBC.

	VF	UNC
a. 1.8.1945-1.3.1957.	650	1,250
b. 1.9.1957-1.3.1962; 1.6.1963; 1.3.1965.	120	375
c. 1.7.1966.	90.00	300
s. As c. Specimen.	—	—

44 5 Pounds   VF   UNC
1956; 1965-66. Green and blue. Flowers at left. Printer: PBC.

	VF	UNC
a. 1.12.1956.	650	1,500
b. 1.3.1965.	650	1,500
c. 1.7.1966.	650	1,500

1969; 1975 ND Issue
#45-47 Replacement notes: Serial # prefix *Z*.

45 1 Pound   VF   UNC
ND (1969-75). Olive on pink and yellow underprint. Arms at center. Back: Castle Cornet. Printer: BWC.

	VF	UNC
a. Signature Guillemette.	25.00	110
b. Signature Hodder.	12.00	50.00
c. Signature Bull.	12.00	45.00

46 5 Pounds   VF   UNC
ND (1969-75). Purple on light brown underprint. Arms at right. Back: City view and harbor wall. Printer: BWC.

	VF	UNC
a. Signature Guillemette.	85.00	325
b. Signature Hodder.	60.00	200
c. Signature Bull.	40.00	150
s. As a. Specimen.	—	900

47 10 Pounds   VF UNC
ND (1975-80). Blue, green and multicolor. Britannia with lion and shield at left. Signature; Hodder. Back: Sir I. Brock and Battle of Queenston Heights. Printer: BWC.   150 575

1980 ND Issue

48 1 Pound   VF UNC
ND (1980-89). Dark green and black on multicolor underprint. Market square scene of 1822 at lower center in underprint. Guernsey States seal at lower left. Back: D. De Lisle Brock and Royal Court of St. Peter Port. Watermark: Guernsey States seal. Printer: TDLR. 135x67mm.

		VF	UNC
a. Signature W. C. Bull.		FV	23.00
b. Black signature M. J. Brown.		FV	25.00
r. As a. Replacement note.		—	30.00
s. Specimen.		—	—
ct. Color trial.		—	—

49 5 Pounds   VF UNC
ND (1980-89). Purple, dark brown and olive-brown on multicolor underprint. Guernsey States seal at lower left. Fort Grey at lower center in underprint. signature W. C. Bull. Back: Thomas de la Rue and Fountain Street at center, workers at envelope making machine at lower right. Watermark: Guernsey States seal. Printer: TDLR. 146x78mm.

	VF	UNC
a. Issued note.	15.00	55.00
r. Replacement note.	—	110
s. Specimen.	—	—
ct. Color trial.	—	—

50 10 Pounds   VF UNC
ND (1980-89). Purple, blue and blue-black on multicolor underprint. Guernsey States seal. Castle Cornet at lower center. Back: Major Sir Isaac Brock and battle of Queenston Heights. Watermark: Guernsey States seal. Printer: TDLR. 151x85mm.

	VF	UNC
a. Signature W. C. Bull.	30.00	110
b. Black signature M. J. Brown.	27.50	95.00
r. As a. Replacement note.	—	130
s. Specimen.	—	—
ct. Color trial.	—	—

51 20 Pounds   VF UNC
ND (1980-89). Red, red-violet, brown and orange on multicolor underprint. Guernsey States seal, 1815 scene of Saumarez Park at lower center in underprint. Back: Adm. Lord de Saumarez and ships on back. Watermark: Guernsey States seal. Printer: TDLR. 161x90mm.

	VF	UNC
a. Signature W. C. Bull.	75.00	210
b. Black signature M. J. Brown.	75.00	190
r. As a. Replacement note.	—	—
s. Specimen.	—	—
ct. Color trial.	—	—

1990; 1991 ND Issue

#52-55 similar to #40-51 but reduced size. Replacement notes: Serial # prefix Z.

52 1 Pound   VF UNC
ND (ca.1991-). Dark green and black on multicolor underprint. Market square scene of 1822 at lower center in underprint. Guernsey States seal at lower left. Back: D. De Lisle Brock and Royal Court of St. Peter Port. Watermark: Guernsey States seal. Printer: (T)DLR. 128x65mm.

		VF	UNC
a. Green signature M. J. Brown.		FV	9.00
b. Signature D. P. Trestain.		FV	8.00
c. Signature D. M. Clark.		FV	7.00
r. As b. Replacement note.		FV	12.00

53 5 Pounds   VF UNC
ND (1990-95). Purple, dark brown and olive-brown on multicolor underprint. Guernsey States seal at lower left. Fort Grey at lower center in underprint. signature W. C. Bull. Back: Thomas de la Rue and Fountain Street at center, workers at envelope making machine at lower right. Watermark: Guernsey States seal. Printer: DLR. 136x70mm.

	VF	UNC
a. Brown signature M. J. Brown.	15.00	50.00
b. Signature D. P. Trestain.	12.50	40.00

54 10 Pounds   VF UNC
ND (ca.1991-95). Purple, blue and blue-black on multicolor underprint. Guernsey States seal. Castle Cornet at lower center. Back: Major Sir Isaac Brock and battle of Queenston Heights. Watermark: Guernsey States seal. Printer: DLR. 142x75mm.

	VF	UNC
a. Blue signature M. J. Brown.	25.00	85.00
r. Replacement note.	—	—

55   20 Pounds

	VF	UNC

ND (ca.1991-95). Red, red-violet, brown and orange on multicolor underprint. Guernsey States seal, 1815 scene of Saumarez Park at lower center in underprint. Back: Adm. Lord de Saumarez and ships on back. Watermark: Guernsey States seal. Printer: DLR. 149x80mm.

	VF	UNC
a. Red-orange signature M. J. Brown.	60.00	150
b. Signature D. P. Trestain.	60.00	130
r. As a. Replacement note.	65.00	165

1994-96 ND Issue

56   5 Pounds

	VF	UNC

ND (1996). Dark brown and purple on multicolor underprint. Queen Elizabeth II at right, Brown Guernsey States seal at bottom center right. St. Peter Port Town Church at lower left. Back: Fort Grey at upper left center, Hanois Lighthouse at center right. Watermark: Queen Elizabeth II. Printer: TDLR. 135x70mm.

	VF	UNC
a. Signature D. P. Trestain.	FV	30.00
b. Signature D. M. Clark.	FV	30.00
r. As a. Replacement note.	FV	40.00

57   10 Pounds

	VF	UNC

ND (1995). Violet, blue and dark blue on multicolor underprint. Queen Elizabeth II at right, Guernsey States seal at bottom center right. Elizabeth College at lower left. Back: Saumarez Park above Le Niaux Watermill and Le Trepid Dolmen at left center. Watermark: Queen Elizabeth II. Printer: TDLR. 142x75mm.

	VF	UNC
a. Signature D. P. Trestain.	FV	60.00
b. Signature D. M. Clark.	FV	55.00
c. As b. Stardust thread above serial #D900001.	FV	45.00
r. As a, b. Replacement note.	FV	70.00

58   20 Pounds

	VF	UNC

ND (1996). Pink, dark brown and orange on multicolor underprint. Queen Elizabeth II at right, Guernsey States seal at bottom center right. St. James Concert Hall at lower left. Back: Flowers at lower left, St. Sampson's Church at left center, sailboats below Vale Castle at center right, ship at upper right. Watermark: Queen Elizabeth II. Printer: TDLR. 142x79mm.

	VF	UNC
a. Signature D. P. Trestain.	FV	90.00

	VF	UNC
b. Signature D. M. Clark.	FV	80.00
c. Signature Bethan Haines. Signature title: *CHIEF ACCOUNTANT*. Segmented security thread, foil device added top center.	FV	80.00
r. As a,b . Replacement note.	FV	110

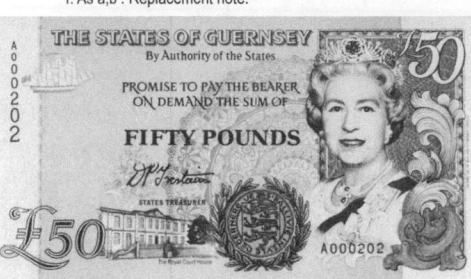

59   50 Pounds

	VF	UNC
	FV	220

ND (1994). Dark brown, dark green and blue-black on multicolor underprint. Queen Elizabeth II at right, Guernsey States seal at bottom center right. Royal Court House at lower left. Back: Stone carving, letter of Marque at lower left, St. Andrew's Church at center right. Watermark: Queen Elizabeth II. Printer: TDLR. 156x85mm.

2000 Issue

#60, Millennium Commemorative

60   5 Pounds

	VF	UNC
	FV	30.00

2000. Dark brown and purple on multicolor underprint. Queen Elizabeth II at right, Blue Guernsey States seal at bottom center. St. Peter Port Town Church at lower left, commemorative text at left. Back: Fort Grey at upper left center, Hanois Lighthouse at center right. Printer: DLR. 135x70mm.

2012 Commemorative Issue

61   20 Pounds

	VF	UNC
	FV	90.00

2012. Rose and orange on multicolor underprint. Queen Elizabeth II bust at right, St. James Concert Hall at lower left. Anniversary seal at bottom center. Back: Vale Castle at top center, St. Sampson's Church at center, small sailing boats, flower at lower left. Printer: DLR. 149x80mm.

2013 Commemorative Issue

62   1 Pound

	VF	UNC
	FV	12.00

2013. 300,000 notes printed. Dark green and black on multicolor underprint. Market square scene of 1822 at lower center in underprint. Guernsey States seal at lower left. Signature Bethan Haines. Back: Thomas de la Rue. Printer: TDLR.

Commemorates the 200th Anniversary of Thomas de la Rue's first commercial venture.

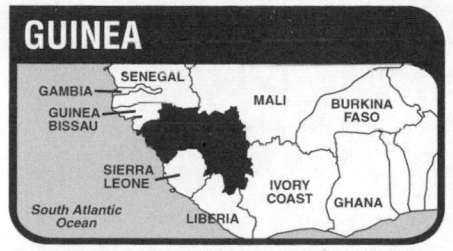

GUINEA

The Republic of Guinea (formerly French Guinea), situated on the Atlantic coast of Africa between Sierra Leone and Guinea-Bissau, has an area of 245,857 sq. km. and a population of 9.8 million. Capital: Conakry. Although Guinea contains one-third of the world's reserves of bauxite and significant deposits of iron ore, gold and diamonds, the economy is still dependent on agriculture. Aluminum, bananas, copra and coffee are exported.

Guinea has had only two presidents since gaining its independence from France in 1958. Lansana Conte came to power in 1984 when the military seized the government after the death of the first president, Sekou Toure. Guinea did not hold democratic elections until 1993 when Gen. Conte (head of the military government) was elected president of the civilian government. He was reelected in 1998 and again in 2003, though all the polls have been marred by irregularities. Guinea has maintained its internal stability despite spillover effects from conflict in Sierra Leone and Liberia. As those countries have rebuilt, Guinea's own vulnerability to political and economic crisis has increased. Declining economic conditions and popular dissatisfaction with corruption and bad governance prompted two massive strikes in 2006; a third nationwide strike in early 2007 sparked violent protests in many Guinean cities and prompted two weeks of martial law. To appease the unions and end the unrest, Conte named a new prime minister in March 2007.

RULERS:
French to 1958

MONETARY SYSTEM:
1 Franc = 100 Centimes to 1971
1 Cyli = 10 Francs, 1971-1980
Franc System, 1985-

REPUBLIC

Banque Centrale de la République de Guinée
1960 Issue

12   50 Francs   VF   UNC
1.3.1960. Brown on multicolor underprint. President Sekou Toure at left. Back: Heavy machinery. Watermark: Dove.
    a. Issued note.   4.00   20.00
    s. Specimen.   —   25.00

13   100 Francs   VF   UNC
1.3.1960. Dark brown on pale olive-green, pale orange, pink and lilac underprint. President Sekou Toure at left. Back: Pineapple field workers. Watermark: Dove.
    a. Issued note.   6.00   35.00
    s. As a. Specimen.   —   25.00
    x. (Error). dark brown and pale olive-green, light blue and pale yellow-orange underprint. Back dark brown on yellow underprint.   —   —

14   500 Francs   VF   UNC
1.3.1960. Blue on multicolor underprint. President Sekou Toure at left. Back: Men pulling long boats ashore. Watermark: Dove.
    a. Issued note.   20.00   150
    s. Specimen.   —   35.00

15   1000 Francs   VF   UNC
1.3.1960. Green on multicolor underprint. President Sekou Toure at left. Back: Banana harvesting. Watermark: Dove.
    a. Issued note.   15.00   75.00
    s. Specimen.   —   35.00

15A   5000 Francs   VF   UNC
1.3.1960. (Not issued). Specimen. Purple on green and multicolor underprint. Pres. Sekou Toure at left. Back: Woman in headdress at left, huts at right. Watermark: Dove.
                                                       —   400

1971 Issue

#16-19 issued under Law of 1960.

16   10 Sylis   **VF   UNC**
1971. Brown on multicolor underprint. Patrice Lumumba at right.   1.50   3.00
Back: People with bananas.

17   25 Sylis   **VF   UNC**
1971. Dark brown on multicolor underprint. Man smoking a pipe at right.   2.00   5.00
Back: Man and cows.

18   50 Sylis   **VF   UNC**
1971. Green on multicolor underprint. Bearded man at left. Back: Landscape with   2.00   10.00
large dam and reservoir.

19   100 Sylis   **VF   UNC**
1971. Purple on multicolor underprint. A. S. Toure at left. Back: Steam shovel and   2.00   9.00
two dump trucks.

1980; 1981 Issue

#20-27 issued under Law of 1960.

20   1 Syli   **VF   UNC**
1981. Olive on green underprint. Mafori Bangoura at right.
   a. Issued note.   0.15   0.50
   s. Specimen.   6.00

21   2 Sylis   **VF   UNC**
1981. Black and brown on orange underprint. Green guilloche at center, King
Mohammed V of Morocco at left.
   a. Issued note.   0.25   0.75
   s. Specimen.   —   7.00

22   5 Sylis   **VF   UNC**
1980. Blue on pink underprint. Kwame Nkrumah at right. Back: People with
bananas.
   a. Issued note.   0.50   2.00
   s. Specimen.   —   8.00

23   10 Sylis   **VF   UNC**
1980. Red and red-orange on multicolor underprint. Patrice Lumumba at right.
Back: People with bananas.
   a. Issued note.   0.50   2.50
   s. Specimen.   —   9.00

24   25 Sylis   **VF   UNC**
1980. Dark green on multicolor underprint. Man smoking a pipe at right. Back:
Man and cows.
   a. Issued note.   0.50   4.00
   s. Specimen.   —   10.00

1985 Issue
#28-33 Issued under Law of 1960.

28   25 Francs   VF   UNC
1985. Blue on multicolor underprint. Young boy at left, arms at center. Back: Girl by huts at center right.
    a. Issued note.   0.20   1.25
    s. Specimen.   —   3.00

25   50 Sylis   VF   UNC
1980. Dark red and brown on multicolor underprint. Bearded man at left. Back: Landscape with large dam and reservoir.
    a. Issued note.   1.50   7.00
    s. Specimen.   —   10.00

29   50 Francs   VF   UNC
1985. Red-violet on multicolor underprint. Bearded man at left, arms at center. Back: Plowing with water buffalo at center.
    a. Issued note.   0.25   1.50
    s. Specimen.   —   50.00

26   100 Sylis   VF   UNC
1980. Blue on multicolor underprint. A. S. Toure at left. Back: Steam shovel and two dump trucks.
    a. Issued note.   4.00   17.50
    s. Specimen.   —   15.00

30   100 Francs   VF   UNC
1985. Purple on multicolor underprint. Young woman at left, arms at center. Back: Harvesting bananas at center.
    a. Issued note.   0.25   1.75
    s. Specimen.   —   50.00

27   500 Sylis   VF   UNC
1980. Dark brown on multicolor underprint. J. Broz Tito at left. Back: Modern building.
    a. Issued note.   2.00   12.50
    s. Specimen.   —   20.00
Note: #27 is purported to commemorate Marshal Tito's visit to Guinea.

31   500 Francs   VF   UNC
1985. Green on multicolor underprint. Woman at left, arms at center. Back: Minehead at center.
    a. Issued note.   1.00   4.50
    s. Specimen. Red overprint: SPECIMEN once on each side.   —   65.00

32 **1000 Francs**
1985. Brown and blue on multicolor underprint. Girl at left, arms at center.
Back: Shovel loading ore into open end dump trucks at center, mask at right.
150x80mm.

	VF	UNC
a. Issued note.	1.50	6.50
s. Specimen.	—	65.00

33 **5000 Francs**
1985. Blue and brown on multicolor underprint. Woman at left, arms at center.
Back: Dam at center, mask at right. 156x86mm.

	VF	UNC
a. Issued note.	4.50	20.00
s. Specimen.	—	100

#34 not assigned.

1998 Issue

35 **100 Francs**
1998; 2012. Multicolor. Young woman at left, arms at center. Back: Harvesting
bananas at center.

	VF	UNC
a. 1998.	FV	1.50
b. 2012.	FV	1.50

36 **500 Francs**   VF   UNC
1998. Multicolor. Woman at left, arms at center. 2 signature varieties. Back: FV   3.50
Minehead at center. 132x62mm.

37 **1000 Francs**   VF   UNC
1998. Brown and red-brown on multicolor underprint. Female head at left, arms at   FV   5.00
center. Back: Mining scene. 146x73mm.

38 **5000 Francs**   VF   UNC
1998. Multicolor. Female at left, arms at center; thick security thread. Back: Dam   FV   17.50
at center, mask at right. 158x79mm.

2006-07 Issue

39 **500 Francs**   VF   UNC
2006; 2012. Green on multicolor underprint. Female at left. Back: Industrial scene.
132x63mm.

	VF	UNC
a. 2006.	FV	3.50
b. 2012.	FV	1.50

40   1000 Francs   **VF   UNC**
2006. Brown, orange and red on multicolor underprint. Girls at left, drum at lower   FV   5.00
right. Back: Ore loading. 138x67mm.

41   5000 Francs   **VF   UNC**
2006; 2012. Violet, blue and brown on multicolor underprint. Female at left,
sculpture at lower right. Back: Dam at center, mask at right. 150x75mm.
    a. 2006.   FV   10.00
    b. 2012.   FV   7.50
42   10,000 Francs   **VF   UNC**
2007; 2008. Blue-green on multicolor underprint. Young male head at left, pineapple at lower right. Back: Cultivated field.
    a. 2007.   FV   35.00
    b. 2008.   FV   35.00

2010 Commemorative issue

43   1000 Francs   **VF   UNC**
1.3.2010. Brown, orange and red on multicolor underprint. Girls at left, drum at   FV   6.00
lower right. Back: Ore loading. 139x68mm.

44   5000 Francs   **VF   UNC**
1.3.2010. Violet, blue and brown on multicolor underprint. Female at left, sculpture   FV   10.00
at lower right. Back: Dam at center, mask at right. 151x76mm.

45   10,000 Francs   **VF   UNC**
1.3.2010. Blue-green on multicolor underprint. Young male head at left, pineapple   FV   17.50
at lower right. Back: Cultivated field.

2012 Issue

46   10,000 Francs   **VF   UNC**
2012. Purple, green and multicolor Young male head at left, hologram nearby.   FV   35.00
Pineapple at lower right. Back: Cultivated field.

2015 Issue

47   500 Francs   **VF   UNC**
2015.   FV   1.50
48   5000 Francs   **VF   UNC**
2015.   FV   10.00
49   20000 Francs   **VF   UNC**
2015. Printer: DLR. 148x70mm.   FV   70.00

GUINEA-BISSAU

The Republic of Guinea-Bissau, a former Portuguese overseas province on the west coast of Africa between Senegal and Guinea, has an area of 36,120 sq. km. and a population of 1.5 million. Capital: Bissau. The country has undeveloped deposits of oil and bauxite. Peanuts, oil-palm kernels and hides are exported.

Since independence from Portugal in 1974, Guinea-Bissau has experienced considerable political and military upheaval. In 1980, a military coup established authoritarian dictator Joao Bernardo 'Nino' Vieira as president. Despite setting a path to a market economy and multiparty system, Vieira's regime was characterized by the suppression of political opposition and the purging of political rivals. Several coup attempts through the 1980s and early 1990s failed to unseat him. In 1994 Vieira was elected president in the country's first free elections. A military mutiny and resulting civil war in 1998 eventually led to Vieira's ouster in May 1999. In February 2000, a transitional government turned over power to opposition leader Kumba Yala, after he was elected president in transparent polling. In September 2003, after only three years in office, Yala was ousted by the military in a bloodless coup, and businessman Henrique Rosa was sworn in as interim president. In 2005, former President Vieira was re-elected president pledging to pursue economic development and national reconciliation.

RULERS:
Portuguese until 1974

MONETARY SYSTEM:
1 Peso = 100 Centavos, 1975-1997
1 Franc = 65 Pesos, 1997-

REPUBLIC
Banco Nacional da Guiné-Bissau
1975 Issue

		VF	UNC
1	**50 Pesos**		

24.9.1975. Blue and brown on multicolor underprint. P. Nalsna at left, group at center. Back: Field workers at center, woman at right. Watermark: A. Cabral. Printer: Algerian.

    a. Issued note. — 6.00 40.00
    s. Specimen. Red overprint: *SPECIMEN*. — 100

		VF	UNC
2	**100 Pesos**		

24.9.1975. Brown (shades) on multicolor underprint. D. Ramos at left, group in open hut at lower left center. Back: Objects and woman. Watermark: A. Cabral. Printer: Algerian.

    a. Issued note. 5.00 30.00
    s. Specimen. Red overprint: *SPECIMEN*. — 200

		VF	UNC
3	**500 Pesos**		

24.9.1975. Green, black and brown on multicolor underprint. Pres. A. Cabral at left, arms at center, soldier at right. Back: Carving and two youths. Watermark: A. Cabral. Printer: Algerian.

    a. Issued note. 30.00 150
    s. Specimen. Red overprint: *SPECIMEN*. — 250

#4 *Deleted*. See #8.

1978-84 Issue
#5-9 Replacement notes: Serial # prefix *Z*.

		VF	UNC
5	**50 Pesos**		

28.2.1983. Orange on blue and multicolor underprint. Artifact at left center, P. Nalsna at right, arms at lower right. Back: Local scene. Watermark: A. Cabral. Printer: BWC.

    a. Issued note. 2.50 12.00
    s. Specimen. Red overprint: *ESPECIMEN* on each side. — 55.00

		VF	UNC
6	**100 Pesos**		

28.2.1983. Red on multicolor underprint. Carving at left, D. Ramos at right, arms at lower right. Back: Building at left center. Watermark: A. Cabral. 1.25 4.50

		VF	UNC
7	**500 Pesos**		

28.2.1983. Deep blue on multicolor underprint. Carving at left, F. Mendes at right, arms at lower right. Back: Slave trade scene. Watermark: A. Cabral. 154x65mm.

    a. Issued note. 2.00 6.00
    s. Specimen. Overprint: *SPECIMEN* in back on both sides. — 35.00

8 **1000 Pesos** VF UNC
24.9.1978. Green on brown and multicolor underprint. Weaver and loom at lower left center, Pres. A. Cabral at right, arms at lower right. Back: Allegory with title: *Apoteose ao Triunfo* Watermark: A. Cabral. Printer: BWC.
    a. Signature titles: *COMISSARIO PRINCIPAL, COMISSARIO DE ESTADO* 20.00 85.00
        DAS FINANCAS and *GOVERNADOR.*
    b. Signature titles: *PRIMEIRO MINISTRO, MINISTRO DE ECONOMIA E* 3.00 8.00
        FINANCAS and *GOVERNADOR.*
    s. As a. Specimen. — 185

9 **5000 Pesos** VF UNC
12.9.1984. Brown and black on multicolor underprint. Map at left center, Pres. A. Cabral at right, arms at lower right. Back: Harvesting grain at center. Watermark: A. Cabral. 4.00 15.00
Note: Date on #9 is the 60th birthday of President Cabral.

1990 Issue

#10-15 Replacement notes: Serial # prefixes *AZ; BZ; CZ; DZ; ZA* or *ZZ.*

10 **50 Pesos** VF UNC
1.3.1990. Reduced size. UV: security strip fluoresces orange. Pale red on multicolor underprint. Artifact at left center, P. Nalsna at right, arms at lower right. Signature titles: *MINISTRO-GOVERNADOR and VICE-GOVERNADOR.* Back: Local scene. Watermark: BCG. Printer: TDLR. 0.25 1.00

11 **100 Pesos** VF UNC
1.3.1990. Reduced size. Olive-gray on multicolor underprint. Carving at left, D. Ramos at right, arms at lower right. Signature titles: *MINISTRO-GOVERNADOR and VICE-GOVERNADOR.* Back: Building at left center. Watermark: BCG. Printer: TDLR. 0.25 1.00

12 **500 Pesos** VF UNC
1.3.1990. Reduced size. Deep blue on multicolor underprint. Carving at left, F. Mendes at right, arms at lower right. Signature titles: *MINISTRO-GOVERNADOR and VICE-GOVERNADOR.* Back: Slave trade scene. Watermark: BCG. Printer: TDLR. 0.50 2.50

13 **1000 Pesos** VF UNC
1990; 1993. Dark brown, brown-violet and orange on multicolor underprint. Weaver and loom at lower left center, Pres. A. Cabral at right, arms at lower right. Back: Allegory with title: *Apoteose ao Triunfo.* Watermark: A. Cabral. Printer: TDLR.
    a. Signature titles: *MINISTRO-GOVERNADOR* and *VICF-GOVERNADOR.* 0.50 3.50
        1.3.1990.
    b. Signature titles: *GOVERNADOR* and *VICE-GOVERNADOR.* 1.3.1993. 0.50 2.50

14 **5000 Pesos** VF UNC
1990; 1993. Purple, violet and brown on multicolor underprint. Map at left center, Pres. A. Cabral at right, arms at lower right. Back: Harvesting grain at center. Watermark: A. Cabral. Printer: TDLR.
    a. Signature titles: *MINISTRO-GOVERNADOR* and *VICE-GOVERNADOR.* 1.00 8.00
    b. Signature titles: *GOVERNADOR* and *VICE-GOVERNADOR.* 1.3.1993. 1.00 5.00

15 **10,000 Pesos** VF UNC
1990; 1993. Green, olive-brown and blue on multicolor underprint. Statue at lower left center, outline map at center, A. Cabral at right. Back: Local people fishing with nets in river at center. Watermark: A. Cabral. Printer: TDLR.
    a. Signature titles: *MINISTRO-GOVERNADOR* and *VICE-GOVERNADOR.* 2.00 15.00
        1.3.1990.
    b. Signature titles: *GOVERNADOR* and *VICE-GOVERNADOR.* 1.3.1993. 1.00 12.50

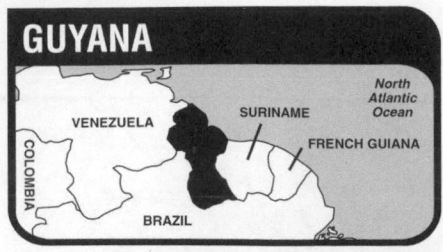

The Cooperative Republic of Guyana, an independent member of the British Commonwealth situated on the northeast coast of South America, has an area of 214,970 sq. km. and a population of 770,800. Capital: Georgetown. The economy is basically agrarian. Sugar, rice and bauxite are exported.

Originally a Dutch colony in the 17th century, by 1815 Guyana had become a British possession. The abolition of slavery led to black settlement of urban areas and the importation of indentured servants from India to work the sugar plantations. This ethnocultural divide has persisted and has led to turbulent politics. Guyana achieved independence from the UK in 1966, and since then it has been ruled mostly by socialist-oriented governments. In 1992, Cheddi Jagan was elected president in what is considered the country's first free and fair election since independence. After his death five years later, his wife, Janet JAGAN, became president but resigned in 1999 due to poor health. Her successor, Bharrat Jagdeo, was reelected in 2001 and again in 2006.

Notes of the British Caribbean Currency Board circulated from 1950-1965.

RULERS:
British to 1966

MONETARY SYSTEM:
1 Joe = 22 Guilders to 1836
1 Dollar = 4 Shillings 2 Pence, 1837-1965
1 Dollar = 100 Cents, 1966-

SIGNATURE VARIETIES

1 GOVERNOR MINISTER OF FINANCE		**2** GOVERNOR MINISTER OF FINANCE	
3 GOVERNOR MINISTER OF FINANCE		**4** GOVERNOR MINISTER OF FINANCE	
4A GOVERNOR MINISTER OF FINANCE		**5** GOVERNOR MINISTER OF FINANCE	
6 GOVERNOR VICE PRESIDENT ECONOMIC MINISTER OF FINANCE		**7** GOVERNOR MINISTER OF FINANCE	
8 GOVERNOR MINISTER OF FINANCE		**9** GOVERNOR MINISTER OF FINANCE	
10 GOVERNOR MINISTER OF FINANCE		**11** GOVERNOR MINISTER OF FINANCE	
12 GOVERNOR MINISTER OF FINANCE		**13**	
14			

REPUBLIC

Bank of Guyana

1966 ND Issue

#21-27 Color shading variations.

---

21 1 Dollar

	VF	UNC
ND (1966-92). Red on multicolor underprint. Arms at center, Kaieteur Falls at right. Back: Black bush polder at left, rice harvesting at right. Watermark: Macaw's (parrot) head. Printer: TDLR. 156x65mm.		
a. Signature 1; 2.	3.00	15.00
b. Signature 3; 4.	6.00	30.00
c. Signature 4A.	0.25	1.50
d. Signature 5.	1.00	4.00
e. Signature 6 (1983).	0.25	1.50
f. Serial # prefix B/1 or higher. Signature 7 (1989).	FV	1.00
g. Signature 8 (1992); 9. Back darker red.	FV	0.75
s. As a. Specimen.	—	25.00

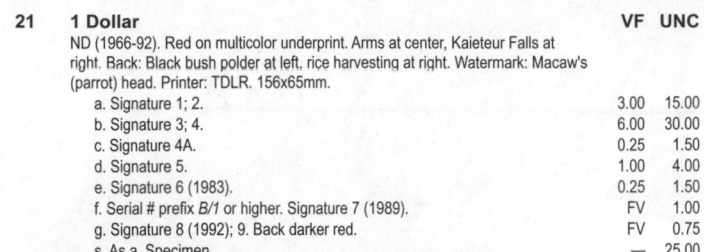

22 5 Dollars

	VF	UNC
ND (1966-92). Dark green on multicolor underprint. Arms at center, Kaieteur Falls at right. Back: Cane sugar harvesting at left, conveyor at right. Watermark: Macaw's (parrot) head. Printer: TDLR. 156x65mm.		
a. Signature 1; 2.	9.00	45.00
b. Signature 3.	10.00	55.00
c. Signature 5.	1.00	7.50
d. Signature 6 (1983).	0.50	5.00
e. Serial # prefix A/27 or higher. Signature 7 (1989).	FV	3.00
f. Signature 8 (1992); 9.	FV	0.75
s. As a. Specimen.	—	25.00

23 10 Dollars

	VF	UNC
ND (1966-92). UV: shiled fluoresces yellow and blue. Dark brown on multicolor underprint. Arms at center, Kaieteur Falls at right. Back: Bauxite mining at left, aluminum plant at right. Watermark: Macaw's (parrot) head. Printer: TDLR. 156x65mm.		
a. Signature 1; 2; 3.	10.00	75.00
b. Signature 4; 5.	2.50	15.00
c. Signature 6 (1983).	1.25	7.50
d. Serial # prefix A/16 or higher. Signature 7 (1989).	FV	1.00
e. Signature 8 (1992).	FV	1.50
f. Signature 9.	FV	1.00
s. As a. Specimen.	—	25.00

24 20 Dollars

	VF	UNC
ND (1966-89). Brown and purple on multicolor underprint. Arms at center, Kaieteur Falls at right. Back: Shipbuilding at left, ferry *Malali* at right. Watermark: Macaw's (parrot) head. Printer: TDLR. 156x65mm.		
a. Signature 1; 2; 4; 4A.	10.00	50.00
b. Signature 5.	3.00	15.00
c. Signature 6 (1983).	2.50	12.50
d. Serial # prefix A/42 or higher. Signature 7 (1989).	FV	1.50
s. As a. Specimen.	—	25.00

#25 and 26 not assigned.

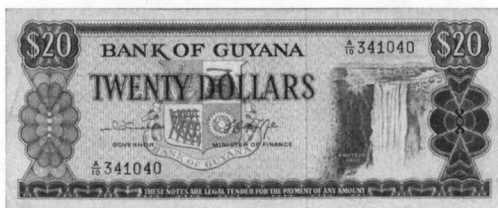

1989; 1992 ND Issue

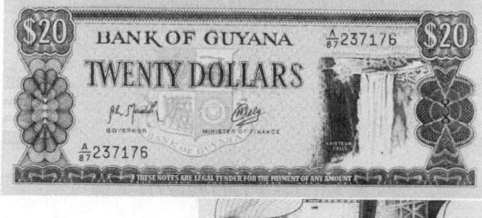

27 20 Dollars   **VF UNC**
ND (1989). Brown and purple on multicolor underprint. Arms at center, Kaieteur   FV   2.50
Falls at right. Signature 7; 9. Back: Shipbuilding at left, ferry *Malali* at right. Design
element in colored border at ends. Watermark: Macaw's (parrot) head. Printer.
TDLR. 156x65mm.

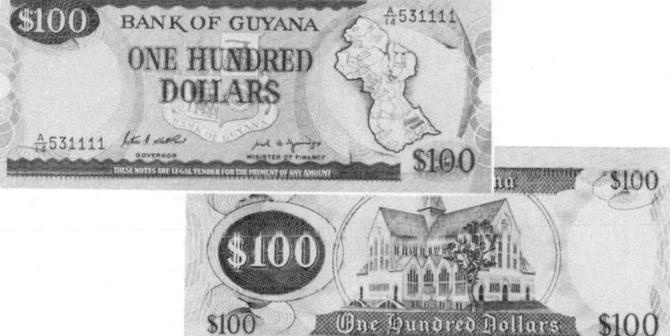

28 100 Dollars   **VF UNC**
ND (1989). Blue on multicolor underprint. Map of Guyana at right, bank arms at   FV   6.00
center. Signature 7; 8. Back: Cathedral at center. Watermark: Macaw's (parrot)
head. Printer: TDLR. 156x65mm.

29 500 Dollars   **VF UNC**
ND (ca. 1992). Lilac-brown and purple on multicolor underprint. Map of Guyana
at right, bank arms at center. Back: Public buildings in Georgetown. Watermark:
Macaw's (parrot) head. Printer: TDLR. 156x65mm.
    a. Signature 8.   FV   35.00
    b. Signature 9.   FV   10.00

1996; 1999 ND Issue

30 20 Dollars   **VF UNC**
ND (1996). Brown and purple on multicolor underprint. Map of Guyana at
right, bank arms at center. Ascending size serial number at upper right. Back:
Shipbuilding at left, ferry *Malali* at right. Design element in colored border at ends.
Watermark: Macaw's (parrot) head. 156x65mm.
    a. Signature 10.   FV   1.00
    b1. Signature 11.   FV   1.00
    b2. Signature 12.   FV   1.00
    c. Signature 13. Signature title as Acting Governor.   FV   1.00
    d. Signature 13. Signature title as Governor.   FV   1.00
    e. Signature 14.   FV   1.00

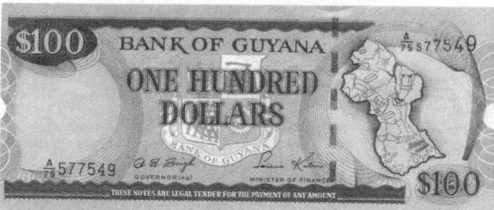

31 100 Dollars   **VF UNC**
ND (1999). Blue on multicolor underprint. Map of Guyana at right, bank arms at   FV   4.00
center. Ascending size serial number at upper right. Signature 10; 11; 12. Back:
Cathedral at center. Watermark: Macaw's (parrot) head. 156x65mm.

32 500 Dollars   **VF UNC**
ND (1996). Lilac-brown and purple on multicolor underprint. Map of Guyana at   FV   10.00
right, bank arms at center. Ascending size serial number at upper right. Silver
OVD map at right. Segmented foil over security thread. Signature 10. Back: Public
buildings in Georgetown. Watermark: Macaw's (parrot) head. 156x65mm.

33 1000 Dollars   **VF UNC**
ND (1996). Dark green, deep red and brown on multicolor underprint. Map of   FV   15.00
Guyana at right, bank arms at center. Ascending size serial number at upper right.
Gold OVD map at right. Segmented foil over security thread. Signature 10. Back:
Bank building at center. Watermark: Macaw's (parrot) head. 156x65mm.

2000 ND Issue

34 500 Dollars   **VF UNC**
ND (2002). Lilac-brown and purple on multicolor underprint. Map of Guyana at
right, bank arms at center. Ascending size serial number at upper right. OVD in
watermark area at right. Segmented foil over security thread. Back: Public buildings in Georgetown. Watermark: Macaw's (parrot) head. 156x65mm.
    a. Signature 11.   FV   8.50
    b. Signature 12.   FV   8.50

35 1000 Dollars — VF **UNC**
ND (2000). Dark green, deep red and brown on multicolor underprint. Map of Guyana at right, bank arms at center. Ascending size serial number at upper right. Gold OVD shield at right. Signature 11, 12. Back: Bank building at center. Watermark: Macaw's (parrot) head. 156x65mm. — FV 15.00

2006 ND Issue

36 100 Dollars — VF **UNC**
ND (2006) Green-blue on green, tan and multicolor underprint. Island map at right. Back: St. George's Cathedral at center. Printer: DLR. 156x65mm.
- a. Signature 13. — FV 2.00
- b. Signature 14. — FV 1.75
- s. Specimen. — — 50.00

37 500 Dollars — VF **UNC**
ND (2011). Lilac-brown and purple on multicolor underprint. Map of Guyana at right. Wide security foil with Macaw bird. Back: Public buildings in Georgetown at center. Segmented security foil. Printer: G&D. 156x65mm. — FV 8.50

38 1000 Dollars — VF **UNC**
ND (2006). Olive green on orange and rose multicolor underprint. Arms at center, island map at right. Wide security strip with Macaw bird. Back: Bank of Guyana building at center. Segmented security strip at center left. Printer: DLR. 156x65mm.
- a. Signature 13. — FV 15.00
- b. Signature 14. — FV 15.00

39 1000 Dollars — VF **UNC**
ND (2011). Lilac-brown and purple on multicolor underprint. Map of Guyana at right, different from that on #37. Arms at center. Back: Public buildings in Georgetown at center. Printer: G&D. 156x65mm. — FV 15.00

40 5000 Dollars — VF **UNC**
ND (2013). Map at right. Holographic stripe. Printer: Oberthur. — FV 30.00

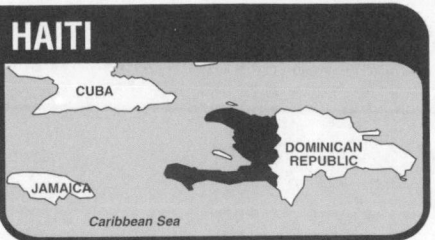

HAITI

The Republic of Haiti, occupying the western one third of the island of Hispañola in the Caribbean Sea between Puerto Rico and Cuba, has an area of 27,750 sq. km. and a population of 8.92 million. Capital: Port-au-Prince. The economy is based on agriculture, light manufacturing and tourism which is becoming increasingly important. Coffee, bauxite, sugar, essential oils and handicrafts are exported.

The native Taino Amerindians - who inhabited the island of Hispañiola when it was discovered by Columbus in 1492 - were virtually annihilated by Spanish settlers within 25 years. In the early 17th century, the French established a presence on Hispaniola, and in 1697, Spain ceded to the French the western third of the island, which later became Haiti. The French colony, based on forestry and sugar-related industries, became one of the wealthiest in the Caribbean, but only through the heavy importation of African slaves and considerable environmental degradation. In the late 18th century, Haiti's nearly half million slaves revolted under Toussaint L'Ouverture. After a prolonged struggle, Haiti became the first black republic to declare its independence in 1804. The poorest country in the Western Hemisphere, Haiti has been plagued by political violence for most of its history. After an armed rebellion led to the forced resignation and exile of President Jean-Bertrand Aristide in February 2004, an interim government took office to organize new elections under the auspices of the United Nations Stabilization Mission in Haiti (Minustah). Continued violence and technical delays prompted repeated postponements, but Haiti finally did inaugurate a democratically elected president and parliament in May of 2006.

MONETARY SYSTEM:
5 Gourdes = 1 U.S. Dollar, 1919-89

REPUBLIC (SECOND)
Banque Nationale de la République d'Haiti
Convention du 12 Avril 1919 - Sixth Issue (ca.1951-64)

178 1 Gourde — VF **UNC**
L.1919. Dark brown on light blue and multicolor underprint. Closeup view of Citadel Rampart at center. Prefix letters AS-BM. 5 signature varieties. First signature title: *Le President*. Back: Arms at center. Printer: ABNC.
- a. Issued note. — 2.00 17.50
- s. Specimen. Punch hole cancelled. — — 35.00

179 2 Gourdes — VF **UNC**
L.1919. Blue and multicolor. Light green in underprint. Citadel rampart at center. Prefix letters Y-AF. 6 signature varieties. First signature title: *Le President*. Back: Arms at center. Printer: ABNC.
- a. Issued note. — 4.00 25.00
- s. Specimen. Punch hole cancelled. SPECIMEN twice on face. — — 65.00

180 5 Gourdes — VF **UNC**
L.1919. Orange and multicolor. Green in underprint. Woman harvesting coffee at left. Prefix letters G-M. 3 signature varieties. First signature title:*Le President*. Back: Arms at center. Printer: ABNC.
- a. Issued note. — 6.00 35.00
- s. Specimen. Punch hole cancelled. — — 55.00

181 10 Gourdes — VF **UNC**
L.1919. Green on multicolor underprint. Coffee plant at center. Prefix letters B-D. 2 signature varieties. First signature title: *Le President*. Back: Arms at center. Printer: ABNC.
- a. Issued note. — 12.50 55.00
- s. Specimen, punch hole cancelled. — — 70.00

#182 not assigned.

183 50 Gourdes VF UNC
L.1919. Specimen. Olive-green on multicolor underprint. Cotton bolls at center. — 225
First signature title: *Le President.* Back: Arms at center. Printer: ABNC.

184 100 Gourdes VF UNC
L.1919. Purple on multicolor underprint. Field workers at loft. Prefix letter A. First
signature title: *Le President.* Back: Arms at center. Printer: ABNC.
  a. Issued note. 125 350
  s. Specimen, punch hole cancelled. — 175

Convention du 12 Avril 1919 - Seventh Issue (ca 1964)

#185-189 like #178-180 but incorporating new guilloche patterns without green in underprint.

185 1 Gourde VF UNC
L.1919. Dark brown on light blue and multicolor underprint. Citadel rampart at
center. Like #178. Serial # prefix letters: *BK-BT.*
  a. Issued note. 1.50 7.50
  s. Specimen. Red overprint: *SPECIMEN* twice on face. — 40.00

186 2 Gourdes VF UNC
L.1919. Blue on light blue and multicolor underprint. Citadel rampart at center.
Like #179. Serial # prefix letters: *AE-AJ.*
  a. Issued note. 1.50 7.50
  s. Specimen. Red overprint: *SPECIMEN* twice on face. — 45.00

187 5 Gourdes VF UNC
L.1919. Orange on light blue and multicolor underprint. Woman harvesting coffee
beans at left. Like #180. Serial # prefix letter: *N.*
  a. Issued note. 1.00 7.00
  s. Specimen. Punch hole cancel. Black overprint SPECIMEN on face. — 55.00
Note: It is reported that the entire shipment of #187 was stolen and never officially released.

Convention du 12 Avril 1919 - Eighth Issue (ca.1967)

190 1 Gourde VF UNC
L.1919. Brown on multicolor underprint. Citadel rampart at center, new guilloche
patterns, without green in underprint. Prefix letters DA-DL. Second signature title:
LE DIRECTEUR. Back: Arms at center. Printer: TDLR.
  a. Issued note. 1.00 7.50
  s. Specimen. — 27.50

191 2 Gourdes VF UNC
L.1919. Grayish blue on multicolor underprint. Citadel rampart at center. New guilloche patterns, without green in underprint. Prefix letters DA-DF. 6 signature varieties. Second signature title: *LE DIRECTEUR.* Back: Arms at center. Printer: TDLR.
  a. Issued note. 1.50 10.00
  s. Specimen. — 27.50

192 5 Gourdes VF UNC
L.1919. Orange on light blue and multicolor underprint. Woman harvesting coffee
at left, new guilloche patterns, without green in underprint. Prefix letters DA-DK. 3
signature varieties. Second signature title: *LE DIRECTEUR.* Back: Arms at center.
Printer: TDLR.
  a. Issued note. 4.00 12.50
  s. Specimen. — 27.50

193 10 Gourdes VF UNC
L.1919. Green on multicolor underprint. Coffee plant at center. Prefix letters DA. 2
signature varieties. Second signature title: *LE DIRECTEUR.* Back: Arms at center.
Printer: TDLR.
  a. Issued note. 8.00 30.00
  s. Specimen. — 35.00

194 50 Gourdes VF UNC
L.1919. Olive-green on multicolor underprint. Cotton bolls at center. Prefix letters
DA. Second signature title: *UN DIRECTEUR.* Back: Arms at center. Printer: TDLR.
  a. Issued note. 17.50 80.00
  s. Specimen. — 170

195 100 Gourdes

		VF	UNC
L.1919. Purple on multicolor underprint. Field workers at left, with new guilloche patterns, without green in underprint. Prefix letters DA. Second signature title: *LE DIRECTEUR.* Back: Arms at center. Printer: TDLR.			
	a. Issued note.	35.00	150
	s. Specimen.	—	—

Convention du 12 Avril 1919 - Ninth Issue

196 1 Gourde

		VF	UNC
L.1919. Dark brown on multicolor underprint. Pres. Dr. François Duvalier at center. Prefix letters DK-DT. Back: Arms at center. Printer: TDLR.			
	a. Issued note.	0.75	3.50
	s. Specimen.	—	20.00

197 2 Gourdes

		VF	UNC
L.1919. Grayish blue on multicolor underprint. Pres. Dr. François Duvalier at center. Prefix letters DG-DK. Back: Arms at center. Printer: TDLR.			
	a. Issued note.	1.25	4.50
	s. Specimen.	—	25.00

198 5 Gourdes

		VF	UNC
L.1919. Orange on multicolor underprint. Pres. Dr. François Duvalier at left. Prefix letters DG-DK. Back: Arms at center. Printer: TDLR.			
	a. Issued note.	2.50	7.50
	s. Specimen.	—	25.00

#199 not assigned.

Convention du 12 Avril 1919 - Tenth Issue

200 1 Gourde

		VF	UNC
L.1919. Dark brown on multicolor underprint. Portrait President Dr. François Duvalier at center. Prefix letters A-Z; AA-CR. Three signature varieties. Back: Arms at center. Printer: ABNC.			
	a. Issued note.	0.75	3.00
	s. Specimen.	—	20.00

201 2 Gourdes

		VF	UNC
L.1919. Blue on multicolor underprint. Portrait of Dr. François Duvalier at center. Three signature varieties. First issued without prefix, then letters A-Q. Back: Arms at center, with 4 lines of text on back. Printer: ABNC.		1.50	5.00

202 5 Gourdes

		VF	UNC
L.1919. Orange on multicolor underprint. Portrait President Dr. François Duvalier at left. First issued without prefix, then letters A-Z; AA-AP. Three signature varieties. Back: Arms at center, with 4 lines of text on back. Printer: ABNC.			
	a. Issued note.	3.00	12.50
	s. Specimen.	—	25.00

203 10 Gourdes

		VF	UNC
L.1919. Dark green on multicolor underprint. Portrait President Dr. François Duvalier at center. First issued without prefix, then letter A. Back: Arms at center, with 4 lines of text on back. Printer: ABNC.			
	a. Issued note.	5.00	15.00
	s. Specimen.	—	30.00

204 50 Gourdes

		VF	UNC
L.1919. Dark gray on multicolor underprint. Portrait President Lysius Fèlicitè Salomon Jeune at center. First issued without prefix, then letters A-C. Two signature varieties. Back: Arms at center, with 4 lines of text on back. 162x70mm.			
	a. Issued note.	17.50	30.00
	s. Specimen. Overprint: *SPECIMEN* twice in red. Punch hole cancelled.	—	40.00

205 100 Gourdes

		VF	UNC
L.1919. Purple on multicolor underprint. Portrait Henri Christophe (Pres., later King) at left. Without prefix letter. Two signature varieties. Back: Arms at center, with 4 lines of text on back.			
	a. Issued note.	40.00	75.00
	s. Speicmen. Red overprint: *SPECIMEN* on face. Punch hole cancelled. With or without serial #.	—	100

206 250 Gourdes

		VF	UNC
L.1919. Dark yellow-green on multicolor underprint. Jean-Jacques Dessalines at right. Back: Arms at center, with 4 lines of text on back.			
	a. Issued note.	110	225
	s. Specimen. Red overprint: *SPECIMEN* on face. Punch hole cancelled.	—	200

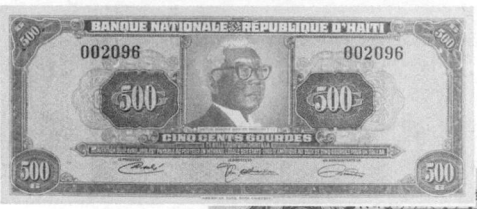

207 500 Gourdes

L.1919. Red on multicolor underprint. Portrait President Dr. François Duvalier at center. Issued without prefix Back: Arms at center, with 4 lines of text on back.

	VF	UNC
a. Issued note.	165	350
s. Specimen.	—	350

#208 and 209 not assigned.

Eleventh Issue (ca.1973)

Lois des 21 Mai 1935 et 15 Mai 1953 et au Décret du 22 Novembre 1973 (issued 1979).

210 1 Gourde

L.1973, etc. UV: Duvalier and 1G fluoresce orange. Dark brown on multicolor underprint. Portrait of President Dr. François Duvalier at center. Prefix letters A-Z; AA-AC. Back: Arms at center. Printer: ABNC.

	VF	UNC
	0.60	4.00

211 2 Gourdes

L.1973, etc. Blue on multicolor underprint. Portrait of Dr. François Duvalier at center. Prefix letters A-J. Three signature varieties Back: Arms at center with 3 lines of text. Printer: ABNC.

	VF	UNC
	1.25	7.50

212 5 Gourdes

L.1973, etc. Orange on multicolor underprint. Portrait Pres. Dr. François Duvalier at left. First issued without prefix, then letters A-AA. Three signature varieties. Back: Arms at center with 3 lines of text. Printer: ABNC.

	VF	UNC
	3.00	12.50

213 50 Gourdes

L.1973, etc. Dark gray on multicolor underprint. Portrait Pres. Lysius Félicité Salomon Jeune at center. Prefix letter A. Two signature varieties. Two serial number varieties. Back: Arms at center with 3 lines of text. Printer: ABNC.

	VF	UNC
a. Issued note.	17.50	35.00
s. Specimen. Overprint: SPECIMEN twice on face. Punch hole cancelled	—	75.00

214 100 Gourdes

L.1973, etc. Purple on multicolor underprint. Portrait Henri Christophe (Pres., later King) at left. Without prefix letter. Two signature varieties. Two serial number varieties. Back: Arms at center with 3 lines of text. Printer: ABNC.

	VF	UNC
a. Issued note.	35.00	70.00
s. Specimen. Black overprint: SPECIMEN on face. Punch hole cancelled.	—	70.00

#215-217 not assigned.

Twelfth Issue

Lois des 21 Mai 1935 et 15 Mai 1953 et au Décret du 22 Novembre 1973

218 25 Gourdes

L.1973, etc. Dark blue and brown-violet on multicolor underprint. President Jean-Claude Duvalier at left, antenna at right. Prefix letters DA-DD. Back: National Palace. Printer: TDLR.

	VF	UNC
a. Issued note.	7.50	22.50
s. Specimen.	—	30.00

#219-229 not assigned.

Banque de la République d'Haiti

Loi du 17 Aout 1979 (1980-82)

230 1 Gourde

L.1979. UV: planchettes fluoresce yellow, red and blue. Duvalier and 1G green, design elements yellow and green. Dark brown on multicolor underprint. Portrait of President Dr. François Duvalier at center. Without prefix letter. Signature titles: *LE GOUVERNEUR, LE GOUVERNEUR ADJOINT* and *LE DIRECTEUR.* Small size numerals in serial #. Planch Back: Arms at center. Printer: ABNC.

	VF	UNC
	0.50	2.75

230A 1 Gourde

L.1979. Printed on Tyvek. UV: Duvalier and IG and central design fluourese orange. Dark brown on multicolor underprint. Portrait of Pres. Dr. François Duvalier at center. Without prefix letter. Larger size numerals in serial number. Signature titles: *LE GOUVERNEUR, LE GOUVERNEUR ADJOINT* and *LE DIRECTEUR.* Back: Arms at center. Printer: ABNC.

	VF	UNC
a. Issued note.	0.50	4.00
s. Specimen. Overprinted: SPECIMEN and punch hole cancelled.	—	250

231 2 Gourdes

L.1979. Printed on paper with planchettes. Blue on multicolor underprint. Portrait of President Dr. François Duvalier at center. Without prefix letter. Signature titles: *LE GOUVERNEUR, LE GOUVERNEUR ADJOINT* and *LE DIRECTEUR.* Small size serial #. Back: Arms at center. Printer: ABNC.

	VF	UNC
	0.50	4.00

231A 2 Gourdes

L.1979. Printed on Tyvek. Blue on multicolor underprint. Portrait of Pres. Dr. François Duvalier at center. Without prefix letter. Signature titles: *LE GOUVERNEUR, LE GOUVERNEUR ADJOINT* and *LE DIRECTEUR.* Larger size serial #. Back: Arms at center. Printer: ABNC.

	VF	UNC
a. Issued note.	1.00	7.50
s. Specimen. Overprinted: SPECIMEN and punch hole cancelled.	—	300

232 5 Gourdes

L.1979. Orange on multicolor underprint. Portrait President Dr. François Duvalier at left. Prefix letters A-T, AA-. Signature titles: *LE GOUVERNEUR, LE GOUVERNEUR ADJOINT* and *LE DIRECTEUR.* Back: Arms at center. Printer: ABNC.

	VF	UNC
	1.25	10.00

#233 and 234 not assigned.

235 50 Gourdes

L.1979. Dark brown on green and multicolor underprint. Portrait President Lysius Félicité Salomon Jeune at center. Two signature varieties. Without prefix letter or with A, B, E, G. Signature titles: *LE GOUVERNEUR, LE GOUVERNEUR ADJOINT* and Back: Arms at center. Printer: ABNC.

	VF	UNC
a. Issued note.	12.50	30.00
s. Specimen. Black overprint: SPECIMEN twice on face. Punch hole cancelled.	—	35.00

235A 50 Gourdes

	VF	UNC

L.1979. Printed on Tyvek. Dark brown on green and multicolor underprint. Portrait Pres. Lysius Fèlicitè Salomon Jeune at center. Two serial number varieties. Without prefix letter or with A, B, G. Signature titles: *LE GOUVERNEUR, LE GOU-VERNEUR ADJOINT* and Back: *Arms at center.* Printer: ABNC.

a. Prefix letter C. Watermark: American bald eagle symbol of ABNC.	12.50	45.00
b. Without watermark. Prefix letter D; E; F.	12.50	40.00
s. Specimen. Red overprint: *SPECIMEN*. Punch hole cancelled.	—	450

236 100 Gourdes

	VF	UNC

L.1979. Printed on paper with planchettes. Purple on multicolor underprint. Portrait Henri Christophe (Pres., later King) at left. Prefix letters A; B. Signature titles: *LE GOUVERNEUR, LE GOUVERNEUR ADJOINT* and *LE DIRECTEUR*. Back: Arms at center. Printer: ABNC.

a. Issued note.	20.00	55.00
s. Specimen. Black overprint: *SPECIMEN* on face. Punch hole cancelled.	—	50.00

236A 100 Gourdes

	VF	UNC
	20.00	55.00

L.1979. Printed on Tyvek. Purple on multicolor underprint. Portrait Henri Christophe (Pres., later King) at left. Prefix letters C, D, E. Signature titles: *LE GOUVERNEUR, LE GOUVERNEUR ADJOINT* and *LE DIRECTEUR*. Back: Arms at center. Printer: ABNC.

237 250 Gourdes

	VF	UNC

L.1979. Printed on Tyvek. Dark yellow-green on multicolor underprint. Jean-Jacques Dessalines at right. Without prefix letter. Signature titles: *LE GOUVER-NEUR, LE GOUVERNEUR ADJOINT* and *LE DIRECTEUR*. Back: Arms at center. Printer: ABNC.

a. Issued note.	45.00	125
p. Proof. Without serial numbers, date, signatures.	—	300
s. Specimen.	—	100

238 500 Gourdes

	VF	UNC

L.1979. Printed on Tyvek. Red on multicolor underprint. Portrait Pres. Dr. François Duvalier at center. Issued without prefix. Signature titles: *LE GOUVERNEUR, LE GOUVERNEUR ADJOINT* and *LE DIRECTEUR*. Back: Arms at center. Printer: ABNC.

a. Issued note.	90.00	250
p. Proof. Without serial #, date, signatues.	—	300
s. Specimen.	—	300

1984; 1985 ND Issue

#239-240 Replacement notes: Serial # prefix ZZ.

239 1 Gourde

	VF	UNC
	0.25	2.75

L.1979 (1984). Dark brown on multicolor underprint. President Dr. François Duvalier at center. Double prefix letters. Signature titles: *LE GOUVERNEUR, LE GOUVER-NEUR ADJOINT* and *LE DIRECTEUR*. Back: Arms at center. Printer: TDLR.

240 2 Gourdes

	VF	UNC
	0.50	4.75

L.1979 (1985). Grayish blue on multicolor underprint. Citadel rampart at center. New guilloche patterns, without green in underprint. Prefix letters DA-DF. 6 signature varieties. Second signature title: *LE DIRECTEUR*. Back: Arms at center. Printer: TDLR.

241 5 Gourdes

	VF	UNC

L.1979 (1985). Orange on multicolor underprint. Jean-Claude Duvalier at left. Signature title at right: *LE DIRECTEUR GENERAL*. Back: Arms at center. Watermark: Jean-Claude Duvalier. Printer: G&D.

a. Issued note.	1.00	7.50
s. Specimen.	—	35.00

242 10 Gourdes

	VF	UNC

L.1979 (1984). Green on multicolor underprint. Portrait President Dr. François Duvalier at center. Signature title at right: *LE DIRECTEUR GENERAL*. Back: Arms at center. Printer: ABNC.

a. Issued note.	2.00	12.50
s. Specimen.	—	27.50

243 25 Gourdes

	VF	UNC

L.1979 (1985). Blue on pink and multicolor underprint. Jean-Claude Duvalier at left. Signature title at right: *LE DIRECTEUR GENERAL*. Back: Arms at center. Printer: G&D.

a. Issued note.	4.50	20.00
s. Specimen.	—	30.00

#244 Renumbered, see #240.

1986-88 Issue

245 1 Gourde VF UNC
1987. UV: back 1G arms legends fluoresce yellow. Dark brown and brown-black
on multicolor underprint. Toussaint L'Ouverture with long hair at center. Signature
title at right: *LE DIRECTEUR GENERAL*. Back: Arms at center. Printer: G&D.
  a. Issued note.   FV 2.00
  s. Specimen.   — 22.50

245A 2 Gourdes VF UNC
L.1979. UV: serial # fluoresce orange. Grayish blue on multicolor underprint. Cita-
del rampart at center. Two prefix letters. Signature title at right: *LE DIRECTEUR
GENERAL*. Back: Arms at center. Printer: TDLR.   0.25 3.00

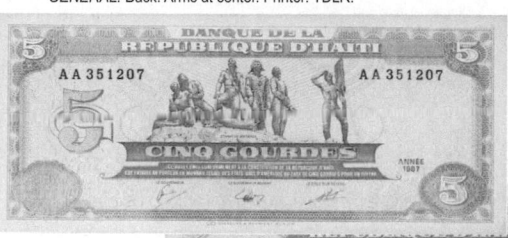

246 5 Gourdes VF UNC
1987. UV: bank name, left, right and center elements and 5 fluoresce orange. Back
shield and 5 orange, fibers orange. Orange and brown on multicolor underprint. Statue of Combat de Vertiéres at upper center. Signature title at right: *LE DIRECTEUR
GENERAL*. Back: Arms at center. Watermark: Palm tree. Printer: G&D.
  a. Issued note.   FV 5.00
  s. Specimen.   — 25.00

247 10 Gourdes VF UNC
1988. Green, red and blue on multicolor underprint. Catherine Flon Arcahaie
seated sewing the first flag of the Republic at right. Signature title at right: *LE
DIRECTEUR GENERAL*. Back: Arms at center. Printer: ABNC.
  a. Issued note.   FV 9.00
  s. Specimen.   — 27.50

248 25 Gourdes VF UNC
1988. Dark blue and purple on multicolor underprint. Palace of Justice at center.
Signature title at right: *LE DIRECTEUR GENERAL*. Back: Arms at center. Watermark: Palm tree. Printer: G&D.
  a. Issued note.   FV 15.00
  s. Specimen.   — 28.50

249 50 Gourdes VF UNC
1986. Dark brown on green and multicolor underprint. Portrait President Lysius
Félicité Salomon Jeune at center. Signature titles: *LE GOUVERNEUR, LE DI-
RECTEUR GENERAL* and *LE Arms at center*. Back: Arms at center. Printer: ABNC.
  a. Issued note.   FV 30.00
  s. Specimen.   — 25.00

250 100 Gourdes VF UNC
1986. Similar to #236 (but more colorful). Purple on multicolor underprint. Portrait
Henri Christophe (Pres., later King) at left. Signature title at right: *LE DIRECTEUR
GENERAL*. Back: Arms at center. Printer: TDLR.
  a. Issued note.   FV 45.00
  s. Specimen.   — 35.00

251 250 Gourdes VF UNC
1988. Tan on multicolor. Jean-Jacques Dessalines at right. Signature title at right:
LE DIRECTEUR GENERAL. Back: Arms at center. Printer: ABNC.
  a. Issued note.   FV 80.00
  s. Specimen.   — 70.00

252 500 Gourdes VF UNC
1988. Red on multicolor underprint. President Alexandre Pétion at right. Signature
title at right: *LE DIRECTEUR GENERAL*. Back: Arms at center. Printer: ABNC.
  a. Issued note.   FV 150
  s. Specimen.   — 85.00

1989-91 Issue

253 1 Gourde VF UNC
1989. Legal clause includes reference to the United States. Dark brown and
brown-black on multicolor underprint. Toussaint L'Ouverture with short hair at
center. Back: Arms at center. Printer: USBC.
  a. Issued note.   FV 1.50
  s. Specimen.   — 22.50

254 2 Gourdes VF UNC
1990. Legal clause without reference to the United States. Blue-black on multicolor underprint. Citadel rampart at center. Back: Arms at center. Printer: USBC.
  a. Issued note.   0.50 3.50
  s. Specimen.   — 25.00

255   5 Gourdes   VF   UNC
1989. Legal clause includes reference to the United States. Orange and brown on
multicolor underprint. Statue of Combat de Vertiéres at upper center. Back: Arms
at center. Watermark: Palm tree. Printer: USBC.

a. Issued note.	FV	5.00
s. Specimen.	—	25.00

256   10 Gourdes   VF   UNC
1991; 1998; 1999. Legal clause on face and back without reference to the United
States. Dark green, red and blue on multicolor underprint. Catherine Flon Arcahaie seated sewing the first flag of the Republic at center. Back: Arms at center.
Watermark: Palm tree. Printer: G&D. 162x70mm.

a. Issued note.	FV	4.00
s. Specimen.	—	25.00

257   50 Gourdes   VF   UNC
1991; 1999. Legal clause on face and back without reference to the United States.
Dark olive-green on multicolor underprint. Portrait President L. F. Salomon Jeune
at center. Back: Arms at center. Watermark: Palm tree. Printer: G&D. 162x70mm.

a. Issued note.	FV	10.00
s. Specimen.	—	50.00

258   100 Gourdes   VF   UNC
1991. Legal clause on face and back without reference to the United States.
Purple on multicolor underprint. Portrait H. Christophe at left. Back: Arms at
center. Watermark: Palm tree. Printer: G&D. 162x70mm

a. Issued note.	FV	20.00
s. Specimen.	—	25.00

1992-94 Issue
#259-261 Replacement notes: Serial # prefix ZZ.

259   1 Gourde   VF   UNC
1992; 1993. Shortened clause on face and back: *CE BILLET EST EMIS CON-
FORMEMENT...* Dark brown and brown-black on multicolor underprint. Toussaint
L'Ouverture with long hair at center, without laws. Back: Arms at center. Printer:
TDLR.

a. Issued note.	FV	1.00
s. Specimen.	FV	25.00

260   2 Gourdes   VF   UNC
1992. Shortened clause on face and back: *CE BILLET EST EMIS CONFORME-
MENT...* Blue-black on multicolor underprint. Citadel rampart at center, without
laws. Back: Arms at center. Printer: TDLR.

a. Issued note.	FV	1.75
s. Specimen. Red overprint:SPECIMEN. and perforated *SPECIMEN* twice.	—	25.00

261   5 Gourdes   VF   UNC
1992. Shortened clause on face and back: *CE BILLET EST EMIS CONFORME-
MENT...* Orange and brown on multicolor underprint. Statue of Combat de
Vertières at upper center, without laws. Back: Arms at center. Printer: TDLR.
162x70mm.

a. Issued note.	FV	3.00
s. Specimen.	—	22.50

262 25 Gourdes
VF UNC

1993. Shortened clause on face and back: *CE BILLET EST EMIS CONFORME-MENT...* Dark blue and purple on multicolor underprint. Palace of Justice at center, without laws. Back: Arms at center. Printer: G&D. 162x70mm.

    a. Issued note.   FV 4.50
    s. Specimen.   — 25.00

263 250 Gourdes
VF UNC

1994. Shortened clause on face and back: *CE BILLET EST EMIS CONFORME-MENT...* Olive-brown and dark brown on multicolor underprint. Portrait J. J. Dessalines at left, without laws. Back: Arms at center. Printer: G&D. 162x70mm.

    a. Issued note.   FV 35.00
    s. Specimen.   — 100

264 500 Gourdes
VF UNC

1993. Shortened clause on face and back: *CE BILLET EST EMIS CONFORME-MENT...* Red-violet on multicolor underprint. Portrait President A. Pétion at left, without laws. Back: Arms at center. Printer: G&D. 162x70mm.

    a. Issued note.   FV 60.00
    s. Specimen.   — 200

2000 Issue

265 10 Gourdes
VF UNC

2000; 2004. Colorful, especially on borders. Dark green and multicolor. Catherine Flon Arcahaie seated sewing the first flag of the Republic at center. Ascending size serial number. Letters BRH at right in various color combinations. Back: Arms at center. Watermark: Palm tree. Printer: (T)DLR. 162x70mm.

    a. 2000.   FV 1.25
    b. 2004.   FV 1.25
    s. Specimen. Red overprint: *SPECIMEN.*   — 50.00

266 25 Gourdes
VF UNC

2000; 2004; 2006; 2009. Dark blue and black on multicolor underprint. Palace of Justice at center. Ascending size serial number. Letters BRH at right in various color combinations. Back: Arms at center. Watermark: Palm tree. Printer: G&D. 162x70mm.

    a. 2000.   FV 3.50
    b. 2004.   FV 3.50
    c. 2006.   FV 3.50
    d. 2009.   FV 3.00
    e. 2014.   FV 3.50
    s. Specimen. Red overprint: *SPECIMEN.*   — 100

267 50 Gourdes
VF UNC

2000; 2003. Colorful, especially on borders. Dark olive-green and black on multicolor underprint. Portrait Pres. L. F. Salomon Jeune at center. Ascending size serial number. Letters BRH at right in various color combinations. Back: Arms at center. Printer: (T)DLR. 162x70mm.

    a. 2000.   FV 8.00
    b. 2003.   FV 8.00

268 100 Gourdes
VF UNC

2000. Colorful, especially on borders. Purple on multicolor underprint. Portrait H. Christophe at left. Ascending size serial number. Letters BRH at right in various color combinations. Back: Arms at center. Printer: G&D. 162x70mm.
    FV 18.00

269 250 Gourdes
VF UNC

2000; 2003; 2005. Colorful, especially on borders. Olive-brown and dark brown on multicolor underprint. Portrait J. J. Dessalines at left. Ascending size serial number. Letters BRH at right in various color combinations. Back: Arms at center. Printer: (T)DLR. 162x70mm.

    a. 2000.   FV 30.00
    b. 2003.   FV 30.00
    s. Specimen. Red overprint: *SPECIMEN.*   — 100

2004 Commemorative Issue

#272-277 Bicentennial of Haiti. Signature titles in Frence French and Haitian Creole.

270　500 Gourdes　　　　　　　　　　　　　　**VF　UNC**

2000; 2003; 2005. Colorful, especially on borders. Red and violet on multicolor underpint. Portrait Pres. A. Pétion at left. Ascending size serial number. Letters BRH at right in various color combinations. Back: Arms at center. Printer: (T)DLR. 162x70mm.

a. 2000.	FV	45.00
b. 2003.	FV	45.00
s. Speciemn. Red overprint: *SPECIMEN*.	—	100

2001 Commemorative Issue

Bicentennial of the Constitution, 1801-2001

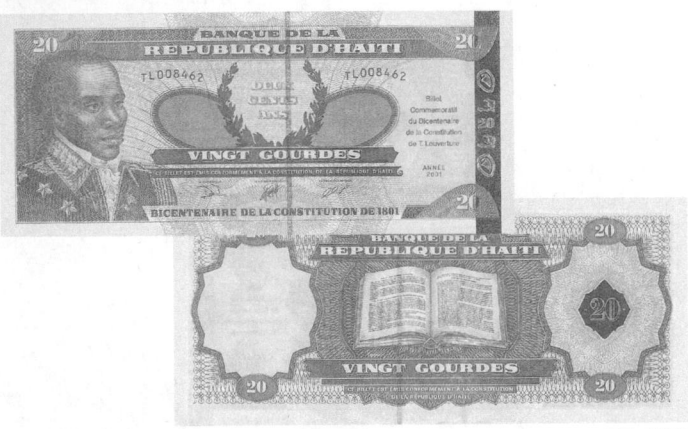

272　10 Gourdes　　　　　　　　　　　　　　**VF　UNC**

2004-. UV: fibers fluoresce red, blue and yellow. 10s in a box yellow. Blue. Sanite Belair at left. Back: Fort Cap-Rouge (Jacmel). Printer: DLR (without imprint). 130x65mm.

a. 2004.	FV	2.00
b. 2006.	FV	1.50
c. 2008.	FV	1.25
d. 2010.	FV	1.25
e. 2012.	FV	1.25
f. 2014.	FV	1.25
s. Specimen.	—	—

271　20 Gourdes　　　　　　　　　　　　　　**VF　UNC**

2001. Brown, orange and yellow. Bust at left. Foil impressions flank center wreath. Back: Open Constitution book. 162x70mm.　　　FV　4.00

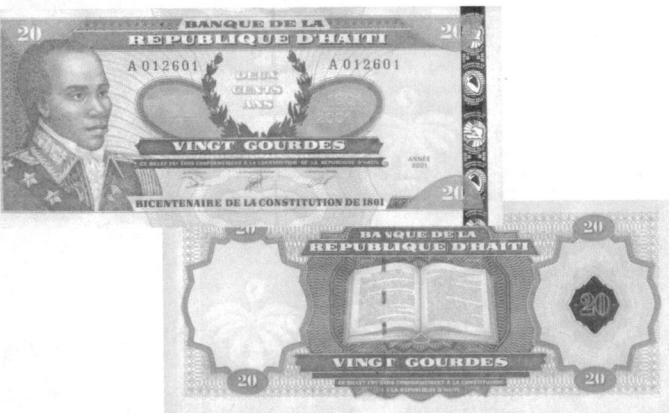

273　25 Gourdes　　　　　　　　　　　　　　**VF　UNC**

2004. Purple on tan and green underprint. Nicolas Gieffrard at left. Back: Fortress des Plantons (Dussio). 155x65mm.

a. Issued note.	FV	3.00
s. Specimen.	—	—

271A　20 Gourdes　　　　　　　　　　　　　**VF　UNC**

2001. Brown, orange and yellow. Bust at left. Foil impressions flank center wreath. Without commemorative legent at right. Back: Open Constitution book at center.

a. Issued note.	FV	4.00
s. Specimen.	—	—

274　50 Gourdes　　　　　　　　　　　　　　**VF　UNC**

2004-. Purple. Francois Cappoix at left. Back: Fort Jalousiere (Marmelade). Printer: DLR (without imprint). 155x65mm.

a. 2004.	FV	9.00
b. 2008. Reinforced corners.	FV	9.00
c. 2010.	FV	8.00
d. 2013.	FV	8.00
e. 2014.	FV	8.00
s. Specimen.	—	—

275 100 Gourdes

2004; 2008; 2010. Blue and gray. Henry Christophé at left. Back: Citadelle Henry (Milot). 155x65mm.

		VF	UNC
a. 2004.		FV	18.00
b. 2008. Reinforced corners.		FV	18.00
c. 2010.		FV	18.00
d. 2013.		FV	18.00
e. 2014.		FV	18.00
s. Specimen.		—	—

276 250 Gourdes

2004; 2007; 2008; 2010. Blue on tan and brown underprint. Jean-Jacques Dessalines at left. Back: Fort Decidé (Marchand). Printer: DLR (without imprint). 155x65mm.

		VF	UNC
a. 2004.		FV	17.50
b. 2007. Reinforced corners.		FV	15.00
c. 2008.		FV	12.50
d. 2010.		FV	12.50
e. 2013.		FV	12.50
s. Specimen.		—	—

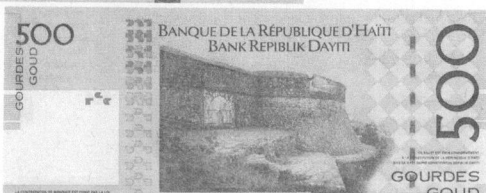

277 500 Gourdes

2004-. Purple on tan underprint. Alexandre Petion at left. Back: Fort Jacques (Fermathe). 155x65mm.

		VF	UNC
a. 2004.		FV	45.00
b. 2007. Reinforced corners.		FV	45.00
c. 2008.		FV	45.00
d. 2010.		FV	45.00
e. 2014.		FV	45.00
s. Specimen.		—	—

2006 Issue

278 1000 Gourdes

ND (2000); 2004; 2007; 2009. Violet, blue and lilac on multicolor underprint. Florvil Hyppolito at left. Back: Marche Valliere at right.

		VF	UNC
a. ND (2000). Series AA.		FV	85.00
b. 2004. Series AB.		FV	85.00
c. 2007. Series AF. Reinforced corners.		FV	85.00
d. 2009.		FV	85.00
e. 2014.		FV	85.00
s1. Specimen. Series AA.		—	—
s2. Specimen. Series AB.		—	—
s3. Specimen. Series AF.		—	—

Certificat de Liberation Economique

The C.L.E. was an internal loan made by the Haitian government. A certain percentage of an employee's wage was paid in C.L.E. notes.

Loi du 17 Septembre 1962

501 1 Gourde

	VF	UNC
1.10.1962. Green with black text.	25.00	65.00

502 5 Gourdes

	VF	UNC
1.10.1962. Red with black text.		
a. Series A.	25.00	65.00
b. Series B.	25.00	65.00
c. Series C.	25.00	65.00

503 25 Gourdes

	VF	UNC
1.10.1962. Yellow-orange with black text.	30.00	80.00

504 100 Gourdes

	VF	UNC
1.10.1962. Blue with black text.	100	250

HONDURAS

The Republic of Honduras, situated in Central America between El Salvador, Nicaragua and Guatemala, has an area of 43,277 sq. mi. (112,088 sq. km.) and a population of 6.48 million. Capital: Tegucigalpa. Tourism, agriculture, mining (gold and silver), and logging are the chief industries. Bananas, timber and coffee are exported.

Once part of Spain's vast empire in the New World, Honduras became an independent nation in 1821. After two and a half decades of mostly military rule, a freely elected civilian government came to power in 1982. During the 1980s, Honduras proved a haven for anti-Sandinista contras fighting the Marxist Nicaraguan Government and an ally to Salvadoran Government forces fighting leftist guerrillas. The country was devastated by Hurricane Mitch in 1998.

MONETARY SYSTEM:
 l Peso = 100 Centavos, 1871-1926
 1 Lempira = 100 Centavos, 1926-

BANKS:
 Aguan Navigation and Improvement Company #S101-S107
 Banco Atlantida #S111-S125
 Banco Centro-Americano #S131-S139
 Banco de Comercio #S141-S145
 Banco Nacional de Honduras #S148
 Banco Nacional Hondureño #S151-S159

REVOLUTION
 Banco Territorial de Honduras #S161-S161A

REPUBLIC
 Billete Aduanero (Customs Notes) #S162-S171

REPÚBLICA DE HONDURAS

Banco Central de Honduras
Established July 1, 1950 by merger of Banco Atlantida and Banco de Honduras. Various date and sign. varieties.

1950-51 Issue

49 100 Lempiras

		VF	UNC
1951-73. Yellow on multicolor underprint. Valle at left, arms at right. Back: Village and bridge.

		VF	UNC
a.	Without security thread, lilac-pink underprint. Printer: W&S. 16.3.1951; 8.3.1957.	300	1,500
b.	Without security thread, With fibers at right center, light green and light orange underprint. Printer: W&S. 5.2.1964; 5.11.1965; 22.3.1968; 10.12.1969.	300	1,500
c.	With security thread, yellow underprint. 13.10.1972. Reported not confirmed.	—	—
d.	As c. but without security thread. 13.10.1972; 23.3.1973.	175	500
s.	Specimen, punch hole cancelled.	—	250

#50 not assigned.

1953-56 Issue

51 5 Lempiras

		VF	UNC
1953-68. Gray on multicolor underprint. Morazán at left, arms at right. Serial # at upper left and upper right. Back: Battle of Trinidad. Printer: ABNC. 156x67mm.

a.	Date horizontal. 17.3.1953; 19.3.1954; 26.3.1954; 7.5.1954.	50.00	300
b.	Date horizontal. 22.11.1957-7.1.1966.	35.00	225
c.	Date vertical. 15.4.1966; 29.9.1967; 22.3.1968.	20.00	150
s.	Specimen.	—	300

52 10 Lempiras

		VF	UNC
1954-69. Date and signature style varieties. Brown on multicolor underprint. Cabañas at left, arms at right. Back: Old bank building. Printer: TDLR. 156x67mm.

| a. | Right signature title: *MINISTRO DE HACIENDA...* 19.11.1954. | 75.00 | 550 |
| b. | Right signature title: *MINISTRO DE ECONOMIA...* 19.2.1960-10.1.1969. | 50.00 | 400 |

53 20 Lempiras

		VF	UNC
1954-72. Green. D. de Herrera at left, arms at right. Back: Waterfalls. Printer: TDLR. 156x67mm.

a.	4.6.1954; 26.11.1954; 5.4.1957; 6.3.1959; 8.5.1959.	90.00	600
b.	19.2.1960; 27.4.1962; 19.4.1963; 6.3.1964.	60.00	450
c.	7.1.1966; 3.3.1967; 8.3.1968; 5.4.1968; 10.1.1969; 11.4.1969; 13.1.1970; 2.4.1971; 18.2.1972.	60.00	400

1961 Issue

54A 1 Lempira

		VF	UNC
1961; 1965. Red on multicolor underprint. Lempira at left, modified design of #45 with black serial #. Two signature varieties. Back: Dios del Maiz/Idolo Maya and Mayan artifacts. Printer: TDLR.

a.	10.2.1961.	4.00	25.00
b.	30.7.1965.	4.00	25.00
s.	Specimen. Punched hole cancelled. 10.2.1961.	—	50.00

1968; 1970 Issue

55 1 Lempira   VF   UNC
1968; 1972. Red-orange on green and pink underprint. Lempira at left, design
different from #45 and 54A. Back: *Ruinas de Copan Juego de Pelota.* Printer:
TDLR. 156x67mm.
    a. Right signature title: *MINISTRO DE ECONOMIA...* 25.10.1968.   3.00   17.50
    b. Right signature title: *MINISTRO DE HACIENDA...* 21.1.1972.   1.00   12.50

56 5 Lempiras   VF   UNC
1968-74. Black on multicolor underprint. Morazan at left, arms at right. Serial
number at lower left and upper right. Back: Battle scene of Trinidad at center.
Printer: ABNC. 156x67mm.
    a. Date horizontal. 29.11.1968; 11.4.1969; 10.3.1970.   20.00   65.00
    b. Date vertical. 20.11.1970-24.8.1974.   10.00   60.00

57 10 Lempiras   VF   UNC
27.8.1970-13.11.1975. Brown on multicolor underprint. Cabañas at left, arms at
right. Back: Ruins and new bank. Printer: ABNC. 156x67mm.   20.00   100

1973; 1974 Issue

58 1 Lempira   VF   UNC
11.3.1974. Red on green and lilac underprint. Lempira without feather at left, arms   2.00   10.00
at right. Back: Different view of Ruinas de Copan. Printer: TDLR. 156x67mm.

59 5 Lempiras   VF   UNC
1974-78. Black on multicolor underprint. Morazán at left, arms at right. Back:
Battle of Trinidad at left. Printer: ABNC. 156x67mm.
    a. Date vertical. 24.10.1974.   10.00   50.00
    b. Date horizontal. 12.12.1975; 26.2.1976; 16.9.1976; 9.12.1976; 13.1.1977;   5.00   30.00
     3.6.1977; 25.11.1977; 13.2.1978.

60 20 Lempiras   VF   UNC
1973-77. Date placement varieties. Green on multicolor underprint. D. de Herrera
at left, arms at right. Back: Presidential residence. Printer: (T)DLR. 156x67mm.
    a. 2.3.1973.   40.00   150
    b. 13.8.1973.   40.00   150
    c. 30.11.1973.   40.00   150
    d. 1.3.1974.   40.00   150
    e. 22.4.1974.   40.00   150
    f. 5.6.1975.   40.00   150
    g. 15.1.1976.   40.00   150
    h. 18.3.1976.   40.00   150
    i. 13.1.1977.   40.00   150
    j. 3.6.1977.   40.00   150

1976 Commemorative Issue
#61, Centennial of the Marco Aurelio Soto Government

61 2 Lempiras   VF   UNC
23.9.1976. Purple on multicolor underprint. Arms at left, M. A. Soto at right. Back: 1.50   9.00
Island and Port of Amapala. Printer: TDLR. 156x67mm.

1975-78 Regular Issue

62   1 Lempira
30.6.1978. Red. Lempira without feather at left, arms at right. Back: View of
Ruinas de Copan. Indian symbols below bank name. Printer: TDLR. 156x67mm.

	VF	UNC
	0.75	7.00

63   5 Lempiras
1978-94. UV: fibers fluoresce orange and blue, serial #s orange, central design
elements and 5s yellow. Black, dark blue, and deep olive-green on multicolor
underprint. Arms at left, Morazán at right. Back: Battle of Trinidad scene (Nov. 11,
1827). Printer: TDLR. 156x67mm.

	VF	UNC
a. 4.10.1978; 8.5.1980.	4.00	15.00
b. 8.12.1985; 30.3.1989.	1.50	12.50
c. Red serial # at upper left in ascending size. 14.1.1993; 25.2.1993.	FV	7.50
d. Brown serial # as c. 12.5.1994.	FV	5.00
s. As d. Specimen. *MUESTRA SIN VALOR.*	—	—

64   10 Lempiras
1976-89. Brown on multicolor underprint. Cabañas at left. Back: City University.
Printer: ABNC. 156x67mm.

	VF	UNC
a. 18.3.1976-10.5.1979.	5.00	30.00
b. 23.6.1982-10.11.1989.	3.00	17.50

65   20 Lempiras
1978-93. Date placement varieties. Green on multicolor underprint. D. de Herrera
at right. Back: Port of Puerto Cortes. Watermark: D. de Herrera. Printer: ABNC.
156x67mm.

	VF	UNC
a. 2.11.1978; 10.9.1979.	8.00	40.00
b. Vertical date at right. 8.1.1981-10.2.1989.	4.00	25.00
c. Horizontal date at upper left. 22.6.1989-2.10.1992.	3.50	15.00
d. 10.12.1992; 18.3.1993; 1.7.1993.	FV	10.00

66   50 Lempiras
1976-93. Deep blue on multicolor underprint. J. M. Galvez D. at left. Back: National Agricultural Development Bank. Watermark: Tree. Printer: ABNC. 156x67mm.

	VF	UNC
a. Vertical date at right. 29.1.1976; 13.1.1977; 3.6.1977; 13.2.1978; 10.9.1979.	15.00	55.00
b. 5.1.1984; 3.7.1986; 24.9.1987; 10.2.1989.	10.00	40.00
c. Horizontal date at upper left. 1.3.1990; 13.12.1990; 29.8.1991.	7.00	30.00
d. 18.3.1993; 1.7.1993.	FV	25.00

67   100 Lempiras
1975-79. Brown-orange on multicolor underprint. Valle at left. Back: Signatepeque
school of forestry. Printer: TDLR. 156x67mm.

	VF	UNC
a. 16.1.1975.	25.00	150
b. 29.1.1976.	25.00	150
c. 18.3.1976.	25.00	150
d. 13.1.1977.	25.00	150
e. 12.1.1978.	25.00	150
f. 10.9.1979.	25.00	150

1980-81 Issue

68   1 Lempira
1980; 1984; 1989. UV: security strip fluoresces blue. Red on multicolor underprint.
Arms at left, Lempira at right. Back: Ruins of Copan. Printer: TDLR. 156x67mm.

	VF	UNC
a. Without security thread. 29.5.1980.	0.75	6.00
b. As a. 18.10.1984.	0.75	5.00
c. With security thread. 30.3.1989.	FV	4.00

69   100 Lempiras
1981-94. Brown-orange, dark olive-green, and deep purple on multicolor underprint. J. C. del Valle at right. Back: Forestry school. Watermark: J. C. del Valle.
Printer: TDLR. 156x67mm.

	VF	UNC
a. Regular serial #. 8.1.1981; 23.6.1982; 8.9.1983.	15.00	75.00
b. 5.1.1984-13.12.1989.	12.50	50.00
c. 21.12.1989-1.7.1993.	FV	40.00

1989 Issue

70   10 Lempiras

VF   UNC

21.9.1989. UV: fibers and serial #s fluoresce orange, central design yellow. Back, elements orange. Dark brown and red on multicolor underprint (of vertical stripes). Arms at left, Cabañas at right. Back: City University. Printer: TDLR. 156x67mm.

		VF	UNC
a. Issued note.		2.50	12.50
s. Specimen. *MUESTRA SIN VALOR.*		—	—

1992-93 Issue

71   1 Lempira

VF   UNC

10.9.1992. Dark red on multicolor underprint. Arms at left, Lempira at right. Back: Ruins of Copan. Printer: CNBC. 156x67mm.

FV   2.50

72   2 Lempiras

VF   UNC

1993-94. Like #61 but with light blue underprint at left. UV. fibers fluoresce orange and blue, serial #s orange. Purple on multicolor underprint. Arms at left, M. A. Soto at right. Ascending size serial number at upper left. Back: Island and Port of Amapala. Printer: TDLR. 156x67mm.

		VF	UNC
a. 14.1.1993. Red serial #.		FV	4.50
b. 25.2.1993. As a.		FV	4.50
c. 12.5.1994. Brown serial #.		FV	4.50
s. Specimen. *MUESTRA SIN VALOR.*		—	—

73   20 Lempiras

VF   UNC

1993-97. Deep green and dark brown on multicolor underprint. D. de Herrera at right. Back: Vertical; Presidential House at center. Watermark: D. de Herrera. Printer: TDLR. 156x67mm.

		VF	UNC
a. 14.1.1993. Red serial #.		FV	7.50
b. 25.2.1993.		FV	7.50
c. 12.5.1994. Brown Serial #.		FV	7.50
d. 12.12.1996.		FV	7.50
e. 18.9.1997.		FV	7.50
s. Specimen. *MUESTRA SIN VALOR.* 12.5.1994.		—	—

73A   20 Lempiras

VF   UNC

3.9.1998. Deep green and dark brown on multicolor underprint. D. de Herrera at right. Back: Vertical; Presidential House at center. Watermark: D. de Herrera. Printer: FC-O.

FV   7.50

74   50 Lempiras

VF   UNC

1993-98. Blue-black and dark brown on multicolor underprint. J. M. Galvez D. at right. Back: Vertical; Central Bank Annex at center. Watermark: J. M. Galvez D. Printer: TDLR. 156x67mm.

		VF	UNC
a. 14.1.1993. Red serial #.		FV	17.50
b. 25.2.1993.		FV	17.50
c. 12.5.1994.		FV	17.50
d. 12.12.1996.		FV	17.50
e. 18.9.1997.		FV	17.50
f. 3.9.1998.		FV	17.50
s. Specimen. *MUESTRA SIN VALOR.* 12.5.1994.		—	—

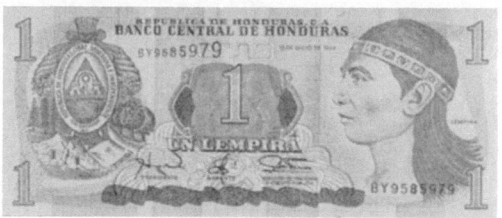

75   100 Lempiras

VF   UNC

1993-94. Brown-orange, dark olive-green and dark brown on multicolor underprint. J. C. del Valle at right. Red serial number at upper left in ascending size. Black signature. Back: Forestry school. Enhanced underprint in watermark area. Watermark: J. C. del Valle. Printer: (T)DLR. 156x67mm.

		VF	UNC
a. 14.1.1993.		FV	30.00
b. 25.2.1993.		FV	30.00
c. 12.5.1994.		FV	30.00
s. Specimen. *MUESTRA SIN VALOR.* 12.5.1994.		—	—

1994; 1995 Issue

76 1 Lempira VF UNC

12.5.1994. UV: serial #s and 1 in box fluoresce yellow, fibers orange and green. Red on multicolor underprint. Arms at left, Lempira at right. Brown ascending size serial number at upper left Printer: TDLR. 156x67mm.

    a. Issued note. FV 1.50

    s. Specimen. *MUESTRA SIN VALOR.* — —

79 1 Lempira VF UNC

1996; 1998. UV: fibers fluoresce blue and yellow, 1 in box yellow. Dark red on multicolor underprint. Arms at left, Lempira at right, brown serial number with ascending size serial number at upper left. Back: Ruins of Copan. Printer: F-CO. 156x67mm.

    a. 12.12.1996. FV 1.00

    b. 3.9.1998. FV 1.00

79A 1 Lempira VF UNC

18.9.1997. Dark red on multicolor underprint. Arms at left, Lempira at right, brown serial number with ascending size serial number at upper left. Back: Ruins of Copan. Printer: TDLR (without imprint). FV 1.00

80 2 Lempiras VF UNC

18.9.1997. Purple on multicolor underprint. Arms at left, M. A. Soto at right, brown serial number with ascending size serial number at upper left. Back: Port of Amapala. Printer: TDLR. 156x67mm. FV 1.50

77 100 Lempiras VF UNC

1994-2004. Brown-orange, black and olive-green on multicolor underprint. J. C. del Valle at center right, bridge over the Choluteca River at right. Brown serial number. Back: Valle's house at left. Watermark: J. C. del Valle. Printer: TDLR (without imprint). 156x67mm.

    a. Signature titles: *MINISTRO DE HACIENDA Y CREDITO PUBLICO.* 12.5.1994. FV 25.00

    b. Signature titles: *SECRETARIO DE FINANZAS.* 18.9.1997. FV 20.00

    c. 3.9.1998. FV 20.00

    d. 14.12.2000. FV 20.00

    e. 30.8.2001. FV 15.00

    f. 23.1.2003. FV 15.00

    g. 26.8.2004. FV 15.00

    h. 17.4.2008. FV 12.50

80A 2 Lempiras VF UNC

1998-2008. Purple on multicolor underprint. Arms at left, M. A. Soto at right, brown serial number with ascending size serial number at upper left. Back: Port of Amapala. Printer: F-CO.

    a. 3.9.1998. FV 1.50

    b. 14.12.2000. FV 1.50

    c. 30.8.2001. FV 1.50

    d. 23.1.2003. FV 1.50

    e. 13.7.2006. FV 1.50

    e. 26.8.2004. FV 1.50

    f. 17.4.2008. FV 1.50

78 500 Lempiras VF UNC

1995-2010. Violet and purple on multicolor underprint. Dr. R. Rosa at right, National Gallery of Art in background. Back: View of Rosario de San Juancito at left center. Watermark: Dr. R. Rosa. 156x67mm.

    a. Signature titles: *MINISTRO DE HACIENDA Y CREDITO PUBLICO.* 16.11.1995. FV 95.00

    b. Signature titles: *SECRETARIO DE FINANZAS.* 3.9.1998. FV 90.00

    c. 14.12.2000. FV 90.00

    d. 30.8.2001. FV 90.00

    e. 23.1.2003. FV 90.00

    f. 26.8.2004. FV 90.00

    g. 6.5.2010. FV 90.00

1996-98 Issue

81 5 Lempiras VF UNC

1996-98. Black, dark blue and deep olive-green on multicolor underprint. Arms at left, Morazán at right, brown serial number with ascending size serial number at upper left. Back: Battle of Trinidad scene (Nov. 11. 1827). Printer: TDLR. 156x67mm.

    a. 12.12.1996. FV 2.00

    b. 18.9.1997. FV 2.00

    c. 3.9.1998. FV 2.00

82   10 Lempiras

		VF	UNC
1996-2008. Dark brown and red on multicolor underprint. Arms at left, Cabañas at right. Back: City University. Printer: TDLR. 156x67mm.			
a. 12.12.1996.		FV	3.50
b. 18.9.1997.		FV	3.50
c. 3.9.1998.		FV	3.50
d. 14.12.2000.		FV	3.50
e. 17.4.2008.		FV	3.50

2000 Commemorative Issue

#83, 50th Anniversary of the Central Bank and Year 2000

83   20 Lempiras

	VF	UNC
30.3.2000. Dark green and brown on multicolor underprint. D. Herrera and Government House at right. Back: Work, effort and unity sculpture. 156x67mm.	FV	5.00

2000-03 Issue

84   1 Lempira

		VF	UNC
2000-06. Dark red on multicolor underprint. Arms at left, Lempira at right. Back: Ruins of Copán. Printer: CBNC. 156x67mm.			
a. 14.12.2000.		FV	1.00
b. 30.8.2001.		FV	1.00
c. 23.1.2003.		FV	1.00
d. 26.8.2004.		FV	1.00
e. 13.7.2006.		FV	1.00

85   5 Lempiras

		VF	UNC
2000-04. Multicolor. Arms at left, Morazán at right. Back: Battle of Trinidad scene (Nov. 11. 1827). Printer: CBNC. 156x67mm.			
a. 14.12.2000.		FV	1.75
b. 30.8.2001.		FV	1.75
c. 23.1.2003.		FV	1.75
d. 26.8.2004.		FV	1.75

86   10 Lempiras

		VF	UNC
2001-10. Multicolor. Arms at left, Cabañas at right. Back: City University. Printer: FC-O. 156x67mm.			
a. 30.8.2001.		FV	2.75
b. 23.1.2003.		FV	2.75
c. 26.8.2004.		FV	2.75
d. 13.7.2006.		FV	2.75
e. 6.5.2010.		FV	2.75

87   20 Lempiras

		VF	UNC
2001; 2003. Green and violet on multicolor underprint. Printer: G&D. 156x67mm.			
a. 30.8.2001.		FV	4.50
b. 23.1.2003.		FV	4.50

88   50 Lempiras

		VF	UNC
2001; 2003; 2006. Multicolor. J. M. Galvez D. at right, vertical serial number at left. Back: Central Bank Annex at center. Printer: TDLR. 156x67mm.			
a. 30.8.2001.		FV	9.50
b. 23.1.2003.		FV	9.50
c. 13.7.2006.		FV	9.50

2004-06 Issue

89   1 Lempira

		VF	UNC
17.4.2008; 6.5.2010. Dark red on multicolor underprint. Arms at left, Lempira at right. Back: Ruins of Copán. 156x67mm.			
a. 17.4.2008. Printer: F-CO.		FV	1.00
b. 6.5.2010. Printer: Oberthur.		FV	1.00

90 **2 Lempiras** VF UNC
17.4.2008; 1.3.2012. Purple on multicolor underprint. Marco Aurello Soto at right. FV 1.50
Printer: F-CO 156x67mm.

91 **5 Lempiras** VF UNC
2006; 2008; 2010. Printer: FC-O. 156x67mm.
    a. 13.7.2006. FV 1.75
    b. 17.4.2008. FV 1.75
    c. 6.5.2010. FV 1.75

92 **20 Lempiras** VF UNC
26.8.2004. Similar to #87 but redesigned. Green and tan on multicolor underprint. FV 4.50
Bust at right, arms at left. Back: Presidential palace at center. Printer: G&D.
156x67mm.

93 **20 Lempiras** VF UNC
2006; 2008. Green on multicolor underprint. Bust at right, arms at left Back:
Presidential manision. Printer: (T)DLR. 156x67mm.
    a. 13.7.2006. FV 4.50
    b. 31.7.2008. FV 4.50

94 **50 Lempiras** VF UNC
2004; 2008; 2010. Blue on multicolor underprint. Juan Manuel Galvez D. at right
with building. Back: Central Bank building at left. Printer: G&D. 156x67mm.
    a. 26.8.2004. FV 9.50
    b. 17.4.2008. FV 7.50
    c. 6.5.2010. FV 6.00
94A **50 Lempiras** VF UNC
2006; 2008. Blue on multicolor underprint. Printer: TDLR. 156x67mm.
    a. 13.7.2006. FV 9.50
    b. 17.4.2008. FV 9.50

2008 Polymer Issue

95 **20 Lempiras** VF UNC
31.7.2008. Polymer plastic. Green on multicolor underprint Dionisio de Herrera at FV 4.50
right. Signature varieties. Back: Presidential mansion. 156x67mm.

96 **1 Lempira** VF UNC
1.3.2012. Like #89 but with vertical bar in top and bottom margin and braille at FV 1.00
right. Printer: FC-O 156x67mm.

97 **2 Lempiras** VF UNC
1.3.2012. Like #90 but with two bars at top and bottom margin and braille at right FV 1.50
end. Printer: FC-O. 156x67mm.

98   5 Lempiras

	VF	UNC
1.3.2012. Like #91 but with three bars at top and bottom margin and braille at right end. Printer: FC-O. 156x67mm.	FV	1.75

99   10 Lempiras

	VF	UNC
1.3.2012. Like # 86 but with vertical bars in top and bottom margin and braille at right end. Printer: FC-O. 156x67mm.	FV	3.00

100   20 Lempiras

	VF	UNC
1.3.2012. Like #93 but vertical bars at top and bottom margin and braille at right end. Printer: FC-O. 156x67mm.	FV	4.50

101   50 Lempiras

	VF	UNC
1.3.2012. Like #94 but with vertical ars at top and bottom margin and braille at right end. Printer: FC-O. 156x67mm.	FV	9.50

102   100 Lempiras

	VF	UNC
1.3.2012. Like #77 but with vertical bars at top and bottom margin and braille at right end. Printer: FC-O. 156x67mm.	FV	15.00

HONG KONG

Hong Kong S.A.R., a former British Colony, is situated at the mouth of the Canton or Pearl River 90 miles (145 km.) southeast of Canton, has an area of 1,092 sq. km. and a population of 7.01 million. Capital: Central (formerly Victoria). The port of Hong Kong had developed as the commercial center of the Far East, a transshipment point for goods destined for China and the countries of the Pacific rim. Light manufacturing and tourism are important components of the economy.

Occupied by the UK in 1841, Hong Kong was formally ceded by China the following year; various adjacent lands were added later in the 19th century. Pursuant to an agreement signed by China and the UK on 19 December 1984, Hong Kong became the Hong Kong Special Administrative Region (SAR) of China on 1 July 1997. In this agreement, China promised that, under its "one country, two systems" formula, China's socialist economic system would not be imposed on Hong Kong and that Hong Kong would enjoy a high degree of autonomy in all matters except foreign and defense affairs for the next 50 years.

RULERS:
  British (1842-1997)

MONETARY SYSTEM:
  1 Dollar = 100 Cents

NOTE ON VALUATIONS:
  Most valuations are for issued notes. At times specimen or proof notes are listed w/valuations, but these are only cases where a regularly issued example is not known to exist.

BRITISH ADMINISTRATION
Chartered Bank

行銀打渣[1]

Cha Ta Yin Hang

Prior to December 1956, it was in business as The Chartered Bank of India, Australia & China. In the 1980s it became the Standard Bank, then later became the Standard Chartered Bank.

1961; 1967 ND Issues

68   5 Dollars

1961-62; ND. Black and green on multicolor underprint. Arms at lower left. Back: Chinese junk and sampan at center. Watermark: Helmeted warrior's head. Printer: TDLR.

	VF	UNC
a. 1.7.1961.	80.00	500
b. 3.3.1962.	125	600
c. ND (1962-70).	40.00	180
s. Specimen. As a.	—	—

69   5 Dollars

	VF	UNC
ND (1967). Black and yellow-brown on multicolor underprint. Arms at lower left. Back: Chinese junk and sampan at center. Watermark: Helmeted warrior's head. Printer: TDLR.	30.00	180

70   10 Dollars

1961-62; ND. Black and red-violet on red underprint. Arms at left. Back: Chartered Bank building at center. Watermark: Helmeted warrior's head. Printer: TDLR.

	VF	UNC
a. 1.7.1961.	125	400
b. 3.3.1962.	60.00	500
c. ND (1962-70).	25.00	80.00
s. Specimen. As a, c.	—	—

74   10 Dollars   **VF   UNC**

ND; 1975; 1977. Dark green on multicolor underprint. Bank building at left, bank crest at center. Back: Ocean terminal at center. Watermark: Helmeted warrior's head. Printer: TDLR.

		VF	UNC
a. Signature titles: *ACCOUNTANT* and *MANAGER*. ND (1970-75).		10.00	50.00
b. Signature titles: *ACCOUNTANT* and *CHIEF MANAGER IN HONG KONG*. ND; 1.6.1975.		20.00	60.00
c. Signature titles as b. 1.1.1977.		6.00	30.00
s. Specimen. As b.		—	350

71   100 Dollars   **VF   UNC**

1961; ND. Dark green and brown on multicolor underprint. Arms at center. Back: Harbor view. Watermark: Helmeted warrior's head. Printer: TDLR.

	VF	UNC
a. 1.7.1961.	750	2,800
b. ND (1961-70).	425	1,500

72   500 Dollars   **VF   UNC**

1961-77. Black and dark brown on multicolor underprint. Male portrait at left. Back: Ship, harbor view at center. Watermark: Helmeted warrior's head. Printer: TDLR.

	VF	UNC
a. Signature titles: *ACCOUNTANT* and *MANAGER*. 1.7.1961.	1,500	3,375
b. Signature titles as a. ND (1962-?).	650	3,000
c. Signature titles: *ACCOUNTANT* and *CHIEF MANAGER IN HONG KONG*. ND (1962-1975).	600	2,600
d. Signature titles as c. 1.1.1977.	350	1,500
s. Specimen. As a, d.	—	1,000

75   50 Dollars   **VF   UNC**

ND (1970-75). Blue on multicolor underprint. Bank building at left, bank crest at center. Back: City Hall at center right. Watermark: Helmeted warrior's head. Printer: TDLR.

	VF	UNC
a. Issued note.	200	700
s. Specimen.	—	1,500

1970 ND; 1975-77 Issue

73   5 Dollars   **VF   UNC**

ND (1970-75); 1975. Dark brown on multicolor underprint. Bank building at left, bank crest at center. Back: City Hall at center right. Watermark: Helmeted warrior's head. Printer: TDLR.

	VF	UNC
a. Signature titles: *ACCOUNTANT* and *MANAGER*. ND (1970-75).	4.00	25.00
b. Signature titles: *ACCOUNTANT* and *CHIEF MANAGER IN HONG KONG* at right. ND; 1.6.1975.	10.00	20.00
s. Specimen. As b.	—	—

76   100 Dollars   **VF   UNC**

ND; 1977. Red on multicolor underprint. Bank building at left, bank crest at center. Watermark: Helmeted warrior's head. Printer: TDLR.

	VF	UNC
a. ND (1970-75).	125	550
b. 1.1.1977.	60.00	350
s. Specimen. As a.	—	350

1979; 1980 Issue

77   10 Dollars
1980-81. Green on multicolor underprint. Stylistic carp at right. Back: Bank building at left, arms at center. Watermark: Helmeted warrior's head. Printer: TDLR.

		VF	UNC
a.	1.1.1980.	4.00	15.00
b.	1.1.1981.	4.00	10.00

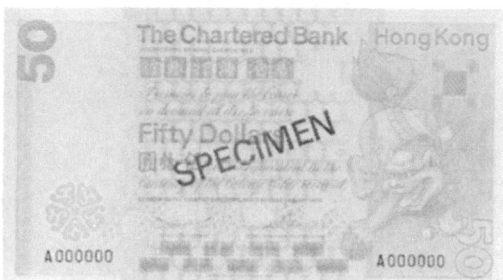

78   50 Dollars
1979-82 Blue on multicolor underprint. Chinze at right. Back: Bank building at left, arms at center. Watermark: Helmeted warrior's head. Printer: TDLR.

		VF	UNC
a.	1.1.1979.	25.00	150
b.	1.1.1981.	FV	60.00
c.	1.1.1982.	FV	90.00
s.	Specimen.	—	450

79   100 Dollars
1979-82. Red on multicolor underprint. Mythical horse *Qilin* at right. Back: Bank building at left, arms at center. Watermark: Helmeted warrior's head. Printer: TDLR.

		VF	UNC
a.	1.1.1979.	40.00	180
b.	1.1.1980.	35.00	120
c.	1.1.1982.	30.00	95.00
s.	Specimen.	—	300

80   500 Dollars
1979; 1982. Brown on multicolor underprint. Mythical phoenix at right. Back: Bank building at left, arms at center. Watermark: Helmeted warrior's head. Printer: TDLR.

		VF	UNC
a.	1.1.1979.	FV	800
b.	1.1.1982.	FV	650
s.	Specimen.	—	700

81   1000 Dollars
1979; 1982. Yellow-orange on multicolor underprint. Dragon at right. Back: Bank building at left, arms at center. Watermark: Helmeted warrior's head. Printer: TDLR.

		VF	UNC
a.	1.1.1979.	250	2,000
b.	1.1.1982.	160	1,500
s.	Specimen	—	1,000

Hong Kong & Shanghai Banking Corporation

行銀理滙海上港香

Hsiang K'ang Shang Hai Hui Li Yin Hang

Hong Kong
#96-101 arms at upper ctr. Printer: Ashby & Co.

1932-35 Issue

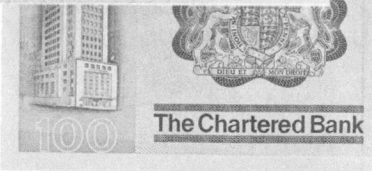

179   500 Dollars
1935-69. Brown and blue. Arms at top center, Sir T. Jackson at right. Back: Allegorical female head at left, bank building at center. Printer: BWC. 201x123mm.

		VF	UNC
a.	11.7.1960-1.8.1966.	700	2,500
b.	31.7.1967.	300	1,800
c.	11.2.1968.	180	700
d.	27.3.1969.	180	750

1959 Issue

181 5 Dollars   VF   UNC

1959-75. Brown on multicolor underprint. Woman seated at right. Back: New bank building at center. Watermark: Helmeted warrior's head. Printer: BWC, 142x79mm.

	VF	UNC
a. Signature titles: *CHIEF ACCOUNTANT* and *CHIEF MANAGER*. 2.5.1959-29.6.1960.	15.00	60.00
b. 1.5.1963.	175	1,500
c. 1.5.1964-27.3.1969.	5.00	30.00
d. Signature titles: *CHIEF ACCOUNTANT* and *GENERAL MANAGER*. 1.4.1970-18.3.1971.	5.00	25.00
e. 13.3.1972; 31.10.1972.	2.00	13.00
f. Small serial #. 31.10.1973; 31.3.1975.	1.25	11.00
s. Specimen.	—	—

182 10 Dollars   VF   UNC

1959-83. Dark green on multicolor underprint. Dark green on multicolor underprint. Back: New bank building at left center. Watermark: Helmeted warrior's head. Printer: BWC. 152x85mm.

	VF	UNC
a. Signature titles: *CHIEF ACCOUNTANT* and *CHIEF MANAGER*. 21.5.1959-1.9.1962.	15.00	60.00
b. 1.5.1963; 1.9.1963.	20.00	70.00
c. 1.5.1964; 1.9.1964.	15.00	60.00
d. 1.10.1964.	200	700
e. 1.2.1965; 1.8.1966; 31.7.1967.	6.00	35.00
f. 20.3.1968; 23.11.1968; 27.3.1969.	6.00	35.00
g. Signature titles: *CHIEF ACCOUNTANT* and *GENERAL MANAGER*. 1.4.1970-31.3.1976.	3.75	15.00
h. Signature titles: *CHIEF ACCOUNTANT* and *EXECUTIVE DIRECTOR*. 31.3.1977; 31.3.1978; 31.3.1979.	3.00	15.00
i. Signature titles: *CHIEF ACCOUNTANT* and *GENERAL MANAGER*. 31.3.1980; 31.3.1981.	3.00	12.50
j. Signature titles: *MANAGER* and *GENERAL MANAGER*. 31.3.1982; 31.3.1983.	3.00	12.50
s. Specimen.	—	—

183 100 Dollars   VF   UNC

1959-72. Red on multicolor underprint. Woman seated at left with open book, arms at upper center. Watermark: Helmeted warrior's head and denomination. Printer: BWC. 160x89mm.

	VF	UNC
a. Signature titles: *CHIEF ACCOUNTANT* and *CHIEF MANAGER*. 12.8.1959-1.10.1964.	100	650
b. 1.2.1965-27.3.1969.	50.00	400
c. Signature titles: *CHIEF ACCOUNTANT* and *GENERAL MANAGER*. 1.4.1970; 18.3.1971; 13.3.1972.	40.00	250

1968-73 Issue

184 50 Dollars   VF   UNC

1968-83. Dark blue on light blue and multicolor underprint. Arms at right. Back: New bank building at left center. Watermark: Helmeted warrior's head and denomination. Printer: BWC.

	VF	UNC
a. Signature titles: *CHIEF ACCOUNTANT* and *CHIEF MANAGER*. 31.5.1968; 27.3.1969.	45.00	150
b. Signature titles: *CHIEF ACCOUNTANT* and *GENERAL MANAGER*. 31.10.1973, 31.3.1975, 31.3.1978.	35.00	120
c. Signature titles as b. 31.3.1977.	35.00	110
d. Signature titles: *CHIEF ACCOUNTANT* and *EXECUTIVE DIRECTOR*. 31.3.1977.	35.00	110
e. 31.3.1979.	175	400
f. Signature titles: *CHIEF ACCOUNTANT* and *GENERAL MANAGER*. 31.3.1980.	12.50	50.00
g. 31.3.1981.	15.00	40.00
h. Signature titles: *MANAGER* and *GENERAL MANAGER*. 31.3.1982; 31.3.1983.	12.50	45.00
s. Specimen.	—	—

185 100 Dollars   VF   UNC

1972-76. Red on multicolor underprint. Arms at left. Back: Facing lions at lower left and right, bank building at center, dragon in medallion at right. Printer: BWC.

	VF	UNC
a. With 4 Large serial # on back. 13.3.1972; 31.10.1972.	50.00	200
b. Smaller electronic sorting serial # on face. without serial # on back. 31.10.1972.	60.00	250
c. 31.10.1973.	35.00	200
d. 31.3.1975; 31.3.1976.	35.00	150

186 500 Dollars

VF UNC

1973-76. Brown on multicolor underprint. Arms at left. Back: Bank building at left, lion's head at right. Printer: BWC.

a. 31.10.1973.	225	950
b. 31.3.1975.	300	1,100
c. 31.3.1976.	250	900

1977; 1978 Issue

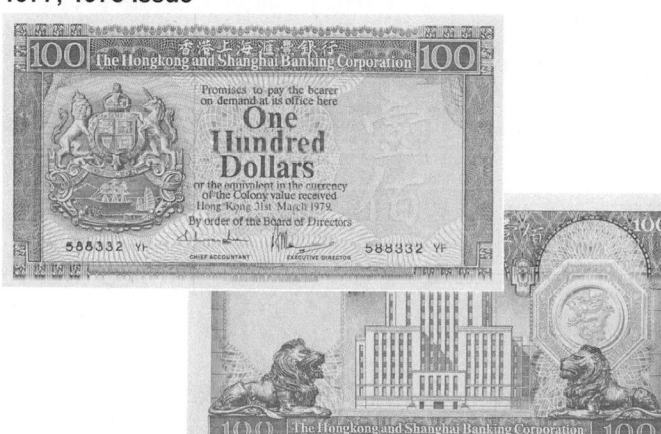

187 100 Dollars

VF UNC

1977-83. Red on lighter multicolor underprint. Arms at left. Back: Facing lions at lower left and right, bank building at center, dragon in medallion at right. Watermark: Lion's head. Printer: BWC.

a. Signature titles: *CHIEF ACCOUNTANT* and *EXECUTIVE DIRECTOR*. 31.3.1977; 31.3.1978.	25.00	100
b. Signature titles as a. 31.3.1979.	25.00	125
c. 31.3.1980; 31.3.1981.	FV	60.00
d. Signature titles: *MANAGER* and *GENERAL MANAGER*. 31.3.1982; 31.3.1983.	FV	45.00

#188 *Deleted*. See #186.

189 500 Dollars

VF UNC

1978-83. Modified frame designs. Brown and black on multicolor underprint. Arms at left. Back: Bank building at left, lion's head at right. Watermark: Lion's head. Printer: BWC.

a. 31.3.1978.	FV	500
b. 31.3.1980.	FV	400
c. 31.3.1981.	FV	350
d. 31.3.1983.	FV	300

190 1000 Dollars

VF UNC

1977-83. Gold and black on multicolor underprint. Arms at right. Back: Lion at left, bank building at center right. Watermark: Lion's head. Printer: BWC.

a. 31.3.1977.	FV	1,100
b. 31.3.1979.	FV	1,300
c. 31.3.1980.	FV	1,300
d. 31.3.1981.	FV	900
e. 31.3.1983.	FV	800

1985-87 Issue

#191-196 Replacement notes: Serial # prefix *ZZ*.

191 10 Dollars

VF UNC

1985-92. Deep green on multicolor underprint. Arms at left. Back: Sampan and ship at right. Facing lions at lower left and right with new bank building at center. Watermark: Lion's head. Printer: TDLR. 138x69mm.

a. Signature title: *GENERAL MANAGER*. 1.1.1985; 1.1.1986; 1.1.1987.	1.50	7.50
b. Signature title: *EXECUTIVE DIRECTOR*. 1.1.1988.	0.75	6.00
c. Signature title: *GENERAL MANAGER*. 1.1.1989; 1.1.1990; 1.1.1991; 1.1.1992.	0.50	5.00
s. Specimen. As a.	—	250

192 20 Dollars

VF UNC

1986-89. Deep gray-green and brown on purple and multicolor underprint. Arms at left. Back: Clock tower, ferry in harbor view at right. Facing lions at lower left and right with new bank building at center. Watermark: Lion's head. Printer: TDLR. 131x95mm.

a. Signature title: *GENERAL MANAGER*. 1.1.1986; 1.1.1987.	2.50	15.00
b. Signature title: *EXECUTIVE DIRECTOR*. 1.1.1988.	1.50	10.00
c. Signature title: *GENERAL MANAGER*. 1.1.1989.	FV	7.50
s. Specimen. As a.	—	300

193   50 Dollars

1985-92. Purple on multicolor underprint. Arms at left. Back: Men in boats at right. Facing lions at lower left and right with new bank building at center. Watermark: Lion's head. Printer: TDLR. 148x74mm.

		VF	UNC
a.	Signature title: *GENERAL MANAGER*. 1.1.1985; 1.1.1986; 1.1.1987.	FV	40.00
b.	Signature title: *EXECUTIVE DIRECTOR*. 1.1.1988.	FV	40.00
c.	Signature title: *GENERAL MANAGER*. 1.1.1989; 1.1.1990; 1.1.1991; 1.1.1992.	FV	15.00
s.	Specimen.	—	600

194   100 Dollars

1985-88. Red on multicolor underprint. Arms at left. Back: Tiger Balm Garden pagoda at right. Facing lions at lower left and right with new bank building at center. Watermark: Lion's head. Printer: TDLR. 154x77mm.

		VF	UNC
a.	Signature title: *GENERAL MANAGER*. 1.1.1985; 1.1.1986; 1.1.1987.	FV	30.00
b.	Signature title: *EXECUTIVE DIRECTOR*. 1.1.1988.	FV	25.00
s.	Specimen.	—	600

195   500 Dollars

1987-92. Brown on multicolor underprint. Arms at left. Back: Old tower at right. Facing lions at lower left and right with new bank building at center. Watermark: Lion's head. Printer: TDLR. 158x79mm.

		VF	UNC
a.	Signature title: *GENERAL MANAGER*. 1.1.1987.	FV	200
b.	Signature title: *EXECUTIVE DIRECTOR*. 1.1.1988.	FV	180
c.	Signature title: *GENERAL MANAGER*. 1.1.1989; 1.1.1990; 1.1.1991; 1.1.1992.	FV	160

196   1000 Dollars

1985-87. Red, brown and orange on multicolor underprint. Arms at left. Back: Old Supreme Court building at right. Facing lions at lower left and right with new bank building at center. Watermark: Lion's head. Printer: TDLR. 164x82mm.

		VF	UNC
a.	1.1.1985.	FV	1,000
b.	1.1.1986.	FV	900
c.	1.1.1987.	FV	800

1988-90 Issue

#197-199 Replacement notes: Serial # prefix ZZ.

197   20 Dollars

1990-92. Gray and black on orange, pink and multicolor underprint. Arms at left. Signature title: *GENERAL MANAGER*. Back: Clock tower, ferry in harbor view at right. Facing lions at lower left and right with new bank building at center. Watermark: Lion's head. Printer: TDLR. 144x72mm.

		VF	UNC
a.	1.1.1990.	FV	6.00
b.	1.1.1991.	FV	6.00
c.	1.1.1992.	FV	6.00

198   100 Dollars

1989-92. Red on multicolor underprint. Arms at left. Signature title: *GENERAL MANAGER*. Back: Tiger Balm Garden pagoda at right. Facing lions at lower left and right with new bank building at center. Watermark: Lion's head. Printer: TDLR. 154x77mm.

		VF	UNC
a.	1.1.1989.	FV	25.00
b.	1.1.1990.	FV	20.00
c.	1.1.1991.	FV	20.00
d.	1.1.1992.	FV	20.00

199   1000 Dollars

1988-91. Red, brown and orange on multicolor underprint. Arms at left. Back: Old Supreme Court building at right. Facing lions at lower left and right with new bank building at center. Printer: TDLR. 164x82mm.

		VF	UNC
a.	Signature title: *EXECUTIVE DIRECTOR*. 1.1.1988.	FV	450
b.	Sign title: *GENERAL MANAGER*. 1.1.1989.	FV	650
c.	1.1.1991.	FV	250

Hong Kong & Shanghai Banking Corporation Limited
1993; 1995 Issue

#201-205 Replacement notes: Serial # prefix ZZ. #200 not assigned.

201   20 Dollars

	VF	UNC
1993-2002. Gray on brown on multicolor underprint. Lion's head at left, city view in underprint at center. Back: Latent image of value in box at lower right, new bank building at center between facing lions. Watermark: Lion's head. Printer: TDLR. 144x72mm.		
a. Signature title: *EXECUTIVE DIRECTOR*. 1.1.1993; 1.1.1994.	FV	8.00
b. Signature titles as a. Copyright clause on both sides. 1.1.1995; 1.1.1996.	FV	7.00
c. Signature title: *GENERAL MANAGER*. 1.1.1997; 1.7.1997.	FV	5.00
d. Signature title as c. 1.1.1998; 1.1.1999; 1.1.2000; 1.1.2001; 1.1.2002.	FV	4.00

202   50 Dollars

	VF	UNC
1993-99. Purple, violet and black on multicolor underprint. Lion's head at left, city view in underprint at center. Back: New bank building at center between facing lions, latent image of value in box at lower right. Watermark: Lion's head. Printer: TDLR. 148x74mm.		
a. Signature title: *EXECUTIVE DIRECTOR*. 1.1.1993; 1.1.1994.	FV	15.00
b. Signature title as a. Copyright clause on both sides. 1.1.1995; 1.1.1996.	FV	12.00
c. Signature title: *GENERAL MANAGER*. 1.1.1997; 1.7.1997.	FV	10.00
d. Signature title as a. 1.1.1998; 1.1.2000; 1.1.2001.	FV	10.00
e. Signature title as c. 1.1.2002.	FV	10.00

203   100 Dollars

	VF	UNC
1993-99. Red, orange and black on multicolor underprint. Lion's head at left, city view in underprint at center. Back: New bank building at center between facing lions, latent image of value in box at lower right. Ten t Watermark: Lion's head. Printer: TDLR. 154x77mm.		
a. Signature title: *EXECUTIVE DIRECTOR*. 1.1.1993; 1.1.1994; 1.1.1996.	FV	30.00
b. Signature title: *GENERAL MANAGER*. 1.1.1997; 1.7.1997; 1.1.1998.	FV	20.00
c. Signature title as a. 1.1.1999; 1.2.2000.	FV	20.00
d. Signature title as b. 1.1.2001; 1.1.2002.	FV	20.00

204   500 Dollars

	VF	UNC
1993-99. Brown and red-orange on multicolor underprint. Lion's head at left, city view in underprint at center. Back: New bank building at center between facing lions, latent image of value in box at lower right. Gover Watermark: Lion's head. Printer: TDLR. 158x79mm.		
a. Signature title: *EXECUTIVE DIRECTOR*. 1.1.1993; 1.1.1994.	FV	120
b. Signature title as a. Copyright clause on both sides. 1.1.1995; 1.1.1996.	FV	120
c. Signature title: *GENERAL MANAGER*. 1.1.1997; 1.7.1997.	FV	120
d. Signature title as c. 1.1.1998; 1.1.1999.	FV	100
e. Signature title as c. 1.1.2002.	FV	150

205   1000 Dollars

	VF	UNC
1993-99. Orange, red-brown and olive-green on pink and multicolor underprint. Lion's head at left, city view in underprint at center. Back: New bank building at center between facing lions, latent image of value in box at lower right. Legis Watermark: Lion's head. Printer: TDLR. 164x82mm.		
a. Signature title: *EXECUTIVE DIRECTOR*. 1.1.1993; 1.1.1994; 1.1.1995.	FV	250
b. Signature title: *GENERAL MANAGER*. 1.1.1997; 1.7.1997.	FV	220
c. Signature titles as a. 1.1.1998; 1.1.1999.	FV	220

2000 Issue

206   1000 Dollars

	VF	UNC
2000; 2002. Wide security thread added. Orange, red-brown and olive-green on pink and multicolor underprint. Signature title: *GENERAL MANAGER*. 164x82mm.		
a. 1.9.2000.	FV	190
b. 1.1.2002.	FV	190

2003 Issue

207   20 Dollars

	VF	UNC
2003-09. Dark blue on light blue and multicolor underprint. Back: The Peak Tram. 144x72mm.		
a. 1.7.2003. Signature title: *GENERAL MANAGER*.	FV	6.00
b. 1.1.2005. As a.	FV	5.00
c. 1.1.2006. As a.	FV	5.00
d. 1.1.2007. Signature title: *EXECUTIVE DIRECTOR*.	FV	5.00
e. 1.1.2008.	FV	4.00
f. 1.1.2009. As d.	FV	4.00

208   50 Dollars
2003-09. Green on multicolor underprint. Back: Po Lin Temple. 148x74mm.

	VF	UNC
a. 1.7.2003. Signature title: *GENERAL MANAGER*.	FV	10.00
b. 1.1.2005. As a.	FV	10.00
c. 1.1.2006. As a.	FV	10.00
d. 1.1.2007. Signature title: *EXECUTIVE DIRECTOR*.	FV	10.00
e. 1.1.2008.	FV	8.00
f. 1.1.2009.	FV	8.00

209   100 Dollars
2003-08. Red on multicolor underprint. Back: Tsing-Ma Bridge. 154x77mm.

	VF	UNC
a. 1.7.2003. Signature title: *GENERAL MANAGER*.	FV	20.00
b. 1.1.2005. As a.	FV	20.00
c. 1.1.2006. As a.	FV	20.00
d. 1.1.2007. Signature title: *EXECUTIVE DIRECTOR*.	FV	20.00
e. 1.1.2008. As d.	FV	20.00
f. 1.1.2009	FV	20.00

210   500 Dollars
2003-09. Brown on multicolor underprint. Back: Hong Kong Airport. 158x79mm.

	VF	UNC
a. 1.7.2003. Signature title: *GENERAL MANAGER*.	FV	125
b. 1.1.2005. As a.	FV	125
c. 1.1.2006. As a.	FV	100
d. 1.1.2007. Signature title: *EXECUTIVE DIRECTOR*.	FV	95.00
e. 1.1.2008. Signature title as d.	FV	95.00
f. 1.1.2009.	FV	85.00

211   1000 Dollars
2003; 2005. Orange, red-brown and olive-green on multicolor underprint. Back: Hong Kong Convention and Exhibition Center. 164x82mm.

	VF	UNC
a. 1.7.2003. Signature title: *GENERAL MANAGER*.	FV	240
b. 1.1.2005.	FV	200
c. 1.1.2006. Signature title: *EXECUTIVE DIRECTOR*.	FV	130
d. 1.1.2007.	FV	170
e. 1.1.2008.	FV	150
f. 1.1.2009.	FV	140

2010 Issue

212   20 Dollars
2010-. Dark blue and blue on multicolor underprint. Lion and Bank headquarters at right. Back: Mid-Autumn festival at right. 144x72mm.

	VF	UNC
a. 1.1.2010.	FV	5.00
b. 1.1.2012.	FV	5.00
c. 1.1.2013.	FV	5.00
d. 1.1.2014.	FV	5.00

213   50 Dollars
2010-. Green on multicolor underprint. Lion and Bank headquarters at right. Back: Spring Lantern Festival. 148x74mm.

	VF	UNC
a. 1.1.2010.	FV	10.00
b. 1.1.2012.	FV	10.00
c. 1.1.2013.	—	10.00

214   100 Dollars
2010-. Red on multicolor underprint. Lion and Bank headquarters at right. 154x77mm.

	VF	UNC
a. 1.1.2010.	FV	20.00
b. 1.1.2012.	FV	20.00
c. 1.1.2013.	FV	20.00
d. 1.1.2014.	FV	20.00

Mercantile Bank Limited

行銀利有港香

Hsiang K'ang Yu Li Yin Hang

1964 Issue

215 500 Dollars   **VF UNC**
2010-. Brown on multicolor underprint. Lion and Bank headquarters at right.
158x79mm.
a. 1.1.2010.		FV	95.00
b. 1.1.2012.		FV	95.00
c. 1.1.2013.		FV	95.00
d. 1.1.2014.		FV	95.00

244 100 Dollars   **VF UNC**
1964-73. Red-brown on multicolor underprint. Aerial view of coastline. Back:
Woman standing with pennant and shield at center. Watermark: Dragon. Printer:
TDLR.
		VF	UNC
a. 28.7.1964.		900	3,500
b. 5.10.1965.		600	2,500
c. 27.7.1968.		750	2,700
d. 16.4.1970.		400	2,500
e. 1.11.1973.		350	1,500

1974 Issue

216 1000 Dollars   **VF UNC**
2010-. Orange on multicolor underprint. Lion and Bank headquarters at right.
164x82mm.
a. 1.1.2010.		FV	130
b. 1.1.2012.		FV	130
c. 1.1.2013.		FV	130
d. 1.1.2014.		FV	130

2015 Commemorative Issue

245 100 Dollars   **VF UNC**
4.11.1974. Red, purple and brown on multicolor underprint. Woman standing with   65.00   200
pennant and shield. Back: City view at center. Watermark: Dragon. Printer: TDLR.

Standard Chartered Bank

府政港香

Hong Kong Cha Ta Yin Hang

1985-89 Issues

217 150 Dollars   **VF UNC**
3.3.2015. Purple on multicolor underprint. 150th anniversary of HSBC. Queen's
Road Central at left. Gold 150 at right. Back: Overlooking the city throughout
history. Large lion with two children at right. Printer: HKNP.
a. Serial number AA prefix.		FV	45.00
b. Serial number HK prefix.		FV	45.00
c. Serial number HSBC prefix.		FV	45.00
d. Serial number AB prefix.		FV	45.00

278	**10 Dollars**	VF	UNC

1985-91. Dark green on yellow-green and multicolor underprint. Mythological carp at right. Back: Bank building at left, bank arms at center. Watermark: Helmeted warrior's head. 138x69mm.

		VF	UNC
a. Signature titles: *FINANCIAL CONTROLLER* and *AREA GENERAL MANAGER.* 1.1.1985.		FV	10.00
b. Signature titles: *AREA FINANCIAL CONTROLLER* and *AREA GENERAL MANAGER.* 1.1.1986; 1.1.1987; 1.1.1988; 1.1.1989.		FV	7.00
c. Signature titles: *AREA FINANCIAL CONTROLLER* and *GENERAL MANAGER.* 1.1.1990.		FV	6.00
d. Signature titles: *CHIEF FINANCIAL OFFICER* and *GENERAL MANAGER.* 1.1.1991.		FV	6.00

1985-89 Issues

279	**20 Dollars**	VF	UNC

1985; 1992. Dark gray, orange and brown on multicolor underprint. Mythological tortoise at right. Back: Bank building at left, bank arms at center. Watermark: Helmeted warrior's head. 144x72mm.

	VF	UNC
a. Signature titles: *FINANCIAL CONTROLLER* and *AREA GENERAL MANAGER.* 1.1.1985.	FV	15.00
b. Signature titles: *CHIEF FINANCIAL OFFICER* and *AREA GENERAL MANAGER.* 1.1.1992.	FV	9.00

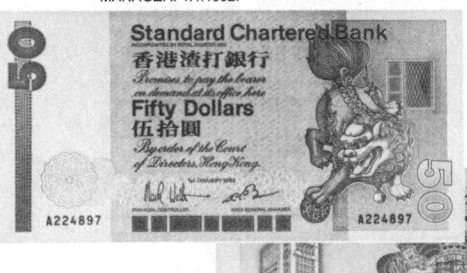

280	**50 Dollars**	VF	UNC

1985-92. Purple, violet and dark gray on multicolor underprint. Mythological lion at right. Back: Bank building at left, bank arms at center. Watermark: Helmeted warrior's head. 148x74mm.

	VF	UNC
a. Signature titles: *FINANCIAL CONTROLLER* and *AREA GENERAL MANAGER.* 1.1.1985.	FV	80.00
b. Signature titles: *AREA FINANCIAL CONTROLLER* and *AREA GENERAL MANAGER.* 1.1.1987; 1.1.1988.	FV	70.00
c. Signature titles: *AREA FINANCIAL CONTROLLER* and *GENERAL MANAGER.* 1.1.1990.	FV	70.00
d. Signature titles: *CHIEF FINANCIAL OFFICER* and *GENERAL MANAGER.* 1.1.1991; 1.1.1992.	FV	60.00

281	**100 Dollars**	VF	UNC

1985-92. Red on multicolor underprint. Mythological horse (unicorn) at right. Back: Bank building at left, bank arms at center. Watermark: Helmeted warrior's head. 154x77mm.

	VF	UNC
a. Signature titles: *FINANCIAL CONTROLLER* and *AREA GENERAL MANAGER.* 1.1.1985.	FV	70.00

	VF	UNC
b. Signature titles: *AREA FINANCIAL CONTROLLER* and *AREA GENERAL MANAGER.* 1.1.1986-1.1.1989.	FV	60.00
c. Signature titles: *FINANCIAL CONTROLLER* and *AREA GENERAL MANAGER.* 1.1.1990.	FV	60.00
d. Signature titles: *FINANCIAL CONTROLLER* and *AREA GENERAL MANAGER.* 1.1.1991; 1.1.1992.	FV	50.00

282	**500 Dollars**	VF	UNC

1988-92. Maroon, gray and green on multicolor underprint. Mythological phoenix at right. Back: Bank building at left, bank arms at center. Watermark: Helmeted warrior's head. 158x79mm.

	VF	UNC
a. Signature titles: *FINANCIAL CONTROLLER* and *AREA GENERAL MANAGER.* 1.1.1988; 1.1.1989; 1.10.1989.	FV	280
b. Signature titles: *FINANCIAL CONTROLLER* and *AREA GENERAL MANAGER.* 1.1.1990.	FV	250
c. Signature titles: *FINANCIAL CONTROLLER* and *AREA GENERAL MANAGER.* 1.1.1991; 1.1.1992.	FV	220

283	**1000 Dollars**	VF	UNC

1985-92. Yellow-orange on multicolor underprint. Mythological dragon at right. Back: Bank building at left, bank arms at center. Watermark: Helmeted warrior's head. 164x82mm.

	VF	UNC
a. Signature titles: *FINANCIAL CONTROLLER* and *AREA GENERAL MANAGER.* 1.1.1985.	FV	350
b. Signature titles: *AREA FINANCIAL CONTROLLER* and *AREA GENERAL MANAGER.* 1.1.1987.	FV	320
c. Signature titles as b. 1.1.1988.	FV	270
d. Signature titles: *FINANCIAL CONTROLLER* and *AREA GENERAL MANAGER.* 1.1.1992.	FV	240

1993 Issue

284	**10 Dollars**	VF	UNC

1993-95. Dark green on yellow-green underprint. Mythological carp at right. Back: Bank building at left, Bauhinia flower at center. Watermark: SCB above helmeted warrior's head. 138x69mm.

	VF	UNC
a. Signature titles: *CHIEF FINANCIAL OFFICER* and *AREA GENERAL MANAGER.* 1.1.1993.	FV	6.00
b. Signature titles: *HEAD OF FINANCE* and *GENERAL MANAGER.* 1.1.1994; 1.1.1995.	FV	5.00

285	**20 Dollars**	VF	UNC

1993-2002. . Dark gray, orange and brown on multicolor underprint. Mythological tortoise at right. Back: Bank building at left, Bauhinia flower at center. Watermark: SCB above helmeted warrior's head. 144x72mm.

	VF	UNC
a. Signature titles: *CHIEF FINANCIAL OFFICER* and *AREA GENERAL MANAGER.* 1.1.1993.	FV	10.00

b. Signature titles: *HEAD OF FINANCE* and *GENERAL MANAGER*. 1.1.1994; 1.1.1995; 1.1.1996; 1.1.1997; 1.7.1997.   FV   7.50

c. Signature titles: *HEAD OF FINANCE* and *CHIEF EXECUTIVE*. 1.1.1998; 1.1.1999; 1.1.2000; 1.1.2001.   FV   6.00

d. Signature titles: *CHIEF FINANCIAL OFFICER* and CHIEF EXECUTIVE & GENERAL MANAGER. 1.1.2002.   FV   5.00

286   50 Dollars   VF   UNC

1993-2002. Purple, violet and dark gray on multicolor underprint. Mythological lion at right. Back: Bank building at left, Bauhinia flower at center. Watermark: SCB above helmeted warrior's head. 148x74mm.

   a. Signature titles: *CHIEF FINANCIAL OFFICER* and *AREA GENERAL MANAGER*. 1.1.1993.   FV   17.50

   b. Signature titles: *HEAD OF FINANCE* and *GENERAL MANAGER*. 1.1.1994; 1.1.1995; 1.1.1996; 1.1.1997; 1.7.1997.   FV   15.00

   c. Signature titles: *HEAD OF FINANCE* and *CHIEF EXECUTIVE*. 1.1.1998; 1.1.1999; 1.1.2000; 1.1.2001; 1.1.2002.   FV   15.00

287   100 Dollars   VF   UNC

1993-2002. Red and purple on multicolor underprint. Mythological horse (unicorn) at right. Back: Bank building at left, Bauhinia flower at center. Watermark: SCB above helmeted warrior's head. 154x77mm.

   a. Signature titles: *CHIEF FINANCIAL OFFICER* and *AREA GENERAL MANAGER*. 1.1.1993.   FV   33.00

   b. Signature titles: *HEAD OF FINANCE* and *GENERAL MANAGER*. 1.1.1994; 1.1.1995; 1.1.1996; 1.1.1997; 1.7.1997.   FV   27.50

   c. Signature titles: *HEAD OF FINANCE* and *CHIEF EXECUTIVE*. 1.1.1998; 1.1.1999; 1.1.2000; 1.1.2001.   FV   27.50

   d. Signature titles: *CHIEF FINANCIAL OFFICER* and *CHIEF EXECUTIVE & GENERAL MANAGER*. 1.1.2001; 1.1.2002.   FV   25.00

288   500 Dollars   VF   UNC

1993-2002. Brown and blue-green on multicolor underprint. Mythological phoenix at right. Back: Bank building at left, Bauhinia flower at center. Watermark: SCB above helmeted warrior's head. 158x79mm.

   a. Signature titles: *CHIEF FINANCIAL OFFICER* and *AREA GENERAL MANAGER*. 1.1.1993.   FV   150

   b. Signature titles: *HEAD OF FINANCE* and *GENERAL MANAGER*. 1.1.1994; 1.1.1995; 1.1.1996; 1.1.1997; 1.7.1997; 1.1.1998; 1.1.1999; 1.1.2000.   FV   135

   c. Signature titles: *CHIEF FINANCIAL OFFICER* and CHIEF EXECUTIVE & GENERAL MANAGER. 1.1.2001; 1.1.2002.   FV   130

289   1000 Dollars   VF   UNC

1993-2002. Yellow-orange on multicolor underprint. Mythological dragon at right. Back: Bank building at left, Bauhinia flower at center. Watermark: SCB above helmeted warrior's head. 164x82mm.

   a. Signature titles: *CHIEF FINANCIAL OFFICER* and *AREA GENERAL MANAGER*. 1.1.1993.   FV   250

   b. Signature titles: *HEAD OF FINANCE* and *GENERAL MANAGER*. 1.1.1994; 1.1.1995; 1.1.1996; 1.1.1997; 1.7.1997; 1.1.1998.   FV   225

   c. Signature titles: *HEAD OF FINANCE* and *CHIEF EXECUTIVE*. 1.1.1999; 1.1.2000.   FV   200

   d. Signature titles: *CHIEF FINANCIAL OFFICER* and CHIEF EXECUTIVE & GENERAL MANAGER. 1.1.2001; 1.1.2002.   FV   200

2002 Issue

290   1000 Dollars   VF   UNC

1.1.2002. Enhanced security features. Yellow-orange and blue-green on multicolor underprint. Mythological dragon at right. Signature title: *CHIEF FINANCIAL OFFICER* and CHIEF EXECUTIVE & GENERAL MANAGER. Back: Bank building at left, Bauhinia flower at center. Watermark: SCB above helmeted warrior's head. 164x82mm.   FV   180

2003 Issue

291   20 Dollars   VF   UNC

1.7.2003. Dark Blue on multicolor underprint. Signature titles: *CHIEF FINANCIAL OFFICER* and *DIRECTOR*. Back: Victoria Harbor view ca. 1850. 144x72mm.   FV   5.00

292   50 Dollars   VF   UNC

1.7.2003. Dark green and brown on multicolor underprint. Back: Victoria Harbor view ca. 1800. 148x74mm.   FV   12.00

293   100 Dollars   VF   UNC

1.7.2003. Red and brown on multicolor underprint. Back: Victoria Harbor view ca. 1930. 154x77mm.   FV   25.00

294 500 Dollars

1.7.2003. Dark brown and dark blue on multicolor underprint. Back: Harbor view ca. 1970. 158x79mm.

	VF	UNC
	FV	100

298 50 Dollars

2010-. 148x74mm.

	VF	UNC
a. 1.1.2010.	FV	10.00
b. 1.1.2012.	FV	10.00
c. 1.1.2013.	FV	10.00
d. 1.1.2014.	FV	10.00

295 1000 Dollars

1.7.2003. Red-brown, orange and olive on multicolor underprint. Back: Victoria Harbor view ca. 2003. 164x82mm.

	VF	UNC
	FV	160

2009 Commemorative Issue

296 150 Dollars

9.9.2009. Bank Building at left, satelite image of Victoria Harbor Back: Historical views of Hong Kong.

	VF	UNC
a. Issued note.	FV	120
b. 4-note sheet.	—	800
c. 35-note sheet.	—	5,000

2010 Issue

297 20 Dollars

2010-. Blue on multicolor underprint. Back: History and Technology - Abicus and Binary code. 144x72mm.

	VF	UNC
a. 1.1.2010.	FV	5.00
b. 1.1.2012.	FV	5.00
c. 1.1.2013.	FV	5.00
d. 1.1.2014.	FV	5.00

299 100 Dollars

2010-. 154x77mm.

	VF	UNC
a. 1.1.2010.	FV	15.00
b. 1.1.2012.	FV	15.00
c. 1.1.2013.	FV	15.00
d. 1.1.2014.	FV	15.00

300 500 Dollars

2010-.

	VF	UNC
a. 1.1.2010.	FV	95.00
b. 1.1.2012.	FV	95.00
c. 1.1.2013.	FV	95.00
d. 1.1.2014.	FV	95.00

301 1000 Dollars

2010-. 164x82mm.

	VF	UNC
a. 1.1.2010.	FV	140
b. 1.1.2012.	FV	140
c. 1.1.2013.	FV	140

Government of Hong Kong

香港政府

Hsiang K'ang Cheng Fu

1961 ND Issue

SIGNATURE VARIETIES			
1	J.J. Cowperthwaite, 1961-71	4	Sir Piers Jacobs, 1986-92
2	C.P. Haddon-Cave, 1971-81	5	Sir Hamish Macleod, 1992-95
3	Sir J.H. Bremridge, 1981-86		

325 1 Cent VF UNC
ND (1961-95). Uniface. Brown on light blue underprint. Queen Elizabeth at right.

	VF	UNC
a. Signature 1. (1961-71).	0.10	1.00
b. Signature 2. (1971-81).	0.25	0.50
c. Signature 3. (1981-86).	0.75	2.00
d. Signature 4. (1986-92).	0.10	0.25
e. Signature 5. (1992-95).	0.25	0.50

326 5 Cents VF UNC
ND (1961-65). Uniface. Green on lilac underprint. Queen Elizabeth at right. 1.75 8.00

327 10 Cents VF UNC
ND (1961-65). Uniface. Red on grayish underprint. Queen Elizabeth at right. 1.00 5.00

Hong Kong Special Administration Region
Bank of China (Hong Kong) Limited

中國銀行

Chung Kuo Yin Hang

1994 Issue

329 20 Dollars VF UNC
1994-2000. Blue-black, blue and purple on multicolor underprint. Bank of China Tower at left. Narcissus flowers at lower center right. Back: Aerial view of Wanchai and Central Hong Kong at center right. Watermark: Chinze. Printer: TDLR (HK) Ltd. (Without imprint). 144x72mm.

	VF	UNC
a. 1.5.1994.	FV	6.00
b. 1.1.1996.	FV	6.00
c. 1.7.1997.	FV	6.00
d. 1.1.1998.	FV	6.00
e. 1.1.1999.	FV	6.00
f. 1.1.2000.	FV	6.00

330 50 Dollars VF UNC
1994-2000. Purple and blue on violet and multicolor underprint. Bank of China Tower at left. Chrysanthemum flowers at lower center right. Back: Aerial view of cross-harbor tunnel at center right. Watermark: Chinze. Printer: TDLR (HK) Ltd. (Without imprint). 148x74mm.

	VF	UNC
a. 1.5.1994.	FV	18.00
b. 1.1.1996.	FV	18.00
c. 1.7.1997.	FV	18.00
d. 1.1.1998.	FV	18.00
e. 1.1.1999.	FV	18.00
f. 1.1.2000.	FV	18.00

331 100 Dollars VF UNC
1994-2000. Red-violet, orange and red on multicolor underprint. Bank of China Tower at left. Lotus flowers at lower center right. Back: Aerial view of Tsimshatsui, Kowloon Peninsula at center right. Watermark: Chinze. Printer: TDLR (HK) Ltd. (Without imprint). 154x77mm.

	VF	UNC
a. 1.5.1994.	FV	30.00
b. 1.1.1996.	FV	30.00
c. 1.7.1997.	FV	30.00
d. 1.1.1998.	FV	30.00
e. 1.1.1999.	FV	30.00
f. 1.1.2000.	FV	30.00

332 **500 Dollars**

1994-2000. Dark brown and blue on multicolor underprint. Bank of China Tower at left. Peony flowers at lower center right. Back: Hong Kong Container Terminal in Kwai Chung at center right. Watermark: Chinze. Printer: TDLR (HK) Ltd. (Without imprint). 158x79mm.

	VF	UNC
a. 1.5.1994.	FV	160
b. 1.1.1995.	FV	160
c. 1.1.1996.	FV	160
d. 1.7.1997.	FV	160
e. 1.1.1998.	FV	160
f. 1.1.1999.	FV	160
g. 1.1.2000.	FV	160

333 **1000 Dollars**

1994-2000. Reddish brown, orange and pale olive-green on multicolor underprint. Bank of China Tower at left. Bauhinia flowers at lower center right. Back: Aerial view overlooking the Central district at center right. Watermark: Chinze. Printer: TDLR (HK) Ltd. (Without imprint). 164x82mm.

	VF	UNC
a. 1.5.1994.	FV	220
b. 1.1.1995.	FV	230
c. 1.1.1996.	FV	230
d. 1.7.1997.	FV	300
e. 1.1.1998.	FV	270
f. 1.1.1999.	FV	270
g. 1.1.2000.	FV	270

2001 Issue

334 **1000 Dollars**

1.1.2001. Enhanced security features. Reddish brown, orange and pale olive-green on multicolor underprint. Bank of China Tower at left. Bauhinia flowers at lower center right. Back: Aerial view overlooking the Central district at center right. Watermark: Chinze. Printer: TDLR (HK) Ltd. (Without imprint). 164x82mm.

	VF	UNC
	FV	220

2003 Issue

335 **20 Dollars**

2003-07. Dark blue on multicolor underprint. Signature title: *CHIEF EXECUTIVE*. Back: The Peak. 144x72mm.

	VF	UNC
a. 1.7.2003.	FV	4.00
b. 1.1.2005.	FV	4.00

	VF	UNC
c. 1.1.2006.	FV	4.00
d. 1.1.2007.	FV	4.00
e. 1.1.2008.	FV	4.00
f. 1.1.2009.	FV	4.00

336 **50 Dollars**

2003-09. Dark green on multicolor underprint. Back: Aerial view of Tsimshatsui, Kowloon Peninsula. 148x74mm.

	VF	UNC
a. 1.7.2003.	FV	10.00
b. 1.1.2005.	FV	10.00
c. 1.1.2006.	FV	10.00
d. 1.1.2007.	FV	10.00
e. 1.1.2008.	FV	10.00
f. 1.1.2009.	FV	10.00

337 **100 Dollars**

2003; 2005-09. Red on pink and multicolor underprint. Back: Tsing-Ma Bridge. 154x77mm.

	VF	UNC
a. 1.7.2003.	FV	20.00
b. 1.1.2005.	FV	20.00
c. 1.1.2006.	FV	20.00
d. 1.1.2007.	FV	20.00
e. 1.1.2008.	FV	20.00
f. 1.1.2009.	FV	20.00

338 **500 Dollars**

2003; 2005-08. Dark brown on multicolor underprint. Back: Hong Kong Airport. 158x79mm.

	VF	UNC
a. 1.7.2003.	FV	90.00
b. 1.1.2005.	FV	90.00
c. 1.1.2006.	FV	90.00
d. 1.1.2007.	FV	90.00
e. 1.1.2008.	FV	90.00

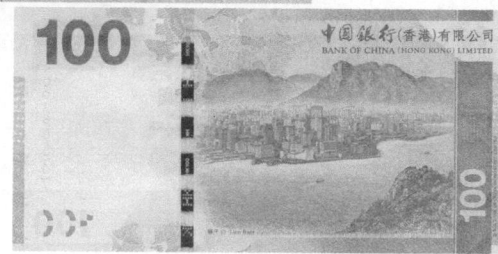

339   1000 Dollars

2003; 2005-08. Reddish-brown, orange and olive-green on multicolor underprint.
Back: Hong Kong Convention and Exhibition Center. 164x82mm.

		VF	UNC
a. 1.7.2003.		FV	160
b. 1.1.2005.		FV	160
c. 1.1.2006.		FV	160
d. 1.1.2007.		FV	160
e. 1.1.2008.		FV	160

2008 Commemorative Issue

340   20 Dollars

1.1.2008. Light blue on multicolor underprint. Bank of China building, classical
Greek column, Bejing Olympic logo. Back: Bejing Olympic Stadium, *the Bird's
Nest*, at left. Watermark: Stadium and value. 144x72mm.

		VF	UNC
a. Two letter serial # prefix.		FV	80.00
b. Serial number without prefix letters.		FV	80.00
c. In folder of issue with matching serical # note from Macau.		—	250

2010 Issue

341   20 Dollars

2010-.

		VF	UNC
a. 1.1.2010.		FV	4.00
b. 1.1.2012.		FV	4.00
c. 1.1.2013.		FV	4.00
d. 1.1.2014.		FV	4.00

342   50 Dollars

2010-. 148x74mm.

		VF	UNC
a. 1.1.2010.		FV	10.00
b. 1.1.2013.		FV	10.00
c. 1.1.2013.		FV	10.00
d. 1.1.2014.		FV	10.00

343   100 Dollars

2010-. 154x77mm.

		VF	UNC
a. 1.1.2010.		FV	20.00
b. 1.1.2012.		FV	20.00
c. 1.1.2013.		FV	20.00
d. 1.1.2014.		FV	20.00

344   500 Dollars

2010-.

		VF	UNC
a. 1.1.2010.		FV	80.00
b. 1.1.2012.		FV	80.00
c. 1.1.2014.		FV	80.00
d. 1.1.2016.		FV	80.00

345   1000 Dollars

2010-. 164x82mm.

		VF	UNC
a. 1.1.2010.		FV	150
b. 1.1.2012.		FV	150
c. 1.1.2013.		FV	150
d. 1.1.2014.		FV	150

2012 Commemorative Issue

346   100 Dollars

	VF	UNC
5.2.2012. Red. Painted 100 at center. Bank building at right. Great Wall at left.	FV	3.00

Back: Bank building at left. City skyline at center.

Government of Hong Kong
2002 Issue

400	10 Dollars	VF	UNC
	2002-03; 2005. Purple, blue and multicolor. Geometric patterns. 138x69mm.		
	a. 1.7.2002.	FV	3.00
	b. 1.1.2003.	FV	3.00
	c. 1.1.2005.	FV	3.00

2007 Issue

401	10 Dollars	VF	UNC
	2007; 2012. Polymer plastic. UV: square with 10 fluoresces green. Purple, blue and multicolor. Geometric patterns. 138x69mm.		
	a. 1.4.2007. Signatures: of Henry Tang Ying-yen and Joseph Yam Chi-kwong.	FV	3.00
	b. 1.10.2007. Signatures: John Tsang Chun-wah and Joseph Yam Chi-kwong.	FV	3.00
	c. 1.1.2012. Signatures: John Tsang Chun-Wah and Norman Chan Tak-lam.	FV	3.00
	d. 1.1.2014.	FV	3.00

HUNGARY

The Hungarian Republic, located in central Europe, has an area of 93,030 sq. km. and a population of 9.93 million. Capital: Budapest. The economy is based on agriculture and a rapidly expanding industrial sector. Machinery, chemicals, iron and steel, and fruits and vegetables are exported.

Hungary became a Christian kingdom in A.D. 1000 and for many centuries served as a bulwark against Ottoman Turkish expansion in Europe. The kingdom eventually became part of the polyglot Austro-Hungarian Empire, which collapsed during World War I. The country fell under Communist rule following World War II. In 1956, a revolt and an announced withdrawal from the Warsaw Pact were met with a massive military intervention by Moscow. Under the leadership of Janos Kadar in 1968, Hungary began liberalizing its economy, introducing so-called *Goulash Communism*. Hungary held its first multiparty elections in 1990 and initiated a free market economy. It joined NATO in 1999 and the EU in 2004.

RULERS:
Austrian to 1918

MONETARY SYSTEM:
1 Korona = 100 Fillér to 1926
1 Pengö = 100 Fillér to 1946
1 Milpengö = 1 Million Pengö
1 B(illió) Pengö = 1 Billion Pengö
1 Adopengö = 1 Tax Pengö
1 Forint = 100 Fillér 1946- 1 Forint (Florin) = 60 Krajczar

PEOPLES REPUBLIC

Magyar Nemzeti Bank
HUNGARIAN NATIONAL BANK
1957-83 Issue
#168-171 The variety in the serial # occurs in 1975 when the letter and numbers are narrower and larger.

168	10 Forint	VF	UNC
	1957-75. Green and slate black on orange and lilac underprint. Portrait Sándar Petöfi at right. Value at left. Arms of 3-bar shield. Back: Trees and river, *Birth of the Song* by János Jankó at center. 174x80mm.		
	a. 23.5.1957.	4.00	10.00
	b. 24.8.1960.	2.00	12.00
	c. 12.10.1962.	2.00	8.00
	d. 30.6.1969. Blue-green center on back.	2.00	8.00
	e. 26.10.1975. Serial # varieties.	2.00	8.00
	s1. As a, b, c. Specimen with red overprint and perforated: *MINTA*.	—	45.00
	s2. As d, e. Specimen.	—	27.50

169 20 Forint

1957-80. Blue and green on light green and pink underprint. Arms of 3-bar shield. Portrait György Dózsa at right. Value at left. Back: Penthathlete Csaba Hegedüs with hammer and wheat at center. 174x80mm.

	VF	UNC
a. 23.5.1957.	5.00	15.00
b. 24.8.1960.	10.00	50.00
c. 12.10.1962.	2.00	15.00
d. 3.9.1965.	2.00	15.00
e. 30.6.1969.	2.00	15.00
f. 28.10.1975. Serial # varieties.	2.00	15.00
g. 30.9.1980.	2.00	15.00
s1. As a; c; d. Specimen with red overprint and perforated: *MINTA*.	—	27.50
s2. As b. Specimen.	—	35.00
s3. As e; f; g. Specimen.	—	25.00

170 50 Forint

1965-89. Brown on blue and orange underprint. Value at left. Arms of 3-bar shield with star. Portrait Prince Ferencz Rákóczi II at right. Back: Battle of the Hungarian insurrectionists (Kuruc) against pro-Austrian soldiers (Labanc) scene at center. 174x80mm.

	VF	UNC
a. 3.9.1965.	3.00	30.00
b. 30.6.1969.	3.00	30.00
c. 28.10.1975. Serial # varieties.	5.00	15.00
d. Serial # prefix D. 30.9.1980.	3.00	12.50
e. Serial # prefix H. 30.9.1980.	4.00	20.00
f. 10.11.1983.	1.00	12.00
g. 4.11.1986.	1.00	30.00
h. 10.1.1989.	1.00	20.00
s1. As a. Specimen. Overprint *MINTA*.	—	50.00
s2. As b-h. Specimen. Overprint: MINTA.	—	25.00

171 100 Forint

1957-89. Red-violet on blue and orange underprint. Arms of 3-bar shield with star. Value at left, portrait Lajos Kossuth at right. Back: Horse-drawn wagon from *Took Refuge from the Storm* by Károly Lotz at center. 174x80mm.

	VF	UNC
a. 23.5.1957.	5.00	18.00
b. 24.8.1960.	5.00	18.00
c. 12.10.1962.	5.00	15.00
d. 24.10.1968.	2.00	15.00
e. 28.10.1975. Serial # varieties.	3.00	12.00
f. 30.9.1980.	2.00	12.00
g. 30.10.1984.	2.00	12.00
h. 10.1.1989.	2.00	12.00
s1. As a. Specimen with red overprint and perforted: *MINTA*.	—	65.00
s2. As b; c. Specimen.	—	—
s3. As d; e. Specimen.	—	35.00
s4. As f; g. Specimen.	—	30.00
s5. As h. Specimen.	—	30.00

172 500 Forint

1969-80. Purple on multicolor underprint. Portrait Endre Ady at right, arms of 3-bar shield with star. Back: Aerial view of Budapest and Danube river. 174x80mm.

	VF	UNC
a. 30.6.1969.	FV	12.50
b. Serial # varieties. 28.10.1975.	FV	12.50
c. 30.9.1980.	FV	10.00
s. As a-c. Specimen.	—	30.00

173 1000 Forint

1983. Deep green and olive-green on multicolor underprint. Béla Bartók at right, arms of 3-bar shield with star. Back: *Anya* sculpture, mother nursing child by F. Medgyessy at center. 172x80mm.

	VF	UNC
a. Serial # prefix: A; B. 25.3.1983.	FV	17.50
b. Serial # prefix: B; C; D;. 10.11.1983.	FV	17.50
s. As a, b. Specimen with red overprint and perforated: *MINTA*.	—	45.00

REPUBLIC

Magyar Nemzeti Bank

Hungarian National Bank

1990; 1992 Issue

#174-177 numerous photocopy counterfeits began appearing in mid-1999.

174 100 Forint

1992-95. Red-violet on multicolor underprint. Value at left, portrait of L. Kossuth at right, St. Stephan's Crown over Hungarian Arms at top center. Back: Horse-drawn wagon from *Took Refuge from the Storm* by Károly Lotz at center. 174x80mm.

	VF	UNC
a. 15.1.1992.	FV	3.00
b. 16.12.1993.	FV	3.00
c. 20.12.1995.	FV	12.50
s1. As a, b. Specimen with red. overprint and perforated *MINTA*.	—	25.00
s2. As c. Specimen.	—	65.00

175 500 Forint | VF | UNC

31.7.1990. Purple on multicolor underprint. Portrait of E. Ady at right, St. Stephan's Crown over Hungarian Arms. Back: Aerial view of Budapest and Danube river. 174x80mm.

		VF	UNC
a. Issued note.		FV	10.00
s. Specimen.		—	30.00

176 1000 Forint | VF | UNC

1992-96. Deep green and olive-green on multicolor underprint. Béla Bartók at right, St. Stephan's Crown over Hungarian Arms. Back: *Anya* sculpture, mother nursing child by F. Medgyessy at center. 174x80mm.

	VF	UNC
a. Serial # prefix: *D.* 30.10.1992.	FV	17.50
b. Serial # prefix: *D; E.* 16.12.1993.	FV	17.50
c. Serial # prefix: *E; F.* 15.1.1996.	FV	17.50
s. Specimen. Serial # prefix: *A-F.*	—	30.00

177 5000 Forint | VF | UNC

1990-95. Deep brown and brown on orange and multicolor underprint. Portrait Count Istvan Széchenyi at right, St. Stephan's Crown over Hungarian Arms Back: Academy of Science at center. 174x80mm.

	VF	UNC
a. Serial # prefix: *H; J.* 31.7.1990.	7.50	60.00
b. Serial # prefix: *J.* 30.10.1992.	7.50	60.00
c. Serial # prefix: *J.* 16.12.1993.	7.50	60.00
d. Serial # prefix: *J; K.* 31.8.1995.	7.50	60.00
s. As a-d. Specimen with red overprint and perforated: *MINTA.*	—	75.00

1997-99 Issue

178 200 Forint | VF | UNC

1998. Dark green and grayish purple on multicolor underprint. King Robert Károly, crowned arms at left center, latent image in cartouche at upper left. Serial number prefix *FA-FH.* Back: Diósgyóri Castle ruins at left. Watermark: King Robert Károly. 154x70mm.

		VF	UNC
a. Issued note.		FV	5.00
s. Specimen.		—	25.00

179 500 Forint | VF | UNC

1998. Brown-violet and brown on multicolor underprint. Ferenc Rákóczi II, crowned arms at left center, latent image in cartouche at upper left. Serial # prefix *EA-EF.* Back: Sárospatak Castle. Watermark: Ferenc Rákóczi II. 154x70mm.

		VF	UNC
a. Issued note.		FV	10.00
s. Specimen.		—	30.00

180 1000 Forint | VF | UNC

1998; 1999. Blue and blue-green on multicolor underprint. King Mátyás, crowned arms at left center, latent image in cartouche at upper left. Back: Fountain in the palace at Visegrád. Watermark: King Mátyás. 154x70mm.

	VF	UNC
a. 1998. Serial # prefix: *DA-DJ.*	FV	17.50
b. 1999. Serial # prefix: *DA-DD.*	FV	17.50
s. As a, b. Specimen.	—	30.00

181 2000 Forint | VF | UNC

1998. Dark brown and brown on multicolor underprint. Prince Gabor Bethlen at right with hologram, crowned arms at left center, latent image in cartouche at upper left. Serial # prefix: *CA-CG.* Back: Bethlen amongst scientists at left center. Watermark: Gabor Bethlen. 154x70mm.

		VF	UNC
a. Issued note.		FV	30.00
s. Specimen. Red overprint: MINTA on both sides.		—	75.00

182 5000 Forint | VF | UNC

1999. Deep violet and purple on multicolor underprint. István Széchenyi at right, crowned arms at left center, latent image in cartouche at upper left with hologram. Serial # prefixes: *BA-BJ.* Back: Széchenyi's home at Nagycenk. Watermark: István Széchenyi. 154x70mm.

		VF	UNC
a. Issued note.		FV	60.00
s. Specimen.		—	75.00

183 10,000 Forint

1997-1999. Violet, dull purple and blue-black on multicolor underprint. King St. Stephan at right, crowned arms at left center, latent image in cartouche at upper left with hologram. Back: View of Esztergom at left center. Watermark: King St. Stephan. 154x70mm.

		VF	UNC
a. Serial # prefixes: AA-AK. 1997.		FV	120
b. Serial # prefixes: AA-AC with additional security devices. 1998.		FV	120
c. Serial # prefix: AA-AE. 1999.		FV	120
s. As a-c. Specimen.		—	120

184 20,000 Forint

1999. Slate gray on red and multicolor underprint. Ferenc Deák at right. Serial number prefix: GA-GE. Back: Old House of Commons in Budapest. Watermark: Ferenc Deák. 154x70mm.

	VF	UNC
a. Issued note.	FV	200
s. Specimen.	—	225

2000 Commemorative Issues

185 1000 Forint

2000. Blue, light yellow brown on multicolor underprint. King Mátyás at right, MNB in seal at upper left and MILLENNIUM at lower left. Serial number prefix: DA-DE. Back: Fountain in the palace at Visegrád. Large letter illustration from illuminated manuscript. Millenium Celebration. 154x70mm.

	VF	UNC
a. Issued note.	FV	17.50
s. Specimen.	—	30.00

186 2000 Forint

20.8.2000. Brown on tan and multicolor underprint. Crown of St. Stephan at right. Serial # prefix: MM. Back: St. Stephan as bishop baptizing. 1000 Years of the Hungarian State. 154x70mm.

	VF	UNC
a. Issued note.	FV	45.00
s. Specimen.	—	50.00

2001-02 Issue

187 200 Forint

2001-05. Enhanced security features. Green and multicolor. King Robert Károly, crowned arms at left center, latent image in cartouche at upper left. Back: Diósgyóri Castle ruins at left. Watermark: Robert Károly. 154x70mm.

	VF	UNC
a. 2001. Serial # prefix: FA-FE.	FV	5.00
b. 2002. Serial # prefix: FA-FC.	FV	5.00
c. 2003. Serial # prefix: FA-FC.	FV	9.00
d. 2004. Serial # prefix: FA-FC.	FV	9.00
e. 2005. Serial # prefix: FA-FD.	FV	9.00
f. 2006. Serial # prefix: FA-FC.	FV	9.00
g. 2007. Serial # prefix: FA-FD.	FV	9.00
s. Specimen.	—	25.00

188 500 Forint

2001-10. Enhanced security features. Brown-violet and brown on multicolor underprint. Ferenc Rákóczi II, crowned arms at left center, latent image in cartouche at upper left. Back: Sárospatak Castle. Watermark: Ferenc Rákóczi II. 154x70mm.

	VF	UNC
a. 2001. Serial # prefix: EA-EC.	FV	7.50
b. 2002. Serial # prefix: EA-EB.	FV	7.50
c. 2003. Serial # prefix: EA-EC.	FV	6.00
d. 2005. Serial # prefix: EA-EC.	FV	6.00
e. 2007.	FV	5.00
f. 2008.	FV	5.00
g. 2010.	FV	5.00
s. Specimen.	—	30.00

189 1000 Forint

2002-04; 2008. Enhanced security features. Blue and light yellow brown on multicolor underprint. King Mátyás, crowned arms at left center, latent image in cartouche at upper left. Back: Fountain in the palace at Visegrád. Watermark: King Mátyás. 154x70mm.

	VF	UNC
a. 2002. Serial # prefix: DA, DB.	FV	12.50
b. 2003. Serial # prefix: DA-DC.	FV	10.00
c. 2004. Serial # prefix: DA-DC.	FV	10.00
s. Specimen.	—	30.00

190 2000 Forint

2002-05. Enhanced security features. Dark brown and brown on multicolor underprint. Prince Gabor Bethlen at right, crowned arms at left center, latent image in cartouche at upper left. Back: Bethlen amongst scientists at left center. Watermark: Gabor Bethlen. 154x70mm.

	VF	UNC
a. 2002. Serial # prefix: CA, CB.	FV	25.00
b. 2003. Serial # prefix: CA.	FV	25.00
c. 2004. Serial # prefix: CA-CC.	FV	25.00
d. 2005. Serial # prefix: CA-CB.	FV	25.00
s. Specimen.	—	50.00

191 5000 Forint

2005-06. Enhanced security features. Multicolor. István Széchenyi at right. Back: Széchenyi's home at Nagycenk. 154x70mm.

	VF	UNC
a. 2005. Serial # prefix: BA-BC.	FV	60.00
b. 2006. Serial # prefix: BA-BC.	FV	60.00
s. Specimen.	—	75.00

192 10,000 Forint

2001-07. Enhanced security features. Multicolor. King St. Stephan at right. Back: View of Esztergom at left center. 154x70mm.

	VF	UNC
a. 2001. Serial # prefix: AA-AC.	FV	120
b. 2003. Serial # prefix: AA-AC.	FV	120
c. 2004. Serial # prefix: AA-AD.	FV	120
d. 2005. Serial # prefix: AA-AC.	FV	120
e. 2006. Serial # prefix: AA-AC.	FV	120
f. 2007. Serial # prefix: AA-AC.	FV	120
s. Specimen.	—	120

193 20,000 Forint

2004-07. Multicolor. Ferenc Deák at right. Back: Old house of Commons in Budapest. 154x70mm.

	VF	UNC
a. 2004. Serial # prefix: GA-GB.	FV	200
b. 2005. Serial # prefix: GA-GC.	FV	200
c. 2006. Serial # prefix: GA.	FV	200
d. 2007. Serial # prefix: GA-GD.	FV	200
s. Specimen.	—	225

2006 Commemorative Issue

194 500 Forint

2006 (23.10.1956). 50th Anniversary of uprising. Brown-violet and brown on multicolor underprint. Ferenc Rákóczi at right. Serial # prefix EB-EC. Back: Parliament building and tri-color national flag, with a hole thru it. 154x70mm.

	VF	UNC
	FV	10.00

2008-2010 Issue

196 500 Forint

2007-. Omron rings added. 154x70mm.

	VF	UNC
a. 2007	FV	5.00
b. 2008.	FV	5.00
c. 2010.	FV	5.00
d. 2011.	FV	5.00
e. 2013.	FV	5.00

2005 Issue

195 1000 Forint

2005-. Blue on light blue and multicolor underprint. King Mátyás at right, crowned arms at left center. Holographic foil strip. Back: Fountain in the palace at Visegrád. 154x70mm.

	VF	UNC
a. 2005. Gold holographic strip. Serial # prefix: DA-DD.	FV	15.00
b. 2006. Serial # prefix: DA-DF.	FV	15.00
c. 2007. Serial # prefix: DA-DC.	FV	15.00
d. 2008. Silver holographic strip.	FV	15.00

2008-2010 Issue

197 1000 Forint
2009-12. Omron rings added. 154x70mm.

		VF	UNC
a. 2009.		FV	7.50
b. 2010.		FV	7.50
c. 2011.		FV	7.50
d. 2012.		FV	7.50
e. 2015.		FV	7.50

198 2000 Forint
2007-. Omron rings added. 154x70mm.

		VF	UNC
a. 2007.		FV	17.50
b. 2008.		FV	17.50
c. 2010.		FV	15.00
d. 2013.		FV	15.00

199 5000 Forint
2008; 2010. Omron rings added. 154x70mm.

		VF	UNC
a. 2008.		FV	35.00
b. 2010.		FV	35.00

200 10,000 Forint
2008; 2009; 2012. Omron rings added. 154x70mm.

		VF	UNC
a. 2008.		FV	80.00
b. 2009.		FV	75.00
c. 2012.		FV	60.00

202 10,000 Forint
2014.

		VF	UNC
		FV	60.00

201 20,000 Forint
2008; 2009. Omron rings added. 154x70mm.

		VF	UNC
a. 2008.		FV	145
b. 2009.		FV	145

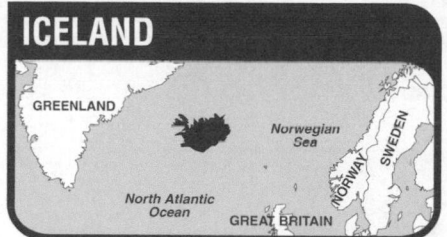

ICELAND

The Republic of Iceland, an island of recent volcanic origin in the North Atlantic east of Greenland and immediately south of the Arctic Circle, has an area of 103,000 sq. km. and a population of 304,367. Capital: Reykjavík. Fishing is the chief industry and accounts for more than 60 percent of the exports.

Settled by Norwegian and Celtic (Scottish and Irish) immigrants during the late 9th and 10th centuries A.D., Iceland boasts the world's oldest functioning legislative assembly, the Althing, established in 930. Independent for over 300 years, Iceland was subsequently ruled by Norway and Denmark. Fallout from the Askja volcano of 1875 devastated the Icelandic economy and caused widespread famine. Over the next quarter century, 20% of the island's population emigrated, mostly to Canada and the US. Limited home rule from Denmark was granted in 1874 and complete independence attained in 1944. Literacy, longevity, income, and social cohesion are first-rate by world standards.

MONETARY SYSTEM:
1 Krona = 100 Aurar, 1874-

SIGNATURE VARIETIES

31	V. Thor - J.G. Mariasson, 1961-64	32	J. Nordal - V. Thor, 1961-64
33	J.G. Mariasson - J. Nordal, 1961-67	34	J. Nordal - J.G. Mariasson, 1961-67
35	S. Klemenzson - J.G. Mariasson, 1966-67	36	J. Nordal - S. Klemenzson, 1966-67
37	J. Nordal - D. Olafsson, 1967-86	38	D. Olafsson - J. Nordal, 1967-86
39	S. Klemenzson - D. Olafsson, 1967-71	40	S. Frimannsson - D. Olafsson, 1971-73
41	J. Nordal - S. Frimannsson, 1971-73	42	G. Hjartarson - D. Olafsson, 1974-84
43	J. Nordal - G. Hjartarson, 1974-84	44	G. Hjartarson - T. Arnason, 1984
45	T. Arnason - J. Nordal, 1984-93	46	T. Arnason - D. Olafsson, 1984-93
47	J. Nordal - T. Arnason, 1984-93	48	G. Hallgrimsson - T. Arnason, 1986-90
49	J. Nordal - G. Hallgrimsson, 1986-90	50	B. I. Gunnarsson - T. Arnason, 1991-93
51	J. Nordal - B. I. Gunnarsson, 1991-93	52	J. Sigurthsson - B. I. Gunnarsson, 1994
53	B. I. Gunnarsson - J. Sigurthsson, 1994	54	E. Guthnason - S. Hermansson, 1994
55	S. Hermansson - E. Guthnason, 1994	56	E. Guthnason - S. Hermansson, 1994

REPUBLIC
Sedlabanki Íslands
CENTRAL BANK OF ICELAND
Law of 29.3.1961

42   10 Krónur VF UNC
L.1961. Brown-violet on green and orange underprint. Jón Eriksson at left, ships   10.00   20.00
in Port of Reykjavík at lower center. Signature 33; 34. Back: Ships moored at pier.
Printer: BWC (without imprint).

43   25 Krónur VF UNC
L.1961. Purple on multicolor underprint. Magnús Stephensen at left, Fjord at   6.00   14.00
center. Signature 34. Back: Fishing boats near Westmen Islands. Watermark: S.
Bjornsson. Printer: BWC (without imprint).

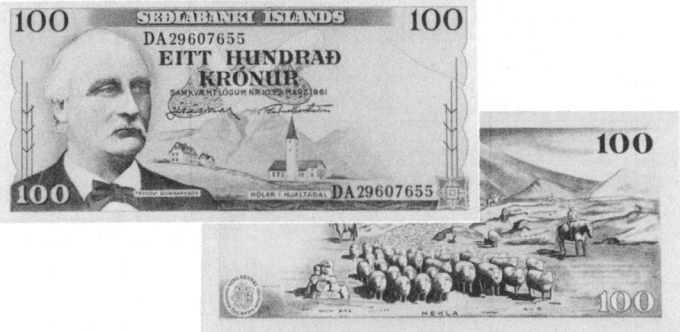

44   100 Krónur VF UNC
L.1961. Dark blue-green on multicolor underprint. Tryggvi Gunnarsson at left.
Signature 31-36; 38-44. Back: Tryggvi Gunnarsson at left. Sheepherders on
horseback, sheep in foreground, Mt. Hekla in background. Watermark: S. Bjornsson. Printer: BWC (without imprint).
    a. Issued note.   10.00   20.00
    s. Specimen.   —   165

45   500 Krónur VF UNC
L.1961. Green on lilac and multicolor underprint. Hannes Hafstein at left. Signature
36; 38-43. Back: Sailors. Watermark: S. Bjornsson. Printer: BWC (without imprint).
    a. Issued note.   10.00   20.00
    s. Specimen.   —   235

46   1000 Krónur VF UNC
L.1961. Blue on multicolor underprint. Jón Sigurthsson at right, building at lower
center. Signature 31-34; 36; 38-43. Back: Rock formations. Watermark: S. Bjornsson. Printer: BWC (without imprint).
    a. Issued note.   15.00   30.00
    s. Specimen.   —   325

47   5000 Krónur VF UNC
L.1961. Brown on multicolor underprint. Einer Benediktsson at left, dam at lower
center. Signature 36; 38-43. Back: Man overlooking waterfall. Watermark: S.
Bjornsson. Printer: BWC (without imprint).
    a. Issued note.   30.00   60.00
    s. Specimen.   —   375

Law 29 March 1961 (1981-86) Issue

48   10 Krónur VF UNC
L.1961 (1981). Blue on multicolor underprint. Arngrimúr Jónsson at right.
Signature 37; 38; 42; 43. Back: Old Icelandic household scene. Watermark: J.
Sigurthsson. Printer: BWC, then later by TDLR (both without imprint).
    a. Issued note.   1.00   3.00
    s. Specimen.   —   105

49   50 Krónur   VF   UNC

L.1961 (1981). Brown on multicolor underprint. Bishop Guthbranthur Thorláksson
at left. Signature 37; 38; 42; 43. Back: Two printers. Watermark: J. Sigurthsson.
Printer: BWC, then later by TDLR (both without imprint).

    a. Issued note.   2.00   5.00
    s. Specimen.   —   105

50   100 Krónur   VF   UNC

L.1961 (1981). Dark green on multicolor underprint. Proffessor Arni Magnússon
at right. Signature 37; 38; 42; 43; 45-53. Back: Monk with illuminated manuscript.
Watermark: J. Sigurthsson. Printer: BWC, then later by TDLR (both without imprint).

    a. Issued note.   3.00   8.00
    s. Specimen.   —   105

51   500 Krónur   VF   UNC

L.1961 (1981). Red on multicolor underprint. Jón Sigurthsson at left center.
Signature 37; 38; 42; 43; 45; 48-53. Back: Sigurthsson working at his desk.
Watermark: J. Sigurthsson. Printer: BWC, then later by TDLR (both without
imprint). 145x70mm.

    a. Issued note.   FV   22.00
    s. Specimen.   —   160

52   1000 Krónur   VF   UNC

L.1961 (1984-91). Purple on multicolor underprint. Bishop Byrnijólfur Sveinsson
with book at right. Signature 38; 42; 43; 45; 48-51. Back: Church at center.
Watermark: J. Sigurthsson. Printer: BWC, then later by TDLR (both without
imprint). 150x70mm.

    a. Issued note.   FV   35.50
    s. Specimen.   —   160

53   5000 Krónur   VF   UNC

L.1961 (1986-95). Blue on multicolor underprint. Ragnheithur Jónsdóttir at center.
Bishop G. Thorláksson with two previous wives at right. Back: Jónsdóttir teaching
two girls embroidery. Watermark: J. Sigurthsson. Printer: BWC, then later by
TDLR (both without imprint). 155x70mm.

    a. Signature 38; 46; 47.   FV   215
    b. Signature 54-56. (1995).   FV   160
    s. Specimen.   —   260

Law 5 Mai 1986 (1994-00) Issue

54   100 Krónur   VF   UNC

L.1986 (1994). Dark green on multicolor underprint. Proffessor Arni Magnússon
at right. Signature 52; 53. Back: Monk with illuminated manuscript. Watermark: J.
Sigurthsson.

    a. Issued note.   FV   6.60
    s. Specimen.   —   120

55   500 Krónur   VF   UNC

L.1986 (1994). Red on multicolor underprint. Jón Sigurthsson at left center.
Signature 45; 50-53. Back: Sigurthsson working at his desk. Watermark: J.
Sigurthsson. 145x70mm.

    a. Issued note.   FV   15.50
    s. Specimen.   —   110

56   1000 Krónur   VF   UNC

L.1986 (1994). Purple on multicolor underprint. Bishop Byrnijólfur Sveinsson
with book at right. Signature 45; 50; 51; 54-56. Serial # prefix *E*. Back: Church at
center. Watermark: J. Sigurthsson. 150x70mm.

    a. Issued note.   FV   28.00
    s. Specimen.   —   160

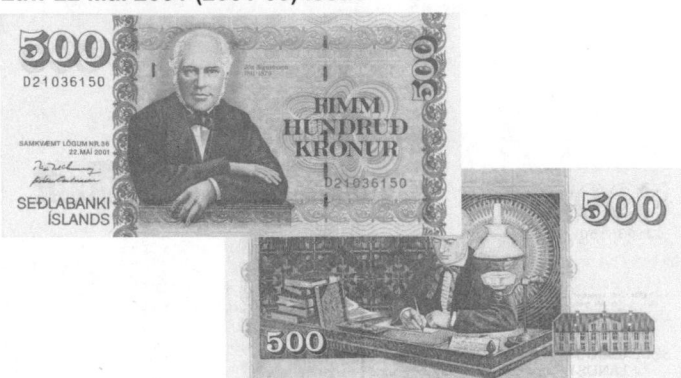

57 2000 Krónur VF UNC
L.1986 (1995). Brown and blue-violet on multicolor underprint. Painting *Inside, Outside* at center, Johannes S. Kjarval at right. Signature 54-56. Serial # prefix *G*. Back: Painting *Yearning for Flight* (Leda and the Swan) and *Woman with Flower*. 150x70mm.
    a. Issued note.   FV   55.00
    s. Specimen.   —   265

Law 22 Mai 2001 (2001-05) Issue

58 500 Krónur VF UNC
L. 1986. (2004); 22.5.2001. Designs to edge of paper. Red on multicolor underprint. Jón Sigurthsson at left center. Signature 45; 50-53. Back: Sigurthsson working at his desk. Watermark: J. Sigurthsson. 145x70mm.
    a. L.1986.   FV   13.00
    b. 22.5.2001.   FV   13.00

59 1000 Krónur VF UNC
L. 1986. (2005). Designs to edge of paper. Red on multicolor underprint. Jón Sigurthsson at left center. Signature 45; 50-53. Back: Sigurthsson working at his desk. Watermark: J. Sigurthsson. 150x70mm. FV 20.50

60 5000 Krónur VF UNC
22.5.2001. Enhanced security decives. Blue on multicolor underprint. Ragnheithur Jónsdóttir at center. Bishop G. Thorláksson with two previous wives at right. Serial # prefix: *F*. Back: Jónsdóttir teaching two girls embroidery. Watermark: J. Sigurthsson. 155x70mm. FV 120

INDIA

The Republic of India, a subcontinent jutting southward from the mainland of Asia, has an area of 3,287,590 sq. km. and a population of 1,147.9 million, second only to that of the Peoples Republic of China. Capital: New Delhi. India's economy is based on agriculture and industrial activity. Engineering goods, cotton apparel and fabrics, handicrafts, tea, iron and steel are exported.

Aryan tribes from the northwest infiltrated onto the Indian subcontinent about 1500 B.C.; their merger with the earlier Dravidian inhabitants created the classical Indian culture. The Maurya Empire of the 4th and 3rd centuries B.C. - which reached its zenith under Ashoka - united much of South Asia. The Golden Age ushered in by the Gupta dynasty (4th to 6th centuries A.D.) saw a flowering of Indian science, art, and culture. Arab incursions starting in the 8th century and Turkic in the 12th were followed by those of European traders, beginning in the late 15th century. By the 19th century, Britain had assumed political control of virtually all Indian lands. Indian armed forces in the British army played a vital role in both World Wars. Nonviolent resistance to British colonialism led by Mohandas Gandhi and Jawaharlal Nehru brought independence in 1947. The subcontinent was divided into the secular state of India and the smaller Muslim state of Pakistan. A third war between the two countries in 1971 resulted in East Pakistan becoming the separate nation of Bangladesh. India's nuclear weapons testing in 1998 caused Pakistan to conduct its own tests that same year. The dispute between the countries over the state of Kashmir is ongoing, but discussions and confidence-building measures have led to decreased tensions since 2002. Despite impressive gains in economic investment and output, India faces pressing problems such as significant overpopulation, environmental degradation, extensive poverty, and ethnic and religious strife.

Note: Staple holes and condition: Perfect uncirculated notes are rarely encountered without having at least two tiny holes made by staples, stick pins or stitching having been done during age old accounting practices before and after a note is released to circulation. Staples were officially discontinued in 1998.

COLONIAL OFFICES

	Allahabad	K	Karachi
B	Bombay	L	Lahore
C	Calcutta	M	Madras
	Calicut	R	Rangoon, refer to Myanmar listings
A	Cawnpore		

DENOMINATION LANGUAGE PANELS

Bengali	Marathi
Burmese	Tamil
Gujarati	Telugu
Gujarati (variation)	Persian (Farsi)
Hindi	Urdu
Kannada	

SIGNATURE VARIETIES

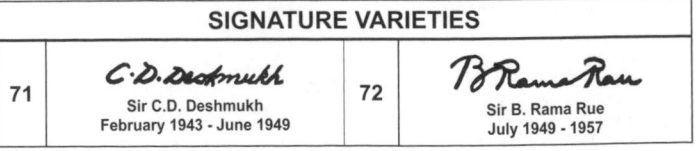

71	Sir C.D. Deshmukh February 1943 - June 1949	72	Sir B. Rama Rue July 1949 - 1957

SIGNATURE VARIETIES

73	*K. G. Ambegoankar* K. G. Ambegoankar January 1957 - February 1957	74	*H. V. R. Iengar* H. V. R. Iengar March 1957 - February 1962
75	*P. C. Bhattacharyya* P. C. Bhattacharyya March 1962 - June 1967	76	*L. K. Jha* L. K. Jha July 1967 - May 1970
77	*B. N. Adarkar* B. N. Adarkar May 1970 - June 1970	78	*S. Jaganathan* S. Jaganathan May 1970 - June 1970
79	*N. C. Sengupta* N. C. Sengupta May 1975 - August 1975	80	*K. R. Puri* K. R. Puri August 1975 - May 1975
81	*M. Narasimham* M. Narasimham May 1977 - November 1977	82	*I. G. Patel* I. G. Patel December 1977 - September 1982
83	*Manmohan Singh* Manmohan Singh September 198. January 1984 - February 1985	84	*Abhitam Ghosh* Abhitam Ghosh January 1985 - February 1985
85	*R. N. Malhotra* R. N. Malhotra February 1985 - December 1990	86	*S. Venkitaramanan* S. Venkitaramanan November 1997 -
87	*C. Rangarajan* C. Rangarajan December 1992 - 97 November 1987 - 88	88	*Bimal Jalan* Bimal Jalan November 1997 -

REPUBLIC OF INDIA

Reserve Bank of India

First Series

रूपया
Error Singular Hindi = *RUPAYA*

रूपये
Corrected plural Hindi = *RUPAYE*

VARIETIES: #27-28, 33, 38, 42, 46, 48 and 50 have large headings in Hindi expressing the value incorrectly in the singular form as: *Rupaya*. **Note:** For similar notes but in different colors, please see the Haj Pilgrim or the Persian Gulf listings at the end of this country listing.

27 2 Rupees — VF 75.00 / UNC 150
ND. Red-brown on violet and green underprint. Hindi numeral *2* at upper right. Signature 72. Asoka column at right. Large letters in underprint beneath serial number. Back: Tiger head at left. 8 value text lines. Watermark: Asoka column.

28 2 Rupees — VF 6.00 / UNC 16.00
ND. Red-brown on violet and green underprint. English *2* at upper left and right. Redesigned panels. Asoka column at right. Large letters in underprint beneath serial number. Signature 72. Back: 7 value text lines; third line 18mm long. Watermark: Asoka column.

29 2 Rupees — VF / UNC
ND. Red-brown on violet and green underprint. Value in English and corrected Hindi on both sides. Asoka column at right. Large letters in underprint beneath serial number. Back: Tiger head at left looking to left, third value text line 24mm long. Watermark: Asoka column.
　a. Signature 72. — 12.00 / 40.00
　b. Signature 74. — 5.00 / 18.00

30 2 Rupees — VF 9.00 / UNC 30.00
ND. Red-brown on green underprint. Value in English and corrected Hindi. Signature 75. Back: Tiger head at left looking to right, with 13 value text lines at center.

31 2 Rupees — VF 8.00 / UNC 25.00
ND. Olive on tan underprint. Value in English and corrected Hindi. Signature 75. Back: Tiger head at left looking to right, with 13 value text lines at center. Watermark: Asoka column.

32 5 Rupees — VF 30.00 / UNC 125
ND. Green on brown underprint. English value only on face, serial number at center. Signature 72. Back: *Rs. 5* and antelope. Watermark: Asoka column.

33 5 Rupees — VF 10.00 / UNC 35.00
ND. Value in English and error Hindi, serial number at right. Signature 72. Back: 8 value lines; fourth line 21mm long. Watermark: Asoka column.

34 5 Rupees — VF 35.00 / UNC 150
ND. Hindi corrected. Signature 72. Back: Fourth value text line 26mm long. Watermark: Asoka column.

35   5 Rupees   **VF   UNC**

ND. Green on brown underprint. Hindi corrected, redesigned panels at left and right. Asoka columns at right. Large letters in underprint beneath serial number. Watermark: Asoka column.

    a. Without letter. Signature 74.   10.00 35.00
    b. Letter A. Signature 74.   6.00 20.00

Note: For similar note but in orange, see #R2 (Persian Gulf listings in the Specialized edition).

36   5 Rupees   **VF   UNC**

ND (1962-67). Green on brown underprint. Hindi corrected, redesigned panels at left and right. Asoka column at right. Large letters in underprint beneath serial number. Signature title: *GOVERNOR* centered. Back: Thirteen value text lines. Watermark: Asoka column.

    a. Letter A. Signature 75.   6.00 20.00
    b. Letter B. Signature 75.   7.00 25.00

37   10 Rupees   **VF   UNC**

ND. Purple on multicolor underprint. English value. Asoka column at right. Large letters in underprint beneath serial number. Back: *Rs. 10* at lower center, 1 serial number. English in both lower corners, dhow at center. Watermark: Asoka column.

    a. Signature 71.   225 750
    b. Signature 72.   30.00 125

38   10 Rupees   **VF   UNC**

ND. Value in English and error Hindi. Asoka column at right. Large letters in underprint beneath serial number. 2 serial numbers. Signature 72. Back: Third value text line 24mm long. Watermark: Asoka column.   6.00 20.00

39   10 Rupees   **VF   UNC**

ND. Purple on multicolor underprint. Hindi corrected. Asoka column at right. Large letters in underprint beneath serial number. Back: Third value text line 29mm long. Watermark: Asoka column.

    a. Without letter. Signature 72.   9.00 30.00
    b. Without letter. Signature 74.   9.00 30.00
    c. Letter A. Signature 74.   5.00 18.00

Note: For similar note but in red, see #R3 (Persian Gulf listings in the Specialized edition); in blue, see #R5 (Haj Pilgrim listings in the Specialized edition).

40   10 Rupees   **VF   UNC**

ND. Green on brown underprint. Hindi corrected. Asoka column at right. Large letters in underprint beneath serial number. Title: *GOVERNOR* centered. Back: Thirteen value text lines. Watermark: Asoka column.

    a. Letter A. Signature 75.   7.00 25.00
    b. Letter B. Signature 75.   4.50 15.00

41   100 Rupees   **VF   UNC**

ND. Blue on multicolor underprint. English value. Asoka column at right. Large letters in overprint beneath serial number. Back: Two elephants at center, 8 value text lines below and bank emblem at left. Watermark: Asoka column.

    a. Dark blue. Signature 72.   140 375
    b. Light blue. Signature 72.   140 375

42   100 Rupees   **VF   UNC**

ND. Purplish-blue on multicolor underprint. Value in English and error Hindi. Asoka column at right. Large letters in underprint beneath serial number. Back: Value in English and error Hindi. 7 value text lines; third 27mm long. Watermark: Asoka column.

    a. Black serial #. Signature 72.   120 325
    b. Red serial #. Signature 72.   120 325

43   100 Rupees   **VF   UNC**

ND. Purplish blue on multicolor underprint. Hindi corrected. Asoka column at right. Large letters in underprint beneath serial number. Back: Third value text line 40mm long. Watermark: Asoka column.

    a. Without letter, thin paper. Signature 72.   120 325
    b. Without letter, thin paper. Signature 74.   100 275
    c. Without letter, thick paper. Signature 74.   140 375

Note: For similar note but in green, see #R4 (Persian Gulf listings in the Specialized volume); in red, see #R6 (Haj Pilgrim listings in the Specialized volume).

44 100 Rupees VF UNC
ND. Purple and multicolor. Heading in rectangle at top, serial numberat upper left and lower right. Asoka column at right. Large letters in underprint beneath serial number. Signature 74. Title: *GOVERNOR* at center right Back: Dam at center with 13 value text lines at left. Watermark: Asoka column. 90.00 250

45 100 Rupees VF UNC
ND. Violet and multicolor. Heading in rectangle at top, serial numberat upper left and lower right. Asoka column at right. Large letters in underprint beneath serial number. Signature 75. Title: *GOVERNOR* centered. Back: Dam at center with 13 value text lines at left. Watermark: Asoka column. 90.00 250

46 1000 Rupees VF UNC
ND. Brown on green and blue underprint. Value in English and error Hindi. Asoka column at right. Large letters in underprint beneath serial number. Back: Value in English and error Hindi. Tanjore Temple at center with 7 value text lines at left. Watermark: Asoka column.
a. *BOMBAY*. signature 72. 1,000 —
b. *CALCUTTA*. signature 72. 1,000 —
c. *DELHI*. signature 72. 2,500 —
d. *KANPUR*. signature 72. 2,000 —
e. *MADRAS*. signature 72. 2,000 —
s. Like a. Specimen. — 7,000

47 1000 Rupees VF UNC
ND. Brown on green and blue underprint. Value in English and Hindi corrected. Asoka column at right. Large letters in underprint beneath serial number. Back: Value in English and Hindi corrected. Tanjore Temple at center. Thirteen value text lines. Watermark: Asoka column.
a. *BOMBAY*. Signature 72. 2,000 —
b. *CALCUTTA*. Signature 72. 2,000 —
c. *DELHI*. Signature 72. 4,000 0.00
d. *MADRAS*. Signature 72. 3,000 0.00
e. *BOMBAY*. Signature 74. 4,000 —
f. *BOMBAY*. Signature 75. 3,000 —

48 5000 Rupees VF UNC
ND. Green, violet and brown. Asoka column at left. Value in English and error Hindi. Back: Gateway of India. Value in English and error Hindi.
a. *BOMBAY*. Signature 72. Rare. 30,000 50,000
b. *CALCUTTA*. Signature 72. Rare. 30,000 50,000
c. *DELHI*. Signature 72. Rare. 30,000 50,000

49 5000 Rupees VF UNC
ND. Green, violet and brown. Value in English. Hindi corrected. Back: Gateway of India.
a. *BOMBAY*. Signature 74. 30,000 50,000
b. *MADRAS*. Signature 74. 30,000 50,000
s. As a. Specimen. Red overprint:*SPECIMEN*. — 17,500

50 10,000 Rupees VF UNC
ND. Blue, violet and brown. Asoka column at center. Value in English and error Hindi. Back: Value in English and error Hindi.
a. *BOMBAY*. Signature 72. 35,000 60,000
b. *CALCUTTA*. Signature 72. 35,000 60,000
s. As B. Specimen. Signature 72. — —

50A 10,000 Rupees Fine XF
ND. Asoka column at center. Value in English. Hindi corrected. Back: Value in English. Hindi corrected.
a. *BOMBAY*. Signature 74. 45,000 60,000
b. *MADRAS*. Signature 74. 45,000 60,000
c. *NEW DELHI*. Signature 74. 45,000 60,000
d. *BOMBAY*. Signature 76. 45,000 60,000

Second Series
Most notes are of reduced size. Large letters found in underprint beneath serial number.

Urd Incorrect   Corrected Urdu (actually Farsi)

51 2 Rupees VF UNC
ND. Brown and multicolor. Numeral 2 at center 7mm high. Large letters found in underprint beneath serial number. Asoka column at right. Back: Incorrect Urdu inscription at bottom left, tiger at center.
a. Signature 75 with title: *GOVERNOR* centered at bottom. 4.00 14.00
b. Signature 76 with title: *GOVERNOR* at center right 4.00 14.00

52 2 Rupees VF UNC
ND. Deep pink and multicolor. Numeral 2 at center 15mm high. Large letters found in underprint beneath serial number. Asoka column at right. Signature 78. Back: Incorrect Urdu inscription at bottom left, tiger at center. 2.00 8.00

53   2 Rupees

ND. Deep pink and multicolor. English text at left. Large letters found in underprint beneath serial number. Asoka column at right. Back: Corrected Urdu inscription at bottom left, tiger at center.

		VF	UNC
a.	Without letter. Signature 78.	1.75	7.00
b.	Without letter. Signature 80.	2.00	8.00
c.	Letter A. Signature 80.	1.75	7.00
d.	Letter A. Signature 82.	1.50	5.00
e.	Letter B. Signature 82.	1.50	5.00
f.	Letter C. Signature 82.	1.50	5.00
g.	Letter C. Signature 83.	1.50	5.00
s.	Specimen.	—	300

53A   2 Rupees

ND. Deep pink and multicolor. English text at right. Large letters found in underprint beneath serial number. Asoka column at right. Smaller size serial number. Back: Corrected Urdu inscription at bottom left, tiger at center.

		VF	UNC
a.	Without letter. Signature 83.	1.25	4.50
b.	Without letter. Signature 84.	4.00	12.50
c.	Letter A. Signature 85.	1.25	4.50
d.	Letter B. Signature 85.	1.25	4.50
e.	Letter B. Signature 86.	1.25	4.50
s.	Specimen.	—	300

54   5 Rupees

ND. Green and multicolor. Numeral *5* at center 11mm high. Large letters found in underprint beneath serial number. Asoka column at right. Back: Incorrect Urdu inscription at bottom left, antelope at center.

		VF	UNC
a.	Signature 75 with title: *GOVERNOR* centered at bottom.	9.00	30.00
b.	Signature 76 with title: *GOVERNOR* at center right.	9.00	30.00

55   5 Rupees

ND. Dark green on multicolor underprint. Numeral *5* at center 17mm high. Large letters found in underprint beneath serial number. Asoka column at right. Signature 78. Back: Incorrect Urdu inscription at bottom left, antelope at center.

VF	UNC
7.00	25.00

56   5 Rupees

ND. Dark green on multicolor underprint. Numeral *5* at center 17mm high. Large letters found in underprint beneath serial number. Asoka column at right. Back: Corrected Urdu inscription at bottom left, antelope at center.

		VF	UNC
a.	Without letter. Signature 78.	6.00	20.00
b.	Letter A. Signature 78.	6.00	20.00

57   10 Rupees

ND. Purple and multicolor. Numeral *10* at center 30mm broad. Large letters found in underprint beneath serial number. Asoka column at right. Back: Dhow at center, incorrect Urdu inscription at bottom left.

		VF	UNC
a.	Signature 75 with title: *GOVERNOR* centered at bottom.	6.00	20.00
b.	Signature 76 with title: *GOVERNOR* at center right.	6.00	20.00

58   10 Rupees

ND. Black on brown and pale green underprint. Numeral *10* at center 18mm broad. Large letters found in underprint beneath serial number. Asoka column at right. Signature 76. Back: Heading in English and Hindi. Incorrect Urdu inscription at bottom left.

VF	UNC
8.00	27.50

59   10 Rupees

ND. Dark brown on multicolor underprint. Numeral *10* at center 18mm broad. Large letters found in underprint beneath serial number. Asoka column at right. Back: Dhow at center. Heading in Hindi. Incorrect Urdu inscription at bottom left.

		VF	UNC
a.	Without letter. Signature 78.	3.00	10.00
b.	Letter A. Signature 78.	3.00	10.00

60   10 Rupees

ND. Dark brown on multicolor underprint. Numeral *10* at center 18mm broad. Large letters found in underprint beneath serial number. Asoka column at right. Back: Heading in Hindi. Corrected Urdu inscription at bottom left.

		VF	UNC
a.	Letter A. Signature 78.	4.00	14.00
b.	Letter B. Signature 78.	20.00	70.00
c.	Letter B. Signature 80.	4.00	14.00
d.	Letter B. Signature 81.	1.75	7.00
e.	Letter C. Signature 81.	1.75	7.00
f.	Letter C. Signature 82.	1.75	7.00
g.	Letter D. Signature 82.	1.75	7.00
h.	Letter D. Signature 83.	1.75	7.00
i.	Letter E. Signature 83.	1.75	7.00
j.	Letter E. Signature 84.	1.75	7.00
k.	Letter F. Signature 85.	1.75	7.00
l.	Letter G. Signature 85.	1.75	7.00

60A   10 Rupees

ND. Dark brown on multicolor underprint. Hindi title above *RESERVE BANK OF INDIA* and Hindi text at left of *10* and *I PROMISE...* at right. Sanskrit title added under Asoka column at right. Back: Dhow at center.

		VF	UNC
a.	Signature 85.	1.75	7.00
b.	Signature 86. Large serial #.	1.75	7.00
c.	Signature 86. Small serial #.	1.75	7.00

Incorrect Kashmiri   Corrected Kashmiri (actually Farsi)

61 20 Rupees
VF UNC

ND. Orange and multicolor. Large letters found in underprint beneath serial number, Asoka column at right. Signature 78. Back: Parliament House at center.
- a. Dark colors under signature, error in Kashmiri in fifth line on back. — 7.00 — 25.00
- b. Light colors under signature, error in Kashmiri in fifth line on back. — 4.00 — 14.00

61A 20 Rupees
VF UNC

ND. Orange and multicolor. Large letters found in underprint beneath serial number, Asoka column at right. Signature 78. Back: Like #61b but corrected Kashmiri in fifth line. — 4.00 — 14.00

62 100 Rupees
VF UNC

ND. Blue and multicolor. Numeral *100* at center 43mm broad. Large letters found in underprint beneath serial number. Asoka column at right. Back: Dam at center with only English heading.
- a. Signature 75. — 20.00 — 70.00
- b. Signature 76. — 20.00 — 70.00

63 100 Rupees
VF UNC

ND. Blue and multicolor. Numeral *100* at center 28mm broad. Large letters found in underprint beneath serial number. Asoka column at right. Signature 78. Back: Dam at center with only Hindi heading. — 12.50 — 45.00

64 100 Rupees
VF UNC

ND. Blue and multicolor. Numeral *100* at center 28mm broad. Large letters found in underprint beneath serial number. Asoka column at right. Back: Like #63 but corrected Urdu value line.
- a. Without letter. Signature 78. — 12.50 — 45.00
- b. Without letter. Signature 80. — 12.50 — 45.00
- c. Without letter. Signature 81. — 12.50 — 45.00
- d. Letter A. Signature 82. — 12.50 — 45.00

65 1000 Rupees
VF UNC

ND. Brown on multicolor underprint. Text in English and Hindi. Large letters found in underprint beneath serial number. Asoka column at right. *BOMBAY.* at lower right. Back: Temple at center.
- a. Signature 79. — 250 — 800
- b. Signature 80. — 250 — 800

Government of India

SIGNATURE VARIETIES	
SECRETARIES, MINISTRY OF FINANCE (1 Rupee notes only)	
K.R.K.Menon	*A.K.Roy*
K. R. K. Menon, 1944	A. K. Roy, 1957
K.G.Ambegaonkar	*L.K.Jha*
K. G. Ambegaonkar, 1949-1951	L. K. Jha, 1957-1963
H.M.Patel	
H. M. Patel, 1951-1957	

1969 ND Commemorative Issue

#66, Centennial - Birth of M. K. Gandhi

66 1 Rupee
VF UNC

ND (1969-70). Violet and multicolor. Coin with Gandhi and *1869-1948* at right. Signature 82. Back: Reverse of Gandhi coin at left. — 2.00 — 7.00

Reserve Bank of India
1969 ND Commemorative Issue
#67-70, Centennial - Birth of M. K. Gandhi

67 2 Rupees

	VF	UNC
ND (1969-70). Red-violet and multicolor. Numeral *2* at center 15mm high. Large letters found in underprint beneath serial number. Asoka column at right. Back: Gandhi seated at center.

	VF	UNC
a. Signature 76.	3.00	10.00
b. Signature 77.	4.00	14.00

68 5 Rupees

ND (1969-70). Dark green on multicolor underprint. Numeral *5* at center 17mm high. Large letters found in underprint beneath serial number. Asoka column at right. Back: Gandhi seated at center.

	VF	UNC
a. Signature 76.	4.50	15.00
b. Signature 77.	6.00	20.00

69 10 Rupees

ND (1969-70). Brown and multicolor. Numeral *10* at center 18mm broad. Large letters found in underprint beneath serial number. Asoka column at right. Back: Gandhi seated at center.

	VF	UNC
a. Signature 76.	6.00	20.00
b. Signature 77.	7.00	25.00
s. Specimen.	—	—

70 100 Rupees

ND (1969-70). Blue and multicolor. Numeral *100* at center 28mm broad. Large letters found in underprint beneath serial number. Asoka column at right. Back: Gandhi seated at center.

	VF	UNC
a. Signature 76.	40.00	140
b. Signature 77.	40.00	140
s. Specimen.	—	—

Government of India
1957; 1963 Issue

75 1 Rupee

	VF	UNC
1957. Violet on multicolor underprint. Redesigned coin with Asoka column at right. Back: Coin dated 1957 and *100 Naye Paise* in Hindi, 7 value text lines. Watermark: Asoka column.

	VF	UNC
a. Letter A. Signature H. M. Patel with signature title: *SECRETARY...* (1957).	2.00	10.00
b. Letter A. Signature H. M. Patel with signature title: *PRINCIPAL SECRE-TARY...* 1957.	3.00	12.00
c. Letter B. Signature A. K. Roy. 1957.	1.00	4.00
d. Letter B. Signature L. K. Jha. 1957.	50.00	125
e. Letter C. Signature L. K. Jha. 1957.	0.60	3.00
f. Letter D. Signature L. K. Jha. 1957.	0.60	3.00

Note: For similar note but in red, see #R1 (Persian Gulf listings in the Specialized edition).

76 1 Rupee

	VF	UNC
1963-65. Violet on multicolor underprint. Redesigned note. Back: Coin with various dates and *1 Rupee* in Hindi, thirteen value text lines.

	VF	UNC
a. Letter A. Signature 35. 1963.	2.50	9.00
b. Letter B. Signature 36. 1964.	35.00	120
c. Letter B. Signature 36. 1965.	2.50	9.00

77 1 Rupee

	VF	UNC
1966-80. Violet on multicolor underprint. Redesigned note, serial number at left. Back: Coin with various dates.

	VF	UNC
a. Without letter. Signature 36. 1966.	2.50	9.00
b. Letter A. Signature 37. 1967.	4.00	14.00
c. Letter A. Signature 37. 1968.	3.50	12.00
d. Letter B. Signature 38 with signature title: *SPECIAL SECRETARY...* 1968.	1.75	7.00
e. Letter B. Signature 38 with signature title: *SPECIAL SECRETARY...* 1969.	1.75	7.00
f. Letter C. Signature 38 with title: *SPECIAL SECRETARY...* 1969.	1.75	7.00
g. Letter C. Signature 38. 1970.	1.75	7.00
h. Letter C. Signature 38. 1971.	1.75	7.00
i. Letter D. Signature 38. 1971.	1.75	7.00
j. Letter D. Signature 38. 1972.	1.75	7.00
k. Letter E. Signature 38. 1972.	1.75	7.00
l. Letter E. Signature 38. 1973.	1.75	7.00
m. Letter F. Signature 39. 1973.	1.75	7.00
n. Letter F. Signature 39. 1974.	1.75	7.00
o. Letter G. Signature 39. 1974.	1.25	5.00
p. Letter G. Signature 39. 1975.	1.25	5.00
q. Letter H. Signature 39. 1975.	1.25	5.00
r. Letter H. Signature 39. 1976.	1.25	5.00
s. Letter I. Signature 39. 1976.	1.25	5.00
t. Without letter. Small serial #. Signature 40. 1976.	1.25	5.00
u. Small serial #. Signature 40. 1977.	1.25	5.00
v. Letter A. Signature 40. 1978.	1.25	5.00
w. Letter A. Signature 40. 1979.	1.25	5.00
x. Letter A. Signature 40. 1980.	1.25	5.00
y. Letter A. Signature 41. 1980.	1.25	5.00
z. Letter B. Signature 41. 1980.	1.25	5.00

78 1 Rupee   VF   UNC
1981. Purple and violet on light blue, brown and multicolor underprint. Coin with Asoka column at upper right. Back: Offshore oil drilling platform and reverse of coin with date.
    a. Signature 41. 1981.   1.00   4.00
    b. Signature 42. 1981.   1.50   6.00

78A 1 Rupee   VF   UNC
1983-1994. Coin with Asoka column at upper right. New coin design. Back: Offshore oil drilling platform and reverse of coin with date. New coin design.
    a. Signature 43 with title: *SECRETARY...* 1983-85.   1.00   4.00
    b. Signature 44 with title: *FINANCE SECRETARY...* 1985.   1.00   4.00
    c. Letter A. Signature 44. 1986-89.   1.00   4.00
    d. Letter B. Signature 45. 1989.   1.25   5.00
    e. Letter B. Signature 46. 1990.   1.25   5.00
    f. Letter B. Signature 47. 1991.   1.25   5.00
    g. Letter B. Signature 48 with title: *SECRETARY...* 1991.   1.25   5.00
    h. Letter B. Signature 48. 1992.   1.25   5.00
    i. Letter B. Signature 48 with title: *FINANCE SECRETARY...* 1993.   1.25   5.00
    j. Letter B. Signature 48. 1994.   1.50   6.00

Reserve Bank of India
Third Series

Large letters in underprint beneath serial #.

79 2 Rupees   VF   UNC
ND(1976). Orange on multicolor underprint. Large letters in underprint beneath serial number. Asoka column at right. Back: Space craft at center. Watermark: Asoka column.
    a. Signature 80.   0.75   3.00
    b. Signature 81.   0.75   3.00
    c. Without letter. Without watermark. Signature 82.   0.75   3.00
    d. Without letter. With watermark: 6 wheels surrounding Asoka column. signature 82.   0.75   3.00
    e. Letter A. Signature 82.   0.75   3.00
    f. Letter A. Signature 83.   0.75   3.00
    g. Letter A. Signature 84.   0.75   3.00
    h. Letter A. Signature 85.   0.75   3.00
    i. Letter B. Signature 85.   0.75   3.00
    j. Without letter. Signature 85 With *Satyameva Jayate* added below the Ashoka Pillar.   0.75   3.00
    k. Letter A. Signature 85 with *Satyameva Jayate* added below the Ashoka Pillar.   0.75   3.00
    l. Letter B. Signature 86.   0.75   3.00
    m. Letter B. Signature 87.   0.75   3.00

80 5 Rupees   VF   UNC
ND(1975). Grayish green on light blue and orange underprint. Large letters in underprint beneath serial number. Asoka column at right. Back: Farmer plowing with tractor at center. Watermark: Asoka column.
    a. Without letter. Signature 78.   2.00   8.00
    b. Without letter. Signature 80.   1.50   6.00
    c. Letter A. Signature 80.   1.00   4.00
    d. Letter A. Signature 81.   1.00   4.00
    e. Letter A. Signature 82.   1.00   4.00
    f. Letter B. Signature 82.   1.00   4.00
    g. Letter C. Signature 82.   1.00   4.00
    h. Letter C. Signature 83.   1.00   4.00
    i. Letter D. Signature 83.   1.00   4.00
    j. Letter D. Signature 84.   1.00   4.00

                                 VF   UNC
    k. Letter D. Signature 85.   1.00   4.00
    l. Letter E. Signature 85.   1.00   4.00
    m. Letter F. Signature 85.   1.00   4.00
    n. Letter G. Signature 85.   1.00   4.00
    o. Without letter. New Seal in Hindi & English. Signature 85.   1.00   4.00
    p. Letter A. New Seal - do - Signature 85.   1.00   4.00
    q. Letter B. Signature 86.   1.00   4.00
    r. Letter B. Signature 87.   1.00   4.00
    s. Without letter. Signature 88.   0.75   3.00

81 10 Rupees   VF   UNC
ND. Brown on multicolor underprint. Large letters in inprint beneath serial number. Asoka column at right. Back: Tree with peacocks at center. Watermark: Asoka column. 137x63mm.
    a. Without letter. Signature 78.   3.50   12.50
    b. Without letter. Signature 80.   3.50   12.50
    c. Without letter. Signature 81.   6.00   20.00
    d. Letter A. Signature 82.   2.50   8.00
    e. Without letter. Signature 82.   2.50   8.00
    f. Letter A. Signature 83.   2.50   8.00
    g. Letter B. Signature 85.   2.50   8.00
    h. Letter C. Signature 85.   2.50   8.00

82 20 Rupees   VF   UNC
ND. Red and purple on multicolor underprint. Large letters in inprint beneath serial number. Asoka column at right. Back: Hindu Wheel of Time at lower center. Watermark: Asoka column. 147x63mm.
    a. Signature 78.   10.00   35.00
    b. Signature 80.   2.75   9.00
    c. Signature 81.   20.00   70.00
    d. Without letter. Signature 82.   7.00   25.00
    e. Letter A. Signature 82.   2.75   9.00
    f. Letter A. Signature 83.   2.75   9.00
    g. Letter A. Signature 85.   2.75   9.00
    h. Letter B. Signature 85.   2.75   9.00
    i. Letter B. Signature 87.   2.50   8.00
    j. Letter C. Signature 87.   2.50   8.00
    k. Letter C. Signature 88.   2.50   8.00
    l. Letter C. Signature 89.   2.50   8.00

83 50 Rupees VF UNC
ND(1975). Black and purple on lilac and multicolor underprint. Large letters in inprint beneath serial number. Asoka column at right. Back: Parliament House at center without flag at top of flagpole. Watermark: Asoka column. 147x73mm.

a. Signature 78.	6.00	20.00
b. Signature 80.	4.50	15.00
c. Signature 81.	10.00	35.00
d. Signature 82.	4.00	14.00

84 50 Rupees VF UNC
ND(1978). Black and purple on orange, lilac and multicolor underprint. Large letters in inprint beneath serial number. Asoka column at right. Back: Parliament House at center with flag at top of flagpole. Watermark: Asoka column. 147x73mm.

a. Signature 82.	3.50	12.50
b. Signature 83.	3.50	12.50
c. Signature 85.	3.50	12.50
d. Letter A. Signature 85.	3.50	12.50
e. Letter B. Signature 85.	3.50	12.50
f. Letter A. Signature 86.	3.00	10.00
g. Letter B. Signature 86.	3.00	10.00
h. Letter A. Signature 87.	2.75	9.00
i. Letter B. Signature 87.	2.75	9.00
j. Letter C. Signature 87.	2.75	9.00
k. Without letter. Signature 87. Requires confirmation.	—	—
l. Letter B. Signature 88.	2.75	9.00

85 100 Rupees VF UNC
ND(1975). Black and blue-violet on brown and multicolor underprint (tan at center). Large letters in inprint beneath serial number. Asoka column at right. Denomination above bar at lower right. Black signature. Back: Dam, agricultural work at center. Watermark: Asoka column. 157x73mm.

a. Signature 78.	45.00	150
b. Signature 80.	12.00	40.00
c. Signature 81.	20.00	65.00
d. Signature 82.	12.00	30.00

85A 100 Rupees VF UNC
ND. Black and blue-violet on brown and multicolor underprint (tan at center). Like #85 but without bar under denomination at lower right. Signature 85. Back: Dam, agricultural work at center. Watermark: Asoka column. 157x73mm.
    12.00   30.00

86 100 Rupees VF UNC
ND(1979). Black, deep red and purple on multicolor underprint, (pink at center). Like #85 but without bar under denomination at lower right. Signature 85. Deep red signature. Back: Dam, agricultural work at center. Watermark: Asoka column. 157x73mm.

a. Signature 82.	12.00	30.00
b. Signature 83.	12.00	30.00
c. Signature 85.	10.00	27.50
d. Signature 86.	7.00	20.00
e. Letter A. Signature 86.	7.00	20.00
f. Without letter. Signature 87.	7.00	20.00
g. Letter A. Signature 87.	7.00	20.00
h. Letter B. Signature 87.	9.00	25.00

87 500 Rupees VF UNC
ND (1987). Brown, deep blue-green and deep blue on multicolor underprint. M. K. Gandhi at center right. Electronic sorting marks at lower left. Large letters in underprint beneath serial number. Asoka column at right. Back: Gandhi leading followers across. Watermark: Asoka column. 167x73mm.

a. Signature 85.	30.00	75.00
b. Signature 86.	27.50	70.00
c. Signature 87.	25.00	65.00

1992 Issue

88 10 Rupees VF UNC
ND (1992). Dull brown-violet on orange, green and multicolor underprint. Large letters in underprint beneath serial number. Asoka column at right. Back: Rural temple at left center. Watermark: Asoka column. 137x63mm.

a. Signature 86.	1.25	4.00
b. Letter A. Signature 86.	1.25	4.00
c. Letter A. Signature 87.	1.25	4.00
d. Letter B. Signature 87.	1.25	4.00
e. Letter C. Signature 87.	1.25	4.00
f. Letter D. Signature 87.	1.25	3.00
g. Letter E. Signature 87.	1.25	3.00

1996-2002 ND Issue

#89-93 Starting in 1999 the name was spelled out as Mahatma Gandhi.

	88A	5 Rupees	VF	UNC

ND(2002)-2011. Green-orange on multicolor underprint. Mahatma Gandhi at right, Reserve Bank seal at lower right. Back: Farmer plowing with tractor at center. Watermark: Mahatma Gandhi.

		VF	UNC
a. Without letter. Signature 88.		FV	2.50
b. Letter L. Signature 88.		FV	2.50
c. Letter R. Signature 88.		FV	2.50
d. Without letter. Signature 89.		FV	2.50
e. Letter L. Signature 89.		FV	2.50
f. Letter R. Signature 89.		FV	2.50
g. 2010.		FV	2.50
h. 2011. Letter R.		FV	2.50

	89	10 Rupees	VF	UNC

ND (1996). Pale brown-violet on multicolor underprint. Mahatma Gandhi at right, Reserve Bank seal at lower right. Back: Ornamented rhinoceros and elephant heads behind tiger at left center. Watermark: Mahatma Gandhi. 137x63mm.

	VF	UNC
a. Without letter. Signature 87.	1.25	3.00
b. Letter L; M; R. Signature 87.	1.25	3.00
c. Letter R; N; A; P; Q; S; T; L; B; M. Signature 88.	1.25	3.00
d. Without letter. Signature 89.	1.25	3.00
e. Letter A, R. Signature 89.	1.25	3.00

	89A	20 Rupees	VF	UNC

ND(2002). Red-orange on multicolor underprint. Mahatma Gandhi at right, Reserve Bank seal at lower right. Back: Coconut trees. Watermark: Mahatma Gandhi. 147x63mm.

	VF	UNC
a. Without letter. Signature 88.	FV	4.00
b. Letter A; R. Signature 88.	FV	4.00
c. Without letter. Signature 89.	FV	4.00
d. Letter A; R. Signature 89.	FV	4.00

	90	50 Rupees	VF	UNC

ND (1997). Black and purple on multicolor underprint. Mahatma Gandhi at right, Reserve Bank seal at lower right. Back: Parliament house at left center. Watermark: Mahatma Gandhi. 147x73mm.

	VF	UNC
a. Without letter. Signature 87.	FV	6.00
b. Without letter. Signature 88.	FV	5.00
c. Letter A. Signature 88.	FV	5.00
d. Letter R. Signature 88.	FV	5.00
e. Letter A. Signature 88.	FV	5.00
f. Letter E. Signature 88.	FV	5.00
g. Letter L. Signature 88.	FV	5.00
h. Without letter. Signature 89.	FV	5.00
i. Letter A. Signature 89.	FV	5.00
j. Letter E. Signature 89.	FV	5.00
k. Letter R. Signature 89.	FV	5.00

	91	100 Rupees	VF	UNC

ND (1996). Segmented foil over security thread. Black, purple and dark olive-green on pale blue-green and multicolor underprint. Mahatma Gandhi at right, Reserve Bank seal at lower right. Back: Himalaya mountains at left center. Watermark: Mahatma Gandhi. 157x73mm.

	VF	UNC
a. Without letter. Signature 87.	2.50	9.00
b. Letter E. Signature 87.	2.50	9.00
c. Letter L. Signature 87.	2.50	9.00
d. Letter A. Signature 87.	FV	8.00
e. Letter L. Signature 88.	FV	8.00
f. Letter E. Signature 88.	FV	8.00
g. Without letter. Signature 88.	FV	8.00
h. Letter R. Signature 88.	FV	8.00
i. Letter F. Signature 88.	FV	8.00
j. Letter B. Signature 88.	FV	8.00
k. Without letter. Signature 89.	FV	8.00
l. Letter L. Signature 89.	FV	8.00
m. Letter R. Signature 89.	FV	8.00

	92	500 Rupees	VF	UNC

ND (1997). Segmented foil over security thread. Dark brown, olive-green and purple on multicolor underprint. Mahatma Gandhi at right, Reserve Bank seal at lower right. Back: Gandhi leading followers across. Watermark: Mahatma Gandhi. 167x73mm.

	VF	UNC
a. Without letter. Signature 87.	FV	50.00
b. Without letter. Signature 88.	FV	50.00
c. Letter A. Signature 88.	FV	50.00
d. Letter C. Signature 88.	FV	50.00

2000-02 ND Issue

	93	500 Rupees	VF	UNC

ND (2000-02). Pale yellow, mauve and brown. Mahatma Gandhi at right, Reserve Bank seal at lower right. Value at center in optical variable ink. Back: Gandhi leading followers. Watermark: Mahatma Gandhi. 167x73mm.

	VF	UNC
a. Without letter. Signature 88.	FV	40.00
b. Letter A. Signature 88.	FV	40.00
c. Letter B. Signature 88.	FV	40.00
d. Letter C. Signature 88.	FV	40.00
e. Without letter. Signature 89.	FV	37.50
f. Letter A. Signature 89.	FV	37.50
g. Letter B. Signature 89.	FV	37.50
h. Letter C. Signature 89.	FV	37.50

94   1000 Rupees   **VF   UNC**

ND (2000). Pink and gray. Mahatma Gandhi at right, Reserve Bank seal at lower right. Back: Allegory of Indian economy. 177x73mm.

a. Without letter. Signature 88.	FV	75.00
b. Letter A. Signature 88.	FV	75.00
c. Without letter. Signature 89.	FV	75.00
d. Letter A. Signature 89.	FV	75.00

2005; 2006 Issue

94A   5 Rupees   **VF   UNC**

2009-. Green on orange underprint. Mahatma Gandi at right. Back: Farmer plowing with tractor at center. Watermark: Mahatma Gandhi   FV   2.50

95   10 Rupees   **VF   UNC**

2006-. Pale brown-violet on multicolor underprint. Mahatma Gandhi at right. Back: Tiger, rhino and elephant. 137x63mm.

a. 2006. Signature Y. V. Reddy.	FV	1.00
b. 2006. Letter L.	FV	1.00
c. 2007	FV	1.00
d. 2007. Letter M.	FV	1.00
e. 2008	FV	1.00
f. 2008. Letter M.	FV	1.00
g. 2008. Letter N.	FV	1.00
h. 2008. Signature D. Subarao.	FV	0.75
i. 2008. Letter R.	FV	0.75
j. 2009	FV	0.75
k. 2009. Letter L.	FV	0.75
l. 2009. Letter P.	FV	0.75
m. 2009. Letter R.	FV	0.75
n. 2010	FV	0.75
o. 2010. Letter L	FV	0.75
p. 2010. Letter M.	FV	0.75
q. 2010. Letter R.	FV	0.75
r. 2010. Letter S.	FV	0.75
s. 2011. Letter A.	FV	0.75
t. 2011. Letter B.	FV	0.75
u. 2011. Letter N.	FV	0.75
v. 2011. Letter P.	FV	0.75
w. 2011. Letter S.	FV	0.75

96   20 Rupees   **VF   UNC**

2006-. Red-orange on multicolor underprint. Mahatma Gandhi at right. Back: Coconut trees. 147x63mm.

a. 2006. Signature Y. V. Reddy.	FV	1.50
b. 2007.	FV	1.50
c. 2008.	FV	1.50
d. 2009. Signature D. Subarao.	FV	1.00
e. 2009. Letter E.	FV	1.00
f. 2009. Letter R.	FV	1.00
g. 2010	FV	1.00
h. 2010. Letter E.	FV	1.00
i. 2010. Letter R.	FV	1.00
j. 2011.	FV	1.00
k. 2011. Letter E.	FV	1.00
l. 2011. Letter F.	FV	1.00
m. 2011. Letter R.	FV	1.00
n. 2012.	FV	1.00
o. 2012. Letter E.	FV	1.00
p. 2012. Letter F.	FV	1.00
q. 2012. Letter R.	FV	1.00

97   50 Rupees   **VF   UNC**

2005-2011. Black and purple on multicolor underprint. Mahatma Gandhi at right. Back: Parliament house at left center. 147x73mm.

a. 2005. Signature Y. V. Reddy.	FV	2.50
b. 2006.	FV	2.00
c. 2007.	FV	2.00
d. 2008.	FV	1.50
e. 2008. Letter E.	FV	1.50
f. 2009. Signature D. Subarao.	FV	1.50
g. 2009. Letter E.	FV	1.50
h. 2009. Letter R.	FV	1.50
i. 2010.	FV	1.50
j. 2010. Letter E.	FV	1.50
k. 2010. Letter L.	FV	1.50
l. 2010. Letter R.	FV	1.50
m. 2011.	FV	1.50
n. 2011. Letter L.	FV	1.50
o. 2011. Letter R.	FV	1.50
p. 2012.	FV	1.50
q. 2012. Letter L.	FV	1.50
r. 2012. Letter R.	FV	1.50

98   100 Rupees   **VF   UNC**

2005-. Black, purple and dark olive-green on pale blue-green and multicolor underprint. Mahatma Gandhi at right. Back: Himalaya mountains at left center. 157x73mm.

a. 2005. Signature Y. V. Reddy.	FV	5.00
b. 2006.	FV	5.00
c. 2007.	FV	3.50
d. 2008.	FV	3.50
e. 2009. Signature D. Subarao.	FV	3.00
f. 2009. Letter F.	FV	3.00
g. 2009. Letter R.	FV	2.75

		VF	UNC
h. 2010.		FV	2.75
i. 2010. Letter F.		FV	2.75
j. 2010. Letter R.		FV	2.75
k. 2011.		FV	2.75
l. 2011. Letter F.		FV	2.75
m. 2011. Letter L.		FV	2.75
n. 2011. Letter R.		FV	2.75

99   500 Rupees

2006-. Multicolor. Mahatma Gandhi at right. Back: Gandhi leading followers. 167x73mm.

	VF	UNC
a. 2006.	FV	20.00
b. 2007.	FV	20.00
c. 2008. Letter R.	FV	17.50
d. 2009.	FV	17.50
e. 2010. Letter R.	FV	17.50

100   1000 Rupees

2006-10. Pink and grey. Mahatma Gandhi at right. Back: Allegory of Indian economy. 177x73mm.

	VF	UNC
a. 2006.	FV	40.00
b. 2007.	FV	35.00
c. 2008.	FV	30.00
d. 2009. Letter L.	FV	30.00
e. 2009. Letter R.	FV	30.00
f. 2010.	FV	30.00
g. 2010. Letter L.	FV	30.00

2011 Issue, New Rupee Symbol

101   5 Rupees

	VF	UNC
2011. Green-orange on multicolor underprint. Mahatma Gandhi at right. Back: Farmer plowing with tractor at center.	FV	2.50

102   10 Rupees

2011-. Pale brown-violet on multicolor underprint. Mahatma Gandhi at right. Back: Tiger, rhino and elephant. 137x63mm.

	VF	UNC
a. 2010. Letter A.	FV	0.75
b. 2011.	FV	0.75
c. 2011. Letter R.	FV	0.75
d. 2012.	FV	0.75
e. 2012. Letter L.	FV	0.75
f. 2012. Letter P.	FV	0.75
g. 2013.	FV	0.75
h. 2014.	FV	0.75

103   20 Rupees

2012-. Orange and red brown on multicolor underprint. Mahatma Gandhi at right. Back: Landscape with coconut trees. 147x63mm.

	VF	UNC
a. 2012.	FV	1.25
b. 2012. Letter R.	FV	1.25
c. 2013.	FV	1.25
d. 2014.	FV	1.25

104   50 Rupees

Lilac and purple on yellow and multicolor udnerprint. Mahatma Gandhi at right. Back: Parliament house. 147x73mm.

	VF	UNC
a. 2012.	FV	2.00
b. 2013.	FV	2.00
c. 2014.	FV	2.00

105   100 Rupees

2011-. Black, purple and dark olive-green on pale blue-green and multicolor underprint. Mahatma Gandhi at right. Back: Himalaya mountains at left center. Watermark: Mahatma Gandhi. 157x73mm.

		VF	UNC
a. 2011.		FV	3.50
b. 2011. Letter R.		FV	3.50
c. 2012.		FV	3.50
d. 2012. Letter L.		FV	3.50
e. 2012. Letter R.		FV	3.50
f. 2014.		FV	3.50

106   500 Rupees

2011-. Brown on multicolor underprint. Mahatma Gandhi at right. Back: Gandhi leading folowers. Watermark: Mahatma Gandhi. 167x73mm.

		VF	UNC
a. 2012.		FV	17.50
b. 2012. Letter R.		FV	17.50
c. 2014.		FV	17.50
d. 2015. Letter R.		FV	17.50

107   1000 Rupees

2011-. Slate black on multicolor underprint. Mahatma Gandhi at right. Back: Allegory of the development of the Indian economy. Watermark: Mahatma Gandhi 177x73mm.

		VF	UNC
a. 2011.		FV	30.00

2015 Issue

108   1 Rupee

2015. Pink and green. Coin with Asoka column at upper right. New rupee sign. Inset letter L. Signature of finance secretary, not the governor of the Reserve Bank of India. Back: Offshore oil drilling platform and reverse of coin with date.

	VF	UNC
	FV	1.00

The Republic of Indonesia, the world's largest archipelago, extends for more than 4,827 km. along the equator from the mainland of southeast Asia to Australia. The 13,667 islands comprising the archipelago have a combined area of 1,919,440 sq. km. and a population of 237.5 million, including East Timor. Capital: Jakarta. Petroleum, timber, rubber and coffee are exported.The Dutch began to colonize Indonesia in the early 17th century; the islands were occupied by Japan from 1942 to 1945. Indonesia declared its independence after Japan's surrender, but it required four years of intermittent negotiations, recurring hostilities, and UN mediation before the Netherlands agreed to relinquish its colony. Indonesia is the world's largest archipelagic state and home to the world's largest Muslim population. Current issues include: alleviating poverty, preventing terrorism, consolidating democracy after four decades of authoritarianism, implementing financial sector reforms, stemming corruption, holding the military and police accountable for human rights violations, and controlling avian influenza. In 2005, Indonesia reached a historic peace agreement with armed separatists in Aceh, which led to democratic elections in December 2006. Indonesia continues to face a low intensity separatist movement in Papua.

MONETARY SYSTEM:
1 Rupiah = 100 Sen, 1945-

REPUBLIC
Republik Indonesia
1961 Issue

78   1 Rupiah

1961. Dark green on orange underprint. Rice field workers at left. Back: Farm produce.

	VF	UNC
	0.25	0.75

79   2 1/2 Rupiah

1961. Black, dark blue and brown on blue-green underprint. Corn field work at left.

	VF	UNC
	0.25	0.75

1961 Borneo Issue

79A   1 Rupiah

1961. Green on orange underprint. President Sukarno at left. Back: Javanese dancers at right.

	VF	UNC
	4.00	10.00

79B   2 1/2 Rupiah

1961. Blue on gray-brown underprint. President Sukarno at left. Back: Javanese dancers at right.

	VF	UNC
	4.00	10.00

1964 Issue (1960 dated)

80	1 Rupiah		VF	UNC
	1964. Black, red and brown. President Sukarno at left. Back: Javanese dancer at right. Watermark: Arms at center.			
	a.	Imprint: *Pertjetakan Kebajoran* at bottom center on face.	1.00	3.00
	b.	Without imprint.	2.00	6.00
	c.	Imprint: *PN Pertjetakan Kebajoran.*	4.00	10.00

81	2 1/2 Rupiah		VF	UNC
	1964. Black, blue and brown. President Sukarno at left. Watermark: Arms at center.			
	a.	Imprint like #80a.	2.50	7.50
	b.	Without imprint.	3.00	8.00

82	5 Rupiah		VF	UNC
	1960. Lilac on yellow underprint. President Sukarno at left. Back: Female dancer at right.			
	a.	Watermark: Sukarno.	1.50	5.00
	b.	Watermark: Water buffalo.	0.60	6.00

Bank Indonesia

1960 Dated (1964) Issue

83	10 Rupiah	VF	UNC
	1960. Green on light blue underprint. President Sukarno at left. Back: Two female dancers. Watermark: Sukarno.	2.00	6.50

84	25 Rupiah		VF	UNC
	1960. Green on yellow underprint. President Sukarno at left. Back: Female dancer. Watermark: Sukarno.			
	a.	Printer: TDLR. Watermark: Sukarno. 3 Letter varieties.	4.00	10.00
	b.	Printer: Pertjetakan. Watermark: Water buffalo.	4.00	10.00

85	50 Rupiah		VF	UNC
	1960. Dark blue on light blue underprint. President Sukarno at left. Back: Female dancer and two men.			
	a.	Printer: TDLR. Watermark: Sukarno. 3 Letter varieties.	8.00	20.00
	b.	Printer: Pertjetakan. Watermark: Water buffalo.	4.50	12.50

86	100 Rupiah		VF	UNC
	1960. Red-brown. President Sukarno at left. Back: Batak Man and woman dancer.			
	a.	Printer: Pertjetakan. Watermark: Sukarno.	10.00	22.50
	b.	Watermark: Water buffalo. Requires confirmation.	—	—

87	500 Rupiah		VF	UNC
	1960. Black on green underprint. President Sukarno at left. Back: Two Javanese dancers.			
	a.	Printer: TDLR. Watermark: Sukarno. 3 Letter varieties.	15.00	75.00
	b.	Printer: Pertjetakan. Watermark: Sukarno.	15.00	75.00
	c.	Printer like b. Watermark: Water buffalo.	15.00	75.00
	d.	Printer like b. Watermark: Arms.	20.00	80.00
	e.	Specimen. As a.	—	—

88	1000 Rupiah		VF	UNC
	1960. Dark green on yellow. President Sukarno at left. Back: Two Javanese dancers.			
	a.	Printer: TDLR. Watermark: Sukarno. 3 Letter varieties.	60.00	175
	b.	Printer: Pertjetakan. Watermark: Water buffalo.	40.00	125

88A	5000 Rupiah		VF	UNC
	1960. Back: Female dancer at right. Printer: TDLR.			
	p.	Uniface back proof.	—	—

1963 Issue

89   10 Rupiah   **VF   UNC**
1963. Pale blue and brown on multicolor underprint. Balinese wood carver at left.   0.50   1.50
Back: Balinese houses at center, mythical figure at right. Watermark: Water buffalo.

1964 Issue

90   1 Sen   **VF   UNC**
1964. Green-blue and brown. Peasant with straw hat at right.
    a. Issued note.   0.05   0.10
    s. Specimen. Serial # prefix X.   —   15.00

 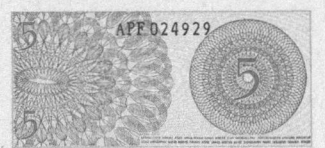

91   5 Sen   **VF   UNC**
1964. Lilac-brown. Female volunteer in uniform at right.
    a. Issued note.   0.05   0.10
    s. Specimen. Serial # prefix X.   —   15.00

92   10 Sen   **VF   UNC**
1964. Dark blue on yellow-green underprint. Female volunteer in uniform at right.
    a. Issued note.   0.05   0.10
    s. Specimen. Serial # prefix X.   —   15.00

93   25 Sen   **VF   UNC**
1964. Red on yellow-green underprint. A volunteer man in uniform at right.
    a. Issued note.   0.05   0.15
    s. Specimen. Serial # prefix X.   —   15.00

94   50 Sen   **VF   UNC**
1964. Purple and red. A volunteer man in uniform at right.
    a. Issued note.   0.10   0.25
    s. Specimen. Serial # prefix X.   —   15.00

95   25 Rupiah   **VF   UNC**
1964. Green on light brown underprint. Batak woman weaver at left, printed arms
in brown at right. Back: Batak house at center.
    a. Issued note.   0.50   2.00
    s. Specimen. Serial # prefix X.   —   15.00

96   50 Rupiah   **VF   UNC**
1964. Black-green on aqua underprint. Timor woman spinner at left, printed arms   0.50   1.50
in pale green at right. Back: Rice barns at center.

97   100 Rupiah   **VF   UNC**
1964. Red on light tan underprint. Rubber tapper at left. Back: Kalimantan house
at center. Watermark: Water buffalo.
    a. Printer's name: *P. T. Pertjetakan Kebajoran Imp.* 16mm. long at right on   2.00   6.00
        back. 2 Serial # prefix letter type varieties.
    b. Printer's name: *PN Pertjetakan Kebajoran Imp.* 22mm. long at right on back.   1.25   4.00

98   100 Rupiah
1964. Blue on light tan underprint. Rubber tapper at left. Back: Kalimantan house at center. Printer's name: *PN Pertjetakan Kebajoran Imp.* 22mm long at right. Watermark: Water buffalo.

VF UNC
1.50 5.00

99   10,000 Rupiah
1964. Red and dark brown on multicolor underprint. Two fishermen at left. Back: Floating houses on Barito river at center. Watermark: Water buffalo.

VF UNC
5.00 20.00

100   10,000 Rupiah
1964. Green. Two fishermen at left. Back: Floating houses at center. Watermark: Water buffalo.

VF UNC
3.00 10.00

101   10,000 Rupiah
1964. Green. Two fishermen at left. Back: Floating houses at center, with printed arms in pale green at right. Watermark: Row of arms.
 a. Watermark in paper at center.
 b. Watermark in paper at left and right.

VF UNC
10.00 25.00
10.00 25.00

1968 Issue

102   1 Rupiah
1968. Light red on light blue and purple underprint. General Sudirman at left. Arms at right. Back: Woman collecting copra at left. Watermark: Arms at center.
 a. Issued note.
 s. Specimen. Serial # prefix *X.*

VF UNC
0.75 2.25
— 15.00

103   2 1/2 Rupiah
1968. Dark blue on light green underprint. General Sudirman at left. Arms at right. Back: Woman gathering paddy rice stalks at left. Watermark: Arms at center.
 a. Issued note.
 s. Specimen. Serial # prefix *X.*

VF UNC
0.75 2.25
— 15.00

104   5 Rupiah
1968. Pale purple on multicolor underprint. General Sudirman at left. Back: Jatiluhur Dam under construction. Watermark: Arms at right upper center.
 a. Issued note.
 s. Specimen. Serial # prefix *X.*

VF UNC
1.50 4.50
— 15.00

105   10 Rupiah
1968. Green on multicolor underprint. General Sudirman at left. Back: Oil refinery. Watermark: Arms at upper right center.
 a. Issued note.
 s. Specimen. Serial # prefix *X.*

VF UNC
1.00 3.00
— 15.00

106   25 Rupiah
1968. Dark green on light brown and multicolor underprint. General Sudirman at left. Back: Ampera lift bridge over Musi River at center right. Watermark: Arms at right upper center.
 a. Issued note.
 s. Specimen. Serial # prefix *X.*

VF UNC
1.50 4.50
— 15.00

107 50 Rupiah VF UNC

1968. Purple and dark blue on multicolor underprint. General Sudirman at left. Back: Airplanes in repair hangar at center right. Watermark: Arms at right upper center.

  a. Issued note. 2.50 7.50

  s. Specimen. — 15.00

108 100 Rupiah VF UNC

1968. Deep red on multicolor underprint. General Sudirman at left. Back: Coal mining transport facility at the port of Tanjung Priok at center right. Watermark: Arms at right upper center.

  a. Issued note. 1.50 5.00

  s. Specimen. Serial # prefix X. — 15.00

109 500 Rupiah VF UNC

1968. Black and dark green on multicolor underprint. General Sudirman at left. Back: Yarn spinning in cotton mill. Watermark: Arms at right upper center.

  a. Issued note. 2.50 7.50

  s. Specimen. — 15.00

110 1000 Rupiah VF UNC

1968. Dark orange and black on multicolor underprint. General Sudirman at left. Back: P.T. Pusri fertilizer plant at center right. Watermark: Arms at right upper center.

  a. Issued note. 3.00 12.00

  s. Specimen. Serial # prefix X. — 15.00

Deceptive forgeries of #110 exist.

111 5000 Rupiah VF UNC

1968. Blue-green on multicolor underprint. General Sudirman at left. Two serial # varieties. Back: Tonasa cememt plant at center right. Watermark: Prince Diponegoro.

  a. Issued note. 22.50 70.00

  s1. Specimen. Serial # prefix X. — 80.00

  s2. Specimen. Serial # prefix DA. — 150

112 10,000 Rupiah VF UNC

1968. Red-brown and dark brown on multicolor underprint. General Sudirman at left. Two serial # varieties. Back: Tin mininig facility in Bangla at center right. Watermark: Prince Diponegoro.

  a. Issued note. 20.00 60.00

  s1. Specimen. Serial # prefix X. — 70.00

  s2. Specimen. Serial # prefix DA. — 150

1975; ND Issue

112A 100 Rupiah VF UNC

ND. (Not issued.) Red on multicolor underprint. Prince Diponegoro at left. Back: Mountain scene at left center. Watermark: Prince Diponegoro.

  a. Normal serial #. — —

  s. Specimen. — —

112B 500 Rupiah VF UNC

ND. (Not issued.) Green on multicolor underprint. Prince Diponegoro at left. Back: Terraced rice fields in Sianok Gorge. Watermark: Prince Diponegoro.

  a. Normal serial #. — —

  s. Specimen. — —

113 1000 Rupiah

VF UNC

ND; 1975. . Blue-green and blue on multicolor underprint. Prince Diponegoro at
left. Back: Farmer plowing in terraced rice fields.

a. 1975. watermark: Majapahit statue.	2.00	7.50
s1. ND. Specimen. (Not issued.)	—	—
s2. 1975. Specimen. Serial # prefix X.	—	9.00

113A 5000 Rupiah

VF UNC

ND. (Not issued.) Brown on multicolor underprint. Prince Diponegoro at right.
Back: Three sailing ships. Watermark: Prince Diponegoro.

a. Normal serial #.	—	—
s. Specimen.	—	—

114 5000 Rupiah

VF UNC

1975. Brown and red-brown on multicolor underprint. Fisherman with net at right.
Back: Three sailing ships. Watermark: Tjut Njak Din.

a. Issued note.	7.50	25.00
s. Specimen. Serial # prefix X.	—	—

114A 10,000 Rupiah

VF UNC

ND. (Not issued.) Green and red on multicolor underprint. Prince Diponegoro at
right. Back: Peasants at center. Watermark: Prince Diponegoro.

a. Normal serial #.	—	—
s. Specimen.	—	—

115 10,000 Rupiah

VF UNC

1975. Brown, red and multicolor. Stone relief at BorobudurTemple. Back: Large 25.00 75.00
mask from Bali at left. Watermark: General Soedirman.

1977 Issue

116 100 Rupiah

VF UNC

1977. Red on multicolor underprint. Javanese Rhinoceros at left. Back: Javanese 0.50 2.00
Rhinoceros in jungle scene at center. Watermark: Arms.

117 500 Rupiah

VF UNC

1977. Green on pink and multicolor underprint. Woman with orchids at left. Back: 1.00 4.00
Bank of Indonesia at center. Watermark: Bank of Indonesia.

1979 Issue

118 **10,000 Rupiah**   **VF** **UNC**
1979. Purple on multicolor underprint. Javanese Gamelan Orchestra at center.   9.00 25.00
Back: Prambanan Temple. Watermark: Dr. Soetomo.

1980 Issue

119 **1000 Rupiah**   **VF** **UNC**
1980. Dark blue on multicolor underprint. Dr. Soetomo at center right. Back: 1.00   3.50
Mountain scene in Sianok Valley. Watermark: Sultan Hasanudin.

120 **5000 Rupiah**   **VF** **UNC**
1980. Brown on multicolor underprint. Diamond cutter at center. Back: Three
Torajan houses from Celebes at center.
    a. Watermark: D. Sartika.   6.00 20.00
    p. Proof. Watermark: Prince Diponegoro.   —   —

1982 Issue

121 **500 Rupiah**   **VF** **UNC**
1982. Dark green on multicolor underprint. Man standing by Amorphophallus.   0.75   2.50
Titanum giant flower at left. Back: Bank of Indonesia. Watermark: General A. Yani.

1984-88 Issue

122 **100 Rupiah**   **VF** **UNC**
1984. Red on multicolor underprint. Goura Victoria (Crowned pigeon) at left. Back:
Asahan Dam. Watermark: Arms.
    a. Engraved.   0.30   1.25
    b. Litho.   0.25   0.75
    s. As a. Specimen. Serial # prefix X.   — 15.00

123 **500 Rupiah**   **VF** **UNC**
1988. Brown and dark green on multicolor underprint. Timorese stag at left. Back:
Bank of Indonesia Cirebon branch at right. Watermark: General A. Yani.
    a. Issued note.   0.50   1.50
    s. Specimen.   — 15.00

124 **1000 Rupiah**   **VF** **UNC**
1987. Blue-black on multicolor underprint. Raja Sisingamangaraja XII at center,
arms at left. Back: Yogyakarta Court at center. Watermark: Sultan Hasanuddin.
    a. Issued note.   1.00   2.00
    s. Specimen.   — 15.00

125 **5000 Rupiah**   **VF** **UNC**
1986. Dark brown on multicolor underprint. Teuku Umar at center. Back: Minaret
of Kudus mosque at right. Watermark: C. Martha Tijahahu.
    a. Issued note.   3.50 10.00
    s. Specimen.   — 15.00

126 10,000 Rupiah   **VF UNC**

1985. Purple on multicolor underprint. R. A. Kartini at left. Prambanan Temple in background. Back: Female graduate at center right. Watermark: Dr. T. Mangoen-koesoemo.

	VF	UNC
a. Issued note.	6.00	15.00
s. Specimen.	—	15.00

1992 Issue

#127-129 second date appears after imprint.

127 100 Rupiah   **VF UNC**

1992-2000. UV: fibers fluoresce yellow and red. Pale red on orange and multicolor underprint. Sailboat *Pinisi* at left. Arms at upper right area. Back: Volcano *Anak Krakatau* at right. Watermark: Ki Hajar Dewantara. Printer: Perum Percetakan Uang.

	VF	UNC
a. 1992.	FV	0.75
b. 1992/1993.	FV	0.50
c. 1992/1994.	FV	0.50
d. 1992/1995.	FV	0.45
e. 1992/1996.	FV	0.25
f. 1992/1997.	FV	0.25
g. 1992/1999.	FV	0.25
h. 1992/2000.	FV	0.20

128 500 Rupiah   **VF UNC**

1992-99. UV: fibers fluoresce yellow and red. Brown and green on multicolor underprint. Orangutan resting on limb at left. Arms at upper right area. Back: Native huts at E. Kalimantan at right. Watermark: H. O. S. Tjokroaminoto. Printer: Perum Percetakan Uang.

	VF	UNC
a. 1992.	FV	1.25
b. 1992/1993.	FV	1.00
c. 1992/1994.	FV	1.00
d. 1992/1995.	FV	1.00
e. 1992/1996.	FV	0.50
f. 1992/1997.	FV	0.40
g. 1992/1998.	FV	0.30
h. 1992/1999.	FV	0.20

129 1000 Rupiah   **VF UNC**

1992-2000. UV: fibers fluoresce yellow and red. Back lower left serial # orange. Deep blue on light blue and multicolor underprint. Aerial view of Lake Toba at left center. Arms at upper right area. Back: Stone jumping attraction on Nias Island at center. Watermark: Tjut Njak Meutia. Printer: Perum Percetakan Uang.

	VF	UNC
a. 1992.	FV	2.00
b. 1992/1993.	FV	1.75
c. 1992/1994.	FV	1.75
d. 1992/1995.	FV	1.50
e. 1992/1996.	FV	1.00
f. 1992/1997.	FV	0.75
g. 1992/1998.	FV	0.75
h. 1992/1999.	FV	0.50
i. 1992/2000.	FV	0.50

130 5000 Rupiah   **VF UNC**

1992-2001. Black, brown and dark brown on multicolor underprint. Sasando musical instrument and Rote Island tapestry at center. Arms at upper right area. Back: Volcano with three-color Lake Kelimutu at center. Watermark: Tjut Njak Din. Printer: Perum Percetakan Uang.

	VF	UNC
a. 1992.	FV	7.50
b. 1992/1993.	FV	7.00
c. 1992/1994.	FV	7.00
d. 1992/1995.	FV	6.50
e. 1992/1996.	FV	3.50
f. 1992/1997.	FV	2.50
g. 1992/1998.	FV	1.50
h. 1992/1999.	FV	1.25
i. 1992/2000.	FV	1.25
j. 1999/2001.	FV	1.25
s. Specimen.	—	—

131 10,000 Rupiah   **VF UNC**

1992-98. Purple and red on multicolor underprint. Sri Sultan Hamengku Buwono IX at left, girl scouts camping at center right. Arms at upper right area. Back: Borobudur Temple on hillside. Watermark: W. R. Soepratman. Printer: Perum Percetakan Uang.

	VF	UNC
a. 1992.	6.00	12.50
b. 1992/1993.	6.00	12.00
c. 1992/1994.	5.00	12.00
d. 1992/1995.	5.00	10.00
e. 1992/1996.	3.00	6.00
f. 1992/1997.	2.00	4.00
g. 1992/1998 & letter prefix.	7.50	15.00
s. Specimen.	—	—

132   20,000 Rupiah

1992-95. Black, dark grayish green and red on multicolor underprint. Red bird of paradise at center. Arms at upper right area. Back: Cloves flower at center, map of Indonesian Archipelago at right. Watermark: K. H. Dewantara. Printer: Perum Percetakan Uang.

	VF	UNC
a. 1992.	10.00	22.50
b. 1992/1993.	10.00	20.00
c. 1992/1994.	8.00	17.50
d. 1992/1995.	12.50	25.00
s. Specimen.	—	—

1993 Commemorative Issues

#133 and 134, 25 Years of Development

133   50,000 Rupiah

1993-94. Greenish blue, tan and gray on multicolor underprint. President Soeharto at left center surrounded by various scenes of development activities. Anti-counterfeiting design at right. Back: Jet plane over Soekarno-Hatta International Airport at center. Watermark: W. R. Soepratman.

	VF	UNC
a. 1993.	20.00	40.00
b. 1993/1994.	17.50	35.00

134   50,000 Rupiah

1993. Polymer plastic. Pale gray. President Soeharto at left center, surrounded by various scenes of development activities. President Soeharto in OVD at right. Back: Jet plane over Soekarno-Hatta International Airport at center.

	VF	UNC
a. Note alone.	20.00	40.00
b. Included in souvenir folder.	—	50.00

1995 Issue

135   20,000 Rupiah

1995-98. Black, dark grayish green and red on multicolor underprint. Red bird of paradise at center, arms at upper right area. Back: Cloves flower at center, map of Indonesian Archipelago at right. Watermark: K. H. Dewantara.

	VF	UNC
a. 1995.	5.00	15.00
b. 1995/1996.	4.00	9.00
c. 1995/1997.	3.00	8.00
d. 1995/1998.	3.00	8.00

136   50,000 Rupiah

1995-98. Greenish blue, tan and gray on multicolor underprint. President Soeharto at left center, surrounded by various scenes of development activities. Segmented foil over security thread. Back: Jet plane over Soekarno-Hatta International Airport at center. Watermark: W. R. Soepratman.

	VF	UNC
a. 1995.	7.00	42.50
b. 1995/1996.	5.00	25.00
c. 1995/1997.	5.00	15.00
d. 1995/1998.	5.00	15.00

1998-99 Issue

137   10,000 Rupiah

1998-2005. Deep brownish purple and black on multicolor underprint. Tjut Njak Dhien at right, arms at upper right, bank monogram at lower right. Back: Segara Anak Volcanic Lake at center right. Watermark: W. R. Soepratman. Printer: Perum Peruri.

	VF	UNC
a. 1998.	FV	3.25
b. 1998/1999.	FV	3.25
c. 1998/2000.	FV	3.25
d. 1998/2001.	FV	3.25
e. 1998/2002.	FV	3.25
f. 1998/2003.	FV	3.25
g. 1998/2004.	FV	3.25
h. 1998/2005.	FV	3.25

138   20,000 Rupiah

1998-2005. Deep green and dark brown on multicolor underprint. Ki Hadjar Dewantara at center, arms at upper left, Ganesha at left, bank monogram at right. Back: Classroom at center right. Watermark: Ki Hadjar Dewantara. Printer: Perum Peruri.

	VF	UNC
a. 1998.	FV	6.00
b. 1998/1999.	FV	5.00
c. 1998/2000.	FV	5.00
d. 1998/2001.	FV	5.00
e. 1998/2002.	FV	5.00
f. 1998/2003.	FV	5.00
g. 1998/2004.	FV	5.00

139 50,000 Rupiah

		VF	UNC
1999-2007. Grayish brown on multicolor underprint. W. R. Soepratman at center. Back: Students guarded by two soldiers, hoisting flag on Independence Day.

	VF	UNC
a. 1999.	FV	22.50
b. 1999/2000.	FV	20.00
c. 1999/2001.	FV	20.00
d. 1999/2002.	FV	20.00
e. 1999/2003.	FV	20.00
f. 1999/2004.	FV	20.00
g. 1999/2005.	FV	20.00
h. 1999/2007.	FV	20.00

140 100,000 Rupiah

	VF	UNC
1999. Polymer plastic. Lilac brown, green and orange. Soekarno and Hatta at center. Back: Peoples Consultative Assembly and Parliament building. Printer. Note Printing, Australia and Thailand.	FV	30.00

2000 Issue

141 1000 Rupiah

	VF	UNC

2000-. UV: upper right serial # fluoresces orange. Blue-green and red on multicolor underprint. Kapitan Pattimura at center. Back: Fishing boat and volcano. Watermark: Tjut Njak Dien. 141x65mm.

	VF	UNC
a. 2000.	FV	0.60
b. 2000/2001.	FV	0.50
c. 2000/2002.	FV	0.50
d. 2000/2003.	FV	0.50
e. 2000/2004.	FV	2.50
f. 2000/2005.	FV	0.50
g. 2000/2006.	FV	0.50
h. 2000/2007.	FV	0.50
i. 2000/2008.	FV	0.50
j. 2000/2009.	FV	0.50
k. 2000/2011.	FV	0.50
l. 2000/2012.	FV	0.50

2001 Issue

142 5000 Rupiah

	VF	UNC

2001-. Brown and green on multicolor underprint. Tuanku Imam Bonjol at center. Back: Western Sumartran female at hand loom at center. Watermark: Tjut Njak Meutia. 143x65mm.

	VF	UNC
a. 2001.	FV	2.50
b. 2001/2002.	FV	2.50
c. 2001/2003.	FV	2.50
d. 2001/2004.	FV	2.00
e. 2001/2005.	FV	2.00
f. 2001/2006.	FV	2.00
g. 2001/2007.	FV	1.50
h. 2001/2008.	FV	1.50
i. 2001/2009.	FV	1.50
j. 2001/2010.	FV	1.50
k. 2001/2011.	FV	1.50
l. 2001/2012.	FV	1.50
m. 2001/2013.	FV	1.50

143 10,000 Rupiah

	VF	UNC

2005-. Violet on multicolor underprint. Sultan Mahmud Badaruddin II Back: Rumah Limab, Palembang. 143x65mm.

	VF	UNC
a. 2005.	FV	2.50
b. 2005/2006.	FV	2.50
c. 2005/2007.	FV	2.25
d. 2005/2008.	FV	2.25

144 20,000 Rupiah

	VF	UNC

2004-. Blue-green on multicolor underprint. Oto Iskandar Dinata at center. Back: Tea pickers, West Java. 149x65mm.

	VF	UNC
a. 2004.	FV	8.00
b. 2004/2005.	FV	5.50
c. 2004/2006.	FV	5.50
d. 2004/2007.	FV	5.00
e. 2004/2008.	FV	5.00
f. 2004/2009.	FV	4.00
g. 2004/2011.	FV	4.00
h. 2004/2012.	FV	0.00

145 50,000 Rupiah

VF UNC

2005-. Dark blue on multicolor underprint. I Gusti Ngurah Rai at center. Back: Beratan Lake, Bali. 149x65mm.

a. 2005.	FV	15.00
b. 2005/2007.	FV	15.00

146 100,000 Rupiah

VF UNC

2004-. Similar to #140 but paper. Red-brown on multicolor underprint. Soekarno and Hatta at center. Back: Parliament building. 151x65mm.

a. 2004.	FV	20.00
b. 2004/2005.	FV	20.00
c. 2004/2007.	FV	17.50
d. 2004/2008.	FV	17.50
e. 2004/2009.	FV	17.50
f. 2004/2010.	FV	17.50
g. 2004/2011.	FV	17.50
h. 2004/2013.	FV	17.50

#147 not assigned.

2009-2011 Issue

148 2000 Rupiah

VF UNC

2009-. Gray-brown on multicolor underprint. Prince Antasari at center. Back: Traditional Dayak dance at center. 140x65mm.

a. 2009/2009.	FV	1.00
b. 2009/2011.	FV	1.00
c. 2009/2012.	FV	1.00
d. 2009/2013.	FV	1.00
e. 2009/2015.	FV	1.00

149 5000 Rupiah

VF UNC

Expected new issue.

— —

150 10,000 Rupiah

VF UNC

2010-. Purple on multicolor underprint. Sultan Mahmud Badaruddin II at center. Tactile marks added at left edge. Back: Limas House in Palembang. 143x65mm.

a. 2005/2010.	FV	3.00
b. 2005/2011.	FV	2.00
c. 2005/2012.	FV	2.00
d. 2005/2013. Signature at right is series of up and down strokes, large to small.	FV	2.00
e. 2005/2013. Signature at right starts and end with a horizontal line.	FV	2.00
f. 2005/2014.	FV	2.00
f. 2005/2014.	FV	2.00
g. 2005/2015.	FV	2.00

151 20,000 Rupiah

VF UNC

2011-. Light and dark green on blue and multicolor underprint. Oto Iskandar Di Nata at center. Tactile squares at left end, omcron dots at right. Back: Tea picker, West Java. 149x65mm.

a. 2004/2011.	FV	5.50
b. 2004/2012.	FV	5.50
c. 2004/2013.	FV	5.50
d. 2004/2014.	FV	5.50
e. 2004/2015.	FV	5.50

152 50,000 Rupiah

VF UNC

2011-. Light and dark blue on multicolor underprint. I Gusti Ngurah Ral at center. Tactile triangles added at left edge, omcron dots at right. Back: Beratan Lake, Bali. 149x65mm.

a. 2005/2009.	FV	15.00
b. 2005/2011.	FV	15.00
c. 2005/2012.	FV	15.00
d. 2005/2013.	FV	15.00
e. 2005/2014.	FV	15.00
f. 2005/2015.	FV	15.00

153 100,000 Rupiah

VF UNC

2011-. Red on multicolor underprint. Soekarno and M. Hatta at center. Tactile circles at left edge, omcron dots at right. BANK INDONESIA at lower left. Back: Parliament building. 151x65mm.

a. 2004/2011.	FV	17.50
b. 2004/2012.	FV	17.50
c. 2004/2013.	FV	17.50
d. 2004/2014.	FV	17.50
e. TE 2014.	FV	17.50

The Islamic Republic of Iran, located between the Caspian Sea and the Persian Gulf in southwestern Asia, has an area of 1,648,000 sq. km. and a population of 65.87 million. Capital: Tehran. Although predominantly an agricultural state, Iran depends heavily on oil for foreign exchange. Crude oil, carpets and agricultural products are exported.

Known as Persia until 1935, Iran became an Islamic republic in 1979 after the ruling monarchy was overthrown and the shah was forced into exile. Conservative clerical forces established a theocratic system of government with ultimate political authority vested in a learned religious scholar referred to commonly as the Supreme Leader who, according to the constitution, is accountable only to the Assembly of Experts. US-Iranian relations have been strained since a group of Iranian students seized the US Embassy in Tehran on 4 November 1979 and held it until 20 January 1981. During 1980-88, Iran fought a bloody, indecisive war with Iraq that eventually expanded into the Persian Gulf and led to clashes between US Navy and Iranian military forces between 1987 and 1988. Iran has been designated a state sponsor of terrorism for its activities in Lebanon and elsewhere in the world and remains subject to US and UN economic sanctions and export controls because of its continued involvement in terrorism and conventional weapons proliferation. Following the election of reformer Hojjat ol-Eslam Mohammad Khatami as president in 1997 and similarly a reformer Majles (parliament) in 2000, a campaign to foster political reform in response to popular dissatisfaction was initiated. The movement floundered as conservative politicians, through the control of unelected institutions, prevented reform measures from being enacted and increased repressive measures. Starting with nationwide municipal elections in 2003 and continuing through Majles elections in 2004, conservatives reestablished control over Iran's elected government institutions, which culminated with the August 2005 inauguration of hardliner Mahmud Ahmadi-Nejad as president.

RULERS:
Pahlavi Dynasty
Mohammad Reza Pahlavi, SH1320-58/1941-79AD

PRESIDENTS:
Islamic Republic of Iran
Abolhassan Bani Sadr, SH1358-60 (AD1979-Jun 81)
Muhammad Ali Rajai, SH1360 (AD-1981 Jun-Oct)
Hojjatoleslam Ali Khamene'i, SH1360-(AD1981-)

MONETARY SYSTEM:
1 Toman = 10 Rials SH1310- (1932-)

SIGNATURE AND TITLE VARIETIES
Kingdom: Mohammad Reza Pahlavi

	GENERAL DIRECTOR	MINISTER OF FINANCE
7	Ebrahim Kashani	Abholbagi Shoaii
8	Dr. Ali Asghar Pouhomayoun	Abduhl Hossein Behnia
9	Medhi Samii	Abduhl Hossein Behnia
10	Medhi Samii	Amir Abbas Hoveyda
11	Medhi Samii	Dr. Jamishid Amouzegar
12	Khodadad Famanfarmaian	Dr. Jamishid Amouzegar
13	Abdul Ali Jahanshahi	Dr. Jamishid Amouzegar
14	Mohammad Yeganeh	Dr. Jamishid Amouzegar
	GENERAL DIRECTOR	MINISTER OF ECONOMIC AND FINANCIAL AFFAIR
15	Mohammad Yeganeh	Hushang Ansary

SIGNATURE AND TITLE VARIETIES
Kingdom: Mohammad Reza Pahlavi

16	Hassan Ali Mehran	Hushang Ansary
17	Hassan Ali Mehran	Mohammad Yeganeh

Shah Mohammad Reza Pahlavi, SH1323-58/1944-79 AD

Type V. Imperial Iranian Army (IIA) uniform. Full face. SH1337-40.

Type VI. Imperial Iranian Air Force (IIAF) uniform. Three quarter face. SH1341-44

Type VII. Imperial Iranian Army (IIA) uniform. Full face. SH1347-48.

Type VIII. Commander in Chief of Iran's Armed Forces. Three quarter face. Large portrait. MS2535 to SH1358.

Type IX. Shah Pahlavi in CinC uniform and his father Shah Reza in Imperial Iranian Army (IIA) uniform. MS2535.

KINGDOM OF IRAN
Bank Markazi Iran
1961; 1962 Issue

71   10 Rials   **VF UNC**
SH1340 (1961). Yellow security thread runs vertically. Blue on green and orange underprint. Geometric design at center. Type V portrait of Shah Pahlavi in army uniform at right. Signature 7. Back: Amir Kabir Dam near Karaj. Watermark: Young Shah Pahlavi. Printer: H&S (without imprint).   5.00 12.00

72   20 Rials   **VF UNC**
SH1340 (1961). Yellow security thread runs vertically. Dark brown on green and pink underprint. Geometric design at center. Type V portrait of Shah Pahlavi in army uniform at right. Signature 7. Back: Statue of Shah and Ramsar Hotel. Watermark: Young Shah Pahlavi. Printer: H&S (without imprint).   7.00 16.00

76 50 Rials VF UNC
SH1343 (1964). Yellow security thread. Dark green on orange and blue underprint. Ornate design at center. Type VI portrait of Shah Pahlavi in armed forces uniform at right. Signature 9. Back: Koohrang Dam and tunnel. Watermark: Young Shah Pahlavi. Printer: H&S (without imprint).
12.00 22.00

73 50 Rials VF UNC
SH1341 (1962). Yellow security thread runs vertically. Green on orange and blue underprint. Type VI portrait of Shah Pahlavi in air force uniform at right. Signature 8. Back: Koohrang Dam and tunnel. Watermark: Young Shah Pahlavi. Printer: H&S (without imprint).
a. Small date 2.5mm high. 7.00 16.00
b. Large date 4.0mm high. 9.00 18.00

77 100 Rials VF UNC
SH1342 (1963). Yellow security thread. Maroon on light green and multicolor underprint. Ornate design at center. Type VI portrait of Shah Pahlavi in armed forces uniform at right. Signature 9. Back: Oil refinery at Abadan. Watermark: Young Shah Pahlavi. Printer: H&S (without imprint).
12.00 25.00

1965 ND Issue

74 500 Rials VF UNC
SH1341 (1962). Yellow security thread runs vertically. Black on pink and multicolor underprint. Type VI portrait of Shah Pahlavi in air force uniform at center. Signature 8. Back: Winged horses. Watermark: Young Shah Pahlavi. Printer: H&S (without imprint).
110 275

78 20 Rials VF UNC
ND (1965). Yellow security thread. Dark brown on pink and green underprint. Ornate design at center. Type VI portrait of Shah Pahlavi in armed forces uniform at right. Back: Oriental hunters on horseback. Watermark: Young Shah Pahlavi. Printer: H&S (without imprint).
a. Signature 9. 3.00 7.00
b. Signature 10. 3.00 7.00

75 1000 Rials VF UNC
SH1341 (1962). Yellow security thread runs vertically. Brown on red and blue underprint. Type VI portrait of Shah Pahlavi in air force uniform at center. Signature 8. Back: Tomb of Hafez in Shiraz. Watermark: Young Shah Pahlavi. Printer: H&S (without imprint).
135 375

1963; 1964 Issue

79 50 Rials VF UNC
ND (1965). Yellow security thread. Dark green on orange and blue underprint. Ornate design at center. Type VI portrait of Shah Pahlavi in armed forces uniform at right. Back: Koohrang Dam and tunnel. Watermark: Young Shah Pahlavi. Printer: H&S (without imprint).
a. Signature 9. 8.00 20.00
b. Signature 10. 8.00 20.00

80   100 Rials

	VF	UNC
	9.00	22.00

ND (1965). Yellow security thread. Maroon on olive-green and multicolor underprint. Ornate design at center. Type VI portrait of Shah Pahlavi in armed forces uniform at right. Signature 10. Back: Oil refinery at Abadan. Watermark: Young Shah Pahlavi. Printer: H&S (without imprint).

81   200 Rials

	VF	UNC
	25.00	55.00

ND (1965). Yellow security thread. Dark blue on orange and lavender underprint. Multicolor ornate design at center. Type VI portrait of Shah Pahlavi in armed forces uniform at right. Signature 9. Back: Railroad bridge. Watermark: Young Shah Pahlavi. Printer: H&S (without imprint).

82   500 Rials

	VF	UNC
	110	260

ND (1965). Yellow security thread. Black on pink and purple underprint. Type VI portrait of Shah Pahlavi in armed forces uniform at center. Signature 9. Back: Winged horses. Watermark: Young Shah Pahlvi. Printer: H&S (without imprint.

83   1000 Rials

	VF	UNC
	125	350

ND (1965). Yellow security thread. Brown on red and blue underprint. Type VI portrait of Shah Pahlavi in armed forces uniform at center. Signature 9. Back: Tomb of Hafez at Shiraz. Watermark: Young Shah Pahlavi. Printer: H&S (without imprint).

1969 ND Issue

#84-89A are called *Dark Panel* **notes. The bank name is located on a contrasting dark ornamental panel at the top center.**

84   20 Rials

	VF	UNC
	4.00	10.00

ND (1969). Yellow security thread runs vertically. Dark brown on pink and green underprint. Ornate design at center. Type VII portrait of Shah Pahlavi in army uniform at right. Signature 11. Back: Oriental hunters on horseback. Watermark: Young Shah Pahlavi. Printer: H&S (without imprint).

85   50 Rials

	VF	UNC
a. Signature 11.	5.00	10.00
b. Signature 12.	5.00	10.00

ND (1969-71). Yellow security thread runs vertically. Green on orange and blue underprint. Ornate design at center. Type VII portrait of Shah Pahlavi in army uniform at right. Back: Koohrang Dam and tunnel. Watermark: Young Shah Pahlavi. Printer: Harrison (without imprint).

86   100 Rials

	VF	UNC
a. Signature 11.	7.00	15.00
b. Signature 12.	7.00	15.00

ND (1969-71). Yellow security thread runs vertically. Maroon on light green and multicolor underprint. Ornate design at center. Type VII portrait of Shah Pahlavi in army uniform at right. Back: Oil refinery at Abadan. Watermark: Young Shah Pahlavi. Printer: H&S (without imprint).

87   200 Rials

	VF	UNC
a. Signature 11.	15.00	35.00
b. Signature 12.	20.00	50.00

ND (1969-71). Yellow security thread runs vertically. Dark blue on orange and purple underprint. Multicolor ornate design at center. Type VII portrait of Shah Pahlavi in army uniform at right. Back: Railroad bridge. Watermark: Young Shah Pahlavi. Printer: H&S (without imprint).

88 500 Rials VF UNC
ND (1969). Black on pink and purple underprint. Ornate frame at center. Type VII 25.00 80.00
portrait of Shah Pahlavi in army uniform at center. Signature 11. Back: Winged
horses.

89 1000 Rials VF UNC
ND (1969). Brown on red and blue underprint. Ornate frame at center. Type VII 44.00 160
portrait of Shah Pahlavi in army uniform at center. Signature 11. Back: Tomb of
Hafez at Shiraz.

89A 5000 Rials VF UNC
ND (1969). Purple on red and multicolor underprint. Ornate frame at center. 1,000 2,000
Type VII portrait of Shah Pahlavi in army uniform at center. Signature 11. Back:
Golestan Palace in Tehran. Printer: Printed in Pakistan.

1971 ND Issue

#90-96 are called *Light Panel* **notes. The bank name is located on a contrasting light ornamental background panel at the top center.**

90 50 Rials VF UNC
ND (1971). Yellow security thread runs vertically. Dark green on orange and blue 4.00 10.00
underprint. Type VII portrait of Shah Pahlavi in army uniform at right. Signature 13.
Back: Koohrang Dam and tunnel. Light panel. Watermark: Young Shah Pahlavi.
Printer: H&S (without imprint).

91 100 Rials VF UNC
ND (1971-73). Yellow security thread runs vertically. Maroon on olive-green and
multicolor underprint. Ornate design at center. Type VII portrait of Shah Pahlavi in
army uniform at right. Light panel. Back: Oil refinery at Abadan. Watermark: Young
Shah Pahlavi. Printer: H&S (without imprint).
   a. Signature 11. 5.00 15.00
   b. Signature 12. 8.00 18.00
   c. Signature 13. 5.00 15.00

92 200 Rials VF UNC
ND (1971-73). Yellow security thread runs vertically. Dark blue on orange and
lavender underprint. Multicolor ornate design at center. Type VII portrait of Shah
Pahlavi in army uniform at right. Light panel. Back: Railroad bridge. Watermark:
Young Shah Pahlavi. Printer: H&S (without imprint).
   a. Signature 11. 16.00 50.00
   b. Signature 12. 20.00 60.00
   c. Signature 13. 10.00 22.50

93 500 Rials VF UNC
ND (1971-73). Black on orange, green and multicolor underprint. Ornate frame
at center. Type VII portrait of Shah Pahlavi in army uniform at center. Light panel.
Back: Winged horses. Watermark: Young Shah Pahlavi.
   a. Signature 11. 20.00 50.00
   b. Signature 12. 40.00 150
   c. Signature 13. 30.00 100

94 1000 Rials VF UNC
ND (1971-73). Brown on red, blue and multicolor underprint. Ornate frame at
center. Type VII portrait of Shah Pahlavi in army uniform at center. Light panel.
Back: Tomb of Hafez at Shiraz. Watermark: Young Shah Pahlavi.
   a. Signature 11. 60.00 200
   b. Signature 12. 50.00 150
   c. Signature 13. 40.00 125

95 5000 Rials VF UNC
ND (1971-72). Purple on red and multicolor underprint. Ornate frame at center.
Type VII portrait of Shah Pahlavi in army uniform at center. Light panel. Back:
Golestan Palace in Tehran. Watermark: Young Shah Pahlavi.
   a. Signature 12. 300 900
   b. Signature 13. 200 600

96   10,000 Rials

ND (1972-73). Dark green and brown. Ornate frame at center. Type VII portrait
of Shah Pahlavi in army uniform at center. Back: National Council of Ministries in
Tehran. Watermark: Young Shah Pahlavi.

		VF	UNC
a. Signature 11.		000	2,000
b. Signature 13.		400	1,250

1971 ND Commemorative Issue

#97 and 98, 2,500th Anniversary of the Persian Empire.

97   50 Rials

SH1350 (1971). Yellow security thread runs vertically. Green on blue, brown and
multicolor underprint. Floral design at center. Type VIII portrait of Shah Pahlavi in the
"Commander in Chief " of Iranian armed forces uniform at right. Back: Shah Pahlavi
giving land deeds to villager. Watermark: Young Shah Pahlavi. Printer: TDLR.

		VF	UNC
a. Signature 11.		7.00	15.00
b. Signature 13.		10.00	20.00

98   100 Rials

SH1350 (1971). Yellow security thread runs vertically. Maroon on orange and
multicolor underprint. Floral and multicolor geometric design . Type VIII portrait
of Shah Pahlavi in the "Commander in Chief " of Iranian armed forces uniform at
right. Signature 11. Back: Three vignettes labeled: *HEALTH, AGRICULTURE* and
EDUCATION. Watermark: Young Shah Pahlavi. Printer: TDLR.

	VF	UNC
	10.00	22.50

#99 *Renumbered*. See #101a.

1974 ND Issue

#100-107 Replacement notes: For signatures 14, 15, 16 where the prefix for regular notes is a whole
number such as 1, 2, 3 or 4, the replacemnt is 01, 02, 03 or 04. For signatures 17 and 18 where the
prefix for regular notes is a fraction, the replacement is 99/9, 98/9 or 97/9.

100   20 Rials

ND (1974-79). Yellow security thread runs vertically. Brown on orange, lilac and
multicolor underprint. Persian carpet design, shepherd and ram. Type VIII portrait
of Shah Pahlavi at right. Back: Amir Kabir Dam near Karaj. Watermark: Young
Shah Pahlavi. Printer: TDLR.

	VF	UNC
a1. Signature 16. Farsi denomination short.	3.00	7.00
a2. Signature 16. Farsi denomination long.	3.00	7.00
b. Signature 17.	5.00	10.00
c. Signature 18.	6.00	12.00

101   50 Rials

ND (1974-79). Yellow security thread runs vertically. Green on brown, blue and
multicolor underprint. Persian carpet design. Type VIII portrait of Shah Pahlavi
at right. Back: Tomb of Cyrus the Great at Pasargarde at left center. Watermark:
Young Shah Pahlavi. Printer: TDLR.

	VF	UNC
a. Yellow security thread. Signature 14.	5.00	12.00
b. Yellow security thread. Signature 15.	5.00	10.00
c. Yellow security thread. Signature 16.	5.00	10.00
d. Black security thread. Signature 17.	5.00	10.00
e. Black security thread. Signature 18.	5.00	12.00

102   100 Rials

ND (1974-79). Yellow security thread runs vertically. Maroon on orange, green and
multicolor underprint. Persian carpet design. Type VIII portrait of Shah Pahlavi
at right. Back: Pahlavi Museum at left center. Watermark: Young Shah Pahlavi.
Printer: TDLR.

	VF	UNC
a. Yellow security thread. Signature 15.	6.00	15.00
b. Yellow security thread. Signature 16.	7.00	18.00
c. Black security thread. Signature 17.	7.50	20.00
d. Black security thread. Signature 18.	7.00	18.00

103 200 Rials VF UNC

ND (1974-79). Blue on green and multicolor underprint. Persian carpet design. Type VIII portrait of Shah Pahlavi at right. Back: Shahyad Square in Tehran. Watermark: Young Shah Pahlavi. Printer: TDLR.

a. 6 point star in design on back. Yellow security thread. Monument name as Maidane Shahyad at lower left on back. Signature 15.	20.00	55.00
b. 12 point star in design on back. Yellow security thread. Monument name as Maidane Shahyad. Signature 16.	10.00	35.00
c. 12 point star in design on back. Yelow security thread. Monument name changed to Shahyard Aryamed. Signature 16.	8.00	30.00
d. 12 point star in design on back. Black security thread and Shahyad Aryamer monument. Signature 17.	8.00	30.00
e. 12 point star in design on back. Black security thread and Shahyad Aryamer monument. Signature 18.	8.00	30.00
h. 12 point star in design on back. Yellow security thread. Monument name changed to Shahyad Aryamer. Signature 16.	8.00	30.00

104 500 Rials VF UNC

ND (1974-79). Yellow security thread runs vertically. Black, dark brown and green on orange and multicolor underprint. Persian carpet design. Type VIII portrait of Shah Pahlavi at right. Back: Winged horses. Watermark: Young Shah Pahlavi. Printer: TDLR.

a. 6 point star in design below Shah Pahlavi. Yellow security thread. Signature 15.	20.00	45.00
b. 6 point star in design below Shah Pahlavi. Yellow security thread. Signature 16.	12.00	30.00
c. Diamond design below Shah Pahlavi. Black security thread. Signature 17.	18.00	40.00
d. Diamond design below Shah Pahlavi. Black security thread. Signature 18.	12.50	35.00

105 1000 Rials VF UNC

ND (1974-79). Yellow security thread runs vertically. Brown on green, red, yellow and multicolor underprint. Persian carpet design. Type VIII portrait of Shah Pahlavi at right. Back: Tomb of Hafez in Shiraz. Watermark: Young Shah Pahlavi. Printer: TDLR.

a. Yellow security thread. Signature 15.	35.00	110
b. Yellow security thread. Signature 16.	12.50	35.00
c. Black security thread. Signature 17.	12.50	35.00
d. Black security thread. Signature 18.	12.50	35.00

106 5000 Rials VF UNC

ND (1974-79). Yellow security thread runs vertically. Purple on pink, green and multicolor underprint. Persian carpet design. Type VIII portrait of Shah Pahlavi at right. Back: Golestan Palace in Tehran. Watermark: Young Shah Pahlavi. Printer: TDLR.

a. Yellow security thread. Signature 15.	100	300
b. Yellow security thread. Signature 16.	10.00	50.00
c. Black security thread. Signature 17.	75.00	200
d. Black security thread. Signature 18.	100	250

107 10,000 Rials VF UNC

ND (1974-79). Yellow security thread runs vertically. Dark brown and green on multicolor underprint. Persian carpet design. Type VIII portrait of Shah Pahlavi at right. Back: National Council of Ministries in Tehran. Watermark: Young Shah Pahlavi. Printer: TDLR.

a. Yellow security thread. Signature 15.	200	550
b. Yellow security thread. Signature 16.	30.00	100
c. Black security thread. Signature 17.	100	300
d. Black security thread. Signature 18.	125	350
s. As a. Specimen.	—	750

1976 ND Commemorative Issue

#108, 50th Anniversary of the Founding of the Pahlavi Dynasty.

108 100 Rials VF UNC

ND (1976). Yellow security thread runs vertically. Maroon on orange, green and multicolor underprint. Persian carpet design with old Bank Melli at bottom center. Type IX portrait of Shah Pahlavi with Shah Reza at right. Signature 16. Back: 50th anniversary design in purple and lavender consisting of fifty suns surrounding Pahlavi Crown. Watermark: Young Shah Pahlavi. Printer: TDLR.

10.00 25.00

ISLAMIC REPUBLIC

Government

Type 1 ND Provisional Issue

#110-116 Type I overprint: Arabesque design over Shah at right. Watermark area at left without overprint. Replacement notes: Refer to #100-107.

REVOLUTIONARY OVERPRINTS

After the Islamic Revolution of 1978-79, the Iranian government used numerous overprints on existing stocks of unissued paper money to obliterate Shah Pahlavi's portrait. There were many unauthorized and illegal crude stampings such as a large "X" and hand obliterations used by zealous citizens which circulated freely, but only three major types types of official overprints were used by the government.

PROVISIONAL ISSUES

All provisional government ovpt. were placed on existing notes of Shah Pahlavi already printed. Overprinting was an interim action meant to discredit and disgrace the deposed Shah as well as to publicize and give credence to the new Islamic Republic. The overprints themselves gave way to more appropriate seals and emblems, changes of watermarks and finally to a complete redesigning of all denominations of notes. In all cases the Shah's portr. was covered by an arabesque design. Eight different styles and varieties of this ovpt. were used. Watermark ovpt., when used, are either the former Iranian national emblem of Lion and Sun or the calligraphic Persian text of JUMHURI-YE-ISLAMI-YE-IRAN (Islamic Republic of Iran) taken from the obverse of the country's new emblem. All ovpt. colors are very dark and require careful scrutiny to distinguish colors other than black.

PORTRAIT OVERPRINT

Obverse 1

Reverse 1

Obverse 2

Obverse 3

Overprint A

Overprint B

Overprint C

Overprint D

Overprint E

Overprint F

Overprint G

Overprint H

110   20 Rials   **VF   UNC**

ND. Brown on orange, lilac and multicolor underprint. Persian carpet design, shepherd and ram. Type VIII portrait of Shah Pahlavi at right. Watermark area at left without overprint. Back: Amir Kabir Dam near Karaj. Watermark: Young Shah Pahlavi. Printer: TDLR.

		VF	UNC
a.	Black type A overprint on #100a1 (short Farsi).	8.00	15.00
b.	Black type A overprint on #100a2 (long Farsi).	8.00	30.00
c.	Black type C overprint on #100a2.	400	800
d.	Black type A overprint on #100c.	500	1,000
e.	Black type A overprint on #100b.	500	1,000

111   50 Rials   **VF   UNC**

ND. Green on brown, blue and multicolor underprint. Persian carpet design. Type VIII portrait of Shah Pahlavi at right. Yellow security thread. Signature 15. Watermark area at left without overprint. Back: Tomb of Cyrus the Great at Pasargarde at left center. Watermark: Young Shah Pahlavi. Printer: TDLR.

		VF	UNC
a.	Black type B overprint.	5.00	12.00
b.	Green type B overprint.	6.00	20.00

112   100 Rials   **VF   UNC**

ND. Maroon on orange, green and multicolor underprint. Persian carpet design. Type VIII portrait of Shah Pahlavi at right. Black security thread. Signature 17. Watermark area at left without overprint. Back: Pahlavi Museum at left center. Watermark: Young Shah Pahlavi. Printer: TDLR.

		VF	UNC
a.	Black type C overprint.	10.00	25.00
b.	Maroon type C overprint.	10.00	25.00
c.	Black type G overprint.	150	300

113   200 Rials

ND. Blue on green and multicolor underprint. Persian carpet design. Type VIII portrait of Shah Pahlavi at right. Watermark area at left without overprint. Back: Shahyad Square in Tehran. Watermark: Young Shah Pahlavi. Printer: TDLR.

		VF	UNC
a. Black type E overprint on #103a.		400	1,200
b. Black type E overprint on #103b.		500	1,400
c. Black type E overprint on #103d.		12.00	30.00
d. Black type G overprint on #103d.		150	300

114   500 Rials

ND. Black, dark brown and green on orange and multicolor underprint. Persian carpet design. Type VIII portrait of Shah Pahlavi at right. Watermark area at left without overprint. Back: Winged horses. Watermark: Young Shah Pahlavi. Printer: TDLR.

		VF	UNC
a. Black type F overprint on #104b.		15.00	50.00
b. Black type F overprint on #104c.		400	900
c. Black type F overprint on #104d.		16.00	60.00

115   1000 Rials

ND. Brown on green, red, yellow and multicolor underprint. Persian carpet design. Type VIII portrait of Shah Pahlavi at right. Watermark area at left without overprint. Back: Tomb of Hafez in Shiraz. Watermark: Young Shah Pahlavi. Printer: TDLR.

		VF	UNC
a. Black type G overprint on #105b.		15.00	50.00
b. Black type G overprint on #105d.		20.00	65.00
c. Brown type G overprint on #105d.		20.00	100

116   5000 Rials

ND. Purple on pink, green and multicolor underprint. Persian carpet design. Type VIII portrait of Shah Pahlavi at right. Black security thread. Signature 18. Black type H overprint. Watermark area at left without overprint. Back: Golestan Palace in Tehran. Watermark: Young Shah Pahlavi. Printer: TDLR.

VF 1,000   UNC 2,000

Type 2 ND Provisional Issue

#117-122 Type II overprint: Arabesque design over Shah at right. Lion and sun national emblem over watermark area at left.

117   50 Rials

ND. Green on brown, blue and multicolor underprint. Persian carpet design. Type VIII portrait of Shah Pahlavi at right. Lion and sun national emblem over watermark area. Back: Cyrus the Great at Pasargarde at left center. Watermark: Young Shah Pahlavi. Printer: TDLR.

		VF	UNC
a. Black type B overprint on #101c.		12.00	30.00
b. Black type B overprint on #101d.		400	1,000
c. Black type B overprint on #101e.		200	600

118   100 Rials

ND. Maroon on orange, green and multicolor underprint. Persian carpet design. Type VIII portrait of Shah Pahlavi at right. Lion and sun national emblem over watermark area. Back: Pahlavi Museum at left center. Watermark: Young Shah Pahlavi. Printer: TDLR.

		VF	UNC
a. Black type C overprint on #102c.		150	400
b. Black type D overprint on #102d.		4.00	10.00

119   200 Rials

ND. Blue on green and multicolor underprint. Persian carpet design. Type VIII portrait of Shah Pahlavi at right. Lion and sun national emblem over watermark area. Back: Shahyad Square in Tehran. Watermark: Young Shah Pahlavi. Printer: TDLR.

		VF	UNC
a. Black Type E overprint on #103d.		25.00	60.00

120   500 Rials

ND. Black, dark brown and green on orange and multicolor underprint. Persian carpet design. Type VIII portrait of Shah Pahlavi at right. Lion and sun national emblem over watermark area. Back: Winged horses. Watermark: Young Shah Pahlavi. Printer: TDLR.

		VF	UNC
a. Black type F overprint on #104b.		700	2,000
b. Black type F overprint on #104d.		30.00	80.00

121   1000 Rials

ND. Brown on green, red, yellow and multicolor underprint. Persian carpet design. Type VIII portrait of Shah Pahlavi at right. Lion and sun national emblem over watermark area. Back: Tomb of Hafez in Shiraz. Watermark: Young Shah Pahlavi. Printer: TDLR.

		VF	UNC
a. Black type G overprint on #105b.		800	3,000
b. Brown type G overprint on #105b.		20.00	75.00
c. Black type G overprint on #105d.		20.00	75.00

122 5000 Rials   VF   UNC
ND. Purple on pink, green and multicolor underprint. Persian carpet design. Type VIII portrait of Shah Pahlavi at right. Lion and sun national emblem over watermark area. Back: Golestan Palace in Tehran. Watermark: Young Shah Pahlavi. Printer: TDLR.
    a. Black type H overprint on #106b.   1,000   2,750
    b. Black type H overprint on #106c.   1,500   3,000
    c. Black type H overprint on #106d.   800   1,750

Type 3 ND Provisional Issue

#123-126 Type III overprint: Arabesque design over Shah at right. Calligraphic Persian text *JUMHURI-YE ISLAMI-YE-IRAN* (Islamic Republic of Iran) over watermark area at left.

123 50 Rials   VF   UNC
ND. Green on brown, blue and multicolor underprint. Persian carpet design. Type VIII portrait of Shah Pahlavi at right. calligraphic Persian text*JUMHURI-YE ISL-AMI YE-IRAN* over watermark area at left. Back: Tomb of Cyrus the Great at Pasargarde at left center. Watermark: Young Shah Pahlavi. Printer: TDLR.
    a. Black type B overprint, dark green script on #101c.   6.00   20.00
    b. Black type D overprint, black script on #101e.   4.00   10.00

124 500 Rials   VF   UNC
ND. Black, dark brown and green on orange and multicolor underprint. Persian carpet design. Type VIII portrait of Shah Pahlavi at right. Calligraphic Persian text*JUMHURI-YE ISL-AMI YE-IRAN* over watermark area at left. Back: Winged horses. Watermark: Young Shah Pahlavi. Printer. TDLR.
    a. Black type F overprint, black script on #104b.   15.00   50.00
    b. Black type D overprint, black script on #104d.   10.00   30.00

125 1000 Rials   VF   UNC
ND. Brown on green, red, yellow and multicolor underprint. Persian carpet design. Type VIII portrait of Shah Pahlavi at right. Calligraphic Persian text*JUMHURI-YE ISL-AMI YE-IRAN* over watermark area at left. Back: Tomb of Hafez in Shiraz. Watermark: Young Shah Pahlavi. Printer: TDLR.
    a. Black type G overprint, black script on #105b.   15.00   50.00
    b. Black type G overprint, black script on #105d.   15.00   50.00
    c. Brown type G overprint, violet script on #105b.   20.00   75.00
    d. Brown type G overprint, brown script on #105b.   20.00   75.00

126 5000 Rials   VF   UNC
ND. Purple on pink, green and multicolor underprint. Persian carpet design. Type VIII portrait of Shah Pahlavi at right. Calligraphic Persian text*JUMHURI-YE ISL-AMI YE-IRAN* over watermark area at left. Back: Golestan Palace in Tehran. Watermark: Young Shah Pahlavi. Printer: TDLR.
    a. Purple type H overprint, purple script on #106b.   1,000   2,500
    b. Black type H overprint, purple script on #106d.   150   350

Note: Some notes with Shah portrait are found with unofficial overprint, i.e. large purple or black stamped X oover the portrait and watermark area.

1980 Emergency Circulating Check Issue

The emergency checks were issed by Bank Melli, the National Bank and not Bank Markazi, the Central Bank, which is only authorized to issue currency. The checks were valid in the country only, not abroad. No English text on the checks.

126A 10,000 Rials   VF   UNC
ND (1980). Uniface. Dark blue with black text on green underprint. Bank Melli building at left and center. Watermark: Bank name repeated.   250   600

Note: These Emergency Checks were issued by Bank Melli the National Bank, and not Bank Markazi, the Central Bank which is only authorized to issue currency. The checks were valid in Iran and not abroad. No English text on the check.

Bank Markazi Iran

	SIGNATURE VARIETIES	
	Notes of the Islamic Republic of Iran	
18	Youset Khoshkish (on ovpt.)	Mohammad Yeganeh (on ovpt.)
19	Mohammad Ali Mowiavi	Ali Ardalan
20	Ali Reza Nobarl	Abol Hassas Bani-Sadr
21	Dr. Mohsen Nourbakhsh	Hossein Nemazi
22	Dr. Mohsen Nourbakhsh	Iravani
23	Ghaseml	Iravani
24	Ghaseml	Dr. Mohsen Nourbakhsh
25	Mohammad Hosein Adeli	Dr. Mohsen Nourbakhsh
26	Mohammad Hosein Adeli	Mohammad Khan
27	Dr. Mohsen Nourbakhsh	Mohammad Khan
28	Dr. Mohsen Nourbakhsh	Hossein Nemazi
29	Dr. Mohsen Nourbakhsh	
30		
31		
32		
33		
34		

SIGNATURE VARIETIES

Notes of the Islamic Republic of Iran		
35	مسی	ک
36	سبحانی	ک

1981 ND First Issue

#127 and #130 have calligraphic seal printed in the same color as the note (blue and lavender, respectively) and with no variation. #128, 129 and 131 had the calligraphic seal applied locally after notes were printed. Numerous color varieties, misplacement or total omission can be seen on face or back, or both.

127 200 Rials **VF UNC**
ND (1981). Yellow security thread with *BANK MARKAZI IRAN* in black runs vertically. Blue and green on multicolor underprint. Calligraphic Persian (Farsi) text from circular republic seal at left, Imam Reza mosque at right without watermark. Signature 19. Back: Circular shield with stars and points at right. Tomb of Ibn-E-Sina in Hamadan at left. Printer: TDLR (without imprint).
   a. Overprint on watermark: Shah profile. 2.00 6.00
   b. Overprint on watermark: Lion & Sun. 4.00 10.00

127A 200 Rials **VF UNC**
ND (1981). Yellow security thread with *BANK MARKAZI IRAN* in black runs 5,000 12,000
vertically. Blue, blue-violet and deep green on multicolor underprint. Calligraphic Persian (Farsi) text from circular republic seal at left with overprint. Imam Reza mosque at right without watermark. Signature 19. Back: Victory Monument renamed *Banaye Azadi* at left. Printer: TDLR (without imprint).

128 500 Rials **VF UNC**
ND (1981). Yellow security thread with *BANK MARKAZI IRAN* in black runs verti- 5.00 15.00
cally. Dark brown on orange, green and multicolor underprint. Calligraphic Persian (Farsi) text from circular republic seal at left, Imam Reza mosque at right without watermark. Signature 19. Back: Winged horses. Printer: TDLR (without imprint).

129 1000 Rials **VF UNC**
ND (1981). Yellow security thread with *BANK MARKAZI IRAN* in black runs 8.00 25.00
vertically. Rust and brown on green and multicolor underprint. Calligraphic Persian (Farsi) text from circular republic seal at left, Imam Reza mosque at right without watermark. Signature 19. Back: Tomb of Hafez in Shiraz. Printer: TDLR (without imprint).

130 5000 Rials **VF UNC**
ND (1981). Yellow security thread with *BANK MARKAZI IRAN* in black runs verti-
cally. Lavender on green and multicolor underprint. Calligraphic Persian (Farsi) text from circular republic seal at left, Imam Reza mosque at right without watermark. Signature 19. Back: Oil refinery at Tehran. Printer: TDLR (without imprint).
   a. Security thread. 30.00 80.00
   b. Without security thread. 50.00 100

131 10,000 Rials **VF UNC**
ND (1981). Yellow security thread with *BANK MARKAZI IRAN* in black runs vertically. Deep green, olive-brown and dark brown on multicolor underprint. Calligraphic Persian (Farsi) text from circular republic seal at left, Imam Reza mosque at right without watermark. Signature 19. Back: National Council of Ministries in Tehran. Printer: TDLR (without imprint).
   a. dark brown circular seal at left. dark brown circular shield seal at right on 50.00 200
     back.

Note: #131 first overprint with circular gray-yellow lion and sun on both sides, then additional overprint regular black calligraphic seal on top of first overprint. Notes without black seal, or misplaced seal, are errors.

1981 ND Second Issue

#132-134 Replacement notes: Serial # prefix *99/99; 98/99; 97/99;* etc.

132 100 Rials
ND (1981). White security thread with *BANK MARKAZI IRAN* in black Persian script runs vertically. Maroon and light brown on multicolor underprint. Ima Reza shrine at Mashad at right. Signature 20. Back: Madressa Chahr-Bagh in Isfahan. Watermark: Republic seal. Printer: TDLR (without imprint).

VF 2.00 **UNC** 5.00

133 5000 Rials
ND (1981). White security thread with *BANK MARKAZI IRAN* in black Persian script runs vertically. Violet, red-orange and brown on multicolor underprint. Mullahs leading marchers carrying posters of Ayatollah Khomeini at center. Signature 20. Back: Hazrat Masoumeh shrine at left center. Watermark: Arms. Printer: TDLR (without imprint).

VF 25.00 **UNC** 80.00

134 10,000 Rials
ND (1981). White security thread with *BANK MARKAZI IRAN* in black Persian script runs vertically. Dark blue and green on yellow and multicolor underprint. Mullahs leading marchers carrying posters of Ayatollah Khomeini at center. Signature 20. Back: Imam Reza shrine in Mashad at center. Printer: TDLR (without imprint).

	VF	UNC
a. Signature 20. Watermark: Republic seal.	30.00	125
b. Signature 21. Watermark: Arms.	30.00	125
c. Signature 22. Watermark: Arms.	30.00	125

1982; 1983 ND Issue

135 100 Rials
ND (1982). Maroon on light brown and multicolor underprint. Ima Reza shrine at Mashad at right. Signature 21. White security thread with *BANK MARKAZI IRAN* in black Persian letters repeatedly runs vertically. Back. Madressa Chahr-Bagh in Isfahan. Printer: TDLR (without imprint).

VF 2.00 **UNC** 4.00

136 200 Rials
ND (1982-). UV: security strip fluoresces blue, serial #s orange. Aqua and blue-black on multicolor underprint. Mosque at center. White security thread with *BANK MARKAZI IRAN* in black Persian letters repeatedly runs vertically. Back: Farmers and farm tractor at left center. Printer: TDLR (without imprint).

	VF	UNC
a. Signature 21. Watermark: Arms.	3.00	6.00
b. Signature 23. Watermark: Arms.	FV	4.00
c. Signatrue 28. Watermark: Arms.	FV	4.00
d. Signature 28. Watermark: Khomeini.	FV	3.00
e. Signature 31. Watermark: Khomeini.	FV	3.00

137 500 Rials
ND (1982-2002). UV: fibers fluoresce yellow and blue, security strip rainbow, serial #s orange. Gray and olive. Feyzich Madressa Seminary at lower left, large prayer gathering at center. White security thread with *BANK MARKAZI IRAN* in black Persian letters repeatedly runs vertically. Back: Tehran University. Printer: TDLR (without imprint).

	VF	UNC
a. Signature 21. Watermark: Arms.	FV	12.00
b. Signature 22.	15.00	40.00
c. Signature 23.	FV	10.00
d. Signature 23. Watermark: Mohd. H. Fahmideh (youth).	FV	8.00
e. Signature 24.	FV	6.00
f. Signature 25.	FV	4.00
g. Signature 25. Watermark: Arms. Known as a replacement prefix only.	FV	20.00
h. Signature 27. Watermark: Arms.	FV	3.00
i. Signature 27. Watermark: Mohd. H. Fahmideh (youth).	FV	3.00
j. Signature 28. Watermark: Khomeini.	FV	3.00
k. Signature 30. Watermark: Khomeini.	FV	3.00
l. Signatrue 31. Watermark: Khomeini.	FV	3.00
s. As a. Specimen. Red Arabic overprint.	—	500

137A 500 Rials   VF   UNC

ND (2003-). Gray and olive. Feyzieh Madressa Seminary at lower left, prayer gathering at center. Architectural image at lower left in different position than number 137. White security thread with *BANK MARKAZI IRAN* in bla Back: Tehran University. Watermark: Khomeini Printer: TDLR (without imprint).

	VF	UNC
a. Signature 30.	FV	3.00
b. Signature 31.	FV	3.00
c. Signature 28.	FV	3.00
d. Signature 33.	FV	3.00

138 1000 Rials   VF   UNC

ND (1982-2002). UV: fibers fluoresce yellow, blue and red. Serial #s orange. Dark olive-green, red-brown and brown on multicolor underprint. Feyzieh Madressa Seminary at center. White security thread with *BANK MARKAZI IRAN* in black Persian letters repeatedly runs vertically. Back: Dome of the Rock in Jerusalem. Printer: TDLR (without imprint).

	VF	UNC
a. Signature 21. With short line of text under mosque (Error name "Masjed al-Aqsa" on back. Watermark: Arms.	FV	20.00
b. Signature 21. Without line of text under mosque on back. Watermark: Arms.	FV	50.00
c. Signature 22. Watermark: Arms.	FV	25.00
d. Signature 23. Watermark: Arms.	FV	15.00
e. Signature 23. Watermark: Mohd. H. Fahmideh (youth).	FV	7.00
f. Signature 25. Watermark: Mohd. H. Fahmideh (youth).	FV	4.00
g. Signature 25. Watermark: Arms.	FV	4.00
h. Signature 26. Watermark: Mohd. H. Fahmideh (youth).	FV	4.00
i. Signature 27. Watermark: Mohd. H. Fahmideh (youth).	FV	4.00
j. Signature 28. Watermark: Mohd. H. Fahmideh (youth).	FV	4.00
k. Signature 28. Watermark: Arms.	FV	4.00

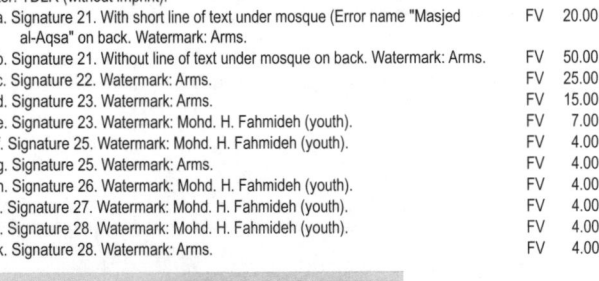

139 5000 Rials   VF   UNC

ND (1983-93). White security thread with *BANK MARKAZI IRAN* in black Persian letters repeatedly runs vertically. Violet, red-orange and brown on multicolor underprint. Mullahs leading marchers carrying posters of Ayatollah Khomeini at center. Reduced crowd, radiant sun removed from upper left, two playcards of Khomeini added to crowd. Two different signatures. Back: Hazrat Masoumeh shrine at left center. Watermark: Arms. Printer: TDLR (without imprint).

	VF	UNC
a. Signature 21. Two signature style varieties.	FV	75.00
b. Signature 22.	FV	75.00

Central Bank of the Islamic Republic of Iran
1985; 1986 ND Issue

140 100 Rials   VF   UNC

ND (1985-). Purple on multicolor underprint. Ayatollah Moddaress at right. Back: Parliament at left. Printer: TDLR (without imprint).

	VF	UNC
a. Signature 21. Watermark: Arms.	FV	3.00
b. Signature 22. Watermark: Arms.	FV	2.50
c. Signature 23. Watermark: Arms.	FV	2.00
d. Signature 25. Watermark: Arms.	FV	2.00
e. Signature 26. Watermark: Arms.	FV	2.00
f. Signature 28. Watermark: Khomeini.	FV	2.00
g. Signature 31. Watermark: Khomeini.	FV	2.00
h. Signature 31. Watermark: Arms.	FV	2.00

141 2000 Rials   VF   UNC

ND(1986-2005). UV: serial #s fluoresce orange, fibers yellow, blue and red, security thread blue, yellow, red. Purple, olive-green and dark brown on multicolor underprint. Revolutionists before mosque at center right. Back: Kaaba in Mecca. 148x73mm.

	VF	UNC
a. Signature 21. Watermark: Arms.	FV	10.00
b. Signature 22. Watermark: Arms.	FV	10.00
c. Signature 23. Watermark: Arms.	FV	10.00
d. Signature 23. Watermark: Mohd. H. Fahmideh (youth).	FV	6.00
e. Signature 24. Watermark: Mohd. H. Fahmideh (youth).	FV	4.00
f. Signature 25. Watermark: Mohd. H. Fahmideh (youth).	FV	4.00
g. Signature 25. Watermark: Arms.	25.00	125
h. Signature 26. Watermark: Moh. H. Fahmideh (youth).	FV	4.00
i. Signature 27. Watermark: Arms.	FV	4.00
j. Signature 27. Watermark: Mohd. H. Fahmideh (youth).	FV	4.00
k. Signature 28. Watermark: Khomeini.	FV	4.00
l. Signature 28. Watermark: Mohd. H. Fahmideh (youth).	FV	4.00

1992; 1993 ND Issue
#142 not assigned.

143 1000 Rials   VF   UNC

ND (1992-). UV: fibers fluoresce yellow and blue, serial #s orange. Brown and dark green on multicolor underprint. Khomeini at right. Back: Dome of the Rock in Jerusalem at center. 148x73mm.

	VF	UNC
a. Signature 25. Watermark: Mohd. Fahmideh (youth).	FV	12.50
b. Signature 27. Watermark: Mohd. Fahmideh (youth).	FV	5.00
c. Signature 28. Watermark: Mohd. Fahmideh (youth).	FV	3.00
d. Signature 31. Watermark: Khomeini.	FV	3.00
e. Signature 32.	FV	3.00
f. Signature 34.	FV	3.00

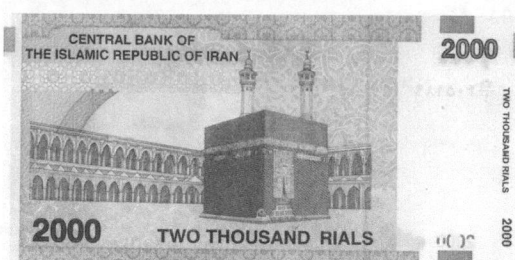

144 2000 Rials

ND (2005-). Lilac and green on multicolor underprint. Khomeini at right. Back: Mosque interior in Mecca. Watermark: Khomeini. 148x73mm.

	VF	UNC
a. Signature 33.	FV	4.50
b. Signature 34.	FV	4.50
c. Signature 35.	FV	4.50
d. Signature 36.	FV	4.50

145 5000 Rials

ND (1993-). Dark brown, brown and olive-green on multicolor underprint. Khomeini at right. Back: Flowers and birds at center right. Watermark: Khomeini. 154x75mm.

	VF	UNC
a. Signature 25.	FV	10.00
b. Signature 27.	FV	0.00
c. Signature 28.	FV	6.00
d. Signature 29.	FV	6.00
e. Signature 30.	FV	6.00

146 10,000 Rials

ND (1992-). Deep blue-green, blue and olive-green on multicolor underprint. Khomeini at right. Back: Mount Damavand at center right. Watermark: Khomeini. 160x77mm.

	VF	UNC
a. Signature 25.	FV	20.00
b. Signature 26.	FV	20.00
c. Signature 27.	FV	12.50
d. Signature 28.	FV	12.50
e. Signature 29.	FV	9.00
f. Signature 30.	FV	9.00
g. Signature 33.	FV	9.00
h. Signature 37.	FV	9.00

147 20,000 Rials

ND (2004-5). Blue and green on multicolor underprint. Large Imam Khomeini bust at right. Back: Khomeini square in Isfahan. Watermark: Khomeini. 164x77mm.

	VF	UNC
a. Signature 30.	FV	20.00
b. Signature 31.	FV	20.00
c. Signature 32.	FV	20.00

148 20,000 Rials

2005. Blue and green on multicolor underprint. Smaller Iman Khomeini bust at right. Back: Khomeini square in Isfahan. Watermark: Khomeini. 104x77mm.

	VF	UNC
a. Signature 32.	FV	15.00
b. Signature 33.	FV	15.00
c. Signature 34.	FV	15.00
d. Signature 36.	FV	15.00
e. Signature 37.	FV	15.00

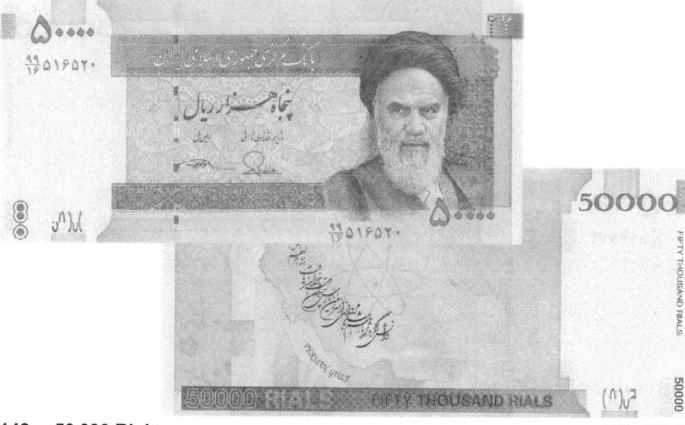

149 50,000 Rials

2006-. Purple on brown, green, orange and multicolor underprint. Iman Khomeini at right. Back: Map and atomic emblems. Watermark: Khomeini. 166x79mm.

	VF	UNC
a. Signature 33.	FV	45.00
b. Signature 34.	FV	45.00
c. Signature 36.	FV	45.00
d. Signature 37.	FV	45.00

2009-2010 Issue

150 5000 Rials

2009. Lilac and green on multicolor underprint. Iman Khomeini bust at right. Back: Omid Satellite. Watermark: Khomeni. 154x75mm.

	VF	UNC
a. Signature 36.	FV	6.00

151   100,000 Rials   VF   UNC
2010. Olive green and green on multicolor underprint. Iman Khomeini at right.   FV   75.00
Back: Tomb of poet Muslih al-din Sa'di. 166x79mm.

2013-2014 Issue

152   5000 Rials   VF   UNC
2013. Brown and green on multicolor underprint. Iman Khomeini bust at right.   FV   4.00
Back: Ancient painted bowl and plate. Watermark: Khomeini.

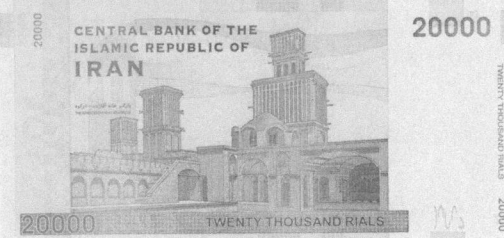

153   20,000 Rials   VF   UNC
ND (2014). Blue and green on multicolor underprint. Large Imam Khomeini bust at   FV   20.00
right. Back: Windcatchers at Abarkooh. Watermark: Khomeini. 163x78mm.

154   500,000 Rials (Cheque)   VF   UNC
2014-2015. Purple, green, yellow. Imam Reza Holy Shrine entrance, dome with   FV   50.00
flag and minaret in Mashhad. Back: Flying dove, Esmail Talayi fountain in the
shrine's court. Watermark: Flying dove and electrotype 50. Printer: (Iranian).
140x68mm.

2015 Commemorative Issue

155   50,000 Rials   VF   UNC
ND (2015). 80th anniversary of the University of Tehran. Purple, brown, green,   FV   45.00
orange. Ayatollah Ruhollah Khomeini. Back: Tree, entrance to Tehran University,
Ferdowsi quote, double-helix strand of DNA, chemical symbol, planet Saturn.
Watermark: Ruhollah Khomeini. 166x79mm.

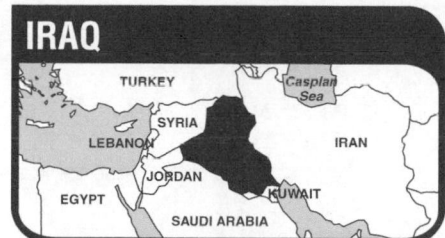

IRAQ

The Republic of Iraq, historically known as Mesopotamia, is located in the Near East and is bordered by Kuwait, Iran, Turkey, Syria, Jordan and Saudi Arabia. It has an area of 437,072 sq. km. and a population of 28.22 million. Capital: Baghdad. The economy of Iraq is based on agriculture and petroleum. Crude oil accounts for 94 percent of the exports before the war with Iran began in 1980.

Formerly part of the Ottoman Empire, Iraq was occupied by Britain during the course of World War I; in 1920, it was declared a League of Nations mandate under UK administration. In stages over the next dozen years, Iraq attained its independence as a kingdom in 1932. A "republic" was proclaimed in 1958, but in actuality a series of military strongmen ruled the country until 2003. The last was Saddam Husayn. Territorial disputes with Iran led to an inconclusive and costly eight-year war (1980-88). In August 1990, Iraq seized Kuwait but was expelled by US-led, UN coalition forces during the Gulf War of January-February 1991. Following Kuwait's liberation, the UN Security Council (UNSC) required Iraq to scrap all weapons of mass destruction and long-range missiles and to allow UN verification inspections. Continued Iraqi noncompliance with UNSC resolutions over a period of 12 years led to the US-led invasion of Iraq in March 2003 and the ouster of the Saddam Husayn regime. Coalition forces remain in Iraq under a UNSC mandate, helping to provide security and to support the freely elected government. The Coalition Provisional Authority, which temporarily administered Iraq after the invasion, transferred full governmental authority on 28 June 2004 to the Iraqi Interim Government, which governed under the Transitional Administrative Law for Iraq (TAL). Under the TAL, elections for a 275-member Transitional National Assembly (TNA) were held in Iraq on 30 January 2005. Following these elections, the Iraqi Transitional Government (ITG) assumed office. The TNA was charged with drafting Iraq's permanent constitution, which was approved in a 15 October 2005 constitutional referendum. An election under the constitution for a 275-member Council of Representatives (CoR) was held on 15 December 2005. The CoR approval in the selection of most of the cabinet ministers on 20 May 2006 marked the transition from the ITG to Iraq's first constitutional government in nearly a half-century.

RULERS:
Faisal I, 1921-1933
Ghazi I, 1933-1939
Faisal II, 1939-1958

MONETARY SYSTEM:
1 Dirham = 50 Fils
1 Riyal = 200 Fils
1 Dinar = 1000 Fils

SIGNATURE AND GOVERNOR VARIETIES

	GENERAL DIRECTOR		
12		13	
14		15	
16		17	
18		19	
20		21	
22		23	
24		25	
26		27	

REPUBLIC

Central Bank of Iraq

1959 Issue

51 1/4 Dinar

ND (1959). Green on multicolor underprint. Republic arms with 1958 at right. Back. Palm trees at center. Watermark: Republic arms with 1958.

		VF	UNC
a. Without security thread. Signature 13.		5.00	15.00
b. With security thread. Signature 14, 16.		5.00	10.00
s. Specimen. Punched hole cancelled.		—	500

52 1/2 Dinar

ND (1959). Brown on multicolor underprint. Republic arms with 1958 at right. Back: Ruins of the mosque and spiral minaret at Samarra. Watermark: Republic arms.

		VF	UNC
a. Without security thread. Signature 13.		100	150
b. With security thread. Signature 14, 16.		7.50	30.00
s. Specimen. Punched hole cancelled.		—	500

53 1 Dinar

ND (1959). Blue on multicolor underprint. Republic arms with 1958 at right. Back: The *Harp of Ur* at center. Watermark: Republic arms.

		VF	UNC
a. Without security thread. Signature 13.		8.00	30.00
b. With security thread. Blue lines over watermark area. Signature 14, 15.		8.00	30.00
s. Specimen. Punched hole cancelled.		—	500

54   5 Dinars　　　　　　　　　　　　　　　　　　**VF   UNC**

ND (1959). Light purple on multicolor underprint. Republic arms with 1958 at right.
Back: Ancient carving of Hammurabi receiving the laws. Watermark: Symbol of
the Immortal Revolution.

a. Without security thread. 1 signature variety.	15.00	45.00
b. With security thread.	15.00	45.00
s. Specimen. Punched hole cancelled.	—	500

58   1 Dinar　　　　　　　　　　　　　　　　　　**VF   UNC**

ND (1971). Blue and brown on multicolor underprint. Oil refinery at center.　6.00　17.50
Signature 16, 17. Back: Entry to the al-Mustansiriyah School at center, *1 Dinar* at
left. Watermark: Falcon's head.

55   10 Dinars　　　　　　　　　　　　　　　　　**VF   UNC**

ND (1959). Purple on multicolor underprint. Republic arms with 1958 at right.
Signature 10, 11 and 12. Back: Carvings of a winged Assyrian ox and an Assyrian
priest. Watermark: Symbol of the Immortal Revolution.

a. Without security thread. 1 signature variety.	12.00	65.00
b. With security thread. 2 signature varieties.	12.00	65.00
s. Specimen. Punched hole cancelled.	—	500

59   5 Dinars　　　　　　　　　　　　　　　　　**VF   UNC**

ND (1971). Lilac on brown and multicolor underprint. Parliament building.　15.00　45.00
Signature 16, 17. Back: Hammurabi (left) in conversation with sun god Shamash
at center *5 Dinars* at left. Watermark: Falcon's head.

1971 ND Issue

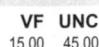

56   1/4 Dinar　　　　　　　　　　　　　　　　　**VF   UNC**

ND (1971). Green and brown on multicolor underprint. Harbor at center. Signature　3.00　9.00
16. Back: *1/4 Dinar* at left, palm trees at center. Watermark: Falcon's head.

60   10 Dinars　　　　　　　　　　　　　　　　　**VF   UNC**

ND (1971). Purple, blue and brown on multicolor underprint. Dockdan dam at　15.00　45.00
center. Signature 17. Back: Winged statues from the palace complex of Sargon II
at Khorsabad at center, *10 Dinars* at left Watermark: Falcon's head.

1973 ND; 1978 Issue

57   1/2 Dinar　　　　　　　　　　　　　　　　　**VF   UNC**

ND (1971). Brown and blue on multicolor underprint. Cement factory at center.　7.50　25.00
Signature 16. Back: *1/2 Dinar* at left, spiral minaret and ruins of mosque at
Samarra at center. Watermark: Falcon's head.

61 1/4 Dinar VF UNC
ND (1973). Green and black on multicolor underprint. Harbor at center. Signature 1.50 5.00
17, 18. Back: Palm trees at center, *Quarter Dinar* at bottom right. Watermark:
Falcon's head.

62 1/2 Dinar VF UNC
ND (1973). Brown on multicolor underprint. Cement factory at center. Signature 1.00 20.00
17, 18. Back: *Half Dinar* below Minaret of the Great Mosque at Samarra at center.
Watermark: Falcon's head.

63 1 Dinar VF UNC
ND (1973). Dark blue and aqua on multicolor underprint. Oil refinery at center.
Signature 17, 18. Back: Entry to the al-Mustansiriyah School at center, *One Dinar*
at bottom right. Watermark: Falcon's head.
    a. 1 line of Arabic caption (factory name) below. 4.50 32.50
    b. Without Arabic caption below factory. 3.00 12.00

64 5 Dinars VF UNC
ND (1973). Deep lilac on multicolor underprint. Parliament building. Signature 17, 3.00 10.00
18. Back: Hammurabi (left) in conversation with sun god Shamash at center *5
Dinars* at bottom. Watermark: Falcon's head.

65 10 Dinars VF UNC
ND (1973). Purple and red-brown on blue and multicolor underprint. Dockdan 5.00 15.00
dam at right. Signature 17, 18. Back: Winged statues from the palace complex of
Sargon II at Khorsabad at center, *Ten Dinars* at bot Watermark: Falcon's head.

66 25 Dinars VF UNC
1978; 1980. Green and brown on multicolor underprint. Three Arabian horses at
center, date below signature at lower right. Back: Abbasid Palace. Watermark:
Falcon's head. 182x88mm.
    a. 1978/AH1398. Signature 19. 10.00 30.00
    b. 1980/AH1400. Signature 21. 7.50 22.50
    s. Specimen. — —

1979-86 Issue

67 1/4 Dinar VF UNC
1979/AH1399. Green and multicolor. Palm trees at center. Signature 20. Back:
Building. Watermark: Arabian horse's head.
    a. Issued note. 0.50 1.50
    s. Specimen. — —

68   1/2 Dinar   VF   UNC

1980/AH1400; 1985/AH1405. Brown and multicolor. Astrolabe at right. Signature
21, 22. Back: Minaret of Samarra. Watermark: Arabian horse's head.

    a. Issued note.   0.50   1.50

    s. Specimen.   —   —

69   1 Dinar   VF   UNC

1979/AH1399; 1980/AH1400; 1984/AH1405. UV: fibers fluoresce blue, Arabic 1s
green. Olive-green and deep blue on multicolor underprint. Coin design at center.
Signature 21. Back: Mustansiriyah School in Baghdad. Watermark: Arabian
horse's head.

    a. Issued note.   0.50   1.50

    s. Specimen.   —   —

70   5 Dinars   VF   UNC

1980/AH1400; 1981/AH1401; 1982/AH1402. Brown-violet and deep blue on multicolor underprint. Gali-Ali Beg waterfall at center. Signature 21. Back: Al-Ukhether
castle at center. Watermark: Arabian horse's head.

    a. Issued note.   1.50   4.00

    s. Specimen.   —   450

71   10 Dinars   VF   UNC

1980/AH1400; 1981/AH1401; 1982/AH1402. Purple on blue, violet and multicolor
underprint. Al-Hassan ibn al-Haitham (scientist) at right. Signature 21. Back:
Hadba minaret in Mosul. Watermark: Arabian horse's head.

    a. Issued note.   1.50   5.00

    s. Specimen. Red overprint in Arabic.   —   450

72   25 Dinars   VF   UNC

1981/AH1401; 1982/AH1402. Reduced size. Green and brown. Three Arabian
horses at center, date below. Signature 21. Back: Abbasid Palace. Watermark:
Arabian horse's head. 175x80mm.   1.00   2.00

73   25 Dinars   VF   UNC

1986. UV: Arabic 2s fluoresce yellow. Brown, green and black on blue and
multicolor underprint. Charging horsemen at center, Saddam Hussein at right.
Signature 22. Back: City gate at left, Martyr's monument at center. Watermark:
Saddam Hussein.

    a. Issued note.   1.50   4.50

    s. Specimen. Red overprint in Arabic.   —   750

Note: In a sudden economic move during summer of 1993, it was announced that all previous 25
    Dinar notes issued before #74 had become worthless.

1990 Emergency Gulf War Issue

**#74-76 Iraq printing. Many color shade varieties exist because of poor print-
ing quality.**

74   25 Dinars   VF   UNC

1990/AH1411. Lithograph, without watermark. Green and gray. Three Arabian
horses at center, date below signature at lower right. Date below horses. Signature 23. Back: Abbasid Palace.

    a. Green underprint with pink highlights and brown ink.   0.50   1.00

    b. Green underprint without pink highlights and black ink.   0.50   1.00

    c. Green and pink underprint. with pink highlights and brown ink. 0.50   1.00

75   50 Dinars   **VF   UNC**
1991/AH1411. Lithograph. Brown and blue-green on peach and multicolor under-   0.50   2.00
print. Saddam Hussein at right. Signature 23. Back: Minaret of the Great Mosque
at Samarra at center right.

76   100 Dinars   **VF   UNC**
1991/AH1411. Dark blue-green on lilac and multicolor underprint. Saddam   15.00   40.00
Hussein at right. Signature 23. Back: Victory Arch Monument of crossed swords
at center.

1992-93 Emergency Issue

#77-79 dull lithograph printing. With faint indelible ink wmk.

77   1/4 Dinar   **VF   UNC**
1993/AH1413. Green on multicolor underprint. Palm trees at center. Signature 24.   —   0.50
Back: Building. Printer: Chinese.

78   1/2 Dinar   **VF   UNC**
1993/AH1413. Brown on multicolor underprint. Astrolabe at right. Signature 24.
Back: Minaret of Samarra. Printer: Chinese.
    a. Dark brown underprint.   —   0.50
    b. Light lilac underprint.   —   0.50

79   1 Dinar   **VF   UNC**
1992/AH1412. Green and blue-black on multicolor underprint. Coin design at   —   0.50
center. Signature 24. Back: Mustansiriyah School in Baghdad. Printer: Chinese.

80   5 Dinars   **VF   UNC**
1992/AH1412. UV: threads fluoresce blue and orange. Dull red-brown on pale
orange, lilac and multicolor underprint. Color shade varieties. Temple at center.
Saddam Hussein at right. Signature 24. Back: Hammurabi in conversation with the
sun god Shamash at left. Tomb of the unknown soldier in center. Printer: Chinese.
    a. With border around embossed text at center.   —   4.00
    b. Without border around embossed text at center.   —   4.00
    c. As b. without embossed text at center.   —   1.00

81   10 Dinars   **VF   UNC**
1992/AH1412. UV: threads fluoresce yellow and blue, Arabic 10 yellow. Purplish   —   2.50
black, blue-green and multicolor. Saddam Hussein at right. Signature 24. Back:
Statue of winged beast from the palace complex of Sargon II at Khorsabad at left.
Printer: Chinese.

#82 not assigned.

1994-95 Issue

83   50 Dinars   VF UNC
1994/AH1414. Brown and pale green on multicolor underprint. Ancient statuette,
monument at left center. Suddam Hussein at right. Signature 24. Back: Aljahad
Project" double deck Saddam bridge at center.   —   1.50

84   100 Dinars   VF UNC
1994/AH1414. Dark blue on light blue and pale ochre underprint. Al-Ukhether
castle at center. Saddam Hussein at right. Signature 24. Back: Baghdad clock at
center. Watermark: Printed Falcon's head.
- a1. First diacritical mark in the text of the denomination is above the first letter
(from the right). Printed on white paper which fluoresces.   —   1.00
- a2. As a. but printed on dark paper which does not fluoresce under UV light.   —   1.00
- b. First diacritical mark in the text of the denomination is below the second
letter (from the right).   —   1.00

85   250 Dinars   VF UNC
1995/AH1415. Shade varieties exist. Lavender on blue and multicolor underprint.
Hydroelectric dam at left center. Saddam Hussein at right. Signature 25. Back:
Friese from the Liberty Monument across back.
- a1. First word of the text for the denomination has its second letters as a long
'a.' Printed on white paper which fluoresces.   —   1.25
- a2. As a. but printed on dark paper which does not fluoresce under UV light.   —   1.25
- b. First word of the text for the denomination has its second last letters as a
long 'i', also with different diacritical marks.   —   1.25

2001-02 Issue

86   25 Dinars   VF UNC
2001/AH1422. UV: fibers fluoresce blue and yellow. Brown on light green underprint. Saddam Hussein at right. Signature 25.   —   1.50

87   100 Dinars   VF UNC
2002/AH1422. UV: fibers fluoresce blue and yellow Blue on blue and yellow underprint. Saddam Hussein at right. Signature 25. Back: Shenashils of old Baghdad.   —   3.00

88   250 Dinars   VF UNC
2002/AH1422. UV: fibers fluoresce green, red and blue, security strip orange.
Purple on rose and blue underprint. Saddam Hussein at right. Signature 25. Back:
Dome of the Rock in Jerusalem.   —   1.50

89   10,000 Dinars   VF UNC
2002/AH1423. Tomb of unknown soldier in center, Saddam Hussein at right.
Signature 25. Back: Al-Mustansiriyah University in Baghdad and Arabic astrolobe.   —   7.00
Uncut sheets and partial sheets exist of this note.

DEMOCRATIC REPUBLIC
Central Bank of Iraq
2003-04 Issue

90   50 Dinars   VF UNC
2003/AH1424. Purple on multicolor underprint. Grain silo at Basrah. Signature 26.   FV   1.00
Back: Date palms. Printer: TDLR.

91   250 Dinars   VF   UNC

2003/AH1424. Light and dark blue on multicolor underprint. Astrolobe. Signature 26. Back: Spiral Minaret in Samarra. Printer: TDLR. 130x66mm.

a. 2003/AH1424.	FV	1.50
b. 2012./AH1433.	FV	1.50

92   500 Dinars   VF   UNC

2004/AH1425. Green and blue on multicolor underprint. Ducan Dam at center. Signature 27. Back: Winged bull statue. Printer: TDLR. 142x66mm.   FV   2.00

93   1000 Dinars   VF   UNC

2003/AH1424. Light and dark brown. Medieval dinar coin. Signature 26. Back: Al-Mustansiriyah University in Baghdad. Printer: TDLR. 142x66mm.

a. 2003/AH1424.	FV	2.50
b. 2013/AH1434.	FV	2.50

94   5000 Dinars   VF   UNC

2003/AH1424-. UV: solid rectangle with Arabic 5000 fluoresces yellow. Dark blue on multicolor underprint. Gali Ali Beg and waterfall. Back: Al-Ukhether fortress. Printer: TDLR. 158x79mm.

a. 2003/AH1424. Signature 26.	FV	14.00
b. 2006/AH1427. Signature 27.	FV	10.00
c. 2010/AH1431.	FV	10.00

95   10,000 Dinars   VF   UNC

2003/AH1424-. Green on multicolor underprint. Abu Ali Hasan Ibn al-Haitham (known as Alhazen), physicist and mathematician. Back: Hadba Minaret at the Great Nurid Mosque in Mosul. Printer: TDLR. 170x78mm.

a. 2003/AH1424. Signature 26.	FV	20.00
b. 2004/AH1425. Signature 27.	FV	17.00
c. 2006/AH1427. Signature 27.	FV	15.00
d. 2010/AH1431.	FV	15.00

96   25,000 Dinars   VF   UNC

2003/AH1424-. Red, purple and tan on multicolor underprint. Kurdish farmer holding sheaf of wheat, tractor in background. Back: Ancient Babylonian King Hammurabi. Printer: TDLR.

a. 2003/AH1424. Signature 26.	FV	35.00
b. 2004/AH1425. Signature 27.	FV	30.00
c. 2006/AH1427. Signature 27.	FV	27.50
d. 2008/AH1429.	FV	27.50
e. 2010/AH1431.	FV	27.50

2013 Issue

97   250 Dinars   VF   UNC

2013/AH1435. Blue on multicolor underprint. Astrolabe at right, tactile circle at left end. Back: Spiral Minaret in Samarra. 130x66mm.   FV   1.50

98　500 Dinars

2013/AH1435. Blue and green on multicolor underprint. Ducan Dam at center, two tactile circles at left end. Back: Winged bull statue. 142x66mm.

VF UNC
FV 2.00

99　1000 Dinars

2013/AH1435. Brown and tan on multicolor underprint. Medieval dinar coin at center. Three tactile circles at left end. Back: Al-Mustaniriyah University in Baghdad. 142x66mm.

VF UNC
FV 2.50

100　5000 Dinars

2013/AH1435. Dark blue on multicolor underprint. Gali Ali Beg and waterfall at center. One tactile bar at left end, color ink design at lower left corner. Back: Al-Ukhether fortress at center. 158x79mm.

VF UNC
FV 10.00

101　10,000 Dinars

2013/AH1435. Light and dark green on multicolor underprint. Freedom Monument in Baghdad, two tactile bars at left end. Color shifting ink design at lower left. Back: Al-Hadba' (the hunchback) minaret at the Great Nur al-Din mosque in Mosul. Watermark: Horse head. 170x78mm.

VF UNC
FV 15.00

102　25,000 Dinars

2013/AH1435. Red and tan on multicolor underprint. Figure at lower left center, tractor plowing at center, coin at right. Three tactile bars at left end. Back: Ancient Babylonian King Hammurabi at center. 175x78mm.

VF UNC
FV 27.50

IRELAND REPUBLIC

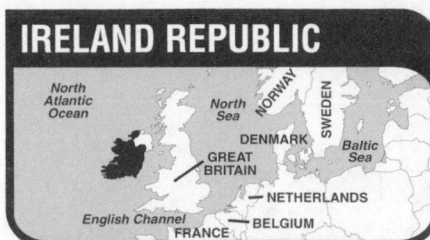

The Republic of Ireland, occupying five-sixths of the island of Ireland located in the Atlantic Ocean west of Great Britain, has an area of 70,280 sq. km. and a population of 4.16 million. Capital: Dublin.Celtic tribes arrived on the island between 600-150 B.C. Invasions by Norsemen that began in the late 8th century were finally ended when King Brian Boru defeated the Danes in 1014. English invasions began in the 12th century and set off more than seven centuries of Anglo-Irish struggle marked by fierce rebellions and harsh repressions. A failed 1916 Easter Monday Rebellion touched off several years of guerrilla warfare that in 1921 resulted in independence from the UK for 26 southern counties; six northern (Ulster) counties remained part of the UK. In 1949, Ireland withdrew from the British Commonwealth; it joined the European Community in 1973.

Additional information on bank notes of Northern Ireland can be found in *Paper Money of Ireland* by Bob Blake and Jonathan Callaway, published by Pam West.

RULERS:
British to 1921

MONETARY SYSTEM:
1 Shilling = 12 Pence
1 Pound = 20 Shillings to 1971
1 Pound = 100 Pence, 1971-2001
1 Euro = 100 Cent, 2002-

REPUBLIC

Banc Ceannais na hÉireann

CENTRAL BANK OF IRELAND

1961-63 Issue

#63-69 Replacement notes: From 1974-1976 single letter prefix plus 6-digit serial number for 1-20. For 1 and 5 dated 1975 a "OO" was used in front of a prefix letter.

63　10 Shillings

3.1.1962-6.6.1968. Orange on light green and lilac underprint. Portrait of Lady Hazel Lavery at left, denomination at bottom center. Signature M. O'Muimhneacháin and T. K. Whitaker. Back: Representation of river gods at center. 78x138mm.

		VF	UNC
a. Issued note.		30.00	100
s. Specimen.		—	350

64　1 Pound

1962-76. Green on pale gold underprint. Portrait of Lady Hazel Lavery at left, denomination at bottom center. Back: Representation of river gods at center. 84x151mm.

	VF	UNC
a. Signature M. O'Muimhneacháin and T. K. Whitaker. 16.3.1962-8.10.1968.	25.00	85.00
b. Signature T. K. Whitaker and C. H. Murray. 1.3.1969-17.9.1970.	22.50	75.00
c. Signature like b, but metallic security thread at left center 8.7.1971-21.4.1975.	20.00	60.00
d. Signature C. H. Murray and M. O'Murchu. 30.9.1976.	20.00	60.00
r1. Replacement note. As c. 17.5.1974. Serial # prefix: S.	35.00	95.00
r2. Replacement note. As c. 21.4.1975. Serial # prefix: OOA.	35.00	130
r3. Replacement note. As d. 30.9.1976. Serial # prefix: OOA.	35.00	130
s. Specimen.	—	—

65   5 Pounds VF UNC

1961-75. Dark brown on light gold and orange underprint. Portrait of Lady Hazel Lavery at left, denomination at bottom center. Back: Representation of river gods at center. 92x165mm.

a. Signature M. O'Muimhneacháin and T. K. Whitaker. 15.8.1961-12.8.1968.	50.00	400
b. Signature T. K. Whitaker and C. H. Murray. 12.5.1969; 27.2.1970.	50.00	350
c. Signature like b., but metallic security thread at left center 18.1.1971-5.9.1975.	50.00	300
r1. Replacement note. As c. 10.1.1975. Serial # prefix: *R*.	150	600
r2. Replacement note. As c. 5.9.1975. Serial # prefix: *OOK*.	90.00	450
s. As a. Specimen. Red overprint: *SPECIMEN* and TDLR oval on both sides. Punch hole cancelled.	—	750

66   10 Pounds VF UNC

1962-76. Blue on multicolor underprint. Lady Hazel Lavery in Irish national costume with chin resting on her hand and leaning on an Irish harp. Back: Representation of river gods at center. 108x191mm.

a. Signature M. O'Muimhneacháin and T. K. Whitaker. 2.5.1962-16.7.1968.	60.00	485
b. Signature T. K. Whitaker and C. H. Murray. 5.5.1969; 9.3.1970.	60.00	425
c. Signature like b, but metallic security thread at left center 19.5.1971-10.2.1975.	60.00	385
d. Signature C. H. Murray and M. O'Murchu. 2.12.1976.	55.00	350
r1. Replacement note. As c. 10.2.1975. Serial # prefix: *T*.	100	600
r2. Replacement note. As d. 2.12.1976. Serial # prefix: *T*.	100	600

67   20 Pounds VF UNC

1961-76. Red on multicolor underprint. Lady Hazel Lavery in Irish national costume with chin resting on her hand and leaning on an Irish harp. Back: Representation of river gods at center. 203x114mm.

a. Signature M. O'Muimhneacháin and T. K. Whitaker. 1.6.1961-15.6.1965.	200	850
b. Signature T. K. Whitaker and C. H. Murray. 3.3.1969-6.1.1975.	190	750
c. Signature C. H. Murray and M. O'Murchu. 24.3.1976.	190	650
r. Replacement note. As c. 34.3.1976. Serial # prefix: *V*.	600	2,000

68   50 Pounds VF UNC

1962-77. Purple on multicolor underprint. Lady Hazel Lavery in Irish national costume with chin resting on her hand and leaning on an Irish harp. Back: Representation of river gods at center. 203x114mm.

a. Signature M. O'Muimhneachain and I. K. Whitaker. 1.2.1962-6.9.1968.	850	2,300
b. Signature T. K. Whitaker and C. H. Murray. 4.11.1970-16.4.1975.	750	2,100
c. Signature C. H. Murray and M. O'Murchu. 4.4.1977.	675	1,900

69   100 Pounds VF UNC

1963-77. Green on multicolor underprint. Lady Hazel Lavery in Irish national costume with chin resting on her hand and leaning on an Irish harp. Back: Representation of river gods at center. 114x203mm.

a. Signature M. O'Muimhneacháin and T. K. Whitaker. 16.1.1963-9.9.1968.	800	2,200
b. Signature T. K. Whitaker and C. H. Murray. 26.10.1970; 3.3.1972; 20.2.1973; 10.4.1975.	700	2,000
c. Signature C. H. Murray and M. O'Murchu. 4.4.1977.	650	1,850

1976-82 Issue

#70-74 replacement notes: Serial # prefixes *AAA; BBB;* etc.

70   1 Pound VF UNC

1977-89. Dark olive-green and green on multicolor underprint. Queen Medb at right. Back: Old writing. Watermark: Lady Lavery. 148x78mm.

a. Signature C. H. Murray and M. O'Murchu. 10.6.1977-29.11.1977.	12.00	35.00
b. Signature C. H. Murray and T. F. O'Cofaigh. 30.8.1978-30.10.1981.	10.00	30.00
c. Signature T. F. O'Cofaigh and M. F. Doyle. 30.6.1982-24.4.1987.	9.00	25.00
d. Signature M. F. Doyle and S. P. Cromien. 23.3.1988-17.7.1989.	8.00	20.00
r1. Replacement note. As a. Serial # prefix: *BBB*.	25.00	100
r2. Replacement note. As b. Serial # prefix: *BBB; DDD; GGG*.	25.00	100
r3. Replacement note. As c. Serial # prefix: *BBB; GGG*.	25.00	100
r4. Replacement note. As d. Serial # prefix: *BBB*.	20.00	80.00
s. Specimen. As a, c.	—	550

71 5 Pounds

1976-93. Brown and red-violet on multicolor underprint. John Scotus Eriugena at right. Back: Old writing. 156x82mm.

	VF	UNC
a. Signature T. K. Whitaker and C. H. Murray. 26.2.1976.	35.00	100
b. Signature C. H. Murray and M. O'Murchu. 18.5.1976-17.10.1977.	30.00	90.00
c. Signature C. H. Murray and T. F. O'Cofaigh. 25.4.1979-29.10.1981.	25.00	65.00
d. Signature T. F. O'Cofaigh and M. F. Doyle. 1982; 17.10.1983-22.4.1987.	22.50	60.00
e. Signature M. F. Doyle and S. P. Cromien. 12.8.1988-7.5.1993.	20.00	55.00
r1. Replacement note. As a. Serial # prefix: *AAA*.	100	250
r2. Replacement note. As b. Serial # prefix: *AAA*.	70.00	100
r3. Replacement note. As c. Serial # prefix: *AAA*.	70.00	200
r4. Replacement note. As d. Serial # prefix: *AAA*.	70.00	200
r5. Replacement note. As e. Serial # prefix: *AAA*.	100	250
r6. Replacement note. As e. Serial # prefix: *FFF*.	20.00	170
s. Specimen. As b, d.	—	650

72 10 Pounds

1978-92. Violet and purple on multicolor underprint. Jonathan Swift at right. Back: Old street map of Dublin. 164x86mm.

	VF	UNC
a. Signature C. H. Murray and T. F. O'Cofaigh. 1.6.1978-28.10.1981.	50.00	150
b. Signature T. F. O'Cofaigh and M. F. Doyle. 1982; 25.2.1983-9.2.1987.	45.00	140
c. Signature M. F. Doyle and S. P. Cromien. 22.12.1987-15.4.1992.	40.00	130
r1. Replacement note. As a. Serial # prefix: *CCC*.	130	300
r2. Replacement note. As b. Serial # prefix: *HHH*.	130	300
r3. Replacement note. As c. Serial # prefix: *HHH*.	130	300
s. Specimen. As a, b. Overprint: *SPECIMEN*.	—	750

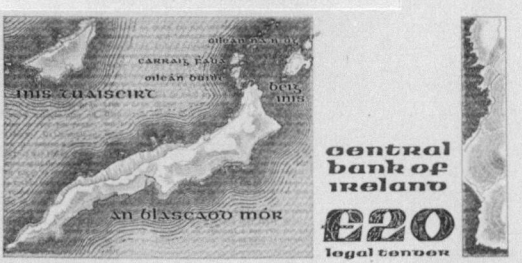

73 20 Pounds

1980-92. Blue on multicolor underprint. William Butler Yeats at right, Abbey Theatre symbol at center. Back: Map. 172x90mm.

	VF	UNC
a. Signature C. H. Murray and T. F. O'Cofaigh. 7.1.1980-28.10.1981.	90.00	225
b. Signature T. F. O'Cofaigh and M. F. Doyle. 11.7.1983-28.8.1986.	80.00	200
c. Signature M. F. Doyle and S. P. Cromien. 12.8.1987-14.2.1992.	75.00	185
r1. Replacement note. As a. Serial # prefix: *EEE*.	300	600
r2. Replacement note. As b. Serial # prefix: *EEE*.	300	600
r3. Replacement note. As c. Serial # prefix: *EEE*.	300	600
r4. Replacement note. As c. Serial # prefix: *LLL*.	450	800
s. Specimen. As b.	—	850

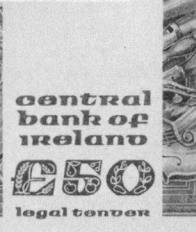

74 50 Pounds

1982; 1991. Red and brown on multicolor underprint. Turlough O'Carolan playing harp in front of group. Back: Musical instruments. 180x94mm.

	VF	UNC
a. Signature T. F. O'Cofaigh and M. F. Doyle. 1.11.1982.	200	550
b. Signature M. F. Doyle and S. P. Cromien. 5.11.1991.	185	500
r1. Replacement note. As a. Serial # prefix: *KKK*.	800	2,600
r2. Replacement note. As b. Serial # prefix: *KKK*.	450	1,300
s. Specimen. As a.	—	950

1992-96 Issue

#75-78 Replacement notes: Serial # prefixes *BBB; CCC,* **etc.**

75 5 Pounds

1994-99. Dark brown, reddish brown, and grayish purple on multicolor underprint. Mater Misericordiae Hospital at bottom left center, Sister Catherine McAuley at right. Back: School children at center. Watermark: Lady Lavery and value. 120x64mm.

	VF	UNC
a. Signature M. F. Doyle and S. P. Cromien. 15.3.1994-28.4.1994.	FV	47.50
b. Signature M. O'Conaill and P. H. Mullarkey. 21.12.1994-15.10.1999.	FV	40.00
r1. Replacement note. As a. Serial # prefix: *HHH*.	10.00	80.00
r2. Replacement note. As b. Serial # prefix: *HHH*.	18.00	80.00
r3. Replacement note. As b. Serial # prefix: *MMM*.	25.00	100

76 10 Pounds

1993-99. Dark green and brown on multicolor underprint. Aerial view of Dublin at center, James Joyce at right. Back: Sculpted head representing Liffey River at left, map in underprint. Watermark: Lady Lavery and value. 128x68mm.

	VF	UNC
a. Signature M. F. Doyle and S. P. Cromien. 14.7.1993-27.4.1994.	FV	80.00
b. Signature M. O'Conaill and P. H. Mullarkey. 13.3.1995-2.7.1999.	FV	75.00
r1. Replacement note. As a. Serial # prefix JJJ.	35.00	180
r2. Replacement note. As b. Serial # prefix JJJ.	35.00	200
r3. Replacement note. As b. Serial # prefix NNN.	35.00	200

77 20 Pounds

1992-99. Violet, brown and dark grayish blue on multicolor underprint. Derrynane Abbey at left center, Daniel O'Connell at right. Back: Writings and Four Courts building, Dublin. Watermark: Lady Lavery and value. 136x72mm.

		VF	UNC
a.	Signature M. F. Doyle and S. P. Cromien. 10.9.1992-29.4.1994.	FV	140
b.	Signature M. O'Conaill and P. H. Mullarkey. 14.6.1995-9.12.1999.	FV	125
r1.	Replacement note. 10.9.1992. As a. Serial # prefix: BBB. (Date exists only as a replacement).	400	800
r2.	Replacement note. As a, (other dates). Serial # prefix: BBB.	50.00	260
r3.	Replacement note. As a. Serial # prefix: FFF.	50.00	200
r4.	Replacement note. As a. Serial # prefix: CCC.	100	350
r5.	Replacement note. As b. Serial # prefix PPP.	90.00	350

78 50 Pounds

1995-2001. Dark blue and violet on multicolor underprint. Douglas Hyde at right, Áras an Uachtaráin building in background at center. Back: Uilinn Piper at left, crest of *Conradh na Gaeilge* at upper center right. Watermark: Lady Lavery and value. 144x76mm.

		VF	UNC
a.	Signature M. O'Conaill and P. H. Mullarkey. 6.10.1995; 14.2.1996; 19.3.1999.	FV	325
b.	Signature M. O'Conaill and J. A. Hurley. 8.3.2001.	FV	300
r1.	Replacement note. As a. Serial # prefix: EEE.	250	700
r2.	Replacement note. As b. Serial # prefix: RRR.	150	550

79 100 Pounds

22.8.1996. Lilac brown, light orange-brown and slate. Charles Stewart Parnell at right, Avondale House and gardens in Rathdrum at lower left center, Irish Wolfhound at lower left. Signature M. O'Conaill and P. H. Mullarkey. Back: Parts of the Parnell monument in Dublin. 152x80mm.

		VF	UNC
a.	Issued note.	230	800
r1.	Replacement note. As a. Serial # prefix: KKK.	400	1,200

Note: For later issues made for use in the Republic of Ireland, see European Union listings.

ISLE OF MAN

The Isle of Man, a dependency of the British Crown located in the Irish Sea equidistant from Ireland, Scotland and England, has an area of 572 sq. km. and a population of 76,220. Capital: Douglas. Agriculture, dairy farming, fishing and tourism are the chief industries.

Part of the Norwegian Kingdom of the Hebrides until the 13th century when it was ceded to Scotland, the isle came under the British crown in 1765. Current concerns include reviving the almost extinct Manx Gaelic language. Isle of Man is a British crown dependency but is not part of the UK. However, the UK Government remains constitutionally responsible for its defense and international representation. The Sovereign of the United Kingdom (currently Queen Elizabeth II) holds the title Lord of Man. The Isle of Man is ruled by its own legislative council and the House of Keys, one of the oldest legislative assemblies in the world. Acts of Parliament passed in London do not affect the island unless it is specifically mentioned. United Kingdom bank notes and coinage circulate concurrently with Isle of Man money as legal tender.

RULERS:
British

MONETARY SYSTEM:
1 Pound = 20 Shillings to 1971
1 Pound = 100 Pence, 1971-

SIGNATURE VARIETIES					
1	Garvey	2	Stallard		
3	Paul (28mm)	4	Paul (20mm)		
5	Dawaon	6	Cashen		
7	Shimmin				

BRITISH ADMINISTRATION

Lloyds Bank Limited

1955 Issue

13 1 Pound

21.1.1955-14.3.1961. Black on green underprint. Bank arms at upper center. Signature varieties. Back: Bank title enlarged.

		Fine	XF
a.	Issued note.	350	750
r.	Unsigned remainder. ND.	—	200

Westminster Bank Limited

Formerly the London County Westminster and Parr's Bank Limited.

1955 Issue

23A 1 Pound

	Fine	XF
1955-61. Black on light yellow underprint. Crowned triskele supported by lion left, unicorn right at upper center. Text: *INCORPORATED IN ENGLAND* added below bank name. Signature varieties. Printer: W&S.		
a. 23.11.1955.	200	500
b. 4.4.1956-10.3.1961.	100	225

Isle of Man Government
1961 ND Issue

24 10 Shillings

	VF	UNC
ND (1961). Red on multicolor underprint. Triskele arms at lower center, young portrait of Queen Elizabeth II at right. Back: Old sailing boat. Watermark: Triskele arms. Printer: BWC.		
a. Signature 1.	25.00	85.00
b. Signature 2.	20.00	75.00
s1. Signature 1. Specimen. 00000 serial #. (150 issued).	—	250
s2. Signature 2. Specimen.	—	260

25 1 Pound

	VF	UNC
ND (1961). Purple on multicolor underprint. Triskele arms at lower center, young portrait of Queen Elizabeth II at right. Back: Tynwald Hill. Watermark: Triskele arms. Printer: BWC.		
a. Signature 1. Without serial # prefix, or Serial # prefix *B*.	40.00	180
b. Signature 2.	30.00	135
s1. Signature 1. Specimen. 00000 serial #. (150 issued).	—	280
s2. Signature 2. Specimen.	—	200

26 5 Pounds

	VF	UNC
ND (1961). Green and blue on multicolor underprint. Triskele arms at lower center, young portrait of Queen Elizabeth II at right. Back: Castle Rushen. Watermark: Triskele arms. Printer: BWC.		
a. Signature 1.	200	1,500
b. Signature 2.	185	1,350
s1. Specimen with normal serial #.	—	500
s2. Signature 1. Specimen with normal serial # blocked out, punch hole cancelled. (50 issued).	—	400
s3. Signature 1. Specimen. 000000 serial #. (150 issued).	—	350
s4. Signature 2. Specimen.	—	400

1969 ND Issue

27 50 New Pence

	VF	UNC
ND (1969). 139 x 66mm. Blue on multicolor underprint. Triskele arms at lower center, young portrait of Queen Elizabeth II at right. Signature 2. Back: Old sailing boat. Watermark: Triskele arms. Printer: BWC.		
a. Issued note.	10.00	45.00
s. Specimen.	—	300

1972 ND Issue

28 50 New Pence

	VF	UNC
ND (1972). 126 x 62mm. Blue on multicolor underprint. Triskele arms at center, mature portrait of Queen Elizabeth II at right. Signature title: *LIEUTENANT GOVERNOR*. Back: Old sailing boat. Watermark: Triskele arms. Printer: BWC.		
a. Signature 2.	20.00	60.00
b. Signature 3.	12.50	35.00
c. Signature 4.	12.50	30.00
s1. As a. Specimen. Punched hole cancelled.	—	220
s2. As b, c. Specimen.	—	220

29 1 Pound

	VF	UNC
ND (1972). Purple on multicolor underprint. Triskele arms at center, mature portrait of Queen Elizabeth II at right. Signature title: *LIEUTENANT GOVERNOR*. Back: Tynwald Hill. Watermark: Triskele arms. Printer: BWC.		
a. Signature 2.	25.00	110
b. Signature 3. Series D.	150	550
c. Signature 3. Series E.	25.00	100
d. Signature 4.	7.50	50.00
s1. As a. Specimen. Punched hole cancelled.	—	240
s2. As b, c. Specimen.	—	240

30 5 Pounds

	VF	UNC
ND (1972). Blue-black and violet on multicolor underprint. Triskele arms at center, mature portrait of Queen Elizabeth II at right. Signature title: *LIEUTENANT GOVERNOR*. Back: Castle Rushen. Watermark: Triskele arms. Printer: BWC.		
a. Signature 2.	75.00	600
b. Signature 3.	40.00	300
s. As a, b. Specimen. Punched hole cancelled.	—	340

31 10 Pounds

	VF	UNC
ND (1972). Brown and dark green on multicolor underprint. Triskele arms at center, mature portrait of Queen Elizabeth II at right. Signature title: *LIEUTENANT GOVERNOR*. Back: Peel Castle ca.1830 at center. Watermark: Triskele arms. Printer: BWC.		
a. Signature 2.	600	2,000
b. Signature 3.	150	550
s. As a, b. Specimen, punched hole cancelled.	—	700

1979 Commemorative Issue

#32, Millennium Year 1979

		VF	UNC
32	**20 Pounds**	150	450

1979. Red-orange, orange and dark brown on multicolor underprint. Triskele at center. Queen Elizabeth II at right. Island outline at upper right. Commemorative text at lower right of triskele. Back: Laxey wheel ca. 1854, crowd of people with hills in background. Printer: BWC.

1979 ND Issue

#33s-38s were mounted on a board for bank display

			VF	UNC
33	**50 New Pence**			

ND. Blue on multicolor underprint. Queen Elizabeth II at right, arms at center. Signature title: *TREASURER OF THE ISLE OF MAN*. Signature 5. Back: Old sailing boat. Watermark: Triskele arms. Printer: BWC.

			VF	UNC
	a. Issued note.		FV	15.00
	s. Specimen. Normal serial #, punched hole cancelled.		—	185
34	**1 Pound**		**VF**	**UNC**

ND. Purple on multicolor underprint. Queen Elizabeth II at right, arms at center. Signature title: *TREASURER OF THE ISLE OF MAN*. Signature 5. Back: Tynwald Hill. Watermark: Triskele arms. Printer: BWC.

		VF	UNC
a. Issued note.		FV	20.00
s. Specimen. Normal serial #, punched hole cancelled.		—	175

		VF	UNC
35	**5 Pounds**		

ND. Blue-black and violet on multicolor underprint. Queen Elizabeth II at right, arms at center. Signature title: *TREASURER OF THE ISLE OF MAN*. Back: Castle Rushen. Watermark: Triskele arms. Printer: BWC.

		VF	UNC
a. Signature 5. Series B-C.		50.00	175
b. Signature 5. Series D. Large 'D' with serifs.		75.00	300
35A	**5 Pounds**	**VF**	**UNC**

ND. Blue-black and violet on multicolor underprint. Queen Elizabeth II at right, arms at center. Signature title: *TREASURER OF THE ISLE OF MAN*. Modified guilloche. Series D. Narrow 'D' without serifs. Back: Castle Rushen. Watermark: Triskele arms. Printer: BWC.

		VF	UNC
a. Issued note.		50.00	200
s. Specimen. Normal serial #, punched hole cancelled.		—	275

		VF	UNC
36	**10 Pounds**		

ND. Brown and dark green on multicolor underprint. Queen Elizabeth II at right, arms at center. Signature title: *TREASURER OF THE ISLE OF MAN*. Signature 5. Back: Peel Castle ca.1830 at center. Watermark: Triskele arms. Printer: BWC.

		VF	UNC
a. Without prefix.		90.00	400
b. Prefix A.		100	425
c. Prefix B. (10,000 printed).		600	2,000
s1. As a. Specimen. Without prefix.		—	900
s2. Specimen. Prefix A, normal serial #, punched hole cancelled.		—	400

		VF	UNC
37	**20 Pounds**		

ND (1979). Red-orange, orange and dark brown on multicolor underprint. Queen Elizabeth II at right, arms at center. Signature title: *TREASURER OF THE ISLE OF MAN*. Without commemorative text. Back: Laxey wheel ca. 1854, crowd of people with hills in background. Watermark: Triskele arms. Printer: BWC.

		VF	UNC
a. Issued note.		125	500
s. Specimen. Normal serial #, punched hole cancelled.		—	510

1983 ND Issue

		VF	UNC
38	**1 Pound**		

ND (1983). Printed on Bradvek, a plastic. Green on multicolor underprint. Triskele arms at lower center, young portrait of Queen Elizabeth II at right. Back: Tynwald Hill. Watermark: Triskele arms. Printer: BWC.

		VF	UNC
a. Issued note.		5.00	45.00
s. Specimen.		—	220

		VF	UNC
39	**50 Pounds**		

ND (1983). Blue gray, deep green and olive-green on multicolor underprint. Back: Douglas Bay.

		VF	UNC
a. Issued note.		100	180
s. Specimen. Normal serial #, punched hole cancelled.		—	700

1983 ND Reduced Size Issue

40 **1 Pound** **VF** **UNC**

ND. Purple on multicolor underprint. Queen Elizabeth II at right, arms at center.
Back: Tynwald Hill. Watermark: Triskele. Printer: TDLR. 128x65mm.

a. Signature 5.	4.00	15.00
b. Signature 6.	FV	5.00
c. Signature 7.	FV	5.00
r1. As a. Replacement note.	150	—
r2. As b. Replacement note.	10.00	45.00
s. As a. Specimen.	—	575

41 **5 Pounds** **VF** **UNC**

ND. Greenish blue and lilac-brown on multicolor underprint. Queen Elizabeth II at
right, arms at center. Back: Castle Rushen. Watermark: Triskele. Printer: TDLR.
135x70mm.

a. Signature 5.	20.00	85.00
b. Signature 6.	FV	20.00
r. As b. Replacement note.	20.00	70.00

42 **10 Pounds** **VF** **UNC**

ND. Brown and green on multicolor underprint. Queen Elizabeth II at right, arms
at center. Signature 6. Back: Peel Castle ca.1830 at center. Watermark: Triskele.
Printer: TDLR. 142x75mm.

FV 55.00

43 **20 Pounds** **VF** **UNC**

ND. Brown and red-orange on multicolor underprint. Queen Elizabeth II at right,
arms at center. Back: Laxey wheel ca. 1854, crowd of people with hills in background. Watermark: Triskele. Printer: TDLR. 150x80mm.

a. Signature 5.	125	450
b. Signature 6. Without prefix, prefix B, C.	FV	90.00
r. As b. Replacement note.	50.00	120

1998; 2000 ND Issue

44 **10 Pounds** **VF** **UNC**

ND (1998). Brown and green on multicolor underprint. Queen Elizabeth II at right,
arms at center. Back: Peel Castle ca.1830 at center. Watermark: Triskele. Printer:
TDLR. 142x75mm.

a. Signature 6.	FV	37.50
b. Signature 7.	FV	22.50
r. Replacement note.	50.00	90.00

45 **20 Pounds** **VF** **UNC**

ND (2000). Brown and red-orange on multicolor underprint. Elizabeth II at right,
arms at center. Signature 6. Without prefix, prefix B, C. Back: Laxey wheel (ca.
1854), crowd of people with hills in background. Watermark: Triskele. Printer:
TDLR. 150x80mm.

a. Signatrue 6, Cashen.	FV	70.00
b. Signature 7, Shimmin.	FV	60.00
s. Specimen. Serial # *D000000*. Punch hole cancelled.	—	200

ISRAEL

The State of Israel, at the eastern end of the Mediterranean Sea, bounded by Lebanon on the north, Syria on the northeast, Jordan on the east, and Egypt on the southwest, has an area of 20,770 sq. km. and a population of 7.11 million. Capital: Jerusalem. Diamonds, chemicals, citrus, textiles, and minerals are exported, local tourism to religious sites.

Following World War II, the British withdrew from their mandate of Palestine, and the UN partitioned the area into Arab and Jewish states, an arrangement rejected by the Arabs. Subsequently, the Israelis defeated the Arabs in a series of wars without ending the deep tensions between the two sides. The territories Israel occupied since the 1967 war are not included in the Israel country profile, unless otherwise noted. On 25 April 1982, Israel withdrew from the Sinai pursuant to the 1979 Israel-Egypt Peace Treaty. In keeping with the framework established at the Madrid Conference in October 1991, bilateral negotiations were conducted between Israel and Palestinian representatives and Syria to achieve a permanent settlement. Israel and Palestinian officials signed on 13 September 1993 a Declaration of Principles (also known as the "Oslo Accords") guiding an interim period of Palestinian self-rule.

MONETARY SYSTEM:

1 Lira = 100 Agorot, 1958-1980
1 Sheqel = 10 "old" Lirot, 1980-85
1 Sheqel = 100 New Agorot, 1980-1985
1 New Sheqel = 1000 "old" Sheqalim, 1985-
1 New Sheqel = 100 Agorot, 1985-

STATE OF ISRAEL

Bank of Israel

1958-60 / 5718-20 Issue

29   1/2 Lira   **VF   UNC**
1958/5718. UV: fibers fluoresce blue. Green on green and peach underprint.
Woman soldier with basket full of oranges at left. Back: Tombs of the Sanhedrin at
right. Watermark: Woman soldier. Printer: JEZ (without imprint).

a. Issued note.	1.50	5.00
s. Specimen.	—	275

30   1 Lira   **VF   UNC**
1958/5718. UV: fibers fluoresce blue. Blue on light blue and peach underprint.
Fisherman with net and anchor at left. Back: Synagogue mosaic at right. Watermark: Fisherman. Printer: JEZ (without imprint).

a. Paper with security thread at left. Black serial #.	1.25	4.00
b. Red serial #.	1.25	4.00
c. Paper with security thread and morse tape, brown serial #.	1.00	3.00
s. Specimen.	—	275

31   5 Lirot   **VF   UNC**
1958/5718. UV: fibers fluoresce yellow. Brown on multicolor underprint. Worker
with hammer in front of factory at left. Back: Seal of Shema at right. Watermark:
Worker with hammer. Printer: TDLR (without imprint).

a. Issued note.	2.00	5.00
s. Specimen.	—	500

32   10 Lirot   **VF   UNC**
1958/5718. Lilac and purple on multicolor underprint. Scientist with microscope
and test tube at left. Back: Dead Sea scroll and vases at right. Watermark:
Scientist. Printer: TDLR (without imprint).

a. Paper with security thread. Black serial #.	2.00	12.00
b. Paper with security thread and morse tape. Red serial #.	2.00	15.00
c. Paper with security thread and morse tape. Blue serial #.	2.00	15.00
d. Paper with security thread and morse tape. Brown serial #.	1.50	6.00
s. Specimen.	—	500

33   50 Lirot   **VF   UNC**
1960/5720. Brown and multicolor. Boy and girl at left. Back: Mosaic of menorah at
right. Watermark: Boy and girl. Printer: JEZ (without imprint).

a. Paper with security thread. Black serial #.	10.00	45.00
b. Paper with security thread. Red serial #.	10.00	45.00
c. Paper with security thread and morse tape. Blue serial #.	6.00	45.00
d. Paper with security thread and morse tape. Green serial #.	6.00	30.00
e. Paper with security thread and morse tape. Brown serial #.	5.00	30.00
s. Specimen.	—	600

1968 / 5728 Issue

34 5 Lirot

<table>
<tr><th></th><th>VF</th><th>UNC</th></tr>
</table>

1968/5728. Gray-green and blue on multicolor underprint. Albert Einstein at right. Back: Atomic reactor at Nahal Sorek. Watermark: Albert Einstein. Printer: JEZ (without imprint).

	VF	UNC
a. Black serial #.	3.00	9.00
b. Red serial #.	3.00	9.00
s. Specimen.	—	225

35 10 Lirot

1968/5728. UV: fluoresce blue. Brown, purple and multicolor. Chaim Nahman Bialik at right. Back: Bialik's house in Tel Aviv. Watermark: Chaim Nahman Bialik. Printer: JEZ (without imprint).

	VF	UNC
a. Black serial #.	1.00	5.00
b. Green serial #.	1.00	5.00
c. Blue serial #.	1.00	5.00
s. Specimen.	—	225

36 50 Lirot

1968/5728. Light and dark brown and green on multicolor underprint. President Chaim Weizmann at right. Back: Knesset building in Jerusalem. Watermark: President Chaim Weizmann. Printer: JEZ (without imprint).

	VF	UNC
a. Black serial #.	2.00	7.00
b. Blue serial #.	2.00	7.00
s. Specimen.	—	225

37 100 Lirot

1968/5728. Blue and light green on multicolor underprint. Dr. Theodor Herzl at right. Back: Menorah and symbols of the twelve tribes of Israel at left center. Watermark: Dr. Theodor Herzl. Printer: JEZ (without imprint).

	VF	UNC
a. Watermark: Profile. Black serial #. 3.5mm.	10.00	30.00
b. Watermark: 3/4 profile rright. Red serial #.	10.00	45.00
c. Watermark: Profile. Black serial #. 2.8mm. Without series letter.	10.00	25.00
d. Watermark: Profile. Brown serial #.	10.00	35.00
s. Specimen.	—	225

1973-75 / 5733-35 Issue

38 5 Lirot

1973/5733. UV: back barcodes fluoresce orange. Light and dark brown. Henrietta Szold at right. Marks for the blind. Back: Lion's Gate. Barely discernible bar code strips at lower left and upper right. Watermark: Henrietta Szold. Printer: JEZ (without imprint).

	VF	UNC
	0.50	1.50

39 10 Lirot

1973/5733. UV: back barcodes fluoresce orange. Purple on lilac underprint. Sir Moses Montefiore at right. Marks for the blind. Back: Jaffa Gate. Barely discernible bar code strips at lower left and upper right. Watermark: Sir Moses Montefiore. Printer: JEZ (without imprint).

	VF	UNC
a. Issued note.	0.50	1.50
s. Specimen.	—	—

40 50 Lirot

1973/5733. Green on olive-green underprint. Chaim Weizmann at right. Marks for the blind. Back: Sichem Gate. Barely discernible bar code strips at lower left and upper right. Watermark: Chaim Weizmann. Printer: JEZ (without imprint).

	VF	UNC
	1.00	5.00

41 100 Lirot VF UNC
1973/5733. Blue on blue and brown underprint. Dr. Theodor Herzl at right. Back: 1.50 7.00
Zion Gate. Barely discernible bar code strips at lower left and upper right. Watermark: Dr. Theodor Herzl. Printer: JEZ (without imprint).

42 500 Lirot VF UNC
1975/5735. Black on tan and brown underprint. David Ben-Gurion at right. Marks 10.00 45.00
for the blind. Back: Golden Gate. Barely discernible bar code strips at lower left
and upper right. Watermark: David Ben-Gurion. Printer: JEZ (without imprint).

1978-84 / 5738-44 Issue

Sheqel system

43 1 Sheqel VF UNC
1978/5738 (1980). UV: back upper and lower barcodes fluoresce orange. Purple
on lilac underprint. Sir Moses Montefiore at right. Marks for the blind. Back: Jaffa
Gate. Barely discernible bar code strips at lower left and upper right. Watermark:
Sir Moses Montefiore. Printer: JEZ (without imprint).
    a. Issued note. 0.50 1.50
    s. Specimen. — —

44 5 Sheqalim VF UNC
1978/5738 (1980). UV: back barcodes fluoresce orange. Green on olive-green 0.75 3.00
underprint. Chaim Weizmann at right. Marks for the blind. Back: Sichem Gate.
Barely discernible bar code strips at lower left and upper right. Watermark: Chaim
Weizmann. Printer: JEZ (without imprint).

45 10 Sheqalim VF UNC
1978/5738 (1980). Blue on blue and brown underprint. Dr. Theodor Herzl at right. 1.50 5.00
Back: Zion Gate. Barely discernible bar code strips at lower left and upper right.
Watermark: Dr. Theodor Herzl. Printer: JEZ (without imprint).

46 50 Sheqalim VF UNC
1978/5738 (1980). UV: back serial #s fluoresce orange. Black on tan and brown
underprint. David Ben-Gurion at right. Marks for the blind. Back: Golden Gate.
Barely discernible bar code strips at lower left and upper right. Watermark: David
Ben-Gurion. Printer: JEZ (without imprint).
    a. Without small bars below serial # or barely discernible bar code strips on 0.50 2.00
       back.
    b. Without small bars below serial #, but with bar code strips on back. 4.00 30.00
    c. 2 green bars below serial # on back. 60.00 250
    d. 4 black bars below serial # on back. 35.00 200
    e. As a. 12-subject sheet. — 20.00
Note: Colored bars were used to identify various surface-coated papers, used experimentally.

47 100 Sheqalim VF UNC
1979/5739. Red-brown on light tan underprint. Ze'ev Jabotinsky at right. Marks for
the blind. Back: Herod's Gate. Watermark: Ze'ev Jabotinsky. Printer: JEZ (without
imprint).
    a. Without bars below serial # on back. 1.50 10.00
    b. 2 bars below serial # on back. 30.00 125

48 500 Sheqalim VF UNC
1982/5742. Red on multicolor underprint. Farm workers at center, Baron Edmond 1.50 6.00
de Rothschild at right. Marks for the blind. Back: Vine leaves. Watermark: Baron
Edmond de Rothschild. Printer: JEZ (without imprint).

49 1000 Sheqalim

1983/5743. Green on multicolor underprint. Rabbi Moses Maimonides at right. Marks for the blind. Back: View of Tiberias at left. Watermark: Rabbi Moses Maimonides. Printer: JEZ (without imprint).

		VF	UNC
a. Error in first letter *he* of second word at right. in vertical text (right to left), partly completed letter resembling 7.		7.50	25.00
b. Corrected letter resembling *17*.		5.00	20.00
c. As a. Uncut sheet of 3 (3,610 sheets).		—	45.00
d. As b. Uncut sheet of 3 (3.365 sheets).		—	35.00

50 5000 Sheqalim

1984/5744. Blue on multicolor underprint. City view at center, Levi Eshkol at right. Marks for the blind. Back: Water pipe and modern design. Watermark: Levi Eshkol. Printer: JEZ (without imprint).

	VF	UNC
a. Issued note.	7.50	45.00
b. Uncut sheet of 3 (2,755 sheets).	—	55.00

51 10,000 Sheqalim

1984/5744. Brown, black, orange and dark green on multicolor underprint. Stylized tree at center, Golda Meir at right. Marks for the blind. Back: Gathering in front of Moscow synagogue. Watermark: Golda Meir. Printer: JEZ (without imprint).

	VF	UNC
a. Issued note.	10.00	30.00
b. Uncut sheet of 3 (2,720 sheets).	—	75.00

SIGNATURE VARIETIES

5	Mandelbaum, 1986	6	Shapira and Mandelbaum, 1985
7	Lorincz and Bruno, 1987-91	**8**	Lorincz and Frankel, 1992
9			

1985-92 / 5745-52 Issue

51A 1 New Sheqel

1986/5746. Green on multicolor underprint. Rabbi Moses Maimonides at right. Marks for the blind. Signature 5. Back: View of Tiberias at left. Watermark: Rabbi Moses Maimonides. Printer: JEZ (without imprint). 138x76mm.

	VF	UNC
a. Issued note.	0.50	2.00
b. Uncut sheet of 3 (2,017 sheets).	—	7.00
c. Uncut sheet of 12 (1,416 sheets).	—	35.00
d. Uncut sheet of 18 (1.503 sheets).	—	50.00

52 5 New Sheqalim

1985/5745; 1987/5747. Blue on multicolor underprint. City view at center, Levi Eshkol at right. Marks for the blind. Back: Water pipe and modern design. Watermark: Levi Eshkol. Printer: JEZ (without imprint). 138x76mm.

	VF	UNC
a. Signature 6. 1985/5745.	3.00	15.00
b. Signature 7. 1987/5747.	2.50	18.00
c. As a. Uncut sheet of 3 (1,630 sheets).	—	40.00

53 10 New Sheqalim

1985/5745; 1987/5747; 1992/5752. Brown, black, orange and dark green on multicolor underprint. Stylized tree at center, Golda Meir at right. Marks for the blind. Back: Gathering in front of Moscow synagogue. Watermark: Golda Meir. Printer: JEZ (without imprint). 138x76mm.

	VF	UNC
a. Signature 6. 1985/5745.	6.00	35.00
b. Signature 7. 1987/5747.	4.00	30.00
c. Signature 8. 1992/5752.	2.00	20.00
d. As a. Uncut sheet of 3 (1,571 sheets).	—	40.00

54 20 New Sheqalim

1987/5747; 1993/5753. Dark gray on multicolor underprint. Moshe Sharett standing holding flag at center, his bust at right. Marks for the blind. Back: Herzlya High School at center. Watermark: Moshe Sharett. Printer: JEZ (without imprint). 138x76mm.

	VF	UNC
a. Without sm. double circle With dot in watermark. area face and back. signature 7. 1987/5747.	FV	45.00
b. With sm. double circle With dot in watermark. area face and back. signature 7. 1987/5747.	FV	20.00
c. Signature 8. 1993/5753.	FV	18.00

55   50 New Sheqalim   **VF   UNC**
1985/5745-1992/5752. Purple on multicolor underprint. Shmuel Yosef Agnon at
right. Marks for the blind. Back: Various buildings and book titles. Watermark:
Shmuel Yosef Agnon. Printer: JEZ (without imprint). 138x76mm.
    a. Signature 6. 1985/5745.   FV   90.00
    b. Signature 7. Slight color variations. 1988/5748.   FV   90.00
    c. Signature 8. 1992/5752.   FV   50 00

56   100 New Sheqalim   **VF   UNC**
1986/5746; 1989/5749; 1995/5755. Brown on multicolor underprint. Itzhak Ben-Zvi
at right. Marks for the blind. Back: Stylized village of Peki'in and carob tree.
Watermark: Itzhak Ben-Zvi. Printer: JEZ (without imprint). 138x76mm.
    a. Signature 5. Plain security thread and plain white paper. 1986/5746.   FV   95.00
    b. with security thread inscribed: *Bank Israel,* paper with colored   FV   95.00
       threads. 1989/5749.
    c. Signature 8. 1995/5755.   FV   85.00

57   200 New Sheqalim   **VF   UNC**
1991/5751; 1994/5754. Deep red, purple and blue-green on multicolor underprint.
Zalman Shazar at right. Back: School girl writing at center. Watermark: Zalman
Shazar. 138x76mm.
    a. Signature 7. 1991/5751.   FV   135
    b. Signature 8. 1994/5754.   FV   120

1998 Commemorative Issue
#58, 50th Anniversary - State of Israel

58   50 New Sheqalim   **VF   UNC**
1998/5758. Purple on multicolor underprint. Shmuel Yosef Agnon at right. Marks
for the blind. OVI *50* at upper left, 5-digit serial number below. Signature 8. Back:
Various buildings and book titles. Watermark: Shmuel Yosef Agnon. Printer: JEZ
(without imprint). 138x/6mm.
    a. Issued note.   FV   45.00
    b. Sheetlet of three in folder. (10,001 sets)   —   100

1998 Dated 1999 Issue

59   20 New Sheqalim   **VF   UNC**
1998; 2001. Dark green on multicolor underprint. Moshe Sharett at bottom, flags
in background. Vertical format. Back: Scenes of his life and work. 71x138mm.
    a. 1998 (1999).   FV   20.00
    b. 2001 (2003). Signatures of Klein, Lorincz.   FV   18.00

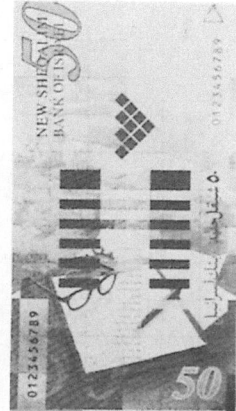

60   50 New Sheqalim   **VF   UNC**
1998; 2001; 2007. Purple on multicolor underprint. Shmuel Yosef Agnon at bottom, library shelves in background. Vertical format. Back: Western "wailing" Wall
and Dome of the Rock. Book titles. 71x138mm.
    a. 1998.   FV   40.00
    b. 2001 (2003). Signatures of Klein, Lorincz.   FV   28.00
    c. 5767/2007. Signatures of Fischer, Fogel.   FV   28.00

61 100 New Sheqalim
1998; 2002; 2007. Dark brown on multicolor underprint. Itzhak Ben-Zvi at bottom. Vertical format. Back: Scenes of his life and work. 71x138mm.

		VF	UNC
a. 1998.		FV	50.00
b. 2002 (2003). Signatures of Klein, Lorincz.		FV	50.00
c. 5767/2007. Signatures of Fischer, Fogel.		FV	50.00

62 200 New Sheqalim
1999, 2002; 2006; 2010. Red and red-orange on multicolor underprint. Zalman Shazar at bottom, classroom in background. Vertical format. Back: Scenes of his life and work. 71x138mm.

		VF	UNC
a. 1999.		FV	100
b. 5761/2002 (2003). Signatures of Klein, Lorincz.		FV	90.00
c. 5766/2006. Signatures of Fischer, Fogel.		FV	90.00
d. 5770/2010.		FV	75.00

2008 Commemorative Issue

 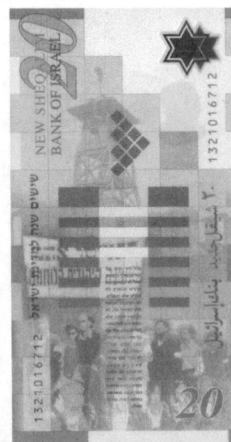

63 20 New Sheqalim — VF UNC — FV 25.00
Vertical format. Polymer Plastic. Dark green on multicolor underprint. Moshe Sharett at bottom, flags in background. Commemorative inscription in red honoring the 60th Anniversary of the State of Israel. Back: Scenes of his life and work. 71x138mm.

2008 Polymer Plastic Issue

 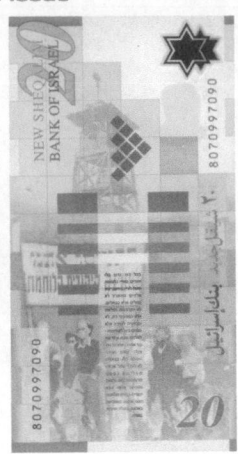

64 20 New Sheqalim — VF UNC — FV 18.00
2008. Vertical format. Polymer plastic. Dark green on multicolor underprint. Moshe Sharett at bottom, flags in background. Back: Scenes of his life and work. 71x138mm.

65 20 New Sheqalim — VF UNC — — —
Expected new issue.

2013-2015 Issue

66 50 New Sheqalim — VF UNC — FV 28.00
2014. Green. Shaul Tchernichovsky at right.

67 200 New Sheqalim — VF UNC — FV 75.00
2015. Blue. Menorah as registration device. Open book in gold-to-green SPARK. Fall leaves. Natan Alterman. Microprinted poem, "Eternal Meeting." Back: Moonlit tree branches, menorah. Windowed color-changing security thread with demetalized 200 and portrait of Natan Alterman. Watermark: Natan Alterman and electrotype 200. 150x71mm.

COLLECTOR SERIES

Bank of Israel

1990 Issue

CS1 (1990). 1-50 New Sheqalim — Mkt. Value — 95.00
1985-87. #51Aa-55a with matching serial #. Issued in special packaging. (2,000).

1991 Issue

CS2 (1991). 100, 200 New Sheqalim — Mkt. Value — 150
1985-86. #56a and 57a with matching serial # issued in special packaging. (2,000).

The Italian Republic, a 700-mile-long peninsula extending into the heart of the Mediterranean Sea, has an area of 301,230 sq. km. and a population of 58.14 million. Captal: Rome. The economy centers about agriculture, manufacturing, forestry and fishing. Machinery, textiles, clothing and motor vehicles are exported.

Italy became a nation-state in 1861 when the regional states of the peninsula, along with Sardinia and Sicily, were united under King Victor Emmanuel II. An era of parliamentary government came to a close in the early 1920s when Benito Mussolini established a Fascist dictatorship. His alliance with Nazi Germany led to Italy's defeat in World War II. A democratic republic replaced the monarchy in 1946 and economic revival followed. Italy was a charter member of NATO and the European Economic Community (EEC). It has been at the forefront of European economic and political unification, joining the Economic and Monetary Union in 1999. Persistent problems include illegal immigration, organized crime, corruption, high unemployment, sluggish economic growth, and the low incomes and technical standards of southern Italy compared with the prosperous north.

MONETARY SYSTEM:
1 Lira = 100 Centesimi, to 2001
1 Euro = 100 Cents, 2001-

DECREES:
There are many different dates found on the following notes of the Banca d'Italia. These include ART. DELLA LEGGE (law date) and the more important DECRETO MINISTERIALE (D. M. date). The earliest D.M. date is usually found on the back of the note while later D.M. dates are found grouped together. The actual latest date (of issue) is referred to in the following listings.

FACE SEAL VARIETIES:

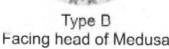

Type B
Facing head of Medusa

Type C
Winged lion of St. Mark of Venice above 3 shields of Genoa, Pisa and Amalfi

REPUBLIC

Repubblica Italiana - Biglietto di Stato
1966 Issue

93	**500 Lire**	**VF**	**UNC**
	1966-75. Dark gray on blue and multicolor underprint. Eagle with snake at left, Arethusa at right. Three signature varieties.		
	a. 20.6.1966; 20.10.1967; 23.2.1970.	1.25	28.50
	b. 23.4.1975.	80.00	455

Decreto Ministeriale 14.2.1974

94	**500 Lire**	**VF**	**UNC**
	14.2.1974; 2.4.1979. Grayish purple on blue and multicolor underprint. Mercury at right. Three signature varieties. Watermark: Star in wreath.	—	7.00

Decreto Ministeriale 5.6.1976

95	**500 Lire**	**VF**	**UNC**
	20.12.1976. Grayish purple on blue and multicolor underprint. Mercury at right. Three signature varieties. Watermark: Star in wreath.	—	7.00

Banca d'Italia
BANK OF ITALY
1962 Issue
Decreto Ministeriale 12.4. 1962; Decreto Ministeriale 28.6.1962.

96	**1000 Lire**	**VF**	**UNC**
	1962-68. Seal: Type B. Blue on red and light brown underprint. G. Verdi at right. Watermark: Laureate head.		
	a. Signature Carli and Ripa. 14.7.1962.	17.00	115
	b. Signature Carli and Ripa. 15.7.1963 14.1.1964.	28.00	220
	c. Signature Carli and Ripa. 25.7.1964	34.00	395
	d. Signature Carli and Febbraio. 10.8.1965; 20.5.1966.	17.00	115
	e. Signature Carli and Pacini. 4.1.1968.	30.00	395

97	**10,000 Lire**	**VF**	**UNC**
	1962-73. Brown, purple, orange and red-brown with dark brown text on multicolor underprint. Michaelangelo at right. Seal: Type B. Back: Piazza del Campidoglio in Rome. Watermark: Roman head.		
	a. Signature Carli and Ripa. 3.7.1962.	12.00	90.00
	b. Signature Carli and Ripa. 14.1.1964; 27.7.1964.	17.00	165
	c. Signature Carli and Febbraio. 20.5.1966.	12.00	90.00
	d. Signature Carli and Pacini. 4.1.1968.	14.00	95.00
	e. Signature Carli and Lombardo. 8.6.1970.	12.00	90.00
	f. Signature Carli and Barbarito. 15.2.1973; 27.11.1973.	12.00	90.00

1964 Issue
Decreto Ministeriale 20.8.1964.

98	**5000 Lire**	**VF**	**UNC**
	1964-70. Green on pink underprint. Columbus at right. Seal: Type B. Back: Ship at left center.		
	a. Signature Carli and Ripa. 3.9.1964.	50.00	320
	b. Signature Carli and Pacini. 4.1.1968.	50.00	320
	c. Signature Carli and Lombardo. 20.1.1970.	50.00	320

1967 Issue

Decreto Ministeriale 27.6.1967.

99   50,000 Lire

1967-74. Brownish black, dark brown and reddish brown with black text on multicolor underprint. Leonardo da Vinci at right. Seal: Type B. Back: City view at center. Watermark: Bust of Madonna.

		VF	UNC
a. Signature Carli and Febbrajo. 3.7.1967.		205	1,870
b. Signature Carli and Lombardo. 19.7.1970.		170	1,190
c. Signature Carli and Barbarito. 16.5.1972; 4.2.1974.		165	1,120

100   100,000 Lire

1967-74. Brownish black, brown and deep olive-green on multicolor underprint. A. Manzoni at right. Seal: Type B. Back: Mountain lake scene at center. Watermark: Archaic female bust.

		VF	UNC
a. Signature Carli and Febbrajo. 3.7.1967.		205	1,930
b. Signature Carli and Lombardo. 19.7.1970.		205	1,360
c. Signature Carli and Barbarito. 6.2.1974.		205	1,475

1969; 1971 Issue

Decreto Ministeriale 26.2.1969; Decreto Ministeriale 15.5.1971.

101   1000 Lire

1969-81. Paper with security thread. Black and brown on light blue and lilac underprint. Harp at left center, G. Verdi at right. Seal: Type B. Back: Milan's La Scala opera house at left center. Watermark: Vertical row of laureate heads.

		VF	UNC
a. Signature Carli and Lombardo. 25.3.1969.		1.25	11.50
b. Signature Carli and Lombardo. 11.3.1971.		1.25	11.50
c. Signature Carli and Barbarito. 15.2.1973.		1.25	11.50
d. Signature Carli and Barbarito. 5.8.1975.		1.25	11.50
e. Signature Baffi and Stevani. 10.1.1977.		1.25	11.50
f. Signature Baffi and Stevani. 10.5.1979.		2.00	15.00
g. Signature Ciampi and Stevani. 20.2.1980; 6.9.1980.		2.00	15.00
h. Signature Ciampi and Stevani. 30.5.1981.		1.50	11.50

1969; 1971 Issue

Decreto Ministeriale 26.2.1969; Decreto Ministeriale 15.5.1971.

102   5000 Lire

1971-77. Olive, blue and brown on light olive underprint. Mythical seahorse at center, Columbus at right. Seal: Type C. Back: Three sailing ships of Columbus' at left center.

		VF	UNC
a. Signature Carli and Lombardo. 20.5.1971.		22.50	115
b. Signature Carli and Barbarito. 11.4.1973.		22.50	115
c. Signature Baffi and Stevani. 10.11.1977.		28.50	205

1973; 1974 Issue

Decreto Ministeriale 10.9.1973; Decreto Ministeriale 20.12.1974.

103   2000 Lire

1973; 1976; 1983. Brown and green on light tan and olive underprint. Galileo at center, ornate arms at left, buildings and leaning tower of Pisa at right. Seal: Type C. Back: Signs of the Zodiac. Watermark: Man's head.

		VF	UNC
a. Signature Carli and Barbarito. 8.10.1973.		1.50	23.00
b. Signature Baffi and Stevani. 22.10.1976.		1.50	16.00
c. Signature Ciampi and Stevani. 24.10.1983.		1.00	11.50

104   20,000 Lire

	VF	UNC
21.2.1975. Brownish black and dark brown on red-brown and pale olive-green underprint. Titian at center. Seal: Type C. Signature Carli and Barbarito. Back: Titian's painting *Amor Sacro e Amor Profano* at left center. Watermark: Woman's head.	115	395

1976-79 Issue

Decreto Ministeriale 2.3.1979; Decreto Ministeriale 25.8.1976; Decreto Ministeriale 20.6.1977; Decreto Ministeriale 16.6.1978.

105   5000 Lire   VF   UNC
1979-83. Brown and green. Man at left. Seal: Type C. Back: Building and statuary at center right. Watermark: Man with cap.
   a. Signature Baffi and Stevani. 9.3.1979.   5.00   28.00
   b. Signature Ciampi and Stevani. 1.7.1980; 3.11.1982.   5.00   28.00
   c. Signature Ciampi and Stevani. 19.10.1983.   6.00   40.00

100   10,000 Lire   VF   UNC
1976-84. Black and multicolor. Man at left. Seal: Type C. Back: Column at right. Watermark: Man.
   a. Signature Baffi and Stevani. 30.10.1976; 29.12.1978. 3.00   28.00
   b. Signature Ciampi and Stevani. 6.9.1980; 3.11.1982.   3.00   28.00
   c. Signature Ciampi and Stevani. 8.3.1984.   5.00   51.00

107   50,000 Lire   VF   UNC
1977-82. Blue, red and green. Young women and lion of St. Mark at left. Seal: Type C. Back: Modern design of arches.
   a. Signature Baffi and Stevani. 20.6.1977; 23.10.1978. 12.00   115
   b. Signature Baffi and Stevani. 12.6.1978.   17.00   375
   c. Signature Ciampi and Stevani. 11.4.1980.   12.00   115
   d. Signature Ciampi and Stevani. 2.11.1982.   12.00   225

108   100,000 Lire   VF   UNC
D.1978. Red-violet and black on multicolor underprint. Woman's bust at left. Seal: Type C. Back: Modern building design at right. Watermark: Woman's bust.
   a. Signature Baffi and Stevani. 20.6.1978.   23.00   225
   b. Signature Ciampi and Stevani. 1.7.1980.   23.00   225
   c. Signature Ciampi and Stevani. 10.5.1982.   23.00   285

1982; 1983 Issue

Decreto Ministeriale 6.1.1982; Decreto Ministeriale 1.9.1983.

109   1000 Lire   VF   UNC
D.1982. UV: fibers fluoresce green. Dark green and tan. Marco Polo at right. Seal: Type C. Back: Façade of the Doge's Palace in Venice at bottom of vertical format. Watermark: Marco Polo. Printer: ODBI. 113x61mm.
   a. Signature Ciampi and Stevani. 6.1.1982.   —   2.50
   b. Signature Ciampi and Speziali. 6.1.1982.   —   2.50

110   100,000 Lire   VF   UNC
D.1983. Dark brown and brown on green and olive-green underprint. Couple at center, Caravaggio at right. Seal: Type C. Back: Fruit basket at left, castle at upper center. Watermark: Caravaggio. 157x70mm.
   a. Signature Ciampi and Stevani. 1.9.1983.   22.00   115
   b. Signature Ciampi and Speziali. 1.9.1983.   22.00   95.00

1984; 1985 Issue

Decreto Ministeriale 4.1.1985; Decreto Ministeriale 3.9.1984; Decreto Ministeriale 6.2.1984.

111   5000 Lire   VF   UNC
D.1985. Olive-green and blue on multicolor underprint. Coliseum at center, V. Bellini at right. Seal: Type C. Back: Scene from opera *Norma* at left center. Watermark: V. Bellini. 126x70mm.
   a. Signature Ciampi and Stevani. 4.1.1985.   —   13.50
   b. Signature Ciampi and Speziali. 4.1.1985.   —   8.50
   c. Signature Fazio and Amici. 4.1.1985.   —   5.50

112   10,000 Lire
D.1984. Dark blue on multicolor underprint. Lab instrument at center, A. Volta
at right. Seal: Type C. Back: Mausoleum at left center. Watermark: A. Volta.
133x70mm.

	VF	UNC
a. Signature Ciampi and Stevani. 3.9.1984.	—	17.00
b. Signature Ciampi and Speziali. 3.9.1984.	—	13.00
c. Signature Fazio and Speziali. 3.9.1984.	—	10.00
d. Signature Fazio and Amici. 3.9.1984.	—	9.00

113   50,000 Lire
D.1984. Red-violet and multicolor. Figurine at center, G.L. Bernini at right.
Seal: Type C. Back: Equestrian statue at left center. Watermark: G.L. Bernini.
149x70mm.

	VF	UNC
a. Signature Ciampi and Stevani. 15.03.1984; 28.10.1985; 1.12.1986.	11.50	60.00
b. Signature Ciampi and Speziali. 25.1.1990.	11.50	57.00
c. Signatures Ciampi and Speziali. 06.03.92. Second letter in the serial number "E". Rare.	57.00	625

1990-94 Issue

Decreto Ministeriale 3.10.1990; Decreto Ministeriale 27.5.1992; Decreto Ministeriale 6.5.1994.

114   1000 Lire
D.1990. UV: fibers fluoresce yellow. Red-violet and multicolor. M. Montessori
at right. Seal: Type C. Back: Teacher and student at left center. Watermark: M.
Montessori. 113x61mm.

	VF	UNC
a. Signature Ciampi and Speziali.	—	1.25
b. Signature Fazio and Speziali.	—	1.25
c. Signature Fazio and Amici.	—	1.25

115   2000 Lire
D.1990. Dark brown on multicolor underprint. Arms at left center, G. Marconi at
right. Seal: Type C. Signature Ciampi and Speziali. Back: Marconi's yacht *Elettra*
at upper left center, radio towers at left, early radio set at center. Watermark: G.
Marconi. 119x61mm.

	VF	UNC
	—	2.50

116   50,000 Lire
D.1992. 27.5.1992. Violet and dull green on multicolor underprint. Figurine at
center, G. L. Bernini at right. Seal: Type C. Back: Equestrian statue at left center.
Watermark: G. L. Bernini. 149x70mm.

	VF	UNC
a. Signature Ciampi and Speziali.	11.50	45.00
b. Signature Fazio and Speziali.	11.50	45.00
c. Signature Fazio and Amici.	11.50	40.00

117   100,000 Lire
D.1994. Dark brown, reddish brown and pale green on multicolor underprint.
Couple at center, Caravaggio at right. Seal: Type C. Back: Fruit basket at left,
castle at upper center. Watermark: Caravaggio. 157x70mm.

	VF	UNC
a. Signature Fazio and Speziali. 6.5.1994.	13.50	90.00
b. Signature Fazio and Amici.	13.50	80.00

1997 Issue

Decreto Ministeriale 6.5.1997.

118   500,000 Lire
D.1997. Deep purple, dark blue and bright green on multicolor underprint.
Raphaël at right, painting of *Triumph of Galatée* at center. Seal: Type C. Signature
Fazio and Amici. Back: *The School of Athens* at left center. 163x78mm.

	VF	UNC
	145	360

Note: For later issues made for use in Italy, see European Union listings.

JAMAICA

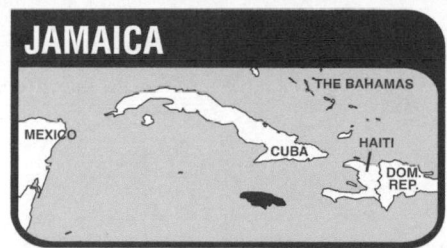

Jamaica, a member of the British Commonwealth situated in the Caribbean Sea 90 miles south of Cuba, has an area of 10,991 sq. km. and a population of 2.8 million. Capital: Kingston. The economy is founded chiefly on mining, tourism and agriculture. Alumina, bauxite, sugar, rum and molasses are exported.

The island - discovered by Christopher Columbus in 1494 - was settled by the Spanish early in the 16th century. The native Taino Indians, who had inhabited Jamaica for centuries, were gradually exterminated and replaced by African slaves. England seized the island in 1655 and established a plantation economy based on sugar, cocoa, and coffee. The abolition of slavery in 1834 freed a quarter million slaves, many of whom became small farmers. Jamaica gradually obtained increasing independence from Britain, and in 1958 it joined other British Caribbean colonies in forming the Federation of the West Indies. Jamaica gained full independence when it withdrew from the Federation in 1962. Deteriorating economic conditions during the 1970s led to recurrent violence as rival gangs affiliated with the major political parties evolved into powerful organized crime networks involved in international drug smuggling and money laundering. Violent crime, drug trafficking, and poverty pose significant challenges to the government today. Nonetheless, many rural and resort areas remain relatively safe and contribute substantially to the economy.

Jamaica is a member of the Commonwealth of Nations. Elizabeth II is the Head of State, as Queen of Jamaica. A decimal standard currency system was adopted on Sept. 8, 1969.

RULERS:
British

MONETARY SYSTEM:
1 Shilling = 12 Pence
1 Pound = 20 Shillings to 1969
1 Dollar = 100 Cents, 1969-

SIGNATURE VARIETIES

1	Stanley W. Payton, 1960-64	2	Richard T.P. Hall Acting Governor, 1964-66
3	Richard T.P. Hall Governor, 1966-67	4	G. Arthur Brown, 1967-77
5	Herbert Samuel Walker, 1977-81	6	Dr. Owen C. Jefferson, Acting Governor, 1981-83
7	Horace G. Barber, 1983-86	8	Headley A. Brown, 1986-89
9	Dr. Owen C. Jefferson, Acting Governor, 1989-90	10	G.A. Brown, 1990-93
11	R. Rainsford, 1993	12	J. Bussieres, 1994-96
13	D.M. Lat. Ibeaudiere		

BRITISH ADMINISTRATION

Bank of Jamaica
Law 1960
1961 ND Issue
Pound System.

49 5 Shillings — VF / UNC
L.1960. (1961). Red on multicolor underprint. Queen Elizabeth II at left. Latin motto below arms. Signature 1. Back: River rapids. Printer: TDLR. 145x68mm. — 25.00 / 150

50 10 Shillings — VF / UNC
L.1960. (1961). Purple on multicolor underprint. Queen Elizabeth II at left. Latin motto below arms. Signature 1. Back: Men with bananas. Printer: TDLR. 145x68mm. — 50.00 / 375

51 1 Pound — VF / UNC
L.1960. (1961). Green on multicolor underprint. Queen Elizabeth II at left. Latin motto below arms. Signature 1. Back: Harvesting. Printer: TDLR. 145x68mm. — 50.00 / 325

1964 ND Issue

51A 5 Shillings — VF / UNC
L.1960. (1964). Red on multicolor underprint. Queen Elizabeth II at left. English motto below arms. Signature 1. Back: River rapids. Printer: TDLR. 145x68mm.
- a. Signature 1. Gothic serial #. — 15.00 / 100
- b. Signature 1. Roman numeral serial #. — 25.00 / 135
- c. Signature 2. — 15.00 / 120
- d. Signature 4. — 10.00 / 95.00
- e. Specimen. As b. — — / —

51B 10 Shillings — VF / UNC
L.1960. (1964). Purple on multicolor underprint. Queen Elizabeth II at left. English motto below arms. Signature 1. Back: Men with bananas. Printer: TDLR. 145x68mm.
- a. Signature 1. Gothic serial #. — 12.50 / 200
- b. Signature 1. Roman numeral serial #. — 15.00 / 225
- c. Signature 2. — 15.00 / 250
- d. Signature 3. — 17.50 / 275
- e. Signature 4. — 12.00 / 165

51C 1 Pound   VF   UNC

L.1960. (1964). Green on multicolor underprint. Queen Elizabeth II at left. English motto below arms. Signature 1. Back: Harvesting. Printer: TDLR. 145x68mm.

	VF	UNC
a. Signature 1. Gothic serial #.	25.00	285
b. Signature 1. Roman numeral serial #.	35.00	325
c. Signature 2.	20.00	250
d. Signature 3.	35.00	325
e. Signature 4.	25.00	250
s. Specimen. As c.	—	—

52 5 Pounds   VF   UNC

L.1960. Blue on multicolor underprint. Queen Elizabeth II at left. English motto below arms. Back: Storage plant at center, woman with fruit basket at right. Printer: TDLR. 145x68mm.

	VF	UNC
a. Signature 1. Gothic serial #.	450	2,000
b. Signature 1. Roman numeral serial #.	550	2,500
c. Signature 3.	500	2,350
d. Signature 4.	400	2,000

Law 1960

1970 ND Issue

Dollar System. Replacement notes: Serial # prefix ZZ.

53 50 Cents   VF   UNC

L.1960 (1970). Red on multicolor underprint. Marcus Garvey at left, arms in underprint at center. Signature 4. Back: National shrine at right. Watermark: Pineapple. Printer: TDLR. 145x68mm.

	VF	UNC
a. Issued note.	2.00	8.00
s. Specimen.	—	—

54 1 Dollar   VF   UNC

L.1960 (1970). Purple on multicolor underprint. Sir Alexander Bustamante at left, arms at bottom center right. Signature 4. Back: Tropical harbor at right. Watermark: Pineapple. Printer: TDLR. 145x68mm.   2.00   8.00

55 2 Dollars   VF   UNC

L.1960 (1970). Dark green and red-brown on multicolor underprint. Paul Bogle, arms at left, Red-billed streamer trail at center. Signature 4. Back: Group of people. Watermark: Pineapple. Printer: TDLR. 145x68mm.

	VF	UNC
a. Issued note.	4.00	15.00
s. Specimen.	—	—

Note: For #54 and 55 w/red serial # see #CS1-CS3.

56 5 Dollars   VF   UNC

L.1960 (1970). Dark brown, green and blue-gray on multicolor underprint. Norman Manley at left, arms at bottom center. Signature 4. Back: Old Parliament at center right. Watermark: Pineapple. Printer: TDLR. 145x68mm.   10.00   55.00

57 10 Dollars   VF   UNC

L.1960 (1970). Blue-black, brown and black on multicolor underprint. George William Gordon at left, arms in underprint at center. Signature 4. Back: Bauxite mining scene at center right. Watermark: Pineapple. Printer: TDLR. 145x68mm.   30.00   175

1973 FAO Commemorative Issue

#58, 25th Anniversary Declaration of Human Rights 1948-73

58 2 Dollars   VF   UNC

1973. Dark green and red-brown on multicolor underprint. Paul Bogle, arms at left, Red-billed streamer trail at center. Signature 4. *Universal Declaration of Human Rights/1948 - 10 December - 1973. Serial number double prefix FA-O.* Back: Group of people. Toward Food Education Employment for All/Articles 23-26 added. Watermark: Pineapple. Printer: TDLR. 145x68mm.   3.00   15.00

1976; 1977 ND Issue

#59-63 Replacement notes: Serial # prefix ZY or ZZ.

59 1 Dollar   VF   UNC

L.1960 (1976). Purple on multicolor underprint. Sir Alexander Bustamante at left, arms at bottom center right. Back: Tropical harbor at right. Watermark: Pineapple. Printer: TDLR. 145x68mm.

	VF	UNC
a. Signature 4.	1.50	7.50
b. Signature 5.	1.00	6.50

60   2 Dollars   VF   UNC
L.1960 (1976). Dark green on multicolor underprint. Paul Bogle, arms at left,
Red-billed streamer trail at center. Back: Group of people. Watermark: Pineapple.
Printer: TDLR. 145x68mm.
    a. Signature 4.   2.00   12.50
    b. Signature 5.   1.50   10.00

61   5 Dollars   VF   UNC
L.1960 (1976). Dark brown, green and blue-green on multicolor underprint. Nor-
man Manley at left, arms at bottom center. Back: Old Parliament at center right.
Watermark: Pineapple. Printer: TDLR. 145x68mm.
    a. Signature 4.   5.00   32.50
    b. Signature 5.   3.50   20.00

62   10 Dollars   VF   UNC
L.1960 (1976). Blue-black and black on multicolor underprint. George William
Gordon at left, arms in underprint at center. Back: Bauxite mining scene at center
right. Watermark: Pineapple. Printer: TDLR. 145x68mm.   20.00   175

67   10 Dollars   VF   UNC
1978-81. Bluish purple on multicolor underprint. George William Gordon at left,
arms in underprint at center. Back: Bauxite mining scene at center right. Watermark: Pineapple. Printer: TDLR. 145x68mm.
    a. Signature 5. 1.10.1978; 1.10.1979.   2.50   25.00
    b. Signature 9. 1.12.1981.   1.00   7.50

63   20 Dollars   VF   UNC
L.1960 (1976). Maroon on multicolor underprint. Noel Nethersole at left, flag in
underprint at center, arms below. Back: Bank of Jamaica building. Watermark:
Pineapple. Printer: TDLR. 145x68mm.   35.00   200

68   20 Dollars   VF   UNC
1978-83. Red and purple on multicolor underprint. Noel Nethersole at left, flag
in underprint at center, arms below. Back: Bank of Jamaica building. Watermark:
Pineapple. Printer: TDLR. 145x68mm.
    a. Signature 5. 1.10.1978; 1.10.1979; 1.10.1981. 5.00   40.00
    b. Signature 6. 1.12.1981.   3.00   30.00
    c. Signature 7. 1.12.1983.   2.50   25.00

1978-84 Issue

Replacement notes: Serial # prefix ZY or ZZ.

1985 Reduced Size Issue

#68A-72 note size: 144 x 68mm. Replacement notes: Serial # prefix ZY or ZZ.

64   1 Dollar   VF   UNC
ND (1982-86). Purple on multicolor underprint. Sir Alexander Bustamante at left,
arms at bottom center right. Back: Tropical harbor at right. Watermark: Pineapple.
Printer: TDLR. 145x68mm.
    a. Signature 6.   0.50   2.50
    b. Signature 7.   0.25   1.50

65   2 Dollars   VF   UNC
ND (1982-86). Dark green and red-brown on multicolor underprint. Paul Bogle,
arms at left, Red-billed streamer trail at center. Back: Group of people. Watermark:
Pineapple. Printer: TDLR. 145x68mm.
    a. Signature 6.   1.50   7.50
    b. Signature 7.   1.00   6.00

66   5 Dollars   VF   UNC
ND (1984). Dark brown, green and blue-gray on multicolor underprint. Norman
Manley at left, arms at bottom center. Signature 7. Back: Old Parliament at center
right. Watermark: Pineapple. Printer: TDLR. 145x68mm.   2.00   10.00

68A   1 Dollar   VF   UNC
1985-90. UV: rays around sailfish, value 1 in broken box all fluoresce orange.
Purple on multicolor underprint. Sir Alexander Bustamante at left, arms at bottom
center right. Back: Tropical harbor at right. Watermark: Pineapple. Printer: TDLR.
    a. Signature 7. 1.1.1985.   FV   4.00
    b. Signature 8. 1.3.1986; 1.2.1987; 1.9.1987.   FV   2.25
    c. Signature 9. 1.7.1989.   FV   2.00
    d. Signature 10. 1.1.1990.   FV   1.00

69 2 Dollars

		VF	UNC
1985-93. UV: Hummingbirds and value $2 in broken box fluoresce yellow. Dark green and red-brown on multicolor underprint. Paul Bogle, arms at left, Red-billed streamer trail at center. Horizontal sorting bar at right. Back: Group of people. Watermark: Pineapple. Printer: TDLR. 145x68mm.

		VF	UNC
a. Signature 7. 1.1.1985.		FV	3.00
b. Signature 8. 1.3.1986; 1.2.1987; 1.9.1987.		FV	2.25
c. Signature 9. 1.7.1989.		FV	2.00
d. Signature 10. 1.1.1990; 29.5.1992.		FV	1.25
e. Signature 11. 1.2.1993.		FV	1.25

70 5 Dollars

		VF	UNC
1985-92. Dark brown, green and blue-gray on multicolor underprint. Norman Manley at left, arms at bottom center. Two horizontal blue-green sorting bars at left and right. Back: Old Parliament at center right. Watermark: Pineapple. Printer: TDLR. 145x68mm.

		VF	UNC
a. Signature 7. 1.1.1985.		FV	5.00
b. Signature 8. 1.9.1987.		FV	3.50
c. Signature 9. 1.5.1989.		FV	3.00
d. Signature 10. 1.7.1991; 1.8.1992.		FV	1.75

71 10 Dollars

		VF	UNC
1985-94. Bluish purple on multicolor underprint. George William Gordon at left, arms in underprint at center. Three horizontal sorting bars at left and right. Back: Bauxite mining scene at center right. Watermark: Pineapple. Printer: TDLR. 145x68mm.

		VF	UNC
a. Signature 7. 1.1.1985.		FV	7.50
b. Signature 8. 1.9.1987.		FV	6.00
c. Signature 9. 1.8.1989.		FV	3.00
d. Signature 10. 1.5.1991; 1.8.1992.		FV	1.50
e. Signature 12. 1.3.1994.		FV	1.50

72 20 Dollars

		VF	UNC
1985-99. Red-orange, purple and black on multicolor underprint. Noel Nethersole at left, flag in underprint at center, arms below. Circular electronic sorting mark at left. Back: Bank of Jamaica building. Watermark: Pineapple. Printer: TDLR. 145x68mm.

		VF	UNC
a. Signature 7. 1.1.1985.		FV	10.00
b. Signature 8. 1.3.1986; 1.2.1987; 1.9.1987.		FV	8.00
c. Signature 9. 1.9.1989.		FV	7.00
d. Signature 10. 1.10.1991.		FV	4.50
e. Signature 12. 1.2.1995.		FV	3.50
f. Signature 13. 24.5.1996.		FV	3.00
g. Signature 13. 12.1.1998.		FV	3.00
h. Signature 13. 15.2.1999.		FV	3.00

1986-91 Issue

#73-75 Replacement notes: Serial # prefix *ZZ; ZY.*

73 50 Dollars

		VF	UNC
1988-99. UV: parrots and value $50 in broken box fluoresce yellow. Brown, purple and red-violet on multicolor underprint. Sam Sharpe at left. Back: Doctor's Cave Beach, Mointego Bay. Watermark: Pineapple. Printer: TDLR. 145x68mm.

		VF	UNC
a. Signature 8. 1.8.1988.		FV	12.00
b. Signature 11. 1.2.1993.		FV	7.50
c. Signature 12. 1.2.1995.		FV	5.00
d. Signature 13. 24.5.1996.		FV	4.50
e. Signature 13. 12.1.1998.		FV	4.50
f. Signature 13. 15.2.1999.		FV	4.50

74 100 Dollars

		VF	UNC
1.12.1986; 1.9.1987. Black and purple on multicolor underprint. Sir Donald Sangster at left. Signature 8. Back: Dunn's River Falls, St. Ann, at right. Watermark: Pineapple. Printer: TDLR. 145x68mm. | | 7.00 | 35.00 |

75 100 Dollars

		VF	UNC
1991-93. Black and purple on lilac underprint. Sir Donald Sangster at left. Signature 8. Two circles at right, each with vertical orange bar. Back: Dunn's River Falls, St. Ann, at right. More silver waves added to both *$100* and across bottom. Watermark: Pineapple. Printer: TDLR. 145x68mm.

		VF	UNC
a. Signature 10. 1.7.1991.		FV	12.50
b. 1.6.1992.		FV	10.00
c. Signature 11. 1.2.1993.		FV	10.00

1994 Issue

#76-78 Replacement notes: Serial # prefix ZY or ZZ.

76 100 Dollars   VF   UNC
1994-2002. Black and purple on lilac underprint. Sir Donald Sangster at left. Signature 8. Two circles at right, each with vertical orange bar. Ascending size serial number and segmented foil over security thread. Back: Dunn's River Falls, St. Ann, at right. More silver waves added to both $100 and across bottom. Watermark: Pineapple. Printer: TDLR. 145x68mm.

		VF	UNC
a. Signature 12. 1.3.1994.		FV	8.50
b. Signature 13. 24.5.1996; 12.1.1998; 12.2.1998; 15.2.1999.		FV	7.50
c. 15.3.2000. watermark: swallow-tailed hummingbird. Improved security thread.		FV	7.00

77 500 Dollars   VF   UNC
1994-99. Purple, violet and brown on multicolor underprint. Nanny of the Maroons at left. Back: Historical map of the islands above Port Royal architecture at center right. Watermark: Pineapple. Printer: TDLR. 145x68mm.

		VF	UNC
a. Signature 12. 1.5.1994.		FV	25.00
b. Signature 13. 24.5.1996; 12.2.1998; 15.2.1999.		FV	25.00

2000 Issue

78 1000 Dollars   VF   UNC
2000-01. Dark blue, green and purple on multicolor underprint. Michael Manley at left. Signature 13. Back: Jamaica House. Printer: TDLR. (without imprint). 145x68mm.

		VF	UNC
a. 15.2.2000.		FV	45.00
b. 15.10.2000.		FV	45.00
c. 15.1.2001.		FV	45.00

2001; 2002 Issue

---

79 50 Dollars   VF   UNC
2000-04. UV: parrot, $50 and security strip all fluoresce green. Multicolor. Sam Sharpe at left. Signature 13. Back: Doctor's Cave Beach, Mointego Bay. Watermark: Swallow-tailed Hummingbird. Printer: TDLR. 145x68mm.

		VF	UNC
a. 15.3.2000.		FV	4.00
b. 15.1.2001.		FV	4.00
c. 15.1.2002.		FV	4.00
d. 15.1.2003.		FV	4.00
e. 15.1.2004.		FV	4.00

80 100 Dollars   VF   UNC
2001-04. Black and purple on lilac underprint. 145x68mm.

		VF	UNC
a. 15.1.2001.		FV	7.00
b. 15.1.2002.		FV	7.00
c. 15.1.2003.		FV	7.00
d. 15.1.2004.		FV	7.00

81 500 Dollars   VF   UNC
15.1.2002. Purple, violet and brown on multicolor underprint. Nanny of the Maroons at left. Back: Historical map of the islands above Port Royal architecture at center right. Watermark: Swallow-Tailed Hummingbird. Printer: TDLR. 145x68mm.   FV   22.50

82 1000 Dollars   VF   UNC
15.1.2002. Dark blue, green and purple on multicolor underprint. Michael Manley at left. Signature 13. Back: Jamaica House. Printer: (T)DLR. 145x68mm.   FV   40.00

2003 Issue

83 50 Dollars   VF   UNC
2005-. Multicolor. Sam Sharpe at left. Back: Doctor's Cave Beach, Mointego Bay. Watermark: Sam Sharpe and value Printer: TDLR. 145x68mm.

		VF	UNC
a. 15.1.2005.		FV	2.50
b. 15.1.2007.		FV	2.50
c. 15.1.2008. Cornerstone watermarks.		FV	2.00
d. 15.1.2009.		FV	2.00
e. 15.1.2010.		FV	2.00

84 100 Dollars   VF   UNC
2003-. Black and purple on lilac and multicolor underprint. Donald Sagster at left. Back: Dunn's River Falls, St. Ann, at right. Watermark: Donald Sagster and value. Printer: TDLR. 145x68mm.

		VF	UNC
a. 15.1.2005.		FV	3.00
b. 15.1.2006.		FV	3.00
c. 15.1.2007.		FV	3.00
d. 15.1.2009.		FV	2.50
e. 15.1.2010. (two signature varieties.		FV	2.50
f. 15.1.2011.		FV	2.50

85 500 Dollars
2003-. Purple, violet and brown on multicolor underprint. Nanny of the Maroons at left. Back: Historical map of the islands above Port Royal architecture at center right. Watermark: Nanny of the Narrons and value. Printer: TDLR. 145x68mm.

	VF	UNC
a. 15.1.2003.	FV	12.50
b. 15.1.2004.	FV	12.50
c. 15.1.2005.	FV	12.50
d. 15.1.2006.	FV	10.00
e. 15.1.2007.	FV	10.00
f. 15.1.2008. Cornerstone watermarks added.	FV	10.00
g. 15.1.2009.	FV	10.00
h. 15.1.2011.	FV	10.00

86 1000 Dollars
2003-. Dark blue, green and purple on multicolor underprint. Michael Manley at left. Back: Jamaica House at center right. Watermark: Michael Manley and value. Printer: TDLR. 145x68mm.

	VF	UNC
a. 15.1.2003.	FV	22.50
b. 15.1.2004.	FV	20.00
c. 15.1.2005.	FV	20.00
d. 15.1.2006.	FV	20.00
e. 15.1.2007.	FV	17.50
f. 15.1.2008.	FV	17.50
g. 15.1.2009.	FV	17.50
h. 15.1.2010.	FV	17.50
i. 15.1.2011.	FV	17.50
j. 01.01.2014.	FV	17.50

87 5000 Dollars
15.1.2009; 15.1.2010. Multicolor. High. Lawson Shearer at left. Back: Highway 2000 and frangipani blossoms. Printer: TDLR. 145x68mm.

	VF	UNC
a. 15.1.2009.	FV	80.00
b. 15.1.2010.	FV	80.00

2010 Commemorative Issue

88 50 Dollars
1.1.2010. Multicolored. Samuel Sharpe at left. Back: Bank of Jamaca building at center. Printer: DLR. 145x68mm.

VF UNC
FV 15.00

2012 Issue

89 50 Dollars
6.8.2012. Multicolor. Samuel Sharpe at left, 50th Anniversary overprint at right. Back: Group of youngsters. Printer: DLR.

VF UNC
FV 2.50

90 100 Dollars
6.8.2012. Multicolor. Sir Donald Sangster at left, 50th Anniversary overprint at right. Back: Group of youngsters. Printer: DLR.

VF UNC
FV 3.00

91 500 Dollars
6.8.2012. Multicolor. Nanny of the Maroons at left, 50th Anniversary overprint at right. Back: Group of youngsters. Printer: DLR.

VF UNC
FV 12.50

92 1000 Dollars
6.8.2012. Multicolor. Michael Manley at left, 50th Anniversary overprint at right. Back: Group of youngsters. Printer: DLR.

VF UNC
FV 20.00

93 5000 Dollars
6.8.2012. Multicolor. Hugh Shearer at left, 50th Anniversary overprint at right. Back: Group of youngsters. Printer: DLR.

VF UNC
FV 80.00

2013-2014 Issue

94 50 Dollars
1.6.2013. Polymer. Multicolor. Sam Sharpe at left. Back: Doctor's Cave Beach, Montego Bay. Watermark: Sam Sharpe and value. Printer: G&D. 145x68mm.

VF UNC
FV 2.00

95 100 Dollars
1.1.2014. Black and purple on lilac and multicolor underprint. Donald Sagster at left. Back: Dunn's River Falls, St. Ann, at right. Watermark: Donald Sagster and value. Printer: G&D. 145x68mm.

VF UNC
FV 3.00

COLLECTOR SERIES

Bank of Jamaica

1976 Issue

CS1 1976 1-10 Dollars
#54-57 with matching red star prefix serial # and *SERIES 1976*. (5000 sets issued).

Mkt. Value
20.00

1977 Issue

CS2 1977 1-10 Dollars
#59a-61a, 62 with matching red star prefix serial # and *SERIES 1977*. (7500 sets issued).

Mkt. Value
15.00

1978 Issue

CS3 1978 1-10 Dollars
#54-57 in double set. One is like #CS1-2 with *SERIES 1978* and the other with additional overprint: *Twenty-fifth Anniversary of the Coronation June 2, 1953* and *SERIES 1978* at right. All with matching red star prefix serial #. (6250 sets issued).

Mkt. Value
30.00

JAPAN

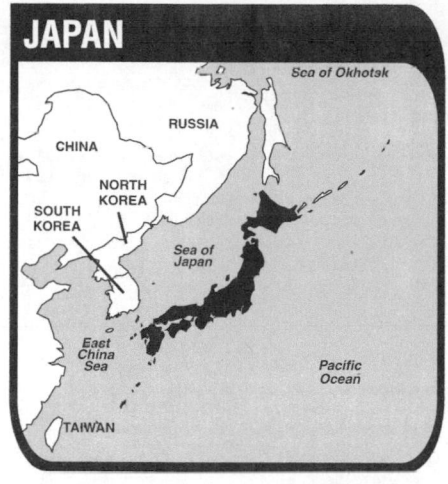

Japan, a constitutional monarchy situated off the east coast of Asia, has an area of 377,835 sq. km. and a population of 127.29 million. Capital: Tokyo. Japan, one of the three major industrial nations of the free world, exports machinery, motor vehicles, textiles and chemicals.

In 1603, a Tokugawa shogunate (military dictatorship) ushered in a long period of isolation from foreign influence in order to secure its power. For more than two centuries this policy enabled Japan to enjoy stability and a flowering of its indigenous culture. Following the Treaty of Kanagawa with the US in 1854, Japan opened its ports and began to intensively modernize and industrialize. During the late 19th and early 20th centuries, Japan became a regional power that was able to defeat the forces of both China and Russia. It occupied Korea, Formosa (Taiwan), and southern Sakhalin Island. In 1931-32 Japan occupied Manchuria, and in 1937 it launched a full-scale invasion of China. Japan attacked US forces in 1941 - triggering America's entry into World War II - and soon occupied much of East and Southeast Asia. After its defeat in World War II, Japan recovered to become an economic power and a staunch ally of the US. While the emperor retains his throne as a symbol of national unity, elected politicians - with heavy input from bureaucrats and business executives - wield actual decisionmaking power. The economy experienced a major slowdown starting in the 1990s following three decades of unprecedented growth, but Japan still remains a major economic power, both in Asia and globally.

See also Burma, China (Japanese military issues, Central Reserve Bank, Federal Reserve Bank, Hua Hsing Commercial Bank, Mengchiang Bank, Chanan Bank, Chi Tung Bank and Manchukuo), Hong Kong, Indochina, Malaya, Netherlands Indies, Oceania, the Philippines, Korea and Taiwan.

RULERS:
Hirohito (Showa), 1926-1989
Akihito (Heisei), 1989-

MONETARY SYSTEM:
1 Yen = 100 Sen, 1870-

REPLACEMENT NOTES:
#49, 50, 51, 57, 89, notes w/first digit 9 are replacements. #62-75, H prefix, #67b, B prefix but no suffix letter.

CONSTITUTIONAL MONARCHY

Bank of Japan

日 本 銀 行 券
Nip-pon Gin-ko Ken

1963-69 ND Issue

95 500 Yen

	VF	UNC
ND (1969). Blue on multicolor underprint. Tomomi Iwakura at right. Back: Mt. Fuji at left center. Watermark: 5-petaled flowers. 160x72mm.		
a. Single letter serial # prefix.	10.00	30.00
b. Double letter serial # prefix.	FV	12.00
s. As b. Specimen.	—	—

96 1000 Yen

	VF	UNC
ND (1963). Dark green and brown on multicolor underprint. Hirobumi Ito at right. Back: Bank of Japan at center. Watermark: Hirobumi Ito. 164x76mm.		
a. Single letter serial # prefix. Black serial #.	25.00	80.00
b. As a., but with double letter serial # prefix.	FV	25.00
c. Single letter serial # prefix. Blue serial #.	15.00	40.00
d. As c., but with double letter serial # prefix.	FV	22.00
s. As b. Specimen.	—	—

1984 ND Issue

#97s-99s were released in a special booklet by Printing Bureau, Ministry of Finance.

97 1000 Yen

	VF	UNC
ND (1984-93). Blue on multicolor underprint. Soseki Natsume at right. Back: Two Manchurian cranes. Watermark: Soseki Natsume. 150x76mm.		
a. Single letter serial # prefix. Black serial #. (1984).	15.00	35.00
b. As a., but with double letter serial # prefix.	FV	22.00
c. Single letter serial # prefix. Blue serial #. (1990).	FV	25.00
d. As c., but with double letter serial # prefix.	FV	22.00
s. As b. Specimen. Perforated *mihon*.	—	1,500

98 5000 Yen

	VF	UNC
ND (1984-93). Purple on multicolor underprint. Inazo Nitobe at right. Back: Lake and Mt. Fuji at center. Watermark: Inazo Nitobe. 155x76mm.		
a. Single letter serial # prefix. Black serial #.	75.00	110
b. As a., but with double letter serial # prefix.	FV	95.00
s. As b. Specimen. Perforated *mihon*.	—	1,500

99   10,000 Yen   **VF   UNC**

ND (1984-93). Light brown on multicolor underprint. Yukichi Fukuzawa at right.
Back: Pheasant at left and right. Watermark: Yukichi Fukuzawa. 160x76mm.

a. Single letter serial # prefix.	145	220
b. As a., but with double letter serial # prefix.	FV	170
s. As b. Specimen. Perforated *mihon*.	—	1,500

1993 ND Issue

**Due to a government reorganization, the Okurasho (Finance Ministry) was
renamed Zaimusho (Ministry of Finance). The imprint on the notes (made at
the Finance Ministry Pinting Bureau) was changed accordingly in 2001. In
2003 the imprint was changed again, to National Printing Bureau.**

Printer a. 8 characters starting *O*.

大藏省印刷局製造

Printer b. 8 characters starting *Zai*.

財務省印刷局製造

Printer c. 7 characters.

國立印刷局製造

100   1000 Yen   **VF   UNC**

ND (1993-). Microprinting added to upper and lower right corner. Blue on
multicolor underprint. Soseki Natsume at right. Back: Two Manchurian cranes.
Watermark: Soseki Natsume. 150x76mm.

a. Single letter serial # prefix. Brown serial #. Printer a. (1993).	FV	25.00
b. As a. Double letter serial # prefix.	FV	20.00
c. Single letter serial # prefix. Green serial #. Printer a (2000).	FV	25.00
d. As c. Double letter serial # prefix.	FV	20.00
e. As d. Double letter serial #. Printer b. (2001).	FV	22.00
f. As d, printer c. (2003).	FV	22.00

101   5000 Yen   **VF   UNC**

ND (1993-). Microprinting added to upper and lower right corner. Violet on
multicolor underprint. Inazo Nitobe at right. Back: Lake and Mt. Fuji at center.
Watermark: Inazo Nitobe. 155x76mm.

a. Single letter serial # prefix. Brown serial # Printer a. (1993).	75.00	110
b. As a., but with double letter serial # prefix.	FV	90.00
c. As b. Printer b. (2001).	FV	95.00
d. As b. Printer c. (2003).	FV	95.00

102   10,000 Yen   **VF   UNC**

ND (1993-). Microprinting added to upper and lower right corner. Light brown on
multicolor underprint. Yukichi Fukuzawa at right. Back: Pheasant at left and right.
Watermark: Yukichi Fukuzawa. 160x76mm.

a. Single letter serial # prefix. Brown serial # (1993).	145	215
b. As a., but with double letter serial # prefix.	FV	165
c. As b. printer b. (2001).	FV	170
d. As b. Printer c. (2003).	FV	170

2000 Commemorative Issue

#103, G-8 Economic Summit in Okinawa

103   2000 Yen   **VF   UNC**

ND (2000). Slate, green and brown on multicolor underprint. Shureimon Gate
in Naha, Okinawa at right. Back: Scene from *Genji Monogatari* (Tale of Genji).
Watermark: Shureimon Gate 154x76mm.

a. Single letter serial # prefix.	FV	38.00
b. Double letter serial # prefix.	FV	38.00

2004 ND Issue

**#104-106 include enhanced security features and bars added to portrait
watermark. The iridescent ink feature (introduced at #103) is observed by
holding the note at a shallow angle to incident light. The iridescent ink glis-
tens like pink mother of pearl from the surface of the ends of the face of the
note; it is otherwise virtually invisible and impossible to copy using available
copying technologies.**

104   1000 Yen   **VF   UNC**

ND (2004). Enhanced security features. Blue on multicolor underprint. Hideo
Noguchi (bacteriologist) at right. Back: Mt. Fuji. Watermark: Hideo Noguchi and
bar. 150x76mm.

a. Single letter serial # prefix. Black serial #.	FV	25.00
b. Double letter serial # prefix.	FV	20.00
c. Brown serial #.	FV	18.00

105   5000 Yen   **VF   UNC**
ND (2004). Enhanced security features. Violet on multicolor underprint. Ichiyo Higuchi (novelist) at right. Back: Irises (painting by Korin Ogata). Watermark: Ichiyo Higuchi and 2 bars. 155x76mm.

   a. Single letter serial # prefix.   70.00   100
   b. Double letter serial # prefix.   FV   90.00

106   10,000 Yen   **VF   UNC**
ND (2004). Enhanced security features. Brown on multicolor underprint. Yukichi Fukuzawa (educator, futurist) at right. Back: Phoenix from Byohdoh-in Temple. Watermark: Yukichi Fukuzawa and 3 bars. 160x76mm.

   a. Single letter serial # prefix. Black serial #.   135   210
   b. Double letter serial # prefix.   FV   170
   c. Brown serial #.   FV   155

JERSEY

The Bailiwick of Jersey, a British Crown dependency located in the English Channel 12 miles (19 km.) west of Normandy, France, has an area of 45 sq. mi. (117 sq. km.) and a population of 90,000. Capital: St. Helier. The economy is based on agriculture and cattle breeding - the importation of cattle is prohibited to protect the purity of the island's world-famous strain of milk cows. Jersey and the other Channel Islands represent the last remnants of the medieval Dukedom of Normandy that held sway in both France and England. These islands were the only British soil occupied by German troops in World War II. Jersey is a British crown dependency but is not part of the UK. However, the UK Government is constitutionally responsible for its defense and international representation.

RULERS:
  British

MONETARY SYSTEM:
  1 Shilling = 12 Pence
  1 Pound = 20 Shillings to 1971
  1 Pound = 100 Pence, 1971-

SIGNATURE VARIETIES			
1	*F.N. Padgham, 1963-72*	**2**	*J. Clennett, 1972-83*
3	*Leslie May, 1983-93*	**4**	*Baird, 1993-*
5	*Ian Black*		

BRITISH ADMINISTRATION
States of Jersey, Treasury
1963 ND Issue
#7-10 Replacement notes: Serial # prefix Z.

7   10 Shillings   **VF   UNC**
ND (1963). Brown on multicolor underprint. Queen Elizabeth II at right looking left, wearing cape. Signature 3. Back: St. Ouen's Manor. Watermark: Jersey cow's head. Printer: TDLR.

   a. Issued note.   30.00   75.00
   s. Specimen.   —   250

8 1 Pound   **VF UNC**

ND (1963). Green on multicolor underprint. Queen Elizabeth II at right looking left, wearing cape. Two signature varieties. Back: Mont Orgueil Castle. Watermark: Jersey cow's head. Printer: TDLR.

	VF	UNC
a. Signature 1.	50.00	135
b. Signature 2.	35.00	90.00
c. Without signature.	200	500
s1. As a. Specimen. Black or red overprint. Serial # prefix A-E.	—	250
s2. As b. Specimen. Red overprint. Serial # prefix F-K.	—	100

9 5 Pounds   **VF UNC**

ND (1963). Dark red on multicolor underprint. Queen Elizabeth II at right looking left, wearing cape. Signature 3. Back: St. Aubin's Fort. Watermark: Jersey cow's head. Printer: TDLR.

	VF	UNC
a. Signature 1.	175	500
b. Signature 2.	50.00	135
r. As b. Replacement note.	—	250
s1. As a. Specimen. Black or red overprint	—	125
s2. As b. Specimen. Red overprint.	—	100

10 10 Pounds   **VF UNC**

ND (1972). Purple on multicolor underprint. Queen Elizabeth II at right looking left, wearing cape. Signature 3. Back: St. Ouen's Manor. Watermark: Jersey cow's head. Printer: TDLR.

	VF	UNC
a. Signature 2.	70.00	185
r. As a. Replacement note.	85.00	250
s. Specimen. Red overprint.	—	225

1976 ND Issue

#11-14 Replacement notes: Serial # prefixes *ZB; ZC.*

11 1 Pound   **VF UNC**

ND (1976-88). Blue on multicolor underprint. Queen Elizabeth II at center right looking left, wearing tiara. Back: Battle of Jersey scene. Watermark: Jersey cow's head. Printer: TDLR.

	VF	UNC
a. Signature 2.	6.00	17.50
b. Signature 3.	4.00	12.00
r. As a. Replacement note.	10.00	30.00
s. As a. Specimen.	—	17.50

12 5 Pounds   **VF UNC**

ND (1976-88). Brown on multicolor underprint. Queen Elizabeth II at center right looking left, wearing tiara. Back: Elizabeth Castle, sailing ships in foreground. Watermark: Jersey cow's head. Printer: TDLR.

	VF	UNC
a. Signature 2.	25.00	75.00
b. Signature 3.	20.00	50.00
r. As a. Replacement note.	45.00	120
s. As a, b. Specimen.	—	45.00

13 10 Pounds   **VF UNC**

ND (1976-88). Green on multicolor underprint. Queen Elizabeth II at center right looking left, wearing tiara. Back: Victoria College. Watermark: Jersey cow's head. Printer: TDLR.

	VF	UNC
a. Signature 2.	50.00	120
b. Signature 3.	45.00	100
r. As b. Replacement note.	75.00	180
s. As a, b. Specimen.	—	85.00

14 20 Pounds   **VF UNC**

ND (1976-88). Red-brown on multicolor underprint. Queen Elizabeth II at center right looking left, wearing tiara. Back: Sailing ship, Gorey Castle. Watermark: Jersey cow's head. Printer: TDLR.

	VF	UNC
a. Signature 2.	90.00	225
b. Signature 3.	90.00	225
r. As b. Replacement note.	140	350
s. As a, b. Specimen.	—	150

1989 ND Issue

#15-19 Replacement notes: Serial # prefix CZ.

15	**1 Pound**	**VF**	**UNC**

ND (1989). UV: value 1 in box fluoresces orange. Back center light orange. Dark green and violet on multicolor underprint. Birds at left corner, arms at center, mature Queen Elizabeth II at right, facing, wearing cape. Treecreepers at lower left. Signature 3. Back: Church at left center. Watermark: Jersey cow's head. 128x65mm.

		VF	**UNC**
a.	Issued note.	5.00	12.00
s.	Specimen.	—	9.00

16	**5 Pounds**	**VF**	**UNC**

ND (1989). . Rose on multicolor underprint. Birds at left corner, arms at center, mature Queen Elizabeth II at right, facing, wearing cape. Whitethroat at lower left. Signature 3. Back: La Corbiere lighthouse. Watermark: Jersey cow's head. 135x70mm.

		VF	**UNC**
a.	Issued note.	14.00	32.50
r.	Replacement note.	20.00	50.00
s.	Specimen.	—	20.00

17	**10 Pounds**	**VF**	**UNC**

ND (1989). Orange-brown on multicolor underprint. Birds at left corner, arms at center, mature Queen Elizabeth II at right, facing, wearing cape. Oyster catchers at lower left. Signature 3. Back: Battle of Jersey. Watermark: Jersey cow's head. 142x75mm.

		VF	**UNC**
a.	Issued note.	27.50	65.00
s.	Specimen.	—	50.00

18	**20 Pounds**	**VF**	**UNC**

ND (1989). Blue on multicolor underprint. Birds at left corner, arms at center, mature Queen Elizabeth II at right, facing, wearing cape. Brent goose at lower left. Signature 3. Back: St. Ouen's Manor. Watermark: Jersey cow's head. 150x80mm.

		VF	**UNC**
a.	Issued note.	55.00	125
r.	Replacement note.	70.00	160
s.	Specimen.	—	100

19	**50 Pounds**	**VF**	**UNC**

ND (1989). Dark gray on multicolor underprint. Birds at left corner, arms at center, mature Queen Elizabeth II at right, facing, wearing cape. Fulmers at lower left. Signature 3. Back: Government House. Watermark: Jersey cow's head. 156x86mm.

		VF	**UNC**
a.	Issued note.	FV	300
s.	Specimen.	—	225

1993 ND Issue

20	**1 Pound**	**VF**	**UNC**

ND (1993). Dark green on multicolor underprint. Birds at left corner, arms at center, mature Queen Elizabeth II at right, facing, wearing cape. Treecreepers at lower left. Signature 3. Solid color denomination at upper right. Back: Church at left center. Watermark: Jersey cow's head. 128x65mm.

		VF	**UNC**
a.	Signature 4.	FV	6.00
s.	Specimen.	—	20.00

21	**5 Pounds**	**VF**	**UNC**

ND (1993). Rose on multicolor underprint. Birds at left corner, arms at center, mature Queen Elizabeth II at right, facing, wearing cape. Whitethroat at lower left. Signature 3. Solid color denomination at upper right. Back: La Corbiere lighthouse. Watermark: Jersey cow's head. 135x70mm.

		VF	**UNC**
a.	Signature 4.	FV	25.00
s.	Specimen.	—	20.00

22	**10 Pounds**	**VF**	**UNC**

ND (1993). Orange-brown on multicolor underprint. Birds at left corner, arms at center, mature Queen Elizabeth II at right, facing, wearing cape. Oyster catchers at lower left. Signature 3. Solid color denomination at upper right. Back: Battle of Jersey. Watermark: Jersey cow's head. 142x75mm.

		VF	**UNC**
a.	Signature 4.	FV	45.00
s.	Specimen.	—	35.00

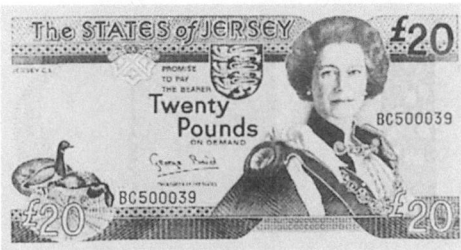

23	**20 Pounds**	**VF**	**UNC**

ND (1993). Blue on multicolor underprint. Birds at left corner, arms at center, mature Queen Elizabeth II at right, facing, wearing cape. Brent goose at lower left. Signature 3. Solid color denomination at upper right. Back: St. Ouen's Manor. Watermark: Jersey cow's head. 150x80mm.

		VF	**UNC**
a.	Signature 4.	FV	85.00
r.	Replacement note.	FV	100
s.	Specimen.	—	70.00

24 50 Pounds   VF UNC

ND (1993). Dark gray on multicolor underprint. Birds at left corner, arms at center, mature Queen Elizabeth II at right, facing, wearing cape. Fulmers at lower left. Signature 3. Solid color denomination at upper right. Back: Government House. Watermark: Jersey cow's head. 156x86mm.

    a. Signature 4   FV   200
    s. Specimen.   —   175

1995 Commemorative Issue

#25, 50th Anniversary Liberation of Jersey

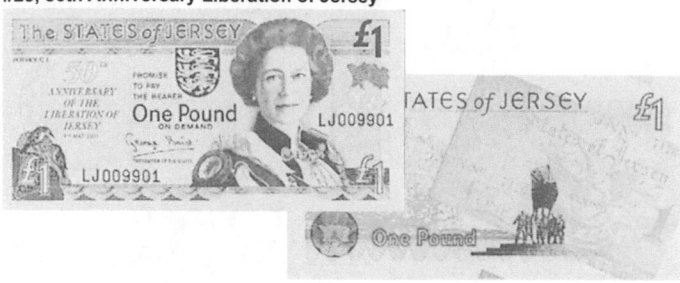

25 1 Pound   VF UNC

9.5.1995. Dark green and purple on multicolor underprint. Face like #20 with island outline at upper right, with text: *50th Anniversary...* at left in watermark area. Serial number prefix: *LJ*. Signature 4. Back: Face and back of German occupation 1 Pound #6. Watermark: Jersey cow's head. Printer: TDLR. 128x65mm.

    a. Issued note.   FV 14.00
    s. Specimen.   — 25.00

Note: #25 also issued in a special wallet w/commemorative 2 coin. (6000 pcs.). Current market value: $20.00.

2000 ND Issue

26 1 Pound   VF UNC

ND (2000). Dark green on multicolor underprint. Birds at left corner, arms at center, mature Queen Elizabeth II at right, facing, wearing cape. Treecreepers at lower left. Solid color denomination at upper right. Signature: Ian Black. Back: Church at left center. Watermark: Jersey cow's head. 128x65mm.

    a. Two letter serial # prefix.   FV   5.00
    b. Three letter serial # prefix.   FV   5.00
    s. Specimen. Red overprint: *SPECIMEN* on both sides.   — 12.50

27 5 Pounds   VF UNC

ND (2000). Rose on multicolor underprint. Birds at left corner, arms at center, mature Queen Elizabeth II at right, facing, wearing cape. Whitethroat at lower left. Solid color denomination at upper right. Signature: Ian Black. Back: La Corbiere lighthouse. Watermark: Jersey cow's head. 135x70mm.

    a. Issued note.   FV 20.00
    s. Specimen.   — 17.50

28 10 Pounds   VF UNC

ND (2000). Orange-brown on multicolor underprint. Birds at left corner, arms at center, mature Queen Elizabeth II at right, facing, wearing cape. Oyster catchers at lower left. Signature: Ian Black. Back: Battle of Jersey. Watermark: Jersey cow's head. 142x75mm.

    a. Issued note.   FV 37.50
    s. Specimen.   — 35.00

29 20 Pounds   VF UNC

ND (2000). Blue on multicolor underprint. Birds at left corner, arms at center, mature Queen Elizabeth II at right, facing, wearing cape. Brent goose at lower left. Solid color denomination at upper right. Signature: Ian Black. Back: St. Ouen's Manor. Watermark: Jersey cow's head. 150x80mm.

    a. Issued note.   FV 70.00
    s. Specimen.   — 65.00

30 50 Pounds   VF UNC

ND (2000). Dark gray on multicolor underprint. Birds at left corner, arms at center, mature Queen Elizabeth II at right, facing, wearing cape. Fulmers at lower left. Solid color denomination at upper right. Signature: Ian Black. Back: Government House. Watermark: Jersey cow's head. 156x86mm.

    a. Issued note.   FV 185
    r. Replacement note.   —   300
    s. Specimen.   —   175

2004 Commemorative Issue

800th Anniversary of the special relationship between Jersey and the British Crown.

31 1 Pound   VF UNC

2004. Dark green and purple on multicolor underprint. Queen Elizabeth II at right. Back: Mount Orgueil Castle. 128x65mm.

    a. Issued note.   FV   9.00
    s. Specimen.   — 25.00

2010 ND Issue

32 1 Pound   VF UNC

ND (2010). Green on multicolor underprint. Queen Elizabeth II facing at right, Monument to Freedom in Liberation Square at center. Back: La Hougue Bei Neolithic burial mount, Le Hocq in St. Clement. Watermark: Jersey cow head. Printer: (T)DLR. 130x65mm.

    a. Issued note.   FV   7.50
    s. Specimen.   — 50.00

33 5 Pounds   VF UNC

ND (2010). Blue on multicolor underprint. Queen Elizabeth II facing at right, Le Rat Cottage in St. Lawrence at center. Back: Archirondel Tower at left, Les Augres Manor at center. Watermark: Jersey cow head. Printer: (T)DLR. 135x70mm.

    a. Issued note.   FV 15.00
    s. Specimen.   — 50.00

34 10 Pounds   VF UNC

ND (2010). Redish-brown on multicolor underprint. Queen Elizabeth II facing at right, Hermitage of Elizabeth Castle in St. Aubin's Bay at center. Back: Seymour Tower in Groville Bay at left, Lalique glass sculptures in St. Matthew's Church in St. Lawrence at center. Watermark: Jersey cow head. Printer: (T)DLR. 145x75mm.

    a. Issued note.   FV 30.00
    s. Specimen.   — 50.00

35 20 Pounds   VF UNC

ND (2010). Violet on multicolor underprint. Queen Elizabeth II facing at right, The States (Parliament building) at center. Back: La Rocco Tower in St. Jean at left, interior of States chamber at center. Watermark: Jersey cow head. Printer: (T)DLR. 150x80mm.

    a. Issued note.   FV 70.00
    s. Specimen.   —   100

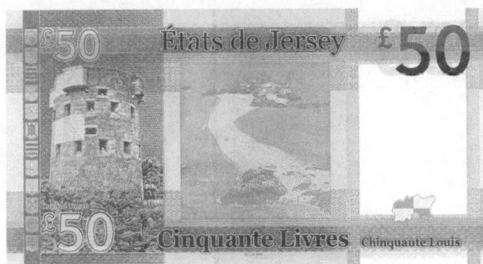

36   50 Pounds   VF   UNC

ND (2010). Red on multicolor underprint. Queen Elizabeth II facing at right, Mont Orgueil Castle at center. Back: Ouaisne Tower at left, houses on La Marmotiere island in Les Ecrehous at center. Watermark: Jersey cow head. Printer: (T)DLR. 155x85mm.

    a. Issued note.   FV   175
    s. Specimen.   —   200

2012 Commemorative Issue

37   100 Pounds   VF   UNC

2012. Violet on multicolor underprint. Queen Elizabeth II bust facing at right. Back: Royal Mace of Jersey at left, flag at lower right. Vertical format.

    a. Issued note.   FV   250
    s. Specimen.   —   350

COLLECTOR SERIES

States of Jersey, Treasury

1978 Issue

CS1   ND (1978) 1-20 Pounds   Mkt. Value

#11a-14a with overprint: *SPECIMEN* and Maltese cross prefix serial #.   75.00

JORDAN

The Hashemite Kingdom of Jordan, a constitutional monarchy in southwest Asia, has an area of 37,738 sq. ml. (97,740 sq. km.) and a population of 5.46 million. Capital: Amman. Agriculture and tourism comprise Jordan's economic base. Chief exports are phosphates, tomatoes and oranges. Following World War I and the dissolution of the Ottoman Empire, the UK received a mandate to govern much of the Middle East. Britain separated out a semi-autonomous region of Transjordan from Palestine in the early 1920s, and the area gained its independence in 1946; it adopted the name of Jordan in 1950. The country's long-time ruler was King Hussein (1953-99). A pragmatic leader, he successfully navigated competing pressures from the major powers (US, USSR, and UK), various Arab states, Israel, and a large internal Palestinian population. Jordan lost the West Bank to Israel in the 1967 war and barely managed to defeat Palestinian rebels who threatened to overthrow the monarchy in 1970. Hussen in 1988 permanently relinquished Jordanian claims to the West Bank. In 1989, he reinstituted parliamentary elections and initiated a gradual political liberalization; political parties were legalized in 1992. In 1994, he signed a peace treaty with Israel. King Abdullah II, the son of King Hussein, assumed the throne following his father's death in February 1999. Since then, he has consolidated his power and undertaken an aggressive economic reform program. Jordan acceded to the World Trade Organization in 2000, and began to participate in the European Free Trade Association in 2001. In 2003, Jordan staunchly supported the Coalition ouster of Saddam in Iraq and following the outbreak of insurgent violence in Iraq, absorbed hundreds of thousands of displaced Iraqis, most of whom remain in the country. Municipal elections were held in July 2007 under a system in which 20% of seats in all municipal councils were reserved by quota for women. Parliamentary elections were held in November 2007 and saw independent pro-government candidates win the vast majority of seats. In November 2007, King Abdullah instructed his new prime minister to focus on socioeconomic reform, developing a healthcare and housing network for civilians and military personnel, and improving the educational system.

RULERS:
    Hussein I, 1952-1999
    Abdullah II, 1999-

MONETARY SYSTEM:
    1 Dinar – 10 Dirhams
    1 Dirham – 10 Piastres – 10 Qirsh
    1 Piastre = 1 Qirsh = 10 Fils

REPLACEMENT NOTES:
    #9-27, jj prefix (YY).

SIGNATURE VARIETIES					
9			10		
11			12A		
12			13		
14			15		
16			17		
18			19		
20			21		
22			23		
24			25		
26			27		
28			29		

KINGDOM
Central Bank of Jordan
First Issue - Law 1959

9   500 Fils　　　　　　　　　　　　　　**VF   UNC**
L.1959. (1965). Brown on multicolor underprint. King Hussein at left with law date 1959 (in Arabic *1909.*) Signature 10. Back: Jerash Forum. *FIVE HUNDRED FILS* at bottom margin. 140x70mm.
　　a. Issued note.　　　　　　　　　　　　60.00　　250
　　s. Specimen.　　　　　　　　　　　　　—　　500

10   1 Dinar　　　　　　　　　　　　　　**VF   UNC**
L.1959. (1965). Green on multicolor underprint. King Hussein at left with law date 1959 (in Arabic *1909.*) Signature 10. Back: Dome of the Rock at center with columns at right. 150x75mm.
　　a. Issued note.　　　　　　　　　　　　25.00　　200
　　s. Specimen.　　　　　　　　　　　　　—　　500

11   5 Dinars　　　　　　　　　　　　　**VF   UNC**
L.1959. (1965). Red-brown on multicolor underprint. Hussein at left with law date 1959 (in Arabic *1909.*) Back: Al-Hazne, Treasury of Pharaoh at Petra at center right. 164x82mm.
　　a. Signature 10.　　　　　　　　　　　45.00　　200
　　b. Signature 11.　　　　　　　　　　　45.00　　200
　　c. Signature 12.　　　　　　　　　　　45.00　　200
　　s. Specimen. Signature 10, 11, 12.　　　—　　500

12   10 Dinars　　　　　　　　　　　　**VF   UNC**
L.1959. (1965). Blue-gray on multicolor underprint. King Hussein at left with law date 1959 (in Arabic *1909.*) Back: Baptismal site on River Jordan. 175x88mm.
　　a. Signature 10.　　　　　　　　　　　95.00　　275
　　b. Signature 11.　　　　　　　　　　　95.00　　275
　　c. Signature 12.　　　　　　　　　　　95.00　　275
　　s. As a, b, c. Specimen. Red overprint: *SPECIMEN* on both sides. Punch hole cancelled.　　—　　750

Second Issue - Law 1959

13   1/2 Dinar　　　　　　　　　　　　**VF   UNC**
ND. Brown on multicolor underprint. King Hussein at left. Back: Jerash Forum. *HALF DINAR* at bottom margin. Watermark: King Hussein wearing kuffiyeh. 140x70mm.
　　a. Signature 12.　　　　　　　　　　　10.00　　40.00
　　b. Signature 12A.　　　　　　　　　　10.00　　40.00
　　c. Signature 14.　　　　　　　　　　　10.00　　25.00
　　s. As a, b, c. Specimen. Black overprint: *SPECIMEN* on both sides.　　—　　500

14   1 Dinar　　　　　　　　　　　　　**VF   UNC**
ND. Green on multicolor underprint. King Hussein at left. Back: Dome of the Rock at center with columns at right. Watermark: King Hussein wearing kuffiyeh. 150x75mm.
　　a. Signature 13.　　　　　　　　　　　20.00　　70.00
　　b. Signature 14.　　　　　　　　　　　15.00　　50.00
　　s. Specimen. Signature 13, 14.　　　　　—　　500

15   5 Dinars   **VF   UNC**

ND. Red-brown on multicolor underprint. King Hussein at left. Back: Al-Hazne,
Treasury of Pharaoh at Petra at center right. Watermark: King Hussein wearing
kuffiyeh. 164x82mm.

    a. Signature 12.   25.00   80.00
    b. Signature 15.   25.00   70.00
    s. Specimen. Signature 12, 13.   —   700

16   10 Dinars   **VF   UNC**

ND. Blue-gray on multicolor underprint. King Hussein at left. Back: Baptismal site
on River Jordan. Watermark: King Hussein wearing kuffiyeh. 175x88mm.

    a. Signature 12.   70.00   200
    b. Signature 12A.   65.00   190
    c. Signature 13.   100   275
    d. Signature 14.   90.00   250
    e. Signature 15.   40.00   160
    s. Specimen. Signature 12, 12A, 13, 14, 15.   —   850
    x. Forgery. Signature 13.   50.00

Third Issue

17   1/2 Dinar   **VF   UNC**

ND (1975-92). Brown on multicolor underprint. King Hussein at left. Back: Jerash
at right. Watermark: King Hussein wearing kuffiyeh. 136x67mm.

    a. Signature 15. Serial # prefix starts with arabic 'l.'   4.00   10.00
    b. Signature 15. Serial # prefix starts with arabic 'u.'   9.00   20.00
    c. Signature 16.   5.00   11.00
    d. Signature 17.   5.00   11.00
    e. Signature 18.   4.00   8.00
    s1. As a. Specimen. Signature 15.   —   200
    s2. As b. Specimen. Signature 15.   —   200
    s3. Specimen. Signature 16.   —   200
    s4. Specimen. Signature 17.   —   200
    s5. Specimen. Signature 18.   —   200

18   1 Dinar   **VF   UNC**

ND (1975-92). Dark green on multicolor underprint. King Hussein at left. Back:
Dome of the Rock in Jerusalem, behind columns at right. Watermark: King Hussein wearing kuffiyeh. 144x71mm.

    a. Text above doorway on back. Signature 15.   10.00   27.00
    b. Without text above doorway on back. Signature 15.   9.00   20.00
    c. Text above doorway on back. Signature 16.   8.00   18.00
    d. Signature 17.   5.00   12.00
    e. Signature 18.   5.00   12.00
    f. Signature 19.   4.00   10.00
    s1. Specimen. As a. Signature 15.   —   250
    s2. Specimen. As b. Signature 15.   —   250
    s3. Specimen. Signature 16.   —   250
    s4. Specimen. Signature 17.   —   250
    s5. Specimen. Signature 18.   —   250
    s6. Specimen. Signature 19.   —   250

19   5 Dinars   **VF   UNC**

ND (1975-92). Red on multicolor underprint. King Hussein at left. Back: Al-Hazne,
Treasury of the Pharaoh at Petra at right. Watermark: King Hussein wearing
kuffiyeh. 152x76mm.

    a. Signature 15.   10.00   60.00
    b. Signature 16.   10.00   55.00
    c. Signature 18.   10.00   55.00
    d. Signature 19.   10.00   50.00
    s1. Specimen. Signature 15.   —   300
    s2. Specimen. Signature 16.   —   300
    s3. Specimen. Signature 18.   —   300
    s4. Specimen. Signature 19.   —   300

20   10 Dinars   **VF   UNC**

ND (1975-92). Blue on multicolor underprint. King Hussein at left. Back: Cultural
palace above and Roman amphitheater at center right. Watermark: King Hussein
wearing kuffiyeh. 160x80mm.

    a. Signature 15.   25.00   120
    b. Signature 16.   22.00   100
    c. Signature 18.   22.00   92.00
    d. Signature 19.   22.00   74.00
    s1. Specimen. As a. Signature 15.   —   275
    s2. Specimen. As b. Signature 16.   —   300
    s3. Specimen. As c. Signature 18.   —   300
    s4. Specimen. As d. Signature 19.   —   300

21 20 Dinars
1977-1988. Deep brown on multicolor underprint. King Hussein at left. Back: Electric power station of Zerga. Watermark: King Hussein wearing kuffiyeh. 168x84mm.

	VF	UNC
a. Signature 16. 1977; 1981.	50.00	125
b. Signature 17. 1985.	50.00	115
c. Signature 18. 1987; 1988.	45.00	105
s1. Specimen. Signature 16. 1977.	—	375
s2. Specimen. Signature 16. 1981.	—	375
s3. Specimen. Signature 17. 1985.	—	375
s4. Specimen. Signature 18. 1987.	—	375
s5. Specimen. Signature 18. 1988.	—	375
x. Forgery. 1985.	—	50.00

22 20 Dinars
1977-85. Blue on multicolor underprint. King Hussein at left. Back: Electric power station of Zerga. Watermark: King Hussein wearing kuffiyeh. 168x84mm.

	VF	UNC
a. Signature 16. 1977 (1991).	70.00	140
b. Signature 15. 1982 (1991).	60.00	125
c. Signature 17. 1985 (1992).	60.00	110
s1. Specimen. Signature 16. 1977 (1991).	—	2,500
s2. Specimen. Signature 15. 1982.	—	2,500
s3. Specimen. Signature 17. 1985 (1992).	—	2,500

Fourth Issue (1992-93)

23 1/2 Dinar
AH1412/1992; AH1413/1993. Lilac-brown and dark brown on multicolor underprint. King Hussein wearing kuffiyeh at center right. Signature 19. Back: Qusayr Amra fortress at right. Watermark: King Hussein wearing kuffiyeh. 131x62mm.

	VF	UNC
a. AH1412/1992.	FV	8.00
b. AH1413/1993.	FV	6.00
s1. As a. Specimen.	—	75.00
s2. As b. Specimen.	—	50.00

24 1 Dinar
AH1412/1992; AH1413/1993. Green on olive and multicolor underprint. King Hussein wearing kuffiyeh at center right. Signature 19. Back: Ruins of Jerash at center right. Watermark: King Hussein wearing kuffiyeh. 137x66mm.

	VF	UNC
a. AH1412/1992.	FV	9.00
b. AH1413/1993.	FV	8.00
s1. As a. Specimen.	—	85.00
s2. As b. Specimen.	—	60.00

25 5 Dinars
AH1412/1992; AH1413/1993. Red and violet-brown on multicolor underprint. King Hussein wearing kuffiyeh at center right. Signature 19. Back: Treasury of Petra. Watermark: King Hussein wearing kuffiyeh. 143x70mm.

	VF	UNC
a. AH1412/1992.	FV	55.00
b. AH1413/1993.	FV	40.00
s1. As a. Specimen.	—	100
s2. As b. Specimen.	—	70.00

26 10 Dinars
AH1412/1992. Blue, gray-violet and green on multicolor underprint. King Hussein wearing kuffiyeh at center right. Signature 19. Back: Al-Rabadh Castle ruins. Watermark: King Hussein wearing kuffiyeh. 149x74mm.

	VF	UNC
a. Issued note.	FV	70.00
s. Specimen.	—	125

27 20 Dinars   **VF UNC**

AH1412/1992. Dark brown, green and red-brown on multicolor underprint. King Hussein wearing kuffiyeh at center right. Signature 19. Back: Dome of the Rock at left center. Watermark: King Hussein wearing kuffiyeh. 155x78mm.

    a. Issued note.   FV   125

    s. Specimen.   —   150

King Hussein financed the restoration of the Dome of the Rock, as well as the gold-leaf treatment on the dome.

Fifth Issue (1995-2002)

28 1/2 Dinar   **VF UNC**

AH1415/1995, AH1417/1997. Lilac-brown and dark brown on multicolor underprint. King Hussein wearing kuffiyeh at center right. Signature 19. Back: Qusayr Amra fortress at right. Title: *THE HASHEMITE KINGDOM OF JORDAN*. Watermark: King Hussein wearing kuffiyeh. 131x62mm.

    a. AH1415/1995. Signature 19.   FV   6.00

    b. AH1417/1997. Signature 21.   FV   4.50

    s1. As a. Specimen.   —   50.00

    s2. As b. Specimen.   —   35.00

29 1 Dinar   **VF UNC**

AH1415/1995-AH1423/2002. Green and olive on multicolor underprint. King Hussein wearing kuffiyeh at center right. Back: Ruins of Jerash at center right. Title: *THE HASHEMITE KINGDOM OF JORDAN*. Watermark: King Hussein wearing kuffiyeh. 137x66mm.

    a. AH1415/1995. Signature 19.   FV   9.00

    b. AH1416/1996. Signature 21.   FV   8.00

    c. AH1422/2001. Signature 24.   FV   7.00

    d. AH1423/2002. Signature 24.   FV   6.50

    s1. As a. Specimen.   —   70.00

    s2. As b. Specimen.   —   85.00

30 5 Dinars   **VF UNC**

AH1415 / 1995-AH1423 / 2001. Red-violet, purple and orange on multicolor underprint. King Hussein wearing kuffiyeh at center right. Signature 19. Back: Treasury of Petra. Title: *THE HASHEMITE KINGDOM OF JORDAN*. Watermark: King Hussein wearing kuffiyeh. 143x70mm.

    a. AH1415/1995. Signature 19.   FV   35.00

    b. AH1417/1997. Signature 22.   FV   28.00

    s1. As a. Specimen.   —   125

    s2. As b. Specimen.   —   100

31 10 Dinars   **VF UNC**

AH1416/1996; AH1422/2001. Purple, dark blue and black on multicolor underprint. King Hussein wearing kuffiyeh at center right. Signature 19. Back: Castle ruins. *AJLOUN CASTLE*. Title: *THE HASHEMITE KINGDOM OF JORDAN*. Watermark: King Hussein wearing kuffiyeh. 149x74mm.

    a. AH1416/1996. Signature 20.   FV   55.00

    b. AH1422/2001. Signature 24.   FV   45.00

    s1. As a. Specimen.   —   150

    s2. As b. Specimen.   —   150

32 20 Dinars   **VF UNC**

AH1415/1995; AH1422/2001. Dark brown, green and red-brown on multicolor underprint. King Hussein wearing kuffiyeh at center right. Signature 19. Back: Dome of the Rock at left center. Title: *THE HASHEMITE KINGDOM OF JORDAN*. Watermark: King Hussein wearing kuffiyeh. 155x78mm.

    a. AH1415/1995. Signature 19.   FV   90.00

    b. AH1422/2001. Signature 24.   FV   65.00

    s1. As a. Specimen.   —   185

    s2. As b. Specimen.   —   200

32A 50 Dinars   **VF UNC**

1994. Portrait of King Hussein waring kuffiyeh at center right within arch frame. Back: King Abdullah I at left, Raghadan Palace at right center. 149x74mm.

    a. Unissued specimen. Red color.   —   10,000

    b. Unissued specimen. Orange color.   —   10,000

32B 50 Dinars

1995. Portrait of King Hussein wearing kuffiyeh at right. no arch frame. Segmented security thread. Back: King Abdullah I at left, Raghadan Palace at right center. 149x74mm.

	VF	UNC
a. Unissued specimen. Green color.	—	10,000
b. Unissued specimen. Blue color.	—	10,000

33 50 Dinars

AH1420/1999. Light green, blue, red and brown on multicolor underprint. King Abdullah II at right wearing business suit. Segmented security thread. Signature 23. Back: Raghadan Palace at right center. Coat of Arms at left. 149x74mm.

	VF	UNC
a. Issued note.	FV	150
s. Specimen.	—	1,250

Sixth Issue (2002-)

34 1 Dinar

AH1423/2002-. Green, gold and brown on multicolor underprint. Sherif Hussein ibn Ali at right. Silver coins. Back: Great Arab Revolt scene. Watermark: Sherif Hussein ibn Ali. Printer: (T)DLR. 133x74mm.

	VF	UNC
a. AH1423/2002. Signature 24.	FV	5.00
b. AH1426/2005. Signature 26.	FV	5.00
c. AH1427/2006. Signature 27.	FV	4.50
d. AH1429/2008. Signature 28.	FV	4.50
e. AH1430/2009. Signature 29.	FV	4.50
f. AH1432/2011. Signature 30.	FV	4.50
g. AH1434/2013.	FV	4.50
s. As a, b, c, d, e, f. Specimen.	—	250

35 5 Dinars

AH1423/2002-. Orange, brown and gold on multicolor underprint. King Abdullah I at right, calvary at center. Back: Ma'an Palace. Watermark: King Abdullah I. Printer: (T)DLR. 137x74mm.

	VF	UNC
a. AH1423/2002. Signature 24.	FV	18.00
b. AH1427/2006. Signature 27.	FV	15.00
c. AH1429/2008. Signature 28.	FV	15.00
d. AH1431/2010. Signature 30.	FV	15.00
e. AH1433/2012. Signature 31.	FV	15.00
f. AH1435/2014.	FV	15.00
s. As a, b, c, d, e. Specimen.	—	275

36 10 Dinars

AH1423/2002-. Blue, green and red on multicolor underprint. King Talal ibn Abdullah at right. First Parliament at center. Back: Camels at Petra. Watermark: King Talal ibn Abdullah. Printer: (T)DLR. 141x74mm.

	VF	UNC
a. AH1423/2002. Signature 24. Foil on vertical serial #.	FV	38.00
b. AH1425/2004. Signature 25. Foil to left of vertical serial #.	FV	32.00
c. AH1428/2007. Signature 27.	FV	32.00
d. AH1433/2012. Signature 31.	FV	32.00
s. As a, b, c, d. Specimen.	—	300

37 20 Dinars
AH1423/2002-. Blue-green and grey on multicolor underprint. King Hussein at right. Back: Dome of the Rock in Jerusalem. Watermark: King Hussein. Printer: (T)DLR. 145x74mm.

		VF	UNC
a. AH1423/2002. Signature 24.		FV	68.00
b. AH1427/2006. Signature 27.		FV	62.00
c. AH1430/2009. Signature 28.		FV	70.00
d. AH1434/2013.		FV	70.00
e. AH1435/2014.		FV	70.00
s. As a, b, c. Specimen.		—	325

38 50 Dinars
AI I1423/2002; AH1425/2004; AH1427/2006; AH1428/2007; AH1430/2009. Light green, blue, red and brown on multicolor underprint. King Abdullah II at right. Back: Raghadan Palace. Watermark: Portrait of King Abdullah II. Printer: (T)DLR. 149x74mm.

		VF	UNC
a. AH1423/2002. Signature 24.		FV	140
b. AH1425/2004. Signature 25.		FV	120
c. AH1427/2006. Signature 27.		FV	120
d. AH1428/2007. Signature 27.		FV	120
e. AH1429/2008.		FV	120
f. AH1430/2009. Signature 28.		FV	120
g. AH1433/2012.		FV	120
h. AH1435/2014.		ГV	120
s. As a, b, c, d, e. Specimen.		—	325

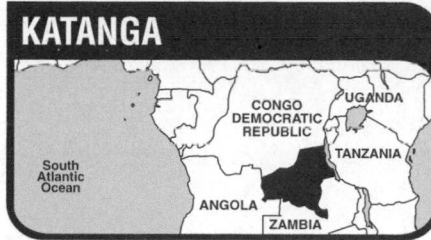

Katanga, the southern province of the former Zaïre extends northeast to Lake Tanganyika, east and south to Zambia, and west to Angola. It was inhabited by Luba and Bantu peoples, and was one of Africa's richest mining areas. In 1960, Katanga, under the leadership of provincial president Moise Tshombe and supported by foreign mining interests, seceded from newly independent Republic of the Congo. A period of political confusion and bloody fighting involving Congolese, Belgian and United Nations forces ensued. At the end of the rebellion in 1962, Katanga was reintegrated into the republic, and is known as the Shaba region. For additional history, see Zaïre.

MONETARY SYSTEM:
1 Franc = 100 Centimes

INDEPENDENT
Government Katanga
1961 ND Provisional Issue

#1-4 with red overprint: *GOUVERNEMENT KATANGA* **on face and back of Banque D'Emission du Rwanda et du Burundi notes.**

		Fine	XF
1	**5 Francs**	**Fine**	**XF**
	ND (1961 - old date 15.5.1961).Overprint on Rwanda & Burundi #1. Rare.	—	—
2	**10 Francs**	**Fine**	**XF**
	ND (1961 - old date 15.9.1960; 5.10.1960).Overprint on Rwanda & Burundi #2. Rare.	—	—

		Fine	XF
3	**20 Francs**	**Fine**	**XF**
	ND (1961 - old date/15.9.1960; 5.10.1960).Overprint on Rwanda & Burundi #3. Rare.	—	—

		Fine	XF
4	**50 Francs**	**Fine**	**XF**
	ND (1961 - old date 1.10.1960).Overprint on Rwanda & Burundi #4. Rare.	—	—

Banque Nationale du Katanga
1960 Issue

5   10 Francs   VF   UNC

1.12.1960; 15.12.1960. Lilac and yellow. Moise Tshombe at right. Signature 1.
Back: Building at left.

    a. Issued note.   135   300
    r. Remainder, without serial #.   —   185
    s. Specimen.   —   200

5A   10 Francs   VF   UNC

1.12.1960. Green, brown and red. Moise Tshombe at left, reservoir at center, flag
at right. Back: Foundry at center. Printer: W&S. (not issued).

    r. Remainder without date or serial #. Rare.   —   —
    s. Specimen. Rare.   —   —

6   20 Francs   VF   UNC

1960. Blue-green and brown. Moise Tshombe at right. Signature 1. Back: Building
at left.

    a. 21.11.1960.   100   300
    b. 1.12.1960.   225   550
    r. Remainder, without serial #.   —   275
    s. Specimen.   —   300

6A   20 Francs   VF   UNC

1.12.1960. Specimen. Rare. Multicolor. Aerial view at center. Moise Tshombe at   —   —
left, flag at right. Back: Miners at center. Printer: W&S. (Not issued).

7   50 Francs   VF   UNC

10.11.1960. Red-brown and blue. Moise Tshombe at right. Signature 1. Back:
Building at left.

    a. Issued note.   100   400
    r. Remainder, without serial #.   —   325
    s. Specimen.   —   375

8   100 Francs   VF   UNC

31.10.1960. Brown, green and yellow. Moise Tshombe at right. Signature 1. Back:
Building at left.

    a. Issued note.   200   500
    r. Remainder, without serial #.   —   400
    s. Specimen.   —   425

9   500 Francs   VF   UNC

31.10.1960. Green, violet and olive. Moise Tshombe at right. Signature 1. Back:
Building at left.

    a. Issued note.   400 1,200
    r. Remainder, without serial #.   —   700
    s. Specimen.   —   400

10   1000 Francs   VF   UNC

31.10.1960. Blue and brown. Moise Tshombe at right. Signature 1. Back: Building
at left.

    a. Issued note.   500 1,500
    r. Remainder, without serial #.   —   700
    s. Specimen.   —   800

#11 Not assigned.

1962 Issue

12   100 Francs   VF   UNC

1962-63. Dark green and brown on multicolor underprint. Woman carrying ears
of corn at right. Signature 2, 3. Back: Wheel of masks and spears. Watermark:
Elephant.

a. 18.6.1962, 15.8.1962; 15.9.1962.	150	400
b. 15.1.1963.	235	575
s. Specimen.	—	350

13   500 Francs   VF   UNC

17.4.1962. Purple and multicolor. Man with fire at right. Signature 2, 3. Back:
Wheel of masks and spears. Watermark: Elephant.

a. Issued note.	250	800
s. Specimen.	—	600

14   1000 Francs   VF   UNC

26.2.1962. Dark blue, red and brown on multicolor underprint. Woman carrying
child on back while picking cotton at right. Ornate wheel at left. Signature 2, 3.
Back: Wheel of masks and spears. Watermark: Elephant.

a. Issued note.	300	850
s. Specimen.	—	500

KAZAKHSTAN

The Republic of Kazakhstan is bordered to the west by the Caspian Sea and Russia, to the north by Russia, in the east by the Peoples Republic of China and in the south by Uzbekistan and Kyrgyzstan. It has an area of 1,049,155 sq. mi. (2,717,300 sq. km.) and a population of 16.93 million. Capital: Astana. The country is rich in mineral resources including coal, tungsten, copper, lead, zinc and manganese with huge oil and natural gas reserves. Agriculture is important also non-ferrous metallurgy, heavy engineering and chemical industries are leaders in its economy.Native Kazakhs, a mix of Turkic and Mongol nomadic tribes who migrated into the region in the 13th century, were rarely united as a single nation. The area was conquered by Russia in the 18th century, and Kazakhstan became a Soviet Republic in 1936. During the 1950s and 1960s agricultural "Virgin Lands" program, Soviet citizens were encouraged to help cultivate Kazakhstan's northern pastures. This influx of immigrants (mostly Russians, but also some other deported nationalities) skewed the ethnic mixture and enabled non-Kazakhs to outnumber natives. Independence in 1991 caused many of these newcomers to emigrate. Kazakhstan's economy is larger than those of all the other Central Asian states combined, largely due to the country's vast natural resources and a recent history of political stability. Current issues include: developing a cohesive national identity; expanding the development of the country's vast energy resources and exporting them to world markets; achieving a sustainable economic growth; diversifying the economy outside the oil, gas, and mining sectors; enhancing Kazakhstan's competitiveness; and strengthening relations with neighboring states and other foreign powers.

MONETARY SYSTEM:

1 Tengé = 100 Tyin = 500 Rubles (Russian), 1993 -

REPUBLIC

КАЗАКСТАН УЛТТЫК БАНКІ

Kazakhstan National Bank

1993-98 Issue

1   1 Tyin   VF   UNC

1993. Three watermark varieties. Two serial # positions. Red, blue and purple
on yellow and multicolor underprint. Ornate denomination in circle at right. Serial
number at left. Back: Circular arms at left.

a. Watermark: large diamond lattice pattern. Low serial # position.	0.50	1.00
b. Watermark: large diamond lattice pattern. Upper serial # position.	0.50	1.00
c. Watermark: small snowflake pattern. Low serial # position.	0.50	1.00
d. Watermark: small snowflake pattern. Upper serial # position.	0.50	1.00
e. No watermark. Low serial # position.	0.50	1.00

2   2 Tyin   VF   UNC

1993. Three watermark varieties. Two serial # positions. Blue-violet on light blue
and multicolor underprint. Ornate denomination in circle at right. Serial number at
left. Back: Circular arms at left.

a. Watermark: large diamond pattern. Low serial # position.	0.50	1.00
b. Watermark: large diamond pattern. Upper serial # position.	0.50	1.00
c. Watermark: small snowflake pattern. Low serial # position.	0.50	1.00
d. Watermark: small snowflake pattern. Upper serial # position.	0.50	1.00
e. Without watermark. Low serial # position.	0.50	1.00

3   5 Tyin   VF   UNC

1993. Violet on light blue and multicolor underprint. Ornate denomination in circle
at right. Serial number at left. Back: Circular arms at left.

a. Watermark: small snowflake pattern. Low serial # position.	0.50	1.00
b. Watermark: small snowflake pattern. Upper serial # position.	0.50	1.00

4   10 Tyin   **VF   UNC**

1993. Deep red on pink and multicolor underprint. Ornate denomination in circle at right. Serial number at left. Back: Circular arms at left.

    a. Watermark: small snowflake pattern. Low serial # position.   0.50   1.50
    b. Watermark: small snowflake pattern. Upper serial # position.   0.50   1.50

5   20 Tyin   **VF   UNC**

1993. Black and blue-gray on yellow and multicolor underprint. Ornate denomination in circle at right. Serial number at left. Back: Circular arms at left.

    a. Watermark: small snowflake pattern. Low serial # position.   0.50   1.50
    b. Watermark: small snowflake pattern. Upper serial # position.   0.50   1.50

6   50 Tyin   **VF   UNC**

1993. Dark brown and black on multicolor underprint. Ornate denomination in circle at right. Serial number at left. Back: Circular arms at left. Watermark: Design.

    a. Watermark: small snowflake pattern. Low serial # position.   0.50   3.00
    b. Watermark: small snowflake pattern. Upper serial # position.   0.50   3.00

7   1 Tengé   **VF   UNC**

1993. Dark blue on multicolor underprint. Al-Farabi at center right. Back: Architectural drawings of mosque at left center, arms at upper right. Watermark: Symmetrical design repeated.

    a. Issued note.   1.00   3.00
    s. Specimen.   —   100

8   3 Tengé   **VF   UNC**

1993. Dark green on multicolor underprint. Suinbai at center right. Back: Mountains, forest, and river at left center. Arms at upper center right. Watermark: Symmetrical design repeated.

    a. Issued note.   1.00   4.00
    s. Specimen.   —   100

9   5 Tengé   **VF   UNC**

1993. Dark brown-violet on multicolor underprint. Kurmangazy at center right. Back: Cemetery at left center, arms at upper center right. Watermark: Symmetrical design repeated.

    a. Issued note.   1.00   4.00
    s. Specimen.   —   100

10   10 Tengé   **VF   UNC**

1993. Dark green on multicolor underprint. Shoqan Valikhanov at center right. Back: Mountains, forest, and lake at left center, arms at upper center right. Watermark: Shoqan Valikhanov.

    a. Issued note.   1.00   6.00
    s. Specimen.   —   100

11   20 Tengé   **VF   UNC**

1993. Brown on multicolor underprint. Abai Kunanbrev at center right. Back: Equestrian hunter at left center, arms at upper center right. Watermark: Abai Kunanbrev.

    a. Issued note.   2.00   10.00
    s. Specimen.   —   100

12   50 Tengé   **VF   UNC**

1993. Red-brown and deep violet on multicolor underprint. Abilkhair Khan at center right. Back: Native artwork at left center, arms at upper center right. Watermark: Abilkhair Khan.

    a. Issued note.   3.00   12.00
    s. Specimen.   —   125

17 2000 Tengé   **VF UNC**
1996. Dark brown and green on multicolor underprint. Al-Farabi at right. Back:
Gate. Watermark: Al-Farabi.   25.00   80.00

13 100 Tengé   **VF UNC**
1993. Purple and dark blue on multicolor underprint. Abylai Khan at center right.
Back: Domed building at left center, arms at upper center right. Watermark: Abylai
Khan.

		VF	UNC
a.	1993. Silver colored OVD ink.	3.00	18.00
b.	2004. Golden colored OVD ink.	2.00	15.00
s.	Specimen.	—	125

18 5000 Tengé   **VF UNC**
1998. Light brown on multicolor underprint. Al Farabi at center. Back: Mausoleum.   35.00   100

#19 *Not assigned.*

1999-2001 Issue

14 200 Tengé   **VF UNC**
1993. Red and brown on multicolor underprint. Al-Farabi at right. Back: Domes of
building at left, arms at upper center right. Watermark: Al-Farabi.

		VF	UNC
a.	Issued note.	FV	20.00
s.	Specimen.	—	135

20 200 Tengé   **VF UNC**
1999. Brown and tan on multicolor underprint. Al-Farabi at right. Back: Domes of
building at left, arms at upper center right. Watermark: Al-Farabi.

		VF	UNC
a.	Security device at lower right with white linear design within.	FV	12.00
b.	Security device at lower right solid.	FV	12.00

15 500 Tengé   **VF UNC**
1994. Blue-black and violet on multicolor underprint. Al-Farabi at right. Back:
Ancient building, arms at upper center right. Watermark: Al-Farabi.

		VF	UNC
a.	Issued note.	FV	27.50
s.	Specimen.	—	150

21 500 Tengé   **VF UNC**
1999. Dark blue and violet on multicolor underprint. Al-Farabi at right. Back:
Ancient building, arms at upper center right. Watermark: Al-Farabi.

		VF	UNC
a.	Security device at lower right. with white linear designature	FV	20.00
b.	Security device at lower right. solid.	FV	20.00

16 1000 Tengé   **VF UNC**
1994. Deep green, red and orange on multicolor underprint. Al-Farabi at right.
Back: Ancient building. Watermark: Al-Farabi.

		VF	UNC
a.	Issued note.	FV	40.00
s.	Specimen.	—	150

22 1000 Tengé
2000. Dark green, red and slate blue on multicolor underprint. Al-Farabi at right.
Back: Ancient building. Watermark: Al-Farabi.

	VF	UNC
	FV	40.00

23 2000 Tengé
2000. Green, brown and purple on multicolor underprint. Al-Farabi at right. Back:
Mausoleum of Khodka Akhemd Yassavi. Watermark: Al-Farabi.

	VF	UNC
	FV	60.00

24 5000 Tengé
2001. Light brown and red on multicolor underprint. Al Farabi at center. Back:
Mausoleum.

	VF	UNC
	FV	90.00

25 10,000 Tengé
2003. Blue and dark brown on multicolor underprint. Back: Snow leopard with
mountains in background.

	VF	UNC
	FV	170

2001 Commemorative Issue

26 5000 Tengé
2001. Light brown and red on multicolor underprint. Blue overprint at top of
watermark area on face of number 18.

	VF	UNC
	FV	80.00

2004 Issue

27 500 Tengé
1999 (2004). Dark blue and blue on violet and multicolor underprint. Al-Farabi at
right. Additional security features at right. Back: Mausoleum of Khodka Akhmed
Yassavi. Watermark: Al-Farabi.

	VF	UNC
	FV	10.00

2006 Issue

28 200 Tengé
2006. Multicolor. Hand at left, tower. Back: Map, birds in flight. 126x64mm.

	VF	UNC
	FV	4.00

29 500 Tengé
2006. Blue and multicolor. Hand at left, tower. Back: Map, birds in flight.
130x67mm.

	VF	UNC
a. 2006.	FV	8.00
b. 2006/2015.	FV	8.00

30 1000 Tengé
  VF UNC
  2006. Yellow and multicolor. Hand at left, tower. Back: Map and mountains. 134x69mm.
  FV 16.00

31 2000 Tengé
  VF UNC
  2006. Green and multicolor. Hand at left, tower. Back: Map and mountain lake. 138x72mm.
  a. Error spelling in bank name.   FV 30.00
  b. Corrected spelling of bank name.   FV 35.00

32 5000 Tengé
  VF UNC
  2006. Reddish brown and multicolor. Hand at left, tower. Back: Map and statue. 144x76mm.
  a. Error spelling of bank name.   FV 50.00
  b. Corrected spelling of bank name.   FV 45.00

33 10,000 Tengé
  VF UNC
  2006. Multicolor. Hand at left, tower. Back: Map and building. 149x74mm.
  FV 90.00

2008 Commemorative Issue

34 5000 Tengé
  VF UNC
  8.7.2008. Red and brown on multicolor underprint. Hand at left, tower. Eagle in device at top left. Back: Map, statue and Kazakhstan hotel in Almaty. Watermark: Snow leopard and value. Printer: TDLR. 144x76mm.
  a. Issued note.   FV 75.00
  s. Specimen.   FV 150

2010 Commemorative Issue

35 1000 Tengé
  VF UNC
  2010. Blue, green and red on multicolor underprint. Value at left within ornate design. Back: Domed building at center. 134x69mm.
  FV 20.00

36 2000 Tengé
  VF UNC
  2011. Green on multicolor underprint. Hand at botom, tower. Back: Mountain and Ski Jumper.
  FV 35.00
  Kazakhstan to chair the OSSE.

2011 OIC Commememorative Issue

37 1000 Tengé   **VF UNC**
2011. Dome of the mausoleum of Hodja Akhmed Yassavi. Back: Mausoleum of   FV 16.00
Hodja Akhmed Yassavi at center. 134x69mm.
Kazaakhstan to chair the OIC.

38 5000 Tengé   **VF UNC**
2011. Red, blue, yellow and green on multicolor underprint. Stylized snow   FV 75.00
leopards, birds, Kazakh Eli monument in Astana. Back: Outline of Kazakhstan,
Zailijsky Alatau ridge of Tjan-Shan, Independence monument and Kazakhstan
hotel in Almaty. 144x76mm.

39 10,000 Tengé   **VF UNC**
2011. National emblem, birds, Kazakh Eli monument in Astana. Back: Outline map   FV 130
of Kazakhstan, Akorda Palace (Presidential residence in Astana). Watermark:
Eagle with spread wings. 149x79mm.
Kazakhstan Independence, 20th Anniversary

2011 Commemorative Issue

40 10,000 Tengé   **VF UNC**
2011. Blue and multicolor.   FV 90.00

2011-12 Issue

41 2000 Tengé   **VF UNC**
2012. Dark and light green on multicolor underprint. Monument at right and   FV 35.00
flying doves at bottom center. Back: Kazakhstan map and Irtysh River image.
139x73mm.

42 5000 Tengé   **VF UNC**
2011. Orange and multicolor.   FV 45.00

43 10,000 Tengé   **VF UNC**
2012. Blue and multicolor.   FV 125

2013 Commemorative Issue

44   1000 Tengé   **VF   UNC**
ND (2013) Red-brown and tan on multicolor underprint. Monument of Kazak Eli   FV   16.00
on right, a fragment of the Kultegin sculpture and doves and column at left. Back:
Segment of Kultegin, Turkic runic designs. 134x70mm.

45   20,000 Tengé   **VF   UNC**
2013. Blue-gray and violet. 20th anniversary of the tenge. Vertical. National
emblem, SPARK pegasus patch, monumental arch, flying doves and Kazakh Eli
monument in Astana, flag. Back: Outline of Kazakhstan, Akorda Palace, doves.
Watermark: Mythic Samruk bird with electrotype 20000. Printer. (BFoNBK).
155x79mm.
    a. Introduced 01.12.2015.   FV   90.00

2014 Issue

46   1000 Tengé   **VF   UNC**
2014. Yellow, brown, blue. Doves, Kazakh Eli monument, flag. Back: Deer, draw-   FV   16.00
ings of warriors on horseback. 134x70mm.

KENYA

The Republic of Kenya, located on the east coast of Central Africa, has an area of 224,961 sq. mi. (582,646 sq. km.) and a population of 30.34 million. Capital: Nairobi. The predominantly agricultural country exports coffee, tea and petroleum products. Founding president and liberation struggle icon Jomo Kenyatta led Kenya from independence in 1963 until his death in 1978, when President Daniel Toroitich arap Moi took power in a constitutional succession.

The country was a de facto one-party state from 1969 until 1982 when the ruling Kenya African National Union (KANU) made itself the sole legal party in Kenya. Moi acceded to internal and external pressure for political liberalization in late 1991. The ethnically fractured opposition failed to dislodge KANU from power in elections in 1992 and 1997, which were marred by violence and fraud, but were viewed as having generally reflected the will of the Kenyan people. President Moi stepped down in December 2002 following fair and peaceful elections. Mwai Kibaki, running as the candidate of the multiethnic, united opposition group, the National Rainbow Coalition (NARC), defeated KANU candidate Uhuru Kenyatta and assumed the presidency following a campaign centered on an anticorruption platform. Kibaki's NARC coalition splintered in 2005 over the constitutional review process. Government defectors joined with KANU to form a new opposition coalition, the Orange Democratic Movement, which defeated the government's draft constitution in a popular referendum in November 2005. Kibaki's reelection in December 2007 brought charges of vote rigging from ODM candidate Raila Odinga and unleashed two months of violence in which as many as 1,500 people died. UN-sponsored talks in late February produced a powersharing accord bringing Odinga into the government in the restored position of prime minister. Notes of the East African Currency Board were in use during the first years.

RULERS:
   British to 1964

MONETARY SYSTEM:
   1 Shilling (Shilingi) = 100 Cents

SIGNATURE VARIETIES		
	GOVERNOR	MEMBER
1	*Dr. Leon Barawski*	*Gevau*
2	*Duncan Ndegwa*	*Gevau*
3	*Duncan Ndegwa*	
4	*Duncan Ndegwa*	*Iganaga*
5	*Duncan Ndegwa*	*L. Mutenge*
6	*Duncan Ndegwa*	*Harry Mule*
7	*Philip Ndegwa*	*Harry Mule*
8	*Philip Ndegwa*	*Subiudyo*

SIGNATURE VARIETIES

9a	Eric Kotut	Subiudyo
9b	Eric Kotut	Subiudyo
10a	Eric Kotut	Kamotho
10b	Eric Kotut	Kamotho
11	Micah D. Cheserem	Kamotho
12	Micah D. Cheserem	B.K. Kipkulei
13	Micah D. Cheserem	B.K. Kipkulei
14	Micah D. Cheserem	S.S. Lesima
15	Micah D. Cheserem	Emengich
16	Micah D. Cheserem	
17	Nahashon Nyagah	
18	Nahashon Nyagah	
19		

REPUBLIC

Banki Kuu Ya Kenya
CENTRAL BANK OF KENYA
1966 Issue

1   5 Shillings   VF   UNC

1966-68. Values in Arabic numerals and letters. Brown on multicolor underprint. Mzee Jomo Kenyatta at left, arms at center in underprint. Back: Woman picking coffee beans at right. Watermark: Lion's head.

		VF	UNC
a.	1.7.1966.	20.00	95.00
b.	1.7.1967.	17.50	90.00
c.	1.7.1968.	17.50	85.00
s.	As a. Specimen, punched hole cancelled.	—	150

2   10 Shillings   VF   UNC

1966-68. Values in Arabic numerals and letters. Green on multicolor underprint. Mzee Jomo Kenyatta at left, arms at center in underprint. Back: Tea pickers in field. Watermark: Lion's head.

		VF	UNC
a.	1.7.1966.	25.00	95.00
b.	1.7.1967.	27.50	140
c.	1.7.1968.	20.00	120
s.	As a. Specimen, punched hole cancelled.	—	200

3   20 Shillings   VF   UNC

1966-68. Values in Arabic numerals and letters. Blue on multicolor underprint. Mzee Jomo Kenyatta at left, arms at center in underprint. Back: Plants and train with sisal. Watermark: Lion's head.

		VF	UNC
a.	1.7.1966.	50.00	250
b.	1.7.1967.	60.00	275
c.	1.7.1968.	50.00	250
s.	As a. Specimen, punched hole cancelled.	—	300

4 50 Shillings

1966-68. Values in Arabic numerals and letters. Dark brown on multicolor underprint. Mzee Jomo Kenyatta at left, arms at center in underprint. Back: Cotton picking below Mt. Kenya. Watermark: Lion's head.

		VF	UNC
a. 1.7.1966.		300	950
b. 1.7.1967.		400	1,500
c. 1.7.1968.		350	1,450
s. As a. Specimen, punched hole cancelled.		—	1,250

5 100 Shillings

1966; 1968. Values in Arabic numerals and letters. Purple on multicolor underprint. Mzee Jomo Kenyatta at left, arms at center in underprint. Back: Workers at pineapple plantation. Watermark: Lion's head.

		VF	UNC
a. 1.7.1966.		55.00	525
b. 1.7.1968.		60.00	575
s. As a. Specimen, punched hole cancelled.		—	750

1969 Issue

6 5 Shillings

1969-73. Value without Arabic numerals and letters. Brown on multicolor underprint. Mzee Jomo Kenyatta at left. Back: Woman picking coffee beans at right. Watermark: Lion's head.

		VF	UNC
a. Signature 2. 1.7.1969.		5.00	25.00
b. Signature 3. 1.7.1971.		6.00	30.00
c. Signature 3. 1.7.1972.		2.00	25.00
d. Signature 3. 1.7.1973.		4.00	22.50

7 10 Shillings

1969-74. Value without Arabic numerals and letters. Green on multicolor underprint. Mzee Jomo Kenyatta at left. Back: Tea pickers in field. Watermark: Lion's head.

		VF	UNC
a. Signature 2. 1.7.1969.		8.00	60.00
b. Signature 3. 1.7.1971.		6.00	50.00
c. Signature 3. 1.7.1972.		7.00	55.00
d. Signature 3. 1.7.1973.		7.00	55.00
e. Signature 3. 1.7.1974.		7.00	57.50

8 20 Shillings

1969-73. Value without Arabic numerals and letters. Blue on multicolor underprint. Mzee Jomo Kenyatta at left. Back: Plants and train with sisal. Watermark: Lion's head.

		VF	UNC
a. Signature 2. 1.7.1969.		20.00	160
b. Signature 3. 1.7.1971.		40.00	275
c. Signature 3. 1.7.1972.		25.00	180
d. Signature 3. 1.7.1973.		30.00	200

9 50 Shillings

1909, 1971. Value without Arabic numerals and letters. Dark brown on multicolor underprint. Mzee Jomo Kenyatta at left. Back: Cotton picking below Mt. Kenya. Watermark: Lion's head.

		VF	UNC
a. Signature 2. 1.7.1969.		175	750
b. Signature 3. 1.7.1971.		65.00	200

10 100 Shillings

1969-73. Value without Arabic numerals and letters. Purple on multicolor underprint. Mzee Jomo Kenyatta at left. Back: Workers at pineapple plantation. Watermark: Lion's head.

		VF	UNC
a. Signature 2. 1.7.1969.		100	500
b. Signature 3. 1.7.1971.		40.00	350
c. Signature 3. 1.7.1972.		40.00	350
d. Signature 3. 1.7.1973.		75.00	375

1974 Issue

11 5 Shillings

1974-77. Values in latent images at bottom left. Brown-orange on multicolor underprint. Mzee Jomo Kenyatta at left. Back: Woman picking coffee beans at right. Watermark: Lion's head.

		VF	UNC
a. Signature 3. 12.12.1974.		2.00	15.00
b. Signature 4. 1.1.1975.		2.00	15.00
c. Signature 4. 1.7.1976.		3.00	20.00
d. Signature 5. 1.7.1977.		2.00	15.00

12   10 Shillings

1975-77. Values in latent images at bottom left. Dark green and dark brown on multicolor underprint. Mzee Jomo Kenyatta at left. Back: Cattle at center right. Watermark: Lion's head.

		VF	UNC
a.	Signature 4. 1.1.1975.	3.00	15.00
b.	Signature 4. 1.7.1976.	6.00	30.00
c.	Signature 5. 1.7.1977.	4.00	17.50

13   20 Shillings

1974-77. Values in latent images at bottom left. Dark blue on multicolor underprint. Mzee Jomo Kenyatta at left. Back: Lions. Watermark: Lion's head.

		VF	UNC
a.	Signature 3. 12.12.1974.	15.00	60.00
b.	Signature 4. 1.1.1975.	7.50	35.00
c.	Signature 4. 1.7.1976.	12.50	65.00
d.	Signature 5. 1.7.1977.	9.00	45.00

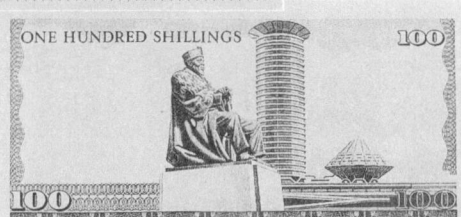

14   100 Shillings

1974-77. 153 x 79mm. Values in latent images at bottom left. Purple on light green and multicolor underprint. Mzee Jomo Kenyatta at left. Back: Kenyatta statue and tower. Watermark: Lion's head.

		VF	UNC
a.	Signature 3. 12.12.1974.	35.00	150
b.	Signature 4. 1.1.1975.	17.50	125
c.	Signature 4. 1.7.1976.	25.00	140
d.	Signature 5. 1.7.1977.	30.00	200

1978 Issue

Note: #15-18 were withdrawn soon after Kenyatta's death. However, a shortage of currency resulted in a reissue during Dec. 1993 - Jan. 1994 of mostly circulated notes.

15   5 Shillings

1.7.1978. Brown-orange on multicolor underprint. Mzee Jomo Kenyatta at left with English value only in third line. Signature 5. Back: Woman picking coffee beans at right. Watermark: Lion's head.

VF	UNC
1.50	3.00

16   10 Shillings

1.7.1978. Dark green and dark brown on multicolor underprint. Mzee Jomo Kenyatta at left with English value only in third line. Signature 5. Back: Cattle at center right. Watermark: Lion's head.

VF	UNC
1.00	5.00

17   20 Shillings

1.7.1978. Blue-black and blue on multicolor underprint. Mzee Jomo Kenyatta at left with English value only in third line. Signature 5. Back: Lions. Watermark: Lion's head.

VF	UNC
2.75	7.50

18 100 Shillings VF UNC
1.7.1978. Purple, dark brown and dark blue on multicolor underprint. Mzee Jomo
Kenyatta at left with English value only in third line. Signature 5. Different colors in
guilloches. Back: Kenyatta statue and tower. Watermark: Lion's head. 157x81mm. 7.50 20.00

1980-81 Issue

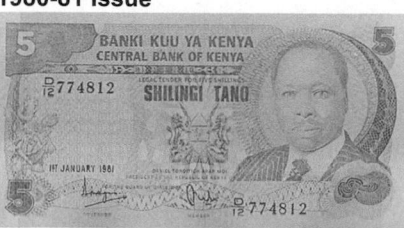

19 5 Shillings VF UNC
1981-84. Orange-brown on multicolor underprint. Arms at center. President
Daniel Toroitich Arap Moi at right. Back: Three rams with giraffes and mountain in
background. Watermark: Lion's head.

		VF	UNC
a.	Signature 6. 1.1.1981.	1.00	6.00
b.	Signature 6. 1.1.1982.	1.00	5.00
c.	Signature 7. 1.7.1984.	1.50	7.00

20 10 Shillings VF UNC
1981-88. UV: bottom front fluoresces yellow and orange. Green, blue and
brown on multicolor underprint. Arms at center. President Daniel Toroitich Arap
Moi at right. Back: Two cows at left, two school children drinking milk at center.
Watermark: Lion's head.

		VF	UNC
a.	Signature 6. 1.1.1981.	1.50	8.00
b.	Signature 6. 1.1.1982.	1.25	7.00
c.	Signature 7. 1.7.1984.	1.75	9.00
d.	Signature 7. 1.7.1985.	2.00	10.00
e.	Signature 7. 14.9.1986.	1.50	8.00
f.	Signature 8. 1.7.1987.	1.25	8.00
g.	Signature 9a. 1.7.1988.	1.25	7.00

21 20 Shillings VF UNC
1981-87. Blue on multicolor underprint. Arms at center. President Daniel Toroitich
Arap Moi at right. Back: Four women reading newspaper at center. Watermark:
Lion's head.

		VF	UNC
a.	Signature 6. 1.1.1981.	1.75	14.00
b.	Signature 6. 1.1.1982.	1.50	10.00
c.	Signature 7. 1.7.1984.	1.50	12.00
d.	Signature 7. 1.7.1985.	2.00	16.00
e.	Signature 7. 14.9.1986.	2.25	17.50
f.	Signature 8. 1.7.1987.	1.75	14.00

22 50 Shillings VF UNC
1980-88. Dark red and multicolor. Arms at center. President Daniel Toroitich Arap
Moi at right. Back: Jet aircraft flying over Jomo Kenyatta airport. Watermark: Lion's
head.

		VF	UNC
a.	Signature 4. 1.6.1980.	3.00	12.50
b.	Signature 7. 1.7.1985.	3.50	17.50
c.	Signature 7. 14.9.1986.	3.50	18.00
d.	Signature 8. 1.7.1987.	5.00	20.00
e.	Signature 9a. 1.7.1988.	5.00	20.00

23 100 Shillings VF UNC
1980-88. Purple and multicolor. Arms at center. President Daniel Toroitich Arap
Moi at right. Back: Kenyatta statue, tower and mountains. Watermark: Lion's head.

		VF	UNC
a.	Signature 4. 1.6.1980.	5.00	25.00
b.	Signature 6. 1.6.1981.	6.00	35.00
c.	Signature 7. 1.7.1984.	5.00	30.00
d.	Signature 7. 14.9.1986.	6.50	40.00
e.	Signature 8. 1.7.1987.	7.00	50.00
f.	Signature 9a. 1.7.1988.	4.00	22.00

23A 200 Shillings

	VF	UNC

1986-88. Dark brown on multicolor underprint. Arms at center. President Daniel Toroitich Arap Moi at right. Triangle in lower left border. No silvering on value at upper right. Back: Fountain at center. Watermark: Lion's head.

a. Signature 7. 14.9.1986.	10.00	55.00
b. Signature 8. 1.7.1987.	25.00	225
c. Signature 9a. 1.7.1988.	50.00	325

1986-90 Issue

#24-30 Replacement notes: Serial # prefix ZZ.

24 10 Shillings

	VF	UNC

1989-94. UV: vertical serial # fluoresces orange, lower left, upper right, middle devices yellow, Back middle design yellow. Dark green, dark blue and brown on multicolor underprint. President Daniel Toroitich Arap Moi at right center, arms at left center. Vertical seial number at left. Back: University at left center. Watermark: Lion's head.

a. Signature 9a. 14.10.1989.	FV	3.00
b. Signature 9a. 1.7.1990.	FV	2.50
c. Signature 9a. 1.7.1991.	FV	1.75
d. Signature 10a. 2.1.1992. Small date font. Printer: H&S.	1.00	4.50
e. Signature 10a. 1.7.1993. Large date font.	1.00	4.50
f. Signature 11. 1.1.1994.	1.00	6.00

25 20 Shillings

	VF	UNC

1988-92. Dark blue and multicolor. President Daniel Toroitich Arap Moi at right center, arms at left center. Vertical seial number at left. Back: Moi International Sports Complex. Watermark: Lion's head.

a. Signature 9b. 12.12.1988.	5.00	22.50
b. Signature 9b. 1.7.1989.	1.00	5.00
c. Signature 9b. 1.7.1990.	1.00	3.50
d. Signature 9b. 1.7.1991.	2.00	6.00
e. Signature 10a. 2.1.1992. Large date font.	2.00	6.00
s. Specimen.	—	—

#25a, which is dated 12.12.1988 is believed to be a commemorative for the 25th Anniversary of Independence.

26 50 Shillings

	VF	UNC

1990; 1992. Red-brown on multicolor underprint. President Daniel Toroitich Arap Moi at right center, arms at left center. Vertical seial number at left. Back: Modern buildings at left, flag at right. Watermark: Lion's head.

a. Signature 9b. 10.10.1990.	4.00	16.00
b. Signature 10b. 1.7.1992.	3.00	14.00
s. Specimen. As b.	—	—

27 100 Shillings

	VF	UNC

1989-95. Purple, dark green and red on multicolor underprint. President Daniel Toroitich Arap Moi at right center, arms at left center. Vertical seial number at left. Back: Monument to 25th Anniversary of Independence with Mt. Kenya. Watermark: Lion's head.

a. Signature 9a. 14.10.1989.	3.00	12.50
b. Signature 9a. 1.7.1990.	3.00	12.50
c. Signature 9a. 1.7.1991.	2.00	10.00
d. Signature 10a. 2.1.1992. Small date font. Printer: H&S.	3.00	12.50
e. Signature 10a. 1.7.1992. Large date font.	4.00	15.00
f. Signature 11. 1.1.1994.	3.00	15.00
g. Signature 12. 1.1.1995.	4.00	17.50

#28 Deleted. See #23A.

29 200 Shillings

	VF	UNC

1989-94. President Daniel Toroitich Arap Moi at right center, arms at left center. Rose replaces colored triangle to right of 200 at lower left. Additional silver diamond design under 200 at upper right Back: Fountain at center. Watermark: Lion's head.

a. Signature 9a. 14.10.1989.	4.50	27.50
b. Signature 9a. 1.7.1990.	4.50	25.00
c. Signature 10a. 2.1.1992. Small date font. Printer: H&S.	5.00	37.50
d. Signature 10a. 1.7.1992. Large date font.	4.00	25.00
e. Signature 11. 14.9.1993.	3.50	22.50
f. Signature 11. 1.1.1994.	4.00	25.00

30   500 Shillings

1988-95. Black, deep green and red on multicolor underprint. President Daniel Toroitich Arap Moi at right center, arms at left center. Vertical seial number at left. Roses at left. Back: Parliament building, Mt. Kenya. Watermark: Lion's head.

		VF	UNC
a.	Signature 9b. 14.10.1988.	50.00	250
b.	Signature 9b. 1.7.1989.	25.00	100
c.	Signature 9b. 1.7.1990.	15.00	55.00
d.	Signature 10a. 2.1.1992. Small date font. Printer: H&S.	20.00	75.00
e.	Signature 10a. 1.7.1992. Large date font.	15.00	55.00
f.	Signature 11. 14.9.1993.	17.50	65.00
g.	Signature 12. 1.1.1995.	17.50	70.00

1993 Issue

31   20 Shillings

1993-94. Dark blue and multicolor. President Daniel Toroitich Arap Moi at center right. Roses added to left border, vertical red serial number. Back: Moi International Sports Complex. Male runner and other artistic enhancements added.

		VF	UNC
a.	Signature 11. 14.9.1993.	2.00	5.00
b.	Signature 11. 1.1.1994.	2.00	6.00

1994-95 Issue

32   20 Shillings

1.7.1995. Dark blue, brown and blue-green on multicolor underprint. President Daniel Toroitich Arap Moi at left center, arms at upper center right. Ascending size serial number. Signature 13. Back: Baton at left, Moi Int'l Sports Complex at left center, runner at center right. Watermark: Lion head facing.

	VF	UNC
	FV	3.00

33   500 Shillings

1.7.1995. Black, green and red on multicolor underprint. President Daniel Toroitich Arap Moi at left center, arms at upper center right. Ascending size serial number. Back: Parliament building at left center. Watermark: Lion head facing.

	VF	UNC
	7.50	25.00

34   1000 Shillings

1994-95. Brown on multicolor underprint. President Daniel Toroitich Arap Moi at left center, arms at upper center right. Ascending size serial number. Back: Water buffalo, elephants and egret. Watermark: Lion head facing.

		VF	UNC
a.	12.12.1994.	FV	50.00
b.	1.7.1995.	FV	50.00

1996-97 Issue

35   20 Shillings

1996-2001. Segmented foil over security thread. Dark blue on multicolor underprint. President Daniel Toroitich Arap Moi at left center, arms at upper center right. Ascending size serial number. Back: Baton at left, Moi Int'l Sports Complex at left center, runner at center right. Watermark: Lion head facing.

		VF	UNC
a1.	1.1.1996. Dark blue signature.	FV	3.00
a2.	1.1.1996. Black signatrue.	FV	5.00
b.	1.7.1997.	FV	5.00
c.	1.7.1998.	FV	7.00

36   50 Shillings

1996-2002. Segmented foil over security thread. Brown-violet and blue-black on multicolor underprint. President Daniel Toroitich Arap Moi at left center, arms at upper center right. Ascending size serial number. Back: Dromedary caravan. 138x72mm.

		VF	UNC
a1.	1.1.1996. Brown signatures.	FV	5.00
a2.	1.1.1996. Black signatures.	FV	8.50
b.	1.7.1997.	FV	7.00
c.	1.7.1998.	FV	4.00
d.	1.7.1999.	FV	5.00
e.	1.7.2000.	FV	3.00
f.	1.7.2001.	FV	15.00
g.	1.7.2002.	FV	2.50

37   100 Shillings

1996-2002. Segmented foil over security thread. Purple, red and deep green on multicolor underprint. President Daniel Toroitich Arap Moi at left center, arms at upper center right. Ascending size serial number. Back: People by Monument to 25th Anniversary of Independence at center, branch of fruit at left. 142x74mm.

	VF	UNC
a. 1.7.1996.	FV	6.00
b. 1.7.1997.	FV	12.00
c. 1.7.1998.	FV	5.00
d. 1.7.1999.	FV	7.50
e. 1.7.2000.	FV	4.00
f. 1.7.2001.	FV	8.00
g. 1.7.2002.	FV	4.00
h. 1.9.2002.	FV	5.00

38   200 Shillings

1996-2002. Segmented foil over security thread. Dark brown, blue-gray and dark green on multicolor underprint. President Daniel Toroitich Arap Moi at left center, arms at upper center right. Ascending size serial number. Back: Unity monument at center, women harvesting at left. 144x76mm.

	VF	UNC
a. 1.7.1996.	FV	16.00
b. 1.7.1997.	FV	12.50
c. 1.7.1998.	FV	16.00
d. 1.7.1999.	FV	16.00
e. 1.7.2000.	FV	16.00
f. 1.7.2001.	FV	8.00
g. 1.9.2002.	FV	7.00

39   500 Shillings

1997-2002. Segmented foil over security thread. Black, green and red on multi-color underprint. President Daniel Toroitich Arap Moi at left center, arms at upper center right. Ascending size serial number. Back: Parliament building at left center. Watermark: Lion head facing. 148x78mm.

	VF	UNC
a. 1.7.1997.	7.50	28.00
b. 1.7.1999.	FV	26.00
c. 1.7.2000.	FV	24.00
d. 1.7.2001.	FV	18.00

40   1000 Shillings

1997-2002. Segmented foil over security thread. Brown-violet and olive-green on multicolor underprint. President Daniel Toroitich Arap Moi at left center, arms at upper center right. Ascending size serial number. Back: Water buffalo, elephants and egret. Watermark: Lion head facing. 150x80mm.

	VF	UNC
a. 1.7.1997.	FV	60.00
b. 1.7.1999.	FV	45.00
c. 1.7.2000.	FV	35.00
d. 1.7.2001.	FV	40.00
e. 1.7.2002.	FV	35.00

2003-04 Issue

#41-45 2003 dates have thin security thread, 2004 onwards have a thick thread.

41   50 Shillings

2003-06. With enhanced security features. Brown violet and blue-black on multicolor underprint. President Kenyatta at left center, arms at upper center right. Ascending size serial number. Back: Dromedary caravan. 138x72mm.

	VF	UNC
a. 1.4.2003. Narrow segmented security foil.	FV	2.50
b. 2.2.2004. Wide segmented security foil.	FV	2.50
c. 2.8.2004.	FV	2.50
s. Specimen.	—	—

42   100 Shillings

2004-06. With enhanced security features. Purple, orange and green on multicolor underprint. President Kenyatta at left center, arms at upper center right. Ascending size serial number. Back: Nyayo monument. 142x74mm.

	VF	UNC
a. 2.2.2004. Wide segmented security foil.	FV	3.50
b. 2.8.2004.	FV	3.50

43   200 Shillings

2004-06. With enhanced security features. Brown, blue and light green on multi-color underprint. President Kenyatta at left center, without commemorative text. Back: Cotton pickers. 144x76mm.

	VF	UNC
a. 2.2.2004. Wide segmented security foil.	FV	6.50
b. 2.8.2004.	FV	6.50

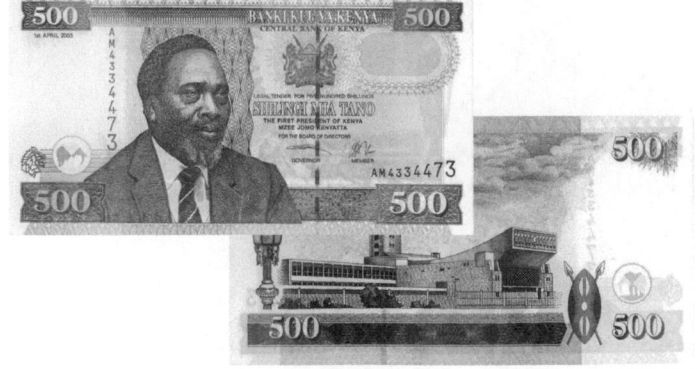

44 500 Shillings
               VF UNC

2003-06. With enhanced security features. Black and green on multicolor under-print. President Kenyatta at left center, arms at upper center right. Ascending size serial number. Back: National Assembly building. 148x78mm.

    a. 1.4.2003. Narrow segmented security foil.   FV 16.00
    b. 2.2.2004. Wide segmented security foil.   FV 16.00
    c. 8.2.2004.   FV 16.00

45 1000 Shillings
               VF UNC

2003-06. With enhanced security features. Brown, lilac and light olive on multicolor underprint. President Kenyatta at left center, arms at upper center right. Ascending size serial number. Back: Elephants and other animals. 150x80mm.

    a. 1.4.2003. Narrow segmented security foil.   FV 32.50
    b. 2.2.2004. Wide segmented security foil.   FV 32.50
    c. 2.8.2004. Value added to watermark.   FV 32.50

2003 Commemorative Issue

40th Anniversary of Independence.

46 200 Shillings
               VF UNC

12.12.2003. Brown, blue and light green on multicolor underprint. Jomo Kenyatta at left center, commemorative text in watermark area at left. Back: Cotton pickers. 144x76mm.   FV 8.00

2005 Issue

47 50 Shillings
               VF UNC

2005-. Brown-violet and blue-black on multicolor underprint. President Jomo Kenyatta at left center. Back: Dromedary caravan. Watermark: Value and Corner-stone stripes added Printer: DLR. 138x72mm.

    a. 1.6.2005.   FV 2.50
    b. 1.4.2006.   FV 2.50
    c. 3.3.2008.   FV 2.50
    d. 17.6.2009.   FV 2.50
    e. 16.7.2010.   FV 2.50

48 100 Shillings
               VF UNC

2005-. Purple, orange and green on multicolor underprint. President Jomo Kenyatta at left center. Back: Nyayo monument. Watermark: Value and Cornerstone stripes added DLR. 142x74mm.

    a. 1.6.2005.   FV 3.50
    b. 1.4.2006.   FV 3.50
    c. 3.3.2008.   FV 3.50
    d. 17.6.2009.   FV 3.50
    e. 16.7.2010.   FV 3.50

49 200 Shillings
               VF UNC

2005-. Brown, blue and light green on multicolor underprint. President Jomo Kanyatta at left center. Back: Cotton pickers. Watermark: Value and Cornerstone stripes added Printer: DLR.

    a. 1.6.2005.   FV 6.50
    b. 1.4.2006.   FV 6.50
    c. 3.3.2008.   FV 6.50
    d. 17.6.2009.   FV 6.50
    e. 16.7.2010.   FV 6.50

50 500 Shillings
               VF UNC

2006-. Black and green on multicolor underprint. President Jomo Kenyatta at left center. Back: National Assembly building at left center. Watermark: Value and Cornerstone stripes added Printer: DLR.

    a. 1.6.2005.   FV 16.00
    b. 1.4.2006.   FV 16.00
    c. 3.3.2008.   FV 16.00
    d. 17.6.2009.   FV 16.00
    e. 16.7.2010.   FV 16.00

51 1000 Shillings
               VF UNC

2005-. Brown, lilac and light olive on multicolor underprint. President Jomo Kenyatta at left center. Back: Elephants and other animals Watermark: Value and Cornerstone stripes added Printer: DLR. 150x80mm.

    a. 1.6.2005.   FV 32.50
    b. 1.4.2006.   FV 32.50
    c. 3.3.2008.   FV 30.00
    d. 17.6.2009.   FV 30.00
    e. 16.7.2010.   FV 25.00

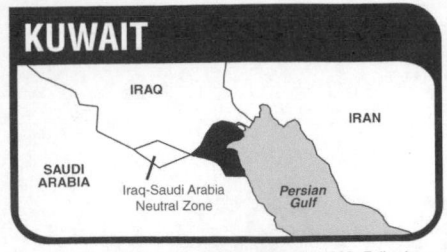

The State of Kuwait, a constitutional monarchy located on the Arabian Peninsula at the northwestern corner of the Persian Gulf, has an area of 6,880 sq. mi. (17,818 sq. km.) and a population of 1.97 million. Capital: Kuwait. Petroleum, the basis of the economy, provides 95 per cent of the exports. Britain oversaw foreign relations and defense for the ruling Kuwaiti Al-Sabah dynasty from 1899 until independence in 1961. Kuwait was attacked and overrun by Iraq on 2 August 1990. Following several weeks of aerial bombardment, a US-led, UN coalition began a ground assault on 23 February 1991 that liberated Kuwait in four days. Kuwait spent more than $5 billion to repair oil infrastructure damaged during 1990-91. The Al-Sabah family has ruled since returning to power in 1991 and reestablished an elected legislature that in recent years has become increasingly assertive.

RULERS:

British to 1961
Abdullah, 1961-1965
Sabah Ibn Salim Al Sabah, 1965-1977
Jabir Ibn Ahmad Al Sabah, 1977-2006
Sabah Al Ahmad Al Sabah, 2006-

MONETARY SYSTEM:

1 Dinar = 1000 Fils

SIGNATURE VARIETIES				
1	Amir Sheikh Jaber al-Ahmed			
	BANK GOVERNOR	FINANCE MINISTER	BANK GOVERNOR	FINANCE MINISTER
2	Hamza Abbas	A.R. al-Atiquel	3 — Hamza Abbas	A.L. al-Hamad
4	A. al-Tammar	A.K. al-Sabah	5 — A. al-Tammar	J.M. al-Kharafi
6	S.A. al-Sabah	N.A. al-Rodhan	7 — S.A. al-Sabah	A.S. al-Sabah
8	S.A. al-Sabah	N.A. al-Rodhan	9 — S.A. al-Sabah	A.S. al-Sabah
10	S.A. al-Sabah	A.A. al-Sabah	11 — S.A. al-Sabah	Y.H. al-Ibrahim
12	S.A. al-Sabah	M.A. Al Nouri	13 — S.A. al-Sabah	B.Y. Al Houmaithy
14	S.A. al-Sabah			

STATE

Kuwait Currency Board
Law of 1960, 1961 ND Issue

1   1/4 Dinar   **VF   UNC**
L.1960 (1961). Brown on multicolor underprint. Amir Shaikh Abdullah at right. Signature 1. Back: Aerial view, Port of Kuwait at center. Watermark: Amir Shaikh Abdullah.   25.00   75.00

2   1/2 Dinar   **VF   UNC**
L.1960 (1961). Purple on multicolor underprint. Amir Shaikh Abdullah at right. Signature 1. Back: School at center. Watermark: Amir Shaikh Abdullah.   35.00   125

3   1 Dinar   **VF   UNC**
L.1960 (1961). Red-brown on multicolor underprint. Amir Shaikh Abdullah at right. Signature 1. Back: Cement plant at center. Watermark: Amir Shaikh Abdullah.   50.00   175

4   5 Dinars   **VF   UNC**
L.1960 (1961). Blue on multicolor underprint. Amir Shaikh Abdullah at right. Signature 1. Back: Street scene. Watermark: Amir Shaikh Abdullah.   250   800

5   10 Dinars   **VF   UNC**
L.1960 (1961). Green on multicolor underprint. Amir Shaikh Abdullah at right. Signature 1. Back: Dhow. Watermark: Amir Shaikh Abdullah.   200   750

Central Bank of Kuwait
Law #32 of 1968, First ND Issue

6   1/4 Dinar

L.1968. Brown on multicolor underprint. Amir Shaikh Abdullah at right. Signature 2. Back: Aerial view, Port of Kuwait at center. Watermark: Amir Shaikh Abdullah.

		VF	UNC
a. Black signature		10.00	30.00
b. Brown signature		10.00	30.00
s. As a. Specimen.		—	250

7   1/2 Dinar

L.1968. Purple on multicolor underprint. Amir Shaikh Abdullah at right. Signature 2. Back: School at center. Watermark: Amir Shaikh Abdullah.

		VF	UNC
a. Black signature		10.00	40.00
b. Purple signature		10.00	40.00
s. As a. Specimen.		—	250

8   1 Dinar

L.1968. Red-brown and blue on multicolor underprint. Amir Shaikh Abdullah at right. Signature 2. Back: Oil refinery. Watermark: Amir Shaikh Abdullah.

		VF	UNC
a. Issued note.		9.00	45.00
s. Specimen.		—	350

9   5 Dinars

L.1968. Blue and aqua on multicolor underprint. Amir Shaikh Abdullah at right. Signature 2. Back: View of Kuwait. Watermark: Amir Shaikh Abdullah.

		VF	UNC
a. Issued note.		75.00	175
s. Specimen.		—	350

10   10 Dinars

L.1968. Green and brown on multicolor underprint. Amir Shaikh Abdullah at right. Signature 2. Back: Dhow. Watermark: Amir Shaikh Abdullah.

		VF	UNC
a. Issued note.		70.00	175
s. Specimen.		—	475

Law #32 of 1968, Second ND Issue

11   1/4 Dinar

L.1968 (1980-91). Brown and purple on multicolor underprint. Oil rig at left. Arms at right. Black serial number. Back: Oil refinery. Watermark: Dhow.

		VF	UNC
a. Overall ornate underprint. Signature 2.		4.00	12.00
b. Signature 3.		3.00	10.00
c. Signature 4.		3.00	8.00
d. Clear margins at top and bottom. Signature 6.		1.50	8.00
s. Specimen.		—	80.00

Contraband stolen by invading Iraqi forces included prefix denominators #54-68. Unc. value $4.00.

12   1/2 Dinar

L.1968 (1980). Purple on multicolor underprint. Kuwait Towers at left. Arms at right. Black serial number. Back: Harbor scene. Watermark: Dhow.

		VF	UNC
a. Overall ornate underprint. Signature 2.		4.00	14.00
b. Signature 3.		3.00	12.00
c. Signature 4.		3.00	10.00
d. Clear margins at top and bottom. Signature 6.		3.00	8.00
s. Specimen.		—	80.00

Contraband stolen by invading Iraqi forces included prefix denominators #30-37. Unc. value $4.00

13   1 Dinar

L.1968 (1980-91). Red-violet and purple on multicolor underprint. Telecommunications Center in Kuwait City at left. Arms at right. Black serial number. Back: Old fortress. Watermark: Dhow.

	VF	UNC
a. Overall ornate underprint. Signature 2.	7.00	25.00
b. Signature 3.	4.00	20.00
c. Signature 4.	3.50	14.00
d. Clear margins at top and bottom. Signature 6.	3.00	8.00
s. As a. Specimen.	—	100

Contraband stolen by invading Iraqi forces included prefix denominators #47-53. Unc. value $4.00

14   5 Dinars

L.1968 (1980-91). Deep blue and black on multicolor underprint. Minaret at left. Arms at right. Black serial number. Back: The Seif Palace (the Amir's Administration HQ). Watermark: Dhow.

	VF	UNC
a. Overall ornate underprint. Signature 2.	15.00	60.00
b. Signature 4.	10.00	40.00
c. Clear margins at top and bottom. Signature 6.	7.50	30.00
s. Specimen.	—	—

Contraband stolen by invading Iraqi forces included prefix denominators #18-20. Unc. value 12.50.

15   10 Dinars

L.1968 (1980-91). Green on multicolor underprint. Falcon at left. Arms at right. Black serial number. Back: Sailing boat. Watermark: Dhow.

	VF	UNC
a. Overall ornate underprint. Signature 2.	20.00	80.00
b. Signature 3.	12.50	50.00
c. Signature 4.	12.50	40.00
d. Clear margins at top and bottom. Signature 6.	12.50	40.00

Contraband stolen by invading Iraqi forces included prefix denominators #70-87. Unc. value $15.

16   20 Dinars

L.1968 (1986-91). Brown and olive-green on multicolor underprint. Façade of Kuwait Stock Exchange at left. Arms at right. Black serial number. Back: The Justice Center of Kuwait at left center. Watermark: Eagle's head.

	VF	UNC
a. Signature 5.	80.00	200
b. Signature 6.	12.00	50.00
s. Specimen.	—	—

Contraband stolen by invading Iraqi forces included prefix denominators #9-13. Unc. value $20.

Law #32 of 1968, 1992 ND Post Liberation Issue

Note: After the 1991 Gulf War, Kuwait declared all previous note issues worthless.

17   1/4 Dinar

L.1968 (1992). Violet and black on silver and multicolor underprint. Oil rig at left. Arms at right. Red serial number at top right. Signature 7. Back: Oil refinery. Watermark: Dhow.

	VF	UNC
	FV	4.00

18   1/2 Dinar

L.1968 (1992). Deep blue, blue-green and deep violet on silver and multicolor underprint. Kuwait Towers at left. Arms at right. Red serial number at top right. Signature 7. Back: Harbor scene. Watermark: Dhow.

	VF	UNC
	FV	7.00

19   1 Dinar

L.1968 (1992). Deep olive-green, green and deep blue on silver and multicolor underprint. Telecommunications Center in Kuwait City at left. Arms at right. Red serial number at top right. Signature 7. Back: Old fortress. Watermark: Dhow.

	VF	UNC
	FV	10.00

20   5 Dinars

L.1968 (1992). Olive-brown, green and pink on multicolor underprint. Minaret at left. Arms at right. Red serial number at top right. Signature 7. Back: The Seif Palace (the Amir's Administration HQ). Watermark: Dhow.

	VF	UNC
	FV	55.00

21   10 Dinars

L.1968 (1992). Orange-red, olive-brown on multicolor underprint. Falcon at left. Arms at right. Red serial number at top right. Back: Sailing boat. Watermark: Dhow.

		VF	UNC
a. Signature 7.		FV	100
b. Signature 8.		60.00	130

22   20 Dinars

L.1968 (1992). Violet-brown on multicolor underprint. Façade of Kuwait Stock Exchange at left. Arms at right. Red serial number at top right. Back: The Justice Center of Kuwait at left center. Watermark: Eagle's head.

		VF	UNC
a. Signature 7.		FV	140
b. Signature 8.		70.00	200

Law #32 of 1968, 1994 ND Issue

#23-27 Signature 8, were withdrawn in early 1995 because of the word *Allah* being present.

23   1/4 Dinar

L.1968 (1994). Brown, grayish purple and deep orange on multicolor underprint. Ship at bottom center right, arms at left, segmented silver vertical thread at center right. Outline of falcon's head at lower right near value. Back: Girls playing game. Watermark: Falcon's head. 110x67mm.

		VF	UNC
a. Signature 8.		FV	5.50
b. Signature 10.		FV	5.50
c. Signature 11.		FV	5.00
d. Signature 12.		FV	4.50
e. Signature 13.		FV	4.50
f. Signature 14.		FV	4.50
s. Specimen. Red overprint in Arabic.		—	100

24   1/2 Dinar

L.1968 (1994). Brown and dark grayish green on multicolor underprint. Souk shops at lower right. Arms at left , segmented silver vertical thread at center right. Outline of falcon's head at upper left near value. Back: Boys playing game. Watermark: Falcon's head. 120x67mm.

		VF	UNC
a. Signature 8.		FV	10.00
b. Signature 10.		FV	10.00
c. Signature 11.		FV	9.00
d. Signature 12.		FV	8.00
e. Signature 13.		FV	8.00
f. Signature 14.		FV	8.00
s. Specimen. Red overprint in Arabic.		—	150

25   1 Dinar

L.1968 (1994). Deep brown, purple and dark gray on blue and multicolor underprint. Kuwait Tower at center right. Arms at left, segmented silver vertical thread at center right. Outline of falcon's head at upper left near value. Back: Aerial view of harbor docks. Watermark: Falcon's head. 130x67mm.

		VF	UNC
a. Signature 8.		FV	15.00
b. Signature 10.		FV	15.00
c. Signature 11.		FV	13.00
d. Signature 12.		FV	12.00
e. Signature 13.		FV	12.00
f. Signature 14.		FV	12.00
s. Specimen. Red overprint in Arabic.		—	250

26   5 Dinars

L.1968 (1994). Dark red and grayish green on multicolor underprint. Liberation Tower at right. Arms at left, segmented silver vertical thread at center right. Silver foiling of falcon's head at left center. Signature 8, 9, 11, 12, 13. Back: Oil refinery at center. Watermark: Falcon's head. 140x67mm.

		VF	UNC
a. Signature 8.		FV	55.00
b. Signature 9.		FV	55.00
c. Signature 11.		FV	50.00
d. Signature 12.		FV	45.00
e. Signature 13.		FV	45.00
f. Signature 14.		FV	45.00
s. Specimen. Red overprint in Arabic.		—	250

27   10 Dinars

L.1968 (1994). Purple, dark blue and dark brown on multicolor underprint. Mosque at lower right. Arms at left, segmented silver vertical thread at center right. Silver foiling of falcon's head at left center. Signature 8, 10, 11, 13, 14. Back: Pearl fisherman at left center, dhow at right. Watermark: Falcon's head. 150x67mm.

		VF	UNC
a. Issued note.		FV	90.00
s. Specimen. Red overprint in Arabic.		—	500

28   20 Dinars

VF   UNC

L.1968 (1994). Dark olive-green, orange and olive-brown on multicolor underprint. Fortress at lower right. Arms at left. segmented silver vertical thread at center right. Silver foiling of falcon's head at left center. Signature 8, 9, 10, 11, 12, 13. Back: Central Bank at bottom left center, old city gate. Watermark: Falcon's head. 160x67mm.

    a. Issued note.   FV   130
    s. Specimen. Red overprint in Arabic.   —   750

29   1/4 Dinar

VF   UNC

ND (2014). Brown and tan on multicolor underprint. Liberation tower in Kuwait City. Back: Traditional Kuwaiti door, plaster carving, first Kuwaiti coin. Watermark: Falcon and value. 110x68mm.

    a. Signature 15.   FV   2.50
    s. Specimen. Overprint in Arabic.   —   100

30   1/2 Dinar

VF   UNC

ND (2014). Green on multicolor underprint. Kuwait Towers. Back: Hawksbill sea turtle and silver pomfret fish. Watermark: Falcon and value. 120x68mm.

    a. Signature 15.   FV   4.00
    s. Specimen. Overprint in Arabic.   —   150

31   1 Dinar

VF   UNC

ND (2014). Gray on multicolor underprint. Grand Mosque at center left, boat. Back: Ionic column from the island of Failaka. Watermark: Falcon and value. 130x68mm.

    a. Signature 15.   FV   7.00
    s. Specimen. Overprint in Arabic.   —   7.00

32   5 Dinars

VF   UNC

ND (2014). Purple on multicolor underprint. Central Bank building at left center. boat. Back: Oil refineries and tanker. Watermark: Falcon and value. 140x68mm.

    a. Signature 15.   FV   35.00
    s. Specimen. Overprint in Arabic.   FV   250

33   10 Dinars

VF   UNC

ND (2014). Reddish-orange on multicolor underprint. Kuwait National Assembly building at left center, ship Back: Falcon, seated camel with sadu saddle. Watermark: Falcon and value. 150x68mm.

    a. Signature 15.   FV   70.00
    s. Specimen. Overprint in Arabic.   —   500

34   20 Dinars

VF   UNC

ND (2014). Blue on multicolor underprint. Seif Palace at left center, ship. Back: The Boom, a large traditional dhow; pearl diver. Watermark: Falcon and value. 160x68mm.

    a. Signature 15.   FV   140
    s. Specimen. Overprint in Arabic.   FV   750

COLLECTOR SERIES

Central Bank of Kuwait

1993 Issue

#CS1 Issued in a special folder for "Second Anniversary of Liberation of Kuwait."

CS1 1 Dinar   **Mkt. Value**
  Polymer plastic with silver foil window. 26.2.1993. Orange-red, violet-blue and   20.00
  blue. Back: Text: *THIS IS NOT LEGAL TENDER.*

Note: Replacement notes for #CS1 have serial # CK000091 and a market value of $175.

2001 Issue

#CS2 Issued in a special folder for "10th Anniversary of the Liberation of the State of Kuwait."

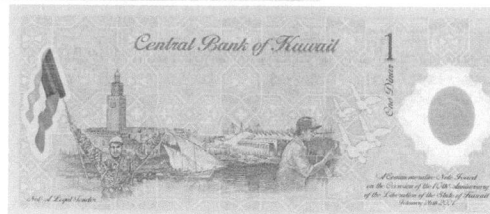

CS2 1 Dinar   **Mkt. Value**
  Polymer plastic with silver foil window. 26.2.2001. Light blue and lilac. Arms at   17.50
  right. Back: Military man holding flag, town view. Text: *NOT A LEGAL TENDER...*
  at lower left.

The Republic of Kyrgyzstan, an independent state since Aug. 31, 1991, is a member of the UN and of the C.I.S. It was the last state of the Union Republics to declare its sovereignty. Capital: Bishkek (formerly Frunze). Population of 4.54 million. A Central Asian country of incredible natural beauty and proud nomadic traditions, most of Kyrgyzstan was formally annexed to Russia in 1876. The Kyrgyz staged a major revolt against the Tsarist Empire in 1916 in which almost one-sixth of the Kyrgyz population was killed. Kyrgyzstan became a Soviet republic in 1936 and achieved independence in 1991 when the USSR dissolved. Nationwide demonstrations in the spring of 2005 resulted in the ouster of President Askar Akaev, who had run the country since 1990. Subsequent presidential elections in July 2005 were won overwhelmingly by former prime minister Kurmanbek BAKIEV. The political opposition organized demonstrations in Bishkek in April, May, and November 2006 resulting in the adoption of a new constitution that transferred some of the president's powers to parliament and the government. In December 2006, the Kyrgyzstani parliament voted to adopt new amendments, restoring some of the presidential powers lost in the November 2006 constitutional change. By late-September 2007, both previous versions of the constitution were declared illegal, and the country reverted to the Akaev-era 2003 constitution, which was subsequently modified in a flawed referendum initiated by Bakiev. The president then dissolved parliament, called for early elections, and gained control of the new parliament through his newly-created political party, Ak Jol, in December 2007 elections. Current concerns include: privatization of state-owned enterprises, negative trends in democracy and political freedoms, reduction of corruption, improving interethnic relations, electricity generation, rising food prices, and combating terrorism.

MONETARY SYSTEM:
  1 СОЬ = 100 Туиун

REPUBLIC

КЫIРгЫЗ РНСПУБЛИКАСЫ

Kyrgyz Republic

1993 ND Issue

1   1 Tyiyn   **VF   UNC**
  ND (1993). Dark brown on pink and brown-orange underprint. Bald eagle at
  center. Back: Ornate design at center.
      a. Watermark: Stylized eagle.   0.30   1.00
      b. Watermark: pattern   0.30   1.00

2   10 Tyiyn   **VF   UNC**
  ND (1993). Brown on pale green and brown-orange underprint. Bald eagle at
  center. Back: Ornate design at center.
      a. Watermark: stylized eage.   0.40   1.00
      b. Watermark: pattern.   0.40   1.00

3   50 Tyiyn   **VF   UNC**
  ND (1993). Gray on blue and brown-orange underprint. Bald eagle at center.
  Back: Ornate design at center.
      a. Watermark: stylized eagle.   0.50   3.00
      b. Watermark: pattern.   0.50   3.00

КЫРГЫЗСТАН БАНКЫ

KYRGYZSTAN BANK

1993; 1994 ND Issue

4   **1 Som**   **VF**   **UNC**
ND (1993). Red on multicolor underprint. Equestrian statue of Manas the Noble   1.00   3.00
at center right. Back: Manas Mausoleum at left center. Watermark: Eagle in
repeating pattern.

5   **5 Som**   **VF**   **UNC**
ND (1993). Deep grayish green on multicolor underprint. Equestrian statue of Ma-   2.00   5.00
nas the Noble at center right. Back: Manas Mausoleum at left center. Watermark:
Eagle in repeating pattern. 140x70mm.

6   **20 Som**   **VF**   **UNC**
ND (1993). Purple on multicolor underprint. Equestrian statue of Manas the Noble   3.00   20.00
at center right. Back: Manas Mausoleum at left center. Watermark: Eagle in
repeating pattern. 140x70mm.

КЫРГЫЗ БАНКЫ

KYRGYZ BANK

1994 ND Issue

Replacement notes: Serial # prefix ZZ.

7   **1 Som**   **VF**   **UNC**
ND (1994). Brown on yellow and multicolor underprint. A. Maldybayev at right.
Back: String musical instruments, Bishkek's Philharmonic Society and Manas
Architectural Ensemble at left. Watermark: A. Maldybayev.
    a. Issued note.   1.00   2.00
    r. Replacement note. Serial # prefix ZZ.   1.00   4.00

8   **5 Som**   **VF**   **UNC**
ND (1994). Dark blue on yellow and multicolor underprint. B. Beishenaliyeva at
right. Back: National Opera Theatre at left center. Watermark: B. Beishenaliyeva.
135x65mm.
    a. Issued note.   2.00   6.00
    r. Replacement note. Serial # prefix ZZ.   2.00   12.00

9   **10 Som**   **VF**   **UNC**
ND (1994). Green and brown on multicolor underprint. Kassim at right. Back:
Mountains. Watermark: Kassim. 135x65mm.
    a. Issued note.   2.00   10.00
    r. Replacement note. Serial # prefix ZZ.   2.00   17.50

10   **20 Som**   **VF**   **UNC**
ND (1994). Red-orange on multicolor underprint. T. Moldo at right. Back: Manas
Mausoleum. Watermark: T. Moldo. 135x65mm.
    a1. Issued note.   2.00   6.00
    r. Replacement note. Serial # prefix ZZ.   2.00   12.50

11   **50 Som**   **VF**   **UNC**
ND (1994). Reddish brown on multicolor underprint. Czarina Kurmanjan Datka at
right. Back: Uzgen Architectural Ensemble, mausoleum and minaret. Watermark:
Czarina Kurmanjan Datka. 135x65mm.
    a. Issued note.   5.00   15.00
    r. Replacement note. Serial # prefix ZZ.   5.00   25.00

12   100 Som   VF   UNC

ND (1994). Dark brown on multicolor underprint. Toktogul at right. Back: Hydroelectric dam at left center. Watermark: Toktogul.

    a. Issued note.   5.00   25.00
    r. Replacement note. Serial # prefix ZZ.   5.00   40.00

1997 Issue

Replacement notes: Serial # prefix *BZ.*

13   5 Som   VF   UNC

1997. Dark blue and violet on multicolor underprint. B. Beishenaliyeva at right.
Back: National Opera Theatre at left center. Watermark: B. Beishenaliyeva.
135x65mm.

    a. Issued note.   FV   3.00
    r. Replacement note. Serial # prefix BZ.   FV   6.00

14   10 Som   VF   UNC

1997. Dark green, purple and red on multicolor underprint. Kassim at right. Back:
Mountains Watermark: Kassim. 135x65mm.

    a. Issued note.   FV   5.00
    r. Replacement note. Serial # prefix BZ.   FV   10.00

2000 ND Issue

15   1 Som   VF   UNC

1999. Brown and tan on multicolor underprint. Abdilas Maldibayeff at left. Back:
Musical instruments.

    a. Issued note.   FV   2.00
    r. Replacement note. Serial # prefix BZ.   FV   5.00

16   200 Som   VF   UNC

2000. Brown and tan on multicolor underprint. Alikul Osmonov at right. Back:
Poetry verse and lake scene.   3.00   10.00

17   500 Som   VF   UNC

2000. Rose, brown and olive on multicolor underprint. Sayakbal Karalalev at right.
Back: Karalaiev seated, in background horseman chasing an eagle. 160x76mm. 5.00   20.00

18   1000 Som   VF   UNC

2000. Olive, slate, brown and multicolor. Jusul Balasagbin at right. Back: Gate,   6.00   30.00
tree and mountains. 165x78mm.

2002 ND Issue

19   20 Som   VF   UNC

2002. Dark brown and orange on multicolor underprint. Togolok Moldo at right.   1.00   5.00
Back: Manas Mausoleum. Watermark: Togolok Moldo. 135x78mm.

20 50 Som | **VF** | **UNC**

2002. Brown and blue on multicolor underprint. Czarina Krumanjan-Datka at right. Back: Uzgen Architectural ensemble: mausoleum and minaret. Watermark: Czarina Krumanjan-Datka. 145x70mm. | 2.00 | 10.00

21 100 Som | **VF** | **UNC**

2002. Green, pink and blue on multicolor underprint. Toktogul at right. Back: Khan Tenyiri Mountains at left center. Watermark: Toktogu. 150x72mm. | 1.00 | 12.50

22 200 Som | **VF** | **UNC**

2004. Brown and tan on multicolor underprint. Alikul Osmonov at right. Back: Poetry verse and lake scene. Watermark: Alikul Osmonov. 155x74mm. | 4.00 | 8.00

23 500 Som | **VF** | **UNC**

2005. Purple 160x76mm.
  a. Issued note. | FV | 20.00
  s. Specimen. Overprint: *MINTA*. | — | —

2009 ND Issue

24 20 Som | **VF** | **UNC**

2009. Red and multicolor. Togolok Moldo at left. Back: Tash-Rabat at center. Watermark: Togolok Moldo. Printer: FC-O.
  a. Issued note. | FV | 2.50
  r. Replacement note. Serial # prefix ZZ. | FV | 5.00
  s. Specimen. | — | 50.00

25 50 Som | **VF** | **UNC**

2009. Orange and multicolor. Czarina Kurmanjan Datka at left. Back: 11th century complex, Uzgen. Watermark: Kurmanjan Datka. Printer: FC-O. 126x61mm.
  a. Issued note. | FV | 4.00
  s. Specimen. | — | 50.00

26 100 Som | **VF** | **UNC**

2009. Blue and multicolor. Toktogul Satylganov at left. Back: Toktogul hydroelectric power station. Watermark: Toktogul Satylganov. Printer: FC-O. 132x63mm.
  a. Issued note. | FV | 7.50
  s. Specimen. | FV | 50.00

27 200 Som | **VF** | **UNC**

2010. Yellow and tan on multicolor underprint. Alykul Osmonov at left, sun waves. Back: Lines from Osmonov's "Jenishbek", lake, mountains. Printer: DLR. 138x66mm.
  a. Issued note. | FV | 12.50
  s. Specimen. | FV | 50.00

28 500 Som | **VF** | **UNC**

2010. Printer: DLR. 144x68mm.
  a. Issued note. | FV | 22.50
  s. Specimen. | — | 100

29 1000 Som | **VF** | **UNC**

2010. Printer: DLR. 150x71mm.
  a. Issued note. | FV | 45.00
  s. Specimen. | — | 100

30 5000 Som | **VF** | **UNC**

2010. Green and multicolor. Suimenkul Chokmorov at left. Back: Ala-too cinima in Bishkek. Watermark: Sayakbai Karalaev. Printer: FC-O. 156x73mm.
  a. Issued note. | FV | 220
  s. Specimen. | — | 225

2009-2010 Commemorative Issue

31 100 Som | **VF** | **UNC**

2009/2014. 3000 pieces issued in a fold. Blue on multicolor underprint. Toktogul Satylganov at left. Profile and commemorative text at right in watermark area. Signatrue: M.O. Alapaev. Back: Toktogul hydroelectric power station, mountains. 132x63mm. | — | 70.00

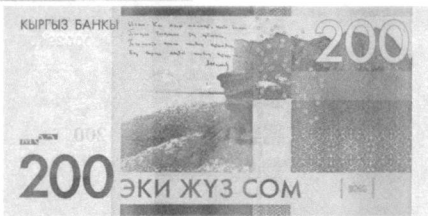

32 200 Som | **VF** | **UNC**

2010 (ND 2014). 3000 notes printed, sold in a folder. Yellow and tan on multicolor underprint. Alykul Osmonov at left, sun and waves, gold quill and commemorative legend in watermark area at right. Back: Lines from Osmonov's "Jenishbek" lake, mountains. 138x66mm. | — | 70.00

LAO

The Lao People's Democratic Republic is located on the Indo-Chinese Peninsula between the Socialist Republic of Viet Nam and the Kingdom of Thailand, has an area of 91,429 sq. mi. (236,800 sq. km.) and a population of 5.69 million. Captial: Vientiane. Agriculture employs 95 percent of the people. Tin, lumber and coffee are exported.

Modern-day Lao has its roots in the ancient Lao Kingdom of Lan Xang, established in the 14th Century under King Fa Ngum. For 300 years Lan Xang had influence reaching into present-day Cambodia and Thailand, as well as over all of what is now Lao. After centuries of gradual decline, Lao came under the domination of Siam (Thailand) and Viet Nam from the late 18th century until the late 19th century when it became part of French Indochina.

The Kingdome of Laos became fully independent of the French in 1955, and war soon ensued with the communist Pathet Lao. In 1975, the communist Pathet Lao took control of the government ending a six-century-old monarchy and instituting a strict socialist regime closely aligned to Viet Nam. A gradual return to private enterprise and the liberalization of foreign investment laws began in 1986. Lao became a member of ASEAN in 1997.

RULERS:
Sisavang Vong, 1949-1959
Savang Vatthana, 1959-1975

MONETARY SYSTEM:
1 Piastre = 100 Cents to 1955
1 Kip = 100 At, 1955-1975
1 (new) Kip = 100 Att, 1975-

SIGNATURE VARIETIES		
	ຜູ້ອຳນວຍການ LE GOUVERNEUR	ຜູ້ກວດກາຜູ້ນຶ່ງ UN CENSEUR
1		
2		
3		
4		
5		
6		

KINGDOM OF LAOS

Banque Nationale du Laos
1962-63 ND Issue

8   1 Kip

ND (1962). Brown on pink and bue underprint. Stylized figure at left. Back: Tricephalic elephant arms at center.

		VF	UNC
a. Signature 3; 4.		0.20	0.50
s. Specimen. Signature 3.		—	40.00
ct. Color trial. Blue. Signature 3.		—	—

la

9   5 Kip

ND (1962). Green on multicolor underprint. S. Vong at right. Back: Temple at left, man on elephant at center Watermark: Tricephalic elephant arms.

		VF	UNC
a. Signature 2.		17.50	50.00
b. Signature 5.		0.50	1.25
s. As a. Specimen.		—	50.00
ct. Color trial. Brown or Brown and blue.		—	—

10   10 Kip

ND (1962). Blue on yellow and green underprint. Woman at left. (like back of French Indochina #102). Back: Stylized sunburst on back (like face of #102). Watermark: Elephant's head.

		VF	UNC
a. Signature 1.		100	200
b. Signature 5.		0.50	1.75
s1. As a. Specimen. Overprint: *SPECIMEN*.		—	100
s2. As b. Specimen. TDLR oval overprint.		—	100

11   20 Kip

ND (1963). Brown on tan and blue underprint. King Savang Vatthana at left. Temple or pagoda at center. Back: Pagoda at center. Watermark: Tricephalic elephant arms.

		VF	UNC
a. Signature 5.		0.40	2.00
b. Signature 6.		0.30	1.50
r. Replacement notes: Serial # prefix *S9* (=Z9 in English).		—	—
s1. As a. Specimen. Overprint: *SANS VALEUR*.		—	40.00
s2. As a. Specimen. Overprint: TDLR oval.		—	40.00

12   50 Kip   **VF   UNC**

ND (1963). Purple on brown and blue underprint. King Savang Vatthana at left.
Pagoda at center. Back: Building at right. Watermark: Tricephalic elephant arms.

- a. Signature 5; 6.   0.25   2.00
- r. Replacement notes: Serial # prefix S9 (=Z9 in English).   —   —
- s1. Signature 5. Specimen. Overprint: SANS VALEUR.   —   40.00
- s2. Signature 5. Specimen. Overprint: TDLR oval.   —   40.00

13   200 Kip   **VF   UNC**

ND (1963). Blue on green and gold underprint. King Savang Vatthana at left. Temple
of That Luang at center. Back: Waterfalls. Watermark: Tricephalic elephant arms.

- a. Signature 4.   1.00   6.00
- b. Signature 6.   0.50   3.00
- r. Replacement notes: Serial # prefix S9 (=Z9 in English).   —   —
- s1. As a. Specimen. Overprint: SANS VALEUR.   —   50.00
- s2. As a. Specimen. Overprint: TDLR oval.   —   60.00

14   1000 Kip   **VF   UNC**

ND (1963). Brown on blue and gold underprint. King Savang Vatthana at left.
Temple at center. Back: Three long canoes. Watermark: Tricephalic elephant arms.

- a. Signature 5.   1.00   6.00
- b. Signature 6.   0.75   4.00
- r. Replacement notes: Serial # prefix S9 (=Z9 in English).   —   —
- s1. As a. Specimen. Overprint: SANS VALEUR.   —   60.00
- s2. As a. Specimen. Overprint: TDLR oval.   —   60.00

1974; 1975 ND Issue

15   10 Kip   **VF   UNC**

ND (1974). Blue on multicolor underprint. King Savang Vatthana at center right.
Signature 6. Back: Ox cart.

- a. Normal serial #. (Not issued).   —   10.00
- s. Specimen. Overprint: SANS VALEUR.   —   600
- ct. Color trial. Red.   —   —

16   100 Kip   **VF   UNC**

ND (1974). Brown on blue, green and pink underprint. King Savang Vatthana at left.
Pagoda at center. Signature 6. Back: Ox cart. Watermark: Tricephalic elephant arms.

- a. Issued note.   0.50   3.00
- r. Replacement note. Serial # prefix (9).   —   —
- s. Specimen. Overprint: SANS VALEUR.   —   50.00

17   500 Kip   **VF   UNC**

ND (1974). Red on multicolor underprint. King Savang Vatthana at left. Pagoda at
center. Signature 6. Back: Hydroelectric dam. Watermark: Tricephalic elephant arms.

- a. Issued note.   0.75   4.00
- r. Replacement note. Serial # prefix (9).   —   —
- s. Specimen. Overprint: SANS VALEUR.   —   75.00

18   1000 Kip   **VF   UNC**

ND. Black on multicolor underprint. King Savang Vatthana at left. Back: Elephant.
Watermark: Tricephalic elephant arms.

- a. Normal serial #. (Not issued.)   —   15.00
- s. Specimen. Overprint: SANS VALEUR.   —   900

19   5000 Kip   **VF   UNC**

ND (1975). Blue-gray on multicolor underprint. King Savang Vatthana at left.
Pagoda at center. Back: Musicians with instruments. Watermark: Tricephalic
elephant arms.

- a. Issued note.   2.25   9.00
- s. Specimen. Overprint: SANS VALEUR.   —   75.00

STATE OF LAO

Pathet Lao Government

ND Issue

#19A-24 printed in Peoples Republic of China and circulated in areas under control of the Pathet Lao insurgents. These same notes became the accepted legal tender for the entire country in 1975.

19A   1 Kip   VF   UNC

ND. Green and blue on yellow and pink underprint. Threshing grain at center. Back: Medical clinic scene.

a. Issued note.	—	10.00
s. Specimen.	—	150

20   10 Kip   VF   UNC

ND. Red on light blue and gold underprint. Medical examination scene. Back: Fighters in the brush.

a. Watermark: Temples.	0.15	2.00
b. Watermark: 5-pointed stars.	0.15	1.00
s. As b. Specimen. Overprint in Lao.	—	50.00

21   20 Kip   VF   UNC

ND. Brown on light pink and olive-brown underprint. Rice distribution. Back: Forge workers.

a. Watermark: Temples.	0.20	3.00
b. Watermark: 5-pointed stars.	0.20	2.00
s. As b. Specimen. Overprint in Lao.	—	50.00

22   50 Kip   VF   UNC

ND. Purple on multicolor underprint. Factory workers. Back: Plowing ox.

a. Watermark: Temples.	0.25	3.00
b. Watermark: 5-pointed stars.	0.25	2.00
s. As b. Specimen. Overprint in Lao.	—	50.00

23   100 Kip   VF   UNC

ND. Blue on multicolor underprint. Long boats on lake. Back: Scene in textile store. Watermark: Temples.

a. Issued note.	3.00	6.00
s. Specimen. Overprint in Lao.	—	50.00

23A   200 Kip   VF   UNC

ND. Green on multicolor underprint. Road and trail convoys. Back: Factory scene. Watermark: Temples

a. Issued note.	4.00	12.00
s. Specimen. Overprint in Lao.	—	50.00
x. Lithograph counterfeit (1974) on plain paper, without serial #. Ho Chi Minh at right on back.	500	800

24   500 Kip   VF   UNC

ND. Brown on multicolor underprint. Armsed field workers in farm scene. Back: Soldiers shooting down planes. Watermark: Temples.

a. Issued note.	5.00	15.00
s. Specimen. Overprint in Lao.	—	50.00

LAO PEOPLES DEMOCRATIC REPUBLIC

Government

1979 Provisional Issue

24A   50 Kip on 500 Kip   **VF   UNC**

ND. New legends and denomination overprint on #24. (Not issued).   400   800

Bank of the Lao PDR

1979 ND; 1988 Issue

25   1 Kip   **VF   UNC**

ND (1979). Blue-gray on multicolor underprint. Militia unit at left, arms at upper right. Back: Schoolroom scene at left. Watermark: Stars, hammer and sickles.

a. Issued note.	0.35	1.00
s. Specimen. Overprint in Lao.	—	15.00

26   5 Kip   **VF   UNC**

ND (1979). Green on multicolor underprint. Shoppers at a store, arms at upper right. Back: Logging elephants at left. Watermark: Stars, hammer and sickles.

a. Issued note.	0.35	1.00
r. Replacement note. Block letters CA.	4.00	7.50
s. Specimen. Red overprint in Lao on face and English on back.	—	25.00

27   10 Kip   **VF   UNC**

ND (1979). Dark brown on multicolor underprint. Lumber mill at left, arms at upper right. Back: Medical scenes at left. Watermark: Stars, hammer and sickles.

a. Issued note.	0.15	1.00
r. Replacement note. Block letters DA.	4.00	7.50
s. Specimen. Overprint in Lao.	—	20.00

28   20 Kip   **VF   UNC**

ND (1979). Brown and red-brown on underprint. Arms at left, tank with troop column at center. Back: Textile mill at center. Watermark: Stars, hammer and sickles.

a. Issued note.	0.20	1.00
r. Replacement note. Block letters EA.	4.00	7.50
s. Specimen. Red overprint in Lao on face and in English on back.	—	25.00

29   50 Kip   **VF   UNC**

ND (1979). Violet on multicolor underprint. Rice planting at left center, arms at upper right. Back: Hydroelectric dam at center. Watermark: Stars, hammer and sickles.

a. Issued note.	0.20	1.00
r. Replacement note. Block letters AQ, DF, YC and YA.	4.00	7.50
s. Specimen. Red overprint in Lao on face and in English on back.	—	25.00

30   100 Kip   **VF   UNC**

ND (1979). Deep blue-green and deep blue on multicolor underprint. Grain harvesting at left, arms at upper right. Back: Bridge, storage tanks, and soldier. Watermark: Stars, hammer and sickles.

a. Issued note.	0.75	2.00
r. Replacement note. Block letters: TT, XA, YM, ZB.	4.00	7.50
s. Specimen. Red overprint in Lao on face and English on back.	—	30.00

31   500 Kip   **VF   UNC**

1988. Dark brown, purple and deep blue on multicolor underprint. Modern irrigation systems at center, arms above. Back: Harvesting fruit at center. Watermark: Stars, hammer and sickles.

a. Issued note.	1.50	3.00
r. Replacement note. Block letters: DD, WW, XC.	4.00	7.50
s. Specimen. Red overprint in Lao on face, English on back.	—	35.00

1998-2003 Issue

32   1000 Kip   **VF   UNC**

1992-96. Dark green, deep purple and green on multicolor underprint. Three women at left, temple at center right, arms at upper right. Underprint in sweeping arc. Back: Cattle at center. Watermark: Star. 152x68mm.

a. 1992. Without security thread. Red serial #.	1.00	6.00
b. 1994. With security thread.	1.00	3.50
c. 1995. With security thread.	1.00	3.50
d. 1996. With security thread.	1.00	3.50
r. Replacement note. Block letters: VA, VB and ZK.	4.00	7.50
s. As a (overprint in Lao); a, b (overprint in English). Specimen.	—	27.50

32A 1000 Kip

1998; 2003. Dark green, deep purple and green on multicolor underprint. Three women at left, temple at center right, arms at upper right. Underprint design as three lobes. Back: Cattle at center. Watermark: Star. 152x68mm.

	VF	UNC
a. 1998.	1.00	3.50
b. 2003.	1.00	3.50
r1. Replacement note. 1998. Block DD.	4.00	7.50
r2. Replacement note. 2003. Block EE, II and KK.	4.00	7.50
s. Specimen. As a. Overprint: SPECIMEN.	—	15.00

32B 1000 Kip

2008. Dark green. Three women.

	VF	UNC
a. Issued note. Recalled.	2.00	4.00
r. Replacement note. Recalled.	4.00	7.50

33 2000 Kip

1997; 2003. Blue-black and purple on multicolor underprint. Kaysone Phomvihane at left, arms at upper right. Temple in underprint at center right. Back: Hydroelectric complex at center. 152x68mm.

	VF	UNC
a. 1997.	1.00	3.50
b. 2003.	1.00	3.50
r1. Replacement note. As a. Block AA, QI.	4.00	7.50
r2. Replacement note. As b. Block EE, PP and QI.	4.00	7.50
s. Specimen. As a. Red overprint: SPECIMEN on both sides.	—	25.00

34 5000 Kip

1997; 2003. Dark brown and purple on multicolor underprint. Kaysone Phomvihane at left, arms at upper right. Temple in underprint at center right. Back: Cement factory at center. Watermark: Temple. 152x68mm.

	VF	UNC
a. 1997.	FV	4.50
b. 2003.	FV	4.50
r1. Replacement note. As a. Block LH.	4.00	7.50
r2. Replacement note. As b. Block DD, NN.	4.00	7.50
s. As a. Specimen. Red overprint: SPECIMEN on both sides.	—	30.00

35 10,000 Kip

2002; 2003; 2008. Slate blue and brown on multicolor underprint. Kaysone Phomuihane at left, temple at center. Bridge over Mekong river at center. Brown and green serial number. Back: Road at contor. 152x68mm.

	VF	UNC
a. 2002.	FV	5.00
b. 2003.	FV	5.00
c. 2008.	FV	5.00
r1. Replacement note. As a. Block AD.	4.00	7.50
r2. Replacement note. As b. Block CC.	4.00	7.50
r3. Replacement note. As c. Block FF, HH.	4.00	7.50
s. As a. Specimen. Overprint: SPECIMEN.	—	20.00

36 20,000 Kip

2002; 2003; 2008. Red-brown on multicolor underprint. Brown and green serial number. Back: Theun-Hinboune Hydroelectric complex at center. 152x68mm.

	VF	UNC
a. 2002.	4.00	10.00
b. 2003.	4.00	10.00
c. 2008.	4.00	10.00
r1. Replacement note. Block BY.	6.00	12.50
r2. Replacement note. Block DD, EE.	6.00	12.50
r3. Replacement note. Block GE.	6.00	12.50
s. Specimen. As a.	—	20.00

#37 has been determined to be an error listing.

38 50,000 Kip

2004. Purple on red, blue and multicolor underprint. Kaysone Phomvihane at left. Back: Building at left center. 156x70mm.

	VF	UNC
	FV	20.00

2008 Issue

39   1000 Kip
2008. Blue on green underprint. Three women at left center. Back: Grazing cattle and power lines in distance. Watermark: Coat of arms 144x66mm.

		VF	**UNC**
a. Issued note.		FV	1.50
s. Specimen.		—	—

2010 Issue

40   100,000 Kip
2010. Dark blue, yellow and orange on multicolor underprint. Chao Zaysettha at center. Back: Building 159x68mm.

	VF	**UNC**
	FV	45.00

2011 Issue

41   2000 Kip
2011. Slate blue on multicolor underprint. Kaysonne Phomvihane at left center, Xieng Thong temple at center. Back: Seset 2 Hydropower plant at right center. Printer: BOL. 141x65mm.

	VF	**UNC**
	FV	2.00

42   100,000 Kip
2011. Dark green on multicolor underprint. Kaysonne Phomvihane at left center, Wat That Luang stupa (temple) in Vietiane at center. Back: Kaysone Phomvihane Museum and statue at right center. Watermark: Kaysone Phomvihane. Printer: Goznak. 152x68mm.

	VF	**UNC**
	FV	25.00

LATVIA

The Republic of Latvia, the central Baltic state in east Europe, has an area of 24,595 sq. mi. (43,601 sq. km.) and a population of 2.4 million. Capital: Riga. Livestock raising and manufacturing are the chief industries. Butter, bacon, fertilizers and telephone equipment are exported. The name "Latvia" originates from the ancient Latgalians, one of four eastern Baltic tribes that formed the ethnic core of the Latvian people (ca. 8th-12th centuries A.D.). The region subsequently came under the control of Germans, Poles, Swedes, and finally, Russians. A Latvian republic emerged following World War I, but it was annexed by the USSR in 1940 - an action never recognized by the US and many other countries. Latvia reestablished its independence in 1991 following the breakup of the Soviet Union. Although the last Russian troops left in 1994, the status of the Russian minority (some 30% of the population) remains of concern to Moscow. Latvia joined both NATO and the EU in the spring of 2004.

MONETARY SYSTEM:
- 1 Rublis = 100 Kapeikas, 1919-22
- 1 Lats = 100 Santimu, 1923-40; 1992
- 1 Lats = 200 Rublu, 1993
- 1 Rublis = 1 Russian Ruble, 1992

REPUBLIC

Government

1992 Issue

35   1 Rublis
1992. UV: fibers flouresce blue. Violet on yellow and ochre underprint. Watermark: Symmetrical design.

	VF	**UNC**
	0.50	1.00

36   2 Rubli
1992. Purple on brown-orange and yellow underprint. Watermark: Symmetrical design.

	VF	**UNC**
	0.50	2.00

37   5 Rubli
1992. Deep blue on light blue and light yellow-orange underprint. Watermark: Symmetrical design.

	VF	**UNC**
	2.00	5.00

38   10 Rublu
1992. Purple on red-orange and pale orange underprint. Watermark: Symmetrical design.

	VF	**UNC**
	1.00	4.00

39   20 Rublu
VF   UNC
1992. Violet on lilac and pink underprint. Watermark: Symmetrical design.
2.00   6.00

40   50 Rublu
VF   UNC
1992. Gray-green on light blue and pink underprint. Watermark: Symmetrical design
3.00   10.00

41   200 Rublu
VF   UNC
1992. Greenish black on yellow and blue-green underprint.
8.00   18.00

42   500 Rublu
VF   UNC
1992. Violet-brown on gray and dull orange underprint.
10.00   30.00

Latvijas Bankas Naudas Zime
1992 Dated 1993-1998 Issue

43   5 Lati
VF   UNC
1992 (1993). Varied shades of green on tan and pale green underprint. Oak tree at center right. Thin foil strip. Back: Local art at center. 130x65mm.
FV   20.00

44   10 Latu
VF   UNC
1992 (1993). Violet and purple on multicolor underprint. Panoramic view of Daugava River at center. Back: Traditional bow broach at center. 130x65mm.
FV   30.00

45   20 Latu
VF   UNC
1992 (1993). Brown and dark brown on multicolor underprint. Rural homestead at right. Back: Traditional ornamented woven linen at left center. 130x65mm.
FV   60.00

46   50 Latu
VF   UNC
1992 (1994). Deep blue on multicolor underprint. Sailing ship at right. Back: Two crossed keys and a cross on back (Historical seal of Riga) superimposed on medieval fortification. 130x65mm.
FV   120

47   100 Latu
VF   UNC
1992 (1994). Red and dark brown on multicolor underprint. Krisjanis Barons at right. Back: Lielvarde belt ornaments. 130x65mm.
FV   260

48   500 Latu
VF   UNC
1992 (1998). Purple on multicolor underprint. Young woman in national costume at right. Back: Small ornamental brass crowns. 130x65mm.
FV   1,200

1996-2001 Issue

49   5 Lati
VF   UNC
1996; 2001. Varied shades of green on tan and pale green underprint. Oak tree at center. Back: Local art at center. 130x65mm.
a. 1996. Wide security strip.   FV   14.00
b. 2001   FV   14.00

50   10 Latu
VF   UNC
2000. Engraving and color modifications. Violet and purple on multicolor underprint. Panoramic view of Daugava River at center. Back: Traditional bow broach at center. 130x65mm.
FV   25.00

51   20 Latu   VF   UNC
2004. Brown and dark brown on multicolor underprint. Rural homestead at right.
Back: Traditional ornamented woven linen at left center. 130x65mm.
  a. 2004   FV   48.00
52   100 Latu   VF   UNC
2006. Brown and red on multicolor underprint.
  a. 2006   FV   275

2006-09 Issue

53   5 Lati   VF   UNC
2006-07; 2009. Green and tan on pale green underprint. Oak tree at center right.
Back: Local art at center. 130x65mm.
  a. 2006   FV   17.50
  b. 2007   FV   17.50
  c. 2009   FV   17.50
54   10 Latu   VF   UNC
2008. Violet and purple on multicolor underprint. Panoramic view of Daugava
River at center. Back: Traditional bow broach at center.   FV   30.00
55   20 Latu   VF   UNC
2007; 2009. Brown and dark brown on multicolor underprint. Rural homestead at
center right. Back: Traditional ornamented woven linen at left center.
  a. 2007   FV   55.00
  b. 2009   FV   55.00
56   50 Latu   VF   UNC
2010.   —   —

57   100 Latu   VF   UNC
2007. Brown and red on multicolor underprint. Krisjanis Barons at right center.
Back: Leilvarde belt ornaments at left center.
  a. Issued note.   FV   260
  s. Specimen.   —   200
58   500 Latu   VF   UNC
2008. Purple on multicolor underprint. Young woman in national costume at center
right. Back: Small ornamental brass crowns.   FV   1,000

LEBANON

The Republic of Lebanon, situated on the eastern shore of the Mediterranean Sea between Syria and Israel, has an area of 4,015 sq. mi. (10,400 sq. km.) and a population of 3.29 million. Capital: Beirut. The economy is based on agriculture, trade and tourism. Fruit, other foodstuffs and textiles are exported. Following the capture of Syria from the Ottoman Empire by Anglo-French forces in 1918, France received a mandate over this territory and separated out the region of Lebanon in 1920. France granted this area independence in 1943. A lengthy civil war (1975-1990) devastated the country, but Lebanon has since made progress toward rebuilding its political institutions. Under the Ta'if Accord - the blueprint for national reconciliation - the Lebanese established a more equitable political system, particularly by giving Muslims a greater voice in the political process while institutionalizing sectarian divisions in the government. Since the end of the war, Lebanon has conducted several successful elections. Most militias have been disbanded, and the Lebanese Armed Forces (LAF) have extended authority over about two-thirds of the country. Hizballah, a radical Shia organization listed by the US State Department as a Foreign Terrorist Organization, retains its weapons. During Lebanon's civil war, the Arab League legitimized in the Ta'if Accord Syria's troop deployment, numbering about 16,000 based mainly east of Beirut and in the Bekaa Valley. Israel's withdrawal from southern Lebanon in May 2000 and the passage in October 2004 of UNSCR 1559 - a resolution calling for Syria to withdraw from Lebanon and end its interference in Lebanese affairs - encouraged some Lebanese groups to demand that Syria withdraw its forces as well. The assassination of former Prime Minister Rafiq Hariri and 22 others in February 2005 led to massive demonstrations in Beirut against the Syrian presence ("the Cedar Revolution"), and Syria withdrew the remainder of its military forces in April 2005. In May-June 2005, Lebanon held its first legislative elections since the end of the civil war free of foreign interference, handing a majority to the bloc led by Saad HARIRI, the slain prime minister's son. Lebanon continues to be plagued by violence - Hizballah kidnapped two Israeli soldiers in July 2006 leading to a 34-day conflict with Israel. The LAF in May-September 2007 battled Sunni extremist group Fatah al-Islam in the Nahr al-Barid Palestinian refugee camp; and the country has witnessed a string of politically motivated assassinations since the death of Rafiq Hariri. Lebanese politicians in November 2007 were unable to agree on a successor to Emile Lahud when he stepped down as president, creating a political vacuum until the election of Army Commander Michel Sulaymanin May 2008 and the formation of a new unity government in July 2008.

RULERS
  French to 1943

MONETARY SYSTEM
  1 Livre (Pound) = 100 Piastres

RÉPUBLIQUE LIBANAISE
Banque de Syrie et du Liban
1952; 1956 Issue

55   1 Livre   VF   UNC
1.1.1952-1.1.1964. Crusader Castle at Saida (Sidon) at left. Signature varieties.
Back: Columns of Baalbek. Printer: TDLR.
  a. Without security strip.   10.00   60.00
  b. With security strip.   10.00   60.00
  s1. Specimen. Oval TDLR stamp, punch hole cancelled.   —   30.00
  s2. Specimen. Perforated: *SPECIMEN* and large double lined X inked on face.   —   150

56   5 Livres   VF   UNC

1.1.1952-1.1.1964. Blue on multicolor underprint. Courtyard of the Palais de Beit-ed-Din. Signature varieties. Back: Snowy mountains with trees. Printer: TDLR.

    a. Without security strip.   45.00   160
    b. With security strip.   45.00   160
    s1. Specimen. Oval TDLR stamp, punch hole cancelled.   —   40.00
    s2. Specimen. Perforated: *SPECIMEN* and large double lined X inked on face.   —   250

57   10 Livres   VF   UNC

1.1.1956; 1.1.1961; 1.1.1963. Green on multicolor underprint. Ruins of Temple of Bacchus temple at Baalbek. Signature varieties. Back: Shoreline with city in hills. Printer: TDLR.

    a. Issued note.   60.00   230
    s1. Specimen. Oval TDLR stamp, punch hole cancelled.   —   100
    s2. Specimen. Perforated: *SPECIMEN* and large double lined X inked on face.   —   500

58   25 Livres   VF   UNC

1.1.1952; 1.1.1953. Blue-gray on multicolor underprint. Harbor town. Signature varieties. Back: Stone arch bridge at center right. Watermark: Lion's head. Printer: TDLR.

    a. Issued note.   210   900
    s1. Specimen. Oval TDLR stamp, punch hole cancelled.   —   1,000
    s2. Specimen. Perforated: *SPECIMEN* and large double lined X inked on face.   —   1,250

59   50 Livres   VF   UNC

1.1.1952; 1.1.1953; 1.1.1964. Deep brown on multicolor underprint. Coast landscape. Signature varieties. Back: Large rock formations in water. Watermark: Lion's head. Printer: TDLR.

    a. Issued note.   200   900
    s1. Specimen. Oval TDLR stamp, punch hole cancelled.   —   1,000
    s2. Specimen. Perforated: *SPECIMEN* and large double lined X inked on face.   —   1,250

60   100 Livres   VF   UNC

1.1.1952, 1.1.1953; 1.1.1958; 1.1.1963. Blue on multicolor underprint. View of Beirut and harbor. Signature varieties. Back: Cedar tree at center. Watermark: Cedar tree. Printer: TDLR.

    a. Issued note.   50.00   250
    s1. Specimen. Oval TDLR stamp, punch hole cancelled.   —   1,000
    s2. Specimen. Perforated: *SPECIMEN* and large double lined X inked on face.   —   1,250

REPUBLIC

Banque du Liban
1964; 1978 Issue

61   1 Livre   VF   UNC

1964-80. Brown or light blue underprint. Columns of Baalbek. Back: Jeita Cavern. Watermark: Two eagles. Printer: TDLR.

    a. 1964; 1968.   6.00   30.00
    b. 1971; 1972; 1973; 1974.   6.00   30.00
    c. 1980.   3.00   4.50

62   5 Livres   VF   UNC

1964-86. UV: Arabic 5 fluoresce yellow, fibers blue. Green on blue and light yellow underprint. Buildings. Back: Bridge over Kalb at center right. Watermark: Ancient galley. Printer: TDLR.

    a. 1964.   8.00   40.00
    b. 1967; 1968.   5.00   25.00
    c. 1972; 1974; 1.2.1978; 1.4.1978.   3.00   10.00
    d. 1986.   1.50   2.00

63 10 Livres

1964-86. Purple on multicolor underprint. Ruins of Anjar. Back: Large rocks in water near Beirut. Watermark: Man's head. Printer: TDLR.

	VF	UNC
a. 1964.	10.00	50.00
b. 1967; 1968.	8.00	35.00
c. 1971; 1972; 1973; 1974.	4.00	20.00
d. 1.2.1978.	8.00	25.00
e. 1.4.1978.	4.00	16.00
f. 1986.	1.50	2.50

64 25 Livres

1964-83. Brown on gold underprint. Crusader Castle at Saida (Sidon). Back: Ruins on rocks. Watermark: Lion's head. Printer: TDLR.

	VF	UNC
a. 1964; 1968.	20.00	90.00
b. 1972; 1974; 1978.	13.00	55.00
c. 1983.	2.00	3.50

65 50 Livres

1964-88. Dark gray, purple and dark olive-green on multicolor underprint. Ruins of Temple of Bacchus at Baalbek. Back: Building. Watermark: Cedar tree. Printer: TDLR.

	VF	UNC
a. 1964; 1967; 1968.	22.00	95.00
b. 1972; 1973; 1974; 1978.	18.00	60.00
c. Guilloche added above temple ruins with 10-petaled rosette at left in underprint. Clear watermark area on back. 1983; 1985.	2.00	4.00
d. Without control # above ruins on face. 1988.	1.50	4.00

66 100 Livres

1964-88. Blue on light pink and light blue underprint. Palais Beit-ed-din with inner courtyard. Back: Snowy cedars on Lebanon mountains. Watermark: Bearded male elder. Printer: TDLR.

	VF	UNC
a. 1964; 1967; 1968.	35.00	120
b. 1972; 1973; 1974; 1977; 1978.	20.00	80.00
c. Guilloche added under bank name on face and back. Clearer watermark area on back. 1983; 1985.	2.00	5.00
d. Without control # at upper center 1988.	2.00	4.50

67 250 Livres

1978-88. Deep gray-green and blue-black on multicolor underprint. Ruins at Tyras. Back: Ruins at Tyras. Watermark: Ancient circular sculpture with head at center from the Grand Temple Podium. Printer: TDLR.

	VF	UNC
a. 1978.	30.00	110
b. 1983. Control # at top center.	8.00	25.00
c. 1985.	2.00	6.00
d. 1986.	1.50	5.00
e. Without control # above signature at archway on face. 1986; 1987; 1988.	1.00	4.50

1988; 1993 Issue

Law of 1988.

68 500 Livres

1988. Brown and olive-green on multicolor underprint. Beirut city view at center. Back: Ruins at left center. Watermark: Lion's head. Printer: TDLR.

	VF	UNC
	1.50	3.50

69   1000 Livres   **VF   UNC**
1988; 1990-92. Dark blue, blue-black and green on multicolor underprint. Map at
right. Back: Ruins at center, modern building at center right. Watermark: Cedar
tree. Printer: TDLR. 157x67mm.

    a. 1988.   FV   4.00
    b. 1990; 1991.   FV   3.00
    c. 1992.   FV   3.00

70   10,000 Livres   **VF   UNC**
1993. Purple and olive-brown on multicolor underprint. Ancient ruins at Tyros at   15.00   40.00
center. Back: City ruins with five archaic statues. Watermark: Ancient circular
sculpture with head at center from the Grand Temple Podium.

1994 Issue

71   5000 Livres   **VF   UNC**
1994; 1995. Dark purple and red on pink and multicolor underprint. Arabic serial
number and matching bar code number. Ornate block designs as underprint.
Back: Geometric designs. Watermark: Cedar tree. Printer: BABN.

    a. 1994.   12.00   24.00
    b. 1995.   10.00   22.00

72   20,000 Livres   **VF   UNC**
1994; 1995. Red-brown and orange on yellow and multicolor underprint. Arabic   25.00   55.00
serial number and matching bar code number. Ornate block designs as underprint. Back: Geometric designs with large *LIBAN* left center Watermark: Cedar
tree. Printer: BABN. 150x80mm.

73   50,000 Livres   **VF   UNC**
1994; 1995. Ornate block designs as underprint. Blue-black and brown-violet on   55.00   120
multicolor underprint. Cedar tree at upper left, artistic boats at lower left center.
Arabic serial number and matching bar code number. Back: Large diamond with
BDL at left center, cedar tree at lower left. Watermark: Cedar tree. Printer: BABN.
155x85mm.

74   100,000 Livres   **VF   UNC**
1994; 1995. Dark blue-green and dark green on multicolor underprint. Cedar tree   85.00   170
at upper right. Arabic serial number and matching bar code number. Back: Artistic
bunch of grapes and grain stalks at left center. Watermark: Cedar tree. Printer:
BABN. 160x90mm.

1998-99 Issue

75   5000 Livres   **VF   UNC**
1999. Like #71 but smaller size. Dark purple and red on multicolor underprint.   FV   18.00
Arabic serial number and matching bar code number. Back: Geometric designs.
Watermark: Cedar tree. Printer: BABN. 140x70mm.

76　10,000 Livres　　　　　　　　　　　　　　　**VF　UNC**
1998. Iridescent planchets in paper. Orange and green on yellow and multicolor　　FV　24.00
underprint. Back: Patriotic Monument, stylized landscape. 145x73mm.

This number issued on Martyr's Day 1998.

77　50,000 Livres　　　　　　　　　　　　　　　**VF　UNC**
1999. Blue-black and brown-violet on multicolor underprint. Cedar tree at upper　　FV　95.00
left, artistic boats at lower left center. Arabic serial # and matching bar code
number. Enhanced security features and holographic foil strip at left. Back: Large
diamond with BDL at left center, cedar tree at lower left. Watermark: Cedar tree.
Printer: BABN. 155x85mm.

78　100,000 Livres　　　　　　　　　　　　　　**VF　UNC**
1999. Dark blue-green and dark green on multicolor underprint. Cedar tree at　　FV　140
lower right. Arabic serial # and matching bar code number. Enhanced security
features. Back: Artistic bunch of grapes and grain stalks at left center. 160x90mm.

2001 Issue

79　5000 Livres　　　　　　　　　　　　　　　　**VF　UNC**
2001. Wide security thread. Dark purple and red on multicolor underprint. Printer:　FV　12.00
BABN. 140x70mm.

80 *Not assigned.*

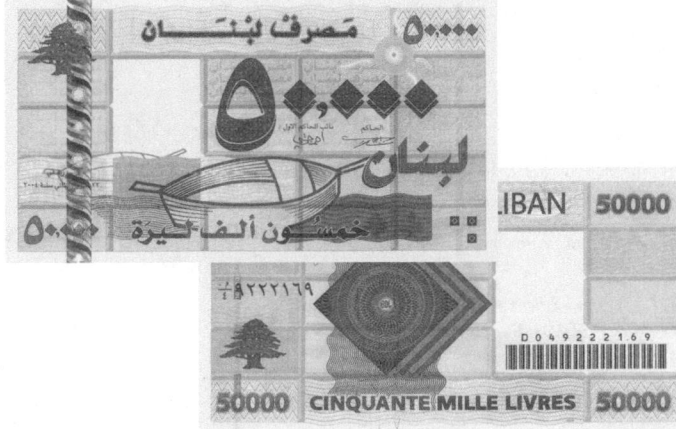

81　20,000 Livres　　　　　　　　　　　　　　**VF　UNC**
2001. Wide security thread. Red-brown and orange on multicolor underprint.　　FV　60.00
Printer: BABN. 150x80mm.

82　50,000 Livres　　　　　　　　　　　　　　**VF　UNC**
2001. Wide security thread. Blue-black and brown-violet on multicolor underprint.　FV　95.00
Printer: G&D. 155x85mm.

83　100,000 Livres　　　　　　　　　　　　　　**VF　UNC**
2001. Dark blue-green and dark green on multicolor underprint. Printer: BABN.　　FV　130
160x90mm.

2004 Issue

84　1000 Livres　　　　　　　　　　　　　　　　**VF　UNC**
2004; 2008. Green. Alphabet development in arc. Back: Numeral development.
116x60mm.
　a. 2004 (2006).　　　　　　　　　　　　　　　　FV　3.00
　b. 2008.　　　　　　　　　　　　　　　　　　　FV　2.00

85   5000 Livres   **VF   UNC**
2004; 2008. Dark purple and red on multicolor underprint. 120x62mm.
    a. 2004.   FV   10.00
    b. 2008.   FV   7.50

86   10,000 Livres   **VF   UNC**
2004; 2008. Orange and green on yellow and multicolor underprint. 128x66mm.
    a. 2004.   FV   18.00
    b. 2008.   FV   14.00

87   20,000 Livres   **VF   UNC**
2004. Red-brown and orange on multicolor underprint. 131x72mm.   FV   42.00
88   50,000 Livres   **VF   UNC**
2004. Blue-black and brown-violet on multicolor underprint. 140x77mm. FV   85.00
89   100,000 Livres   **VF   UNC**
2004. Dark blue-green and dark green on multicolor underprint. 147x82mm. FV 120

2011 Issue

90   1000 Livres   **VF   UNC**
2011-2012. Green and tan. Value in Arabic at center. Wide segmented security
thread. Back: Value. Printer: Goznak (without imprint). 115x60mm.
    a. 2011.   FV   2.00
    b. 2012.   FV   2.00
91   5000 Livres   **VF   UNC**
2012. Pink, purple, orange and green. Cedar tree, geometric block design. Arabic
value. Back: Geometric block design, cedar tree. Watermark: Cedar tree and
value Printer: Goznak (without imprint). 120x62mm.
    a. 2012.   FV   7.50
    b. 2014.   FV   7.50

92   10,000 Livres   **VF   UNC**
2012. Yellow, orange and green. Cedar tree, geometric block design. Value in
Arabic. Back: Geometric block design, statue by Renato Marino Mazzacurati of
three Lebanese nationalists in Martyr's Square, Beirut. Watermark: Cedar tree and
value. Printer: OT. 127x66mm.
    a. 2012.   FV   17.50
    b. 2014.   FV   17.50

93   20,000 Livres   **VF   UNC**
2012, 2014. Value in Arabic. Back: Value. 131x72mm.
    a. 2012.   FV   25.00
    b. 2014.   FV   25.00

94   50,000 Livres   **VF   UNC**
2011. Violet, green, blue and multicolor. Value in Arabic. Back: Diamond
shaped square at left center, value in corners. Printer: Goznak (without imprint).
140x77mm.
    a. 2011.   FV   55.00
    b. 2012.   FV   50.00

95 100,000 Livres

2011; 2012. Green, light blue, yellow and multicolor. Value in Arabic. Wide security thread. Back: Grapes, grain and thread at center, value in corners. Printer: Goznak (without imprint). 147x82mm.

		VF	UNC
a. 2011.		FV	95.00
b. 2012.		FV	95.00

2013-14 Commemorative Issue

96 50,000 Livres

2013. Polymer plastic. Blue and tan. Citadel of Independence in Rashaya, flag. Back: Map and flag of Lebanon, 70th Anniversary logo, flag, cedar tree. Printer: DLR. 140x77mm.

VF UNC
FV 100

97 50,000 Livres

2014. Polymer plastic. Gray and tan. Front view of Bank building. Back: Upward view of Bank building. 140x77mm.

VF UNC
FV 50.00

2015 Commemorative Issue

98 50,000 Livres

2015. Polymer plastic. Blue, green, brown, red. 70 years of Lebanese army. Two soldiers in silhouette, coat of arms, soldier carrying flag. Back: Vertical. Monument to martyrs in Yarze, soldier soluting, wheat stalk. Printer: TDLR. 140x77mm.

VF UNC
FV 100

LESOTHO

The Kingdom of Lesotho, a constitutional monarchy located within the east-central part of the Republic of South Africa, has an area of 11,716 sq. mi. (30,355 sq. km.) and a population of 2.29 million. Capital: Maseru. The economy is based on subsistence agriculture and livestock raising. Wool, mohair, water through Katse Dam, and cattle are exported. Basutoland was renamed the Kingdom of Lesotho upon independence from the UK in 1966. The Basuto National Party ruled for the first two decades. King Moshoeshoe was exiled in 1990, but returned to Lesotho in 1992 and was reinstated in 1995. Constitutional government was restored in 1993 after seven years of military rule. In 1998, violent protests and a military mutiny following a contentious election prompted a brief but bloody intervention by South African and Botswanan military forces under the aegis of the Southern African Development Community. Subsequent constitutional reforms restored relative political stability. Peaceful parliamentary elections were held in 2002, but the National Assembly elections of February 2007 were hotly contested and aggrieved parties continue to periodically demonstrate their distrust of the results.

RULERS:
King Motlotlehi Moshoeshoe II, 1966-1996
King Letsi III, 1997-

MONETARY SYSTEM:
1 Loti = 100 Lisente

KINGDOM

Lesotho Monetary Authority

1979 Issue

#1-3A Dating: Partial date given in the 2 numbers of the serial # prefix for #1-8.

1 2 Maloti

(19)79. Dark brown on multicolor underprint. Arms at center, military bust of King Moshoeshoe II at right. Signature 1. Back: Building and Lesotho flag at left. Watermark: Basotho hat.

	VF	UNC
a. Blue and brown underprint at right of King	4.50	24.00
s. Specimen. Serial # prefix R/79.	—	135

2 5 Maloti

(19)79. Deep blue on multicolor underprint. Arms at center, military bust of King Moshoeshoe II at right. Signature 1. Back: Craftsmen weaving at left center. Watermark: Basotho hat.

	VF	UNC
a. Issued note.	12.50	37.00
s. Specimen. Serial # prefix J/79.	—	135

3 10 Maloti

(19)79. Red and purple on multicolor underprint. Arms at center, military bust of King Moshoeshoe II at right. Signature 1. Back: Basotho horseman in maize field at center. Watermark: Basotho hat.

	VF	UNC
a. Issued note.	30.00	145
s. Specimen. Serial # prefix C/79.	—	135

4 2 Maloti
VF UNC

(19)81; 84. Dark brown on multicolor underprint. Arms at center, military bust of King Moshoeshoe II at right. Signature 1. Back: Building and Lesotho flag at left. Watermark: Basotho hat.

		VF	UNC
a. Signature 1 (19)81.		4.00	15.00
b. Signature 2A (19)84.		3.00	12.50
s1. Specimen. Serial # prefix A/81.		—	135
s2. Specimen. Serial # prefix D/84.		—	135

3A 20 Maloti
VF UNC — —

(19)79. Specimen (Not issued.) Arms at center, military bust of King Moshoeshoe II at right. Signature 1. Back: Herdsmen with cattle at left center. Watermark: Basotho hat.

SIGNATURE VARIETIES

	MINISTER OF FINANCE	GOVERNOR
1	E.R. Sekhonyana	E.K. Molemohi
2A	K. Rakhetla	S. Schoenbeg 08.11.1982 - 08.11.1985
2B	K. Rakhetla	S. Schoenbeg 08.11.1982 - 08.11.1985
2C	K. Rakhetla	S. Schoenbeg 08.11.1982 - 08.11.1985
1985-1988	K. Rakhetla	Mr. E.L. Karlsson 09.11.1985 - 30.06.1988
3	E.R. Sekhonyana	Dr. A.M. Maruping 01.07.1988 - 15.05.1988
4	E.L. Thoahlane	Dr. A.M. Maruping 01.07.1988 - 15.05.1988
5	Dr. L.V. Ketso	Dr. A.M. Maruping 01.07.1988 - 15.05.1988
6	Dr. L.V. Ketso	S.M. Swaray 9.9.1988

5 5 Maloti
VF UNC

(19)81 Deep blue on multicolor underprint. Arms at center, military bust of King Moshoeshoe II at right. Signature 1. Back: Waterfalls at center. Watermark: Basotho hat.

		VF	UNC
a. Issued note.		5.00	22.00
s. Specimen. Serial # prefix A/81		—	135

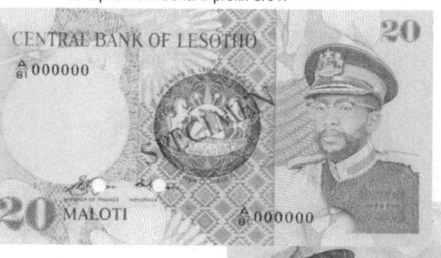

6 10 Maloti
VF UNC

(19)81. Red and purple on multicolor underprint. Arms at center, military bust of King Moshoeshoe II at right. Signature 1. Back: Basotho horseman in maize field at center. Watermark: Basotho hat.

		VF	UNC
a. Signature 1 (19)81.		15.00	55.00
b. Signature 2A (19)81 (1984).		5.00	22.50
s1. Specimen. Serial # prefix A/81.		—	135
s2. Specimen. Serial # prefix C/81.		—	135

Central Bank of Lesotho
1981; 1984 Issue

#4-8 Partial year date given as the denominator of the serial # prefix.

7 20 Maloti
VF UNC

(19)81; 84. Dark green and olive-green on multicolor underprint. Arms at center, military bust of King Moshoeshoe II at right. Back: Mosotho herdsboy with cattle at left center. Watermark: Basotho hat.

		VF	UNC
a. Signature 1 (19)81.		30.00	110
b. Signature 2A (19)84.		12.50	50.00
s1. Specimen. Serial # prefix A/81.		—	135
s2. Specimen. Serial # prefix A/84.		—	135

8   50 Maloti   VF   UNC

(19)81. Purple and deep blue on multicolor underprint. Arms at center, military bust of King Moshoeshoe II at right. Signature 1. Back: Qiloane" mountain at left. Watermark: Basotho hat.

a. Issued note.	80.00	375
s. Specimen. Serial # prefix A/81.	—	175

1989 Issue

9   2 Maloti   VF   UNC

1989. Dark brown on multicolor underprint. Arms at center, civilian bust of King Moshoeshoe II at right. Signature 3. Back: Building and Lesotho flag at left. Watermark: King Moshoeshoe II.

a. Issued note.	1.25	2.75
s. Specimen. Serial # prefix G.	—	115

10   5 Maloti   VF   UNC

1989. Deep blue on multicolor underprint. Arms at center, civilian bust of King Moshoeshoe II at right. Signature 3. Back: Waterfalls at center. Watermark: King Moshoeshoe II.

a. Issued note.	2.00	7.50
s. Specimen. Serial # prefix C.	—	115

11   10 Maloti   VF   UNC

1990. Red and purple on multicolor underprint. Arms at center, civilian bust of King Moshoeshoe II at right. Signature 3. Back: Basotho horseman in maize field at center. Watermark: King Moshoeshoe II.

a. Issued note.	3.50	12.50
s. Specimen. Serial # prefix R.	—	115

12   20 Maloti   VF   UNC

1990. Dark green and blue-black on multicolor underprint. Arms at center, civilian bust of King Moshoeshoe II at right. Signature 3. Back: Mosotho herdsboy with cattle at left center. Watermark: King Moshoeshoe II.

a. 1990.	10.00	40.00
b. 1993.	100	400
s1. As a. Specimen. Serial # prefix F.	—	115
s2. As b. Specimen. Serial # prefix J.	—	160

13   50 Maloti   VF   UNC

1989. Purple and deep blue on multicolor underprint Arms at center, civilian bust of King Moshoeshoe II at right. Signature 3. Back: Sheep by shed and home at center right. Watermark: King Moshoeshoe II.

a. Issued note.	30.00	135
s. Specimen. Serial # prefix A.	—	115

1992 Issue

14   50 Maloti   VF   UNC

1992. Purple, dark olive-green and dark blue on multicolor underprint. Seated King Moshoeshoe I at right. Signature 4. Back: *Qiloane* mountain at left center.

a. Issued note.	20.00	90.00
s1. As a. 1992. Specimen. Serial # prefix A.	—	110
s2. As a. 1993. Specimen. Serial # prefix B.	—	160

1994-2000 Issue

15 10 Maloti   **VF UNC**

2000-. Red and purple on multicolor underprint. Seated King Moshoeshoe I at left, arms at center. Back: Traditionally dressed Masotho on horseback, maize crops and mountain. Watermark: Arms. Printer: TDLR. 128x70mm.

	VF	UNC
a. Signature 6. 2000.	FV	4.50
b. Signature 7. 2003.	FV	3.50
c. Signature 7. 2005.	FV	3.50
d. Signature 7. 2006.	FV	3.50
e. 2007.	FV	3.50
f. 2009.	FV	3.50
s. Specimen. Serial # prefix A.	—	100

16 20 Maloti   **VF UNC**

1994-. Deep olive green and blue black on multicolor underprint. Seated King Moshoeshoe I at left, arms at center. Back: Masotho herdsboy with cattle near huts at center right. Watermark: Arms. Printer: TDLR. 135x70mm.

	VF	UNC
a. Signature 5. 1994.	6.00	20.00
b. Signature 6. 1999.	FV	9.00
c. Signature 6. 2001.	FV	6.50
d. Signature 7. 2006.	FV	6.50
e. Signature 7. 2006.	FV	6.50
f. Signature 8. 2007. Thin security foil.	FV	6.50
g. 2009.	FV	6.50
s1. As a. Specimen. Serial # prefix A.	—	100
s2. As b. Specimen. Serial # prefix F.	—	100

17 50 Maloti   **VF UNC**

1994-. Purple, olive-green and dark blue on multicolor underprint. Seated King Moshoeshoe I at left, arms at center. Back: Herdsman on horseback with pack mule at center, *Qiloane* mountain at right. Watermark: Arms. Printer: TDLR. 138x70mm.

	VF	UNC
a. Signature 5. 1994.	12.50	50.00
b. Signature 5. 1997.	0.00	30.00
c. Signature 6. 1999.	FV	20.00
d. Signature 6. 2001.	FV	17.00
e. 2009.	FV	17.00
s1. As a. Specimen. Serial # prefix A.	—	100
s2. As b. Specimen. Serial # prefix C.	—	100
s3. As c. Specimen. Serial # prefix F.	—	100

18 100 Maloti   **VF UNC**

1994. Dark olive-green, orange and brown on multicolor underprint. Seated King Moshoeshoe I at left, arms at center. Back: Sheep by shed and home at center right. Watermark: Arms. Printer: BABN. 141x70mm.

	VF	UNC
a. Signature 5.	20.00	65.00
s. Specimen. Serial # prefix AA.	—	100

19 100 Maloti   **VF UNC**

1999-. Dark olive-green, orange and brown on multicolor underprint. Seated King Moshoeshoe I at left, arms at center. Back: Sheep by shed and home at center right. Watermark: Arms. Printer: TDLR. 141x70mm.

	VF	UNC
a. Signature 6. 1999.	15.00	55.00
b. Signature 6. 2001.	FV	45.00
c. Signature 7. 2006. Thin security foil.	FV	45.00
d. Signature 8. 2007.	FV	45.00
e. 2009.	FV	45.00
s. As a. Specimen. Serial # prefix A.	—	100

20 200 Maloti   **VF UNC**

1994; 2001. Dark brown, brown and orange on multicolor underprint. Seated King Moshoeshoe I at left, arms at center. Kinegram strip vertically at right. Back: Herdsman with sheep. Watermark: Arms. Printer: TDLR. 144x70mm.

	VF	UNC
a. Signature 5. 1994.	FV	80.00
b. Signature 6. 2001.	FV	100
s. As a. Specimen. Serial # prefix A.	—	100

2010 Issue

21 10 Maloti   **VF UNC**

2010. Red and lilac on multicolor underprint. Portraits of Kings Moshoeshoe II, Letsie III and Morena Moshoeshoe I. Back: Flowers.   FV   3.50

22 20 Maloti   **VF UNC**

2010. Blue and light blue on multicolor underprint. Portraits of Kings Moshoeshoe II, Letsie III and Morena Moshoeshoe I. Back: Small houses.   FV   6.50

23 50 Maloti   **VF UNC**

2010. Brown and purple on multicolor underprint. Portraits of Kings Moshoeshoe II, Letsie III and Morena Moshoeshoe I. Back: Horsemen.   FV   17.00

24 100 Maloti   **VF UNC**

2010. Green on multicolor underprint. Portraits of Kings Moshoeshoe II, Letsie III and Morena Moshoeshoe I. Back: Goats.   FV   45.00

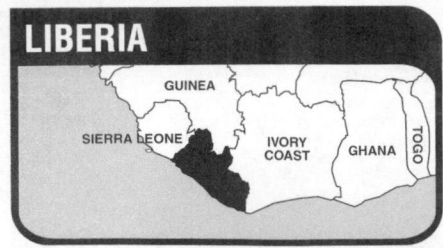

LIBERIA

The Republic of Liberia, located on the southern side of the west African bulge between Sierra Leone and the Ivory Coast, has an area of 38,250 sq. mi. (111,369 sq. km.) and a population of 3.26 million. Capital: Monrovia. The major industries are agriculture, mining and lumbering. Iron ore, diamonds, rubber, coffee and cocoa are exported. Settlement of freed slaves from the US in what is today Liberia began in 1822; by 1847, the Americo-Liberians were able to establish a republic. William Tubman, president from 1944-71, did much to promote foreign investment and to bridge the economic, social, and political gaps between the descendents of the original settlers and the inhabitants of the interior. In 1980, a military coup led by Samuel Doe ushered in a decade of authoritarian rule. In December 1989, Charles Taylor launched a rebellion against Doe's regime that led to a prolonged civil war in which Doe himself was killed. A period of relative peace in 1997 allowed for elections that brought Taylor to power, but major fighting resumed in 2000. An August 2003 peace agreement ended the war and prompted the resignation of former president Charles Taylor, who faces war crimes charges in The Hague related to his involvement in Sierra Leone's civil war. After two years of rule by a transitional government, democratic elections in late 2005 brought President Ellen Johnson Sirleaf to power. The UN Mission in Liberia (UNMIL) maintains a strong presence throughout the country, but the security situation is still fragile and the process of rebuilding the social and economic structure of this war-torn country will take many years.

MONETARY SYSTEM:
   1 Dollar = 100 Cents

REPLACEMENT NOTES:
   #19, 20: ZZ prefix.

REPUBLIC
National Bank of Liberia
1989 Issue

#19 replacement note: Serial # prefix *ZZ*.

19	5 Dollars		VF	UNC

12.4.1989. Black and deep green on multicolor underprint. Latent image star at left, portrait J. J. Roberts at center, tapping trees at right. Back: National Bank building at center. Printer: TDLR. 157x67mm.   2.50   7.00

1991 Issue

#20 replacement note: Serial # prefix *ZZ*.

20	5 Dollars		VF	UNC

6.4.1991. Black and deep green on multicolor underprint. Latent image star at left, arms at center, tapping trees at right. Back: National Bank building. Printer: TDLR. 157x67mm.   2.00   6.00

Central Bank of Liberia
1999 Issue

21	5 Dollars		VF	UNC

1999. Date for establishment of Central Bank shown as 1974. Red and brown on yellow underprint. Edward J. Roye at center. 2 signature varieties. Back: Female farmer harvesting rice, arms at left. *REPUBLIC OF LIBERIA* at top. 157x67mm.   FV   2.50

22	10 Dollars		VF	UNC

1999. Purple and black on multicolor underprint. Joseph Jenkins Roberts at center. Back: Worker tapping rubber, *REPUBLIC OF LIBERIA*. at top. 157x67mm.   FV   3.50

23	20 Dollars		VF	UNC

1999; 2002. Brown, black and olive on multicolor underprint. William V. S. Tubman, Sr. at center. Back: Market, *REPUBLIC OF LIBERIA*. at top. 157x67mm.
   a. 1999.   FV   3.00
   b. 2002.   FV   2.50

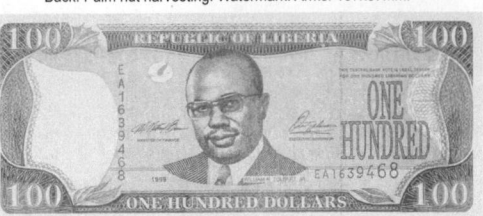

24	50 Dollars		VF	UNC

1999. Purple; red and blue on multicolor underprint. Samuel Kayon Doe at center. Back: Palm nut harvesting. Watermark: Arms. 157x67mm.   FV   7.50

25   100 Dollars   VF   UNC
1999. Green, brown and black on multicolor underprint. William R. Tolbert, Jr. at   FV   15.00
center. Back: Market woman and child. Watermark: Arms. 157x67mm.

2003 Issue

#26-30, *CENTRAL BANK OF LIBERIA* **at trop on back. 2 sign. varieties.**

26   5 Dollars   VF   UNC
2003-. Red and brown on yellow underprint. 2 signature varieties. Back: CEN-
TRAL BANK OF LIBERIA at top. Printer: FC-O 157x67mm.
a. 2003.	FV	2.00
b. 2004.	FV	2.00
c. 2006.	FV	1.50
d. 2008.	FV	1.50
e. 2009.	FV	1.50

27   10 Dollars   VF   UNC
2003-. . Purple and black on multicolor underprint. 2 signature varieties. Back:
CENTRAL BANK OF LIBERIA at top. 157x67mm.
a. 2003.	FV	3.50
b. 2004.	FV	3.50
c. 2006.	FV	3.50
d. 2008.	FV	3.50
e. 2009.	FV	3.50
f. 2011.	FV	3.50

28   20 Dollars   VF   UNC
2003-. Brown, black and olive on multicolor underprint. 2 signature varieties. Back:
CENTRAL BANK OF LIBERIA at top. 157x67mm.
a. 2003.	FV	2.50
b. 2004.	FV	2.50
c. 2006.	FV	2.00
d. 2008.	FV	2.00
e. 2009.	FV	2.00
f. 2011.	FV	2.00

29   50 Dollars   VF   UNC
2003-. Purple, red and blue on multicolor underprint. 2 signatures. Back: CEN-
TRAL BANK OF LIBERIA at top. 157x67mm.
a. 2003.	FV	4.50
b. 2004.	FV	4.00
c. 2008.	FV	3.00
d. 2009.	FV	3.00
e. 2011.	FV	3.00

30   100 Dollars   VF   UNC
2003-. Green, brown and black on multicolor underprint. 2 signature varieties.
Back: CENTRAL BANK OF LIBERIA at top. 157x67mm.
a. 2003.	FV	6.00
b. 2004.	FV	6.00
c. 2006.	FV	5.50
d. 2008.	FV	5.00
e. 2009.	FV	5.00

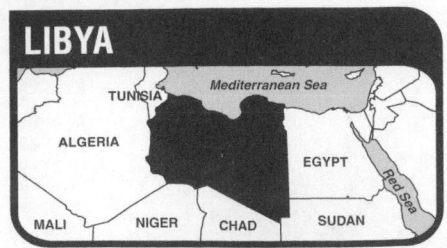

LIBYA

The Socialist People's Libyan Arab Jamahiriya, located on the north central coast of Africa between Tunisia and Egypt, has an area of 679,359 sq. mi. (1,759,540 sq. km.) and a population of 6.39 million. Capital: Tripoli. Crude oil, which accounts for 90 percent of the export earnings, is the mainstay of the economy. The Italians supplanted the Ottoman Turks in the area around Tripoli in 1911 and did not relinquish their hold until 1943 when defeated in World War II. Libya then passed to UN administration and achieved independence in 1951. Following a 1969 military coup, Col. Muammar Abu Minyar al-Qadhafi began to espouse his own political system, the Third Universal Theory. The system is a combination of socialism and Islam derived in part from tribal practices and is supposed to be implemented by the Libyan people themselves in a unique form of "direct democracy." Qadhafi has always seen himself as a revolutionary and visionary leader. He used oil funds during the 1970s and 1980s to promote his ideology outside Libya, supporting subversives and terrorists abroad to hasten the end of Marxism and capitalism. In addition, beginning in 1973, he engaged in military operations in northern Chad's Aozou Strip - to gain access to minerals and to use as a base of influence in Chadian politics - but was forced to retreat in 1987. UN sanctions in 1992 isolated Qadhafi politically following the downing of Pan AM Flight 103 over Lockerbie, Scotland. During the 1990s, Qadhafi began to rebuild his relationships with Europe. UN sanctions were suspended in April 1999 and finally lifted in September 2003 after Libya accepted responsibility for the Lockerbie bombing. In December 2003, Libya announced that it had agreed to reveal and end its programs to develop weapons of mass destruction and to renounce terrorism. Qadhafi has made significant strides in normalizing relations with Western nations since then. He has received various Western European leaders as well as many working-level and commercial delegations, and made his first trip to Western Europe in 15 years when he traveled to Brussels in April 2004. The US rescinded Libya's designation as a state sponsor of terrorism in June 2006. In January 2008, Libya assumed a nonpermanent seat on the United Nations Security Council for the 2008/09 term. In August 2008, the US and Libya signed a bilateral comprehensive claims settlement agreement to compensate claimants in both countries who allege injury or death at the hands of the other country, including the Lockerbie bombing, the LaBelle disco bombing, and the UTA 772 bombing. In October 2008, the US Government received $1.5 billion pursuant to the agreement to distribute to US national claimants, and as a result effectively normalized its bilateral relationship with Libya. The two countries then exchanged ambassadors for the first time since 1973 in January 2009.

RULERS:
Idris I, 1951-1969

MONETARY SYSTEM:
1 Piastre = 10 Milliemes
1 Pound = 100 Piastres = 1000 Milliemes, 1951-1971
1 Dinar = 1000 Dirhams, 1971-

CONSTITUTIONAL MONARCHY

Bank of Libya
Law of 5.2.1963 - First Issue
Pound System.

			VF	UNC
23	**1/4 Pound**			
	L.1963/AH1382. Red on multicolor underprint. Crowned arms at left. Watermark: Arms.			
	a. Issued note.		20.00	150
	s. Specimen.		—	—
24	**1/2 Pound**		VF	UNC
	L.1963/AH1382. Purple on multicolor underprint. Crowned arms at left. Watermark: Arms.		37.50	250
25	**1 Pound**		VF	UNC
	L.1963/AH1382. Blue on multicolor underprint. Crowned arms at left. Watermark: Arms.		65.00	475

		VF	UNC
26	**5 Pounds**	250	—
	L.1963/AH1382. Green on multicolor underprint. Crowned arms at left. Watermark: Arms.		

		VF	UNC
27	**10 Pounds**	350	—
	L.1963/AH1382. Brown on multicolor underprint. Crowned arms at left. Watermark: Arms.		

Law of 5.2.1963 - Second Issue
#28-32 Reduced size notes.

		VF	UNC
28	**1/4 Pound**	25.00	175
	L.1963/AH1382. Red on multicolor underprint. Crowned arms at left. Watermark: Arms.		
29	**1/2 Pound**	35.00	325
	L.1963/AH1832. Purple on multicolor underprint. Crowned arms at left. Watermark: Arms.		
30	**1 Pound**	50.00	425
	L.1963/AH1382. Blue on multicolor underprint. Crowned arms at left. Watermark: Arms.		

		VF	UNC
31	**5 Pounds**	150	700
	L.1963/AH1382. Green on multicolor underprint. Crowned arms at left. Watermark: Arms.		

32   10 Pounds   VF   UNC
L.1963/AH1382. Brown on multicolor underprint. Crowned arms at left. Water-   250   1,650
mark: Arms.

SOCIALIST PEOPLES REPUBLIC

SIGNATURE VARIETIES			
1		2	
3		4	
5		6	
7		8	
9		10	

Central Bank of Libya
1971 Issue - Series 1

Dinar System.The series is indicated by the digit placed before the serial
number prefix fraction.

33   1/4 Dinar   VF   UNC
ND. Orange-brown on multicolor underprint. Arms at left, Arabic inscription at
bottom of watermark area at lower right. Signature 1. Back: Doorway. Watermark:
Arms (Heraldic eagle).
    a. Without inscription (1971).   20.00   150
    b. With inscription (1972).   10.00   35.00
    s. Specimen. Red overprint in Arabic.   —   100

34   1/2 Dinar   VF   UNC
ND. Purple on multicolor underprint. Arms at left, Arabic inscription at bottom of
watermark area at lower right. Signature 1. Back: Oil refinery. Watermark: Arms
(Heraldic eagle).
    a. Without inscription (1971).   35.00   225
    b. With inscription (1972).   15.00   60.00
    s. Specimen. Red overprint in Arabic.   —   250

35   1 Dinar   VF   UNC
ND. Blue on multicolor underprint. Gate and minatet at left, Arabic inscription at
botto9m of watermark area at lower right. Signature 1.. Back: Hilltop fortress.
Watermark: Arms (Heraldic eagle).
    a. Without inscription (1971).   45.00   425
    b. With inscription (1972).   25.00   100
    s. Specimen. Red overprint in Arabic.   —   500

36   5 Dinars   VF   UNC
ND. Olive on multicolor underprint. Arms at left, Arabic inscription at bottom of
watermark area at lower right. Signature 1. Back: Fortress at center. Watermark:
Arms (Heraldic eagle).
    a. Without inscription (1971).   75.00   600
    b. With inscription (1972).   15.00   125
    s. Specimen. Red overprint in Arabic.   —   750

37   10 Dinars   VF   UNC

ND. Blue-gray on multcolor underprint. Omar El Mukhtar at left, without Arabic
inscription. Signature 1. Back: Three horsemen at center. Watermark: Arms
(Heraldic eagle).

    a. Without inscription (1971).   100   750
    b. With inscription (1972).   12.50   50.00
    s. Specimen. Red overprint in Arabic.   —   1,000

#38-42 *Deleted. See #33b-37b.*

1980-81 Issue - Series 2

42A   1/4 Dinar   VF   UNC

ND (1981). Green on multicolor underprint. Ruins at left. Back: Fortress and palms
at center right. Watermark: Heraldic falcon.

    a. Signature 1.   1.75   6.00
    b. Signature 2.   1.50   4.50

43   1/2 Dinar   VF   UNC

ND (1981). Green on multicolor underprint. Petroleum refinery at left. Back: Irrigation system above wheat field. Watermark: Heraldic falcon.

    a. Signature 1.   3.00   7.50
    b. Signature 2.   2.25   6.00

44   1 Dinar   VF   UNC

ND (1981). Green on multicolor underprint. Mosque at left. Back: Interior of
mosque at center right. Watermark: Heraldic falcon.

    a. Signature 1.   4.00   11.50
    b. Signature 2.   3.00   10.00

45   5 Dinars   VF   UNC

ND (1980). Green on multicolor underprint. Camels at left. Back: Crowd around
monument at center right. Watermark: Heraldic falcon.

    a. Signature 1.   12.00   50.00
    b. Signature 2.   10.00   40.00

46   10 Dinars   VF   UNC

ND (1980). Green on multicolor underprint. Omar El Mukhtar at left. Back: Large
crowd below hilltop fortress at center. Watermark: Heraldic falcon.

    a. Signature 1.   25.00   100
    b. Signature 2.   20.00   80.00

1984 Issue - Series 3

47   1/4 Dinar   VF   UNC

ND (1984). Green and brown on multicolor underprint. Ruins at left. Signature 2.   2.50   10.00
Back: Fortress and palms at center right. Watermark: Heraldic falcon.

48 1/2 Dinar VF UNC
ND (1984). Green and purple on multicolor underprint. Petroleum refinery at 4.00 15.00
left. Signature 2. Back: Irrigation system above wheat field. Watermark: Heraldic
falcon.

49 1 Dinar VF UNC
ND (1984). Green and dark blue on multicolor underprint. Mosque at left. Signa- 5.00 20.00
ture 2. Back: Interior of mosque at center right. Watermark: Heraldic falcon.

50 5 Dinars VF UNC
ND (1984). Dark olive-green and light green on multicolor underprint. Camels 12.50 50.00
at left. Signature 2. Back: Crowd around monument at center right. Watermark:
Heraldic falcon.

51 10 Dinars VF UNC
ND (1984). Dark green and blue-green on multicolor underprint. Omar El Mukhtar 20.00 70.00
at left. Signature 2. Back: Large crowd below hilltop fortress at center. Watermark:
Heeraldic falcon.

1988-90 Issue - Series 4

52 1/4 Dinar VF UNC
ND (ca.1990). Green, blue and black on multicolor underprint. Ruins at center. 1.00 4.00
Signature 3. Back: English text at top, fortress with palm trees at left center.
Watermark: Heraldic falcon.

53 1/2 Dinar VF UNC
ND (ca.1990). Deep purple and aqua on multicolor underprint. Oil refinery at 1.75 7.50
left center. Signature 3. Back: English text at top, irrigation system at left center.
Watermark: Heraldic falcon.

54 1 Dinar VF UNC
ND (1988). Blue and green on multicolor underprint. Muammar Qaddafi at left 2.50 10.00
center. Signature 3. Back: Temple at lower center right. Watermark: Heraldic
falcon.

55 5 Dinars VF UNC
ND (ca.1991). Brown and violet on multicolor underprint. Camel at center. Sig- 8.00 35.00
nature 3. Back: Crowd and monument. English text at top. Watermark: Heraldic
falcon.

56 10 Dinars VF UNC
ND (1989). Green on multicolor underprint. Omar el-Mukhtar at left. Signature 3. 15.00 60.00
Back: Arabic text; large crowd before hilltop fortress at center. Octagonal frame
without underprint at upper right. Watermark: Heraldic falcon.

1991-93 Issue - Series 4

57 1/4 Dinar

ND (ca.1991). Green, blue and black on multicolor underprint, more pink in underprint. Ruins at center. Back: Arabic text at top, fortress with palm trees at left center. Watermark: Heraldic falcon. 142x71mm.

	VF	UNC
a. Signature 3.	1.00	5.00
b. Signature 4.	1.00	4.00
c. Signature 5.	0.75	3.00

58 1/2 Dinar

ND (ca. 1991). More color in underprint at upper corners. Deep purple and blue on multicolor underprint. Oil refinery at left center. Back: All Arabic text, irrigation system at left center. Watermark: Heraldic falcon. 152x76mm.

	VF	UNC
a. Signature 3.	1.50	6.00
b. Signature 4.	1.00	5.00
c. Signature 5.	1.00	4.00

59 1 Dinar

ND (1993). Modified green and pink underprint. Blue and green on multicolor underprint. Muammar Qaddafi at left center. Back: Temple at lower center right. Watermark: Heraldic falcon. 162x81mm.

	VF	UNC
a. Signature 4.	2.00	8.50
b. Signature 5.	1.50	8.00

60 5 Dinars

ND (ca. 1991). Brown and violet on multicolor underprint. Camel at center. Back: Crowd and monument, Arabic text at top. Watermark: Heraldic falcon. 172x86mm.

	VF	UNC
a. Signature 3.	8.00	35.00
b. Signature 4.	7.00	30.00
c. Signature 5.	6.00	25.00

61 10 Dinars

ND (1991). Green on multicolor underprint. Omar el-Mukhtar at left. Back: Large crowd before hilltop fortress at center, octagonal frame with underprint at upper right. 182x91mm.

	VF	UNC
a. Signature 4.	12.00	50.00
b. Signature 5.	12.00	50.00

2002 Issue - Series 5

62 1/4 Dinar

ND (2002). Ochre on multicolor underprint. Ruins at center. Signature 4. Back: Walled compound. 142x71mm.

VF	UNC
0.75	2.50

63 1/2 Dinar

ND (2002). Dark blue on blue and multicolor underprint. Oil refinery at center. Signature 4. Back: Irrigation system. 152x76mm.

VF	UNC
1.00	4.00

64 1 Dinar

ND (2002). Blue and green on multicolor underprint. Muammar Qaddafi at center. Back: Mosque. 162x81mm.

	VF	UNC
a. Signature 4.	1.50	7.50
b. Signature 5.	1.50	7.50

65 5 Dinars   **VF UNC**
ND (2002). Green and yellow on multicolor underprint. Camels at center. Back: Monument and crowd. 172x86mm.
   a. Signature 4.   6.00   22.50
   b. Signature 5.   7.00   25.00

66 10 Dinars   **VF UNC**
ND (2002). Green and dark green on multicolor underprint. Omar el-Mukhtar at center left. Signature 4. Back: Fortress and crowd. 182x91mm.   9.00   35.00

67 20 Dinars   **VF UNC**
ND (2002). Green, blue and brown on multicolor underprint. Map with water tunnels at center. Signature 6. Series 1. Back: Muammar Qaddafi with OAU members at center, map of Africa at right. 9.9.1999 meeting date. 166x83mm.
   a. Signatrue 9.   12.50   45.00
   b. Signature 10.   10.00   40.00

2004 Issue - Series 6

#68-70 are reduced in size.

68 1 Dinar   **VF UNC**
ND (2004). Purple and blue on multicolor underprint. Muammar Qaddafi at center. Back: Mosque. 142x71mm.
   a. Signature 9.   FV   7.50
   b. Signatrue 10.   FV   6.00

69 5 Dinars   **VF UNC**
ND (2004). Black and violet on multicolor underprint. Camels at center. Back: Monument and crowd. 149x75mm.
   a. Signature 9.   FV   15.00
   b. Signature 10.   FV   12.50

70 10 Dinars   **VF UNC**
ND (2004). Multicolor. Omar el-Mukhtar at center. Back: Fortress and crowd. 157x79mm.
   a. Signature 9.   FV   25.00
   b. Signature 10.   FV   22.50

2008 Issue - Series 7

71 1 Dinar   **VF UNC**
ND (2009). Blue and multicolor. Muammar Qaddafi. Signature 10. Back: Mosque.   FV   5.00
Watermark: Qaddafi and 1. 140x70mm.

72 5 Dinars   **VF UNC**
ND (2009). Red and multicolor. Two camels at right. Signature 10. Back: Monument. Watermark: Camels and 5. 150x75mm.   FV   11.50

73 10 Dinars   **VF UNC**
ND (2009). Bank name on back in Upper and Lower case English letters. Green and multicolor. Omar el-Mukhtar at right. Signature 10. Back: Fortress and crowd. Watermark: Omar el-Mukhtar and 10. 156x78mm.   FV   20.00

73A 10 Dinars
17.2.2011. Similar to #73 but different security hologram and name of bank and value in English (all capital letters) on back. Printer: F-CO.

	VF	UNC
	FV	17.50

74 20 Dinars
ND (2009). Purple and tan on multicolor underprint. Map of Northern Africa. Signature 10. Back: Organization of African Unity leaders. 166x81mm.

	VF	UNC
	10.00	35.00

75 50 Dinars
ND (2008). Brown and tan on multicolor underprint. Muammar Qaddafi at right. Signature 10. Back: Building.

	VF	UNC
	20.00	75.00

POST REVOLUTIONARY
Central Bank of Libya
2012-13 Issue

76 1 Dinar
ND (2013). Purple, violet and multicolor. Citizens with flags in celebration at lower right. Cornerstone devices. Back: Lybian flag and flock of doves. Watermark: Omar al-Mukhtar and value. Printer: DLR. 130x65mm.

	VF	UNC
	FV	6.00

77 5 Dinars
ND (2012). Similar to #72 but name of bank and value in English on back. Printer: DLR.

	VF	UNC
	FV	10.00

78 10 Dinars
ND (2012). Similar to #73 but name of bank and value in English on back. Printer: DLR.

	VF	UNC
	FV	20.00

78A 10 Dinars
17.2.2011. Like #78, but with date and Series 1.

	VF	UNC
a. Bank name in Arabic at Mukhtar's eye level.	FV	20.00
b. Bank name in Arabic above Mukhtar's eye level.	FV	20.00

79 20 Dinars
2012. Red and orange on multicolor underprint. School in Ghadames. Back: Al-Ateeq mosque in Oujlah. Watermark: Omar al-Mukhtar. 148x74mm.

	VF	UNC
	FV	35.00

80 50 Dinars
ND (2013). Green on multicolor underprint. 1922 Italian lighthouse in Benghazi. SPARK patch with crescent moon and star, cornerstone devices. Back: Rock arch in Tadrart Acacus. Watermark: Omar el-Mukhtar and value. Printer: TDLR. 155x77mm.

	VF	UNC
	FV	95.00

81 5 Dinars
ND (2015). Ottoman clock tower. Foil band at right showing variable images of denomination and palm tree. Optical print with "5" at lower left. Microprinting below bank name. Back: Zeus Temple in Cyrene. Pearlescent stripe with octagon stars containing "5" and cresent & star, foil segmented security thread with demetalized "5." Watermark: Cornerstones, bust of Omar Al-Mukhtar with electrotype palette with "5." 137x68mm.

	VF	UNC
	3.60	7.50

82 10 Dinars
ND (2015). Portrait of Omar Al-Mukhtar. Foil band at right showing variable images of Omar Al-Mukhtar/rearing horse and crescent & star/denomination. Optical print with "10" at lower left. Microprinting below bank name. Back: Al-Mukhtar horsemen. Pearlescent stripe with octagon stars containing "10" and crescent & star, foil segmented security thread with demetalized rearing horse and Arabic text. Watermark: Cornerstones, bust of Omar Al-Mukhtar with electrotype palette with "10." 143x71mm.

	VF	UNC
	7.20	15.00

LITHUANIA

The Republic of Lithuania southernmost of the Baltic states in east Europe, has an area of 26,173 sq. mi. (65,301 sq. km.) and a population of 3.69 million. Capital: Vilnius. The economy is based on livestock raising and manufacturing. Hogs, cattle, hides and electric motors are exported. Lithuanian lands were united under Mlinfaugas in 1236; over the next century, through alliances and conquest, Lithuania extended its territory to include most of present-day Belarus and Ukraine. By the end of the 14th century Lithuania was the largest state in Europe. An alliance with Poland in 1386 led the two countries into a union through the person of a common ruler. In 1569, Lithuania and Poland formally united into a single dual state, the Polish-Lithuanian Commonwealth. This entity survived until 1795, when its remnants were partitioned by surrounding countries. Lithuania regained its independence following World War I but was annexed by the USSR in 1940 - an action never recognized by the US and many other countries. On 11 March 1990, Lithuania became the first of the Soviet republics to declare its independence, but Moscow did not recognize this proclamation until September of 1991 (following the abortive coup in Moscow). The last Russian troops withdrew in 1993. Lithuania subsequently restructured its economy for integration into Western European institutions; it joined both NATO and the EU in the spring of 2004.

MONETARY SYSTEM:
1 Litas = 100 Centu

REPUBLIC
Lietuvos Bankas
BANK OF LITHUANIA
1991 Issue
Talonas System.

29 0.10 Talonas
1991. Brown on green and gold underprint. Plants. Back: Arms at center in gray. Watermark: Design.

	VF	UNC
a. Without 3 lines of black text at center.	1.00	3.00
b. With 3 lines of black text at center.	1.00	2.00
x. Error. As b. but with text: *PAGAL ISTATYMA* repeated.	5.00	10.00

30 0.20 Talonas
1991. Lilac on green and gold underprint. Plants, three lines of black text at center. Back: Arms at center in gray. Watermark: Design.

	VF	UNC
	1.00	4.00

31 0.50 Talonas
1991. Blue-green on green and gold underprint. Plants. Back: Arms at center in gray. Watermark: Design.

	VF	UNC
a. Without 3 lines of black text at center.	1.00	2.00
b. With 3 lines of black text at center.	1.00	4.00
x1. As b. but first word of text: *VALSTYBINIS.* (error).	—	3.00
x2. As x1 but with inverted text. (contemporary counterfeit).	—	—

32   1 (Talonas)   VF   UNC

1991. Brown on yellow-gold underprint. Value with cranberry branch at center, arms in gray at right. Counterfeiting clause at bottom. Back: Two lizards. Watermark: Large squarish diamond with symbol of the republic throughout paper.

     a. Without counterfeit text at bottom.   1.50   4.00
     b. With counterfeit text at bottom.   1.50   3.00

33   3 (Talonas)   VF   UNC

1991. Dark green and gray on blue-green, ochre and brown underprint Value with Juniper branch at center, arms in gray at right. Back: Two Grey Herons. Watermark: Large squarish diamond with symbol of the republic throughout paper.

     a. Without counterfeit text at bottom.   3.00   7.00
     b. With counterfeit text at bottom.   2.00   5.00

34   5 (Talonas)   VF   UNC

1991. Dark purple and gray on blue and gray underprint. Value with oak tree branch at center, arms in gray at right. Back: Osprey at center. Watermark: Large squarish diamond with symbol of the republic throughout paper.

     a. Without counterfeit text at bottom.   5.00   20.00
     b. With counterfeit text at bottom.   3.00   5.00

35   10 (Talonas)   VF   UNC

1991. Brown on pinkish underprint. Value with walnut tree branch at center, arms in gray at right. Counterfeiting clause at bottom. Back: Two martens. Watermark: Large squarish diamond with symbol of the republic throughout paper.

     a. Without counterfeit text at bottom.   10.00   50.00
     b. With counterfeit text at bottom.   5.00   10.00

36   25 (Talonas)   VF   UNC

1991. Purplish gray on blue and orange underprint. Value with pine tree branch at center, arms in gray at right. Counterfeiting clause at bottom. Back: Lynx. Watermark: Large squarish diamond with symbol of the republic throughout paper.

     a. Without counterfeit text at bottom.   15.00   50.00
     b. With counterfeit text at bottom.   5.00   10.00

37   50 (Talonas)   VF   UNC

1991. Green and orange on orange underprint. Value with seashore plant at center, arms in gray at right. Counterfeiting clause at bottom. Back: Moose. Watermark: Large squarish diamond with symbol of the republic throughout paper.

     a. Without counterfiet text at bottom.   10.00   40.00
     b. With counterfeit text at bottom.   5.00   10.00

38   100 (Talonas)   VF   UNC

1991. Green and brown on brown underprint. Value and dandelions at center, arms in gray at right. Counterfeiting clause at bottom. Back: European bison. Watermark: Large squarish diamond with symbol of the republic throughout paper.

     a. Without counterfeit text at bottom.   15.00   45.00
     b. With counterfeit text at bottom.   5.00   10.00
     s. Specimen. Red overprint: *PAVYZDYS*.   —   100

1992 Issue

#39-44 Smaller size

39   1 (Talonas)   VF   UNC

1992. Brown on orange and ochre underprint. Value on plant at center, dark brown shield of arms at right. Back: Two Eurasian lapwings. Watermark: Large squarish diamond with symbol of the republic throughout paper.   1.00   3.00

40   10 (Talonas)   VF   UNC

1992. Brown on tan and ochre underprint. Value on plant at center, gray shield of arms at right. Back: Nest of mistle thrush. Watermark: Large squarish diamond with symbol of the republic throughout paper.   6.00   15.00

41   50 (Talonas)   VF   UNC

1992. Dark grayish green on light green and gray underprint. Value on plant at center, dark gray-green shield of arms at right. Back: Two black grouse. Watermark: Large squarish diamond with symbol of the republic throughout paper.   15.00   45.00

42   100 (Talonas)

1992. Grayish purple on blue and red-orange underprint. Value on plant at center, gray. shield of arms at right. Back: Two otters. Watermark: Large squarish diamond with symbol of the republic throughout paper.

	VF	UNC
	8.00	18.00

43   200 (Talonas)

1992. Dark brown on red and brown underprint. Value on plant at center, gray shield of arms at right. Back: Two Red deer. Watermark: Large squarish diamond with symbol of the republic throughout paper.

	VF	UNC
a. Issued note.	8.00	18.00
x. Error. Without gray shield at right.	—	—

44   500 (Talonas)

1992. Brown-violet on blue underprint. Value on plant at center, brown shield of arms at right. Back: Bear. Watermark: Large squarish diamond with symbol of the republic throughout paper.

	VF	UNC
	3.00	8.00

1993 Issue

45   200 Talonu

1993. Brown and red on blue underprint. Value with branches at center, brown arms at left. Back: Two Red Deer. Watermark: Circle with design inside, repeated.

	VF	UNC
	2.00	8.00

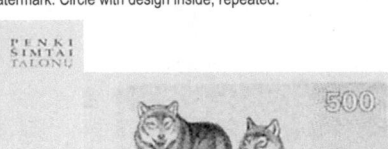

46   500 Talonu

1993. Brown on blue and brown underprint. Value with branches at center, brown arms at left. Back: Two wolves. Watermark: Circle with design inside, repeated.

	VF	UNC
	2.00	4.00

Note: #46 was withdrawn after 6 weeks.

1991 Dated Issue (1993)

47   10 Litu

1991 (1993). Brownish black and brown on tan underprint. Aviators Steponas Darius and Stasys Girénas at center. Back: Monoplane *Lituanica* at upper center, arms "Vytis" at upper right. Watermark: Arms "Vytis". Printer: USBNC (without imprint). 135x65mm.

	VF	UNC
a. *GIRENAS* name without accent dot on E (error).	10.00	30.00
b. *GIRÉNAS* name with accent dot on E.	10.00	35.00
x. Quadrupled engraved face printing. Error.	—	300

48   20 Litu

1991 (1993). Dark brown and green on violet and tan underprint. Jonas Maironis at right. Back: Liberty at left, Museum of History in Kaunas at center, arms "Vytis" at upper right. Watermark: Arms "Vytis". Printer: USBNC (without imprint). 135x65mm.

	VF	UNC
	15.00	50.00

49   50 Litu

1991 (1993). Yellowish black and brown on ochre and tan underprint. Jonas Basanavicius at right. Back: Cathedral at Vilnius at left, arms "Vytis" at upper right. Watermark: Arms "Vytis". Printer: USBNC (without imprint). 135x65mm.

	VF	UNC
a. VALDYBOS with regular L.	30.00	90.00
b. VALDYBOS with heel on L (error).	35.00	90.00

50   100 Litu

1991 (1993); 1994. Deep green, blue and brown on multicolor underprint. Arms "Vytis" at center, Simonas Daukantas at right. Back: Aerial view of University of Vinius at left center. 135x65mm.

	VF	UNC
a. 1991. One signature.	70.00	180
b. 1994. Two signatures (Not issued.)	—	—

51   500 Litu

1991. (Not issued). Arms "Vytis" at center, Vincas Kudirka at right. Back: Liberty bell. 135x65mm.

	VF	UNC
	—	—

52   1000 Litu

1991. (Not issued). Arms "Vytis" at center, Mykolas Ciurlionis at right. Back: Two Kings. 135x65mm.

	VF	UNC
a. Unissued note.	—	—
s. Specimen. Overprint: *SPECIMEN* and serial #0000000.	—	2,100

1993; 1994 Issue

53　1 Litas　　VF　UNC

1994. UV: value 1 in box fluoresce yellow, right design yellow, fibers red and green. Black and dark brown on orange and multicolor underprint. Julija Zemaite at right. Back: Shield with "Vytis" at center, old church at left. Watermark: Arms "Vytis. Printer: TDLR (without imprint). 135x65mm.

a.	Issued note.	2.00	7.00
b.	Uncut sheet of 40.	—	170
r.	Replacement note, ZZ serial # prefix.	3.00	14.00

54　2 Litai　　VF　UNC

1993. Black and dark green on pale green and multicolor underprint. Samogitian Bishop Motiejus Valancius at center right. Back: Shield with "Vytis" at center. Trakai castle at left. Watermark: Arms "Vytis. Printer: TDLR (without imprint). 135x65mm.

a.	Issued note.	5.00	12.00
b.	Uncut sheet of 40.	—	300
r.	Replacement note, ZZ serial # prefix.	5.00	20.00

55　5 Litai　　VF　UNC

1993. Purple, violet and dark blue-green on multicolor underprint. Jonas Jablonskis at center right. Back: Shield with "Vytis" at center. Mother and daughter at spinning wheel at left center. Watermark: Arms "Vytis. Printer: TDLR (without imprint). 135x65mm.

a.	Issued note.	10.00	35.00
b.	Uncut sheet of 40.	—	600
r.	Replacement note, ZZ serial # prefix.	10.00	40.00

56　10 Litu　　VF　UNC

1993. Dark blue, dark green, and brown-violet on multicolor underprint. Aviators Steponas Darius and Stasys Girénas at right. Back: Shield with "Vytis" at center, monoplane "Lituanica" at upper center. Watermark: Arms "Vytis. Printer: TDLR (without imprint). 135x65mm.

a.	Issued note.	10.00	25.00
r.	Replacement note, *(letter) as serial # prefix.	15.00	30.00

57　20 Litu　　VF　UNC

1993. Dark brown, purple and deep blue-green on multicolor underprint. Jonas Maironis at right. Back: Shield with "Vytis" at center. Liberty at left, Museum of History in Kaunas at center. Watermark: Arms "Vytis. Printer: TDLR (without imprint). 135x65mm.

a.	Issued note.	15.00	40.00
r.	Replacement note, *(letter) as serial # prefix.	20.00	45.00

58　50 Litu　　VF　UNC

1993. Dark brown, red-brown and blue-black on multicolor underprint. Jonas Basanavicius at right. Back: Shield with "Vytis" at center, Cathedral at Vilnius at left. Watermark: Arms "Vytis. Printer: TDLR (without imprint). 135x65mm.

a.	Issued note.	30.00	75.00
r.	Replacement note, *(letter) as serial # prefix.	40.00	85.00

1997-2000 Issue

59　10 Litu　　VF　UNC

1997. Dark blue, dark green and brown-violet on multicolor underprint. Aviators Steponas Darius and Stasys Girénas at right. One signature. Back: Shield with "Vytis" at center, monoplane Lituanica at upper center. Watermark: Arms "Vytis". Printer: G&D (without imprint). 135x65mm.　10.00　25.00

60   20 Litu   VF   UNC

1997. Dark brown, purple and deep green on multicolor underprint. Jonas
Maironis at right, one signature. Back: Shield with "Vytis" at center. Liberty at left,
Museum of History in Kaunas at center. Watermark: Jonas Maironis. Printer: G&D
(without imprint). 135x65mm.

10.00   35.00

61   50 Litu   VF   UNC

1998. Brown and green on ochre and multicolor underprint. Jonas Basanavicius
at right. Back: Vilnius Cathedral, belfry and Gediminas hill. Printer: G&D (without
imprint). 135x65mm.

30.00   80.00

62   100 Litu   VF   UNC

2000. Dark green and green on multicolor underprint. Simonas Daukantas at right.
Back: Vilnius's Old Town view. Printer: OFZ. 135x62mm.

FV   140

63   200 Litu   VF   UNC

1997. Dark blue on blue and multicolor underprint. Vilius Vydūnas at right, "Vytis"
at lower left center. Back: Lighthouse at left. Printer: G&D. 135x65mm.

FV   260

64   500 Litu   VF   UNC

2000. Brown and rose on multicolor underprint. Vincas Kudirka at right. Back: Bell
of Freedom of Lithuania against landscape view. Printer: G&D. 135x65mm.

FV   650

2001-03 Issue

#65-67 Replacement notes AZ serial # prefix.

65   10 Litu   VF   UNC

2001. Violet and blue on multicolor underprint. Aviators Steponas Darius and Stasys Girénas at right. One signature. Security features and an airplane hologram at
lower left. Back: Shield with "Vytis" at center, monoplane *Lituanica* at upper center.
Watermark: Vytis. Printer: OFZ. 135x65mm.

FV   18.00

66   20 Litu   VF   UNC

2001. Dark brown on multicolor underprint. Jonas Maironis at right, additional
security features. Back: Book and quill hologram at lower left. Watermark: Jonas
Maironis. Printer: OFZ. 135x65mm.

FV   33.00

67   50 Litu   VF   UNC

2003. Brown and green on ochre and multicolor underprint. Jonas Basanavicius at
right, added security features. Back: Vilnius Cathedral, belfry and Gediminas hill.
Watermark: Jonas Basanavicius. Printer: OFZ. 135x65mm.

FV   70.00

2007 Issue

68   10 Litu   **VF   UNC**
2007. Slate Blue and blue, green on multicolor underprint. Aviators Steponas   FV   12.00
Darius and Stasys Girėnas at right. Back: Monoplane *Lituabica* above clouds,
maps of North America and Europe. Watermark: Vytis Printer: G&D. 135x65mm.

69   20 Litu   **VF   UNC**
2007. Brown and lilac on multicolor underprint. Jonas Maironis at right. Back: FV   17.00
Liberty statue, Museum of History in Kaunas at center. Watermark: Jonas Maironis
Printer: G&D. 135x65mm.

70   100 Litu   **VF   UNC**
2007. Brown adn green on multicolor underprint. Simonas Daukantas at right.   FV   80.00
Back: Vilnius's old town view. Watermark: Simonas Daukantas Printer: G&D.
135x65mm.

LUXEMBOURG

The Grand Duchy of Luxembourg is located in western Europe between Belgium, Germany and France. It has an area of 998 sq. mi. (2,586 sq. km.) and a population of 430,000. Capital: Luxembourg. The economy is based on steel - Luxembourg's per capita production of 16 tons is the highest in the world. Founded in 963, Luxembourg became a grand duchy in 1815 and an independent state under the Netherlands. It lost more than half of its territory to Belgium in 1839, but gained a larger measure of autonomy. Full independence was attained in 1867. Overrun by Germany in both World Wars, it ended its neutrality in 1948 when it entered into the Benelux Customs Union and when it joined NATO the following year. In 1957, Luxembourg became one of the six founding countries of the European Economic Community (later the European Union), and in 1999 it joined the euro currency area

RULERS:
   Charlotte, 1919-64
   Jean, 1964-

MONETARY SYSTEM:
   1 Thaler = 30 Groschen
   1 Mark = 100 Pfennig = 1 Franc (Frankon) 25 Centimes
   1 Franc = 100 Centimes, to 2001
   1 Euro = 100 Cents, 2001-

GRAND DUCHY
Banque Internationale a Luxembourg
INTERNATIONAL BANK IN LUXEMBOURG
1968 Issue

14   100 Francs   **VF   UNC**
1.5.1968. Green-blue and blue on multicolor underprint. Tower at left, portrait Grand
Duke Jean at right. Back: Steelworks and dam. Watermark: *BIL*. Printer: F-CO.
   a. Issued note.   4.00   15.00
   s. Specimen.   —   65.00

1981 Issue

14A   100 Francs   **VF   UNC**
8.3.1981. Brown and tan on multicolor underprint. Bridge to Luxembourg City at left,   3.50   12.50
Grand Duke Jean at right, Prince Henry of the Netherlands in the background. Back:
Two stylized female figures swirling around watermark area. Watermark: *BIL*.

Grand Duché de Luxembourg
1961; 1963 Issue

51   50 Francs   **VF   UNC**

6.2.1961. Brown on multicolor underprint. Portrait of Grand Duchess Charlotte
at right. Back: Landscape with combine harvester. Watermark: Grand Duchess
Charlotte.

    a. Issued note.   4.00   10.00
    s. Specimen, punched hole cancelled.   —   45.00

52   100 Francs   **VF   UNC**

18.9.1963. Dark red on multicolor underprint. Portrait of Grand Duchess Charlotte
at right. Back: Hydroelectric dam. Watermark: Grand Duchess Charlotte.

    a. Issued note.   10.00   30.00
    s. Specimen, punched hole cancelled.   —   65.00

54   20 Francs   **VF   UNC**

7.3.1966. Blue on multicolor underprint. Grand Duke Jean at left center. Back:
Moselle River with dam and lock.

    a. Issued note.   2.25   5.00
    s. Specimen, punched hole cancelled.   —   250

52A   500 Francs   **VF   UNC**

ND. Specimen only. Portrait of Grand Duchess Charlotte at right. Back: Ducal
Palace. Watermark: Grand Duchess Charlotte.   —   2,400

55   50 Francs   **VF   UNC**

25.8.1972. . Dark brown on multicolor underprint. Grand Duke Jean at left center,
guilloche underprint at left. Back: Factory.

    a. Signature title: *LE MINISTRE DES FINANCES.*   4.00   8.50
    b. Signature title: *LE MINISTRE D'ÉTAT.*   3.50   7.00
    s. As a. Specimen, punched hole cancelled.   —   175

52B   1000 Francs   **VF   UNC**

ND. Specimen only. Portrait of Grand Duchess Charlotte at right. Back: Crowned
and mantled arms at center. Watermark: Grand Duchess Charlotte.   —   3,000

56   100 Francs   **VF   UNC**

15.7.1970. Red on multicolor underprint. Grand Duke Jean at left center Back:
View of Adolphe Bridge.

    a. Issued note.   4.00   12.50
    s. Specimen, punched hole cancelled.   —   50.00

1966-72 Issue

1980 Issue

53   10 Francs   **VF   UNC**

20.3.1967. Green on mujlticolor underprint. Grand Duke Jean at left center. Back:
Grand Duchess Charlotte Bridge in city.

    a. Issued note.   2.25   5.00
    s. Specimen, punched hole cancelled.   —   75.00

57 100 Francs   **VF UNC**
14.8.1980. Brownish red on multicolor underprint. Grand Duke Jean at center right, building at left. Signature varieties. Back: City of Luxembourg scene.
     a. Issued note.   4.50   7.50
     s. Specimen.   —   140

Institut Monetaire Luxembourgeois

SIGNATURE VARIETIES		
MINISTRE DU TRESOR		
1	J. Poos	2 J. Santer

1985-93 ND Issue

58 100 Francs   **VF UNC**
ND (1986). Red on multicolor underprint. Grand Duke Jean at center right, building at left. Back: City of Luxembourg scene. Watermark: Grand Duke Jean. 142x76mm.
     a. Without symbol. Signature 1. Series A-K.   FV   6.50
     b. With symbol. Signature 2. Series L-.   FV   4.50

59 1000 Francs   **VF UNC**
ND (1985). Brown on multicolor underprint. Grand Duke Jean at center right. Castle of Vianden at left. Back: Building sketches at center right. Watermark: Grand Duke Jean. 153x76mm.
     a. Issued note.   FV   65.00
     s. Specimen.   —   300

60 5000 Francs   **VF UNC**
ND(1993); 1996. Green, orange and olive-green on brown and multicolor underprint. Grand Duke Jean at center right. Chateau de Clevaux at left. Two signature varieties. Back: 17th century map, European Center at Luxembourg-Kirchberg at center right on back. Watermark: Grand Duke Jean. 160x76mm.
     a. Serial # prefix A. ND.   200   325
     b. Serial # Prefix B. 10.1996.   FV   235

Note: For later issues used in Luxembourg see European Union listings.

MACAU

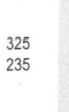

The Macau R.A.E.M., a former Portuguese overseas province located in the South China Sea 35 miles (56 km.) southwest of Hong Kong, consists of the peninsula and the islands of Taipa and Coloane. It has an area of 14 sq. mi. (21.45 sq. km.) and a population of 415,850. Capital: Macau. The economy is based on tourism, gambling, commerce and gold trading - Macau is one of the few entirely free markets for gold in the world. Cement, textiles, vegetable oils and metal products are exported. Established by the Portuguese in 1557, Macau is the oldest European settlement in the Far East. Pursuant to an agreement signed by China and Portugal on 13 April 1987, Macau became the Macau R.A.E.M. of the People's Republic of China on 20 December 1999. In this agreement, China promised that, under its *one country, two systems* formula, China's socialist economic system would not be practiced in Macau, and that Macau would enjoy a high degree of autonomy in all matters except foreign and defense affairs for the next 50 years.

RULERS:
     Portuguese from 1849-1999

MONETARY SYSTEM:
     1 Dollar = 100 Cents
     1 Pataca = 100 Avos

PORTUGUESE ADMINISTRATION

Banco Nacional Ultramarino

大西洋國海外滙理銀行

Ta Hsi Yang Kuo Hai Wai Hui Li Yin Hang

1963-68 Issue

49 5 Patacas   **VF UNC**
21.3.1968. Brown on multicolor underprint. Portrait of Bishop D. Belchior Carneiro at lower right. Bank seal with sailing ship at left. Signature varieties. Back: Woman and sailing ships at center. Watermark: Bishop D. Belchior Carneiro. Printer: BWC.
     a. Issued note.   50.00   350
     s. Specimen.   —   495

50 10 Patacas   **VF UNC**
8.4.1963. Deep blue-violet on multicolor underprint. Portrait of Bishop D. Belchior Carneiro at lower right. Bank seal with sailing ship at left. Signature varieties. Back: Woman and sailing ships at center. Watermark: Bishop D. Belchior Carneiro. Printer: BWC.
     a. Issued note.   30.00   180
     s. Specimen.   —   250

51   100 Patacas

18.1966. Brown on multicolor underprint. Portrait M. de Arriaga Brum da Silveira at right. Back: Arms at left, flag atop archway at center. Printer: TDLR.

	VF	UNC
a. Issued note.	600	3,000
s. Specimen.	—	1,500

52   500 Patacas

8.4.1963. Green on multicolor underprint. Portrait of Bishop D. Belchior Carneiro at lower right. Bank seal with sailing ship at left. Back: Woman and sailing ships at center. Watermark: Bishop D. Belchior Carneiro. Printer: BWC.

	VF	UNC
a. Issued note.	300	2,500
s. Specimen.	—	1,200

1973 Issue

53   100 Patacas

13.12.1973. Deep blue-violet on multicolor underprint. Ruins of S. Paulo Cathedral at right. Signature titles: *GOVERNADOR* and *ADMINISTRADOR* above signs. Back: Junk at left, bank seal with sailing ship at center. Watermark: S. Paulo Cathedral.

	VF	UNC
a. Issued note.	200	1,500
s. Specimen.	—	800

1976-79 Issue

54   5 Patacas

18.11.1976. Brown on multicolor underprint. Portrait of Bishop D. Belchior Carneiro at lower left. Bank seal with sailing ship at left, with text: *CONSELHO DE GESTAO* at center. Signature varieties. Back: Woman and sailing ships at center. Watermark: Bishop D. Belchior Carneiro. Printer: BWC.

	VF	UNC
a. Issued note.	23.00	125
s. Specimen.	—	380

55   10 Patacas

7.12.1977. Deep blue-violet on multicolor underprint. Portrait of Bishop D. Belchior Carneiro at lower right. Bank seal with sailing ship at left, with text: *CONSELHO DE GESTAO* at center. Back: Woman and sailing ships at center. Watermark: Bishop D. Belchior Carneiro. Printer: BWC.

	VF	UNC
a. Issued note.	25.00	130
s. Specimen.	—	220

56   50 Patacas

1.9.1976. Greenish-gray on multicolor underprint. Portrait L. de Camoes at right, with text: *CONSELHO DE GESTAO* at center. Back: Bank seal with sailing ship at left, woman and sailing ships at center.

	VF	UNC
a. Issued note.	250	900
s. Specimen.	—	600

57   100 Patacas

8.6.1979. Blue on multicolor underprint. Ruins of S. Paulo Cathedral at right, with text: *CONSELHO DE GESTAO* at center. Signature title: *PRESIDENTE* at left signature. Back: Junk at left, bank seal with sailing ship at center. Watermark: Ruins of S. Paulo Cathedral.

	VF	UNC
a. Issued note.	160	1,100
s. Specimen.	—	1,000

60   50 Patacas

8.8.1981. Purple on multicolor underprint. Portrait of L. de Camoes at right. Back: Bank seal with sailing ship at left, 19th century harbor scene. Watermark: L. de Camoes.

	VF	UNC
a. With signature title: *PRESIDENTE* at left.	50.00	200
b. Without signature title: *PRESIDENTE* at left.	30.00	160
s1. As a. Specimen.	—	300
s2. As b. Specimen.	—	300

57A   500 Patacas

	VF	UNC

24.4.1979. Green on multicolor underprint. Portrait of Bishop D. Belchior Carneiro at lower right. Bank seal with sailing ship at left. Back: Woman and sailing ships at center. Watermark: Portrait of Bishop D. Belchior Carneiro. Printer: BWC.

	VF	UNC
a. Issued note.	300	2,200
s. Specimen. 2 different signature varieties at right hand side.	—	1,100

1981; 1988 Issue

58   5 Patacas

8.8.1981. Green on multicolor underprint. Temple at right. Back: Bank seal with sailing ship at left, 19th century harbor scene.

	VF	UNC
a. With signature title: *PRESIDENTE* at left.	13.00	70.00
b. With signature title: *VICE-PRESIDENTE* at left.	13.00	60.00
c. Without signature title: *PRESIDENTE* at left.	13.00	60.00
s. As b. Specimen.	—	200

61   100 Patacas

1981; 1984. Blue and purple on multicolor underprint. Portrait of C. Pessanha at right. Back: Bank seal with sailing ship at left, 19th century harbor scene. Watermark: C. Pessanha.

	VF	UNC
a. With signature title: *PRESIDENTE* at left. 8.8.1981; 12.5.1984.	70.00	350
b. Without signature title: *PRESIDENTE* at left. 8.8.1981; 12.5.1984.	30.00	250
s1. As a. Specimen. 8.8.1981; 12.5.1984.	—	350
s2. As b. Specimen. 2 signature varieties. 8.8.1981.	—	350

59   10 Patacas

1981; 1984. Brown on multicolor underprint. Lighthouse with flag at right. Back: Bank seal with sailing ship at left, 19th century harbor scene.

	VF	UNC
a. With signature title: *PRESIDENTE* at left. 2 decrees at upper left. 8.8.1981.	20.00	60.00
b. As a. Without signature title at left. 8.8.1981.	16.00	60.00
c. Signature title as a. 3 decrees at upper left. 12.5.1984.	16.00	30.00
d. With signature title: *VICE-PRESIDENTE* at left. 8.8.1981, 12.5.1984.	16.00	30.00
e. Without signature title under signature at left. 3 signature varieties. 12.5.1984.	16.00	30.00
s1. As a. Specimen.	—	220
s2. As d. Specimen.	—	220

62   500 Patacas

1981; 1984. Olive-green on multicolor underprint. Portrait V. de Morais at right. Back: Bank seal with sailing ship at left, 19th century harbor scene.

	VF	UNC
a. 8.8.1981; 12.5.1984. Signature title: *PRESIDENTE* at left.	110	900
a1. 8.8.1981. Signature title: *VICE-PRESIDENTE*.	110	900
b. 8.8.1981; 12.5.1984. Signature title: *ADMINISTRADOR* at left.	110	750
s1. As a. Specimen.	—	550
s2. As b. Specimen.	—	550
s3. Specimen. 12.5.1984. Signature title: *VICE-PRESIDENTE* at left.	—	800

63 1000 Patacas VF UNC
1988. Brown and yellow-orange on multicolor underprint. Stylized dragon at right.
Back: Modern view of bridge to Macau.

    a. Issued note. 170 645
    s. Specimen. — 850

1988 Commemorative Issue
#64, 35th Anniversary Grand Prix

64 10 Patacas VF UNC
11.26-27.1988 (- old date 1984). Issued in a small folder. Black overprint at left on
face of #59c. Back: Black overprint at center. 140x69mm. 15.00 50.00

1990-96 Issue

65 10 Patacas VF UNC
8.7.1991. Brown and olive-green on multicolor underprint. Building at right.
Back: Bank seal with sailing ship at left, bridge and city view. Watermark: Junk.
140x69mm.

    a. Issued note. 6.00 10.00
    s. Specimen. — 120

66 20 Patacas VF UNC
1.9.1996. Lilac and purple on light green and multicolor underprint. B.N.U. building
at right, facing dragons in border at left and right. Back: Bank seal with sailing ship
at left, bridge and city view. Watermark: Junk. 143x71mm.

    a. Issued note. 6.00 15.00
    s. As a. Specimen. — 300

67 50 Patacas VF UNC
13.7.1992. Olive-brown on multicolor underprint. Holiday marcher with dragon
costume at center right, man at right. Back: Bank seal with sailing ship at left,
bridge and city view. Watermark: Junk. 149x75mm.

    a. Issued note. 15.00 25.00
    s. As a. Specimen. — 350

68 100 Patacas VF UNC
13.7.1992. Black on multicolor underprint. Early painting of Settlement at center,
junk at right. Back: Bank seal with sailing ship at left, bridge and city view.
Watermark: Junk. 154x76mm.

    a. Issued note. FV 40.00
    s. As a. Specimen. — 500

69 500 Patacas VF UNC
3.9.1990. Olive-green on multicolor underprint. Building at right. Two signature
varieties. Back: Bank seal with sailing ship at left, bridge and city view. Watermark:
Junk. 160x80mm.

    a. Issued note. FV 280
    s1. Specimen. Signature as a. Serial # AA00000. — 500
    s2. Specimen. Signature different. Serial # AW00000. — 500

70 1000 Patacas | VF UNC

8.7.1991. Brown and yellow-orange on multicolor underprint. Stylized dragon at right. Two signature varieties. Back: Bank seal with sailing ship at left, bridge and city view. Watermark: Junk. 164x82mm.

    a. 8.7.1991. Signature title at left: *ADMINISTRATOR*. Serial # prefix AP. — FV 400

    b. 8.7.1991. Signature title at left: *PRESIDENTE*. Serial # prefix AQ. — FV 350

    s. As b. Specimen but different signature. Serial # AF00000. — — 700

SPECIAL ADMINISTRATIVE REGION

Banco Nacional Ultramarino

Ta Hsi Yang Kuo Hai Wai Hui Li Yin Hang

1999 Issue

All notes issued since 20 December 1999 are issued under Macau as a Special Administrative Region in China.

71 20 Patacas | VF UNC

20.12.1999. Lilac and purple on light green and multicolor underprint. B.N.U. building at right, facing dragons in border at left and right. Back: Bank seal with sailing ship at left, bridge and city view. Watermark: Junk.

    a. Issued note. — FV 25.00

    b. Uncut sheet of 12. Serial # prefix *JJ* or *KK*. — — 255

    s. As a. Specimen. — — 150

72 50 Patacas | VF UNC

10.12.1999. Olive-brown on multicolor underprint. Holiday marcher with dragon costume at center right, man at right. Back: Bank seal with sailing ship at left, bridge and city view. Watermark: Junk.

    a. Issued note. — FV 25.00

    b. Uncut sheet of 12. Serial # prefix: *CC*. — — 450

    s. As a. Specimen. — — 200

73 100 Patacas | VF UNC

20.12.1999. Black on multicolor underprint. Early painting of Settlement at center, junk at right. Back: Bank seal with sailing ship at left, bridge and city view. Watermark: Junk.

    a. Issued note. — FV 120

    s. Specimen. — — 250

74 500 Patacas | VF UNC

20.12.1999. Olive-green on multicolor underprint. Building at right. Two signature varieties. Back: Bank seal with sailing ship at left, bridge and city view. Watermark: Junk.

    a. Issued note. — FV 200

    s. Specimen. — — 450

75 1000 Patacas | VF UNC

20.12.1999. Brown and yellow-orange on multicolor underprint. Stylized dragon at right. Back: Bank seal with sailing ship at left, bridge and city view. Watermark: Junk.

    a. Signature title: *PRESIDENTE*. — FV 450

    b. Signature title: *ADMINISTRADOR*. — FV 440

    s. Specimen. As a. — — 500

2001 Issue

76 10 Patacas | VF UNC

8.1.2001. Dark red and orange with multicolor underprint. Building at right. Back: Bank seal with sailing ship at left, bridge and city view. Watermark: Junk.

    a. Signature title: *PRESIDENTE*. — FV 10.00

    b. Signature title: *ADMINISTRATOR* — FV 8.00

    c. Uncut sheet of 4. Archive use only. — — —

    d. Uncut sheet of 40. — — 350

    s. As a. Specimen. Overprint on both sides. — — 200

2003 Issue

77   10 Patacas   **VF   UNC**

8.6.2003. Dark red and orange on multicolor underprint. Building at right. Back: FV   8.00
Bank seal with sailing ship at left, bridge and city view. Watermark: Junk.

78   100 Patacas   **VF   UNC**

8.6.2003. Black on multicolor underprint. Early painting of Settlement at center,   FV   30.00
junk at right. Back: Bank seal with sailing ship at left, bridge and city view.
Watermark: Junk.

79   500 Patacas   **VF   UNC**

8.6.2003. Olive-green on multicolor underprint. Building at right. Back: Bank seal   FV   180
with sailing ship at left, bridge and city view. Watermark: Junk.

2005; 2009 Issue

80   10 Patacas   **VF   UNC**

2005; 2010; 2013. Orange and rose. Goddess A-ma at left. Back: B.N.U. headquarters building at left.
   a. 8.8.2005 (2006).   FV   8.00
   b. 8.8.2010.   FV   8.00
   c. 11.11.2013.   FV   8.00

81   20 Patacas   **VF   UNC**

8.8.2005; 8.8.2010; 11.11.2013. Blue and grey. Macau International Airport runway
and terminal. Back: B.N.U. headquarters building at left.
   a. 8.8.2005.   FV   10.00
   b. 8.8.2010.   FV   10.00
   c. 11.11.2013.   FV   10.00

81A   50 Patacas   **VF   UNC**

2009; 2013. Olive-brown on multicolor underprint. Holiday Marcher with dragon
costume at center right, amn at right. Back: Bank seal with sailing ship at left,
bridge and city view. Watermark: Junk.
   a. 8.8.2009.   FV   12.00
   b. 11.11.2013.   FV   45.00

82   100 Patacas   **VF   UNC**

8.8.2005 (2006); 11.11.2013. Purple and blue. *Largo do Senado* at right. Back:
B.N.U. headquarters building at left.
   a. 8.8.2005 (2006).   FV   20.00
   b. 8.8.2010.   FV   20.00
   c. 11.11.2013.   FV   20.00

83   500 Patacas   **VF   UNC**

8.8.2005 (2006); 8.8.2010. Green and aqua. *Torre de Macau* at left. Back: B.N.U.
headquarters building at left.
   a. 8.8.2005 (2006).   FV   180
   b. 8.8.2010.   FV   180

84 1000 Patacas   **VF UNC**
8.8.2005 (2006); 8.8.2010. Orange and yellow. Cultural Center at right. Back:
B.N.U. headquarters building at left.
    a. 8.8.2005 (2006).   FV 200
    b. 8.8.2010.   FV 200

85 10 Patacas   **VF UNC**
1.1.2012. Year of the Dragon Commemorative. 140x69   FV 8.00

86 10 Patacas   **VF UNC**
1.1.2013. Year of the Snake Commemorative. 140x69mm.   FV 8.00

2012-Present Lunar Year Commemorative Issue

87 10 Patacas   **VF UNC**
1.1.2014. Year of the Horse Commemorative. 140x69mm.   FV 8.00

88 10 Patacas   **VF UNC**
1.1.2015. Year of the Goat commemorative. 140x69mm.   FV 8.00

Banco da China

Chung Kuo Yin Hang

1995; 1996 Issue

90 10 Patacas   **VF UNC**
16.10.1995. Dark brown and deep green on multicolor underprint. Farel de Guia   FV 15.00
lighthouse at right. Back: Bank of China - Macau building at left, lotus blossom at
lower center. Watermark: Lotus blossom(s). 140x69mm.

91 20 Patacas   **VF UNC**
1.9.1996. Purple and violet on multicolor underprint. Ama Temple at right. Back:
Bank of China - Macau building at left, lotus blossom at lower center. Watermark:
Lotus blossom(s). 143x72mm.
    a. Issued note.   FV 15.00
    r. Replacement note. Serial # prefix CZ.   FV 30.00

92 50 Patacas   **VF UNC**
1995; 1997. Black, dark brown and brown on multicolor underprint. University
of Macao at right. Back: Bank of China - Macau building at left, lotus blossom at
lower center. Watermark: Lotus blossom(s). 149x74mm.
    a. 16.10.1995.   FV 35.00
    b. 1.11.1997.   FV 30.00

93 100 Patacas   **VF UNC**
16.10.1995. Black, brown and purple on multicolor underprint. New terminal of   FV 35.00
Port Exterior at right. Back: Bank of China - Macau building at left, lotus blossom
at lower center. Watermark: Lotus blossom(s). 152x76mm.

94 500 Patacas   **VF UNC**
16.10.1995. Dark green and dark blue on multicolor underprint. Ponte de Amizade   FV 300
bridge at right. Back: Bank of China - Macau building at left, lotus blossom at
lower center. Watermark: Lotus blossom(s). 158x80mm.

95 1000 Patacas   **VF UNC**
16.10.1995. Brown, orange and red on multicolor underprint. Aerial view of Praia   FV 350
Oeste at right. Back: Bank of China - Macau building at left, lotus blossom at lower
center. Watermark: Lotus blossom(s). 164x82mm.

1999 Issue

All notes issued since 20 December 1999 are issued under Macau as a Special Administrative Region in China.

96   20 Patacas — VF UNC — FV 12.00
20.12.1999. Purple and violet on multicolor underprint. Ama Temple at right. Back: Bank of China - Macau building at left, lotus blossom at lower center. Watermark: Lotus blossom(s).

97   50 Patacas — VF UNC — FV 20.00
20.12.1999. Black, dark brown and brown on multicolor underprint. University of Macao at right. Back: Bank of China - Macau building at left, lotus blossom at lower center. Watermark: Lotus blossom(s).

98   100 Patacas — VF UNC
1999; 2002. Black, brown and purple on multicolor underprint. New terminal of Port Exterior at right. Back: Bank of China - Macau building at left, lotus blossom at lower center. Watermark: Lotus blossom(s).
- a. 20.12.1999. — FV 75.00
- b. 2.2.2002. — FV 70.00

99   500 Patacas — VF UNC
1999; 2002. Dark green and dark blue on multicolor underprint. Ponte de Amizade bridge at right. Back: Bank of China - Macau building at left, lotus blossom at lower center. Watermark: Lotus blossom(s).
- a. 20.12.1999. — FV 260
- b. 2.2.2002. — FV 280

100   1000 Patacas — VF UNC — FV 400
20.12.1999. Brown, orange and red on multicolor underprint. Aerial view of Praia Oeste at right. Back: Bank of China - Macau building at left, lotus blossom at lower center. Watermark: Lotus blossom(s).

2001 Issue

101   10 Patacas — VF UNC
2001; 2002. Red and orange on multicolor underprint. Farel de Guia lighthouse at right. Back: Bank of China - Macau building at left, lotus blossom at lower center. Watermark: Lotus blossom(s).
- a. 8.1.2001. — FV 6.00
- b. 2.2.2002. — FV 5.00
- c. Uncut sheet of 30. 8.1.2001. — — 300

2003 Issue

102   10 Patacas — VF UNC — FV 5.00
8.12.2003 (2004). Red and orange on multicolor underprint. Ama Temple at right. Back: Bank of China - Macau building at left, lotus blossom at lower center. Watermark: Lotus blossom(s).

103   20 Patacas
8.12.2003 (2005). Black, dark brown and brown on multicolor underprint. University of Macao at right. Back: Bank of China - Macau building at left, lotus blossom at lower center. Watermark: Lotus blossom(s).

VF   UNC
FV   10.00

104   100 Patacas
8.12.2003 (2005). Black, brown and purple on multicolor underprint. New terminal of Port Exterior at right. Back: Bank of China - Macau building at left, lotus blossom at lower center. Watermark: Lotus blossom(s).

VF   UNC
FV   60.00

105   500 Patacas
8.12.2003 (2005). Dark green and dark blue on multicolor underprint. Ponte de Amizade bridge at right. Back: Bank of China - Macau building at left, lotus blossom at lower center. Watermark: Lotus blossom(s).

VF   UNC
FV   200

106   1000 Patacas
8.12.2003 (2005). Brown, orange and red on multicolor underprint. Aerial view of Praia Oeste at right. Back: Bank of China - Macau building at left, lotus blossom at lower center. Watermark: Lotus blossom(s).

VF   UNC
FV   520

2008 Commemorative Issue

107   20 Patacas
3.5.2008. Lilac and blue on multicolor underprint. Bank of China Headquarters, calassical Greek column, Beijing olympic logo in red. Back: Beijing Olympic stadium *the Bird's Nest* at left. Watermark: Stadium and value.

VF   UNC

a. Issued note   FV   20.00
b. In original folder with matching serial # Hong Kong note.   —   175

2008 Issue

108   10 Patacas
2008; 2013. Rose on yellow underprint. A-Ma Miu temple of Barra at right center. Back: Bank of China - Macau building at left center. 140x69mm.

VF   UNC

a. 8.8.2008.   FV   5.00
b. 1.7.2013.   FV   5.00

109   20 Patacas
2008; 2013. Purple. São Paulo Cathedral ruins. Back: Bank of China - Macau building at left center. 143x72mm.

VF   UNC

a. 8.8.2008.   FV   6.00
b. 1.7.2013.   FV   6.00

110 50 Patacas   VF   UNC
2008; 2013. Purple. Dom Pedro V theatre at center right. Back: Bank of China -
Macau building at left center. 149x75mm.
    a. 8.8.2008.   FV   20.00
    b. 1.7.2013.   FV   20.00

111 100 Patacas   VF   UNC
2008; 2013. Light blue on green underprint. Lighthouse at right center. Back: Bank
of China - Macau building at left center. 152x76mm.
    a. 8.8.2008.   FV   25.00
    b. 1.7.2013.   FV   25.00

112 500 Patacas   VF   UNC
8.8.2008. Green on blue underprint. Mandarin House at right center. Back: Bank   FV   195
of China - Macau building at left center. 158x80mm.

113 1000 Patacas   VF   UNC
2008; 2013. Yellow orange on multicolor underprint. Senate's palace at right.
Back: Bank of China - Macau building at left center. 163x81mm.
    a. 8.8.2008.   FV   200
    b. 1.7.2013.   FV   200

2012 Commemorative Issue

114 10 Patacas   VF   UNC
1.1.2012. Year of the Dragon Commemorative. 140x69mm.   FV   8.00

115 10 Patacas   VF   UNC
2012. Orange on multicolor underprint. Bank of China building. Back: (Vertical.)   FV   8.00
Lotus flowers center. Watermark: Lotus flower and 100. 153x76mm.

2013-Present Lunar Year Commemorative Issue

116 10 Patacas   VF   UNC
1.1.2013. Year of the Snake Commemorative. 138x69mm.   FV   8.00

117 10 Patacas   VF   UNC
1.1.2014. Year of the Horse Commemorative. 138x69mm.   FV   8.00

118 10 Patacas   VF   UNC
1.1.2015. Year of the Goat Commemorative. 138x69mm.   FV   8.00

COLLECTOR SERIES

Banco Nacional Ultramarino
1999 Issue

CS1 20-1000 Patacas   Mkt. Value
One each of #71-74 in a special folder. Matching serial #.   930

Banco Da China and Banco Nacional Ultramarino
2001 Issue

CS2 10 Pataca Sheetlets of 4   Mkt. Value
One mini-sheet from each bank in a special folder.   230

2011 Issue

CS3 100 Patacas   VF   UNC
2011. 100th anniversary of Bank of China.   FV   130

MACEDONIA

The Republic of Macedonia is land-locked, and is bordered in the north by Yugoslavia, to the east by Bulgaria, in the south by Greece and to the west by Albania. It has an area of 9,923 sq. mi. (25,713 sq. km.) and its population at the 1991 census was 2.23 million. of which the predominating ethnic groups were Macedonians. The capital is Skopje.Macedonia gained its independence peacefully from Yugoslavia in 1991, but Greece's objection to the new state's use of what it considered a Hellenic name and symbols delayed international recognition, which occurred under the provisional designation of "the Former Yugoslav Republic of Macedonia." In 1995, Greece lifted a 20-month trade embargo and the two countries agreed to normalize relations. The United States began referring to Macedonia by its constitutional name, Republic of Macedonia, in 2004 and negotiations continue between Greece and Macedonia to resolve the name issue. Some ethnic Albanians, angered by perceived political and economic inequities, launched an insurgency in 2001 that eventually won the support of the majority of Macedonia's Albanian population and led to the internationally-brokered Framework Agreement, which ended the fighting by establishing a set of new laws enhancing the rights of minorities. Fully implementating the Framework Agreement and stimulating economic growth and development continue to be challenges for Macedonia, although progress has been made on both fronts over the past several years.

MONETARY SYSTEM:
1 дННАР (Denar) = 100 дННИ (Deni)

REPUBLIC

НАРОДНА БАНКА НА ЬАКНдОНИЈА
National Bank of Macedonia
1992 Issue

1 10 (Denar)   VF   UNC
1992. Pale blue on lilac underprint. Farmers harvesting at left. Back: Ilenden
monument in Krushevo at left. Watermark: Design.
    a. Issued note.   0.20   0.75
    s. Specimen. Red overprint ПРИЬНРОК.   —   —

2 25 (Denar)   VF   UNC
1992. Red on lilac underprint. Farmers harvesting at left. Back: Ilenden monument
in Krushevo at left. Watermark: Design.
    a. Issued note.   0.20   1.00
    s. Specimen.   —   —

3   50 (Denar)   VF   UNC
1992. Brown on ochre underprint. Farmers harvesting at left. Back: Ilenden monument in Krushevo at left. Watermark: Design.
    a. Issued note.   0.20   1.00
    s. Specimen.   —   —

4   100 (Denar)   VF   UNC
1992. Blue-gray on light blue underprint. Farmers harvesting at left. Back: Ilenden monument in Krushevo at left. Watermark: Design.
    a. Issued note.   0.20   1.00
    s. Specimen.   —   —

5   500 (Denar)   VF   UNC
1992. Bright green on ochre underprint. Farmers harvesting at left. Back: Ilenden monument in Krushevo at left. Watermark: Design.
    a. Issued note.   0.20   1.25
    s. Specimen.   —   —

6   1000 (Denar)   VF   UNC
1992. Dull blue-violet on pink underprint. Farmers harvesting at left. Back: Ilenden monument in Krushevo at left. Watermark: Design.
    a. Issued note.   0.75   1.75
    s. Specimen.   —   —

7   5000 (Denar)   VF   UNC
1992. Deep brown and dull red on multicolor underprint. Woman at desk top computer at center. Back: Ilenden monument at left. Watermark: Design.
    a. Issued note.   1.50   6.00
    s. Specimen.   —   —

8   10,000 (Denar)   VF   UNC
1992. Blue-black on pink and gray underprint. Buildings at center right. Back: Musicians at left of Ilenden monument at center right. Watermark: Design.
    a. Issued note.   2.50   8.50
    s. Specimen.   —   —

НАРОДНА БАНКА НА РНПУБЛИКА ЬАКНДОНИЈА
National Bank of the Republic of Macedonia
1993 Issue
Currency Reform 1 "New" Denar = 100 "Old" Denars

9   10 Denari   VF   UNC
1993. Light blue on multicolor underprint. Houses on mountainside in Krushevo at center right. Back: Ilenden monument at left center Watermark: Ilenden monument.
    a. Issued note.   FV   1.50
    s. Specimen.   —   15.00

10 20 Denari VF UNC

1993. Wine-red on multicolor underprint. 16th century Tower in Skopje in vertical
format. Back: Turkish bath in Skopje at left center. Watermark: Ilenden monument.

a. Issued note.	FV	2.50
s. Specimen.	—	15.00

11 50 Denari VF UNC

1993. Light red on multicolor underprint. National Bank building in Skopje at right.
Back: 12th century Orthodox Church of St. Pantileimon at left. Watermark: Ilenden
monument.

a. Issued note.	FV	4.00
s. Specimen.	—	15.00

12 100 Denari VF UNC

1993. Brown on multicolor underprint. Bovev Palace, National Museum in Ohrid
at right. Back: 11th century Monastery of St. Sophia in Ohrid at left. Watermark:
Ilenden monument.

a. Issued note.	FV	8.00
s. Specimen.	—	15.00

13 500 Denari VF UNC

1993. Greenish on multicolor underprint. Ohrid castle ruins at upper center. Back:
12th century Orthodox church of St. John in Ohrid at left. Watermark: 12th century
Orthodox church of St. John in Ohrid.

a. Issued note.	FV	35.00
s. Specimen.	—	15.00

1996 Issue

14 10 Denari VF UNC

8.9.1996-12.2011. UV: fibers fluoresce yellow, blue and green. Deep olive-green
with black text on multicolor underprint. Statue torso of Goddess Isida at right.
Back: Mosaic of branch over peacock and duck. Watermark: Statue torso of
Goddess Isida. 140x70mm.

a. 8.9.1996. Two signatrues at bottom left.	FV	1.75
b. 8.1997.	FV	1.50
c. 1.2001. One signature at bottom left.	FV	1.50
d. 1.2003.	FV	1.50
e. 1.2005. New signature.	FV	1.50
f. 1.2006.	FV	1.00
g. 1.2007.	FV	1.00
h. 1.2008.	FV	1.00
i. 12.2011.	FV	1.00
Specimen.	—	20.00

15 50 Denari VF UNC

8.9.1996-1.2007. UV: fibers fluoresce yellow, blue and green. Brown with black
text on multicolor underprint. Byzantine copper follis of Anastasia at center right.
Back: Archangel Gabriel at left center. Watermark: Byzantine copper follis of
Anastasia. 143x70mm.

a. 8.9.1996. Two signatures at bottom left.	FV	3.00
b. 8.1997.	FV	3.00
c. 1.2001. One signature at bottom left.	FV	3.00
d. 1.2003.	FV	3.00
e. 1.2007. New signature.	FV	3.00
s. Specimen.	—	20.00

16 100 Denari VF UNC

8.9.1996-2009. Brown with purple text on multicolor underprint. Large baroque wooden ceiling rosette in Debar town house at center right. Back: J. Harevin's engraving of Skopje "seen" through town house window frame at left center. Watermark: Large baroque wooden ceiling rosette. 146x70mm.

a. 8.9.1996. Two signatures at bottom left.	FV	5.00
b. 8.1997.	FV	5.00
c. 1.2000.	FV	5.00
d. 1.2002. One signature at bottom left.	FV	5.00
e. 5.2004.	FV	5.00
f. 1.2005. New Signature.	FV	5.00
g. 1.2007.	FV	5.00
h. 9.2008.	FV	5.00
i. 1.2009.	FV	5.00
j. 12.2013.	FV	5.00
s. Specimen.	—	25.00

17 500 Denari VF UNC

1996; 2014. Black and violet on multicolor underprint. 6th century golden death mask, Trebenista, Ohrid at right. Back: Violet poppy flower and plant at left center. Watermark: 6th century golden death mask, Trebenista, Ohrid. 149x70mm.

a. 8.9.1996.	FV	22.50
b. 12.2014.	FV	22.50
s. Specimen.	—	25.00

18 1000 Denari VF UNC

8.9.1996. Brown and orange on multicolor underprint. 14th century icon of Madonna Episkepsis and Christ Child, church of St. Vrach-Mali, Ohrid at center right. Back: Partial view of the St. Sophia church in Ohrid at left center. Watermark: Madonna. 152x70mm.

a. Issued note.	FV	40.00
s. Specimen.	—	30.00

19 5000 Denari VF UNC

8.9.1996. Black and violet on olive-green and multicolor underprint. 6th century bronze figurine of Tetovo Maenad VI (horizontally) at center right. Back: 6th century mosaic of Cerberus the Dog tied to a fig tree, representing the watcher of Heaven (horizontally) at left center. Watermark: 6th century bronze figurine of Tetovo Maenad VI (horizontally). 155x70mm.

a. Issued note.	FV	175
s. Specimen.	—	60.00

2000 Commemorative Issue

20 100 Denari VF UNC

1.2000. Brown with purple text on multicolor underprint. Large baroque wooden ceiling rosette in Debar town house at center right, 2000 added at left. Back: J. Harevin's engraving of Skopje "seen" through town house window frame at left center. Watermark: Large baroque wooden ceiling rosette. 146x70mm. 35.00 80.00

2003 Issue

21 500 Denari VF UNC

1.2003; 1.2009. Black and violet on multicolor underprint. 6th century golden death mask, Trebenista, Ohrid at right. Gold foil at center. Back: Violet poppy flower and plant at left center. Watermark: Golden death mask. 149x70mm.

a. 1.2003. One signature at bottom left.	FV	22.50
b. 1.2009.	FV	22.50
s. Specimen.	FV	25.00

22 1000 Denari VF UNC

1.2003; 1.2009; 10.2013. Brown and orange on multicolor underprint. 14th century icon of Madonna Episkepsis and Christ Child, church of St. Vrach-Mali, Ohrid at center right. Hologram on center top. Back: Partial view of the St. Sophia church in Ohrid at left center. Watermark: Madonna. 152x70mm.

a. 1.2003. One signature at bottom left.	FV	40.00
b. 1.2009.	FV	40.00
c. 10.2013. Signature Dimitar Bogov.	FV	40.00
s. Specimen.	—	25.00

MADAGASCAR

The Democratic Republic of Madagascar, an independent member of the French Community located in the Indian Ocean 250 miles (402 km.) off the southeast coast of Africa, has an area of 226,658 sq. mi. (587,041 sq. km.) and a population of 17.39 million. Capital: Antananarivo. The economy is primarily agricultural; large bauxite deposits are presently being developed. Coffee, vanilla, graphite and rice are exported.Formerly an independent kingdom, Madagascar became a French colony in 1896 but regained independence in 1960. During 1992-93, free presidential and National Assembly elections were held ending 17 years of single-party rule. In 1997, in the second presidential race, Didier Ratsiraka, the leader during the 1970s and 1980s, was returned to the presidency. The 2001 presidential election was contested between the followers of Didier Ratsiraka and Marc Ravalomanana, nearly causing secession of half of the country. In April 2002, the High Constitutional Court announced Ravalomanana the winner. Ravalomanana is now in his second term following a landslide victory in the generally free and fair presidential elections of 2006.

MONETARY SYSTEM:
1 CFA Franc = 0.02 French Franc, 1959-1961
5 Malagasy Francs (F.M.G.) = 1 Ariary, 1961-2003
1 Ariary = 5 Francs, 2003-

MALAGASY

Institut d'Emission Malgache
1961 ND Provisional Issue

#51-55 new bank name and new Ariary denominations overprint on previous issue of Banque de Madagascar et des Comores.

51	**50 Francs = 10 Ariary**	VF	UNC
	ND (1961). Multicolor. Woman with hat at center right. Back: Man at center. Watermark: Woman's head.		
	a. Signature title: *LE CONTROLEUR GENERAL.*	17.50	70.00
	b. Signature title: *LE DIRECTEUR GENERAL ADJOINT.*	20.00	75.00

52	**100 Francs = 20 Ariary**	VF	UNC
	ND (1961). Multicolor. Woman at center right, palace of the Queen of Tananariva in background. Back: Woman, boats and animals. Watermark: Woman's head.	30.00	110

53	**500 Francs = 100 Ariary**	VF	UNC
	ND (1961 - old date 9.10.1952). Multicolor. Man with fruit at center. Watermark: Woman's head.	90.00	400

54	**1000 Francs = 200 Ariary**	VF	UNC
	ND (1961 - old date 9.10.1952). Multicolor. Man and woman at left center. Back: Ox cart at center right. Watermark: Woman's head.	175	500

55	**5000 Francs = 1000 Ariary**	VF	UNC
	ND (1961). Multicolor. Gallieni at upper left, woman at right. Back: Woman and baby. Watermark: Woman's head.	325	800

Note: #53-55 some notes also have old dates of intended or original issue (1952-55).

1963 ND Regular Issue

56	**1000 Francs = 200 Ariary**	VF	UNC
	ND (1963). Multicolor. Portrait President P. Tsiranana, people in canoes at left. Back: Ox cart at center right. Watermark: Woman's head.		
	a. Without signature and title.	375	800
	b. With signature and title.	250	700

1966 ND Issue

57	**100 Francs = 20 Ariary**	VF	UNC
	ND (1966). Multicolor. Three women spinning. Two signature varieties. Back: Trees. Watermark: Woman's head.		
	a. Issued note.	10.00	30.00
	s. Specimen.	—	25.00

58	**500 Francs = 100 Ariary**	VF	UNC
	ND (1966). Multicolor. Woman at left, landscape in background. Two signature varieties. Back: River scene. Watermark: Woman's head.		
	a. Issued note.	45.00	185
	s. Specimen.	—	35.00

59   1000 Francs = 200 Ariary   VF   UNC
ND (1966). Multicolor. Woman and man at left. Back: Ox cart at center right.
Watermark: Woman's head. 150x80mm.
    a. Issued note.   65.00   250
    s. Specimen.   —   35.00

63   100 Francs = 20 Ariary   VF   UNC
ND. Brown on multicolor underprint. Old man at right. Signature 1. Back: Rice
planting. Watermark: Zebu's head.
    a. Issued note.   3.00   10.00
    s. Specimen.   —   25.00

60   5000 Francs = 1000 Ariary   VF   UNC
ND (1966). Portrait President P. Tsiranana at left, workers in rice field at right.
Back: Woman and boy. Watermark: Woman's head.
    a. Issued note.   45.00   200
    s. Specimen.   —   45.00

1969 ND Issue

64   500 Francs = 100 Ariary   VF   UNC
ND. Green on multicolor underprint. Butterfly at left, young woman at center right
holding ornate bag on head. Signature 1. Back: Dancers at center. Watermark:
Zebu's head.
    a. Issued note.   6.00   30.00
    s. Specimen.   —   25.00

61   50 Francs = 10 Ariary   VF   UNC
ND (1969). Multicolor. Woman with hat at center right, like #51 but different   7.50   25.00
signature title. Back: Man at center. Watermark: Woman's head.

MADAGASCAR DEMOCRATIC REPUBLIC

Banky Foiben'ny Repoblika Malagasy

Banque Centrale de la République Malgache

1974 ND Issue

#62-66 replacement notes: Serial # prefix Z/.

65   1000 Francs = 200 Ariary   VF   UNC
ND. Bue on multicolor underprint. Ring-tailed Lemurs at left, man in straw hat at
right. Signature 1. Back: Trees and designs. Watermark: Zebu's head.
    a. Issued note.   8.00   45.00
    s. Specimen.   —   25.00

62   50 Francs = 10 Ariary   VF   UNC
ND (1974-75). Purple on multicolor underprint. Young man at center right. Signature 1. Back: Fruit stand under umbrella at left center. Watermark: Zebu's head.
    a. Issued note.   4.00   12.50
    s. Specimen.   —   25.00

66 **5000 Francs = 1000 Ariary** **VF** **UNC**
ND. Red and violet on multicolor underprint. Oxen at left, young woman at center right. Back: Tropical plants and African carving at center. Watermark: Zebu's head.
    a. Issued note.   30.00   80.00
    s. Specimen.   —   25.00

Banky Foiben'i Madagasikara
1983 ND Issue
#67-70 Replacement notes: Serial # prefix Z/ .

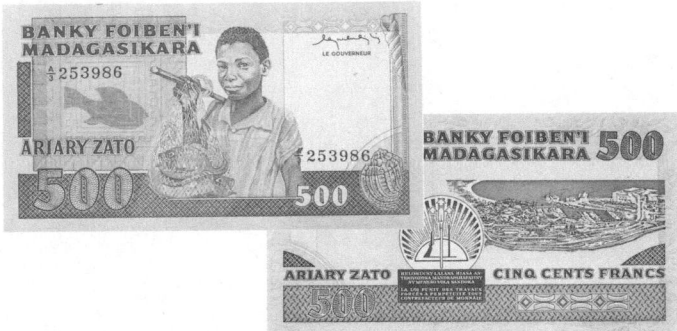

67 **500 Francs = 100 Ariary** **VF** **UNC**
ND (1983-87). Brown and red on multicolor underprint. Boy with fish in net at center. Back: Aerial view of port at right. Watermark: Zebu's head.
    a. Signature 1.   1.50   5.00
    b. Signature 2.   2.50   10.00

68 **1000 Francs = 200 Ariary** **VF** **UNC**
ND (1983-87). Violet and brown on multicolor underprint. Man with hat playing flute at center. Back: Fruits and vegetables at right. Watermark: Zebu's head.
    a. Signature 1.   2.00   7.50
    b. Signature 2.   2.50   10.00

69 **5000 Francs = 1000 Ariary** **VF** **UNC**
ND (1983-87). Blue on multicolor underprint. Woman and child at center. Back: Book at upper center, school at center right, monument at lower right. Watermark: Zebu's head.
    a. Signature 1.   10.00   35.00
    b. Signature 2.   12.50   50.00

70 **10,000 Francs = 2000 Ariary** **VF** **UNC**
ND (1983-87). Green on multicolor underprint. Young girl with sheaf at center. Back: Harvesting rice at center right. Watermark: Zebu's head.
    a. Signature 1.   20.00   65.00
    b. Signature 2.   25.00   85.00

1988 ND Issue
#71-74 Replacement notes: Serial # prefix ZZ.

71 **500 Francs = 100 Ariary** **VF** **UNC**
ND (1988-93). Brown and red on multicolor modified underprint Boy with fish in net at center, vertical serial number at right. Signature varieties. Back: Aerial view of port at right. Watermark: Zebu's head.
    a. Signature 2.   1.50   5.00
    b. Signature 3.   1.50   5.00

72 **1000 Francs = 200 Ariary** **VF** **UNC**
ND (1988-93). Violet and brown on multicolor modified underprint. Man with hat playing flute at center, vertical serial number at right. Back: Fruits and vegetables at right. Watermark: Zebu's head.
    a. Signature 2.   2.00   7.50
    b. Signature 3.   2.00   7.50

72A **2500 Francs = 500 Ariary** **VF** **UNC**
ND (1993). Red, green, blue and black on multicolor underprint. Older woman at center, vertical serial number at right. Back: Grey heron, tortoise, Verreaux's Sifaka and butterfly in foliage on vertical format. Watermark: Zebu's head.
    a. Signature 3.   0.75   2.50
    b. Signature 5.   0.75   2.50

73   5000 Francs = 1000 Ariary   VF   UNC

ND (1988-94). Blue on multicolor modified underprint. Woman and child at center, vertical serial number at right. Back: Book at upper center, school at center right, monument at lower right. Watermark: Zebu's head.

    a. Signature 2.   4.00   15.00
    b. Signature 3.   4.00   15.00

75   500 Francs = 100 Ariary   VF   UNC

ND (1994). UV: value 500 fluoresces yellow, security strip blue. Dark brown and dark green on multicolor underprint. Girl at center right, village in underprint at upper center. Back: Herdsmen with Zebus, village in upper background at left center. Watermark: Zebu's head.

    a. Signature 4.   0.50   1.75
    b. Signature 5.   0.50   1.75

74   10,000 Francs = 2000 Ariary   VF   UNC

ND (1988-94). Green on multicolor modified underprint. Young girl with sheaf at center, vertical serial number at right. Back: Harvesting rice at center right. Watermark: Zebu's head.

    a. Signature 2.   10.00   30.00
    b. Signature 3.   10.00   30.00

76   1000 Francs = 200 Ariary   VF   UNC

ND (1994). UV: value 1000 fluoresces yellow, security strip blue. Dark brown and dark blue on multicolor underprint. Young man at center right, boats in background. Back: Young woman with basket of shellfish at center, fisherman with net at left center. Watermark: Zebu's head.

    a. Signature 4.   0.50   1.50
    b. Signature 5.   0.50   1.00

#77 renumbered to 72A.

74A   25,000 Francs = 5000 Ariary   VF   UNC

ND (1993). Olive-green and green on multicolor underprint. Old man at center, island outline at left. Signature 3. Back: Scene of traditional bullfighting at right. Watermark: Zebu's head.   5.00   17.50

78   5000 Francs = 1000 Ariary   VF   UNC

ND (1995). Dark brown and purple on lilac and multicolor underprint. Young male head at right, ox cart, cane cutters at center. Back: Ringtailed Lemur, Diademed Sifaka, Red-ruffed Lemur and birds - Madagascar pigmy kingfisher, Madagascar fody and helmet vanga, plus seashells. Watermark: Zebu's head.

    a. Signature 4.   1.25   6.00
    b. Signature 5.   1.25   6.00

79 10,000 Francs = 2000 Ariary
ND (1995). Dark brown on tan and multicolor underprint. Old man at right, statuette, local artifacts at center. Back: Artisans at work. Watermark: Zebu's head.

		VF	UNC
a. Signature 4.		2.50	10.00
b. Signature 5.		2.50	10.00

#80 renumbered to #74A.

1998 ND Issue

81 2500 Francs = 500 Ariary
ND (1998). Multicolor. Woman at right, village in background. Signature 5. Back: Woman weaving at left center.

VF 0.75 UNC 3.50

82 25,000 Francs = 5000 Ariary
ND (1998). Multicolor. Mother with child at center right, fruit trees in background. Signature 5. Back: Woman harvesting at center.

VF 3.00 UNC 25.00

2003 Issue

83 2000 Ariary
ND (2003). Green on multicolor underprint. Baobabs trees at left. Signature 5. Back: Terrace farming. 120x60mm.

VF FV UNC 10.00

84 5000 Ariary
ND (2003). Violet, dark blue and yellow on multicolor underprint. Fishing boats. Signature 5. Back: Fort Dauphin Bay. 150x75mm.

VF FV UNC 20.00

85 10,000 Ariary
ND (2003). Green on multicolor underprint. Palais d'Argent at left. Signature 5. Back: Road construction. 156x78mm.

VF FV UNC 35.00

2004-06 Issue

86 100 Ariary
2004. Blue and tan on multicolor underprint. Ravinala and Tsingi plants. Back: Sugarloaf mountain at Antsiranana Bay. 120x60mm.

		VF	UNC
a. Signature 5.		FV	1.00
b. Signature 6.		FV	1.00

87 200 Ariary   VF   UNC
2004. Green and tan on multicolor underprint. Village entrance. Back: Aloalo"
(wooden monuments). 126x63mm.
   a. Signature 5.   FV   1.50
   b. Signature 6.   FV   1.50

88 500 Ariary   VF   UNC
2004. Tan on blue underprint. Man weaving basket at left. Back: Zebu cattle.
132x66mm.
   a. Signature 5.   FV   3.00
   b. Signature 6.   FV   3.00

89 1000 Ariary   VF   UNC
2004. Purple on multicolor underprint. Lemur on tree branch at left. Back: Cactus
and sisal plants. 138x69mm.
   a. Signature 5.   FV   3.50
   b. Signature 6.   FV   3.50

90 2000 Ariary   VF   UNC
2006, 2009. Green on multicolor underprint. Baobabs trees at right. Signature 6.
Omron rings. Back: Terrace farming. 144x72mm.
   a. 2006. With Francs equivalent.   FV   7.00
   b. 2009. Without Francs equivalent.   FV   7.00

91 5000 Ariary   VF   UNC
2006, 2009. Dark blue, violet and yellow on multicolor underprint. Fishing boats at
left. Signature 5. Omron rings. Back: Fort Dauphin Bay. 150x75mm.
   a. 2006. With Francs equivalent.   FV   12.50
   b. 2009. Without Francs equivalent.   FV   12.50

92 10,000 Ariary   VF   UNC
2006; 2009. Green on multicolor underprint. Palais d'Argent at left. Signature 5.
Omron rings. Back: Road construction. 156x78mm.
   a. 2006. With Francs equivalent.   FV   25.00
   b. 2009. Without Francs equivalent.   FV   25.00

2007 Commemorative Issue

93 2000 Ariary   VF   UNC
2007. Multicolor. Signature 6. 144x72mm.
   a. Issued note.   FV   9.00
   s. Specimen. Red overprint.   —   50.00

94 5000 Ariary   VF   UNC
ND. (2008). Multicolor. Sailing ship. Signature 6. Back: Beach. 150x75mm.
   a. Issued note.   FV   35.00
   s. Specimen. Red overprint.   —   50.00

2014 ND Issue

95 500 Ariary   VF   UNC
ND (2014). Polymer hybrid.   FV   3.00

96 2000 Ariary   VF   UNC
ND (2014). Polymer hybrid.   FV   7.00

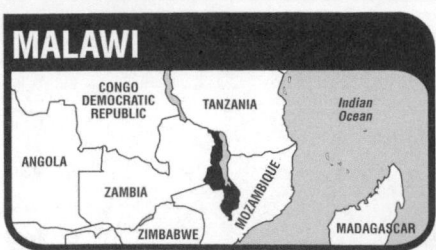

MALAWI

The Republic of Malawi (formerly Nyasaland), located in southeastern Africa to the west of Lake Malawi (Nyasa), has an area of 45,747 sq. mi. (118,484 sq. km.) and a population of 10.98 million. Capital: Lilongwe. The economy is predominantly agricultural. Tobacco, tea, peanuts and cotton are exported.Established in 1891, the British protectorate of Nyasaland became the independent nation of Malawi in 1964. After three decades of one-party rule under President Hastings Kamuzu Banda the country held multiparty elections in 1994, under a provisional constitution that came into full effect the following year. Current President Bingu wa Mitharika, elected in May 2004 after a failed attempt by the previous president to amend the constitution to permit another term, struggled to assert his authority against his predecessor and subsequently started his own party, the Democratic Progressive Party (DPP) in 2005. As president, Mutharika has overseen substantial economic improvement but because of political deadlock in the legislature, his minority party has been unable to pass significant legislation, and anti-corruption measures have stalled. Population growth, increasing pressure on agricultural lands, corruption, and the spread of HIV/AIDS pose major problems for Malawi.

RULERS:
British to 1964

MONETARY SYSTEM:
1 Pound = 20 Shillings to 1971
1 Kwacha = 100 Tambala 1971-

REPLACEMENT NOTES:
#13-17, ZZ prefix. #18-22, V/1, W/1, X/1, Y/1, Z/1 prefix by denomination.
#23-27, ZZ prefix.

REPUBLIC

Reserve Bank of Malawi

1964 Reserve Bank Act; First Issue

		VF	UNC
1	**5 Shillings**		
	L.1964. Blue-gray on multicolor underprint. Portrait of Dr. Hastings Kamuzu Banda at left, fishermen in boat on Lake Malawi at center. Signature title: *GOVERNOR* only. Back: Arms with bird. Watermark: Rooster.	17.50	100

		VF	UNC
2	**10 Shillings**		
	L.1964. Brown on multicolor underprint. Portrait of Dr. Hastings Kamuzu Banda at left, fishermen in boat on Lake Malawi at center. Signature title: *GOVERNOR* only. Back: Workers in tobacco field. Watermark: Rooster.	60.00	250
3	**1 Pound**		
	L.1964. Green on multicolor underprint. Portrait of Dr. Hastings Kamuzu Banda at left, fishermen in boat on Lake Malawi at center. Signature title: *GOVERNOR* only. Back: Workers picking cotton at center right. Watermark: Rooster.	85.00	350

		VF	UNC
4	**5 Pounds**		
	L.1964. Blue and brown on multicolor underprint. Portrait of Dr. Hastings Kamuzu Banda at left, fishermen in boat on Lake Malawi at center. Signature title: *GOVERNOR* only. Back: Tea pickers below Mt. Mulanje. Watermark: Rooster.	300	1,500

1964 Reserve Bank Act; Second Issue

		VF	UNC
1A	**5 Shillings**		
	L.1964. Blue-gray on multicolor underprint. Portrait of Dr. Hastings Kamuzu Banda at left, fishermen in boat on Lake Malawi at center. Signature titles: *GOVERNOR* and *GENERAL MANAGER*. Back: Arms with bird. Watermark: Rooster.		
	a. Issued note.	15.00	85.00
	s. Specimen.	—	—

		VF	UNC
2A	**10 Shillings**		
	L.1964. Brown on multicolor underprint. Portrait of Dr. Hastings Kamuzu Banda at left, fishermen in boat on Lake Malawi at center. Signature titles: *GOVERNOR* and *GENERAL MANAGER*. Back: Workers in tobacco field. Watermark: Rooster.		
	a. Issued note.	20.00	120
	s. Specimen.	—	—

		VF	UNC
3A	**1 Pound**		
	L.1964. Green on multicolor underprint. Portrait of Dr. Hastings Kamuzu Banda at left, fishermen in boat on Lake Malawi at center. Signature titles: *GOVERNOR* and *GENERAL MANAGER*. Back: Worders picking cotton at center right. Watermark: Rooster.		
	a. Issued note.	40.00	225
	s. Specimen.	—	—

1964 Reserve Bank Act; 1971 Issue

Kwacha System

5 50 Tambala
L.1964 (1971). Blue-gray on multicolor underprint. Portrait of Dr. Hastings Kamuzu Banda at left, fishermen in boat on Lake Malawi at center. Signature titles: *GOVERNOR* and *GENERAL MANAGER*. Back: Independence Arch in Blantyre at right.

	VF	UNC
a. Issued note.	50.00	325
s. Specimen.		

6 1 Kwacha
L.1964 (1971). Brown on multicolor underprint. Portrait of Dr. Hastings Kamuzu Banda at left, fishermen in boat on Lake Malawi at center. Signature titles: *GOVERNOR* and *GENERAL MANAGER*. Back: Workers in tobacco field. Watermark: Rooster.

	VF	UNC
a. Issued note.	50.00	350
s. Specimen.	—	—

7 2 Kwacha
L.1964 (1971). Green on multicolor underprint. Portrait of Dr. Hastings Kamuzu Banda at left, fishermen in boat on Lake Malawi at center. Signature titles: *GOVERNOR* and *GENERAL MANAGER*. Back: Workers picking cotton at center right. Watermark: Rooster.

	VF	UNC
a. Issued note.	50.00	300
s. Specimen.	—	—

8 10 Kwacha
L.1964 (1971). Blue and brown on multicolor underprint. Portrait of Dr. Hastings Kamuzu Banda at left, fishermen in boat on Lake Malawi at center. Signature titles: *GOVERNOR* and *GENERAL MANAGER*. Back: Tea pickers below Mount Mulanje.

	VF	UNC
a. Issued note.	175	1,200
s. Specimen.	—	—

1973-74 Issue

9 50 Tambala
L.1964 (ND); 1974-75. Blue-gray on multicolor underprint. Portrait Dr. Hastings Kamuzu Banda as Prime Minister at right, fishermen in boat on Lake Malawi and palm tree at center. Back: Sugar cane harvesting. Watermark: Rooster.

	VF	UNC
a. ND (1973).	30.00	200
b. 30.6.1974.	15.00	100
c. 31.1.1975.	5.00	40.00
s. As a. Specimen.	—	—
ct. Color trial. Purple on multicolor underprint.	—	275

10 1 Kwacha
L.1964 (ND); 1974-75. Red-brown on multicolor underprint. Portrait Dr. Hastings Kamuzu Banda as Prime Minister at right, fishermen in boat on Lake Malawi and palm tree at center. Back: Plantation worker, hill in background. Watermark: Rooster.

	VF	UNC
a. ND (1973).	20.00	135
b. 30.6.1974.	15.00	85.00
c. 31.1.1975.	7.00	75.00
ct. Color trial. Orange on multicolor underprint.	—	250

11 5 Kwacha
L.1964 (ND); 1974-75. Red-orange on multicolor underprint. Portrait Dr. Hastings Kamuzu Banda as Prime Minister at right, fishermen in boat on Lake Malawi and palm tree at center. Back: Worker with basket at center, *K5* at upper left. Watermark: Rooster.

	VF	UNC
a. ND (1973).	55.00	350
b. 31.1.1975.	40.00	300
ct. Color trial. Green on multicolor underprint.	—	550

12 10 Kwacha
L.1964 (ND); 1974-75. Blue and brown on multicolor underprint. Portrait Dr. Hastings Kamuzu Banda as Prime Minister at right, fishermen in boat on Lake Malawi and palm tree at center. Back: Plantation workers with mountains in background. Watermark: Rooster.

	VF	UNC
a. ND (1973).	65.00	500
b. 30.6.1974.	75.00	550
c. 31.1.1975.	45.00	425

1976; 1983 Issue

13 50 Tambala
1976-84. Blue-gray on multicolor underprint. Portrait of Dr. Hastings Kamuzu Banda as President at right. Signature varieties. Back: Cotton harvest. Watermark: Rooster.

	VF	UNC
a. 31.1.1976.	3.00	25.00
b. 1.7.1978.	4.50	30.00
c. 1.1.1981.	5.00	40.00
d. 1.5.1982.	2.50	15.00
e. 1.1.1983.	5.00	35.00
f. 1.11.1984.	7.50	60.00
s. As a. Specimen.	—	35.00

14 1 Kwacha

1976-84. Red-brown on multicolor underprint. Portrait of Dr. Hastings Kamuzu Banda as President at right. Signature varieties. Back: Workers harvesting, mountains in background. Watermark: Rooster.

	VF	UNC
a. 31.1.1976.	3.00	22.50
b. 1.7.1978.	3.00	25.00
c. 30.6.1979.	20.00	150
d. 1.1.1981.	2.00	20.00
e. 1.5.1982.	2.75	20.00
f. 1.1.1983.	3.00	25.00
g. 1.4.1984.	1.50	12.50
h. 1.11.1984.	2.00	15.00
s. Specimen. 31.1.1976.	—	40.00

15 5 Kwacha

1976-84. Red on multicolor underprint. Portrait of Dr. Hastings Kamuzu Banda as President at right. Signature varieties. Back: Field workers, *K5* at upper right. Watermark: Rooster.

	VF	UNC
a. 31.1.1976.	27.50	200
b. 1.7.1978.	27.50	200
c. 30.6.1979.	40.00	325
d. 1.1.1981.	10.00	85.00
e. 1.1.1983.	7.50	75.00
f. 1.11.1984.	20.00	250
s. Specimen. 31.1.1976.	—	50.00

16 10 Kwacha

1976-85. Deep blue and brown on multicolor underprint. Portrait of Dr. Hastings Kamuzu Banda as President at right. Signature varieties. Back: Capital building at Lilongwe. Watermark: Rooster.

	VF	UNC
a. 31.1.1976.	37.50	450
b. 1.7.1978.	37.50	450
c. 30.6.1979.	55.00	550
d. 1.1.1981.	35.00	400
e. 1.1.1983.	35.00	400
f. 1.4.1984.	35.00	400
g. 1.11.1984.	45.00	525
h. 1.8.1985.	50.00	500
s. Specimen. 31.1.1976.	—	45.00

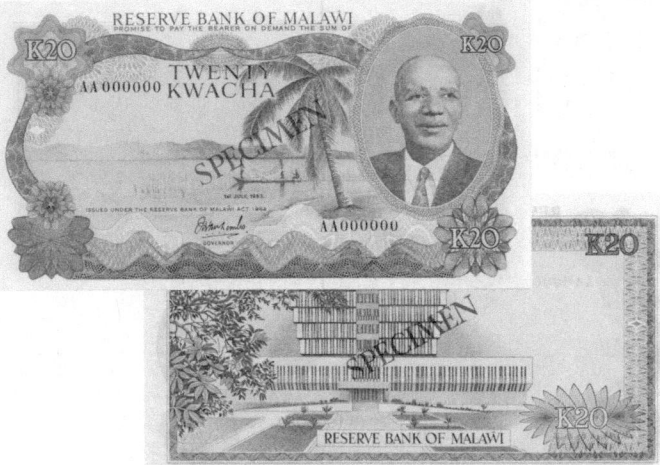

17 20 Kwacha

1983; 1984. Green, brown-violet on multicolor underprint. Portrait of Dr. Hastings Kamuzu Banda as President at right. Signature varieties. Back: Reserve Bank in Lilongwe at center. Watermark: Rooster.

	VF	UNC
a. 1.7.1983.	15.00	125
b. 1.11.1984.	35.00	325
s. Specimen.	—	240

1986 Issue

18 50 Tambala

1.3.1986. Black and dark brown on multicolor underprint. Portrait of President Dr. Hastings Kamuzu Banda at right. Back: Picking corn. Watermark: Rooster.

VF 2.00 UNC 12.50

19 1 Kwacha

1986; 1988. Red-brown on multicolor underprint. Portrait of President Dr. Hastings Kamuzu Banda at right. Back: Cultivating tobacco. Watermark: Rooster.

	VF	UNC
a. 1.3.1986.	2.50	15.00
b. 1.4.1988.	1.50	10.00

20   5 Kwacha   **VF   UNC**
1986; 1988. Red-orange on multicolor underprint. Portrait of President Dr. Hastings
Kamuzu Banda at right. Back: University of Malawi at Zomba Watermark: Rooster.

	VF	UNC
a. 1.3.1986.	7.00	40.00
b. 1.4.1988.	5.00	30.00

21   10 Kwacha   **VF   UNC**
1986; 1988. Deep blue and brown on multicolor underprint. Portrait of President Dr.
Hastings Kamuzu Banda at right. Back: Lilongwe, capital city. Watermark: Rooster.

	VF	UNC
a. 1.3.1986.	15.00	95.00
b. 1.4.1988.	10.00	50.00

22   20 Kwacha   **VF   UNC**
1986; 1988. Deep green on multicolor underprint. Portrait of President Dr. Hastings
Kamuzu Banda at right. Back: Kamuzu International Airport . Watermark: Rooster.

	VF	UNC
a. 1.3.1986.	35.00	285
b. 1.4.1988.	20.00	160

1989 Act; 1990; 1993 Issue

23   1 Kwacha   **VF   UNC**
1990; 1992. UV: fibers fluoresce yellow, four 1s yellow. Red-brown on multicolor
underprint. Portrait of Dr. Hastings Kamuzu Banda as President at right, palm
tree, man in dugout canoe and rayed silver circle at center. Ascending size serial
number at left and lower right. Back: Cultivating tobacco. Watermark: Rooster.

	VF	UNC
a. 1.12.1990.	FV	5.00
b. 1.5.1992.	FV	2.00

24   5 Kwacha   **VF   UNC**
1990; 1994. Red-orange and olive-green on multicolor underprint. Portrait of Dr.
Hastings Kamuzu Banda as President at right, palm tree, man in dugout canoe
and rayed silver circle at center. Ascending size serial number at left and lower
right. Back: University of Malawi at left center. Watermark: Rooster.

	VF	UNC
a. 1.12.1990.	FV	6.50
b. 1.1.1994.	FV	4.50

25   10 Kwacha   **VF   UNC**
1990-94. Blue-gray, blue-violet and dark brown on multicolor underprint. Portrait of
Dr. Hastings Kamuzu Banda as President at right, palm tree, man in dugout canoe
and rayed silver circle at center. Ascending size serial number at left and lower
right. Back: Lilongwe City municipal building at left center. Watermark: Rooster.

	VF	UNC
a. 1.12.1990.	FV	12.50
b. 1.9.1992.	FV	6.00
c. Smaller signature as b. 1.1.1994.	FV	4.00
s. As b. Specimen.	—	135

26   20 Kwacha   **VF   UNC**
1.9.1990. Green, orange and blue on multicolor underprint. Portrait of Dr. Hastings   10.00   60.00
Kamuzu Banda as President at right, palm tree, man in dugout canoe and rayed
silver circle at center. Ascending size serial number at left and lower right. Back:
Kamuzu International Airport at left center. Watermark: Rooster.

27　20 Kwacha　　　　　　　　　　　　　**VF　UNC**
1.7.1993. Green, orange and blue on multicolor underprint. Portrait of Dr. Hastings
Kamuzu Banda as President at right, palm tree, man in dugout canoe and rayed
silver circle at center. Ascending size serial number at left and lower right. Back:
Like #26 but with larger airplane. Watermark: Rooster.　　　　　　　　FV　10.00

28　50 Kwacha　　　　　　　　　　　　　**VF　UNC**
1990; 1994. Pale purple, violet and blue on multicolor underprint. Portrait of Dr.
Hastings Kamuzu Banda as President at right, palm tree, man in dugout canoe
and rayed silver circle at center. Ascending size serial number at left and lower
right. Back: Independence Arch at Blantyre at center. Watermark: Rooster.
　　a. 1.6.1990.　　　　　　　　　　　　　　　　　　　　12.50　55.00
　　b. 1.1.1994.　　　　　　　　　　　　　　　　　　　　5.00　35.00

29　100 Kwacha　　　　　　　　　　　　**VF　UNC**
1993; 1994. Blue, green and dark brown on multicolor underprint. Portrait of Dr.
Hastings Kamuzu Banda as President at right, palm tree, man in dugout canoe
and rayed silver circle at center. Ascending size serial number at left and lower
right. Back: Trucks hauling maize to storage facility at center.
　　a. 1.4.1993.　　　　　　　　　　　　　　　　　　　　30.00　75.00
　　b. 1.1.1994.　　　　　　　　　　　　　　　　　　　　10.00　50.00

1995 Issue

30　5 Kwacha　　　　　　　　　　　　　**VF　UNC**
1.6.1995. Red and orange-brown on multicolor underprint. President Muluzi at right,
sunrise above fisherman in boat on Lake Malawi at center, Spoonbill at upper left,
silver segmented sunburst at lower left. Back: Zebras at left. Watermark: Fish.　　FV　1.75

31　10 Kwacha　　　　　　　　　　　　**VF　UNC**
1.6.1995. Black, dark blue and dark brown on multicolor underprint. President Muluzi at right, sunrise above fisherman in boat on Lake Malawi at center, Crowned
Crane at upper left, silver segmented sunburst at lower left. Back: Capital Hill,
Lilongwe at left center. Watermark: Fish.　　　　　　　　　　　　　FV　4.00

32　20 Kwacha　　　　　　　　　　　　**VF　UNC**
1.6.1995. Deep green and dark brown on multicolor underprint. President Muluzi
at right, sunrise above fisherman in boat on Lake Malawi at center, Lesser Striped
Swallow at upper left, silver segmented sunburst at lower left. Back: Harvesting
tea leaves at left center. Watermark: Fish.　　　　　　　　　　　　FV　7.50

33　50 Kwacha　　　　　　　　　　　　**VF　UNC**
1.6.1995. Purple and violet on multicolor underprint. President Muluzi at right,
sunrise above fisherman in boat on Lake Malawi at center, Pink-backed Pelican
at upper left, silver segmented sunburst at lower left. Back: Independence Arch in
Blantyre at left center. Watermark: Fish.　　　　　　　　　　　　FV　12.00

34   100 Kwacha — VF UNC

1.6.1995. Purple and deep ultramarine on multicolor underprint. President Muluzi at right, sunrise above fisherman in boat on Lake Malawi at center, Sacred Ibis at upper left, silver segmented sunburst at lower left. Back: Trucks hauling maize to storage facility at left center. Watermark: Fish.

FV 25.00

35   200 Kwacha — VF UNC

1.6.1995. Brown-violet and blue-green and silver on multicolor underprint. President Muluzi at right, sunrise above fisherman in boat on Lake Malawi at center, African Fish Eagle at upper left, silver segmented sunburst at lower left. Back: Elephants. Watermark: Fish.

10.00 45.00

1989 Act; 1997 Issue

36   5 Kwacha — VF UNC

1997; 2004-05. UV: fibers fluoresce blue, green and red. Security strip rainbow. Deep olive-green, green and olive-brown on multicolor underprint. J. Chilembwe at right, sunrise, fishermen at center, bank stylized logo at lower left. Back: Villagers mashing grain at left, bank seal at top center right. Watermark: J. Chilembwe.

a. 1.7.1997.   FV 1.25
b. 1.3.2004.   FV 0.50
c. 1.12.2005.   FV 0.50

37   10 Kwacha — VF UNC

1.7.1997. Dark brown and brown-violet on multicolor underprint. J. Chilembwe at right, sunrise, fishermen at center, bank stylized logo at lower left. Back: Children in "bush" school at left center, bank seal at top center right. Watermark: J. Chilembwe.

FV 1.50

38   20 Kwacha — VF UNC

1.7.1997. Blackish purple, purple and violet on multicolor underprint. J. Chilembwe at right, sunrise, fishermen at center, bank stylized logo at lower left. Back: Workers harvesting tea leaves, mountains in background at left, bank seal at top center right. Watermark: J. Chilembwe. 138x70mm.

a. Even height serial #s.   FV 3.50
b. Ascending size serial #.   FV 3.25

39   50 Kwacha — VF UNC

1.7.1997. Dark green, deep blue and aqua on multicolor underprint. J. Chilembwe at right, sunrise, fishermen at center, bank stylized logo at lower left. Back: Independence arch in Blantyre at left center, bank seal at top center right. Watermark: J. Chilembwe. 144x72mm.

FV 5.00

40   100 Kwacha — VF UNC

1.7.1997. Purple, red and violet on multicolor underprint. J. Chilembwe at right, circular kinegram bank seal at right, sunrise, fishermen at center, bank stylized logo at lower left. Back: Capital Hill Lilongwe at left center. Watermark: J. Chilembwe. 150x75mm.

FV 12.50

41   200 Kwacha   VF   UNC

1.7.1997. Dark gray, dull blue and deep blue-green on multicolor underprint. J. Chilembwe at right, oval kinegram bank seal at right, sunrise, fishermen at center, bank stylized logo at lower left. Back: Reserve Bank building in Lilongwe at left center. Watermark: J. Chilembwe. 156x78mm.

FV   17.50

#42 has been merged into #48.

2001-03 Issue

43   10 Kwacha   VF   UNC

2003. UV: fibers fluoresce red, blue and green, Chilembwe's face yellow in a box, security strip rainbow. Dark brown and brown-violet on multicolor underprint. J. Chilembwe at right. Ascending size serial number. Back: Children in "bush" school at left center.
    a. 1.1.2003.   FV   1.50
    b. 1.10.2003.   FV   1.50

44   20 Kwacha   VF   UNC

2001-07. Black and purple on multicolor underprint. J. Chilembwe at right. Ascending size serial number. 138x70mm.
    a. 1.10.2001.   FV   3.00
    b. 1.4.2004.   FV   2.00

45   50 Kwacha   VF   UNC

2001-03. Dark green, deep blue and aqua on multicolor underprint. J. Chilembwe at right. Ascending size serial number. 144x72mm.
    a. 1.10.2001.   FV   4.00
    b. 1.1.2003.   FV   2.75

46   100 Kwacha   VF   UNC

2001-03. Dark purple and red on red and multicolor underprint. J. Chilembwe at right. Ascending size serial number. 150x75mm.
    a. 1.10.2001.   FV   10.00
    b. 1.1.2003.   FV   5.00
    c. 1.10.2003.   FV   4.00

47   200 Kwacha   VF   UNC

2001-03. Multicolor. J. Chilembwe at right, oval kinegram bank seal at right, sunrise, fishermen at center, bank stylized logo at lower left. Ascending size serial number. Back: Reserve Bank building in Lilongwe at left center. 156x78mm.
    a. 1.7.2001.   FV   15.00
    b. 1.10.2003.   FV   9.00

48   500 Kwacha   VF   UNC

2001. Multicolor. J. Chilembwe at right. Holographic square at left center. Ascending size serial number. 163x81mm.
    a. 1.12.2001.   FV   30.00

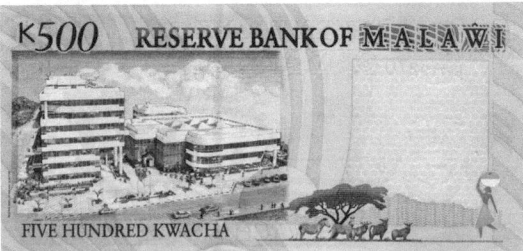

48A   500 Kwacha   VF   UNC

2003. Multicolor. J. Chilembwe at right. Holographic strip at right. 163x81mm.
    a. 1.6.2003.   FV   17.50

2004 Commemorative Issue
#49, 40th Anniversary of Independence.

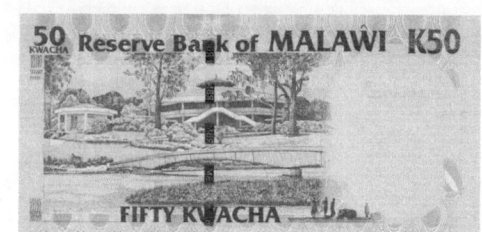

49   50 Kwacha   VF   UNC
6.7.2004. Blue on yellow-orange underprint. Back: Modern buildings. 144x72mm.   FV   5.00

2004 Regular Issue

51   10 Kwacha   VF   UNC
2004-. Black and purple on multicolor underprint. J. Chilembwe at right.
    a. 1.6.2004.   FV   1.50
    b. 31.10.2006.   FV   1.50

52   20 Kwacha   VF   UNC
2004-. Black purple, purple and violet on multicolor underprint. J. Chilembwe at right. 138x70mm.
    a. 1.6.2004.   FV   1.00
    b. 31.10.2005.   FV   1.00
    c. 31.10.2006.   FV   1.00
    d. 31.10.2007.   FV   0.75
    e. 31.10.2009.   FV   0.75

53   50 Kwacha   VF   UNC
2005-. Dark green, deep blue and aqua on multicolor underprint. J. Chilrmbwe at right. 144x72mm.
    a. 31.10.2005.   FV   1.50
    b. 31.10.2006.   FV   1.50
    c. 31.10.2007.   FV   1.00
    d. 31.10.2009.   FV   1.00
    e. 30.0.2011.   FV   1.00

54   100 Kwacha   VF   UNC
2005-. Purple, red and violet on multicolor underprint. J. Chilembwe at right. 150x75mm.
    a. 31.10.2005.   FV   3.00
    b. 31.10.2006.   FV   3.00
    c. 31.10.2007.   FV   2.50
    d. 31.10.2009.   FV   2.50
    e. 30.6.2011.   FV   2.50

55   200 Kwacha   VF   UNC
2004-. Dark gray, dull blue and deep blue-green on multicolor underprint. J. Chilembwe at right. 156x78mm.
    a. 1.6.2004.   FV   9.00
    b. 31.10.2007.   FV   9.00

56   500 Kwacha   VF   UNC
2005-. J. Chilembwe at right. 163x81mm.
    a. 1.11.2005.   FV   15.00
    b. 31.1.2011.   FV   9.00

2012-15 Issue

57   20 Kwacha   VF   UNC
2012. Purple and orange on multicolor underprint. Fishermen in boat, Reserve Bank building, Inkosi ya Makhosi M'mbelwa II. Back: Domadi Teachers Training College building and tree Watermark: Inkosi ya Makhosi M'mbelwa II. 128x64mm.
    a. 1.1.2012.   FV   1.00
    b. 6.1.2012.   FV   1.00

58   50 Kwacha   VF   UNC
2012. Light blue, orange and green on multicolor underprint. Fishermen in boat, Reserve Bank building, Inkosi Ya Mokhosi Gomani II. Back: Elephants, tree and safari vehicle in Kasungu National Park. Watermark: Inkosi Ya Mokhosi Gomani II. 128x64mm.
    a. 1.1.2012.   FV   2.00
    b. 6.1.2012.   FV   2.00

59   100 Kwacha   VF   UNC
2012-2013. Red-brown and orange on multicolor underprint. Fishermen in boat, Reserve Bank building, James Federick Sangala. Back: College of Medicine in Blantyre. Watermark: James Federick Sangala. 128x64mm.
    a. 1.1.2012.   FV   3.00
    b. 6.1.2012.   FV   3.00
    c. 1.1.2013.   FV   3.00

60   200 Kwacha   VF   UNC
1.1.2012. Blue, violet and orange on multicolor underprint. Fishermen in boat, Reserve Bank building, Rose Lomathinda Chibambo. Back: New Parliament building in Lilongwe. Watermark: Rose Lomathinda Chibambo. 132x66mm.   FV   5.00

61 500 Kwacha
2012-2013. Brown, orange and light blue on multicolor underprint. Fishermen in boat, Reserve Bank building, Rev. John Chilembwe. Back: Mulunguzi dam in Zomba. Watermark: John Chilembwe 132x66mm.

		VF	UNC
a. 1.1.2012.		FV	6.00
b. 1.1.2013.		FV	6.00

62 1000 Kwacha
2012-2014. Green and orange on multicolor underprint. Fishermen in boat, Reserve Bank building, Dr. Hastings Kamuzu Banda. Back: Mzuzu maize silos, stalk of maize (corn), silhouette of 2 people mashing maize into flower with poles Watermark: Hastings Kamuzu Banda. 132x66mm.

		VF	UNC
a. 1.1.2012.		FV	12.50
b. 1.1.2013.		FV	12.50
c. 1.1.2014.		FV	12.50

63 20 Kwacha
2014-2015. Purple and orange on multicolor underprint. Fishermen in boat, Reserve Bank building, Inkosi ya Makhosi M'mbelwa II. Back: Domadi Teachers Training College building and tree. Watermark: Inkosi ya Makhosi M'mbelwa II. 128x64mm.

		VF	UNC
a. 1.1.2014.		FV	1.00
b. 1.1.2015.		FV	1.00

64 50 Kwacha
2014-2015. Light blue, orange and green on multicolor underprint. Fishermen in boat, Reserve Bank building, Inkosi Ya Mokhosi Gomani II. Back: Elephants, tree and safari vehicle in Kasungu National Park. Watermark: Inkosi Ya Mokhosi Gomani II. 128x64mm.

		VF	UNC
a. 1.1.2014.		FV	2.00
b. 1.1.2015.		FV	2.00

65 100 Kwacha
1.1.2014. Red-brown and orange on multicolor underprint. Fishermen in boat, Reserve Bank building, James Federick Sangala. Blind recognition feature (three dots) at lower left. Back: College of Medicine in Blantyre. Watermark: James Federick Sangala.

	VF	UNC
	FV	3.00

66 500 Kwacha
2014. Brown, orange and light blue on multicolor underprint. Fishermen in boat, Reserve Bank building, Rev. John Chilembwe. Blind recognition feature (rectangle) at lower left. Back: Mulunguzi dam in Zomba. Watermark: John Chilembwe. 132x66mm.

	VF	UNC
	FV	6.00

67 1000 Kwacha
2014. Green and orange on multicolor underprint. Fishermen in boat, Reserve Bank building, Dr. Hastings Kamuzu Banda. Blind recognition feature (four dots) at lower left. Back: Mzuzu maize silos, stalk of maize (corn), silhouette of 2 people mashing maize into flower with poles. Watermark: Hastings Kamuzu Banda. 132x66mm.

	VF	UNC
	FV	12.50

2014 Commemorative Issue

68 1000 Kwacha
1.1.2014 years of independence. Green and orange on multicolor underprint. Fishermen in boat, Reserve Bank building, Dr. Hastings Kamuzu Banda. Blind recognition feature (four dots) at lower left. Back: Mzuzu maize silos, stalk of maize (corn), silhouette of 2 people mashing maize into flower with poles. Watermark: Hastings Kamuzu Banda. 132x66mm.

	VF	UNC
	FV	12.50

MALAYA & BRITISH BORNEO

Malaya and British Borneo, a Currency Commission named the Board of Commissioners of Currency, Malaya and British North Borneo, was initiated on Jan. 1, 1952, for the purpose of providing a common currency for use in Johore, Kelantan, Kedah, Perlis, Trengganu, Negri Sembilan, Pahang, Perak, Salangor, Penang, Malacca, Singapore, North Borneo, Sarawak and Brunei. For later issues see Brunei, Malaysia and Singapore.

RULERS:
British

MONETARY SYSTEM:
1 Dollar = 100 Cents

BRITISH ADMINISTRATION
Board of Commissioners of Currency
1959-61 Issue

8 1 Dollar
1.3.1959. Blue on multicolor underprint. Sailing boat at left. Back: Men with boat and arms of five states. Watermark: Tiger's head. Printer: W&S.

		VF	UNC
a. Issued note.		50.00	250
s. Specimen.		—	—

8A 1 Dollar
1.3.1959. Blue on multicolor underprint. Sailing boat at left. Back: Men with boat and arms of five states. Watermark: Tiger's head. Printer: TDLR.

	VF	UNC
	50.00	150

9 10 Dollars
1.3.1961. Red and dark brown on multicolor underprint. Farmer plowing with ox at right. Watermark: Tiger's head. Printer: TDLR.

	VF	UNC
a. Small serial #. Series A.	125	550
b. Large serial #. Series A.	225	800
c. Large serial #. Series B.	400	1,500
s. As a. Specimen.	—	—

MALAYSIA

Malaysia, an independent federation of southeast Asia consisting of 11 states of West Malaysia on the Malay Peninsula and two states of East Malaysia on the island of Borneo, has an area of 127,316 sq. mi. (329,747 sq. km.) and a population of 22.3 million. Capital: Kuala Lumpur. The federation came into being on Sept. 16, 1963. Rubber, timber, tin, iron ore and bauxite are exported. During the late 18th and 19th centuries, Great Britain established colonies and protectorates in the area of current Malaysia; these were occupied by Japan from 1942 to 1945. In 1948, the British-ruled territories on the Malay Peninsula formed the Federation of Malaya, which became independent in 1957. Malaysia was formed in 1963 when the former British colonies of Singapore and the East Malaysian states of Sabah and Sarawak on the northern coast of Borneo joined the Federation. The first several years of the country's history were marred by a Communist insurgency, Indonesian confrontation with Malaysia, Philippine claims to Sabah, and Singapore's secession from the Federation in 1965. During the 22-year term of Prime Minister Mahathir bin Mohamad (1981-2003), Malaysia was successful in diversifying its economy from dependence on exports of raw materials to expansion in manufacturing, services, and tourism.

MONETARY SYSTEM:
1 Ringgit (Dollar) = 100 Sen

DEMONETIZED NOTES:
All 500 and 1000 Ringgitt notes ceased to be legal tender on July 1, 1999.

FEDERATION

Bank Negara Malaysia
All notes w/Yang Di-Pertuan Agong, Tunku Abdul Rahman, first Head of State of Malaysia (died 1960).

1967 ND Issue

1   1 Ringgit   **VF   UNC**
ND (1967-72). Blue on multicolor underprint. T. A. Rahman at right. Old spelling of DI-PERLAKUKAN. Signature Ismail Md. Ali with title: GABENOR. Back: Arms Watermark: Arms Printer: BWC.
    a. Solid security thread.   3.00   25.00

2   5 Ringgit   **VF   UNC**
ND (1967-72). Green on multicolor underprint. T. A. Rahman at right. Old spelling of DI-PERLAKUKAN. Signature Ismail Md. Ali with title: GABENOR. Back: Arms. Watermark: Tiger's head. Printer: BWC.
    a. Solid security thread.   12.00   60.00
Replacement notes: Serial # prefix Z/.

3   10 Ringgit   **VF   UNC**
ND (1967-72). Red-orange on multicolor underprint. T. A. Rahman at right. Old spelling of DI-PERLAKUKAN. Signature Ismail Md. Ali with title: GABENOR (SA-PULOH). Back: Arms. Watermark: Tiger's head. Printer: TDLR.
    a. Solid security thread.   17.50   80.00

4   50 Ringgit   **VF   UNC**
ND (1967-72). Blue and greenish gray on multicolor underprint. T. A. Rahman at right. Old spelling of DI-PERLAKUKAN. Signature Ismail Md. Ali with title: GABENOR(LIMA PULOH). Back: Arms. Watermark: Tiger's head. Printer: TDLR.
    a. Solid security thread.   70.00   350

5   100 Ringgit   **VF   UNC**
ND (1967-72). Purple and brown on multicolor underprint. T. A. Rahman at right. Old spelling of DI-PERLAKUKAN. Signature Ismail Md. Ali with title: GABENOR (SA-RATUS). Back: Arms. Watermark: Tiger's head. Printer: TDLR.
    a. Solid security thread.   330   850

6   1000 Ringgit   **VF   UNC**
ND (1967-72). Brown-violet on multicolor underprint. T. A. Rahman at right. Old spelling of DI-PERLAKUKAN. Signature Ismail Md. Ali with title: GABENOR (SA-RIBU). Back: Arms. Watermark: Tiger's head. Printer: BWC.
                                                  3,500   6,500

1972; 1976 ND Issue

7   1 Ringgit   **VF   UNC**
ND (1972-76). Blue on multicolor underprint. T. A. Rahman at right. New spelling of DIPERLAKUKAN. Signature Ismail Md. Ali with title: GABENUR. Back: Arms. Watermark. Tiger's head. Printer. BWC.   2.50   12.50

8   5 Ringgit   **VF   UNC**
ND (1976). . Green on multicolor underprint. T. A. Rahman at right. New spelling of DIPERLAKUKAN. Signature Ismail Md. Ali with title: GABENUR. Back: Arms. Watermark: Tiger's head. Printer: BWC.
    a. Issued note.   7.50   37.50
    s. Specimen.   —   —

9   10 Ringgit   **VF   UNC**
ND (1972-76). Red-orange and brown on multicolor underprint. T. A. Rahman at right. New spelling of DIPERLAKUKAN. Signature Ismail Md. Ali with title: GABENUR(SEPULUH). Back: Arms. Watermark: Tiger's head. Printer: TDLR.
    a. Solid security thread.   15.00   75.00
    s. Specimen.   —   —

10   50 Ringgit VF UNC
ND (1972-76). Blue and greenish gray on multicolor underprint. T. A. Rahman
at right. New spelling of *DIPERLAKUKAN*. Signature Ismail Md. Ali with title:
GABENUR(LIMA PULUH). Back: Arms. Watermark: Tiger's head. Printer: TDLR.
    a. Solid security thread. 100 300

11   100 Ringgit VF UNC
ND (1972-76). Purple and brown on multicolor underprint. T. A. Rahman at 250 800
right. New spelling of *DIPERLAKUKAN*. Signature Ismail Md. Ali with title:
GABENUR(SERATUS). Back: Arms. Watermark: Tiger's head. Printer: BWC.

12   1000 Ringgit VF UNC
ND (1972-76). Brown-violet on multicolor underprint. T. A. Rahman at 1,000 4,000
right. New spelling of *DIPERLAKUKAN*. Signature Ismail Md. Ali with title:
GABENUR(SERIBU). Back: Arms. Watermark: Tiger's head. Printer: BWC.

1976; 1981 ND Issues

13   1 Ringgit VF UNC
ND (1976-81). Blue on multicolor underprint. T. A. Rahman at right. Signature title:
GABENUR. Back: Arms, different guilloche with latent image numeral at lower left.
Watermark: Tiger's head. Printer: BWC.
    a. Signature Ismail Md. Ali. (1976). 1.00 10.50
    b. Signature Abdul Aziz Taha. (1981). 1.00 12.50
    s. Specimen.

14   5 Ringgit VF UNC
ND (1976-81). Green on multicolor underprint. T. A. Rahman at right. Signature
title: *GABENUR*. Back: Arms, different guilloche with latent image numeral at
lower left. Watermark: Tiger's head. Printer: BWC.
    a. Signature Ismail Md. Ali. (1976). 8.00 38.00
    b. Signature Abdul Aziz Taha. (1981). 8.00 38.00
    s. Specimen. — —

15   10 Ringgit VF UNC
ND (1976-81). Red-orange and brown on multicolor underprint. T. A. Rahman 15.00 50.00
at right. Signature Ismail Md. Ali with title: *GABENUR(SEPULUH)*. Back: Arms,
different guilloche with latent image numeral at lower left. Watermark: Tiger's
head. Printer: BWC.

#15A, 16A and 17b replacement notes: Serial # prefix *X/*.

15A   10 Ringgit VF UNC
ND (1976-81). T. A. Rahman at right. Signature Abdul Aziz Taha. *(SEPULUH)*.
Back: Arms, different guilloche with latent image numeral at lower left. Watermark:
Tiger's head. Printer: TDLR.
    a. Issued note. 15.00 50.00
    s. Specimen. — —

16   50 Ringgit VF UNC
ND (1976). Blue and greenish gray on multicolor underprint. T. A. Rahman at right. 100 260
Signature Ismail Md. Ali. *(LIMA PULUH)*. Back: Arms, different guilloche with latent
image numeral at lower left. Watermark: Tiger's head. Printer: BWC.

16A   50 Ringgit VF UNC
ND (1981). Blue and greenish gray on multicolor underprint. T. A. Rahman at right. 100 350
Signature Abdul Aziz Taha. Printer: TDLR.

17   100 Ringgit VF UNC
ND (1976). Purple and brown on multicolor underprint. T. A. Rahman at right.
Signature title: *GABENUR (SERATUS)*. Back: Arms. Watermark: Tiger's head.
Printer: BWC.
    a. Signature Ismail Md. Ali. (1976). 100 300

17A   100 Ringgit VF UNC
ND (1981). Purple and brown on multicolor underprint. T.A. Rahman at right. 300 800
Signature Abdul Aziz Taha. Printer: TDLR.

18   1000 Ringgit VF UNC
ND (1976-81). Purple and green on multicolor underprint. T. A. Rahman at right. 700 3,000
Signature Ismail Md. Ali with title: *GABENUR (SERIBU)*. Back: Arms, Parliament
building in Kuala Lumpur. Watermark: Tiger's head. Printer: BWC.

1981-83 ND Issues

#19-26 Replacement notes: Serial # prefixes *BA; WA; UZ; ZZ.*

19   1 Ringgit VF UNC
ND (1982-84). Dark blue and brown on pink and multicolor underprint. T. A. 2.00 10.00
Rahman at right. Signature Abdul Aziz Taha. Back: National Monument Kuala
Lumpurate at center. Watermark: T. A. Rahman. Printer: BWC.

19A   1 Ringgit VF UNC
ND (1981-83). Dark blue and brown on pink and multicolor underprint. T. A. 4.00 20.00
Rahman at right. Signature Abdul Aziz Taha. Back: National Monument Kuala
Lumpurate at center. Watermark: T. A. Rahman. Printer: TDLR.

20   5 Ringgit VF UNC
ND (1983-84). Dark green and blue on multicolor underprint. T. A. Rahman at 8.00 25.00
right. Signature Abdul Aziz Taha. Back: King's Palace at Kuala Lumpur. Watermark: T. A. Rahman. Printer: TDLR.

21 10 Ringgit

ND (1983-84). Red and brown on multicolor underprint. T. A. Rahman at right.
Signature Abdul Aziz Taha. Back: Railway station at Kuala Lumpur. Watermark: T.
A. Rahman. Printer: TDLR.

	VF	UNC
	15.00	42.50

22 20 Ringgit

ND (1982-84). Deep brown and dark blue on multicolor underprint. T. A. Rahman
at right. Signature Abdul Aziz Taha. Back: Bank Negara Malaysia building in Kuala
Lumpur. Watermark: T. A. Rahman. Printer: BWC.

	VF	UNC
	15.00	60.00

23 50 Ringgit

ND (1983-84). Black and blue-gray on multicolor underprint. T. A. Rahman at right.
Signature Abdul Aziz Taha. Back: National Museum at Kuala Lumpur. Watermark:
T. A. Rahman. Printer: TDLR.

	VF	UNC
	60.00	120

24 100 Ringgit

ND (1983-84). Red-brown and violet on multicolor underprint. T. A. Rahman
at right. Signature Abdul Aziz Taha. Back: National Mosque in Kuala Lumpur.
Watermark: T. A. Rahman. Printer: TDLR.

	VF	UNC
	80.00	160

25 500 Ringgit

ND (1982-84). Dark red and purple on multicolor underprint. T. A. Rahman at
right. Signature Abdul Aziz Taha. Back: High Court building in Kuala Lumpur.
Watermark: T. A. Rahman. Printer: BWC.

	VF	UNC
	400	800

26 1000 Ringgit

ND (1983-84). Gray green on multicolor underprint. T. A. Rahman at right. Signature Abdul Aziz Taha. Back: Parliament building in Kuala Lumpur. Watermark: T. A.
Rahman. Printer: TDLR.

	VF	UNC
	700	1,400

1986-95 ND Issues

#27-31, 32, 33 and 34 Replacement notes: Serial # prefixes *BA; WA; UZ or ZZ.*

27 1 Ringgit

ND (1986; 1989). Dark blue and purple on multicolor underprint. T. A. Rahman
at right. Signature Datuk Jaafar Hussein. Vertical serial number. Back: National
Monument Kuala Lumpurate at center. Watermark: T. A. Rahman. Printer: TDLR.

	VF	UNC
a. Solid security thread (1986).	FV	5.00
b. Segmented foil over security thread (1989).	FV	5.00

28 5 Ringgit

ND (1986-91). Dark green and green on multicolor underprint. T. A. Rahman at
right. Signature Datuk Jaafar Hussein. Vertical serial number. Back: King's Palace
at Kuala Lumpur. Watermark: T. A. Rahman. Printer: TDLR.

	VF	UNC
a. Solid security thread (1986).	FV	35.00
b. Segmented foil over security thread (1989).	FV	15.00
c. Flagpole without crossbar at top of back (1991).	FV	12.50

29　10 Ringgit　　　　　　　　　　　　　　　　　　**VF　UNC**
ND (1989). Red-orange and brown on multicolor underprint. T. A. Rahman at　　FV　18.00
right. Signature Datuk Jaafar Hussein. Vertical serial number. Segmented foil over
security thread. Back: Railway station at Kuala Lumpur. Watermark: T. A. Rahman.
Printer: TDLR.

29A　10 Ringgit　　　　　　　　　　　　　　　　　　**VF　UNC**
ND (1989). Brown, red-orange and violet on multicolor underprint. T. A. Rahman　　FV　17.50
at right. Signature Datuk Jaafar Hussein. Vertical serial number. Segmented foil
over security thread. Back: Railway station at Kuala Lumpur. Watermark: T. A.
Rahman. Printer: BABN.

30　20 Ringgit　　　　　　　　　　　　　　　　　　**VF　UNC**
ND (1989). Deep brown and olive on multicolor underprint. T. A. Rahman at right.　　FV　30.00
Signature Datuk Jaafar Hussein. Vertical serial number. Back: Bank Negara
Malaysia building in Kuala Lumpur. Watermark: T. A. Rahman. Printer: TDLR.

31　50 Ringgit　　　　　　　　　　　　　　　　　　**VF　UNC**
ND (1987). Blue and black on multicolor underprint. T. A. Rahman at right.　　FV　60.00
Signature Jafar Hussein. Vertical serial number. Segmented foil over security
thread. Back: National Museum at Kuala Lumpur. Watermark: T. A. Rahman.
Printer: TDLR.

31A　50 Ringgit　　　　　　　　　　　　　　　　　　**VF　UNC**
ND (1991-92). Blue and black on multicolor underprint. T. A. Rahman at right.　　FV　70.00
Signature Datuk Jafar Hussein. Vertical serial number. Segmented foil over
security thread. Back: National Museum at Kuala Lumpur. Watermark: T. A. Rahman. Printer: BABN.

31B　50 Ringgit　　　　　　　　　　　　　　　　　　**VF　UNC**
ND (1995). Blue and black on multicolor underprint. T. A. Rahman at right.　　FV　70.00
Signature Ahmad M. Don. Vertical serial number. Segmented foil over security
thread. Back: National Museum at Kuala Lumpur. Watermark: T. A. Rahman.
Printer: F-CO.

31C　50 Ringgit　　　　　　　　　　　　　　　　　　**VF　UNC**
ND (1995). Blue and black on multicolor underprint. T. A. Rahman at right.　　FV　65.00
Signature Ahmad M. Don. Vertical serial number. Segmented foil over security
thread. Back: National Museum at Kuala Lumpur. Watermark: T. A. Rahman.
Printer: TDLR.

31D　50 Ringgit　　　　　　　　　　　　　　　　　　**VF　UNC**
ND (1997). Blue and black on multicolor underprint. T. A. Rahman at right.　　FV　55.00
Signature Ahmad M. Don. Vertical serial number. Segmented foil over security
thread. Back: National Museum at Kuala Lumpur. Watermark: T. A. Rahman.
Printer: BABN.

32　100 Ringgit　　　　　　　　　　　　　　　　　　**VF　UNC**
ND (1989). Purple on multicolor underprint. T. A. Rahman at right. Signature Datuk　　FV　120
Jaafar Hussein. Vertical serial number. Segmented foil over security thread. Back:
National Mosque in Kuala Lumpur. Watermark: T. A. Rahman. Printer: TDLR.

32A　100 Ringgit　　　　　　　　　　　　　　　　　　**VF　UNC**
ND (1992). Purple on multicolor underprint. T. A. Rahman at right. Signature　　FV　180
Jafar Hussein. Vertical serial number. Segmented foil over security thread. Back:
National Mosque in Kuala Lumpur. Watermark: T. A. Rahman. Printer: USBNC.

32B　100 Ringgit　　　　　　　　　　　　　　　　　　**VF　UNC**
ND (1995). Purple on multicolor underprint. T. A. Rahman at right. Signature　　FV　100
Ahmad M. Don. Vertical serial number. Segmented foil over security thread. Back:
National Mosque in Kuala Lumpur. Watermark: T. A. Rahman. Printer: TDLR.

32C　100 Ringgit　　　　　　　　　　　　　　　　　　**VF　UNC**
ND (1988). Purple on multicolor underprint. T. A. Rahman at right. Signature　　FV　90.00
Ahmad M. Don. Vertical serial number. Segmented foil over security thread. Back:
National Mosque in Kuala Lumpur. Watermark: T. A. Rahman. Printer: H&S.

33　500 Ringgit　　　　　　　　　　　　　　　　　　**VF　UNC**
ND (1989). Red and brown on yellow and multicolor underprint T. A. Rahman at　　325　1,000
right. Signature Datuk Jaafar Hussein. Vertical serial number. Segmented foil
over security thread. Back: HIgh Court building in Kuala Lumpur. Watermark: T. A.
Rahman. Printer: TDLR.

33A　500 Ringgit　　　　　　　　　　　　　　　　　　**VF　UNC**
ND (1989). Red and brown on yellow and multicolor underprint. T. A. Rahman　　350　1,100
at right. Signature Datuk Jaafar Hussein. Vertical serial number. Segmented foil
over security thread. Back: HIgh Court building in Kuala Lumpur. Watermark: T. A.
Rahman. Printer: H&S.

34　1000 Ringgit　　　　　　　　　　　　　　　　　　**VF　UNC**
ND (1987). Blue, green and purple on multicolor underprint. T. A. Rahman at right.　　550　1,200
Signature Jafar Hussein. Vertical serial number. Segmented foil over security
thread. Back: Parliament building in Kuala Lumpur. Watermark: T. A. Rahman.
Printer: TDLR.

34A　1000 Ringgit　　　　　　　　　　　　　　　　　　**VF　UNC**
ND (1995). Blue, green and purple on multicolor underprint. T. A. Rahman at right.　　550　1,200
Signature Ahmad M. Don. Vertical serial number. Segmented foil over security
thread. Back: Parliament building in Kuala Lumpur. Watermark: T. A. Rahman.
Printer: G&D.

1995 ND Issues

35　5 Ringgit　　　　　　　　　　　　　　　　　　**VF　UNC**
ND (1995). Dark blue on multicolor underprint. T. A. Rahman at right. Signature　　FV　5.00
Ahmed Mohd. Don. Vertical serial number. Back: Parliament building in Kuala
Lumpur. Watermark: T. A. Rahman. Printer: TDLR.

35A　5 Ringgit　　　　　　　　　　　　　　　　　　**VF　UNC**
ND (1998). Dark green. T. A. Rahman at right. Signature Ahmed Mohd. Don. Verti-　　FV　5.00
cal serial number. Segmented security thread. Back: Parliament building in Kuala
Lumpur. Watermark: T. A. Rahman. Printer: CBN.

36 10 Ringgit   **VF UNC**

ND (1995). Dark brown, red-orange and violet on multicolor underprint. T. A. Rahman at right. Signature A. M. Don. Vertical serial number. Segmented foil over security thread. Back: Railway station in Kuala Lumpur. Watermark: T. A. Rahman. Printer: F-CO.   FV   10.00

#37 not assigned.

38 10 Ringgit   **VF UNC**

ND (1995). Dark brown, red-orange and violet on multicolor underprint. T. A. Rahman at right. Signature Ahmed Mohd. Don. Vertical serial number. Segmented foil over security thread. Back: Railway station in Kuala Lumpur. Watermark: T. A. Rahman. Printer: G&D.   FV   8.00

1990-2000 ND Issue

39 1 Ringgit   **VF UNC**

ND (1998-). Blue and multicolor. T. A. Rahman at right. Ascending size serial number. Back: Flora and mountain landscape with lake. Watermark: T. A. Rahman. Printer: TDLR. 120x65mm.

		VF	UNC
a. Unissued note. Signature Ali Abu Hassen, horizontal.		—	450
b. Issued note. Signature Zeti Akhtar Aziz, horizontal.		FV	1.00
s. Specimen. Overprinted: *SPECIMEN* in red.		—	200

40 2 Ringgit   **VF UNC**

ND (1996-99). Purple and red-violet on multicolor underprint. T. A. Rahman at right. Ascending size serial number. Back: Modern tower at left, communications satellite at upper center. Watermark: T. A. Rahman. Printer: NBM (without imprint). 130x65mm.

		VF	UNC
a. Signature Ahmad M. Don vertical at left. Long arabic text on back.		FV	3.00
b. Signature Ali Abu Hassan vertical at left. Long Arabic text on back.		FV	2.50
c. Signature Ali Abu Hassan horizontal at lower center. Short Arabic text on back.		FV	2.00
s. As a. Specimen. Overprint in red.		—	200

41 5 Ringgit   **VF UNC**

ND (1999; 2001). Green on multicolor underprint. T. A. Rahman at right. Ascending size serial number. Short Arabic text on back. Back: Modern buildings. Watermark: T. A. Rahman. 135x65mm.

		VF	UNC
a. ND (1999). Signature Ali Abu Hassan. Printer: TDLR.		FV	3.50
b. ND (2001). Signature Zeti Akhtar Aziz. Printer: CBNC.		FV	3.50
s. As a. Specimen. Overprinted *SPECIMEN* in red.		—	250

42 10 Ringgit   **VF UNC**

ND (1997-). Red on multicolor underprint. T. A. Rahman at right. Ascending size serial number. Back: Modern passenger train at left, passenger jet airplane, freighter ship at center. Watermark: T. A. Rahman. 140x65mm.

		VF	UNC
a. ND (1997). Signature Ahmad M. Don vertical at left. Long arabic text on back. Printer: TDLR.		FV	7.50
b. ND (1999). Signature Ali Abu Hassan vertical at left. Long Arabic text on back. Printer: BABN.		FV	7.50
c. ND (1999). Signature Ali Abu Hassan at center. Short Arabic text on back. Printer: TDLR.		FV	6.00
d. ND (2001). Signature Zeti Akhtar Aziz. Short Arabic text on back. Printer: TDLR.		FV	6.00
s. As a. Specimen. Overprint in red.		—	250

43 50 Ringgit   **VF UNC**

ND (1998-). Dark green and green on multicolor underprint. T. A. Rahman at right. Ascending size serial number. Back: Offshore oil platform at left. Watermark: T. A. Rahman. 145x69mm.

		VF	UNC
a. ND (1998). Signature Ahmad M. Don vertical at left. Long Arabic text on back. Printer: G&D.		FV	35.00
b. ND (1999). Signature Ali Abu Hassan vertical at left. Long Arabic text on back. Printer: G&D.		FV	35.00
c. ND (1999). Signature Ali Abu Hassan at center. Short Arabic text on back. Printer: TDLR.		FV	25.00
d. ND (2001). Signature Zeti Akhtar Aziz. Short Arabic text on back. Printer: TDLR.		FV	25.00

44 100 Ringgit VF UNC
ND (1998-). Purple and brown on multicolor underprint. T. A. Rahman at right.
Ascending size serial number. Back: Automobile production themes. Watermark:
T. A. Rahman. 150x69mm.
  a. ND (1998). Signature Ahmad M. Don vertical at left. Long Arabic text on FV 55.00
     back. Printer: TDLR.
  b. ND (1999). Signature Ali Abu Hassan vertical at left. Long Arabic text on FV 60.00
     back. Printer: G&D.
  c. ND (1999). Signature Ali Abu Hassan at center. Short Arabic text on back. FV 50.00
     Printer: G&D.
  d. ND (2001). Signature Zeti Akhtar Aziz. Short Arabic text on back. PrinterL FV 50.00
     G&D.

1998 Commemorative Issue
#45, XVI Commonwealth Games, Kuala Lumpur, 1998.

45 50 Ringgit VF UNC
(19)98. Polymer plastic. Black and purple on multicolor underprint. T. A. Rahman FV 45.00
at right, Petronas Towers at center, multimedia corridor in underprint at right.
Serial number prefix: *KL/98*. Back: Utama Bukit Jalil Stadium at center, games
logo at left. 145x69mm.

2004 ND First Issue

46 10 Ringgit VF UNC
ND (2004). Red and orange on multicolor underprint. T. A. Rahman at right. FV 8.00
Wide holographic strip at far right. Back: Train, ship and jet plane. Printer: G&D.
140x65mm.

2004 ND Polymer Issue

47 5 Ringgit VF UNC
ND (2004). Polymer plastic. Green on multicolor underprint. T.A. Rahman at right. FV 3.00
Back: Petronas Towers at center. 135x65mm.
#48 not assigned.

2007 Commemorative Issue
49 50 Ringgit VF UNC
2007. Issued in a folder. Blue, green and multicolor underprint. T. A. Rahman FV 30.00
at right, wide holographic strip at far right. Flower at lower center. Gold bands
at both ends. Back: Malaysia's first Prime Minister declaring Independence.
Commemorative 50 Logo at top right, and small commemorative dates at lower
center. 145x69mm.
Commemorative of the 50th Anniversary of Independence.

2009 Issue

50 50 Ringgit VF UNC
ND (2009). Green-blue on multicolor underprint. Tuanku Abdul Rahman at right. FV 30.00
Back: Malaysia's first Prime Minister declairing independence at right. Printer:
G&D. 145x69mm.
55 50 Ringgit VF UNC
ND (2009). Like #50, but serial # has 3-letter prefix. Blue. Tuanku Abdul Rahman FV 30.00
at right. Back: Malaysia's first Prime Minister declairing independence at right.
145x69mm.

2012 Issue
51 1 Ringgit VF UNC
ND (2012). Polymer plastic. Blue and multicolor. Tuanku Abdul Rahman at right, FV 1.00
flower at lower center. Back: *Wau bulan,* a moon kite.
52 5 Ringgit VF UNC
ND (2012). Polymer plastic. Green and multicolor. Tuanku Abdul Rahman at right, FV 2.00
flower at lower center. Back: Pair of Rhinocerus hornbills.
53 10 Ringgit VF UNC
ND (2012). Red and multicolor. Tuanku Abdul Rahman at right, flower at lower FV 6.50
center. Segmented security thread. Back: Rafflesia
54 20 Ringgit VF UNC
ND (2012). Orange and multicolor. Tuanku Abdul Rahman at right, flower at lower FV 12.50
center. Segmented security thread. Back: Hawksbill and Leatherback turtle.
56 100 Ringgit VF UNC
ND (2012). Purple, brown and multicolor. Tuanku Abdul Rahman at right, flower at FV 50.00
lower center. Segmented security thread. Back: Mount Kinabalu and rock formations of Gunung Api Valley

THE MALDIVES

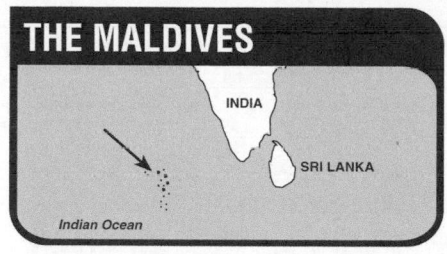

The Republic of Maldives, an archipelago of about 2,000 coral islets in the northern Indian Ocean 417 miles (671 km.) southwest of Ceylon, has an area of 115 sq. mi. (298 sq. km.) and a population of 302,000. Capital: Malé. Fishing employs 95 percent of the work force. Dried fish, copra and coir yarn are exported. The Maldives was long a sultanate, first under Dutch and then under British protection. It became a republic in 1968, three years after independence. President Maumoon Abdul Gayoom dominated the islands' political scene for 30 years, elected to six successive terms by single-party referendums. Following riots in the capital Male in August 2004, the president and his government pledged to embark upon democratic reforms including a more representative political system and expanded political freedoms. Progress was sluggish, however, and many promised reforms were slow to be realized. Nonetheless, political parties were legalized in 2005. In June 2008, a constituent assembly - termed the "Special Majlis" - finalized a new constitution, which was ratified by the president in August. The first-ever presidential elections under a multi-candidate, multi-party system were held in October 2008. Gayoom was defeated in a runoff poll by Mohamed Nasheed, a political activist who had been jailed several years earlier by the former regime. Challenges facing the new president include strengthening democracy and combating poverty and drug abuse.

RULERS:
British to 1965

MONETARY SYSTEM:
1 Rufiyaa (Rupee) = 100 Lari

REPUBLIC

Maldivian State, Government Treasurer
1951; 1960; 1980 Issue

6   50 Rupees   **VF   UNC**
1951-80. Blue on multicolor underprint. Palm tree and dhow at left, dhow at right. Back: Royal Embarkation Gate at Malé at center.
    a. 1951/AH1371.   150   400
    b. 4.6.1960/AH1379.   20.00   90.00
    c. Lithographed 1.8.1980/AH17.7.1400.   25.00   100
    s. As c. Specimen.   —   175

7   100 Rupees   **VF   UNC**
1951; 1960. Green on multicolor underprint. Palm tree and dhow at left, dhow at right. Back: Park and building complex at center.
    a. 1951/AH1371.   175   500
    b. 4.6.1960/AH1379.   50.00   200

#8 not assigned.

Maldives Monetary Authority
1983 Issue

9   2 Rufiyaa   **VF   UNC**
7.10.1983/AH1404. Dark olive green on multicolor underprint. Dhow at right. Back: Shoreline village. Watermark: Arms. Printer: BWC. 150x70mm.
    a. Issued note.   FV   4.00
    s. Specimen. Red overprint: SPECIMEN on both sides.   —   50.00

10   5 Rufiyaa   **VF   UNC**
7.10.1983/AH1404. Deep purple on green and multicolor underprint. Dhow at right. Back: Fishing boats at center. Watermark: Arms. Printer: BWC. 150x70mm.
    a. Issued note.   FV   4.00
    s. Specimen. Red overprint: SPECIMEN on both sides.   —   50.00

11   10 Rufiyaa   **VF   UNC**
7.10.1983/AH1404. Brown on green and multicolor underprint. Dhow at right. Back: Villagers working at center. Watermark: Arms. Printer: BWC. 150x70mm.
    a. Issued note.   FV   4.00
    s. Specimen. Red overprint: SPECIMEN on both sides.   —   50.00

12 20 Rufiyaa

VF   UNC

1983; 1987. Red-violet on multicolor underprint. Dhow at right. Back: Fishing
boats at dockside in Malé Harbour. Watermark: Arms. Printer: BWC. 150x70mm.

    a. 7.10.1983/AH1404. Imprint at bottom center on back.   FV 7.00

    b. 25.8.1987/AH1408. Without imprint at bottom center on back.   FV 5.50

    s. Specimen. As a. Red overprint: SPECIMEN on both sides.   — 50.00

13 50 Rufiyaa

VF   UNC

1983; 1987. Blue-violet on multicolor underprint. Dhow at right. Back: Village
market in Malé at center. Watermark: Arms. Printer: BWC. 150x70mm.

    a. 7.10.1983/AH1404. Imprint at bottom center on back.   FV 25.00

    b. 25.8.1987/AH1408. Without imprint at bottom center on back.   FV 17.50

    s. Specimen. Red overprint: SPECIMEN on both sides.   — 50.00

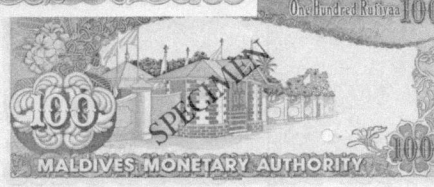

14 100 Rufiyaa

VF   UNC

1983; 1987. Dark green and brown on multicolor underprint. Dhow at right. Back:
Tomb of Medhuziyaaraiy at center. Watermark: Arms. Printer: BWC. 150x70mm.

    a. 7.10.1983/AH1404. Imprint at bottom center on back.   FV 35.00

    b. 25.8.1987/AH1408. Without imprint at bottom center on back.   FV 27.50

    s. Specimen. Red overprint: SPECIMEN on both sides.   — 50.00

1990 Issue

15 2 Rufiyaa

VF   UNC

26.7.1990/AH1411. Dark olive-green on multicolor underprint. Dhow at right. Back: FV 2.50
Shoreline village. Watermark: Arms. Printer: TDLR. 150x70mm.

16 5 Rufiyaa

VF   UNC

26.7.1990/AH1411. Deep purple on multicolor underprint. Dhow at right. Back: FV 3.00
Fishing boats at center. Watermark: Arms. Printer: TDLR. 150x70mm.

17 500 Rufiyaa

VF   UNC

26.7.1990/AH1411. Orange and green on multicolor underprint. Back: Grand   FV 120
Friday Mosque and Islamic Center. Watermark: Arms. Printer: TDLR. 150x70mm.

1995-98 Issue

18 5 Rufiyaa

VF   UNC

1988; 2000; 2006; 2011. Deep purple, dark blue and violet on multicolor underprint. Design to edge of paper. Dhow at right. Ascending size serial numbers at left
and lower right. Back: Fishing boats at center. Watermark: Arms. Printer: TDLR.
150x70mm.

    a. 27.4.1998/AH1419.   FV 2.00

    b. 2000/AH1421. With De La Rue imprint.   FV 2.00

    c. 2000/AH1421. Without imprint.   FV 2.00

    d. 2006/AH1427.   FV 2.00

    e. 2011/AH1432.   FV 2.00

19 10 Rufiyaa

VF   UNC

1998; 2006. Dark brown, green and orange on multicolor underprint. Design to
edge of paper. Dhow at right. Ascending size serial numbers at left and lower
right. Back: Vilagers working at center. Watermark: Arms. 150x70mm.

    a. 25.10.1998/AH1419. Series C. DLR imprint.   FV 3.00

    b. 25.10.1998/AH1419. Series D. Without imprint.   FV 3.00

    c. 2006/AH1427.   FV 3.00

20 20 Rufiyaa   **VF UNC**

2000/AH1421; 2008/AH1430. Design into borders. Red-violet and green on multicolor underprint. Dhow at right. Ascending size serial numbers at left and lower right. Back: Fishing boats at dockside in Malé Harbor. Watermark: Arms. 150x70mm.

    a. 2000/AH1421. Series B. With DLR imprint   FV 5.00
    b. 2000/AH1421 Series C. Without imprint.   FV 5.00
    c. 2008/AH1430.   FV 3.50

21 50 Rufiyaa   **VF UNC**

2000/AH1421; 2008/AH1430. Design into borders. Blue-violet and light green on multicolor underprint. Dhow at right. Ascending size serial numbers at left and lower right. Back: Village market in Malé at center. Watermark: Arms. Printer: TDLR. 150x70mm.

    a. 2000/AH1421.   FV 12.50
    b. 2008/AH1430.   FV 12.50

22 100 Rufiyaa   **VF UNC**

1995; 2000. Dark green and brown on multicolor underprint. Dhow at right. Back: Tomb of Modhuziyaaraiy at center. Watermark: Arms. 160x70mm.

    a. 29.7.1995/AH1416. Series D. Printer BWC, without imprint.   FV 25.00
    b. 2000/AH1421. Series G. Enhanced UV features.   FV 22.50

23 500 Rufiyaa   **VF UNC**

1996. Orange and green on multicolor underprint. Dhow at right. Back: Grand Friday Mosque and Islamic Center. Watermark: Arms. Printer: TDLR. 150x70mm.

    a. 1.5.1996/AH1416.   FV 90.00

24 500 Rufiyaa   **VF UNC**

2006/AH1426; 2008/AH1430. Red, orange and green on multicolor underprint. Dhow at right. Back: Grand Friday Mosque and Islamic Center. Watermark: Arms Printer. TDLR. 150x70mm.

    a. 2006/AH1426.   FV 90.00
    b. 2008/AH1430.   FV 90.00

2015 Commemorative Issue

25 5000 Rufiyaa   **VF UNC**

2015/AH1436. 50th anniversary of independence.   FV 650

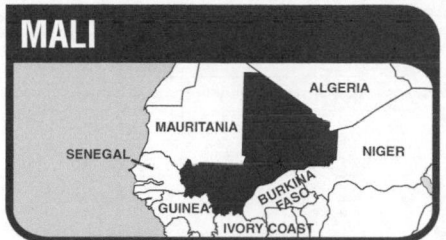

MALI

The Republic of Mali, a landlocked country in the interior of West Africa southwest of Algeria, has an area of 478,764 sq. mi. (1,240,000 sq. km.) and a population of 12.56 million. Capital: Bamako. Livestock, fish, cotton and peanuts are exported. The Sudanese Republic and Senegal became independent of France in 1960 as the Mali Federation. When Senegal withdrew after only a few months, what formerly made up the Sudanese Republic was renamed Mali. Rule by dictatorship was brought to a close in 1991 by a military coup - led by the current president Amadou Toure - enabling Mali's emergence as one of the strongest democracies on the continent. President Alpha Konare won Mali's first democratic presidential election in 1992 and was reelected in 1997. In keeping with Mali's two-term constitutional limit, Konare stepped down in 2002 and was succeeded by Amadou Toure, who was subsequently elected to a second term in 2007. The elections were widely judged to be free and fair. Mali seceded from the African Financial Community in 1962, then rejoined in 1984. Issues specially marked with letter D for Mali were made by the Banque des Etats de l'Afrique de l'Ouest. See also French West Africa, and West African States.

MONETARY SYSTEM:
    1 Franc = 100 Centimes

SIGNATURE VARIETIES		
1	Ministre Des Finances	Gouverneur de La Banque
2	Ministre d'Etat — Ministre Des Finances	Gouverneur de La Banque
3	Le Président du Council d'Administration	Le Directeur Général
4	Le Président du Council d'Administration	Le Directeur Général
5	Le Président du Council d'Administration	Le Directeur Général
6	Le Président du Council d'Administration	Le Directeur Général
7	Le Président du Council d'Administration	Le Directeur Général
8	Le Président du Council d'Administration	Le Directeur Général
9	Le Président du Council d'Administration	Le Directeur Général

REPUBLIC

Banque de la République du Mali

First 1960 (1962) Issue

Note: Post-dated to Day of Independence.

1   50 Francs   **VF UNC**
22.9.1960. Purple on multicolor underprint. President Modibo Keita at left. 100 350
Signature 1. Back: Village.

7   100 Francs   **VF UNC**
22.9.1960 (1967). Brown on green and lilac underprint. Modibo Keita at right,
tractors at lower left. Signature 2. Back: Old man at right, canoes at center, city
view behind. Printer: TDLR.
 a. Issued note.   90.00 325
 s. Specimen. Red overprint: *SPECIMEN* and TDLR logo on both sides. — 1,250

2   100 Francs   **VF UNC**
22.9.1960. Brown on yellow underprint. President Modibo Keita at left. Signature 90.00 325
1. Back: Cattle.

3   500 Francs   **VF UNC**
22.9.1960. Red on light blue and orange underprint. President Modibo Keita at 500 1,300
left. Signature 1. Back: Woman and tent.

8   500 Francs   **VF UNC**
22.9.1960 (1967). Green on yellow, blue and red underprint. Modibo Keita at right,
building at lower left. Signature 2. Back: Longhorn cattle. Printer: TDLR.
 a. Issued note.   235 750
 s. Specimen. Red overprint: *SPECIMEN* and TDLR logo on both sides. — 1,250

4   1000 Francs   **VF UNC**
22.9.1960. Blue on light green and orange underprint. President Modibo Keita at 180 600
left. Signature 1. Farmers with oxen at lower right. Back: Man and huts.

5   5000 Francs   **VF UNC**
22.9.1960. Green on multicolor underprint. President Modibo Keita at left. Signa- 450 —
ture 1. Farmers with oxen at lower right. Two farmers plowing with oxen at right.
Back: Market scene and building.

Second 1960 (1967) Issue
Note: Post-dated to Day of Independence.

9   1000 Francs   **VF UNC**
22.9.1960 (1967). Blue on lilac and brown underprint. Modibo Keita at right, bank
at lower left. Signature 2. Back: People and Djenne mosque. Printer: TDLR.
 a. Issued note.   550 1,400
 s. Specimen. Red overprint: *SPECIMEN* and TDLR logo on both sides. — 1,250

6   50 Francs   **VF UNC**
22.9.1960 (1967). Purple on blue and light green underprint. Modibo Keita at right,
dam at lower left. Signature 2. Back: Woman and village. Printer: TDLR.
 a. Issued note.   100 350
 s. Specimen. Red overprint: *SPECIMEN* and TDLR logo on both sides. — 1,250

10   5000 Francs
22.9.1960 (1967). Dark red on green underprint. Modibo Keita at right, farmers at
center. Signature 2. Back: Market scene and buildings. Printer: TDLR.

		VF	UNC
a. Issued note.		450	1,200
s. Specimen. Red overprint: *SPECIMEN* and TDLR logo on both sides.		—	1,250

Banque Centrale du Mali
1970-73 ND Issues

11   100 Francs
ND (1972-73). Brown and multicolor. Woman at left, hotel at right. Signature 4.
Back: Woman at left, boats docking at center.

	VF	UNC
	70.00	275

12   500 Francs
ND (1973-84). Brown and multicolor. Soldier at left, tractors at right. Back: Man
and camels. Watermark: Man's head.

	VF	UNC
a. Signature 4.	35.00	120
b. Signature 5.	25.00	80.00
c. Signature 6.	20.00	70.00
d. Signature 7.	20.00	70.00
e. Signature 8.	20.00	70.00
f. Signature 9.	75.00	250

13   1000 Francs
ND (1970-84). Brownish black, purple and multicolor. Building at left, older man at
right. Back: Carvings at left, mountain village at center. Watermark: Man's head.

	VF	UNC
a. Signature 4.	27.50	90.00
b. Signature 5.	27.50	90.00
c. Signature 6.	25.00	80.00
d. Signature 7.	25.00	80.00
e. Signature 8.	25.00	80.00

14   5000 Francs
ND (1972-84). Blue, brown and multicolor. Cattle at lower left, man with turban at
right. Back: Woman and flowers at left center, woman at textile machinery at right.
Watermark: Man's head.

	VF	UNC
a. Signature 4.	200	700
b. Signature 5.	185	650
c. Signature 6.	185	650
d. Signature 7.	185	650
e. Signature 8.	175	600

15   10,000 Francs
ND (1970-84). Multicolor. Man with fez at left, factory at lower right. Back: Weaver
at left, young woman with coin headband at right. Watermark: Man's head.

	VF	UNC
a. Signature 3.	275	900
b. Signature 4.	235	800
c. Signature 5.	250	850
d. Signature 6.	235	800
e. Signature 7.	235	800
f. Signature 8.	235	800
g. Signature 9.	250	850

The Republic of Malta, an independent parliamentary democracy within the British Commonwealth, is situated in the Mediterranean Sea between Sicily and North Africa. With the islands of Gozo and Comino, Malta has an area of 122 sq. mi. (316 sq. km.) and a population of 379,000. Capital: Valletta. With the islands of Gozo (Ghawdex), Comino, Cominetto and Filfla, Malta has no proven mineral resources, an agriculture insufficient to its needs and a small but expanding, manufacturing facility. Clothing, textile yarns and fabrics, and knitted wear are exported.Great Britain formally acquired possession of Malta in 1814. The island staunchly supported the UK through both World Wars and remained in the Commonwealth when it became independent in 1964. A decade later Malta became a republic. Since about the mid-1980s, the island has transformed itself into a freight transshipment point, a financial center, and a tourist destination. Malta became an EU member in May 2004 and began to use the euro as currency in 2008.

RULERS:
British to 1974

MONETARY SYSTEM:
1 Shilling = 12 Pence
1 Pound = 20 Shillings to 1971
1 Lira = 100 Centesimi, 1972-2007
1 Euro = 100 Cents, 2008-

REPUBLIC
Government of Malta
1949 Ordinance; 1963 ND Issue

25	10 Shillings	VF	UNC
	L.1949 (1963). Green and blue on multicolor underprint. Queen Elizabeth II at right, cross at center. Signature R. Soler. Back: Mgarr Harbor, Gozo. Printer: BWC.		
	a. Issued note.	175	475
	s. Specimen.	—	600
	ct. Color trial. Red on multicolor underprint.	—	650

26	1 Pound	VF	UNC
	L.1949 (1963). Brown and violet on multicolor underprint. Queen Elizabeth II at right, cross at center. Signature R. Soler. Back: Industrial Estate, Marsa. Printer: BWC.		
	a. Issued note.	115	350
	s. Specimen.	—	500
	ct. Color trial. Blue on multicolor underprint.	—	600

27	5 Pounds	VF	UNC
	L.1949 (1961). Blue on multicolor underprint. Queen Elizabeth II at right, cross at center. Back: Grand Harbor. Printer: BWC.		
	a. Signature D. A. Shepherd (1961).	375	1,600
	b. Signature R. Soler (1963).	600	2,000
	s. As a. Specimen, punch hole cancelled.	—	850
	ct. Color trial. Brown and violet on multicolor underprint.	—	1,000

Central Bank of Malta
1967 Central Bank Act; 1968-69 ND Issue

28	10 Shillings	VF	UNC
	L.1967 (1968). Red on multicolor underprint. Similar to #25. Signature P.L. Hogg. Printer: BWC.		
	a. Issued note.	100	225
	s. Specimen.	—	400
	ct. Color trial. Dark olive on multicolor underprint.	—	500

29	1 Pound	VF	UNC
	L.1967 (1969). Olive-green on multicolor underprint. Similar to #26. Signature P.L. Hogg. Printer: BWC.		
	a. Issued note.	125	300
	s. Specimen.	—	400
	ct. Color trial. Blue on multicolor underprint.	—	500

30	**5 Pounds**		**VF**	**UNC**

L.1967 (1968). Brown and violet on multicolor underprint. Similar to #27. Signature P.L. Hogg. Printer: BWC

	a. Issued note.	175	450
	s. Specimen.	—	700
	ct. Color trial. Red on multicolor underprint.	—	800

Bank Centrali ta' Malta
1967 Central Bank Act; 1973 ND Issue
#31-33 Replacement notes: Serial # prefix *X/1, Y/1 or Z/1* (by denomintation).

31	**1 Lira**		**VF**	**UNC**

L.1967 (1973). Green on multicolor underprint. Arms at right, map at center, War Memorial at left. Back: PrehistoricTemple in Tarxien at left, old capital city of Medina at center. Watermark. Allegorical head of Malta. Printer: TDLR.

	a. Signature J. Sammut and A. Camilleri.	25.00	60.00
	b. Signature H. de Gabriele and J. Laspina.	25.00	60.00
	c. Signature H. de Gabriele and A. Camilleri.	25.00	60.00
	d. Signature J. Laspina and J. Sammut.	25.00	60.00
	e. Signature A. Camilleri and J. Laspina.	25.00	60.00
	f. Signature J. Sammut and H. de Gabriele.	25.00	60.00
	s. Specimen.	—	200

32	**5 Liri**		**VF**	**UNC**

L.1967 (1973). Blue on multicolor underprint. Arms at right, map at center, Neptune at left. Back: Marina at left, boats at center right. Watermark: Allegorical head of Malta. Printer: TDLR.

	a. Signature H. de Gabriele and J. Laspina.	60.00	130
	b. Signature H. de Gabriele and A. Camilleri.	60.00	130
	c. Signature J. Laspina and J. Sammut.	60.00	130
	d. Signature A. Camilleri and J. Laspina.	60.00	130
	e. Signature J. Sammut and H. de Gabriele.	60.00	130
	f. Signature J. Sammut and A. Camilleri.	60.00	130
	s. Specimen.	—	300

33	**10 Liri**		**VF**	**UNC**

L.1967 (1973). Brown on multicolor underprint. Arms at right, map at center, Neptune at left. Back: View of Grand Harbour and boats. Watermark: Allegorical head of Malta. Printer: TDLR.

	a. Signature H. de Gabriele and A. Camilleri.	90.00	300
	b. Signature J. Laspina and J. Sammut.	90.00	300
	c. Signature A. Camilleri and J. Laspina.	90.00	300
	d. Signature J. Sammut and H. de Gabriele.	90.00	300
	e. Signature L. Spiteri with title: *DEPUTAT GOVERNATUR.*	90.00	225
	s. Specimen.	—	400

1979 ND Issue
Central Bank Act, 1967 #34-36 Replacement notes: Serial prefix *X/2, Y/2 or Z/2* (by denomination).

34	**1 Lira**		**VF**	**UNC**

L.1967 (1979). Brown on multicolor underprint. Map at upper left, arms at upper right. Watch tower "Gardjola" at center. Back: New University at left center. Watermark: Allegorical head of Malta. Printer: TDLR.

	a. Without dot.	25.00	50.00
	b. With 1 dot added for blind at upper right.	25.00	50.00
	s. Specimen. Red overprint: *SPECIMEN.*	—	60.00

35	**5 Liri**		**VF**	**UNC**

L.1967 (1979). Purple and violet on multicolor underprint. Map at upper left, arms at upper right. Statue of "Culture" at center. Back: Aerial view of Marsa Industrial Estate at left center. Watermark: Allegorical head of Malta. Printer: TDLR.

	a. Without 2 dots.	25.00	75.00
	b. With 2 dots added for blind at upper right.	90.00	180
	s. Specimen. Red overprint: *SPECIMEN.*	—	130

36	**10 Liri**		**VF**	**UNC**

L.1967 (1979). Gray and pink on multicolor underprint. Map at upper left, arms at upper right.Statue of "Justice" at center. Back: Aerial view of Malta drydocks at left center. Watermark: Allegorical head of Malta. Printer: TDLR.

	a. Without 3 dots.	50.00	125
	b. With 3 dots added for blind at upper right.	60.00	150
	s. Specimen. Red overprint: *SPECIMEN.*	—	300

1986 ND Issue

#37-40 Replacement notes: Serial # prefix *W/2, X/2, Y/2* or *Z/2* **(by denomination).**

37 2 Liri

VF UNC

L.1967 (1986). Red-orange on multicolor underprint. Sailing craft and map of malta at center, A. Barbara at right. Back: Dockside crane at left, aerial harbor view at right. Watermark: Allegorical head of Malta. Printer: TDLR. 138x69mm.

   a. Issued note.   17.50   50.00

   s. Specimen. Red overprint: *SPECIMEN.*   —   60.00

38 5 Liri

VF UNC

L.1967 (1986). Gray-green and blue on multicolor underprint, with two black horizontal accounting bars at lower rig Sailing craft and map of malta at center, A. Barbara at right. Back: Sailboats in harbor and repairing of fishing nets. Watermark: Allegorical head of Malta. Printer: TDLR. 145x69mm.

   a. Issued note.   30.00   85.00

   s. Specimen. Red overprint: *SPECIMEN.*   —   130

39 10 Liri

VF UNC

L.1967 (1986). Olive and dark green on multicolor underprint, with three dark green horizontal accounting bars at l Sailing craft and map of malta at center, A. Barbara at right. Back: Shipbuilding. Watermark: Allegorical head of Malta. Printer: TDLR. 152x73mm.

   a. Issued note.   55.00   165

   s. Specimen. Red overprint: *SPECIMEN.*   —   300

40 20 Lira

VF UNC

L.1967 (1986). Brown and red-brown on multicolor underprint, with four brown horizontal accounting bars at lower ri Sailing craft and map of malta at center, A. Barbara at right. Back: Statue and government building at center. Watermark: Allegorical head of Malta. Printer: TDLR. 179x76mm.

   a. Issued note.   125   300

   s. Specimen. Red overprint: *SPECIMEN.*   —   400

1989 ND Issue

#41-44 Replacement notes: Serial # prefix *W/2, X/2, Y/2* or *Z/2* **(by denomination).**

41 2 Liri

VF UNC

L.1967 (1989). Purple on multicolor underprint. Doves at left, Malta standing with rudder at center. Back: Buildings in Malta and Gozo. Watermark: Turreted head of Malta. Printer: TDLR. 138x69mm.

   a. Issued note.   15.00   35.00

   s. Specimen. Red overprint: *SPECIMEN.*   —   60.00

42 5 Liri

VF UNC

L.1967 (1989). Blue on multicolor underprint. Doves at left, Malta standing with rudder at center. Back: Historical tower. Watermark: Turreted head of Malta. Printer: TDLR. 145x69mm.

   a. Issued note.   20.00   60.00

   s. Specimen. Red overprint: *SPECIMEN.*   —   130

43 10 Liri

VF UNC

L.1967 (1989). Green on multicolor underprint. Doves at left, Malta standing with rudder at center. Back: Wounded people being brought into National Assembly. Watermark: Turreted head of Malta. Printer: TDLR. 159x73mm.

   a. Issued note.   40.00   115

   s. Specimen. Red overprint: *SPECIMEN.*   —   300

44 20 Lira

VF UNC

L.1967 (1989). Brown on multicolor underprint. Doves at left, Malta standing with rudder at center. Back: Prime Minister Dr. G. B. Olivier. Watermark: Turreted head of Malta. Printer: TDLR. 179x76mm.

   a. Issued note.   85.00   220

   s. Specimen. Red overprint: *SPECIMEN.*   —   400

1994 ND Issue

45 2 Liri

VF UNC

L.1967 (1994). Purple on multicolor underprint. Doves at left, Malta standing with rudder at center. Segmented foil over security threads and ascending size serial numbers at upper left. Back: Buildings in Malta and Gozo. Watermark: Turreted head of Malta. Printer: TDLR. 138x69mm.

   a. Signature Anthony P. Galdes.   FV   40.00

   b. Signature Francis J. Vasallo.   FV   40.00

   c. Signature Emanuel Ellul.   FV   40.00

   d. Signature Michael P. Bonello.   FV   40.00

   s. Specimen. Red overprint: *SPECIMEN.*   —   60.00

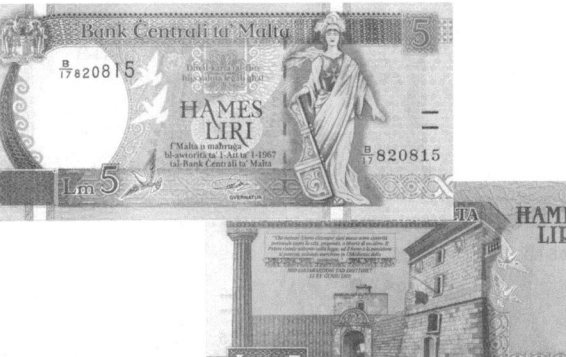

46 5 Liri

VF UNC

L.1967 (1994). Blue on multicolor underprint. Doves at left, Malta standing with rudder at center. Segmented foil over security threads and ascending size serial numbers at upper left. Back: Historical tower. Watermark: Turreted head of Malta. Printer: TDLR. 145x69mm.

   a. Signature Anthony P. Galdes.   FV   85.00

   b. Signature Francis J. Vassallo.   FV   80.00

   c. Signature Emanuel Ellul.   FV   75.00

   d. Signature Michael P. Bonello.   FV   70.00

   s. Specimen. Red overprint: *SPECIMEN.*   —   130

47 10 Liri

L.1967 (1994). Green on multicolor underprint. Doves at left, Malta standing with rudder at center. Segmented foil over security threads and ascending size serial numbers at upper left. Back: Wounded people being brought into National Assembly. Watermark: Turreted head of Malta. Printer: TDLR. 159x73mm.

		VF	UNC
a.	Signature Anthony P. Galdes.	FV	110
b.	Signature Emanuel Ellul.	FV	90.00
c.	Signature Michael P. Bonello.	FV	70.00
s.	Specimen. Red overprint: *SPECIMEN*.	—	300

48 20 Lira

L.1967 (1994). Brown on multicolor underprint. Doves at left, Malta standing with rudder at center. Segmented foil over security threads and ascending size serial numbers at upper left. Signature; Anthony P. Galdes. Back: Prime Minister Dr. G. B. Olivier. Watermark: Turreted head of Malta. Printer: TDLR. 159x76mm.

		VF	UNC
a.	Issued note.	FV	100
s.	Specimen. Red overprint: *SPECIMEN*.	—	400

2000 Issue

#49-51 Millennium Commemorative issue.

49 2 Liri

2000 (L. 1967.) Purple on multicolor underprint. Doves at left, Malta standing with rudder at center. Segmented foil over security threads and ascending size serial numbers at upper left. Map and clock hologram on watermark area. Back: Buildings in Malta and Gozo. Watermark: Turreted head of Malta. Printer: TDLR. 138x69mm.

VF UNC
FV 50.00

50 5 Liri

2000 (L. 1967). Blue on multicolor underprint. Doves at left, Malta standing with rudder at center. Segmented foil over security threads and ascending size serial numbers at upper left. Map and clock hologram on watermark area. Back: Historical tower. Watermark: Turreted head of Malta. Printer: TDLR. 145x69mm.

VF UNC
FV 100

51 10 Liri

2000 (L. 1967.) Green on multicolor underprint. Doves at left, Malta standing with rudder at center. Segmented foil over security threads and ascending size serial numbers at upper left. Map and clock hologram on watermark area. Back: Wounded people being brought into National Assembly. Watermark: Turreted head of Malta. Printer: TDLR. 152x73mm.

VF UNC
FV 150

As of January 2008 Malta has converted to Euro notes.

COLLECTOR SERIES

Bank Centrali ta' Malta

1979 Issue

CS1 ND (1979) 1-10 Liri

#34a-36a with overprint: *SPECIMEN* and Maltese cross prefix serial #.

Mkt. Value
180

2000 Issue

CS2 ND (2000) 2-5-10 Liri

#49-51 in individual folders titled: *Special Millennium Issue*. Hologram on watermark area: *1999 Towards a New Millennium 2000*. 25,000 sets issued.

Mkt. Value
300

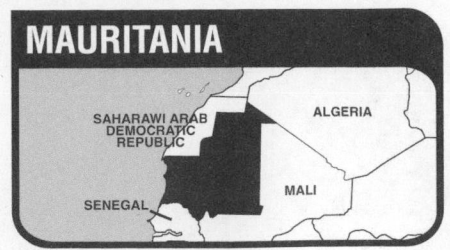

MAURITANIA

The Islamic Republic of Mauritania, located in northwest Africa bounded by Spanish Sahara, Mali, Algeria, Senegal and the Atlantic Ocean, has an area of 397,955 sq. mi. (1,030,700 sq. km.) and a population of 2.58 million. Capital: Nouakchott. The economy centers on herding, agriculture, fishing and mining. Iron ore, copper concentrates and fish products are exported. Independent from France in 1960, Mauritania annexed the southern third of the former Spanish Sahara (now Western Sahara) in 1976, but relinquished it after three years of raids by the Polisario guerrilla front seeking independence for the territory. Maaouya Ould Sid Ahmed Taya seized power in a coup in 1984 and ruled Mauritania with a heavy hand for over two decades. A series of presidential elections that he held were widely seen as flawed. A bloodless coup in August 2005 deposed President TAYA and ushered in a military council that oversaw a transition to democratic rule. Independent candidate Sidi Ould Cheikh Abadallahi was inaugurated in April 2007 as Mauritania's first freely and fairly elected president. His term ended prematurely in August 2008 when a military junta deposed him and ushered in a military council government. Meanwhile, the country continues to experience ethnic tensions among its black population (Afro-Mauritanians) and White and Black Moor (Arab-Berber) communities. On June 28, 1973, in a move designed to emphasize its non-alignment with France, Mauritania converted its currency from the old French-supported CFA franc unit to a new unit called the Ouguiya.

MONETARY SYSTEM:
   1 Ouguiya = 5 Khoum
   100 Ouguiya = 500 CFA Francs, 1973-
Note: Issues specially marked with letter E for Mauritania were issued by the Banque Centrale des Etats de l'Afrique de l'Ouest. These issues were used before Mauritania seceded from the French Community of the West African States in 1973. For those listings see West African States.

REPUBLIC

Banque Centrale de Mauritanie
1973 Issue

		VF	UNC
1	**100 Ouguiya**		
	20.6.1973. Blue on multicolor underprint. Mauritanian girl at center. Back: Men loading boat. Printer: Algerian.		
	a. Issued note.	25.00	100
	s. Specimen. Red overprint SPECIMEN on face.	—	75.00

		VF	UNC
2	**200 Ouguiya**		
	20.6.1973. Brown on multicolor underprint. Bedouin woman at left, tents in background. Back: Camels and huts. Printer: Algerian.		
	a. Issued note.	50.00	200
	s. Specimen.	—	120

		VF	UNC
3	**1000 Ouguiya**		
	20.6.1973. Green and multicolor. Woman weaving on loom at left, metal worker at right center. Back: Local musicians and scenes. Printer: Algerian.		
	a. Issued note.	150	500
	s. Specimen. Red overprint on face.	—	300

1975, 1977, 1981 Unissued Notes

		VF	UNC
3A	**100 Ouguiya**		
	28.11.1975. Unissued Specimen. Rare. Blue and purple on multicolor underprint. Man facing at left, two women at lower center preparing tea service. Back: Bearded man standing with large fish at center, fishing boats in background. Printer: TDLR. 145x70mm.	—	—
3B	**200 Ouguiya**		
	6.29.1977. Violet on multicolor underprint. Man with goatee, camel, woman. Printer: TDLR.	—	—

		VF	UNC
3C	**1000 Ouguiya**		
	26.6.1977. Unissued Specimen. Rare. Multicolor. Female at left. Back: Mine shaft. Printer: TDLR.	—	—
3D	**1000 Ouguiya**		
	28.11.1981. Red and orange on multicolor underprint. Bearded man at left. Back: Camel and palm tree at right center, mine at center, men working field at right center. Printer: G&D.	—	—

1974; 1979 Issue

		VF	UNC
4	**100 Ouguiya**		
	1974-2002. Purple, violet and brown on multicolor underprint. Back: Musical instruments at left, cow and tower at right. Watermark: Old man with beard. Printer: G&D (without imprint).		
	a. 28.11.1974. Narrow black security thread. Two signature varieties.	10.00	25.00
	b. 28.11.1983.	15.00	40.00
	c. 28.11.1985.	7.50	20.00
	d. 28.11.1989. Wide green security thread.	5.00	12.50
	e. 28.11.1992.	4.00	10.00
	f. 28.11.1993.	3.00	10.00

	VF	UNC
g. 28.11.1995.	2.50	10.00
h. 28.11.1996.	2.00	8.00
i. 28.11.1999.	2.00	8.00
j. 28.11.2001.	2.00	8.00
k. 28.11.2002	2.00	8.00
s. As a. Specimen.	—	35.00

5   200 Ouguiya

1974-2002. Brown, dark olive-green and brown-orange on multicolor underprint. Back: Bowl and rod at left, dugout canoe and palm tree at right. Watermark: Old man with beard. Printer: G&D (without imprint).

	VF	UNC
a. 28.11.1974. Thin security thread. Two signature varieties.	15.00	30.00
b. 28.11.1985.	10.00	25.00
c. 28.11.1989. Thick security thread.	6.00	22.50
d. 28.11.1992.	5.00	20.00
e. 28.11.1993.	5.00	15.00
f. 28.11.1995.	4.00	10.00
g. 28.11.1996.	4.00	10.00
h. 28.11.1999.	3.00	10.00
i. 28.11.2001.	3.00	10.00
j. 28.11.2002.	3.00	10.00
s. As a. Specimen.	—	55.00

6   500 Ouguiya

1979-1996. Green, brown and dark green on multicolor underprint. Back: Field workers at left, mine entrance complex at right. Watermark: Old man with beard. Printer: G&D (without imprint).

	VF	UNC
a. 28.11.1979. Thin security thread.	40.00	90.00
b. 28.11.1983.	40.00	100
c. 28.11.1985.	15.00	35.00
d. 28.11.1989. Thick security thread.	12.00	40.00
e. 28.11.1991.	10.00	40.00
f. 28.11.1992.	8.00	30.00
g. 28.11.1993.	8.00	25.00
h. 28.11.1995.	8.00	25.00
i. 28.11.1996.	8.00	25.00
s. As a. Specimen.	—	100

7   1000 Ouguiya

1974-1996. Blue, violet and blue-black on multicolor underprint. Back: Bowl of fish at left, camel, hut and tower at right. Watermark: Old man with beard. Printer: G&D (without imprint).

	VF	UNC
a. 28.11.1974. Thin security thread. Two signature varieties.	40.00	85.00
b. 28.11.1985.	30.00	75.00
c. 28.11.1989. Thick security thread.	25.00	50.00
d. 28.10.1991.	20.00	45.00
e. 28.11.1992.	15.00	45.00
f. 28.11.1993.	15.00	35.00
g. 28.11.1995.	15.00	35.00
h. 28.11.1996.	12.50	30.00
s. As a. Specimen.	—	150

1999 Issue

8   500 Ouguiya

28.11.1999; 28.11.2001; 28.11.2002. Similar to #6 but hologram image added to right center. Green, brown and dark green on multicolor underprint. Signature varieties. Back: Field workers at left, mine entrance complex at right. Watermark: Old man with beard.

	VF	UNC
a. 28.11.1999.	7.50	25.00
b. 28.11.2001.	7.50	20.00
c. 28.11.2002.	7.50	20.00

9   1000 Ouguiya

28.11.1999; 28.11.2001; 28.11.2002. Similar to #7 but with hologram value added at right center. Blue on tan underprint. Signature varieties. Back: Bowl of fish at left, camel, hut and tower at right. Watermark: Old man with beard.

	VF	UNC
a. 28.11.1999.	10.00	30.00
b. 28.11.2001.	10.00	30.00
c. 28.11.2002.	10.00	30.00

2004 Issue

#10-14 Replacement notes: Second letter of serial # prefix: *Z*.

10	**100 Ouguiya**	**VF**	**UNC**

28.11.2004; 28.11.2006; 11.28.2011. Green and purple on multicolor underprint. Geometric design at right. Back. Musical instruments at left, cow feeding before tower at center. Printer: G&D (without imprint). 130x65mm.

	a. 28.11.2004.	FV	4.00
	b. 28.11.2006.	FV	3.00
	c. 28.11.2008.	FV	3.00

11	**200 Ouguiya**	**VF**	**UNC**

28.11.2004; 28.11.2006. Brown and blue on multicolor underprint. Geometric pattern at right. Back: Bowl at left, canoe at center. Printer: G&D (without imprint). 136x68mm.

	a. 28.11.2004.	FV	5.00
	b. 28.11.2006.	FV	4.00
	c. 28.11.2008.	FV	4.00

12	**500 Ouguiya**	**VF**	**UNC**

28.11.2004; 28.11.2006. Green and brown on multicolor underprint. Geometric patern at right. Back: Men harvesting at left, factory at center. Printer: G&D (without imprint). 142x71mm.

	a. 28.11.2004.	FV	10.00
	b. 28.11.2006.	FV	8.00

13	**1000 Ouguiya**	**VF**	**UNC**

28.11.2004; 28.11.2006. Multicolor. Printer: G&D (without imprint). 148x74mm.

	a. 28.11.2004.	FV	15.00
	b. 28.11.2006.	FV	12.50

14	**2000 Ouguiya**	**VF**	**UNC**

28.11.2004; 28.11.2006. Multicolor. Printer: G&D (without imprint). 154x78mm.

	a. 28.11.2004.	FV	25.00
	b. 28.11.2006.	FV	22.50

15	**5000 Ouguiya**	**VF**	**UNC**

28.11.2009. Olive green on multicolor underprint. Ibn Abbas Mosque in Nouakchott at center. Back: Diesel locomotive at center. Watermark: Bearded man. Printer: G&D. 150x70mm.

	a. Issued note.	FV	50.00
	r. Replacement note. Second letter in serial # prefix: Z.	FV	75.00
	s. Specimen. Red overprint.	—	75.00

2011 Issue

16	**100 Ouguiya**	**VF**	**UNC**

2011; 2015. Green and purple on multicolor underprint. Watermark: Bearded male head and 100 130x65mm.

	a. 28.11.2011.	FV	2.50
	b. 28.11.2015.	FV	2.50

17	**200 Ouguiya**	**VF**	**UNC**

28.11.2013. Expected new issue. — —

18	**500 Ouguiya**	**VF**	**UNC**

28.11.2013. Light and dark green on tan and brown underprint. Geometric pattern at right, without holographic patch at right. Back: Men harvesting at left, factory at center. Watermark: Male head and 500. 138x65mm. FV 6.00

19	**1000 Ouguiya**	**VF**	**UNC**

28.11.2014. Polymer plastic. FV 12.00

20	**2000 Ouguiya**	**VF**	**UNC**

28.11.2011. Blue on multicolor underprint. Watermark: Bearded male head and 2000. 146x70mm. FV 30.00

21	**5000 Ouguiya**	**VF**	**UNC**

28.11.2011. Olive and multicolor. Mosque. Back: Airport tower at left, desiel locomotive at left center. FV 50.00

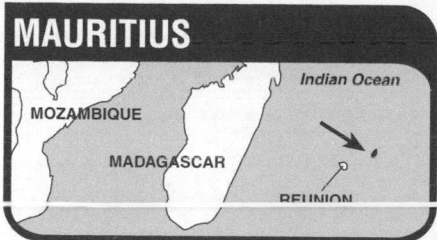

MAURITIUS

Indian Ocean
MOZAMBIQUE
MADAGASCAR
REUNION

The island of Mauritius, a member of the British Commonwealth located in the Indian Ocean 500 miles (805 km.) east of Madagascar, has an area of 790 sq. mi. (2,045 sq. km.) and a population of 1.18 million. Capital: Port Louis. Sugar provides 90 percent of the export revenue. Although known to Arab and Malay sailors as early as the 10th century, Mauritius was first explored by the Portuguese in the 16th century and subsequently settled by the Dutch - who named it in honor of Prince Maurits van Nassau - in the 17th century. The French assumed control in 1715, developing the island into an important naval base overseeing Indian Ocean trade, and establishing a plantation economy of sugar cane. The British captured the island in 1810, during the Napoleonic Wars. Mauritius remained a strategically important British naval base, and later an air station, playing an important role during World War II for anti-submarine and convoy operations, as well as the collection of signals intelligence. Independence from the UK was attained in 1968. A stable democracy with regular free elections and a positive human rights record, the country has attracted considerable foreign investment and has earned one of Africa's highest per capita incomes. Recent poor weather, declining sugar prices, and declining textile and apparel production, have slowed economic growth, leading to some protests over standards of living in the Creole community.

NOTE: Certain listings encompassing issues circulated by various bank and regional authorities are contained in Volume 1.

SIGNATURE VARIETIES

	GOVERNOR	MANAGING DIRECTOR
1	Mr. A. Beejadhur 1.7.1967 - 31.12.1972	Mr. D.G.H. Cook 1.7.1967 - 27.7.1968
2	Mr. A. Beejadhur 1.7.1967 - 31.12.1972	Mr. D.C. Keys 28.2.1970 - 31.12.1972
3	Mr. A. Beejadhur 1.7.1967 - 31.12.1972	Mr. C. Bunwaree 28.2.1970 - 31.12.1972
4	Mr. G. Bunwaree 1.1.1973 - 9.6.1982	Sir I. Ramphul 1.1.1973 - 9.6.1982
5	Sir I. Ramphul 10.6.1982 - 31.3.1996	Mr. R. Tacouri 10.6.1982 - 28.2.1997
6	Mr. D. Maraye 1.4.1996 - 30.11.1998	Mr. B. Gujadhur 1.3.1997 - 1.12.1998
7	Mr. R. Basant Roi 1.12.1998 -	Mr. B.R. Gujadhur 17.12.1998 -

BRITISH ADMINISTRATION

Bank of Mauritius

1967 ND Issue

#30-33 Replacement notes: Serial # prefix Z/#.

30	**5 Rupees**	VF	UNC
	ND (1967). Blue on multicolor underprint. Queen Elizabeth II at right. Back: Sailboat. Watermark: Dodo bird. Printer: TDLR.		
	a. Signature 1.	12.00	45.00
	b. Signature 3.	15.00	70.00
	c. Signature 4.	4.00	15.00
	s. As a Specimen.	—	—

31	**10 Rupees**	VF	UNC
	ND (1967). Red on multicolor underprint. Queen Elizabeth II at right. Back: Government building. Watermark: Dodo bird. Printer: TDLR.		
	a. Signature 1.	15.00	60.00
	b. Signature 2.	25.00	100
	c. Signature 4.	3.50	12.50

32	**25 Rupees**	VF	UNC
	ND (1967). Green on multicolor underprint. Queen Elizabeth II at right. Back: Ox cart. Watermark: Dodo bird. Printer: TDLR.		
	a. Signature 1.	25.00	110
	b. Signature 4.	20.00	90.00

33   50 Rupees   **VF   UNC**
ND (1967). Purple on multicolor underprint. Queen Elizabeth II at right. Back:
Ships docked at Port Louis harbor. Watermark: Dodo bird. Printer: TDLR.

a. Signature 1.	65.00	250
b. Signature 2.	75.00	300
c. Signature 4.	30.00	120

1985-91 ND Issue

#34-41 replacement notes: Serial # prefix *Z/#.*

34   5 Rupees   **VF   UNC**
ND (1985). Dark brown. Arms at lower left center, building with flag at right.
Signature 5. Back: Bank, outline of Mauritius map at right. Watermark: Dodo bird.
Printer: TDLR.

	1.50	5.00

35   10 Rupees   **VF   UNC**
ND (1985). Green on multicolor underprint. Arms at lower left center, building with
flag at center right. Signature 5. Back: Bridge, outline of Mauritius map at right.
Watermark: Dodo bird. Printer: TDLR.

a. Orange UV latent printing. Dark green printing.	2.00	8.00
b. Dark green printing. Green UV latent printing.	2.00	7.00

The light green variety formerly listed is the result of fading.

36   20 Rupees   **VF   UNC**
ND. Bluish purple, blue-green, blue and orange on multicolor underprint. Lady   2.50   9.00
Jugnauth at left, arms at center, building with flag at lower right. Signature 5. Back:
Satellite dishes at center, outline of Mauritius map at right. Watermark: Dodo bird.
Printer: TDLR.

37   50 Rupees   **VF   UNC**
ND (1986). Dark blue on multicolor underprint. Arms at lower center, building
with flag at right. Signature 5. Back: Two deer, butterfly and Mauritius Kestrel.
Watermark: Dodo bird. Printer: BWC (without imprint).

a. Printer's imprint on back.	4.00	15.00
b. Without printer's imprint on back.	4.00	15.00

38   100 Rupees   **VF   UNC**
ND (1986). Red on multicolor underprint. Arms at lower center, building with flag   7.50   25.00
at right. Signature 5. Back: Landscape. Watermark: Dodo bird. Printer: BWC
(without imprint).

39   200 Rupees   **VF   UNC**
ND (1985). Blue on multicolor underprint. Sir Seewoodsagur Ramgoolam at left.
Signature 5. Back: Large home (Le Réduit). Printer: TDLR.

a. Orange UV latent printing.	18.00	50.00
b. Green UV latent printing.	15.00	40.00

40 500 Rupees VF UNC
ND (1988). Brown and orange on multicolor underprint. Building with flag at center, arms below, Sir A. Jugnaurh (Prime Minister) at right. Signature 5. Back: Sugar cane field workers loading wagon with mountains in background. Watermark: Dodo bird. Printer: TDLR (without imprint).
    a. Orange UV latent printing.   40.00   110
    b. Green UV latent printing.   35.00   100

44 100 Rupees VF UNC
1998. Black, blue and deep blue-green on multicolor underprint. R. Seeneevassen at left, arms at lower left, building façades at center, standing Justice with scales at lower right in underprint. Ascending size serial number. Back: Building at left. Watermark: Dodo bird's head.   FV   20.00

41 1000 Rupees VF UNC
ND (1991). Blue and red on multicolor underprint. Sir V. Ringadoo at left, palm trees and building with flag at center. Signature 5. Back: Port Louis harbor. Watermark: Dodo bird. Printer: TDLR.   65.00   180

45 200 Rupees VF UNC
1998. Black, deep green and violet on multicolor underprint. Sir A. R. Mohamed at left, arms at lower left, building façades at center, standing Justice with scales at lower right in underprint. Ascending size serial number. Back: Market street scene at right. Watermark: Dodo bird's head.   FV   32.50

1998 Issue

#42-48 raised much public controversy when the values were printed in the order of English/ Sanskrit/ Tamil instead of the usual order of English/ Tamil/ Sanskrit. The note were withdrawn and replaced with #49-55.

42 25 Rupees VF UNC
1998. UV: value 25 in box fluoresces yellow, left design faint yellow. Black, violet and brown on multicolor underprint. Sir M. J. Ah-chuen at left, arms at lower left, building façades at center, standing Justice with scales at lower right in underprint. Ascending size serial number. Back: Building façade at center, worker at right. Watermark: Dodo bird's head.   FV   7.00

46 500 Rupees VF UNC
1998. Black, brown and orange on multicolor underprint. S. Bissoondoyal at left., arms at lower left, building façades at center, standing Justice with scales at lower right in underprint. Ascending size serial number. Back: University of Mauritius at center right. Watermark: Dodo bird's head.   FV   60.00

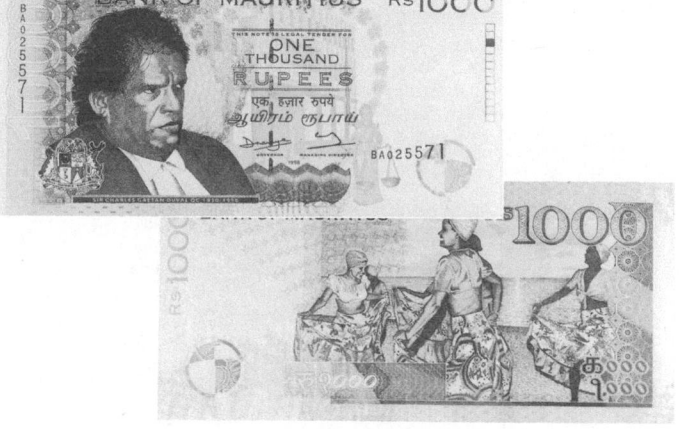

43 50 Rupees VF UNC
1998. Black, purple and deep blue on multicolor underprint. J. M. Paturau at left, arms at lower left, building façades at center, standing Justice with scales at lower right in underprint. Ascending size serial number. Back: Building complex at center right. Watermark: Dodo bird's head.   FV   12.00

47   1000 Rupees

1998. Black and blue on multicolor underprint. Sir Charles G. Duval at left., arms at lower left, building façades at center, standing Justice with scales at lower right in underprint. Ascending size serial number. Back: Women dancing at center right. Watermark: Dodo bird's head.

	VF	UNC
	FV	110

48   2000 Rupees

1998. Rose, orange, black, yellow-brown on multicolor underprint. Seewoosagur Ramgoolam at left., arms at lower left, building façades at center, standing Justice with scales at lower right in underprint. Ascending size serial number. Back: Ox cart. Watermark: Dodo bird's head.

	VF	UNC
	FV	200

1999 Issue

#49-55 language text correctly ordered as: English/ Tamil/ Sanskrit.

49   25 Rupees

1999; 2003; 2006; 2009. UV: 25 in box fluoresces yellow. Black, violet and brown on multicolor underprint. Sir M. J. Ah-chuen at left, arms at lower left, building facades at center, standing Justice with scales at lower right in underprint. Ascending size serial number. Signature 7. Back: Building facade at center, worker at right. Watermark: Dodo bird's head. 135x67mm.

		VF	UNC
a. 1999.		FV	3.00
b. 2003.		FV	2.50
c. 2006.		FV	2.25
d. 2009.		FV	2.25

50   50 Rupees

1999; 2001; 2003; 2006; 2009; 2012. Black, purple and deep blue on multicolor underprint. J. M. Paturau at left, arms at lower left, building facades at center, standing Justice with scales at lower right in underprint. Ascending size serial number. Signature 7. Back: Building complex at center right. Watermark: Dodo bird's head. 140x68mm.

		VF	UNC
a. 1999.		FV	6.00
b. 2001.		FV	4.50
c. 2003.		FV	4.00
d. 2006.		FV	3.25
e. 2009.		FV	3.25
f. 2012.		FV	3.25

51   100 Rupees

1999; 2001. Black, blue and deep blue-green on multicolor underprint. R. Seeneevassen at left, arms at lower left, building façades at center, standing Justice with scales at lower right in underprint. Ascending size serial number. Signature 7. Back: Building at left. Watermark: Dodo bird's head. 145x70mm.

		VF	UNC
a. 1999.		FV	12.00
b. 2001.		FV	10.00

52   200 Rupees

1999; 2001. Black, deep green and violet on multicolro underprint. Sir A. R. Mohamed at left, arms at lower left, building façades at center, standing Justice with scales at lower right in underprint. Ascending size serial number. Signature 7. Back: Market street scene at right. Watermark: Dodo bird's head. 150x72mm.

		VF	UNC
a. 1999.		FV	20.00
b. 2001.		FV	17.50

53   500 Rupees

1999. Black, brown and orangeon multicolor underprint. S. Bissoondoyal at left, arms at lower left, building façades at center, standing Justice with scales at lower right in underprint. Ascending size serial number. Signature 7. Back: University of Mauritius at center right. Watermark: Dodo bird's head. 155x75mm.

		VF	UNC
a. 1999.		FV	45.00
b. 2001		FV	45.00

54 **1000 Rupees** VF UNC
1999. Slate black, light blue and red underprint. Sir Charles Duval at left. Signature 7. Back: Building at center. 160x76mm.
    a. 1999. FV 75.00
    b. 2001. FV 75.00

55 **2000 Rupees** VF UNC
1999. Rose, orange, black, yellow-brown on multicolor underprint. Seewoosagur Ramgoolam at left., arms at lower left, building façades at center, standing Justice with scales at lower right in underprint. Ascending size serial number. Signature 7. Back: Ox cart. Watermark: Dodo bird's head. 165x79mm.   FV 140

2001 Issue

56 **100 Rupees** VF UNC
2004; 2007; 2009; 2012. Similar to #51 but iridescent strip added. Black, blue and deep blue-green on multicolor underprint. R. Seeneevassen at left, arms at lower left, building façades at center, standing Justice with scales at lower right in underprint. Ascending size serial number. Signature 7. Back: Building at left. Watermark: Dodo bird's head. 145x70mm.
    a. 2004. FV 6.00
    b. 2007. FV 5.00
    c. 2009. FV 5.00
    d. 2012. FV 5.00

57 **200 Rupees** VF UNC
2004; 2007. Similar to #52 but iridescent strip added. Black, deep green and violet on multicolor underprint. Sir A. R. Mohamed at left, arms at lower left, building façades at center, standing Justice with scales at lower right in underprint. Ascending size serial number. Signature 7. Back: Market street scene at right. Watermark: Dodo bird's head. 150x72mm.
    a. 2004. FV 15.00
    b. 2007. FV 15.00

58 **500 Rupees** VF UNC
2007. Green and brown on multicolor underprint. Bust at left. Back: Building. 155x75mm.
    a. 2007. FV 37.50

59 **1000 Rupees** VF UNC
2004; 2006; 2007. Slate black, light blue and red munticolor underprint. Sir Charles Duval at left. Back: Building at center. 160x76mm.
    a. 2004. FV 65.00
    b. 2006. FV 62.50
    c. 2007. 3 Signatures. FV 60.00

60 **2000 Rupees** VF UNC

2010 Enhanced issue

61 **200 Rupees** VF UNC
2010; 2013. Black, deep green and violet on multicolor underprint. Sir A.R. Mohamed at left. Building façades at center. Hologram at top right. Back: Market street scene at right.
    a. 2010. FV 15.00
    b. 2013. FV 15.00

62 **500 Rupees** VF UNC
2010. Green and brown on multicolor underprint. S. Bissoondoyal at left. Building façades at center. Hologram at top right. Back: University of Mauritus at center right.   FV 37.50

63 **1000 Rupees** VF UNC
2010. Slate black, light blue and red on multicolor underprint. Sir Charles Duval at left. Building façades at center. Hologram at top right. Back: Building at center.   FV 60.00

2013 Issue

64 **25 Rupees** VF UNC
2013. Polymer plastic. Violet and brown on multicolor underprint. Coat of arms, Milin Jean ah-Chuen. Building façades at center. Back: Dodo bird, buildign façade, Rodrigues Island map.   FV 3.50

65 **50 Rupees** VF UNC
2013. Polymer plastic. Blue on multicolor underprint. Coat of arms, Joseph Maurice Paturau. Building façades at center. Back: Dodo bird, Le Caudan waterfront buildings. Printer: OT.   FV 5.00

66 **500 Rupees** VF UNC
2013. Polymer plastic.   FV 37.50

COLLECTOR SERIES

Bank of Mauritius
1978 ND Issue

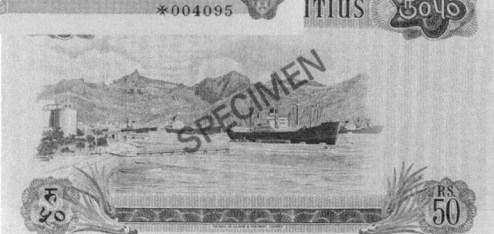

CS1 **ND (1978) 5-50 Rupees** Mkt. Value
#30c, 31c, 32b, 33c with overprint.: SPECIMEN and Maltese cross prefix serial #.   80.00

MEXICO

The United States of Mexico, located immediately south of the United States, has an area of 1,222,612 sq. mi. (1,967,183 sq. km.) and a population of 98.88 million. Capital: Mexico City. The economy is based on agriculture, manufacturing and mining. Cotton, sugar, coffee and shrimp are exported.

Mexico was the site of highly advanced Indian civilizations 1,500 years before conquistador Hernando Cortes conquered the wealthy Aztec empire of Montezuma, 1519-1521, and founded a Spanish colony which lasted for nearly 300 years. During the Spanish period, Mexico, then called New Spain, stretched from Guatemala to the present states of Wyoming and California, it's present northern boundary having been established by the secession of Texas (1836) and the war of 1846-1848 with the United States.

Independence from Spain was declared by Father Miguel Hidalgo on Sept. 16, 1810, Mexican Independence Day, and was acheived by General Agustin de Iturbide in 1821. Iturbide became emperor in 1822 but was deposed when a republic was established a year later. For more than half a century following the birth of the republic, the political scene of Mexico was characterized by turmoil which saw two emperors (including the unfortunate Maximilliam), several dictators and an average of one new government every nine months passing swiftly from obscurity to oblivion. The land, social, economic and labor reforms promulgated by the reform Constitution of Feb. 5, 1917 established the basis for a sustained economic development and participative democracy that have made Mexico one of the most politically stable countries of modern Latin America.

ESTADOS UNIDOS MÉXICANOS
UNITED STATES OF MEXICO

Banco de México
1945-51 Issue

49   50 Pesos

1948-72. Engraved. Blue on multicolor underprint. Portrait I.de Allende at left. Middle signature title: *INTERVENTOR DE LA COM. NAC. BANCARIA*. Signature varieties. Back: Independence Monument at center. Printer: ABNC.

	VF	UNC
a. 22.12.1948. Black series letters. Series: BA-BD.	6.00	15.00
b. 23.11.1949. Series: BU-BX.	6.00	15.00
c. 26.7.1950. Series: BY-CF.	5.00	15.00
d. 27.12.1950. Series: CS-DH.	5.00	15.00
e. 19.1.1953. Series: DK-DV.	4.00	15.00
f. 10.2.1954. Series: DW-EE.	4.00	15.00
g. 8.9.1954. Series: EF-FF.	4.00	15.00
h. 11.1.1956. Series: FK-FV.	4.00	15.00
i. 19.6.1957. Series: FW-GP.	4.00	15.00
j. 20.8.1958. Series: HC-HR.	4.00	15.00
k. 18.3.1959. 2 red series letters. Series: HS-IP.	4.00	15.00
l. 20.5.1959. Series: IQ-JN.	4.00	15.00
m. 25.1.1961. Series: JO-LB.	3.00	8.00
n. 8.11.1961. Series: LC-AID.	3.00	8.00
o. 24.4.1963. Series: AIE-BAP.	3.00	6.00
p. 17.2.1965. Series: BAQ-BCD.	2.50	6.00
q. 10.5.1967. Series: BCY-BEN.	2.50	6.00
r. 19.11.1969. Series: BGK-BIC.	2.50	4.00
s. 22.7.1970. Series: BIG-BKN.	2.50	4.00
t. 27.6.1972. Series: BLI-BMG.	2.50	3.00
u. 29.12.1972. Series: BMO-BRB.	2.00	3.00
v. Specimen, punch hole cancelled.	—	135

50   100 Pesos

17.1.1945. Printed. Brown on multicolor underprint. Portrait M. Hidalgo at left, series letters above serial #. Middle signature title: *INTERVENTOR DEL GOBIERNO*. Signature varieties. Back: Coin with national coat-of-arms at center. Series: S-Z. Printer: ABNC.

	VF	UNC
a. Issued note.	15.00	70.00
s. Specimen, punch hole cancelled.	—	200

51   500 Pesos

1948-78. Black on multicolor underprint. Like #43 but without *No.* above serial #. Middle signature title: *INTERVENTOR DE LA COM. NAC. BANCARIA*. Signature varieties. Back: Palace of Mining at center. Printer: ABNC.

	VF	UNC
a. 22.12.1948. Series: BA.	40.00	125
b. 27.12.1950. Series: CS; CT.	12.00	30.00
c. 3.12.1951. Series: DI; DJ.	12.00	30.00
d. 19.1.1953. Series: DK-DN.	12.00	30.00
e. 31.8.1955. Series: FG-FJ.	12.00	30.00
f. 11.1.1956. Series: FK-FL.	12.00	30.00
g. 19.6.1957. Series: FW-GB.	12.00	30.00
h. 20.8.1958. Series: HC-HH.	12.00	30.00
i. 18.3.1959. Series: HS-HX.	12.00	30.00
j. 20.5.1959. Series: IQ-IV.	12.00	30.00
k. 25.1.1961. Series: JO-JT.	8.00	25.00
l. 8.11.1961. Series: LC-MP.	7.00	20.00
m. 17.2.1965. Series: BAQ-BCN.	12.00	25.00
n. 24.3.1971. Series: BKO-BKT.	5.00	12.50
o. 27.6.1972. Series: BLI-BLM.	5.00	12.50
p. 29.12.1972. Series: BNG-BNP.	5.00	12.50
q. 18.7.1973. Series: BUY-BWB.	5.00	12.50
r. 2.8.1974. Series: BXV-BZI.	3.50	10.00
s. 18.2.1977. Series: BZJ-CCK.	3.50	10.00
t. 18.1.1978. Series: CCL-CDY.	3.50	8.50

52   1000 Pesos

1948-77. Black on multicolor underprint. Cuauhtemoc at left. Middle signature title: *IN-TERVENTOR DE LA COM. NAC. BANCARIA*. Signature varieties. Back: Chichen itza pyramid at center. Printer: ABNC.

	VF	UNC
a. 22.12.1948. Series: BA.	15.00	60.00
b. 23.11.1949. Series: BU.	15.00	60.00
c. 27.12.1950. Series: CS.	15.00	60.00
d. 3.12.1951. Series: DI; DJ.	15.00	60.00
e. 19.1.1953. Series: DK; DL.	15.00	60.00
f. 31.8.1955. Series: FG; FH.	15.00	60.00
g. 11.1.1956. Series: FK; FL.	15.00	60.00
h. 19.6.1957. Series: FW-FZ.	15.00	60.00
i. 20.8.1958. Series: HC-HE.	15.00	60.00
j. 18.3.1959. Series: HS-HU.	15.00	60.00
k. 20.5.1959. Series: IQ-IS.	15.00	60.00
l. 25.1.1961. Series: JO-JQ.	15.00	60.00
m. 8.11.1961. Series: LC-LV.	10.00	20.00
n. 17.2.1965. Series: BAQ-BCN.	8.00	15.00
o. 24.3.1971. Series: BKO-BKT.	6.00	10.00
p. 27.6.1972. Series: BLI-BLM.	6.00	10.00
q. 29.12.1972. Series: BNG-BNK.	3.00	5.00
r. 18.7.1973. Series: BUY-BWB.	6.00	10.00
s. 2.8.1974. Series: BXV-BYY.	5.00	8.00
t. 18.2.1977. Series: BZJ-CBQ.	5.00	8.00
x. Error: *EERIE HD* rather than SERIE at left.	45.00	85.00

1950; 1951 Issue

53   10 Pesos

1951; 1953. Black on multicolor underprint. Portrait E. Ruiz de Velazquez at right. Like #47 but without *No.* above serial #. Signature varieties. Printer: ABNC.

	VF	UNC
a. 3.12.1951. Series: DI, DJ.	2.00	5.00
b. 19.1.1953. Series: DK, DL.	2.00	5.00

1950 Issue

54 20 Pesos VF UNC

1950-70. Black on multicolor underprint. Portrait J. Ortiz de Dominguez at left.
Like number 48 but without *No.* above serial #. Signature varieties. Back: Federal
Palace courtyard at center. Printer: ABNC.

	VF	UNC
a. 27.12.1950. Black series letters. Series: CS; CT.	3.00	15.00
b. 19.1.1953. Serles: dark	3.00	15.00
c. 10.2.1954. Red series letters. Series: DW.	2.00	10.00
d. 11.1.1956. Series: FK.	2.00	10.00
e. 10.6.1957. Series: FW.	2.00	10.00
f. 20.8.1958. Series: HC, HD.	2.00	10.00
g. 18.3.1959. Series: HS, HT.	2.00	10.00
h. 20.5.1959. Series: IQ, IR.	2.00	10.00
i. 25.1.1961. Series: JO, JP.	1.50	10.00
j. 8.11.1961. Series: LC-LG.	1.50	10.00
k. 24.4.1963. Series: AIE-AIH.	1.50	5.00
l. 17.2.1965. Series: BAQ-BAV.	1.50	5.00
m. 10.5.1967. Series: BCY-BDB.	1.50	5.00
n. 27.8.1969. Series: BGA, BGB.	1.50	5.00
o. 18.3.1970. Series: BID-RIF	1.50	5.00
p. 22.7.1970. Series: BIG-BIK.	1.50	5.00
s. Specimen, punch hole cancelled.	—	135

55 100 Pesos VF UNC

1950-61. Engraved. Brown on multicolor underprint. Portrait M. Hidalgo at left,
series letters above serial #. Middle signature title: *INTERVENTOR DE LA COM.
NAC. BANCARIA.* Signature varieties. Back: Coin with national seal at center.
Printer: ABNC.

	VF	UNC
a. 27.12.1950. Black series letters. Series: CS-CZ.	8.00	30.00
b. 19.1.1953. Series: DK-DP.	7.00	25.00
c. 10.2.1954. Series: DW-DZ.	7.00	25.00
d. 8.9.1954. Series: EI-ET.	7.00	25.00
e. 11.1.1956. Series: FK-FV.	7.00	25.00
f. 19.6.1957. Series: FW-GH.	7.00	25.00
g. 20.8.1958. Series: HC-HR.	7.00	25.00
h. 18.3.1959. Series: HS-IH.	7.00	25.00
i. 20.5.1959. Series: IQ-JF.	7.00	25.00
j. 25.1.1961. Series: JO-KL.	7.00	25.00

1954 Issue

58 10 Pesos VF UNC

1954-67. Black on multicolor underprint. Portrait E. Ruiz de Velazquez at right.
Like #53 but with text: *MEXICO D.F.* above series letters. Signature varieties.
Back: Road to Guanajuato at center. Printer: ABNC.

	VF	UNC
a. 10.2.1954. Series: DW, DX.	1.50	5.00
b. 8.9.1954. Series: EI-EN.	1.50	5.00
c. 19.6.1957. Series: FW, FX.	1.50	5.00
d. 24.7.1957. Series: GQ.	1.50	5.00
e. 20.8.1958. Series: HC-HF.	1.50	6.00
f. 18.3.1959. Series: HS-HU.	1.00	5.00
g. 20.5.1959. Series: IQ-IS.	1.00	4.00
h. 25.1.1961. Series: JO-JT.	1.00	4.00
i. 8.11.1961. Series: LC-LV.	1.00	4.00
j. 24.4.1963. Series: AIE-AIT.	1.00	3.00
k. 17.2.1965. Series: BAQ-BAX.	1.00	3.00
l. 10.5.1967. Series: BCY-BDA.	1.00	3.00
s. Specimen, punch hole cancelled.	—	150

1957; 1961 Issue

59 1 Peso VF UNC

1957-70. Black on multicolor underprint. Aztec calendar stone at center. Like #56
but with text: *MEXICO D.F.* added above date at lower left. Back: Independence
monument at center. Printer: ABNC.

	VF	UNC
a. 19.6.1957. Series: FW-GF.	1.00	4.50
b. Deleted.	—	—
c. 4.12.1957. Series: GS-HB.	1.00	4.50
d. 20.8.1958. Series: HC-HL.	0.75	2.50
e. 18.3.1959. Series: HS-IB.	0.50	2.50
f. 20.5.1959. Series: IQ-IZ.	0.50	2.50
g. 25.1.1961. Series: JO-KC.	0.25	2.00
h. 8.11.1961. Series: LC; LD.	0.50	2.00
i. 9.6.1965. Series: BCO-BCX.	0.25	2.00
j. 10.5.1967. Series: BCY-BEB.	0.25	1.00
k. 27.8.1969. Series: BGA-BGJ.	0.25	1.00
l. 22.7.1970. Series: BIL-BIR.	0.20	1.00
s. Specimen.	—	—

60 5 Pesos VF UNC

1957-70. Black on multicolor underprint. Portrait gypsy at center. Like #57 but
with Text: *MEXICO D.F.* before date. Back: Independence Monument at center.
Printer: ABNC.

	VF	UNC
a. 19.6.1957. Series: FW, FX.	2.00	7.00
b. 24.7.1957. Series: GQ, GR.	2.00	7.00
c. 20.8.1958. Series: HC-HJ.	1.50	6.00
d. 18.3.1959. Series: HS-HV.	1.50	6.00
e. 20.5.1959. Series: IQ-IT.	1.50	6.00
f. 25.1.1961. Series: JO-JV.	0.50	4.00
g. 8.11.1961. Series: LC-MP.	0.50	3.00
h. 24.4.1963. Series: AIE-AJJ.	0.50	2.50
i. 27.8.1969. Series BGJ.	0.50	2.50
j. 19.11.1969. Series: BGK-BGT.	0.50	2.50
k. 22.7.1970. Series: BIG-BII.	0.50	2.50

61   100 Pesos   VF   UNC

1961-73. Brown on multicolor underprint. Portrait M. Hodalgo at left. Like #55
but series letters below serial #. Back: Coin with national seal at center. Printer:
ABNC.

	VF	UNC
a. 8.11.1961. Red series letters. Series: LE-ZZ; AAA-AEG.	5.00	12.50
b. 24.4.1963. Series: AIK-AUG.	5.00	12.50
c. 17.2.1965. Series: BAQ-BCD.	3.00	8.00
d. 10.5.1967. Series: BCY-BFZ.	3.00	8.00
e. 22.7.1970. Series: BIO-BJK.	3.00	8.00
f. 24.3.1971. Series: BKP-BLH.	3.00	8.00
g. 27.6.1972. Series: BLI-BNF.	3.00	8.00
h. 29.12.1972. Series: BNG-BUX.	1.50	5.00
i. 18.7.1973. Series: BUY-BXU.	1.50	5.00

1969-74 Issue

62   5 Pesos   VF   UNC

1969-72. Black on multicolor underprint. J. Ortiz de Dominguez at right, bank
titie with S. A. 3 signatures and signature varieties. Back: Yucca plant, aqueduct,
village of Queretaro and national arms. Printer: BdM.

	VF	UNC
a. 3.12.1969.	0.50	3.00
b. 27.10.1971.	0.25	2.00
c. 27.6.1972.	0.25	1.50

63   10 Pesos   VF   UNC

1969-77. Dark green on multicolor underprint. Bell at left, M. Hidalgo y Castilla
at right, bank titie with S. A. 3 signatures and signature varieties. Back: National
arms and Dolores Cathedral. Printer: BdM.

	VF	UNC
a. 16.9.1969. (This is Mexican Independence Day).	0.50	5.00
b. 3.12.1969.	0.25	1.50
c. 22.7.1970.	0.25	1.50
d. 3.2.1971.	0.25	1.25
e. 29.12.1972.	0.25	1.25
f. 18.7.1973.	0.20	1.25
g. 16.10.1974.	0.20	1.00
h. 15.5.1975.	0.20	0.75
i. 18.2.1977.	0.20	0.75
s. Specimen.	—	—

64   20 Pesos   VF   UNC

1972-77. Red and black on multicolor underprint. J. Morelos y Pavon at right with
building in background, bank titie with S. A. 3 signatures and signature varieties.
Back: Pyramid of Quetzalcoatl. Printer: BdM.

	VF	UNC
a. 29.12.1972.	0.50	3.00
b. 18.7.1973.	0.30	2.25
c. 8.7.1976.	0.20	2.00
d. 8.7.1977.	0.20	1.50

65   50 Pesos   VF   UNC

1973-78. Blue on multicolor underprint. Government palace at left, Benito Juárez
at right, bank titie with S. A. 3 signatures and signature varieties. red and black series letters and serial number. Back: Temple and Zapotec figural urn. Printer: BdM.

	VF	UNC
a. 18.7.1973.	1.00	4.00
b. 8.7.1976.	0.50	3.00
c. 5.7.1978.	0.50	3.00

66   100 Pesos   VF   UNC

1974; 1978. Purple on multicolor underprint. V. Carranza at left, *La Trinchera*
painting at center, bank titie with S. A. 3 signatures and signature varieties. red
and black series letters and serial number. Back: Stone figure. Printer: BdM.

	VF	UNC
a. 30.5.1974.	1.00	3.00
b. 5.7.1978.	1.00	3.00
s. Specimen.	—	—

1978-80 Issue

67   50 Pesos   VF   UNC

1978; 1979. Blue on multicolor underprint. Government palace at left, Benito
Juárez at right, bank titie with S. A. Red series letters and black serial number. 3
signatures. Back: Temple and Zapotec figural urn. Printer: BdM.

	VF	UNC
a. 5.7.1978.	0.75	2.00
b. 17.5.1979.	0.40	1.50

68   100 Pesos   VF   UNC

1978-79. UV: fibers fluoresce green. Back left design green. Purple on multicolor
underprint. V. Carranza at left, *La Trinchera* painting at center, bank titie with S.
A. Red series letters and a black serial number. 3 signatures. Back: Stone figure.
Printer: BdM.

	VF	UNC
a. 5.7.1978.	0.40	1.50
b. 17.5.1979. Engraved and litho back. Series before LL.	0.40	1.00
c. 17.5.1979. Litho back. Series LM and later.	0.40	1.00

74 100 Pesos　　　　　　　　　　　　　　　**VF UNC**
1981-82. UV: fibers fluoresce green and blue. Purple on multicolor underprint. V. Carranza at left, *La Trinchera* painting at center, bank titile with S. A. Red series letters and a black serial number. 4 signatures and signature varieties. Back: Stone figure. Printer: BdM.

a. 27.1.1981.	0.30	1.50
b. 3.9.1981.	0.30	1.50
c. 25.3.1982.	0.20	0.75

69 500 Pesos　　　　　　　　　　　　　　**VF UNC**
29.6.1979. Black on dark olive-green on multicolor underprint. F. I. Madero at left, bank titile with S. A. 3 signatures. Back: Aztec calendar stone. Watermark: F. I. Madero. Printer: BdM. 　3.00　11.00

70 1000 Pesos　　　　　　　　　　　　　**VF UNC**
1978-79. Dark brown and brown on multicolor underprint. J. de Asbaje at right, bank titile with S. A. 3 signatures. Back: Santo Domingo plaza at left center. Watermark: J. de Asbaje. Printer: BdM.

a. 5.7.1978	4.50	20.00
b. 17.5.1979.	4.00	12.50
c. 29.6.1979.	3.00	10.00

75 500 Pesos　　　　　　　　　　　　　**VF UNC**
1981-82. Green on multicolor underprint. F. I. Madero at left, bank titile with S. A. 4 signatures and signature varieties, narrow serial number style. Back: Aztec calendar stone. Watermark: F. I. Madero. Printer: BdM.

a. 27.1.1981.	1.25	4.50
b. 25.3.1982.	1.25	4.50

71 5000 Pesos　　　　　　　　　　　　**VF UNC**
25.3.1980. Red on multicolor underprint. Cadets at left center, bank titile with S. A. 3 signatures. Back: Chapultepec castle. Watermark: Cadet. Printer: BdM. 　15.00　45.00

72 10,000 Pesos　　　　　　　　　　　**VF UNC**
18.1.1978. Purple on multicolor underprint. Portrait M. Romero at left. Series CCL-CES. Back: National Palace at center. Printer: ABNC. 　20.00　75.00

1981 Issue

73 50 Pesos　　　　　　　　　　　　　　**VF UNC**
27.1.1981. Blue on multicolor underprint. Government palace at left, Benito Juárez at right, bank titile with S. A. Red series letters and black serial number. 4 signatures and signature varieties. Back: Temple and Zapotec figural urn. Printer: BdM. 　0.25　1.00

76 1000 Pesos　　　　　　　　　　　　**VF UNC**
1981-82. Dark brown and brown on multicolor underprint. J. de Asbaje at right, bank titile with S. A. 4 signatures and signature varieties, narrow serial number style. Back: Santo Domingo plaza at left center. Watermark: J. de Asbaje. Printer: BdM.

a. Engraved buildings on back. 27.1.1981. Black or red serial #.	2.00	10.00
b. Litho buildings on back. 27.1.1981.	2.00	10.00
c. 3.9.1981.	2.00	9.00
d. 25.3.1982.	1.50	7.00

77 5000 Pesos　　　　　　　　　　　　**VF UNC**
1981; 1982. Red and black on multicolor underprint. Cadets at left center, bank titile with S. A. 4 signatures and signature varieties, narrower serial number. Back: Chapultepec castle. Watermark: Cadet. Printer: BdM.

a. 27.1.1981.	6.00	30.00
b. 25.3.1982.	6.00	30.00

78   10,000 Pesos   VF   UNC

1981-82. Blue-black, brown and deep blue-green on multicolor underprint. Power plant at center, General Lazaro Cardenas at right, bank titile with S. A. 4 signatures and signature varieties. Back: Coyolxauhqui stone carving at center. Watermark: General Lazaro Cardenas. Printer: BdM.

a. 8.12.1981.	25.00	55.00
b. 25.3.1982.	15.00	50.00
c. Red and blue serial #. 30.9.1982.	15.00	50.00
d. Green and red serial #. 30.9.1982.	15.00	50.00
e. Green and blue serial #. 30.9.1982. Series CJ.	15.00	50.00

1983-84 Issues

79   500 Pesos   VF   UNC

1983; 1984. UV: fibers fluoresce blue and green. Green on multicolor underprint. F. I. Madero at left, bank titile without S. A., narrow serial number style. 4 signatures. Like #75, but with threads. Design over watermark area, no watermark.. Back: Aztec calendar stone. Printer: BdM.

a. 14.3.1983.	1.00	4.00
b. 7.8.1984.	0.75	2.50

80   1000 Pesos   VF   UNC

1983; 1984. Dark brown and brown on multicolor underprint. J. de Asbaje at right, bank title without S. A. 4 signatures and signature varieties, narrow serial number style. Back: Santo Domingo plaza at left center. Watermark: J. de Asbaje. Printer: BdM.

a. 13.5.1983.	2.00	5.00
b. 7.8.1984.	2.00	5.00

81   1000 Pesos   VF   UNC

30.10.1984. Similar to #80 but radiant quill pen printed over watermark area at left. Dark brown and brown on multicolor underprint. J. de Asbaje at right, bank titile without S. A. 4 signatures and signature varieties, narrow serial number style. Back: Santo Domingo plaza at left center. Watermark: J. de Asbaje. Printer: BdM.   0.75   3.00

82   2000 Pesos   VF   UNC

1983-84. Black, dark green and brown on multicolor underprint. J. Sierra at left center, University building at right. 4 signatures. Back: 19th century courtyard. Printer: BdM.

a. 26.7.1983.	3.00	10.00
b. 7.8.1984.	1.25	5.00
c. 30.10.1984.	1.25	5.00

83   5000 Pesos   VF   UNC

1983. Red and black on multicolor underprint. Cadets at left center, bank titile without S. A. 4 signatures and signature varieties, narrower serial number. Back: Chapultepec castle. Watermark: Cadet. Printer: BdM.

a. 13.5.1983.	3.50	12.50
b. 26.7.1983.	3.00	9.00
c. 5.12.1983. Series FB; FC.	10.00	25.00

84   10,000 Pesos   VF   UNC

1983. Blue-black, brown and deep blue-green on multicolor underprint. Power plant at center, General Lazaro Cardenas at right, bank titile without S. A. 4 signatures and signature varieties. Back: Coyolxauhqui stone carving at center. Watermark: General Lazaro Cardenas Printer: BdM.

a. Serial # upper left on face and lower left on back. 13.5.1983.	4.50	15.00
b. Serial # upper right and lower left on back. Red and dark blue serial #. 26.7.1983.	4.50	15.00
c. Green and blue serial #. 26.7.1983.	4.50	15.00
d. Purple and blue serial #. 26.7.1983.	4.50	17.50
e. 5.12.1983.	5.00	20.00

1985 Issues

85   1000 Pesos   VF   UNC

19.7.1985. Dark brown and brown on multicolor underprint. J. de Asbaje at right, bank titile without S. A. 3 signatures and signature varieties, narrow serial number style. Back: Santo Domingo plaza at left center. Watermark: J. de Asbaje. Printer: BdM.   0.75   2.50

86   2000 Pesos   VF   UNC

1985-89. UV: fibers fluoresce red, security strip green. Black, dark green and brown on multicolor underprint. J. Sierra at left center, University building at right. 3 signatures. Back: 19th century courtyard. Printer: BdM.

a. With *SANTANA* at lower left 2 date positions. 19.7.1985.	1.25	4.00
b. As a. 24.2.1987.	1.25	3.00
c. Without *SANTANA*. 28.3.1989.	1.00	2.25

87   5000 Pesos   **VF   UNC**

19.7.1985. Red on multicolor underprint. Cadets at left center, bank titile without   2.25   7.50
S. A. 4 signatures and signature varieties, narrower serial number. Back:
Chapultepec castle. Watermark: Cadet. Printer: BdM.

88   5000 Pesos   **VF   UNC**

1985-89. Purple and brown-orange on multicolor underprint. Cadets at left
center, bank titile without S. A. 3 signatures and signature varieties, narrower
serial number. Without watermark, design continued over watermark area. Back:
Chapultepec castle. Printer: BdM.

    a. With *SANTANA* vertically at lower left 19.7.1985.   2.00   6.00
    b. As a. 24.2.1987.   1.75   5.00
    c. Without *SANTANA*. 28.3.1989.   1.50   3.00

89   10,000 Pesos   **VF   UNC**

1985; 1987. Blue-black, brown and deep blue-green on multicolor underprint.
Power plant at center, General Lazaro Cardenas at right, bank titile without S. A.
3 signatures and signature varieties. Back: Coyolxauhqui stone carving at center.
Printer: BdM.

    a. Purple and blue serial #. 19.7.1985.   5.00   12.50
    b. Green and blue serial #. 19.7.1985.   5.00   12.50
    c. Red and blue serial #. 19.7.1985; 24.2.1987.   5.00   12.50
    d. Green and blue serial #. 24.7.1987.   5.00   12.50

90   10,000 Pesos   **VF   UNC**

1987-91. Similar to #89 but watermark area filled in. Deep blue-black on brown
and blue-green underprint. Power plant at center, General Lazaro Cardenas at
right, bank titile without S. A. 3 signatures and signature varieties. Back: Coyolxauhqui stone carving at center. Printer: BdM.

    a. With *SANTANA.* at lower left under refinery designature 24.2.1987.   3.00   10.00
    b. Without *SANTANA*. 1.2.1988.   2.50   7.00
    c. 28.3.1989.   2.50   6.00
    d. 16.5.1991.   2.00   6.00

91   20,000 Pesos   **VF   UNC**

1985-87. Deep blue on blue and multicolor underprint. Fortress above coastal
cliffs at center, Don A. Quintana Roo at right. 3 signature titles, S. A. remoned
from bank title. Back: Artwork. Watermark: Don A. Quintana Roo. Printer: BdM.

    a. 19.7.1985.   7.00   22.50
    b. 24.2.1987.   6.50   17.50
    c. 27.8.1987.   6.50   17.50

92   20,000 Pesos   **VF   UNC**

1988; 1989. Similar to #91 but design continued over watermark area. Blue-black
on blue and pink underprint. Fortress above coastal cliffs at center, Don A.
Quintana Roo at right. 3 signatures, S. A. removed from bank titile. Back: Artwork.
Printer: BdM.

    a. 1.2.1988.   5.00   15.00
    b. 28.3.1989.   5.00   12.50

93   50,000 Pesos   **VF   UNC**

1986-90. Purple on multicolor underprint. Aztec symbols at center, Cuauhtémoc
at right. 3 signatures, S.A. removed from bank titile. Back: Aztec and Spaniard
fighting at left center. Watermark: Cuauhtémoc. Printer: BdM.

    a. 12.5.1986; 24.2.1987; 27.8.1987; 1.2.1988.   17.50   60.00
    b. 28.3.1989; 10.1.1990; 20.12.1990.   15.00   45.00

94   100,000 Pesos

1988; 1991. Blue-black and maroon on multicolor underprint. P. E. Calles at left, Banco de Mexico at center. 3 signatures, S.A. removed from bank title. Back: Desert Mule Deer, cactus, lake and mountain at center right. Watermark: P. E. Calles. Printer: BdM.

	VF	UNC
a. 4.1.1988.	27.50	85.00
b. 2.9.1991.	27.50	85.00

1992 First Issue

Nuevos Pesos System 1000 "old" Pesos = 1 Nuevo Peso

95   10 Nuevos Pesos   VF UNC

31.7.1992. Blue-black, brown and deep blue-green on multicolor underprint. Power plant at center, General Lazaro Cardenas at right, bank titile without S. A. 3 signatures and signature varieties. Series A-Y. Back: Coyolxauhqul stone carving at center. Printer: BdM.   FV 7.50

96   20 Nuevos Pesos   VF UNC

31.7.1992. Deep blue on blue and multicolor underprint. Fortress above coastal cliffs at center, Don A. Quintana Roo at right. 3 signatures and signature varieties, S. A. removed from bank titile. Series A-Q. Back: Artwork. Printer: Bdm.   FV 12.50

97   50 Nuevos Pesos   VF UNC

31.7.1992. Purple on multicolor underprint. Aztec symbols at center, Cuauhtémoc at right. 3 signatures and signature titiles, S.A. removed from bank title. Series A-P. Back: Aztec and Spaniard fighting at left center. Printer: BdM.   FV 27.50

98   100 Nuevos Pesos   VF UNC

31.7.1992. Blue-black and maroon on multicolor underprint. P. E. Calles at left, Banco de Mexico at center. 3 signatures and signature titles, S.A. removed from bank title. Series A-Q. Back: Desert Mule Deer, cactus, lake and mountain at center right. Printer: BdM.   FV 40.00

1992 (1994) Second Issue

99   10 Nuevos Pesos   VF UNC

10.12.1992. (1994). Deep blue-green and gold on multicolor underprint. E. Zapata at right, hands holding corn at center. Series A-T. Back: Machinery at lower left, statue of Zapata on horseback near peasant at center right, building in background. Printer: BdM.   FV 4.00

100   20 Nuevos Pesos   VF UNC

10.12.1992 (1994). Purple and dark blue on multicolor underprint. B. Juárez at right, eagle on cactus with snake (arms) at center. Back: Monument, statues "Hemiciclo a Juárez. Printer: BdM.   FV 6.50

101   50 Nuevos Pesos   VF UNC

10.12.1992 (1994). Red-violet and black on multicolor underprint. J. M. Morelos at right, crossed cannons on outlined bow and arrow below his flag at left center. Series A-AF. Back: Butterflies at left, boat fishermen at center. Printer: BdM.   FV 15.00

102   100 Nuevos Pesos   VF UNC

10.12.1992 (1994). Red and brown on multicolor underprint. Nezahualcóyotl at right, Aztec figure at center. Series A-V. Back: Xochipilli statue. Watermark: Nezahualcóyotl. Printer: BdM.   FV 25.00

103 200 Nuevos Pesos

10.12.1992 (1994). Dark olive-green, dark brown and olive-brown on multicolor underprint. J. de Asbaje at right, open book and quill pen at center. Series A-E. Back: Temple de San Jerónimo. Watermark: J. de Asbaje. Printer: BdM.

	VF	UNC
	FV	45.00

104 500 Nuevos Pesos

10.12.1992 (1994). Red-brown, deep purple and dark brown-violet on multicolor underprint. I. Zaragoza at center right, Battle of Puebla at left center. Series A-C. Back: Cathedral at Puebla at center. Watermark: I. Zaragoza. Printer: BdM.

	VF	UNC
	FV	110

1994; 1995 (1996) Issue

105 10 Pesos

1994 (1996); 1996. Deep blue-green and gold on multicolor underprint. E. Zapata at right, hands holding corn at center. El omitted from bank title. 2 signatures. Series A-. Back: Machinery at lower left, statue of Zapata on horseback near peasant at center right, building in background. Printer: BdM.

		VF	UNC
a.	6.5.1994.	FV	3.00
b.	10.5.1996.	FV	3.00

106 20 Pesos

1994 (1996); 1996; 1998-99. Purple and dark blue on multicolor underprint. B. Juárez at right, eagle on cactus with snake (arms) at center. El omitted from bank title. 2 signatures. Series A-. Back: Monument, statues Hemiciclo a Juárez. Printer: BdM. 120x66mm.

		VF	UNC
a.	6.5.1994.	FV	6.00
b.	10.5.1996.	FV	5.50
c.	3.17.1998.	FV	5.50
d.	23.4.1999.	FV	5.50

107 50 Pesos

1994 (1996); 1998-99. Red-violet and black on multicolor underprint. J. M. Morelos at right, crossed cannons on outlined bow and arrow below his flag at left center. El omitted from bank title. 2 signatures. Series A-. Back: Butterflies at left, boat fishermen at center. Printer: BdM. 127x65mm.

		VF	UNC
a.	6.5.1994.	FV	15.00
b.	10.5.1996.	FV	10.00
c.	17.3.1998.	FV	10.00
d.	23.4.1999.	FV	10.00

108 100 Pesos

1994 (1996); 1996; 1998-99. Red and brown-orange on multicolor underprint. Nezahualcóyotl at right, Aztec figure at center. El omitted from bank title. Series A-BS. 2 signatures. Series A-. Back: Xochipilli statue. Printer: BdM. 155x66mm.

		VF	UNC
a.	6.5.1994.	FV	22.50
b.	10.5.1996.	FV	22.50
c.	17.03.1998. Series AX-BG.	FV	22.50
d.	23.4.1999. Series BC-BS.	FV	22.50

109 200 Pesos

1995 (1996); 1996; 1998-99. Dark olive-green, dark brown and olive-brown on multicolor underprint. J. de Asbaje at right, open book and quill pen at center. El omitted from bank title. Series A-E. 2 signatures. Series A-. Back: Temple de San Jerónimo. Watermark: J. de Asbaje. Printer: BdM. 155x66mm.

		VF	UNC
a.	7.2.1995.	FV	45.00
b.	10.5.1996.	FV	37.50
c.	17.3.1998.	FV	37.50
d.	23.4.1999.	FV	37.50

110 500 Pesos VF UNC

1995 (1996); 1996. Red-brown, deep purple and dark brown-violet on multicolor underprint. I. Zaragoza at center right, Battle of Puebla at left center. *El* omitted from bank title. Series A-C. 2 signatures. Back: Cathedral at Puebla at center. Watermark: I. Zaragoza. Printer: BdM. 155x66mm.

a. 7.2.1995.	FV	95.00
b. 10.5.1996.	FV	95.00
c. 17.3.1998.	FV	95.00
d. 23.4.1999.	FV	95.00

2000 Commemorative Issue

#111-115, 75th Anniversary Banco de Mexico. Commemorative text immediately below bank name.

111 20 Pesos VF UNC

25.8.2000. Purple and dark blue on multicolor underprint. B. Juárez at right, eagle on cactus with snake (arms) at center. Commemorative text immediately below bank name. Back: Monument, statues *Hemiciclo a Juárez*. Printer: BdM. 120x66mm. 3.50 9.50

112 50 Pesos VF UNC

25.8.2000. Red-violet and black on multicolor underprint. J. M. Morelos at right, crossed cannons on outlined bow and arrow below his flag at left center. Commemorative text immediately below bank name. Back: Butterflies at left, boat fishermen at center. Printer: BdM. 127x65mm. 9.00 17.50

113 100 Pesos VF UNC

25.8.2000. Red and brown-orange on multicolor underprint. Nezahualcóyotl at right, Aztec figure at center. Commemorative text immediately below bank name. Back: Xochipilli statue. Printer: BdM. 155x66mm. 15.00 35.00

114 200 Pesos VF UNC

25.8.2000. Dark olive-green, dark brown and olive-brown on multicolor underprint. J. de Asbaje at right, open book and quill pen at center. Commemorative text immediately below bank name. Back: Temple de San Jerónimo. Watermark: J. de Asbaje. Printer: BdM. 155x66mm. 30.00 70.00

115 500 Pesos VF UNC

25.8.2000. Red-brown, deep purple and dark brown-violet on multicolor underprint. I. Zaragoza at center right, Battle of Puebla at left center. Commemorative text immediately below bank name. Back: Cathedral at Puebla at center. Watermark: I. Zaragoza. Printer: BdM. 155x66mm. 65.00 150

2000-01 Issue

116 20 Pesos VF UNC

2001; 2002; 2003; 2005. Polymer plastic. Blue and multicolor underprint. B. Juárez at right, eagle on cactus with snake (arms) at center. 2 signatures. Back: Monument, statues "Hemiciclo a Juárez." Printer: NPA and BdM. 120x66mm.

a. 17.5.2001. Series A-F. Two electronic sorting bars at upper left.	FV	5.50
b. 17.5.2001. Series G-T. Three electronic sorting bars at upper left.	FV	4.50
c. 26.3.2002. Two electronic sorting bars. Series U.	FV	4.50
d. 23.5.2003. Two electronic sorting bars. Series V-.	FV	4.50
e. 9.11.2005.	FV	4.50

117 50 Pesos VF UNC

2000 (2001); 2002-03. Vertical iridescent strip at left. Additional enhanced security features. Red-violet and black on multicolor underprint. J. M. Morelos at right, crossed cannons on outlined bow and arrow below his flag at left center. 2 signatures. Back: Butterflies at left, boat fishermen at center. 127x65mm.

a. 18.10.2000.	FV	10.00
b. 26.3.2002.	FV	10.00
c. 21.11.2003.	FV	10.00

118   100 Pesos   VF UNC

2000-05; 2007-08. Vertical iridescent strip at left. Additional enhanced security features. Red and brown-orange on multicolor underprint. Nezahualcóyotl at right, Aztec figure at center. 2 signatures. Back: Xochipilli statue. 155x66mm.

	VF	UNC
a. 18.10.2000.	FV	15.00
b. 26.3.2002.	FV	15.00
c. 23.5.2003.	FV	15.00
d. 21.11.2003.	FV	15.00
e. 31.5.2004.	FV	12.50
f. 5.11.2004.	FV	12.50
g. 31.5.2005. Series DM.	FV	12.50
h. 7.9.2005.	FV	12.50
i. 19.6.2006. Series DT.	FV	12.50
j. 20.11.2007. Series DY.	FV	12.50
k. 28.4.2008.	FV	12.50
l. 28.4.2008. Series DZ.	FV	12.50
m. 28.4.2008. Series EA.	FV	12.50
n. 28.4.2008. Series EB.	FV	12.50

119   200 Pesos   VF UNC

2000-07. Vertical iridescent strip at left. Additional enhanced security features. Dark olive-green, dark brown and olive-brown on multicolor underprint. J. de Asbaje at right, open book and quill pen at center. Series A-E. 2 signatures. Back: Temple de San Jerónimo. Watermark: J. de Asbaje. 155x66mm.

	VF	UNC
a. 18.10.2000.	FV	27.50
b. 26.3.2002.	FV	27.50
c. 3.6.2004. Blind markings added at top right.	FV	25.00
d. 23.5.2006.	FV	25.00
e. 19.6.2006.	FV	22.50
f. 14.5.2007. Series DM, DN.	FV	22.50

120   500 Pesos   VF UNC

2000; 2005-06; 2008. Vertical iridescent strip at left. Additional enhanced security features. Red-brown, deep purple and dark brown-violet on multicolor underprint. I. Zaragoza at center right, Battle of Puebla at left center. Series A-C. 2 signatures. Back: Cathedral at Puebla at center. Watermark: Zaragoza. 155x66mm.

	VF	UNC
a. 18.10.2000.	FV	65.00
b. 7.9.2005.	FV	60.00
c. 19.6.2006.	FV	60.00
d. 28.10.2008. Series AW.	FV	55.00

121   1000 Pesos   VF UNC

26.3.2002. Multicolor. Miguel Hidalgo at right, eagle on cactus with snake (arms) at center. 2 signatures. Back: Monument, statues *Hemiciclo a Juárez*. 155x66mm.

	VF	UNC
a. Issued note.	FV	150
s. Specimen. Overprinted: *ESPECIMEN*.	—	750

2004-06 Polymer & Paper Issue

122   20 Pesos   VF UNC

2006-12. Polymer plastic. Blue. Benito Juarez at right center, book and scales at center. Back: View of Cocijo. 122x66mm.

	VF	UNC
a. 29.3.2006.	FV	4.00
b. 19.6.2006.	FV	4.00
c. 22.11.2006. Series C.	FV	4.00
d. 14.5.2007. Series E.	FV	4.00
e. 3.5.2010.	FV	4.00
f. 24.6.2011. Series Q.	FV	4.00
g. 10.1.2012. Series R.	FV	4.00

123   50 Pesos   VF UNC

2004-. Polymer plastic. Lilac, red and violet. Jose Maria Morelos at right center. Back: Morelia Aqueduct. 127x65mm.

	VF	UNC
a. 5.11.2004.	FV	7.50
b. 7.9.2005.	FV	7.50
c. 19.6.2006.	FV	7.50
d. 22.11.2006.	FV	7.50
e. 28.4.2008. Series J.	FV	7.50
f. 28.10.2008. Series K.	FV	7.50
g. 23.4.2009.	FV	7.50
h. 3.5.2010. Series Q.	FV	6.00
i. 3.5.2010. Series R; S.	FV	6.00
j. 24.6.2011. Series T; U.	FV	6.00
k. 10.1.2012. Series V.	FV	6.00
l. 12.6.2012.	FV	6.00

123A   50 Pesos   VF UNC

2012-. Polymer plastic. Lilac, red and violet. Like #123, but design is different. Jose Maria Morelos at right center. Back: Morelia Aqueduct. 127x65mm.

	VF	UNC
a. 12.6.2012. Series B.	FV	6.00
b. 12.6.2012. Series C.	FV	6.00
c. 25.4.2013. Series G.	FV	6.00
d. 10.6.2013. Series K.	FV	6.00

2010 Independence and Revolution Commemorative Issues

124   100 Pesos   VF   UNC
2008-13. Red and yellow on multicolor underprint. Ear of corn at left, Nezahualcóyotl at right. Back: Temple and central square of Tenochtitlán. Watermark:
Nezahualcóyotl and 100. 148x66mm.

		VF	UNC
a. 28.10.2008. Series A.		FV	18.00
b. 23.4.2009. Series E.		FV	18.00
c. 5.10.2009.		FV	15.00
d. 3.5.2010.		FV	15.00
e. 4.11.2010. Series M.		FV	12.50
f. 12.6.2012. Series V.		FV	12.50
g. 19.12.2012. Series X.		FV	12.50
h. 24.4.2013. Series AB.		FV	12.50

125   200 Pesos   VF   UNC
15.2.2007-. Green and brown on multicolor underprint. Juana de Asbaje at right
center. Back: Hacienda de Panoayán. Watermark: Asbaje and 200. 141x66mm.

		VF	UNC
a. 15.2.2007. Serie A, B.		FV	25.00
b. 14.5.2007. Serie C, D, E, F.		FV	25.00
c. 20.11.2007. Serie G, H.		FV	25.00
d. 5.10.2009.		FV	25.00

126   500 Pesos   VF   UNC
8.3.2010; 4.11.2010; 12.6.2012. Brown on tan underprint. Diego Rivera at center.
Back: Two of Rivera's paintings at center. Watermark: Rivera and 500. Printer:
BdM. 148x66mm.

		VF	UNC
a. 8.3.2010.		FV	70.00
b. 8.3.2010. Three signature varieties.		FV	70.00
c. 12.6.2012. Series V.		FV	70.00
s. Specimen.		—	100

127   1000 Pesos   VF   UNC
2006. Violet and brown on multicolor underprint. Miguel Hidalgo at right center.
Back: Universidad de Guanajato.

		VF	UNC
a. 8.5.2006. Series A.		FV	150
b. 28.11.2006.		FV	150

128   100 Pesos   VF   UNC
2007. Brown and multicolor. Steam Locomotive at center. Back: Revolutionary
crowd at center. 134x66mm.

		VF	UNC
a. Series A/A-A/E. Error in microprinted text: *SUFRAGIO ELECTIVO.*		FV	20.00
b. Corrected microprinted text: *SUFRAGIO EFECTIVO.*		FV	15.00

129   200 Pesos   VF   UNC
15.9.2008. Brown on green underprint. Miguel Hidalgo with standard at lower   FV   25.00
center. Back: Statue of the Angel of Independence. Watermark: Angel of Independence and 200. 141x66mm.

MOLDOVA

The area of Moldova is bordered in the north, east, and south by the Ukraine and on the west by Romania. The historical Romanian principality of Moldova was established in the 14th century. It fell under Turkish suzerainty in the 16th century. From 1812 to 1918, Russians occupied the eastern portion of Moldova which they named Bessarabia. In March 1918, the Bessarabian legislature voted in favor of reunification with Romania.

Part of Romania during the interwar period, Moldova was incorporated into the Soviet Union at the close of World War II. Although independent from the USSR since 1991, Russian forces have remained on Moldovan territory east of the Dniester River supporting the Slavic majority population, mostly Ukrainians and Russians, who have proclaimed a "Transnistria" republic. One of the poorest nations in Europe, Moldova became the first former Soviet state to elect a Communist as its president in 2001.

MONETARY SYSTEM:
3 Ducati = 100 Lei
100 Rubles = 1000 Cupon, 1992
1 Leu = 1000 Cupon, 1993-

REPUBLIC

Minister of Finance

Ruble Control Coupons, March 1992 Issue

			VF	UNC
A11	**20 Rubles**		**VF**	**UNC**
	Martie 1992.			
	a. Full sheet.		1.00	5.00
	b. One coupon.		FV	0.15
A12	**50 Rubles**		**VF**	**UNC**
	Martie 1992.			
	a. Full sheet.		1.00	5.00
	b. One coupon.		—	0.13
A13	**75 Rubles**		**VF**	**UNC**
	Martie 1992.			
	a. Full sheet.		1.00	5.00
	b. One coupon.		—	0.15
A14	**100 Rubles**		**VF**	**UNC**
	Martie 1992.			
	a. Full sheet.		1.00	5.00
	b. One coupon.		—	0.15

Ruble Control Coupons, April 1992 Issues

			VF	UNC
A15	**20 Rubles**		**VF**	**UNC**
	April 1992. Brown.			
	a. Full sheet.		1.00	5.00
	b. One coupon.		—	0.15
A16	**20 Rubles**		**VF**	**UNC**
	April 1992. Violet.			
	a. Full sheet.		1.00	5.00
	b. One coupon.		—	0.15
A17	**50 Rubles**		**VF**	**UNC**
	April 1992. Brown.			
	a. Full sheet.		1.00	5.00
	b. One coupon.		—	0.15
A18	**50 Rubles**		**VF**	**UNC**
	April 1992. Violet.			
	a. Full sheet.		1.00	5.00
	b. One coupon.		—	0.15
A19	**75 Rubles**		**VF**	**UNC**
	April 1992. Brown.			
	a. Full sheet.		1.00	5.00
	b. One coupon.		—	0.15
A20	**75 Rubles**		**VF**	**UNC**
	April 1992. Violet.			
	a. Full sheet.		1.00	5.00
	b. One coupon.		—	0.15

			VF	UNC
A21	**100 Rubles**		**VF**	**UNC**
	1992. Brown.			
	a. Full sheet.		1.00	5.00
	b. Coupon.		—	0.10
A22	**100 Rubles**		**VF**	**UNC**
	April 1992. Violet.			
	a. Full sheet.		1.00	5.00
	b. One coupon.		—	0.15

Banca Nationala a Moldovei
1992; 1993 "Cupon" Issue

		VF	UNC
1	**50 Cupon**	**VF**	**UNC**
	1992. Gray-green on gray underprint. Arms at left. Back: Castle at right. Watermark: Design (varies).	2.00	6.00

		VF	UNC
2	**200 Cupon**	**VF**	**UNC**
	1992. Purple on gray underprint. Arms at left. Back: Castle at right. Watermark: Design (varies).	4.00	8.00

3   1000 Cupon   **VF   UNC**
1993. Brown on pale blue-green and ochre underprint. Bank monogram at upper   5.00   10.00
left, arms at left. Back: Castle at right. Watermark: Design (varies).

4   5000 Cupon   **VF   UNC**
1993. Pale brown-violet on orange and pale olive-green underprint. Bank mono-   7.00   15.00
gram at upper left, arms at left. Back: Castle at right. Watermark: Design (varies).

1992 (1993) Issue

5   1 Leu   **VF   UNC**
1992 (1993). Brown and dark olive-green on ochre underprint. King Stefan at left,   3.00   6.00
arms at upper center right. Signature L. Talmaci. Back: Soroca Fortress at center
right. Printer: Romanian.

6   5 Lei   **VF   UNC**
1992 (1993). Purple on light blue and ochre underprint. King Stefan at left, arms   5.00   10.00
at upper center right. Signature L. Talmaci. Back: Soroca Fortress at center right.
Watermark: Design.

7   10 Lei   **VF   UNC**
1992 (1993). Red brown and olive-green on pale orange underprint. King Stefan   4.00   15.00
at left, arms at upper center right. Signature L. Talmaci. Back: Soroca Fortress at
center right. Watermark: Design. Printer: Romanian.

1992; 1994 Issue

8   1 Leu   **VF   UNC**
1994-2010. Brown on ochre, pale yellow-green and multicolor underprint. King Stefan at left, arms at upper center right. Bank monogram at upper right corner. Back:
Monastery at Capriana at center right. Watermark: King Stefan. Printer: BdF.

	VF	UNC
a. 1994.	0.50	2.50
b. 1995.	0.50	2.50
c. 1998.	0.50	2.50
d. 1999.	0.50	2.50
e. 2002.	0.50	2.50
f. 2005.	0.50	2.00
g. 2006.	0.50	1.50
h. 2010.	0.50	1.50
i. 2013.	FV	1.50

9   5 Lei   **VF   UNC**
1994-. Blue-green on lilac and pale aqua underprint. King Stefan at left, arms at
upper center right. Bank monogram at upper right corner. Back: Basilica of St.
Dumitru in Orhei at center right. Watermark: King Stefan. Printer: BdF. 114x58mm.

	VF	UNC
a. 1994.	1.00	3.50
b. 1995.	1.00	3.00
c. 1999.	1.00	3.00
d. 2005.	1.00	2.50
e. 2006.	1.00	2.50
f. 2009.	FV	2.00
g. 2013.	FV	2.00

10   10 Lei   **VF   UNC**
1994-. Red-brown on pale blue and gold underprint. King Stefan at left, arms at
upper center right. Bank monogram at upper right corner. Back: Monastery at
Hrjauca at center right. Watermark: King Stefan. 120x61mm.

	VF	UNC
a. 1994.	FV	5.00
b. 1995.	FV	5.00
c. 1998.	FV	8.00
d. 2005.	FV	4.50
e. 2006.	FV	4.00
f. 2009.	FV	3.00
g. 2013. Signature Dorin Dragutanu.	FV	3.00

#11 and 12 not assigned.

13   20 Lei   **VF   UNC**
1992-. Blue-green on light green, aqua and ochre underprint. King Stefan at left,
arms at upper center right. Bank monogram at upper right corner. Back: Soroca
Fortress at center right. Watermark: King Stefan. 121x61mm.

	VF	UNC
a. 1992.	FV	8.00
b. 1995.	FV	15.00
c. 1997.	FV	8.00
d. 1999.	FV	8.00
e. 2002.	FV	8.00
f. 2004.	FV	7.00
g. 2005.	FV	7.00
h. 2006.	FV	6.00
i. 2010.	FV	5.00
j. 2013.	FV	5.00

14   50 Lei   **VF   UNC**

1992-. Red-violet on lilac and multicolor underprint. King Stefan at left, arms at upper center right. Bank monogram at upper right corner. Back: Monastery at Hrbovet at center right. Watermark: King Stefan. 121x61mm.

a. 1992.	FV	12.00
b. 2002.	FV	10.00
c. 2005.	FV	10.00
d. 2006.	FV	10.00
e. 2008. Caption on back corrected.	FV	8.00
f. 2013. Signature Dorin Dragutanu.	FV	7.50

1992 (1995) Issue

15   100 Lei   **VF   UNC**

1992 (1995); 2008; 2013. Brown on multicolor underprint. King Stefan at left, arms at upper center right. Back: Thighina Fortress. Watermark: King Stefan. 121x61mm.

a. 1992.	10.00	25.00
b. 2008. Caption on back corrected: CETATEA TIGHINA.	FV	20.00
c. 2013. Signature Dorin Dragutanu.	FV	15.00

16   200 Lei   **VF   UNC**

1992 (1995); 2007; 2008; 2013. Purple on multicolor underprint. King Stefan at left, arms at upper center right. Back: Chisinau City Hall. Watermark: King Stefan. 133x66mm.

a. 1992	FV	45.00
b. 2007.	FV	35.00
c. 2008.	FV	30.00
d. 2013.	FV	30.00

1992 (1999) Issue

17   500 Lei   **VF   UNC**

1992 (1999). Slate black, orange and green on multicolor underprint. Back: Chisinau Cathedral. 133x66mm.   60.00   100

18   1000 Lei   **VF   UNC**

1992 (2003). Blue and purple on multicolor underprint. King Stefan at left. 133x66mm.   100   180

2006; 2013 Commemorative Issue

19   1 Lei   **VF   UNC**

2006. Banca Nationala i Moldovei declared note as a private, unofficial product.   FV   1.50
15th anniversary of leu currency.

20   200 Lei   **VF   UNC**

2013. 20th anniversary of leu currency.   FV   30.00

2015 Issue with New Security Features

21   1 Lei   **VF   UNC**
2015.   FV   1.50
22   10 Lei   **VF   UNC**
2015.   FV   3.00
23   20 Lei   **VF   UNC**
2015.   FV   5.00
24   50 Lei   **VF   UNC**
2015.   FV   7.50

25   100 Lei   **VF   UNC**

2015. Larger size. Brown on multicolor underprint. King Stefan at left, arms at   FV   15.00
upper center right. Demetalized BNM on the solid security thread, denomination
as registration device at lower right front, intaglio printing and blind embossing of
denomination. Back: Thighina Fortress. Watermark: King Stefan with electrotype
BNM. 133x66mm.

26   200 Lei   **VF   UNC**
2015.   FV   30.00
27   500 Lei   **VF   UNC**
2015.   FV   100

The State of Mongolia, a landlocked country in central Asia between Russia and the Peoples Republic of China, has an area of 604,247 sq. mi. (1,565,000 sq. km.) and a population of 2.74 million. Capital: Ulan Bator. Animal herds and flocks are the chief economic asset. Wool, cattle, butter, meat and hides are exported. The Mongols gained fame in the 13th century when under Chinggis Khan they established a huge Eurasian empire through conquest. After his death the empire was divided into several powerful Mongol states, but these broke apart in the 14th century. The Mongols eventually retired to their original steppe homelands and in the late 17th century came under Chinese rule. Mongolia won its independence in 1921 with Soviet backing and a Communist regime was installed in 1924. The modern country of Mongolia, however, represents only part of the Mongols' historical homeland; more Mongols live in the Inner Mongolia Autonomous Region in the People's Republic of China than in Mongolia. Following a peaceful democratic revolution, the ex-Communist Mongolian People's Revolutionary Party (MPRP) won elections in 1990 and 1992, but was defeated by the Democratic Union Coalition (DUC) in the 1996 parliamentary election. The MPRP won an overwhelming majority in the 2000 parliamentary election, but the party lost seats in the 2004 election and shared power with democratic coalition parties from 2004-2008. The MPRP regained a solid majority in the 2008 parliamentary elections; the prime minister and a majority of cabinet members are currently MPRP members.

RULERS:
Chinese to 1921

MONETARY SYSTEM:
1 Tugrik (Tukhrik) = 100 Mongo

STATE
УЛСЫН БАНК

STATE BANK
1966 Issue

		VF	UNC
35	**1 Tugrik**		
	1966. Brown on pale green and yellow underprint. Socialist arms at upper left. Watermark: Circles forming a 6-petaled flower-like pattern.		
	a. Issued note.	0.40	0.75
	s. Specimen. Red overprint on face.	—	40.00
36	**3 Tugrik**	**VF**	**UNC**
	1966. Dark green on light green and pink underprint. Socialist arms at upper left, portrait of Sukhe-Bataar at right. Watermark: Circles forming a 6-petaled flower-like pattern.		
	a. Issued note.	0.50	1.00
	s. Specimen. Red overprint on face.	—	40.00
37	**5 Tugrik**	**VF**	**UNC**
	1966. Dark blue on light blue and pale green underprint. Socialist arms at upper left, portrait of Sukhe-Bataar at right. Watermark: Circles forming a 6-petaled flower-like pattern.		
	a. Issued note.	0.50	1.00
	s. Specimen. Red overprint on face.	—	40.00
38	**10 Tugrik**	**VF**	**UNC**
	1966. Red on pale red and blue underprint. Socialist arms at upper left, portrait of Sukhe-Bataar at right. Watermark: Circles forming a 6-petaled flower-like pattern.		
	a. Issued note.	0.75	1.25
	s. Specimen. Red overprint on face.	—	40.00
39	**25 Tugrik**	**VF**	**UNC**
	1966. Brown-violet on pale green underprint. Socialist arms at upper left, portrait of Sukhe-Bataar at right. Watermark: Circles forming a 6-petaled flower-like pattern.		
	a. Issued note.	1.00	1.50
	s. Specimen.	—	15.00
40	**50 Tugrik**	**VF**	**UNC**
	1966. Dark green on light green and gold underprint. Socialist arms at upper left, portrait of Sukhe-Bataar at right. Back: Government Building at Ulan-Bator. Watermark: Circles forming a 6-petaled flower-like pattern.		
	a. Issued note.	2.50	3.00
	s. Specimen.	—	15.00

		VF	UNC
41	**100 Tugrik**		
	1966. Dark brown on ochre and blue-green underprint. Socialist arms at upper left, portrait of Sukhe-Bataar at right. Back: Government Building at Ulan-Bator. Watermark: Circles forming a 6-petaled flower-like pattern.		
	a. Issued note.	4.00	7.50
	s. Specimen.	—	15.00

1981-83 Issue
Replacement notes: Serial # prefix ЯАЁ

		VF	UNC
42	**1 Tugrik**		
	1983. Brown on pale green and yellow underprint. Socialist arms at upper left. Watermark: Circles forming a 6-petaled flower-like pattern.	0.25	1.00

		VF	UNC
43	**3 Tugrik**		
	1983. Dark green on light green and pink underprint. Socialist arms at upper left, portrait of Sukhe-Bataar at right. Watermark: Circles forming a 6-petaled flower-like pattern.	0.25	1.25

		VF	UNC
44	**5 Tugrik**		
	1981. Blue on light blue and pale green underprint. Socialist arms at upper left, portrait of Sukhe-Bataar at right. Watermark: Circles forming a 6-petaled flower-like pattern.	0.25	1.75

		VF	UNC
45	**10 Tugrik**		
	1981. Red on pale red and blue underprint. Socialist arms at upper left, portrait of Sukhe-Bataar at right. Watermark: Circles forming a 6-petaled flower-like pattern.	0.25	2.00

		VF	UNC
46	**20 Tugrik**		
	1981. Yellow-green on light green and brown underprint. Sukhe-Bataar at center, arms at left. Back: Power station at Ulan-Bator at center right.	0.35	2.25

47 50 Tugrik
	VF	UNC
1981. Dark green on light green and gold underprint. Socialist arms at upper left, portrait of Sukhe-Bataar at right. Back: Government Building at Ulan-Bator. Watermark: Circles forming a 6-petaled flower-like pattern. | 1.00 | 5.00

40 100 Tugrik
	VF	UNC
1981. Dark brown on ochre and blue-green underprint. Socialist arms at upper left, portrait of Sukhe-Bataar at right. Back: Government Building at Ulan-Bator. Watermark: Circles forming a 6-petaled flower-like pattern. | 0.10 | 9.00

ЬОНГОЛ БАНК
Mongol Bank
1993 ND; 1994-95 Issue
#41-51 Replacement notes: Serial # prefix ZZ.

49 10 Mongo
	VF	UNC
ND (1993). Red-violet on pale red-orange underprint. Soemba" arms at upper center, two archers at lower center. Back: Two archers at lower center. | 0.10 | 0.75

50 20 Mongo
	VF	UNC
ND (1993). Brown on ochre and yellow-brown underprint. Soemba" arms at upper center, two athletes at lower center. Back: Two athletes at lower center. | 0.15 | 0.75

51 50 Mongo
	VF	UNC
ND (1993). Greenish-black on blue and pale green underprint. Soemba" arms at upper center, two horsemen at lower center. Back: Two horsemen at lower center. | 0.50 | 0.75

52 1 Tugrik
	VF	UNC
ND (1993). UV: left design as a square with Mongolian 1 fluoresces yellow, upper serial # orange. Back central design orange. Dull olive-green and brown-orange on ochre underprint. Chinze at left. Back: Soemba" arms at center right. Watermark: Genghis Khan. | 0.15 | 1.00

53 5 Tugrik
	VF	UNC
ND (1993). UV: left design as a square with Mongolian 5 fluoresces yellow, upper serial # orange. Back portions of scene yellow. Deep orange, ochre and brown on multicolor underprint. Youthful portrait Sukhe-Bataar at left, "Soemba" arms at center. Back: Horses grazing in mountainous landscape at center right. Watermark: Genghis Khan. | 0.25 | 1.25

54 10 Tugrik
	VF	UNC
ND (1993). UV: left design as a square with Mongolian 10 fluoresces green, upper serial # orange. Back central design green. Green, blue and light green on multicolor underprint. Youthful portrait Sukhe-Bataar at left, "Soemba" arms at center. Back: Horses grazing in mountainous landscape at center right. Watermark: Genghis Khan. | 0.25 | 1.25

55 20 Tugrik
	VF	UNC
ND (1993). UV: left design as a square with Mongolian 20 fluoresces green, upper serial # orange. Back central design green. Violet, orange and red on multicolor underprint. Youthful portrait Sukhe-Bataar at left, "Soemba" arms at center. Back: Horses grazing in mountainous landscape at center right. Watermark: Genghis Khan. | 0.25 | 1.25

56   50 Tugrik   **VF   UNC**
ND (1993). Dark brown on multicolor underprint. Youthful portrait Sukhe-Bataar at   0.25   1.50
left, "Soemba" arms at center. Back: Horses grazing in mountainous landscape at
center right. Watermark: Genghis Khan.

57   100 Tugrik   **VF   UNC**
ND (1993); 1994. Purple, brown and dark blue on multicolor underprint. Youthful   0.50   2.00
portrait Sukhe-Bataar at left, "Soemba" arms at center. Back: Horses grazing in
mountainous landscape at center right. Watermark: Genghis Khan.

58   500 Tugrik   **VF   UNC**
ND (1993); 1997. Dark green, brown and yellow-green on multicolor underprint.   1.00   5.00
Genghis Khan at left, "Soemba" arms at center. Back: Ox drawn yurte, village at
center right. Watermark: Genghis Khan. 145x70mm.

59   1000 Tugrik   **VF   UNC**
ND (1993); 1997-98. Blue-gray, brown and blue on multicolor underprint. Genghis
Khan at left, "Soemba" arms at center. Back: Ox drawn yurte, village at center
right. Watermark: Genghis Khan. 150x72mm.
a. ND (1993).	5.00	10.00
b. 1997.	5.00	10.00
c. 1998.	5.00	10.00

60   5000 Tugrik   **VF   UNC**
1994. Purple, violet and red on multicolor underprint. Genghis Khan at left,   7.50   17.50
"Soemba" arms at center. Back: Building with fountain. Watermark: Genghis Khan.
150x72mm.

61   10,000 Tugrik   **VF   UNC**
1995. Black, dark olive-green and orange on multicolor underprint. Genghis Khan   16.00   35.00
at left, "Soemba" arms at center. Back: Ox drawn yurte, village at center right.
Building complex, tree, people. Watermark: Genghis Khan. 150x72mm.

2000; 2003 Issue

61A   1 Tugrik   **VF   UNC**
2008. Dull olive-green and brown-orange on ochre underprint. Chinze at left   0.15   1.00
center. Back: Soemba" arms at center right. 115x57mm.

61B   5 Tugrik   **VF   UNC**
2008. Deep orange, ochre and brown on multicolor underprint. Youthful portrait of   0.25   1.25
Sukhe-Bataar at left, "Soemba" arms at center. Back: Horses grazing in mountainous landscape at center right. 120x60mm.

62   10 Tugrik   **VF   UNC**
2000-. Dark green and multicolor. Youthful portrait Sukhe-Bataar at left, "Soemba"
arms at center. 128x60mm.
a. 2000.	FV	0.50
b. 2002.	FV	0.50
c. 2005.	FV	0.50
d. 2007.	FV	0.50
e. 2009.	FV	0.50
f. 2011.	FV	0.50
g. 2013.	FV	0.50
h. 2014.	FV	0.50

63 20 Tugrik

2000-. Red on rose, green and orange underprint. Youthful portrait Sukhe-Bataar at left, "Soemba" arms at center. 150x72mm.

		VF	UNC
a.	2000.	FV	0.75
b.	2002.	FV	0.75
c.	2005.	FV	0.75
d.	2007.	FV	0.75
e.	2009.	FV	0.75
f.	2011.	FV	0.75
g.	2013.	FV	0.75
h.	2014.	FV	0.75

64 50 Tugrik

2000; 2008; 2013. Brown-gold. Sukhe-Bataar at left. Segmented security thread. Microprinting, UV ink and embossed *50* below arms.

		VF	UNC
a.	2000.	FV	1.25
b.	2008.	FV	1.25
c.	2013.	FV	1.25

65 100 Tugrik

2000; 2008. Multicolor. Youthful portrait Sukhe-Bataar at left, "Soemba" arms at center.

		VF	UNC
a.	2000.	FV	2.00
b.	2008.	FV	2.00
c.	2014.	FV	2.00

65A 500 Tugrik

2000. Dark green, brown and yellow-green on multicolor underprint. Genghis Khan at left. Back: Ox drawn yurte, village at center right. 145x70mm.

	VF	UNC
	FV	5.00

66 500 Tugrik

2003; 2007; 2011; 2013. Wide security thread added to #65A. Blue and brown on multicolor underprint. Genghis Khan at left. Back: Ox drawn yurte, village at center right. 145x70mm.

		VF	UNC
a.	2003.	FV	5.00
b.	2007.	FV	5.00
c.	2011.	FV	5.00
d.	2013.	FV	5.00

67 1000 Tugrik

2003; 2007; 2011; 2013. Blue and brown on multicolor underprint. Genghis Khan at left. Back: Ox drawn yurtle, village at upper left 145x70mm.

		VF	UNC
a.	2003.	FV	10.00
b.	2007.	FV	10.00
c.	2011.	FV	10.00
d.	2013.	FV	10.00

68 5000 Tugrik

2003; 2013. Purple and orange on multicolor underprint. Genghis Khan at left. Back: Building with fountain. 150x72mm.

		VF	UNC
a.	2003.	FV	17.50
b.	2013. Signature Naidansuren Zoljargal.	FV	12.50

69 10,000 Tugrik   **VF UNC**
2002; 2009. Dark green and orange on multicolor underprint. Genghis Khan at
left. Back: Large old building, tree and groups of people. 150x72mm.
   a. 2002.   FV 35.00
   b. 2009.   FV 35.00
   c. 2014.   FV 35.00

70 20,000 Tugrik   **VF UNC**
2006. Green on purple, yellow and multicolor underprint. Genghis Khan at left.
Back: Pennants. 150x72mm.
   a. 2006.   FV 60.00

A variety with an overprint honoring the Great Mongol Empire, 1206-1806, may be official but
  requires confirmation.

71 20,000 Tugrik   **VF UNC**
2009; 2013. Green on purple, yellow and multicolor underprint. Genghis Khan at
left, transparent window at bottom. Back: Nine white banners. Watermark: Khan
and letters. Printer: G&D. 150x72mm.
   a. 2009.   FV 55.00
   b. 2013. Modified security thread.   FV 50.00

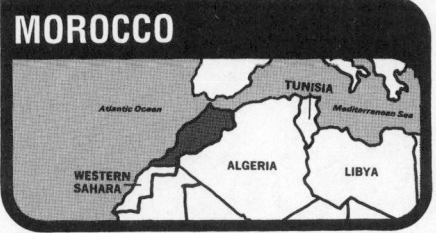

MOROCCO

The Kingdom of Morocco, situated on the northwest corner of Africa south of Spain, has an area of 172,413 sq. mi. (712,550 sq. km.) and a population of 28.98 million. Capital: Rabat. The economy is essentially agricultural. Phosphates, fresh and preserved vegetables, canned fish and raw material are exported. In 788, about a century after the Arab conquest of North Africa, successive Moorish dynasties began to rule in Morocco. In the 16th century, the Sa'adi monarchy, particularly under Ahmad Al-Mansur (1578-1603), repelled foreign invaders and inaugurated a golden age. In 1860, Spain occupied northern Morocco and ushered in a half century of trade rivalry among European powers that saw Morocco's sovereignty steadily erode; in 1912, the French imposed a protectorate over the country. A protracted independence struggle with France ended successfully in 1956. The internationalized city of Tangier and most Spanish possessions were turned over to the new country that same year. Morocco virtually annexed Western Sahara during the late 1970s, but final resolution on the status of the territory remains unresolved. Gradual political reforms in the 1990s resulted in the establishment of a bicameral legislature, which first met in 1997. The country has made improvements in human rights under King Mohammed VI and its press is moderately free. Despite the continuing reforms, ultimate authority remains in the hands of the monarch.

RULERS:
  Muhammad V, AH1346-1380/1927-1961AD
  Hassan II, AH1380-1420 /1961-1999AD
  Muhammad VI, AH1420- /1999- AD

MONETARY SYSTEM:
  1 Franc = 100 Centimes
  1 Dirham = 100 Francs, 1921-1974
  1 Dirham = 100 Centimes = 100 Santimat, 1974-
  1 Riffan = 1 French Gold Franc = 10 British Pence

SIGNATURE VARIETIES		
	GOVERNMENT COMISSIONER	**GOVERNOR**
1	Mohamed Tahiri, 1960	M'hamed Zeghari
2	Ahmed Ben Nani, 1963-65	M'hamed Zeghari
3	Ahmed Ben Nani	Driss Slaovi
4	Mohamed Lemniai, 1996	Driss Slaovi
5	Abdelaziz El Alami, 1967	Driss Slaovi
6	Abdelkrim Lazrek, 1968	M'hamed Zeghari
7	Abdelkrim Lazrek, 1968	Prince Moulay Hassan Ben Medhdi El Alaovi
8	Mohamed El Mdaghri, 1970	Prince Moulay Hassan Ben Medhdi El Alaovi
9	Hassan Lukash, 1985-89	Ahmed Ben Nani
10	Hassan Lukash	Mohamed Es Sakat
11	Abdul el Fatah ben Mansour	Mohamed Es Sakat
12	Noureddin Omary	Mohamed Es Sakat

KINGDOM

Banque du Maroc
Established June 30, 1959

1960 (ND); 1965 Issue

53 5 Dirhams   VF UNC

ND (1960); 1965-69. Brown and multicolor. King Muhammad V wearing a fez at right. Back: Harvesting at left, man holding sheaf at right. Watermark: Lion's head. Printer: Banque de France.

	VF	UNC
a. Signature 1. ND (1960).	25.00	100
b. Signature 2. ND (1963).	20.00	00.00
c. Signature 3. 1965/AH1384.	15.00	65.00
d. Signature 4. 1966/AH1386.	15.00	65.00
e. Signature 6. 1968/AH1387.	16.00	60.00
f. Signature 7. 1969/AH1389.	15.00	60.00

54 10 Dirhams   VF UNC

ND (1960); 1965-69. Brown and multicolor. King Muhammad V wearing fez at left, Hassan Tower in Rabat at center. Back: Orange picking. Watermark: Lion's head. Printer: Banque de France.

	VF	UNC
a. Signature 1. ND (1960).	20.00	75.00
b. Signature 2. ND (1963).	20.00	75.00
c. Signature 3. 1965/AH1384.	15.00	65.00
d. Signature 6. 1968/AH1387.	15.00	60.00
e. Signature 7. 1969/AH1389.	15.00	60.00

55 50 Dirhams   VF UNC

1965-69. Brown and multicolor. King Hassan II at right. Back: Miners at work. Watermark: Lion's head. Printer: Banque de France.

	VF	UNC
a. Signature 3. 1965/AH1385.	120	500
b. Signature 6. 1966/AH1386.	100	400
c. Signature 6. 1968/AH1387.	100	400
d. Signature 7. 1969/AH1389.	100	400

1970 Issue

56 5 Dirhams   VF UNC

1970/AH1390. Replacement notes: Serial # prefix Z. Purple on light blue and multicolor underprint. King Hassan II at left, castle at center. Signature 8. Back: Industrial processing. Watermark: King Hassan II. Printer: TDLR.

	VF	UNC
a. Issued note.	2.50	10.00
s. Specimen.	—	32.50

57 10 Dirhams   VF UNC

1970; 1985. Replacement notes: Serial # prefix Y. Brown on light green and multicolor underprint. King Hassan II at left, Villa at center. Back: Processing oranges. Watermark: King Hassan II. Printer: TDLR.

	VF	UNC
a. Signature 8. 1970/AH1390.	2.50	10.00
b. Signature 9. 1985/AH1405.	2.50	10.00
s. As a. Specimen.	—	35.00

58 50 Dirhams   VF UNC

1970; 1985. Replacement notes: Serial # prefix X. Green and brown on multicolor underprint. King Hassan II at left, city at center. Back: Dam. Watermark: King Hassan II. Printer: TDLR.

	VF	UNC
a. Signature 8. 1970/AH1390.	10.00	30.00
b. Signature 9. 1985/AH1405.	8.00	30.00
s. As b. Specimen.	—	50.00

59 100 Dirhams   VF   UNC

1970; 1985. Replacement notes: Serial # prefix *W*. Brown and blue on light green and multicolor underprint. King Hassan II at left, building at center. Back: Oil refinery. Watermark: King Hassan II. Printer: TDLR.

a. Signature 8. 1970/AH1390.		15.00	60.00
b. Signature 9. 1985/AH1405.		15.00	60.00
s. As b. Specimen.		—	70.00

Bank al-Maghrib

1987 Issue

60 10 Dirhams   VF   UNC

1987/AH1407. Red-brown and red on multicolor underprint. King Hassan II facing at right. Back: Musical instrument and pillar at left center. Watermark: King Hassan II. 142x70mm.

a. Signature 9.		3.00	12.50
b. Signature 10.		2.50	10.00

61 50 Dirhams   VF   UNC

1987/AH1407. Green on multicolor underprint. King Hassan II facing at right. Back: Mounted militia charging, flowers at center. Watermark: King Hassan II. 148x70mm.

a. Signature 9.		12.00	50.00
b. Signature 10.		10.00	40.00

62 100 Dirhams   VF   UNC

1987/AH1407. . Brown on multicolor underprint. King Hassan II facing at right. Back: Demonstration. Watermark: King Hassan II. 153x75mm.

a. Signature 9.		15.00	65.00
b. Signature 10.		FV	50.00

1987 (1991) Issue

63 10 Dirhams   VF   UNC

1987/AH407 (ca.1991). Brown-violet and purple on multicolor underprint. Older bust of King Hassan II at right facing half left. Back: Like #60, but different colors of underprint. Watermark: King Hassan II facing. 142x70mm.

a. Signature 10.		FV	7.50
b. Signature 11.		FV	6.00

64 50 Dirhams   VF   UNC

1987/AH1407 (ca.1991). Green on multicolor underprint. Older bust of King Hassan II at right facing half left. Back: Mounted militia charging, flowers at center. Watermark: King Hassan II facing. 148x70mm.

a. Signature 10.		FV	30.00
b. Signature 11.		FV	25.00
c. Signature 12.		FV	20.00
d. Signature 13.		FV	20.00
e. Signature 16.		FV	20.00

65 100 Dirhams   VF   UNC

1987/AH1407 (ca.1991). Brown and blue on multicolor underprint. Older bust of King Hassan II at right facing half left. Back: Demonstration. Watermark: King Hassan II facing. 153x75mm.

a. Signature 10.		FV	45.00
b. Signature 11.		FV	40.00
c. Signature 12.		FV	35.00
d. Signature 13.		FV	35.00
e. Signature 16.		FV	30.00

66 200 Dirhams   VF   UNC

1987/AH1407 (ca.1991). Blue-violet and blue on multicolor underprint. Older bust of King Hassan II at right facing half left. Mausoleum of King Muhammad V at center. Back: Sailboat, shell and coral. Watermark: King Hassan II facing. 158x75mm.

a. Signature 10.		FV	75.00
b. Signature 11.		FV	65.00
c. Signature 12.		FV	60.00
d. Signature 13.		FV	55.00
e. Signature 16.		FV	50.00

1996 Issue

67   20 Dirhams   **VF   UNC**
1996. Multicolor. King Hassan II at left, Great Mosque of Casablanca at center.
Back: Fountain. 130x68mm.

a. Signature 12.	FV	7.50
b. Signature 13.	FV	6.00
c. Signature 14.	FV	6.00
d. Signature 15.	FV	6.00
e. Signature 16.	FV	6.00

2002 (2004-) Issue

68   20 Dirhams   **VF   UNC**
2005/AH1426. Black and purple on multicolor underprint. Mohammed VI at left,   FV   5.00
city gate at center. Signature 16. Back: Ancient seaside city. 140x70mm.

69   50 Dirhams   **VF   UNC**
2002/AH1423. Green on multicolor underprint. Mohammed VI at left, dam at
center. Signature 16. Back: Old building in ksour and wheat. 148x70mm.

a. With dash between dates.	FV	12.50
b. Without dash between dates.	FV	12.50

70   100 Dirhams   **VF   UNC**
2002/AH1423. Brown on multicolor underprint. Mohammed VI, Hassan II and   FV   20.00
Mohammed V at right, building at center. Signature 16. Back: People marching
with flags. 150x78mm.

71   200 Dirhams   **VF   UNC**
2002/AH1423. Dark blue, blue and multicolor underprint. Mohammed VI and   FV   35.00
Hassan II at left, building at center. Signature 16. Back: Window of the Theological
School at the Hassan II Mosque. 158x78mm.

2009 Commemorative Issue

72   50 Dirhams   **VF   UNC**
AH1430/2009. Green on multicolor underprint. Kings Mohammed VI, Hassan II   FV   15.00
and Mohammed V at left center. Holographic stripe with three portraits. Back:
Bank al-Maghrib building in Rabat. Watermark: Mohammed VI and 50. Printer:
TK. 147x70mm.

#72 Commemorates the 50th Anniversary of Bank al-Maghrib.

2012 Commemorative Issue

73   25 Dirhams   **VF   UNC**
2012. Vertical format. 25th Anniversary of Dar As Sikkah. Red and multicolor   FV   7.50
Mohammed VI facing left. 145x70mm.

2012-14 Issue

74   20 Dirhams   **VF   UNC**
AH1433-2012. Purple, orange and blue on multicolor underprint. Mohammed   FV   6.00
VI, Moroccan door, arms. Back: Train crossing Hassan II Bridge over Bou River
in Rabat; Hassan II Mosque in Casablanca. Watermark: Mohammed VI and 20.
131x70mm.

75   50 Dirhams   **VF   UNC**
AH1433-2012. Green, yellow and blue on multicolor underprint. Mohammed VI,   FV   12.00
Moroccan door, arms Watermark: Mohammed VI and 50. 138x7mm.

76   100 Dirhams   **VF   UNC**
2012. Brown, pink and beige. Archway, coat mof arms, King Mohammed VI.   FV   30.00
SPARK crown and star. Back: Camels with riders, touareg tent, desert tema.
Watermark: Mohammed VI and 100. 145x70mm.

77   200 Dirhams   **VF   UNC**
2012. Blue and dark violet. King Mohammed VI at right. Royal crown at upper   FV   45.00
right Back: Tangier harbor at left, lighthouse at center. Watermark: Mohammed VI
and 200. 151x70mm.

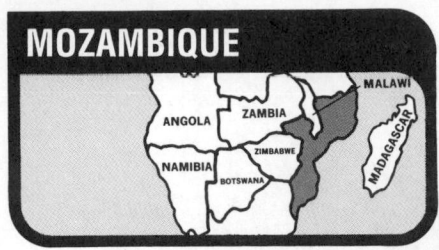

MOZAMBIQUE

The People's Republic of Mozambique, a former overseas province of Portugal stretching for 1,430 miles (2,301 km.) along the southeast coast of Africa, has an area of 309,494 sq. mi. (783,030 sq. km.) and a population of 19.56 million. Capital: Maputo. Agriculture is the chief industry. Cashew nuts, cotton, sugar, copra and tea are exported. Almost five centuries as a Portuguese colony came to a close with independence in 1975. Large-scale emigration by whites, economic dependence on South Africa, a severe drought, and a prolonged civil war hindered the country's development until the mid 1990's. The ruling Front for the Liberation of Mozambique (FRELIMO) party formally abandoned Marxism in 1989, and a new constitution the following year provided for multiparty elections and a free market economy. A UN-negotiated peace agreement between FRELIMO and rebel Mozambique National Resistance (RENAMO) forces ended the fighting in 1992. In December 2004, Mozambique underwent a delicate transition as Joaquim Chissano stepped down after 18 years in office. His elected successor, Armando Emilio Guebuza, promised to continue the sound economic policies that have encouraged foreign investment. Mozambique has seen very strong economic growth since the end of the civil war largely due to post-conflict reconstruction.

RULERS:
Portuguese to 1975

MONETARY SYSTEM:
1 Escudo = 100 Centavos, 1911-1975
1 Escudo = 1 Metica = 100 Centimos, 1975-

REPLACEMENT NOTES:
#116, 117, 119: Z prefix.
#125-133, ZA, ZB, ZC prefix.
#134-137, AW, BW, CY, DZ prefix by denomination.

PORTUGUESE ADMINISTRATION

Banco Nacional Ultramarino
Moçambique Branch
1961; 1967 Issue

109	100 Escudos	VF	UNC
	27.3.1961. Green on multicolor underprint. Portrait A. de Ornelas at right, arms at upper center. Back: Bank steamship seal at left. Printer: BWC without imprint.		
	a. Watermark: Arms.	4.00	17.50
	b. Without watermark.	3.00	10.00
	s. As a. Specimen.	—	140

110	500 Escudos	VF	UNC
	22.3.1967. Purple on multicolor underprint. Portrait C. Xavier at right, arms at upper center. Printer: BWC without imprint.		
	a. Issued note.	20.00	75.00
	s. Specimen.	—	150

1970 Issue

111	50 Escudos	VF	UNC
	27.10.1970. Black on multicolor underprint. J. de Azevedo Coutinho at left center, arms at upper center right. Signature varieties. Back: Bank steamship seal at left. Watermark: Arms.	3.00	15.00

First 1972 Issue

112	1000 Escudos	VF	UNC
	16.5.1972. Black-blue on multicolor underprint. King Afonso V at right, arms at upper center. 3 signature varieties. Back: Allegorical woman with ships at left on back, bank steamship seal at upper center. Watermark: King Afonso V.		
	a. Serial number without prefix. 2.5mm tall.	22.50	125
	b. Serial number with three letter prefix. 3mm tall.	22.50	125

Second 1972 Issue

113	100 Escudos	VF	UNC
	23.5.1972. Blue on multicolor underprint. G. Coutinho and S. Cabral at left center. Back: Surveyor at center. Watermark: G. Coutinho.	7.50	50.00

114 500 Escudos VF UNC
23.5.1972. Purple on multicolor underprint. G. Coutinho at left. Back: Cabral and 15.00 85.00
airplane. Watermark: G. Coutinho.

115 1000 Escudos VF UNC
23.5.1972. Green on multicolor underprint. G. Coutinho at left center. Back: Two 25.00 120
mon in oookpit of airplane at left center.

PEOPLES REPUBLIC

Banco de Moçambique
1976 ND Provisional Issue

116 50 Escudos VF UNC
ND (1976 - old date 27.10.1970). Black on multicolor underprint. J. de Azevedo 1.00 2.00
Coutinho at left center, arms at upper center right. Signature varieties. Overprint.
Back: Bank steamship seal at left.

117 100 Escudos VF UNC
ND (1976 - old date 27.3.1961). Green on multicolor underprint. Portrait A. de Or-
nelas at right, arms at upper center. Overprint. Back: Bank steamship seal at left.
   a. Issued note. 1.00 3.00
   s. Specimen. — 100

118 500 Escudos VF UNC
ND (1976 - old date 22.3.1967). Purple on multicolor underprint. Portrait C. Xavier
at right, arms at upper center. Overprint.
   a. Issued note. 1.00 5.00
   s. Specimen. — 115

119 1000 Escudos VF UNC
ND (1976 - old date 23.5.1972). Green on multicolor underprint. G. Coutinho at 1.00 6.00
left center. Overprint. Back: Two men in cockpit of airplane at left center.

1976 Issue
 # 120-124 These appear to be unadopted designs.

120 5 Meticas VF UNC
25.6.1976. Specimen, punch hole cancelled. Brown and multicolor. President S. — —
Machel at left center. Back: Kudu. Printer: TDLR.

121 10 Meticas VF UNC
25.6.1976. Specimen, punch hole cancelled. Blue on multicolor. President S. — —
Machel at left center. Back: Lions. Printer: TDLR.

122 20 Meticas VF UNC
25.6.1976. Specimen, punch hole cancelled. Red and multicolor. President S. — —
Machel at left center. Back: Giraffes. Printer: TDLR.

123 50 Meticas VF UNC
25.6.1976. Specimen, punch hole cancelled. Purple and multicolor. President S. — —
Machel at left center. Back: Cape buffalo. Printer: TDLR.

124 100 Meticas   VF   UNC
25.6.1976. Specimen, punch hole cancelled. Green and multicolor. President S.   —   —
Machel at left center. Back: Elephants. Printer: TDLR.

República Popular de Moçambique
1980 Issue

125 50 Meticais   VF   UNC
16.6.1980. Dark brown and brown on multicolor underprint. Soldiers at left, flag   0.50   2.00
ceremony at right, arms at center. Large size serial number. Back: Soldiers in
training.

126 100 Meticais   VF   UNC
16.6.1980; 16.6.1983. Green on multicolor underprint. Soldiers at flagpole at   0.75   3.00
left, E. Mondlane at right, arms at center. Large size serial number. Back: Public
ceremony.

127 500 Meticais   VF   UNC
16.6.1980. Deep blue-violet and dark blue-green on multicolor underprint. Govern-   1.00   5.00
ment assembly at left, chanting crowd at right, arms at center. Large size serial
number. Back: Chemists and school scene.

128 1000 Meticais   VF   UNC
16.6.1980. Deep red on multicolor underprint. President S. Machel with three   1.75   8.50
young boys at right, revolutionary monument at left, arms at center. Large size
serial number. Back: Mining and harvesting scenes.

1983-88 Issue

129 50 Meticais   VF   UNC
16.6.1983; 16.6.1986. Dark brown and brown on multicolor underprint. Soldiers at
left, flag ceremony at right, modified arms at center. Smaller size serial number.
Back: Soldiers in training.
  a. 16.6.1983.   0.25   1.50
  b. 16.6.1986.   0.25   1.50

130 100 Meticais   VF   UNC
16.6.1983; 16.6.1986; 16.6.1989. Green on multicolor underprint. Soldiers at
flagpole at left, E. Mondlane at right, modified arms at center. Smaller size serial
number. Back: Public ceremony.
  a. 16.6.1983.   0.50   2.00
  b. 16.6.1986.   0.50   2.00
  c. 16.6.1989.   0.50   2.00

131 500 Meticais
16.6.1983; 16.6.1986; 16.6.1989. Deep blue-violet and dark blue-green on multi-color underprint. Government assembly at left, chanting crowd at right, modified arms at center. Smaller size serial number. Back: Chemists and school scene.

		VF	UNC
a.	16.6.1983.	1.00	3.00
b.	16.6.1986.	1.00	3.00
c.	16.6.1989.	1.00	3.00

132 1000 Meticais
16.6.1983; 16.6.1986; 16.6.1989. Deep red on multicolor underprint. President S. Machel with three young boys at right, revolutionary monument at left, modified arms at center. Smaller size serial number. Back: Mining and harvesting scene.

		VF	UNC
a.	16.6.1983.	1.50	6.00
b.	16.6.1986.	2.00	7.50
c.	16.6.1989.	1.00	3.00

133 5000 Meticais
3.2.1988; 3.2.1989. Purple, brown and violet on multicolor underprint. Carved statues at left, painting at right. Back: Dancers and musicians.

		VF	UNC
a.	3.2.1988.	1.75	5.00
b.	3.2.1989.	1.75	5.00

1991-93 Issue

134 500 Meticais
16.6.1991. Brown and blue on multicolor underprint. Native carving of couple in grief at left center, native art at right, arms at upper center right printed on silver or gold underlay. Back: Dancing warriors at center, bank seal at lower left. Watermark: J. Chissano. Printer: TDLR.

	VF	UNC
	1.00	2.00

135 1000 Meticais
16.6.1991. Brown and red on multicolor underprint. E. Mondlane at left center, military flag raising ceremony at right, arms at upper center right printed on silver or gold underlay. Back: Monument at left center, bank seal at lower left. Watermark: J. Chissano. Printer: TDLR.

	VF	UNC
	1.00	3.00

136 5000 Meticais
16.6.1991. Purple, violet and orange-brown on multicolor underprint. S. Machel at left center, monument to the Socialist vanguard at right, arms at upper center right printed on silver or gold underlay. Back: Foundry workers at center, bank seal at lower left. Watermark: J. Chissano. Printer: TDLR.

	VF	UNC
	1.00	3.00

137 10,000 Meticais
16.6.1991. Blue-green, brown and orange on multicolor underprint. J. Chissano at left center, high tension electrical towers at right, with farm tractor in field and high-rise city view in background at right, arms at upper center right printed on silver or gold underlay. Back: Plowing with oxen at center, bank seal at lower left. Watermark: J. Chissano. Printer: TDLR. 150x69mm.

	VF	UNC
	1.00	4.00

138 50,000 Meticais
16.6.1993 (1994). Dark brown, red-brown on multicolor underprint. Bank of Mozambique building at left center, arms at upper right. Back: Cabora Bassa hydroelectric dam. Watermark: Bank monogram. 157x69mm.

	VF	UNC
	2.00	8.00

139 **100,000 Meticais** VF UNC
16.6.1993 (1994). Red, brown-orange and olive-brown on multicolor underprint. 2.00 14.00
Bank of Mozambique building at left center, arms at upper right. Back: Cabora
Bassa hydroelectric dam. Watermark: Bank monogram. 135x69mm.

1999 Issue

140 **20,000 Meticais** VF UNC
16.6.1999. Green on multicolor underprint. Young woman seated writing at center. 1.00 4.00
Back: Maputo city hall. 153x69mm.

2004 Issue

141 **200,000 Meticais** VF UNC
16.6.2003 (2004). Dark blue and aqua on multicolor underprint. Banco de Moçam- FV 25.00
bique building at center. Back: Dancing warriors. 154x65mm.

142 **500,000 Meticais** VF UNC
16.6.2003 (2004). Purple, tan and multicolor. Banco de Moçambique building FV 55.00
at center. Holographic seal at right. Serial numbers in green and black. Back:
Steelworkers. 157x65mm.

Banco de Moçambique
2006 Issue

143 **20 Meticais** VF UNC
16.6.2006. Purple on multicolor underprint. Samora Moises Machel at left center.
Back: Rhinoceros at left center. 141x65mm.
   a. Issued note. FV 2.50
   s. Specimen. Red overprint: *ESPECIMEN*. — 100

144 **50 Meticais** VF UNC
16.6.2006 Brown and tan on multicolor underprint. Samora Moises Machel at left
center. Back: Impalas at left center. 144x65mm.
   a. Issued note. FV 5.00
   s. Specimen. Red overprint: *ESPECIMEN*. — 100

145 **100 Meticais** VF UNC
16.6.2006 Brown and orange on multicolor underprint. Samora Moises Machel at
left center. Back: Giraffes at left center. 147x65mm.
   a. Issued note. FV 10.00
   s. Specimen. Red overprint: *ESPECIMEN*. — 100

146 **200 Meticais** VF UNC
16.6.2006. Dark blue and green on multicolor underprint. Samora Moises Machel
at left center. Back: Lions at left center. 150x65mm.
   a. Issued note. FV 15.00
   s. Specimen. Red overprint: *ESPECIMEN*. — 100

147 **500 Meticais** VF UNC
16.6.2006. Red-brown and lilac on multicolor underprint. Samora Moises Machel
at left center. Back: Buffaloes at left center. 153x65mm.
   a. Issued note. FV 20.00
   s. Specimen. Red overprint: *ESPECIMEN*. — 100

148   1000 Meticais   VF   UNC
16.6.2006. Dark green and green on multicolor underprint. Samora Moises
Machel at left center. Back: Elephants at left center. 156x65mm.
   a. Issued note.   FV   50.00
   s. Specimen. Red overprint: *ESPECIMEN*.   —   100

2011 Issue

149   20 Meticas   VF   UNC
1.10.2011. Polymer plastic. Violet. Samora Moises Machel at left center. Back: FV   2.50
Rhinoceros.

150   50 Meticais   VF   UNC
1.10.2011. Polymer plastic. Brown and multicolor. Samora Moises Machel at left   FV   5.00
center. Back: Impalas

151   100 Meticais   VF   UNC
1.10.2011. Polymer plastic. Red, brown and multicolor. Samora Moises Machel at   FV   10.00
left center. Back: Giraffes
152   200 Meticais   VF   UNC
16.6.2011.   FV   15.00
153   500 Meticais   VF   UNC
16.6.2011.   FV   20.00
154   1000 Meticais   VF   UNC
16.6.2011.   FV   50.00

MYANMAR

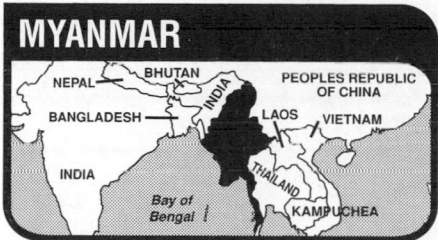

The Socialist Republic of the Union of Myanmar (formally called Burma), a country of Southeast Asia fronting on the Bay of Bengal and the Andaman Sea, has an area of 261,789 sq. mi. (676,552 sq. km.) and a population of 49.34 million. Capital: Rangoon. Myanmar is an agricultural country heavily dependent on its leading product (rice) which embodies two-thirds of the cultivated area and accounts for 40 percent of the value of exports. Petroleum, lead, tin, silver, zinc, nickel, cobalt and precious stones are exported.Britain conquered Burma over a period of 62 years (1824-1886) and incorporated it into its Indian Empire. Burma was administered as a province of India until 1937 when it became a separate, self-governing colony; independence from the Commonwealth was attained in 1948. Gen. Ne Win dominated the government from 1962 to 1988, first as military ruler, then as self-appointed president, and later as political kingpin. In September 1988, the military deposed Ne Win and established a new ruling junta. Despite multiparty legislative elections in 1990 that resulted in the main opposition party - the National League for Democracy (NLD) - winning a landslide victory, the junta refused to hand over power. NLD leader and Nobel Peace Prize recipient Aung San Suu Kyi, who was under house arrest from 1989 to 1995 and 2000 to 2002, was imprisoned in May 2003 and subsequently transferred to house arrest. After the ruling junta in August 2007 unexpectedly increased fuel prices, tens of thousands of Burmese marched in protest, led by prodemocracy activists and Buddhist monks. In late September 2007, the government brutally suppressed the protests, killing at least 13 people and arresting thousands for participating in the demonstrations. Since then, the regime has continued to raid homes and monasteries and arrest persons suspected of participating in the pro-democracy protests. The junta appointed Labor Minister Aung Kyi in October 2007 as liaison to Aung San Suu Kyi, who remains under house arrest and virtually incommunicado with her party and supporters. Burma In early May 2008 was struck by Cyclone Nargis which official estimates claimed left over 80,000 dead and 50,000 injured. Despite this tragedy, the junta proceeded with its May constitutional referendum, the first vote in Burma since 1990, setting the stage for the 2010 parliamentary elections. The country name in English was changed to Union of Myanmar in 1989.

RULERS:
   British to 1948
   Japanese, 1942-1945

MONETARY SYSTEM:
   1 Rupee (Kyat) = 10 Mu = 16 Annas (Pe) to 1942, 1945-1952
   1 Rupee = 100 Cents, 1942-1943
   1 Kyat = 100 Pyas, 1943-1945, 1952-

REPUBLIC

Central Bank of Myanmar

1990 ND Issue

67   1 Kyat   VF   UNC
ND (1990). UV: fibers fluoresce blue. Pale brown and orange on multicolor   FV   0.30
underprint. General Aung San at left. Back: Dragon carving at left. Watermark:
General Aung San.

1991-98 ND Issue

68   50 Pyas   VF   UNC
ND (1994). Dull purple and dull brown on gray and tan underprint. Musical string   FV   0.30
instrument at center. Printer: B/CM.

69 1 Kyat
ND (1996). Gray, blue and purple on multicolor underprint. Chinze at right. Printer: B/CM.

	VF	UNC
	FV	0.30

70 5 Kyats
ND (1996). UV: fibers fluoresce blue. Dark brown and blue-green on multicolor underprint. Chinze at left center. Back: Ball game scene.

	VF	UNC
a. Watermark: Chinze. (1996).	FV	0.75
b. Watermark: Chinze bust over value. (1997).	FV	0.50

71 10 Kyats
ND (1996). Deep purple and violet on multicolor underprint. Chinze at right center. Back: Elaborate barge.

	VF	UNC
a. Watermark: Chinze. (1996).	FV	1.00
b. Watermark: Chinze bust over value. (1997).	FV	0.50

72 20 Kyats
ND (1994). Deep olive-green, brown and blue-green on multicolor underprint. Watermark: Chinze bust over value.

	VF	UNC
	FV	1.00

73 50 Kyats
ND (1994-). Red-brown, tan and dark brown on multicolor underprint. Chinze at right. Back: Coppersmith at left center. Watermark: Chinze.

	VF	UNC
a. Watermark: Chinze. (1994).	FV	3.00
b. Watermark: Chinze bust over value. (1997).	FV	2.00

74 100 Kyats
ND (1994). Blue-violet, blue-green and dark brown on multicolor underprint. Chinze at left. Back: Workers restoring temple and grounds at center right.

	VF	UNC
a. Security thread in negative script. Watermark: Chinze.	FV	4.00
b. Security thread in positive script. Watermark: Chinze above value.	FV	3.00

75 200 Kyats
ND (ca.1991; 1998). Dark blue and green on multicolor underprint. Chinze at right. Back: Elephant pulling log at center right. Watermark: Chinze head. 167x80mm.

	VF	UNC
a. Security thread in negative script. Watermark: Chinze.	FV	8.00
b. Security thread in positive script. Watermark: Chinze above value.	FV	6.00

76 500 Kyats
ND (1994). Brown, purple and brown-orange on multicolor underprint. Chinze at left. Back: Workers restoring medieval statue, craftsman and water hauler at center right. 167x80mm.

	VF	UNC
a. Security thread in negative script. Watermark: Chinze.	FV	14.00
b. Security thread in positive script. Watermark: Chinze above value.	FV	10.00

77   1000 Kyats
ND (1998). Deep green and purple on multicolor underprint. Chinze at right. Back: Central Bank building at left center. 177x70mm.

		VF	UNC
a. Security thread in negative script. Watermark: Chinze.		FV	15.00
b. Security thread in positive script. Watermark: Chinze above value.		FV	15.00

2004 ND Reduced Size Issue

78   200 Kyats   VF   UNC
ND (2004). Greenish blue on multicolor underprint. Chinze at right center. Back: Elephant pulling log at center. 150x70mm.   FV   6.00

79   500 Kyats   VF   UNC
ND (2004). Brown, purple brown and ochre on multicolor underprint. Chinze at left. Back: Workers restoring medieval statue, craftsman and water hauler at right center. 150x70mm.   FV   6.00

80   1000 Kyats   VF   UNC
ND (2004). Green, purple-brown on multicolor underprint. Chinze at right center. Back: Central Bank building at left center. 150x70mm.   FV   7.50

81   5000 Kyats   VF   UNC
ND (2009). Purple on multicolor underprint. Windowed security thread. Elephant at center. Back: Building complex. Printer: Security Printing Wazi CBM. 150x70mm.   FV   10.00

82   10000 Kyats   VF   UNC
ND (2012). Blue, red, purple, green, brown, yellow on multicolor underprint. Two elephants facing at right. Small 10000 at bottom right. Back: Buildings with reflections in water. 150x70mm.   FV   15.00

2015 ND Issue

83   5000 Kyats   VF   UNC
ND (2015). Purple on multicolor underprint. Color-changing security thread. Elephant at center. Back: Building complex. 150x70mm.   FV   10.00

84   10000 Kyats   VF   UNC
ND (2015). Protective layer of varnish on both sides. Blue, red, purple, green, brown, yellow on multicolor underprint. Two elephants facing at right. Large 10000 at bottom right in Burmese numerals printed in SPARK. Back: Buildings with reflections in water. 150x70mm.   FV   20.00

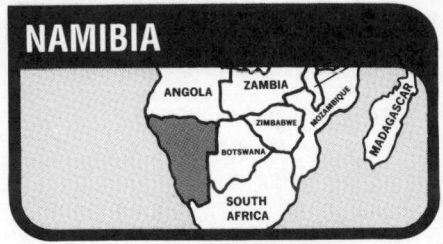

The Republic of Namibia, once the German colonial territory of German South West Africa, is situated on the Atlantic coast of southern Africa, bounded on the north by Angola, on the east by Botswana, and on the south by South Africa. It has an area of 318,261 sq. mi. (824,290 sq. km.) and a population of 1.73 million. Capital: Windhoek. Diamonds, copper, lead, zinc and cattle are exported. South Africa occupied the German colony of South-West Africa during World War I and administered it as a mandate until after World War II, when it annexed the territory. In 1966 the Marxist South-West Africa People's Organization (SWAPO) guerrilla group launched a war of independence for the area that became Namibia, but it was not until 1988 that South Africa agreed to end its administration in accordance with a UN peace plan for the entire region. Namibia has been governed by SWAPO since the country won independence in 1990. Hifikepunye Pohamba was elected president in November 2004 in a landslide victory replacing Sam Nujoma who led the country during its first 14 years of self rule.

MONETARY SYSTEM:
1 Namibia Dollar = 1 South African Rand
1 Namibia Dollar = 100 Cents

REPUBLIC

Namibia Reserve Bank

1990 Issue

#A1-E1 Unadopted designs.

A1   2 Kalahar   VF   UNC
ND. Unissued specimen. Red on multicolor underprint. Zebra head at left. Back: Plant at center, rock formation at right. Printer: BWC.   —   —

B1   5 Kalahar   VF   UNC
ND. Unissued specimen. Red and purple on multicolor underprint. Oryx head at left. Back: Road graders at center. Printer: BWC.   —   —

C1   10 Kalahar   VF   UNC
ND. Unissued specimen. Red and purple on multicolor underprint. Oryx head at left. Back: Commercial fishing boat at center. Printer: BWC.   —   —

D1   20 Kalahar   VF   UNC
ND. Unissued specimen. Purple on multicolor underprint. Lion head in round frame at left, watermark circle at right. Back: Sheep herd, herdsman on horseback. Printer: BWC.   —   —

E1   20 Kalahar   VF   UNC
ND. Unissued specimen. Purple on multicolor underprint. Lion head at left, flag at center. Back: Sheep heerd on back, walking herdsman. Printer: BWC. —   —

SIGNATURE VARIETIES	
	Dr. W.L. Benard 16 July 1990 - 31 August 1991
1	*Erik L. Karlsson (signature)* Mr. Erik L. Karlsson Acting: 1 September 1991 - 24 November 1992 25 November 1992 - 31 December 1993
2	*Jaafar B Ahmad (signature)* Dr. Jaafar B. Ahmad 1 January 1994 - 31 December 1966
3	*Alweendo (signature)* Mr. Tom K. Alweendo 1 January 1997 -

Bank of Namibia

1993 ND Issue

#1-3 Replacement notes: Serial # prefix X; Y; Z for #1, 2 and 3 respectively.

1 10 Namibia Dollars VF UNC
ND (1993). Blue-black on multicolor underprint. Captain H. Wittbooi at left center, arms at upper left. Back: Springbok at right. Watermark: Captain H. Wittbooi. Printer: Tumba Bruk A.B. (without imprint). 129x70mm.
 a. Signature 1.   2.00   8.25
 s. Specimen. Serial # prefix S.   —   150

2 50 Namibia Dollars VF UNC
ND (1993). Blue-green and dark brown on multicolor underprint. Captain H. Wittbooi at left center, arms at upper center. Back: Kudu at right. Watermark: Captain H. Wittbooi. Printer: Tumba Bruk A.B. (without imprint). 140x70mm.
 a. Signature 1.   11.00   38.50
 s. Specimen. Serial # prefix S.   —   150

3 100 Namibia Dollars VF UNC
ND (1993). Red, brown and red-brown on multicolor underprint. Captain H. Wittbooi at left center, arms at upper center right. Back: Oryx a right. Watermark: Captain H. Wittbooi. Printer: Tumba Bruk A.B. (without imprint). 146x70mm.
 a. Signature 1.   20.00   70.00
 s. Specimen. Serial # prefix S.   —   150

1996-2001 ND Issue

#4-8 Replacement notes: Serial # prefix X; V; Y; Z; W respectively for #4-8.

4 10 Namibia Dollars VF UNC
ND (2001). Blue on multicolor underprint. Captain H. Wittbooi at left center, arms at upper left. Segmented foil over security thread and ascending size serial number. Back: Springbok at right. Watermark: Captain H. Wittbooi. Printer: F-CO. 129x70mm.
 a. Signature 3. 7-digit serial #.   FV   3.75
 b. 8-digit serial #. Prefix A.   FV   3.75
 c. 8-digit serial #. Prefix B. No UV 10 at right.   FV   3.50
 s. Specimen. Serial # prefix A.   —   120

5 20 Namibia Dollars VF UNC
ND (1996). Orange and violet on multicolor underprint. Captain H. Wittbooi at left center, arms at upper left. Segmented foil over security thread. Ascending size serial number. Back: Red hartebeest at right. Watermark: Captain H. Wittbooi. Printer: TDLR. 133x70mm.
 a. Signature 2. 7-digit serial #.   FV   15.00
 Specimen. Serial # prefix H.   —   140

6 20 Namibia Dollars VF UNC
ND (2002). Orange and violet on multicolor underprint. Captain H. Wittbooi at left center, arms at upper left. Segmented foil over security thread and ascending size serial number. Back: Red hartebeest at right. Watermark: Captain H. Wittbooi. Printer: SABN. 133x70mm.
 a. Signature 3. 8-digit serial #.   FV   6.75
 b. 8-digit serial #. Prefix H, J.   FV   6.50
 s. Specimen. Serial # prefix J.   —   120

7 50 Namibia Dollars VF UNC
ND (1999). Blue-green and dark brown on multicolor underprint. Captain H. Wittbooi at left center, arms at upper left. Segmented foil over security thread and ascending size serial number. Back: Kudu at right. Watermark: Captain H. Wittbooi. Printer: TDLR. 140x70mm.
 a. Signature 3. 7-digit serial #.   FV   23.00
 s. Specimen. Serial # prefix P.   —   130

8 50 Namibia Dollars VF UNC
ND (2003). Blue green and dark brown on multicolor underprint. Captain H. Wittbooi at left center, arms at upper left. Segmented foil over security thread and ascending size serial number. Back: Kudu at right. Watermark: Captain H. Wittbooi. Printer: SABN. 140x70mm.
 a. Signature 3. 8-digit serial #.   FV   17.00
 s. Specimen. Serial # prefix N.   —   120

9 100 Namibia Dollars VF UNC
ND (1999). Red, brown and red-brown on multicolor underprint. Captain H. Wittbooi at left center, arms at upper center right. Back: Oryx at right. Printer: TDLR. 146x70mm.
 a. Signature 3. 7-digit serial #.   FV   47.50
 c. Signature 3. 7-digit serial #. Prefix TT.   30.00   100
 s. Specimen. Serial # prefix T.   —   130

9A 100 Namibia Dollars VF UNC
ND (2003). Red, brown and red-brown on multicolor underprint. Captain H. Wittbooi at left center. 8-digit serial number. Back: Oryz at right. Printer: SABN. 146x70mm.   FV   30.00

10 200 Namibia Dollars VF UNC
ND (1996). Purple and violet on multicolor underprint. Captain H. Wittbooi at left center. Arms at upper center. Back: Roan antelope at right. Printer: TDLR. 152x70mm.
 a. Signature 2.   FV   80.00
 b. Signature 3.   FV   80.00
 s. Specimen. Serial # prefix U.   —   130

2012 Issue

11 10 Namibia Dollars   **VF UNC**
2012-. Blue and green on multicolor underprint. Dr. Sam Nujoma at left, Parliament building in Windhoek at center. Signature Ipumbu Shiimi. Back: Three Springbok antelope (Antidorcas marsupialis) at center. Watermark: Sam Nujoma and 10. Printer: OT. 129x70mm.
     a. 2012. Diamond shape OVI device at top center.   FV   3.75
     b. 2013. Diamond shape OVI device at side.   FV   3.75

12 20 Namibia Dollars   **VF UNC**
2012-. Brown and orange on multicolor underprint. Dr. Sam Nujoma at left, Parliament building in Windhoek at center. Signature Ipumbu Shiimi. Back: Three standing red hartebeest at center. Watermark: Sam Nujoma and 20. Printer: OT 134x70mm.
     a. 2012. Diamond shape OVI device at top center.   FV   6.50
     b. 2013. Diamond shape OVI device at side.   FV   6.50

13 50 Namibia Dollars   **VF UNC**
2012. Green on multicolor underprint. Captian Hendrik Witbooi, Parliament building in Windhoek. Back: Five standing kudo antelope (Tragelaphus stepsiceros) at center. Watermark: Hendrik Witbooi and 50. Printer: OT. 140x70mm.   FV   17.00

14 100 Namibia Dollars   **VF UNC**
2012. Purple on multicolor underprint. Captian Hendrik Witbooi at left; Parliament building in Windhoek at center. Back: Three standing oryx (Oryx gazella) at center. Watermark: Hendrik Witbooi and 100. Printer: OT 147x70mm.   FV   30.00

15 200 Namibia Dollars   **VF UNC**
2012; 2015. Violet on multicolor underprint. Captian Hendrik Witbooi at left, Parliament building in Windhoek at center. Back: Three standing roan antelope at center. Watermark: Hendrik Witbooi and 200. Printer: OT. 152x70mm.
     a. 2012.   FV   60.00
     b. 2015.   FV   60.00

16 10 Namibia Dollars   **VF UNC**
2013. Blue and green on multicolor underprint. Like #11, but without large OVI diamond at center. Watermark: Sam Nujoma and 10. 129x70mm.   FV   3.75

17 20 Namibia Dollars   **VF UNC**
2013. Brown and orange on multicolor underprint. Like #12, but without large OVI diamond at center. Watermark: Sam Nujoma and 20. 134x70mm.   FV   6.50

COLLECTOR SERIES

Bank of Namibia

1993 ND Issue

CS1 10, 50, 100 Dollars   **Mkt. Value**
#1-3 with matched serial # mounted in a special plexiglass frame. ND (1993).   225

1996; 1999 ND Issue

CS2 20, 50, 100, 200 Dollars   **Mkt. Value**
#5, 7, 9, 10 with matched serial #. ND (1996; 1999).   330

Note: Issued only to current owners of #CS1 to complete matched serial sets.

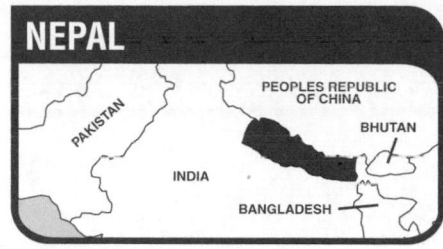

NEPAL

The Kingdom of Nepal, the world's only Hindu kingdom, is a landlocked country located in central Asia along the southern slopes of the Himalayan Mountains. It has an area of 56,136 sq. mi. (140,797 sq. km.) and a population of 24.35 million. Capital: Káthmandu. Nepal has substantial deposits of coal, copper, iron and cobalt but they are largely unexploited. Agriculture is the principal economic activity. Livestock, rice, timber and jute are exported. In 1951, the Nepalese monarch ended the century-old system of rule by hereditary premiers and instituted a cabinet system of government. Reforms in 1990 established a multiparty democracy within the framework of a constitutional monarchy. An insurgency led by Maoist extremists broke out in 1996. The ensuing nine-year civil war between insurgents and government forces witnessed the dissolution of the cabinet and parliament and assumption of absolute power by the king. Several weeks of mass protests in April 2006 were followed by several months of peace negotiations between the Maoists and government officials, and culminated in a November 2006 peace accord and the promulgation of an interim constitution. The newly formed interim parliament declared Nepal a democratic federal republic at its first meeting in May 2008, the king vacated the throne in mid-June 2008, and parliament elected the country's first president the following month.

RULERS:
Mahendra Vlra Vikrama Shahi Deva, 1955-1972
Birendra Bir Bikram Shahi Deva, 1972-2001
Ginendra, 2001-

MONETARY SYSTEM:
1 Mohru = 100 Paisa to 1961
1 Rupee = 100 Paisa. 1961-

SIGNATURE VARIETIES

1	जनक राज Janak Raj	2	भरतराज Bharat Raj
3	नरेन्द्रराज Narendra Raj	4	Himalaya Shamsher (J.B. Rama)
5	Lekshmi Nath Gautam	6	Pradhumna Lai (Rajbhandari)
7	Bekh Bahadur Thapa	8	Yadav Prasad Pant
9	Kul Shekhar Sharma	10	Kalyan Dikram Adhikary
11	Ganesh Bahadur Thapa	12	Harishankar Trfipathi
13	Satyendra Pyara Shrestha	14	Dipendra Purush Dhakal
15	Dr. Tilak Rawal	16	Bijay Nath Bhattarai

KINGDOM

Central Bank of Nepal
1961; 1965 ND Issue

12   1 Rupee   VF UNC
ND (1965). Lilac and olive-green. Coin at left, temple at center. Signature 8. Back: Arms at center, coin at right. Watermark: Plumed crown.   2.00 7.00

13   5 Rupees   VF UNC
ND (1961). Purple and aqua. Portrait of King Mahendra Vira Vikrama at upper left, Stupa at center. Signature 5; 7; 8. Back: Himalayas. Watermark: Plumed crown.   3.00 12.00

14   10 Rupees   VF UNC
ND (1961). Dark brown and red. Portrait of King Mahendra Vira Vikrama at upper left, temple at center. Signature 5; 6; 7; 8. Back: Arms at center. Watermark: Plumed crown.   3.00 15.00

15   100 Rupees   VF UNC
ND (1961). Green and brown. Portrait of King Mahendra Vira Vikrama at upper left. Temple at Lalitpor at center. Signature 5; 6; 7; 8. Back: Indian rhinoceros at center. Watermark: Plumed crown.   10.00 35.00

1972 ND Issue

16   1 Rupee   VF UNC
ND (1972). Light brown on blue underprint. King Mahendra Vira Vikrama wearing military uniform with white cap at left. Signature 8. Back: Lashing pioneering project rotary swing at center right, arms at upper right. Watermark: Plumed crown.   2.00 6.00

17   5 Rupees

	VF	UNC
ND (1972). Light green on lilac underprint. King Mahendra Vira Vikrama wearing military uniform with white cap at left. Signature 8. Back: Terraced hillside with himalayas in background. Watermark: Plumed crown. — 3.00 — 8.00

18   10 Rupees

VF   UNC

ND (1972). Light brown on dull olive-green and light blue underprint. King Mahendra Vira Vikrama wearing military uniform with white cap at left. Signature 8. Back: Singha Dunbar at Kathmandu at center. Watermark: Plumed crown.   2.00   5.00

19   100 Rupees

VF   UNC

ND (1972). Green on lilac underprint. King Mahendra Vira Vikrama wearing military uniform with white cap at left, Himalayas at center. Signature 8. Back: Ornate building, temple and arms at right. Watermark: Plumed crown.   7.00   30.00

20   500 Rupees

VF   UNC

ND (1972). Brown and violey. King Mahendra Vira Vikrama wearing military uniform with white cap at left. Signature 8. Back: Two tigers. Watermark: Plumed crown.   75.00   200

21   1000 Rupees

VF   UNC

ND (1972). Blue and multicolor. King Mahendra Vira Vikrama wearing military uniform with white cap at left, Great Stupa at Bodhnath. Signature 8. Back: House and mountains. Watermark: Plumed crown.   60.00   175

1974 ND Issue

22   1 Rupee

VF   UNC

ND (1974). Blue on purple and gold underprint. King Birendra Bir Bikram in military uniform with dark cap at left, temple at center. Signature 9; 10; 11; 12. Back: Two musk deer at center, arms at upper right. Watermark: Plumed crown.   1.00   2.00

23   5 Rupees

VF   UNC

ND (1974). Red, brown and green. King Birendra Bir Bikram in military uniform with dark cap at left, temple at center. signature 9; 10; 11. Back: Two yaks at center. Watermark: Plumed crown.

	VF	UNC
a. Issued note.	6.00	12.00
s. Specimen.	—	100
ct. Color trial. Green and purple face, back blue.	—	165

24   10 Rupees

VF   UNC

ND (1974). Dark and light brown on multicolor underprint. King Birendra Bir Bikram in military uniform with dark cap at left, Vishnu on Garnda at center. signature 9; 10; 11. Back: Buck Antelope at center, arms at right. Watermark: Plumed crown.

	VF	UNC
a. Issued note.	2.00	5.00
s. Specimen.	—	100
ct. Color trial. Green and purple on multicolor underprint.	—	165

25   50 Rupees

VF   UNC

ND (1974). Purple on green and multicolor underprint. King Birendra Bir Bikram in military uniform with dark cap at left, building at center. Signature 9. Back: Himalayan Tahr standing facing right at center, arms at right. Watermark: Plumed crown.

	VF	UNC
a. Issued note.	5.00	10.00
s. Specimen.	—	135

26 100 Rupees

	VF	UNC
ND (1974). Green and purple on multicolor underprint. King Birendra Bir Bikram in military uniform with dark cap at left, mountains at center, temple at right. Signature 9. Back: Indian Rhinoceros walking left, "eye" at upper left corner, arms at upper right. Watermark: Plumed crown.	7.00	20.00

27 500 Rupees

	VF	UNC
ND (1974). Brown on multicolor underprint. King Birendra Bir Bikram in military uniform with dark cap at left, monastery at center. Signature 9; 10. Back: Two tigers at center right, arms at upper right. Watermark: Plumed crown.	75.00	200

28 1000 Rupees

	VF	UNC
ND (1974). Blue on multicolor underprint. King Birendra Bir Bikram in military uniform with dark cap at left, temple and Great Stupa at center. Back: Elephant at center, arms at upper right on back. Watermark: Plumed crown.		
a. Issued note.	100	250
s. Specimen.	—	—

1981-87 ND Issue

29 2 Rupees

	VF	UNC
ND (1981-). Green on light blue and lilac underprint. King Birendra Bir Bikram wearing plumed crown at left, temple at center. Back: Leopard at center. Watermark: Plumed crown.		
a. Line from king's lower lip extending downward. Serial # 24mm long. Signature 10.	0.50	2.00
b. No line from king's lower lip. Signature 10; 11; 13.	0.50	1.00
c. As b. Serial # 20mm long. Signature 11.	0.50	1.00
d. As b. Serial # 20mm long. Signature 12.	0.50	1.00

30 5 Rupees

	VF	UNC
ND (1987-). Brown on red and multicolor underprint. King Birendra Bir Bikram wearing plumed crown at left, temple at center. Back: Two yaks at center right. Watermark: Plumed crown.		
a. Serial # 24mm long. Signature 11; 12; 13.	0.50	2.00
b. Serial # 20mm long. Signature 12.	0.50	2.00

31 10 Rupees

	VF	UNC
ND (1985-87). Dark brown and orange on lilac and multicolor underprint. King Birendra Bir Bikram wearing plumed crown at left, Vishnu on Garnda at center. Back: Antelopes at center, arms at right. Watermark: Plumed crown.		
a. Serial # 24mm long. Signature 11; 12.	1.00	3.00
b. Segmented foil over security thread. Signature 13, 14.	1.00	2.00

32 20 Rupees

	VF	UNC
ND (1982-87). Orange on multicolor underprint. King Birendra Bir Bikram wearing plumed crown at left, Janakpur Temple at center. Signature 10; 11. Serial # 24mm long. Back: Sambar Deer at center, arms at right. Watermark: Plumed crown.		
a. Issued note.	1.00	5.00
s. Specimen.	—	135

33 50 Rupees

	VF	UNC
ND (1983-). Blue on multicolor underprint. King Birendra Bir Bikram wearing plumed crown at left, Palace at center. Back: Himalayan Tahr at center, arms at right. Watermark: Plumed crown.		
a. With title at right. Serial # 24mm long. Signature 10. (1983).	1.00	7.00
b. With title at center. Serial # 20mm long. Signature 11; 12.	1.00	5.00
c. Segmented foil over security thread. Signature 13, 14.	1.00	5.00

1988-96 ND Issue

37 1 Rupee VF UNC
ND (1991-). Purple and dull blue on multicolor underprint. King Birendra Bir Bikram wearing plumed crown at left. Signature 12; 13. Back: Two musk deer at center, arms at upper right. Watermark: Crown. — FV 0.40

34 100 Rupees VF UNC
ND (1981-). UV: value 100 in box, serial #, signatures fluoresce green. Green on pale lilac and multicolor underprint. King Birendra Bir Bikram wearing plumed crown at left, temple at right. Back: Rhinoceros walking left, arms at upper right, without "eye" at upper left. Watermark: Plumed crown.

		VF	UNC
a.	Line from king's lower lip extending downward. With security thread. Serial # 24mm long. signature 10.	2.00	8.00
b.	No line from king's lower lip. Serial # at lower left. Signature 10.	2.00	8.00
c.	Serial # 20mm long. Signature 11.	2.00	7.00
d.	As b. Segmented foil over security thread. Signature 12.	2.00	7.00
e.	Serial # 20mm long. Signature 13.	1.00	6.00
f.	Serial # 24mm long. Signature 13.	1.00	6.00

38 20 Rupees VF UNC
ND (1988-). Orange on multicolor underprint. King Birendra Bir Bikram wearing plumed crown at left. Janakpur Temple at center. Multicolor border. Back: Sambar Deer at center, arms at right. Multicolor border. Watermark: Crown.

		VF	UNC
a.	Serial # 24mm long. Signature 11; 12.	1.00	3.00
b.	Segmented foil over security thread. Serial # 20mm long. Signature 13.	1.00	3.00
s.	As a. Specimen.	—	115

Note: #39 and 40 have been renumbered 35d and 36d respectively.

1997 ND Commemorative Issue

#41 and 42, Silver Jubilee of Accession, 1972-1997

35 500 Rupees VF UNC
ND (1981-). . Brown and blue-violet on multicolor underprint. King Birendra Bir Bikram wearing plumed crown at left, temple at center. Back: Two tigers at center right, arms at upper right. Watermark: Plumed crown.

		VF	UNC
a.	Line from King's lip extending downwards. Serial # 24mm long. Signature 10.	5.00	45.00
b.	Serial # 20mm long. Signature 11.	3.00	25.00
c.	Segmented foil over security thread. Signature 12.	3.00	20.00
d.	Signature 13. (1996).	3.00	20.00

41 25 Rupees VF UNC
ND (1997). Black and dark brown on multicolor underprint. King Birenda Bir Bikram wearing plumed crown at left, Royal palace at center right. Back: Pillars with chinze at left, steer at center, arms at right. Watermark: Plumed crown. 140x70mm. 1.00 4.00

42 250 Rupees VF UNC
ND (1997). Dark gray and blue-gray on multicolor underprint. King Birenda Bir Bikram wearing plumed crown at left, House of Representatives in underprint at center, royal palace at center right. Back: Pillars with chinze at left, steer at center, arms at right. Watermark: Plumed crown. 4.00 25.00

#42 was also issued in a special folder.

2000 ND Issue

43 500 Rupees VF UNC
ND (2000). Brown, blue-violet and silver on multicolor underprint. Large portrait of King Birendra Bir Bikram wearing plumed crown at left, temple at center. Back: Two tigers at center right, arms at upper right. Watermark: Plumed crown. 3.00 20.00

36 1000 Rupees VF UNC
ND (1981-). Red-brown and gray on multicolor underprint. King Birendra Bir Bikram wearing plumed crown at left, Stupa and temple on face. Back: Elephant at center, arms at upper right. Watermark: Plumed crown.

		VF	UNC
a.	Line from King's lip extending downwards. Serial # 24mm long. Signature 10.	10.00	85.00
b.	Serial # 20mm long. Signature 11.	5.00	45.00
c.	Segmented foil over security thread. Signature 12.	5.00	45.00
d.	Signature 13. (1996).	5.00	45.00

44   1000 Rupees   **VF   UNC**
ND (2000). Blue, brown and silver on multicolor underprint. Large portrait of King   5.00   40.00
Birendra Bir Bikram wearing plumed crown at left, Stupa and temple on face.
Back: Elephant at center, arms at upper right.

2002 ND Commemorative Issue

Accession to the throne of King Gyanendra Bir Bikram

45   10 Rupees   **VF   UNC**
ND (30.9.2002). Multicolor. King Gyanendra Bir Bikram wearing plumed crown   FV   2.00
at left. Commemorative text in horse-shoe shaped window: *This is issued on the
occasion of King Gyanendra Bir Bikram Shah Dev's accession to the throne in BS
2058.* Back: Two antelopes at center. Printer: NPA. 133x70mm.

2002 ND Issue

46   5 Rupees   **VF   UNC**
ND (2002). UV: value 5 in box fluoresce green. Red and brown on multicolor un-   FV   3.00
derprint. Darkly engraved portrait of King Gyanendra Bir Bikram at left. Signature
Tilak Rawal. Back: Two yaks at center.

47   20 Rupees   **VF   UNC**
ND (2002). Portrait King Gyanendra Bir Bikram at right. Signature Tilak Rawal.
Back: Deer at center. 138x70mm.
  a. Center title looks like 3 characters. Short signature 15.   FV   4.00
  b. Center title looks like 4 characters. Long signature 15.   FV   4.00

48   50 Rupees   **VF   UNC**
ND (2002). Black and blue on multicolor underprint. Portrait King Gyanendra Bir
Bikram at right, building at center. Signature Tilak Rawal. Back: Himalayan Tahr at
center. 142x70mm.
  a. Hat in black.   FV   5.00
  b. Hat in blue.   FV   5.00

49   100 Rupees   **VF   UNC**
ND (2002). Green, light purple and blue on multicolor underprint. Portrait King   FV   8.00
Gyanendra Bir Bikram at right. Signature Tilak Rawal. Back: Rhinocerous walking
left at center. 145x70mm.

50   500 Rupees   **VF   UNC**
ND (2002). Black and orange on multicolor underprint. Portrait King Gyanendra   FV   25.00
Bir Bikram at right, building at center. Signature Tilak Rawal. Back: Two tigers at
center. 158x70mm.

51   1000 Rupees   **VF   UNC**
ND (2002). Black and red on multicolor underprint. Portrait King Gyanendra Bir   FV   40.00
Bikram at right, temple at center. Signature Tilak Rawal. Back: Elephant at center.
172x70mm.

2005 Commemorative Issue

52 50 Rupees   VF UNC

2005 Green, yellow and red-orange. King Gyanendra Bir Bikram at left. Nepal Rastra Bank building at left center. Back: Two quail, mountains in background. 142x70mm.   FV 5.00

2005 Issue

53 5 Rupees   VF UNC

2005 Red brown on multicolor underprint. King Gyanendra Bir Bikram at left. Back: Two Oxen at center. 119x69mm.
- a. Signature 15.   FV 3.00
- b. Top line center text with three characters. Signature 16.   FV 3.00
- c. Top line center text with four characters.   FV 3.00

54 10 Rupees   VF UNC

ND (2005). Polymer plastic. Brown, light blue and green on multicolor underprint. King Gyanendra Bir Bikram at left. Back: Two antelopes at center. 133x70mm.   FV 3.00

55 20 Rupees   VF UNC

ND (2005). Orange on multicolor underprint. King Gyanendra Bir Bikram at left. Signature 16. Back: Stag at center. 138x70mm.   FV 4.00

57 100 Rupees   VF UNC

ND (2005). Brown and green on multicolor underprint. King Gyanendra Bir Bikram at right. Signature 16. Back: Rhinocerous walking left at center. 145x70mm.   FV 4.00

#58-59 not assigned.

FEDERAL DEMOCRATIC REPUBLIC

Central Bank of Nepal

2008 Issue

60 5 Rupees   VF UNC

2008. Red and multicolor. Mt. Everest at left, temple at center. Back: Yaks at center. Watermark: Rhododendron. 119x69mm.   — —

61 10 Rupees   VF UNC

2008. Brown on green and multicolor underprint. Mt. Everest at left. Statue at center. Back: Two antelopes at center. Watermark: Rhododendron. 133x70mm.
- a. Signature 17.   FV 1.00
- b. Signature 18.   FV 1.00

62 20 Rupees   VF UNC

2008. Orange on multicolor underprint. Mt. Everest at left. Back: Stag at center. Watermark: Rhododendron. 138x70mm.   FV 1.50

63 50 Rupees   VF UNC

2008. Purple, green and blue on multicolor underprint. Mr. Everest at left, Rama-Janaki temple of Janakpur at center. Back: Himalayan Tahr at center, mountains.. Watermark: Rhododendron. 142x70mm.   FV 2.50

64 100 Rupees   VF UNC

2008. Green on multicolor underprint. Mt. Everest at left. Back: Rhinocerous at center. Watermark: Rhododendron. 140x70mm.
- a. Signature 15.   FV 3.00
- b. Signatrue 16.   FV 3.00
- c. Signature 17.   FV 3.00

65 500 Rupees   VF UNC

2008. Brown and blue-violet on multicolor underprint. Mt. Everest at left center. Red rhododedrum covers watermark area. Back: Two tigers at center. Watermark: Gyanendra Bir Bikram. 160x70mm.   FV 10.00

		VF	UNC
66	**500 Rupees**		

ND (2009). Brown and violet on multicolor underprint. Mt. Everest at left Mt. Amadablam and Thyangboche monastery at center. Wide windowed security thread. Back: Two tigers at center drinking. 160x70mm. — FV 20.00

		VF	UNC
67	**1000 Rupees**		

2008. Blue and brown on multicolor underprint. Mt. Everest at left. Red rhododendron in watermark area. Back: Elephant at center. Watermark: King Gyanendra Bir Bikram.

	VF	UNC
a. Signature 16.	100	200
b. Signature 17.	FV	30.00
s. Specimen.	—	100

		VF	UNC
68	**1000 Rupees**	120	200

ND (2010). Blue and brown on multicolor underprint. Mt. Everest at left, Swayambhunath stupa at center. Signature 16. Back: Elephant at center. Watermark: Rhododendron. 172x70mm.

2012-13 Issue

		VF	UNC
69	**5 Rupees**	FV	0.75

2012 (2013). Lilac, brown and green. Mt. Everest, temple of Taleju, obverse of coin. Signature Yuba Raj Khatiwada. Back: Bank logo, two yaks grazing, Mt. Everest. Watermark: Rhododendron. Printer: TDLR. 120x70mm.

		VF	UNC
70	**10 Rupees**	FV	1.00

2012 (2013). Brown, green and lilac. Mt. Everest, Garud Narayan of Changu Narayan temple, obverse of coin. Back: Three black bucks grazing. Watermark: Rhododendron Printer: TDLR. 133x70mm.

		VF	UNC
71	**20 Rupees**	FV	1.25

2012 (2013). Orange and brown. Mt. Everest, temple of Krishna of Patan, Garuda atop pillar, obverse of coin. Back: Swamp deer, trees, mountain. Watermark: Rhododendron Printer: TDLR. 138x70mm.

		VF	UNC
72	**50 Rupees**	FV	2.00

2012 (2013). Purple, green and blue. Mt. Everest, Rama-Janaki temple of Janakpur, obverse of coin. Back: Male thar, mountains, bank logo. Watermark: Rhododendron Printer: TDLR. 142x70mm.

		VF	UNC
73	**100 Rupees**	FV	3.25

2012 (2013). Green and lilac. Mt. Everest, Mayadevi inside silver metallic oval. Map of Nepal, Ashoka pillar, wood carvings from temple of Tremple of Taleju in Kathmandu, clouds, obverse of coin. Back: One horned rhinoceros in grassy plain, bank logo. Watermark: Rhododendron Printer: TDLR. 146x70mm.

		VF	UNC
74	**500 Rupees**	FV	15.00

2012 (2013). Brown and violet. Mt. Everest, god Indra, Mt. Amadablam and Thyangboche monastery, wood carvings, clouds. Signature Yuba Raj Khatiwada. Back: Two tigers drinking melted snow. Watermark: Rhododendron. Printer: TDLR. 160x70mm.

		VF	UNC
75	**1000 Rupees**	—	—

2012 (2013). Expected new issue. Watermark: Rhododendron Printer: TDLR.

		VF	UNC
76	**1000 Rupees**	FV	30.00

2013. Dated at lower center. Back: Bank name appears in English. Dated at lower center. Watermark: Rhododendron

NETHERLANDS

The Kingdom of the Netherlands, a country of western Europe fronting on the North Sea and bordered by Belgium and Germany, has an area of 15,770 sq. mi. (40,844 sq. km.) and a population of 15.87 million. Capital: Amsterdam, but the seat of government is at The Hague. The economy is based on dairy farming and a variety of industrial activities. Chemicals, yarns and fabrics, and meat products are exported. The Dutch United Provinces declared their independence from Spain in 1579; during the 17th century, they became a leading seafaring and commercial power, with settlements and colonies around the world. After a 20-year French occupation, a Kingdom of the Netherlands was formed in 1815. In 1830 Belgium seceded and formed a separate kingdom. The Netherlands remained neutral in World War I, but suffered invasion and occupation by Germany in World War II. A modern, industrialized nation, the Netherlands is also a large exporter of agricultural products. The country was a founding member of NATO and the EEC (now the EU), and participated in the introduction of the euro in 1999.

RULERS:
William I, 1815-1840
Juliana, 1948-1980
Beatrix, 1981-

MONETARY SYSTEM:
1 Gulden = 20 Stuivers
1 Gulden = 100 Cents, to 2001
1 Rijksdaalder = 2 1/2 Gulden
1 Euro = 100 Cents, 2002-

REPLACEMENT NOTES:
#37-60, 72-74, 77-79, 81-82, 84-89. JEZ-printed notes only, serial numbers starting with "1" instead of normal "o".

KONINKRIJK - KINGDOM
De Nederlandsche Bank
NETHERLANDS BANK
1966-72 Issue

		VF	UNC
90	**5 Gulden**		

26.4.1966. Green on multicolor underprint. Joost van den Vondel at right. Back: Modern design of Amsterdam Play-house. Watermark: Inkwell, quill pen and scroll. 136x76mm.

	VF	UNC
a. Serial # at upper left and lower right. Gray paper with clear watermark.	FV	40.00
b. Serial # at upper left and lower right. White paper with vague watermark. Series XA/XM.	50.00	200
c. Serial # at upper left and center right in smaller type. (Experimental issue; circulated initally in the province of Utrecht.) Series 6AA.	125	750

		VF	UNC
91	**10 Gulden**		

25.4.1968. UV: fibers fluoresce yellow. Dark blue on violet and multicolor underprint. Stylized self-portrait of Frans Hals at right. Back: Modern design. Watermark: Cornucopia. 136x76mm.

	VF	UNC
a. O in "bullseye" at upper left on back.	30.00	100
b. Plain "bullseye" at upper left on back.	FV	25.00

92 25 Gulden

10.2.1971. Red on orange and pink underprint. Jan Pietersz Sweelinck at right. Back: Modern design. Watermark: Rectangular wave design. 148x76mm.

	VF	UNC
a. Issued note. 10 digit serial #.	FV	80.00
b. Issued note. 11 digit serial #.	FV	90.00
s. Specimen.	—	950

93 100 Gulden

14.5.1970. Dark brown on multicolor underprint. Michiel Adriaensz de Ruyter at right. Back: Compass-card or rhumbcard design at center. 154x76mm.

	VF	UNC
a. Issued note.	FV	300
s. Specimen.	—	1,100

94 1000 Gulden

30.3.1972. Black and dark green on multicolor underprint. Baruch d' Espinoza at right. Back: Graphic design. Watermark: Pyramid in bowl on slab. 160x76mm.

	VF	UNC
a. Issued note.	FV	1,000
s. Specimen.	—	1,400

1973 Issue

95 5 Gulden

28.3.1973. Dark green on green and multicolor underprint. Joost van den Vondel at right. Back: Graphic design. Watermark: Inkwell, quill pen and scroll. 136x76mm.

	VF	UNC
a. Issued note.	FV	20.00
s. Specimen.	—	1,300

1977-85 Issue

96 50 Gulden

4.1.1982. Orange and yellow on multicolor underprint. Sunflower with bee at lower center. Vertical format. Back: Map and field of sun flowers. Watermark: Bee. 148x76mm.

	VF	UNC
	FV	80.00

97 100 Gulden

28.7.1977 (1981). Dark brown on multicolor underprint. Snipe at right. Back: Head of Great Snipe. Watermark: Head of Great Snipe. 154x76mm.

	VF	UNC
a. Issued note.	FV	175
s. Specimen.	—	1,200

98 250 Gulden

25.7.1985 (1986). Violet on multicolor underprint. Lighthouse. Vertical format. Back: Lighthouse and map. Watermark: Rabbit and *VHP*. 160x76mm.

	VF	UNC
a. Issued note.	FV	350
s. Specimen.	—	1,700

1989-97 Issue

99   10 Gulden   **VF UNC**
     1.7.1997. Purple and blue-violet on multicolor underprint. Value and geometric   FV   20.00
     designs. Back: Value and geometric designs. Watermark: Bird. 136x76mm.

100   25 Gulden   **VF UNC**
     5.4.1999. Red on multicolor underprint. Value and geometric designs. Back. Value   FV   50.00
     and geometric designs. Watermark: Robin. 141x76mm.

101   100 Gulden   **VF UNC**
     9.1.1992 (7.9.1993). Dark and light brown, gray and gold on multicolor underprint.   FV   125
     Value and geometric designs. Back: Value and geometric designs. Watermark:
     Little owl. 154x76mm.

102   1000 Gulden   **VF UNC**
     2.6.1994 (1996). Dark gray and green. Geometric designs. Back: Geometric   FV   1,200
     designs. Watermark: Lapwing's head. 166x76mm.

Note: For later issues used in the Netherlands see European Union listings.

The Netherlands Antilles, part of the Netherlands realm, comprise two groups of islands in the West Indies: Bonaire and Curaçao near the Venezuelan coast; St. Eustatius, Saba, and the southern part of St. Maarten (St. Martin) southeast of Puerto Rico. The island group has an area of 385 sq. mi. (961 sq. km.) and a population of 210,000. Capital: Willemstad. Chief industries are the refining of crude oil, and tourism. Petroleum products and phosphates are exported.

Once the center of the Caribbean slave trade, the island of Curaçao was hard hit by the abolition of slavery in 1863. Its prosperity (and that of neighboring Aruba) was restored in the early 20th century with the construction of oil refineries to service the newly discovered Venezuelan oil fields. The island of St. Martin is shared with France; its southern portion is named Sint Maarten and is part of the Netherlands Antilles; its northern portion, called Saint Martin, is an overseas collectivity of France. On Dec. 15, 1954, the Netherlands Antilles were given complete domestic autonomy and granted equality within the Kingdom with Surinam and the Netherlands. The island of Aruba gained independence in 1986.

In October 2010 Curaçao and Saint Marten became autonomous entities of the Netherlands with the guilder being a valid currency until 31.12.2011. The islands of Bonaire, Saba, and St. Eustatius became direct dependencies of the Netherlands and will use the U.S. dollar starting 1.1.2011.

RULERS:
    Dutch

MONETARY SYSTEM:
    1 Gulden = 100 Cents

DUTCH ADMINISTRATION

Nederlandse Antillen

1955 Muntbiljet Note Issue

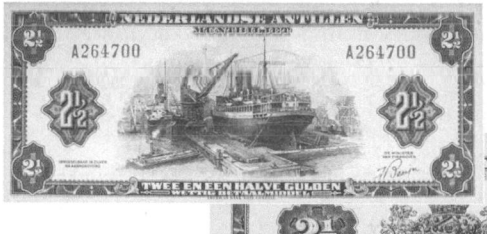

A1   2 1/2 Gulden   **VF UNC**
     1955; 1964. Blue. Ship in dry dock at center. Back: Crowned supported arms at
     center. Printer: ABNC.
         a. 1955.   70.00   330
         b. 1964.   55.00   280
         s. As a or b. Specimen.   —   340

1962 Issue

1   5 Gulden   **VF UNC**
     2.1.1962. Blue on multicolor underprint. View of Curaçao at center, woman seated
     with scroll and flag in oval at left. Back: Crowned arms at center right. Watermark:
     NA monogram. Printer: JEZ.
         a. Issued note.   35.00   165
         s. Specimen.   —   115

2   10 Gulden   VF   UNC
2.1.1962. Green on multicolor underprint. High-rise building (Aruba) at center,
woman seated with scroll and flag in oval at left. Back: Crowned arms at center
right. Watermark: *NA* monogram. Printer: JEZ.
    a. Issued note.   45.00   230
    s. Specimen.   —   130

6   250 Gulden   VF   UNC
2.1.1962. Olive-green on multicolor underprint. Boats on the beach (Saba) at
center, woman seated with scroll and flag in oval at left. Back: Crowned arms at
center right. Watermark: *NA* monogram. Printer: JEZ.
    a. Issued note.   900   —
    s. Specimen.   —   300

3   25 Gulden   VF   UNC
2.1.1962. Black-gray on multicolor underprint. View of Bonaire at center, woman
seated with scroll and flag in oval at left. Back: Crowned arms at center right.
Watermark: *NA* monogram. Printer: JEZ.
    a. Issued note.   60.00   310
    s. Specimen.   —   160

7   500 Gulden   VF   UNC
2.1.1962. Red on multicolor underprint. Oil refinery (Curaçao) at center, woman
seated with scroll and flag in oval at left. Back: Crowned arms at center right.
Watermark: *NA* monogram. Printer: JEZ.
    a. Issued note.   450   1,200
    s. Specimen.   —   550

1967 Issue

4   50 Gulden   VF   UNC
2.1.1962. Brown on multicolor underprint. City by the seaside (St. Maarten) at
center, woman seated with scroll and flag in oval at left. Back: Crowned arms at
center right. Watermark: *NA* monogram. Printer: JEZ.
    a. Issued note.   125   500
    s. Specimen.   —   190

8   5 Gulden   VF   UNC
1967; 1972. Dark blue and green on multicolor underprint. View of Curaçao at
center, monument *Steunend op eigen Kracht...*at left. Back: Crowned arms at
center. Watermark: *NA* monogram. Printer: JEZ.
    a. 28.8.1967.   25.00   130
    b. 1.6.1972.   20.00   100
    s. As a. Specimen.   —   240

5   100 Gulden   VF   UNC
2.1.1962. Violet on multicolor underprint. Monument (St. Eustatius) at center,
woman seated with scroll and flag in oval at left. Back: Crowned arms at center
right. Watermark: *NA* monogram. Printer: JEZ.
    a. Issued note.   210   700
    s. Specimen.   —   230

9   10 Gulden   **VF   UNC**
1967; 1972. Green on multicolor underprint. View of Aruba at center, monument
*Steunend op eigen Kracht...*at left. Back: Crowned arms at center. Watermark: *NA*
monogram. Printer: JEZ.
    a. 28.8.1967.   25.00   140
    b. 1.6.1972.   20.00   110
    s. As a. Specimen.   —   240

10   25 Gulden   **VF   UNC**
1967; 1972. Black-gray on multicolor underprint. View of Bonaire at center,
monument *Steunend op eigen Kracht...*at left. Back: Crowned arms at center.
Watermark: *NA* monogram. Printer: JEZ.
    a. 28.8.1967.   50.00   260
    b. 1.6.1972.   37.50   205
    s. As a. Specimen.   —   240

11   50 Gulden   **VF   UNC**
1967; 1972. Brown on multicolor underprint. Beach (St. Maarten) at center,
monument *Steunend op eigen Kracht...*at left. Back: Crowned arms at center.
Watermark: *NA* monogram. Printer: JEZ.
    a. 28.8.1967.   85.00   390
    b. 1.6.1972.   65.00   300
    s. As a. Specimen.   —   240

12   100 Gulden   **VF   UNC**
1967; 1972. Violet on multicolor underprint. Boats and fishermen on the beach (St.
Eustatius) at center, monument *Steunend op eigen Kracht...*at left. Back: Crowned
arms at center. Watermark: *NA* monogram. Printer: JEZ.
    a. 28.8.1967.   110   550
    b. 1.6.1972.   100   490
    s. As a. Specimen.   —   240

13   250 Gulden   **VF   UNC**
28.8.1967. Olive-green on multicolor underprint. Mountains (Saba) at center,
monument *Steunend op eigen Kracht...*at left. Back: Crowned arms at center.
Watermark: *NA* monogram. Printer: JEZ.
    a. Issued note.   170   675
    s. Specimen.   —   470
#14 *Deleted.* See #A1.

1979; 1980 Issue

15   5 Gulden   **VF   UNC**
1980; 1984. Purplish blue on multicolor underprint. View of Curaçao at center,
monument *Steunend op eigen Kracht...*at left. Back: Crowned arms at center.
Watermark: *NA* monogram. Printer: JEZ.
    a. 23.12.1980.   17.50   85.00
    b. 1.6.1984.   FV   45.00

16   10 Gulden   **VF   UNC**
1979; 1984. Green and blue-green on multicolor underprint. View of Aruba at
center, monument *Steunend op eigen Kracht...*at left. Back: Crowned arms at
center. Watermark: *NA* monogram. Printer: JEZ.
    a. 14.7.1979.   23.00   125
    b. 1.6.1984.   14.00   75.00

17   25 Gulden   **VF   UNC**
14.7.1979. Blue and blue-green on multicolor underprint. View of Bonaire at center, monument *Steunend op eigen Kracht...*at left. Back: Crowned arms at center.
Watermark: *NA* monogram. Printer: JEZ.   65.00   300

18   50 Gulden   **VF   UNC**
23.12.1980. Red on multicolor underprint. Beach (St. Maarten) at center,
monument *Steunend op eigen Kracht...*at left. Back: Crowned arms at center.
Watermark: *NA* monogram. Printer: JEZ.   90.00   430

19   100 Gulden   **VF   UNC**
14.7.1979. Red-brown and violet on multicolor underprint. Boats and fishermen on
the beach (St. Eustatius) at center, monument *Steunend op eigen Kracht...*at left.
Back: Crowned arms at center. Watermark: *NA* monogram. Printer: JEZ.
    a. 14.7.1979.   140   670
    b. 9.12.1981.   FV   425

1970 Muntbiljet Issue

20   1 Gulden

8.9.1970. Red on orange underprint. Aerial view of harbor at left center. Back: Crowned arms at right. Printer: JEZ.

		VF	UNC
a. Issued note.		FV	10.00
s. Specimen. Black overprint: *SPECIMEN* on both sides.		—	225

21   2 1/2 Gulden

8.9.1970. Blue on light blue underprint. Jetliner at left center. Back: Crowned arms at right. Printer: JEZ.

		VF	UNC
a. Issued note.		FV	17.50
s. Specimen. Red overprint: *SPECIMEN* on both sides.		—	225

1986 Bank Issue

22   5 Gulden

1986; 1990; 1994. Dark blue on multicolor underprint. Troupial at center. Back: Shield-like bank logo. Watermark: Shield-like bank logo. Printer: JEZ. 147x60mm.

		VF	UNC
a. Signature titles: *SEKRETARIS; PRESIDENT.* 31.3.1986.		FV	70.00
b. Signature titles: *DIRECTEUR SEKRETARIS; PRESIDENT.* 1.1.1990.		FV	60.00
c. 1.5.1994.		FV	55.00
s. As a. Specimen.		—	220

23   10 Gulden

1986; 1990; 1994. Dark green on multicolor underprint. Purple-throated carib at left center. Back: Shield-like bank logo. Watermark: Shield-like bank logo. Printer: JEZ. 147x66mm.

		VF	UNC
a. 31.3.1986. Signature titles as 22a.		FV	100
b. 1.1.1990. Signature titles as 22b.		FV	85.00
c. 1.5.1994.		FV	75.00
s. As a. Specimen.		—	220

24   25 Gulden

1986; 1990; 1994. Red on multicolor underprint. Flamingo at left center. Back: Shield-like bank logo. Watermark: Shield-like bank logo. Printer: JEZ. 147x66mm.

		VF	UNC
a. 31.3.1986. Signature titles as 22a.		FV	220
b. 1.1.1990. Signature titles as 22b.		FV	175
c. 1.5.1994.		FV	150
s. As a. Specimen.		—	250

25   50 Gulden

1986; 1990; 1994. Brown and orange on multicolor underprint. Rufous-collared sparrow at left center. Back: Shield-like bank logo. Watermark: Shield-like bank logo. Printer: JEZ. 147x66mm.

		VF	UNC
a. 31.3.1986. Signature titles as 22a.		FV	280
b. 1.1.1990. Signature titles as 22b.		FV	230
c. 1.5.1994.		FV	210
s. As a. Specimen.		—	280

26   100 Gulden

1986; 1990; 1994. Brown on multicolor underprint. Bananaquit at left center. Back: Shield-like bank logo. Watermark: Shield-like bank logo. Printer: JEZ. 147x66mm.

		VF	UNC
a. 31.3.1986. Signature titles as 22a.		FV	400
b. 1.1.1990. Signature titles as 22b.		FV	360
c. 1.5.1994.		FV	320
s. As a. Specimen.		—	390

27   250 Gulden

31.3.1986. Purple and red-violet on multicolor underprint. Caribbean mockingbird at left center. Back: Shield-like bank logo. Watermark: Shield-like bank logo. Printer: JEZ. 147x66mm.

		VF	UNC
a. Issued note.		FV	760
s. Specimen.		—	520

1998-2012 Issue

28 10 Gulden

1998-. Dark and light green on multicolor underprint. Purple-throated carib at left center with gold foil at lower right. Additional enhanced security devices include surface overlays. 2 signature varieties. Back: Shield-like bank logo. Additional enhanced security devices include small sparkling dots at top and bottom. Watermark: Shield-like bank logo. 147x66mm

		VF	UNC
a.	1.1.1998.	FV	60.00
b.	1.12.2001.	FV	55.00
c.	1.12.2003.	FV	45.00
d.	1.1.2006.	FV	37.50
e.	1.6.2011.	FV	30.00
f.	1.6.2012.	FV	29.00
g.	1.2.2014.	FV	29.00

29 25 Gulden

1998-. Red on multicolor underprint. Flamingo at left center with gold foil at lower right. Additional enhanced security devices include surface overlays. 2 signature varieties. Back: Shield-like bank logo. Additional enhanced security devices include small sparkling dots at top and Watermark: Shield-like bank logo. 147x66mm.

		VF	UNC
a.	1.1.1998.	FV	135
b.	1.12.2001.	FV	105
c.	1.12.2003.	FV	85.00
d.	1.1.2006.	FV	65.00
e.	1.1.2008.	FV	57.50
f.	1.6.2011.	FV	50.00
g.	1.6.2012.	FV	48.00
h.	1.2.2014.	FV	48.00

30 50 Gulden

		VF	UNC
		FV	105

1998-. Brown-ornage on multicolor underprint. Rufous-collared sparrow at left center with gold foil at lower right. Additional enhanced security devices include surface overlays. 2 signature varieties. Back: Shield-like bank logo. Additional enhanced security devices include small sparkling dots at top and Watermark: Shield-like bank logo. 147x66mm.

1998-. Brown-ornage on multicolor underprint. Rufous-collared sparrow at left center with gold foil at lower right. Additional enhanced security devices include surface overlays. 2 signature varieties. Back: Shield-like bank logo. Additional enhanced security devices include small sparkling dots at top and Watermark: Shield-like bank logo. 147x66mm.

		VF	UNC
a.	1.1.1998.	FV	190
b.	1.12.2001.	FV	150
c.	1.12.2003.	FV	130
d.	1.1.2006.	FV	120
e.	1.6.2011.	FV	110
f.	1.6.2012.	FV	105

31 100 Gulden

1998-. Brown on multicolor underprint. Bananaquit at left center with gold foil at lower right. Additional enhanced security devices include surface overlays. 2 signature varieties. Back: Shield-like bank logo. Additional enhanced security devices include small sparkling dots at top and Watermark: Shield-like bank logo. 147x66mm.

		VF	UNC
a.	1.1.1998.	FV	280
b.	1.12.2001.	FV	220
c.	1.12.2003.	FV	200
d.	1.1.2006.	FV	190
e.	1.1.2008.	FV	180
f.	1.6.2012.	FV	170
g.	1.12.2013.	FV	170

The French Overseas Territory of New Caledonia, a group of about 25 islands in the South Pacific, is situated about 750 miles (1,207 km.) east of Australia. The territory, which includes the dependencies of Ile des Pins, Loyalty Islands, Ile Huon, Isles Belep, Isles Chesterfield, and Ile Walpole, has a total land area of 6,530 sq. mi. (19,058 sq. km.) and a population of 152,000. Capital: Noumea. The islands are rich in minerals; New Caledonia has the world's largest known deposit of nickel. Nickel, nickel castings, coffee and copra are exported. Settled by both Britain and France during the first half of the 19th century, the island was made a French possession in 1853. It served as a penal colony for four decades after 1864. Agitation for independence during the 1980s and early 1990s ended in the 1998 Noumea Accord, which over a period of 15 to 20 years will transfer an increasing amount of governing responsibility from France to New Caledonia. The agreement also commits France to conduct as many as three referenda between 2013 and 2018, to decide whether New Caledonia should assume full sovereignty and independence.

RULERS:
French

MONETARY SYSTEM:
1 Franc = 100 Centimes

SIGNATURE VARIETIES		
	DIRECTEUR GÉNÉRAL	PRÉSIDENT DU CONSEIL DE SURVEILLANCE
1	*signature* André Postel-Vinay, 1967 - 1972	*signature* Bernard Clappier, 1966 - 1972
2	*signature* Claude Panouillot, 1972 - 1973	*signature* André De Lattre, 1973
3	*signature* Claude Panouillot, 1974 - 1978	*signature* Marcel Theron, 1974 - 1979
4	*signature* Yves Roland-Billecart, 1979 - 1984	*signature* Gabriel Lefort, 1980 - 1984
5	*signature* Yves Roland-Billecart, 1985 - 1993	*signature* Jaques Waitzenegger, 1985 -

FRENCH ADMINISTRATION

Institut d'Emission d'Outre-mer
Nouméa
1969 ND Issue

59 100 Francs VF UNC
ND (1969). Intaglio. Brown on multicolor underprint. Girl wearing wreath and playing guitar at right. Without overprint: *RÉPUBLIQUE FRANÇAISE* at lower center. Signature 1. Back: Girl at left, harbor scene at center.   70.00 225

60 500 Francs VF UNC
ND (1969-92). Blue, brown and multicolor. Dugout canoe with sail at center, fisherman at right. *RÉPUBLIQUE FRANÇAISE* at lower left. Back: Man at left, rock formation at left center, native art at right.
    a. Signature 1.   55.00 125
    b. Signature 2.   45.00 110
    c. Signature 3.   40.00 100
    d. Signature 4.   40.00 100
    e. Signature 5.   40.00 100

61 1000 Francs VF UNC
ND (1969). Orange, brown and multicolor. Hut under palm tree at left, girl at right.   120 285
Without overprint: *RÉPUBLIQUE FRANÇAISE* at lower left. Signature 1. Back: Building, Kagu bird at left, deer near hut at right.

#62 *Deleted*. See #65.

1971 ND Issue

63 100 Francs VF UNC
ND (1971; 1973). Brown on multicolor underprint. Girl wearing wreath and playing guitar at right, overprint at lower center. Signature 1. Back: Girl at left, harbor scene at center.
    a. Intaglio. Signature 1 (1971).   65.00 150
    b. Lithographed. Series beginning #H2, from #51,000. Signature 1 (1973).   55.00 135
    c. As b. Signature 2 (1975).   35.00 85.00
    d. As b. Signature 3 (1977).   20.00 60.00
    s. As a. Specimen.   — —

64 1000 Francs VF UNC
ND (1971; 1983). Orange, brown and multicolor. Hut under palm tree at left, girl at right. Signature 1. *RÉPUBLIQUE FRANÇAISE* at lower left. Back: Building, Kagu bird at left, deer near hut at right.
    a. Signature 1 (1971).   90.00 200
    b. Signature 4 (1983).   55.00 125

65 5000 Francs VF UNC
ND (1971-84). Multicolor. Bougainville at left, sailing ships at center, *RÉPUBLIQUE FRANÇAISE* at top center. Back: Admiral Febvrier-Despointes at right, sailboat at center right.
    a. Signature 1 (1971).   165 350
    b. Signature 2 (1975).   150 325
    c. Signature 4 (1982-84).   140 300
    s. As a. Specimen.   — 400

Note: For current 500 and 10,000 Francs see French Pacific Territories.

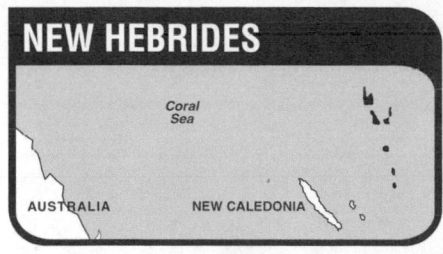

NEW HEBRIDES

New Hebrides Condominium, a group of islands located in the South Pacific 500 miles (800 km.) west of Fiji, were under the joint sovereignty of Great Britain and France. The islands have an area of 5,700 sq. mi. (14,763 sq. km.) and a population of mainly Melanesians of mixed blood. Capital: Port-Vila. The volcanic and coral islands, while malarial and subject to frequent earthquakes, are extremely fertile, and produce copra, coffee, tropical fruits and timber for export. The New Hebrides were discovered by Portuguese navigator Pedro de Quiros in 1606, visited by French explorer Bougainville in 1768, and named by British navigator Capt. James Cook in 1774. Ships of all nations converged on the islands to trade for sandalwood, prompting France and Britain to relinquish their individual claims and declare the islands a neutral zone in 1878. The New Hebrides were placed under the control of a mixed Anglo-French commission of naval officers during the native uprisings of 1887, and established as a condominium under the joint sovereignty of France and Great Britain in 1906.

RULERS:
British and French to 1980

MONETARY SYSTEM:
1 Franc = 100 Centimes

SIGNATURE VARIETIES		
	DIRECTEUR GENERAL	PRÉSIDENT DU CONSEIL DE SURVEILLANCE
1	André Postel-Vinay, 1967 - 1972	Bernard Clappier, 1966 - 1972
2	Claude Panouillot, 1972 - 1973	André De Lattre, 1973
3	Claude Panouillot, 1974 - 1978	Marcel Theron, 1974 - 1979
3A	Yves Roland-Billecart, 1979 - 1984	Marcel Theron, 1974 - 1979
4	Yves Roland-Billecart, 1979 - 1984	Gabriel Lefort, 1980 - 1984
5	Yves Roland-Billecart, 1985 - 1993	Jaques Waitzenegger, 1985 -

BRITISH AND FRENCH ADMINISTRATION

Institut d'Emission d'Outre-Mer, Nouvelles Hébrides
1965; 1967 ND Issue

16   100 Francs   **VF   UNC**
Multicolor. Printer: TDLR.   120   275

17   1000 Francs   **VF   UNC**
ND (1967-71). Red. Hut under palm tree at left, girl at right. Signature 1.   160   400
NOUVELLES HÉBRIDES. Back: Building, Kagu bird at left, deer near hut at right, overprint in capital letters at upper center.

1970 ND Issue

18   100 Francs   **VF   UNC**
ND (1970; 1972; 1977). Multicolor. Like #16, but red and blue underprint. *Nouvelles Hébrides* in script. Back: *Nouvelles Hébrides* in script.
    a. Intaglio plates. Signature 1. (1970).   75.00   175
    b. Lithographed series beginning E1, from no. 51,000. Signature 1. (1972).   70.00   160
    c. As b. Signature 2. (1975).   40.00   105
    d. As b. Signature 3. (1977).   35.00   80.00

19   500 Francs   **VF   UNC**
ND (1970-80). Blue, brown and multicolor. Dugout canoe with sail at center, fisherman at right. Back: Man at left, rock formation at left center, native art at right.
    a. Signature 1. (1970).   75.00   175
    b. Signature 3. (1979).   60.00   135
    c. Signature 3A. (1979).   60.00   135
    d. Signature 4. (1980).   40.00   100

20   1000 Francs   **VF   UNC**
ND (1970-80). Orange, brown and multicolor. Hut under palm tree at left, girl at right. *Nouvelles Hébrides* in script. Back: Building , Kagu bird at left, deer near hut at right. *Nouvelles Hébrides* in script.
    a. Signature 1. (1970).   95.00   225
    b. Signature 2. (1975).   80.00   185
    c. Signature 3A (1979).   80.00   185
    d. Signature 3. (1980).   65.00   150

Note: For later issues see Vanuatu.

NEW ZEALAND

New Zealand, a parliamentary state located in the southwestern Pacific 1,250 miles (2,011 km.) east of Australia, has an area of 103,736 sq. mi. (269,056 sq. km.) and a population of 4.3 million. Capital: Wellington. Wool, meat, dairy products and some manufactured items are exported. The Polynesian Maori reached New Zealand in about A.D. 800. In 1840, their chieftains entered into a compact with Britain, the Treaty of Waitangi, in which they ceded sovereignty to Queen Victoria while retaining territorial rights. In that same year, the British began the first organized colonial settlement. A series of land wars between 1843 and 1872 ended with the defeat of the native peoples. The British colony of New Zealand became an independent dominion in 1907 and supported the UK militarily in both World Wars. New Zealand's full participation in a number of defense alliances lapsed by the 1980s. In recent years, the government has sought to address longstanding Maori grievances.

RULERS:
British

MONETARY SYSTEM:
1 Shilling = 12 Pence
1 Pound = 20 Shillings (also 2 Dollars) to 1967
1 Dollar = 100 Cents, 1967-

BRITISH ADMINISTRATION
Reserve Bank of New Zealand
1940 ND Issue

158	10 Shillings	VF	UNC
	ND (1940-67). Brown on multicolor underprint. Arms at upper center. Portrait of Capt. James Cook at lower right. Signature title: *CHIEF CASHIER*. Back: Kiwi at left, Waitangi Treaty signing scene at center. Watermark: Maori chief. Printer: TDLR.		
	a. Signature T. P. Hanna. (1940-55).	80.00	600
	b. Signature G. Wilson. (1955-56).	150	1,000
	c. Signature R. N. Fleming. Without security thread. (1956-60).	60.00	500
	d. As c. With security thread. (1960-67).	20.00	100

159	1 Pound	VF	UNC
	ND (1940-67). Purple on multicolor underprint. Arms at upper center. Portrait of Capt. James Cook at lower right. Signature title: *CHIEF CASHIER*. Back: Sailing ship on sea at left. Watermark: Maori chief. Printer: TDLR.		
	a. Signature T. P. Hanna. (1940-55).	80.00	500
	b. Signature G. Wilson. (1955-56).	80.00	600
	c. Signature R. N. Fleming. Without security thread. (1956-60).	40.00	300
	d. As c. With security thread. (1960-67).	12.50	70.00

160	5 Pounds	VF	UNC
	ND (1940-67). Blue on multicolor underprint. Crowned arms at upper center. Portrait of Capt. James Cook at lower right. Signature title: *CHIEF CASHIER*. Back: Lake Pukaki and Mt. Cook. Watermark: Maori chief. Printer: TDLR.		
	a. Signature T. P. Hanna. (1940-55).	100	700
	b. Signature G. Wilson. (1955-56).	100	750
	c. Signature R. N. Fleming. Without security thread. (1956-60).	70.00	500
	d. As c. With security thread. (1960-67).	40.00	150
	s. As a. Specimen. Black overprint of TDLR oval.	—	750

161	10 Pounds	VF	UNC
	ND (1940-67). Green on multicolor underprint. Crowned arms, sailing ship at left. Portrait of Capt. James Cook at lower right. Signature title: *CHIEF CASHIER*. Back: Flock of sheep at left center. Watermark: Maori chief. Printer: TDLR.		
	a. Signature T. P. Hanna. (1940-55).	300	1,500
	b. Signature G. Wilson. (1955-56).	400	1,600
	c. Signature R. N. Fleming. (1956-60).	200	1,500
	d. As c. With security thread. (1960-67).	150	500

162	50 Pounds	VF	UNC
	ND (1940-67). Red on multicolor underprint. Crowned arms, sailing ship at left. Portrait of Capt. James Cook at lower right. Signature title: *CHIEF CASHIER*. Back: Dairy farm and Mt. Egmont. Printer: TDLR.		
	a. Signature T. P. Hanna. (1940-55).	4,000	12,000
	b. Signature G. Wilson. (1955-56).	4,000	10,000
	c. Signature R. N. Fleming. (1956-67).	2,000	5,000

1967 ND Issue

#163b-168b replacement notes: Special serial # prefix and * suffix.

163   1 Dollar

	VF	UNC
ND (1967-81). Brown on multicolor underprint. Queen Elizabeth II at right. Back: Pied fantail at center and plants. Watermark: Capt. James Cook. Printer: TDLR.		
a. Signature R. N. Fleming. (1967-68).	20.00	50.00
b. Signature D. L. Wilks. (1968-75).	10.00	25.00
c. Signature R. L. Knight. (1975-77).	10.00	20.00
d. Signature H. R. Hardie. (1977-81).	10.00	20.00
s. Specimen.	—	—

164   2 Dollars

	VF	UNC
ND (1967-81). Purple on multicolor underprint. Queen Elizabeth II at right. Back: Riffleman at center and plants. Watermark: Capt. James Cook. Printer: TDLR.		
a. Signature R. N. Fleming. (1967-68).	15.00	50.00
b. Signature D. L. Wilks. (1968-75).	15.00	40.00
c. Signature R. L. Knight. (1975-77).	10.00	30.00
d. Signature H. R. Hardie. (1977-81).	10.00	25.00
s. Specimen.	—	—

165   5 Dollars

	VF	UNC
ND (1967-81). Orange on multicolor underprint. Queen Elizabeth II at right. Back: Tui at center and plants. Watermark: Capt. James Cook. Printer: TDLR.		
a. Signature R. N. Fleming. (1967-68).	20.00	85.00
b. Signature D. L. Wilks. (1968-75).	40.00	275
c. Signature R. L. Knight. (1975-77).	20.00	65.00
d. Signature H. R. Hardie. (1977-81).	20.00	60.00
s. Specimen.	—	—

166   10 Dollars

	VF	UNC
ND (1967-81). Blue on multicolor underprint. Queen Elizabeth II at right. Back: Kea at center and plants. Watermark: Capt. James Cook. Printer: TDLR.		
a. Signature R. N. Fleming. (1967-68).	35.00	150
b. Signature D. L. Wilks. (1968-75.)	30.00	200
c. Signature R. L. Knight. (1975-77).	30.00	200
d. Signature H. R. Hardie. (1977-81).	20.00	100
s. Specimen.	—	—

167   20 Dollars

	VF	UNC
ND (1967-81). Green on multicolor underprint. Queen Elizabeth II at right. Back: New Zealand pigeon at center and plants. Watermark: Capt. James Cook. Printer: TDLR.		
a. Signature R. N. Fleming. (1967-68).	70.00	200
b. Signature D. L. Wilks. (1968-75).	80.00	400
c. Signature R. L. Knight. (1975-77).	70.00	300
d. Signature H. R. Hardie. (1977-81).	40.00	120
s. Specimen.	—	—

168   100 Dollars

	VF	UNC
ND (1967-77). Red on multicolor underprint. Queen Elizabeth II at right. Back: Takahe at center and plants. Watermark: Capt. James Cook. Printer: TDLR.		
a. Signature R. N. Fleming. (1967-68).	300	1,600
b. Signature R. L. Knight. (1975-77).	300	800
s. Specimen.	—	—

1981-92 ND Issue

#169a, 170a, 171a, 171b, 172a, 172b and 173a replacement note: Special serial # prefix and * suffix.

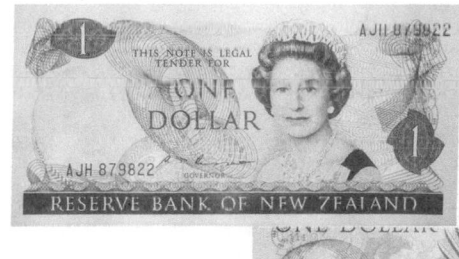

169   1 Dollar

	VF	UNC
ND (1981-92). UV: central design fluoresce orange, security strip blue. Back left and value 1 orange. Dark brown on multicolor underprint Mature portrait of Queen Elizabeth II. Back: Pied fantail at center and plants. Watermark: Capt. James Cook. Printer: BWC.		
a. Signature H. R. Hardie with title: *CHIEF CASHIER*. (1981-85).	4.00	8.00
b. Signature S. T. Russell with title: *GOVERNOR*. (1985-89).	4.00	7.00
c. Signature D. T. Brash. (1989-92).	3.00	6.00

170   2 Dollars

	VF	UNC
ND (1981-92). Purple on multicolor underprint. Mature portrait of Queen Elizabeth II. Back: Riffleman at center and plants. Watermark: Capt. James Cook. Printer: BWC.		
a. Signature H. R. Hardie with title: *CHIEF CASHIER*. (1981-85).	6.00	10.00
b. Signature S. T. Russell with title: *GOVERNOR*. (1985-89).	5.00	10.00
c. Signature D. T. Brash. (1989-92).	4.00	8.00

171 5 Dollars   **VF UNC**

ND (1981-92). Orange on multicolor underprint. Mature portrait of Queen Elizabeth II. Back: Tui at center and plants. Watermark: Capt. James Cook. Printer: BWC.

	VF	UNC
a. Signature H. R. Hardie with title: *CHIEF CASHIER.* (1981-85).	20.00	40.00
b. Signature S. T. Russell with title: *GOVERNOR.* (1985-89).	15.00	30.00
c. Signature D. T. Brash. (1989-92).	12.00	20.00

172 10 Dollars   **VF UNC**

ND (1981-92). Blue on multicolor underprint. Mature portrait of Queen Elizabeth II. Back: Kea at center and plants. Watermark: Capt. James Cook. Printer: BWC.

	VF	UNC
a. Signature H. R. Hardie with title: *CHIEF CASHIER.* (1981-85).	25.00	50.00
b. Signature S. T. Russell with title: *GOVERNOR.* (1985-89).	20.00	40.00
c. Signature D. T. Brash. (1989-92).	20.00	40.00
s. As b. Specimen. Overprinted: *SPECIMEN* and TDLR oval.	—	750

173 20 Dollars   **VF UNC**

ND (1981-92). Green on multicolor underprint. Mature portrait of Queen Elizabeth II. Back: New Zealand pigeon at center and plants. Watermark: Capt. James Cook. Printer: BWC.

	VF	UNC
a. Signature H. R. Hardie with title: *CHIEF CASHIER.* (1981-85).	45.00	120
b. Signature S. T. Russell with title: *GOVERNOR.* (1985-89).	40.00	70.00
c. Signature D. T. Brash. (1989-92).	40.00	70.00

174 50 Dollars   **VF UNC**

ND (1983-92). Yellow-orange on multicolor underprint. Mature portrait of Queen Elizabeth II. Back: Morepork Owl at center and plants. Watermark: Capt. James Cook. Printer: BWC.

	VF	UNC
a. Signature H. R. Hardie, with title: *CHIEF CASHIER.* (1981-85).	100	220
b. Signature D. T. Brash, with title: *GOVERNOR.* (1989-92).	70.00	140

175 100 Dollars   **VF UNC**

ND (1981-89). Red on multicolor underprint. Mature portrait of Queen Elizabeth II. Back: Takahe at center and plants. Watermark: Capt. James Cook. Printer: BWC.

	VF	UNC
a. Signature H. R. Hardie with title: *CHIEF CASHIER.* (1981-85).	150	350
b. Signature S. T. Russell with title: *GOVERNOR.* (1985-89).	150	300

1990 Commemorative Issue

#176, 150th Anniversary - Treaty of Waitangi, 1840-1990

176 10 Dollars   **VF UNC**

1990. Blue-violet and pale blue on multicolor underprint. Mature portrait of Queen Elizabeth II with addition of 1990 Commission logo, the White Heron (in red and white with date 1990) at right of Queen. Serial # prefix *BBB; CCC; DDD.* Back: Special inscription and scene of treaty signing. Watermark: Capt. James Cook. Printer: BWC.   15.00 25.00

Note: #176 w/prefix letters *AAA* was issued in 2, 4, 8, 16 and 32 subject panes. Market value is 10% over face value.

Note: #176 w/serial # prefix *BBB* was also issued in a special folder.

1992-97 ND Issue

#177-181 Replacement notes: Serial # prefix ZZ.

177	5 Dollars	VF	UNC

ND (1992-97). UV: value 5 in box fluoresce green. Back central design yellow. Brown and brown-orange on multicolor underprint. Mt. Everest at left, Sir Edmund Hillary at center. Signature D.T. Brash. Back: Flora with Yellow-eyed Penguin at center. Watermark: Queen Elizabeth II. Printer: TDLR. 135x66mm.

		VF	UNC
a. Issued note.		15.00	40.00
b. Uncut block of 4 in special folder.		—	60.00
c. Uncut block of 8 in special folder.		—	250

178	10 Dollars	VF	UNC

ND (1992-97). Blue and purple on multicolor underprint. Camellia flowers at left, K. Sheppard at center right. Signature D.T. Brash. Back: Pair of green ducks at center right. Watermark: Queen Elizabeth II. Printer: TDLR. 140x68mm.

		VF	UNC
a. Green ducks. Series AA-BI.		25.00	60.00
c. Uncut pair in special folder.		—	40.00
d. Uncut block of 4 in special folder.		—	70.00

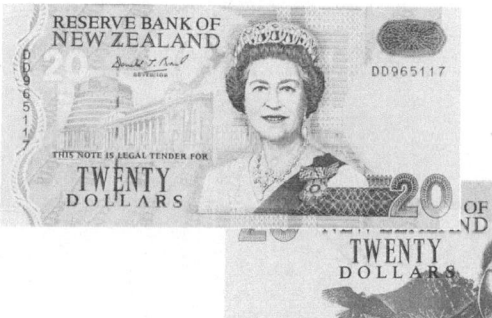

179	20 Dollars	VF	UNC

ND (1992). Green on multicolor underprint. Queen Elizabeth II at right, government building at left in underprint. Signature D.T. Brash. Back: New Zealand falcons at center. Watermark: Queen Elizabeth II. Printer: TDLR. 145x70mm.

		VF	UNC
a. Blue background. Series AA-CK.		27.50	60.00
c. Uncut block of 4 in special folder.		—	120

180	50 Dollars	VF	UNC

ND (1992). Purple, violet and deep blue on multicolor underprint. Sir A. Ngata at right, Maori meeting house at left in underprint. Signature D.T. Brash. Back: Kokako at right. Watermark: Queen Elizabeth II. Printer: TDLR. 150x72mm.

		VF	UNC
a. Issued note.		55.00	80.00
b. Uncut block of 4 in special folder.		—	300

181	100 Dollars	VF	UNC

ND (1992). Violet-brown and red on multicolor underprint. Lord Rutherford of Nelson at center, Nobel prize medal in underprint at left. Signature D.T. Brash. Back: Yellowhead on tree trunk at center right, moth at lower left. Watermark: Queen Elizabeth II. Printer: TDLR. 155x74mm.

		VF	UNC
a. Issued note.		140	250
b. Uncut block of 4 in special folder.		—	500
s. Specimen.		—	—

1994 ND Issue

#182 and 183 replacement notes: Serial # prefix ZZ.

182	10 Dollars	VF	UNC

ND (1994). Blue and purple on multicolor underprint. Camellia flowers at left, K. Sheppard at center right. Signature D.T. Brash. Back: Bright blue at center behind Whio ducks. Watermark: Queen Elizabeth II. Printer: TDLR. 140x68mm.

		VF	UNC
a. Thin paper. Series BM-DH.		12.50	20.00
b. Thick paper. Series DJ-EX.		12.50	20.00

183	20 Dollars	VF	UNC
		25.00	45.00

ND (1994). Green on multicolor underprint. Queen Elizabeth II at right, government building at left in underprint. Signature D.T. Brash. Series CY-HK. Back: Karearea falcon, bright green background. Watermark: Queen Elizabeth II. Printer: TDLR. 145x70mm.

1996 Commemorative Issue

#184, 70th Birthday - Queen Elizabeth II

184	20 Dollars	VF	UNC
		75.00	215

ND (1996). Green on multicolor underprint. Commemorative overprint on number 183. Serial # prefix *ER*. 145x70mm.

Note: Issued in a special folder w/a $5 Commemorative coin (3000).

1999 Issue

Note: See Collector Series for special sets.

185	5 Dollars	VF	UNC

(19)99; (20)04; (20)05 (20)06. Polymer plastic. Brown and brown-orange on multicolor underprint. Mt. Everest at left, Sir Edmund Hillary at center. Signature D.T. Brash. Back: Flora with Yellow-eyed Penguin at center. Watermark: Queen Elizabeth II. Printer: NPA (without imprint). 135x66mm.

		VF	UNC
a. Signature Donald T. Brash.		FV	15.00
b. Signature Alan Bollard.		FV	9.00

186 10 Dollars

(19)99; (20)03; (20)04; (20)05; (20)06 (20)07. Polymer plastic. Blue and multi-
color. Camellia flowers at left, K. Sheppard at center right. Signature D.T. Brash.
Back: Pair of blue ducks at center right. Watermark: Queen Elizabeth II. Printer:
NPA (without imprint). 140x68mm.

		VF	UNC
a. Signature Donald T. Brash.		FV	15.00
b. Signature Alan Bollard.		FV	15.00

187 20 Dollars

(19)99; (20)02; (20)04; (20)05. Polymer plastic. Gray and multicolor. Queen Elizabeth II at right, government building at left in underprint. Signature D.T. Brash.
Back: New Zealand falcons at center. Watermark: Queen Elizabeth II. Printer: NPA
(without imprint). 145x70mm.

		VF	UNC
a. Signature Donald T. Brash.		FV	40.00
b. Signature Alan Bollard.		FV	27.50

188 50 Dollars

(19)99; (20)04; (20)05; (20)07. Polymer plastic. Purple and multicolor. Sir A. Ngata
at right, Maori meeting house at left in underprint. Signature D.T. Brash. Back:
Kokako at right. Watermark: Queen Elizabeth II. Printer: NPA (without imprint).
150x72mm.

		VF	UNC
a. Signature Donald T. Brash.		FV	100
b. Signatrue Alan Bollard.		FV	80.00

189 100 Dollars

(19)99; (20)05. Polymer plastic. Brownish red and multicolor. Lord Rutherford of
Nelson at center, Nobel prize medal in underprint at left. Signature D.T. Brash.
Back: Yellowhead on tree trunk at center right, moth at lower left. Watermark:
Queen Elizabeth II. Printer: NPA (without imprint). 155x74mm.

		VF	UNC
a. Signature Donald T. Brash.		FV	150
b. Signature Alan Bollard.		FV	140

2000 Commemorative Issue

#190, Millennium Commemorative.

190 10 Dollars

2000. Polymer plastic. Blue, orange and multicolor. Earth, map of New Zealand
at left, ceremonial boat at center. Back: Five sport activities. Printer: NPA (without
imprint). 140x68mm.

		VF	UNC
a. Black serial #. Serial # prefix *AA; AB*.		FV	25.00
b. Red serial #. Serial # prefix *NZ*.		FV	25.00

2015-16 Issue

		VF	UNC
191 5 Dollars		**VF**	**UNC**
(20)15. 135x66mm.		FV	9.00
192 10 Dollars		**VF**	**UNC**
(20)15. 140x68mm.		FV	15.00
193 20 Dollars		**VF**	**UNC**
(20)15. Expected new issue. 145x70mm.		—	—
194 50 Dollars		**VF**	**UNC**
(20)15. Expected new issue. 150x72mm.		—	—
195 100 Dollars		**VF**	**UNC**
(20)15. Expected new issue.		—	—

NICARAGUA

GUATEMALA HONDURAS

EL SALVADOR

Pacific Ocean

Caribbean Sea

COSTA RICA

The Republic of Nicaragua, situated in Central America between Honduras and Costa Rica, has an area of 50,193 sq. mi (130,000 sq. km.) and a population of 4.69 million. Capital: Managua. Agriculture, mining (gold and silver) and hardwood logging are the principal industries. Cotton, meat, coffee, tobacco and sugar are exported.The Pacific coast of Nicaragua was settled as a Spanish colony from Panama in the early 16th century. Independence from Spain was declared in 1821 and the country became an independent republic in 1838. Britain occupied the Caribbean Coast in the first half of the 19th century, but gradually ceded control of the region in subsequent decades. Violent opposition to governmental manipulation and corruption spread to all classes by 1978 and resulted in a short-lived civil war that brought the Marxist Sandinista guerrillas to power in 1979. Nicaraguan aid to leftist rebels in El Salvador caused the US to sponsor anti-Sandinista contra guerrillas through much of the 1980s. Free elections in 1990, 1996, and 2001, saw the Sandinistas defeated, but voting in 2006 announced the return of former Sandinista President Daniel Ortega Saavedra. Nicaragua's infrastructure and economy - hard hit by the earlier civil war and by Hurricane Mitch in 1998 - are slowly being rebuilt.

MONETARY SYSTEM:
1 Peso = 100 Centavos to 1912
1 Córdoba = 100 Centavos, 1912-1987
1 New Córdoba = 1000 Old Córdobas, 1988-90
1 Córdoba Oro = 100 Centavos, 1990-

REPLACEMENT NOTES:
1985-dated issues printed by TDLR, ZA; ZB prefix.

REPUBLIC

Banco Central de Nicaragua
Decreto 26.4.1962

107   1 Córdoba
D.1962. Blue on multicolor underprint. Banco Central at upper center. Back: Portrait of F. Hernandez Córdoba at center. Printer: ABNC.

	VF	UNC
	1.00	7.50

108   5 Córdobas
D.1962. Green on multicolor underprint. C. Nicarao at upper center. Back: Portrait of F. Hernandez Córdoba at center. Printer: ABNC.

	VF	UNC
a. Issued note.	3.00	15.00
s. Specimen.	—	125

109   10 Córdobas
D.1962. Red on multicolor underprint. Portrait of M. de Larreynaga at upper center. Back: Portrait of F. Hernandez Córdoba at center. Printer: ABNC.

	VF	UNC
a. Issued note.	5.00	22.50
s. Specimen.	—	—

110   20 Córdobas
D.1962. Orange-brown on multicolor underprint. Portrait of T. Martinez at upper center. Back: Portrait of F. Hernandez Córdoba at center. Printer: ABNC.

	VF	UNC
	10.00	45.00

111   50 Córdobas
D.1962. Purple on multicolor underprint. Portrait of M. Jerez at upper center. Back: Portrait of F. Hernandez Córdoba at center. Printer: ABNC.

	VF	UNC
	25.00	85.00

112   100 Córdobas
D.1962. Red-brown on multicolor underprint. Portrait of J. D. Estrada at upper center. Back: Portrait of F. Hernandez Córdoba at center. Printer: ABNC.

	VF	UNC
	12.50	60.00

113   500 Córdobas
D.1962. Black on multicolor underprint. Portrait of R. Dario at upper center. Back: Portrait of F. Hernandez Córdoba at center. Printer: ABNC.

	VF	UNC
a. Issued note.	175	425
s. Specimen.	—	500

114   1000 Córdobas
D.1962. Brown on multicolor underprint. Portrait of A. Somoza at upper center. Back: Portrait of F. Hernandez Córdoba at center. Printer: ABNC.

	VF	UNC
a. Issued note.	200	550
s. Specimen.	—	500

Decreto 25.5.1968

115 1 Córdoba   VF   UNC
D.1968. Blue on multicolor underprint. Banco Central at upper center. Series B.
Back: Portrait of F. Hernandez Córdoba. Printer: TDLR.
    a. With 3 signatures.   1.00   6.00
    b. Pres. A. Somoza hand signed at left.   —   —

116 5 Córdobas   VF   UNC
D.1968. Green on multicolor underprint. C. Nicarao at upper center. Series B.
Back: Portrait of F. Hernandez Córdoba. Printer: TDLR.
    a. Issued note.   3.00   15.00
    s. Specimen. Without right hand signature. Overprint: *MUESTRA SIN VALOR*   —   —
      twice.

117 10 Córdobas   VF   UNC
D.1968. Red on multicolor underprint. Portrait of M. de Larreynaga at upper
center. Series B. Back: Portrait of F. Hernandez Córdoba. Printer: TDLR.
    a. Issued note.   4.00   22.50
    s. Specimen. Without right hand signature. Overprint: *MUESTRA SIN VALOR*   —   —
      twice.
Note: Some of #118-120 were apparently released w/ithout the right hand signature after the
    Managua earthquake of 1972 damaged the Central Bank building.

118 20 Córdobas   VF   UNC
D.1968. Orange-brown on multicolor underprint. Portrait of T. Martinez at upper
center. Series B. Back: Portrait of F. Hernandez Córdoba. Printer: TDLR.
    a. With 3 signatures.   5.00   30.00
    b. Without right hand signature.   —   —
    s. Specimen. Without right hand signature. Overprint: *MUESTRA SIN VALOR*   —   —
      twice.

119 50 Córdobas   VF   UNC
D.1968. Purple on multicolor underprint. Portrait of M. Jerez at upper center.
Series B. Back: Portrait of F. Hernandez Córdoba. Printer: TDLR.
    a. With 3 signatures.   12.50   50.00
    b. Without right hand signature.   —   —

120 100 Córdobas   VF   UNC
D.1968. Red-brown on multicolor underprint. Portrait of J. D. Estrada at upper
center. Series B. Back: Portrait of F. Hernandez Córdoba. Printer: TDLR.
    a. With 3 signatures.   17.50   75.00
    b. Without right hand signature.   —   —

Decreto 27.4.1972

121 2 Córdobas   VF   UNC
D.1972. Olive-green on multicolor underprint. Banco Central at right. Series C.
Back: Furrows at left. Printer: TDLR.
    a. 3 signatures.   1.00   6.00
    b. 2 signatures (without right hand signature).   —   400
    s. As a. Specimen.   —   35.00

122 5 Córdobas   VF   UNC
D.1972. Dark green on multicolor underprint. C. Nicarao standing at right with   1.50   10.00
bow. Series C. Back: Fruitseller at left. Printer: TDLR.

123 10 Córdobas   VF   UNC
D.1972. Red on multicolor underprint. A. Castro standing at right atop rocks.   3.00   12.50
Series C. Back: Hacienda at left Printer: TDLR.

124 20 Córdobas   VF   UNC
D.1972. Orange-brown on multicolor underprint. R. Herrera igniting cannon at   4.00   17.50
right. Series C. Back: Signing ceremony of abrogation of Chamorro-Bryan Treaty
of 1912, Somoza at center. Printer: TDLR.
Note: #124 was issued on the 60th anniversary of the Chamorro-Bryan Treaty of 1912.

125 50 Córdobas

		VF	UNC
D.1972. Purple on multicolor underprint. M. Jerez at right. Series C. Back: Cows at left. Printer: TDLR.		30.00	85.00

126 100 Córdobas

		VF	UNC
D.1972. Violet on multicolor underprint. J. Dolores Estrada at right. Series C. Back: National flower at left. Printer: TDLR.		2.50	10.00

127 500 Córdobas

		VF	UNC
D.1972. Black on multicolor underprint. R. Darío at right. Series C. Back: National Theater at left. Printer: TDLR.		35.00	115

128 1000 Córdobas

		VF	UNC
D.1972. Brown on multicolor underprint. A. Somoza G. at right. Series C. Back: View of Managua at left. Printer: TDLR.			
a. 3 signatures.		40.00	135
b. 2 signatures (without right hand signature).		—	90.00

Decreto 20.2.1978

129 20 Córdobas

		VF	UNC
D.1978. Orange-brown on multicolor underprint. R. Herrera igniting cannon at right. Series D. Back: Signing ceremony of abrogation of Chamorro-Bryan Treaty of 1912, Somoza at center. Printer: TDLR.		1.50	7.50

130 50 Córdobas

		VF	UNC
D.1978. Purple on multicolor underprint. M. Jerez at right. Series D. Back: Cows at left. Printer: TDLR.		2.50	9.00

Decreto 16.8.1979

Series E, first issue.

131 50 Córdobas

		VF	UNC
D.1979. With square outer frame. Engraved. Purple on multicolor underprint. Comdt. C. F. Amador at right. Series E. Back: Liberation of 19.7.1979. Printer: TDLR.		1.50	5.00

132 100 Córdobas

		VF	UNC
D.1979. With square outer frame. Engraved. Dark brown on multicolor underprint. J. Dolores Estrada at right. Series E. Back: National flower at left. Printer: TDLR.		1.50	5.00

133   500 Córdobas

	VF	**UNC**

D.1979. With square outer frame. Engraved. Deep blue on multicolor underprint. R. Dario at right. Series E. Back: National Theater at left. Printer: TDLR.   2.50   7.00

1979 ND Second Issue

Series E, second issue.

134   10 Córdobas

	VF	**UNC**

D.1979. Underprint to paper edge. Lithographed. Red on multicolor underprint. A. Castro standing atop rocks at right. Series E. Back: Miners. Watermark: Sandino. Printer: TDLR.   0.75   4.00

135   20 Córdobas

	VF	**UNC**

D.1979. Underprint to paper edge. Lithographed. Orange-brown on multicolor underprint. Comdt. G. P. Ordoñez at right. Series E. Back: Marching troops. Watermark: Sandino. Printer: TDLR.   1.00   5.00

136   50 Córdobas

	VF	**UNC**

D.1979. Underprint to paper edge. Lithographed. Purple on multicolor underprint. Comdt. C. F. Amador at right. Series E. Back: Liberation of 19.7.1979. Watermark: Sandino. Printer: TDLR.   1.00   7.50

137   100 Córdobas

	VF	**UNC**

D.1979. Underprint to paper edge. Lithographed. Brown on multicolor underprint. J. D. Estrada at right. Series E. 2 signature varieties. Back: Flower. Watermark: Sandino. Printer: TDLR.   1.00   10.00

138   500 Córdobas

	VF	**UNC**

D.1979. Underprint to paper edge. Engraved. Deep olive-green on multicolor underprint. R. Darío at right. Series E. 2 signature varieties. Back: Teatro Popular at left. Watermark: Sandino. Printer: TDLR.   2.50   17.50

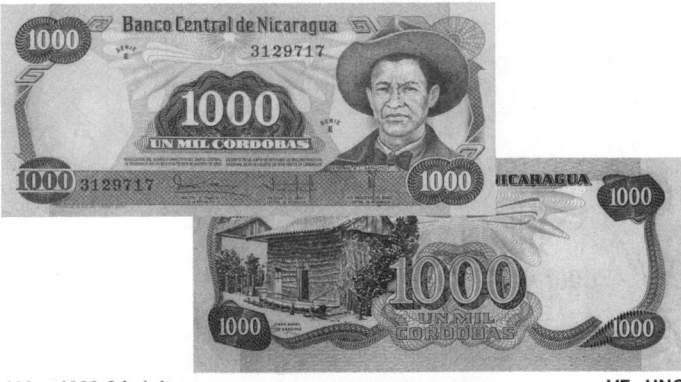

139   1000 Córdobas

	VF	**UNC**

D.1979. Underprint to paper edge. Engraved. Blue-gray on multicolor underprint. General A. C. Sandino at right. Series E. 2 signature varieties. Back: Hut (Sandino's birthplace). Watermark: Sandino. Printer: TDLR.   15.00   45.00

Resolution of 6.8.1984

140   50 Córdobas

	VF	**UNC**

L.1984 (1985). Purple on multicolor underprint. Comdt. C. F. Amador at right. Series F. Back: Liberation of 19.7.1979. Watermark: Sandino. Printer: TDLR.   0.50   2.00

141   100 Córdobas

	VF	**UNC**

L.1984 (1985). Brown on multicolor underprint. J. D. Estrada at right. Series F. Back: Flower. Watermark: Sandino. Printer: TDLR.   1.00   3.00

142 500 Córdobas
VF UNC
L.1984 (1985). Deep olive-green on multicolor underprint. R. Dario at right. Series F. Back: Teatro Popular at left. Watermark: Sandino. Printer: TDLR. 156x67mm.
1.00 5.00

143 1000 Córdobas
VF UNC
L.1984 (1985). Blue-gray on multicolor underprint. General A. C. Sandino at right. Series F. Back: Hut (Sandino's birthplace). Watermark: Sandino. Printer: TDLR.
2.00 9.00

Resolution of 11.6.1985

Replacement notes: Serial # prefix *ZA; ZB.*

144 500 Córdobas
VF UNC
L.1985 (1987). Lithographed. Deep olive-green on multicolor underprint. R. Dario at right. Series G. Back: Teatro Popular at left. Watermark: Sandino. Printer: TDLR. 156x67mm.
1.00 5.00

145 1000 Córdobas
VF UNC
L.1985 (1987). Dark gray on multicolor underprint. General A. C. sandino at right. Series G. Back: Hut (Sandino's birthplace). Watermark: Sandino. Printer: TDLR.
  a. Engraved. 1.00 5.00
  b. Lithographed. 0.50 3.50

146 5000 Córdobas
VF UNC
L.1985 (1987). Brown, orange and black on multicolor underprint. Map at upper center, General B. Zeledon at right. Series G. Back: National Assembly building. Watermark: Sandino. Printer: TDLR.
1.00 7.50

A.P.E. Del 26 Oct.

147 20,000 Córdobas on 20 Córdobas
VF UNC
D.1987 (1987). Orange-brown on multicolor underprint. Comdt. G. P. OrdoÔez at right. Overprint on unissued 20 Cordobas Series F. Back: Marching troops. Watermark: Sandino. Printer: TDLR.
0.75 5.00

148 50,000 Córdobas on 50 Córdobas
VF UNC
D.1987 (1987). Purple on multicolor underprint. Comdt C. F. Amador at right. Back. Liberation of 19.7.1979. Watermark: Sandino. Printer: TDLR.
0.75 7.50

149 100,000 Córdobas on 500 Córdobas
VF UNC
D.1987 (1987). Lithographed. Deep olive-green on multicolor underprint. R. Dario at right. Back: Teatro Popular at left. Watermark: Sandino. Printer: TDLR.
0.75 10.00

150 500,000 Córdobas on 1000 Córdobas
VF UNC
D.1987 (1987). Lithographed. (Not issued). Dark gray on multicolor underprint. General A. C. Sandino at right. Back: Hut (Sandino's birthplace). Watermark: Sandino. Printer: TDLR.
2.50 12.50

1985 (1988) Issue

#151-156 Replacement notes: Serial # prefix *ZA; ZB.*

151 10 Córdobas

		VF	UNC
1985 (1988). Green and olive on multicolor underprint. Comdt. C. F. Amador at right. Back: Troop formation marching at left. Watermark: Sandino. | | 1.00 | 3.50

152 20 Córdobas

		VF	UNC
1985 (1988). Blue-black and blue on multicolor underprint. Comdt. G. P. Ordoñez at right. Back: Demonstration for agrarian reform at left. Watermark: Sandino. | | 1.00 | 5.00

153 50 Córdobas

		VF	UNC
1985 (1988). Brown and dark red on multicolor underprint. General J. D. Estrada at right. Back: Medical clinic scene at left. Watermark: Sandino. | | 1.25 | 7.50

154 100 Córdobas

		VF	UNC
1985 (1988). Deep blue, blue and gray on multicolor underprint. R. Lopez Perez at right. Back: State council building at left. Watermark: Sandino. | | 1.25 | 10.00

155 500 Córdobas

		VF	UNC
1985 (1988). UV: fibers fluoresce blue. Purple, blue and brown on multicolor underprint. R. Dario at right. Back: Classroom with students at left. Watermark: Sandino. | | 1.25 | 15.00

156 1000 Córdobas

		VF	UNC
1985 (1988). Brown on multicolor underprint. General A. C. Sandino at right. Back: Liberation of 19.7.1979. Watermark: Sandino. | | | |
a. Engraved with watermark. Serial # prefix FA. | | 1.25 | 20.00
b. Lithographed without watermark. Serial # prefix FC. | | 0.75 | 4.00

1988-89 ND Provisional Issue

157 5000 Córdobas

		VF	UNC
ND (1988). Brown, orange and black on multicolor underprint. Map at upper center, Gen. Zeledon at right with black overprint elements. Overprint: signature and title: *PRIMER VICE PRESIDENTE BANCO CENTRAL DE NICARAGUA* at left, two lines of text at lower center blocked out, guilloche added at right. Back: National Assembly building. | | 0.50 | 2.50

Overprint errors exist and are rather common.

158 10,000 Córdobas on 10 Córdobas

		VF	UNC
ND (1989). Green and loive on multicolor underprint. Comdt. C. F. Amador at right. Back: Troop formation marching at left. Watermark: Sandino. | | 0.75 | 3.00

159   100,000 Córdobas on 100 Córdobas

	VF	UNC
ND (1989). Deep blue, blue and gray on multicolor underprint. R. Lopez Perez at right. Back: State council building at left. Watermark: Sandino.	1.25	6.00

1989 ND Emergency Issue

160   20,000 Córdobas

	VF	UNC
ND (1989). Black on blue, yellow and multicolor underprint. Comdt. Cleto Ordoñez at right, grid map of Nicaragua at center. Back: Church of San Francisco Granada at left, grid map of Nicaragua at center. Watermark: Sandino.	1.00	4.50

161   50,000 Córdobas

	VF	UNC
ND (1989). Brown on purple, orange and multicolor underprint. General J. D. Estrada at right, grid map of Nicaragua at center. Back: Hacienda San Jacinto at left, grid map of Nicaragua at center. Watermark: Sandino.	1.00	4.00

1990 ND Provisional Issue

162   200,000 Córdobas on 1000 Córdobas

	VF	UNC
ND (1990). Lithographed without watermark. Brown on multicolor underprint. General A. C. Sandino at right. Serial number prefix FC. Back: Liberation of 19.7.1979.	0.40	1.75

163   500,000 Córdobas on 20 Córdobas

	VF	UNC
ND (1990). Blue-black and blue on multicolor underprint. Comdt. G. P. Ordoñez at right. Back: Demonstration for agrarian reform at left.	1.00	3.50

164   1 Million Córdobas on 1000 Córdobas

	VF	UNC
ND (1990). Lithographed without watermark. Brown on multicolor underprint. General A. C. Sandino at right. Serial number prefix FC. Back: Liberation of 19.7.1979.	1.00	3.50

1990 ND Emergency Issue

165   5 Million Córdobas

	VF	UNC
ND (1990). Purple and orange on red and multicolor underprint. Comdt. Cleto Ordoñez at right, grid map of Nicaragua at center. Back: Church of San Francisco Granada at left, grid map of Nicaragua at center. Watermark: Sandino head, repeated.	0.50	2.00

166   10 Million Córdobas

	VF	UNC
ND (1990). Purple and lilac on blue and multicolor underprint. General J. D. Estrada at right, grid map of Nicaragua at center. Back: Hacienda San Jacinto at left, grid map of Nicaragua at center. Watermark: Sandino head, repeated.	0.75	2.50

1990; 1991-92 ND Issues

#173-177, 2 sign. varieties.

167   1 Centavo

	VF	UNC
ND (1991). UV: fibers and value 1 fluoresce yellow. Purple on pale green and multicolor underprint. F. H. Córdoba at right. Back: Arms at left, flower at right. Printer: Harrison.	0.05	0.15

168 5 Centavos

ND (1991). UV: fibers and value 5 fluoresce yellow. Red-violet on pale green and multicolor underprint. F. H. Córdoba at right. 2 signature varieties. Back: Arms at left, flower at right. Printer: Harrison.

	VF	UNC
a. Issued note.	0.05	0.20
s. Specimen.	—	100

169 10 Centavos

ND (1991). UV: fibers and value 10 fluoresce yellow. Olive-green on light green and multicolor underprint. F. H. Córdoba at right. 2 signature varieties. Back: Arms at left, flower at right. Printer: Harrison.

	VF	UNC
a. Issued note.	0.10	0.25
b. Specimen.	—	100

170 25 Centavos

ND (1991). UV: fibers and value 25 fluoresce yellow. Blue on pale green and multicolor underprint. F. H. Córdoba at right. 2 signature varieties. Back: Arms at left, flower at right. Printer: Harrison.

	VF	UNC
a. Issued note.	0.00	0.25
s. Specimen.	—	100

171 1/2 Córdoba

ND (1991). UV: right design and value 1/2 fluoresce green. Back center design and legends green. Brown and green on multicolor underprint. F. H. de Córdoba at left, plant at right. Back: Arms at center. Printer: CBNC. 156x67mm.

VF FV UNC 0.50

172 1/2 Córdoba

ND (1992). UV: right design and valyue 1/2 fluoresce green; fibers red, yellow and green. Back background legend green. F. H. de Córdoba at left, plant at right. Back: Arms at left, national flower at right. Printer: CBNC. 156x67mm.

VF FV UNC 0.50

173 1 Córdoba

1990 UV: left and right designs fluoresce yellow. Maize and sun yellow and green, Serial # and series green. Back corners green. Blue on purple and multicolor underprint. Sunrise over field of maize at left, F. H. Córdoba at right. 2 signature varieties. Back: Arms at center. Printer: TDLR. 156x67mm.

VF FV UNC 1.00

174 5 Córdobas

ND (1991). Red-violet and deep olive-green on multicolor underprint. Indian Chief Diriangén at left, sorghum plants at right. 2 signature varieties. Back: R. Herrera firing cannon at British warship. Printer: CBNC. 156x67mm.

VF FV UNC 2.00

175 10 Córdobas

1990 Green on blue and multicolor underprint. Sunrise over rice field at left, M. de Larreynaga at right. 2 signature varieties. Back: Arms at center. Printer: TDLR. 156x67mm.

VF FV UNC 3.50

176 20 Córdobas

ND (1990). Pale red-orange and dark brown on multicolor underprint. Sandino at left, coffee plant at right. Two signature varieties. Back: E. Mongalo at left, fire in the Mesón de Rivas (1854) at center. Printer: CBNC. 156x67mm.

VF FV UNC 6.00

177   50 Córdobas   VF   UNC
ND (1990-91). Purple and violet on multicolor underprint. Dr. P. J. Chamorro at
left, banana plants at right. Back: Toppling of Somoza's statue and scene at polling place. Printer: CBNC. 156x67mm.
   a. Series A. Three signatures. Two signature varieties.   FV   12.50

178   100 Córdobas   VF   UNC
1990 Blue and red on multicolor underprint. Sunrise over cotton field at left, R. Dario   FV   25.00
at right. Two signatures. Series A. Back: Arms at center. Printer: TDLR. 156x67mm.

178A   500 Córdobas   VF   UNC
1991 Brown and red on multicolor underprint. Estrada at right, cattle and sunrise
at left. Back: Arms at center. Printer: H&S. 156x67mm.
   a. Issued note. Rare.   —   2,500
   s. Specimen.   —   175

178B   1000 Córdobas   VF   UNC
1991 Purple and brown on multicolor underprint. Coffee plants at left, peace
demonstration at right. Back: Arms at center Printer: H&S. 156x67mm.
   a. Issued note. Rare.   —   2,500
   s. Specimen.   —   200

1992-96 Issue

179   1 Córdoba   VF   UNC
1995 Blue on purple and multicolor underprint. Sunrise over field of maize at   FV   1.00
left, F. H. Córdoba at right. 2 signature varieties. Series B. Back: Arms at center.
Printer: BABN. 156x67mm.

180   5 Córdobas   VF   UNC
1995 Red, deep olive-green and brown on multicolor underprint. Indian Chief   FV   1.75
Diriangén at left, sorghum plants at right. 2 signature varieties. Back: R. Herrera
firing cannon at British warship. Printer: F-CO. 156x67mm.

181   10 Córdobas   VF   UNC
1996 Green on blue and mlticolor underprint. Sunrise over rice field at left, M. de   FV   3.00
Larreynaga at right. 2 signature varieties. Back: Arms at center. Printer: G&D.
156x67mm.

182   20 Córdobas   VF   UNC
1995 Pale red-orange and dark brown on multicolor underprint. Sandino at left,   FV   5.00
coffee plant at right. Back: E. Mongalo at left, fire in the Mesón de Rivas (1854) at
center. Printer: F-CO. 156x67mm.

183   50 Córdobas   VF   UNC
1995 Purple and brown on multicolor underprint. Dr. P. J. Chamorro at left, banana   FV   10.00
plants at right. Series B. 2 signatures. Back: Arms at center. Printer: F-CO.
156x67mm.

184   100 Córdobas   VF   UNC
1992 Blue and red multicolor underprint. Sunrise over cotton field at left, R. Darío   FV   22.50
at right. 2 signatures. Series B. Back: Arms at center. 156x67mm.

1997 Issue

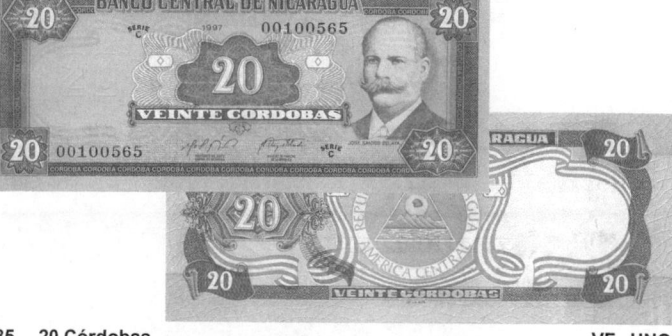

185   20 Córdobas   VF   UNC
1997 Orange-brown, green and multicolor. J. Santos Zelaya at right. Series C.   FV   6.00
Back: Arms at center. Printer: TDLR. 156x67mm.
#186 Not assigned.

187 100 Córdobas   **VF UNC**
1997 Blue and red on multicolor underprint. Sunrise over cotton field at left, R. Darío   FV   17.50
at right. 2 signatures. Series C. Back: Arms at center. Printer: TDLR. 156x67mm.

1999 Issue

188 10 Córdobas   **VF UNC**
1999 Green on blue and multicolor underprint. Sunrise over rice field at left, M. de   FV   2.50
Larreynaga at right. Series D. Back: Arms at center. Printer: F-CO. 156x67mm.

189 20 Córdobas   **VF UNC**
1999 Pale red-orange and dark brown on multicolor underprint. Sandino at left,   FV   5.00
coffee plant at right. Two signature varieties. Back: E. Mongalo at left, fire in the
Mesón de Rivas (1854) at center. Printer: F-CO. 156x67mm.

189A 50 Córdobas   **VF UNC**
2001 Denomination added to watermark. Windowed security thread. Purple and
brown on multicolor underprint. Dr. P. J. Chamorro at right. Back: Arms at center.
Printer: G&D. 156x67mm.
   a. Issued note.   FV   7.50
   s1. Specimen. Red overprint:*SPECIMEN* on both sides.   —   80.00
   s2. Specimen. Red overprint:*SPECIMEN* on face and *ESPECIMEN* on back.   —   150

190 100 Córdobas   **VF UNC**
1999 With windowed security thread. Blue and red on multicolor underprint.   FV   15.00
Sunrise over cotton field at left, R. Darío at right. Two signatures. Series D. Back:
Arms at center. 156x67mm.

2002 Issue

191 10 Córdobas   **VF UNC**
2002 Green on blue and multicolor underprint. Miguel de Larreynaga at right.   FV   3.00
Back: Isletas de Granada at left, arms at center. 156x67mm.

192 20 Córdobas   **VF UNC**
2002 Pale red-orange and dark brown on multicolor underprint. José Santos   FV   5.00
Zelaya at right. Back: Playa del Caribe at left, arms at center. 156x67mm.

193 50 Córdobas   **VF UNC**
2002 Purple and brown on multicolor underprint. Pedro Joaquin Chamorro at right.   FV   10.00
Back: Castillo de la Inmaculada Concepcion at left, arms at center. 156x67mm.

194 100 Córdobas   **VF UNC**
2002 Blue and red on multicolor underprint. Rubén Darío at right. Back: Teatro   FV   15.00
Nacional Rubén Darío at left, arms at center. 156x67mm.

195 500 Córdobas   **VF UNC**
2002 Brown and red on multicolor underprint. José Dolores Estrada at right. Back: FV   50.00
Hacienda San Jacinto at left, arms at center. 156x67mm.

2006 Issue

197 20 Córdobas
10.3.2006. Denomination added to watermark. Orange and brown on light green underprint. José Santos Zelaya at right. Back: Rlaya del Caribe. 156x67mm.

	VF	UNC
	FV	4.00

198 50 Córdobas
10.3.2006. Denomination added to watermark. Purple on yellow underprint. Pedro Joaquin Chamorro at right. Back: Castillo des la Inmaculada Conception. 156x67mm.

	VF	UNC
	FV	9.00

199 100 Córdobas
10.3.2006. Golden security ink band added. Blue on light blue underprint. Rubén Dario at right. Back: Teatro Nacional Rubén Dario. 156x67mm.

	VF	UNC
	FV	15.00

200 500 Córdobas
10.3.2006. Rose and brown on multicolor underprint. José Dolores Estrada at right, wide security foil at right. Back: Hacienda San Jacinto. 156x67mm.

	VF	UNC
	FV	70.00

2007 Polymer Issue

201 10 Córdobas
L. 12.9.2007 (2012). Polymer plastic. Green and light blue on multicolor underprint. Castillo Inmaculada Concepción in San Juan at right center. Back: Hacienda San Jacinto in Managua. 131x67mm.
  a. Embossed 10 in see-thru window.
  b. White 10 in see-thru window.

	VF	UNC
a.	FV	2.00
b.	FV	2.00

202 20 Córdobas
L. 12.9.2007 (2012) Polymer plastic. Brown, green and multicolor Costa Caribe (native hut) at center. Back: Palo de Mayo, group of women dancing. 136x67mm.
  a. Embossed 20 in see-thru window.
  b. White 20 in see-thru window.

	VF	UNC
a.	FV	3.00
b.	FV	3.00

203 50 Córdobas
L. 12.9.2007 (2012). Black and purple on multicolor underprint. Four vases in a bowl. Back: Cañon de Somoto. Watermark: Pottery and 50. 140x67mm.

	VF	UNC
	FV	9.00

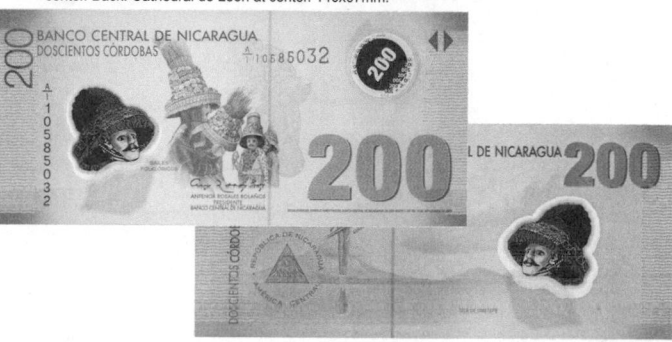

204 100 Córdobas
L. 12.9.2007 (2012). Blue, green and multicolor. Monumento a Rubén Darío at center. Back: Cathedral de León at center. 146x67mm.

	VF	UNC
	FV	15.00

205 200 Córdobas
L. 12.9.2007 (2012). Polymer plastic. Olive, brown and multicolor. Bailes Folklóricos at center. Back: Guardabarranco bird. Ometepe island. 151x67mm.
  a. Embossed 200 in see-thru window.
  b. White 200 in see-thru window.

	VF	UNC
a.	FV	20.00
b.	FV	20.00

206 500 Córdobas
L. 12.9.2007 (2012). Red and orange on multicolor underprint. House where Sandino was born. Bank logo in OVI. Back: Line art and statues at center. Watermark: Sandino and 500. 156x67mm.
  a. Bank logo at top right an OVI, thin security thread.
  b. Bank logo at top right is a hologram, wide window security thread.

	VF	UNC
a.	FV	45.00
b.	FV	45.00

2007 Commemorative Issue

208 100 Córdobas
18.9.2007. 100th anniversary of cordoba currency.

	VF	UNC
	FV	15.00

2011 Commemorative Issue

207 50 Córdobas
1.1.2011. Polymer plastic. Black and purple on multicolor underprint. Central Bank building. Back: Canon de Somoto.

	VF	UNC
	FV	9.00

2012 Commemorative Issue

		VF	UNC
209	**100 Córdobas**	**VF**	**UNC**
	2012 OVI for 35th anniversary of Banco Central de Nicaragua. Blue, green and multicolor. 146x67mm.	FV	0.00

2014 Issue

		VF	UNC
210	**10 Córdobas**	**VF**	**UNC**
	26.3.2014. Polymer. Green.	FV	2.00
211	**20 Córdobas**	**VF**	**UNC**
	26.3.2014. Polymer. Orange.	FV	3.00
212	**50 Córdobas**	**VF**	**UNC**
	26.3.2014. Polymer. Purple.	FV	9.00
213	**100 Córdobas**	**VF**	**UNC**
	26.3.2014. Polymer. Blue.	0.00	0.00
	26.3.2014. Polymer. Blue.	FV	15.00
214	**200 Córdobas**	**VF**	**UNC**
	26.3.2014. Polymer. Brown.	FV	20.00
215	**500 Córdobas**	**VF**	**UNC**
	26.3.2014. Paper. Red.	FV	45.00

2015 Issue

		VF	UNC
216	**10 Córdobas**	**VF**	**UNC**
	26.10.2015. Signature Ovidio Reyes Ramírez and Iván Adolfo Acosta Montalván.	FV	2.00

		VF	UNC
217	**20 Córdobas**	**VF**	**UNC**
	26.10.2015. Signature Ovidio Reyes Ramírez and Iván Adolfo Acosta Montalván.	FV	3.00

		VF	UNC
218	**50 Córdobas**	**VF**	**UNC**
	26.10.2015. Signature Ovidio Reyes Ramírez and Iván Adolfo Acosta Montalván.	FV	9.00

		VF	UNC
219	**100 Córdobas**	**VF**	**UNC**
	26.10.2015. Signature Ovidio Reyes Ramírez and Iván Adolfo Acosta Montalván.	FV	15.00

		VF	UNC
220	**200 Córdobas**	**VF**	**UNC**
	26.10.2015. Signature Ovidio Reyes Ramírez and Iván Adolfo Acosta Montalván.	FV	20.00

		VF	UNC
221	**500 Córdobas**	**VF**	**UNC**
	26.10.2015. Signature Ovidio Reyes Ramírez and Iván Adolfo Acosta Montalván.	FV	45.00

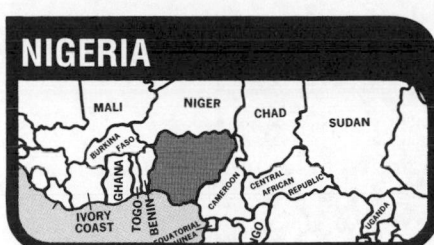

NIGERIA

The Federal Republic of Nigeria, situated on the Atlantic coast of Africa between Benin and Cameroon, has an area of 356,667 sq. mi. (923,768 sq. km.) and a population of 128.79 million. Capital: Abuja. The economy is based on petroleum and agriculture. Crude oil, cocoa, tobacco and tin are exported. British influence and control over what would become Nigeria and Africa's most populous country grew through the 19th century. A series of constitutions after World War II granted Nigeria greater autonomy; independence came in 1960. Following nearly 16 years of military rule, a new constitution was adopted in 1999, and a peaceful transition to civilian government was completed. The government continues to face the daunting task of reforming a petroleum-based economy, whose revenues have been squandered through corruption and mismanagement, and institutionalizing democracy. In addition, Nigeria continues to experience longstanding ethnic and religious tensions. Although both the 2003 and 2007 presidential elections were marred by significant irregularities and violence, Nigeria is currently experiencing its longest period of civilian rule since independence. The general elections of April 2007 marked the first civilian-to-civilian transfer of power in the country's history.

RULERS:
British to 1963

MONETARY SYSTEM:
1 Shilling = 12 Pence
1 Pound = 20 Shillings to 1973
1 Naira (10 Shillings) = 100 Kobo, 1973-

SIGNATURE VARIETIES

	GOVERNOR	CHIEF OF BANKING OPERATIONS		GOVERNOR	CHIEF OF BANKING OPERATIONS
1	*(signature)*	F.Algerume	2	*(signature)*	*(signature)*
3	OlaVincent	*(signature)*			DIRECTOR OF DOMESTIC OPERATIONS
			4	OlaVincent	*(signature)*
5	OlaVincent	*(signature)*	6	Ahmed	*(signature)*
		DIRECTOR OF CURRENCY OPERATIONS			DIRECTOR OF CURRENCY OPERATIONS
7	Ahmed	*(signature)*	8	Ahmed	*(signature)*
9	Ahmed	*(signature)*	10	*(signature)*	*(signature)*
11	*(signature)*	*(signature)*	12	*(signature)*	*(signature)*
13	*(signature)*	*(signature)*	14		

FEDERAL REPUBLIC OF NIGERIA

Central Bank of Nigeria
1967 ND Issue
Pound System

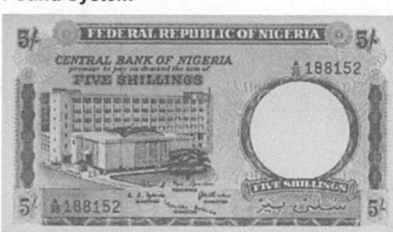

		VF	UNC
6	**5 Shillings**		
	ND (1967). Lilac and blue. Bank building at left. Back: Log cutting. Watermark: Lion's head.	20.00	140
7	**10 Shillings**	VF	UNC
	ND (1967). Green and brown. Bank building at left. Back: Stacking grain sacks. Watermark: Lion's head.	35.00	200

		VF	UNC
8	**1 Pound**		
	ND (1967). Red and dark brown. Bank building at left. Back: Man beating cluster from date palm at right. Watermark: Lion's head.	2.00	8.00
9	**5 Pounds**	VF	UNC
	ND (1967). Blue-gray and blue-green on multicolor underprint. Bank building at left. Back: Food preparation. Watermark: Lion's head.	30.00	350

1968 ND Issue

		VF	UNC
10	**5 Shillings**		
	ND (1968). Green and orange on multicolor underprint. Bank building at left. Back: Log cutting. Watermark: Lion's head.		
	a. Right signature title: *GENERAL MANAGER*.	15.00	150
	b. Right signature title: *CHIEF OF BANKING OPERATIONS*.	25.00	200
	s. As a. Specimen.	—	25.00

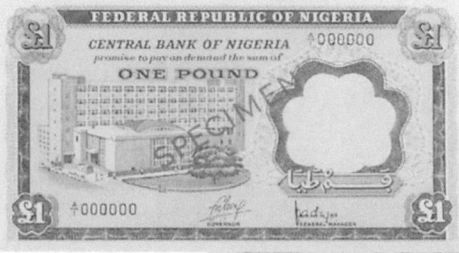

		VF	UNC
11	**10 Shillings**		
	ND (1968). Blue and black on multicolor underprint. Bank building at left. Back: Stacking grain sacks. Watermark: Lion's head.		
	a. Right signature title: *GENERAL MANAGER*.	25.00	200
	b. Right signature title: *CHIEF OF BANKING OPERATIONS*.	35.00	325
	s. As a. Specimen.	—	25.00

12 1 Pound | | VF | UNC

ND (1968). Olive-brown and purple on multicolor underprint. Bank building at left. Back: Man beating cluster from date palm at right. Watermark: Lion's head.

	VF	UNC
a. Right signature title: *GENERAL MANAGER.*	25.00	200
b. Right signature title: *CHIEF OF BANKING OPERATIONS.*	35.00	325
s. As a. Specimen.	—	25.00

13 5 Pounds | | VF | UNC

ND (1968). Red-brown and blue on multicolor underprint. Bank building at left. Back: Food preparation. Watermark: Lion's head.

	VF	UNC
a. Right signature title: *GENERAL MANAGER.*	75.00	500
b. Right signature title: *CHIEF OF BANKING OPERATIONS.*	100	550
s. As a. Specimen.	—	60.00

1973; 1977 ND Issue

 # 14-17 Naira System. Replacement notes: Serial # prefix DZ/.

14 50 Kobo | | VF | UNC

ND (1973-78). Blue and purple on multicolor underprint. Bank building at left center. Back: Logging at right. Watermark: Heraldic eagle.

	VF	UNC
a. Signature 1.	4.00	8.00
b. Signature 2.	5.00	35.00
c. Signature 3.	2.00	15.00
d. Signature 4.	2.00	15.00
e. Signature 5.	2.00	15.00
f. Signature 6.	1.75	10.00
g. Signature 7.	FV	1.50
h. Signature 8.	FV	1.50
j. Signature 9.	FV	1.50

15 1 Naira | | VF | UNC

ND (1973-78). Red and brown on multicolor underprint. Bank building at left center. Back: Stacking grain sacks. Watermark: Heraldic eagle.

	VF	UNC
a. Signature 1.	5.00	12.50
b. Signature 2.	4.00	12.50
c. Signature 3.	4.00	12.50
d. Signature 4.	17.50	50.00

16 5 Naira | | VF | UNC

ND (1973-78). Blue-gray and olive-green on multicolor underprint. Bank building at left center. Back: Man beating cluster from date palm at right. Watermark: Heraldic eagle.

	VF	UNC
a. Signature 1.	15.00	70.00
b. Signature 2.	10.00	50.00
c. Signature 3.	60.00	275
d. Signature 4.	75.00	325

17 10 Naira | | VF | UNC

ND (1973-78). Carmine and dark blue on multicolor underprint. Bank building at left center. Back: Dam at center. Watermark: Heraldic eagle.

	VF	UNC
a. Signature 1.	35.00	110
b. Signature 2.	22.50	85.00
c. Signature 3.	125	400
d. Signature 4.	150	475

18 20 Naira | | VF | UNC

ND (1977-84). Yellow-green and black on red and multicolor underprint. General M. Muhammed at left. Back: Arms at center right.

	VF	UNC
a. Signature 2.	100	325
b. Signature 3.	60.00	200
c. Signature 4.	20.00	65.00
d. Signature 5.	15.00	45.00
e. Signature 6.	10.00	35.00

1979 ND Issue

19 1 Naira | | VF | UNC

ND (1979-84). Red on orange and multicolor underprint. H. Macaulay at left. Signature titles: *GOVERNOR* and *DIRECTOR OF DOMESTIC OPERATIONS.* Back: Mask at center right. Watermark: Heraldic eagle.

	VF	UNC
a. Signature 4.	2.00	7.50
b. Signature 5.	1.00	5.00
c. Signature 6.	0.75	3.00

20   5 Naira

ND (1979-84). Green on multicolor underprint. Sir AbubakarTafawa Balewa Alaji at left. Signature titles: *GOVERNOR* and *DIRECTOR OF DOMESTIC OPERA-TIONS*. Back: Dancers at center right. Watermark: Heraldic eagle.

	VF	UNC
a. Signature 4.	5.00	15.00
b. Signature 5.	4.00	12.50
c. Signature 6.	3.00	10.00

21   10 Naira

ND (1979-84). Brown, purple and violet on multicolor underprint. A. Ikoku at left Signature titles: *GOVERNOR* and *DIRECTOR OF DOMESTIC OPERATIONS*. Back: Two women with bowls on heads at center right. Watermark: Heraldic eagle.

	VF	UNC
a. Signature 4.	12.00	30.00
b. Signature 5.	8.00	25.00
c. Signature 6.	20.00	—

1984; 1991 ND Issue

23   1 Naira

ND (1984-). Reduced size. Red, violet and green. H. Macaulay at left. Signature titles: *GOVERNOR* and *DIRECTOR OF DOMESTIC OPERATIONS*. Back: Mask at center right. Watermark: Heraldic eagle.

	VF	UNC
a. Signature title at right: *DIRECTOR OF DOMESTIC OPERATIONS*. Signature 6.	1.00	3.00
b. Signature title at right: *DIRECTOR OF CURRENCY OPERATIONS*. Signature 7.	FV	2.50
c. Titles as b. Signature 8.	FV	2.50
d. Titles as b. Signature 9.	FV	2.50

24   5 Naira

ND (1984-); 2001-5. Reduced size. UV: fibers fluoresce red and blue; security strip red; value 5, serial #s yellow. Purple and brown-violet on multicolor underprint. Sir Abubakar Tafawa Balewa alhaji at left. Back: Dancers at center right. Watermark: Heraldic eagle.

	VF	UNC
a. Signature title at right: *DIRECTOR OF DOMESTIC OPERATIONS*. Signature 6.	2.00	6.50
b. Signature title at right: *DIRECTOR OF CURRENCY OPERATIONS*. Signature 7.	1.00	4.00
c. Titles as b. Signature 8.	FV	2.00
d. Titles as b. Signature 9.	FV	2.00
e. Titles as b. Signature 10.	FV	1.75
f. Titles as b. Signature 11.	FV	1.75
g. 2001; 2002. Signature 11.	FV	1.75
h. 2004; 2005. Signature 12.	FV	1.75
i. 2005. Signature 13.	FV	1.75
j. 2005. Signature 14.	FV	1.75

25   10 Naira

ND (1984-); 2001-2005. Reduced size. Red-violet and orange on multicolor underprint. A. Ikoku at left. Back: Two women with bowls on heads at center right. Watermark: Heraldic eagle.

	VF	UNC
a. Signature title at right: *DIRECTOR OF DOMESTIC OPERATIONS*. Signature 6.	2.50	9.00
b. Signature title at right: *DIRECTOR OF CURRENCY OPERATIONS*. Signature 7.	2.50	6.00
c. Titles as b. Signature 8.	FV	3.25
d. Titles as b. Signature 9.	FV	3.00
e. Titles as b. Signature 10.	FV	3.00
f. 2001; 2002; 2003.Titles as b. Signature 11.	FV	3.00
g. 2003; 2004; 2005. Signature 12.	FV	3.00
h. 2005. Signature 13.	FV	3.00
I. 2005. Signature 14.	FV	3.00

26   20 Naira

ND (1984-); 2001-05. UV: value 20 and serial #s fluoresce yellow; fibers blue. Dark blue-green, dark green and green on multicolor underprint. General M. Muhammed at left. Back: Arms at center right. Watermark: Heraldic eagle.

	VF	UNC
a. ND (1984). Signature title at right: *DIRECTOR OF DOMESTIC OPERATIONS*. Signature 6.	5.00	20.00
b. ND. Signature title at right: *DIRECTOR OF CURRENCY OPERATIONS*. Signature 7.	FV	6.00
c. ND. Titles as b. Signature 8.	FV	4.00
d. ND. Titles as b. Signature 9.	FV	4.00
e. ND. *Serie* in big letters.Titles as b. Signature 10.	FV	3.00
f. ND. *Serie* in small letters. Titles as b. Signature 10.	FV	3.00
g. 2001; 2002; 2003. Signature 11.	FV	3.00
h. 2003; 2004. Signature 12.	FV	3.00
i. 2005. Signature 13.	FV	3.00
j. 2005. Signature 14.	FV	3.00
k. 2006.	FV	3.00

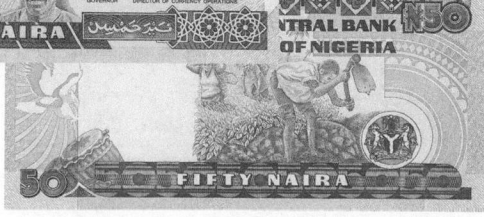

27   50 Naira

ND (1991-); 2001-2005. Dark blue, black and gray on multicolor underprint. Four busts reflecting varied citizenry at left center. Back: Three farmers in field at center right, arms at lower right. Watermark: Heraldic eagle.

	VF	UNC
a. ND (1991). Signature 8.	3.50	12.50
b. ND. Signature 9.	FV	7.50
c. ND. Signature 10.	FV	6.50
d. 2001. Signature 11.	FV	6.50
e. 2004. Signature 12.	FV	6.50
f. 2005. Signature 14.	FV	6.50

1999-2001 ND Issue

28   100 Naira VF UNC

1999-. Brown and red on multicolor underprint. Chief Obafemi Awolowo at left. Back: Zuma rock.

a. 1999. Back with *Abuja Province* identification by rock. Signature 11.   FV   4.00
b. 1999. Back modified without identification. Signature 11.   FV   3.50
c. 2001. Signature 11.   FV   3.50
d. 2004. Signature 12.   FV   3.00
e. 2005. Signature 13.   FV   3.00
f. 2005. Signature 14.   FV   3.00
g. 2006.   FV   2.50
h. 2007.   FV   2.50
i. 2009.   FV   2.50
j. 2010.   FV   2.50
k. 2011.   FV   2.50
l. 2012. Two signature varieties.   FV   2.50
m. 2013.   FV   2.50
n. 2014.   FV   2.50

29   200 Naira VF UNC

2000-. Brown, dark blue and green on multicolor underprint. Sir Ahmadu Bello at left. Back: Two cows and agricultural products. Watermark: Sir Ahmadu Bello. 151x78mm.

a. 2000; 2001; 2002. Signature 11.   FV   4.00
b. 2003. Signature 12.   FV   3.50
c. 2004; 2005. *Serie* in big letters. Signature 13.   FV   3.50
d. 2005. *Serie* in small letters. Signature 13.   FV   3.50
e. 2006. Signature 14.   FV   3.50
f. 2007.   FV   3.00
g. 2008.   FV   3.00
h. 2009.   FV   3.00
i. 2010.   FV   3.00
j. 2011.   FV   3.00
k. 2012. Signature 16.   FV   3.00
l. 2012. Signature 17.   FV   3.00
m. 2013.   FV   3.00
n. 2014.   FV   3.00

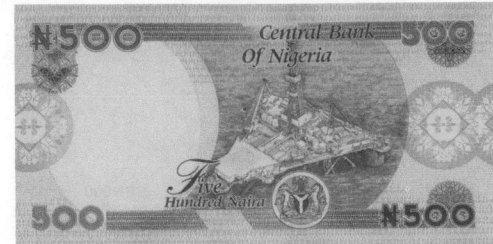

30   500 Naira VF UNC

2001-. Purple and olive-green on rose and multicolor underprint. Dr. Nnamdi Azikiwe at left. Wide segmented security thread at left center. Back: Oil platform at center right. Watermark: Dr. Nnamdi Azikiwe. 151x78mm.

a. 2001; 2002. Signature 11.   FV   7.50
b. 2004. Signature 12.   FV   6.50
c. 2005. Signature 12.   FV   6.50
d. 2005. Signature 13.   FV   6.50
e. 2005. Signature 14.   FV   6.50
f. 2006. Signature 14.   FV   6.50
g. 2007.   FV   6.50
h. 2009.   FV   6.00
i. 2010.   FV   6.00
j. 2011.   FV   6.00
k. 2012.   FV   6.00
l. 2013.   FV   6.00
m. 2014.   FV   6.00
n. 2015.   FV   6.00

2005-06 Issue

31   2 Naira VF UNC

2006.   FV   1.50

32   5 Naira VF UNC

2006-2008. Paper. Brown and orange. Alhaji Sir Abubakar Tafawa Salewa at left. Back: Drum players.

a. 2006.   FV   1.50
b. 2007.   FV   1.50
c. 2008   FV   1.50

 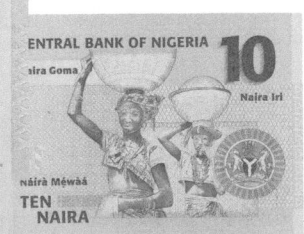

33   10 Naira VF UNC

2006-. Paper. Red-brown and orange. Aslvan Ikoku at left. Back: Two women carrying baskets on their heads.

a. 2006.   FV   1.50
b. 2007.   FV   1.25
c. 2008.   FV   1.25
d. 2009. Signatures Chukwuma Soludo and Benjamin Onyido.   FV   1.25

34 20 Naira

2006-. Plastic. Dark green and green. General Murtalla R. Muhammed Back: Potter. 121x72mm.

	VF	UNC
a. 2006.	FV	2.00
b. 2007. 7-Digit serial #. Printer: G&D.	FV	1.50
c. 2007. 6-Digit serial #. Printer: Nigeria Security Printing. Matte or Glossy finish.	FV	1.50
d. 2008.	FV	1.00
e. 2009.	FV	1.00
f. 2010.	FV	1.00
g. 2011.	FV	1.00
h. 2012.	FV	1.00
i. 2013.	FV	1.00
j. 2014.	FV	1.00
k. 2015.	FV	1.00

35 50 Naira

2006-. Paper. Slate blue and blue. Four portraits. Signature 14. Back: Fishermen. 121x72mm.

	VF	UNC
a. 2006. Signature 14.	FV	2.50
b. 2007. 7-digit serial #.	FV	2.00
c. 2008. 6-digit serial #.	FV	2.00

36 1000 Naira

2005-. Brown, lilac and multicolor underprint. Alhaji Aliyu Mai-Bornu and Dr. Clement Isong at left center. Signature 14. Back: Central Bank building. 151x78mm.

	VF	UNC
a. 2005.	FV	12.50
b. 2006.	FV	10.00
c. 2007.	FV	10.00
d. 2010.	FV	10.00
e. 2012.	FV	10.00
f. 2013.	FV	10.00
g. 2014.	FV	10.00

2010 Commemorative Issue

37 50 Naira

2010. Slate blue and blue on multicolor underprint. Four portraits. Back: Fishermen. 130x72mm.

	VF	UNC
	FV	5.00

2009 Polymer Issue

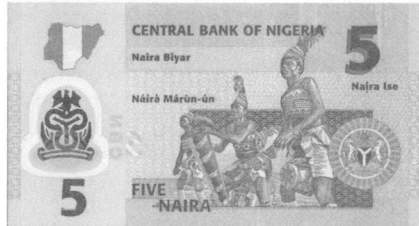

38 5 Naira

2009-. Plastic. Mauve on multicolor underprint. Alhaji Dir Abubakar Tafawa Balewa at left. Back: Four Nkpokiti dancers with drums. 130x72mm.

	VF	UNC
a. 2009. 6-digit serial #. Printer NSP&M.	FV	1.00
b. 2009. 7-digit serial #. Printer G&D.	FV	1.00
c. 2011	FV	1.00
d. 2013	FV	1.00
e. 2014	FV	1.00
f. 2015	FV	1.00

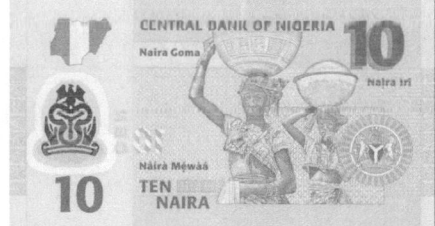

39 10 Naira

2009-. Plastic. Red on multicolor underprint. Alvan Ikoku at left. Back: Two females carrying bowls on their heads. Watermark: Coat-of-arms and CBN 130x72mm.

	VF	UNC
a. 2009	FV	2.50
b. 2010	FV	2.50
c. 2011	FV	2.50
d. 2013	FV	2.50
e. 2014	FV	2.50
f. 2015	FV	2.50

40 50 Naira

2009-. Plastic. Blue on multicolor underprint. Four portraits at left. Back: Three fishermen and two fish. Watermark: Coat-of-arms and CBN 130x72mm.

	VF	UNC
a. 2009	FV	5.00
b. 2010	FV	5.00
c. 2011	FV	5.00
d. 2013	FV	5.00
e. 2015	FV	5.00

2014 Commemorative Issue

41 100 Naira

2014. 100th anniversary of united nation.

	VF	UNC
	FV	10.00

NORTH KOREA

The Democratic Peoples Republic of Korea, situated in in northeastern Asia on the northern half of the Korean peninsula between the Peoples Republic of China and the Republic of Korea, has an area of 46,540 sq. mi. (120,538 sq. km.) and a population of 23.26 million. Capital: Pyongyang. The economy is based on heavy based on heavy industry and agriculture. Metals, minerals and farm produce are exported. Japan replaced China as the predominant foreign influence in Korea in 1895 and annexed the peninsular country in 1910. Defeat in World War II brought an end to Japanese rule. U.S. troops entered Korea from the south and Soviet forces entered from the north. The Cairo conference (1943) had established that Korea should be "free and independent." The Potsdam conference (1945) set the 38th parallel as the line dividing the occupation forces of the United States and Russia. When Russia refused to permit a U.N. commission designated to supervise reunification elections to enter North Korea, an election was held in South Korea which established the Republic of Korea on Aug. 15, 1948. North Korea held an unsupervised election on Aug. 25, 1948, and on the following day proclaimed the establishment of the Democratic Peoples Republic of Korea.

MONETARY SYSTEM:
1 Won = 100 Chon

DEMOCRATIC PEOPLES REPUBLIC

Korean Central Bank

1959 Issue

12	50 Chon		VF	UNC
	1959. With watermark. Blue on multicolor underprint. Arms at upper left.		2.50	8.00

13	1 Won		VF	UNC
	1959. With watermark. Red-brown on multicolor underprint. Fishing boat at center. Arms at upper left.		1.75	6.00

14	5 Won		VF	UNC
	1959. With watermark. Green on multicolor underprint. Large building at center. Arms at upper left.		2.00	7.00

15	10 Won		VF	UNC
	1959. With watermark. Red on multicolor underprint. Fortress gateway at center right. Arms at upper left. Back: Woman picking fruit.		2.25	8.00

16	50 Won		VF	UNC
	1959. With watermark. Purple on multicolor underprint. Bridge and city at center. Arms at upper left. Back: Woman with wheat.		3.50	10.00

17	100 Won		VF	UNC
	1959. With watermark. Green on multicolor underprint. Steam freight train in factory area at center. Arms at upper left. Back: River with cliffs.		4.50	15.00

1978 Issue

Note: Circulation of varieties #18-21: a. For general circulation.b. For Socialist visitors. c. For non-Socialist visitors.d. Replaced a for general circulation. e. Use not known.

18   1 Won

	VF	UNC
1978. Olive-green on multicolor underprint. Two adults and two children at center, arms at upper left. Back: Soldier at left, woman with flowers at center, woman at right.		
a. Red and black serial #. No seal on back.	0.75	2.50
b. Black serial #. Green seal at left. on back.	0.25	1.25
c. Red serial #. Red seal at left. on back.	0.25	1.25
d. Red serial #. Large numeral 1 in red guilloche on back.	0.25	1.25
e. Black serial #. Large numeral 1 in blue guilloche on back.	0.25	1.25
s. Specimen.	—	—

19   5 Won

	VF	UNC
1978. Blue-gray on multicolor underprint. Worker with book and gear, and woman with wheat at center, arms at upper left. Back: Mount gumgang.		
a. Red and black serial #. No seal on back.	0.50	1.50
b. Black serial #. Green seal at left. on back.	0.50	1.50
c. Red serial #. Red seal at left. on back.	0.50	1.50
d. Red serial #. Large numeral 5 in red guilloche on back.	0.50	1.50
e. Black serial #. Large numeral 5 in blue guilloche on back.	0.50	1.50
s. Specimen.	—	—

20   10 Won

	VF	UNC
1978 Brown on multicolor underprint. Winged equestrian statue "Chonllima" at center, arms at upper left. Back: Waterfront factory.		
a. Red and black serial #. No seal on back.	0.50	2.50
b. Black serial #. Green seal at upper right on back.	0.50	2.00
c. Red serial #. Red seal at upper right on back.	0.50	2.00
d. Red serial #. Large numeral 10 in red guilloche on back.	0.50	2.00
e. Black serial #. Large numeral 10 in blue guilloche on back.	0.50	2.00
s. Specimen.	—	—

21   50 Won

	VF	UNC
1978. Olive-green on multicolor underprint. Soldier with man holding torch, woman with wheat, man with book at center, arms at upper left. Back: Lake scene.		
a. Red and black serial #. No seal on back.	0.50	3.00
b. Black serial #. Green seal at lower right on back.	0.50	2.50
c. Red serial #. Red seal at lower right on back.	0.50	2.50
d. Red serial #. Large numeral 50 in red guilloche on back.	0.50	2.50
e. Black serial #. Large numeral 50 in blue guilloche on back.	0.50	2.50
s. Specimen.	—	—

22   100 Won

	VF	UNC
1978. Brown on lilac and multicolor underprint. Kim Il Sung at center right, arms at upper left. Red and black serial number. Back: House with trees. No seal.		
a. Issued note.	1.00	5.00
s. Specimen. Overprint in red on face.	—	200

1988 "Capitalist Visitor" Issue

23   1 Chon

	VF	UNC
1988. Blue on purple underprint. Arms at upper left, red serial number. Back: Value.	0.20	0.40

24   5 Chon

	VF	UNC
1988. Blue on pink underprint. Arms at upper left, red serial number. Back: Value.	0.75	1.00

25   10 Chon

	VF	UNC
1988. Blue and black on green-yellow underprint. Arms at upper left, red serial number. Back: Value.	0.40	1.00

26   50 Chon

	VF	UNC
1988. Blue on yellow underprint. Arms at upper left, red serial number. Back: Value.	0.50	1.00

27   1 Won

	VF	UNC
1988. Dark green on blue and pink underprint. Winged equestrian statue "Chonllima" at center, arms at upper right. Red serial number.	0.75	2.50

28　5 Won　　　　　　　　　　　　　　　　　　**VF　UNC**
1988. Dark green on blue and pink underprint. Winged equestrian statue "Chonl-　1.50　7.50
lima" at center, arms at upper right. Red serial number.

29　10 Won　　　　　　　　　　　　　　　　　**VF　UNC**
1988. Dark green on blue and pink underprint. Winged equestrian statue "Chonl-　3.00　12.50
lima" at center, arms at upper right. Red serial number.

30　50 Won　　　　　　　　　　　　　　　　　**VF　UNC**
1988. Dark green on blue and pink underprint. Winged equestrian statue "Chonl-　8.00　40.00
lima" at center, arms at upper right. Red serial number.

1988 "Socialist Visitor" Issue

31　1 Chon　　　　　　　　　　　　　　　　　**VF　UNC**
1988. Red-brown on pink and blue underprint. Arms at upper right. Black serial　FV　1.25
number. Back: Value.

32　5 Chon　　　　　　　　　　　　　　　　　**VF　UNC**
1988. Purple on pink and blue underprint. Arms at upper right. Black serial　FV　1.75
number. Back: Value.

33　10 Chon　　　　　　　　　　　　　　　　**VF　UNC**
1988. Olive-green on pink and blue underprint. Arms at upper right. Black serial　FV　2.50
number. Back: Value.

34　50 Chon　　　　　　　　　　　　　　　　**VF　UNC**
1988. Brown-violet on pink and blue underprint. Arms at upper right. Black serial　FV　3.00
number. Back: Value.

35　1 Won　　　　　　　　　　　　　　　　　**VF　UNC**
1988. Red on blue and ochre underprint. Temple at center, olive sprig on globe at　FV　3.50
right, arms at upper right. Black serial number. Back: Olive sprig on globe, value.

36　5 Won　　　　　　　　　　　　　　　　　**VF　UNC**
1988. Red on blue and ochre underprint. Temple at center, olive sprig on globe at　FV　12.50
right, arms at upper right. Black serial number. Back: Olive sprig on globe, value.

37　10 Won　　　　　　　　　　　　　　　　　**VF　UNC**
1988. Red on blue and ochre underprint. Temple at center, olive sprig on globe at　3.50　15.00
right, arms at upper right. Black serial number. Back: Olive sprig on globe, value.

38　50 Won　　　　　　　　　　　　　　　　　**VF　UNC**
1988. Red on blue and ochre underprint. Temple at center, olive sprig on globe at　15.00　60.00
right, rms at upper right. Black serial number. Back: Olive sprig on globe, value.

1992; 1998 Issue

39　1 Won　　　　　　　　　　　　　　　　　**VF　UNC**
1992; 1998. Grayish olive-green and olive-brown on multicolor underprint. Young
woman with flower basket at center right, arms at upper left. Back: Mount Gum-
gang. Watermark: Winged equestrian statue "Chonllima".
　　a. Issued note.　　　　　　　　　　　　　　　　　1.00　2.00
　　s. 1992. Specimen. Red overprint at left face.　　　—　15.00

40　5 Won　　　　　　　　　　　　　　　　　**VF　UNC**
1992; 1998. Blue-black and deep purple on multicolor underprint. Students at
center right with modern building and factory in background, arms at upper left.
Back: Palace. Watermark: Winged equestrian statue "Chonllima".
　　a. Issued note.　　　　　　　　　　　　　　　　　1.00　3.00
　　s. 1998. Specimen. Red overprint at left face.　　　—　12.50

41   10 Won   **VF   UNC**

1992; 1998. Deep brown and red-brown on multicolor underprint. Factory worker,
winged equestrian statue "Chonllima" at center, factories in background at right,
arms at upper left. Back: Flood gates. Watermark: Winged equestrian statue
"Chonllima".

 a. Issued note.   1.00   4.00
 s. 1992. Specimen. Red overprint at right face.   0.00   15.00

42   50 Won   **VF   UNC**

1992; 1998. Deep brown and deep olive-brown on multicolor underprint. Monument to five year plan at left, young professionals at center right, arms at upper
right. Back: Landscape of pine trees and mountains. Watermark: Monument to
five year plan.

 a. Issued note.   2.00   5.00
 s. 1992. Specimen. Red overprint at left face.   —   15.00

43   100 Won   **VF   UNC**

1992; 1998. Deep brown and brown-violet on multicolor underprint. Arms at lower
left center, Kim II Sung at right. Back: Rural home at center. Watermark: Arched
gateway.

 a. Issued note.   3.00   7.50
 s. Specimen. Red overprint at left face.   —   35.00

44   500 Won   **VF   UNC**

1998. Slate gray on light blue and purple underprint. Assembly Hall. Back:
Suspension bridge.

 a. Issued note.   5.00   12.50
 s1. Specimen. Red overprint at left center. Regular serial #s.   —   50.00
 s2. Specimen. Serial # as 000000.   —   50.00

2002 Issue

45   1000 Won   **VF   UNC**

2002, 2006. Dark green on multicolor underprint. Arms at lower left center, Kim II
Sung at right. Back: Rural home at center. Watermark: Arched gateway.

 a. 2002.   5.00   10.00
 b. 2006.   5.00   10.00
 s1. Specimen. Red overprint at upper left. Regular serial #.   —   40.00
 s2. Specimen. Serial # as 000000.   —   40.00

46   5000 Won   **VF   UNC**

2002. Purple on multicolor underprint. Arms at lower left center, Kim II Sung at
right. Back: Rural home at center.

 a. Orange *5000* in upper left measures 19x9mm.   10.00   30.00
 b. Orange *5000* in upper left measures 20x10.   10.00   30.00
 s1. Specimen. Red overprint at upper left. Regular serial #.   —   50.00
 s2. Specimen. Serial # as 000000.   —   50.00
 s3. Specimen. Uncut sheet of 20 notes, regular serial #.   —   275

2002 Commemorative Issue

47   500 Won   **VF   UNC**
2002.   FV   17.50

2005 Issue

48   200 Won   **VF   UNC**
2005 Green on multicolor underprint. Flower. Back: Large 200.

 a. Issued note.   FV   12.50
 s. Specimen. Red overprint at left face.   —   22.50

2007 Commemorative Overprint Issue

		VF	UNC
49	**1 Won**	VF	UNC
	(2007). Grayish olive-green and olive brown on multicolor underprint. As #39.	FV	1.00
50	**5 Won**	VF	UNC
	(2007). Blue-black and deep purple on multicolor underprint. As #40.	FV	2.00
51	**10 Won**	VF	UNC
	(2007). Deep brown and red-brown on multicolor underprint. As #41.	FV	3.00
52	**50 Won**	VF	UNC
	(2007). Deep brown and deep olive-brown on multicolor underprint. As #42.		
	a. Issued note.	FV	5.00
	s. Specimen.	—	50.00
53	**100 Won**	VF	UNC
	(2007). Deep brown and brown-violet on multicolor underprint. As #43.	FV	7.50
54	**200 Won**	VF	UNC
	(2007). Green on multicolor underprint. As #48.	FV	12.50
55	**500 Won**	VF	UNC
	(2007). Slate gray on light blue and purple underprint. As #44.	FV	15.00
56	**1000 Won**	VF	UNC
	(2007). Dark green on multicolor underprint. As #45.	FV	20.00
56A	**5000 Won**	VF	UNC
	(2007). Purple on multicolor underprint As #46.	FV	50.00

2002 (2009) Issue

		VF	UNC
57	**1 Won**	VF	UNC
	2002 (2009).	FV	0.25
58	**5 Won**	VF	UNC
	2002 (2009). Slate black on multicolor underprint. Man with glasses, boy with cap at right center. Back: Dam. Watermark: Flowers. 145x65mm.	FV	0.25
59	**10 Won**	VF	UNC
	2002 (2009). Blue, green and purple on multicolor underprint. Pilot, sailor and solder at right center. Back: Military statue group. 145x65mm.	FV	0.25
60	**50 Won**	VF	UNC
	2002 (2009). Purple on multicolor underprint. Man in suit, man in overalls, female at right center. Back: Party Foundation Monument in Pyongyang 145x65mm.	FV	0.25
	2002 (2009). Purple on multicolor underprint. Man in suit, man in overalls, female at right center. Back: Party Foundation Monument in Pyongyang 145x65mm.	0.00	0.00
61	**100 Won**	VF	UNC
	2002 (2009). Green on multicolor underprint. Seibold magnolia at center. Back: Value at center. 145x65mm.	FV	7.50
62	**200 Won**	VF	UNC
	2002 (2009). Violet and lilac on multicolor underprint. Equestrian statue at center. Back: Value at center. 145x65mm.	FV	12.50
63	**500 Won**	VF	UNC
	2002 (2009). Gray and purple on multicolor underprint. Arch of Triumph. Back: Value at center. 145x65mm.	FV	12.50

		VF	UNC
64	**1000 Won**	VF	UNC
	2002 (2009). Red on lilac underprint. Birthplace of Kim Jong Suk in Hoeryong. Back: Birch tree forest along Lake Samji. 145x65mm.		
	a. Issued note.	FV	12.50
	s. Specimen. Red overprint.	—	75.00

		VF	UNC
65	**2000 Won**	VF	UNC
	2002 (2009). Gray and blue on multicolor underprint. Cabin birthplace of Kim Hong Il and Jong Il peak. Back: Forest and Baekdu Mountains. 145x65mm.		
	a. Issued note.	FV	20.00
	s. Specimen. Red overprint.	—	75.00

		VF	UNC
66	**5000 Won**	VF	UNC
	2002 (2009). Brown on pink underprint. Kim Il Sung at right center with Seibold's magnolia wreath at right. Back: Birthplace of Kim Il Sung in Mangyongdae. 145x65mm.		
	a. Issued note.	FV	50.00
	s. Specimen. Red overprint.	—	75.00

COLLECTOR SERIES

Korean Central Bank

1978 Issue

			Mkt. Value
CS1	**1978 1-100 Won.**		60.00
	Red overprint Korean characters for specimen on #18a-21a, 22 (with all zero serial #).		

1992 Issue

			Mkt. Value
CS2	**1992 1-100 Won.**		50.00
	Red, rectangular overprint Korean characters for specimen on #39-43. (39, 42 and 43 with all zero serial #, 40-41 with normal serial #).		

2000 Issue

#CS3-CS8 ovpt. in Korean or English: *The 55th Anniversary of Foundation of the Workers' Party of Korea 10th.10.Juche 89 (2000).*

			Mkt. Value
CS3	**1 Won**		3.00
	Overprint: *The 55th Anniversary of Foundation of the Worders' Party of korea 10th. 10. juche 89 (2000). Black overprint in English on face of #18e.*		
CS4	**5 Won**		3.00
	Overprint: *The 55th Anniversary of Foundation of the Worders' Party of korea 10th. 10. juche 89 (2000). Red overprint in Korean on face of #19d.*		
CS5	**10 Won**		3.00
	Overprint: *The 55th Anniversary of Foundation of the Worders' Party of korea 10th. 10. juche 89 (2000). Black overprint in English on face of #20e.*		

CS6   50 Won
Overprint: *The 55th Anniversary of Foundation of the Worders' Party of korea 10th. 10. juche 89 (2000)*. Red overprint in Korean on face of #21b.

Mkt. Value
3.00

CS7   50 Won
Overprint: *The 55th Anniversary of Foundation of the Worders' Party of korea 10th. 10. juche 89 (2000)*. Red overprint in English on face of #21b.

Mkt. Value
3.00

CS8   50 Won
Overprint: *The 55th Anniversary of Foundation of the Worders' Party of korea 10th. 10. juche 89 (2000)*. Black overprint in English on face of #21b.

Mkt. Value
3.00

2013 Issue

CS9   5000 Won
2013. Overprint: *The 100th birthday of Kim Il Sung*. 145x65mm.

Mkt. Value
5.00

CS10   5000 Won
2013. Overprint: *The 70th anniversary of the ruling Workers' Party*. All-zero serial number.

Mkt. Value
5.00

NORTHERN IRELAND

From 1800 to 1921 Ireland was an integral part of the United Kingdom. The Anglo-Irish treaty of 1921 established the Irish Free State of 26 counties within the Commonwealth of Nations and recognized the partition of Ireland. The six predominantly Protestant counties of northeast Ulster chose to remain a part of the United Kingdom with a limited self-government. Up to 1928 banknotes issued by six of the nine joint stock commercial banks were circulating in the whole of Ireland. After the establishment of the Irish Free State, the commercial notes were issued for circulation only in Northern Ireland, with the Consolidated Banknotes being issued by the eight commercial banks operating in the Irish Free State.

Additional information on bank notes of Northern Ireland can be found in *Paper Money of Ireland* by Bob Blake and Jonathan Callaway, published by Pam West.

RULERS:
British

MONETARY SYSTEM:
1 Shilling = 12 Pence
1 Pound = 20 Shillings to 1971
1 Pound = 100 New Pence, 1971-

BRITISH ADMINISTRATION

Allied Irish Banks Ltd.
Formerly Provincial Bank of Ireland Ltd., later became First Trust Bank.

1982 Issue
#1-5 designs similar to Provincial Bank of Ireland Ltd. (#247-251) except for bank title and signature.

		VF	UNC
1	**1 Pound**		
	1.1.1982; 1.7.1983; 1.12.1984. Green on multicolor underprint. Young girl at right. Back: Sailing ship *Girona* at center. Printer: TDLR.		
	a. 1.1.1982.	15.00	45.00
	b. 1.7.1983.	15.00	45.00
	c. 1.12.1984.	15.00	45.00

		VF	UNC
2	**5 Pounds**		
	1.1.1982; 1.7.1983. Blue and purple on multicolor underprint. Young woman at right. Back: Dunluce Castle at center. Printer: TDLR.		
	a. 1.1.1982.	35.00	95.00
	b. 1.7.1983.	35.00	95.00

8   20 Pounds

	VF	UNC
1.1.1987; 1.4.1987; 1.1.1990. Purple and green. Elderly woman at right. Back: Chimney at Lacada Point at center. Printer: TDLR.		
a. 1.1.1987.	70.00	180
b. 1.4.1987.	65.00	140
c. 1.1.1990.	65.00	140

3   10 Pounds

	VF	UNC
1.1.1982; 1.12.1984. Brown and gray-green on multicolor underprint. Young man at right. Back: Wreck of the *Girona* at center. Printer: TDLR.		
a. 1.1.1982.	50.00	160
b. 1.12.1984.	50.00	160

4   20 Pounds

	VF	UNC
1.1.1982; 1.7.1983; 1.12.1984. Purple and green. Elderly woman at right. Back: Chimney at Lacada Point at center. Printer: TDLR.		
a. 1.1.1982.	75.00	325
b. 1.7.1983.	75.00	325
c. 1.12.1984.	75.00	325

5   100 Pounds

	VF	UNC
1.1.1982. Black, olive and green. Elderly man at right. Back: The *Armada* at center. Printer: TDLR.	400	850

Allied Irish Banks Public Limited Company
Formerly Allied Irish Banks Ltd., later became First Trust Bank.

1987-88 Issue
#6-9 like #2-5 except for bank title and signatrue.

6   5 Pounds

	VF	UNC
1.1.1987; 1.1.1990. Blue and purple on multicolor underprint. Young woman at right. Back: Dunluce castle at center. Printer: TDLR.		
a. 1.1.1987.	30.00	75.00
b. 1.1.1990.	30.00	75.00

7   10 Pounds

	VF	UNC
1.6.1988; 1.1.1990; 18.5.1993. Brown and gray-green on multicolor underprint. Young man at right. Back: Wreck of the *Girona* at center. Printer: TDLR.		
a. 1.6.1988.	45.00	110
b. 1.1.1990.	45.00	110
c. 18.5.1993.	40.00	90.00

9   100 Pounds

	VF	UNC
1.12.1988. Black, olive and green. Elderly man at right. Back: The *Armada* at center. Printer: TDLR.	350	700

Bank of Ireland
Belfast

1967 ND Issue

56   1 Pound

	VF	UNC
ND (1967). Black on green and lilac underprint. Mercury at left, woman with harp at right. Signature W. E. Guthrie. Signature title as *Agent*. Back: Airplane, bank building and boat. 151x72mm.	20.00	70.00

57   5 Pounds

	VF	UNC
ND (1967-68). Brown-violet. Mercury at left, woman with harp at right. Signature title as *Agent*. Back: Airplane, bank building and boat.		
a. Signature W. E. Guthrie. (1967).	200	700
b. Signature H. H. M. Chestnutt. (1968).	200	700

58   10 Pounds

	VF	UNC
ND (1967). Brown and yellow. Mercury at left, woman with harp at right. Signature W. E. Guthrie. Signature title as *Agent*. Back: Airplane, bank building and boat.	400	1,100

#59 and 60 not assigned.

1971-74 ND Issues
#61-63 replacement notes: Serial # prefix *Z*.

61   1 Pound

	VF	UNC
ND (1972-77). Like # 56 but smaller size. Black on light green and lilac underprint. Mercury at left, woman with harp at right. Back: Airplane, bank building and boat. 134x66mm.		
a. Signature H. H. M. Chestnutt. (1972).	30.00	60.00
b. Signature A. S. J. O'Neill. (1977).	25.00	45.00

62   5 Pounds | VF | UNC
ND (1971-77). Blue on light green and lilac underprint. Mercury at left, woman with harp at right. Back: Airplane, bank building and boat. 146x78mm.
    a. Signature H. H. M. Chestnutt. (1971). | 90.00 | 160
    b. Signature A. S. J. O'Neill. (1977). | 75.00 | 150

63   10 Pounds | VF | UNC
ND (1971-77). Brown on light green and pale orange underprint. Mercury at left, woman with harp at right. Back: Airplane, bank building and boat.
    a. Signature H. H. M. Chestnutt. (1971). | 300 | 600
    b. Signature A. S. J. O'Neill. (1977). | 200 | 375
    s. Specimen. As a. | — | —

64   100 Pounds | VF | UNC
ND (1974-78). Red on multicolor underprint. Mercury at left, woman with harp at right. Back: Airplane, bank building and boat.
    a. Signature H. H. M. Chestnutt. (1974). | 950 | 1,400
    b. Signature A. S. J. O'Neill. (1978). | 600 | 950

1980s ND Issue

65   1 Pound | VF | UNC
ND. Black on light green and lilac underprint. Mercury at left, woman with harp at right. *STERLING* added below value. Signature A. S. J. O'Neill. Back: Airplane, bank building and boat. Watermark: Bank name repeated.
    a. Issued note. | 12.50 | 20.00
    r. Replacement note. | — | —

66   5 Pounds | VF | UNC
ND. Blue on light green and lilac underprint. Mercury at left, woman with harp at right. signs added in corners, *STERLING.* added below value. Back: Airplane, bank building and boat.
    a. Signature A. S. J. O'Neill. | 65.00 | 120
    b. Signature D. F. Harrison. | 45.00 | 80.00

67   10 Pounds | VF | UNC
ND (1984). Dark brown on light green and pale orange underprint. Mercury at left, woman with harp at right. *STERLING* added below value. Back: Airplane, bank building and boat.
    a. Signature A. S. J. O'Neill. | 120 | 190
    b. Signature D. F. Harrison. | 100 | 140

67A   20 Pounds | VF | UNC
ND. Dark olive-green on multicolor underprint. Mercury at left, woman with harp at right. *STERLING* added below value. Back: Airplane, bank building and boat.
    a. Signature A. S. J. O'Neill. | 180 | 275
    b. Signature D. F. Harrison. | 170 | 225

68   100 Pounds | VF | UNC
ND. Red on multicolor underprint. Mercury at left, woman with harp at right. sign at upper right and lower left corners. *Sterling* added at lower center. Back: Airplane, bank building and boat.
    a. Signature A. S. J. O'Neill. | 525 | 750
    b. Signature D. F. Harrison. | 400 | 650

1983 Commemorative Issue
#69, Bank of Ireland Bicentenary, 1783-1983

69   20 Pounds | VF | UNC
1983. Dark olive green on multicolor underprint. Like number 67A but commemorative text below bank title. Signature A. S. J. O'Neill. Back: Airplane, bank building and boat. | 000 | 1,200

1990-95 Issue

70   5 Pounds | VF | UNC
28.8.1990; 18.1.1992; 1.7.1994. Blue and purple on multicolor underprint. Bank seal (Hibernia seated) at left, six county shields at upper center. Signature D. F. Harrison. Back: Queen's University in Belfast. Watermark: Medusa head.
    a. 28.8.1990. | 22.50 | 40.00
    b. 18.1.1992. | 22.50 | 40.00
    c. 1.7.1994. | 22.50 | 40.00
    s. Specimen. | — | 150

71   10 Pounds | VF | UNC
14.5.1991; 24.5.1992. Purple and maroon on multicolor underprint. Bank seal (Hibernia seated) at left, six county shields at upper center. Signature D. F. Harrison. Back: Queen's University in Belfast. Watermark: Medusa head.
    a. 14.5.1991. | 35.00 | 65.00
    b. 24.5.1992. | 35.00 | 65.00
    s. Specimen. | — | 190

72 20 Pounds

VF UNC

9.5.1991; 1.5.1993. Green and brown on multicolor underprint. Bank seal (Hibernia seated) at left, six county shields at upper center. Signature D. F. Harrison. Back: Queen's University in Belfast. Watermark: Medusa head.

		VF	UNC
a. 9.5.1991.		80.00	130
b. 1.5.1993.		80.00	130
s. Specimen.		—	250

73 100 Pounds

VF UNC

28.8.1992. Red on multicolor underprint. Bank seal (Hibernia seated) at left, six county shields at upper center. Signature D. F. Harrison. Back: Queen's University in Belfast. Watermark: Medusa head.

		VF	UNC
a. Issued note.		275	600
s. Specimen.		—	400

Note: Specimens and 3-subject sheets were sold to collectors. Low numbers were also available in special folders.

1995; 1998 Issue

74 5 Pounds

VF UNC

1.7.1997; 4.8.1998; 5.9.2000. Blue and purple on multicolor underprint. Bank seal (Hibernia seated) at left, six county shields at upper center. Signature D. F. Harrison. Ascending size seial number at lower right. Back: Queen's University in Belfast. Watermark: Medusa head.

		VF	UNC
a. 1.7.1997.		15.00	30.00
b. 4.8.1998.		15.00	30.00
c. 5.9.2000.		15.00	30.00
s. Specimen. 1.3.2003.		—	—

75 10 Pounds

VF UNC

1.7.1995; 1.7.1998; 5.9.2000. Purple and maroon on multicolor underprint. Bank seal (Hibernia seated) at left, six county shields at upper center. Signature D. F. Harrison. Ascending size serial number at lower right. Back: Queen's University in Belfast. Watermark: Medusa head.

		VF	UNC
a. 1.7.1995.		27.50	45.00
b. 1.7.1998.		27.50	45.00
c. 5.9.2000.		27.50	45.00
s. Specimen. 1.7.1995.		—	400

76 20 Pounds

VF UNC

1.7.1995; 1.1.1999; 5.9.2000. Green and brown on multicolor underprint. Bank seal (Hibernia seated) at left, six county shields at upper center. Signature D. F. Harrison. Ascending size serial number at lower right. Back: Queen's University in Belfast. Watermark: Medusa head.

		VF	UNC
a. 1.7.1995.		55.00	85.00
b. 1.1.1999.		55.00	85.00
c. 5.9.2000.		55.00	85.00
s. Specimen. 5.9.2000.		—	—

77 50 Pounds

VF UNC

1.7.1995; 1.9.1999. Brown, olive and multicolor. Bank seal (Hibernia seated) at left, six county shields at upper center. Signature D. F. Harrison. Ascending size serial number at lower right. Back: Queen's University in Belfast. Watermark: Medusa head.

		VF	UNC
a. 1.7.1995.		140	190
b. 1.9.1999.		140	190
s. Specimen. 1.7.1995.		—	—

78 100 Pounds

VF UNC

1.7.1995. Red on multicolor underprint. Bank seal (Hibernia seated) at left, six county shields at upper center. Signature D. F. Harrison. Ascending size serial number at lower right. Back: Queen's University in Belfast. Watermark: Medusa head.

		VF	UNC
a. Issued note.		225	480
s. Specimen. 1.7.1995.		—	—

2003 Issue

79 5 Pounds

VF UNC

1.3.2003. Blue and violet on multicolor underprint. Back: Queen's University in Belfast.

		VF	UNC
a. 1.3.2003. Signature Sowden.		FV	25.00
s. As a. Specimen.		—	400

80 20 Pounds

VF UNC

1.1.2003; 1.5.2005; 22.2.2007. Multicolor. Signature D. McGowan.

		VF	UNC
a. 1.1.2003.		FV	65.00
b. 1.5.2005.		FV	65.00
c. 22.2.2007.		FV	65.00

81 50 Pounds

VF UNC

5.4.2004. Multicolor. Signature R. Keenan.   FV   160

82 100 Pounds   **VF UNC**
1.3.2005. Multicolor. Signature D. McGowan.   FV 275

2008 Issue

83 5 Pounds   **VF UNC**
20.4.2008. Bank seal (Hibernia seated) at left. Signature D. McGowan. Back: Old
Bushmills distillery.
  a. Issued note.   FV 20.00
  r. Replacement note. Serial # prefix ZZ.   — —

84 10 Pounds   **VF UNC**
20.4.2008. Signature S. Kirkpatrick. Back: Old Bushmills distillery.
  a. Issued note.   FV 45.00
  r. Replacement note. Serial # prefix: ZZ.   — —
85 20 Pounds   **VF UNC**
20.4.2008. Bank seal (Hibernia seated) at left. Signature S. Kirkpatrick. Back: Old
Bushmills distillery.
  a. Issued note.   FV 85.00
  r. Replacement note. Serial # prefix ZZ.   — —

2013 Issue

86 5 Pounds   **VF UNC**
1.1.2013. Blue on multicolor underprint. Bank seal (Hibernia seated) at left..
Signature Stephen Matchett. Back: Old Bushmills distillery.
  a. Issued note.   FV 15.00
  r. Replacement note. Serial # prefix ZZ.   20.00 70.00
87 10 Pounds   **VF UNC**
1.1.2013. Brown-red on multicolor underprint. Bank seal (Hibernia seated) at left.
Signature Stephen Matchett. Back: Old Bushmills distillery.
  a. Issued note.   FV 30.00
  r. Replacement note. Serial # prefix ZZ.   40.00 100
88 20 Pounds   **VF UNC**
1.1.2013. Green on multicolor underprint. Bank seal (Hibernia seated) at left.
Signature Stephen Matchett. Back: Old Bushmills distillery.
  a. Issued note.   FV 60.00
  r. Replacement note.   80.00 140
89 50 Pounds   **VF UNC**
1.1.2013. Violet on multicolor underprint. Bank seal (Hibernia seated) at left.   FV 150
Signatrue: Stephen Matchett Back: Old Bushmills distillery.

Belfast Banking Company Limited
Note: See also Ireland.

Belfast
1922-23 Issue

127 5 Pounds   **VF UNC**
1923-66. Black on red underprint. Arms at top center with payable text...*at our
Head Office, Belfast.*
  a. Black serial #. 3.1.1923; 3.5.1923; 7.9.1927.   350 850
  b. Red serial #. 8.3.1928-2.10.1942.   60.00 200
  c. Red serial #. 6.1.1966.   50.00 140
  p. Proof.   — 300

128 10 Pounds   **VF UNC**
1923-65. Black on green underprint. Arms at top center with payable text...*at our
Head Office, Belfast.*
  a. Black serial #. 3.1.1923.   625 —
  b. Green serial #. 9.1.1929-1.1.1943.   275 625
  c. Green serial #. 3.12.1963; 5.6.1965.   70.00 170
  p. Proof.   — 300
129 20 Pounds   **VF UNC**
1923-65. Black on purple underprint. Arms at top center with payable text...*at our
Head Office, Belfast.*
  a. Black serial #. 3.1.1923.   900 1,825
  b. Mauve serial #. 9.11.1939; 10.8.1940.   500 1,200
  c. Black serial #. 3.2.1943.   500 1,200
  d. Black serial #. 5.6.1965.   550 1,400
  p. Proof.   — 600

130 50 Pounds   **VF UNC**
1923-63. Black on orange underprint. Arms at top center with payable text...*at our
Head Office, Belfast.*
  a. Black serial #. 3.1.1923; 3.5.1923.   1,200 2,100
  b. Yellow serial #. 9.11.1939; 10.8.1940.   550 1,400
  c. Black serial #. 3.2.1943.   500 1,400
  d. Black serial #. 3.12.1963.   700 1,750
  p. Proof.   — 600

131   100 Pounds   **VF   UNC**

1923-68. Black on red underprint. Arms at top or upper center with payable text...
at our Head Office, Belfast.

a. 3.1.1923; 3.5.1923.	1,000	2,000
b. 9.11.1939; 3.2.1943.	700	1,700
c. 3.12.1963.	700	1,700
d. 8.5.1968.	700	1,700
p. Proof.	—	600

First Trust Bank

Formerly Allied Irish Banks PLC, which acquired the Trustee Savings Bank. Member AIB Group Northern Ireland PLC.

1994 Issue

132   10 Pounds   **VF   UNC**

10.1.1994; 1.3.1996. Dark brown and purple. Five shields at bottom center. Young man at right. Signature title: *GROUP MANAGING DIRECTOR.* Back: Sailing ship Girona at center. Watermark: Young woman. Printer: TDLR.

a. 10.1.1994.	50.00	80.00
b. 1.3.1996.	60.00	110
s1. As a. Specimen.	—	260
s2. As b. Specimen.	—	300

133   20 Pounds   **VF   UNC**

10.1.1994; 1.3.1996. Violet, dark brown and red-brown on multicolor underprint. Five shields at bottom center. Elderly woman at right. Signature title: *GROUP MANAGING DIRECTOR.* Back: Chimney at Lacada Point at center. Watermark: Young woman. Printer: TDLR.

a. 10.1.1994.	75.00	120
b. 1.3.1996.	85.00	140
s1. As a. Specimen.	—	450
s2. As b. Specimen.	—	500

134   50 Pounds   **VF   UNC**

10.1.1994. Black, dark olive-green and blue on multicolor underprint. Five shields at bottom center. Elderly man at right. Signature title: *GROUP MANAGING DIRECTOR.* Back: Cherubs holding Armada medallion at center. Watermark: Young woman. Printer: TDLR.

a. Issued note.	160	300
s. Specimen.	—	500

135   100 Pounds   **VF   UNC**

10.1.1994; 1.3.1996. Black and olive-brown on multicolor underprint. Five shields at bottom center. Elderly couple at right. Signature title:*GROUP MANAGING DIRECTOR.* Back: The *Armada* at center. Watermark: Young woman. Printer: TDLR.

a. 10.1.1994.	275	500
b. 1.3.1996.	275	600
s1. As a. Specimen.	—	500
s2. As b. Specimen.	—	700

1998 Issue

136   10 Pounds   **VF   UNC**

1.1.1998. Dark brown and purple. Five shields at bottom center. Young man at right. Signature title: *GROUP MANAGING DIRECTOR.* Scalloped gold seal over value at upper right. Back: Sailing ship Girona at center. Watermark: Young woman. Printer: TDLR.

a. Signature Dennis Licence.	25.00	50.00
b. Signature John Kilty.	FV	30.00
r. Replacement note. Serial # prefix: ZZ.	—	—
s. Specimen.	—	300

137   20 Pounds   **VF   UNC**

1998; 1.5.2007. Violet, dark brown and red-brown on multicolor underprint. Six shields at bottom center. Elderly woman at right. Signature title: *MANAGING DIRECTOR, FIRST TRUST BANK.* Windowed security thread and gold seal at upper right. Back: Chimney at Lacada Point at center. Watermark: Young woman. Printer: TDLR.

a. 1.1.1998.	55.00	90.00
b. 1.5.2007.	55.00	90.00
s1. Specimen. 1.1.1998. With gold seal and windowed security thread.	—	400
s2. Specimen. 1.3.1996. Without gold seal, with windowed security thread.	—	400

138   50 Pounds   **VF   UNC**

1998; 2009. Black, dark olive-green and blue on multicolor underprint. Five shields at bottom center. Elderly man at right. Signature title: *GROUP MANAGING DIRECTOR.* Windowed security thread and silver seal at upper right. Back: Cherubs holding Armada medallion at center. Watermark: Young woman. Printer: TDLR.

a. 1.1.1998. Signature Dennis Licence.	110	175
b. 1.6.2009. Signature Terry McDaid.	FV	150
s. Specimen.	—	440

139   100 Pounds

1998. Black and olive-brown on multicolor underprint. Five shields at bottom center. Elderly couple at right. Windowed security thread and gold seal at upper right. Signature Dennis Licence. Back: The *Armada* at center. Watermark: Young woman. Printer: TDLR. 163x90mm.

	VF	UNC
a. Signature title: *GROUP MANAGING DIRECTOR.*	250	350
b. Signature title: *MANAGING DIRECTOR FIRST TRUST BANK.*	250	350
s. Specimen.	—	475

Northern Bank Limited

1929 Regular Issue

178   1 Pound

1929-68. Black. Blue guilloche. Sailing ship, plow and man at grindstone at upper center.

	VF	UNC
a. Red serial #. 6.5.1929; 1.7.1929; 1.8.1929.	85.00	175
b. Black prefix letters and serial #. 1.1.1940.	45.00	70.00
c. 1.10.1968.	40.00	85.00
p. Proof. 1.9.1940.	—	350

181   10 Pounds

1930-68. Black on red underprint. Sailing ship, plow and man at grindstone at upper center.

	VF	UNC
a. Red serial #. 1.1.1930-1.1.1940.	125	350
b. Black serial #. 1.8.1940; 1.9.1940.	85.00	175
c. Red serial #. 1.1.1942-1.11.1943.	50.00	140
d. Imprint on back below central signature 1.10.1968.	50.00	240
p. Proof.	—	175
s. Specimen.	—	250

1968 Issue

184   5 Pounds

	VF	UNC
1.10.1968. Black on green underprint.	70.00	200

185   50 Pounds

1.10.1968. Black on dark blue underprint. Back: *NBLD* monogram.

	VF	UNC
a. Issued note.	500	160
s. Specimen.	—	1,200

186   100 Pounds

1.10.1968. Black on dark blue underprint. Back: *NBLD* monogram.

	VF	UNC
a. Issued note.	900	1,400
s. Specimen.	—	1,400

1970 Issue

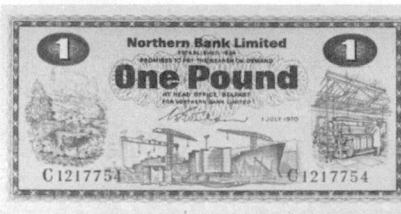

187   1 Pound

1970-82. Green on pink underprint. Cows at left, shipyard at bottom center, loom at right. Back: Stylized arms at center. Printer. BWC.

	VF	UNC
a. Signature Wilson.	27.50	50.00
b. Signature Gabbey.	25.00	50.00
c. Signature Ervin.	22.50	40.00

188   5 Pounds

1.7.1970-1.4.1982. Light blue. Cows at left, shipyard at bottom center, loom at right. Back: Stylized arms at center.

	VF	UNC
a. Signature Wilson.	90.00	200
b. Signature Gabbey.	90.00	180
c. Signature Newland.	60.00	100
d. Signature Ervin.	50.00	80.00
e. Signature Roberts.	60.00	100

189   10 Pounds

1970-88. Brown. Cows at left, shipyard at bottom center, loom at right. Back: Stylized arms at center.

	VF	UNC
a. Signature Wilson.	90.00	400
b. Signature Gabbey.	200	375
c. Signature Newland.	150	300
d. Signature Ervin.	120	225
e. Signature Roberts.	100	190
f. Signature Torrens.	90.00	150

190   20 Pounds

1.7.1970; 1.3.1981; 2.3.1987; 15.6.1988. Purple. Cows at left, shipyard at bottom center, loom at right. Back: Stylized arms at center.

	VF	UNC
a. Signature Wilson.	300	600
b. Signature Ervin.	225	400
c. Signature Roberts.	200	375
d. Signature Torrens.	130	200

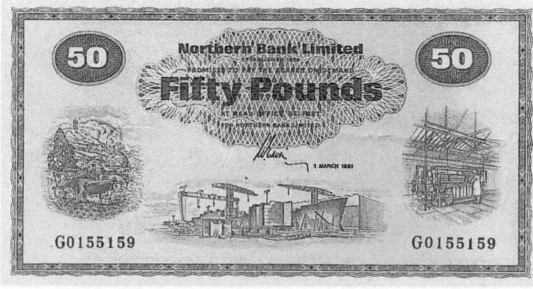

191   50 Pounds

1.7.1970; 1.3.1981. Orange. Cows at left, shipyard at bottom center, loom at right. Back: Stylized arms at center.

	VF	UNC
a. Signature Wilson.	450	850
b. Signature Newland.	450	700
c. Signature Ervin.	275	600

192   100 Pounds

1.7.1970; 1.10.1971; 1.1.1975; 1.7.1976; 1.1.1980. Red. Cows at left, shipyard at bottom center, loom at right. Back: Stylized arms at center.

	VF	UNC
a. Signature Wilson.	500	1,400
b. Signature Gabbey.	450	1,300
c. Signature Newland.	375	750
d. Signature Ervin.	375	800

1988-90 Issue

193   5 Pounds   **VF   UNC**

24.8.1988; 24.8.1989; 24.8.1990. Blue and multicolor. Station above trolley car at center, W. A. Traill at right. Back: Dish antenna at left, stylized N at center and computer. Printer: TDLR.

a. 24.8.1988; 24.8.1989.	22.50	50.00
b. 24.8.1990.	20.00	40.00
s. Specimen. 24.8.1988.	—	300

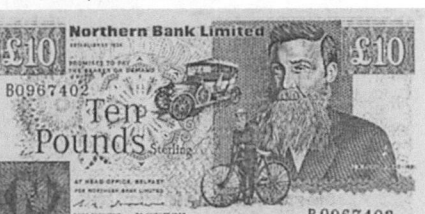

194   10 Pounds   **VF   UNC**

24.8.1988; 14.5.1991; 24.8.1993. Red and brown on multicolor underprint. Early automobile above bicyclist at center, J. B. Dunlop at right. Back: Dish antenna at left, stylized N at center and computer. Printer: TDLR.

a. 24.8.1988; 24.8.1990.	100	160
b. 14.5.1991; 24.8.1993.	80.00	160
c. 30.8.1996.	50.00	100
r. 24.8.1990. Replacement note.	40.00	140
s. Specimen. 24.8.1988.	—	400

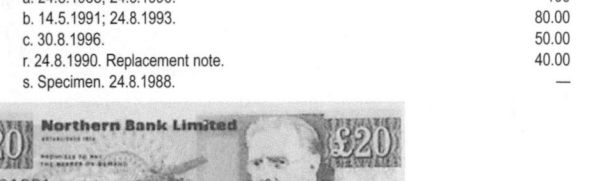

195   20 Pounds   **VF   UNC**

24.8.1988; 24.8.1989; 24.8.1990; 9.5.1991; 30.3.1992; 8.24.1993. Purple-brown, red and multicolor. Airplane at center, H. G. Ferguson at right, tractor at bottom right. Back: Dish antenna at left, stylized N at center and computer. Printer: TDLR.

a. 24.8.1988.	140	225
b. 24.8.1989; 24.8.1990; 9.5.1991; 30.3.1992; 8.24.1993.	110	200
c. 30.8.1996.	90.00	150
s. Specimen.	—	400

196   50 Pounds   **VF   UNC**

1.11.1990. Bluish green, black and multicolor. Tea dryer, centrifugal machine at center, Sir S. Davidson at right. Back: Dish antenna at left, stylized N at center and computer. Printer: TDLR.

a. Issued note.	180	275
s. Specimen. 1.11.1990.	—	450

197   100 Pounds   **VF   UNC**

1.11.1990. Lilac, black, blue and multicolor. Airplanes and ejection seat at center, Sir J. Martin at right. Back: Dish antenna at left, stylized N at center and computer. Printer: TDLR.

a. Issued note.	375	500
s. Specimen. 1.11.1990.	—	450

1997; 1999 Issue

198   10 Pounds   **VF   UNC**

24.2.1997. Dark brown and violet on multicolor underprint. J. B. Dunlop at right, bicycle at lower left. Back: City Hall in Belfast at center, buildings and architectural drawings in underprint. Watermark: J. B. Dunlop.

a. 24.2.1997. Signature Savage.	32.50	60.00
b. 8.10.1999. Signature Price.	27.50	60.00
s. Specimen. As a.	—	400

199   20 Pounds   **VF   UNC**

24.2.1997; 8.10.1999. Purple and dark brown on multicolor underprint. H. Ferguson at right, farm tractor at lower left. Back: City Hall in Belfast at center, buildings and architectural drawings in underprint. Watermark: H. Ferguson.

a. 24.2.1997. Signature Savage.	50.00	80.00
b. 8.10.1999. Signature Price.	55.00	80.00
s. As a or b. Specimen.	—	420

200   50 Pounds

8.10.1999. Olive brown on multicolor underprint. Sir Samuel Davidson at right. Back: City Hall in Belfast at center, buildings and architectural drawings in underprint.

		VF	UNC
a.	Issued note.	160	225
s.	Specimen.	—	500

201   100 Pounds

8.10.1999. Brown olive on multicolor underprint. Sir James Martin at right. Martin Baker ejection seat at left. Back: City Hall in Belfast at center, buildings and architectural drawings in underprint.

		VF	UNC
a.	Issued note.	250	400
s.	Specimen.	—	550

1999 Commemorative Issue

#202, 175 Years of Banking, 1824-1999

202   20 Pounds

1.9.1999. Purple and dark brown on multicolor underprint. H. Ferguson at right, farm tractor at lower left. Commemorative text and gold rectangle at upper left center. Back: City Hall in Belfast at center, buildings and architectural drawings in underprint. Watermark: H. Ferguson.

		VF	UNC
a.	Issued note.	65.00	100
s.	Specimen.	—	400

2000 Commemorative Issue

#203, Millennium and Y2K Commemoratives

 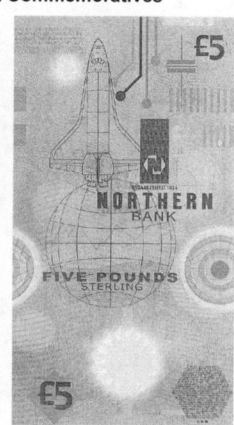

203   5 Pounds

1999; 2000. Polymer plastic. Blue, red and multicolor. Ovals, globe pattern. Back: Space shuttle, electronics.

		VF	UNC
a.	8.10.1999. Serial # prefix MM.	12.50	25.00
b.	1.1.2000. Serial # prefix Y2K.	17.50	32.50
s.	As a. Specimen.	—	600

#204 not assigned.

2004 Issue

205   10 Pounds

29.4.2004. Green and blue on multicolor underprint. J. B. Dunlop at right, bicycle at lower left. Signature Price. Back: Pediment of City Hall, Belfast at center, buildings and architectural drawings in underprint. Watermark: J. B. Dunlop.

VF	UNC
37.50	80.00

This note made up the "take" in the largest bank robbery in Irish history, and was quickly replaced with #206.

2005 Issue

206   10 Pounds

19.1.2005. Green and blue on multicolor underprint. J. B. Dunlop at right, bicycle at lower left. Signature Price. Back: Pediment of City Hall, Belfast at center, buildings and architectural drawings in underprint. Watermark: J. B. Dunlop.

		VF	UNC
a.	Issued note.	FV	30.00
s.	Specimen.	—	400

207   20 Pounds

19.1.2005; 6.11.2006. Blue and rose on multicolor underprint. H. Ferguson at right, farm tractor at lower left. Signature Price. Back: Pediment of City Hall, Belfast at center, buildings and architectural drawings in underprint. Watermark: H. Ferguson.

		VF	UNC
a.	19.1.2005.	FV	65.00
b.	6.11.2006. Signature D. Price.	FV	65.00
r.	Replacement note. Serial # prefix: YY.	—	—
s.	Specimen.	—	400

208 50 Pounds
19.1.2005. Viloet on multicolor underprint. Sir Samuel Davidson at right. Signature Price. Back: Pediment of City Hall, Belfast at center, buildings and architectural drawings in underprint. Watermark: Sir Samuel Davidson.

		VF	UNC
a. Issued note.		FV	160
s. Specimen.		—	400

209 100 Pounds
19.1.2005. Rose and blue on multicolor underprint. Sir James Martin at right. Signature Price. Back: Pediment of City Hall, Belfast at center, buildings and architectural drawings in underprint. Watermark: Sir James Martin.

		VF	UNC
a. Issued note.		FV	275
s. Specimen.		—	400

2008 Issue

210 10 Pounds
2008. Bank logo area redesigned to reflect Danske Bank takeover of Northern Bank.

		VF	UNC
a. 9.11.2008. Signature Gerry Mallon.		30.00	100
r. Replacement note. Serial # prefix YY.		30.00	100

211 20 Pounds
2009. Bank logo area redesigned to reflect Danske Bank takeover of Northern Bank.

		VF	UNC
a. 15.4.2009.		60.00	150
r. Replacement note. Serial # prefix YY.		60.00	150

2011 Issue Danske Bank

212 10 Pounds
25.1.2013. Bank title change from Northern Bank to Danske Bank. Other minor changes. Signature Gerry Mallon.

	VF	UNC
	FV	30.00

213 20 Pounds
2012. Bank title changed from Northern Bank to Danske Bank. Other minor changes.

		VF	UNC
a. 16.10.2012. Signature Gerry Mallon.		FV	60.00
r. Replacement note. Serial # prefix YY.		60.00	120

Provincial Bank of Ireland Limited
Belfast
1948; 1951 Issue

240 10 Pounds
10.1.1948. Green on red underprint and green and pink mesh.

		VF	UNC
a. Signature Clarke.		280	775
p. Proof. 1946; 1948.		—	300

1954 Issue

241 1 Pound
1.10.1954. Green. 148x84mm.

VF	UNC
280	525

1965 Issue

243 1 Pound
1.12.1965. Green. Cameo portrait of archaic woman at upper center. Back: Bank building at center. Printer: TDLR.

VF	UNC
300	500

244 5 Pounds
6.12.1965. Brown. Cameo Portrait of archaic woman at upper center. Back: Bank building at center. Printer: TDLR.

VF	UNC
200	300

1968 Issue

245 1 Pound
1.1.1968-1.1.1972. Green. Cameo portrait of archaic woman at upper center. Back: Bank building at center. Printer: TDLR. 150x71mm.

VF	UNC
60.00	110

246 5 Pounds
5.1.1968; 5.1.1970; 5.1.1972. Brown. Cameo portrait of archaic woman at upper center. Back: Bank building at center. Printer: TDLR. 139x84mm.

VF	UNC
50.00	90.00

1977; 1981 Issue

247 1 Pound   VF   UNC

1977; 1979. Green on multicolor underprint. Young girl at right. Back: Sailing ship *Girona* at center.

     a. Signature J. G. McClay. 1.1.1977.   25.00   45.00
     b. Signature F. H. Hollway. 1.1.1979.   25.00   37.50
     r. As b. Replacement note.   —   180

248 5 Pounds   VF   UNC

1977; 1979. Blue and purple on multicolor underprint. Young woman at right. Back: Dunluce Castle at center.

     a. Signature J. G. McClay. 1.1.1977.   52.50   125
     b. Signature F. H. Hollway. 1.1.1979.   42.50   100

249 10 Pounds   VF   UNC

1977, 1979. Brown and gray-green on multicolor underprint. Young man at right. Back: Wreck of the *Girona* at center.

     a. Signature J. G. McClay. 1.1.1977.   100   175
     b. Signature F. H. Hollway. 1.1.1979.   90.00   150

250 20 Pounds   VF   UNC

1.3.1981. Purple and green. Elderly woman at right. Back: Chimney at Lacada Point at center.   150   350

251 100 Pounds   VF   UNC

1.3.1981. Black, olive and green. Elderly man at right. Back: The *Armada* at center.   450   950

Ulster Bank Limited

Belfast

NOTE: Sheets of 3 specimen notes of Bank of Ireland 1989-90 issue were sold to collectors.

1966-70 Issue

321 1 Pound   VF   UNC

4.10.1966. Blue-black on multicolor underprint. Rural and urban views of Belfast at lower left and right. Port with bridge at lower center. Signature: Jno. J. A. Leitch. Back: Arms at center. Printer: BWC. 151x72mm.

     a. Issued note.   35.00   65.00
     s. Specimen.   —   400

322 5 Pounds   VF   UNC

4.10.1966. Brown on multicolor underprint. Rural and urban views of Belfast at lower left and right. Port with bridge at lower center. Signature: Jno. J. A. Leitch. Back: Arms at center. Printer: BWC. 140x85mm.

     a. Issued note.   90.00   350
     s. Specimen, punch hole cancelled.   —   600

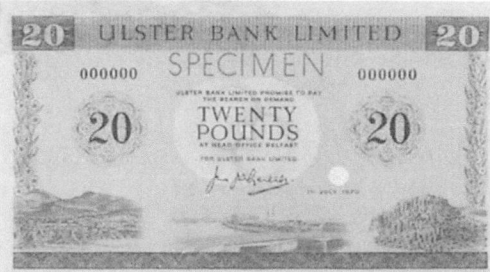

323 10 Pounds   VF   UNC

4.10.1966. Green on multicolor underprint. Rural and urban views of Belfast at lower left and right. Port with bridge at lower center. Signature: Jno. J. A. Leitch. Back: Arms at center. Printer: BWC. 151x93mm.

     a. Issued note.   120   400
     s. Specimen, punch hole cancelled.   —   750

324 20 Pounds   VF   UNC

1.7.1970. Lilac on multicolor underprint. Rural and urban views of Belfast at lower left and right. Port with bridge at lower center. Signature: Jno. J. A. Leitch. Back: Arms at center. Printer: BWC. 161x90mm.

     a. Issued note. Rare.   —   4,000
     s. Specimen. Punch hole cancelled.   —   900

1971-82 Issue

325   1 Pound

1971-76. Blue-black on multicolor underprint. Rural and urban views of Belfast at lower left and right. Port with bridge at lower center. Back: Arms at center. Watermark: Bank name repeated. Printer: BWC. 135x67mm.

	VF	UNC
a. Signature A. E. G. Brain. 15.2.1971.	22.50	60.00
b. Signature R. W. Hamilton. 1.3.1973; 1.3.1976.	12.50	30.00
s. As a. Specimen.	—	100

326   5 Pounds

1971-86. Brown on multicolor underprint. Rural and urban views of Belfast at lower left and right. Port with bridge at lower center. Back: Arms at center. Printer: BWC. 146x78mm.

	VF	UNC
a. Signature A. E. G. Brain. 15.2.1971.	125	300
b. Signature R. W. Hamilton. 1.3.1973; 1.3.1976.	45.00	130
c. Signature V. Chambers. 1.10.1982; 1.10.1983; 1.9.1986; 1.2.1988.	30.00	65.00

327   10 Pounds

1971-89. Green on multicolor underprint. Rural and urban views of Belfast at lower left and right. Port with bridge at lower center. Back: Arms at center. Printer: BWC. 151x86mm.

	VF	UNC
a. Signature A. E. G. Brain. 15.2.1971.	200	350
b. Signature R. W. Hamilton. 1.3.1973; 1.3.1976; 2.6.1980.	80.00	160
c. Signature V. Chambers. 1.10.1982; 1.10.1983; 1.2.1988.	75.00	140
d. Signature D. Went. 1.12.1989.	60.00	120

328   20 Pounds

1976-83. Violet on multicolor underprint. Rural and urban views of Belfast at lower left and right. Port with bridge at lower center. Back: Arms at center. Printer: BWC.

	VF	UNC
a. Signature A. E. G. Brain. 15.2.1971.	1,300	2,000
b. Signature R. W. Hamilton. 1.3.1976.	150	250
c. Signature V. Chambers. 1.10.1982; 1.10.1983; 1.2.1988.	140	200

329   50 Pounds

1.10.1982. Brown on multicolor underprint. Rural and urban views of Belfast at lower left and right. Port with bridge at lower center. Signature: V. Chambers. Back: Arms at center. Printer: BWC.

	VF	UNC
a. Issued note.	275	450
s. Specimen.	—	550

330   100 Pounds

1973; 1982. Red on multicolor underprint. Rural and urban views of Belfast at lower left and right. Port with bridge at lower center. Back: Arms at center. Printer: BWC.

	VF	UNC
a. Signature R. W. Hamilton. 1.3.1973; 1.3.1977.	400	700
b. Signature Chambers. 1.10.1982.	400	700
s. Specimen.	—	650

1989-90 Issue

Note: The Bank of Ireland sold to collectors matched serial # sets of 5-10-20 notes as well as 100 sets of replacement serial # prefix Z.

331   5 Pounds

1.12.1989; 1.1.1992; 4.1.1993. Smaller size notes. Brown on multicolor underprint. Rural and urban views of Belfast at lower left and right. Port with bridge at lower center. Signature: D. Went. Back: Arms at center. Printer: TDLR.

	VF	UNC
a. 1.12.1989	22.50	50.00
b. 1.1.1992; 4.1.1993.	20.00	40.00
s. Specimen. 4.1.1993	—	300

332   10 Pounds

1.12.1990. Smaller size notes. Green on multicolor underprint. Rural and urban views of Belfast at lower left and right. Port with bridge at lower center. Signature: D. Went. Back: Arms at center. Printer: TDLR.

	VF	UNC
a. Issued note.	35.00	85.00
s. Specimen.	—	375

333   20 Pounds

1.11.1990. Smaller size notes. Violet on multicolor underprint. Rural and urban views of Belfast at lower left and right. Port with bridge at lower center. Signature: D. Went. Back: Arms at center. Printer: TDLR.

	VF	UNC
a. Issued note.	75.00	160
s. Specimen.	—	450

334   100 Pounds

1.12.1990. Smaller size notes. Red on multicolor underprint. Rural and urban views of Belfast at lower left and right. Port with bridge at lower center. Signature: D. Went. Back: Arms at center. Printer: TDLR.

	VF	UNC
a. Issued note.	400	750
s. Specimen.	—	700

1996; 1998 Issue

335   5 Pounds

2.1.1998; 1.7.1998; 1.1.2001. Brown on multicolor underprint. Rural and urban views of Belfast at lower left and right. Port with bridge at lower center below signature at center right, date at left. Ascending size serial numbers. Signature Wilson. Back: Arms at center. Printer: TDLR.

	VF	UNC
a. 2.1.1998.	12.50	27.50
b. 1.7.1998.	12.50	27.50
c. 1.1.2001.	10.00	17.50

336   10 Pounds

1.1.1997' 1.7.1999. Blue and green on multicolor underprint. Rural and urban views of Belfast at lower left and right. Port with bridge at lower center below signature at center right, date at left. Ascending size serial numbers. Back: Arms at center. Printer: TDLR.

	VF	UNC
a. 1.1.1997. Signature Kells.	22.50	40.00
b. 1.7.1999. Signature Wilson.	20.00	32.50
s. Specimen. As a.	—	400

337 20 Pounds   **VF**   **UNC**

1.1.1996; 1.7.1999; 1.7.2002; 6.1.2004; 1.1.2007. Purple and violet on multicolor underprint. Rural and urban views of Belfast at lower left and right. Port with bridge at lower center below signature at center right, date at left. Ascending size serial numbers. Back: Arms at center. Printer: TDLR.

	VF	UNC
a. 1.1.1996. Signature Kells.	75.00	150
b. 1.7.1999. Signature Wilson.	47.50	80.00
c. 1.7.2002. Signature Wilson.	42.50	70.00
d. 6.1.2004. Signature McCarthy	FV	66.00
e. 1.1.2007.	FV	65.00

338 50 Pounds   **VF**   **UNC**

1.1.1997. Brown on multicolor underprint. Rural and urban views of Belfast at lower left and right. Port with bridge at lower center below signature at center right, date at left. Signature: V. Chambers. Ascending size serial numbers. Back: Arms at center. Printer: TDLR.   120   220

2006 Commemorative Issue

339 5 Pounds   **VF**   **UNC**

25.11.2006. Brown on multicolro underprint. Rural and urban views of Belfast at lower left and right. Back: George Best.   FV   20.00

2007 Issue

340 5 Pounds   **VF**   **UNC**

1.7.2007. Violet and brown on multicolor underprint. Rural and urban vews of Belfast at left and right. Port with bridge at lower center.   0.00   17.50

341 10 Pounds   **VF**   **UNC**

1.1.2007; 1.1.2008; 1.1.2012. Blue and green on multicolor underprint. Rural and urban views of Belfast at lower left and right.

	VF	UNC
a. 1.1.2007; 1.1.2008. Signature L. McCarthy.	FV	30.00
b. 1.1.2012. Signature J. Brown.	FV	30.00
r. Replacement note. Serial # prefix Z.	—	—

342 20 Pounds   **VF**   **UNC**

1.1.2007; 1.1.2010; 3.1.2012. Purple and violet on multicolor underprint. Rural and urban views of Belfast at lower left and right.

	VF	UNC
a. 1.1.2007; 1.1.2010. Signature L. McCarthy.	FV	60.00
b. 3.1.2012. Signature J. Brown.	FV	60.00

COLLECTOR SERIES

Bank of Ireland

Note: The Bank of Ireland sold to collectors matched serial # sets of 5-10-20 notes as well as 100 sets of replacement serial # prefix Z.

1978 ND Issue

CS1 ND (1978). 1, 5, 10, 100 Pounds   **Mkt. Value**

#61b-64b overprint: SPECIMEN and Maltese cross prefix serial #.   85.00

Provincial Bank of Ireland Limited

1978 Issue

CS2 1978 1, 5, 10 Pounds   **Mkt. Value**

#247a-249a dated 1.1.1977. Overprint: SPECIMEN and Maltese cross prefix serial #.   60.00

Bank of Ireland

Note: The Bank of Ireland sold to collectors matched serial # sets of 5-10-20 notes as well as 100 sets of replacement serial # prefix Z.

1995 ND Issue

CS3 ND (1995). 5, 10, 100 Pounds   **Mkt. Value**

#62b-64b overprint: SPECIMEN.   300

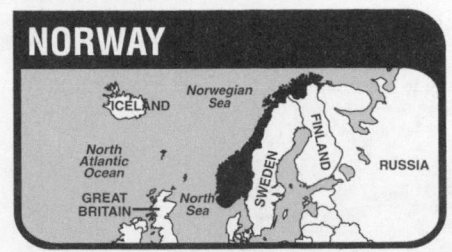

NORWAY

The Kingdom of Norway, a constitutional monarchy located in northwestern Europe, has an area of 150,000 sq. mi. (388,500 sq. km.) including the island territories of Spitzbergen (Svalbard) and Jan Mayen, and a population of 4.46 million. Capital: Oslo. The diversified economic base of Norway includes shipping, fishing, forestry, agriculture and manufacturing. Nonferrous metals, paper and paperboard, paper pulp, iron, steel and oil are exported. Two centuries of Viking raids into Europe tapered off following the adoption of Christianity by King Olav Tryggvason in 994. Conversion of the Norwegian kingdom occurred over the next several decades. In 1397, Norway was absorbed into a union with Denmark that lasted more than four centuries. In 1814, Norwegians resisted the cession of their country to Sweden and adopted a new constitution. Sweden then invaded Norway but agreed to let Norway keep its constitution in return for accepting the union under a Swedish king. Rising nationalism throughout the 19th century led to a 1905 referendum granting Norway independence. Although Norway remained neutral in World War I, it suffered heavy losses to its shipping. Norway proclaimed its neutrality at the outset of World War II, but was nonetheless occupied for five years by Nazi Germany (1940-45). In 1949, neutrality was abandoned and Norway became a member of NATO. Discovery of oil and gas in adjacent waters in the late 1960s boosted Norway's economic fortunes. The current focus is on containing spending on the extensive welfare system and planning for the time when petroleum reserves are depleted. In referenda held in 1972 and 1994, Norway rejected joining the EU.

RULERS:
Olav V, 1957-1991
Harald V, 1991-

MONETARY SYSTEM:
1 Speciedaler = 96 Skilling to 1816
1 Speciedaler = 120 Skilling, 1816-1873
1 Krone = 100 re, 1873-

KINGDOM

Norges Bank - Post WW II

1948-55 Issue

#30-33 Replacement notes: Serial # prefix *Z*.

30   5 Kroner

1955-63. Blue on gray and multicolor underprint. Portrait Fridtjof Nansen at left. Back: Fishing scene. Watermark: Value repeated.

	VF	UNC
a. Signature Brofoss - Thorp. 1955-56. Prefix A-D.	40.00	100
b. Signature Brofoss - Thorp. 1957. Prefix D.	40.00	100
c. Signature Brofoss - Thorp. 1957. Prefix E.	17.50	65.00
d. Signature Brofoss - Thorp. 1957. Prefix F.	40.00	100
e. Signature Brofoss - Ottesen. 1959. Prefix F.	17.50	65.00
f. Signature Brofoss - Ottesen. 1959. Prefix G.	40.00	105
g. Signature Brofoss - Ottesen. 1960-63. Prefix G-L.	17.50	65.00
s1. As a. Specimen. 1955. Overprint: *SPECIMEN.* Punch hole cancelled.	150	300
s2. Specimen. Perforated.	—	750

31   10 Kroner

1954-73. Yellow-brown on gray underprint. Portrait Christian Michelsen at left. Back: Mercury with ships. Watermark: Value repeated.

	VF	UNC
a. Signature Jahn - Thorp. 1954. Prefix A-D.	8.50	45.00
b1. Signature Brofoss - Thorp. 1954-55. Prefix D-G.	8.00	40.00
b2. Signature Brofoss - Thorp. 1955. Prefix H.	375	825
b3. Signature Brofoss - Thorp. 1956. Prefix H-I.	8.00	40.00
b4. Signature Brofoss - Thorp. 1957. Prefix I.	40.00	115
b5. Signature Brofoss - Thorp. 1957-58. Prefix J-M.	8.00	40.00

	VF	UNC
b6. Signature Brofoss - Thorp. 1958. Prefix N.	35.00	105
c. Signature Brofoss - Ottesen. 1959-65. Prefix N-E.	4.50	25.00
d. Signature Brofoss - Petersen. 1965-69. Prefix F-V.	3.00	12.50
e. Signature Brofoss - Odegaard. 1970. Prefix W-.	2.00	10.00
f. Signature Wold - Odegaard. 1971-73. Prefix Å-R.	1.75	7.50
p. Face or back proof. Uniface. Blue.	—	500
s. As a, d, f. Specimen. Punch hole cancelled.	150	750

#31 Replacement notes: Serial # prefix *X* (1966-72) *Z* (1954-73).

32   50 Kroner

1950-65. Dark green. Portrait Bjørnstjerne Björnson at upper left. Crowned arms at upper center. Back: Harvesting. Watermark: Bjørnstjerne Björnson.

	VF	UNC
a1. Signature Jahn - Thorp. 1950-52. Prefix A.	55.00	200
a2. Signature Jahn - Thorp. 1952. Prefix B.	120	550
a3. Signature Jan - Thorp. 1953-54. Prefix B.	55.00	200
b1. Signature Brofoss - Thorp. 1954. Prefix B.	150	650
b2. Signature Brofoss - Thorp. 1955-58. Prefix B; C.	50.00	170
b3. Signature Brofoss - Thorp. 1958. Prefix D.	95.00	350
c. Signature Brofoss - Ottesen. 1959-65. Prefix D-F.	35.00	130
s. As a. 1951. Specimen. Punch hole cancelled.	—	—

33   100 Kroner

1949-62. Red. Portrait Henrik Wergeland at upper left. Crowned arms at upper center. Back: Logging. Watermark: Henrik Wergeland.

	VF	UNC
a1. Signature Jahn - Thorp. 1949-52. Prefix A.	50.00	175
a2. Signature Jahn - Thorp. 1952. Prefix C.	1,250	—
a3. Signature Jahn - Thorp. 1953-54. Prefix C.	50.00	175
b. Signature Brofoss - Thorp. 1954-58. Prefix D-G.	50.00	175
c. Signature Brofoss - Ottesen. 1959-62. Prefix G-I.	40.00	140
s. As a. 1950. Specimen. Punch hole cancelled.	—	200

		VF	UNC
35	**1000 Kroner**		

1949-74. Red-brown. Portrait H. Ibsen at left. Crowned supported arms at upper center. Prefix A. Back: Old man and child. Watermark: Portrait H. Ibsen.

	VF	UNC
a. Signature Jahn - Thorp. 1949; 1951; 1953.	425	800
b. Signature Brofoss - Thorp. 1955; 1958.	290	600
c. Signature Brofoss - Ottesen. 1961; 1962.	225	500
d. Signature Brofoss - Petersen. 1965-70.	210	400
e. Signature Brofoss - Odegaard. 1971-74.	200	325
s. As a. Specimen. Punch hole cancelled.	600	850

Replacement note: Serial # prefix G.

1962-78 Issue

		VF	UNC
36	**10 Kroner**		

1972-84. Dark blue on multicolor underprint. Fridtjof Nansen at left, arms at center. Back: Fisherman and cargo ship at right. Watermark: Value 10 repeated.

	VF	UNC
a. 1972. Replacement note. Prefix Q.	50.00	100
b. Signature Wold and Odegaard. 1973-76.	4.00	11.00
c. Signature Wold and Sagård. 1977-79; 1981-84.	2.00	6.50
s. As a. Specimen.	500	900

#37-40 replacement notes: Serial # prefix X or Z.

		VF	UNC
34	**500 Kroner**		

1948-76. Dark green. Portrait Niels Henrik Abel at upper left. Crowned supported arms at upper center. Prefix A. Back: Factory workers. Watermark: Niels Henrik Abel.

	VF	UNC
a. Signature Jahn - Thorp. 1948; 1951.	350	1,000
b1. Signature Brofoss - Thorp. 1954; 1956.	350	1,000
b2. Signature Brofoss - Thorp. 1958.	200	675
c. Signature Brofoss - Ottesen. 1960-64.	160	550
d. Signature Brofoss - Petersen. 1966-69.	140	400
e. Signature Brofoss - Ödegaard. 1970.	130	325
f. Signature Wold - Odegaard. 1971-76.	120	275
s. As a. Specimen. 1948. Punch hole cancelled.	600	850

Replacement note: Serial # prefix G.

		VF	UNC
37	**50 Kroner**		

1966-83. Green on multicolor underprint. Bjørnstjerne Björnson at left, arms at left center. Back: Old church at right. Watermark: Bjørnstjerne Björnson.

	VF	UNC
a. Signature Brofoss and Petersen. 1966-67; 1969. Prefix A-C.	25.00	80.00
b. Signature Wold and Odegaard. 1971-73. Prefix C-E.	17.50	60.00
c. As b. with security thread. 1974-75. Prefix F-G.	15.00	40.00
d. Signature Wold and Sagård. 1976-83. Prefix H-R.	12.50	35.00
s. As a. Specimen.	450	750

38 100 Kroner

1962-77. Red-violet on multicolor underprint. H. Wergeland at left, arms at left center. Back: Establishment of Constitution in 1814 at right. Watermark: H. Wergeland.

	VF	UNC
a. Signature Brofoss and Óttesen. 1962-65. Prefix A-D.	20.00	80.00
b. Signature Brofoss and Petersen. 1965-69. Prefix D-L.	17.50	80.00
c. Signature Brofoss and Petersen. 1969. Prefix M.	90.00	350
d. Signature Brofoss and degaard. 1970. Prefix M-P.	17.50	55.00
e. Signature Wold and degaard. 1971-72. Prefix P-T.	17.50	50.00
f. Signature Wold and degaard. 1972. Prefix U.	45.00	180
g. Signature Wold and degaard. 1973-76. Prefix U-C.	17.50	45.00
h. Signature Wold and Sagård. 1977. Prefix D-K.	FV	40.00
s. As a. Specimen.	450	800

39 500 Kroner

1978-85. Green on brown underprint. Niels Henrik Abel at left, arms at left center. Back: University of Oslo at right. Watermark: Niels Henrik Abel.

	VF	UNC
a. Signature Wold and Sagård. 1978; 1982.	100	200
b. Signature Skånland and Sagård. 1985.	100	200
s. As a. Specimen.	1,000	1,900

40 1000 Kroner

1975-87. Brown and violet on multicolor underprint. Henrik Ibsen at left, arms at left center. Back: Scenery. Watermark: Henrik Ibsen.

	VF	UNC
a. Signature Wold and Odegaard. 1975. Prefix A.	200	275
b. Signature Wold and Sagård. 1978; 1980; 1982-85. Prefix A-C.	160	250
c. Signature Skånland and Sagård. 1985-87. Prefix C-E.	140	225
s. As a. Specimen.	800	1,400

1977 Issue

41 100 Kroner

1977-82. . Purple on pink and multicolor underprint. Cahilla Collett at left, date at top left center. Signature Wold and Sagård. Back. Filigree design.

	VF	UNC
a. Brown serial #. 1977.	17.50	55.00
b. Black serial #. 1979; 1980.	17.50	45.00
c. 1981; 1982.	17.50	45.00
s. As a. Specimen.	800	1,400

1983-91 Issue

42 50 Kroner

1984-95. Green on multicolor underprint. Aasmund Olavsson Vinje at left. Back: Stone carving with soldier slaying dragon. Watermark: 50 repeated within diagonal bars.

	VF	UNC
a. Signature Wold and Sagård. 1984.	15.00	30.00
b. Signature Skånland and Sagård. 1985.	9.00	22.50
c. Signature Skånland and Sagård. 1986.	12.00	25.00
d. Signature Skånland and Sagård. 1987.	9.00	22.50
e. Signature Skånland and Johansen. 1989-90; 1993.	9.00	17.50
f. Signature Moland and Johansen. 1995.	FV	15.00
s. As a. Specimen.	800	1,400

Note: #42d was also issued in a special "Last Edition" folder w/50 re coin dated 1996. (8400 pieces), Value $50.00.

43   100 Kroner   VF   UNC

1983-94. Red-violet on pink and multicolor underprint. Similar to number 41 but
smaller print area, and date at lower right. Back: Filigree design. Watermark:
Cahilla Collett.

a. Signature Wold and Sagard. 1983.		17.50	40.00
b. As a. but large date. 1904.		17.50	40.00
c. Signature Skånland and Sagård. 1985-87.		17.50	35.00
d. Signature Skånland and Johansen. 1988-93.		15.00	27.50
e. Signature Moland and Johansen. 1994.		FV	27.50

Note: #43e was also issued in a special "Last Edition" folder w/1 Krone coin dated 1996. (6000
issued). Value $50.

47   100 Kroner   VF   UNC

1995; 1997-99. Deep brown-violet and red-violet on multicolor underprint. Kirsten
Flagstad at right. Signature: K. Storvik and S. Johansen. Back: Theatre layout.
Watermark: Kirsten Flagstad repeated vertically.

a. Signature Storvik and Johansen. 1995; 1997; 1998. 10-digit serial # upper left and lower right on face. Date on back.		FV	30.00
b. Signature Gjedrem and Johansen. 1999. 10-digit serial # upper left, 8-digit # lower right on face, where last four digits are the date.		FV	27.50

Issued on the 100th birthday of famed singer Kirsten Flagstad.

44   500 Kroner   VF   UNC

1991; 1994; 1996; 1997. Blue-violet on multicolor underprint. Edvard Grieg at left.
Back: Floral mosaic at center. Watermark: Grieg repeated vertically.

a. Signature Skånland and Johansen. 1991.		FV	140
b. Signature Moland and Johansen. 1994.		FV	120
c. Signature Storvik and Johansen. 1996; 1997.		FV	120

48   200 Kroner   VF   UNC

1994; 1998; 1999; 2000. Blue-black and dark blue on multicolor underprint. Kristian Birkeland at right. Back: Map of the North Pole; North America and Northern
Europe at left center. Watermark: Kristian Birkeland repeated vertically.

a. Signature Moland and Johansen. 1994.		FV	50.00
b. Signature Storvik and Johansen. 1998.		FV	45.00
c. Signature Gjedrem and Johansen. 1999; 2000.		FV	42.50

1999-2002 Issue

45   1000 Kroner   VF   UNC

1989; 1990. Purple and dark blue on multicolor underprint. C. M. Falsen at left.
Back: 1668 royal seal.

a. Signature Skånland and Johansen. 1989; 1990.		FV	275
b. Signature Storvik and Johansen. 1998.		FV	225

49   100 Kroner   VF   UNC

2003-04; 2006-07. Deep brown-violet and red-violet on multicolor underprint.
Kirsten Flagstad at right. Wide holographic strip at right. Signature: Gjdren and
Eklund. Back: Theatre layout. Watermark: Kirsten Flagstad repeated vertically.

a. 2003.		FV	27.50
b. 2004.		FV	27.50
c. 2006.		FV	27.50
d. 2007.		FV	27.50

1994-96 Issue

46   50 Kroner   VF   UNC

1996-. Dark green on pale green and multicolor underprint. P. C. Asbjörnsen at
right. Back: Water lilies and dragonfly. Watermark: P. C. Asbjörnsen repeated
vertically.

a. Signature Storvik and Johansen. 1996; 1998.		FV	17.50
b. Signature Gjedrem and Johansen. 1999; 2000; 2003.		FV	15.00
c. Signature Gjedrem and Eklund. 2003; 2005.		FV	15.00
d. Signature Olsen and Eklund. 2011.		FV	15.00

50 200 Kroner

2002-. Blue-black and dark blue on multicolor underprint. Kristian Birkeland at right, wide holographic strip at right. Back: Map of the North Pole; North America and Northern Europe at left center. Watermark: Birkeland repeated vertically.

	VF	UNC
a. 2002. Signature Gjedrem and Johansen.	FV	45.00
b. 2003. Signature Gjedrem and Eklund.	FV	42.50
c. 2004.	FV	42.50
d. 2006.	FV	42.50
e. 2009.	FV	42.50

51 500 Kroner

1999-. Brown on tan and multicolor underprint. Sigrid Undste and wide holographic strip at right. Signature: Gjedrem and Johansen. Back: Wreath of wheat and roses.

	VF	UNC
a. 1999.	FV	125
b. 2000.	FV	125
c. 2002.	FV	125
d. 2005.	FV	125

52 1000 Kroner

2001; 2004. Lilac, blue, yellow and multicolor. Edvard Munch at right, wide holographic strip at right edge, part of his painting *Melancholy* at left center. Signature: Gjedrem and Johansen. Back: Munch's great work *The Sun*.

	VF	UNC
a. 2001.	FV	275
b. 2004.	FV	275

Listings for Nouméa, see New Caledonia

OMAN

The Sultanate of Oman (formerly Muscat and Oman), an independent monarchy located in the southeastern part of the Arabian Peninsula, has an area of 82,030 sq. mi. (212,457 sq. km.) and a population of 2.72 million. Capital: Muscat. The economy is based on agriculture, herding and petroleum. Petroleum products, dates, fish and hides are exported. The inhabitants of the area of Oman have long prospered on Indian Ocean trade. In the late 18th century, a newly established sultanate in Muscat signed the first in a series of friendship treaties with Britain. Over time, Oman's dependence on British political and military advisors increased, but it never became a British colony. In 1970, Qaboos bin Said al-Said overthrew the restrictive rule of his father; he has ruled as sultan ever since. His extensive modernization program has opened the country to the outside world while preserving the longstanding close ties with the UK. Oman's moderate, independent foreign policy has sought to maintain good relations with all Middle Eastern countries.

RULERS:
Sa'id bin Taimur, AH1351-1390/1932-1970 AD
Qaboos bin Sa'id, AH1390-1419/1970-1999AD

MONETARY SYSTEM:
1 Rial Omani = 1000 Baiza (Baisa)
1 Rial Saidi = 1000 Baiza (Baisa)

MUSCAT AND OMAN
Sultanate of Muscat and Oman
1970 ND Issue

1 100 Baiza

ND (1970). Brown on blue-green and multicolor underprint. Arms at right. Watermark: Arms.

	VF	UNC
a. Issued note.	15.00	40.00
s. Specimen.	—	150
ct. Color trial in violet.	—	200

2 1/4 Rial Saidi

ND (1970). Blue and brown on multicolor underprint. Arms at right. Back: Jalali Fortress. Watermark: Arms.

	VF	UNC
a. Issued note.	18.00	40.00
s. Specimen.	—	150
ct. Color trial in green.	—	200

3 1/2 Rial Saidi

ND (1970). Green and purple on multicolor underprint. Arms at right. Back: Sumail Fortress. Watermark: Arms.

	VF	UNC
a. Issued note.	30.00	85.00
s. Specimen.	—	180
ct. Color trial in purple.	—	250

OMAN
Oman Currency Board
1973 ND Issue

7   100 Baiza

VF   UNC

ND (1973). Brown on blue-green and multicolor underprint. Arms at right.
Watermark: Arms.

a. Issued note.	7.50	20.00
s. Specimen.	—	125
ct. Color trial. Violet-brown on multicolor underprint.	—	150

4   1 Rial Saidi

VF   UNC

ND (1970). Red and olive-green on multicolor underprint. Arms at right. Back:
Sohar Fort. Watermark: Arms.

a. Issued note.	45.00	120
s. Specimen.	—	225
ct. Color trial in blue.	—	300

8   1/4 Rial Omani

VF   UNC

ND (1973). Blue and brown on multicolor underprint. Arms at right. Back: Jalali
Fortress. Watermark: Arms.

a. Issued note.	10.00	30.00
s. Specimen.	—	125
ct. Color trial. Green on multicolor underprint.	—	150

5   5 Rials Saidi

VF   UNC

ND (1970). Purple and blue on multicolor underprint. Arms at right. Back: Nizwa
Fort. Watermark: Arms.

a. Issued note.	125	350
s. Specimen.	—	400
ct. Color trial in red.	—	500

9   1/2 Rial Omani

VF   UNC

ND (1973). Green and purple on multicolor underprint. Arms at right. Back: Sumail
Fortress. Watermark: Arms.

a. Issued note.	20.00	50.00
s. Specimen.	—	150
ct. Color trial. Black and purple on multicolor underprint.	—	200

6   10 Rials Saidi

VF   UNC

ND (1970). Dark brown and blue on multicolor underprint. Arms at right. Back:
Mirani Fort. Watermark: Arms.

a. Issued note.	225	650
s. Specimen.	—	700
ct. Color trial in blue-green.	—	800

10   1 Rial Omani

VF   UNC

ND (1973). Red and olive-green on multicolor underprint. Arms at right. Back:
Sohar Fort. Watermark: Arms.

a. Issued note.	35.00	95.00
s. Specimen.	—	200
ct. Color trial. Blue on multicolor underprint.	—	250

11 5 Rials Omani VF UNC
ND (1973). Purple and blue on multicolor underprint. Arms at right. Back: Nizwa Fort. Watermark: Arms.

    a. Issued note. 100 285
    s. Specimen. — 350
    ct. Color trial. Red and blue on multicolor underprint. — 425

12 10 Rials Omani VF UNC
ND (1973). Dark brown and blue on multicolor underprint. Arms at right. Back: Mirani Fort. Watermark: Arms.

    a. Issued note. 200 550
    s. Specimen. — 600
    ct. Color trial in blue-green. — 700

Central Bank of Oman
1977; 1985 ND Issue

13 100 Baisa VF UNC
ND (1977). Light brown on multicolor underprint. Arms at right. Back: Port of Qaboos.

    a. Issued note. 3.00 8.00
    s. Specimen. — 120

14 200 Baisa VF UNC
ND (1985). Purple on multicolor underprint. Arms at right. Back: Rustaq Fortress. Watermark: Arms. 4.50 10.00

15 1/4 Rial VF UNC
ND (1977). Blue and brown on multicolor underprint. Arms at right. Back: Jalali Fortress. Watermark: Arms.

    a. Issued note. 7.50 18.00
    s. Specimen. — 120

16 1/2 Rial VF UNC
ND (1977). Green and purple on multicolor underprint. Arms at right. Back: Sumail fortress. Watermark: Arms.

    a. Issued note. 15.00 35.00
    s. Specimen. — 135

17 1 Rial VF UNC
ND (1977). Red and brown on multicolor underprint. Arms at right. Back: Rustaq Fortress. Watermark: Arms.

    a. Issued note. 25.00 55.00
    s. Specimen. — 150

18 5 Rials

VF UNC

ND (1977). Lilac and blue on multicolor underprint. Arms at right. Back: Jalali Fortress. Watermark: Arms.

		VF	UNC
a. Issued note.		60.00	125
s. Specimen.		—	225

19 10 Rials

VF UNC

ND (1977). Brown and blue on multicolor underprint. Arms at right. Back: Sumail Fortress. Watermark: Arms.

	VF	UNC
a. Issued note.	100	200
s. Specimen.	—	275

20 20 Rials

VF UNC

ND (1977). Gray-blue and orange on multicolor underprint. Sultan Qaboos bin Sa'id at right. Back: Central Bank at left center. Watermark: Arms.

	VF	UNC
a. Issued note.	190	400
s. Specimen.	—	350

21 50 Rials

VF UNC

ND. Olive-brown, blue and dark brown on multicolor underprint. Sultan at right. Back: Jabreen Fort at left center.

	VF	UNC
a. Issued note.	400	850
s. Specimen.	—	700

1985-90 Issue

22 100 Baisa

VF UNC

AH1408-1414/1987-1994AD. UV: center design elements fluoresce yellow. Light brown on multicolor underprint. Sultan Qaboos bin Sa'id at right. Back: Port of Qaboos. Watermark: Sultan Qaboos bin Sa'id.

	VF	UNC
a. 1987//AH1408.	3.50	8.00
b. 1989/AH1409.	3.00	7.00
c. 1992/AH1413.	15.00	35.00
d. 1994/AH1414.	2.50	6.00

23 200 Baisa

VF UNC

AH1407-1414/1987-1994AD. Purple on multicolor underprint. Sultan Qaboos bin Sa'id at right. Back: Rustaq Fort. Watermark: Sultan Qaboos bin Sa'id.

	VF	UNC
a. 1987/AH1407.	6.00	14.00
b. 1993/AH1413.	5.00	11.00
c. 1994/AH1414.	4.00	9.00

24 1/4 Rial

VF UNC

1989/AH1409. Blue, brown and red on multicolor underprint. Sultan Qaboos bin Sa'id at right. Back: Modern fishing industry. Watermark: Sultan Qaboos bin Sa'id. 7.50 18.00

25   1/2 Rial

	VF	UNC
1987/AH1408. Green on multicolor underprint. Sultan Qaboos bin Sa'id at right. Back: Aerial view of Sultan Qaboos University. Watermark: Sultan Qaboos bin Sa'id. | 10.00 | 22.50 |

26   1 Rial

	VF	UNC
AH1407-1414/1987-1994AD. Red, black and olive-brown on multicolor underprint. Sultan Qaboos bin Sa'id at right. Back: Sohar Fort at left. Watermark: Sultan Qaboos bin Sa'id. | | |
a. 1987/AH1407. | 16.00 | 37.50 |
b. 1989/AH1409. | 15.00 | 35.00 |
c. 1994/AH1414. | 14.00 | 30.00 |

27   5 Rials

	VF	UNC
1990/AH1411. Dark rose, brown-violet and multicolor underprint. Sultan Qaboos bin Sa'id at right. Back: Fort Nizwa. Watermark: Sultan Qaboos bin Sa'id. | 55.00 | 120 |

28   10 Rials

	VF	UNC
AH1408/1987AD; AH1413/1993AD. Dark brown, red-brown and blue on multicolor underprint. Sultan Qaboos bin Sa'id at right. Back: Fort Mirani at left center. Watermark: Sultan Qaboos bin Sa'id. | | |
a. 1987/AH1408. | 90.00 | 190 |
b. 1993/AH1413. | 85.00 | 180 |

29   20 Rials

	VF	UNC
AH1407/1987AD; AH1414/1994AD. Brown, dark olive-brown and blue-gray on multicolor underprint. Sultan Qaboos bin Sa'id at right. Back: Central Bank at left center. Watermark: Sultan Qaboos bin Sa'id. | | |
a. 1987/AH1408. | 140 | 300 |
b. 1994/AH1414. | 135 | 285 |

30   50 Rials

	VF	UNC
AH1405/1985AD; AH1413/1992AD. Olive-brown, blue and dark brown on multicolor underprint. Sultan Qaboos bin Sa'id at right. Back: Jabreen Fort at left center, *Jabreen Fort* added at lower right. Watermark: Sultan Qaboos bin Sa'id. | | |
a. 1985/AH1405. | 450 | 1,000 |
b. 1992/AH1413. | 300 | 650 |
s. As a. Specimen. | — | 750 |

Note: For note with similar design but w/o date, see #21.

1995 Issue

31   100 Baisa

	VF	UNC
1995/AH1416. Deep olive-green, dark green-blue and purple on multicolor underprint. Sultan Qaboos bin Sa'id at right, Faslajs irrigation system at center, arms at upper left. Back: Verreaux's eagle and white oryx at center. Watermark: Sultan Qaboos bin Sa'id. 122x64mm. | FV | 1.00 |

32   200 Baisa   VF   UNC
1995/AH1416. Black, deep blue and green on multicolor underprint. Sultan   FV   4.00
Qaboos bin Sa'id at right, Seeb & Salalah Airports at left center, arms at upper left.
Back: Raysut Port and Marine Science & Fisheries Center at lower left, aerial view
of Sultan Qaboos port at center. Watermark: Sultan Qaboos bin Sa'id. 128x64mm.

33   1/2 Rial   VF   UNC
1995/AH1416. Dark brown and gray on multicolor underprint. Sultan Qaboos bin   FV   3.00
Sa'id at right, Bahla Castle at center, arms at upper left. Back: Nakhl Fort and
Al-Hazm castle at lower left, Nakhl Fort at center. Watermark: Sultan Qaboos bin
Sa'id. 135x64mm.

34   1 Rial   VF   UNC
1995/AH1416. Deep purple, purple and blue-green on multicolor underprint.   FV   10.00
Sultan Qaboos bin Sa'id at right, Sultan Qaboos Sports Complex, Burj al-Sahwa,
road overpass at center, arms at upper left. Back: Omani Khanjar, traditional silver
bracelets and ornaments with shipbuilding in background underprint. Watermark:
Sultan Qaboos bin Sa'id. 145x76mm.

35   5 Rials   VF   UNC
1995/AH1416. Red on pale blue and multicolor underprint. Sultan Qaboos bin
Sa'id at right, Sultan Qaboos University building with clock tower at center, arms
at upper left. Back: Nizwa city view at left center. Watermark: Sultan Qaboos bin
Sa'id. 152x76mm.
a. Without reflective pattern of Khanjars (State Emblem) on back.   30.00   65.00
b. With reflective pattern of Khanjars on back.   22.00   52.00

36   10 Rials   VF   UNC
1995/AH1416. Dark brown on pale blue and multicolor underprint. Sultan Qaboos   35.00   80.00
bin Sa'id at right, al-Nahdha in Salalah Tower, Jabreen coconut palm and frankincense tree at center, arms at upper left. Back: Mutrah Fort and Corniche at left
center. Watermark: Sultan Qaboos bin Sa'id. 159x27mm.

37   20 Rials   VF   UNC
1995/AH1416. Dark blue-green and olive-green on multicolor underprint. Sultan   70.00   150
Qaboos bin Sa'id at right, Central Bank of Oman building at center, minaret at
right. Back: Muscat Security Market at left, aerial view of Rysayl Industrial Area at
center, Oman Chamber of Commerce building at upper right. Watermark: Sultan
Qaboos bin Sa'id. 166x77mm.

38   50 Rials   VF   UNC
1995/AH1416. Purple and violet on multicolor underprint. Sultan Qaboos bin   FV   350
Sa'id at right, Ministry of Finance and Economy building at center, Mirani Fort at
right, arms at upper left. Back: Cabinet building at left, Ministry of Commerce and
Industry building at center right. Watermark: Sultan Qaboos bin Sa'id. 174x77mm.

2000 Issue

39　5 Rials　VF　UNC

2000/AH1420. Red on multicolor underprint. Sultan Qaboos bin Sa'id at right, Sultan Qaboos University building with clock tower at center, arms at upper left. Holographic strip at right. Back: Nizwa city view at left center. Watermark: Sultan Qaboos bin Sa'id. 152x76mm.　FV　27.50

40　10 Rials　VF　UNC

2000/1420AH. Brown on multicolor underprint. Sultan Qaboos bin Sa'id at right, al-Nahdha in Salalah Tower, Jabreen coconut palm and frankincense tree at center, arms at upper left. Holographic strip at right. Back: Mutrah Fort and Corniche at left center. Watermark: Sultan Qaboos bin Sa'id. 159x77mm.　FV　50.00

41　20 Rials　VF　UNC

2000/1420AH. Green on multicolor underprint. Sultan Qaboos bin Sa'id at right, Central Bank of Oman building at center, minaret at right. Holographic strip at right. Back: Muscat Security Market at left, aerial view of Rysayl Industrial Area at center, Oman Chamber of Commerce building at upper right. Watermark: Sultan Qaboos bin Sa'id. 166x77mm.　FV　100

42　50 Rials　VF　UNC

2000/1420AH. Purple on multicolor underprint. Sultan Qaboos bin Sa'id at right, Ministry of Finance and Economy building at center, Mirani Fort at right, arms at upper left. Holographic strip at right. Back: Cabinet building at left, Ministry of Commerce and Industry building at center right. Watermark: Sultan Qaboos bin Sa'id. 174x77mm.　FV　225

2005 Commemorative Issue

43　1 Rial　VF　UNC

2005/AH1426. Red. Sultan Qaboos at right Back: Sailing ship at left. 145x76mm.
　　a. Issued note.　FV　10.00
　　s. Specimen　—　75.00

2010 Commemorative Issue

44　5 Rials　VF　UNC

AH 1431/2010. Red on multicolor underprint. Sultan Qaboos bin Said at center, Sultan Qaboos University building with clock tower at center. Back: Nizwa buildings, 40th National day logo. Watermark: Sultan Qaboos and 5. Printer: G&D. 153x76mm.　FV　30.00

45　10 Rials　VF　UNC

2010. Brown on multicolor underprint. Salalah Tower, palm trees, Sultan Qaboos bin Said. Back: Muttrah Fort and town with harbor, 40th National Day log. Watermark: Suntan and 10. Printer: G&D. 160x76mm.
　　a. Issued note.　FV　60.00
　　b. Replacement note. Serial # prefix: /99.　FV　90.00

46   20 Rials

AH1431/2010. Blue, olive and multicolor. Sultan Qaboos at right center, mosque at lower left. Back: Palace. Watermark: Sultan and 20. Printer: G&D. 166x77mm.

	VF	UNC
	FV	130

47   50 Rials

AH1431/2010. Purple on multicolor underprint. Ministry of Finance and Economy building, Sultan Qaboos bin Said. Mirani fort. Back: Cabinet building, Ministry of Commerce and Industry building. 40th National Day logo. Watermark: Sultan and 50. Printer: G&D. 174x76mm.

	VF	UNC
	FV	240

48   1 Rial

AH1437/2015G. Purple. Sultan Qaboos bin Said, coat of arms with crossed swords and khanjar (dagger), Al Alam Palace in Muscat, khanjar as registration device. Back: Flowers, khanjar, desert white butterflies (Pontia glauconome), 45th National Day logo, Sultan Qaboos University in Al Khoudh in the Muscat Governorate. Two-tone windowed security thread. Watermark: Sultan. 140x71mm.

	VF	UNC
	FV	50.00

The Islamic Republic of Pakistan, located on the Indian subcontinent between India and Afghanistan, has an area of 310,404 sq. mi. (803,943 sq. m.) and a population of 170 million. Capital: Islamabad. Pakistan is mainly an agricultural land. Yarn, cotton, rice and leather are exported. The Indus Valley civilization, one of the oldest in the world and dating back at least 5,000 years, spread over much of what is presently Pakistan. During the second millennium B.C., remnants of this culture fused with the migrating Indo-Aryan peoples. The area underwent successive invasions in subsequent centuries from the Persians, Greeks, Scythians, Arabs (who brought Islam), Afghans, and Turks. The Mughal Empire flourished in the 16th and 17th centuries; the British came to dominate the region in the 18th century. The separation in 1947 of British India into the Muslim state of Pakistan (with West and East sections) and largely Hindu India was never satisfactorily resolved, and India and Pakistan fought two wars - in 1947-48 and 1965 - over the disputed Kashmir territory. A third war between these countries in 1971 - in which India capitalized on Islamabad's marginalization of Bengalis in Pakistani politics - resulted in East Pakistan becoming the separate nation of Bangladesh. In response to Indian nuclear weapons testing, Pakistan conducted its own tests in 1998. The dispute over the state of Kashmir is ongoing, but discussions and confidence-building measures have led to decreased tensions since 2002. Mounting public dissatisfaction with President Musharraf, coupled with the assassination of the prominent and popular political leader, Benazir Bhutto, in late 2007, and Musharraf's resignation in August 2008, led to the September presidential election of Asif Zardari, Bhutto's widower. Pakistani government and military leaders are struggling to control Islamist militants, many of whom are located in the tribal areas adjacent to the border with Afghanistan. The November 2008 Mumbai attacks again inflamed Indo-Pakistan relations. The Pakistani Government is also faced with a deteriorating economy as foreign exchange reserves decline, the currency depreciates, and the current account deficit widens.

MONETARY SYSTEM:
    1 Rupee = 16 Annas to 1961
    1 Rupee = 100 Paisa (Pice), 1961-

REPLACEMENT NOTES:
    #24, 24A, 24B, 1/X or 2/X prefix. #25-33, X as first of double prefix letters.

REPUBLIC

Government of Pakistan
1951-73 ND Issues

8   1 Rupee

ND (1951). Blue on multicolor underprint. Crescent moon and star at right. 2 signature varieties. Back: Archway at left center.

	VF	UNC
	100	150

9   1 Rupee

ND (1953-63). Blue on multicolor underprint. Crescent moon and star at right. Like #8 but larger size serial #. 6 signature varieties. Back: Archway at left center.

	VF	UNC
	7.00	12.00

Note: The scarce signatrue in this variety is Abdul Qadir, valued at $50. in Unc.

9A   1 Rupee

ND (1964). Blue on multicolor underprint. Crescent moon and star at right. Like #8 but different font for serial #. 3 signature varletles. Back: Archway at left center.

	VF	UNC
	4.00	7.00

10 1 Rupee VF UNC
ND (1973). Brown on multicolor underprint. Crescent moon and star at right. Like #8 but larger size serial #. 6 signature varieties. Back: Archway at left center.

		VF	UNC
a. Signature 1. *Aftab Qazi.*		1.50	3.50
b. Signature 2. *Abdul Rauf.*		1.50	3.00

State Bank of Pakistan
CITY OVERPRINT VARIETIES

ঢাকা کراچی করাচী کراچی লাহোর لاہور

Dacca   Karachi   Lahore

Some notes exist w/Urdu and some w/Bengali ovpt. denoting city of issue, Dacca, Karachi or Lahore.

1957-66 ND Issue

15 5 Rupees VF UNC
ND (1966). Purple on light blue and maroon underprint. Portrait of Mohammed Ali Jinnah at center. Three signature varieties. Back: Terraces. Watermark: Portrait of Mohammed Ali Jinnah. 3.50 6.00

19 500 Rupees VF UNC
ND (1964). Red on gold and light green underprint. Portrait of Mohammed Ali Jinnah at center. Back: State Bank of Pakistan building. Watermark: Mohammed Ali Jinnah.

		VF	UNC
a. overprint: *Dhaka.*		25.00	45.00
b. overprint: *Karachi.* 2 signature varieties.		20.00	30.00
c. overprint: *Lahore.*		20.00	30.00

1973 ND Issue

16 10 Rupees VF UNC
ND (1970). Brown on multicolor underprint. Portrait of Mohammed Ali Jinnah at left. Back: Gardens. Watermark: Mohammed Ali Jinnah.

		VF	UNC
a. Latin signature		7.50	15.00
b. Urdu & Bengali signature		6.00	12.50

20 5 Rupees VF UNC
ND (1972-78). Orange-brown on pale blue and dull green underprint. Mohammed Ali Jinnah at center. Three signature varieties. Back: Terraces. Watermark: Mohammed Ali Jinnah.

		VF	UNC
a. Serial # prefix of single or double letters.		5.00	8.00
b. Serial # prefix fractional with double letters over numerals.		5.00	8.00

17 50 Rupees VF UNC
ND (1964). Blue-green on peach underprint. Portrait of Mohammed Ali Jinnah at center. Back: Sailing ships. Watermark: Mohammed Ali Jinnah.

		VF	UNC
a. Latin signature 2 signature varieties.		6.00	10.00
b. 1 Urdu and 1 Bengali signature of the same signatory.		6.00	10.00

Note: The sacrce signature is S. U. Durazi, valued at $150 in Unc.

21 10 Rupees VF UNC
ND (1972-75). Green on multicolor underprint. Mohammed Ali Jinnah at left. Two signature varieties. Back: Shalimar Gardens, Lahore. Watermark: Mohammed Ali Jinnah.

		VF	UNC
a. Sans-serif font for serial #.		5.00	10.00
b. Serif font for serial #. Printer: TDLR (without imprint.)		10.00	20.00
c. Serial # prefix with two **.		40.00	100

18 100 Rupees VF UNC
ND (1957). Green on violet and peach underprint. Portrait of Mohammed Ali Jinnah at center. Back: Badshahi Mosque in Lahore. Watermark: Mohammed Ali Jinnah.

		VF	UNC
a. Without overprint. 2 signature varieties.		6.00	10.00
b. Overprint: *Dhaka.* 2 signature varieties.		6.00	12.00
c. Overprint: *Karachi.* 2 signature varieties.		6.00	10.00
d. Overprint: *Lahore.* 2 signature varieties.		6.00	10.00

22 50 Rupees VF UNC
ND (1972-78). Blue on multicolor underprint. Mohammed Ali Jinnah at center. 12.50 25.00
Three signature varieties. Back: Sailing ships. Watermark: Mohammed Ali Jinnah.

23 100 Rupees VF UNC
ND (1973-70). Dark blue on multicolor underprint. Mohammed Ali Jinnah at left. 20.00 55.00
Two signature varieties. Back: Badshahi Mosque, Lahore. Watermark: Mohammed Ali Jinnah.

Note: The signature variety of Osman Ali is valued at $150 in Unc.

Government of Pakistan

	SIGNATURE VARIETIES		
1	عبدالرزت	2	آغا شاہب احمد خان
3	نیب الله نیک	4	اظہار الحسن
5	سعید احمد قریشی	6	رفیق اختر
7	تنویر علیم السمرائی	8	خالہ جاوید
9	جاوید طلعت	10	میاں طیب حسن
11	معین افضل	12	احتشام عالم حنفی

1975 ND Issue

24 1 Rupee VF UNC
ND (1974). Blue on light green and lilac underprint. Arms at right. Lower border on 10.00 35.00
face is 14mm high and includes text in four languages. Signature 1. Back: Minar-i-
Pakistan monument at left. Watermark: Arms.

24A 1 Rupee VF UNC
ND (1975-81). Blue on light green and lilac underprint. Arms at right. Signature 2.00 3.50
1-3. New broader panel is 22mm. high and without four-language text along bottom. Back: Minar-i-Pakistan monument at left. Watermark: Arms.

1981-83 ND Issue

رزق حلال عین عبادت ہے
URDU TEXT LINE A

حصول رزق حلال عبادت ہے
URDU TEXT LINE B

25 1 Rupee VF UNC
ND (1981-82). Dull brown on multicolor underprint. Arms at right. Signature 3. 2.00 3.50
Serial number at upper center. Back: Tomb of Allama Mohammed Iqbal, no Urdu
text line at bottom.

26 1 Rupee VF UNC
ND (1982). Dull brown on multicolor underprint. Arms at right. Back: Tomb of
Allama Mohammed Iqbal. Urdu text line A at bottom. Watermark: Arms.
a. Serial # at upper center. Signature 3. 2.00 3.00
b. Serial # at lower right. Signature 3. 2.00 3.00

27 1 Rupee VF UNC
ND (1983-). Dull brown on multicolor underprint. Arms at right. Back: Tomb of
Allama Mohammed Iqbal. Urdu text line B at bottom. Watermark: Arms.
a. Serial # at upper center. Signature 3. 1.00 2.00
b. Serial # at lower right. Signature 3. 0.50 1.00
c. As a. Signature 4. 1.00 2.00
d. As b. Signature 4. 0.50 1.00
e. As a. Signature 5. 1.00 2.00
f. As b. Signature 5. 0.50 1.00
g. As a. Signature 6. 1.00 2.00
h. As b. Signature 6. 0.50 1.00
i. As a. Signature 7. 1.00 2.00
j. As b. Signature 7. 0.50 1.00
k. As b. Signature 8. 0.50 1.00
l. As b. Signature 9. 0.50 1.00
m. As b. Signature 10. 0.50 1.00
n. As b. Signature 11 0.50 1.00
o. As b. Signature 12. 0.50 1.00

State Bank of Pakistan

	GOVERNORS OF THE BANK		
1	زاہد حسین	2	عبدالقادر
3	شجاعت علی	4	
5	محبوب الرشید	6	
7	غلام اسحاق خان	8	عثمان علی
9	آغا شاہب قاصر	10	وسیم عون جعفری
11	احتشام عالم حنفی	12	قاسم پارکیھ
13	محمد یعقوب	14	عشرت حسین
15	شمشاد اختر	16	سلیم رضا

1976-77 ND Issue

28   5 Rupees

	VF	UNC
	2.50	4.00

ND (1976-84). Dark brown on tan and pink underprint. Mohammed Ali Jinnah at right. Two signature varieties. Serial number varieties. Back: Khajak railroad tunnel. No Urdu text line beneath upper title. Watermark: Mohammed Ali Jinnah.

29   10 Rupees

	VF	UNC
	2.50	4.00

ND (1976-84). Pale olive-green on multicolor underprint. Mohammed Ali Jinnah at right. Two signature varieties. Serial number varieties. Back: View of Moenjodaro. No Urdu text line beneath upper title. Watermark: Mohammed Ali Jinnah.

30   50 Rupees

	VF	UNC
	5.00	12.50

ND (1977-84). Purple on multicolor underprint. Mohammed Ali Jinnah at right. Two signature varieties. Serial number varieties. Back: Main gate of Lahore fort. No Urdu text line beneath upper title. Watermark: Mohammed Ali Jinnah.

31   100 Rupees

	VF	UNC
	12.50	25.00

ND (1976-84). Red and orange on multicolor underprint. Mohammed Ali Jinnah at right. Two signature varieties. Serial number varieties. Back: Islamic College, Peshawar. No Urdu text line beneath upper title. Watermark: Mohammed Ali Jinnah.

1981-82 ND Issue

#32 Not assigned.

33   5 Rupees

	VF	UNC
	2.50	5.00

ND (1981-82). Dark brown on tan and pink underprint. Mohammed Ali Jinnah at right. Back: Khajak railroad tunnel. Urdu text line A beneath upper title. Watermark: Mohammed Ali Jinnah.

34   10 Rupees

	VF	UNC
	2.50	5.00

ND (1981-82). Pale olive-green on multicolor underprint. Mohammed Ali Jinnah at right. Back: View of Moenjodaro. Urdu text line A beneath upper title. Watermark: Mohammed Ali Jinnah.

35   50 Rupees

	VF	UNC
	7.50	12.50

ND (1981-82). Purple on multicolor underprint. Mohammed Ali Jinnah at right. Back: Main gate of Lahore fort. Urdu text line A beneath upper title. Watermark: Mohammed Ali Jinnah.

36   100 Rupees

	VF	UNC
	12.50	25.00

ND (1981-82). Purple on multicolor underprint. Mohammed Ali Jinnah at right. Back: Islamic College, Peshawar. Urdu text line A beneath upper title. Watermark: Mohammed Ali Jinnah.

1983-88 ND Issue

37   2 Rupees

	VF	UNC
	2.00	4.00

ND (1985-99). Pale purple on multicolor underprint. Shade varieties exist. Arms at right. Five signature varieties. Back: Badshahi mosque. Urdu text line B beneath upper title. Watermark: Arms.

38   5 Rupees

	VF	UNC
	FV	1.00

ND (1983-84). Dark brown on tan and pink underprint. Mohammed Ali Jinnah at right. Six signature varieties. Back: Khajak railroad tunnel. Urdu text line B beneath upper title. Watermark: Mohammed Ali Jinnah.

39   10 Rupees

	VF	UNC
	FV	1.50

ND (1983-84). Pale olive-green on multicolor underprint. Mohammed Ali Jinnah at right. Six signature varieties. Back: View of Moenjodaro. Urdu text line B beneath upper title. Watermark: Mohammed Ali Jinnah. 141x73mm.

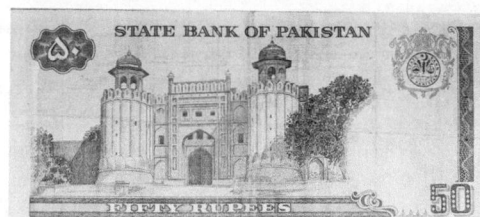

40 50 Rupees

ND (1986-). Purple on multicolor underprint. Mohammed Ali Jinnah at right. Six signatue varieties. Back: Main gate of Lahore fort. Urdu text line B beneath upper title. Watermark: Mohammed Ali Jinnah. 154x73mm.

VF UNC
FV 6.00

41 100 Rupees

ND (1986-). Red and orange on multicolor underprint. Mohammed Ali Jinnah at right. Six signature varieties. Back: Islamic College, Peshawar. Urdu text line B beneath upper title. Watermark: Mohammed Ali Jinnah. 165x73mm.

VF UNC
FV 7.50

42 500 Rupees

ND (1986-). Deep blue-green and olive-green on multicolor underprint. Mohammed Ali Jinnah at right. Six signature varieties. Back: State Bank of Pakistan building at center. Watermark: Mohammed Ali Jinnah. 175x73mm.

VF UNC
FV 30.00

43 1000 Rupees

ND (1988-). Deep purple and blue-black on multicolor underprint. Mohammed Ali Jinnah at right. Four signature varieties. Back: Tomb of Jahangir. Watermark: Mohammed Ali Jinnah. 175x73mm.

VF UNC
FV 50.00

1997 Commemorative Issue

#44, Golden Jubilee of Independence, 1947-1997

44 5 Rupees

1997. Dull violet on light green and pale orange-brown underprint. Star-burst with text and dates at left, Mohammed Ali Jinnah at right. Back: Tomb of Shah Ruke-e-Alam at left center, bank seal at upper right. Watermark: Mohammed Ali Jinnah.

VF UNC
3.50 5.00

2005 Reduced Size Issue

45 10 Rupees

2006-. Light olive green. Muhammad Ali Jinnah at right center. Back: Khyber Pass, Peshawar. 114x65mm.

		VF	UNC
a.	2006.	FV	1.50
b.	2007.	FV	1.50
c.	2008.	FV	1.50
d.	2009.	FV	1.50
e.	2010.	FV	0.50
f.	2011.	FV	0.50
g.	2012.	FV	0.50
h.	2013.	FV	0.50
i.	2014.	FV	0.50
j.	2015.	FV	0.50

46 20 Rupees

2005; 2006, 2007. Brown and tan. Muhammad Ali Jinnah at right center. Back: View of Mohen jo Daro complex, Larkana. 123x65mm.

		VF	UNC
a.	2005.	FV	6.00
b.	2006.	FV	6.00
c.	2007. Slight change to face/back registration device at top left.	FV	6.00

47 50 Rupees

2007-. Muhammad Ali Jinnah at right center.

		VF	UNC
a.	2007.	FV	7.00
b.	2008.	FV	7.00
c.	2009.	FV	7.00
d.	2010.	FV	7.00
e.	2011.	FV	7.00
f.	2012.	FV	7.00
g.	2013.	FV	7.00
h.	2014.	FV	7.00
i.	2015.	FV	7.00

48   100 Rupees

2006-. Rose red. Muhammad Ali Jinnah at right center. Back: Quaid-e-Azam residence. 149x64mm.

	VF	UNC
a. 2006.	FV	7.50
b. 2007.	FV	7.50
c. 2008.	FV	7.50
d. 2009.	FV	7.50
e. 2010.	FV	2,010
f. 2011.	FV	7.50
g. 2012.	FV	7.50
h. 2013.	FV	7.50
i. 2014.	FV	7.50
j. 2015.	FV	7.50

49   500 Rupees

2006-. Green and olive on multicolor underprint. Muhammad Ali Jinnah at right center. Back: Badshahi Mosque, Lahore. 146x65mm.

	VF	UNC
a. 2006.	FV	30.00
b. 2007.	FV	30.00
c. 2008.	FV	10.00

49A   500 Rupees

2009-. Green and olive on multicolor underprint. Muhammad Ali Jinnah at right center; flag added at right end. Back: Basshahi Mosque, Lahore. 146x65mm.

	VF	UNC
a. 2009.	FV	10.00
b. 2010.	FV	10.00
c. 2011.	FV	10.00
d. 2012.	FV	10.00
e. 2013.	FV	10.00
f. 2014.	FV	10.00
g. 2015.	FV	10.00

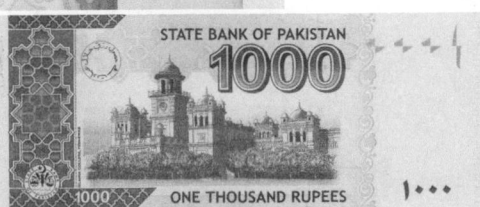

50   1000 Rupees

2006-. Dark blue and light blue on multicolor underprint. Muhammad Ali Jinnah at right center. Back: Islamia College, Peshawar. 154x64mm.

	VF	UNC
a. 2006.	FV	25.00
b. 2007.	FV	25.00
c. 2008.	FV	20.00
d. 2009.	FV	20.00
e. 2010.	FV	20.00
f. 2011.	FV	20.00
g. 2012.	FV	20.00
h. 2013.	FV	20.00
i. 2014	FV	20.00
j. 2015.	FV	20.00

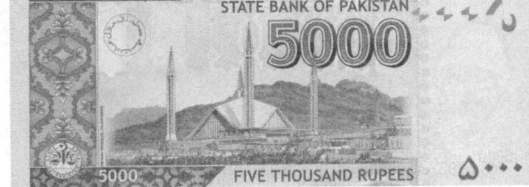

51   5000 Rupees

2006-. Brown and tan on multicolor underprint. Muhammad Ali Jinnah at right center. Back: Faisalo Mosque, Islamabad. 164x65mm.

	VF	UNC
a. 2006.	FV	120
b. 2007.	FV	115
c. 2008.	FV	115
d. 2009.	FV	110
e. 2012.	FV	110
f. 2013.	FV	110
g. 2014.	FV	110

2008 Issue

53   5 Rupees

2008-. Brown on light blue and olive underprint. Muhammad Ali Jinnah at right center. Back: Gwadar Sea Port at center. 115x65mm.

	VF	UNC
a. 2008.	FV	1.00
b. 2009.	FV	1.00
c. 2010.	FV	1.00
s. As a. Specimen.	—	50.00

55   20 Rupees

2008-. Orange and red. Muhammad Ali Jinnah. Back: Mohen Jo Daro, Larkana

	VF	UNC
a. 2007.	FV	3.00
b. 2008.	FV	3.00
c. 2009.	FV	2.00
d. 2010.	FV	2.00
e. 2011.	FV	2.00
f. 2012.	FV	2.00
g. 2013.	FV	2.00
h. 2014.	FV	2.00
i. 2015.	FV	2.00

PAPUA NEW GUINEA

Papua New Guinea, an independent member of the British Commonwealth, occupies the eastern half of the island of New Guinea. It lies north of Australia near the equator and borders on West Irian. The country, which includes nearby Bismarck Archipelago, Buka and Bougainville, has an area of 462,820 sq. km. and a population of 5.93 million. Capital: Port Moresby. The economy is agricultural, and exports include copra, rubber, cocoa, coffee, tea, gold and copper. The eastern half of the island of New Guinea - second largest in the world - was divided between Germany (north) and the UK (south) in 1885. The latter area was transferred to Australia in 1902, which occupied the northern portion during World War I and continued to administer the combined areas until independence in 1975. A nine-year secessionist revolt on the island of Bougainville ended in 1997 after claiming some 20,000 lives.

RULERS:
British

MONETARY SYSTEM:
1 Kina = 100 Toea, 1975-
1 Shilling = 12 Pence
1 Crown = 5 Shillings
1 Pound = 4 Crowns

SIGNATURE VARIETIES

1		
2		
3		
4		
5		
6		
7		
8		
9		
10		

BRITISH ADMINISTRATION

Bank of Papua New Guinea

1975 Issue

1	**2 Kina**		**VF**	**UNC**
	ND (1975). Black on light green and multicolor underprint. Stylized Bird of Paradise at left center. Signature 1. Back: Artifacts. Watermark: Bird of Paradise.			
	a. Issued note.		6.00	17.50
	s1. Specimen. Overprint: *SPECIMEN*. Serial # all zeros.		—	35.00
	s2. Specimen. Serial # all zeros, without overprint.		—	250

2	**5 Kina**		**VF**	**UNC**
	ND (1975). Violet and purple on multicolor underprint. Stylized Bird of Paradise at left center. Signature 1. Back: Mask at center right. Watermark: Bird of Paradise.			
	a. Issued note.		8.50	27.50
	s1. Specimen. Overprint: *SPECIMEN*. Serial # all zeros.		—	75.00
	s2. Specimen. Sperial # all zeros, without overprint.		—	250

3	**10 Kina**		**VF**	**UNC**
	ND (1975). Dark blue-green and purple on multicolor underprint. Stylized Bird of Paradise at left center. Signature 1. Back: Bowl, ring and other artifacts. Watermark: Bird of Paradise.			
	a. Issued note.		20.00	60.00
	s1. Specimen. Overprint: *SPECIMEN*. Serial # all zeros.		—	125
	s2. Specimen. Serial # all zeros, without overprint.		—	250

4	**20 Kina**		**VF**	**UNC**
	ND (1977). Dark brown and deep red on multicolor underprint. Stylized Bird of Paradise at left center. Signature 1. Back: Boar's head. Watermark: Bird of Paradise.			
	a. Issued note.		25.00	80.00
	s1. Specimen. Overprint: *SPECIMEN*. Serial # all zeros.		—	150
	s2. Specimen. Serial # all zeros, without overprint.		—	180

1981-85 Issues

5   2 Kina   VF   UNC
ND (1981). Black and dark green on light green and multicolor underprint. Stylized
Bird of Paradise at left center. Signature 1. White strip 16mm wide at right. Back:
Artifacts. Watermark: Bird of Paradise.
   a. Signature 1.   FV   10.00
   b. Signature 2.   7.50   30.00
   c. Signature 3.   FV   7.50

6   5 Kina   VF   UNC
ND (1981). Violet and purple on multicolor underprint. Stylized Bird of Paradise.
White strip 22mm wide at right. Back: Mask at center. Watermark: Bird of
Paradise.
   a. Signature 1.   6.50   30.00
   b. Signature 2.   7.00   32.50

7   10 Kina   VF   UNC
ND (1985). Dark blue, purple and green on multicolor underprint. Stylized Bird of   10.00   50.00
Paradise at left center. White strip 18mm wide at right. Signature 1. Back: Bowl,
ring and other artifacts. Watermark: Bird of Paradise.

#8 Not assigned.

9   10 Kina   VF   UNC
ND (1988). Ornate corner designs omitted on both sides. Dark blue, dark green
and brown-violet on multicolor underprint. Stylized Bird of Paradise at left center,
design elements in underprint aerial view of Parliament House. Back: Bowl, ring
and other artifacts. Watermark: Bird of Paradise.
   a. Signature 2.   15.00   85.00
   b. Signature 3.   FV   25.00
   c. Signature 5.   FV   22.50
   d. Signature 7.   FV   22.50
   e. Signature 8.   FV   22.50
   s. As a. Specimen. Overprint: SPECIMEN.   —   150

10   20 Kina   VF   UNC
ND. Dark brown and deep red on multicolor underprint. Stylized Bird of Paradise,
similar to # 4 but different design elements in underprint. Back: Boar's head,similar
to number 4 but different design elements in underprint. Watermark: Bird of
Paradise.
   a. Signature 3.   FV   50.00
   b. Signature 6.   FV   40.00
   c. Signature 8.   FV   30.00
   d. Signature 10. Signature title: SECRETARY DEPARTMENT OF FINANCE.   FV   35.00
   e. (20)02. Signature 10.   FV   35.00

11   50 Kina   VF   UNC
ND (1989). Brown, red, blue and multicolor underprint. National Parliament building at center. Signature 3. Back: Foreign Affairs Minister M. Somare at left center,
ceremonial masks at right. Watermark: Central Bank logo.
   a. Issued note.   FV   75.00
   s. Specimen. Overprint: SPECIMEN.   —   150

1991 Commemorative Issue
#12, 9th South Pacific Games 1991

12   2 Kina   VF   UNC
1991. Polymer plastic. UV: serial # and logo fluoresce yellow. Black and dark
green on light green and multicolor underprint. Stylized Bird of Paradise in clear
circle at lower right. Signature 3. Back: Artifacts. Printer: NPA (without imprint).
   a. Issued note.   FV   6.50
   s. Specimen. Overprint: SPECIMEN.   —   100

1992; 1993 ND Regular Issues

12A   2 Kina   VF   UNC
ND (1992). Like #5 but most design elements much lighter. Serial # darker and   FV   6.00
heavier type face. Black and dark green on light green and multicolor underprint.
Stylized Bird of Paradise at left center. Signature 3. Back: Artifacts. Watermark:
Bird of Paradise.

13   5 Kina   VF   UNC
ND (1992). Like #6 but most design elements much lighter. Serial # darker,
heavier type face. Violet and purple on multicolor underprint. Stylized Bird of
Paradise at left center. Back: Mask at center right. Watermark: Bird of Paradise.
   a. Signature 3. Signature title: SECRETARY DEPARTMENT OF FINANCE.   FV   15.00
   b. Signature 7.   FV   15.00
   c. Signature 9. Signature title: SECRETARY DEPARTMENT OF TREASURY.   FV   7.50
   d. Signature 10.   FV   5.00
   e. (20)02. Signature 10.   FV   5.00
   f. (20)05. Serial # prefix: STK. Signature 11.   FV   7.50

14   5 Kina   **VF   UNC**
ND (1993). Violet and purple on multicolor underprint. Stylized Bird of Paradise at
left center, with segmented security thread and new signature title: *Secretary for
Finance and Planning.* Back: Mask at center right. Watermark: Bird of Paradise.
- a. Signature 4.   FV   20.00
- b. Signature 5.   FV   20.00
- s. Specimen. Overprint: *SPECIMEN.*   —   125

1995 ND Commemorative Issue

#15, 20th Anniversary of Independence

15   2 Kina   **VF   UNC**
ND (1995). Polymer plastic. Black and dark green on light green and multicolor   FV   7.50
underprint. Similar to number 12 but with ornate *20 ANNIVERSARY* logo at left,
PNG 20 at lower left. Signature 5. Back: Artifacts. Printer: NPA (without imprint).

1996 ND Regular Issue

16   2 Kina   **VF   UNC**
ND (1996). Polymer plastic. Black and dark green on light green and multicolor
underprint. Stylized Bird of Paradise at left center. Back: Artifacts.
- a. Signature 5.   FV   5.50
- b. Signature 7.   FV   5.50
- c. Signature 10. Signature title: *SECRETARY DEPARTMENT OF FINANCE.*   FV   5.00
- d. (20)02. Signature 10.   FV   5.00
- s. As b. Specimen. Serial # all zeros, without overprint.   —   100

1998 Commemorative Issue

#17, Bank's 25th Anniversary

17   10 Kina   **VF   UNC**
1998. Dark blue, dark green and brown-violet on multicolor underprint. Stylized
Bird of Paradise at left center, design elements representing a modern building.
Signature 8. Silver Jubilee foil with arms and commemorative dates *1973-1998* at
left, and *SJ XXV* Back: Bowl, ring and other artifacts at lower left center.
- a. Issued note.   FV   20.00
- s1. Specimen. Overprint: SPECIMEN.   —   150
- s2. Specimen. Serial # all zeros, without overprint.   —   150

1999 Issue

18   50 Kina   **VF   UNC**
1999; 2002. Polymer plastic. Black and red on orange, yellow and multicolor
underprint. Similar to #11 but with ornate window design. Printer: NPA (without
imprint).
- a. Signature 9.   FV   70.00
- b. Signature 10.   FV   65.00
- s. Specimen. Serial # all zeros, without overprint.   —   150

2000 Commemorative Issue

19   5 Kina   **VF   UNC**
2000; 2002. Violet and purple on multicolor underprint. Similar to #14 but with   FV   11.00
YEAR 2000 at lower left center in dull gold and serial # prefix: *PNG20.* Signature
9. Back: Mask at center right.

2000 Second Commemorative Issue

#20 Currency Silver Jubilee

20   5 Kina   **VF   UNC**
2000. Similar to #19 but with silver imprint at lower center right and red inscription
overprint at lower center: *PNG1942000 (19 4 2000 date).* Signature 10. Back:
Mask at center right.
- a. Issued note.   FV   10.00
- s. Specimen. Overprint: *SPECIMEN.*   —   150

2000 Third Commemorative Issue
#21-25, 25th Anniversary, of Papua New Guinea.

21 2 Kina VF UNC
(20)00. Polymer plastic. Black and dark green on light green and multicolor
underprint. Stylized Bird of Paradise at left center. Signature 10. 25th Anniversary
logo at left. Back: Artifacts. Watermark: Bird of Paradise.
FV 5.00

22 5 Kina VF UNC
ND (2000). Violet and purple on multicolor underprint. Stylized Bird of Paradise at
left center. Signature 10. 25th Anniversary logo at left. Back: Mask at center right.
Watermark: Bird of Paradise.
  a. Issued note. FV 10.00
  s. Specimen. Overprint: *SPECIMEN*. — 150

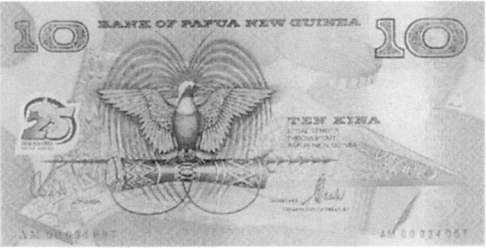

23 10 Kina VF UNC
(20)00. Polymer plastic. Dark blue, dark green and brown-violet on multicolor underprint. Stylized Bird of Paradise at left center, aerial view of Parliament House.
Signature 10. 25th Anniversary logo at left. Back: Bowl, ring and other artifacts.
Watermark: Bird of Paradise.
  a. Issued note. FV 18.50
  s. Specimen. Overprint: SPECIMEN. — 150

24 20 Kina VF UNC
(20)00. Orange-red and brown on multicolor underprint. Stylized Bird of Paradise,
similar to #4 but different design elements in underprint. Signature 10. 25th Anniversary logo at left. Back: Boar's head at right. Watermark: Bird of Paradise.
FV 35.00

25 50 Kina VF UNC
(20)00. Polymer plastic. National Parliament building at center. Signature 10. 25th
Anniversary logo at upper left center. Back: Foreign Affairs Minister M. Somare at
left center, ceremonial masks at right.
FV 65.00

2000 Issue

26 10 Kina VF UNC
July 2000; (20)02. Polymer plastic. Stylized Bird of Paradise at left center, aerial
view of Parliament House. Signature 10. Back: Bowl, ring and other artifacts.
Watermark: Bird of Paradise.
  a. ND (2000). FV 20.00
  b. (20)02. Signature 10. FV 20.00

26A 20 Kina VF UNC
ND (2006). Polymer plastic. Coat of arms with Bird of Paradise on drum and
spear. Back: Boar's head. Watermark: Bank logo. Printer: NPA. 150x75mm.
FV 35.00

2003 Commemorative Issue
#27, 30th Anniversary of the Bank.

27A 5 Kina VF UNC
2003. Coat of arms with Bird of Paradise on drum and spear, gold overprint of
bank logo right. Back: Mask right. Printer: (TDLR). 148x73mm.
FV 10.00

27 20 Kina VF UNC
2003. Polymer plastic. Printer: (NPA). 150x75mm.
FV 35.00

2005-08; ND Issue

28 2 Kina VF UNC
(20)07; (20)08; (20)13; (20)14. Polymer plastic. Light and dark green. Bird of
Paradise at left and Parliament building at center. Printer: (NPA). 140x70mm.
  a. (20)07. FV 5.00
  b. (20)08. FV 5.00
  c. (20)13. FV 5.00
  d. (20)14. FV 5.00
  s. Specimen. Red overprint: *SPECIMEN*. — 250

29   5 Kina   VF   UNC
(20)08; (20)09. Polymer plastic. Violet, purple and tan. Bird of Paradise at left and
Parliament building at center. Printer: (NPA). 140x70mm.

    a. (20)08.   FV   10.00
    b. (20)09.   FV   10.00

30   10 Kina   VF   UNC
(20)08; (20)13. Polymer plastic. Blue and tan. Bird of Paradise at left and Parliament building at center. Printer: (NPA). 145x73mm.

    a. (20)08.   FV   18.50
    b. (20)13.   FV   18.50

31   20 Kina   VF   UNC
(20)07; (20)13; (20)14. Polymer plastic. Bird of Paradise at left and Parliament
building at center. Printer: (NPA). 150x75mm.

    a. (20)07.   FV   35.00
    b. (20)13.   FV   35.00
    c. (20)14.   FV   35.00
    s. Specimen. Overprint: *SPECIMEN*.   —   125

32   50 Kina   VF   UNC
(20)08; (20)12. Polymer plastic. Black, orange and multicolor Bird of Paradise at
left, Parliament building at center. Back: M. Somare at center, headdresses and
masks at right. Printer: (NPA). 150x75mm.

    a. (20)08.   FV   50.00
    b. (20)12.   FV   50.00
    s. Specimen. Overprint: *SPECIMEN*.   —   150

33   100 Kina   VF   UNC
(20)05; (20)07. Polymer plastic. Bird of Paradise at left and Parliament building at
center. 150x75mm.

    a. (20)05.   FV   120
    b. (20)07.   FV   120
    c. (20)14.   FV   120
    s. Specimen. Overprint: *SPECIMEN*.   FV   225

2007 Commemorative Issue

34   5 Kina   VF   UNC
2007. XIII South Pacific Games logo at left end. Violet on multicolor underprint.   FV   8.00
Bird of Paradise. 140x73mm.

2008 Commemorative Issue

35   2 Kina   VF   UNC
(20)08. Polymer plastic. Green on multicolor underprint. Parliament house in   FV   3.00
center. 140x70mm.

36   20 Kina   VF   UNC
(20)08. Orange-red and brown on multicolor underprint. Parliament house at
center. Back: Boar's head. Printer: TDLR.

    a. Issued note.   FV   17.50
    s. Specimen.   —   100

37   100 Kina   VF   UNC
(20)08. Paper. Green and brown on multicolor underprint. Parliament house at
center. Back: Palm tree, fishing boat, mining truck. Printer: TDLR. 150x75mm.

    a. Issued note.   FV   110
    s. Specimen.   —   150

2010 Commemorative Issue

38   2 Kina   VF   UNC
(20)10. Polymer plastic. Green. National Parliament building at center. 35th An-   FV   4.00
niversary of independence logo at top center. Printer: NPA. 140x70mm.

39   5 Kina   VF   UNC
(20)10. Polymer plastic. Violet. National Parliament building at center. 35th An-   FV   6.50
niversary of independence logo at top center. Printer: NPA. 148x73mm.

40   10 Kina   VF   UNC
(20)10. Polymer plastic. Blue. National Parliament building at center. 35th Anniver- FV   10.00
sary of independence logo at top center. Printer: NPA. 150x75mm.

41   20 Kina   VF   UNC
(20)10. Polymer plastic. Red-brown. National Parliament building at center. 35th   FV   15.00
Anniversary of independence logo at top center. Printer: NPA. 150x75mm.

42   50 Kina   VF   UNC
(20)10. Polymer plastic. Orange. National Parliament building at center. 35th   FV   40.00
Anniversary of independence logo at top center. Back: Prime Minister Michael
Somare at center. Printer: NPA. 150x75mm.

43   100 Kina   VF   UNC
(20)10. Polymer plastic. Green and gold. National Parliament building at   FV   75.00
center. 35th Anniversary of independence logo at top center. Back: Ship, plane, oil
rig, dump truck, communications tower. Printer: NPA. 150x75mm.

2012-2013 Commemorative Issue

45   2 Kina   VF   UNC
2013. Polymer plastic. Green. National Parliament building. Printer: NPA.   FV   4.00
140x70mm.

44   100 Kina   VF   UNC
(20)12. Green and gold on multicolor underprint. National Parliament building.   FV   75.00
150x75mm.

46   100 Kina   VF   UNC
2013. Polymer plastic. Green and gold. National Parliament building. 150x75mm.   FV   75.00

2005-2014 Issue

47   100 Kina   VF   UNC
(20)12. Polymer plastic. Green and gold. Coat of arms with Bird of Paradise on   FV   75.00
drum and spear, National Parliament building in Port Moresby. Window at right
looks like a bird. Like #44 but without 35th Anniversary logo. Printer: (NPA).
150x75mm.

2015 Commemorative Issue

48   10 Kina   **VF   UNC**
(20)15. Polymer plastic. South Pacific Games. Blue. National Parliament building   FV   10.00
at center. XV Pacific Games logo at top right. Watermark: Bank logo. Printer:
(NPA). 135x70mm.

49   20 Kina   **VF   UNC**
(20)15. Polymer plastic. 40th anniversary of Independence. Red-brown. National   FV   15.00
Parliament building at center. 40th anniversary logo at top center. Watermark:
Bank logo. Printer: (NPA). 140x70mm.

The Republic of Paraguay, a landlocked country in the heart of South America surrounded by Argentina, Bolivia and Brazil, has an area of 157,042 sq. mi. (406,752 sq. km.) and a population of 5.5 million, 95 percent of whom are of mixed Spanish and Indian descent. Capital: Asunción. The country is predominantly agrarian, with no important mineral deposits or oil reserves. Meat, timber, oilseeds, tobacco and cotton account for 70 percent of Paraguay's export revenue. In the disastrous War of the Triple Alliance (1865-70) - between Paraguay and Argentina, Brazil, and Uruguay - Paraguay lost two-thirds of all adult males and much of its territory. It stagnated economically for the next half century. In the Chaco War of 1932-35, Paraguay won large, economically important areas from Bolivia. The 35-year military dictatorship of Alfredo Stroessner ended in 1989, and, despite a marked increase in political infighting in recent years, Paraguay has held relatively free and regular presidential elections since then.

MONETARY SYSTEM:
1 Peso = 100 Centavos to 1870
1 Peso = 8 Reales to 1872
1 Peso = 100 Centésimos to 1870
1 Peso = 100 Centavos (Centésimos) to 1944
1 Guaraní = 100 Céntimos, 1944-

REPUBLIC

Banco Central del Paraguay
Decreto Ley de No. 18 del 25 de Marzo de 1952 (from Aug.1963)

#192-201 Replacement notes: Serial # prefix *Z*.

192   1 Guaraní   **VF   UNC**
L.1952. Green on multicolor underprint. Soldier at right, arms at left. Black serial #   1.00   4.00
at lower left and lower right. Back: Banco Central. Printer: TDLR. 157x67mm.

193   1 Guaraní   **VF   UNC**
L.1952. Green on multicolor underprint. Soldier at right, arms at left. Two signature
varieties. Back: Palacio Legislativo. Printer: TDLR. 157x67mm.
    a. Black serial # at lower left and lower right.   0.25   1.75
    b. Black serial # at upper left and lower right.   0.25   1.25
    s. As a. Specimen.   —   25.00

194 5 Guaraníes   VF UNC

L.1952. Blue on multicolor underprint. Girl holding jug at right, arms at left.
Black serial # at lower left and lower right. Back: Hotel Guarani. Printer: TDLR.   1.50 6.00
157x67mm.

195 5 Guaraníes   VF UNC

L.1952. UV: value fluoresce yellow. Black on multicolor underprint. Girl holding
jug at right, arms at left. Black serial number at lower left and lower right. Two
signature varieties. Back: Hotel Guarani. Printer: TDLR. 157x67mm.
  a. Red serial # at lower left and lower right.   0.25 1.50
  b. Red serial # at upper left and lower right.   0.25 1.25
  s. As a. Specimen.   — 25.00

106 10 Guaraníes   VF UNC

L.1952. Deep red on multicolor underprint. General Eugenio A. Garay at right,
arms at left. Two signature varieties. Back: International bridge. Printer: TDLR.
157x67mm.
  a. Black serial # at lower left and lower right.   0.40 2.25
  b. Black serial # at upper left and lower right.   0.40 2.00
  s. As a. Specimen. Overprint: *SPECIMEN* in black.   — 35.00

197 50 Guaraníes   VF UNC

L.1952. Brown on multicolor underprint. Mariscal José F. Estigarribia at right, arms
at left. Two signature varieties. Back: Country road. Printer: TDLR. 157x67mm.
  a. Black serial # at lower left and lower right.   1.75 7.00
  b. Black serial # at upper left and lower right.   0.75 4.00
  s. As a. Specimen.   — 25.00

198 100 Guaraníes   VF UNC

L.1952. Green on multicolor underprint. General José E. Diaz at right, arms at left.
Black serial number at lower left and lower right. Back: Ruins of Humaita. Printer:
TDLR. 157x67mm.
  a. Issued note.   3.00 15.00
  s. Specimen.   — 25.00

Note: Do not confuse green #198 with later issue #205 also in green. #198 has value: *CIEN GUA-RANIES* at bottom on back.

199 100 Guaraníes   VF UNC

L.1952. Orange on multicolor underprint. General José E. Diaz at right, arms
at left. Black serial number at lower left and lower right. Two signature varieties
(small size signature). Back: Ruins of Humaita. Printer: TDLR. 157x67mm.
  a. Black serial # at lower left and lower right.   2.50 7.00
  b. Black serial # at upper left and lower right.   1.00 3.00

200 500 Guaraníes   VF UNC

L.1952. Blue-gray on multicolor underprint. General Bernardino Caballero at right,
arms at left. Two signature varieties. Back: Federal merchant ship. Printer: TDLR.
157x67mm.
  a. Black serial # at lower left and lower right.   4.00 10.00
  b. Black serial # at upper left and lower right.   2.00 6.00
  s. As a. Specimen. Red overprint: *SPECIMEN* on both sides. Perforated   — 75.00
    number.

201 1000 Guaraníes   VF UNC

L.1952. Purple on multicolor underprint. Mariscal Francisco Solano Lopez right,
arms at left. Two signature varieties. Back: National shrine. Printer: TDLR.
157x67mm.
  a. Black serial # at lower left and lower right.   7.50 20.00
  b. Black serial # at upper left and lower right.   6.00 15.00
  s. As a. Specimen.   — 75.00

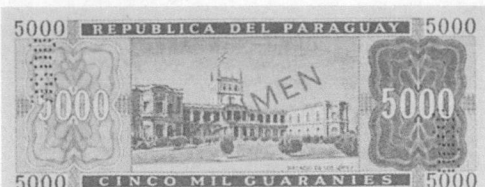

202 5000 Guaraníes

	VF	UNC

L.1952. Red-orange on multicolor underprint. Arms at center, Don Carlos Antonio López at right. Two signature varieties. Back: López Palace. Printer: TDLR. 157x67mm.

a. Black serial # at lower left and lower right.	25.00	60.00
b. Black serial # at upper left and lower right.	75.00	45.00
s1. As a. Specimen. Red overprint:*SPECIMEN* on both sides.	—	70.00
s2. Specimen. Overprint SPECIMEN in red. Punch hole cancel. TDLR oval.	—	175

203 10,000 Guaraníes

	VF	UNC

L.1952. Dark brown on multicolor underprint. Arms at center, Dr. José Caspar Rodríguez de Francia at right, black serial # at lower left and lower right. Back: Historical scene from 14.5.1811. Printer: TDLR. 157x67mm.

a. Issued note.	40.00	100
s. Specimen. Red overprint: SPECIMEN on each side. Perforated number.	—	80.00

204 10,000 Guaraníes

	VF	UNC

L.1952. Dark brown on multicolor underprint. Like number 203 but *CASPAR* changed to *GASPAR* below Francia. Two signature varieties. Back: Historical scene from 14.5.1811. Printer: TDLR. 157x67mm.

a. Black serial # at lower left and lower right.	40.00	100
b. Black serial # at upper left and lower right.	30.00	75.00

1982; 1990 ND Issue

#205-210 replacement notes: Serial # prefix *Z*.

205 100 Guaraníes

	VF	UNC

L.1952 (1982). Green on multicolor underprint. General José E. Díaz at right, arms at left. Black serial number at lower left and lower right. Four signature varieties (small size signature). Back: Ruins of Humaita, value stated as: *SA GUARANI*. Printer: TDLR. 157x67mm.

0.25   1.25

206 500 Guaraníes

	VF	UNC

L.1952. Blue-gray on multicolor underprint. General Bernardino Caballero at right, arms at left. Six signature varieties. Back: Federal merchant ship, value stated as: *PO SA GUARANI*. Printer: TDLR. 157x67mm.

FV   1.75

207 1000 Guaraníes

	VF	UNC

L.1952 (1982). Purple on multicolor underprint. Mariscal Francisco Solano Lopez right, arms at left. Six signature varieties. Back: National shrine, value stated as: *SU GUARANI*. Printer: TDLR. 157x67mm.

FV   2.00

208 5000 Guaraníes

	VF	UNC

L.1952 (1982). Red-orange on multicolor underprint. Arms at center, Don Carlos Antonio López at right. Six signature varieties. Back: López Palace, value stated as: *PO SU GUARANI*. Printer: TDLR. 157x67mm.

FV   7.50

209 10,000 Guaraníes

	VF	UNC

L.1952 (1982). Dark brown on multicolor underprint. Arms at center, Dr. José Caspar Rodriguez de Francia at right, black serial # at lower left and lower right. Five signature varieties. Back: Historical scene from 14.5.1811, value stated as: *PA SU GUARANI*. Printer: TDLR. 157x67mm.

FV   10.00

210 50,000 Guaraníes   VF UNC
L.1952 (1990). Deep purple and light blue on multicolor underprint. Soldier at   FV 45.00
right, outline map of Paraguay at center. Plain security thread. Three signature
varieties. Back: House of Independence at center. Watermark: Bust of soldier.
Printer: TDLR. 157x67mm.

1994 ND Issue

211 50,000 Guaraníes   VF UNC
L.1952 (1994). Purple and light blue on multicolor underprint. Soldier at right, out-   FV 40.00
line map of Paraguay at center. Segmented foil over plain security thread. Three
signature varieties. Series A. Back: House of Independence at center. Watermark:
Bust of soldier. Printer: TDLR. 157x67mm.

1995 ND Issue

212 500 Guaraníes   VF UNC
L.1952 (1995). Blue-gray on multicolor underprint. General Bernardino Caballero   FV 1.25
at right, arms at left. Two signature varieties. Back: Federal merchant ship, value
stated as: PO SA GUARANI. Printer: F-CO. 157x67mm.

213 1000 Guaraníes   VF UNC
L.1952 (1995). Purple on multicolor underprint. Mariscal Francisco Solano Lopez   FV 2.00
right, arms at left. Six signature varieties. Back: National shrine, value stated as:
SU GUARANI. Printer: F-CO. 157x67mm.

Ley 489 del 29 de Junio de 1995; 1997-98 Issue

214 1000 Guaraníes   VF UNC
1998; 2001; 2003. Purple on multicolor underprint. Mariscal Francisco Solano
Lopez right, arms at left. Series B. Back: National shrine, value stated as: SU
GUARANI. 157x67mm.
     a. 1998. Printer: Ciccone Calcografica S.A.   FV 2.00
     b. 2001. Printer: De La Rue.   FV 2.00
     c. 2003. Printer: F-CO.   FV 2.00

215 5000 Guaraníes   VF UNC
1997. Red-orange on multicolor underprint. Arms at center, Don Carlos Antonio   FV 5.00
López at right. Two signature varieties. Series B. Silver foil over security thread.
Back: López Palace, value stated as: PO SU GUARANI. Printer: TDLR.
157x67mm.

216 10,000 Guaraníes   VF UNC
1998; 2003. Brown. Arms at center, Dr. José Caspar Rodríguez De Francia at
right, black serial # at lower left and lower right. Series B. Back: Historical scene
from 14.5.1811, value stated as: PA SU GUARANI. Printer: Ciccone Calcografica,
S.A. 157x67mm.
     a. 1998. Lower left corner has 10000.   FV 7.50
     b. 2003. Lower left corner has: Triangles.   FV 7.50

217 50,000 Guaraníes   VF   UNC

1997. Purple and light blue on multicolor underprint. Soldier at right, outline map of Paraguay at center. Segmented foil over plain security thread. Three signature varieties. Series B. Back: House of Independence at center. Printer: TDLR. 157x67mm.   FV   35.00

218 50,000 Guaraníes   VF   UNC

1998. Purple and light blue on multicolor underprint. Like # 217 but with staircase metallic impression at lower left corner. Series B. Back: House of Independence at center. Printer: (T)DLR. 157x67mm.   FV   27.50

219 100,000 Guaraníes   VF   UNC

1998. Green, yellow-brown and multicolor. San Rogue González de Santa Cruz at right. Series A. Back: *Represa de Itaipu*, Itaipu Hydroelectric Dam. Printer: TDLR. 157x67mm.   FV   45.00

2000 Issue

220 5000 Guaraníes   VF   UNC

2000; 2003. Red-orange on multicolor underprint. Arms at center, Don Carlos Antonio López at right. Two signature varieties. Series C. Silver foil over security thread. Back: López Palace, value stated as: *PO SU GUARANI.* Printer: Ciccone Calcografica S.A. 157x67mm.

   a. 2000. Lower left corner: small diamond.   FV   4.00
   b. 2003. Lower left corner: large diamond.   FV   4.00

2002 Commemorative Issue

50th Anniversary of the Banco Cenral del Paraguay

221 1000 Guaraníes   VF   UNC

2002. Purple on multicolor underprint. Mariscal Francisco Solano Lopez right, arms at left, anniversary text below date. Series B. Back: National shrine, value stated as: *SU GUARANI.* Printer: F-CO. 157x67mm.   FV   2.00

2004 Issue

222 1000 Guaraníes   VF   UNC

2004; 2005. Purple on multicolor underprint. Mariscal Francisco Solano Lopez right, arms at left, without anniversary text below date. Six signature varieties. Series B. Back: National shrine, value stated as: *SU GUARANI.* Printer: DLR. 157x67mm.

   a. 2004. 1 MIL at upper left and right corners on face. Series C.   FV   2.00
   b. 2005. Series D.   FV   2.00

223 5000 Guaraníes   VF   UNC

2005; 2008; 2010. Red-orange on multicolor underprint. 5 MIL at upper left and right corner on face. 157x67mm.

   a. 2005. Series D. Printer De La Rue.   FV   4.00
   b. 2008. Series E. Segmented security thread. Printer G&D.   FV   4.00
   c. 2010. Series F. Wide segmented security thread. Printer CMB.   FV   4.00

224 10,000 Guaraníes   VF   UNC

2004; 2005; 2008; 2010-11. Brown on multicolor underprint. 10 MIL at upper left corner on face. 157x67mm.

   a. 2004. Series C. Printer: De La Rue.   FV   6.00
   b. 2005. Series D. Printer: De La Rue.   FV   6.00
   c. 2008. Series E. Segmented security thread. Printer: Oberthur.   FV   6.00
   d. 2010. Printer CMB.   FV   6.00
   e. 2011. Printer: PWPN.   FV   6.00

228 2000 Guaranies   VF UNC
2008-. Polymer plastic. Purple on multicolor underprint. Adela and Celsa Speratti at right. Back: Parade with flags. 157x67mm.

		VF	UNC
a. 2008. Printer: Oberthur Technologies.		FV	2.00
b. 2009. Printer: G&D.		FV	2.00
c. 2011. Printer: CBNC.		FV	2.00
s. Specimen. Red overprint *MUESTRA SIN VALOR.*		—	75.00

#229 not assigned.

225 20,000 Guaranies   VF UNC
2005. La Mujer Paraguaya at right. 20 MIL at upper left corner. Series A. Back: Banco Central building at center. 20 MIL at upper left and right. Printer: G&D. 157x67mm.   FV 10.00

2005 Issue

230 20,000 Guaranies   VF UNC
2007; 2009; 2011. Blue and green on multicolor. Paraguayan woman holding vase at right. Back: Modern Bank building at center. Printer: G&D. 157x67mm.

		VF	UNC
a. 2007.		FV	10.00
b. 2009.		FV	10.00
c. 2011.		FV	10.00
d. 2011.		FV	10.00

225A 50,000 Guaranies   VF UNC
2005. Purple and light blue on multicolor underprint. Soldier at right. Series C. Back: House of Independence at center. 157x67mm.   FV 27.50

231 50,000 Guaranies   VF UNC
2005; 2007. Thin segmented security strip. Blue, green and orange on multicolor underprint. Map of Paraguay at center, Paraguayan soldier at right. Back: *Casa de la Independencia* at center. Printer: F-CO. 157x67mm.

		VF	UNC
a. 2005. Note: 250,000 notes were stolen during shipment and thus the bank cancelled their release.		—	100
b. 2007.		FV	22.50

226 100,000 Guaranies   VF UNC
2004. Purple on multicolor underprint. Francisco Solano Lopez at right. 100 MIL at upper left and right corners. Holographic silver florette, lion face-to-back registery device. Series B. Back: Church of the Assuncion at center. 100 MIL at lower right. Printer: (T)DLR. 157x67mm.   FV 40.00

227 100,000 Guaranies   VF UNC
2005. Brown holographic florette. Series C. Printer: F-CO. 157x67mm.   FV 40.00

2007 Issue

232 50,000 Guaranies   VF UNC
2008-. Wide segmented security strip. Purple, green and light brown on multicolor underprint. Agustín Pío Barros at center. Series E. Back: Guitar. Printer: G&D. 157x67mm.

		VF	UNC
a. 2008.		FV	22.50
b. 2009.		FV	20.00
c. 2011.		FV	20.00
s. Specimen. Red overprint *MUESTRA SIN VALOR.*		—	100

233 100,000 Guaraníes
2007-11. Printer: Oberthur Technologies. 157x67mm.

		VF	UNC
a. 2007.		FV	40.00
b. 2008.		FV	40.00
c. 2011.		FV	35.00
d. 2013.		FV	40.00
s. Specimen.		—	125

2011 Polymer Issue

234 5000 Guaraníes   VF   UNC
2011 (2013). Red-orange. Printer: CBNC (without imprint).   FV   5.00

2013 Issue

235 20,000 Guaraníes   VF   UNC
2013. Blue and green. Circle symbol for blind, BCP registration device, round coat   FV   9.00
of arms with star, round emblem with lion and cap, woman holding vase. Back:
Modern bank headquarters building in Asunción. Motion windowed security thread
with star in circle pattern. Watermark: Paraguayan woman and electrotype 20 MIL.
Printer: Joh. Eschedé. 157x67mm.

236 50,000 Guaraníes   VF   UNC
2013. Printer: Joh. Eschedé. 157x67mm.   FV   20.00

237 100,000 Guaraníes   VF   UNC
2013. Printer: Joh. Eschedé. 157x67mm.   FV   40.00

2015 Issue

238 20,000 Guaraníes   VF   UNC
2015. Printer: PWPN. 157x67mm.   FV   10.00

239 50,000 Guaraníes   VF   UNC
2015. Purple, peach and green. Pentagon symbol for blind, map, guitar registra-   FV   20.00
tion device, Agustín Pío Barrios, round coat of arms with star, round emblem with
lion and cap. Back: Guitar. Motion windowed security thread. Watermark: Agustín
Pío Barrios Printer: Oberthur. 157x67mm.

240 100,000 Guaraníes   VF   UNC
2015. Green, blue and yellow. Semicircle symbol for blind, round coat of arms with   FV   40.00
star, lion and cap registration device, round emblem with lion and cap, San Roque
González de Santa Cruz. Back: Itaipu hydroelectric dam on the Parana River.
Printer: TDLR. 157x67mm.

COLLECTOR SERIES

Banco Central del Paraguay
1979 Issue

CS1 100-10,000 Guaraníes   Mkt. Value
199b-202b, 204b overprint: *SPECIMEN* and with serial # prefix Maltese cross.   25.00
L.1972 (1979).

PERU

The Republic of Perú, located on the Pacific coast of South America, has an area of 496,222 sq. mi. (1,285,216 sq. km.) and a population of 25.66 million. Capital: Lima. The diversified economy includes mining, fishing and agriculture. Fish meal, copper, sugar, zinc and iron ore are exported. Ancient Peru was the seat of several prominent Andean civilizations, most notably that of the Incas whose empire was captured by the Spanish conquistadors in 1533. Peruvian independence was declared in 1821, and remaining Spanish forces defeated in 1824. After a dozen years of military rule, Peru returned to democratic leadership in 1980, but experienced economic problems and the growth of a violent insurgency. President Alberto Fujimori's election in 1990 ushered in a decade that saw a dramatic turnaround in the economy and significant progress in curtailing guerrilla activity. Nevertheless, the president's increasing reliance on authoritarian measures and an economic slump in the late 1990s generated mounting dissatisfaction with his regime, which led to his ouster in 2000. A caretaker government oversaw new elections in the spring of 2001, which ushered in Alejandro Toledo Manrique as the new head of government - Peru's first democratically elected president of Native American ethnicity. The presidential election of 2006 saw the return of Alan Garcia Perez who, after a disappointing presidential term from 1985 to 1990, returned to the presidency with promises to improve social conditions and maintain fiscal responsibility.

MONETARY SYSTEM:
- 1 Sol = 1 Sol de Oro = 100 Centavos, 1879-1985
- 1 Libra = 10 Soles
- 1 Inti = 1000 Soles de Oro, 1986-1991
- 1 Nuevo Sol = 100 Centimes = 1 Million Intis, 1991-
- 1 Sol = 100 Centavos (10 Dineros)

REPÚBLICA DEL PERÚ

Banco Central de Reserva del Peru

Ley 10535, 1956 Issue

76   5 Soles VF UNC
22.3.1956; 18.3.1960. Green on patterned light blue underprint. Seated Liberty holding shield and staff at center. Like #70. Signature varieties. Back: Arms at center. Printer: TDLR.   1.50   5.00

77   10 Soles VF UNC
9.7.1956. Orange on multicolor underprint. Seated Liberty holding shield and staff at center. Similar to #71. Signature varieties. Back: Arms at center. Printer: G&D.   6.00   20.00

78   50 Soles VF UNC
22.3.1956; 24.10.1957; 13.5.1959. Dark blue on lilac underprint. Seated Liberty holding shield and staff at center. Serial # at upper left and right. Like #72. Signature varieties. Back: Arms at center. Printer: TDLR.
a. Issued note.   4.50   17.50
s. Specimen.   —   —

79   100 Soles VF UNC
1956-61. Black on light blue underprint. Seated Liberty holding shield and staff at center. Like #73 but different guilloche. Signature varieties. Back: Arms at center. Printer: TDLR.
a. LIMA at lower left. 22.3.1956; 24.10.1957.   12.00   30.00
b. LIMA at lower right. 13.5.1959.   12.00   30.00
c. As b. Series and serial # at lower left and upper right. 1.2.1961.   12.00   30.00
s. As a. Specimen.   —   —

80   500 Soles VF UNC
1956-61. Brown on light brown and lilac underprint. Seated Liberty holding shield and staff at center. Similar to #74. Signature varieties. Back: Arms at center. Printer: TDLR.
a. Series and serial # at upper corners. 22.3.1956; 24.10.1957.   25.00   75.00
b. Series and serial # at lower left and upper right. 10.12.1959; 10.0.1901   30.00   75.00
s. As b. Specimen.   —   —

1958 Issue

81   5 Soles VF UNC
21.8.1958. Green. Seated Liberty holding shield and staff at center. Back: Arms at center. Like #70 but different guilloche. Printer: W&S.   4.00   7.50

82   10 Soles VF UNC
21.8.1958. Orange on multicolor underprint. Seated Liberty holding shield and staff at center. Similar to #71. Back: Arms at center. Printer: W&S.   4.00   15.00

1960 Issue

82A   10 Soles VF UNC
8.7.1960, 1.2.1961. Orange on multicolor underprint. Liberty seated holding shield and staff at center. Serial # and series at lower left and upper right. Printer: TDLR.   1.50   6.00

REPUBLIC

Banco Central de Reserva del Perú

Ley 13958, 1962; 1964 Issue

83   5 Soles de Oro   **VF UNC**
9.2.1962; 20.9.1963; 18.6.1965; 18.11.1966; 23.2.1968. Green on multicolor underprint. Liberty seated holding shield and staff at center. Serial number at lower
left and upper right. Series J. Back: Arms at center. Printer: TDLR.
   a. Issued note.   1.00   4.00
   s. Specimen.   —   25.00

84   10 Soles de Oro   **VF UNC**
8.6.1962; 20.9.1963; 20.5.1966; 25.5.1967; 23.2.1968. Orange on multicolor
underprint. Liberty seated holding shield and staff at center. Series I. Back: Arms
at center. Printer: TDLR.
   a. Issued note.   1.50   4.00
   s. Specimen.   —   25.00

85   50 Soles de Oro   **VF UNC**
9.2.1962; 20.9.1963; 23.2.1968. Blue on multicolor underprint. Liberty seated
holding shield and staff at center. Serial number at lower left and upper right.
Series H. Back: Arms at center. Printer: TDLR.
   a. Issued note.   3.50   12.50
   s. Specimen.   —   25.00

86   100 Soles de Oro   **VF UNC**
13.3.1964; 23.2.1968. Black on light blue and multicolor underprint. Liberty seated
holding shield and staff at center. Series G. Back: Arms at center. Printer: TDLR.
   a. Issued note.   6.00   20.00
   s. Specimen.   —   25.00

87   500 Soles de Oro   **VF UNC**
9.2.1962; 20.9.1963; 20.5.1966; 23.2.1968. Brown on light brown and multicolor
underprint. Liberty seated holding shield and staff at center. Series L. Back: Arms
at center. Printer: TDLR.
   a. Issued note.   10.00   40.00
   s. Specimen.   —   25.00

1962; 1965 Issue

88   10 Soles de Oro   **VF UNC**
26.2.1965. Red-orange on light green and multicolor underprint. Liberty seated   2.00   7.50
holding shield and staff at center. Series C. *Pagar· al Portador* added under bank
name at top center. Back: Arms at center. Printer: ABNC.

89   50 Soles de Oro   **VF UNC**
20.8.1965. Blue on multicolor underprint. Liberty seated holding shield and staff at
center. Series B. *Pagar· al Portador* added under bank name at top center. Back:
Arms at center. Printer: ABNC.
   a. Issued note.   5.00   20.00
   s. Specimen.   —   100

90 100 Soles de Oro   **VF** **UNC**
12.9.1962; 20.8.1965. Black on light blue and multicolor underprint. Liberty seated
holding shield and staff at center. Series A. *Pagar· al Portador* added under bank
name at top center. Back: Arms at center. Printer: ABNC.
    a. Issued note.   6.50   22.50
    s. Specimen.   —   100

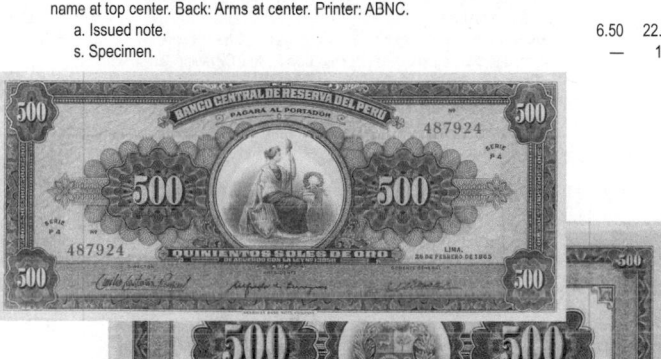

91 500 Soles de Oro   **VF** **UNC**
26.2.1965. Brown on multicolor underprint. Liberty seated holding shield and staff
at center. Series P. *Pagar· al Portado* added under bank name at top center.
Back: Arms at center. Printer: ABNC.   25.00   70.00

Ley 13 958 1968 Issue

#92-98 Replacement notes: Serial # Z999 . . .

92 5 Soles de Oro   **VF** **UNC**
23.2.1968. Green on multicolor underprint. Artifacts at left, Inca Pachacútec at
right, arms at center. 3 signatures. Series J. Back: *Fortaleza de Sacsahuaman.*
Printer: TDLR.
    a. Issued note.   0.75   3.00
    s. Specimen.   —   25.00

93 10 Soles de Oro   **VF** **UNC**
23.2.1968. Red-orange on multicolor underprint. Building at left, Garcilaso Inca de
la Vega at right, arms at center. 3 signatures. Series I. Back: Lake Titicaca, boats.
Printer: TDLR.
    a. Issued note.   0.50   2.00
    s. Specimen.   —   25.00

94 50 Soles de Oro   **VF** **UNC**
23.2.1968. Blue-gray on multicolor underprint. Workers at left, Tupac Amaru II at
right, arms at center. 3 signatures. Series H. Back: Scene of historic town of Tinta.
Printer: TDLR.
    a. Issued note.   1.00   5.00
    s. Specimen.   —   25.00

95 100 Soles de Oro   **VF** **UNC**
23.2.1968. Black on multicolor underprint. Dock workers at left, *Hipolito Unanue*
at right, arms at center. 3 signatures. Series G. Back: Church, site of first National
Congress. Printer: TDLR.
    a. Issued note.   1.50   6.50
    s. Specimen.   —   25.00

96 200 Soles de Oro   **VF** **UNC**
23.2.1968. Purple on multicolor underprint. Fishermen at left, Ramon Castilla at
right, arms at center. 3 signatures. Series Q. Back: Frigate *Amazonas* at center.
Printer: TDLR.
    a. Issued note.   3.50   12.50
    s. Specimen.   —   25.00

97 500 Soles de Oro   **VF** **UNC**
23.2.1968. Brown on multicolor underprint., tan near center. Builders at left,
Nicolas de Pierola at right, arms at center. 3 signatures. Series L. Back: National
mint. Printer: TDLR.
    a. Issued note.   3.00   20.00
    s. Specimen.   —   25.00

98 1000 Soles de Oro VF UNC

23.2.1968. Violet on multicolor underprint. Miguel Grau at left, Francisco Bolognesi (misspelled *BOLOGÑESI*) at right, arms at center. 3 signatures. Series R. Back: Scene of Machu Picchu. Printer: TDLR.

a. Issued note.	12.50	30.00
s. Specimen.	—	25.00

1969 Issue

#99-105 Replacement notes: Serial # Z999 . . .

105 1000 Soles de Oro VF UNC

1969-73. Violet on multicolor underprint. Like #98 but *BOLOGNESI* correctly spelled at right and text changed to: *De Acuerdo Con Su Ley Organica*. 2 signatures. Series R. Back: Scene of Macchu Picchu. Printer: TDLR.

a. 20.6.1969; 16.10.1970.	7.50	30.00
b. 9.9.1971; 4.5.1972; 24.5.1973.	5.00	25.00

1975 Issue

#106-111 Replacement notes: Serial # Z999 . . .

106 10 Soles de Oro VF UNC

2.10.1975. Red-orange on multicolor underprint. Building at left, Garcilaso Inca de la Vega at right, arms at center. 3 signatures. Series I. Back: Lake Titicaca, boats. Printer: TDLR. 0.25 1.50

99 5 Soles de Oro VF UNC

1969-74. Green on multicolor underprint. Like #92 but text changed to: *De Acuerdo Con Su Ley Organica*. 2 signatures. Series J. Back: *Fortaleza de Sacsahuaman*. Printer: TDLR.

a. 20.6.1969.	0.25	2.50
b. 16.10.1970; 9.9.1971; 4.5.1972.	0.25	2.00
c. 24.5.1973; 16.5.1974; 15.8.1974.	0.25	1.25

100 10 Soles de Oro VF UNC

1969-74. Red-orange on multicolor underprint. Like #93 but text changed to: *De Acuerdo Con Su Ley Organica*. 2 signatures. Series I. Back: Lake Titicaca, boats. Printer: TDLR.

a. 20.6.1969.	0.25	2.00
b. 16.10.1970; 9.9.1971.	0.25	1.50
c. 4.5.1972; 24.5.1973; 16.5.1974.	0.25	1.50

101 50 Soles de Oro VF UNC

1969-74. Blue-gray on multicolor underprint. Like #94 but text changed to: *De Acuerdo Con Su Ley Organica*. 2 signatures. Series H. Back: Scene of historic town of Tinta. Printer: TDLR.

a. 20.6.1969.	0.50	5.00
b. 16.10.1970; 9.9.1971; 4.5.1972.	0.50	4.00
c. 24.5.1973; 16.5.1974; 15.8.1974.	0.50	2.50

102 100 Soles de Oro VF UNC

1969-74. Black on multicolor underprint. Like #95 but text changed to: *De Acuerdo Con Su Ley Organica*. 2 signatures. Series G. Back: Church, site of first National Congress. Printer: TDLR.

a. 20.6.1969.	1.00	5.00
b. 16.10.1970; 9.9.1971; 4.5.1972.	0.50	3.50
c. 24.5.1973; 16.5.1974; 15.8.1974.	0.50	3.00

103 200 Soles de Oro VF UNC

1969-74. Purple on multicolor underprint. Like #96 but text changed to: *De Acuerdo Con Su Ley Organica*. 2 signatures. Series Q. Back: Frigate *Amazonas* at center. Printer: TDLR.

a. 20.6.1969.	3.00	10.00
b. 24.5.1973; 16.5.1974; 15.8.1974.	2.00	9.00

107 50 Soles de Oro VF UNC

2.10.1975. Blue-gray on multicolor underprint. Workers at left, Tupac Amaru II at right, arms at center. 3 signatures. Series H. Back: Scene of historic town of Tinta. Printer: TDLR. 0.25 1.50

108 100 Soles de Oro VF UNC

2.10.1975. Black on multicolor underprint. Dock workers at left, *Hipolito Unanue* at right, arms at center. 3 signatures. Series G. Back: Church, site of first National Congress. Printer: TDLR. 0.50 2.50

#109 Not assigned.

104 500 Soles de Oro VF UNC

1969-74. Brown on multicolor underprint. Like #97 but text changed to: *De Acuerdo Con Su Ley Organica*. 2 signatures. Series L. Back: National mint. Printer: TDLR.

a. 20.6.1969.	5.00	20.00
b. 16.10.1970; 9.9.1971; 4.5.1972; 24.5.1973.	4.00	15.00
c. 16.5.1974; 15.8.1974.	2.50	10.00

110 500 Soles de Oro VF UNC

2.10.1975. Brown on multicolor underprint, pale green underprint near center. Builders at left, Nicolas de Pierola at right, arms at center. 3 signatures. Series L. Back: National mint. Printer: TDLR. 3.00 15.00

111 1000 Soles de Oro
2.10.1975. Miguel Grau at left, Francisco Bolognesi, name spelled correctly at right, arms at center. 3 signatures. Series R. Back: Scene of Macchu Picchu. Printer: TDLR.

	VF	UNC
	5.00	27.50

1976-77 Issues

#112 and 113 Replacement notes: Serial # Z999....

112 10 Soles de Oro
17.11.1976. Red-orange on multicolor underprint. Like #106 but without *Pagará al Portador* at top and without security thread. 3 signatures. Series I. Back: Lake Titicaca. Printer: TDLR.

	VF	UNC
	0.25	1.50

113 50 Soles de Oro
15.12.1977. Blue-gray on multicolor underprint. Like #107 but without *Pagará al Portador* at top and without security thread. 3 signatures. Series H. Back: Scene of historic town of Tinta. Printer: TDLR.

	VF	UNC
	0.25	1.25

114 100 Soles de Oro
22.7.1976. Green, brown and multicolor. Arms at left, Tupac Amaru II at right. Back: Machu Picchu. Printer: IPS-Roma.

	VF	UNC
	0.25	1.25

115 500 Soles de Oro
22.7.1976. Green, blue and yellow. Arms at center, Jose Quiñones at right. Back: Logging scene. Printer: IPS-Roma.

	VF	UNC
	0.25	1.50

116 1000 Soles de Oro
22.7.1976. Black, green, brown and multicolor. Arms at center, Miguel Grau at right. Back: Fishermen. Printer: BDDK.

	VF	UNC
	2.00	7.50

Replacement notes: Serial # prefix Y, and suffix letter A.

117 5000 Soles de Oro
1976-85. Brown and maroon on multicolor underprint. Arms at center, Colonel Bolognesi at right. Back: Two miners in mine at left. Watermark: Colonel Bolognesi. Printer: BDDK.

	VF	UNC
a. 22.7.1976.	2.50	10.00
b. 5.11.1981.	0.50	2.50
c. 21.6.1985.	0.25	1.50

Replacement notes: Serial # prefix Y, and suffix letter A.

1979 Issue

#118-120 Replacement notes: Serial # prefix Y and suffix letter A.

118 1000 Soles de Oro
1.2.1979; 3.5.1979. Black, green and multicolor. Admiral Grau at right, arms at center, denominations below coat of arms. Back: Fishermen and boats at left. Watermark: Admiral Grau. Printer: TDLR.

	VF	UNC
	1.00	3.00

119 5000 Soles de Oro
1.2.1979. Brown-violet and multicolor. Colonel Bolognese at right, arms at center, denominations below coat of arms. *CINCO MIL* added at bottom. Back: Miners. Watermark: Colonel Bolognese. Printer: TDLR.

	VF	UNC
	1.50	7.50

120 10,000 Soles de Oro
1.2.1979; 5.11.1981. Black, blue-violet and purple on multicolor underprint. Garcilaso Inca de la Vega, arms at center, denominations below coat of arms. Back: Indian digging at left, woman with flowers at center. Watermark: Garcilaso Inca de la Vega. Printer: TDLR.

	VF	UNC
	3.00	15.00

1981 Issue

#121 *Deleted*. See #125B. #122-125 Replacement notes: Serial # prefix Y, suffix A.

122　1000 Soles de Oro　　　　　　　　　　　　　　　　VF　UNC
5.11.1981. Black, green and multicolor. Similar to #118 but slightly modified
guilloche in underprint at center. Back: Fishermen and boats. Watermark: Admiral
Grau. Printer: ABNC.
　　a. Issued note.　　　　　　　　　　　　　　　　　0.30　1.50
　　s. Specimen.　　　　　　　　　　　　　　　　　　—　75.00

123　5000 Soles de Oro　　　　　　　　　　　　　　　　VF　UNC
5.11.1981. Black and red-brown on multicolor underprint. Similar to #119 but　1.00　5.00
denomination is above signatures at center. Back: Miners. Watermark: Colonel
Bolognesi. Printer: ABNC.

124　10,000 Soles de Oro　　　　　　　　　　　　　　　VF　UNC
5.11.1981. Black, blue-violet and purple on multicolor underprint. Similar to #120　2.00　7.00
but slight variations on borders. Back: Indian digging at left, woman with flowers at
center. Watermark: Garcilaso Inca de la Vega. Printer: ABNC.

125　50,000 Soles de Oro　　　　　　　　　　　　　　　VF　UNC
5.11.1981; 2.11.1984. Black and orange on multicolor underprint. Arms at center,
Nicolas de Pierola at right. Back: Drilling rig at left on back, helicopter approaching. Watermark: Nicolas de Pierola. Printer: ABNC.
　　a. Issued note.　　　　　　　　　　　　　　　　　3.00　12.50
　　s. Specimen.　　　　　　　　　　　　　　　　　　—　125

1982; 1985 Issue

Replacement notes: Serial # prefix *Y*, suffix *A* and *ZZ* respectively.

125A　500 Soles de Oro　　　　　　　　　　　　　　　VF　UNC
18.3.1982 Green, blue and yellow. Arms at center, Jose Quiñones at right. Back:　0.50　3.00
Logging scene. Printer: (T)DLR.

125B　50,000 Soles de Oro　　　　　　　　　　　　　VF　UNC
23.8.1985. Black, orange and multicolor. Arms at center, Nicolas de Pierola at　2.25　6.50
right. Back: Drilling rig at left on back, helicopter approaching. Watermark: Nicolas
de Pierola. Printer: TDLR.

1985 Provisional Issue

126　100,000 Soles de Oro　　　　　　　　　　　　　VF　UNC
23.8.1985. Black, green and multicolor. Admiral Grau at right, arms at center.　150　375
Back: Fishermen and boats. Watermark: Admiral Grau. Printer: ABNC.

127　500,000 Soles de Oro　　　　　　　　　　　　　VF　UNC
23.8.1985. Black and red-brown on multicolor underprint. Colonel Bolognesi at　—　—
right, arms at center. Back: Miners. Watermark: Colonel Bolognesi. Printer: ABNC.

1985-91 Issues

During the period from around 1984 and extending beyond 1990, Perú suffered from a hyperinflation that saw the Sol depreciate in value dramatically
and drastically. A sudden need for new Inti banknotes caused the government to approach a number of different security printers in order to satisfy
the demand for new notes. #128-150 involve 7 different printers: BdM, BDDK,
CdM-B, FNMT, G&D, IPS-Roma and TDLR. Listings proceed by denomination
and in chronological order. Replacement notes:

　BdM - Serial # prefix *Y; Z*.
　BDDK - Serial # prefix *Y*.
　FNMT - Serial # prefix *Y*.
　IPS-Roma - Serial # prefix *Y; Z*.
　TDLR - Serial # prefix *Y; Z*.

128　10 Intis　　　　　　　　　　　　　　　　　　　VF　UNC
3.4.1985; 17.1.1986. Black, dark blue and purple on multicolor underprint. Ricardo　0.20　0.50
Palma at right, arms at center. Back: Indian farmer digging at left and another
picking cotton at center. Watermark: Ricardo Palma. Printer: TDLR.

129　10 Intis　　　　　　　　　　　　　　　　　　　VF　UNC
26.6.1987. UV: fibers fluoresce yellow and blue. Black, dark blue and purple on　0.15　0.75
multicolor underprint. Ricardo Palma at right, arms at center. Back: Indian farmer
digging at left and atother picking cotton at center. Watermark: Ricardo Palma.
Printer: IPS-Roma.

130 50 Intis VF UNC
3.4.1985. Black, orange and green on multicolor underprint. Nicolas de Pierola at
right. Back: Drilling rig at left on back, helicopter approaching. Watermark: Nicolas
de Pierola. Printer: TDLR. 0.50 2.00

131 50 Intis VF UNC
1986; 1987 UV: fibers fluoresce green and orange. Black, orange and green on
multicolor underprint. Nicolas de Pierola at right, arms at center. Back: Drilling rig
at left, hilicopter approaching. Watermark: Nicolas de Pierola. Printer: CdM-Brazil.
  a. 6.3.1986. 0.25 1.50
  b. 26.6.1987. 0.25 1.25

132 100 Intis VF UNC
1985; 1986. Black and dark brown on multicolor underprint. Ramon Castilla at
right, arms at center. Back: Women workers by cotton spinning frame at left
center. Watermark: Ramon Castilla. Printer: CdM-Brazil
  a. 1.2.1985; 1.3.1985. 2.00 12.00
  b. 6.3.1986. With additional pink and light green vertical underprint at right. 0.75 0.50

133 100 Intis VF UNC
26.6.1987. UV: fibers fluoresce yellow and blue, security strip yellow. Black and 0.10 0.35
dark brown on multicolor underprint. Ramon Castilla at right, arms at center with
additional pink and light green vertical underprint at right. Back: Women workers by
cotton spinning frame at left center. Watermark: Ramon Castilla. Printer: BDDK.

134 500 Intis VF UNC
1985; 1987. UV: fibers and security thread fluoresce yellow and blue. Deep
brown-violet and olive-brown on multicolor underprint. Jose Cabriel Condorcanqui
Tupac Amaru II at right, arms at center. Back: Mountains and climber at center.
Watermark: Jose Cabriel Condorcanqui Tupac Amaru II. Printer: BDDK.
  a. 1.3.1985. 0.30 3.00
  b. 26.6.1987. 0.20 0.50

135 500 Intis VF UNC
6.3.1986 Deep brown-violet and olive-brown on multicolor underprint. Jose Cabriel 3.50 12.50
Condorcanqui Tupac Amaru II at right, arms at center. Ornate red-orange vertical
strip at left end of design with added security thread underneath. Back: Mountains
and climber at center. Watermark: Jose Cabriel Condorcanqui Tupac Amaru II.
Printer: FNMT.

136 1000 Intis VF UNC
1986-88. UV: fibers fluoresce green adn blue; signatures green; security strip
yellow. Deep green, olive-brown and red on multicolor underprint. Mariscal Andres
Avelino Caceres at right, arms at center. Back: Ruins of Chan Chan. Watermark:
Mariscal Andres Avelino Caceres. Printer: TDLR.
  a. 6.3.1986. 0.50 2.00
  b. 26.6.1987; 28.6.1988. 0.25 1.50

137 5000 Intis VF UNC
28.6.1988. UV: security strip fluoresces red, blue and yellow; fibers yellow and 0.20 1.00
blue, center design yellow. Pruple, deep brown and red-orange on multicolor underprint. Admiral Miguel Grau at right, arms at center. Back: Fishermen repairing
nets. Watermark: Admiral Miguel Grau. Printer: G&D.

138 5000 Intis VF UNC
28.6.1988. . Purple, deep brown and red-orange on multicolor underprint. Admiral 1.00 3.50
Miguel Grau at right, arms at center. Back: Fishermen repairing nets. Watermark:
Admiral Miguel Grau. Printer: IPS-Roma.

139 5000 Intis
9.9.1988. Purple, deep brown and red-orange on multicolor underprint. Admiral Miguel Grau at right, arms at center. Back: Fishermen repairing nets. Printer: TDLR.

	VF	UNC
	1.00	4.50

140 10,000 Intis
28.6.1988. UV: fibers fluoresce blue and green; value yellow; security strip multicolor; some notes have vertical serial # red and signatures green. Aqua, blue and orange on light green and multicolor underprint. Cesar Vallejo at right, arms at center. Black and red increasing size serial # (anti-counterfeiting device). Back: Santiago de Chuco street scene. Watermark: Cesar Vallejo. Printer: IPS-Roma.

	VF	UNC
	0.20	1.00

141 10,000 Intis
28.6.1988. Dark blue and orange on light green and multicolor underprint. Like # 140 but with broken silver security thread. Cesar Vallejo at right, arms at center. Black and red increasing size serial # (anti-counterfeiting device). Back: Santiago de chuco street scene. Watermark: Cesar Vallejo. Printer: TDLR.

	VF	UNC
	0.75	3.00

142 50,000 Intis
28.6.1988. Red, violet and dark blue on multicolor underprint. Victor Raul Haya de la Torre at right, arms at center. Back: Chamber of National Congress. Watermark: Victor Raul Haya de la Torre. Printer: IPS-Roma.

	VF	UNC
	1.00	4.00

143 50,000 Intis
28.6.1988. Red, violet and dark blue on multicolor underprint. Like #142 but with segmented foil security thread. Victor Raul Haya de la Torre at right, arms at center. Back: Chamber of National Congress. Watermark: Victor Raul Haya de la Torre. Printer: TDLR.

	VF	UNC
	1.50	5.00

144 100,000 Intis
21.11.1988. Brown and black on multicolor underprint. Francisco Bolognesi at right, arms at center. Back: Local boats in Lake Titicaca. Watermark: Francisco Bolognesi. Printer: TDLR.

	VF	UNC
	0.75	2.25

144A 100,000 Intis
21.12.1988. Brown and black on multicolor underprint. Francisco Bolognesi at right, arms at center. Segmented foil over security thread. Back: Local boats in Lake Titicaca. Watermark: Francisco Bolognesi. Printer: TDLR.

	VF	UNC
	0.75	2.50

145 100,000 Intis
21.12.1989. Brown and black on multicolor underprint. Francisco Bolognesi at right, arms at center, black security thread at right of arms. Back: Local boats in Lake Titicaca. Printer: BdeM.

	VF	UNC
	0.75	3.00

146 500,000 Intis
21.11.1988. Blue and blue-violet on multicolor underprint. Ricardo Palma at right, arms at center. Back: Church of *La Caridád* (charity), site of first National Congress. Watermark: Ricardo Palma's printed image. Printer: TDLR.

	VF	UNC
	1.00	6.50

146A 500,000 Intis
21.12.1988. Blue and blue-violet on multicolor underprint. Ricardo Palma at right, arms at center. Segmented foil over security thread. Back: Indian farmer digging at left and another picking cotton at center. Watermark: Ricardo Palma. Printer: TDLR.

	VF	UNC
	1.75	7.50

147 500,000 Intis
21.12.1989. Blue and blue-violet on multicolor underprint. Ricardo Palma at right, arms at center, black security thread at right. Back: Indian farmer digging at left and another picking cotton at center. Watermark: Picardo Palma. Printer: BdeM.

	VF	UNC
	1.25	5.50

148 1,000,000 Intis   **VF**   **UNC**
5.1.1990. Red-brown, green and multicolor. Hipolito Unanue at right, arms at 1.00   5.00
center. Back: Medical college at San Fernando at left center. Watermark: Hipolito
Unanue. Printer: TDLR.

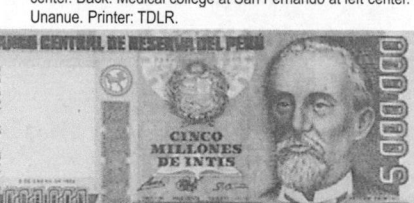

149 5,000,000 Intis   **VF**   **UNC**
5.1.1990. Brown, red and multicolor. Antonio Raimondi at right, arms at center. 7.50 20.00
Back: Indian comforting Raimundi. Watermark: Antonio Raimondi. Printer: BdeM.

150 5,000,000 Intis   **VF**   **UNC**
16.1.1991. Brown, red and multicolor. Antonio Raimondi at right, arms at center,
plants printed on watermark area at left. Back: Old building at right. Watermark:
Antonio Raimondi. Printer: IPS-Roma.
    a. Issued note.   2.00   7.50
    s. Specimen. Red overprint: SPECIMEN on face.   —   150

1991; 1992 Issues

MONETARY REFORM:
   1 Nuevo Sol = 1 Million Intis

151 10 Nuevos Soles   **VF**   **UNC**
1.2.1991. Dark green and blue-green on multicolor underprint. WW II era fighter
plane as monument at upper center, José Abelardo Quiñones at right, arms at upper right. Back: Biplane inverted (signifying pilot's death) at left center. Watermark:
José Abelardo Quiñones. Printer: TDLR. 140x65mm.
    a. Issued note.   FV   9.50
    s. Specimen. Overprint: MUESTRA SIN VALOR on both sides.   —   175

151A 10 Nuevos Soles   **VF**   **UNC**
10.9.1992. Dark green and blue-green on multicolor underprint. WW II era fighter FV   9.50
plane as monument at upper center, José Abelardo Quiñones at right, arms at upper right. Back: Biplane inverted (signifying pilot's death) at left center. Watermark:
José Abelardo Quiñones. Printer: IPS-Roma. 140x65mm.

152 20 Nuevos Soles   **VF**   **UNC**
1.2.1991. Black, brown and orange on multicolor underprint. Patio of San Marcos FV 22.50
University at center, Raul Porras B. at right, arms at upper right. Back: Palace of
TorreTagle at left center. Watermark: Raul Porras B. Printer: TDLR. 140x65mm.

153 20 Nuevos Soles   **VF**   **UNC**
25.6.1992. Black, brown and orange on multicolor underprint. Patio of San FV 17.50
Marcos University at center, Raul Porras B. at right, arms at upper right. Back:
Palace of TorreTagle at left center. Watermark: Raul Porras B. Printer: IPS-Roma.
140x65mm.

154 50 Nuevos Soles   **VF**   **UNC**
1.2.1991; 25.6.1992. Red-brown, blue-violet and black on multicolor underprint.
Building at center, Abraham Valdelomar at right, arms at upper right. Back:
Laguna de Huacachina at left center. Watermark: Abraham Valdelomar. Printer:
IPS-Roma. 140x65mm.
    a. Issued note.   FV 40.00
    s. Specimen. Overprint: SPECIMEN on face.   —   175

155 100 Nuevos Soles   **VF**   **UNC**
1.2.1991; 25.6.1992; 10.9.1992. Black, blue-black, red-violet and deep green on
multicolor underprint. Arch monument at center, Jorge Basadre (Grohmann) at
right. Back: National Library at left center. Watermark: Jorge Basadre (Grohmann).
Printer: IPS-Roma. 140x65mm.
    a. Name as: *Jorge Basadre.* 1.2.1991.   FV 75.00
    b. Name as: *Jorge Basadre Grohmann.* 10.9.1992.   FV 70.00
    s. Specimen. Overprint in red on face.   FV   175

1994; 1995 Issue
#156-161 similar to #151-155 but w/clear wmk. area.

		VF	UNC
156	**10 Nuevos Soles**	FV	7.50

16.6.1994. Dark green and blue-green on multicolor underprint. WW II era fighter plane as monument at upper center, José Abelardo Quiñones at right, arms at upper right. Back: Biplane inverted (signifying pilot's death) at left center. Printer: TDLR. 140x65mm.

		VF	UNC
157	**10 Nuevos Soles**	FV	7.00

20.4.1995. Dark green and blue-green on multicolor underprint. WW II era fighter plane as monument at upper center, José Abelardo Quiñones at right, arms at upper right. Back: Biplane inverted (signifying pilot's death) at left center. Printer: G&D. 140x65mm.

		VF	UNC
158	**20 Nuevos Soles**	FV	15.00

16.6.1994. Black, brown and orange on multicolor underprint. Patio of San Marcos University at center, Raul Porras B. at right, arms at upper right. Back: Palace of Torre Tagle at left center. Printer: TDLR. 140x65mm.

		VF	UNC
159	**20 Nuevos Soles**	FV	14.00

20.4.1995. Black, brown and orange on multicolor underprint. Patio of San Marcos University at center, Raul Porras B. at right, arms at upper right. Back: Palace of Torre Tagle at left center. Printer: TDLR. 140x65mm.

		VF	UNC
160	**50 Nuevos Soles**	FV	37.50

16.6.1994; 20.4.1995. Brown, deep blue and black on multicolor underprint. Building at center, Abraham Valdelomar at right, arms at upper right. Back: Laguna de Huacachina at left center. Printer: IPS-Roma. 140x65mm.

		VF	UNC
161	**100 Nuevos Soles**	FV	65.00

20.4.1995. Black, blue-black, red-violet and deep green on multicolor underprint. Like #155b. Arch monument at center, Jorge Basadre (Grohmann) at right, arms at upper right. Back: National Library at left center. Printer: IPS-Roma. 140x65mm.

		VF	UNC
162	**200 Nuevos Soles**		

20.4.1995. Red, brown-violet and dark blue on multicolor underprint. Isabel Flores de Oliva, St. Rose of Lima at right, well in underprint at center. Back: Convent of Santo Domingo at left. Watermark: Isabel Flores de Oliva, St. Rose of Lima. Printer: IPS-Roma. 140x65mm.

		VF	UNC
	a. Issued note.	FV	120
	s. Specimne.	—	150

1996 Issue

		VF	UNC
163	**10 Nuevos Soles**	FV	10.00

24.4.1996. Dark green and blue-green on multicolor underprint. WW II era fighter plane as monument at upper center, José Abelardo Quiñones at right, arms at upper right. Back: Biplane inverted (signifying pilot's death) at left center. Printer: IPS-Roma. 140x65mm.

		VF	UNC
164	**20 Nuevos Soles**	FV	15.00

25.4.1996; 11.6.1997. Black, brown and orange on multicolor underprint. Patio of San Marcos University at center, Raul Porras B. at right, arms at upper right. Back: Palace of Torre Tagle at left center. Printer: IPS-Roma. 140x65mm.

		VF	UNC
165	**100 Nuevos Soles**	FV	65.00

25.4.1996. Black, blue-black, red-violet and deep green on multicolor underprint. Like #155b. Arch monument at cetnr, Jorge Basadre (Grohmann) at right, arms at upper right. Back: National Library at left. Printer: IPS-Roma. 140x65mm.

1997 Issue

		VF	UNC
166	**10 Nuevos Soles**	FV	9.00

11.6.1997; 6.8.1998; 20.5.1999. Dark green and blue-green on multicolor underprint. WW II era fighter plane as monument at upper center, José Abelardo Quiñones at right, arms at upper right. Back: Biplane inverted (signifying pilot's death) at left center. Printer: BABN. 140x65mm.

		VF	UNC
167	**20 Nuevos Soles**		

11.6.1997; 6.8.1998. Black, brown and orange on multicolor underprint. Patio of San Marcos University at center, Raul Porras B. at right, arms at upper right. Back: Palace of TorreTagle at left center. Printer: BABN. 140x65mm.

		VF	UNC
	a. 11.6.1997.	FV	15.00
	b. 6.8.1998.	FV	15.00

		VF	UNC
168	**50 Nuevos Soles**	FV	37.50

11.6.1997. Red-brown, blue-violet and black on multicolor underprint. Building at center, Abraham Valdelomar at right, arms at upper right. Back: Laguna de Huacachina at left center. Printer: IPS-Roma. 140x65mm.

1998 Issue

		VF	UNC
169	**50 Nuevos Soles**	FV	37.50

6.8.1998. Red-brown, blue-violet and black on multicolor underprint. Building at center. Abraham Valdelomar at right, arms at upper right. Back: Laguna de Huacachina. Printer: BABN. 140x65mm.

1999 Issue

170   20 Nuevos Soles   VF   UNC
20.5.1999. Black, blue-black, red-violet and deep green on multicolor underprint.   FV   15.00
Patio of San Marcos University at center. Raúl Porras Barrenechea at right, arms at
upper right. Back: Palace of Torre Tagle at left center. Printer: FNMT. 140x65mm.

171   50 Nuevos Soles   VF   UNC
20.5.1999. Red-brown, blue-violet and black on multicolor underprint. Building   FV   37.50
at center. Abraham Valdelomar at right, arms at upper right. Back: Laguna de
Huacachina. Printer: (T)DLR. 140x65mm.

172   100 Nuevos Soles   VF   UNC
20.5.1999. Black, blue-black, red-violet and green on multicolor underprint. Arch   FV   65.00
monument at center, Jorge Basadre Grohmann at right, arms at upper center.
Back: National Library. Printer: BABN. 140x65mm.

2000 Series

173   20 Nuevos Soles   VF   UNC
20.5.1999; 12.10.2000. Black, brown and orange on multicolor underprint. Patio of
San Marcos University at center. Raúl Porras Barrenechea at right. Back: Palace
of Torre Tagle at left center. Printer: BABN. 140x65mm.
    a. 20.5.1999.   FV   15.00
    b. 12.10.2000.   FV   12.50

2001; 2004 Issue

174   10 Nuevos Soles   VF   UNC
1.3.2001. Dark green and blue-green on multicolor underprint. WW II era fighter   FV   9.00
plane as monument at upper center. José Abelardo Quiñones at right, arms at
upper center. Back: Biplane inverted (signifying pilot's death). Printer: F-CO.
140x65mm.

175   10 Nuevos Soles   VF   UNC
27.9.2001. Dark green and blue-green on multicolor underprint. WW II era fighter   FV   9.00
plane as monument at upper center. José Abelardo Quiñones at right, arms at
upper center. Back: Biplane inverted (signifying pilot's death). Printer: (T)DLR.
140x65mm.

176   20 Nuevos Soles   VF   UNC
2001; 2004; 2006. Black, brown and orange on multicolor underprint. Patio of
San Marcos University at center. Raúl Porras Barrenechea at right, arms at upper
right. Back: Palace of Torre Tagle at left center. 140x65mm.
    a. 27.9.2001. Printer: F-CO.   FV   15.00
    b. 28.10.2004. Printer: F-CO.   FV   15.00
    c. 21.12.2006. Printer: (T)DLR.   FV   15.00

177   50 Nuevos Soles   VF   UNC
27.9.2001. Red-brown, blue-violet and black on multicolor underprint. Building   FV   37.50
at center. Abraham Valdelomar at right, arms at upper center. Back: Laguna de
Huacachina. Printer: JEZ. 140x65mm.

178   100 Nuevos Soles   VF   UNC
2001; 2004. Black, blue-black, red-violet and green on multicolor underprint. Arch
monument at center, Jorge Basadre Grohman at right, arms at upper right. Back:
National Library. Printer: F-CO. 140x65mm.
    a. 27.9.2001.   FV   65.00
    b. 28.10.2004.   FV   65.00

2005 Issue

179   10 Nuevos Soles   VF   UNC
11.8.2005; 21.12.2006. Without colored planchettes as on #174. Dark green and
blue-green on multicolor underprint. WW II era fighter plane as monument at
upper center, José Abelardo Quiñones at right, arms at upper right. Back: Biplane
inverted (signifying pilot's death). Printer: F-CO. 140x65mm.
    a. 11.8.2005.   FV   7.50
    b. 21.12.2006.   FV   6.50

180   50 Nuevos Soles   VF   UNC
11.8.2005; 21.12.2006. Red brown, blue violet and black on multicolor underprint.
Building at center. Abraham Valdelomar at right, arms at upper right. Back:
Laguna de Huacachina. 140x65mm.
    a. 11.8.2005. Printer: BDDK.   FV   37.50
    b. 21.12.2006. Printer: F-CO.   FV   37.50

181   100 Nuevos Soles   VF   UNC
21.12.2006. Black, blue-black, red-violet and green on multicolor underprint. Arch   FV   65.00
monument at center, Jorge Basadre Grohmann at right, arms at upper right. Back:
National Library. Printer: G&D. 140x65mm.

2009 Issue

182   10 Nuevos Soles   VF   UNC
13.8.2009. Green, orange, brown and multicolor underprint. José Abelardo   FV   10.00
Quiñones Gonzales at right. Back: Inca site of Machu Picchu mountian top ruins
at left. 140x65mm.

183   20 Nuevos Soles   VF   UNC
13.8.2009. Brown, orane, green, red and multicolor underprint. Raúl Porras Bar-   FV   15.00
renechea at right. Back: Chan Chan archaeological complex at left. 140x65mm.

184   50 Nuevos Soles   VF   UNC
13.8.2009. Rose and green on multicolor underprint. Abraham Valdelomar at right.   FV   37.50
Back: Templo Nuevo at left. Watermark: Valdelomar and 50. 140x65mm.

185   100 Nuevos Soles   VF   UNC
13.8.2009. Blue on multicolor underprint. Jorge Basadre Grohman at right. Back: FV   65.00
Gran Pajatén. Watermark: Grohmann and 100. 140x65mm.

186   200 Nuevos Soles   **VF   UNC**
13.8.2009. Black and rose on multicolor underprint. St. Rose of Lima at right.   FV   120
Back: Ciudad Sagrada de Caral at left. Watermark: St. Rose and 200. 140x65mm.

2012 Issue

190   100 Nuevos Soles   **VF   UNC**
22.3.2012. Blue on multicolor underprint. Jorge Basadre Grohman at right.   FV   65.00
Watermark: Grohman and 100 140x65mm.

2013 Issue

187   10 Nuevos Soles   **VF   UNC**
17.1.2013. Dark green on multicolor underprint. Jose Abelardo Quinones Gonza-   FV   10.00
les at right. 140x65mm.

188   20 Nuevos Soles   **VF   UNC**
17.1.2013. Brown, orange, green, red and multicolor. Raul Porras Barrenechea at   FV   15.00
right. 140x65mm.

189   50 Nuevos Soles   **VF   UNC**
Expected new issue. 140x65mm.   —   —

Banco de Credito del Perú / Banco Central de Reserva del Perú

1985 Emergency Check Issue

R2   100,000 Soles   **VF   UNC**
2.9.1985. Black text on light blue text underprint. Two signature varieties.   150   —

Banco de la Nación / Banco Central de Reserva del Perú

1985 Cheques Circulares de Gerencia Issue

#R6-R8 bank monogram at upper l.

R6   50,000 Soles   **VF   UNC**
9.9.1985; 16.9.1985. Black text on tan underprint. Bank at center, bank monogram   125   —
at upper left.

R7   100,000 Soles   **VF   UNC**
2.9.1985. Black text on light blue underprint. Bank at center, bank monogram at   125   —
upper left.

R8   200,000 Soles   **VF   UNC**
2.9.1985. Black text on pink underprint. Bank at center, bank monogram at upper   125   —
left.

PHILIPPINES

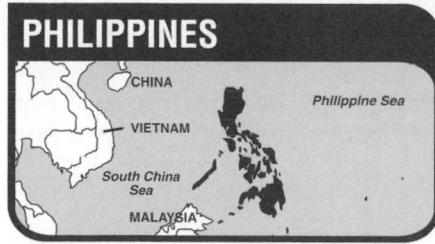

The Republic of the Philippines, an archipelago in the western Pacific 500 miles (805 km.) from the southeast coast of Asia, has an area of 115,830 sq. mi. (300,000 sq. km.) and a population of 75.04 million. Capital: Manila. The economy of the 7,000-island group is based on agriculture, forestry and fishing. Timber, coconut products, sugar and hemp are exported. The Philippine Islands became a Spanish colony during the 16th century; they were ceded to the US in 1898 following the Spanish-American War. In 1935 the Philippines became a self-governing commonwealth. Manuel Quezon was elected president and was tasked with preparing the country for independence after a 10-year transition. In 1942 the islands fell under Japanese occupation during World War II, and US forces and Filipinos fought together during 1944-45 to regain control. On 4 July 1946 the Republic of the Philippines attained its independence. The 20-year rule of Ferdinand Marcos ended in 1986, when a "people power" movement in Manila ("EDSA 1") forced him into exile and installed Corazon Aquino as president. Her presidency was hampered by several coup attempts, which prevented a return to full political stability and economic development. Fidel Ramos was elected president in 1992 and his administration was marked by greater stability and progress on economic reforms. In 1992, the US closed its last military bases on the islands. Joseph Estrada was elected president in 1998, but was succeeded by his vice-president, Gloria Macapagal-Arroyo, in January 2001 after Estrada's stormy impeachment trial on corruption charges broke down and another "people power" movement ("EDSA 2") demanded his resignation. Macapagal-Arroyo was elected to a six-year term as president in May 2004. The Philippine Government faces threats from three terrorist groups on the US Government's Foreign Terrorist Organization list, but in 2006 and 2007 scored some major successes in capturing or killing key wanted terrorists. Decades of Muslim insurgency in the southern Philippines have led to a peace accord with one group and on-again/off-again peace talks with another.

RULERS:
Spanish to 1898
United States, 1898-1946

MONETARY SYSTEM:
1 Peso = 100 Centavos to 1967
1 Piso = 100 Sentimos, 1967-

Type 1	Type 2	Type 3	Type 4	Type 5

SIGNATURE VARIETIES

1	E. Quirino	M. Cuaderno
2	R. Magsaysay	M. Cuaderno
3	C. Garcia	M. Cuaderno
4	C. Garcia	A. Castillo
5	D. Macapagal	A. Castillo
6	F. Marcos	A. Castillo
7	F. Marcos	A. Calalang
8	F. Marcos	G. Licaros
9	F. Marcos	J. Laya

SIGNATURE VARIETIES

10	F. Marcos	J. Fernandez
11	C. Aquino	J. Fernandez
12	C. Aquino	J. Cuisia
13	M. Ramos	J. Cuisia
14	M. Ramos	G.C. Singson
15	J.E. Estrada	G.C. Singson
16	J.E. Estrada	R.B. Buenaventura
17	G. Macapagal-Arroyo	R.B. Buenaventura

REPUBLIC

Central Bank of the Philippines
1949 ND "English" Issues

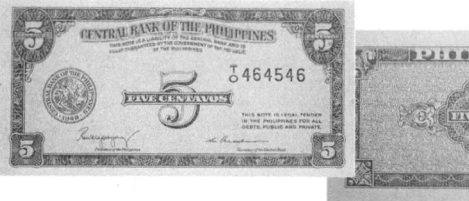

125 5 Centavos
ND (1949). Red on tan underprint. Central Bank Seal Type 1 at left. Signature 1. Printer: SBNC.

	VF	UNC
a. Issued note.	0.50	2.00
s. Specimen. Punch hole cancelled.	—	200
ct. Color trial. Black on green underprint.	—	150

126 5 Centavos
ND. Red on tan underprint. Central Bank Seal Type 1 at left. Signature 2. Like #125. Printer: W&S.

	VF	UNC
a. Issued note.	0.25	2.50
p. Proof.	—	250
s. Specimen.	—	250

127 10 Centavos
ND. Brownish purple on tan underprint. Central Bank Seal Type 1 at left. Signature 1. Printer: SBNC.

	VF	UNC
a. Issued note.	0.50	1.75
r. Remainder without serial #.	75.00	125
s. Specimen.	—	250

128 10 Centavos
ND. Brownish purple on tan underprint. Central Bank Seal Type 1 at left. Signature 2. LIke #127. Printer: W&S.

		VF	UNC
a. Issued note.		0.50	1.25
s. Specimen.		—	250

129 20 Centavos
ND. Green on light green underprint. Central Bank Seal Type 1 at left. Signature 1. Printer: SBNC.

		VF	UNC
a. Issued note.		1.00	3.50
r. Remainder without serial #.		75.00	125
s. Specimen.		—	300

130 20 Centavos
ND. Green on light green underprint. Printer: TDLR.

		VF	UNC
a. Signature 2.		0.50	2.00
b. Signature 3.		0.50	2.00
s1. Specimen. Pin perforated.		—	300
s2. Specimen. Red overprint.		—	500

131 50 Centavos
ND. Blue on light blue underprint. Signature 2. Printer: TDLR.

		VF	UNC
a. Issued note.		0.50	3.00
p. Proof.		—	250
s. Specimen.		—	150
ct. Color trial. Brown on tan underprint.		—	150

132 1/2 Peso
ND. Green on yellow and blue underprint. Ox-cart with Mt. Mayon in background at center. Large Central Bank Seal Type 1 at lower right. Signature 2. Printer: TDLR.

		VF	UNC
a. Issued note.		2.50	14.00
s. Specimen.		—	550

133 1 Peso
ND. Black on light gold and blue underprint. Portrait of A. Mabini at left. Large Central Bank Seal Type 1 at lower right. Back: Barasoain Church at center. Printer: TDLR.

	VF	UNC
a. Signature 1. *GENUINE* in very light tan letters just beneath top heading on face.	30.00	110
b. Signature 1. Without *GENUINE* on face.	2.00	12.50
c. Signature 2.	2.50	15.00
d. Signature 3.	2.00	10.00
e. Signature 4.	1.25	8.00
f. Signature 5.	1.00	2.50
g. Signature 6.	0.50	2.00
h. Signature 7.	1.00	1.50
s1. Signature as a. Specimen.	—	200
s2. Signature as b. Specimen. (De La Rue).	—	200
s3. Signature as c. Specimen. (De La Rue).	—	200
s4. Signature as d. Specimen. (De La Rue).	—	200
s5. Signature as e. Specimen. (De La Rue).	—	200
s6. Signature as f. Specimen.	—	45.00
s7. Signature as f. Specimen. (De La Rue).	—	250
s8. Signature as g. Specimen.	—	40.00
s9. Signature as g. Specimen. (De La Rue).	—	250
10. Signature as h. Specimen.	—	25.00
11. Signature as h. Specimen. (De La Rue).	—	250

134 2 Pesos
ND. Black on blue and gold underprint. Portrait of J. Rizal at left. Large Central Bank Seal Type 1 at lower right. Back: Landing of Magellan in the Philippines. Printer: TDLR.

	VF	UNC
a. Signature 1.	7.50	15.00
b. Signature 2.	2.00	5.00
c. Signature 4.	2.50	10.00
d. Signature 5.	0.50	2.00
p. Signature as b. Proof.	—	250
s1. Signature as a. Specimen. (De La Rue) Cancelled.	—	250
s2. Signature as b. Specimen.	—	60.00
s3. Signature as b. Specimen. (De La Rue).	—	250
s4. Signature as c. Specimen. (De La Rue).	0.00	250
s5. Signature as d. Specimen.	—	60.00

135 5 Pesos
ND. Black on yellow and gold underprint. Portrait of M. H. del Pilar at left, Lopez Jaena at right. Large Central Bank Seal Type 1 at lower right. Back: Newspaper *La Solidaridad*. Printer: TDLR.

	VF	UNC
a. Signature 1.	7.50	40.00
b. Signature 2.	3.50	10.00
c. Signature 3.	7.50	40.00
d. Signature 4.	3.00	10.00
e. Signature 5.	0.50	2.50
f. Signature 8.	0.50	2.00
p. Proof.	—	150
s1. Signature as a. Specimen. (De La Rue).	—	250
s2. Signature as b. Specimen. (De La Rue).	—	250
s3. Signature as d. Specimen. (De La Rue).	—	250
s4. Signature as e. Specimen.	—	30.00
s5. Signature as e. Specimen. (De La Rue).	—	200
s6. Signature as f. Specimen. Red overprint *SPCEIMEN* on each side.	—	25.00

136 10 Pesos

ND. Black on tan and light red underprint. Fathers Burgos, Gomez and Zamora at left. Large Central Bank Seal Type 1 at lower right. Back: Monument. Printer: TDLR.

		VF	UNC
a.	Signature 1.	500	5,775
b.	Signature 2.	5.00	25.00
c.	Signature 3.	5.00	25.00
d.	Signature 4.	5.00	30.00
e.	Signature 5.	1.00	3.00
f.	Signature 8.	1.00	2.00
s1.	Signature as b. Specimen.	—	70.00
s2.	Signature as c. Specimen.	—	70.00
s3.	Signature as c. Specimen. (De La Rue)	—	250
s4.	Signature as d. Specimen	—	75.00
s5.	Signature as d. Specimen. (De La Rue).	—	250
s6.	Signature as e. Specimen.	—	75.00
s7.	Signature as e. Specimen. (De La Rue).	—	200
s8.	Signature as f. Specimen.	—	15.00

137 20 Pesos

ND. Black on yellow underprint. Portrait of A. Bonifacio at left, E. Jacinto at right. Large Central Bank Seal Type 1 at lower right. Back: Flag and monument. Printer: TDLR.

		VF	UNC
a.	Signature 1.	375	1,000
b.	Signature 2.	20.00	50.00
c.	Signature 4.	10.00	20.00
d.	Signature 5.	1.50	3.00
e.	Signature 8.	1.00	2.50
p.	Signature as d. Proof.	—	150
s1.	Signature as a. Specimen.	—	175
s2.	Signature as c. Specimen. (De La Rue).	—	200
s3.	Signature as d. Specimen.	—	35.00
s4.	Signature as d. Specimen (De La Rue).	—	175
s5.	Signature as e. Specimen. Red overprint: *SPECIMEN* on both sides.	—	20.00

138 50 Pesos

ND. Black on pink and light tan underprint. Portrait of A. Luna at left. Large Central Bank Seal Type 1 at lower right. Back: Scene of blood compact of Sikatuna and Legaspi. Printer: TDLR.

		VF	UNC
a.	Signature 1.	500	—
b.	Signature 2.	50.00	125
c.	Signature 3.	12.50	25.00
d.	Signature 5.	1.50	5.00
p.	Signature as d. Proof.	—	200
s1.	Signature as a. Specimen. (De La Rue).	—	700
s2.	Signature as b. Specimen. (De La Rue).	—	300
s3.	Signature as d. Specimen.	—	50.00
s4.	Signature as d. Specimen. (De La Rue).	—	500

139 100 Pesos

ND. Black on gold underprint. Portrait of T. Sora at left. Large Central Bank Seal Type 1 at lower right. Signature 1. Back: Regimental flags. Printer: TDLR. 160x66mm.

		VF	UNC
a.	Issued note.	6.00	10.00
s.	Specimen.	—	250
ct.	Color trial. Green on tan and light blue underprint.	—	550

140 200 Pesos

ND. Green on pink and light blue underprint. Portrait of President Manuel Quezon at left. Large Central Bank Seal Type 1 at lower right. Signature 1. Back: Legislative building. Printer: TDLR. 160x66mm.

		VF	UNC
a.	Issued note.	5.00	15.00
s.	Specimen (De La Rue).	—	350

141 500 Pesos

ND. Black on purple and light tan underprint. Portrait of President Manuel Roxas at left. Large Central Bank Seal Type 1 at lower right. Signature 1. Back: Central Bank. Printer: TDLR.

		VF	UNC
a.	Issued note.	40.00	75.00
s.	Specimen. (De La Rue).	—	750
ct.	Brown on light green and tan underprint.	—	1,300

Bangko Sentral ng Pilipinas
1969 ND "Pilipino" Issue

#142-147 Replacement notes: Serial # prefix "+".

142 1 Piso

ND (1969). Blue and black on multicolor underprint. J. Rizal at left, heading at top in double outline. Central Bank Seal Type 2. Back: Scene of Aguinaldo's Independence Declaration of June 12, 1898. 160x66mm.

	VF	UNC
a. Signature 7.	0.50	2.50
b. Signature 8.	0.50	1.50
s1. Signature as a. Specimen.	—	40.00
s2. Signature as a. Specimen. (De La Rue)	—	45.00
s3. Signature as b. Specimen. Red overprint: *SPECIMEN* on face.	—	40.00

143 5 Piso

ND (1969). Green and brown on multicolor underprint. A. Bonifacio at left in brown, heading at top in double outline. Central Bank Seal Type 3. Back: Scene of the Katipunan organization. Watermark: A. Bonifacio. Printer: G&D (without imprint). 160x66mm.

	VF	UNC
a. Signature 7.	1.50	2.00
b. Signature 8.	1.00	3.00
s1. Signature as a. Specimen.	—	125
s2. Signature as b. Specimen.	—	30.00

144 10 Piso

ND (1969). Brown on multicolor underprint. A. Mabini at left, heading at top in double outline. Central Bank Seal Type 3. Back: Barasoain Church. Watermark: A. Mabini. Printer: G&D (without imprint). 160x66mm.

	VF	UNC
a. Signature 7.	1.50	3.00
b. Signature 8.	1.50	3.00
s1. Signature as a. Specimen.	—	75.00
s2. Signature as b. Specimen.	—	50.00

145 20 Piso

ND (1969). Orange and brown on multicolor underprint. M. L. Quezon at left in brown, heading at top in double outline. Central Bank Seal Type 3. Back: Malakanyang Palace. Watermark: M. L. Quezon. Printer: G&D (without imprint). 160x66mm.

	VF	UNC
a. Signature 7.	2.00	5.00
b. Signature 8.	2.00	5.00
s1. Signature as a. Specimen.	—	100
s2. Signature as b. Specimen. Red overprint: *SPECIMEN* on face.	—	75.00

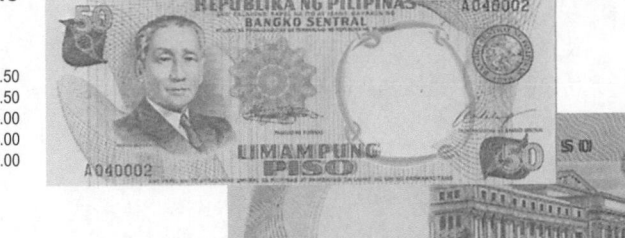

146 50 Piso

ND (1969). Red on multicolor underprint. S. Osmeña at left, heading at top in double outline. Central Bank Seal Type 2. Back: Legislative Building. Watermark: S. Osmeña. 160x66mm.

	VF	UNC
a. Signature 7.	4.00	8.00
b. Signature 8.	3.00	9.00
s1. Signature as a. Specimen. (De La Rue).	—	200
s2. Signature as b. Specimen.	—	30.00
s3. Signature as b. Specimen. (De La Rue).	—	225

147 100 Piso

ND (1969). Purple on multicolor underprint. M. Roxas at left, heading at top in double outline. Central Bank Seal Type 2. Back: Old Central Bank. Watermark: M. Roxas. 160x66mm.

	VF	UNC
a. Signature 7.	7.50	20.00
b. Signature 8.	7.50	20.00
p. Signature as a. Proof.	—	475
s1. Signature as a. Specimen.	—	50.00
s2. Signature as a. Specimen. (De La Rue).	—	175
s3. Signature as b. Specimen.	—	50.00
s4. Signature as b. Specimen. (De La Rue).	—	200

1970's ND First Issue

#148-151 Replacement notes: Serial # prefix "+".

148 5 Piso

ND. Green on multicolor underprint. A. Bonifacio at left in green. Central Bank Seal Type 2. Heading at top in single outline, left and right ends completely filled in. Signature 8. Back: Scene of the Katipunan organization. Watermark: A. Bonifacio. Printer: G&D (without imprint). 160x66mm.

	VF	UNC
a. Issued note.	0.75	2.00
s. Specimen.	—	20.00

149 10 Piso

ND. Brown on multicolor underprint. A. Mabini at left. Central Bank Seal Type 2. Heading at top in single outline, left and right ends completely filled in without white paper showing at sides. Signature 8. Back: Barasoain Church, without white paper showing at sides. Watermark: A. Mabini at left. Printer: G&D (without imprint). 160x66mm.

	VF	UNC
a. Issued note.	3.00	8.00
s. Specimen.	—	35.00

150 20 Piso   VF   UNC

ND. Orange and blue on multicolor underprint. M. L. Quezon at left in orange.
Central Bank Seal Type 2. Heading at top in single outline, left and right ends
completely filled in. Signature 8. Back: Malakanyang Palace. Watermark: M. L.
Quezon. Printer: G&D (without imprint). 160x66mm.

    a. Issued note.   1.00   5.00
    s. Specimen.   —   75.00

151 50 Piso   VF   UNC

ND. Red on multicolor underprint. Similar to #146. Seal under denomination
instead of over, signature closer, *LIMAMPUNG PISO* in one line, and other
modifications. Central Bank Seal Type 2. Heading at top in single outline, left adn
right ends completely filled in. Signature 8. Back: Legislative building. Watermark:
S. Osmeña. 160x66mm.

    a. Issued note.   4.00   9.00
    s. Specimen.   —   70.00

1970's ND Second Issue

#152-158 Central Bank Seal Type 2. Ovpt: *ANG BAGONG LIPUNAN* **(New Society) on wmk. area, 1974-85. Replacement notes: Serial # prefix "+".**

152 2 Piso   VF   UNC

ND. UV: legend in curve over Rizal portrait fluoresce orange. Blue on multicolor
underprint. J. Rizal at left. Central Bank Seal Type 2. Signature 8. Back: Scene
of Aguinaldo's Independence Declaration of June 12, 1898. Watermark: J. Rizal.
160x66mm.

    a. Issued note.   0.50   1.00
    s1. Specimen.   —   12.00
    s2. Specimen. (De La Rue).   —   225

153 5 Piso   VF   UNC

ND. Green on multicolor underprint. A. Bonifacio in green at left. Central Bank
Seal Type 2. Signature 8. Back: Scene of the Katipunan organization. Watermark:
A. Bonifacio. Printer: G&D (without imprint). 160x66mm.

    a. Dark overprint.   1.00   5.00
    b. Light overprint.   1.00   3.00
    s1. Specimen.   —   15.00
    s2. Specimen. (De La Rue).   —   225

154 10 Piso   VF   UNC

ND. Brown on multicolor underprint. A. Mabini at left. Heading at top in single
outline, left and right ends completely filled in without white paper showing at
sides. Central Bank Seal Type 2. Signature 8. Back: Barasoain Church, without
white paper showing at sides. Watermark: A. Mabini at left. Printer: G&D (without
imprint). 160x66mm.

    a. Issued note.   1.00   3.50
    s1. Specimen.   —   26.00
    s2. Specimen. (De La Rue).   —   225

Note. Varieties of light or dark overprints.

155 20 Piso   VF   UNC

ND. Orange on multicolor underprint. M. L. Quezon at left in orange. Heading at
top in single outline, left and right ends completely filled in. Central Bank Seal
Type 2. Signature 8. Back: Malakanyang Palace. Watermark: M. L. Quezon.
Printer: G&D (without imprint). 160x66mm.

    a. Issued note.   1.50   4.00
    s1. Specimen.   —   35.00
    s2. Specimen. (De La Rue).   —   250

156 50 Piso   VF   UNC

ND. Red on multicolor underprint. Similar to #146. Seal under denomination,
signature closer, *LIMAMPUNG PISO* in one line, and other modifications. Heading
at top in single outline, left and right. Central B Back: Legislative building. Watermark: S. Osmeña. Printer: G&D (without imprint). 160x66mm.

    a. Brown signature title.   4.00   6.00
    b. Red signature title.   7.50   10.00
    s1. Signature as b. Specimen.   —   45.00
    s2. Signature as b. Specimen. (De La Rue). —   250

157 100 Piso
ND. Purple on multicolor underprint. M. Roxas at left, heading at top in double outline. Central Bank Seal Type 2 in purple at left. Back: Old Central Bank. Printer: G&D (without imprint). 160x66mm.

	VF	UNC
a. Signature 7.	15.00	30.00
b. Signature 8.	10.00	20.00
s1. Signature as a. Specimen.	—	200
s2. Signature as b. Specimen.	—	50.00

158 100 Piso
ND. Purple on multicolor underprint. M. Roxas at left, heading at top solid letters, denomintaion near upper right. Green Central Bank Seal Type 2 at lower right. Signature 8. Back: Old Central Bank, denomination at bottom. Watermark: M. Roxas. Printer: G&D (without imprint). 160x66mm.

	VF	UNC
a. Issued note.	25.00	45.00
s. Specimen.	—	175

1978 ND Issue

#159-167 Replacement notes: Serial # prefix "+".

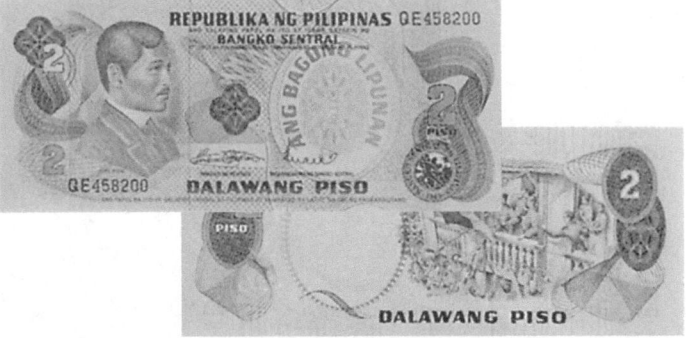

159 2 Piso
ND. UV: legend in curve over Rizal portrait fluoresce orange. Blue on multicolor underprint. J. Rizal at left. Signature 8. Central Bank Seal Type 4. Back: Scene of Aguinaldo's Independence Declaration of June 12, 1898. Watermark: J. Rizal. 160x66mm.

	VF	UNC
a. Signature 8.	0.30	2.50
b. Signature 9. Black serial #.	0.50	2.50
c. Signature 9. Red serial #. Single and double letter serial # prefix varieties.	0.30	1.00
d. Signature as b. Uncut sheet of 4.	—	15.00
s1. Signature as a. Specimen.	—	15.00
s2. Signature as b. Specimen.	—	15.00

160 5 Piso
ND. UV: legend in curve over Bonifacio portrait fluoresce orange. Green on multicolor underprint. A. Bonifacio in green at left. Signature 8. Central Bank Seal Type 4. Back: Scene of the Katipunan organization. Watermark: A. Bonifacio. Printer: G&D (without imprint). 160x66mm.

	VF	UNC
a. Signature 8.	0.50	1.75
b. Signature 9. Black serial #.	1.00	7.00
c. Signature 9. Red serial #.	0.40	1.00
d. Signature 10.	0.40	1.25
e. Signature as b. Uncut sheet of 4.	—	30.00
f. Signature as d. Uncut sheet of 4.	—	30.00
s1. Signature as a. Specimen.	—	15.00
s2. Signature as b. Specimen.	—	20.00

161 10 Piso
ND. Brown on multicolor underprint. A. Mabini at left. Heading at top in single outline, left and right ends completely filled in without white paper showing at sides. Signature 8. Central Bank Seal Type 4. Back: Barasoain Church, without white paper showing at sides. Printer: G&D (without imprint). 160x66mm.

	VF	UNC
a. Signature 8.	0.75	2.00
b. Signature 9.	1.00	3.00
c. Signature 10. Black serial #.	0.50	2.00
d. Signature 10. Red serial #.	1.00	8.00
e. Signature as b. Uncut sheet of 4.	—	35.00
f. Signature as c. Uncut sheet of 4.	—	35.00
s1. Signature as a. Specimen.	—	15.00
s2. Signature as b. Specimen.	—	15.00

162 20 Piso
ND. Orange and blue on multicolor underprint. M. L. Quezon at left in orange. Heading at top in single outline, left and right ends completely filled in. Signature 8. Central Bank Seal Type 4. Back: Malakanyang Palace. Watermark: M. L. Quezon. Printer: G&D (without imprint). 160x66mm.

	VF	UNC
a. Signature 8.	1.00	3.00
b. Signature 9.	1.00	4.00
c. Signature 10.	1.00	4.50
d. Signature as b. Uncut sheet of 4.	—	40.00
e. Signature as d. Uncut sheet of 4.	—	40.00
s1. Signature as a. Specimen.	—	20.00
s2. Signature as b. Specimen.	—	30.00

163 50 Piso
ND. Red on multicolor underprint. Like #156. Central Bank Seal Type 4. Back: Legislative building. Watermark: S. Osmeña. Printer: G&D (without imprint). 160x66mm.

	VF	UNC
a. Signature 8.	2.00	5.50
b. Signature 9.	2.00	4.00
c. Signature 10.	1.50	5.00
s1. Signature as a. Specimen.	—	35.00
s2. Signature as b. Specimen.	—	35.00

164 100 Piso
ND. Purple and deep olive-green on multicolor underprint. M. Roxas at left, heading at top solid letters, denominaion near upper right. Green Central Bank Seal Type 4 at lower right. Signature 8. Back: New Central Bank complex with ships behind. 160x66mm.

	VF	UNC
a. Signature 8.	10.00	27.50
b. Signature 9.	4.00	7.00
c. Signature 10. Black serial #.	5.00	16.50
s1. Signature as a. Specimen.	—	35.00
s2. Signature as b. Specimen.	—	40.00

1978 Commemorative Issue
#165, Centennial - Birth of Pres. Osmeña, 1978

165 50 Piso
1978. Red on multicolor underprint. Black circular commemorative overprint at left on #163a. Central Bank Seal Type 4. Back: Legislative building. Watermark: S. Osmeña. 160x66mm.

	VF	UNC
	4.00	10.00

1981 Commemorative Issues
#166, Papal Visit of John Paul II, 1981

166 2 Piso
1981. Blue on multicolor underprint. Black commemorative overprint at center right on #159b. Central Bank Seal Type 4. Back: Scene of Aguinaldo's Independence Declaration of June 12,1898. 160x66mm.

	VF	UNC
a. Regular prefix letters before serial #.	0.50	3.00
b. Special prefix letters *JP* and all zero numbers (presentation).	—	100

#167, Inauguration of Pres. Marcos, 1981

167 10 Piso
1981. Brown on multicolor underprint. Black commemorative overprint at center right on #161b. Central Bank Seal Type 4. Back: Barasoain Church, without white paper showing at sides. 160x66mm.

	VF	UNC
a. Regular prefix letters before serial #. Wide and narrow collar varieties.	0.50	2.00
b. Special prefix letters *FM* and all zero numbers (presentation).	—	35.00
s. As a. Specimen. Wide or narrow collar.	—	50.00

1985-91 ND Issue
#168-173 replacement notes: Serial # prefix "+".

168 5 Piso
ND (1985-94. Deep green and brown on multicolor underprint. Aguinaldo at left center, plaque with cannon at right. Back: Aguinaldo's Independence Declaration of June 12, 1898. Watermark: Aguinaldo. 160x66mm.

	VF	UNC
a. Signature 10. Black serial #.	FV	2.00
b. Signature 11. Black serial #.	FV	1.25
c. Signature as b. Red serial # (1990).	FV	1.25
d. Signature 12. Red serial #.	FV	1.00
e. Signature 13. Red serial #.	FV	1.00
f. Signature as b. Uncut sheet of 4.	—	30.00
g. Signature as d. Uncut sheet of 4.	—	30.00
h. Signature as e. Uncut sheet of 4.	—	15.00
s1. Signature as b. Specimen.	—	15.00
s2. Signature as c. Specimen.	—	15.00
s3. Signature as d. Specimen.	—	20.00

169 10 Piso
ND (1985-94). UV: legend in curve over Mabini portrait fluoresce orange. Dark brown, brown and blue-gray on multicolor underprint. Mabini at left center, handwritten scroll at right. Back: Barasoain church. Watermark: Mabin. 160x66mm.

	VF	UNC
a. Signature 10.	0.50	3.00
b. Signature 11.	FV	1.50
c. Signature 12. Black serial #.	FV	2.00
d. Signature as c. Red serial #.	0.50	5.00
e. Signature 13.	—	2.00
f. Signature as b. Uncut sheet of 4.	—	25.00
g. Signature as b. Uncut sheet of 32.	—	100
s. Signature as b. Specimen.	—	25.00

170 20 Piso
ND (1986-94). Orange and blue on multicolor underprint. President M. Quezon at left center, arms at right. Back: Malakanyang Palace. Watermark: President M. Quezon. 160x66mm.

	VF	UNC
a. Signature 10. Black serial #.	1.50	8.00
b. Signature 11. Black serial #.	FV	3.00
c. Signature 12. Black serial #.	1.00	3.50
d. Signature as c. Red serial #. Not confirmed.	—	—
e. Signature 13. Red serial #.	1.00	5.00
f. Signature as e. Black serial #.	FV	4.00
g. Signature as e. Uncut sheet of 4.	—	45.00
s. Signature as b. Specimen.	—	35.00

171 50 Piso   **VF**   **UNC**

ND (1987-94). Red and purple on multicolor underprint. President Sergio Osmeña at left center, gavel at right. Back: Legislative building. Watermark: Sergio Osmeña. 160x66mm.

a. Signature 11. Black serial #.	1.00	6.00
b. Signature 12. Black serial #.	FV	4.50
c. Signature 13. Black serial #.	FV	4.00
s1. Signature as a. Specimen.	—	75.00
s2. Signature as b. Specimen.	—	60.00
s3. Signature as b. Uncut sheet of 4. Specimen.	—	30.00
s4. Signature as c. Specimen.	—	35.00

172 100 Piso   **VF**   **UNC**

ND (1987-94). Purple on multicolor underprint. President M. Roxas at left center, USA and Philippine flags at right. Back: New Central Bank complex at left center with old building facade above. Watermark: M. Roxas. 160x66mm.

a. Signature 11. Black serial #.	FV	7.50
b. Signature 11. Red serial #.	FV	35.00
c. Signature 12. Black serial #.	FV	11.00
d. Signature as b. Red serial #.	FV	12.50
e. Signature 13. Red serial #.	FV	9.00
f. Signature as d. Blue serial #.	FV	7.50
s1. Signature as a. Specimen.	—	120
s2. Signature as b. Specimen.	—	100
s3. Signature as c. Specimen.	—	50.00
s4. Signature as d. Specimen.	—	50.00
s5. Signature as d. Specimen. Uncut sheet of 4.	—	25.00
s6. Signature as b. Specimen. Uncut sheet of 4.	—	75.00
s7. Signature as b. Specimen. Uncut sheet of 32.	—	200
s8. Signature as e. Specimen. Blue serial #.	—	75.00
cr. Replacement note. Sign. as a. Red serial #. Rare.	—	—

173 500 Piso   **VF**   **UNC**

ND (1987-94). Black and brown on multicolor underprint. Aquino at left center, flag in underprint at center, typewriter at lower right. Back: Various scenes and gatherings of Aquino's career. Watermark: Aquino. 160x66mm.

a. Signature 11.	FV	30.00
b. Signature 12.	FV	40.00
c. Signature 13.	FV	30.00
s1. Signature as a. Specimen.	—	80.00
s2. Signature as b. Specimen.	—	55.00
s3. Signature as b. Specimen. Uncut sheet of 4.	—	75.00

174 1000 Piso   **VF**   **UNC**

ND (1991-94). Dark blue and blue-black on multicolor underprint. J. A. Santos, J. L. Escoda and V. Lim at left center, flaming torch at right. Back: Banawe rice terraces at left, to center, local carving and hut at center right. Watermark: J. A. Santos, J. L. Escoda and V. Lim. 160x66mm.

a. Signature 12.	FV	85.00
b. Signature 13.	FV	60.00

1986-91 Commemorative Issues

Commemorative overprints not listed were produced privately in the Philippines.

#175, Visit of President Aquino to the United States

175 5 Piso   **VF**   **UNC**

1986. Deep green and brown on multicolor underprint. Aguinaldo at left center, plaque with cannon at right, with commemorative text, seal and visit dates in watermark area. Prefix letters CA. Signature 11. Back: Aguinaldo's Independence Declaration of June 12, 1898. Watermark: Aguinaldo. 160x66mm.

a. Serial #1-20,000 in special folder.	FV	12.50
b. Serial # above 20,000.	FV	1.00
c. Uncut sheet of 4.	—	30.00

#176, Canonization of San Lorenzo Ruiz

176 5 Piso   **VF**   **UNC**

18.10.1987. Deep green and brown on multicolor underprint. Aguinaldo at left center, plaque with cannon at right, commemorative design, text and date in watermark area. Signature 11. Back: Aguinaldo's Independence Declaration of June 12, 1898. Watermark: Aguinaldo. 160x66mm.

a. Issued note.	FV	1.00
b. Uncut sheet of 8 in special folder.	—	20.00

#177, 40th Anniversary of Central Bank

177 5 Piso   **VF**   **UNC**

1989. Deep green and brown on multicolor underprint. Aguinaldo at left center, plaque with cannon at right, red commemorative design, text and date in watermark area. Signature 11. Back: Aguinaldo's Independence Declaration of June 12, 1898. 160x66mm.

a. Issued note.	FV	1.00
b. Uncut sheet of 8 in special folder.	—	20.00

#178, Women's Rights, 1990

178 5 Piso

1990. Deep green and brown on multicolor underprint. Aguinaldo at left center, plaque with cannon at right, black commemorative design, text and date in watermark area. Signature 11. Back: Aguinaldo's Independence Declaration of June 12, 1898. 160x66mm.

		VF	UNC
a.	Black serial #.	FV	1.00
b.	Red serial #.	FV	4.00

#179, II Plenary Council, 1991

179 5 Piso

	VF	UNC
1991. Deep green and brown on multicolor underprint. Aguinaldo at left center, plaque with cannon at right, black commemorative design and date in watermark area. Signature 12. Red serial #. Back: Aguinaldo's Independence Declaration of June 12, 1898. 160x66mm.	FV	1.25

1995 ND; 1998-99 Issue

180 5 Piso

	VF	UNC
ND (1995). Deep green and rown on multicolor underprint. Aguinaldo at left center, plaque with cannon at right. Cental Bank Seal Type 5. Signature 14. Back: Aguinaldo's Independence Declaration of June 12, 1898. Watermark: Aguinaldo. 160x66mm.	FV	1.00

181 10 Piso

ND (1995-97). Dark brown and blue-gray on multicolor underprint. Mabini at left center, handwritten scroll at right. Cental Bank Seal Type 5. Signature 14. Back: Barasoain church. Watermark: Mabini. 160x66mm.

		VF	UNC
a.	Red serial #.	FV	1.50
b.	Signature as a. Black serial #.	FV	1.50

182 20 Piso

ND (1997); 1998-. Orange and blue on multicolor underprint. President M. Quezon at left center, arms at right. Cental Bank Seal Type 5. Back: Malakanyang Palace. Watermark: M. Quezon. 160x66mm.

		VF	UNC
a.	Signature 14. Red serial #. ND.	FV	2.00
b.	Signature 14. Black serial #.	FV	2.25
c.	Signature 15. Black serial #. 1998; 1999.	FV	2.75
d.	Signature 15. Blue serial #. 1999.	FV	6.50
e.	Signature 16. Blue serial #. 1999, 2000.	FV	15.00
f.	Signature 16. Blue serial #. 2001.	FV	6.50
g.	Signature 17. Blue serial #. 2001.	FV	4.00
h.	Signature 17. Black serial #. 2001; 2002; 2003; 2004, 2005.	FV	3.50
i.	Signature 18. Black serial #. 2005; 2006; 2007; 2008; 2008A; 2009; 2010.	FV	4.00
j.	Signature 19. 2010; 2011.	FV	4.00
s1.	As a. Specimen.	—	50.00
s2.	Uncut sheet of 4. Specimen.	—	100

183 50 Piso

ND; 1998-2001. Red and purple on multicolor underprint. President Sergio Osmeña at left center, gavel at right. Cental Bank Seal Type 5. Back: Legislative building. Watermark: Sergio Osmeña. 160x66mm.

		VF	UNC
a.	Signature 14. ND (1995).	FV	4.00
b.	Signature as a. Red serial #. 1998.	FV	5.00
c.	Signature 16. Red serial #. 1999; 2000; 2001.	FV	4.00
d.	Signature 16. Black serial #. 2001.	FV	8.00
s.	Specimen.	—	—

184 100 Piso

ND; 1998-. Purple on multicolor underprint. President M. Roxas at left center, USA and Philippine flags at right. Cental Bank Seal Type 5. Back: New Central Bank complex at left center with old building facade above. Watermark: M. Roxas. 160x66mm.

		VF	UNC
a.	Signature 14. ND.	FV	10.00
b.	Signature as a. 1998.	FV	8.00
c.	Signature 15. Red serial #. 1998.	FV	5.00
d.	Signature as c. Black serial #. 1998; 1999.	FV	6.00
e.	Signature 16. 1999; 2000.	FV	6.00
f.	Signature 16. 2001.	FV	12.50
s.	Signature as a. Specimen.	—	30.00

185 500 Piso — VF UNC
ND; 1998-2001. Black on multicolor underprint. Aquino at left center, flag in underprint at center, typewriter at lower right. Cental Bank Seal Type 5. Back: Various scenes and gatherings of Aquino's career. Watermark: Aquino. 160x66mm.

a. Signature 14. ND; 1998. — FV 30.00
b. Signature 15. 1998; 1999. — FV 25.00
c. Signature 16; 1999; 2000; 2001. — FV 40.00
s. As a. Specimen. — — 50.00

186 1000 Piso — VF UNC
ND; 1998-2001. Dark blue on multicolor underprint. J. A. Santos, J. L. Escoda and V. Lim at left center, flaming torch at right. Cental Bank Seal Type 5. Back: Banawe rice terraces at left, to center, local carving and hut at center right. Watermark: J. A. Santos, J. L Escoda and V. Lim. 160x66mm.

a. Signature 14. ND; 1998. — FV 45.00
b. Signature 15. 1998; 1999. — FV 45.00
c. Signature 16. 1999; 2000. — FV 45.00
d. Signature 17. 2001. Red serial #. — FV 85.00
s1. Signature as a. Specimen. — — 125
s2. Signature as c. Specimen. 1999. — — 125

1997 Issue

187 10 Piso — VF UNC
1997-. Dark brown and blue-gray on multicolor underprint. A. Mabini and A. Bonifacio at left center; flag, book, declaration and quill pen at right. Back: Barasoain church at left, blood *Pacto de Sangre* meeting at lower right. 160x66mm.

a. Signature 14. Single figure watermark. 1997. — FV 2.00
b. Signature 14. Single figure watermark. 1998. — FV 2.00
c. Signature 14. Double figures as watermark. Black serial #. 1998. — FV 3.00
d. Signature 14. Double figures as watermark. Red serial #. 1998. — 5.00 20.00
e. Signature 15. Red serial #. 1999. — FV 2.50
f. Signature 16. Red serial #. 1999; 2000; 2001. — FV 3.00
g. Signature 16. Red serial #. — FV 7.00
h. Signature 17. Red serial #. 2001. — FV 2.00
i. Signature 17. Black serial #. 2001. — FV 2.00

1998 Commemorative Issue

#188-190, Centennial of First Republic, 1898-1998

188 100 Piso — VF UNC
ND (1997); 1998. Purple on multicolor underprint. Like #184 but with centennial design and inscription in rectangular frame at left in watermark area. Signature 14. Back: New Central Bank complex at left center with old building facade above. 160x66mm.

a. Without date at upper left. (1997). — FV 6.00
b. 1998 under value at left. — FV 12.00

189 2000 Piso — VF UNC
1998; 2001. Multicolor. President J. E. Estrada taking his oath of office on June 30, 1998 in the Barasoain Church at center. Back: Re-enactment of the declaration of Philippine Independence at the Aguinaldo Shrine in Kawit, Cavit. Watermark: Estrada and Ramos. 160x66mm.

a. 1998. Signature 15. Issued in folder. 216x133mm. — — 115
b. 2001. Signature 15. Limited release. — — 200

190 100,000 Piso — VF UNC
1998; 2001. Only 1,000 pieces issued. Green, yellow and brown. President F. V. Ramos being greated by crowd, Bank seal at right. Back: President Ramos greeting crowd from inside enclosed porch.

a. 1998. Signature 14. — — 3,500
b. 2001. Signature 16. — FV 3,000

1999 Commemorative Issue

#191, 50th Anniversary Bangko Sentral

191 50 Piso — VF UNC
ND; 1999. Red and purple on multicolor underprint. Overprint on #183. Iridescent denomination strip at left center and metallic segmented security strip at center right. Back: Legislative building. 160x66mm.

a. Without date at upper left. Signature 14. — FV 3.50
b. 1999 at upper left. Signature 15. — FV 7.50

#192-194 not assigned.

2001-02 Issue

#195-196 like #185-186 but w/iridescent denomination strip at l. ctr. and metallic segmented security strip at ctr. r.

193 50 Piso — VF UNC
2001-. Red and purple on multicolor underprint. President Sergio Osmeña at left center, gavel at right. Cental Bank Seal Type 5 with date 1993 at right. Back: National Museum.

a. 2001; 2002; 2003; 2004. Signature 17. — FV 4.00
b. 2005; 2006; 2007; 2008; 2009. Signature 18. Black serial #. — FV 4.50
c. 2010. Signature 19. Black serial #. — FV 4.00
d. 2011; 2012; 2013. — FV 6.00

194 100 Piso — VF UNC
2001-. Purple on multicolor underprint. Like #184. Black serial number. Back: New Central Bank complex at left center with old building facade above. 160x65mm.

a. 2001; 2002; 2003; 2004. Signature 16, 17. — FV 6.50
b. 2005; 2006; 2007; 2008 (wide and narrow date); 2009; 2010; 2010A. Signature 18. — FV 6.00
c. 2005. Signature 18. Signature spelled Arrovo. — FV 8.25
d. 2010A; 2011; 2012; 2013. Signature 19. — FV 7.50

195   200 Piso
2002-. Green and purple on multicolor underprint. Diosdado Macapagal at left, Aguinaldo shrine at lower right. Back: Scene of swearing in of Gloria Macapagal-Arroyo. 160x66mm.

		VF	UNC
a. 2002; 2003; 2004. Signature 17.		FV	9.00
b. 2007-09. Signature 18.		FV	9.00
c. 2010. Signature 19.		FV	10.00

196   500 Piso

	VF	UNC
2001-. Black on multicolor underprint. Like #185 but with iridescent denomination strip at left center and metallic segmented security strip at center right. Back: Various scenes and gatherings of Aquino's career. 160x66mm.		
a. 2001; 2002; 2003; 2004; 2005. Signature 17.	FV	17.50
b. 2005; 2007; 2008; 2008A; 2009. Signature 18. Black serial #.	FV	20.00
c. 2010-13. Signature 19.	FV	18.00

197   1000 Piso

	VF	UNC
2001-. Dark blue on multicolor underprint. Like #186 but with iridescent denomination strip at left center and metallic segmented security strip at center right. Back: Banawe rice terraces at left, to center, local carving and hut at center right. 160x66mm.		
a. 2001; 2002; 2003; 2004. Signature 17.	FV	30.00
b. 2005; 2006; 2008; 2009, 2010. Signatrue 18.	FV	35.00
c. 2007. Signature 18. (limited printing).	35.00	50.00
d. 2009; 2010, 2011; 2012. Signature 19.	FV	30.00

2008 Commemorative overpritnts

198   50 Piso

	VF	UNC
2008 Red and purple on multicolor underprint.	FV	5.00

199   100 Piso

	VF	UNC
2011. Purple on multicolor. 160x66mm.	FV	5.00

2009 Commemorative Issue

200   20 Piso

	VF	UNC
2009. Orange and blue on multicolor underprint. Signature 18. 160x66mm.	FV	3.00

201   50 Piso

	VF	UNC
2009. Red and purple on multicolor underprint. Signature 18. 160x66mm.	FV	4.00

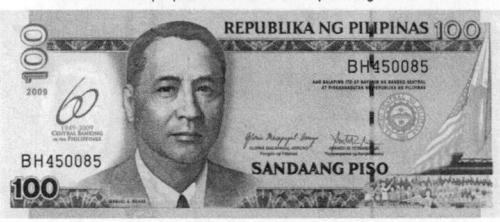

202   100 Piso

	VF	UNC
2009. Purple on multicolor underprint. Signature 18. 160x66mm.	FV	10.00

203   200 Piso

	VF	UNC
2009. Green adn purple on multicolor underprint. Signature 18. 160x66mm.		
a. Issued note.	FV	12.50
s. Specimen. Red overprint SPECIMEN on each side.	—	50.00

204   500 Piso

	VF	UNC
2009. Black on multicolor underprint. Signature 18. 160x66mm.	FV	25.00

205   1000 Piso

	VF	UNC
2009. Dark blue on multicolor underprint. Signature 18. 160x66mm.	FV	35.00

2010 Issue

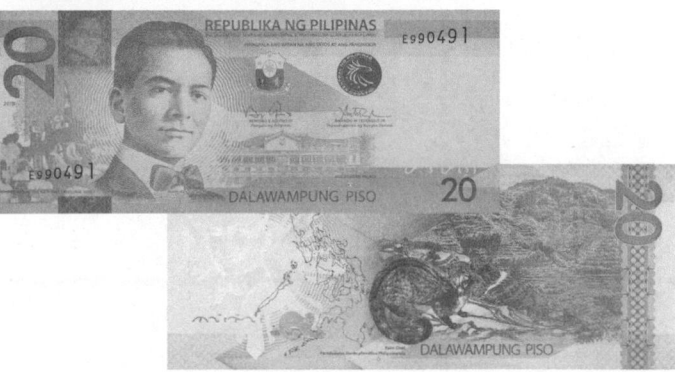

206   20 Piso

	VF	UNC
2010. Orange on multicolor underprint. Manuel Luis Quezón at left center. Presidential palace at lower center. Back: Map, palm civet, Banaue rice terraces. Watermark: Quezón and 20. 160x66mm.		
a. 2010; 2012; 2013. Signature 19.	FV	3.50

207 50 Piso
VF UNC

2010-. Red on multicolor underprint. Sergio Osmeña at left center, MacArthur's
Leyte landing of 1944, National Assembly interior. Back: Map, maliputo fish, Taal
lake. Watermark: Osmeña and 50. 160x66mm.

    a. 2010; 2012; 2014. Signature 19.   FV   6.50

208 100 Piso
VF UNC

2010-. Purple on multicolor underprint. Manuel Acuña Rozas at left center, Central   FV   10.00
Bank building at left. Back: Map, white shark, Mayon Volcano in Legazpi City.
Watermark: Roxas and 100. 160x66mm.

2010-. Purple on multicolor underprint. Manuel Acuña Rozas at left center, Central
Bank building at left. Back: Map, white shark, Mayon Volcano in Legazpi City.
Watermark: Roxas and 100. 160x66mm.

    a. 2010. Signature 19.   FV   10.00
    b. 2012.   FV   10.00

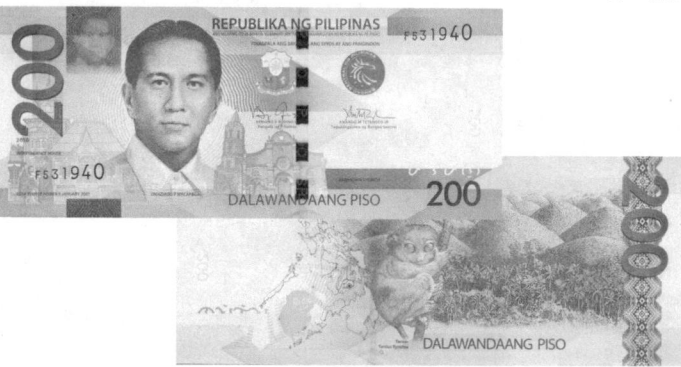

209 200 Piso
VF UNC

2010. Green on multicolor underprint. Diosdado Macapagal at left center,
Aguinaldo Shrine at left, Malolos City Catholic Church. Back: Map, tarsier, Bohol
Chocolate Hills. Watermark: Macapagal and 200. 160x66mm.

    a. 2010. Signature 19.   FV   10.00

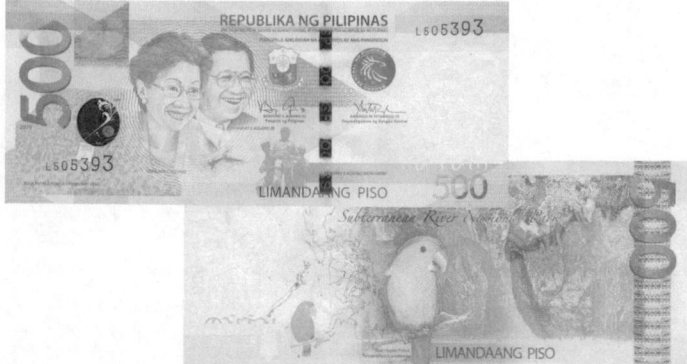

210 500 Piso
VF UNC

2010-15. Yellow on multicolor underprint. Corazon and Benigno Aquino at left
center. Back: Map, blue-naped parrot, Puerto Princesa Subterranean River Park.
Watermark: Aquinos and 500. 160x66mm.

    a. 2010-15. Signature 19.   FV   22.00

211 1000 Piso
VF UNC

2010-15. Blue on multicolor underprint. José Santos, Josefa Escoda and Vicente
Lim. Back: Map, South sea pearl in shell, turtle, Tubbataha Reefs Natural Park.
Watermark: Santos, Escoda, Lim and 1000. 166x60mm.

    a. 2010-15. Signature 19.   FV   35.00

2011 Commemorative Issue

211A 50 Piso
VF UNC

2012. 45th ASEAN Day celebration at the Department of Foreign Affairs. Red and   FV   4.00
purple on multicolor underprint. President Sergio Osmeña at left center, gavel at
right, commemorative design overprint, text and date in watermark area on #193d.
Back: National Museum.

212 100 Piso
VF UNC

2011. 75th Anniversary of Ateneo Law School. Purple on multicolor underprint.   FV   8.00
President M. Roxas at left center, USA and Philippine flags at right, commemora-
tive design overprint, text and date in watermark area on #194d. Back: New
Central Bank Complex at left center with old building façade above. 160x65mm.

212A 100 Piso
VF UNC

2011. 100th Anniversary of De La Salle. Purple on multicolor underprint. President   FV   10.00
M. Roxas at left center, USA and Philippine flags at right, commemorative design
overprint, text and date in watermark area on #194d. Signature 19. Back: New
Central Bank Complex at left center with old building façade above.

212B 100 Piso
VF UNC

2011. Centenary of University of the Philippines College of Law. Purple on mul-   FV   5.00
ticolor underprint. President M. Roxas at left center, USA and Philippine flags at
right, commemorative design overprint, text and date in watermark area on #194d.
Signature 19. Back: New Central Bank Complex at left center with old building
façade above. 160x65mm.

212C 200 Piso
VF UNC

2011. 400th Anniversary of Pontifical and Royal University of Santo Tomas. Green   FV   12.50
and purple on multicolor underprint. Diosdado Macapagal at left, Aguinaldo shrine
at lower right, commemorative design overprint, text and date in watermark area.
Back: Scene of swearing in of Gloria Macapagal-Arroyo.

2012 Commemorative Issue

213 100 Piso
VF UNC

2012. 100 years Manila Hotel. Purple on multicolor underprint. President M.   FV   8.00
Roxas at left center, USA and Philippine flags at right, commemorative design
overprint, text and date in watermark area on #194d. Back: New Central Bank
Complex at left center with old building façade above. 160x65mm.

214 100 Piso
VF UNC

2012. 100 years Grand Lodge of Free and Accepted Masons. Purple on multicolor
underprint. President M. Roxas at left center, USA and Philippine flags at right,
commemorative design overprint, text and date in watermark area on #194d.
Back: New Central Bank Complex at left center with old building façade above.

    a. Issued note.   FV   8.00
    b. Uncut sheet of 4 in folder.   —   30.00

214A 500 Piso
VF UNC

2012. 45th Annual Meeting of Asian Development Bank in Manila. Black on   FV   60.00
multicolor underprint. Aquino at left center, flag in underprint at center, typewriter
at lower right, commemorative design overprint, text and date in watermark area
on #196c. Back: Various scenes and gatherings of Aquino's career.

2013 Commemorative Issue

215 50 Piso
VF UNC

2013. Canonization of San Pedro Calungsod. Red and purple on multicolor   FV   8.00
underprint. President Sergio Osmeña at left center, gavel at right, commemorative design overprint, text and date in watermark area on #193d. Back: National
Museum.

216 50 Piso
VF UNC

2013. 50 years Trinity University of Asia. Red and purple on multicolor underprint.   FV   4.00
President Sergio Osmeña at left center, gavel at right, commemorative design
overprint, text and date in watermark area on #193d. Back: National Museum.

217 50 Piso — VF UNC
2013. 50 years Philippine Deposit Insurance Corporation (PDIC). Red and purple on multicolor underprint. President Sergio Osmeña at left center, gavel at right, commemorative design overprint, text and date in watermark area on #193d. Back: National Museum. — FV 7.50

218 100 Piso — VF UNC
2013. 20 years Bangko Sentral ng Pilipinas. Purple on multicolor underprint. President M. Roxas at left center, USA and Philippine flags at right, commemorative design overprint, text and date in watermark area on #194d. Back: New Central Bank Complex at left center with old building façade above. 160x65mm. — FV 8.00

219 100 Piso — VF UNC
2013. 100 years Shell Oil in the Philippines. Purple on multicolor underprint. President M. Roxas at left center, USA and Philippine flags at right, commemorative design overprint, text and date in watermark area on #194d. Back: New Central Bank Complex at left center with old building façade above. 160x65mm. — FV 8.00

220 100 Piso — VF UNC
2013. National Year of Rice - 2013. Purple on multicolor underprint. President M. Roxas at left center, USA and Philippine flags at right, commemorative design overprint, text and date in watermark area on #194d. Back: New Central Bank Complex at left center with old building façade above. 160x65mm. — FV 8.00

221 100 Piso — VF UNC
2013. Centennial Iglesia ni Cristo. Purple on multicolor underprint. President M. Roxas at left center, USA and Philippine flags at right, commemorative design overprint, text and date in watermark area on #194d. Back: New Central Bank Complex at left center with old building façade above. 160x65mm. — FV 8.00

COLLECTOR SERIES
Bangko Sentral ng Pilipinas
1978 ND Issue

CS1 1978 ND 2-100 Piso — Mkt. Value
#159a-164a overprint: *SPECIMEN* and with serial # prefix Maltese cross. — 45.00

POLAND

The Republic of Poland, formerly the Polish Peoples Republic, located in central Europe, has an area of 120,725 sq. mi. (312,677 sq. km.) and a population of 38.73 million. Capital: Warsaw. The economy is essentially agricultural, but industrial activity provides the products for foreign trade. Machinery, coal, coke, iron, steel and transport equipment are exported. Poland is an ancient nation that was conceived near the middle of the 10th century. Its golden age occurred in the 16th century. During the following century, the strengthening of the gentry and internal disorders weakened the nation. In a series of agreements between 1772 and 1795, Russia, Prussia, and Austria partitioned Poland amongst themselves. Poland regained its independence in 1918 only to be overrun by Germany and the Soviet Union in World War II. It became a Soviet satellite state following the war, but its government was comparatively tolerant and progressive. Labor turmoil in 1980 led to the formation of the independent trade union "Solidarity" that over time became a political force and by 1990 had swept parliamentary elections and the presidency. A "shock therapy" program during the early 1990s enabled the country to transform its economy into one of the most robust in Central Europe, but Poland still faces the lingering challenges of high unemployment, underdeveloped and dilapidated infrastructure, and a poor rural underclass. Solidarity suffered a major defeat in the 2001 parliamentary elections when it failed to elect a single deputy to the lower house of Parliament, and the new leaders of the Solidarity Trade Union subsequently pledged to reduce the Trade Union's political role. Poland joined NATO in 1999 and the European Union in 2004. With its transformation to a democratic, market-oriented country largely completed, Poland is an increasingly active member of Euro-Atlantic organizations.

RULERS:
Stanislaw Augustus, 1764-1795
Fryderyk August I, King of Saxony, as Grand Duke, 1807-1814
Alexander I, Czar of Russia, as King, 1815-1825
Nikolaj (Mikolay) I, Czar of Russia, as King, 1825-1855

MONETARY SYSTEM:
1 Marka = 100 Fenigow to 1919
1 Zloty = 100 Groszy, 1919-

PEOPLES REPUBLIC
Narodowy Bank Polski
POLISH NATIONAL BANK
1962; 1965 Issue

140A 20 Zlotych — VF UNC
2.1.1965. (Not issued). Multicolor. Man at right, arms at upper left center. — — —

141 1000 Zlotych — VF UNC
1962; 1965. Orange, red and green on multicolor underprint. Copernicus at center right, arms at upper right. Back: Zodiac signs in ornate sphere at left. Watermark: Copernicus. 150x74mm.

	VF	UNC
a. 29.10.1965.	5.00	20.00
b. 29.10.1965. Serial # prefix: X.	25.00	120
s1. Specimen overprint: *WZOR*. 24.5.1962. (Not issued).	—	200
s2. Specimen overprint: *WZOR* with regular serial #. 29.10.1965.	—	30.00

1974-76 Issue

142 50 Zlotych   VF   UNC

1975-88. Olive-green on multicolor underprint. K. Swierczewski at center, eagle arms at lower right. Signature varieties. Back: Order of Grunwald at left. Watermark: Eagle arms. 138x63mm.

	VF	UNC
a. 9.5.1975.	1.50	10.00
b. 1.6.1979; 1.6.1982.	0.30	2.75
c. 1.6.1986; 1.12.1988.	0.20	0.75
s1. Specimen overprint: *WZOR.* 1975; 1986; 1988.	—	8.00
s2. Specimen overprint: *WZOR.* 1979.	—	7.00
s3. Specimen overprint: *WZOR.* 1982.	—	10.00

143 100 Zlotych   VF   UNC

1975-88. Brown on lilac and multicolor underprint. L. Warynski at right, eagle arms at lower center. Signature varieties. Back: Old paper at left. Watermark: Eagle arms. 138x63mm.

	VF	UNC
a. 15.1.1975.	4.00	25.00
b. 17.5.1976.	2.00	8.00
c. 1.6.1979.	0.75	3.00
d. 1.6.1982.	0.20	2.00
e. 1.6.1986; 1.5.1988.	—	0.50
s1. Specimen overprint: *WZOR.* 1975; 1982.	—	8.00
s2. Specimen overprint: *WZOR.* 1976.	—	7.00
s3. Specimen overprint: *WZOR.* 1979.	—	10.00

144 200 Zlotych   VF   UNC

1976-88. Purple on orange and multicolor underprint. J. Dabrowski at right, eagle arms at lower center. Signature varieties. Back: Standing woman at wall. Watermark: Eagle arms. 138x63mm.

	VF	UNC
a. 25.5.1976.	4.00	20.00
b. 1.6.1979; 1.6.1982.	0.30	4.50
c. 1.6.1986; 1.12.1988.	0.25	1.00
s1. Specimen overprint: *WZOR.* 1976; 1986.	—	8.00
s2. Specimen overprint: *WZOR.* 1979.	—	7.00
s3. Specimen overprint: *WZOR.* 1982.	—	10.00

145 500 Zlotych   VF   UNC

1974-82. . Brown on tan and multicolor underprint. T. Kosciuszko at right, eagle arms at lower center. Signature varieties. Back: Arms and flag at left center. Watermark: Eagle arms. 138x63mm.

	VF	UNC
a. 16.12.1974.	7.00	30.00
b. 15.6.1976.	3.00	10.00
c. 1.6.1979.	0.75	7.00
d. 1.6.1982.	0.25	1.00
s1. Specimen overprint: *WZOR.* 1974; 1976.	—	8.00
s2. Specimen overprint: *WZOR.* 1979.	—	7.00
s3. Specimen overprint: *WZOR.* 1982.	—	10.00

146 1000 Zlotych   VF   UNC

1975-82. Blue on olive-green and multicolor underprint. Copernicus at right, eagle arms at lower center. Signature varieties. Back: Atomic symbols. Watermark: Eagle arms. 138x63mm.

	VF	UNC
a. 2.7.1975.	4.00	35.00
b. 1.6.1979.	1.25	10.00
c. 1.6.1982.	0.50	1.50
s1. Specimen overprint: *WZOR.* 1975; 1982.	—	10.00
s2. Specimen overprint: *WZOR.* 1979.	—	7.00

POLSKA RZECZPOSPOLITA LUDOWA
POLISH PEOPLES REPUBLIC
Narodowy Bank Polski
POLISH NATIONAL BANK
1977 Issue

147 2000 Zlotych   VF   UNC

1977-82. Dark brown on multicolor underprint. Mieszko I at right, arms at lower center. Back: B. Chrobry. Watermark: Arms. 63x138mm.

	VF	UNC
a. 1.5.1977.	1.00	5.00
b. 1.6.1979.	1.75	13.50
c. 1.6.1982.	0.50	1.00
s1. Specimen overprint: *WZOR.* 1977.	—	10.00
s2. Specimen overprint: *WZOR.* 1979.	—	7.00
s3. Specimen overprint: *WZOR.* 1982.	—	15.00

1982 Issue

148 10 Zlotych   VF   UNC

1.6.1982. Blue and green on multicolor underprint. J. Bem at left center, arms at lower right. Back: Large value. Watermark: Arms. 138x63mm.

	VF	UNC
a. Issued note.	0.25	1.50
s. Specimen overprint: *WZOR.*	—	10.00

149 20 Zlotych
1.6.1982. Brown and purple on multicolor underprint. R. Traugutt at left center, arms at lower right. Back: Large value. Watermark: Arms. 138x63mm.

	VF	UNC
a. Issued note.	0.25	0.75
s. Specimen overprint: *WZOR*.	—	10.00

150 5000 Zlotych
1982-88. Dark green, purple and black on multicolor underprint. F. Chopin at right, arms at lower center. Back: *Polonaise* music score at center. Watermark: Arms.

	VF	UNC
a. 1.6.1982.	1.00	4.00
b. 1.6.1986.	2.00	7.00
c. 1.12.1988.	FV	2.50
s. Specimen overprint: *WZOR*.	—	12.50

1987-90 Issue

151 10,000 Zlotych
1.2.1987; 1.12.1988. Dark blue and red on green and multicolor underprint. S. Wyspianski at left center, arms at lower right. Back: Trees and city scene. Watermark: Arms.

	VF	UNC
a. 1.2.1987.	2.25	10.00
b. 1.12.1988.	0.50	3.00
s. Specimen overprint: *WZOR*.	—	10.00

152 20,000 Zlotych
1.2.1989. Dark brown on tan and gold underprint. M. Curie at right, arms at lower center. Back: Scientific instrument. Watermark: Arms.

	VF	UNC
a. Issued note.	1.25	4.00
s. Specimen overprint: *WZOR*.	—	10.00

153 50,000 Zlotych
1.2.1989. Dark brown and greenish black on multicolor underprint. S. Staszic at left center, arms at lower right. Back: S. Staszic at left center. Watermark: Arms.

	VF	UNC
a. Issued note.	5.00	10.00
s. Specimen overprint: *WZOR*.	—	10.00

154 100,000 Zlotych
1.2.1990. Black and grayish blue on multicolor underprint. S. Moniuczko at right, arms at lower center. Back: Warsaw Theatre at left. Watermark: Arms.

	VF	UNC
a. Issued note.	5.00	12.50
s. Specimen overprint: *WZOR*.	—	10.00

155 200,000 Zlotych
1.2.1989. Dark purple on red, tan and multicolor underprint. Coin of Sigismund III at lower center, arms at right. Back: Warsaw shield at left, view of Warsaw. Watermark: Geometric design repeated.

	VF	UNC
a. Issued note.	10.00	30.00
s. Specimen overprint: *WZOR*.	—	75.00

RZECZPOSPOLITA POLSKA

REPUBLIC OF POLAND

Narodowy Bank Polski

POLISH NATIONAL BANK

1990-92 Issue

156 500,000 Zlotych
20.4.1990. Dark blue-green and black on multicolor underprint. H. Sienkiewicz at left center, arms at lower right. Back: Shield with three books, also four flags.

	VF	UNC
a. Issued note.	25.00	65.00
s. Specimen overprint: *WZOR*.	—	75.00

157 1,000,000 Zlotych VF UNC

15.2.1991. Brown-violet, purple and red on multicolor underprint. W. Reymont at right, arms. Back: Tree with rural landscape in background. Watermark: Arms.

    a. Issued note. 50.00 150
    s. Specimen overprint: *WZOR*. — 150

158 2,000,000 Zlotych VF UNC

14.8.1992. Black and deep brown-violet on multicolor underprint. I. Paderewski at left center, arms at lower right. Back: Imperial eagle at left. Watermark: Arms.

    a. Issued note, misspelling *KONSTYTUCYJY* on back. Series A. — 250
    b. As a, but corrected spelling *KONSTYTUCYJNY* on back. Series B. 90.00 200
    s. Specimen. Overprint: *WZOR*. — 225

1993 Issue

159 50,000 Zlotych VF UNC

16.11.1993. Dark blue-green and brown on multicolor underprint. S. Staszic at left center, arms at lower right with color in watermark area. Back: S. Staszic at left center. Watermark: Eagle's head.

    a. Issued note. 3.00 7.00
    s. Specimen overprint: *WZOR*. — 8.50

160 100,000 Zlotych VF UNC

16.11.1993. Black and grayish blue on multicolor underprint. S. Moniuszko at right, arms at lower center with color in watermark area. Back: Scientific instrument. Watermark: Eagle's head.

    a. Issued note. 5.00 10.00
    s. Specimen overprint: *WZOR*. — 10.00

161 500,000 Zlotych VF UNC

16.11.1993. Dark blue-green and black on multicolor underprint. H. Sienkiewicz at left center, eagle with crown at lower right with color in watermark area. Back: Shield with three books, also four flags. Watermark: Eagle's head.

    a. Issued note. 20.00 30.00
    s. Specimen overprint: *WZOR*. — 75.00

162 1,000,000 Zlotych VF UNC

16.11.1993. Brown-violet, purple and red on multicolor underprint. W. reymont at right, eagle with crown with color in watermark area. Back: Tree with rural landscape in background. Watermark: Eagle's head.

    a. Issued note. 45.00 100
    s. Specimen overprint: *WZOR*. — 150

163 2,000,000 Zlotych VF UNC

16.11.1993. Black and deep brown on multicolor underprint. I. Paderewski at left center, eagle with crown at lower right with color in watermark area. Back: Staszic Palace in Warsaw. Watermark: Eagle's head.

    a. Issued note. 95.00 200
    s. Specimen overprint: *WZOR*. — 100

1990 (1996) "Cancelled" Issue

Currency Reform 1 "new" Zloty = 10,000 "old" Zlotych #164-172 arms at l. and as wmk. These notes were printed in Germany (w/o imprint). Before their release, it was decided a more refined issue of notes should be prepared and these notes were later overprinted: *NIEOBIEGOWY* (non-negotiable) in red and released to the collecting community. Specimens are also known.

164 1 Zloty VF UNC

1.3.1990. Blue-gray and brown on multicolor underprint. Building in Gdynia at right, arms at left. Back: Sailing ship at left. Watermark: Arms.

    a. Cancelled note. — 3.00
    s. Specimen overprint: *WZOR*. — 25.00

165 2 Zlote VF UNC

1.3.1990. Dark brown and brown on multicolor underprint. Mining conveyor tower at Katowice at right, arms at left. Back: Battle of Upper Silesia (1921) monument at left. Watermark: Arms.

    a. Cancelled note. — 3.00
    s. Specimen overprint: *WZOR*. — 25.00

166 5 Zlotych VF UNC

1.3.1990. Deep green on multicolor underprint. Building in Zamosc at right, arms at left. Back: Order of Grunwald at left. Watermark: Arms.

    a. Cancelled note. — 3.00
    s. Specimen overprint: *WZOR*. — 25.00

167 10 Zlotych VF UNC
1.3.1990. Red and purple on multicolor underprint. Building in Warsaw at right, arms at left. Back: Statue of Warszawa at left. Watermark: Arms.
    a. Cancelled note. — 3.00
    s. Specimen overprint: WZOR. — 25.00

168 20 Zlotych VF UNC
1.3.1990. Brownish black and deep violet on multicolor underprint. Grain storage facility in Gdansk at right, arms at left. Back: Male statue at left. Watermark: Arms.
    a. Cancelled note. — 3.00
    s. Specimen overprint: WZOR — 25.00

169 50 Zlotych VF UNC
1.3.1990. Purple on lilac and multicolor underprint. Church in Wroclaw at right, arms at left. Back: Medallion at left. Watermark: Arms.
    a. Cancelled note. — 3.00
    s. Specimen overprint: WZOR. — 35.00

170 100 Zlotych VF UNC
1.3.1990. Dark brown and black on orange and multicolor underprint. Building in Poznan at right, arms at left. Back: Medieval seal at left. Watermark: Arms.
    a. Cancelled note. — 3.00
    s. Specimen overprint: WZOR. — 35.00

171 200 Zlotych VF UNC
1.3.1990. Black and deep purple on multicolor underprint. Buildings in Krakow at right, arms at left. Back: Medieval coin at left. Watermark: Arms.
    a. Cancelled note. — 3.00
    s. Specimen overprint: WZOR. — 25.00

172 500 Zlotych VF UNC
1.3.1990. Black on green and multicolor underprint. Church in Gniezno at right, arms at left. Back: Medieval seal at left. Watermark: Arms.
    a. Cancelled note. — 3.00
    s. Specimen overprint: WZOR. — 25.00

1994 (1995) Regular Issue

#173-177 Replacement notes: Serial # prefix ZA.

173 10 Zlotych VF UNC
25.3.1994 (1995). UV: value in box and circle under eagle fluoresce yellow; serial # orange. Dark brown, brown and olive-green on multicolor underprint. Prince Mieszko I at center right, arms at upper left center. Back: Medieval denar of Mieszko I at left center. 120x60mm.
    a. Issued note. FV 6.50
    r. Replacement. FV 17.00
    s. Specimen overprint: WZOR. — 7.50

174 20 Zlotych VF UNC
25.3.1994 (1995). UV: value in box fluoresce yellow; serial # orange. Purple and deep blue on multicolor underprint. King Boleslaw I Chrobry at center right, arms at upper left center. Back: Medieval denar of Boleslaw II at left center. 126x63mm.
    a. Issued note. FV 10.00
    r. Replacement. FV 27.00
    s. Specimen overprint: WZOR. — 12.50

175 50 Zlotych VF UNC
25.3.1994 (1995). Blue-violet and deep blue and green on multicolor underprint. King Kazimierz III Wielki at center right, arms at upper left center. Back: Eagle from seal, orb and sceptre at left center, town views of Cracow and Kazimierz. 132x66mm.
    a. Issued note. FV 22.50
    r. Replacement. FV 50.00
    s. Specimen overprint.: WZOR. — 35.00

176   100 Zlotych   **VF   UNC**
25.3.1994 (1995). Olive-green on multicolor underprint. Wladyslaw II Jagiello at
center right. Back: Arms and Teutonic Knights' castle in Malbork. 138x69mm.

   a. Issued note.   FV   45.00
   r. Replacement.   FV   100
   s. Specimen overprint: *WZOR.*   —   65.00

177   200 Zlotych   **VF   UNC**
25.3.1994. Brown on multicolor underprint. King Zygmunt I the old at center
right. Back: Arms and eagle in hexagon from the Zygmunt's chapel in the Wawel
Cathedral and Wawel's court. 144x72mm.

   a. Issued note.   FV   85.00
   r. Replacement.   FV   170
   s. Specimen overprint: *WZOR.*   —   100

2006 Commemorative Issue

178   50 Zlotych   **VF   UNC**
16.10.2006. Light blue and yellow. Pope John Paul II at right center, hand raised   —   65.00
in blessing. World map as background. Pope John Paul II seated at left, kissing
hand of kneeling Cardinal Stefan Wyszynski at right. Back: Text from letter to
Poles, and rendering of Jasna Góra Monastery. 144x72mm.

#178 originally sold in a folder for 90 Zlotych.

2008 Commemorative Issue

179   10 Zlotych   **VF   UNC**
4.6.2008. 90th Anniversary of the Restoration of Independence. 80,000 notes   FV   25.00
printed. Olive, tan and rose on multicolor underprint. Jozef Pilsudski at right, Bel-
weder Palace at center. Back: Eagle and monument of four soldiers. 138x69mm.

2009 Commemorative Issue

180   20 Zlotych   **VF   UNC**
23.9.2009. Brown and tan on yellow underprint. Juliusz Slowacki at right, his   FV   10.00
house in Krzemieniec at center. Back: Sigismund III column at Warsaw's castle
square at left, fragment of the poem *Uspokojenie* at right. Printer: PSPW

2010 Commemorative Issue

181   20 Zlotych   **VF   UNC**
29.3.2009. Released in special folder. 120,000 pieces issued. Brown and tan on   FV   10.00
yellow underprint. Frédéric Chopin profile at center, home in Zelazowa Wola and
score of the *Mazurka in B-flat major, Op 7 #1.* Back: Score fragment of *Etude in
F-minor, Op 10 #9. Willow tree landscape.* Printer: PSPW.

2011 Commemorative Issue

182   20 Zlotych   **VF   UNC**
20.4.2011. Brown on multicolor underprint. Marie Sklodowska Curie at left;
Sorbonne school building in Paris at bottom center. Back: Nobel prize medal at
right, Radium Institute building in Warsaw at lower center. Printer: PWPW S.A.
138x69mm.

   a. Issued note.   FV   10.00
   b. Note in commemorative folder.   —   25.00

2012 Commemorative Issue

183   10 Zlotych   **VF   UNC**
5.1.2012. Dark brown. Prince Mieszko. Omron rings added. Printer: PWPW S.A.   FV   7.50
120x60mm.

184   20 Zlotych   **VF   UNC**
5.1.2012. Purple and deep blue on multicolor underprint. King Boleslaw I Chrobry.   FV   15.00
Omron rings added.

185 50 Zlotych   **VF UNC**
5.1.2012. Blue-violet and deep blue on multicolor underprint. King Kazimierz III. Omron rings added. 132x68mm.   FV 35.00

186 100 Zlotych   **VF UNC**
5.1.2012. Olive-green on multicolor underprint. Wladyslaw II. Omron rings added. 138x69mm.   FV 70.00

2014 Commemorative Issue

187 20 Zlotych   **VF UNC**
16.1.2014. Polymer. Commemorative for the Polish Legions. Green, brown, yellow and blue. Commander Jozef Klemens Pilsudksi. Printer: PWPW S.A.
   a. Issued note.   FV 10.00
   b. Note in commemorative folder.   — 30.00

2015 Commemorative Issue

188 20 Zlotych   **VF UNC**
24.6.2015. Brown, green and gold. Open book and arms at center. Jan Dlugosz at right. Back: Wawel Cathedral. Watermark: Arms. 138x69mm.   FV 10.00

2016 Commemorative Issue

189 200 Zlotych   **VF UNC**
3.3.2015 (2016). Brown and yellow on multicolor underprint. King Sigismund I at center. Watermark: King Sigismund I. 144x72mm.   — —

COLLECTOR SERIES

Narodowy Bank Polski

ND (1948; 1965) Issue

CS1 Collector Set   **Mkt. Value**
Deep red overprint: *WZOR* on 1948-dated 20, 50, 100, 500 Zlotych #137, 138, 139 and on 1965-dated 1000 Zlotych #141a. All with normal serial #.   75.00

1967 Issue

CS2 Collector Set   **Mkt. Value**
Red overprint: *WYSTAWA PIENIEDZY RADZIECKICH - LISTOPAD 1967* and *50 LAT WIELKIEGO PAZDZIERNIKA.* with *NBP* monogram at corners on faces of 1937 Russian 1, 3, 5, 10 Chervonetz #202-205. Made for the 50th anniversary of the Socialist revolution of 1917. Released by the National Bank of Poland in a special booklet.   50.00

1974 Issue

CS3 Collector Set   **Mkt. Value**
Reprints of 1944 Russian issue from 50 Groszy-500 Zlotych #104b-119b. Indicated as reprints of 1974 but without other overprint. Made for the 30th anniversary of the Polish Peoples Republic.   20.00

1978 Issue

CS4 Collector Set   **Mkt. Value**
Dark blue-black overprint: *150 LAT BANKU POLSKIEGO 1828-1978* on faces of 1948-dated 20, 100 Zlotych #137, 139a. Made for 150th anniversary of Polish banknotes. Issued in a folder.   25.00

1979 Issues

CS5 Collector Set   **Mkt. Value**
Reprints of 1944 Soviet issue as #C3, but dated 1979 and with red overprint on face: *XXXV - LECIE PRL 1944-1979.* Made for the 35th anniversary of the Polish Peoples Republic.   25.00

CS6 Collector Set   **Mkt. Value**
Reprint of 1919-dated 100 Marek with red overprint on face: *60-LECIE POLSKIEGO BANKNOTU PO ODZY SANIU NIEPODLEGLOSCI 1919-1979.* Made for 60th anniversary of modern Polish bank notes. Released by National Bank of Poland in a folder.   15.00

CS7 Collector Set   **Mkt. Value**
Red overprint: *WYSTAWA WSPOLCZESNE MONETY I BANKNOTY POLSKIE I OBCE NBP 1979* on 1948 dated 2 Zlote #134. Issued in a small leatherette folder by the National Bank of Poland for a numismatic exposition.   10.00

1979-92 Issue

CS8 Collector Set   **Mkt. Value**
#142-157a, 148a with red overprint: *WZOR* on face; all zero serial # and additional black specimen # with star suffix. Red overprint: *SPECIMEN* on back.   300

Note: Originally #CS8 was sold in a special booklet by Pekao Trading Company at its New York City, NY, and Warsaw offices.

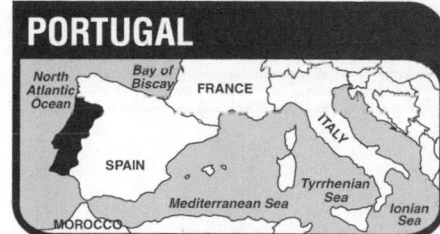

PORTUGAL

The Portuguese Republic, located in the western part of the Iberian Peninsula in southwestern Europe, has an area of 35,553 sq. mi. (91,905 sq. km.) and a population of 9.79 million. Capital: Lisbon. Portugal's economy is based on agriculture and a small but expanding industrial sector. Textiles, machinery, chemicals, wine and cork are exported. Following its heyday as a global maritime power during the 15th and 16th centuries, Portugal lost much of its wealth and status with the destruction of Lisbon in a 1755 earthquake, occupation during the Napoleonic Wars, and the independence of its wealthiest colony of Brazil in 1822. A 1910 revolution deposed the monarchy; for most of the next six decades, repressive governments ran the country. In 1974, a left-wing military coup installed broad democratic reforms. The following year, Portugal granted independence to all of its African colonies. Portugal is a founding member of NATO and entered the EC (now the EU) in 1986.

MONETARY SYSTEM:
   1 Mil Reis = 1000 Reis to 1910
   1 Escudo = 100 Centavos, 1910-2001
   1 Euro = 100 Cents, 2002-
Note: Prata = Silver, Ouro = Gold.

REPUBLIC

Banco de Portugal

1960; 1961 Issue

163 20 Escudos   **VF UNC**
26.7.1960. Dark green and purple on multicolor underprint. Portrait of Dom Antonio Luiz de Menezes at right. Chapa 6A. 8 signature varieties. Back: Bank seal at left. Watermark: Portrait of Dom Antonio Luiz de Menezes. Printer: BWC (without imprint).
   a. Issued note.   25.00 80.00
   ct. Color trial. Blue and brown on multicolor underprint.   — 500

164 50 Escudos   **VF UNC**
24.6.1960. Blue on multicolor underprint. Arms at upper center, Fontes Pereira de Mello at right. Chapa 7A. 8 signature varieties. Back: Bank seal at upper left, statue *The Thinker* at left. Watermark: Fontes Pereira de Mello. Printer: TDLR (without imprint).   90.00 250

165 100 Escudos   VF   UNC
19.12.1961. Deep violet and purple on orange, green and multicolor underprint.
Pedro Nunes at right, arms at upper center. Ch. 6A. 7 signature varieties. Back:
Fountain and arches at left, bank seal at center. Watermark: Pedro Nunes. Printer:
BWC (without imprint).
    a. Issued note.   70.00 200
    ct. Color trial. Deep green and purple on multicolor underprint. —   650

166 1000 Escudos   VF   UNC
30.5.1961. Purple on multicolor underprint. Queen Filipa de Lancastre at right. Ch. 225 600
8A. 8 signature varieties. Watermark: Queen Filipa de Lancastre. Printer: BWC
(without imprint).

1964-66 Issue

167 20 Escudos   VF   UNC
26.5.1964. Olive-green and purple on multicolor underprint. Santo Antonio of
Padua at right. Ch. 7. 7 signature varieties. Back: Church of Santo Antonio de
Lisboa at left. Watermark: Santo Antonio of Padua.
    a. Olive-brown underprint at left and right.   6.00 20.00
    b. Green underprint at left and right.   4.50 15.00
    ct. Color trial. Blue and purple on multicolor underprint. —   275

168 50 Escudos   VF   UNC
28.2.1964. Dark brown on multicolor underprint. Queen Isabella at right. Ch. 8. 15 4.00 14.00
signature varieties. Back: Old city Conimbria. Watermark: Queen Isabella.

169 100 Escudos   VF   UNC
1965; 1978. Blue on light tan and multicolor underprint. Camilo Castello Branco at
right. Ch. 7. Back: City of Porto in 19th century at left. Watermark: Camilo Castello
Branco.
    a. 22 signature varieties. 30.11.1965.   7.00 20.00
    b. 6 signature varieties. 20.9.1978.   8.00 25.00

170 500 Escudos   VF   UNC
1966; 1979. Brown on multicolor underprint. Old map at center, João II at right.
Ch. 10. Back: Compass-card or Rhumb-card and double statue. Watermark: João
II. Printer: JEZ (without imprint).
    a. 7 signature varieties. 25.1.1966.   47.50 110
    b. 9 signature varieties. 6.9.1979.   42.50 95.00

171 1000 Escudos   VF   UNC
2.4.1965. Gray-blue on red-brown and multicolor underprint. Pillar at left, arms 2,000 5,000
at upper center, Dom Diniz at right. Ch. 9. 7 signature varieties. Back: Scene of
founding of University of Lisbon in 1290. Watermark: Dom Diniz. Printer: JEZ
(without imprint).

1967 Issue

172 1000 Escudos

VF UNC

19.5.1967. Blue, dark brown and violet on multicolor underprint. Queen Maria II at right. Ch. 10. 24 signature varieties. Back: Her medallion portrait at left, Banco de Portugal in 1846 building at lower right. Watermark: Queen Maria II. Printer: JEZ (without imprint).

a. Signature titles: *O GOVERNADOR* and *O ADMINISTRADOR*.	50.00	125
b. Signature titles: *O VICE-GOVERNADOR* and *O ADMINISTRADOR*.	50.00	125

1968; 1971 Issue

173 20 Escudos

VF UNC

27.7.1971. Green (shades) on multicolor underprint. Garcia de Orta at right. Ch. 8. 15 signature varieties. Back: 16th century market in Goa. Watermark: Garcia de Orta.

2.25 8.00

174 50 Escudos

VF UNC

1968; 1980. Dark brown on multicolor underprint. Arms at left, Infante Dona Maria at right. Ch. 9. Back: Cintra in 1507. Watermark: Infante Dona Maria.

a. 7 signature varieties. 28.5.1968.	5.00	18.00
b. 9 signature varieties. 1.2.1980.	4.50	16.00

175 1000 Escudos

VF UNC

1968-82. Blue and black on multicolor underprint. Dom Pedro V at right. Ch. 11. Back: Conjoined busts at left, ceremonial opening of the first railway at bottom center and right. Watermark: Dom Pedro V. Printer: Printer: BWC (without imprint).

a. 24 signature varieties. 28.5.1968.	30.00	70.00
b. 8 signature varieties. 16.9.1980.	20.00	50.00
c. 9 signature varieties. 3.12.1981.	20.00	50.00
d. 9 signature varieties. 21.9.1982.	85.00	175
e. 11 signature varieties. 26.10.1982.	20.00	50.00
ct. Color trial. Purple and green.	—	450

1978; 1979 Issue

176 20 Escudos

VF UNC

1978. Green (shades) on multicolor underprint. Admiral Gago Coutinho at right. Ch. 9. Large or small size numerals in serial number. Back: Airplane. Watermark: Admiral Gago Coutinho.

a. 6 signature varieties. 13.9.1978.	2.50	9.00
b. 6 signature varieties. 4.10.1978.	2.25	8.00

177 500 Escudos

VF UNC

4.10.1979 (1982). Brown on multicolor underprint. Old street layout of part of Braga at center, Francisco Sanches at right. Ch. 11. 9 signature varieties. Back: 17th century street scene in Braga. Watermark: Francisco Sanches. Printer: JEZ (without imprint).

a. Issued note.	17.50	40.00
s. Specimen. Overprinted: ESPECIMEN on both sides.	—	750

1980-89 Issues

178 100 Escudos

VF UNC

1980-85. Dark blue on multicolor underprint. Manuel M. B. du Bocage seated at right. Ch. 8. Back: Early 19th century scene of Rossio Square in Lisbon. Watermark: Manuel M. B. du Bocage.

a. 8 signature varieties. Darker underprint through center 2.9.1980.	7.00	30.00
b. 8 signature varieties. Light underprint through center 24.2.1981.	5.00	20.00
c. 7 signature varieties. 31.1.1984.	3.50	16.00
d. 6 signature varieties. 12.3.1985.	3.50	15.00
e. 6 signature varieties. 4.6.1985.	3.25	14.00
s. Specimen.	—	195
ct. Color trial. Blue and green on multicolor underprint.	—	250

179 100 Escudos

1986-88. Blue (shades) on multicolor underprint. Fernando Antonio Pessoa at center right. Ch. 9. Back: Rosebud. Watermark: Fernando Antonio Nogueira Pessoa.

	VF	UNC
a. 5 signature varieties. 16.10.1986.	3.75	16.00
b. 8 signature varieties. 12.2.1987.	5.00	20.00
c. Prefix letters *FIL*. 12.2.1987.	—	200
d. 8 signature varieties. 3.12.1987.	3.75	16.00
e. 6 signature varieties. 26.5.1988.	3.25	12.00
f. 6 signature varieties. 24.11.1988.	3.25	12.00
s. As a. Specimen. Overprinted: *ESPECIMEN* on both sides.	—	150

Note: #179c was issued in a special folder with an adhesive postage stamp affixed on the upper right corner of the folder commemorating the 300th Anniversary of Portuguese Paper Money.

180 500 Escudos

1987-94. Brown and multicolor. José Xavier Mouzinho da Silveira at center right, arms at upper left. Ch. 12. Back: Sheaf. Watermark: José Xavier Mouzinho da Silveira.

	VF	UNC
a. 8 signature varieties. 20.11.1987.	17.50	40.00
b. 6 signature varieties. 4.8.1988.	20.00	45.00
c. 6 signature varieties. 4.10.1989.	15.00	35.00
d. 5 signature varieties. 13.2.1992.	15.00	35.00
e. 7 signature varieties. 18.3.1993.	15.00	35.00
f. 6 signature varieties. 4.11.1993.	15.00	35.00
g. 5 signature varieties. 29.9.1994.	17.50	40.00
s. As a. Specimen.	—	250

181 1000 Escudos

1983-94. Purple and dark brown on multicolor underprint. Teofilo Braga at center right. Ch. 12. Back: Museum artifacts. Watermark: Teofilo Braga.

	VF	UNC
a. 9 signature varieties. 2.8.1983.	22.50	50.00
b. 5 signature varieties. 12.6.1986.	25.00	60.00
c. 8 signature varieties. 26.2.1987.	25.00	60.00
d. 8 signature varieties. 3.9.1987.	25.00	60.00
e. 6 signature varieties. 22.12.1988.	25.00	60.00
f. 6 signature varieties. 9.11.1989.	25.00	60.00
g. 5 signature varieties. 26.7.1990.	22.50	50.00
h. 5 signature varieties. 20.12.1990.	20.00	45.00
i. 5 signature varieties. 6.2.1992.	25.00	55.00
j. 6 signature varieties. 17.6.1993.	20.00	45.00
k. 6 signature varieties. 3.3.1994.	20.00	45.00
s. As a. Specimen.	—	400

182 5000 Escudos

1980-86. Brown and multicolor. Antonio Sergio de Sousa at left center. Ch. 1. Back: Antonio Sergio de Sousa walking at center. Watermark: Antonio Sergio de Sousa. Printer: TDLR (without imprint).

	VF	UNC
a. 8 signature varieties. 10.9.1980.	90.00	200
b. 8 signature varieties. 27.1.1981.	85.00	190
c. 10 signature varieties. 24.5.1983.	80.00	180
d. 6 signature varieties. 4.6.1985.	110	240
e. 6 signature varieties. 7.1.1986.	90.00	200
s. Specimen.	—	500

183 5000 Escudos

1987. Olive-green and brown on multicolor underprint. Antero de Quental at center right. Ch. 2. Back: Six hands with rope and chain at center. Watermark: Antero de Quental.

	VF	UNC
a. 8 signature varieties. 12.2.1987.	60.00	140
b. 8 signature varieties. 3.12.1987.	60.00	140
s. As a. Specimen.	—	400

184 5000 Escudos

1988-93. Olive-green and brown on multicolor underprint. Antero de Quental at center right. Ch. 2A. Back: Six hands with rope and chain at center. Watermark: Antero de Quental.

	VF	UNC
a. 6 signature varieties. 28.10.1988.	60.00	140
b. 6 signature varieties. 6.7.1989.	65.00	150
c. 6 signature varieties. 19.10.1989.	55.00	130
d. 5 signature varieties. 31.10.1991.	60.00	140
e. 7 signature varieties. 18.3.1993.	60.00	140
f. 7 signature varieties. 2.9.1993.	60.00	140

185   10,000 Escudos   VF   UNC
1989-91. Orange, light brown and yellow. Dr. Antonio Gaetano de Abreu Preire
Egas Moniz by human brain at center. Ch. 1. Back: Nobel Prize medal, snakes,
tree at center. Watermark: Dr. Antonio Gaetano de Abreu Preire Egas Moniz.

		VF	UNC
a. 6 signature varieties. 12.1.1989.		130	300
b. 6 signature varieties. 14.12.1989.		120	260
c. 5 signature varieties. 16.5.1991.		120	260
s. As a. Specimen.		—	500

1991 Issue

186   2000 Escudos   VF   UNC
1991-93. . Dark brown and blue on multicolor underprint. Bartholomeu Dias at left,
astrolabe at center. Ch. 1. Back: Sailing ship at center, arms at right. Watermark:
Bartholomeu Dias.

		VF	UNC
a. 5 signature varieties. 23.5.1991.		35.00	85.00
b. 5 signature varieties. 29.8.1991.		50.00	125
c. 6 signature varieties. 16.7.1992.		30.00	70.00
d. 6 signature varieties. 21.10.1993.		45.00	100
s. As a. Specimen.		—	400

1995-97 Issue

Note: #187-191, Quincentenary of Portuguese Discoveries Series

187   500 Escudos   VF   UNC
1997; 2000. Violet and brown on multicolor underprint. João de Barros at right,
crowned shields on global view at upper center, angels below at left and right in
underprint. Ch. 13. Back: Allegory of the Portuguese Discoveries at left center,
illustrations from the *Grammer* at left in underprint. Watermark: João de Barros.
125x68mm.

		VF	UNC
a. 6 signature varieties. 17.4.1997.		FV	18.00
b. 6 signature varieties. 11.9.1997.		FV	15.00
c. 7.11.2000.		FV	14.00
s. As a. Specimen.		—	200

188   1000 Escudos   VF   UNC
1996; 1998; 2000. Purple and brown on multicolor underprint. Pedro Alvares
Cabral wearing helmet at right, Brazilian arms at center. Ch. 13. Back: Old sailing
ship at center, birds and animals of Brazilian jungle in underprint. Watermark:
Pedro Alvares Cabral. 132x68mm.

		VF	UNC
a. 6 signature varieties. 18.4.1996.		FV	32.50
b. 6 signature varieties. 31.10.1996.		FV	30.00
c. 6 signature varieties. 12.3.1998; 21.5.1998.		FV	25.00
d. 7.11.2000.		FV	22.50
s. As a. Specimen.		—	250

189   2000 Escudos   VF   UNC
1995-97. Blue-violet and deep blue-green on multicolor underprint. Bartholomeu
Dias at right, cruzado coin of Dom João II at upper center, sailing instrument
below. Ch. 2. Back: Old sailing ship at center right, compass, map at left center.
Watermark: Bartholomeu Dias. 140x68mm.

		VF	UNC
a. 5 signature varieties. 21.9.1995.		FV	60.00
b. 6 signature varieties. 1.2.1996.		FV	55.00
c. 31.7.1997; 11.9.1997.		FV	50.00
d. 7.11.2000.		FV	55.00
s. As a. Specimen.		—	300

190   5000 Escudos   VF   UNC
1995-98. Deep olive-green and brown-violet on underprint. Vasco da Gama at
right, medallion at upper center. Ch. 3. Back: Old sailing ship at center right, da
Gama with authorities in Calcutta at left. Watermark: Vasco da Gama. 147x75mm.

		VF	UNC
a. 5 signature varieties. 5.1.1995.		FV	130
b. 6 signature varieties. 12.9.1996.		FV	120
c. 6 signature varieties. 20.2.1997.		FV	120
d. 6 signature varieties. 11.9.1997.		FV	110
e. 2.7.1998.		FV	110
s. As a. Specimen.		—	400

191   10,000 Escudos   VF   UNC
1996-98. Violet and dark brown on multicolor underprint. Infante Dom Henrique at
right, arms at center. Ch. 2. 6 signature varieties. Back: Old sailing ship at center.
Watermark: Infante Dom Henrique. 153x75mm.

		VF	UNC
a. 2.5.1996.		FV	200
b. 10.7.1997.		FV	190
c. 12.2.1998; 12.7.1998.		FV	190
s. As a. Specimen.		—	500

Note: For later issues used in Portugal see European Union listings.

Portuguese Guinea (now Guinea-Bissau), a former Portuguese province off the west coast of Africa bounded on the north by Senegal and on the east and southeast by Guinea, had an area of 13,948 sq. mi. (36,125 sq. km.). Capital: Bissau. The province exported peanuts, timber and beeswax. Portuguese Guinea was discovered by Portuguese navigator Nuno Tristao in 1446. Trading rights in the area were granted to Cape Verde islanders but few prominent posts were established before 1851, and they were principally coastal installations. The chief export of this colony's early period was slaves for South America, a practice that adversely affected trade with the native people and retarded subjection of the interior. Territorial disputes with France delayed final demarcation of the colony's frontiers until 1905. The African Party for the Independence of Guinea-Bissau was founded in 1956, and several years later began a guerrilla warfare that grew in effectiveness until 1974, when the rebels controlled most of the colony. Portugal's costly overseas wars in her African territories resulted in a military coup in Portugal in April 1974, that appreciably brightened the prospects for freedom for Guinea-Bissau. In August, 1974, the Lisbon government signed an agreement granting independence to Portuguese Guinea effective Sept. 10, 1974. The new republic took the name of Guinea-Bissau.

RULERS:
Portuguese to 1974

MONETARY SYSTEM:
1 Mil Reis = 1000 Reis to 1910
1 Escudo = 100 Centavos, 1910-1975

STEAMSHIP SEALS

Type I	Type II	Type III
LOANDA	LISBOA	C,C,A

C,C,A = Colonias, Commercio, Agricultura.

PORTUGUESE ADMINISTRATION

Banco Nacional Ultramarino, Guiné

Decretos - Leis 39221 E 44891; 1964 Issue

40 50 Escudos
30.6.1964. Dark green on lilac and multicolor underprint. Texeira Pinto at left, bank ship seal at right. Back: Woman sitting, ships through the ages in background at center.

	VF	UNC
a. Issued note.	125	350
s. Specimen, punch hole cancelled.	—	250

41 100 Escudos
30.6.1964. Blue-green on multicolor underprint. Texeira Pinto at left, bank ship seal at right. Back: Woman sitting, ships through the ages in background at center.

	VF	UNC
a. Issued note.	175	450
s. Specimen, punch hole cancelled.	—	325

42 500 Escudos
30.6.1964. Brown on multicolor underprint. Texeira Pinto at left, bank ship seal at right. Back: Woman sitting, ships through the ages in background at center.

	VF	UNC
a. Issued note.	350	850
s. Specimen, punch hole cancelled.	—	500

43 1000 Escudos
30.6.1964. Red-orange on multicolor underprint. Portrait of H. Barreto at right, bank ship seal at upper center. Back: Woman standing, ships through the ages in background at left center. Printer: BWC.

	VF	UNC
a. Issued note.	275	650
s. Specimen.	—	375
ct. Color trial. Brown on multicolor underprint.	—	350

Decretos - Leis 39221 E 44891; 1971 Issue

44 50 Escudos   **VF UNC**

17.12.1971. Olive-green on multicolor underprint. Portuguese arms at upper center, N. Tristao at right. Back: Woman standing, ships through the ages in background at left center, bank ship seal at lower left. Watermark: N. Tristao.

a. Issued note.	35.00	80.00
s. Specimen.	—	175
ct. Color trial. Green on multicolor underprint.	—	195

45 100 Escudos   **VF UNC**

17.12.1971. Blue on multicolor undderprint. Portuguese arms at upper center, portrait of N.Tristaoat right. Back: Woman standing, ships through the ages in background at left center, bank ship seal at lower left. Watermark: N. Tristao.

a. Issued note.	37.50	90.00
s. Specimen.	—	200
ct. Color trial. Olive on multicolor underprint.	—	195

46 500 Escudos   **VF UNC**

27.7.1971. Purple on multicolor underprint. Portuguese arms at upper center, portrait H. Barreto at right. Back: Woman standing, ships through the ages in background at left center, bank ship seal at lower left.

a. Issued note.	225	600
ct. Color trial. Brown on multicolor underprint.	—	450

QATAR

The State of Qatar, an emirate in the Persian Gulf between Bahrain and the United Arab Emirates, has an area 4,247 sq. mi. (11,437 sq. km.) and a population of 700,000. Capital: Doha.Ruled by the al-Thani family since the mid-1800s, Qatar transformed itself from a poor British protectorate noted mainly for pearling into an independent state with significant oil and natural gas revenues. During the late 1980s and early 1990s, the Qatari economy was crippled by a continuous siphoning off of petroleum revenues by the Amir, who had ruled the country since 1972. His son, the current Amir Hamad bin Khalifa al-Thani, overthrew him in a bloodless coup in 1995. In 2001, Qatar resolved its longstanding border disputes with both Bahrain and Saudi Arabia. As of 2007, oil and natural gas revenues had enabled Qatar to attain the highest per capita income in the world. Also see Qatar and Dubai.

MONETARY SYSTEM:
1 Riyal = 100 Dirhem

EMIRATE

Qatar Monetary Agency

1973 ND Issue

1 1 Riyal   **VF UNC**

ND (1973). Red on lilac and multicolor underprint. Arms in circle at right. Back: Port of Doha at left. Watermark: Falcon's head.

a. Issued note.	12.00	60.00
s. Specimen.	—	200

2 5 Riyals   **VF UNC**

ND (1973). Dark brown on lilac and multicolor underprint. Arms in circle at right. Back: National Museum at left. Watermark: Falcon's head.

a. Issued note.	30.00	120
s. Specimen.	—	300

3 10 Riyals   **VF UNC**

ND (1973). Green on multicolor underprint. Arms in circle at right. Back: Qatar Monetary Agency building at left. Watermark: Falcon's head.

a. Issued note.	40.00	170
s. Specimen.	—	400

4 50 Riyals

VF UNC

ND (1976). Blue on multicolor underprint. Arms in circle at right. Back: Offshore oil drilling platform at left. Watermark: Falcon's head.

    a. Issued note.   400   1,400

    s. Specimen.   —   1,000

5 100 Riyals

VF UNC

ND (1973). Olive-green and orange-brown on multicolor underprint. Arms in circle at right. Back: Ministry of Finance building at left. Watermark: Falcon's head.

    a. Issued note.   220   850

    s. Specimen.   —   1,500

6 500 Riyals

VF UNC

ND (1973). Blue-green on multicolor underprint. Arms in circle at right. Back: Mosque of the Sheikhs and minaret at left. Watermark: Falcon's head.

    a. Issued note.   850   2,700

    s. Specimen.   —   2,000

1980's ND Issue

7 1 Riyal

VF UNC

ND. Brown on multicolor underprint. Arms at right. Back: City street scene in Doha at left center. Watermark: Falcon's head.   6.00   12.00

8 5 Riyals

VF UNC

ND. Dark red and purple on multicolor underprint. Arms at right. Back: Sheep and plants at left center. Watermark: Falcon's head.

    a. Watermark: Hawk, nostril visible, and top bill overlaps bottom.   7.00   15.00

    b. Watermark: Hawk, without nostril, beak even.   7.00   12.00

9 10 Riyals

VF UNC

ND. Green on blue and multicolor underprint. Arms at right. Back: National   12.00   30.00
Museum at left center. Watermark: Falcon's head.

10 50 Riyals

VF UNC

ND (1989). Blue on multicolor underprint. Arms at right. Back: Furnace at a steel   45.00   100
factory. Watermark: Falcon's head.

11 100 Riyals

VF UNC

ND. Green on multicolor underprint. Arms at right. Back: Qatar Monetary Agency   85.00   140
building at left center. Watermark: Falcon's head.

12   500 Riyals   VF   UNC

ND. Blue and green on multicolor underprint. Arms at right. Back: Offshore oil drilling platform on vertical format. Watermark: Falcon's head.

     a. Issued note.   365   650
     s. Specimen.   —   1,500

1985 ND Issue

13   1 Riyal   VF   UNC

ND (1985). Brown on multicolor underprint. Arms at right. Back: Boat beached at left, Ministry of Finance, Emir's Palace in background at center. Watermark: Falcon's head. 134x66mm.

     a. Watermark: Hawk, nostril visible, and top bill overlaps bottom.   FV   6.00
     b. Watermark: Hawk, without nostril, beak even.   FV   5.00

Qatar Central Bank
1996 ND Issue

14   1 Riyal   VF   UNC

ND (1996). Brown on multicolor underprint. Arms at right. 2 signatures. Back: Boat beached at left, Ministry of Finance, Emir's Palace in background at center. Watermark: Falcon's head. 134x66mm.

     a. Security thread reads: *QATAR MONETARY AGENCY.*   FV   5.00
     b. Security thread reads: *QATAR CENTRAL BANK.*   FV   4.00

15   5 Riyals   VF   UNC

ND (1996). Red and purple on multicolor underprint. Arms at right. 2 signatures. Back: Sheep and plants at left center. Watermark: Falcon's head. 140x67mm.

     a. Security thread reads: *QATAR MONETARY AGENCY.*   FV   14.00
     b. Security thread reads: *QATAR CENTRAL BANK.*   FV   10.00

16   10 Riyals   VF   UNC

ND (1996). Green and blue on multicolor underprint. Arms at right. 2 signatures. Back: National Museum at left center. Watermark: Falcon's head. 145x69mm.

     a. Security thread reads: *QATAR MONETARY AGENCY.*   FV   20.00
     b. Security thread reads: *QATAR CENTRAL BANK.*   FV   12.00

17   50 Riyals   VF   UNC

ND (1996). Blue on multicolor underprint. Arms at right. 2 signatures. Back: Furnace at a steel factory. Watermark: Falcon's head. 152x70mm.   FV   60.00

18   100 Riyals   VF   UNC

ND (1996). Green on multicolor underprint. Arms at right. 2 signatures. Back: Qatar Monetary Agency building at left center. Watermark: Falcon's head. 152x72mm.   FV   100

FIVE HUNDRED RIYALS

19 500 Riyals
ND (1996). Blue on multicolor underprint. Arms at right. 2 signatures. Silver foil emblem at upper left. Back: Offshore oil drilling platform. Watermark: Falcon's head. 165x74mm.

VF UNC
FV 475

2003 ND Issue

20 1 Riyal
ND (2003). UV: fibers fluoresce yellow and blue; left serial # orange; central design elements yellow. Purple and blue on multicolor underprint. Back: Three native birds - Crested Lark, Eurasian Bee Eater and lesser Sand Plover at left. Watermark: Falcon's head. 134x66mm.

VF UNC
FV 2.00

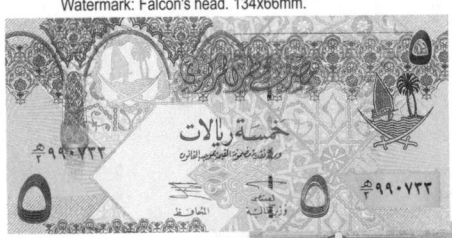

21 5 Riyals
ND (2003). Light and dark green on multicolor underprint. Back: National Museum and native animals at left. Watermark: Falcon's head. 140x67mm.

VF UNC
FV 6.00

22 10 Riyals
ND (2003). Orange-brown and tan on multicolor underprint. Back: Traditional Dhow and sand dunes Khor Al-Udeid at left. Watermark: Falcon's head. 146x69mm.

VF UNC
FV 11.00

23 50 Riyals
ND (2003). Rose on multicolor underprint. Back: Qatar Central Bank building and Oyster and Pearl Monument at left. Watermark: Falcon's head. 152x70mm.

VF UNC
FV 62.50

24 100 Riyals
ND (2003). Green on multicolor underprint. Back: Mosque of the Sheikhs and Al-Shaqab Institute at left. Watermark: Falcon's head. 158x72mm.

VF UNC
FV 95.00

25 500 Riyals
ND (2003). Light and dark blue on multicolor underprint. Back: Royal Palace, Al-Wajbah Fort and Falcon's head at left. Watermark: Falcon's head. 164x74mm.

VF UNC
FV 425

2007 ND Issue

26   100 Riyals — VF UNC
ND (2007). Green on multicolor underprint. Solid security thread at left and — FV 50.00
windowed foil thread with QCB 100 repeatedly cut out. Foil over clear window at
center. 158x72mm.

27   500 Riyals — VF UNC
ND (2007). Light and dark blue on multicolor underprint. Solid security thread at — FV 225
left and windowed foil thread with QCB 500 repeatedly cut out. Clear window at
center. 164x74mm.

2008 ND Issue

28   1 Riyal — VF UNC
ND (2008-15). Purple and blue on multicolor underprint. Two signature varieties. — FV 2.00
Tactile markings for visually impaired added at center left edge.

29   5 Riyals — VF UNC
ND (2008-15). Light and dark green on multicolor underprint. Two signature variet- — FV 6.00
ies. Tactile markings for visually impaired added at center left edge.

30   10 Riyals — VF UNC
ND (2008). Orange-brown and tan on multicolor underprint. Tactile markings for — FV 11.00
visually impaired added at center left edge.

31   50 Riyals — VF UNC
ND (2008). Rose on multicolor underprint. Tactile markings for visually imparred — FV 35.00
added at center left edge. Back: Qatar Central Bank building and Oyster and Pearl
Monument at left.

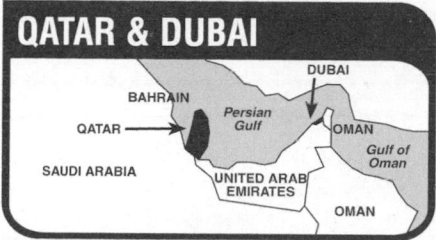

The State of Qatar, which occupies the Qatar Peninsula jutting into the Persian Gulf from eastern Saudi Arabia, has an area of 4,247 sq. mi. (11,000 sq. km.) and a population of 382,000. Capital: Doha. The traditional occupations of pearling, fishing and herding have been replaced in economics by petroleum-related industries. Crude oil, petroleum products, and tomatoes are exported.

Dubai is one of the seven sheikhdoms comprising the United Arab Emirates (formerly Trucial States) located along the southern shore of the Persian Gulf. It has a population of about 60,000. Qatar, which initiated protective treaty relations with Great Britain in 1820, achieved independence on Sept. 3, 1971, upon withdrawal of the British military presence from the Persian Gulf, and replaced its special treaty arrangement with Britain with a treaty of general friendship. Dubai attended independence on Dec. 1, 1971, upon termination of Britain's protective treaty with the trucial sheikhdoms, and on Dec. 2, 1971, entered into the union of the United Arab Emirates.

Despite the fact that the sultanate of Qatar and the sheikhdom of Dubai were merged under a monetary union, the two territories were governed independently from each other. Qatar now uses its own currency while Dubai uses the United Arab Emirates currency and coins.

The Department of Reunion, an overseas department of France located in the Indian Ocean 400 miles (640 km.) east of Madagascar, has an area of 969 sq. mi. (2,510 sq. km.) and a population of 556,000. Capital: Saint-Denis. The island's volcanic soil is extremely fertile. Sugar, vanilla, coffee and rum are exported. Although first visited by Portuguese navigators in the 16th century, Reunion was uninhabited when claimed for France by Capt. Goubert in 1638. It was first colonized as Isle de Burbon by the French in 1662 as a layover station for ships rounding the Cape of Good Hope to India. It was renamed Reunion in 1793. The island remained in French possession except for the period of 1810-15, when it was occupied by the British. Reunion became an overseas department of France in 1946, and in 1958 voted to continue that status within the now French Union. Baque du France notes were introduced 1.1.1973.

MONETARY SYSTEM:
1 Riyal = 100 Dirhem

SULTANATE AND SHEIKHDOM
Qatar and Dubai Currency Board
1960s ND Issue

1   1 Riyal — VF UNC
ND. Dark green on multicolor underprint. Dhow, derrick and palm tree at left.
Watermark: Falcon's head.
  a. Issued note. — 150 450
  s. Specimen, punch hole cancelled. — — 2,500

2   5 Riyals — VF UNC
ND. Purple on multicolor underprint. Dhow, derrick and palm tree at left. Watermark: Falcon's head.
  a. Issued note. — 1,000 3,500
  s. Specimen, punch hole cancelled. — — 3,500

3   10 Riyals — VF UNC
ND. Gray-blue on multicolor underprint. Dhow, derrick and palm tree at left.
Watermark: Falcon's head.
  a. Issued note. — 500 3,000
  s. Specimen, punch hole cancelled. — — 3,000

4   25 Riyals   **VF   UNC**
ND. Blue on multicolor underprint. Dhow, derrick and palm tree at left. Watermark:
Falcon's head.
    a. Issued note.   6,000 75,000
    s. Specimen, punch hole cancelled. Rare.   —   —

5   50 Riyals   **VF   UNC**
ND. Red on multicolor underprint. Dhow, derrick and palm tree at left. Watermark:
Falcon's head.
    a. Issued note.   4,500 60,000
    s. Specimen, punch hole cancelled. Rare.   —   —

6   100 Riyals   **VF   UNC**
ND. Olive on multicolor underprint. Dhow, derrick and palm tree at left. Watermark:
Falcon's head.
    a. Issued note.   2,500 7,500
    s. Specimen, punch hole cancelled. Rare.   —   —

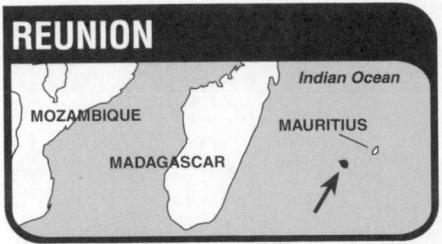

REUNION

The Department of Reunion, an overseas department of France located in the Indian Ocean 400 miles (640 km.) east of Madagascar, has an area of 969 sq. mi. (2,510 sq. km.) and a population of 556,000. Capital: Saint-Denis. The island's volcanic soil is extremely fertile. Sugar, vanilla, coffee and rum are exported. Although first visited by Portuguese navigators in the 16th century, Reunion was uninhabited when claimed for France by Capt. Goubert in 1638. It was first colonized as Isle de Bourbon by the French in 1662 as a layover station for ships rounding the Cape of Good Hope to India. It was renamed Reunion in 1793. The island remained in French possession except for the period of 1810-15, when it was occupied by the British. Reunion became an overseas department of France in 1946, and in 1958 voted to continue that status within the new French Union. Banque de France notes were introduced 1.1.1973.

MONETARY SYSTEM:
    1 Franc = 100 Centimes
    1 Nouveau Franc = 50 Old Francs, 1960

FRENCH ADMINISTRATION

Institut d'Emission des Départements d'Outre-Mer, République Française

Department de la Réunion

1964; 1965 ND Issue

51   500 Francs   **VF   UNC**
ND (1964). Multicolor. Two girls at right, sailboat at left. Back: Farmers with
ox-carts.
    a. Signature A. Postel-Vinay and P. Calvet.   325   900
    b. Signature A. Postel-Vinay and B. Clappier.   275   800
    s. As a. Specimen. Overprint and perforated: *SPECIMEN*.   —   450

52 **1000 Francs** VF UNC
ND (1964). Multicolor. Two women (symbol of the *Union Française*) at right.
Signature A. Postel-Vinay and P. Calvet. Back: Two men in canoe at left, female
at right.
    a. Issued note. 350 1,000
    s. Specimen. — 600

53 **5000 Francs** VF UNC
ND (1965). Brown on multicolor underprint. General Schoelcher at center right.
Signature A. Postel-Vinay and P. Calvet.
    a. Issued note. 600 1,500
    s. Specimen. — 900

1967 ND Provisional Issue

54 **10 Nouveaux Francs on 500 Francs** VF UNC
ND (1967-71). Multicolor. Two girls at right, sailboat at left with overprint. Back:
Farmers with ox-carts.
    a. Signature A. Postel-Vinay and P. Calvet. (1967). 175 650
    b. Signature A. Postel-Vinay and B. Clappier. (1971). 140 500
    s. Specimen. FV 700

55 **20 Nouveaux Francs on 1000 Francs** VF UNC
ND (1967-71). Multicolor. Two women (symbol of the *Union Française*) at right.
Signature A. Postel-Vinay and P. Calvet. With overprint.
    a. Signature A. Postel-Vinay and P. Calvet. (1967). 200 750
    b. Signature A. Postel-Vinay and B. Clappier. (1971). 160 600
    s. Specimen. — 900

56 **100 Nouveaux Francs on 5000 Francs** VF UNC
ND (1967-71). Multicolor. General Schoelcher at center right. Signature A. Postel-
Vinay and P. Calvet. With overprint.
    a. Signature A. Postel-Vinay and P. Calvet. (1967). 450 1,250
    b. Signature A. Postel-Vinay and B. Clappier. (1971). 375 1,000
    s. Specimen. — 1,500

RHODESIA

The "Republic of" Rhodesia (never recognized by the British government and was referred to as Southern Rhodesia, now Zimbabwe) located in the east-central part of southern Africa, has an area of 150,804 sq. mi. (390,580 sq. km.) and a population of 9.9 million. Capital: Harare. The economy is based on agriculture and mining. Tobacco, sugar, asbestos, copper and chrome ore and coal are exported. The Rhodesian area, the habitat of paleolithic man, contains extensive evidence of earlier civilizations, notably the world-famous ruins of Zimbabwe, a gold-trading center that flourished about the 14th or 15th century AD. The Portuguese of the 16th century were the first Europeans to attempt to develop south-central Africa, but it remained for Cecil Rhodes and the British South Africa Co. to open the hinterlands. Rhodes obtained a concession for mineral rights from local chiefs in 1888 and administered his African empire (named Southern Rhodesia in 1895) through the British South Africa Co. until 1923, when the British government annexed the area after the white settlers voted for existence as a separate entity, rather than for incorporation into the Union of South Africa. From Sept. of 1953 through 1963 Southern Rhodesia was joined with the British protectorates of Northern Rhodesia and Nyasaland into a multiracial federation. When the federation was dissolved at the end of 1963, Northern Rhodesia and Nyasaland became the independent states of Zambia and Malawi. Britain was prepared to grant independence to Southern Rhodesia but declined to do so when the politically dominant white Rhodesians refused to give assurances of representative government. In November 1965, the white minority government of Southern Rhodesia unilaterally declared Southern Rhodesia an independent dominion. The United Nations and the British Parliament both proclaimed this unilateral declaration of independence null and void. Following a conference in London in December 1979, the opposition government conceded and it was agreed that the British government should resume control. In 1970, the government proclaimed a republic, but this too received no recognition. In 1979, the government purported to change the name of the Colony to Zimbabwe Rhodesia, but again this was never recognized. A British governor soon returned to Southern Rhodesia. One of his first acts was to affirm the nullification of the purported declaration of independence. On April 18, 1980, pursuant to an act of the British Parliament, the colony of Southern Rhodesia became independent within the commonwealth as the Republic of Zimbabwe.

RULERS:
    British to 1970 (1000)

MONETARY SYSTEM:
    1 Shilling = 12 Pence
    1 Pound = 20 Shillings to 1970
    1 Dollar = 100 Cents, 1970-80

REPLACEMENT NOTES:
    #30-33 later dates, W/1, X/1, Y/1 and Z/1, respectively.

SIGNATURE VARIETIES		
	GOVERNOR	TERM OF OFFICE
1	*N.H.B. Bruce*	1964 - 1974
2	*Dr. D.C. Krogh*	1974 - 1982

BRITISH ADMINISTRATION

Reserve Bank of Rhodesia

1964 Issue

Pound System

24 **10 Shillings** VF UNC
30.9.1964-16.11.1964. Blue on multicolor underprint. Blue portrait of Queen
Elizabeth II at right, arms at upper center, black serial number. Signature 1. Back:
Tobacco field at left center. Watermark: C. Rhodes. Printer: BWC.
    a. Issued note. 250 850
    ct. Color trial. Brown on multicolor underprint. — 1,100

29 5 Pounds VF UNC

1.7.1966. Blue-green on multicolor underprint. Purple portrait of Queen Elizabeth II at right, arms at upper center, red serial number. Sable antelope at lower left. Various dates and signature varieties. Lithographed. Back: Zimbabwe ruins at left center. Watermark: C. Rhodes. Printer: Rhodesian (without imprint).

a. 1.7.1966.	285	1,000
s. Specimen.	—	—

Note: Before the issue of #27-29, a series of Rhodesian banknotes was printed in Germany by Giesecke and Devrient, Munich. An injunction prevented delivery of this issue and it was never released. Subsequently it was destroyed.

25 1 Pound VF UNC

3.9.1964-16.11.1964. Red on multicolor underprint. Red portrait of Queen Elizabeth II at right, arms at upper center, black serial number. Signature 1. Back: Victoria Falls at left center. Watermark: C. Rhodes. Printer: BWC.

a. Issued note.	225	750
ct. Color trial. Green on multicolor underprint.	—	900

REPUBLIC

Reserve Bank of Rhodesia

1970-75 Issue

Dollar System #30-33 Replacement notes: Serial # prefixes *W/1, X/1, Y/1, Z/1* **respectively.**

26 5 Pounds VF UNC

10.11.1964; 12.11.1964; 16.11.1964. Blue-green on multicolor underprint. Blue portrait of Queen Elizabeth II at right, arms at upper center, black serial number. Sable antelope at lower left. Signature 1. Back: Zimbabwe ruins at left center. Watermark: C. Rhodes. Printer: BWC.

a. Issued note.	275	900
ct. Color trial. Light blue on multicolor underprint.	—	1,250

1966 Issue

27 10 Shillings VF UNC

1.6.1966; 10.9.1968. Blue on multicolor underprint. Black portrait of Queen Elizabeth II at right, arms at upper center, Red serial number. Signature 1. Lithographed. Back: Tobacco field at left center. Watermark: C. Rhodes. Printer: Rhodesian (without imprint).

a. 1.6.1966.	120	425
b. 10.9.1968.	100	325
s. Specimen.	—	—

30 1 Dollar VF UNC

1970-74. Blue on multicolor underprint. Bank logo at upper center, arms at right. Back: Tobacco field at left center. Watermark: C. Rhodes.

a. 17.2.1970.	45.00	120
b. 16.4.1971.	45.00	120
c. 14.5.1971.	45.00	120
d. 17.6.1971.	45.00	120
e. 19.7.1971.	45.00	120
f. 18.8.1971.	20.00	55.00
g. 14.2.1973.	20.00	55.00
h. 2.3.1973.	20.00	55.00
i. 12.8.1974.	20.00	55.00
j. 2.9.1974.	20.00	55.00
k. 15.10.1974.	20.00	55.00
s. Specimen.	—	—

28 1 Pound VF UNC

15.6.1966-14.10.1968. Pale red on multicolor underprint. Brown portrait of Queen Elizabeth II at right, arms at upper center, red serial number. Signature 1. Lithographed. Back: Victoria Falls at left center. Watermark: C. Rhodes. Printer: Rhodesian (without imprint).

a. 15.6.1966.	150	550
b. 18.8.1967.	125	500
c. 1.9.1967.	100	450
d. 14.10.1968.	80.00	400
s. Specimen.	—	900

31   2 Dollars

1970-75. Red on multicolor underprint. Bank logo at upper center, arms at right. Back: Victoria Falls at left center. Watermark: C. Rhodes.

	VF	UNC
a. 17.2.1970.	35.00	100
b. 15.8.1970.	35.00	100
c. 8.9.1970.	35.00	100
d. 10.11.1970.	35.00	100
e. 12.11.1971.	35.00	100
f. 4.1.1972.	35.00	100
g. 29.6.1973.	32.50	90.00
h. 10.1.1974.	32.50	90.00
i. 20.1.1975.	32.50	90.00
j. 4.3.1975.	32.50	90.00
k. 7.4.1975.	32.50	90.00
s. As b, d. Specimen.	—	—

32   5 Dollars

16.10.1972. Brown on multicolor underprint. Bank logo at upper center, arms at right. Giraffe at lower left. Back: Two lions. Watermark: C. Rhodes.

	VF	UNC
a. 16.10.1972.	37.50	110
s. Specimen.	—	—

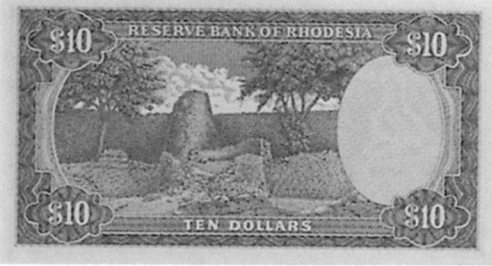

33   10 Dollars

1970-75. Black on blue-green and multicolor underprint. Bank logo at upper center, arms at right. Sable antelope at lower left. Back: Zimbabwe ruins at left center. Watermark: C. Rhodes.

	VF	UNC
a. 17.2.1970.	110	300
b. 25.1.1971.	110	300
c. 24.2.1971.	110	300
d. 8.5.1972.	110	300
e. 20.11.1973.	50.00	140
f. 15.12.1973.	50.00	140
g. 15.9.1975.	50.00	140
h. 19.11.1975.	50.00	140
i. 3.12.1975.	50.00	140
s. Specimen.	—	—

1976-79 Issue

34   1 Dollar

1976-78. Watermark: C. Rhodes.

	VF	UNC
a. 1.3.1976.	20.00	55.00
b. 1.11.1976.	20.00	55.00
c. 18.4.1978.	20.00	55.00

35   2 Dollars

1976-79. Watermark: C. Rhodes.

	VF	UNC
a. 1.3.1976.	32.50	90.00
b. 15.4.1977.	32.50	90.00
c. 5.8.1977.	32.50	90.00
d. 10.4.1979.	200	500

36   5 Dollars

1976-78. Watermark: C. Rhodes.

	VF	UNC
a. 1.3.1976.	35.00	100
b. 20.10.1978.	35.00	100

37   10 Dollars

1976. Watermark: C. Rhodes.

	VF	UNC
a. 1.3.1976.	50.00	140

1979 Issue

38   1 Dollar

2.8.1979. Signature 2. Watermark: Zimbabwe bird.

	VF	UNC
a. Issued note.	16.00	45.00

39   2 Dollars

10.4.1979; 24.5.1979. Signature 2. Watermark: Zimbabwe bird.

	VF	UNC
a. 10.4.1979.	25.00	70.00
b. 24.5.1979.	25.00	70.00

40   5 Dollars

15.5.1979. Signature 2. Watermark: Zimbabwe bird.

	VF	UNC
a. 15.5.1979.	32.50	90.00

41   10 Dollars

2.1.1979. Signature 2. Watermark: Zimbabwe bird.

	VF	UNC
a. 2.1.1979.	45.00	125

Rhodesia and Nyasaland (now the Republics of Malawi, Zambia and Zimbabwe) was located in the east-central part of southern Africa, had an area of 487,133 sq. mi. (1,261,678 sq. km.). Capital: Salisbury. The area was the habitat of paleolithic man, contains extensive evidence of earlier civilizations, notably the world-famous ruins of Zimbabwe, a gold-trading center that flourished about the 14th or 15th century AD. The Portuguese of the 16th century were the first Europeans to attempt to develop south-central Africa, but it remained for Cecil Rhodes and the British South Africa Co. to open the hinterlands. Rhodes obtained a concession for mineral rights from local chiefs in 1888 and administered his African empire (named Southern Rhodesia in 1895) through the British South Africa Co. until 1923, when the British government annexed the area after the white settlers voted for existence as a separate entity, rather than for incorporation into the Union of South Africa. From Sept. of 1953 through 1963 Southern Rhodesia was joined with the British protectorates of Northern Rhodesia and Nyasaland into a multiracial federation. When the federation was dissolved at the end of 1963, Northern Rhodesia and Nyasaland became the independent states of Zambia and Malawi.

RULERS:
British to 1963

MONETARY SYSTEM:
1 Shilling = 12 Pence
1 Pound = 20 Shillings to 1963

BRITISH ADMINISTRATION

Bank of Rhodesia and Nyasaland
1956 Issue

		VF	UNC
20	**10 Shillings**		

1956-61. Reddish brown on multicolor underprint. Fish eagle at lower left. Portrait of Queen Elizabeth II at right. Back: River scene. Watermark: Cecil Rhodes. Printer: BWC.

		VF	UNC
a. Signature A. P. Grafftey-Smith. 3.4.1956-17.6.1960.		550	2,300
b. Signature B. C. J. Richards. 30.12.1960-1.2.1961.		600	2,400
s. As a. Specimen punch hole cancelled. 3.4.1956.		—	1,600
ct. Color trial. Green on pink underprint.		—	2,150

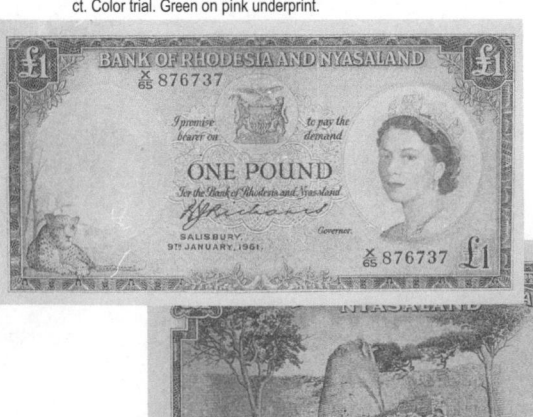

		VF	UNC
21	**1 Pound**		

1956-61. Green on multicolor underprint. Leopard at lower left. Portrait of Queen Elizabeth II at right. Back: Zimbabwe ruins at center. Watermark: Cecil Rhodes. Printer: BWC.

		VF	UNC
a. Signature A. P. Grafftey-Smith. 3.4.1956-17.6.1960.		575	2,400
b. Signature B. C. J. Richards. 28.11.1960-1.2.1961.		625	2,500
s. As a. Specimen punch hole cancelled. 2.5.1956.		—	1,750
ct. Color trial. Blue on orange underprint.		—	2,250

		VF	UNC
22	**5 Pounds**		

1956-61. Blue on multicolor underprint. Sable antelope at lower left. Portrait of Queen Elizabeth II at right. Back: Victoria Falls. Watermark: Cecil Rhodes. Printer: BWC.

		VF	UNC
a. Signature A. P. Grafftey-Smith. 3.4.1956-17.6.1960.		1,200	3,600
b. Signature B. C. J. Richards. 23.1.1961-3.2.1961.		1,300	4,000
s. As a. Specimen punch hole cancelled. 3.4.1956.		—	2,500
ct. Color trial. Red-brown on blue underprint.		—	3,000

		VF	UNC
23	**10 Pounds**		

1956-61. Brown on multicolor underprint. Portrait of Queen Elizabeth II at right. Back: Elephants at center. Watermark: Cecil Rhodes. Printer: BWC.

		VF	UNC
a. Signature A. P. Grafftey-Smith. 3.4.1956-17.6.1960.		3,000	—
b. Signature B. C. J. Richards. 1.2.1961; 3.1.1961.		3,500	—
s. As a. Specimen punch hole cancelled. 3.4.1956.		—	4,500
ct. Color trial. Green on multicolor underprint.		—	5,000

Note: For earlier issues refer to Southern Rhodesia in Volume 2. For later issues refer to Malawi, Zambia, Rhodesia and Zimbabwe in Volume 3.

Romania, located in southeast Europe, has an area of 91,699 sq. mi. (237,500 sq. km.) and a population of 22.5 million. Capital: Bucharest. Machinery, foodstuffs, raw minerals and petroleum products are exported. The principalities of Wallachia and Moldavia - for centuries under the suzerainty of the Turkish Ottoman Empire - secured their autonomy in 1856; they united in 1859 and a few years later adopted the new name of Romania.

The country gained recognition of its independence in 1878. It joined the Allied Powers in World War I and acquired new territories - most notably Transylvania - following the conflict. In 1940, Romania allied with the Axis powers and participated in the 1941 German invasion of the USSR. Three years later, overrun by the Soviets, Romania signed an armistice. The post-war Soviet occupation led to the formation of a Communist "people's republic" in 1947 and the abdication of the king. The decades-long rule of dictator Nicolae Ceausescu, who took power in 1965, and his Securitate police state became increasingly oppressive and draconian through the 1980s. Ceausescu was overthrown and executed in late 1989. Former Communists dominated the government until 1996 when they were swept from power. Romania joined NATO in 2004 and the EU in 2007.

MONETARY SYSTEM:
10,000 "old" Lei = 1 "new" Leu, 1.7.2005
1 Leu = 100 Bani

SOCIALIST REPUBLIC

Banca Nationala a Republicii Socialiste România

1966 Issue

91   1 Leu   **VF   UNC**
1966. Olive-brown and tan. Arms at center. Back: Value at center. Watermark: Rhombuses.
  a. Issued note.   2.00   5.00
  s. Specimen.   —   12.50

92   3 Lei   **VF   UNC**
1966. Blue on orange and multicolor underprint. Arms at center. Back: Value at center. Watermark: Rhombuses.
  a. Issued note.   5.00   85.00
  s. Specimen.   —   12.50
This note was soon replaced by a coin.

93   5 Lei   **VF   UNC**
1966. Brown and dark blue on multicolor underprint. Arms at center. Back: Cargo ships at dockside. Watermark: Rhombuses.
  a. Issued note.   1.50   4.50
  s. Specimen.   —   12.50

94   10 Lei   **VF   UNC**
1966. Purple on multicolor underprint. Arms at center. Back: Harvest scene. Watermark: Rhombuses.
  a. Issued note.   2.50   6.00
  s. Specimen.   —   12.50

95   25 Lei   **VF   UNC**
1966. Dark green on multicolor underprint. Portrait of Tudor Vladimirescu at left. Arms at center right. Back: Large refinery. Watermark: Rhombuses.
  a. Issued note.   3.00   7.50
  s. Specimen.   —   17.50

96   50 Lei   **VF   UNC**
1966. Dark green on multicolor underprint. Portrait of Alexandru Ioan Cuza at left. Arms at center right. Back: Culture Palace in Iasi at center right. Watermark: Rhombuses.
  a. Issued note.   5.00   15.00
  s. Specimen.   —   17.50

97   100 Lei   **VF   UNC**
1966. Dark blue and purple on multicolor underprint. Portrait of Nicolae Balcescu at left. Arms at center right. Back: The Athenaeum in Bucharest at center right. Watermark: Rhombuses.
  a. Issued note.   3.00   12.00
  s. Specimen.   —   20.00

REPUBLIC
Banca Nationala a României
1991 Issue

98 500 Lei VF UNC
1991. Dark brown on multicolor underprint. Constantin Brâncusi at right. Signature
Isarescu. Back: Brâncusi seated with statue at left center. Watermark: Constantin
Brâncusi.
  a. Jan. 1991. 8.00 23.00
  b. April 1991. 3.00 10.00
  x. As b, with *APRILIED* (error). Requires confirmation. — —

#99 has been renumbered to #101A.

1991-94 Issue

100 200 Lei VF UNC
Dec. 1992. Dull deep brown and brown-violet on multicolor underprint. Square-
topped shield at left center, steamboat *Tudor Vladimirescu* above grey heron
and Sulina Lighthouse in underprint at center, Grigore Antipa at right. Back:
Herons, fish, and net on outline of Danube Delta at left center. Watermark: Bank
monogram repeated.
  a. Issued note. 1.00 4.00
  s. Specimen. — 50.00

101 500 Lei VF UNC
Dec. 1992. Dull deep green, reddish brown and violet on multicolor underprint.
Square topped shield at left center, sculptures at center, Constantin Brâncusi at
right. Back: Sculptures at left center. Watermark: C. Brâncusi.
  a. Watermark: C. Brâncusi facing as #98. 4.00 12.50
  b. Watermark: C. Brâncusi right. 1.25 3.50

101A 1000 Lei VF UNC
Sept. 1991. Red-brown, blue-green and brown-orange on multicolor underprint.
Circular shield at left center, sails of sailing ships at lower center, Mihai Eminescu
at right. Signature: Isarescu and Florescu. Back: Putna monastery at left center.
Watermark: Mihai Eminescu.
  a. Issued note. 4.50 17.50
  s. Specimen. Serial # prefix as: A.001 or A001. — 50.00

102 1000 Lei VF UNC
May 1993. Dull deep green, reddish brown and violet on multicolor underprint.
Square topped shield at left center, sculptures at center, Constantin Brâncusi at
right. Back: Sculptures at left center. Watermark: Bust right. 2.00 5.00

103 5000 Lei VF UNC
March 1992. Pale purple on multicolor underprint. Round seal at left center,
church at center, Avram Iancu at right. Back: Church at left, the gate of Alba Iulia
stronghold at left center, seal at center right. Watermark: Avram Iancu.
  a. Issued note. 5.00 20.00
  s. Specimen. — 50.00

104 5000 Lei VF UNC
May 1993. Pale purple on multicolor underprint. Square-topped shield at left
center, church at center, Avram Iancu at right. Back: Church at left, the gate
of Alba Iulia stronghold at left center, seal at center right. Watermark: Avram Iancu.
  a. Issued note. 2.00 7.50
  s. Specimen. — 50.00

105 10,000 Lei   **VF**   **UNC**
Feb. 1994. Dull violet and reddish brown on multicolor underprint. Nicolae Iorga at right, snake god Glycon at center. Back: Statue of Fortuna at left, historical Museum in Bucharest at center, The Thinking Man of Hamangia at Watermark: Nicolae Iorga.

   a. Issued note.   3.00   12.50
   s. Specimen.   —   50.00

1996-2000 Paper Issue

106 1000 Lei   **VF**   **UNC**
1000. UV. security strip fluoresces blue. Back value 1000 in box yellow. Blue-violet, dark green and olive-brown on multicolor underprint. Mihai Eminescu at right, lily flower and quill pen at center. Arms at top left, bank monogram at top right. Back: Lime and blue flowers at left center, ruins of ancient fort of Histria at center, bank monogram at t Watermark: Mihai Eminescu.   1.00   2.50

107 5000 Lei   **VF**   **UNC**
1998. Violet, dark brown and brown-orange on multicolor underprint. Lucian Blaga at right, daffodil at center. Arms at top left, bank monogram at upper center right. Back: Vine leaf at left center, roadside crucifix at center, bank monogram at top right. Watermark: Lucian Blaga.

   a. Issued note. BNR watermark vertical only.   1.50   3.75
   b. Issueed note. BNR watermark vertical and partially horizontal.   —   15.00
   s. Specimen.   —   50.00

108 10,000 Lei   **VF**   **UNC**
1999. Green-yellow and blue on multicolor underprint. Nicolae Iorga at right, gentian flower at center. Arms at top left, bank monogram at upper center right. Back: The church of Curtea de Arges monastery at center, Wallachian arms of Prince Brancoveanu at left. Watermark: Nicolae Iorga.

   a. Issued note. BNR watermark vertical only.   2.25   7.50
   b. Issued note. BNR watermark vertical and partially horizontal.   —   15.00
   s. Specimen.   —   50.00

109 50,000 Lei   **VF**   **UNC**
1996. Purple and red-violet on lilac and multicolor underprint. George Enescu at right, floral ornament, musical notes at center, arms at upper left. Bank monogram at upper center right. Back: Sphinx of Carpathian mountains at left center, musical chord from *Oedip King* above, bank monogram at top right. Watermark: George Enescu.

   a. Issued note.   5.00   25.00
   s. Specimen.   —   50.00

109A 50,000 Lei   **VF**   **UNC**
2000. Purple and red-violet on lilac and multicolor underprint. Like #109 but violin shaped bronze area near portrait, and changed underprint design. Back: Sphinx of Carpathian mountains at left center, musical chord from *Oedip King* above, bank mon Watermark: George Enescu.

   a. Issued note.   3.00   15.00
   s. Specimen.   —   50.00

110 100,000 Lei   **VF**   **UNC**
1998. Dull red on olive-green and multicolor underprint. Nicolae Grigorescu at right, mallow flowers and artist's brush at center. Arms at top left, bank monogram at upper center right. Back: Peasant girl with ewe at left, cottage at center, bank monogram at top right. Watermark: Nicolae Grigorescu.   6.00   24.00

1999 Commemorative Issue
#111, Total Solar Eclipse, August 11, 1999

111 2000 Lei

1999. Polymer plastic. UV: value in box fluoresce green, vertical serial # blue, horizontal serial # red with blue frame. The clear window is a latent hologram, shine a lazer pointer thru it and view a solar eclipse on a sheet of paper or a wall. Blue on multicolor underprint. Imaginative reproduction of the Solar System at right, with mention of the ecilpse. Back: The map of Romania having the colors of the national flag, (blue, yellow, red) marking the route of the solar eclipse where it was total at center.

	VF	UNC
a. Issued note.	0.75	4.00
b. Serial # prefix 001A in folder. (One million pieces.)	—	12.00
s. As a. Specimen.	—	50.00

2000-01 Polymer Issue

112 10,000 Lei

2000. Polymer plastic. UV: value 10000 fluoresce yellow. Green and blue on multi-color underprint. Nicolae Igora at right, gentian flower at center. Signature Ghizari; Nitu. Back: The church of Curtea de Arges monastery at center. Wallachian arms of Prince Brancoveanu at left. Watermark: George Enescu.

	VF	UNC
a. Issued note.	1.00	7.00
b. Uncut sheet of 4 (5000 sheets).	—	17.50
s. Specimen.	—	50.00

113 50,000 Lei

2001. Polymer plastic. Purple and red-violet on lilac and multicolor underprint. George Enescu at right, floral ornament, musical notes at center, arms at upper left. Bank monogram at upper center right. Back: Rumanian Athenaeum and piano at left center. Watermark: George Enescu.

	VF	UNC
a. Issued note.	3.50	12.00
b. Uncut sheet of 4 (500 sheets).	—	60.00
s. Specimen.	—	50.00

114 100,000 Lei

2001. Polymer plastic. Dull red on olive-green and multicolor underprint. Nicolae Grigorescu at right, mallow flowers and artist's brush at center. Arms at top left, bank monogram at upper center right. Signature Isarescu; Nitu. Back: Peasant girl with ewe at left, cottage at center, bank monogram at top right. Watermark: Nicolae Grigorescu.

	VF	UNC
a. Issued note.	6.00	10.00
s. Specimen.	—	50.00

115 500,000 Lei

2000. Polymer plastic. Brown on yellow and multicolor underprint. Aurel Vlaicu at right, edelweiss flower at center. Back: Imperial Eagle head at center, *Vlaicu II* plane and *Gnome* engine sketch at left center.

	VF	UNC
a. Issued note.	30.00	45.00
b. Uncut sheet of 4 (2000 sheets).	—	150
s. Issued note.	—	100

116 1,000,000 Lei

2003. Blue, green, violet and yellow. Luca Caragiale at right. Back: Statue and building.

	VF	UNC
a. Issued note.	50.00	80.00
s. Specimen.	—	100

2005 Revaluation Issue

117 1 Leu

1.7.2005; (20)11; (20)12; (20)13; (20)14. Green and blue on multicolor underprint. Nicolae Iorga at right, gentain flower at center. Back: Church of Curtea de Arges monastery at center. 120x62mm.

	VF	UNC
a. 1.7.2005.	FV	1.25
b. (20)11.	FV	1.25
c. (20)12.	FV	1.25
d. (20)13.	FV	1.25
e. (20)14.	FV	1.25

118   5 Lei   **VF   UNC**

1.7.2005; (20)11. Polymer plastic. Violet and purple on blue and multicolor underprint. George Enescu at right. Back: Romanian Athenaeum and piano. 127x67mm.

a. 1.7.2005.	FV	3.75
b. (20)06.	FV	3.75
c. (20)07.	FV	3.75
d. (20)08.	FV	3.75
e. (20)11.	FV	3.75
f. (20)13.	FV	3.75
g. (20)14.	FV	3.75

119   10 Lei   **VF   UNC**

1.7.2005; 1.12.2008; (20)11; (20)12. Polymer plastic. Blue and yellow on rose and
multicolor underprint. Nicolae Grigorescu at right, paintbrush and flower at center.
Artist palate in window. Back: Female with canister on shoulder, house at center.
133x72mm.

a. 1.7.2005; (20)06; (20)07. Artist pallet in window, only white brush present.	FV	7.00
b. 1.12.2008; (20)09; (20)10. Artist pallet in window, one white brush and two yellow brushes.	FV	6.00
c. (20)11.	FV	5.00
d. (20)12.	FV	5.00
e. (20)13.	FV	5.00

120   50 Lei   **VF   UNC**

1.7.2005; (20)06; (20)07; (20)08; (20)09. Polymer plastic. Yellow, light green, light   FV   30.00
blue and orange. Aurel Vlaicu at right. Back: Eagle and airplane. 140x77mm.

121   100 Lei   **VF   UNC**

1.7.2005; (20)06; (20)07; (20)08; (20)09; (20)15. Polymer plastic. Blue, green,   FV   55.00
violet and yellow. Luca Caragiale at right. Back: Old national Theatre in Bucharest,
statue of Caragiale at left. 147x82mm.

122   200 Lei   **VF   UNC**

1.12.2006; (20)09. Polymer plastic. Brown, tan and multicolor. Lucian Blaga at
right. Back: Neolithic statues. 150x82mm.

a. 1.12.2006; (20)07.	FV	105
b. (20)09.	FV	105
c. (20)12.	FV	105
d. (20)13.	FV	105
e. (20)14.	FV	105

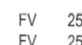

123   500 Lei   **VF   UNC**

1.7.2005; (20)09. Polymer plastic. Blue, violet, green and multicolor. Mihai Eminescu at right. Back: Iasi University Library and page from Timpul. 153x82mm.

a. 1.7.2005.	FV	250
b. (20)09.	FV	250

RUSSIA (U.S.S.R.)

Russia, (formerly the central power of the Union of Soviet Socialist Republics and now of the Commonwealth of Independent States) occupying the northern part of Asia and the far eastern part of Europe, has an area of 17,075,200 sq. km. and a population of 140.7 million. Capital: Moscow. Exports include machinery, iron and steel, oil, timber and nonferrous metals. Founded in the 12th century, the Principality of Muscovy, was able to emerge from over 200 years of Mongol domination (13th-15th centuries) and to gradually conquer and absorb surrounding principalities. In the early 17th century, a new Romanov Dynasty continued this policy of expansion across Siberia to the Pacific. Under Peter I (ruled 1682-1725), hegemony was extended to the Baltic Sea and the country was renamed the Russian Empire. During the 19th century, more territorial acquisitions were made in Europe and Asia. Defeat in the Russo-Japanese War of 1904-05 contributed to the Revolution of 1905, which resulted in the formation of a parliament and other reforms. Repeated devastating defeats of the Russian army in World War I led to widespread rioting in the major cities of the Russian Empire and to the overthrow in 1917 of the imperial household. The Communists under Vladimir Lenin seized power soon after and formed the USSR. The brutal rule of Iosif STALIN (1928-53) strengthened Communist rule and Russian dominance of the Soviet Union at a cost of tens of millions of lives. The Soviet economy and society stagnated in the following decades until General Secretary Mikhail Gorbachev (1985-91) introduced glasnost (openness) and perestroika (restructuring) in an attempt to modernize Communism, but his initiatives inadvertently released forces that by December 1991 splintered the USSR into Russia and 14 other independent republics. Since then, Russia has shifted its post-Soviet democratic ambitions in favor of a centralized semi-authoritarian state whose legitimacy is buttressed, in part, by carefully managed national elections, former President Putin's genuine popularity, and the prudent management of Russia's windfall energy wealth. Russia has severely disabled a Chechen rebel movement, although violence still occurs throughout the North Caucasus.

MONETARY SYSTEM:
1 Ruble = 100 Kopeks, until 1997
1 Chervonetz = 10 Gold Rubles
1 Ruble = 1000 "old" Rubles, 1998-

А	а	*A*	*a*	A	С	с	*C*	*c*	S
Б	б	*Бо*	*б*	ABV	Т	т	*Т*	*т*	TUF
В	в	*В*	*в*	V	У	у	*У*	*у*	U
Г	г	*Г*	*г*	G	Ф	ф	*Ф*	*ф*	F
Д	д	*D*	*д*	D	Х	х	*Х*	*х*	Kh
Е	е	*Е*	*е*	ye	Ц	ц	*Ц*	*ц*	C
Ё	ё	*Ё*	*ё*	yo	Ч	ч	*Ч*	*ч*	ch
Ж	ж	*Ж*	*ж*	zh	Ш	ш	*Ш*	*ш*	sh
З	з	*З*	*з*	Z	Щ	щ	*Щ*	*щ*	shch
И	и	*И*	*и*	I	Ъ *)	ъ *)	—	*ъ*	'
Й	й	*Й*	*й*	J	Ы	ы	—	*ы*	i
К	к	*К*	*к.к*	K	Ь**)	ь**)	—	*ь*	'
Л	л	*Л*	*л*	L	Э	э	*Э*	*э*	E
М	м	*М*	*м*	M	Ю	ю	*Ю*	*ю*	yu
Н	н	*Н*	*н*	N	Я	я	*Я*	*я*	ya
О	о	*О*	*о*	O	І	і	*І*	*і*	I
П	п	*П*	*п*	P	Ѣ	ѣ	*Ѣ*	*ѣ*	ye
Р	р	*Р*	*р*	R					

*) "hard", and **) "soft" signs; both soundless. I and Ѣ were dropped in 1918.

U.S.S.R. - UNION OF SOVIET SOCIALIST REPUBLICS

гОСУДАРСТВННННЫЙ КАЗНАЧНЙСКИЙ БИЛНТ
STATE TREASURY NOTE
1961 Issue

222 1 Ruble   VF   UNC
1961. Brown on pale green underprint. Arms at upper left. Watermark: Stars. 104x54mm.

	VF	UNC
a. Issued note.	0.50	2.00
s. Specimen.	—	150

223 3 Rubles   VF   UNC
1961. Dark green on multicolor underprint. View of Kremlin at center. Arms at upper left. Watermark: Stars. 113x53mm.

	VF	UNC
a. Issued note.	1.00	3.00
s. Specimen.	—	150

224 5 Rubles   VF   UNC
1961. Blue on peach underprint. Kremlin Spasski tower at left. Arms at upper left. Watermark: Stars.

	VF	UNC
a. Issued note.	2.00	5.00
s. Specimen.	—	150

БИЛНТ гОСУДАРСТВНННОгО БАНКА С.С.С.Р.
STATE BANK NOTE U.S.S.R.
1961 Issue

233 10 Rubles   VF   UNC
1961. Red-brown on pale gold underprint. Arms at upper left, portrait of V. I. Lenin at right. Watermark: Stars. 121x62mm.

	VF	UNC
a. Issued note.	1.00	3.00
s. Specimen.	—	150

234 25 Rubles   VF   UNC
1961. Purple on pale light green underprint. Portrait of V. I. Lenin at upper left, arms at upper center. Watermark: Stars.

	VF	UNC
a. Lilac tinted paper. 124 x 61mm.	15.00	30.00
b. White paper. 121 x 62mm.	2.00	4.00
s. Specimen.	—	150

235 50 Rubles

1961. Dark green and green on green and pink underprint. Portrait of V. I. Lenin at upper left, arms at upper center. Back: Kremlin at upper center. 140x70mm.

		VF	UNC
a. Issued note.		7.00	18.00
s. Specimen.		—	150

236 100 Rubles

1961. Brown on light blue underprint. Portrait of V. I. Lenin at upper left, arms at upper center. Back: Kremlin tower at center with date. Watermark: V. I. Lenin. 140x70mm.

		VF	UNC
a. Issued note.		7.00	15.00
s. Specimen.		—	150

1991 Issue

237 1 Ruble

1991. Dark green and red-brown on tan underprint. Arms at upper left. Watermark: Star in circle repeated. 104x54mm.

		VF	UNC
a. Issued note.		0.50	2.00
s. Specimen.		—	150

238 3 Rubles

1991. Green on blue and multicolor underprint. View of Kremlin at center. Arms at upper left. Watermark: Star in circle repeated. 113x57mm.

		VF	UNC
a. Issued note.		0.50	3.00
s. Specimen.		—	150

239 5 Rubles

1991. Blue-gray on light blue, pale green and pink underprint. Kremlin Spasski tower at left. Arms at upper left. Watermark: Star in circle repeated. 113x57mm.

		VF	UNC
a. Issued note.		0.50	2.00
s. Specimen.		—	150

240 10 Rubles

1991. Red-brown and green on multicolor underprint. Arms at upper left, portrait of V. I. Lenin at right. Watermark: Stars. 124x62mm.

		VF	UNC
a. Issued note.		1.00	3.00
s. Specimen.		—	150

241 50 Rubles

1991. Dark brown, green and red on multicolor underprint. Portrait of V. I. Lenin at upper left, arms at upper center. Back: Kremlin at upper center. Watermark: V. I. Lenin. 145x70mm.

		VF	UNC
a. Issued note.		2.00	12.00
s. Specimen.		—	150

242 100 Rubles

1991. Deep red-brown and blue on multicolor underprint. Portrait of V. I. Lenin at upper left, arms at upper center. Date at right. Back: Kremlin tower at center with date. Watermark: V. I. Lenin. 145x70mm.

		VF	UNC
a. Issued note.		2.00	15.00
s. Specimen.		—	150

243 100 Rubles

1991. Deep red-brown and blue on multicolor underprint. Portrait of V. I. Lenin at upper left, arms at upper center. Pink and green guilloche at right in watermark area. Date at right. Back: Kremlin tower at center with date. Blue guilloche added at upper left. Watermark: Stars.

		VF	UNC
a. Issued note.		2.00	10.00
s. Specimen.		—	150

244   200 Rubles

1991. Green and brown on multicolor underprint. Portrait of V. I. Lenin at upper left, arms at upper center. Back: View of Kremlin. Watermark: V. I. Lenin. 145x70mm.

		VF	UNC
a. Issued note.		10.00	40.00
s. Specimen.		—	150

245   500 Rubles

1991. Red and green on multicolor underprint. Portrait of V. I. Lenin at upper left, arms at upper center. Back: View of Kremlin. Watermark: V. I. Lenin. 145x70mm.

		VF	UNC
a. Issued note.		20.00	55.00
s. Specimen.		—	150

246   1000 Rubles

1991. Brown and blue on green and multicolor underprint. Portrait of V. I. Lenin at upper left, arms at upper center. Back: View of Kremlin. Watermark: V. I. Lenin. 145x70mm.

		VF	UNC
a. Issued note.		20.00	60.00
s. Specimen.		—	150

RUSSIAN FEDERATION
РОССИЙСКАЯ ФНДНРАЦИЯ

RUSSIAN FEDERATION
1992 Issue

247   50 Rubles

1992. Brown and gray on green and multicolor underprint. Portrait of V. I. Lenin at upper left, arms at upper center. Back: Kremlin at upper center. Watermark: Star in circle repeated.

		VF	UNC
a. Issued note.		2.00	4.00
s. Specimen.		—	150

248   200 Rubles

1992. Green and brown on multicolor underprint. Portrait of V. I. Lenin at upper left, arms at upper center. Back: View of Kremlin with guilloche in watermark area. Watermark: Star in circle repeated.

		VF	UNC
a. Issued note.		2.00	5.00
s. Specimen.		—	150

249   500 Rubles

1992. Red, violet and dark green on multicolor underprint. Portrait of V. I. Lenin at upper left, arms at upper center. Back: View of Kremlin with guilloche in watermark area. Watermark: Stars.

		VF	UNC
a. Issued note.		2.00	6.00
s. Specimen.		—	150

250   1000 Rubles

1992. Dark brown and deep green on multicolor underprint. Portrait of V. I. Lenin at upper left, arms at upper center. Back: View of Kremlin with guilloche in watermark area. Watermark: Stars.

		VF	UNC
a. Issued note.		2.00	5.00
s. Specimen.		—	150

1992 Government Privatization Check Issue

251 10,000 Rubles   **VF UNC**

1992. Valid until Dec. 31, 1993. Dark brown on multicolor underprint. Parliament
White House in Moscow. Back: Text indicating method of redemption into shares
of government-owned property. Handstamp from bank added at bottom.

    a. Issued note.   20.00 50.00

    s. Specimen.   — 150

While not regular banknote, # 251 was easily negotiable and was widely distributed by the government. It was to provide funds to allow citizens to "buy into" an business. Worth about $35. at
time of issue (early 1992), inflation then cut its real value dramatically.

БАНК РОССИИ

BANK OF RUSSIA

1992 Issue

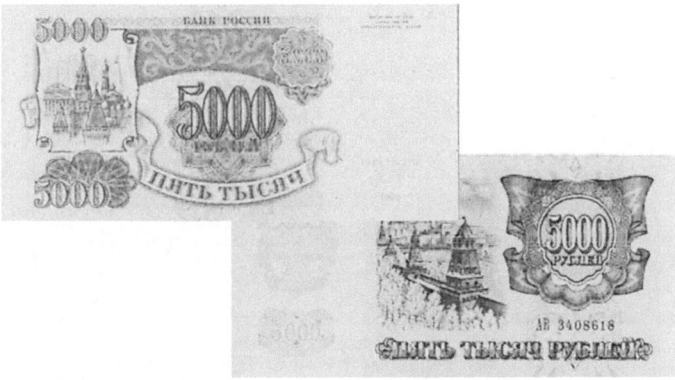

252 5000 Rubles   **VF UNC**

1992. Blue and maroon on multicolor underprint. St. Basil's Cathedral at left.
Signature Georgui Matiukhin. Back: Kremlin. Watermark: Stars. 145x79mm.

    a. Issued note.   1.00 4.00

    s. Specimen.   — 150

253 10,000 Rubles   **VF UNC**

1992. Brown, black and red on multicolor underprint. Kremlin with new tricolor flag
at left center. Back: Kremlin towers at center right. Watermark: Kremlin with new
tricolor flag. 145x79mm.

    a. Issued note.   1.00 4.00

    s. Specimen.   — 150

1993 Issue

254 100 Rubles   **VF UNC**

1993. Blue-black on pink and light blue underprint. Tricolor flag over stylized   0.50 2.00
Kremlin at left, monogram at upper right. Back: Kremlin, Spasski Tower at center
right. Watermark: Stars within wavy lines repeated. 130x53mm.

255 200 Rubles   **VF UNC**

1993. UV: fibers fluoresce yellow and red. Brown on pink and multicolor under-   0.50 3.00
print. Tricolor flag over stylized Kremlin at left, monogram at upper right. Back:
Kremlin gate at center. Watermark: Stars within wavy lines repeated. 130x53mm.

256 500 Rubles   **VF UNC**

1993. Green, blue and purple on multicolor underprint. Tricolor flag over stylized   1.00 2.00
Kremlin at left, monogram at upper right. Back: Kremlin at left center. Watermark:
Stars within wavy lines repeated. 130x53mm.

257 1000 Rubles   **VF UNC**

1993. Green, olive-green and brown on multicolor underprint. Tricolor flag over   1.00 8.00
stylized Kremlin at left, monogram at upper right. Back: Kremlin at center. Watermark: Stars. 151x68mm.

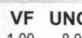

258 5000 Rubles
1993; 1993/94. Blue, brown and violet on multicolor underprint. Tricolor flag over house of Government in the Kremlin at left, monogram at upper center. Back: Kremlin at center. Watermark: Flag over House of Goverment. 152x68mm.

	VF	UNC
a. 1993.	5.00	25.00
b. 1993//94.	5.00	20.00

259 10,000 Rubles
1993; 1993//94. Violet, greenish blue, brownish purple and multicolor. Tricolor flag over house of Goverment in the Kremlin at left, monogram at upper right. Back: Kremlin at center right. Watermark: Flag over house of Goverment. 152x68mm.

	VF	UNC
a. 1993.	10.00	30.00
b. 1993//94.	12.00	35.00

260 50,000 Rubles
1993; 1993//94. Olive-green, black and reddish brown on multicolor underprint. Tricolor flag over house of Government in the Kremlin at left, monogram at upper right. Back: Kremlin at center right. Watermark: Flag over house of Goverment. 152x68mm.

	VF	UNC
a. 1993.	15.00	120
b. 1993//94.	15.00	100

1995 Issue

261 1000 Rubles
1995. Dark brown and brown on multicolor underprint. Seaport of Vladivostok at left center, memorial column at center right. Back: Entrance to Vladivostok Bay at center. Watermark: *1000* and memorial column.

	VF	UNC
	1.00	6.00

262 5000 Rubles
1995. Deep blue-green and dark olive-green on multicolor underprint. Monument of the Russian Millennium in Novgorod at left center. Cathedral of St. Sophia at center. Back: Old towered city wall of Novgorod at upper left center. Watermark: Cathedral of St. Sophia. 137x60mm.

	VF	UNC
	2.00	15.00

263 10,000 Rubles
1995. Dark brown and dark gray on multicolor underprint. Arch bridge over Yenisei River in Krasnoyarsk at left center, steeple at center right. Back: Hydroelectric dam at Krasnoyarsk at center. Watermark: Steeple. 150x65mm.

	VF	UNC
	3.00	20.00

264 50,000 Rubles
1995. Dark brown, grayish purple and black on multicolor underprint. Personification of river Neva on foot of Rostral Column, Peter and Paul Fortress in St. Petersburg. Back: Rostral Column and Naval Museum at upper left center. Watermark: Building with steeple. 150x65mm.

	VF	UNC
	10.00	50.00

265 100,000 Rubles
1995. Purple and brown on multicolor underprint. Apollo and chariot freize on Bolshoi (Great) Theatre in Moscow at center. Back: Bolshoi Theatre. Watermark: Building over value. 150x65mm.

	VF	UNC
	20.00	70.00

266 500,000 Rubles

	VF	UNC
1995 (1997). Brown-violet on multicolor underprint. Statue of Peter the Great, sailing ship dockside in port of Arkhangelsk at center. Back: Monastery in Solovetsky Island. 150x65mm.	100	250

1997 (1998) "New Ruble" Issue

1 Ruble = 1000 "old" Rubles

267 5 Rubles

	VF	UNC
1997 (1998). Deep blue-green and dark olive-green on multicolor underprint. Monument of the Russian Millennium in Novgorod at left center. Cathedral of St. Sophia at center. Back: Old towered city wall in Novgorod at upper left center. Watermark: Cathedral of St. Sophia. 138x60mm.	FV	3.00

268 10 Rubles

	VF	UNC
1997 (1998); 2001; 2004. UV: fibers fluoresce red and yellow. Dark brown and dark gray on multicolor underprint. Arch bridge over Yenisei River in Krasnoyarsk at left center, steeple at center right. Back: Hydroelectric dam in Krasnoyarsk at center. Watermark: Steeple. 150x65mm.		
a. 1997.	FV	6.00
b. 2001. Date vertically in very small text to left of bridge.	FV	5.00
c. 2004.	FV	2.00

269 50 Rubles

	VF	UNC
1997 (1998); 2001; 2004. Dark brown, grayish purple and black on multicolor underprint. Personification of river Neva on foot of Rostral Column, Peter and Paul Fortress in St. Petersburg. Back: Rostral Column and Naval Museum at upper left center. Watermark: Building with steeple. 150x65mm.		
a. 1997.	FV	12.50
b. 2001. Date vertically in very small text to left of bridge.	FV	8.00
c. 2004. Segmented security thread right center on back.	FV	5.00

270 100 Rubles

	VF	UNC
1997 (1998); 2001; 2004. UV: fibers fluoresce red and yellow. Violet and brown on multicolor underprint. Apollo and chariot freize on Bolshoi (Great) Theatre in Moscow at center. Back: Bolshoi Theatre. Watermark: Building over value. 150x65mm.		
a. 1997.	FV	20.00
b. 2001. Date vertically in very small text to left of bridge.	FV	15.00
c. 2004. Segmented security thread right center on back.	FV	10.00

271 500 Rubles

	VF	UNC
1997 (1998); 2001; 2004; 2010. Brown-violet on multicolor underprint. Statue of Peter the Great, sailing ship dockside in port of Arkhangelsk at center. Back: Monastery in Solovetsky Island. 150x65mm.		
a. 1997.	FV	50.00
b. 2001. Date vertically in very small text to left of bridge.	FV	40.00
c. 2004. Segmented security thread right center on back.	FV	35.00
d. 2010.	FV	35.00

272 1000 Rubles

	VF	UNC
1997 (2000); 2004; 2010. Multicolor. Statue at left. Back: St. Basil Cathedral. 157x69mm.		
a. 1997.	32.00	85.00
b. 2004. Segmented security thread at left center on back.	FV	70.00
c. 2010.	FV	70.00

273 5000 Rubles

	VF	UNC
2006; 2007; 2010. Orange on multicolor underprint. Statue of N. N. Muravyov at center. Back: Khavarkovsk city view at center. 157x69mm.		
a. 2006.	FV	220
b. 2007.	FV	220
c. 2010.	FV	220

2014 Sochi Olympics Commemorative

274 100 Rubles

	VF	UNC
2013. Vertical format. Serial # prefix: AA, Aa and aa. Blue, purple, green and orange on multicolor underprint. Snowboarder, mountains, Olympic venues in Sochi. Back: Fischt Stadium in Sochi, skier, ski jumper, skaters, hockey player, curler, bobsled team. Printer: Goznak. 150x65mm.	FV	10.00

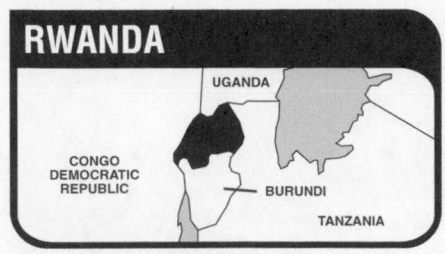

RWANDA

The Republic of Rwanda, located in central Africa between the Republic of the Congo and Tanzania, has an area of 26,338 sq. km. and a population of 10.186 million. Capital: Kigali. The economy is based on agriculture and mining. Coffee and tin are exported.In 1959, three years before independence from Belgium, the majority ethnic group, the Hutus, overthrew the ruling Tutsi king. Over the next several years, thousands of Tutsis were killed, and some 150,000 driven into exile in neighboring countries. The children of these exiles later formed a rebel group, the Rwandan Patriotic Front (RPF), and began a civil war in 1990. The war, along with several political and economic upheavals, exacerbated ethnic tensions, culminating in April 1994 in the genocide of roughly 800,000 Tutsis and moderate Hutus. The Tutsi rebels defeated the Hutu regime and ended the killing in July 1994, but approximately 2 million Hutu refugees - many fearing Tutsi retribution - fled to neighboring Burundi, Tanzania, Uganda, and Zaire. Since then, most of the refugees have returned to Rwanda, but several thousand remained in the neighboring Democratic Republic of the Congo (DRC; the former Zaire) and formed an extremist insurgency bent on retaking Rwanda, much as the RPF tried in 1990. Despite substantial international assistance and political reforms - including Rwanda's first local elections in March 1999 and its first post-genocide presidential and legislative elections in August and September 2003 - the country continues to struggle to boost investment and agricultural output, and ethnic reconciliation is complicated by the real and perceived Tutsi political dominance. Kigali's increasing centralization and intolerance of dissent, the nagging Hutu extremist insurgency across the border, and Rwandan involvement in two wars in recent years in the neighboring DRC continue to hinder Rwanda's efforts to escape its bloody legacy. Also see Belgian Congo, Rwanda-Burundi.

MONETARY SYSTEM:
1 Franc (Amafranga, Amafaranga) = 100 Centimes

REPLACEMENT NOTES:
#6e, 17:ZZ prefix. #12, VV prefix. Others probably exist.

REPUBLIC

Banque Nationale du Rwanda

Banki Nasiyonali Y'u Rwanda

1962 Provisional Issue

1	20 Francs	Fine	XF
	ND (1962 -old date 5.10.1960). Green on tan and pink underprint. Maroon or black stamped overprint on Rwanda-Burundi # 3. Signature title: *LE GOUVERNEUR*.	175	—

2	50 Francs	Fine	XF
	ND (1962 -old dates 15.9.1960; 1.10.1960). Red on multicolor underprint. Maroon stamped overprint on Rwanda-Burundi # 4. Signature title: *LE GOUVERNEUR*.	300	—

3	100 Francs	Fine	XF
	ND (1962 -old dates 15.9.1960; 1.10.1960; 31.7.1962). Blue on light green and tan underprint. Stamped overprint on Rwanda-Burundi # 5. Signature title: *LE GOUVERNEUR*.		
	a. Black overprint.	250	2,000
	b. Purple overprint.	250	2,000
4	**500 Francs**	**Fine**	**XF**
	ND (1962 -old dates 15.9.1960; 15.9.1961). Lilac-brown on multicolor underprint. Embossed overprint and blind embossed facsimile signature on Rwanda-Burundi # 6. Signature title: *LE GOUVERNEUR*.	1,250	5,000
5	**1000 Francs**	**Fine**	**XF**
	ND (1962 -old dates 15.5.1961; 1.7.1962). Green on multicolor underprint. Embossed overprint and blind facsimile signature on Rwanda-Burundi # 7. Signature title: *LE GOUVERNEUR*.	1,000	4,000

1964 Issue

#6-10 Replacement notes: Serial # prefix ZZ.

6	20 Francs	VF	UNC
	1964-76. Brown on multicolor underprint. Flag of Rwanda at left. Various date and signature title varieties. Back: Four young boys at left center with pipeline in background at center.		
	a. Signature titles: *VICE-GOUVERNEUR* and *GOUVERNEUR*, with security thread. 1.7.1964; 31.3.1966; 15.3.1969; 1.9.1969.	15.00	48.00
	b. Signature titles: *VICE GOUVERNEUR* and *ADMINISTRATEUR*, with security thread. 1.7.1965.	12.50	40.00
	c. Signature titles: *GOUVERNEUR* and *ADMINISTRATEUR*, with security thread. 1.7.1971.	3.00	7.50
	d. Signature titles: *ADMINISTRATEUR* and *ADMINISTRATEUR*, with security thread. 30.10.1974.	1.50	22.50
	e. Signature titles: *ADMINISTRATEUR* and *GOUVERNEUR*, without security thread. 1.1.1976.	0.75	5.25
	s1. As a. Specimen. 1.7.1964; 1.7.1965; 31.3.1966; 15.3.1969.	—	60.00
	s2. As b. Specimen. 1.7.1965.	—	50.00
	s3. As c. Specimen. 1.7.1971.	—	15.00
	s4. As d. Specimen. 30.10.1974.	—	15.00

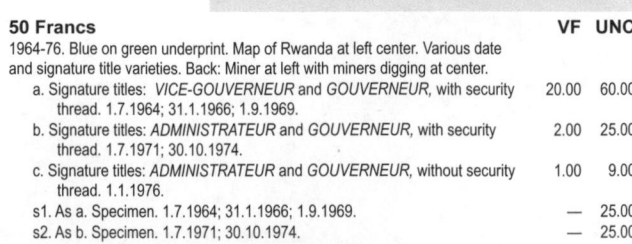

7	50 Francs	VF	UNC
	1964-76. Blue on green underprint. Map of Rwanda at left center. Various date and signature title varieties. Back: Miner at left with miners digging at center.		
	a. Signature titles: *VICE-GOUVERNEUR* and *GOUVERNEUR*, with security thread. 1.7.1964; 31.1.1966; 1.9.1969.	20.00	60.00
	b. Signature titles: *ADMINISTRATEUR* and *GOUVERNEUR*, with security thread. 1.7.1971; 30.10.1974.	2.00	25.00
	c. Signature titles: *ADMINISTRATEUR* and *GOUVERNEUR*, without security thread. 1.1.1976.	1.00	9.00
	s1. As a. Specimen. 1.7.1964; 31.1.1966; 1.9.1969.	—	25.00
	s2. As b. Specimen. 1.7.1971; 30.10.1974.	—	25.00

8   100 Francs   VF   UNC

1964-76. Purple on multicolor underprint. Map of Rwanda at left. Various date and signature title varieties. Back: Woman with basket on head at left, banana trees at center.

   a. Signature titles: *VICE-GOUVERNEUR* and *GOUVERNEUR*, with security thread. 1.7.1964; 31.3.1966; 31.10.1969.   12.50   50.00

   b. Signature titles: *VICE-GOUVERNEUR* and *ADMINISTRATEUR*, with security thread. 1.7.1965.   8.00   20.00

   c. Signature titles: *ADMINISTRATEUR* and *GOUVERNEUR*, with security thread. 1.7.1971; 30.10.1974.   3.50   10.00

   d. Signature titles: *ADMINISTRATEUR* and *GOUVERNEUR*, without security thread. 1.1.1976.   1.50   15.00

   s1. As a. Specimen. 1.7.1964; 1.7.1965; 31.3.1966; 31.10.1969. Red overprint: *SPECIMEN* on both sides.   —   50.00

   s2. As c. Specimen. 1.7.1971; 30.10.1974. Black overprint: *SPECIMEN*. on both sides.   —   25.00

9   500 Francs   VF   UNC

1964-76. Dark green and multicolor. Arms of Rwanda at left. Various date and signature title varieties. Back: Man with basket on head at left, rows of plants in background.

   a. Signature titles: *VICE-GOUVERNEUR* and *GOUVERNEUR*. 1.7.1964; 31.3.1966; 31.10.1969.   12.50   50.00

   b. Signature titles: *ADMINISTRATEUR* and *GOUVERNEUR*. 1.7.1971; 30.10.1974; 1.1.1976.   10.00   40.00

   s1. As a. Specimen. 1.7.1964; 31.3.1966; 31.10.1969. Black overprint: *SPECIMEN* on both sides.   —   30.00

   s2. As b. Specimen. 1.7.1971; 30.10.1974   —   30.00

10   1000 Francs   VF   UNC

1964-76. Red and multicolor. Arms of Rwanda at left. Various date and signature title varieties. Back: Man and terraced hills at center.

   a. Signature titles: *VICE-GOUVERNEUR* and *GOUVERNEUR*. 1.7.1964; 31.3.1966; 15.3.1969.   35.00   300

   b. Signature titles: *ADMINISTRATEUR* and *GOUVERNEUR*. 1.7.1971; 30.10.1974.   20.00   45.00

   c. Printed signature titles like b. 1.1.1976.   15.00   85.00

   s1. As a. Specimen. 1.7.1964; 31.3.1966; 15.3.1969. Black overprint: *SPECIMEN* on both sides.   —   45.00

   s2. As b. Specimen. 1.7.1971.   —   45.00

1974 Issue

11   500 Francs   VF   UNC

19.4.1974. Green and multicolor. General Habyarimana at left. Back: Man with basket on head at left, rows of plants in background.

   a. Issued note.   10.00   20.00

   s. Specimen.   —   45.00

1978 Issue

12   100 Francs   VF   UNC

1.1.1978. Gray on light blue and multicolor underprint. Zebras. Back: Woman carrying child at left, mountains in background at center right.

   a. Issued note.   4.00   15.00

   s. Specimen.   —   12.50

13   500 Francs   VF   UNC

1.1.1978. Brown, orange and multicolor. Impalas. Back: Eight drummers at left, strip mining at right.

   a. Watermark: Impala's head.   10.00   50.00

   b. Without watermark.   60.00   150

   s. As a. Specimen.   —   20.00

14   1000 Francs   VF   UNC
1.1.1978. Green and multicolor. Boys picking tea leaves at left. Back: Tribal
dancer at right. Watermark: Impala's head.
   a. Issued note.   15.00 55.00
   s. Specimen.   —   25.00

15   5000 Francs   VF   UNC
1.1.1978. Green, blue and multicolor. Female with basket on her head at left, field
workers at center. Back: Lake and mountains. Watermark: Impala's head.
   a. Issued note.   65.00 150
   s. Specimen.   —   200

1981 Issue

16   500 Francs   VF   UNC
1.7.1981. Brown and multicolor. Arms at left, three Impalas at right. Back: Men
working in field at left. Watermark: Crowned crane's head.
   a. Issued note.   10.00 52.00
   s. Specimen.   —   20.00

17   1000 Francs   VF   UNC
1.7.1981. Green, brown and multicolor. Two Watusi warriors at right. Back: Two
Eastern Gorillas at left, canoe in lake at right. Watermark: Crowned crane's head.
   a. Issued note.   12.00 55.00
   s. Specimen. Black overprint: SPECIMEN on both sides.   —   45.00

1982 Issue

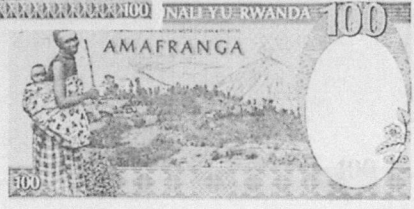

18   100 Francs   VF   UNC
1.8.1982. Black on lilac and multicolor underprint. Zebras at center and right.
Back: Woman carrying baby at left, view of mountains at center. Watermark:
Impala's head.   1.50   9.50

1988-89 Issue

19   100 Francs   VF   UNC
24.4.1989. Black on lilac and multicolor underprint. Zebras at center and right.
Signature titles: 2E VICE-GOUVERNEUR and GOUVERNEUR. Back: Woman
carrying baby at left, view of mountains at center. New spelling AMAFARANGA.
   a. Issued note.   1.25   4.00
   s. Specimen. Overprint: SPECIMEN on both sides. —   25.00
#20 Not assigned.

21   1000 Francs   VF   UNC
1.1.1988; 24.4.1989. Green, brown and multicolor. Two Watusi warriors at right.
Signature titles: 2E VICE-GOUVERNEUR and GOUVERNEUR. Back: Two
Eastern Gorillas at left, canoe in lake at right. New spelling AMAFARANGA.
   a. Issued note.   2.50   5.00
   s. Specimen. Black overprint: SPECIMEN on both sides.   —   75.00

22 5000 Francs   VF   UNC
1.1.1988; 24.4.1989. Green, blue and multicolor. Female with basket on her head at left, field workers at center. Signature titles: *2E VICE-GOUVERNEUR* and *GOUVERNEUR*. Back: Lake and mountains. New spelling *AMAFARANGA*.
    a. Issued note.   3.00   6.00
    s. Specimen. Overprint: *SPECIMEN* on both sides.   —   25.00

1994 Issue

23 500 Francs   VF   UNC
1.12.1994. Blue-black, black and dark blue-green on multicolor underprint. Mountainous landscape at center right. Back: Female Waterbuck at left center. Watermark: Impala's head. Printer: G&D (without imprint).
    a. Issued note.   FV   17.00
    s. Specimen. Black overprint: *SPECIMEN* on both sides.   —   25.00

24 1000 Francs   VF   UNC
1.12.1994. Purple, red-brown and dark brown on multicolor underprint. Mountainous landscape at center right. Back: Vegetation at left, African Buffalo at center. Watermark: Impala's head. Printer: G&D (without imprint).
    a. Issued note.   FV   22.00
    s. Specimen. Black overprint: *SPECIMEN* on both sides.   —   25.00

25 5000 Francs   VF   UNC
1.12.1994. Dark brown, violet and purple on multicolor underprint. Mountainous landscape at center right. Back: Reclining lion at left center. Watermark: Impala's head. Printer: G&D (without imprint).
    a. Issued note.   FV   32.00
    s. Specimen. Black overprint: *SPECIMEN* on both sides.   —   35.00

1998 Issue

26 500 Francs   VF   UNC
1.12.1998. Blue and green on multicolor underprint. Mountain gorillas at right. Back: National Museum of Butare and schoolchildren.
    a. Issued note.   FV   6.00
    s. Specimen. Red overprint: *SPECIMEN* on both sides.   —   40.00

27 1000 Francs   VF   UNC
1.12.1998. Blue and brown on multicolor underprint. Volcano range at right. Back: Tea plantation and cattle.
    a. Issued note.   FV   5.50
    s. Specimen. Red overprint: *SPECIMEN* on both sides.   —   40.00

28 5000 Francs   VF   UNC
1.12.1998. Black, red and green on multicolor underprint. *Intore* dancers at right. Back: National Bank building.
    a. Issued note.   FV   15.00
    s. Specimen. Red overprint: *SPECIMEN* on both sides.   —   50.00

2003-04 Issue

29 100 Francs   VF   UNC
1.5.2003; 1.9.2003. UV: fibers fluoesce yellow and blue; design elements yellow
and orange. Green, brown and blue on yellow underprint. Oxen and farmer plowing at center. Back: Mountain and lake. 129x65mm.

   a. 1.5.2003. Bank name in English.   FV   4.00
   b. 1.9.2003. Bank name in English and French.   FV   2.50
   s. As a or b. Specimen. Red overprint.   —   25.00

30 500 Francs   VF   UNC
1.7.2004. Green on tan and blue underprint. 136x72mm.
   a. 1.7.2004.   FV   6.00

31 1000 Francs   VF   UNC
1.7.2004. Blue on tan underprint. Doggett's Guenon. 141x72mm.
   a. 1.7.2004.   FV   4.50
#32 renumbered to #36.

33 5000 Francs   VF   UNC
1.4.2004. Purple on tan and multicolor underprint. Baskets. Back: Gorilla.
145x72mm.
   a. 1.4.2004.   FV   45.00

Banki Nkuru Y'u Rwanda

2007-2009 Issue

34 500 Francs   VF   UNC
   1.2.2008.   FV   3.50
35 1000 Francs   VF   UNC
   1.2.2008.   FV   7.00
36 2000 Francs   VF   UNC
   31.10.2007.   FV   12.00
37 5000 Francs   VF   UNC
   1.2.2009.   FV   22.00

2013 Issue

38 500 Francs   VF   UNC
1.1.2013. Blue-gray on multicolor underprint. Three cows. Back: Students in
computer class. Watermark: Coat of arms 135x72mm.   FV   3.00
39 1000 Francs   VF   UNC
   1.5.2015.   —   —
40 2000 Francs   VF   UNC
   1.12.2014.   FV   12.00
41 5000 Francs   VF   UNC
   1.12.2014.   FV   22.00

2015 Issue

42 1000 Francs   VF   UNC
2015. Blue, green and orange. Green-to-blue flying dove SPARK orbital patch,
National Museum of Rwanda buildings in Butare. Back: Golden monkey in Volcanoes National Park. Red-to-green windowed security thread with demetalized
BNR1000. Watermark: Coat of arms and electrotype BNR. 140x72mm.
   a. 01.05.2015. Prefix AA - BV.   FV   7.00

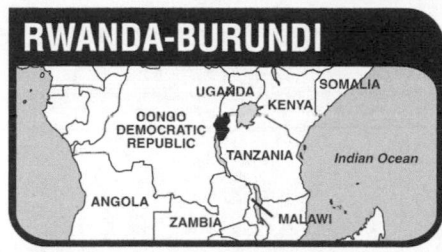

RWANDA-BURUNDI

Rwanda-Burundi, a Belgian League of Nations mandate and United Nations trust territory comprising the provinces of Rwanda and Burundi of the former colony of German East Africa, was located in central Africa between the present Republic of the Congo, Uganda and mainland Tanzania. The mandate-trust territory had an area of 20,916 sq. mi. (54,272 sq. km.). For specific statistics and history of Rwanda and Burundi see individual entries. When Rwanda and Burundi were formed into a mandate for administration by Belgium, their names were changed to Ruanda and Urundi and they were organized as an integral part of the Belgian Congo, during which time they used a common banknote issue with the Belgian Congo. After the Belgian Congo acquired independence as the Republic of the Congo, the provinces of Ruanda and Urundi reverted to their former names of Rwanda and Burundi and issued notes with both names on them. In 1962, both Rwanda and Burundi became separate independent states. Also see Belgian Congo, Burundi and Rwanda.

MONETARY SYSTEM:
1 Franc = 100 Centimes

MANDATE - TRUST TERRITORY
Banque d'Emission du Rwanda et du Burundi
1960 Issue

1	5 Francs	VF	UNC
	1900-03. Light brown on green underprint. Impala at left. Signature varieties.		
	a. 15.9.1960; 15.5.1961.	150	450
	b. 15.4.1963.	120	450

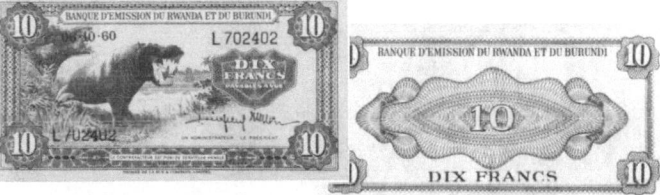

2	10 Francs	Fine	XF
	15.9.1960; 5.10.1960. Dull gray on pale blue and pale orange underprint. Hippopotamus at left. Signature varieties. Printer: TDLR.		
	a. Issued note.	250	550
	s. Specimen.	—	—

3	20 Francs	Fine	XF
	15.9.1960; 5.10.1960. Green on tan and pink underprint. Crocodile at right. Signature varieties. Printer: TDLR.		
	a. Issued note.	250	525
	s. Specimen.	—	—

4	50 Francs	Fine	XF
	15.9.1960; 1.10.1960. Red on multicolor underprint. Lioness at center right. Signature varieties.		
	a. Issued note.	450	900
	s. Specimen.	—	—
	ct. Color trial. Green on multicolor underprint.	—	—

5	100 Francs	Fine	XF
	15.9.1960; 1.10.1960; 31.7.1962. Blue on light green and tan underprint. Zebu at left. Signature varieties.		
	a. Issued note.	300	1,400
	s. Specimen.	—	—
	ct. Color trial. Brown on multicolor underprint.	—	—

6	500 Francs	Fine	XF
	15.9.1960; 15.5.1961; 15.9.1961. Lilac-brown on multicolor underprint. Black Rhinoceros at center right. Signature varieties.		
	a. Issued note.	850	3,000
	s. Specimen.	—	—

7	1000 Francs	Fine	XF
	15.9.1960; 15.5.1961; 31.7.1962. Green on multicolor underprint. Zebra at right. Signature varieties.		
	a. Issued note.	1,100	2,500
	s. Specimen.	—	—
	ct. Color trial. Purple on multicolor underprint.	0.00	0.00

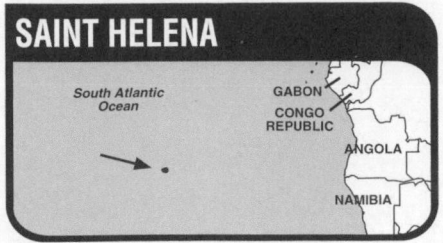

SAINT HELENA

South Atlantic Ocean

GABON
CONGO REPUBLIC
ANGOLA
NAMIBIA

The British Overseas Territory of St. Helena, is located about 1,150 miles (1,850 km.) from the west coast of Africa, has an area of 413 sq. km. and a population of 7,600. Capital: Jamestown. Flax, lace and rope are produced for export. Ascension and Tristan da Cunha are dependencies of St. Helena.Saint Helena was uninhabited when first discovered by the Portuguese in 1502, it was garrisoned by the British during the 17th century.

It acquired fame as the place of Napoleon Bonaparte's exile, from 1815 until his death in 1821, but its importance as a port of call declined after the opening of the Suez Canal in 1869. During the Anglo-Boer War in South Africa, several thousand Boer prisoners were confined on the island between 1900 and 1903. St. Helena banknotes are also used on the islands of Assencion and Tristan de Cunia.

RULERS:
British

MONETARY SYSTEM:
1 Pound = 20 Shillings to 1971
1 Pound = 100 New Pence, 1971-

	SIGNATURE VARIETIES		
1	C.B. Kendall	R. J. Adams	G. B. Lawrence
2	R. J. Adams	B. Quinn	M. B. Lawrence
3	H. Perry	J. Caldwell	Quinn
4	T.F. Brooks	Quinn	P.C. Knipe	
5	H.T. Abney	M.J. Young	Kieth D Awade
6		Linda Clemett	Kieth C Lee	D Awade

BRITISH ADMINISTRATION

Government of St. Helena
1976; 1979 ND Issue

5	50 Pence		VF	UNC
	ND (1979). Purple on pink and pale yellow-green underprint. Views of the island at left, Queen Elizabeth II at right. Signature 2. Back: Royal arms with motto at left, shield with ship at right. Correctly spelled *ANGLIAE* in motto 140x60mm.			
	a. Issued note.		11.00	60.00
	s. Specimen.		—	140

Note: #5 w/serial #170,001-200,000 are non-redeemable.

6	1 Pound		VF	UNC
	ND (1976). Deep olive-green on pale orange and ochre underprint. Views of the island at left, Queen Elizabeth II at right. Back: Royal arms with motto at left, shield with ship at right. Incorrect spelling *ANGLAE* in motto. 153x67mm.			
	a. Issued note.		20.00	110
	s. Specimen.		—	170

7	5 Pounds		VF	UNC
	ND (1976). Blue on light brown underprint. Views of the island at left, Queen Elizabeth II at right. Back: Royal arms with motto at left, shield with ship at right. 153x72mm.			
	a. Incorrect spelling *ANGLAE* in motto. Signature 1. (1976).		25.00	170
	b. Corrected spelling *ANGLIAE* in motto. Signature 2. (1981).		18.00	100
	s. As a. Specimen.		—	270

8	10 Pounds		VF	UNC
	ND (1979). Pale red on multicolor underprint. Views of the island at left, Queen Elizabeth II at right. Back: Arms, correctly spelled *ANGLIAE* in motto. 159x80mm.			
	a. Signature 2. (1979).		40.00	230
	b. Signature 3. (1985).		FV	110
	c. As a. Uncut sheet of 3.		—	500
	r. Remainder without signature or serial #.		—	320
	s. As a. Specimen.		—	300

1981; 1986 ND Issue

9   1 Pound   **VF   UNC**
ND (1981). Reduced size. Deep olive-green on pale orange and ochre underprint.
Queen Elizabeth II at right. Signature 2. Back: Royal arms with motto at left, cor-
rected spelling *ANGLIAE* in motto. 147x66mm.
    a. Issued note.   5.00   32.50
    s. Specimen.   —   160
Note: #9 w/serial #*A/1* 350,000 - *A/1* 400,000 are non-redeemable.

10   20 Pounds   **VF   UNC**
ND (1986). Dark brown on multicolor underprint. Harbor view at left center, Queen
Elizabeth II at right. Four signatures in block form. Signature 4. Back: Arms at
center. 164x85mm.
    a. Issued note.   FV   165
    s. Specimen.   —   275

1998 ND Issue

11   5 Pounds   **VF   UNC**
ND (1998). Blue on light brown underprint. Views of the island at left, Queen
Elizabeth II at right. Four signatures in block form. Signature 5. Back: Royal arms
with motto at left, shield with ship at right. 135x71mm.
    a. Issued note.   FV   50.00
    s. Specimen.   —   190

2004 Issue

12   10 Pounds   **VF   UNC**
2004. Rose on multicolor underprint. Historic harbor view at left. Queen Elizabeth
II at right. Signature 6, four signatures in block form. Back: Arms at left, large 10 at
right, year date. 135x71mm.
    a. Issued note.   FV   90.00
    s. Specimen (300 issued). Red overprint: *SPECIMEN* on both sides.   —   220

13   20 Pounds   **VF   UNC**
2004. Brown on multicolor underprint. Modern harbor view. Queen Elizabeth II
at right. Signature 6, four signatures in block form. Back: Arms at left, large 20 at
right, year date. 135x71mm.
    a. Issued note.   FV   150
    s. Specimen (300 issued). Red overprint: *SPECIMEN* on both sides.   —   290

The Territorial Collectivity of St. Pierre and Miquelon, a French overseas territory located 10 miles (16 km.) off the south coast of Newfoundland, has an area of 242 sq. km. and a population of 7,045. Capital: St. Pierre. The economy of the barren archipelago is based on cod fishing and fur farming Fish and fish products, and mink and silver fox pelts are exported. The islands, occupied by the French in 1604, were captured by the British in 1702 and held until 1763 when they were returned to the possession of France and employed as a fishing station. They passed between France and England on six more occasions between 1778 and 1814 when they were awarded permanently to France by the Treaty of Paris. The rugged, soil-poor granite islands, which will support only evergreen shrubs, are all that remain to France of her extensive colonies in North America. In 1958 St. Pierre and Miquelon voted in favor of the new constitution of the Fifth Republic of France, thereby choosing to remain within the French Community. Notes of the Banque de France circulated 1937-1942; afterwards notes of the Caisse Centrale de la France Libre and the Caisse Centrale de la France d'Outre-Mer were in use.

RULERS:
French

MONETARY SYSTEM:
1 Nouveau Franc = 100 "old" Francs, 1960-

FRENCH ADMINISTRATION
Caisse Centrale de la France d'Outre-Mer
Saint-Pierre-et-Miquelon
1960 ND Provisional Issue
#30-35 overprint: *SAINT-PIERRE-ET-MIQUELON* and new denomination.

30	1 Nouveau Franc on 50 Francs	VF	UNC
	ND (1960). Multicolor. Overprint on Reunion number 25.		
	a. Special series *A.1-Y.1* with 3 digit serial # and 5 digit control #.	40.00	200
	b. Normal series with 5 digit serial # and 9 digit control #.	20.00	75.00
	s. As a, b. Specimen.	—	—

1961; 1964 ND Provisional Issue

31	1 Nouveau Franc on 50 Francs	VF	UNC
	ND (1961). Multicolor. B. d'Esnambuc at left, ship at right. Back: Woman.	200	650

32	2 Nouveaux Francs on 100 Francs	VF	UNC
	ND (1963). Multicolor. La Bourdonnais at left, two women at right. Back: Woman looking at mountains.	25.00	90.00

33	10 Nouveaux Francs on 500 Francs	VF	UNC
	ND (1964). Multicolor. Buildings and sailboat at left, two women at right. Back: Ox-carts with wood and plants.		
	a. Issued note.	175	425
	s. Specimen. Overprinted and perforated: *SPECIMEN*.	—	1,250

34	20 Nouveaux Francs on 1000 Francs	VF	UNC
	ND (1964). Multicolor. Two women at right. Back: Women at right, two men in small boat.		
	a. Issued note.	225	700
	s. Specimen. Overprinted and perforated: *SPECIMEN*.	—	1,250
35	100 Nouveaux Francs on 5000 Francs	VF	UNC
	ND (1961). Multicolor. General Schoelcher at center right. Back: Family.		
	a. Issued note.	450	2,000
	s. Specimen.	—	—

SAINT THOMAS & PRINCE

The Democratic Republic of Sao Tomé and Príncipe (formerly the Portuguese overseas province of St. Thomas and Prince Islands) is located in the Gulf of Guinea 150 miles (241 km.) off the West African coast. It has an area of 372 sq. mi. (960 sq. km.) and a population of 149,000. Capital: São Tomé. The economy of the islands is based on cocoa, copra and coffee. Discovered and claimed by Portugal in the late 15th century, the islands' sugar-based economy gave way to coffee and cocoa in the 19th century - all grown with plantation slave labor, a form of which lingered into the 20th century. While independence was achieved in 1975, democratic reforms were not instituted until the late 1980s. The country held its first free elections in 1991, but frequent internal wrangling between the various political parties precipitated repeated changes in leadership and two failed coup attempts in 1995 and 2003. The recent discovery of oil in the Gulf of Guinea promises to attract increased attention to the small island nation.

RULERS:
Portuguese to 1975

MONETARY SYSTEM:
1 Escudo = 100 Centavos, 1911-1976
1 Dobra = 100 Centimos, 1977-

STEAMSHIP SEALS

Type I
LOANDA

Type II
LISBOA

Type III
C.C.A

C.C.A = Colonias, Commercio, Agricultura.

PORTUGUESE ADMINISTRATION
Banco Nacional Ultramarino
S. Tomé e Príncipe
1956-64 Issue

			VF	UNC
40	**1000 Escudos**			
	11.5.1964. Green on multicolor underprint. J. de Santarem at right, bank arms at upper center. Back: Woman, sailing ships at left center, arms at upper right.			
		a. Issued note.	95.00	250
		s. Specimen, punch hole cancelled.	—	150
		ct. Color trial. Purple on multicolor underprint.	—	300

1974 Circulating Bearer Check Issue

		VF	UNC
41	**100 Escudos**		
	31.3.1974.	—	—
42	**500 Escudos**		
	28.4.1974.	—	—
43	**500 Escudos**		
	31.12.1974.	85.00	160
43A	**1000 Escudos**		
	23.12.1974; 31.12.1974 Red.	85.00	160

DEMOCRATIC REPUBLIC
Banco Nacional de S. Tomé e Príncipe
1976 Provisional Issue

			VF	UNC
44	**20 Escudos**			
	1.6.1976 (- old date 20.11.1958). Brown on multicolor underprint. Bank seal at left, Portuguese arms at lower center, King D. Afonso V at right. Overprint on #36. Printer: BWC.			
		a. Issued note.	10.00	25.00
		s. Specimen.	—	—

			VF	UNC
45	**50 Escudos**			
	1.6.1976 (- old date 20.11.1958). Brown-violet on multicolor underprint. Bank seal at left, Portuguese arms at lower center, King D. Afonso V at right.Overprint on #37. Printer: BWC.		10.00	30.00

			VF	UNC
46	**100 Escudos**			
	1.6.1976 (- old date 20.11.1958). Purple on multicolor underprint. Bank seal at left, Portuguese arms at lower center, King D. Afonso V at right. Overprint on #38. Printer: BWC.			
		a. Issued note.	15.00	45.00
		s. Specimen.	—	—

47 500 Escudos — VF UNC
1.6.1976 (- old date 18.4.1956). Blue on multicolor underprint. Overprint on #39.
   a. Issued note. — 40.00 150
   s. Specimen. — — —

48 1000 Escudos — VF UNC
1.6.1976 (- old date 11.5.1964). Green on multicolor underprint. Overprint on #40. — 40.00 120
#49 renumbered, see #43A.

1976 Circulating Bearer Check Issue

50 500 Escudos — VF UNC
21.6.1976. Black on pink and light aqua underprint. 167x75mm.
   a. Issued note. — 27.50 85.00
   ct. Uniface. Signatures mauve and blue, or blue and blue. — — —

51 1000 Escudos — VF UNC
21.6.1976. 167x75mm. — 35.00 100

Decreto-Lei No. 50/76; 1977 Issue

52 50 Dobras — VF UNC
12.7.1977. Red and multicolor. African grey parrot at center in underprint. Rei
Amador at right, arms at lower left. Signature titles: *O MINISTRO DA COORDE-
NACO ECONOMICA* and *O GOVERNADOR*. Back: Scene with two fishermen in
boats. Watermark: Rei Amador. Printer: BWC.
   a. Issued note. — 3.00 8.00
   s. Specimen. — — 125

53 100 Dobras — VF UNC
12.7.1977. Green and multicolor. Flower at center in underprint. Rei Amador
at right, arms at lower left. Signature titles: *O MINISTRO DA COORDENACO
ECONOMICA* and *O GOVERNADOR*. Back: Group of people preparing food.
Watermark: Rei Amador. Printer: BWC.
   a. Issued note. — 4.00 10.00
   s. Specimen. — — 125

54 500 Dobras — VF UNC
12.7.1977. Purple and multicolor. Sea Turtle at center in underprint. Rei Amador
at right, arms at lower left. Signature titles: *O MINISTRO DA COORDENACO
ECONOMICA* and *O GOVERNADOR*. Back: Waterfall. Watermark: Rei Amador.
Printer: BWC.
   a. Issued note. — 10.00 25.00
   s. Specimen. — — 150

55 1000 Dobras — VF UNC
12.7.1977. Blue and multicolor. Bananas at center in underprint. Rei Amador
at right, arms at lower left. Signature titles: *O MINISTRO DA COORDENACO
ECONOMICA* and *O GOVERNADOR*. Back: Fruit gatherer. Watermark: Rei
Amador. Printer: BWC.
   a. Issued note. — 35.00 90.00
   s. Specimen. — — 200

Decreto-Lei No. 6/82; 1982 Issue

56 50 Dobras — VF UNC
30.9.1982. Red and multicolor. African grey parrot at center in underprint. Rei — 2.50 6.50
Amador at right, arms at lower left. Signature titles: *O MINISTRO DO PLANO* and
O GOVERNADOR. Back: Scene with two fishermen in boats. Watermark: Rei
Amador. Printer: BWC.

57 100 Dobras — VF UNC
30.9.1982. Green and multicolor. Flower at center in underprint. Rei Amador — 3.50 9.00
at right, arms at lower left. Signature titles: *O MINISTRO DO PLANO* and *O
GOVERNADOR*. Back: Group of people preparing food. Watermark: Rei Amador.
Printer: BWC.

58 500 Dobras — VF UNC
30.9.1982. Purple and multicolor. Sea Turtle at center in underprint. Rei Amador — 9.00 22.50
at right, arms at lower left. Signature titles: *O MINISTRO DO PLANO* and *O
GOVERNADOR*. Back: Waterfall. Watermark: Rei Amador. Printer: BWC.

59   1000 Dobras
30.9.1982. Blue and multicolor. Bananas at center in underprint. Rei Amador at right, arms at lower left. Signature titles: *O MINISTRO DO PLANO* and *O GOVERNADOR*. Back: Fruit gatherer. Watermark: Rei Amador. Printer: BWC,

	VF	UNC
	12.00	32.50

Decreto-Lei No. 1/88; 1989 Issue

60   100 Dobras
4.1.1989. Green and multicolor. Flower at center in underprint. Rei Amador at right, arms at lower left. Signature title at left: *O MINISTRO DA ECONOMIA E FINANÇAS*. Back: Group of people preparing food. Watermark: Rei Amador. Printer: TDLR.

	VF	UNC
	2.50	6.00

61   500 Dobras
4.1.1989. Violet, red, orange and tan on multicolor underprint. Sea Turtle at center in underprint. Rei Amador at right, arms at lower left. Signature title at left: *O MINISTRO DA ECONOMIA E FINANÇAS*. Back: Waterfall. Watermark: Rei Amador. Printer: TDLR.

	VF	UNC
	4.00	9.00

62   1000 Dobras
4.1.1989. Blue, green and multicolor underprint. Bananas at center in underprint. Rei Amador at right, arms at left. Signature title at left: *O MINISTRO DA ECONOMIA E FINANÇAS*. Back: Fruit gatherer. Watermark: Rei Amador. Printer: TDLR.

	VF	UNC
	7.00	17.50

Banco Central de S.Tomé e Príncipe
Decreto Lei No. 29/93; 1993 Issue
#63 and 64 like #61 and 62. Ascending size serial #. Printer: TDLR.

63   500 Dobras
26.8.1993. UV: arms over turtle fluoresce yellow. Violet, red, orange and tan on blue and multicolor underprint. Sea Turtle at center in underprint. Rei Amador at right, blue arms at lower left. Green ascending size serial number at right. Signature title at left: *O MINISTRO DA ECONOMIA E FINANÇAS*. Back: Waterfall. Watermark: Rei Amador. Printer: TDLR.

	VF	UNC
	1.00	4.00

64   1000 Dobras
26.8.1993. Purple and deep blue and blue-green on multicolor underprint. Bananas at center in underprint. Rei Amador at right, arms at left. Red serial number at right. Signature title at left: *O MINISTRO DA ECONOMIA E FINANÇAS*. Back: Fruit gatherer. Watermark: Rei Amador. Printer: TDLR.

	VF	UNC
	2.00	10.00

Decreto Lei No. 42/96; 1996 Issue
#65-68 Replacement notes: Serial # prefix ZZ.

65   5000 Dobras
22.10.1996-. Purple, lilac and olive-green on multicolor underprint. Papa Figo bird (Principe Glossy Starling) at left center, Rei Amador at right, arms at upper center right. Back: Esplanade, modern building at left center. Watermark: Rei Amador. Printer: TDLR. 129x67mm.

	VF	UNC
a. 22.10.1996. One security thread.	FV	10.00
b. 22.10.1996. Two security threads.	FV	8.00
c. 26.8.2004. Two security threads.	FV	8.00
d. 31.12.2013.	FV	8.00
s. Specimen.	—	75.00

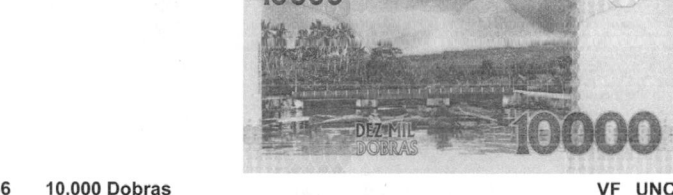

66   10,000 Dobras
22.10.1996-. Dark green, blue-violet and tan on multicolor underprint. Emerald Cuckoo at left center, Rei Amador at right, arms at upper center right. Back: Bridge over river at left center. Watermark: Rei Amador. Printer: TDLR. 136x67mm.

	VF	UNC
a. 22.10.1996. One security threads.	FV	17.50
b. 22.10.1996. Two security threads.	FV	17.50
c. 26.8.2004. Two security threads.	FV	15.00
d. 31.12.2013.	FV	15.00
s. Specimen.	—	75.00

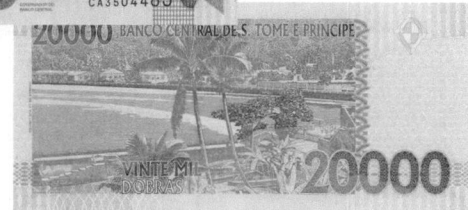

67   20,000 Dobras
22.10.1996; 26.8.2004; 10.12.2010. Red, olive-brown and blue-black on multicolor underprint. Sao Tome Oriole at left center, Rei Amador at right, arms at upper center right. Back: Beach scene at left center. Watermark: Rei Amador. Printer: TDLR. 143x67mm.

	VF	UNC
a. 22.10.1996. One security thread.	FV	25.00
b. 22.10.1996. Two security threads.	FV	25.00
c. 26.8.2004. Two security threads.	FV	22.50
d. 10.12.2010.	FV	22.50
s. Specimen.	—	75.00

68 50,000 Dobras VF UNC
22.10.1996; 26.8.2004; 10.12.2010; 31.12.2013. Brown, purple and red on
multicolor underprint. Black-winged Kingfisher at left center, Rei Amador at right,
arms at upper center right. Back: Central Bank building at left center. Watermark:
Rei Amador. Printer: TDLR. 150x67mm.
  a. 22.10.1996. One security thread. FV 50.00
  b. 22.10.1996. Two security threads. FV 50.00
  c. 26.8.2004. Two security threads. FV 50.00
  d. 10.12.2010. FV 50.00
  e. 31.12.2013. FV 50.00
  s. Specimen overprint: ESPECIME, 0's in serial #. — 75.00

69 100,000 Dobras VF UNC
2.6.2005; 10.12.2010; 31.12.2013. Green on multicolor underprint. Francisco José
Tenreiro at right, bird at center. Back: Auto de Floripes. Printer: TDLR. 150x67mm.
  a. 2.6.2005. FV 100
  b. 10.12.2010. FV 100
  c. 31.12.2013. FV 100

70 20,000 Dobras VF UNC
31.12.2013. Like previous date, but with new signatures and new date. Red, olive- FV 22.50
brown and blue-black on multicolor underprint. Sao Tome Oriole at left center,
Rei Amador at right, arms at upper center right. Back: Beach scene at left center.
Watermark: Rei Amador. 143x67mm.

71 50,000 Dobras VF UNC
31.12.2013. Like previous date, but with new date and signatures (Hélio Silva Vaz FV 50.00
de Almeida and Maria do Carmo Trovoada Pires de Carvalho Silveira). Brown,
purple and red on multicolor underprint. Black-winged Kingfisher at left center, Rei
Amador at right, arms at upper center right. Back: Central Bank building at left
center. Watermark: Rei Amador. 150x67mm.

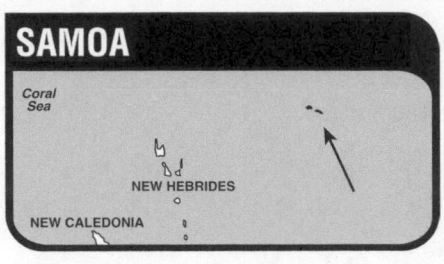

SAMOA

The Independent State of
Western Samoa (formerly German
Samoa), located in the Pacific Ocean
1,600 miles (2,574 km.) northeast of
New Zealand, has an area of 1,097
sq. mi. (2,860 sq. km.) and a population of 157,000. Capital: Apia. The
economy is based on agriculture,
fishing and tourism. Copra, cocoa and
bananas are exported. The Samoan
group of islands was discovered by
Dutch navigator Jacob Roggeveen in
1772. Great Britain, the United States
and Germany established consular representation at Apia in 1847, 1853 and 1861 respectively. The conflicting
interests of the three powers produced the Berlin agreement of 1889 which declared Samoa neutral and had
the effect of establishing a tripartite protectorate over the islands. A further agreement, 1899, recognized the
rights of the United States in those islands east of 171 deg. west longitude (American Samoa) and of Germany
in the other islands (Western Samoa). New Zealand occupied Western Samoa at the start of World War I and
administered it as a League of Nations mandate and U.N. trusteeship until Jan. 1, 1962, when it became an independent state. Western Samoa is a member of the Commonwealth of Nations. The Chief Executive is Chief
of State. The prime minister is the Head of Government. The present Head of State, Malietoa Tanumafili II,
holds his position for life. Future Heads of State will be elected by the Legislature Assembly for five-year terms.

RULERS:
  British, 1914-1962
  Malietoa Tanumafili II, 1962-2007

MONETARY SYSTEM:
  1 Pound = 20 Shillings to 1967
  1 Tala = 100 Sene, 1967-

Faletupe Tutotonu O Samoa

CENTRAL BANK OF SAMOA

1985 ND Issue

25 2 Tala VF UNC
ND (1985). Deep blue-violet on multicolor underprint. Woodcarver at right, national FV 4.00
flag at left center. Back: Arms at lower center right, national flag at left center, hut
with palms on small island at left cen Watermark: M. Tanumafili II.

26 5 Tala VF UNC
ND (1985). Red on multicolor underprint. Child writing at right, national flag at left
center. Back: Small port city at left center, arms at lower center, national flag at
center right. Watermark: M. Tanumafili II.
  a. Issued note. FV 6.50
  s. Specimen. Red overprint: SPECIMEN on each side. — 50.00

27 10 Tala VF UNC
ND (1985). Dark brown and purple on multicolor underprint. Man picking bananas
at right, national flag at left center. Back: Shoreline landscape, arms at lower
center, national flag at center right. Watermark: M. Tanumafili II.
  a. Issued note. FV 10.00
  s. Specimen. — 50.00

28 20 Tala VF UNC
ND (1985). Brown and orange-brown on multicolor underprint. Fishermen with
net at right, national flag at left center. Back: Arms at lower center, national flag at
center right, round building at left. Watermark: M. Tanumafili II.
  a. Issued note. FV 20.00
  s. Specimen. Red overprint: SPECIMEN on both sides. — 50.00

29 50 Tala VF UNC
ND (ca.1990). Green on multicolor underprint. Former home of Robert Louis
Stevenson, current residence of Head of State at center, M. Tanumafili II at right.
Back: Man performing traditional knife dance. Watermark: M. Tanumafili II.
  a. Issued note. FV 40.00
  s. Specimen. Red overprint: SPECIMEN on both sides. — 50.00

30 100 Tala
	VF	UNC

ND (ca.1990). Violet and light brown on multicolor underprint. Flag and Parliament building at center, M. Tanumafili II at right. Back: Harvest scene. Watermark: M. Tanumafili II.
a. Issued note.	FV	65.00
s. Specimen. Red overprint: SPECIMEN on both sides.	—	50.00

1990 Commemorative Issue

#31, Golden Jubilee of Service of the Head of State, Susuga Malletoa Tanumafili II, 1990

31 2 Tala
	VF	UNC

ND (1990). Polymer plastic. UV: serial # fluoresces orange. Brown, blue and purple on multicolor underprint. Samoan village at center, M. Tanumafili II at right. Clear area at lower right containing a Rava bowl visible from both sides. Back: Family scene at center, arms at upper right. Printer: NPA (without imprint). 140x72mm.
a. Text on face partly engraved. Serial # prefix AAA.	FV	6.50
b. Printing as a. Uncut sheet of 4 subjects. Serial # prefix AAB.	—	25.00
c. Face completely lithographed, deeper blue, purple and dull brown. Serial # prefix AAC.	FV	3.50
d. Serial # prefix: AAD.	FV	3.50
e. Serial # prefix: AAE-AAK.	FV	3.50
s. Specimen. Red overprint: SPECIMEN on each side.	—	65.00

Note: #31a was also issued in a special folder.

2002-2006 ND Issue

33 5 Tala
	VF	UNC

ND (2002). Red on multicolor underprint. Child writing at right, national flag at left center. Back: Small port city at left center, arms at lower center, national flag at center right. Watermark: M. Tanumafili II. 140x72mm.
a. Signature title: MINISTER OF FINANCE.	FV	6.50
b. Signature titles: MINISTER OF FINANCE and Governor.	FV	6.50

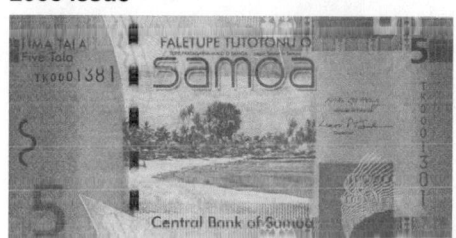

34 10 Tala
	VF	UNC

ND (2002). Dark brown and purple on multicolor underprint. Man picking bananas at right, national flag at left center. Back: Shoreline landscape, arms at lower center, national flag at center right. Watermark: M. Tanumafili II. 140x72mm.
a. Signatrue title: MINISTER OF FINANCE.	FV	10.00
b. Signature titles: MINISTER OF FINANCE and GOVERNOR.	FV	10.00

35 20 Tala
	VF	UNC

ND (2002). Brown and orange-brown on multicolor underprint. Fishermen with net at right, national flag at left center. Back: Arms at lower center, national flag at center right, round building at left. Watermark: M. Tanumafili II. 140x72mm.
a. Signature title: MINISTER OF FINANCE.	FV	20.00
b. Signature titles: MINISTER OF FINANCE and GOVERNOR.	FV	20.00

36 50 Tala
	VF	UNC

ND (2006). Green on multicolor underprint. Malietoa Tanumafili II at right, National Museum at center. Back: Man performing traditional knife dance. 140x72mm.
	FV	40.00

37 100 Tala
	VF	UNC

ND (2006). Olive and brown on multicolor underprint. Malietoa Tanumafili at right, flag and Fono House (Parliament) at center. Back: Harvest scene. 140x72mm.
	FV	65.00

2008 Issue

38 5 Tala
	VF	UNC

2008. Rose and purple on multicolor underprint. Beach scene at center. Back: Home of Robert Louis Stevenson. 140x70mm.
a. Issued note.	FV	6.00
r. Replacement note. Serial # prefix: ZZ.	FV	10.00
s. Specimen. Red overprint: SPECIMEN on both sides.	—	50.00

39 10 Tala
	VF	UNC

2008. Blue and green on multicolor underprint. Championship rugby team at center. Back: Group of children. 140x70mm.
a. Issued note.	FV	10.00
r. Replacement note. Serial # prefix: ZZ.	FV	17.50
s. Specimen. Red overprint: SPECIMEN on both sides.	—	50.00

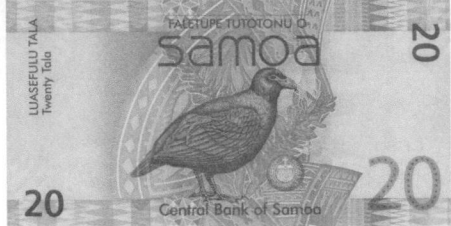

40 20 Tala VF UNC

2008. Brown, yellow and orange on multicolor underprint. Waterfall. Back: Bird. 140x70mm.

    a. Issued note. FV 20.00
    r. Replacement note. Serial # prefix: ZZ. FV 30.00
    s. Specimen. Red overprint: *SPECIMEN* on both sides. — 50.00

41 50 Tala VF UNC

2008. Purple, blue and multicolor. Government building at center. Back: Central Bank building. 140x70mm.

    a. Issued note. FV 40.00
    r. Replacement note. Serial # prefix: ZZ. FV 60.00
    s. Specimen. Red overprint: *SPECIMEN* on both sides. — 100

2012 Commemorative Issue

42 100 Tala VF UNC

2008. Dark green and light green on multicolor underprint. Malietoa Tanumfili II at center. Back: Church. 140x70mm.

    a. Issued note. FV 65.00
    r. Replacement note. Serial # prefix: ZZ. FV 100
    s. Specimen. Red overprint: *SPECIMEN* on both sides. — 125

43 100 Tala VF UNC

ND (2012). Like #42 but new designs at top and bottom. 140x70mm. FV 65.00

44 50 Tala VF UNC

2012. Independence, 50th Anniversary. Purple, blue and multicolor. Government building at center. Back: Central Bank building. 140x70mm. FV 40.00

SAUDI ARABIA

The Kingdom of Saudi Arabia, an independent and absolute hereditary monarchy comprising the former sultanate of Nejd, the old kingdom of Hejaz, Asir and el Hasa, occupies four-fifths of the Arabian peninsula. The kingdom has an area of 2,149,690 sq. km. and a population of 28.15 million. Capital: Riyadh. The economy is based on oil, which provides 85 percent of Saudi Arabia's revenue.

Saudi Arabia is the birthplace of Islam and home to Islam's two holiest shrines in Mecca and Medina. The king's official title is the Custodian of the Two Holy Mosques. The modern Saudi state was founded in 1932 by Abd al-Aziz bin Abd al-Rahman al Saud (Ibn Saud) after a 30-year campaign to unify most of the Arabian Peninsula. A male descendent of Ibn Saud, his son Abdallah bin Abd al-Aziz, rules the country today as required by the country's 1992 Basic Law.

Following Iraq's invasion of Kuwait in 1990, Saudi Arabia accepted the Kuwaiti royal family and 400,000 refugees while allowing Western and Arab troops to deploy on its soil for the liberation of Kuwait the following year. The continuing presence of foreign troops on Saudi soil after the liberation of Kuwait became a source of tension between the royal family and the public until all operational US troops left the country in 2003. Major terrorist attacks in May and November 2003 spurred a strong on-going campaign against domestic terrorism and extremism. King Abdallah has continued the cautious reform program begun when he was crown prince. To promote increased political participation, the government held elections nationwide from February through April 2005 for half the members of 179 municipal councils. In December 2005, King Abdallah completed the process by appointing the remaining members of the advisory municipal councils. The country remains a leading producer of oil and natural gas and holds more than 20% of the world's proven oil reserves. The government continues to pursue economic reform and diversification, particularly since Saudi Arabia's accession to the WTO in December 2005, and promotes foreign investment in the kingdom. A burgeoning population, aquifer depletion, and an economy largely dependent on petroleum output and prices are all ongoing governmental concerns.

RULERS:

Sa'ud Ibn Abdul Aziz, AH1373-1383/1953-1964AD
Faisal, AH1383-1395/1964-1975AD
Khaled, AH1395-1402/1975-1982AD
Fahd, AH1402-1432/1982-2005AD
Abdullah, 2005-2015AD
Salman, 2015AD-

MONETARY SYSTEM:

1 Riyal = 20 Ghirsh

REPLACEMENT NOTES:

#1-4, serial number starting with an Arabic zero.

SIGNATURE VARIETIES		
	GOVERNOR OF SAMA	**MINISTER OF FINANCE**
1	Anwar Ali	Tallal bin Abdul Aziz
2	Anwar Ali	Musa'id bin Abdul Rahman
3	Abdul Aziz al-Qurashi	Musa'id bin Abdul Rahman
4	Abdul Aziz al-Qurashi	Muhammad Ali Aba Al-Khail
5	Hamad Saud al-Sayyari	Muhammad Ali Aba Al-Khail
6	Hamad Saud al-Sayyari	Ibrahim bin Abdulaziz bin Abdullah al-Assaf

KINGDOM

Saudi Arabian Monetary Agency
Law of 1.7. AH1379; 1961 ND Issue

6   1 Riyal   VF   UNC

L. AH1379 (1961). Embedded security thread. Brown on light blue and green underprint. Hill of Light at center. Signature 1. Back: Arms (palm tree and crossed swords). Watermark: Arms (palm tree and crossed swords).

a. Issued note.	25.00	125
s. Specimen.	—	2,000

7   5 Riyals   VF   UNC

L. AH1379 (1961). Embedded security thread. Blue and green on multicolor underprint. Fortress at center. Back: Arms (palm tree and crossed swords). Watermark: Arms (palm tree and crossed swords).

a. Signature #1.	150	700
b. Signature #2.	175	800
s. Specimen.	—	2,750

8   10 Riyals   VF   UNC

L. AH1379 (1961). Embedded security thread. Green on pink and multicolor underprint. Dhows in Jedda harbor. Back: Arms (palm tree and crossed swords). Watermark: Arms (palm tree and crossed swords).

a. Signature #1.	150	650
b. Signature #2.	200	850
s. Specimen.	—	2,500

9   50 Riyals   VF   UNC

L. AH1379 (1961). Embedded security thread. Violet and olive-green on multicolor underprint. Derrick at center right. Back: Arms (palm tree and crossed swords). Watermark: Arms (palm tree and crossed swords).

a. Signature #1.	450	1,500
b. Signature #2.	550	1,750
s. Specimen.	—	3,000

10   100 Riyals   VF   UNC

L. AH1379 (1961). Embedded security thread. Red on multicolor underprint. Building at left, archway in background at center, building at right. Back: Arms (palm tree and crossed swords). Watermark: Arms (palm tree and crossed swords).

a. Signature #1.	1,250	3,250
b. Signature #2.	1,100	3,000
s. Specimen.	—	3,250

Law of 1.7. AH1379; 1968 ND Issue

11   1 Riyal   VF   UNC

L. AH1379 (1968). Embedded security thread. Purple on multicolor underprint. Goverment building at center right. Back: Saudi arms. Watermark: Arms.

a. Signature #2.	8.00	40.00
b. Signature #3.	10.00	50.00
s. As a. Specimen.	—	—

12   5 Riyals   VF   UNC

L. AH1379 (1968). Embedded security thread. Green on multicolor underprint. Airport. Back: Oil loading on ships at dockside. Watermark: Arms.

a. Signature #2.	30.00	125
b. Signature #3.	150	500

13   10 Riyals

VF   UNC

L. AH1379 (1968). Embedded security thread. Gray-blue on multicolor underprint. Mosque. Signature 2. Back: Al-Masa Wall with arches. Watermark: Arms.

30.00   125

17   5 Riyals

VF   UNC

L. AH1379 (1977). Green and brown on multicolor underprint. Portrait of King Faisal at right, Irrigation canal at center. Signature 4. Back: Dam at left center. Watermark: King Faisal.

		VF	UNC
a.	Incorrect Khamsa (five) in lower center panel of text.	8.00	30.00
b.	Correct Khamsa (five) in lower center panel of text.	4.00	20.00

14   50 Riyals

VF   UNC

L. AH1379 (1968). Embedded security thread. Brown on multicolor underprint. Courtyard of mosque at right. Back: Saudi arms at left, row of palms at center. Watermark: Arms.

		VF	UNC
a.	Signature #2.	95.00	340
b.	Signature #3.	85.00	310

18   10 Riyals

VF   UNC

L. AH1379 (1977). Lilac and brown on multicolor underprint. Portrait of King Faisal at right, oil drilling platform at center. Signature 4. Back: Oil refinery. Watermark: King Faisal.

6.00   30.00

15   100 Riyals

VF   UNC

L. AH1379 (1966). Embedded security thread. Red on multicolor underprint. Government Building at center right. Back: Derricks at left center. Watermark: Arms.

		VF	UNC
a.	Signature #2.	110	400
b.	Signature #3.	90.00	350

Law of 1.7. AH1379; 1976; 1977 ND Issue

خمسة ريالات   خمسة ريالات

Incorrect   Correct

16   1 Riyal

VF   UNC

L. AH1379 (1977). Red-brown on multicolor underprint. Portrait of King Faisal at right, Hill of Light at center. Signature 4. Back: Airport at left center. Watermark: King Faisal.

1.00   6.00

19   50 Riyals

VF   UNC

L. AH1379 (1976). Green, purple and brown on multicolor underprint. Portrait of King Faisal at right, Arches of mosque at center. Signature 4. Back: Courtyard of mosque at left center. Watermark: King Faisal.

32.50   95.00

20	100 Riyals		VF	UNC

L. AH1379 (1976). Blue and turquoise on multicolor underprint. Mosque at center, King 'Abd al-'Aziz Ibn Saud at right. Back: Long building with arches. — 48.50 — 150

Law of 1.7. AH1379; 1983; 1984 ND Issue

#21-26 wmk: Kg. Fahd. Lower l. serial # fluoresces gold under UV light. Non-visible portr. of King fluoresces yellow under UV light. #21-24 upper l. panel also exists w/unnecessary upper accent mark in "Monetary." at ctr. r. in text.

21	1 Riyal	VF	UNC

L. AH1379 (1984). Dark brown on multicolor underprint. 7th century gold dinar at left, portrait King Fahd at center right. Two signature varieties. Back: Flowers and landscape. Watermark: King Fahd. UV: fibers fluoresce yellow, lower serial # orange, King's face yellow. 134x62mm.

   a. Incorrect text. Signature 5 with acting in title. — 1.00 — 4.00
   b. Correct "Monetary" text. Signature 5 with acting in title. — FV — 3.00
   c. As b, but without acting in title. — FV — 2.00
   d. Signature 6. — FV — 2.00

22	5 Riyals	VF	UNC

L. AH1379 (1983). Purple, brown, and blue-green on multicolor underprint. Dhows at left, portrait King Fahd at center right. Back: Oil refinery at center right. Watermark: King Fahd. 145x66mm.

   a. Incorrect text. Signature 5 with acting in title. — 2.50 — 10.00
   b. Correct "Monetary" text. Signature 5 with acting in title. — FV — 8.00
   c. Like b, but without acting in title. — FV — 5.00
   d. Signature 6. — FV — 4.50

23	10 Riyals	VF	UNC

L. AH1379 (1983). Black, brown and purple on multicolor underprint. Fortress at left, portrait King Fahd at center right. Back: Palm trees at center right. Watermark: King Fahd. 150x68mm.

   a. Incorrect text. Signature 5 with acting in title. — FV — 18.00
   b. Correct "Monetary" text. Signature 5 with acting in title. — FV — 13.00
   c. As b. without acting in title. — FV — 10.00
   d. Signature 6. — FV — 9.00
   s. Specimen. Red overprint in Arabic on face and English on back. — — — 1,250

24	50 Riyals		VF	UNC

L. AH1379 (1983). Dark green and dark brown on multicolor underprint. Dome of the Rock in Jerusalem at left, portrait King Fahd at center right. Back: Al-Aqsa Mosque at center. Watermark: King Fahd. 155x70mm.

   a. Incorrect text. Signature 5 with acting in title. — FV — 60.00
   b. Correct "Monetary" text. Signature 5 with acting in title. — FV — 52.00
   c. Signature 6. — FV — 42.00
   s. As b. Specimen. Red overprint in English on both sides. Punch hole cancelled. — — — 2,000

25	100 Riyals	VF	UNC

L. AH1379 (1984). Brown-violet and olive-green on multicolor underprint. Mosque at left, portrait King Fahd at center right. Saudi arms in blind embossed latent image area at left center. Watermark: King Fahd. 160x72mm.

   a. Signature 5 with acting in title. — FV — 85.00
   b. Signature 5 without acting in title. — FV — 70.00
   c. Signature 6. — FV — 70.00
   s. Specimen. Red overprint in Arabic on face and English on back. — — — 2,000

Incorrect   Correct

26	500 Riyals	VF	UNC

L. AH1379 (1983). Purple and green on multicolor underprint. Ka'aba at left, portrait King 'Abd al-'Aziz Ibn Saud at center right. Saudi arms in blind embossed latent image area at left center. Back: Courtyard of Great Mosque at center. Watermark: King Fahd. 163x73mm.

   a. Incorrect "Five Hundred Riyals" in lower center panel of text. Signature 5 with acting in title. — 150 — 420
   b. Correct "Five Hundred Riyals" in lower center panel of text. Signature 5 with acting in title. — FV — 350
   c. As b. without acting in title. — FV — 275
   d. Signature 6. — FV — 275
   s. As a. Specimen. Red overprint in Arabic on face and English on back. — — — 2,000

2000 Commemorative Issue

#27 and 28, Centennial of Kingdom

27	20 Riyals	VF	UNC

AH1419, 1999. Brown, red, gray and blue on multicolor underprint. Abdul Aziz at left center. Signature 6. Back: Annur Mouuntain at center, commemorative logo and text at left. Watermark: Abdul Aziz. 152x69mm. — FV — 15.00

28	200 Riyals	VF	UNC

2000 Red, brown, gray and green on multicolor underprint. Abdul Aziz at left center. Signature 6. Back: Al Mussmack Palace at lower right and its gate. Commemorative logo and text at right. Watermark: Abdul Aziz. 163x73mm. — FV — 130

2003 Issue

29　100 Riyals
2003 Brown, violet and multicolor. Hologram added at upper center. Back: Mosque at center. 160x72mm.

	VF	UNC
	FV	68.50

30　500 Riyals
2003 Purple, green and peach on multicolor underprint. King 'Abd al-'Aziz Ibn Saud at right, Ka'aba at left. Back: Couryard of Great Mosque at center. 166x74mm.

	VF	UNC
	FV	255

2007 Issue

31　1 Riyal
2007; 2009; 2012. Black, green and peach on multicolor underprint. King Abdullah at right, coin at center. Back: Saudi Arabian Monetary Authority building. 133x63mm.

	VF	UNC
a. 2007	FV	1.25
b. 2009	FV	1.25
c. 2012	FV	1.25
s. Specimen.	—	75.00

32　5 Riyals
2007; 2009; 2012. Violet, blue and multicolor. King 'Abd al-'Aziz ibn Saud at right, Ras Tanura refinery at center. Back: Oil tanker at pier in the port of Jubayl. 145x66mm.

	VF	UNC
a. 2007.	FV	5.00
b. 2009.	FV	5.00
c. 2012.	FV	5.00
s. Specimen.	—	75.00

33　10 Riyals
2007; 2009; 2012. Black and brown on multicolor underprint. King Abdullah at right, palace at center. Back: King Abdullah Historical Center in Riyadh. 150x68mm.

	VF	UNC
a. 2007.	FV	8.00
b. 2009.	FV	8.00
c. 2012.	FV	8.00
s. Specimen.	—	100

#34 has been deleted.

34　50 Riyals
2007; 2009; 2012. Black, green and yellow on multicolor underprint. King Abdullah at right, Dome of the Rock at center. Back: Mosque. 155x70mm.

	VF	UNC
a. 2007.	FV	35.00
b. 2009.	FV	35.00
c. 2012.	FV	35.00
s. Specimen.	—	150

35　100 Riyals
2007; 2009; 2012. Violet and light blue on multicolor underprint. King Abdullah at right, Green Dome Mosque in Medina at center. Back: Mosque. 160x72mm.

	VF	UNC
a. 2007.	FV	55.00
b. 2009.	FV	55.00
c. 2012.	FV	55.00
s. Specimen	—	200

36　500 Riyals
2007; 2009; 2012. Black and blue on multicolor underprint. King Abdullah at right, Ka'aba at center. Back: Great Mosque in Mecca. 166x74mm.

	VF	UNC
a. 2007.	FV	250
b. 2009.	FV	250
c. 2012.	FV	250
s. Specimen.	—	400

SCOTLAND

North Atlantic Ocean / NORWAY / NORTHERN IRELAND / North Sea / DENMARK / IRELAND / ENGLAND / WALES

Scotland, a part of the United Kingdom of Great Britain and Northern Ireland, consists of the northern part of the island of Great Britain. It has an area of 30,414 sq. mi. (78,772 sq. km.). Capital: Edinburgh. Principal industries are agriculture, fishing, manufacturing and ship-building. In the 5th century, Scotland consisted of four kingdoms; that of the Picts, the Scots, Strathclyde, and Northumbria. The Scottish kingdom was united by Malcolm II (1005-34), but its ruler was forced to payo homage to the English crown in 1174. Scotland won independence under Robert Bruce at Bannockburn in 1314 and was ruled by the house of Stuart from 1371 to 1688. The personal union of the kingdoms of England and Scotland was achieved in 1603 by the accession of King James VI of Scotland as James I of England. Scotland was united with England by Parliamentary act in 1707.

RULERS:
British

MONETARY SYSTEM:
1 Pound = 20 Shillings to 1971
1 Pound = 100 New Pence, 1971-1981
1 Pound = 100 Pence, 1982-
1 Pound = 20 Shillings to 1971

BRITISH ADMINISTRATION
Bank of Scotland
Most notes from 1695 to 1856 are black and uniface.

1935; 1938 Issue

91	1 Pound	VF	UNC
	1937-43. Yellow-brown, dark brown and gray-blue. Arms of the bank at left. Back: Bank building.		
	a. Signature Lord Elphinstone and A. W. M. Beveridge. 15.1.1935-15.9.1937.	90.00	280
	b. Signature Lord Elphinstone and J. Macfarlane. 5.1.1939-7.5.1941.	80.00	260
	c. Signature Lord Elphinstone and J. B. Crawford. 2.6.1942; 16.10.1943.	80.00	240
	s. As c. Specimen.	—	225
92	**5 Pounds**	**VF**	**UNC**
	1935-44. Yellow-brown, dark brown and gray-blue. Thistle motif at left. Back: Bank building.		
	a. Signature Lord Elphinstone and A. W. M. Beveridge. 17.1.1935-17.3.1938.	300	975
	b. Signature Lord Elphinstone and J. Macfarlane. Black value panels. 24.4.1939-16.10.1941.	300	975
	c. Signature Lord Elphinstone and J. B. Crawford. 5.6.1942-26.9.1944.	250	850
	s. As c. Specimen.	—	350
93	**10 Pounds**	**VF**	**UNC**
	1938-63. Scottish arms in panel at left, medallion of Goddess of fortune below arms at right. Back: Bank building.		
	a. Signature Lord Elphinstone and A. W. M. Beveridge. 24.1.1935; 28.6.1938.	1,200	2,500
	b. Signature Lord Elphinstone and J. B. Crawford. 16.7.1942; 15.10.1942.	1,100	2,250
	c. Signature Lord Bilsland and Sir Wm. Watson. 26.9.1963; 27.9.1963.	700	1,600
94	**20 Pounds**	**VF**	**UNC**
	1935-65. Scottish arms in panel at left, medallion of Goddess of fortune below arms at right. Back: Bank building.		
	a. Signature Lord Elphinstone and A. W. M. Beveridge. 11.1.1935-22.7.1938.	500	1,400
	b. Signature Lord Elphinstone and J. Macfarlane. 16.5.1939; 12.7.1939.	550	1,600
	c. Signature Lord Elphinstone and J. B. Crawford. 5.6.1942-11.8.1952.	425	1,200
	d. Signature Lord Elphinstone and Sir Wm. Watson. 5.12.1952; 14.4.1953.	500	1,400
	e. Signature Sir J. Craig and Sir Wm. Watson. 6.4.1955-12.6.1956.	350	1,000
	f. Signature Lord Bilsland and Sir Wm. Watson. 21.3.1958-3.10.1963.	300	900

95	100 Pounds	VF	UNC
	1935-62. Scottish arms in panel at left, medallion of Goddess of fortune below arms at right. Back: Bank building.		
	a. Signature Lord Elphinstone and A. W. M. Beveridge. 8.1.1935-12.8.1937.	2,000	5,000
	b. Signature Lord Elphinstone and J. Macfarlane. 2.4.1940; 15.7.1940.	1,750	4,200
	c. Signature Lord Elphinstone and J. B. Crawford. 10.6.1942; 14.12.1951.	1,500	3,800
	d. Signature John Craig and Sir Wm. Watson. 14.9.1956-3.12.1956.	1,500	3,500
	e. Signature Lord Bilsland and Sir Wm. Watson. 24.3.1959-30.11.1962.	1,500	3,500

1961 Issue

102	1 Pound	VF	UNC
	1961-65. Light brown and pale blue. Medallion at center, date below. Back: Ship at contor.		
	a. Imprint ends: LD. Signature Lord Bilsland and Sir Wm. Watson. 10.5.1961-13.2.1964.	25.00	80.00
	b. Imprint ends: LTD. Signature Lord Bilsland and Sir Wm. Watson. 4.5.1965; 11.5.1965.	20.00	70.00
	c. Magnetic ink encoded experimental note. Four short parallel lines overprinted at right and left borders. (1963-64).	—	400
103	**5 Pounds**	**VF**	**UNC**
	14.9.1961-22.9.1961. Reduced size. Light brown and pale blue. Medallion at center, date below. Signature Lord Bilsland and Sir Wm. Watson. Back: Arms at left, ship at right.	70.00	250

#104 deleted, see #102.

1961; 1966 Issue

105	1 Pound	VF	UNC
	1966; 1967. Light brown and pale blue. Similar to #102 but *EDINBURGH* and date at right. Signature Lord Polwarth and J. Letham with titles: *GOVERNOR* and *TREASURER & GENERAL MANAGER*. Two watermark varieties. Back: Ship at center.		
	a. Without electronic sorting marks on back. 1.6.1966.	18.50	65.00
	b. With electronic sorting marks on back. 3.3.1967.	17.50	60.00
	s. As b. Specimen.	—	250

106 5 Pounds | VF | UNC

1961-67. Blue and light brown. Medallion of fortune at center, numerals of value filled in at base. Back: Arms at left, ship at right.

    a. Signature Lord Bilsland and Sir Wm. Watson with titles: *GOVERNOR* and | 50.00 | 180
       TREASURER. 25.9.1961-12.1.1965.
    b. Signature Lord Polwarth and Sir Wm. Watson. 7.3.1966-8.3.1966. | 55.00 | 200
    c. Lighter shades of printing. Signature Lord Polwarth and J. Letham with | 50.00 | 180
       titles: *GOVERNOR* and *TREASURER & GENERAL MANAGER.* 1.2.1967;
       2.2.1967.
    d. Signature titles as b. with electronic sorting marks on back. 1.11.1967. | 60.00 | 200
    s. As c. Specimen. | — | 300

1968; 1969 Issue

109 1 Pound | VF | UNC

1968; 1969. Ochre on blue and multicolor underprint. Arms at center flanked by two women. Back: Arms at upper left, shield at upper center, sailing ship at upper right.

    a. *EDINBURGH* 19mm in length. 17.7.1968. | 20.00 | 80.00
    b. *EDINBURGH* 24mm in length. 18.8.1969. | 20.00 | 80.00
    s. As b. Specimen. | — | 400

110 5 Pounds | VF | UNC

1968-69. Green on multicolor underprint. Arms at center flanked by two women. Back: Arms at upper left, shield at upper center, sailing ship at upper right.

    a. *EDINBURGH* 19mm in length. 1.11.1968; 4.11.1968. | 80.00 | 250
    b. *EDINBURGH* 24mm in length. 8.12.1969; 9.12.1969. | 80.00 | 250

110A 20 Pounds | VF | UNC

5.5.1969. Scottish arms in panel at left, medallion of Goddess of Fortune below | 175 | 425
arms at center right. Signature: Lord Polwarth and J. Letham. With security
thread. Watermark: Thistle.

Note: #110A was an emergency printing of 25,000 bank notes.

1970-74 Issue

#111-113 Replacement notes: #111 - Serial # prefix *Z/1, Z/2* **or** *Z/3;* **#112 - Serial # prefix** *ZA* **or** *ZB;* **#113 - Serial # prefix** *ZB.*

111 1 Pound | VF | UNC

1970-88. Green on multicolor underprint. Arms at center flanked by two women, Sir W. Scott at right. Back: Sailing ship at left, arms at upper center, medallion of Pallas seated at right.

    a. Signature Lord Polwarth and T. W. Walker. 10.8.1970; 31.8.1971. | 17.50 | 55.00
    b. Signature Lord Clydesmuir and T. W. Walker. 1.11.1972; 30.8.1973. | 17.50 | 55.00
    c. Signature Lord Clydesmuir and A. M. Russell. 28.10.1974-3.10.1978. | 6.00 | 22.50
    d. Signature Lord Clydesmuir and D. B. Pattullo. 15.10.1979; 4.11.1980. | 6.00 | 15.00
    e. Signature T. N. Risk and D. B. Pattullo. 30.7.1981. | 8.00 | 18.00
    f. Without sorting marks on back. Signature like e. 7.10.1983; 9.11.1984; | 5.00 | 16.00
       12.12.1985; 18.11.1986.
    g. Signature T. N. Risk and L. P. Burt. 19.8.1988. | 4.00 | 12.50
    s. As a (1970); c (1974). Specimen. | — | 225

112 5 Pounds | VF | UNC

1970-88. Blue on multicolor underprint. Arms at center flanked by two women, Sir W. Scott at right. Back: Sailing ship at let, arms at upper center, medallion of Pallas seated at right.

    a. Signature Lord Polwarth and T. W. Walker. 10.8.1970; 2.9.1971. | 60.00 | 175
    b. Signature Lord Clydesmuir and T. W. Walker. 4.12.1972; 5.9.1973. | 40.00 | 125
    c. Signature Lord Clydesmuir and A. M. Russell. 4.11.1974; 1.12.1975; | 35.00 | 105
       21.11.1977; 19.10.1978.
    d. Signature Lord Clydesmuir and D. B. Pattullo. 28.9.1979; 28.11.1980. | 30.00 | 90.00
    e. Signature T. N. Risk and D. B. Pattullo. 27.7.1981; 25.6.1982. | 25.00 | 85.00
    f. Without encoding marks. 13.10.1983; 3.12.1985; 29.2.1988. | 25.00 | 60.00
    s. As a (1970); c (1974). Specimen. | — | 225

113 10 Pounds

1974-90. Brown on multicolor underprint. Arms at center flanked by two women,
Sir W. Scott at right. Back: Medallions of sailing ship at lower left, Pallas seated at
upper left center, arms at right.

	VF	UNC
a. Signature Lord Clydesmuir and A. M. Russell. 1.5.1974-10.10.1979.	50.00	190
b. Signature Lord Clydesmuir and D. B. Pattullo. 5.2.1981.	50.00	175
c. Signature T. N. Risk and D. B. Pattullo. 22.7.1981; 16.6.1982; 14.10.1983;	35.00	70.00
17.9.1984; 8.1.1986; 20.10.1986; 6.8.1987.		
d. Signature T. N. Risk and P. Burt. 1.9.1989; 31.10.1990.	35.00	70.00
cr. As c. Replacement.	60.00	200

114 20 Pounds

1970-87. Purple on multicolor underprint. Arms at center flanked by two women,
Sir W. Scott at right. Back: Arms at upper left, above sailing ship with medallion of
Pallas seated below, head office building at center.

	VF	UNC
a. Signature Lord Polwarth and T. W. Walker. 1.10.1970.	175	500
b. Signature Lord Clydesmuir and T. W. Walker. 3.1.1973.	150	450
c. Signature Lord Clydesmuir and A. M. Russell. 8.11.1974; 14.1.1977.	120	425
d. Signature Lord Clydesmuir and D. B. Pattullo. 16.7.1979; 2.2.1981.	125	325
e. Signature T. N. Risk and D. B. Pattullo. 4.8.1981-15.12.1987.	85.00	300
s. As a. Specimen. 1.10.1970.	—	475

115 100 Pounds

1971-86. Red on multicolor underprint. Arms at center flanked by two women, Sir
W. Scott at right. Back: Arms at upper left, medallions of sailing ship at lower left,
Pallas seated at lower right, head office building at center.

	VF	UNC
a. Signature Lord Polwarth and T. W. Walker. 6.12.1971.	625	1,500
b. Signature Lord Clydesmuir and T. W. Walker. 6.9.1973.	600	1,400
c. Signature Lord Clydesmuir and A. M. Russell. 11.10.1978.	550	1,200
d. Signature Lord Clydesmuir and D. B. Pattullo. 26.1.1981.	525	1,100
e. Signature T. N. Risk and D. B. Pattullo. 11.6.1982; 26.11.1986.	450	900
s. As a. Specimen.	—	600

1990-92 Sterling Issue

116 5 Pounds

1990-94. Blue on multicolor underprint. Arms at center flanked by two women, Sir
W. Scott at right. STERLING added below value. Back: Sailing ship at left, arms at
upper center, medallion of Pallas seated at right. 135x70mm.

	VF	UNC
a. Signature T. N. Risk and P. Burt. 20.6.1990.	17.50	40.00
b. Signature D. B. Pattullo and P. Burt. 6.11.1991; 18.1.1993; 7.1.1994.	17.50	40.00

117 10 Pounds

7.5.1992; 9.3.1993; 13.4.1994. Deep brown on multicolor underprint. Arms at cen-
ter flanked by two women, Sir W. Scott at right. STERLING added below value.
Signature D. B. Pattullo and P. Burt. Back: Medallions of sailing ship at lower left,
Pallas seated at upper left center, arms at right. 142x75mm.

	VF	UNC
a. Issued note.	25.00	70.00
r. Replacement.	30.00	90.00

118 20 Pounds

1.7.1991; 3.2.1992; 12.1.1993. Purple on multicolor underprint. Arms at center
flanked by two women, Sir W. Scott at right. STERLING added below value.
Signature D. B. Pattullo and P. Burt. Back: Arms at upper left, above sailing ship
with medallion of Pallas seated below, head office building at center. 148x81mm.

	VF	UNC
	50.00	100

118A 100 Pounds

14.2.1990; 22.1.1992; 2.12.1992; 9.2.1994. Similar to #115. Red on multicolor
underprint. STERLING added below value.

	VF	UNC
a. 14.2.1990. Signature T.N. Risk and Peter Burt.	350	750
b. 22.1.1992; 2.12.1992; 9.2.1994. Signature D.B. Pattullo and Peter Burt.	325	700
s. Specimen.	—	600

1995 Commemorative Issue

#119-122, Tercentenary - Bank of Scotland

119 5 Pounds		VF	UNC
1995-2006. Dark blue and purple on multicolor underprint. Sir Walter Scott at left, bank arms at center. Back: Bank head office building at lower left, medallion of Pallas seated, arms and medallion of sailing ship at right. Watermark: Sir Walter Scott. Printer: TDLR (without imprint). 135x70mm.		
a. Signature D. Bruce Pattullo and Peter A. Burt. 4.1.1995. Signature titles as: *GOVERNOR* and *TREASURER & CHIEF GENERAL MANAGER.*		FV	40.00
b. Signature D. Bruce Pattullo and Gavin Masterton. 13.9.1996.		FV	35.00
c. Signature Alistair Grant and Gavin Masterton. 5.8.1998.		FV	20.00
d. Signature Peter Burt and George Mitchell. 25.6.2002. Signature titles as: *GOVERNOR* and *TREASURER & MANAGING DIRECTOR.*		FV	18.50
e. Signature Dennis Stevenson and Colin Matthew. 1.1.2006.		FV	18.50

120 10 Pounds		VF	UNC
1995-2006. Dark brown and deep olive-green on multicolor underprint. Sir Walter Scott at left, bank arms at center. Back: Workers by distilling equipment at center. Bank head office building at lower left, medallion of Pallas seated, arms and medallion of sailing ships at right. Watermark: Sir Walter Scott. Printer: TDLR (without imprint). 142x72mm.		
a. Signature D. Bruce Pattullo and Peter A. Burt. 1.2.1995. Signature titles as: *GOVERNOR and TREASURER & CHIEF GENERAL MANAGER.*		FV	50.00
b. Signature Bruce Pattullo and Gavin Masterton. 5.8.1997.		FV	45.00
c. Signature Alistair Grant and Gavin Masterton. 18.8.1998.		FV	40.00
d. Signature John Shaw and George Mitchell. 18.6.2001. Signature titles as: *GOVERNOR and TREASURER & MANAGING DIRECTOR.*		FV	40.00
e. Signature George Mitchell. 26.11.2003; 24.9.2004. Signature title as: *GOVERNOR.*		FV	37.50
f. Signature Lord Stevenson adn Colin Matthew. 1.1.2006. Signature titles as: *GOVERNOR* and *TREASURER.*		FV	35.00

121 20 Pounds		VF	UNC
1995-2004. Violet and brown on multicolor underprint. Sir Walter Scott at left, bank arms at center. Back: Woman researcher at laboratory station at center. Bank head office building at lower left, medallion of Pallas seated, arms and medallion of sailing ships at right. Watermark: Sir Walter Scott. Printer: TDLR (without imprint). 150x80mm.		
a. Signature D. Bruce Pattullo and Peter A. Burt. 1.5.1995. Signature titles as: *GOVERNOR and TREASURER & CHIEF GENERAL MANAGER.*	50.00	100
b. Signature Bruce Pattullo and Gavin Masterton. 25.10.1996; 1.4.1998.	FV	90.00
c. Signature Alistair Grant and Gavin Masterton. 22.3.1999. Signature titles as: *GOVERNOR* and *TREASURER & MANAGING DIRECTOR.*	FV	85.00
d. Signature John Shaw and George Mitchell. 18.6.2001. Signature title as: *GOVERNOR.*	FV	75.00
e. Signature George Mitchell. 26.11.2003; 24.9.2004. Signature title as: *GOVERNOR.*	FV	70.00

122 50 Pounds		VF	UNC
1995-2006. Dark green and olive-brown on multicolor underprint. Sir W. Scott at left, bank arms at center. Back: Music director and violinists at center. Bank head office building at lower left, medallion of Pallas seated, arms and medallion of sailing ships at right. Watermark: Sir W. Scott. Printer: TDLR (without imprint). 155x85mm.		
a. Signature D. Bruce Pattullo and Peter A. Burt. 1.5.1995. Signature titles as: *GOVERNOR* and *CHIEF GENERAL MANAGER.*	110	250
b. Signature Alistar Grant and Gavin Masterton. 15.4.1999. Signature titles as: *GOVERNOR* and *TREASURER & MANAGING DIRECTOR.*	FV	200
c. Signature George Mitchell. 29.1.2003. Signature title as *GOVERNOR.*	FV	170
d. Signature Dennis Stevenson and Colin Matthew. 1.1.2006.	FV	160

123 100 Pounds		VF	UNC
1995-2006. Red-violet and red-orange on multicolor underprint. Sir Walter Scott at left, bank arms at center. Back: Golf outing at center. Bank head office building at lower left, medallion of Pallas seated, arms and medallion of sailing ships at right. Watermark: Sir Walter Scott. Printer: TDLR (without imprint). 164x90mm.		
a. Signature D. Bruce Pattullo and Peter A. Burt. 17.7.1995. Signature titles as: *GOVERNOR* and *TREASURER & CHIEF GENERAL MANAGER.*	300	700
b. Signature D. Bruce Pattullo and Gavin Masterton. 18.8.1997.	250	500
c. Signature Alistair Grant and Gavin Masterton. 19.5.1999. Signature titles as: *GOVERNOR and TREASURER & MANAGING DIRECTOR.*	FV	400
d. Signature George Mitchell. 26.11.2003. Signature title as: *GOVERNOR.*	FV	375
e. Signature Dennis Stevenson and Colin Matthew. 1.1.2006.	FV	350

2007 Issue

124 5 Pounds		VF	UNC
2007-. Dark blue on multicolor underprint. Sir Walter Scott at center. Back: Statue and Brig o'Doon in South Ayrshire. Watermark: Sir Walter Scott. Printer: TDLR (without imprint). 135x70mm.		
a. Signature Lord Stevenson and Colin Matthew. 17.9.2007. Signature titles as: *GOVERNOR* and *TREASURER.*	FV	17.50
s. Specimen.	—	125

125 10 Pounds		VF	UNC
2007-. Dark brown and deep olive green on multicolor underprint. Sir Walter Scott at center. Back: Glenfinnan Viaduct, West Highlands. Watermark: Sir Walter Scott. Printer: TDLR (without imprint). 142x75mm.		
a. Signature Lord Stevenson and Colin Matthew. 17.9.2007. Signature titles as: *GOVERNOR* and *TREASURER.*	FV	35.00
s. Specimen.	—	125

126 20 Pounds		VF	UNC
2007-. Violet on multicolor underprint. Sir Walter Scott at center. Back: Firth of Forth rail and road bridges as seen from South Queensferry. Watermark: Sir Walter Scott. Printer: TDLR (without imprint). 150x80mm.		
a. Signature Lord Stevenson and Colin Matthew. 17.9.2007. Signature titles as: *GOVERNOR* and *TREASURER.*	FV	70.00
s. Specimen.	—	150

127 50 Pounds   VF   UNC
2007-. Dark green on multicolor underprint. Sir Walter Scott at center. Back: Falkirk Wheel. Watermark: Sir Walter Scott. Printer: TDLR (without imprint). 155x85mm.
   a. Signature Lord Stevenson and Colin Matthew. 17.9.2007. Signature titles as: *GOVERNOR* and *TREASURER*.   FV   150
   s. Specimen.   —   200

128 100 Pounds   VF   UNC
2007-. Red-violet and orange on multicolor underprint. Sir Walter Scott at center. Back: Kessock Bridge, Inverness. Watermark: Sir Walter Scott. Printer: TDLR (without imprint). 164x90mm.
   a. Signature Lord Stevenson and Colin Matthew. 17.9.2007. Signature titles as: *GOVERNOR* and *TREASURER*.   FV   300
   s. Specimen.   —   400

British Linen Bank

Note: Formerly the British Linen Company. See Vol. I. Merged with the Bank of Scotland in 1970.

1961; 1962 Issue

162 1 Pound   VF   UNC
30.9.1961. Blue and red. Sideview of seated Britannia in emblem at left, arms at upper right. Printer: TDLR.   30.00   85.00

163 5 Pounds   VF   UNC
2.1.1961; 3.2.1961. Blue and red. Sideview of seated Britannia in emblem at left, arms at upper right. Printer: TDLR.   125   325

164 20 Pounds   VF   UNC
14.2.1962; 5.3.1962; 4.4.1962. Blue and red. Sideview of seated Britannia in emblem at left, arms at upper right. Printer: TDLR.   275   800

165 100 Pounds   VF   UNC
9.5.1962; 1.6.1962. Blue and red. Sideview of seated Britannia in emblem at left, arms at upper right. Printer: TDLR.   550   1,850

1962 Issue

166 1 Pound   VF   UNC
1962-67. Blue and red. Sideview of seated Britannia in emblem at left, arms at upper right. Printer: TDLR. 155x85mm.
   a. Signature A. P. Anderson. 31.3.1962.   27.50   75.00
   b. Test note with lines for electronic sorting on back. 31.3.1962.   —   350
   c. Signature T. W. Walker. 1.7.1963-13.6.1967.   20.00   60.00
   s. As a, c. Specimen.   —   250

167 5 Pounds   VF   UNC
21.9.1962-18.8.1964. Blue and red. Sir Walter Scott at right, sideview of seated Britannia in emblem at left, arms at upper right. Printer: TDLR. 140x85mm.
   a. Signature A. P. Anderson. 21.9.1962; 20.10.1962; 16.6.1962.   30.00   100
   b. Signature T. W. Walker. 16.6.1964; 17.7.1964; 18.8.1964.   30.00   100
   c. As b. Test note with lines for electronic sorting. 17.7.1964.   150   400

1967 Issue

168 1 Pound   VF   UNC
13.6.1967. Blue on multicolor underprint. Sideview of seated Britannia in emblem at left, arms at upper right. Back: Similar to number 166 but modified design and with lines for electronic sorting. Printer: TDLR.   20.00   60.00

1968 Issue

169 1 Pound   VF   UNC
1968-70. Blue on multicolor underprint. Sir W. Scott at right, sideview of seated Britannia in emblem at left, supported arms at top center. Printer: TDLR.
   a. 29.2.1968; 5.11.1969.   20.00   60.00
   b. 20.7.1970.   40.00   120

170 5 Pounds   VF   UNC
22.3.1968; 23.4.1968; 24.5.1968. Similar to #167, but reduced size and many plate changes. Blue and red. Sideview of seated Britannia in emblem at left, arms at upper right. Printer: TDLR. 146x78mm.   40.00   120

Clydesdale and North of Scotland Bank Ltd.

Formerly, and later to become the Clydesdale Bank Ltd. again.

1950-51 Issue

191 1 Pound   VF   UNC
1950-60. Blue, red and orange. Ships at dockside at left, landscape (sheaves) at right. Back: River scene with trees.
   a. 1.11.1950-1.11.1956.   45.00   150
   b. 1.5.1958-1.11.1960.   40.00   125
   s. As a. Specimen.   —   250

192 5 Pounds   VF   UNC
2.5.1951-1.3.1960. Purple. King's College at Aberdeen at lower left, Glasgow Cathedral at lower right.
   a. Signature J. J. Campbell.   90.00   300
   b. Signature R. D. Fairbairn.   90.00   300
   s. As a. Specimen. TDLR oval overprint.   —   500

193 20 Pounds

2.5.1951-1.8.1962. Green on multicolor underprint. King's College at Aberdeen at lower left, Glasgow Cathedral at lower right. 180x97mm.

	VF	UNC
a. Signature J. J. Campbell.	160	550
b. Signature R. D. Fairbairn.	150	500

194 100 Pounds

2.5.1951. Blue. King's College at Aberdeen at lower left, Glasgow Cathedral at lower right. Signature J. J. Campbell. 180x97mm.

VF	UNC
1,200	3,000

1961 Issue

195 1 Pound

1.3.1961; 2.5.1962; 1.2.1963. Green on multicolor underprint. Arms at right. Back: Ship and tug at center.

	VF	UNC
a. Issued note.	35.00	100
s. Specimen.	—	160

196 5 Pounds

20.9.1961; 1.6.1962; 1.2.1963. Dark blue on multicolor underprint. Arms at right. Back: King's College at Aberdeen.

VF	UNC
75.00	200

Clydesdale Bank Limited

Formerly the Clydesdale and North of Scotland Bank Ltd. Later became Clydesdale Bank PLC.

1963-64 Issue

197 1 Pound

2.9.1963-3.4.1967. Green on multicolor underprint. Arms at right. Back: Ship and tug at center.

VF	UNC
25.00	80.00

198 5 Pounds

2.9.1963-1.9.1969. Blue and violet. Arms at right. Back: King's College at Aberdeen.

VF	UNC
60.00	200

199 10 Pounds

20.4.1964; 1.12.1967. Brown on multicolor underprint. Arms at right. Back: University of Glasgow.

VF	UNC
200	700

200 20 Pounds

19.11.1964; 1.12.1967. Carmine on multicolor underprint. Arms at right. Back: George Square in Glasgow.

VF	UNC
200	650

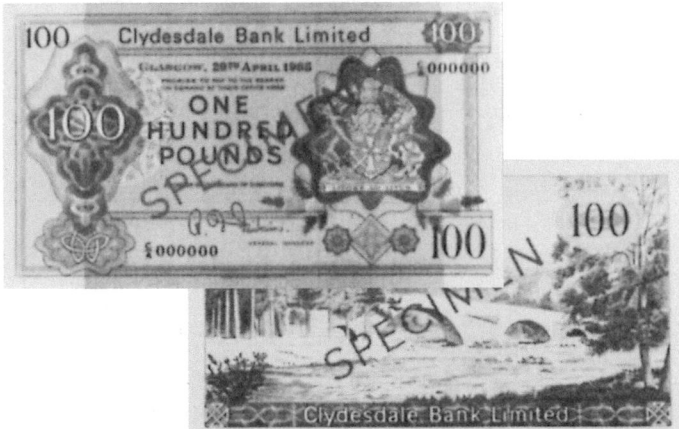

201 100 Pounds

1.2.1965; 29.4.1965; 1.2.1968. Violet on multicolor underprint. Back: Multiple arch bridge across river at center.

VF	UNC
600	1,750

1967 Issue

202 1 Pound

3.4.1967; 1.10.1968; 1.9.1969. Green on multicolor underprint. Arms at right. Back: Like number 197 but lines for electronic sorting.

VF	UNC
20.00	80.00

203 5 Pounds

	VF	UNC
1.5.1967; 1.11.1968; 1.9.1969. Blue and violet on multicolor underprint. Arms at right. Back: Like number 198 but lines for electronic sorting.	60.00	200

1971-81 Issue

204 1 Pound

VF UNC

1971-81. Dark olive-green on multicolor underprint. Robert the Bruce at left. Back: Scene of Battle of Bannockburn, 1314. Watermark: Old sailing ships.

		VF	UNC
a.	Signature R. D. Fairbairn, with title: *GENERAL MANAGER.* 1.3.1971.	12.00	50.00
b.	Signature A. R. Macmillan, with title: *GENERAL MANAGER.* 1.5.1972; 1.8.1973.	12.00	55.00
c.	Signature A. R. Macmillan, with title: *CHIEF GENERAL MANAGER.* 1.3.1974-27.2.1981.	10.00	35.00
s.	As c. Specimen.	—	—

205 5 Pounds

VF UNC

1971-80. Grayish lilac on multicolor underprint. Robert Burns at left. Back: Harvest Mouse and rose from Burns' poems. Watermark: Old sailing ships.

		VF	UNC
a.	Signature R. D. Fairbairn, with title: *GENERAL MANAGER.* 1.3.1971.	65.00	200
b.	Signature A. R. Macmillan, with title: *GENERAL MANAGER.* 1.5.1972; 1.8.1973.	65.00	200
c.	Signature A. R. Macmillan, with title: *CHIEF GENERAL MANAGER.* 1.3.1974; 6.1.1975; 2.2.1976; 31.1.1979; 1.2.1980.	45.00	120
s.	As c. Specimen.	—	—

#206 *Deleted.* See #205.

207 10 Pounds

VF UNC

1972-81. Brown and pale purple on multicolor underprint. David Livingstone at left. Back: Dromedary Camel and African scene. Watermark: Old sailing ships.

		VF	UNC
a.	Signature A. R. MacMillan, with title: *GENERAL MANAGER.* 1.3.1972; 1.8.1973.	150	500
b.	Signature A. R. MacMillan, with title: *CHIEF GENERAL MANAGER.* 1.3.1974-27.2.1981.	130	450

208 20 Pounds

VF UNC

1972-81. Lilac on multicolor underprint. Lord Kelvin at left. Back: Kelvin's lecture room at Glasgow University. Watermark: Old sailing ships.

		VF	UNC
a.	Signature A. R. MacMillan, with title: *GENERAL MANAGER.* 1.3.1972.	175	500
b.	Signature A. R. MacMillan, with title: *CHIEF GENERAL MANAGER.* 2.2.1976; 27.2.1981.	165	450

209 50 Pounds

	VF	UNC
1.9.1981. Olive on multicolor underprint. A. smith at left. Back: Sailing ships, blacksmith implements and farm. Watermark: Old sailing ships.	275	650

210 100 Pounds

VF UNC

1972; 1975; 1976. Red on multicolor underprint. Lord Kelvin at left. Back: Kelvin's lecture room at Glasgow University. Watermark: Old sailing ships.

		VF	UNC
a.	Signature A. R. MacMillan, with title: *GENERAL MANAGER.* 1.3.1972.	600	1,400
b.	Signature A. R. MacMillan, with title: *CHIEF GENERAL MANAGER.* 6.1.1975; 2.2.1976.	500	1,250

Clydesdale Bank PLC

Formerly the Clydesdale Bank Limited.

1982-89 "Sterling" Issues

211 1 Pound

VF UNC

1982-88. Dark olive-green on multicolor underprint. Robert the Bruce at left. Back: Scene of Battle of Bannockburn, 1314. Watermark: Old sailing ship repeated vertically.

		VF	UNC
a.	With sorting marks. Signature A. R. Macmillan. 29.3.1982.	8.00	25.00
b.	Like a. signature A. R. Cole Hamilton. 5.1.1983.	8.00	25.00
c.	Without sorting marks. Signature A. R. Cole Hamilton. 8.4.1985; 25.11.1985.	6.00	22.50
d.	Signature title: *CHIEF EXECUTIVE.* 18.9.1987; 9.11.1988.	5.00	17.50

212 5 Pounds

1982-89. Blue on multicolor underprint. Robert Burns at left. Back: Harvest Mouse and rose from Burns' poems. Watermark: Old sailing ship repeated vertically.

		VF	UNC
a. Signature A. R. Macmillan. 29.3.1982.		40.00	125
b. Signature A. R. Cole Hamilton. 5.1.1983.		35.00	110
c. Without sorting marks. Signature A. R. Cole Hamilton. 18.9.1986.		35.00	100
d. Signature title: *CHIEF EXECUTIVE*. 18.9.1987; 2.8.1988; 28.6.1989.		25.00	70.00
s. As d. Specimen.		—	200

213 10 Pounds

1982-87. Brown and pale purple on multicolor underprint. David Livingstone at left. Back: Dromedary Camel and African scene. Watermark: Old sailing ship repeated vertically.

		VF	UNC
a. Signature A. R. Macmillan. 29.3.1982; 5.1.1983.		80.00	325
b. Signature A. R. Cole Hamilton. 8.4.1985; 18.9.1986.		75.00	300
c. Signature title: *CHIEF EXECUTIVE*. 18.9.1987.		75.00	275
s. As d. Specimen.		—	—

214 10 Pounds

7.5.1988; 3.9.1989; 1.3.1990; 9.11.1990. Dark brown on multicolor underprint. D. Livingstone in front of map at left. Back: Blantyre (Livingstone's birthplace). Watermark: Old sailing ship repeated vertically.

	VF	UNC
	45.00	120

215 20 Pounds

1982-90. Lilac on multicolor underprint. Lord Kelvin at left. Back: Kelvin's lecture room at Glasgow University. Watermark: Old sailing ship repeated vertically.

		VF	UNC
a. Signature A. R. Macmillan. 29.3.1982.		150	450
b. Signature A. R. Cole Hamilton. 5.1.1983; 8.4.1985.		140	425
c. Signature title: *CHIEF EXECUTIVE*. 18.9.1987; 2.8.1990.		150	450

#216 renumbered, see #222.

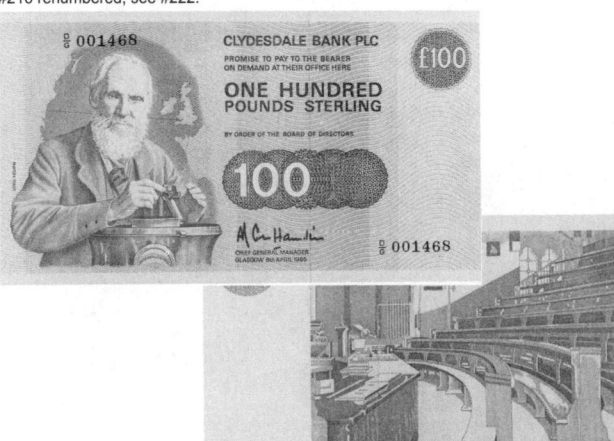

217 100 Pounds

1985; 1991. Red on multicolor underprint. Lord Kelvin at left. Back: Kelvin's lecture room at Glasgow University. Watermark: Old sailing ship repeated vertically. 163x90mm.

		VF	UNC
a. Signature title: *CHIEF GENERAL MANAGER*. 8.4.1985.		550	1,150
b. Signature title: *CHIEF EXECUTIVE*. 9.11.1991.		500	1,050

1989-96 "Sterling" Issue

218 5 Pounds

1990-. Black and gray on multicolor underprint. Robert Burns at left. Back: Harvest Mouse and rose from Burns' poems. Watermark: Old sailing ship repeated vertically. 135x70mm.

		VF	UNC
a. Signature A. R. Cole Hamilton. 2.4.1990.		17.50	35.00
b. Signature F. Cicutto. 1.9.1994.		15.00	30.00
c. Signature F. Goodwin. 21.7.1996; 1.12.1997.		FV	25.00
d. Signature G. Savage. 19.6.2002. Larger size date and title.		FV	22.50

219 10 Pounds VF UNC

1992-97. Deep brown and green on multicolor underprint. Similar to number 214 but with modified sailing ship outlines at right. Back: Blantyre (Livingston's birthplace) Watermark: Old sailing ship repeated vertically. 142x75mm.

   a. Signature A. R. Cole Hamilton. 3.9.1992.   32.50   85.00
   b. Signature Charles Love. 5.1.1993.   30.00   100
   c. Signature F. Goodwin. 22.3.1996; 27.2.1997.   30.00   65.00

220 20 Pounds VF UNC

1990-93. Violet, purple, brown and brown-orange on multicolor underprint. Robert the Bruce at left. Back: His equestrian statue, Monymusk reliquary, Stirling Castle and Wallace Monument. Watermark: Old sailing ship repeated vertically. 148x80mm.

   a. Signature A. R. Cole Hamilton. 30.11.1990; 2.8.1991; 3.9.1992.   70.00   175
   b. Signature Charles Love. 5.1.1993.   75.00   180

221 20 Pounds VF UNC

1994; 1996. Reduced size. Purple, dark brown and deep orange on multicolor underprint. Robert the Bruce at left. Back: His equestrian statue, Monymusk reliquary, Stirling Castle and Wallace Monument. Watermark: Old sailing ship repeated vertically. Ascending size serial number at upper left.

   a. Signature F. Cicutto. 1.9.1994.   60.00   120
   b. Signature F. Goodwin. 2.12.1996.   55.00   100

222 50 Pounds VF UNC

3.9.1989; 20.4.1992. Olive-green on multicolor underprint. A. Smith at left. Signature A. R. Cole Hamilton. Back: Sailing ships, blacksmith implements and farm. Watermark: Old sailing ships.   250   700

223 100 Pounds VF UNC

2.10.1996. Olive-green on multicolor underprint. Lord Kelvin at left. signature F. Goodwin. Vertical serial number at right. Back: Glasgow University.   250   400

1996 Commemorative Issue

#224, Poetry of Robert Burns

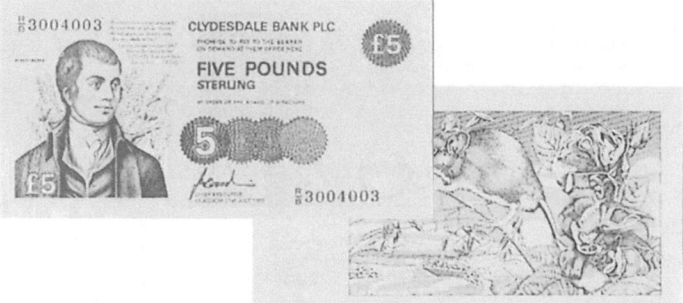

224 5 Pounds VF UNC

21.7.1996. Black and gray on multicolor underprint. Robert Burns at left, lines of poetry. Back: Harvest Mouse and rose from Burns' poems. Watermark: Sailing ship. 135x70mm.

   a. A man's a man for a'that - Then let us...   12.50   25.00
   b. Tam O'Shanter - Now, wha this...   12.50   25.00
   c. Ae Fond Kiss - But to see...   12.50   25.00
   d. Scots wha hae - By oppressions woes...   12.50   25.00

Note: For sets w/matching serial # see Collector Series - CS1.

1996 Regular Issue

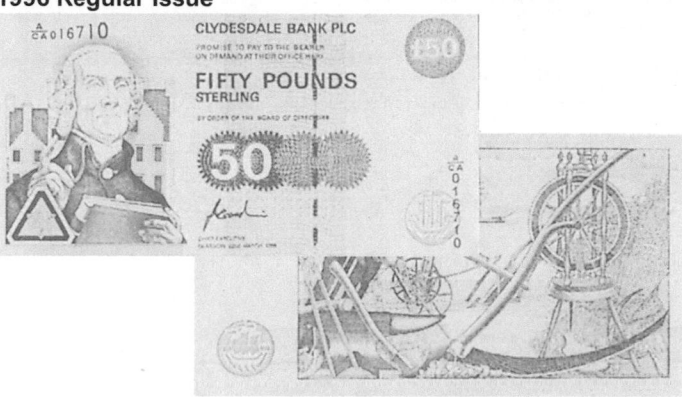

225 50 Pounds VF UNC

1996; 2003; 2005. Olive-green on multicolor underprint. A. Smith at left. Back: Sailing ships, blacksmith implements and farm. Watermark: Sailing ships. 157x85mm.

   a. 22.3.1996. Signature F. Goodwin.   150   250
   b. 25.4.2003. Signature Ross Pinney as *Chief Operating Officer*.   FV   200
   c. 9.1.2006. Signature David Thorburn.   FV   200

1997 Commemorative Issues

#226, Work of Mary Slessor

226 10 Pounds VF UNC

1997. Dark brown and brown on multicolor underprint. Mary Slessor at left. Back: Map of Calabar in Nigeria in wreath at center, sailing ship at upper left, Slessor seated below and with children at right. Watermark: Mary Slessor. 142x75mm.

   a. Signature F. Goodwin. 1.5.1997.   25.00   55.00
   b. Signature J. Wright. 5.11.1998; 20.10.1999.   25.00   42.50
   c. Signature S. Targett. 26.1.2003.   25.00   40.00
   d. Signature Ross Pinney. 25.4.2003.   FV   35.00
   e. Signature David Thorburn as *Chief Operating Officer*. 21.11.2004.   FV   32.50
   f. Signature David Thorburn, larger CB bank emblem. 14.3.2006; 16.4.2007.   FV   32.50

Note: #226 exists w/serial # prefix *NAB* encapsulated in acrylic plastic w/text: *1987-1997 THE FIRST DECADE*. Market value $150.
Non-encapsulated *NAB* market value in Unc. $70.

#227, Commonwealth heads of government meeting in Edinburgh, Oct. 1997

227 20 Pounds VF UNC

30.9.1997. Purple, dark brown and deep orange on multicolor underprint. Robert the Bruce at left. Signature F. Goodwin. Back: Edinburgh International Conference Centre at lower right, Clydesdale Bank plaza and Edinburgh Castle 150x80mm.   55.00   100

Note: #227 was issued w/serial # prefix: *CHG* (Special Commemorative prefix). Market value $70.

1997 Regular Issue

228   20 Pounds   **VF   UNC**

1.11.1997-. Purple, dark brown and deep orange on multicolor underprint. Like
number 221 but square design replaces *20* at lower left, segmented foil over security thread, bank logo added to value panel at lower center right. 150x80mm.

a. Signature Fred Goodwin. 1.11.1997.	FV	100
b. Signature John Wright. 12.10.1999.	FV	70.00
c. Signature Grahm Savage. 19.6.2002.	FV	90.00
d. Signature Steve Targett. 26.1.2003; 26.4.2003.	FV	75.00
e. Signature Ross Pinney. 25.4.2003.	FV	62.50
f. Signature David Thorburn as *Chief Operating Officer.* 21.11.2004.	FV	62.50
g. Signature David Thorburn, larger CB emblem. 24.6.2006.	FV	62.50

1999 Commemorative Issue

#229, Glasgow as UK City of Architecture and Design

229   20 Pounds   **VF   UNC**

9.4.1999. Purple, brown and multicolor. Alex "Greek" Thompson at left. Special   FV   95.00
text at lower right. Back: Holmwood House. Special text at lower right. 150x80mm.

2000 Commemorative Issues

#229A and 229B, special text: *COMMEMORATING THE YEAR 2000.*

229A   10 Pounds   **VF   UNC**

1.1.2000. Special text: *COMMEMORATING THE YEAR 2000.* Brown and green   25.00   55.00
on multicolor underprint. Mary Slessor at left, commemorative text added at
right. Back: Map of Calabar in Nigeria in wreath at center, sailing ship at upper
left, Slessor seated below and with children at right. Watermark: Mary Slessor.
142x75mm.

229B   20 Pounds   **VF   UNC**

1.1.2000. Special text: *COMMEMORATING THE YEAR 2000.* Purple, dark brown   50.00   100
and deep orange on multicolor underprint. Like #221 but square design replaces
20 at lower left, segmented foil over security thread, bank logo added to value
panel at lower center right. Back: Similar to #228 but commemorative text added
at right. 150x80mm.

#229C and 229D, Commemorating the 550th Anniversary of the University of Glasgow

2001 Commemorative Issues

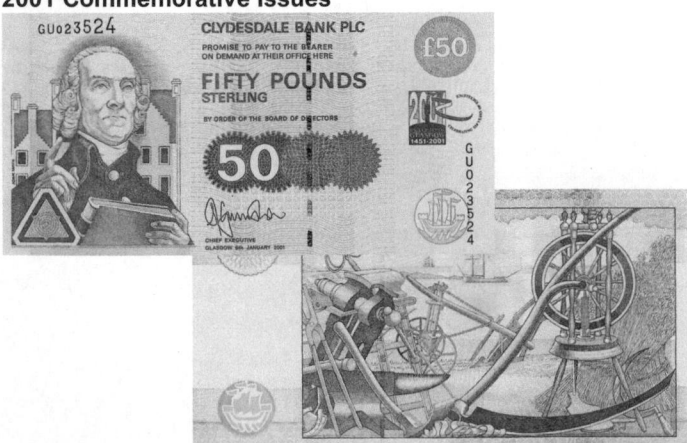

229C   50 Pounds   **VF   UNC**

6.1.2001. Olive-green on multicolor underprint. Like #225 but with commemorative   FV   200
emblem and text at right. 155x85mm.

Commemorating the 550th Anniversary of the University of Glasgow.

229D   100 Pounds   **VF   UNC**

6.1.2001. Purple, red and violet on multicolor underprint. Like #223 but with com-   FV   375
memorative emblem and text at right. 164x90mm.

Commemorating the 550th Anniversary of the University of Glasgow.

2005 Commemorative Issues

229E   10 Pounds   **VF   UNC**

2005. Dark brown and brown on multicolor underprint. Mary Slessor at left. Serial   FV   68.00
#prefix *CG.* Back: Commonwealth Games. Athletics - Montage of sports events.
Watermark: Mary Slessor. 142x75mm.

229F   20 Pounds   **VF   UNC**

2005. Like #221 but square design replaces *20* at lower left, segmented foil over   FV   70.00
security thread, bank logo added to value panel at lower center right. Signature
David Thorburn. Back: Clysesdale Bank Exchange in Glasgow. 150x80mm.

2006 Commemorative Issue

229G   20 Pounds   **VF   UNC**

25.3.2006 Like #228 but with addition of "700th Anniversary 1306 / 2006" and   FV   70.00
shield. Serial # prefix *RB.* Back: Bruce on horseback right. 150x80mm.

2006 Issue

229H   20 Pounds   **VF   UNC**

24.6.2006. Back: Like #221 150x80mm.   FV   50.00

2009 Issue

229I 5 Pounds   **VF UNC**
2009. Black and blue on multicolor underprint. Sir Alexander Fleming at right   FV   15.00
center, microscope at right. Back: St. Kilda. 135x70mm.

229J 10 Pounds   **VF UNC**
2009. Brown and tan on multicolor underprint. Robert Burns at right center. Back: FV   22.50
Old and new views of Edinburgh. 142x75mm.

229K 20 Pounds   **VF UNC**
2009. Purple and brown on multicolor underprint. Robert the Bruce at right center.   FV   50.00
Back: New Lanark. 150x80mm.

229L 50 Pounds   **VF UNC**
2009. Olive and green on multicolor underprint. Elsie Inglis at right center. Back: FV   100
Antonine Wall. 155x85mm.

229M 100 Pounds   **VF UNC**
2009. Rose on multicolor underprint. Charmes Rennie Mackintosh at right center.   FV   200
Back: Neart of Neolithic Orkney. 164x90mm.

National Commercial Bank of Scotland Limited

Formed by an amalgamation of The Commercial Bank of Scotland Ltd. and The National Bank of Scotland Ltd. in 1959. In 1969 it amalgamated with The Royal Bank of Scotland.

1961 Issue

269 1 Pound   **VF UNC**
1.11.1961-4.1.1966. Reduced size. Green on multicolor underprint. Forth Railway
bridge. Back: Arms at center. Printer: BWC. 151x72mm.
  a. Issued note.   20.00   60.00
  s. Specimen.   —   200

270 5 Pounds   **VF UNC**
3.1.1961. Reduced size. Green on multicolor underprint. Arms at bottom center   90.00   325
right. Back: Forth Railway bridge. Printer: W&S. 159x90mm.

1963-67 Issue

271 1 Pound   **VF UNC**
4.1.1967. Green on multicolor underprint. Forth Railway bridge. Back: Arms at
center, electronic sorting lines. Printer: BWC. 152x72mm.
  a. Issue note.   25.00   80.00
  s. Specimen.   —   —

272 5 Pounds   **VF UNC**
2.1.1963; 1.8.1963; 1.10.1964; 4.1.1966; 1.8.1966. Blue on multicolor underprint.
Arms at lower center. Back: Landscape with Edinburgh Castle, National Gallery
Printer: BWC. 142x85mm.
  a. Issued note.   45.00   120
  s. Specimen.   —   260

273 10 Pounds   **VF UNC**
18.8.1966. Brown on multicolor underprint. Arms at lower center. Back: Forth   350   1,100
Railway bridge. Printer: BWC. 151x94mm.

1967; 1968 Issue

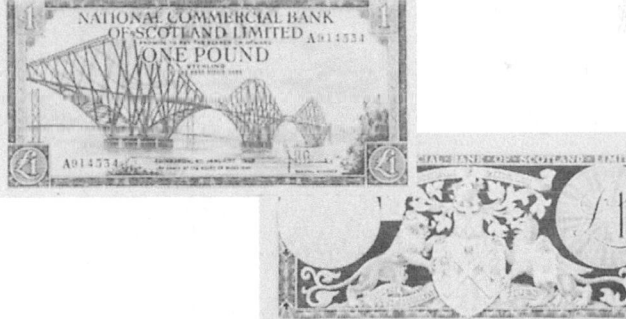

274 1 Pound   **VF UNC**
4.1.1968. Green on multicolor underprint. Forth Railway Bridge and road bridge.
Back: Arms at center, electronic sorting lines. Printer: BWC. 136x67mm.
  a. Issued note.   17.50   70.00
  s. Specimen.   —   160

275 5 Pounds   **VF UNC**
4.1.1968. Blue, red and green on multicolor underprint. Arms at lower center.
Back: Landscape with Edinburgh Castle, National Gallery; electronic sorting
marks. Printer: BWC.
  a. Issued note.   50.00   160
  s. Specimen.   —   225

275A 20 Pounds   **VF UNC**
1.6.1967. Red on multicolor underprint. Arms at lower right. Back: Bridge. Printer:
TDLR.
  a. Issued note.   4,000   6,000
  s. Specimen.   —   600

275B 100 Pounds   **VF UNC**
1.6.1967. Specimen. Purple on multicolor underprint. Arms at lower right. Back: —   1,500
Bridge. Printer: TDLR.

Royal Bank of Scotland
Later became the Royal Bank of Scotland Limited.

1875; 1887 Issue

319	20 Pounds	Fine	XF
	1877-1969. Blue and brown. Uniface.		
	a. Plate C. 1877-1911.	950	2,850
	b. Plate D. Yellow underprint. Imprint: W. & A. K. Johnston 1931-47.	600	1,400
	c. Plates E; F; G; H. Underprint without red. Imprint: W. & A. K. Johnston & G. W. Bacon Ltd. Both signatures printed 1947-66.	325	700

320	100 Pounds	Fine	XF
	1877-1969. Blue and red. Uniface.		
	a. Plate C. 1877-1918.	4,500	—
	b. Plates D; E. Yellow underprint. 1918-60.	1,250	3,000
	c. Plates F; G. Imprint: W. & A. K. Johnston & G. W. Bacon Ltd. Both signatures printed. 1960-66.	1,000	2,750

1952 Issue

323	5 Pounds	VF	UNC
	1952-63. Blue and red on yellow underprint. Like number 317 but reduced size. Uniface.		
	a. 2 signatures. Imprint: W. & A.K. Johnston Ltd. 2.1.1952-1.7.1953.	125	325
	b. 3 signatures. Imprint: W. & A. K. Johnston & G. W. Bacon Ltd. 1.7.1953-1.2.1954.	150	400
	c. 2 signatures. Imprint: W. & A. K. Johnston & G. W. Bacon. 1.4.1955-3.1.1963.	100	250

1955 Issue

324	1 Pound	VF	UNC
	1955-64. Dark blue on yellow and brown underprint. Signature W. R. Ballantyne with title: General Manager. 152x85mm.		
	a. Without engraver's name on back. 1.4.1955-1.11.1955.	40.00	125
	b. With engraver's name W. H. Egan upside down and in very small letters below the right hand bank building on back. 1.2.1956-1.7.1964.	30.00	80.00
	s. As a. Specimen.	—	—

1964 Issue

325	1 Pound	VF	UNC
	1964-67. Black and brown on yellow underprint. Like number 324, but 150 x 71mm.		
	a. Signature W. R. Ballantyne. 1.8.1964-1.6.1965.	32.50	85.00
	b. Signature G. P. Robertson. 2.8.1965-1.11.1967.	25.00	75.00
	s. As a. Specimen.	—	250

326	5 Pounds	VF	UNC
	1964-65. Dark blue, orange-brown and yellow. Like number 323, but 140 x 85mm. Uniface.		
	a. 2.11.1964. Signature W. R. Ballantyne & A. G. Campbell.	100	250
	b. 2.8.1965. Signature G. P. Robertson & A. G. Campbell.	100	250
	s1. As a. Specimen.	—	600
	s2. As b. Specimen.	—	275

1966; 1967 Issue

327	1 Pound	VF	UNC
	1.9.1967. Green on multicolor underprint. Portrait of D. Dale at left, bank arms at lower right. Back: Bank head office building at center and upper right. Watermark: D. Dale.		
	a. Issued note.	25.00	70.00
	s. Specimen.	—	260

328	5 Pounds	VF	UNC
	1.11.1966; 1.3.1967. Blue on multicolor underprint. Portrait of D. Dale at left, bank arms at lower right. Back: Bank head office building at center and upper right. Watermark: D. Dale.	75.00	200

Royal Bank of Scotland Limited

Formerly the Royal Bank of Scotland. Later became the Royal Bank of Scotland PLC.

1969 Issue

		VF	UNC
329	**1 Pound**		

19.3.1969. Green on multicolor underprint. Forth Road Bridge at left center, old Forth Railway bridge in background. Signature G. P. Robertson and J. B. Burke. Back: Arms at center right. Watermark: D. Dale. Printer: BWC.

	VF	UNC
a. Issued note.	25.00	60.00
s. Specimen.	—	180

		VF	UNC
330	**5 Pounds**		

19.3.1969. Blue on multicolor underprint. Arms at left. Signature G. P. Robertson and J. B. Burke. Back: Edinburgh Castle. Watermark: D. Dale. Printer: BWC.   75.00   200

		VF	UNC
331	**10 Pounds**		

19.3.1969. Brown on mjulticolor underprint. Arms at center. Signature G. P. Robertson and J. B. Burke. Back: Tay road bridge. Watermark: D. Dale. Printer: BWC.   125   450

		VF	UNC
332	**20 Pounds**		

19.3.1969. Purple on multicolor underprint. Signature G. P. Robertson and J. B. Burke. Back: Forth Road Bridge. Watermark: D. Dale. Printer: BWC.   150   550

		VF	UNC
333	**100 Pounds**		

19.3.1969. Red on multicolor underprint. Signature G. P. Robertson and J. B. Burke. Back: Forth Road Bridge. Watermark: D. Dale. Printer: BWC.

	VF	UNC
a. Issued note.	700	1,800
s. Specimen.	—	—

1970 Issue

		VF	UNC
334	**1 Pound**		

15.7.1970. Green on multicolor underprint. Forth Road Bridge at left center, old Forth Railway bridge in background. Signature; J. D. Durke. Dack: Arms at center right. Printer: BWC.

	VF	UNC
a. Issued note.	15.00	55.00
s. Specimen.	—	—

		VF	UNC
335	**5 Pounds**		

15.7.1970. Blue on multicolor underprint. Arms at left. Signature; J. B. Burke. Back: Edinburgh Castle. Printer: BWC.   65.00   175

1972 Issue

		VF	UNC
336	**1 Pound**		

5.1.1972-1.5.1981. Dark green on multicolor underprint. Arms at right. Back: Edinburgh Castle at left center. Watermark: A. Smith. Printer: BWC.

	VF	UNC
a. Issued note.	9.00	32.50
s. Specimen.	—	250

337 5 Pounds   VF   UNC

5.1.1972; 2.4.1973; 1.5.1975; 3.5.1976; 1.5.1979; 1.5.1980; 1.5.1981. Blue on multicolor underprint. Arms at right. Back: Culzean Castle at left center. Watermark: A. Smith. Printer: BWC.

a. Issued note.   35.00   100

s. Specimen.   —   260

338 10 Pounds   VF   UNC

5.1.1972; 1.3.1974; 15.12.1975; 2.5.1978; 10.1.1981. Brown on multicolor underprint. Arms at right. Back: Glamis Castle at left center. Watermark: A. Smith. Printer: BWC.

a. Issued note.   75.00   225

s. Specimen.   —   380

339 20 Pounds   VF   UNC

5.1.1972; 1.5.1981. Purple on multicolor underprint. Arms at right. Back: Brodick Castle. Watermark: A. Smith. Printer: BWC.   150   350

340 100 Pounds   VF   UNC

5.1.1972; 1.5.1979; 1.5.1981. Red on multicolor underprint. Arms at right. Back: Balmoral Castle. Watermark: A. Smith. Printer: BWC.

a. Issued note.   550   1,400

s. Specimen.   —   800

Royal Bank of Scotland PLC

Formerly the Royal Bank of Scotland Limited.

1982-86 Issues

REPLACEMENT NOTE

#341. Replacement note: Serial # prefix *Y/1*.

341 1 Pound   VF   UNC

1982-85. Dark green on multicolor underprint. Arms at right. Signature C. Winter. Back: Edinburgh Castle at left center. Watermark: A. Smith. Printer: BWC.

a. With sorting marks. 3.5.1982.   20.00   60.00

b. Without sorting marks. 1.10.1983; 4.1.1984; 3.1.1985.   10.00   30.00

341A 1 Pound   VF   UNC

1986. Dark green on multicolor underprint. Arms at right. Signature C. Winter. Back: Edinburgh Castle at left center. Watermark: A. Smith. Printer: TDLR.

a. Signature C. Winter. 1.5.1986.   10.00   30.00

b. Signature R. M. Maiden. 17.12.1986.   10.00   35.00

342 5 Pounds   VF   UNC

1982-86. Blue on multicolor underprint. Arms at right. Signature title varies. Back: Culzean Castle at left center. Watermark: A. Smith. Printer: BWC.

a. Signature C. M. Winter. With electronic sorting marks. 3.5.1982; 5.1.1983.   40.00   130

b. Without sorting marks. 4.1.1984.   40.00   125

c. Signature C. M. Winter title larger size. 3.1.1985.   40.00   130

d. Signature R. M. Maiden. 17.12.1986.   40.00   120

#342A *Deleted*. See #342d.

343 10 Pounds   VF   UNC

1982-86. Brown on multicolor underprint. Arms at right. Signature titile varies. Back: Glamis Castle at left center. Watermark: A. Smith. Printer: BWC.

a. Signature C. M. Winter. 3.5.1982; 4.1.1984; 3.1.1985.   65.00   200

b. Signature R. M. Maiden. 17.12.1986.   65.00   190

344 20 Pounds   VF   UNC

3.5.1982; 3.1.1985. Purple on multicolor underprint. Arms at right. Signature title varies. Back: Brodick Castle. Watermark: A. Smith. Printer: BWC.   125   325

345 100 Pounds   VF   UNC

3.5.1982; 3.1.1985. Red on multicolor underprint. Arms at right. Signature title varies. Back: Balmoral Castle. Watermark: A. Smith. Printer: BWC.   400   1,000

1987 Issue

346 1 Pound   VF   UNC

25.3.1987. Dark green and green on multicolor underprint. Lord Ilay at right. Back: Edinburgh Castle at left center. Watermark: Lord Ilay. Printer: TDLR.

a. Issued note   5.00   15.00

r. Replacement note. Serial # prefix: Z/1.   15.00   50.00

347 5 Pounds   VF   UNC

25.3.1987; 22.6.1988. Black and blue-black on multicolor underprint. Lord Ilay at right. Back: Culzean Castle at left center. Watermark: Lord Ilay. Printer: TDLR.

a. Issued note.   17.50   35.00

r. Replacement note. Serial # prefix: Z/1.   20.00   100

348   10 Pounds   VF   UNC

25.3.1987; 24.2.1988; 22.2.1989; 24.1.1990. Deep brown and brown on multicolor underprint. Lord Ilay at right. Signature right. M. Maiden. Back: Glamis Castle at left center. Watermark: Lord Ilay. Printer: TDLR.

a. Issued note	40.00	90.00
r. Replacement note. Serial # prefix: Z/1.	40.00	200

349   20 Pounds   VF   UNC

25.3.1987; 24.1.1990. Black and purple on multicolor underprint. Lord Ilay at right. Signature right. M. Maiden. Back: Brodick Castle at left center. Watermark. Lord Ilay. Printer: TDLR.   70.00   175

350   100 Pounds   VF   UNC

1987-. Red on multicolor underprint. Lord Ilay at right. Back: Balmoral Castle at left center. Watermark: Lord Ilay. Printer: TDLR. 170x96mm.

a. Signature R. M. Maiden, with title: *MANAGING DIRECTOR*. 25.3.1987; 24.1.1990.	300	700
b. Signature G. R. Mathewson, with title: *CHIEF EXECUTIVE*. 28.1.1992; 23.3.1994; 24.1.1996; 26.3.1997; 30.9.1998.	260	600
c. Signature G. R. Matthewson, with title: *GROUP CHIEF EXECUTIVE*. 30.3.1999.	FV	500
d. Signature Fred Goodwin. 27.6.2000.	FV	350

1988-92 Issue

#351-355 similar to #346-350, but reduced size. Replacement notes: Serial # prefix: Z/1.

351   1 Pound   VF   UNC

1988-. UV: left part of castle and central design fluoresce yellow. Dark green and green on multicolor underprint. Lord Ilay at right. Back: Edinburgh Castle. Watermark: Lord Ilay. Printer: TDLR. 128x65mm.

a. Signature R. M. Maiden with title: *MANAGING DIRECTOR*. 13.12.1988; 26.7.1989; 19.12.1990.	4.00	11.00
b. Signature C. Winter with title: *CHIEF EXECUTIVE*. 24.7.1991.	3.00	8.00
c. Signature G. R. Mathewson with title: *CHIEF EXECUTIVE*. 24.3.1992; 24.2.1993; 24.2.1994; 24.1.1996; 1.10.1997.	3.00	7.00
d. Signature G. R. Mathewson with title: *GROUP CHIEF EXECUTIVE*. 30.3.1999.	FV	6.00
e. Signature Fred Goodwin. 27.6.2000; 1.10.2001.	FV	5.00

352   5 Pounds   VF   UNC

1988-. Black and blue-black on multicolor underprint. Lord Ilay at right. Back: Culzean Castle at left center. Watermark: Lord Ilay. Printer: TDLR. 135x70mm.

a. Signature R. M. Maiden, with title: *MANAGING DIRECTOR*. 13.12.1988; 24.1.1990.	17.50	45.00
b. Signature G. R. Mathewson. with title: *CHIEF EXECUTITIVE*. 23.3.1994; 24.1.1996; 26.3.1997; 29.4.1998.	12.00	30.00
c. Signature G. R. Matthewson, with title: *GROUP CHIEF EXECUTIVE*. 30.3.1999.	15.00	35.00
d. Signature Fred Goodwin. 27.6.2000; 20.1.2005.	FV	17.50

353   10 Pounds   VF   UNC

1992 . Deep brown and brown on multicolor underprint. Lord Ilay at right. Signature right, M. Maiden. Back: Glamis Castle at left center. Watermark: Lord Ilay. Printer: TDLR. 142x75mm.

a. Signature G. R. Mathewson, with title: *CHIEF EXECUTIVE*. 28.1.1992; 7.5.1992; 24.2.1993; 23.3.1994.	FV	40.00
b. Signature Fred Goodwin, with title: *GROUP CHIEF EXECUTIVE*. 27.6.2000; 1.10.2001; 19.9.2006.	FV	35.00

354   20 Pounds   VF   UNC

1991-. Black and purple on multicolor underprint. Lord Ilay at right. Signature right, M. Maiden. Back: Brodick Castle at left center. Watermark: Lord Ilay. Printer: TDLR. 150x81mm.

a. Signature C. Winter with title: *CHIEF EXECUTIVE*. 27.3.1991.	45.00	120
b. Signature G. R. Mathewson. 28.1.1992; 24.2.1993; 26.3.1997; 29.4.1998.	45.00	105
c. Signature G. R. Mathewson, with title: *GROUP CHIEF EXECUTIVE*. 30.3.1999.	45.00	110
d. Signature Fred Goodwin. 27.6.2000; 19.9.2006.	FV	70.00

#355 not assigned.

1992 Commemorative Issue

#356, European Summit at Edinburgh, Dec. 1992

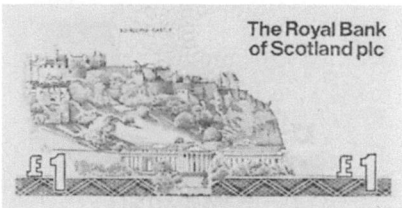

356 **1 Pound**   **VF UNC**
8.12.1992. Dark green and green on multicolor underprint. Like number 351c but with additional blue-violet overprint containing commemorative inscription at left. Serial # prefix: EC. 128x65mm.
     a. Issued note.   FV   7.00
     s. Specimen.   —   180

1994 Regular Issue

#357, Replacement note: Serial # prefix *Y/1*.

357 **1 Pound**   **VF UNC**
23.3.1994. Dark green and green on multicolor underprint. Lord Ilay at right. Back: 20.00   60.00
Edinburgh Castle at left center. Printer: BABN. 128x65mm.

1994 Commemorative Issue

#358, Centennial - Death of Robert Louis Stevenson

358 **1 Pound**   **VF UNC**
3.12.1994. Dark green and green on multicolor underprint. Commemorative overprint in watermark area on #351c. Serial number prefix: RLS. Back: Portrait R. L. Stevenson and images of his life and works. 128x65mm.
     a. Issued note.   3.00   7.50
     s. Specimen.   —   180

1997 Commemorative Issue

#359, 150th Anniversary - Birth of Alexander Graham Bell, 1847-1997

359 **1 Pound**   **VF UNC**
3.3.1997. UV: Back central design fluoresces yellow and green. Dark green and   FV   6.50
green on multicolor underprint. Overprint telephone, text and OVD on watermark area of face like #351c. Serial number prefix: AGB. Back: Portrait Alexander Graham Bell and images of his life and work. 128x65mm.

1999 Commemorative Issue

#360, Opening of the Scottish Parliament

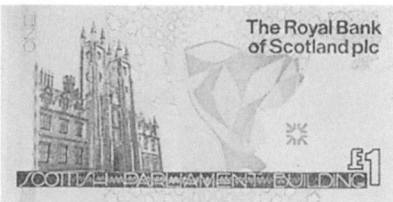

360 **1 Pound**   **VF UNC**
12.5.1999. UV: central design fluoresces yellow. Dark green on multicolor   FV   6.00
underprint. Overprint Scottish Parliament text at left at watermark area of face like #351c. Serial number prefix: SP. Back: Scottish Parliament building. 128x65mm.

2000 Commemorative Issue

#361, Birth centennial of the Queen Mother

361 **20 Pounds**   **VF UNC**
4.8.2000. Black and purple on multicolor underprint. Gold crown with inscription   FV   70.00
beneath at left. Serial number prefix: QETQM. Back: Queen Mother. 150x80mm.

361A **100 Pounds**   **VF UNC**
4.8.2000. Special presentation item for the Queen Mother. Black and purple on   —   —
multicolor underprint.

2002 Commemorative Issue

#362, Queen's Golden Jubilee. Printer: TDLR.

362 **5 Pounds**   **VF UNC**
6.2.2002. Black and dark blue on multicolor underprint. Gold crown overprint   FV   25.00
at left. Back: 1952 and 2002 portraits of Queen Elizabeth II. Printer: TDLR. 135x70mm.

2004 Commemorative Issue

#363 250th Anniversary of St. Andrews Royal & Ancient Golf Club.

363 **5 Pounds**   **VF UNC**
14.5.2004. Black and blue-black on multicolor underprint. Similar to number 352   FV   30.00
but shield and 1754 at left. Serial number prefix: *R&A*. Back: Tom Morris and images of St. Andrews. 135x70mm.

Note: Also available in a presentation folder.

2005 Commemorative Issues

500th Anniversary, College of Surgeons.

364 5 Pounds — VF UNC
1.7.2005. Commemorative overprint at left. Serial number prefix RCS. 135x70mm. — FV 17.50
#365 Jack Nicholas' retirement from golf commemorative. RBS's sponsorship of the British Open at St. Andrew's.

365 5 Pounds — VF UNC
14.7.2005. Commemorative overprint at left. Serial number prefix JWN. Back: Jack Nicklaus. 135x70mm. — FV 19.00
#366 New Bank Neadquarters at Gogarburn.

366 50 Pounds — VF UNC
14.9.2005. Serial number prefix RBS. Back: New Bank headquarters at Gogarburn. 155x85mm. — FV 200

2005 Regular Issue

367 50 Pounds — VF UNC
14.9.2005. Back: Inverness Castle. 155x85mm. — FV 150

2012 Commemorative Issue

368 10 Pounds — VF UNC
2012. Deep brown and tan on multicolor underprint. Lord Ilay at right. Back: Four portraits of Queen Elizabeth II, crowned text at right. 142x76mm. — FV 60.00

2015 Commemorative Issue

369 5 Pounds — VF UNC
2015. Polymer. Smaller size than paper note. 125th anniversary of the Forth Bridge. Prefix FB. 137x70mm. — FV 27.50

COLLECTOR SERIES

Clydesdale Bank Plc

1996 Issue

CS1 1996 5 Pounds — Mkt. Value
Matched serial # (prefix R/B 0 - R/B 3) set #224a-224d. — 90.00

SERBIA

Serbia, a former inland Balkan kingdom (now a federated republic with Montenegro) has an area of 34,116 sq. mi. (88,361 sq. km.) Capital: Belgrade. The Kingdom of Serbs, Croats, and Slovenes was formed in 1918; its name was changed to Yugoslavia in 1929. Various paramilitary bands resisted Nazi Germany's occupation and division of Yugoslavia from 1941 to 1945, but fought each other and ethnic opponents as much as the invaders. The military and political movement headed by Josip Tito (Partisans) took full control of Yugoslavia when German and Croatian separatist forces were defeated in 1945. Although Communist, Tito's government and his successors (he died in 1980) managed to steer their own path between the Warsaw Pact nations and the West for the next four and a half decades. In 1989, Slobodan Milosevic became president of the Serbian Republic and his ultranationalist calls for Serbian domination led to the violent breakup of Yugoslavia along ethnic lines. In 1991, Croatia, Slovenia, and Macedonia declared independence, followed by Bosnia in 1992. The remaining republics of Serbia and Montenegro declared a new Federal Republic of Yugoslavia in April 1992 and under Milosevic's leadership, Serbia led various military campaigns to unite ethnic Serbs in neighboring republics into a "Greater Serbia." These actions led to Yugoslavia being ousted from the UN in 1992, but Serbia continued its - ultimately unsuccessful - campaign until signing the Dayton Peace Accords in 1995. Milosevic kept tight control over Serbia and eventually became president of the FRY in 1997. In 1998, an ethnic Albanian insurgency in the formerly autonomous Serbian province of Kosovo provoked a Serbian counterinsurgency campaign that resulted in massacres and massive expulsions of ethnic Albanians living in Kosovo. The Serbian government's rejection of a proposed international settlement led to NATO's bombing of Serbia in the spring of 1999 and to the eventual withdrawal of Serbian military and police forces from Kosovo in June 1999. UNSC Resolution 1244 in June 1999 authorized the stationing of a NATO-led force (KFOR) in Kosovo to provide a safe and secure environment for the region's ethnic communities, created a UN interim Administration Mission in Kosovo (UNMIK) to foster self-governing institutions, and reserved the issue of Kosovo's final status for an unspecified date in the future. In 2001, UNMIK promulgated a constitutional framework that allowed Kosovo to establish institutions of self-government and led to Kosovo's first parliamentary election. FRY elections in September 2000 led to the ouster of Milosevic and installed Vojislav Kostunica as president. A broad coalition of democratic reformist parties known as DOS (the Democratic Opposition of Serbia) was subsequently elected to parliament in December 2000 and took control of the government. DOS arrested Milosevic in 2001 and allowed for him to be tried in The Hague for crimes against humanity. (Milosevic died in March 2006 before the completion of his trial.) In 2001, the country's suspension from the UN was lifted. In 2003, the FRY became Serbia and Montenegro, a loose federation of the two republics with a federal level parliament. Widespread violence predominantly targeting ethnic Serbs in Kosovo in March 2004 caused the international community to open negotiations on the future status of Kosovo in January 2006. In May 2006, Montenegro invoked its right to secede from the federation and - following a successful referendum - it declared itself an independent nation on 3 June 2006. Two days later, Serbia declared that it was the successor state to the union of Serbia and Montenegro. A new Serbian constitution was approved in October 2006 and adopted the following month. After 15 months of inconclusive negotiations mediated by the UN and four months of further inconclusive negotiations mediated by the US, EU, and Russia, on 17 February 2008, the UNMIK-administered province of Kosovo declared itself independent of Serbia.

MONETARY SYSTEM:
1 Dinar = 100 Para

FEDERATION OF SERBIA AND MONTENEGRO

Narodna Banka Srbija

NATIONAL BANK OF SERBIA

2003 Issue

40 50 Dinara — VF UNC
2005. Purple and tan on multicolor underprint. Stevan Stojanovic Mokranjac at left center, violin, keyboard and music score at center. Back: Mokranjac standing, scores and linear art from Gospel of Miroslav illuminated manuscript. 139x66mm.
a. Issued note. — FV 2.00
s. Specimen. — — —

41   100 Dinara   VF UNC

2003; 2004. Light and dark blue on multicolor underprint. NikolaTesla at left. Back:
Detail from theTesla electromagnetic induction engine at center, Tesla at left on
vertical format. 143x68mm.

$$T = \frac{Wb}{m^2}$$

a. 2003.	FV	4.00
b. 2004.	FV	4.00
s. Specimen.		

42   200 Dinara   VF UNC

2005. Black and blue on tan underprint. Nadezda Petrovic at left center, Petrovic
sculpture and Gracanica monastery at center. Back: Petrovic photo as WWI
nurse, Gracanica monastery and painting detail on vertical format. 147x70mm.

a. Issued note.	FV	8.50
s. Specimen.	—	—

43   500 Dinara   VF UNC

2004. Blue and green on multicolor underprint. 147x69mm.

a. Issued note.	FV	17.50
s. Specimen.	—	—

44   1000 Dinara   VF UNC

2003; 2005. Red on multicolor underprint. Dorde Vajfert at left. Back: Vajfert
seated, details of National Bank's interior on vertical format. 151x72mm.

a. Signature Mladjan Dinkic.	FV	35.00
b. Signature Kori Udovicki.	FV	30.00
s. Specimen.	—	—

45   5000 Dinara   VF UNC

2003. Green on multicolor underprint. Slibodan Jovanovic at left. Back: Jovanovic
and Parliament building views on vertical format. 151x76mm.

a. Signature Mladjan Dinkic	FV	150
b. Signature Kori Udovicki. Expected new issue.	—	—
s. Specimen.	—	—

2006 Issue

46   10 Dinara   VF UNC

2006. Black and tan on multicolor underprint. Vuk Stefanovic Karadzic at left.
Back: First Slavic Congress, Prague, 1848. 131x62mm.

a. 2006.	FV	0.75
s. Specimen.	—	15.00

47   20 Dinara   **VF UNC**
2006. Green on multicolor underprint. Petar II Petrovic Njegos at left. Back:
Mausoleum Statue. 135x64mm.

a. 2006.		FV	0.75
s. Specimen.		FV	15.00

49   100 Dinara   **VF UNC**
2006. Light and dark blue on multicolor underprint. Nikola Tesla at left. Back:
Details from Tesla's electromagnetic induction machine. 143x68mm.

a. 2006.		FV	4.00
s. Specimen.		—	25.00

51   500 Dinara   **VF UNC**
2007. Olive and green on multicolor underprint. Jovan Cvijic at left. Back: Cvijic
and ethnographic motifs. 147x70mm.

a. 2007.		FV	17.50
s. Specimen.		—	50.00

52   1000 Dinara   **VF UNC**
2006. Rose on multicolor underprint. Dorde Vajfert at left. 151x72mm.

a. 2006.		FV	35.00
s. Specimen.		—	100

53   5000 Dinara   **VF UNC**
2010. Green and lilac on multicolor underprint. Slobodan Javanovic at left, female
sculpture at center. Back: Interior of Parliament, Jovanovic wearing hat and coat.
155x76mm.

a. 2010.		FV	150

2011 Issue

54   10 Dinara   **VF UNC**
2011, 2013. Brown and tan on multicolor underprint. Vuk Stefanovic Karadzic at
left. Back: First Slavic Congress, Prague, 1848. Vertical format. 131x62mm.

a. 2011.		FV	0.75
b. 2013.		FV	0.75
s. Specimen. Red overprint.		—	50.00

55   20 Dinara   **VF UNC**
2011; 2013. Green on multicolor underprint. Petar II Petrovic Njegos at left. Back:
Mausoleum Statue.

a. 2011.		FV	1.00
b. 2013.		FV	1.00
s. Specimen. Red overprint.		—	50.00

56   50 Dinara   **VF UNC**
2011; 2014. Violet and tan on multicolor underprint. Stevan Stojanovic Mokranjac
at left. Back: Photograph of Mokranjac.

a. 2011.		FV	2.00
b. 2014. Signature of Jorgovanka Tabakovic.		FV	2.00
s. Specimen. Red overprint.		—	50.00

57   100 Dinara   **VF UNC**
2012; 2013.

a. 2012. Signature Dejan Soskic.		FV	5.00
b. 2013.		FV	5.00

58   200 Dinara   **VF UNC**
2011; 2013. Brown and purple on multicolor underprint. Nadezda Petrovic at left.
Back: Gracanica Monastery

a. 2011.		FV	8.00
b. 2013.		FV	8.00
s. Specimen. Red overprint.		—	50.00

59   500 Dinara   **VF UNC**
2011; 2012. 147x69mm.

a. 2011.		FV	17.50
b. 2012.		FV	17.50
r. Replacement note. Serial # prefix ZA.		FV	30.00

60   1000 Dinara   **VF UNC**
2011; 2014.

a. 2011.		FV	35.00
b. 2014. Signature Jorgovanka Tabakovic.		FV	35.00
r. Replacement note. Serial # prefix ZA.		FV	50.00

61   2000 Dinara   **VF UNC**
2011; 2012. Mulutin Milankovic at left. 155x74mm.

a. 2011.		FV	75.00
b. 2012.		FV	70.00

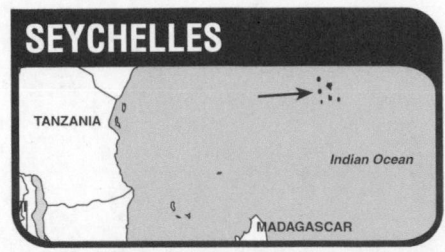

SEYCHELLES

The Republic of Seychelles, an archipelago of 85 granite and coral islands situated in the Indian Ocean 600 miles (965 km.) northeast of Madagascar, has an area of 156 sq. mi. (455 sq. km.) and a population of 82,400. Among these islands are the Aldabra Islands, the Farquhar Group, and Ile Desroches, which the United Kingdom ceded to the Seychelles upon its independence. Capital: Victoria, on Mahe. The economy is based on fishing, a plantation system of agriculture and tourism. Copra, cinnamon and vanilla are exported. A lengthy struggle between France and Great Britain for the islands ended in 1814, when they were ceded to the latter. Independence came in 1976. Socialist rule was brought to a close with a new constitution and free elections in 1993. President France-Albert Rene, who had served since 1977, was re-elected in 2001, but stepped down in 2004. Vice President James Michel took over the presidency and in July 2006 was elected to a new five-year term.

RULERS:
British to 1976

MONETARY SYSTEM:
1 Rupee = 100 Cents

BRITISH ADMINISTRATION
Government of Seychelles
1954 Issue

11	**5 Rupees**	**VF**	**UNC**
	1954; 1960. Lilac and green. Portrait Queen Elizabeth II in profile at right. Signature varieties. Back: Denomination. Printer: TDLR. 160x98mm.		
	a. 1.8.1954.	85.00	500
	b. 1.8.1960.	75.00	450

12	**10 Rupees**	**VF**	**UNC**
	1954-67. Green and red. Portrait Queen Elizabeth II in profile at right. Signature varieties. Back: Denomination. Printer: TDLR. 157x98mm.		
	a. 1.8.1954.	225	1,750
	b. 1.8.1960.	150	1,500
	c. 1.5.1963.	125	1,250
	d. 1.1.1967.	125	1,250

13	**50 Rupees**	**VF**	**UNC**
	1954-67. Black. Portrait Queen Elizabeth II in profile at right. Signature varieties. Back: Denomination. Printer: TDLR.		
	a. 1.8.1954.	500	4,500
	b. 1.8.1960.	400	3,750
	c. 1.5.1963.	400	3,500
	d. 1.1.1967.	400	3,500

1968 Issue

14	**5 Rupees**	**VF**	**UNC**
	1.1.1968. Dark brown on multicolor underprint. Queen Elizabeth II at right. Various signature varieties. Back: Seychelles black parrot at left. Watermark: Black parrot's head.		
	a. Issued note.	45.00	150
	s. Specimen.	—	—
	ct. Color trial. Blue-green on multicolor underprint.	—	575

15	**10 Rupees**	**VF**	**UNC**
	1968; 1974. Light blue on multicolor underprint. Queen Elizabeth II at right. Various signature varieties. Back: Sea tortoise at left center. Letters *SCUM* discernible beneath tortoise's rear flipper at left. Watermark: Black parrot's head.		
	a. 1.1.1968.	125	525
	b. 1.1.1974.	100	400
	s. As a. Specimen.	—	—

16   20 Rupees

1968-74. Purple on multicolor underprint. Queen Elizabeth II at right. Various signature varieties. Back: Bridled tern at left center. Watermark: Black parrot's head.

		VF	UNC
a. 1.1.1968.		185	800
b. 1.1.1971.		100	675
c. 1.1.1974.		140	625
s. As c. Specimen.		—	—

17   50 Rupees

1968-73. Olive on multicolor underprint. Queen Elizabeth II at right. Various
signature varieties. Back: Sailing ship at left. Word *SEX* discernible in trees at
right. Watermark: Black parrot's head.

		VF	UNC
a. 1.1.1968.		425	1,650
b. 1.1.1969.		550	2,250
c. 1.10.1970.		450	1,750
d. 1.1.1972.		225	900
e. 1.8.1973.		250	1,000
s. As d. Specimen.		—	—
ct. Color trial. Green on multicolor underprint.		—	2,350

18   100 Rupees

1968-75. Red on multicolor underprint. Queen Elizabeth II at right. Various signature varieties. Back: Land turtles at left center. Watermark: Black parrot's head.

		VF	UNC
a. 1.1.1968.		1,400	5,000
b. 1.1.1969.		2,000	7,000
c. 1.1.1972.		1,250	4,500
d. 1.8.1973.		1,200	4,000
e. 1.6.1975.		1,200	4,000
s. Specimen.		—	—
ct. Color trial. Blue on multicolor underprint.		—	6,000

REPUBLIC

Republic of Seychelles

1976; 1977 ND Issue

19   10 Rupees

ND (1976). Dark blue and blue on multicolor underprint. President J. R. Mancham
at right, seashell at lower left. Back: Hut with boats and cliffs. Watermark: Black
parrot's head.

		VF	UNC
a. Issued note.		5.00	17.50
s. Specimen.		—	175

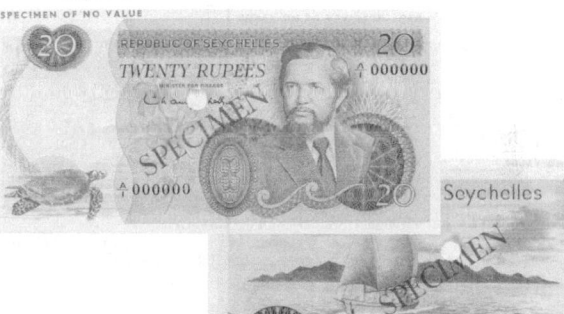

20   20 Rupees

ND (1977). Purple on multicolor underprint. President J. R. Mancham at right, Sea
Tortoise at lower left. Back: Sailboat at left center. Watermark: Black parrot's head.

		VF	UNC
a. Issued note.		10.00	30.00
s. Specimen.		—	125

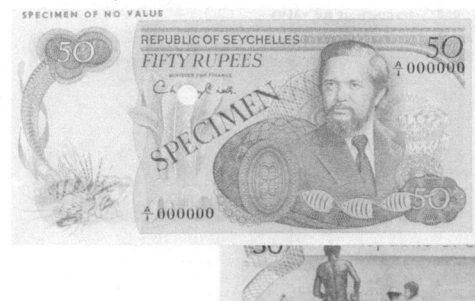

21   50 Rupees

ND (1977). . Olive on multicolor underprint. President J. R. Mancham at right, fish
at lower left. Back: Fishermen at left center. Watermark: Black parrot's head.

		VF	UNC
a. Issued note.		25.00	80.00
s. Specimen.		—	165

22 100 Rupees
ND (1977). Red and multicolor. President J. R. Mancham at right, Fairy Terns at
lower left. Back: Dock area and islands. Watermark: Black parrot's head.

		VF	UNC
a. Issued note.		40.00	150
s. Specimen.		—	235

Seychelles Monetary Authority
1979 ND Issue

23 10 Rupees
ND (1979). Blue, green and light red on multicolor underprint. Red-footed booby
at center. Back: Girl picking flowers in vertical format. Watermark: Black parrot's
head.

		VF	UNC
a. Issued note.		4.00	15.00
s. Specimen.		—	125

24 25 Rupees
ND (1979). Brown, purple and gold on multicolor underprint. Coconuts at center.
Back: Man and basket in vertical format. Watermark: Black parrot's head.

		VF	UNC
a. Issued note.		10.00	25.00
s. Specimen.		—	125

25 50 Rupees
ND (1979). Olive-green, brown and lilac on multicolor underprint. Turtle at center.
Back: Buildings and palm trees in vertical format. Watermark: Black parrot's head.

		VF	UNC
a. Issued note.		20.00	55.00
s. Specimen.		—	150

26 100 Rupees
ND (1979). Red and light blue on multicolor underprint. Tropical fish at center.
Back: Man with tools, swordfish in vertical format. Watermark: Black parrot's head.

		VF	UNC
a. Issued note.		40.00	120
s. Specimen.		—	250

Note: A shipment of #26 was lost at sea; only serial # A000,001 - A300,000 are valid numbers for
exchange.

1980 ND Issue

27 100 Rupees   VF   UNC
ND (1980). Brown and light blue on multicolor underprint. Tropical fish at center.
Back: Man with tools, swordfish in vertical format. Watermark: Black parrot's head.
    a. Issued note.   35.00 90.00
    s. Specimen, punch hole cancelled.   —   175

Central Bank of Seychelles
1983 ND Issue

28 10 Rupees   VF   UNC
ND (1983). Blue, green and light red on multicolor underprint. Red-footed booby
at center, new bank name and signature title. Back: Girl picking flowers in vertical
format. Watermark: Black parrot's head.
    a. Issued note.   FV   7.00
    s. Specimen.   125

29 25 Rupees   VF   UNC
ND (1983). Brown, purple and gold on multicolor underprint. Coconuts at center,
new bank name and signature title. Back: Man and basket in vertical format.
Watermark: Black parrot's head.
    a. Issued note.   FV   17.00
    s. Specimen.   —   125

30 50 Rupees   VF   UNC
ND (1983). Olive-green, brown and lilac on multicolor underprint. Turtle at center,
new bank name and signature title. Back: Buildings and palm trees in vertical
format. Watermark: Black parrot's head.
    a. Issued note.   FV   35.00
    s. Specimen.   —   150

31 100 Rupees   VF   UNC
ND (1983). Brown and light blue on multicolor underprint. Tropical fish at center,
new bank name and signature title. Back: Man with tools, swordfish in vertical
format. Watermark: Black parrot's head.
    a. Issued note.   FV   65.00
    s. Specimen.   —   175

Labank Santral Sesel
Central Bank of Seychelles
1989 ND Issue

32 10 Rupees   VF   UNC
ND (1989). Blue-black and deep blue-green on multicolor underprint. Boy Scouts   FV   7.00
at lower left, image of man with flags and broken chain at right, bank at center, flying fish at left and center right. Back: Local people dancing to drummer at center.
Watermark: Black parrot's head.

33 25 Rupees   VF   UNC
ND (1989). Purple on multicolor underprint. Two men with coconuts at lower left,   FV   16.00
boy near palms at upper right, bank at center, flying fish at left and center right.
Back: Primitive ox-drawn farm equipment. Watermark: Black parrot's head.

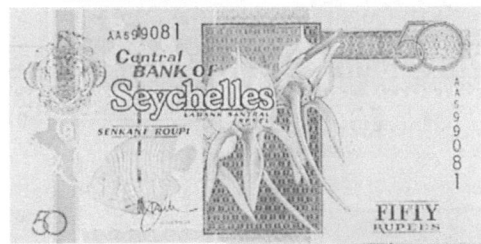

37　25 Rupees　　　　　　　　　　　　　　　　　VF　UNC
ND (1998). Purple, violet and blue-violet on multicolor underprint. *Wrights gardenia* flower at center, Lion fish at lower left, arms at upper left. Ascending size serial number. Back: Cowry shells at upper left, Bi-Centennary monument at lower left, coconut crab at center, Seychelles blue Pigeon at right. Watermark: Sea Turtle. 150x75mm.　　FV　14.00

34　50 Rupees　　　　　　　　　　　　　　　　　VF　UNC
ND (1989). Dark green and brown on multicolor underprint. Two men in boat, Seychelles man at lower left, prow of boat in geometric outline at upper right, bank at center, flying fish at left and center right. Back: Lesser noddy at lower left, fishermen with nets at center, modern cargo ships at right. Watermark: Black parrot's head.　　FV　30.00

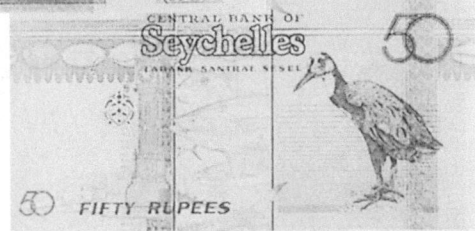

38　50 Rupees　　　　　　　　　　　　　　　　　VF　UNC
ND (1998). Dark green, deep olive-green and brown on multicolor underprint. *Paille en Que* orchids at center, Angel fish at lower left, arms at upper left. Ascending size serial number. Back: Cowry shells at upper left. Clock tower, autos at lower left, Yellow fin tuna at center, Flightless white throated rail or tiomitio at right. Watermark: Sea Turtle. 150x75mm.　　FV　30.00

35　100 Rupees　　　　　　　　　　　　　　　　VF　UNC
ND (1989). Red and brown on multicolor underprint. Men in ox-cart at lower left, girl with shell at upper right, bank at center, flying fish at left and center right. Back: Building at center. Watermark: Black parrot's head.　　FV　55.00

1998 ND Issue

39　100 Rupees　　　　　　　　　　　　　　　　VF　UNC
ND (1998). Red, brown-orange and violet on multicolor underprint. Pitcher plant at center, Vielle Babone Cecile fish at lower left, arms at upper left. Ascending size serial number. Back: Cowry shells at upper left, shoreline at lower left, Bridled terns at center, giant land tortoise at lower right. Watermark: Sea Turtle. 150x75mm.　　FV　47.50

2001 ND Issue

39A　50 Rupees　　　　　　　　　　　　　　　　VF　UNC
ND (2004). Silver foil impression of sailfish added at top right.　　FV　30.00

40　100 Rupees　　　　　　　　　　　　　　　　VF　UNC
ND (2001). Red, brown-orange and violet on multicolor underprint. Pitcher plant at center, Vielle Babone Cecile fish at lower left. Gold foil impression of sailfish at top right. Signature varieties. Back: Cowry shells at top left, shoreline at lower left, Bridled terns at center, giant land tortoise at lower right. 150x75mm.　　FV　45.00

36　10 Rupees　　　　　　　　　　　　　　　　　VF　UNC
ND (1998; 2010). Deep blue, dark green and green on multicolor underprint. *Coco-de-Mer* palm at center, black-spotted trigger fish at lower left, arms at upper left. Ascending size serial number. Back: Cowry shells at upper left, Coco-de-Mer palm fruit at lower left, FairyTerns at center, Hawksbill turtle at lower right. Watermark: Sea Turtle. 150x75mm.
　　a. Signature 1.　　　　　　　　　　　　　　　FV　5.00
　　b. Signature 2.　　　　　　　　　　　　　　　FV　5.00

41   500 Rupees   **VF   UNC**
ND (2005). Brown and red orange on tan and multicolor underprint. *Coco de Mer*   FV   150
fish. Gold foin sailfish at top right. Back: Owl at right. 150x75mm.

2011 ND Issue

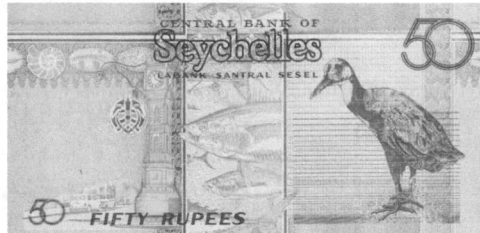

42   50 Rupees   **VF   UNC**
2011 Dark green and lavender on multicolor underprint. Paile en Que orchids at   FV   25.00
center, angel fish at lower left. Back: Yellowfin tuna at center, flightless bird at
right.

43   100 Rupees   **VF   UNC**
2011; 2013. Rose on multicolor underprint. Pitcher plant at center, Vielle Babone
Cecile fish at lower left. Back: Brided terns at center, giant land tortoise at right.
    a. 2011.   FV   47.50
    b. 2013.   FV   47.50

44   500 Rupees   **VF   UNC**
2011 Brown and red orange on multicolor underprint. Coco de Mer at center, foil   FV   150
sailfish at top right. Back: Owl at right.

SIERRA LEONE

The Republic of Sierra Leone, a British Commonwealth nation located in western Africa between Guinea and Liberia, has an area of 71,740 sq. km. and a population of 6.29 million. Capital: Freetown. The economy is predominantly agricultural but mining contributes significantly to export revenues. Diamonds, iron ore, palm kernels, cocoa and coffee are exported. Democracy is slowly being reestablished after the civil war from 1991 to 2002 that resulted in tens of thousands of deaths and the displacement of more than 2 million people (about one-third of the population). The military, which took over full responsibility for security following the departure of UN peacekeepers at the end of 2005, is increasingly developing as a guarantor of the country's stability. The armed forces remained on the sideline during the 2007 presidential election, but still look to the UN Integrated Office in Sierra Leone (UNIOSIL) - a civilian UN mission - to support efforts to consolidate peace. The new government's priorities include furthering development, creating jobs, and stamping out endemic corruption.

RULERS:
British to 1971

MONETARY SYSTEM:
1 Leone = 100 Cents
1 Pound = 20 Shillings

REPUBLIC

Bank of Sierra Leone

1964 ND Issue

1   1 Leone   **VF   UNC**
ND (1964-70). Green on multicolor underprint. 300-Year old cottonwood tree and
court building at left. Signature varieties. Back: Diamond mining at the city of
Hangha. Watermark: Lion's head. Printer: TDLR.
    a. ND (1964). Prefix A/1-A/6.   12.50   65.00
    b. ND (1969). Prefix A/7-A/8.   18.50   85.00
    c. ND (1970). Prefix A/9-A/12.   7.50   45.00
    s. As a. Specimen.   —   —
#2d replacement notes: Serial # prefix Z1.

2   2 Leones   **VF   UNC**
ND (1964-70). Red on multicolor underprint. 300-Year old cottonwood tree and
court building at left. Signature varieties. Back: Village scene. Watermark: Lion's
head. Printer: TDLR.
    a. ND (1964). Prefix B/1-B/21.   15.00   60.00
    b. ND (1967). Prefix B/22-B/25.   17.50   85.00
    c. ND (1969). Prefix B/26-B/30.   17.50   85.00
    d. ND (1970). Prefix B/31-B/41.   15.00   70.00
    s. As a. Specimen.   —   —

3 5 Leones VF UNC
ND (1964). Purple on multicolor underprint. 300-Year old cottonwood tree and
court building at left. Signature varieties. Prefix C/1. Back: Dockside at Freetown
at center right with boats in harbor. Watermark: Lion's head. Printer: TDLR.
a. Issued note. 75.00 450
s. Specimen. — —

1974-80 Issue

#4-8 Replacement notes: Serial # prefix Z/1.

4 50 Cents VF UNC
ND; 1979-84. . Dark brown on multicolor underprint. President S. Stevens at left,
arms at upper left, flowers in underprint at right. Back: Central Bank building at
center. Printer: TDLR.
a. ND (1972). Prefix D/1-D/2. 2.00 6.00
b. ND (1974). Prefix D/3-D/5. 1.50 4.00
c. Prefix D/6-D/8. 1.7.1979. 1.00 3.00
d. Prefix D/9; D/10. 1.7.1981. 0.50 1.50
e. 4.8.1984. 0.25 0.75
s. As a. Specimen, without prefix.

5 1 Leone VF UNC
1974-84. Olive-green and dark green on multicolor underprint. President S.
Stevens at left. Back: Central Bank building at center right, arms at upper right.
Watermark: Lion's head. Printer: TDLR.
a. Prefix A/1-A/7. 19.4.1974. 2.25 7.50
b. Prefix A/8-A/12. 1.1.1978. 4.00 10.00
c. Prefix A/13-A/17. 1.3.1980. 1.00 4.00
d. Prefix A/18-A/26. 1.7.1981. 0.50 2.00
e. 4.8.1984. 0.50 1.00

6 2 Leones VF UNC
1974-85. Red, deep red-orange and dark brown on multicolor underprint. President S. Stevens at left. Back: Central Bank building at center right, arms at upper
right. Watermark: Lion's head. Printer: TDLR.
a. Prefix B/1-B/20. 19.4.1974. 3.50 10.00
b. Prefix B/21-B/22. 1.1.1978. 15.00 65.00
c. Prefix B/23-B/27. 1.7.1978. 4.00 12.50
d. Prefix B/28-B/31. 1.7.1979. 2.00 7.50
e. Prefix B/32-B/37. 1.5.1980. 2.00 7.00
f. 1.7.1983. 0.75 3.00
g. 4.8.1984. 0.45 1.25
h. 4.8.1985. 0.45 1.25

7 5 Leones VF UNC
1975-85. Purple and blue-black on multicolor underprint. President S. Stevens at
left, plant leaves at center. Back: Parliament building at center right, arms at upper
right. Watermark: Lion's head. Printer: TDLR.
a. Prefix C/1. 4.8.1975. 10.00 35.00
b. Prefix C/2. 1.7.1978. 7.00 25.00
c. Prefix C/3. 1.3.1980. 4.00 12.50
d. Prefix C/4-C/6. 1.7.1981. 3.00 7.50
e. 19.4.1984. 1.00 3.50
f. 4.8.1984. 1.00 3.50
g. 4.8.1985. 1.00 3.25

8 10 Leones VF UNC
1980; 1984. Blue-gray, black and blue-green on multicolor underprint. President
S. Stevens at left. Back: Dredging operation at center right, arms at upper right.
Watermark: Lion's head. Printer: TDLR.
a. 1.7.1980. Prefix E/1-E/4. 4.00 12.50
b. 19.4.1984. 1.00 3.00
c. 4.8.1984. 1.00 3.00

1980 Commemorative Issue

**#9-13, Commemorating The Organisation of African Unity Conference in
Freetown**

Note: #9-13 were prepared in special booklets (1800 sets).

9 50 Cents VF UNC
1.7.1980. Dark brown on multicolor underprint. President S. Stevens at left, arms 4.00 15.00
at upper left, flowers in underprint at right. Back: Central Bank building at center.
Printer: TDLR.

10 1 Leone VF UNC
1.7.1980. Olive-green and dark green on multicolor underprint. President S. 5.00 15.00
Stevens at left, date below overprint. Back: Central Bank building at center right,
arms at upper right. Printer: TDLR.

11   2 Leones

	VF	UNC
1.7.1980. Red, deep red-orange and dark brown on multicolor underprint. President S. Stevens at left, date below overprint. Back: Central Bank building at center right, arms at upper right. Printer: TDLR.	7.50	20.00

12   5 Leones

	VF	UNC
1.7.1980. Purple and blue-black on multicolor underprint. President S. Stevens at left, plant leaves at center, date below overprint. Back: Parliament building at center, arms at upper right Printer: TDLR.	7.50	22.50

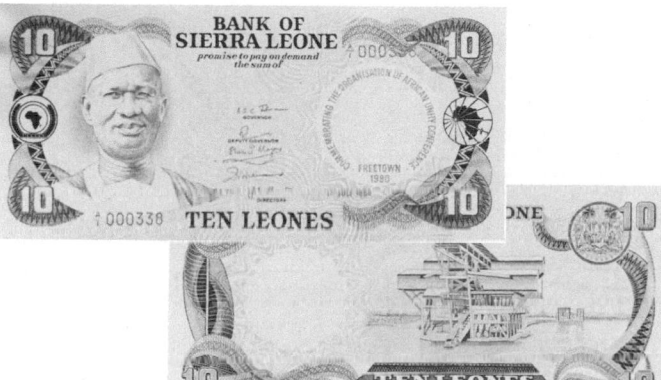

13   10 Leones

	VF	UNC
1.7.1980. Blue-gray, black and blue-green on multicolor underprint. President S. Stevens at left, date below overprint. Back: Dredging operation at center right, arms at upper right. Printer: TDLR.	10.00	30.00

1982 Issue

14   20 Leones

	VF	UNC
1982; 1984. UV: Bank name, value and crest fluoresce orange. Brown, red and green on multicolor underprint. Tree at center, President S. Stevens at right. Back: Two youths pan mining (gold or diamonds). Watermark: Lion's head. Printer: BWC. 160x74mm.		
a. 24.8.1982.	2.50	10.00
b. 24.8.1984.	1.00	4.00
s. As a, b. Specimen.	—	100

1988-93 Issue

#15-21 Replacement notes: Serial # prefix Z/1.

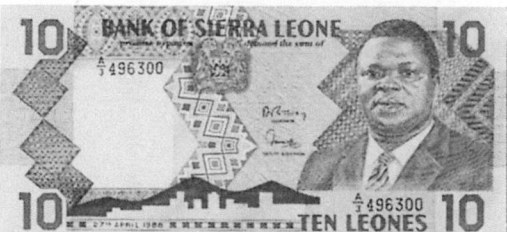

15   10 Leones

	VF	UNC
27.4.1988. Dark green and purple on multicolor underprint. President Dr. Joseph Saidu Momoh at right, arms at upper center. Back: Steer at left, farmer harvesting at center. Watermark: Lion's head. 160x74mm.	0.50	2.00

16   20 Leones

	VF	UNC
27.4.1988. Brown, red and green on multicolor underprint. President Dr. Joseph Saidu Momoh at right, arms at upper center. Back: Two youths pan mining (gold or diamonds). Watermark: Lion's head. 160x74mm.	0.75	2.50

17   50 Leones

	VF	UNC
1988-89. Purple, blue and black on multicolor underprint. President Dr. Joseph Saidu Momoh at right, sports stadium at center, arms at upper center. Back: Dancers at left center. Watermark: Lion's head. 160x74mm.		
a. Without imprint. 27.4.1988.	1.50	3.00
b. Printer: TDLR. 27.4.1989.	0.75	2.00

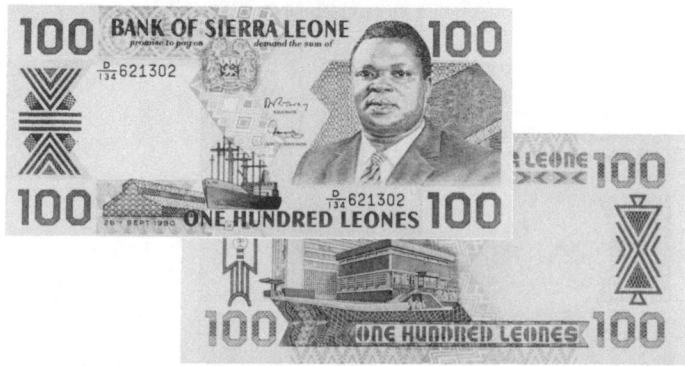

18   100 Leones

	VF	UNC
1988-90. Blue and black on multicolor underprint. President Dr. Joseph Saidu Momoh at right, building and ship at left center, arms at upper center. Back: Local designs at left and right, Central Bank building at left center. Watermark: Lion's head. 160x74mm.		
a. Without imprint. 27.4.1988.	1.00	5.00
b. Printer: TDLR. 27.4.1989.	0.75	2.00
c. 26.9.1990.	FV	2.00

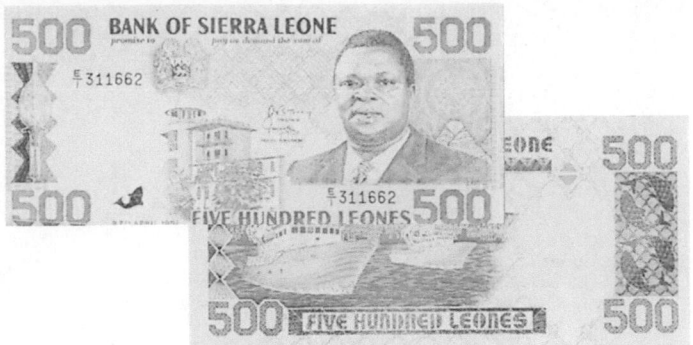

19   500 Leones
27.4.1991. Red-brown and dark green on multicolor underprint. President Dr. Joseph Saidu Momoh at right, arms at upper center, modern building below arms at left center. Back: Two fishing boats at left center, artistic carp at right. Watermark: Lion's head. 160x74mm.

	VF	UNC
	1.00	3.75

20   1000 Leones
1993-98. Black, red and yellow on multicolor underprint. Bai Bureh at right, carving at lower center, arms at upper center. Back: Dish antenna at left center. Watermark: Lion's head. Printer: TDLR. 160x74mm.

	VF	UNC
a. 4.8.1993.	1.50	5.00
b. 27.4.1996.	1.50	5.00
c. 27.4.1997.	1.50	5.00
d. 27.4.1998.	1.50	5.00

21   5000 Leones
1993-98. Blue and violet on multicolor underprint. Sengbe Pieh at right, building at lower center, arms at upper center. Back: Dam at left center. Watermark: Lion's head. Printer: TDLR. 160x74mm.

	VF	UNC
a. 4.8.1993.	6.00	22.50
b. 27.4.1996.	6.00	22.50
c. 27.4.1997.	6.00	22.50
d. 15.7.1998.	6.00	22.50

1995-2000 Issues

#22 Not assigned.

23   500 Leones
27.4.1995 (1996); 15.7.1998; 1.3.2003. Blue-green, brown and green on multicolor underprint. K. Londo at right, arms at upper center, spearhead at left, building at lower center. Back: Fishing boats at left center, artistic carp at right. Watermark: Lion's head. Printer: TDLR. 160x74mm.

	VF	UNC
a. 27.4.1995 (1996).	FV	3.00
b. 15.7.1998.	FV	3.00
c. 1.3.2003.	FV	3.00

24   1000 Leones
1.2.2002; 1.3.2003; 4.8.2006. Brown and red on multicolor underprint. Bai Bureh at left. Back: Antenna. 160x74mm.

	VF	UNC
a. 1.2.2002.	FV	5.00
b. 1.3.2003.	FV	5.00
c. 4.8.2006.	FV	5.00

25   2000 Leones
1.1.2000. Brown and blue on multicolor underprint. I. T. A. Wallace-Johnson at right, cargo ship and storage shed at center. Back: Modern building at left center. Printer: TDLR. 160x74mm.

	VF	UNC
	FV	9.00

2002-2004 Issue

26   2000 Leones
1.2.2002; 1.3.2003; 4.8.2006. Metallic printing. Brown and blue on multicolor underprint. I. T. A. Wallace-Johnson at righ, cargo ship and storage shed at center. Back: Modern building at left center. Printer: TDLR. 160x74mm.

	VF	UNC
a. 1.2.2002.	FV	9.00
b. 1.3.2003.	FV	9.00
c. 4.8.2006.	FV	9.00

27 5000 Leones   VF   UNC

1.2.2002; 1.3.2003; 4.8.2006. Blue and violet on multicolor underprint. Serge Pieh at right. Back: Dam. 160x74mm.

     a. 1.2.2002.   FV   22.50
     b. 1.3.2003.   FV   22.50
     c. 4.8.2006.   FV   22.50

29 10,000 Leones   VF   UNC

4.8.2004; 4.8.2007. Blue, green and multicolor. Dove at center, flag at right center. Back: Tree at center. 160x74mm.

     a. 4.8.2004.   FV   7.50
     b. 4.8.2007.   FV   6.00

2010 Issue

30 1000 Leones   VF   UNC

27.4.2010. Brown and red on multicolor underprint. Bai Bureh at right. Back: Antenna. Printer: TDLR. 160x74mm.   FV   5.00

31 2000 Leones   VF   UNC

27.4.2010. Brown and blue on multicolor underprint. I.T.A. Wallace-Johnson at right. Back: Modern building at center. Printer: TDLR. 160x74mm.   FV   9.00

32 5000 Leones   VF   UNC

27.4.2010. Blue and violet on multicolor underprint. Serge Pieh at right. Back: Dam. Printer: TDLR. 160x74mm.   FV   22.50

33 10,000 Leones   VF   UNC

27.4.2010. Blue and green on multicolor underprint. Dove and Flag at center. Back: Tree. Printer: TDLR. 160x74mm.   FV   40.00

COLLECTOR SERIES

Bank of Sierra Leone

1972 ND Issue

#CS1, First Anniversary of Republic, 1972

CS1 ND (19.4.1972) - 50 Cents   Mkt. Value

#4 laminated in plastic with two 50 cent coins in special maroon case.   10.00

Note: #CS1 note has serial # all zeros but w/o specimen overprint

1979 ND Issue

CS2 ND (1979) 50 Cents - 5 Leones   Mkt. Value

#4, 5b-7b with overprint: *SPECIMEN* and serial # prefix Maltese cross.   20.00

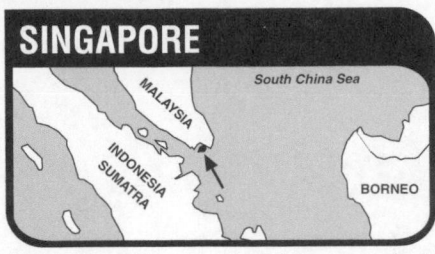

The Republic of Singapore, a British Commonwealth nation situated at the southern tip of the Malayan peninsula, has an area of 712 sq. km. and a population of 5.1 million. Capital: Singapore. The economy is based on electronics production, petrochemicals, pharmaceuticals and shipbuilding/repairs. It is a world financial, business E-commerce, oil refining and air services center, besides having the busiest port in terms of shipping tonnage and containers handled. Singapore was founded as a British trading colony in 1819. It joined the Malaysian Federation in 1963 but separated two years later and became independent. Singapore subsequently became one of the world's most prosperous countries with strong international trading links (its port is one of the world's busiest in terms of tonnage handled) and with per capita GDP equal to that of the leading nations of Western Europe.

MONETARY SYSTEM:
1 Dollar = 100 Cents

SIGNATURE SEAL VARIETIES

Type I: Dragon, seal script, lion   Type II: Seal script w/symbol

REPUBLIC

Board of Commissioners of Currency
Type I: Dragon and lion flanking seal script   Type II: Seal script w/symbols

1967-73 ND Issue

1   **1 Dollar**   **VF**   **UNC**
ND (1967-72). UV: left design, leaves, watermark area legend fluoresce yellow. Blue on multicolor underprint. Light red flowers (Janet Kaneali Orchid) at center, arms at right. Back: Apartment buildings. Watermark: Lion's head. Printer: BWC.

	VF	UNC
a. Without red seal. Signature Lim Kim San (1967).	10.00	30.00
b. Red signature seal Type I at center. Signature Dr. Goh Keng Swee (1970).	17.50	50.00
c. Without red seal. Signature Hon Sui Sen (1971).	8.00	35.00
d. Red signature seal Type II at center. Signature Hon Sui Sen (1972).	5.00	20.00

2   **5 Dollars**   **VF**   **UNC**
ND (1967-73). Light orange flowers (T. M. A. Orchid) at center, arms at upper right. Back: Busy scene on the Singapore River. Watermark: Lion's head. Printer: BWC.

	VF	UNC
a. Without red seal. Signature Lim Kim San (1967).	75.00	150
b. Red signature seal Type I at center. Signature Dr. Goh Keng Swee (1970).	225	1,200
c. Without red seal. Signature Hon Sui Sen (1972).	60.00	220
d. Red signature seal Type II at center. Signature Hon Sui Sen (1973).	20.00	140

3   **10 Dollars**   **VF**   **UNC**
ND (1967-73). Red on multicolor underprint. Lilac flowers (Dendrobium Marjorie Orchid) at center, arms at lower right. Back: Four hands clasping wrists over map of Singapore at left center. Watermark: Lion's head. Printer: TDLR.

	VF	UNC
a. Without red seal. Signature Lim Kim San (1967).	50.00	150
b. Red signature seal Type I at center. Signature Dr. Goh Keng Swee (1970).	55.00	180
c. Without red seal. Signature Hon Sui Sen (1972).	45.00	170
d. Red signature seal Type II at center. Signature Hon Sui Sen (1973).	40.00	120
s. As d. Specimen.	—	300

4   **25 Dollars**   **VF**   **UNC**
ND (1972). Dark brown on multicolor underprint. Yellow flowers (Renanthopsis Aurora Orchid) at center, arms at upper right. Back: Supreme Court building. Watermark: Lion's head. Printer: TDLR.   100   250

5   **50 Dollars**   **VF**   **UNC**
ND (1967-73). Blue on multicolor underprint. Violet flowers (Vanda Rothschildiana Orchid) at center, arms at lower right. Back: Singapore seafront and Clifford Pier. Watermark: Lion's head. Printer: TDLR.

	VF	UNC
a. Without red seal. Signature Lim Kim San (1967).	200	400
b. Red signature seal Type I at center. Signature Dr. Goh Keng Swee (1970).	225	600
c. Without red seal. Signature Hon Sui Se Sen (1972).	85.00	350
d. Red signature seal Type II at center. Signature Hon Sui Sen (1973).	75.00	300
s. As d. Specimen.	—	530

6 100 Dollars

	VF	UNC

ND (1967-73). Blue and violet on multicolor underprint. Red flowers (Cattleya Orchid) at center, arms at right. Back: Sailing vessels along Singapore waterfront. Watermark: Lion's head. Printer: BWC.

	VF	UNC
a. Without red seal. Signature Lim Kim San (1967).	150	600
b. Red signature seal Type I at center. Signature Dr. Goh Keng Swee (1970).	750	2,500
c. Without red seal. Signature Hon Sui Sen (1972).	175	600
d. Red signature seal Type II at center. Signature Hon Sui Sen (1973).	100	400
s. Specimen.	—	700

10 5 Dollars

	VF	UNC
	FV	20.00

ND (1976). Green and brown on multicolor underprint. Red-whiskered bulbul at left, city skyline along bottom, arms at upper right. Back: Ariel tram cars and view of harbor. Watermark: Lion's head. Printer: BWC.

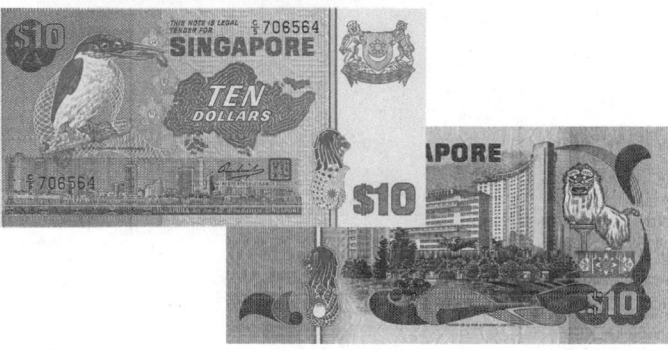

11 10 Dollars

	VF	UNC

ND (1979). Red and dark blue on multicolor underprint. White collared kingfisher at left, city skyline along bottom, arms at upper right. Back: Garden City with high rise public housing in background. Watermark: Lion's head. Printer: TDLR.

	VF	UNC
a. With security thread (1979).	20.00	90.00
b. With segmented foil over security thread (1980).	15.00	50.00

7 500 Dollars

	VF	UNC
ND (1972). Dark green, lilac on multicolor underprint. Pink flowers (Dendrobium Shangri-la) at center. Back: Government offices at St. Andrew's road. Watermark: Lion's head. Printer: TDLR.	700	2,000

8 1000 Dollars

	VF	UNC

ND (1967-75). Purple on multicolored underprint. Lilac-brown colored flowers (Dendroblum Klmlyo Kondo) at center, arms at right. Back: Victoria Theatre and Empress Palace. Watermark: Lion's head. Printer: TDLR.

	VF	UNC
a. Without red seal. Signature Lim Kim San (1967).	1,200	2,500
b. Red signature seal Type I at center. Signature Dr. Goh Keng Swee (1970).	1,500	3,500
c. Without red seal. Signature Hon Sui Sen (1973).	1,300	3,000
d. Red signature seal Type II at center. Signature Hon Sui Sen (1975).	900	2,250

12 20 Dollars

	VF	UNC
	40.00	75.00

ND (1979). Brown, yellow and blue on multicolor underprint. Yellow-breasted Sunbird at left, city skyline along bottom, arms at upper right. Back: Dancer at left, Concorde over Changi International airport center right. Watermark: Lion's head. Printer: BWC.

8A 10,000 Dollars

	VF	UNC
ND (1973). Green on multicolor underprint. Orchids (Aranda Majulah) at center, arms at at right. Signature Hon Sui Sen. Back: The Istana (Presidential residence) at left center. Watermark: Lion's head. Printer: TDLR.	8,000	17,000

1976-80 ND Issue

9 1 Dollar

	VF	UNC
	3.00	8.00

ND (1976). Blue-black on multicolor underprint. Black-naped tern at left, city skyline along bottom, arms at upper right. Back: National Day parade passing large building at center right. Watermark: Lion's head. Printer: BWC.

13 50 Dollars

	VF	UNC

ND (1976). Dark blue on multicolor underprint. White-rumped shama at left, city skyline along bottom, arms at upper right. Back: School band on parade. Watermark: Lion's head. Printer: TDLR.

	VF	UNC
a. With security thread.	40.00	150
b. With segmented foil over security thread.	35.00	125

14   100 Dollars   VF   UNC
ND (1977). Blue on multicolor underprint. Blue-throated bee eater at left, city sky-   100   300
line along bottom, arms at upper right. Back: Various ethnic dancers. Watermark:
Lion's head. Printer: BWC.

15   500 Dollars   VF   UNC
ND (1977). Green and multicolor. Black-naped oriole at left, city skyline along
bottom, arms at upper right. Back: View of island and oil refinery at center. Watermark: Lion's head. Printer: TDLR.
    a. Issued note.   500   1,000
    s. Specimen.   —   —

16   1000 Dollars   VF   UNC
ND (1978). Violet and brown on multicolor underprint. Brahminy Kite bird at left,   1,000   2,000
city skyline along bottom, arms at upper right. Back: Container ship terminal.
Watermark: Lion's head. Printer: TDLR.

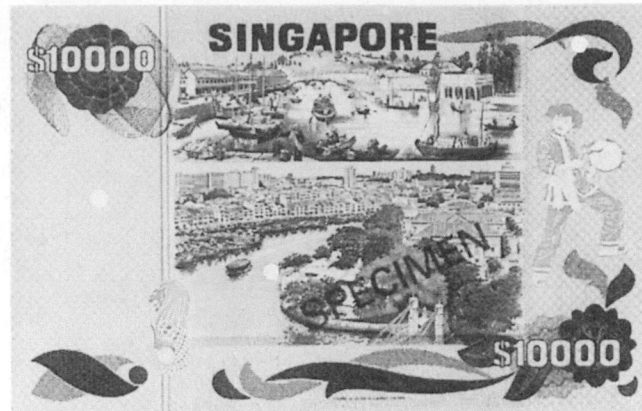

17   10,000 Dollars   VF   UNC
ND (1980). Green on multicolor underprint. White-bellied Sea Eagle at left, city
skyline along bottom, arms at upper right. Back: 19th century Singapore River scene
above, modern view below on back. Watermark: Lion's head. Printer: TDLR.
    a. Issued note.   10,000   20,000
    s. Specimen, punched hole cancelled.   —   1,500

1984-89 ND Issue

#18-25 Replacement notes: Serial # prefix *Z/1, Z/2,* **etc.**

18   1 Dollar   VF   UNC
ND (1987). UV: Chop fluoresce orange. Deep blue and green. Sailing ship *Sha
Chuan* at left. Chinese Crasse and carp at lower right, arms at upper left. Back:
Orchids and satellite tracking station at center. Watermark: Lion's head. Printer:
TDLR. 160x74mm.
    a. Signature Goh Keng Swee.   FV   6.00
    b. Signature Hu Tsu Tau.   FV   5.00
19   5 Dollars   VF   UNC
ND (1989). Green and red-violet on multicolor underprint. Chinese lion with ball and   FV   15.00
Commerson's Anchovy at right, arms at upper left. Back: *Twkow* boats at left, View
of the PSA container terminal at right. Watermark: Lion's head. Printer: TDLR.

20   10 Dollars   VF   UNC
ND (1988). Red-orange and violet on multicolor underprint. Trader vessel *Palari* at   FV   20.00
left, Phoenix and round scad at lower right, arms at upper left. Back: Stylized map
at center, public housing at right. Watermark: Lion's head. Printer: TDLR.
#21 Not assigned.

22   50 Dollars

ND (1987). Blue on multicolor underprint. Coastal vessel *Perak* at left. Mountain ducks and six-banded grouper at lower right, two raised areas in circles at lower right, arms at upper left. Back: Benjamin Sheares Bridge and city view. Watermark: Lion's head. Printer: TDLR.

		VF	UNC
a. With security thread.		FV	125
b. With segmented foil over security thread.		FV	110

23   100 Dollars

ND (1985; 1995). Dark brown, violet and orange-brown on multicolor underprint. Passenger liner *Chusan* at left center, slender shad and three raised areas in circles at lower right, arms at upper left. Back: Airplane above with Changi air terminal at center right. Watermark: Lion's head. Printer: TDLR.

		VF	UNC
a. With security thread. Signature Dr. Goh Keng Swee. (1985).		FV	200
b. With segmented foil over "Cleartext" security thread with $100 *SINGAPORE* in four languages. (1995)		FV	175
c. As b. signature Hu Tsu Tau.		FV	150

24   500 Dollars

ND (1988). Green on multicolor underprint. Cargo vessel *Neptune Sardonyx* at left, arms at upper left. Back: Members of the three Armed Forces and the Civil Defence Force with outline map of Singapore. Watermark: Lion's head. Printer: TDLR.

VF FV   UNC 900

25   1000 Dollars

ND (1984). Purple and red on multicolor underprint. Container ship *Neptune Garnet* at left center, Phoenix and Polka-dot grouper at lower right, arms at upper left. Back: Shipyard. Watermark: Lion's head. Printer: TDLR.

		VF	UNC
a. Signature Dr. Goh Keng Swee.		FV	1,600
b. Signature Dr. Hu Tsu Tau.		FV	1,500
s. As a. Specimen.		—	—

26   10,000 Dollars

ND (1987). Red and purple on multicolor underprint. General bulk carrier *Neptune Canopus* at left, Chinese dragon at center right. Back: 1987 National Day parade.

VF 10,000   UNC 15,000

1990 ND Issue

#27 and 28. Replacement notes: Serial prefix *ZZ*.

27   2 Dollars

ND (ca.1990). Orange and red on yellow-green underprint. Arms at upper left, *Tongkang* boat and two smaller boats at center. Back: Chingay procession. Watermark: Lion's head. Printer: TDLR.

VF FV   UNC 8.00

28   2 Dollars

ND (1992). UV: Chop fluoresce orange. Deep purple and brown-violet on multicolor underprint. Arms at upper left, *Tongkang* boat and two smaller boats at center. Ascending size serial number. Back: Chingay procession. Printer: TDLR.

VF FV   UNC 7.00

Note: #28 also issued in various uncut sheets from 2 to 40 subjects.

1992 Commemorative Issues

#29, 25th Anniversary - Board of Commissioners of Currency

29 2 Dollars   **VF UNC**
ND(1992). Deep purple and brown-violet on multicolor underprint. Overprint on #28. (5000).
    a. Issued note.   —   400
    x. Without overprint text: *COMMISSONERS* (error).   —   50.00
#30 and 31, 25th Anniversary of Independence

30 50 Dollars   **VF UNC**
9.8.1990. Polymer plastic. 300,000 pieces printed. Red and purple on multicolor   FV   125
underprint. Silver hologram of Yusof bin Ishak at center. Old harbor scene at left,
modern buildings at right. Back: First parliament at left, group of people below flag
and arms at right.

Note: A number of notes exist without the printed date.

31 50 Dollars   **VF UNC**
ND (1990). 4.817 million pieces printed. Red and purple on multicolor underprint.   FV   100
Silver hologram of Yusof bin Ishak at center. Old harbor scene at left, modern
buildings at right, without date. Back: First parliament at left, group of people
below flag and arms at right, without date.

1994 ND Commemorative Issue

#31A, 25th Anniversary - Board of Commissioners of Currency

31A 2 Dollars   **VF UNC**
ND (1994). Deep purple and brown-violet on multicolor underprint. *Tongkang* boat   —   150
and twl smaller boats at center.

Note: #31A was issued in the book *Prudence at the Helm, 1967-1992.*

1994 Regular Issue

32 50 Dollars   **VF UNC**
ND (1994). Deep blue-black and red on multicolor underprint. Coastal vessel   FV   100
Perak at left. Mountain ducks and six-banded grouper at lower right, two raised
areas in circles at lower right, arms at upper left, with segmented foil over security
thread. Back: Benjamin Sheares Bridge and city view. Printer: TDLR.

1996 Commemorative Issue

#33, 25th Anniversary of Monetary Authority, 1971-1996

33 25 Dollars   **VF UNC**
1.1.1996. Red-brown and green on multicolor underprint. Arms at upper left,   FV   125
Monetary Authority building at center. Optical variable device at left center in addition to many other security features. Signature Hu Tsu Tau. Back: Financial sector
skyline. Watermark: Lion's head.

Note: #33 was offered in 2 varieties of special booklets, wide, narrow and uncut sheets of 20
subjects.

1997 ND Regular Issue

34 2 Dollars   **VF UNC**
ND (1997). Deep purple and brown-violet on multicolor underprint. Arms at upper   FV   9.00
left, *Tongkang* boat and two smaller boats at center. Ascending size serial number.
Back: Chingay procession. Watermark: Lion's head. Printer: H&S.

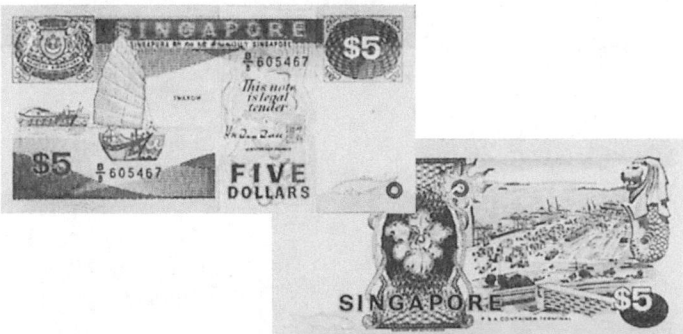

35 5 Dollars   **VF UNC**
ND (1997). Green and red-violet on multicolor underprint. Chinese lion with ball   FV   12.50
and Commerson's Anchovy at right, arms at upper left. Back: *Twkow* boats at left,
View of the PSA container terminal at right. Watermark: Lion's head. Printer: H&S.

36 50 Dollars   **VF UNC**
ND (1997). Slate gray and red on multicolor underprint. Like #32. Segmented foil   FV   100
over "Cleartext" security thread with $50 *SINGAPORE* in four languages. Back:
Benjamin Sheares Bridge and city view. Watermark: Lion's head.

1998 ND Issue

37   2 Dollars   VF   UNC
ND(1998). Deep purple and brown-violet on multicolor underprint. Arms at upper   FV   7.00
left, *Tongkang* boat and two smaller boats at center. Ascending size serial number.
Back: Chingay procession. Watermark: Lion's head. Printer: BABN. 126x63mm.

1999 ND Issue

38   2 Dollars   VF   UNC
ND (1999). UV: value in box and vertical serial # fluoresce yellow. Purple, brown   FV   6.00
and multicolor underprint. President Encik Yusof bin Ishak at right. Back: Education - Victoria Bridge School, Raffles Institue, College of Medicine views with
children. Watermark: Encik Yusof bin Ishak. 126x63mm.

39   5 Dollars   VF   UNC
ND (1999). Green, red and multicolor. President Encik Yusof bin Ishak at right.   FV   12.00
Back: Garden City - trees and flowers, skyline in background. Watermark: Encik
Yusof bin Ishak. 133x66mm.

40   10 Dollars   VF   UNC
ND (1999). . Red, brown and multicolor. President Encik Yusof bin Ishak at right.   FV   20.00
Back: Sports - swimming, tennis, soccer, sailing, running. Watermark: Encik Yusof
bin Ishak. 141x69mm.

41   50 Dollars   VF   UNC
ND (1999). Slate blue and multicolor. President Encik Yusof bin Ishak at right.
Back: Arts - music, graphics. Watermark: Encik Yusof bin Ishak. 156x74mm.
  a. Signature as illustration.   55.00   100
  b. Signature Lee Hsieh Loong.   75.00   125

42   100 Dollars   VF   UNC
ND (1999). Orange, brown and multicolor. President Encik Yusof bin Ishak at right.   FV   150
Back: Youth - Members of the Singapore Red Cross, St. John's Ambulance Bri-
gade, National Police Cadet Corp Watermark: Encik Yusof bin Ishak. 162x77mm.

43   1000 Dollars   VF   UNC
ND (1999). Purple, lilac and multicolor. President Encik Yusof bin Ishak at right.   FV   1,400
Back: Parliament House at left, Istana (Presidential residence) at center, Supreme
Court at right. Watermark: Encik Yusof bin Ishak. 170x83mm.

44   10,000 Dollars   VF   UNC
ND (1999). Light brown and multicolor. President Encik Yusof bin Ishak at right.
Back: Technology - computer chip research lab. Watermark: Encik Yusof bin
Ishak. 180x90mm.
  a. Issued note.   FV   13,000
  s. Specimen.   —   1,250

2000 Issue

45 **2 Dollars**   **VF UNC**
2000. Purple, brown and multicolor. President Encik Yusof bin Ishak at right. #38 with 2000 overprint in red at upper right and lower left. Watermark: Encik Yusof bin Ishak. 126x63mm.   4.00   7.00

Monetary Authority of Singapore

2004-5 ND Paper Issue

45A **2 Dollars**   **VF UNC**
ND (2004). President Encik Yuosf at right. "Flag" at bottom center. Paper   FV   5.00

2005 ND Second Issue

46 **2 Dollars**   **VF UNC**
ND (2005). Polymer plastic. Purple, brown and multicolor underprint. President Encik Yusof bin Ishak at right. Without "flag" at lower center. Back: Education - Victoria Bridge School, Raffles Institue, College of Medicine views with children. 126x63mm.

		VF	UNC
a. No symbol below EDUCATION on back.		FV	5.00
b. One square below EDUCATION on back.		FV	5.00
c. Two squares below EDUCATION on back.		FV	5.00
d. One triangle below EDUCATION on back.		FV	5.00
e. Two triangles below EDUCATION on back.		FV	5.00
f. One diamond below EDUCATION on back.		FV	5.00
g. Two diamonds below EDUCATION on back.		FV	5.00

47 **5 Dollars**   **VF UNC**
ND (2005). Polymer plastic. Green, red and multicolor. President Encik Yusof bin Ishak at right, without "flag" at bottom center. Back: Garden City - trees and flowers, skyline in background. 133x66mm.

		VF	UNC
a. No symbol below GARDEN CITY on back.		FV	9.00
b. One square below GARDEN CITY on back.		FV	9.00
c. Two triangles below GARDEN CITY on back.		FV	9.00
d. One triangle below GARDEN CITY on back.		FV	9.00

47A **5 Dollars**   **VF UNC**
ND (2005). Like #47, except paper. 133x66mm.   FV   9.00

48 **10 Dollars**   **VF UNC**
ND (2005). Polymer plastic. Red, brown and multicolor. President Encik Yusof bin Ishak at right. Back: Sports - swimming, tennis, soccer, sailing, running. 141x69mm.

		VF	UNC
a. No symbol below SPORTS on back.		FV	15.00
b. One square below SPORTS on back.		FV	15.00
c. Two squares below SPORTS on back.		FV	15.00
d. One triangle below SPORTS on back.		FV	15.00
e. Two triangles below SPORTS on back.		FV	15.00
f. One diamond below SPORTS on back.		FV	15.00
g. Two diamonds below SPORTS on back.		FV	15.00
h. One star below SPORTS on back.		FV	15.00
i. Signature T. Shanmugaratnam. Solid house below SPORTS on back.		FV	15.00
j. Signature T. Shanmugaratnam. Hollow house below SPORTS on back.		FV	15.00

48A **10 Dollars**   **VF UNC**
ND (2005). Like #48, except paper. 141x69mm.   FV   15.00

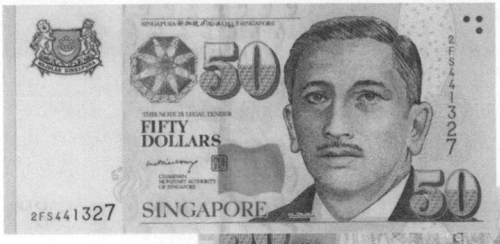

49 **50 Dollars**   **VF UNC**
ND (2008). Slate blue and multicolor. President Encik Yusof bin Ishak at right. "Flag" at bottom center. Back: Arts - music graphics Watermark: Encik Yusof bin Ishak 156x74mm.

		VF	UNC
a. No symbol below ARTS on back.		FV	80.00
b. One square below ARTS on back.		FV	80.00
c. Two squares below ARTS on back.		FV	80.00
d. One triangle below ARTS on back.		FV	80.00
e. Two triangles below ARTS on back.		FV	80.00
f. One diamond below ARTS on back.		FV	80.00
g. Two diamonds below ARTS on back.		FV	80.00
h. One star below ARTS on back.		FV	80.00

50 **100 Dollars**   **VF UNC**
President Encik Yusof bin Ishak at right. "Flag" at bottom center. Back: Youth - Members of the Singapore Red Cross, St. John's Ambulance Brigade, National Police Cadet Corp. Watermark: Encik Yusof bin Ishak. 170x83mm.

		VF	UNC
a. No symbol below YOUTH on back.		FV	150
b. One square below YOUTH on back.		FV	150
c. Two squares below YOUTH on back.		FV	150
d. One triangle below YOUTH on back.		FV	150
e. Two triangles below YOUTH on back.		FV	150

51 **1000 Dollars**   **VF UNC**
ND (2009). Purple on multicolor underprint. Encik Yusof bin Ishak at right. "Flag" at bottom center. Back: Government buildings: Parliament House, Istana and the Old Supreme Court Building. Watermark: Encik Yusof bin Ishak and braille codes 170x83mm.

		VF	UNC
a. No symbol below GOVERNMENT on back.		FV	1,300
b. One triangle below GOVERNMENT on back.		FV	1,300
c. Two triangles below GOVERNMENT on back.		FV	1,300
d. One diamond below GOVERNMENT on back.		FV	1,300
e. Two diamonds below GOVERNMENT on back.		FV	1,300
f. One star below GOVERNMENT on back.		FV	1,300

52 **10,000 Dollars**   **VF UNC**
Expected new issue.   —   —

2007 Singapore-Brunei Commemorative Issue

53 **20 Dollars**   **VF UNC**
6.2007. Polymer plastic. Brown, yellow and multicolor underprint. President Yusof bin Ishak at right. Back: 40th Anniversary of Currency Interchangeability with Buruni. 141x69mm.   FV   25.00

2004 MAS Commemorative Issue

54 **10 Dollars**   **VF UNC**
ND (2004). Purple, brown and multicolor. President Encik Yusof bin Ishak at right. Watermark: Encik Yusof bin Ishak. 141x69mm.   FV   40.00

55 **50 Dollars**   **VF UNC**
50 Dollars BCCS + 50 Dollars MAS ND (2002). Slate blue and multicolor. BCCS note signed by Hu Hsu Tau. MAS note signed by Lee Hsien Loong and with additional overprint of MAS logo at right. Both notes bear identical numbers. Back: Arts - Music and Graphics. 156x74mm.   FV   500

2015 Commemorative Issue: 50 Years of Nation-Building

56   10 Dollars   VF   UNC

2015 Polymer plastic. Red on multicolor underprint. President Encik Yusof bin Ishak at right. Back. "...regardless of race, language or religion..." Eight children at center. 141x69mm.

    a. One diamond on back.   FV   15.00
    b. Two diamonds on back.   FV   15.00

57   10 Dollars   VF   UNC

2015. Polymer plastic. Red on multicolor underprint. President Encik Yusof bin Ishak at right. Back: "Opportunities for All." Large group of people all doing different tasks. 141x69mm.

    a. One diamond on back.   FV   15.00
    b. Two diamonds on back.   FV   15.00

58   10 Dollars   VF   UNC

2015. Polymer plastic. Red on multicolor underprint. President Encik Yusof bin Ishak at right. Back: "Strong Families." Several families sharing various activities. 141x69mm.

    a. One diamond on back.   FV   15.00
    b. Two diamonds on back.   FV   15.00

59   10 Dollars   VF   UNC

2015. Polymer plastic. Red on multicolor underprint. President Encik Yusof bin Ishak at right. Back: "Safe and Secure." Various military personnel. 141x69mm.

    a. One diamond on back.   FV   15.00
    b. Two diamonds on back.   FV   15.00

60   10 Dollars   VF   UNC

2015. Polymer plastic. Red on multicolor underprint. President Encik Yusof bin Ishak at right. Back: "Caring Community, Active Citizenry." People working together. 141x69mm.

    a. One diamond on back.   FV   15.00
    b. Two diamonds on back.   FV   15.00

61   50 Dollars   VF   UNC

2015. Polymer plastic. Gold, green and red. Lee Kuan Yew shouting "Merdeka!", four children at left and President Encik Yusof bin Ishak at right. Back: Modern buildings, bridge and soldiers marching during First National Day Parade 1966.

    a. Brown vertical serial # at right.   FV   65.00
    b. Blue vertical serial # at right (limited edition).   FV   65.00

COLLECTOR SERIES

Singapore

1989 ND Issues

CS1   ND (1989). 1 Dollar - 100 Dollars   Mkt. Value

#1a-3a, 5a and 6a overprint: *SPECIMEN.* (77 sets)   2,500

CS2   ND (1989). 1 Dollar - 100 Dollars   Mkt. Value

#1c-3c, 5c and 6c overprint: *SPECIMEN.* (89 sets).   3,500

CS3   ND (1989). 1 Dollar - 100 Dollars   Mkt. Value

#1d-3d, 4, 5d and 6d overprint: *SPECIMEN.* (82 sets).   4,000

CS4   ND (1989). 1-100 Dollars   Mkt. Value

#9-11, 13 and 14 overprint: *SPECIMEN.* (311 sets).   1,200

2000 Issue

CS5   2 Dollars   Mkt. Value

Twin sets of albums, each with 3 Two Dollar notes that bear identical serial #s for the last 6 digits. Albums titled: *The Twin Collection of the Millennium Dragon Circa 2000 Singapore.*   20.00

Slovakia as a republic has an area of 18,923 sq. mi. (49,011 sq. km.) and a population of 5.37 million. Capital: Bratislava. Textiles, steel, and wood products are exported. The dissolution of the Austro-Hungarian Empire at the close of World War I allowed the Slovaks to join the closely related Czechs to form Czechoslovakia. Following the chaos of World War II, Czechoslovakia became a Communist nation within Soviet-dominated Eastern Europe. Soviet influence collapsed in 1989 and Czechoslovakia once more became free. The Slovaks and the Czechs agreed to separate peacefully on 1 January 1993. Slovakia joined both NATO and the EU in the spring of 2004 and the Eurozone on 1 January 2009.

MONETARY SYSTEM:
1 Korun = 100 Halierov, 1945-2008
1 Euro = 100 Euro Cent, 2009-

REPUBLIC

Slovenska Republika

REPUBLIC OF SLOVAKIA

1993 ND Provisional Issue

#15-19 Czechoslovakian issue w/affixed adhesive stamps w/*SLOVENSKA / arms / REPUBLIKA*.

15	20 Korun	VF	UNC
	ND (1993- old date 1988). Black and light blue adhesive stamp on Czechoslovakia number 95.	2.50	5.50

16	50 Korun	VF	UNC
	ND (1993- old date 1987). Black and yellow adhesive stamp on Czechoslovakia number 96. Serial number prefixes: *F* and *I*.	3.50	25.00

17	100 Korun	VF	UNC
	ND (1993- old date 1961). Black and orange adhesive stamp on Czechoslovakia # 91. Series G37-.		
	a. Stamp on Czechoslovakia #91a.	25.00	150
	b. Stamp on Czechoslovakia #91b.	5.00	22.50
	c. Stamp on Czechoslovakia #91c.	4.00	20.00
18	**500 Korun**	**VF**	**UNC**
	ND (1993- old date 1973). Adhesive stamp on Czechoslovakia number 93. Serial number prefixes: *Z, V* and *W*.	25.00	65.00
19	**1000 Korun**	**VF**	**UNC**
	ND (1993- old date 1985). Adhesive stamp on Czechoslovakia number 98.	45.00	110

Národná Banka Slovenska

SLOVAK NATIONAL BANK

1993 Issue

20	20 Korun		VF	UNC
	1993-2006. Black and green on multicolor underprint. Prince Pribina at right. Signature varieties. Back: Nitra Castle at left, shield of arms at lower center right. Watermark: Prince Pribina. 128x65mm.			
	a. Pale green underprint. 1.9.1993. Serial # prefix B. Printer BABN.		FV	5.00
	b. As a. but with green underprint at right. Security thread closer to center. 1.6.1995. Serial # prefix B. Printer: BABN.		FV	6.00
	c. 31.10.1997. Serial # prefix B, J. Printer: BABN.		FV	2.50
	d. 1.7.1999. Serial # prefix B, J. Printer: BABN.		FV	2.00
	e. 31.8.2001. Serial # prefix J, S. Printer: BABN.		FV	2.50
	f. 6.9.2004. Serial # prefix S. Printer: BAI Ottawa.		FV	2.50
	g. 20.10.2006. Serial # prefix S, V. Printer: PWPW Warszawa.		FV	2.50
	h. As a. Serial # prefix A. Uncut sheet of 60 (6000 sheets).		—	120
	r1. Replacement note. As a. Serial # prefix A.		FV	5.00
	r2. Replacement note. As b. Serial # prefix A.		5.00	13.00
	r3. Replacement note. As c. Serial # prefix A.		10.00	25.00
	r4. Replacement note. As d. Serial # prefix A.		5.00	13.00
	r5. Replacement note. As e. Serial # prefix A.		5.00	13.00
	r6. Replacement note. As f. Serial # prefix A.		5.00	13.00
	r7. Replacement note. As g. Serial # prefix A.		5.00	13.00

21	50 Korun		VF	UNC
	1993-2005. Black, blue and aqua on multicolor underprint. St. Cyril and St. Method at right, Signature varieties. Back: Medieval church at Drazovce and first 7 letters of Slavic alphabet, shield of arms at lower center right. Watermark: St. Cyril and St. Method. Printer: BABN. 134x68mm.			
	a. 1.8.1993. Serial # prefix A, C. 7 or 8 digit serial #.		FV	10.00
	b. Security thread closer to center. 1.6.1995. Serial # prefix A, C.		FV	20.00
	c. 1.7.1999. Serial # prefix A, C.		FV	12.00
	d. 2.5.2002. Serial # prefix A, C, K.		FV	8.00
	e. 16.11.2005. Serial # prefix K.		FV	5.00
	f. As a. Serial # prefix A. Uncut sheet of 45 (4000 sheets).		—	220
	r1. Replacement note. As a. Serial # A.		FV	10.00
	r2. Replacement note. As b. Serial # A.		20.00	50.00
	r3. Replacement note. As c. Serial # prefix A.		10.00	40.00
	r4. Replacement note. As d. Serial # prefix A.		10.00	40.00
	r5. Replacement note. As e. Serial # prefix A.		4.00	20.00

22   100 Korun   **VF   UNC**

1.9.1993. Red and black on orange and multicolor underprint. Madonna (by master woodcarver Pavol) from the altar of the Birth in St. Jacob's Church in Levoca at right. Signature varieties. Back: Levoca town view, shield of arms at lower center right. Watermark: Madonna. Printer: TDLR. 140x71mm.

a. Serial # prefix D.	FV	18.00
b. Serial # prefix A. Uncut sheet of 35 (4000 sheets).	—	300
r. Replacement note. Serial # prefix A.	FV	18.00

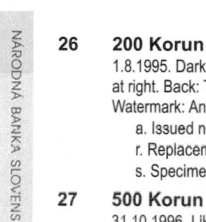

23   500 Korun   **VF   UNC**

1.10.1993. Dark gray and brown on multicolor underprint. Ludovit Stúr at right. Signature varieties. Back: Bratislava Castle and St. Michael's Church at left, shield of arms at lower center right. Watermark: Ludovit Stúr. Printer: TDLR. 152x77mm.

a. Serial # prefix F.	FV	150
b. Serial # prefix A. Uncut sheet of 28 (2500 sheets).	—	1,050
r. Replacement note. Serial # prefix A.	FV	100
s. Specimen. Perforated: *SPECIMEN.*	—	—

24   1000 Korun   **VF   UNC**

1993; 1995; 1997. Dark gray and purple on red-violet and multicolor underprint. Andrej Hlinka at right. Signature varieties. Back: Madonna of the Church of Liptovké Sliace near Ruzomberok and Church of St. Andrew in Ruzomberok at left center. Watermark: Andrej Hlinka. Printer: TDLR. 158x80mm.

a. 1.10.1993. Serial # prefix G.	FV	200
b. Security thread closer to center 1.6.1995. Serial # prefix G.	FV	120
c. 1.7.1997. Serial # prefix G.	FV	90.00
d. As a. Serial # prefix A. Uncut sheet of 28 (1500 sheets).	—	2,100
r1. Replacement note. As a. Serial # prefix A.	70.00	175
r2. Replacement note. As b. Serial # prefix A.	100	250
r3. Replacement note. As c. Serial # prefix A.	100	250
s. Specimen. Perforated: *SPECIMEN.*	—	—

1995; 1996 Issue

25   100 Korun   **VF   UNC**

1996-2001. Red and black on orange and multicolor underprint. Madonna (by master woodcarver Pavol) from the altar of the Birth in St. Jacob's Church in Levoca at right. Signature varieties. Back: Levoca town view, shield of arms at lower center right, red-orange replaces dull orange in corners. Watermark: Madonna. Printer: TDLR. 140x71mm.

a. Printer as: *TDLR.* 1.7.1996. Serial # prefix D.	FV	18.00
b. Serial # prefix: *D, L.* 1.10.1997.	FV	18.00
c. Printer as: *DLR.* 1.7.1999. Serial # prefix L.	FV	9.00
d. 10.10.2001. Serial # prefix L, U.	FV	8.00
r1. Replacement note. As a. Serial # prefix A.	10.00	30.00
r2. Replacement note. As b. Serial # prefix A.	10.00	30.00
r3. Replacement note. As c. Serial # prefix A.	15.00	40.00
r4. Replacement note. As d. Serial # prefix A.	10.00	30.00
s. Specimen. Perforated: *SPECIMEN.*	—	—

26   200 Korun   **VF   UNC**

1.8.1995. Dark gray and blue-green on multicolor underprint. Anton Bernolák at right. Back: Trnava town view at left center, shield of arms at lower center. Watermark: Anton Bernolák. Printer: G&D. 146x74mm.

a. Issued note. Serial # prefix E.	FV	45.00
r. Replacement note. Serial # prefix A.	20.00	50.00
s. Specimen. Perforated: *SPECIMEN.*	—	—

27   500 Korun   **VF   UNC**

31.10.1996. Like #23 but blue underprint at left center and in corners. Ludovit Stúr at right. Signature varieties. Back: Bratislava Castle and St. Michael's Church at left, shield of arms at lower center. Watermark: Ludovit Stúr. Printer: TDLR. 152x77mm.

a. Issued note. Serial # prefix F.	FV	55.00
r. Replacement note. Serial # prefix A.	80.00	200
s. Specimen. Perforated: *SPECIMEN.*	—	—

#28 not assigned.

29   5000 Korun   **VF   UNC**

3.4.1995. Brown-violet and pale yellow-brown on multicolor underprint. Milan Rastislav Stefánik at right, sun and moon at center. Back: Stefánik's grave at Bradlo Hill, part of *Ursa Major* constellation, and a pasque flower at left center. Watermark: Milan Rastislav Stefánik. Printer: G&D. 164x82mm.

a. Issued note. Serial # prefix H.	FV	420
r. Replacement note. Serial # prefix A.	270	380
s. Specimen. Perforated: *SPECIMEN.*	—	—

1999-2000 Issue

30   200 Korun   **VF   UNC**

31.3.1999. Dark gray and blue-green on multicolor underprint. Anton Bernolák at right, but with optical variable ink and champagne dots in watermark area. Back: Trnava town view at left center, shield of arms at lower center. Watermark: Anton Bernolák. Printer: G&D. 146x74mm.

a. Issued note. Serial # prefix E.	FV	20.00
r. Replacement note. Serial # prefix A.	40.00	100

31 500 Korun   **VF UNC**

20.10.2000. Dark gray and brown on multicolor underprint. Ludovit Stúr at right, optical variable device and champagne dots in watermark area. Signature varieties. Back: Bratislava Castle and St. Michael's Church at left, shield of arms at lower center. Watermark: Ludovit Stúr. Printer: TDLR. 152x77mm.

    a. Issued note. Serial # prefix F.   FV 55.00
    r. Replacement note. Serial # prefix A.   80.00 100

32 1000 Korun   **VF UNC**

1.10.1999. Dark gray and purple on red-violet and multicolor underprint. Andrej Hlinka at right, optical variable device and champagne dots in watermark area. Signature varieties. Back: Madonna of the Church of Liptovké Sliace near Ruzomberok and Church of St. Andrew in Ruzomberok at left center. Watermark: Andrej Hlinka. Printer: TDLR. 158x80mm.

    a. Issued note. Serial # prefix G, P.   FV 65.00
    r. Replacement note. Serial # prefix A.   80.00 200

33 5000 Korun   **VF UNC**

11.5.1999. Orange-brown and olive on multicolor underprint. Milan Rastislav Stefánik at right, sun and moon at center. Optical variable device and champagne dots in watermark area and Kinegram at left center. Back: Stefánik's grave at Bradlo Hill, part of *Ursa Major* constellation, and a pasque flower at left center. Printer: G&D. 164x82mm.

    a. Issued note. Serial # prefix H.   FV 330
    r. Replacement note. Serial # prefix A.   260 330

2000 Commemorative Issue

Previously Series *A* notes were available only as uncut sheets. These overprints caused problems with bank counting machines and were not in circulation for an extended period of time.

34 20 Korun   **VF UNC**

1.9.1993. 330,000 pieces. Black and green on multicolor underprint. 128x65mm.   FV 4.25

35 50 Korun   **VF UNC**

1.8.1993. 168,750 pieces. Black, blue and aqua on multicolor underprint. 134x68mm.   FV 9.00

36 100 Korun   **VF UNC**

1.9.1993. 133,000 pieces. Red and black on orange and multicolor underprint. 140x71mm.   FV 16.00

37 200 Korun   **VF UNC**

1.8.1995. 108,000 pieces. Dark gray and blue green on multicolor underprint. 146x74mm.   FV 32.50

38   500 Korun   **VF   UNC**
1.10.1993. 67,200 pieces. Dark gray and brown on multicolor underprint.   FV   60.00
152x77mm.

39   1000 Korun   **VF   UNC**
1.10.1993. 40,600 pieces. Dark gray and purple on red-violet and multicolor   FV   110
underprint. 158x80mm.

40   5000 Korun   **VF   UNC**
3.4.1995. 10,800 pieces. Orange-brown and olive on multicolor underprint.   FV   400
164x82mm.

2002 Issue

41   200 Korun   **VF   UNC**
30.8.2002. Dark gray and blue-green on multicolor underprint. Anton Bernolák
at right, but with optical variable ink in watermark area and additional security
features. Serial # prefix E. Back: Trnava town view at left center, shield of arms at
lower center. Watermark: Anton Bernolák. Printer: F-CO. 146x74mm.
     a. Issued note. Serial # prefix E.   FV   17.50
     r. Replacement note. Serial # prefix A.   20.00   50.00

42   1000 Korun   **VF   UNC**
10.6.2002. Dark gray and purple on red-violet and multicolor underprint. Andrej
Hlinka at right, optical variable device in watermark area; additional security
features added. Signature varieties. Back: Madonna of the Church of Liptovké
Sliace near Ruzomberok and Church of St. Andrew in Ruzomberok a Watermark:
Andrej Hlinka. Printer: (T)DLR. 158x80mm.
     a. Issued note. Serial # prefix P.   FV   85.00
     r. Replacement note. Serial # prefix A.   80.00   200

43   5000 Korun   **VF   UNC**
17.11.2003. Orange-brown and olive on multicolor underprint. Milan Rastislav
Stefánik at right, sun and moon at center. Optical variable device in watermark
area and Kinegram at left center, also additional security features. Back: Stefánik's grave at Bradlo Hill, part of *Ursa Major* constellation, and a pasque flower.
Watermark: Milan Rastislav Stefánik. Printer: DeBS, Wein. 164x82mm.
     a. Issued note. Serial # prefix H.   FV   330
     r. Replacement note. Serial # prefix A.   250   300

2004-2006 Issue

44   100 Korun   **VF   UNC**
5.11.2004. Red and black on orange and multicolor underprint. Madonna (by master woodcarver Pavol) from the altar of the Birth in St. Jacob's Church in Levoca
at right. Back: Levoca town view, shield of arms at lower center right. Watermark:
Madonna. Printer: PWPW, Warszawa. 140x71mm.
     a. Issued note. Serial # prefix U.   FV   7.00
     r. Replacement note. Serial # prefix A.   6.00   13.00

45   200 Korun   **VF   UNC**
1.6.2006. Dark gray and blue-green on multicolor underprint. Anton Bernolák
at right. Back: Trnava town view at left center, shield of arms at lower center.
Watermark: Anton Bernolák. Printer: F-CO. 146x74mm.
     a. Issued note. Serial # prefix E.   FV   15.00
     r. Replacement note. Serial # prefix A.   120   300

46   500 Korun   **VF   UNC**
10.7.2006. Dark gray and brown on multicolor underprint. Ludovit Stúr at right.
Back: Bratislava Castle and St. Michael's Chruch at left, shield of arms at lower
center. Watermark: Ludovit Stúr. Printer: TDLR. 152x77mm.
     a. Issued note. Serial # prefix F.   FV   40.00
     r. Replacement note. Serial # prefix A.   160   400

47   1000 Korun   **VF   UNC**
25.8.2005; 1.8.2007. Dark gray and purple on red-violet and multicolor underprint.
Andrej Hinka at right. Back: Madonna of the Church of Liptovké Sliace near Ruzomberok and Church of St. Andrew in Ruzomberok a Watermark: Andrej Hinka.
Printer: TDLR. 158x80mm.
     a. 25.8.2005. Serial # prefix P.   FV   62.50
     b. 1.8.2007. Serial # prefix W.   FV   62.50
     ar. As a. Replacement note. Serial # prefix A.   80.00   200
     br. As b. Replacement note. Serial # prefix A.   70.00   175

Slovakia adopted the Euro in January 2009.

The Republic of Slovenia is bounded in the north by Austria, northeast by Hungary, southeast by Croatia and to the west by Italy. It has an area of 20,251 sq. km. and a population of 2.01 million. Capital: Ljubljana. The economy is based on electricity, minerals, forestry, agriculture and fishing. Small industries are being developed during privatization. The Slovene lands were part of the Austro-Hungarian Empire until the latter's dissolution at the end of World War I. In 1918, the Slovenes joined the Serbs and Croats in forming a new multinational state, which was named Yugoslavia in 1929. After World War II, Slovenia became a republic of the renewed Yugoslavia, which though Communist, distanced itself from Moscow's rule. Dissatisfied with the exercise of power by the majority Serbs, the Slovenes succeeded in establishing their independence in 1991 after a short 10-day war. Historical ties to Western Europe, a strong economy, and a stable democracy have assisted in Slovenia's transformation to a modern state. Slovenia acceded to both NATO and the EU in the spring of 2004.

MONETARY SYSTEM:
1 (Tolar) = 1 Yugoslavian Dinar
1 Tolar = 100 Stotinas
REPLACEMENT NOTES:
#11-19, ZA prefix.

REPUBLIC

Banka Slovenije (First)

1989 Issue

A1   1 Lipa   VF   UNC
29.11.1989 (1990). Green. Plants at left, Dr. France Preseren at right. Back: Slovenian Parliament.
    a. Issued note.   8.00   20.00
    s. Specimen.   —   20.00
Note: reportedly 25,000 notes issued, of which more than 10,000 were distributed.

Republika Slovenija

1990-92 Issue

Note: About 500 sets of Specimens #1s-10s were released to the general collecting public. Specimens exist with normal serial #'s and with O's as serial #'s. Zero serial #'s are valued up to $20.00 each.

1A   .50 (Tolar)   VF   UNC
(19)90. Dark olive-green on light gray and light olive-green underprint. Pedimented beehive at lower left, denomination numeral in guilloche over a representation of the dance of the Catrniolan bee on an underprint of honeycomb at center right. Back: Mountain ridge of Triglav at left center. Watermark: Symmetrical designs repeated.
                                                    —   50.00

1   1 (Tolar)   VF   UNC
(19)90. UV: fibers fluoresce yellow. Dark olive-green on light gray and light olive-green underprint. Pedimented beehive at lower left, denomination numeral in guilloche over a representation of the dance of the Catrniolan bee on an underprint of honeycomb at center right. Back: Mountain ridge of Triglav at left center. Watermark: Symmetrical designs repeated.
    a. Issued note.   0.10   0.30
    s1. Specimen overprint: VZOREC.   —   4.00
    s2. Specimen overprint SPECIMEN.   —   4.00

2   2 (Tolarjev)   VF   UNC
(19)90. Brown on tan and ochre underprint. Pedimented beehive at lower left, denomination numeral in guilloche over a representation of the dance of the Catrniolan bee on an underprint of honeycomb at center right. Back: Mountain ridge of Triglav at left center. Watermark: Symmetrical designs repeated.
    a. Issued note.   0.10   0.40
    s1. Specimen overprint: VZOREC.   —   4.00
    s2. Specimen overprint: SPECIMEN.   —   4.00

3   5 (Tolarjev)   VF   UNC
(19)90. Maroon on pale maroon and pink underprint. Pedimented beehive at lower left, denomination numeral in guilloche over a representation of the dance of the Catrniolan bee on an underprint of honeycomb at center right. Back: Mountain ridge of Triglav at left center. Watermark: Symmetrical designs repeated.
    a. Issued note.   0.15   0.50
    s1. Specimen overprint: VZOREC.   —   4.00
    s2. Specimen overprint: SPECIMEN.   —   4.00

4   10 (Tolarjev)   VF   UNC
(19)90. Dark blue-green and grayish purple on light blue-green underprint. Pedimented beehive at lower left, denomination numeral in guilloche over a representation of the dance of the Catrniolan bee on an underprint of honeycomb at center right. Back: Mountain ridge of Triglav at left center. Watermark: Symmetrical designs repeated.
    a. Issued note.   FV   3.00
    s1. Specimen overprint: VZOREC.   —   4.00
    s2. Specimen overprint: SPECIMEN.   —   4.00

5   50 (Tolarjev)   VF   UNC
(19)90. Dark gray on tan and light gray underprint. Pedimented beehive at lower left, denomination numeral in guilloche over a representation of the dance of the Catrniolan bee on an underprint of honeycomb at center right. Back: Mountain ridge of Triglav at left center. Watermark: Symmetrical designs repeated.
    a. Issued note.   FV   5.00
    s1. Specimen overprint: VZOREC.   —   3.50
    s2. Specimen overprint: SPECIMEN.   —   4.00

6   100 (Tolarjev)   VF   UNC
(19)90. Reddish brown and violet on orange and light violet underprint. Pedimented beehive at lower left, denomination numeral in guilloche over a representation of the dance of the Catrniolan bee on an underprint of honeycomb at center right. Back: Mountain ridge of Triglav at left center. Watermark: Symmetrical designs repeated.
    a. Issued note.   FV   8.00
    s1. Specimen overprint: VZOREC.   —   3.50
    s2. Specimen overprint: SPECIMEN.   —   4.00

7   200 (Tolarjev)   VF   UNC
(19)90. Greenish black and dark brown on light gray and light green underprint. Pedimented beehive at lower left, denomination numeral in guilloche over a representation of the dance of the Catrniolan bee on an underprint of honeycomb at center right. Back: Mountain ridge of Triglav at left center. Watermark: Symmetrical designs repeated.
    a. Issued note.   FV   25.00
    s. Specimen overprint: SPECIMEN.   —   4.00

8 500 (Tolarjev)   VF UNC

(19)90; (19)92. Deep lilac and red on pink and pale blue underprint. Pedimented beehive at lower left, denomination numeral in guilloche over a representation of the dance of the Catrniolan bee on an underprint of honeycomb at center right. Back: Mountain ridge of Triglav at left center. Watermark: Symmetrical designs repeated.

a. 1990.	FV	25.00
b. 1992.	FV	40.00
s1. Specimen overprint: *VZOREC*.	—	3.50
s2. Specimen overprint: *SPECIMEN*.	—	4.00

9 1000 (Tolarjev)   VF UNC

(19)91; (19)92. Dark blue-gray and gray on light gray and pale blue underprint. Pedimented beehive at lower left, denomination numeral in guilloche over a representation of the dance of the Catrniolan bee on an underprint of honeycomb at center right. Back: Mountain ridge of Triglav at left center. Watermark: Symmetrical designs repeated.

a. 1991.	FV	35.00
b. 1992.	FV	45.00
s1. Specimen overprint: *VZOREC.*. Watermark: Column pedestal.	—	7.50
s2. Specimen overprint: *SPECIMEN*. Watermark: Column pedestal.	—	7.50
s3. Specimen overprint: *SPECIMEN*. Watermark: Snowflake (error).	—	150

9A 2000 (Tolarjev)   VF UNC

(19)91. (Not issued). Multicolor. Pedimented beehive at lower left, denomination numeral in guilloche over a representation of the dance of the Catrniolan bee on an underprint of honeycomb at center right. Back: Mountain ridge of Triglav at left center. Watermark: Symmetrical designs repeated.   — 60.00

Note: #9A was not released into circulation, but sold along with #B1 to collectors about twelve years later.

10 5000 (Tolarjev)   VF UNC

(19)92. Purple and lilac on pink underprint. Pedimented beehive at lower left, denomination numeral in guilloche over a representation of the dance of the Catrniolan bee on an underprint of honeycomb at center right. Back: Mountain ridge of Triglav at left center. Watermark: Symmetrical designs repeated.

a. Issued note.	FV	130
s1. Specimen overprint: *VZOREC*.	—	20.00
s2. Specimen overprint: *SPECIMEN*.	—	10.00

Banka Slovenije
1992-93 Issue

#11-20 replacement notes: Serial # prefix *AZ* and possibly others.

11 10 Tolarjev   VF UNC

15.1.1992. UV: fibers and box over feather fluoresce yellow; back value 10 yellow; serial # orange. Black, brown-violet and brown-orange on multicolor underprint. P. Trubar at right, quill pen at left center. Back: Ursuline church in Ljubljana at center. Watermark: P. Trubar.

a. Issued note.	FV	0.50
s. Specimen overprint: *SPECIMEN* and *VZOREC*.	—	8.50

12 20 Tolarjev   VF UNC

15.1.1992. Brownish black, deep brown and brown-orange on multicolor underprint. J. Vajkard Valvasor at right, compass at left. Back: Topographical outlines at left center, cherub arms at right.

a. Issued note.	FV	0.75
s. Specimen overprint: *SPECIMEN* and *VZOREC*.	—	10.00

13 50 Tolarjev   VF UNC

15.1.1992. Black, purple and brown-orange on multicolor underprint. J. Vega at right, geometric design and calculations at left center. Back: Academy at upper left, planets and geometric design at center. Watermark: J. Vega.

a. Issued note.	FV	1.50
s. Specimen overprint: *SPECIMEN* and *VZOREC*.	—	12.50

14 100 Tolarjev

15.1.1992. Black, blue-black and brown-orange on multicolor underprint. R. Jakopic at right. Back: Outline of the Jakopicev Pavilion at center right. Watermark: R. Jakopic.

		VF	UNC
a. Issued note.		FV	2.75
s. Specimen overprint: *SPECIMEN* and *VZOREC*.		—	15.00

15 200 Tolarjev

1992; 1997; 2001; 2004. Black, violet-brown and brown-orange on multicolor underprint. I. Gallus at right, musical façade at left. Back: Drawing of Slovenia's Philharmonic building at upper left, five lines of medieval music at upper center. Watermark: I. Gallus.

	VF	UNC
a. 15.1.1992.	FV	20.00
b. 8.10.1997.	FV	3.25
c. 15.1.2001.	FV	3.00
d. 15.1.2004.	FV	3.00
s. Specimen overprint: *SPECIMEN* and *VZOREC*.	—	17.50

16 500 Tolarjev

1992; 2001; 2005. Black, red and brown-orange on multicolor underprint. J. Plecnik at right. Back: Drawing of the National and University Library of Ljubljana at left center. Watermark: J. Plecnik.

	VF	UNC
a. 15.1.1992.	FV	9.00
b. 15.1.2001.	FV	8.00
c. 15.1.2005.	FV	8.00
s. Specimen overprint: *SPECIMEN* and *VZOREC*.	—	20.00

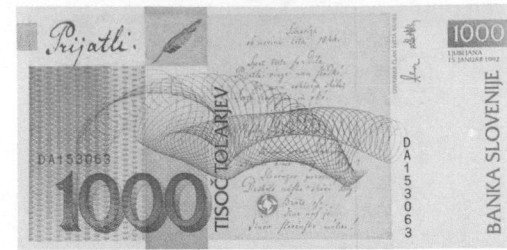

17 1000 Tolarjev

15.1.1992. Brownish black, deep green and brown-orange on multicolor underprint. F. Preseren at right. Back: The poem *Drinking Toast* at center. Watermark: F. Preseren.

	VF	UNC
a. Issued note.	FV	22.50
s. Specimen overprint: *SPECIMEN* and *VZOREC*.	—	50.00

18 1000 Tolarjev

1.6.1993. Black, deep blue-green and brown-orange on multicolor underprint. F. Preseren at right. Like #17 but modified portrait and other changes including color. Back: The poem *Drinking Toast* at center. Watermark: F. Preseren.

	VF	UNC
a. Without *1000* in UV ink on back.	FV	15.00
b. With *1000* in UV ink on back.	FV	15.00
s. Specimen overprint: *SPECIMEN* and *VZOREC*.	—	50.00

19 5000 Tolarjev

1.6.1993. Brownish black, dark brown and brown-orange on multicolor underprint. I. Kobilika at right. Back: National Gallery in Ljubljana at upper left. Watermark: I. Kobilika.

	VF	UNC
a. Issued note.	FV	80.00
s. Specimen overprint: *SPECIMEN* and *VZOREC*.	—	30.00

20 10,000 Tolarjev — VF UNC
28.6.1994. Black, purple and brown-orange on multicolor underprint. I. Cankar at right. Back: Chrysanthemum blossom at left. Watermark: I. Cankar.
  a. Issued note. — FV 110
  s. Specimen overprint: *SPECIMEN* and *VZOREC*. — — 35.00

1997 Issue

21 5000 Tolarjev — VF UNC
8.10.1997. Brownish black, dark brown and brown-orange on multicolor underprint. I. Kobilika at right. Like #19 but with scalloped kinegram. Back: National Gallery in Ljubljana at upper left. Watermark: I. Kobilika.
  a. Kinegram 5000 vertical. — FV 50.00
  b. Kinegram 5000 horizontal. — FV 50.00
  o. Specimen. Red overprint: *SPECIMEN* and *VZOREC*. — — 50.00

2000 Issue

22 1000 Tolarjev — VF UNC
15.1.2000. Black, green and yellow. F. Preseren at left. Like #17 with modified portrait and other changes. Back: The poem *Drinking Toast* at center. Watermark: F. Preseren.
  a. Issued note. — FV 10.00
  s. Specimen overprint: *SPECIMEN* and *VZOREC*. — — —

23 5000 Tolarjev — VF UNC
15.1.2000. Black, green, red and orange. I. Kobilika at right. Similar to #21a. Back: National Gallery in Ljubljana at upper left. Watermark: I. Kobilika.
  a. Issued note. — FV 45.00
  s. Specimen overprint: *SPECIMEN* and *VZOREC*. — — —

24 10,000 Tolarjev — VF UNC
15.1.2000. Brown-black, purple and red. I. Cankar at right, holographic band at right edge. Back: Chrysanthemum blossom at left. Watermark: I. Cankar.
  a. Issued note. — FV 80.00
  s. Specimen overprint: *SPECIMEN* and *VZOREC*. — — —

2000 Commemorative Issue

#25-27, 10th Anniversary of Bank Slovenije

25 100 Tolarjev — VF UNC
2001. 10,000 pieces. Black, blue-black and brown-orange on multicolor underprint. R. Jakopic at right. Back: Outline of the Jakopicev Pavilion at center right. Watermark: R. Jakopic. — FV 3.00

26 100 Tolarjev — VF UNC
2001. 5,000 pieces. Black, green and yellow. F. Preseren at right. Back: The poem *Drinking Toast* at center. Watermark: F. Preseren. — FV 10.00

27 10,000 Tolarjev — VF UNC
2001. 1,000 pieces. Brown'black, purple and red. I. Cankar at right, holographic band at right edge. Back: Chrysanthemum blossom at left. Watermark: I. Cankar. — FV 80.00

2004 Commemorative Issue

#28-30 EU entry on May 1, 2004.

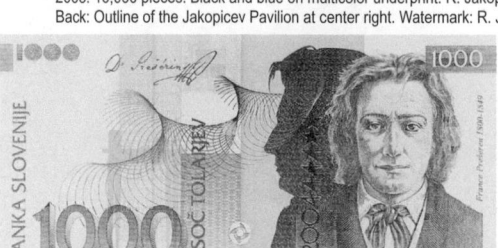

28 100 Tolarjev — VF UNC
2003. 10,000 pieces. Black and blue on multicolor underprint. R. Jakopic at right. Back: Outline of the Jakopicev Pavilion at center right. Watermark: R. Jakopic. — FV 7.50

29 1000 Tolarjev — VF UNC
2003. 5,000 pieces. Black, green and yellow. F. Preseren at right. Back: The poem *Drinking Toast* at center. Watermark: F. Preseren. — FV 25.00

30 **10,000 Tolarjev** VF UNC
2003. 1,000 pieces. Brown, black, purple and red. I. Cankar at right, holographic FV 125
band at right edge. Back: Chrysanthemum blossom at left. Watermark: I. Cankar.

2003 Issue

31 **100 Tolarjev** VF UNC
15.1.2003. . Black and blue on multicolor underprint. R. Jakopic at right. Watermark: R. Jakopic.
   a. Issued note. FV 3.50
   s. Specimen overprint: *SPECIMEN* and *VZOREC*. — —

32 **1000 Tolarjev** VF UNC
2003-05. Black and green on multicolor underprint. F. Preseren at right. Back: The
poem *Drinking Toast* at center. Watermark: F. Preseren.
   a. 15.1.2003. FV 12.00
   b. 15.1.2004. FV 12.00
   c. 15.1.2005. FV 12.00
   s. Specimen overprint: *SPECIMEN* and *VZOREC*. — —

33 **5000 Tolarjev** VF UNC
15.1.2002; 15.1.2004. Black, green, red and orange. I. Kobilika at right. Similar to
#21a. Back: National Gallery in Ljubljana at upper left. Watermark: I. Kobilika.
   a. 15.1.2002. FV 50.00
   b. 15.1.2004. FV 50.00
   s. Specimen. — —

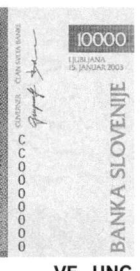

34 **10,000 Tolarjev** VF UNC
15.1.2003; 15.1.2004. Black and purple on multicolor underprint. I. Cankar at right,
holographic band at right edge. Back: Chrysanthemum blossom at left, Iridescent
ink added onto it. Watermark: I. Cankar.
   a. 15.1.2003. FV 95.00
   b. 15.1.2004. FV 95.00
   s. Specimen overprint: *SPECIMEN* and *VZOREC*. — —

Slovenia adopted the Euro in January 2007.

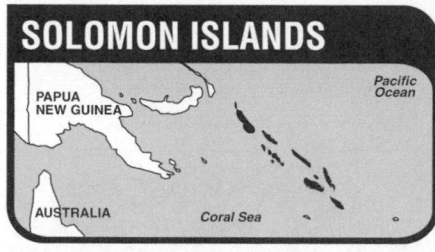

SOLOMON ISLANDS

The Solomon Islands, located in the Southwest Pacific east of Papua New Guinea, has an area of 28,450 sq. km. and a population of 581,300. Capital: Honiara. The most important islands of the Solomon chain are Guadalcanal (scene of some of the fiercest fighting of World War II), Malaitia, New Georgia, Florida, Vella Lavella, Choiseul, Rendova, San Cristobal, the Lord Howe group, the Santa Cruz islands, and the Duff group. Copra is the only important cash crop but it is hoped that timber will become an economic factor. The UK established a protectorate over the Solomon Islands in the 1890s. Some of the bitterest fighting of World War II occurred on this archipelago. Self-government was achieved in 1976 and independence two years later. Ethnic violence, government malfeasance, and endemic crime have undermined stability and civil society. In June 2003, then Prime Minister Sir Allan Kemakeza sought the assistance of Australia in reestablishing law and order; the following month, an Australian-led multinational force arrived to restore peace and disarm ethnic militias. The Regional Assistance Mission to the Solomon Islands (RAMSI) has generally been effective in restoring law and order and rebuilding government institutions.

RULERS:
British

MONETARY SYSTEM:
1 Shilling = 12 Pence
1 Pound = 20 Shillings to 1966
1 Dollar = 100 Cents, 1966-

SIGNATURE VARIETIES

	BANK GOVERNOR	FINANCE MINISTER		BANK GOVERNOR	FINANCE MINISTER
1			4	A.V. Hughes	
2			5	A.V. Hughes	
3	P. N. Tovey		6		
	GOVERNOR	SEC. OF FINANCE		GOVERNOR	SEC. OF FINANCE
7	Rick N. Houenipwela	George Kiriau	8	Rick N. Houenipwela	

BRITISH ADMINISTRATION

Solomon Islands Monetary Authority

1977; 1981 ND Issue

Replacement notes: Serial # prefix: *Z/1.*

5   2 Dollars   VF   UNC
ND (1977). Dark green on pink and pale green underprint. Queen Elizabeth II at right. Signature 1. Back: Fishermen. Watermark: Falcon. Printer: TDLR (without imprint). 139x70mm.

		VF	UNC
a. Issued note.		2.00	10.00
s. Specimen.		—	30.00

6   5 Dollars   VF   UNC
ND (1977). Dark blue on multicolor underprint. Queen Elizabeth II at right. Back: Long boats and hut. Watermark: Falcon. Printer: TDLR (without imprint). 144x72mm.

a. Signature 1.	5.00	27.50
b. Signature 2.	6.00	30.00
s. As a. Specimen.	—	30.00

7   10 Dollars   VF   UNC
ND (1977). Purple and violet on multicolor underprint. Queen Elizabeth II at right. Back: Weaver. Watermark: Falcon. Printer: TDLR (without imprint). 147x74mm.

a. Signature 1.	7.50	35.00
b. Signature 2.	8.00	40.00
s. As a. Specimen.	—	30.00

8   20 Dollars   VF   UNC
ND (1981). Brown and deep orange on multicolor underprint. Queen Elizabeth II at right. Signature 3. Back: Line of people. Watermark: Falcon. Printer: TDLR (without imprint). 153x77mm.   20.00   65.00

#9-10 not assigned.

Central Bank of Solomon Islands

1984 ND Issue

#11 and 12. Replacement notes: Serial # prefix *Z/1.*

11   10 Dollars   VF   UNC
ND (1984). Purple and violet on multicolor underprint. Queen Elizabeth II at right, new bank name. Signature 4. Back: Weaver. Watermark: Falcon. 147x74mm.   7.50   30.00

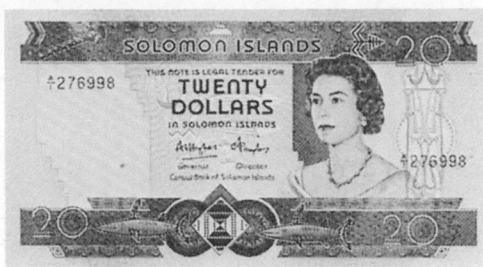

12   20 Dollars

	VF	UNC
ND (1984). Brown and dark orange on multicolor underprint. Queen Elizabeth II at right, new bank name. Signature 4. Back: Line of people. Watermark: Falcon. 154x77mm.	15.00	55.00

1986 ND Issue

#13-17 Replacement notes: Serial # prefix *Y/1*.

13   2 Dollars

	VF	UNC
ND (1986). UV: central design fluoresces yellow. Green on multicolor underprint. Arms at right. Signature 5. Back: Fishermen. Watermark: Falcon. 139x70mm.		
a. Issued note.	FV	2.25
s. Specimen.	—	25.00

14   5 Dollars

	VF	UNC
ND (1986). Dark blue, deep purple and violet on multicolor underprint. Arms at right. Signature 5. Back: Long boats and hut. Watermark: Falcon. 144x72mm.		
a. Issued note.	FV	5.00
s. Specimen.	—	25.00

15   10 Dollars

	VF	UNC
ND (1986). Purple and violet on multicolor underprint. Arms at right. Signature 5. Back: Weaver. Watermark: Falcon. 147x74mm.		
a. Issued note.	FV	10.00
s. Specimen.	—	10.00

16   20 Dollars

	VF	UNC
ND (1986). Brown and deep orange on multicolor underprint. Arms at right. Signature 5. Back: Line of people. Watermark: Falcon. 153x77mm.		
a. Issued note.	FV	20.00
s. Specimen.	—	25.00

17   50 Dollars

	VF	UNC
ND (1986). Blue-green and purple on multicolor underprint. Arms at right. Signature 5. Back: Butterflies and reptiles. Watermark: Falcon. 160x80mm.		
a. Issued note.	FV	45.00
s. Specimen.	—	30.00

1996; 1997 ND Issue

#18-22. Replacement notes: Serial # prefix *X/1*.

18   2 Dollars

	VF	UNC
ND (1997). Greenish black and olive-green on multicolor underprint. Queen Elizabeth II at right, security thread. Ascending size serial number. Back: Fishermen. Printing in watermark area. Watermark: Falcon.	FV	2.00

19   5 Dollars

ND (1997). Dark blue, deep purple and violet on multicolor underprint. Queen
Elizabeth II at right, security thread. Ascending size serial number. Back: Long
boats and hut. Printing in watermark area. Watermark: Falcon. 144x72mm.

VF UNC
FV 4.00

20   10 Dollars

ND (1996). Purple and red-violet on multicolor underprint. Queen Elizabeth II at
right, security thread. Ascending size serial number. Back: Weaver. Printing in
watermark area. Watermark: Falcon. 147x74mm.

VF UNC
FV 7.00

21   20 Dollars

ND (1996). Brown and brown-orange on multicolor underprint. Queen Elizabeth
II at right, security thread. Ascending size serial number. Back: Line of people.
Printing in watermark area. Watermark: Falcon. 154x77mm.

VF UNC
FV 12.50

22   50 Dollars

ND (1996). Green, Blue-gray and purple on multicolor underprint. Queen Elizabeth II at right, security thread. Ascending size serial number. Back: Butterflies
and reptiles. Printing in watermark area. Watermark: Falcon. 160x80mm.

VF UNC
FV 30.00

2001 Commemorative Issue

#23, 25th Anniversary Central Bank of Solomon Islands

23   2 Dollars

(20)01. Polymer plastic. Dark and light green on multicolor underprint. Queen
Elizabeth II at right; with ornate window design. Silver imprint *CBSI Silver Jubilee.*
Back: Fishermen, silver imprint; *COMMEMORATING CBSI SILVER JUBILEE.*
139x70mm.

VF UNC
FV 2.50

2001 ND Issue

24   50 Dollars

ND (2001). Smaller size in width. Green, blue-gray and purple on multicolor
underprint. Similar to #22 but flag added at left center, segmented silver security
strip at center right, and vertical serial # at right. 160x72mm.

VF UNC
FV 30.00

2004-2006 ND Issue

25   2 Dollars

ND (2004). Polymer plastic. Green. Signature varieties. 139x70mm.

VF UNC
FV 2.50

26   5 Dollars

ND (2006). Blue. Signature varieties. Back: Long boats and hut. 144x72mm.

VF UNC
FV 4.00

27 10 Dollars — VF UNC
ND (2006). Purple. Signature varieties. Back: Shell money manufacturing. — FV 7.50
147x74mm.

28 20 Dollars — VF UNC
ND (2006). Brown. Back: Dancers. 154x72mm. — FV 15.00
29 50 Dollars — VF UNC
ND (2004). Green. Back: Butterflies and reptiles. 160x72mm. — FV 30.00
30 100 Dollars — VF UNC
ND (2006). Brown on tan and multicolor underprint. Signature varieties. Back: — FV 75.00
Coconut harvest. 160x72mm.

2013 Issue

31 2 Dollars — VF UNC
  Expected new issue. 139x70mm. — — —
32 5 Dollars — VF UNC
  Expected new issue. 144x72mm. — — —
33 10 Dollars — VF UNC
  Expected new issue. 147x74mm. — — —
34 20 Dollars — VF UNC
  Expected new issue. 154x72mm. — — —
35 50 Dollars — VF UNC
ND (2013) Local basket weave design representing the swirling movement of — FV 17.50
shoals of fish. Back: Iguana, lizard and snake. Printer: DLR. 160x72mm.

36 100 Dollars — VF UNC
ND (2013). Local basket weave design representing the swirling movement of — FV 27.50
shoals of fish. Printer: DLR. 160x72mm.

COLLECTOR SERIES
Solomon Islands Monetary Authority
1979 ND Issue

CS1 ND (1979) 2-10 Dollars — Mkt. Value
  #5, 6b, 7b with overprint: *SPECIMEN* and serial # prefix Maltese cross. — 25.00

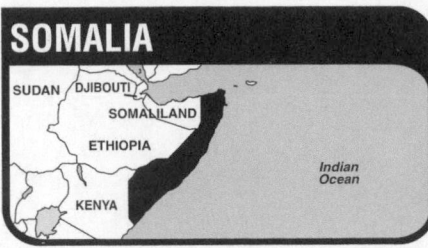

SOMALIA

Somalia, the Somali Democratic Republic, comprising the former Italian Somaliland, is located on the coast of the eastern projection of the African continent commonly referred to as the *Horn*. It has an area of 178,201 sq. mi. (461,657 sq. km.) and a population of 11.53 million. Capitol Mogadishu. The economy is pastoral and agricultural. Livestock, bananas and hides are exported. The area of the British Somaliland Protectorate was known to the Egyptians at least 1,500 years B.C., and was occupied by the Arabs and Portuguese before British sea captains obtained trading and anchorage rights in 1827. The land of sandy clay and sporadic rainfall acquired a strategic importance with the opening of the Suez Canal in 1869. After negotiating treaties with the tribes, Britain declared the area a protectorate in 1888. Italy acquired Italian Somaliland in 1895 by purchase from the sultan of Zanzibar. Britain occupied Italian Somaliland in 1941 and administered it until April 1, 1950, when it was returned to Italy as a U.N. trusteeship. The British Somaliland protectorate became independent on June 26, 1960. Five days later it joined with Italian Somaliland to form the Somali Republic. The country was under a revolutionary military regime installed Oct. 21, 1969. After 11 years of civil war rebel forces fought their way into the capital. A. M. Muhammad became president in Aug. 1991 but interfactional fighting continued. A UN-sponsored truce was signed in March 1992 and a peace plan and pact was signed Jan. 15, 1993. The northern Somali National Movements (SNM) declared a secession of the northwestern Somaliland Republic on May 17, 1991 which is not recognized by the Somali Democratic Republic.

MONETARY SYSTEM:
  1 Scellino = 1 Shilling = 100 Centesimi
  1 Shilin = 1 Shilling = 100 Centi

REPUBLIC
Banca Nazionale Somala
1962 Issue

1 5 Scellini = 5 Shillings — VF UNC
1962. Red on green and orange underprint. Antelope at left. Signature title: *IL PRESI-DENTE* at left. Back: Dhow at center. Watermark: Leopard's head. Printer: OCV.
  a. Issued note. — 35.00 200
  s. Specimen. — — 110

2 10 Scellini = 10 Shillings — VF UNC
1962. Green oon red-brown and green underprint. Flower at left. Signature title: *IL PRESIDENTE* at left. Back: River scene at center right. Watermark: Leopard's head. Printer: OCV.
  a. Issued note. — 55.00 325
  s. Specimen. — — 185

3 20 Scellini = 20 Shillings VF UNC
1962. Brown on blue and gold underprint. Banana plant at left.Signature title: *IL PRESIDENTE* at left. Back: Bank building at center right. Watermark: Leopard's head. Printer: OCV.
   a. Issued note. 75.00 600
   s. Specimen. — 750

4 100 Scellini = 100 Shillings VF UNC
1962. Blue on green and orange underprint. Artcraft at left.Signature title: *IL PRESIDENTE* at left. Back: Building. Watermark: Leopard's head. Printer: OCV.
   a. Issued note. 125 750
   s. Specimen 400

1966 Issue

5 5 Scellini = 5 Shillings VF UNC
1966. Red on green and orange underprint. Antelope at left, different guilloche in underprint. Signature title: *IL PRESIDENTE* at left. Back: Dhow at center. Watermark: Leopard's head. Printer: OCV (without imprint).
   a. Issued note. 30.00 175
   s. Specimen perforated: *ANNULLATO*. — 100

6 10 Scellini = 10 Shillings VF UNC
1966. Green on red-brown and green underprint. Flower at left, different guilloche in underprint. Signature title: *IL PRESIDENTE* at left. Back: River scene at center right. Watermark: Leopard's head. Printer: OCV (without imprint).
   a. Issued note. 50.00 325
   s. Specimen perforated: *ANNULLATO*. — 225

7 20 Scellini = 20 Shillings VF UNC
1966. Brown on pink, blue and green underprint. Banana plant at left. Signature title: *IL PRESIDENTE* at left. Back: Brown bank building at center right. Watermark: Leopard's head. Printer: OCV (without imprint).
   a. Issued note. 65.00 450
   s. Specimen perforated: *ANNULLATO*. — 325

8 100 Scellini = 100 Shillings VF UNC
1966. Blue on green, purple and tan underprint. Artcraft at left.Signature title: *IL PRESIDENTE* at left. Back: Building. Watermark: Leopard's head. Printer: OCV (without imprint).
   a. Issued note. 120 600
   s. Specimen perforated: *ANNULLATO*. — 435

1968 Issue

9 5 Scellini = 5 Shillings VF UNC
1968. Red on green and orange underprint. Antelope at left, different guilloche in underprint. Signature title: *IL GOVERNATORE* at left. Back: Dhow at center. Watermark: Leopard's head. Printer: OCV (without imprint). 40.00 250

10 10 Scellini = 10 Shillings VF UNC
1968. . Green on red-brown and green underprint Flower at left, different guilloche in underprint. Signature title: *IL GOVERNATORE* at left. Back: River scene at center right. Watermark: Leopard's head. Printer: OCV (without imprint). 55.00 450

11 20 Scellini = 20 Shillings VF UNC
1968. Brown on blue and gold underprint. Banana plant at left. Signature title: *IL GOVERNATORE* at left. Back: Brown bank building. Watermark: Leopard's head. Printer: OCV (without imprint). 85.00 575

12 100 Scellini = 100 Shillings VF UNC
1968. Blue on green and orange underprint. Artcraft at left. Signature title: *IL GOVERNATORE* at left. Back: Building. Watermark: Leopard's head. Printer: OCV (without imprint). 125 850

DEMOCRATIC REPUBLIC

Banca Nazionale Somala

1971 Issue

13 5 Scellini = 5 Shillings VF UNC
1971. Purple-brown on blue, green and gold underprint. Artcraft at left. Signature title: *IL GOVERNATORE* and *IL CASSIERE* at right. Back: Building. Watermark: Leopard's head. Printer: OCV (without imprint).
   a. Issued note. 25.00 200
   s. Specimen. — 110

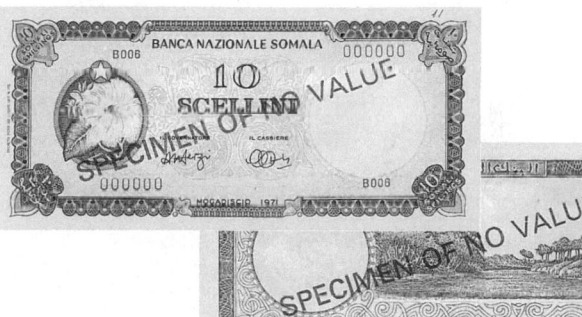

14 10 Scellini = 10 Shillings VF UNC
1971. Green on red-brown and green underprint. Flower at left, different guilloche in underprint. Signature title: *IL GOVERNATORE* and *IL CASSIERE* at right. Back: River scene at center right. Watermark: Leopard's head. Printer: OCV (without imprint).
   a. Issued note. 30.00 325
   s. Specimen. — 175

15 20 Scellini = 20 Shillings VF UNC
1971. Brown on blue and gold underprint. Banana plant at left. Signature title: *IL GOVERNATORE* and *IL CASSIERE* at right. Back: Brown bank building at center right. Watermark: Leopard's head. Printer: OCV (without imprint).
   a. Issued note. 70.00 500
   s. Specimen. — 275

16   100 Scellini = 100 Shillings   VF   UNC

1971. Blue on green and orange underprint. Artcraft at left. Signature title: *IL GOVERNATORE* and *IL CASSIERE* at right. Back: Building. Watermark: Leopard's head. Printer: OCV (without imprint).

a. Issued note.	85.00	650
s. Specimen.	—	375

Bankiga Qaranka Soomaaliyeed

SOMALI NATIONAL BANK
Law of 11.12.1974

17   5 Shilin = 5 Shillings   VF   UNC

1975. Purple on gold and multicolor underprint. Gnus and zebras at bottom center, arms at left. Back: Banana harvesting at center right. Watermark: Sayyid Mohammed Aabdullah Hassan.

a. Issued note.	12.50	50.00
s. Specimen.	—	—

18   10 Shilin = 10 Shillings   VF   UNC

1975. Dark green on pink and multicolor underprint. Minaret at left center, arms at left. Back: Shipbuilders at work at center right. Watermark: Sayyid Mohammed Aabdullah Hassan.

15.00   60.00

19   20 Shilin = 20 Shillings   VF   UNC

1975. Brown on multicolor underprint. Bank building at center, arms at left. Back: Cattle. Watermark: Sayyid Mohammed Aabdullah Hassan.

15.00   125

20   100 Shilin = 100 Shillings   VF   UNC

1975. Blue on gold and multicolor underprint. Womam with baby, rifle and farm tools at left center, Dagathur Monument at center right, arms at left. Back: Workers in factory. Watermark: Sayyid Mohammed Aabdullah Hassan.

35.00   160

Bankiga Dhexe ee Soomaaliya

CENTRAL BANK OF SOMALIA
Law of 6.12.1977

20A   5 Shilin = 5 Shillings   VF   UNC

1978. Purple on gold and multicolor underprint. Gnus and zebras at bottom center, arms at left. Black series and serial number. Back: Banana harvesting at center right. Watermark: Sayyid Mohammed Aabdullah Hassan.

a. Issued note.	25.00	85.00
s. Specimen.	—	25.00

21   5 Shilin = 5 Shillings   VF   UNC

1978. Purple on gold and multicolor underprint. Cape Buffalo herd at bottom left center, arms at left. Black series and serial number. Back: Banana harvesting at center right. Watermark: Sayyid Mohammed Aabdullah Hassan.

10.00   42.50

22   10 Shilin = 10 Shillings   VF   UNC

1978. Dark green on pink and multicolor underprint. Minaret at left center, arms at left. Black series and serial number. Back: Shipbuilders at work at center right. Watermark: Sayyid Mohammed Aabdullah Hassan.

a. Issued note.	8.00	45.00
s. Specimen.	—	25.00

23   20 Shilin = 20 Shillings   VF   UNC

1978. Brown on multicolor underprint. Bank building at center, arms at left. Black series and serial number. Back: Cattle. Watermark: Sayyid Mohammed Aabdullah Hassan.

a. Issued note.	15.00	85.00
s. Specimen.	—	40.00

24 100 Shilin = 100 Shillings VF UNC
1978. Blue on gold and multicolor underprint. Woman with baby, rifle and farm tools at left center, Dagathur Monument at center right, arms at left. Black series and serial number. Back: Workers in factory. Watermark: Sayyid Mohammed Aabdullah Hassan.
a. Issued note. 22.50 130
s. Specimen. — 25.00

Law of 5.4.1980
#26-28. Replacement ntoes: Serial # prefix *Z001*. #25 not assigned.

26 10 Shilin = 10 Shillings VF UNC
1980. Dark green on pink and multicolor underprint. Minaret at left center, arms at left. Red series and serial number. Back: Shipbuilders at work at center right. Watermark: Sayyid Mohammed Abdullah Hassan. 8.00 27.50

27 20 Shilin = 20 Shillings VF UNC
1980. Brown on multicolor underprint. Bank building at center, arms at left. Red series and serial number. Back: Cattle. Watermark: Sayyid Mohammed Aabdullah Hassan. 9.00 55.00

28 100 Shilin = 100 Shillings VF UNC
1980. Blue on gold and multicolor underprint. Woman with baby, rifle and farm tools at left center, Dagathur Monument at center right, arms at left. Red series and serial number. Back: Workers in factory. Watermark: Sayyid Mohammed Aabdullah Hassan. 17.50 85.00

Law of 9.12.1981
#29-30 Replacement notes: Serial # prefix *ZZ001*.

29 20 Shilin = 20 Shillings VF UNC
1981. Brown on multicolor underprint. Bank building at center, arms at left. Red series and serial number. Back: Cattle. Watermark: Sayyid Mohammed Aabdullah Hassan. 17.50 55.00

30 100 Shilin = 100 Shillings VF UNC
1981. Blue on gold and multicolor underprint. Woman with baby, rifle and farm tools at left center, Dagathur Monument at center right, arms at left. Red series and serial number. Back: Workers in factory. Watermark: Sayyid Mohammed Aabdullah Hassan. 15.00 50.00

Law of 30.12.1982; 1983 Issue
#31-35 Replacement notes: Serial # prefix *Z001*.

31 5 Shilin = 5 Shillings VF UNC
1983 87. Reduced size. Brown violet. Cape Buffalo herd at left center, arms at top left center, star near lower center. Back: Harvesting bananas
a. 1983. 3.00 7.00
b. 1986. 3.00 6.00
c. 1987. 3.00 5.00

32 10 Shilin = 10 Shillings VF UNC
1983-87. Reduced size. Green and multicolor. Lighthouse at left, arms at top left center, star at lower center. Back: Shipbuilders at center right. Watermark: Sayyid Mohammed Abdullah Hassan.
a. 1983. 3.00 8.00
b. 1986. 3.00 6.00
c. 1987. 2.50 5.00

33 20 Shilin = 20 Shillings VF UNC
1983-89. Reduced size. Brown and multicolor. Bank at left, arms at top left center, star at lower center. Back: Cattle. Watermark: Sayyid Mohammed Abdullah Hassan.
a. 1983. 5.00 15.00
b. 1986. 4.00 12.50
c. 1987. 3.00 10.00
d. 1989. 3.00 6.00

34 50 Shilin = 50 Shillings VF UNC
1983-89. Reduced size. Red-brown and multicolor underprint. Walled city at left and center, arms at top left center, star near lower center. Back: Watering animals at center right. Watermark: Sayyid Mohammed Aabdullah Hassan.
a. 1983. 3.00 12.00
b. 1986; 1987. 2 signature varieties for 1987. 2.00 8.00
c. 1988. 2.00 5.00
d. 1989. 2.00 4.00

35 100 Shilin = 100 Shillings

1983-89. Reduced size. Blue-black, dark blue and dark green on multicolor underprint. Woman with baby, rifle and farm tools at left center, Dagathur Monument at center right, arms at top left center, star at lower center. Back: Workers in factory. Watermark: Sayyid Mohammed Aabdullah Hassan.

		VF	UNC
a.	1983.	5.00	12.00
b.	1986; 1987. Two signature varieties for 1987.	2.00	10.00
c.	1988.	2.00	7.00
d.	1989.	2.00	4.00

Law of 1.1.1989

36 500 Shilin = 500 Shillings

1989; 1990; 1996. Green and aqua on multicolor underprint. Fishermen mending net at left center, arms at top left center. Two signature varieties. Back: Mosque at left center. Watermark: Sayyid Mohammed Aabdullah Hassan.

		VF	UNC
a.	1989.	2.00	9.00
b.	1990.	2.00	8.00
c.	1996.	2.00	8.00

Law of 1.1.1990; 1990 Issue

37 1000 Shilin = 1000 Shillings

1990; 1996. UV: value 1000 fluoresce yellow; serial # orange. Back design elements yellow. Violet and orange on multicolor underprint. Women seated weaving baskets at left center; arms above at top left center. Back: City view at bottom, Port of Mogadishu at upper center right. Watermark: Sayyid Mohammed Aabdullah Hassan.

		VF	UNC
a.	1990.	2.00	5.00
b.	1996.	2.00	7.00

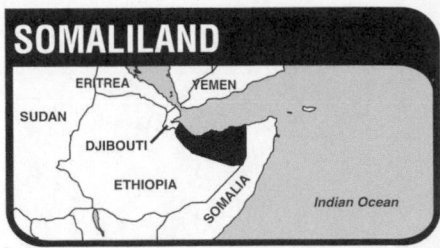

SOMALILAND

The Somaliland Republic, comprising the former British Somaliland Protectorate, is located on the coast of the northeastern projection of the African continent commonly referred to as the "Horn" on the southwestern end of the Gulf of Aden. Bordered by Eritrea to the west, Ethiopia to west and south and Somalia to the east, it has an area of 68,000* sq. mi. (176,000* sq. km). Capital: Hargeysa. It is mostly arid and mounainous except for the gulf shoreline. The Protectorate of British Somaliland was established in 1888 and from 1905 the territory was administered by a commissioner under the British Colonial Office. Italian Somaliland was administered as a colony from 1893 to 1941, when the territory was occupied by British forces. In 1950 the United Nations allowed Italy to resume control of Italian Somaliland under a trusteeship. In 1960 British and Italian Somaliland were united as Somalia, an independent republic outside the Commonwealth. Civil War erupted in the late 1970's and continued until the capital of Somalia was taken in 1990. The United Nations provided aid and peacekeepers. A UN sponsored truce was signed in March 1992 and a peace plan and pact was signed Jan. 15, 1993. The northern Somali National Movement (SMN) declared a secession of the Somaliland Republic on May 17, 1991 which is not recognized by the Somali Democratic Republic. The currency issued by the East African Currency Board was used in British Somaliland from 1945 to 1961. Somali currency was then used until 1995.

MONETARY SYSTEM:
   1 Somaliland Shilling = 1 Shilin

REPUBLIC

Baanka Somaliland
1994 Issue

1 5 Shillings = 5 Shilin

1994. Bright green, olive-green and red-brown on multicolor underprint. Greater Kudu at right, building at center. Back: Trader with camels.

		VF	UNC
a.	Issued note.	FV	1.00
s.	Specimen.	—	100

2 10 Shillings = 10 Shilin

1994-96. Violet, purple and red-brown on multicolor underprint. Greater Kudu at right, building at center. Back: Trader with camels.

		VF	UNC
a.	1994.	FV	1.25
b.	1996.	FV	1.00
s.	Specimen.	—	100

3 20 Shillings = 20 Shilin

1994-96. Brown and red-brown on multicolor underprint. Greater Kudu at right, building at center. Back: Trader with camels.

		VF	UNC
a.	1994.	FV	2.25
b.	1996.	FV	2.00
s.	Specimen.	—	110

4   50 Shillings = 50 Shilin   VF UNC
1994-96. Blue-violet, blue-gray and red-brown on multicolor underprint. Greater
Kudu at right, building at center. Back: Trader with camels.
    a. 1994.   FV 4.00
    b. 1996.   FV 3.50
    s. Specimen.   —   110

5   100 Shillings = 100 Shilin   VF UNC
1994-. Brownish black and red-violet on multicolor underprint. Building at
center. Back: Ship dockside in background, herdsmen w/sheep at front center.
135x61mm.
    a. 1994.   FV 6.50
    b. 1996.   FV 5.00
    c. 1999. Signature 3.   FV 5.00
    d. 2002.   FV 5.00
    s. Specimen. As a, b.   —   110

6   500 Shillings = 500 Shilin   VF UNC
1994-. Purple, blue-black and blue-green on multicolor underprint. Building at
center. Back: Ship dockside in background, herdsmen w/sheep at front center.
145x66mm.
    a. 1994.   FV 15.00
    b. 1996.   FV 10.00
    c. 1999.   FV 10.00
    d. 2002.   FV 10.00
    e. 2005.   FV 10.00
    f. 2006.   FV 10.00
    g. 2008.   FV 10.00
    h. 2011.   FV 10.00
    s. Specimen. As a, b.   —   125

1996 Issue

7   50 Shillings = 50 Shilin   VF UNC
1996; 1999; 2002. Increased size. Blue-violet, blue-gray and violet on multicolor
underprint. Greater Kudu at right, building at center. Back: Trader with camels.
130x58mm.
    a. Signature 1.   FV 0.75
    b. Signature 2.   FV 0.75
    c. Signature 3. 1999.   FV 0.50
    d. 2002.   FV 0.50
    s. Specimen.   —   125

1996 "Bronze" Commemorative Issue
#8-13, 5th Anniversary of Independence

8   5 Shillings = 5 Shilin   VF UNC
18.5.1996 (- old date 1994). Bright green, olive-green and red-brown on multicolor FV 1.75
underprint. Overprint on #1. Back: Traders with camels.

9   10 Shillings = 10 Shilin   VF UNC
18.5.1996 (- old date 1994). Violet, purple and red-brown on multicolor underprint. FV 2.00
Overprint on #2a. Back: Traders with camels.

10   20 Shillings = 20 Shilin   VF UNC
18.5.1996 (- old date 1994). Brown and red-brown on multicolor underprint. FV 3.00
Overprint on #3a. Back: Traders with camels.

11   50 Shillings = 50 Shilin   VF UNC
18.5.1996.
    a. Overprint on #4a. (- old date 1994).   FV 4.25
    b. Overprint on #4b. 1996.   FV 3.00

11A 50 Shillings = 50 Shilin   VF UNC
18.5.1996. Blue-violet, blue-gray and violet on multicolor underprint. Bronze FV 3.50
overprint on #7a. Back: Traders with camels.

12   100 Shillings = 100 Shilin

18.5.1996 (- old date 1994). Brownish black and red-violet on multicolor underprint. Overprint on #5a. Back: Ship dockside in background, herdsmen with sheep at front center.

	VF	UNC
	FV	7.50

13   500 Shillings = 500 Shilin

18.5.1996 (- old date 1994). Purple, blue-black and blue-green on multicolor underprint. Overprint on #6a. Back: Ship dockside in background, herdsmen with sheep at front center.

	VF	UNC
	FV	25.00

1996 "Silver" Commemorative Issue

#14-19, 5th Anniversary of Independence

14   5 Shillings = 5 Shilin

18.5.1996 (- old date 1994). Bright green, olive-green and red-brown on multicolor underprint. Overprint on #1. Back: Traders with camels.

	VF	UNC
	FV	1.75

15   10 Shillings = 10 Shilin

18.5.1996 (- old date 1994). Violet, purple and red-brown on multicolor underprint. Overprint on #2a. Back: Traders with camels.

	VF	UNC
	FV	2.00

16   20 Shillings = 20 Shilin

18.5.1996 (- old date 1994). Brown and red-brown on multicolor underprint. Overprint on #3a. Back: Traders with camels.

	VF	UNC
	FV	3.00

17   50 Shillings = 50 Shilin

18.5.1996.
a. overprint on #4a. (- old date 1994).
b. overprint on #4b. 1996.

	VF	UNC
a.	FV	4.25
b.	FV	3.00

17A   50 Shillings = 50 Shilin

1996. Blue-violet, blue-gray and violet on multicolor underprint. Overprint on number 7b. Back: Ship dockside in background, herdsmen with sheep at front center.

	VF	UNC
	FV	3.50

18   100 Shillings = 100 Shilin

18.5.1996 (- old date 1994). Brownesh black and red-violet on multicolor underprint. Overprint on #5a. Back: Ship dockside in background, herdsmen with sheep at front center.

	VF	UNC
	FV	7.50

19   500 Shillings = 500 Shilin

18.5.1996 (- old date 1994). Purple, blue-black and blue-green on multicolor underprint. Overprint on #6a. Back: Ship dockside in background, herdsmen with sheep at front center.

	VF	UNC
	FV	25.00

2011 Issue

20   1000 Shillings

2011; 2012. Red and purple on multicolor underprint. Bank of Somaliland building in Hargeisa. Back: Heardsman with flock of sheep and goats. 145x66mm.
a. 2011.
b. 2012.

	VF	UNC
a.	FV	35.00
b.	FV	35.00

21   5000 Shillings   **VF   UNC**
   2011. Green on multicolor underprint. Bank of Somaliland building in Hargeisa.
   Back: Three camels and three goats. 145x66mm.
   a. 2011. Signature Abdi Dirir Abdi and Abdi Mohamoud Gullet.   FV   60.00
   b. 2012.   FV   60.00

COLLECTOR SERIES

Baanka Somaliland
2006 Issue

CS1   1000 Shillings   **VF   UNC**
   2006 Purple on tan and purple underprint. Young girl at right, lion at left. Back:
   Lion standing at center, camel at right. 159x76mm.
   a. Issued note   —   5.00
   b. Uncut sheet, 3 notes.   —   10.00
   r. Replacement note. Serial # prefix AX.   —   7.50
   s. Specimen. Red overprint: SPECIMEN on both sides.   —   30.00

SOUTH AFRICA

The Republic of South Africa, located at the southern tip of Africa, has an area, including the enclave of Walvis Bay, of 1,219,912 sq. km. and a population of 48.78 million. Capital: Administrative, Pretoria; Legislative, Cape Town; Judicial, Bloemfontein. Manufacturing, mining and agriculture are the principal industries. Exports include wool, diamonds, gold and metallic ores.Dutch traders landed at the southern tip of modern day South Africa in 1652 and established a stopover point on the spice route between the Netherlands and the East, founding the city of Cape Town. After the British seized the Cape of Good Hope area in 1806, many of the Dutch settlers (the Boers) trekked north to found their own republics. The discovery of diamonds (1867) and gold (1886) spurred wealth and immigration and intensified the subjugation of the native inhabitants. The Boers resisted British encroachments but were defeated in the Boer War (1899-1902); however, the British and the Afrikaners, as the Boers became known, ruled together under the Union of South Africa. In 1948, the National Party was voted into power and instituted a policy of apartheid - the separate development of the races. The first multi-racial elections in 1994 brought an end to apartheid and ushered in black majority rule under the African National Congress (ANC). ANC infighting, which has grown in recent years, came to a head in September 2008 after President Thabo Mneki resigned. Kgalema Motlanthe, the party's General-Secretary, succeeded as interim president until general elections scheduled for 2009. South African currency carries inscriptions in both Afrikaans and English.

RULERS:
   British to 1961

MONETARY SYSTEM:
   1 Shilling = 12 Pence
   1 Pound = 20 Shillings to 1961
   1 Rand = 100 Cents (= 10 Shillings), 1961-

REPLACEMENT NOTES:
   #77b, 78b, Y/1 prefix. #83c, 84c, Z/1 prefix.
   The major areas comprising this section are covered individually according to the following outline:

SIGNATURE VARIETIES			
3	M.H. de Kock, 1.7.1945 - 30.6.1962	4	G. Rissik, 1.7.1962 - 30.6.1967
5	T.W. de Jongh, 1.7.1967 - 31.12.1980	6	G.P.C. de Kock, 1.1.1981 - 7.8.1989
7	C.L. Stals, 8.8.1989 - 7.8.1999	8	T.T. Mboweni, 8.8.1999 -

REPUBLIC OF SOUTH AFRICA

South African Reserve Bank

SUID-AFRIKAANSE RESERWEBANK
1961 ND Issue

#102-105 replacement notes: Serial # prefix Z/1; Y/1; X/1; W/1 respectively.

102   1 Rand   **VF   UNC**
   ND (1961-65). Rust brown on multicolor underprint. Portrait of Jan van Riebeeck
   at left, first line of bank name and value in English. Watermark: Jan van Riebeeck.
   135x77mm.
   a. Signature 3. (1961).   22.50   65.00
   b. Signature 4. (1962-65).   11.00   28.00
   s. As a. Specimen.   —   550

103 1 Rand

	VF	UNC
ND (1961-65). Rust brown on multicolor underprint. Portrait of Jan van Riebeeck at left, first line of bank name and value in Afrikaans. Watermark: Jan van Riebeeck. 137x78mm.		
a. Signature 3. (1961).	22.50	65.00
b. Signature 4. (1962-65).	11.00	27.50

106 10 Rand

	VF	UNC
ND (1961-65). Green and brown on multicolor underprint. Portrait of Jan van Riebeeck at left, first line of bank name and value in English. Back: Sailing ship. Watermark: Jan van Riebeeck. 170x97mm.		
a. Signature 3. (1961).	25.00	65.00
b. Signature 4. (1962-65).	17.50	37.50
s. Specimen. Punch hole cancel.	—	—

107 10 Rand

	VF	UNC
ND (1961-65). Green and brown on multicolor underprint. Portrait of Jan van Riebeeck at left, first line of bank name and value in Afrikaans. Watermark: Jan van Riebeeck. 170x97mm.		
a. Signature 3. (1961).	25.00	65.00
b. Signature 4. (1962-65).	17.50	37.50
s. Specimen.	—	550

104 2 Rand

	VF	UNC
ND (1961-65). Blue on multicolor underprint. Portrait of Jan van Riebeeck at left, first line of bank name and value in English. Watermark: Jan van Riebeeck. 150x85mm.		
a. Signature 3. (1961).	12.50	36.00
b. Signature 4. (1962-65).	6.50	20.00

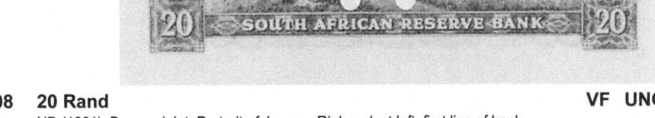

108 20 Rand

	VF	UNC
ND (1961). Brown-violet. Portrait of Jan van Riebeeck at left, first line of bank name and value in English. Signature 3. Back: Machinery. Watermark: Jan van Riebeeck.		
a. Issued note.	50.00	160
s. Specimen.	—	550

108A 20 Rand

	VF	UNC
ND (1962-65). Brown-violet. Portrait of Jan van Riebeeck at left, first line of bank name in Afrikaans. Signature 4. Watermark: Jan van Riebeeck.	50.00	160

1966 ND Issue

#109-114 Replacement notes: Serial # prefix *Z/1; Y/1; X/1; W/1* respectively.

105 2 Rand

	VF	UNC
ND (1961-65). Blue on multicolor underprint. Portrait of Jan van Riebeeck at left, first line of bank name and value in Afrikaans. Watermark: Jan van Riebeeck. 150x85mm.		
a. Signature 3. (1961).	12.50	36.00
b. Signature 4. (1962-65).	6.50	20.00
s. As a. Specimen.	—	550

109 1 Rand

	VF	UNC
ND (1966-72). Dark reddish brown on multicolor underprint. Jan van Riebeeck at left, first lines of bank name and value in English. Back: Rams in field. Watermark: Springbok. 126x64mm.		
a. Signature 4. (1966).	2.50	13.50
b. Signature 5. (1967).	1.50	8.00
s1. As a. Specimen.	—	35.00
s2. As b. Specimen.	—	35.00

110 1 Rand VF UNC
ND (1966-72). Dark reddish brown on multicolor underprint. Jan van Riebeeck at left,first lines of bank name and value in Afrikaans. Back: Rams in field. Watermark: Springbok. 126x64mm.
    a. Signature 4. (1966).   2.50   13.50
    b. Signature 5. (1967).   1.50   8.00
    s1. As a. Specimen.   —   35.00
    s2. As b. Specimen.   —   35.00

111 5 Rand VF UNC
ND (1966-76). Purple on multicolor underprint. Jan van Riebeeck at left, covered wagons on trail at right corner, first lines of bank name and value in English. Back: Ore mine with train. 133x70mm.
    a. Signature 4. Watermark: Springbok (1966).   15.00   90.00
    b. Signature 5. Watermark: Springbok (1967-74).   6.00   17.50
    c. Signature 5. Watermark: J. van Riebeeck (1975).   6.50   20.00
    s1. As a. Specimen.   —   35.00
    s2. As b. Specimen.   —   35.00

112 5 Rand VF UNC
ND (1966-76). Purple on multicolor underprint. Jan van Riebeeck at left, first lines of bank name and value in Afrikaans. Back: Ore mine with train.
    a. Signature 4. Watermark: Springbok (1966).   15.00   90.00
    b. Signature 5. Watermark: Springbok (1967-74).   6.00   17.50
    c. Signature 5. Watermark: J. van Riebeeck (1975).   6.50   20.00
    s1. As a. Specimen.   —   35.00
    s2. As b. Specimen.   —   0.00

113 10 Rand VF UNC
ND (1966-76). Dark green and brown on multicolor underprint. Jan van Riebeeck at left, Capital building at center, first lives of bank name and value in English. Back: Old sailing ships. 140x76mm.
    a. Signature 4. Watermark: Springbok (1966).   10.00   35.00
    b. Signature 5. Watermark: Springbok (1967-74).   5.00   16.50
    c. Signature 5. Watermark: J. van Riebeeck (1975).   5.00   16.50
    s1. As a. Specimen.   —   50.00
    s2. As b. Specimen.   —   50.00

114 10 Rand VF UNC
ND (1966-76). Dark green and brown on multicolor underprint. Jan van Riebeeck at left, Capital building at center, first lines of bank name and value in Afrikaans. Back: Old sailing ships. 140x76mm.
    a. Signature 4. Watermark: Springbok (1966).   10.00   35.00
    b. Signature 5. Watermark: Springbok (1967-74).   5.00   16.50
    c. Signature 5. Watermark: J. van Riebeeck (1975).   5.00   16.50
    s1. As a. Specimen.   —   50.00
    s2. As b. Specimen.   —   50.00

1973-84 ND Issue

115 1 Rand VF UNC
ND (1973-75). Dark reddish brown on multicolor underprint. Jan van Riebeeck at left, first lines of bank name and value in English. Signature 5. Back: Rams in field. 120x57mm.
    a. Watermark: Springbok (1973).   1.75   5.00
    b. Watermark: J. van Riebeeck (1975).   2.00   6.00

116 1 Rand VF UNC
ND (1973-75). Dark reddish brown on multicolor underprint. Jan van Riebeeck at left,first lines of bank name and value in Afrikaans. Signature 5. Back: Rams in field. Watermark: Springbok. 120x57mm.
    a. Watermark: Springbok (1973).   1.75   5.00
    b. Watermark: J. van Riebeeck (1975).   2.00   6.00

117 2 Rand VF UNC
ND (1974-76). Blue on multicolor underprint. Jan van Riebeek at left, first lines of bank name and value in Afrikaans. Signature 5. Back: Hydroelectric dam. 127x62mm.
    a. Watermark: Springbok (1974).   3.00   15.00
    b. Watermark: J. van Riebeeck (1976).   4.50   16.00

118 2 Rand VF UNC
ND (1978-90). Blue on multicolor underprint. Jan van Riebeek at left, electrical tower at center. Back: Refinery at left center. Watermark: Jan van Riebeek. 120x57mm.
    a. Signature 5. (1978-81).   1.00   6.50
    b. Signature 6. Fractional numbering system. Without security thread (1981).   3.00   20.00
    c. As b. With security thread. (1981-83).   1.00   4.50
    d. As c. Alpha-numeric system. (1983-90).   0.50   3.50
    e. Signature 7. (1990).   2.00   6.50
Note: #118b exists with serial # which has a small fractional letters and large numerals or large letters with small numerals.

119 5 Rand VF UNC

ND (1978-94). Purple on multicolor underprint. Jan van Riebeek at left, first lines of bank name and value in English, diamond at center. Back: Grain storage at left center. Watermark: Jan van Riebeek. 127x63mm.

a. Signature 5. (1978-81). 2.50 13.50
b. Signature 6. Fractional numbering system. Without security thread (1981). 40.00 165
c. As b. With security thread. (1981-89). 1.50 14.00
d. As c. Alpha-numeric system. (1989-90). 2.50 12.00
e. Signature 7. (1990-94). 2.50 12.50

120 10 Rand VF UNC

ND (1978-93). Green on multicolor underprint. Jan van Riebeek at left, flower at center. Back: Bull and ram at left center. Watermark: Jan van Riebeek. 134x70mm.

a. Signature 5. (1978-81). 4.50 17.00
b. Signature 6. Fractional numbering system. Without security thread (1981). 12.50 55.00
c. As b. With security thread. (1982-85). 3.25 16.50
d. As c. Alpha-numeric system. (1985-90). 3.00 20.00
e. Signature 7. (1990-93). 2.00 12.50

121 20 Rand VF UNC

ND (1984-93). Brown on multicolor underprint. Jan van Riebeek at left, building in underprint at center. Back: Three sailing ships at left center with arms at right. Watermark: Jan van Riebeek. 144x77mm.

a. Signature 5. (1978-81). 7.00 27.50
b. Signature 6. Fractional numbering system. Without security thread (1981). 22.50 80.00
c. As b. With security thread. (1982-85). 5.00 25.00
d. As c. Alpha-numeric system. (1985-90). 10.00 50.00
e. Signature 7. (1990-93). 6.00 16.50

122 50 Rand VF UNC

ND (1984-90). Red on multicolor underprint. Jan van Riebeek at left, lion in underprint at center. Back: Local animals at lower left, mountains at center, plants at right. Watermark: Jan van Riebeek. 147x83mm.

a. Signature 6. (1984). 15.00 40.00
b. Signature 7. (1990). 22.50 50.00

1992-94 Issue

123 10 Rand VF UNC

ND (1993; 1999). Dark green and dark blue on brown and multicolor underprint. White rhinoceros at center, large white rhino at right. Back: Ram's head over sheep at left. Watermark: White rhinoceros. 128x70mm.

a. Signature 7. (1993). FV 10.00
b. Signature 8. (1999). 2.50 4.50

124 20 Rand VF UNC

ND (1993; 1999). Deep brown and red-brown on multicolor underprint. Elephants at center, large elephant head at right. Back: Open pit mining at left center. Watermark: Elephant head. 134x70mm.

a. Signature 7. (1993). FV 10.00
b. Signature 8. (1999). FV 7.50

125 50 Rand VF UNC

ND (1992; 1999). Maroon, brown and deep blue-green on multicolor underprint. Lions with cub drinking water at center, male lion head at right. Back: Sasol oil refinery at lower left center. Watermark: Male lion head. 140x70mm.

a. Signature 7 (1992). Reddish lion drinking water (serial # prefix lower than AL). 25.00 85.00
b. Signature 7. (1992). Brownish blue lion drinking water. (serial # prefix greater than AL). FV 25.00
c. Signature 8 (1999). FV 17.50
x. Like a. Watermark on wrong side. Serial # prefix: BP. 22.50 50.00

126 100 Rand VF UNC
ND (1994; 1999). Blue-violet and dark gray on multicolor underprint. Cape buffalo
at center and large water buffalo head at right. Back: Zebras along bottom from
left to center. Watermark: Water buffalo head. 146x70mm.
    a. Signature 7 (1994). FV 72.50
    b. Signature 8 (1999). FV 30.00

127 200 Rand VF UNC
ND (1994; 1999). Orange on multicolor underprint. Leopard at center, large
leopard's head at right. Back: Dish antenna at upper left, modern bridge at lower
left. 152x70mm.
    a. Signature 7 (1994). FV 85.00
    b. Signature 8 (1999). FV 60.00

2005 Issue

128 10 Rand VF UNC
2005. Green on multicolor underprint. White rhinoceros at center, large white rhino
head at right, coat of arms at top left, various geometric shapes at lower portion.
Back: Ram's head over sheep at left. Watermark: Rhino head. 128x70mm.
    a. Signature: Tito Mboweni. FV 4.00
    b. Signature: Gill Marcus. FV 3.50

129 20 Rand VF UNC
2005. Brown on tan underprint. Elephants at center, large elephant head at right,
coat of arms at top left, various geometric shapes at lower portion. Back: Open pit
mining at left center. Watermark: Elephant head. 134x70mm.
    a. Signature: Tito Mboweni. FV 7.00
    b. Signature: Gill Marcus. FV 5.00

130 50 Rand VF UNC
2005. Red on multicolor underprint. Lions with cub drinking water at center, male
lion head at right, coat of arms at top left, various geometric shapes at lower
portion. Back: Sasol oil refinery at lower left center. Watermark: Male lion head.
140x70mm.
    a. Signature: Tito Mboweni. FV 13.00
    b. Signature: Gill Marcus. FV 12.50

131 100 Rand VF UNC
2005. Blue on multicolor underprint. Cape buffalo at center and large water buffalo
head at right, coat of arms at top left, various geometric shapes at lower portion.
Back: Zebras along bottom from left to center. Watermark: Water buffalo head.
146x70mm.
    a. Signature: Tito Mboweni. FV 27.50
    b. Signature: Gill Marcus. FV 22.50

132 200 Rand VF UNC
2005. Brown on green and multicolor underprint. Leopard at center, large FV 60.00
leopard's head at right, coat of arms at top left, various geometric shapes at lower
portion. Back: Dish antenna at upper left, modern bridge at lower left. 152x70mm.

2012 Issue

133 10 Rand VF UNC
ND (2012). Green and multicolor. Nelson Mandela at right. Back: Rhinoceros head FV 3.50
at center. 128x70mm.

134   20 Rand
ND (2012). Brown, tan and multicolor. Nelson Mandela at right. Back: Elephant head at center. 134x70mm.

	VF	UNC
	FV	5.00

135   50 Rand
ND (2012). Red and multicolor. Nelson Mandela at right. Back: Lion head at center. 140x70mm.

	VF	UNC
	FV	12.50

136   100 Rand
ND (2012). Blue and multicolor. Nelson Mandela at right. Back: Cape buffalo head at center. 146x70mm.

	VF	UNC
	FV	22.50

137   200 Rand
ND (2012). Brown, green and multicolor. Nelson Mandela at right. Back: Leopard head at center. 152x70mm.

	VF	UNC
	FV	60.00

2013 Issue

138   10 Rand
NS (2013). Brown, tan and multicolor. Nelson Mandela at right, Omron rings. 134x70mm.

	VF	UNC
	FV	5.00

139   20 Rand
NS (2013). Brown, tan and multicolor. Nelson Mandella at right. Omron rings. Back: Elephant. 134x70mm.

	VF	UNC
	FV	5.00

140   50 Rand
ND (2013). Red and multicolor. Nelson Mandela at right. Omron rings. Back: Lion head at center. 140x70mm.

	VF	UNC
	FV	12.50

141   100 Rand
ND (2013). Blue and multicolor. Nelson Mandela at right. Omron rings. Back: Cape buffalo head at center.

	VF	UNC
	FV	22.50

142   200 Rand
ND (2013). Brown, green and multicolor. Nelson Mandela at right. Omron rings. Back: Leopard head at center. 152x72mm.

	VF	UNC
	FV	60.00

SOUTH KOREA

The Republic of Korea, situated in northeastern Asia on the southern half of the Korean peninsula between North Korea and the Korean Strait, has an area of 38,025 sq. mi. (98,484 sq. km.) and a population of 44.61 million. Capital: Seoul. The economy is based on agriculture and textiles. Clothing, plywood and textile products are exported. Japan replaced China as the predominant foreign influence in Korea in 1895 and annexed the peninsular country in 1910. Defeat in World War II brought an end to Japanese rule. U.S. troops entered Korea from the south and Soviet forces entered from the north. The Cairo Conference (1943) had established that Korea should be "free and independent." The Potsdam Conference (1945) set the 38th parallel as the line dividing the occupation forces of the United States and Russia. When Russia refused to permit a U.N. commission designated to supervise reunification elections to enter North Korea, an election was held in South Korea on May 10, 1948. By its determination, the Republic of Korea was inaugurated on Aug. 15, 1948.

MONETARY SYSTEM:
 1 Won (Hwan) = 100 Chon
 1 new Won = 10 old Hwan, 1962-

REPLACEMENT NOTES:
 #30-32, 34, 36-37, sm. crosslet design in front of serial #. #35, 38, 38A, 39, 43-49: notes w/first digit 9 in serial number.

DATING:
 The modern notes of Korea are dated according to the founding of the first Korean dynasty, that of the house of Tangun, in 2333 BC.

REPUBLIC

Bank of Korea
1958-60 Issue

23   50 Hwan
4291 (1958). Green-blue on olive-green underprint. Archway at left. Back: Statue at center, medieval tortoise warship at right.

	VF	UNC
	60.00	350

24   500 Hwan
4291 (1958); 4292 (1959). Dark green. Portrait Syngman Rhee at right.

	VF	UNC
	40.00	350

25   1000 Hwan   VF   UNC
4293 (1960); 4294 (1961); 1962. Black on olive underprint. King Sejong the Great
at right. Back: Flaming torch at center.
   a. 4293 (1960).   10.00   100
   b. 4294 (1961).   6.00   60.00
   c. 1962.   7.00   65.00

1961-62 Issue

26   100 Hwan   VF   UNC
1962. Green on orange and multicolor underprint. Woman reading to child at right.   60.00   325
Back: Archway at left, date at bottom right margin.

27   500 Hwan   VF   UNC
4294 (1961). Eight-character imprint. Blue-green on multicolor underprint. King   80.00   475
Sejong the Great at right. Back: Building at right.

1962 ND Issues

Won System

28   10 Jeon   VF   UNC
1962. Deep blue on pale blue and pink underprint.
   a. Issued note.   0.10   0.40
   s. Specimen.   —   50.00

29   50 Jeon   VF   UNC
1962. Black on pale green and ochre underprint.
   a. Issued note.   0.10   0.50
   s. Specimen.   —   50.00

30   1 Won   VF   UNC
ND (1962). Violet on brown underprint.
   a. Issued note.   0.10   1.00
   s. Specimen.   —   100

31   5 Won   VF   UNC
ND (1962). Black on gray-green underprint.
   a. Issued note.   10.00   90.00
   s. Specimen.   —   150

32   10 Won   VF   UNC
ND (1962). Brown on green underprint.
   a. Issued note.   2.00   10.00
   s. Specimen.   —   200

33   10 Won   VF   UNC
1962-65; ND. Brown on lilac and green underprint. Tower at left. Back: Medieval
tortoise warship at center, date at lower right.
   a. 1962.   8.00   50.00
   b. 1963.   8.50   52.50
   c. 1964.   4.50   27.50
   d. 1965.   3.00   20.00
   e. ND.   0.50   3.00

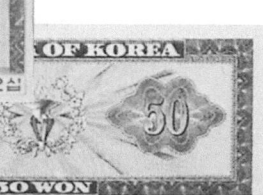

34   50 Won   VF   UNC
ND (1962). Red-brown on blue and lilac underprint. Rock in the sea at left. Back:
Torch at center.
   a. Issued note.   15.00   95.00
   s. Specimen.   —   —

35   100 Won   VF   UNC
1962-69. Green on olive underprint. Archway at left. Underprint: *100 Won* at
center. Back: Pagoda and date.
   a. 1962.   17.50   110
   b. 1963.   12.50   80.00
   c. 1964.   12.50   75.00
   d. 1965.   12.50   75.00
   e. 1969.   15.00   90.00

36   100 Won   VF UNC
ND (1962). Green on blue and gold underprint. Archway at left. Five-petaled blossom at center in underprint. Back: Torch at center.
  a. Issued note.   12.50 80.00
  s. Specimen.   —   —

37   500 Won   VF UNC
ND (1962). Blue on lilac and green underprint. Pagoda portal at left. Back: Torch at center.
  a. Issued note.   22.50 135
  s. Specimen.   —   —

1965; 1966 ND Issue

38   100 Won   VF UNC
ND (1965). Dark green and blue on multicolor underprint. Bank name and denomination in red. King Sejong the Great at right. Back: Building.
  a. Issued note.   1.75 5.50
  s. Specimen.   —   —

38A   100 Won   VF UNC
ND (1965). Dark blue-green. Bank name and denomination in brown, King Sejong the Great at right. Back: Building.   2.25 10.00

39   500 Won   VF UNC
ND (1966). Black on multicolor underprint. City gate at left. Back: Medieval turtle warships.
  a. Issued note.   1.50 9.00
  s. Specimen.   —   —

1969-73 ND Issue

40   50 Won   VF UNC
ND (1969). Black on green and brown underprint. Pavilion at left. Back: Torch at center.
  a. Issued note.   1.00 4.00
  s. Specimen.

41   5000 Won   VF UNC
ND (1972). Brown on green and multicolor underprint. Yi I at right. Back: Large building. Watermark: Yi I.   12.50 40.00

42   10,000 Won   VF UNC
ND (1973). Dark brown on multicolor underprint. King Sejong the Great at left center. Back: Buildings and pavilion. Watermark: Woman with headdress.   25.00 60.00

1973-79 ND Issue

43   500 Won   VF UNC
ND (1973). Blue and green on multicolor underprint. Admiral Yi Sun-shin at left, medieval turtle warship at center. Back: Building with steps.   1.00 3.50

44 **1000 Won**
ND (1975). UV: threads fluoresce green. Purple on multicolor underprint. Yi
Hwang at right. Back: Toansowon Academy at center. Watermark: Flowers.

	VF	UNC
	2.00	5.00

45 **5000 Won**
ND (1977). Brown on multicolor underprint. Yi I at right. Back: Ojukon, birthplace
of Yi I. Watermark: Yi I.

	VF	UNC
	8.50	20.00

46 **10,000 Won**
ND (1979). Black and dark green on multicolor underprint. Water clock at left, King
Sejong at right. Back: Kyonghoeru Pavilion at center. Watermark: King Sejong.

	VF	UNC
	20.00	40.00

1983 ND Issue

47 **1000 Won**
ND (1983). UV: threads fluoresce green, central design in shades of green. Purple
on multicolor underprint. Yi Hwang at right. One raised colored dot for visually
impaired at lower left. Back: Buildings of Tosansowon Academy. Watermark: Yi
Hwang. 151x76mm.

	VF	UNC
	FV	4.00

48 **5000 Won**
ND (1983). UV: threads fluoresce green, central design shades of green. Brown
on multicolor underprint. Yi I at right. Two raised colored dots for visually impaired
at lower left. Back: Ojukon, birthplace of Yi I. Watermark: Yi I. 156x76mm.

	VF	UNC
	FV	12.00

49 **10,000 Won**
ND (1983). Dark green on multicolor underprint. Water clock at left, King Sejong
at right.Three raised colored dots in green for visually impaired at lower left. Back:
Kyonghoeru Pavilion at center. Watermark. King Sejong. 161x76mm.

	VF	UNC
	FV	22.50

50 **10,000 Won**
ND (1994). UV: threads fluoresce green. Dark green on multicolor underprint. Like
number 49, but with circular dark green lines over watermark area at left, microprinting added under water clock, segmented silver security thread at left center.
Back: Kyonghoeru Pavilion at center. Watermark: King Sejong. 161x76mm.

	VF	UNC
	FV	20.00

2000-2002 Issue

51 **5000 Won**
2002. Brown and orange on multicolor underprint. Scholar Yi I at right. Date below
two raised dots in variable ink at lower left. Back: Ojukon, the house where Yi I
was born. 156x76mm.

	VF	UNC
	FV	9.00

52	**10,000 Won**		**VF**	**UNC**
	2000. (c) 2000 in Korean at lower left on face, in English at lower right. Dark green on multicolor underprint. Water clock at left, King Sejong at right. Date below three raised dots in variable ink at lower left. Back: Kyonghoeru Pavilion at center. 161x76mm.			
	a. Issued note.		FV	20.00
	s. Specimen. Red overprint.		—	750

2004 Bank Check Issue

52A	**100,000 Won**		**VF**	**UNC**
	6.2004.		FV	7.50
53	**1,000,000 Won**		**VF**	**UNC**
	6.2004.		FV	20.00

2006; 2007 Issue

54	**1000 Won**		**VF**	**UNC**
	ND (2007). Purple and blue on multicolor underprint. Yi Hwang at right, Myeong-nyundang at center. 136x68mm.			
	a. Issued note.		FV	4.00
	s. Specimen.		—	75.00

55	**5000 Won**		**VF**	**UNC**
	ND (2006). UV: Security strip fluoresces yellow, threads yellow and blue. Brown, rose and green on multicolor underprint. Scholar Yi I at right and the house where he was born at center. Hologram at left center. Back: Tree branch and flowers at left. 142x68mm.			
	a. Issued note.		FV	5.00
	s. Specimen.		—	75.00

56	**10,000 Won**		**VF**	**UNC**
	ND (2007). Dark Green on light green and multicolor underprint. King Sejong at right. Hologram at left center. Back: Astrolabe. 148x68mm.			
	a. Issued note.		FV	10.00
	s. Specimen.		—	75.00
57	**50,000 Won**		**VF**	**UNC**
	ND (2009). Brown and yellow on multicolor underprint. Wide hologram foil at left face, wide windowed thread at right of watermark window. Shin Saim-dang at right. Back: Painting of Bamboo and Apricot trees. Watermark: Shin and 5 within pentagon. 154x68mm.		FV	80.00

SOUTH SUDAN

Egypt attempted to colonize the region of southern Sudan by establishing the province of Equatoria in the 1870s. Islamic Mahdist revolutionaries overran the region in 1885, but in 1898 a British force was able to overthrow the Mahdist regime. An Anglo-Egyptian Sudan was established the following year with Equatoria being the southernmost of its eight provinces. The isolated region was largely left to itself over the following decades, but Christian missionaries converted much of the population and facilitated the spread of English. When Sudan gained its independence in 1956, it was with the understanding that the southerners would be able to participate fully in the political system. When the Arab Khartoum government reneged on its promises, a mutiny began that led to two prolonged periods of conflict (1955-1972 and 1983-2005) in which perhaps 2.5 million people died - mostly civilians - due to starvation and drought. Ongoing peace talks finally resulted in a Comprehensive Peace Agreement, signed in January 2005. As part of this agreement the south was granted a six-year period of autonomy to be followed by a referendum on final status. The result of this referendum, held in January 2011, was a vote of 98% in favor of secession. Independence was attained on 9 July 2011.

MONETARY SYSTEM:
100 Piasters = 1 South Sudanese Pound

REPUBLIC

Bank of South Sudan

2011 Issue

1	**5 Piasters**	**VF**	**UNC**
	ND (2011). Dr. John Garang de Mabior at right. Printer: TLDR (without imprint).	5.00	20.00
2	**10 Piasters**	**VF**	**UNC**
	ND (2011). Dr. John Garang de Mabior at right. Printer: TLDR (without imprint).	5.00	20.00
3	**25 Piasters**	**VF**	**UNC**
	ND (2011). Dr. John Garang de Mabior at right. Printer: TLDR (without imprint).	5.00	20.00

#4 held in reserve.

5	**1 Pound**	**VF**	**UNC**
	ND (2011). Brown and green on multicolor underprint. Dr. John Garang de Mabior at left. Back: Giraffe heard at right. Printer: TDLR (without imprint).	1.00	4.00

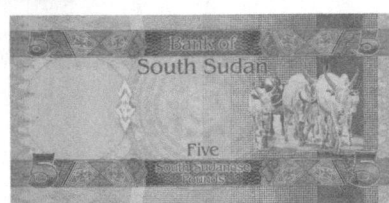

6	**5 Pounds**	**VF**	**UNC**
	ND (2011). Brown and rose on multicolor underprint. Dr. John Garang de Mabior at left. Back: Water buffalo pair ar right. Printer: TLDR (without imprint). 120x60mm.	2.00	8.00
7	**10 Pounds**	**VF**	**UNC**
	ND (2011). Brown and aqua on multicolor underprint. Dr. John Garang de Mabior at left. Back: Water buffalo pair at right. Printer: TDLR (without imprint). 120x60mm.	4.00	15.00
8	**25 Pounds**	**VF**	**UNC**
	ND (2011). Brown and tan on multicolor underprint. Dr. John Garang de Mabior at left. Back: Ibex pair at right. Printer: TDLR (without imprint). 120x60mm.	8.00	25.00
9	**50 Pounds**	**VF**	**UNC**
	ND (2011). Brown and purple on multicolor underprint. Dr. John Garang de Mabior at left. Back: Elephant line at right. Printer: TDLR (without imprint).	12.00	45.00
10	**100 Pounds**	**VF**	**UNC**
	ND (2011). Brown and blue on multicolor underprint. Dr. John Garang de Mabior at left. Back: Lion lying on ground at right. Printer: TDLR (without imprint).	20.00	90.00

SOUTH VIET NAM

South Viet Nam (the former Republic of Viet Nam), located in Southeast Asia, bounded by North Viet Nam on the north (the former Democratic Republic of Viet Nam), Laos and Cambodia on the west, and the South China Sea on the east and south, had an area of 66,280 sq. mi. (171,665 sq. km.) and a population of 20 million. Capital: Saigon. The economy of the area was predominantly agricultural. South Viet Nam, the direct successor to the French-dominated regime (also known as the State of Viet Nam), was created after the first Indochina War (between the French and the Viet-Minh) by the Geneva agreement of 1954 which divided Viet Nam at the 17th parallel of latitude.

The elections which would have reunified North and South Viet Nam in 1956 never took place, and the North restarted their war for unification of the country in 1959. In 1975, North Vietnamese forces overran the South reuniting the country under communist rule. There followed a short period of co-existence of the two Vietnamese states, but the South was now governed by the North through the Peoples Revolutionary Government (PRG). On July 2, 1976, South and North Viet Nam joined to form the Socialist Republic of Viet Nam. See also Viet Nam.

MONETARY SYSTEM
1 Dng = 100 Xu

VIET NAM - REPUBLIC
Ngân-Hàng Quô'c-Gia Viêt-Nam
NATIONAL BANK OF VIET NAM
1962 ND Issue

5   10 Dông   VF   UNC
ND (1962). Shade varieties. Red. Young farm couple at left. Back: Ornate arch. Printer: SBNC.
- a. Issued note.   2.00   8.00
- p. Proof. Uniface face and back pair.   —   450
- s. Specimen. Overprint: *GIAY MAU*   —   300

6   20 Dông   VF   UNC
ND (1962). Brown. Ox cart at left. Back: Woman digging. Printer: SBNC.
- a. Issued note.   6.00 35.00
- p. Proof. Uniface face and back pair.   —   450
- s. Specimen. Overprint: *GIAY MAU*.   —   350
- x. Counterfeit.   —   —

6A   500 Dông   VF   UNC
ND (1962). Green-blue on gold and pinkish underprint. Dragon at left, palace-like building at left center. Back: Farmer with two water buffalos at right. Watermark: Ngo Dinh Diem.
- a. Issued note.   200   700
- s1. Specimen. Overprint: *GIAY MAU*.   —   1,000
- s2. Specimen. TDLR oval.   —   1,000

1964; 1966 ND Issues

15   1 Dông   VF   UNC
ND (1964). Light and dark brown on orange and light blue underprint. Back: Farm tractor at right. Watermark: Plant.
- a. Issued note.   3.00   5.00
- s1. Specimen. *GIAY MAU*.   —   1,200
- s2. Specimen. TDLR oval.   —   1,200

16   20 Dông   VF   UNC
ND (1964). Green on multicolor underprint. Back: Stylized fish at center. Watermark: Dragon's head.
- a. Issued note.   0.75   9.00
- s. Specimen. *GIAY MAU*.   —   300

Note: Three different #16 specimens have been reported. This indicates that more varieties of issued notes may exist. Please report all new varieties to the editors.

17   50 Dông   VF   UNC
ND (1966). Purple on multicolor underprint. Leaf tendrils at right
- a. Issued note.   5.00 25.00
- s. Specimen. *GIAY MAU*.   —   300

18 100 Dông VF UNC
ND (1966). Light and dark brown on light blue underprint. Building with domed roof at right. Back: Power plant, water reservoir and dam. Watermark: Plant.
  a. Issued note. 5.00 35.00
  s1. Specimen. Red overprint *GIAY MAU*. — 300
  s2. Specimen. Black overprint — 300

19 100 Dông VF UNC
ND (1966). Red on multicolor underprint. Le Van Duyet in national costume at left. Back: Building and ornate gateway at center right.
  a. Watermark: Demon's head. 10.00 40.00
  b. Watermark: Le Van Duyet's head. 3.00 15.00
  s1. As a. Specimen. TDLR oval. — 500
  s2. As b. Specimen. — 500

20 200 Dông VF UNC
ND (1966). Dark brown on multicolor underprint. Nguyen-Hue, warrior, at left. Back: Warrior on horseback leading soldiers.
  a. Watermark: Demon's head. 10.00 45.00
  b. Watermark: Nguyen Hue's head. 3.00 25.00
  s1. As a. Specimen. — 500
  s2. As b. Specimen. — 500

#21 renumbered, see #6A.

22 500 Dông VF UNC
ND (1964). Brown on multicolor underprint. Museum in Saigon at center. Back: Stylized creatures at center. Watermark: Demon's head.
  a. Issued note. 12.50 50.00
  s1. Specimen. — 300
  s2. Specimen. TDLR oval. — 600

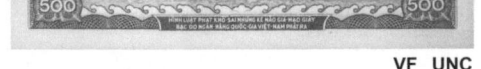

23 500 Dông VF UNC
ND (1966). Blue on multicolor underprint. Tr,'n-Hu'ng-Dao, warrior, at left. Back: Sailboat and rocks in water at center right. Watermark: Tr,'n-Hu'ng-Dao, warrior.
  a. Issued note. 5.00 25.00
  s. Specimen. TDLR oval. — 500
  x. Counterfeit. Series S; U; X. — 15.00

1969-71 ND Issue

24 20 Dông VF UNC
ND (1969). Red on multicolor underprint. Bank building at right. Back: Lathework. Watermark: Tr,'n-Hu'ng-Dao, warrior.
  a. Issued note. 0.50 5.00
  s. Specimen. *GIAY MAU*. — 175

25 50 Dông VF UNC
ND (1969). Blue-green on multicolor underprint. Bank building at right. Back: Lathework. Watermark: Tr,'n-Hu'ng-Dao, warrior.
  a. Issued note. 0.50 5.00
  s. Specimen. *GIAY MAU*. — 175

26 100 Dông VF UNC
ND (1970). Dark green on multicolor underprint. Bank building at right. Back: Lathework. Watermark: Tr,'n-Hu'ng-Dao, warrior.
  a. Issued note. 0.75 5.00
  s. Specimen. *GIAY MAU*. — 175

27 200 Dông VF UNC
ND (1970). Purple on multicolor underprint. Bank building at right. Back: Lathework. Watermark: Tr,'n-Hu'ng-Dao, warrior.
  a. Issued note. 1.25 25.00
  s. Specimen. Overprint: *GIAY MAU*. — 300

31   100 Dông   VF   UNC

ND (1972). Green on multicolor underprint. Palace of Independence at right.
Back: Farmer with two water buffalo at left center. Watermark: Young woman's
head in profile.

    a. Issued note.   0.75   5.00
    s. Specimen.   —   400

28   500 Dông   VF   UNC

ND (1970). Orange and dark brown on multicolor underprint. Bank building at
right. Back: Lathework. Watermark: Tr,'n-Hu'ng-Dao, warrior.

    a. Issued note.   0.75   5.00
    s. Specimen. Overprint: *GIAY MAU*.   —   200

#28A renumbered, see #28.
  Note: The brown and black variety previously listed as #28A is believed to be the result of oxidation.

32   200 Dông   VF   UNC

ND (1972). Wine red on multicolor underprint. Palace of Independence at right.
Back: Three deer at left center. Watermark: Young woman's head in profile.

    a. Issued note.   2.50   15.00
    s. Specimen. TDLR oval.   —   500

29   1000 Dông   VF   UNC

ND (1971). Turquoise on multicolor underprint. Bank building at right. Back:
Lathework. Watermark: Tr,'n-Hu'ng-Dao, warrior.

    a. Issued note.   5.00   15.00
    s. Specimen. *GIAY MAU*.   —   250

1972; 1975 ND Issue

33   500 Dông   VF   UNC

ND (1972). Orange and olive-brown on multicolor underprint. Palace of Independence at right. Back: Tiger at left center. Watermark: Young woman's head
in profile.

    a. Issued note.   1.25   6.00
    s. Specimen.   —   500

Note: The brown and olive-brown variety previously listed as #33A is current believed by leading
          authorities to be caused by oxidation.
#33A renumbered, see #33.

30   50 Dông   VF   UNC

ND (1972). Blue-gray on multicolor underprint. Palace of Independence at right.
Back: Three horses at left center. Watermark: Young woman's head in profile.

    a. Issued note.   0.50   4.00
    s. Specimen.   —   400
    ct. Color trial. Purple Palace on face.   —   —

34 1000 Dông
VF UNC

ND (1972). . Blue on multicolor underprint. Palace of Independence at right. Back: Three elephants carrying loads at left center. Watermark: Young woman's head in profile.

    a. Issued note.   1.25   5.00
    s. Specimen.   —   500

34A 1000 Dông
VF UNC

ND (1975). Specimen. (Not issued). Green and multicolor. Stylized fish at left, Truong Cong Dinh at right. Back: Dinh's tomb at upper left, stylized fish at right.
        — 5,000

35 5000 Dông
VF UNC

ND (1975). (Not issued). Brown, blue and multicolor. Palace of Independence at right. Back: Leopard at left center. Watermark: Young woman's head in profile. Printer: TDLR.

    a. Normal serial #.   80.00 500
    s. Specimen. Overprint: *GAIY MAU.* — 700

36 10,000 Dông
VF UNC

ND (1975). (Not issued). Violet and multicolor. Palace of Independence at right. Back: Water buffalo at left center. Watermark: Young woman's head in profile. Printer: TDLR.

    a. Normal serial #.   80.00 500
    s. Specimen. Overprint: *GIAY MAU.* — 700

Ngân Hàng Viêt Nam
1966 Dated (1975) Transitional Issue

#37-44 were printed in the People's Republic of China for use in South Viet Name after liberation by the National Liberation Front. The Republic of Viet Name notes were converted to these notes before there was another conversion to unite the currency for the entire country.

37 10 Xu
VF UNC

1966 (1975). Brown on multicolor underprint. Drying salt at center. Back: Unloading boats.

    a. Issued note.   1.25   3.00
    s. Specimen.   —   40.00

38 20 Xu
VF UNC

1966 (1975). Blue on multicolor underprint. Workers on rubber plantation at center. Back: Soldiers greeting farmers with oxen.

    a. Issued note.   1.25   3.00
    s. Specimen.   —   40.00

39 50 Xu
VF UNC

1966 (1975). Brownish purple on multicolor underprint. Harvesting cane at center. Back: Women weaving rugs.

    a. Issued note.   2.50   8.00
    s. Specimen.   —   40.00

40 1 Dông
VF UNC

1966 (1975). Red-orange on multicolor underprint. Boats on canal at center. Back: Workers in field.

    a. Issued note.   3.00 10.00
    s. Specimen.   —   40.00

41 2 Dông
VF UNC

1966 (1975). Blue and green on multicolor underprint. Houseboats under a bridge at center. Back: Soldiers and workers.

    a. Issued note.   5.00 15.00
    s. Specimen.   —   41.00

42 5 Dông
VF UNC

1966 (1975). . Purple on multicolor underprint. Four women in textile factory at center. Back: Armed soldiers with downed helicopters.

    a. Issued note.   6.00 20.00
    s. Specimen.   —   40.00

43 10 Đồng   **VF UNC**
1966 (1975). Red on multicolor underprint. Three women and train at center.
Back: Soldiers and people with flag. 148x75mm.
    a. Issued note.   20.00   40.00
    s. Specimen. Overprint: *GIAY MAU* in black on both sides.   —   40.00

44 50 Đồng   **VF UNC**
1966 (1975). Green and blue on multicolor underprint. Workers in factory at
center. Back: Combine harvester.
    a. Issued note.   75.00   200
    s. Specimen.   —   50.00

The Spanish State, forming the greater part of the Iberian Peninsula of southwest Europe, has an area of 504,782 sq. km. and a population of 40.5 million. Capital: Madrid. The economy is based on agriculture, industry and tourism. Machinery, fruit, vegetables and chemicals are exported. Spain's powerful world empire of the 16th and 17th centuries ultimately yielded command of the seas to England. Subsequent failure to embrace the mercantile and industrial revolutions caused the country to fall behind Britain, France, and Germany in economic and political power. Spain remained neutral in World Wars I and II but suffered through a devastating civil war (1936-39). A peaceful transition to democracy following the death of dictator Francisco Franco in 1975, and rapid economic modernization (Spain joined the EU in 1986) gave Spain a dynamic and rapidly growing economy and made it a global champion of freedom and human rights. The government continues to battle the Basque Fatherland and Liberty (ETA) terrorist organization, but its major focus for the immediate future will be on measures to reverse the severe economic recession that started in mid-2008.

RULERS:
    Francisco Franco, regent, 1937-1975
    Juan Carlos I, 1975-

MONETARY SYSTEM:
    1 Peseta = 100 Centimos 1874-2001
    1 Euro = 100 Cents, 2002-

REPLACEMENT NOTES:
    #150 and later, *9A, 9B, 9C* type prefix.

REPUBLIC

Banco de España
1965 (1970; 1971) Issue

150 100 Pesetas   **VF UNC**
19.11.1965 (1970). Brown on multicolor underprint. Gustavo Adolfo Bécquer   7.50   20.00
at center right, couple near fountain at lower left. Back: Woman with parasol at
center, Cathedral of Sevilla at left. Watermark: Woman's head. Printer: FNMT.

151 1000 Pesetas
19.11.1965 (1971). Green on multicolor underprint. San Isidoro at left. Back: Imaginary figure with basilica behind. Watermark: San Isidoro. Printer: FNMT.

	VF	UNC
	40.00	140

1970-71 Issue

152 100 Pesetas
17.11.1970 (1974). Brown on pale orange and multicolor underprint. Manuel de Falla at right. Back: The summer residence of the Moorish kings in Granada at left center. Watermark: Manuel de Falla. Printer: FNMT.

	VF	UNC
a. Issued note.	4.00	15.00
s. Specimen.	—	—

153 500 Pesetas
23.7.1971 (1973). Blue-gray and black on multicolor underprint. Jacinto Verdaguer at right. Back: View of Mt. Canigó with village of Vignolas d'Oris. Watermark: Jacinto Verdaguer. Printer: FNMT.

	VF	UNC
a. Issued note.	22.50	50.00
s. Specimen.	—	—

1974 Commemorative Issue

#154, Centennial of the Banco de España's becoming the sole issuing bank, 1874-1974

154 1000 Pesetas
17.9.1971 (1974). Green and black on multicolor underprint. José Echegaray at right. Back: Bank of Spain in Madrid and commemorative legend. Watermark: José Echegaray. Printer: FNMT.

	VF	UNC
	40.00	100

1976 Issue

155 5000 Pesetas
6.2.1976 (1978). Purple and brown on multicolor underprint. King Carlos III at right. Back: Museum of Prado in Madrid at left center. Watermark: King Carlos III.

	VF	UNC
	80.00	275

1982-87 Issue

156 200 Pesetas
16.9.1980 (1984). Brown and orange on multicolor underprint. Leopoldo Garcí de las Alas, known as *Clarín* at right, cross at lower center. Back: Tree at left, cross at center. Watermark: Leopoldo Garcí de las Alas. Printer: FNMT.

	VF	UNC
	12.00	30.00

157 500 Pesetas
23.10.1979 (1983). Dark blue and black on multicolor underprint. Rosalia de Castro at right. Back: Villa at left center. Watermark: Rosalia de Castro. Printer: FNMT.

	VF	UNC
	14.00	35.00

158 1000 Pesetas
23.10.1979 (1982). Gray-blue and green on multicolor underprint. Tree at center, Benito Pérez Galdos at right. Back: Rock formations, mountains and map of Canary Islands. Watermark: Benito Pérez Galdos. Printer: FNMT. 138x76mm.

	VF	UNC
	22.50	55.00

159 2000 Pesetas
22.7.1980 (1983). Deep red and orange on multicolor underprint. Rose at center, Juan Ramón Jiménez at right. Back: Villa de la Rosa at left center. Watermark: Juan Ramón Jiménez. Printer: FNMT. 147x79mm.

	VF	UNC
	35.00	85.00

160   5000 Pesetas
23.10.1979 (1982). Brown and purple on multicolor underprint. Fleur-de-lis at
center, King Juan Carlos I at right. Back: Royal Palace in Madrid at left center.
Watermark: Juan Carlos I. Printer: FNMT. 156x85mm.

VF UNC
80.00 180

164   2000 Pesetas
24.4.1992 (1996). Red-violet and orange on multicolor underprint. Modified
portrait of José Celistino Mutis observing flower at right, with blurred *BANCO
DE ESPAÑA* at right margin. One serial number. Back: Royal Botanical Garden
and title page of Mutis' work on vertical format. Watermark: José Celistino Mutis.
138x68mm.

VF UNC
25.00 60.00

161   10,000 Pesetas
24.9.1985 (1987). Gray-black on multicolor underprit. Arms at center, King Juan
Carlos I at rigfht. Back: Felipe, Prince of Asturias at left, view of the Escorial at
center. Watermark: Juan Carlos I. Printer: FNMT. 165x85mm.

VF UNC
120 250

165   5000 Pesetas
12.10.1992 (1996). Violet-brown, brown and red-brown on multicolor underprint.
Christopher Columbus at right, with blurred *BANCO DE ESPAÑA* at right margin.
Back: Astrolabe at lower center on vertical format. Watermark: Christopher
Columbus. 146x71mm.

VF UNC
55.00 135

1992 Issue

162   2000 Pesetas
24.4.1992. Red-violet and orange on multicolor underprint. José Celistino Mutis
observing flower at right. Two serial numbers. Back: Royal Botanical Garden
and title page of Mutis' work on vertical format. Watermark: José Celistino Mutis.
147x79mm.

VF UNC
27.50 65.00

1992 (1996) Issue

**Issued for the 500th Centennial Anniversary of the Discovery of America by
Spain.**

163   1000 Pesetas
12.10.1992 (1996). Dark green, purple and red-brown on multicolor underprint.
Hernán Cortes at right, with blurred *BANCO DE ESPAÑA* at right margin. Back:
Francisco Pizarro on vertical format. Watermark: Francisco Pizarro. 130x65mm.

VF UNC
15.00 37.50

166   10,000 Pesetas
12.10.1992 (1996). Slate blue on multicolor underprint. King Juan Carlos I at right,
Casa de América in Madrid at lower center, with blurred *BANCO DE ESPAÑA* at
right margin. Back: A. de Ulloa y de Jorge Juan above astronomical navigation
diagram on vertical format. Watermark: Juan Carlos I. 154x74mm.

VF UNC
110 225

Note: For later issues used in Spain, see European Union listings.

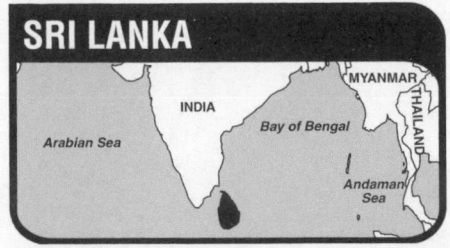

SRI LANKA

The Democratic Socialist Republic of Sri Lanka is situated in the Indian Ocean 18 miles (29 km.) southeast of India, has an area of 65,610 sq. km. and a population of 21.13 million. Capital: Colombo. The economy is chiefly agricultural. Tea, coconut products and rubber are exported. The first Sinhalese arrived in Sri Lanka late in the 6th century B.C. probably from northern India. Buddhism was introduced in about the mid-third century B.C., and a great civilization developed at the cities of Anuradhapura (kingdom from circa 200 B.C. to circa A.D. 1000) and Polonnaruwa (from about 1070 to 1200). In the 14th century, a south Indian dynasty established a Tamil kingdom in northern Sri Lanka. The coastal areas of the island were controlled by the Portuguese in the 16th century and by the Dutch in the 17th century. The island was ceded to the British in 1796, became a crown colony in 1802, and was united under British rule by 1815. As Ceylon, it became independent in 1948; its name was changed to Sri Lanka in 1972. Tensions between the Sinhalese majority and Tamil separatists erupted into war in 1983. Tens of thousands have died in the ethnic conflict that continues to fester. After two decades of fighting, the government and Liberation Tigers of Tamil Eelam (LTTE) formalized a cease-fire in February 2002 with Norway brokering peace negotiations. Violence between the LTTE and government forces intensified in 2006 and the government regained control of the Eastern Province in 2007. In January 2008, the government officially withdrew from the ceasefire, and has begun engaging the LTTE in the northern portion of the country.

See also Ceylon for earlier listings.

RULERS:
    Dutch to 1796
    British, 1796-1948

MONETARY SYSTEM:
    1 Rupee = 100 Cents, since 1870

REPUBLIC

Central Bank of Ceylon
Issues After May 22, 1972

72A   2 Rupees   VF   UNC
1973; 1974; 1977. Light brown on lilac, light green and blue underprint. Statue of King Parakkrama at right. Back: Pavilion. Watermark: Chinze. Printer: BWC. 114x59mm.
    a. Signature N. M. Perera and W. Tennekoon. 21.8.1973; 27.8.1974.   2.00   6.00
    b. Signature R. J. G. de Mel and H. E. Tennekoon. 26.8.1977.   1.50   5.00

For notes issued before May 22, 1972, see Ceylon #72.

73A   5 Rupees   VF   UNC
1973; 1974; 1977. Orange and brown on multicolor underprint. Statue of King Parakkrama at right. Back: Standing Figure. Watermark: Chinze. Printer: BWC. 125x64mm.
    a. Signature N. M. Perera and W. Tennekoon. 21.8.1973; 16.7.1974; 27.8.1974.   4.00   10.00
    b. Signature F.R.D. Bandaranaike and H. E. Tennekoon. 26.8.1977.   4.00   10.00

For notes issued before May 22, 1972, see Ceylon #73.

74A   10 Rupees   VF   UNC
1973; 1974; 1975; 1977. Green and purple on orange and blue underprint. Statue of King Parakkrama at right. Back: Ceremonial figures. Watermark: Chinze. Printer: BWC. 140x70mm.
    a. Signature N. M. Perera and W. Tennekoon.   4.00   10.00
    b. Signature Felix R. Dias Bandaranaike and H. E. Tennekoon. 6.10.1975.   4.00   10.00
    c. Signature R. J. G. de Mel and H. E. Tennekoon. 26.8.1977.   2.00   10.00

For notes issued before May 22, 1972, see Ceylon #74.

79A   50 Rupees   VF   UNC
1972; 1974. Purple and multicolor. Smiling President S.W.R.D. Bandaranaike without raised hand. Signatures: N.M. Perera and Herbert Tennekoon. Back: Landscape. Watermark: Chinze. Printer: BWC. 151x79mm.
    a. Issued note.   12.50   75.00
    s. Specimen.   —   175

80A   100 Rupees   VF   UNC
1974; 1975. Brown and purple on multicolor underprint. Smiling President W. R. D. Bandaranaike without raised hand. Back: Ornate stairway. Watermark: Chinze. Printer: BWC. 162x86mm.
    a. Signature N. M. Perera and H. E. Tennekoon. 16.7.1974; 27.8.1974.   17.50   100
    b. Signature F. R. D. Bandaranaike and H. E. Tennekoon. 6.10.1975.   15.00   80.00

For notes issued before May 22, 1972, see Ceylon #80.

1977 Issue

81   50 Rupees   VF   UNC
26.8.1977. Purple and green on multicolor underprint. Sri Lanka arms at right. Signature: Ronnie de Mel and Herbert Tennekoon. Serial # prefix: *N*. Back: Terraced hillside. Watermark: Lion with sword. Printer: BWC. 151x79mm.   15.00   50.00

82   100 Rupees   VF   UNC
26.8.1977. Purple and brown on multicolor underprint. Sri Lanka arms at right. Signature: Ronnie de Mel and Herbert Tennekoon. Serial # prefix: *W*. Back: Shrine at left center. Watermark: Lion with sword. Printer: BWC. 162x86mm.
    a. Issued note.   20.00   95.00
    s. Specimen.   —   150

1979 Issue

#83-88 Replacement notes: Serial # prefix *Z/1*.

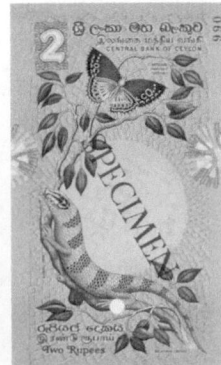

83   2 Rupees   VF   UNC
26.3.1979. Red on multicolor underprint. Fish at right. Signatures: Ronnie de Mel and Warnasena Rasaputram. Serial # prefix: *A*. Back: Butterfly and lizard. Vertical format. Watermark: Lion with sword. 108x60mm.
    a. Issued note.   1.25   6.00
    s. Specimen.   —   100

84   5 Rupees   VF   UNC

26.3.1979. Gray on multicolor underprint. Butterfly and lizard at right. Signatures: Ronnie de Mel and Warnasena Rasaputram. Serial # prefix: *F*. Back: Flying squirrel and White-faced Starling. Vertical format. Watermark: Lion with sword. 117x64mm.

    a. Issued note.   4.00   15.00
    s. Specimen.   —   100

87   50 Rupees   VF   UNC

26.3.1979. Blue and brown on multicolor underprint. Butterfly at center, Red-faced Malcoha at right. Signatures: Ronnie de Mel and Warnasena Rasaputram. Serial # prefix: *T*. Back: Lizard and Ceylon Spurfowl. Vertical format. Watermark: Lion with sword. 146x73mm.

    a. Issued note.   25.00   100
    s. Specimen.   —   220

85   10 Rupees   VF   UNC

26.3.1979. Green, brown and black on multicolor underprint. Sri Lanka Grey Hornbill in tree at center. Signatures: Ronnie de Mel and Warnasena Rasaputram. Serial # prefix: *H*. Back: Flowers and Yellow-eared Bulbul. Vertical format. Watermark: Lion with sword. 127x67mm.

    a. Issued note.   7.50   30.00
    s. Specimen.   —   125

88   100 Rupees   VF   UNC

26.3.1979. Gold, green and black on multicolor underprint. Snakes and tree at center, Sri Lanka Myna at right. Signatures: Ronnie de Mel and Warnasena Rasaputram. Serial # prefix: *Z*. Back: Yellow-fronted Barbet in tree, butterfly below. Vertical format. Watermark: Lion with sword. 156x76mm.

    a. Issued note.   30.00   150
    s. Specimen.   —   325

1981 Issue

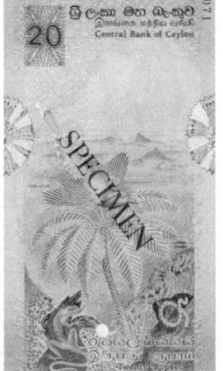

86   20 Rupees   VF   UNC

26.3.1979. Brown and green on multicolor underprint. Ceylon Wood Pigeon at center, monkey at right. Signatures: Ronnie de Mel and Warnasena Rasaputram. Serial # prefix: *K*. Back: Bird, tree and animals. Vertical format. Watermark: Lion with sword. 137x70mm.

    a. Issued note.   10.00   40.00
    s. Specimen.   —   150

89　500 Rupees

1981; 1985. Brown and purple on multicolor underprint. Elephant with rider at right. Signatures: Ronnie de Mel and Warnasena Rasaputram. Serial # prefix: *J.* Back: Abhayagiri Stupa, Anuradhapura temple on hill in vertical format. Watermark: Lion with sword. 165x79mm.

	VF	UNC
a. 1.1.1981.	30.00	150
b. 1.1.1985.	50.00	200

90　1000 Rupees

1.1.1981. Green on multicolor underprint. Dam at right. Signatures: Ronnie de Mel and Warnasena Rasaputram. Serial # prefix: *P.* Back: Peacock and mountains in vertical format. Watermark: Lion with sword. 75x250mm.

	VF	UNC
a. Issued note.	75.00	250
s. Specimen.	—	—

1982 Issue

91　5 Rupees

1.1.1982. Light red on multicolor underprint. Ruins at right. Signatures: Ronnie de Mel and Warnasena Rasaputram. Serial # prefix: *A.* Back: Stone carving of deity and child in vertical format. Watermark: Lion with sword. Printer: BWC. 119x64mm.

	VF	UNC
a. Issued note.	0.75	5.00
s. Specimen.	—	100

92　10 Rupees

1982; 1985. Olive-green on multicolor underprint. Temple of the Tooth in Kandy at right.Signatures: Ronnie de Mel and Warnasena Rasaputram. Serial # prefix: *D.* Back: Shrine in vertical format. Watermark: Lion with sword. Printer: BWC. 127x67mm.

	VF	UNC
a. 1.1.1982.	1.00	7.50
b. 1.1.1985.	1.00	6.00
s. Specimen.	—	100

93　20 Rupees

1982; 1985. Purple and red on multicolor underprint. Moonstone at right. Signatures: Ronnie de Mel and Warnasena Rasaputram. Serial # prefix: *F.* Back: Dagoba Shrine in vertical format. Watermark: Lion with sword. Printer: BWC. 137x70mm.

	VF	UNC
a. 1.1.1982.	2.00	12.50
b. 1.1.1985.	2.00	11.00
s. Specimen.	—	110

94　50 Rupees

1.1.1982. Dark blue and dark brown on multicolor underprint. Building in Kelaniya at right. Signatures: Ronnie de Mel and Warnasena Rasaputram. Serial # prefix: *H.* Back: Ruins of temple at Polonnaruwa at center in vertical format. Watermark: Lion with sword. Printer: BWC. 146x73mm.

	VF	UNC
a. Issued note.	4.00	20.00
s. Specimen.	—	125

95 100 Rupees   VF   UNC

1.1.1982. Orange and brown on multicolor underprint. Stone carving of lion at lower right. .Signatures: Ronnie de Mel and Warnasena Rasaputram. Serial # prefix: S. Back: Parliament building in vertical format. Watermark: Lion with sword. Printer: BWC. 146x76mm.

a. Issued note.	5.00	37.50
s. Specimen.	—	160

Srí Lanká Maha Bänkuva
CENTRAL BANK OF SRI LANKA
1987-89 Issue

#96-100 similar to #89 and 92-95 but with bank name changed in English from *Ceylon* to *Sri Lanka*. **Printer: BWC.**

96 10 Rupees   VF   UNC

1987-90. UV: value 10 and lion with sword fluoresces yellow. Back leaves yellow. Green on multicolor underprint. Temple of the Tooth in Kandy at right. Serial # prefix: Γ. Back: Shrine in vertical format. Watermark: Lion with sword. Printer: BWC. 127x67mm.

a. Signature: Ronnie de Mel and warnasena Rasaputram. 1.1.1987.	0.75	4.00
b. Signature: M. H. M. Nainamarikkar & H. N. S. Karunatellake. 21.11.1988.	0.75	4.00
c. Signature: D. B. Wijethunga & H. N.S. Karunatillake. 21.2.1989.	0.75	4.00
d. As c. Dot after second signature. 21.2.1989.	0.75	4.00
e. Signature: D. B. Wijethunga and H. N. S. Karunatillake. 5.4.1990.	0.75	4.00
r. Replacement note. Serial # prefix: R/1.	—	6.00

97 20 Rupees   VF   UNC

1988-90. Purple and red on multicolor underprint. Moonstone at right. Serial # prefix: E. Back: Dagoba Shrine in vertical format. Watermark: Lion with sword. Printer: BWC. 137x70mm.

a. Signature: M. H. M. Nainamarikkar and H. N. S. Karunatillake. 21.11.1988.	4.00	25.00
b. Signature: D. B. Wijethunga and H. N. S. Karunatillake. 21.2.1989	1.00	6.00
c. Signature: D. B. Wijethunga and H. N. S. Karunatillake. 5.4.1990.	1.00	6.00
r. Replacement note. Serial # prefix: R/3.	—	11.00

98 50 Rupees   VF   UNC

1988-90. Blue and brown on multicolor underprint. Building in Kelaniya at right. Serial # prefix D. Back: Ruins of temple at Polonnaruwa at center in vertical format. Watermark: Lion with sword. Printer: BWC. 146x73mm.

a. Signature: M. H. M. Nainamarikkar and H. N. S. Karunatillake. 21.11.1988.	2.00	12.50
b. Signature: D. B. Wijethunga and H. N. S. Karunatillake. 21.2.1989.	2.00	12.50
c. As b. 5.4.1990.	2.00	12.50

99 100 Rupees   VF   UNC

1987-90. Orange and brown on multicolor underprint. Stone carving of lion at lower right. Serial # prefix: C. Back: Parliament building in vertical format. Watermark: Lion with sword. Printer: BWC. 146x73mm.

a. Signature: Ronnie de Mel and Warnasena Rasaputram. 1.1.1987.	2.00	20.00
b. Signature: M. H. M. Nainamarikkar and Warnasena Rasaputram. 1.2.1988.	3.00	20.00
c. Signature: D. B. Wijethunga & H. N. S. Karunatillake. 21.2.1989	3.00	20.00
d. As c. 5.4.1990.	3.00	20.00

100 500 Rupees   VF   UNC

1987-90. Brown and purple on multicolor underprint. Similar to #89 but with larger watermark area, vertical silver segmented security strip, bird and borders deeper red brown. Serial # prefix: B. Back: Hill and temple in purple in vertical format. Watermark: Lion with sword. Printer: BWC. 165x79mm.

a. Signature: Ronnie de Mel and Warnasena Rasaputram. 1.1.1987.	14.00	75.00
b. Signature: M. H. M. Nainamarikkar & H. N. S. Karunatellake. 21.11.1988.	14.00	75.00
c. Signature: D. B. Wijethunga & H. N. S. Karunatillake. 21.2.1989	14.00	75.00
d. As c. 5.4.1990.	14.00	75.00
r. Replacement note: Serial # prefix: R/7.	—	80.00

101 1000 Rupees   VF   UNC

1987-90. Deep green and purple on multicolor underprint. Victoria Dam at right. Serial # prefix: A. Back: Peacock and University of Ruhuna in vertical format. Watermark: Lion with sword. Printer: BWC. 175x83mm.

a. Signature: Ronnie de Mel and Warnasena Rasaputram. 1.1.1987.	25.00	35.00
b. Signature: D. B. Wijethunga and H. N. S. Karunatillake. 21.2.1989.	25.00	100
c. As b. 5.4.1990.	25.00	100

1991 Issue

#102-107 Replacement notes: Serial # prefix Z/1.

102   10 Rupees

		VF	UNC

1991-94. UV: value 10 in box fluoresce yellow. Deep brown and green on multicolor underprint. Sinhalese Chinze at right. Serial # prefix: M. Back: Painted stork at top left, Presidential Secretariat building in Colombo, flowers in lower foreground Watermark: Lion with sword. Printer: TDLR. 122x61mm.

		VF	UNC
a.	Signature: D. B. Wijethunga and H. N. S. Karunatillake. 1.1.1991.	0.50	2.00
b.	Signature: D. B. Wijethunga and H. B. Disanayaka. 1.7.1992.	0.50	2.00
c.	Signature: C. B. Kumaratunga and H. B. Disanayaka. 19.8.1994.	0.50	2.00
r.	Replacement note: Serial # prefix: Z/1.	—	7.00

103   20 Rupees

1991-94. Purple and red on multicolor underprint. Native bird mask at right. Serial # prefix: L. Back: Two youths fishing, sea shells in vertical format. Watermark: Lion with sword. Printer: TDLR. 129x64mm.

		VF	UNC
a.	Signatures: D. B. Wijethunga & H. N. S. Karunatillake. 1.1.1991.	0.75	3.50
b.	Signatures: D. B. Wijethunga & H. B. Disanayaka. 1.7.1992.	0.75	3.50
c.	Signatures: C. B. Kumaratunga and H. B. Disanayaka. 19.8.1994.	5.00	20.00
r.	Replacement note: Serial # prefix: Z/2.	—	8.00

104   50 Rupees

1991-94. Brown-violet, deep blue and blue-green on multicolor underprint. Male dancer with local headdress at right. Serial # prefix: K. Back: Butterflies above temple ruins, with shield and ornamental sword hilt in lower foreground in vertical format. Watermark: Lion with sword. Printer: TDLR. 136x68mm.

		VF	UNC
a.	Signature: D. B. Wijethunga and H. N. S. Karunatillake. 1.1.1991.	1.00	6.00
b.	Signatures: D. B. Wijethunga and H. B. Disanayaka. 1.7.1992.	1.00	6.00
c.	Signatures: C. B. Kumaratunga and H. B. Disanayaka. 19.8.1994.	1.00	6.00
r.	Replacement note: Serial # prefix: Z/3.	—	11.00

105   100 Rupees

		VF	UNC

1991-92. Orange and dark brown on multicolor underprint. Decorative urn at right. Serial # prefix: J. Back: Tea leaf pickers, two Rose-ringed Parakeets at bottom in vertical format. Watermark: Lion with sword. Printer: TDLR. 143x72mm.

		VF	UNC
a.	Signature: D. B. Wijethunga and H. N. S. Karunatillake. Without dot on value in Tamil at left. 1.1.1991.	20.00	100
b.	As a. With dot on value in Tamil at left. 1.1.1991.	4.00	15.00
c.	Signatures: D. B. Wijethunga and H. B. Disanayaha. 1.7.1992.	4.00	15.00
r.	Replacement note: Serial # prefix: Z/4.	—	20.00

105A   100 Rupees

	VF	UNC

1.7.1992. Orange and dark brown on multicolor underprint. Decorative urn at right. Signatures: D. B. Wijethunga and H. B. Disanayaka. Serial # prefix: J. Back: Tea leaf pickers, two Rose-ringed Parakeets at bottom in vertical format. Watermark: Chinze. 3x9mm.

VF	UNC
3.00	10.00

106   500 Rupees

		VF	UNC

1991-92. Dark brown, purple and brown-orange on multicolor underprint. Musicians at right, dancer at left center. Serial # prefix: H. Back: Stork-billed Kingfisher above temple and orchids in vertical format. Watermark: Lion with sword. Printer: TDLR. 150x75mm.

		VF	UNC
a.	Signatures: D. B. Wijethunga and H. N. S. Karunatillake. 1.1.1991.	10.00	45.00
b.	Signatures: D. B. Wijethunga and H. B. Disanayaka. 1.7.1992.	15.00	60.00
r.	Replacement note. Serial # perfix: Z/5.	—	65.00

107 1000 Rupees VF UNC

1991-92. Brown, dark green and purple on multicolor underprint. Chinze at lower left, two headed bird at bottom center, elephant with trainer at right. Serial # prefix: G. Back: Peacocks on palace lawn; lotus flowers above and Octagon Temple of the Tooth in Kandy in vertical format. Watermark: Lion with sword. Printer: TDLR. 157x79mm.

		VF	UNC
a. Signatures: D. B. Wijethunga and H. N. S. Karunatillake. 1.1.1991.		15.00	65.00
b. Signatures: D. B. Wijethunga and H. B. Disanayaka. 1.7.1992.		20.00	65.00
r. Replacement note: Serial # prefix: Z/6.		—	70.00

1995 Issue

#108-113 backs have a vertical format. Enhanced latent image security feature at lower ctr. on face. Printer: TDLR.

108 10 Rupees VF UNC

1995; 2001; 2004, 2005, 2006. UV: value 10 in box and central design fluoresce yellow. Back flowers and bird beak yellow. Deep brown and green on multicolor underprint. Sinhalese Chinze at right. Enhanced latent image security feature at lower center. Back: Painted stork at top left, Presidential Secretariat building in Colombo, flowers in lower foreground Watermark: Lion with sword. Printer: TDLR. 122x61mm.

		VF	UNC
a. Signatures: K. N. Choksy and A. S. Jayawardena. 12.12.2001.		FV	2.00
b. Signatures: Sarath Amunugama and A. S. Jayawardena. 10.4.2004.		FV	1.00
c. Signatures: Sarath Amunugama and Sunil Mendis. 1.7.2004.		FV	1.00
d. Signatures: Mahinda Rajapaksa and Sunil Mendis. 19.11.2005.		FV	1.00
e. Signatures: Mahinda Rahapaksa and Ajith Nivard Cabral. 3.7.2006.		FV	1.00
r. Replacement note. Serial # prefix: Z/1.		—	6.00

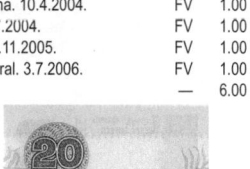

109 20 Rupees VF UNC

1995; 2001; 2004; 2005; 2006. UV: value 20 in box fluoresce yellow. Back fish and design elements orange. Purple and red on multicolor underprint. Native bird mask at right. Enhanced latent image security feature at lower center. Serial # prefix: L. Back: Two youths fishing, sea shells on vertical format. Watermark: Lion with sword. Printer: TDLR. 130x65mm.

		VF	UNC
a. Signatures: K. N. Choksy and A. S. Jayawardena. 12.12.2001.		FV	2.50
b. Signatures: Sarath Amunugama and Sunil Mendis. 1.7.2004.		FV	1.00
c. Signatures: Mahinda Rajapaksa and Sunil Mendis. 19.11.2005.		FV	1.00
d. Signatures: Mahinda Rajapaksa and Ajith Nivard Cabral. 7.3.2006.		FV	1.00
r. Replacement note. Serial # prefix: Z/2.		—	—

110 50 Rupees VF UNC

1995; 2001; 2004; 2005; 2006. Brown-violet, deep blue and bleu-green on multicolor underprint. Male dancer with local headdress at right. Enhanced latent image security feature at lower center. Serial # prefix: K. Back: Butterflies above temple ruins, with shield and ornamental sword hilt in lower foreground on vertical format. Watermark: Lion with sword. Printer: TDLR. 136x68mm.

		VF	UNC
a. Signatures: K. N. Choksy and A. S. Jayawardena. 12.12.2001.		FV	3.00
b. Signatures: Sarath Amunugama and A. S. Jayawardena. 10.4.2004.		FV	2.00
c. Signatures: Sarath Amunugama and Sunil Mendis. 1.7.2004.		FV	2.00
d. Signatures: Mahinda Rajapaksa and Sunil Mendis. 19.11.2005.		FV	2.00
e. Signatures: Mahinda Rajapaksa and Ajith Nivard Cabral. 3.7.2006.		FV	2.00
r. Replacement note. Serial # prefix: Z/3.		—	—

111 100 Rupees VF UNC

1995; 2001; 2004; 2005; 2006. UV: value 100 in box fluoresce yellow. Back portions of flowerand upper design yellow. Dark brown and orange on multicolor underprint. Decorative urn at right. Enhanced latent image security feature at lower center. Serial # prefix: J. Back: Tea leaf pickers, two Rose-ringed Parakeets at bottom on vertical format. Watermark: Lion with sword. Printer: TDLR. 144x72mm.

		VF	UNC
a. Signatures: K. N. Choksy and A. S. Jayawardena. 12.12.2001.		FV	5.00
b. Signatures: Sarath Amunugama and A. S. Jayawardena. 1.7.2004.		FV	4.00
c. Signatures: Mahinda Rajapaksa and Sunil Mendis. 19.11.2005.		FV	4.00
r. Replacement note. Serial # prefix: Z/4.		—	—

112 500 Rupees VF UNC

15.11.1995. . Dark brown, purple and brown-orange on multicolor underprint. Musicians at right, dancer at left center. Enhanced latent image security feature at lower center. Signatrues: C. B. Kumaratunga and A. S. Jayawardena. Serial # prefix: H. Back: Stork-billed Kingfisher above temple and orchids in vertical format. Watermark: Lion with sword. Printer: TDLR. 150x75mm.

		VF	UNC
a. Issued note.		FV	35.00
r. Replacement note. Serial # prefix: Z/5.		—	40.00

113 1000 Rupees VF UNC

15.11.1995. Brown, dark green and purple on multicolor underprint. Chinze at lower left, two-headed bird at bottomcenter, elephant with trainer at right. Enhanced latent image security feature at lower center. Signatures: C. B. Kumaratunga and A. S. Jayawardena. Serial # prefix: G. Back: Peacocks on palace lawn; lotus flowers above and Octagon Temple of the Tooth in Kandy in vertical format. Watermark: Lion with sword. Printer: TDLR. 157x79mm.

		VF	UNC
a. Issued note.		FV	50.00
r. Replacement note: Serial # prefix: Z/6.		—	55.00

1998 Commemorative Issue
#114, 50th Anniversary of Independence, 1948-1998

114　200 Rupees　　　　　　　　　　　　　　　　　　　　　　VF　UNC
4.2.1998. Polymer plastic. Greenish black on blue, orange and multicolor
underprint. Temple at upper center right above a collage of modern scenes across
bottom. Signatures: C. B. Kumaratunga and A. S. Jayawardena. Back: Palace
at upper left center above collage of medieval scenes of British landing across
bottom right. 146x74mm.

　　a. Red serial # in folder.　　　　　　　　　　　　　　　　FV　20.00
　　b. Black serial #.　　　　　　　　　　　　　　　　　　　　FV　10.00

#115-118 not assigned.

2001 Issue

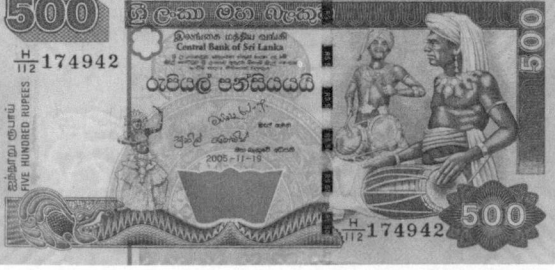

119　500 Rupees　　　　　　　　　　　　　　　　　　　　　　VF　UNC
2001; 2004; 2005. Dark brown, purple and brown-orange on multicolor underprint.
Musicians at right, dancer at left center. Enhanced latent image security feature at
lower center. Serial # prefix: H. Back: Stork-billed Kingfisher above temple and orchids on vertical format. Watermark: Lion with sword. Printer: TDLR. 150x75mm.

　　a. Signatures: K. N. Choksy and A. S. Jayawardena. 12.12.2001.Monogram　FV　17.50
　　　 on wide security band.
　　b. Signatures: Sarath Amunugama and A. S. Jayawardena. 10.4.2004.　　　　FV　15.00
　　　 Monogram on wide security band.
　　c. Signatures: Sarath Amunugama and Sunil Mendis. 1.7.2004. Monogram on　FV　15.00
　　　 wide security band.
　　d. Signatures: Mahinda Rajapaksa and Sunil Mendis. 19.11.2005. Text on　　FV　14.00
　　　 wide security band.
　　r. Replacement note. Serial # prefix: Z/5.　　　　　　　　　　—　　—

120　1000 Rupees　　　　　　　　　　　　　　　　　　　　　VF　UNC
2001; 2004; 2006. Brown, dark green and purple on multicolor underprint. Chinze
at lower left, two-headed bird at bottomcenter, elephant with traineer at right.
Enhanced latent image security feature at lower center. Serial # prefix: G. Back:
Peacocks on palace lawn; lotus flowers above and Octagon Temple of the Tooth in
Kandy on vertical format. Watermark: Lion with sword. Printer: TDLR. 156x78mm.

　　a. Signatures: K. N. Choksy and A. S. Jayawardena. 12.12.2001.Monogram　FV　22.50
　　　 on wide security band.
　　b. Signatures: Sarath Amunugama and A. S. Jayawardena. 10.4.2004.　　　　FV　20.00
　　　 Monogram on wide security band.
　　c. Signatures: Sarath Amunugama and Sunil Mendis. 1.7.2004. Monogram on　FV　20.00
　　　 wide security band.
　　d. Signatures: Mahinda Rajapaksa and Ajith Nivard Cabral. 7.3.2006. Text on　FV　20.00
　　　 wide security band.
　　r. Replacement note: Serial # prefix: Z/6.　　　　　　　　　—　　—

121　2000 Rupees　　　　　　　　　　　　　　　　　　　　　VF　UNC
2005; 2006. Green on orange and yellow on multicolor underprint. Sirigiya mountain top, elephants and forest. Serial # prefix: P. Back: Maiden of Sirigiya Frescoe.
Vertical format. Watermark: Lion with sword. Printer: TDLR 164x82mm.

　　a. Signature Sarath Amunugama and Sunil Mendis. 2.11.2005.　　　　　　　FV　35.00
　　b. Signatures: Mahinda Rajapaksa and Ajith Nivard Cabral. 3.7.2006.　　　　FV　30.00
　　r. Replacement note: Serial # prefix: Z/7.　　　　　　　　　—　　—

2009 Commemorative Issue
122　1000 Rupees　　　　　　　　　　　　　　　　　　　　　VF　UNC
20.5.2009. Light blue and multicolor. President Mahinda Rajapaksa with arms
raised at right. Signatures: Mahinda Rajapaksa and Ajith Nivard Cabral. Serial
prefix Q. Back: Security forces raising flag. Watermark: Lion with sword.
156x82mm.

　　a. Issued note.　　　　　　　　　　　　　　　　　　　　　FV　15.00
　　b. Low serial # in a commemorative folder.　　　　　　　　　—　　20.00
　　r. Replacement note: Serial # prefix: X/1.　　　　　　　　12.00　50.00

2010-15 Issue

123 20 Rupees

VF UNC

2010; 2015. Maroon and multicolor Port of Colombo at center, owl at right. Signatures: Mahinda Rajapaksa and Ajith Nivard Cabral. Serial # prefix: *W*. Back: Ves Netuma dancer and Geta Bera drummer. Vertical format. Watermark: Owl and 20. Printer: DLR. 128x67mm.

		VF	UNC
a.	1.1.2010.	FV	0.50
b.	Low serial # in a commemorative folder.	—	2.00
c.	4.2.2015. Signatures Ravi Karunanayake and A. Mahendran.	FV	0.50
r.	Replacement note: Serial # prefix: *Z/2*.	—	4.00

124 50 Rupees

VF UNC

2010; 2015. Blue and multicolor Manampitlya bridges at center, dull blue flycatcher at right. Signatures: Mahinda Rajapaksa and Ajith Nivard Cabral. Serial # prefix: *V*. Back: Yakbera drummer and Vadiga Patuna dancer. Vertical format. Watermark: Flycatcher bird and 50. Printer: DLR. 133x67mm.

		VF	UNC
a.	1.1.2010.	FV	2.00
b.	Low serial # in a commemorative folder.	—	2.50
c.	4.2.2015. Signatures Ravi Karunanayake and A. Mahendran.	FV	2.00
r.	Replacement note: Serial # prefix: *Z/3*.	—	6.00

125 100 Rupees

VF UNC

1.1.2010. Orange and yellow. Norochocholai Power plant at center, orange billed babbler at right. Signature Mahinda Rajapaksa and Ajith Nivard Cabral. Serial # prefix: *U*. Back: Bharatanatyam dancer and Mridirangam drummer. Vertical format. Watermark: Babbler and 100. Printer: DLR. 138x67mm.

		VF	UNC
a.	Issued note.	FV	1.50
b.	Low serial # in commemorative folder.	—	3.00
c.	Uncut sheet of 40 notes. Serial # prefix: *CB/60*.	—	125
d.	4.2.2015. Signatures Ravi Karunanayake and A. Mahendran.	FV	1.50
r.	Replacement note: Serial # prefix: *Z/4*.	—	5.00

126 500 Rupees

VF UNC

1.1.2010. Purple and green. World Trade Center, Bank of Ceylon building at center, parakeet at right. Signatures: Mahinda Rajapaksa and Ajith Nivard Cabral. Serial # prefix: *T*. Back: Thelma dancer and Yak Bera drummer. Vertical format. Watermark: Parakeet and 500. 143x67mm.

		VF	UNC
a.	Issued note.	FV	5.50
b.	Low serial # in commemorative folder.	—	8.00
c.	4.2.2015. Signatures Ravi Karunanayake and A. Mahendran.	FV	5.50
r.	Replacement note. Serial # prefix: *Z/5*.	—	11.00

127 1000 Rupees

VF UNC

1.1.2010. Green and multicolor. Ramboda tunnel at center, parrot at right. Signature Mahinda Rajapaksa and Ajith Nivard Cabral. Serial # prefix: *S*. Back: Malpadaya dancer and Dawul Bera drummer. Vertical format. Watermark: Parrot and 1000. 148x67mm.

		VF	UNC
a.	Issued note.	FV	11.00
b.	Low serial # in a commemorative folder.	—	13.50
c.	4.2.2015. Signatures Ravi Karunanayake and A. Mahendran.	FV	11.00
r.	Replacement note: Serial # prefix: *Z/6*.	—	16.00

128   5000 Rupees
    2010; 2015. Tan and golden multicolor. Weheragala dam at center, yellow eastern
bulbyl at right. Signature: Mahinda Rajapaksa and Ajith Nivard Cabral. Serial #
prefix: R. Back: Nagaraksha dancer and Guruluraksha dancer. Vertical format.
Watermark: Bulbul bird and 5000. 153x67mm.

		VF	UNC
a.	1.1.2010.	FV	55.00
b.	Low serial # in a commemorative folder.	—	60.00
c.	4.2.2015. Signatures Ravi Karunanayake and A. Mahendran.	FV	55.00
r.	Replacement note: Serial # prefix: Z/8.	—	65.00

2013 Commemorative Issue

129   500 Rupees
    15.11.2013. Purple and green World Trade Center, Bank of Ceylon building at
center, parakeet at right. Signatures Mahinda Rajapaksa and Ajith Nivard Cabral.
Serial # prefix V. Watermark: Parakeet and 500 143x67mm.

		VF	UNC
a.	Issued note.	FV	7.50
b.	Low serial # in commemorative folder.	—	10.00

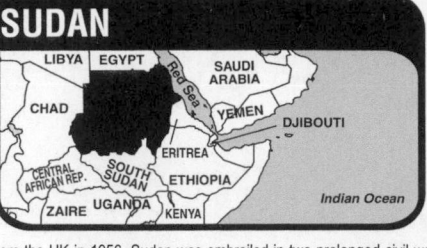

SUDAN

The Democratic Republic of the Sudan, was located in northeast Africa on the Red Sea between Egypt and Ethiopia, it had an area of 2,505,810 sq. km. and a population of 40.22 million. Capital: Khartoum. Agriculture and livestock raising are the chief occupations. Cotton, gum arabic and peanuts are exported. Military regimes favoring Islamic-oriented governments have dominated national politics since independence from the UK in 1956. Sudan was embroiled in two prolonged civil wars during most of the remainder of the 20th century. These conflicts were rooted in northern economic, political, and social domination of largely non-Muslim, non-Arab southern Sudanese. The first civil war ended in 1972 but broke out again in 1983. The second war and famine-related effects resulted in more than four million people displaced and, according to rebel estimates, more than two million deaths over a period of two decades. Peace talks gained momentum in 2002-04 with the signing of several accords. The final North/South Comprehensive Peace Agreement (CPA), signed in January 2005, granted the southern rebels autonomy for six years. After which, a referendum for independence is scheduled to be held. A separate conflict, which broke out in the western region of Darfur in 2003, has displaced nearly two million people and caused an estimated 200,000 to 400,000 deaths. The UN took command of the Darfur peacekeeping operation from the African Union on 31 December 2007. As of early 2009, peacekeeping troops were struggling to stabilize the situation, which has become increasingly regional in scope, and has brought instability to eastern Chad, and Sudanese incursions into the Central African Republic. Sudan also has faced large refugee influxes from neighboring countries, primarily Ethiopia and Chad. Armed conflict, poor transport infrastructure, and lack of government support have chronically obstructed the provision of humanitarian assistance to affected populations. After an election, the country voted to split, forming North Sudan and South Sudan in 2011.

MONETARY SYSTEM:
    1 Ghirsh (Piastre) = 10 Millim (Milliemes)
    1 Sudanese Pound = 100 Piastres to 1992
    1 Dinar = 10 Old Sudanese Pounds, 1992

REPUBLIC

Bank of Sudan
1961-64 Issue

6   25 Piastres
    1964-68. Red on multicolor underprint. Soldiers in formation at left, date and
signature varieties. Back: Arms (desert camel rider).

		VF	UNC
a.	6.3.1964; 20.1.1966.	25.00	225
b.	25.1.1967.	22.50	200
c.	Without Arabic text al-Khartoum. 7.2.1968.	25.00	225

7   50 Piastres
    1964-68. Green on multicolor underprint. Elephants at left, date and signature
varieties. Back: Arms (desert camel rider).

		VF	UNC
a.	6.3.1964.	150	950
b.	25.1.1967.	130	900
c.	Without Arabic text al-Khartoum. 7.2.1968.	135	950

8   1 Pound
    1961-68. Blue on yellow and multicolor underprint. Dam at left, date and signature
varieties. Back: Arms (desert camel rider).

		VF	UNC
a.	8.4.1961.	35.00	325
b.	2.3.1965.	35.00	325
c.	20.1.1966.	25.00	300
d.	25.1.1967.	25.00	300
e.	Without Arabic text al-Khartoum. 7.2.1968.	30.00	320
s.	As a. Specimen. Punch hole cancel. Overprint: CANCELLED.	—	150

9   5 Pounds

		VF	UNC
1962-68. Lilac-brown on multicolor underprint. Dhow at left, date and signature varieties. Back: Arms (desert camel rider).			
a. 1.7.1962.		150	1,350
b. 2.3.1965.		150	1,200
c. 20.1.1966.		140	1,100
d. 25.1.1967.		140	1,100
e. Without Arabic text *al-Khartoum*. 7.2.1968.		150	1,200

10   10 Pounds

		VF	UNC
1964-68. Gray-black on multicolor underprint. Bank of Sudan building at left, date and signature varieties. Back: Arms (desert camel rider).			
a. 6.3.1964.		85.00	900
b. 20.1.1966.		100	1,000
c. 25.1.1967.		135	1,200
d. Without Arabic text *al-Khartoum*. 7.2.1968.		150	1,250

1970 Issue

11   25 Piastres

		VF	UNC
1970-80. Red on multicolor underprint. Bank of Sudan at left. Various date and signature varieties. Back: Textile industry. Printer: TDLR.			
a. Jan. 1970; Jan. 1971; Jan. 1972.		15.00	75.00
b. 1.4.1973-28.5.1978.		3.50	15.00
c. 2.1.1980.		1.50	10.00

12   50 Piastres

		VF	UNC
1970-80. Green on multicolor underprint. Bank of Sudan at left. Various date and signature varieties. Back: University of Khartoum. Printer: TDLR.			
a. Jan. 1970; Jan. 1971; Jan. 1972.		25.00	90.00
b. 1.4.1973-28.5.1978.		4.00	18.00
c. 2.1.1980.		5.00	20.00

13   1 Pound

		VF	UNC
1970-80. Blue on multicolor underprint. Bank of Sudan at left. Various date and signature varieties. Back: Ancient temple. Printer: TDLR.			
a. Watermark: Rhinoceros head. Jan. 1970.		20.00	100
b. Watermark: Arms (secretary bird) .Jan 1971-28.5.1978.		3.00	32.50
c. 2.1.1980.		4.00	35.00

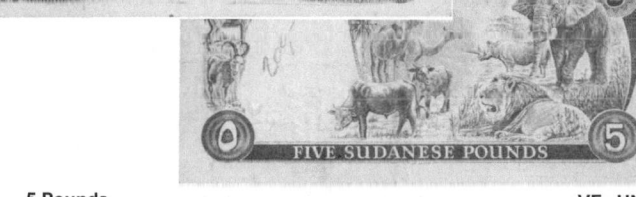

14   5 Pounds

		VF	UNC
1970-80. Brown on lilac on multicolor underprint. Bank of Sudan at left. Various date and signature varieties. Back: Domestic and wild animals. Printer: TDLR.			
a. Watermark: Rhinoceros head. Jan. 1970.		50.00	325
b. Watermark: Arms. Jan. 1971-28.5.1978.		37.50	275
c. 2.1.1980.		37.50	275

15   10 Pounds

		VF	UNC
1970-80. Purple and green on multicolor underprint. Bank of Sudan at left. Various date and signature varieties. Back: Transportation elements (ship, plane, etc.). Printer: TDLR.			
a. Watermark: Rhinoceros head. Jan. 1970.		50.00	275
b. Watermark: Arms. Jan. 1971-28.5.1978.		20.00	90.00
c. 2.1.1980.		15.00	40.00

1981 Issue

16   25 Piastres

		VF	UNC
1.1.1981. Brown on multicolor underprint. President J. Nimeiri wearing national headdress at left, arms at center. Back: Kosti bridge.		1.00	2.50
1.1.1981. Brown on multicolor underprint. President J. Nimeiri wearing national headdress at left, arms at center. Back: Kosti bridge.			
s. Specimen. Red overprint in Arabic.		—	100

17   50 Piastres

	VF	UNC
1.1.1981. Purple on brown underprint. President J. Nimeiri wearing national headdress at left, arms at center. Back: Bank of Sudan.		
a. Issued note.	1.50	6.00
s. Specimen. Red overprint in Arabic.	—	150

18   1 Pound

	VF	UNC
1.1.1981. Blue on multicolor underprint. President J. Nimeiri wearing national headdress at left, arms at center. Back: People's Assembly. Watermark: Arms.		
a. Issued note.	4.00	20.00
s. Specimen. Red overprint in Arabic.	—	150

19   5 Pounds

	VF	UNC
1.1.1981. Green and brown on multicolor underprint. President J. Nimeiri wearing national headdress at left, arms at center. Back: Islamic Centre Mosque in Khartoum. Watermark: Arms.	6.00	40.00

20   10 Pounds

	VF	UNC
1.1.1981. Blue and brown on multicolor underprint. President J. Nimeiri wearing national headdress at left, arms at center. Back: Kenana sugar factory. Watermark: Arms.		
a. Issued note.	20.00	90.00
s. Specimen. Red overprint in Arabic.	—	150

21   20 Pounds

	VF	UNC
1.1.1981. Green on multicolor underprint. President J. Nimeiri wearing national headdress at left, arms at center; without commemorative text. Back: Unity Monument at left, People's Palace at center right. Watermark: Arms.		
a. Issued note.	35.00	150
s. Specimen. Red overprint in Arabic.	—	150

1981 Commemorative Issue

#22, 25th Anniversary of Independence

22   20 Pounds

	VF	UNC
1.1.1981. Green on multicolor underprint. President J. Nimeiri with native headdress at left, map at center, commemorative legend in circle at right around watermark, monument at right. Back: Unity Monument at left, People's Palace at center right.	22.50	90.00

1983-84 Issue

23   25 Piastres

	VF	UNC
1.1.1983. Red-orange on pale yellow underprint. President J. Nimeiri wearing national headdress at left, arms at center. Back: Kosti bridge. Watermark: Arms.		
a. Issued note.	0.50	1.50
s. Specimen. Red overprint in Arabic.	—	150

24   50 Piastres

	VF	UNC
1.1.1983. Purple on brown underprint. President J. Nimeiri wearing national headdress at left, arms at center. Back: Bank of Sudan. Watermark: Arms.	1.25	2.00

25   1 Pound

	VF	UNC
1.1.1983. Blue on multicolor underprint. President J. Nimeiri wearing national headdress at left, arms at center. Back: People's Assembly, building is blue. Watermark: Arms.	2.00	4.50

26   5 Pounds

	VF	UNC
1.1.1983. Green. President J. Nimeiri wearing national headdress at left, arms at center. Back: Islamic Centre Mosque in Khartoum at right. Watermark: Arms.		
a. Issued note.	4.00	17.50
s. Specimen. Red overprint in Arabic.	—	150

27   10 Pounds

	VF	UNC
1.1.1983. Purple and red-brown on multicolor underprint. President J. Nimeiri wearing national headdress at left, arms at center. Back: Kenana sugar factory. Watermark: Arms.		
a. Issued note.	10.00	50.00
s. Specimen. Red overprint in Arabic.	—	200

28   20 Pounds

	VF	UNC
1.1.1983. Green on multicolor underprint. President J. Nimeiri with native headdress at left, map at center, without commemorative legend in circle at right around watermark, monument at right. Back: Unity Monument at left, People's Palace at center right. Watermark: Arms.	12.50	75.00

29   50 Pounds

	VF	UNC
25.5.1984. Brown-orange, blue and olive-brown on multicolor underprint. President Nimeiri at left. Back: Sailing ship at center, modern oil tanker at right. Watermark: Arms.		
a. Issued note.	20.00	90.00
s. Specimen. Red overprint in Arabic.	—	200

Law of 30.6.1985/AH1405

Replacement notes: Serial # prefix Z/1; Z/11; Z/21; Z/31; Z/41; Z/51; Z/61; Z/71.

30 25 Piastres
VF UNC
L.1985. Purple on multicolor underprint. Camels at left, outline map of Sudan at center. Signature title with 2 lines of Arabic text (Acting Governor). Back: Bank of Sudan at center right. Watermark: Arms.
0.40 1.50

31 50 Piastres
VF UNC
L.1985. Red on lilac and peach underprint. Lyre and drum at left, peanut plant at right, outline map of Sudan at center. Signature title with 2 lines of Arabic text (Acting Governor). Back: Bank of Sudan at center right. Watermark: Arms.
0.50 2.50

32 1 Pound
VF UNC
L.1985. Green and blue on multicolor underprint. Cotton boll at left, outline map of Sudan at center. Signature title with 2 lines of Arabic text (Acting Governor). Back: Bank of Sudan at center right. Watermark: Arms.
0.75 3.00

33 5 Pounds
VF UNC
L.1985. Olive and brown on multicolor underprint. Cattle at left, outline map of Sudan at center. Signature title with 2 lines of Arabic text (Acting Governor). Back: Bank of Sudan at center right. Watermark: Arms.
5.00 30.00

34 10 Pounds
VF UNC
L.1985. Brown on multicolor underprint. City gateway at left, outline map of Sudan at center. Signature title with 2 lines of Arabic text (Acting Governor). Back: Bank of Sudan at center right. Watermark: Arms.
10.00 50.00

35 20 Pounds
VF UNC
L.1985. Green and purple on multicolor underprint. Feluka at left, outline map of Sudan at center. Signature title with 2 lines of Arabic text (Acting Governor). Back: Bank of Sudan at center right. Watermark: Arms.
45.00 250

36 50 Pounds
VF UNC
L.1985. Brown, purple and red-orange on multicolor underprint. Columns along pool below National Museum at left, spear at right, outline map of Sudan at center. Signature title with 2 lines of Arabic text (Acting Governor). Back: Bank of Sudan at center right. Watermark: Arms.
37.50 225

1987-90 Issue

37 25 Piastres
VF UNC
1987. UV: Arabic 25 and 25 in box fluoresce yellow. Purple on multicolor underprint. Camels at left, outline map of Sudan at center. Signature title in 1 lines of Arabic text (Governor). Back: Bank of Sudan at center right. Watermark: Arms.
0.20 1.00

38 50 Piastres
VF UNC
1987. Red on lilac and peach underprint. Lyre and drum at left, peanut plant at right, outline map of Sudan at center. Signature title in 1 lines of Arabic text (Governor). Back: Bank of Sudan at center right. Watermark: Arms.
0.25 1.00

39   1 Pound

1987. UV: Arabic value 1 and in a box fluoresce yellow. Green and blue on multicolor underprint. Cotton boll at left, outline map of Sudan at center. Signature title in 1 lines of Arabic text (Governor). Back: Bank of Sudan at center right. Watermark: Arms.

	VF	UNC
	0.50	1.50

40   5 Pounds

1987-90. Olive and brown on multicolor underprint. Cattle at left, outline map of Sudan at center. Signature title in 1 lines of Arabic text (Governor). Back: Bank of Sudan at center right. Watermark: Arms.

		VF	UNC
a.	1987.	1.00	8.50
b.	1989.	1.50	7.50
c.	1990.	2.00	17.50

41   10 Pounds

1987-90. Brown on multicolor underprint. City gateway at left, outline map of Sudan at center. Signature title in 1 lines of Arabic text (Governor). Back: Bank of Sudan at center right. Watermark: Arms.

		VF	UNC
a.	1987.	2.00	25.00
b.	1989.	3.00	30.00
c.	1990.	3.00	25.00

42   20 Pounds

1987-90. Green and purple on multicolor underprint. Feluka at left, outline map of Sudan at center. Signature title in 1 lines of Arabic text (Governor). Back: Bank of Sudan at center right. Watermark: Arms.

		VF	UNC
a.	1987.	5.00	25.00
b.	1989.	4.00	20.00
c.	1990.	6.00	27.50

43   50 Pounds

1987; 1989; 1990. Brown, purple and red-orange on multicolor underprint. Columns along pool below national Museum at left, spear at right, outline map of Sudan at center. Signature title in 1 lines of Arabic text (Governor). Back: Bank of Sudan at center right. Watermark: Arms.

		VF	UNC
a.	1987.	4.00	20.00
b.	1989.	3.50	15.00
c.	1990.	3.50	17.50

44   100 Pounds

1988-90. Brown, purple and deep green on multicolor underprint. Shield, University of Khartoum building at left, open book at lower right. Back: Bank of Sudan and shiny coin design. Watermark: Arms.

		VF	UNC
a.	1988.	3.00	20.00
b.	1989.	1.50	5.00
c.	1990.	1.50	5.00

1991 Issue

45   5 Pounds

1991/AH1411. Red, orange and violet on multicolor underprint. Cattle at left, outline map of Sudan at center. Signature title in 1 lines of Arabic text (Governor). Back: Bank of Sudan at center right. Watermark: Arms.

	VF	UNC
	0.50	2.00

46 10 Pounds

VF UNC

1991/AH1411. Black and deep green on multicolor underprint. City gateway at left, outline map of Sudan at center. Signature title in 1 lines of Arabic text (Governor). Back: Bank of Sudan at center right. Watermark: Arms.

0.75 3.00

47 20 Pounds

VF UNC

1991/AH1411. Purple and violet on multicolor underprint. Feluka at left, outline map of Sudan at center. Signature title in 1 lines of Arabic text (Governor). Back: Bank of Sudan at center right. Watermark: Arms.

1.00 4.00

48 50 Pounds

VF UNC

1991/AH1411. Yellow-orange, brownish black and dark brown on multicolor underprint. Columns along pool below national Museum at left, spear at right, outline map of Sudan at center. Signature title in 1 lines of Arabic text (Governor). Back: Bank of Sudan at center right. Watermark: Arms.

1.50 6.00

49 100 Pounds

VF UNC

1991/AH1411. Ultramarine and blue-green on multicolor underprint. Ultramarine shield at left, light blue-green map image at center, University of Khartoum building at left, open book at lower right. Back: Shiny light green coin design at right on back (partially engraved), Bank of Sudan at center right. Watermark: Arms.

5.00 15.00

50 100 Pounds

VF UNC

1991/AH1411; 1992/AH1412. Similar to number 49 but colors rearranged. Blue green shield at left, darker details on building and ultramarine map image at center. Back: Bank of Sudan at center right, pink coin design at right. (litho). Watermark: Arms.

    a. 1991/AH1411.   1.50   5.00
    b. 1992/AH1412.   1.00   4.00

1992-98 Issue

Note: First issues w/fractional serial # prefix (Type I) replaced w/local printings w/double letter serial # prefix (Type II).

51 5 Dinars

VF UNC

1993/AH1413. Dark brown and red-orange on multicolor underprint. People's Palace at lower right. Serial # Type II. Replacement note: *GZ*. Back: Plants including sunflowers at center. Watermark: Domed building with tower.

    a. Issued note.   1.00   3.00
    s. Specimen.   —   85.00

52 10 Dinars

VF UNC

1993/AH1413. Deep red and dark brown on multicolor underprint. People's Palace at lower right. Serial # Type II. Replacement note: *HZ*. Back: Domed building with tower at left center. Watermark: Domed building with tower.

    a. Issued note.   1.00   4.00
    s. Specimen.   —   85.00

53 25 Dinars — VF UNC

1992/AH1412. Brownish black and green on multicolor underprint. People's Palace at lower right. Back: Circular design at left. Watermark: Domed building with tower.

	VF	UNC
a. With artist's name *DOSOUGI* at lower right. Serial # Type I.	3.00	10.00
b. Without artist's name. Serial # Type I. Replacement note: *IZ*.	2.00	6.00
c. As b. Serial # Type II.	1.00	3.00
s. Specimen.	—	50.00

57 200 Dinars — VF UNC

1998/AH1419. Green and black on multicolor underprint. Peoples Palace at right, crop line art at center. Back: Building at upper center, line art at lower center.

	VF	UNC
a. 7 digit serial #. Embedded security thread.	2.00	6.50
b. 8 digit serial #. Segmented security thread.	2.00	5.50

54 50 Dinars — VF UNC

1992/AH1412. Dark blue-green, black and purple on multicolor underprint. People's Palace at lower right. Watermark: Domed building with tower.

	VF	UNC
a. With artist's name *DOSOUGI* at lower right below palace. Serial # Type I.	5.00	20.00
b. Without artist's name. 2 signature varieties. Serial # Type I.	1.50	5.00
c. As b. Serial # Type II. Replacement note: *JZ*.	1.50	6.00
d. As c. Segmented security thread. 7 or 8 digit serial #.	1.50	4.00
s. Specimen.	—	50.00

58 500 Dinars — VF UNC

1998/AH1419. Red, black and green on multicolor underprint. Serial number Type II.. Back: Oil well and building.

	VF	UNC
a. 7 digit serial #. Embedded security thread.	2.50	7.50
b. 8 digit serial #. Segmented security thread.	2.50	7.50
s. Specimen.	—	50.00

55 100 Dinars — VF UNC

1994/AH1414. Black and deep brown-violet on multicolor underprint. People's Palace at center or lower right, double doorway at center. Serial # Type I. Replacement note: *KZ*. Back: Building at left center. Watermark: Domed building with tower.

	VF	UNC
a. Issued note.	3.00	10.00
s. Specimen.	—	50.00

59 1000 Dinars — VF UNC

1996/AH1416. Green, yellow-brown and purple. Seal at left center, building in background at center. Serial # Type II. Replacement note: *MZ*. Back: Building.

	VF	UNC
a. 8 digit serial #. Signature 11.	4.00	15.00
b. 7 digit serial #. Signature 12.	4.00	15.00
c. 8 digit serial #. Signature 12.	4.00	15.00
s. Specimen.	—	50.00

60 10,000 Dinars — VF UNC

1996. Unissued specimen. Brown and multicolor. Presidential Palace in Khartoum at center, leaf and front at right. Back: Building at center. Watermark: Domed building. 140x65mm.   — 1,000

#61 not assigned.

2002-03 Issue

56 100 Dinars — VF UNC

1994/AH1414. Black and deep brown-violet on multicolor underprint. Like number 55 but with segmented foil over security thread. 7 or 8 digit serial #. Serial # Type II. Replacement note: *LZ*. Back: Building at left center. Watermark: Domed building with tower.

	VF	UNC
a. Issued note.	1.50	4.00
s. Specimen.	—	50.00

62   2000 Dinars   VF   UNC
2002/AH1422. Tan, blue, maroon and black on multicolor underprint. Back: Dam,
oil rig and Bank of Sudan building.
    a. Issued note.   7.00   32.50
    s. Specimen.   —   50.00

63   5000 Dinars   VF   UNC
2002. Orange and multicolor. Foil at left.
    a. Issued note.   10.00   50.00
    s. Specimen.   —   50.00

Central Bank of Sudan

2006 Issue

64   1 Pound   VF   UNC
9.7.2006. Brown and yellow on multicolor underprint. Dove and modern buildings
at right center. Back: Two doves. 139x64mm.
    a. Issued note.   1.00   4.00
    s. Specimen.   —   50.00

65   2 Pounds   VF   UNC
9.7.2006. Blue on multicolor underprint. Objects at right center. Back: Musical
instruments. 144x64mm.
    a. 9.7.2006.   1.50   7.00
    s. Specimen.   —   50.00

66   5 Pounds   VF   UNC
9.7.2006. Rose and brown on multicolor underprint. Building at right center. Back:
Dam. 150x69mm.
    a. Issued note.   2.50   10.00
    s. Specimen.   —   50.00

67   10 Pounds   VF   UNC
9.7.2006. Purple on multicolor underprint. Tree, ox and cart at right center. Back:
Building. 155x69mm.
    a. Issued note.   4.00   17.50
    s. Specimen.   —   50.00

68   20 Pounds   VF   UNC
9.7.2006. Rose, brown and yellow on multicolor underprint. Machine and oil rig at
right center. Back: Factories, antenna and fruits. 160x75mm.
    a. Issued note.   7.50   30.00
    s. Specimen.   —   50.00

69   50 Pounds   VF   UNC
9.7.2006. Greenish yellow, brown and multicolor. Rhinoceros, elephant, gnu,
zebras, giraffe and primate at right center. Back: Cattle and camels. 165x74mm.
    a. Issued note.   10.00   55.00
    s. Specimen.   —   75.00

2011 Issue

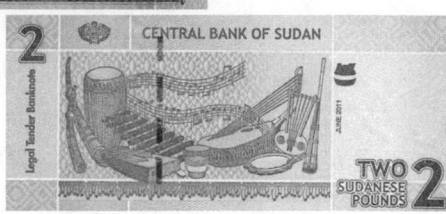

71   2 Pounds   VF   UNC
6.2011. Red brown and ochre. Dove in flight above map, Central Bank of Sudan   FV   2.50
building in Khartoum, drums. Back: Two doves in flight. Watermark: Dove and
LS1. Printer: Sudan Currency Printing Press. 139x64mm.

72   5 Pounds   VF   UNC
6.2011. 144x64mm.
    a. Segmented foil security thread on back.   FV   5.00
    b. Segmented foil security thread on face.   FV   5.00

73   10 Pounds   VF   UNC
6.2011. Green, blue and multicolor. Tree at center, camel at right Back: Building at   FV   10.00
center. 155x69mm.

74   20 Pounds   **VF   UNC**

2011; 2015. Tan, blue and multicolor. Costal city and oil rig. Back: Ancient ruins.
160x75mm.

    a. Segmented foil security thread on back.   FV   18.00
    b. Segmented foil security thread on face.   FV   18.00
    c. 3.2015.   FV   18.00

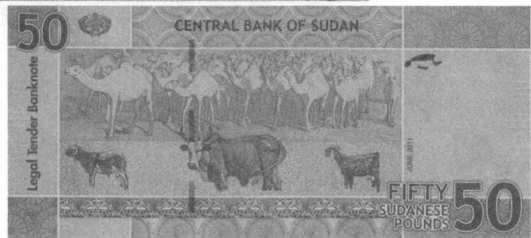

75   50 Pounds   **VF   UNC**

2011; 2015. Blue, brown and multicolor. Heard of animals at center. Back: Camels
at top, animals at lower center. 165x74mm.

    a. Segmented foil security thread on back.   FV   40.00
    b. Segmented foil security thread on face.   FV   40.00
    c. 3.2015. Signature: Abdelrahman Hassan Abdelrahman Hashim. Prefix FH.   FV   40.00

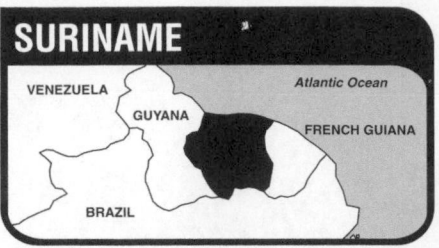

SURINAME

The Republic of Surinam, formerly known as Dutch Guiana, located on the north central coast of South America between Guyana and French Guiana, has an area of 163,270 sq. km. and a population of 476,000. Capital: Paramaribo. The country is rich in minerals and forests, and self-sufficient in rice, the staple food crop. The mining, processing and exporting of bauxite is the principal economic activity.First explored by the Spaniards in the 16th century and then settled by the English in the mid-17th century, Suriname became a Dutch colony in 1667. With the abolition of slavery in 1863, workers were brought in from India and Java. Independence from the Netherlands was granted in 1975. Five years later the civilian government was replaced by a military regime that soon declared a socialist republic. It continued to exert control through a succession of nominally civilian administrations until 1987, when international pressure finally forced a democratic election. In 1990, the military overthrew the civilian leadership, but a democratically elected government - a four-party New Front coalition - returned to power in 1991 and has ruled since; the coalition expanded to eight parties in 2005.

RULERS:
    Dutch to 1975

MONETARY SYSTEM:
    1 Gulden = 1 Florin = 100 Cents, to 2004
    1 Dollar = 1000 "old" Gulden, 2004-

DUTCH ADMINISTRATION

Muntbiljet

Law 8.4.1960

Replacement notes: 6-digit serial number beginning with "1".

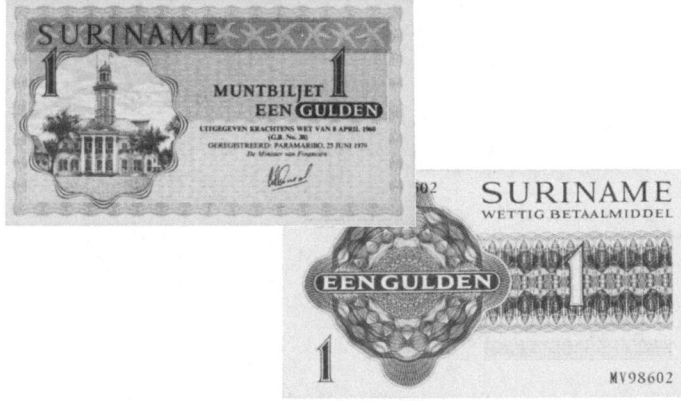

116   1 Gulden   **VF   UNC**

1961-86. Dark green with black text on pale olive-green and brown underprint.
Building with tower and flag at left. Signature varieties. Printer: JEZ.

    a. Signature title: *De Minister van Financien* with printed Signature but without   2.00   10.00
       name. 1.8.1961-1.4.1969.
    b. Signature in facsimile with printed name below. 1.4.1971.   2.00   7.00
    c. Similar to b., but printed name of signer at right. 1.11.1974.   2.00   5.50
    d. Like c. without printed name at right. 1.11.1974.   2.00   5.50
    e. Similar to a., but shorter text, and signature title centered. 1.11.1974;   1.50   7.00
       25.6.1979.
    f. Similar to d., but signature title: *De Minister van Financien en Planning.*   0.50   2.50
       1.9.1982.
    g. 2.1.1984.   0.50   2.25
    h. 1.12.1984.   0.50   2.25
    i. 1.10.1986.   0.50   2.00

117   2 1/2 Gulden   **VF   UNC**

1961; 1967. Red-brown. Girl wearing hat at left. Signature varieties. Printer: JEZ.

    a. 2.1.1961.   3.00   12.50
    b. 2.7.1967.   2.25   7.50

118   2 1/2 Gulden   **VF   UNC**

1973; 1978. Red-brown, light blue and multicolor. Blue-gray Tanager on branch at left. Three lines of text above signature title at center. Back: Lizard and Afobaka Dam. Printer: BWC.

    a. Signature title: *De Minister van Financien.* Printed name below Signature   2.25   9.00
        1.9.1973.
    b. Without printed name below signature 1.8.1978.   0.75   4.50
    s1. As a. Specimen.   —   —
    s2. As b. Specimen.   —   —

119   2 1/2 Gulden   **VF   UNC**

1.11.1985. UV: fibers fluoresce yellow. Back design green and yellow. Red-brown, light blue and multicolor. Blue-gray Tanager on branch at left. four lines of text above signature with signature title: *De Minister van Financien en Planning* . Back: Lizard and Afobaka Dam. Printer: BWC.

    a. Issued note.   0.75   3.50
    s. Specimen.   0.00   0.00

Centrale Bank van Suriname
1963 Issue

#30-34 Replacement notes: Serial # prefix ZZ.

120   5 Gulden   **VF   UNC**

1.9.1963. Blue on multicolor underprint. Two serial number varieties. Back: Different arms than 1957 issue. Watermark: Toucan's head. Printer: JEZ.

    a. Serial # first three digits smaller than last three digits.   0.25   0.75
    b. Serial # digits of equal height.   0.25   0.75

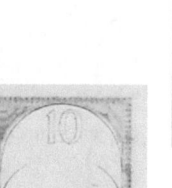

121   10 Gulden   **VF   UNC**

1.9.1963. Orange on multicolor underprint. Back: Different arms than 1957 issue. Watermark: Toucan's head. Printer: JEZ.

    a. Serial # first three digits smaller than last three digits.   0.25   1.00
    b. Serial # digits of equal height.   0.25   1.00

122   25 Gulden   **VF   UNC**

1.9.1963. Green on multicolor underprint. Back: Different arms than 1957 issue.   3.00   10.00
Watermark: Toucan's head. Printer: JEZ.

123   100 Gulden   **VF   UNC**

1.9.1963. Purple on multicolor underprint. Back: Different arms than 1957 issue.   5.00   12.50
Watermark: Toucan's head. Printer: JEZ.

124   1000 Gulden   **VF   UNC**

1.9.1963. Brown on multicolor underprint. Back: Different arms than 1957 issue.   5.00   12.50
Watermark: Toucan's head. Printer: JEZ.

Note: #124 was sold in quantity by the Central Bank to the numismatic community.

REPUBLIC
Centrale Bank van Suriname
1982 Issue

125   5 Gulden   **VF   UNC**

1.4.1982. Blue on multicolor underprint. Soldiers and woman at right. Back: Build-   0.50   1.00
ing with flag. Watermark: Toucan's head. Printer: JEZ.

126   10 Gulden   **VF   UNC**

1.4.1982. Red on multicolor underprint. Soldiers and woman at right. Back: Build-   0.40   1.25
ing with flag. Watermark: Toucan's head. Printer: JEZ.

127　25 Gulden　　　　　　　　　　　　　　　　　　**VF　UNC**
1982; 1985. Green on multicolor underprint. Soldiers and woman at right. Back:
Building with flag. Watermark: Toucan's head. Printer: JEZ.
　　　a. 1.4.1982.　　　　　　　　　　　　　　　2.50　5.00
　　　b. 1.11.1985.　　　　　　　　　　　　　　　0.25　0.75

128　100 Gulden　　　　　　　　　　　　　　　　　**VF　UNC**
1982; 1985. Purple on multicolor underprint. Soldiers and woman at right. Back:
Building with flag. Watermark: Toucan's head. Printer: JEZ.
　　　a. 1.4.1982.　　　　　　　　　　　　　　　10.00　20.00
　　　b. 1.11.1985.　　　　　　　　　　　　　　　1.25　3.50

129　500 Gulden　　　　　　　　　　　　　　　　　**VF　UNC**
1.4.1982. Brown on multicolor underprint. Soldiers and woman at right. Back:　1.00　7.50
Building with flag on back. Watermark: Toucan's head. Printer: JEZ.

Note: 1000 uncirculated examples of #129 were sold by the Central Bank to the numismatic community for USA $2.00 each. Although absorbed into the collector marketplace, they are still
commonly available.

1986-88 Issue

130　5 Gulden　　　　　　　　　　　　　　　　　　**VF　UNC**
1986; 1988. Blue on multicolor underprint. Anton DeKom at left, militia at right,
row of buildings across bottom. Back: Toucan at left, speaker with people at right.
Watermark: Toucan. Printer: TDLR.
　　　a. 1.7.1986.　　　　　　　　　　　　　　　0.75　3.00
　　　b. 9.1.1988.　　　　　　　　　　　　　　　FV　2.00

131　10 Gulden　　　　　　　　　　　　　　　　　**VF　UNC**
1986; 1988. Orange and red on multicolor underprint. Anton DeKom at left, militia
at right, row of buildings across bottom. Back: Toucan at left, speaker with people
at right. Watermark: Toucan. Printer: TDLR.
　　　a. 1.7.1986.　　　　　　　　　　　　　　　1.25　4.00
　　　b. 9.1.1988.　　　　　　　　　　　　　　　FV　2.00

132　25 Gulden　　　　　　　　　　　　　　　　　**VF　UNC**
1986; 1988. Green on multicolor underprint. Anton DeKom at left, militia at right,
row of buildings across bottom. Back: Toucan at left, speaker with people at right.
Watermark: Toucan. Printer: TDLR.
　　　a. 1.7.1986.　　　　　　　　　　　　　　　2.00　8.00
　　　b. 9.1.1988.　　　　　　　　　　　　　　　FV　3.50

133　100 Gulden　　　　　　　　　　　　　　　　　**VF　UNC**
1986; 1988. Purple on multicolor underprint. Anton DeKom at left, militia at right,
row of buildings across bottom. Two serial number varieties. Back: Toucan at left,
speaker with people at right. Watermark: Toucan. Printer: TDLR.
　　　a. 1.7.1986.　　　　　　　　　　　　　　　7.50　20.00
　　　b. 9.1.1988.　　　　　　　　　　　　　　　FV　2.50

134　250 Gulden　　　　　　　　　　　　　　　　　**VF　UNC**
9.1.1988. Blue-gray on multicolor underprint. Anton DeKom at left, militia at right,　2.00　8.00
row of buildings across bottom. Back: Toucan at left, speaker with people at right.
Watermark: Toucan. Printer: TDLR.

135 500 Gulden   **VF UNC**
1.7.1986; 9.1.1988. Brown and orange on multicolor underprint. Anton DeKom at
left, militia at right, row of buildings across bottom. Back: Toucan at left, speaker
with people at right. Watermark: Toucan. Printer: TDLR.

a. 1.7.1986.   15.00   50.00
b. 9.1.1988.   3.50   12.50

1991-97 Issue

136 5 Gulden   **VF UNC**
1991; 1995-96; 1998. UV: fibers fluoresce blue; CBVS In box yellow; serial #
orange. Back top central design yellow. Deep blue and green on multicolor underprint. Central Bank building, Paramaribo at center, log trucks at upper left. Back:
Arms at upper right, logging at center right. Watermark: Toucan. Printer: TDLR.

a. 9.7.1991.   FV   1.50
b. 1.6.1995; 1.12.1996; 10.2.1998.   FV   0.25

137 10 Gulden   **VF UNC**
1991; 1995; 1998. Red and dark green on multicolor underprint. Central Bank
building, Paramaribo at center, bananas at upper left. Back: Arms at upper right,
banana harvesting at center right. Watermark: Toucan. Printer: TDLR.

a. 9.7.1991.   FV   3.00
b. 1.6.1995; 1.12.1996; 10.2.1998.   FV   0.25

138 25 Gulden   **VF UNC**
1991; 1995; 1996; 1998. Green and brown-orange on multicolor underprint.
Central Bank building, Paramaribo at center, Track participants at upper left. Back:
Arms at upper right, Competition swimmer (Olympian Anthony Neste) in butterfly
Watermark: Toucan. Printer: TDLR.

a. 9.7.1991.   FV   4.00
b. 1.6.1995.   FV   3.50
c. 1.12.1996.   FV   2.50
d. 10.2.1998.   FV   2.50

139 100 Gulden   **VF UNC**
9.7.1991; 10.2.1998. Violet and purple on multicolor underprint. Central Bank
building, Paramaribo at center, factory at upper left. Back: Arms at upper right,
strip mining at cetner right. Watermark: Toucan. Printer: TDLR.

a. 9.7.1991.   FV   6.50
b. 10.2.1998.   FV   6.50

140 500 Gulden   **VF UNC**
9.7.1991. Brown and red-orange on multicolor underprint. Central Bank building,   FV   10.00
Paramaribo at center, crude oil pump at upper left. Back: Arms at upper right,
drilling for crude oil at center right. Watermark: Toucan. Printer: TDLR.

141 1000 Gulden   **VF UNC**
1993; 1995. Black and red on multicolor underprint. Central Bank building,
Paramaribo at center, combine at upper left. Back: Arms at upper right, combining
grain at center right. Watermark: Toucan. Printer: TDLR.

a. 1.7.1993.   FV   10.00
b. 1.3.1995.   FV   5.00

142 2000 Gulden   **VF UNC**
1.6.1995. Purple and green on multicolor underprint. Central Bank building, Para-   FV   10.00
maribo at center. Back: Arms at upper right, logging at center right. Watermark:
Toucan. Printer: TDLR.

143 5000 Gulden

5.10.1997; 1.2.1999. Purple on multicolor underprint. Central Bank building, Paramaribo at center. Back: Long Billed Gnatwren, banana bunches. Watermark: Toucan. Printer: TDLR.

	VF	UNC
a. 5.10.1997.	FV	20.00
b. 1.2.1999.	FV	20.00

144 10,000 Gulden

5.10.1997. Green, red and multicolor. Central Bank building, silver segmented security thread. Back: Bird, industrial complex. Watermark: Toucan. Printer: TDLR.

	VF	UNC
	FV	37.50

145 10,000 Gulden

5.10.1997. Green, red and multicolor. Central Bank building, Purple segmented security thread. Back: More red used on buildings at center and arms at left center on back than with #144.

	VF	UNC
	FV	37.50

2000 Issue

146 5 Gulden

1.1.2000. UV: value 5 in box, butterflies, batwings, trees fluoresce green. Blue and multicolor. Red-necked Woodpecker at left center, arms at upper center. Ascending size serial number. Back: Flower. Printer: TDLR.

	VF	UNC
	FV	1.50

147 10 Gulden

1.1.2000. UV: value 10 in box, right of bird fluoresce yellow; beetle wings, trees orange. Green, purple, brown on multicolor underprint. Black-throated mango at left center, arms at upper center. Ascending size serial number. Back: Flower. Printer: TDLR.

	VF	UNC
	FV	2.00

148 25 Gulden

1.1.2000. UV: value 25 in box, mantis wings, trees fluoresce yellow. Blue and black on multicolor underprint. Red-billed Toucan at left center, arms at upper center. Ascending size serial number. Back: Flower. Printer: TDLR.

	VF	UNC
	FV	3.00

149 100 Gulden

1.1.2000. UV: value 100 in box, chameleon, trees fluoresce yellow. Rose on multicolor underprint. Long-tailed Hermit at left center, arms at upper center. Ascending size serial number. Back: Flower. Printer: TDLR.

	VF	UNC
	FV	4.00

150 500 Gulden

1.1.2000. Orange and green on multicolor underprint. Guianan Cock-of-the-Rock at left center, arms at upper center. Ascending size serial number. Back: Flower. Printer: TDLR.

	VF	UNC
	FV	6.00

151 1000 Gulden

1.1.2000. Green and red on multicolor underprint. Royal Flycatcher at left center, arms at upper center. Ascending size serial number. Back: Flower. Printer: TDLR.

	VF	UNC
	FV	8.00

152 5000 Gulden VF UNC
1.1.2000. Green, yellow, blue and orange on multicolor underprint. Sun Parakeet   FV   15.00
at left center, arms at upper center. Ascending size serial number. Back: Flowers.
Printer: TDLR.

153 10,000 Gulden VF UNC
1.1.2000. Brown, black and red on multicolor underprint. Ornate Hawk-eagle at   FV   22.50
left center, arms at upper center. Ascending size serial number. Back: Flower.
Printer: TDLR.

154 25,000 Gulden VF UNC
1.1.2000. Brown and green on multicolor underprint. Specktacled Owl at left   FV   45.00
center, arms at upper center. Ascending size serial number. Back: Flower and long
leaves. Printer: TDLR.

Suriname Wettig Betaalmiddel
2004 Issue

155 1 Dollar VF UNC
1.1.2004. Green. Central Bank building at left. Back: Value. 168x73mm.   FV   1.00

156 2 1/2 Dollars VF UNC
1.1.2004. Violet blue and red-brown. Central Bank building at left. Back: Value.   FV   2.00
168x73mm.

2004 Issue

157 5 Dollars VF UNC
1.1.2004; 4.1.2006. Orange and brown on multicolor underprint. Central Bank
building at center. Back: Gran - Rio Suia. 140x70mm.
  a. 1.1.2004.   FV   2.00
  b. 4.1.2006.   FV   2.00
  c. 5.1.2009.   FV   2.00

158 10 Dollars VF UNC
1.1.2004; 11.1.2004; 4.1.2006; 9.1.2009. Olive green on multicolor underprint.
Central Bank building at center. Back: Surinam river. 140x70mm.
  a. 1.1.2004.   FV   2.50
  b. 11.1.2004.   FV   2.50
  c. 4.1.2006.   FV   2.50
  d. 9.1.2009.   FV   2.50

159 20 Dollars VF UNC
1.1.2004; 11.1.2004; 4.1.2006; 9.1.2009. Slate black and lilac on multicolor underprint. Central Bank building at center. Back: Volzberg mountain. 140x70mm.
  a. 1.1.2004.   FV   10.00
  b. 11.1.2004.   FV   10.00
  c. 4.1.2006.   FV   10.00
  d. 5.1.2009.   FV   10.00

160 50 Dollars VF UNC
1.1.2004; 11.1.2004; 4.1.2006. Olive and lilac on multicolor underprint. Central Bank building at center. Back: Kasi Kasima rock formation. 140x70mm.
a. 1.1.2004. FV 20.00
b. 11.1.2004. FV 20.00
c. 4.1.2006. FV 20.00

161 100 Dollars VF UNC
1.1.2004; 4.1.2006. 140x70mm.
a. 1.1.2004. FV 40.00
b. 4.1.2006. FV 40.00

2010 Issue

162 5 Dollars VF UNC
9.1.2010; 4.1.2012. Rose and brown on multicolor underprint. Central Bank building at center. Wide security strip at right. Back: Cocos nucifera tree; Forest and rapids near Gran-Rio in Sula Watermark: Bank headquarters and CBvS. 140x70mm.
a. 9.1.2009. FV 2.00
b. 4.1.2006. FV 2.00

163 10 Dollars VF UNC
1.9.2010. Green and yellow on multicolor underprint. Central Bank building at center. Wide security strip at right. Back: Tabebuia serratifolia tree and Surinam river. Watermark: Bank headquarters and CBvS. 140x70mm. FV 2.50

164 20 Dollars VF UNC
1.9.2010. Slate black and lilac on multicolor underprint. Central Bank building at center. Wide security strip at right. Back: Rhizophora mangle tree; Volzberg mountain and waterfalls. Watermark: Bank headwuarters and CBvS. 140x70mm. FV 10.00

165 50 Dollars VF UNC
1.9.2010. Slate black and lilac on multicolor underprint. Central Bank building at center. Wide security strip at right. Back: Kasi Kasima rock formation. Watermark: Bank headquarters and CBvS. 140x70mm. FV 20.00

166 100 Dollars VF UNC
9.1.2010; 4.1.2012. Slate black and lilac on multicolor underprint. Central Bank building at center. Wide security strip at right. Back: Aruba-tabbetje, Marowijne river. Watermark: Bank Headquarters and CBvS. 140x70mm.
a. 9.1.2010. FV 40.00
b. 4.1.2012. FV 40.00

2012 Commemorative Issue

167 50 Dollars VF UNC
01.04.2012. Signature: Gillmore A. Hoefdraad. Centrale Bank van Suriname sold note packaged in a folder. Issue was limited to 50,000 notes. Brown and green. Coat of arms, LOOK serial #, Central Bank building, bougainvillea flower, bank logo SPOT patch. Back: Names and terms of service of bank's presidents, man at lecturn addressing crowd, bank's mission statement. LEAD holographic stripe with bougainvillea flower, bank logo and 50. RollingStar magenta-to-green windowed security thread with demetalized SRD. Watermark: Bank headquarters and electrotype CBvS. Printer: Giesecke & Devrient. 140x70mm. FV 175

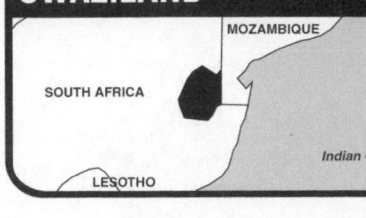

SWAZILAND

The Kingdom of Swaziland, located in southeastern Africa, has an area of 6,704 sq. mi. (17,360 sq. km.) and a population of 984,000. Capital: Mbabane (administrative); Lobamba (legislative). The diversified economy includes mining, agriculture and light industry. Asbestos, iron ore, wood pulp and sugar are exported. Autonomy for the Swazis of southern Africa was guaranteed by the British in the late 19th century; independence was granted in 1968. Student and labor unrest during the 1990s pressured King Mswati III, the world's last absolute monarch, to grudgingly allow political reform and greater democracy, although he has backslid on these promises in recent years. A constitution came into effect in 2006, but political parties remain banned. The African United Democratic Party tried unsuccessfully to register as an official political party in mid 2006. Talks over the constitution broke down between the government and progressive groups in 2007. Swaziland recently surpassed Botswana as the country with the world's highest known HIV/AIDS prevalence rate.

RULERS:
British to 1968
Sobhuza II, 1968-82
Queen Ntombi, as regent, 1982-86
King Mswati III, 1986-

MONETARY SYSTEM:
1 Lilangeni = 100 Cents (plural: Emalangeni)

SIGNATURE VARIETIES		
	MINISTER FOR FINANCE	GOVERNOR
1	R.P. Stephens 1.6.1972 - 11.1.1979	E.A.Z. Mayisela 1.4.1974 - 31.10.1976
	J.F.L. Simelane 12.1.1979 - 20.11.1983	Deputy Governor H.B.B. Oliver 1.11.1976 - 30.6.1978 Acting Governor A.D. Ockenden 1.6.1978 - 30.6.1981
2	J.L.F. Simelane 12.1.1979 - 20.11.1983	H.B.B. Oliver 1.7.1981 - 30.6.1992
3	Dr. S.S Nxumalo 21.11.1983 - 8.6.1984	H.B.B. Oliver 1.7.1981 - 30.6.1992
4	B.S. Dlamini 27.8.1984 - 5.11.1993	H.B.B. Oliver 1.7.1981 - 30.6.1992
5	B.S. Dlamini 27.8.1984 - 5.11.1993	J. Nxumalo 1.7.1992 - 30.6.1997
6	I.S. Shabangu 10.11.1993 - 3.3.1995	J. Nxumalo 1.7.1992 - 30.6.1997
7A	Dr. D. von Wissell 3.3.1995 - 12.11.1996	J. Nxumalo 1.7.1992 - 30.6.1997
7B	Dr. D. von Wissell 3.3.1995 - 12.11.1996	J. Nxumalo 1.7.1992 - 30.6.1997

SIGNATURE VARIETIES

	MINISTER FOR FINANCE	GOVERNOR
8	*(signature)* T. Masuku 12.11.1996 - 19.11.1998	*(signature)* J. Nxumalo 1.7.1992 - 30.6.1997
9A	*Themba N Masuku* T. Masuku 12.11.1996 - 19.11.1998	*(signature)* M.G. Dlamini 1.7.1997 →
9B	*Themba N Masuku* T. Masuku 12.11.1996 - 19.11.1998	*(signature)* M.G. Dlamini 1.7.1997 →
	J Carmichael 20.11.1998 - 14.2.2001	M.G. Dlamini 1.7.1997 →
10A	*Majozi V. Sithole* Majozi V. Sithole 15.2.2001 →	*(signature)* M.G. Dlamini 1.7.1997 →
10B	*Majozi V. Sithole* Majozi V. Sithole 15.2.2001 →	*(signature)* M.G. Dlamini 1.7.1997 →
11	*Majozi V. Sithole* Majozi V. Sithole	*(signature)* M.G. Dlamini

KINGDOM

Monetary Authority of Swaziland

1974-78 ND Issue

Replacement notes: Serial # prefix Z.

1   1 Lilangeni　　　　　　　　　　　　　　　　**VF   UNC**

ND (1974). Red-brown on multicolor underprint. King Sobhuza II at left, Parliament House at bottom center right. Signature 1. Back: Princesses taking part in the Ncwala (kingship ceremony). Watermark: Shield and spears. Printer: TDLR.

　　a. Issued note.　　　　　　　　　　　　　　　0.75　6.00
　　s. Specimen. Serial # prefix A; G. Red overprint: SPECIMEN on both sides.　—　65.00

2   2 Emalangeni　　　　　　　　　　　　　　　**VF   UNC**

ND (1974). Dark brown on pink and multicolor underprint. King Sobhuza II at left, Parliament House at bottom center right. Signature 1. Back: Sugar mill. Watermark: Shield and spears. Printer: TDLR.

　　a. Issued note.　　　　　　　　　　　　　　　1.75　12.00
　　s. Specimen. Serial # prefix A; C. Red overprint: SPECIMEN on both sides.　—　65.00

3   5 Emalangeni　　　　　　　　　　　　　　　**VF   UNC**

ND (1974). Dark green on yellow-green and multicolor underprint. King Sobhuza II at left, Parliament House at bottom center right. Signature 1. Back: Mantenga Falls and landscape. Watermark: Shield and spears. Printer: TDLR.

　　a. Issued note.　　　　　　　　　　　　　　　5.00　37.50
　　s. Specimen. Serial # prefix A; B. Red overprint: SPECIMEN on both sides.　—　65.00

4   10 Emalangeni　　　　　　　　　　　　　　**VF   UNC**

ND (1974). Blue-black on blue and multicolor underprint. King Sobhuza II at left, Parliament House at bottom center right. Signature 1. Back: Asbestos mine. Watermark: Shield and spears. Printer: TDLR.

　　a. Issued note.　　　　　　　　　　　　　　　10.00　80.00
　　s. Specimen. Serial # prefix A; B.　　　　　　—　65.00

5   20 Emalangeni　　　　　　　　　　　　　　**VF   UNC**

ND (1978). Purple and green on multicolor underprint. King Sobhuza II at left, Parliament House at bottom center right. Signature 1. Back: Agricultural products and cows. Watermark: Shield and spears. Printer: TDLR.

　　a. Issued note.　　　　　　　　　　　　　　　35.00　185
　　s. Specimen. Serial # prefix A.　　　　　　　—　65.00

Central Bank of Swaziland
1981 Commemorative Issue
#6 and 7, Diamond Jubilee of King Sobhuza II

6	10 Emalangeni	VF	UNC

1981. Blue-black on blue and multicolor underprint. Black commemorative text on watermark area. Signature 2. Back: Asbestos mine. Watermark: Shield and spears. Printer: TDLR.

a. Issued note.		85.00	300
s. Specimen. Serial # prefix K.		—	185

7	20 Emalangeni	VF	UNC

1981. Purple and green on multicolor underprint. King Sobhuza II at left, Parliament House at bottom center right. Black commemorative text on watermark area. Signature 2. New issuer's name at top. Back: Agricultural products and cows. Watermark: Shield and spears. Printer: TDLR.

a. Issued note.		100	335
s. Specimen. Serial # prefix C.		—	185

1982; 1983 ND Issue
Replacement notes: Serial # prefix Z.

8	2 Emalangeni	VF	UNC

ND (1983-86). Dark brown on pink and multicolor underprint. King Sobhuza II at left, Parliament House at bottom center right. Signature 2. New issuer's name at top. Back: Sugar mill. Watermark: Shield and spears. Printer: TDLR.

a. Signature 2. (1983).		3.75	22.50
b. Signature 4. (1984).		1.50	6.00
s1. As a. Specimen. Serial # prefix F. Red overprint: SPECIMEN on both sides.		—	65.00
s2. As b. Specimen. Serial # prefix G, J. Red overprint: SPECIMEN on each side.		—	65.00

9	5 Emalangeni	VF	UNC

ND (1982-86). Dark green on yellow-green and multicolor underprint. King Sobhuza II at left, Parliament House at bottom center right. Signature 1. New issuer's name at top. Back: Mantenga Falls and landscape. Watermark: Shield and spears. Printer: TDLR.

a. Signature 2. (1982).		5.00	37.50
b. Signature 4. (1984).		2.00	11.00
s1. As a. Specimen. Serial # prefix D; E. Red overprint: SPECIMEN on each side.		—	65.00
s2. As b. Specimen. Serial # prefix F. Red overprint: SPECIMEN on both sides.		—	65.00

10	10 Emalangeni	VF	UNC

ND (1982-86). Blue-black on blue and multicolor underprint. King Sobhuza II at left, without commemorative inscription. Back: Asbestos mine. Watermark: Shield and spears. Printer: TDLR.

a. Signature 2. (1982).		25.00	135
b. Signature 3. (1984).		22.50	120
c. Signature 4. (1985).		4.00	16.50
s1. As a. Specimen. Serial # prefix Q.		—	65.00
s2. As b. Specimen. Serial # prefix U.		—	65.00
s3. As c. Specimen. Serial # prefix W.		—	65.00

11	20 Emalangeni	VF	UNC

ND (1984-86). Purple and green on multicolor underprint. King Sobhuza II at left, Parliament House at bottom center right. Signature 2. New issuer's name at top. Without commemorative inscription. Back: Agricultural products and cows. Watermark: Shield and spears. Printer: TDLR.

a. Signature 3. (1984).		45.00	200
b. Signature 4. (1985).		8.00	38.50
s1. As a. Specimen. Serial # prefix E.		—	65.00
s2. As b. Specimen. Serial # prefix F.		—	65.00

1986 ND Issue

12	20 Emalangeni	VF	UNC

ND (1986). Purple and green on multicolor underprint. King Mswati III at left, Parliament House at bottom center right. Signature 4. New issuer's name at top. Without commemorative inscription. Back: Agricultural products and cows. Watermark: Shield and spears. Printer: TDLR.

a. Issued note.		6.50	30.00
s. Specimen. Serial # prefix A.		—	110

1986; 1987 ND Issues
Replacement notes: Serial # prefix Z.

13	2 Emalangeni	VF	UNC

ND (1987). Dark brown and orange on multicolor underprint. Facing portrait of young King Mswati III at left, arms at lower center. Signature 4. Back: Grey lourie, blue crane, hippos and other wildlife. Watermark: Shield and spears. Printer: TDLR.

a. Issued note.		1.50	7.00
s. Specimen. Serial # prefix A.		—	110

14 **5 Emalangeni** VF UNC
ND (1987). Dark green, dark brown and bright green on multicolor underprint.
Facing portrait of young King Mswati III at left, arms at lower center. Signature 4.
Back: Warriors. Watermark: Shield and spears. Printer: TDLR.
    a. Issued note. 2.50 12.50
    s. Specimen. Serial # prefix A. — 110

19 **5 Emalangeni** VF UNC
ND (1990-95). Dark green, dark brown and bright green on multicolor underprint.
Older portrait of King Mswati III at left facing half right, arms at lower center.
Signature 4. Back: Warriors. Watermark: Shield and spears. Printer: TDLR.
    a. Signature 4. (1990). 2.50 8.50
    b. Signature 6. (1994). 7.50 37.50
    s1. As a. Specimen. Serial # prefix D. — 100
    s2. As b. Specimen. Serial # prefix J. — 90.00

15 **10 Emalangeni** VF UNC
ND (1986). Dark blue and black on multicolor underprint. Facing portrait of young
King Mswati III at left, arms at lower center. Signature 4. Back: Hydroelectric plant
at Luphohlo and bird. Watermark: Shield and spears. Printer: TDLR. 144x66mm.
    a. Issued note. 6.00 20.00
    s. Specimen. Serial # prefix A; F. — 110

16 **20 Emalangeni** VF UNC
ND (1986). Violet, brown and purple on multicolor underprint. Facing portrait of
young King Mswati III at left, arms at lower center. Signature 4. Back: Cattle and
truck. Watermark: Shield and spears. Printer: TDLR. 150x69mm.
    a. Issued note. 32.50 160
    s. Specimen. Serial # prefix A. — 110

20 **10 Emalangeni** VF UNC
ND (1990-95). Dark blue and black on multicolor underprint. Older portrait of
King Mswati III at left facing half right, arms at lower center. Signature 4. Back:
Hydroelectric plant at Luphohlo and bird. Watermark: Shield and spears. Printer:
TDLR. 148x67mm.
    a. Signature 4. (1990). 4.50 22.50
    b. Signature 5. (1992). 5.00 25.00
    s1. As a. Specimen. Serial # prefix J. — 100
    s2. As b. Specimen. Serial # prefix N. — 100

1989 Commemorative Issue
#17, 21st Birthday of King Mswati III

17 **20 Emalangeni** VF UNC
19.4.1989. Violet, brown and purple on multicolor underprint. Like number 16, with
silver commemorative text and dates overprint on watermark area. Signature 4.
Back: Cattle and truck. Watermark: Shield and spears. Printer: TDLR.
    a. Issued note. 7.50 27.50
    s. Specimen. Serial # prefix A. — 100

1990; 1992 ND Issue
Replacement notes: Serial # prefix Z.

18 **2 Emalangeni** VF UNC
ND (1992-95). Dark brown on multicolor underprint. Older portrait of King Mswati
III at left facing half right, arms at lower center. Signature 4. Back: Grey lourie,
blue crane, hippos and other wildlife. Watermark: Shield and spears. Printer:
TDLR.
    a. Signature 4. (1992). 1.50 5.00
    b. Signature 6. (1994). 4.00 15.00
    s1. As a. Specimen. Serial # prefix M. — 100
    s2. As b. Specimen. Serial # prefix S. — 100

21 **20 Emalangeni** VF UNC
ND (1990-95). Violet, brown and purple on multicolor underprint. Older portrait of
King Mswati III at left facing half right, arms at lower center. Signature 4. Back:
Cattle and truck. Watermark: Shield and spears. Printer: TDLR. 150x69mm.
    a. Signature 4. (1990). 9.00 37.50
    b. Signature 5. (1992). 8.00 35.00
    s1. As a. Specimen. Serial # prefix D. — 100
    s2. As b. Specimen. Serial # prefix G. — 100

22 **50 Emalangeni** VF UNC
ND (1990-95). Dull red-brown, orange and dark green on multicolor underprint.
King Mswati III at left. Back: Central Bank seal at left center, head office building
at right. Watermark: Shield and spears. Printer: TDLR. 157x72mm.
    a. Signature 4. (1990). 20.00 80.00
    b. Signature 6. (1995). 60.00 240
    s1. As a. Specimen. Serial # prefix A. — 90.00
    s2. As b. Specimen. Serial # prefix C. — 85.00

1995 ND; 1995-98 Issue

23   5 Emalangeni

VF   UNC

ND (1995). UV: right of King's face, value 5 and vertical bars fluoresce yellow. Dark green, dark brown and bright green on multicolor underprint. Older portrait of King Mswati III at left facing half right, arms at lower center. Ascending size serial number. Signature 7a. Segmented foil over security thread. Back: Warriors in dark brown. Printer: H&S.

a. Issued note.	2.00	7.00
s. Specimen. Serial # prefix *AA*.	—	85.00

24   10 Emalangeni

VF   UNC

ND (1995); 1997; 1998. Dark blue and black on multicolor underprint. Older portrait of King Mswati III at left facing half right, arms at lower center. Signature 4. Segmented foil over security thread. Back: Hydroelectric plant at Luphohlo and bird. Printer: F-CO. 148x67mm.

a. Signature 7a. ND.	13.00	32.50
b. Signature 8. 8.4.1997.	4.50	18.50
c. Signature 9a. 1.4.1998.	1.75	5.00
s1. As a. Specimen. Serial # prefix *AA*.	—	85.00
s2. As b. Specimen. Serial # prefix *AG*.	—	85.00
s3. As c. Specimen. Serial # prefix *AK, AL, AN*.	—	85.00

25   20 Emalangeni

VF   UNC

ND (1995); 1997; 1998. Violet, brown and purple on multicolor underprint. Facing portrait of young King Mswati III at left, arms at lower center. Signature 4. Segmented foil over security thread. Back: Cattle and truck. Printer: F-CO. 150x69mm.

a. Signature 7a. ND.	5.00	22.50
b. Signature 8. 8.4.1997.	8.25	32.50
c. Signature 9a. 1.4.1998.	FV	8.50
s1. As a. Specimen. Serial # prefix *AA*.	—	85.00
s2. As b. Specimen. Serial # prefix *AF; AG*.	—	85.00
s3. As c. Specimen. Serial # prefix *AK, AL*.	—	85.00

26   50 Emalangeni

VF   UNC

1995; 1998. Dull red-brown and dark green on multicolor underprint King Mswati III at left. OVD strip at right with C B of S repeated. Back: Central Bank seal at let center, head office building at right. Printer: G&D. 152x70mm.

a. Signature 7b. 1.4.1995.	12.00	50.00
b. Signature 9b. 1.4.1998.	FV	24.00
s1. As a. Specimen. Serial # prefix *AA*.	—	85.00
s2. As b. Specimen. Serial # prefix *AA*.	—	85.00

27   100 Emalangeni

VF   UNC

6.9.1996. Dark brown on multicolor underprint. King Mswati III at left. OVD strip at right with C B of S repeated. Signature 7b. Back: Central Bank seal at upper left center, rock formation at center. Printer: G&D. 156x70mm.

a. Issued note.	FV	40.00
s. Specimen. Serial # prefix *AA*.	—	85.00

1998 Commemorative Issue

#28, 30th Anniversary of Independence

28   200 Emalangeni

VF   UNC

6.9.1998. Dark green and green on multicolor underprint. King Mswati III at left, OVD strip at right with C B of S repeated. Commemorative text vertically at left and right. Signature 9b. Back: Swazi villagers by thatched circular domed and fenced huts at center. Printer: G&D. 161x70mm.

a. Issued note.	FV	65.00
s. Specimen. Serial # prefix *AA*.	—	85.00

2001 Issue

29 10 Emalangeni
1.4.2001; 1.4.2004; 1.4.2006. Dark blue and black on multicolor underprint. Older
portrait of King Mswati III at left facing half right, arms at lower center. Signature
10. Segmented foil over security thread. Back: Hydroelectric plant at Luphohlo
and bird. Motto; *GOD IS OUR SOURCE* added. Printer: F-CO. 148x67mm.

		VF	UNC
a. 1.4.2001. Signature 10a.		FV	3.75
b. 1.4.2004. Signature 11.		FV	3.75
c. 1.4.2006. Signature 11.		FV	3.75
s. Specimen.		—	80.00

30 20 Emalangeni
2001; 2004; 2006. Violet, brown and purple on multicolor underprint. Facing
portrait of young King Mswati III at left, arms at lower center. Signature 10.
Segmented foil over security thread. Back: Rice, corn, cotton, pineapple, cattle,
lumber on truck. Motto; *GOD IS OUR SOURCE* added. Printer: F-CO. 150x70mm.

		VF	UNC
a. 1.4.2001. Signature 10a.		FV	6.50
b. 1.4.2006. Signature 11.		FV	6.50
c. 1.4.2006.		FV	6.50
s. Specimen.		—	80.00

31 50 Emalangeni
1.4.2001. Dull red-brown and dark green on multicolor underprint. King Mswati III
at left. OVD strip at right with C B of S repeated. Signature 10. Back: Central Bank
seal at left center, hed office building at right. Motto; *GOD IS OUR SOURCE* adde
Printer: G&D. 152x70mm.

		VF	UNC
a. Signature 10b.		FV	12.50
s. Specimen.		—	80.00

32 100 Emalangeni
1.4.2001. Dark brown on multicolor underprint. King Mswati III at left. OVD strip at
right with C B of S repeated. Signature 10. Back: Central Bank seal at upper left
center, rock formation at center. Motto; *GOD IS OUR SOURCE* add Printer: G&D.
156x70mm.

		VF	UNC
a. 1.4.2001. Signature 10b.		FV	17.50
s. Specimen.		—	80.00

2004 Commemorative Issue

33 100 Emalangeni
2004. Dark brown on multicolor underprint. King Mswati III at left, commemorative
overprint in center. OVD strip at right with C B of S repeated. Signature 11. Back:
Central Bank seal at upper left center, rock formation at center. Motto; *GOD IS
OUR SOURCE* add 156x70mm.

		VF	UNC
		FV	17.50

2008 Commemorative Issue

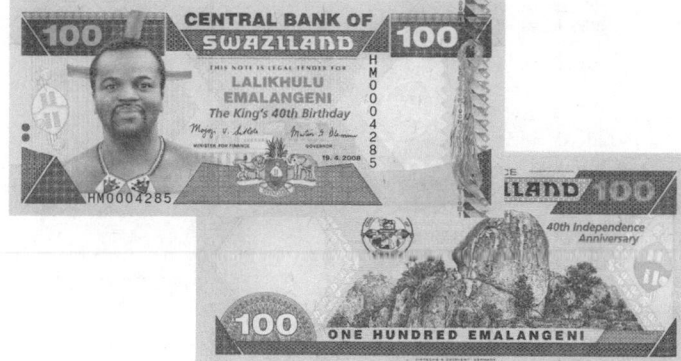

34 100 Emalangeni
19.4.2008. Dark brown on multicolor underprint. King Mswati III facing at left.
Signature 11. Back: Rock formation at center. 157x70mm.

	VF	UNC
	FV	17.50

35 200 Emalangeni
19.4.2008. Green and multicolor. King Mswati III facing at left. Back: Parliament
House in Lobamba at center. Watermark: Shield and spears. Printer: G&D.
160x70mm.

	VF	UNC
	FV	35.00

2010 Issue

36 10 Emalangeni
6.9.2010; 7.1.2014. Blue on multicolor underprint. King Mswati III at left. Back:
Nine princesses taking part in the Ncwala (kingship ceremony). Watermark:
Mswati and 10. Printer: G&D. 148x70mm.

		VF	UNC
a. 6.9.2010.		FV	3.00
b. 7.1.2014. Signatories' titles changed after office switch.		FV	3.00
s. Specimen. Red overprint.		—	75.00

37 20 Emalangeni
6.9.2010; 7.1.2014. Purple on multicolor underprint. King Mswati III at left. Back:
Flower, corn, pineapple, steer, refinery. Watermark: Mswati and 20. Printer: G&D.
151x70mm.

		VF	UNC
a. 6.9.2010.		FV	6.00
b. 7.1.2014. Signatories' titles changed after office switch.		FV	6.00
s. Specimen. Red overprint.		—	80.00

38 50 Emalangeni VF UNC
6.9.2010. Violet on multicolor underprint. King Mswati III at left. Back: Central Bank building at center. Watermark: Mswati and 50. Printer: G&D. 154x70mm.
    a. Issued note. FV 15.00
    s. Specimen. Red overprint. — 100

39 100 Emalangeni VF UNC
6.9.2010. Brown on multicolor underprint. King Mswati III at left. Back: Elephant, rhinoceros, lion, flowers, bird. Watermark: Mswati and 100. Printer: G&D. 157x70mm.
    a. Issued note. FV 30.00
    s. Specimen. Red overprint. — 100

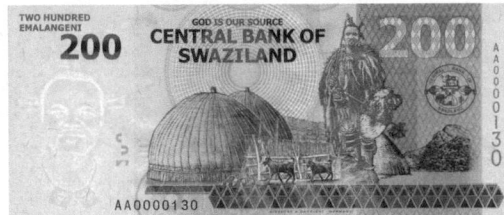

40 200 Emalangeni VF UNC
6.9.2010; 7.1.2014. Green on multicolor underprint. King Mswati III at left. Back: Straw huts, goats, warrior, rock formation. Watermark: Mswati and 200. Printer: G&D. 160x70mm.
    a. 6.9.2010. FV 60.00
    b. 7.1.2014. Signatories' titles changed after office switch. FV 60.00
    s. Specimen. Red overprint. — 125

COLLECTOR SERIES

Monetary Authority of Swaziland

1974 Issue

CS1 ND (1974). 1-20 Emalangeni Mkt. Value
#1-5 with overprint: SPECIMEN and serial # prefix Maltese cross. 80.00

SWEDEN

The Kingdom of Sweden, a limited constitutional monarchy located in northern Europe between Norway and Finland, has an area of 449,964 sq. km. and a population of 9.04 million. Capital: Stockholm. Mining, lumbering and a specialized machine industry dominate the economy. Machinery, paper, iron and steel, motor vehicles and wood pulp are exported. A military power during the 17th century, Sweden has not participated in any war in almost two centuries. An armed neutrality was preserved in both World Wars. Sweden's long-successful economic formula of a capitalist system interlarded with substantial welfare elements was challenged in the 1990s by high unemployment and in 2000-02 by the global economic downturn, but fiscal discipline over the past several years has allowed the country to weather economic vagaries. Sweden joined the EU in 1995, but the public rejected the introduction of the euro in a 2003 referendum.

RULERS:
    Gustaf VI Adolf, 1950-1973
    Carl XVI Gustaf, 1973-

MONETARY SYSTEM:
    1 Krona = 100 Öre

REPLACEMENT NOTES:
    Issues since 1956 with asterisk following serial number. Asterisk following the serial number for note issued since 1956.

KINGDOM

Sveriges Riksbank

1952-55 Issue

42 5 Kronor VF UNC
1954-61. Dark brown on red and blue underprint. Portrait King Gustaf VI Adolf at right center. Back: Svea standing with shield at left center. Watermark: Gustaf VI Adolf.
		VF	UNC
a. 1954.		3.00	6.00
b. 1955.		3.00	5.00
c. 1956.		3.00	5.00
d. 1959.		3.00	7.50
e. 1960.		3.00	5.50
f. 1961.		3.00	4.00
r1. Replacement note: Serial # suffix with star. 1956.		30.00	120
r2. Replacement note: Serial # suffix with star. 1959.		20.00	80.00
r3. Replacement note: Serial # suffix with star. 1960. Rare.		—	—
r4. Replacement note: Serial # suffix with star. 1961		20.00	80.00

43 10 Kronor VF UNC
1953-62. Gray-blue on multicolor underprint. Portrait King Gustav Vasa at left. Blue date and serial #. Like #40. Back: Arms at center. Watermark: Gustav Vasa.
		VF	UNC
a. 1953.		2.50	6.00
b. 1954.		2.50	5.50
c. 1955.		2.50	5.50
d. 1956.		2.50	5.00
e. 1957.		2.50	5.00
f. 1958.		2.50	5.00
g. 1959.		2.50	5.00
h. 1960.		2.00	10.00
i. 1962.		2.00	6.00
r1. Replacement note: Serial # suffix with star. 1956.		40.00	150
r2. Replacement note: Serial # suffix with star. 1957.		25.00	100
r3. Replacement note: Serial # suffix with star. 1958.		25.00	100
r4. Replacement note: Serial # suffix with star. 1959.		25.00	100
r5. Replacement note: Serial # suffix with star. 1960.		40.00	150
r6. Replacement note: Serial # prefix with star. 1962.		25.00	100

46   1000 Kronor

	VF	UNC
1952-73. Brown and multicolor. Svea standing. Back: King Gustaf V. Watermark: Gustaf V.		
a. Blue and red safety fibers. 1952.	200	600
b. 1957.	200	600
o. 1962.	150	500
d. 1965.	150	450
e. With security thread. 1971.	150	450
f. 1973.	150	400

1958; 1959 Issue

47   50 Kronor

	VF	UNC
1959-62. Seated Svea at lower right. Second signature at left. Small date and serial number. Back: King Gustaf Vasa at center.		
a. 1959.	25.00	60.00
b. 1960.	25.00	60.00
c. 1961.	100	200
d. 1962.	25.00	60.00
r1. Replacement note: Serial # suffix with star. 1959.	100	200
r2. Replacement note: Serial # suffix with star. 1960. Rare.	—	—
r3. Replacement note: Serial # suffix with star. 1961.	200	400
r4. Replacement note: Serial # suffix with star. 1962.	75.00	150

48   100 Kronor

	VF	UNC
1959-63. Seated Svea at lower right. Second signature at left. Small date and serial number. Back: King Gustaf Vasa at center.		
a. 1959.	30.00	100
b. 1960.	25.00	80.00
c. 1961.	25.00	80.00
d. 1962.	20.00	60.00
e. 1963.	20.00	60.00
r1. Replacement note: Serial # suffix with star. 1959. Rare.	—	—
r2. Replacement note: Serial # suffix with star. 1960.	100	200
r3. Replacement note: Serial # suffix with star. 1961.	100	200
r4. Replacement note: Serial # suffix with star. 1962.	100	200
r5. Replacement note: Serial # suffix with star. 1963. Rare.	—	—

49   10,000 Kronor

	VF	UNC
1958. Green and multicolor. King Gustaf VI Adolf at right. Back: Svea standing with shield at center. Watermark: Gustaf VI Adolf.	3,000	5,000

1962 Issue

50   5 Kronor

	VF	UNC
1962-63. Dark brown on red and blue underprint. Portrait King Gustaf VI Adolf at center. With security thread. Back: Svea standing with shield. Watermark: Esaias Tegnér (repeated).		
a. 1962.	2.00	6.00
b. 1963.	2.00	4.00
r1. Replacement note: Serial # suffix with star. 1962.	15.00	40.00
r2. Replacement note: Serial # suffix with star. 1963.	—	12.00

1963-76 Issue

#51-55 replacement notes: Serial # suffix star.

51   5 Kronor

	VF	UNC
1965-81. Purple, green and orange. King Gustav Vasa at right. Back: Abstract design of rooster crowing at left. Watermark: Square with 5 repeated.		
a. With year in dark red letter press. 1965-69.	2.00	5.00
b. With year in deep red offset. 1970.	2.00	3.00
c. As a. 1972-74; 1976-77.	2.00	3.00
d. With year in pale red offset. 1977-79; 1981.	2.00	3.00

	VF	UNC
r1. Replacement note. Serial # suffix with star. 1965-67.	25.00	50.00
r2. Replacement note. Serial # suffix with star. 1972.	100	200
r3. Replacement note. Serial # suffix with star. 1974.	5.00	10.00
r4. Replacement note. Serial # suffix with star. 1979.	40.00	75.00

52   10 Kronor

1963-90. Dark green, with red and blue guilloche at center. King Gustaf VI Adolf at right, arms at center. Back: Northern lights and snowflakes at left center. Watermark: August Strindberg (repeated).

	VF	UNC
a. With year in dark red letter press. 1963.	3.00	6.00
b. As a. 1966; 1968.	2.00	5.00
c. As a. 1971; 1972; 1975.	2.00	4.00
d. With year in pale red offset. Engraved signature. 1976-77; 1979; 1983; 1985.	2.00	4.00
e. As d. but with signature printed by offset. 1980-81; 1983-84; 1987-90.	1.00	3.00
r1. Replacement note. Serial # suffix with star. 1963; 1966; 1968; 1971; 1972; 1975.	6.00	12.00
r2. Replacement note. Serial # suffix with star. 1976; 1979; 1983.	5.00	10.00
r3. Replacement note. Serial # suffix with star. 1980.	5.00	10.00
r4. Replacement note. Serial # suffix with star. 1984.	25.00	50.00

53   50 Kronor

1965-90. Blue on green and brown underprint. King Gustaf III at right. Back: Carl von Linné (Linnaeus) at center. Watermark: Anna Maria Lenngren (repeated).

	VF	UNC
a. Small watermark. 1965; 1967; 1970.	10.00	30.00
b. Large watermark with year in dark red letter press. 1974; 1976.	10.00	25.00
c. Large watermark as b. with year in red-brown offset. 1978; 1979; 1981.	10.00	20.00
d. As c. Black serial #. 1982; 1984; 1986; 1989; 1990.	10.00	20.00
r1. Replacement note. Serial # suffix with star. 1965; 1967; 1970.	25.00	50.00
r2. Replacement note. Serial # suffix with star. 1974; 1976.	15.00	30.00
r3. Replacement note. Serial # suffix with star. 1979; 1981.	12.00	25.00
r4. Replacement note. Serial # suffix with star. 1989.	35.00	70.00

54   100 Kronor

1965-85. Red-brown, blue and gray. King Gustav II Adolf at right. Back: Figure head at left, Admiral ship *Vasa* of 1628 in center. Watermark: Axel Oxenstierna (repeated).

	VF	UNC
a. Small watermark. 22mm. 1965; 1968; 1970.	20.00	40.00
b. Large watermark. 27mm. with year in dark blue letter press. 1971; 1972; 1974; 1976.	20.00	30.00
c. Large watermark. as b. with year in blue-green offset. 1978; 1980-83; 1985.	20.00	27.50
r1. Replacement note. Serial # suffix with star. 1965; 1968; 1970.	30.00	60.00
r2. Replacement note. Serial # suffix with star. 1971; 1974; 1976.	20.00	40.00
r3. Replacement note. Serial # suffix with star. 1972.	200	350
r4. Replacement note. Serial # suffix with star. 1978; 1980; 1981.	20.00	40.00

55   1000 Kronor

1976-88. Red-brown on green and violet underprint. King Carl XIV Johan at right. Back: Bessemer steel process. Watermark: Jacob Berzelius.

	VF	UNC
a. 1976-78.	200	400
b. 1980; 1981; 1983-86; 1988.	200	300
r1. Replacement note. Serial # suffix with star. 1976-1978; 1981.	250	450
r2. Replacement note. Serial # suffix with star. 1983; 1985.	250	350

1968 Commemorative Issue

#56, 300th Anniversary Sveriges Riksbank, 1668-1968

56   10 Kronor

1968. Deep blue on multicolor underprint. Svea standing with ornaments at right. Back: Old Riksbank building at left center. Watermark: Charles XI crowned monogram.

	VF	UNC
a. Issued note.	3.00	8.00
b. In printed banquet program folder with bank name, date and seal.	—	50.00

1985-89 Regular Issues

#57-65 the last digit of the year is first digit of the serial #. All notes have 2 sign. but only the right one is mentioned. Replacement notes: Serial # suffix star.

57 100 Kronor   VF   UNC
(198)6-(200)0. Blue-green and brown-violet on multicolor underprint. Carl von
Linné (Linnaeus) at right, building in background. Plants at left center. Back: Bee
pollinating flowers at center. Watermark: Carl von Linné. 140x72mm.
   a. Watermark: Large portrait. Signature Bengt Dennis. (198)6; 7; 8; (199)2.   FV   30.00
   b. Watermark: Small portrait repeated vertically. Signature Urban Bäckström.   FV   25.00
     (199)6; 8; 9; (200)0.
   r1. Replacement note. Serial # suffix with star. (198)6; 8.   20.00   35.00
   r2. Replacement note. Serial # suffix with star. (199)6.   40.00   75.00

58 500 Kronor   VF   UNC
(198)5-(198)6. Gray-blue and red-brown. King Carl XI at right. Back: Christopher
Polhem seated at left center. Watermark: King Carl XI. 150x82mm.
   a. (198)5.   FV   160
   b. (198)6.   FV   170
   r. Replacement note. Serial # suffix with star. (198)5.   175   300

59 500 Kronor   VF   UNC
(198)9-(200)0. Red and multicolor underprint. King Carl XI at right; without white
margin. Back: Christopher Polhem seated at left center. Watermark: Carl XI.
150x82mm.
   a. Signature Bengt Dennis. (198)9; (199)1; 2.   FV   120
   b. Signature Urban Bäckström. (199)4; 5; 7; 8; 9; (200)0.   FV   120
   r. Replacement note. Serial # suffix with star. (198)9; (199)4; 9; (200)0.   150   200

60 1000 Kronor   VF   UNC
(198)9-(199)2. Brownish black on multicolor underprint. King Gustav Vasa at right.
Back: Medieval harvest and threshing scene at left center. Watermark: Gustav
Vasa. 160x82mm.
   a. Issued note.   FV   220
   r. Replacement note. Serial # suffix with star. (198)9; (199)1.   200   300

1991; 1996 Issue

61 20 Kronor   VF   UNC
(199)1-(199)5. Dark blue on multicolor underprint. Horse-drawn carriage at lower
center, Selma Lagerlöf at right. Back: Story scene with boy riding a snow goose in
flight at left center. Watermark: Selma Lagerlöf. 130x72mm.
   a. Signature Bengt Dennis. (199)1; 2.   FV   12.00
   b. Signature Urban Bäckström. (199)4; 5.   FV   10.00
   r. Replacement note. Serial # suffix with star. (199)1.   15.00   25.00

62 50 Kronor   VF   UNC
(199)6-(200)3. Deep olive-brown on multicolor underprint. Jenny Lind at center,
music lines at left, stage at right. Back: Violin, treble clef with line of notes,
abstract musical design. Watermark: Jenny Lind (repeated). 120x77mm.
   a. Signature Urban Bäckström. (199)6; 7; 9; (200)0; 2.   FV   17.00
   b. Signature Lars Heikensten. (200)3.   FV   14.00
   r. Replacement note. Serial # suffix with star. (199)6.   40.00   75.00

1997 Issue

63 20 Kronor   VF   UNC
(199)7-(201)1. Purple on multicolor underprint. Horse-drawn carriage at lower
center, Selma Lagerlöf at right. Back: Story scene with boy riding a snow goose in
flight at left center. Watermark: Selma Lagerlöf. 120x67mm.
   a. Signature Urban Bäckström. (199)7; (199)8; (199)9; (200)1; 2.   FV   6.00
   b. Signature Lars Heikensten. (200)3; (200)5.   FV   5.00
   c. Signature Stefan Ingves. (200)6; (200)8; (201)1.   FV   5.00
   r. Replacement note. Serial # suffix with star. (199)7.   30.00   50.00

2001-06 Issue

64 50 Kronor   VF   UNC

(200)4; (200)8. Deep olive-brown on multicolor underprint. Jenny Lind at right center, music lines at center, stage at right. Wide Foil hologram at left. Back: Violin, treble clef with line of notes, abstract musical design. Watermark: Jenny Lind. 120x77mm.

a. Signature Lars Heikensten.(200)4.	FV	12.50
b. Signature Stefan Ingves. (200)8.	FV	12.00
c. Signature Stefan Ingves. (201)1.	FV	12.00

65 100 Kronor   VF UNC

(200)1-(20)10. Blue-green and brown-violet on multicolor underprint. Carl von Linné (Linnaeus) at right, building in background. Plants at left center. Foil hologram. Back: Bee pollinating flowers at center. Watermark: Carl von Linné. 140x72mm.

a. Signature Urban Bäckström. (200)1; 2.	FV	27.00
b. Signature Lars Heikensten. (200)3.	FV	22.50
c. Signature Stefan Ingves. (200)6; 8; 9; (201)0.	FV	22.50

66 500 Kronor   VF UNC

(200)1-(200)9. Red on multicolor underprint. King Carl XI at right; without white margin. Foil hologram. Back: Christopher Polhem seated at left center. Watermark: Carl XI. 150x82mm.

a. Signature Urban Bäckström. (200)1; 2.	FV	110
b. Signature Lars Heikensten. (200)3.	FV	100
c. Signature Stefan Ingves. (200)7; (200)9.	FV	100

67 1000 Kronor   VF UNC

(200)5. Brown, black on multicolor underprint. Gustav Vasa at right. Wide foil hologram. Back: Harvest and threshing scene from *History of the Nordic Peoples* by Olaus Magnus. Watermark: Gustav Vasa 160x82mm.   FV 200

2005 Commemorative Issue

#66 250th anniversary of the Tumba Paper Mill.

68 100 Kronor   VF UNC

2005. Issued in a folder. Green on multicolor underprint. Seated Svea. Back: Paper production and old map.   — 50.00

2015-16 ND Issue

69 20 Kronor   VF UNC

ND (2015). Violet and multicolor. Astrid Lindgren at center. Gold foil device at upper right, denomination with three crowns at lower right. Back: Forested landscape in Småland, provincial map of Sweden. 120x67mm.   FV 6.00

70 50 Kronor   VF UNC

ND (2015). Yellow-brown and multicolor. Evert Taube at center. Gold foil device at upper right, denomination with three crowns at lower right. Back: Lighthouse on coastline, provincial map of Sweden. 126x66mm.   FV 15.00

71 100 Kronor   VF UNC

ND (2016). Expected new issue. Blue and multicolor. Greta Garbo at center. Gold foil device at upper right, denomination with three crowns at lower right. Back: View of Stockholm, provincial map of Sweden.   — —

72   200 Kronor
ND (2015). Green and multicolor. Ingmar Bergman at center. Gold foil device at upper right, denomination with three crowns at lower right. Back: Rock formations on Gotland Island, provincial map of Sweden. 140x66mm.

	VF	UNC
	FV	60.00

73   500 Kronor
ND (2016). Expected new issue. Red-brown, orange and multicolor. Birgit Nilsson at center. Gold foil device at upper right, denomination with three crowns at lower right. Back. Öresund Bridge, provincial map of Sweden.

	VF	UNC
	—	—

74   1000 Kronor
ND (2015). Brown and multicolor. Dag Hammarskiöld at center. Gold foil device at upper right, denomination with three crowns at lower right. Back: Mountain range, provincial map of Sweden. 154x66mm.

	VF	UNC
	FV	300

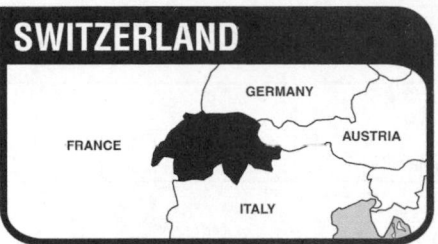

SWITZERLAND

The Swiss Confederation, located in central Europe north of Italy and south of Germany, has an area of 15,941 sq. mi. (41,290 sq. km.) and a population of 7.41 million. Capital: Beme. The economy centers about a well developed manufacturing industry, however the most important economic factor is services (banks and insurance).

Switzerland, the habitat of lake dwellers in prehistoric times, was peopled by the Celtic Helvetians when Julius Caesar made it a part of the Roman Empire in 58 BC. After the decline of Rome, Switzerland was invaded by Teutonic tribes who established small temporal holdings which, in the Middle Ages, became a federation of fiefs of the Holy Roman Empire. As a nation, Switzerland originated in 1291 when the districts of Nidwalden Schwyz and Uri united to defeat Austria and attain independence as the Swiss Confederation. After aquiring new cantons in the 14th century, Switzerland was made independent from the Holy Roman Empire by the 1648 Treaty of Westphalia. The revolutionary armies of Napoleonic France occupied Switerland and set up the Helvetian Republic, 1798-1803. After the fall of Napoleon, the Congress of Vienna, 1815, recognized the independence of Switzerland and guaranteed its neutrality. The Swiss Constitutions of 1848, 1874, and 1999 established a union modeled upon that of the United States.

MONETARY SYSTEM:
1 Franc (franken) = 10 Batzen = 100 Centimes (Rappen)
Plural: Francs, Franchi or Franken

SIGNATURE VARIETIES

	PRESIDENT, BANK COUNCIL	DIRECTOR	CASHIER
39	Dr. Brenno Galli 1959-78	Dr. Walter Schweigler	Otto Kunz 1954-66
40	Dr. Brenno Galli	Dr. Riccardo Motta 1955-66	Otto Kunz
41	Dr. Brenno Galli	Dr. Max Iklé 1956-68	Otto Kunz
42	Dr. Brenno Galli 1959-78	Dr. Edwin Stopper 1966-74	Rudolph Aebersold 1954-66
43	Dr. Brenno Galli	Alexandre Hay 1966-74	Rudolph Aebersold
44	Dr. Brenno Galli	Max Iklé	Rudolph Aebersold
45	Dr. Brenno Galli	Dr. Fritz Leutwiler 1968-84	Rudolph Aebersold
46	Dr. Brenno Galli	Dr. Leo Schürmann 1974-80	Rudolph Aebersold
47	Dr. Brenno Galli	Dr. Pierre Languetin 1976-88	Rudolph Aebersold

NOTE: From #180 onward w/o the Chief Cashier's signature.

SIGNATURE VARIETIES

	PRESIDENT, BANK COUNCIL	DIRECTOR
48	Dr. Brenno Galli	Dr. Leo Shü
49	Dr. Brenno Galli	Alexandre Hay

	SIGNATURE VARIETIES	
	PRESIDENT, BANK COUNCIL	DIRECTOR
50	Dr. Brenno Galli	Dr. Fritz Leutwiler
51	Dr. Brenno Galli	Dr. Pierre Languetin
52	Dr. Edmund Wyss, 1978 - 86	Dr. Leo Schürmann
53	Dr. Edmund Wyss	Dr. Pierre Languetin
54	Dr. Edmund Wyss	Dr. Fritz Leutwiler
55	Dr. Edmund Wyss	Dr. Markus Lusser, 1981 - 96
56	Dr. Edmund Wyss	Dr. Hans Meyer, 1985 - 2000
57	Dr. Francois Schaller, 1986 - 89	Dr. Markus Lusser
58	Dr. Francois Schaller	Dr. Pierre Languetin
59	Dr. Francois Schaller	Dr. Hans Meyer
60	Dr. Francois Schaller	Jean Zwahlen (18mm), 1988 - 96
61	Peter Gerber, 1989 - 93	Dr. Markus Lusser
62	Peter Gerber	Jean Zwahlen (18mm)
63	Peter Gerber	Jean Zwahlen (15mm)
64	Peter Gerber	Dr. Hans Meyer
65	Dr. Jakob Schönenberger, 1993 - 99	Jean Zwahlen (12mm)
66	Dr. Jakob Schönenberger	Dr. Hans Meyer
67	Dr. Jakob Schönenberger	Jean Zwahlen (12mm)

	SIGNATURE VARIETIES	
	PRESIDENT, BANK COUNCIL	DIRECTOR
68	Dr. Jakob Schönenberger	Dr. Jean-Pierre Roth, 1996 -
69	Dr. Jakob Schönenberger	Dr. Bruno Gehrig, 1996 - 2003
70	Eduard Belser, 1999 - 2002	Dr. Hans Meyer
71	Eduard Belser	Dr. Jean-Pierre Roth
72	Eduard Belser	Dr. Bruno Gehrig
73	Eduard Belser	Dr. Niklaus Blattner, 2001 -
74	Dr. Hansueli Raggenbass, 2002 -	Dr. Jean-Pierre Roth
75	Dr. Hansueli Raggenbass	Dr. Bruno Gehrig
76	Dr. Hansueli Raggenbass	Dr. Niklaus Blattner
77	Dr. Hansueli Raggenbass	Dr. Philipp Hildebrand, 2003

CONFEDERATION
Schweizerische Nationalbank
SWISS NATIONAL BANK
1954-61 Issue

45   10 Franken

VF   UNC

1955-77. Purple on red-brown underprint. Gottfried Keller at right. Back: Carnation flower at left center. Printer: OFZ.

	VF	UNC
a. 25.8.1955. (34, 36, 37).	10.00	50.00
b. 20.10.1955 (34, 36, 37).	10.00	50.00
c. 29.11.1956 (34, 37, 38).	10.00	45.00
d. 18.12.1958 (34, 37, 38).	30.00	125
e. 23.12.1959 (34, 37, 38).	3.50	30.00
f. 22.12.1960 (39, 40, 41).	3.50	30.00
g. 26.10.1961 (39, 40, 41).	3.50	20.00
h. 28.3.1963 (39, 40, 41).	3.50	20.00
i. 2.4.1964 (39, 40, 41).	3.50	20.00
j. 21.1.1965 (39, 40, 41).	3.50	20.00
k. 23.12.1965 (39, 40, 41).	3.50	20.00
l. 1.1.1967 (42, 43, 44).	15.00	40.00
m. 30.6.1967 (42, 43, 44).	3.50	15.00
n. 15.5.1968 (42, 43, 45).	3.50	15.00
o. 15.1.1969 (42, 43, 45).	3.50	15.00
p. 5.1.1970 (42, 43, 45).	3.50	15.00
q. 10.2.1971 (42, 43, 45).	3.50	15.00
r. 24.1.1972 (42, 43, 45).	3.50	15.00
s. 7.3.1973 (42, 43, 45).	3.50	14.00
s1. Specimen.	—	750
t. 7.2.1974 (42, 43, 45).	3.50	14.00
u. 6.1.1977 (45, 46, 47).	3.00	14.00

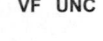

46   20 Franken

VF   UNC

1954-76. Blue on multicolor underprint. General Guillaume-Henri Dufour at right. Back: Silver thistle at left center. Printer: OFZ.

	VF	UNC
a. 1.7.1954 (34, 35, 36).	22.50	120
b. 7.7.1955 (34, 36, 37).	22.50	120
c. 20.10.1955 (34, 36, 37).	22.50	120
d. 5.7.1956 (34, 37, 38).	22.50	120
e. 4.10.1957 (34, 37, 38).	25.00	110
f. 18.12.1958 (34, 37, 38).	40.00	150
g. 23.12.1959 (39, 40, 41).	8.00	30.00
h. 22.12.1960 (39, 40, 41).	8.00	30.00
i. 26.10.1961 (39, 40, 41).	8.00	30.00
j. 28.3.1963 (39, 40, 41).	8.00	30.00
k. 2.4.1964 (39, 40, 41).	8.00	30.00
l. 21.1.1965 (39, 40, 41).	8.00	30.00
m. 23.12.1965 (39, 40, 41).	8.00	30.00
n. 1.1.1967 (42, 43, 44).	10.00	30.00
o. 30.6.1967 (42, 43, 44).	8.00	30.00
p. 15.5.1968 (42, 43, 45).	8.00	25.00
q. 15.1.1969 (42, 43, 45).	8.00	25.00
r. 5.1.1970 (42, 43, 45).	8.00	25.00
s. 10.2.1971 (42, 43, 45).	8.00	25.00
s1. As a. Specimen.	—	800
t. 24.1.1972 (42, 43, 45).	8.00	25.00
u. 7.3.1973 (42, 43, 45).	8.00	22.50
v. 7.2.1974 (42, 43, 45).	8.00	22.50
w. 9.4.1976 (45, 46, 47).	7.50	22.50

47   50 Franken

VF   UNC

1955-58. Green and red-brown on yellow-green underprint. Girl at upper right. Back: Apple harvesting scene (symbolizing fertility). Printer: W&S.

	VF	UNC
a. 7.7.1955 (34, 36, 37).	42.50	175
b. 4.10.1957 (34, 37, 38).	37.50	175
c. 18.12.1958 (34, 37, 38).	500	800

48   50 Franken

VF   UNC

1961-74. Green and red on multicolor underprint. Girl at upper right. Like #47. Back: Apple harvesting scene (symbolizing fertility).

	VF	UNC
a. 4.5.1961 (39, 40, 41).	60.00	200
b. 21.12.1961 (39, 40, 41).	30.00	90.00
c. 28.3.1963 (39, 40, 41).	85.00	220
d. 2.4.1964 (39, 40, 41).	90.00	250
e. 21.1.1965 (39, 40, 41).	30.00	90.00
f. 23.12.1965 (39, 40, 41).	30.00	90.00
g. 30.6.1967 (42, 43, 44).	30.00	90.00
h. 15.5.1968 (42, 43, 45).	30.00	90.00
i. 15.1.1969 (42, 43, 45).	30.00	75.00
j. 5.1.1970 (42, 43, 45).	30.00	75.00
k. 10.2.1971 (42, 43, 45).	30.00	75.00
l. 24.1.1972 (42, 43, 45).	30.00	75.00
m. 7.3.1973 (42, 43, 45).	30.00	75.00
n. 7.2.1974 (42, 43, 45).	30.00	75.00
s. Specimen.	—	800

49 100 Franken

1956-73. Dark blue and brown-olive on multicolor underprint. Boy's head at upper right with lamb. Back: St. Martin cutting his cape (to share) at center right. Printer: TDLR.

	VF	UNC
a. 25.10.1956 (34, 37, 38).	57.50	350
b. 4.10.1957 (34, 37, 38).	55.00	350
c. 18.12.1958 (34, 37, 38).	60.00	500
d. 21.12.1961 (39, 40, 41);	30.00	200
e. 28.3.1963 (39, 40, 41).	30.00	200
f. 2.4.1964 (39, 40, 41).	30.00	200
g. 21.1.1965 (39, 40, 41).	32.50	200
h. 23.12.1965 (39, 40, 41).	35.00	200
i. 1.1.1967 (42, 43, 44).	35.00	200
j. 30.6.1967 (42, 43, 44).	27.50	200
k. 15.1.1969 (42, 43, 45).	25.00	200
l. 5.1.1970 (42, 43, 45).	35.00	175
m. 10.2.1971 (42, 43, 45).	25.00	175
n. 24.1.1972 (42, 43, 45).	25.00	175
o. 7.3.1973 (42, 43, 45).	25.00	175
s. Specimen.	—	1,000

50 500 Franken

1957-58. Red-brown and olive on multicolor underprint. Woman looking in mirror at right. Back: Elders with four girls bathing at center right (Fountain of Youth). Printer: W&S.

	VF	UNC
a. 31.1.1957 (34, 37, 38).	400	1,650
b. 4.10.1957 (34, 37, 38).	350	1,650
c. 18.12.1958 (34, 37, 38).	500	2,000
s. Specimen. Red overprint: *SPECIMEN* and punch hole cancelled.	—	2,250

51 500 Franken

1961-74. Brown-orange and olive on multicolor underprint. Woman looking in mirror at right. Like #50. Back: Elders with four girls bathing at center right (Fountain of Youth).

	VF	UNC
a. 21.12.1961 (39, 40, 41).	275	1,250
b. 28.3.1963 (39, 40, 41).	240	1,250
c. 2.4.1964 (39, 40, 41).	250	1,250
d. 21.1.1965 (39, 40, 41).	250	1,250
e. 1.1.1967 (42, 43, 44).	250	1,250
f. 15.5.1968 (42, 43, 45).	250	1,250
g. 15.1.1969 (42, 43, 45).	250	1,250
h. 5.1.1970 (42, 43, 45).	235	950
i. 10.2.1971 (42, 43, 45).	235	950
j. 24.1.1972 (42, 43, 45).	235	950
k. 7.3.1973 (42, 43, 45).	230	950
l. 7.2.1974 (42, 43, 45).	225	950
s. As a. Specimen.	—	2,200

52 1000 Franken

1954-74. Red-violet and turquoise on green and light violet underprint. Female head at upper right. Back: Allegorical scene *Dance Macabre*. Printer: TDLR.

	VF	UNC
a. 30.9.1954 (34, 35, 36).	500	2,500
b. 4.10.1957 (34, 37, 38).	500	2,500
c. 18.12.1958 (34, 37, 38).	1,000	3,500
d. 22.12.1960 (39, 40, 41).	500	2,800
e. 21.12.1961 (39, 40, 41).	500	2,500
f. 28.3.1963 (39, 40, 41).	400	2,200
g. 21.1.1965 (39, 40, 41).	400	2,200
h. 1.1.1967 (42, 43, 44).	400	2,200
i. 5.1.1970 (42, 43, 45).	400	2,000
j. 10.2.1971 (42, 43, 45).	400	1,950
k. 24.1.1972 (42, 43, 45).	400	1,950
l. 1.10.1973 (42, 43, 45).	400	1,950
m. 7.2.1974 (42, 43, 45).	400	1,950
s. Specimen.	—	2,750

1976-79 Issue; 6th Series

#53-59 series of notes printed in 4 languages - the traditional German, French and Italian plus Romansch; (Rhaeto - Romanic), the language of the mountainous areas of Graubünden Canton. Wmk. as portr. The first 2 numerals before the serial # prefix letter are date (year) indicators. Printer: OFZ. Note: Sign. varieties listed after date.

53 10 Franken **VF UNC**

(19)79-92. Orange-brown and multicolor. Leonhard Euler at right. Back: Water turbine, light rays through lenses and Solar System in vertical format. Watermark: Leonhard Euler. Printer: OFZ. 137x66mm.

a. 1979 (52, 53, 54).	FV	35.00
b. 1980 (52, 53, 54).	FV	40.00
c. 1981 (53, 54, 55).	FV	40.00
d. 1982 (53, 54, 55).	FV	35.00
e. 1983 (53, 54, 55).	FV	35.00
f. 1986 (53, 55, 56).	FV	30.00
g. 1987 (57, 58, 59).	FV	30.00
h. 1990 (61, 63, 64).	FV	30.00
i. 1990 (62).	FV	200
j. 1991 (61, 63, 64).	FV	30.00
k. 1992 (61, 62, 64).	FV	35.00

54 20 Franken **VF UNC**

1978 (52, 53, 54). Light blue on multicolor underprint. Horace-Bénédict de Saussure at right, hygrometer at left. Underprint on face ends 2mm before the margin, only plain blue underprint visible within the 2mm. Back: Fossel and early mountain expedition team hiking in the Alps. Watermark: Horace-Bénédict de Saussure. Printer: OHZ. 148x70mm.

	FV	55.00

55 20 Franken **VF UNC**

(19)78-92. Blue and multicolor. Horace-Bénédict de Saussure at right, hygrometer at left. Similar to #54, but underprint at upper margin on face goes to the margin. Back: Fossel and early mountain expedition team hiking in the Alps on vertical format. Watermark: Horace-Bénédict de Saussure. Printer: OHZ. 148x70mm.

a. 1978 (52, 53, 54).	FV	110
b. 1980 (52, 53, 54).	FV	65.00
c. 1981 (53, 54, 55).	FV	80.00
d. 1982 (53, 54, 55).	FV	55.00
e. 1983 (53, 54, 55).	FV	55.00
f. 1986 (57, 58, 59).	FV	55.00
g. 1987 (57, 58, 59).	FV	55.00
h. 1989 (61, 62, 64).	FV	50.00
i. 1990 (61, 63, 64).	FV	45.00
j. 1992 (61, 63, 64).	FV	50.00
s. Perforated: *SPECIMEN*.	—	1,650

56 50 Franken **VF UNC**

(19)78-88. Green and multicolor. Konrad Gessner at right. Back: Eagle owl, *Primula auricu-la* plant and stars on vertical format. Watermark: Konrad Gessner. Printer: OHZ. 159x74mm.

a. 1978 (48, 50, 51).	FV	120
b. 1979 (52, 53, 54).	FV	145
c. 1980 (52, 53, 54).	FV	120
d. 1981 (53, 54, 55).	FV	120
e. 1983 (53, 54, 55).	FV	135
f. 1985 (53, 55, 56).	FV	165
g. 1987 (57, 58, 59).	FV	100
h. 1988 (57, 59, 60).	FV	95.00
s. Perforated: *SPECIMEN*.	—	1,950

57 100 Franken **VF UNC**

(19)75-93. Blue and multicolor. Francesco Borromini at right. Back: Baroque architectural drawing and view of S. Ivo alla Sapienza on vertical format. Watermark: Francesco Borromini. Printer: OHZ. 170x78mm.

a. 1975 (48, 49, 50).	FV	220
b. 1977 (48, 50, 51).	FV	280
c. 1980 (52, 53, 54).	FV	220
d. 1981 (53, 54, 55).	FV	190
e. 1982 (53, 54, 55).	FV	190
f. 1983 (53, 54, 55).	FV	240
g. 1984 (53, 54, 55).	FV	280
h. 1986 (57, 58, 59).	FV	220
i. 1988 (57, 59, 60).	FV	190
j. 1989 (57, 59, 60).	FV	190
k. 1991 (61, 63, 64).	FV	180
l. 1992 (61, 63, 64).	FV	180
m. 1993 (61, 63, 64).	FV	180
s. Perforated: *SPECIMEN*.	—	2,200

58   500 Franken   VF   UNC

(19)76-92. Brown and multicolor. Albrecht von Haller at right, mountains (Gemmi Pass) at left. Back: Anatomical muscles of the back, schematic blood circulation and a purple orchid flower on vertical format. Watermark: Albrecht von Haller. Printer: OHZ. 181x82mm.

    a. 1976 (48, 50, 51).   FV   1,050
    b. 1986 (57, 58, 59).   FV   1,200
    c. 1992 (61, 63, 64).   FV   1,050
    s. Perforated: *SPECIMEN*.   —   2,750

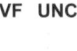

59   1000 Franken   VF   UNC

(19)77-93. Purple on multicolor underprint. Auguste Forel at right, diagrams through a brain and a nerve cell at left. Back: Ants and ant-hill schematic on vertical format. Watermark: Auguste Forel. Printer: OFZ. 192x96mm.

    a. 1977 (48, 50, 51).   FV   1,950
    b. 1980 (52, 53, 54).   FV   2,050
    c. 1984 (53, 54, 55).   FV   2,050
    d. 1987 (57, 58, 59).   FV   2,150
    e. 1988 (57, 59, 60).   FV   1,750
    f. 1993 (61, 63, 64).   FV   1,700
    s. Perforated: *SPECIMEN*.   —   3,000

1983-85 Reserve Issue

60   10 Franken   VF   UNC

1983. Orange-brown and multicolor. Leonhard Euler at right. Back: Polyhedron in center, calculations, table for calculation of numbers and solar system diagram.   —   —

61   20 Franken   VF   UNC

1985. Blue on multicolor underprint. Horace-Bénédict de Saussure at right, crystal in center. Back: Hair hygrometer, mountains and mountain team hiking.   —   —

62   50 Franken   VF   UNC

1985. Olive-green and multicolor. Konrad Gessner at right. Back: Cherry tree branch, eagle, animals.   —   —

63   100 Franken   VF   UNC

1985. Violet-blue and multicolor. Francesco Borromini at right, architectural motif at center. Back: Drawing and tower of S. Ivo.   —   —

64   500 Franken   VF   UNC

1985. Brown and multicolor. Albrecht von Haller at right, hexagonal structure of a cell in center. Back: Anatomy plate and X-ray of a human thorax.   —   —

65   1000 Franken   VF   UNC

1985. Violet and multicolor. Louis Agassiz at right, structure of the surface of a shellfish. Back: Perch in three parts: head, skeleton and fossil, fishscales and ammonite.   —   —

1994-98 Issue; 8th Series

#66-71 vertical format, reduced size. First two numerals before serial # prefix letter indicates the year of printing. Many sophisticated security features added.

66   10 Franken   VF   UNC

(19)95; (19)96. Brown-orange, dark brown and blue on multicolor underprint. Architect Le Corbusier (Charles Édouard Jeanneret-Gris) at upper left and bottom center. Vertical format. Back: Modular" measuring system and buildings in Chandigarh designed by Le Corbusier. Vertical format. Watermark: Le Corbusier. 74x126mm.

    a. 1995. (65, 66, 67).   FV   20.00
    b. 1996. (65, 66, 67).   FV   23.00

67   10 Franken   VF   UNC

2000; 2006; 2008; 2010; 2013. Like #66 but with microperforation '10' added. Brown-orange, dark brown and blue on multicolor underprint. Architect Le Corbusier (Charles Édouard Jeanneret-Gris) at upper left and bottom center. Vertical format. Back: Modular" measuring system and buildings in Chandigarh designed by Le Corbusier. Vertical format. Watermark: Le Corbusier. 74x126mm.

    a. 2000. (70, 71, 72).   FV   28.00
    b. 2006. (74, 75, 76).   FV   25.00
    c. 2008. (74, 77, 78).   FV   15.00
    d. 2010. (77, 78, 79).   FV   15.00
    e. 2013. (80, 81, 82).   FV   15.00

68   20 Franken   VF   UNC

(19)94; (19)95. Red-violet and green on multicolor underprint. Composer Arthur Honegger at upper left and bottom center. Vertical format. Back: Trumpet valves at top, steam locomotive wheel at center, musical score and piano keys at bottom. Vertical format. Watermark: Arthur Honegger. 74x137mm.

    a. 1994. (65, 66, 67).   FV   31.00
    b. 1995. (65, 66, 67).   FV   35.00

69   20 Franken   VF   UNC

(20)00-. Like #68 but with microperforation '20' added. Red-violet and green on multicolor underprint. Composer Arthur Honegger at upper left and bottom center. Vertical format. Back: Trumpet valves at top, steam locomotive wheel at center, musical score and piano keys at bottom. Watermark: Arthur Honegger. 74x137mm.

    a. 2000. (71, 72, 73).   FV   40.00
    b. 2003. (74, 75, 76).   FV   40.00
    c. 2004. (74, 76, 77).   FV   40.00
    d. 2005. (74, 76, 77).   FV   32.00
    e. 2008. (74, 77, 78).   FV   28.00
    f. 2012. (80, 81, 82).   FV   28.00
    g. 2013. (80, 81, 82).   FV   28.00
    h. 2014. (80, 81, 82).   FV   28.00

70   50 Franken
(19)94 (1995). Deep olive-green and purple on multicolor underprint. Artist Sophie Taeuber-Arp at upper left, bottom. Back: Examples of her abstract art works. Signatures (65, 66, 67). Vertical format. Watermark: Sophie Taeuber-Arp. 74x148mm.

	VF	UNC
	FV	85.00

71   50 Franken
2002 (2003)-. Like #70 but with microperforation '50' added. Deep olive-green and purple on multicolor underprint. Artist Sophie Taeuber Arp at upper left, bottom. Vertical format. Back: Examples of her abstract works. Ver Watermark: Sophie Taeuber-Arp. 74x148mm.

	VF	UNC
a. 2002 (71, 72, 73).	FV	85.00
b. 2004 (85, 76, 77).	FV	85.00
c. 2006. (74, 76, 77).	FV	72.00
d. 2010. (77, 78, 79).	FV	65.00
e. 2012. (80, 81, 82).	FV	65.00

72   100 Franken
(19)96-. Dark blue, purple and brown-orange on multicolor underprint. Alberto Giacometti (artist) at upper left and bottom. Vertical format. Back: Bronze bust *Lotar II* at top, sculpture *Homme Qui Marche I* repeated at center, time-space relationship scheme at lower center. Vertical format. Watermark: Alberto Giacometti. 74x159mm.

	VF	UNC
a. (19)96. (66, 68, 69).	FV	165
b. (19)97. (66, 68, 69).	FV	165
c. (19)98. (66, 68, 69).	FV	165
d. (19)99. (66, 68, 69).	FV	165
e. (20)00. (71, 72, 73).	FV	150
f. (20)03. (74, 75, 76).	FV	165
g. (20)04. (74, 76, 77).	FV	140
h. (20)07. (74, 76, 77).	FV	125
i. (20)10. (77, 78, 78).	FV	125

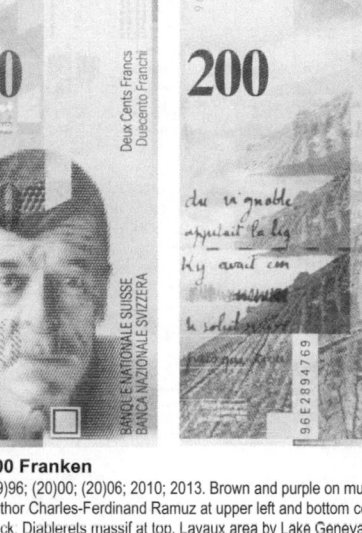

73   200 Franken
(19)96; (20)00; (20)06; 2010; 2013. Brown and purple on multicolor underprint. Author Charles-Ferdinand Ramuz at upper left and bottom center. Vertical format. Back: Diablerets massif at top, Lavaux area by Lake Geneva repeated at center to bottom with partial manuscript overlay. Vertical format. Watermark: Charles-Ferdinand Ramuz. 74x170mm.

	VF	UNC
a. 1996 (66, 68, 69).	FV	280
b. 2002 (71, 72, 73).	FV	300
c. 2006. (74, 76, 77).	FV	260
d. 2010. (77, 78, 78).	FV	250
e. 2013. (80, 81, 82).	FV	250

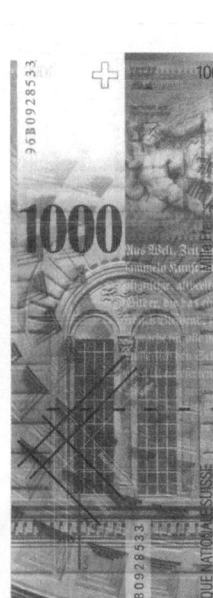

74   1000 Franken
(19)96 (1998); (19)99; (20)06. Purple and violet on multicolor underprint. Jacob Burckhardt (art historian) at upper left and bottom. Vertical format. Back: Window and the Pergamon Altar at top, the Rotunda of the Pantheon in Rome and a section of the fa Watermark: Jacob Burckhardt. 74x181mm.

	VF	UNC
a. 1996 (1998). (66; 67; 68).	FV	1,250
b. 1999. (66, 68, 69).	FV	1,200
c. 2006. (74, 76, 77).	FV	1,200
d. 2012. (79, 80, 81).	FV	1,200

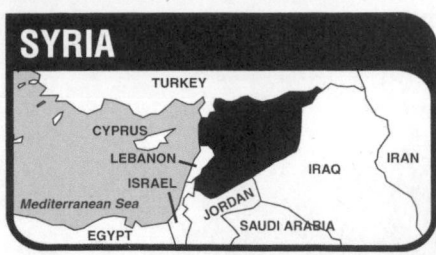

The Syrian Arab Republic, located in the Near East at the eastern end of the Mediterranean Sea, has an area of 185,180 sq. km. and a population of 19.75 million. Capital: Damascus. Agriculture and animal breeding are the chief industries. Cotton, crude oil and livestock are exported.Following the breakup of the Ottoman Empire during World War I, France administered Syria until its independence in 1946. The country lacked political stability, however, and experienced a series of military coups during its first decades. Syria united with Egypt in February 1958 to form the United Arab Republic. In September 1961, the two entities separated, and the Syrian Arab Republic was reestablished. In November 1970, Hafiz al-Asad, a member of the Socialist Ba'th Party and the minority Alawite sect, seized power in a bloodless coup and brought political stability to the country. In the 1967 Arab-Israeli War, Syria lost the Golan Heights to Israel. During the 1990s, Syria and Israel held occasional peace talks over its return. Following the death of President al-Asad, his son, Bashar al-Asad, was approved as president by popular referendum in July 2000. Syrian troops - stationed in Lebanon since 1976 in an ostensible peacekeeping role - were withdrawn in April 2005. During the July-August 2006 conflict between Israel and Hizballah, Syria placed its military forces on alert but did not intervene directly on behalf of its ally Hizballah.

MONETARY SYSTEM:
1 Pound (Livre) = 100 Piastres

REPUBLIC

Banque Centrale de Syrie

CENTRAL BANK OF SYRIA

1958 Issue

86 1 Pound
1958/AH1377. Brown on multicolor underprint. Worker at right. Back: Water wheel of Hama. Bank name in English. Watermark: Arabian horse's head. Printer: Pakistan Security Printing Corp. Ltd.

		VF	UNC
a. Issued note.		7.50	30.00
s. Specimen.		—	35.00

87 5 Pounds
1958/AH1377. Green on multicolor underprint. Worker at right. Similar to #86. Back: Citadel of Aleppo. Bank name in English. Watermark: Arabian horse's head. Printer: Pakistan Security Printing Corp. Ltd.

		VF	UNC
a. Issued note.		20.00	100
s. Specimen.		—	50.00

88 10 Pounds
1958/AH1377. Purple on multicolor underprint. Worker at right. Similar to #86. Back: Courtyard of Omayad Mosque. Bank name in English. Watermark: Arabian horse's head. Printer: Pakistan Security Printing Corp. Ltd.

		VF	UNC
a. Issued note.		30.00	135
s. Specimen.		—	100

89 25 Pounds
1958/AH1377. Blue on multicolor underprint. Girl with basket at right. Back: Interior view of Azem Palace in Damascus. Bank name in English. Watermark: Arabian horse's head. Printer: JEZ.

		VF	UNC
a. Issued note.		35.00	150
s. Specimen.		—	150

90 50 Pounds
1958/AH1377. Red and brown on multicolor underprint. Girl with basket at right. Similar to #89. Back: Mosque of Sultan Selim. Bank name in English. Watermark: Arabian horse's head. Printer: JEZ.

		VF	UNC
a. Issued note.		40.00	175
s. Specimen.		—	175

91 100 Pounds
1958;1962. Olive-green on multicolor underprint. Girl with basket at right. Similar to #89. Back: Old ruins of Palmyra. Bank name in English. Watermark: Arabian horse's head. Printer: JEZ.

		VF	UNC
a. 1958.		70.00	250
b. 1962.		60.00	210
s. Specimen.		—	200

92 500 Pounds
1958/AH1377. Brown and purple on multicolor underprint. Motifs from ruins of Kingdom of Ugarit, head at right. Back: Ancient religious wheel and cuneiform clay tablet. Bank name in English. Watermark: Arabian horse's head. Printer: JEZ.

		VF	UNC
a. Issued note.		160	410
s. Specimen.		—	400

1963-66 Issue

93 1 Pound
1963-82/AH1383-1402. Brown on multicolor underprint. Worker at right. Back: Water wheel of Hama. Bank name in English. Watermark: Arabian horse's head.

		VF	UNC
a. Without security thread. 1963/AH1383.		4.00	20.00
b. 1967/AH1387.		4.00	16.00
c. 1973/AH1393.		3.00	10.00
d. Security thread with *Central Bank of Syria* in small letters. 1978/AH1398.		2.00	8.00
e. 1982/AH1402.		1.00	4.00
s. As a. Specimen.		—	85.00

94 5 Pounds
1963-73/AH1383-93. Green on multicolor underprint. Worker at right. Back: Citadel of Aleppo on back. Bank name in English. Watermark: Arabian horse's head.

		VF	UNC
a. 1963/AH1383.		18.00	75.00
b. 1967/AH1387.		12.00	60.00
c. 1970.		10.00	55.00
d. 1973/AH1393.		8.00	50.00

95   10 Pounds VF UNC
1965-73/AH138x-93. Purple on multicolor underprint. Worker at right. Back:
Courtyard of Omayad Mosque. Bank name in English. Watermark: Arabian
horse's head.

	VF	UNC
a. 1965.	15.00	85.00
b. 1968.	12.00	65.00
c. 1973/AH1393.	8.00	55.00

96   25 Pounds VF UNC
1966-73/AH1386-93. Blue and brown on multicolor underprint. Worker at the loom
at left. Back: Bosra theater at center right. Watermark: Arabian horse's head.

	VF	UNC
a. 1966/AH1386.	32.00	220
b. 1970.	30.00	160
c. 1973/AH1393.	25.00	140

97   50 Pounds VF UNC
1966-73/AH1386-93. Brown and olive-green on multicolor underprint. Arab driving
combine at left. Back: Fortress. Watermark: Arabian horse's head.

	VF	UNC
a. 1966/AH1386; 1970.	55.00	250
b. 1973/AH1393.	45.00	145

98   100 Pounds VF UNC
1966-74/AH1386-139x. Green and blue on multicolor underprint. Port installation
at left. Back: Dam at center. Watermark: Arabian horse's head.

	VF	UNC
a. 1966/AH1386.	55.00	165
b. 1968.	70.00	200
c. 1971/AH1391.	45.00	130
d. 1974.	35.00	100

1976-77 Issue

99   1 Pound VF UNC
1977/AH1397. Orange and brown on multicolor underprint. Omayyad Mosque at
center, craftsman at right. Back: Combine at center. Watermark: Arabian horse's
head.

	VF	UNC
a. Issued note.	4.00	16.00
s. Specimen.	—	—

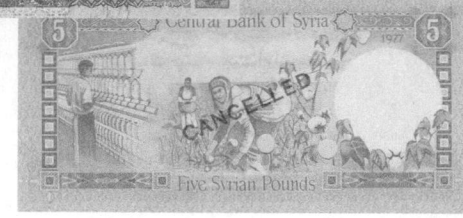

100   5 Pounds VF UNC
1977-91/AH1397-1412. Dark green on multicolor underprint. Bosra theater
and statue of female warrior at right. Back: Cotton picking and spinning frame.
Watermark: Arabian horse's head.

	VF	UNC
a. Security thread. 1977/AH1397.	4.00	12.00
b. Security thread. With *Central Bank of Syria* in small letters. 1978/AH1398.	FV	4.00
c. 1002/AH1402.	FV	3.00
d. 1988/AH1408.	FV	2.00
e. 1991/AH1412.	FV	1.50
s. As a. Specimen.	—	—

101   10 Pounds VF UNC
1977-91/AH1397-1412. UV: Arabic 10, horse head, central design, fibers all
fluoresce yellow. Purple and violet on multicolor underprint. Al-Azem Palace
in Damascus at center, dancing woman at right. Back: Water treatment plant.
Watermark: Arabian horse's head.

	VF	UNC
a. Like #100a. 1977/AH1397.	6.00	16.00
b. Like #100b. 1978/AH1398.	FV	5.00
c. 1982/AH1402.	FV	3.00
d. 1988/AH1408.	FV	2.00
e. 1991/AH1412.	FV	1.50

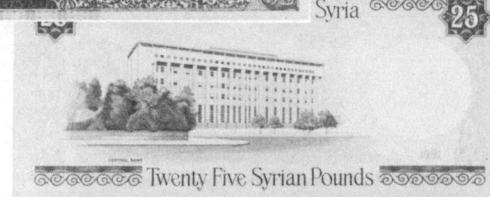

102   25 Pounds VF UNC
1977-91/AH1397-1412. Dark blue and dark green on multicolor underprint. Krak
des Chevaliers castle at center, Saladdin at right. Back: Central Bank building.
Watermark: Arabian horse's head.

	VF	UNC
a. Like #100a. 1977/AH1397.	12.00	32.00
b. Like #100b. 1978/AH1398.	3.00	15.00
c. 1982/AH1402.	2.50	10.00
d. 1988/AH1408.	1.00	6.00
e. 1991/AH1412.	FV	4.00

1997-98 Issue

103　50 Pounds　　　　　　　　　　　　　　　　　**VF　UNC**

1977-91/AH1397-1412. Brown, black and green on multicolor underprint. Dam at center, ancient statue at right. Back: Citadel of Aleppo. Watermark: Arabian horse's head. 155x75mm.

		VF	UNC
a.	Like #100a. 1977/AH1397.	12.00	42.00
b.	Like #100b. 1978/AH1398.	5.00	21.00
c.	1982/AH1402.	4.00	16.00
d.	1988/AH1408.	3.00	8.00
e.	1991/AH1412.	2.00	6.00

107　50 Pounds　　　　　　　　　　　　　　　　　**VF　UNC**

1998/AH1419. UV: value 50SP in rectangle and horse head fluoresce yellow; fibers fluoresce yellow, red and blue. Dark and light brown, green and lilac on multicolor underprint. Aleppo Citadel at center, water wheel of Hama at right. Back: Al-Assad library, Abbyssian stadium and students. Watermark: Arabian horse's head. 150x75mm. — FV 4.50

104　100 Pounds　　　　　　　　　　　　　　　　**VF　UNC**

1977-90/AH1397-1411. Dark blue, dark green and dark brown on multicolor underprint. Ancient Palmyra ruins at center, Queen Zenobia bust at right. Back: Grain silos at Lattakia. Watermark: Arabian horse's head. 167x80mm.

		VF	UNC
a.	Like #100a. 1977/AH1397.	21.00	65.00
b.	Like #100b. 1978/AH1398.	12.00	40.00
c.	1982/AH1402.	4.00	20.00
d.	1990/AH1411.	3.00	10.00

108　100 Pounds　　　　　　　　　　　　　　　　**VF　UNC**

1998/AH1419. Light blue, red-brown and purple on multicolor underprint. Bosra theater at center, ancient bust of Philip at right. Back: Hajaz railway locomotive; Damascus station and road. Watermark: Arabian horse's head. 155x80mm. — FV 6.50

105　500 Pounds　　　　　　　　　　　　　　　　**VF　UNC**

1976-90/AH1396-1411. Dark violet-brown and brown on multicolor underprint. Motifs from ruins of Kingdom of Ugarit, head at right. Back: Ancient religious wheel and cuneiform clay tablet. Bank name in English. Watermark: Arabian horse's head. 180x85mm.

		VF	UNC
a.	1976/AH1396.	25.00	75.00
b.	1979.	45.00	200
c.	1982/AH1402.	25.00	80.00
d.	1986.	20.00	75.00
e.	1990/AH1411.	15.00	50.00
f.	1992/AH1413.	15.00	40.00

#106 not assigned.

109　200 Pounds　　　　　　　　　　　　　　　　**VF　UNC**

1997/AH1418. Red-orange, purple and light brown on multicolor underprint. Monument to the Unknown soldier at center, Islamic coin at lower center right, Statue of Saladdin at right. Back: Cotton weaving and energy plant. Watermark: Arabian horse's head. 160x75mm. — FV 11.00

110 500 Pounds   **VF UNC**

1998/AH1419 (2000). Gray and bluish-green on multicolor underprint. Queen Zenobia at right, Palmyra theater at center. Back: Eufrate dam, irrigation and agricultural products. 165x75mm.

    a. Without map of Syria on back.   FV 30.00
    b. Map of Syria added to back.   FV 25.00
    c. "500" added to back bottom right.   FV 25.00

111 1000 Pounds   **VF UNC**

1997/AH1418. Green, blue and light brown on multicolor underprint. Omayyad Mosque main entrance at center, Islamic dinar coin and clay tablet at lower center, H. Assad at right. Back: Oil industry workers at left, harvesting machinery and fishing boat. Watermark: H. Assad. 170x75mm.

    a. Without map of Syria on back.   FV 48.00
    b. With map of Syria on back.   FV 40.00

2009 Issue

112 50 Pounds   **VF UNC**

2009. Blue and ton on multicolor underprint. Clay tablets from Ebla. Back: Hafiz al Assad Library in Damascus. Watermark: Horse head and 50. 135x65mm.   FV 3.00

113 100 Pounds   **VF UNC**

2009. Red and tan on multicolor underprint. Ancient Roman theater and archway of Bosra gate. Back: Umayyad Mosque in Damascus safe; Central Bank building, coin. Watermark: Horse head and 100 141x65mm.   FV 6.00

114 200 Pounds   **VF UNC**

2009. Tan and green on multicolor underprint. Norias (waterwheels) of Hama. Back: Bel Temple ceiling in Palmyra. Watermark: Horse head and 200. 146x65mm.   FV 8.00

115 500 Pounds   **VF UNC**

2010. Blue, brown and multicolor. Opera house at right. Back: Painting of artists and musicians. Watermark: Arms and 500.   FV 17.50

2013 Issue

116 1000 Pounds   **VF UNC**

2013. Green, purple, red and yellow. Ancient Roman amphitheater in Bosra. Back: Tile mosaic of grape harvest from ancient Roman ruins in As-Suwayda, olive branches. 4mm wide windowed security thread with demetalized SP1000 and Arabic text. Watermark: Electrotype 1000 and eagle coat of arms. Printer: (Goznak). 155x65mm.   FV 13.00

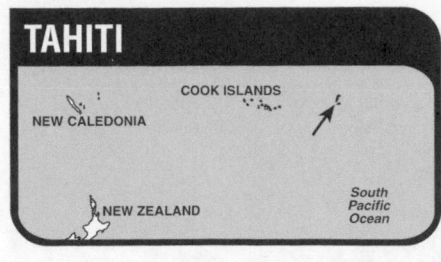

TAHITI

Tahiti, the largest island of the central South Pacific French overseas territory of French Polynesia, has an area of 402 sq. mi. (1,042 sq. km.) and a population of 79,024. Papeete on the northwest coast is the capital and administrative center of French Polynesia. Copra, sugar cane, vanilla and coffee are exported. Tourism is an important industry. Capt. Samuel Wallis of the British Navy discovered Tahiti in 1768 and named it King George III Island. Louis-Antoine de Bougainville arrived the following year and claimed it for France. Subsequent English visits were by James Cook in 1769 and William Bligh in the HMS "Bounty" in 1788. Members of the Protestant London Missionary Society established the first European settlement in 1797, and with the aid of the local Pomare family gained control of the entire island and established a "missionary kingdom" with a scriptural code of law. Nevertheless, Tahiti was subsequently declared a French protectorate (1842) and a colony (1880), and since 1958 is part of the overseas territory of French Polynesia.

RULERS:
French

MONETARY SYSTEM:
1 Franc = 100 Centimes

SIGNATURE VARIETIES

	DIRECTEUR GÉNÉRAL	PRÉSIDENT DU COUNSEIL DE SURVEILLANCE
1	André Postel-Vinay, 1967 - 1972	Bernard Clappier, 1966 - 1972
2	Claude Panouillot, 1972 - 1973	André de Lattre, 1973
3	Claude Panouillot, 1974 - 1978	Marcel Theron, 1974 - 1979
3A	Yves Roland-Billecart, 1979 - 1984	Marcel Theron, 1974 - 1979
4	Yves Roland-Billecart, 1979 - 1984	Gabriel Lefort, 1980 - 1984
5	Yves Roland-Billecart, 1985 -	Jacques Waitzenegger, 1985 -

FRENCH ADMINISTRATION

Banque de l'Indochine
Papeete
1939-40 ND Issue

14   100 Francs   Fine   XF

ND (1939-65). Brown and multicolor. Woman wearing wreath and holding small figure of Athena at center. Back: Angkor statue.

a. Signature M. Borduge and P. Baudouin with titles: *LE PRÉSIDENT* and *LE ADMINISTRATEUR DIRECTEUR GÉNÉRAL.*   85.00   300

b. Signature titles: *LE PRÉSIDENT* and *LE ADMINISTRATEUR DIRECTEUR GÉNÉRAL.*   75.00   250

c. Signature titles: *LE PRÉSIDENT* and *LE VICE-PRÉSIDENT DIRECTEUR GÉNÉRAL.*   60.00   225

d. Signature titles: *LE PRÉSIDENT* and *LE DIRECTEUR GÉNÉRAL.*   50.00   200

1951 ND Issue

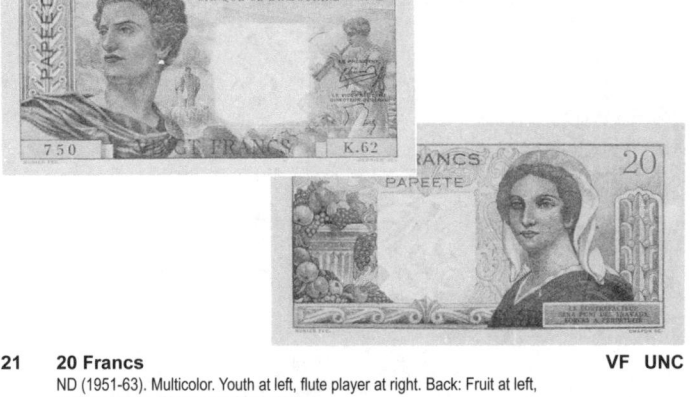

21   20 Francs   VF   UNC

ND (1951-63). Multicolor. Youth at left, flute player at right. Back: Fruit at left, woman at right. Watermark: Man with hat.

a. Signature titles: *LE PRÉSIDENT* and *LE DIRECTEUR GAL.* (1951).   50.00   125

b. Signature titles: *LE PRÉSIDENT* and *LE VICE-PRÉSIDENT DIRECTEUR GÉNÉRAL* (1954-1958).   30.00   75.00

c. Signature titles: *LE PRÉSIDENT* and *LE DIRECTEUR GÉNÉRAL.* (1963).   20.00   50.00

s. As b, c. Specimen. Pin hole perforated *SPECIMEN.*   —   250

Institut d'Emission d'Outre-Mer
1969-71 ND Issues

23   100 Francs   VF   UNC

ND (1969). Printed from engraved copper plates. Brown and multicolor. Girl wearing wreath holding guitar at right, without *REPUBLIQUE FRANCAISE* near bottom center. Signature 1. Back: Girl at left, town scene at center.   10.00   75.00

24 100 Francs

ND. (1971; 1973). Multicolor. Girl wearing wreath holding guitar at right, with overprint *REPUBLIQUE FRANCAISE* near bottom center. Signature 1. Back: Girl at left, town scene at center.

		VF	UNC
a. Printed from engraved copper plates. (1971).		25.00	65.00
b. Offset printing. (1973).		20.00	55.00

25 500 Francs

ND (1970-85). Blue and multicolor. Harbor view with boat in background at center, fisherman at lower right. Back: Man at left, objects at right.

		VF	UNC
a. Signature 1. (1970).		40.00	95.00
b1. Signature 3. (1977).		32.50	80.00
b2. Signature 3A.		35.00	85.00
c. Signature 4. (1983).		27.50	70.00
d. Signature 5. (1985).		20.00	55.00

26 1000 Francs

ND (1969). Dark brown on red and multicolor underprint. Hut under palms at left, girl at right. Without *REPUBLIQUE FRANCAISE* overprint at bottom center. Signature 1. Back: Kagu, deer, buildings, native carvings. Watermark: Marianne.

	VF	UNC
	90.00	225

27 1000 Francs

ND (1971-85). Dark brown on multicolor underprint. Hut under palms at left, girl at right. With overprint *REPUBLIQUE FRANCAISE* overprint at bottom center. Signature 1. Back: Kagu, deer, buildings, native carvings. Watermark: Marianne.

		VF	UNC
a. Signature 1. (1971).		55.00	125
b. Signature 3. (1977).		45.00	100
c. Signature 4. (1983).		40.00	100
d. Signature 5. (1985).		35.00	90.00

28 5000 Francs

ND (1971-85). Brown with black text on olive-green and multicolor underprint. Bougainville at left, sailing ships at center. Back: Admiral Febvrier-Despointes at right, sailboat at center right.

		VF	UNC
a. Signature 1. (1971).		120	250
b. Signature 2. (1975).		100	225
c. Signature 4. (1982; 1984).		95.00	190
d. Signature 5. (1985).		85.00	165

The Republic of Tajikistan, was formed from those regions of Bukhara and Turkestan where the population consisted mainly of Tajiks. It is bordered in the north and west by Uzbekistan and Kyrgyzstan, in the east by China and in the south by Afghanistan. It has an area of 143,100 sq. km. and a population of 7.21 million. It includes 2 provinces of Khudzand and Khatlon together with the Gorno-Badakhshan Autonomous Region. Capital: Dushanbe.The Tajik people came under Russian rule in the 1860s and 1870s, but Russia's hold on Central Asia weakened following the Revolution of 1917. Bolshevik control of the area was fiercely contested and not fully reestablished until 1925. Much of present-day Sughd province was transferred from the Uzbekistan SSR to newly formed Tajikistan SSR in 1929. Ethnic Uzbeks form a substantial minority in Sughd province. Tajikistan became independent in 1991 following the breakup of the Soviet Union, and it is now in the process of strengthening its democracy and transitioning to a free market economy after its 1992-97 civil war. There have been no major security incidents in recent years, although the country remains the poorest in the former Soviet sphere. Attention by the international community in the wake of the war in Afghanistan has brought increased economic development and security assistance, which could create jobs and increase stability in the long term. Tajikistan is in the early stages of seeking World Trade Organization membership and has joined NATO's Partnership for Peace.

MONETARY SYSTEM:
1 Ruble = 100 Tanga, to 2000
1 Somoni = 1,000 Rubles
1 Somoni = 100 Diram

REPUBLIC

БОНКИ ЫИЛЛИИ ЧУЬХУРИИ ТОЧИКИСТОН

NATIONAL BANK OF THE REPUBLIC OF TAJIKISTAN

1994 Issue

1 **1 Ruble**   **VF** **UNC**
1994. Brown on multicolor underprint. Arms at upper left. Back: *Majlisi Olii* (Parliament). Watermark: Multiple stars. Printer: Goznak (without imprint).
  a. Issued note.   0.50   1.00
  s. Specimen.   —   —

2 **5 Rubles**   **VF** **UNC**
1994. Deep blue on multicolor underprint. Arms at upper left. Back: *Majlisi Olii* (Parliament). Watermark: Multiple stars. Printer: Goznak (without imprint).
  a. Issued note.   0.50   2.00
  s. Specimen.   —   —

3 **10 Rubles**   **VF** **UNC**
1994. Deep red on multicolor underprint. Arms at upper left. Back: *Majlisi Olii* (Parliament). Watermark: Multiple stars. Printer: Goznak (without imprint).
  a. Issued note.   1.00   3.00
  s. Specimen.   —   —

4 **20 Rubles**   **VF** **UNC**
1994. Purple on multicolor underprint. Arms at upper left. Back: *Majlisi Olii* (Parliament). Watermark: Multiple stars. Printer: Goznak (without imprint).
  a. Issued note.   1.00   3.00
  s. Specimen.   —   —

5 **50 Rubles**   **VF** **UNC**
1994. Dark olive-green on multicolor underprint. Arms at upper left. Back: *Majlisi Olii* (Parliament). Watermark: Multiple stars. Printer: Goznak (without imprint).
  a. Issued note.   1.00   4.00
  s. Specimen.   —   —

6 **100 Rubles**   **VF** **UNC**
1994. Blue-black and brown on multicolor underprint. Arms at left. Back: *Majlisi Olii* (Parliament). Watermark: Multiple stars. Printer: Goznak (without imprint).
  a. Issued note.   1.00   5.00
  s. Specimen. Red overprint: *SPECIMEN* on both sides.   —   27.50

7 **200 Rubles**   **VF** **UNC**
1994. Deep olive-green and pale violet on multicolor underprint. Arms at left. Back: *Majlisi Olii* (Parliament). Watermark: Multiple stars. Printer: Goznak (without imprint).
  a. Issued note.   1.00   6.00
  s. Specimen.   —   —

8 **500 Rubles**   **VF** **UNC**
1994. Brown-violet on multicolor underprint. Arms at upper left. Back: *Majlisi Olii* (Parliament). Watermark: Multiple stars. Printer: Goznak (without imprint).
  a. Issued note.   2.00   8.00
  s. Specimen. Red overprint: *SPECIMEN* on both sides.   —   30.00

9 **1000 Rubles**   **VF** **UNC**
1994 (1999). Brown and purple on multicolor underprint.
  a. Issued note.   0.50   10.00
  s. Specimen. Black overprint: *НАМУНА* on both sides.   —   35.00

9A 5000 Rubles   VF   UNC

1994. (Not issued). Dark green and blue on multicolor underprint. Coat of Arms at left. Back: Parliament building with flag.   —   50.00

9B 10,000 Rubles   VF   UNC

1994. Pink and brown on multicolor underprint. Coat of Arms at center. Back: Parliament building with flag.
- a. Unissued note.   —   50.00
- s. Specimen.   —   —

БОНКИ ЬИЛЛИИ ТОЧИКИСТОН

NATIONAL BANK OF TAJIKISTAN

1999 Issue

10 1 Diram   VF   UNC

1999 (2000). Brown on tan and red underprint. Sadriddin Ayni Theatre and Opera house at center. Back: Pamir mountains. Watermark: Two mountains over rectangle. Printer: German. 110x60mm.
- a. Issued note.   FV   2.00
- s. Specimen. Red overprint: *SPECIMEN* on both sides.   —   20.00

11 5 Diram   VF   UNC

1999 (2000). Blue on tan underprint. Arbob Culture Palace at center. Back: Shrine of Mirzo Tursunzoda. Watermark: Two mountains over rectangle. Printer: German. 110x60mm.
- a. Issued note.   FV   2.00
- s. Specimen. Red overprint: *SPECIMEN* on both sides.   —   20.00

12 20 Diram   VF   UNC

1999 (2000). Green on tan underprint. *Majlisi Olii,* Meeting Hall of the National Bank. Back: Road pass in the mountains. Watermark: Two mountains over rectangle. Printer: German. 110x60mm.
- a. Issued note.   FV   3.00
- s. Specimen. Red overprint: *SPECIMEN* on both sides.   —   20.00

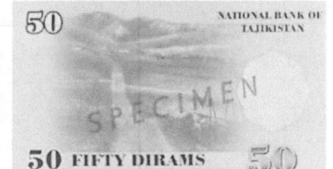

13 50 Diram   VF   UNC

1999 (2000). Purple on tan underprint. Statue of Ismoili Somoni at center. Back: Road in a valley. Watermark: Two mountains over rectangle. Printer: German. 100x60mm.
- a. Nominal value and bank name reflect UV.   FV   4.00
- b. Nominal value and bank name does not reflect UV.   FV   4.00
- s. Specimen. Red overprint: *SPECIMEN* on both sides.   —   20.00

14 1 Somoni   VF   UNC

1999 (2000). Green and blue on multicolor underprint. Mirzo Tursunzoda (poet) at right. Globe at center is green and orange. Back: National Bank of Tajikistan building. Watermark: Mirzo Tursunzoda. 141x65mm.
- a. Globe green-yellow and glows under UV light.   FV   4.00
- b. Globe green-yellow and does not glow UV. Series AK.   FV   4.00
- r. Replacement note. Series AZ.   —   —
- s. Specimen. Red overprint: *SPECIMEN* on both sides.   —   40.00

14A 1 Somoni   VF   UNC

1999 (2010). Green and blue on multicolor underprint. Mirzo Tursunzoda at right. Globe at center is green. Back: National Bank building at center. Watermark: Tursunzoda. 141x65mm.   FV   4.00

15 5 Somoni   VF   UNC

1999 (2000). Blue and green on multicolor underprint. Sadriddin Ayni at right. Back: Tomb of Abuabdullo Rudaki in Panjakent. Watermark: Sadriddin Ayni. 144x65mm.
- a. Gray table on face, right number is not UV reflective. Back middle element is UV reflective.   FV   8.00
- b. Blue table on face, right number is not UV reflective. Series BG.   FV   8.00
- c. Blue table on face. Right number is UV reflective. Series BK.   FV   8.00
- r. Replacement note. Series BZ.   —   —
- s. Specimen. Red overprint: *SPECIMEN* on both sides.   —   40.00

16   10 Somoni   **VF   UNC**

1999 (2000). Purple and orange-red. Mir Saiid Alii Hamadoni at right. Back: Tomb of Mir Said Alii Hamadoni in Kulob Watermark: Mir Saiid Alii Hamadoni. 147x65mm.

a. Back middle element glows under UV light.		FV	15.00
b. Back middle does not glow under UV light. Series CG.		FV	15.00
r. Replacement note. Series CZ.		—	—
s. Specimen. Red overprint: *SPECIMEN* on both sides.		—	40.00

17   20 Somoni   **VF   UNC**

1999 (2000). Brown and blue on multicolor underprint. Abuali Ibn Sino at right. Holographic strip at right. Back: Hissar fortress near Dushanbe. Watermark: Abuali Ibn Sino. 150x65mm.

a. Bowl on face glows under UV light.		FV	20.00
b. Bowl on face does not glow under UV light.		FV	20.00
r. Replacement note. Series DZ.		—	—
s. Specimen. Red overprint: *SPECIMEN* on both sides.		—	40.00

18   50 Somoni   **VF   UNC**

1999 (2000). Dark blue and black on multicolor underprint. Bobojon Gafurov at right. Holographic strip at right. Back: *Choikhanai Sina*, a tea house in Dushanbe. Watermark: Bobojon Gafurov. 153x65mm.

a. Issued note. Serial # not on kinegram foil.		FV	25.00
r. Replacement note. Series EZ.		0.00	—
s. Specimen. Red overprint: *SPECIMEN* on both sides.		—	40.00

19   100 Somoni   **VF   UNC**

1999 (2000). Brown and blue on multicolor underprint. Ismoili Somoni at right. Holographic strip at right. Back: Presidential Palace in Dushanbe. Watermark: Ismoili Somoni. 156x65mm.

a. Issued note. Serial # not on kinegram foil.		FV	85.00
r. Replacement note. Series FZ.		—	—
s. Specimen. Red overprint: *SPECIMEN* on both sides.		—	50.00

2010 Commemorative Issue

20   3 Somoni   **VF   UNC**

2010. Violet on multicolor underprint. Shirinsho Shotemur at right. Back: Majlisi Oli (parliament) building at center. 142x65mm.   FV   1.25

21   200 Somoni   **VF   UNC**

2010. Brown and yellow on multicolor underprint. Nusratullo Makhsum at right. Back: National Library in Dushanbe. Watermark: Makhsum. 159x65mm.   FV   90.00

22   500 Somoni   **VF   UNC**

2010. Purple and gray on multicolor underprint. Abuabdullo Rudaki at right. Back: Palace of Nations in Dushanbe. Watermark: Rudaki. 162x65mm.   FV   300

1999 (2013 enhanced) Issue

23   5 Somoni   **VF   UNC**

1999 (2013). Blue on multicolor underprint. Sadriddin Ayni at right, blue central design. Series BN. Wide security foil at right. Back: Tomb of Abuabdullo Rudaki in Panjakent. 144x65mm.   FV   3.00

24   10 Somoni   **VF   UNC**

1999 (2013). Purple and orange-red on multicolor underprint. Mir Saiid Alii Hamadoni at right. Series CM. Wide foil strip at right. Back: Tomb of Mir Said Alii Hamadoni in Kulob. 147x65mm.   FV   5.00

25   20 Somoni   **VF   UNC**

1999 (2013).   FV   10.00

26   50 Somoni   **VF   UNC**

1999 (2013).   FV   20.00

27   100 Somoni   **VF   UNC**

1999 (2013).   FV   40.00

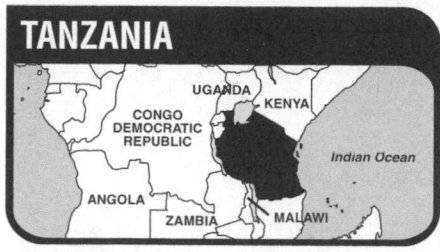

TANZANIA

The United Republic of Tanzania, located on the east coast of Africa between Kenya and Mozambique, consists of Tanganyika and the islands of Zanzibar and Pemba. It has an area of 945,090 sq. km. and a population of 40.21 million. Capital: Dodoma. The chief exports are cotton, coffee, diamonds, sisal, cloves, petroleum products and cashew nuts. Shortly after achieving independence from Britain in the early 1960s, Tanganyika and Zanzibar merged to form the nation of Tanzania in 1964. One-party rule came to an end in 1995 with the first democratic elections held in the country since the 1970s. Zanzibar's semi-autonomous status and popular opposition have led to two contentious elections since 1995, which the ruling party won despite international observers' claims of voting irregularities.

MONETARY SYSTEM:

1 Shilingi (Shilling) = 100 Senti

SIGNATURE VARIETIES

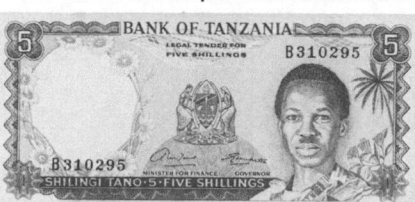

	MINISTER FOR FINANCE	GOVERNOR		MINISTER FOR FINANCE	GOVERNOR
1			2		
3			4		
5			6	WAZIRI WA FEDHA	GAVANA
7	WAZIRI WA FEDHA	GAVANA	7A		
8			9		
10			11		
12			13		
14					

REPUBLIC

Bank of Tanzania

1966 ND Issue

Note: Signature 3-5 with English titles on #2 and 3, changed to Swahili titles for later issues. #1-5 Replacement notes: Serial # prefix ZZ; ZY.

2 10 Shillings VF UNC

ND (1966). Green on multicolor underprint. Arms at center, President J. Nyerere at right. Back: Sisal drying. Watermark: Giraffe's head.

		VF	UNC
a. Signature 1.		3.00	9.00
b. Signature 2.		4.00	10.00
c. Signature 3.		30.00	225
d. Signature 4.		2.00	7.50
e. Signature 5.		2.00	6.00
s. As a. Specimen		—	25.00

3 20 Shillings VF UNC

ND (1966). Blue on multicolor underprint. Arms at center, President J. Nyerere at right. Back: Work buildings. Watermark: Giraffe's head.

		VF	UNC
a. Signature 1.		5.00	12.50
b. Signature 2.		5.00	12.50
c. Signature 3.		7.00	20.00
d. Signature 4.		5.00	15.00
e. Signature 5.		3.00	9.00
s. As a. Specimen.		—	25.00

4 100 Shillings VF UNC

ND (1966). Red on multicolor underprint. Arms at center, President J. Nyerere at right. Signature 1. Back: Masai herdsman with animals. Watermark: Giraffe's head.

		VF	UNC
a. Issued note.		60.00	375
s. Specimen.		—	85.00

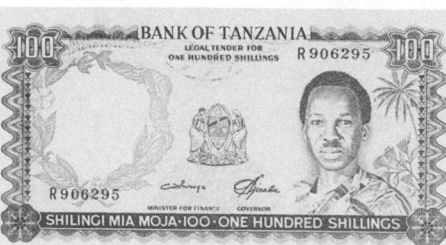

1 5 Shillings VF UNC

ND (1966). Brown on multicolor underprint. Arms at center, President J. Nyerere at right. Signature 1. Back: Mountain view. Watermark: Giraffe's head.

		VF	UNC
a. Issued note.		3.00	12.50
s. Specimen.		—	25.00

5   100 Shillings

	VF	UNC

ND (1966). Red on multicolor underprint. Arms at center, President J. Nyerere at right. Back: Various animals. Watermark: Giraffe's head.

	VF	UNC
a. Signature 1.	50.00	350
b. Signature 3.	40.00	275

Benki Kuu Ya Tanzania
1977-78 ND Issue

#6-8 Replacement notes: Serial # prefix *ZZ; ZY.* **Note: For #6-8, sign. are shown in chronological order of appearance. It seems sign. 3 was used again following several later combinations.**

6   10 Shilingi

	VF	UNC

ND (1978). Green on multicolor underprint. Arms at top center, President J. Nyerere at right. Back: Monument and mountain at center. Watermark: Giraffe's head.

	VF	UNC
a. Signature 5.	1.50	7.50
b. Signature 6.	1.25	4.50
c. Signature 3. Signature titles: *WAZIRI WA FEDHA* and *GAVANA*.	0.75	3.00

7   20 Shilingi

	VF	UNC

ND (1978). Blue on multicolor underprint. Arms at top center, President J. Nyerere at right. Back: Cotton knitting machine. Watermark: Giraffe's head.

	VF	UNC
a. Signature 5.	2.25	10.00
b. Signature 6.	2.25	7.00
c. Signature 3. Signature titles: *WAZIRI WA FEDHA* and *GAVANA*.	2.25	6.00

8   100 Shilingi

	VF	UNC

ND (1977). Purple on multicolor underprint. Arms at top center, President J. Nyerere at right. Back: Teacher and students at left, farmers at center. Watermark: Giraffe's head.

	VF	UNC
a. Signature 4.	6.00	40.00
b. Signature 5.	5.00	35.00
c. Signature 6.	4.00	27.50
d. Signature 3. Signature titles: *WAZIRI WA FEDHA* and *GAVANA*.	4.50	20.00

1985 ND Issue

#9-11 Replacement notes: Serial # prefix *ZZ; ZY.*

9   20 Shilingi

	VF	UNC

ND (1985). Purple, brown on multicolor underprint. Arms at center, torch at left, portrait of an older President J. Nyerere at right. Signature 3. Back: Tire factory scene, islands of Mafia, Pemba and Zanzibar are omitted from map. Watermark: Giraffe's head.

	VF	UNC
	0.50	2.50

10   50 Shilingi

	VF	UNC

ND (1985). UV: value 50 in box fluoresce orange. Back torch and wreath yellow. Red-orange, light brown on multicolor underprint. Arms at center, torch at left, portrait of an older President J. Nyerere at right. Signature 3. Back: Brick making, islands of Mafia, Pemba and Zanzibar are omitted from map. Watermark: Giraffe's head.

	VF	UNC
	1.50	5.00

11   100 Shilingi

	VF	UNC

ND (1985). Blue, purple on multicolor underprint. Arms at center, torch at left, portrait of an older President J. Nyerere at right. Signature 3. Back: Graduation procession, islands of Mafia, Pemba and Zanzibar are omitted from map. Watermark: Giraffe's head.

	VF	UNC
	3.00	12.00

1986 ND Issue

#12-14 Replacement notes: Serial # prefix *ZZ; ZY.*

12 20 Shilingi   VF   UNC

ND (1986). Purple, brown on multicolor underprint. Arms at center, torch at left, portrait of an older President J. Nyerere at right. Signature 3. Signature titles: WAZIRI WA FEDHA and *GAVANA*. Back: Tire factory scene, islands of Mafia, Pemba and Zanzibar are included in map.   0.50   2.00

13 50 Shilingi   VF   UNC

ND (1986). Red-orange, light brown on multicolor underprint. Arms at center, torch at left, portrait of an older President J. Nyerere at right. Signature 3. Signature titles: *WAZIRI WA FEDHA* and *GAVANA*. Back: Brick making, islands of Mafia, Pemba and Zanzibar are included in map.   1.00   3.50

14 100 Shilingi   VF   UNC

ND (1986). Blue, purple on multicolor underprint. Arms at center, torch at left, portrait of an older President J. Nyerere at right. Signature 3. Back: Graduation procession, islands of Mafia, Pemba and Zanzibar are included in map.

a. Signature 3 with titles: *WAZIRI WA FEDHA* and *GAVANA*.   1.50   7.50
b. Signature 8.   1.00   5.00

1986-90 ND Issue

#15-18 Replacement notes: Serial # prefix *ZZ; ZY.*

15 20 Shilingi   VF   UNC

ND (1987). Purple, red-brown on multicolor underprint. Arms at center, President Mwinyi at right. Signature 3 but with titles: *WAZIRI WA FEDHA* and *GAVANA*. Back: Tire factory scene, islands of Mafia, Pemba and Zanzibar are included in map. Watermark: Giraffe's head.   0.25   2.00

16 50 Shilingi   VF   UNC

ND (1986). Red-orange, light brown on multicolor underprint. Arms at center, President Mwinyi at right. Back: Brick making, islands of Mafia, Pemba and Zanzibar are included in map. Watermark: Giraffe's head.

a. Signature 3 but with titles: *WAZIRI WA FEDHA* and *GAVANA*.   1.00   4.00
b. Signature 7.   0.75   3.00
c. Signature 7B.   1.25   8.00

#17 not assigned.

18 200 Shilingi   VF   UNC

ND (1986). Black, orange and ochre on multicolor underprint. Arms at center, President Mwinyi at right. Back: Two fishermen. Watermark: Giraffe's head.

a. Signature 3 but with titles: *WAZIRI WA FEDHA* and *GAVANA*.   2.00   9.00
b. Signature 7.   4.00   20.00

1989-92 ND Issue

#19-22 Replacement notes: Serial # prefix *ZZ; ZY.*

19 50 Shilingi   VF   UNC

ND (1992). Red-orange and light brown on multicolor underprint. Arms at center, modified portrait of President Mwinyi at right. Signature 8. Back: Brick making, islands of Mafia, Pemba and Zanzibar are included in map. Watermark: Giraffe's head.   0.50   1.75

20 200 Shilingi   VF   UNC

ND (1992). Black, orange and ochre on multicolor underprint. Arms at center, modified portrait of President Mwinyi at right. Signature 7, 8. Back: Two fishermen. Watermark: Giraffe's head.   1.50   6.00

21 500 Shilingi

	VF	UNC
ND (1989). Dark blue on multicolor underprint. Arms at center, modified portrait of President Mwinyi at right. Zebra at lower left. Back: Harvesting. Watermark: Giraffe's head.		
a. Signature 3 but with titles: *WAZIRI WA FEDHA* and *GAVANA*.	10.00	40.00
b. Signature 7.	5.00	25.00
c. Signature 8.	3.00	17.50

22 1000 Shilingi

	VF	UNC
ND (1990). Green and brown on multicolor underprint. Arms at center, modified portrait of President Mwinyi at right. Elephants at lower left. Signature 8. Back: Kiwira Coal Mine at left center, door to the Peoples Bank of Zanzibar at lower right. Watermark: Giraffe's head.	5.00	35.00

1993; 1995 ND Issue

#23, 25-27 Reduced size. Replacement notes: Serial # prefix *ZZ; ZY.*

23 50 Shilingi

	VF	UNC
ND (1993). Red-orange and brown on multicolor underprint. Arms at center, President Mwinyi at right. Wildebeest grazing at left. Signature 9. Back: Men making bricks. Watermark: Giraffe's head.	FV	1.00

24 100 Shilingi

	VF	UNC
ND (1993). Blue and aqua on multicolor underprint. Kudu at left, arms at center, J. Nyerere at right. Signature 9. Back: Graduation procession.	FV	2.00

Note: #24 honors the 70th birthday of Julius Nyerere.

25 200 Shilingi

	VF	UNC
ND (1993). Black and orange on multicolor underprint. Arms at center, President Mwinyi at right. Leopards at left. Back: Two fishermen. Watermark: Giraffe's head.		
a. Signature 9.	FV	3.50
b. Signature 11.	FV	3.00

26 500 Shilingi

	VF	UNC
ND (1993). Back similar to #21 with arms at lower right. Purple, blue-green and violet on multicolor underprint. Arms at center, President Mwinyi at right. Zebra at lower left. Back: Harvesting. Watermark: Giraffe's head.		
a. Signature 9.	FV	9.00
b. Signature 10.	FV	5.00
c. Signature 11.	FV	5.00

27 1000 Shilingi

	VF	UNC
ND (1993). Dark green, brown and orange-brown on multicolor underprint. Arms at center, President Mwinyi at right. Elephants at lower left. Back: Kiwira Coal Mine at left center, door to the Peoples Bank of Zanzibar at lower right. Watermark: Giraffe's head.		
a. Signature 9.	FV	15.00
b. Signature 10.	FV	10.00
c. Signature 11.	FV	7.50

28 5000 Shilingi
ND (1995). Brown on multicolor underprint. Arms at center, President Mwinyi at right. Rhinoceros at lower left. Signature 10. Back: Giraffes with Mt. Kilimanjaro in background.

VF UNC
FV 40.00

29 10,000 Shilingi
ND (1995). Multicolor. Lion at lower left. Signature 10. Back: Bank of Tanzania Head Office building at left center, Zanzibar House of Wonder at lower right.

VF UNC
FV 50.00

1997 ND Issue

30 500 Shilingi
ND (1997). Blue-black and dark green on multicolor underprint. Zebra at lower left. Arms at upper center, giraffe's head at right. Signature 12. Back: Woman harvesting cloves at left center. Watermark: Giraffe's head.

VF UNC
FV 2.50

31 1000 Shilingi
ND (1997). Deep olive-green, red-orange and dark brown on multicolor underprint. Elephants at lower left. Arms at upper center, giraffe's head at right. Signature 12. Back: Industrial buildings at left center, door to the Peoples Bank of Zanzibar at lower right. Watermark: Giraffe's head.

VF UNC
FV 5.00

32 5000 Shilingi
ND (1997). Segmented foil over security thread. Dark brown and purple on multicolor underprint. Rhinoceros at lower left. Arms at upper center, giraffe's head at right. Signature 12. Back: Giraffes with Mt. Kilimanjaro in background. Watermark: Giraffe's head.

VF UNC
FV 17.50

33 10,000 Shilingi
ND (1997). Blue-black and dark gray on multicolor underprint. Lion at lower left. Arms at upper center, giraffe's head at right. Vertical foil strip at right. Signature 12. Back: Bank of Tanzania Head Office building at left center, Zanzibar House of Wonder at lower right. Watermark: Giraffe's head.

VF UNC
FV 35.00

2000 ND Issue

34 1000 Shilingi
ND (2000). Brown and green on multicolor underprint. Elephants at lower left, Julius Nyerere at right. Signature 13. Back: Industrial buildings at left center, door to the Peoples Bank of Zanzibar at lower right. Watermark: Giraffe's head.

VF UNC
FV 5.00

2003 ND Issue

35   500 Shilingi   **VF   UNC**
ND (2003). Green and blue on multicolor underprint. Cape Buffalo at center   FV   1.50
right. Signature 14. Back: Hospital at center, boats in background. Printer: G&D.
130x63mm.

36   1000 Shilingi   **VF   UNC**
ND (2003). Blue and slate blue on multicolor underprint. Julius Nyerere at center
right. Signature 14. Back: Palace. Printer: G&D. 135x66mm.
   a. ND (2003). Button on Nyerere's jacket on right side of split.   FV   3.50
   b. ND (2006). Button on Nyerere's jacket on left side of spilt.   FV   3.00

37   2000 Shilingi   **VF   UNC**
ND (2003); 2009. Brown, tan and green on multicolor underprint. Lion and Mt.
Kilimanjaro at center. Back: Fort. Printer: G&D. 140x69mm.
   a. ND (2003). Signature 14.   FV   6.00
   b. ND (2009). Signature 15.   FV   4.00

38   5000 Shilingi   **VF   UNC**
ND (2003). Purple on multicolor underprint. Black Rhinoceros at center left. Signa-   FV   14.00
ture 14. Back: Mining and House of Wonder. Printer: G&D. 145x72mm.

39   10,000 Shilingi   **VF   UNC**
ND (2003). Rose and green on multicolor underprint. Elephant at center left.   FV   28.00
Signature 14. Back: Central Bank building. Printer: G&D. 150x75mm.

2010 ND Issue

40   500 Shilingi   **VF   UNC**
ND (2010). Green on multicolor underprint. Sheikh Abeid Amani Karume at center.   FV   1.50
Back: Central Hall at Dar es Salaam University. Printer: TDLR. 120x60mm.

41   1000 Shilingi   **VF   UNC**
ND (2010; 2015). Blue on multicolor underprint. Julius Kambarage Nyerere
at center. Back: Coffee plant and State House (Ikulu) building. Printer: TDLR.
124x65mm.
   a. ND (2010). Signature 15.   FV   1.25
   b. ND (2015). Signature 16. Prefix DH.   FV   1.00

42   2000 Shilingi   **VF   UNC**
ND (2010; 2015). Tan and brown on multicolor underprint. Lion head at center.
Back: Omani Arab fort (Ngome Kongwe) at left. Printer: TDLR. 130x66mm.
   a. ND (2010). Signature 15.   FV   2.25
   b. ND (2015). Signature 16. Prefix EQ - EX.   FV   2.00

43   5000 Shilingi   **VF   UNC**
ND (2010, 2015). Purple on multicolor underprint. Black Rhinoceros head at
center. Back: Mining machinery, diamonds. Printer: TDLR. 135x67mm.
   a. ND (2010). Signature 15.   FV   7.50
   b. ND (2015). Signature 16. Prefix CL.   FV   70.00

44   10,000 Shilingi   **VF   UNC**
ND (2010; 2015). Red and yellow on multicolor underprint. Elephant head at
center. Back: Bank of Tanzania building at center. Printer: TDLR. 140x68mm.
   a. ND (2010). Signature 15.   FV   13.00
   b. ND (2015). Signature 16. Prefix DF.   FV   12.50

Tatarstan, an autonomous republic in the Russian Federation, is situated between the middle of the Volga River and its tributary Kama, extends east to the Ural mountains, covering 26,500 sq. mi. (68,000 sq. km.) and as of the 1970 census has a population of 3,743,600. Captial: Kazan. Tatarstan's economy combines its ancient traditions in the craftsmanship of wood, leather, cloth and ceramics with modern engineering, chemical, and food industries. Colonized by the Bulgars in the 5th century, the territory of the Volga-Kama Bulgar State was inhabited by Turks. In the 13th century, Ghengis Khan conquered the area and established control until the 15th century when residual Mongol influence left Tatarstan as the Tatar Khanate, seat of the Kazar (Tatar) Khans. In 1552, under Ivan IV (the Terrible), Russia conquered, absorbed and controlled Tatarstan until the dissolution of the U.S.S.R. Constituted as an autonomous republic on May 27, 1990, and as a sovereign state equal with Russia in April, 1992, Tatarstan, signed a treaty in February, 1994, defining it as a state united with the Commonwealth of Independent States.

MONETARY SYSTEM:
   1 Ruble = 100 Kopeks

ТАТАРСКАЯ С.С.Р.

Treasury

1992 ND КУРОН - Ruble Control Coupon Issues

#1-3 red and green stripes w/black ТАТАРСКАЯ repeated on back.

1   50 Rubles   **VF   UNC**
ND (1992). Black text on green underprint. With month: СіЧеньЁ (January).
   a. Issued full sheet.   10.00   15.00
   b. Remainder full sheet.   6.00   10.00
   c. Coupon.   0.20   0.50

2   50 Rubles   **VF   UNC**
ND (1992). Black text on pink underprint. With month: ЛютийЁ (February).
   a. Issued full sheet.   7.50   15.00
   b. Remainder full sheet.   5.00   9.00
   c. Coupon.   0.20   0.50

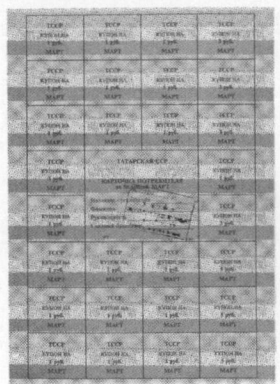

3   50 Rubles

	VF	**UNC**
ND (1992). Black text on blue underprint. With month: березеьЁ (March).		
a. Issued full sheet.	7.50	15.00
b. Remainder full sheet.	4.00	8.00
c. Coupon.	0.20	0.50

Government
1993 Privatization Check Issue

4A   30,000 Rubles

	VF	**UNC**
1993. Black text on green underprint. Arms with number. Printer: USBN.		
a. Issued note. With registration and without privatization book.	25.00	40.00
b. Issued note. With registration and with privatization book.	40.00	80.00
c. Not issued. All with coupons and without registration.	—	50.00

4B   40,000 Rubles

	VF	**UNC**
1993. Black text on green. Arms with number. Printer: USBN.		
a. Issued note. With registration and without privatization book.	17.50	30.00
b. Issued note. With registration and with privatization book.	30.00	50.00
c. Not issued. All with coupons and without registration.	—	50.00

4C   60,000 Rubles

	VF	**UNC**
1993. Black text on green underprint. Arms with number. Printer: USBN (without imprint).		
a. Issued note. With registration and without privatization book.	20.00	35.00
b. Issued note. With registration and with privatization book.	35.00	60.00
c. Not issued. All with coupons and without registration.	—	50.00

4D   80,000 Rubles

	VF	**UNC**
1993. Black text on green. Arms with number. Printer: USBN.		
a. Issued note. With registration and without privatization book.	25.00	40.00
b. Issued note. With registration and with privatization book.	40.00	75.00
c. Not issued. All with coupons and without registration.	—	50.00

4E   90,000 Rubles

	VF	**UNC**
1993. Black text on green. Arms with number. Printer: USBN.		
a. Issued note. With registration and without privatization book.	30.00	50.00
b. Issued note. With registration and with privatization book.	40.00	80.00
c. Not issued. All with coupons and without registration.	—	50.00

4F   100,000 Rubles

	VF	**UNC**
1993. Black text on green. Arms with number. Printer: USBN.		
a. Issued note. With registration and without privatization book.	35.00	60.00
b. Issued note. With registration and with privatization book.	45.00	85.00
c. Not issued. All with coupons and without registration.	—	—

1991; 1993 ND First Currency Check Issue

5   (100 Rubles)

	VF	**UNC**
ND (1991-92). Uniface. Blue-gray. State flag inside circle at left, stylized image of old castle Suumbeky in Kazan (ca. 16th century) in ornate frame at right. Watermark: Lozenges. 138x66mm.		
a. Gray underprint.	3.00	15.00
b. Red underprint.	10.00	25.00
c. Yellow underprint.	12.50	25.00
d. Orange underprint.	12.50	25.00

Note: Issued statewide. Checks probably printed in 1991, as coat of arms was accepted later than flag, but issued to circulation in 1992.

6   (100 Rubles)

	VF	**UNC**
ND (1993). Uniface. Red and pink. Red and green arms at left, stylized image of old castle Suumbeky in ornate frame at right. Watermark: Lozenges. 138x66mm.		
a. Gray underprint.	10.00	22.00
b. Violet on pink underprint.	10.00	22.00
c. dark blue on pale blue underprint.	10.00	22.00
d. Brown underprint.	10.00	22.00
e. Olive-green underprint.	10.00	22.00

Note: Issued for circulation in Kazan.

1994 ND Second Currency Check Issue

7   (200 Rubles)

	VF	**UNC**
ND (1994). Uniface. Medical emblem inside oval at right, stylized image of old castle Suumbeky in Kazan (ca. 16th century) at left. Watermark: Lozenges. 138x66mm.		
a. Blue-black and pale blue on multicolor underprint.	10.00	20.00
b. Deep olive-green and green on tan and pale green underprint.	10.00	20.00

Note: Circulated in the republic from 3.10.1994 to 1.7.1995.

1993-95 ND Third Currency Check Issue

8   (500 Rubles)

	VF	**UNC**
ND (1993). Red-brown on multicolor underprint. Arms at top center, Kazan Kremlin (ca. 16th century) at lower left. Arabic *TATAR* at right. Back: Woman feeding geese. Watermark: Mosaic. 105x53mm.	10.00	20.00

9   (500 Rubles)

	VF	**UNC**
ND (1993). Green on multicolor underprint. Arms at top center, Kazan Kremlin (ca. 16th century) at lower left. Arabic *TATAR* at right. Back: Horses galloping at center. Watermark: Mosaic. 150x53mm.	10.00	20.00

10   (1000 Rubles)

	VF	**UNC**
ND (1994). Pink on multicolor underprint. Arms at top center, Kazan Kremlin (ca. 16th century) at lower left. Arabic *TATAR* at right. Back: Gulls flying over raging waves. Watermark: Mosaic. 105x53mm.	10.00	20.00

11 (1000 Rubles)
ND (1995). Blue on multicolor underprint. Arms at top center, Kazan Kremlin (ca. 16th century) at lower left. Arabic *TATAR* at right. Back: Deer at watering hole. Watermark: Mosaic. 105x53mm.

	VF	UNC
	10.00	20.00

Note: Checks #8-11 found in circulation before Aug. 1996.

1996 ND Fourth Currency Check Issue

12 (50 Shamil = 5000 Rubles)
ND (1996). Kazan Kremlin (ca. 16th century) with English and Russian text "Tatarstan" in frame below. Back: Women from national epic. Watermark: Light lines. 135x65mm.

	VF	UNC
a. dark blue on pale blue-gray underprint.	15.00	40.00
b. Deep green on pale green underprint.	10.00	30.00

Note: Check #12 found in circulation from Aug. 1996 to date.

THAILAND

The Kingdom of Thailand, a constitutional monarchy located in the center of mainland southeast Asia between Burma and Lao, has an area of 514,000 sq. km. and a population of 65.49 million. Capital: Bangkok. The economy is based on agriculture and mining. Rubber, rice, teakwood, tin and tungsten are exported. A unified Thai kingdom was established in the mid-14th century. Known as Siam until 1939, Thailand is the only Southeast Asian country never to have been taken over by a European power. A bloodless revolution in 1932 led to a constitutional monarchy. In alliance with Japan during World War II, Thailand became a US treaty ally following the conflict. A military coup in September 2006 ousted then Prime Minister Thaksin Chinnawat. The interim government held elections in December 2007 that saw the pro-Thaksin People's Power Party (PPP) emerge at the head of a coalition government. The anti-Thaksin People's Alliance for Democracy (PAD) in May 2008 began street demonstrations against the new government, eventually occupying the prime minister's office in August. Clashes in October 2008 between PAD protesters blocking parliament and police resulted in the death of at least two people. The PAD occupied Bangkok's international airports briefly, ending their protests in early December 2008 following a court ruling that dissolved the ruling PPP and two other coalition parties for election violations. The Democrat Party then formed a new coalition government with the support of some of Thaksin's former political allies, and Abhisit Wetchachlwa became prime minister. Since January 2004, thousands have been killed as separatists in Thailand's southern ethnic Malay-Muslim provinces increased the violence associated with their cause.

RULERS:
Rama IX (Bhumiphol Adulyadej), 1946-

MONETARY SYSTEM:
1 Baht (Tical) = 100 Satang
1 Tamlung = 4 Baht

REPLACEMENT NOTES:
#63-67, notes w/o suffix letter.

SIGNATURE VARIETIES		
	MINISTER OF FINANCE	**GOVERNOR OF THE BANK OF THAILAND**
34		
35		
36		
37		
38		
39	Chote Kvnakasem - no error -	Chote Kvnakasem
40		Puey Ungpakom
41	S. Vinichchaikul	Puey Ungpakom
42	S. Vinichchaikul	Bisudhi Nimmanhaemin
43	Boonma Wongesesawan	Bisudhi Nimmanhaemin
44	Sommai Hoontrakul	Bisudhi Nimmanhaemin
45	Sawet Piempongsarn	Bisudhi Nimmanhaemin
46	Boonchu Rojanasathien	Bisudhi Nimmanhaemin

SIGNATURE VARIETIES		
	MINISTER OF FINANCE	GOVERNOR OF THE BANK OF THAILAND
47	Boonchu Rojanasathien	Sanoh Unakul
48	Sawet Piempongsarn	Sanoh Unakul
49	Suphat Suthatham	Sanoh Unakul
50	Gen. K. Chomanan	Sanoh Unakul
51	Gen. K. Chomanan	Nukul Prachuabmoh
52	Amnuey Virawan	Nukul Prachuabmoh
53	Sommai Hoontrakul	Nukul Prachuabmoh
54	Sommai Hoontrakul	Kamchorn Sathirakul
55	Suthee Singsaneh	Kamchorn Sathirakul
56	Pramual Sabhavasu	Kamchorn Sathirakul
57	Pramual Sabhavasu	Chavalit Thanachanan
57a	Virabongsa Ramangkul	Chavalit Thanachanan
58	Virabongsa Ramangkul	Vigit Supinit
59	Banharn Silpa-acha	Vigit Supinit
60	Suthee Singsaneh	Vigit Supinit
61	Phanas Simasathien	Vigit Supinit
62	Pedro Malan, 1999 -	Vigit Supinit
63		
64	Surakiart Satirathai	Vigit Supinit
65	Bhodi Joonanond	Vigit Supinit
66	Bhodi Joonanond	Rerngchai Marakanond

SIGNATURE VARIETIES		
	MINISTER OF FINANCE	GOVERNOR OF THE BANK OF THAILAND
67	Amnuey Virawan	Rerngchai Marakanond
68	Thanon Pithaya	Rerngchai Marakanond
69	Thanon Pithaya	Chaiwat Viboonswat
70	Kosit Pampiernras	Chaiwat Viboonswat
71	Tharin Nimahaemin	Chaiwat Viboonswat
72	Tharin Nimahaemin	Jatumongkol Sonakul
73	Somkid Chatursripitak	Jatumongkol Sonakul
74	Somkid Chatursripitak	Preeyadhorn Dhevakul
75	Suchart Chaovisit	Preeyadhorn Dhevakul
76		Preeyadhorn Dhevakul
77		
78		

KINGDOM

Government of Thailand
1953-56 ND Issue

Small Letters in 2-line text on back

Large letters in 2-line text on back

74	**1 Baht**		VF	UNC
	ND (1955). Blue on multicolor underprint. Portrait of King in Field Marshal's uniform with collar insignia and three decorations. Black serial number. Printer: TDLR.			
	a. Watermark: Constitution. Red and blue security threads. Signature 34.		1.00	4.00
	b. Watermark: Constitution. Metal security strip. Signature 34; 35 (Large size).		1.00	3.50
	c. Watermark: King profile. Small letters in 2-line text on back. Signature 35.		0.75	3.00
	d. Watermark: King profile. Larger letters in 2-line text on back. Signature 36; 37; 38; 39; 40; 4l.		0.75	2.50
	s. As a; d. Specimen.		—	250

75   5 Baht   **VF   UNC**

ND (1956). Purple on multicolor underprint. Portrait of King in Field Marshal's uniform with collar insignia and three decorations. Black serial number. Printer: TDLR.

		VF	UNC
a.	Watermark: Constitution. Red and blue security threads. Signature 34.	15.00	50.00
b.	Watermark: Constitution. Metal security strip. Signature 34; 35 (Large size).	2.50	10.00
c.	Watermark: King profile. Small letters in 2-line text on back. Signature 35; 36.	2.50	10.00
d.	Watermark: King profile. Larger letters in 2-line text on back. Signature 38; 39; 40; 41.	1.50	4.50
s.	As a. Specimen.	—	250

76   10 Baht   **VF   UNC**

ND (1953). Brown on multicolor underprint. Portrait of King in Field Marshal's uniform with collar insignia and three decorations. Black serial number. Printer: TDLR.

		VF	UNC
a.	Watermark: Constitution. Red and blue security threads. Signature 34.	2.50	8.00
b.	Watermark: Constitution. Metal security strip. Signature 34; 35 (Large size).	2.50	8.00
c.	Watermark: King profile. Small letters in 2-line text on back. Signature 35; 36; 37; 38; 39.	4.00	12.00
d.	Watermark: King profile. Larger letters in 2-line text on back. Signature 39; 40; 41; 44.	1.00	4.00
s.	As a. Specimen.	—	250

77   20 Baht   **VF   UNC**

ND (1953). Olive-green on multicolor underprint. Portrait of King in Field Marshal's uniform with collar insignia and three decorations. Black serial number. Printer: TDLR.

		VF	UNC
a.	Watermark: Constitution. Red and blue security threads. Signature 34.	4.00	15.00
b.	Watermark: Constitution. Metal security strip. Signature 34; 35 (Large size).	8.00	20.00
c.	Watermark: King profile. Small letters in 2-line text on back. Signature 35; 37; 38.	6.00	15.00
d.	Watermark: King profile. Larger letters in 2-line text on back. Signature 38; 39; 40; 41; 44.	2.00	6.00
s.	As a. Specimen.	—	250

78   100 Baht   **VF   UNC**

ND (1955). Red on multicolor underprint. Portrait of King in Field Marshal's uniform with collar insignia and three decorations. Black serial number. Printer: TDLR.

		VF	UNC
a.	Watermark: Constitution. Red and blue security threads. Signature 34.	20.00	60.00
b.	Watermark: Constitution. Metal security strip. Signature 34; 35; 37.	12.50	30.00
c.	Watermark: King profile. Small letters in 2-line text on back. Signature 38.	10.00	35.00
d.	Watermark: King profile. Larger letters in 2-line text on back. Signature 38 41.	6.00	15.00
s.	As a; c. Specimen.	—	250

Bank of Thailand
1968 Issue; Series 10

79   100 Baht   **VF   UNC**

ND (1968). Red, blue and multicolor. Rama IX in uniform at right. Signature 41; 42. Back: Royal barge. Watermark: Rama IX in uniform. Printer: TDLR.

		VF	UNC
a.	Issued note.	6.50	13.00
s.	Specimen.		

1969 Commemorative Issue
Reportedly 6,000 or 7,000 sets issued.

80   5 Baht   **VF   UNC**

24.6.1969. Purple and multicolor. King Rama IX wearing traditional robes at right. Signature of Finance Minister above, Governor of the Bank of Thailand below at center. Serial number prefix 00A. Signature 41. Back: Aphonphimok Prasat Pavilion. Watermark: King Rama IX. Printer: Thai Banknote Printing Works
                                                                    — 150

81   10 Baht

	VF	UNC
24.6.1969. Brown on multicolor underprint. King Rama IX wearing traditional robes at right. Signature of Finance Minister above, Governor of the Bank of Thailand below at center. Serial number prefix 00A. Signature 41. Back: Wat Benchamabophitr temple. Watermark: King Rama IX. Printer: Thai Banknote Printing Works	—	175

1969-75 ND Issue; Series 11

#82-86 replacement notes: Serial # prefix *S-(W).*

82   5 Baht

	VF	UNC
ND (1969). Purple and multicolor underprint. Like #80 but without commemorative line at bottom. Signature 41; 42. Back: Aphonphimok Prasat Pavilion. Watermark: King Rama IX. Printer: Thai Banknote Printing Works.		
a. Issued note.	0.50	2.00
s. Specimen.	—	—

83   10 Baht

	VF	UNC
ND (1969-78). Brown and multicolor. Like #81 but without commemorative line at bottom. Signature 41; 42; 43; 44; 45; 46; 47; 48; 49; 50; 51; 52; 53. Back: Wat Benchamabophitr temple. Watermark: King Rama IX. Printer: Thai Banknote Printing Works.		
a. Issued note.	0.50	2.00
s. Specimen.	—	—

84   20 Baht

	VF	UNC
ND (1971-81). Dark green, olive-green and multicolor. King Rama IX wearing traditional robes at right. Signature of Finance Minister above, Governor of the Bank of Thailand below at center. Signature 41; 42; 43; 44; 45; 46; 47; 48; 49; 50; 51; 52; 53. Back: Royal barge at left center. Watermark: King Rama IX. Printer: Thai Banknote Printing Works.		
a. Issued note.	1.00	4.00
s. Specimen.	—	—

85   100 Baht

	VF	UNC
ND (1969-78). Red-brown and multicolor. King Rama IX wearing traditional robes at right. Signature of Finance Minister above, Governor of the Bank of Thailand below at center. Back: Emerald Buddha section of Grand Palace. Watermark: King Rama IX. Printer: Thai Banknote Printing Works.		
a. Without black Thai overprint on face. Signature 42; 43; 44; 45; 46; 47; 48; 49.	4.00	8.00
b. Black Thai overprint line just below upper signature for change of title. Signature 43.	10.00	20.00
s. As a. Specimen.	—	40.00

86   500 Baht

	VF	UNC
ND (1975-88). Purple and multicolor. King Rama IX wearing traditional robes at right. Signature of Finance Minister above, Governor of the Bank of Thailand below at center. Signature 47; 49; 50; 51; 52; 53; 54; 55. Back: Pra Prang Sam Yod Lopburi (three towers). Watermark: King Rama IX. Printer: Thai Banknote Printing Works.		
a. Issued note.	10.00	20.00
s. Specimen.	—	—

1978-81 ND Issue; Series 12

#87-89 Kg. Rama IX wearing dk. Field Marshal's uniform at r. and as wmk. Sign. of Finance Minister (upper) and Governor of the Bank of Thailand (lower) at ctr. Replacement notes: Serial # prefix *S-(W).*

87   10 Baht

	VF	UNC
BE2523 (1980). Dark brown on multicolor underprint. King Rama IX wearing dark Field Marshal's uniform at right. Signature of Finance Minister above, Governor of the Bank of Thailand below at center. Signature 52; 53; 54; 55; 56; 57; 58; 59; 60; 61; 63 Back: Mounted statue of King Chulalongkorn. Watermark: King Rama IX.	0.50	1.25

88   20 Baht

VF   UNC

BE2524 (1981). Dark green on multicolor underprint. King Rama IX wearing dark   0.75   2.00
Field Marshal's uniform at right. Signature of Finance Minister above, Governor
of the Bank of Thailand below at center. Signature 53-61; 63; 64; 66; 67; 72-74.
Back: King Taksin's statue at Chantaburi with three armed men. Watermark: King
Rama IX. 139x72mm.

89   100 Baht

VF   UNC

ND (1978). Violet, red and orange on multicolor underprint. King Rama IX wear-   2.00   5.00
ing dark Field Marshal's uniform at right. Signature of Finance Minister above,
Governor of the Bank of Thailand below at center. Signature 49-63. Back: King
Narasuan the Great atop elephant. Watermark: King Rama IX.

1985-92 ND Issue; Series 13

#90-92 replacement notes: Serial # prefix *S-(W)*.

90   50 Baht

VF   UNC

ND (1985-96). Dark blue and purple on multicolor underprint. King Rama IX facing
at right, wearing traditional robe. Back: Palace at left, statue of King Rama VII at
center, his arms and signature at upper left. Watermark: King Rama IX.

a. King with pointed eartips. Signature 54.   2.00   6.00
b. Darker blue color obscuring pointed eartips. Signature 54-60; 63.   1.50   3.00

91   500 Baht

VF   UNC

ND (1988-96). Purple and violet on multicolor underprint. King Rama IX at right in   8.50   20.00
Field Marshal's uniform. Signature 55-61; 63. Back: Statue at center right, palace
in background in underprint at left center. Watermark: King Rama IX.

92   1000 Baht

VF   UNC

BE2535 (1992). Gray, brown, orange and multicolor. King Rama IX at center right.   17.50   35.00
Signature 62-64; 66-67; 69; 71-72. Back: King Rama IX and Queen Sirikit greeting
children at left center in underprint, viewing map at center right. Watermark: King
Rama IX.

1987 Commemorative Issue

#93, King's 60th Birthday

93   60 Baht   **VF   UNC**
BE2530 (5.12.1987). UV: fibers and security strip fluoresce blue. Dark brown on
multicolor underprint. King Rama IX seated on throne at center, Victory crown at
left, Royal regalia at right. Signature 55. Back: Royal family seated with subjects.
a. Issued note.   —   4.00
s. Specimen in blue folder.   —   100

Note: A 40 Baht surcharge was added to issue price of #93, for charity work and the expense of the
special envelope which came with each issued note.

1992 Commemorative Issue
#94 and 95, 90th Birthday of Princess Mother

94   50 Baht   **VF   UNC**
ND (1992). Blue on multicolor underprint. King Rama IX facing at right, wearing
traditional robe over Field Marshall's uniform. Two lines of text added under
watermark. Signature 57. Back: Palace at left, statue of King Rama VII at center,
his arms and signature at upper left. Watermark: Princess Mother's portrait.

95   500 Baht   **VF   UNC**
ND (1992). Purple and multicolor. King Rama IX facing at right, wearing dark Field
Marshall's uniform. Two lines of text added under watermark. Signature 57. Back:
Palace at left, statue of King Rama VII at center, his arms and signature at upper
left. Watermark: Princess Mother's portrait.

#96, Queen Sirikit's 60th Birthday

96   1000 Baht   **VF   UNC**
ND (1992). Black, deep olive-green and yellow-brown on multicolor underprint.   FV   32.50
King Rama IX facing at right. Three lines of commemorative text added under
watermark. Signature 61. Back: King Rama IX and Queen Sirikit greeting children
at left center in underprint, viewing map at center Watermark: Queen Sirikit's
portrait. 166x80mm.

1994 ND Issue

97   100 Baht   **VF   UNC**
BE2537 (1994). Violet, red and brown-orange on multicolor underprint. King Rama   FV   4.00
IX at right. Signature 63-65; 67-75. Back: Statue of King Rama V and Rama VI
with children; Royal initial emblem in center. 150x72mm.

1995 Commemorative Issue
Text at lower margin:

๑๒๐ ปี กระทรวงการคลัง วันที่ ๑๔ เมษายน พุทธศักราช ๒๕๓๘

98   10 Baht   **VF   UNC**
ND (1995). Dark brown on multicolor underprint. King Rama IX wearing dark Field   —   2.00
Marshal's uniform at right. Signature of Finance Minister above, Governor of the
Bank of Thailand below at center. Commemorative text in lower margin. Signature
63. Back: Mounted statue of King Chulalongkorn. Watermark: King Rama IX.

1996 Commemorative Issue
#99 and 101, 50th Anniversary of Reign

99   50 Baht   **VF   UNC**
ND (1996). Polymer plastic. Purple on light blue and multicolor underprint. King FV   4.00
Rama IX wearing Field Marshal's uniform at right and as a shadow design in clear
area at left, royal seal of kingdom at upper right. Signature 66, 67. Back: Palace
at left, statue of King Rama VII at center, his arms and signature at upper left.
Printer: NPA (without imprint).

100 500 Baht VF UNC

ND (1996). Purple and red-violet on multicolor underprint. King Rama IX at right with Crowned Royal seal with 50 at center right, arms above dancers at right replacing crowned radiant Chakra at left center. Signature 64. Back: Temple of the Emerald Buddha at left, King Rama I and Rama II at left center. FV 20.00

101 500 Baht VF UNC

ND (1996). Polymer plastic. Multicolor. King Rama IX seated in royal attire at center right, hologram of King at upper right. Signature 64; 66. Back: King holding map at center, waterfalls at left, farmers in terraced landscape at right. Printer: NPA (without imprint).

    a. Issued note. — 60.00

    s. Specimen. Red overprint. Issued in folder. — 300

Note: #101 was also issued in a box with booklet about the king. Issue price was $60.00.

1996-97 ND Regular Issue

102 50 Baht VF UNC

BE2540. (1997). Polymer plastic. Black on light blue and multicolor underprint. King Rama IX in Field Marshal's uniform at center right, arms at upper left. Signature 67, 71; 72; 74. Back: King Rama VI seated at table at center right, royal arms at upper left center, medieval ship's prow at lower right. Printer: NPA (without imprint). 144x72mm.

    a. Issued note. FV 2.00

    s. Specimen. — 400

103 500 Baht VF UNC

BE2539 (1996). Purple and red-violet on multicolor underprint. King Rama IX at right in Field Marshall's uniform. Arms at upper left, radiant crowned Chakra seal on platform at left center. Signature 64; 66; 67; 69; 72. Back: Temple of the Emerald Buddha at left, King Rama I and Rama II at left center. Watermark: King Rama IX. 156x71mm FV 20.00

1999 Commemorative Issue

#104, 72nd Birthday of King

104 1000 Baht VF UNC

BE2542. 1000. Brown, orange and yellow on multicolor underprint. King Rama IX at right center in Field Marshall's uniform. Green seal has scroll below. Signature 72. Back: King with camera at right, Pa Sak Jolasid Dam at left. 162x72mm. FV 32.50

2000 Commemorative Issue

#105, 106 Golden Wedding Anniversary

105 50 Baht VF UNC

ND (2000). Issued in special folder. Brown and tan on multicolor underprint. Conjoined profiles of King Rama IX and Queen Sirikit. Signature 72. Back: Views of their family life. 126x205mm. — 60.00

106 500,000 Baht VF UNC

ND (2000). (1998 pieces printed). Brown and tan on multicolor underprint. Conjoined profiles of King Rama IX and Queen Sirikit. Signature 72. Back: Views of their family life. — 31,000

2000-01 ND Issue

107	**500 Baht**	VF	UNC
	ND (2001). Blue and rose on multicolor underprint. King Rama IX at right in Field Marshall's unifrom. Signature 74; 75; 76; 78. Back: Statue and palace. 156x72mm.	FV	22.50

108	**1000 Baht**	VF	UNC
	ND (2000). Brown, orange and yellow on multicolor underprint. King Rama IX at right center in Field Marshall's uniform. Center green seal set on an octagonal base. Signature 72; 73; 74; 75; 76; 78. Back: King with camera at right, Pa Sak Jolasid Dam at left. 162x72mm.	FV	45.00

2002 ND Issue

109	**20 Baht**	VF	UNC
	ND (2003). Green on green and tan multicolor underprint. King Rama IX wearing Field Marshal's uniform at center right. Signature 74; 75; 76; 77; 78. Back: Procession with King in military uniform and new bridge.	FV	1.50

2002 Commemorative Issue

110	**100 Baht**	VF	UNC
	ND (2002). Brown and slate blue on green and multicolor underprint. Kings Rama V and Rama IX at right. Signature 74; 75. Back: Facsimile print of #12a.	—	7.00

2004 Commemorative Issue

#111, Queen's 72nd Birthday. Issued in a folder.

111	**100 Baht**	VF	UNC
	2004. Multicolor. King Rama IX standing and Queen Sirikit seated. Signature 72.. Signature 74. Back: Queen standing, views of her life.	—	10.00

2004 Second Commemorative Issue

Commemorating the opening of the Printing Works.

111A	**50 Baht**	VF	UNC
	ND (2004). Slate black on light blue and multicolor underprint. King Rama IX wearing uniform. Red overprint above emblem at left center, and line of text below portrait. Back: King Rama IV seated. Printer: NPW. 144x72mm.	FV	25.00
118	**100 Baht**	VF	UNC
	ND (2010). Red and orange on multicolor underprint. King Rama IX wearing uniform. Back: King Rama IX and Queen Sirikit at center. Rama IX seated at right wearing crown. Printer: NPW.	FV	5.00

2004 Issue

112	**50 Baht**	VF	UNC
	ND (2004). Like #102 but paper. Slate black on light blue and multicolor. King Rama IX in Field Marshall's uniform at center right, arms at upper left. Signature 74; 75; 76. Back: King Rama VI seated at table at center right, telescope and globe at center left, royal arms at upp Printer: NPA (without imprint). 144x72mm.	FV	2.00

113 100 Baht VF UNC
ND (2004). Holographic strip at left. Like #97. Violet, red and brown orange on FV 3.50
multicolor underprint. King Rama IX at right. Back: Statue of King Rama V and
Rama VI with children. Royal emblem at center. 150x83mm.

2005 Issue

115 1000 Baht VF UNC
ND (2005). Like #108. Brown, orange and yellow on multicolor underprint. King FV 35.00
Rama IX at rigth center in Field Marshal uniform. Wide security foil at left. Back:
King with camera at right, Pa Sak Jolasid Dam at left.

2006 Commemorative Issue

116 60 Baht VF UNC
9.6.2006. Red and orange. King Rama IX seated on royal throne at left. Back: FV 8.00
King visiting his people, Khun Dan Prakan Chon Dam in Nakon Nayok province in
background. 162x81mm.

2007 Commemorative Issue

117 16 Baht VF UNC
2007. Blue, purple, brown on multicolor underprint. Three early notes of 1, 5 and
10 Bhat. Back: Full design forming a montage of important events in king's life
   a. Issued note in commemorative folder. — 25.00
   b. Issued note without folder. — 10.00
   s. Specimen. — 100

2010-15 Issue

		VF	UNC
119	**100 Baht**	**VF**	**UNC**
	2010.	FV	3.50
120	**50 Baht**	**VF**	**UNC**
	2011.	FV	2.00
122	**80 Baht**	**VF**	**UNC**
	2012.	FV	3.00
123	**100 Baht**	**VF**	**UNC**
	2012.	FV	3.50
124	**20 Baht**	**VF**	**UNC**
	2013.	FV	1.50
125	**500 Baht**	**VF**	**UNC**
	ND (2013).	FV	20.00
127	**100 Baht**	**VF**	**UNC**
	ND (2015).		
	a. Issued note.	FV	3.50
	r. Replacement note.	FV	3.50

2011 Commemorative Issue

121 100 Baht VF UNC
2011. King's 7th Cycle Birthday. FV 3.50

2014 Commemorative Issue

126 100 Baht

	VF	UNC
	FV	8.00

2015. Princess Maha Chakri Sirindhorn's 5th Cycle Birthday Anniversary. Red, orange, brown and green. Royal Garuda emblem, King Rama IX in the Royal House of Chakri gown. Back: Royal Garuda embem, Kind Rama IX walking with Princess Maha Chakri Sirindhorn, flower. Holographic stripe, gold-to-green windowed security thread with demetalized 1100 บาท 100 BAHT. Watermark: King Rama IX and electrotype ๑๐๐. Printer: (NPW). 150x72mm.

Collector Series
1991 Commemorative Issue
#CS1, World Bank Group / International Monetary Fund Annual Meetings

CS1 1991 10, 20, 50, 100, 500 Baht

	Mkt. Value
	600

#87-91 with overprint: 1991 World Bank Group/IMF Annual Meetings in English and Thai. Specimen. (Issued in blue hanging folder).

TIMOR

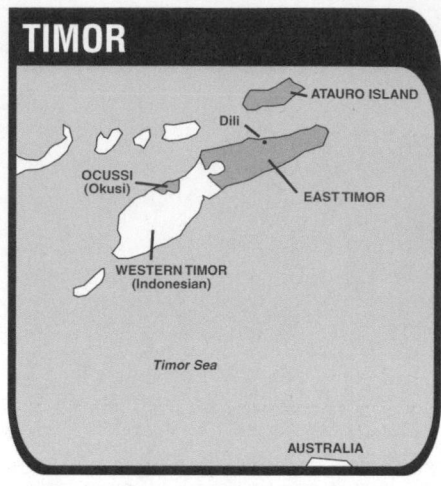

Timor, is an island between the Savu and Timor Seas, has an area, including the former colony of Portuguese Timor, of 11,883 sq. mi. (30,775 sq. km.) and a population of 1.5 million. Western Timor is administered as part of Nusa Tenggara Timur (East Nusa Tenggara) province. Capital: Kupang. The eastern half of the island, the former Portuguese colony, forms a single province, Timor Timur (East Timor). Originally the Portuguese colony also included the area around Ocussi-Ambeno and the small island of Atauro (Pulau Kambing) located north of Dili. Capital: Dili. Timor exports sandalwood, coffee, tea, hides, rubber and copra. Portuguese traders reached Timor about 1520, and moved to the north and east when the Dutch established themselves in Kupang, a sheltered bay at the southwestern tip, in 1613. Treaties effective in 1860 and 1914 established the boundaries between the two colonies. Japan occupied the entire island during World War II. The former Portuguese Province of Timor attained independence as the People's Democratic Republic of East Timur. In Dec., 1975 or early in 1976 the government of the People's Democratic Republic was seized by a guerilla faction sympathetic to the Indonesian territorial claim to East Timur which ousted the constitutional government and replaced it with the Provisional Government of East Timur. On July 17, 1976, the Provisional Government enacted a law which dissolved the free republic and made East Timur the 24th province of Indonesia. In 1999 a revolution suceeded, and it is once again an independent country.

Note: For later issues see Indonesia.

MONETARY SYSTEM:
 1 Escudo = 100 Centavos, 1958-1975

SIGNATURE VARIETIES		
	O ADMINISTRADOR	O GOVERNADOR
1		
2		
3		
4		
5		
6		
7		
8		

PORTUGUESE ADMINISTRATION
Banco Nacional Ultramarino
Decretos - Lei 39221e 44891; 1963-68 Issue

26 20 Escudos

	VF	UNC

24.10.1967. Olive-brown on multicolor underprint. Portrait of R. D. Aleixo at right. Signature 3; 8. Back: Bank ship seal at left, crowned arms at center. Printer: BWC.

		VF	UNC
a. Issued note.		2.50	7.50
s. Specimen.		—	—

27 50 Escudos VF UNC

24.10.1967. Blue on multicolor underprint. Portrait of R. D. Aleixo at right.
Signature 2; 4; 5; 6; 8. Back: Bank ship seal at left, crowned arms at center.
Printer: BWC.

    a. Issued note.   4.00   12.50
    s. Specimen.   —   160

28 100 Escudos VF UNC

25.4.1963. Brown on multicolor underprint. Portrait of R. D. Aleixo at right. Signature 1-3; 8. Back: Bank ship seal at left, crowned arms at center. Printer: BWC.

    a. Issued note.   4.50   15.00
    s1. Specimen. Punched hole cancelled. Without signatures.   —   300
    s2. Specimen. Punch hole cancel with signatures. Overprint: ESPECIME. — 350

29 500 Escudos VF UNC

25.4.1963. Dark brown on multicolor underprint. Portrait of R. D. Aleixo at right.
Signature 1-3; 8; 9. Back: Bank ship seal at left, crowned arms at center. Printer: BWC.

    a. Issued note.   10.00   30.00
    s. Specimen.   —   175

30 1000 Escudos VF UNC

21.3.1968. Green on multicolor underprint. Portrait of R. D. Aleixo at right.
Signature 2; 8. Back: Bank ship seal at left, crowned arms at center. Printer: BWC.

    a. Issued note.   20.00   55.00
    s. Specimen.   —   185

1969 ND Provisional Issue

31 20 Escudos VF UNC

ND. Specimen. Green on multicolor underprint. Régulo Jose Nunes at left. Back: Bank seal at center, local huts on pilings at right.   —   —

32 500 Escudos VF UNC

ND (1969 - old date 22.3.1967). Brown and violet on multicolor underprint. Overprint: *PAGAVEL EM TIMOR* on Mozambique #110. Back: Overprint: *PAGAVEL EM TIMOR* on Mozambique #110.   350   750

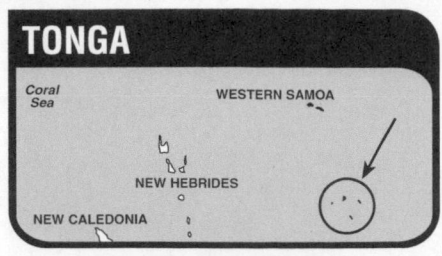

TONGA

The Kingdom of Tonga (or Friendly Islands), a member of the British Commonwealth, is an archipelago situated in the southern Pacific Ocean south of Western Samoa and east of Fiji comprising 150 islands. Tonga has an area of 748 sq. km. and a population of 119,000. Capital: Nuku'alofa. Primarily agricultural, the kingdom exports bananas and copra. Tonga - unique among Pacific nations - never completely lost its indigenous governance. The archipelagos of "The Friendly Islands" were united into a Polynesian kingdom in 1845. Tonga became a constitutional monarchy in 1875 and a British protectorate in 1900; it withdrew from the protectorate and joined the Commonwealth of Nations in 1970. Tonga remains the only monarchy in the Pacific.

RULERS:
Queen Salote III, 1918-1965
King Taufa'ahau IV, 1967-2005
King Taufa'ahau V, 2005-2012
King Tupoutoia Lavaka Ata, 2012-

MONETARY SYSTEM:
1 Pound = 20 Shillings to 1967
1 Pa'anga = 100 Seniti, 1967-

REPLACEMENT NOTES:
#18-24, Z/1 prefix.

KINGDOM

Government of Tonga
1939-42 Issue

9   4 Shillings

1941-66. Brown on multicolor underprint. *FOUR SHILLINGS* at left and right. Arms at center. Printer: TDLR.

	VF	UNC
a. 1.12.1941-8.9.1947. 3 signatures.	125	450
b. 7.2.1949; 15.2.1951; 20.7.1951; 6.9.1954.	100	375
c. 19.9.1955-30.11.1959.	25.00	150
d. 24.10.1960-27.9.1966.	25.00	85.00
e. 3.11.1966. 2 signatures.	20.00	50.00

10   10 Shillings

1939-66. Green on multicolor underprint. *TEN SHILLINGS* at left and right. Arms at center. Printer: TDLR.

	VF	UNC
a. 3.5.1940; 17.10.1941-28.11.1944. 3 signatures.	250	—
b. 9.7.1949-1955.	150	450
c. 2.5.1956; 22.7.1957; 10.12.1958; 13.10.1959.	35.00	300
d. 24.10.1960; 28.11.1962; 29.7.1964; 22.6.1965.	30.00	125
e. 3.11.1966. 2 signatures.	22.50	65.00
s. Specimen. As b, d. Perforated: *CANCELLED*.	—	300

11   1 Pound

1940-66. Red on multicolor underprint. *ONE POUND* at left and right. Arms at center. Printer: TDLR.

	VF	UNC
a. 3.5.1940-7.11.1944. 3 signatures.	275	—
b. 15.6.1951; 11.9.1951; 19.9.1955.	175	550
c. 2.5.1956; 10.12.1958; 30.11.1959; 12.12.1961.	70.00	425
d. 28.11.1962; 30.10.1964; 2.11.1965; 3.11.1966.	40.00	150
e. 2.12.1966. 2 signatures.	15.00	100
s. Specimen. Perforated: *CACNELLED*.	—	500

12   5 Pounds

1942-66. Dark blue on multicolor underprint. *FIVE POUNDS* at left and right. Arms at center. Printer: TDLR.

	VF	UNC
a. 11.3.1942-1945. 3 signatures.	2,000	—
b. 15.6.1951; 5.7.1955; 11.9.1956; 26.6.1958.	1,500	—
c. 30.11.1959; 2.11.1965.	500	1,000
d. 2.12.1966. 2 signatures.	60.00	150

Pule' Anga 'o Tonga
GOVERNMENT OF TONGA
1967 Issue

13   1/2 Pa'anga

1967-73. Dark brown on pink underprint. Arms at lower left. Queen Salote III at right. Various date and signature varieties. Back: Coconut workers at left.

		VF	UNC
a.	3.4.1967.	20.00	100
b.	19.5.1969; 27.10.1969.	35.00	125
c.	10.3.1970; 16.6.1970.	32.50	125
d.	4.2.1971; 14.4.1971; 24.7.1972.	35.00	150
e.	13.6.1973; 2.8.1973. 2 signatures.	50.00	250
s.	ND. Specimen.	—	70.00

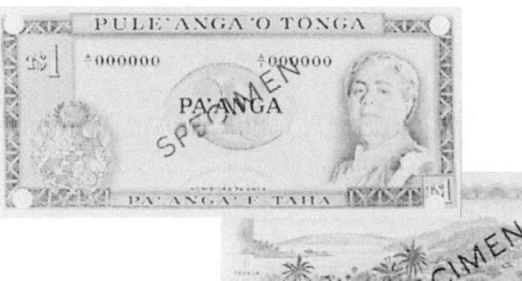

14   1 Pa'anga

1967; 1970-71. Olive-green on multicolor underprint. Arms at lower left. Queen Salote III at right. Various date and signature varieties. Back: River scene, palm trees.

		VF	UNC
a.	3.4.1967.	20.00	125
b.	12.4.1967; 2.10.1967; 8.12.1967.	40.00	150
c.	10.3.1970; 16.6.1970.	45.00	165
d.	4.2.1971; 19.10.1971.	60.00	235
s.	ND. Specimen.	—	70.00

15   2 Pa'anga

1967-73. Red on multicolor underprint. Arms at lower left. Queen Salote III at right. Various date and signature varieties. Back: Women making Tapa cloth.

		VF	UNC
a.	3.4.1967.	35.00	200
b.	2.10.1967; 8.12.1967.	50.00	250
c.	19.5.1969; 10.3.1970; 19.10.1971.	60.00	250
d.	24.7.1972; 10.11.1972; 2.8.1973.	60.00	300
e.	12.11.1973. 2 signatures.	100	500
s.	ND. Specimen.	—	70.00

16   5 Pa'anga

1967; 1973. Purple on multicolor underprint. Arms at lower left. Queen Salote III at right. Various date and signature varieties. Back: Ha'amonga stone gateway.

		VF	UNC
a.	3.4.1967.	80.00	350
b.	13.6.1973.	100	550
c.	4.9.1973; 6.12.1973. 2 signatures.	150	600
s.	ND. Specimen.		100

17   10 Pa'anga

1967; 1973. Dark blue on multicolor underprint. Arms at lower left. Queen Salote III at right. Various date and signature varieties. Back: Royal Palace.

		VF	UNC
a.	3.4.1967.	125	600
b.	2.10.1967; 8.12.1967.	200	775
c.	13.6.1973; 16.7.1973.	250	1,200
s.	ND. Specimen.	—	150

1974; 1985 Issue

#18-22 Replacement notes: Serial # prefix Z/1.

18   1/2 Pa'anga

1974-83. Dark brown on pink underprint. Arms at lower left. King Taufa'ahau at right. Signature varieties. Back: Coconut workers at left.

		VF	UNC
a.	2 signatures. 2.10.1974; 19.6.1975.	6.00	17.50
b.	3 signatures. 12.1.1977; 17.5.1977; 10.9.1979.	4.00	15.00
c.	As b. 28.11.1979; 27.8.1980; 31.7.1981; 17.8.1982; 29.7.1983.	3.00	12.00
s.	As a. Specimen.	—	—

19   1 Pa'anga

1974-89. Olive-green on multicolor underprint. Arms at lower left. King Taufa'ahau at right. Signature varieties. Back: River scene, palm trees.

		VF	UNC
a.	6.12.1973.	25.00	100
b.	2 signatures. 31.7.1974; 19.6.1975; 21.8.1975; 5.8.1976; 21.1.1981; 18.5.1983.	3.50	12.50
c.	3 signatures. 5.8.1976-11.6.1980; 31.7.1981-28.10.1982; 27.7.1983-30.6.1989.	2.00	7.50
s.	As a. Specimen.	—	—

20　2 Pa'anga　　　　　　　　　　　　　　　**VF　UNC**
1974-89. Red on multicolor underprint. Arms at lower left. King Taufa'ahau at right.
Signature varieties. Back: Women making Tapa cloth.

a. 2 signatures. 2.10.1974; 19.6.1975; 21.8.1975; 21.1.1981.	3.50	15.00
b. 3 signatures. 12.1.1977-27.8.1980;	4.00	17.50
c. 3 signatures. 31.7.1981-30.6.1989.	2.75	12.00
s. As a. Specimen.	—	—

21　5 Pa'anga　　　　　　　　　　　　　　　**VF　UNC**
1974-89. Purple on multicolor underprint. Arms at lower left. King Taufa'ahau at
right. Signature varieties. Back: Ha'amonga stone gateway.

a. 2 signatures. 3.9.1974; 2.10.1974; 19.6.1975; 21.1.1981.	7.50	37.50
b. 3 signatures. 21.12.1976-28.11.1980.	6.50	27.50
c. 3 signatures. 27.5.1981-30.6.1989.	5.00	20.00
s. As a. Specimen.	—	—

22　10 Pa'anga　　　　　　　　　　　　　　**VF　UNC**
1974-89. Dark blue on multicolor underprint. Arms at lower left. King Taufa'ahau at
right. Signature varieties. Back: Royal Palace.

a. 2 signatures. 3.9.1974; 31.7.1974; 3.9.1974; 19.6.1975; 21.1.1981.	12.00	65.00
b. 3 signatures. 12.12.1976-28.11.1980.	10.00	50.00
c. 3 signatures. 27.5.1981-30.6.1989.	7.50	35.00
s. As a. Specimen.	—	—

23　20 Pa'anga　　　　　　　　　　　　　　**VF　UNC**
1985-89. Orange on green and multicolor underprint. King in new design at center
right, arms at right. Back: Tonga Development Bank. Watermark: King in new
design.

a. 4.7.1985.	35.00	150
b. 18.7.1985; 3.10.1985; 8.1.1986; 27.2.1987; 28.9.1987.	27.50	55.00
c. 20.5.1988; 14.12.1988; 23.1.1989; 30.6.1989.	25.00	50.00

Note: #23a was made in limited quantities in celebration of the king's birthday.

Kingdom of Tonga
1988 Issue

24　50 Pa'anga　　　　　　　　　　　　　　**VF　UNC**
1988-89. Brown and green on multicolor underprint. King in new design at center
right, arms at right. Back: Vava'u Harbor. Watermark: Portrait of King in new design.

a. 4.7.1988.	65.00	225
b. 14.12.1988; 30.6.1989.	55.00	100

Note: #24a was issued in celebration of the king's birthday. (5,000 pcs.).

National Reserve Bank of Tonga
1992 ND Issue

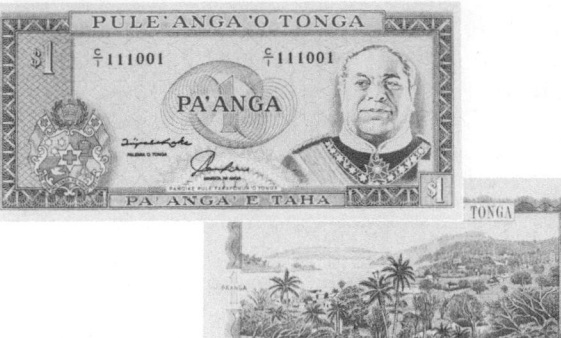

25　1 Pa'anga　　　　　　　　　　　　　　　**VF　UNC**
ND (1992-95). Olive-green on multicolor underprint. Arms at lower left. King　　FV　3.50
Taufa'ahau at right. Two signatures with Tongan titles beneath. Back: River scene,
palm trees.

26　2 Pa'anga　　　　　　　　　　　　　　　**VF　UNC**
ND (1992-95). Red on multicolor underprint. Arms at lower left. King Taufa'ahau at　FV　6.00
right. Two signatures with Tongan titles beneath. Back: Women making Tapa cloth.

27　5 Pa'anga　　　　　　　　　　　　　　　**VF　UNC**
ND (1992-95). Purple on multicolor underprint. Arms at lower left. King Taufa'ahau　FV　15.00
at right. Two signatures with Tongan titles beneath. Back: Ha'amonga stone
gateway.

28　10 Pa'anga　　　　　　　　　　　　　　**VF　UNC**
ND (1992-95). Dark blue on multicolor underprint. Arms at lower left. King　　FV　30.00
Taufa'ahau at right. Two signatures with Tongan titles beneath. Back: Royal
Palace.

29　20 Pa'anga　　　　　　　　　　　　　　**VF　UNC**
ND (1992-95). Orange and green on multicolor underprint. King in new design at　FV　45.00
center right, arms at right. Two signatures with Tongan titles beneath. Back: Tonga
Development Bank. Watermark: Portrait of King.

1989 Commemorative Issue
#30, Inauguration of National Reserve Bank of Tonga

30　20 Pa'anga　　　　　　　　　　　　　　**VF　UNC**
1.7.1989. Orange on green and multicolor underprint. King in new design at center
right, arms at right, commemorative text in circle on watermark area. Back: Vava'u
Harbour, commemorative text in circle on watermark area. Watermark: King in
new design.

a. Issued note.	20.00	65.00
s. Specimen. Red overprint: SPECIMEN once on each side.	—	75.00

1995 ND Issue

31 1 Pa'anga VF UNC
ND (1995). UV: value 1 in box fluorese yellow. Olive-green and green on multi-color underprint. King Taufa'ahau at upper center right, arms at right. Signature varieties. Back: River scene, palm trees. Watermark: King Taufa'ahau. Printer: TDLR. 150x70mm.

	VF	UNC
a. Signature N-D.	2.00	6.00
b. Signature U-F.	FV	3.00
c. Signature U-U.	FV	3.00

32 2 Pa'anga VF UNC
ND (1995). Red and reddish-brown on multicolor underprint. King Taufa'ahau at upper center right, arms at right. Signature varieties. Back: Women making Tapa cloth. Watermark: King Taufa'ahau. Printer: TDLR. 150x70mm.

	VF	UNC
a. Signature N-D.	3.00	7.50
b. Signature U-F.	FV	4.50

33 5 Pa'anga VF UNC
ND (1995). Purple and violet on multicolor underprint. King Taufa'ahau at upper center right, arms at right. Signature varieties. Back: Ha'amonga stone gateway. Watermark: King Taufa'ahau. Printer: TDLR. 150x70mm.

	VF	UNC
a. Signature N-F. Series A.	FV	10.00
b. Signature U-U. Series B.	FV	8.00
c. Series C.	FV	8.00

34 10 Pa'anga VF UNC
ND (1995). Dark blue on multicolor underprint. King Taufa'ahau at upper center right, arms at right. Signature varieties. Back: Royal Palace. Watermark: King Taufa'ahau. Printer: TDLR. 150x70mm.

	VF	UNC
a. Signature N-D.	20.00	35.00
b. Signature U-F.	FV	22.50
c. Signature U-U.	FV	17.50

35 20 Pa'anga VF UNC
ND. Orange and multicolor. King in new design at center right, arms at right. Two signatures with Tongan titles beneath. Back: Tonga Development Bank. Watermark: Portrait of King in new design. 150x70mm.

	VF	UNC
a. Signature N-D.	40.00	35.00
b. Signature N-F.	FV	40.00
c. Signature U-U.	FV	30.00
d. Signature U-F.	FV	30.00

36 50 Pa'anga VF UNC
ND. Brown and green on multicolor underprint. King in new design at center right. Signature U-U. Back: View of the harbor. 150x70mm.

FV 85.00

2008 Issue

37 1 Pa'anga VF UNC
ND (2008). Green on multicolor underprint. King Tupou V at right. Back: Whale.

FV 2.50

38   2 Pa'anga

ND (2008). Red and reddish brown on multicolor underprint. King Tupou V at right. Back: Education and sports.

	VF	UNC
	FV	5.00

39   5 Pa'anga

ND (2008). Purple and violet on multicolor underprint. King Tupou V at right. Back: Langi (large ceremonial tomb).

	VF	UNC
	FV	8.50

40   10 Pa'anga

ND (2008). Blue and olive green on multicolor underprint. King Tupou V at right. Back: Royal tomb.

	VF	UNC
	FV	15.00

41   20 Pa'anga

ND (2008). Brown and light olive green on multicolor underprint. King Tupou V at right. Back: National Reserve Bank of Tonga building.

	VF	UNC
	FV	27.50

42   50 Pa'anga

ND (2008). Green and tan on multicolor underprint. King Tupou V at right. Back: Palace.

	VF	UNC
	FV	70.00

43   100 Pa'anga

ND (2008). Maroon and red on multicolor underprint. King Tupou V at right. Back: Vava'u harbor.

	VF	UNC
	FV	135

2015 Issue

44   2 Pa'anga

ND (2015). Light red. King Tupou VI, coat of arms. Back: Whale leaping out of water, medallion. Prefix A. Watermark: King Tupou VI, electrotype NRBT and Cornerstones. Printer: TDLR. 150x70mm.

	VF	UNC
	FV	7.00

45   5 Pa'anga

ND (2015). Purple. King Tupou VI, coat of arms. Back: Langi, medallion. 1.4mm windowed security thread with demetalized NRBT. Prefix A. Watermark: King Tupou VI, electrotype NRBT and Cornerstones. Printer: TDLR. 150x70mm.

	VF	UNC
	FV	10.00

46 10 Pa'anga

VF UNC
FV 15.00

ND (2015). Blue. King Tupou VI, coat of arms. Back: Royal tomb, medallion. 2.0mm red-to-green windowed security thread with demetalized NRBT. Prefix A. Watermark: King Tupou VI, electrotype NRBT and Cornerstones. Printer: TDLR. 150x70mm.

47 20 Pa'anga

VF UNC
FV 28.00

ND (2015). Brown. King Tupou VI, coat of arms. Back: NRBT building medallion. 2.0mm red-to-green windowed security thread with demetalized NRBT. Prefix A. Watermark: King Tupou VI, electrotype NRBT and Cornerstones. Printer: TDLR. 150x70mm.

48 50 Pa'anga

VF UNC
FV 45.00

ND (2015). Light green and yellow. King Tupou VI, coat of arms. Back: Royal Palace building, medallion. Optiks security thread. Prefix A. Watermark: King Tupou VI, electrotype NRBT and Cornerstones. Printer: TDLR. 150x70mm.

49 100 Pa'anga

VF UNC
FV 145

ND (2015). Cherry red and white. King Tupou VI, coat of arms. Back: Vava'u Harbor, medallion. Optiks security thread. Watermark: King Tupou VI, electrotype NRBT and Cornerstones. Printer: TDLR. 150x70mm.

COLLECTOR SERIES

Government of Tonga

1978 Issue

CS1 1978 1-10 Pa'anga

Mkt. Value

#19b-22b overprint: *SPECIMEN* and prefix serial # Maltese cross. 70.00

TRANSNISTRIA

The Transnistria Moldavian Republic was formed in 1990, even before the separation of Moldavia from Russia. It has an area of 11,544 sq. mi. (29,900 sq. km.) and a population of 700,000. Capital: Tiraspol. The area was conquered from the Turks in the last half of the 18th Century, and in 1792 the capital city of Tiraspol was founded. After 1812, the area called Bessarabia (present Moldova and part of the Ukraine) became part of the Russian Empire. During the Russian Revolution, in 1918, the area was taken by Romanian troops, and in 1924 the Moldavian Autonomous SSR was formed on the left bank of the Dniester River. A Romanian occupation area between the Dniester and Bug Rivers called *Transnistria* was established in October 1941. Its center was the port of Odessa. A special issue of notes for use in Transnistria was made by the Romanian government. In 1944 the Russians recaptured Transnistria. Once the Moldavian SSR declared independence in August 1991. Transnistria did not want to be a part of Moldova. In 1992, Moldova tried to solve the issue militarily. Transnistria has a president, parliament, army and police forces, but as yet is lacking international recognition.

MONETARY SYSTEM:

1 Ruble = 1,000 old Rubles (August 1994)
1 Ruble = 1,000,000 old Rubles (January 2001)

REPUBLIC

Government

1994 ND Provisional Issues

#1-15 issued 24.1.1994, invalidated on 1.12.1994. The Bank purchased used Russian notes and placed stickers on them. Most collectors feel that "uncirculated" notes currently available were made after 1994.

1 10 Rublei

VF UNC
2.00 4.00

ND (1994- old date 1961). Green on pink tint adhesive stamp on Russia #233.

2 10 Rublei

VF UNC
2.00 4.00

ND (1994- old date 1991). Green on pink tint adhesive stamp on Russia # 240.

3 25 Rublei

VF UNC
2.00 5.00

ND (1994- old date 1961). Red-violet on buff tint adhesive stamp on Russia # 234.

4 50 Rublei   **VF UNC**
ND (1994- old date 1991). Red on pale green tint adhesive stamp on Russia #241.   6.00   12.00
5 50 Rublei   **VF UNC**
ND (1994- old date 1992). Red on pale green tint adhesive stamp on Russia #247.   3.00   8.00

6 100 Rublei   **VF UNC**
ND (1994- old date 1991). Black on pale blue tint adhesive stamp on Russia #242.   6.00   12.00
7 100 Rublei   **VF UNC**
ND (1994- old date 1991). Black on pale blue tint adhesive stamp on Russia #243.   3.00   8.00

8 200 Rublei   **VF UNC**
ND (1994- old date 1991). Green on yellow tint adhesive stamp on Russia # 244.   10.00   30.00

9 200 Rublei   **VF UNC**
ND (1994- old date 1992). Green on yellow tint adhesive stamp on Russia #248.   3.00   6.00

10 500 Rublei   **VF UNC**
ND (1994- old date 1991). Blue adhesive stamp on Russia #245.   20.00   40.00
11 500 Rublei   **VF UNC**
ND (1994- old date 1992). Blue adhesive stamp on Russia # 249.   2.00   7.00

12 1000 Rublei   **VF UNC**
ND (1994- old date 1991). Violet on yellow tint adhesive stamp on Russia #246.   20.00   50.00
13 1000 Rublei   **VF UNC**
ND (1994- old date 1992). Violet on yellow tint adhesive stamp on Russia #250.   3.00   8.00
14 5000 Rublei   **VF UNC**
ND (1994- old date 1992). Dark brown on pale blue-gray tint adhesive stamp on Russia #252.   2.00   6.00

14A 5000 Rublei   **VF UNC**
ND (1994 -old date 1961). Adhesive stamp on Russia 5 Rubles #224.   2.00   4.00

14B 5000 Rublei   **VF UNC**
ND (1994 -old date 1991). Adhesive stamp on Russia 5 Rubles # 239.   2.00   5.00
15 10,000 Rublei   **VF UNC**
ND (1994- old date 1992). Purple on yellow tint adhesive stamp on Russia #253.   2.00   5.00

БАНКА НИСТРЯНЭ

Banka Nistriana

1993; 1994 КУПОН Kupon Issue

#16-18 Note: Postal adhesive stamps have been seen affixed to #16-18 to imitate revalidated notes.

16 1 Ruble   **VF UNC**
1994. UV: fibers fluoresce yellow and red. Dark green on multicolor underprint. Alexander Vassilievitch Suvurov at right. Back: Parliament building at center. Watermark: Block design.   0.50   1.00

17 5 Rublei
1994. UV: fibers fluoresce yellow and red. Blue on multicolor underprint. Alexander Vassilievitch Suvurov at right. Back: Parliament building at center. Watermark: Block design.

	VF	UNC
	0.50	1.00

18 10 Rublei
1994. UV: fibers fluoresce yellow and red. Red-violet on multicolor underprint. Alexander Vassilievitch Suvurov at right. Back: Parliament building at contor. Watermark: Block design.

	VF	UNC
	0.50	1.00

19 50 Rublei
1993 (1994). Green on multicolor underprint. Equestrian statue of Alexander Vassilievitch Suvurov at right. Back: Parliament building at center. Watermark: Block design

	VF	UNC
	1.00	2.00

20 100 Rublei
1993 (1994). Dark brown on multicolor underprint. Equestrian statue of Alexander Vassilievitch Suvurov at right. Back: Parliament building at center. Watermark: Block design.

	VF	UNC
	1.00	2.00

21 200 Rublei
1993 (1994). Red-violet on multicolor underprint. Equestrian statue of Alexander Vassilievitch Suvurov at right. Back: Parliament building at center. Watermark: Block design.

	VF	UNC
	1.00	4.00

22 500 Rublei
1993 (1994). Blue on multicolor underprint. Equestrian statue of Alexander Vassilievitch Suvurov at right. Back: Parliament building at center. Watermark: Block design.

	VF	UNC
	2.00	5.00

23 1000 Rublei
1993 (1994). Purple and red violet on multicolor underprint. Equestrian statue of Alexander Vassilievitch Suvurov at right. Back: Parliament building at center. Watermark: Block design.

	VF	UNC
	2.00	5.00

24 5000 Rublei
1993 (1995). Black on deep olive-green and multicolor underprint. Equestrian statue of Alexander Vassilievitch Suvurov at right. Back: Parliament building at center. Watermark: Block design.

	VF	UNC
	2.00	6.00

#25 Not assigned

1994 (1995) Issue

1 Ruble = 1000 "Old" Rublei

26 1000 Rublei = 100,000 Rublei
1994 (1995). Blue-violet and purple. Alexander Vassilievitch Suvurov at right. Back: Parliament building. Printer: German.

	VF	UNC
	3.00	7.00

1995; ND (1996) Provisional Issue

27 50,000 Rublei on 5 Rublei
ND (1996 - old date 1994). Blue on multicolor underprint. Alexander Vassilievitch Suvurov at right. Hologram with *50,000* at upper left. Back: Parliament building at center.

	VF	UNC
	2.00	4.00

28 50,000 Rublei = 500,000 Rublei
1995 (1996). Brown-violet and brown on multicolor underprint. Bogdan Khmelnitsky at right. Signature Vyacheslav Zagryatsky. Back: Drama and comedy theatre. Printer: German.

	VF	UNC
a. Issued note.	8.00	15.00
s. Specimen. Red overprint.	—	40.00

1996 ND Provisional Issue

29 10,000 Rublei on 1 Ruble
ND (1996 - old date 1994). Dark green on multicolor underprint. General Alexander Vassilievitch Suvurov at right, with overprint. Back: Parliament building at center, with overprint.

	VF	UNC
	1.00	2.00

29A 10,000 Rublei on 1 Ruble
1998. Green and tan on multicolor underprint. General Alexander Vassilievitch Suvurov at right, with overprint. Back: Parliament building at center.

	VF	UNC
	1.00	2.00

30 50,000 Rublei on 5 Rublei
ND (1996 - old date 1994). Blue on multicolor underprint. General Alexander Vassilievitch Suvurov at right, with overprint. Back: Parliament building at center with overprint.

	VF	UNC
	1.00	3.00

31 100,000 Rublei on 10 Rublei
ND (1996 - old date 1994). Red-violet on multicolor underprint. General Alexander Vassilievitch Suvurov at right, with overprint. Back: Parliament building at center with overprint.

	VF	UNC
	1.00	3.00

#32 Not assigned.

1997; 1999 Issue

33 500,000 Rublei
1997. Purple and violet on multicolor underprint. Equestrian statue of Alexander Vassilievitch Suvurov at right. Back: Parliament building at center. Watermark: Block design.

	VF	UNC
	3.00	5.00

2000 Issue

34   1 Ruble   VF   UNC
2000. Orange-brown on multicolor underprint. General Alexander Vassilievitch
Suvurov at left. Back: Kitskansky Bridgehead Memorial complex. 129x56mm.
    a. Issued note.   0.50   1.00
    s. Specimen.   —   —

35   5 Rublei   VF   UNC
2000. Blue on multicolor underprint. General Alexander Vassilievitch Suvurov at
left. Back: *Kvint* destillery administrative building. 129x56mm.
    a. Issued note.   1.00   3.00
    s. Specimen. ОБРАЗНЦ.   —   —

36   10 Rublei   VF   UNC
2000. Brown on multicolor underprint. General Alexander Vassilievitch Suvurov at
left. Back: Novo Nyametsky Monastery in Kitzkansk. 129x56mm.
    a. Issued note.   FV   5.00
    s. Specimen.   —   —

37   25 Rublei   VF   UNC
2000. Rose on multicolor underprint. General Alexander Vassilievitch Suvurov at
left. Back: Bendery fortress and a Russian soldiers' Memorial. 129x56mm.
    a. Issued note.   FV   10.00
    s. Specimen.   —   —

38   50 Rublei   VF   UNC
2000. Deep green on multicolor underprint. Taras Shevchenko (poet) at left. Back:
Transnistria Parliament building. 129x60mm.
    a. Issued note.   FV   15.00
    s. Specimen.   —   —

39   100 Rublei   VF   UNC
2000. Purple on multicolor underprint. Prince Dimitrie Cantemir at left. Back: The
Christmas Church. 129x60mm.
    a. Issued note.   FV   30.00
    s. Specimen.   —   —

40   200 Rublei   VF   UNC
2004. Brown. Peter Rumyantsev-Zadunaisky at left. Back: 1757 Battle scene.
135x64mm.
    a. Incorrect spelling of bank name in Ukrainian. Serles AA.   FV   60.00
    b. Correct spelling of bank name in Ukrainian. From Series AB. FV   40.00
    c. Modikatsiya 2012.   FV   40.00

41   500 Rublei   VF   UNC
2004. Green. Catherine II at left. Back: Fort. 140x68mm.
    a. Incorrect spelling of bank name in Ukrainian. Series AA.   FV   150
    b. Correct spelling of bank name in Ukrainian. Series AB.   FV   75.00
    c. Modikatsiya 2012.   FV   75.00

2007 Issue

42   1 Ruble   VF   UNC
2007. Orange-brown on multicolor underprint. General Alexander Vassilievitch
Suvurov at left. Security band. Back: Kitskansky Bridgehead memorial complex.
129x56mm.
    a. 2007.   FV   1.00
    b. Modikatsiya 2012.   FV   1.00

43   5 Rublei   VF   UNC
2007. Blue on multicolor underprint. General Alexander Vassilievitch Suvurov at
left. Secureaty band. Back: *Kvint* destiliery administrative building. 129x56mm.
    a. 2007.   FV   2.00
    b. Modikatsiya 2012.   FV   2.00

44   10 Rublei   **VF   UNC**

2007. Brown on multicolor underprint. General Alexander Vassilievitch Suvurov at left. Secureaty band. Back: Novo Nyametssky Monastery in Kitzkansk. 129x56mm.

    a. 2007.   FV   3.50
    b. Modikatsiya 2012.   FV   3.50

45   25 Rublei   **VF   UNC**

2007. Rose on multicolor underprint. General Alexander Vassilievitch Suvurov at left. Secureaty band. Back: Bendery Fortress and a Russian soldier's memorial. 129x56mm.

    a. 2007.   FV   6.00
    b. Modikatsiya 2012.   FV   6.00

46   50 Rublei   **VF   UNC**

2007. Deep green on multicolor underprint.. Taras Shevchenko (poet) at left. Security band. Back: Transnistria Parliament building. 129x56mm.

    a. 2007.   FV   12.50
    b. Modikatsiya 2012.   FV   14.00

47   100 Rublei   **VF   UNC**

2007. Purple on multicolor underprint. Prince Dimitrie Cantemir at left. Security foil. Back: The Christmas Church. 129x56mm.

    a. 2007.   FV   25.00
    b. Modikatsiya 2012.   FV   22.50

48   1 Ruble   **VF   UNC**

2014. Brown and orange. General Alexander Vassilievitch Suvurov and value.   FV   1.00
Back: Bank monogram on argyle pattern. 26mm.

49   1 Ruble   **VF   UNC**

2014. Square with rounded corners. Dark green on light green. F. P. de Volan bust   FV   1.00
left and large value. Back: Bank monogram on argyle pattern. 26mm.

50   5 Rublei   **VF   UNC**

 Pentagon shape with rounded corners. Dark blue on light blue underprint. Peter   FV   3.00
Rumyantsev-Zadunaisky at right, large value. Back: Bank monogram on argyle pattern. 28

51   10 Rublei   **VF   UNC**

2014. Hexagon with rounded corners. Red on rose underprint. Catherine II bust   FV   5.00
and large value Back: Bank monogram on argyle pattern. 28

2015 Commemorative Issue

52   1 Ruble   **VF   UNC**

28.4.2015. 70th Anniversary of Victory in World War II. 7,070 pieces is-   FV   20.00
sued into circulation. 2,000 sets of 1- and 10-Ruble notes in folders sold as numismatic products. Overprint at lower right with 70 ЛЕТ ВЕЛИКОЙ ПОБЕДЫ (70 Years of Great Victory) above Saint George's Ribbon and 1945-2015 below.

53   10 Rubles   **VF   UNC**

28.4.2015. 70th Anniversary of Victory in World War II. 7,070 pieces is-   FV   30.00
sued into circulation. 2,000 sets of 1- and 10-Ruble notes in folders sold as numismatic products. Overprint at lower right with 70 ЛЕТ ВЕЛИКОЙ ПОБЕДЫ (70 Years of Great Victory) above Saint George's Ribbon and 1945-2015 below.

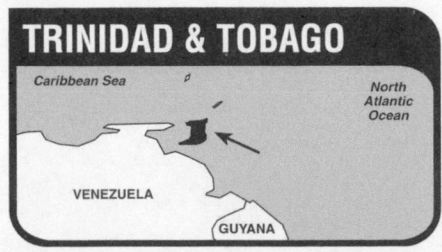

TRINIDAD & TOBAGO

Caribbean Sea

North Atlantic Ocean

VENEZUELA

GUYANA

The Republic of Trinidad and Tobago, a member of the British Commonwealth situated 11 km. off the coast of Venezuela, has an area of 5,128 sq. km. and a population of 1.23 million. Capital: Port-of-Spain. The Island of Trinidad contains the world's largest natural asphalt bog. Birds of Paradise live on little Tobago, the only place outside of their native New Guinea where they can be found in a wild state. Petroleum and petroleum products are the mainstay of the economy. Petroleum products, crude oil and sugar are exported. First colonized by the Spanish, the islands came under British control in the early 19th century. The islands' sugar industry was hurt by the emancipation of the slaves in 1834. Manpower was replaced with the importation of contract laborers from India between 1845 and 1917, which boosted sugar production as well as the cocoa industry. The discovery of oil on Trinidad in 1910 added another important export. Independence was attained in 1962. The country is one of the most prosperous in the Caribbean thanks largely to petroleum and natural gas production and processing. Tourism, mostly in Tobago, is targeted for expansion and is growing. Notes of the British Caribbean Territories circulated between 1950-1964.

RULERS:
British to 1976

MONETARY SYSTEM:
1 Dollar = 100 Cents
5 Dollars = 1 Pound 10 Pence

SIGNATURE VARIETIES			
1	J.F. Pierce	2	A.N. McLeod
3	J.E. Bruce	4	Linn OHB
5	W. Demas	6	N. Hareward
7		8	

REPUBLIC
Central Bank of Trinidad and Tobago
1964 Central Bank Act

26   1 Dollar   VF   UNC
L.1964. Red on multicolor underprint. Arms at left, portrait of Queen Elizabeth II at center. Back: Central Bank building at center right. Oil rig in water at upper right. Watermark: Bird of Paradise. 156x66mm.

a. Signature 1.	8.00	55.00
b. Signature 2. Serial # single letter or fractional letters prefix.	10.00	75.00
c. Signature 3.	7.00	45.00
s. As a, c. Specimen.	—	200
ct. Color trial. As a, c. Purple on multicolor underprint.	—	300

27   5 Dollars   VF   UNC
L.1964. Green on multicolor underprint. Arms at left, portrait of Queen Elizabeth II at center. Back: Central Bank building at center right. Crane loading sugar cane at upper right. Watermark: Bird of Paradise. 156x66mm.

a. Signature 1.	125	500
b. Signature 2.	75.00	375
c. Signature 3.	35.00	150
s. As a, c. Specimen.	—	300
ct. Color trial, As a, c. Brown on multicolor underprint.	—	450

28   10 Dollars   VF   UNC
L.1964. Dark brown on multicolor underprint. Arms at left, portrait of Queen Elizabeth II at center. Back: Central Bank building at center right. Factory at upper right. Watermark: Bird of Paradise. 156x66mm.

a. Signature 1.	300	1,350
b. Signature 2.	265	1,150
c. Signature 3.	150	600
s. As a, c. Specimen.	—	350
ct. Color trial. As a, c. Olive-green on multicolor underprint.	—	600

29   20 Dollars   VF   UNC
L.1964. Purple on multicolor underprint. Arms at left, portrait of Queen Elizabeth II at center. Back: Central Bank building at center right. Cocoa pods at upper right. Watermark: Bird of Paradise. 156x66mm.

a. Signature 1.	275	1,250
b. Signature 2.	250	1,100
c. Signature 3.	140	550
s. As a, c. Specimen.	—	400
ct. Color trial. As a, c. Red on multicolor underprint.	—	750

1977 ND Issue
#30-35 authorization date 1964. Replacement notes: Serial # prefix *XX*.

30   1 Dollar   VF   UNC
L.1964 (1977). Red on multicolor underprint. Arms at center, two scarlet Ibis at
left. Back: Central bank building at center right. Oil rig in water at upper right.
Watermark: Bird of Paradise. 156x66mm.
    a. Signature 3.   0.50   2.50
    b. Signature 4.   1.00   4.00
    s. As a. Specimen.   —   150

31   5 Dollars   VF   UNC
L.1964 (1977). Dark green on multicolor underprint. Arms at center, branches and
leaves at left. Back: Central Bank building at center right. Crane loading sugar
cane at upper right. Watermark: Bird of Paradise. 156x66mm.
    a. Signature 3.   1.00   6.00
    b. Signature 4.   4.00   20.00
    s. As a. Specimen.   —   —

32   10 Dollars   VF   UNC
L.1964 (1977). Dark brown on multicolor underprint. Arms at center. Piping guan
on branch at left. Signature 3. Back: Central Bank building at center right. Factory
at upper right. Watermark: Bird of Paradise. 156x66mm.
    a. Issued note.   2.50   12.50
    s. Specimen.   —   —

33   20 Dollars   VF   UNC
L.1964 (1977). Purple on multicolor underprint. Arms at center, flowers at left.
Signature 3. Back: Central Bank building at center right, cocoa pods at upper
right. Watermark: Bird of Paradise. 156x66mm.
    a. Issued note.   5.00   25.00
    s. Specimen, punch hole cancelled.   —   —

34   50 Dollars   VF   UNC
L.1964 (1977). Dark brown on multicolor underprint. Arms at center, long-billed
starthroat at left. Signature 3. Back: Central Bank building at center right, net
fishing at upper right. Watermark: Bird of Paradise. 156x66mm.
    a. 1963 (error date in authorization).   75.00   350
    b. 1964 (corrected authorization date). 175   900
    s. As b. Specimen.   —   —

35   100 Dollars   VF   UNC
L.1964 (1977). Deep blue on multicolor underprint. Arms at center, branch with
leaves and berries at left. Back: Central Bank building at center right. Huts and
palm trees at upper right. Watermark: Bird of Paradise. 156x66mm.
    a. Signature 3.   30.00   125
    b. Signature 4.   35.00   150
    s. As a. Specimen.   —   —

Central Bank Act Chap. 79.02; 1985 ND Issue
#36-40 Replacement notes: Serial # prefix _XX_.

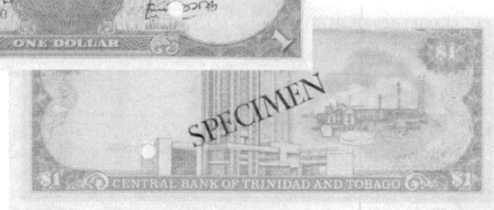

36   1 Dollar   VF   UNC
ND (1985). UV: Back two vertical stripes at left fluoresce blue. Red-orange and
purple on multicolor underprint. Arms at center, scarlet Ibis at left. Back: Eric
Williams Financial Complex in Port of Spain, oil refinery at right. Watermark: Bird
of Paradise. 156x66mm.
    a. Signature 4.   FV   1.50
    b. Signature 5.   FV   1.50
    c. Signature 6.   FV   1.00
    d. Signature 7.   FV   1.00
    s. Specimen.   —   150

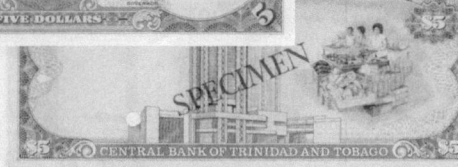

37   5 Dollars   VF   UNC
ND (1985). Dark green and blue on multicolor underprint. Arms at center,
blue crowned motmot at left. Back: Eric Williams Financial Complex in Port of
Spain, woman at roadside produce stand at right. Watermark: Bird of Paradise.
156x66mm.
    a. Signature 4.   FV   5.00
    b. Signature 5.   FV   3.00
    c. Signature 6.   FV   2.00
    d. Signature 7.   FV   2.00
    s. Specimen.   —   150

38   10 Dollars   VF   UNC

ND (1985). Dark green and brown on multicolor underprint. Arms at center, piping guan on branch at left. Back: Eric Williams Financial Complex in Port of Spain, cargo ship dockside at right. Watermark: Bird of Paradise. 156x66mm.

a. Signature 4.	FV	7.50
b. Signature 5.	FV	6.00
c. Signature 6.	FV	4.00
d. Signature 7.	FV	4.00
s. Specimen.	—	175

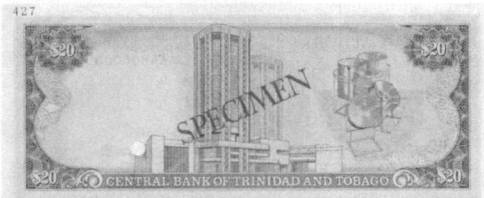

39   20 Dollars   VF   UNC

ND (1985). Purple and green on multicolor underprint. Arms at center, white-tailed Saberwing in flowers at left. Back: Eric Williams Financial Complex in Port of Spain, steel drums at right. Watermark: Bird of Paradise. 156x66mm.

a. Signature 4.	FV	12.50
b. Signature 5.	FV	7.50
c. Signature 6.	FV	6.00
d. Signature 7.	FV	6.00
s. Specimen.	—	175

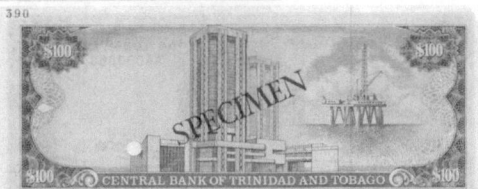

40   100 Dollars   VF   UNC

ND (1985). Deep blue on multicolor underprint. Arms at center, Greater Bird of Paradise at left. Back: Eric Williams Financial Complex in Port of Spain, oil rig at right. Watermark: Bird of Paradise. 156x66mm.

a. Signature 4.	FV	50.00
b. Signature 5.	FV	37.50
c. Signature 6.	FV	30.00
d. Signature 7.	FV	30.00
s. Specimen.	—	225

2002 Issue

41   1 Dollar   VF   UNC

2002. Red on multicolor underprint. Arms at center, scarlet Ibis at left. Segmented security foil. Back: Eric Williams Financial Complex in Port of Spain, oil refinery at right. Watermark: Bird of Paradise. 156x66mm.

a. Signature 7.	FV	1.00
b. Signature 8.	FV	1.00

42   5 Dollars   VF   UNC

2002. Green and blue on multicolor underprint. Arms at center, blue crowned motmot at left. Segmented security foil. Back: Eric Williams Financial Complex in Port of Spain, woman at roadside produce stand at right. Watermark: Bird of Paradise. 156x66mm.

a. Signature 7.	FV	2.00
b. Signature 8.	FV	2.00

43   10 Dollars   VF   UNC

2002. Dark green on multicolor underprint. Arms at center, piping guan on branch at left. Segmented security foil. Back: Eric Williams Financial Complex in Port of Spain, cargo ship dockside at right. Watermark: Bird of Paradise. 156x66mm.

a. Signature 7.	FV	4.00
b. Signature 8.	FV	4.00

44 20 Dollars   **VF   UNC**
2002. Purple on multicolor underprint. Arms at center, white-tailed Saberwing in flowers at left. Segmented security foil. Back: Eric Williams Financial Complex in Port of Spain, steel drums at right. Watermark: Bird of Paradise. 156x66mm.
   a. Signature 7.   FV   6.00
   b. Signature 8.   FV   6.00

45 100 Dollars   **VF   UNC**
2002. Deep blue on multicolor underprint. Arms at center, Greater Bird of Paradise at left. Segmented security foil. Back: Eric Williams Financial Complex in Port of Spain, oil rig at right. Watermark: Bird of Paradise. 145x66mm.
   a. Signature 7.   FV   30.00
   b. Signature 8.   FV   30.00

2006 Issue

46 1 Dollar   **VF   UNC**
2006. Red on multicolor underprint. Arms at center, scarlet ibis at left. Back: Twin towered bank building at center, oil refinery at right. Watermark: Bird of Paradise. Printer: TDLR (without imprint).   FV   1.00

46A 1 Dollar   **VF   UNC**
ND (2009). Red on multicolor underprint. Arms at center, scarlet Ibis at left. Back: Twin towered bank building at center, refinery at right. Watermark: Bird of Paradise. Printer: TDLR (without imprint).   FV   1.00

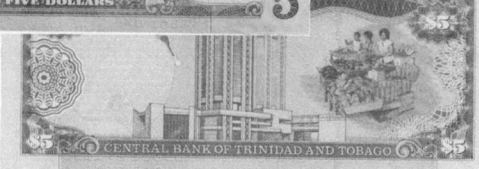

47 5 Dollars   **VF   UNC**
2006. Green and blue on multicolor underprint. Arms at center, blue crowned motmot at left. Back: Twin towered bank building at center, women at roadside produce stand at right. Watermark: Bird of Paradise. Printer: TDLR (without imprint).   FV   2.00

48 10 Dollars   **VF   UNC**
2006. Dark green on multicolor underprint. Arms at center, piping guan at left. Back: Twin towered bank building at center, cargo ship dockside at right. Watermark: Bird of Paradise. Printer: TDLR (without imprint).   FV   4.00

49 20 Dollars   **VF   UNC**
ND (2009). Purple on multicolor underprint. Arms at center, white-tailed Saberwing at left. Back: Twin towered bank building at center, Steel drum at right. Watermark: Bird of Paradise. Printer: TDLR (without imprint).   FV   6.00

49A 20 Dollars   **VF   UNC**
2006 (2014). Purple on multicolor underprint. Arms at center, white-tailed Saberwing at left. Horizontal bars at ends. Back: Eric Williams Financial Complex in Port of Spain, steel drum at right. 156x66mm.   FV   6.00

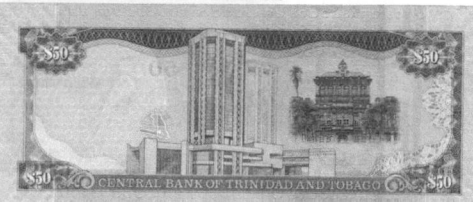

50 50 Dollars   **VF   UNC**
2006. Gold and olive green on multicolor. Red-capped cardinal on branch at left, Coat of Arms at center. Back: Eric Williams Financial Complex in Port of Spain; Red House (Parliament building) at right. Watermark: Red-capped cardinal and 50. 152x70mm.   FV   22.50

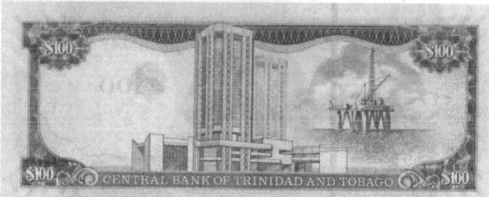

51 100 Dollars   **VF   UNC**
2006. Deep blue on multicolor underprint. Arms at center, Greater Bird of Paradise at left. Wreath around face-to-back register. Blue serial #. Back: Twin towered modern bank building at center, oil rig at right. Watermark: Bird of Paradise and value. 156x66mm.   FV   30.00

2009 Commemorative Issue

52 100 Dollars   **VF   UNC**
ND (2009). Deep blue on multicolor underprint. Arms at center, Great Bird of Paradise at left. Back: Twin towered bank building at center, oil rig at right. Watermark: Bird of Paradise. Printer: TDLR (without imprint).   FV   35.00

2012 Commemorative Issue

53 50 Dollars
2012. Gold and olive green on multicolor underprint. Red-capped cardinal bird on branch at left. Commemorative legend around central Coat of Arms. Back: Eric Williams Financial complex in Port of Spain, Red house (Parliament building). Watermark: Red-capped Cardinal and 50. Printer: TDLR. 152x70mm.

	VF	UNC
	FV	32.50

54 50 Dollars
2014. Gold and green on multicolor. Red-capped cardinal bird, red hibiscus flower, coat of arms at center. Serial # prefix CB. Polymer plastic. Central Bank, 50th Anniversary. Back: Eric Williams Financial complex in Port of Spain. Female masquerader in Carnival Costume.

	VF	UNC
	FV	35.00

2015 Issue

55 10 Dollars
2006. Like #48, but new signature of Jwala Rambarran and raised horizontal bars at upper left and right to assist visually impaired.

	VF	UNC
	FV	2.50

56 50 Dollars
2015. Polymer plastic. Gold, brown, purple, red and green. Coat of arms, hibiscus flower, SPARK Orbital hibiscus, red-capped cardinal in flight. Prefix CH. Back: Cardinal in flight, Eric Williams Financial Complex in Port of Spain, female masquerader in Carnival costume. No security thread. Watermark: None. Printer: TDLR. 152x70mm.

	VF	UNC
	FV	35.00

TUNISIA

The Republic of Tunisia, located on the northern coast of Africa between Algeria and Libya, has an area of 163,610 sq. km. and a population of 10.38 million. Capital: Tunis. Agriculture is the backbone of the economy. Crude oil, phosphates, olive oil, and wine are exported. Rivalry between French and Italian interests in Tunisia culminated in a French invasion in 1881 and the creation of a protectorate. Agitation for independence in the decades following World War I was finally successful in getting the French to recognize Tunisia as an independent state in 1956. The country's first president, Habib Bourguiba, established a strict one-party state. He dominated the country for 31 years, repressing Islamic fundamentalism and establishing rights for women unmatched by any other Arab nation. In November 1987, Bourguiba was removed from office and replaced by Zine el Abidine Ben Ali in a bloodless coup. Ben Ali served well into his fifth consecutive five-year term but was overthrown as part of the *Arab Spring* events of 2011. Elections are expected soon.

RULERS:
French, 1881-1956

MONETARY SYSTEM:
1 Dinar = 1000 Millimes, 1960-

REPLACEMENT NOTES:
#61-89 with second prefix letter *R* added after regular letter.

REPUBLIC

Banque Centrale de Tunisie

1962 Issue

61 5 Dinars
20.3.1962. Blue on multicolor underprint. Habib Bourguiba at right, bridge at left. Back: Archways. Watermark: Arms. Printer: TDLR.

	VF	UNC
	100	450

1965-69 Issue

62 1/2 Dinar
1.6.1965. Blue on multicolor underprint. Habib Bourguiba at left, mosque at right. Back: Mosaic from Monastir. Watermark: Habib Bourguiba. Printer: TDLR.

	VF	UNC
a. Issued note.	35.00	150
s. Specimen.	—	100

63 1 Dinar
1.6.1965. Blue on purple and multicolor underprint. Habib Bourguiba at right. Factory at left. Back: Mosaic. Watermark: Habib Bourguiba. Printer: TDLR.

	VF	UNC
a. Issued note.	35.00	150
s. Specimen.	—	100

67 **1 Dinar** **VF UNC**
3.8.1972. Purple on multicolor underprint. Habib Bourguiba at right. Old fortin
Sousse at left. Back: Minaret at left, girl at center. Watermark: Habib Bourguiba.
Printer: (T)DLR.
    a. Issued note.   6.00   30.00
    s. Specimen.   —   40.00

64 **5 Dinars** **VF UNC**
1.6.1965. Lilac-brown and green on multicolor underprint. Habib Bourguiba at
right. Sadiki College at left. Back: Mosaic with woman in sprays at left, Roman
arch in Sbeitla at center, Sunface at lower right. Watermark: Habib Bourguiba.
    a. Issued note.   40.00   175
    s. Specimen.   —   100

68 **5 Dinars** **VF UNC**
3.8.1972. Green on multicolor underprint. Habib Bourguiba at right. Modern
building at left. Back: Amphitheater at El-Djem. Watermark: Habib Bourguiba.
Printer: (T)DLR.
    a. Issued note.   15.00   50.00
    s. Specimen.   —   40.00

65 **10 Dinars** **VF UNC**
1.6.1969. Multicolor. Habib Bourguiba at right, refinery at left. Back: Palm trees in
field. Watermark: Habib Bourguiba.
    a. Issued note.   35.00   125
    s. Specimen.   —   100

1973 Issue

1972 Issue

69 **1/2 Dinar** **VF UNC**
15.10.1973. Green on multicolor underprint. Habib Bourguiba at left center. Man
with camel and trees at left. Back: Landscape with sheep and assorted produce.
Watermark: Habib Bourguiba.
    a. Issued note.   2.50   7.50
    r. Replacement note. Serial # prefix: *AR/1*.   4.00   12.50

66 **1/2 Dinar** **VF UNC**
3.8.1972. Brown on multicolor underprint. Habib Bourguiba at right. City with river
at left. Back: View of Tunis. Watermark: Habib Bourguiba. Printer: (T)DLR.
    a. Issued note.   4.00   15.00
    s. Specimen.   —   40.00

70 **1 Dinar** **VF UNC**
15.10.1973. Blue and green on multicolor underprint. Habib Bourguiba at left   4.00   12.50
center, building at right. Back: Industrial scenes. Watermark: Habib Bourguiba.

71   5 Dinars

	VF	UNC
15.10.1973. Dark brown on multicolor underprint. Habib Bourguiba at left center. City view at left. Back: Montage of old and new. Watermark: Habib Bourguiba.	10.00	40.00

72   10 Dinars

	VF	UNC
15.10.1973. Purple and brown on multicolor underprint. Habib Bourguiba at left center. Refinery in background at center. Back: Montage with students, column, train and drummers. Watermark: Habib Bourguiba.	17.50	70.00

#73 not assigned.

1980 Issue

74   1 Dinar

	VF	UNC
15.10.1980. Red-brown and brown on red and multicolor underprint. Habib Bourguiba at right. Amphitheater at center. Back: Village of Korbous in the "Cap Bon". Watermark: Habib Bourguiba.	2.00	7.50

75   5 Dinars

	VF	UNC
15.10.1980. Brown, red-brown and olive-green on multicolor underprint. Habib Bourguiba at right. Buildings at center. Back: Ruins and hills at left. Watermark: Habib Bourguiba.	7.50	35.00

76   10 Dinars

	VF	UNC
15.10.1980. Blue-green on bistre and multicolor underprint. Habib Bourguiba at left, building at center. Back: Reservoir at center. Watermark: Habib Bourguiba.	20.00	70.00

77   20 Dinars

	VF	UNC
15.10.1980. Dark blue-green and brown on multicolor underprint. Habib Bourguiba at right. Amphitheater at center. Back: Harbor of Sousse. Watermark: Habib Bourguiba.	25.00	90.00

#78 not assigned.

1983 Issue

79   5 Dinars

	VF	UNC
3.11.1983. Red-brown and purple on lilac underprint. Habib Bourguiba at left, desert scene at bottom center. Back: Hydroelectric dam at center right. Watermark: Habib Bourguiba.	7.50	25.00

80   10 Dinars

3.11.1983. Blue and lilac on multicolor underprint. Workers at lower left center, Habib Bourguiba at center, offshore oil rig at right. Back: Modern building at center, old city gateways at right. Watermark: Habib Bourguiba.

	VF	UNC
	12.50	40.00

81   20 Dinars

3.11.1983. Light blue and dark blue on green and multicolor underprint. Habib Bourguiba at left, building at bottom center. Back: Building at lower left, aerial view of harbor at right. Watermark: Habib Bourguiba.

	VF	UNC
	22.50	70.00

1986 Issue

#82 and 83 Held in reserve.

84   10 Dinars

20.3.1986. Yellow-brown on green underprint. Habib Bourguiba at left center, agricultural scene at bottom center. Back: Offshore oil rig at left center. Watermark: Habib Bourguiba. 170x84mm.

	VF	UNC
	10.00	35.00

#85 not assigned.

1992-97 Dated Issues

#86-89 replacement notes: *R* in denominator of lserial # at the lower right or lower left.

86   5 Dinars

7.11.1993. Green, olive-brown and black. Head of Hannibal at left center, Carthage harbor fortress at right. Back: Nov. 7, 1987 collage at left center. Watermark: Head of Hannibal. 130x70mm.

	VF	UNC
	FV	20.00

87   10 Dinars

7.11.1994. Purple, blue-green and red-brown on multicolor underprint. Ibn Khaldoun at center. Back: Open book of 7 Novembre 1987 at left center. Watermark: Ibn Khaldoun. 145x73mm.

	VF	UNC
	FV	30.00

87A   10 Dinars

7.11.1994 (2005). Brown on multicolor underprint. Ibn Khaldoun at center. Back: Open book of '7 Novembre 1987' at left center. Watermark: Ibn Khaldoun. 145x73mm.

	VF	UNC
	FV	25.00

88   20 Dinars

7.11.1992. Deep purple, blue-black and red-brown on multicolor underprint. Kheoreddeme ET-Tounsi on horseback at left center, buildings in background. Back: Montage of city view; a "7" with 1987 date over flag on stylized dove at center. Watermark: Head of Kheireddine ET-Tounsi. 153x76mm.

	VF	UNC
	FV	40.00

89   30 Dinars

7.11.1997. Green and yellow on multicolor underprint. Abou EL Kacem Chebbi at right. Back: Schoolgirls, sheep and weaver. Watermark: Abou EL Kacem Chebbi. 161x79mm.

	VF	UNC
	FV	60.00

2005 Issue

90   10 Dinars   **VF   UNC**
7.11.2005. Blue on multicolor underprint. Mosque. Elissa, Queen of Carthage.   FV   17.50
145x73mm.

2008 Commemorative Issue

91   50 Dinars   **VF   UNC**
7.11.2008. Green and grey-violet on multicolor underprint. Ibn Rashiq al Qirwani,
Cité de la Culture in Tunis in background. Back: Rades-La Goulette bridge over
Rades Harbor, the former Zin El Abridine Ben Ali airport in Enfidha. Watermark:
Ibn Rachiq and 50. 167x80mm.
     a. Issued note.   FV   65.00
     s. Specimen.   —   100

2008 Issue

92   5 Dinars   **VF   UNC**
2008. Omron rings added. Green on multicolor underprint. Hannibar head right,   FV   8.50
Carthage harbor fortress at right. Back: Nov. 7, 1987 collage at left center. Watermark: Hannibal and 5. Printer: TDLR (without imprint). 130x70mm.

93   20 Dinars   **VF   UNC**
3.20.2011. Red and blue on multicolor underprint. K. Et-tounsi on horseback
at left center, Ksar Ouled Soltane fortress in backgorund. Back: Sadiki School.
153x76mm.
     a. Text on back below building: L'École Sadiki (error).   FV   22.50
     b. Text on back below building: College Sadiki (correction).   FV   22.50

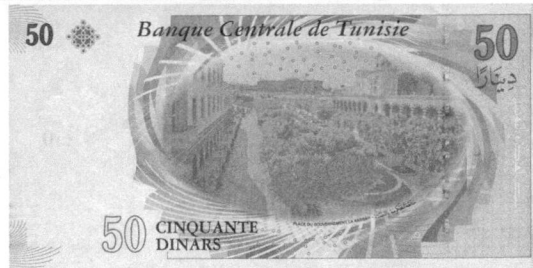

94   50 Dinars   **VF   UNC**
20.3.2011. Blue and green on multicolor underprint. Rashiq al Qirwani at left cen-   FV   45.00
ter, Musee de la Monnaie in Tunis at left. Back: Place Gouvernement la Kasbah,
central square in Tunis. 168x81mm.

2013 Issue

95   5 Dinars   **VF   UNC**
3.20.2013. Green and multicolor. City of Carthage; General Hannibal wearing   FV   6.00
helmet. Back: Carthaginian ships. Watermark: Olive trees and 5. 143x73mm.

96   10 Dinars   **VF   UNC**
3.20.2013. Light blue and yellow on multicolor underprint. Aboul el Kacem Chebbi,   FV   15.00
poet. Back: Arches of Medesa Bacchia school in Tunis. Watermark: Olive tree and
10. 148x73mm.

TURKEY

The Republic of Turkey, a parliamentary democracy of the Near East located partially in Europe and partially in Asia between the Black and the Mediterranean seas, has an area of 301,302 sq. mi. (780,580 sq. km.) and a population of 65.73 million. Capital: Ankara. Turkey exports cotton, hazelnuts and tobacco, and enjoys a virtual monopoly in meerschaum. Modern Turkey was founded in 1923 from the Anatolian remnants of the defeated Ottoman Empire by national hero Mustafa Kemal, who was later honored with the title Ataturk or "Father of the Turks." Under his authoritarian leadership, the country adopted wide-ranging social, legal, and political reforms. After a period of one-party rule, an experiment with multi-party politics led to the 1950 election victory of the opposition Democratic Party and the peaceful transfer of power. Since then, Turkish political parties have multiplied, but democracy has been fractured by periods of instability and intermittent military coups (1960, 1971, 1980), which in each case eventually resulted in a return of political power to civilians. In 1997, the military again helped engineer the ouster - popularly dubbed a "post-modern coup" - of the then Islamic-oriented government. Turkey intervened militarily on Cyprus in 1974 to prevent a Greek takeover of the island and has since acted as patron state to the "Turkish Republic of Northern Cyprus," which only Turkey recognizes. A separatist insurgency begun in 1984 by the Kurdistan Workers' Party (PKK) - now known as the People's Congress of Kurdistan or Kongra-Gel (KGK) - has dominated the Turkish military's attention and claimed more than 30,000 lives. After the capture of the group's leader in 1999, the insurgents largely withdrew from Turkey mainly to northern Iraq. In 2004, KGK announced an end to its ceasefire and attacks attributed to the KGK increased. Turkey joined the UN in 1945 and in 1952 it became a member of NATO; it holds a non-permanent seat on the UN Security Council from 2009-2010. In 1964, Turkey became an associate member of the European Community. Over the past decade, it has undertaken many reforms to strengthen its democracy and economy; it began accession membership talks with the European Union in 2005.

MONETARY SYSTEM:
1 Lira (Livre, Pound) = 100 Piastres

REPUBLIC

Türkiye Cümhuriyet Merkez Bankasi
CENTRAL BANK OF TURKEY
Law 11 Haziran 1930; 1961-65 ND Issue

173	5 Lira	VF	UNC
L.1930 (25.10.1961). Blue with orange, blue and multicolor guilloche. Portrait of President Kemal Ataturk at right. Back: Three women with baskets of hazelnuts at center. Watermark: Kemal Ataturk. Printer: DBM-A (without imprint).
	a. Issue note.	100	300
	s. Specimen.	—	200

174	5 Lira	VF	UNC
L.1930 (4.1.1965). Blue-green. Portrait of President Kemal Ataturk at right. Back: Three women with baskets of hazelnuts at center. Watermark: Kemal Ataturk. Printer: DBM-A (without imprint).
	a. Issued note.	60.00	180
	s. Specimen.	—	200

175	50 Lira	VF	UNC
L.1930 (1.6.1964). Brown on multicolor underprint. Portrait of President Kemal Ataturk at right. Three signatures. Back: Soldier holding rifle figure from the Victory statue at Ulus Square in Ankara at center. Watermark: Kemal Ataturk. Printer: DBM-A (without imprint).
	a. Issued note.	30.00	100
	s. Specimen.		250

176	100 Lira	VF	UNC
L.1930 (15.3.1962). Olive on orange and multicolor guilloche. Portrait of President Kemal Ataturk at right. Back: Youth Park with bridge in Ankara. Watermark: Kemal Ataturk. Printer: DBM-A (without imprint).
	a. Issued note.	200	600
	s. Specimen.	—	350

177	100 Lira	VF	UNC
L.1930 (1.10.1964). Olive on blue, lilac and multicolor guilloche. Portrait of President Kemal Ataturk at right. Different signature. Back: Youth Park with bridge in Ankara. Watermark: Kemal Ataturk. Printer: DBM-A (without imprint).
	a. Issued note.	75.00	225
	s. Specimen.	—	350

178	500 Lira	VF	UNC
L.1930 (1.12.1962). Purple and brown on multicolor underprint. Portrait of President Kemal Ataturk at right. Back: Sultan Ahmet Mosque, the Obelisc and the Hippodrome in Istanbul. Watermark: Kemal Ataturk. Printer: DBM-A (without imprint).
	a. Issued note.	130	400
	s. Specimen.	—	500

Law 11 Haziran 1930; 1966-69 ND Issue

			VF	UNC
185	**5 Lira**		**VF**	**UNC**

L.1970 (1976). Grayish purple on multicolor underprint. President Kemal Atatürk at right. Two signatures. Back: Manavgat waterfall in Antalya at left center. Watermark: Kemal Atatürk. Printer: DBM-A (without imprint). — 0.50 / 2.00

179 **5 Lira** — **VF** **UNC**

L.1930 (8.1.1968). Grayish purple on multicolor underprint. President Kemal Atatürk at right. Three signatures. Back: Manavgat waterfall in Antalya at left center. Watermark: Kemal Atatürk. Printer: DBM-A (without imprint). — 1.00 / 4.00

186 **10 Lira** — **VF** **UNC**

L.1970 (1975). Green on multicolor underprint. President Kemal Atatürk at right. Two signatures. Back: Maiden's Tower on the Bosphorus in Istanbul at center. Watermark: Kemal Atatürk. Printer: DBM-A (without imprint). — 1.50 / 5.00

180 **10 Lira** — **VF** **UNC**

L.1930 (4.7.1966). Green on multicolor underprint. President Kemal Atatürk at right. Three signatures. Back: Bosporus Tower in Istanbul at center. Watermark: Kemal Atatürk. Printer: DBM-A (without imprint). — 8.00 / 20.00

187 **20 Lira** — **VF** **UNC**

L.1970 (1974). Orange-brown on multicolor underprint. President Kemal Atatürk at right. Two signatures. Back: Mausoleum of of Atatürk in Ankara at center. Watermark: Kemal Atatürk. Printer: DBM-A (without imprint).
- a. Black signature. 2 varieties. Prefix C to H. — 1.00 / 5.00
- b. Brown signature. Prefix I. — 0.50 / 1.00

181 **20 Lira** — **VF** **UNC**

L.1930 (15.6.1966). Orange-brown on multicolor underprint. President Kemal Atatürk at right. Three signatures. Back: Mausoleum of of Atatürk in Ankara at center. Watermark: Kemal Atatürk. Printer: DBM-A (without imprint).
- a. 7-digit serial #. Prefix A and B. — 300 / 900
- b. 8-digit serial #. Prefix A and B. — 20.00 / 60.00

182 **100 Lira** — **VF** **UNC**

L.1930 (17.3.1969). President Kemal Atatürk at right. Modified guilloche in pinkish red, blue and multicolor underprint. Different signature. Back: Youth Park with bridge in Ankara. Watermark: Kemal Atatürk. Printer: DBM-A (without imprint).
- a. — 75.00 / 225
- b. Prefix C to F27. — 8.00 / 20.00
- c. Prefix F28 to I. — 1.00 / 4.00

183 **500 Lira** — **VF** **UNC**

L.1930 (3.6.1968). Purple, brown and multicolor. President Kemal Atatürk at right. Three signatures. Back: Sultan Ahmet Mosque, the Obelisc and the Hippodrome in Istanbul. Watermark: Kemal Atatürk. Printer: DBM-A (without imprint). — 60.00 / 180

#184 Not assigned.

Law Ocak 14 (Jan. 26), 1970; 1971-82 ND Issues

#185, 188, 190 and 191 replacement notes: Serial # prefix *Z91-Z95*.

187A **50 Lira** — **VF** **UNC**

L.1970 (2.8.1971). Series O-Y. Brown on multicolor underprint. President Kemal Atatürk at right. Different inscription at center. Two signature varieties. Back: Soldier figure from Statue of Victory at Ulus Square in Ankara. Watermark: Kemal Atatürk. Printer: Devlet Banknot Matbaasi (without imprint).
- a. Issued note. Prefix A to I36. — 3.00 / 10.00
- b. Issued note. Prefix I37 to J. — 2.00 / 6.00
- s. Specimen. — — / —

Law Ocak 14 (Jan. 26), 1970; 1984-97 ND Issues
Some sign. varieties.

188   50 Lira   VF   UNC
L.1970 (1976). Dark brown on multicolor underprint. President Kemal Atatürk   0.50   2.00
at right. Two signature varieties. Back: Marble Fountain in Topkapi Palace in
Istanbul. Watermark: Kemal Atatürk.

192   10 Lira   VF   UNC
L.1970 (1979). UV: security thread fluoresces blue. Dull gray-green on multicolor   0.20   0.50
underprint. President Kemal Atatürk at right. Young boy and girl in medallion in
underprint at center. Back: Children presenting flowers to Atatürk. Watermark:
Kemal Atatürk.

193   10 Lira   VF   UNC
L.1970 (1982). UV: security thread fluoresces blue, serial # yellow. Black on
multicolor underprint. President Kemal Atatürk at right. Back: Children presenting
flowers to Atatürk. Watermark: Kemal Atatürk.
    a. Back is dark olive green. (1979).   0.20   0.50
    b. Back is black. (1982).   0.20   0.50

189   100 Lira   VF   UNC
L.1970 (15.5.1972). Blue-green on multicolor underprint. President Kemal Atatürk
at right. Three signature varieties. Back: Mt. Ararat at center. Watermark: Kemal
Atatürk.
    a. Issued note. Prefix A, B.   20.00   60.00
    s. Specimen.   —   —

194   100 Lira   VF   UNC
L.1970 (1984). Violet and brown on multicolor underprint. President Kemal Atatürk
at right. Back: Fort of Ankara, Mehmet Akif Ersoy, his home and document.
Watermark: Kemal Atatürk.
    a. Watermark: Head small, bust facing right, dotted security thread.   0.30   1.25
    b. Watermark: Head large, bust facing 3/4 right.   0.25   1.00

190   500 Lira   VF   UNC
L.1970 (1.9.1971). Dark blue and dark green on multicolor underprint. President
Kemal Atatürk at right. Two signature varieties. Back: Main Gate of Istanbul
University. Watermark: Kemal Atatürk.
    a. Prefix A to C.   100   300
    b. Prefix D and K.   400   1,200
    c. Prefix E to H.   30.00   90.00
    d. Prefix I, J, L, M, N, O.   10.00   30.00

195   500 Lira   VF   UNC
L.1970 (1983). Blue on multicolor underprint. President Kemal Atatürk at right. Two   0.50   1.50
signature varieties. Back: Clock Tower in Izmir at left center. Watermark: Variety.

191   1000 Lira   VF   UNC
L.1970. Deep purple and brown-violet on multicolor underprint. President Kemal   10.00   30.00
Atatürk at right. Three signature varieties. Back: Bosphorus River with boat and
suspension bridge. Watermark: Kemal Atatürk.

196   1000 Lira   VF   UNC
L.1970 (1986). UV: fibers fluoresce blue and red; security thread red. Purple and   0.75   1.75
blue on multicolor underprint. President Kemal Atatürk at right. Two signature
varieties. One dot for visually impaired at lower left. Back: Istanbul coastline at left,
Fathi Sultan Mehmet at center right. Watermark: Kemal Atatürk.

196A   5000 Lira   VF   UNC
L.1970 (1981). Dark brown and olive-green on multicolor underprint. Portrait of   30.00   90.00
President Kemal Ataturk at right. Back: Mevlana Museum in Konya and figure of
Mevlana at right. Watermark: Kemal Ataturk.

197 5000 Lira

L.1970 (1985). Dark brown, red-brown and blue on multicolor underprint. President Kemal Atatürk at right. Two signature varieties. Back: Seated Mevlana at left center, Mevlana Museum at center. Watermark: Kemal Atatürk.

	VF	UNC
	3.00	10.00

198 5000 Lira

L.1970 (1990). UV: fibers fluoresce blue and red. Deep brown and deep green on multicolor underprint. President Kemal Atatürk at right. Back: Afsin-Elbistan thermal power plant at left center. Watermark: Kemal Atatürk.

	VF	UNC
	1.00	3.00

199 10,000 Lira

L.1970 (1982). UV: fibers fluoresce blue and red. Purple and deep green on multicolor underprint. President Kemal Atatürk at right. Three dots for visally impaired at lower left. Back: Selimiye Mosque in Edirne, Mimar Sinan (architect) at center. Watermark: Kemal Atatürk.

	VF	UNC
a. Prefix A, B.	70.00	200
b. Prefix C to F.	7.00	20.00
c. Prefix G to H.	2.00	6.00

200 10,000 Lira

L.1970 (1989). UV: fibers fluoresce blue and red. Purple and deep green on multicolor underprint. President Kemal Atatürk at right. Three dots for visally impaired at lower left. Back: Selimiye Mosque in Edirne, Mimar Sinan (architect) at center. Watermark: Kemal Atatürk.

	VF	UNC
	1.00	3.00

201 20,000 Lira

L.1970 (1988). UV: fibers fluoresce blue and red; serial # yellow. Red-brown and purple on multicolor underprint. President Kemal Atatürk at right. Back: New Central Bank building in Ankara at left center. Watermark: Kemal Atatürk

	VF	UNC
a. Prefix A, B. Black signatures.	5.00	15.00
b. Prefix C to F. Black signatures.	3.00	9.00

202 20,000 Lira

L.1970 (1995). President Kemal Atatürk at right. Lighter underprint at center. Red signature. Series G-. Back: New Central Bank building in Ankara at left center. Watermark: Kemal Atatürk.

	VF	UNC
	1.00	3.00

203 50,000 Lira

L.1970 (1989). Blue-green and dark green on multicolor underprint. President Kemal Atatürk at right. Back: National Parliament House in Ankara at left center. Watermark: Kemal Atatürk.

	VF	UNC
a. Prefix A, B, C, D, E, F, G, I, J.	3.00	10.00
b. Serial # prefix H.	400	1,200

204 50,000 Lira

L.1970 (1995). Blue-green and dark green on multicolor underprint. President Kemal Atatürk at right. Series K-. Back: National Parliament House in Ankara at left center. Value in gray. Watermark: Kemal Atatürk

	VF	UNC
	1.00	3.00

205 100,000 Lira

L.1970 (1991). Reddish brown, dark brown and dark green on multicolor underprint. President Kemal Atatürk facing at center right. Equestrian statue of Atatürk at lower left center. Security device at upper right. Signature varieties. Back: Children presenting flowers to Atatürk at left center. Watermark: Kemal Atatürk.

	VF	UNC
a. Prefix A, B, C.	1.00	40.00
b. Prefix D, E.	2.00	6.00
c. Prefix G to H.	1.00	3.00

206 100,000 Lira

L.1970 (1997). Multicolor. President Kemal Atatürk facing at center right. Without security device at upper right. Signature varieties. Back: Children presenting flowers to Atatürk at left center. Watermark: Kemal Atatürk.

	VF	UNC
	FV	4.00

207 250,000 Lira

L.1970 (1992). Blue-gray, dark green and violet on multicolor underprint. President Kemal Atatürk facing at center right. Triangular security device at upper right. Signature varieties. Back: Kizilkale Fortress at Alunya at center. Watermark: Kemal Atatürk

	VF	UNC
	5.00	15.00

208 500,000 Lira

L.1970 (1993). UV: fibers fluoresce blue, red and pink. Purple, blue-black and violet on multicolor underprint. President Kemal Atatürk facing at center right. Square security device at upper right. Signature varieties. Back: Aerial view of Canakkale Martyrs Monument. Watermark: Kemal Atatürk

	VF	UNC
a. Prefix A, B, C.	8.00	25.00
b. Prefix D.	100	300
c. Prefix E to G.	3.00	9.00

209 1,000,000 Lira

L.1970 (1995). Claret red and blue-gray on multicolor underprint. President Kemal Atatürk facing at center right. Signature varieties. Back: Atatürk dam in Sanliurfa. Watermark: Kemal Atatürk.

	VF	UNC
a. Prefix A to L.	8.00	24.00
b. Prefix M, N.	2.00	6.00

210 5,000,000 Lira

L.1970 Ocak (January) 1997 (at bottom left). Dark brown and red-brown on multicolor underprint. President Kemal Atatürk facing at center right. Gold oval seal with AH1329 date at right. Signature varieties. Back: Anitkabir complex (mausoleum of Ataturk) in Ankara at left center. Watermark: Kemal Atatürk.

	VF	UNC
a. Prefix A to C.	15.00	50.00
b. Prefix D to N.	4.00	12.00

Law Ocak 14 (Jan. 26), 1970; 1998-2002 ND Issue

211 250,000 Lira

L.1970 (1998). Blue-gray and violet on multicolor underprint. President Kemal Atatürk facing at center right. Triangular security device at upper right printed in gold ink. Signature varieties. Back: Kizilkale Fortress at Alunya at center. Watermark: Kemal Atatürk

	VF	UNC
	FV	3.00

212 500,000 Lira

L.1970 (1998). Lithograph. Purple, blue-black and violet on multicolor underprint. President Kemal Atatürk facing at center right. Without square security device at upper right. Signature varieties. Back: Aerial view of Canakkale Martyrs Monument. Watermark: Kemal Atatürk

	VF	UNC
	2.00	6.00

213 1,000,000 Lira

L.1970 (2002). Claret red and blue-gray on multicolor underprint. President Kemal Atatürk facing at center right. Signature varieties. Back: Sanliurfa-Adiyaman dam in Sanliurfa. Watermark: Kemal Atatürk

	VF	UNC
	3.00	3.00

214 10,000,000 Lira

	VF	UNC
L.1970 (1999). Red and purple on multicolor underprint. President Kemal Atatürk at left center. Square security device in gold at right. Back: World map of 1513 by Piri Reis.	10.00	35.00

215 20,000,000 Lira

	VF	UNC
L.1970 (2000). Green and red. Kemal Atatürk at center globe and olive branch behind. Back: Efes ancient city.	15.00	45.00

2005 New Lira Issue

#216-221 Atatürk at ctr. or r. and as wmk. Monetary reform: 100,000 "old" lira = 1 "new" lira

216 1 New Lira

	VF	UNC
2005. Claret red and blue. President Kemal Atatürk at center or right. Back: Atatürk Dam in Sanliurfa-Adiyaman. Watermark: Kemal Atatürk. 156x76mm.	1.00	3.00

217 5 New Lira

	VF	UNC
2005. Greenish brown. President Kemal Atatürk at center or right. Back: Mausolem of Atatürk. Watermark: Kemal Atatürk. 162x76mm.	4.00	12.00

218 10 New Lira

	VF	UNC
2005. Red on multicolor underprint. President Kemal Atatürk at center or right. Back: World map of 1513 by Piri Reis. Watermark: Kemal Atatürk. 162x76mm.	6.00	18.00

219 20 New Lira

	VF	UNC
2005. Green. President Kemal Atatürk at center or right. Back: Ancient city of Ephesus. Watermark: Kemal Atatürk. 162x76mm.	12.00	36.00

220 50 New Lira

	VF	UNC
2005. Orange. President Kemal Atatürk at center or right. Back: Goreme National Park, Capadoccia. Watermark: Kemal Atatürk. 152x81mm.	20.00	60.00

221   100 New Lira   **VF   UNC**
2005. Blue. President Kemal Atatürk at center or right. Back: Ishak Pasha Palace,   40.00   120
Dogu Bayazit. Watermark: Kemal Atatürk. 152x81mm.

Law Ocak 14 (Jan. 26), 1970; 2009 ND Issue

222   5 Lira   **VF   UNC**
ND (2009). Brown and yellow on multicolor underprint. Kemal Atatürk at right.
Back: Aydin Sayili, historical scientist, at left. 130x64mm.
    a. 2009. Prefix A. Brown.   FV   7.00
    b. 2009. Prefix B. Purple.   FV   5.00

222A   5 Lira   **VF   UNC**
2009 Purple Kemal Ataturk at right. Back: Aydin Saylli, historical scientist at left.   FV   4.50
130x64mm.

223   10 Lira   **VF   UNC**
ND (2009). Rose on multicolor underprint. Kemal Atatürk at right. Back: Cahit Arf,
mathematician, at right. 136x64mm.
    a. 2009. Prefix A.   FV   9.00
    b. 2009. Prefix B.   FV   9.00

224   20 Lira   **VF   UNC**
ND (2009). Green and brown on multicolor underprint. Kemal Atatürk at right.
Back: Kemaleddin, architect, at right. 142x68mm.
    a. 2009. Prefix A.   FV   16.00
    b. 2009. Prefix B.   FV   16.00

225   50 Lira   **VF   UNC**
ND (2009). Light brown and green on multicolor underprint. Kemal Atatürk at right.
Back: Fatma Aliye, writer, at right. 148x68mm.
    a. 2009. Prefix A.   FV   40.00
    b. 2009. Prefix B.   FV   40.00

226   100 Lira   **VF   UNC**
ND (2009). Light blue and rose on multicolor underprint. Kemal Atatürk at right.
Back: Itri, composer, at right. 154x72mm.
    a. 2009. Prefix A.   FV   70.00
    b. 2009. Prefix B.   FV   70.00

227   200 Lira   **VF   UNC**
ND (2009). Purple and light blue on multicolor underprint. Kemal Atatürk at right.
Back: Yunus Emre, writer, at right. 160x72mm.
    a. 2009. Prefix A.   FV   180
    b. 2009. Prefix B.   FV   145

TURKMENISTAN

The Turkmenistan Republic covers the territory of the Trans-Caspian Region of Turkestan, the Charjiui Vilayet of Bukhara and the part of Khiva located on the right bank of the Oxus. Bordered on the north by the Autonomous Kara-Kalpak Republic (a constituent of Uzbekistan), by Iran and Afghanistan on the south, by the Uzbek Republic on the east and the Caspian Sea on the west. It has an area of 488,100 sq. km. and a population of 5.18 million. Capital: Ashgabat (formerly Poltoratsk). Main occupation is agricultural products including cotton and maize. It is rich in minerals, oil, coal, sulphur and salt,and is also famous for it's carpets, Turkoman horses and Karakul sheep. Eastern Turkmenistan for centuries formed part of the Persian province of Khurasan; in medieval times Merv (today known as Mary) was one of the great cities of the Islamic world and an important stop on the Silk Road. Annexed by Russia between 1865 and 1885, Turkmenistan became a Soviet republic in 1924. It achieved independence upon the dissolution of the USSR in 1991. Extensive hydrocarbon/natural gas reserves could prove a boon to this underdeveloped country if extraction and delivery projects were to be expanded. The Turkmenistan Government is actively seeking to develop alternative petroleum transportation routes to break Russia's pipeline monopoly. President for Life Saparmurat Nyyazow died in December 2006, and Turkmenistan held its first multi-candidate presidential electoral process in February 2007. Gurbanguly Berdimuhamedow, a vice premier under Nyyazow, emerged as the country's new president.

REPUBLIC

Türkmenistanyñ Merkezi Döwlet Banky

CENTRAL BANK OF TURKMENISTAN

1993 ND; 1995-98 Issue

#1-9 Replacement notes: Serial # prefix ZZ.

1   1 Manat VF UNC
ND (1993). Brown and tan on orange and multicolor underprint. Ylymlar Academy at center, native craft at right. Signature Khudaiberdy Orazov. Back: Arms at left, Temple at center. Watermark: Rearing Arabian horse. 0.50 1.00

2   5 Manat VF UNC
ND (1993). UV: value 5 in blx fluoresce yellow; right serial # orange. Blue and green on multicolor underprint. Building at center. Signature Khudaiberdy Orazov. Back: Arms at left, building at center. Watermark: Rearing Arabian horse. 1.00 2.00

3   10 Manat VF UNC
ND (1993). Brown and pale orange on multicolor underprint. President S. Niazov at right. Government Building at center. Signature Khudaiberdy Orazov. Back: Government Building at center, arms at left. Watermark: Rearing Arabian horse. 1.00 3.00

4   20 Manat VF UNC
ND (1993); 1995. Blue-gray and blue on multicolor underprint. President S. Niazov at right. National library at center. Signature Khudaiberdy Orazov. Back: Large Building at center, arms at left. Watermark: Rearing Arabian horse.
   a. ND (1993). 3.00 6.00
   b. 1995. 1.00 3.00

5   50 Manat VF UNC
ND (1993); 1995. Brown and green on multicolor underprint. President S. Niazov at right. Monument at center. Signature Khudaiberdy Orazov. Back: Mosque ruins, arms at left. Watermark: Rearing Arabian horse.
   a. ND (1993). 5.00 10.00
   b. 1995. 2.00 4.00

6   100 Manat VF UNC
ND (1993); 1995. Dark blue and dark gray on multicolor underprint. President S. Niazov at right. Presidential Palace at center. Signature Khudaiberdy Orazov. Back: Sultan Sanjaryn mausoleum, arms at left. Watermark: Rearing Arabian horse.
   a. ND (1993). 7.00 15.00
   b. 1995. 2.00 5.00

7   500 Manat VF UNC
ND (1993); 1995. Violet, dark brown and orange on multicolor underprint. President S. Niazov at right. National theatre at center. Signature Khudaiberdy Orazov. Back: Hanymyn mausoleum, arms at left. Watermark: Rearing Arabian horse.
   a. ND (1993). 10.00 24.00
   b. 1995. 4.00 10.00

8   1000 Manat VF UNC
1995. Green on multicolor underprint. President S. Niazov at right. Building at center. Signature Khudaiberdy Orazov. Back: Arms at center. Watermark: Rearing Arabian horse. 5.00 12.00

9   5000 Manat VF UNC
1996. Violet, purple and red on multicolor underprint. President S. Niazov at right. Building at center. Signature Khudaiberdy Orazov. Back: Arms. Watermark: Rearing Arabian horse. 6.00 14.00

10   10,000 Manat VF UNC
1996. Dark brown on multicolor underprint. President S. Niazov at right. Presidential palace at center. Back: Arms. 156x78mm. 5.00 15.00

11 10,000 Manat
1998. Light blue, light brown, and red on multicolor underprint. President S. Niazov at right. Palace of Turkmenbashy. Back: Mosque of Saparmurat at center. 156x78mm.

VF 5.00 UNC 15.00

1999-2005 Issues

12 5000 Manat
1999; 2000. Violet, purple and red on multicolor underprint. President S. Niazov at right. Building at center. Signature Khudaiberdy Orazov. Back: Arms. Watermark: Rearing Arabian horse. 156x78mm.

	VF	UNC
a. 1999. Signature Khudaiberdy Orazov.	4.00	12.00
b. 2000. Signature S. Kandymov.	4.00	12.00

13 10,000 Manat
1999. Light blue and light brown on multicolor underprint. President Niyazov with medals at right. Palace of Turkmenbashy at center. Signature Khudaiberdy Orazov. Back: Mosque of Saparmurat at center. 156x78mm.

VF 3.00 UNC 10.00

14 10,000 Manat
2000. Light blue and light brown on multicolor underprint. President Niyazov with medals at right. Palace of Turkmenbashy at center. Stars and crescent at upper left. Signature S. Kandymov. Back: Circular design at upper right. 156x78mm.

VF FV UNC 15.00

15 10,000 Manat
2003. Light blue and light brown on multicolor underprint. President Niyazov with medals at right. Palace of Turkmenbashy at center. Stars and crescent at upper left. Signature S. Kandymov. Back: Circular design at upper right. Arms at upper left. 156x78mm.

VF FV UNC 15.00

16 10,000 Manat
2005. Black and green on multicolor underprint. President Niyazov at center. Back: Monument. 156x78mm.

VF FV UNC 15.00

2005 Issue

17 50 Manat
2005. Slate black on multicolor underprint. President Niyazov at center. Back: Horse standing left, racetrack stands in background. 156x78mm.

VF FV UNC 1.00

18 100 Manat
2005. Rose on multicolor underprint President Niyazov at center. Back: Building at left. 156x78mm.

VF FV UNC 3.00

19   500 Manat   **VF UNC**

2005. Purple on brown and multicolor underprint. President Niyazov at center.   FV   5.00
Back: Traditional jewelry designs at left. 156x78mm.

20   1000 Manat   **VF UNC**

2005. Blue on multicolor underprint. President Niyazov at center. Back: Palace of   FV   7.50
Turkmenbasy at left. 156x78mm.

21   5000 Manat   **VF UNC**

2005. Blue. President Niyazov at center. 156x78mm.   FV   10.00

2009 Issue

22   1 Manat   **VF UNC**

2009. Slate black and green on tan and multicolor underprint. Togrul Beg Türkmen
Back: Beyik Sparmyrat Türkmenbasynyn 120x60mm.

a. 2009.   FV   2.00

23   5 Manat   **VF UNC**

2009. Brown and green on multicolor underprint. Soltan Sanjar Türkmen at right.
Back: Bitaraplyk Binasy. Printer: TDLR (without imprint). 126x63mm.

a. 2009.   FV   7.00

24   10 Manat   **VF UNC**

2009. Rose and carmine on multicolor underprint. Magtymguy Pyragy at right.
Back: Turkmenistan National Bank building. Printer: TDLR (without imprint).
132x66mm.

a. 2009.   FV   12.00

25   20 Manat   **VF UNC**

2009. Purple on multicolor underprint. Gorogly Beg Türkmen at right. Back:
Ruhyyet Palace. Printer: TDLR (without imprint). 138x69mm.

a. 2009.   FV   22.50

26 50 Manat

VF UNC

2009. Green on multicolor underprint. Gorkut Ata Türkmen at right. Back: National Assembly building. Printer: TDLR (without imprint). FV 45.00

27 100 Manat

VF UNC

2009. Violet and blue on multicolor underprint. Oguz Han Türkmen at right. Back: Presidential Palace. Printer: TDLR (without imprint). FV 90.00

28 500 Manat

VF UNC

2009. Not issued. Blue on multicolor underprint. President Sasparmyrat Nijjazow at right center. Back: Kipchak mosque. Printer: TDLR (without imprint). 0.00 700

2012 Issue

29 1 Manat

VF UNC

2012. Green and multicolor. Togrul Beg Turkmen at right center. Back: National Cultural Centre. Printer: TDLR. FV 2.00

30 5 Manat

VF UNC

2012. FV 7.00

31 10 Manat

VF UNC

2012. FV 12.00

32 20 Manat

VF UNC

2012. FV 22.00

2014 Issue

33 50 Manat

VF UNC

2014. FV 50.00

34 100 Manat

VF UNC

2014. FV 100

UGANDA

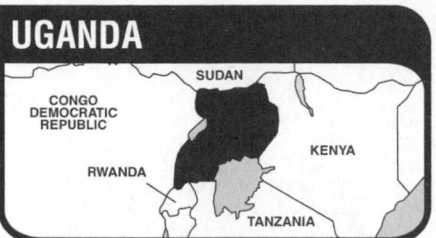

The Republic of Uganda, a former British protectorate located astride the equator in east-central Africa, has an area of 236,040 sq. km. and a population of 31.37 million. Capital: Kampala. Agriculture, including livestock, is the basis of the economy; there is some mining of copper, tin, gold and lead. Coffee, cotton, copper and tea are exported. The colonial boundaries created by Britain to delimit Uganda grouped together a wide range of ethnic groups with different political systems and cultures. These differences prevented the establishment of a working political community after independence was achieved in 1962. The dictatorial regime of Idi Amin (1971-79) was responsible for the deaths of some 300,000 opponents; guerrilla war and human rights abuses under Milton Obote (1980-85) claimed at least another 100,000 lives. The rule of Yoweri Museveni since 1986 has brought relative stability and economic growth to Uganda. During the 1990s, the government promulgated non-party presidential and legislative elections. Notes of East African Currency Board circulated before Bank of Uganda notes were available. Also see East Africa.

MONETARY SYSTEM:

1 Shilling = 100 Cents

Caution: Several years ago the Bank of Uganda sold quantities of demonetized notes, most of which were made available for only $1.00 per note. Condition of notes thus sold is not reported. A listing of some pieces NOT available from the bank includes #4, 6a, 7a, 8a and b, 9a and b, 13a, 14a, 21, 23, and 24a and b.

REPUBLIC

Bank of Uganda

1966 ND Issue

#1-5 Replacement notes. Serial # prefix Z/1 (5/ and 10/); Y/1; X/1; W/1 respectively.

1 5 Shillings

VF UNC

ND (1966). Dark blue on multicolor underprint. Arms at right. Signature titles: *GOVERNOR* and *SECRETARY*. Back: River and waterfall. Watermark: Hand.

		VF	UNC
a. Issued note.		1.50	5.00
s. Specimen.		—	25.00
ct. Color trial.		—	75.00

2 10 Shillings

VF UNC

ND (1966). Brown on multicolor underprint. Arms at center. Signature titles: *GOVERNOR* and *SECRETARY*. Back: Workers picking cotton. Watermark: Hand.

		VF	UNC
a. Issued note.		2.50	5.00
s. Specimen.		—	25.00
ct. Color trial.		—	125

3 20 Shillings

VF UNC

ND (1966). Purple on multicolor underprint. Arms at upper left. Signature titles: *GOVERNOR* and *SECRETARY*. Back: Marabou stork, Green Monkey, Lion, Elephants, Zebra and Impala. Watermark: Hand.

		VF	UNC
a. Issued note.		2.00	6.00
s. Specimen.		—	25.00
ct. Color trial.		—	250

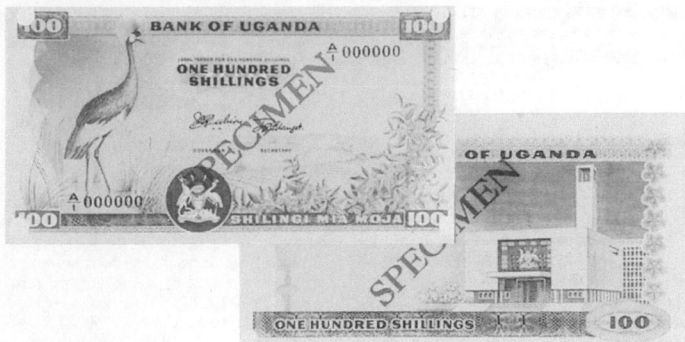

4 100 Shillings   VF   UNC

ND (1966). Green on multicolor underprint. Crowned crane at left, without *FOR BANK OF UGANDA* just below value at center. Signature titles: *GOVERNOR* and *SECRETARY*. Back: Building at right. Watermark: Hand.

    a. Issued note.   75.00   750

    s. Specimen.   —   125

    ct. Color trial.   —   500

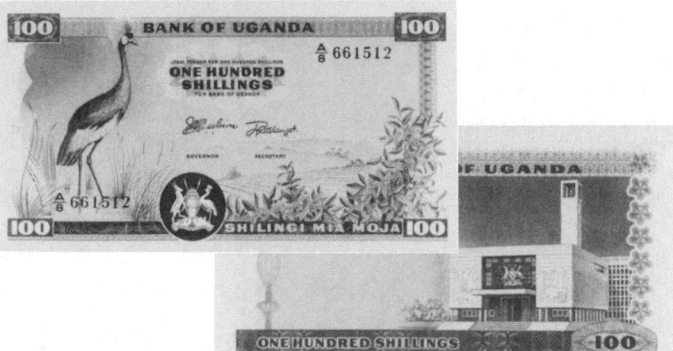

5 100 Shillings   VF   UNC

ND (1966). Green on multicolor underprint. Crowned crane at left, wih text: *FOR BANK OF UGANDA* just below value at center. Signature titles: *GOVERNOR* and *SECRETARY*. Back: Building at right. Watermark: Hand.

    a. Issued note.   1.50   6.00

    s. Specimen.   —   25.00

1973-77 ND Issue

#5A-9 Replacement notes: Serial # prefix *Z/1* **(5/ and 10/);** *Y/1; X/1; W/1* **respectively.**

5A 5 Shillings   VF   UNC

ND (1977). Blue on multicolor underprint. President Idi Amin at left, arms at lower   0.50   2.50
right. Back: Woman picking coffee beans. Watermark: Crested crane.

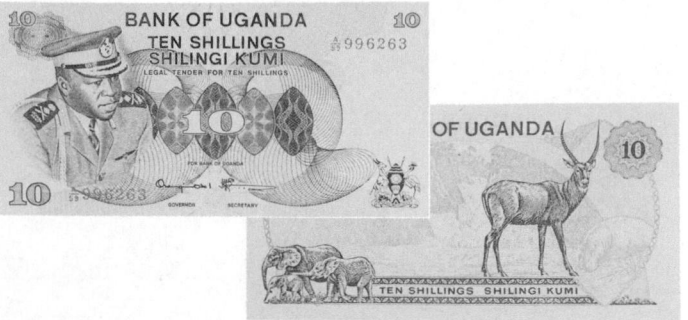

---

6 10 Shillings   VF   UNC

ND (1973). Brown on multicolor underprint. President Idi Amin at left, arms at lower right. Back: Elephants, antelope and hippopotamus. Watermark: Crested crane.

    a. Signature titles: *GOVERNOR* and *DIRECTOR*.   40.00   285

    b. Signature titles: *GOVERNOR* and *SECRETARY*. Signature 1.   2.50   12.50

    c. Signature titles as b. Signature 2.   1.00   6.00

    s. As a. Specimen.   —   80.00

7 20 Shillings   VF   UNC

ND (1973). Purple and brown on multicolor underprint. President Idi Amin at left, arms at lower right. Back: Large building. Watermark: Crested crane.

    a. Signature titles: *GOVERNOR* and *DIRECTOR*.   50.00   300

    b. Signature titles: *GOVERNOR* and *SECRETARY*. Signature 1.   10.00   75.00

    c. Signature titles as b. Signature 2.   2.00   7.50

    s. As a. Specimen.   —   90.00

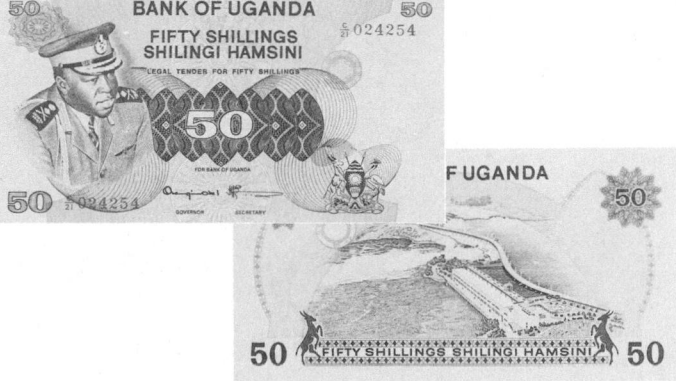

8 50 Shillings   VF   UNC

ND (1973). Blue (shade) on multicolor underprint. President Idi Amin at left, arms at lower right. Back: Hydroelectric dam. Watermark: Crested crane.

    a. Signature titles: *GOVERNOR* and *DIRECTOR*.   40.00   275

    b. Signature titles: *GOVERNOR* and *SECRETARY*. Signature 1.   8.00   85.00

    c. Signature titles as b. Signature 2.   2.00   7.00

    s. As a. Specimen.   —   135

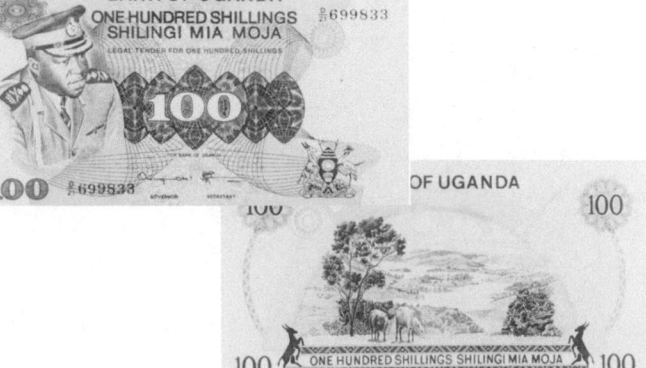

9 100 Shillings   VF   UNC

ND (1973). Green (shades) on multicolor underprint. President Idi Amin at left, arms at lower right. Back: Scene of lake and hills. Watermark: Crested crane.

    a. Signature titles: *GOVERNOR* and *DIRECTOR*.   30.00   150

    b. Signature titles: *GOVERNOR* and *SECRETARY*. Signature 1.   12.50   85.00

    c. Signature titles as b. Signature 2.   2.00   8.50

    s. As a. Specimen.   —   110

1979 Issue

#10-14 Replacement notes: Serial # prefix *Z/1 (5/ and 10/)*; *Y/1; X/1; W/1* **respectively.**

10   5 Shillings

	VF	UNC
	0.20	1.00

ND (1979). Blue on multicolor underprint. Bank of Uganda at left. Signature titles: *GOVERNOR* and *DIRECTOR.* Back: Woman picking coffee beans. Watermark: Crested crane's head.

11   10 Shillings

	VF	UNC

ND (1979). Brown on multicolor underprint. Bank of Uganda at left. Signature titles: *GOVERNOR* and *DIRECTOR.* Back: Elephants, antelope and hippopotamus. Watermark: Crested crane's head.

	VF	UNC
a. Light printing on bank.	1.50	5.00
b. Dark printing on bank.	0.50	2.00

12   20 Shillings

ND (1979). Purple and brown on multicolor underprint. Bank of Uganda at left. Signature titles: *GOVERNOR* and *DIRECTOR.* Back: Large building. Watermark: Crested crane's head.

	VF	UNC
a. Light printing on bank.	2.00	7.50
b. Dark printing on bank.	0.50	2.50

13   50 Shillings

	VF	UNC

ND (1979). Dark blue and purple on multicolor underprint. Bank of Uganda at left. Signature titles: *GOVERNOR* and *DIRECTOR.* Back: Hydroelectric dam. Watermark: Crested crane's head.

	VF	UNC
a. Light printing on bank.	17.50	100
b. Dark printing on bank.	1.00	4.50

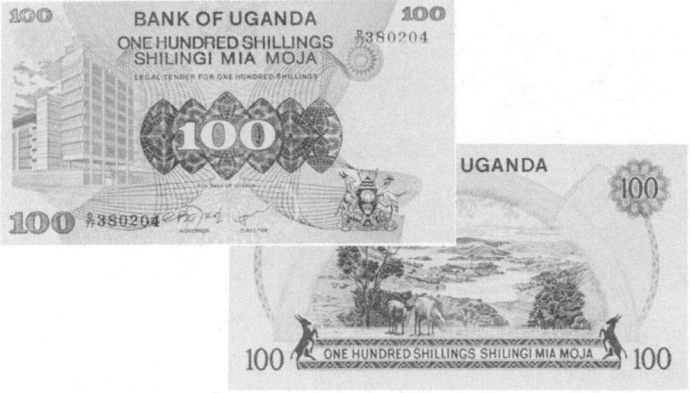

14   100 Shillings

	VF	UNC

ND (1979). Green (shades) on multicolor underprint. Bank of Uganda at left. Signature titles: *GOVERNOR* and *DIRECTOR.* Back: Scene of lake and hills. Watermark: Crested crane's head.

	VF	UNC
a. Light printing on bank.	3.00	12.00
b. Dark printing on bank.	2.50	8.50

1982 Issue

#15-19 Replacement notes: Serial # prefix *Z/1 (5/ and 10/)*; *Y/1; X/1; W/1* **respectively.**

15   5 Shillings

	VF	UNC
	0.25	1.50

ND (1982). Olive-green on multicolor underprint. Arms at left. Signature titles: *GOVERNOR* and *SECRETARY.* Back: Woman picking coffee beans. Watermark: Crested crane's head.

16   10 Shillings

	VF	UNC
	0.50	3.00

ND (1982). Purple on multicolor underprint. Arms at left. Signature titles: *GOVERNOR* and *SECRETARY.* Back: Elephants, antelope and hippopotamus. Watermark: Crested crane's head.

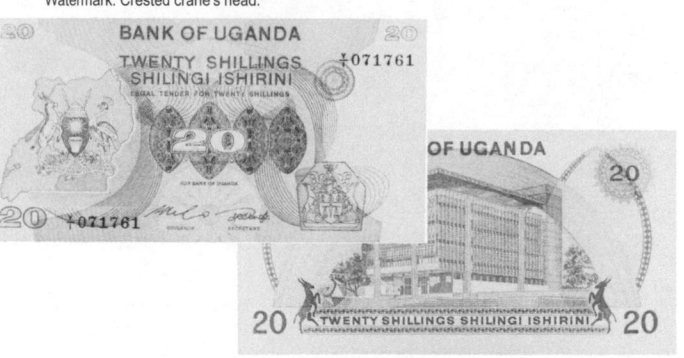

17 20 Shillings VF UNC
ND (1982). Green, dark red and multicolor. Arms at left. Signature titles: *GOVER-* 2.00 7.00
NOR and *SECRETARY*. Back: Large building. Watermark: Crested crane's head.

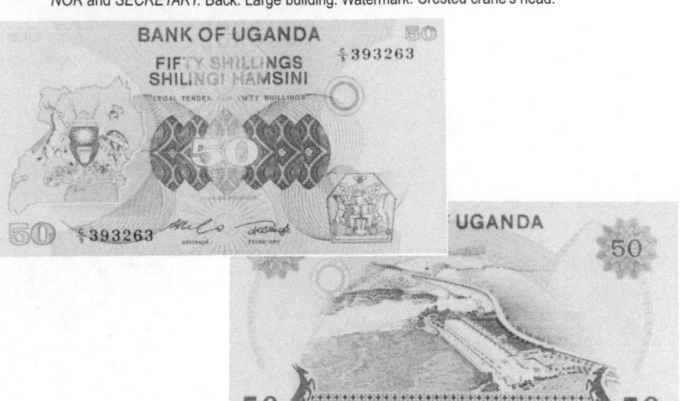

18 50 Shillings VF UNC
ND (1982). Brown, orange and multicolor. Arms at left. Signature titles: *GOVERNOR*
and *SECRETARY*. Back: Hydroelectric dam. Watermark: Crested crane's head.
   a. Signature titles: *GOVERNOR* and *SECRETARY*. 0.75 4.00
   b. Signature titles: *GOVERNOR* and *DEPUTY GOVERNOR*. 1.00 10.00
   s. Specimen. Red overprint: SPECIMEN on both sides. — 60.00

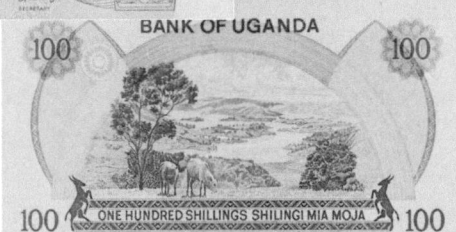

19 100 Shillings VF UNC
ND (1982). Red-violet, orange and multicolor. Arms at left. Signature titles: *GOV-*
ERNOR and *SECRETARY*. Back: Scene of lake and hills. Watermark: Crested
crane's head.
   a. Signature titles: *GOVERNOR* and *SECRETARY*. 1.00 4.50
   b. Signature titles: *GOVERNOR* and *DEPUTY GOVERNOR*. Small or large 1.50 7.50
      prefix letter and # before serial #.
   s. Specimen. Red overprint: SPECIMEN on both sides. — 50.00

1983-85 Issue

#20-23 Replacement notes: Serial # prefix *X/1; W/1; U/1; T/1; S/1* **respectively.**

20 50 Shillings VF UNC
ND (1985). Brown and orange on multicolor underprint. President Milton Obote at 1.00 4.50
left. Signature titles: *GOVERNOR* and *DEPUTY GOVERNOR*. Back: Hydroelectric dam. Watermark: Hand.

21 100 Shillings VF UNC
ND (1985). Red-violet and orange on multicolor underprint. President Milton 4.00 22.50
Obote at left. Signature titles: *GOVERNOR* and *DEPUTY GOVERNOR*. Back:
Scene of lake and hills. Watermark: Hand.

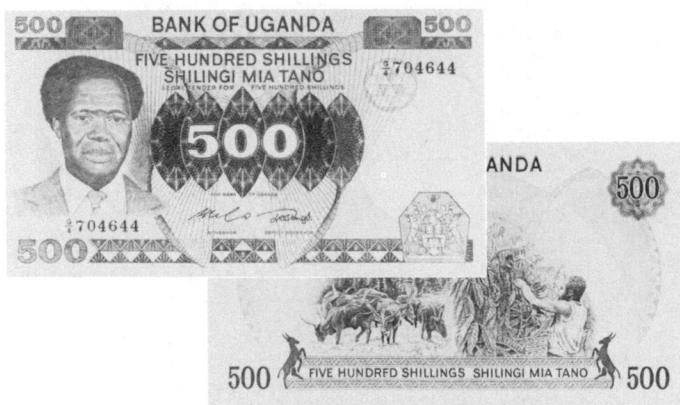

22 500 Shillings VF UNC
ND (1983). Blue, purple and multicolor. President Milton Obote at left. Signature
titles: *GOVERNOR* and *DEPUTY GOVERNOR*. Serial number prefix varieties as
#19b. Back: Cattle and harvesting. Watermark: Hand.
   a. Issued note. 1.00 5.00
   s. Specimen. — 10.00

23 1000 Shillings VF UNC
ND (1983). Red and multicolor. President Milton Obote at left. Signature titles:
GOVERNOR and *DEPUTY GOVERNOR*. Serial number prefix varieties as #19b.
Back: Building. Watermark: Hand.
   a. Issued note. 4.00 22.50
   s. Specimen. — 12.50

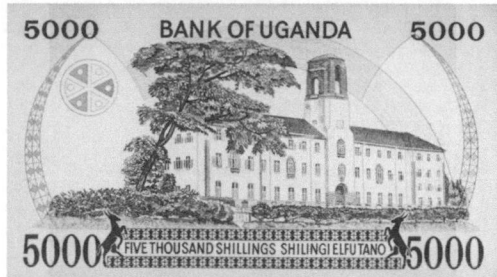

24 5000 Shillings VF UNC
1985-86. Purple and multicolor. Arms at left. Back: Building with clock tower at
center right.
  a. Watermark: Hand. 1985. 6.00 30.00
  b. Watermark: Crested crane. 1986. 1.50 5.00
  s. Specimen. Red overprint: SPECIMEN on each side. — 60.00

1985-86 Issue

#25 and 26 Replacement notes: Serial # prefix U/1; T/1 respectively.

25 500 Shillings VF UNC
1986. Blue, purple and multicolor. Arms at left. Back: Cattle and harvesting. 0.75 3.00
Watermark: Crested crane's head.

26 1000 Shillings VF UNC
1986. Red and multicolor. Arms at left. Back: Building. Watermark: Crested 1.00 4.50
crane's head.

1987 Issue

#27-34 Replacement notes: Serial # prefix ZZ.

27 5 Shillings VF UNC
1987. UV: value 5 in box fluoresces orange. Back design elements green. Brown 0.30 2.00
on multicolor underprint. Arms at right and upper left. Map at center. Back:
Crowned crane, hippo, elephant and waterbuck. Printer: TDLR.

28 10 Shillings VF UNC
1987. UV: value 10 fluoresces orange. back design elements green. Green on 0.30 2.50
multicolor underprint. Arms at right and upper left. Map at center. Back: Two
antelope grazing, two men fishing in canoe at center. Printer: TDLR.

29 20 Shillings VF UNC
1987-88. Purple, blue-black and violet on multicolor underprint. Arms at upper left,
map at center. Back: Modern buildings at center right. Watermark: Crested crane's
head. Printer: TDLR.
  a. Imprint on back. 1987. 0.50 2.50
  b. Without imprint. 1988. 0.25 1.50

30 50 Shillings VF UNC
1987-98. UV: value 50 fluoresce yellow. Back design elements yellow. Red,
orange and dark brown on multicolor underprint. Arms at upper left, map at center.
Back: Parliament building at center right. Watermark: Crested crane's head.
Printer: TDLR.
  a. Imprint on back. 1987. 0.50 2.50
  b. Without imprint. 1988; 1989. 0.50 2.00
  c. 1994; 1996; 1997; 1998. 0.25 1.00

31 100 Shillings VF UNC
1987-98. Deep blue-violet, black and aqua on multicolor underprint. Arms at upper
left, map at center. Back: High Court building with clock tower at center right.
Watermark: Crested crane's head. Printer: TDLR.
  a. Signature titles: GOVERNOR and SECRETARY, TREASURY. Imprint on 1.00 4.50
    back. 1987.
  b. As a. but without imprint on back. 1988. 0.75 2.00
  c. As b. but with signature titles: GOVERNOR and SECRETARY. 1994; 1996; 0.25 1.50
    1997; 1998.

32 200 Shillings
1987-98. Brown, orange and olive-brown on multicolor underprint. Arms at upper left, map at center. Back: Worker in textile factory at center right. Watermark: Crested crane's head. Printer: TDLR.

		VF	UNC
a. 1987.		0.50	4.00
b. 1991; 1994; 1996; 1998.		0.50	2.50

1991 Issue

33 500 Shillings
1991. Dark brown and deep purple on multicolor underprint. Elephant at left, arms at upper center and lower right. Back: Uganda Independence Monument at left, municipal building with clock tower at center. Watermark: Crested crane's head.

		VF	UNC
a. Signature titles: *GOVERNOR* and *SECRETARY, TREASURY*.		1.00	4.00
b. Signature titles: *GOVERNOR* and *SECRETARY*.		1.00	4.50
s. As a. Specimen.		—	30.00

34 1000 Shillings
1991. Black, deep brown-violet and dark green on multicolor underprint. Farmers at left, arms at upper center and lower right. Back: Grain storage facility at center. Watermark: Crested crane's head.

		VF	UNC
a. Signature titles: *GOVERNOR* and *SECRETARY, TREASURY*.		2.50	5.00
b. Signature titles: *GOVERNOR* and *SECRETARY*.		1.25	4.00

1993-95 Issue

#35-38 Replacement notes: Serial # prefix *ZZ*.

35 500 Shillings
1994; 1996-98. UV: fibers fluoresce blue and yellow; value 500 in rectangle yellow; serial # orange. Dark brown and deep purple on multicolor underprint. Arms at upper center. Ascending size serial number vertically at left. Segmented foil over security thread. Back: Uganda Independence Monument at left, municipal building with clock tower at center. Watermark: Crested crane's head.

		VF	UNC
a. 1994; 1996.		2.00	4.00
b. 1997; 1998.		2.50	5.00

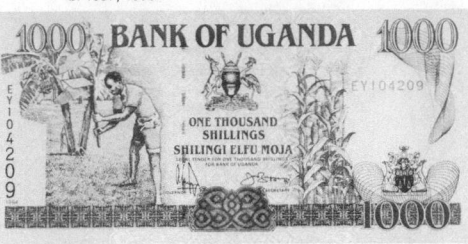

36 1000 Shillings
1994; 1996; 1998; 1999. Segmented foil over security thread. Black, deep brown-violet and dark green on multicolor underprint. Arms at upper center. Ascending size serial number vertically at left. Back: Grain storage facility at center. Watermark: Crested crane's head. 152x74mm.

	VF	UNC
	1.25	3.50

37 5000 Shillings
1993; 1998. Red-violet, deep purple and dark green on multicolor underprint. Arms at upper center. Lake Bunyonyi, terraces at left. Ascending size serial number vertically at left. Back: Railroad cars being loaded onto Kaawa Ferry at center, plant at lower right. Watermark: Crested crane's head. 152x74mm.

		VF	UNC
a. 1993.		5.00	12.50
b. 1998.		FV	12.00

38 10,000 Shillings
1995; 1998. Green and red on multicolor underprint. Arms at upper center. Musical instruments at left. Ascending size serial number vertically at left. Back: Owen Falls dam, kudu. Watermark: Crested crane's head. 152x74mm.

		VF	UNC
a. 1995.		10.00	25.00
b. 1998.		FV	22.50

1999-2002 Issue

39 1000 Shillings VF UNC

2000; 2003. Black, deep brown-violet and dark green on multicolor underprint. Arms at upper center in brown and green. Numerals of value at lower right all in dark brown. Ascending size serial number vertically at left. Back: Grain storage facility at center. Watermark: Crested crane's head. 152x74mm.

a. 2000.		FV	3.00
b. 2003.		FV	3.00

39A 1000 Shillings VF UNC

2001. Black, deep brown-violet and dark green on multicolor underprint. Arms at upper center in brown and green. Numerals of value at lower right all in dark brown. Ascending size serial number vertically at left. Different security devices. Back: Grain storage facility at center. Different security devices. Watermark: Crested crane's head.

FV 3.00

40 5000 Shillings VF UNC

2000; 2002. Red-violet, deep purple and dark green on multicolor underprint. Arms at upper center. Lake Bunyonyi, terraces at left. Ascending size serial number vertically at left. Silver leaf overlay at upper left center and security V symbol at lower right. Back: Railroad cars being loaded onto Kaawa Ferry at center, plant at lower right. Watermark: Crested crane's head. 152x74mm.

FV 10.00

40A 5000 Shillings VF UNC

2002. Red-violet, deep purple and dark green on multicolor underprint. Like #40 but different devices added. Back: Railroad cars being loaded onto Kaawa Ferry at center, plant at lower right. Watermark: Crested crane's head. 152x74mm.

FV 10.00

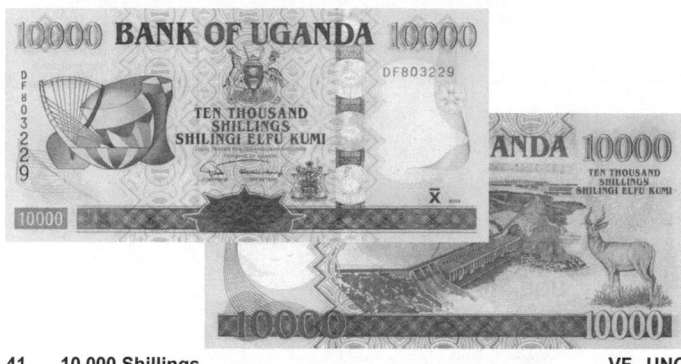

41 10,000 Shillings VF UNC

2001; 2003; 2004. Red, green, brown and multicolor. Arms at upper center. Musical instruments at left. Ascending size serial number vertically at left. Changes in security devices. Back: Owen Falls dam, kudu. Changes in security devices. Watermark: Crested crane's head. 157x76mm.

a. 2001.		FV	17.50
b. 2003.		FV	17.50
c. 2004.		FV	17.50

42 20,000 Shillings VF UNC

1999; 2002. Green on multicolor underprint. Crested crane at left, arms at upper center. Silver vertical OVD strip with repeated value at right. Two signature varieties. Back: Modern building. Watermark: Arms. 160x78mm.

FV 30.00

2003-04 Issue

43 1000 Shillings VF UNC

2005; 2008; 2009. Black, deep brown-violet and dark green on multicolor underprint. Farmer at left. Silver OVD strip at right. Back: Grain storage facility at center. 152x74mm.

a. 2008.		FV	3.00
a. 2005.		FV	3.00
c. 2009.		FV	3.00

44   5000 Shillings

2004; 2005; 2008; 2009. Red-violet, deep purple and dark green on multicolor underprint. Lake Bunyonyi , terraces at left. Arms at upper center. Back: Railroad cars being loaded onto Kaawa Ferry at center. 152x74mm.

		VF	UNC
a. 2004.		FV	7.50
b. 2005.		FV	7.50
c. 2008.		FV	7.50
d. 2009.		FV	7.50

45   10,000 Shillings

2005; 2008; 2009. Red, green, brown and multicolor. Musical instruments at left. Back: Owen Falls Dam at center, kudu at right. 157x76mm.

		VF	UNC
a. 2005.		FV	12.50
b. 2008.		FV	12.50
c. 2009.		FV	12.50

46   20,000 Shillings

2004; 2005; 2008; 2009. Multicolor. Crested crane at left, arms at upper center. Silver vertical OVD strip with repeated value at right. Two signature varieties. Different security devices. Back: Modern building. Different security devices. Watermark: Arms. 160x78mm.

		VF	UNC
a. 2004.		FV	20.00
b. 2005.		FV	20.00
c. 2008.		FV	20.00
d. 2009.		FV	20.00

47   50,000 Shillings

2003; 2007; 2008. Brown. Monument at left. Back: Cotton harvest. 164x80mm.

		VF	UNC
a. 2003.		FV	45.00
b. 2007.		FV	45.00
c. 2008.		FV	45.00

2007 Commemorative Issue

48   10,000 Shillings

23-25.11.2007. For the Commonwealth Heads of Goverment Meeting. Orange, brown, green and multicolor CHOGM logo at left center. Back: Own Falls dam and gorillas. 157x76mm.

	VF	UNC
	FV	15.00

2010 Issue

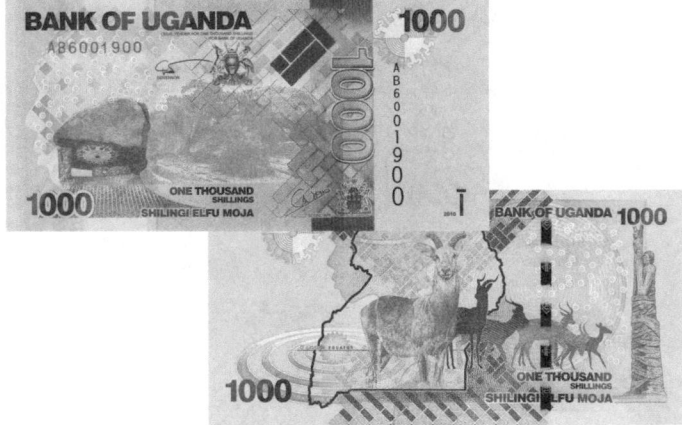

49   1000 Shillings

2010; 2013; 2015. Brown and orange on multicolor underprint. One variant of signatures (14).

		VF	UNC
a. 2010.		FV	3.00
b. 2013.		FV	3.00
c. 2015.		FV	3.00

50   2000 Shillings

2010; 2013; 2015. Blue on multicolor underprint. One variant of signatures (14).

		VF	UNC
a. 2010.		FV	5.00
b. 2013.		FV	5.00
c. 2015.		FV	5.00

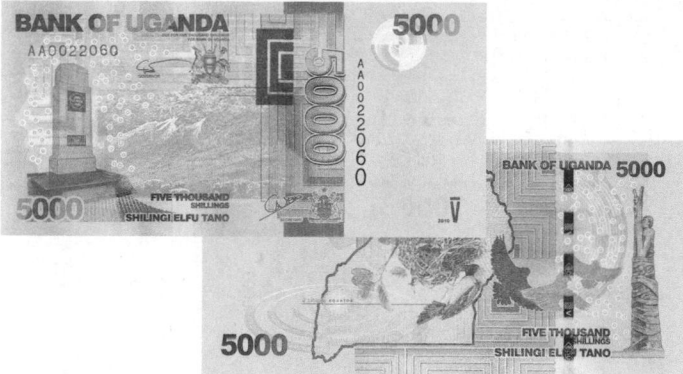

51   5000 Shillings **VF   UNC**

2010; 2011; 2013; 2015. Green on multicolor underprint. One variant of signatures (14).

a. 2010. FV   7.50
b. 2011. FV   7.50
c. 2013. FV   7.50
d. 2015. FV   7.50

52   10,000 Shillings **VF   UNC**

2010; 2011; 2013. Purple on multicolor underprint. One variant of signatures (14).

a. 2010. FV   12.50
b. 2011. FV   12.50
c. 2013. FV   12.50

53   20,000 Shillings **VF   UNC**

2010; 2013. Rose on multicolor underprint. One variant of signatures (14).

a. 2010. FV   20.00
b. 2013. FV   20.00

54   50,000 Shillings **VF   UNC**

2010; 2013. Yellow and ochre on multicolor underprint. One variant of signatures (14).

a. 2010. FV   45.00
b. 2013. FV   45.00

UKRAINE

Ukraine is bordered by Russia to the east, Russia and Belarus to the north, Poland, Slovakia and Hungary to the west, Romania and Moldova to the southwest and in the south by the Black Sea and the Sea of Azov. It has an area of 603,700 sq. km. and a population of 45.99 million. Capital: Kyiv (Kiev). Coal, grain, vegetables and heavy industrial machinery are major exports. The territory of Ukraine has been inhabited for over 30,000 years.

As the result of its location, Ukraine has served as the gateway to Europe for millennia and its early history has been recorded by Arabic, Greek, Roman, as well as Ukrainian historians.Ukraine was the center of the first eastern Slavic state, Kyivan Rus, which during the 10th and 11th centuries was the largest and most powerful state in Europe. Weakened by internecine quarrels and Mongol invasions, Kyivan Rus was incorporated into the Grand Duchy of Lithuania and eventually into the Polish-Lithuanian Commonwealth. The cultural and religious legacy of Kyivan Rus laid the foundation for Ukrainian nationalism through subsequent centuries. A new Ukrainian state, the Cossack Hetmanate, was established during the mid-17th century after an uprising against the Poles. Despite continuous Muscovite pressure, the Hetmanate managed to remain autonomous for well over 100 years. During the latter part of the 18th century, most Ukrainian ethnographic territory was absorbed by the Russian Empire. Following the collapse of czarist Russia in 1917, Ukraine was able to bring about a short-lived period of independence (1917-20), but was reconquered and forced to endure a brutal Soviet rule that engineered two artificial famines (1921-22 and 1932-33) in which over 8 million died. In World War II, German and Soviet armies were responsible for some 7 to 8 million more deaths. Although final independence for Ukraine was achieved in 1991 with the dissolution of the USSR, democracy remained elusive as the legacy of state control and endemic corruption stalled efforts at economic reform, privatization, and civil liberties. A peaceful mass protest "Orange Revolution" in the closing months of 2004 forced the authorities to overturn a rigged presidential election and to allow a new internationally monitored vote that swept into power a reformist slate under Viktor Yushchenko. Subsequent internal squabbles in the Yushchenko camp allowed his rival Viktor Yanukovych to stage a comeback in parliamentary elections and become prime minister in August of 2006. An early legislative election, brought on by a political crisis in the spring of 2007, saw Yuliya Tymoshenko, as head of an "Orange" coalition, installed as a new prime minister in December 2007.

MONETARY SYSTEM:

1 Karbovanets (Karbovantsiv) = 2 Hryven
1917-1920 = 200 Shahiv
1 Karvovanets (Karbovantsiv) = 1 Russian Ruble, 1991-96
1 Hryvnia (Hryvni, Hryven) = 100,000 Karbovantsiv, 1996-

УКРАЇНСЬКА Р.С.Р.

Treasury

1990-92 КУПОН Ruble Control Coupon Issue

#68-72 are Consumer cards (coupons) were not legal tender on their own but were required to be used in conjunction with U.S.S.R. rubles and only then could they perform the function of money within the Ukraine. Tehse cards were issued once a month, with the month preprinted. Various authorization handstamps are used in central registry square. Uniface.

68   20 Karbovantsiv **VF   UNC**

1990-92. Sheet of 28 coupons and registry.

a. 1990. November. Листопад. —   4.00
b. 1990. December. Грудень. —   4.00
c. 1991. January. Січень.   4.00
d. 1991. February. Лютий —   4.00
e. 1991. March. Березень. —   4.00
f. 1991. April. Квітень. —   4.00
g. 1991. May. Травень. —   4.00
h. 1991. June. Червень. —   4.00
i. 1991. July. Липень. —   4.00
j. 1991. August. Серпень. —   4.00
k. 1991. September. Вересень. —   4.00
l. 1991. October. Жовтень. —   4.00
m. 1991. November. Листопад. —   4.00
n. 1991. December. Грудень. —   4.00
o. 1992. January. Січень. —   4.00

<table>
</table>

		VF	UNC
j. 1991. August. Серпень.		—	4.00
k. 1991. September. Вересень.		—	4.00
l. 1991. October. Жовтень.		—	4.00
m. 1991. November. Листопад.		—	4.00
n. 1991. December. Грудень.		—	4.00
o. 1992. January. СіЧень.		—	4.00

72   200 Karbovantsiv

1990-92. Sheet of 28 coupons and registry.

	VF	UNC
a. 1990. November. Листопад.	—	4.00
b. 1990. December. Грудень.	—	4.00
c. 1991. January. СіЧень.	—	4.00
d. 1991. February. Лютий.	—	4.00
e. 1991. March. Березень.	—	4.00
f. 1991. April. Квітень.	—	4.00
g. 1991. May. Травень.	—	4.00
h. 1991. June. Червень.	—	4.00
i. 1991. July. Липень.	—	4.00
j. 1991. August. Серпень.	—	4.00
k. 1991. September. Вересень.	—	4.00
l. 1991. October. Жовтень.	—	4.00
m. 1991. November. Листопад.	—	4.00
n. 1991. December. Грудень.	—	4.00
o. 1992. January. СіЧень.	—	4.00

#73-80 not assigned.

НАЦІОНАЛЬНИЙ БАНК УКРАЇНИ

UKRAINIAN NATIONAL BANK

1991 КУПОН Control Coupon Issue

Karbovanets System Originally issued at par and temporarily to be used jointly with Russian rubles in commodity purchases as a means of currency control (similar to Ruble Control Coupons above). They soon became more popular while the ruble slowly depreciated in exchange value. This did not last very long and the karbovanets has since suffered a higher inflation rate than the Russian ruble.

81   1 Karbovanets   VF   UNC

1991. 1 KRB printed sideways with fluorescent ink at left. Dull brown and pale orange on yellow underprint. Lybid, Viking sister of the founding brothers at left. All notes without serial number. Back: Cathedral of St. Sophia in Kiev at left center. Watermark: Paper. Printer: ISPB (France).

	VF	UNC
a. Issued note.	0.50	1.00
s1. Specimen. Perforated *SPECIMEN*.	—	200
s2. Specimen. Overprint *SPECIMEN*.	—	200

82   3 Karbovantsi   VF   UNC

1991. 3 KRB printed sideways with fluorescent ink at left. Greenish gray and pale orange on yellow underprint. Lybid, Viking sister of the founding brothers at left. All notes without serial number. Back: Cathedral of St. Sophia in Kiev at left center. Watermark: Paper. Printer: ISPB (France).

	VF	UNC
a. Issued note.	1.00	2.00
b. Issued note with imprint 3 *Kpe* at left.	1.00	2.00
s1. Specimen. Perforated *SPECIMEN*.	—	200
s2. Specimen. Overprint *SPECIMEN*.	—	200

83   5 Karbovantsiv   VF   UNC

1991. 5 KRB printed sideways with fluorescent ink at left. Dull blue-violet and pale orange on yellow underprint. Lybid, Viking sister of the founding brothers at left. All notes without serial number. Back: Cathedral of St. Sophia in Kiev at left center. Watermark: Paper. Printer: ISPB (France).

	VF	UNC
a. Issued note.	1.00	2.00
s1. Specimen. Perforated *SPECIMEN*.	—	200
s2. Specimen. Overprint *SPECIMEN*.	—	200
x. Error. No printing on face.	—	10.00

69   50 Karbovantsiv   VF   UNC

1990-92. Sheet of 28 coupons and registery.

	VF	UNC
a. 1990. November. Листопад.	—	4.00
b. 1990. December. Грудень.	—	4.00
c. 1991. January. Січень.	—	4.00
d. 1991. February. Лютий.	—	4.00
e. 1991. March. Березень.	—	4.00
f. 1991. April. Квітень.	—	4.00
g. 1991. May. Травень.	—	4.00
h. 1991. June. Червень.	—	4.00
i. 1991. July. Липень.	—	4.00
j. 1991. August. Серпень.	—	4.00
k. 1991. September. Вересень.	—	4.00
l. 1991. October. Жовтень.	—	4.00
m. 1991. November. Листопад.	—	4.00
n. 1991. December. Грудень.	—	4.00
o. 1992. January. Січень.	—	4.00

70   75 Karbovantsiv   VF   UNC

1990-92. Sheet of 28 coupons and registery.

	VF	UNC
a. 1990. November. Листопад.	—	4.00
b. 1990. December. Грудень.	—	4.00
c. 1991. January. СіЧень.	—	4.00
d. 1991. February. Лютий.	—	4.00
e. 1991. March. Березень.	—	4.00
f. 1991. April. Квітень.	—	4.00
g. 1991. May. Травень.	—	4.00
h. 1991. June. Червень.	—	4.00
i. 1991. July. Липень.	—	4.00
j. 1991. August. Серпень.	—	4.00
k. 1991. Sptember. Вересень.	—	4.00
l. 1991. October. Жовтень.	—	4.00
m. 1991. November. Листопад.	—	4.00
n. 1991. December. Грудень.	—	4.00
o. 1991. January. Січень.	—	4.00

71   100 Karbovantsiv   VF   UNC

1990-92. Sheet of 28 coupons plus registery.

	VF	UNC
a. 1990. November. Листопад.	—	4.00
b. 1990. December. Грудень.	—	4.00
c. 1991. January. СіЧень.	—	4.00
d. 1991. February. Лютий.	—	4.00
e. 1991. March. Березень.	—	4.00
f. 1991. April. Квітень.	—	4.00
g. 1991. May. Травень.	—	4.00
h. 1991. June. Червень.	—	4.00
i. 1991. July. Липень.	—	4.00

84 10 Karbovantsiv — VF UNC

1991. 10 KRB printed sideways with fluorescent ink at left. Pink and pale orange on yellow underprint. Lybid, Viking sister of the founding brothers at left. All notes without serial number. Back: Cathedral of St. Sophia in Kiev at left center. Watermark: Paper. Printer: ISPB (France).

- a. Issued note. — 1.00 2.00
- s1. Specimen. Perforated *SPECIMEN*. — — 200
- s2. Specimen. Overprint *SPECIMEN*. — — 200

85 25 Karbovantsiv — VF UNC

1991. 25 KRB printed sideways with fluorescent ink at left. Purple and pale orange on yellow underprint. Lybid, Viking sister of the founding brothers at left. All notes without serial number. Back: Cathedral of St. Sophia in Kiev at left center. Watermark: Paper. Printer: ISPB (France).

- a. Issued note. — 2.00 5.00
- s1. Specimen. Perforated *SPECIMEN*. — — 200
- s2. Specimen. Overprint *SPECIMEN*. — — 200

86 50 Karbovantsiv — VF UNC

1991. 50 KRB printed sideways with fluorescent ink at left. Blue-green and pale orange on yellow underprint. Lybid, Viking sister of the founding brothers at left. All notes without serial number. Back: Cathedral of St. Sophia in Kiev at left center. Watermark: Paper. Printer: ISPB (France).

- a. Issued note. — 1.00 3.00
- b. Issued note with *50 Kps* at left. — 0.70 1.00
- s1. As a. Specimen. Perforated *SPECIMEN*. — — 200
- s2. As a. Specimen. Overprint *SPECIMEN*. — — 200

87 100 Karbovantsiv — VF UNC

1991. 100 KRB printed sideways with fluorescent ink at left. Brown-violet and pale orange on yellow underprint. Lybid, Viking sister of the founding brothers at left. All notes without serial number. Back: Cathedral of St. Sophia in Kiev at left center. Watermark: Paper. Printer: ISPB (France).

- a. Issued note. — 3.00 7.00
- s1. Specimen. Perforated *SPECIMEN*. — — 200
- s2. Specimen. Overprint *SPECIMEN*. — — 200

87A 250 Karbovantsiv — VF UNC

1991. Proof perforated: *SPECIMEN*. Unissued. Eight color varieties. Blue and red. — — 500

87B 500 Karbovantsiv — VF UNC

1991. Proof perforated *SPECIMEN*. Unissued. Eight color varieties. — — 500

1992 Issue

#88-91 Replacement notes: Serial # prefix *.../99* in denominator.

88 100 Karbovantsiv — VF UNC

1992. Orange on lilac and ochre underprint. Founding Viking brothers Kyi, Shchek and Khoryv with sister Libyd in bow of boat at left. All notes with serial number. Back: Cathedral of St. Sophia in Kiev at left center. Watermark: Paper. Printer: TDLR (without imprint).

- a. Issued note. — 1.00 4.00
- r. Replacement note. — 3.00 6.00
- s. Specimen. Red overprint on both sides. — — 25.00

89 200 Karbovantsiv — VF UNC

1992. Dull brown and silver on lilac and ochre underprint. Founding Viking brothers Kyi, Shchek and Khoryv with sister Libyd in bow of boat at left. All notes with serial number. Back: Cathedral of St. Sophia in Kiev at left center. Watermark: Paper. Printer: TDLR (without imprint).

- a. Issued note. — 2.00 6.00
- r. Replacement note. — 2.50 7.00
- s. Specimen. Red overprint on both sides. — — 25.00

00 500 Karbovantsiv — VF UNC

1992. Blue-green and silver on lilac and ochre underprint. Founding Viking brothers Kyi, Shchek and Khoryv with sister Libyd in bow of boat at left. All notes with serial number. Back: Cathedral of St. Sophia in Kiev at left center. Watermark: Paper. Printer: TDLR (without imprint).

- a. Issued note. — 1.00 5.00
- r. Replacement note. — 3.00 7.00
- s. Specimen. Red overprint on both sides. — — 25.00

91 1000 Karbovantsiv — VF UNC

1992. Red-violet and light green on lilac and ochre underprint. Founding Viking brothers Kyi, Shchek and Khoryv with sister Libyd in bow of boat at left. All notes with serial number. Back: Cathedral of St. Sophia in Kiev at left center. Watermark: Paper. Printer: TDLR (without imprint).

- a. Issued note. — 0.75 2.00
- r. Replacement note. — 2.50 6.00
- s. Specimen. Red overprint on both sides. — — 25.00

GOVERNMENT

Treasury

1992 СЕРТИФІКАТ - Compensation Certificate Issue

#91A and 91B The exact use of these notes has come into question.

91A 1,000,000 Karbovantsiv — VF UNC

1992. Dull blue-green, orange and gray on pale orange and pale green underprint. Church at left, small arms at upper right. Back: Text. — 2.00 7.00

91B 2,000,000 Karbovantsiv

VF UNC

1992. Green, orange and pink with black text on light blue, pink and multicolor underprint. Church at left, small arms at upper right. Back: Text.

6.00 10.00

НАЦІОНАЛЬНИЙ БАНК УКРАЇНИ

Ukrainian National Bank

1993 Issue

#92 and 93 Replacement notes: Serial # prefix *001/92-001/99; 001/99* for notes dated 1993.

92 2000 Karbovantsiv

VF UNC

1993. Blue and olive-green on aqua and gold underprint. Founding Viking brothers Kyi, Shchek and Khoryv with sister Libyd in bow of boat at left. All notes with serial number. Trident shield added at left. Back: Cathedral of St.Sophia in Kiev at left center. Trident shield added at right. Watermark: Paper. Printer: TDLR (without imprint).

a. Issued note.	2.00	5.00
s. Specimen.	—	10.00

93 5000 Karbovantsiv

VF UNC

1993; 1995. Red-orange and olive-brown on pale blue and ochre underprint. Founding Viking brothers Kyi, Shchek and Khoryv with sister Libyd in bow of boat at left. All notes with serial number. Trident shield added at left. Back: Cathedral of St.Sophia in Kiev at left center. Trident shield added at right. Watermark: Paper. Printer: TDLR (without imprint).

a. 1993.	1.00	3.00
b. 1995.	2.50	5.00
r. Replacement note. 1993.	3.00	6.00
s1. Specimen. 1993.	—	25.00
s2. Specimen. 1995.	—	25.00

#94-97 Printer: TDLR (Serial # as a fraction) or Banknote Printing and Minting works of the National Bank of Ukraine, Kyiv (BPMW) (serial # prefix is 2 letters) (Both w/o imprint).

94 10,000 Karbovantsiv

VF UNC

1993-96. Apple green and tan on pale blue and ochre underprint. Statue of St. Volodymyr standing with long cross at left. Trident shield at left. Back: Building facade at left, trident shield at right. Watermark: Ornamental shield repeated vertically.

a. 1993.	1.00	2.00
b. 1995.	0.50	1.00
c. 1996. Watermark: Zig-zag of 4 bars. (parquet-paper).	1.00	2.00
s1. Specimen. 1993. Red overprint on both sides.	—	25.00
s2. Specimen. 1995. Red overprint on both sides.	—	25.00
s3. Specimen. 1996. Red overprint on both sides.	—	25.00

95 20,000 Karbovantsiv

VF UNC

1993-96. Lilac and tan on blue and yellow underprint. Statue of St. Volodymyr standing with long cross at left. Trident shield at left. Back: Building façade at left, trident shield at right. Watermark: Ornamental shield repeated vertically.

a. 1993.	1.00	4.00
b. 1994.	1.00	4.00
c. 1995.	1.00	3.00
d. 1996. Watermark: Zig-zag of 4 bars. (parquet-paper).	1.00	3.00
s1. Specimen. 1993. Red overprint on both sides.	—	25.00
s2. Specimen. 1994. Red overprint on both sides.	—	25.00
s3. Specimen. 1995. Red overprint on both sides.	—	25.00
s4. Specimen. 1996. Red overprint on both sides.	—	25.00

96 50,000 Karbovantsiv

VF UNC

1993-95. Dull orange and blue on multicolor underprint. Statue of St. Volodymyr standing with long cross at left. Trident shield at left. Back: Building façade at left, trident shield at right. Watermark: Ornamental shield repeated vertically.

a. 1993.	2.00	6.00
b. 1994.	1.00	4.00
c. 1995.	1.00	4.00
s1. Specimen. 1993.	—	25.00
s2. Specimen. 1994.	—	25.00
s3. Specimen. 1995.	—	25.00

97 100,000 Karbovantsiv

VF UNC

1993; 1994. Gray-green and ochre on multicolor underprint. Statue of St. Volodymyr standing with long cross at left. Trident shield at left. Back: Building façade at left, trident shield at right. Watermark: Trident shield repeated.

a. Prefix fraction before serial #. 1993.	4.00	10.00
b. Prefix letters with serial #. 1994.	2.00	6.00
s1. Specimen. 1993.	—	30.00
s2. Specimen. 1994.	—	17.50

#98 and 99 Replacement notes: Serial # prefix *001/92-001/99; 001-99* for notes dated 1994.

98 200,000 Karbovantsiv

VF UNC

1994. Dull red-brown and light blue on aqua and gray underprint. Statue of St. Volodymyr standing with long cross at right. Back: Opera house at left center. Watermark: Trident shield repeated.

		VF	UNC
a.	Prefix fraction before serial #. 1994.	5.00	15.00
b.	Prefix letters with serial #. 1994.	5.00	10.00
s1.	Specimen. 1994. Serial # prefix as a fraction.	—	30.00
s2.	Specimen. 1994. Serial # prefix as letter.	—	17.50

99 500,000 Karbovantsiv

VF UNC

1994. Light blue and lilac on yellow and gray underprint. Statue of St. Volodymyr standing with long cross at right. Back: Opera house at left center. Watermark: Trident shield repeated.

		VF	UNC
a.	Issued note.	10.00	20.00
s.	Specimen.	—	30.00

1995 Issue

100 1,000,000 Karbovantsiv

VF UNC

1995. Dark brown on pale orange, light blue and multicolor underprint. Statue of T. G. Shevchenko at right, arms at lower left. Back: Kiev State University at left center, arms at lower right.

		VF	UNC
a.	Issued note.	15.00	30.00
s.	Specimen.	—	30.00

1995 Privatization Certificate Issue

101 1,050,000 Karbovantsiv

VF UNC

1995. Dark gray on light gray and ochre underprint. Arms at upper left. Back: Text. 15.00 35.00

#102 not assigned.

1992 (1996) Regular Issue

#103-107 wmk: Trident repeated. Printer: CBNC (w/o imprint). Replacement notes: First digit of serial # is 9.

103 1 Hryvnia

VF UNC

1992 (1996). Olive-brown on multicolor underprint. Ruins of Kherson at center. Back: St. Volodymr at center.

		VF	UNC
a.	Signature 1.	1.00	2.00
b.	Signature 3.	1.00	2.00
s.	As a or b. Specimen.	—	25.00

104 2 Hryvni

VF UNC

1992 (1996). Brown on multicolor underprint. Cathedral of St. Sophia at center. Back: Prince Yaroslav at center.

		VF	UNC
a.	Signature 1.	FV	3.00
b.	Signature 2.	FV	5.00
c.	Signature 3.	FV	3.00
s.	As a, b, c. Specimen.	—	25.00

105 5 Hryven

VF UNC

1992 (1996). Blue-gray on multicolor underprint. Illinska Church in Subotiv at center. Back: B. Khmelnytsky at center.

		VF	UNC
a.	Signature 1.	FV	4.00
b.	Signature 2.	FV	6.00
c.	Signature 3.	FV	3.00
s.	As a, b, c. Specimen.	—	25.00

106 10 Hryven

1992 (1996). Purple on multicolor underprint. Kyiv-Pecherska Monastery at center. Back: I. Mazepa at center.

		VF	UNC
a. Signature 1.		FV	9.00
b. Signature 3.		FV	9.00
s. As a, b. Specimen.		—	50.00

107 20 Hryven

1992 (1996). Brown on multicolor underprint. Lviv Opera House at center. Back: Ivan Franko at center.

		VF	UNC
a. Signature 1.		5.00	25.00
b. Signature 3.		5.00	25.00
s. As a, b. Specimen.		—	50.00

107A 50 Hryven

1992. (Not issued). Back: Man at center. Printer: CBNC.

VF UNC

— —

107B 100 Hryven

1992. (Not issued). Back: Man at center. Printer: CBNC.

VF UNC

— —

1994-98 ND and Dated Issue

108 1 Hryvnia

1994; 1995. Grayish brown and green on multicolor underprint. St. Volodymyr at center right. Signature 3. Back: City of Khersonnes at center. Watermark: St. Volodymyr. 133x66mm.

	VF	UNC
a. 1994 (1996).	FV	1.00
b. 1995 (1997).	FV	1.00
s. Specimen. 1994; 1995.	—	35.00

109 2 Hryvni

1995; 2001. Multicolor. Prince Yaroslav at center right. Back: Cathedral of St. Sophia in Kyiv. Watermark: Prince Yaroslav. 133x66mm.

	VF	UNC
a. 1995 (1997).	FV	2.00
b. 2001.	FV	2.00
s. Specimen. 1995; 2001.	—	30.00

110 5 Hryven

1994; 1997; 2001. Multicolor. Bohdan Khmelnytsky at center right. Back: Illinska Church in Subotiv at center. Printer: TDLR (without imprint). 133x66mm.

	VF	UNC
a. 1994 (1997).	FV	4.00
b. 1997 (1998).	FV	4.00
c. 2001.	FV	4.00
s. Specimen. 1994; 1997; 2001.	—	30.00

111 10 Hryven

1994; 2000. Multicolor. L. Mazepa at center right. Back: Kyiv-Pecherska Monastery at center. Watermark: L. Mazepa. 133x66mm.

	VF	UNC
a. 1994 (1997). Series in "Arial" font. Printer: TDLR.	FV	6.00
b. 1994 (1997). Series in "Times Roman" font. Ukrainian printer.	FV	6.00
c. 2000. Ukrainian printer.	FV	6.00
s. As b, c. Specimen.	—	40.00

112 20 Hryven VF UNC
1995; 2000. Multicolor. Ivan Franko at right. Back: Opera House in Lviv. Watermark: Ivan Franko. 133x66mm.
    a. 1995. With segmented security thread.   FV   12.00
    b. 2000.   FV   12.00
    s. As a, b. Specimen.   —   30.00

113 50 Hryven VF UNC
ND (1996). Purple and dark blue-gray on multicolor underprint. M. Hrushevsky at right. Back: Parliament building at center. Watermark: M. Hrushevsky. 133x66mm.
    a. Signature 1.   FV   30.00
    b. Signature 3.   FV   30.00
    s. As a, b. Specimen.   —   150
    x. Watermark: T. Shevchenko (error). Rare.   —   200

114 100 Hryven VF UNC
ND (1996). Brown and dark green on multicolor underprint. T. Shevchenko at right. Back: Cathedral of St. Sophia in Kyiv at center, statue of St. Volodymyr standing at left. Watermark: T. Shevchenko. 133x66mm.
    a. Signature 1.   FV   45.00
    b. Signature 3.   FV   45.00
    s. As a, b. Specimen.   —   175
    x. Watermark: M. Hrushevsky (error).   —   200

115 200 Hryven VF UNC
ND (2001). Black and blue on multicolor underprint. Lesia Ukrainka (L. P. Kosach) at right. Signature 1. Back: Castle gate. Watermark: Lesia Ukrainka (L. P. Kosach). 133x66mm.
    a. Issued note.   FV   80.00
    s. Specimen.   —   200

2003-07 Issue

116 1 Hryvnia VF UNC
2004; 2005. Green and blue on multicolor underprint. Prince Volodymyr at right. Back: Volodymyr's fortress in Kyiv. Watermark: Prince Volodymyr 118x63mm.
    a. 2004.   FV   1.00
    b. 2005.   FV   1.00
    s. Specimen.   —   50.00

116A 1 Hryvnia VF UNC
2006; 2011; 2014. Yellow and blue on multicolor. Prince Volodymyr at right. Back: Volodymyr's fortress in Kyiv. Watermark: Prince Volodymyr 118x63mm.
    a. 2006.   FV   1.00
    b. 2011.   FV   1.00
    c. 2014.   FV   1.00

117 2 Hryven VF UNC
2004-. Brown on multicolor underprint. Yaroslav the Wise at right. Back: Cathedral of St. Sophia in Kyiv. Watermark: Yaroslav the Wise. 118x63mm.
    a. 2004.   FV   2.00
    b. 2005.   FV   2.00
    c. 2011.   FV   2.00
    d. 2013.   FV   2.00
    s. Specimen.   —   50.00

118 5 Hryven VF UNC
2004-. Blue on multicolor underprint. Bohdan Khmelnytsky at center. Back: Iliynska Church in Subotiv. Watermark: Bohdan Khmelnytsky 118x63mm.
    a. 2004.   FV   4.00
    b. 2005.   FV   4.00
    c. 2011.   FV   4.00
    d. 2013.   FV   4.00
    e. 2015. Signature: Valeriia O. Gontareva.   0-2   4.00
    s. Specimen.   —   50.00

119　10 Hryven

	VF	UNC

2004; 2005. Black, red and multicolor. Ivan Mazepa at right. Back: Pecherska Monastery in Kyiv at center. Watermark: Ivan Mazepa 123x65mm.

a. 2004.	FV	6.00
b. 2005.	FV	6.00
s. Specimen.	—	75.00

119A　10 Hryven

	VF	UNC

2006; 2011; 2013. Gray on multicolor. Ivan Mazepa at right. Back: Pecherska Monastery in Kyiv at center. Watermark: Ivan Mazepa. 123x65mm.

a. 2006.	FV	6.00
b. 2011.	FV	6.00
c. 2013.	FV	6.00

120　20 Hryven

	VF	UNC

2003-. Slate black and green on multicolor underprint. Ivan Franko at right. Back: Opera House in Lviv. Watermark: Ivan Franko. 133x69mm.

a. 2003.	FV	12.00
b. 2005.	FV	12.00
c. 2011.	FV	12.00
d. 2013.	FV	12.00
s. Specimen.	—	75.00

121　50 Hryven

	VF	UNC

2004-. Brown and lilac on multicolor underprint. Mikhaylo Hrushevsky at right. Back: Parliament building at cetner. Watermark: Mikhaylo Hrushevsky. 136x72mm.

a. 2004.	FV	17.50
b. 2005.	FV	15.00
c. 2011.	FV	15.00
d. 2013.	FV	15.00
e. 2014. Kubiv signature.	FV	15.00
f. 2014. Gontareva signature.	FV	15.00
s. Specimen.	—	50.00

122　100 Hryven

	VF	UNC

2005; 2011; 2014. Green and burgundy on multicolor underprint. Taras Shevchenko at right. Back: Shevchenko playing instrument. Watermark: Taras Shevchenko. 142x75mm.

a. 2005.	FV	40.00
b. 2011.	FV	40.00
c. 2014	FV	40.00
s. Specimen.	—	50.00

123　200 Hryven

	VF	UNC

2007-. Purple and rose on multicolor underprint. Lesia Ukrainka at right. Back: Kutsk Castle Gate Tower at right. Watermark: Lesia Ukrainka. 148x74mm.

a. 2007.	FV	50.00
b. 2011.	FV	50.00
c. 2013.	FV	50.00
d. 2014.	FV	50.00
e. 2014. Signature Gontareva.	FV	50.00
s. Specimen.	—	75.00

124 500 Hryven VF UNC
2006; 2011; 2014; 2015. Brown, tan and green on multicolor underprint. Grigori Skovoroda at right. Back: Kyiv Mohyla Academy at center. Watermark: Grigori Skovoroda. 154x75mm.

a. 2006.	FV	110
b. 2011.	FV	110
c. 2014.	FV	110
d. 2015.	FV	90.00
s. Specimen.	—	125

2011 Commemorative Issue

125 50 Hryven VF UNC
2011. HBY hologram. 20th Anniversary of Bank. 1,000 pieces issued in folder. Mikhailo Hrushevskiy. Back: Tsentralna Rada (House of the Teacher) building, Kiev

2014 Issue

126 100 Hryven VF UNC
2014 (2015). Olive green, brown, red and purple. Artist Taras Shevchenko, coat of arms, painter's palette and brushes as gold-to-green SPARK patch. Back: Taras Shevchenko National University building in Kyiv. Motion windowed security thread with demetalized 100. Solid security thread with demetalized 100 ГРН and trident. Watermark: Taras Shevchenko and electrotype 100. Printer: NBU. 142x75mm.   FV 16.00

COLLECTOR SERIES

НАЦІОНАЛЬНИЙ БАНК УКРАЇНИ

Ukrainian National Bank

1996 Issue

CS1 1 Hryvnia Mkt. Value
#103 and 2 Karbovantsiv 1996 Independence coins in a folder.   —

The seven United Arab Emirates (formerly known as the Trucial Sheikhdoms or States), located along the southern shore of the Persian Gulf, are comprised of the Sheikhdoms of Abu Dhabi, Dubai, Sharjah, Ajman, Umm al Qaiwain, Ras al-Khaimah and Fujairah. They have a combined area of 83,600 sq. km. and a population of 4.62 million. Capital: Abu Dhabi. Since the oil strikes of 1958-60, the economy has centered on petroleum. The Trucial States of the Persian Gulf coast granted the UK control of their defense and foreign affairs in 19th century treaties. In 1971, six of these states - Abu Zaby, 'Ajman, Al Fujayrah, Ash Shariqah, Dubayy, and Umm al Qaywayn - merged to form the United Arab Emirates (UAE). They were joined in 1972 by Ra's al Khaymah. The UAE's per capita GDP is on par with those of leading West European nations. Its generosity with oil revenues and its moderate foreign policy stance have allowed the UAE to play a vital role in the affairs of the region.

MONETARY SYSTEM:
1 Dirham = 1000 Fils

SHEIKHDOMS

United Arab Emirates Currency Board

1973; 1976 ND Issue

1 1 Dirham VF UNC
ND (1973). Green on multicolor underprint. Dhow, camel caravan, palm tree and oil derrick at left. Back: Police station at center right. Watermark: Arabian horse's head. Printer: (T)DLR.

a. Issued note.	12.00	60.00
s. Specimen.	—	75.00

2 5 Dirhams VF UNC
ND (1973). Purple on multicolor underprint. Dhow, camel caravan, palm tree and oil derrick at left. Back: Fortress Fujairah at center right. Watermark: Arabian horse's head. Printer: (T)DLR.

a. Issued note.	25.00	90.00
s. Specimen.	—	75.00

3 10 Dirhams

ND (1973). Gray-blue on multicolor underprint. Dhow, camel caravan, palm tree and oil derrick at left. Back: Aerial view of Umm al-Qaiwan at center right. Watermark: Arabian horse's head. Printer: (T)DLR.

VF UNC

a. Issued note.   16.00 90.00
s. Specimen.   —   100

4 50 Dirhams

VF UNC

ND (1973). Red on multicolor underprint. Dhow, camel caravan, palm tree and oil derrick at left. Back: Sheikh's Palace of Ajman at center right. Watermark: Arabian horse's head. Printer: (T)DLR.

a. Issued note.   85.00 450
s. Specimen.   —   225

5 100 Dirhams

VF UNC

ND (1973). Olive-green on multicolor underprint. Dhow, camel caravan, palm tree and oil derrick at left. Back: Ras al-Khaimah city at center right. Watermark: Arabian horse's head. Printer: (T)DLR.

a. Issued note.   80.00 450
s. Specimen.   —   325

6 1000 Dirhams

VF UNC

ND (1976). Blue on multicolor underprint. Dhow, camel caravan, palm tree and oil derrick at left. Back: Fortress at center right. Watermark: Arabian horse's head. Printer: (T)DLR.

a. Issued note.   850   3,000
s. Specimen.   —   1,000

United Arab Emirates Central Bank
1982; 1983 ND Issue

7 5 Dirhams

VF UNC

ND (1982). UV: value 5, eagle and shield fluoresce orange. Brown on multicolor underprint. Sharjah Market at right. Arms at upper center. Back: Seacoast cove with tower. Sparrowhawk at left. Watermark: Sparrowhawk's head.

a. Issued note.   5.00 16.00
s. Specimen.   —   50.00

8 10 Dirhams

VF UNC

ND (1982). Green on multicolor underprint. Arab dagger at right. Arms at upper center. Back: Ideal farm with trees at left center. Sparrowhawk at left. Watermark: Sparrowhawk's head.

a. Issued note.   7.00 30.00
s. Specimen.   —   50.00

9 50 Dirhams

VF UNC

ND (1982). Purple, dark brown and olive on multicolor underprint. Oryx at right, arms at upper center. Back: Al Jahilie Fort at left center. Sparrowhawk at left. Watermark: Sparrowhawk's head.

a. Issued note.   50.00 120
s. Specimen.   —   95.00

10 100 Dirhams VF UNC
ND (1982). Red, violet and black on multicolor underprint. Al Fahidie Fort at right, arms at upper center. Back: Dubai Trade center at left center. Sparrowhawk at left. Watermark: Sparrowhawk's head.
    a. Issued note. 70.00 130
    s. Specimen. — 100

11 500 Dirhams VF UNC
ND (1983). Dark blue, purple and brown on multicolor underprint. Sparrowhawk at right, arms at upper center. Back: Mosque in Dubai at left center. Sparrowhawk at left. Watermark: Sparrowhawk's head.
    a. Issued note. 275 650
    s. Specimen. — 350

1989-96 Issues

12 5 Dirhams VF UNC
1993/AH1414-1995/AH1416. Dark brown, red-orange and violet on multicolor underprint. Sharjah market at right. Condensed Arabic text in titles, modified designs and slight color variations. Large value outline type in watermark area. Silver arms at upper center. Arabic serial number in red at left. Electronic sorting style in black at right. Back: Seacoast cove with tower. Sparrowhawk at left. Watermark: Sparrowhawk's head.
    a. 1993/AH1414. 6.00 13.00
    b. 1995/AH1416. FV 7.50

13 10 Dirhams VF UNC
1993/AH1414-199/AH1416. Green and pale olive-green on multicolor underprint. Arab dagger at right. Condensed Arabic text in titles, modified designs and slight color variations. Large value outline type in watermark area. Silver arms at upper center. Arabic serial number in red at left. Electronic sorting style in black at right. Back: Ideal farm with trees at left. Sparowhawk at left. Watermark: Sparrowhawk's head.
    a. 1993/AH1414. 10.00 20.00
    b. 1995/AH1416. 7.00 15.00

14 50 Dirhams VF UNC
1995/AH1415-1996/AH1417. With segmented foil over security thread. Purple, black and violet on multicolor underprint. Oryx at right. Condensed Arabic text in titles, modified designs and slight color variations. Large value outline type in watermark area. Silver arms at upper center. Arabic serial number in red at left. Electronic sorting style in black at right. Back: Al Jahilie Fort at left center. Sparrowhawk at left. Watermark: Sparrowhawk's head.
    a. 1995/AH1415. 20.00 85.00
    b. 1996/AH1417. 20.00 75.00

15 100 Dirhams VF UNC
1993/AH1414-1995/AH1416. With segmented foil over security thread. Red, red-violet and black on multicolor underprint. Al Fahidie Fort at right. Condensed Arabic text in titles, modified designs and slight color variations. Large value outline type in watermark area. Silver arms at upper center. Arabic serial number in red at left. Electronic sorting style in black at right. Back: Dubai Trade center at left center. Sparrowhawk at left. Watermark: Sparrowhawk's head.
    a. 1993/AH1414. FV 100
    b. 1995/AH1416. FV 90.00

16 200 Dirhams VF UNC
1989/AH 1410. With segmented foil over security thread. Brown, green and multicolor. Sharia Court building and Zayed Sports City. Back: Central Bank building at left center. 90.00 240

17 500 Dirhams VF UNC
1993/AH1414. With segmented foil over security thread. Dark blue, black, purple and silver on multicolor underprint. Sparrowhawk at right. Back: Mosque in Dubai at left center. Sparrowhawk at left. Watermark: Sparrowhawk's head. 300 825

18 500 Dirhams VF UNC
1996/AH1416. Dark blue, black, purple and silver on multicolor underprint. Sparrowhawk at right. Kinegram added at lower left. Back: Mosque in Dubai at left center. Sparrowhawk at left. Watermark: Sparrowhawk's head. 250 650

1997-2000 Issue

19   5 Dirhams

2000/AH1420-. Brown and orange. Similar to #12 but with color and minor design variations. Watermark area shaded. Back: Seacoast cove with tower. Sparrowhawk at left. Watermark: Sparrowhawk's head. 143x60mm.

	VF	UNC
a. 2000/AH1420.	FV	8.00
b. 2001/AH1422.	FV	7.00
c. 2004/AH1425.	FV	7.00
d. 2007/AH1428.	FV	7.00

20   10 Dirhams

1998/AH1419-. Green and pale olive-green on multicolor underprint. Arab dagger at right. Condensed Arabic text in titles, modified designs and slight color variations. Large value outline type in watermark area. Silver arms at upper center. Arabic serial number in red at left. Electronic sorting style in black at right. Back: Ideal farm with trees at left. Sparrowhawk at left. Watermark: Sparrowhawk's head. 145x62mm.

	VF	UNC
a. 1998/AH1419.	FV	12.00
b. 2001/AH1422.	FV	10.00
c. 2004/AH1425.	FV	10.00
d. 2007/AH1428.	FV	9.00

21   20 Dirhams

1997/AH1418-. Green, blue and multicolor. Dubai Creek Golf and Yacht Club at right. Watermark area shaded. Back: Dhow. Sparrowhawk at left. Watermark: Sparrowhawk's head. 150x63mm.

	VF	UNC
a. 1997/AH1418.	FV	25.00
b. 2000/AH1420.	FV	20.00
c. 2007/AH1428.	FV	16.00
s. As a. Specimen. Perforated: *SPECIMEN*.	—	350

22   50 Dirhams

1998/AH1419. Purple, black and violet on multicolor underprint. Oryx at right. Condensed Arabic text in titles, modified designs and slight color variations. Large value outline type in watermark area. Silver arms at upper center. Arabic serial number in red at left. Electronic sorting style in black at right. Back: Al Jahilie Fort at left center. Sparrowhawk at left. Watermark: Sparrowhawk's head. 150x63mm.

	VF	UNC
	FV	50.00

23   100 Dirhams

1998/AH1419. Red, red-violet and black on multicolor underprint. Al Fahidie Fort at right. Condensed Arabic text in titles, modified designs and slight color variations. Silver arms at upper center. Arabic serial number in red at left, electronic sorting style in black at right. Back: Dubai Trade center at left center. Sparrowhawk at left. Watermark: Sparrowhawk's head. 155x66mm.

	VF	UNC
	FV	85.00

24   500 Dirhams

1998-. Dark blue, black, purple and silver on multicolor underprint. Sparrowhawk at right. Kinegram added at lower left. Wide silver foil at right, silver seal at left. Watermark area shaded. Back: Mosque in Dubai at left center. Sparrowhawk at left. Watermark: Sparrowhawk's head. 160x68mm.

	VF	UNC
a. 1998/AH1419.	FV	350
b. 2000/AH1420.	FV	320
c. 2004/AH1425.	FV	300

25   1000 Dirhams

1998-2000. Brown, green and multicolor. Palace corner tower at right. Holographic strip vertically at right. Watermark area shaded. Back: City view. Sparrowhawk at left. Watermark: Sparrowhawk's head. 163x70mm.

	VF	UNC
a. 1998/AH1419.	FV	850
b. 2000/AH1420.	FV	700

2004-13 New State Arms Issue

26   5 Dirhams | | **VF** | **UNC**

2009; 2013; 2015. Brown and orange on multicolor underprint. Dallah (coffee pot) added to watermark area. 143x60mm.

a. 2009/AH1430.		FV	5.00
b. 2013/AH1434. Left serial # vertical.		FV	5.00
c. 2015/AH1436. Bars left and right.		2.00	5.00

27   10 Dirhams | | **VF** | **UNC**

2009; 2013; 2015. Green and pale-olive-green on multicolor underprint. Arab dagger at right. 145x62mm.

a. 2009/AH1430.		FV	8.00
b. 2013/AH1434.		FV	8.00
c. 2013/AH1434. Serial # at left is vertical.		FV	6.00
d. 2015/AH1436. Bars left and right.		FV	6.00

28   20 Dirhams | | **VF** | **UNC**

2009; 2013; 2015. Green, blue and multicolor. Dubai Creek Golf and Yacht Club at right. 150x63mm.

a. 2009/AH1430.		FV	16.00
b. 2013/AH1434.		FV	14.00
c. 2015/AH1436. Bars left and right.		FV	14.00

29   50 Dirhams | | **VF** | **UNC**

2004-. Purple, black and violet on multicolor underprint. Oryx at right. Condensed Arabic text in titles, modified designs and slight color variations. Large value outline type in watermark area. Silver arms at upper center. Arabic serial number in red at le Back: Al Jahilie Fort at left center. Watermark: Sparrowhawk's head. 150x63mm.

a. 2004/AH1425.		FV	45.00
b. 2006/AH1427.		FV	40.00
c. 2008/AH1429.		FV	35.00
d. 2011/AH1432. Omron rings added.		FV	35.00
e. 2014/AH1436. Bars left and right.		FV	35.00

30   100 Dirhams | | **VF** | **UNC**

2003; 2004; 2006; 2012. Red, red-violet and black on multicolor underprint. Similar to #23 but with silver overprint of tower at upper right. Dallah (coffee pot) added to watermark area. Back: Dubai Trade center at left center. Watermark: Sparrowhawk's head. 155x66mm.

a. 2003/AH1424.		FV	60.00
b. 2004/AH1425.		FV	55.00
c. 2006/AH1427.		FV	50.00
d. 2008/AH1429.		FV	50.00
e. 2012/AH1433.		FV	50.00
f. 2014/AH1436. Bars left and right.		FV	50.00

31   200 Dirhams | | **VF** | **UNC**

2004/AH1425-. Brown and black on yellow and multicolor underprint. Sharia Court building and Zayed Sports City at right. Back: U.A.E. Central Bank building at center, falcon at left end. 157x67mm.

a. 2004/AH1425.		FV	225
b. 2008/AH1429.		FV	240

32   500 Dirhams | | **VF** | **UNC**

2004/AH1425-. Security foil strip with denomination. Dark blue, black, purple and silver on multicolor underprint. Al Hosn palace in Abu Dhabi at right. Back: Abu Dhabi cornice. 160x68mm.

a. 2004/AH1424.		FV	280
b. 2006/AH1427.		FV	280
c. 2008/AH1429.		FV	240
d. 2011/AH1432.		FV	225
e. 2015/AH1436. Bars left and right.		FV	225

33   1000 Dirhams | | **VF** | **UNC**

2006/AH1427-. Security foil strip with alternating arms and denomination in Arabic. Brown, green and multicolor. Al Hosn palace in Abu Dhabi. Back: Abu Dhabi cornice. 163x70mm.

a. 2006/AH1427.		FV	500
b. 2008/AH1429. Slighly modified arms on face.		FV	475
c. 2012/AH1433.		FV	475
d. 2015/AH1436. Bars left and right.		FV	475

The area of the North American continent currently controlled by the United States of America was originally inhabited by numerous groups of Indian tribes. Some of these groups settled in particular areas, creating permanent settlements, while others were nomadic, traveling great distances and living off the land.

English explorers John and Sebastian Cabot reached Nova Scotia in what is today Canada in 1497; in 1534 the French gained a foothold with the explorations of Jacques Cartier. In 1541 the Spanish explorer Coronado traversed the south central portion of the country in what was to become the states of New Mexico, Texas, Nebraska and Oklahoma. In 1542 another Spaniard, Juan Cabrillo navigated north from Mexico along the Pacific coastline to California. The Spanish set up the first permanent settlement of Europeans in North America at St. Augustine, Florida in 1565. In 1607 the English settled in Jamestown, Virginia, and in 1620 at Plymouth, Massachusetts. This was followed closely by Dutch settlements in Albany and New York in 1624, and in 1638 the Swedes arrived in Delaware. From their foothold in Canada, French explorers pushed inland through the Great Lakes. Jean Nicolet explored what was to become Wisconsin in 1634, and in 1673 explorers Marquette and Joliet reached Iowa. In the 1650s the Dutch won the Swedish lands, and in 1664 the English gained control of the Dutch lands, thus giving the English control all along the Atlantic Coast. The resulting thirteen British colonies; New Hampshire, Vermont, Massachusetts, Rhode Island, Connecticut, New York, Pennsylvania, Delaware, Maryland, Virginia, North Carolina, South Carolina and Georgia formed the nucleus of what would become the United States of America.

From this point on tensions grew between the English, who could not expand westward from their settlements along the Atlantic Coast, and the French who had settled inland into the Ohio river valley. This dispute ended in 1763 after a war with the French loosing control of lands east of the Mississippi river. Manufacturing, textiles and other industry was developing at this time, and by 1775 about one-seventh of the world's production of raw iron came from the colonies. From 1771-1783 the war for American Independence was fought by the colonists against the English, and settled by the Peace of Paris in 1783. Americans gained control of lands south of the St. Lawrence and Great Lakes, and east of the Mississippi, with the exception of Florida which would remain under Spanish control until 1821. At the close of the war, the population was about 3 million, many of whom lived on self-sufficient family farms. Fishing, lumbering and the production of grains for export were becoming major economic endeavors. The newly independent states formed a loose confederation, but in 1787 approved the Constitution of the United States which is the framework for the goverment today. In 1789 it's first president, George Washington was elected, and the capitol was set up in New York City. In 1800 the capitol was moved to a planned city, Washington, D.C. where it remains.

Westward expansion was an inevitability as population grew. French territory west of the Mississippi, stretching to the northern Pacific was purchased in 1804 under the presidency of Thomas Jefferson, who then sent out Lewis and Clark on expedition of discovery. Spain granted independence to Mexico in 1821, which included lands which would become the states of California, New Mexico, Arizona and Texas. From 1836-1845 Texas was an independent republic, not joining the United States until 1845. Upon losing a war with the United States, Mexico ceded California (including most of Arizonia and New Mexico) to the United States in 1848. Gold was discovered in California that year, and western migration took off on overland wagon trains or around-the-horn sail and steam ships. Hawaii came under U.S. protection in 1851. As the country developed in the 19th century, the northern states increased in commerce and industry while the southern states developed a vast agricultural base through the use of slave labor. Northern political and social threats to slavery lead twelve southern states to secede from the Union in 1860 forming the Confederate States of America. The ensuing Civil War lasted until 1865, at which time slavery was abolished and the States reunited.

In 1867 Alaska was purchased from Russia. The transcontinental railroad was completed in 1869. The central region of the country west of the Mississippi River and east of the Rocky Mountains was the last to be developed, beginning after the Civil War, with the establishment of cattle ranches and farms. Between 1870 and 1891 the nomadic Native American population clashed with settlers and federal troops. By 1891 the Native Americans were confined to reservations.

At the close of the 19th century the United States embarked on a colonial mission of its own, with advances into Cuba, Puerto Rico, Panama, Nicaragua and the Philippines. This resulted in the Spanish-American War which was quickly decided, ending Spanish colonial dominance, and signaling the rise of the United States as a world power. Slow to enter both World Wars of the 20th century, it was a major contributor to the conclusion of both, making it one of the major nations of the 20th century.

MONETARY SYSTEM:
1 Dollar = 100 Cents

SIGNATURE VARIETIES		
SERIES	TREASURER	SECRETARY
1963	Kathryn O'Hay Granahan	C. Douglas Dillon
1963A	Kathryn O'Hay Granahan	Henry H. Fowler
1963B	Kathryn O'Hay Granahan	Joseph W. Barr
1969	Dorothy Andrews Elston	David M. Kennedy
1969A	Dorothy Andrews Kabis	David M. Kennedy
1969B	Dorothy Andrews Kabis	John B. Connally
1969C	Romana Acosta Banuelos	John B. Connally
1969D	Romana Acosta Banuelos	George P. Schultz
1974	Francine I. Neff	William E. Simon
1977	Azie Taylor Morton	W. Michael Blumenthal
1977A	Azie Taylor Morton	J. William Miller
1981	Angela M. Buchanan	Donald T. Regan
1981A	Katherine Davalos Ortega	Donald T. Regan
1985	Katherine Davalos Ortega	John A. Baker III
1988	Katherine Davalos Ortega	Nicholas F. Brady
1988A-1990	Catalina Vasquez Villalpando	Nicholas F. Brady
1993	Mary Ellen Withrow	Lloyd Bentson
1995, 1996	Mary Ellen Withrow	Robert E. Rubin
1999	Mary Ellen Withrow	Lawrence Summers
2001	Rosario Marin	Paul H. O'Neill
2003, 2004	Rosario Marin	John Snow

REPUBLIC

United States Notes - Small Size
Red Treasury seal.

Series of 1963
Replacement Notes: Serial # suffix is an *.

382   2 Dollars   VF   UNC
1963. Thomas Jefferson at center. Red Treasury seal. Back: Monticello.
    a. 1963   5.00   12.00
    b. 1963A.   5.00   15.00

383   5 Dollars   VF   UNC
1963. Abraham Lincoln at center. Red Treasury seal. Back: Lincoln Memorial.   10.00   20.00

Series of 1966

384   100 Dollars   VF   UNC
1966 Benjamin Franklin at center. Back: Independence Hall.
    a. 1966   125   550
    b. 1966A.   250   1,250

Federal Reserve Notes - Small Size

Imprinted #, letter and name (in seal at l.) of 1 of the 12 Federal Reserve-Banks:

A-1: Boston   E-5: Richmond   I-9: Minneapolis
B-2: New York   F-6: Atlanta   J-10: Kansas City
C-3: Philadelphia   G-7: Chicago   K-11: Dallas
D-4: Cleveland   H-8: St. Louis   L-12: San Francisco

1963 Series

443   1 Dollar   VF   UNC
1963. George Washington at center. Back: Great Seal flanking ONE.
    a. 1963. (A-L).   FV   5.00
    b. 1963A. (A-L).   FV   5.00
    c. 1963B. (B; E; G; J; L).   FV   6.00

444   5 Dollars   VF   UNC
1963. Abraham Lincoln at center. Back: Lincoln Memorial.
    a. 1963. (A-D; F-H; J-L).   9.00   20.00
    b. 1963A. (A-L).   7.00   15.00

445   10 Dollars   VF   UNC
1963. Alexander Hamilton at center. Back: Treasury Building.
    a. 1963. (A-H; J-L).   FV   50.00
    b. 1963A. (A-L).   FV   37.50

446   20 Dollars   VF   UNC
1963. Andrew Jackson at center. Back: White House.
    a. 1963. (A-B; D-H; J-L).   FV   75.00
    b. 1963A. (A-L).   FV   60.00

447   50 Dollars   VF   UNC
1963A. (A-L). Ulysses Grant at center. Back: Unites States Capital Building.   FV   150

448   100 Dollars   VF   UNC
1963A. (A-L). Benjamin Franklin at center. Back: Independence Hall.   FV   275

1969 Series

449   1 Dollar   VF   UNC
1969 George Washington at center. Back: Great Seal flanking ONE.
    a. 1969. (A-L).   FV   4.00
    b. 1969A. (A-L).   FV   4.00
    c. 1969B. (A-L).   FV   4.00
    d. 1969C. (B; D-L).   FV   4.00
    e. 1969D. (A-L).   FV   4.00

450   5 Dollars   VF   UNC
1969. Abraham Lincoln at center. Back: Lincoln Memorial.
    a. 1969. (A-L).   6.00   15.00
    b. 1969A. (A-L).   6.00   20.00
    c. 1969B. (A-L).   8.00   50.00
    d. 1969C. (A-L).   7.00   20.00

451   10 Dollars   VF   UNC
1969. Alexander Hamilton at center. Back: Treasury Building.
   a. 1969. (A-L).   FV   35.00
   b. 1969A. (A-L).   FV   35.00
   c. 1969B. (A-L).   15.00   100
   d. 1969C. (A-L).   FV   40.00

452   20 Dollars   VF   UNC
1969. Andrew Jackson at center. Back: White House.
   a. 1969. (A-L).   FV   60.00
   b. 1969A. (A-L).   FV   75.00
   c. 1969B. (B; D-L).   FV   150
   d. 1969C. (A-L).   FV   50.00

453   50 Dollars   VF   UNC
1969. Ulysses Grant at center. Back: United States Capital Building.
   a. 1969. (A-L).   FV   200
   b. 1969A. (A-L).   FV   200
   c. 1969B. (A-B; E-G; K).   FV   120
   d. 1969C. (A-L).   FV   150

454   100 Dollars   VF   UNC
1969. Benjamin Franklin at center. Back: Independence Hall.
   a. 1969. (A-L).   FV   225
   b. 1969A. (A-L).   FV   225
   c. 1969C. (A-L).   FV   225

1974 Series

455   1 Dollar   VF   UNC
1974. (A-L). George Washington at center. Back: Great Seal flanking ONE.   FV   4.00

456   5 Dollars   VF   UNC
1974. (A-L). Abraham Lincoln at center. Back: Lincoln Memorial.   6.00   15.00

457   10 Dollars   VF   UNC
1974. (A-L). Alexander Hamilton at center. Back: Treasury Building. FV   35.00

458   20 Dollars   VF   UNC
1974. (A-L). Andrew Jackson at center. Back: White House.   FV   60.00

459   50 Dollars   VF   UNC
1974. (A-L). Ulysses Grant at center. Back: United States Capital Building.   FV   200

460   100 Dollars   VF   UNC
1974. (A-L). Benjamin Franklin at center. Back: Independence Hall.   FV   200

1976 Series

#461, U.S. Bicentennial - Trumbull's painting *Signing of the Declaration of Independence*

461   2 Dollars   VF   UNC
1976. (A-L). Thomas Jefferson at center. Back: Signing of the Declaration of Independence.   3.00   10.00

1977 Series

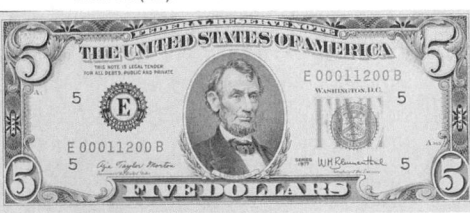

462   1 Dollar   VF   UNC
1977. George Washington at center. Back: Great Seal flanking ONE.
   a. 1977. (A-L).   FV   4.00
   b. 1977A. (A-L).   FV   4.00

463   5 Dollars   VF   UNC
1977. Abraham Lincoln at center. Back: Lincoln Memorial.
   a. 1977. (A-L).   6.00   10.00
   b. 1977A. (A-L).   6.00   18.00

464   10 Dollars   VF   UNC
1977. Alexander Hamilton at center. Back: Treasury Building.
   a. 1977. (A-L).   FV   40.00
   b. 1977A. (A-L).   FV   35.00

465   20 Dollars   VF   UNC
1977. (A-L). Andrew Jackson at center. Back: White House.   FV   60.00

466   50 Dollars   **VF   UNC**
1977. (A-L). Ulysses Grant at center. Back: United States Capital Building.   FV   175

467   100 Dollars   **VF   UNC**
1977. (A-L). Benjamin Franklin at center. Back: Independence Hall.   FV   225

1981 Series

Note: Since Oct. 1981 the Bureau of Engraving and Printing has made available to collectors uncut sheets of 4, 16, and 32 notes of the $1.00 and $2.00 denominations.

468   1 Dollar   **VF   UNC**
1981. George Washington at center. Back: Great Seal flanking ONE.
   a. 1981. (A-L).   FV   4.00
   b. 1981A. (A-L).   FV   4.00

469   5 Dollars   **VF   UNC**
1981. Abraham Lincoln at center. Back: Lincoln Memorial.
   a. 1981. (A-L).   FV   20.00
   b. 1981A. (A-L).   FV   20.00

470   10 Dollars   **VF   UNC**
1981. Alexander Hamilton at center. Back: Treasury Building.
   a. 1981. (A-L).   FV   40.00
   b. 1981A. (A-L).   FV   40.00

471   20 Dollars   **VF   UNC**
1981. Andrew Jackson at center. Back: White House.
   a. 1981. (A-L).   FV   75.00
   b. 1981A. (A-L).   FV   60.00

472   50 Dollars   **VF   UNC**
1981. Ulysses Grant at center. Back: United States Capital Building.
   a. 1981. (A-L).   FV   200
   b. 1981A. (A-L).   FV   225

473   100 Dollars   **VF   UNC**
1981. Benjamin Franklin at center. Back: Independence Hall.
   a. 1981. (A-L).   FV   275
   b. 1981A. (A-L).   FV   250

1985 Series

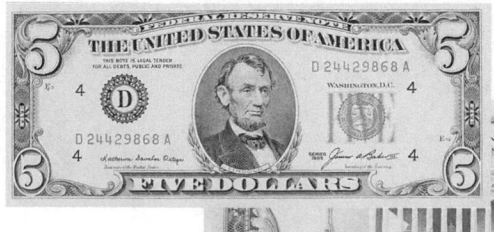

474   1 Dollar   **VF   UNC**
1985. (A-L). George Washington at center. Back: Great Seal flanking ONE.   FV   4.00

475   5 Dollars   **VF   UNC**
1985. (A-L). Abraham Lincoln at center. Back: Lincoln Memorial.   FV   15.00

		VF	UNC
476	**10 Dollars** 1985. (A-L). Alexander Hamilton at center. Back: Treasury Building.	FV	30.00

		VF	UNC
477	**20 Dollars** 1985. (A-L). Andrew Jackson at center. Back: White House.	FV	50.00

		VF	UNC
478	**50 Dollars** 1985. (A-L). Ulysses Grant at center. Back: United States Capital Building.	FV	120

		VF	UNC
479	**100 Dollars** 1985. (A-L). Benjamin Franklin at center. Back: Independence Hall.	FV	200

1988 Series

		VF	UNC
480	**1 Dollar** 1988. George Washington at center. Back: Great Seal flanking ONE.		
	a. 1988. (A-L).	FV	4.00
	b. 1988A. (A-L).	FV	4.00
	c. 1988A Web Press. (A-C; E-G).	8.00	40.00

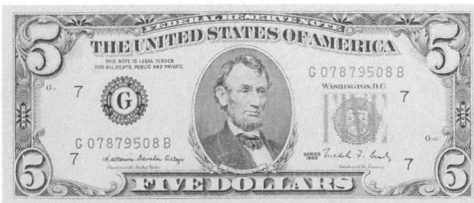

		VF	UNC
481	**5 Dollars** 1988. Abraham Lincoln at center. Back: Lincoln Memorial.		
	a. 1988. (A-L).	FV	15.00
	b. 1988A. (A-L).	FV	15.00

		VF	UNC
482	**10 Dollars** 1988A (A-L). Alexander Hamilton at center. Back: Treasury Building.	FV	30.00

		VF	UNC
483	**20 Dollars** 1988A (A-L). Andrew Jackson at center. Back: White House.	FV	50.00

		VF	UNC
484	**50 Dollars** 1988 (A-L). Ulysses Grant at center. Back: United States Capital Building.	FV	150

		VF	UNC
485	**100 Dollars** 1988 (A-L). Benjamin Franklin at center. Back: Independence Hall.	FV	200

1990 Series

#486-489 w/additional row of micro-printing: *THE UNITED STATES OF AMERICA* **repeated around portr. Filament w/value and** *U.S.A.* **repeated inversely at l.**

		VF	UNC
486	**10 Dollars** 1990. (A-L). Alexander Hamilton at center. Back: Treasury Building.	FV	20.00

		VF	UNC
487	**20 Dollars** 1990. (A-L). Andrew Jackson at center. Back: White House.	FV	35.00
488	**50 Dollars** 1990. (A-L). Ulysses Grant at center. Back: United States Capital Building.	FV	100
489	**100 Dollars** 1990. (A-L). Benjamin Franklin at center. Back: Independence Hall.	FV	150

1993 Series

		VF	UNC
490	**1 Dollar** 1993. George Washington at center. Back: Great Seal flanking ONE.		
	a. 1993. (A-G; L).	FV	2.00
	b. 1993. Web Press. (G-I; K; L).	5.00	15.00
491	**5 Dollars** 1993 (A-C; E-L). Abraham Lincoln at center. Back: Lincoln Memorial.	FV	15.00

492 10 Dollars VF UNC
1993 (A-D, F-H, J, L). Alexander Hamilton at center. Back: Treasury Building. FV 20.00

493 20 Dollars VF UNC
1993. (A-L). Andrew Jackson at center. Back: White House. FV 40.00

494 50 Dollars VF UNC
1993 (A, B, D, E, G, H, J, K). Ulysses Grant at center. Back: Unites States Capital Building. FV 135

495 100 Dollars VF UNC
1993. (A-L). Benjamin Franklin at center. Back: Independence Hall. FV 150

1995 Series

496 1 Dollar VF UNC
1995. George Washington at center. Back: Great Seal flanking ONE.
a. 1995. (A-L). FV 2.00
b. 1995. Web Press. (A; B; D; F). 5.00 17.50

497 2 Dollars VF UNC
1995. (F). Thomas Jefferson at center. Back: Signing of the Declaration of Independence. FV 6.00

498 5 Dollars VF UNC
1995 (A-L). Abraham Lincoln at center. Back: Lincoln Memorial. FV 11.00

499 10 Dollars VF UNC
1995 (A-L). Alexander Hamilton at center. Back: Treasury Building. FV 25.00

500 20 Dollars VF UNC
1995 (B-L). Andrew Jackson at center. Back: White House. FV 40.00

1996 Series

#501-503 redesigned and enlarged portr. on face at l. ctr. and as wmk. Green value at lower r. Security thread at l. Backs similar to #493-495.

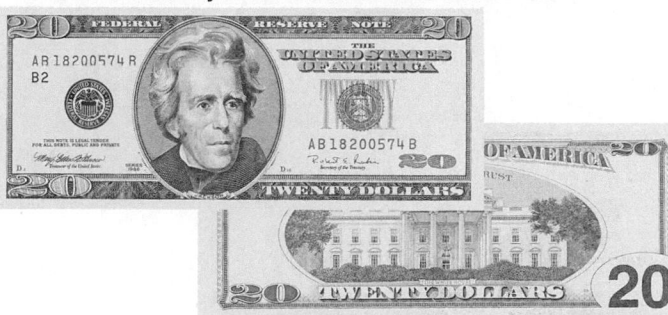

501 20 Dollars VF UNC
1996. (A1-L12). Andrew Jackson at left center. Green value at lower right. Security thread at left. Back: White House. Watermark: Andrew Jackson. FV 30.00

502 50 Dollars VF UNC
1996 (A1-L12). Ulysses Grant at left center. Green value at lower right. Security thread at left. Back: United States Capital Building. Watermark: Ulysses Grant. FV 60.00

503 100 Dollars VF UNC
1996 (A1-L12). Benjamin Franklin at left center. Green value at lower right. Security thread at left. Back: Independence Hall. Watermark: Benjamin Franklin. FV 115

1999 Series

#505-507 redesigned and enlarged portr. on face at l. ctr. and as wmk.

504 1 Dollar VF UNC
1999 (A-L). Black. George Washington at left center. Back: Great Seal flanking ONE. FV 2.00

505   5 Dollars
1999 (A1-L12). Abraham Lincoln at left center. Back: Lincoln Memorial. Watermark: Abraham Lincoln.

VF   UNC
FV   10.00

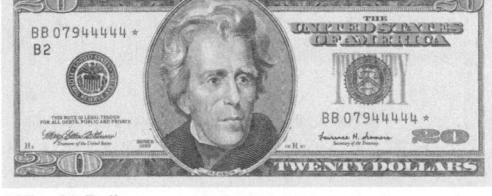

506   10 Dollars
1999 (A1-L12). Alexander Hamilton at left center. Redesigned and enlarged portrait at left center. Back: Treasury Building. Watermark: Alexander Hamilton.

VF   UNC
FV   15.00

507   20 Dollars
1999 (A1-L12). Andrew Jackson at left center. Back: White House. Watermark: Andrew Jackson.

VF   UNC
FV   30.00

508   100 Dollars
1999(A1-L12). Benjamin Franklin at center. Back: Independence Hall.

VF   UNC
FV   120

2001 Series

509   1 Dollar
2001 (A-L). George Washington at center. Back: Great Seal flanking ONE.

VF   UNC
FV   2.00

510   5 Dollars
2001 (A1-L12). Abraham Lincoln at center. Back: Lincoln Memorial. Watermark: Abraham Lincoln.

VF   UNC
FV   10.00

511   10 Dollars
2001 (A1-L12). Alexander Hamilton at center. Back: Treasury Building. Watermark: Alexander Hamilton.

VF   UNC
FV   20.00

512   20 Dollars
2001 (A1-L12). Andrew Jackson at center. Back: White House. Watermark: Andrew Jackson.

VF   UNC
FV   30.00

513   50 Dollars
2001 (A1-L12). Ulysses Grant at center. Back: United States Capital Building. Watermark: Ulysses Grant.

VF   UNC
FV   60.00

514   100 Dollars
2001 (A1-L12). Benjamin Franklin at center. Back: Independence Hall. Watermark: Benjamin Franklin.

VF   UNC
FV   115

2003 Series

515   1 Dollar
2003. George Washington at center. Back: Great Seal flanking ONE.
a. 2003 (A-L).
b. 2003A (A-L).

VF   UNC
FV   2.00
FV   2.00

516 2 Dollars VF UNC
2003. Thomas Jefferson at center. Back: Signing of the Declaration of Independence.
    a. 2003. (A-L). FV 7.00
    b. 2003A. (A-L). FV 7.00

517 5 Dollars VF UNC
2003. Abraham Lincoln at center. Back: Lincoln Memorial. Watermark: Abraham Lincoln.
    a. 2003. (A1-L12). FV 10.00
    b. 2003A. (A1-L12). FV 10.00

518 10 Dollars VF UNC
2003 (A1-L12). Alexander Hamilton at center. Back: Treasury Building. Watermark. Alexander Hamilton. FV 17.50

519 100 Dollars VF UNC
2003. Benjamin Franklin at center. Back: Indepence Hall. Watermark: Benjamin Franklin.
    a. 2003. (A1-L12). FV 120
    b. 2003A. (A1-L12). FV 120

2004 Series

#519-520 redesigned face and back, color underprint.

520 10 Dollars VF UNC
2004A (A1-L12). Black on beige underprint. Alexander Hamilton at left center. Back: Treasury Building. Watermark: Alexander Hamilton. FV 15.00

521 20 Dollars VF UNC
2004. Black on light green, blue and tan underprint. Andrew Jackson at left center. Back: White House. Watermark: Andrew Jackson.
    a. 2004 (A1-L12). FV 27.50
    b. 2004A (A1-A12). FV 27.50

522 50 Dollars VF UNC
2004. Black on multicolor underprint. Ulysses Grant at center. Back: United States Capital Building. Watermark: Ulysses Grant.
    a. 2004 (A1-L12). FV 60.00
    b. 2004A (A1-A12). FV 60.00

2006 Series

523 1 Dollar VF UNC
2000. Black. George Washington at center. Back: Great Seal flanking ONE.
    a. 2006 (A-L). FV 2.00
    b. 2006A (A-E, F-H, K-L). FV 2.00

523A 5 Dollars VF UNC
2006. Black. Abraham Lincoln at center. Back: Lincoln Memorial. Watermark: Abraham Lincoln FV 10.00

524 5 Dollars VF UNC
2006. Black on blue underprint. Abraham Lincoln at left center. Back: Lincoln Memorial. Watermark: Large 5. FV 7.50

525 10 Dollars VF UNC
2006. Black on beige underprint. Alexander Hamilton at left center. Back: Treasury Building. Watermark: Alexander Hamilton. 15.00

526 20 Dollars   **VF**   **UNC**
2006. Black on light green underprint. Andrew Jackson at left center. Back: White   FV   27.50
House. Watermark: Andrew Jackson.

527 50 Dollars   **VF**   **UNC**
2006. Black on red and blue underprint. Ulysses Grant at left center. Back: United   FV   60.00
States Capital Building. Watermark: Ulysses Grant.

528 100 Dollars   **VF**   **UNC**
2006. Black. Benjamin Franklin at center. Back: Independence Hall. Watermark: FV   120
Benjamin Franklin.

2009A Colorized Series

529 100 Dollars   **VF**   **UNC**
2006A. Black and multicolor. Benjamin Franklin at left center. Back: Independence   FV   120
Hall. Watermark: Benjamin Franklin

2009 Series

530 1 Dollar   **VF**   **UNC**
2009. Black. George Washington at center. Back: Great Seal flanking ONE.   FV   2.00

531 5 Dollars   **VF**   **UNC**
2009. Black on blue underprint. Abraham Lincoln at left center. Back: Lincoln   FV   10.00
Memorial. Watermark: Large 5.

532 10 Dollars   **VF**   **UNC**
2009. Black on beige underprint. Alexander Hamilton at left center. Back: Treasury   FV   15.00
Building. Watermark: Alexander Hamilton.

533 20 Dollars   **VF**   **UNC**
2009. Black on light green underprint. Andrew Jackson at left center. Back: White   FV   27.50
House. Watermark: Andrew Jackson.

534 50 Dollars   **VF**   **UNC**
2009. Black on red and blue underprint. Ulysses Grant at left center. Back: United   FV   60.00
States Capital Building. Watermark: Ulysses Grant.

535 100 Dollars   **VF**   **UNC**
2009. Black. Benjamin Franklin at left center. Back: Independence Hall. Water-   FV   125
mark: Benjamin Franklin.

URUGUAY

The Oriental Republic of Uruguay (so called because of its location on the east bank of the Uruguay River) is situated on the Atlantic coast of South America between Argentina and Brazil. This most advanced of South American countries has an area of 176,220 sq. km. and a population of 3.48 million. Capital: Montevideo. Uruguay's chief economic asset is its rich, rolling grassy plains. Meat, wool, hides and skins are exported. Montevideo, founded by the Spanish in 1726 as a military stronghold, soon took advantage of its natural harbor to become an important commercial center. Claimed by Argentina but annexed by Brazil in 1821, Uruguay declared its independence four years later and secured its freedom in 1828 after a three-year struggle. The administrations of President Jose Battle in the early 20th century established widespread political, social, and economic reforms that established a statist tradition. A violent Marxist urban guerrilla movement named the Tupamaros, launched in the late 1960s, led Uruguay's president to cede control of the government to the military in 1973. By year end, the rebels had been crushed, but the military continued to expand its hold over the government. Civilian rule was not restored until 1985. In 2004, the left-of-center Frente Amplio Coalition won national elections that effectively ended 170 years of political control previously held by the Colorado and Blanco parties. Uruguay's political and labor conditions are among the freest on the continent.

MONETARY SYSTEM:
    1 Peso = 100 Centésimos, 1860-1975
    1 Nuevo Peso = 1000 Old Pesos, 1975-1993
    1 Peso Uruguayo = 1000 Nuevo Pesos, 1993-

OFFICE TITLES:
    1 - Gerente General, Secretario General, Presidente
    2 - Co-Gerente General, Secretario General, Presidente
    3 - p.Gerente General, Secretario General, Presidente
    4 - Gerente General, Secretario General, Vicepresidente
    5 - Gerente General, Secretario General, 2o Vicepresidente
    6 - p.Gerente General, Secretario General, Vicepresidente
    7 - Secretario General, Presidente

REPUBLIC

Banco Central del Uruguay

1967 ND Provisional Issue

#42-45 Banco Central was organized in 1967 and used notes of previous issuing authority with Banco Central signature title overprint.

42 10 Pesos   **VF**   **UNC**
L.1939 (1967). Purple on multicolor underprint. J. G. Artigas at lower center, arms
at upper left. Series D. Signature title 1. Back: Farmer with 3-team ox-cart. Printer:
TDLR.
    a. Bank name below title: *Banco Central de la República.*   3.00   10.00
    b. Bank name below title: *Banco Central del Uruguay.*   2.50   7.50

42A 50 Pesos   **VF**   **UNC**
L.1939 (1967). Blue and brown on multicolor underprint. Warrior wearing helmet at
right, arms at upper left. Series D. Back: Group of people with flag. Printer: TDLR.
    a. Bank name below all 3 signatures. Signature title: 1.   3.00   7.50
    b. Bank name below 2 signatures at right. Signature title: 3.   3.00   10.00

43 100 Pesos

VF UNC

L.1939. (1967). Red and brown. Constitution" at right, arms at center. Series D.
Back: People in town square. Printer: TDLR.
- a. Bank name below 3 signature *Banco Central del Uruguay.* Signature title: 1, 3; *PRESIDENTE* at right — 3.50 / 12.00
- b. Bank name below 2 signature at l.: *Banco Central del Uruguay.* Signature title: 4; 6 *VICE PRESIDENTE* at right. — 3.50 / 12.00
- c. Bank name below 2 signature at right. Signature title: 3. — 3.50 / 12.00

44 500 Pesos

VF UNC

L.1939. Green and blue. Industry" at right, arms at upper left. Series D. Back:
People with symbols of agriculture. Printer: TDLR.
- a. Signature Like #42a. — 6.00 / 17.50
- b. Signature like #42b. — 6.00 / 17.50

45 1000 Pesos

VF UNC

L.1939. Purple and black on pale yellow underprint. Jose Gervasio Artigas at right,
arms at upper left. Series D. Signature like # 42a. Back: Man on horseback at
center. Printer: TDLR. — 8.00 / 25.00

1967 ND Issue

#46-51 Jose Gervasio Artigas at ctr.

46 50 Pesos

VF UNC

ND (1967). UV: rays around Artigas head fluoresce green. Deep blue on light
green and lilac underprint. Arms at left. Jose Gervasio Artigas at center. Signature
titles: 1; 2; 4. Series A. Back: Group of 33 men with flag. Printer: TDLR.
- a. Issued note. — 0.25 / 1.75
- s. Specimen. — — / 55.00

47 100 Pesos

VF UNC

ND (1967). Red on lilac and light gold underprint. Arms at left. Jose Gervasio
Artigas at center. Signature titles: 1; 2; 3. Back: Man presiding at independence
meeting. Printer: TDLR.
- a. Issued note. — 0.25 / 1.75
- s. Specimen. — — / 55.00

48 500 Pesos

VF UNC

ND (1967). Green and blue on orange and light green underprint. Jose Gervasio
Artigas at center. Signature titles: 1; 2. Back: Dam. Watermark: Arms. Printer: TDLR.
- a. Issued note. — 1.25 / 7.00
- s. Specimen. — — / 55.00

49 1000 Pesos   VF   UNC
ND (1967). Purple and black on blue and yellow underprint. Jose Gervasio Artigas
at center. Signature titles: 1; 2; 3; 4. Back: Large building. Watermark: Arms.
Printer: TDLR.
    a. Issued note.   1.25   6.00
    s. Specimen.   —   60.00

50 5000 Pesos   VF   UNC
ND (1967). Brown and blue-green on lilac and light blue underprint. Jose Gervasio
Artigas at center. Signature title varieties. Back: Bank. Watermark: Arms. Printer:
TDLR.
    a. Series A; B. Signature titles: 1, 4, 5, 6.   5.00   25.00
    b. Series C. Signature title: 2.   1.00   4.50
    s. Specimen.   —   60.00

51 10,000 Pesos   VF   UNC
ND (1967). Dark green and black on yellow and light orange underprint. Jose
Gervasio Artigas at center. Signature title varieties. Back: Building. Watermark:
Arms. Printer: TDLR.
    a. Series A. Signature title: 1.   12.50   35.00
    b. Series A. Signature title: 6.   15.00   40.00
    c. Series B. Signature titles: 2, 3, 4.   12.50   30.00
    s. Specimen.   —   65.00

1974 ND Issue

#52 replacement notes: Serial # prefix *R*.

52 1000 Pesos   VF   UNC
ND (1974). Violet and dark green on multicolor underprint. Arms at upper left   1.00   3.00
center, Artigas at right. Signature title: 2. Back: Building. Watermark: Artigas.
Printer: CdeM-A.

#53 replacement notes: First digit of 8 digit serial # is *9*.

53 10,000 Pesos   VF   UNC
ND (1974). Orange on multicolor underprint. Arms at upper left center, J. G. Arti-
gas at right. Signature varieties. Back: Palace Esteze at left center. Watermark:
Artigas. Printer: TDLR.
    a. Series A. Signature titles: 2.   3.00   10.00
    b. Series B. Signature titles: 2.   2.50   7.00
    c. Series C. Signature titles: 1.   2.00   6.00

1975 ND Provisional Issue

#54-58 new value ovpt. in black on wmk. area on face only.

54 0.50 Nuevo Peso on 500 Pesos   VF   UNC
ND (1975). Green and blue on orange and light green underprint. Jose Gervasio   0.25   1.50
Artigas at center with overprint. Signature titles: 1. Back: Dam. Watermark: Arms.
Printer: TDLR.

55 1 Nuevo Peso on 1000 Pesos   VF   UNC
ND (1975). Purple and black on blue and yellow underprint. Jose Gervasio Artigas   1.00   3.50
at center with overprint. Signature titles: 1. Back: Large building. Watermark:
Arms. Printer: TDLR.

#56 and 57 replacement notes: 8 digit serial # prefix *R*.

56 1 Nuevo Peso on 1000 Pesos   VF   UNC
ND (1975). Violet and dark green on multicolor underprint. Arms at upper left   1.00   4.00
center, Artigas at right with overprint. Signature title: 2. Back: Building. Watermark:
Artigas. Printer: CdeM-A.

57 5 Nuevos Pesos on 5000 Pesos

ND (1975). Brown on multicolor underprint. J. G. Artigas at right, arms at left center, overprint new value at left. Signature titles: 2. Back: Old Banco de la República. Printer: CdM-A.

	VF	UNC
	1.25	5.00

58 10 Nuevos Pesos on 10,000 Pesos

ND (1975). Orange on multicolor underprint. Arms at upper left center, J. G. Artigas at right with overprint. Series C. Signature titles: 1. Back: Palace Esteze at left center. Watermark: J. G. Artigas. Printer: TDLR.

	VF	UNC
	4.00	16.00

Ley No. 14.316; 1975 ND Issue

59 50 Nuevos Pesos

ND (1975). Deep blue on multicolor underprint. Arms near center, J. G. Artigas at right. Series A.Three signatures. Signature titles: 1. Back: Old Government palace. Watermark: J. G. Artigas. Printer: TDLR.

	VF	UNC
	5.00	9.00

60 100 Nuevos Pesos

ND (1975). Olive-green on multicolor underprint. Arms near center, J. G. Artigas at right. Series A.Three signatures. Signature titles: 1. Back: Old Government palace. Watermark: J. G. Artigas. Printer: TDLR.

	VF	UNC
a. Issued note.	6.00	15.00
s. Specimen.	—	—

Ley No. 14.316; 1978-88 ND Issues

#61-64A Replacement notes: 8 digit serial # starting w/9.

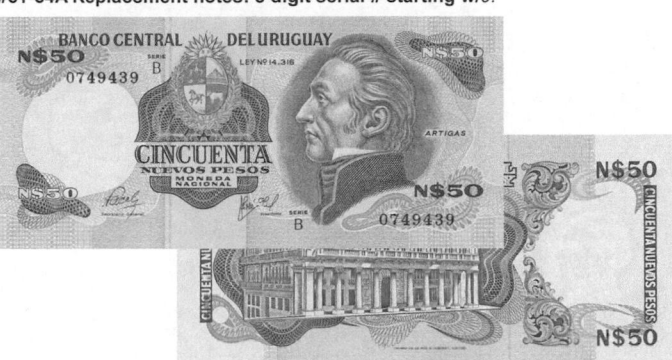

61 50 Nuevos Pesos

ND (1978-87). Deep blue on multicolor underprint. Arms near center, J. G. Artigas at right, without text: *PAGARA....A LA VISTA* at center. Series A.Three signatures. Back: Old Government palace. Watermark: J. G. Artigas. Printer: TDLR.

	VF	UNC
a. 2 Signatures. Series B (1978). Signature titles: 7.	1.50	6.00
b. 3 Signatures. Series C (1980). Signature titles: 1.	1.00	5.00
c. 2 Signatures. Series D (1981). Signature titles: 7.	0.75	3.00
d. 3 Signatures. Series E (1987). Signature titles: 1.	0.50	2.00

61A 50 Nuevos Pesos

ND (1988-89). Arms near center, J. G. Artigas at right, portrait of Artigas in watermark area, without text *PAGARA....A LA VISTA* at center. Series F (1988); Series G (1989). Three signatures. Signature titl Back: Old Government palace. Watermark: J. G. Artigas. Printer: TDLR.

	VF	UNC
	0.20	0.75

62 100 Nuevos Pesos

ND (1978-86). Olive-green on multicolor underprint. Arms near center, J. G. Artigas at right, without text: *PAGARA....A LA VISTA* at center. Series A.Three signatures. Back: Old Government palace. Watermark: J. G. Artigas. Printer: TDLR.

	VF	UNC
a. 2 Signature. Series B (1978). Signature titles: 7.	2.50	7.50
b. 3 Signature. Series C (1980); Series D (1981). Signature titles: 1.	0.50	3.00
c. Series E (1985); Series F (1986). Signature titles: 1.	0.25	1.00
s. Specimen. As c. Series E. Black overprint: *MUESTRA SIN VALOR* on both sides.	—	75.00

62A   100 Nuevos Pesos VF   UNC
ND (1987). Olive-green on multicolor underprint. Arms near center, J. G. Artigas at right, without text: *PAGARA....A LA VISTA* at center. Portrait of Artigas printed in watermark area. Series G (1987). Three signatures. Signature titles: 1. Back: Old Government palace. Watermark: J. G. Artigas. Printer: TDLR.   0.50   2.00

63   500 Nuevos Pesos VF   UNC
ND (1978-85). Red on multicolor underprint. Arms near center, J. G. Artigas at right, without text: *PAGARA....A LA VISTA* at center. Series A.Three signatures. Signature titles: 1. Back: Old Government palace. Watermark: J. G. Artigas. Printer: TDLR.
a. 2 Signature. Series A (1978). Signature titles: 7.   4.00   12.50
b. 3 Signature. Series B (1978); Series C (1985). Signature titles: 1.   0.75   3.50
s. Specimen. As b. Series C. Black overprint: *MUESTRA SIN VALOR* on both sides.   —   75.00

63A   500 Nuevos Pesos VF   UNC
ND (1991). Red on multicolor underprint. Arms near center, J. G. Artigas at right, without text: *PAGARA....A LA VISTA* at center. Portrait of Artigas printed in watermark area. Series D (1991). Three signatures. Signature titles: 1. Back: Old Government palace. Printer: TDLR.   0.50   1.50

64   1000 Nuevos Pesos VF   UNC
ND(1978-81). Purple on multicolor underprint. Arms near center, J. G. Artigas at right, without text: *PAGARA....A LA VISTA* at center. Series A.Three signatures. Back: Old Government palace. Watermark: J. G. Artigas. Printer: TDLR.
a. 2 Signature. Series A (1978). Signature titles: 7.   4.50   12.50
b. 3 Signature. Series B (1981). Signature titles: 1.   1.50   5.00

64A   1000 Nuevos Pesos VF   UNC
ND (1991-92). Purple on multicolor underprint. Arms near center, J. G. Artigas at right, without text: *PAGARA....A LA VISTA* at center. Portrait of Artigas printed in watermark area. Series A. Three signatures. Back: Old Government palace. Printer: TDLR.
a. Series C (1991). Signature titles: 1.   1.00   3.50
b. Series D (1992). Signature titles: 1.   0.50   2.50

65   5000 Nuevos Pesos VF   UNC
ND (1983). Deep brown, orange-brown and blue on multicolor underprint. Arms at top left center, Brig. General Juan Antonio Lavalleja at right. Series A; B; C. Signature titles: 1. Back: 1830 scene of pledging allegiance at center. Printer: TDLR.
a. Issued note.   1.50   5.00
s. Specimen. Black overprint: *MUESTRA SIN VALOR* on both sides.   —   75.00

Ley No. 14.316; 1986; 1987 ND Issue
#66 replacement notes: Series A-R.

66   200 Nuevos Pesos VF   UNC
1986. Dark and light green on brown and multicolor underprint. Quill and scroll at left, arms at center, J. E. Rodo at right. Series A. Signature titles: 1. Back: Rodo Monument at center, statuary at left and center. Watermark: J. G. Artigas. Printer: C. Ciccone S.A.
a. Isused note.   0.25   1.50
s. Specimen. Red overprint: *SIN VALOR* on face.   —   75.00

67 10,000 Nuevos Pesos   **VF UNC**
ND (1987). Purple, dark blue, dark olive-green and violet on multicolor underprint.
Plaza of Democracy with flag at left center. Signature titles: 1. Back: 19 depart-
mental arms. Printer: ABNC.

    a. Overprint gold gilt bars on description and law designation. Series A.   25.00   75.00
    b. No overprint bars on new inscription at left, *DECRETO-LEY NO. 14.316* at   2.00   7.50
       upper right. Series B; C.
    s1. Note as printed but without gold bar overprint. Series A. Specimen.   —   1,250
    s2. Note as printed, with gold bar overprint. Specimen. Red overprint: *MUES-*   —   1,250
       TRA SIN VALOR on face. Punch hole cancelled.
    s3. Specimen. As b. Series B. Red overprint: *MUESTRA SIN VALOR* on face,   —   250
       punch hole cancelled.

Note: On #67 the description *Plaza de la Nacionalidad Oriental/Monumento a la bandera* and
LEY 14.316 ovpt. was being blocked out because of a change of government from military
to elected civil administration before the notes were released. The new government took the
prepared notes, ovpt. the legend relating to the old government and issued them (Series A).
Only Specimen notes are known w/o the ovpt.

1989-92 Issue

67A 1000 Nuevos Pesos   **VF UNC**
1989. Specimen. (Not issued.) Brown and orange on multicolor underprint. Pedro   —   35.00
Figari at right. Back: Allegory of Music.

68 2000 Nuevos Pesos   **VF UNC**
1989. UV: value 2000 in box fluoresces orange, BCU yellow; vertical serial #
orange. Back right design yellow. Dark brown and orange on multicolor underprint.
Arms at upper left. Latent image with letters B/CU at upper right. J. M. Blanes at
center right. Series A. Signature titles: 1. Back: Altar of the Homeland (allegory of
the Republic). Watermark: J. G. Artigas. Printer: TDLR.

    a. Issued note.   0.50   2.00
    b. Specimen. Black overprint: *NUESTRA SIN VALOR* on both sides.   —   75.00

68A 5000 Nuevos Pesos   **VF UNC**
1989. Specimen. (Not issued.) Brown and orange on multicolor underprint. Pedro   —   35.00
Figari at right. Arms at upper left, latent image at upper right with letters B/CU.
Signature titles: 1. Back: *Baile Antiguo* (old dance). Watermark: J.G. Artigas.
Printor: TDLR.

68B 10,000 Nuevos Pesos   **VF UNC**
1989. Specimen. (Not issued.) Brown and orange on multicolor underprint. Arms
at upper left. Latent image at upper right with letters B/CU. Alfredo Vasquez
Acevedo at right. Signature titles: 1. Back: University of the Republic. Watermark:
J. G. Artigas. Printer: TDLR.

    a. Issued note.   —   35.00
    s. Specimen. Handstamped: NO EMITIDO. Regular serial #.   —   80.00

69 20,000 Nuevos Pesos   **VF UNC**
1989; 1991. Dark green and violet on multicolor underprint. Arms at upper left.
Latent image (silver oval) at upper right with letters B/CU. Dr. J. Zorrilla de San
Martin at center right. Series A. Signature titles: 1. Back: Manuscript and allegory
of the legend of the homeland (Victory with wings). Watermark: J.G. Artigas.
Printer: TDLR.

    a. 1989.   3.50   8.00
    b. 1991.   3.50   8.00
    s. Specimen. As a. Black overprint: *NUESTRA SIN VALOR* on both sides.   —   100

70 50,000 Nuevos Pesos   **VF UNC**

1989; 1991. Black, violet and red on multicolor underprint. Arms at upper left.
Latent image (silver oval) at upper right with letters B/CU. José Pedro Varela at
center right. Series A. Signature titles: 1. Back: Varela Monument at left. Watermark: J. G. Artigas. Printer: TDLR.

a. 1989.	7.50	17.50
b. 1991.	7.50	17.50
s. Specimen. As a, b. Black overprint: *MUESTRA SIN VALOR* on both sides.	—	100

71 100,000 Nuevos Pesos   **VF UNC**

1991. Purple and dark brown on multicolor underprint. Arms at upper left. Latent
image (silver oval) at upper right with letters B/CU. Eduardo Fabini at right center.
Series A. Signature titles: 1. Back: Musical allegory. Watermark: J. G. Artigas.
Printer: TDLR.

a. Issued note.	15.00	32.50
s. Specimen. Black overprint: *MUESTRA SIN VALOR* on both sides.	—	125

72 200,000 Nuevos Pesos   **VF UNC**

1992. Dark brown and violet and orange on multicolor underprint. Arms at upper
left. Latent image (silver oval) at upper right with letters B/CU. Pedro Figari at
center right. Series A. Signature titles: 1. Back: Old dance at left. Watermark: J. G.
Artigas. Printer: TDLR.

a. Issued note.	27.50	65.00
s. Specimen. Black overprint: *MUESTRA SIN VALOR* on both sides.	—	150

73 500,000 Nuevos Pesos   **VF UNC**

1992. Blue-gray, violet and pale red on multicolor underprint. Arms at upper left.
Latent image (silver oval) at upper right with letters B/CU. Alfredo Vaquez Acevedo at center right. Series A. Signature titles: 1. Back: University of Montevideo at
left. Watermark: J. G. Artigas. Printer: TDLR.

a. Issued note.	65.00	125
s. Specimen. Black overprint: *MUESTRA SIN VALOR* on both sides.	—	150

1994-97 Issue

1 Peso Uruguayo = 1000 Nuevos Pesos, 1993-

73A 5 Pesos Uruguayos   **VF UNC**

ND (1997). Dark brown, red-brown and blue on multicolor underprint. Arms at top
left center, Brig. General Juan Antonio Lavalleja at right. Series A. Signature titles:
1. Back: 1830 scene of pledging allegiance at center. Printer: TDLR.

a. Issued note.	FV	2.00
s. Specimen. Red overprint: *MUESTRA SIN VALOR* on both sides.	—	75.00

73B 10 Pesos Uruguayos   **VF UNC**

ND (1995). Purple, dark blue, dark olive-green and violet on multicolor underprint.
Plaza of Democracy with flag at left center. Signature titles: 1. Back: 19 depart-
mental arms. Printer: G&D.

a. With Decreto-Ley No.14.316 (error). Series A.	FV	4.00
b. Without Ley. Series B.	FV	3.50
s. Specimen. As a. Red overprint: *MUESTRA SIN VALOR* on each side.	—	75.00

74 20 Pesos Uruguayos   **VF UNC**

1994; 1997. Dark green and violet on multicolor underprint. Arms at upper left.
Latent image (silver oval) at upper right with letters B/CU. Dr. J. Zorrilla de San
Martin at center right. Signature titles: 1. Back: Manuscript and allegory of the leg-
end of the homeland (Victory with wings). Watermark: J. G. Artigas. Printer: TDLR.

a. 1994. Series A.	FV	4.50
b. 1997. Series B.	FV	4.50
s. Specimen. As a. Pin hole cancelled.	—	75.00

75   50 Pesos Uruguayos   VF   UNC

1994; 2000. Black, red and violet on multicolor underprint. Arms at upper left.
Latent image (silver oval) at upper right with letters B/CU. José Pedro Varela
at center right. Series A, B. Signature titles: 1. Back: Varela Monument at left.
Watermark: J. G. Artigas. Printer: TDLR.

a. 1994.	FV	10.00
b. 2000.	FV	10.00
s. Specimen. As a. Pin hole cancelled SPECIMEN.	—	100

76   100 Pesos Uruguayos   VF   UNC

1994; 1997; 2000. Purple and dark brown on multicolor underprint. Arms at upper
left. Latent image (silver oval) at upper right with letters B/CU. Eduardo Fabini at
right center. Series A; B; C. Signature titles: 1. Back: Musical allegory. Watermark:
J. G. Artigas. Printer: TDLR.

a. 1994.	FV	17.50
b. 1997.	FV	17.50
c. 2000.	FV	17.50
s. Specimen. As a. Pin hole cancelled.	—	100

77   200 Pesos Uruguayos   VF   UNC

1995; 2000. Dark brown-violet on multicolor underprint. Arms at upper left. Latent
image (silver oval) at upper right with letters B/CU. Pedro Figari at center right.
Series A; B. Signature titles: 1. Back: Old dance at left. Watermark: J. G. Artigas.
Printer: TDLR.

a. 1995.	FV	35.00
b. 2000.	FV	35.00
s. Specimen. As a. Pin hole cancelled.	—	150

78   500 Pesos Uruguayos   VF   UNC

1994. Blue-gray, violet and pale red on multicolor underprint. Arms at upper left.
Latent image (silver oval) at upper right with letters B/CU. Alfredo Vaquez Acevedo at center right. Series A. Signature titles: 1. Back: University of Montevideo at
left. Watermark: J. G. Artigas. Printer: TDLR.

a. Issued note.	FV	75.00
s. Specimen. Pin hole cancelled: SPECIMEN.	—	175

79   1000 Pesos Uruguayos   VF   UNC

1995; 2004. Brown and olive-green on multicolor underprint. Arms at upper right.
Latent image at upper right with letters B/CU. Juana de Ibarbourou at right. Signa-
ture titles: 1. Back: Palm tree in Ibarbourou Square at left, books. Watermark: J.
G. Artigas. Printer: TDLR.

a. 1995. Series A. Imprint as TDLR.	FV	140
s. Specimen. As a. Pin hole cancelled.	—	175

Note. #79 issued in celebration of the 100th birthday of Juana de Ibarbourou.

1998 Issue

80   5 Pesos Uruguayos   VF   UNC

1998. Brown and orange-brown on blue and multicolor underprint. Joaquín Torres
Garcia at right center. Series A. Signature titles: 1. Back: Garcia's painting at left.
Printer: (T)DLR.

a. Issued note.	FV	2.00
s. Specimen. Red overprint: *MUESTRA SIN VALOR* one both sides.	—	75.00

81   10 Pesos Uruguayos   **VF   UNC**
1998. Slate black and light rose on multicolor underprint. Eduardo Acevedo
Vásquez at right. Series A. Signature titles: 1. Back: Agronomy building at left.
Printer: (T)DLR.
    a. Issued note.   FV   3.00
    s. Specimen. Red overprint: *MUESTRA SIN VALOR* on both sides.   —   75.00

1999 Issue

82   500 Pesos Uruguayos   **VF   UNC**
1999. Blue on multicolor underprint. Arms at upper left. Latent image (silver oval)   FV   75.00
at upper right with letters B/CU. Alfredo Vaquez Acevedo at center right. Series
B. Signature titles: 1. Back: University of Montevideo at left. Watermark: J. G.
Artigas. Printer: FC-O.

2000 Issue

83   20 Pesos Uruguayos   **VF   UNC**
2000; 2003. Dark green and violet on multicolor underprint. Arms at upper left.
Latent image (silver oval) at upper right with letters B/CU. Dr. J. Zorrilla de San
Martin at center right. Series C. Signature titles: 1. Back: Manuscript and allegory
of the legend of the homeland (Victory with wings). Watermark: J. G. Artigas.
Printer: TDLR.
    a. 2000.   FV   4.50
    b. 2003.   FV   4.50
83A 20 Pesos Uruguayos   **VF   UNC**
2003. Dark green and violet on multicolor underprint. Dr. J. Zorrille de San Martin   FV   4.50
at center right. Arms at upper left. Latent image (silver oval) at upper right with
letters B/CU. Seríes D. Signature titles: 1. Back: Manuscript and allegory of the
legend of the homelaqnd (Victory with wings). Watermark: J. G. Artigas. Printer:
F-CO.

84   50 Pesos Uruguayos   **VF   UNC**
2003. Black, red and violet on multicolor underprint. Arms at upper left. Latent   FV   10.00
image (silver oval) at upper right with letters B/CU. José Pedro Varela at center
right. Series C. Signature titles: 1. Back: Varela Monument at left. Watermark: J.
G. Artigas. Printer: F-CO.

85   100 Pesos Uruguayos   **VF   UNC**
2003. Purple and dark brown on multicolor underprint. Arms at upper left. Latent   FV   35.00
image (silver oval) at upper right with letters B/CU. Eduardo Fabini at right center.
Series D. Signature titles: 1. Back: Musical allegory. Watermark: J. G. Artigas.
Printer: F-CO.

85A 100 Pesos Uruguayos   **VF   UNC**
2006. Purple and dark brown on multicolor underprint. Arms at upper left. Latent   FV   35.00
image (silver oval) at upper right with letters B/CU. Eduardo Fabini at right center.
Back: Musical allegory. Printer: G&D.

2003-2011 Issue

86   20 Pesos Uruguayos   **VF   UNC**
2008; 2011. Green on multicolor underprint. Dr. Juan Zorrilla de San Martin at
right center. Back: Allegory of the homeland at left. Printer: TDLR. 159x74mm.
    a. 2008. Series E.   FV   3.50
    b. 2011. Series F.   FV   3.50

87   50 Pesos Uruguayos

2008; 2011. Black and rose on multicolor underprint. Jose Pedro Varela at right. 159x74mm.

		VF	UNC
a.	2008. Series D. Printer: F-CO.	FV	7.50
b.	2011. Series E. Printer: DLR.	FV	7.50

88   100 Pesos Uruguayos

2008; 2011. Pruple on multicolor underprint. Eduardo Fabani at left center. Back: Musical muse seated under tree. 159x74mm.

		VF	UNC
a.	2008. Series E. Printer G&D.	FV	15.00
b.	2011. Series F. Printer: DLR.	FV	15.00

89   200 Pesos Uruguayos

2006; 2009; 2011. Brown and orange on multicolor underprint. Pedro Figari. Signatrue titles: 1. Watermark: Figari and value. 159x74mm.

		VF	UNC
a.	2006. Series C. Printer: F-CO.	FV	25.00
b.	2009. Series D. Printer: Oberthur.	FV	22.50
c.	2011. Series E. Printer: DLR.	FV	22.50

90   500 Pesos Uruguayos

2006. Alfredo Vaquez Acevedo. Similar to #82. Series C. Signatrue titles: 1. Watermark: Alfredo Acevedo and value. 159x74mm.

		VF	UNC
a.	2006. Series C. Printer: F-CO.	FV	60.00
b.	2009. Series D. Printer: Oberthur.	FV	60.00

91   1000 Pesos Uruguayos

2004; 2008; 2011. Brown and green on multicolor underprint. Juana de Ibarbourou at right. 159x74mm.

		VF	UNC
a.	2004. Series B. Printer: DLR.	FV	100
b.	2008. Series C. Printer: FCO.	FV	100
c.	2011. Series D. Printer: Oberthur.	FV	100

92   2000 Pesos Uruguayos

2003. Gray and light olive-green. Dámaso Antonio Larrañaga at right. Series A. Signature titles: 1. Back: National Library. Printer: G&D. 159x74mm.

		VF	UNC
a.	Issued note.	FV	250
s.	Specimen. Red overprint: *MUESTRA SIN VALOR* on both sides.	—	300

2014 Issue

93   500 Pesos Uruguayos

2014. Blue, purple, red, green and multicolor. Alfdrredo Vasquez Acevedo at right. Back: University of the Republic in Montevideo. Watermark: Jose Gervasio Artigas. Printer: Oberthur. 159x74mm.

	VF	UNC
	FV	40.00

UZBEKISTAN

The Republic of Uzbekistan (formerly the Uzbek S.S.R.), is bordered on the north by Kazakhstan, to the east by Kirghizia and Tajikistan, on the south by Afghanistan and on the west by Turkmenistan. The republic is comprised of the regions of Andizhan, Bukhara, Dzhizak, Ferghana, Kashkadar, Khorezm (Khiva), Namangan, Navoi, Samarkand, Surkhan-Darya, Syr-Darya, Tashkent and the Karakalpak Autonomous Republic. It has an area of 447,400 sq. km. and a population of 27.34 million. Capital: Tashkent. Crude oil, natural gas, coal, copper and gold deposits make up the chief resources, while intensive farming, based on artificial irrigation, provides an abundance of cotton. Russia conquered Uzbekistan in the late 19th century. Stiff resistance to the Red Army after World War I was eventually suppressed and a socialist republic set up in 1924. During the Soviet era, intensive production of "white gold" (cotton) and grain led to overuse of agrochemicals and the depletion of water supplies, which have left the land poisoned and the Aral Sea and certain rivers half dry. Independent since 1991, the country seeks to gradually lessen its dependence on agriculture while developing its mineral and petroleum reserves. Current concerns include terrorism by Islamic militants, economic stagnation, and the curtailment of human rights and democratization.

Monetary System:
- 1 THHbrA (Tenga) = 20 КОПЬНКъ (Kopeks)
- 5 THHbrОВъ (Tengov) = 1 РЧЬПЙ (Ruble)
- 1 Sum (Ruble) = 100 Kopeks, 1991
- 1 Sum = 1,000 Sum Coupon, 1994
- 1 Сўь (Sum) = 100 ТИЙИН (Tiyin)

REPUBLIC

Government

КУПОНГА КАРТОЧКА - 1993 Ruble Control Coupons

		VF	UNC
43	**10 and 25 Coupons**		
	ND (1993). Uniface. Black on pale blue underprint.		
	a. Full sheet of 35 coupons with 2 registries.	—	5.00
	b. Top half sheet of 10 coupons with registry.	—	5.00
	c. Bottom half sheet of 25 coupons with registry.	—	5.00
	d. Coupon.	—	0.10
44	**10 and 25 Coupons**	**VF**	**UNC**
	ND (1993). Uniface. Black on orange underprint.		
	a. Full sheet of 35 coupons with 2 registries.	—	3.00
	b. Top half sheet of 10 coupons with registry.	—	2.00
	c. Bottom half sheet of 25 coupons with registry.	—	2.00
	d. Coupon.	—	0.10
45	**10 and 25 Coupons**	**VF**	**UNC**
	ND (1993). Uniface. Black on pink underprint.		
	a. Full sheet of 35 coupons with 2 registries.	—	7.00
	b. Top half sheet of 10 coupons with registry.	—	5.00
	c. Bottom half sheet of 25 coupons with registry.	—	5.00
	d. Coupon.	—	0.10
46	**50 Coupons**	**VF**	**UNC**
	ND (1993). Uniface. Black on pale ochre underprint.		
	a. Full sheet of 28 coupons with registry.	—	5.00
	b. Coupon.	—	0.10
47	**100 Coupons**	**VF**	**UNC**
	ND (1993). Uniface. Black on violet underprint.		
	a. Full sheet of 100 coupons with registry.	—	5.00
	b. Coupon.	—	0.10

		VF	UNC
48	**100 Coupons**		
	ND (1993). Uniface. Black on tan underprint.		
	a. Full sheet of 100 coupons with registry.	—	5.00
	b. Coupon.	—	0.10
49	**100 Coupons**	**VF**	**UNC**
	ND (1993). Uniface. Black on light blue underprint.		
	a. Full sheet of 100 coupons with registry.	—	5.00
	b. Coupon.	—	0.10
50	**150 Coupons**	**VF**	**UNC**
	ND (1993). Uniface. Red on pale gray underprint.		
	a. Full sheet of 150 coupons with registry.	—	5.00
	b. Coupon.	—	0.10
51	**200 Coupons**	**VF**	**UNC**
	ND (1993). Uniface. Black on pink underprint.		
	a. Full sheet of 200 coupons with registry.	—	5.00
	b. Coupon.	—	0.10
52	**200 Coupons**	**VF**	**UNC**
	ND (1993). Uniface. Black on tan underprint.		
	a. Full sheet of 200 coupons with registry.	—	0.10
	b. Coupon.	—	0.10

#53-57 not assigned.

		VF	UNC
58	**2000 Coupons**		
	ND (1993). Uniface. Blue on pink underprint.		
	a. Full sheet of 28 coupons with registry.	—	8.00
	b. Coupon.	—	0.10

#59-60 not assigned.

УЗБНКИСТОН ДАВЛАТ БАНКИ
BANK OF UZBEKISTAN
1992 (1993) Issue

61   1 Sum   **VF   UNC**

1992 (1993). Blue-gray on light blue and gold underprint. Arms at left. Back: Mosque at center. Watermark: Flower pattern repeated. Printer: H&S (without imprint).

a. Issued note.	1.00	2.00
s. Specimen.	—	25.00

62   3 Sum   **VF   UNC**

1992 (1993). Green on light blue and gold underprint. Arms at left. Back: Mosque at center. Watermark: Flower pattern repeated. Printer: H&S (without imprint).

a. Issued note.	1.00	2.50
s. Specimen.	—	25.00

63   5 Sum   **VF   UNC**

1992 (1993). Purple on light blue and gold underprint. Arms at left. Back: Mosque at center. Watermark: Flower pattern repeated. Printer: H&S (without imprint).

a. Issued note.	1.00	3.00
s. Specimen.	—	25.00

64   10 Sum   **VF   UNC**

1992 (1993). Red on light blue and gold underprint. Arms at left. Back: Mosque at center. Watermark: Flower pattern repeated. Printer: H&S (without imprint).

a. Issued note.	1.00	3.50
s. Specimen.	—	25.00

65   25 Sum   **VF   UNC**

1992 (1993). Blue-green on light blue and gold underprint. Arms at left. Back: Mosque at center. Watermark: Flower pattern repeated. Printer: H&S (without imprint).

a. Issued note.	1.50	4.50
s. Specimen.	—	25.00

66   50 Sum   **VF   UNC**

1992 (1993). Rose on light blue and gold underprint. Arms at left. Back: Mosque at center. Watermark: Large detailed cotton flower. Printer: H&S (without imprint).

a. Issued note.	2.00	6.00
s. Specimen.	—	25.00

67   100 Sum   **VF   UNC**

1992 (1993). Dark brown on light blue and gold underprint. Arms at left. Back: Mosque at center. Watermark: Large detailed cotton flower. Printer: H&S (without imprint).

a. Issued note.	2.50	7.50
s. Specimen.	—	25.00

68   200 Sum   **VF   UNC**

1992 (1993). Violet on light blue and gold underprint. Arms at left. Back: Mosque at center. Watermark: Large detailed cotton flower. Printer: H&S (without imprint).

a. Issued note.	4.50	10.00
s. Specimen.	—	25.00

69   500 Sum   **VF   UNC**

1992 (1993). Orange on light blue and gold underprint. Arms at left. Back: Mosque at center. Watermark: Large detailed cotton flower. Printer: H&S (without imprint).

a. Larger and italicized serial #, 8 digits.	6.00	15.00
b. Smaller and regular serial #. 7 digits.	6.00	15.00
s. Specimen.	—	25.00

70   1000 Sum   **VF   UNC**

1992 (1993). Brown on lilac and pale green underprint. Arms at left. Back: Mosque at center. Watermark: Large detailed cotton flower. Printer: H&S (without imprint).

a. Low and wide serial #.	7.00	18.00
b. High and narrow serial #.	7.00	18.00
s. Specimen.	—	30.00

71   5000 Sum   **VF   UNC**

1992 (1993). Blue-gray on lilac and pale green underprint. Arms at left. Back: Mosque at center. Watermark: Large detailed cotton flower. Printer: H&S (without imprint).

a. 3mm high serial #.	10.00	25.00
b. 4mm high serial #.	10.00	25.00
s. Specimen.	10.00	25.00

72   10,000 Sum   **VF   UNC**

1992 (1993). Red-orange on lilac and pale green underprint. Arms at left. Back: Mosque at center. Printer: H&S (without imprint).

a. 4mm high serial #. Watermark simple outline of cotton flower.	10.00	25.00
b. 4mm high serial #. Watermark: detailed cotton flower.	10.00	25.00
c. 3mm high serial #. Watermark: detailed cotton flower.	10.00	25.00
s. Specimen.	—	30.00

ЎЗБНКИСТОН РНСПУБЛИКАСИ ЬАРКАЗИЙ БАНКИ
CENTRAL BANK OF UZBEKISTAN REPUBLIC
1994; 1997 Issue
#73-80 Replacement notes: serial # prefix ZZ.

73   1 Sum   **VF   UNC**

1994. Dark green on multicolor underprint. Arms at left. Back: Building, fountain at center right. Watermark: Design.

a. Issued note.	FV	2.00
r. Replacement note. Serial # prefix: ZZ.	—	—

74   3 Sum VF UNC
1994. Violet and red-violet on multicolor underprint. Arms at left. Back: Mosque of Çaçma Ayub Mazar in Bukhara. Watermark: Design.
  a. Issued note. FV 3.00
  r. Replacement note. Serial # prefix: ZZ. — —

75   5 Sum VF UNC
1994. Dark blue and red-violet on multicolor underprint. Arms at upper center. Back: Ali Shir Nawai Monument in Tashkent at center right. Watermark: Arms.
  a. Issued note. FV 4.00
  r. Replacement note. Serial # prefix: ZZ. — —

76   10 Sum VF UNC
1994. Purple and blue-gray on multicolor underprint. Arms at upper center. Back: Tomb of Tamerlane in Samarkand at center right. Watermark: Arms.
  a. Issued note. FV 5.00
  r. Replacement note. Serial # prefix: ZZ. — —

77   25 Sum VF UNC
1994. Dark blue and brown on multicolor underprint. Arms at upper center. Back: Mausoleum Kazi Zadé Rumi in the necropolis Shakhi-Zinda in Samarkand at center right. Watermark: Arms.
  a. Issued note. FV 6.00
  r. Replacement note. Serial # prefix: ZZ. — —

78   50 Sum VF UNC
1994. Dark brown, olive-brown and dull brown-orange on multicolor underprint. Arms at upper center. Back: Esplanade in Reghistan and the two Medersas in Samarkand at center right. Watermark: Arms.
  a. Issued note. FV 6.00
  r. Replacement note. Serial # prefix: ZZ. — —

79   100 Sum VF UNC
1994. Purple and blue on multicolor underprint. Stylized facing peacocks at left. Arms at upper center. Back: *Drubja Narodov* palace in Tashkent at center right. Watermark: Arms.
  a. Issued note. FV 7.00
  r. Replacement note. Serial # prefix: ZZ. — —

80   200 Sum VF UNC
1997. Dark blue, black, deep purple on green and multicolor underprint. Arms at left. Back: Sunface over mythological tiger at center. Watermark: Arms. FV 7.00

81   500 Sum VF UNC
1999. Red, blue and green on multicolor underprint. Arms at left. Back: Equestrian statue at center right. Watermark: Arms. FV 7.00

82   1000 Sum VF UNC
2001. Brown & purple. Arms at left. Back: Amir Temur Museum. Watermark: Arms. FV 7.00

83   5000 Sum VF UNC
2013. Green, blue and brown. Coat of arms. Back: Oliy Majlis parliament building in Tashkent. Watermark: Coat of arms and 5000. 144x77mm. FV 9.00

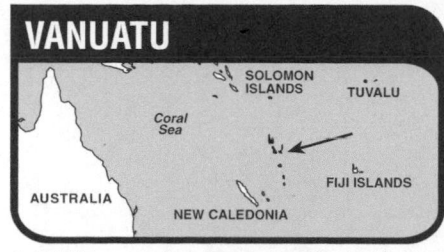

VANUATU

Vanuatu (formerly the New Hebrides Condominium), a group of islands located in the South Pacific 800 km. west of Fiji, were under the joint sovereignty of Great Britain and France. The islands have an area of 12,200 sq. km. and a population of 215,450. Capital: Vila. The volcanic and coral islands, while malarial and subject to frequent earthquakes, are extremely fertile, and produce copra, coffee, tropical fruits and timber for export. Multiple waves of colonizers, each speaking a distinct language, migrated to the New Hebrides in the millennia preceding European exploration in the 18th century. This settlement pattern accounts for the complex linguistic diversity found on the archipelago to this day. The British and French, who settled the New Hebrides in the 19th century, agreed in 1906 to an Anglo-French Condominium, which administered the islands until Independence in 1980, when the new name of Vanuatu was adopted.

RULERS:
British and French to 1982

MONETARY SYSTEM:
100 Vatu = 100 Francs

SIGNATURE VARIETIES					
	PRESIDENT	**GENERAL MANAGER**		**GOVERNOR**	**MINISTER OF FINANCE**
1			2		
3			4		

INDEPENDENT
Banque Centrale de Vanuatu

CENTRAL BANK OF VANUATU / CENTRAL BANK BLONG VANUATU
1982; 1989 ND Issue

1 100 Vatu   **VF UNC**
ND (1982). Dark green on multicolor underprint. Arms with Melanesian chief standing with spear at center right. Signature 1. Back: Cattle among palm trees at left center. Watermark: Melanesian male head. Printer: BWC.
    a. Issued note.   2.50 15.00
    s. Specimen.   — 160

2 500 Vatu   **VF UNC**
ND (1982). Light red on multicolor underprint. Arms with Melanesian chief standing with spear at center right. Signature 1. Back: Three carvings at left, two men beating upright hollow log drums at left center. Watermark: Melanesian male head. Printer: BWC. 140x70mm.
    a. Issued note.   5.00 20.00
    s. Specimen.   — 180

3 1000 Vatu   **VF UNC**
ND (1982). Black on light orange, green and multicolor underprint. Arms with Melanesian chief standing with spear at center. Signature 1. Back: Three carvings at lower left, three men in outrigger sailboat at center. Watermark: Melanesian male head. Printer: BWC. 150x75mm.
    a. Issued note.   12.50 35.00
    s. Specimen.   — 225

4 5000 Vatu   **VF UNC**
ND (1989). Brown and lilac on multicolor underprint. Arms with Melanesian chief standing with spear at center right. Signature 2. Back: Man watching another *Gol* diving from log tower at center. Watermark: Melanesian male head. Printer: BWC. 160x79mm.   50.00 95.00

Banque de Reserve de Vanuatu

RESERVE BANK OF VANUATU / RESERVE BANK BLONG VANUATU
1993 ND Issue

5 500 Vatu   **VF UNC**
ND (1993). Light red on multicolor underprint. Arms with Melanesian chief standing with spear at center right, new bank name. Signature 3. Back: Three carvings at left, two men beating upright hollow log drums at left center. Watermark: Melanesian male head. 140x70mm.
    a. Printer as: TDLR.   FV 12.50
    b. Printer as: DLR.   FV 12.50

6 1000 Vatu   **VF UNC**
ND (1993). Black on light orange, green and multicolor underprint. Arms with Melanesian chief standing with spear at center right, new bank name. Signature 3. Back: Three carvings at lower left, three men in outrigger sailboat at center. Watermark: Melanesian male head. Printer: TDLR. 150x75mm.   FV 22.50

7 5000 Vatu   **VF UNC**
ND. Arms with Melanesian chief standing with spear at center right, new bank name. Signature 3. Back: Man watching another *Gol* diving from log tower at center. Watermark: Melanesian male head. Printer: DLR. 160x79mm.   FV 100

1995 ND Issue

8   200 Vatu   **VF   UNC**
ND (1995). Purple and violet on multicolor underprint. Arms with Melanesian chief standing with spear at center right. Signature varieties. Back: Statue of family life, "Traditional parliament in session" and flag. Watermark: Melanesian male head. Printer: TDLR. 135x68mm.

		VF	UNC
a. Imprint at left end as TDLR.		FV	7.50
b. Imprint at left end as DLR.		FV	7.50

1995 Commemorative Issue

#9, 15th Anniversary of Independence

9   200 Vatu   **VF   UNC**
ND (1995). Purple and violet on multicolor underprint. Commemorative text overprint in watermark area at left on #8. Printer: TDLR. 135x68mm.   FV   7.50

2002 ND Issue

10   1000 Vatu   **VF   UNC**
ND (2002). Black and green on orange underprint. Arms with Melanesian chief standing with spear at center right. Back: Outrigger sailboat. Printer: (T)DLR. 150x75mm.

		VF	UNC
a. Signature 3.		FV	25.00
b. Signature 5.		FV	25.00

2006 Commemorative Issue

11   1000 Vatu   **VF   UNC**
2006. Black and green on orange underprint. Signature 5. 150x75mm.   FV   22.50

2006; 2014 Regular Issue

12   5000 Vatu   **VF   UNC**
ND (2006). Red on yellow and multicolor underprint. Arms with Melanesian chief standing with spear at center right. Signature 5. Back: "Goi" diver.   FV   100

14   200 Vatu   **VF   UNC**
2014. Pink, brown, blue and green. Conch shell, waterway, Melanesian chief standing with spear, map of Vanuatu islands. Back: Map of Vanuatu islands, family seated outside house with palm trees, conch shell. No security thread. Prefix AA. Watermark: None. Printer: Oberthur. 130x65mm.   FV   6.50

15   1000 Vatu   **VF   UNC**
2014. Polymer plastic. Brown, purple, blue and green. Conch shell, waterway, Melanesian chief standing holding spear, map of Vanuatu islands. Back: Map of Vanuatu islands, flower, farmers with crops, rancher riding horse among cattle with palm trees, conch shell. No security thread. Prefix AA. Watermark: None. Printer: Oberthur. 140x65mm.   FV   24.00

16   2000 Vatu   **VF   UNC**
2014. Polymer. Prefix AA. Green, blue, orange and brown. Conch shell, waterway, Melanesian chief standing with spear, map of Vanuatu islands. Back: Map of Vanuatu islands, flower, three birds, tree, waterfall, conch shell. No security thread. Watermark: None. Printer: Oberthur. 145x65mm.   FV   46.00

2010 Commemorative Issue

13   10,000 Vatu   **VF   UNC**
2010. Polymer. Commemorative: 30th Anniversary of Independence. Prefix AA - MN. Light blue, brown, green. Melanesian chief. Back: Building, totems. Printer: De La Rue, London.   FV   205

VENEZUELA

The Republic of Venezuela, located on the northern coast of South America between Colombia and Guyana, has an area of 912,050 sq. km. and a population of 26.41 million. Capital: Caracas. Petroleum and mining provide 90 percent of Venezuela's exports although they employ less than 2 percent of the work force. Coffee, grown on 60,000 plantations, is the chief crop. Venezuela was one of three countries that emerged from the collapse of Gran Colombia in 1830 (the others being Ecuador and New Granada, which became Colombia). For most of the first half of the 20th century, Venezuela was ruled by generally benevolent military strongmen, who promoted the oil industry and allowed for some social reforms. Democratically elected governments have held sway since 1959. Hugo Chavez, president since 1999, seeks to implement his "21st Century Socialism," which purports to alleviate social ills while at the same time attacking globalization and undermining regional stability. Current concerns include: a weakening of democratic institutions, political polarization, a politicized military, drug-related violence along the Colombian border, increasing internal drug consumption, overdependence on the petroleum industry with its price fluctuations, and irresponsible mining operations that are endangering the rain forest and indigenous peoples.

REPUBLIC

Banco Central de Venezuela

Established in 1940. Sign. and date varieties. Notes from 1940-53 bear the legend E E UU de Venezuela in the coat of arms and after 1953 República de Venezuela. Note: Many specimen notes entered the market about 1982. Up to 200 of each are known for many of the types.

1940-45 Issues

		VF	UNC
31	**10 Bolívares**		
	19.7.1945-11.3.1960. Purple on multicolor underprint. Portrait Simon Bolívar at left, Antonio Jose de Sucre at right. Back: Arms at right. Printer: ABNC.		
	a. 19.7.1945-17.5.1951.	40.00	125
	b. 31.7.1952. Serial # prefix F-G.	50.00	100
	c. 23.7.1953-17.4.1958.	30.00	60.00
	d. 18.6.1959-11.3.1960.	20.00	45.00
	s. As a. Specimen. Without signature. Punched hole cancelled.	—	250
32	**20 Bolívares**	**VF**	**UNC**
	15.2.1941-18.6.1959. Dark green on multicolor underprint. Portrait Simon Bolívar at right. Back: Arms at left. Printer: ABNC.		
	a. 15.2.1941-17.1.1952.	60.00	125
	b. 21.8.1952. Serial # prefix G-H.	50.00	100
	c. 23.7.1953-18.6.1959.	30.00	75.00
	s. As a. Specimen. Without signature. Punched hole cancelled.	—	125
33	**50 Bolívares**	**VF**	**UNC**
	12.12.1940-11.3.1960. Black on multicolor underprint. Portrait Simon Bolívar at left. Back: Arms at right. Printer: ABNC.		
	a. 12.12.1940-17.1.1952.	100	250
	b. 23.7.1953. Serial # prefix C.	125	225
	c. 22.4.1954-11.3.1960.	65.00	125
	s. As a. Specimen. Without signature. Punched hole cancelled.	—	175
35	**500 Bolívares**	**VF**	**UNC**
	10.12.1940-21.12.1940. Blue on multicolor underprint. Portrait Simon Bolívar at right. Back: Arms at left. Printer: ABNC.		
	a. Issued note.	1,000	—
	s. Specimen.	—	2,000
36	**500 Bolívares**	**VF**	**UNC**
	21.1.1943-29.11.1946. Red on multicolor underprint. Portrait Simon Bolívar at right. Like #35. Back: Arms at left. Printer: ABNC.		
	a. Issued note.	1,000	—
	s. As a or ND. Specimen.	—	1,250

1947 Issue

		VF	UNC
37	**500 Bolívares**		
	1947-71. Orange on multicolor underprint. Portrait Simon Bolívar at right. Like #35. Back: Arms at left. Printer: ABNC.		
	a. 14.8.1947-21.8.1952.	250	—
	b. 23.7.1953-29.5.1958.	125	300
	c. 11.3.1960-17.8.1971.	80.00	200
	s. As b or ND. Specimen. Without signature. Punched hole cancelled.	—	500

1952-53 Issue

		VF	UNC
38	**10 Bolívares**		
	31.7.1952. Purple on multicolor underprint. Portrait Simon Bolívar at left, Antonio Jose de Sucre at right. Similar to #31. Series E, F. 7 digit serial #. Back: Arms at center. Printer: TDLR.	125	350
39	**20 Bolívares**	**VF**	**UNC**
	21.8.1952. Dark green on multicolor underprint. Portrait Simon Bolívar at right, bank name in 1 line. Series G. 7 digit serial #. Similar to #43. Back: Arms at left. Monument at center. Printer: TDLR.	175	450

		VF	UNC
40	**50 Bolívares**		
	26.2.1953; 23.7.1953. Simon Bolívar at left, *CINCUENTA BOLÍVARES* at right. Series C. 7 digit serial #. Back: Arms at right. Monument at center. Printer: TDLR.	135	450
41	**100 Bolívares**	**VF**	**UNC**
	23.7.1953. Portrait Simon Bolívar at right. Series C, D. 7 digit serial #. Back: Arms at left. Monument at center. Printer: TDLR.	125	425

1960-61 Issue

		VF	UNC
42	**10 Bolívares**		
	6.6.1961. Purple on multicolor underprint. Portrait Simon Bolívar at left, Antonio Jose de Sucre at right. Similar to #31. Series E-J. 7 digit serial #. Back: Arms at right, monument to Battle of Carabobo at center. Like #38. Printer: TDLR.		
	a. Issued note.	15.00	35.00
	s. Specimen with black overprint: *SPECIMEN*. Serial # prefix E.	—	12.50

		VF	UNC
43	**20 Bolívares**		
	1960-66. Dark green on multicolor underprint. Portrait Simon Bolívar at right, bank name in 1 line. 7 digit serial #. Similar to #32. Back: Arms at left, monument at center. Printer: TDLR.		
	a. 11.3.1960. Serial # prefix U-X.	20.00	50.00
	b. 6.6.1961. Serial # prefix X-Z.	15.00	40.00
	c. 7.5.1963. Serial # prefix A-B.	0.00	40.00
	d. 2.6.1964. Serial # prefix C-D.	15.00	40.00
	e. 10.5.1966. Serial # preifx E-G.	15.00	40.00
	s1. Specimen with red overprint: *SPECIMEN*. Paper with colored planchettes. Serial # prefix X.	—	15.00
	s2. Specimen with red overprint: *ESPECIMEN SIN VALOR*. Paper with security thread. Punched hole cancelled.	—	15.00
	s3. Specimen with black overprint: *SPECIMEN*. Serial # prefix U.	—	15.00

		VF	UNC
44	**50 Bolívares**		
	6.6.1961; 7.5.1963. Black on multicolor underprint. Modified portrait of Simon Bolívar at left, value *CINCUENTA BOLIVARES* at right. 7 digit serial #. Serial # prefix H-J; J-K. Back: Monument at center, arms at right. Printer: TDLR.		
	a. Issued note.	50.00	125
	s. Specimen with red overprint: *SPECIMEN SIN VALOR*. Punched hole cancelled.	—	75.00

1963-67 Issue

45   10 Bolívares   VF   UNC

1963-70. Purple on multicolor underprint. Similar to #42 but much different portrait of Antonio Jose de Sucre at right. 7-digit serial number. Back: Monument to Battle of Carabobo. Printer: TDLR.

		VF	UNC
a. 7.5.1963. Serial # prefix K-N.		2.50	15.00
b. 2.6.1964. Serial # prefix P-T.		2.50	12.50
c. 10.5.1966. Serial # prefix T-V; X-Z.		2.50	12.50
d. 8.8.1967. Serial # prefix A-D.		2.50	10.00
e. 5.3.1968. Serial # prefix G-H; J-K.		2.50	10.00
f. 19.11.1968. Serial # prefix E-F.		2.50	7.50
g. 27.1.1970. Serial # preifx L-N; P-U.		2.50	7.50
s. Specimen with red overprint: ESPECIMEN SIN VALOR. ND. Punched hole cancelled.		—	30.00

46   20 Bolívares   VF   UNC

1967-74. Green on orange and blue underprint. Portrait Simon Bolívar at right, bank name in three lines. Back: Arms without circle at left, Monument to Battle of Carabobo. Watermark: Simon Bolívar. Printer: TDLR.

		VF	UNC
a. 8.8.1967. Serial # prefix H-J.		4.00	20.00
b. 5.3.1968. Serial # prefix L-M.		3.50	17.50
c. 30.9.1969. Serial # prefix K.		3.50	17.50
d. 27.1.1970. Serial # prefix N; P-R.		3.00	15.00
e. 29.1.1974. Serial # prefix Y-Z (7 digits); A-C (7 or 8 digits).		3.00	15.00
s1. Specimen with red overprint: ESPECIMEN SIN VALOR. ND. Punched hole cancelled.		—	15.00
s2. Specimen with red overprint as S1. 27.1.1970.		—	15.00

47   50 Bolívares   VF   UNC

1964-72. Black on orange and green underprint. Portrait Simon Bolívar at left. CINCUENTA BOLÍVARES above 50 at center. Back: Monument to Battle of Carabobo at center, arms at right. Printer: TDLR.

		VF	UNC
a. 2.6.1964. Serial # prefix K-L.		6.00	40.00
b. 27.7.1965. Serial # preifx L-M.		6.00	30.00
c. 10.5.1966. Serial # prefix M-N.		6.00	30.00
d. 8.8.1967. Serial # prefix P.		6.00	30.00
e. 18.3.1969. Serial # prefix P-Q.		6.00	30.00
f. 7.4.1970. Serial # prefix Q-S.		6.00	30.00
g. 22.2.1972. Serial # prefix T-U.		6.00	30.00
s. Specimen with red overprint: ESPECIMEN SIN VALOR. ND.		—	37.50

48   100 Bolívares   VF   UNC

1963-73. Brown on multicolor underprint. Portrait Simon Bolívar at right. Back: Monument to Battle of Carabobo, arms at left. Watermark: Simon Bolívar. Printer: TDLR.

		VF	UNC
a. 7.5.1963. Serial # prefix M-N.		5.00	40.00
b. 2.6.1964. Serial # prefix P-Q.		5.00	40.00
c. 27.7.1965. Serial # prefix Q.		5.00	40.00
d. 10.5.1966. Serial # prefix Q-R.		5.00	40.00
e. 8.8.1967. Serial # prefix S-T.		5.00	40.00
f. 18.3.1969. Serial # prefix U-V.		5.00	40.00
g. 26.5.1970. Serial # prefix X-Y.		5.00	40.00
h. 17.8.1971. Serial # prefix Z; A-B.		5.00	40.00
i. 24.10.1972. Serial # prefix C-D.		5.00	40.00
j. 6.2.1973. Serial # prefix E-F.		5.00	40.00
s1. Specimen with red overprint: ESPECIMEN SIN VALOR. ND.		—	60.00
s2. Specimen with red overprint: SPECIMEN and TDLR oval stampings. ND. Punched hole cancelled.		—	95.00

1966 Commemorative Issue

#49, 400th Anniversary Founding of Caracas 1567-1967

49   5 Bolívares   VF   UNC

10.5.1966. Blue on green and yellow underprint. Scene of the founding and commemorative text at center and left, portrait Simon Bolívar at right. Serial number prefix A-D. Back: City arms at left, early map (1578) of the city at center, national arms at right. Printer: ABNC.   3.00   22.50

1968-71 Issue

50   5 Bolívares   VF   UNC

1968-74. Red on multicolor underprint. Simon Bolívar at left, Francisco de Miranda at right. Back: Arms at left, National Pantheon at center. Printer: TDLR.

		VF	UNC
a. 24.9.1968. Serial # prefix E; F.		2.25	12.50
b. 29.4.1969. Serial # prefix H-J.		2.00	12.00
c. 30.9.1969. Serial # prefix G; H.		2.00	12.00
d. 27.1.1970. Serial # prefix J-M.		1.50	9.00

		VF	UNC
e. 22.6.1971. Serial # prefix *M-P*.		1.50	7.50
f. 11.4.1972. Serial # prefix *P; R*.		1.50	7.50
g. 13.3.1973. Serial # prefix *S; T*.		1.00	6.00
h. 29.1.1974. Serial # prefix *U-Z* (7 digits); *A-E* (7 or 8 digits).		1.00	5.50
r. Remainder without date, signature or serial #.		—	8.00
s. Specimen.		—	10.00

51 10 Bolívares

1971-79. Purple on green and lilac underprint. Similar to #42 but much different portrait of Antonio Jose de Sucre at right. 7-digit serial number. Back: Monument to Battle of Carabobo. Printer: ABNC.

	VF	UNC
a. 22.6.1971. dark blue serial # with prefix *U-A*.	2.50	12.50
b. 11.4.1972. Serial # prefix *A-H*.	2.00	10.00
c. 13.3.1973. Serial # prefix *H-R*.	1.50	9.00
d. 29.1.1974. Serial # prefix *R-Z; A-H*.	1.50	9.00
e. 27.1.1976. Serial # prefix *J-Y*.	1.50	8.00
f. 7.6.1977. Serial # prefix *Y-C*.	1.50	7.00
g. 18.9.1979. Black serial # with prefix *C; D*.	1.50	7.50
s1. Specimen with red overprint: *MUESTRA*. Punch hole cancelled. 11.4.1972.	—	125
s2. Specimen with red overprint: *MUESTRA*, twice on each side. Punch hole cancelled. 27.1.1976.	—	125
s3. Specimen with red overprint: *MUESTRA*. Punch hole cancelled. 7.6.1977.	—	125
s4. Specimen with red overprint: *MUESTRA*. Punch hole cancelled. 18.9.1979.	—	125

52 20 Bolívares

1971; 1972. Dark green on multicolor underprint. Portrait Simon Bolívar at right, bank name in three lines. Back: Arms without circle at left, Monument to Battle of Carabobo. Watermark: Simon Bolívar. Printer: ABNC.

	VF	UNC
a. 22.6.1971. Serial # prefix *S-T*.	2.00	12.50
b. 11.4.1972. Serial # prefix *U-V; X-Y*.	2.00	12.50
s. Specimen with red overprint: *MUESTRA*. Punched hole cancelled. 11.4.1972.	—	125

1971-74 Issue

53 20 Bolívares

1974-79. Dark green on multicolor underprint. Jose Antonio Paez at right. 7 or 8 digit serial number. Back: Arms at left, monument to Battle of Carabobo at center. Watermark: Jose Antonio Paez. Printer: ABNC.

	VF	UNC
a. 23.4.1974. Serial # prefix *A-H; J*.	1.50	9.00
b. 7.6.1977. Serial # prefix *J-N; P-T*.	1.50	8.00
c. 18.9.1979. Serial # prefix *T-V; X-Z; A-D*. 7 or 8-digit serial #.	1.50	9.00
s1. Specimen with red overprint: *ESPECIMEN SIN VALOR*. 23.4.1974.	—	150
s2. Specimen with red overprint: *MUESTRA*. Punched hole cancelled. 7.6.1977.	—	150
s3. Specimen with red overprint: *MUESTRA*. Punched hole cancelled. 18.9.1979.	—	150

54 50 Bolívares

1972-77. Purple, orange and multicolor. Academic building at center, Andres Bello at right. Back: Arms at left, bank at center. Watermark: Andres Bello. Printer: TDLR.

	VF	UNC
a. 21.11.1972. Serial # prefix *A-B*.	4.00	15.00
b. 29.1.1974. Serial # prefix *B-D*.	4.00	14.50
c. 27.1.1976. Serial # prefix *D-F*.	4.00	15.00
d. 7.6.1977. Serial # prefix *F-H; J-N*.	3.00	12.50
s. Specimen with red overprint: *ESPECIMEN SIN VALOR*. 21.11.1972.	—	17.50

55 100 Bolívares

1972-81. Dark brown and brown-violet on multicolor underprint. Simon Bolívar at right. Back: National Capitol at left, arms at right. Watermark: Simon Bolívar. Printer: BDDK.

	VF	UNC
a. Red serial #. 21.11.1972. Serial # prefix *A-D*.	12.50	65.00
b. Watermark: Bolívar. 5.3.1974. Serial # prefix *D-H; J*.	10.00	45.00
c. Blue serial #. *B-C* added to watermark. 27.1.1976.	5.00	27.50
d. 23.11.1976. Serial # prefix *Q-V; X-Z; A* (8 digit serial #.)	5.00	27.50
e. 12.12.1978. Serial # prefix *A-H; J-M*.	5.00	25.00
f. 18.9.1979. Serial # prefix *N; P-V; X-Z; A-F*.	5.00	25.00
g. 1.9.1981. Serial # prefix *F-H; J-N; P-R*.	4.50	20.00
s1. Specimen with red overprint: *ESPECIMEN SIN VALOR*. 21.11.1972.	—	100
s2. Specimen. 27.1.1976.	—	100

56 500 Bolívares VF UNC
1971-72. Brown and blue on multicolor underprint. Simon Bolívar at left, horsemen with rifles riding at center. Serial number prefix A. Back: Dam at center, arms at right. Watermark: Simon Bolívar. Printer: TDLR.
a. 9.11.1971. 15.00 50.00
b. 11.1.1972. 8.50 45.00
s. Specimen with red overprint: *ESPECIMEN SIN VALOR*. ND. — 22.50

1980 Issue

57 10 Bolívares VF UNC
29.1.1980. Purple on multicolor underprint. Antonio Jose de Sucre at right. Serial number prefix A. 7 or 8 digit serial number. Back: Arms at left, officers on horseback at center right. Printer: ABNC.
a. Issued note. 1.00 3.00
p. Uniface Proofs, face and back. 29.1.1980. — 150
s. Specimen with red overprint: *MUESTRA*, once on face, twice on back. Punch hole cancelled. — 200

1980-81 Commemorative Issues

#58, Bicentennial Birth of Andres Bello, 1781-1981

58 50 Bolívares VF UNC
27.1.1981. Dark brown and green on multicolor underprint. Andres Bello at right. Serial number prefix A. Back: Arms at left, scene showing Bello teaching young Bolívar. Watermark: Andres Bello. Printer: TDLR.
a. Issued note. 3.00 12.50
s. Specimen. — —

#59, 150th Anniversary Death of Simon Bolívar, 1830-1980

59 100 Bolívares VF UNC
29.1.1980. Red, purple and black on multicolor underprint. Simon Bolívar at right, his tomb at center right. Serial number prefix A. Back: Arms at left, scene of hand to hand combat aboard ship. Watermark: Simon Bolívar. Printer: TDLR.
a. Issued note. 5.00 27.50
s. Specimen with red overprint: *ESPECIMEN SIN VALOR*. — 15.00

1981-88 Issues

60 10 Bolívares VF UNC
6.10.1981. Purple on light blue and multicolor underprint. Similar to #57 but underprint is different, and there are many significant plate changes. Back: Arms at left, officers on horseback at center right. Printer: CdM-B (without imprint). 157x69mm.
a. 7 or 8 digit serial #. Serial # prefix: *B-D*. 0.50 4.50
s. Specimen. Red overprint: *MUESTRA* on both sides. — 60.00

61 10 Bolívares VF UNC
1986-95. UV: fibers fluoresce red and green. value 10 and central design elements orange. Back: central design elements, bank name and 10 orange. Purple on light green and lilac underprint. Like #51, but *CARACAS* removed from upper center beneath bank title. Back: Monument to Battle of Carabobo. Printer: ABNC (without imprint).
a. 18.3.1986. Serial # prefix: *D-F*. FV 2.50
b. 31.5.1990. Serial # prefix: *G-H, J-L*. FV 1.50
c. 8.12.1992. Serial # prefix: *L-N, P*. FV 1.00
d. 5.6.1995. Serial # prefix: *P-U*. FV 1.00
s. Specimen. Overprint: *MUESTRA SIN VALOR*. — —

62 10 Bolívares VF UNC
3.11.1988. Purple on ochre underprint. Like #45, but *CARACAS* removed from upper center beneath bank title. Serial number prefix *F-G*. Printer: TDLR (without imprint). FV 1.50

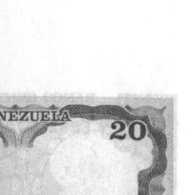

63 20 Bolívares   VF UNC

1981-95. UV: fibers fluoresce yellow; value 20 green; central design elements orange. Back: bank name and 20 orange. Dark green on multicolor underprint. Similar to #53 but *CARACAS* deleted under bank title. Title 82mm, horizontal central design in left center guilloche. Back: Arms at left, monument to Battle of Carabobo at center. Watermark: Jose Antonio Paez. Printer: TDLR (without imprint).

a. 6.10.1981. Serial # prefix: *D-H, J.*	FV	5.00
b. 7.9.1989; 31.3.1990. Serial # prefix: *X-Z, A-H, J, Y.*	FV	3.50
c. 31.5.1990. Serial # prefix: *X.*	FV	2.50
d. 8.12.1992. Short design in guilloche. Serial # prefix: *D-H, J-N, P-Z, A.*	FV	2.00
e. 5.6.1995. Serial # prefix: *A-E.*	FV	1.00
f. 10.2.1998. Serial # prefix: *E-F.*	FV	1.00
s. Specimen. As a. Red overprint: *ESPECIMEN SIN VALOR.* on both sides.	—	35.00

64 20 Bolívares   VF UNC

25.9.1984. Dark green on multicolor underprint. Like #63, but title 84mm and without central design in left center guilloche, also other minor plate differences. Latent image *BCV* in guilloches easily seen. Serial # prefix *J* (8 Watermark: Jose Antonio Paez. Printer: CdM-B (without imprint).

    FV 3.00

64A 20 Bolívares   VF UNC

7.7.1987. Dark green on multicolor underprint. Similar to #53 but *CARACAS* deleted under bank title. Title 82mm, horizontal central design in left center guilloche. Serial number prefix *T-X.* 7 or 8 digit serial number. Back: Arms at left, monument to Battle of Carabobo at center. Watermark. Jose Antonio Paez. Printer: ABNC (without imprint).

    FV 2.50

65 50 Bolívares   VF UNC

1985-98. Purple, black and orange on multicolor underprint. Like #54, but *CARACAS* removed under bank name. Back: Arms at left, bank at center. Watermark: Andres Bello.

a. 10.12.1985. Serial # prefix: *N, P-S.* Printer BDDK (without imprint).	FV	4.00
b. 3.11.1988. Serial # prefix: *S-V, X-Z, A.*	FV	4.00
c. 31.5.1990. Serial # prefix: *A-H, J-K.*	FV	3.00
d. 8.12.1992. Serial # prefix: *K, L-N, P-V, X-Z.* 7 or 8 digit serial #. Printer TDLR.	FV	2.50
e. 5.6.1995. Serial # prefix: *Q-U.* Printer BDDK (without imprint).	FV	2.00
f. 5.2.1998. Serial # prefix: *U-V.*	FV	1.50
g. 13.10.1998. Serial # prefix: *V-Z.*	FV	1.50
s. Specimen. 10.12.1985. Serial # prefix *N.*	—	20.00

66 100 Bolívares   VF UNC

1987-98. Dark brown and brown-violet on multicolor underprint. Simon Bolívar at right. Back: National Capitol at left, arms at right. Watermark: Simon Bolívar. Printer: BDDK (without imprint).

a. 3.2.1987. Serial # prefix: *R-V, X-Z, A-H, J-K.*	FV	5.00
b. 16.3.1989. Serial # prefix: *K-N, P-V, X-Z, A-G.*	FV	3.50
c. 31.5.1990. Serial # prefix: *G-H, J-N, P-V, X-Y.*	FV	3.50
d. 12.5.1992. Serial # prefix: *Y-Z, A-E.*	FV	2.00
e. 8.12.1992. Serial # prefix: *F-H, K-N.*	FV	2.00
f. 5.2.1998. Serial # prefix: *E-G.*	FV	2.00
g. 13.10.1998.	FV	2.00

67 500 Bolívares   VF UNC

1981-98. UV: fibers fluoresce yellow. Purple and black on multicolor underprint. Simon Bolívar at right. Back: Arms at left, orchids at center. Watermark: Simon Bolívar. Printer: BDDK (without imprint).

a. 25.9.1981. Serial # prefix: *A.*	5.00	30.00
b. 3.2.1987. Serial # prefix: *B-C.*	FV	15.00
c. 16.3.1989. Serial # prefix: *C-F.*	FV	15.00
d. 31.5.1990. Serial # prefix: *F-H, J-N, P-V, X-Z, A-C.*	FV	5.00
e. 5.6.1995. Serial # prefix: *C-H, J-N, P-Q.*	FV	5.00
f. 5.2.1998. Serial # prefix: *Q-Z.*	FV	2.50

1989 Issue

#68 and 69 replacement notes: Serial # prefix *X XX* and *W.*

68 1 Bolívar   VF UNC

5.10.1989. UV: fibers fluoresce green. Purple on blue and green underprint. Large *1* at left, coin with Simon Bolívar at right. Serial number prefix: *A-D; X.* Back: Arms at left, rosette at right. Printer: BDDK (without imprint).

    FV 0.25

69 2 Bolívares   VF UNC

5.10.1989. UV: value 2 and DES fluoresce yellow. Blue and brownish gray on light blue underprint. Coin head of Simon Bolívar at right. Serial number prefix: *AA-AH, AJ-AM, AW-AZ, BA, BJ, BL, BN, BP, BU-BW, XX.* Back: Large 2 at left, arms at right. Printer: USBNC (without imprint).

    FV 0.50

70 5 Bolívares **VF UNC**

21.9.1989. UV: fibers fluoresce red and green; serial # and signatures green. Red on multicolor underprint. Like #50, but *CARACAS* removed from upper center beneath bank title. Lithographed. Back: Like #50, but *CARACAS* removed from upper center beneath bank title. Printer: TDLR (without imprint).

    a. 7 digit serial #. Serial # prefix: *F-Z (no I or O).* FV 1.00

    b. 8 digit serial #. Serial # prefix: *A-E, J, W.* FV 0.50

1989 Commemorative Issue

#71, Bicentennial Birth of General Rafael Urdaneta, 1789-1989

71 20 Bolívares **VF UNC**

20.10.1987 (1989). Deep green and black on multicolor underprint. General Rafael Urdaneta at right. Serial number prefix *A-C.* Back: Battle of Lake Maracaibo at left center. Watermark: Rafael Urdaneta. FV 2.00

1990-94 Issue

72 50 Bolívares **VF UNC**

31.5.1990. Purple, black and orange on multicolor underprint. Similar to #65 but modified plate design, ornaments in "50's". Serial number prefix *A-H; J-K.* Back: Arms at left, bank at center. Watermark: Andres Bello. Printer: BDDK (without imprint). FV 2.50

73 1000 Bolívares **VF UNC**

1991-92. Without imprint. Red-violet on multicolor underprint. Part of independence text at far left, Simon Bolívar at left. Back: Signing of the Declaration of Independence at center right, arms at upper right. Watermark: Simon Bolívar.

    a. Dot instead of accent above *i* (error) in *Bolívares* on face and back. 10.00 45.00
       8.8.1991. Serial # prefix: *A.*

    b. Accent above *i* in *Bolívares* on face and back. 30.7.1992. Serial # prefix: *A.* FV 25.00

    c. As b. 8.12.1992. Serial # prefix: *A* (8-digits); *B* (8 or 9-digits). FV 4.00

    s1. As a. Specimen. — 40.00

    s2. As b. Specimen. — 40.00

74 2000 Bolívares **VF UNC**

1994; 1995. Dark green and black on multicolor underprint. Antonio Jose de Sucre at right. Value at lower left in green. Back: Scene of Battle of Ayacucho at left center, arms at upper right. Watermark: Antonio Jose de Sucre.

    a. 12.5.1994. Serial # prefix: *A.* FV 7.50

    b. Serial # prefix: *A-B.* 21.12.1995. Large serial #. FV 6.00

75 5000 Bolívares **VF UNC**

1994; 1996. Dark brown and brown-violet on multicolor underprint. Simon Bolívar at right. Back: Gathering at palace for Declaration of Independence at center, arms at upper right. Watermark: Simon Bolívar.

    a. 12.5.1994. Serial # prefix *A.* FV 15.00

    b. 14.3.1996. Serial # prefix *A-B.* FV 15.00

1994 Issue

76 1000 Bolívares **VF UNC**

1994-98. Red-violet on multicolor underprint. Part of independence text at far left, Simon Bolívar at left, green OVD *1000* at lower right. Back: Signing of the Declaration of Independence at center right, arms at upper right. Watermark: Simon Bolívar.

    a. 17.3.1994. Serial # prefix: *C-E.* (8 or 9-digits). FV 3.00

    b. 5.6.1995. Serial # prefix: *E-H, J, W.* (9 digits). FV 3.00

    c. 5.2.1998. Serial # prefix: *J-M, Z.* (8 or 9 digits). FV 2.50

    d. 6.8.1998. Serial # prefix: *M-Q, Z.* (8 or 9 digits) FV 2.50

    e. 10.9.1998. FV 2.50

1997 Issue

77   2000 Bolívares   **VF   UNC**
1997; 1998. Dark green, brown and black on multicolor underprint. Antonio Jose
de Sucre at right, with *2000* at lower left in black. Back: Scene of Battle of Ayacucho at left center, arms at upper right. Watermark: Antonio Jose de Sucre.
- a. 16.6.1997. Serial # prefix *B-C.*   FV   9.00
- b. 10.2.1998 Serial # prefix *C-D.*   FV   9.00
- c. 6.8.1998. Serial # prefix: *D-F.*   FV   9.00

78   5000 Bolívares   **VF   UNC**
1997-98. Brown and red-brown on multicolor underprint. Simon Bolívar at left
center. Back: Gathering at palace for Declaration of Independence at center, arms
at upper right.
- a. 16.6.1997. Serial # prefix: *B-C.*   FV   17.50
- b. 10.2.1998. Serial # prefix: *C-D.*   FV   15.00
- c. 6.8.1998. Serial # prefix: *D-F.*   FV   15.00

1998 Issue

Replacement notes are indicated by a *Z* serial # prefix for all notes dated
1998 but for the 5.6.1998 1000 Bolívares which uses a *W.*

79   1000 Bolívares   **VF   UNC**
10.9.1998. Violet and multicolor underprint. Simon Bolívar at right. Serial number   FV   2.50
prefix; *A.* Back: Panteon Nacional at right center.

80   2000 Bolívares   **VF   UNC**
29.10.1998. Olive green and gray. Andrea Bello at right. Serial number prefix; *A.*   FV   5.00
Back: Pico Bolívar mountain range at right center.

81   10,000 Bolívares   **VF   UNC**
10.2.1998. Black, red and olive-brown on multicolor underprint. Simon Bolívar at   FV   27.50
right. Serial number prefix: *Z, A-B.* Back: Teresa Carreño Theatre at left center,
arms at top center right. Watermark: Simon Bolívar.

82   20,000 Bolívares   **VF   UNC**
24.8.1998. Green on multicolor underprint. Simon Rodriguez at right. Serial number   FV   45.00
prefix: *Z, A-B.* Back: Arms at left, parrot at left center, Angel Falls at center right.

83   50,000 Bolívares   **VF   UNC**
24.8.1998. Orange and multicolor. Dr. Jose Maria Vargas at center. Serial number   FV   50.00
prefix; *A.* Back: Central University at center, araguaney flower at left. Printer: CMV.

REPUBLICA BOLIVARIANA DE VENEZUELA

Banco Central de Venezuela

2000-01 Issue

84   5000 Bolívares   **VF   UNC**

2000-04. Blue and multicolor. Francisco de Miranda at right. Back: Electric power dam at Guri at center. Watermark: Francisco de Miranda. Printer: CMV.

a. 25.5.2000.	FV	7.50
b. 13.8.2002.	FV	7.50
c. 25.4.2004.	FV	7.50

85   10,000 Bolívares   **VF   UNC**

2000-06. Black on brown and multicolor underprint. Antonio J. Sucre at center right. Serial number prefix; A. Back: Supreme Court building at center. Printer: CMV.

a. 25.5.2000.	FV	20.00
b. 16.8.2001.	FV	20.00
c. 13.8.2002.	FV	20.00
d. 25.4.2004.	FV	20.00
e. 25.4.2006.	FV	20.00

86   20,000 Bolívares   **VF   UNC**

2001-06. Green on multicolor underprint. Simon Rodriguez at right. Back: Arms at left, parrot at left center, Angel Falls at center right. Printer: CMV.

a. 16.8.2001.	FV	30.00
b. 13.8.2002.	FV	30.00
c. 25.5.2004.	FV	30.00
d. 25.4.2006.	FV	30.00

87   50,000 Bolívares   **VF   UNC**

2002-06. Orange and multicolor. Dr. Jose Maria Vargas at center. Serial # prefix: A. Back: Central University at center, araguaney flower at left. Printer: CMV.

a. 29.9.2005.	FV	45.00
b. 25.4.2006.	FV	45.00

2007 Issue

88   2 Bolívares   **VF   UNC**

2007-2012. Dark blue and light brown on multicolor underprint. Francisco de Miranda. Back: Two porpose. Printer: CMV 69x157mm.

a. 20.3.2007.	FV	1.50
b. 24.5.2007.	FV	1.50
c. 19.12.2008.	FV	1.50
d. 31.1.2012.	FV	1.50
e. 27.12.2012.	FV	1.50

89   5 Bolívares   **VF   UNC**

2007-2013. Brown and orange on multicolor underprint. Negro Primero. Back: Two armadillos. Printer: CMV 69x157mm.

a. 20.3.2007.	FV	2.50
b. 24.5.2007.	FV	2.50
c. 19.12.2008.	FV	2.50
d. 3.2.2011.	FV	2.50
e. 29.10.2013.	FV	2.50

90   10 Bolívares   VF   UNC

2007-2014. Red-brown and tan on multicolor underprint. Cacique Guaicaipuro.
Back: Harpy eagle. Printer: CMV 69x157mm.

a. 20.3.2007.	FV	4.00
b. 3.9.2009.	FV	4.00
c. 3.2.2011.	FV	4.00
d. 29.10.2013.	FV	4.00
e. 19.8.2014.	FV	4.00

91   20 Bolívares   VF   UNC

2007-2011. Purple, green and lilac on multicolor underprint. Luisa Cáceres de
Arismendi. Back: Two sea turtles. Printer: CMV 69x157mm.

a. 20.3.2007.	FV	7.00
b. 24.5.2007.	FV	7.00
c. 19.12.2008.	FV	7.00
d. 3.9.2009.	FV	7.00
e. 3.2.2011.	FV	7.00

92   50 Bolívares   VF   UNC

2007-2015. Green and yellow on multicolor underprint. Simon Rodrigues. Back:
Bear. Printer: CMV 69x157mm.

a. 20.3.2007.	FV	16.50
b. 24.5.2007.	FV	16.50
c. 19.12.2008.	FV	16.50
d. 3.9.2009.	FV	16.50
e. 3.2.2011.	FV	16.50
f. 31.1.2012.	FV	16.50
g. 27.12.2012.	FV	16.50
h. 29.10.2013.	FV	16.50
i. 19.8.2014.	FV	16.50
j. 23.6.2015.	FV	16.50

93   100 Bolívares   VF   UNC

2007-2015. Brown and tan on multicolor underprint. Simon Bolívar. Back: Two
birds. Printer: CMV 69x157mm.

a. 20.3.2007.	FV	30.00
b. 19.12.2008.	FV	30.00
c. 3.9.2009.	FV	30.00
d. 3.2.2011.	FV	30.00
e. 31.1.2012.	FV	30.00
f. 27.12.2012.	FV	30.00
g. 29.10.2013.	FV	30.00
h. 19.8.2014.	FV	30.00
i. 23.6.2015.	FV	30.00

VIET NAM

The Socialist Republic of Viet Nam, located in Southeast Asia west of the South China Sea, has an area of 329,560 sq. km. and a population of 86.12 million. Capital: Hanoi. Agricultural products, saltwater fish, shellfish, coal, mineral ores and electronic products are exported.

The conquest of Viet Nam by France began in 1858 and was completed by 1884. It became part of French Indochina in 1887. Viet Nam declared independence after World War II, but France continued to rule until its 1954 defeat by communist forces under Ho Chi Minh. Under the Geneva Accords of 1954, Viet Nam was divided into the communist North and anti-communist South. The US and its allies' sent economic and military aid to South Viet Nam and the Soviety Union and its allies sent their aid to the North. The US and its allies were withdrawn following a cease-fire agreement in 1973. Two years later, North Vietnamese forces overran the South reuniting the country under Communist rule. Despite the return of peace, for over a decade the country experienced limited economic growth because of the communist leadership policies. However, since the enactment of Viet Nam's *doi moi* (renovation) policy in 1986, Vietnamese authorities have committed to increased economic liberalization and enacted structural reforms needed to modernize the economy and to produce more competitive, export-driven industries, which greatly reduced inflation and greatly increased economic growth.

MONETARY SYSTEM:
1 Hao = 10 Xu
1 Dng = 100 Xu
1 Dng = 100 "Old" Dong, 19511 Dong = 100 Xu = 100 Su to 1975 1 New Dong = 500 Old Dong, 1975-76

REPLACEMENT NOTES:
#5-7, 11-14, star instead of series prefix of letter and number.
Note: HCM = Ho Chi Minh

DEMOCRATIC REPUBLIC
Ngân Hàng Nhà Nu'ó'c Viêt Nam
STATE BANK OF VIET NAM
1964 ND; 1972; 1975 Issue

74A   20 Dông   VF   UNC

1969. (Not issued). Olive on dark green underprint. HCM at left. Coat of arms at
right. Back: Tractor.

	—	400

75   2 Xu   VF   UNC

ND (1964). Purple on green underprint. Arms at center.

a. Issued note.	15.00	75.00
s. Specimen.	—	200

76   5 Xu   VF   UNC

1975 (date in light brown above *VIET* at lower left center). Purple on brown
underprint. Arms at upper right.

a. Watermark: 15mm stars.	3.00	10.00
b. Watermark: 30mm radiant star.	3.00	10.00
s1. Specimen. Without watermark.	—	15.00
s2. Specimen. As a. Red overprint: *MAU BAC.NI>*	—	20.00

77   1 Hao   VF   UNC

1972. Violet on multicolor underprint. Arms at center. Back: Woman feeding pigs.
103x57mm.

a. Watermark: 15mm stars. Series KG-?.	3.00	10.00
b. Watermark: 32mm encircled stars. Series MK-?.	3.00	10.00
c. Without watermark. Series ML.	3.00	10.00
s1. Specimen. Without watermark.	—	15.00
s2. Specimen. As a. Red overprint: *MAU BAC.NI>*	—	20.00

78   2 Hao   VF   UNC

1975. Brownish gray on green and peach underprint. Arms at center. Back: Two
men spraying rice field.

a. Issued note.	3.00	10.00
s. Specimen.	—	15.00

SOCIALIST REPUBLIC
Ngân Hàng Nhà Nu'ó'c Viêt Nam
STATE BANK OF VIET NAM
1976 Dated Issue

Northern 1958 and Southern 1966-dated notes were exchanged in 1978 for 1976-dated notes to unify the currency of North and South Viet Nam. All of the old northern and southern Xu and Hao notes continued as legal tender, but the old Dong notes were overstamped with *Da Thu*, marked with an *X*, and/or destroyed.

79   5 Hao   VF   UNC
1976. Purple on multicolor underprint. Back: Coconut palms and river scene.
    a. Issued note.   1.00   3.00
    s. Specimen. Reported not confirmed.   —   —

80   1 Dông   VF   UNC
1976. Brown on multicolor underprint. Arms at center. Back: Factory.
    a. Issued note.   1.00   3.00
    s. Specimen.   —   30.00

81   5 Dông   VF   UNC
1976. Blue-gray and green on pink underprint. Back: Two women with fish in foreground, boats in harbor in background.
    a. Watermark: Flower. Block letter at left, six digit serial # at right.   1.00   4.00
    b. Block letter and seven digit serial # together. Without watermark.   1.00   3.00
    s. Specimen. As b. Red overprint: *SPECIMEN* on face.   —   25.00

82   10 Dông   VF   UNC
1976. Purple and brown on multicolor underprint. Back: Elephants logging at center.
    a. Issued note.   1.00   5.00
    s. Specimen.   —   30.00
Counterfeits exist.

---

83   20 Dông   VF   UNC
1976. Blue on pink and green underprint. HCM at right, arms at left. Back: Tractors and dam.
    a. Issued note.   2.00   10.00
    s. Specimen.   —   30.00
84   50 Dông   VF   UNC
1976. Red-brown on pink and green underprint. HCM at right, arms at left. 2 serial number varieties. Back: Hong Gay open pit mining scene.
    a. Large block letters and serial #.   1.25   7.00
    b. Small block letters and serial #.   1.25   7.00
    s. Specimen.   —   25.00

SOCIALIST REPUBLIC OF VIET NAM
Ngân Hàng Nhà Nu'ó'c Viêt Nam
STATE BANK OF VIET NAM
1980; 1981 Issue

85   2 Dông   VF   UNC
1980 (1981). Brown on multicolor underprint. Arms at center. Back: River scene.
    a. Issued note.   0.75   2.00
    s. Specimen. Red overprint: *SPECIMEN* on face.   —   30.00

86   10 Dông   VF   UNC
1980 (1981). Brown on multicolor underprint. Arms at right. Back: House and trees.
    a. Issued note.   0.75   4.00
    s1. Specimen. Serial # of zeroes.   —   50.00
    s2. Specimen. Serial # of 1's.   —   15.00

87   30 Dông   VF   UNC
1981 (1982). Purple, brown and multicolor. Arms at left center, HCM at right. Large and small serial number varieties. Back: Harbor scene.
    a. Small block letters and serial #.   1.50   8.00
    b. Large block letters and serial #.   15.00   30.00
    s1. Specimen overprint: *SPECIMEN*. Small block letters and serial #.   30.00   60.00
    s2. Specimen overprint: *GIAY MU*. Large Block letters and serial #.   —   40.00

88 100 Dông VF UNC

1980 (1981). Brown, dark blue and multicolor. Portrait HCM at right, arms at center. Large or small digits in serial number. Back: Boats and rock formations in sea cove. Watermark: HCM.

	VF	UNC
a. Small block letters and serial #.	1.00	8.00
b. Large block letters and serial #.	2.00	10.00
s. Specimen.	—	40.00

1985 Issue

89 5 Hao VF UNC

1985. Red-violet on light blue underprint. Tower of Ha Noi at left center, arms at right. Back: Large 5 at center.

	VF	UNC
a. Issued note.	2.00	4.00
s. Specimen. Red overprint: SPECIMEN on face.	—	20.00

90 1 Dông VF UNC

1985. UV: fibers fluoresce blue. Blue-green on multicolor underprint. Tower of Ha Noi at left center, arms at right. Back: Sampans along rocky coastline.

	VF	UNC
a. Issued note.	0.50	2.00
s. Specimen. Red overprint: SPECIMEN on face. Serial # prefix AA, AE.	—	25.00

91 2 Dông VF UNC

1985. Purple on multicolor underprint. Tower of Ha Noi at left center, arms at right. Back: Sampans anchored along coastline.

	VF	UNC
a. Issued note.	0.75	2.00
s. Specimen. Red overprint: SPECIMEN on face.	—	20.00

92 5 Dông VF UNC

1985. Green on multicolor underprint. Tower of Ha Noi at left center, arms at right. Back: Sampans anchored in river.

	VF	UNC
a. Issued note.	0.50	2.00
s. Specimen. Red overprint: SPECIMEN on face.	—	20.00

93 10 Dông VF UNC

1985. Brown-violet on multicolor underprint. Tower of Ha Noi at left center, arms at right. Back: Island in the Lake Hoan Kiem in Hanoi

	VF	UNC
a. Issued note.	0.75	3.00
s. Specimen. Red overprint: SPECIMEN on face.	—	25.00

94 20 Dông VF UNC

1985 (1986). Brown, dark purple and multicolor. HCM at right, arms at center right. Back: One pillar pagoda in Hanoi.

	VF	UNC
a. Issued note.	0.75	2.00
s. Specimen. Red overprint: SPECIMEN on face. Serial # prefix AD, AH.	—	30.00

95 30 Dông VF UNC

1985 (1986). Blue and multicolor. HCM at right, arms at left. Back: Large building with clock tower at center.

	VF	UNC
a. Issued note.	1.25	5.00
s. Specimen. Red overprint: SPECIMEN on face.	—	27.50

96 50 Dông VF UNC

1985. Green, brown and multicolor. HCM at right, arms at left center. Back: Thac Ba hydro power plant and reservoir (Hoang Lien Son Province).

	VF	UNC
a. Issued note.	1.50	7.00
s. Specimen.	—	25.00

97   50 Dông   **VF   UNC**

1985 (1987). Blue-gray on orange and multicolor underprint. HCM at right, arms at center. Back: Thang Loing bridge crossing the Red River (north of Ha Noi) at center.

    a. Issued note.   0.75   3.00
    s. Specimen.   —   15.00

98   100 Dông   **VF   UNC**

1985. Brown, green, yellow and multicolor. HCM at right, arms at left center. Back: Planting rice. Watermark: HCM.

    a. Issued note.   2.50   15.00
    s. Specimen.   —   30.00

99   500 Dông   **VF   UNC**

1985. Red on blue and multicolor underprint. HCM at right, arms at upper center. Back: Bim Son Cement plant (Thanh Hoa Province) at left center. Watermark: HCM.

    a. Issued note.   3.00   12.50
    s. Specimen.   —   40.00

1987; 1988 Issue

100   200 Dông   **VF   UNC**

1987. UV: fibers fluoresce red and blue; serial # red. Red-brown and tan on multicolor underprint. HCM at right, arms at left center. Back: Field workers at left and tractor at center right. 131x62mm.

    a. Small sans serif serial # digits.   0.50   1.00
    b. Large sans serif serial # digits.   3.00   5.00
    c. Small serif serial # digits.   0.50   1.00
    s. Specimen. Green overprint: *SPECIMEN* on face.   —   20.00

101   500 Dông   **VF   UNC**

1988 (1989). UV: fibers fluoresce yellow. Red-brown and red on multicolor underprint. HCM at right, arms at left. Back: Dockside view.

    a. Small serial # digits.   0.50   2.00
    b. Large serial # digits.   3.00   5.00
    s1. Specimen. Red overprint: *SPECIMEN* on face.   —   35.00
    s2. Specimen. Blue overprint: *SPECIMEN* on face.   —   25.00

Two watermark varieteis are known, 27mm ornate square, 45mm foliate quatrilobe.

102   1000 Dông   **VF   UNC**

1987 (1988). Dark brown and deep olive-green on multicolor underprint. HCM at right, arms at left center. Back: Open pit mining equipment at left center. Watermark: HCM.

    a. Issued note.   3.00   20.00
    s. Specimen. Red overprint: *SPECIMEN* on each side.   —   27.50

103   2000 Dông   **VF   UNC**

1987 (1988). Dark and light brown on green and multicolor underprint. HCM at right, arms at left center. Back: Pha Lai thermo power plant (Hai Hung Province) at left center. Watermark: HCM.

    a. Issued note.   4.00   40.00
    s. Specimen. Red overprint: *SPECIMEN* on each side.   —   30.00

104   5000 Dông
1987 (1989). Deep blue, purple, brown and green on multicolor underprint. HCM
at right, arms at left center. Back: Offshore oil rigs at left center. Watermark: HCM.

		VF	UNC
a. Issued note.		2.00	10.00
s. Specimen. Red overprint: *SPECIMEN* on each side.		—	32.50

Counterfeits exist.

1988-91 Issue

105   100 Dông
1991 (1992). Light brown on multicolor underprint. Arms at left. Back: Temple and
pagoda at left center.

		VF	UNC
a. Small serif serial # digits. Serif or sans serif.		0.50	1.00
b. Large sans serif serial # digits.		3.00	5.00
s1. Specimen. Red overprint: *TIEN MU* on face.		—	32.50
s2. Specimen. Red overprint: *SPECIMEN*.		—	40.00

109   10,000 Dông
1990 (1992). Red and red-violet on multicolor underprint. HCM at right, arms at
center. Back: Junks along coastline at center. Watermark: HCM. 140x68mm.

		VF	UNC
a. Issued note.		1.50	20.00
s. Specimen. Red overprint: *SPECIMEN* on each side.		—	32.50

106   1000 Dông
1988 (1989). UV: fibers fluoresce red and blue. Purple on gold and multicolor
underprint. HCM at right, arms at left center. Back: Elephant logging at center.

		VF	UNC
a. Small serif serial # digits.		0.25	1.50
b. Large sans serif serial # digits.		3.00	5.00
s. Specimen. Red overprint: *SPECIMEN* on face.		—	45.00

110   20,000 Dông
1991 (1993). Blue-green on multicolor underprint. HCM at right, arms at center.
Back: Packing factory. Watermark: HCM. 140x68mm.

		VF	UNC
a. Issued note.		1.25	8.00
s. Specimen. Red overprint: *SPECIMEN* on each side.		—	35.00

Counterfeits exist.

107   2000 Dông
1988 (1989). UV: fibers fluoresce yellow and blue. Brownish purple on lilac and
multicolor underprint. HCM at right, arms at left. Back: Women workers in textile
factory. 135x65mm.

		VF	UNC
a. Small serif serial # digits.		0.50	2.00
b. Large sans serif serial # digits.		3.00	5.00
s1. Specimen. Red overprint: *TI MU* on face and *SPECIMEN* on back.		—	40.00
s2. Specimen. Red overprint: *SPECIMEN* on face and *TI MU* on back.		—	40.00

111   50,000 Dông
1990 (1993). Dark olive-green and black on multicolor underprint. HCM at right,
arms at upper left center, date at lower right. Back: Dockside view. Watermark:
HCM.

		VF	UNC
a. Issued note.		3.50	25.00
s. Specimen. Red overprint: *SPECIMEN* on each side.		—	32.50

1992 Bank Cheque Issue

#112-114A Negotiable Bank Cheques/Certificates with expiration dates used
for high value merchandise and large transactions. Specimens are valued a
2x the Unc. price.

112   100,000 Dông
1992-94.

		VF	UNC
a. Issued note.		600	1,000
s. Specimen.		—	1,000

108   5000 Dông
1991 (1993). UV: fibers fluoresce blue. Dark blue on multicolor underprint. HCM at
right, arms at left. Back: Electric lines. 134x64mm.

		VF	UNC
a. Issued note.		0.75	3.00
s. Specimen. Red overprint: *SPECIMEN* on face.		—	30.00

Counterfeits exist.

113 500,000 Dông VF UNC
1992-2000.
a. Issued note. 300 450
s. Specimen. — 400

114 1,000,000 Dông VF UNC
1992-2001.
a. Issued note. 300 450
s. Specimen. — 400
114A 5,000,000 Dông VF UNC
1992-2001.
a. Issued note. 300 450
s. Specimen. — 400

1993; 1994 Issue

115 10,000 Dông VF UNC
1993. Red and red-violet on multicolor underprint. HCM at right, arms at center,
optical registry device at lower left, modified underprint color around arms. Back:
Junks along coastline at center. Watermark: HCM. 140x68mm.
a. Issued note. FV 4.00
s. Specimen. Black overprint: *SPECIMEN* on face. — 45.00
Counterfeits exist.

116 50,000 Dông VF UNC
1994. Dark olive-green and black on multicolor underprint. HCM at right with
date below, arms at upper left center. Back: Dockside view. Watermark: HCM.
140x68mm.
a. Issued note. FV 8.00
s. Specimen. Red overprint: *SPECIMEN* on face. — 45.00
Counterfeits exist.

117 100,000 Dông VF UNC
1994 (2000). Brown and light green on multicolor underprint. HCM at right. Back:
HCM's house. 145x71mm.
a. Issued note. FV 20.00
s. Specimen. Red overprint: *SPECIMEN* on face. — 45.00
Counterfeits exist.

2001 Commemorative Issue

**#118, 50th Anniversary National Bank of Viet Nam Released in a special
folder and envelope. Face value is minimal.**

118 50 Dông VF UNC
2001. Polymer plastic. Released in a special folder and envelope. Face value is
minimal. Rose on multicolor underprint. HCM at right center. Back: Bank building.
a. Issued note. — 30.00

2003 Issue

**#118A-9-121 HCM at r. Printed originally at NPA, later printings done at the
National banknote Printing Plant (NBPP) in Viet Nam.**

119 10,000 Dông VF UNC
(20)06-. Polymer plaster. Brown, green and yellow on multicolor underprint. HCM
at right. Back: Sea platform. 132x59mm.
a. (20)06. FV 2.00
b. (20)07. FV 1.50
c. (20)08. FV 1.00
d. (20)09. FV 1.00
e. (20)10. FV 1.00
f. (20)11. FV 1.00
g. (20)13. FV 1.00
h. (20)14. FV 1.00
i. (20)15. FV 1.00
s. Specimen. — 100

120   20,000 Dông   VF   UNC
(20)06-. Polymer plastic. Purple and blue on multicolor underprint. HCM at right.
Back: Palace. 136x65mm.

		VF	UNC
a. (20)06.		FV	4.00
b. (20)07.		FV	3.50
c. (20)08.		ГV	3.00
d. (20)09.		FV	3.00
e. (20)12.		FV	3.00
f. (20)14.		FV	3.00
s. Specimen.		—	100

123   200,000 Dông   VF   UNC
(20)06-. Polymer plastic. Rose on yellow and multicolor underprint. HCM at right.
Back: Lake with rock formations. 148x64mm.

		VF	UNC
a. (20)06.		FV	25.00
b. (20)07.		FV	24.00
c. (20)09.		FV	23.00
d. (20)10.		FV	22.00
e. (20)11.		FV	22.00
f. (20)13.		FV	22.00
g. (20)14.		FV	22.00
s. Specimen.		—	65.00

121   50,000 Dông   VF   UNC
(20)03-. Polymer plastic. Rose on multicolor underprint. HCM at right. Back: Buildings in Hua. 139x65mm.

		VF	UNC
a. (20)03.		FV	7.00
b. (20)04.		FV	6.50
c. (20)05.		FV	6.00
d. (20)06.		FV	5.50
e. (20)07.		FV	5.00
f. (20)08.		FV	5.00
g. (20)09.		FV	5.00
h. (20)11.		FV	5.00
i. (20)12.		FV	5.00
j. (20)13.		FV	5.00
s. Specimen.		—	100

124   500,000 Dông   VF   UNC
(20)03 . Polymer plastic. Blue and green on multicolor underprint. HCM at right.
Back: HCM's birthplace in Kim Lien, Nghean Province. 151x65mm.

		VF	UNC
a. (20)03.		FV	70.00
b. (20)04.		FV	69.00
c. (20)05.		FV	68.00
d. (20)06.		FV	67.00
e. (20)08.		FV	65.00
f. (20)09.		FV	65.00
g. (20)10.		FV	65.00
h. (20)11.		FV	65.00
i. (20)12.		FV	65.00
j. (20)14.		FV	65.00
k. (20)15.		FV	65.00
s. Specimen.		—	70.00

122   100,000 Dông   VF   UNC
(20)04-. Ploymer plastic. Green on multicolor underprint. HCM at right. Back: Van
Mieu Quoc Tu Giam (National University). 144x65mm.

		VF	UNC
a. (20)04.		FV	12.00
b. (20)05.		FV	11.00
c. (20)06.		FV	10.00
d. (20)07.		FV	9.50
e. (20)08.		FV	9.00
f. (20)09.		FV	9.00
g. (20)10.		FV	9.00
h. (20)11.		FV	9.00
i. (20)12.		FV	9.00
j. (20)13.		FV	9.00
s. Specimen.		—	55.00

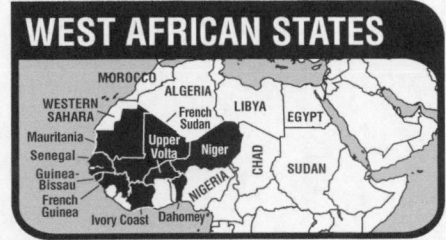

WEST AFRICAN STATES

The West African States, a former federation of eight French colonial territories on the northwest coast of Africa, had an area of 1,813,079 sq. mi. (4,742,495 sq. km.) and a population of about 60 million. Capital: Dakar. The constituent territories were Mauritania, Senegal, Dahomey, French Sudan, Ivory Coast, Upper Volta, Niger and French Guinea. The members of the federation were overseas territories within the French Union until Sept. of 1958 when all but French Guinea approved the constitution of the Fifth French Republic, thereby electing to become autonomous members of the new French Community. French Guinea voted to become the fully independent Republic of Guinea. The other seven attained independence in 1960. The French West Africa territories were provided with a common currency, a practice which was continued as the monetary union of the West African States which provides a common currency to the autonomous republics of Dahomey (now Benin), Mali, Senegal, Upper Volta (now Burkina Faso) Ivory Coast, Togo, Niger, and Guinea-Bissau.

MONETARY SYSTEM:
1 Franc = 100 Centimes

DATING:
The year of issue on the current notes appear in the first 2 digits of the serial number, i.e. (19)91, (19)92, etc.

SIGNATURE VARIETIES

	LE PRÉSIDENT	LE DIRECTEUR GÉNÉRAL	DATE
1		R. Julienne	Various dates - 1959 20.3.1961
2		R. Julienne	20.3.1961
3		R. Julienne	20.12.1964
4		R. Julienne	2.3.1965; ND
5		R. Julienne	ND
6		R. Julienne	ND
7		R. Julienne	ND
8		R. Julienne	ND
9		R. Julienne	ND

	LE PRÉSIDENT DU CONSEIL DES MINISTRES	LE GOUVERNEUR	DATE
10		d'Arding	ND
11		d'Arding	ND (1977); 1977
12		d'Arding	ND (1978); 1978; 1979
13		d'Arding	ND (1980); 1980

SIGNATURE VARIETIES

			DATE
14		d'Arding	ND (1977); 1977; 1988; 1989
15		d'Arding	ND (1981); 1981; 1982
16		d'Arding	ND (1983); 1983
17		d'Arding	1981; 1983; 1984
18		d'Arding	ND (1984); 1984
19		d'Arding	1984; 1985
20		d'Arding	1986; 1987
21		Alassane Ouattara	1989
22		Alassane Ouattara	1991
23		Alassane Ouattara	1992
24		Alassane Ouattara	1992
25		Alassane Ouattara	1993
26		B	1994
27		B	1994; 1995
28		B	1996; 1997
29		B	1999
30		B	2000; 2001
31		B	2002; 2003
32		B	2003

Banque Centrale des Etats de l'Afrique de l'Ouest
A for Cote d'Ivoire (Ivory Coast)
1959-65; ND Issue

101A 100 Francs

1961-65; ND. Design like #201B. Dark brown, orange and multicolor.

	VF	UNC
a. Engraved. Signature 1. 20.3.1961.	18.00	65.00
b. Signature 2. 20.3.1961.	18.00	65.00
c. Litho. Signature 2. 20.3.1961.	18.00	65.00
d. Signature 3. 2.12.1964.	18.00	65.00
e. Signature 4. 2.3.1965.	18.00	65.00
f. Signature 4. ND.	15.00	40.00
g. Signature 5. ND.	15.00	50.00

102A 500 Francs

1959-64; ND. Brown, green and multicolor. Field workers at left, mask carving at right. Back: Woman at left, farmer on tractor at right. Watermark: Woman's head.

	VF	UNC
a. Engraved. Signature 1. 15.4.1959.	66.00	
b. Signature 1. 20.3.1961.	30.00	90.00
c. Signature 2. 20.3.1961.	45.00	—
d. Signature 3. 2.12.1964.	55.00	—
e. Signature 5. ND.	35.00	90.00
f. Signature 6. ND.	25.00	75.00
g. Litho. Signature 6. ND.	30.00	90.00
h. Signature 7. ND.	30.00	90.00
i. Signature 8. ND.	50.00	—
j. Signature 9. ND.	18.00	50.00
k. Signature 10. ND.	15.00	40.00
l. Signature 11. ND.	12.00	35.00
m. Signature 12. ND.	18.00	55.00

103A 1000 Francs

1959-65; ND. Brown, blue and multicolor. Man and woman at center. Back: Man with rope suspension bridge in background and pineapples. Watermark: Man's head.

	VF	UNC
a. Engraved. Signature 1. 17.9.1959.	—	—
b. Signature 1. 20.3.1961.	30.00	90.00
c. Signature 2. 20.3.1961.	25.00	75.00
d. Signature 4. 2.3.1965.	80.00	—
e. Signature 5. ND.	20.00	60.00
f. Signature 6. ND.	20.00	60.00
g. Litho. Signature 6. ND.	20.00	60.00
h. Signature 7. ND.	22.00	65.00
i. Signature 8. ND.	22.00	75.00
j. Signature 9. ND.	20.00	60.00
k. Signature 10. ND.	15.00	40.00
l. Signature 11. ND.	15.00	40.00
m. Signature 12. ND.	15.00	40.00
n. Signature 13. ND.	15.00	40.00

104A 5000 Francs

1961-65; ND. Blue, brown and multicolor. Bearded man at left, building at center. Back: Woman, corn grinders and huts.

	VF	UNC
a. Signature 1. 20.3.1961.	125	—
b. Signature 2. 20.3.1961.	75.00	—
c. Signature 3. 2.12.1964.	100	—
d. Signature 4. 2.3.1965.	125	—
e. Signature 6. ND.	75.00	225
f. Signature 7. ND.	90.00	—
g. Signature 8. ND.	125	—
h. Signature 9. ND.	55.00	200
i. Signature 10. ND.	55.00	200
j. Signature 11. ND.	55.00	200

1977-81; ND Issue
#105A-109A smaller size notes.

105A 500 Francs

1979-80. Lilac, light olive-green and multicolor. Artwork at left, long horn animals at center, man wearing hat at right. Back: Cultivated palm at left, aerial view at center, mask at right. Watermark: Woman in profile.

	VF	UNC
a. Signature 12. 1979.	12.00	30.00
b. Signature 13. 1980.	12.00	30.00

106A 500 Francs

1981-90. Pale olive-green and multicolor. Artwork at left, long horn animals at center, man wearing hat at right. Back: Cultivated palm at left, aerial view at center, mask at right. Watermark: Woman in profile.

	VF	UNC
a. Signature 14. 1988.	3.00	8.00
b. Signature 15. 1981. (BF).	15.00	35.00
c. Signature 15. 1981. (F-CO).	3.00	10.00
d. Signature 15. 1982. (BF).	20.00	50.00
e. Signature 17. 1981. (F-CO).	20.00	50.00
f. Signature 17. 1983.	3.00	10.00
g. Signature 18. 1984.	3.00	9.00
h. Signature 19. 1984.	3.00	9.00
i. Signature 19. 1985.	3.00	9.00
j. Signature 20. 1986.	3.00	8.00
k. Signature 20. 1987.	3.00	8.00
l. Signature 21. 1988.	3.00	8.00
m. Signature 21 (reversed order). 1989.	3.00	8.00
n. Signature 22. 1990.	3.00	8.00

Note: #106A w/10-digit small serial # were printed by Banque de France (BF) while those w/9-digit large serial # were printed by F-CO.

107A 1000 Francs

1981-90. Brown on multicolor underprint. Artwork at left, open pit mine at center, woman at right. Back: Wood carver with finished works. Watermark: Woman.

	VF	UNC
a. Signature 14. 1988.	4.00	10.00
b. Signature 15. 1981.	4.00	15.00
c. Signature 17. 1981.	5.00	15.00
d. Signature 18. 1984.	5.00	12.00
e. Signature 19. 1984.	10.00	30.00
f. Signature 19. 1985.	4.00	12.00
g. Signature 20. 1986.	4.00	10.00
h. Signature 20. 1987.	4.00	10.00
i. Signature 21. 1989.	4.00	10.00
j. Signature 22. 1990.	4.00	10.00

108A 5000 Francs

1977-91. Black and red on multicolor underprint. Woman at left, fish and boats on shore at center, carving at right. Back: Carvings, fishing boats and mask.

	VF	UNC
a. Signature 11. 1977.	25.00	65.00
b. Signature 12. 1978.	25.00	65.00
c. Signature 12. 1979.	35.00	90.00
d. Signature 13. 1980.	35.00	90.00
e. Signature 14. 1977.	35.00	—
f. Signature 14. 1988.	10.00	35.00
g. Signature 14. 1989.	10.00	35.00
h. Signature 15. 1981.	20.00	50.00
i. Signature 15. 1982.	20.00	50.00
j. Signature 16. 1983.	—	—
k. Signature 17. 1983.	—	—
l. Signature 18. 1984.	22.00	55.00
m. Signature 19. 1984.	20.00	50.00
n. Signature 19. 1985.	20.00	50.00
o. Signature 20. 1986.	35.00	—
p. Signature 20. 1987.	10.00	35.00
q. Signature 21. 1990.	10.00	35.00
r. Signature 22. 1991.	10.00	35.00

109A 10,000 Francs

ND (1977-92). Red-brown on multicolor underprint. Two men seated operating primitive spinning apparatus, woman with headwear at right. Back: Figurine and girl at left, modern textile spinning machine at center. Watermark: Woman with headwear.

	VF	UNC
a. Signature 11. ND.	35.00	100
b. Signature 12. ND.	90.00	—
c. Signature 13. ND.	35.00	100
d. Signature 14. ND.	20.00	90.00
e. Signature 15. ND.	20.00	70.00
f. Signature 18. ND.	35.00	0.00
g. Signature 19. ND.	40.00	110
h. Signature 20. ND.	35.00	0.00
i. Signature 21. ND.	20.00	60.00
j. Signature 22. ND.	20.00	60.00
k. Signature 23. ND.	25.00	—

1991-92 Issue

#113A and 114A were first issued on 19.9.1994.

110A 500 Francs

(19)91-(20)02. Dark brown and dark green on multicolor underprint. Man at right, flood control dam at center. Back: Farmer riding spray rig behind garden tractor at center, native art at left. Watermark: Man.

	VF	UNC
a. Signature 22. (19)91.	3.00	8.00
b. Signature 23. (19)92.	3.00	8.00
c. Signature 25. (19)93.	3.00	7.00
d. Signature 26. (19)94.	3.00	7.00
e. Signature 27. (19)95.	3.00	7.00
f. Signature 28. (19)96.	3.00	7.00
g. Signature 28. (19)97. 10-digit serial #.	3.00	7.00
h. Signature 28. (19)97. 11-digit serial #.	5.00	10.00
i. Signature 28. (19)98.	3.00	7.00
j. Signature 28. (19)99.	3.00	6.00
k. Signature 29. (19)99.	9.00	—
l. Signature 30. (20)01.	3.00	6.00
m. Signature 31. (20)02.	3.00	6.00

111A 1000 Francs

(19)91-(20)03. Dark brown-violet on tan, yellow and multicolor underprint. Workmen hauling peanuts to storage at center, woman's head at right. Back: Twin statues and mask at left, two women with baskets, elevated riverside storage bins in background at center. Watermark: Woman's head.

	VF	UNC
a. Signature 22. (19)91.	5.00	10.00
b. Signature 23. (19)92.	5.00	10.00
c. Signature 25. (19)93.	5.00	10.00
d. Signature 26. (19)94.	4.00	9.00
e. Signature 27. (19)95.	4.00	9.00
f. Signature 28. (19)96.	4.00	9.00
g. Signature 28. (19)97.	4.00	9.00
h. Signature 28. (19)98.	3.00	8.00
i. Signature 29. (19)99.	3.00	8.00
j. Signature 30. (20)01.	3.00	8.00
k. Signature 31. (20)02.	3.00	8.00
l. Signature 31. (20)03.	3.00	8.00

112A 2500 Francs

(19)92-(19)94. Deep purple and dark brown on lilac and multicolor underprint. Dam at center, young woman's head at right. Back: Statue at left, harvesting and spraying of fruit at left center. Watermark: Young woman's head.

	VF	UNC
a. Signature 23. (19)92.	7.00	20.00
b. Signature 25. (19)93.	6.00	15.00
c. Signature 27. (19)94.	6.00	15.00

113A 5000 Francs

	VF	UNC
(19)92-(20)03. Dark brown and deep blue on multicolor underprint. Woman wearing headdress adorned with cowrie shells at right, smelting plant at center. Back: Women with children and various pottery at left center. Watermark: Woman wearing headdress adorned with cowrie shells.		
a. Signature 23. (19)92.	9.00	25.00
b. Signature 25. (19)93.	9.00	25.00
c. Signature 27. (19)94.	8.00	20.00
d. Signature 27. (19)95.	8.00	20.00
e. Signature 28. (19)96.	8.00	20.00
f. Signature 28. (19)97.	8.00	20.00
g. Signature 28. (19)98.	8.00	20.00
h. Signature 29. (19)99.	8.00	20.00
i. Signature 29. (19)99.	8.00	20.00
j. Signature 30. (20)00.	20.00	—
k. Signature 30. (20)01.	8.00	20.00
l. Signature 31. (20)02.	8.00	20.00
m. Signature 31. (20)03.	8.00	20.00

114A 10,000 Francs

	VF	UNC
(19)92-(20)01. Dark brown on multicolor underprint. Headman with scepter at right, skyscraper at center. Back: Native art at left, woman crossing vine bridge over river at center. Watermark: Headman with scepter.		
a. Signature 25. (19)92.	15.00	45.00
b. Signature 27. (19)94.	15.00	45.00
c. Signature 27. (19)95.	15.00	45.00
d. Signature 28. (19)96.	15.00	45.00
e. Signature 28. (19)97.	15.00	45.00
f. Signature 28. (19)98.	25.00	—
g. Signature 29. (19)98.	15.00	45.00
h. Signature 29. (19)99.	15.00	45.00
i. Signature 30. (20)00.	25.00	—
j. Signature 30. (20)01.	15.00	45.00

2003 Issue

115A 1000 Francs

	VF	UNC
(20)03-. Red-brown on red and multicolor underprint. 125x65mm.		
a. Signature 32. (20)03.	FV	6.00
b. Signature 32. (20)04.	FV	6.00
c. Signature 33. (20)05.	FV	6.00
d. Signature 34. (20)06.	FV	5.50
e. Signature 34. (20)07.	FV	5.50
f. Signature 34. (20)08.	FV	5.50
g. Signature 34. (20)09.	FV	5.50
h. Signature 38. (20)11.	FV	5.50
i. Signature 39. (20)12.	FV	4.50
j. Signature 40. (20)13.	FV	4.00
k. Signature 40. (20)14.	FV	5.50

116A 2000 Francs

	VF	UNC
(20)03-. Blue on light blue and multicolor underprint. 130x66mm.		
a. Signature 32. (20)03.	FV	10.00
b. Signature 32. (20)04.	FV	8.00
c. Signature 32. (20)05.	FV	8.00
d. Signature 33. (20)06.	FV	8.00
e. Signature 34. (20)07.	FV	7.50
f. Signature 34. (20)08.	FV	6.00
g. Signature 35. (20)08.	FV	6.00
h. Signature 35. (20)09.	FV	6.00
i. Signature 38. (20)11.	FV	6.00
j. Signature 39. (20)12.	FV	4.50
k. Signature 40. (20)13.	FV	4.00
l. Signature 40. (20)14.	FV	3.50

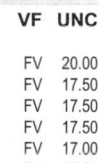

117A 5000 Francs

	VF	UNC
(20)03-. Multicolor. 141x74mm.		
a. Signature 32. (20)03.	FV	20.00
b. Signature 32. (20)04.	FV	17.50
c. Signature 33. (20)05.	FV	17.50
d. Signature 34. (20)06.	FV	17.50
e. Signature 34. (20)07.	FV	17.00
f. Signature 34. (20)08.	FV	17.00
g. Signature 35. (20)08.	FV	17.00
h. Signature 35. (20)09.	FV	17.00
i. Signature 38. (20)10.	FV	16.00
j. Signature 38. (20)11.	FV	16.00
k. Signature 39. (20)12.	FV	16.00
l. Signature 40. (20)13.	FV	15.00
m. Signature 40. (20)14.	FV	15.00
n. Signature 41. (20)15.	FV	14.50

118A   10,000 Francs

(20)03-. Multicolor. 145x74mm.

		VF	UNC
a. Signature 32. (20)03.		FV	40.00
b. Signature 32. (20)04.		FV	35.00
c. Signature 33. (20)05.		FV	35.00
d. Signature 34. (20)06.		FV	35.00
e. Signature 34. (20)07.		FV	35.00
f. Signature 35. (20)08.		FV	30.00
g. Signature 35. (20)09.		FV	30.00
h. Signature 36. (20)10.		FV	28.00
i. Signature 37. (20)11.		FV	28.00
j. Signature 38. (20)11.		FV	28.00
k. Signature 39. (20)12.		FV	24.00
l. Signature 40. (20)13.		FV	24.00
m. Signature 40. (20)14.		FV	23.50
n. Signature 41. (20)15.		FV	23.50

(20)12-(20)14 Issue

119A   500 Francs

(20)12-(20)14. Brown, orange, multicolor. West African symbols. Back: Hippopotami. 125x65mm.

	VF	UNC
a. Signature 40. (20)12.	FV	4.00
b. Signature 40. (20)13.	FV	3.50
c. Signature 40. (20)14.	FV	3.00

B for Benin (Dahomey)
1959-65; ND Issue

201B   100 Francs

1961-65; ND. Like #101A. Dark brown, orange and multicolor.

	VF	UNC
a. Engraved. Signature 1. 20.3.1961.	40.00	120
b. Signature 2. 20.3.1961.	35.00	100
c. Litho. Signature 2. 20.3.1961.	35.00	100
d. Signature 3. 2.12.1964.	65.00	—
e. Signature 4. 2.3.1965.	20.00	65.00
f. Signature 4. ND.	15.00	45.00

202B   500 Francs

1961-64; ND. Brown, green and multicolor. Field workers at left, mask carving at right. Back: Woman at left, farmer on tractor at right. Watermark: Woman's head.

	VF	UNC
a. Signature 1. 20.3.1961.	—	—
b. Engraved signature 2. 20.3.1961.	—	—
d. Signature 3. 2.12.1964.	—	—
e. Signature 4. 2.3.1965.	—	—
f. Signature 5. ND.	70.00	—
g. Signature 6. ND.	30.00	85.00
h. Litho. Signature 7. ND.	35.00	100
i. Signature 8. ND.	70.00	—
j. Signature 9. ND.	30.00	85.00
k. Signature 10. ND.	20.00	60.00
l. Signature 11. ND.	15.00	50.00

203B   1000 Francs

1961-65; ND. Brown, blue and multicolor. Man and woman at center. Back: Man with rope suspension bridge in background and pineapples. Watermark: Man's head.

	VF	UNC
a. Engraved. Signature 1. 17.9.1959.	—	—
b. Signature 1. 20.3.1961.	—	—
c. Signature 2. 20.3.1961.	90.00	—
d. Signature 4. 2.3.1965.	60.00	—
g. Signature 6. ND.	35.00	—
h. Litho. Signature 6. ND.	35.00	75.00
i. Signature 7. ND.	60.00	150
j. Signature 8. ND.	35.00	100
k. Signature 9. ND.	35.00	—
l. Signature 10. ND.	20.00	60.00
m. Signature 11. ND.	15.00	50.00
n. Signature 12. ND.	20.00	60.00

204B   5000 Francs

1961; ND. Blue, brown and multicolor. Bearded man at left, building at center. Back: Woman, corn grinders and huts.

	VF	UNC
a. Signature 1. 20.3.1961.	150	—
b. Signature 2. 20.3.1961.	150	—
h. Signature 6. ND.	75.00	250
j. Signature 7. ND.	75.00	250
k. Signature 9. ND.	50.00	—
l. Signature 10. ND.	50.00	—

1977-81; ND Issue

#205B-209B smaller size notes.

205B   500 Francs

1979-80. Lilac, light olive-green and multicolor. Artwork at left, long horn animals at center, man wearing hat at right. Back: Cultivated palm at left, aerial view at center, mask at right.

	VF	UNC
a. Signature 12. 1979.	65.00	—
b. Signature 13. 1980.	12.00	30.00

206B 500 Francs

1981-90. Pale olive-green and multicolor. Artwork at left, long horn animals at center, man wearing hat at right. Back: Cultivated palm at left, aerial view at center, mask at right. Watermark: Woman in profile.

	VF	UNC
a. Signature 14. 1988.	15.00	—
b. Signature 15. 1981. (BF).	7.00	20.00
c. Signature 15. 1981. (F-CO).	3.00	12.00
d. Signature 15. 1982. (BF).	20.00	50.00
e. Signature 17. 1981. (F-CO).	—	—
f. Signature 17. 1983. (BF).	—	—
g. Signature 18. 1984.	5.00	15.00
h. Signature 19. 1984.	5.00	15.00
i. Signature 19. 1985.	7.00	20.00
j. Signature 20. 1986.	3.00	12.00
k. Signature 20. 1987.	15.00	—
l. Signature 21. 1989.	3.00	10.00
m. Signature 22. 1990.	3.00	10.00

Note: #206B w/10-digit small serial # were printed by Banque de France (BF) while those w/9-digit large serial # were printed by F-CO.

209B 10,000 Francs

ND (1977-92). Red-brown on multicolor underprint. Two men seated operating primitive spinning apparatus, woman with headwear at right. Back: Figurine and girl at left, modern textile spinning machine at center. Watermark: Woman with headwear.

	VF	UNC
a. Signature 11. ND.	75.00	—
b. Signature 12. ND.	75.00	175
c. Signature 14. ND.	35.00	90.00
d. Signature 15. ND.	90.00	—
e. Signature 16. ND.	100	—
f. Signature 18. ND.	75.00	—
g. Signature 19. ND.	35.00	110
h. Signature 20. ND.	65.00	—
l. Signature 21. ND.	20.00	60.00
j. Signature 22. ND.	20.00	60.00
k. Signature 23. ND.	20.00	65.00

1991-92 Issue

207B 1000 Francs

1981-90. Brown on multicolor underprint. Artwork at left, open pit mine at center, woman at right. Back: Wood carver with finished works. Watermark: Woman.

	VF	UNC
a. Signature 14. 1988.	5.00	15.00
b. Signature 15. 1981.	7.00	20.00
c. Signature 18. 1984.	5.00	15.00
d. Signature 19. 1984.	40.00	—
e. Signature 19. 1985.	5.00	15.00
f. Signature 20. 1986.	5.00	15.00
g. Signature 20. 1987.	5.00	15.00
h. Signature 21. 1989.	7.00	20.00
i. Signature 22. 1990.	5.00	15.00

210B 500 Francs

(19)91-(20)02. Dark brown and dark green on multicolor underprint. Man at right, flood control dam at center. Back: Farmer riding spray rig behind garden tractor at center, native art at left. Watermark: Man.

	VF	UNC
a. Signature 22. (19)91.	3.00	8.00
b. Signature 22. (19)92.	30.00	—
c. Signature 23. (19)92.	25.00	—
d. Signature 25. (19)93.	25.00	—
e. Signature 26. (19)94.	3.00	8.00
f. Signature 27. (19)95.	3.00	7.00
g. Signature 28. (19)96.	3.00	7.00
h. Signature 28. (19)97. 10-digit serial #.	—	—
i. Signature 28. (19)97. 11-digit serial #.	3.00	7.00
j. Signature 28. (19)98.	3.00	7.00
k. Signature 29. (19)99.	3.00	6.00
l. Signature 30. (20)00.	3.00	6.00
m. Signature 30. (20)01.	3.00	6.00
n. Signature 31. (20)02.	3.00	6.00

208B 5000 Francs

1977-92. Black and red on multicolor underprint. Woman at left, fish and boats on shore at center, carving at right. Back: Carvings, fishing boats and mask.

	VF	UNC
a. Signature 12. 1979.	55.00	—
b. Signature 14. 1977.	35.00	90.00
c. Signature 14. 1988.	75.00	—
d. Signature 14. 1989.	10.00	40.00
e. Signature 15. 1981.	25.00	65.00
f. Signature 15. 1982.	25.00	60.00
g. Signature 17. 1983.	75.00	—
h. Signature 18. 1984.	75.00	—
i. Signature 19. 1985.	75.00	—
j. Signature 20. 1986.	75.00	—
k. Signature 20. 1987.	20.00	55.00
l. Signature 21. 1990.	10.00	40.00
m. Signature 22. 1991.	15.00	55.00
n. Signature 22. 1992.	10.00	40.00
o. Signature 23. 1992.	10.00	40.00
p. Signature 24. 1992.	40.00	—

211B 1000 Francs

(19)91-(20)02. Dark brown-violet on tan, yellow and multicolor underprint. Work-men hauling peanuts to storage at center, woman's head at right. Back: Twin statues and mask at left, two women with baskets, elevated riverside storage bins in background at center. Watermark: Woman's head.

	VF	UNC
a. Signature 22. (19)91.	5.00	12.00
b. Signature 22. (19)92.	40.00	—
c. Signature 23. (19)92.	30.00	—
d. Signature 25. (19)93.	30.00	—
e. Signature 26. (19)94.	5.00	10.00
f. Signature 27. (19)95.	5.00	10.00
g. Signature 28. (19)96.	5.00	10.00
h. Signature 28. (19)97.	4.00	9.00
i. Signature 28. (19)98.	4.00	9.00
j. Signature 29. (19)99.	4.00	9.00
k. Signature 30. (20)00.	15.00	—
l. Signature 30. (20)01.	4.00	8.00
m. Signature 31. (20)02.	4.00	8.00
n. Signature 31. (20)03.	9.00	—

212B 2500 Francs

(19)92-(19)94. Deep purple and dark brown on lilac and multicolor underprint. Dam at center, young woman's head at right. Back: Statue at left, harvesting and spraying of fruit at left center. Watermark: Young woman's head.

	VF	UNC
a. Signature 23. (19)92.	8.00	20.00
b. Signature 25. (19)93.	8.00	25.00
c. Signature 27. (19)94.	8.00	25.00

213B 5000 Francs

(19)92-(20)02. Dark brown and deep blue on multicolor underprint. Woman wearing headdress adorned with cowrie shells at right, smelting plant at center. Back: Women with children and various pottery at left center. Watermark: Woman wearing headdress adorned with cowrie shells.

	VF	UNC
a. Signature 23. (19)92.	15.00	45.00
b. Signature 25. (19)93.	10.00	35.00
c. Signature 27. (19)94.	9.00	30.00
d. Signature 27. (19)95.	9.00	30.00
e. Signature 28. (19)96.	9.00	25.00
f. Signature 28. (19)97.	9.00	25.00
g. Signature 28 (19)98.	10.00	30.00
h. Signature 29. (19)98.	9.00	25.00
i. Signature 29. (19)99.	9.00	25.00
j. Signature 30. (20)00.	10.00	35.00
k. Signature 30. (20)01.	10.00	35.00
l. Signature 31. (20)02.	9.00	25.00
m. Signature 31. (20)03.	9.00	25.00

214B 10,000 Francs

(19)92-(20)01. Dark brown on multicolor underprint. Headman with scepter at right, skyscraper at center. Back: Native art at left, woman crossing vine bridge over river at center. Watermark: Headman with scepter.

	VF	UNC
a. Signature 25. (19)92.	15.00	50.00
b. Signature 27. (19)94.	15.00	50.00
c. Signature 27. (19)95.	15.00	45.00
d. Signature 28. (19)96.	25.00	—
e. Signature 28. (19)97.	15.00	45.00
f. Signature 28. (19)98.	25.00	—
g. Signature 29. (19)98.	15.00	45.00
h. Signature 29. (19)99.	25.00	—
i. Signature 30. (20)00.	15.00	45.00
j. Signature 30. (20)01.	25.00	—

2003 Issue

215B 1000 Francs

(20)03-. Red-brown on red and multicolor underprint. 125x65mm.

	VF	UNC
a. Signature 32. (20)03.	FV	6.00
b. Signature 32. (20)04.	FV	6.00
c. Signature 33. (20)05.	FV	6.00
d. Signature 34. (20)06.	FV	5.50
e. Signature 34. (20)08.	FV	5.50
f. Signature 35. (20)09.	FV	5.00
g. Signature 39. (20)12.	FV	4.50
h. Signature 40. (20)13.	FV	4.00
i. Signature 40. (20)14.	FV	5.50

216B 2000 Francs

(20)03-. Blue on light blue and multicolor underprint. 130x66mm.

	VF	UNC
a. Signature 32. (20)03.	FV	10.00
b. Signature 32. (20)04.	FV	10.00
c. Signature 33. (20)05.	FV	10.00
d. Signature 34. (20)08.	FV	8.00
e. Signature 35. (20)09.	FV	8.00
f. Signature 38. (20)11.	FV	7.50
g. Signature 39. (20)12.	FV	7.50

217B 5000 Francs

(20)03-. Multicolor. 141x74mm.

	VF	UNC
a. Signature 32. (20)03.	FV	20.00
b. Signature 32. (20)04.	FV	17.50
c. Signature 33. (20)05.	FV	17.50
d. Signature 34. (20)06.	FV	17.50
e. Signature 35. (20)09.	FV	17.00
f. Signature 38. (20)10.	FV	17.00
g. Signature 38. (20)11.	FV	16.00
h. Signature 40. (20)13.	FV	15.00
i. Signature 40. (20)14.	FV	15.00

218B 10,000 Francs

(20)03-. Multicolor. 145x74mm.

	VF	UNC
a. Signature 32. (20)03.	FV	40.00
b. Signature 32. (20)04.	FV	35.00
c. Signature 33. (20)05.	FV	35.00
d. Signature 34. (20)06.	FV	35.00
e. Signature 35. (20)09.	FV	30.00
f. Signature 36. (20)10.	FV	28.00
g. Signature 38. (20)11.	FV	28.00

(20)12-(20)14 Issue

219B 500 Francs

(20)12-(20)14. Brown, orange, multicolor. West African symbols. Back: Hippopotami. 125x65mm.

	VF	UNC
a. Signature 40. (20)12.	FV	4.00
b. Signature 40. (20)13.	FV	3.50
c. Signature 40. (20)14.	FV	3.00

C for Burkina Faso (Upper Volta)

1961; ND Issue

301C 100 Francs

1961-65; ND. Like #101A. Dark brown, orange and multicolor.

	VF	UNC
a. Engraved. signature 1. 20.3.1961.	45.00	140
b. Signature 2. 20.3.1961.	35.00	120
c. Litho. Signature 2. 20.3.1961.	35.00	120
d. Signature 3. 2.12.1964.	20.00	75.00
e. Signature 4. 2.3.1965.	20.00	75.00
f. Signature 4. ND.	15.00	55.00

302C 500 Francs

1961-65; ND. Brown, green and multicolor field workers at left, mask carving at right. Back: Woman at left, farmer on tractor at right. Watermark: Woman's head.

	VF	UNC
a. Signature 1. 15.4.1959.	110	—
b. Signature 1. 20.3.1961.	110	—
c. Engraved. Signature 2. 20.3.1961.	75.00	—
d. Signature 4. 20.3.1961.	65.00	—
e. Signature 4. 2.3.1965.	90.00	—
f. Signature 5. ND.	75.00	—
g. Signature 6. ND.	45.00	—
h. Litho. Signature 6. ND.	35.00	—
i. Signature 7. ND.	45.00	—
k. Signature 8. ND.	45.00	100
l. Signature 9. ND.	35.00	80.00
m. Signature 11. ND.	15.00	45.00
n. Signature 12. ND.	15.00	50.00

303C 1000 Francs

1961; ND. Brown, blue and multicolor. Mand and woman at center. Back: Man with rope suspension bridge in background and pineapples. Watermark: Man's head.

	VF	UNC
a. Engraved. Signature 1. 17.9.1959.	175	—
b. Signature 1. 20.3.1961.	—	—
d. Signature 2. 20.3.1961.	100	—
e. Signature 4. 2.3.1965.	100	—
f. Signature 5. ND.	120	—
g. Signature 6. ND.	40.00	110
h. Litho. Signature 6. ND.	40.00	110
i. Signature 7. ND.	45.00	120
j. Signature 8. ND.	55.00	150
k. Signature 9. ND.	35.00	—
l. Signature 10. ND.	15.00	55.00
m. Signature 11. ND	12.00	45.00
n. Signature 12. ND.	15.00	55.00
o. Signature 13. ND.	15.00	55.00

304C 5000 Francs

1961; ND. Blue, brown and multicolor. Bearded man at left, building at center. Back: Woman, corn grinders and huts.

	VF	UNC
a. Signature 1. 20.3.1961.	100	—
b. Signature 2. 20.3.1961.	—	—
d. Signature 4. 2.3.1965.	150	—
h. Signature 6. ND.	75.00	250
i. Signature 7. ND.	75.00	250
k. Signature 9. ND.	60.00	225
l. Signature 11. ND.	55.00	200

1977-81; ND Issues

#305C-309C smaller size notes.

305C 500 Francs

1979-80. Lilac, light olie-green and multicolor. Artwork at left, long horn animals at center, man wearing hat at right. Back: Cultivated palm at left, aerial view at center, mask at right. Watermark: Woman in profile.

	VF	UNC
a. Signature 12. 1979.	13.00	35.00
b. Signature 13. 1980.	12.00	30.00

306C 500 Francs

1981-90. Pale olive-green and multicolor. Artwork at left, long horn animals at center, man wearing hat at right. Back: Cultivated palm at left, aerial view at center, mask at right. Watermark: Woman in profile.

	VF	UNC
a. Signature 14. 1988.	3.00	10.00
b. Signature 15. 1981. (BF).	3.00	12.00
c. Signature 15. 1981. (F-CO).	3.00	12.00
d. Signature 15. 1982. (BF).	3.00	12.00
e. Signature 17. 1981. (F-CO).	3.00	12.00
f. Signature 17. 1983. (BF).	9.00	—
g. Signature 18. 1984.	3.00	12.00
h. Signature 19. 1984.	3.00	10.00
i. Signature 19. 1985.	3.00	10.00
j. Signature 20. 1986.	3.00	10.00
k. Signature 20. 1987.	3.00	10.00
l. Signature 21. 1989.	3.00	10.00
m. Signature 22. 1990.	3.00	10.00

Note: #306C w/10-digit small serial # were printed by Banque de France (BF) while those w/9-digit large serial # were printed by F-CO.

307C 1000 Francs

1981-90. Brown on multicolor underprint. Artwork at left, open pit mine at center, woman at right. Back: Wood carver with finished works. Watermark: Woman.

	VF	UNC
a. Signature 14. 1988.	5.00	15.00
b. Signature 15. 1981.	7.00	20.00
c. Signature 17. 1981.	9.00	—
d. Signature 18. 1984.	9.00	—
e. Signature 19. 1984.	10.00	—
f. Signature 19. 1985.	9.00	25.00
g. Signature 20. 1986.	5.00	15.00
h. Signature 20. 1987.	5.00	15.00
i. Signature 21. 1989.	10.00	—
j. Signature 22. 1990.	5.00	15.00

308C 5000 Francs

1977-92. Black and red on multicolor underprint. Woman at left, fish and boats on shore at center, carving at right. Back: Carvings, fishing boats and mask.

	VF	UNC
a. Signature 12. 1978.	35.00	85.00
b. Signature 12. 1979.	35.00	85.00
c. Signature 14. 1977.	35.00	85.00
d. Signature 14. 1988.	10.00	40.00
e. Signature 14. 1989.	10.00	40.00
f. Signature 15. 1981.	15.00	60.00
g. Signature 15. 1982.	15.00	65.00
h. Signature 17. 1983.	15.00	65.00
i. Signature 18. 1984.	15.00	65.00
k. Signature 19. 1985.	15.00	65.00
l. Signature 20. 1986.	20.00	80.00
m. Signature 20. 1987.	18.00	75.00
n. Signature 21. 1990.	10.00	40.00
o. Signature 22. 1991.	10.00	40.00
p. Signature 22. 1992.	10.00	40.00
q. Signature 23. 1992.	10.00	40.00
r. Signature 24. 1992.	15.00	—

309C 10,000 Francs

ND (1977-92). Red-brown on multicolor underprint. Two men seated operating primitive spinning appartaus, woman with headwear at right. Back: Figurine and girl at left, modern textile spinning machine at center. Watermark: Woman with headwear.

	VF	UNC
a. Signature 11. ND.	80.00	200
b. Signature 12. ND.	50.00	110
c. Signature 13. ND.	50.00	110
d. Signature 14. ND.	—	—
e. Signature 15. ND.	65.00	—
f. Signature 20. ND.	35.00	80.00
g. Signature 21. ND.	20.00	55.00
h. Signature 22. ND.	20.00	55.00
i. Signature 23. ND.	20.00	55.00

1991 Issue

310C 500 Francs

(19)91-(20)02. Dark brown and dark green on multicolr underprint. Man at right, flood control dam at center. Back: Farmer riding spray rig behind garden tractor at center, native art at left. Watermark: Man.

	VF	UNC
a. Signature 22. (19)91.	3.00	8.00
b. Signature 23. (19)92.	7.00	20.00
c. Signature 25. (19)93.	3.00	8.00
d. Signature 26. (19)94.	3.00	8.00
e. Signature 27. (19)95.	3.00	7.00
f. Signature 28. (19)96.	3.00	7.00
g. Signature 28. (19)97. 10-digit serial #.	3.00	7.00
h. Signature 28. (19)97. 11-digit serial #.	3.00	7.00
i. Signature 28. (19)98.	3.00	7.00
j. Signature 29. (19)99.	3.00	7.00
k. Signature 30. (20)00.	3.00	6.00
l. Signature 30. (20)01.	3.00	6.00
m. Signature 31. (20)02.	3.00	6.00

311C 1000 Francs

(19)91-(20)02. Dark brown-violet on tan, yellow and multicolor underprint. Workmen hauling peanuts to storage at center, woman's head at right. Back: Twin statues and mask at left, two women with baskets, elevated riverside storage bins in background at center. Watermark: Woman's head.

	VF	UNC
a. Signature 22. (19)91.	5.00	12.00
b. Signature 22. (19)92.	40.00	—
c. Signature 23. (19)92.	30.00	—
d. Signature 25. (19)93.	5.00	10.00
e. Signature 26. (19)94.	5.00	10.00
f. Signature 27. (19)95.	5.00	10.00
g. Signature 28. (19)96.	4.00	9.00
h. Signature 28. (19)97.	4.00	9.00
i. Signature 28. (19)98.	4.00	9.00
j. Signature 29. (19)99.	4.00	9.00
k. Signature 30. (20)00.	4.00	8.00
l. Signature 30. (20)01.	4.00	8.00
m. Signature 31. (20)02.	4.00	8.00
n. Signature 31. (20)03.	4.00	8.00

312C 2500 Francs

(19)92-(19)94. Deep purple and dark brown on lilac and multicolor underprint. Dam at center, young woman's head at right. Back: Statue at left, harvesting and spraying of fruit at left center. Watermark: Young woman's head.

	VF	UNC
a. Signature 23. (19)92.	8.00	20.00
b. Signature 25. (19)93.	8.00	20.00
c. Signature 27. (19)94.	8.00	20.00

313C 5000 Francs

(19)92-(20)02. Dark brown and deep blue on multicolor underprint. Woman wearing headdress adorned with cowrie shells at right, smelting plant at center. Back: Women with children and various pottery at left center. Watermark: Woman wearing headdress adorned with cowrie shells.

	VF	UNC
a. Signature 23. (19)92.	9.00	30.00
b. Signature 25. (19)93.	9.00	25.00
c. Signature 27. (19)94.	9.00	25.00
	VF	**UNC**
d. Signature 27. (19)95.	8.00	20.00
e. Signature 28. (19)96.	8.00	20.00
f. Signature 28. (19)97.	8.00	20.00
g. Signature 28. (19)98.	8.00	20.00
h. Signature 29. (19)98.	8.00	20.00
i. Signature 29. (19)99.	7.00	20.00
j. Signature 30. (20)00.	30.00	—
k. Signature 30. (20)01.	7.00	20.00
l. Signature 31. (20)02.	7.00	20.00
m. Signature 31. (20)03.	7.00	20.00

314C 10,000 Francs
(19)92-(20)01. Dark brown on multicolor underprint. Headman with scepter at right, skyscraper at center. Back: Native art at left, woman crossing vine bridgte over river at center. Watermark: Headman with scepter.

	VF	UNC
a. Signature 25. (19)92.	25.00	—
b. Signature 27. (19)94.	15.00	50.00
c. Signature 27. (19)95.	15.00	45.00
d. Signature 28. (19)96.	15.00	45.00
e. Signature 28. (19)97.	15.00	45.00
f. Signature 28. (19)98.	15.00	45.00
g. Signature 29. (19)98.	15.00	45.00
h. Signature 29. (19)99.	15.00	40.00
i. Signature 30. (20)00.	15.00	40.00
j. Signature 30. (20)01.	15.00	40.00

2003 Issue

315C 1000 Francs
(20)03-. Red-brown on red and multicolor underprint. 125x65mm.

	VF	UNC
a. Signature 32. (20)03.	FV	6.00
b. Signature 32. (20)04.	FV	6.00
c. Signature 34. (20)06.	FV	5.50
d. Signature 34. (20)07.	FV	5.50
e. Signature 34. (20)08.	FV	5.50
f. Signature 35. (20)09.	FV	5.00
g. Signature 38. (20)10.	FV	4.50
h. Signature 38. (20)11.	FV	4.50
i. Signature 39. (20)12.	FV	4.50
j. Signature 40. (20)13.	FV	4.00
k. Signature 40. (20)14.	FV	3.50

316C 2000 Francs
(20)03-. Blue on light blue and multicolor underprint. 130x66mm.

	VF	UNC
a. Signature 32. (20)03.	FV	10.00
b. Signature 32. (20)04.	FV	10.00
c. Signature 33. (20)05.	FV	10.00
d. Signature 33. (20)06.	FV	10.00
e. Signature 34. (20)07.	FV	8.00
f. Signature 35. (20)09.	FV	8.00
g. Signature 38. (20)10.	FV	7.50
h. Signature 37. (20)11.	FV	7.50
i. Signature 39. (20)12.	FV	7.50
j. Signature 40. (20)13.	FV	7.50
k. Signature 40. (20)14.	FV	7.00

317C 5000 Francs
(20)03-. Multicolor. 141x74mm.

	VF	UNC
a. Signature 32. (20)03.	FV	20.00
b. Signature 32. (20)04.	FV	17.50
c. Signature 33. (20)05.	FV	17.50
d. Signature 33. (20)06.	FV	17.50
e. Signature 34. (20)07.	FV	17.50
f. Signature 34 (20)08.	FV	17.50
g. Signature 35. (20)09.	FV	17.00
h. Signature 36. (20)10.	FV	16.00
i. Signature 38. (20)11.	FV	16.00
j. Signature 39. (20)12.	FV	15.00
k. Signature 40. (20)13.	FV	15.00
l. Signature 40. (20)14.	FV	15.00

318C 10,000 Francs
(20)03-. Multicolor. 145x74mm.

	VF	UNC
a. Signature 32. (20)03.	FV	40.00
b. Signature 32. (20)04.	FV	35.00
c. Signature 33. (20)05.	FV	35.00
d. Signature 34. (20)06.	FV	35.00
e. Signature 34. (20)07.	FV	35.00
f. Signature 35. (20)08.	FV	30.00
g. Signature 35. (20)09.	FV	30.00
h. Signature 36. (20)10.	FV	28.00
i. Signature 37. (20)11.	FV	28.00
j. Signature 38. (20)11.	FV	28.00
k. Signature 39. (20)12.	FV	24.00
l. Signature 40. (20)13.	FV	24.00
m. Signature 40. (20)14.	FV	23.50

(20)12-(20)14 Issue

319C 500 Francs
(20)12-(20)14. Brown, orange, multicolor. West African symbols. Back: Hippopotami. 125x65mm.

	VF	UNC
a. Signature 40. (20)12.	FV	4.00
b. Signature 40. (20)13.	FV	3.50
c. Signature 40. (20)14.	FV	3.00

D for Mali

1959-61; ND Issue

401D 100 Francs
20.3.1961.Like #101A. Dark brown, orange and multicolor. Signature left.

	Fine	XF
	200	400

402D 500 Francs
1959; 1961. Brown, green and multicolor. Field workers at left, mask carving at right. Like #102A. Back: Woman at left, farmer on tractor at right. Watermark: Woman's head.

	Fine	XF
a. Signature 1. 15.4.1959.	600	—
b. Signature 1. 20.3.1961.	—	—

403D 1000 Francs
1959; 1961. Brown, blue and multicolor. Man and woman at center. Like #103A. Back: Man with rope suspension bridge in background and pineapples. Watermark: Man's head.

	Fine	XF
a. Signature 1. 17.9.1959.	400	1,000
b. Signature 1. 20.3.1961.	400	1,000

404D 5000 Francs
20.3.1961.. Blue, brown and multicolor. Bearded man at left, building at center. Signature left. Back: Woman, corn grinders and huts.

	Fine	XF
	500	1,300

1981; ND Issue

#405D-408D smaller size notes.

405D 500 Francs
1981-90. Pale olive-green and multicolor. Artwork at left, long horn animals at center, man wearing hat at right. Back: Cultivated palm at left, aerial view at center, mask at right. Watermark: Woman in profile.

	VF	UNC
a. Signature 14. 1988.	3.00	9.00
b. Signature 15. 1981. (BF).	3.00	10.00
c. Signature 17. 1981. (F-CO).	3.00	11.00
e. Signature 19. 1985.	4.00	15.00
f. Signature 20. 1986.	3.00	10.00
g. Signature 20. 1987.	3.00	10.00
h. Signature 21. 1989.	3.00	9.00
i. Signature 22. 1990.	3.00	9.00

Note: #405D w/10-digit small serial # were printed by Banque de France (BF) while those w/9-digit large serial # were printed by F-CO.

406D 1000 Francs
1981-90. Brown on multicolor underprint. Artwork at left, open pit mine at center, woman at right. Back: Wood carver with finished works. Watermark: Woman.

	VF	UNC
a. Signature 14. 1988.	5.00	12.00
b. Signature 15. 1981.	5.00	12.00
c. Signature 17. 1981.	6.00	15.00
f. Signature 19. 1985.	6.00	15.00
g. Signature 20. 1986.	6.00	15.00
h. Signature 20. 1987.	6.00	15.00
i. Signature 21. 1989.	5.00	12.00
j. Signature 22. 1990.	20.00	—

407D 5000 Francs   **VF   UNC**

1981-92. Black and red on multicolor underprint. Woman at left, fish and boats on shore at center, carving at right. Back: Carvings, fishing boats and mask.

a. Signature 14. 1988.	15.00	60.00
b. Signature 14. 1989.	40.00	—
c. Signature 15. 1981.	15.00	55.00
d. Signature 17. 1984.	15.00	55.00
e. Signature 18. 1984.	35.00	80.00
f. Signature 19. 1985.	15.00	55.00
g. Signature 20. 1986.	15.00	55.00
h. Signature 20. 1987.	15.00	55.00
i. Signature 21. 1990.	15.00	55.00
j. Signature 22. 1991.	10.00	45.00
k. Signature 23. 1992.	15.00	55.00
l. Signature 24. 1992.	35.00	—

408D 10,000 Francs   **VF   UNC**

ND (1981-92). Red-brown on multicolor underprint. Two men seated operating primitive spinning apparatus, woman with headwear at right. Back: Figurine and girl at left, modern textile spinning machine at center. Watermark: Woman with headwear.

a. Signature 14. ND.	60.00	—
b. Signature 15. ND.	35.00	85.00
c. Signature 18. ND.	55.00	120
d. Signature 19. ND.	—	—
e. Signature 20. ND.	30.00	75.00
f. Signature 21. ND.	20.00	55.00
g. Signature 22. ND.	20.00	55.00

1991-92 Issue

410D 500 Francs   **VF   UNC**

(19)91-(20)02. Dark brown and dark green on multicolor underprint. Man at right, flood control dam at center. Back: Farmer riding spray rig behind garden tractor at center, native art at left. Watermark: Man.

a. Signature 22. (19)91.	3.00	10.00
b. Signature 23. (19)92.	7.00	20.00
c. Signature 25. (19)93.	3.00	8.00
d. Signature 26. (19)94.	3.00	8.00
e. Signature 27. (19)95.	3.00	7.00
f. Signature 28. (19)96.	3.00	7.00
g. Signature 28. (19)97. 10-digit serial #.	3.00	7.00
h. Signature 28. (19)97. 11-digit serial #.	3.00	7.00
i. Signature 28. (19)98.	3.00	7.00
j. Signature 29. (19)99.	3.00	7.00
k. Signature 30. (20)00.	3.00	6.00
l. Signature 30. (20)01.	3.00	6.00
m. Signature 31. (20)02.	3.00	10.00
n. Signature 31. (20)03.	3.00	6.00

411D 1000 Francs   **VF   UNC**

(19)91-(20)02. Dark brown-violet on tan, yellow and multicolor underprint. Workmen hauling peanuts to storage at center, woman's head at right. Back: Twin statues and mask at left, two women with baskets, elevated riverside storage bins in background at center. Watermark: Woman's head.

a. Signature 22. (19)91.	5.00	12.00
b. Signature 23. (19)92.	30.00	—
c. Signature 25. (19)93.	5.00	10.00
d. Signature 26. (19)94.	5.00	10.00
e. Signature 27. (19)95.	5.00	10.00
f. Signature 28. (19)96.	4.00	9.00
g. Signature 28. (19)97.	4.00	9.00
h. Signature 28. (19)98.	4.00	9.00
i. Signature 29. (19)99.	4.00	9.00
j. Signature 30. (20)00.	4.00	8.00
k. Signature 30. (20)01.	4.00	8.00
l. Signature 31. (20)02.	4.00	8.00
m. Signature 31. (20)03.	4.00	8.00

412D 2500 Francs   **VF   UNC**

(19)92-(19)94. Deep purple and dark brown on lilac and multicolor underprint. Dam at center, young woman's head at right. Back: Statue at left, harvesting and spraying of fruit at left center. Watermark: Young woman's head.

a. Signature 23. (19)92.	8.00	20.00
b. Signature 25. (19)93.	20.00	—
c. Signature 27. (19)94.	8.00	20.00

413D 5000 Francs   **VF   UNC**

(19)92-(20)02. Dark brown and deep blue on multicolor underprint. Woman wearing headdress adorned with cowrie shells at right, smelting plant at center. Back: Women with children and various pottery at left center. Watermark: Woman wearing headdress adorned with cowrie shells.

a. Signature 23. (19)92.	9.00	30.00
b. Signature 27. (19)94.	9.00	25.00
c. Signature 27. (19)95.	15.00	35.00
d. Signature 28. (19)96.	8.00	20.00
e. Signature 28. (19)97.	8.00	20.00
f. Signature 28. (19)98.	8.00	20.00
g. Signature 29. (19)98.	15.00	35.00
h. Signature 29. (19)99.	8.00	20.00
i. Signature 30. (20)00.	35.00	—
j. Signature 30. (20)01.	15.00	35.00
k. Signature 31. (20)02.	8.00	20.00
l. Signature 32. (20)03.	8.00	20.00

414D 10,000 Francs   **VF   UNC**

(19)92-(20)02. Dark brown on multicolor underprint. Headman with scepter at right, skyscraper at center. Back: Native art at left, woman crooning vine bridge over river at center. Watermark: Headman with scepter.

a. Signature 25. (19)92.	25.00	—
b. Signature 27. (19)94.	35.00	—
c. Signature 27. (19)95.	15.00	45.00
d. Signature 28. (19)96.	15.00	45.00
e. Signature 28. (19)97.	15.00	45.00
f. Signature 28. (19)98.	15.00	45.00
g. Signature 29. (19)98.	15.00	45.00
h. Signature 29. (19)99.	15.00	45.00
i. Signature 30. (20)00.	35.00	—
j. Signature 30. (20)01.	15.00	45.00

2003 Issue

415D 1000 Francs   **VF   UNC**

(20)03-. . Red on light red and multicolor underprint. 125x65mm.

a. Signature 32. (20)03.	FV	6.00
b. Signature 32. (20)04.	FV	6.00
c. Signature 33. (20)05.	FV	6.00
d. Signature 32. (20)06.	FV	5.50
e. Signature 34. (20)07.	FV	5.50
f. Signature 34. (20)08.	FV	5.50
g. Signature 35. (20)08.	FV	5.00
h. Signature 37. (20)11.	FV	4.50
i. Signature 39. (20)12.	FV	4.50
j. Signature 40. (20)13.	FV	4.00
k. Signature 40. (20)14.	FV	3.50

416D 2000 Francs   **VF   UNC**

(20)03-. Red-brown on red and multicolor underprint. 130x65mm.

a. Signature 32. (20)03.	FV	10.00
b. Signature 32. (20)04.	FV	10.00
c. Signature 32. (20)05.	FV	10.00
d. Signature 33. (20)06.	FV	10.00
e. Signature 34. (20)07.	FV	8.00
f. Signature 34. (20)08.	FV	8.00
g. Signature 35. (20)08.	FV	7.50
h. Signature 35. (20)09.	FV	7.50
i. Signature 38. (20)11.	FV	7.50
j. Signature 39. (20)12.	FV	7.50
k. Signature 40. (20)13.	FV	7.00
l. Signature 40. (20)14.	FV	7.00

417D 5000 Francs		VF	UNC
(20)03-. Multicolor. 141x74mm.			
a. Signature 32. (20)03.		FV	25.00
b. Signature 32. (20)04.		FV	17.50
c. Signature 33. (20)05.		FV	17.50
d. Signature 34. (20)06.		FV	17.50
e. Signature 32. (20)07.		FV	17.50
f. Signature 34. (20)08.		FV	17.50
g. Signature 35. (20)08.		FV	17.50
h. Signature 35. (20)09.		FV	17.00
i. Signature 36. (20)10.		FV	16.00
j. Signature 37. (20)11.		FV	16.00
k. Signature 39. (20)12.		FV	15.00
l. Signature 40. (20)13.		FV	15.00
m. Signature 40. (20)14.		FV	15.00

418D 10,000 Francs		VF	UNC
(20)03-. Multicolor. 145x74mm.			
a. Signature 32. (20)03.		FV	40.00
b. Signature 32. (20)04.		FV	35.00
c. Signature 33. (20)05.		FV	35.00
d. Signature 35. (20)07.		FV	32.50
e. Signature 36. (20)08.		FV	32.50
f. Signature 36. (20)10.		FV	28.00
g. Signature 37. (20)11.		FV	28.00
h. Signature 38. (20)11.		FV	28.00
i. Signature 39. (20)12.		FV	24.00
j. Signature 40. (20)13.		FV	24.00
k. Signature 40. (20)14.		FV	23.50

(20)12-(20)14 Issue

419D 500 Francs		VF	UNC
(20)12-(20)14. Brown, orange, multicolor. West African symbols. Back: Hippopotami. 125x65mm.			
a. Signature 40. (20)12.		FV	4.00
b. Signature 40. (20)13.		FV	3.50
c. Signature 40. (20)14.		FV	3.00

E for Mauritania
1959-64; ND Issue

501E 100 Francs		Fine	XF
1961-65. Like #101A. Dark brown, orange and multicolor.			
b. Engraved. Signature 1. 20.3.1961.		100	300
c. Litho. Signature 3. 2.12.1964.		100	300
e. Signature 4. 2.3.1965.		90.00	275
f. Signature 4. ND.		90.00	275

502E 500 Francs		Fine	XF
1959-64; ND. Brown, green and multicolor. Field workers at left, mask carving at right. Like #102A. Back: Woman at left, farmer on tractor at right. Watermark: Woman's head.			
a. Engraved. Signature 1. 15.4.1959.		—	—
b. Signature 1. 20.3.1961.		200	—
c. Signature 2. 20.3.1961.		175	—
e. Signature 4. 2.3.1965.		200	—
f. Signature 5. ND.		175	650
g. Signature 6. ND.		175	600
h. Litho. Signature 6. ND.		200	—
i. Signature 7. ND.		175	600

503E 1000 Francs		Fine	XF
1961-65. Brown, blue and multicolor. Man and woman at center. Back: Man with rope suspension bridge in background and pineapples. Watermark: Man's head.			
a. Engraved. Signature 1. 17.9.1959.		—	—
b. Signature 1. 20.3.1961.		175	600
e. Signature 4. 2.3.1965.		175	600
g. Signature 6. ND.		175	600
h. Litho. Signature 6. ND.		175	600

504E 5000 Francs		Fine	XF
1961-65; ND. Blue, brown and multicolor. Bearded man at left, building at center. Back: Woman, corn grinders and huts.			
a. Signature 1. 20.3.1961.		350	—
b. Signature 2. 20.3.1961.		275	—
c. Signature 4. 2.3.1965.		275	900
d. Signature 6. ND.		275	900
e. Signature 7. ND.		275	—

H for Niger
1959-65; ND Issue

601H 100 Francs		VF	UNC
1961-65; ND. Like #101A. Dark brown, orange and multicolor.			
a. Engraved. Signature 1. 20.3.1961.		50.00	—
b. Signature 2. 20.3.1961.		65.00	—
c. Litho. Signature 2. 20.3.1961.		50.00	—
d. Signature 3. 2.12.1964.		—	—
e. Signature 4. 2.3.1965.		35.00	100
f. Signature 4. ND.		35.00	100

602H 500 Francs		VF	UNC
1959-65; ND. Brown, green and multicolor. Field workers at left, mask carving at right. Like #102A. Back: Woman at left, farmer on tractor at right. Watermark: Woman's head.			
a. Engraved. Signature 1. 15.4.1959.		—	—
c. Signature 2. 20.3.1961.		125	—
d. Signature 3. 2.12.1964.		75.00	200
e. Signature 4. 2.3.1965.		75.00	200
f. Signature 5. ND.		125	—
g. Signature 6. ND.		40.00	120
h. Litho. Signature 6. ND.		40.00	120
i. Signature 7. ND.		65.00	150
j. Signature 8. ND.		40.00	120
k. Signature 9. ND.		30.00	90.00
l. Signature 10. ND.		—	—
m. Signature 11. ND.		25.00	75.00

603H 1000 Francs		VF	UNC
1959-65; ND. Brown, blue and multicolor. Man and woman at center. Like #103A. Back: Man with rope suspension bridge in background and pineapples. Watermark: Man's head.			
a. Engraved. Signature 1. 17.9.1959.		100	—
b. Signature 1. 20.3.1961.		100	—
c. Signature 2. 20.3.1961.		—	—
e. Signature 4. 2.3.1965.		100	250
f. Signature 5. ND.		100	250
g. Signature 6. ND.		80.00	—
h. Litho. Signature 6. ND.		80.00	200
i. Signature 7. ND.		80.00	200
j. Signature 8. ND.		100	—
k. Signature 9. ND		40.00	120
l. Signature 10. ND.		40.00	120
m. Signature 11. ND.		30.00	90.00
n. Signature 12. ND.		40.00	120
o. Signature 13. ND.		50.00	150

604H 5000 Francs		VF	UNC
1961; 1965; ND. Blue, brown and multicolor. Bearded man at left, building at center. Back: Woman, corn grinders and huts.			
a. Signature 1. 20.3.1961.		—	—
b. Signature 2. 20.3.1961.		200	—
d. Signature 4. 2.3.1965.		200	—
e. Signature 6. ND.		200	—
i. Signature 7. ND.		200	—
k. Signature 9. ND.		150	350
l. Signature 10. ND.		200	—
m. Signature 11. ND.		150	350

1977-81; ND Issue
#605H-608H smaller size notes.

605H 500 Francs		VF	UNC
1979-80. Lilac, light olive-green and multicolor. Artwork at left, long horn animals at center, man wearing hat at right. Back: Cultivated palm at left, aerial view at center, mask at right. Watermark: Woman in profile.			
a. Signature 12. 1979.		20.00	50.00
b. Signature 13. 1980.		12.00	30.00

606H 500 Francs		VF	UNC
1981-90. Pale olive-green and multicolor. Artwork at left, long horn animals at center, man wearing hat at right. Back: Cultivated palm at left, aerial view at center, mask at right. Watermark: Woman in profile.			
a. Signature 14. 1988.		3.00	10.00
b. Signature 15. 1981. (BF).		20.00	5.00
c. Signature 15. 1981. (F-CO).		4.00	12.00
d. Signature 15. 1982. (BF).		—	—

	VF	UNC
e. Signature 17. 1981. (F-CO).	4.00	12.00
f. Signature 18. 1984.	50.00	—
g. Signature 19. 1984.	—	—
h. Signature 19. 1985.	—	—
i. Signature 20. 1986.	3.00	10.00
j. Signature 20. 1987.	3.00	10.00
k. Signature 21. 1989.	3.00	9.00
l. Signature 22. 1990.	3.00	9.00

607H 1000 Francs   VF   UNC

1981-90. Brown on multicolor underprint. Artwork at left, open pit mine at center, woman at right. Back: Wood carver with finished works. Watermark: Woman.

	VF	UNC
a. Signature 14. 1988.	5.00	12.00
b. Signature 15. 1981.	6.00	20.00
c. Signature 17. 1981.	—	—
d. Signature 18. 1984.	20.00	—
e. Signature 19. 1984.	25.00	—
f. Signature 19. 1985.	6.00	20.00
g. Signature 20. 1986.	5.00	12.00
h. Signature 20. 1987.	5.00	12.00
i. Signature 21. 1989.	5.00	12.00
j. Signature 22. 1990.	5.00	12.00

608H 5000 Francs   VF   UNC

1977-90. Black and red on multicolor underprint. Woman at left, fish and boats on shore at center, carving at right. Back: Carvings, fishing boats and mask.

	VF	UNC
a. Signature 12. 1978.	40.00	100
b. Signature 12. 1979.	40.00	100
c. Signature 13. 1980.	50.00	120
d. Signature 14. 1977.	40.00	100
e. Signature 14. 1989.	20.00	50.00
f. Signature 15. 1981.	25.00	60.00
g. Signature 15. 1982.	25.00	60.00
h. Signature 17. 1983.	25.00	60.00
i. Signature 18. 1984.	40.00	100
j. Signature 19. 1985.	30.00	70.00
k. Signature 20. 1986.	25.00	60.00
l. Signature 20. 1987.	20.00	50.00
m. Signature 21. 1990.	20.00	50.00
n. Signature 27. 1995.	20.00	50.00

609H 10,000 Francs   VF   UNC

ND (1977). Red-brown on multicolor underprint. Two men seated operating primitive spinning apparatus, woman with headwear at right. Back: Figurine and girl at left, modern textile spinning machine at center. Watermark: Woman with headwear.

	VF	UNC
a. Signature 11. ND.	75.00	200
b. Signature 12. ND.	—	—
c. Signature 13. ND.	—	—
d. Signature 14. ND.	35.00	100
e. Signature 15. ND.	40.00	110
f. Signature 18. ND.	55.00	140
g. Signature 19. ND.	—	—
h. Signature 20. ND.	35.00	90.00
i. Signature 21. ND.	30.00	75.00
j. Signature 22. ND.	30.00	75.00

1991-92 Issue

610H 500 Francs   VF   UNC

(19)91-(20)02. Dark brown and dark green on multicolor underprint. Man at right, flood control dam at center. Back: Farmer riding spray rig behind garden tractor at center, native art at left. Watermark: Man.

	VF	UNC
a. Signature 22. (19)91.	3.00	8.00
b. Signature 23. (19)92.	25.00	—
c. Signature 25. (19)93.	3.00	8.00
d. Signature 26. (19)94.	3.00	8.00
e. Signature 27. (19)95.	3.00	7.00
f. Signature 28. (19)96.	3.00	7.00
g. Signature 28. (19)97. 10-digit serial #.	3.00	7.00
h. Signature 28. (19)97. 11-digit serial #.	3.00	7.00
i. Signature 28. (19)98.	3.00	7.00
j. Signature 29. (19)99.	5.00	10.00
k. Signature 30 (20)00.	3.00	7.00
l. Signature 30. (20)01.	—	—
m. Signature 31. (20)02.	3.00	7.00

611H 1000 Francs   VF   UNC

(19)91-(20)02. Dark brown-violet on tan, yellow and multicolor underprint. Workmen hauling peanuts to storage at center, woman's head at right. Back: Twin statues and mask at left, two women with baskets, elevated riverside storage bins in background at center. Watermark: Woman's head.

	VF	UNC
a. Signature 22. (19)91.	5.00	12.00
b. Signature 23. (19)92.	5.00	12.00
c. Signature 25. (19)93.	5.00	12.00
d. Signature 26. (19)94.	30.00	—
e. Signature 27. (19)95.	5.00	10.00
f. Signature 28. (19)96.	5.00	10.00
g. Signature 28. (19)97.	4.00	8.00
h. Signature 28. (19)98.	30.00	—
i. Signature 29. (19)99.	4.00	8.00
j. Signature 30. (20)00.	4.00	8.00
k. Signature 30. (20)02.	4.00	8.00
l. Signature 31. (20)03.	4.00	8.00

612H 2500 Francs   VF   UNC

(19)92-(19)94. Deep purple and dark brown on lilac and multicolor underprint. Dam at center, young woman's head at right. Back: Statue at left, harvesting and spraying of fruit at left center. Watermark: Young woman's head.

	VF	UNC
a. Signature 23. (19)92.	9.00	25.00
b. Signature 25. (19)93.	9.00	25.00
c. Signature 27. (19)94.	9.00	25.00

613H 5000 Francs   VF   UNC

(19)92-(20)02. Dark brown and deep blue on multicolor underprint. Woman wearing headdress adorned with cowrie shells at right, smelting plant at center. Back: Women with children and various pottery at left center. Watermark: Woman wearing headdress adorned with cowrie shells.

	VF	UNC
a. Signature 23. (19)92.	9.00	30.00
b. Signature 27. (19)94.	9.00	25.00
c. Signature 27. (19)95.	9.00	25.00
d. Signature 28. (19)96.	9.00	25.00
e. Signature 28. (19)97.	8.00	20.00
f. Signature 28. (19)98.	40.00	—
g. Signature 28. (19)98.	8.00	20.00
h. Signature 29. (19)99.	8.00	20.00
i. Signature 30. (20)00.	40.00	—
j. Signature 30. (20)01.	40.00	—
k. Signature 31. (20)02.	8.00	20.00
l. Signature 31. (20)03.	8.00	20.00

614H 10,000 Francs   VF   UNC

(19)92-(20)01. Dark brown on multicolor underprint. Headman with scepter at right, skyscraper at center. Back: Native art at left, woman crossing vine bridge over river at center. Watermark: Headman with scepter.

	VF	UNC
a. Signature 25. (19)92.	20.00	50.00
b. Signature 27. (19)94.	15.00	45.00
c. Signature 27. (19)95.	15.00	45.00
d. Signature 28. (19)96.	15.00	45.00
e. Signature 28. (19)97.	15.00	45.00
f. Signature 28. (19)98.	25.00	—
g. Signature 29. (19)98.	—	—
h. Signature 29. (19)99.	15.00	45.00
i. Signature 30. (20)00.	—	—
j. Signature 30. (20)01.	15.00	45.00

2003 Issue

615H 1000 Francs   VF   UNC

(20)03-. Red-brown on red and multicolor underprint. 125x65mm.

	VF	UNC
a. Signature 32. (20)03.	FV	6.00
b. Signature 32. (20)04.	FV	6.00
c. Signature 34. (20)06.	FV	5.50
d. Signature 34. (20)07.	FV	5.50
e. Signature 34. (20)08.	FV	5.50
f. Signature 35. (20)08.	FV	5.00
g. Signature 35. (20)09.	FV	5.00
h. Signature 35. (20)09.	FV	4.50
i. Signature 39. (20)12.	FV	4.00
j. Signature 40. (20)13.	FV	4.00
k. Signature 40. (20)14.	FV	3.50

616H 2000 Francs   VF   UNC

(20)03-. Blue on light blue and multicolor underprint. 130x66mm.

	VF	UNC
a. Signature 32. (20)03.	FV	10.00
b. Signature 32. (20)04.	FV	10.00
c. Signature 33. (20)05.	FV	10.00
d. Signature 34. (20)07.	FV	8.00
e. Signature 35. (20)09.	FV	7.50
f. Signature 34. (20)08.	FV	8.00
g. Signature 35. (20)08.	FV	7.50
h. Signature 38. (20)11.	FV	7.50
i. Signature 39. (20)12.	FV	7.50
j. Signature 40. (20)13.	FV	7.00
k. Signature 40. (20)14.	FV	7.00

617H 5000 Francs   VF   UNC

(20)03-. Multicolor. 141x74mm.

	VF	UNC
a. Signature 32. (20)03.	FV	20.00
b. Signature 32. (20)04.	FV	17.50
c. Signature 33. (20)05.	FV	17.50
d. Signature 33. (20)06.	FV	17.50

	VF	UNC
e. Signature 34. (20)07.	FV	17.50
f. Signature 35. (20)09.	FV	17.00
g. Signature 36. (20)10.	FV	16.00
h. Signature 37. (20)11.	FV	16.00
i. Signature 39. (20)12.	FV	15.00
j. Signature 40. (20)13.	FV	15.00
k. Signature 40. (20)14.	FV	15.00

618H 10,000 Francs   VF   UNC

(20)03-. Multicolor. 145x74mm.

	VF	UNC
a. Signature 32. (20)03.	FV	40.00
b. Signature 32. (20)04.	FV	35.00
c. Signature 33. (20)05.	FV	35.00
d. Signature 33. (20)06.	FV	35.00
e. Signature 34. (20)07.	FV	35.00
f. Signature 36. (20)10.	FV	28.00
g. Signature 37. (20)11.	FV	28.00

	VF	UNC
h. Signature 38. (20)11.	FV	28.00
i. Signature 39. (20)12.	FV	24.00
j. Signature 40. (20)13.	FV	24.00
k. Signature 40. (20)14.	FV	23.50

(20)12-(20)14 Issue

619H 500 Francs

	VF	UNC
(20)12-(20)14. Brown, orange, multicolor. West African symbols. Back: Hippopotami. 125x65mm.		
a. Signature 40. (20)12.	FV	4.00
b. Signature 40. (20)13.	FV	3.50
c. Signature 40. (20)14.	FV	3.00

K for Senegal
1959-65; ND Issue

701K 100 Francs

	VF	UNC
1961-65; ND. Like #101A. Dark brown, orange and multicolor.		
a. Engraved. Signature 1. 20.3.1961.	45.00	—
b. Signature 2. 20.3.1961.	25.00	70.00
c. Litho. Signature 2. 20.3.1961.	25.00	70.00
d. Signature 3. 2.12.1964.	30.00	—
e. Signature 4. 2.3.1965.	20.00	65.00
f. Signature 4. ND.	15.00	45.00
g. Signature 5. ND.	45.00	—

702K 500 Francs

	VF	UNC
1959-65; ND. Brown, green and multicolor. Field workers at left, mask carving at right. Like #102A. Back: Woman at left, farmer on tractor at right. Watermark: Woman's head.		
a. Engraved. Signature 1. 15.4.1959.	—	—
b. Signature 1. 20.3.1961.	45.00	120
c. Signature 2. 20.3.1961.	45.00	120
d. Signature 3. 2.12.1964.	45.00	120
e. Signature 4. 2.3.1965.	40.00	100
f. Signature 5. ND.	45.00	120
g. Signature 6. ND.	25.00	85.00
h. Litho. Signature 6. ND.	25.00	85.00
i. Signature 7. ND.	40.00	—
j. Signature 8. ND.	40.00	100
k. Signatur 9. ND.	20.00	60.00
l. Signature 10. ND.	20.00	60.00
m. Signature 11. ND.	15.00	45.00
n. Signature 12. ND.	15.00	45.00

703K 1000 Francs

	VF	UNC
1959-65; ND. Brown, blue and multicolor. Man and woman at center. Like #103A. Back: Man with rope suspension bridge in background and pineapples. Watermark: Man's head.		
a. Engraved. Signature 1. 17.9.1959.	65.00	—
b. Signature 1. 20.3.1961.	65.00	—
c. Signature 2. 20.3.1961.	50.00	—
e. Signature 4. 2.3.1965.	50.00	—
f. Signature 5. ND.	90.00	—
g. Signature 6. ND.	75.00	120
h. Litho. Signature 6. ND.	25.00	60.00
i. Signature 7. ND.	30.00	75.00
j. Signature 8. ND.	35.00	—
k. Signature 9. ND.	15.00	50.00
l. Signature 10. ND.	15.00	50.00
m. Signature 11. ND.	15.00	50.00
n. Signature 12. ND.	15.00	50.00
o. Signature 13. ND.	15.00	50.00

704K 5000 Francs

	VF	UNC
1961-65; ND. Blue, brown and multicolor. Bearded man at left, building at center. Back: Woman, corn grinders and huts.		
b. Signature 1. 20.3.1961.	—	—
c. Signature 2. 20.3.1961.	90.00	—
d. Signature 3. 2.12.1964.	90.00	—
e. Signature 4. 2.3.1965.	75.00	—
h. Signature 6. ND.	55.00	—
i. Signature 7. ND.	75.00	—
j. Signature 8. ND.	—	—
k. Signature 9. ND.	75.00	—
l. Signature 10. ND.	75.00	—
m. Signature 11. ND.	55.00	200

1977-81; ND Issue

#705K-709K smaller size notes.

705K 500 Francs

	VF	UNC
1979-80. Lilac, light olive-green and multicolor. Artwork at left, long horn animals at center, man wearing hat at right. Back: Cultivated palm at left, aerial view at center, mask at right. Watermark: Woman in profile.		
a. Signature 12. 1979.	12.00	35.00
b. Signature 13. 1980.	12.00	30.00

706K 500 Francs

	VF	UNC
1981-90. Pale olive-green and multicolor. Artwork at left, long horn animals at center, man wearing hat at right. Back: Cultivated palm at left, aerial view at center, mask at right. Watermark: Woman in profile.		
a. Signature 14. 1988.	3.00	9.00
b. Signature 15. 1981 (BF).	15.00	35.00
c. Signature 15. 1981. (F-CO).	3.00	10.00
d. Signature 15. 1982. (BF).	4.00	12.00
e. Signature 17. 1981. (F-CO).	3.00	10.00
f. Signature 17. 1983. (BF).	4.00	12.00
g. Signature 18. 1984.	3.00	10.00
h. Signature 19. 1985.	3.00	10.00
i. Signature 20. 1986.	3.00	9.00
j. Signature 20. 1987.	3.00	9.00
k. Signature 21. (reversed order). 1989.	3.00	9.00
l. Signature 22. 1990.	3.00	9.00

Note: #706K w/10-digit small serial # were printed by Banque de France (BF) while those w/9-digit large serial # were printed by F-CO.

707K 1000 Francs

	VF	UNC
1981-90. Brown on multicolor underprint. Artwork at left, open pit mine at center, woman at right. Back: Wood carver with finished works. Watermark: Woman.		
a. Signature 14. 1988.	4.00	10.00
b. Signature 15. 1981.	4.00	14.00
c. Signature 17. 1981.	4.00	14.00
d. Signature 18. 1984.	4.00	14.00
e. Signature 19. 1984.	30.00	—
f. Signature 19. 1985.	4.00	12.00
g. Signature 20. 1986.	4.00	12.00
h. Signature 20. 1987.	4.00	12.00
i. Signature 21. 1989.	4.00	10.00
j. Signature 22. 1990.	4.00	10.00

708K 5000 Francs

1977-92. Black and red on multicolor underprint. Woman at left, fish and boats on shore at center, carving at right. Back: Carvings, fishing boats and mask.

	VF	UNC
a. Signature 12. 1978.	25.00	70.00
b. Signature 12. 1979.	35.00	100
c. Signature 13. 1980.	45.00	110
d. Signature 14. 1977.	25.00	70.00
e. Signature 14. 1989.	15.00	50.00
f. Signature 15. 1982.	45.00	110
g. Signature 16. 1983.	55.00	130
h. Signature 17. 1983.	25.00	65.00
i. Signature 18. 1984.	25.00	65.00
j. Signature 19. 1985.	60.00	—
k. Signature 20. 1986.	50.00	—
l. Signature 20. 1987.	15.00	40.00
m. Signature 21. 1990.	15.00	40.00
n. Signature 22. 1991.	15.00	40.00
o. Signature 22. 1992.	15.00	40.00
p. Signature 23. 1992.	15.00	40.00
q. Signature 24. 1992.	15.00	40.00

709K 10,000 Francs

ND. (1977-92). Red-brown on multicolor underprint. Two men seated operating primitive spinning apparatus, woman with headwear at right. Back: Figurine and girl at left, modern textile spinning machine at center. Watermark: Woman with headwear.

	VF	UNC
a. Signature 11. ND.	40.00	100
b. Signature 12. ND.	40.00	100
c. Signature 13. ND.	45.00	110
d. Signature 14. ND.	25.00	60.00
e. Signature 15. ND.	25.00	70.00
f. Signature 16. ND.	55.00	130
h. Signature 18. ND.	30.00	85.00
i. Signature 19. ND.	40.00	
j. Signature 20. ND.	25.00	65.00
k. Signature 21. ND.	20.00	60.00
l. Signature 22. ND.	20.00	60.00
m. Signature 23. ND.	20.00	60.00

1991-92 Issue

710K 500 Francs

(19)91-(20)02. Dark brown and dark green on multicolor underprint. Man at right, flood control dam at center. Back: Farmer riding spray rig behind garden tractor aat center, native art at left. Watermark: Man.

	VF	UNC
a. Signature 22. (19)91.	3.00	8.00
b. Signature 23. (19)92.	3.00	8.00
c. Signature 25. (19)93.	3.00	8.00
d. Signature 26. (19)94.	3.00	7.00
e. Signature 27. (19)95.	3.00	7.00
f. Signature 28. (19)96.	3.00	7.00
g. Signature 28. (19)97. 10-digit serial #.	3.00	7.00
h. Signature 28. (19)97. 11-digit serial #.	3.00	7.00
i. Signature 28. (19)98.	3.00	7.00
j. Signature 29. (19)99.	3.00	6.00
k. Signature 30. (20)00.	3.00	6.00
l. Signature 30. (20)01.	3.00	6.00
m. Signature 31. (20)02.	3.00	6.00

711K 1000 Francs

(19)91-(20)02. Dark brown-violet on tan, yellow and multicolor underprint. Workmen hauling peanuts to storage at center, woman's head at right. Back: Twin statues and mask at left, two women with baskets, elevated riverside storage bins in background at center. Watermark: Woman's head.

	VF	UNC
a. Signature 22. (19)91.	5.00	12.00
b. Signature 23. (19)92.	5.00	12.00
c. Signature 25. (19)93.	4.00	10.00
d. Signature 26. (19)94.	4.00	10.00
e. Signature 27. (19)95.	4.00	10.00
f. Signature 28. (19)96.	3.00	9.00
g. Signature 28. (19)97.	3.00	9.00
h. Signature 28. (19)98.	3.00	9.00

	VF	UNC
i. Signature 29. (19)99.	3.00	8.00
j. Signature 30. (20)00.	3.00	8.00
k. Signature 30. (20)01.	3.00	8.00
l. Signature 31. (20)02.	3.00	8.00
m. Signature 31. (20)03.	7.00	—

712K 2500 Francs

(19)92-(19)94. Deep purple and dark brown on lilac and multicolor underprint. Dam at center, young woman's head at right. Back: Statue at left, harvesting and spraying of fruit at left center. Watermark: Young woman's head.

	VF	UNC
a. Signature 23. (19)92.	8.00	20.00
b. Signature 25. (19)93.	8.00	20.00
c. Signature 27. (19)94.	8.00	20.00

713K 5000 Francs

(19)92-(20)02. Dark brown and deep blue on multicolor undorprint. Woman wearing headdress adorned with cowrie shells at right, smelting plant at center. Back: Women with children and various pottery at left center. Watermark: Woman wearing headdress adorned with cowrie shells.

	VF	UNC
a. Signature 23. (19)92.	9.00	30.00
b. Signature 25. (19)93.	9.00	30.00
c. Signature 27. (19)94.	9.00	25.00
d. Signature 27. (19)95.	9.00	25.00
e. Signature 28. (19)96.	—	25.00
f. Signature 28. (19)97.	9.00	25.00
g. Signature 28. (19)98.	9.00	25.00
h. Signature 29. (19)98.	9.00	25.00
i. Signature 29. (19)99.	9.00	25.00
j. Signature 30. (20)00.	8.00	20.00
k. Signature 30. (20)01.	8.00	20.00
l. Signature 31. (20)02.	9.00	25.00
m. Signature 31. (20)03.	8.00	20.00

714K 10,000 Francs

(19)92-(20)01. Dark brown on multicolor underprint. Headman with scepter at right, skyscraper at center. Back: Native art at left, woman crossing vine bridge over river at center. Watermark: Headman with scepter.

	VF	UNC
a. Signature 25. (19)92.	15.00	50.00
b. Signature 27. (19)94.	15.00	45.00
c. Signature 27. (19)95.	15.00	45.00
d. Signature 28. (19)96.	15.00	45.00
e. Signature 28. (19)97.	15.00	45.00
f. Signature 28. (19)98.	15.00	45.00
g. Signature 28. (19)98.	15.00	45.00
h. Signature 29. (19)99.	15.00	45.00
i. Signature 30. (20)00.	—	—
j. Signature 30. (20)01.	15.00	45.00

2003 Issue

715K 1000 Francs

(20)03-. Red-brown on red and multicolor underprint. 125x65mm.

	VF	UNC
a. Signature 32. (20)03.	FV	6.00
b. Signature 32. (20)04.	FV	6.00
c. Signature 33. (20)05.	FV	5.50
d. Signature 33. (20)06.	FV	5.50
e. Signature 34. (20)07.	FV	5.50
f. Signature 34. (20)08.	FV	5.50

	VF	UNC
g. Signature 35. (20)08.	FV	5.00
h. Signature 35. (20)09.	FV	5.00
i. Signature 37. (20)11.	FV	4.50
j. Signature 39. (20)12.	FV	4.00
k. Signature 40. (20)13.	FV	4.00
l. Signature 40. (20)14.	FV	3.50

716K 2000 Francs

(20)03-. Blue on light blue and multicolor underprint. 130x66mm.

	VF	UNC
a. Signature 32. (20)03.	FV	10.00
b. Signature 32. (20)04.	FV	10.00
c. Signature 33. (20)05.	FV	10.00
d. Signature 34. (20)07.	FV	8.00
e. Signature 38. (20)08.	FV	8.00
f. Signature 35. (20)09.	FV	7.50
g. Signature 35. (20)10.	FV	7.50
h. Signature 38. (20)11.	FV	7.50
i. Signature 39. (20)12.	FV	7.50
j. Signature 40. (20)13.	FV	7.00
k. Signature 40. (20)14.	FV	7.00

717K 5000 Francs

(20)03-. Multicolor. 141x74mm.

	VF	UNC
a. Signature 32. (20)03.	FV	20.00
b. Signature 32. (20)04.	FV	17.50
c. Signature 33. (20)05.	FV	17.50
d. Signature 33. (20)06.	FV	17.50
e. Signature 34. (20)07.	FV	17.50
f. Signature 34. (20)08.	FV	17.50
g. Signature 35. (20)09.	FV	17.00
h. Signature 36. (20)10.	FV	17.50
i. Signature 37. (20)11.	FV	16.00
j. Signature 39. (20)12.	FV	15.00
k. Signature 40. (20)13.	FV	15.00
l. Signature 40. (20)14.	FV	15.00

718K 10,000 Francs

(20)03-. Multicolor. 145x74mm.

	VF	UNC
a. Signature 32. (20)03.	FV	40.00
b. Signature 32. (20)04.	FV	35.00
c. Signature 33. (20)05.	FV	35.00
d. Signature 33. (20)06.	FV	35.00
e. Signature 34. (20)07.	FV	35.00
f. Signature 35. (20)08.	FV	35.00
g. Signature 35. (20)09.	FV	30.00
h. Signature 36. (20)10.	FV	28.00
i. Signature 37. (20)11.	FV	28.00
j. Signature 38. (20)11.	FV	28.00
k. Signature 39. (20)12.	FV	24.00
l. Signature 40. (20)13.	FV	24.00

(20)12-(20)14 Issue

719K 500 Francs

(20)12-(20)14. Brown, orange, multicolor. West African symbols. Back: Hippopotami. 125x65mm.

	VF	UNC
a. Signature 40. (20)12.	FV	4.00
b. Signature 40. (20)13.	FV	3.50
c. Signature 40. (20)14.	FV	3.00

T for Togo
1959-65; ND Issue

801T 100 Francs

1961-65; ND. Like #101A. Dark brown, orange and multicolor.

	VF	UNC
a. Engraved. Signature 1. 20.3.1961.	35.00	100
b. Signature 2. 20.3.1961.	25.00	70.00
c. Litho. Signature 2. 20.3.1961.	25.00	70.00
d. Signature 3. 2.12.1964.	30.00	85.00
e. Signature 4. 2.3.1965.	20.00	60.00
f. Signature 4. ND.	15.00	45.00
g. Signature 5. ND.	35.00	100

802T 500 Francs

1959-61; ND. Brown, green and multicolor. Field workers at left, mask carving at right. Like #102A. Back: Woman at left, farmer on tractor at right. Watermark: Woman's head.

	VF	UNC
a. Engraved. Signature 1. 15.4.1959.	75.00	—
b. Signature 1. 20.3.1961.	75.00	—
c. Signature 2. 20.3.1961.	75.00	—
f. Signature 5. ND.	85.00	—
g. Signature 6. ND.	30.00	80.00
i. Litho. Signature 7. ND.	50.00	130
j. Signature 8. ND.	50.00	—
k. Signature 9. ND.	20.00	60.00
l. Signature 10. ND.	—	—
m. Signature 11. ND.	10.00	35.00

803T 1000 Francs

1959-65; ND. Brown, blue and multicolor. Man and woman at center. Like #103A. Back: Man with rope suspension bridge in background and pineapples. Watermark: Man's head.

	VF	UNC
a. Engraved. Signature 1. 17.9.1959.	—	—
b. Signature 1. 20.3.1961.	60.00	—
c. Signature 2. 20.3.1961.	75.00	—
e. Signature 4. 2.3.1965.	60.00	—
f. Signature 5. ND.	30.00	80.00
g. Signature 6. ND.	70.00	—
h. Litho. Signature 6. ND.	80.00	—
i. Signature 7. ND.	30.00	80.00
j. Signature 8. ND.	90.00	—
k. Signature 9. ND.	20.00	55.00
l. Signature 10. ND.	15.00	45.00
m. Signature 11. ND.	12.00	40.00
n. Signature 12. ND.	12.00	40.00
o. Signature 13. ND.	15.00	45.00

804T 5000 Francs

1961; ND. Blue, brown and multicolor. Bearded man at left, building at center. Back: Woman, corn grinders and huts.

	VF	UNC
b. Signature 1. 20.3.1961.	125	300
h. Signature 6. ND.	75.00	250
i. Signature 7. ND.	125	—
j. Signature 8. ND.	125	—
k. Signature 9. ND.	65.00	200
m. Signature 11. ND.	50.00	175

1977-81; ND Issue

#805T-809T smaller size notes.

805T 500 Francs

1979. Lilac, light olive-green and multicolor. Artwork at left, long horn animals at center, man wearing hat at right. Back: Cultivated palm at left, aerial view at center, mask at right. Watermark: Woman in profile. Signature 12.

	VF	UNC
	12.00	30.00

806T 500 Francs

1981-90. Pale olive-green and multicolor. Artwork at left, long horn animals at center, man wearing hat at right. Back: Cultivated palm at left, aerial view at center, mask at right. Watermark: Woman in profile.

	VF	UNC
a. Signature 14. 1988.	15.00	—
b. Signature 15. 1981. (BF).	4.00	12.00
c. Signature 15. 1981. (F-CO).	4.00	12.00
d. Signature 15. 1982. (BF).	12.00	30.00
e. Signature 17. 1981. (F-CO).	12.00	30.00
f. Signature 18. 1984.	15.00	40.00
g. Signature 19. 1984.	4.00	12.00
h. Signature 19. 1985.	3.00	9.00
i. Signature 20. 1986.	3.00	9.00
j. Signature 20. 1987.	3.00	9.00
k. Signature 21. 1989.	3.00	9.00
l. Signature 22. 1990.	3.00	9.00

Note: #806T w/10-digit small serial # were printed by Banque de France (BF) while those w/9-digit large serial # were printed by F-CO.

807T 1000 Francs

1981-90. Brown on multicolor underprint. Artwork at left, open pit mine at center, woman at right. Back: Wood carver with finished works. Watermark: Woman.

	VF	UNC
a. Signature 14. 1988.	4.00	12.00
b. Signature 15. 1981.	5.00	15.00
c. Signature 17. 1981.	7.00	—
d. Signature 18. 1984.	4.00	12.00
e. Signature 19. 1984.	15.00	—
f. Signature 19. 1985.	4.00	12.00
g. Signature 20. 1986.	—	—
h. Signature 20. 1987.	4.00	10.00
i. Signature 21. 1989.	4.00	10.00
j. Signature 22. 1990.	4.00	10.00

808T 5000 Francs

1977-92. Black and red on multicolor underprint. Woman at left, fish and boats on shore at center, carving at right. Back: Carvings, fishing boats and mask.

	VF	UNC
a. Signature 12. 1978.	35.00	100
b. Signature 12. 1979.	35.00	100
c. Signature 14. 1977.	35.00	95.00
d. Signature 14. 1989.	10.00	40.00
e. Signature 15. 1981.	50.00	120
f. Signature 15. 1982.	50.00	120
g. Signature 17. 1983.	—	—
h. Signature 18. 1984.	30.00	75.00
i. Signature 20. 1987.	10.00	40.00

	VF	UNC
j. Signature 21. 1990.	10.00	40.00
k. Signature 22. 1991.	—	—
l. Signature 22. 1992.	10.00	40.00
m. Signature 23. 1992.	10.00	40.00
n. Signature 24. 1992.	20.00	50.00

809T 10,000 Francs

ND. (1977-92). Red-brown on multicolor underprint. Two men seated operating primitive spinning apparatus, woman with headwear at right. Back: Figurine and girl at left, modern textile spinning machine at center. Watermark: Woman with headwear.

	VF	UNC
a. Signature 11. ND.	40.00	110
b. Signature 12. ND.	—	—
c. Signature 13. ND.	—	—
d. Signature 14. ND.	65.00	—
e. Signature 15. ND.	30.00	80.00
f. Signature 16. ND.	55.00	125
h. Signature 18. ND.	30.00	80.00
k. Signature 22. ND.	25.00	65.00
l. Signature 23. ND.	25.00	65.00

1991-92 Issue

810T 500 Francs

(19)91-(20)02. Dark brown and dark green on multicolor underprint. Man at right, flood control dam at center. Back: Farmer riding spray rig behind garden tractor at center, native art at left. Watermark: Man.

	VF	UNC
a. Signature 22. (19)91.	3.00	8.00
b. Signature 23. (19)92.	—	—
c. Signature 25. (19)93.	3.00	8.00
d. Signature 26. (19)94.	3.00	7.00
e. Signature 27. (19)95.	3.00	7.00
f. Signature 28. (19)96.	3.00	7.00
g. Signature 28. (19)97. 10-digit serial #.	3.00	7.00
h. Signature 28. (19)97. 11-digit serial #.	3.00	7.00
i. Signature 28. (19)98.	3.00	7.00
j. Signature 29. (19)99.	3.00	7.00
k. Signature 30. (20)00.	3.00	6.00
l. Signature 30. (20)01.	3.00	6.00
m. Signature 31. (20)02.	3.00	6.00

811T　1000 Francs
(19)91-(20)02. Dark brown-violet on tan, yellow and multicolor underprint. Workmen hauling peanuts to storage at center, woman's head at right. Back: Twin statues and mask at left, two women with baskets, elevated riverside storage bins in background at center. Watermark: Woman's head.

	VF	UNC
a. Signature 22. (19)91.	5.00	12.00
b. Signature 23. (19)92.	12.00	—
c. Signature 25. (19)93.	5.00	10.00
d. Signature 26. (19)94.	5.00	10.00
e. Signature 27. (19)95.	4.00	9.00
f. Signature 28. (19)96.	4.00	9.00
g. Signature 28. (19)97.	4.00	9.00
h. Signature 28. (19)98.	4.00	9.00
i. Signature 29. (19)99.	4.00	8.00
j. Signature 30. (20)00.	4.00	8.00
k. Signature 30. (20)01.	4.00	8.00
l. Signature 31. (20)02.	4.00	8.00
m. Signature 31. (20)03.	4.00	8.00

812T　2500 Francs
(19)92-(19)94. Deep purple and dark brown on lilac and multicolor underprint. Dam at center, young woman's head at right. Back: Statue at left, harvesting and spraying of fruit at left center. Watermark: Young woman's head.

	VF	UNC
a. Signature 23. (19)92.	8.00	20.00
b. Signature 25. (19)93.	8.00	20.00
c. Signature 27. (19)94.	8.00	20.00

813T　5000 Francs
(19)92-(20)02. Dark brown and deep blue on multicolor underprint. Woman wearing headdress adorned with cowrie shells at right, smelting plant at center. Back: Women with children and various pottery at left center. Watermark: Woman wearing headdress adorned with cowrie shells.

	VF	UNC
a. Signature 23. (19)92.	9.00	30.00
b. Signature 25. (19)93.	9.00	30.00
c. Signature 27. (19)94.	9.00	25.00
d. Signature 27. (19)95.	9.00	25.00
e. Signature 28. (19)97.	—	—
f. Signature 28. (19)98.	—	—
g. Signature 29. (19)98.	9.00	25.00
h. Signature 29. (19)99.	9.00	25.00
i. Signature 30. (20)00.	9.00	25.00
j. Signature 30. (20)01.	8.00	20.00
k. Signature 31. (20)02.	8.00	20.00
l. Signature 31. (20)03.	—	—

814T　10,000 Francs
(19)92-(20)01. Dark brown on multicolor underprint. Headman with scepter at right, skyscraper at center. Back: Native art at left, woman crossing vine bridge over river at center. Watermark: Headman with scepter.

	VF	UNC
a. Signature 25. (19)92.	15.00	50.00
b. Signature 27. (19)94.	15.00	45.00
c. Signature 27. (19)95.	15.00	45.00
d. Signature 28. (19)96.	15.00	45.00
e. Signature 28. (19)97.	15.00	45.00
f. Signature 28. (19)98.	—	0.00
g. Signature 29. (19)98.	15.00	45.00
h. Signature 29. (19)99.	15.00	45.00
i. Signature 30. (20)00.	15.00	45.00
j. Signature 30. (20)01.	15.00	45.00

2003 Issue

815T　1000 Francs
(20)03-. . Red-brown on red and multicolor underprint.

	VF	UNC
a. Signature 32. (20)03.	FV	6.00
b. Signature 32. (20)04.	FV	6.00
c. Signature 35. (20)08.	FV	5.00
d. Signature 35. (20)09.	FV	5.00
e. Signature 36. (20)10.	FV	4.50
f. Signature 37. (20)11.	FV	4.50
g. Signature 39. (20)12.	FV	4.00
h. Signature 40. (20)13.	FV	4.00
i. Signature 40. (20)14.	FV	3.50

816T　2000 Francs
(20)03-. Blue on light blue and multicolor underprint.

	VF	UNC
a. Signature 32. (20)03.	FV	10.00
b. Signature 32. (20)04.	FV	10.00
c. Signature 34. (20)07	FV	8.00
d. Signature 38. (20)11	FV	7.50
e. Signature 39. (20)12	FV	7.50
f. Signature 40. (20)13	FV	7.00

817T　5000 Francs
(20)03-. Multicolor.

	VF	UNC
a. Signature 32. (20)03.	FV	20.00
b. Signature 32. (20)04.	FV	17.50
c. Signature 33. (20)05.	FV	17.50
d. Signature 33. (20)06.	FV	17.50
e. Signature 34. (20)07.	FV	17.00
f. Signature 35. (20)09.	FV	17.50
g. Signature 36. (20)10.	FV	16.00
h. Signature 37. (20)11.	FV	15.00
i. Signature 39. (20)12.	FV	15.00
j. Signature 40. (20)13.	FV	15.00
k. Signature 40. (20)14.	FV	15.00

818T　10,000 Francs
(20)03-. Multicolor.

	VF	UNC
a. Signature 32. (20)03.	FV	40.00
b. Signature 32. (20)04.	FV	35.00
c. Signature 33. (20)05.	FV	35.00
d. Signature 33. (20)06.	FV	35.00
e. Signature 34. (20)07.	FV	35.00
f. Signature 35. (20)09.	FV	30.00
g. Signature 36. (20)10.	FV	28.00
h. Signature 37. (20)11.	FV	28.00
i. Signature 39. (20)12.	FV	24.00
j. Signature 40. (20)14.	FV	24.00

(20)12-(20)14 Issue

819T　500 Francs
(20)12-(20)14. Brown, orange, multicolor. West African symbols. Back: Hippopotami. 125x65mm.

	VF	UNC
a. Signature 40. (20)12.	FV	4.00
b. Signature 40. (20)13.	FV	3.50
c. Signature 40. (20)14.	FV	3.00

S for Guinea-Bissau

1997 Issue

910S　500 Francs
(19)97-(19)99. Dark brown and dark green on multicolor underprint. Man at right, flood control dam at center. Back: Farmer riding spray rig behind garden tractor at center, native art at left. Watermark: Man.

	VF	UNC
a. Signature 28. (19)97. 10-digit.	3.00	7.00
b. Signature 28. (19)97. 11-digit.	9.00	20.00
c. Signature 28. (19)98.	3.00	7.00
d. Signature 29. (19)99.	10.00	30.00
e. Signature 30. (20)00.	—	—
g. Signature 31. (20)02.	10.00	30.00

911S　1000 Francs
(19)97-(19)99. Dark brown-violet on tan, yellow and multicolor underprint. Workmen hauling peanuts to storage at center, woman's head at right. Back: Twin statues and mask at left, two women with baskets, elevated riverside storage bins in background at center. Watermark: Woman's head.

	VF	UNC
a. Signature 28. (19)97.	4.00	10.00

		VF	UNC
b. Signature 28. (19)98.		4.00	10.00
c. Signature 29. (19)99.		4.00	10.00
e. Signature 30. (20)01.		—	—
f. Signature 31. (20)02.		4.00	10.00

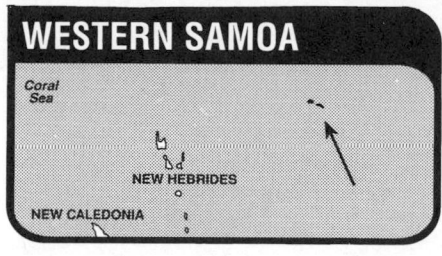

913S 5000 Francs   VF UNC
(19)97-(20)00. Dark brown and deep blue on multicolor underprint. Woman wearing headdress adorned with caowrie shells at right, smelting plant at center. Back: Women with children and various pottery at left center. Watermark: Woman wearing headdress adorned with cowrie shells.

		VF	UNC
a. Signature 28. (19)97.		9.00	30.00
b. Signature 28. (19)98.		9.00	30.00
c. Signature 29. (19)98.		—	—
d. Signature 29. (19)99.		9.00	30.00
e. Signature 30. (20)00.		25.00	45.00
g. Signature 31. (20)02.		8.00	25.00
h. Signature 31. (20)03.		—	—

914S 10,000 Francs   VF UNC
(19)97-(19)98. Dark brown on multicolor underprint. Headman with scepter at right, skyscraper at center. Back: Native art at left, woman crossing vine bridge over river at center. Watermark: Headman with scepter.

		VF	UNC
a. Signature 28. (19)97.		15.00	50.00
b. Signature 28. (19)98.		—	—
c. Signature 29. (19)98.		30.00	65.00
d. Signature 29. (19)99.		—	—
e. Signature 30. (20)00.		—	—

2003 Issue

915S 1000 Francs   VF UNC
(20)03-. Red-brown on red and multicolor underprint. 125x65mm.

		VF	UNC
a. Signature 32. (20)03.		FV	6.00
b. Signature 32. (20)04.		FV	6.00
c. Signature 35. (20)08.		FV	5.00
d. Signature 35. (20)09.		FV	5.00
e. Signature 37. (20)11.		FV	4.50
f. Signature 39. (20)12.		FV	4.00

916S 2000 Francs   VF UNC
(20)03-. Blue on light blue and multicolor underprint. 130x66mm.

		VF	UNC
a. Signature 32. (20)03.		FV	10.00
b. Signature 32. (20)04.		FV	10.00
c. Signature 38. (20)11.		FV	7.50
d. Signature 39. (20)12.		FV	7.50

917S 5000 Francs   VF UNC
(20)03-. Multicolor. 141x74mm.

		VF	UNC
a. Signature 32. (20)03.		FV	20.00
b. Signature 32. (20)04.		FV	17.50
c. Signature 35. (20)09.		FV	17.00
d. Signature 37. (20)11.		FV	16.00
e. Signature 39. (20)12.		FV	15.00

918S 10,000 Francs   VF UNC
(20)03- Multicolor. 145x74mm.

		VF	UNC
a. Signature 32. (20)03.		FV	40.00
b. Signature 32. (20)04.		FV	35.00
c. Signature 33. (20)05.		FV	35.00
d. Signature 33. (20)06.		FV	35.00
e. Signature 35. (20)08.		FV	30.00
f. Signature 35. (20)09.		FV	30.00
g. Signature 36. (20)10.		FV	28.00
h. Signature 37. (20)11.		FV	28.00
i. Signature 39. (20)12.		FV	24.00

(20)12-(20)14 Issue

919S 500 Francs   VF UNC
(20)12-(20)14. Brown, orange, multicolor. West African symbols. Back: Hippopotami. 125x65mm.

		VF	UNC
a. Signature 40. (20)12.		FV	4.00
b. Signature 40. (20)13.		FV	3.50

WESTERN SAMOA

The Independent State of Western Samoa (formerly German Samoa), located in the Pacific Ocean 1,600 miles (2,574 km.) northeast of New Zealand, has an area of 1,097 sq. mi. (2,860 sq. km.) and a population of 157,000. Capital: Apia. The economy is based on agriculture, fishing and tourism. Copra, cocoa and bananas are exported. The Samoan group of islands was discovered by Dutch navigator Jacob Roggeveen in 1772. Great Britain, the United States and Germany established consular representation at Apia in 1847, 1853 and 1861 respectively. The conflicting interests of the three powers produced the Berlin agreement of 1889 which declared Samoa neutral and had the effect of establishing a tripartite protectorate over the islands. A further agreement, 1899, recognized the rights of the United States in those islands east of 171 deg. west longitude (American Samoa) and of Germany in the other islands (Western Samoa). New Zealand occupied Western Samoa at the start of World War I and administered it as a League of Nations mandate and U.N. trusteeship until Jan. 1, 1962, when it became an independent state. Western Samoa is a member of the Commonwealth of Nations. The Chief Executive is Chief of State. The prime minister is the Head of Government. The present Head of State, Malietoa Tanumafili II, holds his position for life. Future Heads of State will be elected by the Legislature Assembly for five-year terms.

RULERS:
British, 1914-1962
Malietoa Tanumafili II, 1962-2007

MONETARY SYSTEM:
1 Shilling = 12 Pence
1 Pound = 20 Shillings to 1967
1 Tala = 100 Sene, 1967-

NEW ZEALAND ADMINISTRATION

Territory of Western Samoa

1920-22 Treasury Note Issue

By Authority of New Zealand Government Note: Some of these hand stamped dated notes may appear to be ND, probably through error or that the date has faded, been washed out or worn off.

7   10 Shillings   VF UNC
1922-59. Black on brown and green underprint. Palm trees along beach at center. Signature varieties. Printer: BWC.

		VF	UNC
a. 3.3.1922.		—	—
b. Signature title: *MINISTER OF EXTERNAL AFFAIRS FOR NEW ZEALAND* at left. 13.4.1938-21.11.1949.		175	650
c. Signature title: *MINISTER OF ISLAND TERRITORIES FOR NEW ZEALAND* at left. 24.5.1951-27.5.1958; 29.10.1959.		250	750
d. Signature title: *HIGH COMMISSIONER* at left. 20.3.1957-22.12.1959.		150	600

8A   1 Pound   VF UNC
1948-61. Purple on multicolor underprint. Hut, palm trees at center. Like #8 but *STERLING* omitted from center. Signature varieties. Printer: BWC.

		VF	UNC
a. Signature title: *MINISTER OF ISLAND TERRITORIES FOR NEW ZEALAND* at left. 6.8.1948-7.8.1958.		450	—
b. Signature title: *HIGH COMMISSIONER* at left. 20.4.1959; 10.12.1959; 1.5.1961.		250	1,600

Bank of Western Samoa

1960-61 Provisional Issue

#10-12 red overprint: *Bank of Western Samoa / Legal Tender in Western Samoa by virtue of the Bank of Western Samoa Ordinance 1959* **on older notes.**

10	**10 Shillings**		**VF**	**UNC**

1960-61; ND. Black on brown and green underprint. Palm trees along beach at center. Signature varieties.

	a. Signature title: *HIGH COMMISSIONER* blocked out at lower left, with *MINISTER OF FINANCE* below. 8.12.1960; 1.5.1961.	150	550
	b. ND. signature title: *MINISTER OF FINANCE* in plate without overprint., at lower left	150	550

11	**1 Pound**	**VF**	**UNC**

1960-61. Purple on multicolor underprint. Hut, palm trees at center. *STERLING* directly appears close beneath spelled out denomination at center. Signature varieties.

	a. Signature title: *HIGH COMMISSIONER* blocked out at lower left, with *MINISTER OF FINANCE* below. 8.11.1960; 1.5.1961.	500	1,500
	b. Signature title: *MINISTER OF FINANCE* in plate without overprint., at lower left 1.5.1961.	400	1,450

12	**5 Pounds**	**VF**	**UNC**

1.5.1961. Purple on multicolor underprint. Boat at lower center. *STERLING* omitted from center. Signature varieties. | 2,000 | 7,500 |

STATE

Fale Tupe o Samoa I Sisifo

BANK OF WESTERN SAMOA
1963 ND Issue

13	**10 Shillings**		**VF**	**UNC**

ND (1963). Dark green on multicolor underprint. Arms at left, boat at right. Back: Hut and two palms at center.

	a. Issued note.	10.00	65.00
	s. Specimen.	—	50.00

14	**1 Pound**		**VF**	**UNC**

ND (1963). Blue on multicolor underprint. Palms and rising sun at left and right, arms at center. Back: Small Building and lagoon at center. 159x83mm.

	a. Issued note.	20.00	100
	s. Specimen.	—	50.00

15	**5 Pounds**		**VF**	**UNC**

ND (1963). Brown on multicolor underprint. Rava bowl at left, red and blue flag over arms at right. Back: Shoreline with trees, sea and islands. 166x89mm.

	a. Issued note.	50.00	200
	s. Specimen.	—	200

1967 ND Issue

Tala System.

SIGNATURE VARIETIES			
1	*signature* MANAGER	2	*signature* MANAGER
3	*signature* MANAGER	4	*signature* SENIOR MANAGER

16	**1 Tala**		**VF**	**UNC**

ND (1967). Dark green on multicolor underprint. Arms at left, boat at right. Signature varieties. Back: Hut and two palms at center. Watermark: BWS repeated.

	a. Signature 1.	8.00	55.00
	b. Signature 2.	7.00	45.00
	c. Signature 3.	7.00	35.00
	d. Signature 4.	8.00	40.00
	s. Signature as a, b, d. Specimen.	—	40.00

17   2 Tala   VF   UNC

ND (1967). Blue on multicolor underprint. Palms and rising sun at left and right, arms at center. Signature varieties. Watermark: BWS repeated. 144x77mm.

    a. Signature 1.   7.50   45.00
    b. Signature 3.   5.00   40.00
    c. Signature 4.   8.00   50.00
    s. Signature as a, c. Specimen.   —   50.00

18   10 Tala   VF   UNC

ND (1967). Brown on multicolor underprint. Tava bowl at left, red and blue flag over arms at right. Back: Shoreline with trees, sea and islands. Watermark: BWS repeated. 150x76mm.

    a. Signature 1.   75.00   300
    b. Signature 2.   90.00   350
    c. Signature 3.   30.00   150
    d. Signature 4.   35.00   165
    s. Signature as a, b, d. Specimen.   —   60.00

Komiti Faatino o Tupe a Samoa I Sisifo

MONETARY BOARD OF WESTERN SAMOA
1980-84 ND Issue

19   1 Tala   VF   UNC

ND (1980). Dark green on multicolor underprint. Two weavers at right, national flag at left center. Back: Two fishermen in canoe at left center, arms at lower center, national flag at center right. Watermark: M. Tanumafili II.   2.00   10.00

20   2 Tala   VF   UNC

ND (1980). Deep blue-violet on multicolor underprint. Woodcarver at right, national flag at left center. Back: Hut with palms on small island at left center, arms at lower center, national flag at center right. Watermark: M. Tanumafili II.   3.00   15.00

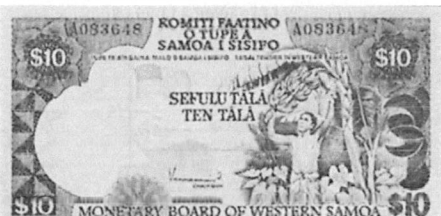

21   5 Tala   VF   UNC

ND (1980). Red on multicolor underprint. Child writing at right, national flag at left   7.00   27.50
center. Back: Small port city at left center, arms at lower center, national flag at center right. Watermark: M. Tanumafili II.

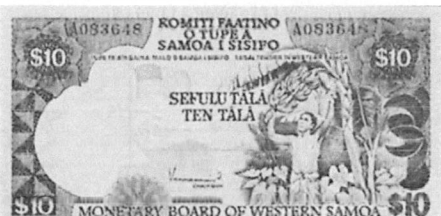

22   10 Tala   VF   UNC

ND (1980). Dark brown and purple on multicolor underprint. Man picking bananas   50.00   150
at right, national flag at left center. Back: Shoreline landscape, arms at lower center, national flag at center right. Watermark: M. Tanumafili II.

23   20 Tala   VF   UNC

ND (1984). Brown and orange-brown on multicolor underprint. Fishermen with   90.00   350
net at right, national flag at left center. Back: Arms at lower center, national flag at center right, round building at left. Watermark: M. Tanumafili II.

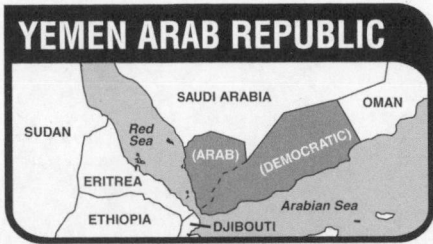

YEMEN ARAB REPUBLIC

The Yemen Arab Republic, located in the southwestern corner of the Arabian Peninsula, has an area of 75,290 sq. mi. (195,000 sq. km.) and a population of 18.12 million. Capital: San'a. The industries of Yemen, one of the world's poorest countries, are agriculture and local handicrafts. Qat (a mildly narcotic leaf), coffee, cotton and rock salt are exported. One of the oldest centers of civilization in the Near East, Yemen was once part of the Minaean Kingdom and of the ancient Kingdom of Sheba, after which it was captured successively by Egyptians, Ethiopians and Romans. It was converted to the Moslem religion in 628 AD and administered as a caliphate until 1538, when it came under Turkish occupation which was maintained until 1918 when autonomy was achieved through revolution. On Feb. 1, 1958, Egypt and Syria formed the United Arab Republic. Yemen joined on March 8 in an association known as the United Arab States. Syria withdrew from the United Arab Republic on Sept. 29, 1961, and on Dec. 26 Egypt dissolved its ties with Yemen in the United Arab States. Provoked by the harsh rule of Imam Mohammed al-Badr, last ruler of the Kingdom of Mutawwakkilite, the National Liberation Front seized control of the government on Sept. 27, 1962. Badr fled to Saudi Arabia. An agreement for a constitution for a unified state was reached in Dec. 1989 uniting the Yemen Arab Republic with the People's Democratic Republic of Yemen into the Republic of Yemen on May 22, 1990. Both currencies circulated for a number of years, but the PDR dinar lost legal tender status on June 11, 1996.

RULERS:
Imam Ahmad, AH1367-1382/1948-1962AD
Imam al-Badr, AH1382-1388/1962-1968AD

MONETARY SYSTEM:
1 Rial = 40 Buqshas
1 Rial = 100 Fils (from April 1, 1995).

SIGNATURE VARIETIES

	Minister of the Treasury		Minister of the Treasury and Economy
1	*(signature)* Abdul Ghani Ali, 1964	**2**	*(signature)* Abdul Ghani Ali, 1967
	Minister of the Treasury		Minister of the Treasury
3	*(signature)* Ahmad al-Ruhumi, 1966 (actually inverted)	**4**	*(signature)* Ahmad Abdu Said, 1968
	Governor & Chairman, CBY		Governor & Chairman, CBY
5	*(signature)* Abdul Aziz Abdul Ghani, 1971 - 85	**6**	*(signature)* Abdulla Mohamed al-Sanabani, 1978 - 85
	Governor & Chairman, CBY		Governor, CBY
7	*(signature)* Abdulla Mohamed al-Sanabani, 1978 - 85	**8**	*(signature)* Muhammad Ahmad Gunaid, 1985 - 94
	Governor, CBY		Governor, CBY
9	*(signature)* Aluwi Salih al-Salami, 1994	**10**	*(signature)* Ahed Adbul Rahman al-Samani, 1997

ARAB REPUBLIC

Yemen Currency Board
1964 ND Issue

1 1 Rial VF UNC
ND (1964; 1967). Green on multicolor underprint. Arms at left. Back: Houses in Sana'a with minaret at center. Watermark: Arms.
a. Signature 1. (1964).	20.00	110
b. Signature 2. (1967).	25.00	135
s. As a. Specimen.	—	225

2 5 Rials VF UNC
ND (1964; 1967). Red on multicolor underprint. Arms at left. Back: Lion of Timna sculpture at right. Watermark: Arms.
a. Signature 1. (1964).	65.00	275
b. Signature 2. (1967).	75.00	300
s. As a. Specimen.	—	300

3 10 Rials VF UNC
ND (1964; 1967). Blue-green on multicolor underprint. Arms at left. Back: Dam at right. Watermark: Arms.
a. Signature 1. (1964).	90.00	375
b. Signature 2. (1967).	90.00	375
s. As a. Specimen.	—	300

1966-71 ND Issue

4 10 Buqshas VF UNC
ND (1966). Brown on multicolor underprint. Lion of Timna sculpture at left. Signature 3. Back: Ancient dedication stone from a temple at Ma'rib at right. Watermark: Arms.
	4.00	25.00

5 20 Buqshas VF UNC
ND (1966). Green on multicolor underprint. Tall alabaster head at left. Signature 3. Back: Ruins of the Bara'an temple at right. Watermark: Arms.
	5.00	35.00

6   1 Rial   **VF   UNC**

ND (1969). Green on multicolor underprint. Alabaster head at left. Signature 4.
Back: Houses in Sana'a with minaret at center. Watermark: Arms.

    a. Issued note.   15.00   75.00
    s. Specimen.   —   175

7   5 Rials   **VF   UNC**

ND (1969). Red on multicolor underprint. Bronze lion's head sculpture at left.
Signature 4. Back: Lion of Timna sculpture at right. Watermark: Arms.

    a. Issued note.   35.00   180
    s. Specimen.   —   250

8   10 Rials   **VF   UNC**

ND (1969). Blue-green on multicolor underprint. Shadhili Mosque at left. Signature
4. Back: Dam at right. Watermark: Arms.

    a. Issued note.   20.00   130
    s. Specimen.   —   250

9   20 Rials   **VF   UNC**

ND (1971). Purple and blue-green on multicolor underprint. Palace on the rock at
Wadi Dahr. Signature 4. Back: City view of Sana'a. Watermark: Arms.

    a. Issued note.   25.00   160
    s. Specimen.   —   —

10   50 Rials   **VF   UNC**

ND (1971). Dark olive-green on multicolor underprint. Crossed *jambiyas* (daggers)   20.00   140
at left. Signature 4. Back: Coffee branch and tree, mountains in background at
center right. Watermark: Arms.

Central Bank of Yemen
1973-77 ND Issues

11   1 Rial   **VF   UNC**

ND (1973). Green on multicolor underprint. Al Baqiliyah Mosque at left. Back:
Coffee plants with mountains in background at center. Watermark: Arms.

    a. Signature 5.   0.50   2.50
    b. Signature 7.   2.50   10.00
    s. Specimen.   —   —
    ct. Color trial.   —   —

See also 16B as these two types are often confused.

12   5 Rials   **VF   UNC**

ND (1973). Red on multicolor underprint. Buildings in Wadi Du'an at left. Signature
5. Back: Beit al Midie on high rock hill at center. Watermark: Arms.

    a. Issued note.   5.00   17.50
    s. Specimen.   —   —

13   10 Rials   **VF   UNC**

ND (1973). Blue-green on multicolor underprint. Bronze head of King Dhamer Ali
at left. Back: Republican Palace in Sana'a at center. Watermark: Arms.

    a. Signature 5.   5.00   20.00
    b. Signature 7.   4.00   16.00
    s. Specimen.   —   —
    ct. Color trial.   —   —

14 20 Rials

	VF	UNC

ND (1973). Purple on multicolor underprint. Marble sculpture of seated figure with grapes at left. Signature 5. Back: Terraced slopes along mountain at center right. Watermark: Arms. 145x75mm.

		VF	UNC
a. Issued note.		7.50	25.00
ct. Color trial.		—	—

15 50 Rials

	VF	UNC

ND (1973). Dark olive-green on multicolor underprint. Bronze statue of Ma'adkarib at left. Back: Bab al Yemen (main gate of Sana'a). Watermark: Arms. 150x75mm.

	VF	UNC
a. Signature 5.	5.00	20.00
b. Signature 7.	3.00	10.00
s. Specimen.	—	—

16 100 Rials

	VF	UNC

ND (1976). Red-violet on multicolor underprint. Marble sculpture of cherub and griffin at left. Signature 5. Back: View of Ta'izz. Watermark: Arms. 150x75mm.

	VF	UNC
a. Issued note.	20.00	75.00
s. Specimen.	—	—

1979-85 ND Issues

16B 1 Rial

	VF	UNC

ND (1983). The rays in all four guilloches are much more pronounced in this note than in P#11, a note with which this is often confused. Darker green on multicolor underprint. Al Baqiliyah Mosque at left. Smaller serial number. Signature 7. Back: Coffee plants with mountains in background at center. Clearer underprint design over watermark area Watermark: Arms.

	VF	UNC
	0.50	1.25

17 5 Rials

	VF	UNC

ND (1981). Red on orange and multicolor underprint. Dhahr al Dahab at left. Back: Fortress Qal'at al Qahira overlooking Ta'izz at center right. Watermark: Arms.

		VF	UNC
a. Signature 5. (1981).		1.00	5.00
b. Signature 7. (1983).		0.75	5.00
c. Signature 8. (1991).		0.40	2.00

18 10 Rials

	VF	UNC

ND (1981). Blue on green and multicolor underprint. Village of Thulla at left. Back: Al Baqiliyah Mosque. Watermark: Arms.

		VF	UNC
a. Signature 5. (1981).		3.00	15.00
b. Signature 7. (1983).		2.50	10.00

19 20 Rials

	VF	UNC

ND (1985). Purple on multicolor underprint. Marble sculpture of seated figure with grapes at left. Signature 5. Back: View of San'a. Watermark: Arms. 145x75mm.

		VF	UNC
a. Bank title on tan underprint. on back. Signature 7. (1983). 4mm serial #.		7.50	25.00
b. As a. Signature 8. 3mm serial #.		5.00	20.00
c. Bank title on light brown underprint of vertical lines on back. Signature 8.		2.00	10.00
s. Specimen.		—	—

#20 renumbered, see #26.

21 100 Rials

	VF	UNC

ND (1979). Red-violet on multicolor underprint. Al Ashrafiya Mosque and Ta'izz city view at left. Signature 6. Back: View of San'a with mountains. Watermark: Arms. 150x75mm.

	VF	UNC
	5.00	25.00

21A   100 Rials   **VF   UNC**
ND (1984). Red-violet on multicolor underprint. Marble sculpture of cherub and
griffin at left. Signature 7. Back: Central Bank of Yemen building at center right.
Watermark: Arms. 150x75mm.
   a. Issued note.   2.50   10.00
   s. Specimen.   —   —

1990-97 ND Issues

23   10 Rials   **VF   UNC**
ND (1990-). Blue and black on multicolor underprint. Al Baqilyah Mosque at left. Signature 8. Back: Ma'rib Dam at center right, *10* at upper corners. Watermark: Arms.
   a. Watermark: Arms have flags with a star at the center.   FV   3.00
   b. Watermark: Arms have flags without star at center.   FV   3.00

24   10 Rials   **VF   UNC**
ND (ca.1992). lue and black on multicolor underprint. Al Baqilyah Mosque at left.   FV   3.00
Signature 8. *10* at upper left and lower right. Back: Ma'rib Dam at center right, *10*
at upper corners with Arabic text: *Sadd Marib* near lowe Watermark: Arms.

25   20 Rials   **VF   UNC**
ND (1995). Dark brown on multicolor underprint. Arch ends straight border across   FV   4.00
upper center Marble sculpture of cupid with grapes at left. Signature 8. Back:
Coastal view of Aden, dhow. Watermark: Arms. 145x75mm.

26   20 Rials   **VF   UNC**
ND (1990). Dark brown on multicolor underprint. Arch ends straight border across
upper center Marble sculpture of cupid with grapes at left. Signature 8. Back:
Different city view of San'a without minarets or dhow at center right. Watermark:
Arms. 145x75mm.
   a. Without shading around title of the bank.   3.00   10.00
   b. With shading around title of the bank.   2.00   3.00

27   50 Rials   **VF   UNC**
ND (1993). Black and deep olive-brown on multicolor underprint. Bronze statue   FV   4.50
of Ma'adkarib at left. Signature 8. Back: Shibam city view at center right. Without
Arabic title at lower left. Watermark: Arms. 150x75mm.

27A   50 Rials   **VF   UNC**
ND (199?). Black and deep olive-brown on multicolor underprint. Bronze statue   FV   4.00
of Ma'adkarib at left. Signature 8, 9. Back: Shibam city view at center right with
Arabic title *Shibam Hadramaut* at lower left. Watermark: Arms. 150x75mm.

28   100 Rials   **VF   UNC**
ND (1993). Violet, purple and black on multicolor underprint. Ancient culvert   FV   3.00
in Aden at left. Signature 8, 9. Back: City view of Sana'a. Watermark: Arms.
150x75mm.

29 200 Rials   **VF UNC**
ND (1996). Deep blue-green on multicolor underprint. Alabaster sculpture of a   FV   8.00
man at left. Signature 9. Back: Harbor view of Mukalla at center right. Watermark:
Arms. 155x75mm.

30 500 Rials   **VF UNC**
ND (1997). Blue-violet and red-brown on multicolor underprint. Central Bank of   FV   16.00
Yemen building at left. Signature 9. Back: Bara'an temple ruins in brown at right.
Watermark: Arms. 155x80mm.

1998-2001 ND Issues

31 500 Rials   **VF UNC**
AH1422/2001. Light blue and gray on beige and multicolor underprint. Palace on   FV   11.00
the Rock at left. Holographic strip with arms repeated at left. Signature 10. Back:
Al Muhdar mosque in Tarim, Hadramaut at center. Watermark: Arms. 155x80mm.

32 1000 Rials   **VF UNC**
ND (1998). Pink and dark green on multicolor underprint. Sultan's palace in Sei-   FV   30.00
yun, Hadramaut at center. Holographic strip with arms repeated at left. Signature
10. Back: Bab al-Yemen and old city of Sana'a. 157x85mm.

2004 Issue

33 1000 Rials   **VF UNC**
2004/AH1424; 2006/AH1426. Brown and dark green on multicolor underprint.
Sultan's palace in Seiym at left. Color changes and date on front at lower right.
Back: Bab al Yemen (main gate of Sana'a). Watermark: Arms. 155x85mm.
     a. 2004/AH1424.   FV   25.00
     b. 2006/AH1426.   FV   25.00

2007 Issue

34 500 Rials   **VF UNC**
2007. Light blue and grey on beige and multicolor underprint. Palace on the Rock   FV   12.00
at left. Holographic strip at left with irregular edge. Back: Al Muhdar Mosque in
Tarim Hadramaut at center. Arms. 155x80mm.

2009 Issue

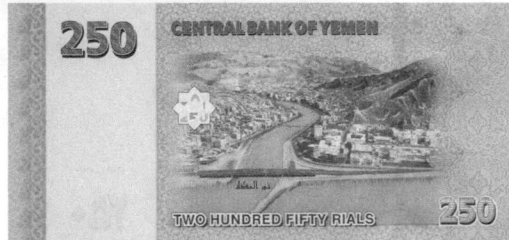

35   250 Rials   **VF   UNC**
2009/AH1430. Tan on blue and multicolor underprint. Al Saleh Mosque in Sana'a   FV   6.00
at center. Back: Mukalla Khor waterway. 155x75mm.

36   1000 Rials   **VF   UNC**
2009/AH1430. Green on multicolor underprint. Castle of Sayoun. Back: View of
old Sana'a.
    a. 2009/AH1430.   FV   10.00
    b. 2012/AH1433.   FV   10.00

The People's Democratic Republic of Yemen, (formerly the Peoples Republic of Southern Yemen) was located on the southern coast of the Arabian Peninsula. It had an area of 128,560 sq. mi. (332,968 sq. km.). Capital: Aden. It consisted of the port city of Aden, 17 states of the former South Arabian Federation, 3 small sheikhdoms, 3 large sultanates, Quaiti, Kathiri and Mahri, which made up the Eastern Aden Protectorate, and Socotra, the largest island in the Arabian Sea. The port of Aden is the area's most valuable natural resource. Cotton, fish, coffee and hides are exported. Between 1200 BC and the 6th century AD, what is now the People's Democratic Republic of Yemen was part of the Minaean kingdom. In subsequent years it was controlled by Persians, Egyptians and Turks. Aden, one of the cities mentioned in the Bible, had been a port for trade between the East and West for 2,000 years. British rule began in 1839 when the British East India Co. seized control to put an end to the piracy threatening trade with India. To protect their foothold in Aden, the British found it necessary to extend their control into the area known historically as the Hadramaut, and to sign protection treaties with the sheikhs of the hinterland. Eventually, 15 of the 16 Western Protectorate states, the Wahidi state of the Eastern Protectorate, and Aden Colony joined to form the Federation of South Arabia. In 1959, Britain agreed to prepare South Arabia for full independence, which was achieved on Nov. 30, 1967, at which time South Arabia, including Aden, changed its name to the People's Republic of Southern Yemen. On Dec. 1, 1970, following the overthrowing of the new government by the National Liberation Front, Southern Yemen changed its name to the People's Democratic Republic of Yemen. On May 22, 1990 the People's Democratic Republic merged with the Yemen Arab Republic into a unified Republic of Yemen. The YDR currency ceased to circulate on June 11, 1996.

MONETARY SYSTEM:
   1 Dinar = 1000 Fils

SIGNATURE VARIETIES			
1		2	
3		4	

FEDERATED STATE

South Arabian Currency Authority
1965 ND Issue

1   250 Fils   **VF   UNC**
ND (1965). Brown on multicolor underprint. Aden harbor, dhow at center. Back:
Date palm at center. Watermark: Camel's head. Printer: TDLR.
    a. Signature 1.   7.50   35.00
    b. Signature 2.   5.00   20.00
    s. As a. Specimen.   —   35.00

2 **500 Fils** VF UNC
ND (1965). Green on multicolor underprint. Aden harbor, dhow at center. Back:
Date palm at center, heads of wheat at lower left. Watermark: Camel's head.
Printer: TDLR.

    a. Signature 1.   20.00   85.00
    b. Signature 2.   6.00   30.00
    s. As a. Specimen.   —   50.00

3 **1 Dinar** VF UNC
ND (1965). Dark blue on multicolor underprint. Aden harbor, dhow at center. Back:
Date palm at center, branch of a cotton plant at left. Watermark: Camel's head.
Printer: TDLR.

    a. Signature 1.   25.00   150
    b. Signature 2.   20.00   60.00
    s. As a. Specimen.   —   75.00

4 **5 Dinars** VF UNC
ND (1965). Red on multicolor underprint. Aden harbor, dhow at center. Back: Date
palm at center, cotton plant branch and millet flanking. Watermark: Camel's head.
Printer: TDLR.

    a. Signature 1.   100   500
    b. Signature 2.   20.00   95.00
    s. As a. Specimen.   —   100

5 **10 Dinars** VF UNC
ND (1967). Deep olive-green on multicolor underprint. Aden harbor, dhow at cen- 90.00   400
ter. Signature 2. Back: Date palm at center, cotton branch, corn cobs and heads of
wheat. Watermark: Camel's head. Printer: TDLR.

PEOPLES DEMOCRATIC REPUBLIC
Bank of Yemen
1984 ND Issue

6 **500 Fils** VF UNC
ND (1984). Green on multicolor underprint. Aden harbor, dhow at center. Without 5.00   20.00
English. Back: Date palm at center, heads of wheat at lower left. New bank name.
Capital *ADEN* added to botto Watermark: Camel's head.

7 **1 Dinar** VF UNC
ND (1984). Dark blue on multicolor underprint. Aden harbor, dhow at center. 8.00   32.00
Without English. Back: Date palm at center, branch of cotton plant at left. New
bank name. Capital *ADEN* added to bot Watermark: Camel's head.

8 5 Dinars VF UNC

ND (1984). Red on multicolor underprint. Aden harbor, dhow at center. Without English. Back: Date palm at center, cotton plant branch and millet flanking. New bank name. Capital *ADEN* add Watermark: Camel's head.

  a. Signature 0.   20.00 75.00
  b. Signature 4.   15.00 52.00

9 10 Dinars VF UNC

ND (1984). Deep olive-green on multicolor underprint. Aden harbor, dhow at center. Without English. Back: Date palm at center, cotton branch, corn cobs and heads of wheat. New bank name. Capital *ADEN* Watermark: Camel's head.

  a. Signature 3.   27.00 110
  b. Signature 4.   22.00 80.00

YUGOSLAVIA

The Federal Republic of Yugoslavia is a Balkan country located on the east shore of the Adriatic Sea bordering Bosnia-Herzegovina and Croatia to the west, Hungary and Romania to the north, Bulgaria to the east, and Albania and Macedonia to the south. It has an area of 39,449 sq. mi. (102,173 sq. km.) and a population of 10.5 million. Capital: Belgrade. The chief industries are agriculture, mining, manufacturing and tourism. Machinery, nonferrous metals, meat and fabrics are exported. The first South-Slavian State - Yugoslavia - was proclaimed on Dec. 1, 1918, after the union of the Kingdom of Serbia, Montenegro and the South Slav territories of Austria-Hungary; it then changed its official name from the Kingdom of the Serbs, Croats, and Slovenes to the Kingdom of Yugoslavia on Oct. 3, 1929. The Royal government of Yugoslavia attempted to remain neutral in World War II but, yielding to German pressure, aligned itself with the Axis powers in March of 1941; a few days later it was overthrown by a military-led coup and its neutrality reasserted. The Nazis occupied the country on April 17, and throughout the remaining years were resisted by a number of guerrilla armies, notably that of Marshal Josip Broz known as Tito. After the defeat of the Axis powers, a leftist coalition headed by Tito abolished the monarchy and, on Jan. 31, 1946, established a "People's Republic". Tito's rival General Draza Mihajlovic, who led the Chetniks against the Germans and Tito's forces, was arrested on March 13, 1946 and executed the following day after having been convicted by a partisan court.

The Federal Republic of Yugoslavia was composed of six autonomous republics: Serbia, Croatia, Slovenia, Bosnia-Herzegovina, Macedonia and Montenegro with two autonomous provinces within Serbia: Kosovo-Metohija and Vojvodina. The collapse of the Socialist Federal Republic of Yugoslavia during 1991-92 has resulted in the autonomous republics of Croatia, Slovenia, Bosnia-Herzegovina and Macedonia declaring their respective independence. The Federal Republic of Yugoslavia was proclaimed in 1992; it consists of the former Republics of Serbia and Montenegro.

MONETARY SYSTEM:
1 Dinar = 100 Para
1 Dinar = 100 *Old* Dinara, 1965
1 Dinar = 10,000 *Old* Dinara, 1990-91
1 Dinar = 10 *Old* Dinara, 1992
1 Dinar = 1 Million *Old* Dinara, 1.10.1993
1 Dinar = 1 Milliard *Old* Dinara, 1.1.1994
1 Novi Dinar = 1 German Mark = 12,000,000 Dinara, 24.1.1994

SIGNATURE VARIETIES		
	VICE GOVERNOR	GOVERNOR
5	Isak Sion	Nikola Maljanich
6	Borivoje Jelich	Nikola Maljanich
7	Branislav Colanovich	Nikola Maljanich
8	Branislav Colanovich	Ivo Perishin
9	Joshko Shtrukelj	Branislav Colanovich
10	Ilija Marjanovich	Ksente Bogoev
11	Miodrag Veljkovich	Radovan Makich
12	Dr. Slobodan Stanojevich	Radovan Makich
13	Dr. Slobodan Stanojevich	Dushan Vlatkovitch
14	Mitja Gaspari	Dushan Vlatkovitch

SIGNATURE VARIETIES

	VICE GOVERNOR	GOVERNOR
15		*Dushan Vlatkovitch*
16		*Vuk Ognjanovich*
17		*Borivoje Atanockovich*
18	*(signature)*	
19	*Bozidar Gazivoda*	
20	*Bozidar Gazivoda*	*Dragoslav Avramovich*

SOCIALIST FEDERAL REPUBLIC

НАРОДНА БАНКА ЈУГОСЛАВИЈН

Narodna Banka Jugoslavije

1963 Issue

#73-76 Replacement notes: Serial # prefix *ZA*.

73   100 Dinara VF   UNC
1.5.1963. Dark red on multicolor underprint. Woman wearing national costume at left. Signature 5. Back: View of Dubrovnik at center.
- a. Issued note.   0.25   3.00
- s. Specimen.   —   40.00

74   500 Dinara VF   UNC
1.5.1963. Dark green on multicolor underprint. Farm woman with sickle at left. Signature 5. Back: Two combine harvesters at center.
- a. Issued note.   1.00   5.00
- s. Specimen.   —   50.00

75   1000 Dinara VF   UNC
1.5.1963. Dark brown on multicolor underprint. Male steelworker at left. Signature 5. Back: Factory complex at center.
- a. Issued note.   1.00   4.00
- s. Specimen.   —   50.00

76   5000 Dinara VF   UNC
1.5.1963. Dark blue on multicolor underprint. Relief of Mestrovic at left. Signature 5. Back: Parliament building in Belgrade at center.
- a. Issued note.   30.00   150
- p. Proof. Without serial #.   125   200
- s. Specimen.   —   80.00

1965 Issue

#77-80 Replacement notes: Serial # prefix *ZA*.

77   5 Dinara VF   UNC
1.8.1965. UV: fibers fluoresce red and yellow. Design elements around value 5 green. Dark green on multicolor underprint. Farm woman with sickle at left. Signature 6. Back: Two combine harvesters at center. 134x64mm.
- a. Small numerals in serial number.   3.00   25.00
- b. Large numerals in serial number.   1.50   15.00
- s. Specimen.   —   40.00

78   10 Dinara VF   UNC
1.8.1965. Dark brown on multicolor underprint. Male steelworker at left. Signature 6. Back: Factory complex at center. 143x66mm.
- a. Small numerals in serial number.   1.50   15.00
- b. Large numerals in serial number.   5.00   25.00
- s. Specimen.   —   40.00

79   50 Dinara VF   UNC
1.8.1965. Dark blue on multicolor underprint. Relief of Mestrovic at left. Signature 6. Back: Parliament building in Belgrade at center. 151x72mm.
- a. Small numerals in serial number.   5.00   40.00
- b. Large numerals in serial number.   5.00   50.00
- s. Specimen.   —   40.00

80   100 Dinara VF   UNC
1.8.1965. Red on multicolor underprint. Equestrian statue "Peace" of Augustincic in garden of United Nations, New York at left. Signature 6.
- a. Small numerals in serial number.   5.00   30.00
- b. Large numerals in serial number, without security thread.   2.00   10.00
- c. Large numerals in serial number, with security thread. 7 digit serial #.   0.75   5.00
- s. Specimen.   —   40.00

1968-70 Issue

#81-84 Replacement notes: Serial # prefix ZA.

			VF	UNC
81	**5 Dinara**		**VF**	**UNC**

1.5.1968. Dark green on multicolor underprint. Farm woman with sickle at left. Signature 7, 8 Back: Large numerals of value at left center. 123x59mm.

		VF	UNC
a. Small numerals in serial number.		0.20	1.00
b. Large numerals in serial number.		0.20	1.00
s. Specimen.		—	30.00

82 10 Dinara　　　　　　　　　　　　　　VF UNC

1.5.1900. UV: fibers fluoresce yellow, security strip green. Design elements orange. Dark brown on multicolor underprint. Male steelworker at left. Signature 7, 0. Back: Large numerals of value at left center. 131x63mm.

	VF	UNC
a. Small numerals in serial number.	1.00	20.00
b. Large numerals in serial number, without security thread.	3.00	25.00
c. Large numerals in serial number, with security thread.	1.00	5.00
s. Specimen.	—	30.00

83 50 Dinara　　　　　　　　　　　　　　VF UNC

1.5.1968. Dark blue on multicolor underprint. Relief of Mestrovic at left. Signature 7, 8. Back: Large numerals of value at left center. 139x66mm.

	VF	UNC
a. Small numerals in serial number.	1.50	20.00
b. Large numerals in serial number, without security thread.	0.50	4.00
c. Large numerals in serial number, with security thread.	0.25	1.00
s. Specimen.	—	45.00

84 500 Dinara　　　　　　　　　　　　　VF UNC

1.8.1970. Dark olive-green on multicolor underprint. Statue of Nicola Tesla seated with open book at left. Signature 7, 8. Back: Large numerals of value at left center.

	VF	UNC
a. Without security thread. Signature 8.	0.50	2.50
b. With security thread.	1.50	6.00

1974 Issue

#85 and 86 Replacement notes: Serial # prefix ZA.

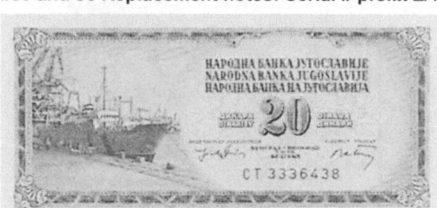

85 20 Dinara　　　　　　　　　　　　　　VF UNC

19.12.1974. Purple on multicolor underprint. Ship dockside at left. Two prefix letters plus 6 or 7-digit serial number. Signature 9.　0.25 1.50

86 1000 Dinara　　　　　　　　　　　　　VF UNC

19.12.1974. Blue-black on multicolor underprint. Woman with fruit at left. Signature 9.　1.00 4.50

1978 Issue

#87-92 Replacement notes: Serial # prefix ZA; ZB; ZC.

87 10 Dinara　　　　　　　　　　　　　　VF UNC

1978; 1981. Dark brown on multicolor underprint. Male steelworker at left. Long, 2-line signature title at left. Back: Large numerals of value at left center.

	VF	UNC
a. Signature 10. 12.8.1978.	0.20	0.75
b. Signature 11. 4.11.1981.	0.20	0.75

88 20 Dinara　　　　　　　　　　　　　　VF UNC

1978; 1981. Purple on multicolor underprint. Ship dockside at left. Two prefix letters plus 6 or 7-digit serial number. Long 2-line signature title at left.

	VF	UNC
a. Signature 10. 12.8.1978.	0.15	0.75
b. Signature 11. 4.11.1981.	0.25	2.00

89 50 Dinara　　　　　　　　　　　　　　VF UNC

1978; 1981. UV: fibers fluoresce yellow, security strip blue. Dark blue on multicolor underprint. Relief of Mestrovic at left. Large 2-line signature title at left. Back: Large numerals of value at left center

	VF	UNC
a. Signature 10. 12.8.1978.	0.20	1.00
b. Signature 11. 4.11.1981.	0.20	1.00

90 100 Dinara　　　　　　　　　　　　　VF UNC

1978; 1981; 1986. UV: fibers fluoresce yellow; serial # and design elements red. Red on multicolor underprint. Equestrian statue "Peace" of Augustincic in garden of United Nations, New York at left. Long 2-line signature title at left.

	VF	UNC
a. Signature 10. 12.8.1978.	0.25	1.25
b. Signature 11. 4.11.1981.	0.25	1.25
c. Signature 13. 16.5.1986.	0.20	1.00

91 500 Dinara　　　　　　　　　　　　　VF UNC

1978; 1981; 1986. Dark olive-green on multicolor underprint. Statue of Nicola Tesla seated with open book at left. Long 2-line signature title at left. Back: Large numerals of value at left center.

	VF	UNC
a. Signature 10. 12.8.1978.	0.50	2.00
b. Signature 11. 4.11.1981.	0.50	1.00
c. Signature 13. 16.5.1986.	0.50	2.00

92   1000 Dinara

1978; 1981. Blue-black on multicolor underprint. Woman with fruit at left. Long 2-line signature title at left.

		VF	UNC
a.	Signature 10 with title at right: *GUVERNE* in Latin without final letter *R* (engraving error). Series AF. 12.8.1978.	1.00	7.50
b.	As a. Series AR.	3.00	15.00
c.	Corrected signature title.	0.50	3.00
d.	Signature 11. 4.11.1981.	0.25	1.00

1985-89 Issue

93   5000 Dinara

1.5.1985. Deep blue on multicolor underprint. Josip Broz Tito at left, arms at center. Signature 12. Back: Jajce in Bosnia at center. Watermark: Josip Broz Tito.

		VF	UNC
a.	Corrected year of Tito's death - *1980*.	0.50	3.50
x.	Error: Tito's death date as *1930* instead of *1980*.	10.00	65.00

#94 not assigned.

95   20,000 Dinara

1.5.1987. Brown on multicolor underprint. Miner at left, arms at center. Signature 13. Back: Mining equipment at center. Watermark: Miner.

VF	UNC
0.25	1.50

96   50,000 Dinara

1.5.1988. Green and blue on multicolor underprint. Girl at left, arms at center. Signature 13. Back: City of Dubrovnik at center. Watermark: Girl.

VF	UNC
1.00	3.50

97   100,000 Dinara

1.5.1989. Violet and red on multicolor underprint. Young girl at left, arms at center. Signature 14. Back: Abstract design with letters and numbers at center right. Watermark: Young girl.

VF	UNC
0.75	3.50

98   500,000 Dinara

Aug. 1989. Deep purple and blue on lilac underprint. Arms at left, Partisan monument "Kozara" at right. Signature 14. Back: Partisan monument "Sutjeska" at center.

		VF	UNC
a.	Issued note.	1.50	7.00
s.	Specimen.	—	50.00

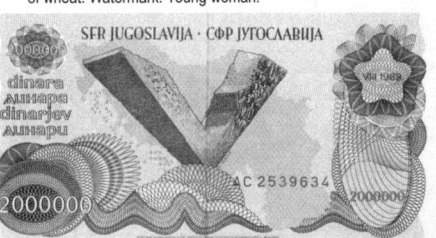

99   1,000,000 Dinara

1.11.1989. UV: fibers fluoresce yellow. Light olive-green on orange and gold underprint. Young woman at left, arms at center. Signature 14. Back: Stylized stalk of wheat. Watermark: Young woman.

VF	UNC
1.50	10.00

100   2,000,000 Dinara

Aug. 1989. Pale olive-green and brown on light orange underprint. Arms at left, Partisan monument "Kozara" at right. Signature 14. Back: Partisan "V3" monument at Kragujevac at center.

		VF	UNC
a.	Issued note.	12.50	65.00
s.	Specimen.	—	50.00

1990 First Issue

#101 and 102 Replacement notes: Serial # prefix *ZA*.

101 50 Dinara

	VF	UNC
1.1.1990. Deep purple and blue on lilac underprint. Arms at left, Partisan monument "Kozara" at right. Signature 14. Back: Partisan monument "Sutjeska" at center.		
a. Issued note.	3.00	25.00
s. Specimen.	—	50.00

101A 100 Dinara

	VF	UNC
ND (1990). (Not issued). Like #98. 7-digit serial #. Proof designed in 1979 and reconsidered for issue in 1990. Black and dark olive-green on pink and yellow-green underprint. Marshal Tito at right, flags in underprint at center, arms at upper left. Back: Partisan monument "Sutjeska" at center.	400	700

102 200 Dinara

	VF	UNC
1.1.1990. Pale olive-green and brown on light orange underprint. Arms at left, Partisan monument "Kozara" at right. Signature 14. Back: Partisan "V3" monument at Kragujevac at center.		
a. Issued note.	4.00	25.00
s. Specimen.	—	50.00

1990 Second Issue

#103-107 Replacement notes: Serial # prefix *ZA*.

103 10 Dinara

	VF	UNC
1.9.1990. Violet and red on multicolor underprint. Young girl at left, arms at center. Signature 14. Back: Abstract design with letters and numbers at center right. Watermark: Young girl.	0.20	1.50

104 50 Dinara

	VF	UNC
1.6.1990. UV: fibers fluoresce yellow. Purple. Young boy at left. Signature 14. Back: Roses at center right. Watermark: Young boy.	0.25	1.50

105 100 Dinara

	VF	UNC
1.3.1990. UV: fibers fluoresce yellow. Light olive-green on orange and gold underprint. Young woman at left, arms at center. Signature 14. Back: Stylized stalk of wheat. Watermark: Young woman.	0.50	7.00

106 500 Dinara

	VF	UNC
1.3.1990. UV: fibers fluoresce yellow. Blue and purple. Young man at left. Arms at center. Signature 14. Back: Mountain scene. Watermark: Young man.	0.50	7.00

106A 500 Dinara

(Not issued). Brown and orange. Young man at left. Arms at center. Signature 14. Back: Mountain scene. Watermark: Young man.

VF	UNC
—	225

107 1000 Dinara

26.11.1990. UV: fibers fluoresce yellow. Brown and orange. Nicola Tesla at left. Arms at center. Signature 14. Back: High frequency transformer. Watermark: Nicola Tesla.

VF	UNC
1.00	12.50

1991 Issue

#107A-111 Replacement notes: Serial # prefix *ZA.*

107A 10 Dinara

1991. (Not issued). Purple, black and lilac. Young girl at left, arms at center. Signature 15. Back: Abstract design with letters and numbers at center right. Watermark: Young girl.

VF	UNC
—	175

107B 50 Dinara

1991. (Not issued). UV: fibers fluoresce yellow. Orange and red. Young boy at left. Signature 15. Back: Roses at center right. Watermark: Young boy.

VF	UNC
—	175

108 100 Dinara

1991. UV: fibers fluoresce yellow. Black and olive-brown on yellow underprint. Young woman at left, arms at center. Signature 15. Back: Stylized stalk of wheat. Watermark: Young woman.

VF	UNC
0.50	1.50

109 500 Dinara

1991. UV: fibers fluoresce yellow. Brown, dark brown and orange on tan underprint. Young man at left. Arms at center. Signature 15. Back: Mountain scene. Watermark: Young man.

VF	UNC
0.50	2.50

110 1000 Dinara

1991. UV: fibers fluoresce yellow. Blue and purple. Nicola Tesla at left. Arms at center. Signature 15. Back: High frequency transformer. Watermark: Nicola Tesla. 165x80mm.

VF	UNC
0.50	7.00

111 5000 Dinara

1991. Purple, red-orange and blue-gray on gray underprint. Ivo Andric at left. Arms at center. Signature 15. Back: Multiple arch stone bridge on the Drina River at Visegrad at center. Watermark: Ivo Andric.

VF	UNC
1.50	7.50

1992 Issue

#112-117 National Bank monogram arms at ctr. Replacement notes: Serial # prefix *ZA.*

112 100 Dinara

1992. UV: fibers fluoresce yellow. Pale blue and purple. Young woman at left. National Bank monogram at center. Signature 15. Back: Stylized stalk of wheat. Watermark: Young woman.

VF	UNC
0.40	1.00

113 500 Dinara

1992. Pale purple and lilac. Young man at left. National Bank monogram at center. Signature 15. Back: Mountain scene. Watermark: Youn man.

VF	UNC
0.50	4.00

114 1000 Dinara

1992. Red, orange and purple on lilac underprint. Nicola Tesla at left. National Bank monogram at center. Signature 15. Back: High frequency transformer. Watermark: Nicola Tesla.

VF	UNC
0.50	7.50

115 5000 Dinara
1992. Deep blue-green, purple and deep olive-brown on gray underprint. Ivo Andric at left. National Bank monogram at center. Signature 15. Back: Multiple arch stone bridge on the Drina River at Visegrad at center. Watermark: Ivo Andric.

	VF	UNC
	1.50	6.00

116 10,000 Dinara
1992. Varied shades of brown and salmon on tan underprint. Young girl at left. National Bank monogram at center. Signature 16. Back: Abstract design with letters and numbers at center right. Watermark: Young girl.

	VF	UNC
a. With dot after date.	0.20	2.00
b. Without dot after date.	0.20	2.00

117 50,000 Dinara
1992. Purple, olive-green and deep blue-green. Young boy at left. National Bank monogram at center. Signature 16. Back: Roses at center right. Watermark: Young boy.

	VF	UNC
	0.75	4.50

1993 Issue

#118-127 replacement notes: Serial # prefix *ZA*.

118 100,000 Dinara
1993. Olive-green on orange and gold underprint. Young woman at left. National Bank monogram at center. Signature 16. Back: Sunflowers at center right.

	VF	UNC
	0.50	3.50

119 500,000 Dinara
1993. Blue-violet and orange on multicolor underprint. Young man at left. National Bank monogram at center. Signature 16. Back: Koponik Sky Center.

	VF	UNC
	2.50	20.00

120 1,000,000 Dinara
1993. Purple on blue, orange and multicolor underprint. Young boy at left. National Bank monogram at center. Signature 16. Back: Iris flowers at center right.

	VF	UNC
	4.00	20.00

121 5,000,000 Dinara
1993. Violet, lilac, turquoise and multicolor. Nicola Tesla at left. National Bank monogram at center. Signature 16. Back: Vertical rendition of high frequency transformer at center, hydroelectric dam at right.

	VF	UNC
	0.50	3.00

122 10,000,000 Dinara
1993. Slate blue, light and dark brown. Ivo Andric at left. National Bank monogram at center. Signature 16. Back: National library at center right.

	VF	UNC
	0.50	3.00

123 50,000,000 Dinara
1993. Black and orange. Young girl at left. National Bank monogram at center. Signature 16. Back: Belgrade University.

	VF	UNC
	0.75	5.00

124 100,000,000 Dinara
1993. Grayish purple and blue. Young man at left. National Bank monogram at center. Signature 17. Back: Academy of Science at center right.

	VF	UNC
	0.50	3.00

125 500,000,000 Dinara
1993. Black and lilac. Young woman at left. National Bank monogram at center. Signature 17. Back: Department of Agriculture building.

	VF	UNC
	1.00	6.00

126 1,000,000,000 Dinara
1993. UV: fibers fluoresce yellow. Red and purple on orange and blue-gray underprint. Young girl at left. National Bank monogram at center. Signature 17. Back: Parliament building (National Assembly) at center.

	VF	UNC
	2.50	12.50

127   10,000,000,000 Dinara

1993. Black, purple and red. Nicola Tesla at left. National Bank monogram at center. Signature 17. Back: High frequency transformer. Watermark: Nicola Tesla.

VF	UNC
1.50	10.00

1993 Reform Issue
#128-137 replacement notes: Serial # prefix ZA.

128   5000 Dinara

1993. UV: fibers fluoresce yellow. Pale reddish brown, pale olive-green and orange. Nicola Tesla at left. National Bank monogram at center. Signature 17. Back: Tesla Museum at center right.

VF	UNC
1.00	6.00

129   10,000 Dinara

1993. Gray and green on orange and olive-green underprint. Vuk. Stefanovic Karadzic at left. National Bank monogram at center.Signature 17. Back: Orthodox church, house.

VF	UNC
0.75	5.00

130   50,000 Dinara

1993. Dark blue on pink and aqua underprint. Petar II Petrovic Niegos Prince-Bishop of Montenegro, at left. National Bank monogram at center. Signature 17. Back: Monastery in Cetinje at right.

VF	UNC
0.50	2.00

131   500,000 Dinara

1993. Dark green on blue-green and yellow-orange underprint. Dositej Obradovic at left. Signature 18. Back: Monastery Hopovo at center right.

VF	UNC
0.50	2.00

132   5,000,000 Dinara

1993. Dark brown on orange, blue-green and pale olive-brown underprint. Karadjordj Petrovich, Prince of Serbia, at left. Signature 18. Back: Orthodox church at center right.

VF	UNC
0.50	2.00

133   50,000,000 Dinara

1993. Red and purple on orange and lilac underprint. Michajlo Pupin at left. Signature 18. Back: Telephone Exchange building at center right.

VF	UNC
0.25	2.00

134   500,000,000 Dinara

1993. Purple on aqua, brown-orange and dull pink underprint. Jovan Cvijich at left. Signature 18. Back: University at center right.

	VF	UNC
a. Issued note.	0.50	3.00
s. Specimen. Red handstamp overprint: SPECIMEN on face.	—	100

135   5,000,000,000 Dinara

1993. Olive-brown on light green, ochre and orange underprint. Djura Jaksich at left. Signature 18. Back: Monastery in Vrazcevsnitza at center right.

	VF	UNC
a. Issued note.	0.50	3.00
s. Specimen with red overprint.	—	60.00

136 50,000,000,000 Dinara   VF UNC

1993. Dark brown on blue-violet, orange, red-violet and gray underprint. Serbian Prince
Milan Obrenovich at left. Signature 18. Back: Villa of Obrenovich at center right. 0.75 5.00

137 500,000,000,000 Dinara   VF UNC

1993. Red-violet on orange, pale blue-gray and olive-brown underprint. Poet J.
Zmaj at left. Signature 18. Back: National Library at center right.
    a. Issued note.   1.50 10.00
    s. Specimen with red overprint.   —   70.00

1994 Issue

138 10 Dinara   VF UNC

1994. Chocolate brown on brown and gray-green underprint. Joseph Panchic at
left. Signature 18. Back: Mountain view, pine trees at center right. Watermark:
Design.
    a. Issued note. Without serial #.   0.50 1.00
    b. Issued note. Privately added serial #, serial # prefix *AR*. —   —
    s. Specimen with red overprint: *SPECIMEN* once on face. Serial #AA —   65.00
       0000000.

**Note: Violet or orange specimen overprints are forgeries. Notes with serial #s were privately
added.**

139 100 Dinara   VF UNC

1994. Grayish purple on pink and pale blue underprint. Nicola Tesla at left.
National Bank monogram arms at center. Signature 18. Back: Tesla Museum at
center right. Watermark: Design.
    a. Issued note. Without serial #.   0.25 1.00
    s. Specimen with red overprint *SPECIMEN* once on face. Serial # AA —   65.00
       0000000.

Note: Examples are known with serial #s privately added.

140 1000 Dinara   VF UNC

1994. Dark olive-gray on red-orange, olive-brown and lilac underprint. Petar II
Petrovic Niegos, Prince-Bishop of Montenegro, at left. Signature 18. Back: Monastery in Cetinje at right. Watermark: Design.
    a. Issued note.   0.50 2.00
    s. Specimen with red overprint.   —   40.00

141 5000 Dinara   VF UNC

1994. Dark blue on lilac, orange and aqua underprint. Dositej Obradovic at left.
Signature 18. Back: Monastery Hopovo at center right. Watermark: Design.
    a. Issued note.   0.50 2.00
    s. Specimen with red overprint.   —   40.00

142 50,000 Dinara   VF UNC

1994. Dull red and lilac on orange underprint. Karadjordj Petrovich, Prince of Serbia,
at left. Signature 18. Back: Orthodox church at center right. Watermark: Design.
    a. Issued note.   0.75 3.00
    s. Specimen with red overprint   —   40.00

142A 100,000 Dinara   VF UNC

1994. (Not issued). Red-brown on ochre and pale olive-green underprint. Michajlo
Pupin at left. Signature 18. Back: Telephone Exchange building. Watermark: Design. —   350

143 500,000 Dinara   VF UNC

1994. Dull olive-green and orange on yellow underprint. Jovan Cvijich at left.
Signature 18. Back: University at center right. Watermark: Design.
    a. Issued note.   0.40 1.50
    s. Specimen. Red handstamp overprint: SPECIMEN.   —   100

1994 Provisional Issue

144	10,000,000 Dinara	VF	UNC

1994 (-old date 1993). Slate blue, light and dark brown. Ivo Andric at left.
National Bank monogram at center. Signature 18. Back: National Library at center right
with signature title.

		VF	UNC
	a. Issued note.	1.00	5.00
	s. Specimen with red overprint.	—	50.00

1994 Reform Issues

Note: #145-147 withdrawn from circulation on 1.1.1995.

145	1 Novi Dinar	VF	UNC

1.1.1994. Blue-gray and brown on pale olive-green and tan underprint. Joseph
Panchic at left. National Bank monogram at center. Signature 19. Back: Mountain
view, pine trees at center right. Watermark: Diamond grid.

VF 1.00 UNC 4.00

146	5 Novih Dinara	VF	UNC

1.1.1994. Red-brown and pink on ochre and pale orange underprint. Nicola Tesla
at left. National Bank monogram at center. Signature 19. Back: Tesla Museum at
center right. Watermark: Diamond grid.

VF 2.50 UNC 15.00

147	10 Novih Dinara	VF	UNC

1.1.1994. Purple and pink on aqua and olive-green underprint. Petar II Petrovic
Niegos Prince-Bishop of Montenegro, at left. National Bank monogram at center.
Signature 19. Back: Monastery in Cetinje at right. Watermark: Diamond grid.

VF 2.50 UNC 15.00

1994; 1996 Issue

#148-152 Replacement notes: Serial # prefix 3A.

148	5 Novih Dinara	VF	UNC

3.3.1994. Black, deep purple and violet. NicolaTesla at left. Arms with double-
headed eagle at upper center. Signature 20. Back: Tesla Museum at center right.
Watermark: Symmetrical design repeated. 131x62mm.

VF 0.25 UNC 2.00

149	10 Novih Dinara	VF	UNC

3.3.1994. Purple, violet and brown. Petar II Petrovic Niegos Prince-Bishop of Montenegro, at left. Arms with double-headed eagle at upper center. Signature 20. Back:
Monastery in Cetinje at right. Watermark: Symmetrical design repeated. 135x64mm.

VF 1.00 UNC 4.00

150	20 Novih Dinara	VF	UNC

3.3.1994. Dark green, brown-orange and brown. D. Jaksich at left. Arms with
double-headed eagle at upper center. Signature 20. Back: Monastery in Vrazcevsnitza at center right. Watermark: Symmetrical design repeated. 139x66mm.

VF 2.00 UNC 6.00

#151 and 152 Replacement notes: Serial # prefix ZA.

151	50 Novih Dinara	VF	UNC

June 1996. Black and blue. Serbian Prince Milan Obrenovich at left. Arms with
double-headed eagle at upper center. Signature 19. Back: Villa of Obrenovich at
center right. Watermark: Symmetrical design repeated. 143x68mm.

VF 3.00 UNC 14.00

152	100 Novih Dinara	VF	UNC

Oct. 1996. Black on olive-brown and grayish green underprint. Dositej Obradovic at
left. Arms with double-headed eagle at upper center. Signature 19. Back: Monastery
Hopovo at center right. Watermark: Symmetrical design repeated. 148x70mm.

VF 2.50 UNC 25.00

152A 200 Dinara   VF   UNC
   1999. Not issued. Blak and dark green on multicolor underprint. Stevàn St.   —   —
   Mokianjac bust at left. Back: Piano.

2000-01 Issue

153 10 Dinara   VF   UNC
   2000. Vertical back. Brown on ochre-yellow and green underprint. Vuk Stefanovich
   Karadzic at left. Back: Karadzic and alphabet. Arms at upper left. Watermark:
   Portrait. 131x62mm.
       a. Signature Dusan Vlatkovic (not issued).   —   150
       b. Signature Mladjan Dinkich.   FV   1.25
       s. Specimen.   —   40.00

157 200 Dinara   VF   UNC
   2001. Vertical back. Black and blue on tan underprint. Nadezda Petrovic at left.
   Back: Figure of the artist and Gracanica monastery. Arms at upper left. Watermark: Portrait. 147x70mm.
       a. Issued note.   FV   14.00
       s. Specimen.   —   40.00

154 20 Dinara   VF   UNC
   2000 (2001). Vertical back. Green and black on tan underprint. Petar II Petrovic
   Njegos, Prince-Bishop of Montenegro at left. Back: Statue from Njegos' mausoleum, mosaic and mountains. Arms at upper left. Watermark: Portrait. 135x64mm.
       a. Issued note.   0.50 2.00
       s. Specimen.   —   40.00

158 1000 Dinara   VF   UNC
   2001. Red on blue and tan underprint. Djordje Vajfert at left. Back: Vajfert portrait
   and Central Bank interior. 151x72mm.
       a. Issued note.   FV   40.00
       s. Specimen.   —   80.00

155 50 Dinara   VF   UNC
   2000. Vertical back. Light and dark violet on tan underprint. Stevan Stojanovic
   Mokranjac at left, piano keyboard at lower center. Back: Full-length photo and
   musical bars. Arms at upper left. Watermark: Portrait. 139x66mm.
       a. Issued note.   FV   4.00
       s. Specimen.   —   40.00

159 5000 Dinara   VF   UNC
   2002. Green, violet and gray on multicolor underprint. Slobodan Jovanovic
   (Serbian historian, 1869-1958) at left. Back: Jovanovic in front of the Federal
   Assembly. 159x76mm.
       a. Issued note.   FV   175
       s. Specimen.   —   200

156 100 Dinara   VF   UNC
   2000. Vertical back. Blue on green and tan underprint. Nikola Tesla at left, motor
   at lower center. Back: Tesla photo, schematic of electro-magnetic induction
   engine, dove. Arms at upper left. Watermark: Portrait. 143x68mm.
       a. Issued note.   FV   6.00
       s. Specimen.   —   40.00

ZAÏRE

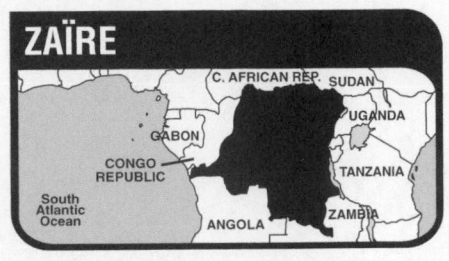

The Republic of Zaïre (formerly the Congo Democratic Republic) located in the south-central part of Africa, has an area of 905,568 sq. mi. (2,345,409 sq. km.) and a population of 43.81 million. Capital: Kinshasa. The mineral-rich country produces copper, tin, diamonds, gold, zinc, cobalt and uranium. In ancient times the territory comprising Zaïre was occupied by Negrito peoples (Pygmies) pushed into the mountains by Bantu and Nilotic invaders. The interior was first explored by the American correspondent Henry Stanley, who was subsequently commissioned by King Leopold II of Belgium to conclude development treaties with the local chiefs. The Berlin conference of 1885 awarded the area to Leopold, who administered and exploited it as his private property until it was annexed to Belgium in 1908. Following the eruption of bloody independence riots in 1959, Belgium granted the Belgian Congo independence as the Republic of the Congo on June 30, 1960. The Belgian Congo attained independence with the distinction of being the most ill-prepared country to ever undertake self-government. Without a single doctor, lawyer or engineer, with no organized unit capable of maintaining law and order, independence disintegrated into an orgy of anarchy. Provinces seceded. Intertribal warfare erupted. Belgian troops intervened to protect Belgian citizens from retributive massacre. By 1961, four groups were fighting for political dominance. The most serious threat to the viability of the country was posed by the secession of mineral-rich Katanga province on July 11, 1960. After two and one-half years of sporadic warfare with a U.N. military force, Katanga's leaders capitulated, Jan. 14, 1963 and the rebellious province was partioned into three provinces. The nation officially changed its name to Zaïre on Oct. 27, 1971. In May 1997, the dictator was overthrown after a three-year rebellion. The country changed its name to the Democratic Republic of the Congo. See also Rwanda, Rwanda-Burundi or Congo Democratic Republic.

MONETARY SYSTEM:
1 Franc = 100 Centimes to 1967
1 Zaïre = 100 Makuta, 1967-1993
1 Nouveau Zaïre = 100 N Makuta = 3 million "old" Zaïres, 1993-1998

BANQUE DU ZAÏRE

	GOVERNOR		GOVERNOR
3	J. Sambwa Mbagui	4	Bofossa W. Amba
5	Emony	6	J. Sambwa Mbagui
7	Pay Pay wa Syakassighe	8	Nyembo Shabanga
9	B. Mushaba	10	Ndiang Kabul
11	L.O. Djamboleka		

REPUBLIC

Banque du Zaïre
1971-80 Issues

#16-25 Replacement notes: Serial # suffix *Z*.

16   50 Makuta

1973-78. Intaglio. Red, dark brown and multicolor. Mobutu at left, leopard at lower right facing right. Various date and signature varieties. Back: Man and structure in water. Watermark: Mobutu. Printer: G&D.

	VF	UNC
a. Red guilloche at left center on back. Signature 3. 30.6.1973; 4.10.1974; 4.10.1975.	6.00	30.00
b. Red and purple guilloche at left center on back. Signature 3. 24.6.1976; 24.6.1977.	7.00	35.00
c. Guilloche as b. Signature 4. 20.5.1978.	5.00	24.00
s. Specimen. As a. Red overprint: *SPECIMEN* on both sides.	—	75.00

17   50 Makuta

1979; 1980. Lithographed. Like #16 but slight color differences. Mobutu at left, leopard at lower right facing right. Various date and signature varieties. Back: Man and structure in water. Watermark: Mobutu. Printer: G&D.

	VF	UNC
a. Signature 5. 24.11.1979.	1.25	7.00
b. Signature 3. 14.10.1980.	1.25	6.00
s. Specimen.	—	75.00

18   1 Zaïre

1972-77. Intaglio. Brown and multicolor. Mobutu at left, leopard at lower right facing right. Various date and signature varieties. Back: Factory, pyramid, flora and elephant tusks at center right. Watermark: Mobutu. Printer: G&D.

	VF	UNC
a. Signature 3 with title: *LE GOUVERNEUR* placed below line. 15.3.1972; 27.10.1974; 20.5.1975; 27.10.1975; 27.10.1976.	2.25	14.00
b. Signature 4 with title: *LE GOUVERNEUR* placed above line. 27.10.1977.	2.00	10.00
s. Specimen. As a. Red overprint: *SPECIMEN* on both sides.	—	75.00

19   1 Zaïre   VF   UNC

1979-81. Lithographed. Like number 18 but slight color differences. Mobutu at left, leopard at lower right facing right. Various date and signature varieties. Back: Factory, pyramid, flora and elephant tusks at center right. Watermark: Mobutu. Printer: G&D.

    a. Signature 5. 22.10.1979.   1.25   5.25
    b. Signature 3. 27.10.1980; 20.5.1981.   1.00   4.50
    s. Specimen.   —   75.00

20   5 Zaïres   VF   UNC

24.11.1972. Like Congo #14. Green, black, brown and multicolor. Mobutu at left, leopard at lower right facing right. Various date and signature varieties. Signature 3. Back: Carving at left, hydroelectric dam at center right. Watermark: Mobutu. Printer: G&D.

    a. Issued note.   50.00   200
    p. Proof. Uniface face and back pasted together. Back overprinted *UNGÜLTIG* in gray.   —   —
    s. Specimen. Red overprint: *SPECIMEN* on both sides.   —   250

21   5 Zaïres   VF   UNC

1974-77. Green, black, brown and multicolor. Mobutu with cap at left, leopard at lower right facing right. Various date and signature varieties. Back: Carving at left, hydroelectric dam at center right. Watermark: Mobutu. Printer: G&D.

    a. Signature 3. 30.11.1974; 30.6.1975; 24.11.1975; 24.11.1976.   7.50   30.00
    b. Signature 4. 24.11.1977.   3.00   14.00
    s. As a. Specimen.   —   75.00

22   5 Zaïres   VF   UNC

1979; 1980. Blue, brown, violet and multicolor. Mobutu at left, leopard at lower right facing right. Various date and signature varieties. Back: Carving at left, hydroelectric dam at center right. Watermark: Mobutu. Printer: G&D.

    a. Signature 5. 20.5.1979.   2.00   9.50
    b. Signature 3. 27.10.1980.   3.00   17.50
    s. Specimen. As a. Red overprint: *SPECIMEN* on both sides.   —   65.00

23   10 Zaïres   VF   UNC

1972-77. Dark brown and blue on multicolor underprint. Mobutu at left, leopard at lower right facing right. Various date and signature varieties. Back: Similar to Congo number 15 but arms with hand holding torch at left center. Watermark: Mobutu. Printer: G&D.

    a. Signature 3. 30.6.1972; 22.6.1974; 30.6.1975; 30.6.1976; 27.10.1976.   12.00   65.00
    b. Signature 4. 27.10.1977.   3.00   15.00
    s. As a. Specimen without serial #.   —   85.00

24   10 Zaïres   VF   UNC

1979; 1981. Green, brown and multicolor. Mobutu at left, leopard at lower right facing right. Various date and signature varieties. Back: Similar to Congo number 15 but arms with hand holding torch at left center. Watermark: Mobutu. Printer: G&D.

    a. Signature 5. 24.6.1979.   4.00   17.50
    b. Signature 3. 4.1.1981.   3.00   15.00
    s. Specimen. As a. Red overprint: *SPECIMEN* on both sides.   —   85.00

25   50 Zaïres   VF   UNC

1980. Red, violet, brown and multicolor. Mobutu at left, leopard at lower right facing right. Various date and signature varieties. Back: Arms at left center. Watermark: Mobutu. Printer: G&D.

    a. Signature 5. 4.2.1980.   12.50   47.50
    b. Signature 3. 24.11.1980.   20.00   70.00
    s. Specimen. 4.2.1980.   —   100

1982-85 Issues

#26-31 replacement notes: Serial # suffix Z.

26   5 Zaïres   VF   UNC

17.11.1982. Blue, black and multicolor. Mobutu in civilian dress at center right, leopard at lower left facing left. Signature 6. Back: Hydroelectric dam at center right. Watermark: Mobutu. Printer: G&D.

    a. Issued note.   1.00   5.00
    s. Specimen.   —   85.00

26A 5 Zaïres

24.11.1985. Blue, black and multicolor. Mobutu in civilian dress at center right, leopard at lower left facing left. Signature 7. Back: Hydroelectric dam at center right. Watermark: Mobutu. Printer: HdMZ.

	VF	UNC
	0.50	1.75

27 10 Zaïres

27.10.1982. Green, black and multicolor. Mobutu in civilian dress at center right, leopard at lower left facing left. Signature 6. Back: Arms with hand holding torch. Watermark: Mobutu. Printer: G&D.

	VF	UNC
a. Issued note.	1.00	5.50
s. Specimen. Red overprint: *SPECIMEN* on both sides.	—	50.00

27A 10 Zaïres

27.10.1985. Green, black and multicolor. Mobutu in civilian dress at center right, leopard at lower left facing left. Signature 7. Back: Arms with hand holding torch. Watermark: Mobutu. Printer: HdMZ.

	VF	UNC
	0.50	1.75

28 50 Zaïres

1982; 1985. Purple, blue and multicolor. Mobutu in civilian dress at center right, leopard at lower left facing left. Back: Men fishing with stick nets at center. Watermark: Mobutu. Printer: G&D.

	VF	UNC
a. Signature 6. 24.11.1982.	2.50	15.00
b. Signature 7. 24.6.1985.	1.50	9.00
s. Specimen.	—	50.00

29 100 Zaïres

1983; 1985. Dark brown, orange and multicolor. Mobutu in civilian dress at center right, leopard at lower left facing left. Back: Bank of Zaïre at center right. Watermark: Mobutu. Printer: G&D.

	VF	UNC
a. Signature 6. 30.6.1983.	3.00	16.50
b. Signature 7. 30.6.1985.	1.00	7.50
s. Specimen. As a. Red overprint: *SPECIMEN* on both sides.	—	50.00

30 500 Zaïres

1984; 1985. Gray, purple and multicolor. Mobutu in military dress at center right, leopard at lower left facing left, arms at lower right. Back: Suspension bridge over river at center right. Watermark: Mobutu. Printer: G&D.

	VF	UNC
a. Signature 6. 14.10.1984.	15.00	70.00
b. Signature 7. 14.10.1985.	6.00	30.00
s. Specimen. As b. Red overprint: *SPECIMEN* on both sides.	35.00	100

31 1000 Zaïres

24.11.1985. Blue-black and green on multicolor underprint. Mobutu in military dress at center right, leopard at lower left facing left, arms at lower right. Signature 7. Back: Civic building, water fountain at center right. Watermark: Mobutu. Printer: G&D.

	VF	UNC
a. Issued note.	6.00	15.00
s. Specimen. Red overprint: *SPECIMEN* on both sides.	65.00	110

1988-92 Issues

#32-46 Replacement notes: serial # suffix *Z*.

32 50 Zaïres

30.6.1988. Green and multicolor. Mobutu in military dress at right, leopard at lower left center facing left, arms at lower right. Signature 7. Back: Men fishing with stick nets at left. Watermark: Mobutu. Printer: HdMZ.

	VF	UNC
a. Issued note.	0.50	1.50
s. Specimen. Red overprint: *SPECIMEN* on both sides.	—	45.00

33 100 Zaïres

14.10.1988. Blue and multicolor. Mobutu in military dress at right, leopard at lower left center facing left, arms at lower right. Signature 7. Back: Bank of Zaïre at left center. Watermark: Mobutu. Printer: HdMZ.

	VF	UNC
a. Issued note.	0.75	3.00
s. Specimen. Red overprint: *SPECIMEN* on both sides.	30.00	50.00

34 500 Zaïres

24.6.1989. Brown, orange and multicolor. Mobutu in military dress at right, leopard at lower left center facing left, arms at lower right. Signature 7. Back: Suspension bridge over river at left center. Watermark: Mobutu. Printer: HdMZ.

	VF	UNC
a. Issued note.	1.25	6.00
s. Specimen. Red overprint: *SPECIMEN* on both sides.	40.00	65.00

35 1000 Zaïres
VF UNC

24.11.1989. Purple, brown and multicolor. Mobutu in military dress at right, leopard at lower left center facing left, arms at lower right. Signature 7. Back: Civic building, fountain at left center. Watermark: Mobutu. Printer: HdMZ.

a. Issued note.		4.00	21.00
s. Specimen. Red overprint: *SPECIMEN* on both sides.		—	70.00

36 2000 Zaïres
VF UNC

1.10.1991. (Smaller size than #35.) Purple and peach on multicolor underprint. Mobutu in military dress at right, leopard at lower left center facing left, arms at lower right. Signature 8. Back: Men fishing with stick nets at left, carved figure at center right. Watermark: Mobutu. Printer: HdMZ.

a. Issued note.		0.75	2.50
s. Specimen. Red overprint: *SPECIMEN* on both sides.		30.00	50.00

#37 and 38 Replacement notes: Serial # suffix Z.

37 5000 Zaïres
VF UNC

20.5.1988. Blue, green and multicolor. Mobutu in military dress at right, leopard at lower left center facing left, arms at lower right. Signature 7. Back: Factory at left, elephant tusks and plants at center. Watermark: Mobutu. Printer: G&D.

a. Brown central diamond to right of Mobutu's ear.		30.00	150
b. Green central diamond to right of Mobutu's ear.		1.25	6.00
s1. Specimen. As a. Red overprint: *SPECIMEN* on both sides.		—	40.00
s2. Specimen. As b. Red overprint: *SPECIMEN* on both sides.		—	40.00

38 10,000 Zaïres
VF UNC

24.11.1989. Purple, brown-orange and red on multicolor underprint. Mobutu in military dress at right, leopard at lower left center facing left, arms at lower right. Signature 7. Back: Government Building complex at left center. Watermark: Mobutu. Printer: G&D.

a. Issued note.		1.25	5.50
s. Specimen. Red overprint: *SPECIMEN* on both sides.		30.00	50.00

39 20,000 Zaïres
VF UNC

1.7.1991. Black on multicolor underprint. Mobutu in military dress at right, leopard at lower left center facing left, arms at lower right. Signature 8. Back: Bank of Zaïre at left, other buildings across center. Watermark: Mobutu. Printer: HdMZ.

a. Issued note.		0.50	3.50
s. Specimen. Red overprint: *SPECIMEN* on both sides.		40.00	60.00

#40 and 41 Replacement notes: Serial # suffix Z.

40 50,000 Zaïres
VF UNC

24.4.1991. Replacement notes: Serial # prefix Z. Wine and blue-black on multicolor underprint. Mobutu in military dress at right, leopard at lower left center facing left, arms at lower right. Signature 7. Back: Family of Western Gorillas. Watermark: Mobutu. Printer: G&D.

a. Issued note.		2.50	8.00
s. Specimen.		60.00	70.00

41 100,000 Zaïres
VF UNC

4.1.1992. Black and deep olive-green on multicolor underprint. Mobutu in military dress at right, leopard at lower left center facing left, arms at lower right. Signature 8. Back: Domed building at left center. Watermark: Mobutu. Printer: G&D.

a. Issued note.		1.25	6.00
s. Specimen. Red overprint: *SPECIMEN* on both sides.		30.00	50.00

42   200,000 Zaïres   VF   UNC

1.3.1992. Deep purple and deep blue on multicolor underprint. Mobutu in military
dress at right, leopard at lower left center facing left, arms at lower right. Signature 8.
Back: Civic building and fountain at left center. Watermark: Mobutu. Printer: HdMZ.

   a. Issued note.   1.00   5.50
   s. Specimen. Red overprint: *SPECIMEN* on both sides.   30.00   60.00

46   5,000,000 Zaïres   VF   UNC

1.10.1992. Deep brown and brown on multicolor underprint. Mobutu in military
dress at right, leopard at lower left center facing left, arms at lower right. Signature
8. Back: Factory, pyramids at center, flora and elephant tusks at left. Watermark:
Mobutu. Printer: H&S.

   a. Issued note.   2.00   8.25
   s. Specimen. Red overprint: *SPECIMEN* on both sides.   40.00   75.00

1993 Issue

#47-58 Replacement notes: serial # suffix *Z*.

47   1 Nouveau Likuta   VF   UNC

24.6.1993. UV: fibers fluoresce yellow, red and blue. Light brown on pink and
multicolor underprint. Mobutu in military dress at right, arms at lower right, leopard
at lower left. Signature 9. Back: Independence Monument at left. Printer: G&D.

   a. Issued note.   0.20   0.75
   s. Specimen. Red overprint: *SPECIMEN* on both sides.   —   15.00

43   500,000 Zaïres   VF   UNC

15.3.1992. Brown and orange on multicolor underprint. Mobutu in military dress at
right, leopard at lower left center facing left, arms at lower right. Signature 8. Back:
Hydroelectric dam at left center. Watermark: Mobutu. Printer: G&D.

   a. Issued note.   1.50   7.75
   s. Specimen. Red overprint: *SPECIMEN* on both sides.   40.00   60.00

48   5 Nouveaux Makuta   VF   UNC

24.6.1993. Black on pale violet and blue-green underprint. Mobutu in military
dress at right, arms at lower right, leopard at lower left. Signature 9. Back:
Independence Monument at left. Printer: G&D.

   a. Issued note.   0.20   1.00
   s. Specimen. Red overprint: *SPECIMEN* on both sides.   —   25.00

44   1,000,000 Zaïres   VF   UNC

31.7.1992. Red-violet and deep red on multicolor underprint. Mobutu in military
dress at right, leopard at lower left center facing left, arms at lower right. Signature
8. Back: Suspension bridge at left center. Watermark: Mobutu. Printer: G&D.

   a. Issued note.   3.00   12.00
   s. Specimen. Red overprint: *SPECIMEN* on both sides.   —   60.00

45   1,000,000 Zaïres   VF   UNC

1993. Red-violet and deep red on multicolor underprint. Mobutu in military dress at
right, leopard at lower left center facing left, arms at lower right. Back: Suspension
bridge at left center. Watermark: Mobutu. Printer: HdMZ.

   a. Signature 8. 15.3.1993.   2.50   13.00
   b. Signature 9. 17.5.1993; 30.6.1993.   1.25   7.00
   s. Specimen. As a, b. Red overprint: *SPECIMEN* on both sides. 50.00 80.00

49   10 Nouveaux Makuta   VF   UNC

24.6.1993. Green on multicolor underprint. Mobutu in military dress at right, arms   0.50   1.75
at lower right, leopard at lower left. Signature 9. Back: Factory, pyramids at center,
flora and elephant tusks at left. Watermark: Mobutu. Printer: HdMZ (CdM-A).

#50. Not assigned.

51 50 Nouveaux Makuta   **VF UNC**
24.6.1993. Brown-orange on light green and multicolor underprint. Mobutu in   0.30   1.25
military dress at right, arms at lower right, leopard at lower left. Signature 9. Back:
Chieftain at left, men fishing with stick nets at center. Watermark: Mobutu. Printer:
HdMZ (CdM-A).

52 1 Nouveau Zaïre   **VF UNC**
24.6.1993. Violet and purple on multicolor underprint. Mobutu in military dress
at right, arms at lower right, leopard at lower left. Signature 9. Back: Banque du
Zaïre at left center. Watermark: Mobutu. Printer: G&D.
     a. Issued note.   0.30   1.75
     s. Specimen. Red overprint: *SPECIMEN* on both sides.   —   30.00

53 5 Nouveaux Zaïres   **VF UNC**
24.6.1993. Brown on multicolor underprint. Mobutu in military dress at right, arms
at lower right, leopard at lower left. Signature Back: Domed building at left center.
Watermark: Mobutu. Printer: G&D.
     a. Signature 9.   0.50   1.75
     b. Signature 10.   1.50   4.00
     s. Specimen. Red overprint: *SPECIMEN* on both sides.   —   40.00

54 10 Nouveaux Zaïres   **VF UNC**
24.6.1993. Dark gray and dark blue-green on multicolor underprint. Mobutu in
military dress at right, arms at lower right, leopard at lower left. Signature 9. Back:
Civic building, water fountain at center right. Watermark: Mobutu. Printer: G&D.
     a. Issued note.   0.75   3.00
     s. Specimen. Red overprint: *SPECIMEN* on both sides.   —   40.00

55 10 Nouveaux Zaïres   **VF UNC**
24.6.1993. Dark gray and dark blue-green on multicolor underprint. Mobutu in
military dress at right, arms at lower right, leopard at lower left. Signature 9. Back:
Civic building, water fountain at center right. Watermark: Mobutu. Printer: HdMZ
(CdM-A).
     a. Issued note.   0.50   1.75
     s. Specimen. Red overprint: SPECIMEN on both sides.   —   55.00

56 20 Nouveaux Zaïres   **VF UNC**
24.6.1993. Brown and blue on pale green and lilac underprint. Mobutu in military   0.75   3.50
dress at right, arms at lower right, leopard at lower left. Signature 9. Back: Civic building and water fountain at left center. Watermark: Mobutu. Printer: HdMZ (CdM-A).

57 50 Nouveaux Zaïres   **VF UNC**
24.6.1993. Brown and deep red on multicolor underprint. Mobutu in military dress   0.75   4.00
at right, arms at lower right, leopard at lower left. Signature 9. Back: Hydroelectric
dam at left center. Watermark: Mobutu. Printer: HdMZ (CdM-A).

58 100 Nouveaux Zaïres   **VF UNC**
1993-94. Grayish purple and blue-violet on aqua and ochre underprint. Mobutu in
military dress at right, arms at lower right, leopard at lower left. Back: Suspension
bridge at left center. Watermark: Mobutu. Printer: G&D.
     a. Signature 9. 24.6.1993.   1.00   4.75
     b. Signature 10. 15.2.1994.   1.25   5.50
     s. Specimen. As a. Red overprint: *SPECIMEN* on both sides.   —   50.00

58A 100 Nouveaux Zaïres   **VF UNC**
1993. Grayish purple and blue-violet on aqua and ochre underprint. Mobutu in   1.00   4.75
military dress at right, arms at lower right, leopard at lower left. Back: Suspension
bridge at left center. Watermark: Mobutu. Printer: HdMZ.

1994-96 Issues

#59-77 Replacement notes: serial # suffix Z.

59 50 Nouveaux Zaïres   **VF UNC**
15.2.1994. Dull red-violet and red on multicolor underprint. Mobutu in military
dress at right, arms at lower right, leopard at lower left center. Signature 10. Back:
Hydroelectric dam at left center. Watermark: Mobutu. Printer: HdMZ.
     a. Issued note.   2.00   8.25
     s. Specimen. Red overprint: *SPECIMEN* on both sides.   —   40.00

60 100 Nouveaux Zaïres   **VF UNC**
15.2.1994. Grayish purple and blue-violet on aqua and ochre underprint. Mobutu   1.00   4.75
in military dress at right, arms at lower right, leopard at lower left center. Signature
10. Back: Suspension bridge at left center. Watermark: Mobutu. Printer: HdMZ.

61 200 Nouveaux Zaïres   **VF UNC**
15.2.1994. Deep olive-brown on orange and multicolor underprint. Mobutu in military
dress at right, arms at lower right, leopard at lower left center. Signature 10. Back:
Men fishing with stick nets at left center. Watermark: Mobutu. Printer: HdMZ.
     a. Issued note.   0.25   3.00
     s. Specimen. Red overprint: *SPECIMEN* on both sides.   —   61.00

62 200 Nouveaux Zaïres   **VF UNC**
15.2.1994. Deep olive-brown on orange and multicolor underprint. Mobutu in
military dress at right, arms at lower right, leopard at lower left center. Back: Men
fishing with stick nets at left center. Watermark: Mobutu. Printer: G&D.
    a. Issued note.   0.50   3.00
    s. Specimen. Red overprint: *SPECIMEN* on both sides.   —   40.00

63 500 Nouveaux Zaïres   **VF UNC**
15.2.1994. Gray and deep olive-green on multicolor underprint. Mobutu in military
dress at right, arms at lower right, leopard at lower left center. Back: Banque du
Zaïre at left center. Watermark: Mobutu. Printer: HdMZ.
    a. Issued note.   0.50   1.75
    s. Specimen. Red overprint: *SPECIMEN* on both sides.   —   40.00

64 500 Nouveaux Zaïres   **VF UNC**
15.2.1994. Gray and deep olive-green on multicolor underprint. Mobutu in military
dress at right, arms at lower right, leopard at lower left center. Back: Banque du
Zaïre at left center. Watermark: Mobutu. Printer: G&D.
    a. Issued note.   0.50   4.00
    s. Specimen. Red overprint: *SPECIMEN* on both sides.   —   45.00

64A 500 Nouveaux Zaïres   **VF UNC**
15.2.1994. Gray and deep loivegreen on multicolor underprint. Mobutu in military
dress at right, arms at lower right, leopard at lower left center. Serial number prefix
X. Back: Banque du Zaïre at left center. Watermark: Mobutu. Printer: Printed in
Argentina.   1.00   4.75

65 500 Nouveaux Zaïres   **VF UNC**
30.1.1995. Blue on multicolor underprint. Mobutu in military dress at right, arms
at lower right, leopard at lower left center. Signature 11. Back: Large value.
Watermark: Mobutu.
    a. Issued note.   0.50   1.75
    s. Specimen. Red overprint: *SPECIMEN* on both sides.   —   45.00

66 1000 Nouveaux Zaïres   **VF UNC**
30.1.1995. Olive-green and olive-gray on multicolor underprint. Mobutu in military
dress at right, arms at lower right, leopard at lower left center. Back: Large value.
Watermark: Mobutu. Printer: G&D.
    a. Issued note.   1.00   4.75
    s. Specimen. Red overprint: *SPECIMEN* on both sides.   —   50.00

67 1000 Nouveaux Zaïres   **VF UNC**
30.1.1995. Olive-green and loive-gray on multicolor underprint. Mobutu in military
dress at right, arms at lower right, leopard at lower left center. Back: Large value.
Watermark: Mobutu. Printer: HdMZ.   0.75   4.00

68 5000 Nouveaux Zaïres   **VF UNC**
30.1.1995. Brown-violet and red-violet on multicolor underprint. Mobutu in military
dress at right, arms at lower right, leopard at lower left center. Signature 11.
Watermark: Mobutu. Printer: G&D.
    a. Issued note.   2.00   9.50
    s. Specimen. Red overprint: *SPECIMEN* on both sides.   —   50.00

69 5000 Nouveaux Zaïres   **VF UNC**
30.1.1995. Brown-violet and red-violet on multicolor underprint. Mobutu in military
dress at right, arms at lower right, leopard at lower left center. Signature 11.
Watermark: Mobutu. Printer: HdMZ.   1.25   7.00

70 10,000 Nouveaux Zaïres   **VF UNC**
30.1.1995. Blue-violet on multicolor underprint. Mobutu in military dress at right,
arms at lower right, leopard at lower left center, OVD vertical band at left. Signature 11. Watermark: Mobutu. Printer: G&D.
    a. Issued note.   1.50   7.50
    s. Specimen. Red overprint: *SPECIMEN* on both sides.   —   50.00

71 10,000 Nouveaux Zaïres   **VF UNC**
30.1.1995. Blue-violet on multicolor underprint. Mobutu in military dress at right,
arms at lower right, leopard at lower left center, OVD vertical band at left. Signature 11. Watermark: Mobutu. Printer: HdMZ.   1.25   6.00

72 20,000 Nouveaux Zaïres   **VF UNC**
30.1.1996. Brown on multicolor underprint. Mobutu in military dress at right, arms
at lower right, leopard at lower left center, OVD vertical band at left. Signature 11.
Watermark: Mobutu. Printer: G&D.
    a. Issued note.   1.50   7.00
    s. Specimen. Red overprint: *SPECIMEN* on both sides.   —   40.00

73 20,000 Nouveaux Zaïres   **VF UNC**
30.1.1996. Brown on multicolor underprint. Mobutu in military dress at right, arms
at lower right, leopard at lower left center, OVD vertical band at left. Signature 11.
Watermark: Mobutu. Printer: HdMZ.   1.50   7.00

74 50,000 Nouveaux Zaïres   **VF UNC**
30.1.1996. Violet and pale blue on multicolor underprint. Mobutu in military dress
at right, arms at lower right, leopard at lower left center, OVD vertical band at left.
Signature 11. Watermark: Mobutu. Printer: G&D.
    a. Issued note.   3.00   12.00
    s. Specimen. Red overprint: SPECIMEN on both sides.   —   50.00

75 50,000 Nouveaux Zaïres   **VF UNC**
30.1.1996. Violet and pale blue on multicolor underprint. Mobutu in military dress
at right, arms at lower right, leopard at lower left center, OVD vertical band at left.
Signature 11. Watermark: Mobutu. Printer: HdMZ.   3.00   12.00

76 100,000 Nouveaux Zaïres   **VF UNC**
30.6.1996. Dull orange on green and multicolor underprint. Mobutu in military
dress at right, arms at lower right, leopard at lower left center, OVD vertical band
at left. Signature 11. Watermark: Mobutu. Printer: G&D.
    a. Issued note.   2.00   9.50
    s. Specimen. Red overprint: *SPECIMEN* on both sides.   —   55.00

77 100,000 Nouveaux Zaïres   **VF UNC**
30.6.1996. Dull orange on green and multicolor underprint. Mobutu in military
dress at right, arms at lower right, leopard at lower left center, OVD vertical band
at left. Signature 11. Watermark: Mobutu. Printer: HdMZ.   2.00   9.50

77A 100,000 Nouveaux Zaïres
30.6.1996. Gray and blue-green on multicolor underprint. Mobutu in military dress at right, arms at lower right, leopard at lower left center. Watermark: Mobutu. Printer: HdMZ.

		VF	UNC
a. Issued note.		4.50	20.00
s. Specimen. Red overprint: *SPECIMEN* on both sides.		—	60.00

78 500,000 Nouveaux Zaïres
25.10.1996. Green and yellow-green on multicolor underprint. Mobutu at right. Signature 11. Back: Map of Zaïre, family in canoe. Watermark: Mobutu. Printer: G&D.

		VF	UNC
a. Issued note.		3.00	12.00
s. Specimen. Red overprint: *SPECIMEN* on both sides.		—	65.00

79 1,000,000 Nouveaux Zaïres
25.10.1996. Light violet and red on multicolor underprint. Mobutu at right, diamonds at lower left center. Signature 11. Back: Map of Zaïre, mining facility. Watermark: Mobutu. Printer: G&D.

		VF	UNC
a. Issued note.		4.00	17.50
s. Specimen. Red overprint: *SPECIMEN* on both sides.		—	80.00

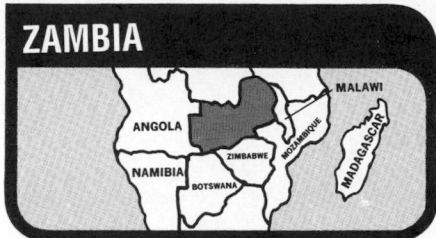

ZAMBIA

The Republic of Zambia is a landlocked country in south-central Africa, has an area of 752,614 sq. km. and a population of 11.67 million. Capital: Lusaka. The economy is based principally on copper, of which Zambia is the world's third largest producer. Copper, zinc, lead, cobalt and tobacco are exported. The territory of Northern Rhodesia was administered by the [British] South Africa Company from 1891 until it was taken over by the UK in 1923. During the 1920s and 1930s, advances in mining spurred development and immigration. The name was changed to Zambia upon independence in 1964. In the 1980s and 1990s, declining copper prices and a prolonged drought hurt the economy. Elections in 1991 brought an end to one-party rule, but the subsequent vote in 1996 saw blatant harassment of opposition parties. The election in 2001 was marked by administrative problems with three parties filing a legal petition challenging the election of ruling party candidate Levy Mwanawasa. The new president launched an anticorruption investigation in 2002 to probe high-level corruption during the previous administration. In 2006-07, this task force successfully prosecuted four cases, including a landmark civil case in the UK in which former President Chiluba and numerous others were found liable for USD 41 million. Mwanawasa was reelected in 2006 in an election that was deemed free and fair. Upon his abrupt death in August 2008, he was succeeded by his Vice-president Rupiah Banda, who subsequently won a special presidential election in October 2008. Also see Rhodesia and Malawi.

RULERS:
British to 1964

MONETARY SYSTEM:
1 Shilling = 12 Pence
1 Pound = 20 Shillings to 1968
1 Kwacha = 100 Ngwee, 1968-

	SIGNATURE VARIETIES		
1	R.C. Hallet, 1964 - 67	2	Dr. J.B. Zulu, 1967 - 70
3	V.S. Musakanya, 1970 - 72	4	B.R. Kuwani, 1972 - 76, 1982 - 84
5	L.J. Mwananshiku, 1967 - 81	6	D.A.R. Phiri, 1984 - 88
7	Dr. L.S. Chivuno, 1986 - 88	8	F. Nkhoma, 1988 - 89
9	J.A. Bussiere, 1991 - (ca. 1993)	10	D. Mulaisho, 1993 - 95
11	Dr. J. Mwanza, 1995 - 2002	12	K. Fundanga, 2002 -

REPUBLIC

Bank of Zambia

1963 ND Issue

A1 1 Pound
1963. Blue on lilac underprint. Fisherman with net and boat at center, portrait Queen Elizabeth II at right. Back: Ross's Turaco at left center. Printer: H&S (Not issued).

	VF	UNC
	—	4,500

Note: #A1 exists in a number of different color varieties.

1964 ND Issue

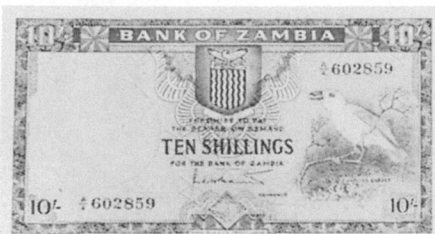

1 10 Shillings
ND (1964). Brown on multicolor underprint. Chaplins Barbet bird at right, arms at upper center. Signature 1. Back: Farmers plowing with tractor and oxen. Watermark: Wildebeest's head. Printer: TDLR.

	VF	UNC
a. Issued note.	150	400
s. Specimen.	—	300

2   1 Pound   VF   UNC
ND (1964). Green on multicolor underprint. Black-cheeked Lovebird at right, arms at upper center. Signature 1. Back: Mining tower and conveyors at left center. Watermark: Wildebeest's head. Printer: TDLR.

    a. Issued note.   200   900
    s. Specimen.   —   300

3   5 Pounds   VF   UNC
ND (1964). Blue on multicolor underprint. Wildebeest at right, arms at upper center. Signature 1. Back: Victoria Falls of Zambezi at left center. Watermark: Wildebeest's head. Printer: TDLR.

    a. Issued note.   450   2,500
    s. Specimen.   —   400

1968 ND Issue

#4-8 Replacement notes: Serial # prefix *1/Z; 1/Y; 1/X; 1/W; 1/V* **respectively.**

4   50 Ngwee   VF   UNC
ND (1968). Red-violet on multicolor underprint. President K. Kaunda at right, arms at left. Dot between letter and value. Signature 2. Back: Two antelope. Printer: TDLR.

    a. Issued note.   27.50   80.00
    s. Specimen. Red overprint: SPECIMEN on both sides.   —   75.00

5   1 Kwacha   VF   UNC
ND (1968). Dark brown on multicolor underprint. President K. Kaunda at right, arms at upper center. Dot between letter and value. Signature 2. Back: Farmers plowing with tractor and oxen. Watermark: Kaunda. Printer: TDLR.

    a. Issued note.   40.00   95.00
    s. Specimen.   —   80.00

6   2 Kwacha   VF   UNC
ND (1968). Green on multicolor underprint. President K. Kaunda at right, arms at upper center. Dot between letter and value. Signature 2. Back: Mining tower and conveyors at left center. Watermark: Kaunda. Printer: TDLR.

    a. Issued note.   50.00   150
    s. Specimen.   —   120

7   10 Kwacha   VF   UNC
ND (1968). Blue on multicolor underprint. President K. Kaunda at right, arms at upper center. Dot between letter and value. Signature 2. Back: Waterfall at center. Watermark: Kaunda. Printer: TDLR.

    a. Issued note.   125   850
    s. Specimen.   —   175

8   20 Kwacha   VF   UNC
ND (1968). Purple on multicolor underprint. President K. Kaunda at right, arms at upper center. Dot between letter and value. Signature 2. Back: National Assembly. Watermark: Kaunda. Printer: TDLR.

    a. Issued note.   200   950
    s. Specimen.   —   225

1969 ND Issue

#9-13 Replacement notes: Serial # prefix *1/Z; 1/Y; 1/X; 1/W; 1/V* **respectively.**

9   50 Ngwee   VF   UNC
ND (1969). Red-violet on multicolor underprint. President K. Kaunda at right, arms at left, without dot between letter and value. Back: Two antelope. Watermark: K. Kaunda. Printer: TDLR.

    a. Signature 3.   20.00   75.00
    b. Signature 4.   10.00   45.00
    s. As c. Specimen.   —   50.00

10   1 Kwacha   VF   UNC
ND (1969). Dark brown on multicolor underprint. President K. Kaunda at right, arms at upper center, without dot between letter and value. Back: Farmers plowing with oxen. Watermark: K. Kaunda. Printer: TDLR.

    a. Signature 2.   20.00   75.00
    b. Signature 3.   9.00   45.00
    s. Specimen.   —   50.00

11   2 Kwacha   VF   UNC
ND (1969). Green on multicolor underprint. President K. Kaunda at right, arms at upper center, without dot between letter and value. Back: Mining tower and conveyors at left center. Watermark: K. Kaunda. Printer: TDLR.

    a. Signature 2.   40.00   200
    b. Signature 3.   30.00   200
    c. Signature 4.   22.50   160
    s. As s. Specimen.   —   90.00

12 10 Kwacha — VF UNC
ND (1969). Blue on multicolor underprint. President K. Kaunda at right, arms at upper center, without dot between letter and value. Back: Waterfall at center. Watermark: K. Kaunda. Printer: TDLR.

		VF	UNC
a.	Signature 2.	75.00	350
b.	Signature 3.	125	700
c.	Signature 4.	60.00	300
s.	Specimen. Red overprint: SPECIMEN.	—	175

13 20 Kwacha — VF UNC
ND (1969). Purple on multicolor underprint. President K. Kaunda at right, arms at upper center, without dot between letter and value. Back: National Assembly. Watermark: K. Kaunda. Printer: TDLR.

		VF	UNC
a.	Signature 2.	100	600
b.	Signature 3.	150	800
c.	Signature 4.	25.00	75.00
s.	Specimen.	—	125

1973 ND Issue

#14 and 15 Replacement notes: Serial # prefix *1/Z; 1/U* **respectively.**

14 50 Ngwee — VF UNC
ND (1973). Black on lilac and multicolor underprint. President K. Kaunda at right, arms at upper center. Signature 4. Back: Miners. Watermark: K. Kaunda. Printer: TDLR.

		VF	UNC
a.	Issued note.	5.00	12.50
s.	Specimen.	—	40.00

15 5 Kwacha — VF UNC
ND (1973). Red-violet on multicolor underprint. President K. Kaunda at right, arms at upper center. Signature 4. Back: Children by school. Watermark: K. Kaunda.

		VF	UNC
a.	Issued note.	150	450
s.	Specimen.	—	200

1973 ND Commemorative Issue

#16, Birth of the Second Republic, December 13, 1972

16 1 Kwacha — VF UNC
ND (1973). Red-orange and brown on multicolor underprint. President K. Kaunda at right. Signature 4. Back: Document signing, commemorative text and crowd. Watermark: K. Kaunda. Printer: TDLR.

		VF	UNC
a.	Issued note.	12.50	45.00
s.	Specimen. Red overprint: SPECIMEN.	—	150

1974 ND Issue

#17 and 18 Replacement notes: Serial # prefix *1/W; 1/V* **respectively.**

17 10 Kwacha — VF UNC
ND (1974). Blue on multicolor underprint. President K. Kaunda at right, arms at upper center. Signature 4. Back: Waterfalls at left center. Watermark: K. Kaunda. Printer: BWC.

		VF	UNC
a.	Issued note.	100	350
s.	Specimen.	—	175

18 20 Kwacha — VF UNC
ND (1974). Purple and red on multicolor underprint. President K. Kaunda at right, arms at upper center. Signature 4. Back: National Assembly. Watermark: K. Kaunda. Printer: BWC.

		VF	UNC
a.	Issued note.	65.00	260
s.	Specimen.	—	220

1974-76 ND Issue

#19-22A Replacement notes: Serial # prefix *1/Y; 1/X; 1/U; 1/W* **respectively.**

19 1 Kwacha — VF UNC
ND (1976). Brown on multicolor underprint. Older President K. Kaunda at right, earlier frame design, arms at upper center. Signature 5. Back: Farmers plowing with tractor and oxen. Watermark: K. Kaunda. Printer: TDLR.

		VF	UNC
a.	Issued note.	6.00	12.50
s.	Specimen.	—	30.00

20 2 Kwacha — VF UNC
ND (1974). Green on multicolor underprint. Older President K. Kaunda at right, earlier frame design, arms at upper center. Signature 4. Back: Mining tower and conveyors at left center. Watermark: K. Kaunda. Printer: TDLR.

		VF	UNC
a.	Issued note.	7.00	22.50
s.	Specimen.	—	30.00

21   5 Kwacha   **VF   UNC**
ND (1976). Brown and violet on multicolor underprint. Older President K. Kaunda
at right, earlier frame design, arms at upper center. Signature 5. Back: Document
signing, commemorative text and crowd. Watermark: K. Kaunda. Printer: TDLR.

	VF	UNC
a. Issued note.	10.00	35.00
s. Specimen.	—	55.00

22   10 Kwacha   **VF   UNC**
ND (1976). Blue on multicolor underprint. Older President K. Kaunda at right,
earlier frame design, arms at upper center. Signature 5. Back: Waterfalls at left
center. Watermark: K. Kaunda. Printer: TDLR.

	VF	UNC
a. Issued note.	20.00	50.00
s. Specimen.	—	75.00

22A   20 Kwacha   **VF   UNC**
ND. (Not issued.) Purple, red and multicolor. Older President K. Kaunda at right,
earlier frame design, arms at upper center. Back: National Assembly. Watermark:
K. Kaunda. Printer: TDLR.

                                     —   —

1980; 1986 ND Issue

#23-28 Replacement notes: Serial # prefix *Z/1*.

23   1 Kwacha   **VF   UNC**
ND (1980-88). Dark brown on multicolor underprint. President K. Kaunda at
right, African fish eagle at left center. Back: Workers picking cotton at left center.
Watermark: K. Kaunda. Printer: TDLR.

	VF	UNC
a. Signature 5.	2.00	8.00
b. Signature 7.	0.40	2.00
s. Specimen.	—	40.00

24   2 Kwacha   **VF   UNC**
ND (1980-88). Olive-green on multicolor underprint. President K. Kaunda at right,
African fish eagle at left center. Back: Teacher with student at left, school building
at center. Watermark: K. Kaunda. Printer: TDLR.

	VF	UNC
a. Signature 5.	4.00	10.00
b. Signature 6.	3.00	8.00
c. Signature 7.	0.60	3.00
s. Specimen.	—	40.00

25   5 Kwacha   **VF   UNC**
ND (1980-88). Brown on multicolor underprint. President K. Kaunda at right,
African fish eagle at left center. Back: Hydroelectric dam at left center. Watermark:
K. Kaunda. Printer: TDLR.

	VF	UNC
a. Signature 5.	2.00	10.00
b. Signature 4.	10.00	45.00
c. Signature 6.	4.00	8.00
d. Signature 7.	1.00	5.00
s. Specimen.	—	40.00

26   10 Kwacha   **VF   UNC**
ND (1980-88). Blue, green and black on multicolor underprint. President K.
Kaunda at right, African fish eagle at left center. Back: Bank at left center. Water-
mark: K. Kaunda. Printer: TDLR.

	VF	UNC
a. Signature 5.	10.00	45.00
b. Signature 4 in black.	18.00	125
c. Signature 4 in blue.	15.00	100
d. Signature 6.	6.00	14.00
e. Signature 7.	1.25	6.00
s. Specimen. As a, d. Red overprint: *SPECIMEN* on both sides.	—	40.00

27   20 Kwacha   **VF   UNC**
ND (1980-88). Green and olive-brown on multicolor underprint. President K.
Kaunda at right, African fish eagle at left center. Back: Woman with basket on
head at center right. Watermark: K. Kaunda. Printer: TDLR.

	VF	UNC
a. Signature 5.	15.00	60.00
b. Signature 4 in black.	20.00	150
c. Signature 4 in dark green.	15.00	100
d. Signature 6.	8.00	17.50
e. Signature 7.	1.75	9.00
s. Specimen. As a. Red overprint: *SPECIMEN* on both sides.	—	60.00

28   50 Kwacha   **VF   UNC**
ND (1986-88). UV: value 50 fluoresce orange. Purple, violet and multicolor.
President K. Kaunda at right, African fish eagle at left center. Signature 7. Back:
Chainbreaker" statue at left, modern building at left center. Watermark: K. Kaunda.
Printer: TDLR.
   a. Issued note.   4.00   20.00
   s. Specimen. Red overprint: *SPECIMEN* on both sides.   —   60.00

1989 ND Issue

29   2 Kwacha   **VF   UNC**
ND (1989). Olive brown on multicolor underprint. President K. Kaunda at right, fish
eagle at lower left, butterfly over arms at center. Signature 8. Back: Rhinoceros
head at lower left facing left, cornfield at center, tool at right, "Chainbreaker" statue
at left. Watermark: K. Kaunda.
   a. Issued note.   1.50   5.00
   s. Specimen.   —   40.00

32   20 Kwacha   **VF   UNC**
ND (1989-91). UV: value 20 fluoresce yellow. Dark olive-green, brown and blue on
multicolor underprint. President K. Kaunda at right, fish eagle at lower left, butterfly
over arms at center. Back: Chainbreaker" statue at left, Dama gazelle head at lower
left, facing 3/4 left, building at center, carving at right. Watermark: K. Kaunda.
   a. Signature 8.   5.00   10.00
   b. Signature 9.   4.00   8.00
   s. Specimen.   —   60.00

30   5 Kwacha   **VF   UNC**
ND (1989). UV: value 5 fluoresce yellow. Brown and red-orange on multicolor underprint. President K. Kaunda at right, fish eagle at lower left, butterfly over arms
at center. Signature 8. Back: Chainbreaker" statue at left, lion cub head facing at
lower left, building at center, jar at right. Watermark: K. Kaunda.
   a. Issued note.   2.00   7.00
   s. Specimen.   —   40.00

33   50 Kwacha   **VF   UNC**
ND (1989-91). Red-violet and purple on multicolor underprint. President K.
Kaunda at right, fish eagle at lower left, butterfly over arms at center. Signature
Back: Zebra head at lower left, facing left, manufacturing at center, carving of
woman's bust at right, "Chainbreaker" statue at left. Watermark: K. Kaunda.
   a. Signature 8.   10.00   30.00
   b. Signature 9.   5.00   15.00
   s. Specimen.   —   60.00

1991 ND Issue

31   10 Kwacha   **VF   UNC**
ND (1989-91). UV: value 10 fluoresce yellow. Black, dark blue and red-violet on
multicolor underprint. President K. Kaunda at right, fish eagle at lower left, butterfly over arms at center. Signature Back: Chainbreaker" statue at left, giraffe head
at lower left, facing left, building at center, carving at right. Watermark: K. Kaunda.
   a. Signature 8.   3.00   8.00
   b. Signature 9.   1.00   4.50
   s. Specimen.   —   40.00

34   100 Kwacha   **VF   UNC**
ND (1991). Purple, red and blue on multicolor underprint. Older President K.
Kaunda at right, gish eagle at left, palm trees at center. Back: Victoria Falls of
Zambezi with rainbow through center. Watermark: K. Kaunda.
   a. Issued note.   6.00   12.00
   s. Specimen.   —   50.00

35   500 Kwacha   VF   UNC

ND (1991). Brown on multicolor underprint. Older President K. Kaunda at right, fish eagle at left, tree over arms at center. Signature 9. Back: Elephant at left, workers picking cotton at center. Watermark: K. Kaunda.

a. Issued note.		10.00	25.00
s. Specimen. Red overprint: SPECIMEN on both sides.		—	60.00

1992; 1996 ND Issue

#36-42 Replacement notes: Serial # prefix *1/X.*

36   20 Kwacha   VF   UNC

1992. UV: value 20 in blox fluoresce yellow; vertical serial # orange. Back design elements orange. Green on multicolor underprint. Fish eagle at right, seal of arms with date at lower left. Back: Fig tree at center, Kudu at left, 3/4 facing left, State House at Lusaka at center, "Chainbreaker" statue at right center. Watermark: Fish eagle's head. Printer: TDLR.

a. Signature 10.		0.50	3.00
b. Signature 11.		0.50	2.50
s. Specimen. As a. Red overprint: SPECIMEN on both sides.		—	65.00

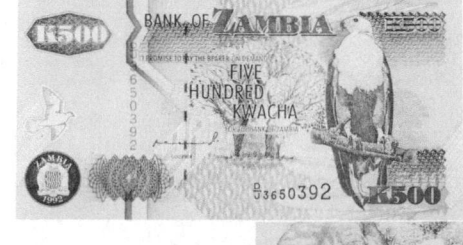

37   50 Kwacha   VF   UNC

1992; 2001; 2003; 2006-08. UV: value 50 in square fluoresces yellow. Red on multicolor underprint. Fish eagle at right, seal of arms with date at lower left, sausage tree at center, zebra at left. Back: Copper refining at Nkana Mine at center, "Chainbreaker" statue at center right. Watermark: Fish eagle's head. Printer: TDLR.

a. 1992. Signature 10.		0.60	3.25
b. 1992. Signature 11.		0.60	3.00
c. 2001. Signature 11.		0.50	2.75
d. 2003. Signature 12.		0.50	2.50
e. 2006. Signature 12.		FV	1.25
f. 2007. Signature 12.		FV	1.00
g. 2008. Signature 12.		FV	0.75
h. 2009. Signature. 12.		FV	0.75
s. Specimen. As a. Red overprint: SPECIMEN on both sides.		—	65.00

38   100 Kwacha   VF   UNC

1992; 2001; 2003; 2005; 2006. Deep purple on multicolor underprint. Fish eagle at right, palm tree at center, seal of arms with date at lower left. Serial # varieties. Back: Water buffalo head facing at left, Victoria falls at center, "Chainbreaker" statue at center right. Watermark: Fish eagle's head. Printer: TDLR.

a. 1992. Signature 10.		0.60	3.00
b. 1992. Signature 11.		0.60	3.00
c. 2001. Signature 11.		FV	2.50
d. 2003. Signature 12.		FV	2.00
e. 2005. Signature 12.		FV	2.00
f. 2006. Signatrue 12.		FV	2.25
g. 2008. Signature 12.		FV	1.00
h. 2009. Signature 12.		FV	1.00
i. 2010. Signature 12.		FV	1.00
s. Specimen. As a. Red overprint: SPECIMEN on both sides.		—	65.00

39   500 Kwacha   VF   UNC

1992; 2001; 2003. Brown on multicolor underprint. Fish eagle at right, seal of arms with date at lower left, Baobab tree. Back: Elephant head at left, workers picking cotton at center, "Chainbreaker" statue at center right. Watermark: Fish eagle's head. Printer: TDLR.

a. 1992. Signature 10.		1.75	6.00
b. 1992. Signature 11.		1.00	5.00
c. 2001. Signature 11.		FV	3.00
d. 2003. Signature 12.		FV	3.00
s. Specimen. As a. Red overprint: SPECIMEN on both sides.		—	65.00

40   1000 Kwacha   VF   UNC

1992 (1996); 2001; 2003. Red-violet, deep orange and dark olive-green on multicolor underprint. Fish eagle at right, seal of arms with date at lower left, Jacaranda tree. Back: Aardvark at left, sorghum farmer on tractor at center, "Chainbreaker" statue at center right. Watermark: Fish eagle's head. Printer: TDLR.

a. 1992 (1996). Signature 11.		1.25	5.50
b. 2001. Signature 11.		0.75	4.50
c. 2003. Signature 12.		FV	3.00
s. Specimen. As a. Red overprint: SPECIMEN on both sides.		—	50.00

41   5000 Kwacha   **VF   UNC**

1992 (1996); 2001. Large zero's in denomination. Purple, dark brown and deep
red on multicolor underprint. Fish eagle at right, Murera / Acacia / Mopani tree at
center, seal of arms with date at lower left. Back: Lion facing at left, root cassava
plant at center, "Chainbreaker" statue at center right. Watermark: Fish eagle's
head. Printer: TDLR.

a. 1992 (1996). Signature 11.	2.50	10.00
b. 2001. Signature 11.	1.75	5.50
s. Specimen. As a. Red overprint: *SPECIMEN* on both sides.	—	50.00

42   10,000 Kwacha   **VF   UNC**

1992 (1996); 2001; 2003. Aqua, brown-violet and yellow-brown on multicolor underprint. Fish eagle at right, Musuku tree at center, seal of arms with date at lower
left. Back: Porcupine at left, harvesting rice paddy at center, "Chainbreaker" statue
at center right. Watermark: Fish eagle's head facing left. Printer: TDLR.

a. 1992 (1996). Signature 11.	5.00	17.50
b. 2001. Signature 11.	3.00	12.00
c. 2003. Signature 12.	3.00	20.00
s. Specimen. As a. Red overprint: *SPECIMEN* on both sides.	—	75.00

2003 Issue

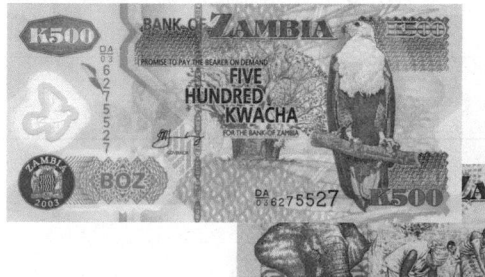

43   500 Kwacha   **VF   UNC**

2003-11. Polymer plastic. Multicolor. Fish eagle at right, Baobab tree at center.
Back: Elephant's head at left, workers picking cotton at center, "Chainbreaker"
statue at center right. Watermark: Fish eagle's head. 145x70mm.

a. 2003. Serial # wears off. Printer CBNC.	—	15.00
b. 2003. Second printing.	FV	1.00
c. 2004. Signature 12.	FV	1.00
d. 2005. Signature 12.	FV	1.00
e. 2006. Signature 12.	FV	1.00
f. 2008. Signature 12. Altered security features.	FV	0.75
g. 2009. Signature 12.	FV	0.75
h. 2011. Signature 12. Printer: G&D.	FV	0.75
s. Specimen.	—	40.00

44   1000 Kwacha   **VF   UNC**

2003-12. Polymer plastic. UV: value 500 in box and design elements fluoresce
yellow; vertical serial # orange. Multicolor. Fish eagle at left, tree at center. Back:
Aardvark at left, sorghum farmer on tractor at center, "Chainbreaker" statue at
center right. 145x70mm.

a. 2003. Serial # wears off. Printer: CBNC.	—	20.00
b. 2003. Second Printing.	FV	3.00
c. 2004. Signature 12.	FV	3.00
d. 2005. Signature 12.	FV	3.00
e. 2006. Signature 12.	FV	3.00
f. 2008. Signature 12.	FV	1.50
g. 2009. Signature 12.	FV	1.50
h. 2011. Signature 12. Printer: G&D.	FV	1.50
i. 2012. Signature 12.	FV	1.50
s. Specimen.	—	40.00

45   5000 Kwacha   **VF   UNC**

2003-12. Small zero's in denomination. Multicolor. Fish eagle at right, Murera /
Acacia / Mopani tree at center, seal of arms with date at lower left. Back: Lion
at left center, root cassava plant at center, "Chainbreaker" statue at center right.
145x70mm.

a. 2003. Signature 12.	FV	4.50
b. 2005. Signature 12.	FV	3.00
c. 2006. Signature 12.	FV	2.00
d. 2008. Signature 12.	FV	1.75
e. 2009. Signature 12.	FV	1.75
f. 2010. Signature 12.	FV	1.75
g. 2011. Signature 12.	FV	1.75
h. 2012. Signature 12.	FV	1.75
s. Specimen.	—	40.00

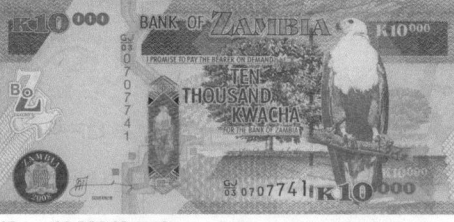

46   10,000 Kwacha   **VF   UNC**

2003-12. Aqua, brown-violet and yellow-brown on multicolor underprint. Fish
eagle at right, Musuku tree at center, seal of arms with date at lower left. Foil fish
eagle head at lower left. Back: Porcupine at left, harvesting rice paddy at center,
"Chainbreaker" statue at center right. Watermark: Fish eagle's head. Printer:
TDLR. 145x70mm.

a. 2003. Date as denominator. Foil fish eagle head points right.	FV	6.00
b. 2005. Signature 12.	FV	6.00
c. 2006. Signature 12.	FV	6.00
d. 2007. Signature 12.	FV	5.00
e. 2008. Signature 12. Altered security features.	FV	4.00
f. 2009. Signature 12.	FV	4.00
g. 2011. Signature 12.	FV	4.00
h. 2012. Signature 12.	FV	4.00
s. Specimen.	—	40.00

47   20,000 Kwacha

2003-12. Multicolor. Fish eagle at right, Murea / Acacia / Mopani tree at center. seal of arms with date at lower left. Back: Lion head at left. Root cassava plant at center, "Chainbreaker" statue at center right. Watermark: Fish eagle's head. 145x70mm.

		VF	UNC
a. 2003. Signature 12.		FV	10.00
b. 2005. Signature 12.		FV	10.00
c. 2006. Signature 12.		FV	10.00
d. 2008. Signature 12.		FV	8.00
e. 2009. Signature 12.		FV	8.00
f. 2010. Signature 12.		FV	8.00
g. 2011. Signature 12.		FV	8.00
h. 2012. Signature 12.		FV	8.00
s. Specimen.		—	50.00

48   50,000 Kwacha

2003-12. Multicolor. Fish eagle at right, tree at center. Back: Leopard at left, Bank of Zambia building at center, "Chainbreaker" statue at right center. 145x70mm.

		VF	UNC
a. 2003. Signature 12.		FV	25.00
b. 2006. Signature 12.		FV	25.00
c. 2007. Signature 12.		FV	22.00
d. 2008. Signature 12.		FV	20.00
e. 2009. Signature 12.		FV	15.00
f. 2010. Signature 12.		FV	15.00
g. 2011. Signature 12.		FV	15.00
h. 2012. Signature 12.		FV	15.00
s. Specimen.		—	60.00

2012 Issue

49   2 Kwacha

2012. Gray and multicolor. Fish eagle at right. Baobab tree at center. Back: Roan antelope; two women and Freedom statue. Watermark: Fish eagle and value. Printer: G&D. 140x70mm.

	VF	UNC
a. 2012.	FV	1.50
b. 2013.	FV	1.50
c. 2014.	FV	1.50

50   5 Kwacha

2012. Purple and multicolor. Fish eagle at right. Baobab tree at center. Back: Lion head at left, plant and Freedom statue. Watermark: Fish eagle and 5. Printer: G&D. 140x70mm.

	VF	UNC
a. 2012.	FV	2.00
b. 2013.	FV	2.00
c. 2014.	FV	2.00

51   10 Kwacha

2012. Blue and multicolor. Fish eagle at right. Baobab tree at center. Back: Porcupine, harvest scene and Freedom Statue. Watermark: Fish eagle and 10. Printer: G&D. 145x70mm.

	VF	UNC
a. 2012.	FV	4.00
b. 2013.	FV	4.00
c. 2014.	FV	4.00

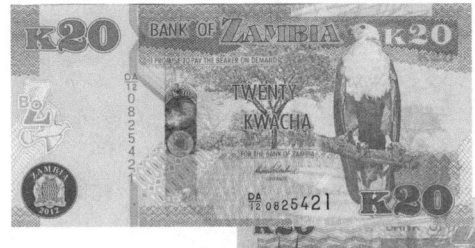

52   20 Kwacha

2012. Brown and multicolor. Fish eagle at right. Baobab tree at center. Back: Black lechwe antelope, men working pneumatic drill in mine. Watermark: Fish eagle and 20. 145x70mm.

	VF	UNC
a. 2012.	FV	8.00
b. 2013.	FV	8.00
c. 2014.	FV	8.00

53   50 Kwacha

2012. Blue and multicolor. Fish eagle at right. Baobab tree at center. Back: Leopard and Bank of Zambia building. Watermark: Fish eagle and 50 Printer: G&D. 145x70mm.

	VF	UNC
a. 2012.	FV	20.00
b. 2013.	FV	20.00
c. 2014.	FV	20.00

54 100 Kwacha   VF UNC
2012. Olive green and multicolor. Fish eagle at right. Baobab tree at center. Back:
Buffalo, National Assembly building and Freedom Statue. Watermark: Fish eagle
and 100. Printer: G&D. 145x70mm.
- a. 2012.   FV 40.00
- b. 2013.   FV 40.00
- c. 2014.   FV 40.00

2014 Commemorative Issue

55 50 Kwacha   VF UNC
2014. 50th Anniversary of Independence.   FV 20.00

2015 Issue

56 2 Kwacha   VF UNC   FV 1.50
2015. Gray and multicolor. Fish eagle at right. Baobab tree at center. Tactile
diagonal lines for the visually impaired intaglio printed at center right. Signature:
Denny Kalyalya. Back: Roan antelope; two women and Freedom statue. Printer
imprint at lower right. Watermark: Fish eagle and value. Printer: OBERTHUR
fiduciaire.

57 5 Kwacha   VF UNC   FV 2.00
2015. Purple and multicolor. Fish eagle at right. Baobab tree at center. Tactile
diagonal lines for the visually impaired intaglio printed at center right. Signature:
Denny Kalyalya. Back: Lion head at left, plant and Freedom statue. Printer imprint
at lower right. Watermark: Fish eagle and 5. Printer: Royal Joh. Enschede.

58 10 Kwacha   VF UNC   FV 4.00
2015. Blue and multicolor. Fish eagle at right. Baobab tree at center. Tactile diagonal lines for the visually impaired intaglio printed at center right. Signature: Denny
Kalyalya. Back: Porcupine, harvest scene and Freedom Statue. Printer imprint at
lower right. Watermark: Fish eagle and 10. Printer: Giesecke & Devrient.

59 20 Kwacha   VF UNC   FV 8.00
2015. Brown and multicolor. Fish eagle at right. Baobab tree at center. Tactile
diagonal lines for the visually impaired intaglio printed at center right. Signature:
Denny Kalyalya. Back: Black lechwe antelope, men working pneumatic drill
in mine. Printer imprint at lower right. Watermark: Fish eagle and 20. Printer:
Giesecke & Devrient.

60 50 Kwacha   VF UNC   FV 20.00
2015. Blue and multicolor. Fish eagle at right. Baobab tree at center. Tactile
diagonal lines for the visually impaired intaglio printed at center right. Signature:
Denny Kalyalya. Back: Leopard and Bank of Zambia building. Printer imprint at
lower right. Watermark: Fish eagle and 50 Printer: Giesecke & Devrient.

61 100 Kwacha   VF UNC   FV 40.00
2015. Olive green and multicolor. Fish eagle at right. Baobab tree at center. Tactile
diagonal lines for the visually impaired intaglio printed at center right. Signature:
Denny Kalyalya. Back: Buffalo, National Assembly building and Freedom Statue.
Printer imprint at lower right. Watermark: Fish eagle and 100. Printer: Giesecke
& Devrient.

ZIMBABWE

The Republic of Zimbabwe is located in the east-central part of southern Africa, has an area of 390,580 sq. km. and a population of 11.35 million. Capital: Harare (formerly Salisbury). The economy is based on agriculture and mining. Tobacco, sugar, asbestos, copper and chrome ore and coal are exported. The UK annexed Southern Rhodesia from the [British] South Africa Company in 1923. A 1961 constitution was formulated that favored whites in power. In 1965 the government unilaterally declared its independence, but the UK did not recognize the act and demanded more complete voting rights for the black African majority in the country (then called Rhodesia). UN sanctions and a guerrilla uprising finally led to free elections in 1979 and independence (as Zimbabwe) in 1980. Robert Mugabe, the nation's first prime minister, has been the country's only ruler (as president since 1987) and has dominated the country's political system since independence. His chaotic land redistribution campaign, which began in 2000, caused an exodus of white farmers, crippled the economy, and ushered in widespread shortages of basic commodities. Ignoring international condemnation, Mugabe rigged the 2002 presidential election to ensure his reelection. The ruling ZANU-PF party used fraud and intimidation to win a two-thirds majority in the March 2005 parliamentary election, allowing it to amend the constitution at will and recreate the Senate, which had been abolished in the late 1980s. In April 2005, Harare embarked on Operation Restore Order, ostensibly an urban rationalization program, which resulted in the destruction of the homes or businesses of 700,000 mostly poor supporters of the opposition. President Mugabe in June 2007 instituted price controls on all basic commodities causing panic buying and leaving store shelves empty for months. General elections held in March 2008 contained irregularities but still amounted to a censure of the ZANU-PF-led government with significant gains in opposition seats in parliament. MDC opposition leader Morgan Tsvangirai won the presidential polls, and may have won an out right majority, but official results posted by the Zimbabwe Electoral Committee did not reflect this. In the lead up to a run-off election in late June 2008, considerable violence enacted against opposition party members led to the withdrawal of Tsvangirai from the ballot. Extensive evidence of vote tampering and ballot-box stuffing resulted in international condemnation of the process. A power sharing agreement has been negoated allowing Mugabe to remain as president and creating the new position of prime minister for Tsvangirai. For earlier issues see Rhodesia.

MONETARY SYSTEM:
1 Dollar = 100 Cents

SIGNATURE/TITLE VARIETIES			
	GOVERNOR		GOVERNOR
1	Dr. D.C. Krogh	2	K. Moyana
3	L. Tsumba	4	Dr. D.C. Krogh
5	Dr. K.J. Moyana	6	Dr. L.L. Tsumba
7	C. Chikaura	8	Dr. G. Gono
	FINANCE DIRECTOR		OPERATIONS DIRECTOR
A	Priscilla P. Mutembwa		Stephen J. Newton-Howes

ZIMBABWEAN BIRD WATERMARK VARIETIES

Type A	Type B	Type C
Profile short neck	3/4 view medium neck	3/4 view long neck

REPUBLIC

Reserve Bank of Zimbabwe

1980 Issue

#1-4 Replacement notes: Serial # prefix: *AW; BW; CW; DW* respectively.

1	2 Dollars	VF	UNC

1980 (1981); 1983; 1994. Blue and multicolor. Water buffalo at left. Chiremba balancing rock formation. Epworth (Harare) at center right. Signature varieties. Back: Tigerfish at center, Kariba Dam and reservoir at right. Watermark: Zimbabwe bird.

		VF	UNC
a. Signature 1. Salisbury. 1980.		2.25	10.00
b. Signature 2. Harare. 1983.		1.25	5.00
c. Signature 3. Watermark: Type A. 1994.		0.75	3.75
d. Signature 3. Watermark: Type B. 1994.		22.50	95.00

2	5 Dollars	VF	UNC

1980 (1981); 1982-83; 1994. Green and multicolor. Zebra at left. Chiremba balancing rock formation. Epworth (Harare) at center right. Signature varieties. Back: Village scene with two workers. Watermark: Zimbabwe bird.

		VF	UNC
a. Signature 1. Salisbury. 1980.		5.50	24.00
b. Signature 1. Harare. 1982.		5.00	22.50
c. Signature 2. 1983.		1.50	6.00
d. Signature 3. 1994. Watermark: Type A.		2.75	11.00
e. Signature 3. 1994. Watermark: Type B.		12.50	50.00

3	10 Dollars	VF	UNC

1980 (1981); 1982-83; 1994. Red and multicolor. Sable antelope at left. Chiremba balancing rock formation. Epworth (Harare) at center right. Signature varieties. Back: View of Harare and Freedom Flame monument. Watermark: Zimbabwe bird.

		VF	UNC
a. Signature 1. Salisbury. 1980.		10.00	50.00
b. Signature 1. Salisbury. 1982 (error).		35.00	125
c. Signature 1. Harare. 1982.		25.00	120
d. Signature 2. 1983.		2.75	11.00
e. Signature 3. 1994.		1.50	6.50

4	20 Dollars	VF	UNC

1980 (1982); 1982-83; 1994. Blue, black and dark green on multicolor underprint. Giraffe at left. Chiremba balancing rock formation. Epworth (Harare) at center right. Signature varieties. Back: Elephant and Victoria Falls. Watermark: Zimbabwe bird.

		VF	UNC
a. Signature 1. Salisbury. 1980.		17.50	70.00
b. Signature 1. Harare. 1982.		75.00	300
c. Signature 2. 1983.		5.00	15.00
d. Signature 3. 1994.		3.50	14.00

1994; 1997; 2001 Issues

5	5 Dollars	VF	UNC

1997. UV: fibers fluoresce blue and red; vertical serial # and central design elements orange. Back 5s and design elements orange. Brown, red-orange and purple on multicolor underprint. Chiremba balancing rock formation. Epworth (Harare) at center right. Signature 3. Back: Terraced hills at center right. Watermark: Zimbabwe bird. Type C.

		VF	UNC
a. Light brown back (litho). Series BA-BL.		0.75	3.00
b. Darker brown back (intaglio). Series BM-BZ.		0.20	1.00
r. Replacement. Serial number prefix AB.		—	—

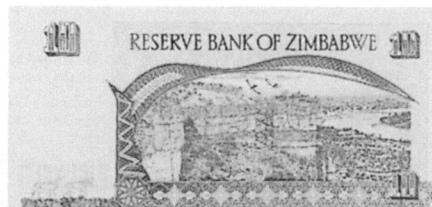

6	10 Dollars	VF	UNC

1997. UV: fibers fluoresce yellow and blue; vertical serial # orange. Red-brown, deep green and blue-black on multicolor underprint. Chiremba balancing rock formation. Epworth (Harare) at center right. Signature 3. Back: Chilolo Cliffs at center right. Watermark: Zimbabwe bird. Type C.

		VF	UNC
a. Issued note.		FV	2.00
r. Replacement note. Serial number prefix AC.		—	—

7	20 Dollars	VF	UNC

1997. Deep blue, purple and gray-green on multicolor underprint. Chiremba balancing rock formation. Epworth (Harare) at right. Back: Victoria Falls at center right.

		VF	UNC
a. Issued note.		FV	2.50
r. Replacement note. Serial number prefix AD.		—	—

		VF	UNC
8	**50 Dollars**		

1994. Dark brown, olive-brown and red-orange on multicolor underprint. Chiremba balancing rock formation. Epworth (Harare) at right. Back: Great Zimbabwe ruins.

	a. Issued note.	FV	3.00
	r. Replacement note. Serial # prefix AE.	—	—

		VF	UNC
9	**100 Dollars**		

1995. Brownish black and purple on multicolor underprint. Chiremba balancing rock formation. Epworth (Harare) at right. Back: Aerial view of Kariba Dam and reservoir at center right.

	a. Issued note.	FV	3.00
	r. Replacement note. Serial # prefix AF.	—	—

		VF	UNC
10	**500 Dollars**	FV	5.00

2001. Dark brown and red on multicolor underprint. Chiremba balancing rock formation. Epworth (Harare) at right. Hologram silver foil at left. Back: Hwange power station. Watermark: Zimbabwe bird and *500*.

		VF	UNC
11	**500 Dollars**		

2001; 2004. Dark brown on tan and multicolor underprint. Chiremba balancing rock formation. Epworth (Harare) at right. Without foil at left. Back: Hwange power station. Watermark: Zimbabwe bird and *500*.

	a. 2001.	FV	5.00
	b. 2004. Signature: Gideon Gono.	FV	5.00

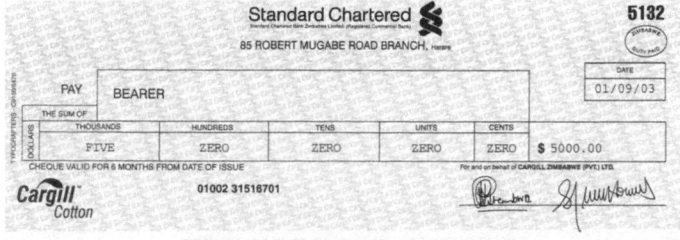

		VF	UNC
12	**1000 Dollars**		

2003. Brown, purple and green on multicolor underprint. Chiremba balancing rock formation at left. Back: Elephants.

	a. Large digits in serial number.	FV	3.00
	b. Small digits in serial number.	FV	6.00

2003 Emergency Cargill Bearer Checks

		VF	UNC
13	**5000 Dollars**		

2003. Pink and green underprint. Reseve Bank of Zimbabwe logo. Signature 4. Back: Wave pattern. Watermark: Cotton plant. Printer: Typocrafters.

	a. 1.6.2003. Green.	35.00	150
	b. 1.9.2003. Blue.	45.00	175

		VF	UNC
14	**10,000 Dollars**		

2003. Blue. Reserve Bank of Zimbabwe logo. Signature 4. Back: Wave pattern. Watermark: Cotton plant. Printer: Typocrafters.

	a. 1.5.2003.	45.00	175
	b. 1.9.2003.	55.00	200

2003 Emergency Travellers' Checks

		VF	UNC
15	**1000 Dollars**	2.50	4.00

2003. Gray. Reserve Bank of Zimbabwe logo. Signature 4. Back: Wave pattern. Watermark: Zimbabwe bird. Type 1.

		VF	UNC
16	**5000 Dollars**	3.00	10.00

2003. Red. Reserve Bank of Zimbabwe logo. Signature 4. Back: Wave pattern. Watermark: Zimbabwe bird. Type 1.

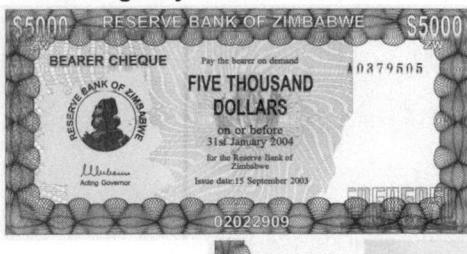

		VF	UNC
17	**10,000 Dollars**	2.50	5.00

2003. Light blue. Reserve Bank of Zimbabwe logo. Signature 4. Back: Wave pattern. Watermark: Zimbabwe bird. Type 1.

		VF	UNC
18	**20,000 Dollars**	2.50	5.00

2003. Olive green. Reserve Bank of Zimbabwe logo. Signature 4. Back: Wave pattern. Watermark: Zimbabwe bird. Type 1.

		VF	UNC
19	**50,000 Dollars**	2.50	7.50

2003. Dark blue. Reserve Bank of Zimbabwe logo. Watermark: Zimbabwe bird. Type 3.

Printed on paper stock from #8, $50.00.

		VF	UNC
20	**100,000 Dollars**	2.50	7.50

2003. Brown. Reserve Bank of Zimbabwe logo. Watermark: Zimbabwe bird. Type 3.

Printed on paper stock from #8, $50.00.

2003 Emergency Bearer Checks

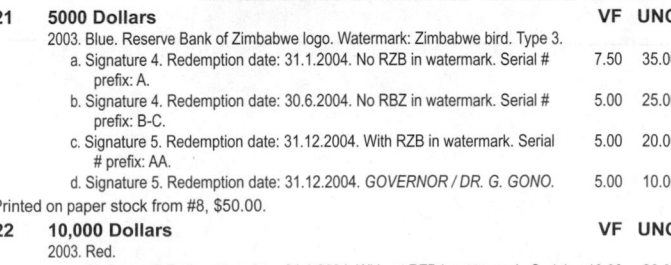

		VF	UNC
21	**5000 Dollars**		

2003. Blue. Reserve Bank of Zimbabwe logo. Watermark: Zimbabwe bird. Type 3.

	a. Signature 4. Redemption date: 31.1.2004. No RZB in watermark. Serial # prefix: A.	7.50	35.00
	b. Signature 4. Redemption date: 30.6.2004. No RBZ in watermark. Serial # prefix: B-C.	5.00	25.00
	c. Signature 5. Redemption date: 31.12.2004. With RZB in watermark. Serial # prefix: AA.	5.00	20.00
	d. Signature 5. Redemption date: 31.12.2004. *GOVERNOR / DR. G. GONO.*	5.00	10.00

Printed on paper stock from #8, $50.00.

		VF	UNC
22	**10,000 Dollars**		

2003. Red.

	a. Signature 4. Redemption date: 31.1.2004. Without RZB in watermark. Serial # prefix: E.	10.00	80.00
	b. Signature 4. Redemption date: 30.6.2004. Without RZB in watermark. Serial # prefix: F-G.	5.00	60.00
	c. Signature 5. Redemption date: 31.12.2004. With RZB in watermark. Serial # prefix: BA.	5.00	50.00
	d. Signature 5. Redemption date: 31.12.2004. With RZB in watermark. *GOVERNOR / DR. G. GONO.*	5.00	20.00

		VF	UNC
23	**20,000 Dollars**		

2003. Brown.

	a. Signature 4. Redemption date: 31.1.2004. Without RZB in watermark. Serial # prefix: J.	12.50	115
	b. Signature 4. Redemption date: 30.6.2004. Without RZB in watermark. Serial # prefix: K-L.	6.25	85.00

c. Signature 5. Redemption date: 31.12.2004. Without RZB in watermark. Serial # prefix: AA.

	VF	UNC
	30.00	125

d. Signature 5. Redemption date: 31.12.2004. *GOVERNOR* with RZB in watermark. Serial # prefix AA.

	VF	UNC
	7.50	60.00

e. Signature 5. Redemption date: 31.12.2004. *GOVERNOR / DR. G. GONO.* with RZB in watermark.

	VF	UNC
	—	35.00

2004 Emergency Cargill Bearer Checks

24   10,000 Dollars

1.4.2004. Blue.

VF	UNC
20.00	75.00

25   20,000 Dollars

1.4.2004. Green.

VF	UNC
35.00	125

26   50,000 Dollars

1.4.2004. Orange.

VF	UNC
65.00	200

27   100,000 Dollars

1.4.2004. Red.

VF	UNC
85.00	250

2005-06 Emergency Bearer Checks

28   50,000 Dollars

1.10.2005. Serial # prefix AA-AB.

VF	UNC
10.00	20.00

29   50,000 Dollars

1.2.2006. Serial # prefiex CA-CK. Printer: G&D.

VF	UNC
10.00	20.00

30   50,000 Dollars

1.2.2006. Redemption date of 31.12.2006. Violet on green and red underprint. Back: Waterfall. 147x74mm.

VF	UNC
3.00	7.50

31   100,000 Dollars

1.10.2005. Serial # prefix: AA-AC.

VF	UNC
15.00	35.00

32   100,000 Dollars

1.6.2006. Green on light green and red underprint. Back: Waterfalls. 147x74mm.

VF	UNC
3.50	10.00

2006-08 Emergency Bearer Checks, Second Dollar (ZWN)

33   1 Cent

1.8.2006. Rose. Back: Large value in circle. 153x78mm.

VF	UNC
0.25	1.00

34   5 Cents

1.8.2006. Green. Back: Large value in circle. 153x78mm.

VF	UNC
0.25	1.00

35   10 Cents

1.8.2006. Brown. Back: Large value in circle. 153x78mm.

VF	UNC
0.25	1.00

36   50 Cents

1.8.2006. Black. Back: Large value in circle. 153x78mm.

VF	UNC
0.35	1.25

37   1 Dollar

1.8.2006. Blue on light blue and rose underprint. Back: Two women mashing grain. 148x75mm.

VF	UNC
0.20	0.75

38   5 Dollars

1.8.2006. Green on brown underprint. Back: Torch in city park. 147x75mm.

VF	UNC
0.20	0.75

39   10 Dollars

1.8.2006. Rose. Back: Two women mashing grain. 148x74mm.

VF	UNC
0.30	0.80

40   20 Dollars

1.8.2006. Brown on light orange and green underprint. Back: Waterfalls. 146x75mm.

VF	UNC
0.25	0.75

41   50 Dollars

1.8.2006. Violet on light tan underpint. Back: Waterfalls. 147x75mm.

VF	UNC
0.35	0.80

42   100 Dollars

1.8.2006. Green on light blue underprint. Back: Mountain. 147x75mm.

VF	UNC
0.35	0.80

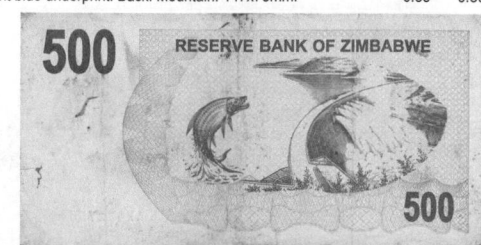

43   500 Dollars

1.8.2006. Brown on light green, blue and rose underprint. Back: Tiger fish at center, Kariba Dam at right. 148x75mm.

VF	UNC
0.30	0.75

44   1000 Dollars

1.8.2006. Brown on light grey, rose and green underprint. Back: Mountain. 148x75mm.

VF	UNC
0.30	0.75

45 5000 Dollars   VF UNC
1.2.2007. Blue on light blue, green and rose underprint. Back: Kariba Dam. 0.60 1.50
147x75mm.

46 10,000 Dollars   VF UNC
1.8.2006. Violet on light blue and green underprint. Back: Great Zimbabwe ruins.
147x75mm.
   a. Without space in value: 10000. Serial # prefix: AA. 15.00 100
   b. With space in value: 10 000. 1.00 3.00

47 50,000 Dollars   VF UNC
1.3.2007. Orange. Back: Elephant at waterfall at right. 0.70 2.00

48 100,000 Dollars   VF UNC
1.8.2006. Blue-green. Back: Great Zimbabwe ruins at right.
   a. Without space in value 100000. Serial # prefix: AA. 15.00 100
   b. With space in value 100 000. 0.90 2.75

49 200,000 Dollars   VF UNC
1.7.2007. Red brown and multicolor. Back: Power plant and cooling towers 0.80 2.50

50 250,000 Dollars   VF UNC
20.12.2007. Black and multicolor. Back: Great Zimbabwe ruins at right. 1.00 3.00

51 500,000 Dollars   VF UNC
1.7.2007. Olive and green on multicolor. Back: Three elephants at right. 0.45 1.50

52 750,000 Dollars   VF UNC
31.12.2007. Purple. Back: Elephant at waterfall at right. 0.50 1.75

53 1 Million Dollars   VF UNC
1.1.2008. Brown and orange. Back: Two women mashing grain. 0.75 2.25

54 5 MillionDollars   VF UNC
1.1.2008. Blue. Back: Mountain range. 2.75 7.00

55 10 Million Dollars   VF UNC
1.1.2008. Red and green. Back: Tiger fish at center, Kariba Dam at right.
   a. Series A. 1.75 4.00
   b. Series D. 0.65 2.00

56 25 Million Dollars   VF UNC
2.4.2008. Green. 1.00 3.00

57   50 Million Dollars VF UNC
2.4.2008. Purple and violet. Back: Three elephants at right.   1.20   3.50

58   100 Million Dollars VF UNC
2.5.2008. Green on multicolor underprint. Back: Two women mashing grain.   1.20   3.50

59   250 Million Dollars VF UNC
2.5.2008. Blue on multicolor underprint. Back: Elephant at waterfall.   1.25   4.00

60   500 Million Dollars VF UNC
2.5.2008. Rose on multicolor underprint. Back: Tiger fish at center, Kariba Dam at right.   0.80   2.50

2008 Special Agro Checks

61   5 Billion Dollars VF UNC
15.5.2008. Violet.   1.00   3.00

62   25 Billion Dollars VF UNC
15.5.2008. Green.   1.50   4.50

63   50 Billion Dollars VF UNC
15.5.2008. Brown.   1.75   5.50

64   100 Billion Dollars VF UNC
1.7.2008. Blue.   2.00   6.50

2007-08 Issue, Third Dollar (ZWR)

65   1 Dollar VF UNC
1.8.2008. Purple and black. Chiremba balanced rock formation. Back: Waterfall and water buffalo. 153x76mm.   0.30   1.00

66   5 Dollars VF UNC
1.8.2008. Brown on green underprint. Chiremba balanced rock formation. Back: Dam and elephant.   0.40   1.25

67   10 Dollars VF UNC
1.8.2008. Dark green on light green underprint. Chiremba balanced rock formation. Back: Tractor in field, cilos.   0.50   1.75

68   20 Dollars VF UNC
1.8.2008. Burgundy on violet underprint. Chiremba balanced rock formation. Back: Mine tower and earth pile, Miner with jack hammer.   0.60   2.25

69   100 Dollars VF UNC
1.8.2008. Blue and black on light blue underprint. Chiremba balanced rock formation. Back: Palm trees and ancient fortification.   1.00   3.00

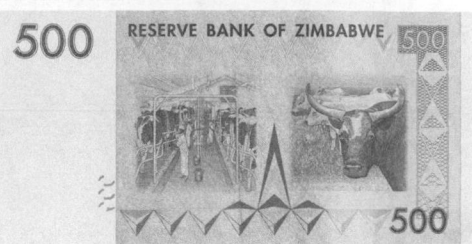

70   500 Dollars VF UNC
1.8.2008. Violet on blue underprint. Chiremba balanced rock formation. Back: Cow milking parlor and cattle. 152x77mm.   0.80   3.00

71 1000 Dollars — **VF UNC**
1.8.2008. Red-brown on tan and light green underprint. Chiremba balanced rock   0.80   3.00
formation. Back: Buildings. 155x79mm.

72 10,000 Dollars — **VF UNC**
29.9.2008. Brown on violet underprint. Chiremba balanced rock formation. Back: 1.25   5.00
Harvester and tractor. 153x76mm.

73 20,000 Dollars — **VF UNC**
29.9.2008. Brown on green underprint. Chiremba balanced rock formation. Back:
Victoria Falls and Kariba Dam. 153x76mm.
  a. Plain paper.   1.25   5.00
  b. Lined (laid) paper.   1.25   5.00

74 50,000 Dollars — **VF UNC**
13.10.2008. Green on pink and yellow underprint. Chiremba balanced rock formation. Back: Tractor in fields and miner with jackhammer. 153x76mm.
  a. Plain paper.   1.00   4.00
  b. Lined (laid) paper.   1.00   4.00

75 100,000 Dollars — **VF UNC**
5.11.2008. Dark blue on light blue underprint. Chiremba balanced rock formation.   1.25   5.00
Back: Water buffalo and elephant. 153x76mm.

76 500,000 Dollars — **VF UNC**
5.11.2008. Dark green light green underprint. Chiremba balanced rock formation.
Back: Palm trees and dairy cow milking parlor. 148x74mm.
  a. Plain paper.   1.50   6.00
  b. Lined (laid) paper.   1.50   6.00

77 1 Million Dollars — **VF UNC**
5.11.2008. Blue on light green underprint. Chiremba balanced rock formation.   0.75   3.00
Back: Great Zimbabwe ruins and cattle. 153x73mm.

78 10 Million Dollars — **VF UNC**
3.12.2008. Blue and tan. Chiremba balanced rock formation. Back: Parliament   1.25   5.00
and Great Zimbabwe ruins. 148x74mm.

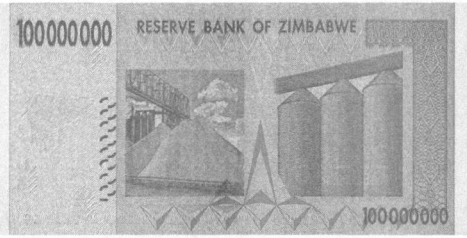

79 50 Million Dollars — **VF UNC**
3.12.2008. Green on blue underprint. Chiremba balanced rock formation. Back: 1.00   3.50
Water buffalo and Great Zimbabew ruins.

80 100 Million Dollars — **VF UNC**
3.12.2008. Red on light green underprint. Chiremba balanced rock formation.   1.00   3.50
Back: Grain pile and cilos. 147x74mm.

81 200 Million Dollars — **VF UNC**
5.12.2008. Brown on light green underprint. Chiremba balanced rock formation.   1.00   3.50
Back: Parliament and Hero's monument. 148x74mm.

82 **500 Million Dollars** VF UNC
12.12.2008. Purple on light blue and green underprint. Chiremba balanced rock 1.10 4.00
formation. Back: Cows in milking parlor and miner with jackhammer. 148x74mm.

83 **1 Billion Dollars** VF UNC
19.12.2008. Green on light green underprint. Chiremba balanced rock formation. 1.25 4.50
Back: Palm trees and elephant.

84 **5 Billion Dollars** VF UNC
19.12.2008. Brown on light blue underprint. Chiremba balanced rock formation. 1.25 5.00
Back: Tractor in fields, dairy cow milking parlor.

85 **10 Billion Dollars** VF UNC
19.12.2008. Blue on tan and light green underprint. Chiremba balanced rock 1.20 4.50
formation. Back: Dam, miner with jack hammer.

86 **20 Billion Dollars** VF UNC
2008. Green on light orange underprint. Chiremba balanced rock formation. Back: 0.80 3.00
Great Zimbabwe ruins and palm trees.

87 **50 Billion Dollars** VF UNC
2008. Light red-brown on light green underprint. Chiremba balanced rock forma- 1.00 4.00
tion. Back: Great Zimbabwe ruins and modern building tower.

88 **10 Trillion Dollars** VF UNC
2008. Green on light green underprint. Chiremba balanced rock formation. Back: 2.25 7.00
Modern building tower and Great Zimbabew ruins.

89 **20 Trillion Dollars** VF UNC
2008. Red-brown on light blue underprint. Chiremba balanced rock formation. 5.75 15.00
Back: Miner with jack hammer, cilos

90 **50 Trillion Dollars** VF UNC
2008. Black and green. Chiremba balanced rock formation. Back: Karba Dam 1.50 5.00
and elephant.

91 **100 Trillion Dollars** VF UNC
2008. Light blue on tan underprint. Chiremba balanced rock formation. Back: 0.75 10.00
Victoria Falls and water buffalo.

2009 Issue, Fourth Dollar (ZWL)

92 **1 Dollar** VF UNC
2.2.2009. Blue on light blue underprint. Chiremba balanved rock formation. Back: 0.35 1.25
Two women mashing grain.

93 **5 Dollars** VF UNC
2.2.2009. Green on tan underprint. Chiremba balanced rock formation. Back: 0.40 1.50
Tiger fish at center, Kariba Dam at right.

94 **10 Dollars** VF UNC
2.2.2009. Rose on tan underprint. Chiremba balanced rock formation. Back: Great 0.50 2.00
Zimbabwe ruins.

95 **20 Dollars** VF UNC
2.2.2009. Rose on light red underprint. Chiremba balanced rock formation. Back: 1.00 3.00
Power plant and cooling towers.

96 **50 Dollars** VF UNC
2.2.2009. Violet on light blue underprint. Chiremba balanced rock formation. Back: 1.50 4.00
Power plant and cooling towers.

97 **100 Dollars** VF UNC
2.2.2009. Brown on tan underprint. Chiremba balanced rock formation. Back: 1.75 5.00
Torch and skyline.

98 **500 Dollars** VF UNC
2009. Green on lime underprint. Chiremba balanced rock formation. Back: Three 3.50 10.00
elephants.